LOUISIANA CIVIL CODE 2014

As Revised and Amended through the
2013 Regular Session of the Legislature

Volume II

Volume I includes:
Text of Civil Code Articles,
Revision Comments, Editor's Notes,
Numerical Analysis of and Index to Civil Code Articles

Volume II includes:
Text of Title 9 of the Revised Statutes,
Revision Comments, Editor's Notes, Tables, Appendices,
Numerical Analysis of and Index to Revised Statutes Title 9

Edited by

A. N. YIANNOPOULOS

Eason-Weinmann Professor of Comparative Law (Emeritus)
Tulane University School of Law

Mat #41265252

© 2014 Thomson Reuters

ISBN: 978-0-314-65671-1

This publication was created to provide you with accurate and authoritative information concerning the subject matter covered; however, this publication was not necessarily prepared by persons licensed to practice law in a particular jurisdiction. The publisher is not engaged in rendering legal or other professional advice and this publication is not a substitute for the advice of an attorney. If you require legal or other expert advice, you should seek the services of a competent attorney or other professional.

West's and Westlaw are registered in the U.S. Patent and Trademark Office.

LOUISIANA

CIVIL CODE

2014

As Revised and Amended through
the 2013 Regular Session of the Legislature

Volume II

WHAT IS NEW IN THIS EDITION

The 2014 Pamphlet Edition of the Louisiana Civil Code has incorporated all changes to the Louisiana Civil Code (Volume I) and Title 9 of the Louisiana Revised Statutes (Volume II) affected by the 2013 Regular Session of the Louisiana Legislature.

In Volume I of the Civil Code, the most important changes are the amendments to the Civil Code by Acts 2013, No. 88. That Act amended and reenacted Civil Code Article 2041 (governing the prescription of the revocatory action) in order to add a second paragraph to that article, and added Articles 3505 to 3505.4 relating to the extension of liberative prescription by juridical act.

In Volume II of the Louisiana Civil Code, among the amendments and enactments of note are those governing funds related to the Crescent City Bridge Connection (R.S. 9:154.2), the online certification of certain electronic records (R.S. 9:2621), and the enactment of R.S. 9:3260.1 governing a lessee's right to notification of a foreclosure action.

In addition to updated articles of the Civil Code and sections of Title 9 of the Revised Statutes, the 2013 amendments necessitated the updating of Tables, Indices, and existing cross references as well as the inclusion of new Editor's notes.

The Revision Comments that accompany articles of the Civil Code are dated and some are either obsolete or misleading. The editor of the Pamphlet Edition lacks authority to edit the Revision Comments. However, in this edition, the editor has added notes updating obsolete references in Revision Comments and indicating needed corrections.

*

CHANGES BY 2013 LEGISLATION

Unless otherwise indicated, the effective date of the 2013 legislation is August 1, 2013

1. LOUISIANA CIVIL CODE

Article	Effect	Act No.	Sec.	Subject	Special eff. date
2041	Amended	88	1	Revocatory action; time for bringing action; cases of fraud	
3505	Added	88	1	Liberative prescription; acts extending	
3505.1	Added	88	1	Liberative prescription; formal requirements of extension	
3505.2	Added	88	1	Liberative prescription; commencement of period of extension	
3505.3	Added	88	1	Liberative prescription; effect of extension	
3505.4	Added	88	1	Liberative prescription; interruption or extension	

2. TITLE 9 OF THE REVISED STATUTES

Section	Effect	Act No.	Sec.	Subject	Special eff. date
9:154.2	Added	247	1	Uniform Unclaimed Property Act; tolls; Crescent City Connection; Geaux Pass accounts and deposits	6/12/13
9:171	Amended	247	2	Uniform Unclaimed Property Act; periods of limitations; federally insured financial institutions	
9:173	Amended	247	2	Uniform Unclaimed Property Act; retention of records federally insured financial institutions	
9:400	Amended	220	2	Parent and child; putative father registry; Department office name correction	6/11/13

v

CHANGES BY 2013 LEGISLATION

Section	Effect	Act No.	Sec.	Subject	Special eff. date
9:2621	Added	176	1	Louisiana Uniform Electronic Transactions Act; certification of electronic records	6/7/13
9:3198	Amended	369	1	Residential property disclosure; notification of proximity of certain salt domes	
9:3260.1	Added	354	1	Leases; lessee's right to notification of foreclosure action	
9:4802	Amended	357	1	Private Works Act; notice; privileges securing improvement; requirements of lessor of movables placed at site of immovable for use in a work	
9:4822	Amended	277	1	Private Works Act; preservation of claims and privileges; content of statement of claim or privilege	

PREFACE

This volume contains the official text of Title 9 of the Louisiana Revised Statutes of 1950, as revised and amended through the 2013 Regular Session of the Louisiana Legislature, with the addition of bracketed words to show the correct spelling or punctuation of what appear almost certainly to be clerical or typographical errors.

The editor wishes to thank Mr. Bradley Schwab, research assistant for the 2012 and 2013 academic years, the editorial staff of Thomson Reuters and, particularly, Ms. Kimberly Trtan for her active participation in the preparation, editing, and publication of this volume. Special thanks are also due to Mr. H. Mark Levy, Coordinator of Research and Revisor of Statutes, Louisiana State Law Institute, for his interest in this publication and Mr. James Carter, Assistant Coordinator of Research, for his cooperation and able assistance in carrying out the Revision of Title X, Book III, of the Louisiana Civil Code—Annuities.

A. N. Yiannopoulos

Baton Rouge, Louisiana
December 15, 2013

*

TABLE OF CONTENTS

Volume I

	Page
What is New in This Edition	III
Changes by 2013 Legislation	V
Preface	VII
1806 Manifesto	XVII
Historical Title Page	XXI
Governor Claiborne's Correspondence	XXIII
1823 Report of the Commissioners	XXV
Historical Title Page	XXXV
Historical Title Page	XXXVI
In Praise of the Civil Code by Justice Fenner and Mitchell Franklin	XXXVII
Foreword by Colonel Tucker	XXXIX
The Civil Codes of Louisiana	XLI
Numerical Analysis of the Civil Code	LXXI

CIVIL CODE OF LOUISIANA

Title

Preliminary Title	1

BOOK I
OF PERSONS

I.	Natural and Juridical Persons	7
II.	Domicile	10
III.	Absent Persons	12
IV.	Husband and Wife	17
V.	Divorce	24
VI.	Of Master and Servant [Repealed]	46
VII.	Parent and Child	46
VIII.	Of Minors, Of Their Tutorship and Emancipation	64
IX.	Persons Unable to Care for Their Persons or Property	76
X.	Of Corporations [Repealed]	80

BOOK II
THINGS AND THE DIFFERENT MODIFICATIONS OF OWNERSHIP

I.	Things	81
II.	Ownership	101
III.	Personal Servitudes	126
IV.	Predial Servitudes	179

TABLE OF CONTENTS

Title

V.	Building Restrictions	221
VI.	Boundaries	226
VII.	Ownership in Indivision	231

BOOK III
OF THE DIFFERENT MODES OF ACQUIRING THE OWNERSHIP OF THINGS

Preliminary Title—General Dispositions		239
I.	Of Successions	239
II.	Donations	298
III.	Obligations in General	362
IV.	Conventional Obligations or Contracts	418
V.	Obligations Arising Without Agreement	470
VI.	Matrimonial Regimes	482
VII.	Sale	516
VIII.	Exchange	563
IX.	Lease	565
X.	Annuities	604
XI.	Partnership	609
XII.	Loan	626
XIII.	Deposit and Sequestration	632
XIV.	Of Aleatory Contracts	639
XV.	Representation and Mandate	640
XVI.	Suretyship	652
XVII.	Compromise	664
XVIII.	Of Respite	667
XIX.	Of Arbitration	670
XX.	Of Pledge	674
XXI.	Of Privileges	682
XXII.	Mortgages	698
XXII-A.	Of Registry	717
XXIII.	Occupancy and Possession	727
XXIV.	Prescription	740
XXV.	Of the Signification of Sundry Terms of Law Employed in This Code	766

BOOK IV
CONFLICT OF LAWS

I.	General Provisions	769
II.	Status	773
III.	Marital Property	776
IV.	Successions	782
V.	Real Rights	789

TABLE OF CONTENTS

Title
VI.	Conventional Obligations	793
VII.	Delictual and Quasi–Delictual Obligations	798
VIII.	Liberative Prescription	808
	Index to Louisiana Civil Code	I–1

Volume II

What is New in This Edition	III
Changes by 2013 Legislation	V
Preface	VII
Revised Statutes Title 9 Numerical Analysis	XVII

APPENDIX

Appendix 1—Title 9, Revised Statutes	1
Appendix 2—Provisions of Civil Code Repealed by Revisions	545
Appendix 3—Civil Law Terms Found in Texts of the Louisiana Civil Code and in Revision Comments	553

TABLES

Table

1. Disposition 569
    1. Former Articles 1 to 23, and Revision of the Preliminary Title, Articles 1 to 15
    2. Former Articles 24 to 37, and Revision of Book I, Title I, Articles 24 to 31
    3. Former Articles 38 to 46, and Revision of Book I, Title II, Articles 38 to 46
    4. Former Articles 47 to 85, and Revision of Book I, Title III, Articles 47 to 59
    5. Former Articles 86 to 119, and Revision of Book I, Title IV, Chapters 1 to 5, Articles 86 to 101
    6. Former Articles 111 to 120, and Revision of Book I, Title V, Chapter 2, Section 1, Articles 111 to 117
    7. Former Articles 131 to 135, 138 to 145, and Revision of Book I, Title V, Chapters 1 and 2
    8. Former Article 178 to 211 and Revision of Book I, Title VII, Chapters 1 and 2
    9. Former Article 214 and Revision of Book I, Title VII, Chapter 4, Articles 212 to 214
    10. Former Articles 365 to 385, and Revision of Book I, Title VIII, Chapter 2, Articles 365 to 371
    11. Former Articles 389 to 426, and Revision of Book I, Title IX, Articles 389 to 399
    12. Former Articles 448 to 855, and Revision of Book II, Articles 448 to 796

TABLE OF CONTENTS

Table

13. Former Articles 870 to 933, and Revision of Book III, Preliminary Title and Title I, Chapters 1 through 3, Articles 870 to 902
14. Former Articles 934 to 1074, and Revision of Book III, Title I, Chapters 4, 5, and 6, Articles 934 to 968
15. Former Articles 1415 to 1466, and Revision of Book III, Title I, Chapter 13, Articles 1415 to 1429
16. Former Articles 1467 to 1469, and Revision of Book III, Title II, Chapter 1, Articles 1467 to 1469
17. Former Articles 1470 to 1492, and Revision of Book III, Title II, Chapter 2, Articles 1470 to 1483; Former Articles 1493 to 1518, and Revision of Book III, Tile II, Chapter 3, Articles 1493 to 1514
18. Former Articles 1523 to 1569, and Revision of Book III, Title II, Chapter 5, Articles 1526 to 1567
19. Former Articles 1570 to 1723, and Revision of Book III, Title II, Chapter 6, Articles 1570 to 1616
20. Former Articles 1734 to 1755, and Revision of Book III, Title II, Chapters 8 and 9, Articles 1734 to 1751
21. Former Articles 1756 to 2291, and Revision of Book III, Titles III and IV, Articles 1756 to 2057
22. Former Articles 2292 to 2313, and Revision of Book III, Title V, Articles 2292 to 2305
23. Former Articles 2325 to 2437, and Revision of Book III, Title VI, Articles 2325 to 2437
24. Former Articles 2438 to 2659, and Revision of Book III, Title VII, Articles 2438 to 2659
25. Former Articles 2660 to 2667, and Revision of Book III, Title VIII, Articles 2660 to 2667
26. Former Articles 2668 to 2744, and Revision of Book III, Title IX, Chapters 1 and 2, Articles 2668 to 2729
27. Former Articles 2778 to 2800, and Revision of Book III, Title X, Articles 2778 to 2791
28. Former Articles 2801 to 2890, and Revision of Book III, Title XI, Articles 2801 to 2848
29. Former Articles 2891 to 2925, and Revision of Book III, Title XII, Articles 2891 to 2913
30. Former Articles 2926 to 2981, and Revision of Book III, Title XIII, Articles 2926 to 2951
31. Former Articles 2985 to 3034, and Revision of Book III, Title XV, Articles 2985 to 3032
32. Former Articles 3035 to 3070, and Revision of Book III, Title XVI, Articles 3035 to 3070
33. Former Articles 3071 to 3083 and Revision of Book III, Title XVII
34. Former Articles 3278 to 3411, and Revision of Book III, Title XXII, Chapter 1, Articles 3278 to 3337 (1991 Revision)
35. Former Articles 3308 to 3310, 3314, 3321 to 3324, 3327 to 3336 and Revision of Title XXII (2005 Revision)

TABLE OF CONTENTS

Table

    36. Former Articles 3412 to 3554, and Revision of Book III, Titles XXIII and XXIV, Articles 3412 to 3504

2. Derivation 590

    1. Revision of the Preliminary Title, Articles 1 through 15, and Former Articles 1 to 23

    2. Revision of Book I, Title I, Articles 24 to 31, and Former Articles 24 to 37

    3. Revision of Book I, Title II, Articles 38 to 46, and Former Articles 38 to 46

    4. Revision of Book I, Title III, Articles 47 to 59, and Former Articles 47 to 85

    5. Revision of Book I, Title IV, Chapters 1 through 5, Articles 86 to 100, and Former Articles 86 to 119

    6. Revision of Book I, Title V, Chapter 2, Section 1, Articles 111 to 117 and Former Articles 111 to 120

    7. Revision of Book I, Title V, Chapters 1 and 2, Articles 102 to 105, 131 to 136, 141, 142, 151, 152, and Former Articles 131 to 158

    8. Revision of Book I, Title VII, Articles 184 to 198 and Former Articles 178 to 211

    9. Revision of Book I, Title VII, Chapter 4, Articles 212 to 214, and Former Article 214

    10. Revision of Book I, Title VIII, Chapter 2, Articles 365 to 371, and Former Articles 365 to 385

    11. Revision of Book I, Title IX, Articles 389 to 399 and Former Articles 389 to 426

    12. Revision of Book II, Articles 448 to 818, and Former Articles 448 to 855

    13. Revision of Book III, Preliminary Title and Title I, Chapters 1 through 3, Articles 870 to 902, and Former Articles 870 to 933

    14. Revision of Book III, Title I, Articles 934 to 968, and Former Articles 934 to 1074

    15. Revision of Book III, Title I, Articles 1415 to 1429, and Former Articles 1415 to 1466

    16. Revision of Book III, Title II, Chapter 1, Articles 1467 to 1469, and Former Articles 1467 to 1469

    17. Revision of Book III, Title II, Chapter 2, Articles 1470 to 1483, and Former Articles 1470 to 1492; Chapter 3, Articles 1493 to 1514 and Former Articles 1493 to 1518

    18. Revision of Book III, Title II, Chapter 5, Articles 1526 to 1567, and Former Articles 1523 to 1569

    19. Revision of Book III, Title II, Articles 1570 to 1616, and Former Articles 1570 to 1723

    20. Revision of Book III, Title II, Chapters 8 and 9, Articles 1734 to 1751 and Former Articles 1734 to 1755

    21. Revision of Book III, Titles III and IV, Articles 1756 to 2057, and Former Articles 1756 to 2291

TABLE OF CONTENTS

Table
  22. Revision of Book III, Title V, Articles 2292 to 2305, and Former Articles 2291 to 2313
  23. Revision of Book III, Title VI, Articles 2325 to 2437, and Former Articles 2325 to 2437
  24. Revision of Book III, Title VII, Articles 2438 to 2659, and Former Articles 2438 to 2659
  25. Revision of Book III, Title VIII, Articles 2660 to 2667, and Former Articles 2660 to 2667
  26. Revision of Book III, Title IX, Articles 2668 to 2729, and Former Articles 2668 to 2744
  27. Revision of Book III, Title X, Articles 2778 to 2791, and Former Articles 2778 to 2800
  28. Revision of Book III, Title XI, Articles 2801 to 2848, and Former Articles 2801 to 2890
  29. Revision of Book III, Title XII, Articles 2891 to 2913, and Former Articles 2891 to 2925
  30. Revision of Book III, Title XIII, Articles 2926 to 2951, and Former Articles 2926 to 2981
  31. Revision of Book III, Title XV, Articles 2985 to 3032, and Former Articles 2985 to 3034
  32. Revision of Book III, Title XVI, Articles 3035 to 3070, and Former Articles 3035 to 3070
  33. Revision of Book I, Title XVII, Articles 3071 to 3083 and Former Articles 3071 to 3083
  34. Revision of Book III, Title XXII, Articles 3278 to 3337, and Former Articles 3278 to 3411 (1991 Revision)
  35. Revision of Book III, Title XXII, Articles 3338 to 3368, and Former Articles 3308 to 3310, 3314, 3321 to 3324, 3327 to 3337 (2005 Revision)
  36. Revision of Book III, Title XXIII and Title XXIV, Articles 3412 to 3504, and Former Articles 3412 to 3554
  37. Book IV, Titles I–VIII, Articles 3515 to 3549
3. Revision 606
  1. Preliminary Title
  2. Book I, Title I
  3. Book I, Title II
  4. Book I, Title III
  5. Book I, Title IV
  6. Book I, Title V
  7. Book I, Title VII, Chapters 1, 2, 3, and 4
  8. Book I, Title IX
  9. Book II
  10. Book III, Preliminary Title, and Title I, Chapters 1 through 6 and 13
  11. Book III, Title II, Chapter 1
  12. Book III, Title II, Chapters 2, 3, 5, and 6
  13. Book III, Title II, Chapters 8 and 9
  14. Book III, Title III
  15. Book III, Title IV

TABLE OF CONTENTS

Table

    16. Book III, Title V

    17. Book III, Title VI

    18. Book III, Title VII

    19. Book III, Title VIII

    20. Book III, Title IX

    21. Book III, Title X

    22. Book III, Title XI

    23. Book III, Title XII

    24. Book III, Title XIII

    25. Book III, Title XV

    26. Book III, Title XVI

    27. Book III, Title XVII

    28. Book III, Title XXII

    29. Book III, Title XXIII

    30. Book III, Title XXIV

    31. Book IV

4. Change—Civil Code of 1870 Articles Amended, Revised, Repealed, Redesignated or Added 612

5. Concordance for the 1976–2013 Revision, the Civil Code of 1870, Civil Code of 1825, Projet, Civil Code of 1808, and Code Napoléon 624

Index to Title 9 of the Louisiana Revised Statutes I–1

*

REVISED STATUTES TITLE 9
NUMERICAL ANALYSIS

CIVIL CODE—ANCILLARIES

PRELIMINARY TITLE [BLANK]

CODE BOOK I—OF PERSONS

CODE TITLE I—NATURAL AND JURIDICAL PERSONS

CHAPTER 1. WOMEN

PART I. IN GENERAL

Section
51. Civil rights and duties.

PART II. MARRIED WOMEN

SUBPART A. EMANCIPATION AND POWERS

101. Emancipation from all disabilities and incapacities; obligations.
102. Suits, judicial proceedings, and judgments.
103. Binding themselves or disposing of or hypothecating property for benefit of husband or community; contracts with husband.
104. Repealed.
105. Laws relating to matrimonial community and separate property not affected.

CHAPTER 2. DEATH

Section
111. Definition of death.

CHAPTER 3. HUMAN EMBRYOS

Section
121. Human embryo; definition.
122. Uses of human embryo in vitro.
123. Capacity.
124. Legal status.
125. Separate entity.
126. Ownership.
127. Responsibility.
128. Qualifications.
129. Destruction.
130. Duties of donors.
131. Judicial standard.
132. Liability.
133. Inheritance rights.

CODE TITLE II—OF DOMICILE AND THE MANNER OF CHANGING THE SAME [BLANK]

CODE TITLE III—ABSENT PERSONS

CHAPTER 1. UNIFORM UNCLAIMED PROPERTY ACT

Section
151. Short title.
152. Uniformity of application and construction.
153. Definitions.
154. Presumptions of abandonment.
154.1. Compensation for expropriation; ownership; town of Berwick.
154.2. Crescent City Connection; Geaux Pass accounts and deposits; tolls; Geaux Pass Transition Fund; disposition.
155. Contents of safe deposit box or other safekeeping depository.
156. Rules for taking custody.
157. Dormancy charge.
158. Burden of proof as to property evidenced by record of check or draft.
159. Report of abandoned property.
160. Payment or delivery of abandoned property.
161. Notice and publication of lists of abandoned property.
162. Custody by state; recovery by holder; defense of holder.
163. Crediting of dividends, interest, and increments to owner's account.
164. Public sale of abandoned property.
165. Deposit of funds.
165.1. Bonds; unclaimed property bonds; completion of I-49.
165.2. Designates first I-49 unclaimed property bond project; "Alvin B. Kessler Memorial Highway".
166. Claim of another state to recover property.
167. Filing claim with administrator; handling of claims by administrator.
168. Action to establish claim.
169. Election to take payment or delivery.

XVII

REVISED STATUTES TITLE 9 NUMERICAL ANALYSIS

Section
170. Destruction or disposition of property having no substantial commercial value; immunity from liability.
171. Periods of limitation.
172. Requests for reports and examination of records.
173. Retention of records.
174. Enforcement.
175. Interstate agreements and cooperation; joint and reciprocal actions with other states; confidentiality.
176. Interest and penalties.
177. Agreement to locate property.
178. Foreign transactions.
179. Applicability of Chapter.
180. Rules.
181. Severability.
182 to 188. [Blank].

CHAPTER 2. DISPOSITION OF UNCLAIMED SPECIMENS BY TAXIDERMISTS

Section
191. Definition.
192. Disposition.

CHAPTER 3. THE CARE OF MINOR CHILDREN

Section
195. Provisional tutor upon death of mother.
196. Limited tutorship by nature.

CODE TITLE IV—HUSBAND AND WIFE

CHAPTER 1. MARRIAGE: GENERAL PRINCIPLES

PART I. OFFICIANTS

Section
201. Definition.
202. Authority to perform marriage ceremony.
202.1. [Blank].
203. Officiant; judges and justices of the peace.
204. Officiant other than judge; registration.
205. Officiant to require marriage license.
206 to 208. [Blank].

PART II. COLLATERAL RELATIONS

211. Relations of the fourth degree.
212 to 214. Repealed.

PART III. APPLICATION FOR MARRIAGE LICENSE

SUBPART A. IN GENERAL

221. Authority to issue marriage license.
222. Place of issuance.
223. Form.
224. Same; information required.
225. Same; attachments.

Section

SUBPART B. BIRTH CERTIFICATE

226. Certified copy of birth certificate.
227. Certified copy unavailable; other proof.
228. Same; court order waiving.

SUBPART C. MEDICAL CERTIFICATE [REPEALED]

229 to 231. Repealed.
232. Repealed.
233. Repealed.

SUBPART D. ISSUANCE AND TIME

234. Time and date; indication of covenant marriage.
235. Valid for thirty days.
236. Reissuance.

SUBPART E. SUMMARY OF MATRIMONIAL REGIMES LAWS

237. Information on matrimonial regime and covenant marriage laws; printed summary.

PART IV. DELAYS AND CEREMONY

SUBPART A. SEVENTY–TWO HOUR DELAY

241. Premature ceremony prohibited.
242. Waiver of delay.
243. Penalty.

SUBPART B. CEREMONY AND MARRIAGE CERTIFICATE

244. Witnesses required.
245. Marriage certificate.

PART V. RECORD KEEPING

251. Consolidated form.
252. Duplicate records of marriage licenses issued; preservation; filing of duplicate copy with state division of vital records; penalty for failure to file.
253. Disposition and recordation of marriage certificates.
254. Penalty for failure to file or complete marriage certificate.
255. Tabulation of marriage statistics; annual report.
256. Penalties.

PART VI. OPPOSITION TO MARRIAGE

261. Opposition to marriage.
262. Hearing on opposition.
263. Persons entitled to oppose.
264. [Blank].
265 to 270. [Blank].
271. [Blank].

REVISED STATUTES TITLE 9 NUMERICAL ANALYSIS

PART VII. COVENANT MARRIAGE

Section
- 272. Covenant marriage; intent; conditions to create.
- 273. Covenant marriage; contents of declaration of intent.
- 273.1. Declaration of intent; form.
- 274. Covenant marriage; other applicable rules.
- 275. Covenant marriage; applicability to already married couples.
- 275.1. Declaration of intent; married couples; form.
- 275.5. [Blank].
- 276. Limitation of liability; pastoral counselor.
- 277 to 280. [Blank].
- 281. Repealed.
- 282 to 284. [Blank].

CHAPTER 2. INCIDENTS AND EFFECTS OF MARRIAGE

PART I. IN GENERAL

Section
- 291. Suits between spouses.
- 292. Surname of married person.

PART II. SPECIAL INCIDENTS AND EFFECTS OF COVENANT MARRIAGE

- 293. Law applicable to spouses in covenant marriage.
- 294. Covenant spouses' love, respect, and community.
- 295. Covenant spouses' obligation to live together.
- 296. Right and duty of covenant spouses to manage household.
- 297. Decisionmaking in interest of family.
- 298. Obligations to children of the marriage.

CODE TITLE V—DIVORCE

CHAPTER 1. DIVORCE

PART I. IN GENERAL

Section
- 301. Court may authorize spouse of military personnel presumed dead to remarry; judgment dissolves marriage.
- 302. Divorce proceedings; hearings in chambers; procedure.
- 303. Income assignment; new orders; deviation.
- 304. Judgment of divorce; waiting periods; accrual of abandonment period.
- 304.1. Court costs; action to make child support executory.
- 305. Repealed.
- 306. Seminar for divorcing parents.
- 307. Divorce or separation from bed and board in a covenant marriage; exclusive grounds.

Section
- 308. Separation from bed and board in covenant marriage; suit against spouse; jurisdiction, procedure, and incidental relief.
- 309. Separation from bed and board in a covenant marriage; effects.
- 310. Retroactivity of spousal support order.
- 311. Modification of support; material change in circumstances; periodic review by DSS; medical support.
- 311.1. [Blank].
- 312. Child support; accounting; requirements.
- 313. Divorce and child support proceedings; special requirements.
- 314. Repealed.

PART I-A. CHILD SUPPORT

SUBPART A. GUIDELINES FOR DETERMINATION OF CHILD SUPPORT

- 315. Economic data and principles; definitions.
- 315.1. Rebuttable presumption; deviation from guidelines by court; stipulations by parties.
- 315.1.1. Determination of income; evidence.
- 315.2. Calculation of basic child support obligation.
- 315.3. Net child care costs; addition to basic obligation.
- 315.4. Health insurance premiums; addition to basic obligation.
- 315.5. Extraordinary medical expenses; addition to basic obligation.
- 315.6. Other extraordinary expenses; addition to basic obligation.
- 315.7. Deductions for income of the child.
- 315.8. Calculation of total child support obligation; worksheet.
- 315.9. Effect of shared custodial arrangement.
- 315.10. Effect of split custodial arrangement.
- 315.11. Voluntarily unemployed or underemployed party.
- 315.12. Second jobs and overtime.
- 315.12.1. [Blank].
- 315.13. Amounts not set forth in or exceeding schedule.
- 315.14. Mandatory minimum child support award.
- 315.15. No change in circumstances intended.
- 315.16. Review of guidelines.
- 315.17. Standard of appellate review.
- 315.18. Schedule; information.
- 315.19. Schedule for support.
- 315.20 Worksheets.

SUBPART B. OTHER CHILD SUPPORT PROVISIONS

- 315.21. Retroactivity of child support judgment.

XIX

REVISED STATUTES TITLE 9 NUMERICAL ANALYSIS

Section
- 315.22. Termination of child support upon majority or emancipation; exceptions.
- 315.23. Suspension or modification of child support obligation; secreting of child.
- 315.24. Child support enforcement; revocatory and oblique actions.
- 315.25. Consideration of custody or visitation matters.
- 315.26. Collection of past due child support.

SUBPART C. JUDICIAL SUSPENSION OF LICENSE FOR NONPAYMENT OF CHILD SUPPORT OR CONTEMPT OF COURT IN CHILD SUPPORT OR PATERNITY PROCEEDINGS

- 315.30. Family financial responsibility; purpose.
- 315.31. Definitions.
- 315.32. Order of suspension of license; noncompliance with support order; contempt of court.
- 315.33. Suspension of license; notice of suspension from licensing board; temporary license.
- 315.34. Subsequent compliance; order of compliance; order of partial compliance.
- 315.35. Reissuance of license.
- 315.36. Suspension of license; pattern of nonpayment.
- 315.37, 315.38. [Blank].

SUBPART D. ADMINISTRATIVE SUSPENSION OF CERTAIN LICENSES FOR NONPAYMENT OF CHILD SUPPORT

- 315.40. Definitions.
- 315.41. Notice of child support delinquency; suspension of license.
- 315.42. Objection to suspension of license.
- 315.43. Administrative hearing.
- 315.44. Certification of noncompliance.
- 315.45. Suspension of license; notice of suspension from licensing authority.
- 315.46. Subsequent compliance with support order; compliance and partial compliance releases.
- 315.47. Reissuance of license.
- 315.48. Repealed.

PART II. SPOUSAL SUPPORT

- 321. Retroactivity of judgment concerning spousal support.
- 322. Judgment or order for support not to be recorded.
- 323. Recordation of judgment or order for amount due.
- 324. Cancellation of record following payment.
- 325. Collection of past due spousal support.
- 326. Determination of income for spousal support; evidence.
- 327. Repealed.

Section

PART III. CHILD CUSTODY

SUBPART A. EVALUATION AND MEDIATION

- 331. Custody or visitation proceeding; evaluation by mental health professional.
- 331.1. Drug testing in custody or visitation proceeding.
- 332. Custody or visitation proceeding; mediation.
- 333. Duties of mediator.
- 334. Mediator qualifications.

SUBPART B. JOINT CUSTODY

- 335. Joint custody decree and implementation order.
- 336. Obligation of joint custodians to confer.
- 337. Repealed.

SUBPART C. PROTECTIVE AND REMEDIAL PROVISIONS

- 341. Restriction on visitation.
- 342. Bond to secure child custody or visitation order.
- 343. Return of child kept in violation of custody and visitation order.
- 344. Visitation rights of grandparents and siblings.
- 345. Appointment of attorney in child custody or visitation proceedings.
- 346. Action for failure to exercise or to allow visitation, custody or time rights pursuant to court-ordered schedule; judgment and awards.
- 347. Repealed.
- 348. Loss of visitation due to military service; compensatory visitation.

SUBPART D. ACCESS TO RECORDS

- 351. Access to records of child.

SUBPART E. RELOCATING A CHILD'S RESIDENCE

- 355.1. Definitions.
- 355.2. Applicability.
- 355.3. Persons authorized to propose relocation of principal residence of a child.
- 355.4. Notice of proposed relocation of child; court authorization to relocate.
- 355.5. Mailing notice of proposed relocation address.
- 355.6. Failure to give notice of relocation.
- 355.7. Objection to relocation of child.
- 355.8. Limitation on objection by non-parents.
- 355.9. Effect of objection or failure to object to notice of proposed relocation.
- 355.10. Burden of proof.
- 355.11. Court authorization to relocate.
- 355.12. Temporary order.

REVISED STATUTES TITLE 9 NUMERICAL ANALYSIS

Section
- 355.13. Priority for trial.
- 355.14. Factors to determine contested relocation.
- 355.15. Mental health expert; appointment.
- 355.16. Application of factors at initial hearing.
- 355.17. Modification of custody.
- 355.18. Posting security.
- 355.19. Sanctions for unwarranted or frivolous proposal to relocate child or objection to relocation.

SUBPART F. OTHER CHILD CUSTODY PROVISIONS

- 356. Consideration of child support.
- 357. Use of technology.

SUBPART G. PARENTING COORDINATOR

- 358.1. Appointment of parenting coordinator; term; costs.
- 358.2. No appointment in family violence cases.
- 358.3. Qualifications.
- 358.4. Authority and duties of parenting coordinator.
- 358.5. Testimony and report.
- 358.6. Communication with court.
- 358.7. Access to information.
- 358.8. Termination of appointment of parenting coordinator.
- 358.9. Limitation of liability.

SUBPART H. MILITARY PARENT AND CHILD CUSTODY PROTECTION ACT

- 359. Short title.
- 359.1. Definitions.
- 359.2. Final order; modification prohibited.
- 359.3. Material change in circumstances.
- 359.4. Temporary modification.
- 359.5. Termination of temporary modification order.
- 359.6. Delegation of visitation.
- 359.7. Testimony; evidence.
- 359.8. Lack of existing order of custody or visitation.
- 359.9. Duty to cooperate; disclosure of information.
- 359.10. Appointment of counsel.
- 359.11. Jurisdiction.
- 359.12. Attorney fees.
- 359.13. Applicability.

PART IV. POST–SEPARATION FAMILY VIOLENCE RELIEF ACT

- 361. Legislative findings.
- 362. Definitions.
- 363. Ordered mediation prohibited.
- 364. Child custody; visitation.
- 365. Qualification of mental health professional.
- 366. Injunctions.
- 367. Costs.

Section
- 368. Other remedies not affected.
- 369. Limitations.

PART V. INJUNCTIONS AND INCIDENTAL ORDERS

- 371. Injunction against alienation or encumbrance; spouse's right to demand.
- 372. Injunction against abuse; form; central Registry.
- 372.1. Injunction against harassment.
- 373. Removal of personal property.
- 374. Possession and use of family residence or community movables or immovables.
- 375. Award of attorney's fees.
- 376. Repealed.

CHAPTER 2. TRANSITIONAL PROVISIONS

PART I. DIVORCE

Section
- 381. Actions pending on effective date of divorce revision act; law governing.
- 382. Present effect of judgment of separation from bed and board.
- 383. Judgment of divorce after judgment of separation.
- 384. Effect of reconciliation on community.

PART II. CHILD CUSTODY AND SUPPORT

- 385. Actions pending on effective date of child custody and support revision act; law governing.

PART III. SPOUSAL SUPPORT

- 386. Actions pending on effective date of spousal support revision act; law governing.
- 387. Spousal support; period of grace after effective date of spousal support revision act.

CODE TITLE VI—OF MASTER AND SERVANT [BLANK]

CODE TITLE VII—PARENT AND CHILD

CHAPTER 1. CHILDREN

PART I. LEGITIMATION

Section
- 391. Repealed.
- 391.1. Child conceived after death of parent.
- 392. Acknowledgment; requirements; content.
- 392.1 Acknowledgment; obligation to support; visitation.
- 393. Full faith and credit of acknowledgments.
- 394. Evidence of hospital bills and tests in paternity action.
- 395. Paternity proceedings; special requirements.

REVISED STATUTES TITLE 9 NUMERICAL ANALYSIS

Section
395.1. Repealed.

PART I–A. BLOOD OR TISSUE SAMPLING FOR DETERMINATION OF PATERNITY

396. Authority for test; ex parte orders; use of results.
397. Selection of expert.
397.1. Compensation of expert witnesses and recovery of testing costs.
397.2. Chain of custody of blood or tissue samples.
397.3. Admissibility and effect of test results.
398. Applicability to criminal actions.
398.1. Award of attorney's fees in actions to establish paternity.
398.2. Petition for order to submit to blood or tissue tests prior to bringing filiation action.

PART I–B. ESTABLISHMENT OF CHILD SUPPORT IN PATERNITY PROCEEDING

399. Establishment of child support; interim order during proceeding; final order following judgment of paternity.
399.1. Dismissal of final order following judgment of paternity; time periods; procedure; effects.

PART I–C. PUTATIVE FATHER REGISTRY

400. Putative father registry.
400.1. Repealed.

PART II. FILIATION

401. Disavowal action under Civil Code Article 186; parties.
402. Effect of disavowal action on prior child support order.
403. Mother's contestation action; procedure.
404. Father's paternity action; time period; exception.
405. Legal effect of acknowledgment.
406. Revocation of authentic act; with and without cause; procedure.
407. Repealed.

PART III. ADOPTION

SUBPART A. MINORS UNDER SEVENTEEN [REPEALED]

421 to 441. Repealed.

SUBPART B. PERSONS OVER SEVENTEEN

461. Effect of adult adoption by stepparent.
462. Adult adoption; effective date of adoption.
463. Adult adoption; recordation.
464. Adult adoption; birth certificate.
465. Adult adoption; change of name.

Section

PART IV. NEGLECT OR ABUSE [REPEALED]

551 to 553. Repealed.

PART V. GENERAL PROVISIONS

571. General rule that child may not sue parent.
572. Uncontested paternity proceedings; proof by affidavit; adoption of court rules.
573, 574. Repealed.
575. Abused parent or grandparent; domestic abuse assistance.

CODE TITLE VIII—OF MINORS, OF THEIR TUTORSHIP AND EMANCIPATION

CHAPTER 1. TUTORSHIP

PART I. APPOINTMENT, RECOGNITION, OR CONFIRMATION

SUBPART A. IN GENERAL

Section
601. Parent's appointment of tutor when spouse insane.
602. Tutor, under tutor, curator, under curator; family meeting dispensed with.
603. Absentee minor or interdict not represented; special representation to effect sale.

PART II. MANAGEMENT AND DISPOSITION OF PROPERTY

SUBPART A. FAMILY MEETING DISPENSED WITH; PROCEDURE [REPEALED]

651 to 653. Repealed.

SUBPART B. PRIVATE SALE; PROCEDURE [REPEALED]

671 to 674. Repealed.
675. Validating provision.

SUBPART C. SALE TO EFFECT PARTITION; PROCEDURE [REPEALED]

691 to 693. Repealed.

SUBPART D. MINERAL LEASES AND CONTRACTS; PROCEDURE [REPEALED]

711 to 713. Repealed.

SUBPART E. MISCELLANEOUS PROVISIONS

731. Sale or lease of right of way.
732. Ratification of sale during minority of person afterwards interdicted.
733. Purchase of federal bonds and debentures by tutors and curators.
734. Investment of funds.
735 to 742. Repealed.

REVISED STATUTES TITLE 9 NUMERICAL ANALYSIS

Section

SUBPART F. UNIFORM TRANSFERS TO MINORS ACT

751.	Definitions.
752.	Scope.
753.	Nomination of custodian.
754.	Transfer by gift.
755.	Transfer authorized by will or trust.
756.	Other transfer by fiduciary.
757.	Transfer by obligor.
758.	Receipt for custodial property.
759.	Manner of creating custodial property and effecting transfer; designation of initial custodian; control.
760.	Single custodianship.
761.	Validity and effect of transfer.
762.	Care of custodial property.
763.	Powers of custodian.
764.	Use of custodial property.
765.	Expenses, compensation, and bond of custodian.
766.	Exemption of third person from liability.
767.	Liability to third persons.
768.	Renunciation, resignation, death, or removal of custodian; designation of successor custodian.
769.	Accounting by and liability of custodian.
770.	Termination of custodianship.
771.	Applicability.
772.	Effect on existing custodianship.
773.	Short title.

PART III. BOND OR SECURITY IN PLACE OF MORTGAGE [REPEALED]

801 to 804. Repealed by Acts 1960, No. 31, 7, eff. Jan. 1, 1961

PART IV. SMALL ESTATES [REPEALED]

821 to 823. Repealed by Acts 1960, No. 31, 7, eff. Jan. 1, 1961

PART V. MISCELLANEOUS PROVISIONS [REPEALED]

841. Repealed by Acts 1960, No. 31, 7, eff. Jan. 1, 1961
842. Repealed by Acts 1979, No. 709, 3, eff. Jan. 1, 1980

CHAPTER 2. EMANCIPATION

PART I. IN GENERAL

Section
901. Judgments and decrees of other states or District of Columbia given full faith and credit; procedure.

CHAPTER 3. PROVISIONAL CUSTODY BY MANDATE

Section
951. Provisional custody by mandate; conferring.
952. Duration of provisional custody; termination.
953. Functions, powers, and duties of agent.
954. Statutory form.

CHAPTER 4. NON-LEGAL CUSTODIAN

Section
975. Non-legal custodian; consent for certain services; affidavit, form of.

CODE TITLE IX—PERSONS UNABLE TO CARE FOR THEIR PERSONS OR PROPERTY

CHAPTER 1. INTERDICTION

PART I. INEBRIATES [REPEALED]

Section
1001 to 1004. Repealed.

PART II. MISCELLANEOUS PROVISIONS

1021. Interdiction of veterans in government institutions; manner of service.
1022. Authorization of curators to continue making donations to descendants.
1023. Donation by curator to charitable and nonprofit organizations; conditions; court approval.
1024. Donations by curator to collaterals; court authorization.
1025. Removal of a curator.
1026 to 1030. [Blank].

PART III. NONPROFIT CURATOR AND CONTINUING TUTOR PROGRAMS

1031. Appointment of nonprofit curatorship services.
1032. Powers, functions, and duties of curator and continuing tutor.
1033. Confidentiality; penalties.
1034. Fees and court costs.

CODE TITLE X—OF CORPORATIONS

CHAPTER 1. CORPORATIONS; UNAUTHORIZED CORPORATIONS; UNINCORPORATED NONPROFIT ASSOCIATIONS

Section
1051. Unauthorized corporations; unincorporated nonprofit associations; powers and liabilities.

REVISED STATUTES TITLE 9 NUMERICAL ANALYSIS

CODE BOOK II—THINGS AND THE DIFFERENT MODIFICATIONS OF OWNERSHIP

CODE TITLE I—THINGS

CHAPTER 1. IMMOVABLES

PART I. IN GENERAL

Section
- 1101. Ownership of waters and beds of bayous, rivers, streams, lagoons, lakes and bays.
- 1102. Batture in cities and towns; right of riparian owner.
- 1102.1. Rights of riparian landowners and their lessees.
- 1102.2. Rights and duties of riparian owners and their lessees; joint usage of certain riparian lands.
- 1103. Carbon sequestration on surface or water bottom.
- 1104. Riparian owners, use of surface water; fees prohibited; legislative finding and intent.
- 1105. Repealed.
- 1106. Storage tanks placed on land by one not owner of land as movable property.
- 1107. Public policy respecting ownership of navigable waters and beds thereof.
- 1108. Invalidity of patent or transfer purporting to include navigable waters and beds thereof.
- 1109. Statutes not to be construed as validating purported transfer of navigable waters or beds thereof.
- 1110. Ownership of land adjacent to False River.
- 1111. Exclusion of certain interests in trust from classification as immovable property.
- 1112. Immovable property held in common; agreement not to alienate, encumber or lease.
- 1113. Partition of immovable property; minority interest; private sale; appraisal

PART I–A. OWNERSHIP OF BEDS OF NON–NAVIGABLE WATERS

- 1115.1. Declaration of purpose.
- 1115.2. Ownership of inland non-navigable water bottoms.
- 1115.3. Interpretation of transfers.

PART II. LOUISIANA CONDOMINIUM ACT

SUBPART A. GENERAL PROVISIONS

- 1121. Repealed.
- 1121.101. Short title.
- 1121.102. Applicability.
- 1121.103. Definitions.
- 1121.104. Attorney fees.
- 1121.105. Separate taxation.

Section
- 1121.106. Applicability of ordinances, zoning, and building restrictions.
- 1121.107. Expropriation.
- 1121.108. Sale of unit; escrow accounts.
- 1121.109. [Blank].
- 1121.110. [Blank].
- 1121.111. [Blank].
- 1121.112. [Blank].
- 1121.113. [Blank].
- 1121.114. [Blank].
- 1122. Repealed.

SUBPART B. CREATION, ALTERATION, AND TERMINATION OF CONDOMINIUMS

- 1122.101. Creation of condominium regimes; condominium declaration; recordation.
- 1122.102. [Blank].
- 1122.103. Construction and validity of declaration and bylaws.
- 1122.104. Description of units.
- 1122.105. Contents of the condominium declaration.
- 1122.106. Reapportionment among unit owners of the percentage ownership interest in the common elements; percentages of sharing common expenses and common surplus; voting power in the association of unit owners.
- 1122.107. Condominiums established on leased land.
- 1122.108. Allocation of common element interest, votes, and common expense liabilities.
- 1122.109. [Blank].
- 1122.110. Plats and plans.
- 1122.111. [Blank].
- 1122.112. Termination; withdrawal.
- 1122.113. Alterations of units.
- 1122.114. Relocation of boundaries between adjoining units.
- 1122.115. Subdivision or conversion of units.
- 1122.116. [Blank].
- 1122.117. [Blank].
- 1122.118. [Blank].
- 1122.119. Amendment of declaration.
- 1122.120. [Blank].
- 1122.121. [Blank].
- 1123. Repealed.

SUBPART C. MANAGEMENT OF THE CONDOMINIUM

- 1123.101. Organization of unit owners' association.
- 1123.102. Powers of unit owners' association.
- 1123.103. [Blank].
- 1123.104. [Blank].
- 1123.105. Termination of contracts and leases of declarant.
- 1123.106. Bylaws.

REVISED STATUTES TITLE 9 NUMERICAL ANALYSIS

Section	
1123.107.	Upkeep of the condominium.
1123.108.	Association Records.
1123.109.	[Blank].
1123.110.	[Blank].
1123.111.	[Blank].
1123.112.	Insurance.
1123.113.	Fidelity bond or equivalent form of insurance required.
1123.114.	[Blank].
1123.115.	Privilege on immovables.
1123.115.1.	[Blank].
1123.116.	Privilege for utility assessments.
1123.117.	[Blank].
1124.	Repealed.

SUBPART D. PROTECTION OF PURCHASERS

1124.101.	Applicability; waiver.
1124.102.	Public offering statement; general provisions.
1124.103.	[Blank].
1124.104.	Public offering statement; conversion condominiums.
1124.105.	Public offering statement; condominium securities.
1124.106.	Purchaser's right to cancel.
1124.107.	Resales of units.
1124.108.	[Blank].
1124.109.	Privileges.
1124.110.	[Blank].
1124.111.	[Blank].
1124.112.	[Blank].
1124.113.	[Blank].
1124.114.	[Blank].
1124.115.	Compliance with condominium declaration, bylaws, and administrative rules and regulations.
1124.116.	[Blank].
1124.117.	[Blank].
1125 to 1131.	Repealed.

PART II–A. LOUISIANA TIMESHARING ACT

1131.1.	Short title.
1131.2.	Definitions.
1131.3.	Applicability and scope.
1131.4.	Creation of a timeshare plan.
1131.5.	Construction and validity of declaration.
1131.6.	Description of timeshare property.
1131.7.	Partition.
1131.8.	Termination.
1131.9.	Tax assessment and payment.
1131.9.1.	Developer supervisory duties.
1131.9.2.	Public offering statement.
1131.10.	Repealed.
1131.10.1.	Contracts for purchase of timeshare interests.
1131.11.	Public offering statement; when not required.

Section	
1131.12.	Regulations of timeshare advertising.
1131.13.	Cancellation.
1131.14.	Repealed.
1131.15.	Repealed.
1131.16.	Repealed.
1131.16.1.	Escrow of payments; escrow accounts; nondisturbance agreements; interests, liens, and encumbrances; alternative assurances.
1131.17.	Escrow account; establishment; claims for damages.
1131.18.	Resales of timeshares.
1131.19.	Privileges.
1131.20.	Management and operation of the timeshare plan.
1131.21.	Assessment for timeshare interest expenses.
1131.22.	Privilege for assessments.
1131.23.	Insurance.
1131.24.	Requirements where developer's interest in the timeshare property is a leasehold interest.
1131.25.	Remedies.
1131.26.	Louisiana Real Estate Recovery Fund; exemption.
1131.27.	Repealed.
1131.28.	Recordation.
1131.29.	Waiver prohibited.
1131.30.	Preservation of claims and defenses.
1132 to 1142.	Repealed.

PART II–B. LOUISIANA HOMEOWNERS ASSOCIATION ACT

SUBPART A. GENERAL PROVISIONS

1141.1.	Short title.
1141.2.	Definitions.
1141.3.	Applicability.

SUBPART B. BUILDING RESTRICTIONS

1141.4.	Building restrictions; matters of interpretation.
1141.5.	Building restrictions; generally, affirmative duty, and common areas.
1141.6.	Establishment, amendment, or termination of building restrictions.
1141.7.	Agreement of owners; voting.

SUBPART C. ENFORCEMENT

1141.8.	Community documents; force of law.
1141.9.	Homeowners association privilege.
1142.	Repealed.

PART III. PRIVILEGES ON IMMOVABLES FOR CHARGES OR DUES OF ASSOCIATION OF OWNERS

1145.	Association of owners; privilege; definition.
1146.	Privilege; sworn detailed statement; filing.

REVISED STATUTES TITLE 9 NUMERICAL ANALYSIS

Section
1147. Privilege; five year period.
1148. Privilege; ranking.

PART IV. MANUFACTURED HOME PROPERTY ACT

1149.1. Short title.
1149.2. Definitions.
1149.3. Classification.
1149.4. Immobilization.
1149.5. Security devices.
1149.6. Deimmobilization.
1149.7. Reference to prior law.

CODE TITLE II—OWNERSHIP
CHAPTER 1. ACCESSION

Section
1151. Change in ownership of land or water bottoms as result of action of navigable stream, bay, lake, sea, or arm of the sea; mineral leases.
1152. Grant of mineral servitude on lands acquired by the state from agencies or political subdivisions by subsidence or erosion.

CODE TITLE III—PERSONAL SERVITUDES
CHAPTER 1. FAMILY HOME

Section
1201. Family home.
1202. Form of security for legal usufruct of surviving spouse

CODE TITLE IV—PREDIAL SERVITUDES
CHAPTER 1. GENERAL PROVISIONS

Section
1251. Passage to or from waters or recreational sites; servitudes or rights of way or passage not acquired.
1252. Creation of real right for educational, charitable, or historic purposes.
1253. Public transportation servitude.
1254. Enclosed estate; right and servitude of passage on certain waterways.
1255. Solar collectors; right of use.

CHAPTER 2. LOUISIANA CONSERVATION SERVITUDE ACT

Section
1271. Short title.
1272. Definitions.
1273. Creation, conveyance, acceptance and duration.
1274. Judicial actions.
1275. Applicability.
1276. Uniformity of application and construction.

CODE TITLE V—BUILDING RESTRICTIONS [BLANK]
CODE TITLE VI—BOUNDARIES [BLANK]
CODE TITLE VII—OWNERSHIP IN INDIVISION [BLANK]

CODE BOOK III—OF THE DIFFERENT MODES OF ACQUIRING THE OWNERSHIP OF THINGS

CODE TITLE I—OF SUCCESSIONS
CHAPTER 1. SUCCESSIONS

Section
1400. [Blank].

PART I. PROCEDURE
SUBPART A. MISCELLANEOUS PROVISIONS

1421. Repealed.
1422. Certified copies of inventories in Parish of Orleans; admission as proof.
1423. Fees of experts and appraisers.
1424. Affixing of seals on succession property; preservation.
1425. Succession judgments affecting real property in Orleans; attorneys to file with assessor.
1426. Retirement plan; usufruct of surviving spouse.

SUBPART B. SMALL SUCCESSIONS

1431. Repealed.

SUBPART C. PRESUMPTIONS

1441. Presumption of death of military personnel.
1442. Succession of military personnel presumed dead.
1443. Proof of presumption of death of military personnel.

CHAPTER 2. ADMINISTRATION OF SUCCESSIONS

PART I. IN GENERAL
SUBPART A. PRIVATE SALE; PROCEDURE

Section
1451 to 1454. Repealed.
1454.1. Prescription against informalities of legal procedure.
1455. Repealed.

SUBPART B. DATION EN PAIEMENT; PROCEDURE [REDESIGNATED]

1471 to 1474. [Blank].

REVISED STATUTES TITLE 9 NUMERICAL ANALYSIS

Section

SUBPART C. MINERAL LEASES; PROCEDURE [REPEALED]

1491 to 1493. Repealed.

SUBPART D. MISCELLANEOUS PROVISIONS

1511. Option for servitudes or flowage rights; perfecting.
1512. Repealed.
1513. Payment to surviving spouse without court proceedings.
1514. Credit unions; payment to surviving spouse without court proceedings.
1515. Payment to surviving spouse or children of deceased; last wages due by employers.
1516. Transfer or payment of monetary proceeds of minerals or mineral products, rentals, accrued royalties, and other funds related to minerals or mineral contracts belonging or payable to deceased person; authority; discharge of holder.
1517. Certain succession representatives; power of attorney.

SUBPART E. PUBLIC SALE OF SUCCESSION PROPERTY

1521. Public sale of succession property for purposes other than payment of estate debts or legacies.

PART II. BURIAL OF UNCLAIMED BODIES; ADMINISTRATION OF SUCCESSIONS OF $500 OR LESS

1551. Burial of unclaimed bodies.
1552. Administration of successions of value of five hundred dollars or less.
1553 to 1557. Repealed.

PART III. PUBLIC ADMINISTRATORS

1581. Public administrators; appointment; terms; powers and duties.
1582. Bond.
1583. Administrators of intestate succession; when.
1584. Dative testamentary executors; when.
1585. Repealed.
1586. Curator of vacant succession; disposition of funds.
1587. Repealed.
1588. Power to represent state in court; costs.
1589. Compensation; employees; expense allowance; cost-of-living increases.
1590. Exemptions.

PART IV. STATE SUCCEEDING TO IMMOVABLE PROPERTY

1611. Retention instead of sale; administration.
1612. Compromise of rights and claims.

Section

1613. Disposition of funds; apportionment and allocation.
1614. Special counsel; patents for interests.
1615. Application of sections.

CHAPTER 3. PARTITIONS

Section

1701. Partition of land in which United States has servitude or real right.
1702. Agreement not to partition by persons holding property in common.

CODE TITLE II—OF DONATIONS INTER VIVOS (BETWEEN LIVING PERSONS) AND MORTIS CAUSA (IN PROSPECT OF DEATH)

CHAPTER 1. LOUISIANA TRUST CODE

PART I. PRELIMINARY PROVISIONS

Section

1721. Title.
1722. Express private trusts authorized; application of Code.
1723. Dispositions containing substitutions.
1724. Construction of Code.
1725. Definitions.

PART II. CREATION OF THE TRUST

SUBPART A. GENERAL PROVISIONS

1731. Trust defined.
1732. Inter vivos and testamentary trusts.
1733. Testamentary trust defined.
1734. Inter vivos trust defined.
1735. Gratuitous and onerous trusts.
1736. Conditions.
1737. Dispositions permitted.

SUBPART B. FORM

1751. Form of testamentary trust.
1752. Form of inter vivos trust.
1753. Technical language not required; interpretation of instrument.
1754. Incorporation by reference.
1755. Acceptance by trustee.

SUBPART C. THE SETTLOR

1761. Settlor defined.
1762. Number of settlors.
1763. Who may be settlor of inter vivos trust.
1764. Who may be settlor of testamentary trust.

SUBPART D. THE TRUST PROPERTY

1771. General rule.

SUBPART E. THE TRUSTEE

1781. Trustee defined.

REVISED STATUTES TITLE 9 NUMERICAL ANALYSIS

Section
- 1782. Number of trustees.
- 1783. Who may be trustee.
- 1784. Jurisdiction over the trustee.
- 1785. Manner in which trustee chosen.
- 1786. Provisional trustee.
- 1787. Provisional trustee; security.
- 1788. Resignation of trustee.
- 1789. Removal of trustee.
- 1790. Effect of resignation or removal of trustee.
- 1791. Appeal from judgment appointing or removing trustee.

SUBPART F. THE BENEFICIARY

- 1801. Beneficiary defined.
- 1802. Sufficiency of designation.
- 1803. Requirement that beneficiary be in being and ascertainable.
- 1804. Settlor as beneficiary.
- 1805. One or several beneficiaries; separate beneficiaries.
- 1806. Concurrent beneficiaries.
- 1807. Successive income beneficiaries.
- 1808. Acceptance by beneficiary.
- 1809. Representation upon predecease of named principal beneficiary.

SUBPART G. EFFECTIVE DATE OF CREATION

- 1821. When testamentary trust created.
- 1822. When inter vivos trust created.
- 1823. Retroactive nature of trustee's acceptance.
- 1824. Consequence of trustee's failure to accept.

SUBPART H. TERM OF THE TRUST

- 1831. Limitations upon stipulated term.
- 1832. Effect of stipulation of excessive term.
- 1833. Term in absence of stipulation.
- 1834. Exceptions.
- 1835. Definitions.

SUBPART I. THE LEGITIME IN TRUST

- 1841. General rule.
- 1842. Effect of improper stipulation.
- 1843. Stipulation restraining alienation.
- 1844. Legitime burdened with income interest or usufruct.
- 1845, 1846. Repealed.
- 1847. Invasion of principal; legitime affected.

SUBPART J. MARITAL PORTION IN TRUST

- 1851. General rule.
- 1852. Marital portion in full property.
- 1853. Marital portion in usufruct.
- 1854. Effect of improper stipulation.

SUBPART K. LIFE INSURANCE IN TRUST

- 1881. General rule.

Section

SUBPART L. CLASS TRUSTS

A. GENERAL RULES

- 1891. Creation of class.
- 1892. Class members.
- 1893. Income and principal designations.
- 1894. Representation.
- 1895. Effect of death of class member during the term of the trust.
- 1896. Closing of the class.
- 1897. Term; general rule.
- 1898. Effect of stipulation of excessive term.

B. RULES GOVERNING WHEN MEMBERS OF A CLASS ARE BENEFICIARIES OF INCOME ONLY

- 1899. Distribution of income; forced heirs.
- 1900. Absence of living members before class closes; treatment of income.
- 1901. Closing of class; members living; effect; termination.

C. RULES GOVERNING WHEN MEMBERS OF A CLASS ARE BENEFICIARIES OF PRINCIPAL ONLY

- 1902. Closing of class; continuation of trust.
- 1903. Class not closed; termination of income interests; effect.

D. RULES GOVERNING WHEN MEMBERS OF ONE CLASS ARE BENEFICIARIES OF INCOME AND MEMBERS OF A DIFFERENT CLASS ARE BENEFICIARIES OF PRINCIPAL

- 1904. General rule.

E. RULES GOVERNING WHEN THE MEMBERS OF THE SAME CLASS ARE BENEFICIARIES OF BOTH INCOME AND PRINCIPAL

- 1905. Interests in income.
- 1906. Term.

SUBPART M. TRUSTS FOR EMPLOYEES

- 1921. General rule.
- 1922. Term of trust.

SUBPART N. ADDITIONS TO THE TRUST PROPERTY

- 1931. General rule.
- 1932. Form.
- 1933. Rights of person who adds property.
- 1934. Modification, termination, rescission, or revocation of trust to which property added.
- 1935. When addition by donation inter vivos effected.

REVISED STATUTES TITLE 9 NUMERICAL ANALYSIS

Section
1936. When addition by donation mortis causa effected.
1937. Definition of annual exclusion.

SUBPART O. TRUSTS FOR MIXED PRIVATE AND CHARITABLE PURPOSES

1951. General rule.
1952. Invasion of principal in mixed trusts.
1953. Assignment of interest in trust and termination of trust for mixed private and charitable purposes.

SUBPART P. COMMUNITY PROPERTY IN TRUST

1955. Power to divide community interests.

PART III. THE INTEREST OF THE BENEFICIARY

SUBPART A. THE INTEREST OF THE INCOME BENEFICIARY

1961. Nature of the interest.
1962. Distribution of income.
1963. Permissible stipulations regulating distribution of income.
1964. Termination of income interest; undistributed income.
1965. Effect of termination of interest.

SUBPART B. THE INTEREST OF THE PRINCIPAL BENEFICIARY

1971. Time of acquisition of interest.
1972. Treatment of interest upon death of principal beneficiary.
1973. Shifting interest in principal.
1974. Substitute beneficiary's interest may be conditional.
1975. Requirement that substitute beneficiary be in being and ascertainable.
1976. Treatment upon death of substitute beneficiary whose interest is not conditioned on survival.
1977. Class as substitute beneficiary.
1978. Shifting interest in principal if beneficiary is descendant of settlor.
1979. Status of potential substitute principal beneficiary.

SUBPART C. REFUSAL

1981. General rule.
1982. Acceptance of interest in inter vivos trust by creditor; effect.
1983. Acceptance of interest in testamentary trust by creditor; effect.
1984. Rights of beneficiary who refuses interest in testamentary trust.
1985. Manner of refusal; effect of conditions.
1986. Retroactive nature of refusal.

Section
1987. Effect of refusal upon trustee.
1988. Partial refusal; refusal in another's favor.
1989. Refusal of addition to trust.
1990. Effect of refusal upon interest refused.

SUBPART D. ALIENATION BY THE BENEFICIARY

2001. General rule.
2002. Restraint upon alienation.
2003. Form.
2004. Seizure by creditor; general rule.
2005. Seizure by creditor; special claims.
2006. Exemption from seizure.
2007. Use of words "spendthrift trust".

SUBPART E. DEFERRED ASCERTAINMENT OF PRINCIPAL BENEFICIARIES OF REVOCABLE TRUSTS

2011. General rule.
2012. Provisional principal beneficiaries.
2013. Settlor as default principal beneficiary.
2014. Number of settlors allowed.

PART IV. MODIFICATION, TERMINATION, REVOCATION, AND RESCISSION OF THE TRUST

SUBPART A. MODIFICATION AND TERMINATION OF THE TRUST

2021. General rule; modification.
2022. Effect of reservation of right to revoke.
2023. Effect of reservation of unrestricted right to modify.
2024. Concurrence of settlors in modification.
2025. Delegation of right to terminate or to modify administrative provisions.
2026. Change of circumstances.
2027. Accomplishment of purposes becoming impossible or illegal.
2028. Concurrence of settlors in termination.
2029. Effect of termination.
2030. Combination and division of trusts.
2031. Delegation of right to amend.

SUBPART B. REVOCATION AND RESCISSION OF THE TRUST

2041. General rule; revocation.
2042. Effect of reservation of right to revoke.
2043. Revocation or rescission under general law.
2044. Concurrence of settlors in revocation; effect.
2045. Delegation of right to revoke.
2046. Effect of revocation or rescission.

SUBPART C. FORMAL REQUIREMENTS

2051. Form.

REVISED STATUTES TITLE 9 NUMERICAL ANALYSIS

Section

PART V. DUTIES AND POWERS OF THE TRUSTEE

SUBPART A. GENERAL DISPOSITIONS

2061. General rule.
2062. Limitation of duties by settlor.
2063. Relief from duties by beneficiary.
2064. Judicial permission or direction to deviate from administrative provisions of trust instrument.
2065. Judicial permission to deviate from administrative provisions of this code.
2066. Judicial permission or direction to deviate from investment provisions of trust instrument.
2067. Invasion of principal; action of court.
2068. Invasion of principal; provisions of trust instrument.
2069. Winding-up duty and powers of trustee.

SUBPART B. DUTIES OF THE TRUSTEE

2081. Breach of trust defined.
2082. Administration in interest of beneficiary; duty of impartiality.
2083. Dealing on own account.
2084. Loan by trustee to himself.
2085. Sale by trustee to himself.
2086. Self-dealing by corporate trustee.
2087. Delegating performance.
2088. Accounting.
2089. Furnishing of information.
2090. Prudent administration.
2091. Control and preservation of trust property.
2092. Recordation of instruments.
2093. Defense of actions.
2094. Separation of trust property.
2095. Bank deposits.
2096. Co-trustees.
2097. Serving as officer of legal entity in which trust funds invested.

SUBPART C. POWERS OF THE TRUSTEE

2111. Extent of powers.
2112. Attachment of powers to office.
2113. Exercise of powers by two trustees.
2114. Three or more trustees; exercise of powers.
2115. Control of discretionary powers.
2116. Repealed.
2117. Expenses that may be incurred.
2118. Lease of trust property.
2119. Sale of trust property.
2120. Mortgage or pledge; borrowing.
2121. Compromise, arbitration, and abandonment of claims.
2122. Powers with respect to shares of stock.
2123. Stock subscription; incorporator; organizer; partnership; joint venture; limited liability company; other legal entities.

Section

2124. Holding stock in name of nominee.
2124.1. [Blank].
2125. Contractual liability of trust.
2126. Tort liability of trust.
2127. Standard of care in investing and management.
2128. Common trust funds.
2129. Corporate trustees; deposit of securities in clearing corporation.
2130. Transfer of fiduciary accounts.
2131. Distributions.

SUBPART D. ALLOCATION TO INCOME AND PRINCIPAL

2141. General rule.
2142. Allocation to beneficiaries of income and principal.
2143. Allocation to beneficiaries of usufruct and naked ownership.
2144. Income and principal distinguished.
2145. When right to income arises.
2146. Apportionment of receipts when right to income arises.
2147. Apportionment of receipts when right to income ceases.
2148. Succession receipts.
2149. Corporate distributions.
2150. Bonds.
2151. Business operations.
2152. Proceeds of mineral interests.
2153. Timber.
2154. Other property subject to depletion.
2155. Underproductive property.
2156. Charges.
2157. Inventory value defined.

SUBPART E. POWER TO ADJUST

2158. Power to adjust.
2159. When the power to adjust is denied.
2160. Adjustment benefiting trustee.
2161. Adjustment beyond percentage limit.
2162. General provisions regarding court orders affecting adjustments.
2163. Remedies.

SUBPART F. THE TRUSTEE'S BOND

2171. Individual and corporate trustees.
2172. Security required by court.
2173. Increasing, diminishing, or dispensing with trustee's security by court.

PART VI. COMPENSATION AND INDEMNITY OF THE TRUSTEE

SUBPART A. COMPENSATION OF THE TRUSTEE

2181. General rule.

REVISED STATUTES TITLE 9 NUMERICAL ANALYSIS

Section
2182. Effect of breach of trust upon compensation.

SUBPART B. INDEMNITY OF THE TRUSTEE

2191. Indemnity for expenses properly incurred.
2192. Indemnity for expenses not properly incurred.
2193. Liability of beneficiary.
2194. Charge on beneficiary's interest.
2195. Charge on beneficiary's interest; advance or loan of trust money.
2196. Indemnity for tort liability.

PART VII. LIABILITIES OF THE TRUSTEE

2201. General rule.
2202. Loss not resulting from breach of trust.
2203. Balancing losses against gains.
2204. Liability of successor trustee.
2205. Liability of co-trustee.
2206. Relief from liability by trust instrument.
2207. Relief from liability by beneficiary.
2208. Relief from liability by proper court.

PART VIII. REMEDIES OF THE BENEFICIARY

2221. Remedies against trustee.
2222. Remedies against third persons.

PART IX. ACTIONS

2231. Causes of action; procedure.
2232. Injunctive relief.
2233. Instructions.
2234. Prescription.
2235. Proper court.

PART X. DESIGNATION OF ATTORNEY OR REGISTERED AGENT

2241. General rule.
2242. Registered agent for service of process.

PART XI. VALIDATION

2251. Severability of provisions of trust instrument.
2252. Saving clause.

CHAPTER 1–A. UNIFORM CUSTODIAL TRUST ACT

Section
2260.1. Definitions.
2260.2. Custodial trust; general.
2260.3. Custodial trustee for future payment or transfer.
2260.4. Form and effect of receipt and acceptance by custodial trustee; jurisdiction.
2260.5. Transfer to custodial trustee by fiduciary or obligor; facility of payment.

Section
2260.6. Multiple beneficiaries; separate custodial trusts; survivorship.
2260.7. General duties of custodial trustee.
2260.8. General powers of custodial trustee.
2260.9. Use of custodial trust property.
2260.10. Determination of incapacity; effect.
2260.11. Exemption of third person from liability.
2260.12. Liability to third person.
2260.13. Declination, resignation, incapacity, death, or removal of custodial trustee; designation of successor custodial trustee.
2260.14. Expenses, compensation, and bond of custodial trustee.
2260.15. Reporting and accounting by custodial trustee; determination of liability of custodial trustee.
2260.16. Limitations of action against custodial trustee.
2260.17. Distribution on termination.
2260.18. Methods and forms for creating custodial trusts.
2260.19. Applicable law.
2260.20. Uniformity of application and construction.
2260.21. Short title.

CHAPTER 1–B. FOREIGN TRUSTS

Section
2262.1. Definitions.
2262.2. Recordation of instruments.
2262.3. Authority to convey.
2262.4. Form.

CHAPTER 2. DONATIONS FOR CHARITABLE PURPOSE

PART I. TRUSTS FOR CHARITABLE PURPOSES

Section
2271. Charitable purpose; beneficiary; conditions.
2271.1. Renumbered.
2272. Trustees.
2273. Who may be trustee.
2274. Application of Louisiana Trust Code.
2275. Trust enforcement.
2276 to 2280. Repealed.
2281. Definition of terms used in R.S. 9:2282.
2282. Method of transfer of control of educational, charitable or religious trusts; grounds.
2283. Governing instrument; contents.

PART II. DURATION OF CHARITABLE TRUSTS

2290. Perpetual duration.
2291. Termination of small trust.
2292 to 2295. Repealed.

REVISED STATUTES TITLE 9 NUMERICAL ANALYSIS

Section

PART III. DONATIONS TO RELIGIOUS ORGANIZATIONS

2321. Title quieted and perfected by lapse of time.
2322. Rights in property after perfection of title.

PART IV. CY PRES

2331. Circumstances authorizing application of doctrine; jurisdiction; petitioners.
2332. Filing of petition; order; notice; service.
2333. Hearing, evidence.
2334. Judgment.
2335. Immunity of trustee acting pursuant to judgment.
2336. Appeal.
2337. Application of Part.

PART V. UNIFORM PRUDENT MANAGEMENT OF INSTITUTIONAL FUNDS ACT

2337.1. Short title.
2337.2. Definitions.
2337.3. Standard of conduct in managing and investing institutional fund.
2337.4. Appropriation for expenditure or accumulation of endowment funds; rules of construction.
2337.5. Delegation of management and investment functions.
2337.6. Release or modification of restrictions on management, investment, or purpose.
2337.7. Reviewing compliance.
2337.8. Application to existing institutional funds.
2337.9. Relation to Electronic Signatures in Global and National Commerce Act.
2337.10. Uniformity of application and construction.

CHAPTER 2-A. PUBLIC TRUSTS

Section

2341. Public trusts authorized; purposes.
2342. Mode of creation; acceptance of beneficial interest; amendments.
2343. Trustees; appointment; powers; duties; term of office; compliance with Public Bid Law, Public Meetings Law, and Public Records Law; legislative oversight.
2344. Liability of trustees and beneficiary.
2345. Termination of public trusts.
2346. Audits; supervision by legislative auditor; operating budget approval.
2347. Bonds of public trust.

CHAPTER 3. DONATIONS INTER VIVOS

PART I. MARRIED PERSON TO SPOUSE

Section

2351. Donation irrevocable; reservation of right to revoke.

Section

2352. Renouncing right to revoke.
2353. Civil Code Art. 156 unaffected.
2354. [Blank].

PART II. PARENT TO CHILD

2361. Parent's right of usufruct.

PART III. EFFECT ON DONEES AND THIRD PARTIES

2371. Recordation of donations inter vivos; effect.

PART IV. CALCULATION OF MASS, REDUCTION AND COLLATION

2372. Donations inter vivos; exempt from reduction and calculation of succession mass.
2373. Donations inter vivos to spouse of previous marriage; exemption from reduction and calculation of succession mass.

CHAPTER 4. DONATIONS MORTIS CAUSA

PART I. UNIFORM WILLS LAW

Section

2401. Will executed outside state.

PART II. UNIFORM PROBATE LAW

2421. Will probated outside state may be allowed and recorded.
2422. Filing of will and proceedings thereon.
2423. Admission to probate; force and effect.
2424. Probate of will operative under laws of state or country not requiring probate.
2425. Short title; interpretation.

PART II–A. ESTATE TAX APPORTIONMENT LAW

2431. Definitions.
2432. Apportionment of tax liability among persons interest in estate.
2433. No apportionment between principal and income beneficiaries of trust and between usufructuaries and naked owners.
2434. Fiduciary's right to withhold or recover proportion of tax attributable to persons interested in estate; security by person interested in estate for payment of tax.
2435. Allowance for exemptions, deductions, and credits.
2436. Action to recover amount of tax or deficiency from person interested in estate; time of filing; liability of fiduciary.
2437. Action by nonresident; reciprocity.
2438. Application of provisions.
2439. Estate tax marital deduction; formula qualifying.

REVISED STATUTES TITLE 9 NUMERICAL ANALYSIS

PART III. MISCELLANEOUS PROVISIONS

Section
- 2440. Continued validity of previously executed testaments.
- 2441. Duration of usufruct in previously executed testament.
- 2442 to 2445. Repealed.
- 2446. Will information registration.
- 2447. Fees.
- 2448. Repealed.
- 2449. Individual retirement accounts; payment of benefits.
- 2450. Succession representatives; liability for distributions.

CHAPTER 5. OF FORCED HEIRS

Section
- 2501. Repealed.
- 2502. Disinherison; retroactivity.
- 2503. Exercise of succession rights; remedial provisions.

CODE TITLE III—OBLIGATIONS IN GENERAL [BLANK]

CHAPTER 1. OF OBLIGATIONS DURING CERTAIN EMERGENCIES AND DISASTERS [BLANK]

Section
- 2551 to 2553. [Blank].
- 2554. [Blank].
- 2555 to 2565. [Blank].

CODE TITLE IV—CONVENTIONAL OBLIGATIONS OR CONTRACTS

CHAPTER 1. LOUISIANA UNIFORM ELECTRONIC TRANSACTIONS ACT

Section
- 2601. Short title.
- 2602. Definitions.
- 2603. Scope.
- 2603.1. Electronic applications for all warrants; signatures; electronic judicial record.s
- 2604. Prospective application; exemption from preemption.
- 2605. Use of electronic records and electronic signatures; variation by agreement.
- 2606. Construction and application.
- 2607. Legal recognition of electronic records, electronic signatures, and electronic contracts.
- 2608. Provision of information in writing; presentation of records.
- 2609. Attribution and effect of electronic record and electronic signature.
- 2610. Effect of change or error.
- 2611. Notarization and acknowledgment.
- 2612. Retention of electronic records; originals.
- 2613. Admissibility in evidence.

Section
- 2614. Automated transaction.
- 2615. Time and place of sending and receipt.
- 2616. Transferable records.
- 2617. Creation and retention of electronic records and conversion of written records by governmental agencies in this state
- 2618. Acceptance and distribution of electronic records by governmental agencies in this state.
- 2619. Interoperability
- 2620. Severability clause.
- 2621. Certification of electronic records.
- 2622 to 2674. Repealed.

CHAPTER 1–A. OF PRESUMPTIONS

Section
- 2701. Judgment in class action concludes all members of class adequately represented.

CHAPTER 1–B. REQUISITES FOR A VALID AGREEMENT

Section
- 2711. Definitions; withdrawal of consent to agreement.
- 2711.1. Consumer's right to cancel noncredit home solicitation sale.
- 2712. Prohibition; counterletters.
- 2713. Contract for surrogate motherhood; nullity.
- 2714. Chiropractors; certain contractual agreements invalid.
- 2715. Transfer of structured settlement rights.
- 2716. Contracts with automatic renewal clauses.
- 2717. Contracts against public policy.

CHAPTER 2. REGISTRY OF INSTRUMENTS AFFECTING IMMOVABLES

PART I. GENERAL PROVISIONS

Section
- 2721. Filing in office of parish recorder.
- 2721.1, 2722. Repealed.
- 2723. Operation.
- 2724. Liens or privileges not dependent upon recordation for existence or priority.
- 2725. Certificates of redemption under Federal Tax Lien Act; filing and recording.
- 2726. Attachment and recordation of plats; definitions; penalty.
- 2727. Attachment and recordation of plats; expropriations.
- 2728. Repealed.
- 2729. Presumption of uniform intent and ownership.

PART II. AGREEMENTS FOR EXPLOITATION OF MINERAL INTERESTS [REPEALED]

2731, 2732. [Blank].

REVISED STATUTES TITLE 9 NUMERICAL ANALYSIS

Section	
2733.	Repealed.

CHAPTER 2–A. REGISTRY UNDER COMMERCIAL LAWS

Section	
2736.	Limitation of liability.
2737.	Repealed.

CHAPTER 2–B. REGISTRY

Section	
2741.	Establishing authenticity.
2742.	Notice of lease; requirements and effect.
2743.	Certificate of encumbrances; procedure; content; liability.
2744.	Repealed.
2745.	Repealed.
2746 to 2757.	Repealed.
2758.	Notarial certified copy of lost original.
2759.	Lost original, certified copy from public record.

CHAPTER 3. PERFORMANCE OF OBLIGATIONS

Section	
2770, 2770.1.	[Blank].
2771.	Non-liability of contractor for destruction or deterioration of work.
2772.	Peremptive period for actions involving deficiencies in surveying, design, supervision, or construction of immovables or improvements thereon.
2773.	Limitations on the responsibility of agents, contractors and representatives.
2774.	Guarantees and warranties in construction specifications.
2775.	Construction projects; equipment and machinery contracts; certain provisions invalid.
2776.	Acceptance of funds to procure legal representation; accounting.
2777.	[Blank].
2778.	Public contracts; certain provisions invalid.
2779.	Construction contracts, subcontracts, and purchase orders; certain provisions invalid.
2780.	Certain indemnification agreements invalid.
2780.1.	Certain contract provisions invalid; motor carrier transportation contracts; construction contracts.
2781.	Open accounts; attorney fees; professional fees; open account owed to the state.
2781.1.	Real estate broker privilege on commercial real estate; definition; recordation; ranking; collection of open account.
2781.2.	Real estate appraiser privilege on commercial real estate; definition; recordation; ranking

Section	
2782.	Nonsufficient fund checks; damages, attorney fees.
2782.1.	Posting of nonsufficient fund checks.
2782.2.	Stop-payment order on checks; damages, attorney fees.
2783.	Public parking meters; public and private parking lots and garages.
2784.	Late payment by contractors to subcontractors and suppliers; penalties.

CHAPTER 4. DEATH OF A PARTY

Section	
2785.	Death of either party when obligation personal as to both.
2786.	Death of legatee before performance of personal obligation imposed on legacy.
2787.	Heritable obligations imposed on legacies.

CHAPTER 5. INTEREST UPON ACCRUED INTEREST; EXCEPTIONS [BLANK]

Section	
2788.	[Blank].

CHAPTER 6. INTEREST–BEARING DEPOSIT ACCOUNTS

Section	
2789.	Interest-bearing deposit accounts.
2789.1 to 2789.10.	[Blank].

CHAPTER 7. UNIFORM FRAUDULENT TRANSFER ACT [REPEALED]

Section	
2790.1. to 2790.4	Repealed.

CODE TITLE V—OF QUASI CONTRACTS, AND OF OFFENSES AND QUASI OFFENSES

CHAPTER 1. DISGORGEMENT

Section	
2790.5.	Legislative intent.
2790.6.	Disgorgement.

CHAPTER 2. OF OFFENSES AND QUASI OFFENSES

Section	
2791.	Liability of owner or occupant of property not used primarily for commercial recreational purposes.
2792.	Limitation of liability of member, director, trustee or officer of any public, charitable or nonprofit hospital, institution or organization.
2792.1.	Limitation of liability of director, officer, or trustee of nonprofit organization.
2792.1.	Limitation of liability of director, officer, or trustee of nonprofit organization.

REVISED STATUTES TITLE 9 NUMERICAL ANALYSIS

Section	
2792.2.	Limitation of liability of board member of downtown development district.
2792.3.	Limitation of liability of director, officer, trustee, or volunteer worker for incorporated and unincorporated nonprofit organizations; civic or historical purpose.
2792.4.	Limitation of liability of members of boards, commissions, or authorities of political subdivisions.
2792.5.	Limitation of liability of officer; federal or state credit union.
2792.6.	Limitation of liability of a trustee of a self-insurance trust fund.
2792.7.	Limitation of liability of director, officer, or trustee of certain homeowners associations.
2792.8.	Limitation of liability; employees of certain nonprofit organizations supervising or coordinating community services.
2792.9.	Limitation of liability of volunteers of area agencies on aging and voluntary councils on the aging; definitions; exceptions.
2793.	Gratuitous service at scene of emergency; limitation on liability.
2793.1.	Immunity from liability for public entities; fire department; law enforcement agency; public emergencies; F.B.I. agents.
2793.2.	Gratuitous emergency services rendered by American Red Cross volunteers; limitation of liability.
2793.3.	Gratuitous services rendered by the United Way; limitation of liability.
2793.4.	Gratuitous services rendered by Southern Mutual Help Association; limitation of liability.
2793.5.	Gratuitous services rendered by PRC Compassion, Inc.; limitation of liability.
2793.6.	Gratuitous services rendered by Catholic charities; limitation of liability.
2793.7.	Gratuitous services rendered by the Louisiana Girl Scout Councils; limitation of liability.
2793.8.	Gratuitous services rendered by National Voluntary Organizations Active in Disaster; limitation of liability.
2793.9.	Gratuitous services rendered by religious organizations; limitation of liability.
2794.	Physicians, dentists, optometrists, and chiropractic physicians; malpractice; burden of proof; jury charge; physician witness expert qualification.
2795.	Limitation of liability of landowner of property used for recreational purposes; property owned by the Department of Wildlife and Fisheries; parks owned by public entities.
2795.1.	Limitation of liability of farm animal activity sponsor or professional; exceptions; required warning.
2795.2.	Limitation of liability for the Audubon Commission; the city of New Orleans; other entities operating facilities of the Audubon Commission; exceptions; required warning.
2795.3.	Limitation of liability of equine activity sponsor; exceptions; required warning
2795.4.	Limitation of liability; motorized off-road vehicle activities; definitions; exceptions; required warning.
2795.5.	Limitation of liability; agritourism activities; definitions; exceptions; required warning.
2796.	Limitation of liability for loss connected with Mardi Gras parades and festivities; fair and festival parades.
2796.1.	Limitation of liability for loss connected with St. Patrick's Day parades or any ethnic parade.
2796.2.	Limitation of liability for loss connected with festivals, programs, or activities sponsored by an animal sanctuary
2796.3.	Limitation for loss related to bonfire presentations on the Mississippi River levee.
2797.	Users of blood or tissue; a medical service.
2797.1.	Certified, nonprofit poison control centers; legislative findings; limitation of liability.
2798.	Limitation of liability of a volunteer athletic coach, manager, team volunteer health care provider, or official; definitions.
2798.1.	Policymaking or discretionary acts or omissions of public entities or their officers or employees.
2798.2.	Limitation of liability for school volunteers.
2798.3.	Limitation of liability for school systems.
2798.4.	Immunity from liability; injuries sustained by persons driving under the influence of alcoholic beverages or drugs.
2798.5.	Limitation of liability; Louisiana Emergency Response Network.
2799.	Limitation of liability for damages from donated food.
2799.1.	Civil liability for theft of goods from merchant.
2799.2.	Institutional vandalism; civil damages.

REVISED STATUTES TITLE 9 NUMERICAL ANALYSIS

Section	
2799.3.	Limitation of liability of restaurants, schools, churches, civic organizations, and certain food donors for damages from donated food.
2799.4.	Liability for unauthorized release of certain animals, birds, or aquatic species.
2799.5.	Limitation of liability for gratuitous service by a health care provider in a community health care clinic or community pharmacy.
2799.6.	Limitation of liability for damages from long-term consumption of food and nonalcoholic beverages.
2800.	Limitation of liability for public bodies.
2800.1.	Limitation of liability for loss connected with sale, serving, or furnishing of alcoholic beverages.
2800.2.	Psychologist, psychiatrist, marriage and family therapist, licensed professional counselor, and social worker; limitation of liability.
2800.3.	Limitation of liability of persons designing, supervising or performing hazardous waste mitigation, abatement, or cleanup and asbestos removal, abatement, or cleanup services.
2800.4.	Limitation of liability of owner of farm or forest land; owner of oil, gas, or mineral property.
2800.5.	Immunity from liability for owners of block safe-houses.
2800.6.	Burden of proof in claims against merchants.
2800.7.	Repealed.
2800.9.	Action against a person for abuse of a minor.
2800.10.	Immunity from liability for injuries sustained while committing a felony offense.
2800.11.	Limitation of liability; municipal or parish airport authority; parked aircraft.
2800.12.	Liability for termination of a pregnancy.
2800.13.	Violation of transportation statute or regulation; determination of causation; evidence.
2800.14.	Limitation of liability for damages to oyster leases.
2800.15.	Limitation of liability for commercial and marine contractors, architects, and engineers, and persons licensed by the Louisiana Manufactured Housing Commission; mold and mold damage.
2800.16.	Limitation of liability; Louisiana Public Defender Board members.
2800.17.	Liability for the diminution in the value of a damaged vehicle.

Section	
2800.18.	Limitation of liability for volunteer medical transportation pilots.
2800.19.	Limitation of liability for used force in defense of certain crimes.
2800.20.	Limitation of liability for a nonprofit health care quality improvement corporation; health care providers; health plans; reporting and disclosure of information.
2800.21.	Limitation of liability for curators and undercurators; acts of interdicts.
2800.22.	Limitation of liability for use of school facilities.

CHAPTER 3. LOUISIANA PRODUCTS LIABILITY ACT

Section	
2800.51.	Short title.
2800.52.	Scope of this Chapter.
2800.53.	Definitions.
2800.54.	Manufacturer responsibility and burden of proof.
2800.55.	Unreasonably dangerous in construction or composition.
2800.56.	Unreasonably dangerous in design.
2800.57.	Unreasonably dangerous because of inadequate warning.
2800.58.	Unreasonably dangerous because of nonconformity to express warranty.
2800.59.	Manufacturer knowledge, design feasibility and burden of proof.
2800.60.	Liability of manufacturers and sellers of firearms.

CHAPTER 4. LOUISIANA DRUG DEALER LIABILITY ACT

Section	
2800.61.	Title; legislative intent.
2800.62.	Definitions.
2800.63.	Action for damages by persons other than the individual user.
2800.64.	Action by individual users.
2800.65.	Third parties not liable; nonassignment of cause of action.
2800.66.	Level of offense; amount of liability.
2800.67.	Joinder of actions.
2800.68.	Comparative fault.
2800.69.	Contribution by tortfeasors.
2800.70.	Proof of liability.
2800.71.	Defense; exclusion.
2800.72.	Writ of attachment.
2800.73.	Prescription.
2800.74.	Stay of action by governmental entity.
2800.75.	Actions between spouses.
2800.76.	Exemplary damages.

REVISED STATUTES TITLE 9 NUMERICAL ANALYSIS

CODE TITLE VI—MATRIMONIAL REGIMES

CHAPTER 1. PARTITION OF COMMUNITY PROPERTY

Section
2801. Partition of community property and settlement of claims arising from matrimonial regimes and co-ownership of former community property.
2801.1. Community property; allocation and assignment of ownership.
2801.2. Community property; valuation of goodwill.
2802. Rendition of judgment of partition; prerequisite.
2803, 2804. Repealed.
2805 to 2820. [Blank].
2821, 2822. Repealed.

CODE TITLE VII—SALE

CHAPTER 1. SALES IN GENERAL

PART I. RESEARCH CERTIFICATES

SUBPART A. TAX CERTIFICATES; NEW ORLEANS EXCEPTED

Section
2901. Payment of taxes prior to transfer of real property.
2902. Receipt or certificate of collector.
2903. Certificate annexed to act; evidence of payment; officer exonerated for nonpayment.
2904. Repealed.

SUBPART B. TAX, LOCAL IMPROVEMENT ASSESSMENT, AND NONALIENATION CERTIFICATES; NEW ORLEANS

2921. Payment of taxes and past due charges for local improvement assessments prior to transfer of real property.
2922. Receipt or certificate of collector.
2923. Content of certificate.
2924. Certificate annexed to act; evidence of payment; officer exonerated for nonpayment.
2925. Assumption by transferee of taxes for current year.
2926. Assumption by transferee of local improvement assessment charges maturing in future.
2927. Penalty for violation; act prima facie proof.
2928. Nonalienation certificate; penalty for violation.

CHAPTER 2. CONVENTIONAL SALES

PART I. BOND FOR DEED CONTRACTS

Section
2941. "Bond for deed" defined.

Section
2941.1. Recordation; subsequent filings; interest prohibited; cancellation of mortgage records.
2942. Unlawful to sell encumbered real property by bond for deed without guarantee to release on payment.
2943. Method of payment.
2944. Timely payment of installments precludes foreclosure; change of description upon foreclosure.
2945. Cancellation of bond for deed upon default.
2946. Unlawful to require mortgage notes when property encumbered; act of sale.
2947. Penalty for violations.
2948. Bond for deed buyer deemed owner for purposes of homestead exemption.
2949. [Blank].

PART II. SALES OF MOTOR VEHICLE DEALERSHIPS

2961. Limited availability of revocatory action.
2962 to 2968. Repealed.

PART III. TRANSFER OF LANDS FRONTING WATERWAYS, HIGHWAYS, ETC.

2971. Presumption of grant of all interest; exceptions.
2972. Nature of Part.
2973. Preservation of rights.

PART IV. TRANSFER OF LANDS ABUTTING ABANDONED ROADS, STREETS OR ALLEYS

2981. Presumption of grant of interest in abandoned road.
2982. Part remedial.
2983. Preservation of rights.
2984. Construction.
2985 to 2987. [Blank].

PART V. DUAL OR FRAUDULENT CONTRACTS

2989. Dual contracts; definition; violations; penalties.

CHAPTER 3. JUDICIAL SALES

PART I. IN GENERAL

Section
3001. Persons authorized to make judicial sales.
3002. Sales on credit; notes; security.
3003. Notes or bonds to be identified with sales.

CHAPTER 4. ASSIGNMENT OR TRANSFER OF CREDITS OR OTHER INCORPOREAL RIGHTS

PART I. IN GENERAL

Section
3051. Transfer of claims for collection.

REVISED STATUTES TITLE 9 NUMERICAL ANALYSIS

Section

PART II. LOUISIANA ASSIGNMENT OF ACCOUNTS RECEIVABLE ACT [REPEALED]

3101 to 3112. Repealed.

PART III. ASSIGNMENT OF PROCEEDS OF CROP FINANCING

3121. Crop financing; assignment of interest by agricultural producer.

PART IV. LOUISIANA EXCHANGE SALE OF RECEIVABLES ACT [BLANK]

CHAPTER 4–A. CORPOREAL IMMOVABLES

Section
3131. Legislative intent.
3131.1. [Blank].
to
3131.9.
3132. Definitions.
3133. Private transfer fee; prohibition.
3134. Violations; liability.
3135. Disclosure.
3136. Existing transfer fee obligations; notice requirements.

CHAPTER 4–B. LOUISIANA EXCHANGE SALE OF RECEIVABLES ACT

Section
3137.1. Short title.
3137.2. Legislative intent.
3137.3. Definitions.
3137.4. Scope.
3137.5. True sales of receivables; not subject to recharacterization; simulation articles not applicable.
3137.6. Binding effectiveness of Louisiana law.
3137.7. Buyer ownership rights; evidence of ownership.
3137.8. Relationship to the UCC.
3137.9. Prohibition of actions.

CHAPTER 5. NEW HOME WARRANTY ACT

Section
3141. Purpose.
3142. Short title.
3143. Definitions.
3144. Warranties; exclusions.
3145. Required notice.
3146. Peremption.
3147. Insurance.
3148. Transfer of warranty and insurance.
3149. Violations; limitations.
3150. Exclusiveness.

CHAPTER 6. AUCTION SALES, JUDICIAL SALES, AND EXPROPRIATION

PART I. AUCTION SALES

Section
3151. Sale by auction, definition.
3152. Voluntary or forced sale.
3153. Auction sale by officers of justice.
3154. General rules governing sales by auction.
3155. Sale through public officer.
3156. Announcement of conditions of sale and demand for bids.
3157. Adjudication to highest bidder.
3158. Adjudication as completion of sale.
3159. Payment of price before delivery.
3160. Sale of immovable, retention of price until execution of act.
3161. Resale for non-compliance with bid; adjudicatee's liability for deficiency.
3162. Resale, bid by first adjudicatee prohibited.
3163. Rejection of indorser of purchase price notes, effect on adjudication.
3164. Liability of seller refusing to accept solvent indorser.
3165. Liability for unauthorized bidding in name of another.

PART II. JUDICIAL SALES

SUBPART A. IN GENERAL

3166. Kinds of judicial sales.
3167. General rules for judicial sales.

SUBPART B. SEIZURE OR EXECUTION

3168. Execution sale, persons authorized to make.
3169. Rescission for fraud or nullity; redhibition not permitted.
3170. Rights acquired at execution sale.
3171. Rights of buyer in case of eviction.

SUBPART C. SUCCESSION PROPERTY

3172. Authority to order succession sale; persons authorized to sell.
3173. Transfer of title.
3174. Warranties.
3175. Purchase of property by heirs of succession.

PART III. EXPROPRIATION

3176 to 3191. Repealed.
3191.1. Thirty-year prescription; return of expropriated residential property.

CHAPTER 7. RELATIONSHIP BETWEEN THE CIVIL CODE TITLE ON SALE AND THE COMMERCIAL LAWS

Section
3192. Rule governing conflict between sale and commercial laws.

REVISED STATUTES TITLE 9 NUMERICAL ANALYSIS

CHAPTER 8. RESIDENTIAL PROPERTY DISCLOSURE

Section
- 3195. [Blank].
- 3196. Definitions.
- 3197. Applicability; exemptions.
- 3198. Duties of the seller; delivery of property disclosure document; termination of real estate contract; information contained in document and inaccuracies; required disclosure of information relative to homeowners' associations; liability of seller.
- 3198.1. Duties of governmental entities; contaminated property.
- 3199. Duty of real estate licensees; liability.
- 3200. Other statutory disclosure obligations.

CODE TITLE VIII—OF EXCHANGE [BLANK]

CODE TITLE IX—OF LEASE

CHAPTER 1. LEASES

PART I. LIABILITY FOR DAMAGES

Section
- 3201. Abandonment or failure to cultivate land.
- 3202. Assisting and enticing lessee to violate lease.
- 3203. Refusal to permit lessee to occupy or cultivate property.
- 3204. Lessor's part of crop considered his property; disposition; penalty.

PART II. LIABILITY FOR INJURIES

- 3221. Assumption of responsibility by lessee; liability of owner.

PART III. LESSOR'S PRIVILEGE

- 3241. Limitation on lessor's privilege upon failure or death of lessee.

PART IV. LESSEE'S DEPOSIT

- 3251. Lessee's deposit to secure lease; retention by lessor; conveyance of leased premises; itemized statement by lessor.
- 3252. Damages; venue.
- 3253. Costs and attorney's fees.
- 3254. Waiver of tenant's rights prohibited.

PART V. LESSORS' RIGHTS

- 3258. Lessor's right to own, control, use, enjoy, protect and dispose of property and things.
- 3259. Unpaid rent; attorney fees.
- 3259.1. Unpaid rent; mobile homes or manufactured housing; notification by lessor.
- 3259.2. Application for or receipt of government funds not a defense to action to evict.

PART VI. OBLIGATIONS AND RIGHTS OF THE LESSEE

Section
- 3260. Premises rendered uninhabitable; mitigation of damages.
- 3260.1. Lessee's right to notification of foreclosure action.
- 3261. Rights of military personnel to terminate lease.

CHAPTER 2. LEASES OF MOVABLES

Section
- 3262 to 3272. Repealed.

PART I. IN GENERAL

- 3301. Short title.
- 3302. Declaration of policy.
- 3303. Scope.
- 3304. Exclusions.
- 3305. Waiver; agreement to forego rights.
- 3306. Definitions.
- 3307. Terms.
- 3308. Construction against implicit repeal.

PART II. CIVIL CODE

- 3309. True leases.
- 3310. Financed leases.
- 3310.1. Constructive delivery and possession in sale/lease-back situations.

PART III. CHARGES

- 3311. Interest rate charges; true leases.
- 3312. Interest rate charges; financed leases.
- 3313. Additional lease related charges.
- 3314. Late charges.
- 3315. Deferral charges.
- 3316. Early termination charges.
- 3317. End of lease charges.

PART IV. REMEDIES FOLLOWING LESSEE'S DEFAULT

- 3318. Options of lessor following lessee's default.
- 3319. Accelerated rental payments.
- 3320. Cancellation of lease following lessee's default.
- 3321. Surrender of leased property after notice.
- 3322. Summary proceeding for surrender of property; rule to show cause; judgment.
- 3323. Appeal from judgment on rule.
- 3324. Ordinary proceedings in addition to summary proceedings.
- 3325. Recovery of liquidated damages.
- 3326. Sequestration in ordinary proceedings.
- 3327. Release to lessee of sequestered property.
- 3328. Release of sequestered property to lessor.
- 3329. Prohibition against self-help repossession.
- 3330. Lessor's right to protect and preserve leased property.

REVISED STATUTES TITLE 9 NUMERICAL ANALYSIS

PART V. INSURANCE

Section
- 3331. Requirement of insurance.
- 3332. Credit life and credit health and accident insurance.
- 3333. Property insurance.
- 3334. Choice of insurer.
- 3335. Limitations on insurance rates; contract requirements.
- 3336. Conditions applying to insurance provided by the lessor.
- 3337. Cancellation of insurance; refund or credit upon cancellation.
- 3338. Gain from insurance.

PART VI. MISCELLANEOUS

- 3339. Referrals.
- 3340. Unauthorized collection practices.
- 3341. Violations.
- 3342. Recordation of leases of movables.

CHAPTER 3. RENTAL–PURCHASE AGREEMENTS

Section
- 3351. Short title.
- 3352. Definitions.
- 3353. Inapplicability of other laws; exempted transactions.
- 3354. General requirements of disclosure.
- 3355. Disclosures.
- 3356. Prohibited practices.
- 3357. Reinstatement.
- 3358. Receipts and accounts.
- 3359. Renegotiations and extensions.
- 3360. Advertising.
- 3361. Enforcement; penalties.
- 3362. Taxes.

CHAPTER 4. SALE/LEASE–BACK COMMERCIAL TRANSACTIONS

Section
- 3370. [Blank].
- 3371. Validity of sale/lease-back commercial transactions
- 3372. Sale/lease-back defined.

CHAPTER 5. REMOVAL AND PRESERVATION OF PROPERTY DURING EMERGENCIES AND DISASTERS [TERMINATED]

Section
- 3391. Terminated.

CODE TITLE X—OF RENTS AND ANNUITIES [BLANK]

CODE TITLE XI—PARTNERSHIP

CHAPTER 1. CENTRAL REGISTRY FOR CONTRACTS OF PARTNERSHIP

Section
- 3401. Central registry; creation.
- 3402. Filing.
- 3403. Contract of partnership; required content.
- 3404. Contract amendment.
- 3405. Registration; endorsement; issuance of certificate; effect.
- 3406. Recorder of mortgages; filings.
- 3407. Delivery in advance of effective date.
- 3408. Filing within five days of execution; effect.
- 3409. Annual report.
- 3410. Filing and copying fees.

CHAPTER 2. QUALIFICATION OF FOREIGN PARTNERSHIPS

Section
- 3421. Foreign partnership; definition.
- 3422. Registration.
- 3423. Ownership of immovable property; limitation of liability.
- 3424. Service of process.
- 3425. Effect of registry.
- 3426. Amendment of statement.
- 3427. Termination.
- 3428. Annual report.

CHAPTER 3. REGISTERED LIMITED LIABILITY PARTNERSHIPS

Section
- 3431. Nature of partner's liability in ordinary partnership and in registered limited liability partnership.
- 3432. Registered limited liability partnerships.
- 3433. Name of registered limited liability partnership.
- 3434. Restrictions on distributions.
- 3435. Provisions applicable to registered limited liability partnerships.

CHAPTER 4. MERGER OR CONSOLIDATION

Section
- 3441. Terms defined.
- 3442. Merger or consolidation.
- 3443. Agreement of merger or consolidation.
- 3444. Approval of merger or consolidation.
- 3445. Certificate of merger or consolidation.
- 3446. Effects of merger or consolidation.
- 3447. Merger or consolidation with foreign entity.

CODE TITLE XII—OF LOAN

CHAPTER 1. INTEREST

PART I. IN GENERAL

Section
- 3500. Rates of legal and conventional interest; usury.
- 3501. Forfeiture of interest.
- 3502. Statement of policy.

REVISED STATUTES TITLE 9 NUMERICAL ANALYSIS

Section	
3503.	Maximum rate of conventional interest on certain loans.
3504.	Certain types of transactions exempt from the application of the laws on usury and interest upon interest; adjustable rate mortgage loan.
3505.	Items or charges not considered interest.
3506.	Application.
3506.1.	Time for accrual of interest; penalties.
3506.2.	Repealed.
3507.	Maximum interest rate on assessments for public improvements on benefited properties.
3508.	Federal Housing Administration insured obligations; interest clause; enforceability.
3509.	Rate of interest paid for commercial, business, or agricultural loans; rate upon default.
3509.1.	Adjustable rate loans for commercial, business, or agricultural purposes.
3509.2.	Interest upon accrued interest; exceptions.
3509.3.	Prepayment of loan.
3509.4.	Deferment of loan payments during declared disaster.

CHAPTER 2. LOUISIANA CONSUMER CREDIT LAW

PART I. GENERAL PROVISIONS AND DEFINITIONS

Section	
3510.	Short title.
3511.	Scope.
3512.	Exclusions.
3513.	Waiver, agreement to forego rights.
3514.	Agreement to contract; disclosures of the contract.
3515.	Conduct of certain business other than making consumer loans prohibited.
3516.	Definitions.
3517.	Terms; construction; additional fees and charges.
3518.	Construction against implicit repeal.
3518.1.	Records of the Office of Financial Institutions.
3518.2.	Credit cards; unsolicited delivery or mailing prohibited; penalty.
3518.3.	Credit cards; printing of accounting numbers on sales receipts; liability.

PART II. MAXIMUM CHARGES

3519.	Consumer loans.
3520.	Consumer credit sale.
3521.	Maximum charges after negotiations.
3522.	Maximum charges after maturity.
3523.	Credit service charge for revolving charge accounts.

Section	
3524.	Loan finance charge on lender credit card accounts.
3524.1.	[Blank].
3524.2.	[Blank].
3525.	Leap years.
3526.	Variable rates.
3526.1.	[Blank].
3526.2.	[Blank].
3526.3.	[Blank].
3527.	Maximum delinquency charges; notice of conversion.
3528.	Maximum deferral charges.
3529.	Installment of consumer credit transaction returned; additional charge to account.
3530.	Fees; origination; notary, documentation; over-the-credit-limit fee.
3530.1.	[Blank].

PART III. PREPAYMENT OF CONSUMER CREDIT TRANSACTIONS

3531.	Right to prepay.
3532.	Rebate upon prepayment.
3532.1.	Prepayment penalties in connection with simple interest real estate secured loans.
3533.	Rebate after acceleration of maturity.

PART IV. LIMITATIONS ON AGREEMENTS AND PRACTICES

3534.	Fees; attorney, collection agency.
3534.1.	Collection agent; registration; assignment of debt to collector.
3534.5.	[Blank].
3535.	Use of multiple agreements.
3536.	Referral sales.
3537.	Repealed.

PART V. HOME SOLICITATION SALES

3538.	Consumer's right to cancel.
3538.1.	[Blank].
3539.	Form of agreement or offer; statement of consumer's right; compliance.
3540.	Restoration of down payment; retention of cancellation fee.
3541.	Duty of consumer; no compensation for services prior to cancellation.
3541.1.	Consumer's right to cancel mail and check solicitation sales.

PART V-A. HOME SOLICITATION OF AGED PERSONS

3541.21.	Definitions.
3541.22.	Prohibited practices.

PART VI. INSURANCE

3542.	Requirement of insurance.
3543.	Property insurance.
3544.	Existing insurance.

REVISED STATUTES TITLE 9 NUMERICAL ANALYSIS

Section	
3545.	Limitations on insurance rates; contract requirements.
3546.	Choice of insurer.
3547.	Conditions applying to insurance provided by the extender of credit.
3548.	Cancellation of insurance; refund or credit upon cancellation.
3549.	Gain from insurance.
3550.	Insurance premium finance companies.

PART VII. REMEDIES AND PENALTIES

3551.	Unconscionability.
3552.	Effect of violations on rights of parties.
3553.	Criminal penalties.

PART VIII. ADMINISTRATION

3554.	Powers of commissioner.
3554.1.	Commissioner's powers; unlicensed persons.
3554.2.	Reapplication after revocation of a license.
3554.3.	Cost of appeal; effect of final decision.
3555.	Injunctions; investigations; enforcement actions; civil penalties; costs.
3556.	Method of procedure.
3556.1.	Records; rules.
3556.2.	Guidance by commissioner; advisory opinions.
3556.3.	Violations; penalties.

PART IX. LICENSING PROVISIONS

3557.	Authority to make consumer loans.
3558.	License to make consumer loans.
3559.	Continuation of licensing.
3559.1.	Regulation of former licensees.
3560.	Licenses not required.
3561.	Single place of business; additional licenses.
3561.1.	License; examination; renewal fees; records.

PART X. COLLECTION PRACTICES

3562.	Unauthorized collection practices.

PART XI. NOTIFICATION AND FEES

3563.	Applicability.
3563.1.	Financial institutions exempt.
3564.	Notification.
3565.	Notification fee.
3566.	Repealed.
3567.	Repealed.

PART XII. IDENTITY THEFT

3568.	Identity theft.

PART XIII. DISCLOSURE OF PERSONAL CREDIT INFORMATION

Section	
3571.	Dissemination of specific credit information; subpoena of records; requirements; penalties.
3571.1.	Credit reporting agency information and reports; consumer access to files; right of correction; dissemination or maintenance of untrue or misleading credit information by credit reporting agency; investigation; right to recovery.
3571.2.	Limitations on use of consumer's credit report.

PART XIV. LOAN BROKERS

3572.1.	Loan broker defined.
3572.2.	Exemptions; licensing and bonding; loan broker.
3572.3.	Licensure required.
3572.4.	Corporation.
3572.5.	Application form.
3572.6.	Restrictions; records.
3572.7.	Examination; rules.
3572.8.	Bond or trust account required.
3572.9.	Rebate upon prepayment.
3572.10.	Right of cancellation.
3572.11.	Loan brokerage statement; disclosure statement required.
3572.12.	Violations; penalties.

PART XV. CREDIT REPAIR SERVICES ORGANIZATIONS ACT

3573.1.	Short title; purpose; license; renewal; application; change of location; change of name; fees.
3573.2.	Definitions; exemptions.
3573.2–A.	[Blank].
3573.3.	Prohibited conduct.
3573.4.	Bond; trust account.
3573.5.	Repealed.
3573.6.	Disclosure statement.
3573.7.	Form and terms of contract.
3573.8.	Waiver.
3573.9.	Repealed.
3573.10.	Action for damages.
3573.11.	Orders, injunctions, and publication.
3573.12.	Statute of limitations.
3573.13.	Criminal penalty.
3573.14.	Burden of proving exemption.
3573.15.	Remedies cumulative.
3573.16.	Civil money penalties.
3573.17.	Repealed.

PART XVI. ADVANCE FEE LOANS

3574.1.	Short title.
3574.2.	Definitions.
3574.3.	Advance fees; prohibited acts.
3574.4.	Responsibility of principals.

REVISED STATUTES TITLE 9 NUMERICAL ANALYSIS

Section
3574.5. Investigations; cease and desist orders; administrative fines.
3574.6. Investigations; examinations; subpoenas; hearings; witnesses.
3574.7. Injunction to restrain violations.
3574.8. Criminal penalties.
3574.9. Actions for damages.
3574.10. Duties and powers of the office.
3575. [Blank].

PART XVII. REFUND ANTICIPATION LOANS [REPEALED]

3575.1 to 3575.4. Repealed.
3575.5. Repealed.
3575.6 to 3575.10. Repealed.

PART XVIII. COLLECTION AGENCY REGULATION ACT [REPEALED]

3576.1 to 3576.24. Repealed.

PART XIX. COLLEGE CAMPUS CREDIT CARD SOLICITATION LAW

3577.1. Short title.
3577.2. Definitions.
3577.3. Registration prior to solicitation; inducements prohibited.
3577.4. Debt collection against parent or guardian prohibited.
3577.5. Violations; penalties.
3577.6 to 3577.8. [Blank].

PART XX. [BLANK]

CHAPTER 2–A. LOUISIANA DEFERRED PRESENTMENT AND SMALL LOAN ACT

Section
3578.1. Short title.
3578.2. Legislative intent.
3578.3. Definitions.
3578.4. Finance charge and fees.
3578.5. Rebate upon prepayment.
3578.6. Prohibited acts.
3578.7. Posting of notice; toll-free number.
3578.8. Powers of the commissioner; adoption of rules and regulations.

CHAPTER 2–B. LOUISIANA TAX REFUND ANTICIPATION LOAN ACT

Section
3579.1. Short title.
3579.2. Definitions.
3579.3. Restriction on acting as facilitator.
3579.4. Disclosure requirements.

CHAPTER 3. LOUISIANA EQUAL CREDIT OPPORTUNITY LAW

Section
3581. Short title.
3582. Scope.
3583. Discrimination prohibited.
3584, 3585. Repealed.

CHAPTER 4. CONFESSION OF JUDGMENT

PART I. IN GENERAL

Section
3590. Limitations on confession of judgment.

CODE TITLE XIII—OF DEPOSIT AND SEQUESTRATION

CHAPTER 1. DEPOSIT IN GENERAL

Section
3601. Payment of interest by newspapers on deposits required of their distributors or dealers.

CODE TITLE XIV—OF ALEATORY CONTRACTS [BLANK]

CODE TITLE XV—OF MANDATE

CHAPTER 1. UNIFORM FIDUCIARIES LAW

Section
3801. Definitions.
3802. Payment or transfer to fiduciary; responsibility for proper application.
3803. Repealed.
3804. Endorsement of negotiable instrument; duty and liability of endorsee.
3805. Payee of check or bill of exchange; duties and liability.
3806. Check or bill of exchange payable to, or transferred to, fiduciary; duties and liability of transferee.
3807. Bank paying check; liability of.
3808. Check upon principal's account; liability of bank paying.
3809. Deposit by fiduciary to his personal credit; duties and liabilities of bank.
3810. Check upon deposit in name of two or more trustees; duties of bank and holder.
3811. Transactions prior to January 1, 1925.
3812. Cases not provided for; rules applicable.
3813. Uniform construction.
3814. Short title.

CHAPTER 2. UNIFORM LAW FOR SIMPLIFICATION OF FIDUCIARY SECURITY TRANSFERS

Section
3831. Definitions.
3832. Registration in the name of a fiduciary.

REVISED STATUTES TITLE 9 NUMERICAL ANALYSIS

Section	
3833.	Assignment by a fiduciary.
3834.	Evidence of appointment or incumbency.
3835.	Adverse claims.
3836.	Non-liability of corporation and transfer agent.
3837.	Non-liability of third persons.
3838.	Territorial application.
3839.	Tax obligations.
3840.	Uniformity of interpretation; short title.
3841 to 3849.	[Blank].
3850.	Express mandate between spouses; revocation.

CHAPTER 3. LOUISIANA MILITARY POWERS OF ATTORNEY

Section	
3861.	Application; military personnel.
3862.	Illustrative form; military power of attorney.
3863.	Requirements for legally sufficient power of attorney; federal preemption.
3864.	Initialed lines on form or designation as general or special; no limitation of powers.
3865.	Repealed.
3866.	Reserved.
3867.	Additional form of power of attorney; application of this Chapter.
3868.	Short title.
3869.	Application and construction of Chapter.
3870.	Powers granted.
3871.	Tangible personal property transactions; powers granted.
3872.	Stock and bond transactions; powers granted.
3873.	Commodity and option transactions; powers granted.
3874.	Banking and other financial institution transactions; powers granted.
3875.	Business operating transactions; powers granted.
3876.	Insurance and annuity transactions; powers granted.
3877.	Estate, trust, and other beneficiary transactions; powers granted.
3878.	Claims and litigations; powers granted.
3879.	Personal and family maintenance; powers granted.
3879.1.	Care, custody, and control of minor child.
3880.	Social security; civil or military benefits; powers granted.
3881.	Retirement plan transactions; powers granted.
3882.	Tax matters; powers granted.
3882.1.	Real or immovable property transactions; powers granted.
3883.	After-acquired property; state where property is located or where power is executed.
3884.	Trust instruments; power to modify or revoke.
3885.	Liability of person acting in good faith reliance upon power of attorney.
3886.	Application of power of attorney to all or portion of property of principal; description of items or parcels.
3887.	Acceptance of military power of attorney.

CHAPTER 3–A. CONDITIONAL PROCURATION

Section	
3890.	Conditional procuration.

CHAPTER 4. AGENCY RELATIONS IN REAL ESTATE TRANSACTIONS

Section	
3891.	Definitions.
3892.	Relationships between licensees and persons.
3893.	Duties of licensees representing clients.
3894.	Licensee's relationship with customers.
3895.	Termination of agency relationship.
3896.	Compensation; agency relationship.
3897.	Dual agency.
3898.	Subagency.
3899.	Vicarious liability.

CODE TITLE XVI—SURETYSHIP

CHAPTER 1. SURETYSHIP

PART I. IN GENERAL

Section	
3901.	Premium on bond, expense of administration.
3902.	Failure of surety to pay; recovery of attorney's fees.
3903.	Subrogation in favor of surety on twelve months' bond.
3904.	Agreement with surety as to deposit of moneys.

PART II. SURETY FOR LEGAL REPRESENTATIVE

Section	
3911.	Withdrawal of surety from bond of administrator, executor, curator or tutor.
3912.	Procedure for release of judicial surety.

CODE TITLE XVII—OF TRANSACTION OR COMPROMISE

CHAPTER 1. TRANSACTION OR COMPROMISE

Section	
3921.	Remission, transaction, compromise, or other conventional discharge of obligations.

REVISED STATUTES TITLE 9 NUMERICAL ANALYSIS

CODE TITLE XVIII—OF RESPITE
[BLANK]

CODE TITLE XIX—OF ALTERNATIVE DISPUTE RESOLUTION

CHAPTER 1. LOUISIANA MEDIATION ACT

Section
4101. Short title; purpose; definitions.
4102. Discussion of mediation with clients.
4103. Referral of a case for mediation; exceptions.
4104. Selection of mediator.
4105. Approved register of mediators.
4106. Qualifications of mediators.
4107. Standard of conduct; disclosure.
4108. Required attendance and participation in mediation.
4109. Cost of mediation.
4110. Nonbinding effect.
4111. Written settlement agreements.
4112. Confidentiality.

CHAPTER 2. LOUISIANA BINDING ARBITRATION LAW

Section
4201. Validity of arbitration agreements.
4202. Stay of proceedings brought in violation of arbitration agreement.
4203. Remedy in case of default; petition and notice; hearing and proceedings.
4204. Appointment of arbitrators.
4205. Application heard as motion.
4206. Witnesses; summoning; compelling attendance; evidence.
4207. Depositions.
4208. Award.
4209. Motion to confirm award; jurisdiction; notice.
4210. Motion to vacate award; grounds; rehearing.
4211. Motion to modify or correct award; grounds.
4212. Judgment upon award.
4213. Notice of motions; when made; service; stay of proceedings.
4214. Record; filing; judgment; effect and enforcement.
4215. Appeals.
4216. Limitation of application of Chapter.
4217. Short title.

CHAPTER 3. ARBITRATION OF MEDICAL AND DENTAL SERVICES OR SUPPLIES CONTRACTS

Section
4230. Definitions.
4231. Voluntary arbitration; medical or dental practitioner and patient.
4232. Voluntary arbitration; patient and medical institution.
4233. Selection of arbitrators; qualifications; restrictions.
4234. Arbitration procedure; controversies involving medical contracts and dental contracts.
4235. Notification to patient.
4236. Expiration of contract.

CHAPTER 4. INTERNATIONAL COMMERCIAL ARBITRATION ACT

Section
4241. Scope of application.
4242. Definitions and rules of interpretation.
4243. Receipt of written communications.
4244. Waiver of right to object.
4245. Extent of court intervention.
4246. Court; functions of arbitration assistance and supervision.
4247. Definition and form of arbitration agreement.
4248. Arbitration agreement and substantive claim before court.
4249. Arbitration agreement and interim measures by court.
4250. Number of arbitrators.
4251. Appointment of arbitrators.
4252. Grounds for challenge.
4253. Challenge procedure.
4254. Failure or impossibility to act.
4255. Appointment of substitute arbitrator.
4256. Competence of arbitral tribunal to rule on its jurisdiction.
4257. Power of arbitral tribunal to order interim measures.
4258. Equal treatment of parties.
4259. Determination of rules of procedure.
4260. Place of arbitration.
4261. Commencement of arbitral proceedings.
4262. Language.
4263. Statements of claim and defense.
4264. Hearings and written proceedings.
4265. Default of a party.
4266. Expert appointed by arbitral tribunal.
4267. Court assistance in taking evidence.
4268. Rules applicable to substance of dispute.
4269. Decisionmaking by panel of arbitrators.
4270. Settlement.
4271. Form and contents of award.
4272. Termination of proceedings.
4273. Correction and interpretation of award; additional award.
4274. Application for setting aside as exclusive recourse against arbitral award.
4275. Recognition and enforcement.
4276. Grounds for refusing recognition or enforcement.

REVISED STATUTES TITLE 9 NUMERICAL ANALYSIS

CODE TITLE XX—OF PLEDGE

CHAPTER 1. PLEDGES

PART I. RIGHTS UNDER MINERAL LEASES AND CONTRACTS [REPEALED]

Section
4301 to 4304. Repealed.
4305. [Blank].

PART II. INCORPOREAL RIGHTS NOT EVIDENCED IN WRITING [REPEALED]

4321 to 4323.1. Repealed.

PART II-A. DISPOSITION OF PLEDGED INCORPOREAL BY PLEDGOR [REPEALED]

4324. Repealed.

PART II-B. SECURITIZED FINANCINGS [REPEALED]

4330 to 4334. Repealed.

PART III. CROP PLEDGES [REPEALED]

SUBPART A. IN GENERAL [REPEALED]

4341 to 4343. Repealed.

SUBPART B. RECORDATION [REPEALED]

4361. Repealed.
4362. Repealed.
4363. Repealed.

SUBPART C. LIABILITY FOR VIOLATIONS [REPEALED]

4381 to 4382. Repealed.

SUBPART D. RELATION TO CHAPTER 9 OF THE LOUISIANA COMMERCIAL LAWS [REPEALED]

4391. Repealed.

PART IV. PLEDGE OR ASSIGNMENT OF LEASES AND RENTS

4401. Conditional or collateral assignment of leases or rents.

PART V. PLEDGE OR ASSIGNMENT OF SECURED INSTRUMENTS

4421. Repealed.
4422. Obligations secured by mortgages or privileges; signatures and writings deemed authentic for purposes of foreclosure.
4423 to 4450. [Blank].
4451. [Blank].

CODE TITLE XXI—OF PRIVILEGES

CHAPTER 1. PRIVILEGES ON MOVABLES

PART I. MAKING AND REPAIRING MOVABLES

Section
4501. Repairman's privilege on automobiles and other machinery.
4502. Privilege for making or repairing movable goods, commodities, equipment, merchandise, machinery, and other movable objects.

PART I-A. AIRCRAFT

4511. Privilege; aircraft.
4512. Notice of privilege.
4513. Privilege; storage of aircraft.

PART II. CROPS

4521. Repealed.
4522. Water furnished to grow crops.
4522.1. Water furnished under crop share agreement; exempt.
4523. Threshermen's, combinemen's, and grain drier's privilege.
4524. Repealed.

PART III. VENDOR'S PRIVILEGE

SUBPART A. IN GENERAL

4541. Seller of agricultural products in chartered cities and towns.
4542. Seller of cotton seed on manufactured products.
4543. Seller of sugar cane on manufactured products.
4544. Vegetables, seafood, and other perishable items.

SUBPART B. SEWING MACHINES AND PIANOS

4561. Sewing machines and pianos subject to seizure.
4562. Repealed.
4563. Entry and removal of property.
4564. Penalty for violation.

SUBPART C. PAYMENTS UNDER POLICIES OF INSURANCE

4581. Holder of vendor's privilege on property destroyed by fire, privilege on insurance.
4582. Notice to insurer and to assured; deposit in court.

PART IV. CARRIER'S CHARGES

4601. Hauling or trucking.

# REVISED STATUTES TITLE 9 NUMERICAL ANALYSIS

PART V. LOGS AND LUMBER

4621. Logs and products manufactured therefrom.
4622. Effective period; rank; sequestration.

PART VI. MOSS

4641. Laborers and furnishers of supplies.

PART VII. HORSES

4661. Feed, medicine, and veterinary services for horses.

PART VIII. RUGS, CARPETS, CLOTHING, AND HOUSEHOLD GOODS

4681. Carpets and rugs, cleaning and storage.
4682. Loss of privilege.
4683. Other remedies.
4684. Satisfaction of privilege; procedure; sale.
4685. Proceeds, disposition of.
4686. Claimant may pay charges and acquire possession.
4687. Clothing or household goods; procedures for sale.
4688. Proceeds, disposition of.
4689. Clothing or household goods; disposition of other than by sale.

PART IX. JEWELRY, GEMS, AND WATCHES

4701. Private sale of unclaimed goods of less than $10.
4702. Notice to owner.
4703. Proceeds, disposition of.

PART X. SUGAR, SYRUP, AND MOLASSES

4721. Sugar refinery and mill employees.

PART XI. SHIPS AND OTHER VESSELS

4741. Canal toll fees.

PART XII. PROCEEDS RECOVERED BY INJURED PERSON

4751. Definitions.
4752. Privilege on net proceeds collected from third party in favor of medical providers for services and supplies furnished injured persons.
4753. Written notice.
4754. Failure to pay over monies after notice.
4755. Itemized statements.

PART XIII. SELF-SERVICE STORAGE FACILITIES

4756. Short title.
4757. Definitions.
4758. Privilege.
4759. Options of owner upon lessee's default.
4760. Supplemental nature of act.

PART XIV. RELATION TO UNIFORM COMMERCIAL CODE

4770. Conflicts with Chapter 9 of the Uniform Commercial Code.

PART XV. MARINA AND BOATYARD STORAGE FACILITIES

4780. Short title.
4781. Definitions.
4782. Privilege.
4783. Notice of privilege.
4784. Enforcement of privilege.
4785. Cessation of enforcement actions.

PART XVI. OTHER PRIVILEGES ON MOVABLES

4790. Child support arrearages; privilege on motor vehicles.

PART XVII. TOWED AND STORED VESSEL ACT

4791. Short title.
4792. Definitions.
4793. Privilege.
4794. Vessel owner information.
4795. Notice of privilege and default.
4796. Advertisement; enforcement of privilege.
4797. Sale and purchasers.
4798. Regulations.

CHAPTER 2. PRIVILEGES ON IMMOVABLES

PART I. PRIVATE WORKS ACT

SUBPART A. LIABILITY OF OWNERS AND CONTRACTORS FOR THE IMPROVEMENT OF AN IMMOVABLE

4801. Improvement of immovable by owner; privileges securing the improvement.
4802. Improvement of immovable by contractor; claims against the owner and contractor; privileges securing the improvement.
4803. Amounts secured by claims and privileges.

SUBPART B. DEFINITIONS

4806. Owner defined; interest affected.
4807. Contractor, general contractor, subcontractor defined.
4808. Work defined.

SUBPART C. WORK PERFORMED BY GENERAL CONTRACTORS

4811. Notice of a contract with a general contractor to be filed.
4812. Bond required; terms and conditions.

REVISED STATUTES TITLE 9 NUMERICAL ANALYSIS

Section	
4813.	Liability of the surety.
4814.	Contractors; misapplication of payments prohibited; civil penalties; payment of claims, attorney fees and costs.
4815.	Escrow of funds due under contract; procedures.

SUBPART D. CLAIMS AND PRIVILEGES; EFFECTIVENESS; PRESERVATION; RANKING; EXTINGUISHMENT

4820.	Privileges; effective date.
4821.	Ranking of privileges.
4822.	Preservation of claims and privileges.
4823.	Extinguishment of claims and privileges.

SUBPART E. FILING; CANCELLATION; PEREMPTION

4831.	Filing; place of filing; contents.
4832.	Cancellation of notice of contract.
4833.	Request to cancel the inscription of claims and privileges; cancellation; notice of pendency of action.
4834.	Notice of contract; cessation of effect, reinscription.
4835.	Filing of bond or other security; cancellation of statement of claim or privilege or notice of pendency of action.

SUBPART F. PROCEDURE FOR ENFORCEMENT; BURDEN OF PROOF

4841.	Enforcement of claims and privileges; concursus.
4842.	Delivery of notice or other documents and materials; burden of proof.

SUBPART G. RESIDENTIAL TRUTH IN CONSTRUCTION ACT

4851.	Scope; definition.
4852.	Notice.
4853.	Copies of notice.
4854.	Lien rights unaffected.
4855.	Penalty for violation.

PART II. OIL, GAS, AND WATER WELLS

SUBPART A. IN GENERAL

4861.	Definitions.
4862.	Privilege for labor, services, or supplies.
4863.	Property subject to the privilege.
4864.	When the privilege is established and when it is extinguished.
4865.	Cessation of effect as to certain third persons.
4866.	Extinction as to movable property.
4867.	Notice to operator.
4868.	Statement of privilege; form and content.
4869.	Purchaser of hydrocarbons; effect of privilege and notices required.

Section	
4870.	Ranking of privileges.
4871.	Enforcement of claims and privileges.
4872.	Filing of bond or other security; cancellation of statement of privilege or notice of pendency of action.
4873.	Delivery of movables to well site; burden of proof.
4874 to 4880.	[Blank].

SUBPART B. PRIVILEGES AND OTHER RIGHTS OF OPERATORS AND NON–OPERATORS

4881.	Definitions.
4882.	Privilege of the operator and non-operator.
4883.	Property subject to the privilege.
4884.	When the privilege is established and when it is extinguished.
4885.	Cessation of effect as to certain third persons.
4886.	Extinction as to movable property.
4887.	Statement of privilege; form and content.
4888.	Ranking of privileges.
4889.	Enforcement of privileges.

PART III. RAILROADS

SUBPART A. IN GENERAL

4901.	Railroad tracks, road-beds, etc., privilege for material or labor.
4902.	Recordation unnecessary; effective period.
4903.	Rank.

PART IV. PUBLIC WORKS

SUBPART A. IN GENERAL

4921.	Feed for livestock used on public works; filing claims for.
4922.	Statement of amount due.
4923.	Feed claims have same rights as those for labor or materials.

SUBPART B. BONDING CLAIMS

4941.	Contractor may bond claims.

PART V. MISCELLANEOUS

4961.	Attorney's fees, limitation for recordation of lien.
4962 to 4965.	Repealed.

CHAPTER 3. PRIVILEGES ON MOVABLES AND IMMOVABLES

PART I. PRIVILEGE FOR ATTORNEY FEES

Section	
5001.	Privilege for fees.

REVISED STATUTES TITLE 9 NUMERICAL ANALYSIS

Section

PART II. PRIVILEGES TO EFFECT SEPARATION OF PATRIMONY

5011. Privilege of succession creditor and particular legatee.
5012. Privilege of creditor of heir or legatee.
5013. Effect of privileges.
5014. Enforcement of privilege on immovables alienated by heirs or legatees.
5015. Peremption of inscription of privilege of succession creditor or particular legatee.
5016. Peremption of inscription of privilege of creditor of heir or legatee.

PART III. PRIVILEGE FOR PRODUCERS OF AGRICULTURAL AND DAIRY PRODUCTS

5021. Privilege on assets of purchaser when purchaser becomes insolvent or bankrupt.

PART IV. RIGHTS OF LIEN OR PRIVILEGE HOLDER

5031. Preservation of rights of lien or privilege holder in sales held in certain proceedings.

CODE TITLE XXII—MORTGAGES

CHAPTER 1. MORTGAGES IN GENERAL

PART I. PROPERTY SUBJECT TO MORTGAGE

SUBPART A. IN GENERAL

Section

5101. Repealed.
5102. Repealed.
5103. Newspaper plant, equipment, name, and good will.
5104. Repealed.
5105. Repealed.
5106 to 5110. [Blank].

SUBPART B. HOME APPLIANCES AND EQUIPMENT [REPEALED]

5121 to 5126. Repealed.

SUBPART C. MINERAL MORTGAGES—APPOINTMENT OF KEEPER

5131. Appointment by court.
5132. Designation in mortgage.
5133. Powers, duties and compensation.
5134. Security.
5135. Requests to court for instructions.

SUBPART D. CONVENTIONAL MORTGAGES, APPOINTMENT OF RECEIVER OR KEEPER

5136. Designation in mortgage or other instrument of keeper of property.

Section

5137. Appointment of person designated by parties.
5138. Powers, duties, and compensation.
5139. Security.
5140. Requests to court for instructions.
5140.1. Effect of Subpart on other provisions of law.
5140.2. Security interests under Chapter 9 of Louisiana Commercial Laws.

PART II. DUTIES OF RECORDERS

SUBPART A. INSCRIPTION

5141. Repealed.
5142. Parish wherein state capitol is located, special mortgages.
5143. Parish wherein state capitol is located, vendor's mortgages or sales with mortgage.

SUBPART B. ERASURE OR CANCELLATION

5161, 5162. Repealed.
5163. United States agencies mortgagees of record; no cancellation or subordination without notice.
5164. Service of notice.
5165. Issuance of release of mortgage by current mortgagee.
5166. Cancellation of mortgage and vendor's lien inscriptions; uniform cancellation affidavit; requirements and effects.
5167. Cancellation of mortgage or vendor's privilege by affidavit of notary or title insurer where paraphed note or other evidence is lost or destroyed.
5167.1. Cancellation of mortgage inscription by affidavit; penalties.
5167.2. Cancellation of mortgage inscription.
5168. Promissory notes; loss or destruction; proof by affidavit.
5169. Cancellation of mortgages and privileges not securing paraphed obligations.
5169.1. Repealed.
5170. Cancellation of mortgages and privileges securing paraphed obligations.
5171. Cancellation; certified copy of order, decree or other instrument.
5172. Cancellation; licensed financial institution.
5173. Mortgage or privilege cancellation by financial institution-standard form.
5174. Liability for incorrect or false request for cancellation.
5175. Order of discharge in bankruptcy; effect.
5176. Extinction of certain rights; acknowledgment by owner or holder.
5177 to 5180.1. Repealed.
5180.2. Repealed.
5180.3. Repealed.
5180.4.

XLIX

REVISED STATUTES TITLE 9 NUMERICAL ANALYSIS

Section

SUBPART C. CERTIFICATES [REPEALED]

5181. Repealed.
5182. Repealed.
5183. Repealed.

SUBPART D. NOTICE OF TAX SALES [REPEALED]

5201 to 5203. Repealed.

SUBPART E. THE OFFICE OF MORTGAGES

5206, 5207. Repealed.
5207. Recorder of mortgages in each parish.
5208. Registers kept by recorder of mortgages in Orleans parish.
5209. Authentication of registers in Orleans parish.
5210. Registers and authentication outside Orleans parish.
5211. Register with title of acts and time of filing.
5212. Prompt recordation and certificate of encumbrances.
5213. Method of recordation; certificate of encumbrances.
5214 to 5216. Repealed.
5217. Recorder's fees for multiple indebtedness mortgages; form.

PART III. RIGHTS OF MORTGAGE HOLDER

5251. Preservation of rights of mortgage holder in sales held in certain proceedings.

CHAPTER 2. CONVENTIONAL MORTGAGES

PART I. MORTGAGES SECURING SEVERAL OBLIGATIONS

Section
5301. Conventional mortgage to secure several obligations.
5302. Fiduciary as mortgagee in trust for creditors.
5303. Creditors' interests under mortgage.
5304. Enforcement of mortgage; limitations.
5305. Paraph unnecessary; proviso.
5306. Act of mortgage may include pledge.
5307. Substitutions, fidei commissa, or trust dispositions; laws not applicable.

PART II. MORTGAGES ON RURAL PROPERTY

5321. Definitions.
5322. Repealed.
5323. Repealed.
5324. Schedule of penalties.
5325. Exclusions.
5326. Repealed.

Section

PART III. CHATTEL MORTGAGES

5351 to 5352. Repealed.
5352.1. Repealed.
5353 to 5363. Repealed.
5363.1. Abandoned mobile homes; secured parties.
5364 to 5366.2. Repealed.

PART IV. MORTGAGE OF MOVABLES USED IN COMMERCIAL OR INDUSTRIAL ACTIVITY [REPEALED]

5367 to 5373. Repealed.

PART V. MISCELLANEOUS PROVISIONS

5381. Ships and other vessels, hypothecation and conveyance; record; effect.
5382. Right of mortgage holder to recover for disposal or conversion of property.
5383. Transfers of more than one parcel of immovable property.
5384. Assumption of a mortgage on immovable property by a third person.
5385. Satisfaction of mortgage; production of promissory note or release for cancellation; liability.
5386. Mortgage including collateral assignment and pledge of certain incorporeal rights.
5387. Repealed.
5388. Authority to carry out and enforce rights.
5389. Additional funds advanced under mortgage or security agreement.
5390. Amendment, renewal, or refinancing of mortgage and mortgage note.
5391. Additions, accessions, and natural increases subject to mortgage.
5392. Continuation of mortgage after judgment.
5393. Combination forms.
5394. Applicability.
5395. Protection of mortgage lenders and fiduciaries from state environmental liability; parity with federal law.
5396. Maintenance of abandoned mortgaged property.

CHAPTER 3. LEGAL MORTGAGES

PART I. IN GENERAL

Section
5501. Affidavit of distinction; acknowledgment; contents; damages.
5501.1. Sworn affidavit; form.
5502. Repealed.
5503. Affidavit of identity; content; effect; penalty for falsifying.
5504. Privileges and liens in favor of state, parish, or municipal bodies.

REVISED STATUTES TITLE 9 NUMERICAL ANALYSIS

CHAPTER 4. SHIP MORTGAGE LAW

Section
- 5521. Short title.
- 5522. Definitions.
- 5523. Identifying numbers.
- 5524. Title to work; materials and components.
- 5525. Mortgage of ships; materials and components.
- 5526. Mortgage to be in writing; description and content.
- 5527. Authentication; filing; fee.
- 5528. Effect of filing; rights and privileges retained.
- 5529. Ship mortgage book; form.
- 5530. Cancellation; reinscription; fee.
- 5531. Failure to affix hull number; removal of hull number; penalty.
- 5532. Mortgaging with fraudulent intent; penalty.
- 5533. Disposal of mortgaged ship with fraudulent intent; penalty.
- 5534. Acceleration of maturity date, grounds for.
- 5535. Fraudulent release of mortgage; penalty.
- 5536. Remedies of creditors.
- 5537. Ship mortgage certificates; fee.
- 5538. Relation to Chapter 9 of the Louisiana Commercial Laws.

CHAPTER 5. COLLATERAL MORTGAGES AND VENDOR'S PRIVILEGES: EFFECTIVE DATE OF COLLATERAL MORTGAGES, RELATIONSHIP OF COLLATERAL MORTGAGES TO CHAPTER 9 OF THE LOUISIANA COMMERCIAL LAWS AND DEFENSES TO ENFORCEMENT

Section
- 5550. Definitions.
- 5551. Effective date of a collateral mortgage.
- 5552. Defenses to enforcement of a collateral mortgage.
- 5553. Defenses to enforcement of a vendor's privilege.
- 5554. No requirement of registry of transfer, assignment, pledge, or security interest in or of the written obligation, collateral mortgage, or vendor's privilege.
- 5555. Executory process in the case of notes or other obligations not paraphed for identification with the mortgage.
- 5556. Repealed.
- 5557. Obligation to grant release of mortgage.

CODE TITLE XXIII—OCCUPANCY AND POSSESSION [BLANK]

CODE TITLE XXIV—PRESCRIPTION

CHAPTER 1. PRESCRIPTION

PART I. PERIODS OF PRESCRIPTION

SUBPART A. ONE YEAR

Section
- 5601. Crops; injury, destruction, or loss of profits; non-delivery or non-acceptance.
- 5602. Contracts for work and labor; New Orleans.
- 5603. Public ways; damages due to grading.
- 5604. Actions for professional accounting liability.
- 5605. Actions for legal malpractice.
- 5605.1. Theft of client funds; prescription.
- 5606. Actions for professional insurance agent liability.
- 5607. Actions against a professional engineer, surveyor, professional interior designer, architect, real estate developer; peremptive periods.
- 5608. Actions against home inspectors.
- 5609. Contracts to buy or sell; peremption of the effect of recordation; prescription for actions.

SUBPART B. TWO YEARS

- 5621. Acts of succession representative.
- 5622. Informalities in auction sales, two and five year prescription.
- 5623. Acts of sheriff; overpayments.
- 5624. Actions for damages to property damaged for public purposes.
- 5625. Violation of zoning restriction, building restriction, or subdivision regulation.
- 5626. Actions and claims for lands and improvements used or destroyed for levees or levee drainage purposes.
- 5627. Building encroaching on public way.
- 5628. Actions for medical malpractice.
- 5628.1. Actions for liability from the use of blood or tissue.
- 5629. Uninsured motorist insurance claims.
- 5630. Actions by unrecognized successor against third persons.
- 5631. Minors, interdicts, and posthumous children.
- 5632. Actions against succession representatives, tutors, and curators; defect in private sales or mortgages.
- 5632.1. Power of attorney; action to set aside under certain conditions.

REVISED STATUTES TITLE 9 NUMERICAL ANALYSIS

SUBPART B-1. THREE YEARS

5633. Blighted property; acquisitive prescription.

SUBPART C. FIVE YEARS

5641. Sale under attachment against foreign corporation.
5642. Sheriffs' deeds.
5643. Right to probate testament.
5644. Prescription of actions involving asbestos abatement.
5645. Prescription of actions involving contract to sell or transfer immovable property.
5646. Sale of immovable property by domestic or foreign corporation or unincorporated association.
5647. Power of attorney; action to set aside under certain conditions.

SUBPART D. SIX YEARS

5661. Land patents.

SUBPART E. TEN YEARS

5681. Redesignated as R.S. 9:5646.
5682. Redesignated as R.S. 9:5632.1.
5683, 5684. Repealed.
5685. Prescription against the state.

SUBPART F. THIRTY YEARS

5701. Debts due charitable or educational institution or fund.

PART II. INTERRUPTION AND SUSPENSION

5801. Involuntary dismissal; failure to timely request service of citation.
5802. Fugitive from justice.
5803. Property adjudicated to state for non-payment of taxes.
5804. Immovable property of municipal corporation.
5805. Minerals, mineral or royalty rights; liberative prescription not suspended by minority or other disability.
5806. Repealed.
5807. Interruption of prescription on pledged obligations by payment on obligation secured by pledge.

PART III. ALTERATION OF PRESCRIPTIVE PERIODS

5811. Prescription of action of revendication.

PART IV. SUSPENSION OR EXTENSION OF PRESCRIPTION, PEREMPTION AND OTHER LEGAL DEADLINES DURING HURRICANES KATRINA OR RITA

5821. Purpose; ratification.
5822. Suspension and extension of prescription and peremption; exceptions.
5823. Suspension of legal deadlines; extension of legal deadlines; contradictory hearing.
5824. Purpose; certain courts; suspension and extension of prescription and peremption and other legal deadlines.
5825. Applicability.
5826 to 5835. Reserved.

CODE TITLE XXV—OF THE SIGNIFICATION OF SUNDRY TERMS OF LAW EMPLOYED IN THIS CODE [BLANK]

CODE BOOK IV—CONFLICT OF LAWS

CODE TITLE I—OF FOREIGN LAW

CHAPTER 1. APPLICATION OF FOREIGN LAW

6000. [Blank].
6001. Application of foreign law.

APPENDIX 1. REVISED STATUTES TITLE 9
CIVIL CODE—ANCILLARIES

PRELIMINARY TITLE [BLANK]

CODE BOOK I—OF PERSONS

CODE TITLE I—NATURAL AND JURIDICAL PERSONS

Chapter		Section
1.	Women	9:51
	Part	
	I. In General	9:51
	II. Married Women	9:101
	Subpart	
	A. Emancipation and Powers	9:101
2.	Death	9:111
3.	Human Embryos	9:121

CODE TITLE II—OF DOMICILE AND THE MANNER OF CHANGING THE SAME [BLANK]

CODE TITLE III—ABSENT PERSONS

1.	Uniform Unclaimed Property Act	9:151
2.	Disposition of Unclaimed Specimens by Taxidermists	9:191
3.	The Care of Minor Children	9:195

CODE TITLE IV—HUSBAND AND WIFE

1.	Marriage: General Principles	9:201
	Part	
	I. Officiants	9:201
	II. Collateral Relations	9:211
	III. Application for Marriage License	9:221
	Subpart	
	A. In General	9:221
	B. Birth Certificate	9:226
	C. Medical Certificate [Repealed]	9.229
	D. Issuance and Time	9:234
	E. Summary of Matrimonial Regimes Laws	9:237
	IV. Delays and Ceremony	9:241
	A. Seventy-two Hour Delay	9:241
	B. Ceremony and Marriage Certificate	9:244
	V. Record Keeping	9:251
	VI. Opposition to Marriage	9:261
	VII. Covenant Marriage	9:272
2.	Incidents and Effects of Marriage	9:291
	Part	
	I. In General	9:291
	II. Special Incidents and Effects of Covenant Marriage	9:293

CODE TITLE V—DIVORCE

1.	Divorce	9:301
	Part	
	I. In General	9:301

For Annotative Materials, see West's Louisiana Statutes Annotated

APPENDIX 1—REVISED STATUTES, TITLE 9

- I–A. Child Support ... 9:315
  - **Subpart**
    - A. Guidelines for Determination of Child Support ... 9:315
    - B. Other Child Support Provisions ... 9:315.21
    - C. Judicial Suspension of License for Nonpayment of Child Support or Contempt of Court in Child Support or Paternity Proceedings ... 9:315.30
    - D. Administrative Suspension of Certain Licenses for Nonpayment of Child Support ... 9:315.40
- II. Spousal Support ... 9:321
- III. Child Custody ... 9:331
  - **Subpart**
    - A. Evaluation and Mediation ... 9:331
    - B. Joint Custody ... 9:335
    - C. Protective and Remedial Provisions ... 9:341
    - D. Access to Records ... 9:351
    - E. Relocating a Child's Residence ... 9:355.1
    - F. Other Child Custody Provisions ... 9:356
    - G. Parenting Coordinator ... 9:358.1
    - H. Military Parent and Child Custody Protection Act ... 9:359
- IV. Post-Separation Family Violence Relief Act ... 9:361
- V. Injunctions and Incidental Orders ... 9:371

2. Transitional Provisions ... 9:381
   - I. Divorce ... 9:381
   - II. Child Custody and Support ... 9:385
   - III. Spousal Support ... 9:386

CODE TITLE VI—OF MASTER AND SERVANT [BLANK]

CODE TITLE VII—PARENT AND CHILD

1. Children ... 9:391
   - **Part**
     - I. Legitimation ... 9:391
     - I–A. Blood or Tissue Sampling for Determination of Paternity ... 9:396
     - I–B. Establishment of Child Support in Paternity Proceeding ... 9:399
     - I–C. Putative Father Registry ... 9:400
     - II. Filiation ... 9:401
     - III. Adoption ... 9:421
       - **Subpart**
         - A. Minors Under Seventeen [Repealed] ... 9:421
         - B. Persons Over Seventeen ... 9:461
     - IV. Neglect or Abuse [Repealed] ... 9:551
     - V. General Provisions ... 9:571

CODE TITLE VIII—OF MINORS, OF THEIR TUTORSHIP AND EMANCIPATION

1. Tutorship ... 9:601
   - **Part**
     - I. Appointment, Recognition, or Confirmation ... 9:601
       - **Subpart**
         - A. In General ... 9:601
     - II. Management and Disposition of Property ... 9:651
       - A. Family Meeting Dispensed With; Procedure [Repealed] ... 9:651
       - B. Private Sale; Procedure ... 9:671
       - C. Sale to Effect Partition; Procedure [Repealed] ... 9:691
       - D. Mineral Leases and Contracts; Procedure [Repealed] ... 9:711
       - E. Miscellaneous Provisions ... 9:731
       - F. Uniform Transfers to Minors Act ... 9:751
     - III. Bond or Security in Place of Mortgage [Repealed] ... 9:801
     - IV. Small Estates [Repealed] ... 9:821
     - V. Miscellaneous Provisions [Repealed] ... 9:841
2. Emancipation ... 9:901

For Annotative Materials, see West's Louisiana Statutes Annotated

APPENDIX 1—REVISED STATUTES, TITLE 9

	I. In General	9:901
3.	Provisional Custody By Mandate	9:951
4.	Non-Legal Custodian	9:975

CODE TITLE IX—PERSONS UNABLE TO CARE FOR THEIR PERSONS OR PROPERTY

1.	Interdiction	9:1001
Part		
I.	Inebriates [Repealed]	9:1001
II.	Miscellaneous Provisions	9:1021
III.	Nonprofit Curator and Continuing Tutor Programs	9:1031

CODE TITLE X—OF CORPORATIONS

1.	Corporations; Unauthorized Corporations; Unincorporated Nonprofit Associations	9:1051

CODE BOOK II—THINGS AND THE DIFFERENT MODIFICATIONS OF OWNERSHIP

CODE TITLE I—THINGS

1.	Immovables	9:1101
Part		
I.	In General	9:1101
I-A.	Ownership of Beds of Non–Navigable Waters	9:1115.1
II.	Louisiana Condominium Act	9:1121
Subpart		
A.	General Provisions	9:1121
B.	Creation, Alteration, and Termination of Condominiums	9:1122.101
C.	Management of the Condominium	9:1123.101
D.	Protection of Purchasers	9:1124.101
II-A.	Louisiana Timesharing Act	9:1131.1
II-B.	Louisiana Homeowners Association Act	9:1141.1
A.	General Provisions	9:1141.1
B.	Building Provisions	9:1141.4
C.	Enforcement	9:1141.8
III.	Privileges on Immovables for Charges or Dues of Association of Owners	9:1145
IV.	Manufactured Home Property Act	9:1149.1

CODE TITLE II—OWNERSHIP

1.	Accession	9:1151

CODE TITLE III—PERSONAL SERVITUDES

1.	Family Home	9:1201

CODE TITLE IV—PREDIAL SERVITUDES

1.	General Provisions	9:1251
2.	Louisiana Conservation Servitude Act	9:1271

For Annotative Materials, see West's Louisiana Statutes Annotated

APPENDIX 1—REVISED STATUTES, TITLE 9

CODE TITLE V—BUILDING RESTRICTIONS [BLANK]

CODE TITLE VI—BOUNDARIES [BLANK]

CODE TITLE VII—OWNERSHIP IN INDIVISION [BLANK]

CODE BOOK III—OF THE DIFFERENT MODES OF ACQUIRING THE OWNERSHIP OF THINGS

CODE TITLE I—OF SUCCESSIONS

1. Successions 9:1421
   Part
      I. Procedure 9:1421
        Subpart
         A. Miscellaneous Provisions 9:1421
         B. Small Successions 9:1431
         C. Presumptions 9:1441
2. Administration of Successions 9:1451
      I. In General 9:1451
         A. Private Sale; Procedure 9:1451
         B. Dation En Paiement; Procedure 9:1471
         C. Mineral Leases; Procedure [Repealed] 9:1491
         D. Miscellaneous Provisions 9:1511
         E. Public Sale of Succession Property 9:1521
      II. Burial of Unclaimed Bodies; Administration of Successions of $500 or Less 9:1551
      III. Public Administrators 9:1581
      IV. State Succeeding to Immovable Property 9:1611
3. Partitions 9:1701
      I. In General 9:1701

CODE TITLE II—OF DONATIONS INTER VIVOS (BETWEEN LIVING PERSONS) AND MORTIS CAUSA (IN PROSPECT OF DEATH)

1. Louisiana Trust Code 9:1721
   Part
      I. Preliminary Provisions 9:1721
      II. Creation of the Trust 9:1731
        Subpart
         A. General Provisions 9:1731
         B. Form 9:1751
         C. The Settlor 9:1761
         D. The Trust Property 9:1771
         E. The Trustee 9:1781
         F. The Beneficiary 9:1801
         G. Effective Date of Creation 9:1821
         H. Term of The Trust 9:1831
         I. The Legitime In Trust 9:1841
         J. Marital Portion In Trust 9:1851
         K. Life Insurance In Trust 9:1881
         L. Class Trusts 9:1891
            A. General Rules 9:1891
            B. Rules Governing When Members of a Class are Beneficiaries of Income Only 9:1899
            C. Rules Governing When Members of a Class are Beneficiaries of Principal Only 9:1902
            D. Rules Governing When Members of One Class are Beneficiaries of Income and Members of a Different Class are Beneficiaries of Principal 9:1904
            E. Rules Governing When the Members of the Same Class are Beneficiaries of Both Income and Principal 9:1905
         M. Trusts for Employees 9:1921
         N. Additions to the Trust Property 9:1931

For Annotative Materials, see West's Louisiana Statutes Annotated

APPENDIX 1—REVISED STATUTES, TITLE 9

		O.	Trusts For Mixed Private And Charitable Purposes	9:1951
		P.	Community Property In Trust	9:1955
	III.		The Interest of The Beneficiary	9:1961
		A.	The Interest of the Income Beneficiary	9:1961
		B.	The Interest of the Principal Beneficiary	9:1971
		C.	Refusal	9:1981
		D.	Alienation by the Beneficiary	9:2001
		E.	Deferred Ascertainment of Principal Beneficiaries of Revocable Trusts	9:2011
	IV.		Modification, Termination, Revocation and Rescission of The Trust	9:2021
		A.	Modification and Termination of The Trust	9:2021
		B.	Revocation and Rescission of The Trust	9:2041
		C.	Formal Requirements	9:2051
	V.		Duties and Powers of The Trustee	9:2061
		A.	General Dispositions	9:2061
		B.	Duties of the Trustee	9:2081
		C.	Powers of the Trustee	9:2111
		D.	Allocation to Income and Principal	9:2141
		E.	Power to Adjust	9:2158
		F.	The Trustee's Bond	9:2171
	VI.		Compensation and Indemnity of the Trustee	9:2181
		A.	Compensation of the Trustee	9:2181
		B.	Indemnity of the Trustee	9:2191
	VII.		Liabilities of the Trustee	9:2201
	VIII.		Remedies of the Beneficiary	9:2221
	IX.		Actions	9:2231
	X.		Designation of Attorney or Registered Agent	9:2241
	XI.		Validation	9:2251
1-A.			Uniform Custodial Trust Act	9:2260.1
1-B.			Foreign Trusts	9:2262.1
2.			Donations for Charitable Purposes	9:2271
	I.		Trusts for Charitable Purposes	9:2271
	II.		Duration of Charitable Trusts	9:2291
	III.		Donations to Religious Organizations	9:2321
	IV.		Cy Pres	9:2331
	V.		Uniform Management of Institutional Funds Act	9:2337.1
2-A.			Public Trusts	9:2341
3.			Donations Inter Vivos	9:2351
	I.		Married Person to Spouse	9:2351
	II.		Parent to Child	9:2361
	III.		Effect on Donees and Third Parties	9:2371
	IV.		Calculation of Mass, Reduction and Collation	9:2372
4.			Donations Mortis Causa	9:2401
	I.		Uniform Wills Law	9:2401
	II.		Uniform Probate Law	9:2421
	II-A.		Estate Tax Apportionment Law	9:2431
	III.		Miscellaneous Provisions	9:2441
5.			Of Forced Heirs	9:2501

CODE TITLE III—OBLIGATIONS IN GENERAL [BLANK]

1.	[Blank]	9:2551

CODE TITLE IV—CONVENTIONAL OBLIGATIONS OR CONTRACTS

1.	Louisiana Uniform Electronic Transactions Act	9:2601
1-A.	Of Presumptions	9:2701
1-B.	Requisites for a Valid Agreement	9:2711
2.	Registry of Instruments Affecting Immovables	9:2721
	Part	
	I. General Provisions	9:2721

For Annotative Materials, see West's Louisiana Statutes Annotated

APPENDIX 1—REVISED STATUTES, TITLE 9

	II. Agreements for Exploitation of Mineral Interests [Repealed]	9:2731
2-A.	Registry Under Commercial Laws	9:2736
2-B.	Registry	9:2741
3.	Performance of Obligations	9:2770
4.	Death of a Party	9:2785
5.	Interest Upon Accrued Interest; Exceptions [Blank]	9:2788
6.	Interest-Bearing Deposit Accounts	9:2789
7.	Uniform Fraudulent Transfer Act [Repealed]	9:2790.1

CODE TITLE V—OF QUASI CONTRACTS, AND OF OFFENSES AND QUASI OFFENSES

1.	Disgorgement	9:2790.5
2.	Of Offenses and Quasi Offenses	9:2791
3.	Louisiana Products Liability Act	9:2800.51
4.	Louisiana Drug Dealer Liability Act	9:2800.61

CODE TITLE VI—MATRIMONIAL REGIMES

1.	Partition of Community Property	9:2801
2.	Matrimonial Regimes [Repealed]	9:2831

CODE TITLE VII—SALE

1.	Sales in General		9:2901
	Part		
	I. Research Certificates		9:2901
	Subpart		
		A. Tax Certificates; New Orleans Excepted	9:2901
		B. Tax, Local Improvement Assessment, and Nonalienation Certificates; New Orleans	9:2921
2.	Conventional Sales		9:2941
	I. Bond for Deed Contracts		9:2941
	II. Sales of Motor Vehicle Dealership		9:2961
	III. Transfer of Lands Fronting Waterways, Highways, Etc.		9:2971
	IV. Transfer of Lands Abutting Abandoned Roads, Streets or Alleys		9:2981
	V. Dual or Fraudulent Contracts		9:2989
3.	Judicial Sales		9:3001
	I. In General		9:3001
4.	Assignment or Transfer of Credits or Other Incorporeal Rights		9:3051
	I. In General		9:3051
	II. Louisiana Assignment of Accounts Receivable Act [Repealed]		9:3101
	III. Assignment of Proceeds of Crop Financing		9:3121
4-A.	Corporeal Immovables		9:3131
4-B.	Louisiana Exchange Sale of Receivables Act		9:3137.1
5.	New Home Warranty Act		9:3141
6.	Auction Sales, Judicial Sales, and Expropriation		9:3151
	I. Auction Sales		9:3151
	II. Judicial Sales		9:3166
		A. In General	9:3166
		B. Seizure or Execution	9:3168
		C. Succession Property	9:3172
	III. Expropriation		9:3191.1
7.	Relationship Between the Civil Code Title on Sale and the Commercial Laws		9:3192
8.	Residential Property Disclosure		9:3195

CODE TITLE VIII—OF EXCHANGE [BLANK]

CODE TITLE IX—OF LEASE

1.	Leases	9:3201
	Part	
	I. Liability For Damages	9:3201

For Annotative Materials, see West's Louisiana Statutes Annotated

APPENDIX 1—REVISED STATUTES, TITLE 9

	II. Liability For Injuries	9:3221
	III. Lessor's Privilege	9:3241
	IV. Lessee's Deposit	9:3251
	V. Lessor's Rights	9:3258
	VI. Obligations and Rights of the Lessee	9:3260
2.	Leases of Movables	9:3261
	I. In General	9:3301
	II. Civil Code	9:3309
	III. Charges	9:3311
	IV. Remedies Following Lessee's Default	9:3318
	V. Insurance	9:3331
	VI. Miscellaneous	9:3339
3.	Rental-Purchase Agreements	9:3351
4.	Sale/Lease–Back Commercial Transactions	9:3370
5.	Removal and Preservation of Property During Emergencies and Disasters [Terminated]	9:3391

CODE TITLE X—OF RENTS AND ANNUITIES [BLANK]

CODE TITLE XI—PARTNERSHIP

1.	Central Registry for Contracts of Partnership	9:3401
2.	Qualification of Foreign Partnerships	9:3421
3.	Registered Limited Liability Partnerships	9:3431
4.	Merger or Consolidation	9:3441

CODE TITLE XII—OF LOAN

1.	Interest	9:3500
	Part	
	I. In General	9:3500
2.	Louisiana Consumer Credit Law	9:3510
	I. General Provisions And Definitions	9:3510
	II. Maximum Charges	9:3519
	III. Prepayment Of Consumer Credit Transactions	9:3531
	IV. Limitations on Agreements And Practices	9:3534
	V. Home Solicitation Sales	9:3538
	V-A. Home Solicitation of Aged Persons	9:3541.21
	VI. Insurance	9:3542
	VII. Remedies And Penalties	9:3551
	VIII. Administration	9:3554
	IX. Licensing Provisions	9:3557
	X. Collection Practices	9:3562
	XI. Notification And Fees	9:3563
	XII. Identity Theft	9:3568
	XIII. Disclosure Of Personal Credit Information	9:3571
	XIV. Loan Brokers	9:3572.1
	XV. Credit Repair Services Organizations Act	9:3573.1
	XVI. Advance Fee Loans	9:3574.1
	XVII. Refund Anticipation Loans [Repealed]	9:3575.1
	XVIII. Collection Agency Regulation Act [Repealed]	9:3576.1
	XIX. College Campus Credit Card Solicitation Law	9:3577.1
	XX. [Blank]	
2-A.	Louisiana Deferred Presentment and Small Loan Act	9:3578.1
2-B.	Louisiana Tax Refund Anticipation Loan Act	9:3579.1
3.	Louisiana Equal Credit Opportunity Law	9:3581
4.	Confession of Judgment	9:3590
	I. In General	9:3590

CODE TITLE XIII—OF DEPOSIT AND SEQUESTRATION

1.	Deposit in General	9:3601

For Annotative Materials, see West's Louisiana Statutes Annotated

APPENDIX 1—REVISED STATUTES, TITLE 9

CODE TITLE XIV—OF ALEATORY CONTRACTS [BLANK]

CODE TITLE XV—OF MANDATE

1. Uniform Fiduciaries Law 9:3801
2. Uniform Law for Simplification of Fiduciary Security Transfers 9:3831
3. Louisiana Military Powers of Attorney 9:3861
3-A. Conditional Procuration 9:3890
4. Agency Relations In Real Estate Transactions 9:3891

CODE TITLE XVI—SURETYSHIP

1. Suretyship 9:3901
   Part
      I. In General 9:3901
      II. Surety for Legal Representative 9:3911

CODE TITLE XVII—OF TRANSACTION OR COMPROMISE

1. Transaction or Compromise 9:3921

CODE TITLE XVIII—OF RESPITE [BLANK]

CODE TITLE XIX—OF ALTERNATIVE DISPUTE RESOLUTION

1. Louisiana Mediation Act 9:4101
2. Louisiana Binding Arbitration Law 9:4201
3. Arbitration of Medical and Dental Services or Supplies Contracts 9:4230
4. International Commercial Arbitration Act 9:4241

CODE TITLE XX—OF PLEDGE

1. Pledges 9:4301
   Part
      I. Rights under Mineral Leases and Contracts [Repealed] 9:4301
      II. Incorporeal Rights Not Evidenced in Writing [Repealed] 9:4321
      II-A. Disposition of Pledged Incorporeal by Pledgor [Repealed] 9:4324
      II-B. Securitized Financings [Repealed] 9:4330
      III. Crop Pledges [Repealed] 9:4341
         Subpart
         A. In General [Repealed] 9:4341
         B. Recordation [Repealed] 9:4361
         C. Liability for Violations [Repealed] 9:4381
         D. Relation to Chapter 9 of the Louisiana Commercial Laws [Repealed] 9:4391
      IV. Pledge or Assignment of Leases and Rents 9:4401
      V. Pledge or Assignment of Secured Instruments 9:4421

CODE TITLE XXI—OF PRIVILEGES

1. Privileges on Movables 9:4501
   Part
      I. Making and Repairing Movables 9:4501
      I-A. Aircraft 9:4511
      II. Crops 9:4521
      III. Vendor's Privilege 9:4541
         Subpart
         A. In General 9:4541
         B. Sewing Machines and Pianos 9:4561
         C. Payments Under Policies of Insurance 9:4581

For Annotative Materials, see West's Louisiana Statutes Annotated

APPENDIX 1—REVISED STATUTES, TITLE 9

		IV.	Carrier's Charges	9:4601
		V.	Logs and Lumber	9:4621
		VI.	Moss	9:4641
		VII.	Horses	9:4661
		VIII.	Rugs, Carpets, Clothing, and Household Goods	9:4681
		IX.	Jewelry, Gems, and Watches	9:4701
		X.	Sugar, Syrup, and Molasses	9:4721
		XI.	Ships and Other Vessels	9:4741
		XII.	Proceeds Recovered by Injured Person	9:4751
		XIII.	Self-Service Storage Facilities	9:4756
		XIV.	Relation to Chapter 9 of the Louisiana Commercial Laws	9:4770
		XV.	Marina and Boatyard Storage Facilities	9:4780
		XVI.	Other Privileges on Movables	9:4790
		XVII.	Towed and Stored Vessel Act	9:4791
2.	Privileges on Immovables			9:4801
	I.	Private Works Act		9:4801
		A.	Liability Of Owners and Contractors for the Improvement of an Immovable	9:4801
		B.	Definitions	9:4806
		C.	Work Performed by General Contractors	9:4811
		D.	Claims and Privileges; Effectiveness; Preservation; Ranking; Extinguishment	9:4820
		E.	Filing; Cancellation; Peremption	9:4831
		F.	Procedure for Enforcement; Burden of Proof	9:4841
		G.	Residential Truth in Construction Act	9:4851
	II.	Oil, Gas, And Water Wells		9:4861
		A.	In General	9:4861
		B.	Privileges and other rights of operators and non-operators	9:4881
	III.	Railroads		9:4901
		A.	In General	9:4901
	IV.	Public Works		9:4921
		A.	In General	9:4921
		B.	Bonding Claims	9:4941
	V.	Miscellaneous		9:4961
3.	Privileges on Movables and Immovables			9:5001
	I.	Privilege for Attorney Fees		9:5001
	II.	Privileges to Effect Separation of Patrimony		9:5011
	III.	Privilege for Producers of Agricultural and Dairy Products		9:5021
	IV.	Rights of Lien or Privilege Holder		9:5031

CODE TITLE XXII—MORTGAGES

1.	Mortgages in General			9:5101
	Part			
	I.	Property Subject to Mortgage		9:5101
		Subpart		
		A.	In General	9:5101
		B.	Home Appliances and Equipment [Repealed]	9:5121
		C.	Mineral Mortgages—Appointment of Keeper	9:5131
		D.	Conventional Mortgages, Appointment of Receiver or Keeper	9:5136
	II.	Duties of Recorders		9:5141
		A.	Inscription	9:5141
		B.	Erasure or Cancellation	9:5161
		C.	Certificates [Repealed]	9:5181
		D.	Notice of Tax Sales [Repealed]	9:5201
		E.	The Office of Mortgages	9:5206
	III.	Rights of Mortgage Holder		9:5251
2.	Conventional Mortgages			9:5301
	I.	Mortgages Securing Several Obligations		9:5301
	II.	Mortgages on Rural Property		9:5321
	III.	Chattel Mortgages		9:5351
	IV.	Mortgage of Movables Used in Commercial or Industrial Activity [Repealed]		9:5367
	V.	Miscellaneous Provisions		9:5381

For Annotative Materials, see West's Louisiana Statutes Annotated

APPENDIX 1—REVISED STATUTES, TITLE 9

3. Legal Mortgages 9:5501
     I. In General 9:5501
4. Ship Mortgage Law 9:5521
5. Collateral Mortgages and Vendor's Privileges: Effective Date of Collateral Mortgages, Relationship of Collateral Mortgages to Chapter 9 of the Louisiana Commercial Laws and Defenses to Enforcement 9:5550

CODE TITLE XXIII—OCCUPANCY AND POSSESSION [BLANK]

CODE TITLE XXIV—PRESCRIPTION

1. Prescription 9:5601
   Part
     I. Periods of Prescription 9:5601
        Subpart
          A. One Year 9:5601
          B. Two Years 9:5621
          B-1. Three Years 9:5633
          C. Five Years 9:5641
          D. Six Years 9:5661
          E. Ten Years 9:5681
          F. Thirty Years 9:5701
     II. Interruption and Suspension 9:5801
     III. Alteration of Prescriptive Periods 9:5811
     IV. Suspension or Extension of Prescription, Peremption, and Other Legal Deadlines During Hurricanes Katrina and Rita 9:5821

CODE TITLE XXV—OF THE SIGNIFICATION OF SUNDRY TERMS OF LAW EMPLOYED IN THIS CODE [BLANK]

CODE BOOK IV—CONFLICT OF LAWS

CODE TITLE I—OF FOREIGN LAW

1. Application of Foreign Law 9:6001

CODE PRELIMINARY TITLE [BLANK]
CODE BOOK I—OF PERSONS
CODE TITLE I—NATURAL AND JURIDICAL PERSONS

CHAPTER 1. WOMEN

PART I. IN GENERAL

Section
51. Civil rights and duties.

PART II. MARRIED WOMEN

SUBPART A. EMANCIPATION AND POWERS

101. Emancipation from all disabilities and incapacities; obligations.
102. Suits, judicial proceedings, and judgments.
103. Binding themselves or disposing of or hypothecating property for benefit of husband or community; contracts with husband.
104. Repealed.
105. Laws relating to matrimonial community and separate property not affected.

PART I. IN GENERAL

§ 51. Civil rights and duties

Women have the same rights, authority, privileges, and immunities, and shall perform the same obligations and duties as men in the holding of office including the civil functions of tutor, under tutor, curator, under curator, administrator, executor, arbitrator, and notary public.

Cross References

C.C. arts. 81, 83, 85, 250, 258, 259, 262, 2336, 3519, 3523 to 3527, 3532, 3536.

PART II. MARRIED WOMEN

SUBPART A. EMANCIPATION AND POWERS

§ 101. Emancipation from all disabilities and incapacities; obligations

All married women, including non-residents so far as they are affected by the laws of this state, are fully emancipated from all the disabilities and relieved from all the incapacities to which, as such, they were formerly subject. They may make contracts of all kinds, and assume or stipulate for obligations of all kinds, in any form or manner now permitted, or which may hereafter be permitted, by law for any person, married or unmarried, of either sex, and in no case shall any act, contract, or obligation of a married woman require, for the validity or effectiveness thereof, the authority of her husband or of the judge.

Cross References

C.C. arts. 81, 250, 258, 2336, 3101, 3290, 3519, 3523 to 3527.

§ 102. Suits, judicial proceedings, and judgments

Married women may institute or defend suits, or otherwise appear in judicial proceedings, and stand in judgment, without the authority of their husbands or of the judge.

Cross References

C.C. arts. 2336, 3101, 3290, 3519, 3523 to 3527.

§ 103. Binding themselves or disposing of or hypothecating property for benefit of husband or community; contracts with husband

Married women may obligate themselves personally in any form, or dispose of or hypothecate their property, as security or otherwise, for the benefit of their husbands or of the community between them and their husbands.

Cross References

C.C. arts. 2336, 2999, 3101, 3290, 3519, 3523 to 3527.

§ 104. Repealed by Acts 1974, No. 89, § 1

§ 105. Laws relating to matrimonial community and separate property not affected

Nothing contained in R.S. 9:101, 9:102, and 9:103 is intended to modify or affect the laws relating to the matrimonial community of acquêts and gains or the laws prescribing what is deemed the separate property of the spouses.

Cross References

C.C. arts. 2334, 2336, 2338, 2339, 2340, 2341, 3101, 3290, 3519, 3523 to 3527.

CHAPTER 2. DEATH

Section
111. Definition of death.

§ 111. Definition of death

A. A person will be considered dead if in the announced opinion of a physician, duly licensed in the state of Louisiana based on ordinary standards of approved medical practice, the person has experienced an irreversible cessation of spontaneous respiratory and circulatory functions. In the event that artificial means of support preclude a determination that these functions have ceased, a person will be considered dead if in the announced opinion of a physician, duly licensed in the state of Louisiana based upon ordinary standards of approved medical practice, the person has experienced an irreversible total cessation of brain function. Death will have occurred at the time when the relevant functions ceased. In any case when organs are to be used in a transplant, then an additional physician, duly licensed in the state of Louisiana not a member of the transplant team, must make the pronouncement of death unless a hospital has adopted a written policy allowing that a single physician, duly licensed in the state of Louisiana, not a member of the transplant team, may make the pronouncement of death. In all cases in which a hospital written policy provides that a single physician makes the pronouncement of death, such policy shall also require an opinion by a second physician, not a member of the transplant team, as to the candidacy of the person for the process of organ donation.

B. The medical pronouncement of death by a coroner may also be based on personal observation, information, or statements obtained from coroner investigators or emergency medical technicians at the scene who are reporting from firsthand observation of the physical condition of the deceased. The time of death shall be reported as the time that the death was reported or discovered. The name of the personnel that the coroner is relying on shall be noted on the coroner's day record or protocol.

Added by Acts 1976, No. 233, § 1. Amended by Acts 2001, No. 317, § 1; Acts 2010, No. 937, § 1, eff. July 1, 2010.

Cross References

C.C. arts. 30, 31, 54, 56, 872, 1493, 3528.

CHAPTER 3. HUMAN EMBRYOS

Section
121. Human embryo; definition.
122. Uses of human embryo in vitro.
123. Capacity.
124. Legal status.
125. Separate entity.
126. Ownership.
127. Responsibility.
128. Qualifications.
129. Destruction.
130. Duties of donors.
131. Judicial standard.
132. Liability.
133. Inheritance rights.

§ 121. Human embryo; definition

A "human embryo" for the purposes of this Chapter is an in vitro fertilized human ovum, with certain rights granted by law, composed of one or more living human cells and human genetic material so unified and organized that it will develop in utero into an unborn child.

Added by Acts 1986, No. 964, § 1.

Cross References

C.C. arts. 24, 25, 81, 216, 252, 479, 880, 940, 3519.

§ 122. Uses of human embryo in vitro

The use of a human ovum fertilized in vitro is solely for the support and contribution of the complete development of human in utero implantation. No in vitro fertilized human ovum will be farmed or cultured solely for research purposes or any other purposes. The sale of a human ovum, fertilized human ovum, or human embryo is expressly prohibited.

Added by Acts 1986, No. 964, § 1.

Cross References

C.C. arts. 7, 2448.

§ 123. Capacity

An in vitro fertilized human ovum exists as a juridical person until such time as the in vitro fertilized ovum is implanted in the womb; or at any other time when rights attach to an unborn child in accordance with law.

Added by Acts 1986, No. 964, § 1.

Cross References

C.C. arts. 24, 25, 252, 940, 3519.

§ 124. Legal status

As a juridical person, the in vitro fertilized human ovum shall be given an identification by the medical facility for use within the medical facility which entitles such ovum to sue or be sued. The confidentiality of the in vitro fertilization patient shall be maintained.

Added by Acts 1986, No. 964, § 1.

Cross References

C.C. arts. 1918, 2315, 3519.

§ 125. Separate entity

An in vitro fertilized human ovum as a juridical person is recognized as a separate entity apart from the medical facility or clinic where it is housed or stored.

Added by Acts 1986, No. 964, § 1.

Cross References

C.C. arts. 24, 25, 252, 940, 3519.

§ 126. Ownership

An in vitro fertilized human ovum is a biological human being which is not the property of the physician which acts as an agent of fertilization, or the facility which employs him or the donors of the sperm and ovum. If the in vitro fertilization patients express their identity, then their rights as parents as provided under the Louisiana Civil Code will be preserved. If the in vitro fertilization patients fail to express their identity, then the physician shall be deemed to be temporary guardian of the in vitro fertilized human ovum until adoptive implantation can occur. A court in the parish where the in vitro fertilized ovum is located may appoint a curator, upon motion of the in vitro fertilization patients, their heirs, or physicians who caused in vitro fertilization to be performed, to protect the in vitro fertilized human ovum's rights.

Added by Acts 1986, No. 964, § 1.

Cross References

C.C. arts. 24, 25, 81 to 85, 215 to 237, 246.

§ 127. Responsibility

Any physician or medical facility who causes in vitro fertilization of a human ovum in vitro will be directly responsible for the in vitro safekeeping of the fertilized ovum.

Added by Acts 1986, No. 964, § 1.

Cross References

C.C. art. 2315.

§ 128. Qualifications

Only medical facilities meeting the standards of the American Fertility Society and the American College of Obstetricians and Gynecologists and directed by a medical doctor licensed to practice medicine in this state and possessing specialized training and skill in in vitro fertilization also in conformity with the standards established by the American Fertility Society or the American College of Obstetricians and Gynecologists shall cause the in vitro fertilization of a human ovum to occur. No person shall engage in in vitro fertilization procedures unless qualified as provided in this Section.

Added by Acts 1986, No. 964, § 1.

§ 129. Destruction

A viable in vitro fertilized human ovum is a juridical person which shall not be intentionally destroyed by any natural or other juridical person or through the actions of any other such person. An in vitro fertilized human ovum that fails to develop further over a thirty-six hour period except when the embryo is in a state of cryopreservation, is considered non-viable and is not considered a juridical person.

Added by Acts 1986, No. 964, § 1.

Cross References

C.C. arts. 24, 25, 252, 940.

§ 130. Duties of donors

An in vitro fertilized human ovum is a juridical person which cannot be owned by the in vitro fertilization patients who owe it a high duty of care and prudent administration. If the in vitro fertilization patients renounce, by notarial act, their parental rights for in utero implantation, then the in vitro fertilized human ovum shall be available for adoptive implantation in accordance with written procedures of the facility where it is housed or stored. The in vitro fertilization patients may renounce their parental rights in favor of another married couple, but only if the other couple is willing and able to receive the in vitro fertilized ovum. No compensation shall be paid or received by either couple to renounce parental rights. Constructive fulfillment of the statutory provisions for adoption in this state shall occur when a married couple executes a notarial act of adoption of the in vitro fertilized ovum and birth occurs.

Added by Acts 1986, No. 964, § 1.

Cross References

C.C. arts. 24, 221, 454, 479.

§ 131. Judicial standard

In disputes arising between any parties regarding the in vitro fertilized ovum, the judicial standard for resolving such disputes is to be in the best interest of the in vitro fertilized ovum.

Added by Acts 1986, No. 964, § 1.

Cross References

C.C. arts. 131, 134.

§ 132. Liability

Strict liability or liability of any kind including actions relating to succession rights and inheritance shall not be applicable to any physician, hospital, in vitro fertilization clinic, or their agent who acts in good faith in the screening, collection, conservation, preparation, transfer, or cryopreservation of the human ovum fertilized in vitro for transfer to the human uterus. Any immunity granted by this Section is applicable only to an action brought on behalf of the in vitro fertilized human ovum as a juridical person.

Added by Acts 1986, No. 964, § 1.

Cross References

C.C. arts. 1759, 1760, 2315.

§ 133. Inheritance rights

Inheritance rights will not flow to the in vitro fertilized ovum as a juridical person, unless the in vitro fertilized ovum develops into an unborn child that is born in a live birth, or at any other time when rights attach to an unborn child in accordance with law. As a juridical person, the embryo or child born as a result of in vitro fertilization and in vitro fertilized ovum donation to another couple does not retain its inheritance rights from the in vitro fertilization patients.

Added by Acts 1986, No. 964, § 1.

Cross References

C.C. arts. 24, 252, 940, 3519.

CODE TITLE II—OF DOMICILE AND THE MANNER OF CHANGING THE SAME [BLANK]

CODE TITLE III—ABSENT PERSONS

CHAPTER 1. UNIFORM UNCLAIMED PROPERTY ACT

Section
151. Short title.
152. Uniformity of application and construction.
153. Definitions.
154. Presumptions of abandonment.
154.1. Compensation for expropriation; ownership; town of Berwick.
154.2. Crescent City Connection; Geaux Pass accounts and deposits; tolls; Geaux Pass Transition Fund; disposition.
155. Contents of safe deposit box or other safekeeping depository.
156. Rules for taking custody.
157. Dormancy charge.
158. Burden of proof as to property evidenced by record of check or draft.
159. Report of abandoned property.

APPENDIX 1—REVISED STATUTES, TITLE 9

Section
160. Payment or delivery of abandoned property.
161. Notice and publication of lists of abandoned property.
162. Custody by state; recovery by holder; defense of holder.
163. Crediting of dividends, interest, and increments to owner's account.
164. Public sale of abandoned property.
165. Deposit of funds.
165.1. Bonds; unclaimed property bonds; completion of I-49.
165.2. Designates first I-49 unclaimed property bond project; "Alvin B. Kessler Memorial Highway".
166. Claim of another state to recover property.
167. Filing claim with administrator; handling of claims by administrator.
168. Action to establish claim.
169. Election to take payment or delivery.
170. Destruction or disposition of property having no substantial commercial value; immunity from liability.
171. Periods of limitation.
172. Requests for reports and examination of records.
173. Retention of records.
174. Enforcement.
175. Interstate agreements and cooperation; joint and reciprocal actions with other states; confidentiality.
176. Interest and penalties.
177. Agreement to locate property.
178. Foreign transactions.
179. Applicability of Chapter.
180. Rules.
181. Severability.
182 to 188. [Blank].

Editor's note. Acts 1997, No. 809, § 2, provides: "The provisions of this Act shall become effective for all reportable periods ending June 30, 1997, and thereafter."

§ 151. Short title

This Chapter may be cited as the "Uniform Unclaimed Property Act of 1997".

Acts 1997, No. 809, § 1, eff. July 10, 1997.

Cross References

C.C. arts. 44, 47, 453, 479, 526, 3412, 3418, 3419, 3421, 3437, 3468, 3491, 3499.

§ 152. Uniformity of application and construction

This Chapter shall be applied and construed to effectuate its general purpose to make uniform the law with respect to the subject of this Chapter among states enacting it.

Acts 1997, No. 809, § 1, eff. July 10, 1997.

Cross References

C.C. arts. 44, 47, 453, 479, 526, 3412, 3418, 3419, 3421, 3437, 3468, 3491, 3499.

§ 153. Definitions

As used in this Chapter:

(1) "Administrator" means the state treasurer.

(2) "Apparent owner" means a person whose name appears on the records of a holder as the person entitled to property held, issued, or owed by the holder.

(3) "Business association" means a corporation, joint stock company, investment company, partnership, unincorporated association, joint venture, limited liability company, business trust, trust company, savings and loan association, building and loan association, savings bank, industrial bank, land bank, safe deposit company, safekeeping depository, bank, banking organization, financial organization, insurance company, mutual fund, credit union, utility, or other business entity consisting of one or more persons, whether or not for profit.

(4) "Domicile" means the state of incorporation of a corporation and the state of the principal place of business of a holder other than a corporation.

(5) "Holder" means a person obligated to hold for the account of, or deliver or pay to, the owner of property that is subject to this Chapter.

(6) "Insurance company" means an association, corporation, or fraternal or mutual benefit organization, whether or not for profit, engaged in the business of providing insurance including accident, burial, casualty, credit life, contract performance, dental, fidelity, fire, health, hospitalization, illness, life insurance, life endowments and annuities, malpractice, marine, mortgage, surety, and wage protection insurance.

(7) "Mineral" means gas, oil, coal, other gaseous liquid and solid hydrocarbons, oil shale, cement material, sand and gravel, road material, building stone, chemical substance, gemstone, fissionable and nonfissionable ores, colloidal and other clay, steam and other geothermal resource, or any other substance defined as a mineral by the law of this state.

(8) "Mineral proceeds" means amounts payable for the extraction, production, or sale of minerals, or, upon the abandonment of those payments, all payments that become payable thereafter. The term includes amounts payable for all of the following:

(a) For the acquisition and retention of a mineral lease, including bonuses, royalties, compensatory royalties, shut-in royalties, minimum royalties, and delay rentals.

(b) For the extraction, production, or sale of minerals, including net revenue interests, royalties, overriding royalties, extraction payments, and production payments.

(c) Resulting from an agreement or option, including a joint operating agreement, unit agreement, pooling agreement, and farm-out agreement.

(9) "Money order" includes an express money order and a personal money order, on which the remitter is the purchaser. The term does not include a bank money order or any other instrument sold by a banking or financial organization if the seller has obtained the name and address of the payee.

(10) "Owner" means a person who has a legal or equitable interest in property subject to this Chapter or the person's legal representative. The term includes a depositor in the case of a deposit, a beneficiary in the case of a trust other than a deposit in trust, and a creditor, claimant, or payee in the case of other property.

(11) "Person" means an individual, business association, estate, trust, partnership, government, governmental subdivision, agency, or instrumentality, public corporation, or any other legal or commercial entity.

(12) "Property" means a fixed and certain interest in intangible property that is held, issued, or owed in the course

of a holder's business, or by a government or governmental entity, and all income or increments therefrom. The term includes property that is referred to as or evidenced by the following:

(a) Money, a check, draft, deposit, interest, or dividend.

(b) Credit balance, customer's overpayment, gift certificate, security deposit, refund, credit memorandum, unpaid wage, unused ticket, mineral proceeds, or unidentified remittance.

(c) Stock or other evidence of ownership of an interest in a business association.

(d) A bond, debenture, note, or other evidence of indebtedness.

(e) Money deposited to redeem stocks, bonds, coupons, or other securities or to make distributions.

(f) An amount due and payable under the terms of an annuity or insurance policy, including policies providing life insurance, property and casualty insurance, workers' compensation insurance, or health and disability insurance.

(g) An amount distributable from a trust or custodial fund established under a plan to provide health, welfare, pension, vacation, severance, retirement, death, stock purchase, profit sharing, employee savings, supplemental unemployment insurance, or similar benefits.

(h) Any certificate, rebate, coupon, or other instrument issued in connection with a class action judgment or court-approved settlement of a class action proceeding which represents a refund on, or reduction of, the purchase price of an item or services purchased or to be purchased shall not constitute property within the meaning of this statute.

(13) "Record" means information that is inscribed on a tangible medium or that is stored in an electronic or other medium and is retrievable in perceivable form.

(14) "State" means a state of the United States, the District of Columbia, the Commonwealth of Puerto Rico, or any territory or insular possession subject to the jurisdiction of the United States.

(15) "Utility" means a person who owns or operates for public use any plant, equipment, real property, franchise, or license for the transmission of communications or the production, storage, transmission, sale, delivery, or furnishing of electricity, water, steam, or gas.

Acts 1997, No. 809, § 1, eff. July 10, 1997. Amended by Acts 2000, 1st Ex.Sess., No. 135, § 2, eff. July 1, 2000.

Cross References

C.C. arts. 44, 47, 453, 479, 526, 3412, 3418, 3419, 3421, 3437, 3468, 3491, 3499.

§ 154. Presumptions of abandonment

A. Property is presumed abandoned if it is unclaimed by the apparent owner during the time set forth below for the particular property for the following:

(1) Travelers check, fifteen years after issuance.

(2) Money order, seven years after issuance.

(3)(a) Stock or other interest in a business association, including a debt obligation other than a bearer bond or original issue discount bond, if either of the following applies:

(i) Three years after the earlier of the date of an unpresented instrument issued to pay interest or a dividend or other cash distribution, or the date of issue of an undelivered stock certificate issued as a stock dividend, split, or other distribution.

(ii) If a dividend or other distribution has not been paid on the stock or other interest for three consecutive years, or the stock or other interest is held pursuant to a plan that provides for the automatic reinvestment of dividends or other distributions, three years after the date of the second mailing of a statement of account or other notification or communication that was returned as undeliverable, or after the holder discontinued mailings to the apparent owner, whichever is earlier.

(b) Any dividend, profit, distribution, interest, redemption, payment on principal, or other sum held or owing by a business association for or to a shareholder, certificate holder, member, bond holder, or other security holder, who has not claimed it, or corresponded in writing with the business association concerning it, within three years after the date prescribed for payment or delivery.

(4) A demand, savings, or matured time deposit, including a deposit that is automatically renewable, five years after the earlier of its maturity or the date of the last indication by the owner of interest in the property; however, property that is automatically renewable is deemed matured for purposes of this Section upon its initial date of maturity, unless the owner has consented to a renewal at or about the time of the renewal and the consent is in writing or is evidenced by a memorandum or other record on file with the holder. However, no property under this Paragraph shall be presumed abandoned if a banking or financial organization has forwarded a statement or other written communication to the owner within the preceding ninety days with regard to the property at the owner's last known address and the statement or communication has not been returned to the banking or financial organization as undeliverable or unclaimed by the forwarding agent.

(5) Money or credits owed to a customer as a result of a retail business transaction, three years after the obligation accrued.

(6) Gift certificate, three years after December thirty-first of the year in which the certificate was sold.

(7) Amount owed by an insurer on a life or endowment insurance policy or annuity contract that has matured or terminated, three years after the obligation to pay arose or, in the case of a policy or contract payable upon proof of death, three years after the insured has attained, or would have attained if living, the limiting age under the mortality table on which the reserve is based.

(8) Property distributable by a business association in a course of dissolution, one year after the property becomes distributable.

(9) Property received by a court as proceeds of a class action, and not distributed to members of the class, one year after the distribution date.

(10) Property held by a court, state or other government, governmental subdivision or agency, public corporation, or other public authority, one year after the property becomes distributable, except as provided in R.S. 15:86.1.

(11) Wages or other compensation for personal services, one year after the compensation becomes payable.

(12) Deposit or refund owed to a subscriber by a utility, one year after the deposit or refund becomes payable.

(13) Property in an individual retirement account or other account or plan that is qualified for tax deferral under the

income tax laws of the United States, three years after the earliest of the date of the distribution or attempted distribution of the property, the date of the required distribution as stated in the plan or trust agreement governing the plan, or the date, if determinable by the holder, specified in the income tax laws of the United States by which distribution of the property must begin in order to avoid a tax penalty.

(14) Mineral proceeds, two years after the property is payable or distributable.

(15) Funds in an education savings account established in accordance with the Louisiana Student Tuition Assistance and Revenue Trust Program as provided in Chapter 22–A of Title 17, during any five-year period subsequent to the beneficiary's thirty-fifth birthday.

(16) Property distributable in the course of a demutualization, rehabilitation, or related reorganization of an insurance company, two years after the date of the demutualization or other event covered herein if, at the time of the demutualization or other event covered herein, the last known address of the owner on the book and records of the holder is known to be incorrect, or distributions or statements are returned by the post office as undeliverable, and the owner has not communicated in writing with the holder or its agent regarding the interest, or otherwise communicated with the holder regarding the interest as evidenced by a memorandum or other record on file with the holder or its agent.

(17) All other property, five years after the obligation to pay or distribute the property arises.

B. At the time that an interest is presumed abandoned under Paragraph A(3) of this Section, any other property right accrued or accruing to the owner as a result of the interest, and not previously presumed abandoned, shall also be presumed abandoned.

C. (1) Property is unclaimed if, for the applicable period of time set forth in Subsection A of this Section, the apparent owner has not communicated, in writing or by other means reflected in a contemporaneous record prepared by or on behalf of the holder, with the holder concerning the property or the account in which the property is held, and has not otherwise indicated an interest in the property. A communication with an owner by a person other than the holder or its representative who has not in writing identified the property to the owner shall not be an indication of interest in the property by the owner.

(2) Property is unclaimed for purposes of Subsection (A)(15) of this Section if, for the applicable period of time set forth in Subsection (A)(15) of this Section, the education savings account owner has not communicated, in writing or by other means reflected in a contemporaneous record prepared by or on behalf of the holder, with the holder concerning the account in which the funds are held, and has not otherwise indicated an interest in the funds and the beneficiary of the account has not requested a disbursement of any of the funds for qualified higher education expenses. A communication with an owner by a person other than the holder or its representative who has not identified the account in writing to the owner shall not be an indication of interest in the property by the owner.

D. An indication of an owner's interest in property includes the following:

(1) The presentment of a check or other instrument of payment of a dividend or other distribution made with respect to an account or underlying stock or other interest in a business association or, in the case of a distribution made by electronic or similar means, evidence that the distribution has been received.

(2) Owner–directed activity in the account in which the property is held, including a direction by the owner to increase, decrease, or change the amount or type of property held in the account.

(3) The making of a deposit to or withdrawal from a bank account.

(4) The payment of a premium with respect to a property interest in an insurance policy; however, the application of an automatic premium loan provision or other nonforfeiture provision contained in an insurance policy does not prevent a policy from maturing or terminating if the insured has died or the insured or the beneficiary of the policy has otherwise become entitled to the proceeds before the depletion of the cash surrender value of a policy by the application of those provisions.

E. Property shall be payable or distributable for purposes of this Chapter notwithstanding the owner's failure to make demand or present an instrument or document otherwise required to obtain payment.

Acts 1997, No. 809, § 1, eff. July 10, 1997. Amended by Acts 2003, No. 221, § 1, eff. June 5, 2003; Acts 2004, No. 839, § 1; Acts 2006, No. 573, § 1.

Cross References

C.C. arts. 44, 47, 453, 479, 526, 3412, 3418, 3419, 3421, 3437, 3468, 3491, 3499.

§ 154.1. Compensation for expropriation; ownership; town of Berwick

A. Notwithstanding the provisions of R.S. 9:154, monetary funds paid by the town of Berwick into the registry of the court for the expropriation of property and which monetary funds would otherwise be deemed abandoned pursuant to R.S. 9:154, and which monetary funds have not been claimed by any person for a period in excess of twelve years, shall revert to being funds of the town of Berwick, and any such monetary funds held by the administrator shall be returned to the town of Berwick.

B. The administrator who returns the funds to the town of Berwick shall be relieved of all liability which may arise with respect to the funds which have been returned to the town of Berwick.

Added by Acts 2001, No. 836, § 1.

§ 154.2. Crescent City Connection; Geaux Pass accounts and deposits; tolls; Geaux Pass Transition Fund; disposition

A. Notwithstanding the provisions of R.S. 9:154 or any other provision of law to the contrary, the provisions of this Section shall apply to account balances and toll tag deposits for all Geaux Pass accounts with the primary designation of the Crescent City Connection Bridge that have had no activity on Louisiana Highway 1 since July 1, 2012, and all tolls paid to cross the Crescent City Connection Bridge for the period beginning January 1, 2013, and continuing through March 5, 2013.

B. On July 1, 2013, any monetary funds remaining in any Geaux Pass account, any monetary funds remaining for toll tag deposits for all Geaux Pass accounts with the primary designation of the Crescent City Connection Bridge that have had no activity on Louisiana Highway 1 on or after July 1, 2012, and any monetary funds paid as a toll to cross the Crescent City Connection Bridge from January 1, 2013, through March 5, 2013, and which monetary funds have not been claimed by any person as of June 15, 2013, shall be deemed abandoned funds for the purposes of treatment as unclaimed property in accordance with the provisions of this Section.

C. Funds that are deemed abandoned funds pursuant to this Section shall be immediately reported and transferred from the Department of Transportation and Development to the state treasurer in his capacity as administrator of the Uniform Unclaimed Property Act. The state treasurer shall deposit these funds into the Geaux Pass Transition Fund as provided in this Section, and shall through June 30, 2014, provide for the return of such funds to their owners in accordance with the Uniform Unclaimed Property Act. The state treasurer shall further provide for the payment of all unexpended and unencumbered funds remaining in the Geaux Pass Transition Fund on June 30, 2014, in accordance with the provisions of this Section.

D. (1) There is hereby created the Geaux Pass Transition Fund as a special fund in the state treasury, hereinafter referred to as the "fund". The source of monies for the fund shall be the monies transferred from the Department of Transportation and Development to the state treasurer in his capacity as administrator of the Uniform Unclaimed Property Act pursuant to the provisions of this Section.

(2) After compliance with the requirements of Article VII, Section 9(B) of the Constitution of Louisiana, relative to the Bond Security and Redemption Fund, an amount equal to that deposited into the state treasury from the foregoing sources shall be deposited in and credited to the fund. The monies in the fund shall be invested by the treasurer in the same manner as the state general fund, and interest earnings shall be deposited into the fund.

(3) All unexpended and unencumbered monies remaining in the fund on June 30, 2014, shall be appropriated as follows:

(a) An amount not to exceed thirty percent of the monies in the fund shall be appropriated to the Department of Transportation and Development for operational and maintenance costs for the New Orleans ferries, formerly operated by its Crescent City Connection Division.

(b) The balance of the monies in the fund as of June 30, 2014, shall be appropriated to the New Orleans Regional Planning Commission for lighting of the eastbank and westbank approaches to the Crescent City Connection Bridge, including General DeGaulle and the Westbank Expressway approach through ground level, improvements to ingress and egress points, lighting, maintenance, grass cutting, and landscaping of the Westbank Expressway and its connecting arteries.

(c) The state treasurer shall be relieved of all liability which may arise with respect to such distribution of funds.

E. All data associated with funds transferred to the state treasurer pursuant to this Section shall be provided to the Unclaimed Property Division in an electronic format as designated by such division.

F. For the purposes of this Section, holder requirements under R.S. 9:159 shall be deemed waived and the Department of Transportation and Development shall be deemed a holder in good faith pursuant to provisions of the Uniform Unclaimed Property Act.

G. The state treasurer in his capacity as administrator of the Uniform Unclaimed Property Act may establish policies and procedures as necessary to implement the provisions of this Section.

H. All books, papers, and records transferred to the state treasurer pursuant to this Section or as a result of Act No. 247 of the 2013 Regular Session of the Legislature shall be retained for a period of no less than five years following such transfer.

I. The provisions of this Section shall supersede and control to the extent of conflict with any other provision of law.

Added by Acts 2013, No. 247, § 1, eff. June 12, 2013.

§ 155. Contents of safe deposit box or other safekeeping depository

Intangible property held in a safe deposit box or other safekeeping depository in this state in the ordinary course of the holder's business, and proceeds resulting from the sale of the property permitted by other law, shall be presumed abandoned if it remains unclaimed by the owner for more than five years after expiration of the lease or rental period on the box or other depository.

Acts 1997, No. 809, § 1, eff. July 10, 1997.

Cross References

C.C. arts. 44, 47, 453, 479, 526, 3412, 3418, 3419, 3421, 3437, 3468, 3491, 3499.

§ 156. Rules for taking custody

Unless otherwise provided in this Chapter or by other statute of this state, property that is presumed abandoned, whether located in this or another state, shall be subject to the custody of this state if any of the following applies:

(1) The last known address of the apparent owner, as shown on the records of the holder, is in this state.

(2) The records of the holder do not reflect the identity of the person entitled to the property and it is established that the last known address of the person entitled to the property is in this state.

(3) The records of the holder do not reflect the last known address of the apparent owner and it is established that any of the following applies:

(a) The last known address of the person entitled to the property is in this state.

(b) The holder is a domiciliary or a government or governmental subdivision or agency of this state and has not previously paid or delivered the property to the state of the last known address of the apparent owner or other person entitled to the property.

(4) The last known address of the apparent owner, as shown on the records of the holder, is in a state that does not provide for the escheat or custodial taking of the property and the holder is a domiciliary or a government or governmental subdivision or agency of this state.

(5) The last known address of the apparent owner, as shown on the records of the holder, is in a foreign country and the holder is a domiciliary or a government or governmental subdivision or agency of this state.

(6) The transaction out of which the property arose occurred in this state, the holder is a domiciliary of a state that does not provide for the escheat or custodial taking of the

property and the last known address of the apparent owner or other person entitled to the property is unknown or is in a state that does not provide for the escheat or custodial taking of the property.

(7) The property is a traveler's check, cashier's check, teller's check, or other official bank issued check, or money order purchased in this state, or the issuer of the traveler's check, cashier's check, teller's check, or other official bank issued check, or money order has its principal place of business in this state and the issuer's records do not show the state in which the instrument was purchased or show that the instrument was purchased in a state that does not provide for the escheat or custodial taking of the property.

Acts 1997, No. 809, § 1, eff. July 10, 1997. Amended by Acts 2009, No. 86, § 1.

Cross References

C.C. arts. 44, 47, 453, 479, 526, 3412, 3418, 3419, 3421, 3437, 3468, 3491, 3499.

§ 157. Dormancy charge

A holder may deduct from property presumed abandoned a charge imposed by reason of the owner's failure to claim the property within a specified time only if there is a valid and enforceable written contract between the holder and the owner pursuant to which the holder may impose the charge and the holder regularly imposes the charge, which is not regularly reversed or otherwise canceled. The amount of the deduction is limited to an amount that is not unconscionable.

Acts 1997, No. 809, § 1, eff. July 10, 1997.

Cross References

C.C. arts. 44, 47, 453, 479, 526, 3412, 3418, 3419, 3421, 3437, 3468, 3491, 3499.

§ 158. Burden of proof as to property evidenced by record of check or draft

A record of the issuance of a check, draft, or similar instrument is prima facie evidence of an obligation. In claiming property from a holder who is also the issuer, the administrator's burden of proof as to the existence and amount of the property and its abandonment is satisfied by showing issuance of the instrument and passage of the requisite period of abandonment. Defenses of payment, satisfaction, discharge, and want of consideration are affirmative defenses that must be established by the holder.

Acts 1997, No. 809, § 1, eff. July 10, 1997.

Cross References

C.C. arts. 44, 47, 453, 479, 526, 3412, 3418, 3419, 3421, 3437, 3468, 3491, 3499.

§ 159. Report of abandoned property

A. A holder of property presumed abandoned shall make a report to the administrator concerning the property.

B. The report shall be verified and shall include all of the following:

(1) Except with respect to a traveler's check or money order, the name if known, and last known address, if any, and the social security number or taxpayer identification number, if readily ascertainable, of the apparent owner of property of the value of fifty dollars or more.

(2) An aggregated amount of items valued under fifty dollars each.

(3) In the case of unclaimed money amounting to fifty dollars or more held or owing under any annuity or life or endowment insurance policy the full name and last known address of the insured or annuitant and of the beneficiary.

(4) In the case of tangible property held in a safe deposit box or other safekeeping depository, a description of the property and the place where it is held and where it may be inspected by the administrator, and any amounts owing to the holder.

(5) The date, if any, on which the property became payable, demandable, or returnable, and the date of the last transaction with the apparent owner with respect to the property.

(6) Other information that the administrator by rule prescribes as necessary for the administration of this Chapter.

C. If a holder of property presumed abandoned is a successor to another person who previously held the property for the apparent owner or the holder has changed its name while holding the property, the holder shall file with the report its former names, if any, and the known names and addresses of all previous holders of the property.

D. The report shall be filed before November first of each year and cover the twelve months next preceding July first of that year.

E. The holder of property presumed abandoned shall send written notice to the apparent owner not more than one hundred twenty days nor less than sixty days before filing the report required by this Section, stating that the holder is in possession of property subject to this Chapter if each of the following applies:

(1) The holder has in its records an address for the apparent owner that the holder's records do not disclose to be inaccurate.

(2) The claim of the apparent owner is not barred by the statute of limitations.

(3) The value of the property is fifty dollars or more.

F. Before the date for filing the report, the holder of property presumed abandoned may request the administrator to extend the time for filing the report. The administrator may grant the extension for good cause. The holder, upon receipt of the extension, may make an interim payment on the amount the holder estimates will ultimately be due, which shall terminate the accrual of additional interest on the amount paid.

G. The holder of property presumed abandoned shall file with the report an affidavit stating that the holder has complied with Subsection E of this Section.

Acts 1997, No. 809, § 1, eff. July 10, 1997.

Cross References

C.C. arts. 44, 47, 453, 479, 526, 3412, 3418, 3419, 3421, 3437, 3468, 3491, 3499.

§ 160. Payment or delivery of abandoned property

A. Upon filing the report required by R.S. 9:159, the holder of property presumed abandoned shall pay, transfer, or cause to be paid or transferred to the administrator the property described in the report as unclaimed, but if the property is an automatically renewable deposit, and a penalty or forfeiture in the payment of interest would result, the time for compliance is extended until a penalty or forfeiture would no longer result.

B. If the property reported to the administrator is a security or security entitlement under Chapter 8 of Title 10 of the Louisiana Revised Statutes of 1950, the administrator is an appropriate person to make an endorsement, instruction, or entitlement order on behalf of the apparent owner to invoke the duty of the issuer or its transfer agent or the securities intermediary to transfer or dispose of the security or the security entitlement in accordance with Chapter 8 of Title 10 of the Louisiana Revised Statutes of 1950.

C. If the holder of property reported to the administrator is the issuer of a certificated security, the administrator has the right to obtain a replacement certificate pursuant to R.S. 10:8–405, but an indemnity bond is not required.

D. An issuer, the holder, and any transfer agent or other person acting on behalf of the issuer or holder pursuant to them in accordance with this Section is not liable to the apparent owner and shall be indemnified against claims of any person in accordance with R.S. 9:162.

Acts 1997, No. 809, § 1, eff. July 10, 1997.

Cross References

C.C. arts. 44, 47, 453, 479, 526, 3412, 3418, 3419, 3421, 3437, 3468, 3491, 3499.

§ 161. Notice and publication of lists of abandoned property

A. The administrator shall cause a notice to be published not later than November thirtieth of the year following the year in which abandoned property has been paid or delivered to the administrator. The notice shall be published in a newspaper of general circulation in the parish of this state in which is located the last known address of any person named in the notice. If a holder does not report an address for the apparent owner, or the address is outside this state, the notice shall be published in the parish in which the holder has its principal place of business within this state or another parish that the administrator reasonably selects. The advertisement shall be in a form that, in the judgment of the administrator, is likely to attract the attention of the apparent owner of the unclaimed property. The form shall contain the following information:

(1) The name of each person appearing to be the owner of the property, as set forth in the report filed by the holder.

(2) The last known address or location of each person appearing to be the owner of the property, if an address or location is set forth in the report filed by the holder.

(3) A statement explaining that property of the owner is presumed to be abandoned and has been taken into the protective custody of the administrator.

(4) A statement that information about the property and its return to the owner is available to a person having a legal or beneficial interest in the property, upon request to the administrator.

B. The administrator is not required to advertise the name and address or location of an owner of property having a total value less than fifty dollars, or information concerning a traveler's check, money order, or similar written instrument.

C. The administrator shall, not less than thirty days prior to any notice of unclaimed property being published in any newspaper, mail each legislator a list of the names and addresses of all unclaimed property owners by parish of last known residence for the parishes in the legislator's district and the amount of property unclaimed. The administrator shall not send any written communication to any unclaimed property owner until thirty days following the notice required by this Subsection.

Acts 1997, No. 809, § 1, eff. July 10, 1997. Amended by Acts 2000, 1st Ex.Sess., No. 135, § 5, eff. July 1, 2000.

Cross References

C.C. arts. 44, 47, 453, 479, 526, 3412, 3418, 3419, 3421, 3437, 3468, 3491, 3499.

§ 162. Custody by state; recovery by holder; defense of holder

A. In this Section, payment or delivery is made in "good faith" if all of the following apply:

(1) Payment or delivery was made in a reasonable attempt to comply with this Chapter.

(2) The holder was not then in breach of a fiduciary obligation with respect to the property and had a reasonable basis for believing, based on the facts then known, that the property was presumed abandoned.

(3) There is no showing that the records under which the delivery was made did not meet reasonable commercial standards of practice in the industry.

B. Upon payment or delivery of property to the administrator, the state assumes custody and responsibility for the safekeeping of the property. A holder who pays or delivers property to the administrator in good faith is relieved of all liability arising thereafter with respect to the property. The administrator shall be responsible for taking all reasonable measures to deliver to the owner any property paid or delivered to the administrator.

C. A holder who has paid money to the administrator pursuant to this Chapter may subsequently make payment to a person reasonably appearing to the holder to be entitled to payment. Upon a filing by the holder of proof of payment and proof that the payee was entitled to the payment, the administrator shall promptly reimburse the holder for the payment without imposing a fee or other charge. If reimbursement is sought for a payment made on a negotiable instrument, including a traveler's check or money order, the holder shall be reimbursed upon filing proof that the instrument was duly presented and that payment was made to a person who reasonably appeared to be entitled to payment. The holder shall be reimbursed for payment made even if the payment was made to a person whose claim was barred under R.S. 9:171(A).

D. A holder who has delivered property other than money to the administrator pursuant to this Chapter may reclaim the property if it is still in the possession of the administrator, without paying any fee or other charge, upon filing proof that the apparent owner has claimed the property from the holder.

E. The administrator may accept a holder's affidavit as sufficient proof of the holder's right to recover money and property under this Section.

F. If a holder pays or delivers property to the administrator in good faith and thereafter another person claims the property from the holder or another state claims the money or property under its laws relating to escheat or abandoned or unclaimed property, the administrator, upon written notice of the claim, shall defend the holder against the claim and indemnify the holder against any liability on the claim.

G. Property removed from a safe deposit box or other safekeeping depository is received by the administrator subject to the holder's right to be reimbursed for the cost of the opening and to any valid lien or contract providing for the holder to be reimbursed for unpaid rent or storage charges. The administrator shall reimburse the holder out of the proceeds remaining after deducting the expense incurred by the administrator in selling the property.

Acts 1997, No. 809, § 1, eff. July 10, 1997. Amended by Acts 1999, No. 206, § 1, eff. June 11, 1999.

Cross References

C.C. arts. 44, 47, 453, 479, 526, 3412, 3418, 3419, 3421, 3437, 3468, 3491, 3499.

§ 163. Crediting of dividends, interest, and increments to owner's account

If property other than money is paid, delivered, or transferred to the administrator under this Chapter, the owner is entitled to receive from the administrator any gain realized or accruing on the property at or before liquidation or conversion of the property into money. If the property was interest bearing to the owner on the date of surrender by the holder, the administrator shall pay interest at a rate of five percent a year or any lesser rate the property earned while in the possession of the holder. Interest begins to accrue when the property is delivered to the administrator and ceases on the earlier of the expiration of ten years after delivery or the date on which payment is made to the owner. Interest on interest bearing property is not payable for any period before the effective date of this Chapter, unless authorized by law superseded by this Chapter.

Acts 1997, No. 809, § 1, eff. July 10, 1997.

Cross References

C.C. arts. 44, 47, 453, 479, 526, 3412, 3418, 3419, 3421, 3437, 3468, 3491, 3499.

§ 164. Public sale of abandoned property

A. Except as otherwise provided in this Section, the administrator, within three years after the receipt of abandoned property, may sell it to the highest bidder at public sale at a location in the state which in the judgment of the administrator affords the most favorable market for the property. The administrator may decline the highest bid and reoffer the property for sale if the administrator considers the bid to be insufficient. The administrator need not offer the property for sale if the administrator considers that the probable cost of sale will exceed the proceeds of the sale. A sale held under this Section shall be preceded by a single publication of notice, at least three weeks before sale, in a newspaper of general circulation in the parish in which the property is to be sold.

B. Securities listed on an established stock exchange shall be sold at prices prevailing on the exchange at the time of sale. Other securities may be sold over the counter at prices prevailing at the time of sale or by any other method the administrator considers reasonable.

C. Securities constituting stock or other interest in a business association shall be held for at least three years before being sold and all other securities shall be held for at least one year before being sold, unless the administrator considers an earlier sale to be in the best interest of the state.

D. If securities constituting stock or other interest in a business association are sold by the administrator before the expiration of three years from their delivery to the administrator, a person making a claim under this Chapter before the end of the three-year period is entitled to the proceeds of the sale of the securities or the market value of the securities at the time the claim is made, whichever is greater, plus dividends, interest, or other increments thereon up to the time the claim is made, less any deduction for expenses of sale. A person making a claim under this Chapter after the expiration of the three-year period is entitled to receive the securities delivered to the administrator by the holder, if they still remain in the custody of the administrator, or the net proceeds received from sale, and is entitled to receive any dividends, interest, or other increments thereon occurring after delivery to the administrator.

E. A purchaser of property at a sale conducted by the administrator pursuant to this Chapter takes the property free of all claims of the owner or previous holder and of all persons claiming through or under them. The administrator shall execute all documents necessary to complete the transfer of ownership.

Acts 1997, No. 809, § 1, eff. July 10, 1997.

Cross References

C.C. arts. 47, 453, 479, 526, 3412, 3418, 3419, 3421, 3437, 3468, 3491, 3499.

§ 165. Deposit of funds

A. Except as otherwise provided by this Section, the administrator shall promptly deposit in the Bond Security and Redemption Fund of this state all funds received under this Chapter, including the proceeds from the sale of abandoned property under R.S. 9:164. The administrator shall retain in a separate trust fund at least five hundred thousand dollars from which the administrator shall pay claims duly allowed. Before making the deposit, the administrator shall record the name and last known address of each person appearing from the holders' reports to be entitled to the property and the name and last known address of each insured person or annuitant and beneficiary and, with respect to each policy or contract listed in the report of an insurance company, its number, the name of the company, and the amount due.

B. The administrator may deduct an amount equal to the costs incurred for authorized external auditing from total gross collections during any fiscal year, and an amount not to exceed seven percent of the total gross collections during any fiscal year for the remaining costs of administering this Chapter.

C. (1) The Unclaimed Property Leverage Fund is created as a special fund in the state treasury for the deposit of a portion of the funds received by the administrator under this Chapter. The state treasurer shall deposit into the Unclaimed Property Leverage Fund each fiscal year fifteen million dollars.

(a) There is hereby created, as a special account in the Unclaimed Property Leverage Fund, the I–49 North Account. The source of monies in the I–49 North Account shall be fifty percent of the funds deposited in the Unclaimed Property Leverage Fund each fiscal year, any monies appropriated to the fund by the legislature, including federal funds, donations, gifts, or grants, and any other monies as may be provided by law.

(b) There is hereby created, as a special account in the Unclaimed Property Leverage Fund, the I–49 South Account. The source of monies in the I–49 South Account shall be fifty percent of the funds deposited in the Unclaimed Property Leverage Fund each fiscal year, any monies appropriated to the fund by the legislature, including federal funds, donations, gifts, or grants, and any other monies as may be provided by law.

(2) Monies appropriated from the funds shall be expended only in accordance with the provisions of this Paragraph:

(a) For transfer to the State Bond Commission, hereinafter referred to as the "commission", to pay the principal, premium, and interest of unclaimed property bonds issued by the commission pursuant to R.S. 9:165.1 as the bonds become due and payable and to fund such reserves for contingencies, costs, and expenses as may be required by the resolution authorizing the issuance of such bonds as well as pay amounts of ongoing expenses associated with the administration, maintenance, or evaluation of the bonds issued for Interstate 49 North and Interstate 49 South. Proceeds of the bonds, except monies needed to fund reserves and pay costs of issuance, and to the extent not needed to pay debt service or other amounts due under the resolution authorizing the bonds, shall be expended utilizing any or all powers granted to the commission including the funding or securitization of revenue bonds. Monies from the I–49 North Account shall be used exclusively to match federal funds to be used by the Department of Transportation and Development for the costs for and associated with the construction of Interstate 49 North from Interstate 20 in the city of Shreveport to the Louisiana/Arkansas border. Monies from the I–49 South Account shall be used exclusively to match federal funds to be used by the Department of Transportation and Development for the costs for and associated with the construction of Interstate 49 South from Interstate 10 in the city of Lafayette to the West Bank Expressway in the city of New Orleans.

(b) For transfer to the Department of Transportation and Development:

(i) Funds from the I–49 North Account to be used exclusively to match federal funds to be used for the costs for and associated with the construction of Interstate 49 North from Interstate 20 in the city of Shreveport to the Louisiana/Arkansas border; provided, however, that the monies in the fund shall be applied first to that portion of the project from I–220 to the Louisiana/Arkansas border; and

(ii) Funds from the I–49 South Account to be used exclusively to match federal funds to be used for the costs for and associated with the construction of Interstate 49 South from Interstate 10 in the city of Lafayette to the West Bank Expressway in the city of New Orleans.

(3) All unexpended and unencumbered monies in the Unclaimed Property Leverage Fund, the I–49 North Account, and the I–49 South Account at the end of the fiscal year shall remain in the Unclaimed Property Leverage Fund, the I–49 North Account, and the I–49 South Account and interest earned on the investment of these monies shall be credited to the Unclaimed Property Leverage Fund, the I–49 North Account, and the I–49 South Account.

Acts 1997, No. 809, § 1, eff. July 10, 1997. Amended by Acts 2004, No. 839, § 1; Acts 2005, No. 256, § 1, eff. June 29, 2005; Acts 2007, No. 320, § 1, eff. July 9, 2007; Acts 2011, No. 413, § 1.

Cross References

C.C. arts. 44, 47, 453, 479, 526, 3412, 3418, 3419, 3421, 3437, 3468, 3491, 3499.

§ 165.1. Bonds; unclaimed property bonds; completion of I–49

A. (1) Without reference to any provision of the Constitution of Louisiana and the laws of Louisiana, and as a grant of power in addition to any other general or special law, the State Bond Commission, hereinafter "commission", is hereby authorized to issue unclaimed property bonds, hereinafter referred to as "unclaimed property bonds" or "bonds", for the I–49 Project and pledge for the payment of the principal and interest of the unclaimed property bonds monies deposited or to be deposited into the Unclaimed Property Leverage Fund, which pledge shall be subject to the appropriation of funds by the legislature. The commission is further authorized, in its discretion, to pledge all or any part of any gift, grant, donation, or other sum of money, aid, or assistance from the United States, the state, or any political subdivision, thereof, unless otherwise restricted by the terms thereof, all or any part of the proceeds of bonds, credit agreements, instruments, or other money of the commission, from whatever source derived, for the further securing of the payment of the principal and interest of the bonds, including any monies provided to the commission from the Department of Transportation and Development. Any bonds shall be payable solely from revenues and bond proceeds, pending their disbursement and investment income thereon.

(2) The unclaimed property receipts which have been deposited into the Unclaimed Property Leverage Fund shall be applied to pay or provide for the payment of debt service and all related costs and expenses associated therewith on unclaimed property bonds issued by the commission. At no time shall bond payments securitized by unclaimed property receipts in the Unclaimed Property Leverage Fund exceed fifteen million dollars per year.

(3) The resolution or resolutions under which unclaimed property bonds are authorized to be issued may contain any or all of the following:

(a) Provisions respecting custody of the proceeds from the sale of the bonds, including any requirements that such proceeds be held separate from or not be commingled with other funds of the state.

(b) Provisions for the investment and reinvestment of unclaimed property bond proceeds until used to pay the costs of financing such unclaimed property bonds and for the disposition of any excess bond proceeds or investment earnings thereon.

(c) Provisions for the execution of reimbursement agreements or similar agreements in connection with credit facilities, including but not limited to letters of credit or policies of bond insurance, remarketing agreements, and credit enhancement devices, for the purpose of moderating interest rate fluctuations.

(d) Provisions for the collection, custody, investment, reinvestment, and use of the pledged revenues or other receipts, funds, or monies pledged therefor and deposited in the Unclaimed Property Leverage Fund.

(e) Provisions regarding the establishment and maintenance of reserves, sinking funds, and any other funds, and accounts as shall be approved by the commission in such amounts as may be established by the commission, and the regulation and disposition thereof, including requirements that any such funds and accounts be held separate from or not be commingled with other funds.

(f) Covenants for the establishment of pledged revenue coverage requirements for the unclaimed property bonds.

(g) Provisions for the issuance of additional unclaimed property bonds on a parity with unclaimed property bonds theretofore issued, including establishment of coverage requirements with respect thereto.

(h) Provisions or covenants of like or different character from the foregoing which are determined in such proceedings as necessary, convenient, or desirable in order to better secure the unclaimed property bonds, or will tend to make the unclaimed property bonds more marketable, and which are in the best interests of the commission.

B. Bonds issued under the provisions of this Section shall not be deemed to constitute a pledge of the full faith and credit of the state or of any governmental unit thereof. All such bonds shall contain a statement on their face substantially to the effect that neither the full faith and credit of the state nor the full faith and credit of any public entity of the state are pledged to the payment of the principal of or the interest on such bonds. The issuance of bonds under the provisions of this Section shall not directly, indirectly, or contingently obligate the state or any governmental unit of the state to levy any taxes whatever therefor or to make any appropriation for their payment, other than obligations to make payments by the state or any public entity to the commission arising out of contracts, including without limitation the bonds, the bond resolution, and trust indentures authorized under this Section.

C. Bonds shall be authorized by a resolution of the commission and shall be of such series, bear such date or dates, mature at such time or times, bear interest at such rate or rates, including but not limited to fixed, variable, or zero rates, be payable at such time or times, be in such denominations, be in such form, carry such registration and exchangeability privilege, be payable in such medium of payment and at such place or places, be subject to such terms of redemption prior to maturity at such price or prices as determined by the commission, and be entitled to such priority on the revenues as such resolution or resolutions may provide.

D. Bonds shall be sold by the commission at public sale by competitive bid or negotiated by private sale and at such price as the commission may determine to be in the best interest of the commission.

E. The issuance of unclaimed property bonds shall not be subject to any limitations, requirements, or conditions contained in any other law, and bonds may be issued without obtaining the consent of the state or any political subdivision, or of any agency, commission, or instrumentality thereof, except that bonds issued hereunder shall be included in the calculation of "net state tax supported debt" as defined in R.S. 39:1367.

F. For a period of thirty days after the date of publication of a notice of intent to issue bonds in the official journal of the state authorizing the issuance of bonds hereunder, any person in interest shall have the right to contest the legality of the resolution and the legality of the bond issue for any cause, but after that time no one shall have any cause or right of action to contest the legality of the resolution or of the bonds or the security therefor for any cause whatsoever. If no suit, action, or proceeding is begun contesting the validity of the resolution, the bonds or the security therefor within the thirty days herein prescribed, the commission to issue the bonds and to provide for the payment thereof, the legality thereof, and of all of the provisions of the resolution authorizing the issuance of the bonds shall be conclusively presumed to be legal and shall be incontestable. Any notice of intent so published shall set forth in reasonable detail the purpose of the bonds, the security therefor, and the parameters of amount, duration, and interest rates. The commission may designate any paper of general circulation in its geographical jurisdiction to publish the notice of intent or may utilize electronic media available to the general public. Any suit to determine the validity of bonds issued by the commission shall be brought only in accordance with the provisions of R.S. 13:5121 et seq.

G. All bonds issued pursuant to this Section shall have all the qualities of negotiable instruments under the commercial laws of the state.

H. Any pledge of revenues or other monies made by the commission shall be valid and binding from the time when the pledge is made. The revenues or monies so pledged and thereafter received by the commission shall immediately be subject to the lien of such pledge without any physical delivery thereof or further act, and the lien of any such pledge shall be valid and binding as against all parties having claims of any kind in tort, contract, or otherwise against the commission irrespective of whether such parties have notice thereof.

I. Neither the members of the commission nor any person executing the bonds shall be liable personally for the bonds or be subject to any personal liability or accountability by reason of the issuance thereof.

J. Bonds of the commission, their transfer, and the income therefrom shall at all times be exempt from all taxation by the state or any political subdivision thereof, and may or may not be exempt for federal income tax purposes. The bonds issued pursuant to this Section shall be and are hereby declared to be legal and authorized investments for banks, savings banks, trust companies, building and loan associations, insurance companies, fiduciaries, trustees, and guardians. Such bonds shall be eligible to secure the deposit of any and all public funds of the state and any and all public funds of municipalities, parishes, school districts, or other political corporations or subdivisions of the state. Such bonds shall be lawful and sufficient security for the deposits to the extent of their value. When any bonds shall have been issued hereunder, neither the legislature, the commission, nor any other entity may discontinue or decrease the revenues pledged to the payment of the bonds authorized hereunder or permit to be discontinued or decreased the revenues in anticipation of the collection of which such bonds have been issued, or in any way make any change in the allocation and dedication of the revenues which would diminish the amount of the revenues to be received by the commission, until all of such bonds shall have been retired as to principal and interest, and there is hereby vested in the holders from time to time of such bonds a contract right in the provisions of this Section.

K. The commission may provide by resolution for the issuance of refunding bonds pursuant to R.S. 39:1444 et seq.

L. The holders of any bonds issued hereunder shall have such rights and remedies as may be provided in the resolution or trust agreement authorizing the issuance of the bonds, including but not by way of limitation appointment of a trustee for the bondholders and any other available civil action to compel compliance with the terms and provisions of the bonds and the resolution or trust agreement.

M. Subject to the agreements with the holders of bonds, all proceeds of bonds and all revenues pledged under a resolution or trust agreement authorizing or securing such bonds shall be deposited and held in trust in a fund or funds separate and apart from all other funds of the state. Subject to the resolution or trust agreement, the trustee shall hold the same for the benefit of the holders of the bonds for the application and disposition thereof solely to the respective uses and purposes provided in such resolution or trust agreement.

N. The commission is authorized to employ all professionals it deems necessary in the issuance of its bonds.

O. The commission shall be deemed to be a public entity for purposes of Chapters 13, 13–A, 14, 14–A, 14–B, and 15–A of Title 39 of the Louisiana Revised Statutes of 1950, as amended, which statutes shall apply to bonds of the commission, provided that in the event of a conflict with the provisions of this Section, the provisions of this Section shall control.

P.(1) The provisions of this Section shall become null, void, and of no effect on the date that all bonds issued by the commission are paid or deemed paid in full and are no longer considered outstanding or the Interstate 49 project is deemed completed by the Department of Transportation and Development, whichever is later.

(2) If bonds for this project are not sold by December 31, 2013, the provisions of this Section shall become, null, void, and of no effect on January 1, 2014.

Added by Acts 2011, No. 413, § 1.

§ 165.2. Designates first I–49 unclaimed property bond project; "Alvin B. Kessler Memorial Highway"

The first project on I–49 North constructed utilizing financing with unclaimed property bonds shall be named and designated as the "Alvin B. Kessler Memorial Highway". The Department of Transportation and Development shall erect appropriate signage indicating this designation.

Added by Acts 2011, No. 413, § 1.

§ 166. Claim of another state to recover property

A. After property has been paid or delivered to the administrator under this Chapter, another state may recover the property if any of the following applies:

(1) The property was delivered to the custody of this state because the records of the holder did not reflect a last known location of the apparent owner within the borders of the other state and the other state establishes that the apparent owner or other person entitled to the property was last known to be located within the borders of that state, and under the laws of that state the property has escheated or become subject to a claim of abandonment by that state.

(2) The property was delivered to the custody of this state because the laws of the other state did not provide for the escheat or custodial taking of the property, and under the laws of that state subsequently enacted the property has escheated or become subject to a claim of abandonment by that state.

(3) The records of the holder were erroneous in that they did not accurately identify the owner of the property and the last known location of the owner within the borders of another state, and under the laws of that state the property has escheated or become subject to a claim of abandonment by that state.

(4) The property was subjected to custody by this state under R.S. 9:156(5) and under the laws of the state of domicile of the holder the property has escheated or become subject to a claim of abandonment by that state.

(5) The property is a sum payable on a traveler's check, money order, or similar instrument that was purchased in the other state and delivered into the custody of this state under R.S. 9:156(6), and under the laws of the other state the property has escheated or become subject to a claim of abandonment by that state.

B. A claim of another state to recover escheated or abandoned property shall be presented in a form prescribed by the administrator, who shall decide the claim within ninety days after it is presented. The administrator shall allow the claim upon determining that the other state is entitled to the abandoned property under Subsection A of this Section.

C. The administrator shall require another state, before recovering property under this Section, to agree to indemnify this state and its officers and employees against any liability on a claim to the property.

Acts 1997, No. 809, § 1, eff. July 10, 1997.

Cross References

C.C. arts. 44, 47, 453, 479, 526, 3412, 3418, 3419, 3421, 3437, 3468, 3491, 3499.

§ 167. Filing claim with administrator; handling of claims by administrator

A. A person, excluding another state, claiming an interest in property paid or delivered to the administrator may file a claim on a form prescribed by the administrator and verified by the claimant.

B. Within ninety days after a claim is filed, the administrator shall allow or deny the claim and give written notice of the decision to the claimant. If the claim is denied, the administrator shall inform the claimant of the reasons for the denial and specify what additional evidence is required before the claim will be allowed. The claimant may refile the claim under Subsection A of this Section or maintain an action under R.S. 9:168.

C. Within thirty days after a claim is allowed, the property or the net proceeds of a sale of the property shall be delivered or paid by the administrator to the claimant, together with any additional amount to which the claimant is entitled under R.S. 9:163 and 164.

D. A holder who pays the owner for property that has been delivered to the state and which, if claimed from the administrator by the owner would be subject to an increment under R.S. 9:163 and 164, may recover from the administrator the amount of the increment.

Acts 1997, No. 809, § 1. eff. July 10, 1997.

Cross References

C.C. arts. 44, 47, 453, 479, 526, 3412, 3418, 3419, 3421, 3437, 3468, 3491, 3499.

§ 168. Action to establish claim

A person aggrieved by a decision of the administrator or whose claim has not been acted upon within ninety days after its filing may maintain an action *de novo* to establish the claim in a court of competent jurisdiction in this state, naming the administrator as a defendant. The action shall be brought within ninety days after the decision of the administrator or, if the administrator has failed to allow or deny the claim, within one hundred eighty days after its filing.

Acts 1997, No. 809, § 1, eff. July 10, 1997.

Cross References

C.C. arts. 44, 47, 453, 479, 526, 3412, 3418, 3419, 3421, 3437, 3468, 3491, 3499.

§ 169. Election to take payment or delivery

A. The administrator may decline to receive property reported under this Chapter that the administrator considers to have a value less than the expenses of notice and sale.

B. A holder, with the written consent of the administrator and upon conditions and terms prescribed by the administrator, may report and deliver property before the property is presumed abandoned. Property so delivered shall be held by the administrator and is not presumed abandoned until it otherwise would be presumed abandoned under this Chapter.

Acts 1997, No. 809, § 1, eff. July 10, 1997.

Cross References

C.C. arts. 44, 47, 453, 479, 526, 3412, 3418, 3419, 3421, 3437, 3468, 3491, 3499.

§ 170. Destruction or disposition of property having no substantial commercial value; immunity from liability

If the administrator determines after investigation that property delivered under this Chapter has no substantial commercial value, the administrator may destroy or otherwise dispose of the property at any time. An action or proceeding may not be maintained against the state or any officer or against the holder for or on account of any acts taken by the administrator under this Section, except for acts constituting intentional misconduct.

Acts 1997, No. 809, § 1, eff. July 10, 1997.

Cross References

C.C. arts. 44, 47, 453, 479, 526, 2924, 3412, 3418, 3419, 3421, 3437, 3468, 3491, 3499.

§ 171. Periods of limitation

A. The expiration, before or after the effective date of this Chapter, of a period of limitation on the owner's right to receive or recover property, whether specified by contract, statute, or court order, does not preclude the property from being presumed abandoned or affect a duty to file a report or to pay or deliver or transfer property to the administrator as required by this Chapter.

B. An action or proceeding may not be maintained by the administrator to enforce this Chapter more than ten years after the holder specifically identified the property reported to the administrator or gave express notice to the administrator of a dispute regarding the property. In the absence of a report, the period of limitation is tolled. The period of limitation is also tolled by the filing of a report that is fraudulent.

C. Notwithstanding the provisions of this Section or any other law to the contrary, an action or proceeding by the administrator to enforce the provisions of this Chapter shall not be maintained against a federally insured financial institution for any violation that occurred more than six years prior to the most recently completed auditable period which ends on June thirtieth of each year as provided by R.S. 9:159(D).

Acts 1997, No. 809, § 1, eff. July 10, 1997. Amended by Acts 2013, No. 247, § 2.

Cross References

C.C. arts. 44, 47, 453, 479, 526, 3412, 3418, 3419, 3421, 3437, 3468, 3491, 3499.

§ 172. Requests for reports and examination of records

A. The administrator may require a person who has not filed a report, or a person who the administrator believes has filed an inaccurate, incomplete, or false report, to file a verified report in a form specified by the administrator. The report shall state whether the person is holding property reportable under this Chapter, describe property not previously reported or as to which the administrator has made inquiry, and specifically identify and state the amounts of property that may be in issue.

B. The administrator, at reasonable times and upon reasonable notice, may examine the records of any person to determine whether the person has complied with this Chapter. The administrator may conduct the examination even if the person believes it is not in possession of any property reportable or deliverable under this Chapter. The administrator may contract with any other person to conduct the examination on behalf of the administrator.

C. The administrator at reasonable times may examine the records of an agent, including a dividend disbursing agent or transfer agent, of a business association that is the holder of property presumed abandoned if the administrator has given the notice required by Subsection B of this Section to both the association and the agent at least ninety days before the examination.

D. Documents and working papers obtained or compiled by the administrator, or the administrator's agents, employees, or designated representatives in the course of conducting an examination, are confidential and are not public records but any of the documents and papers may be used for the following:

(1) Used by the administrator in the course of an action to collect unclaimed property or otherwise enforce this Chapter.

(2) Used in joint examinations conducted with or pursuant to an agreement with another state, the federal government, or any other governmental entity.

(3) Produced pursuant to subpoena or court order.

(4) Disclosed to the abandoned property office of another state for that state's use in circumstances equivalent to those described in Paragraphs (1), (2), and (3) of this Subsection, if the other state is bound to keep the documents and papers confidential.

E. If an examination of the records of a person results in the disclosure of property reportable under this Chapter, the administrator may assess the cost of the examination against the holder at the rate of two hundred dollars a day for each examiner, or a greater amount that is reasonable and was actually incurred, but the assessment may not exceed the value of the property found to be reportable. The cost of examination made pursuant to Subsection C of this Section may be assessed only against the business association.

F. If a holder fails after the effective date of this Chapter to maintain the records required by R.S. 9:173 and the records of the holder available for the periods subject to this Chapter are insufficient to permit the preparation of a report, the administrator may require the holder to report and pay the amount the administrator may reasonably estimate on the basis of any available records of the holder or on the basis of any other reasonable method of estimation that the administrator may select.

Acts 1997, No. 809, § 1, eff. July 10, 1997.

Cross References

C.C. arts. 44, 47, 453, 479, 526, 3412, 3418, 3419, 3421, 3437, 3468, 3491, 3499.

§ 173. Retention of records

A. A holder required to file a report under R.S. 9:159 shall maintain its records containing the information required to be included in the report until the holder files the report and for ten years after the date of filing, unless a shorter time is provided in Subsection B or C of this Section or by rule of the administrator.

B. A business association that sells, issues, or provides to others for sale or issue in this state, traveler's checks, money orders, or similar written instruments other than third-party bank checks, on which the business association is directly liable, shall maintain a record of the instruments while they remain outstanding, indicating the state and date of issue, for three years after the date the property becomes reportable.

C. (1) A federally insured financial institution shall maintain its report filed pursuant to R.S. 9:159 for six years after the date the report is filed.

(2) For purposes of this Chapter, a federally insured financial institution shall maintain its records containing the information required to be included in the report until the holder files the report and for six years after the date of filing.

Acts 1997, No. 809, § 1, eff. July 10, 1997. Amended by Acts 2013, No. 247, § 2.

Cross References

C.C. arts. 44, 47, 453, 479, 526, 3412, 3418, 3419, 3421, 3437, 3468, 3491, 3499.

§ 174. Enforcement

The administrator may maintain an action in this or another state to enforce this Chapter. The court may award reasonable attorney fees to the administrator.

Acts 1997, No. 809, § 1, eff. July 10, 1997. Amended by Acts 2006, No. 573, § 1.

Cross References

C.C. arts. 44, 47, 453, 479, 526, 3412, 3418, 3419, 3421, 3437, 3468, 3491, 3499.

§ 175. Interstate agreements and cooperation; joint and reciprocal actions with other states; confidentiality

A. The administrator may enter into an agreement with another state to exchange information relating to abandoned property or its possible existence. The agreement may permit the other state, or another person acting on behalf of a state, to examine records as authorized in R.S. 9:172. The administrator by rule may require the reporting of information needed to enable compliance with an agreement made under this Section and prescribe the form.

B. The administrator may join with another state to seek enforcement of this Chapter against any person who is or may be holding property reportable under this Chapter.

C. At the request of another state, the attorney general of this state may maintain an action on behalf of the other state to enforce, in this state, the unclaimed property laws of the other state against a holder of property subject to escheat or a claim of abandonment by the other state, if the other state has agreed to pay expenses incurred by the attorney general in maintaining the action.

D. The administrator may request that the attorney general of another state or another attorney commence an action in the other state on behalf of the administrator. With the approval of the attorney general of this state, the administrator may retain any other attorney to commence an action in this state on behalf of the administrator. This state shall pay all expenses, including attorney fees, in maintaining an action under this Subsection. With the administrator's approval, the expenses and attorney fees may be paid from money received under this Chapter. The administrator may agree to pay expenses and attorney fees based in whole or in part on a percentage of the value of any property recovered in the action. Any expenses or attorney fees paid under this Subsection may not be deducted from the amount that is subject to the claim by the owner under this Chapter.

Acts 1997, No. 809, § 1, eff. July 10, 1997.

Cross References

C.C. arts. 47, 453, 479, 526, 3412, 3418, 3419, 3421, 3437, 3468, 3491, 3499.

§ 176. Interest and penalties

A. A holder who fails to report, pay, or deliver property within the time prescribed by this Chapter shall pay to the administrator interest at the annual rate established pursuant to R.S. 13:4202 on the property or value thereof from the date the property should have been reported, paid, or delivered.

B. Except as otherwise provided in Subsection C of this Section, a holder who fails to report, pay, or deliver property within the time prescribed by this Chapter, or fails to perform other duties imposed by this Chapter, shall pay to the administrator, in addition to interest as provided in Subsection A of this Section, a civil penalty of two hundred dollars for each day the report, payment, or delivery is withheld, or the duty is not performed, up to a maximum of five thousand dollars.

C. A holder who willfully fails to report, pay, or deliver property within the time prescribed by this Chapter, or willfully fails to perform other duties imposed by this Chapter, shall pay to the administrator, in addition to interest as provided in Subsection A of this Section, a civil penalty of one thousand dollars for each day the report, payment, or delivery is withheld, or the duty is not performed, up to a maximum of twenty-five thousand dollars, plus twenty-five percent of the value of any property that should have been but was not reported.

D. A holder who renders a fraudulent report shall pay to the administrator, in addition to interest as provided in Subsection A of this Section, a civil penalty of one thousand dollars for each day from the date a report under this Chapter was due, up to a maximum twenty-five thousand dollars, plus twenty-five percent of the value of any property that should have been but was not reported.

E. Upon good cause shown the administrator may waive, in whole or in part, interest and penalties under Subsections B and C of this Section, and shall waive penalties if the holder acted in good faith and without negligence.

Acts 1997, No. 809, § 1, eff. July 10, 1997.

Cross References

C.C. arts. 44, 47, 453, 479, 526, 3412, 3418, 3419, 3421, 3437, 3468, 3491, 3499.

§ 177. Agreement to locate property

A. An agreement by an owner to pay compensation to locate, deliver, recover, or assist in the recovery of property that is presumed abandoned is void and unenforceable if it was entered into during the period commencing on the date the property was presumed abandoned and extending to a time that is twenty-four months after the date the property is paid or delivered to the administrator.

B. Any agreement by an owner to pay compensation to locate, deliver, recover, or assist in the recovery of property is enforceable only if the agreement is in writing, clearly sets forth the nature of the property and the services to be rendered, is signed by the apparent owner, and states the value of the property before and after the fee or other compensation has been deducted.

C. If an agreement covered by this Section is applicable to mineral proceeds and the agreement contains a provision to pay compensation that includes a portion of the underlying minerals or any production payment, overriding royalty, compensating royalty, or similar payment, the provision is void and unenforceable.

D. Any agreement by an owner to pay compensation to locate, deliver, recover, and assist in the recovery of property which is entered into on a date that is twenty-four months or more after the date the property is paid or delivered to the administrator shall not provide for compensation exceeding ten percent of the value of the recoverable property. An owner who has agreed to pay compensation that is unconscionable, or the administrator on behalf of the owner, may maintain an action to reduce the compensation to a conscionable amount. The court may award reasonable attorney fees to an owner who prevails in the action.

E. An owner may at any time assert that an agreement covered by this Section is otherwise invalid.

Acts 1997, No. 809, § 1, eff. July 10, 1997.

Cross References

C.C. arts. 44, 47, 453, 479, 526, 3412, 3418, 3419, 3421, 3437, 3468, 3491, 3499.

§ 178. Foreign transactions

This Chapter does not apply to property held, due, and owing in a foreign country and arising out of a foreign transaction.

Acts 1997, No. 809, § 1, eff. July 10, 1997.

Cross References

C.C. arts. 44, 47, 453, 479, 526, 3412, 3418, 3419, 3421, 3437, 3468, 3491, 3499.

§ 179. Applicability of Chapter

A. An initial report filed under this Chapter for property that was not required to be reported before the effective date of this Chapter but that is subject to this Chapter shall include all items of property that would have been presumed abandoned during the ten-year period next preceding the effective date of this Chapter as if this Chapter had been in effect during that period.

B. This Chapter does not relieve a holder of a duty that arose before the effective date of this Chapter to report, pay, or deliver property. Except as otherwise provided in R.S. 9:171(B), a holder who did not comply with the law in effect before the effective date of this Chapter is subject to the applicable provisions for enforcement and penalties that then existed, that are continued in effect for the purpose of this Section.

Acts 1997, No. 809, § 1, eff. July 10, 1997.

Cross References

C.C. arts. 44, 47, 453, 479, 526, 3412, 3418, 3419, 3421, 3437, 3468, 3491, 3499.

§ 180. Rules

The administrator may adopt necessary rules and regulations in accordance with the Administrative Procedure Act to carry out the provisions of this Chapter.

Acts 1997, No. 809, § 1, eff. July 10, 1997.

Cross References

C.C. arts. 44, 47, 453, 479, 526, 3412, 3418, 3419, 3421, 3437, 3468, 3491, 3499.

§ 181. Severability

If any provision of this Chapter or the application thereof to any person or circumstance is held invalid, the invalidity does not affect other provisions or the application of this Chapter that can be given effect without the invalid provision or application, and to this end the provisions of this Chapter are severable.

Acts 1997, No. 809, § 1, eff. July 10, 1997.

Cross References

C.C. arts. 44, 47, 453, 479, 526, 3412, 3418, 3419, 3421, 3437, 3468, 3491, 3499.

For Annotative Materials, see West's Louisiana Statutes Annotated

§§ 182 to 188. [Blank]

CHAPTER 2. DISPOSITION OF UNCLAIMED SPECIMENS BY TAXIDERMISTS

Section
191. Definition.
192. Disposition.

§ 191. Definition

As used in this Chapter, "taxidermist" means a person who, for a consideration, mounts, preserves, or otherwise prepares the body of any bird, animal, or fish, or any part thereof, for display.

Added by Acts 1983, No. 115, § 1.

§ 192. Disposition

A. Any taxidermist may sell any unclaimed specimen left in his possession in excess of one year, provided that he complies with the following requirements:

(1) Each taxidermist shall receive, upon written request to the Secretary of the Department of Wildlife and Fisheries, a permit to sell an unclaimed specimen. No permit shall be issued by the secretary until receipt by the secretary of proof that the taxidermist has made a reasonable effort to notify the owner of the unclaimed specimen. Such proof shall include a copy of a letter notifying the owner, mailed to him at his last known address by registered or certified mail, and the return receipt of the mailing or, if not delivered, the actual letter and envelope with return receipt attached.

(2) Each taxidermist shall provide the Secretary of the Department of Wildlife and Fisheries with the name, address, and other information as may be required by the secretary relating to the owner of the unclaimed specimen.

(3) Each taxidermist may sell the unclaimed specimen for an amount not to exceed the original price for mounting, preserving, tanning, or otherwise preparing the unclaimed specimen for display.

B. Notwithstanding any provision of this Section to the contrary, any migratory specie or other federally protected animal shall not be sold under the provisions of this Section unless the specimen is accompanied by all the permits required by federal law for disposition or sale of such specie or animal.

Added by Acts 1983, No. 115, § 1.

CHAPTER 3. THE CARE OF MINOR CHILDREN

Section
195. Provisional tutor upon death of mother.
196. Limited tutorship by nature.

§ 195. Provisional tutor upon death of mother

There shall be appointed for the children a provisional tutor in the manner herein directed, if at the time of the disappearance of the father, the mother should be dead, or if she should die before their attaining the age of majority.

C.C. art. 84. Redesignated as R.S. 9:195 by Acts 1990, No. 989, § 6, eff. Jan. 1, 1991.

Editor's note. R.S. 9:195 is former Article 84 of the Louisiana Civil Code of 1870. Book I, Title III, of the Louisiana Civil Code was revised, amended, and re-enacted by Acts 1990, No. 989, § 1. Section 6 of Acts 1990, No. 989 redesignated Article 84 as R.S. 9:195. The redesignation is neither an amendment nor a re-enactment of Article 84 of the 1870 Code.

Cross References

C.C. arts. 221, 246, 250, 263, 270, 3523.

§ 196. Limited tutorship by nature

A tutor who is entitled to tutorship by nature pursuant to the provisions of Section 2 of Chapter 1 of Title VIII of Book I of the Civil Code [1] and without qualification may perform or discharge any act affecting any right or interest of the minor which involves not more than ten thousand dollars actually received by the minor, notwithstanding court costs, attorney fees, and other expenses. For purposes of this Section, the natural tutor need not comply with the provisions of Code of Civil Procedure Articles 4061, 4265 through 4268, 4269.1, and 4270 through 4272.

Added by Acts 1997, No. 851, § 1; Acts 1997, No. 1243, § 1. Amended by Acts 2003, No. 600, § 1.

[1] C.C. art. 250 et seq.

CODE TITLE IV—HUSBAND AND WIFE

CHAPTER 1. MARRIAGE: GENERAL PRINCIPLES

PART I. OFFICIANTS

Section
201. Definition.
202. Authority to perform marriage ceremony.
202.1. [Blank].
203. Officiant; judges and justices of the peace.
204. Officiant other than judge; registration.
205. Officiant to require marriage license.
206 to 208. [Blank]

PART II. COLLATERAL RELATIONS

211. Relations of the fourth degree.
212 to 214. Repealed.

Section

PART III. APPLICATION FOR MARRIAGE LICENSE

SUBPART A. IN GENERAL

221. Authority to issue marriage license.
222. Place of issuance.
223. Form.
224. Same; information required.
225. Same; attachments.

SUBPART B. BIRTH CERTIFICATE

226. Certified copy of birth certificate.
227. Certified copy unavailable; other proof.
228. Same; court order waiving.

APPENDIX 1—REVISED STATUTES, TITLE 9

Section

SUBPART C. MEDICAL CERTIFICATE [REPEALED]
229 to 231. Repealed.
232. Repealed.
233. Repealed.

SUBPART D. ISSUANCE AND TIME
234. Time and date; indication of covenant marriage.
235. Valid for thirty days.
236. Reissuance.

SUBPART E. SUMMARY OF MATRIMONIAL REGIMES LAWS
237. Information on matrimonial regime and covenant marriage laws; printed summary.

PART IV. DELAYS AND CEREMONY
SUBPART A. SEVENTY-TWO HOUR DELAY
241. Premature ceremony prohibited.
242. Waiver of delay.
243. Penalty.

SUBPART B. CEREMONY AND MARRIAGE CERTIFICATE
244. Witnesses required.
245. Marriage certificate.

PART V. RECORD KEEPING
251. Consolidated form.
252. Duplicate records of marriage licenses issued; preservation; filing of duplicate copy with state division of vital records; penalty for failure to file.
253. Disposition and recordation of marriage certificates.
254. Penalty for failure to file or complete marriage certificate.
255. Tabulation of marriage statistics; annual report.
256. Penalties.

PART VI. OPPOSITION TO MARRIAGE
261. Opposition to marriage.
262. Hearing on opposition.
263. Persons entitled to oppose.
264. [Blank].
265 to 270. [Blank].
271. [Blank].

PART VII. COVENANT MARRIAGE
272. Covenant marriage; intent; conditions to create.
273. Covenant marriage; contents of declaration of intent.
273.1. Declaration of intent; form.
274. Covenant marriage; other applicable rules.
275. Covenant marriage; applicability to already married couples.
275.1. Declaration of intent; married couples; form.
275.5. [Blank].
276. Limitation of liability; pastoral counselor.
277 to 280. [Blank].
281. Repealed.
282 to 284. [Blank].

PART I. OFFICIANTS

§ 201. Definition

An officiant is a person authorized by law to perform marriage ceremonies.

Acts 1987, No. 886, § 3, eff. Jan. 1, 1988.

Cross References

C.C. arts. 87, 91, 3523.

§ 202. Authority to perform marriage ceremony

A marriage ceremony may be performed by:

(1) A priest, minister, rabbi, clerk of the Religious Society of Friends, or any clergyman of any religious sect, who is authorized by the authorities of his religion to perform marriages, and who is registered to perform marriages;

(2) A state judge or justice of the peace.

Acts 1987, No. 886, § 3, eff. Jan. 1, 1988. Amended by Acts 1997, No. 73, § 1.

Cross References

C.C. arts. 87, 91, 95, 3520, 3522, 3523.

§ 202.1. [Blank]

§ 203. Officiant; judges and justices of the peace

A. Judges and justices of the peace may perform marriage ceremonies within the following territorial limits:

(1) A justice of the supreme court within the state;

(2) A judge of a court of appeals within the circuit;

(3) A judge of a district court within the district;

(4) A judge of a family court, juvenile court, parish court, city court, or, in Orleans Parish, a municipal or traffic court, within the parish in which the court is situated; and

(5) A justice of the peace within the parish in which the court of that justice of the peace is situated, and in any parish within the same supreme court district which has no justice of the peace court.

B. A judge's authority to perform marriage ceremonies continues after he retires.

C. A retired justice of the peace who has served a total of eighteen years in that capacity shall retain his authority to perform marriage ceremonies within the territorial limits authorized in Subsection A of this Section provided he registers to perform such ceremonies as required by R.S. 9:204.

D. Notwithstanding the provisions of Paragraph (A)(5) of this Section, a justice of the peace within any of the parishes of DeSoto, Bossier, Caddo, Bienville, Webster, or Red River may perform marriage ceremonies within any of these parishes.

E. (1) A United States District Court judge or magistrate judge of the Eastern District of Louisiana, Middle District of Louisiana, or Western District of Louisiana may perform marriage ceremonies in this state upon the adoption of a court rule, resolution, or standing order by a majority of the judges sitting en banc authorizing judges to perform such ceremonies.

(2) A judge of a court of the United States whose official duty station includes a municipality having a population in excess of one hundred five thousand but less than one hundred thirty thousand persons according to the latest decennial census may perform marriage ceremonies within his official duty station. The authority granted by this

Paragraph shall be effective only from August 1, 2012, through September 1, 2012.

Acts 1987, No. 886, § 3, eff. Jan. 1, 1988. Amended by Acts 1991, No. 710, § 1; Acts 1993, No. 105, § 1; Acts 1995, No. 212, § 1; Acts 2001, No. 341, § 1, eff. June 12, 2001; Acts 2001, No. 1103, § 1; Acts 2002, 1st Ex.Sess., No. 60, § 1; Acts 2003, No. 255, § 1, eff. June 6, 2003; Acts 2004, No. 454, § 1, eff. June 24, 2004; Acts 2005, No. 4, § 1, eff. May 27, 2005; Acts 2007, No. 114, § 1; Acts 2008, No. 675, § 2, eff. July 1, 2008; Acts 2008, No. 873, § 2, eff. July 9, 2008; Acts 2008, No. 879, § 3; Acts 2009, No. 15, § 1; Acts 2010, No. 199, § 1; Acts 2010, No. 237, § 1, eff. June 17, 2010; Acts 2012, No. 184, § 1; Acts 2012, No. 286, § 1.

Editor's note. Section 2 of Acts 1991, No. 710 declares: "The marriages of all persons whose marriage ceremonies were performed during the period January 1, 1988, through the effective date of this Act, by a person who had formerly held the office of justice of the peace, but who, through retirement or otherwise, had left the office and was not actually a justice of the peace at the time the wedding ceremony was performed, are hereby declared to be legal and valid, if those marriages would have otherwise been legal and valid."

Acts 2001, No. 341, § 3, effective June 12, 2001, declares that "The provisions of R.S. 9:203(D) as enacted by this Act shall terminate and be null, void, and without effect on July 1, 2001."

Subsection D as added by Acts 2001, No. 341, provided:

"D. A judge of a court of the United States who has an official duty station within the territorial limits of the state may perform marriage ceremonies within his official duty station in the state. For purposes of this Subsection, 'judge' and 'official duty station' shall have the same meaning as provided in 28 U.S.C. 451 and 456, respectively."

Cross References

C.C. arts. 87, 91, 95, 3523.

§ 204. Officiant other than judge; registration

An officiant, other than a judge or justice of the peace, may perform marriage ceremonies only after he registers to do so by depositing with the clerk of court of the parish in which he will principally perform marriage ceremonies, or, in the case of Orleans Parish, with the office of the state registrar of vital records, an affidavit stating his lawful name, denomination, and address.

Acts 1987, No. 886, § 3, eff. Jan. 1, 1988.

Cross References

C.C. arts. 87, 91, 95, 3520, 3522, 3523.

§ 205. Officiant to require marriage license

An officiant may not perform a marriage ceremony until he has received a license authorizing him to perform that marriage ceremony.

Acts 1987, No. 886, § 3, eff. Jan. 1, 1988. Amended by Acts 1988, No. 978, § 1; Acts 1990, No. 81, § 1.

Editor's note. Acts 1990, No. 81, § 1 amended subsec. A of this section to contain no subsection designation. Section 2 of Acts 1990, No. 81 repealed existing subsec. B of this section.

Cross References

C.C. arts. 87, 91, 94, 95, 3520, 3522, 3523.

§§ 206 to 208. [Blank]

PART II. COLLATERAL RELATIONS

§ 211. Relations of the fourth degree

Notwithstanding the provisions of Civil Code Article 90, marriages between collaterals within the fourth degree, fifty-five years of age or older, which were entered into on or before December 31, 1992, shall be considered legal and the enactment hereof shall in no way impair vested property rights.

Added by Acts 1993, No. 7, § 1.

Cross References

C.C. art. 90.

§§ 212 to 214. Repealed by Acts 1991, No. 235, § 17, eff. Jan. 1, 1992

PART III. APPLICATION FOR MARRIAGE LICENSE

SUBPART A. IN GENERAL

§ 221. Authority to issue marriage license

A license authorizing an officiant to perform a marriage ceremony must be issued by:

(1) The state registrar of vital records, or a judge of the city court, in the Parish of Orleans;

(2) The clerk of court, in any other parish; or

(3) A district judge, if the clerk of court is a party to the marriage.

Acts 1987, No. 886, § 3, eff. Jan. 1, 1988.

Cross References

C.C. arts. 87, 91, 3519, 3520, 3522.
R.S. 13:2162.

§ 222. Place of issuance

A marriage license may be issued in any parish, regardless of where the ceremony is to be performed or the parties reside.

Acts 1987, No. 886, § 3, eff. Jan. 1, 1988. Amended by Acts 1988, No. 978, § 1; Acts 1990, No. 81, § 1.

Cross References

C.C. arts. 87, 91, 3519, 3520, 3522.
R.S. 13:2162.

§ 223. Form

An application for a marriage license must be made on a form provided by the state registrar of vital records.

Acts 1987, No. 886, § 3, eff. Jan. 1, 1988.

Cross References

C.C. arts. 3519, 3520, 3522.

§ 224. Same; information required

A. An application for a marriage license must include:

(1) The date and hour of the application.

(2) The full name, residence, race, and age of each party.

(3) The names of the parents of each party.

(4) The number of former marriages of each party, and whether divorced or not.

(5) The relationship of each party to the other.

(6) Each party's social security number or a statement by the applicable party that no social security number has been issued to him. The state registrar of vital records and the officiant shall maintain confidentiality of social security numbers. Notwithstanding the provisions of R.S. 44:1 et seq. the clerk of court shall maintain the confidentiality of a party's social security number in an application for a marriage license provided a request is made to the clerk in writing by the party at the time of application.

B. The applicant must verify the information to the issuing official by affidavit.

C. In cases wherein the parties intend to contract a covenant marriage, the application for a marriage license must also include the following statement completed by at least one of the two parties:

"We, [name of intended husband] and [name of intended wife], do hereby declare our intent to contract a Covenant Marriage and, accordingly, have executed a declaration of intent attached hereto."

D. Upon request, the state registrar shall provide the information required in this Section to the agency charged with implementing a program of family support in accordance with R.S. 46:236.1.1 et seq., which shall maintain the confidentiality of the information.

E. The failure of the application to contain the signatures of both parties shall not affect the validity of the covenant marriage if the declaration of intent and accompanying affidavit have been signed by the parties.

Acts 1987, No. 886, § 3, eff. Jan. 1, 1988. Amended by Acts 1997, No. 1380, § 2; Acts 1998, 1st Ex. Sess., No. 8, § 1, eff. April 24, 1998; Acts 1999, No. 1298, § 1.

Editor's note. Acts 1997, No. 1380, § 5 declares: "The office of attorney general, Department of Justice shall, prior to August 15, 1997, promulgate an informational pamphlet, entitled 'Covenant Marriage Act', which shall outline in sufficient detail the consequences of entering into a covenant marriage. The informational pamphlet shall be made available to any counselor who provides marriage counseling as provided for by this Act."

Cross References

C.C. arts. 87, 91, 3519, 3520, 3522.

§ 225. Same; attachments

A. An application for a marriage license shall be accompanied by:

(1) A certified copy of each party's birth certificate.

(2) The written consent for a minor to marry, or the court's authorization for the minor to marry, or both, as required by Chapter 6 of Title XV of the Children's Code.[1]

(3) If applicable, the declaration of intent for a covenant marriage, as provided in Part VII of this Chapter.

B. It shall be unlawful for any officer authorized to issue a marriage license in this state to issue a license to any male or female unless both parties first present and file with such officer a certified copy of their original birth certificate. A photostatic or photographic reproduction of the certified copy of the birth certificate may be filed with the officer.

Acts 1987, No. 830, § 1, eff. Jan. 1, 1988; Acts 1987, No. 886, § 3, eff. Jan. 1, 1988. Amended by Acts 1988, No. 344, § 1; Acts 1988, No. 345, § 1, eff. July 7, 1988; Acts 1988, No. 808, § 1, eff. July 18, 1988; Acts 1995, No. 415, § 1; Acts 1997, No. 1380, § 2.

[1] Ch.C. art. 1543 et seq.

Editor's note. Section 3 of Acts 1988, No. 808 provides: "In the event of any conflict between the provisions of this Act and those of any other Act adopted by the legislature at its Regular Session in 1988, including but not limited to the provisions of Senate Bill No. 107 [Vetoed by Governor], House Bill No. 278 [Acts 1988, No. 344], and House Bill No. 586 [Acts 1988, No. 345], regardless of which Act is adopted later or signed later by the governor, the provisions of this Act shall prevail."

Acts 1997, No. 1380, § 5 declares: "The office of attorney general, Department of Justice shall, prior to August 15, 1997, promulgate an informational pamphlet, entitled 'Covenant Marriage Act', which shall outline in sufficient detail the consequences of entering into a covenant marriage. The informational pamphlet shall be made available to any counselor who provides marriage counseling as provided for by this Act."

Cross References

C.C. arts. 87, 91, 93, 3519, 3520, 3522.

SUBPART B. BIRTH CERTIFICATE

§ 226. Certified copy of birth certificate

A. A person born in Louisiana may submit a certified copy of his birth certificate. A short-form birth certification card shall be acceptable as a certified copy of a birth certificate.

B. A person born outside of Louisiana may submit a copy of his birth certificate under the raised seal or stamp of the vital statistics registration authority of his place of birth.

C. A certified copy of the birth certificate or letter issued in lieu thereof shall be retained by the official recorder of the marriage for a minimum period of sixty days.

Acts 1987, No. 886, § 3, eff. Jan. 1, 1988. Amended by Acts 1990, No. 362, § 1, eff. Jan. 1, 1991; Acts 1991, No. 462, § 1; Acts 2000, 1st Ex.Sess., No. 118, § 1, eff. April 19, 2000.

Editor's note. Another R.S. 9:226, as added by Acts 1987, No. 330, § 1 and redesignated on authority of the Louisiana State Law Institute from R.S. 9:242(B), was repealed by Acts 1988, No. 344, § 2; Acts 1988, No. 345, § 2, eff. July 7, 1988; and Acts 1988, No. 808, § 2, eff. July 18, 1988.

Cross References

C.C. arts. 3519, 3520, 3522.

R.S. 40:38, 40:39, 40:42.

§ 227. Certified copy unavailable; other proof

A. If no birth certificate is on file for an applicant, a letter signed by the proper registration authority, under his raised seal or stamp, must be submitted in lieu of a birth certificate. The letter must state that a thorough search was made and that no birth record was located for the applicant.

B. The officer issuing the marriage license may demand other proof of birth facts.

Acts 1987, No. 886, § 3, eff. Jan. 1, 1988.

Cross References

C.C. arts. 87, 91, 3519, 3520, 3522.

§ 228. Same; court order waiving

In the event of extenuating circumstances, and after finding that the parties have complied with all other requirements, a judge of the Orleans Parish City Court, a family court judge, a juvenile court judge, or any district court judge of a parish may order an issuing official within the territorial jurisdiction of his court to issue a marriage license without the applicant submitting a birth certificate. In the event of extenuating circumstances, and after finding that the parties have complied with all other requirements, a justice of the peace or city court judge may order an issuing official within the parish where his court is situated to issue a marriage license without the applicant submitting a birth certificate. The order need not state the reasons.

Acts 1987, No. 886, § 3, eff. Jan. 1, 1988. Amended by Acts 1991, No. 692, § 1; Acts 1995, No. 454, § 1; Acts 1999, No. 113, § 1.

Cross References

C.C. arts. 87, 91, 3519, 3520, 3522.

SUBPART C. MEDICAL CERTIFICATE [REPEALED]

§§ 229 to 231. Repealed by Acts 1988, No. 345, § 2, eff. July 7, 1988; Acts 1988, No. 808, § 2, eff. July 18, 1988

§ 232. Repealed by Acts 1988, No. 345, § 2, eff. July 7, 1988; Acts 1988, No. 808, § 2, eff. July 18, 1988; Acts 1988, No. 973, § 1

§ 233. Repealed by Acts 1988, No. 345, § 2, eff. July 7, 1988; Acts 1988, No. 808, § 2, eff. July 18, 1988

SUBPART D. ISSUANCE AND TIME

§ 234. Time and date; indication of covenant marriage

A. The official who issues the marriage license shall show on the face of it the exact time and date of issuance.

B. The official shall also indicate on the marriage license whether the parties intend to enter into a covenant marriage.

Acts 1987, No. 886, § 3, eff. Jan. 1, 1988. Amended by Acts 1997, No. 1380, § 2.

Editor's note. Acts 1997, No. 1380, § 5 declares: "The office of attorney general, Department of Justice shall, prior to August 15, 1997, promulgate an informational pamphlet, entitled 'Covenant Marriage Act', which shall outline in sufficient detail the consequences of entering into a covenant marriage. The informational pamphlet shall be made available to any counselor who provides marriage counseling as provided for by this Act."

Cross References

C.C. arts. 87, 91, 3519, 3520, 3522.

§ 235. Valid for thirty days

A marriage license is valid for thirty days from the date of issuance. No officiant shall perform a marriage after the license has expired.

Acts 1987, No. 886, § 3, eff. Jan. 1, 1988.

Cross References

C.C. arts. 87, 91.

§ 236. Reissuance

A new license may be issued to the parties if they surrender the expired license to the issuing official.

Acts 1987, No. 886, § 3, eff. Jan. 1, 1988. Amended by Acts 1988, No. 345, § 1, eff. July 7, 1988; Acts 1988, No. 808, § 1, eff. July 18, 1988.

Editor's note. For effect of conflict of Acts 1988, No. 808 with other 1988 legislation, see note under R.S. 9:225.

Cross References

C.C. arts. 87, 91, 225.

SUBPART E. SUMMARY OF MATRIMONIAL REGIMES LAWS

§ 237. Information on matrimonial regime and covenant marriage laws; printed summary

A. On receiving an application for a license to marry, the license-issuing officer shall deliver to each prospective spouse, either in person or by registered mail, a printed summary of the then current matrimonial regime laws of this state and the covenant marriage law of this state. These summaries shall be prepared by the attorney general of this state.

B. The summary of matrimonial regime law shall emphasize the possibility of contracting expressly a regime of one's choosing before marriage, that spouses who have not entered into a matrimonial agreement before marriage become subject to the legal regime by operation of law, and the possibility of contracting after marriage to modify the matrimonial regime.

C. The summary of covenant marriage law shall emphasize that premarital counseling is mandatory at which time the necessary documents consisting of the declaration of intent and the affidavit and attestation of the counselor shall be executed, that the couple agrees to take all reasonable steps to preserve their marriage if marital difficulties arise, including marriage counseling, that divorce in a covenant marriage is restricted to fault by a spouse and living separate and apart for two years as provided in R.S. 9:307, and that divorce under the general marriage law of this state differs significantly.

Acts 1987, No. 886, § 3, eff. Jan. 1, 1988. Amended by Acts 2001, No. 561, § 1.

Cross References

C.C. arts. 87, 91, 2325, 2326 to 2329, 2331 to 2334, 3520, 3522 to 3527.

PART IV. DELAYS AND CEREMONY

SUBPART A. SEVENTY-TWO HOUR DELAY

§ 241. Premature ceremony prohibited

An officiant may not perform a marriage ceremony until seventy-two hours have elapsed since the issuance of the marriage license.

Acts 1987, No. 886, § 3, eff. Jan. 1, 1988.

Cross References

C.C. arts. 87, 91, 95, 3522.

§ 242. Waiver of delay

A. A judge or justice of the peace authorized to perform the marriage may waive the seventy-two-hour delay upon application of the parties giving serious and meritorious reasons. His certificate authorizing the immediate performance of the ceremony must be attached to the marriage license.

B. Notwithstanding the provisions of R.S. 9:241, an officiant authorized to perform marriage ceremonies in the parish of Orleans may waive the seventy-two-hour delay for nonresident parties upon application of the parties giving serious and meritorious reasons. His certificate authorizing the immediate performance of the ceremony shall be attached to the marriage license. For purposes of this Subsection, "nonresident" shall mean a person domiciled or residing in a jurisdiction other than the state of Louisiana.

Acts 1987, No. 886, § 3, eff. Jan. 1, 1988. Amended by Acts 2003, No. 255, § 1, eff. June 6, 2003.

Cross References

C.C. arts. 87, 91, 3520, 3522.

§ 243. Penalty

An officiant who violates R.S. 9:241, other than a judge, justice of the peace or an officiant authorized to perform marriage ceremonies in the parish of Orleans and who is authorized to waive the seventy-two-hour delay pursuant to the provisions of R.S. 9:242(B), may have his authority to perform marriage ceremonies revoked by the state registrar of vital records. The revocation may not exceed one year.

Acts 1987, No. 886, § 3, eff. Jan. 1, 1988. Amended by Acts 2003, No. 255, § 1, eff. June 6, 2003.

Editor's note. Former R.S. 9:243 was specifically repealed by Acts 1987, No. 830, § 2.

Cross References

C.C. arts. 87, 91, 95, 3520, 3522.

SUBPART B. CEREMONY AND MARRIAGE CERTIFICATE

§ 244. Witnesses required

The marriage ceremony shall be performed in the presence of two competent witnesses of full age.

Acts 1987, No. 886, § 3, eff. Jan. 1, 1988.

Cross References

C.C. arts. 26, 29, 87, 91, 3520, 3522.

§ 245. Marriage certificate

A. (1) The marriage certificate is the record prepared for every marriage on a form approved by the state registrar of vital records. It shall contain the information prescribed. On the face of the certificate shall appear the certification to the fact of marriage including, if applicable, a designation that the parties entered into a covenant marriage, signed by the parties to the marriage and by the witnesses, and the signature and title of the officiant.

(2) The marriage certificate shall show the place, time, and date of the performance of the ceremony.

B. Every officiant of a marriage ceremony performed in this state shall sign a certificate of marriage in triplicate.

Acts 1987, No. 886, § 3, eff. Jan. 1, 1988. Amended by Acts 1997, No. 1380, § 2.

Editor's note. Acts 1997, No. 1380, § 5 declares: "The office of attorney general, Department of Justice shall, prior to August 15, 1997, promulgate an informational pamphlet, entitled 'Covenant Marriage Act', which shall outline in sufficient detail the consequences of entering into a covenant marriage. The informational pamphlet shall be made available to any counselor who provides marriage counseling as provided for by this Act."

Cross References

C.C. arts. 87, 91, 151, 152, 3520, 3522.

PART V. RECORD KEEPING

§ 251. Consolidated form

The application for a marriage license, the authorization to the officiant to perform the marriage ceremony, and the marriage certificate may be incorporated into a single form approved by the state registrar of vital records.

Acts 1987, No. 886, § 3, eff. Jan. 1, 1988.

Cross References

C.C. arts. 87, 91.

§ 252. Duplicate records of marriage licenses issued; preservation; filing of duplicate copy with state division of vital records; penalty for failure to file

A. Each officer authorized to issue marriage licenses in this state shall keep a duplicate record of all marriage licenses issued, on which he shall note the date and place of the marriage, and the name of the person who performed the ceremony.

B. One copy shall be kept in a loose-leaf book until it has been filled, at which time it shall be permanently bound, and shall be kept open to the inspection of the public during office hours.

C. The other copy shall be filed with the division of vital records of the Department of Children and Family Services within ten days of the expiration of each month, and the failure, neglect, or refusal to do so shall be punished by a fine of not less than ten dollars nor more than fifty dollars.

Acts 1987, No. 886, § 3, eff. Jan. 1, 1988.

Cross References

C.C. arts. 87, 91.

§ 253. Disposition and recordation of marriage certificates

A. The officiant shall give one copy of the marriage certificate to the married parties. Within ten days after the ceremony, he shall file the other two copies of the certificate of marriage with the officer who issued the marriage license.

B. Upon receipt of these copies, this officer shall sign them and note thereon the date the certificate was recorded by him.

C. He shall forward to the state registrar of vital records, on or before the fifteenth day of each calendar month, one copy of each certificate of marriage filed with him during the preceding calendar month.

Acts 1987, No. 886, § 3, eff. Jan. 1, 1988.

Cross References

C.C. arts. 87, 91.

§ 254. Penalty for failure to file or complete marriage certificate

Any person authorized to perform marriages in this state who fails to complete the forms provided by the Department of Children and Family Services, and specifically fails to fill in the date and place the ceremony was performed, or neglects or fails to file the two executed copies with the clerk of court in the parish where the license was issued or, if in Orleans Parish, with the state office of vital records, within ten days after the date of the marriage as provided by law, shall be fined not less than twenty dollars for the first offense, fifty dollars for the second offense, and one hundred dollars for a third offense, and the offender shall be prohibited thereafter from officiating at any marriage in this state.

Acts 1987, No. 886, § 3, eff. Jan. 1, 1988.

Cross References

C.C. arts. 87, 91.

§ 255. Tabulation of marriage statistics; annual report

The state registrar of vital records shall annually prepare, from the information filed with him under the provisions of R.S. 9:224 and 9:252, abstracts and tabular statements of the facts relating to marriages in each parish, and embody them, with the necessary analysis, in his annual report to the state.

Acts 1987, No. 886, § 3, eff. Jan. 1, 1988.

Cross References

C.C. arts. 87, 91.

§ 256. Penalties

Any person who makes a false entry in a marriage license as to the time and date of the issuance of the license or, in a marriage certificate, as to the time and date of the performance of the marriage, shall be guilty of a misdemeanor and upon conviction shall be fined not more than twenty-five dollars.

Acts 1987, No. 886, § 3, eff. Jan. 1, 1988.

Cross References

C.C. arts. 87, 91, 95.

PART VI. OPPOSITION TO MARRIAGE

§ 261. Opposition to marriage

In case of an opposition to the marriage, if it be supported by the oath of the party making it, and by reason sufficient in the opinion of the judge to authorize a suspension of the marriage, it shall be notified to the parties, and a day shall be assigned for a hearing.

Acts 1987, No. 886, § 3, eff. Jan. 1, 1988.

Cross References

C.C. arts. 87, 91, 151, 152.

§ 262. Hearing on opposition

The time fixed for the hearing of the parties and the decision on the opposition shall not exceed ten days from the day on which the opposition was made.

Acts 1987, No. 886, § 3, eff. Jan. 1, 1988.

Cross References

C.C. arts. 87, 91.

§ 263. Persons entitled to oppose

Any person may make opposition to a marriage, but if the opposition be overruled, the party making it shall pay costs.

Acts 1987, No. 886, § 3, eff. Jan. 1, 1988.

Cross References

C.C. arts. 87, 91.

§ 264. [Blank]

§§ 265 to 270. [Blank]

§ 271. [Blank]

PART VII. COVENANT MARRIAGE

§ 272. Covenant marriage; intent; conditions to create

A. A covenant marriage is a marriage entered into by one male and one female who understand and agree that the marriage between them is a lifelong relationship. Parties to a covenant marriage have received counseling emphasizing the nature and purposes of marriage and the responsibilities thereto. Only when there has been a complete and total breach of the marital covenant commitment may the non-breaching party seek a declaration that the marriage is no longer legally recognized.

B. A man and woman may contract a covenant marriage by declaring their intent to do so on their application for a marriage license, as provided in R.S. 9:224(C), and executing a declaration of intent to contract a covenant marriage, as provided in R.S. 9:273. The application for a marriage license and the declaration of intent shall be filed with the official who issues the marriage license.

C. A covenant marriage terminates only for one of the causes enumerated in Civil Code Article 101. A covenant

marriage may be terminated by divorce only upon one of the exclusive grounds enumerated in R.S. 9:307. A covenant marriage agreement may not be dissolved, rescinded, or otherwise terminated by the mutual consent of the spouses.
Added by Acts 1997, No. 1380, § 3. Amended by Acts 2006, No. 249, § 1.

Editor's note. Acts 1997, No. 1380, § 5 declares: "The office of attorney general, Department of Justice shall, prior to August 15, 1997, promulgate an informational pamphlet, entitled 'Covenant Marriage Act', which shall outline in sufficient detail the consequences of entering into a covenant marriage. The informational pamphlet shall be made available to any counselor who provides marriage counseling an provided for by this Act."

§ 273. Covenant marriage; contents of declaration of intent

A. A declaration of intent to contract a covenant marriage shall contain all of the following:

(1) A recitation signed by both parties to the following effect:

"A COVENANT MARRIAGE

We do solemnly declare that marriage is a covenant between a man and a woman who agree to live together as husband and wife for so long as they both may live. We have chosen each other carefully and disclosed to one another everything which could adversely affect the decision to enter into this marriage. We have received premarital counseling on the nature, purposes, and responsibilities of marriage. We have read the Covenant Marriage Act, and we understand that a Covenant Marriage is for life. If we experience marital difficulties, we commit ourselves to take all reasonable efforts to preserve our marriage, including marital counseling.

With full knowledge of what this commitment means, we do hereby declare that our marriage will be bound by Louisiana law on Covenant Marriages and we promise to love, honor, and care for one another as husband and wife for the rest of our lives."

(2)(a) An affidavit by the parties attesting they have received premarital counseling from a priest, minister, rabbi, clerk of the Religious Society of Friends, any clergyman of any religious sect, or a professional marriage counselor, which counseling shall include a discussion of the seriousness of covenant marriage, communication of the fact that a covenant marriage is a commitment for life, a discussion of the obligation to seek marital counseling in times of marital difficulties, and that they have received and read the informational pamphlet developed and promulgated by the office of the attorney general entitled "Covenant Marriage Act" which provides a full explanation of the terms and conditions of a covenant marriage.

(b) An attestation, signed by the counselor and attached to or included in the parties' affidavit, confirming that the parties were counseled as to the nature and purpose of the marriage.

(3)(a) The signature of both parties witnessed by a notary.

(b) If one or both of the parties are minors, the written consent or authorization of those persons required under the Children's Code to consent to or authorize the marriage of minors.

B. The declaration shall contain two separate documents, the recitation and the affidavit, the latter of which shall include the attestation either included therein or attached thereto. The recitation shall be prepared in duplicate originals, one of which shall be retained by the parties and the other, together with the affidavit and attestation, shall be filed as provided in R.S. 9:272(B).
Added by Acts 1997, No. 1380, § 3. Amended by Acts 1999, No. 1298, § 1.

Editor's note. Acts 1997, No. 1380, § 5 declares: "The office of attorney general, Department of Justice shall, prior to August 15, 1997, promulgate an informational pamphlet, entitled 'Covenant Marriage Act', which shall outline in sufficient detail the consequences of entering into a covenant marriage. The informational pamphlet shall be made available to any counselor who provides marriage counseling as provided for by this Act."

§ 273.1. Declaration of intent; form

A. The following is suggested as a form for the recitation which may be used by the couple:

"DECLARATION OF INTENT

We do solemnly declare that marriage is a covenant between a man and a woman who agree to live together as husband and wife for so long as they both may live. We have chosen each other carefully and disclosed to one another everything which could adversely affect the decision to enter this marriage. We have received premarital counseling on the nature, purposes, and responsibilities of marriage. We have read the Covenant Marriage Act, and we understand that a Covenant Marriage is for life. If we experience marital difficulties, we commit ourselves to take all reasonable efforts to preserve our marriage, including marital counseling.

With full knowledge of what this commitment means, we do hereby declare that our marriage will be bound by Louisiana law on Covenant Marriages and we promise to love, honor, and care for one another as husband and wife for the rest of our lives."

B. The following is the suggested form of the affidavit which may be used by the parties, notary, and counselor:

STATE OF LOUISIANA

PARISH OF _____

BE IT KNOWN THAT on this ___ day of _____, _____, before me the undersigned notary, personally came and appeared:

_____

(Insert names of the prospective spouses)

who after being duly sworn by me, Notary, deposed and stated that:

Affiants acknowledge that they have received premarital counseling from a priest, minister, rabbi, clerk of the Religious Society of Friends, any clergyman of any religious sect, or a professional marriage counselor, which marriage counseling included:

A discussion of the seriousness of Covenant Marriage;

Communication of the fact that a Covenant Marriage is a commitment for life;

The obligation of a Covenant Marriage to take reasonable efforts to preserve the marriage if marital difficulties arise, and

That the affiants both read the pamphlet entitled "The Covenant Marriage Act" developed and promulgated by the office of the attorney general, which provides a full explanation of a Covenant Marriage, including the obligation to seek marital counseling in times of marital difficulties and the exclusive grounds for legally terminating a Covenant Marriage by divorce or divorce after a judgment of separation from bed or board.

_____
(Name of prospective spouse)

_____
(Name of prospective spouse)

SWORN TO AND SUBSCRIBED BEFORE ME THIS _____ DAY OF _____, _____.

_____
NOTARY PUBLIC

ATTESTATION

The undersigned does hereby attest that the affiants did receive counseling from me as to the nature and purpose of marriage, which included a discussion of the seriousness of Covenant Marriage, communication of the fact that a Covenant Marriage is for life, and the obligation of a Covenant Marriage to take reasonable efforts to preserve the marriage if marital difficulties arise.

_____
Counselor

Added by Acts 1999, No. 1298, § 1.

§ 274. Covenant marriage; other applicable rules

A covenant marriage shall be governed by all of the provisions of Chapters 1 through 4 of Title IV of Book I of the Louisiana Civil Code and the provisions of Code Title IV of Code Book I of this Title.

Added by Acts 1997, No. 1380, § 3.

Editor's note. Acts 1997, No. 1380, § 5 declares: "The office of attorney general, Department of Justice shall, prior to August 15, 1997, promulgate an informational pamphlet, entitled 'Covenant Marriage Act', which shall outline in sufficient detail the consequences of entering into a covenant marriage. The informational pamphlet shall be made available to any counselor who provides marriage counseling as provided for by this Act."

§ 275. Covenant marriage; applicability to already married couples

A. On or after August 15, 1997, married couples may execute a declaration of intent to designate their marriage as a covenant marriage to be governed by the laws relative thereto.

B. (1) This declaration of intent in the form and containing the contents required by Subsection C of this Section must be presented to the officer who issued the couple's marriage license and with whom the couple's marriage certificate is filed. If the couple was married outside of this state, a copy of the foreign marriage certificate, which need not be certified, with the declaration of intent attached thereto, shall be filed with the officer who issues marriage licenses in the parish in which the couple is domiciled. The officer shall make a notation on the marriage certificate of the declaration of intent of a covenant marriage and attach a copy of the declaration to the certificate.

(2) On or before the fifteenth day of each calendar month, the officer shall forward to the state registrar of vital records each declaration of intent of a covenant marriage filed with him during the preceding calendar month pursuant to this Section.

C. (1) A declaration of intent to designate a marriage as a covenant marriage shall contain all of the following:

(a) A recitation signed by both parties to the following effect:

"A COVENANT MARRIAGE

We do solemnly declare that marriage is a covenant between a man and a woman who agree to live together as husband and wife for so long as they both may live. We understand the nature, purpose, and responsibilities of marriage. We have read the Covenant Marriage Act, and we understand that a Covenant Marriage is for life. If we experience marital difficulties, we commit ourselves to take all reasonable efforts to preserve our marriage, including marital counseling.

With full knowledge of what this commitment means, we do hereby declare that our marriage will be bound by Louisiana law on Covenant Marriage, and we renew our promise to love, honor, and care for one another as husband and wife for the rest of our lives."

(b)(i) An affidavit by the parties that they have discussed their intent to designate their marriage as a covenant marriage with a priest, minister, rabbi, clerk of the Religious Society of Friends, any clergyman of any religious sect, or a professional marriage counselor, which included a discussion of the obligation to seek marital counseling in times of marital difficulties and that they have received and read the informational pamphlet developed and promulgated by the office of the attorney general entitled "Covenant Marriage Act" which provides a full explanation of the terms and conditions of a Covenant Marriage.

(ii) An attestation signed by the counselor confirming that the parties were counseled as to the nature and purpose of the marriage.

(iii) The signature of both parties witnessed by a notary.

(2) The declaration shall contain two separate documents, the recitation and the affidavit, the latter of which shall include the attestation either included therein or attached thereto. The recitation shall be prepared in duplicate originals, one of which shall be retained by the parties and the other, together with the affidavit and attestation, shall be filed as provided in Subsection B of this Section.

Added by Acts 1997, No. 1380, § 3. Amended by Acts 1999, No. 1298, § 1.

Editor's note. Acts 1997, No. 1380, § 5 declares: "The office of attorney general, Department of Justice shall, prior to August 15, 1997, promulgate an informational pamphlet, entitled 'Covenant Marriage Act', which shall outline in sufficient detail the consequences of entering into a covenant marriage. The informational pamphlet shall be made available to any counselor who provides marriage counseling as provided for by this Act."

§ 275.1. Declaration of intent; married couples; form

A. The following is suggested as a form for the recitation which may be used by the couple:

"DECLARATION OF INTENT

We do solemnly declare that marriage is a covenant between a man and a woman who agree to live together as husband and wife for so long as they both may live. We understand the nature, purpose, and responsibilities of marriage. We have read the Covenant Marriage Act, and we understand that a Covenant Marriage is for life. If we experience marital difficulties, we commit ourselves to take reasonable efforts to preserve our marriage, including marital counseling.

With full knowledge of what this commitment means, we do hereby declare that our marriage will be bound by Louisiana law on Covenant Marriage, and we renew our promise to love, honor, and care for one another as husband and wife for the rest of our lives."

B. The following is the suggested form of the affidavit which may be used by the parties, notary, and counselor:

STATE OF LOUISIANA

PARISH OF _____

BE IT KNOWN THAT on this ___ day of _____, _____, before me the undersigned notary, personally came and appeared:

_____
(Insert names of spouses)

who after being sworn by me, Notary, deposed and stated that:

Affiants acknowledge that they have received counseling from a priest, minister, rabbi, clerk of the Religious Society of Friends, any clergyman of any religious sect, or a professional marriage counselor, which counseling included:

A discussion of the seriousness of Covenant Marriage;

Communication of the fact that a Covenant Marriage is a commitment for life;

The obligation of a Covenant Marriage to take reasonable efforts to preserve the marriage if marital difficulties arise, and

That the affiants both read the pamphlet entitled "The Covenant Marriage Act" developed and promulgated by the office of the attorney general, which provides a full explanation of a Covenant Marriage, including the obligation to seek marital counseling in times of marital difficulties and the exclusive grounds for legally terminating a Covenant Marriage by divorce or divorce after a judgment of separation from bed or board.

_____
(Name of Spouse)

_____
(Name of Spouse)

SWORN TO AND SUBSCRIBED BEFORE ME THIS _____ DAY OF _____, _____.

_____
NOTARY PUBLIC

ATTESTATION

The undersigned does hereby attest that the affiants did receive counseling from me as to the nature and purpose of marriage, which included a discussion of the seriousness of Covenant Marriage, communication of the fact that a Covenant Marriage is for life, and the obligation of a Covenant Marriage to take reasonable efforts to preserve the marriage if marital difficulties arise.

_____
Counselor

Added by Acts 1999, No. 1298, § 1.

§ 275.5. [Blank]

§ 276. Limitation of liability; pastoral counselor

A. No person shall have a cause of action against any priest, minister, rabbi, clerk of religious society of friends, or any clergyman of any religious sect, for any action taken or statement made in adherence with the provisions for counseling as provided for in this Part.

B. The immunity from liability provided for in Subsection A of this Section, shall not apply to any action or statement by such priest, minister, rabbi, clerk of religious society of friends, or any clergyman of any religious sect, if such action or statement was maliciously, willfully, and deliberately intended to cause harm to, or harass or intimidate those seeking such counseling.

Added by Acts 2003, No. 778, § 1.

§§ 277 to 280. [Blank]

§ 281. Repealed by Acts 1958, No. 160, § 2

§§ 282 to 284. [Blank]

CHAPTER 2. INCIDENTS AND EFFECTS OF MARRIAGE

PART I. IN GENERAL

Section
291. Suits between spouses.
292. Surname of married person.

PART II. SPECIAL INCIDENTS AND EFFECTS OF COVENANT MARRIAGE

293. Law applicable to spouses in covenant marriage.
294. Covenant spouses' love, respect, and community.
295. Covenant spouses' obligation to live together.
296. Right and duty of covenant spouses to manage household.
297. Decisionmaking in interest of family.
298. Obligations to children of the marriage.

PART I. IN GENERAL

§ 291. Suits between spouses

Spouses may not sue each other except for causes of action pertaining to contracts or arising out of the provisions of Book III, Title VI of the Civil Code;[1] for restitution of separate property; for divorce or declaration of nullity of the marriage; and for causes of action pertaining to spousal support or the support or custody of a child while the spouses are living separate and apart.

Added by Acts 1960, No. 31, § 2, eff. Jan. 1, 1961. Amended by Acts 1978, No. 627, § 4, eff. Sept. 7, 1979; Acts 1979, No. 711, § 2, eff. Jan. 1, 1980; Acts 1990, No. 1009, § 6, eff. Jan. 1, 1991.

[1] C.C. art. 2325 et seq.

Comments—1979

(a) This provision is based on § 291, as modified by the H.C.R. 232 (1978) Joint Legislative Subcommittee. The last sentence reproduces the substance of House Bill No. 194 of 1978, on recommendation of the Louisiana State Law Institute.

(b) This provision does not affect the direct action statute. R.S. 22:1269.

(c) This provision is not intended to suppress a right that a spouse may have under the present law to sue the other spouse.

(d) This provision does not affect the rights of judicially separated or divorced spouses to sue each other.

Cross References

C.C. arts. 86, 101, 103, 131, 151, 152, 2325, 2365, 3336, 3520, 3521, 3522, 3525, 3526.

§ 292. Surname of married person

Notwithstanding any other law to the contrary, a woman, at her option, may use her maiden name, her present spouse's name, or a hyphenated combination thereof. If widowed, divorced, or remarried, a woman may use her maiden name, the surname of her deceased or former spouse, the surname of her present spouse, or any combination thereof.

Added by Acts 2003, No. 852, § 1. Amended by Acts 2004, No. 118, § 1.

PART II. SPECIAL INCIDENTS AND EFFECTS OF COVENANT MARRIAGE

§ 293. Law applicable to spouses in covenant marriage

Spouses in a covenant marriage are subject to all of the laws governing married couples generally and to the special rules governing covenant marriage.

Added by Acts 2004, No. 490, § 1.

§ 294. Covenant spouses' love, respect, and community

Spouses owe each other love and respect and they commit to a community of living. Each spouse should attend to the satisfaction of the other's needs.

Added by Acts 2004, No. 490, § 1.

§ 295. Covenant spouses' obligation to live together

Spouses are bound to live together, unless there is good cause otherwise. The spouses determine the family residence by mutual consent, according to their requirements and those of the family.

Added by Acts 2004, No. 490, § 1.

§ 296. Right and duty of covenant spouses to manage household

The management of the household shall be the right and the duty of both spouses.

Added by Acts 2004, No. 490, § 1.

§ 297. Decisionmaking in interest of family

Spouses by mutual consent after collaboration shall make decisions relating to family life in the best interest of the family.

Added by Acts 2004, No. 490, § 1.

§ 298. Obligations to children of the marriage

The spouses are bound to maintain, to teach, and to educate their children born of the marriage in accordance with their capacities, natural inclinations, and aspirations, and shall prepare them for their future.

Added by Acts 2004, No. 490, § 1.

CODE TITLE V—DIVORCE

CHAPTER 1. DIVORCE

PART I. IN GENERAL

Section	
301.	Court may authorize spouse of military personnel presumed dead to remarry; judgment dissolves marriage.
302.	Divorce proceedings; hearings in chambers; procedure.
303.	Income assignment; new orders; deviation.
304.	Judgment of divorce; waiting periods; accrual of abandonment period.
304.1.	Court costs; action to make child support executory.
305.	Repealed.
306.	Seminar for divorcing parents.
307.	Divorce or separation from bed and board in a covenant marriage; exclusive grounds.
308.	Separation from bed and board in covenant marriage; suit against spouse; jurisdiction, procedure, and incidental relief.
309.	Separation from bed and board in a covenant marriage; effects.
310.	Retroactivity of spousal support order.
311.	Modification of support; material change in circumstances; periodic review by DSS; medical support.
311.1.	[Blank].
312.	Child support; accounting; requirements.
313.	Divorce and child support proceedings; special requirements.
314.	Repealed.

PART I–A. CHILD SUPPORT

SUBPART A. GUIDELINES FOR DETERMINATION OF CHILD SUPPORT

315.	Economic data and principles; definitions.
315.1.	Rebuttable presumption; deviation from guidelines by court; stipulations by parties.
315.1.1.	Determination of income; evidence.
315.2.	Calculation of basic child support obligation.
315.3.	Net child care costs; addition to basic obligation.
315.4.	Health insurance premiums; addition to basic obligation.
315.5.	Extraordinary medical expenses; addition to basic obligation.
315.6.	Other extraordinary expenses; addition to basic obligation.

APPENDIX 1—REVISED STATUTES, TITLE 9

Section
- 315.7. Deductions for income of the child.
- 315.8. Calculation of total child support obligation; worksheet.
- 315.9. Effect of shared custodial arrangement.
- 315.10. Effect of split custodial arrangement.
- 315.11. Voluntarily unemployed or underemployed party.
- 315.12. Second jobs and overtime.
- 315.12.1. [Blank].
- 315.13. Amounts not set forth in or exceeding schedule.
- 315.14. Mandatory minimum child support award.
- 315.15. No change in circumstances intended.
- 315.16. Review of guidelines.
- 315.17. Standard of appellate review.
- 315.18. Schedule; information.
- 315.19. Schedule for support.
- 315.20. Worksheets.

SUBPART B. OTHER CHILD SUPPORT PROVISIONS
- 315.21. Retroactivity of child support judgment.
- 315.22. Termination of child support upon majority or emancipation; exceptions.
- 315.23. Suspension or modification of child support obligation; secreting of child.
- 315.24. Child support enforcement; revocatory and oblique actions.
- 315.25. Consideration of custody or visitation matters.
- 315.26. Collection of past due child support.

SUBPART C. JUDICIAL SUSPENSION OF LICENSE FOR NONPAYMENT OF CHILD SUPPORT OR CONTEMPT OF COURT IN CHILD SUPPORT OR PATERNITY PROCEEDINGS
- 315.30. Family financial responsibility; purpose.
- 315.31. Definitions.
- 315.32. Order of suspension of license; noncompliance with support order; contempt of court.
- 315.33. Suspension of license; notice of suspension from licensing board; temporary license.
- 315.34. Subsequent compliance; order of compliance; order of partial compliance.
- 315.35. Reissuance of license.
- 315.36. Suspension of license; pattern of nonpayment.
- 315.37, 315.38. [Blank].

SUBPART D. ADMINISTRATIVE SUSPENSION OF CERTAIN LICENSES FOR NONPAYMENT OF CHILD SUPPORT
- 315.40. Definitions.
- 315.41. Notice of child support delinquency; suspension of license.
- 315.42. Objection to suspension of license.
- 315.43. Administrative hearing.
- 315.44. Certification of noncompliance.
- 315.45. Suspension of license; notice of suspension from licensing authority.
- 315.46. Subsequent compliance with support order; compliance and partial compliance releases.
- 315.47. Reissuance of license.
- 315.48. Repealed.

PART II. SPOUSAL SUPPORT
- 321. Retroactivity of judgment concerning spousal support.
- 322. Judgment or order for support not to be recorded.
- 323. Recordation of judgment or order for amount due.

Section
- 324. Cancellation of record following payment.
- 325. Collection of past due spousal support.
- 326. Determination of income for spousal support; evidence.
- 327. Repealed.

PART III. CHILD CUSTODY

SUBPART A. EVALUATION AND MEDIATION
- 331. Custody or visitation proceeding; evaluation by mental health professional.
- 331.1. Drug testing in custody or visitation proceeding.
- 332. Custody or visitation proceeding; mediation.
- 333. Duties of mediator.
- 334. Mediator qualifications.

SUBPART B. JOINT CUSTODY
- 335. Joint custody decree and implementation order.
- 336. Obligation of joint custodians to confer.
- 337. Repealed.

SUBPART C. PROTECTIVE AND REMEDIAL PROVISIONS
- 341. Restriction on visitation.
- 342. Bond to secure child custody or visitation order.
- 343. Return of child kept in violation of custody and visitation order.
- 344. Visitation rights of grandparents and siblings.
- 345. Appointment of attorney in child custody or visitation proceedings.
- 346. Action for failure to exercise or to allow visitation, custody or time rights pursuant to court-ordered schedule; judgment and awards.
- 347. Repealed.
- 348. Loss of visitation due to military service; compensatory visitation.

SUBPART D. ACCESS TO RECORDS
- 351. Access to records of child.

SUBPART E. RELOCATING A CHILD'S RESIDENCE
- 355.1. Definitions.
- 355.2. Applicability.
- 355.3. Persons authorized to propose relocation of principal residence of a child.
- 355.4. Notice of proposed relocation of child; court authorization to relocate.
- 355.5. Mailing notice of proposed relocation address.
- 355.6. Failure to give notice of relocation.
- 355.7. Objection to relocation of child.
- 355.8. Limitation on objection by non-parents.
- 355.9. Effect of objection or failure to object to notice of proposed relocation.
- 355.10. Burden of proof.
- 355.11. Court authorization to relocate.
- 355.12. Temporary order.
- 355.13. Priority for trial.
- 355.14. Factors to determine contested relocation.
- 355.15. Mental health expert; appointment.
- 355.16. Application of factors at initial hearing.
- 355.17. Modification of custody.
- 355.18. Posting security.
- 355.19. Sanctions for unwarranted or frivolous proposal to relocate child or objection to relocation.

Section
SUBPART F. OTHER CHILD CUSTODY PROVISIONS
356. Consideration of child support.
357. Use of technology.

SUBPART G. PARENTING COORDINATOR
358.1. Appointment of parenting coordinator; term; costs.
358.2. No appointment in family violence cases.
358.3. Qualifications.
358.4. Authority and duties of parenting coordinator.
358.5. Testimony and report.
358.6. Communication with court.
358.7. Access to information.
358.8. Termination of appointment of parenting coordinator.
358.9. Limitation of liability.

SUBPART H. MILITARY PARENT AND CHILD CUSTODY PROTECTION ACT
359. Short title.
359.1. Definitions.
359.2. Final order; modification prohibited.
359.3. Material change in circumstances.
359.4. Temporary modification.
359.5. Termination of temporary modification order.
359.6. Delegation of visitation.
359.7. Testimony; evidence.
359.8. Lack of existing order of custody or visitation.
359.9. Duty to cooperate; disclosure of information.
359.10. Appointment of counsel.
359.11. Jurisdiction.
359.12. Attorney fees.
359.13. Applicability.

PART IV. POST–SEPARATION FAMILY VIOLENCE RELIEF ACT
361. Legislative findings.
362. Definitions.
363. Ordered mediation prohibited.
364. Child custody; visitation.
365. Qualification of mental health professional.
366. Injunctions.
367. Costs.
368. Other remedies not affected.
369. Limitations.

PART V. INJUNCTIONS AND INCIDENTAL ORDERS
371. Injunction against alienation or encumbrance; spouse's right to demand.
372. Injunction against abuse; form; central Registry.
372.1. Injunction against harassment.
373. Removal of personal property.
374. Possession and use of family residence or community movables or immovables.
375. Award of attorney's fees.
376. Repealed.
377 to 380. Reserved.

PART I. IN GENERAL

Editor's note. Acts 1990, No. 1009, § 9 repealed R.S. 9:301 to 9:304, R.S. 9:305 to 9:308, and R.S. 9:314, effective January 1, 1991. Acts 1990, No. 1009, § 7 enacted new R.S. 9:301 to R.S. 9:302, R.S. 9:371 to R.S. 9:375, and R.S. 9:381 to R.S. 9:384, effective January 1, 1991.

§ 301. Court may authorize spouse of military personnel presumed dead to remarry; judgment dissolves marriage

A. The spouse of a person presumed dead, as provided in R.S. 9:1441, may petition the district court of the parish in which the petitioner is domiciled for authority to contract another marriage. Upon the submission of proof that the petitioner is domiciled in the parish, and that the other spouse is presumed dead, the court may authorize petitioner to contract another marriage. The presumption of the death of petitioner's spouse may be proved as provided in R.S. 9:1443.

B. The judgment of court authorizing the petitioner to contract another marriage has the effect of terminating the marriage to the person presumed dead if he is alive at the time.

Added by Acts 1990, No. 1009, § 7, eff. Jan. 1, 1991.

Editor's note. R.S. 9:301 was repealed by Acts 1990, No. 1009, § 9, effective January 1, 1991. New R.S. 9:301 was enacted by Acts 1990, No. 1009, § 7, effective January 1, 1991.

Cross References
C.C. arts. 47, 54, 101, 3521, 3522.

§ 302. Divorce proceedings; hearings in chambers; procedure

A. In addition to any hearing otherwise authorized by law to be held in chambers, the court by local rule, and only in those instances where good cause is shown, may provide that only with mutual consent, civil hearings before the trial court in divorce proceedings may be held in chambers. Such hearings shall include contested and uncontested proceedings and rules for spousal support, child support, visitation, injunctions, or other matters provisional and incidental to divorce proceedings.

B. A motion for hearing in chambers pursuant to this Section may be made by either party or upon the court's own motion.

C. Except for being closed to the public, the hearings held in chambers pursuant to this Section shall be conducted in the same manner as if taking place in open court. The minute clerk and court reporter shall be present if necessary to perform the duties provided by law.

D. The provisions of this Section shall not be construed to repeal or restrict the authority otherwise provided by law for any hearing to be held in chambers.

Added by Acts 1990, No. 1009, § 7, eff. Jan. 1, 1991.

Editor's note. R.S. 9:302 was repealed by Acts 1990, No. 1009, § 9, effective January 1, 1991. Acts 1990, No. 1009, § 7 enacted new R.S. 9:302, effective January 1, 1991.

Cross References
C.C. arts. 101 to 105, 112, 3521.
R.S. 9:291, 9:381, 13:3491.

§ 303. Income assignment; new orders; deviation

A. In all new child support orders after January 1, 1994, that are not being enforced by the Department of Children and Family Services, the court shall include as part of the order an immediate income assignment unless there is a written agreement between the parties or the court finds good cause not to require an immediate income assignment.

B. For purposes of this Section:

(1) "Written agreement" means a written alternative arrangement signed by both parents, reviewed by the court, and entered into the record of the proceedings.

(2) "Good cause" exists upon a showing by the respondent that any of the following exist:

(a) There has been no delinquency in payment of child support for the six calendar months immediately preceding the filing of the motion for modification of an existing child support order.

(b) The respondent is agreeable to a consent judgment authorizing an automatic ex parte immediate income assignment if he becomes delinquent in child support payments for a period in excess of one calendar month.

(c) The respondent is not likely to become delinquent in the future.

(d) Any other sufficient evidence which, in the court's discretion, constitutes good cause.

C. An income assignment order issued pursuant to this Section shall be payable through the Louisiana state disbursement unit for collection and disbursement of child support payments as provided in R.S. 46:236.11 and shall be governed by the same provisions as immediate income assignment orders that are being enforced by the department, including R.S. 46:236.1.1 et seq. All clerks of court in the state shall provide information to the state disbursement unit on income assignment orders issued pursuant to this Section. The department shall promulgate rules and regulations to implement the provisions of this Section in accordance with the Administrative Procedure Act.

Added by Acts 1993, No. 145, § 1. Amended by Acts 1997, No. 1121, § 1, eff. Oct. 1, 1998; Acts 2010, No. 238, § 1.

Cross References

C.C. arts. 141, 142.

R.S. 9:315, 9:317.

§ 304. Judgment of divorce; waiting periods; accrual of abandonment period

A. (1) In the aftermath of Hurricanes Katrina and Rita, the issuance of Executive Orders KBB 2005–32, 48, and 67 shall not affect the calculation of the one hundred eighty-day waiting period required by Civil Code Article 102, the six-month waiting period required by Civil Code Article 103(1), or the one-year, one-year and six months, or two-year waiting periods required by R.S. 9:307.

(2) Any judgment of divorce rendered during the time periods affected by Executive Orders KBB 2005–32, 48, and 67 shall be a good and valid judgment if no appeal or request for new trial has been filed in accordance with the provisions of the Code of Civil Procedure or any applicable law or by January 3, 2006, whichever is later.

B. Notwithstanding Code of Civil Procedure Article 3954, if the two-year abandonment period would have otherwise accrued during the suspension of all legal deadlines as provided in Executive Orders KBB 2005–32, 48, and 67, the parties shall have thirty days from the effective date of this Section to file a rule to show cause as required by Civil Code Article 102.

Added by Acts 2005, 1st Ex.Sess., No. 31, § 1, eff. Nov. 29, 2005.

Editor's note. For text of Executive Orders, see Editor's note preceding R.S. 9:5821.

A prior R.S. 9:304 was repealed by Acts 1990, No. 1009, § 9.

§ 304.1. Court costs; action to make child support executory

A. An action to make past due child support executory may be filed by any plaintiff, who is unable to utilize the provisions of Chapter 5 of Title I of Book IX of the Code of Civil Procedure, without paying the costs of court in advance or as they accrue or furnishing security therefor, if the court is satisfied that the plaintiff because of poverty or lack of means cannot afford to make payment.

B. When the action has been filed without the payment of costs as provided in Subsection A and the plaintiff is not the prevailing party, except for good cause, the court shall order the plaintiff to pay all costs of court.

Added by Acts 1988, No. 603, § 1.

§ 305. Repealed by Acts 2006, No. 344, § 7, eff. June 13, 2006

§ 306. Seminar for divorcing parents

A. Upon an affirmative showing that the facts and circumstances of the particular case before the court warrant such an order, a court exercising jurisdiction over family matters may require the parties in a custody or visitation proceeding to attend and complete a court-approved seminar designed to educate and inform the parties of the needs of the children.

B. If the court chooses to require participation in such a seminar, it shall adopt rules to accomplish the goals of Subsection A of this Section, which rules shall include but not be limited to the following:

(1) Criteria for evaluating a seminar provider and its instructors.

(2) Criteria to assure selected programs provide and incorporate into the provider's fee structure the cost of services to indigents.

(3) The amount of time a participant must take part in the program, which shall be a minimum of three hours but not exceed four hours nor shall the costs exceed twenty-five dollars per person.

(4) The time within which a party must complete the program.

C. For purposes of this Section, "instructor" means any psychiatrist, psychologist, professional counselor, social worker licensed under state law, or in any parish other than Orleans, means a person working with a court-approved, nonprofit program of an accredited university created for educating divorcing parents with children. All instructors must have received advanced training in instructing co-parenting or similar seminars.

D. The seminar shall focus on the developmental needs of children, with emphasis on fostering the child's emotional health. The seminar shall be informative and supportive and shall direct people desiring additional information or help to appropriate resources. The course content shall contain but not be limited to the following subjects:

(1) The developmental stages of childhood, the needs of children at different ages, and age appropriate expectations of children.

(2) Stress indicators in children adjusting to divorce, the grief process, and avoiding delinquency.

(3) The possible enduring emotional effects of divorce on the child.

(4) Changing parental and marital roles.

(5) Recommendations with respect to visitation designed to enhance the child's relationship with both parents.

(6) Financial obligations of child rearing.

(7) Conflict management and dispute resolution.

E. Nonviolent acts or communications made during the seminar, which are otherwise relevant to the subject matter of a divorce, custody, or visitation proceeding, are confidential, not subject to disclosure, and may not be used as evidence in favor of or against a participant in the pending proceeding. This rule does not require the exclusion of any evidence otherwise discoverable merely because it is presented or otherwise made during the seminar.

Added by Acts 1995, No. 766, § 1, eff. July 1, 1995. Amended by Acts 1999, No. 276, § 1.

Editor's note. Section 2 of Acts 1995, No. 766 provides that the act shall be effective on July 1, 1995, and that it "shall apply to all cases pending on that date."

Cross References

C.C. arts. 105, 131 et seq.

Ch.C. arts. 309, 618.

R.S. 9:331 et seq.

§ 307. Divorce or separation from bed and board in a covenant marriage; exclusive grounds

A. Notwithstanding any other law to the contrary and subsequent to the parties obtaining counseling, a spouse to a covenant marriage may obtain a judgment of divorce only upon proof of any of the following:

(1) The other spouse has committed adultery.

(2) The other spouse has committed a felony and has been sentenced to death or imprisonment at hard labor.

(3) The other spouse has abandoned the matrimonial domicile for a period of one year and constantly refuses to return.

(4) The other spouse has physically or sexually abused the spouse seeking the divorce or a child of one of the spouses.

(5) The spouses have been living separate and apart continuously without reconciliation for a period of two years.

(6)(a) The spouses have been living separate and apart continuously without reconciliation for a period of one year from the date the judgment of separation from bed and board was signed.

(b) If there is a minor child or children of the marriage, the spouses have been living separate and apart continuously without reconciliation for a period of one year and six months from the date the judgment of separation from bed and board was signed; however, if abuse of a child of the marriage or a child of one of the spouses is the basis for which the judgment of separation from bed and board was obtained, then a judgment of divorce may be obtained if the spouses have been living separate and apart continuously without reconciliation for a period of one year from the date the judgment of separation from bed and board was signed.

B. Notwithstanding any other law to the contrary and subsequent to the parties obtaining counseling, a spouse to a covenant marriage may obtain a judgment of separation from bed and board only upon proof of any of the following:

(1) The other spouse has committed adultery.

(2) The other spouse has committed a felony and has been sentenced to death or imprisonment at hard labor.

(3) The other spouse has abandoned the matrimonial domicile for a period of one year and constantly refuses to return.

(4) The other spouse has physically or sexually abused the spouse seeking the divorce or a child of one of the spouses.

(5) The spouses have been living separate and apart continuously without reconciliation for a period of two years.

(6) On account of habitual intemperance of the other spouse, or excesses, cruel treatment, or outrages of the other spouse, if such habitual intemperance, or such ill-treatment is of such a nature as to render their living together insupportable.

C. The counseling referenced in Subsections A and B of this Section, or other such reasonable steps taken by the spouses to preserve the marriage, as required by the Declaration of Intent signed by the spouses, shall occur once the parties experience marital difficulties. If the spouses begin living separate and apart, the counseling or other intervention should continue until the rendition of a judgment of divorce.

D. Notwithstanding the provisions of Subsection C of this Section, the counseling referenced in Subsections A and B of this Section shall not apply when the other spouse has physically or sexually abused the spouse seeking the divorce or a child of one of the spouses.

Added by Acts 1997, No. 1380, § 4. Amended by Acts 2004, No. 490, § 1.

Editor's note. Acts 1997, No. 1380, § 5 declares: "The office of attorney general, Department of Justice shall, prior to August 15, 1997, promulgate an informational pamphlet, entitled 'Covenant Marriage Act', which shall outline in sufficient detail the consequences of entering into a covenant marriage. The informational pamphlet shall be made available to any counselor who provides marriage counseling as provided for by this Act."

Section 2 of Acts 2004, No. 490, declares that the provisions of subsection C of R.S. 9:307 "shall not apply to actions for divorce or separations from bed or board in a covenant marriage instituted before the effective date of this Act," that is, August 15, 2004.

§ 308. Separation from bed and board in covenant marriage; suit against spouse; jurisdiction, procedure, and incidental relief

A. Unless judicially separated, spouses in a covenant marriage may not sue each other except for causes of action pertaining to contracts or arising out of the provisions of Book III, Title VI of the Civil Code; for restitution of separate property; for separation from bed and board in covenant marriages, for divorce, or for declaration of nullity of the marriage; and for causes of action pertaining to spousal support or the support or custody of a child while the spouses are living separate and apart, although not judicially separated.

B. (1) Any court which is competent to preside over divorce proceedings, including the family court for the parish of East Baton Rouge, has jurisdiction of an action for separation from bed and board in a covenant marriage, if:

(a) One or both of the spouses are domiciled in this state and the ground therefor was committed or occurred in this state or while the matrimonial domicile was in this state.

(b) The ground therefor occurred elsewhere while either or both of the spouses were domiciled elsewhere, provided the person obtaining the separation from bed and board was domiciled in this state prior to the time the cause of action accrued and is domiciled in this state at the time the action is filed.

(2) An action for a separation from bed and board in a covenant marriage shall be brought in a parish where either party is domiciled, or in the parish of the last matrimonial domicile.

(3) The venue provided herein may not be waived, and a judgment of separation rendered by a court of improper venue is an absolute nullity.

C. Judgments on the pleadings and summary judgments shall not be granted in any action for separation from bed and board in a covenant marriage.

D. In a proceeding for a separation from bed and board in a covenant marriage or thereafter, a court may award a spouse all incidental relief afforded in a proceeding for divorce, including but not limited to spousal support, claims for contributions to education, child custody, visitation rights, child support, injunctive relief and possession and use of a family residence or community movables or immovables.

Added by Acts 1997, No. 1380, § 4.

Editor's note. Acts 1997, No. 1380, § 5 declares: "The office of attorney general, Department of Justice shall, prior to August 15, 1997, promulgate an informational pamphlet, entitled 'Covenant Marriage Act', which shall outline in sufficient detail the consequences of entering into a covenant marriage. The informational pamphlet shall be made available to any counselor who provides marriage counseling as provided for by this Act."

§ 309. Separation from bed and board in a covenant marriage; effects

A. (1) Separation from bed and board in a covenant marriage does not dissolve the bond of matrimony, since the separated husband and wife are not at liberty to marry again; but it puts an end to their conjugal cohabitation, and to the common concerns, which existed between them.

(2) Spouses who are judicially separated from bed and board in a covenant marriage shall retain that status until either reconciliation or divorce.

B. (1) The judgment of separation from bed and board carries with it the separation of goods and effects and is retroactive to the date on which the original petition was filed in the action in which the judgment is rendered, but such retroactive effect shall be without prejudice to the liability of the community for the attorney fees and costs incurred by the spouses in the action in which the judgment is rendered, or to rights validly acquired in the interim between commencement of the action and recordation of the judgment.

(2) Upon reconciliation of the spouses, the community shall be reestablished between the spouses, as of the date of filing of the original petition in the action in which the judgment was rendered, unless the spouses execute prior to the reconciliation a matrimonial agreement that the community shall not be reestablished upon reconciliation. This matrimonial agreement shall not require court approval.

(3) Reestablishment of the community under the provisions of this Section shall be effective toward third persons only upon filing notice of the reestablishment for registry in accordance with the provisions of Civil Code Article 2332. The reestablishment of the community shall not prejudice the rights of third persons validly acquired prior to filing notice of the reestablishment nor shall it affect a prior community property partition between the spouses.

Added by Acts 1997, No. 1380, § 4.

Editor's note. Acts 1997, No. 1380, § 5 declares: "The office of attorney general, Department of Justice shall, prior to August 15, 1997, promulgate an informational pamphlet, entitled 'Covenant Marriage Act', which shall outline in sufficient detail the consequences of entering into a covenant marriage. The informational pamphlet shall be made available to any counselor who provides marriage counseling as provided for by this Act."

§ 310. Retroactivity of spousal support order

A. An order for spousal support shall be retroactive to the filing date of the petition for spousal support granted in the order.

B. Any support of any kind provided by the judgment debtor from the date the petition for support is filed to the date the support order is issued, to or on behalf of the person for whom support is ordered, shall be credited to the judgment debtor against the amount of the judgment.

C. In the event the court finds good cause for not making the award retroactive, the court may fix the date such award shall become due.

Added by Acts 1984, No. 166, § 1. Amended by Acts 1993, No. 261, § 4, eff. Jan. 1, 1994.

Cross References

C.C. arts. 6, 3521, 3522.

§ 311. Modification of support; material change in circumstances; periodic review by DSS; medical support

A. (1) An award for support shall not be modified unless the party seeking the modification shows a material change in circumstances of one of the parties between the time of the previous award and the time of the rule for modification of the award.

(2) The Department of Children and Family Services shall prepare and distribute information, forms, and rules for the modification of support orders, in accordance with this Subsection, and for proceeding *in forma pauperis*. The information provided by the Department of Children and Family Services shall specifically include what may constitute a material change in circumstances. The clerks of court in all parishes shall make this information available to the public upon request. When the initial support order is entered, either the court or the department, if providing services, shall provide this information to the parties.

B. A judgment for past due support shall not of itself constitute a material change in circumstances of the obligor sufficient to reduce an existing award of support.

C. For purposes of this Section, in cases where the Department of Children and Family Services is providing support enforcement services:

(1) A material change in circumstance exists when a strict application of the child support guidelines, Part I-A of this Chapter, would result in at least a twenty-five percent change in the existing child support award. A material change in circumstance does not exist under this Paragraph if the amount of the award was the result of the court's deviating from the guidelines pursuant to R.S. 9:315.1 and there has not been a material change in the circumstances which warranted the deviation.

(2) Upon request of either party or on its own initiative and if the best interest of the child so requires, the department shall provide for judicial review and, if appropriate, the court may adjust the amount of the existing child support award every three years if the existing award differs from the amount which would otherwise be awarded under the application of the child support guidelines. The review provided hereby does not require a showing of a material change in circumstance nor preclude a party from seeking a reduction or increase under the other provisions of this Section.

D. A material change in circumstance need not be shown for purposes of modifying a child support award to include a court-ordered award for medical support.

E. If the court does not find good cause sufficient to justify an order to modify child support or the motion is dismissed prior to a hearing, it may order the mover to pay all court costs and reasonable attorney fees of the other party if the court determines the motion was frivolous.

F. The provisions of Subsection E of this Section shall not apply when the recipient of the support payments is a public entity acting on behalf of another party to whom support is due.

G. A modified order for support shall be retroactive to the filing date of the rule for modification.

Added by Acts 1985, No. 41, § 1. Amended by Acts 1993, No. 478, § 1; Acts 1997, No. 1245, § 1, eff. July 1, 1997; Acts 2001, No. 1082, § 1; Acts 2008, No. 886, § 1; Acts 2010, No. 913, § 3.

Comments—2001

(a) To obtain a reduction or increase in support the change in circumstances of one of the parties must be *material*, defined as a change in circumstance having real importance or great consequences for the needs of the child or the ability to pay of either party. The amendment specifying that the court first consider the threshold matter of materiality of the change in circumstance overrules Stogner v. Stogner, 739 So.2d 762 (La. 1999), in which the Louisiana Supreme Court held that *any* change in circumstances is sufficient to justify a reduction or increase in child support, a conclusion extended to spousal support by the court of appeal in Council v. Council, 775 So.2d 628 (La. App. 2 Cir. 2000). But see C.C. Art. 114, as amended by Acts 2001, No. 1049.

(b) If (1) either the motion to modify support is dismissed before a hearing or the court finds insufficient cause to modify the existing order and (2) the court also concludes that the motion was frivolous, the court has discretion to order the mover to pay court costs and reasonable attorney fees, unless the recipient is a public entity. See Subsections E and F.

Editor's note. Acts 2001, No. 1082, § 5, declares that this Act applies to actions concerning child support filed after August 15, 2001.

Cross References

C.C. arts. 3521, 3522.

§ 311.1. [Blank]

Editor's note. Acts 1987, No. 745, § 1 enacted R.S. 9:311.1 which was redesignated as R.S. 9:313 pursuant to the statutory revision authority of the Louisiana State Law Institute.

§ 312. Child support; accounting; requirements

A. On motion of the party ordered to make child support payments pursuant to court decree, by consent or otherwise, after a contradictory hearing and a showing of good cause based upon the expenditure of child support for the six months immediately prior to the filing of the motion, the court shall order the recipient of the support payments to render an accounting.

B. The accounting ordered by the court after the hearing shall be in the form of an expense and income affidavit for the child with supporting documentation and shall be provided quarterly to the moving party. The order requiring accounting in accordance with this Section shall continue in effect as long as support payments are made or in accordance with the court order.

C. The movant shall pay all court costs and attorney fees of the recipient of child support when the motion is dismissed prior to the hearing, and the court determines the motion was frivolous, or when, after the contradictory hearing, the court does not find good cause sufficient to justify an order requiring the recipient to render such accounting and the court determines the motion was frivolous.

D. The provisions of this Section shall not apply when the recipient of the support payments is a public entity acting on behalf of another party to whom support is due.

Added by Acts 1997, No. 1197, § 1. Amended by Acts 2001, No. 1082, § 1.

Comments—2001

(a) Louisiana, one of only ten states to do so, permits the obligor who pays child support to seek by contradictory motion an accounting from the obligee of the expenditure of such payments on behalf of the child. The amendments direct the court to consider the expenditure of child support payments during the six months immediately preceding the motion to determine if good cause exists to require future accounting by the obligee. Should the court decide that good cause exists for ordering an accounting, it shall consist of the quarterly submission of an expense and income affidavit for the child accompanied by reasonable documentation. The accounting order under Subsection B continues until the support terminates or until further order of the court.

(b) The movant *shall* pay court costs and attorney fees of the person who receives child support if (1) either the motion for an accounting is dismissed before the hearing or the court fails to find good cause for an accounting *and* (2) the motion was frivolous.

Editor's note. Acts 2001, No. 1082, § 5, declares that this Act applies to actions concerning child support filed after August 15, 2001.

§ 313. Divorce and child support proceedings; special requirements

A. Each party in a divorce proceeding shall provide the court with his social security number or a statement that a social security number is not available. The social security number or statement shall be an attachment to the pleadings. Notwithstanding the provisions of R.S. 44:1 et seq. the clerk of court shall maintain the confidentiality of a party's social security number in a divorce proceeding, provided a request is made to the clerk in writing by the party at the time of the filing of the original petition for divorce or separation or at any time thereafter.

B. (1) Each party in a child support proceeding shall advise the state case registry of his current address and telephone number, social security number, driver's license number, and the name, address, and telephone number of his current employer and of any change in this information during the pendency of the proceeding and thereafter. If any of this information is unavailable, the party shall submit a statement to this effect with the state case registry. Information submitted pursuant to this Subsection shall be available for inspection by the parties in the proceeding but shall otherwise be confidential except as provided in this Subsection.

(2) Any order entered or judgment rendered shall require the parties to provide the state case registry with any change in the information required by this Section which occurs after the date of the entry or rendering.

(3) Upon entry of an order or upon receipt of any change in this information during the pending proceeding, the clerk of court shall forward this information to the state case registry in accordance with R.S. 46:236.10.

(4) In any subsequent child support proceeding between the parties concerning the same minor child, the court may find that an absent party has received sufficient notice of trial or other matter upon a showing of all of the following:

(a) The moving party has made a diligent effort to locate the absentee.

(b) Notice of the proceeding was attempted by personal or domiciliary service in accordance with law to the most recent residence and employment address submitted to the state case registry in accordance with this Subsection and at any current address of the absentee known by the moving party.
Added by Acts 1998, 1st Ex.Sess., No. 8, eff. April 24, 1998.

Editor's note. Acts 1987, No. 745, § 1 enacted R.S. 9:311.1 which was redesignated as R.S. 9:313 pursuant to the statutory revision authority of the Louisiana State Law Institute. R.S. 9:313 was redesignated as R.S. 13:4291 by Acts 1993, No. 261, § 10, effective January 1, 1994.

§ 314. Repealed by Acts 1993, No. 261, § 9, eff. Jan. 1, 1994

PART I–A. CHILD SUPPORT

SUBPART A. GUIDELINES FOR DETERMINATION OF CHILD SUPPORT

§ 315. Economic data and principles; definitions

A. **Basic principles.** The premise of these guidelines as well as the provisions of the Civil Code is that child support is a continuous obligation of both parents, children are entitled to share in the current income of both parents, and children should not be the economic victims of divorce or out-of-wedlock birth. The economic data underlying these guidelines, which adopt the Income Shares Model, and the guideline calculations attempt to simulate the percentage of parental net income that is spent on children in intact families incorporating a consideration of the expenses of the parties, such as federal and state taxes and FICA taxes. While the legislature acknowledges that the expenditures of two-household divorced, separated, or non-formed families are different from intact family households, it is very important that the children of this state not be forced to live in poverty because of family disruption and that they be afforded the same opportunities available to children in intact families, consisting of parents with similar financial means to those of their own parents.

B. **Economic data.**

(1) The Incomes Shares approach to child support guidelines incorporates a numerical schedule of support amounts. The schedule provides economic estimates of child-rearing expenditures for various income levels and numbers of children in the household. The schedule is composed of economic data utilizing a table of national averages adjusted to reflect Louisiana's status as a low-income state and to incorporate a self-sufficiency reserve for low-income obligors to form the basic child support obligation.

(2) In intact families, the income of both parents is pooled and spent for the benefit of all household members, including the children. Each parent's contribution to the combined income of the family represents his relative sharing of household expenses. This same income sharing principle is used to determine how the parents will share a child support award.

C. **Definitions.** As used in this Part:

(1) "Adjusted gross income" means gross income, minus amounts for preexisting child support or spousal support obligations paid to another who is not a party to the proceedings, or on behalf of a child who is not the subject of the action of the court.

(2) "Combined adjusted gross income" means the combined adjusted gross income of both parties.

(3) "Gross income" means:

(a) The income from any source, including but not limited to salaries, wages, commissions, bonuses, dividends, severance pay, pensions, interest, trust income, recurring monetary gifts, annuities, capital gains, social security benefits, workers' compensation benefits, basic and variable allowances for housing and subsistence from military pay and benefits, unemployment insurance benefits, disaster unemployment assistance received from the United States Department of Labor, disability insurance benefits, and spousal support received from a preexisting spousal support obligation;

(b) Expense reimbursement or in-kind payments received by a parent in the course of employment, self-employment, or operation of a business, if the reimbursements or payments are significant and reduce the parent's personal living expenses. Such payments include but are not limited to a company car, free housing, or reimbursed meals; and

(c) Gross receipts minus ordinary and necessary expenses required to produce income, for purposes of income from self-employment, rent, royalties, proprietorship of a business, or joint ownership or a partnership or closely held corporation. "Ordinary and necessary expenses" shall not include amounts allowable by the Internal Revenue Service for the accelerated component of depreciation expenses or investment tax credits or any other business expenses determined by the court to be inappropriate for determining gross income for purposes of calculating child support.

(d) As used herein, "gross income" does not include:

(i) Child support received, or benefits received from public assistance programs, including Family Independence Temporary Assistance Plan, supplemental security income, food stamps, and general assistance.

(ii) Per diem allowances which are not subject to federal income taxation under the provisions of the Internal Revenue Code.

(iii) Extraordinary overtime including but not limited to income attributed to seasonal work regardless of its percentage of gross income when, in the court's discretion, the inclusion thereof would be inequitable to a party.

(iv) Any monetary gift to the domiciliary party when the objective of the gift is to supplement irregular child support payments from the nondomiciliary party.

(v) Any disaster assistance benefits received from the Federal Emergency Management Agency through its Individuals and Households Program or from any other nonprofit organization qualified as a tax-exempt organization under Section 501(c) of the Internal Revenue Code of 1954, as amended.

(4) "Health insurance premiums" means the actual amount paid by a party for providing health insurance on behalf of the child. It does not include any amount paid by an employer or any amounts paid for coverage of any other persons. If more than one dependent is covered by health insurance which is paid through a lump-sum dependent-coverage premium, and not all of such dependents are the subject of the guidelines calculation, the cost of the coverage shall be prorated among the dependents covered before being applied to the guidelines.

(5) "Income" means:

(a) Actual gross income of a party, if the party is employed to full capacity; or

(b) Potential income of a party, if the party is voluntarily unemployed or underemployed. A party shall not be deemed voluntarily unemployed or underemployed if he or she is absolutely unemployable or incapable of being employed, or if the unemployment or underemployment results through no fault or neglect of the party.

(c) The court may also consider as income the benefits a party derives from expense-sharing or other sources; however, in determining the benefits of expense-sharing, the court shall not consider the income of another spouse, regardless of the legal regime under which the remarriage exists, except to the extent that such income is used directly to reduce the cost of a party's actual expenses.

(6) "Medical support" means health insurance and the payment of the medical expenses of the child.

(7) "Net child care costs" means the reasonable costs of child care incurred by a party due to employment or job search, minus the value of the federal income tax credit for child care.

(8) "Ordinary medical expenses" means unreimbursed medical expenses less than or equal to two hundred fifty dollars per child per year. Expenses include but are not limited to reasonable and necessary costs for orthodontia, dental treatment, asthma treatment, physical therapy, chronic health problems, and professional counseling or psychiatric therapy for diagnosed mental disorders not covered by medical insurance. The schedule of support in R.S. 9:315.19 incorporates ordinary medical expenses.

Acts 2001, No. 1082, § 1. Amended by Acts 2003, No. 547, § 1; Acts 2004, No. 251, § 1; Acts 2005, 1st Ex.Sess., No. 59, § 1, eff. Dec. 6, 2005; Acts 2006, No. 315, § 1, eff. June 13, 2006; Acts 2006, No. 481, § 1, eff. Oct. 1, 2006.

Comments—2001

(a) Subsection A enunciates the basic principles of Louisiana's child support guidelines, most prominent of which is that children should not be the economic victims of their parents' divorce or failure to marry and should not suffer a loss of opportunity available to children in intact families.

(b) Louisiana's income shares model of child support guidelines incorporates a numerical schedule of support amounts based upon estimates of child-rearing expenditures of intact families at different income levels. Louisiana's schedule adjusts the national average of such expenditures to reflect Louisiana's status as a low-income state and historically incorporates a self-sufficiency reserve for low-income obligors. The income shares model simulates the percentage of both parents' net income spent on children in intact families. See Subsection A. The legislation assumes that as in an intact family income of both parents is pooled and each parent shares proportionately in household expenses.

Editor's note. Section 3 of Acts 1991, No. 854 declares: "The provisions of this Act shall not be considered in conflict with Chapter 4 of Title XIII of the Louisiana Children's Code and accordingly, the Louisiana State Law Institute shall direct and supervise the printing of Articles 1376(6)(c) and 1390 of the Louisiana Children's Code, if it becomes law, in a manner consistent with the provisions of Section 1 of this Act."

Acts 2001, No. 1082, § 5, declares that this Act applies to actions concerning child support filed after August 15, 2001.

Section 4 of Acts 2005, 1st Ex.Sess. No. 59 provides:

"The provisions of this Act shall apply to all cases pending on its effective date and to all cases filed after its effective date."

Cross References

C.C. arts. 141, 142, 3521, 3522.

§ 315.1. Rebuttable presumption; deviation from guidelines by court; stipulations by parties

A. The guidelines set forth in this Part are to be used in any proceeding to establish or modify child support filed on or after October 1, 1989. There shall be a rebuttable presumption that the amount of child support obtained by use of the guidelines set forth in this Part is the proper amount of child support.

B. (1) The court may deviate from the guidelines set forth in this Part if their application would not be in the best interest of the child or would be inequitable to the parties. The court shall give specific oral or written reasons for the deviation, including a finding as to the amount of support that would have been required under a mechanical application of the guidelines and the particular facts and circumstances that warranted a deviation from the guidelines. The reasons shall be made part of the record of the proceedings.

(2) Notwithstanding the provisions of Paragraph (1), as a direct result of either Hurricane Katrina or Rita, the court may deviate from the guidelines set forth in this Part if the application of the guidelines would not be in the best interest of the child or would be unjust, inequitable, or cause undue hardship to the parties. In determining the amount of the child support, the court may also consider that the parties may have been prevented from timely access to the courts for the exercise of their legal rights. However, the amount of the deviation shall not exceed the consideration the court would have given if the party were able to timely access the court.

C. In determining whether to deviate from the guidelines, the court's considerations may include:

(1) That the combined adjusted gross income of the parties is not within the amounts shown on the schedule in R.S. 9:315.19.

(a) If the combined adjusted gross income of the parties is less than the lowest sum shown on the schedule, the court shall determine an amount of child support based on the facts of the case, except that the amount awarded shall not be less than the minimum child support provided in R.S. 9:315.14.

(b) If the combined adjusted gross income of the parties exceeds the highest sum shown on the schedule, the court shall determine an amount of child support as provided in R.S. 9:315.13(B)(1) and may order the placement of a portion of the amount in a trust in accordance with R.S. 9:315.13.

(2) The legal obligation of a party to support dependents who are not the subject of the action before the court and who are in that party's household.

(3) That in a case involving one or more families, consisting of children none of whom live in the household of the noncustodial or nondomiciliary parent but who have existing child support orders (multiple families), the court may use its discretion in setting the amount of the basic child support obligation, provided it is not below the minimum fixed by R.S. 9:315.14, if the existing child support orders reduce the noncustodial or nondomiciliary parent's income below the lowest income level on the schedule contained in R.S. 9:315.19.

(4) The extraordinary medical expenses of a party, or extraordinary medical expenses for which a party may be responsible, not otherwise taken into consideration under the guidelines.

(5) An extraordinary community debt of the parties.

(6) The need for immediate and temporary support for a child when a full hearing on the issue of support is pending but cannot be timely held. In such cases, the court at the full hearing shall use the provisions of this Part and may redetermine support without the necessity of a change of circumstances being shown.

(7) The permanent or temporary total disability of a spouse to the extent such disability diminishes his present and future earning capacity, his need to save adequately for uninsurable future medical costs, and other additional costs associated with such disability, such as transportation and mobility costs, medical expenses, and higher insurance premiums.

(8) Any other consideration which would make application of the guidelines not in the best interest of the child or children or inequitable to the parties.

D. The court may review and approve a stipulation between the parties entered into after the effective date of this Part as to the amount of child support to be paid. If the court does review the stipulation, the court shall consider the guidelines set forth in this Part to review the adequacy of the stipulated amount and may require the parties to provide the court with the income statements and documentation required by R.S. 9:315.2.

Acts 2001, No. 1082, § 1. Amended by Acts 2005, 1st Ex.Sess., No. 59, § 1, eff. Dec. 6, 2005; Acts 2008, No. 579, § 1.

Comments—2001

(a) Although the amount of child support reflected in the guideline tables is presumed to be the proper amount, the court is permitted to deviate from the guidelines if, as a general proposition, the application of guidelines would not be in the best interest of the child or would be inequitable to the parties. The general ground for deviation, repeated at the end of Paragraph (8) of Subsection C which refers to the best interest of the child, is consistent with the first principles of child support contained in Civil Code Article 141. See the specific reference in R.S. 9:315.13. However, the court is not permitted to deviate in ordering child support below the minimum award established in R.S. 9:315.14, which is one hundred dollars.

(b) Subsection C contains an illustrative list of the reasons for which a court may deviate that, by amendment in 2001, includes the case of multiple families. If the circumstances involve an obligor with multiple families, the court may deviate from the guidelines. Multiple families is defined as one or more families with children not living in the home of the noncustodial or non-domiciliary parent (obligor parent) who have existing child support orders that reduce such obligor parent's income below the lowest amount in the tables.

Editor's notes. Acts 2001, No. 1082, § 5, declares that this Act applies to actions concerning child support filed after August 15, 2001. Section 4 of Acts 2005, 1st Ex.Sess., No. 59 provides:

"The provisions of this Act shall apply to all cases pending on its effective date and to all cases filed after its effective date."

§ 315.1.1. Determination of income; evidence

A. When a party alleges that income is being concealed or underreported, the court shall admit evidence relevant to establishing the actual income of the party, including but not limited to the following:

(1) Redirected income. (a) Loans to the obligor by a business in which the obligor has an ownership interest and whether the loans will be repaid. There shall be a presumption that such loans are income of the obligor which may be rebutted if the obligor demonstrates there is a history of similar past loans being made and repaid in a timely manner with market interest rates, or the current loan is at market interest rates and is fully paid in accordance with a commercially reasonable time. The amount by which a commercially reasonable repayment amount exceeds the amount actually repaid shall be treated as income.

(b) Payment made by the obligor or by a business in which the obligor has an ownership interest to a person related by blood or affinity in the form of wages or salary. There shall be a presumption that such payments are income of the obligor, which may be rebutted if the obligor demonstrates there is a history of payments preceding the separation of the parties or the filing of an action to establish or modify child support, or that the payments are fair market value for services actually performed.

(2) **Deferred income.** Recent reductions in distributions of income, such as salary, bonuses, dividends, or management fees as a percentage of gross income of the business of the obligor. There shall be a presumption that past distributions of income will continue, which may be rebutted if the obligor demonstrates business conditions justify a reduction in distributions.

(3) **Standard of living and assets.** The standard of living and assets of the obligor both prior and subsequent to the establishment of a child support order, to establish the actual income if the amount claimed is inconsistent with his lifestyle.

B. When the income of an obligor cannot be sufficiently established, evidence of wage and earnings surveys distributed by government agencies for the purpose of attributing income to the obligor is admissible.

Added by Acts 2009, No. 378, § 1.

Editor's note. Acts 2009, No. 378, amended R.S. 9:315.2(A) and enacted R.S. 9:315.1.1 and 326. Section 2 of that Act directed the Louisiana State Law Institute to prepare comments. The original recommendations came from the Louisiana Child Support Guidelines Review 2008 Quadrennial Report. These comments come from the Marriage-Persons Committee of the Louisiana State Law Institute.

Comments—2010

[Acts 2009, No. 378, amended R.S. 9:315.2(A) and enacted R.S. 9:315.1.1 and 9:326. The Act was not presented on recommendation of the Louisiana State Law Institute. Section 2 of the Act directed the Law Institute to prepare comments.]

(a) The purpose of this Section is to facilitate the determination of actual income in child support cases when one of the parties is receiving benefits from a business in which he has an ownership interest and the other party alleges that the income of the obligor is being "concealed or underreported". The allegation gives notice to the obligor of his obligation to produce evidence to rebut the presumptions created by this Section.

(b) The presumptions created in this Section are true evidentiary presumptions; they shift the burden of persuasion to the obligor. See Pugh, "Authors' Introductory Note" Chapter 3, Handbook on Louisiana Evidence Law (Thomson–West 2009). If the predicate fact is established by the proponent, the court must find the presumed fact, in the absence of contrary evidence. In order to rebut the presumption, the obligor has the burden of persuasion by a preponderance of the evidence to disprove the fact to be presumed.

(c) Subparagraph (A)(1)(a) of this Section requires the obligor to prove that loans made to him by a business in which he has an ownership interest are not income. The obligor may show that either prior loans have been repaid at market rates, or that the current loan at market interest rates is paid in a commercially reasonable time.

(d) The purpose of Subparagraph (A)(1)(b) of this Section is to prevent an obligor from redirecting income to a relative to reduce his child support obligation. Such payments shall be considered income of the obligor unless he can prove that there was a history of the relative receiving payments prior to the separation of the parties or the filing of the child support action. The obligor may also rebut the presumption by proving that the relative is receiving fair market value for services actually rendered.

(e) Paragraph (A)(2) of this Section addresses the issue of deferred income. See Moncus v. Moncus, 510 So.2d 1271, 1276 (La. App. 3 Cir. 1987) ("One cannot avoid all or part of his child support obligation by exercising exclusive control over a corporation wholly owned by him in order to limit his own salary.") The statute establishes a rebuttable presumption that past distributions of income to the obligee will continue. To invoke the presumption, the obligee must first establish that the obligor received distributions in the past in the form of salary, bonuses, dividends, fees, or other income. The statute does not provide a specific time period for past distributions.

(f) Paragraph (A)(3) of this Section, which is consistent with prior law, allows the court to consider evidence of the standard of living of the obligor when the actual income he claims is inconsistent with his lifestyle. See Sawyer v. Sawyer, 799 So.2d 1226 (La. App. 2 Cir. 2001) (obligor "went on luxury vacations, used private jets, owned an extravagant home, expensive vehicles, a pool house, and a boat—items certainly indicative of greater income than what was reported on the W-2 forms." 799 So.2d at 1332.) Jackson v. Belfield, 725 So. 2d 32 (La. App. 4 Cir. 1998) (argument made that lawyer-obligor's lifestyle was not consistent with limited documents showing minimal 12 income).

(g) Subsection B of this Section allows the court to use governmental wage and earnings surveys to determine the income of an obligor when his income cannot be otherwise established. This provision is an evidentiary tool particularly when the obligor is a wage earner who is voluntarily unemployed or underemployed. Subsection B of this Section makes the survey admissible as against a hearsay objection; however, the survey must still be authenticated and pass the original writings test. In other words, the proponent must introduce evidence sufficient to support a finding that the survey is what it purports to be and that it is an original or accurate copy. See C.E. Art. 901(A) and Art. 1001 et seq.; See also, C.E. Art. 902(10) (labor reports in possession of field officers of the support enforcement services program are self authenticating) and R.S. 13:3712.1 (labor report prima facie proof), discussed in Triche, "Rules of Evidence in Family Law Court", Handbook on Louisiana Family Law (Thomson–West 2009). A court admitting a survey pursuant to Subsection B of this Section is not required to accept the findings in the survey, unlike a labor report admitted under R.S. 13:3712.1 which is prima facie proof and must be accepted by the judge in the absence of contrary evidence.

§ 315.2. Calculation of basic child support obligation

A. Each party shall provide to the court a verified income statement showing gross income and adjusted gross income, together with documentation of current and past earnings. Spouses of the parties shall also provide any relevant information with regard to the source of payments of household expenses upon request of the court or the opposing party, provided such request is filed in a reasonable time prior to the hearing. Failure to timely file the request shall not be grounds for a continuance. Suitable documentation of current earnings shall include but not be limited to pay stubs or employer statements. The documentation shall include a copy of the party's most recent federal tax return. A copy of the statement and documentation shall be provided to the other party. When an obligor has an ownership interest in a business, suitable documentation shall include but is not limited to the last three personal and business state and federal income tax returns, including all attachments and all schedules, specifically Schedule K–1 and W–2 forms, 1099 forms, and amendments, the most recent profit and loss statements, balance sheets, financial statements, quarterly sales tax reports, personal and business bank account statements, receipts, and expenses. A copy of all statements and documentation shall be provided to the other party.

B. If a party is voluntarily unemployed or underemployed, his or her gross income shall be determined as set forth in R.S. 9:315.11.

C. The parties shall combine the amounts of their adjusted gross incomes. Each party shall then determine by percentage his or her proportionate share of the combined amount. The amount obtained for each party is his or her percentage share of the combined adjusted gross income.

D. The court shall determine the basic child support obligation amount from the schedule in R.S. 9:315.19 by using the combined adjusted gross income of the parties and the number of children involved in the proceeding, but in no event shall the amount of child support be less than the amount provided in R.S. 9:315.14.

E. After the basic child support obligation has been established, the total child support obligation shall be determined as hereinafter provided in this Part.

Acts 2001, No. 1082, § 1. Amended by Acts 2009, No. 378, § 1.

Comment—2001

Additional language was added to Subsection A to facilitate the acquisition of information concerning the benefits a party derives from expense-sharing or other sources, which R.S. 9:315(C)(6)(c) defines as "income." The court or the opposing party may request such information as long as the request is filed within a reasonable time prior to the hearing; if not, such an untimely request is not grounds for a continuance.

Comment—2010

[Acts 2009, No. 378, amended R.S. 9:315.2(A) and enacted R.S. 9:315.1.1 and 9:326. The Act was not presented on recommendation of the Louisiana State Law Institute. Section 2 of the Act directed the Law Institute to prepare comments.]

For purposes of implementing the provisions of R.S. 9:315.1.1 (2009), the amendment to Subsection A of this Section specifies in an illustrative list the type of documentation that is suitable for a party with an ownership interest in a business, i.e., the last three federal and state income tax returns.

Editor's note. Acts 2001, No. 1082, § 5, declares that this Act applies to actions concerning child support filed after August 15, 2001.

Acts 2009, No. 378, amended R.S. 9:315.2(A) and enacted R.S. 9:315.1.1 and 326. Section 2 of that Act directed the Louisiana State Law Institute to prepare comments. The original recommendations came from the Louisiana Child Support Guidelines Review 2008 Quadrennial Report. These comments come from the Marriage-Persons Committee of the Louisiana State Law Institute.

Cross References

C.C. arts. 141, 142.

§ 315.3. Net child care costs; addition to basic obligation

Net child care costs shall be added to the basic child support obligation. The net child care costs are determined by applying the Federal Credit for Child and Dependent Care Expenses provided in Internal Revenue Form 2441 to the total or actual child care costs.

Acts 2001, No. 1082, § 1.

Comment—2001

See IRS Form 2441. The form may be downloaded from http://www.irs.gov.

Editor's note. Acts 2001, No. 1082, § 5, declares that this Act applies to actions concerning child support filed after August 15, 2001.

Cross References

C.C. arts. 141, 142.

§ 315.4. Health insurance premiums; addition to basic obligation

A. In any child support case, the court may order one of the parties to enroll or maintain an insurable child in a health benefits plan, policy, or program. In determining which party should be required to enroll the child or to maintain such insurance on behalf of the child, the court shall consider each party's individual, group, or employee's health insurance program, employment history, and personal income and other resources. The cost of health insurance premiums incurred on behalf of the child shall be added to the basic child support obligation.

B. In any case in which the department is providing support enforcement services, the child support order shall require one or both of the parties to provide medical support for the child.

Acts 2001, No. 1082, § 1. Amended by Acts 2006, No. 481, § 1, eff. Oct. 1, 2006.

Editor's note. Acts 2001, No. 1082, § 5, declares that this Act applies to actions concerning child support filed after August 15, 2001.

Cross References

C.C. arts. 141, 142.

§ 315.5. Extraordinary medical expenses; addition to basic obligation

By agreement of the parties or order of the court, extraordinary medical expenses incurred on behalf of the child shall be added to the basic child support obligation. Extraordinary medical expenses are unreimbursed medical expenses which exceed two hundred fifty dollars per child per calendar year.

Acts 2001, No. 1082, § 1. Amended by Acts 2004, No. 251, § 1; Acts 2008, No. 578, § 1.

Editor's note. Acts 2001, No. 1082, § 5, declares that this Act applies to actions concerning child support filed after August 15, 2001.

Cross References

C.C. arts. 141, 142.

§ 315.6. Other extraordinary expenses; addition to basic obligation

By agreement of the parties or order of the court, the following expenses incurred on behalf of the child may be added to the basic child support obligation:

(1) Expenses of tuition, registration, books, and supply fees required for attending a special or private elementary or secondary school to meet the needs of the child.

(2) Any expenses for transportation of the child from one party to the other.

(3) Special expenses incurred for child rearing intended to enhance the health, athletic, social, or cultural development of a child, including but not limited to camp, music or art lessons, travel, and school sponsored extracurricular activities.

Acts 2001, No. 1082, § 1. Amended by Acts 2008, No. 579, § 1.

Comment—2001

Prior to 2001 "any expenses" for attending a special or private elementary or secondary school to meet the "particular educational" needs of the child could be added to the basic child support obligation calculated using the guideline tables. Clarifying language was added to Paragraph (1) to specify the types of school expenses—tuition, registration, books and supply fees *required* for attending the school–permitted to be added to the basic child support amount, but the necessity of showing that attendance at the special or private school was required to meet the "particular educational" needs of the child was eliminated. The needs of the child met by the special or private school need not be particular educational needs but may include such needs of the child as the need for stability or continuity in the child's educational program.

Editor's note. Acts 2001, No. 1082, § 5, declares that this Act applies to actions concerning child support filed after August 15, 2001.

Cross References

C.C. arts. 141, 142.

§ 315.7. Deductions for income of the child

A. Income of the child that can be used to reduce the basic needs of the child may be considered as a deduction from the basic child support obligation.

B. The provisions of this Section shall not apply to income earned by a child while a full-time student, regardless of whether such income was earned during a summer or holiday break.

C. The provisions of this Section shall not apply to benefits received by a child from public assistance programs, including but not limited to Family Independence Temporary Assistance Programs (FITAP), food stamps, or any means-tested program.

D. Notwithstanding the provisions of Subsection C of this Section, social security benefits received by a child due to the earnings of a parent shall be credited as child support to the parent upon whose earning record it is based, by crediting the amount against the potential obligation of that parent.

E. In cases where there is a child support arrearage, the court shall grant an evidentiary hearing before any arrearage is reduced based upon any lump sum payments received by the child.

Acts 2001, No. 1082, § 1. Amended by Acts 2006, No. 386, § 1.

Comment—2001

The 2001 amendment adding Subsection C clarifies that benefits received *by the child* from public assistance or other means-tested programs are not to be considered income of the child for purposes of a deduction from the sum due from the parents.

Editor's note. Acts 2001, No. 1082, § 5, declares that this Act applies to actions concerning child support filed after August 15, 2001.

Cross References

C.C. arts. 141, 142.

§ 315.8. Calculation of total child support obligation; worksheet

A. The total child support obligation shall be determined by adding together the basic child support obligation amount, the net child care costs, the cost of health insurance premiums, extraordinary medical expenses, and other extraordinary expenses.

B. A deduction, if any, for income of the child shall then be subtracted from the amount calculated in Subsection A. The remaining amount is the total child support obligation.

C. Each party's share of the total child support obligation shall then be determined by multiplying his or her percentage share of combined adjusted gross income times the total child support obligation.

D. The party without legal custody or nondomiciliary party shall owe his or her total child support obligation as a money judgment of child support to the custodial or domiciliary party, minus any court-ordered direct payments made on behalf of the child for work-related net child care costs, health insurance premiums, extraordinary medical expenses, or extraordinary expenses provided as adjustments to the schedule.

E. "Joint Custody" means a joint custody order that is not shared custody as defined in R.S. 9:315.9.

(1) In cases of joint custody, the court shall consider the period of time spent by the child with the nondomiciliary party as a basis for adjustment to the amount of child support to be paid during that period of time.

(2) If under a joint custody order, the person ordered to pay child support has physical custody of the child for more than seventy-three days, the court may order a credit to the child support obligation. A day for the purposes of this Paragraph shall be determined by the court; however, in no instance shall less than four hours of physical custody of the child constitute a day.

(3) In determining the amount of credit to be given, the court shall consider the following:

(a) The amount of time the child spends with the person to whom the credit would be applied. The court shall include in such consideration the continuing expenses of the domiciliary party.

(b) The increase in financial burden placed on the person to whom the credit would be applied and the decrease in financial burden on the person receiving child support.

(c) The best interests of the child and what is equitable between the parties.

(4) The burden of proof is on the person seeking the credit pursuant to this Subsection.

(5) Worksheet A reproduced in R.S. 9:315.20, or a substantially similar form adopted by local court rule, shall be used to determine child support in accordance with this Subsection.

Acts 2001, No. 1082, § 1. Amended by Acts 2004, No. 756, § 1.

Comments—2001

(a) A parental joint custody decree may constitute reason for an adjustment in the amount owed by the nondomiciliary parent to the domiciliary parent. Joint custody is defined as a joint custody order that is not shared custody, the latter an arrangement which requires that each parent have physical custody of the child for an approximately equal amount of time. See R.S. 9:315.9.

(b) An adjustment in the form of a credit may be afforded the nondomiciliary parent who has physical custody of the child for more than seventy-three days, the definition of a day to be determined by the court but in no case can a day be less than four hours of physical custody of the child. Physical custody of the child for seventy-three days constitutes physical custody at least twenty percent of the year as a threshold for the discretionary adjustment permitted by this Section. The amendment adds specificity to the meaning of "extraordinary visitation" in Guillot v. Munn, 756 So.2d 290 (La. 2000).

(c) If the threshold of seventy-three days of physical custody is met, the 2001 amendment guides the court in determining whether to exercise its discretion in ordering an adjustment to child support owed by the nondomiciliary parent. The court must consider the amount of time the child spends with the nondomiciliary parent, the effect upon the domiciliary and nondomiciliary parent of the decreasing or increasing, respectively, financial burden occasioned by the physical custody arrangement, and lastly, the best interests of the child and equity between the parties. See Guillot v. Munn, *supra*, comment (b). The nondomiciliary parent who seeks the credit adjustment bears the burden of proof.

(d) The amount of the credit under Subsection (E)(3) should be based on a portion of the costs actually incurred by the nondomiciliary parent while the child is in his or her custody, while excluding the continuing expenses of the custodial parent, such as the housing related expenses of the custodial parent. In determining the amount of the credit, the court should determine the costs incurred by the nondomiciliary parent only when the child is with the nondomiciliary parent including food, transportation and some entertainment. See also New Jersey Child Support Guidelines, Appendix IX–A.

(e) Worksheet A contains a line at the end for "a credit for a joint custodial arrangement" if ordered by the court.

Editor's note. Acts 2001, No. 1082, § 5, declares that this Act applies to actions concerning child support filed after August 15, 2001.

Cross References

C.C. arts. 141, 142.

§ 315.9. Effect of shared custodial arrangement

A. (1) "Shared custody" means a joint custody order in which each parent has physical custody of the child for an approximately equal amount of time.

(2) If the joint custody order provides for shared custody, the basic child support obligation shall first be multiplied by one and one-half and then divided between the parents in proportion to their respective adjusted gross incomes.

(3) Each parent's theoretical child support obligation shall then be cross multiplied by the actual percentage of time the child spends with the other party to determine the basic child support obligation based on the amount of time spent with the other party.

(4) Each parent's proportionate share of work-related net child care costs and extraordinary adjustments to the schedule shall be added to the amount calculated under Paragraph (3) of this Subsection.

(5) Each parent's proportionate share of any direct payments ordered to be made on behalf of the child for net child care costs, the cost of health insurance premiums, extraordinary medical expenses, or other extraordinary expenses shall be deducted from the amount calculated under Paragraph (3) of this Subsection.

(6) The court shall order each parent to pay his proportionate share of all reasonable and necessary uninsured ordinary medical expenses as defined in R.S. 9:315(C)(8) which are under two hundred fifty dollars.

(7) The parent owing the greater amount of child support shall owe to the other parent the difference between the two amounts as a child support obligation. The amount owed shall not be higher than the amount which that parent would have owed if he or she were a domiciliary parent.

B. Worksheet B reproduced in R.S. 9:315.20, or a substantially similar form adopted by local court rule, shall be used to determine child support in accordance with this Subsection.

Acts 2001, No. 1082, § 1. Amended by Acts 2002, 1st Ex.Sess., No. 62, § 1; Acts 2004, No. 668, § 1, eff. July 5, 2004; Acts 2012, No. 255, § 2.

Comments—2001

(a) This Section is entirely new and contains a formula for calculating the basic child support obligation and an adjustment when the parents have *shared* custody, which is defined as equal or approximately equal physical custody under a joint custody decree. The reference in Subsection (A)(3) should be interpreted as one half or an approximately equal amount of time, expressed in percentages such as forty-nine percent/fifty-one percent. See Subsection (A)(1). Worksheet B, which incorporates the statutory formula, is also new and should be used, or a substantially similar form, to calculate child support when the custodial arrangement between the parents is *shared*.

(b) The formula for calculating child support if custody of the child is shared requires first that the basic child support obligation be multiplied by one and one-half times approximating the duplication of costs, such as housing, food, and transportation, incurred by both parents who have physical custody for approximately one-half of the year. Only after recognition of the duplication of costs in a shared custody arrangement is the adjusted basic child support obligation divided between the parents in proportion to their respective adjusted gross incomes. Secondly, each parent's share of the basic support obligation shall be cross-multiplied by fifty percent or the actual percentage of time the child spends with the other parent and the parent owing the greater amount pays the difference to the other parent as support, after deducting each parent's proportionate share of direct payments ordered to be made to a third party on behalf of the child. This calculation reflects the fact that each parent has physical custody of the child for approximately one-half of the year.

Editor's note. Acts 2001, No. 1082, § 5, declares that this Act applies to actions concerning child support filed after August 15, 2001.

Sections 1 and 3 of Acts 2002, 1st Ex.Sess., No. 115 (§ 2 of which amends R.S. 46:236.8, relating to medical support orders) provide:

"Section 1. The calculation of child support in shared custodial arrangements shall be governed by House Bill No. 27 of the 2002 First Extraordinary Session of the Legislature and nothing in this Act shall be construed to supersede the provisions of House Bill No. 27."

"Section 3. The provisions of Section 1 of this Act shall become effective at the same time that House Bill No. 27 of the 2002 First Extraordinary Session of the Legislature becomes effective."

House Bill No. 27 of the 2002 First Extraordinary Session was approved and became Acts 2002, 1st Ex.Sess., No. 62, amending R.S. 9:315.9(A) and Obligation Worksheet B within R.S. 9:315.20, and became effective June 16, 2002. Pursuant to § 4 of Acts 2002, 1st Ex.Sess., No. 115, the amendment of R.S. 46:236.8 by § 2 of Act 115 became effective April 18, 2002, upon signature by the Governor.

§ 315.10. Effect of split custodial arrangement

A. (1) "Split custody" means that each party is the sole custodial or domiciliary parent of at least one child to whom support is due.

(2) If the custody order provides for split custody, each parent shall compute a total child support obligation for the child or children in the custody of the other parent, based on a calculation pursuant to this Section.

(3) The amount determined under Paragraph (2) of this Subsection shall be a theoretical support obligation owed to each parent.

(4) The parent owing the greater amount of child support shall owe to the other parent the difference between the two amounts as a child support obligation.

B. Worksheet A reproduced in R.S. 9:315.20, or a substantially similar form adopted by local court rule, shall be used by each parent to determine child support in accordance with this Section.

Acts 2001, No. 1082, § 1.

Comments—2001

(a) This Subsection providing for the calculation of child support if the parents' custodial arrangement is split custody is new but codifies the jurisprudence. See Nixon v. Nixon, 631 So.2d 42 (La. App. 2 Cir. 1994). *Split custody* occurs when each party is the sole custodial or the domiciliary parent of at least one child to whom support is due.

(b) If each parent has custody or is the domiciliary parent of at least one child of the parties, each parent calculates the total child support obligation owed to the other parent. Thus, this subsection contemplates that each parent will complete Worksheet A or a substantially similar form to calculate the theoretical child support obligation owed to the other parent. Then the parent owing the greater amount as reflected in the two worksheets owes the difference as a child support obligation.

Editor's note. Acts 2001, No. 1082, § 5, declares that this Act applies to actions concerning child support filed after August 15, 2001.

§ 315.11. Voluntarily unemployed or underemployed party

A. If a party is voluntarily unemployed or underemployed, child support shall be calculated based on a determination of income earning potential, unless the party is physically or mentally incapacitated, or is caring for a child of the parties under the age of five years. In determining the party's income earning potential, the court may consider the most recently published Louisiana Occupational Employment Wage Survey.

B. The amount of the basic child support obligation calculated in accordance with Subsection A of this Section shall not exceed the amount which the party paying support would have owed had a determination of the other party's income earning potential not been made.

C. A party shall not be deemed voluntarily unemployed or underemployed if he or she has been temporarily unable to find work or has been temporarily forced to take a lower paying job as a direct result of Hurricane Katrina or Rita.

Acts 2001, No. 1082, § 1. Amended by Acts 2004, No. 156, § 1, eff. June 10, 2004; Acts 2005, 1st Ex.Sess., No. 59, § 1, eff. Dec. 6, 2005; Acts 2010, No. 238, § 1.

Editor's note. Acts 2001, No. 1082, § 5, declares that this Act applies to actions concerning child support filed after August 15, 2001.

Section 4 of Acts 2005, 1st Ex.Sess., No. 59 provides:

"The provisions of this Act shall apply to all cases pending on its effective date and to all cases filed after its effective date."

§ 315.12. Second jobs and overtime

The court may consider the interests of a subsequent family as a defense in an action to modify an existing child support order when the obligor has taken a second job or works overtime to provide for a subsequent family. However, the obligor bears the burden of proof in establishing that the additional income is used to provide for the subsequent family.

Acts 2001, No. 1082, § 1.

Comment—2001

Specific causes for deviation from the guidelines include "the legal obligation of a party to support dependents who are not the subject of the action before the court and who are in that party's household." Such dependents include the obligor's children to whom he owes a legal obligation of support. See R.S. 9:315.1(C)(2). This new Section provides further that if the obligor takes a second job or works overtime to provide for a subsequent family the court may consider the interests of that subsequent family as an affirmative defense in an action to modify an existing child support order. The obligor bears the burden of proving that the income from the second job or overtime is actually "used to provide for the subsequent family."

Editor's note. Acts 2001, No. 1082, § 5, declares that this Act applies to actions concerning child support filed after August 15, 2001.

§ 315.12.1. [Blank]

Editor's note. A prior R.S. 9:315.12.1, enacted by Acts 1989, No. 9, § 1, was redesignated as R.S. 9:315.13 on authority of the statutory revision authority of the Louisiana State Law Institute.

§ 315.13. Amounts not set forth in or exceeding schedule

A. If the combined adjusted gross income of the parties falls between two amounts shown in the schedule contained in R.S. 9:315.19, the basic child support obligation shall be based on an extrapolation between the two amounts.

B. If the combined adjusted gross income of the parties exceeds the highest level specified in the schedule contained in R.S. 9:315.19, the court:

(1) Shall use its discretion in setting the amount of the basic child support obligation in accordance with the best interest of the child and the circumstances of each parent as provided in Civil Code Article 141, but in no event shall it be less than the highest amount set forth in the schedule; and

(2) May order that a portion of the amount awarded be placed in a spendthrift trust for the educational or medical needs of the child. The trust shall be administered, managed, and invested in accordance with the Louisiana Trust Code. The trust instrument shall name the child as sole beneficiary of the trust, shall name a trustee, shall impose maximum spendthrift restraints, and shall terminate when the child attains twenty-four years of age, unless the parties agree to a later date. The trustee shall furnish security unless the court, in written findings of fact, dispenses with security.

Acts 2001, No. 1082, § 1. Amended by Acts 2008, No. 579, § 1.

Comment—2001

If the combined adjusted gross income of the parties exceeds the highest amount provided for in the schedule, the court is to exercise discretion in setting the amount of child support guided by the best interest of the child and the circumstances of each party under Civil Code Article 141. Article 141, which governs the award of child support at divorce, contains first principles: child support is to be determined based upon the needs of the child as measured by the standard of living enjoyed by the child while living with his intact family and upon the ability to pay of each of the parents. In no case, however, may the amount awarded be less than the highest amount specified in the schedule.

Editor's note. This section was enacted as R.S. 9:315.12.1 and was redesignated pursuant to the statutory revision authority of the Louisiana State Law Institute.

Acts 2001, No. 1082, § 5, declares that this Act applies to actions concerning child support filed after August 15, 2001.

§ 315.14. Mandatory minimum child support award

In no event shall the court set an award of child support less than one hundred dollars, except in cases involving shared or split custody as provided in R.S. 9:315.9 and 315.10. In cases when the obligor has a medically documented disability that limits his ability to meet the mandatory minimum, the court may set an award of less than one hundred dollars.

Acts 2001, No. 1082, § 1. Amended by Acts 2003, No. 1202, § 1.

Comment—2001

This Section is new and establishes for the first time a minimum child support order of one hundred dollars. The only exceptions to the minimum order provided for in the legislation are cases of shared or split custody provided for in R.S. 9:315.9 and 315.10. See comment (a) to R.S. 9:315.1.

Editor's note. This section was enacted as R.S. 9:315.13 and was redesignated on authority of the statutory revision authority of the Louisiana State Law Institute.

Acts 2001, No. 1082, § 5, declares that this Act applies to actions concerning child support filed after August 15, 2001.

§ 315.15. No change in circumstances intended

The enactment and subsequent amendment of this Part shall not for that reason alone be considered a material change in the circumstances of either party.

Acts 2001, No. 1082, § 1.

Comment—2001

The 2001 amendments to the child support guidelines made some substantial changes to the rules for the calculation of child support. The changes made by amendment to the guidelines are not for that reason alone to be considered sufficient to constitute a material change in circumstance warranting a modification of an existing child support order.

Editor's note. This section was enacted as R.S. 9:315.14 and was redesignated as R.S. 9:315.15 on authority of the statutory revision authority of the Louisiana State Law Institute.

Acts 2001, No. 1082, § 5, declares that this Act applies to actions concerning child support filed after August 15, 2001.

Cross References

C.C. arts. 141, 142.

§ 315.16. Review of guidelines

A. The guidelines set forth in this Part shall be reviewed by the legislature not less than once every four years. A review of the guidelines shall take place in 2012 and every four years thereafter, and it shall be the responsibility of the office of children and family services, child support enforcement section of the Department of Children and Family Services, and the Louisiana District Attorneys Association, in consultation with the child support review committee provided in Subsection B of this Section, to obtain all information required to comply with the provisions of 42 U.S.C. 667(a) and present the same to the legislature sixty days prior to the beginning of the 2008 Regular Session of the Legislature and every four years thereafter.

B. The child support review committee shall serve without compensation, except for the members of the legislature who shall receive a per diem as provided by law, and shall consist of the following members:

(1) The reporter of the Louisiana State Law Institute Marriage and Persons Advisory Committee.

(2) The chairman or designee of the House Committee on Civil Law and Procedure.

(3) The chairman or designee of Senate Committee on Judiciary A.

(4) The president or designee of the Louisiana District Judges Association.

(5) The executive director or a designee of the Louisiana District Attorneys Association.

(6) The president or designee of the Juvenile and Family Court Judges Association.

(7) The chairman or designee of the Louisiana State Bar Association, Family Law Section.

(8) The chairman or designee of the Louisiana Chapter of American Academy of Matrimonial Lawyers.

(9) The secretary or a designee of the Department of Children and Family Services.

(10) The chairman or designee of the Louisiana Children's Cabinet.

(11) The president or designee of the Louisiana Hearing Officers' Association.

Acts 2001, No. 1082, § 1. Amended by Acts 2004, No. 249, § 1; Acts 2008, No. 578, § 1; Acts 2012, No. 255, § 2.

Editor's note. Acts 2001, No. 1082, § 5, declares that this Act applies to actions concerning child support filed after August 15, 2001.

Cross References

C.C. arts. 141, 142.

§ 315.17. Standard of appellate review

Deviations by the trial court from the guidelines set forth in this Part shall not be disturbed absent a finding of manifest error.

Acts 2001, No. 1082, § 1.

Editor's note. Acts 2001, No. 1082, § 5, declares that this Act applies to actions concerning child support filed after August 15, 2001.

§ 315.18. Schedule; information

A. The amounts set forth in the schedule in R.S. 9:315.19 presume that the custodial or domiciliary party has the right to claim the federal and state tax dependency deductions and any earned income credit. However, the claiming of dependents for federal and state income tax purposes shall be as provided in Subsection B of this Section.

B. (1) The non-domiciliary party whose child support obligation equals or exceeds fifty percent of the total child support obligation shall be entitled to claim the federal and state tax dependency deductions if, after a contradictory motion, the judge finds both of the following:

(a) No arrearages are owed by the obligor.

(b) The right to claim the dependency deductions or, in the case of multiple children, a part thereof, would substantially benefit the non-domiciliary party without significantly harming the domiciliary party.

(2) The child support order shall:

(a) Specify the years in which the party is entitled to claim such deductions.

(b) Require the domiciliary party to timely execute all forms required by the Internal Revenue Service authorizing the non-domiciliary party to claim such deductions.

C. The party who receives the benefit of the exemption for such tax year shall not be considered as having received payment of a thing not due if the dependency deduction allocation is not maintained by the taxing authorities.

D. Repealed by Acts 2004, No. 668, § 2, eff. July 5, 2004.

Acts 2001, No. 501, § 1; Acts 2001, No. 1082, § 1. Amended by Acts 2004, No. 668, § 1, eff. July 5, 2004.

Comment—2001

(a) The guideline schedule presumes the custodial parent claims the tax exemption(s) for the child(ren), unless the appropriate tax forms are completed each year to allow the non custodial parent to claim the exemption. However, the child support guidelines were not updated based on the 1999 personal income tax rates, which are slightly less than the rate in effect when the child support schedule was developed in 1989.

(b) Subsection C was added by 2001 Acts, No. 501.

(c) Subsection D added in 2001 simply contains the substance of R.S. 9:337(B), which was repealed in Act No. 1082.

Editor's note. Acts 2001, No. 1082, § 5, declares that this Act applies to actions concerning child support filed after August 15, 2001.

Cross References

C.C. arts. 141, 142.

§ 315.19. Schedule for support

The schedule of support to be used for determining the basic child support obligation is as follows:

R.S. 9:315.19

APPENDIX 1—REVISED STATUTES, TITLE 9

LOUISIANA CHILD SUPPORT GUIDELINE
SCHEDULE OF BASIC CHILD SUPPORT OBLIGATIONS

COMBINED ADJUSTED MONTHLY GROSS INCOME	ONE CHILD	TWO CHILDREN (TOTAL)	THREE CHILDREN (TOTAL)	FOUR CHILDREN (TOTAL)	FIVE CHILDREN (TOTAL)	SIX CHILDREN (TOTAL)
0–600.00	100	100	100	100	100	100
650.00	102	103	104	106	107	108
700.00	136	138	139	141	142	144
750.00	165	172	174	176	178	179
800.00	174	206	208	211	213	215
850.00	182	240	243	245	248	251
900.00	189	274	277	280	283	286
950.00	197	305	310	313	317	320
1000.00	203	315	339	342	346	350
1050.00	210	325	367	371	375	379
1100.00	216	335	396	400	405	409
1150.00	226	345	425	429	434	439
1200.00	236	354	444	458	463	468
1250.00	245	364	456	487	493	498
1300.00	255	374	469	516	522	528
1350.00	264	385	481	542	551	557
1400.00	273	398	494	556	581	587
1450.00	282	411	506	570	610	617
1500.00	290	423	519	584	637	646
1550.00	299	435	531	598	653	676
1600.00	308	447	545	614	670	717
1650.00	316	459	560	630	688	736
1700.00	325	472	574	647	705	755
1750.00	333	484	588	663	723	774
1800.00	342	497	603	679	741	792
1850.00	351	510	617	695	758	811
1900.00	360	523	631	711	776	830
1950.00	369	536	643	724	790	846
2000.00	378	549	655	737	805	865
2050.00	388	562	667	751	819	885
2100.00	396	575	679	764	834	903
2150.00	405	588	693	778	852	926
2200.00	414	601	709	792	871	946
2250.00	423	614	724	808	889	967
2300.00	432	627	739	825	908	987
2350.00	441	639	753	840	924	1004
2400.00	449	652	768	854	939	1021
2450.00	458	664	782	868	955	1038
2500.00	466	676	796	882	970	1055
2550.00	475	689	811	896	986	1072
2600.00	484	701	825	911	1002	1089
2650.00	492	714	839	925	1017	1106
2700.00	501	726	854	939	1033	1122
2750.00	510	739	868	953	1048	1139
2800.00	518	751	882	967	1064	1156
2850.00	526	763	896	981	1079	1173
2900.00	533	776	911	995	1095	1190
2950.00	540	788	925	1009	1110	1207
3000.00	548	801	939	1023	1126	1224
3050.00	555	813	954	1037	1141	1240
3100.00	563	825	968	1051	1156	1257
3150.00	570	837	982	1065	1172	1274
3200.00	577	850	996	1082	1190	1293
3250.00	585	862	1011	1100	1210	1315
3300.00	592	874	1026	1118	1230	1337
3350.00	600	887	1040	1137	1250	1359

For Annotative Materials, see West's Louisiana Statutes Annotated

APPENDIX 1—REVISED STATUTES, TITLE 9   R.S. 9:315.19

COMBINED ADJUSTED MONTHLY GROSS INCOME	ONE CHILD	TWO CHILDREN (TOTAL)	THREE CHILDREN (TOTAL)	FOUR CHILDREN (TOTAL)	FIVE CHILDREN (TOTAL)	SIX CHILDREN (TOTAL)
3400.00	607	898	1054	1153	1268	1379
3450.00	614	909	1066	1169	1286	1397
3500.00	622	919	1079	1185	1303	1416
3550.00	629	930	1092	1200	1320	1435
3600.00	636	941	1104	1216	1338	1454
3650.00	644	951	1117	1232	1355	1473
3700.00	651	962	1130	1248	1373	1492
3750.00	659	973	1142	1264	1390	1511
3800.00	666	983	1155	1279	1407	1530
3850.00	673	994	1168	1295	1425	1549
3900.00	681	1004	1181	1311	1442	1563
3950.00	688	1015	1193	1327	1459	1583
4000.00	696	1026	1206	1343	1477	1605
4050.00	702	1036	1219	1358	1494	1624
4100.00	708	1047	1231	1374	1512	1643
4150.00	715	1058	1244	1389	1528	1661
4200.00	721	1067	1255	1401	1542	1676
4250.00	728	1077	1266	1414	1555	1690
4300.00	734	1086	1277	1426	1568	1705
4350.00	741	1096	1287	1438	1582	1719
4400.00	748	1105	1298	1450	1595	1734
4450.00	754	1115	1309	1462	1609	1749
4500.00	761	1124	1320	1475	1622	1763
4550.00	767	1134	1331	1487	1636	1778
4600.00	774	1143	1342	1499	1649	1792
4650.00	780	1153	1353	1511	1662	1807
4700.00	787	1163	1364	1523	1676	1822
4750.00	793	1172	1375	1536	1689	1836
4800.00	800	1182	1386	1548	1703	1851
4850.00	806	1188	1393	1556	1711	1860
4900.00	813	1194	1399	1563	1719	1869
4950.00	820	1200	1406	1570	1727	1877
5000.00	826	1206	1412	1577	1735	1886
5050.00	833	1212	1419	1585	1743	1895
5100.00	839	1218	1425	1592	1751	1903
5150.00	846	1224	1432	1599	1759	1912
5200.00	852	1230	1438	1606	1767	1921
5250.00	859	1236	1445	1614	1775	1929
5300.00	865	1242	1451	1621	1783	1938
5350.00	870	1248	1458	1628	1791	1947
5400.00	874	1255	1464	1635	1799	1955
5450.00	879	1261	1471	1643	1807	1964
5500.00	883	1266	1477	1650	1815	1973
5550.00	887	1272	1483	1657	1822	1981
5600.00	891	1277	1490	1664	1830	1989
5650.00	895	1283	1496	1671	1838	1998
5700.00	899	1289	1502	1678	1846	2006
5750.00	903	1294	1508	1685	1853	2015
5800.00	907	1300	1515	1692	1861	2023
5850.00	911	1305	1521	1699	1869	2032
5900.00	915	1311	1527	1706	1877	2040
5950.00	919	1316	1534	1713	1885	2048
6000.00	923	1322	1540	1720	1892	2057
6050.00	927	1328	1546	1727	1900	2065
6100.00	931	1333	1553	1734	1908	2074
6150.00	935	1339	1559	1741	1916	2082
6200.00	939	1344	1565	1748	1923	2091
6250.00	943	1350	1572	1756	1931	2099
6300.00	947	1355	1578	1763	1939	2108

For Annotative Materials, see West's Louisiana Statutes Annotated

R.S. 9:315.19   APPENDIX 1—REVISED STATUTES, TITLE 9

COMBINED ADJUSTED MONTHLY GROSS INCOME	ONE CHILD	TWO CHILDREN (TOTAL)	THREE CHILDREN (TOTAL)	FOUR CHILDREN (TOTAL)	FIVE CHILDREN (TOTAL)	SIX CHILDREN (TOTAL)
6350.00	951	1361	1584	1770	1947	2116
6400.00	955	1367	1591	1777	1954	2124
6450.00	959	1372	1597	1784	1962	2133
6500.00	963	1378	1603	1791	1970	2142
6550.00	968	1384	1610	1799	1978	2151
6600.00	972	1390	1617	1806	1987	2160
6650.00	976	1396	1624	1814	1995	2168
6700.00	980	1402	1630	1821	2003	2177
6750.00	985	1408	1637	1829	2011	2186
6800.00	989	1414	1644	1836	2020	2195
6850.00	993	1419	1650	1843	2028	2204
6900.00	998	1425	1657	1851	2036	2213
6950.00	1002	1431	1664	1858	2044	2222
7000.00	1006	1437	1670	1866	2052	2231
7050.00	1010	1443	1677	1873	2060	2240
7100.00	1014	1449	1683	1880	2068	2248
7150.00	1018	1454	1690	1887	2076	2257
7200.00	1022	1460	1696	1894	2084	2265
7250.00	1027	1465	1702	1901	2092	2274
7300.00	1031	1471	1709	1909	2099	2282
7350.00	1035	1477	1715	1916	2107	2291
7400.00	1039	1482	1721	1923	2115	2299
7450.00	1043	1488	1728	1930	2123	2308
7500.00	1047	1494	1734	1937	2131	2316
7550.00	1051	1499	1741	1944	2139	2325
7600.00	1055	1505	1747	1951	2146	2333
7650.00	1059	1511	1753	1958	2154	2342
7700.00	1063	1516	1760	1966	2162	2350
7750.00	1067	1522	1766	1973	2170	2359
7800.00	1071	1528	1772	1980	2178	2367
7850.00	1075	1533	1779	1987	2186	2376
7900.00	1079	1539	1785	1994	2193	2384
7950.00	1084	1545	1791	2001	2201	2393
8000.00	1088	1550	1798	2008	2209	2401
8050.00	1092	1556	1804	2016	2217	2410
8100.00	1096	1562	1811	2023	2225	2419
8150.00	1100	1568	1818	2031	2234	2428
8200.00	1105	1574	1825	2039	2243	2438
8250.00	1110	1581	1833	2047	2252	2448
8300.00	1114	1587	1840	2056	2261	2458
8350.00	1119	1594	1848	2064	2271	2468
8400.00	1123	1600	1855	2073	2280	2478
8450.00	1128	1607	1863	2081	2289	2488
8500.00	1132	1613	1871	2089	2298	2498
8550.00	1137	1620	1878	2098	2308	2508
8600.00	1142	1626	1886	2106	2317	2519
8650.00	1146	1633	1893	2115	2326	2529
8700.00	1151	1639	1901	2123	2336	2539
8750.00	1155	1646	1908	2132	2345	2549
8800.00	1160	1652	1916	2140	2354	2559
8850.00	1164	1659	1923	2149	2363	2569
8900.00	1169	1665	1931	2157	2373	2579
8950.00	1174	1672	1939	2165	2382	2589
9000.00	1178	1678	1946	2174	2391	2599
9050.00	1183	1685	1954	2182	2400	2609
9100.00	1187	1691	1961	2191	2410	2619
9150.00	1192	1698	1969	2199	2419	2629
9200.00	1196	1704	1976	2208	2428	2640
9250.00	1201	1711	1984	2216	2438	2650

For Annotative Materials, see West's Louisiana Statutes Annotated

APPENDIX 1—REVISED STATUTES, TITLE 9

R.S. 9:315.19

COMBINED ADJUSTED MONTHLY GROSS INCOME	ONE CHILD	TWO CHILDREN (TOTAL)	THREE CHILDREN (TOTAL)	FOUR CHILDREN (TOTAL)	FIVE CHILDREN (TOTAL)	SIX CHILDREN (TOTAL)
9300.00	1205	1717	1991	2224	2447	2660
9350.00	1210	1724	1999	2233	2456	2670
9400.00	1215	1730	2007	2241	2465	2680
9450.00	1219	1737	2014	2250	2475	2690
9500.00	1224	1743	2022	2258	2484	2700
9550.00	1228	1750	2029	2267	2493	2710
9600.00	1233	1756	2037	2275	2503	2720
9650.00	1237	1763	2044	2283	2512	2730
9700.00	1242	1769	2052	2292	2521	2740
9750.00	1246	1776	2059	2300	2530	2751
9800.00	1251	1782	2067	2309	2540	2761
9850.00	1256	1789	2074	2317	2549	2771
9900.00	1260	1795	2082	2326	2558	2781
9950.00	1265	1802	2090	2334	2567	2791
10000.00	1269	1808	2097	2343	2577	2801
10050.00	1274	1815	2105	2351	2586	2811
10100.00	1278	1821	2112	2359	2595	2821
10150.00	1283	1828	2120	2368	2605	2831
10200.00	1287	1834	2127	2376	2614	2841
10250.00	1292	1841	2135	2385	2623	2851
10300.00	1297	1847	2142	2393	2632	2861
10350.00	1301	1854	2150	2402	2642	2872
10400.00	1306	1860	2158	2410	2651	2882
10450.00	1310	1867	2165	2418	2660	2892
10500.00	1315	1873	2173	2427	2670	2902
10550.00	1319	1880	2180	2435	2679	2912
10600.00	1324	1886	2188	2444	2688	2922
10650.00	1329	1893	2195	2452	2697	2932
10700.00	1333	1899	2203	2461	2707	2942
10750.00	1337	1905	2209	2468	2715	2951
10800.00	1341	1910	2215	2474	2722	2959
10850.00	1345	1915	2221	2481	2729	2967
10900.00	1348	1920	2227	2487	2736	2974
10950.00	1352	1926	2233	2494	2743	2982
11000.00	1356	1931	2239	2500	2750	2990
11050.00	1359	1936	2244	2507	2758	2998
11100.00	1363	1941	2250	2513	2765	3005
11150.00	1367	1946	2256	2520	2772	3013
11200.00	1370	1951	2262	2526	2779	3021
11250.00	1374	1956	2268	2533	2786	3029
11300.00	1378	1961	2273	2539	2793	3036
11350.00	1381	1967	2279	2546	2800	3044
11400.00	1385	1972	2285	2552	2808	3052
11450.00	1389	1977	2291	2559	2815	3060
11500.00	1392	1982	2297	2565	2822	3067
11550.00	1396	1987	2302	2572	2829	3075
11600.00	1400	1992	2308	2578	2836	3083
11650.00	1403	1997	2314	2585	2843	3091
11700.00	1407	2002	2320	2591	2850	3098
11750.00	1411	2008	2326	2598	2858	3106
11800.00	1414	2013	2331	2604	2865	3114
11850.00	1418	2018	2337	2611	2872	3122
11900.00	1422	2023	2343	2617	2879	3129
11950.00	1425	2028	2349	2624	2886	3137
12000.00	1429	2033	2355	2630	2893	3145
12050.00	1433	2038	2360	2637	2900	3153
12100.00	1436	2043	2366	2643	2907	3160
12150.00	1440	2049	2372	2650	2915	3168
12200.00	1444	2054	2378	2656	2922	3176

For Annotative Materials, see West's Louisiana Statutes Annotated

R.S. 9:315.19 APPENDIX 1—REVISED STATUTES, TITLE 9

COMBINED ADJUSTED MONTHLY GROSS INCOME	ONE CHILD	TWO CHILDREN (TOTAL)	THREE CHILDREN (TOTAL)	FOUR CHILDREN (TOTAL)	FIVE CHILDREN (TOTAL)	SIX CHILDREN (TOTAL)
12250.00	1447	2059	2384	2663	2929	3184
12300.00	1451	2064	2390	2669	2936	3191
12350.00	1455	2069	2395	2676	2943	3199
12400.00	1458	2074	2401	2682	2950	3207
12450.00	1462	2079	2407	2689	2957	3215
12500.00	1466	2084	2413	2695	2965	3222
12550.00	1469	2090	2419	2702	2972	3230
12600.00	1473	2095	2424	2708	2979	3238
12650.00	1477	2100	2430	2715	2986	3246
12700.00	1480	2105	2436	2721	2993	3254
12750.00	1484	2110	2442	2727	3000	3261
12800.00	1488	2115	2448	2734	3007	3269
12850.00	1491	2120	2453	2740	3015	3277
12900.00	1495	2125	2459	2747	3022	3285
12950.00	1499	2130	2465	2753	3029	3292
13000.00	1502	2136	2471	2760	3036	3300
13050.00	1506	2141	2477	2766	3043	3308
13100.00	1510	2146	2482	2773	3050	3316
13150.00	1513	2151	2488	2779	3057	3323
13200.00	1517	2156	2494	2786	3064	3331
13250.00	1521	2161	2500	2792	3072	3339
13300.00	1524	2166	2506	2799	3079	3347
13350.00	1528	2171	2511	2805	3086	3354
13400.00	1532	2177	2517	2812	3093	3362
13450.00	1536	2182	2523	2818	3100	3370
13500.00	1539	2187	2529	2825	3107	3378
13550.00	1543	2192	2535	2831	3114	3385
13600.00	1547	2197	2541	2838	3122	3393
13650.00	1550	2202	2546	2844	3129	3401
13700.00	1554	2207	2552	2851	3136	3409
13750.00	1558	2212	2558	2857	3143	3416
13800.00	1561	2218	2564	2864	3150	3424
13850.00	1565	2223	2570	2870	3157	3432
13900.00	1568	2227	2575	2876	3164	3439
13950.00	1570	2230	2577	2879	3166	3442
14000.00	1572	2232	2579	2881	3169	3445
14050.00	1574	2234	2581	2883	3172	3448
14100.00	1576	2236	2584	2886	3175	3451
14150.00	1577	2239	2586	2888	3177	3454
14200.00	1579	2241	2588	2891	3180	3456
14250.00	1581	2243	2590	2893	3182	3459
14300.00	1583	2245	2592	2895	3185	3462
14350.00	1584	2247	2594	2897	3187	3465
14400.00	1586	2249	2596	2900	3190	3467
14450.00	1588	2251	2598	2902	3192	3470
14500.00	1590	2253	2600	2904	3195	3473
14550.00	1591	2256	2602	2907	3197	3475
14600.00	1593	2258	2604	2909	3200	3478
14650.00	1595	2260	2606	2911	3202	3481
14700.00	1596	2262	2608	2913	3205	3484
14750.00	1598	2264	2610	2916	3207	3486
14800.00	1600	2266	2612	2918	3210	3489
14850.00	1602	2268	2614	2920	3212	3492
14900.00	1603	2270	2617	2923	3215	3495
14950.00	1605	2272	2619	2925	3217	3497
15000.00	1607	2274	2621	2927	3220	3500
15050.00	1608	2277	2623	2929	3222	3503
15100.00	1610	2279	2625	2932	3225	3506
15150.00	1612	2281	2627	2934	3227	3508

For Annotative Materials, see West's Louisiana Statutes Annotated

APPENDIX 1—REVISED STATUTES, TITLE 9   R.S. 9:315.19

COMBINED ADJUSTED MONTHLY GROSS INCOME	ONE CHILD	TWO CHILDREN (TOTAL)	THREE CHILDREN (TOTAL)	FOUR CHILDREN (TOTAL)	FIVE CHILDREN (TOTAL)	SIX CHILDREN (TOTAL)
15200.00	1614	2283	2629	2936	3230	3511
15250.00	1615	2285	2631	2939	3232	3514
15300.00	1617	2287	2633	2941	3235	3516
15350.00	1619	2289	2635	2943	3238	3519
15400.00	1620	2291	2637	2945	3240	3522
15450.00	1622	2293	2639	2948	3243	3525
15500.00	1624	2295	2641	2950	3245	3527
15550.00	1626	2298	2643	2952	3248	3530
15600.00	1627	2300	2645	2955	3250	3533
15650.00	1629	2302	2647	2957	3253	3536
15700.00	1631	2304	2649	2959	3255	3538
15750.00	1632	2306	2651	2961	3258	3541
15800.00	1634	2308	2653	2964	3260	3544
15850.00	1636	2310	2655	2966	3263	3547
15900.00	1638	2312	2657	2968	3265	3549
15950.00	1639	2314	2659	2971	3268	3552
16000.00	1641	2316	2662	2973	3270	3555
16050.00	1643	2319	2664	2975	3273	3557
16100.00	1644	2321	2666	2977	3275	3560
16150.00	1646	2323	2668	2980	3278	3563
16200.00	1648	2325	2670	2982	3280	3566
16250.00	1650	2327	2672	2984	3283	3568
16300.00	1651	2329	2674	2987	3285	3571
16350.00	1653	2331	2676	2989	3288	3574
16400.00	1655	2333	2678	2991	3290	3577
16450.00	1656	2335	2680	2994	3293	3579
16500.00	1658	2338	2682	2996	3295	3582
16550.00	1660	2340	2684	2998	3298	3585
16600.00	1662	2342	2686	3000	3300	3588
16650.00	1663	2344	2688	3003	3303	3590
16700.00	1665	2346	2690	3005	3305	3593
16750.00	1667	2348	2692	3007	3308	3596
16800.00	1668	2350	2694	3010	3310	3598
16850.00	1670	2352	2696	3012	3313	3601
16900.00	1672	2354	2698	3014	3315	3604
16950.00	1674	2356	2700	3016	3318	3607
17000.00	1675	2359	2702	3019	3321	3609
17050.00	1677	2361	2705	3021	3323	3612
17100.00	1679	2363	2707	3023	3326	3615
17150.00	1680	2365	2709	3026	3328	3618
17200.00	1682	2367	2711	3028	3331	3620
17250.00	1684	2369	2713	3030	3333	3623
17300.00	1686	2371	2715	3032	3336	3626
17350.00	1689	2376	2721	3039	3343	3634
17400.00	1693	2382	2727	3046	3351	3642
17450.00	1697	2387	2733	3053	3359	3651
17500.00	1701	2393	2740	3060	3366	3659
17550.00	1705	2398	2746	3067	3374	3667
17600.00	1708	2403	2752	3074	3382	3676
17650.00	1712	2409	2758	3081	3389	3684
17700.00	1716	2414	2765	3088	3397	3692
17750.00	1720	2420	2771	3095	3405	3701
17800.00	1724	2425	2777	3102	3412	3709
17850.00	1727	2430	2783	3109	3420	3717
17900.00	1731	2436	2790	3116	3428	3726
17950.00	1735	2441	2796	3123	3435	3734
18000.00	1739	2447	2802	3130	3443	3743
18050.00	1743	2452	2808	3137	3451	3751
18100.00	1746	2457	2815	3144	3458	3759

For Annotative Materials, see West's Louisiana Statutes Annotated

R.S. 9:315.19   APPENDIX 1—REVISED STATUTES, TITLE 9

COMBINED ADJUSTED MONTHLY GROSS INCOME	ONE CHILD	TWO CHILDREN (TOTAL)	THREE CHILDREN (TOTAL)	FOUR CHILDREN (TOTAL)	FIVE CHILDREN (TOTAL)	SIX CHILDREN (TOTAL)
18150.00	1750	2463	2821	3151	3466	3768
18200.00	1754	2468	2827	3158	3474	3776
18250.00	1758	2474	2833	3165	3481	3784
18300.00	1762	2479	2840	3172	3489	3793
18350.00	1766	2485	2846	3179	3497	3801
18400.00	1769	2490	2852	3186	3504	3809
18450.00	1773	2495	2858	3193	3512	3818
18500.00	1777	2501	2865	3200	3520	3826
18550.00	1781	2506	2871	3207	3527	3834
18600.00	1785	2512	2877	3214	3535	3843
18650.00	1788	2517	2883	3221	3543	3851
18700.00	1792	2522	2890	3228	3550	3859
18750.00	1796	2528	2896	3235	3558	3868
18800.00	1800	2533	2902	3242	3566	3876
18850.00	1804	2539	2908	3249	3574	3884
18900.00	1807	2544	2915	3256	3581	3893
18950.00	1811	2549	2921	3263	3589	3901
19000.00	1815	2555	2927	3270	3597	3909
19050.00	1819	2560	2933	3277	3604	3918
19100.00	1823	2566	2940	3284	3612	3926
19150.00	1826	2571	2946	3291	3620	3935
19200.00	1830	2576	2952	3298	3627	3943
19250.00	1834	2582	2958	3305	3635	3951
19300.00	1838	2587	2965	3311	3643	3960
19350.00	1842	2593	2971	3318	3650	3968
19400.00	1846	2598	2977	3325	3658	3976
19450.00	1849	2603	2983	3332	3666	3985
19500.00	1853	2609	2990	3339	3673	3993
19550.00	1857	2614	2996	3346	3681	4001
19600.00	1861	2620	3002	3353	3689	4010
19650.00	1865	2625	3008	3360	3696	4018
19700.00	1868	2630	3015	3367	3704	4026
19750.00	1872	2636	3021	3374	3712	4035
19800.00	1876	2641	3027	3381	3719	4043
19850.00	1880	2647	3033	3388	3727	4051
19900.00	1884	2652	3040	3395	3735	4060
19950.00	1887	2657	3046	3402	3742	4068
20000.00	1891	2663	3052	3409	3750	4076
20050.00	1895	2668	3058	3416	3758	4085
20100.00	1899	2674	3065	3423	3766	4093
20150.00	1903	2679	3071	3430	3773	4101
20200.00	1906	2684	3077	3437	3781	4110
20250.00	1910	2690	3083	3444	3789	4118
20300.00	1914	2695	3090	3451	3796	4127
20350.00	1918	2701	3096	3458	3804	4135
20400.00	1922	2706	3102	3465	3812	4143
20450.00	1925	2711	3108	3472	3819	4152
20500.00	1929	2717	3115	3479	3827	4160
20550.00	1933	2722	3121	3486	3835	4168
20600.00	1937	2728	3127	3493	3842	4177
20650.00	1941	2733	3133	3500	3850	4185
20700.00	1945	2738	3140	3507	3858	4193
20750.00	1948	2744	3146	3514	3865	4202
20800.00	1952	2749	3152	3521	3873	4210
20850.00	1956	2755	3158	3528	3881	4218
20900.00	1960	2760	3165	3535	3888	4227
20950.00	1964	2765	3171	3542	3896	4235
21000.00	1967	2771	3177	3549	3904	4243
21050.00	1971	2776	3183	3556	3911	4252

For Annotative Materials, see West's Louisiana Statutes Annotated

APPENDIX 1—REVISED STATUTES, TITLE 9   R.S. 9:315.19

COMBINED ADJUSTED MONTHLY GROSS INCOME	ONE CHILD	TWO CHILDREN (TOTAL)	THREE CHILDREN (TOTAL)	FOUR CHILDREN (TOTAL)	FIVE CHILDREN (TOTAL)	SIX CHILDREN (TOTAL)
21100.00	1975	2782	3190	3563	3919	4260
21150.00	1979	2787	3196	3570	3927	4268
21200.00	1983	2792	3202	3577	3934	4277
21250.00	1986	2798	3208	3584	3942	4285
21300.00	1990	2803	3215	3591	3950	4293
21350.00	1994	2809	3221	3598	3957	4302
21400.00	1998	2814	3227	3605	3965	4310
21450.00	2002	2819	3233	3612	3973	4318
21500.00	2005	2825	3240	3619	3981	4327
21550.00	2009	2830	3246	3626	3988	4335
21600.00	2013	2836	3252	3633	3996	4344
21650.00	2017	2841	3258	3640	4004	4352
21700.00	2021	2846	3265	3647	4011	4360
21750.00	2025	2852	3271	3654	4019	4369
21800.00	2028	2857	3277	3661	4027	4377
21850.00	2032	2863	3283	3668	4034	4385
21900.00	2036	2868	3290	3675	4042	4394
21950.00	2040	2873	3296	3681	4050	4402
22000.00	2044	2879	3302	3688	4057	4410
22050.00	2047	2884	3308	3695	4065	4419
22100.00	2051	2890	3315	3702	4073	4427
22150.00	2055	2895	3321	3709	4080	4435
22200.00	2059	2900	3327	3716	4088	4444
22250.00	2063	2906	3333	3723	4096	4452
22300.00	2066	2911	3340	3730	4103	4460
22350.00	2070	2917	3346	3737	4111	4469
22400.00	2074	2922	3352	3744	4119	4477
22450.00	2078	2927	3358	3751	4126	4485
22500.00	2082	2933	3365	3758	4134	4494
22550.00	2085	2938	3371	3765	4142	4502
22600.00	2089	2944	3377	3772	4149	4510
22650.00	2093	2949	3383	3779	4157	4519
22700.00	2097	2954	3390	3786	4165	4527
22750.00	2101	2960	3396	3793	4173	4536
22800.00	2105	2965	3402	3800	4180	4544
22850.00	2108	2971	3408	3807	4188	4552
22900.00	2112	2976	3415	3814	4196	4561
22950.00	2116	2981	3421	3821	4203	4569
23000.00	2120	2987	3427	3828	4211	4577
23050.00	2124	2992	3433	3835	4219	4586
23100.00	2127	2998	3440	3842	4226	4594
23150.00	2131	3003	3446	3849	4234	4602
23200.00	2135	3008	3452	3856	4242	4611
23250.00	2139	3014	3458	3863	4249	4619
23300.00	2143	3019	3465	3870	4257	4627
23350.00	2146	3025	3471	3877	4265	4636
23400.00	2150	3030	3477	3884	4272	4644
23450.00	2154	3035	3483	3891	4280	4652
23500.00	2158	3041	3490	3898	4288	4661
23550.00	2162	3046	3496	3905	4295	4669
23600.00	2165	3052	3502	3912	4303	4677
23650.00	2169	3057	3508	3919	4311	4686
23700.00	2173	3062	3515	3926	4318	4694
23750.00	2177	3068	3521	3933	4326	4702
23800.00	2181	3073	3527	3940	4334	4711
23850.00	2185	3079	3533	3947	4341	4719
23900.00	2188	3084	3540	3954	4349	4728
23950.00	2192	3089	3546	3961	4357	4736
24000.00	2196	3095	3552	3968	4364	4744

For Annotative Materials, see West's Louisiana Statutes Annotated

R.S. 9:315.19   APPENDIX 1—REVISED STATUTES, TITLE 9

COMBINED ADJUSTED MONTHLY GROSS INCOME	ONE CHILD	TWO CHILDREN (TOTAL)	THREE CHILDREN (TOTAL)	FOUR CHILDREN (TOTAL)	FIVE CHILDREN (TOTAL)	SIX CHILDREN (TOTAL)
24050.00	2200	3100	3558	3975	4372	4753
24100.00	2204	3106	3565	3982	4380	4761
24150.00	2207	3111	3571	3989	4388	4769
24200.00	2211	3116	3577	3996	4395	4778
24250.00	2215	3122	3583	4003	4403	4786
24300.00	2219	3127	3590	4010	4411	4794
24350.00	2223	3133	3596	4017	4418	4803
24400.00	2226	3138	3602	4024	4426	4811
24450.00	2230	3143	3608	4031	4434	4819
24500.00	2234	3149	3615	4038	4441	4828
24550.00	2238	3154	3621	4045	4449	4836
24600.00	2242	3160	3627	4051	4457	4844
24650.00	2245	3165	3633	4058	4464	4853
24700.00	2249	3170	3640	4065	4472	4861
24750.00	2253	3176	3646	4072	4480	4869
24800.00	2257	3181	3652	4079	4487	4878
24850.00	2261	3187	3658	4086	4495	4886
24900.00	2265	3192	3665	4093	4503	4894
24950.00	2268	3197	3671	4100	4510	4903
25000.00	2272	3203	3677	4107	4518	4911
25050.00	2276	3208	3683	4114	4526	4919
25100.00	2280	3214	3690	4121	4533	4928
25150.00	2284	3219	3696	4128	4541	4936
25200.00	2287	3224	3702	4135	4549	4945
25250.00	2291	3230	3708	4142	4556	4953
25300.00	2295	3235	3715	4149	4564	4961
25350.00	2299	3241	3721	4156	4572	4970
25400.00	2303	3246	3727	4163	4580	4978
25450.00	2306	3251	3733	4170	4587	4986
25500.00	2310	3257	3740	4177	4595	4995
25550.00	2314	3262	3746	4184	4603	5003
25600.00	2318	3268	3752	4191	4610	5011
25650.00	2322	3273	3758	4198	4618	5020
25700.00	2325	3278	3765	4205	4626	5028
25750.00	2329	3284	3771	4212	4633	5036
25800.00	2333	3289	3777	4219	4641	5045
25850.00	2337	3295	3783	4226	4649	5053
25900.00	2341	3300	3790	4233	4656	5061
25950.00	2345	3305	3796	4240	4664	5070
26000.00	2348	3311	3802	4247	4672	5078
26050.00	2352	3316	3808	4254	4679	5086
26100.00	2356	3322	3815	4261	4687	5095
26150.00	2360	3327	3821	4268	4695	5103
26200.00	2364	3332	3827	4275	4702	5111
26250.00	2367	3338	3833	4282	4710	5120
26300.00	2371	3343	3840	4289	4718	5128
26350.00	2375	3349	3846	4296	4725	5137
26400.00	2379	3354	3852	4303	4733	5145
26450.00	2383	3359	3858	4310	4741	5153
26500.00	2386	3365	3865	4317	4748	5162
26550.00	2390	3370	3871	4324	4756	5170
26600.00	2394	3376	3877	4331	4764	5178
26650.00	2398	3381	3883	4338	4771	5187
26700.00	2402	3386	3890	4345	4779	5195
26750.00	2405	3392	3896	4352	4787	5203
26800.00	2409	3397	3902	4359	4795	5212
26850.00	2413	3403	3908	4366	4802	5220
26900.00	2417	3408	3915	4373	4810	5228
26950.00	2421	3413	3921	4380	4818	5237

For Annotative Materials, see West's Louisiana Statutes Annotated

APPENDIX 1—REVISED STATUTES, TITLE 9   R.S. 9:315.19

COMBINED ADJUSTED MONTHLY GROSS INCOME	ONE CHILD	TWO CHILDREN (TOTAL)	THREE CHILDREN (TOTAL)	FOUR CHILDREN (TOTAL)	FIVE CHILDREN (TOTAL)	SIX CHILDREN (TOTAL)
27000.00	2425	3419	3927	4387	4825	5245
27050.00	2428	3424	3933	4394	4833	5253
27100.00	2432	3430	3940	4401	4841	5262
27150.00	2436	3435	3946	4408	4848	5270
27200.00	2440	3440	3952	4414	4856	5278
27250.00	2444	3446	3958	4421	4864	5287
27300.00	2447	3451	3965	4428	4871	5295
27350.00	2451	3457	3971	4435	4879	5303
27400.00	2455	3462	3977	4442	4887	5312
27450.00	2459	3467	3983	4449	4894	5320
27500.00	2463	3473	3990	4456	4902	5328
27550.00	2466	3478	3996	4463	4910	5337
27600.00	2470	3484	4002	4470	4917	5345
27650.00	2474	3489	4008	4477	4925	5354
27700.00	2478	3494	4015	4484	4933	5362
27750.00	2482	3500	4021	4491	4940	5370
27800.00	2485	3505	4027	4498	4948	5379
27850.00	2489	3511	4033	4505	4956	5387
27900.00	2493	3516	4040	4512	4963	5395
27950.00	2497	3521	4046	4519	4971	5404
28000.00	2501	3527	4052	4526	4979	5412
28050.00	2505	3532	4058	4533	4986	5420
28100.00	2508	3538	4065	4540	4994	5429
28150.00	2512	3543	4071	4547	5002	5437
28200.00	2516	3548	4077	4554	5010	5445
28250.00	2520	3554	4083	4561	5017	5454
28300.00	2524	3559	4090	4568	5025	5462
28350.00	2527	3565	4096	4575	5033	5470
28400.00	2531	3570	4102	4582	5040	5479
28450.00	2535	3575	4108	4589	5048	5487
28500.00	2539	3581	4115	4596	5056	5495
28550.00	2543	3586	4121	4603	5063	5504
28600.00	2546	3592	4127	4610	5071	5512
28650.00	2550	3597	4133	4617	5079	5520
28700.00	2554	3602	4140	4624	5086	5529
28750.00	2558	3608	4146	4631	5094	5537
28800.00	2562	3613	4152	4638	5102	5546
28850.00	2565	3619	4158	4645	5109	5554
28900.00	2569	3624	4165	4652	5117	5562
28950.00	2573	3629	4171	4659	5125	5571
29000.00	2577	3635	4177	4666	5132	5579
29050.00	2581	3640	4183	4673	5140	5587
29100.00	2584	3646	4190	4680	5148	5596
29150.00	2588	3651	4196	4687	5155	5604
29200.00	2592	3656	4202	4694	5163	5612
29250.00	2596	3662	4208	4701	5171	5621
29300.00	2600	3667	4215	4708	5178	5629
29350.00	2604	3673	4221	4715	5186	5637
29400.00	2607	3678	4227	4722	5194	5646
29450.00	2611	3683	4233	4729	5202	5654
29500.00	2615	3689	4240	4736	5209	5662
29550.00	2619	3694	4246	4743	5217	5671
29600.00	2623	3700	4252	4750	5225	5679
29650.00	2626	3705	4258	4757	5232	5687
29700.00	2630	3710	4265	4764	5240	5696
29750.00	2634	3716	4271	4771	5248	5704
29800.00	2638	3721	4277	4778	5255	5712
29850.00	2642	3727	4283	4784	5263	5721
29900.00	2645	3732	4289	4791	5270	5729

For Annotative Materials, see West's Louisiana Statutes Annotated

R.S. 9:315.19 APPENDIX 1—REVISED STATUTES, TITLE 9

COMBINED ADJUSTED MONTHLY GROSS INCOME	ONE CHILD	TWO CHILDREN (TOTAL)	THREE CHILDREN (TOTAL)	FOUR CHILDREN (TOTAL)	FIVE CHILDREN (TOTAL)	SIX CHILDREN (TOTAL)
29950.00	2649	3737	4296	4798	5278	5737
30000.00	2653	3742	4302	4805	5285	5745

Acts 2001, No. 1082, § 1. Amended by Acts 2008, No. 585, § 1.

Comment—2001

The schedule of parents' combined adjusted gross income up to an amount of ten thousand dollars was retained with some adjustments at the higher levels to facilitate the incorporation of additional amounts. For the same reason, the amounts of parents' combined adjusted gross income from ten thousand dollars per month to twenty thousand dollars per month were adjusted at the lower levels. The principal effect of the 2001 amendment to this Section is to extend the schedule amounts of parents' combined adjusted gross income to twenty thousand dollars.

Editor's note. Acts 2001, No. 1082, § 5, declares that this Act applies to actions concerning child support filed after August 15, 2001.

§ 315.20. Worksheets

Obligation Worksheet A

(The worksheet for calculation of the total support obligation under R.S. 9:315.8 and 315.10)

Court _____   Parish _____ Louisiana
Case Number _____   Div/CtRm _____
_____   and _____
Petitioner   Respondent

Children   Date of Birth   Children   Date of Birth
_____   _____
_____   _____
_____   _____

		A. Petitioner	B. Respondent	C. Combined
1.	MONTHLY GROSS INCOME (R.S. 9:315.2(A))	$_____	$_____	////////
	a. Preexisting child support payment.	–_____	–_____	////////
	b. Preexisting spousal support payment.	–_____	–_____	////////
2.	MONTHLY ADJUSTED GROSS INCOME (Line 1 minus 1a and 1b).	$	$	////////
3.	COMBINED MONTHLY ADJUSTED GROSS INCOME (Line 2 Column A plus Line 2 Column B). (R.S. 9:315.2(C))	////////	////////	$
4.	PERCENTAGE SHARE OF INCOME (Line 2 divided by line 3). (R.S. 9:315.2(C))	%	%	////////
5.	BASIC CHILD SUPPORT OBLIGATION (Compare line 3 to Child Support Schedule). (R.S. 9:315.2(D))	////////	////////	$
	a. Net Child Care Costs (Cost minus Federal Tax Credit). (R.S. 9:315.3)	////////	////////	+_____
	b. Child's Health Insurance Premium Cost. (R.S. 9:315.4)	////////	////////	+_____
	c. Extraordinary Medical Expenses (Uninsured Only). (Agreed to by parties or by order of the court). (R.S. 9:315.5)	////////	////////	+_____
	d. Extraordinary Expenses (Agreed to by parties or by order of the court). (R.S. 9:315.6)	////////	////////	+_____
	e. Optional. Minus extraordinary adjustments (Child's income if applicable). (R.S. 9:315.7)	////////	////////	–_____
6.	TOTAL CHILD SUPPORT OBLIGATION (Add lines 5, 5a, 5b, 5c, and 5d; Subtract line 5e). (R.S. 9:315.8)	////////	////////	$
7.	EACH PARTY'S CHILD SUPPORT OBLIGATION (Multiply line 4 times line 6 for each parent).	$	$	////////
8.	DIRECT PAYMENTS made by the noncustodial parent on behalf of the child for work-related net child care	////////		////////

For Annotative Materials, see West's Louisiana Statutes Annotated

APPENDIX 1—REVISED STATUTES, TITLE 9   R.S. 9:315.20

costs, health insurance premiums, extraordinary medical expenses, or extraordinary expenses.

9. RECOMMENDED CHILD SUPPORT ORDER (Subtract line 8 from line 7). $

Comments, calculations, or rebuttals to schedule or adjustments if made under 8 above or if ordering a credit for a joint custodial arrangement:

Prepared by _____ Date _____

Obligation Worksheet B

(The worksheet for calculation of the total child support obligation under R.S. 9:315.9)

Court _____ Parish _____ Louisiana
Case Number _____ Div/CtRm _____
                                and _____
Petitioner   Respondent

Children   Date of Birth   Children   Date of Birth

	A. Petitioner	B. Respondent	C. Combined
1. MONTHLY GROSS INCOME (R.S. 9:315.2(A))	$	$	
a. Preexisting child support payment.	–	–	
b. Preexisting spousal support payment.	–	–	
2. MONTHLY ADJUSTED GROSS INCOME (Line 1 minus 1a and 1b).	$	$	
3. COMBINED MONTHLY ADJUSTED GROSS INCOME (Line 2 Column A plus Line 2 Column B) (R.S. 9:315.2(C))			$
4. PERCENTAGE SHARE OF INCOME (Line 2 divided by line 3) (R.S. 9:315.2(C))	%	%	
5. BASIC CHILD SUPPORT OBLIGATION (Compare line 3 to Child Support Schedule) (R.S. 9:315.2(D))			$
6. SHARED CUSTODY BASIC OBLIGATION (Line 5 times 1.5) (R.S. 9:315.9(A)(2))			$
7. EACH PARTY'S THEORETICAL CHILD SUPPORT OBLIGATION (Multiply line 4 times line 6 for each party) (R.S. 9:315.9(A)(2))	$	$	
8. PERCENTAGE with each party (Use actual percentage of time spent with each party, if percentage is not 50%) (R.S. 9:315.9(A)(3))	%	%	
9. BASIC CHILD SUPPORT OBLIGATION FOR TIME WITH OTHER PARTY (Cross Multiply line 7 for each party times line 8 for the other party) (R.S. 9:315.9(A)(3)) (For Line 9 Column A, multiply Line 7 Column A times Line 8 Column B) (For Line 9 Column B, multiply Line 7 Column B times Line 8 Column A)	$	$	
a. Net Child Care Costs (Cost minus Federal Tax Credit) (R.S. 9:315.3)			+ _____
b. Child's Health Insurance Premium Cost (R.S. 9:315.4)			+ _____
c. Extraordinary Medical Expenses (Uninsured only) (Agreed to by parties or by order of court) (R.S. 9:315.5)			+ _____
d. Extraordinary Expenses (Agreed to by parties or by order of the court) (R.S. 9:315.6)			+ _____
e. Optional. Minus extraordinary adjustments (Child's income if applicable) (R.S. 9:315.7)			– _____
10. TOTAL EXPENSES/EXTRAORDINARY ADJUST-			$

For Annotative Materials, see West's Louisiana Statutes Annotated

	MENTS (Add lines 9a, 9b, 9c, and 9d; Subtract line 9e)	/////////////	/////////////
11.	EACH PARTY'S PROPORTIONATE SHARE of Expenses/Extraordinary Adjustments (Line 4 times line 10) (R.S. 9:315.9(A)(4))	$	$
12.	DIRECT PAYMENTS made by either party on behalf of the child for work-related net child care costs, health insurance premiums, extraordinary medical expenses, or extraordinary expenses. Deduct each party's proportionate share of an expense owed directly to a third party. If either parent's proportionate share of an expense is owed to the other parent, enter zero. (R.S. 9:315.9(A)(5))	–	–
13.	EACH PARTY'S CHILD SUPPORT OBLIGATION (Line 9 plus line 11 and minus line 12) (R.S. 9:315.9(A)(4) and (5))	$	$
14.	RECOMMENDED CHILD SUPPORT ORDER (Subtract lesser amount from greater amount in line 13 and place the difference in the appropriate column) (R.S. 9:315.9(A)(6))	$	$

Comments, calculations, or rebuttals to schedule or adjustments:

Prepared by _____ Date _____

Acts 2001, No. 1082, § 1. Amended by Acts 2002, 1st Ex.Sess., No. 62, § 1; Acts 2003, No. 617, § 1.

Comments—2001

(a) Worksheet A modifies the worksheet by adding to the calculation a deduction for direct payments to be made by the noncustodial or nondomiciliary parent for certain expenses (line 8) and by adding language to the last line of the worksheet for an adjustment or credit in the case of a joint custody arrangement between parents. R.S. 9:315.8(E).

(b) Worksheet B is new and incorporates a calculation for the statutory language in R.S. 9:315.9 which provides for determining child support when the parents have *shared custody*. Worksheet B also includes a deduction for each party's proportionate share of the expenses owed directly to a third party (line 12).

Editor's note. Acts 2001, No. 1082, § 5, declares that this Act applies to actions concerning child support filed after August 15, 2001.

SUBPART B. OTHER CHILD SUPPORT PROVISIONS

§ 315.21. Retroactivity of child support judgment

A. Except for good cause shown, a judgment awarding, modifying, or revoking an interim child support allowance shall be retroactive to the date of judicial demand, but in no case prior to the date of judicial demand.

B. (1) A judgment that initially awards or denies final child support is effective as of the date the judgment is signed and terminates an interim child support allowance as of that date.

(2) If an interim child support allowance award is not in effect on the date of the judgment awarding final child support, the judgment shall be retroactive to the date of judicial demand, except for good cause shown, but in no case prior to the date of judicial demand.

C. Except for good cause shown, a judgment modifying or revoking a final child support judgment shall be retroactive to the date of judicial demand, but in no case prior to the date of judicial demand.

D. Child support of any kind, except that paid pursuant to an interim child support allowance award, provided by the judgment debtor from the date of judicial demand to the date the support judgment is signed, to or on behalf of the child for whom support is ordered, shall be credited to the judgment debtor against the amount of the judgment.

E. In the event that the court finds good cause for not making the award retroactive to the date of judicial demand, the court may fix the date on which the award shall commence, but in no case shall this date be a date prior to the date of judicial demand.

Text of subsec. F effective upon the amendment of 42 USC 666(a)(9)(c) to permit retroactive modification of child support. See notes following this section.

F. (1) Notwithstanding any other provision of this Section, if a party has been directly affected by Hurricane Katrina, a judgment modifying a final child support judgment may be made retroactive to August 26, 2005, if judicial demand is made prior to April 15, 2006.

(2) Notwithstanding any other provision of this Section, if a party has been directly affected by Hurricane Rita, a judgment modifying a final child support judgment may be made retroactive to September 20, 2005, if judicial demand is made prior to April 15, 2006.

Added by Acts 1993, No. 261, § 7, eff. Jan. 1, 1994. Amended by Acts 2001, No. 459, § 1; Acts 2005, 1st Ex.Sess., No. 59, § 1, eff. Dec. 6, 2005.

Editor's note. Sections 2 and 4 of Acts 2005, 1st Ex.Sess., No. 59 provide:

"Section 2. The provisions of R.S. 9:315.21(F) as enacted in this Act shall not take effect unless 42 USC 666(a)(9)(c), (the Bradley Amendment), which currently provides that any payment or installment of support under any child support order is not subject to retroactive modification, is amended and enacted into law to permit retroactive modification of child support."

"Section 4. The provisions of this Act shall apply to all cases pending on its effective date and to all cases filed after its effective date."

Cross References

C.C. arts. 6, 141, 142.

§ 315.22. Termination of child support upon majority or emancipation; exceptions

A. When there is a child support award in a specific amount per child, the award for each child shall terminate automatically without any action by the obligor upon each child's attaining the age of majority, or upon emancipation relieving the child of the disabilities attached to minority.

B. When there is a child support award in globo for two or more children, the award shall terminate automatically and without any action by the obligor when the youngest child for whose benefit the award was made attains the age of majority or is emancipated relieving the child of the disabilities attached to minority.

C. An award of child support continues with respect to any unmarried child who attains the age of majority, or to a child who is emancipated relieving the child of the disabilities attached to minority, as long as the child is a full-time student in good standing in a secondary school or its equivalent, has not attained the age of nineteen, and is dependent upon either parent. Either the primary domiciliary parent or the major or emancipated child is the proper party to enforce an award of child support pursuant to this Subsection.

D. An award of child support continues with respect to any child who has a developmental disability, as defined in R.S. 28:451.2, until he attains the age of twenty-two, as long as the child is a full-time student in a secondary school. The primary domiciliary parent or legal guardian is the proper party to enforce an award of child support pursuant to this Subsection.

Added by Acts 1993, No. 261, § 7, eff. Jan. 1, 1994. Amended by Acts 2001, No. 408, § 2; Acts 2001, No. 1082, § 1.

Editor's note. Acts 2001, No. 1082, § 5, declares that this Act applies to actions concerning child support filed after August 15, 2001.

Cross References

C.C. arts. 29, 141, 142, 365 et seq.

R.S. 9:335.

§ 315.23. Suspension or modification of child support obligation; secreting of child

If one joint custodial parent or his agent is intentionally secreting a child with the intent to preclude the other joint custodial parent from knowing the whereabouts of the child sufficiently to allow him to exercise his rights or duties as joint custodial parent, the latter may obtain from the court an order suspending or modifying his obligation under an order or judgment of child support. However, such circumstances shall not constitute a defense to an action for failure to pay court-ordered child support or an action to enforce past due child support.

Added by Acts 1993, No. 261, § 7, eff. Jan. 1, 1994.

Cross References

C.C. arts. 105, 131, 141, 142, 227, 240.

§ 315.24. Child support enforcement; revocatory and oblique actions

A. A party to whom child support is owed, including the Department of Children and Family Services when rendering child support enforcement services, may seek enforcement of a child support obligation by any lawful means provided by law, including the use of a revocatory or oblique action brought pursuant to the provisions of Civil Code Article 2036 et seq.

B. In cases wherein the Department of Children and Family Services is providing support enforcement services and has reason to believe that an obligor acted or failed to act in such a way that caused or increased his insolvency, the department shall seek either of the following:

(1) To institute a revocatory or oblique action in a court of competent jurisdiction to annul an act or exercise a right of the obligor which caused or increased the insolvency.

(2) To obtain a settlement in the best interest of the child support obligee.

Added by Acts 1997, No. 1246, § 1, eff. July 1, 1997.

§ 315.25. Consideration of custody or visitation matters

In any proceeding for child support, either party may raise any issue relating to custody of the child, or visitation with the child, or both, and the court may hear and determine that issue if all parties consent. The custody or visitation matter need not be specifically pleaded for the party to raise the issue or for the court to decide the issue.

Added by Acts 1999, No. 447, § 1.

§ 315.26. Collection of past due child support

A. In addition to any other legal remedies provided by law, any party may seek the collection of past due child support from federal tax refunds by sending notice to the federal secretary of the treasury that a person owes past due support. The party shall comply with all rules and regulations imposed by the secretary of the treasury and by the federal secretary of health and human services, including payment of any fee assessed by the secretary of the treasury for the cost of applying the offset procedure.

B. As used in this Part, "past due child support" means the amount of a delinquency determined under a court order under state law for support and maintenance of a child.

C. A court in a civil proceeding has jurisdiction to render a judgment for past due support which has accrued under a civil court order for support and also has limited jurisdiction to render a judgment for past due support which has accrued under any criminal or juvenile court order for support.

Added by Acts 2006, No. 478, § 1, eff. June 22, 2006.

SUBPART C. JUDICIAL SUSPENSION OF LICENSE FOR NONPAYMENT OF CHILD SUPPORT OR CONTEMPT OF COURT IN CHILD SUPPORT OR PATERNITY PROCEEDINGS

Redesignation

Acts 1995, No. 751, § 1, effective on the general effective date of August 15, 1995, and Acts 1995, No. 1078, § 1, effective January 1, 1996, both enacted this Subpart. The Louisiana State Law Institute initially directed that the text of Act 1078 be printed as live text and the text of Act 751 be printed in note type and shown as being effective from August 15, 1995, to January 1, 1996. Upon reconsideration, the Louisiana State Law Institute directed that Subpart C as enacted by Act 751 be redesignated as Subpart D, "Administrative Suspension of Certain Licenses for Nonpayment of Child Support", consisting of R.S. 9:315.40 to 9:315.48 as redesignated from R.S. 9:315.30 to 9:315.38. The Louisiana State Law Institute also revised the heading of Subpart C by inserting "Judicial" preceding "Suspension".

§ 315.30. Family financial responsibility; purpose

The legislature finds and declares that child support is a basic legal right of the state's parents and children, that mothers and fathers have a legal obligation to provide financial support for their children, and that child support payments can have a substantial impact on child poverty and state welfare expenditures. It is therefore the legislature's intent to facilitate the establishment of paternity and child support orders and encourage payment of child support to decrease overall costs to the state's taxpayers while increasing the amount of financial support collected for the state's children. To this end, the courts of this state are authorized to suspend certain licenses of individuals who are found to be in contempt of court for failure to comply with a subpoena or warrant in a child support or paternity proceeding or who are not in compliance with a court order of child support. Added by Acts 1995, No. 1078, § 1, eff. Jan. 1, 1996. Amended by Acts 1997, No. 1249, § 1, eff. July 1, 1997.

§ 315.31. Definitions

As used in this Subpart:

(1) "Board" means any agency, board, commission, or office, public or private, that issues any license for activity specified in Paragraph (6) of this Section.

(2) "Compliance with an order of support" means that the support obligor is no more than ninety days in arrears in making payments in full for current support or in making periodic payments as set forth in a court order of support, and has obtained or maintained health insurance coverage if required by an order of support.

(3) "Contempt of court" means that a person has been found guilty of a direct contempt of court for a contumacious failure to comply with a subpoena, pursuant to Code of Civil Procedure Article 222(5), or a constructive contempt of court for willful disobedience of a lawful order of the court, pursuant to Code of Civil Procedure Article 224(2), in or ancillary to a child support or paternity proceeding.

(4) "Court" means any court exercising jurisdiction over the determination of child support, paternity, or criminal neglect of family proceedings.

(5) "Department" means the Department of Children and Family Services when rendering child support enforcement services in TANF or non–TANF cases.

(6) "License" means any license, certification, registration, permit, approval, or other similar document evidencing admission to or granting authority for any of the following:

(a) To engage in a profession, occupation, business, or industry.

(b) To operate a motor vehicle.

(c) To participate in any sporting activity, including fishing and hunting.

(7) "Licensee" means any individual holding a license, certification, registration, permit, approval, or other similar document evidencing admission to or granting authority to engage in any activity specified in Paragraph (6) hereof. The term "licensee" may be used interchangeably with "obligor".

(8) "Obligee" means any person to whom an award of child support is owed and may include the department.

(9) "Obligor" means any individual legally obligated to support a child or children pursuant to an order of support. The term "obligor" may be used interchangeably with "licensee".

(10) "Order of support" means any judgment or order for the support of dependent children issued by any court of this state or another state, including any judgment or order issued in accordance with an administrative procedure established by state law that affords substantial due process and is subject to judicial review.

(11) "Suspension" means a temporary revocation of a license for an indefinite period of time or the denial of an application for issuance or renewal of a license.

Added by Acts 1995, No. 1078, § 1, eff. Jan. 1, 1996. Amended by Acts 1997, No. 1249, § 1, eff. July 1, 1997.

§ 315.32. Order of suspension of license; noncompliance with support order; contempt of court

A. (1)(a) In or ancillary to any action to make past-due child support executory, for contempt of court for failure to comply with an order of support, or a criminal neglect of family proceeding, the court on its own motion or upon motion of an obligee or the department shall, unless the court determines good cause exists, issue an order of suspension of a license or licenses of any obligor who is not in compliance with an order of child support. The court shall give specific written and oral reasons supporting its determination of good cause including a finding as to the particular facts and circumstances that warrant a determination not to suspend a license or licenses of an obligor who is not in compliance with an order of child support. The reasons shall become part of the record of the proceeding.

(b) An order suspending a license to operate a motor vehicle may provide specific time periods for the suspension at the court's discretion.

(2) In or ancillary to any child support or paternity proceeding, the court on its own motion or upon motion of any party or the department may issue an order of suspension of a license of any person who is guilty of contempt of court for failure to comply with a subpoena or warrant. Provided that before the issuance of an order for a suspension of a license of any person in, or ancillary to, any paternity proceeding where paternity has not yet been established, the court shall notify such person by personal service.

B. The order of suspension shall contain the name, address, and social security number of the obligor, if known, and shall indicate whether the suspension is for a particular, specified license, or all licenses which the obligor may possess, or any combination thereof at the discretion of the court.

C. An order of suspension may include a provision whereby the obligor is required to disclose to the court information concerning the types of licenses which the obligor possesses, which written disclosure when attached to the order of suspension becomes a part thereof.

Added by Acts 1995, No. 1078, § 1, eff. Jan. 1, 1996. Amended by Acts 1997, No. 1249, § 1, eff. July 1, 1997; Acts 1999, No. 559, § 1, eff. July 1, 1999.

§ 315.33. Suspension of license; notice of suspension from licensing board; temporary license

A. Within thirty days of receipt of a certified order of suspension of license for noncompliance with an order of support or contempt of court, sent by first class mail from either the court or the attorney representing the obligee, the board shall suspend all licenses which it issued to the obligor, or other person in contempt, or a particular license as specified in the order.

B. The board shall specify an exact date and hour of suspension, which date shall be within thirty days from the board's receipt of the order of suspension, and shall promptly issue a notice of suspension informing the licensee of all of the following:

(1) His license has been suspended by order of the court, including the suit name, docket number, and court as indicated on the order.

(2) The effective date of the suspension.

(3) To apply for reinstatement, the obligor must obtain an order of compliance from the court.

(4) Any other information prescribed by the board.

C. Upon being presented with a court order of partial compliance and at the request of an obligor whose motor vehicle operator's license, permit, or privilege has been suspended under this Subpart, the office of motor vehicles may issue the obligor a temporary license valid for a period not to exceed one hundred twenty days.

Added by Acts 1995, No. 1078, § 1, eff. Jan. 1, 1996. Amended by Acts 1997, No. 1249, § 1, eff. July 1, 1997.

§ 315.34. Subsequent compliance; order of compliance; order of partial compliance

A. (1) An obligor is in subsequent compliance with an order of support when all of the following occur:

(a) The obligor is up to date with current child support payments.

(b) All past-due support has been paid or, if periodic payment for past-due support has been ordered by the court, the obligor is making such payments in accordance with the court order.

(c) The obligor has fulfilled the required health insurance provisions, if any, in the order of support.

(2) A person is in subsequent compliance with a subpoena or court order when the court rescinds the order of contempt.

B. (1) Upon motion of an obligor who is in subsequent compliance with an order of support and after a contradictory hearing or upon rescission of an order of contempt, the court shall issue an order of compliance indicating that the obligor is eligible to have all licenses reissued. In cases where the department is providing support enforcement services, the court shall issue an ex parte order of compliance upon filing of written certification by the department that the obligor is in compliance.

(2) At the request of an obligor or other individual for whom an undue financial hardship will occur or has occurred as a result of the loss of his driver's license and upon a showing of good faith, the court may issue an order of partial compliance authorizing the issuance of a temporary license in accordance with R.S. 9:315.33(C).

Added by Acts 1995, No. 1078, § 1, eff. Jan. 1, 1996. Amended by Acts 1997, No. 1249, § 1, eff. July 1, 1997; Acts 1999, No. 559, § 1, eff. July 1, 1999.

§ 315.35. Reissuance of license

A. A board shall issue, reissue, renew, or otherwise extend an obligor's or other individual's license in accordance with the board's rules upon receipt of a certified copy of an order of compliance from the court.

B. After receipt of an order of compliance, the board may waive any of its applicable requirements for issuance, reissuance, renewal, or extension if it determines that the imposition of that requirement places an undue burden on the person and that waiver of the requirement is consistent with the public interest.

Added by Acts 1995, No. 1078, § 1, eff. Jan. 1, 1996. Amended by Acts 1997, No. 1249, § 1, eff. July 1, 1997.

§ 315.36. Suspension of license; pattern of nonpayment

Notwithstanding any other provisions to the contrary in this Subpart, the court on its own motion or upon motion of an obligee or the department shall issue an order of suspension of a license or licenses of any obligor upon proof of a pattern of nonpayment evidenced by his failure to pay child support on a regular basis, the remittance of payments of support only after continuous requests or legal action by or on behalf of the obligee, or the remittance of a de minimis amount of the child support owed.

Added by Acts 2003, No. 622, § 1.

§§ 315.37, 315.38. [Blank]

SUBPART D. ADMINISTRATIVE SUSPENSION OF CERTAIN LICENSES FOR NONPAYMENT OF CHILD SUPPORT

Redesignation

Acts 1995, No. 751, § 1, effective on the general effective date of August 15, 1995, and Acts 1995, No. 1078, § 1, eff. January 1, 1996, both enacted a Subpart designated as Subpart C. The Louisiana State Law Institute originally directed that the text of Act 1078 be printed as live text and the text of Act 751 be printed in note type and shown as being effective from August 15, 1995, to January 1, 1996. Upon reconsideration, the Louisiana State Law Institute directed that Subpart C as enacted by Act 751 be redesignated as Subpart D, consisting of R.S. 9:315.40 to 9:315.48 as redesignated from 9:315.30 to 9:315.38. The Louisiana State Law also revised the heading of Subpart D by substituting "Administrative Suspension" for "Revocation" at the beginning of the heading.

§ 315.40. Definitions

As used in this Subpart:

(1) "Administrator" means the administrator of the child support enforcement section, office of children and family services, Department of Children and Family Services.

(2) "Compliance with an order of support" means that the support obligor is no more than ninety days in arrears in making payments in full for current support, or in making periodic payments on a support arrearage pursuant to a court order or written agreement with the department, or in making periodic payments as set forth in a court order of support, and has obtained or maintained health insurance coverage if required by an order of support.

(3) "Department" means the Department of Children and Family Services, office of children and family services.

(4) "License" means any license, certification, registration, permit, approval, or other similar document evidencing admission to or granting authority for any of the following:

(a) To engage in a profession, occupation, business, or industry.

(b) To operate a motor vehicle. For purposes of this Subpart, a license to operate a motor vehicle shall also include the license plate for any vehicle registered in the name of any obligor, as well as the registration for such vehicle.

(c) To participate in any sporting activity, including fishing and hunting.

(d) To operate a motorboat, a sailboat, or a trailer.

(5) "Licensee" means any individual holding a license, certificate, registration, permit, approval, or other similar document evidencing admission to or granting authority to engage in any activity specified in Paragraph (4) of this section. The term "licensee" may be used interchangeably with "obligor".

(6) "Licensing authority" means any state board, commission, department, agency, officer, or other entity which issues, authorizes, or otherwise regulates licenses as defined in Paragraph (4) of this Section.

(7) "Obligor" means any individual legally obligated to support a child or children pursuant to an order of support. The term "obligor" may be used interchangeably with "licensee".

(8) "Order of support" means any judgment or order for the support of dependent children issued by any court of this state or another state, including any judgment or order issued in accordance with an administrative procedure established by state law that affords substantial due process and is subject to judicial review.

(9) "Suspension" means a temporary revocation of a license for an indefinite period of time or the denial of an application for issuance or renewal of a license. With respect to a motor vehicle, personal watercraft, motorboat, sailboat, all-terrain vehicle or trailer, "suspension" includes a temporary suspension of the registration, including the seizure of the vehicle license plate, trailer license plate, or a certificate of identification or registration of a motorboat or sailboat for an indefinite period of time or the denial of an application for issuance or renewal of a registration or license plate.

Added by Acts 1995, No. 751, § 1. Amended by Acts 2001, No. 612, § 1, eff. June 22, 2001; Acts 2003, No. 1068, § 1, eff. July 2, 2003; Acts 2004, No. 319, § 1; Acts 2004, No. 652, § 1; Acts 2012, No. 255, § 2.

§ 315.41. Notice of child support delinquency; suspension of license

A. The department may send by certified mail, return receipt requested, a notice of child support delinquency to an obligor who is not in compliance with an order of support informing the obligor of the department's intention to submit his name to the licensing authority for suspension of his license. If an obligor holds multiple licenses, the department may issue a single notice of its intention to submit multiple suspensions. When the obligor has one or more motor vehicles, personal watercraft, motorboats, sailboats, all-terrain vehicles or trailers registered in his name, the notice shall inform the obligor of the department's intention to suspend the registration of all of them as well. A non-obligor spouse who uses any such vehicle may so inform the department by notarized affidavit, and thereby retain the use of that vehicle and its license.

B. A notice of child support delinquency shall include all of the following:

(1) A summary of the obligor's right to file a written objection to the suspension of his license, including the time within which such objection must be filed and the address where the objection must be filed.

(2) A brief description of the administrative hearing and location of such hearing if the obligor timely files a written objection.

(3) The municipal address and telephone number of the department that issued the notice of child support delinquency.

(4) The docket number and court which issued the order of support.

(5) A statement of the amount of past-due support.

(6) A brief summary of what the obligor must do to come into compliance or to forestall the suspension.

Added by Acts 1995, No. 751, § 1. Amended by Acts 2001, No. 612, § 1, eff. June 22, 2001; Acts 2004, No. 319, § 1.

§ 315.42. Objection to suspension of license

A. Within twenty days after receipt of the notice of child support delinquency, the obligor may file a written objection with the department requesting an administrative hearing to determine whether the obligor is in compliance with an order of support.

B. If the obligor does not timely file a written objection or enter into a written agreement with the department to make periodic payments on a support arrearage and he is not in compliance with an order of support, the department shall certify the obligor's noncompliance to the licensing authority for license suspension.

Added by Acts 1995, No. 751, § 1. Amended by Acts 2001, No. 612, § 1, eff. June 22, 2001.

§ 315.43. Administrative hearing

Upon receipt of a timely written objection, the department shall conduct an administrative hearing in accordance with the Administrative Procedure Act. Such hearing may be conducted telephonically or by means of any other such electronic media. The sole issue at the administrative hearing shall be whether the obligor is in compliance with an order of support.

Added by Acts 1995, No. 751, § 1. Amended by Acts 2001, No. 612, § 1, eff. June 22, 2001.

§ 315.44. Certification of noncompliance

A. The department may certify in writing to the licensing authority that a licensee is not in compliance with an order of support in the event of any of the following:

(1) The obligor has not timely filed an objection to the notice of child support delinquency, he is not in compliance with an order of support, and more than twenty days have passed after service of the notice of child support delinquency.

(2) The obligor has timely filed an objection to the notice of child support delinquency and an adverse decision or order was issued after the administrative hearing, rehearing, or judicial review and all legal delays have lapsed.

(3) The department receives a certified copy of a final judgment in an action to make executory past-due payments under a child support award and the judgment specifically provides for the suspension or revocation of the obligor's license.

(4) The department receives a certified copy of a final judgment or order finding the obligor to be in violation of R.S. 14:74, Criminal neglect of family.

B. An obligor is not entitled to the notice of child support delinquency, required by R.S. 9:315.41, when certification of noncompliance is pursuant to Paragraph A(3) or (4) of this Section.

Added by Acts 1995, No. 751, § 1. Amended by Acts 2001, No. 612, § 1, eff. June 22, 2001.

§ 315.45. Suspension of license; notice of suspension from licensing authority

A. Within thirty days after receipt of a certification of noncompliance from the department, the licensing authority shall suspend the license of all licensees named therein and notify each licensee that his license has been suspended because of noncompliance with an order of support.

B. The licensing authority shall specify a date of suspension, which date shall be within thirty days from the licensing authority's receipt of the order of suspension and shall promptly issue a notice of suspension informing the licensee of all of the following:

(1) His license has been suspended by administrative order for noncompliance with an order of support, including a copy of the certification of nonsupport. However, the office of motor vehicles is not required to include a copy of the certification of nonsupport in its notice of suspension.

(2) The effective date of the suspension.

(3) To apply for reinstatement, the obligor must obtain a compliance release from the department.

(4) Any other information prescribed by the licensing authority.

C. (1) When the license to be suspended is for the operation of a motor vehicle, except for a Class A, Class B, or Class C license, the department may recommend that the suspension be restricted to specific time periods to allow the obligor to travel to and from his place of employment. Upon receipt of such a recommendation with the certification of noncompliance, the office of motor vehicles shall suspend the license for the specific time periods recommended, as provided in Subsection B of this section.

(2) When the suspension involves the registration or license plate of a motor vehicle, the licensing authority shall suspend the registration or seize the license plate, in the same manner as suspensions under R.S. 32:863 et seq.

D. (1) In cases wherein the obligor is an attorney licensed to practice law in this state, a judgment or order indicating noncompliance with an order of support shall be mailed to the state supreme court and the Louisiana State Bar Association.

(2) The legislature hereby recognizes the judicial power vested in the state supreme court pursuant to Article V, Section 1 of the Constitution of Louisiana and, accordingly, urges and requests the supreme court to adopt rules and regulations affecting the suspension of licenses to practice law consistent with the provisions of this Chapter.

Added by Acts 1995, No. 751, § 1. Amended by Acts 2001, No. 612, § 1, eff. June 22, 2001; Acts 2003, No. 947, § 1.

§ 315.46. Subsequent compliance with support order; compliance and partial compliance releases

A. An obligor is in subsequent compliance with an order of support when all of the following occur:

(1) The obligor is up to date with current child support payments.

(2) All past-due support has been paid or either of the following has occurred:

(a) If periodic payment for past-due support has been ordered by the court, the obligor is making such payments in accordance with the court order.

(b) If periodic payment has not been ordered by the court and the obligor is unable to pay all past-due support, the obligor is making periodic payments pursuant to and in accordance with the terms of a written agreement entered into with the department.

(3) The obligor has fulfilled the required health insurance provisions, if any, in the order of support.

B. At the request of an obligor who is in subsequent compliance with an order of support, the department shall issue a compliance release certificate indicating that the obligor is eligible to have his license reissued.

C. At the request of an obligor who provides evidence of his ability to comply with the support order and who enters into a written agreement with the department, the department may issue a certificate of partial compliance requesting that the suspension be lifted or modified. The secretary of the department shall have the authority to promulgate rules and regulations and take such action as may be necessary to implement the provisions of this Section.

Added by Acts 1995, No. 751, § 1. Amended by Acts 2012, No. 613, § 1.

§ 315.47. Reissuance of license

The licensing authority shall issue, reissue, renew, or otherwise extend an obligor's license, in accordance with any applicable reinstatement fees or applicable rules, upon receipt of a certified copy of a compliance or partial compliance release from the department.

Added by Acts 1995, No. 751, § 1. Amended by Acts 2001, No. 612, § 1, eff. June 22, 2001; Acts 2012, No. 613, § 1.

§ 315.48. Repealed by Acts 2001, No. 612, § 3, eff. June 22, 2001

PART II. SPOUSAL SUPPORT

§ 321. Retroactivity of judgment concerning spousal support

A. Except for good cause shown, a judgment awarding, modifying, or revoking an interim spousal support allowance shall be retroactive to the date of judicial demand.

B. (1) A judgment that initially awards or denies final spousal support is effective as of the date the judgment is rendered and terminates an interim spousal support allowance as of that date.

(2) If an interim spousal support allowance award is not in effect on the date of the judgment awarding final spousal support, the judgment shall be retroactive to the date of judicial demand, except for good cause shown.

C. Except for good cause shown, a judgment modifying or revoking a final spousal support judgment shall be retroactive to the date of judicial demand.

D. Spousal support of any kind, except that paid pursuant to an interim allowance award, provided by the debtor from the date of judicial demand to the date the support judgment is rendered, to or on behalf of the spouse for whom support is ordered, shall be credited to the debtor against the amount of the judgment.

E. In the event that the court finds good cause for not making the award retroactive to the date of judicial demand, the court may fix the date on which the award shall commence.

F. A judgment extinguishing an obligation of spousal support owed to a person who has cohabited with another person of either sex in the manner of married persons shall be retroactive to the date of judicial demand.

Acts 1997, No. 1078, § 2, eff. Jan. 1, 1998.

Cross References

C.C. arts. 3299, 3521.

R.S. 9:2721.

§ 322. Judgment or order for support not to be recorded

It is unlawful for any recorder of mortgages in the state of Louisiana to record a judgment or order for spousal or child support by any court, and if such a judgment or order is recorded, it shall not have the effect of a judicial mortgage and shall be forthwith canceled by the clerk upon demand, in writing, by the party against whom it is rendered, without charge, except as provided in R.S. 13:4291.

Acts 1997, No. 1078, § 2, eff. Jan. 1, 1998.

Cross References

C.C. arts. 112, 3299.

§ 323. Recordation of judgment or order for amount due

A recorder of mortgages shall record, at the request of any person in interest, a judgment or order for spousal or child support for the amount that the court has decreed to be due and executory, which judgment or order shall be a judicial mortgage in the amount only found to be due, together with costs and interest.

Acts 1997, No. 1078, § 2, eff. Jan. 1, 1998.

Cross References

C.C. arts. 112, 3299.

§ 324. Cancellation of record following payment

A recorder of mortgages shall forthwith cancel and erase from his records any judgment or order recorded in his office as provided in R.S. 9:323 upon the order of the person in whose favor said judgment or order was rendered or upon proper evidence showing payment in full by the person against whom said judgment or order was rendered.

Acts 1997, No. 1078, § 2, eff. Jan. 1, 1998.

Cross References

C.C. arts. 112, 3299.

§ 325. Collection of past due spousal support

A. In addition to any other legal remedies provided by law, any party may seek the collection of past due spousal support from federal tax refunds by sending notice to the federal secretary of the treasury that a person owes past due support. The party shall comply with all rules and regulations imposed by the secretary of the treasury and by the federal secretary of health and human services, including payment of any fee assessed by the secretary of the treasury for the cost of applying the offset procedure.

B. As used in this Part, "past due spousal support" means the amount of a delinquency determined under a court order under state law for support and maintenance of a spouse.

C. A court in a civil proceeding has jurisdiction to render a judgment for past due spousal support which has accrued under a civil court order for support.

Added by Acts 2006, No. 478, § 1, eff. June 22, 2006.

§ 326. Determination of income for spousal support; evidence

A. Each party shall provide to the court a verified income statement showing gross income and adjusted gross income, together with documentation of current and past earnings. Suitable documentation of current earnings shall include but not be limited to pay stubs or employer statements. The documentation shall include a copy of the party's most recent federal tax return. A copy of the statement and documentation shall be provided to the other party. When an obligor has an ownership interest in a business, suitable documentation shall include but is not limited to the last three personal and business state and federal income tax returns, including all attachments and all schedules, specifically Schedule K–1 and W–2 forms, 1099 forms, and amendments, the most recent profit and loss statements, balance sheets, financial statements, quarterly sales tax reports, personal and business bank account statements, receipts, and expenses. A copy of all statements and documentation shall be provided to the other party.

B. When a party alleges that income is being concealed or underreported, the court shall admit evidence relevant to establishing the actual income of the party, including but not limited to all of the following:

(1) Redirected income. (a) Loans to the obligor by a business in which the obligor has an ownership interest and whether the loans will be repaid. There shall be a presumption that the loans are income of the obligor which may be rebutted if the obligor demonstrates there is a history of similar past loans being made and repaid in a timely manner with market interest rates, or the current loan is at market interest rates and is fully paid in accordance with a commercially reasonable time. The amount by which a commercially reasonable repayment amount exceeds the amount actually repaid shall be treated as income.

(b) Payment made by the obligor or by a business in which the obligor has an ownership interest to a person related by blood or affinity in the form of wages or salary. There shall be a presumption that the payments are income of the obligor, which may be rebutted if the obligor demonstrates there is a history of payments preceding the separation of the parties or the filing of an action to establish or modify spousal support, or that the payments are fair market value for services actually performed.

(2) **Deferred income.** Recent reductions in distributions of income, such as salary, bonuses, dividends, or management fees as a percentage of gross income of the business of the obligor. There shall be a presumption that past distributions of income will continue, which may be rebutted if the obligor demonstrates business conditions justify a reduction in distributions.

(3) **Standard of living and assets.** The current standard of living and assets of the obligor both prior and subsequent to the establishment of a spousal support order, to establish the actual income if the amount claimed is inconsistent with his lifestyle.

C. When the income of an obligor cannot be sufficiently established, evidence of wage and earnings surveys distributed by government agencies for the purpose of attributing income to the obligor is admissible.

Added by Acts 2009, No. 378, § 1.

Comment—2010

[Acts 2009, No. 378, amended R.S. 9:315.2(A) and enacted R.S. 9:315.1.1 and 9:326. The Act was not presented on recommendation of the Louisiana State Law Institute. Section 2 of the Act directed the Law Institute to prepare comments.]

(a) Subsection A of this Section is almost identical to R.S. 9:315.2(A) (child support). It provides a detailed documentation for purposes of establishing income of the parties for spousal support, especially for a spouse who has an ownership interest in a business.

(b) Likewise, Subsection B of this Section is virtually identical to R.S. 9:315.1.1(A) which addresses the evidence admissible to prove actual income when a spouse owns an interest in a business and the other spouse alleges that income is being concealed or underreported. *See* comments to R.S. 9:315.1.1(A) (2009).

Editor's note. Acts 2009, No. 378, amended R.S. 9:315.2(A) and enacted R.S. 9:315.1.1 and 326. Section 2 of that Act directed the Louisiana State Law Institute to prepare comments. The original recommendations came from the Louisiana Child Support Guidelines Review 2008 Quadrennial Report. These comments come from the Marriage-Persons Committee of the Louisiana State Law Institute.

§ 327. Repealed by Acts 1997, No. 1078, § 5, eff. Jan. 1, 1998

PART III. CHILD CUSTODY

SUBPART A. EVALUATION AND MEDIATION

§ 331. Custody or visitation proceeding; evaluation by mental health professional

A. The court may order an evaluation of a party or the child in a custody or visitation proceeding for good cause shown. The evaluation shall be made by a mental health professional selected by the parties or by the court. The court may render judgment for costs of the evaluation, or any part thereof, against any party or parties, as it may consider equitable.

B. The court may order a party or the child to submit to and cooperate in the evaluation, testing, or interview by the mental health professional. The mental health professional shall provide the court and the parties with a written report. The mental health professional shall serve as the witness of the court, subject to cross-examination by a party.

Acts 1993, No. 261, § 5, eff. Jan. 1, 1994.

Cross References

C.C. arts. 131 to 136, 141, 245.

C.C.P. arts. 74.2, 3943.

R.S. 9:335, 9:341 to 9:344, 9:364, 9:365, 9:387.

§ 331.1. Drug testing in custody or visitation proceeding

The court for good cause shown may, after a contradictory hearing, order a party in a custody or visitation proceeding to submit to specified drug tests and the collection of hair, urine, tissue, and blood samples as required by appropriate testing procedures within a time period set by the court. The refusal to submit to the tests may be taken into consideration by the court. The provisions of R.S. 9:397.2 and 397.3(A), (B), and (C) shall govern the admissibility of the test results. The fact that the court orders a drug test and the results of such test shall be confidential and shall not be admissible in any other proceedings. The court may render judgment for costs of the drug tests against any party or parties, as it may consider equitable.

Added by Acts 1999, No. 974, § 1.

§ 332. Custody or visitation proceeding; mediation

A. The court may order the parties to mediate their differences in a custody or visitation proceeding. The mediator may be agreed upon by the parties or, upon their failure to agree, selected by the court. The court may stay any further determination of custody or visitation for a period not to exceed thirty days from the date of issuance of such an order. The court may order the costs of mediation to be paid in advance by either party or both parties jointly. The court may apportion the costs of the mediation between the parties if agreement is reached on custody or visitation. If mediation concludes without agreement between the parties, the costs of mediation shall be taxed as costs of court. The costs of mediation shall be subject to approval by the court.

B. If an agreement is reached by the parties, the mediator shall prepare a written, signed, and dated agreement. A consent judgment incorporating the agreement shall be submitted to the court for its approval.

C. Evidence of conduct or statements made in mediation is not admissible in any proceeding. This rule does not require the exclusion of any evidence otherwise discoverable merely because it is presented in the course of mediation. Facts disclosed, other than conduct or statements made in mediation, are not inadmissible by virtue of first having been disclosed in mediation.

Acts 1993, No. 261, § 5, eff. Jan. 1, 1994.

Cross References

C.C. arts. 131 to 136, 141, 245.

R.S. 9:335, 9:341 to 9:344, 9:363, 9:387.

§ 333. Duties of mediator

A. The mediator shall assist the parties in formulating a written, signed, and dated agreement to mediate which shall identify the controversies between the parties, affirm the parties' intent to resolve these controversies through mediation, and specify the circumstances under which the mediation may terminate.

B. The mediator shall advise each of the parties participating in the mediation to obtain review by an attorney of any agreement reached as a result of the mediation prior to signing such an agreement.

C. The mediator shall be impartial and has no power to impose a solution on the parties.

Acts 1993, No. 261, § 5, eff. Jan. 1, 1994.

Cross References

C.C. arts. 131 to 136.
R.S. 9:363, 9:387.

§ 334. Mediator qualifications

A. In order to serve as a qualified mediator under the provisions of this Subpart, a person shall meet all of the following criteria:

(1)(a) Possess a four-year college degree and complete a minimum of forty hours of general mediation training and twenty hours of specialized training in the mediation of child custody disputes; or

(b) Possess a four-year college degree and hold a license as an attorney, psychiatrist, psychologist, social worker, marriage and family counselor, professional counselor, or clergyman and complete a minimum of twelve hours of general mediation training and twenty hours of specialized training in the mediation of child custody disputes.

(2) Complete a minimum of eight hours of co-mediation training under the direct supervision of a mediator who is qualified in accordance with the provisions of Paragraph (B)(1) of this Section and who has served a minimum of fifty hours as a dispute mediator.

B. (1) Mediators who prior to August 15, 1997, satisfied the provisions of Paragraph (A)(1) of this Section and served a minimum of fifty hours as a child custody dispute mediator are not required to complete eight hours of co-mediation training in order to serve as a qualified mediator and are qualified to supervise co-mediation training as provided in Paragraph (A)(2) of this Section.

(2) Any person who has served as a Louisiana city, parish, family, juvenile, district, appellate, or supreme court judge for at least ten years, and who is no longer serving as a judge shall be deemed qualified to serve as a mediator if:

(a) The former judge has actually served as a judge in a family court of record or statutory family court for at least three years and completes a minimum of twelve hours of general mediation training; or

(b) The former judge completes at least twenty hours of specialized mediation training in child custody and visitation disputes.

C. The training specified in Paragraph (A)(1) of this Section shall include instruction as to the following:

(1) The Louisiana judicial system and judicial procedure in domestic cases.

(2) Ethical standards, including confidentiality and conflict of interests.

(3) Child development, including the impact of divorce on development.

(4) Family systems theory.

(5) Communication skills.

(6) The mediation process and required document execution.

D. A dispute mediator initially qualified under the provisions of this Subpart shall, in order to remain qualified, complete a minimum of twenty hours of clinical education in dispute mediation every two calendar years.

E. A mediator shall furnish satisfactory evidence of his qualifications upon request.

F. The Louisiana State Bar Association, Alternative Dispute Resolution Section, may promulgate rules and regulations governing dispute mediator registration and qualifications and may establish a fee not to exceed one hundred dollars for registration sufficient to cover associated costs. A person denied listing in the approved register may request a review of that decision by a panel of three members of the Louisiana State Bar Association Alternative Dispute Resolution Section.

G. For the purposes of this Section, an "hour" means a period of at least sixty minutes of actual instruction.

Added by Acts 1995, No. 287, § 1. Amended by Acts 1997, No. 1144, § 1; Acts 1999, No. 713, § 1, eff. July 1, 1999; Acts 2004, No. 25, § 1; Acts 2006, No. 471, § 1; Acts 2008, No. 631, § 1.

SUBPART B. JOINT CUSTODY

§ 335. Joint custody decree and implementation order

A. (1) In a proceeding in which joint custody is decreed, the court shall render a joint custody implementation order except for good cause shown.

(2)(a) The implementation order shall allocate the time periods during which each parent shall have physical custody of the child so that the child is assured of frequent and continuing contact with both parents.

(b) To the extent it is feasible and in the best interest of the child, physical custody of the children should be shared equally.

(3) The implementation order shall allocate the legal authority and responsibility of the parents.

B. (1) In a decree of joint custody the court shall designate a domiciliary parent except when there is an implementation order to the contrary or for other good cause shown.

(2) The domiciliary parent is the parent with whom the child shall primarily reside, but the other parent shall have physical custody during time periods that assure that the child has frequent and continuing contact with both parents.

(3) The domiciliary parent shall have authority to make all decisions affecting the child unless an implementation order provides otherwise. All major decisions made by the domiciliary parent concerning the child shall be subject to review by the court upon motion of the other parent. It shall be presumed that all major decisions made by the domiciliary parent are in the best interest of the child.

C. If a domiciliary parent is not designated in the joint custody decree and an implementation order does not pro-

vide otherwise, joint custody confers upon the parents the same rights and responsibilities as are conferred on them by the provisions of Title VII of Book I of the Civil Code.
Acts 1993, No. 261, § 5, eff. Jan. 1, 1994. Amended by Acts 1993, No. 905, § 1; Acts 1995, No. 463, § 1.

Editor's note. Acts 1993, No. 905, § 1 amended Article 131(D) of the Louisiana Civil Code, effective August 15, 1993. Acts 1993, No. 261, effective January 1, 1994, amended and re-enacted Article 131 of the Civil Code and R.S. 9:305.

Acts 1993, No. 261, revised Book I, Title V, Chapter 2, Section 3, formerly containing Articles 131 to 135, to comprise new Articles 131 to 136, effective January 1, 1994. Ordinarily, revision implies a legislative intent to substitute the new legislation in the place of the old, in toto. It would seem, therefore, that the legislature intended, effective January 1, 1994, to replace old Articles 131 to 135, as they may have been amended, by new Articles 131 to 136.

However, argument may be made that, since Acts 1993, No. 905, was enacted last, in case of conflict its provisions prevail over those of Acts 1993, No. 261. See C.C. art. 8. The question of whether Acts 1993, No. 905 and Acts 1993, No. 261, are in conflict or fully reconcilable is a matter of interpretation of laws. Generally, "the repeal of a statute by implication is not favored .... Moreover, where two acts relating to the same subject are passed at the same legislative session, there is a strong presumption against implied repeal, and they are to be construed together, if possible, so as to reconcile them, giving effect to each." Chappuis v. Reggie, 222 La. 35, 62 So. 92, 95 (1952).

It appears that the only substantial difference between Article 131(D), as amended by Acts 1993, No. 905, § 1, and R.S. 9:335, as amended and re-enacted by Acts 1993, No. 261, § 5 is the sentence, "To the extent feasible, physical custody of the children shall be shared equally." This sentence is found in Acts 1993, No. 905, § 1 only. Acting under the authority of R.S. 24:252(B), the Louisiana State Law Institute has transferred the quoted sentence to R.S. 9:335, apparently on the assumption that a reconciliation between the two acts is possible.

Cross References

C.C. arts. 99, 131 to 136, 141, 215 et seq., 245.

R.S. 9:331 to 9:333, 9:341 to 9:344, 9:387.

§ 336. Obligation of joint custodians to confer

Joint custody obligates the parents to exchange information concerning the health, education, and welfare of the child and to confer with one another in exercising decision-making authority.
Acts 1993, No. 261, § 5, eff. Jan. 1, 1994.

Cross References

C.C. arts. 99, 131 to 136, 220, 227.

R.S. 9:335, 9:387.

§ 337. Repealed by Acts 2001, No. 1082, § 3

Editor's note. Acts 2001, No. 1082, § 5, declares that this Act applies to actions concerning child support filed after August 15, 2001.

SUBPART C. PROTECTIVE AND REMEDIAL PROVISIONS

§ 341. Restriction on visitation

A. Whenever the court finds by a preponderance of the evidence that a parent has subjected his or her child to physical abuse, sexual abuse or exploitation, or has permitted such abuse or exploitation of the child, the court shall prohibit visitation between the abusive parent and the abused child until such parent proves that visitation would not cause physical, emotional, or psychological damage to the child. Should visitation be allowed, the court shall order such restrictions, conditions, and safeguards necessary to minimize any risk of harm to the child. All costs incurred in compliance with the provisions of this Section shall be borne by the abusive parent.

B. When visitation has been prohibited by the court pursuant to Subsection A, and the court subsequently authorizes restricted visitation, the parent whose visitation has been restricted shall not remove the child from the jurisdiction of the court except for good cause shown and with the prior approval of the court.

Acts 1993, No. 261, § 5, eff. Jan. 1, 1994.

Cross References

C.C. arts. 131 to 136.

R.S. 9:331, 9:335, 9:342 to 9:345, 9:361 et seq., 9:387.

§ 342. Bond to secure child custody or visitation order

For good cause shown, a court may, on its own motion or upon the motion of any party, require the posting of a bond or other security by a party to insure compliance with a child visitation order and to indemnify the other party for the payment of any costs incurred.

Acts 1993, No. 261, § 5, eff. Jan. 1, 1994.

Cross References

C.C. arts. 105, 131 to 136.

R.S. 9:341, 9:343, 9:574, 9:387.

§ 343. Return of child kept in violation of custody and visitation order

A. Upon presentation of a certified copy of a custody and visitation rights order rendered by a court of this state, together with the sworn affidavit of the custodial parent, the judge, who shall have jurisdiction for the limited purpose of effectuating the remedy provided by this Section by virtue of either the presence of the child or litigation pending before the court, may issue a civil warrant directed to law enforcement authorities to return the child to the custodial parent pending further order of the court having jurisdiction over the matter.

B. The sworn affidavit of the custodial parent shall include all of the following:

(1) A statement that the custody and visitation rights order is true and correct.

(2) A summary of the status of any pending custody proceeding.

(3) The fact of the removal of or failure to return the child in violation of the custody and visitation rights order.

(4) A declaration that the custodial parent desires the child returned.

Acts 1993, No. 261, § 5, eff. Jan. 1, 1994.

Cross References

C.C. arts. 131 to 136.

R.S. 9:335, 9:387.

§ 344. Visitation rights of grandparents and siblings

A. If one of the parties to a marriage dies, is interdicted, or incarcerated, and there is a minor child or children of such marriage, the parents of the deceased, interdicted, or incarcerated party without custody of such minor child or children may have reasonable visitation rights to the child or children of the marriage during their minority, if the court in its discretion finds that such visitation rights would be in the best interest of the child or children.

B. When the parents of a minor child or children live in concubinage and one of the parents dies, or is incarcerated, the parents of the deceased or incarcerated party may have reasonable visitation rights to the child or children during their minority, if the court in its discretion finds that such visitation rights would be in the best interest of the child or children.

C. If one of the parties to a marriage dies or is incarcerated, the siblings of a minor child or children of the marriage may have reasonable visitation rights to such child or children during their minority if the court in its discretion finds that such visitation rights would be in the best interest of the child or children.

D. If the parents of a minor child of the marriage have lived apart for a period of six months, in extraordinary circumstances, the grandparents or siblings of the child may have reasonable visitation rights to the child during his minority, if the court in its discretion finds that such visitation rights would be in the best interest of the child. In determining the best interest of the child the court shall consider the same factors contained in Civil Code Article 136(D). Extraordinary circumstances shall include a determination by a court that a parent is abusing a controlled dangerous substance.

Acts 1993, No. 261, § 5, eff. Jan. 1, 1994. Amended by Acts 1999, No. 1352, § 1; Acts 2012, No. 763, § 2, eff. June 12, 2012.

Cross References

C.C. arts. 136, 238, 245.

R.S. 9:331 to 9:336, 9:341 to 9:343, 9:387.

§ 345. Appointment of attorney in child custody or visitation proceedings

A. In any child custody or visitation proceeding, the court, upon its own motion, upon motion of any parent or party, or upon motion of the child, may appoint an attorney to represent the child if, after a contradictory hearing, the court determines such appointment would be in the best interest of the child. In determining the best interest of the child, the court shall consider:

(1) Whether the child custody or visitation proceeding is exceptionally intense or protracted.

(2) Whether an attorney representing the child could provide the court with significant information not otherwise readily available or likely to be presented to the court.

(3) Whether there exists a possibility that neither parent is capable of providing an adequate and stable environment for the child.

(4) Whether the interests of the child and those of either parent, or of another party to the proceeding, conflict.

(5) Any other factor relevant in determining the best interest of the child.

B. The court shall appoint an attorney to represent the child if, in the contradictory hearing, any party presents a prima facie case that a parent or other person caring for the child has sexually, physically, or emotionally abused the child or knew or should have known that the child was being abused.

C. The order appointing an attorney to represent the child shall serve as his enrollment as counsel of record on behalf of the child.

D. Upon appointment as attorney for the child, the attorney shall interview the child, review all relevant records, and conduct discovery as deemed necessary to ascertain facts relevant to the child's custody or visitation.

E. The appointed attorney shall have the right to make any motion and participate in the custody or visitation hearing to the same extent as authorized for either parent.

F. Any costs associated with the appointment of an attorney at law shall be apportioned among the parties as the court deems just, taking into consideration the parties' ability to pay. When the parties' ability to pay is limited, the court shall attempt to secure proper representation without compensation.

Acts 1993, No. 261, § 5, eff. Jan. 1, 1994.

Cross References

C.C. arts. 131 to 136, 141, 142, 227, 240, 245.

R.S. 9:331, 9:341 to 9:344, 9:387.

§ 346. Action for failure to exercise or to allow visitation, custody or time rights pursuant to court-ordered schedule; judgment and awards

A. An action for the failure to exercise or to allow child visitation, custody or time rights pursuant to the terms of a court-ordered schedule may be instituted against a parent. The action shall be in the form of a rule to show cause why such parent should not be held in contempt for the failure and why the court should not further render judgment as provided in this Section.

B. If the action is for the failure to exercise child visitation, custody or time rights pursuant to the terms of a court-ordered schedule, and the petitioner is the prevailing party, the defendant shall be held in contempt of court and the court shall award to the petitioner:

(1) All costs for counseling for the child which may be necessitated by the defendant's failure to exercise visitation, custody or time rights with the child.

(2) A reasonable sum for any actual expenses incurred by the petitioner by reason of the failure of the defendant to exercise rights pursuant to a court-ordered visitation, custody or time schedule.

(3) A reasonable sum for a caretaker of the child, based upon the hourly rate for caretakers in the community.

(4) All attorney fees and costs of the proceeding.

C. If the action is for the failure to allow child custody, visitation, or time rights pursuant to a court-ordered schedule, and the petitioner is the prevailing party, the defendant shall be held in contempt of court and the court shall award to the petitioner:

(1) A reasonable sum for any actual expenses incurred by the petitioner by the loss of his visitation, custody or time rights.

(2) Additional visitation, custody or time rights with the child equal to the time lost.

(3) All attorney fees and costs of the proceeding.

(4) All costs for counseling for the child which may be necessitated by the defendant's failure to allow visitation, custody, or time rights with the child.

D. The court may award a reasonable penalty to the petitioner against the defendant upon a finding that the failure to allow or exercise visitation, time or custody rights pursuant to the terms of a court-ordered visitation schedule was intended to harass the petitioner.

E. The court may award attorney fees and costs to the defendant if he is the prevailing party, based upon actual expenses incurred.

F. The court may require the prevailing party to submit proof showing the amounts to be awarded pursuant to this Section.

G. It shall be a defense that the failure to allow or exercise child visitation rights pursuant to a court-ordered schedule was by mutual consent, beyond the control of the defendant, or for other good cause shown.

H. A pattern of willful and intentional violation of this Section, without good cause, may be grounds for a modification of a custody or visitation decree.

I. This Section applies to judicial orders involving sole or joint custody.

J. The action authorized by this Section shall be in addition to any other action authorized by law.

Added by Acts 2004, No. 519, § 1. Amended by Acts 2008, No. 671, § 2; Acts 2010, No. 277, § 1, eff. June 17, 2010.

§ 347. Repealed by Acts 2008, No. 671, § 3

§ 348. Loss of visitation due to military service; compensatory visitation

A. As used in this Section, "active duty" shall mean a military service member under any of the following conditions:

(1) A service member on active duty pursuant to an executive order of the president of the United States, an act of the Congress of the United States, presidential recall, or the provisions of R.S. 29:7.

(2) A service member on orders including but not limited to annual training, active duty special work, or individual duty training.

(3) A service member on drill status.

(4) A service member subject to the Uniform Code of Military Justice or the Louisiana Code of Military Justice.

B. (1) When a service member on active duty is unable due to his military obligations to have visitation with a minor child as authorized by a court order, the service member may request a period of compensatory visitation with the child which shall be granted only if the court determines it is in the best interest of the child. Such compensatory visitation shall be negotiated, on a day-for-day basis for each day missed, for the number of compensatory days requested by the service member, not to exceed the total number of days missed. The custodial or domiciliary parent shall negotiate with the service member to develop an equitable schedule for the requested compensatory visitation.

(2)(a) If the parents cannot establish an equitable arrangement for compensatory visitation as required by this Section, the requesting parent may petition the court having jurisdiction to enforce the judicial order for visitation for a temporary alteration to the current visitation order by making an adjustment to require compensatory visitation for visitation days lost as a result of an obligation of active duty. The court may refer the parent to mediation under the provisions of R.S. 9:332.

(b) The court may render judgment for court costs against either party or may apportion such costs between the parties as it may consider equitable.

C. The provisions of this Section shall not apply if either party has a history of physically or sexually abusing a child.

Added by Acts 2006, No. 110, § 1.

SUBPART D. ACCESS TO RECORDS

§ 351. Access to records of child

Notwithstanding any provision of law to the contrary, access to records and information pertaining to a minor child, including but not limited to medical, dental, and school records, shall not be denied to a parent solely because he is not the child's custodial or domiciliary parent.

Acts 1993, No. 261, § 5, eff. Jan. 1, 1994.

Cross References

C.C. arts. 131 to 136, 141, 142, 215, 245.

R.S. 9:331 to 9:336.

SUBPART E. RELOCATING A CHILD'S RESIDENCE

Section 4 of Acts 2012, No. 627, declares that this Act "shall not apply to any litigation pending on the effective date of this Act [August 1, 2012] regarding the relocation of the principal residence of a child, but shall apply to any subsequent relocation after final disposition of that litigation."

§ 355.1. Definitions

As used in this Subpart:

(1) "Principal residence of a child" means:

(a) The location designated by a court to be the primary residence of the child.

(b) In the absence of a court order, the location at which the parties have expressly agreed that the child will primarily reside.

(c) In the absence of a court order or an express agreement, the location, if any, at which the child has spent the majority of time during the prior six months.

(2) "Relocation" means a change in the principal residence of a child for a period of sixty days or more, but does not include a temporary absence from the principal residence.

Acts 2012, No. 627, § 1.

Comments—2012 Revision

(a) This revision moves the geographic threshold for application of the relocation statutes to R.S. 9:355.2.

(b) Absences of more than sixty days which are temporary—including, for instance, a summer holiday-are not relocation as defined in this Subpart.

§ 355.2. Applicability

A. This Subpart shall apply to an order regarding custody of or visitation with a child issued:

(1) On or after August 15, 1997.

(2) Before August 15, 1997, if the existing custody order does not expressly govern the relocation of the child.

B. This Subpart shall apply to a proposed relocation when any of the following exist:

(1) There is intent to establish the principal residence of a child at any location outside the state.

(2) There is no court order awarding custody and there is an intent to establish the principal residence of a child at any location within the state that is at a distance of more than seventy-five miles from the domicile of the other parent.

(3) There is a court order awarding custody and there is an intent to establish the principal residence of a child at any location within the state that is at a distance of more than seventy-five miles from the principal residence of the child at the time the most recent custody decree was rendered.

(4) If either no principal residence of a child has been designated by the court or the parties have equal physical custody, and there is an intent to establish the principal residence of a child at any location within the state that is at a distance of more than seventy-five miles from the domicile of a person entitled to object to relocation.

C. To the extent that this Subpart conflicts with an existing custody order, this Subpart shall not apply to the terms of that order that govern relocation.

D. This Subpart shall not apply when either of the following circumstances exist:

(1) The persons required to give notice of and the persons entitled to object to a proposed relocation have entered into an express written agreement for the relocation of the principal residence of the child.

(2) There is in effect an order issued pursuant to Domestic Abuse Assistance, R.S. 46:2131, et seq., Protection from Dating Violence, R.S. 46:2151, Part II of Chapter 28 of Title 46 or the Post–Separation Family Violence Relief Act or Injunctions and Incidental Orders, Parts IV and V of Chapter 1 of Code Title V of Code Book I of Title 9, except R.S. 9:372.1, all of the Louisiana Revised Statutes of 1950, Domestic Abuse Assistance, Chapter 8 of Title XV of the Children's Code, or any other restraining order, preliminary injunction, permanent injunction, or any protective order prohibiting a person from harming or going near or in the proximity of the other person.

Acts 2012, No. 627, § 1.

Comments—2012 Revision

(a) This revision reduces the threshold distance for application of the relocation statutes from one hundred fifty miles to seventy-five miles in recognition of the likelihood that weekday visitation and the general ability to participate in the child's daily life will be substantially affected by distances of more than seventy-five miles. The relocation laws of a number of other states hinge upon relocations involving even shorter distances. See, e.g., Ala. Code 1975 § 30–3–162 (60 miles); Florida Stat. § 61.13001 (50 miles); Maine Rev. Stat. § 1657 (60 miles); Or. Rev. Stat. § 107.159 (60 miles).

(b) "Equal physical custody" in Paragraph (4) of Subsection B of this Section refers to a custody arrangement under which persons have equal or approximately equal physical custody. It should be interpreted to mean one-half or an approximately equal amount of time, expressed in percentages such as forty-nine percent/fifty-one percent. "Equal physical custody" is distinguished from "shared custody" under R.S. 9:315.9, which Louisiana courts have interpreted to include custody arrangements with a split of sixty-three percent/thirty-seven percent. See, e.g., *Westcott v. Westcott*, 927 So. 2d 377 (La. App. 1st Cir. 2005). Such a split is not "equal physical custody" under this statute.

(c) If a person proposes relocation of a child within the state and within distances shorter than those prescribed under Subsection B of this Section, Louisiana's relocation statutes have no application, and the person seeking to relocate has no obligation to provide notice or seek court approval in advance of the move.

(d) Paragraph (3) of Subsection B of this Section changes the focus of the distance threshold from the domicile of the primary custodian at the time that the custody decree was rendered to the principal residence of the child at the time of the custody decree in light of the notion that the body of relocation statutes focuses on a relocation of the child and not his caregivers.

(e) See R.S. 9:355.7 and 355.8 regarding the persons entitled to object to a proposed relocation. Not all persons entitled to notice of a relocation are permitted to object.

(f) The purpose of Paragraph (2) of Subsection D of this Section is to prevent the application of Louisiana's child relocation statutes, requiring the party proposing relocation to notify a person entitled to receive notice of the details of the proposed move, in situations involving family violence, domestic abuse, and the like. The reference to "Part V of Chapter 1 of Code Title V of Code Book I of Title 9," however, includes R.S. 9:372.1, which governs an injunction prohibiting harassment. When an injunction has been issued only under R.S. 9:372.1, there is insufficient justification for exempting the proposed relocation from the requirements of the child relocation statutes.

§ 355.3. Persons authorized to propose relocation of principal residence of a child

The following persons are authorized to propose relocation of the principal residence of a child by complying with the notice requirements of this Subpart:

(1) A person designated in a current court decree as the sole custodian.

(2) A person designated in a current court decree as a domiciliary parent in a joint custody arrangement.

(3) A person sharing equal physical custody under a current court decree.

(4) A person sharing equal parental authority under Chapter 5 of Title VII of Book I of the Louisiana Civil Code.

(5) A person who is the natural tutor of a child born outside of marriage.

Acts 2012, No. 627, § 1.

Comments—2012 Revision

(a) Persons authorized to propose relocation of a child's principal residence are generally those with legal decision-making authority over the child, including the sole custodian or domiciliary parent in a joint custody arrangement or the natural tutor of a child born outside of marriage. When parents are married and sharing equal parental authority, both are entitled to propose relocation. Regardless of who holds decision-making authority for the child, however, persons who share equal physical custody of the child under a court decree are equally authorized to propose relocation.

(b) For the definition of "equal physical custody," see R.S. 9:355.2, Comment (b).

§ 355.4 Notice of proposed relocation of child; court authorization to relocate

A. A person proposing relocation of a child's principal residence shall notify any person recognized as a parent and any other person awarded custody or visitation under a court decree as required by R.S. 9:355.5.

B. If multiple persons have equal physical custody of a child under a court decree, the person proposing relocation shall notify the other of a proposed relocation of the principal residence of the child as required by R.S. 9:355.5, and before relocation shall obtain either court authorization to relocate, after a contradictory hearing, or the express written consent of the other person.

Acts 2012, No. 627, § 1.

Comments—2012 Revision

(a) See R.S. 9:355.3 for a list of persons authorized to propose relocation of a child's principal residence.

(b) For the definition of "equal physical custody," see R.S. 9:355.2, Comment (b).

(c) A "person recognized as a parent" under this provision includes persons who have been recognized by a court as parents in a filiation or avowal action, persons who are presumed to be parents under Louisiana Civil Code Articles 185 or 195, and persons who have formally acknowledged a child, as set out in Louisiana Civil Code Article 196, though they have not been judicially recognized as such.

§ 355.5 Mailing notice of proposed relocation address

A. Notice of a proposed relocation of the principal residence of a child shall be given by registered or certified mail, return receipt requested, or delivered by commercial courier as defined in R.S. 13:3204(D), to the last known address of the person entitled to notice under R.S. 9:355.4 no later than any of the following:

(1) The sixtieth day before the date of the proposed relocation.

(2) The tenth day after the date that the person proposing relocation knows the information required to be furnished by Subsection B of this Section, if the person did not know and could not reasonably have known the information in sufficient time to provide the sixty-day notice, and it is not reasonably possible to extend the time for relocation of the child.

B. The following information shall be included with the notice of intended relocation of the child:

(1) The current mailing address of the person proposing relocation.

(2) The intended new residence, including the specific physical address, if known.

(3) The intended new mailing address, if not the same.

(4) The home and cellular telephone numbers of the person proposing relocation, if known.

(5) The date of the proposed relocation.

(6) A brief statement of the specific reasons for the proposed relocation of a child.

(7) A proposal for a revised schedule of physical custody or visitation with the child.

(8) A statement that the person entitled to object shall make any objection to the proposed relocation in writing by registered or certified mail, return receipt requested, within thirty days of receipt of the notice and should seek legal advice immediately.

C. A person required to give notice of a proposed relocation shall have a continuing duty to provide the information required by this Section as that information becomes known.

Acts 2012, No. 627, § 1.

Comment—2012 Revision

The proposal for a revised custody and visitation schedule described in Paragraph (7) of Subsection B of this Section has no legal effect. Any existing custody or visitation order remains in effect unless and until a court orders a modification of custody or visitation. The intent, however, is to require the person proposing relocation to consider and describe in writing how all persons entitled to custody or visitation under an existing order may continue to maintain their relationship with the child after the proposed relocation.

§ 355.6. Failure to give notice of relocation

The court may consider a failure to provide notice of a proposed relocation of a child as:

(1) A factor in making its determination regarding the relocation of a child.

(2) A basis for ordering the return of the child if the relocation has taken place without notice or court authorization.

(3) Sufficient cause to order the person proposing relocation to pay reasonable expenses incurred by the person objecting to the relocation.

Acts 2012, No. 627, § 1.

§ 355.7. Objection to relocation of child

Except for a person with equal physical custody of a child under a court decree, a person who is entitled to object to a proposed relocation of the principal residence of a child shall make any objection within thirty days after receipt of the notice. The objection shall be made in writing by registered or certified mail, return receipt requested, or delivered by commercial courier as defined in R.S. 13:3204(D), to the mailing address provided for the person proposing relocation in the notice of proposed relocation.

A person with equal physical custody of a child under a court decree need not make an objection under this Section. The rights of persons with equal physical custody are governed by R.S. 9:355.4(B).

Acts 2012, No. 627, § 1.

Comments—2012 Revision

(a) The objection procedure described in this Section is subject to the limitations described in R.S. 9:355.8. Some persons entitled to receive notice of a proposed relocation of a child's residence are not permitted to object to the proposed relocation.

(b) A person who is entitled to object to a proposed relocation but chooses not to do so may nonetheless commence an action to change legal or physical custody or the visitation schedule in light of the changed circumstances of the relocation.

(c) In the absence of timely objection, retaining an attorney to handle an objection to relocation is not sufficient to require the person proposing relocation to initiate a proceeding.

(d) For the definition of "equal physical custody," see R.S. 9:355.2, Comment (b).

§ 355.8. Limitation on objection by non-parents

A non-parent may object to the relocation only if he has been awarded custody. A non-parent who has been awarded visitation may initiate a proceeding to obtain a revised visitation schedule.

Acts 2012, No. 627, § 1.

Comments—2012 Revision

(a) This Section recognizes the primacy of parental rights over non-parent rights regarding relocation of a child. See generally *Troxel v. Granville*, 530 U.S. 57, 120 S.Ct. 2054, 147 L.Ed. 49 (2000) (holding that Washington's non-parent visitation statute violated mother's fundamental right to raise her children as she saw fit). Although a non-parent who has not been awarded custody may be entitled to notice of a proposed relocation and may not object to a relocation, the non-parent may, if granted visitation, commence an action to revise the visitation schedule in light of the changed circumstances of the relocation.

(b) This provision governs objections by non-parents only. It does not limit the right of a parent to object to a proposed relocation.

§ 355.9. Effect of objection or failure to object to notice of proposed relocation

Except as otherwise provided by R.S. 9:355.4(B), the person required to give notice may relocate the principal residence of a child after providing the required notice unless a person entitled to object does so in compliance with R.S. 9:355.7.

If a written objection is sent in compliance with R.S. 9:355.7, the person proposing relocation of the principal residence of the child shall initiate within thirty days after receiving the objection a summary proceeding to obtain court approval to relocate. Court approval to relocate shall be granted only after a contradictory hearing.

Acts 2012, No. 627, § 1.

Comment—2012 Revision

If, at any time, the person proposing relocation and those entitled to object enter into the express written agreement on relocation described in R.S. 9:355.2(D), no summary proceeding or court approval to relocate is necessary. The relocation statutes do not apply to restrict moves for which the parties agree. R.S. 9:355.2(D).

§ 355.10 Burden of proof

The person proposing relocation has the burden of proof that the proposed relocation is made in good faith and is in the best interest of the child.

Acts 2012, No. 627, § 1.

Comments—2012 Revision

(a) Although the person proposing relocation has the burden to prove that the relocation attempt is made both in good faith and in the best interest of the child, there is no presumption in favor of or against relocation of the child's residence. This Section places the burden of proof on the person proposing relocation. If an objection to the relocation is made in accordance with R.S. 9:355.7, the person wishing to relocate must prove by a preponderance of the evidence, on contradictory hearing, that relocation meets the good faith and best interest standards.

(b) This revision eliminates reference to the court's consideration of an enhancement in the quality of life of the person seeking relocation in determining the best interest of the child. It does not, however, change the law. A detailed list of factors to be considered in determining whether relocation is in the best interest of the child is set out in R.S. 9:355.14, and among them is a consideration of "how the relocation of the child will affect the general quality of life for the child, including but not limited to financial or emotional benefit or education opportunity."

§ 355.11 Court authorization to relocate

If timely objection to a proposed relocation is made by a person entitled to object, the person proposing relocation shall not, absent express written consent of the objecting person, relocate the child pending resolution of the dispute by final order of the court, unless the person proposing relocation obtains a temporary order pursuant to R.S. 9:355.12.

Acts 2012, No. 627, § 1.

§ 355.12 Temporary order

A. The court may grant a temporary order allowing relocation.

B. The court, upon the request of the moving party, may hold an expedited preliminary hearing on the proposed relocation but shall not grant authorization to relocate the child on an ex parte basis.

C. If the court issues a temporary order authorizing relocation, the court shall not give undue weight to the temporary relocation as a factor in reaching its final determination.

D. If temporary relocation of a child is permitted, the court may require the person relocating the child to provide reasonable security guaranteeing that the court-ordered physical custody or visitation with the child will not be interrupted or interfered with or that the relocating person will return the child if court authorization for the relocation is denied at trial.

E. An order not in compliance with the provisions of this Section is not enforceable and is null and void.

Acts 2012, No. 627, § 1.

Comment—2012 Revision

Subsection (E) of this Section tracks the language of C.C.P. Art. 3945(E), which makes temporary custody orders unenforceable and null and void if not issued in compliance.

§ 355.13 Priority for trial

A trial on the proposed relocation shall be assigned within sixty days after the filing of the motion to obtain court approval to relocate.

Acts 2012, No. 627, § 1.

Comments—2012 Revision

(a) The trial referenced here is the final hearing on the merits of the relocation; it is to be distinguished from a preliminary hearing on relocation, described in R.S. 9:355.12.

(b) After entry of an order on relocation, a Louisiana court may retain jurisdiction consistent with Louisiana law and the Uniform Child Custody Jurisdiction and Enforcement Act. (R.S. 13:1814).

§ 355.14 Factors to determine contested relocation

A. In reaching its decision regarding a proposed relocation, the court shall consider all relevant factors in determining whether relocation is in the best interest of the child, including the following:

(1) The nature, quality, extent of involvement, and duration of the relationship of the child with the person proposing relocation and with the non-relocating person, siblings, and other significant persons in the child's life.

(2) The age, developmental stage, needs of the child, and the likely impact the relocation will have on the child's physical, educational, and emotional development.

(3) The feasibility of preserving a good relationship between the non-relocating person and the child through suitable physical custody or visitation arrangements, considering the logistics and financial circumstances of the parties.

(4) The child's views about the proposed relocation, taking into consideration the age and maturity of the child.

(5) Whether there is an established pattern of conduct by either the person seeking or the person opposing the relocation, either to promote or thwart the relationship of the child and the other party.

(6) How the relocation of the child will affect the general quality of life for the child, including but not limited to financial or emotional benefit and educational opportunity.

(7) The reasons of each person for seeking or opposing the relocation.

(8) The current employment and economic circumstances of each person and how the proposed relocation may affect the circumstances of the child.

(9) The extent to which the objecting person has fulfilled his financial obligations to the person seeking relocation, including child support, spousal support, and community property, and alimentary obligations.

(10) The feasibility of a relocation by the objecting person.

(11) Any history of substance abuse, harassment, or violence by either the person seeking or the person opposing relocation, including a consideration of the severity of the conduct and the failure or success of any attempts at rehabilitation.

(12) Any other factors affecting the best interest of the child.

B. The court may not consider whether the person seeking relocation of the child may relocate without the child if relocation is denied or whether the person opposing relocation may also relocate if relocation is allowed.

Acts 2012, No. 627, § 1.

Comments—2012 Revision

(a) This revision changes the opening language of the statute to make it clear that, as in cases requiring the application of the factors of Civil Code Article 134, a court need not make a factual finding on every factor.

(b) In considering the needs of the child and the developmental impact of relocation, the court may take into account not only the general needs of similarly situated children, but also any special needs of the particular child under consideration.

(c) The "logistics" referred to in Paragraph (3) of Subsection A of this Section may include a consideration of the amount of time the child will be required to spend traveling in order to maintain a meaningful relationship with the person objecting to the relocation, the distance involved, and the proximity, availability, and safety of travel arrangements.

(d) A consideration of the child's "preference" is a traditional factor in cases involving custody. The word "views" is used here in order to broaden the inquiry and to decrease the potentially harmful impact of asking a child to choose in a relocation contest.

(e) Because the focus of the best interest inquiry in relocation is on the child, references to improvements in the custodial parent's quality of life and the necessity of improving the circumstances of a parent in Paragraphs (6) and (8) of Subsection A of this Section have been eliminated. A child may benefit or suffer detriment either directly or indirectly from a change in the quality of life or economic circumstances of any person exercising custody or visitation with him, and such benefits and detriments are to be considered by the court. The assessment must focus on the effect of relocation on the child, however, and not the benefit that relocation will provide to the adults exercising custody or visitation rights.

(f) The promotion of or interference with the relationship between the child and the other parent described in Paragraphs (3) and (5) of Subsection A of this Section may include a parent's willingness to make travel arrangements that allow the child meaningful time with both parents and that minimize the negative impact of long-distance parenting on the child.

(g) Paragraph (7) of Subsection A of this Section may lead to a consideration of the mental and emotional well-being of both the person seeking relocation and the person opposing it. The substantial mental and emotional toll of custody proceedings should be considered in the relocation context, just as it is in Civil Code Article 134, on factors affecting the best interest of the child in custody disputes in general.

§ 355.15 Mental health expert; appointment

The court, on motion of either party or on its own motion, may appoint an independent mental health expert to render a report to assist the court in determining the best interest of the child.

Acts 2012, No. 627, § 1.

§ 355.16 Application of factors at initial hearing

If the issue of relocation is presented at the initial hearing to determine custody of and visitation with a child, the court shall consider also the factors set forth in R.S. 9:355.14 in making its initial determination.

Acts 2012, No. 627, § 1.

Comment—2012 Revision

In an initial custody determination, the court will generally consider the factors concerning best interest of the child set out in Civil Code Article 134. This statute requires the court to consider application of the relevant factors specific to relocation in R.S. 9:355.14 as well as the Article 134 factors. Dicta in *McLain v. McLain*, 974 So.2d 726, 733 (La. App. 4th Cir. 2007), stating that the Article 134 factors are "arguably not applicable" when relocation is at issue in the initial custody hearing, are no longer accurate under this revision.

§ 355.17 Modification of custody

Providing notice of a proposed relocation does not constitute a change of circumstance warranting a change of custody. Relocating without prior notice if there is a court order awarding custody or relocating in violation of a court order may constitute a change of circumstances warranting a modification of custody.

Any change in the principal residence of a child, including one not meeting the threshold distance set out in R.S. 9:355.2, may constitute a change of circumstances warranting a modification of custody.

Acts 2012, No. 627, § 1.

Comments—2012 Revision

(a) In accordance with R.S. 9:355.8, not all persons receiving notice of a proposed relocation are entitled to object. Moving without prior notice or in violation of a court order may constitute a change of circumstances warranting a modification of custody, but only in a contest between a person proposing relocation and a person entitled to object to the proposed relocation.

(b) The second paragraph of this Article clarifies that even a move of less than seventy-five miles may warrant a change of custody. Although such a move would not be sufficient to trigger the protection of the relocation statutes, courts have discretion to modify the current custodial arrangement after any move that makes an existing custody order unfeasible.

§ 355.18 Posting security

If relocation of a child is permitted, the court may require the person relocating the child to provide reasonable security guaranteeing that the court-ordered physical custody or visitation with the child will not be interrupted or interfered with by the relocating party.

Acts 2012, No. 627, § 1.

§ 355.19 Sanctions for unwarranted or frivolous proposal to relocate child or objection to relocation

A. After notice and a reasonable opportunity to respond, the court may impose a sanction on a person proposing or objecting to a proposed relocation of a child if it determines that the proposal or objection was made:

(1) For the purpose of harassing the other person or causing unnecessary delay or needless increase in the cost of litigation.

(2) Without a basis in existing law or on the basis of a frivolous argument.

(3) In violation of Code of Civil Procedure Article 863(B).

B. A sanction imposed under this Section shall be limited to what is sufficient to deter repetition of such conduct. The sanction may consist of reasonable expenses and attorney fees incurred as a direct result of the conduct.

Acts 2012, No. 627, § 1.

SUBPART F. OTHER CHILD CUSTODY PROVISIONS

§ 356. Consideration of child support

In any proceeding for child custody or visitation, either party may raise any issue relating to child support and the court may hear and determine that issue if all parties consent. The child support matters need not be specifically pleaded for the party to raise the issue, or the court to decide the issue.

Added by Acts 1999, No. 447, § 1.

§ 357. Use of technology

The court shall consider ordering persons awarded custody or visitation to use technology, including video calling, telephone, text messaging, Internet communications, or other forms of technology, to facilitate communication with the child when it is in the best interest of the child.

Added by Acts 2012, No. 627, § 2.

Editor's note. Section 4 of La.Acts 2012, No. 627, declares that this Act "shall not apply to any litigation pending on the effective date of this Act [August 1, 2012] regarding the relocation of the principal residence of a child, but shall apply to any subsequent relocation after final disposition of that litigation."

SUBPART G. PARENTING COORDINATOR

§ 358.1. Appointment of parenting coordinator; term; costs

A. On motion of a party or on its own motion, the court may appoint a parenting coordinator in a child custody case for good cause shown if the court has previously entered a judgment establishing child custody, other than an ex parte order. The court shall make the appointment on joint motion of the parties.

B. The initial term of the appointment of the parenting coordinator shall not exceed one year. For good cause shown, the court may extend the appointment of the parenting coordinator for additional one year terms.

C. The court shall order each party to pay a portion of the costs of the parenting coordinator. No parenting coordinator shall be appointed by the court if a party has been granted pauper status or is unable to pay his apportioned cost of the parenting coordinator.

Added by Acts 2007, No. 265, § 2.

Comments—2007

(a) Parenting coordination is a child-focused alternate dispute resolution process in which a duly qualified parenting coordinator assists parents or persons exercising parental authority to implement a parenting plan by facilitating the resolution of their disputes in a timely manner and by reducing their child-related conflict so that the children may be protected from the impact of that conflict. The parenting coordinator assists the parties in promoting the best interests of the children by reducing or eliminating child-related conflict through the use of the parenting coordination process.

(b) The court may appoint a parenting coordinator only if there is an existing child custody order. The custody order may be a "considered decree" or an order based on a joint stipulation; however the appointment may not follow an ex-parte custody order. The purpose of this limitation is to prevent the court from using the parenting coordinator process as a means of abdicating its responsibility to make the initial custody determination. The parenting coordinator may not make suggestions that would affect the existing custody arrangement. See R.S. 9:358.4(B). This provision follows the approach taken in Idaho Code 32-717D.

(c) The court may appoint a parenting coordinator on its own motion or on motion of a party only upon a showing of "good cause shown." "Good cause" includes a determination by the court that either or both parties have demonstrated an inability or unwillingness to collaboratively make parenting decisions without assistance of others or insistence of the court. "Good cause" may also include an inability or unwillingness to comply with parenting agreements and orders or a determination by the court that either or both parties have demonstrated an ongoing pattern of unnecessary litigation, refusal to communicate or difficulty in communicating about and cooperation in the care of the children, and refusal to acknowledge the right of each party to have and maintain a continuing relationship with the children.

(d) This Section requires the court to appoint a parenting coordinator if both parties agree. No showing of good cause is required.

(e) The order of appointment must set the term of the parenting coordinator at no more than one year. At the end of the term the court may extend the appointment for good cause shown. The appointment of the parenting coordinator may be terminated as provided in R.S. 9:358.8.

(f) This Section requires that each party must pay some portion of the fee but allows the court to apportion the fee according to the parties' ability to pay. The court may order a particularly obstinate party to pay a larger portion of the fee. The portion of the costs that each party is to pay should be specified in the order of appointment and the court should state its reasons on the record in the event of an appeal. Under normal circumstances each party would pay the costs of his time with the parenting coordinator and would split the cost of other times.

§ 358.2. No appointment in family violence cases

Unless good cause is shown, the court shall not appoint a parenting coordinator if it finds that a party has a history of perpetrating family violence.

Added by Acts 2007, No. 265, § 2.

Comments—2007

(a) The Section follows the policy of this state as set forth in the Post-Separation Family Violence Relief Act, which prohibits mediation in cases when there is family violence. R.S. 9:361 et seq. The term "family violence" as used here has the same meaning as that in R.S. 9:362(3). Under that Section, a parent who has a history of perpetrating family violence may only be allowed supervised visitation conditioned on the parent's completing a treatment program. After completion of the treatment program the parent may petition the court for unsupervised visitation.

(b) A parenting coordinator is required to have training on the effects of domestic violence on children and families. R.S. 9:358.3(B)(8). If a parenting coordinator determines that a party is guilty of domestic violence, he should immediately file a report of his findings. A parenting coordinator is a mandatory reporter of child abuse. See Children's Code Art. 603(13)(h) and Arts. 609–610.

§ 358.3. Qualifications

A. A person appointed as a parenting coordinator shall meet all of the following qualifications:

(1) Possess a master's, Ph.D., or equivalent degree, in a mental health field, such as psychiatry, psychology, social work, marriage and family counseling, or professional counseling, hold a Louisiana license in the mental health profession, and have no less than three years of related professional post-degree experience.

(2) Be qualified as a mediator under R.S. 9:334.

(3) Complete a minimum of forty hours of specialized training on parent coordination. A maximum of fourteen hours of family mediation training may be used towards the total forty hours.

B. The training specified in Paragraph (A)(3) of this Section shall include instruction on all of the following:

(1) The Louisiana judicial system and judicial procedure in domestic cases.

(2) Ethical standards, including confidentiality and conflicts of interest.

(3) Child development, including the impact of divorce on development.

(4) Parenting techniques.

(5) Parenting plans and time schedules.

(6) Family systems theory.

(7) Communication skills.

(8) Domestic violence and its effects on children and families.

(9) The parenting coordination process and required documentation execution.

C. In order to remain qualified, a parenting coordinator shall complete, every two calendar years, a minimum of twenty hours of continuing education in parenting coordination.

D. A court may accept the initial certification of a parenting coordinator or the maintenance of that certification made by a legal or mental health association whose focus includes resolution of child-related conflicts.

E. Upon request of the court, a parenting coordinator shall furnish satisfactory evidence of his qualifications.

Added by Acts 2007, No. 265, § 2.

Comments—2007

Paragraph (A)(1) of this Section allows two categories of persons to qualify as a parenting coordinator: attorneys and mental health care professionals. The list of health care professionals tracks the qualifications required for mediators, but does not include clergymen. In addition, those persons must be qualified as mediators and have an additional forty hours of specialized training.

§ 358.4. Authority and duties of parenting coordinator

A. A parenting coordinator shall assist the parties in resolving disputes and in reaching agreements regarding children in their care including, but not limited to, the following types of issues:

(1) Minor changes or clarifications of access schedules from the existing custody plan.

(2) Exchanges of the children including date, time, place, means of transportation, and the transporter.

(3) Health care management including medical, dental, orthodontic, and vision care.

(4) Child-rearing issues.

(5) Psychotherapy or other mental health care including substance abuse or mental health assessment or counseling for the children.

(6) Psychological testing or other assessments of the children.

(7) Education or daycare including school choice, tutoring, summer school, participation in special education testing and programs, or other educational decisions.

(8) Enrichment and extracurricular activities including camps and jobs.

(9) Religious observances and education.

(10) Children's travel and passport arrangements.

(11) Clothing, equipment, and personal possessions of the children.

(12) Communication between the parties about the children.

(13) Means of communication by a party with the children when they are not in that party's care.

(14) Alteration of appearance of the children including hairstyle and ear and body piercing.

(15) Role of and contact with significant others and extended families.

(16) Substance abuse assessment or testing of either or both parties or the child, including access to results.

(17) Parenting classes or referral for other services of either or both parties.

B. A parenting coordinator shall:

(1) Refrain from facilitating an agreement by the parties that would change legal custody from one party to the other or that would change the physical custody or visitation schedule in a way that may result in a change in child support.

(2) Notify the court of a conflict of interest of the parenting coordinator.

(3) Prepare interim and final reports as ordered by the court and other reports when necessary.

C. When the parties are unable to reach an agreement, the parenting coordinator may make a recommendation in a report to the court for resolution of the dispute.

Added by Acts 2007, No. 265, § 2.

Comments—2007

The purpose of the parenting coordinator process is to assist the parties in implementing a parenting plan by facilitating the resolution of their disputes and by reducing their child-related conflicts so that the children may be protected from the impact of that conflict. The parenting coordinator may not attempt to help the parties reach an agreement that changes the basic child custody and child support orders. If the parties reach an agreement on other matters, the parenting coordinator may state the substance of the agreement in a report to the court and the lawyers; however, it remains the responsibility of the parties' attorneys to prepare a written agreement and incorporate it into a judgment.

§ 358.5. Testimony and report

A. The parenting coordinator shall not be called as a witness in the child custody proceeding without prior court approval.

B. The parenting coordinator shall distribute all reports to the court, the parties, and their attorneys.

Added by Acts 2007, No. 265, § 2.

Comments—2007

(a) Paragraph A allows the parties to call the parenting coordinator as a witness only with permission of the court. The approval of a parenting coordinator to be a witness does not require a contradictory hearing. Compare Evidence Code Article 507 which requires court approval and a hearing before a lawyer may be called as a witness in a criminal case. A judge should not authorize the issuance of a subpoena to a parenting coordinator unless the calling party demonstrates a need for the testimony and that the evidence cannot be adduced from other sources. The court may not call the parenting coordinator as a witness on its own motion. See C.E. Art. 614.

(b) The report of the parenting coordinator is inadmissible hearsay under the general rules of evidence if offered for the truth of the matters asserted. See C.E. Art. 801. However, evidence rules are relaxed in custody cases and the judge has some authority to admit hearsay. See C.E. Art. 1101(B)(2). If the court does admit the report into evidence it should allow the parenting coordinator to be called as a witness and to be subject to cross-examination. See generally, Triche, Handbook on Louisiana Family Law, Rules of Evidence in Family Court (Thomson-West 2007).

(c) There is no confidentiality provision for statements made to the parenting coordinator, unlike the mediation statute. See R.S. 9:332(C). Statements by a party may be admissible as an admission of a party opponent under Evidence Code Article 801(D)(2).

§ 358.6. Communication with court

The parenting coordinator shall not communicate ex parte with the court, except in an emergency situation.

Added by Acts 2007, No. 265, § 2.

§ 358.7. Access to information

The court shall order the parties to cooperate with the parenting coordinator and to provide relevant non-privileged records and information requested by the parenting coordinator. The parenting coordinator may communicate with the child and other persons not a party to the litigation.

Added by Acts 2007, No. 265, § 2.

Comments—2007

(a) This Section authorizes the parenting coordinator to communicate to third persons. Access to such persons, such as a grandparent or teacher, or to documents should be arranged through a cooperative party. If persons not a party to the litigation are not willing to speak to the parenting coordinator, the parenting coordinator may arrange a status conference with the court and the parties to determine whether the court should issue a subpoena.

(b) The pleadings filed in the proceeding are public records and thus accessible to the parenting coordinator. The court may release to the parenting coordinator other information about the case, such as mediator or health professional reports.

(c) The order of appointment should order the parties to cooperate with the parenting coordinator and supply the parenting coordinator with relevant non-privileged information. If a party objects to the release of information he deems confidential or irrelevant, he should file an objection with the court. All communications subject to the attorney-client privilege are exempt from disclosure. The health care provider privilege generally does not cover communications relating to the health condition of a party to a child custody case when that information has a substantial bearing on the fitness of the party. See C.E. Art. 510(B)(2)(d). The spousal privilege does not apply in child custody cases. See C.E. Art. 504(C)(2) and (4) and comment (d). Statements made by the parties to the parenting coordinator are not confidential. Whether the parenting coordinator may have access to information that might not be admissible in the custody case because of relevancy is left to the discretion of the judge.

§ 358.8. Termination of appointment of parenting coordinator

For good cause shown, the court, on its own motion, on motion of a party, or upon request of the parenting coordinator, may terminate the appointment of the parenting coordinator.

Added by Acts 2007, No. 265, § 2.

Comments—2007

This Section allows the court, a party, or the parenting coordinator to request termination of the appointment. "Good cause" for terminating the appointment may include nonpayment of fees, the process has exhausted itself, safety concerns, a lack of reasonable progress despite the best efforts of the parties, one of the parties is a perpetrator of family violence, or the parenting coordinator is unable or unwilling to serve.

§ 358.9. Limitation of liability

No parenting coordinator shall be personally liable for any act or omission resulting in damage, injury, or loss arising out of the exercise of his official duties and within the course and scope of his appointment by the court. However, this limitation of liability shall not be applicable if the damage, injury, or loss was caused by the gross negligence or willful or wanton misconduct of the parenting coordinator.

Added by Acts 2007, No. 265, § 2.

SUBPART H. MILITARY PARENT AND CHILD CUSTODY PROTECTION ACT

§ 359. Short title

This Subpart may be cited as the "Military Parent and Child Custody Protection Act".

Added by Acts 2010, No. 739, § 1.

Cross References

C.C. arts. 99, 131, 132, 134 to 136.

§ 359.1. Definitions

As used in this Subpart, the following terms shall have the following meanings:

(1) "Deploying parent" means a parent of a minor child whose parental rights have not been terminated and whose custody or visitation rights have not been restricted by court order to supervised visitation only, by a court of competent jurisdiction who is deployed or has received written orders to deploy with the United States military or any reserve component thereof.

(2) "Deployment" means military service in compliance with mandatory written orders, unaccompanied by any family member, for combat operations, contingency operations, peacekeeping operations, temporary duty, a remote tour of duty, or other active service.

(3) "Order" means any custody or visitation judgment, decree, or order issued by a court of competent jurisdiction in this state or any judgment of another state which has been made executory in this state.

Added by Acts 2010, No. 739, § 1.

Cross References

C.C. arts. 99, 131, 132, 134 to 136.

§ 359.2. Final order; modification prohibited

The court shall not enter a final order modifying the existing terms of a custody or visitation order until ninety days after the termination of deployment; however, if the matter was fully tried by a court prior to deployment, the court may enter a final order at any time.

Added by Acts 2010, No. 739, § 1.

Cross References

C.C. arts. 99, 131, 132, 134 to 136.

§ 359.3. Material change in circumstances

Deployment or the potential for future deployment alone shall not constitute a material change in circumstances for the permanent modification of a custody or visitation order.

Added by Acts 2010, No. 739, § 1.

Cross References

C.C. arts. 99, 131, 132, 134 to 136.

§ 359.4. Temporary modification

A. An existing order of custody or visitation may be temporarily modified to reasonably accommodate the deployment of a parent. Any such order issued in accordance with the provisions of this Subpart shall be entered as a temporary order by the court.

B. Unless the court determines that it is not in the best interest of the child, a temporary modification order shall grant the deploying parent reasonable custody or visitation during periods of approved military leave if the existing order granted the deploying parent custody or visitation prior to deployment. All restrictions on the custody or visitation in the existing order shall remain in effect in the temporary modification order.

C. A temporary modification order shall specify that deployment is the reason for modification and shall require the other parent to provide the court and the deploying parent with written notice thirty days prior to a change of address or telephone number.

D. The court shall have an expedited hearing on any custody or visitation matters, upon the motion of a parent and for good cause shown, when military duties prevent the deploying parent from personally appearing at a hearing scheduled regularly on the docket.

Added by Acts 2010, No. 739, § 1.

Cross References

C.C. arts. 99, 131, 132, 134 to 136.

§ 359.5. Termination of temporary modification order

A. A temporary modification order terminates by operation of law upon the completion of deployment, and the prior order shall be reinstated. If the other parent has relocated with the child in accordance with the provisions of R.S. 9:355.1 et seq., custody or visitation shall be exercised where the child resides, pending further orders of the court.

B. Notwithstanding the provisions of Subsection A of this Section, the court may, upon motion alleging immediate danger or irreparable harm to the child, grant an expedited hearing on the termination of the temporary modification order and the reinstatement of the prior order, or the court may grant an ex parte order of temporary custody prior to the reinstatement of the prior order. Any ex parte temporary order shall comply with the provisions of Code of Civil Procedure Article 3945.

Added by Acts 2010, No. 739, § 1.

Cross References

C.C. arts. 99, 131, 132, 134 to 136.

§ 359.6. Delegation of visitation

The court may delegate some or all of the deploying parent's visitation, upon motion of the deploying parent, to a family member with a substantial relationship to the child if the court determines it is in the best interest of the child. For the purposes of this Section, the court shall consider Civil Code Article 136 in determining the best interest of the child. Delegated visitation shall not create standing to assert separate visitation rights. Delegated visitation shall terminate by operation of law in accordance with the provisions of R.S. 9:359.5 or upon a showing that the delegated visitation is no longer in the best interest of the child.

Added by Acts 2010, No. 739, § 1.

Cross References

C.C. arts. 99, 131, 132, 134 to 136.

§ 359.7. Testimony; evidence

The court shall permit the presentation of testimony and evidence by affidavit or electronic means, upon motion of a parent and for good cause shown, when military duties prevent the deploying parent from personally appearing.

Added by Acts 2010, No. 739, § 1.

Cross References

C.C. arts. 99, 131, 132, 134 to 136.

§ 359.8. Lack of existing order of custody or visitation

When an order establishing custody or visitation has not been rendered and deployment is imminent, upon the motion of either parent, the court shall expedite a hearing to establish a temporary order in accordance with this Subpart.

Added by Acts 2010, No. 739, § 1.

Cross References

C.C. arts. 99, 131, 132, 134 to 136.

§ 359.9. Duty to cooperate; disclosure of information

A. When military necessity precludes court adjudication prior to deployment, the parties shall cooperate in custody or visitation matters.

B. Within ten days of receipt, a copy of the deployment orders shall be provided to the other parent. When the deployment date is less than ten days after receipt of the orders, a copy shall immediately be provided.

Added by Acts 2010, No. 739, § 1.

Cross References

C.C. arts. 99, 131, 132, 134 to 136.

§ 359.10. Appointment of counsel

When the court declines to grant or extend a stay of proceedings in accordance with the Servicemembers Civil Relief Act, 50 U.S.C. Appendix Section 521–522, upon motion of either parent or upon its own motion, the court shall appoint an attorney to represent the child in accordance with the provisions of R.S. 9:345.

Added by Acts 2010, No. 739, § 1.

Cross References

C.C. arts. 99, 131, 132, 134 to 136.

§ 359.11. Jurisdiction

When a court of this state has issued a custody or visitation order, the absence of a child from this state during the deployment of a parent shall be a "temporary absence" for the purposes of the Uniform Child Custody Jurisdiction and Enforcement Act and this state shall retain exclusive continuing jurisdiction in accordance with the provisions of R.S. 13:1814. The deployment of a parent may not be used as a basis to assert inconvenience of the forum in accordance with the provisions of R.S. 13:1819.

Added by Acts 2010, No. 739, § 1.

Cross References

C.C. arts. 99, 131, 132, 134 to 136.

§ 359.12. Attorney fees

The court may award attorney fees and costs when either party causes unreasonable delays, fails to provide information required in this Subpart, or in any other circumstance in which the court considers it to be appropriate.

Added by Acts 2010, No. 739, § 1.

Cross References

C.C. arts. 99, 131, 132, 134 to 136.

§ 359.13. Applicability

The provisions of this Subpart shall not apply to any custody or visitation order requested in a verified petition alleging the applicability of the Domestic Abuse Assistance Act, R.S. 46:2131 et seq., Children's Code Article 1564 et seq., or the Post–Separation Family Violence Relief Act, R.S. 9:361 et seq.

Added by Acts 2010, No. 739, § 1.

Cross References

C.C. arts. 99, 131, 132, 134 to 136.

PART IV. POST–SEPARATION FAMILY VIOLENCE RELIEF ACT

§ 361. Legislative findings

The legislature hereby reiterates its previous findings and statements of purpose set forth in R.S. 46:2121 and 2131 relative to family violence and domestic violence. The legislature further finds that the problems of family violence do not necessarily cease when the victimized family is legally separated or divorced. In fact, the violence often escalates, and child custody and visitation become the new forum for the continuation of the abuse. Because current laws relative to child custody and visitation are based on an assumption that even divorcing parents are in relatively equal positions of power, and that such parents act in the children's best interest, these laws often work against the protection of the children and the abused spouse in families with a history of family violence. Consequently, laws designed to act in the children's best interest may actually effect a contrary result due to the unique dynamics of family violence

Added by Acts 1992, No. 1091, § 1.

§ 362. Definitions

As used in this Part:

(1) "Abused parent" means the parent who has not committed family violence.

(2) "Court" means any district court, juvenile court, or family court having jurisdiction over the parents and/or child at issue.

(3) "Family violence" includes but is not limited to physical or sexual abuse and any offense against the person as defined in the Criminal Code of Louisiana, except negligent injuring and defamation, committed by one parent against the other parent or against any of the children. Family violence does not include reasonable acts of self-defense utilized by one parent to protect himself or herself or a child in the family from the family violence of the other parent.

(4) "Injunction" means a temporary restraining order or a preliminary or a permanent court ordered injunction, as defined in the Code of Civil Procedure, which prohibits the violent parent from in any way contacting the abused parent or the children except for specific purposes set forth in the injunction, which shall be limited to communications expressly dealing with the education, health, and welfare of the children, or for any other purpose expressly agreed to by the abused parent. All such injunctions shall prohibit the violent parent, without the express consent of the abused parent, from intentionally going within fifty yards of the home, school, place of employment, or person of the abused parent and the children, or within fifty feet of any of

their automobiles, except as may otherwise be necessary for court ordered visitation or except as otherwise necessitated by circumstances considering the proximity of the parties' residences or places of employment. Such injunctions shall be issued in the form of a Uniform Abuse Prevention Order and transmitted to the Louisiana Protective Order Registry, as required by this Part.

(5) "Sexual abuse" includes but is not limited to acts which are prohibited by R.S. 14:41, 42, 42.1, 43, 43.1, 43.2, 43.4, 78, 80, 81, 81.1, 81.2, 89 and 89.1.

(6) "Supervised visitation" means face-to-face contact between a parent and a child which occurs in the immediate presence of a supervising person approved by the court under conditions which prevent any physical abuse, threats, intimidation, abduction, or humiliation of either the abused parent or the child. The supervising person shall not be any relative, friend, therapist, or associate of the parent perpetrating family violence. With the consent of the abused parent, the supervising person may be a family member or friend of the abused parent. At the request of the abused parent, the court may order that the supervising person shall be a police officer or other competent professional. The parent who perpetrated family violence shall pay any and all costs incurred in the supervision of visitation. In no case shall supervised visitation be overnight or in the home of the violent parent.

(7) "Treatment program" means a course of evaluation and psychotherapy designed specifically for perpetrators of family violence, and conducted by licensed mental health professionals.

Added by Acts 1992, No. 1091, § 1. Amended by Acts 1995, No. 888, § 1; Acts 1997, No. 1156, § 4.

§ 363. Ordered mediation prohibited

Notwithstanding any other provision of law to the contrary, in any separation, divorce, child custody, visitation, child support, alimony, or community property proceeding, no spouse or parent who satisfies the court that he or she, or any of the children, has been the victim of family violence perpetrated by the other spouse or parent shall be court ordered to participate in mediation.

Added by Acts 1992, No. 1091, § 1.

§ 364. Child custody; visitation

A. There is created a presumption that no parent who has a history of perpetrating family violence shall be awarded sole or joint custody of children. The court may find a history of perpetrating family violence if the court finds that one incident of family violence has resulted in serious bodily injury or the court finds more than one incident of family violence. The presumption shall be overcome only by a preponderance of the evidence that the perpetrating parent has successfully completed a treatment program as defined in R.S. 9:362, is not abusing alcohol and the illegal use of drugs scheduled in R.S. 40:964, and that the best interest of the child or children requires that parent's participation as a custodial parent because of the other parent's absence, mental illness, or substance abuse, or such other circumstances which affect the best interest of the child or children. The fact that the abused parent suffers from the effects of the abuse shall not be grounds for denying that parent custody.

B. If the court finds that both parents have a history of perpetrating family violence, custody shall be awarded solely to the parent who is less likely to continue to perpetrate family violence. In such a case, the court shall mandate completion of a treatment program by the custodial parent. If necessary to protect the welfare of the child, custody may be awarded to a suitable third person, provided that the person would not allow access to a violent parent except as ordered by the court.

C. If the court finds that a parent has a history of perpetrating family violence, the court shall allow only supervised child visitation with that parent, conditioned upon that parent's participation in and completion of a treatment program. Unsupervised visitation shall be allowed only if it is shown by a preponderance of the evidence that the violent parent has completed a treatment program, is not abusing alcohol and psychoactive drugs, and poses no danger to the child, and that such visitation is in the child's best interest.

D. If any court finds, by clear and convincing evidence, that a parent has sexually abused his or her child or children, the court shall prohibit all visitation and contact between the abusive parent and the children, until such time, following a contradictory hearing, that the court finds, by a preponderance of the evidence, that the abusive parent has successfully completed a treatment program designed for such sexual abusers, and that supervised visitation is in the children's best interest.

Added by Acts 1992, No. 1091, § 1. Amended by Acts 1995, No. 888, § 1.

§ 365. Qualification of mental health professional

Any mental health professional appointed by the court to conduct a custody evaluation in a case where family violence is an issue shall have current and demonstrable training and experience working with perpetrators and victims of family violence.

Added by Acts 1992, No. 1091, § 1.

§ 366. Injunctions

A. All separation, divorce, child custody, and child visitation orders and judgments in family violence cases shall contain an injunction as defined in R.S. 9:362. Upon issuance of such injunction, the judge shall cause to have prepared a Uniform Abuse Prevention Order as provided in R.S. 46:2136.2(C), shall sign such order, and shall forward it to the clerk of court for filing, all without delay. The clerk of the issuing court shall transmit the Uniform Abuse Prevention Order to the Louisiana Protective Order Registry, R.S. 46:2136.2(A) by facsimile transmission, mail, or direct electronic input, where available, as expeditiously as possible, but no later than the end of the next business day after the order is filed with the clerk of court.

B. Any violation of the injunction, if proved by the appropriate standard, shall be punished as contempt of court, and shall result in a termination of all court ordered child visitation.

Added by Acts 1992, No. 1091, § 1. Amended by Acts 1995, No. 888, § 1; Acts 2003, No. 750, § 3.

§ 367. Costs

In any family violence case, all court costs, attorney fees, evaluation fees, and expert witness fees incurred in furtherance of this Part shall be paid by the perpetrator of the family violence, including all costs of medical and psychological care for the abused spouse, or for any of the children, necessitated by the family violence.

Added by Acts 1992, No. 1091, § 1.

§ 368. Other remedies not affected

This Part shall in no way affect the remedies set forth in R.S. 46:2131 through 2142, the Criminal Code, the Children's Code, or elsewhere; however, the court, in any case brought under R.S. 46:2131 et seq., may impose the remedies provided herein.

Added by Acts 1992, No. 1091, § 1.

§ 369. Limitations

No public funds allocated to programs which provide services to victims of domestic violence shall be used to provide services to the perpetrator of domestic violence.

Added by Acts 1992, No. 1091, § 1.

PART V. INJUNCTIONS AND INCIDENTAL ORDERS

§ 371. Injunction against alienation or encumbrance; spouse's right to demand

A. In a proceeding for divorce, a spouse may obtain an injunction restraining or prohibiting the disposition or encumbrance of community property until further order of the court.

B. To be effective against a federally insured financial institution, an injunction granted under the provisions of this Section shall be served in accordance with the provisions of R.S. 6:285(C). An injunction granted pursuant to the provisions of this Section shall be effective only against accounts, safe deposit boxes, or other assets listed or held in the name of the following:

(1) One or both of the spouses named in the injunction.

(2) Another party or business entity specifically named in the injunction.

C. A federally insured financial institution shall not be liable for loss or damages resulting from its actions to comply with the injunction provided that the requirements of this Section have been met.

Added by Acts 1990, No. 1009, § 7, eff. Jan. 1, 1991. Amended by Acts 2012, No. 582, § 1.

Cross References

C.C. arts. 101 to 105, 151, 152, 2357, 2362.1, 3521.

C.C.P. arts. 10, 969, 1701, 1702, 3941, 3942, 3944.

R.S. 9:291, 9:301, 9:302, 9:381 to 9:384, 13:1401, 13:3491.

§ 372. Injunction against abuse; form; central Registry

A. In a proceeding for divorce, a court may grant an injunction prohibiting a spouse from physically or sexually abusing the other spouse or a child of either of the parties.

B. Immediately upon rendering a decision granting relief provided in Subsection A of this Section, the judge shall cause to have prepared a Uniform Abuse Prevention Order, as provided in R.S. 46:2136.2(C), shall sign such order, and shall forward it to the clerk of court for filing, all without delay.

C. The clerk of the issuing court shall transmit the Uniform Abuse Prevention Order to the Louisiana Protective Order Registry, R.S. 46:2136.2(A), by facsimile transmission, mail, or direct electronic input, where available, as expeditiously as possible, but no later than the end of the next business day after the order is filed with the clerk of court.

Added by Acts 1990, No. 1009, § 7, eff. Jan. 1, 1991. Amended by Acts 1997, No. 1156, § 4; Acts 2003, No. 750, § 3.

Cross References

C.C. arts. 101 to 105, 151, 152, 2357, 2362.1, 3521, 3522.

C.C.P. arts. 10, 969, 1701, 1702, 3491, 3492, 3944.

R.S. 9:291, 9:301, 9:302, 9:381 to 9:384, 13:1401, 13:3491.

§ 372.1. Injunction against harassment

In a proceeding for divorce, a court may grant an injunction prohibiting a spouse from harassing the other spouse.

Added by Acts 2003, No. 750, § 3.

§ 373. Removal of personal property

A. In a proceeding for divorce, a court may grant an ex parte order requiring the sheriff or appropriate law enforcement officer to accompany a spouse to the family residence or another location designated by the court so that personal property specified in the order may be obtained by that spouse.

B. Personal property which may be obtained by a court order issued under this Section includes, but is not limited to, the following:

(1) Items of personal wearing apparel belonging to the petitioning spouse or belonging to any children in the custody of the spouse.

(2) Food and eating utensils necessary for the spouse or any children in the custody of the spouse.

(3) Any other item or items deemed necessary by the court for the safety or well-being of the spouse or any children in the custody of the spouse.

Added by Acts 1990, No. 1009, § 7, eff. Jan. 1, 1991.

Cross References

C.C. arts. 101 to 105, 227, 230, 242, 243, 2357, 2362.1, 3522, 3525, 3527.

C.C.P. arts. 10, 969, 1701, 1702, 3941, 3942, 3944, 3521.

R.S. 9:291, 9:301, 9:302, 9:381 to 9:384, 13:1401, 13:3491.

§ 374. Possession and use of family residence or community movables or immovables

A. When the family residence is the separate property of either spouse, after the filing of a petition for divorce or in conjunction therewith, the spouse who has physical custody or has been awarded temporary custody of the minor children of the marriage may petition for, and a court may award to that spouse, after a contradictory hearing, the use and occupancy of the family residence pending the partition of the community property or one hundred eighty days after termination of the marriage, whichever occurs first. In these cases, the court shall inquire into the relative economic status of the spouses, including both community and separate property, and the needs of the children, and shall award the use and occupancy of the family residence to the spouse in accordance with the best interest of the family. The court shall consider the granting of the occupancy of the family residence in awarding spousal support.

B. When the family residence is community property or is owned by the spouses in indivision, or the spouses own community movables or immovables, after or in conjunction with the filing of a petition for divorce or for separation of property in accordance with Civil Code Article 2374, either spouse may petition for, and a court may award to one of the spouses, after a contradictory hearing, the use and occupancy of the family residence and use of community movables or immovables pending partition of the property or further order of the court, whichever occurs first. In these cases, the court shall inquire into the relative economic status of the spouses, including both community and separate property, and the needs of the children, if any, and shall award the use and occupancy of the family residence and the use of any community movables or immovables to the spouse in accordance with the best interest of the family. If applicable, the court shall consider the granting of the occupancy of the family residence and the use of community movables or immovables in awarding spousal support.

C. A spouse who, in accordance with the provisions of Subsection A or B of this Section, uses and occupies or is awarded by the court the use and occupancy of the family residence, a community immovable occupied as a residence, or a community manufactured home as defined in R.S. 9:1149.2 and occupied as a residence, regardless of whether it has been immobilized, shall not be liable to the other spouse for rental for the use and occupancy, except as hereafter provided. If the court awards use and occupancy to a spouse, it shall at that time determine whether to award rental for the use and occupancy and, if so, the amount of the rent. The parties may agree to defer the rental issue for decision in the partition proceedings. If the parties agreed at the time of the award of use and occupancy to defer the rental issue, the court may make an award of rental retroactive to the date of the award of use and occupancy.

D. The court may determine whether a residence is separate or community property, or owned in indivision, in the contradictory hearing authorized under the provisions of this Section.

E. (1) In a proceeding for divorce or thereafter, a summary proceeding shall be undertaken by the court upon request of either party to allocate the use of community property, including monetary assets, bank accounts, savings plans, and other divisible movable property pending partition.

(2) The court shall determine allocation of community property after considering:

(a) The custody of the children and exclusive use and occupancy of the family residence.

(b) The total community property.

(c) The need of a spouse for funds to maintain a household prior to partition.

(d) The need of a spouse to receive legal representation during the course of the proceedings.

(3) Upon court order, each spouse shall provide the other a complete accounting of all allocated community property to demonstrate compliance with Civil Code Article 2369.3.

Added by Acts 1990, No. 1009, § 7, eff. Jan. 1, 1991. Amended by Acts 1995, No. 965, § 1; Acts 1997, No. 614, § 1; Acts 2001, No. 903, § 1; Acts 2001, No. 1082, § 1; Acts 2004, No. 668, § 1, eff. July 5, 2004; Acts 2008, No. 408, § 1; Acts 2009, No. 204, § 2.

Comment—2001

The amendments to Subsections A and B eliminate references to the court's consideration of the use and occupancy of the family home or the use of community movables and immovables in awarding child support. The child support guidelines incorporate the consideration of the cost of housing.

Editor's note. Acts 2001, No. 1082, § 5, declares that this Act applies to actions concerning child support filed after August 15, 2001.

Cross References

C.C. arts. 101 to 105, 2336, 2339, 2351, 2358, 2362.1, 2366, 2369, 2374, 3521, 3522, 3525, 3527.

C.C.P. arts. 10, 969, 1701, 1702, 3941, 3942, 3944.

R.S. 9:291, 9:301, 9:381 to 9:384, 13:1401, 13:3491.

§ 375. Award of attorney's fees

A. When the court renders judgment in an action to make executory past-due payments under a spousal or child support award, or to make executory past-due installments under an award for contributions made by a spouse to the other spouse's education or training, it shall, except for good cause shown, award attorney's fees and costs to the prevailing party.

B. When the court renders judgment in an action to enforce child visitation rights it shall, except for good cause shown, award attorney's fees and costs to the prevailing party.

Added by Acts 1990, No. 1009, § 7, eff. Jan. 1, 1991.

Cross References

C.C. arts. 101 to 105, 2357, 2362.1, 3521, 3522.

C.C.P. arts. 10, 969, 1701, 1702, 3941, 3942, 3944.

R.S. 9:291, 9:301, 9:302, 9:381 to 9:384, 13:1401, 13:3491.

§ 376. Repealed by Acts 1993, No. 261, § 9, eff. Jan. 1, 1994

§§ 377 to 380. Reserved for future legislation

CHAPTER 2. TRANSITIONAL PROVISIONS

PART I. DIVORCE

Section
381. Actions pending on effective date of divorce revision act; law governing.
382. Present effect of judgment of separation from bed and board.
383. Judgment of divorce after judgment of separation.
384. Effect of reconciliation on community.

PART II. CHILD CUSTODY AND SUPPORT

385. Actions pending on effective date of child custody and support revision act; law governing.

PART III. SPOUSAL SUPPORT

386. Actions pending on effective date of spousal support revision act; law governing.
387. Spousal support; period of grace after effective date of spousal support revision act.

PART I. DIVORCE

§ 381. Actions pending on effective date of divorce revision act; law governing

This Act does not apply to actions for separation from bed and board or divorce or actions for incidental relief commenced before January 1, 1991, or to reconventional demands thereto, whenever filed. Such actions are to be governed by the law in effect prior to January 1, 1991.

Added by Acts 1990, No. 1009, § 7, eff. Jan. 1, 1991.

Editor's note. By a 1991 Concurrent Resolution, the legislature declared its intent that "the sole purpose of enacting R.S. 9:381 was to permit parties to an action for separation from bed and board filed before January 1, 1991, to continue to proceed in those suits under the law effective before that date, and was not to preclude such parties from amending their pleadings or filing new pleadings to take advantage of the new ground for divorce under Louisiana Civil Code Article 102."

Cross References

C.C. arts. 101 to 105, 3521, 3522.

C.C.P. arts. 10, 969, 1701, 1702, 3941, 3942, 3944.

R.S. 9:291, 9:301, 9:302, 9:371 to 9:375, 13:1401, 13:3491.

§ 382. Present effect of judgment of separation from bed and board

A judgment of separation from bed and board or divorce rendered before January 1, 1998, or a judgment rendered in an action governed by R.S. 9:381, shall have the same effect that it had prior to January 1, 1998. These effects include but are not limited to:

(1) Spouses who are judicially separated shall retain that status until either reconciliation or divorce.

(2) A judicial determination of fault or freedom from fault made prior to January 1, 1998, shall have the same effect on the right to claim spousal support as it had prior to January 1, 1998.

(3) A judgment of separation or divorce rendered prior to January 1, 1998, without a determination of fault shall not preclude a subsequent adjudication of fault as a bar to spousal support.

Added by Acts 1990, No. 1009, § 7, eff. Jan. 1, 1991. Amended by Acts 1997, No. 1078, § 3, eff. Jan. 1, 1998.

Cross References

C.C. arts. 101 to 105, 3521, 3522.

C.C.P. arts. 10, 969, 1701, 1702, 3941, 3942, 3944.

R.S. 9:291, 9:301, 9:371 to 9:375, 13:3491, 13:1401.

§ 383. Judgment of divorce after judgment of separation

A. Any person who is judicially separated before January 1, 1991, may obtain a judgment of divorce if there has been no reconciliation between the spouses for a period of six months or more from the date the judgment of separation from bed and board was signed. If an appeal is taken from a judgment of separation from bed and board, a suit for divorce pursuant to this Section may not be commenced until the judgment becomes final and definitive as provided by Articles 2166 and 2167 of the Code of Civil Procedure.

B. This Section shall be effective until January 1, 1992, and thereafter spouses who are judicially separated shall be governed by the provisions of this Act in obtaining a judgment of divorce.

Added by Acts 1990, No. 1009, § 7, eff. Jan. 1, 1991.

Cross References

C.C. arts. 101 to 105, 3521, 3522.

C.C.P. arts. 10, 969, 1701, 1702, 3941, 3942, 3944.

R.S. 9:291, 9:301, 9:302, 9:371 to 9:375.

§ 384. Effect of reconciliation on community

A. If spouses who were judicially separated by a judgment signed before January 1, 1991, or by a judgment rendered in an action governed by R.S. 9:381, reconcile after September 6, 1985, their community of acquets and gains shall be reestablished between the spouses, as of the date of filing of the original petition in the action in which the separation judgment was rendered, unless the spouses execute prior to the reconciliation a matrimonial agreement that the community will not be reestablished upon reconciliation. This matrimonial agreement shall not require court approval.

B. Reestablishment of a community property regime under the provisions of this Section shall be effective toward third persons only upon filing notice of the reestablishment for registry in accordance with the provisions of Civil Code Article 2332. The reestablishment of the community shall not prejudice the rights of third persons validly acquired prior to filing notice of the reestablishment nor shall it affect a prior community property partition between the spouses.

Added by Acts 1990, No. 1009, § 7, eff. Jan. 1, 1991. Amended by Acts 1995, No. 1233, § 1.

Editor's note. Section 2 of Acts 1995, No. 1233 provides: "The provisions of this Act are remedial and shall be applied retroactively."

Cross References

C.C. arts. 101 to 105, 2332, 3521, 3522.

C.C.P. arts. 10, 969, 1701, 1702, 3941, 3942, 3944.

R.S. 9:291, 9:301, 9:302, 9:371 to 9:375.

PART II. CHILD CUSTODY AND SUPPORT

§ 385. Actions pending on effective date of child custody and support revision act; law governing

Acts 1993, No. 261 does not apply to actions for separation from bed and board or divorce or actions for incidental relief commenced before January 1, 1994, or to reconventional demands thereto, whenever filed. Such actions are to be governed by the law in effect prior to January 1, 1994.

Added by Acts 1993, No. 261, § 8, eff. Jan. 1, 1994. Redesignated by Acts 1997, No. 1078, § 6, eff. Jan. 1, 1998.

Cross References

C.C. arts. 6, 131 to 136, 141, 142, 245.

R.S. 9:331 to 9:333, 9:335, 9:341 to 9:344.

PART III. SPOUSAL SUPPORT

§ 386. Actions pending on effective date of spousal support revision act; law governing

Acts 1997, No. 1078 does not apply to actions for separation from bed and board or divorce or actions for incidental relief commenced before January 1, 1998, or to reconventional demands thereto, whenever filed. Such actions are to be governed by the law in effect prior to January 1, 1998. Added by Acts 1997, No. 1078, § 4, eff. Jan. 1, 1998.

§ 387. Spousal support; period of grace after effective date of spousal support revision act

A person who is entitled to assert a claim for spousal support, and who is adversely affected by the provisions of Acts 1997, No. 1078, has one year from January 1, 1998, within which to assert a claim under the law in effect prior to that date.

Added by Acts 1997, No. 1078, § 4, eff. Jan. 1, 1998.

CODE TITLE VI—OF MASTER AND SERVANT [BLANK]
CODE TITLE VII—PARENT AND CHILD

CHAPTER 1. CHILDREN

PART I. LEGITIMATION

Section
391. Repealed.
391.1. Child conceived after death of parent.
392. Acknowledgment; requirements; content.
392.1. Acknowledgment; obligation to support; visitation.
393. Full faith and credit of acknowledgments.
394. Evidence of hospital bills and tests in paternity action.
395. Paternity proceedings; special requirements.
395.1. Repealed.

PART I-A. BLOOD OR TISSUE SAMPLING FOR DETERMINATION OF PATERNITY

396. Authority for test; ex parte orders; use of results.
397. Selection of expert.
397.1. Compensation of expert witnesses and recovery of testing costs.
397.2. Chain of custody of blood or tissue samples.
397.3. Admissibility and effect of test results.
398. Applicability to criminal actions.
398.1. Award of attorney's fees in actions to establish paternity.
398.2. Petition for order to submit to blood or tissue tests prior to bringing filiation action.

PART I-B. ESTABLISHMENT OF CHILD SUPPORT IN PATERNITY PROCEEDING

399. Establishment of child support; interim order during proceeding; final order following judgment of paternity.
399.1. Dismissal of final order following judgment of paternity; time periods; procedure; effects.

PART I-C. PUTATIVE FATHER REGISTRY

400. Putative father registry.
400.1. Repealed.

PART II. FILIATION

401. Disavowal action under Civil Code Article 186; parties.
402. Effect of disavowal action on prior child support order.
403. Mother's contestation action; procedure.
404. Father's paternity action; time period; exception.
405. Legal effect of acknowledgment.

Section
406. Revocation of authentic act; with and without cause; procedure.
407. Repealed.

PART III. ADOPTION

SUBPART A. MINORS UNDER SEVENTEEN [REPEALED]

421 to 441. Repealed.

SUBPART B. PERSONS OVER SEVENTEEN

461. Effect of adult adoption by stepparent.
462. Adult adoption; effective date of adoption.
463. Adult adoption; recordation.
464. Adult adoption; birth certificate.
465. Adult adoption; change of name.

PART IV. NEGLECT OR ABUSE [REPEALED]

551 to 553. Repealed.

PART V. GENERAL PROVISIONS

571. General rule that child may not sue parent.
572. Uncontested paternity proceedings; proof by affidavit; adoption of court rules.
573, 574. Repealed.
575. Abused parent or grandparent; domestic abuse assistance.

PART I. LEGITIMATION

§ 391. Repealed by Acts 2004, No. 26, § 15

§ 391.1. Child conceived after death of parent

A. Notwithstanding the provisions of any law to the contrary, any child conceived after the death of a decedent, who specifically authorized in writing his surviving spouse to use his gametes, shall be deemed the child of such decedent with all rights, including the capacity to inherit from the decedent, as the child would have had if the child had been in existence at the time of the death of the deceased parent, provided the child was born to the surviving spouse, using the gametes of the decedent, within three years of the death of the decedent.

B. Any heir or legatee of the decedent whose interest in the succession of the decedent will be reduced by the birth of a child conceived as provided in Subsection A of this Section shall have one year from the birth of such child within which to bring an action to disavow paternity.

Added by Acts 2001, No. 479, § 1. Amended by Acts 2003, No. 495, § 1.

Comments—2003

Despite the requirement in Civil Code Article 939 that a successor must exist at the time of the death of the decedent in order to inherit, this statute specifically grants inheritance rights to children conceived after the death of a parent who authorized in writing his surviving spouse to use his gametes, provided the child is born within three years of the death of the deceased parent and the gametes used for conception were those of the decedent. Paragraph A is written as gender neutral and applies to the death of either parent, thus protecting children born of artificial insemination, in vitro fertilization, and gestational surrogacy. By affording such children the right to inherit by intestacy pursuant to Louisiana law, the statute allows the child to qualify for Social Security benefits of the deceased parent pursuant to 42 U.S.C. § 416(h)(2)(A).

§ 392. Acknowledgment; requirements; content

A. Prior to the execution of an acknowledgment of paternity, the notary shall apprise in writing and orally, which may include directing them to video or audio presentations, the mother and alleged father making the acknowledgment of the following:

(1) Either party has the right to request a genetic test to determine if the alleged father is the biological father of the child.

(2) The alleged father has the right to consult an attorney before signing an acknowledgment of paternity.

(3) If the alleged father does not acknowledge the child, the mother has the right to file a paternity suit to establish paternity.

(4) After the alleged father signs an acknowledgment of paternity, he has the right to pursue visitation with the child and the right to petition for custody.

(5) Once an acknowledgment of paternity is signed, the father may be obligated to provide support for the child.

(6) Once an acknowledgment of paternity is signed, the child will have inheritance rights and any rights afforded children born in wedlock.

(7)(a) An alleged father who executed an authentic act of acknowledgment may revoke the act, without cause, before the earlier of the following:

(i) Sixty days after the signing of the act, in a judicial hearing for the limited purpose of revoking the acknowledgment.

(ii) A judicial hearing relating to the child, including a child support proceeding, wherein the alleged father who executed the authentic act of acknowledgment is a party to the proceeding.

(b) Thereafter, the acknowledgment of paternity may be voided only upon proof, by clear and convincing evidence, that such act was induced by fraud, duress, material mistake of fact, or error, or that the alleged father who executed the authentic act of acknowledgment is not the biological father.

(c) Except for good cause shown, the court shall not suspend any legal responsibilities or obligations, including a support obligation, of the party or parties during the pendency of the proceeding authorized in this Section.

(8) All parties to the action have any other rights and responsibilities which may be afforded by law now or in the future.

B. In addition to the general requirements of the Civil Code, an acknowledgment of a child born outside of marriage shall include the social security numbers of the father and mother, and, in accordance with the provisions of 42 U.S.C. 652(a)(7) and 42 U.S.C. 666(a)(5)(D), shall include all minimum requirements specified by the secretary of the United States Department of Health and Human Services. Failure to recite a party's social security number as required herein shall not affect the validity of the declaration.

Added by Acts 1997, No. 1243, § 1. Amended by Acts 1998, 1st Ex. Sess., No. 6, § 2, eff. July 1, 1998; Acts 2004, No. 26, § 5; Acts 2006, No. 344, § 4, eff. June 13, 2006; Acts 2006, No. 470, § 1, eff. June 22, 2006; Acts 2010, No. 173, § 1.

Editor's note. Section 2 of Acts 2006, No. 470 declares that this Act "shall be applied retroactively to June 29, 2005, as well as prospectively." For the unconstitutionality of retroactive laws that impair the obligation of contracts or divest vested rights, see Yiannopoulos, Civil Law System §§ 110–112 (2d ed. 1999); id., Civil Law Property § 10 (2001).

§ 392.1. Acknowledgment; obligation to support; visitation

In child support, custody, and visitation cases, the acknowledgment of paternity by authentic act is deemed to be a legal finding of paternity and is sufficient to establish an obligation to support the child and to establish visitation without the necessity of obtaining a judgment of paternity.

Added by Acts 2006, No. 344, § 4, eff. June 29, 2005.

Editor's note. Section 8 of Acts 2006, No. 344 declares: "Notwithstanding any provision of law to the contrary, the provisions of Article 196 and R.S. 9:392.1 shall be retroactive to June 29, 2005." For the unconstitutionality of retroactive laws that impair the obligation of contracts or divest vested rights, see Yiannopoulos, Civil Law System §§ 110 to 112 (2d ed. 1999); id., Civil Law Property § 10 (2001)).

§ 393. Full faith and credit of acknowledgments

Full faith and credit shall be given by Louisiana courts to an affidavit acknowledging paternity executed in any state in accordance with the laws and procedures of that state.

Added by Acts 1997, No. 1243, § 1.

§ 394. Evidence of hospital bills and tests in paternity action

In an action to establish paternity, originals or certified copies of bills for pregnancy, childbirth, and genetic testing shall be admissible as an exception to the hearsay rule and shall be prima facie evidence that the amounts reflected on the bills were incurred for such services or testing on behalf of the child. Extrinsic evidence of authenticity of the bills, or their duplicates, as a condition precedent to admissibility shall not be required.

Added by Acts 1997, No. 1242, § 1.

§ 395. Paternity proceedings; special requirements

A. Each party in a paternity proceeding shall advise the state case registry of his current address and telephone number, social security number, driver's license number, and the name, address, and telephone number of his current employer and of any change in this information during the pendency of the proceeding and thereafter. If any of this information is unavailable, the party shall submit a statement to this effect with the state case registry. Information submitted pursuant to this Section shall be available for inspection by the parties in the proceeding but shall otherwise be confidential except as provided in this Section.

B. Any order entered or judgment rendered shall require the parties to provide the state case registry with any change in the information required by this Section which occurs after the date of the entry or rendering.

C. Upon entry of an order or upon receipt of any change in this information during the pending proceeding, the clerk of court shall forward this information to the state case registry in accordance with R.S. 46:236.10.

Added by Acts 1998, 1st Ex.Sess., No. 8, § 1, eff. April 24, 1998.

§ 395.1. Repealed by Acts 2006, No. 344, § 7, eff. June 13, 2006

PART I-A. BLOOD OR TISSUE SAMPLING FOR DETERMINATION OF PATERNITY

§ 396. Authority for test; ex parte orders; use of results

A. (1) Notwithstanding any other provision of law to the contrary, in any civil action in which paternity is a relevant fact, or in an action en desaveu, the court may, on its own initiative, or shall, under either of the following circumstances, order the mother, child, and alleged father, or the mother's husband or former husband in an action en desaveu, to submit to the collection of blood or tissue samples, or both, and direct that inherited characteristics in the samples, including but not limited to blood and tissue type, be determined by appropriate testing procedures:

(a) Upon request made by or on behalf of any person whose blood or tissue is involved, provided that such request is supported by a sworn affidavit alleging specific facts which either tend to prove or deny paternity.

(b) Upon motion of any party to the action made at a time so as not to delay the proceedings unduly.

(2) If any party refuses to submit to such tests, the court may resolve the question of paternity against such party or enforce its order if the rights of others and the interests of justice so require.

B. (1) The district attorney, in assisting the Department of Children and Family Services in establishing paternity as authorized by R.S. 46:236.1.1 et seq., may file a motion with a court of proper jurisdiction and venue prior to and without the necessity of filing any other legal proceeding. Upon ex parte motion of the district attorney and sworn affidavit of the party alleging specific facts tending to prove paternity and other facts necessary to establish the jurisdiction and venue of the court, the court shall issue an ex parte order directing the mother, her husband or former husband, child, and alleged father to appear at a certain date and time to submit to the collection of blood or tissue samples, or both, and shall direct that inherited characteristics in the samples, including but not limited to blood and tissue type, be determined by appropriate testing procedures. The order shall be personally served upon the alleged father. If any party refuses to submit to such tests, the court, in a subsequent civil action in which paternity is a relevant fact, may resolve the question of paternity against such party or enforce its order if the rights of others and the interests of justice so require.

(2) If the written report of the results of the initial testing absolves a party from the allegation of paternity, the district attorney and the department shall be enjoined from initiating any subsequent civil action against that party to establish paternity of the same child. If the written report fails to absolve a party from the allegation of paternity, such report may be used by the district attorney or the department as evidence against the alleged father in any subsequent civil action for the establishment of paternity or by the alleged father in any subsequent proceeding in which filiation is an issue.

C. (1) Prior to ordering the alleged father to submit to paternity testing under the provisions of this Section, the court may, upon motion of the alleged father and after a contradictory hearing, order a person presumed to be the father of the child, pursuant to the provisions of the Civil Code, to produce the results of prior blood or tissue testing or to submit to the collection of blood or tissue samples, or both, and direct that inherited characteristics in the samples, including but not limited to blood and tissue type, be determined by appropriate testing procedures. If the written report of the results of the testing negates the presumption that this person is the father of the child, only then may the court order the alleged father to submit to paternity testing.

(2) If a presumed father is unknown by the parties or unavailable to submit to testing, then the court shall resolve the matter in the interest of justice in chambers.

Added by Acts 1972, No. 521, § 1. Amended by Acts 1985, No. 38, § 1; Acts 1990, No. 789, § 1; Acts 1992, No. 407, § 1; Acts 1998, 1st Ex.Sess., No. 6, § 1, eff. July 1, 1998; Acts 1999, No. 922, § 1; Acts 2006, No. 344, § 4, eff. June 13, 2006.

Cross References

C.C. arts. 3519.

§ 397. Selection of expert

The tests shall be conducted by a court appointed expert or experts qualified as examiners of blood or tissue samples for inherited characteristics, including but not limited to blood and tissue type. The number and qualifications of such expert or experts shall be determined by the court.

Added by Acts 1972, No. 521, § 2. Amended by Acts 1985, No. 38, § 1; Acts 1992, No. 407, § 1.

§ 397.1. Compensation of expert witnesses and recovery of testing costs

A. The costs of the blood or tissue tests conducted by the expert witness appointed by the court shall be fixed at a reasonable amount. The costs shall be advanced by the party who requested that such tests be conducted. If the court orders the blood or tissue tests on its own motion, the petitioner shall advance the costs of the tests. In either case, the court shall tax the costs to the party against whom judgment is rendered. The compensation of each expert witness appointed by the court and called by a party shall be fixed at a reasonable amount. It shall be paid by the party against whom judgment is rendered, which shall be taxed as costs of court.

B. If the state, a political subdivision of the state, or the petitioner pays the initial costs of testing under this Part in a paternity action, the state, political subdivision, or petitioner may recover those costs from an individual only if he is found to be the father of the child in the action. If an income assignment order is issued, the reimbursement for the costs shall be ordered through the income assignment order. If an income assignment order has not been issued, the court shall determine the manner in which the reimbursement for the costs shall be made.

Added by Acts 1972, No. 521, § 3. Amended by Acts 1984, No. 790, § 1; Acts 1985, No. 38, § 1; Acts 1988, No. 425, § 1; Acts 1992, No. 406, § 1; Acts 1992, No. 407, § 1; Acts 2008, No. 444, § 1.

§ 397.2. Chain of custody of blood or tissue samples

The chain of custody of blood or tissue samples taken under this Part may be established if documentation of the chain of custody is submitted with the expert's report and if such documentation was made at or near the time of the chain of custody and was made in the course of regularly conducted business activity.

Added by Acts 1972, No. 521, § 4. Amended by Acts 1985, No. 38, § 1; Acts 1992, No. 407, § 1; Acts 1999, No. 1127, § 1.

§ 397.3. Admissibility and effect of test results

A. (1) A written report of the results of the initial testing, certified by a sworn affidavit by the expert who supervised the tests, shall be filed in the suit record. The affidavit shall state in substance:

(a) That the affiant is qualified as an examiner of blood or tissue samples for inherited characteristics, including but not limited to blood and tissue types, to administer the test and shall give the affiant's name, address, telephone number, qualifications, education, and experience.

(b) How the tested individuals were identified when the samples were obtained.

(c) Who obtained the samples and how, when, and where the samples were obtained.

(d) The chain of custody of the samples from the time obtained until the tests were completed.

(e) The results of the test and the probability of paternity as calculated by an expert based on the test results.

(f) The procedures performed to obtain the test results.

(2) A notice that the report has been filed shall be mailed by certified mail to all parties by the clerk of court or shall be served in accordance with Code of Civil Procedure Article 1314.

(3) A party may challenge the testing procedure within thirty days of the date of receipt or service of the notice.

B. (1) If the court finds there has been a procedural error in the administration of the tests, the court shall order an additional test made by the same laboratory or expert.

(2)(a) If there is no timely challenge to the testing procedure or if the court finds there has been no procedural error in the testing procedure, the certified report shall be admitted in evidence at trial as prima facie proof of its contents, provided that the party against whom the report is sought to be used may summon and examine those making the original of the report as witnesses under cross-examination. The summons for the individual making the original of the report may be served through his employer's agent for service of process listed with the secretary of state or served pursuant to R.S. 13:3201 et seq.

(b) A certified report of blood or tissue sampling which indicates by a ninety-nine and nine-tenths percentage point threshold probability that the alleged father is the father of the child creates a rebuttable presumption of paternity.

C. Any additional testing ordered by the court pursuant to this Part shall be proved by the testimony of the expert.

D. If the court finds that the conclusions of all the experts as disclosed by the reports, based upon the tests, are that the alleged father is not the father of the child, the question of paternity shall be resolved accordingly. If the experts disagree in their findings or conclusions, the question shall be submitted upon all the evidence.

Added by Acts 1972, No. 521, § 5. Amended by Acts 1985, No. 38, § 1; Acts 1988, No. 298, § 1; Acts 1995, No. 1144, § 1; Acts 1999, No. 1127, § 1.

§ 398. Applicability to criminal actions

This part shall apply to criminal cases subject to the following limitations and provisions:

(1) An order for the tests shall be made only upon application of a party or on the court's initiative;

(2) The compensation of the experts shall be paid by the parish of the party's domicile under order of court;

(3) The court may direct a verdict of acquittal upon the conclusions of all the experts under the provisions of R.S. 9:397.3(D), otherwise the case shall be submitted for determination upon all the evidence.

Added by Acts 1972, No. 521, § 6.

§ 398.1. Award of attorney's fees in actions to establish paternity

When the court renders judgment in favor of a party seeking to establish paternity, it shall, except for good cause shown, award attorney's fees costs to the prevailing party. However, the provisions of this Section shall not apply to compensation of expert witnesses and recovery of blood or tissue testing costs in accordance with R.S. 9:397.1.

Added by Acts 1991, No. 854, § 2. Amended by Acts 1992, No. 407, § 1.

Editor's note. Section 3 of Acts 1991, No. 854 declares: "The provisions of this Act shall not be considered in conflict with Chapter 4 of Title XIII of the Louisiana Children's Code and accordingly, the Louisiana State Law Institute shall direct and supervise the printing of Articles 1376(6)(c) and 1390 of the Louisiana Children's Code, if it becomes law, in a manner consistent with the provisions of Section 1 of this Act."

§ 398.2. Petition for order to submit to blood or tissue tests prior to bringing filiation action

A. (1) Notwithstanding any other provision of law to the contrary, the husband of the mother, prior to filing an action of disavowal of a child born or conceived during his marriage to the mother and prior to the expiration of the time required to file an action of disavowal, may petition a court of proper jurisdiction and venue for an order directing the mother, child, and petitioner to submit to the collection of blood or tissue samples, or both, for determination of paternity for the purpose of exercising rights relating to the child. The filing of the petition suspends the period for bringing the disavowal action for a period of one year from the date the petition is filed.

(2) Notwithstanding any other provision of law to the contrary, the alleged biological father of a child born outside of marriage, prior to filing any action to establish filiation of the child, may petition a court of proper jurisdiction and venue for an order directing the mother, child, and petitioner to submit to the collection of blood or tissue samples, or both, for determination of paternity for the purpose of exercising rights relating to the child.

B. The petition authorized in Paragraphs (1) and (2) of Subsection A of this Section shall name the mother as defendant and shall allege specific facts tending to prove the relationship or the circumstances of any physical relationship with the mother, or facts tending to prove paternity, and other facts necessary to establish the jurisdiction and venue of the court.

C. The court, after contradictory hearing, may order the parties to submit to blood or tissue samples, or both, and direct that inherited characteristics in the samples, including but not limited to blood and tissue type, be determined by appropriate testing procedures as provided in this Part.

D. If the court issues an order directing blood or tissue tests, or both, the provisions of R.S. 9:397 through 397.2 and 397.3(A) and (B) shall be applicable to the selection and compensation of experts, payment of testing costs, establishment of chain of custody, filing of test results in the court record, and authority of the court to order additional tests if it finds there has been a procedural error in the administration of the tests.

E. The court shall not make a determination of paternity based on the test results and conclusions of the experts filed in the record; however, the test results shall be admissible in any subsequent action filed by any of the parties relating to filiation of the child.

F. The provisions of this Section shall not in any manner affect the status of a child whose legal father is the husband of the mother who does not timely disavow paternity of the child nor affect any right that a child may have to file an action of filiation as provided by law.

Added by Acts 1995, No. 1206, § 1. Amended by Acts 2004, No. 26, § 5; Acts 2006, No. 344, § 4, eff. June 13, 2006.

Cross References

C.C.P. arts. 10(8), 74.1.

R.S. 9:396 to 9:398.1.

PART I–B. ESTABLISHMENT OF CHILD SUPPORT IN PATERNITY PROCEEDING

§ 399. Establishment of child support; interim order during proceeding; final order following judgment of paternity

A. In a proceeding for the determination of paternity and upon motion of any party, the court presiding over the paternity issue shall issue an order of interim child support if there is clear and convincing evidence of paternity on the basis of genetic testing or other evidence susceptible of independent verification or corroboration.

B. If no interim child support was ordered pursuant to Subsection A of this Section, a judgment for final child support rendered against a defendant who has acknowledged paternity after a paternity suit has been filed or has been adjudged in a suit to establish paternity to be the parent of the child for whom support is ordered shall be effective from the date on which the paternity suit was filed. In the event the court finds good cause for not making the award retroactive to the date of the filing of the paternity suit, the court may make the award retroactive to a date subsequent to the filing of the paternity suit, but in no event shall the award be fixed later than the date of the rendition of the paternity judgment. Any monetary support provided by the judgment debtor, from the date the petition for support is filed to the date the final support order is issued to or on behalf of the person for whom support is ordered, may be credited to the judgment debtor against the amount of the judgment.

Added by Acts 1985, No. 376, § 1. Amended by Acts 1997, No. 1247, § 1, eff. July 1, 1997.

Cross References

C.C. art. 3519.

§ 399.1. Dismissal of final order following judgment of paternity; time periods; procedure; effects

A. Notwithstanding any other provision of law, a judgment establishing paternity may be set aside or vacated by the adjudicated father of a child, the child, the mother of the child, or the legal representative of any of these persons. The proceeding shall be instituted by ordinary process in a court of competent jurisdiction and service shall be made upon the office of children and family services, child support enforcement section of the Department of Children and Family Services, if services are being provided by the department. The burden of proof shall be upon the party seeking to set aside or vacate the judgment of paternity. The proceeding shall be brought within a two-year period commencing with the date on which the adjudicated father knew or should have known of a judgment that established him as the father of the child or commencing with the date the adjudicated father knew or should have known of the existence of an action to adjudicate the issue of paternity, whichever is first.

B. Subsection A of this Section does not apply if the child is presumed to be a child of a marriage between the mother and the legal father.

C. If the court finds there is a substantial likelihood that the adjudicated father is not the biological father, it shall order genetic tests pursuant to R.S. 9:396. Nothing herein shall preclude the introduction of other evidence if it is not possible to conduct genetic testing.

D. The test results certified under oath by an authorized representative of an accredited laboratory shall be filed with the court and shall be admissible on the issue of paternity in accordance with R.S. 9:397.3. If the test results show a statistical probability of paternity of ninety-nine point nine percent or greater, a rebuttable presumption of paternity shall be established. If the adjudicated father is found to be excluded by the tests, the court shall nullify the judgment of paternity.

E. Except for good cause shown, the court shall not suspend, during the pendency of this proceeding, any legal obligations including a support obligation of the adjudicated father.

F. (1) If a judgment of paternity is set aside, vacated, or dismissed, the court shall dismiss any obligation of child support.

(2) A judgment dismissing an established order of support does not affect any child support payment or arrearages paid, due, or owing prior to the date the action to set aside or vacate the judgment of paternity was filed.

(3) The judgment dismissing an established order of support shall be served upon the office of children and family services, child support enforcement section of the Department of Children and Family Services, if services are being provided by the department.

(4) Neither the state of Louisiana, its officers, employees, agents, contractors, nor the office of children and family services, child support enforcement section of the Department of Children and Family Services shall be liable in any case to compensate any person for child support paid or for any other costs as a result of the judgment setting aside or vacating the judgment of paternity or support entered in accordance with this Section.

Added by Acts 2008, No. 533, § 1. Amended by Acts 2010, No. 173, § 1; Acts 2012, No. 255, § 2.

PART I–C. PUTATIVE FATHER REGISTRY

§ 400. Putative father registry

A. The Department of Health and Hospitals, office of public health, shall establish a putative father registry which shall record the names and addresses of the following:

(1) Any person adjudicated by a court of this state to be the father of the child.

(2) Repealed by Acts 2006, No. 344, § 7, eff. June 13, 2006.

(3) Any person adjudicated by a court of another state or territory of the United States to be the father of an out of wedlock child, where a certified copy of the court order has been filed with the registry by such person or any other person.

(4) Any person who has filed with the registry an acknowledgment by authentic act.

(5) Repealed by Acts 2004, No. 26, § 15.

(6) Any person who has filed with the registry a judgment of filiation rendered by a court which recognizes a father as having, either formally or informally, acknowledged a child born outside of marriage and in which the father is adjudged the parent of the child.

B. A person filing a declaration to claim paternity of a child or an acknowledgement of paternity shall include therein his current address and shall notify the registry of any change of address pursuant to procedures prescribed by rules and regulations of the Department of Health and Hospitals, office of public health.

C. A declaration to claim paternity of a child may be introduced in evidence by any party, other than the person who filed such notice, in any proceeding in which such fact may be relevant.

D. The Department of Health and Hospitals, office of public health, shall, upon request, provide the names and addresses of persons listed with the registry to any court or authorized agency, and such information shall not be divulged to any other person, except upon order of a court for good cause shown.

E. The Department of Health and Hospitals, office of public health, shall promulgate all rules and regulations necessary to carry out the purposes of this Part.

Added by Acts 1989, No. 361, § 1. Amended by Acts 1993, No. 634, § 2, eff. June 15, 1993; Acts 2004, No. 26, § 5; Acts 2006, No. 344, § 4, eff. June 13, 2006; Acts 2013, No. 220, § 2, eff. June 11, 2013.

§ 400.1. Repealed by Acts 2006, No. 344, § 7, eff. June 13, 2006

PART II. FILIATION

§ 401. Disavowal action under Civil Code Article 186; parties

A. A person who will be presumed to be the father under Civil Code Article 186 if the plaintiff obtains a judgment of disavowal shall be made a party to the disavowal action and shall be served with process.

B. If the person cannot be served, an attorney shall be appointed to represent him.

Added by Acts 2006, No. 344, § 4, eff. June 13, 2006.

§ 402. Effect of disavowal action on prior child support order

A judgment of disavowal terminates existing child custody and visitation orders in favor of the husband or former husband. The judgment also terminates the obligation to pay child support and revokes any court order enforcing that obligation. However, it does not affect any child support payment or arrearages paid, due, or owing prior to the date the disavowal action was filed.

Added by Acts 2006, No. 344, § 4, eff. June 13, 2006.

§ 403. Mother's contestation action; procedure

A. The mother of the child is the proper party plaintiff and her former husband and present husband are proper party defendants in the contestation action provided for in the Civil Code.

B. The hearing may be closed to the public.

C. (1) A judgment rendered in favor of the mother terminates existing child custody and visitation orders. However, the former husband in extraordinary circumstances may be granted reasonable visitation if the court finds it is in the best interest of the child in accordance with the Civil Code.

(2) A judgment rendered in favor of the mother terminates the obligation of the former husband to pay child support and revokes any court order enforcing that obligation.

(3) A judgment does not affect any child support payment or arrearages paid, due, or owing prior to the date the contestation action was filed.

D. An appeal from a judgment in the contestation action may only be taken within thirty days from the applicable date in accordance with Code of Civil Procedure Article 2087(A). The appeal shall suspend the execution of the judgment.

Added by Acts 2006, No. 344, § 4, eff. June 13, 2006.

§ 404. Father's paternity action; time period; exception

The peremptive periods in Civil Code Article 198 shall apply to the Department of Children and Family Services when providing services in accordance with 42 U.S.C. 666.

Added by Acts 2006, No. 344, § 4, eff. June 13, 2006.

§ 405. Legal effect of acknowledgment

In child support, custody, and visitation cases, the acknowledgment of paternity by authentic act is deemed to be a legal finding of paternity and is sufficient to establish an obligation to support the child and to establish visitation without the necessity of obtaining a judgment of paternity.

Added by Acts 2006, No. 344, § 4, eff. June 13, 2006.

§ 406. Revocation of authentic act; with and without cause; procedure

A. (1) A person who executed an authentic act of acknowledgment may, without cause, revoke it within sixty days of the execution of the authentic act of acknowledgment:

(a) Upon the submission of a sworn statement refuting the named father. The state registrar, office of vital records, shall develop and make available a form and may impose a fee for the filing of revocation of the authentic act of acknowledgment. This form shall be filed in a central repository of the office of vital records of the Department of Health and Hospitals within sixty days of the date of the execution of the authentic act of acknowledgment. The registrar shall send a copy of the revoked acknowledgment to the other party in the original authentic act of acknowledgment. If the party requesting revocation of the authentic act of acknowledgment has been served with a petition for support for the child who is the subject of the act, the party shall also request that the registrar send a copy of the revoked acknowledgment to the agency charged with implementing a program of family support in accordance with R.S. 46:236.1.2; or

(b) In a judicial hearing for the limited purpose of revoking the acknowledgment or declaration; or

(c) In a judicial hearing relating to the child, including a child support proceeding, wherein the affiant to the authentic act of acknowledgment is a party to the proceeding.

(2) If at any time during the hearing, the court has reasonable cause to believe that a party to the authentic act of acknowledgment is or was unable to understand the effects of executing that act, the court shall orally explain to the individual the effects of the execution and the right to revoke the authentic act of acknowledgment in accordance with this Subsection, and the right to genetic tests to determine paternity in accordance with the provisions of R.S. 9:396 in any proceeding relative to the paternity of the child.

B. (1) If the notarial act of acknowledgment has not been revoked within sixty days in accordance with the provisions of Subsection A of this Section, a person who executed an authentic act of acknowledgment may petition the court to revoke such acknowledgment only upon proof, by clear and convincing evidence, that such act was induced by fraud, duress, material mistake of fact or error, or that the person is not the biological parent of the child.

(2) The mover shall institute the proceeding by ordinary process, within a two-year period commencing with the execution of the authentic act of acknowledgment of paternity, in a court of competent jurisdiction upon notice to the other party who executed the notarial act of acknowledgment and other necessary parties including the office of children and family services, child support enforcement section of the Department of Children and Family Services. If the court finds based upon the evidence presented at the hearing that there is substantial likelihood that fraud, duress, material mistake of fact or error existed in the execution of the act or that the person who executed the authentic act of acknowledgment is not the biological father, then, and only then, the court shall order genetic tests pursuant to R.S. 9:396. Nothing herein shall preclude the mover from presenting any other evidence as a substitute for the genetic tests if it is not possible to conduct such tests.

(3) The test results certified under oath by an authorized representative of an accredited laboratory shall be filed with the court and shall be admissible on the issue of paternity pursuant to R.S. 9:397.3. If the test results show a statistical probability of ninety-nine point nine percent or greater, a rebuttable presumption of paternity shall be established. If the acknowledged father is found to be excluded by the tests, an action seeking support or an established order of support shall be dismissed and the acknowledgment of paternity shall be revoked. A judgment dismissing an established order of support does not affect any child support payment or arrearages paid, due or owing prior to the date the revocation action was filed.

(4) The burden of proof in this proceeding shall be upon the party seeking to revoke the authentic act of acknowledgment.

C. (1) Except for good cause shown, the court shall not suspend during the pendency of this proceeding any legal obligations, including a support obligation, of the person who petitions the court to revoke or rescind the authentic act of acknowledgment under this Section.

(2) Neither the state of Louisiana, its officers, employees, agents, contractors, nor the office of children and family services, child support enforcement section of the Department of Children and Family Services shall be liable to compensate any person for child support paid or any other costs as a result of the revocation of any authentic act of acknowledgment or the revocation of any judgment of paternity or support in accordance with this Section.

D. (1) The revocation of the authentic act of acknowledgment pursuant to Subsection A of this Section shall not preclude the initiation of a paternity action against any alleged putative father, or by a man against a mother to establish his paternity.

(2) However, if the voluntary acknowledgment is revoked by order of the court based upon genetic tests conducted in accordance with Subsection B of this Section which excluded a person as a parent and an order of support has not been established, no further action may be initiated against the excluded person.

E. (1) The original form revoking the authentic act of acknowledgment shall be sent by the person revoking it to the state registrar at the office of vital records of the Department of Health and Hospitals in accordance with the provisions of this Section. If the revocation is as a result of a judicial hearing, a certified copy of any judgment revoking an authentic act of acknowledgment shall be sent by the clerk of court to the state registrar at the office of vital records of the Department of Health and Hospitals.

(2) Upon receipt of the form revoking the authentic act of acknowledgment which was executed and filed with the registrar within the sixty-day period or upon receipt of the

judgment which shows that the voluntary acknowledgment has been revoked at the hearing which is held no later than the sixtieth day following the execution of the voluntary acknowledgment, or upon receipt of a certified copy of a judgment with a finding shown clearly in the judgment that the authentic act of acknowledgment was revoked due to fraud, duress, material mistake of fact or error that existed in the execution of the act or that the person who executed the authentic act of acknowledgment is not the biological father, the registrar shall make the appropriate amendments to the birth record of the child who was the subject of the order.

Added by Acts 2006, No. 344, § 4, eff. June 13, 2006. Amended by Acts 2008, No. 533, § 1; Acts 2012, No. 255, § 2.

§ 407. Repealed by Acts 1991, No. 235, § 17, eff. Jan. 1, 1992

PART III. ADOPTION

SUBPART A. MINORS UNDER SEVENTEEN [REPEALED]

§§ 421 to 441. Repealed by Acts 1991, No. 235, § 17, eff. Jan. 1, 1992

SUBPART B. PERSONS OVER SEVENTEEN

§ 461. Effect of adult adoption by stepparent

In an adoption in accordance with the first paragraph of Civil Code Article 212, if the adoptive parent is married to a parent of the adopted child at the time of the adoption or was married to a parent at the time of the death of the parent, the relationship of that parent and his relatives to the adopted child shall remain unaltered and unaffected by the adoption.

Acts 2008, No. 351, § 3, eff. Jan. 1, 2009.

Revision Comment—2008

This provision does not change the law but simply replaces the former Article (C.C. Art. 214, as amended 1995) and explicitly applies to adult adoptions. See Children's Code Art. 1256 (same rule for the adoption of minors by a stepparent). Predecessor C.C. Art. 214, as amended 1995, maintained the legal relationship between the spouse who is a parent and that spouse's relatives and the child who is adopted by the parent's spouse. Without such a provision, the adoption would sever the relationship between both of the parents and their relatives and the child who is adopted, which is not the intended purpose of a "stepparent" adoption, either before or after the death of the parent.

Cross References

C.C. arts. 888, 1493, 1495 et seq.

R.S. 9:130, 9:401 to 9:405, 9:421 to 9:441, 9:461, 9:462, 9:2502, 9:2503, 13:3735, 40:72, 40:75, 40:79.

Const. Art. XII, § 5.

§ 462. Adult adoption; effective date of adoption

Notwithstanding the general provisions of Civil Code Article 214, if the act of adult adoption is filed within five days, exclusive of legal holidays, after the date of the last signature required for validity of the act, the adoption shall be effective as of the date of the last signature.

Acts 2008, No. 351, § 3, eff. Jan. 1, 2009.

§ 463. Adult adoption; recordation

A. An act of adult adoption executed in accordance with the first paragraph of Civil Code Article 212 shall be filed for registry with the clerk of court of any parish. If court authorization is required by the second paragraph of Civil Code Article 212, the judgment with the act of adoption shall be filed for registry with the clerk of court of any parish.

B. The clerk shall record the acts of adoption in the conveyance records. Within two business days of filing the act of adoption, the clerk shall transmit to the Department of Health and Hospitals, office of public health, vital records registry, such information as may be required by the rules of the department for indexing the adoption. The vital records registry shall index the adoption under the name of the adoptive parent or parents and the person being adopted and shall make reference to the day of filing and the parish where the original act of adoption is recorded. The failure of the clerk or the department to comply with the provisions of this Subsection does not affect the adoption.

Acts 2008, No. 351, § 3, eff. Jan. 1, 2009.

Cross References

C.C. arts. 212 to 214.

C.C.P. art. 74.5.

§ 464. Adult adoption; birth certificate

If the person who is adopted in an adult adoption was born in a state which requires a court order prior to issuing a new birth certificate, upon petition of the parent, parents, or the person adopted, a court of proper jurisdiction may grant a judgment recognizing the adoption based upon the authentic act of adoption without further proceedings. In this case, the validity and civil effects of the authentic act of adoption are not affected by the court order and shall continue to be governed by the applicable laws.

Acts 2008, No. 351, § 3, eff. Jan. 1, 2009.

Cross References

C.C. arts. 212 to 214, 1839.

C.C.P. art. 74.5.

§ 465. Adult adoption; change of name

The name of the adopted person may be changed in the act of adult adoption.

Acts 2008, No. 351, § 3, eff. Jan. 1, 2009.

Cross References

C.C. arts. 100, 212 to 214, 1839.

C.C.P. art. 74.5.

PART IV. NEGLECT OR ABUSE [REPEALED]

§§ 551 to 553. Repealed by Acts 1956, No. 111, § 1

PART V. GENERAL PROVISIONS

§ 571. General rule that child may not sue parent

The child who is not emancipated cannot sue:

(1) Either parent during the continuance of their marriage, when the parents are not judicially separated; or

(2) The parent who is entitled to his custody and control, when the marriage of the parents is dissolved, or the parents are judicially separated.

Added by Acts 1960, No. 31, § 3, eff. Jan. 1, 1961.

Cross References

C.C. arts. 215, 228, 250.

§ 572. Uncontested paternity proceedings; proof by affidavit; adoption of court rules

The court vested with jurisdiction may provide, by local rule, that in uncontested proceedings to establish paternity, proof may be submitted by affidavit.

Added by Acts 1999, No. 524, § 1.

§§ 573, 574. Repealed by Acts 1993, No. 261, § 9, eff. Jan. 1, 1994

§ 575. Abused parent or grandparent; domestic abuse assistance

A parent or grandparent who is being abused by an adult child or adult grandchild may file a petition in the district court seeking protection pursuant to the laws governing domestic abuse assistance, R.S. 46:2131 et seq.

Added by Acts 1993, No. 402, § 1.

CODE TITLE VIII—OF MINORS, OF THEIR TUTORSHIP AND EMANCIPATION

CHAPTER 1. TUTORSHIP

PART I. APPOINTMENT, RECOGNITION, OR CONFIRMATION

SUBPART A. IN GENERAL

Section
601. Parent's appointment of tutor when spouse insane.
602. Tutor, under tutor, curator, under curator; family meeting dispensed with.
603. Absentee minor or interdict not represented; special representation to effect sale.

PART II. MANAGEMENT AND DISPOSITION OF PROPERTY

SUBPART A. FAMILY MEETING DISPENSED WITH; PROCEDURE [REPEALED]

651 to 653. Repealed.

SUBPART B. PRIVATE SALE; PROCEDURE

671 to 674. Repealed.
675. Validating provision.

SUBPART C. SALE TO EFFECT PARTITION; PROCEDURE [REPEALED]

691 to 693. Repealed.

SUBPART D. MINERAL LEASES AND CONTRACTS; PROCEDURE [REPEALED]

711 to 713. Repealed.

SUBPART E. MISCELLANEOUS PROVISIONS

731. Sale or lease of right of way.
732. Ratification of sale during minority of person afterwards interdicted.
733. Purchase of federal bonds and debentures by tutors and curators.
734. Investment of funds.
735 to 742. Repealed.

Section

SUBPART F. UNIFORM TRANSFERS TO MINORS ACT

751. Definitions.
752. Scope.
753. Nomination of custodian.
754. Transfer by gift.
755. Transfer authorized by will or trust.
756. Other transfer by fiduciary.
757. Transfer by obligor.
758. Receipt for custodial property.
759. Manner of creating custodial property and effecting transfer; designation of initial custodian; control.
760. Single custodianship.
761. Validity and effect of transfer.
762. Care of custodial property.
763. Powers of custodian.
764. Use of custodial property.
765. Expenses, compensation, and bond of custodian.
766. Exemption of third person from liability.
767. Liability to third persons.
768. Renunciation, resignation, death, or removal of custodian; designation of successor custodian.
769. Accounting by and liability of custodian.
770. Termination of custodianship.
771. Applicability.
772. Effect on existing custodianship.
773. Short title.

PART III. BOND OR SECURITY IN PLACE OF MORTGAGE [REPEALED]

801 to 804. Repealed.

PART IV. SMALL ESTATES [REPEALED]

821 to 823. Repealed.

PART V. MISCELLANEOUS PROVISIONS [REPEALED]

841. Repealed.
842. Repealed.

PART I. APPOINTMENT, RECOGNITION, OR CONFIRMATION

SUBPART A. IN GENERAL

§ 601. Parent's appointment of tutor when spouse insane

If one of the parents is an interdict or notoriously insane, the other may appoint a tutor to the minor children as in the case of the father or mother dying last; however, if the interdicted or notoriously insane parent should be restored to reason, this tutorship by will shall be vacated.

Cross References
C.C. arts. 83, 257, 3519.

§ 602. Tutor, under tutor, curator, under curator; family meeting dispensed with

The judge shall act, without the convocation of a family meeting, in all matters pertaining to the appointment, recognition, or confirmation of all tutors, under tutors, curators, or under curators for minors or interdicts.

Cross References
C.C. arts. 270, 3519.

§ 603. Absentee minor or interdict not represented; special representation to effect sale

When it is desired to sell the whole property in which a minor or interdict owns an undivided interest, or the undivided interest of a minor or interdict in property, and the minor or interdict is an absentee and not represented by a tutor or curator residing in the state, the court having jurisdiction of the property may appoint, on the petition of any co-owner, a tutor or curator and an under tutor or under curator to serve under oath without bond to represent the absentee in the proceedings. A foreign tutor, curator, or guardian who has been recognized as provided in Article 4431 or 4556 of the Code of Civil Procedure may represent the minor or interdict under this section.

Amended by Acts 1960, No. 31, § 2, eff. Jan. 1, 1961.

Cross References
C.C. arts. 47 to 53, 336, 3519.

PART II. MANAGEMENT AND DISPOSITION OF PROPERTY

SUBPART A. FAMILY MEETING DISPENSED WITH; PROCEDURE [REPEALED]

§§ 651 to 653. Repealed by Acts 1960, No. 31, § 7, eff. Jan. 1, 1961

SUBPART B. PRIVATE SALE; PROCEDURE

§§ 671 to 674. Repealed by Acts 1960, No. 31, § 7, eff. Jan. 1, 1961

§ 675. Validating provision

Any person or corporation holding or claiming immovable property the title to which is based on a private sale of minor's property under the provisions of Louisiana Act No. 209 of 1932 [1] in which proceeding the written concurrence of the under-tutor was filed in lieu of the issuance of a rule nisi, shall after sixty days from July 26, 1950, be quieted in said title insofar as the failure to obtain a rule nisi in said proceeding is concerned, unless within said period of sixty days, proceedings to annul said private sale of minor's property are instituted, and said title thereafter shall be deemed good and merchantable for all purposes and against all persons including minors and interdicts.

Added by Acts 1950, No. 495, § 1.

[1] R.S. 9:603, 9:671 to 9:674 [repealed 1960], 9:691 to 9:693 [repealed 1952].

SUBPART C. SALE TO EFFECT PARTITION; PROCEDURE [REPEALED]

§§ 691 to 693. Repealed by Acts 1952, No. 321, § 5

SUBPART D. MINERAL LEASES AND CONTRACTS; PROCEDURE [REPEALED]

§§ 711 to 713. Repealed by Acts 1974, No. 133, § 2

SUBPART E. MISCELLANEOUS PROVISIONS

§ 731. Sale or lease of right of way

The tutor of a minor or the curator of an interdict may sell or lease a right of way over, across, and through lands owned in whole or in part by his ward in the manner provided by the applicable provisions of Articles 4268, 4271, 4341 and 4566 of the Code of Civil Procedure, for any legitimate purpose including, but not limiting the generality of, irrigation canals, drainage canals, navigation canals, railroads, roads, highways, tramways, power and communication lines, and pipe lines for water, oil, gas, and other hydro-carbon substances.

Amended by Acts 1950, No. 281, § 1; Acts 1960, No. 31, § 1, eff. Jan. 1, 1961.

Cross References
C.C. arts. 250, 256, 257.

§ 732. Ratification of sale during minority of person afterwards interdicted

The curator of an interdict may ratify, under Article 4566, and by proceeding in accordance with Article 4271, of the Code of Civil Procedure, any sale made on behalf of his ward while the latter was a minor, if the sale was one which could have been made legally at that time and was made by order of a court of competent jurisdiction. Sales so ratified are as valid and binding upon the interdict and his heirs as if such sales had been authorized and conducted validly.

Amended by Acts 1960, No. 31, § 1, eff. Jan. 1, 1961.

§ 733. Purchase of federal bonds and debentures by tutors and curators

Federal farm loan bonds issued by federal land banks, debentures issued by federal intermediate credit banks, and debentures issued by banks for cooperatives may be pur-

chased by tutors of minors and by curators of interdicts and absentees with funds under their management or control.
Amended by Acts 1958, No. 201, § 1.

§ 734. Investment of funds

Tutors of minors and curators of interdicts may invest the funds of their wards by depositing them at interest in savings accounts or on time deposit in banks domiciled in this state, in amounts not exceeding the amounts insured under the Acts of Congress by the Federal Deposit Insurance Corporation or insured under any other Act of the Congress of the United States.
Added by Acts 1952, No. 292, § 1.

§§ 735 to 742. Repealed by Acts 1987, No. 469, § 2, eff. Jan. 1, 1988

SUBPART F. UNIFORM TRANSFERS TO MINORS ACT

§ 751. Definitions

As used in this Subpart:

(1) "Adult" means an individual who has attained the age of eighteen years.

(2) "Benefit plan" means an employer's plan for the benefit of an employee or partner.

(3) "Broker" means a person lawfully engaged in the business of effecting transactions in securities or commodities for the person's own account or for the account of others.

(4) "Court" means a court of competent jurisdiction in the parish of the domicile of the minor.

(5) "Custodial property" means any interest in property transferred to a custodian under this Subpart and the income from and proceeds of that interest in property.

(6) "Custodian" means a person so designated under R.S. 9:759 or a successor or substitute custodian designated under R.S. 9:768.

(7) "Financial institution" means a bank, trust company, savings institution, or credit union, chartered and supervised under state or federal law.

(8) "Legal representative" means an individual's personal representative or tutor.

(9) "Member of the minor's family" means the minor's parent, stepparent, spouse, grandparent, brother, sister, uncle, or aunt, whether of the whole or half blood or by adoption.

(10) "Minor" means an individual who has not attained the age of eighteen years.

(11) "Person" means an individual, corporation, organization, or other legal entity.

(12) "Personal representative" means an executor, administrator, or representative of a decedent's estate or a person legally authorized to perform substantially the same functions.

(13) "State" includes any state of the United States, the District of Columbia, the Commonwealth of Puerto Rico, and any territory or possession subject to the legislative authority of the United States.

(14) "Transfer" means a transaction that creates custodial property under R.S. 9:759.

(15) "Transferor" means a person who makes a transfer under this Subpart.

(16) "Trust company" means a financial institution, corporation, or other legal entity authorized to exercise general trust powers.

(17) "Tutor" means a person appointed or qualified by a court to act as guardian of a minor's property or a person legally authorized to perform substantially the same functions, including but not limited to a curator.
Added by Acts 1987, No. 469, § 1, eff. Jan. 1, 1988.

§ 752. Scope

A. This Subpart applies to a transfer that refers to this Subpart in the designation under R.S. 9:759(A) by which the transfer is made if at the time of the transfer, the transferor, the minor, or the custodian is a resident of this state or the custodial property is located in this state. The custodianship so created remains subject to this Subpart despite a subsequent change in residence of a transferor, the minor, or the custodian, or the removal of custodial property from this state.

B. A person designated as custodian is subject to personal jurisdiction in this state with respect to any matter relating to the custodianship.

C. A transfer that purports to be made and which is valid under the Uniform Transfers to Minors Act, the Uniform Gifts to Minors Act,[1] or a substantially similar act, of another state is governed by the law of the designated state and may be executed and is enforceable in this state if at the time of the transfer, the transferor, the minor, or the custodian is a resident of the designated state or the custodial property is located in the designated state.
Added by Acts 1987, No. 469, § 1, eff. Jan. 1, 1988.

[1] Louisiana Gifts to Minors Act, R.S. 9:735 et seq. (repealed eff. Jan. 1, 1988).

§ 753. Nomination of custodian

A. A person having the right to designate the recipient of property transferable upon the occurrence of a future event may revocably nominate a custodian to receive the property for a minor beneficiary upon the occurrence of the event by naming the custodian followed in substance by the words: "as custodian for _____ (name of minor) under the Louisiana Uniform Transfers to Minors Act." The nomination may name one or more persons as substitute custodians to whom the property must be transferred, in the order named, if the first nominated custodian dies before the transfer or is unable, declines, or is ineligible to serve. The nomination may be made in a will, a trust, a deed, or in a writing designating a beneficiary of contractual rights which is registered with or delivered to the payor, issuer, or other obligor of the contractual rights.

B. A custodian nominated under this Section must be a person to whom a transfer of property of that kind may be made under R.S. 9:759(A).

C. The nomination of a custodian under this Section does not create custodial property until the nominating instrument becomes irrevocable or a transfer to the nominated custodian is completed under R.S. 9:759. Unless the nomination of a custodian has been revoked, upon the occurrence of the future event the custodianship becomes effective and the custodian shall enforce a transfer of the custodial property pursuant to R.S. 9:759.

Added by Acts 1987, No. 469, § 1, eff. Jan. 1, 1988.

§ 754. Transfer by gift

A person may make a transfer by irrevocable gift to a custodian for the benefit of a minor pursuant to R.S. 9:759.

Added by Acts 1987, No. 469, § 1, eff. Jan. 1, 1988.

§ 755. Transfer authorized by will or trust

A. A personal representative or trustee may make an irrevocable transfer pursuant to R.S. 9:759 to a custodian for the benefit of a minor as authorized in the governing will or trust.

B. If the testator or settlor has nominated a custodian under R.S. 9:753 to receive the custodial property, the transfer shall be made to that person.

C. If the testator or settlor has not nominated a custodian under R.S. 9:753, or all persons so nominated as custodian die before the transfer or are unable, decline, or are ineligible to serve, the personal representative or the trustee, as the case may be, shall designate the custodian from among those eligible to serve as custodian for property of that kind under R.S. 9:759(A).

Added by Acts 1987, No. 469, § 1, eff. Jan. 1, 1988.

§ 756. Other transfer by fiduciary

A. Subject to Subsection C of this Section, a personal representative or trustee may make an irrevocable transfer to another adult or trust company as custodian for the benefit of a minor pursuant to R.S. 9:759, in the absence of a will or under a will or trust that does not contain an authorization to do so.

B. Subject to Subsection C of this Section, a curator or tutor may make an irrevocable transfer to another adult or trust company as custodian for the benefit of the minor pursuant to R.S. 9:759.

C. A transfer under Subsections A or B of this Section may be made only if all of the following occur:

(1) The personal representative, trustee, curator, or tutor considers the transfer to be in the best interest of the minor.

(2) The transfer is not prohibited by or inconsistent with provisions of the applicable will, trust agreement, or other governing instrument.

(3) The transfer is authorized by the court, if it exceeds ten thousand dollars in value.

Added by Acts 1987, No. 469, § 1, eff. Jan. 1, 1988.

§ 757. Transfer by obligor

A. Subject to Subsections B and C of this Section, a person, not subject to the provisions of R.S. 9:755 or 756, who holds property of or owes a liquidated debt to a minor not having a tutor may make an irrevocable transfer to a custodian for the benefit of the minor pursuant to R.S. 9:759.

B. If a person having the right to do so under R.S. 9:753 has nominated a custodian under that Section to receive the custodial property, the transfer shall be made to that person.

C. If no custodian has been nominated under R.S. 9:753, or all persons so nominated as custodian die before the transfer or are unable, decline, or are ineligible to serve, a transfer under this Section may be made to an adult member of the minor's family or to a trust company unless the property exceeds ten thousand dollars in value.

Added by Acts 1987, No. 469, § 1, eff. Jan. 1, 1988.

§ 758. Receipt for custodial property

A written acknowledgment of delivery by a custodian constitutes a sufficient receipt and discharge for custodial property transferred to the custodian pursuant to this Subpart.

Added by Acts 1987, No. 469, § 1, eff. Jan. 1, 1988.

§ 759. Manner of creating custodial property and effecting transfer; designation of initial custodian; control

A. Custodial property is created and a transfer is made whenever:

(1) An uncertificated security or a certificated security in registered form is either of the following:

(a) Registered in the name of the transferor, an adult other than the transferor or a trust company, followed in substance by the words: "as custodian for _____ (name of minor) under the Louisiana Uniform Transfers to Minors Act".

(b) Delivered if in certificated form, or any document necessary for the transfer of an uncertificated security is delivered, together with any necessary endorsement to an adult other than the transferor or to a trust company as custodian, accompanied by an instrument in substantially the form set forth in Subsection B of this Section.

(2) Money is paid or delivered to a broker or financial institution for credit to an account in the name of the transferor, an adult other than the transferor, or a trust company, followed in substance by the words: "as custodian for _____ (name of minor) under the Louisiana Uniform Transfers to Minors Act".

(3) The ownership of a life or endowment insurance policy or annuity contract is either of the following:

(a) Registered with the issuer in the name of the transferor, an adult other than the transferor, or a trust company, followed in substance by the words: "as custodian for _____ (name of minor) under the Louisiana Uniform Transfers to Minors Act".

(b) Assigned in a writing delivered to an adult other than the transferor or to a trust company whose name in the assignment is followed in substance by the words: "as custodian for _____ (name of minor) under the Louisiana Uniform Transfers to Minors Act".

(4) An irrevocable present right to future payment under a contract is the subject of a written notification delivered to the payor, issuer, or other obligor that the right is transferred to the transferor, an adult other than the transferor, or a trust company, whose name in the notification is followed in substance by the words: "as custodian for _____ (name of minor) under the Louisiana Uniform Transfers to Minors Act".

(5) An interest in immovable property is recorded in the name of the transferor, an adult other than the transferor, or a trust company, followed in substance by the words: "as custodian for _____ (name of minor) under the Louisiana Uniform Transfers to Minors Act".

(6) A certificate of title issued by a department or agency of a state or of the United States which evidences title to corporeal movable property is either of the following:

(a) Issued in the name of the transferor, an adult other than the transferor, or a trust company, followed in substance by the words: "as custodian for _____ (name of minor) under the Louisiana Uniform Transfers to Minors Act".

(b) Delivered to an adult other than the transferor or to a trust company, endorsed to that person followed in substance by the words: "as custodian for _____ (name of minor) under the Louisiana Uniform Transfers to Minors Act".

(7) An interest in any property not described in Paragraphs (1) through (6) of this Subsection is transferred to an adult other than the transferor or to a trust company by a written instrument in substantially the form set forth in Subsection B of this Section.

B. An instrument in the following form satisfies the requirements of R.S. 9:759(A)(1)(b) and (7):

"TRANSFER UNDER THE LOUISIANA UNIFORM TRANSFERS TO MINORS ACT

I, _____ (name of transferor or name and representative capacity if a fiduciary) hereby transfer to _____ (name of custodian), as custodian for _____ (name of minor) under the Louisiana Uniform Transfers to Minors Act, the following: (description of the custodial property sufficient to identify it).

Dated: _____

_____
(Signature)

_____ (name of custodian) acknowledges receipt of the property described above as custodian for the minor named above under the Louisiana Uniform Transfers to Minors Act.

Dated: _____

_____"
(Signature of Custodian)

C. A transferor shall place the custodian in control of the custodial property as soon as practicable.

Added by Acts 1987, No. 469, § 1, eff. Jan. 1, 1988.

§ 760. Single custodianship

A transfer may be made only for one minor, and only one person may be the custodian. All custodial property held under this Subpart by the same custodian for the benefit of the same minor constitutes a single custodianship.

Added by Acts 1987, No. 469, § 1, eff. Jan. 1, 1988.

§ 761. Validity and effect of transfer

A. The validity of a transfer made in a manner prescribed in this Subpart is not affected by any of the following:

(1) Failure of the transferor to comply with R.S. 9:759(C) concerning possession and control.

(2) Designation of an ineligible custodian, except designation of the transferor in the case of property for which the transferor is ineligible to serve as custodian under R.S. 9:759(A).

(3) Death or incapacity of a person nominated under R.S. 9:753 or designated under R.S. 9:759 as custodian or the disclaimer of the office by that person.

B. A transfer made pursuant to R.S. 9:759 is irrevocable, and the custodial property is indefeasibly vested in the minor, but the custodian has all the rights, powers, duties, and authority provided by this Subpart, and neither the minor nor the minor's legal representative has any right, power, duty, or authority with respect to the custodial property, except as provided in this Subpart.

C. By making a transfer, the transferor incorporates in the disposition all the provisions of this Subpart and grants to the custodian, and to any third person dealing with a person designated as custodian, the respective powers, rights, and immunities provided in this Subpart.

Added by Acts 1987, No. 469, § 1, eff. Jan. 1, 1988.

§ 762. Care of custodial property

A. A custodian shall do all of the following:

(1) Take control of custodial property.

(2) Register or record title to custodial property if appropriate.

(3) Collect, hold, manage, invest, and reinvest custodial property.

B. In dealing with custodial property, a custodian shall observe the standard of care that would be observed by a prudent person dealing with property of another and is not limited by any other statute restricting investments by fiduciaries. If a custodian has a special skill or expertise or is named custodian on the basis of representations of a special skill or expertise, the custodian shall use that skill or expertise. However, a custodian, in the custodian's discretion and without liability to the minor or the minor's estate, may retain any custodial property received from a transferor.

C. A custodian may invest in or pay premiums on life insurance or endowment policies on either of the following:

(1) The life of the minor only if the minor or the minor's estate is the sole beneficiary.

(2) The life of another person in whom the minor has an insurable interest only to the extent that the minor, the minor's estate, or the custodian in the capacity of custodian, is the irrevocable beneficiary.

D. A custodian at all times shall keep custodial property separate and distinct from all other property in a manner sufficient to identify it clearly as custodial property of the minor. Custodial property subject to recordation is so identified if it is recorded, and custodial property subject to registration is so identified if it is either registered, or held in an account designated, in name of the custodian, followed in substance by the words: "as a custodian for _____ (name of minor) under the Louisiana Uniform Transfers to Minors Act".

E. A custodian shall keep records of all transactions with respect to custodial property, including information necessary for the preparation of the minor's tax returns, and shall make them available for inspection at reasonable intervals by a parent or a legal representative of the minor or by the minor, if the minor has attained the age of fourteen years.

Added by Acts 1987, No. 469, § 1, eff. Jan. 1, 1988.

§ 763. Powers of custodian

A. A custodian, acting in a custodial capacity, has all the rights, powers, and authority over custodial property that unmarried adult owners have over their own property, but a custodian may exercise those rights, powers, and authority in that capacity only.

B. This Section does not relieve a custodian from liability for breach of the provisions of R.S. 9:762.

Added by Acts 1987, No. 469, § 1, eff. Jan. 1, 1988.

§ 764. Use of custodial property

A. A custodian may deliver or pay to the minor or expend for the minor's benefit so much of the custodial property as the custodian considers advisable for the use and benefit of the minor, without court order and without regard to either of the following:

(1) The duty or ability of the custodian personally or of any other person to support the minor.

(2) Any other income or property of the minor which may be applicable or available for that purpose.

B. On petition of an interested person or the minor, if the minor has attained the age of fourteen years, the court may order the custodian to deliver or pay to the minor or expend for the minor's benefit so much of the custodial property as the court considers advisable for the use and benefit of the minor.

C. A delivery, payment, or expenditure under this Section is in addition to, not in substitution for, and does not affect any obligation of a person to support the minor.

Added by Acts 1987, No. 469, § 1, eff. Jan. 1, 1988.

§ 765. Expenses, compensation, and bond of custodian

A. A custodian is entitled to reimbursement from custodial property for reasonable expenses incurred in the performance of the custodian's duties.

B. Except for one who is a transferor under R.S. 9:754, a custodian has a non-cumulative election during each calendar year to charge reasonable compensation for services performed during that year.

C. Except as otherwise provided in R.S. 9:768(F), a custodian need not give a bond.

Added by Acts 1987, No. 469, § 1, eff. Jan. 1, 1988.

§ 766. Exemption of third person from liability

A third person in good faith and without court order may act on the instructions of or otherwise deal with any person purporting to make a transfer or purporting to act in the capacity of a custodian and, in the absence of knowledge, is not responsible for determining any of the following:

(1) The validity of the purported custodian's designation.

(2) The propriety of, or the authority under this Subpart for, any act of the purported custodian.

(3) The validity or propriety, under this Subpart, of any instrument or instructions executed or given either by the person purporting to make a transfer or by the purported custodian.

(4) The propriety of the application of any property of the minor delivered to the purported custodian.

Added by Acts 1987, No. 469, § 1, eff. Jan. 1, 1988.

§ 767. Liability to third persons

A. A claim based on a contract entered into by a custodian acting in a custodial capacity or an obligation arising from the ownership or control of custodial property, or a tort committed during the custodianship, may be asserted against the custodial property by proceeding against the custodian in the custodial capacity, whether or not the custodian or the minor is personally liable therefor.

B. A custodian is not personally liable for either:

(1) A contract properly entered into in the custodial capacity unless the custodian fails to reveal that capacity and to identify the custodianship in the contract.

(2) An obligation arising from control of custodial property or for a tort committed during the custodianship unless the custodian is personally at fault.

C. A minor is not personally liable for an obligation arising from ownership of custodial property or for a tort committed during the custodianship unless the minor is personally at fault.

Added by Acts 1987, No. 469, § 1, eff. Jan. 1, 1988.

§ 768. Renunciation, resignation, death, or removal of custodian; designation of successor custodian

A. A person nominated under R.S. 9:753 or designated under R.S. 9:759 as custodian may decline to serve by delivering a valid disclaimer to the person who made the nomination or to the transferor or the transferor's legal representative. If the event giving rise to a transfer has not occurred and no substitute custodian able, willing, and eligible to serve was nominated under R.S. 9:753, the person who made the nomination may nominate a substitute custodian under R.S. 9:753; otherwise the transferor or the transferor's legal representative shall designate a substitute custodian at the time of the transfer, in either case from among the persons eligible to serve as custodian for that kind of property under R.S. 9:759(A). The custodian so designated has the rights of a successor custodian.

B. A custodian at any time may designate a trust company or an adult other than a transferor under R.S. 9:754 as successor custodian by executing and dating an instrument of designation before a subscribing witness other than the successor. If the instrument of designation does not contain, or is not accompanied by, the resignation of the custodian, the designation of the successor does not take effect until the custodian resigns, dies, becomes incapacitated, or is removed.

C. A custodian may resign at any time by delivering written notice to the minor if the minor has attained the age of fourteen years and to the successor custodian and by delivering the custodial property to the successor custodian.

D. If a custodian is ineligible, dies, or becomes incapacitated without having effectively designated a successor and the minor has attained the age of fourteen years, the minor may designate as successor custodian, in the manner prescribed in Subsection B of this Section, an adult member of the minor's family, a tutor of the minor, or a trust company. If the minor has not attained the age of fourteen years or fails to act within sixty days after the ineligibility, death, or incapacity, the tutor of the minor becomes successor custodian. If the minor has no tutor or the tutor declines to act, the transferor, the legal representative of the transferor or of the custodian, an adult member of the minor's family, or any other interested person may petition the court to designate a successor custodian.

E. A custodian who declines to serve under Subsection A of this Section or resigns under Subsection C of this Section, or the legal representative of a deceased or incapacitated custodian, as soon as practicable, shall put the custodial property and records in the possession and control of the successor custodian. The successor custodian by action may enforce the obligation to deliver custodial property and records and becomes responsible for each item as received.

F. A transferor, the legal representative of a transferor, an adult member of the minor's family, a guardian of the person of the minor, the tutor of the minor, or the minor, if the minor has attained the age of fourteen years, may petition the court to remove the custodian for cause and to designate a successor custodian other than a transferor under R.S. 9:754 or to require the custodian to give appropriate bond.

Added by Acts 1987, No. 469, § 1, eff. Jan. 1, 1988.

§ 769. Accounting by and liability of custodian

A. A minor who has attained the age of fourteen years, the minor's guardian of the person or legal representative, an adult member of the minor's family, a transferor, or a transferor's legal representative may petition the court for an accounting by the custodian or the custodian's legal representative; or for a determination of responsibility, as between the custodial property and the custodian personally, for claims against the custodial property, unless the responsibility has been adjudicated in an action under R.S. 9:767 to which the minor or the minor's legal representative was a party.

B. A successor custodian may petition the court for an accounting by the predecessor custodian.

C. The court, in a proceeding under this Subpart or in any other proceeding, may require or permit the custodian or the custodian's legal representative to account.

D. If a custodian is removed under R.S. 9:768(F), the court shall require an accounting and order delivery of the custodial property and records to the successor custodian and the execution of all instruments required for transfer of the custodial property.

Added by Acts 1987, No. 469, § 1, eff. Jan. 1, 1988.

§ 770. Termination of custodianship

The custodian shall transfer in an appropriate manner the custodial property to the minor or to the minor's estate upon the earlier of the following:

(1) The minor's attainment of eighteen years of age.

(2) The minor's judicial emancipation.

(3) The minor's death.

Added by Acts 1987, No. 469, § 1, eff. Jan. 1, 1988.

§ 771. Applicability

This Subpart applies to a transfer within the scope of R.S. 9:752 made after its effective date if either of the following occur:

(1) The transfer purports to have been made under the Louisiana Gifts to Minors Act.[1]

(2) The instrument by which the transfer purports to have been made uses in substance the designation "as custodian under the Uniform Gifts to Minors Act" or "as custodian under the Uniform Transfers to Minors Act" of any other state, and the application of this Subpart is necessary to validate the transfer.

Added by Acts 1987, No. 469, § 1, eff. Jan. 1, 1988.

[1] R.S. 9:735 et seq. (repealed eff. Jan. 1, 1988).

§ 772. Effect on existing custodianship

A. Any transfer of custodial property, as now defined in this Subpart, made before January 1, 1988, is validated notwithstanding that there was no specific authority in the Louisiana Gifts to Minors Act[1] for the coverage of custodial property of that kind or for a transfer from that source at the time the transfer was made.

B. This Subpart applies to all transfers made before January 1, 1988, in a manner and form prescribed in the Louisiana Gifts to Minors Act, except insofar as the application impairs constitutionally vested rights.

Added by Acts 1987, No. 469, § 1, eff. Jan. 1, 1988.

[1] R.S. 9:735 et seq. (repealed eff. Jan. 1, 1988).

§ 773. Short title

This Subpart may be cited as the "Louisiana Uniform Transfers to Minors Act".

Added by Acts 1987, No. 469, § 1, eff. Jan. 1, 1988.

PART III. BOND OR SECURITY IN PLACE OF MORTGAGE [REPEALED]

§§ 801 to 804. Repealed by Acts 1960, No. 31, § 7, eff. Jan. 1, 1961

PART IV. SMALL ESTATES [REPEALED]

§§ 821 to 823. Repealed by Acts 1960, No. 31, § 7, eff. Jan. 1, 1961

PART V. MISCELLANEOUS PROVISIONS [REPEALED]

§ 841. Repealed by Acts 1960, No. 31, § 7, eff. Jan. 1, 1961

§ 842. Repealed by Acts 1979, No. 709, § 3, eff. Jan. 1, 1980

CHAPTER 2. EMANCIPATION

PART I. IN GENERAL

Section
901. Judgments and decrees of other states or District of Columbia given full faith and credit; procedure.

PART I. IN GENERAL

§ 901. Judgments and decrees of other states or District of Columbia given full faith and credit; procedure

Judgments and decrees of judicial emancipation of nonresident minors over the age of eighteen years, rendered by courts of competent jurisdiction of the minor's domicile in the several states and in the District of Columbia, upon being authenticated according to the Acts of Congress shall be given full faith and credit in this state.

A petition to have recognized the foreign judgment or decree, to which is annexed an authenticated copy, shall be presented to the judge of the district court wherein is situated the minor's principal estate and he shall render judgment thereon either in open court or in chambers.

Cross References

C.C. art. 365.

CHAPTER 3. PROVISIONAL CUSTODY BY MANDATE

Section
951. Provisional custody by mandate; conferring.
952. Duration of provisional custody; termination.
953. Functions, powers, and duties of agent.
954. Statutory form.

§ 951. Provisional custody by mandate; conferring

A. Parents acting jointly or, in the event of divorce, or separation from bed and board, or illegitimacy, the natural tutor, tutrix, or cotutors acting jointly, or a grandparent awarded custody, may authorize any person of legal age to provide for the care, custody, and control of a minor child.

B. For purposes of this Chapter, any person who could qualify as a natural tutor, tutrix, or cotutor pursuant to Section 2 of Chapter 1 of Title VIII of Book I of the Louisiana Civil Code may confer provisional custody by mandate of a child lawfully within his care, custody, and control, although he has not judicially qualified for the office of natural tutor, tutrix, or cotutor.

C. Provisional custody by mandate may not be conferred upon a parent or other person previously denied custody by court order.

Added by Acts 1992, No. 304, § 2. Amended by Acts 1995, No. 235, § 1; Acts 2010, No. 171, § 1.

§ 952. Duration of provisional custody; termination

A. The mandate of provisional custody shall be effective for the duration of time provided therein, but in no case shall it exceed one year from date of execution.

B. Regardless of the duration provided above, the mandate of provisional custody shall terminate:

(1) When revoked by either parent, by a natural tutor or tutrix, by either natural cotutor, or by a grandparent awarded custody.

(2) When the agent resigns or otherwise renounces the mandate.

(3) Fifteen days after the death of either parent, natural tutor or tutrix, natural cotutor, or grandparent awarded custody.

(4) Upon the qualification of a court appointed tutor or provisional tutor.

Added by Acts 1992, No. 304, § 2. Amended by Acts 1995, No. 235, § 1; Acts 2010, No. 171, § 1.

§ 953. Functions, powers, and duties of agent

In addition to the general functions, powers, and duties accorded to tutors pursuant to Chapter 8 of Title VI of Book VII of the Code of Civil Procedure, except those that require court approval, a mandate of child custody may provide for the health, education, and welfare of the child, which, if so indicated, may include the following:

(1) Consenting to and authorizing such medical care, treatment, or surgery as may be deemed necessary for the health, safety, and welfare of the child.

(2) Enrolling the child in such schools or educational institutions as may be deemed necessary for his due and proper education.

(3) Disciplining the child in such reasonable manner as may be necessary for his proper rearing, supervision, and training.

(4) Doing and performing all other such acts as may be necessary for the shelter, support, and general welfare of the child.

Added by Acts 1992, No. 304, § 2.

§ 954. Statutory form

The following is a suggested form which may be used by a parent, natural tutor, tutrix, or cotutors acting jointly, or a grandparent awarded custody, to confer the power of provisional custody for the care, custody, and control of the named minor child as authorized herein:

STATE OF LOUISIANA
PARISH OF _____

BE IT KNOWN THAT on this ___ day of _____, 20___, before me, the undersigned notary, and in the presence of the competent witnesses hereinafter named and undersigned:

Personally came and appeared:

(affiant's name, marital status, and mailing address), who is the (parent(s), or, in the event of divorce, separation, or illegitimacy, the natural (co)tutor or tutrix), or grandparent awarded custody of (minor child(ren)) who, by these presents make, name, constitute, and appoint (agent's name and mailing address) and grant provisional custody of the above named child(ren), to provide for the health, education, and welfare of the child as provided by the law on Provisional Custody by Mandate, specifically including the authority to:

INITIAL ALL APPLICABLE PROVISIONS:

____ (1) Consent to and authorize such medical care, treatment, or surgery as may be deemed necessary for the health, safety, and welfare of the child.

____ (2) Enroll the child in such schools or educational institutions as may be deemed necessary for his due and proper education.

____ (3) Discipline the child in such reasonable manner as may be necessary for his proper rearing, supervision, and training.

____ (4) Do and perform all other such acts as may be necessary for the shelter, support, and general welfare of the child.

This Provisional Custody by Mandate will continue to be effective until _____, 20 ___, or one year from date hereof, whichever period is shorter.

I agree that any third party who receives a copy of this document may rely upon the authority granted the agent as indicated herein and may act in reliance on such authority. Revocation or termination by operation of law is not effective as to a third party until he has actual knowledge thereof. I agree to indemnify and hold harmless the third party for any claims that arise against him because of reliance on this Provisional Custody by Mandate.

The undersigned agent does hereby accept the provisional custody of the children named herein.

THUS DONE AND PASSED at _____, state of _____, in the presence of _____ and _____, competent witnesses, who sign these presents with the appearers and me, notary, after due reading of the whole.

WITNESSES:

_____

_____ (Parent, Tutor, Tutrix, or Grandparent awarded custody)

_____ (Other parent, Cotutor, or Grandparent awarded custody)

_____ (Agent)

_____ NOTARY PUBLIC

Added by Acts 1992, No. 304, § 2. Amended by Acts 1995, No. 235, § 1; Acts 2010, No. 171, § 1.

CHAPTER 4. NON–LEGAL CUSTODIAN

Section
975. Non-legal custodian; consent for certain services; affidavit, form.

§ 975. Non-legal custodian; consent for certain services; affidavit, form

A. (1) A non-legal custodian, who is not a foster parent caring for a child in the custody of the Office of Community Services, shall be authorized to give legal consent for a child in his custody to receive any medical or educational services for which parental consent is usually required by executing the affidavit described in Paragraph (B)(4) of this Section. The affidavit shall not be valid for more than one year after the date on which it is executed.

(2) The decision of a non-legal custodian to consent to or to refuse medical or educational services for a child in his custody shall be superseded by any contravening decision of a parent or a person having legal custody of the child, provided the decision of the legal custodian does not jeopardize the life, health, safety, or welfare of the child.

(3) Nothing in this Section shall apply to, or give authority for, an abortion as provided in R.S. 40:1299.35.5.

B. (1) No person who acts in good faith reliance on a non-legal custodian properly executed affidavit, having no actual knowledge of any facts contrary to those stated in the affidavit, shall be subject to civil liability or criminal prosecution, or to professional disciplinary procedure, for any action which would have been proper if the facts had been as he believed them to be. This Paragraph shall apply even if medical or educational services are rendered to a child in contravention of the wishes of the parent or legal custodian of that child. However, the person rendering the services must not have actual knowledge of the wishes of the parent or legal custodian.

(2) A person who relies on a properly executed affidavit has no obligation to make further inquiry or investigation. Nothing herein shall relieve any person of responsibility for violations of other provisions of law, rules, or regulations.

(3) If the child ceases to live with the non-legal custodian, the non-legal custodian shall notify all parties to whom he has transmitted the affidavit or to whom he has caused the affidavit to be transmitted.

(4) A non-legal custodian's affidavit shall be invalid unless it substantially contains, in not less than ten-point boldface type, or a reasonable equivalent thereof, the warning statement beginning with the word "warning" specified in this Paragraph. The warning statement shall be enclosed in a box with three-point rule lines. The non-legal custodian's affidavit shall be in substantially the following form:

NON–LEGAL CUSTODIAN'S AFFIDAVIT

Use of this affidavit is authorized by R.S. 9:975.

INSTRUCTIONS: Completion of items 1 through 4 and the signing of the affidavit are sufficient to authorize educational services and school-related medical services for the named child. Completion of items 5 through 8 is additionally required to authorize any other medical services. Please print clearly.

The child named below lives in my home and I am 18 years of age or older.

1. Name of child:
2. Child's date of birth:
3. My name (adult giving authorization):
4. My home address:
5. [ ] I am a non-legal custodian.
6. Check one or both (for example, if one parent was advised and the other cannot be located):

[ ] I have advised the parent(s) or legal custodian(s) of the child of my intent to authorize the rendering of educational or medical services, and have received no objection.

[ ] I am unable to contact the parent(s) or legal custodian(s) of the child at this time, to notify them of my intended authorization.

7. Affiant's date of birth:
8. Affiant's Louisiana driver's license number or identification card number:

WARNING: Do not sign this form if any of the statements above are incorrect, or you will be committing a crime punishable by a fine, imprisonment, or both.

I declare under penalty of perjury under the laws of Louisiana that the foregoing is true and correct.

Signed: Date:

NOTICES:

1. This declaration does not affect the rights of the child's parent or legal guardian regarding the care, custody, and control of the child, and does not mean that the non-legal custodian has legal custody of the child.

2. A person who relies on this affidavit has no obligation to make any further inquiry or investigation.

3. This affidavit is not valid for more than one year after the date on which it is executed.

ADDITIONAL INFORMATION:

TO NON–LEGAL CUSTODIANS:

1. If the child stops living with you, you are required to notify anyone to whom you have given this affidavit as well as anyone of whom you have actual knowledge who received the affidavit from a third party.

2. If you do not have the information in item 8 (Louisiana driver's license or identification card), you must provide another form of identification such as your social security card number.

TO SCHOOL OFFICIALS:

The school district may require additional reasonable evidence that the non-legal custodian lives at the address provided in Item 4.

TO HEALTH CARE PROVIDERS AND HEALTH CARE SERVICE PLANS:

1. No person who acts in good faith reliance upon a non-legal custodian's affidavit to render educational or medical services, without actual knowledge of facts contrary to those stated in the affidavit, is subject to criminal prosecution or civil liability to any person, or subject to any professional disciplinary action, for such reliance if the applicable portions of the form are completed.

2. This affidavit does not confer dependency for health care coverage purposes.

Added by Acts 2001, No. 410, § 1, eff. June 15, 2001.

CODE TITLE IX—PERSONS UNABLE TO CARE FOR THEIR PERSONS OR PROPERTY

CHAPTER 1. INTERDICTION

PART I. INEBRIATES [REPEALED]

Section
1001 to 1004. Repealed.

PART II. MISCELLANEOUS PROVISIONS

1021. Interdiction of veterans in government institutions; manner of service.
1022. Authorization of curators to continue making donations to descendants.
1023. Donation by curator to charitable and nonprofit organizations; conditions; court approval.
1024. Donations by curator to collaterals; court authorization.
1025. Removal of a curator.
1026 to 1030. [Blank].

PART III. NONPROFIT CURATOR AND CONTINUING TUTOR PROGRAMS

1031. Appointment of nonprofit curatorship services.
1032. Powers, functions, and duties of curator and continuing tutor.
1033. Confidentiality; penalties.
1034. Fees and court costs.

PART I. INEBRIATES [REPEALED]

§§ 1001 to 1004. Repealed by Acts 2000, 1st Ex.Sess. No. 25, § 4, eff. July 1, 2001

PART II. MISCELLANEOUS PROVISIONS

§ 1021. Interdiction of veterans in government institutions; manner of service

Where it is necessary to interdict a person who is the beneficiary of the War Risk Insurance Act or the National Service Life Insurance Act of 1940, and he is not present in the state and is actually incarcerated in an institution maintained by the United States of America for the care of such persons, citation and service of the petition shall be made in the following manner.

A copy of the petition certified by the clerk of the court having jurisdiction, and a citation shall be served on the defendant by and through the officer in charge of the government institution in which he is confined. A certificate signed by such officer to the fact that such service has been made shall be accepted by the court in lieu of a personal service, provided there shall be produced in the trial of the case proof that the defendant is confined to such a government institution, and a certified copy of the records of the medical examination made by the officers of the United States of America is filed in evidence.

This Section applies solely to the cases of soldiers, sailors, marines, and nurses, beneficiaries under the War Risk Insurance Act or the National Service Life Insurance Act of 1940, and does not amend or repeal the laws relative to interdictions generally.

Cross References

C.C. arts. 389, 390.

§ 1022. Authorization of curators to continue making donations to descendants

The court may authorize a curator, in the name and on behalf of the interdict, to make donations inter vivos from the surplus funds or other surplus property of the interdict, of a value of not more than ten thousand dollars annually to each of the direct descendants of the interdict, when:

(1) There is no known testamentary disposition to the contrary.

(2) These donations are equal with respect to all descendants of the interdict in the same degree, and will not impinge upon the legitime of any forced heir of the interdict.

(3) The court is satisfied from the evidence presented to it that, prior to his interdiction, the interdict had made donations inter vivos to each of his direct descendants in each of at least four calendar years, not necessarily consecutive, of sums of money amounting to, or of property valued at, three thousand dollars or more.

(4) The curator has obtained the consent of the interdict's spouse and heirs of the first degree.

(5) The proposed donations will not discriminate between descendants of the interdict, will not materially impair the financial condition of the interdict and are not likely to deprive him of sufficient funds to care for his future needs and support. In order to establish that the proposed donations will not deprive the interdict of sufficient funds to provide for his future needs and support, the curator must satisfy the court, from the evidence presented to it, that the total fair market value of the interdict's estate, after subtracting the value of the proposed donations, is not less than a sum amounting to: fifty thousand dollars multiplied by the number of years of life expectancy remaining to the interdict at the time of the donation, as determined by his age and the table of life expectancy set out in R.S. 47:2405.

(6) The procedure prescribed by Articles 4271 and 4566 of the Code of Civil Procedure is complied with. When all of the conditions prescribed in Paragraphs (1) through (5) above

have been met, the court may authorize such donations to be made to the curator individually, if he is a direct descendant of the interdict, on the recommendation of the undercurator concurred in by an undercurator ad hoc appointed by the court.

(7) If a contrary testamentary disposition is discovered following the interdict's death, the donee shall restore the donated property to the interdict's estate or pay the estate the value of the gift.

Added by Acts 1966, No. 39, § 1. Amended by Acts 1983, No. 237, § 1; Acts 1991, No. 143, § 1.

Cross References

C.C. art. 389, 390.

§ 1023. Donation by curator to charitable and nonprofit organizations; conditions; court approval

The curator, in the name of and on behalf of the interdict, may make donations inter vivos to charitable and other nonprofit organizations with approval of the court and subject to such conditions or restrictions as the court may direct, if all the following requirements are met:

(1) The court is satisfied from the evidence presented to it that, prior to his interdiction, the interdict had an established history or pattern of donations inter vivos to charitable and other nonprofit organizations.

(2) The donations will not jeopardize the assets of the estate and will not impinge upon the legitime of any forced heir.

(3) The donations will not materially impair the financial condition of the interdict and will not deprive the interdict of sufficient funds to care for his future needs and support, which shall be established in the manner provided in R.S. 9:1022.

Added by Acts 1979, No. 68, § 1, eff. June 26, 1979.

Cross References

C.C. art. 389, 390.

§ 1024. Donations by curator to collaterals; court authorization

A. The court may authorize a curator, in the name and on behalf of an interdict who has no direct descendants and no spouse, to make donations inter vivos of money from surplus funds of the interdict to each of the brothers and sisters of the interdict and to each of the direct descendants of the brothers and sisters of the interdict, or to trusts in which they are the only principal and income beneficiaries, provided that there is no known testamentary disposition to the contrary. Annual donations shall not exceed ten thousand dollars per donee. The total amount donated annually to each of the brothers and sisters of the interdict and to each of the direct descendants of the brothers and sisters of the interdict, or to trusts therefor, shall be equal by roots from the parents of the interdict.

B. (1) The court may authorize such donations only when the procedure prescribed by Code of Civil Procedure Articles 4271 and 4566 is complied with and the proposed donations will not materially impair the financial condition of the interdict and are not likely to deprive him of sufficient funds to care for his future needs and support.

(2) To establish that the proposed donations will not deprive the interdict of sufficient funds to provide for his future needs and support, the curator must satisfy the court that:

(a) Following the proposed donation, the total amount of the difference between the fair market value of the interdict's estate and his total liabilities will exceed six hundred thousand dollars; and

(b) The total fair market value of the interdict's estate, after subtracting the value of the proposed donations, is not less than six hundred thousand dollars.

C. When all of the conditions in Subsections A and B have been met, the court may authorize such donations to be made to the curator individually, if he is a brother or sister or a direct descendant of a brother or sister of the interdict, on the recommendation of the undercurator, concurred in by the undercurator ad hoc appointed by the court.

Added by Acts 1991, No. 299, § 1, eff. July 5, 1991. Amended by Acts 1995, No. 451, § 1.

§ 1025. Removal of a curator

A. Any spouse or relative of an interdict, interested party, or nonprofit organization whose main function it is to serve as an advocate for persons with disabilities, the elderly, or both, may petition a court of competent jurisdiction for the removal of a curator upon a clear showing that neither the curator nor the undercurator are adequately performing their court-appointed duties.

B. A court of competent jurisdiction may remove a curator and appoint a successor, if such removal is deemed to be in the best interest of the interdict, either on its own motion or upon request by any spouse or relative of the interdict, or on the motion of any interested party or nonprofit organization whose main function it is to serve as advocate for persons with disabilities, the elderly, or both, upon contradictory hearing. The court shall consider the following factors in making its ruling:

(1) Whether the curator has, with gross negligence, misapplied, embezzled, or removed from the state, or is about to misapply, embezzle, or remove from the state all or any part of the interdict's property committed to the curator's care.

(2) The curator's failure to render any account required by law.

(3) The curator's failure to obey any proper order of the court having jurisdiction with respect to performance of the curator's duties.

(4) Proof of gross misconduct, or mismanagement in the performance of duties.

(5) Incompetence, incarceration, or any other cause rendering the curator incapable of performing court-appointed duties.

(6) Abuse of the interdict, or failure to educate the interdict or provide the interdict with as much independence as the means of the interdict and the conditions of his estate permit.

C. When the court removes a curator, it may appoint any spouse or relative of the interdict, any interested party, or any nonprofit organization whose main function it is to serve as curator for persons with disabilities, the elderly, or both.

Added by Acts 1993, No. 639, § 1, eff. June 15, 1993.

Cross References

C.C. arts. 47 to 53, 389.1.

§§ 1026 to 1030. [Blank]

PART III. NONPROFIT CURATOR AND CONTINUING TUTOR PROGRAMS

§ 1031. Appointment of nonprofit curatorship services

A. Notwithstanding any law to the contrary, a nonprofit curatorship service program, organized and operating pursuant to the corporation laws of this state, may be appointed the curator for an indigent adult in need of full or limited interdiction or may be appointed the continuing tutor for an indigent in need of continuing tutorship, if no individual seeks the appointment and meets the qualifications of curator. No appointment of a curator or continuing tutor pursuant to this Part shall confer authority to terminate life support or a pregnancy.

B. Any party to an interdiction or tutorship proceeding, including the state of Louisiana and its political subdivisions, may petition the court to appoint the program as curator or continuing tutor.

C. The court may hear such evidence as it deems necessary in order to determine whether the program is an appropriate entity to serve as curator or continuing tutor, including the sufficiency of a bond secured and maintained by the program. If the court desires to make such an appointment, it shall deliver to the program notice of the prospective appointment and information regarding the person in need of program services.

D. Within ten days from delivery of the notice, the program shall notify the court in writing of the decision to provide or decline the rendering of program services.

E. Upon election of the program to provide program services, the court shall appoint the program as curator or continuing tutor for the person in need of such services.

F. Notwithstanding any law to the contrary, in cases wherein the program is appointed curator or continuing tutor, the appointment of an undercurator or undertutor is not required.

Added by Acts 1992, No. 820, § 1, eff. July 8, 1992.

§ 1032. Powers, functions, and duties of curator and continuing tutor

A. Except as otherwise provided in this Part, the relationship between an interdict and his curator or continuing tutor is the same as that between a minor and his tutor, with respect to the person and property of the interdict.

B. The rules provided in Code of Civil Procedure Articles 4101 and 4102, or a sworn statement that the interdict has no inventory, 4171 and 4172, 4231 through 4235, 4237 through 4342, 4391 through 4464, and 4566, apply likewise to the powers, functions, and duties of a curator or continuing tutor, appointed pursuant to this Part.

C. The executive director of the program or his appointee shall have access to all health records and to all court records of persons receiving program services.

Added by Acts 1992, No. 820, § 1, eff. July 8, 1992.

§ 1033. Confidentiality; penalties

A. All communications and records of the program pertaining to persons in need of program services are confidential and may be disclosed only pursuant to a court order by the program in the performance of its program services.

B. Any person who violates the confidentiality of individuals served by the program may be punished by a fine not to exceed one thousand dollars or imprisonment for not more than six months, or both.

Added by Acts 1992, No. 820, § 1, eff. July 8, 1992.

§ 1034. Fees and court costs

The program shall be exempt from the payment of filing fees or taxing of court costs in connection with any judicial proceeding related to its performance of program services for indigent adults.

Added by Acts 1992, No. 820, § 1, eff. July 8, 1992.

CODE TITLE X—OF CORPORATIONS

CHAPTER 1. CORPORATIONS; UNAUTHORIZED CORPORATIONS; UNINCORPORATED NONPROFIT ASSOCIATIONS

Section
1051. Unauthorized corporations; unincorporated nonprofit associations; powers and liabilities.

§ 1051. Unauthorized corporations; unincorporated nonprofit associations; powers and liabilities

A. Corporations unauthorized by law or by an act of the legislature enjoy no public character, although these corporations may acquire and possess estates and have common interests as well as other private societies.

Unless otherwise provided by its constitution, charter, bylaws, rules, or regulations under which it is organized, governed, and exists, any unincorporated nonprofit association may alienate or encumber title to immovable property to any person. For the purposes of this article, immovable property includes, without limitation, mineral rights, predial servitudes, and predial leases, and a transaction to alienate or encumber shall include, without limitation, transactions to mortgage, hypothecate, donate, or transfer title to immovable property. Any such transaction shall be authorized by resolution adopted by a majority of the members of the association who vote on the resolution at a special meeting called and held for that purpose. The resolution may designate a person or persons to act as agent for the purpose of effectuating the transaction. Notice of the special meeting, including the date, time, and place of the meeting and the substance of the contemplated resolution, shall be published, on two separate days at least fifteen days prior to the date of the meeting, in the official journal of the parish in which a majority of the members reside or, if none, in a newspaper of general circulation in the parish. A copy of the resolution and proof of publication as required herein shall be attached to each act effectuating the transaction.

B. The provisions of this article applicable to transfers of immovable property by unincorporated nonprofit associations shall not apply when the transfers are part of an incorporation of the association in which substantially all of the assets of the unincorporated nonprofit association are transferred to the new corporation. In such cases, R.S. 12:207(C) shall govern the transfer.

C.C. art. 446. Amended by Acts 1977, No. 489, § 1; Acts 1978, No. 388, § 1; Acts 1978, No. 459, § 1; Acts 1979, No. 356, § 1; Acts 1980, No. 352, § 1. Redesignated as R.S. 9:1051 by Acts 1987, No. 126, § 2.

Cross References

C.C. arts. 2801 et seq., 3518, 3525, 3526.

C.C.P. arts. 739 to 741.

R.S. 10:9–102, 12:301, 12:304, 12:308, 12:310.

CODE BOOK II—THINGS AND THE DIFFERENT MODIFICATIONS OF OWNERSHIP

CODE TITLE I—THINGS

CHAPTER 1. IMMOVABLES

PART I. IN GENERAL

Section	
1101.	Ownership of waters and beds of bayous, rivers, streams, lagoons, lakes and bays.
1102.	Batture in cities and towns; right of riparian owner.
1102.1.	Rights of riparian landowners and their lessees.
1102.2.	Rights and duties of riparian owners and their lessees; joint usage of certain riparian lands.
1103.	Carbon sequestration on surface or water bottom.
1104.	Riparian owners, use of surface water; fees prohibited; legislative finding and intent.
1105.	Repealed.
1106.	Storage tanks placed on land by one not owner of land as movable property.
1107.	Public policy respecting ownership of navigable waters and beds thereof.
1108.	Invalidity of patent or transfer purporting to include navigable waters and beds thereof.
1109.	Statutes not to be construed as validating purported transfer of navigable waters or beds thereof.
1110.	Ownership of land adjacent to False River.
1111.	Exclusion of certain interests in trust from classification as immovable property.
1112.	Immovable property held in common; agreement not to alienate, encumber or lease.
1113.	Partition of immovable property; minority interest; private sale; appraisal.

PART I–A. OWNERSHIP OF BEDS OF NON–NAVIGABLE WATERS

1115.1.	Declaration of purpose.
1115.2.	Ownership of inland non-navigable water bottoms.
1115.3.	Interpretation of transfers.

PART II. LOUISIANA CONDOMINIUM ACT

SUBPART A. GENERAL PROVISIONS

1121.	Repealed.
1121.101.	Short title.
1121.102.	Applicability.
1121.103.	Definitions.
1121.104.	Attorney fees.
1121.105.	Separate taxation.
1121.106.	Applicability of ordinances, zoning, and building restrictions.
1121.107.	Expropriation.

Section	
1121.108.	Sale of unit; escrow accounts.
1121.109.	[Blank].
1121.110.	[Blank].
1121.111.	[Blank].
1121.112.	[Blank].
1121.113.	[Blank].
1121.114.	[Blank].
1122.	Repealed.

SUBPART B. CREATION, ALTERATION, AND TERMINATION OF CONDOMINIUMS

1122.101.	Creation of condominium regimes; condominium declaration; recordation.
1122.102.	[Blank].
1122.103.	Construction and validity of declaration and by-laws.
1122.104.	Description of units.
1122.105.	Contents of the condominium declaration.
1122.106.	Reapportionment among unit owners of the percentage ownership interest in the common elements; percentages of sharing common expenses and common surplus; voting power in the association of unit owners.
1122.107.	Condominiums established on leased land.
1122.108.	Allocation of common element interest, votes, and common expense liabilities.
1122.109.	[Blank].
1122.110.	Plats and plans.
1122.111.	[Blank].
1122.112.	Termination; withdrawal.
1122.113.	Alterations of units.
1122.114.	Relocation of boundaries between adjoining units.
1122.115.	Subdivision or conversion of units.
1122.116.	[Blank].
1122.117.	[Blank].
1122.118.	[Blank].
1122.119.	Amendment of declaration.
1122.120.	[Blank].
1122.121.	[Blank].
1123.	Repealed.

SUBPART C. MANAGEMENT OF THE CONDOMINIUM

1123.101.	Organization of unit owners' association.
1123.102.	Powers of unit owners' association.
1123.103.	[Blank].
1123.104.	[Blank].
1123.105.	Termination of contracts and leases of declarant.
1123.106.	Bylaws.

Section	
1123.107.	Upkeep of the condominium.
1123.108.	Association records.
1123.112.	Insurance.
1123.113.	Fidelity bond or equivalent form of insurance required.
1123.114.	[Blank].
1123.115.	Privilege on immovables.
1123.115.1.	[Blank].
1123.116.	Privilege for utility assessments.
1123.117.	[Blank].
1124.	Repealed.

SUBPART D. PROTECTION OF PURCHASERS

1124.101.	Applicability; waiver.
1124.102.	Public offering statement; general provisions.
1124.103.	[Blank].
1124.104.	Public offering statement; conversion condominiums.
1124.105.	Public offering statement; condominium securities.
1124.106.	Purchaser's right to cancel.
1124.107.	Resales of units.
1124.108.	[Blank].
1124.109.	Privileges.
1124.110.	[Blank].
1124.111.	[Blank].
1124.112.	[Blank].
1124.113.	[Blank].
1124.114.	[Blank].
1124.115.	Compliance with condominium declaration, by-laws, and administrative rules and regulations.
1124.116.	[Blank].
1124.117.	[Blank].
1125 to 1131.	Repealed.

PART II–A. LOUISIANA TIMESHARING ACT

1131.1.	Short title.
1131.2.	Definitions.
1131.3.	Applicability and scope.
1131.4.	Creation of a timeshare plan.
1131.5.	Construction and validity of declaration.
1131.6.	Description of timeshare property.
1131.7.	Partition.
1131.8.	Termination.
1131.9.	Tax assessment and payment.
1131.9.1.	Developer supervisory duties.
1131.9.2.	Public offering statement.
1131.10.	Repealed.
1131.10.1.	Contracts for purchase of timeshare interests.
1131.11.	Public offering statement; when not required.
1131.12.	Regulations of timeshare advertising.
1131.13.	Cancellation.
1131.14.	Repealed.
1131.15.	Repealed.
1131.16.	Repealed.
1131.16.1.	Escrow of payments; escrow accounts; nondisturbance agreements; interests, liens, and encumbrances; alternative assurances.
1131.17.	Escrow account; establishment; claims for damages.
1131.18.	Resales of timeshares.
1131.19.	Privileges.

Section	
1131.20.	Management and operation of the timeshare plan.
1131.21.	Assessment for timeshare interest expenses.
1131.22.	Privilege for assessments.
1131.23.	Insurance.
1131.24.	Requirements where developer's interest in the timeshare property is a leasehold interest.
1131.25.	Remedies.
1131.26.	Louisiana Real Estate Recovery Fund; exemption.
1131.27.	Repealed.
1131.28.	Recordation.
1131.29.	Waiver prohibited.
1131.30.	Preservation of claims and defenses.
1132 to 1141.	Repealed.

PART II–B. LOUISIANA HOMEOWNERS ASSOCIATION ACT

SUBPART A. GENERAL PROVISIONS

1141.1.	Short title.
1141.2.	Definitions.
1141.3.	Applicability.

SUBPART B. BUILDING RESTRICTIONS

1141.4.	Building restrictions; matters of interpretation.
1141.5.	Building restrictions; generally, affirmative duty, and common areas.
1141.6.	Establishment, amendment, or termination of building restrictions.
1141.7.	Agreement of owners; voting.

SUBPART C. ENFORCEMENT

1141.8.	Community documents; force of law.
1141.9.	Homeowners association privilege.
1142.	Repealed.

PART III. PRIVILEGES ON IMMOVABLES FOR CHARGES OR DUES OF ASSOCIATION OF OWNERS

1145.	Association of owners; privilege; definition.
1146.	Privilege; sworn detailed statement; filing.
1147.	Privilege; five year period.
1148.	Privilege; ranking.

PART IV. MANUFACTURED HOME PROPERTY ACT

1149.1.	Short title.
1149.2.	Definitions.
1149.3.	Classification.
1149.4.	Immobilization.
1149.5.	Security devices.
1149.6.	Deimmobilization.
1149.7.	Reference to prior law.

PART I. IN GENERAL

§ 1101. Ownership of waters and beds of bayous, rivers, streams, lagoons, lakes and bays

The waters of and in all bayous, rivers, streams, lagoons, lakes and bays, and the beds thereof, not under the direct ownership of any person on August 12, 1910, are declared to be the property of the state. There shall never be any charge assessed against any person for the use of the waters of the state for municipal, industrial, agricultural or domestic purposes.

While acknowledging the absolute supremacy of the United States of America over the navigation on the navigable waters within the borders of the state, it is hereby declared that the ownership of the water itself and the beds thereof in the said navigable waters is vested in the state and that the state has the right to enter into possession of these waters when not interfering with the control of navigation exercised thereon by the United States of America. This Section shall not affect the acquisition of property by alluvion or accretion.

All transfers and conveyances or purported transfers and conveyances made by the state of Louisiana to any levee district of the state of any navigable waters and the beds and bottoms thereof are hereby rescinded, revoked and canceled.

This Section is not intended to interfere with the acquisition in good faith of any waters or the beds thereof transferred by the state or its agencies prior to August 12, 1910. Amended by Acts 1954, No. 443, § 1.

Cross References
C.C. arts. 450, 451, 455, 563, 3524.

§ 1102. Batture in cities and towns; right of riparian owner

Whenever the riparian owner of any property in incorporated towns or cities is entitled to the right of accretion, and more batture has been formed in front of his land than is necessary for public use, which the corporation withholds from him, he shall have the right to institute action against the corporation for so much of the batture as may not be necessary for public use. If it be determined by the court that any portion of the batture be not necessary for public use, it shall decree that the owner is entitled to the property, and shall compel the corporation to permit him to enjoy the use and ownership of such portion of it.

Cross References
C.C. arts. 456, 459, 499.

§ 1102.1. Rights of riparian landowners and their lessees

A. Riparian owners and their lessees of property on navigable rivers, lakes, or streams within the limits of any deep water port commission of this state or, in the absence of any such commission, within a municipality having a population in excess of five thousand inhabitants, shall have the right to erect and maintain on the batture or banks owned or leased by them and in the bed of the navigable river, lake, or stream adjacent to or adjoining such batture or banks, such wharves, buildings, or improvements as may be required for the purposes of commerce, navigation, or other public purposes. However, where such owners first have obtained the consent of the governing authority of the deep-water port commission, which consent each deep-water port commission is hereby authorized to grant, or of the municipality, as the case may be, to erect such wharves, buildings, or improvements, and same are erected in conformity to plans and specifications which have been approved by such governing authorities, those governing authorities may expropriate said wharves, buildings, or improvements whenever said improvements or the riparian front shall be required for public purposes, and the owners shall be entitled to claim compensation to the full extent of their loss, but where such consent and approval is not obtained, the owners shall be entitled to be paid compensation therefor to the full extent of their loss or required to remove such wharves, buildings, or improvements at their own expense, in the discretion of the governing authority of the deep-water port commission or of the municipality. In all cases, such wharves, buildings, or improvements shall remain subject to the administration and control of the governing authorities with respect to their maintenance and to the fees and charges to be exacted for their use by the public.

B. Nothing herein shall deprive the levee boards of their authority with respect to levees in their respective districts or their right to appropriate, without compensation, such wharves, buildings, or improvements.

Added by Acts 1975, No. 141, § 1. Amended by Acts 1981, No. 2, § 1, eff. May 18, 1981.

Cross References
C.C. arts. 455, 456, 459, 460.

§ 1102.2. Rights and duties of riparian owners and their lessees; joint usage of certain riparian lands

A. (1)(a) Whenever the governing authority of any port commission, or in the absence of such commission, the governing authority of a municipality having a population in excess of five thousand inhabitants, owns, leases, or otherwise lawfully occupies or uses property on a navigable river, lake, or stream, which is within the territorial limits of such commission or municipality, or the bed of such river, lake, or stream adjacent to such property, and the governing authority in its discretion determines that the needs of commerce, navigation, or other public purposes respecting such property are being satisfied and would not be unduly interfered with, the governing authority may permit and grant to the riparian owner or owners, or their lessees or persons occupying with the riparian owner's consent, the use of such property owned, leased, or otherwise lawfully occupied or used, including the air space above any wharves, buildings, or improvements constructed by the governing authority, for the construction and maintenance of buildings or improvements for any purpose, including residential purposes.

(b) The use and construction of any buildings or improvements on such property by the riparian owner, or owners, or their lessees or persons occupying with the riparian owner's consent, shall be subject to the terms and conditions, including compensation to be paid to the governing authority, which the governing authority in its discretion determines to be appropriate under the circumstances.

(c)(i) These terms and conditions may include arrangements whereby any wharves, buildings, or other improvements made by the governing authority on such property may be made to connect with or provide structural support to buildings or improvements which the riparian owner or owners, or their lessees or persons occupying with the riparian owner's consent, have been granted permission to erect; or

(ii) They may include arrangements whereby separate structural supports may be provided for any building or improvements constructed by the riparian owner or owners, or their lessees or persons occupying with the riparian owner's consent, in the air space over any wharves, buildings, or improvements of the governing authority, whether by extending such supports through the wharves, buildings, or other improvements constructed by the authority, or otherwise.

(d) Unless expressly provided otherwise by the governing authority in writing, any buildings or improvements erected by the owner or owners, or their lessees or persons occupying with the riparian owner's consent, and any use made thereof, or any activity conducted thereupon, shall be the separate property of the owner or owners, or their lessees or persons occupying with the riparian owner's consent.

(e) Any such buildings or improvements erected by the owner or owners, or their lessees or persons occupying with the riparian owner's consent, shall be subject to the administration and control of the governing authority with respect to their maintenance and, should such buildings or improvements be used for purposes of commerce, navigation, or other public purposes, with respect to the fees and charges exacted for their use by the public, and shall also remain subject to expropriation by any such authority should same become required for public purposes.

(2)(a) The governing authority of each port commission of the state shall have the right to lease or sublease any property, whether movable or immovable, that is owned or leased by it, on a long-term basis and without the necessity of public bidding. Any such lease or sublease may be for such purpose or purposes and subject to such terms and conditions, including such compensation to be paid to the governing authority, which the governing authority, in its discretion determines to be in the public interest.

(b) Without limitation, the right herein granted includes the right to lease or sublease for purposes of commerce, navigation or other public purposes, any wharves, buildings, or improvements that are owned or leased by the governing authority that are located on any riparian lands that are subject to the servitude existing in favor of the public for purposes of commerce and navigation.

(3) The provisions of this Subsection shall not be applicable to any river which is part of the Louisiana Natural and Scenic Rivers System as defined in R.S. 56:1841 et seq.

B. Nothing herein shall deprive the levee boards of their authority with respect to levees in their respective districts or their right to appropriate such wharves, buildings, or improvements.

C. The provisions of this Section shall not be applicable in the parish of St. Tammany.

Added by Acts 1981, No. 454, § 1, eff. July 18, 1981. Amended by Acts 1982, No. 858, § 1, eff. Aug. 4, 1982; Acts 1984, No. 498, § 1; Acts 2012, No. 388, § 1.

Cross References

C.C. arts. 459, 460.

§ 1103. Carbon sequestration on surface or water bottom

Any monetary compensation derived from the sequestration of carbon on the surface of land or water bottoms through biological processes, including but not limited to the growth of plants or animals or other natural or induced processes, is the property of the owner of the land or water bottom upon which such sequestration occurs, unless (a) contractually assigned to another party; or (b) the sequestration, uptake, or prevention of emission of greenhouse gases is directly related to the avoided conversion or avoided loss attributable to a project carried out or sponsored by the Coastal Protection and Restoration Authority including use of public resources as provided in R.S. 49:214.5.4. In such instance, the monetary compensation is the property of the state.

Added by Acts 2010, No. 193, § 1.

§ 1104. Riparian owners, use of surface water; fees prohibited; legislative finding and intent

A. The Legislature of Louisiana finds that waters used in agricultural or aquacultural pursuits are not consumed, rather they are merely used, and the movement of the water ultimately provides value to the resource in several ways as these uses provide for additional pathways for integration of the water into the hydrological cycle. Some of these value-adding processes include recharging aquifers by percolation into the groundwater, entry into the cycle as water vapor through the evaporation from movement of the surface water, from the absorption into crops, providing nourishment to living organisms that indirectly support agriculture and aquaculture, from the hydration of livestock, and also through providing habitat and sustenance for the fish and wildlife resources of the state. The direct and indirect effects that result from these uses bring a positive impact on the resource and the environment that yields a value far in excess of the value of the resource as mere running water, and as such the Legislature of Louisiana specifically finds that there is no prohibited donation by agricultural and aquacultural uses of these sorts. The public purpose served by the enactment and implementation of this Section is the protection and conservation of the water as a resource of the state in such a way that the health, safety, and welfare of the people of the state are protected and benefitted.

B. A riparian owner may assign access rights equal to his own for the surface water adjacent to his riparian land for any agricultural or aquacultural purpose within the state of Louisiana by the non-riparian owner without restriction as to the form of any such agreement to another, provided that the withdrawal of running surface waters is environmentally and ecologically sound and is consistent with the required balancing of environmental and ecological impacts with the economic and social benefits found in Article IX, Section 1 of the Constitution of Louisiana. No riparian owner shall authorize the withdrawal of running waters for non-riparian use where the use of the water would significantly adversely impact the sustainability of the water body, or have undue impacts on navigation, public drinking water supplies, stream or water flow energy, sediment load and distribution, and on the environment and ecology balanced against the social and economic benefits of a contract of sale or withdrawal, or sale of agreement, or right to withdraw running surface water for agricultural and aquacultural purposes.

C. For purposes of this Section, "agricultural or aquacultural purpose" means any use by a riparian owner or an assignee of a riparian owner of running surface waters withdrawn and used for the purpose of directly sustaining life or providing habitat to sustain life of living organisms that are customarily or actually intended to be brought to market for sale.

D. The state shall not charge any fee for the water usage, except where the state, including its political subdivisions, contracts or assigns rights for withdrawal as provided for in Subsection B of this Section.

E. This Section shall become null and of no effect on January 12, 2035.

Added by Acts 2010, No. 994, § 1, eff. July 6, 2010.

<small>Editor's note. R.S. 9:1104 was enacted by Acts 2010, No. 994, as R.S. 9:1103. It has been redesignated by the Louisiana State Law Institute as R.S. 9:1104.</small>

§ 1105. Repealed by Acts 1974, No. 50, § 3, eff. Jan. 1, 1975

§ 1106. Storage tanks placed on land by one not owner of land as movable property

A. Tanks placed on land whether urban or rural by other than the owner of the land for the storage or use of butane, propane or other liquefied gases, or for the storage or use of anhydrous ammonia or other liquid fertilizer, be and they are declared to be and shall remain movable property, and the ownership of such tank or tanks shall not be affected by the sale, either private or judicial, of the land on which they are placed.

B. This section is intended to and does affect all such tanks presently on such land which were placed thereon by other than the owner of the land.

Added by Acts 1954, No. 49, §§ 1, 2.

Cross References

C.C. arts. 462, 466, 467, 471, 490, 2461.

§ 1107. Public policy respecting ownership of navigable waters and beds thereof

It has been the public policy of the State of Louisiana at all times since its admission into the Union that all navigable waters and the beds of same within its boundaries are common or public things and insusceptible of private ownership; that no act of the Legislature of Louisiana has been enacted in contravention of said policy, and that the intent of the Legislature of this state at the time of the enactment of Act No. 62 of the year 1912, now appearing as R.S. 9:5661, and continuously thereafter was and is at this present time to ratify and confirm only those patents which conveyed or purported to convey public lands susceptible of private ownership of the nature and character, the alienation or transfer of which was authorized by law but not patents or transfers which purported to convey or transfer navigable waters and the beds of same.

Added by Acts 1954, No. 727, § 1.

Cross References

C.C. arts. 449, 450, 451, 455.

§ 1108. Invalidity of patent or transfer purporting to include navigable waters and beds thereof

Any patent or transfer heretofore or hereafter issued or made is null and void, so far as same purports to include such navigable waters and the beds thereof, as having been issued or made in contravention of the public policy of this state and without any prior authorization by law; provided that the provisions of this Section shall not affect the laws of accretion or apply to lands that were susceptible to private ownership on the date of the patent or transfer by the state or a state agency.

Added by Acts 1954, No. 727, § 2.

Cross References

C.C. arts. 449, 450, 451, 455.

§ 1109. Statutes not to be construed as validating purported transfer of navigable waters or beds thereof

No statute enacted by the legislature of Louisiana shall be construed as to validate by reason of prescription or peremption any patent or transfer issued by the state of any levee district thereof, so far as the same purports to include navigable or tide waters or the beds of same.

Added by Acts 1954, No. 727, § 3.

Cross References

C.C. arts. 449, 450, 451, 455.

§ 1110. Ownership of land adjacent to False River

The title of the owners of land adjacent to that body of water in Pointe Coupee Parish known as False River shall extend to fifteen feet above mean sea level. The boundary line formed at fifteen feet above mean sea level marks the division between land owned by the state and land owned by private persons along the banks of False River.

Added by Acts 1975, No. 285, § 1.

§ 1111. Exclusion of certain interests in trust from classification as immovable property

Notwithstanding any other provision of law to the contrary, no interest in a trust which has five hundred or more beneficiaries or owners of beneficial interests shall be classified as immovable property in this state provided the trust owns an interest in, or is a beneficiary of, another trust which owns property classified in Louisiana as immovable.

Added by Acts 1986, No. 251, § 1.

Cross References

C.C. arts. 462, 473.

§ 1112. Immovable property held in common; agreement not to alienate, encumber or lease

Persons holding immovable property in common may agree not to alienate, encumber, or lease the property held in common for a specific period of time, not to exceed fifteen years. This agreement must be in writing.

Added by Acts 1987, No. 476, § 1.

§ 1113. Partition of immovable property; minority interest; private sale; appraisal

A. If immovable property is susceptible of partition by licitation or private sale pursuant to Civil Code Article 811 and a co-owner or co-owners owning an aggregate interest of fifteen percent or less of the immovable property petition the court to partition the property, the court shall allow the remaining co-owners to purchase at private sale the petitioners' shares at a price determined by a court-appointed appraiser.

B. (1) Each remaining co-owner shall only be entitled to purchase a portion of the property being sold equal to his pro rata share. Each remaining co-owner shall have thirty days from the date the last defendant is served with the petition to partition or thirty days from receipt of written notice, sent by certified mail or commercial courier, from a co-owner waiving his right to purchase, whichever is earlier, in which to file a notice to exercise his option to purchase his pro rata share of the property being sold. The filed notice, which shall be served on all parties, shall be considered a fully binding contract to purchase the property.

(2) Upon the lapse of the thirtieth day, any co-owner who has failed to timely exercise his option to purchase the property shall relinquish his right to purchase his pro rata share. The relinquishment of the right to purchase shall enure to the benefit of the remaining purchasing co-owners, who shall then be entitled to purchase, by pro rata share, the shares made available by the co-owner who relinquished his right to purchase. Each remaining purchasing co-owner shall have an additional ten days from the previous deadline to file his notice to purchase the relinquished shares.

(3) The procedures provided in this Subsection shall continue until there are no outstanding forfeited shares; however, the court may use its discretion in rounding the shares of the co-owners to the nearest hundredth share.

(4) The initial calculation of the pro rata share in Subsection B of this Section shall be based on the percentage of ownership of potential purchasing co-owners, excluding the petitioning co-owners. When a potential purchasing co-owner relinquishes his right to purchase, the pro rata share shall be recalculated to include only the remaining purchasing co-owners, excluding the relinquishing co-owners. Once a purchasing co-owner relinquishes his right to purchase his pro rata share, he shall not be entitled to file any subsequent notice to purchase in the pending action.

Added by Acts 2003, No. 156, § 1, eff. June 2, 2003.

Editor's note. Acts 1999, No. 1074, enacted a prior R.S. 9:1113. The statute has been redesignated as R.S. 33:4777 under the authority of the Louisiana State Law Institute.

PART I–A. OWNERSHIP OF BEDS OF NON–NAVIGABLE WATERS

§ 1115.1. Declaration of purpose

A. The purpose of this Part is to distinguish the law of Louisiana from the state law upon which the United States Supreme Court based its decision in *Phillips Petroleum Co. v. Mississippi*, 108 S.Ct. 791 (1988), and thereby quiet titles to lands which have long been owned by private persons but which titles may have been clouded as a result of that decision.

B. Consistent with the Louisiana State Law Institute Advisory Legal Opinion Relative to Non-navigable Water Bottoms to the Louisiana Legislature on or about January 31, 1992,[1] the legislature hereby finds that as to lands not covered by navigable waters including the sea and its shore, which are subject to being covered by water from the influence of the tide and which have been alienated under laws existing at the time of such alienation, the *Phillips* decision neither reinvests the state, or a political subdivision thereof, with any ownership of such lands nor does the state, or a political subdivision thereof, acquire any new ownership of such property.

C. It is the intent of the legislature by the enactment of this Part to codify and confirm the law of Louisiana as heretofore interpreted by the courts thereof without change and without divesting the state, its agencies, or its political subdivisions of the ownership or rights as to any immovable property and without affecting the provisions of the state Oyster Statutes passed by the legislature since 1886. Furthermore, it is the intent of the legislature by the enactment of this Part that no provision herein shall be interpreted to create, enlarge, restrict, terminate, or affect in any way any right or claim to public access and use of such lands, including but not limited to navigation, crawfishing, shellfishing, and other fishing, regardless of whether such claim is based on existing law, custom and usage, or jurisprudence.

Added by Acts 1992, No. 998, § 1.

[1] See 53 La.L.Rev. 35 (1992) for the Louisiana State Law Institute's advisory opinion relative to non-navigable waterbottoms.

§ 1115.2. Ownership of inland non-navigable water bottoms

A. Inland non-navigable water bodies are those which are not navigable in fact and are not sea, arms of the sea, or seashore.

B. Inland non-navigable water beds or bottoms are private things and may be owned by private persons or by the state and its political subdivisions in their capacity as private persons.

Added by Acts 1992, No. 998, § 1.

§ 1115.3. Interpretation of transfers

Any act by which the state has transferred or hereafter transfers ownership of immovable property which, at the time of the transfer, encompasses inland non-navigable water beds or bottoms within the boundaries of the property transferred, is presumed to convey to the transferee the ownership of the inland non-navigable water bottoms, unless title thereto has been expressly reserved by the state of Louisiana in the act. Nothing contained in this Part shall be construed as conveying to any person title to any lands that have not previously been conveyed or transferred by the state.

Added by Acts 1992, No. 998, § 1.

PART II. LOUISIANA CONDOMINIUM ACT

SUBPART A. GENERAL PROVISIONS

§ 1121. Repealed by Acts 1979, No. 682, § 3

§ 1121.101. Short title

This Part shall be known as the "Louisiana Condominium Act".

Acts 1979, No. 682, § 1.

Cross References

C.C. arts. 462, 464, 476.

§ 1121.102. Applicability

A. This Part shall apply only to property made subject to it by a condominium declaration duly executed and filed for registry.

B. The provisions of this Part shall be applicable from, and after the effective date of this Part, to existing condominium property regimes created pursuant to the provisions of Act No. 502 of 1974 or Act No. 494 of 1962. This Part shall not affect or impair any right that is guaranteed or protected by the constitutions of this state or the United States nor shall this Part be construed to impair or affect any act done or offense committed or right accruing, accrued or acquired, or liability, penalty, forfeiture or punishment incurred, under Act No. 502 of 1974 or Act No. 494 of 1962. This Part shall not be construed to impair or cast a cloud upon the titles to units of any condominium property regime formed prior to the effective date of this Part, notwithstanding any conflicts which may exist between this Part, Act No. 502 of 1974, or Act No. 494 of 1962.

Acts 1979, No. 682, § 1.

Cross References

C.C. arts. 462, 464, 490, 491.

§ 1121.103. Definitions

As used in this Part:

(1) "Condominium" is the property regime under which portions of immovable property are subject to individual ownership and the remainder thereof is owned in indivision by such unit owners.

(2) "Condominium property" means all interests in land, improvements thereon, and all servitudes and rights attaching to the condominium.

(3) "Unit" means a part of the condominium property subject to individual ownership. A unit may include air space only. A unit includes such accessory rights and obligations as are stipulated in the condominium declaration.

(4) "Unit designation" means the number, letter, or combination thereof or any other official designation identifying a particular unit in the condominium declaration.

(5) "Common elements" means the portion of the condominium property not a part of the individual units.

(6) "Limited common elements" means those common elements reserved in the condominium declaration for the exclusive use of a certain unit or certain units.

(7) "Condominium parcel" means a unit together with the undivided interest in the common elements which is an inseparable component part of the unit.

(8) "Association of unit owners" or "association" means a corporation, or unincorporated association, owned by or composed of the unit owners and through which the unit owners manage and regulate the condominium.

(9) "Common expenses" means:

(a) Expenses of administration, maintenance, repair, and replacement of the common elements.

(b) Expenses declared to be common expenses by provisions of this Part or by the condominium declaration or bylaws.

(c) Expenses agreed upon as common expenses by the unit owners.

(10) "Condominium declaration" or "declaration" means the instrument by which immovable property is made subject to this Part.

(11) "Declarant" means:

(a) If the condominium has not yet been created, any person who offers to dispose of or disposes of his interest in a unit not previously disposed of; or

(b) If the condominium has been created, any person who has executed a declaration, or an amendment to a declaration to add additional property to the condominium regime, other than persons holding interests in the property solely as security for a debt or persons whose interest in the property will not be conveyed to unit owners.

(12) "Leasehold condominium" means a condominium in which all or a portion of the condominium property is subject to a lease the expiration or termination of which will terminate the condominium or reduce its size.

Acts 1979, No. 682, § 1.

Cross References

C.C. arts. 462, 464, 476.

§ 1121.104. Attorney fees

Notwithstanding the provisions of R.S. 9:1121.101 and 1122.112 to the contrary, in the event the actions or inactions by the association of unit owners to repair damage to any common element of a unit or portion of a unit which falls under the responsibility of the association, the association of unit owners may be responsible for the payment of any condominium repairs and the court costs and reasonable attorney fees of the individual unit owner incurred during the pendency of a claim when judgment is rendered in favor of the individual unit owner. Any contractual provision that attempts to limit, diminish, or prevent the recovery provided for in this Section shall be prohibited.

Added by Acts 2010, No. 753, § 1.

Cross References

C.C. arts. 1958, 1964, 2000, 2357, 2362.1, 2545, 3052.

§ 1121.105. Separate taxation

All kinds of taxes and special assessments authorized by law shall be assessed against each individual condominium parcel. A multi-unit building, the condominium property as a whole, and any of the common elements shall not be deemed to be an individual parcel for tax purposes. Each unit shall be deemed to contain its percentage of undivided interest in the common elements and computation of taxes and special assessments against the unit shall include the percentage of undivided interest. The taxes and special assessments levied against a condominium parcel shall constitute a basis for claiming a lien only upon the individual condominium parcel assessed. There shall be no forfeiture or sale of a multi-unit building or the common elements as a whole for delinquent taxes or assessments on individual units.

Acts 1979, No. 682, § 1.

Cross References

C.C. arts. 462, 464.

§ 1121.106. Applicability of ordinances, zoning, and building restrictions

A zoning, subdivision, building code, or other land use law, ordinance, or regulation may not prohibit the condominium form of ownership or impose any requirement upon condominium property which it would not impose upon a physically identical development under a different form of ownership. Otherwise, no provision of this Part invalidates or modifies any provision of any zoning, subdivision, building code, or other land use law, ordinance, or regulation.

Acts 1979, No. 682, § 1.

Cross References

C.C. arts. 462, 464.

§ 1121.107. Expropriation

A. If a unit is acquired by eminent domain, unless the order of taking otherwise provides, that unit's entire common element interest, votes in the association, and proportionate liability for common expense assessments are deemed to be reallocated to the remaining units in proportion to the respective common element interests, voting power, and common expense liabilities of those units prior to the taking, and the association shall promptly prepare, execute, and record an amendment to the declaration reflecting the reallocation.

B. If a portion, but less than all of a unit is acquired by expropriation, and the remaining portion of the unit may be practically or lawfully used for those purposes permitted under the declaration, such unit's ownership in the common elements, votes in the association, and proportionate liability for common expenses shall be reduced in proportion to the reduction in the size of the unit, or on any other basis specified in the declaration, and the portion of the ownership interest in the common elements, voting power, and liability for common expense assessments divested from the partially acquired unit shall be deemed to be reallocated to that unit and the remaining units in proportion to the respective common element ownership interest, voting power, and liability for common expenses of those units prior to the taking, with the partially acquired unit participating in the reallocation on the basis of its reduced size.

C. If a portion of the common elements is acquired by expropriation, the award shall be paid to the association. The association shall divide any portion of the award not used for restoration or repair of the remaining common elements among the unit owners in proportion to their respective ownership interest in the common elements before the taking; any portion of the award attributable to the acquisition of a limited common element shall be equally divided among the owners of the unit to which that limited common element appertains, or in such other manner as the declaration may provide.

Acts 1979, No. 682, § 1.

§ 1121.108. Sale of unit; escrow accounts

As part of the initial sale of units, the seller, whether that be the condominium developer, the declarant, or a successor-in-interest, shall collect at least two months of assessments from each unit purchaser, which funds are dedicated for the sole purpose of establishing the association's reserve account. Such funds shall be placed in a reserve escrow account separate from the seller's account. Those funds may be used only for the exclusive benefit of the unit owner's association and shall be turned over to the unit owner's association along with the other condominium assets in accordance with the association declaration or bylaws.

Added by Acts 2010, No. 245, § 1.

Editor's note. R.S. 9:1121.108 was enacted by Acts 2010, No. 245, as R.S. 9:1121.111. It has been redesignated by the Louisiana State Law Institute as R.S. 9:1121.108.

§ 1121.109. [Blank]

§ 1121.110. [Blank]

§ 1121.111. [Blank]

§ 1121.112. [Blank]

§ 1121.113. [Blank]

§ 1121.114. [Blank]

§ 1122. Repealed by Acts 1979, No. 682, § 3

SUBPART B. CREATION, ALTERATION, AND TERMINATION OF CONDOMINIUMS

§ 1122.101. Creation of condominium regimes; condominium declaration; recordation

A condominium regime is established by the execution of a condominium declaration by the owner of the immovable property to be conveyed and by every lessor of a lease the expiration and termination of which will terminate the condominium or reduce its size. The condominium declaration and any instrument by which the condominium regime is altered or terminated shall be effective against third parties when filed for registry in the conveyance records in the parish in which the immovable property is located.

Acts 1979, No. 682, § 1.

§ 1122.102. [Blank]

§ 1122.103. Construction and validity of declaration and bylaws

A. All provisions of the declaration and bylaws are severable.

B. The effectiveness of the condominium declaration and merchantability of title to a condominium parcel is not affected by reason of an insubstantial failure of the declaration to comply with this Part.

Acts 1979, No. 682, § 1.

§ 1122.104. Description of units

After the declaration is properly filed for registry, a description of a unit which sets forth the name of the condominium, the place of recordation of the declaration, the parish in which the condominium is located, and the identifying number of the unit, is a sufficient legal description of that unit and its common element interest even if the common element interest is not described or referred to therein.

Acts 1979, No. 682, § 1.

§ 1122.105. Contents of the condominium declaration

A. The condominium declaration shall contain or provide for the following matters:

(1) A statement submitting the immovable property to a condominium regime.

(2) The name by which the condominium is to be identified, which name shall include the word "condominium" or be followed by the words "a condominium".

(3) A legal description of the land.

(4) An identification of each unit by letter, name or number, or combination thereof, so that no unit bears the same designation as any other unit.

(5) A written description delineating the precise boundaries of each unit and any limited common element appurtenant thereto.

(6) The undivided shares, stated as percentages or fractions, in the common elements which are a component part of each of the units.

(7) The proportions or percentages and the manner of sharing common expenses and owning common surplus.

(8) The proportionate voting rights of the unit owners in the association.

(9) The method of amendment of the condominium declaration.

(10) A plat of survey of the land and plans of the proposed or existing improvements complying with Section 1122.110.

(11) All matters required by Section 1122.106 in the event the declarant or an individual unit owner intends to reserve the right to change with respect to a unit or units, its percentage interest in the common elements, percentage of

sharing of common surplus and common expense, and proportion of voting power in the association of unit owners.

(12) The reconstruction or repair of all or part of the condominium property after casualty and the disposition of the proceeds of casualty insurance required by Section 1123.112 among owners of destroyed or damaged units or to the owners of any common elements destroyed.

(13) The name of the association and the type of legal entity under which it is organized; if the association is not incorporated, the name and residence address of the person designated as agent to receive service of process upon the association, which agent must be a resident of the state of Louisiana; and

(14) The procedure for collecting from the unit owners their respective shares of the common expenses assessed.

B. The condominium declaration may contain other provisions not inconsistent with this Section such as:

(1) Those relating to the withdrawal of damaged or destroyed units from the condominium regime.

(2) The reallocation of the percentage interest in the common elements of the units so withdrawn to the unit owners remaining within the condominium regime, and the basis of the reallocation, and the release of any unit or units so withdrawn from their respective obligations for payment of their percentage share of the common expenses of the condominium property.

(3) The purpose or purposes for which the condominium property and units are intended.

(4) Procedures whereby a unit owner may convey his unit to the association and thereby release himself from any further obligation for the common expenses of the condominium.

(5) Designation of limited common elements.

(6) Responsibility for the maintenance and repair of units.

(7) Use restrictions, and

(8) Limitations upon conveyance, sale, leasing, ownership, and occupancy of units.

C. Whenever additional immovable property is subjected to the condominium regime, an amendment to the condominium declaration shall be executed in accordance with Subsections A and B of this Section and filed for registry in the conveyance records in the parish in which the condominium is located.

Acts 1979, No. 682, § 1.

§ 1122.106. Reapportionment among unit owners of the percentage ownership interest in the common elements; percentages of sharing common expenses and common surplus; voting power in the association of unit owners

If on the date a condominium regime is created, it is the intention of the declarant to add additional units, common elements, or both, to the condominium regime, the declarant shall have the power to change, with respect to individual units in the condominium property, their respective percentage interest in the common elements, their percentage sharing of the common surplus and common expenses and their respective voting rights in the association of unit owners and to reallocate part of said interest to units actually dedicated at a future date upon providing the following particulars in the condominium declaration:

(1) A statement that the respective percentage interest of an individual unit in the common elements, common surplus and common expenses, and the proportionate voting rights of an individual unit in the association, may be changed in the event the declarant actually dedicates additional units, common elements, or both, to the condominium regime.

(2) A formula indicating the method or manner of determining a particular unit's percentage interest in the common elements, percentage sharing of surplus and common expenses and proportion of voting power in the association, dependent upon the total number of units comprising the entire condominium regime.

(3) The maximum time period, not to exceed a period of seven years subsequent to the date of filing the condominium declaration, during which additional units or common elements or both may be dedicated to the condominium regime.

(4) A description of each parcel of additional immovable property which may be later included in the condominium regime.

(5) If parcels of immovable property may be added to the condominium regime at different times, a statement to that effect, together with (i) either a statement fixing the boundaries of the parcels and regulating the order in which they may be added to the condominium regime or a statement that no assurances are made in those regards, and (ii) a statement as to whether, if any portion of additional immovable property is added to the condominium regime, all or any particular portion of that or any other immovable property must be so added.

(6) A statement of:

(a) The maximum number of condominium units that may be created within any parcel of additional immovable property to be added to the condominium regime, the boundaries of which are fixed pursuant to Paragraph (5).

(b) An indication of those units restricted to residential use.

(c) The maximum number of units per acre that may be created within any such parcels, the boundaries of which are not fixed pursuant to Paragraph (5).

(7) A statement of the extent to which any improvements that may be erected upon each parcel of the additional immovable property which may be added to the condominium regime will be compatible with the existing improvements in the condominium in terms of architectural style, quality of construction, principal materials employed in construction, and size, or a statement that no assurances are made in those regards.

(8) A statement that all covenants in the condominium declaration affecting use, occupancy, and alienation of units will apply to units created within additional parcels of immovable property which may be later added to the condominium regime, or a statement of any differentiations which may be made as to those units.

(9) Any additional common elements that may be included within the condominium in the event additional units are included within the condominium at a later date and specifically indicating what common elements will be added if less than the maximum number of units are later included within the condominium regime, and

(10) A statement of any limitations as to the locations of improvements that may be made within parcels of immovable

property to be added to the condominium regime, or a statement that no assurances are made in that regard.
Acts 1979, No. 682, § 1.

§ 1122.107. Condominiums established on leased land

A. With respect to any lease, the expiration or termination of which may terminate the condominium, or reduce its size, the condominium declaration shall state:

(1) The place of recordation of such lease or statement where the complete lease may be inspected.

(2) The date on which the lease is scheduled to expire.

(3) A legal description of the immovable property subject to the lease.

(4) Any rights of a unit owner or owners upon termination of the lease and the manner whereby those rights may be exercised or a statement that they do not have such rights.

(5) Any right of the unit owners to renew such lease including the conditions of any renewal or statement that they do not have such rights.

B. If the expiration or termination of a lease decreases the number of units in a condominium, then the ownership interest in the common elements, voting rights in the association, and obligation for payment of common expense appurtenant to such units shall be equitably reallocated among the remaining units. Such reallocation shall be effected by an amendment to the condominium declaration duly filed for registry.
Acts 1979, No. 682, § 1.

§ 1122.108. Allocation of common element interest, votes, and common expense liabilities

A. The declaration may provide that different allocations of votes shall be made to the units on particular matters specified in the declaration.

B. Except as provided in Section 1121.107, Section 1122.112, Section 1122.114, or Section 1122.115 or in the event a portion of the condominium property is removed from the provisions of this Part following a casualty loss or expropriation, the percentage of undivided interest of such unit owner in the common elements of the condominium as expressed in the condominium declaration shall be an inseparable component of the ownership of the unit and shall not be altered without the consent of all the unit owners expressed in an amended condominium declaration duly filed for registry.

C. The common elements shall remain undivided and shall not be subject to partition, except with respect to that part or all of the condominium property that has been withdrawn from the provisions of this Part.
Acts 1979, No. 682, § 1.

§ 1122.109. [Blank]

§ 1122.110. Plats and plans

A. Each plat shall show:

(1) The name, general location, and horizontal dimensions of the immovable property.

(2) The location and horizontal dimensions of all existing improvements.

(3) The location and dimensions of any immovable property which the declarant has the option to later include within the condominium regime.

(4) The intended location and dimensions of any contemplated improvements to be constructed within the immovable property which may later be added to the condominium regime.

(5) The location and dimensions of all servitudes serving or burdening any portion of the immovable property.

(6) The location and dimensions of any immovable property in which the unit owners will own only an interest as lessee, labeled as "immovable property subject to lease".

(7) The distance between noncontiguous parcels of immovable property comprising the condominiums, and

(8) All other matters customarily shown on land surveys.

B. Plans of every building improvement that contain or comprise all or part of any unit and is located within any portion of the immovable property of the condominium regime other than within the boundaries of any additional immovable property which the declarant has reserved the right to add to the condominium regime at a later date, shall show:

(1) The location and dimensions of the horizontal and vertical boundaries of each unit, with reference to established datum, and that unit's identifying number; and

(2) Any units that may be converted by the declarant to create additional units or common elements, identified appropriately.

C. If additional immovable properties are later included within a condominium regime, the declarant shall record new plats for such immovable property conforming to the requirements of Subsection A and new plans for any buildings on that immovable property conforming to the requirements of Subsection B.

D. If the declarant converts any units into two or more units, common elements, or both, new plans shall be recorded as an amendment to the declaration showing the location of any new units and common elements thus created as well as the location and dimensions of any portions of that space not being converted.

E. Any certification of a plat or plan required by this Section shall be made by a surveyor, architect, or engineer licensed as such in the state of Louisiana.
Acts 1979, No. 682, § 1.

§ 1122.111. [Blank]

§ 1122.112. Termination; withdrawal

A. The condominium property or a portion thereof may be withdrawn from the provisions of this Part by the consent of all or a percentage of the unit owners and unit mortgage creditors as provided in the condominium declaration.

B. To withdraw immovable property from a condominium regime, the association shall prepare, execute, and record an amendment to the condominium declaration containing a legally sufficient description of the immovable property being withdrawn and stating the fact of withdrawal. If only a portion of the condominium property is being withdrawn, the amendment shall reallocate the percentages of common element ownership, voting power in the association, and liability for common expenses to any units remaining in the condominium in proportion to the said respective percentages of those units.

C. Upon withdrawal of the condominium property or a portion thereof from the provisions of this Part, the portion so withdrawn shall be deemed to be owned in indivision by the unit owners in the withdrawn premises. The percentage of undivided ownership of a unit owner in the withdrawn property shall be equal to his former percentage of ownership in the common elements divided by the total former percentages of ownership in such common elements of all withdrawing unit owners. Privileges and mortgages upon individual condominium parcels shall, following their withdrawal, be upon the respective undivided shares of the withdrawing owners in the property withdrawn.

D. Condominium property withdrawn from the provisions of this Part shall be subject to partition by action of a unit owner owning a portion of the withdrawn property. The proceeds from any sale of the withdrawn property shall be paid to a unit owner after all claims secured by privileges and mortgages on his share of the withdrawn property have been satisfied.

Acts 1979, No. 682, § 1.

§ 1122.113. Alterations of units

Subject to the provisions of the condominium declaration and other provisions of law, a unit owner:

(1) May make any improvements or alterations to his unit that does not impair the structural integrity or mechanical systems or lessen the support of any portion of the condominium.

(2) May not change the appearance of the common elements, or the exterior appearance of a unit or any portion of the condominium, without permission of the association, and

(3) After acquiring an adjoining unit or an adjoining part of an adjoining unit, may remove or alter any intervening partition or create apertures therein, even if the partition in whole or in part is a common element, provided those acts do not impair the structural integrity or mechanical systems or lessen the support of any portion of the condominium.

Acts 1979, No. 682, § 1.

§ 1122.114. Relocation of boundaries between adjoining units

A. Subject to the provisions of the condominium declaration and other provisions of law, the boundaries between adjoining units may be reallocated by an amendment to the condominium declaration upon written request to the association by the owners of the adjoining units. Such an amendment shall specify the method of reallocation between the adjoining units of their respective percentage interest in the common elements, voting power in the association, and percentage obligations for common expense assessments. Such an amendment shall identify the units involved, shall be executed by the reallocating unit owners, and shall contain words of conveyance between them.

B. The association, upon the request and at the expense of the reallocating unit owners, shall prepare and record plats or plans showing the altered boundaries, their dimensions, and identifying numbers.

Acts 1979, No. 682, § 1.

§ 1122.115. Subdivision or conversion of units

A. If the condominium declaration expressly so permits, a unit may be subdivided or converted into two or more units, common elements, or combination of one or more units and common elements. Subject to the provisions of the condominium declaration and other provisions of law, upon written request of a unit owner to subdivide a unit, the condominium association shall prepare, execute and record an amendment to the condominium declaration, including the plats and plans, subdividing that unit.

B. An amendment to the condominium declaration must assign an identifying number to each unit created, and reallocate the common elements interests, votes in the association, and common expense assessment liabilities formerly allocated to the subdivided unit to the new units in any reasonable manner prescribed by the owner of the subdivided unit.

Acts 1979, No. 682, § 1.

§ 1122.116. [Blank]

§ 1122.117. [Blank]

§ 1122.118. [Blank]

§ 1122.119. Amendment of declaration

Except in cases of amendments that may be executed by declarant under Sections 1122.110C or 1122.110D, or by the Association under Sections 1121.107, 1122.107B or 1122.114A or 1122.115, the declaration, including the plats and plans, may be amended only by vote or agreement of unit owners of units to which at least sixty-seven percent of the votes of the association are allocated or any other percent of votes which the condominium declaration specifies.

Acts 1979, No. 682, § 1.

§ 1122.120. [Blank]

§ 1122.121. [Blank]

§ 1123. Repealed by Acts 1979, No. 682, § 3

SUBPART C. MANAGEMENT OF THE CONDOMINIUM

§ 1123.101. Organization of unit owners' association

A unit owners' association shall be organized no later than the date the condominium is created. The membership of the association at all times shall consist exclusively of all the unit owners or, following termination of the condominium, of all former unit owners entitled to distributions of proceeds under Section 1122.112, or their heirs, successors, or assigns. The association shall be organized as a profit or nonprofit corporation, or as an unincorporated association.

Acts 1979, No. 682, § 1.

§ 1123.102. Powers of unit owners' association

Subject to the provisions of the declaration, the association, even if unincorporated, may:

(1) Adopt and amend bylaws and rules and regulations.

(2) Adopt and amend budgets for revenues, expenditures, and reserves and make and collect assessments for common expenses from unit owners.

(3) Hire and terminate managing agents and other employees, agents, and independent contractors.

(4) Institute, defend, or intervene in litigation or administrative proceedings in its own name on behalf of itself or two or more unit owners on matters affecting the condominium.

(5) Make contracts and incur liabilities.

(6) Regulate the use, maintenance, repair, replacement, and modification of common elements.

(7) Cause additional improvements to be made as a part of the common elements.

(8) Acquire, hold, encumber, and convey in its own name any right, title, or interest to real or personal property.

(9) Grant easements, leases, licenses, and concessions, through or over the common elements.

(10) Impose and receive any payments, fees, or charges for the use, rental, or operation of the common elements other than limited common elements.

(11) Impose charges for later payment of assessments and, after notice and an opportunity to be heard, levy reasonable fines for violations of the declaration, bylaws, and rules and regulations of the association and, when the violation is a failure to pay for services, interrupt those services until the violation has ceased. No charge for later payment of assessments shall be imposed if the assessment is paid within ten days of the due date. Furthermore, no such charge shall exceed thirty percent of the amount of the monthly assessment. The condominium association shall provide to each unit owner written or electronic notice detailing all of the following:

(a) The amount of the assessment due by the unit owner.

(b) The due date of the assessment due by the unit owner.

(c) Notice that the assessment is due within ten days of the due date.

(12) Impose reasonable charges for the preparation and recordation of amendments to the declaration, resale certificates required by Section 1124.107, or statements of unpaid assessments.

(13) Provide for the indemnification of its officers and executive board and maintain directors' and officers' liability insurance.

(14) Exercise any other powers conferred by the declaration or bylaws.

(15) Exercise all other powers that may be exercised in this state by legal entities of the same type as the association, and

(16) Exercise any other powers necessary and proper for the governance and operation of the association.

Acts 1979, No. 682, § 1. Amended by Acts 1988, No. 979, § 1; Acts 2011, No. 180, § 1, eff. June 24, 2011.

§ 1123.103. [Blank]

§ 1123.104. [Blank]

§ 1123.105. **Termination of contracts and leases of declarant**

A contract for the maintenance, management, or operation of the condominium property or any lease of recreational or parking facilities entered into by the association while the association is controlled by the developer of the condominium shall be subject to cancellation by the association by vote of not less than a majority of the individual unit owners other than the declarant computed with reference to their respective percentage obligations for common expenses within a one year period immediately following the date on which individual unit owners other than the declarant assume or acquire control of the association.

Acts 1979, No. 682, § 1.

§ 1123.106. **Bylaws**

A. The administration and operation of the condominium shall be governed by the bylaws.

B. The bylaws shall provide for the form and manner of administration of the condominium.

C. The bylaws may include other provisions deemed necessary or desirable for the administration of the condominium property consistent with this Part, including but not limited to the following:

(1) The method of adopting and amending administrative rules and regulations concerning the details of the operation and use of the condominium property.

(2) A procedure for submitting disputes among unit owners arising from the administration of the condominium property to arbitration, and

(3) The establishment of reserves to provide for maintenance, improvements, replacements, working capital, bad debts, obsolescence, and other appropriate purposes.

Acts 1979, No. 682, § 1.

§ 1123.107. **Upkeep of the condominium**

Except to the extent provided by the declaration, or Section 1123.112, the association is responsible for maintenance, repair, and replacement of the common elements, and each unit owner is responsible for maintenance, repair and replacement of his unit.

Acts 1979, No. 682, § 1.

§ 1123.108. **Association records**

The association shall keep financial records sufficiently detailed to enable the association to comply with Section 1124.107. All financial and other records shall be made reasonably available for examination by any unit owner and his authorized agents.

Acts 1979, No. 682, § 1.

§ 1123.109. [Blank]

§ 1123.110. [Blank]

§ 1123.111. [Blank]

§ 1123.112. **Insurance**

A. Commencing not later than the time of the first conveyance of a unit to a person other than a declarant, the association shall maintain, to the extent reasonably available:

(1) Property insurance on the common elements and units, exclusive of improvements and betterments installed in units by unit owners, insuring against all risks of direct physical loss commonly insured against. The total amount of insurance after application of any deductibles shall be not less than eighty percent of the actual cash value of the insured property, exclusive of land, excavations, foundations, and other items normally excluded from property policies; and

(2) Comprehensive general liability insurance, including medical payments insurance, in an amount determined by the executive board but not less than any amount specified in the declaration, covering all occurrences commonly insured against for death, bodily injury, and property damage arising out of or in connection with the use, ownership, or maintenance of the common elements.

B. If the insurance described in Subsection A is not maintained, the association promptly shall cause notice of that fact to be hand-delivered or sent prepaid by United

States mail to all unit owners. The declaration may require the association to carry any other insurance, and the association in any event may carry any other insurance it deems appropriate to protect the association or the unit owners.

C. Insurance policies carried pursuant to Subsection A must provide that:

(1) Each unit owner is an insured person under the policy with respect to liability arising out of his ownership of an individual interest in the common elements or membership in the association.

(2) The insurer waives its right to subrogation under the policy against any unit owner of the condominium or members of his household.

(3) No act or omission by any unit owner, unless acting within the scope of his authority on behalf of the association, will void the policy or be a condition to recovery under the policy, and

(4) If, at the time of a loss under the policy, there is other insurance in the name of a unit owner covering the same property covered by the policy, the policy is primary insurance not contributing with the other insurance.

D. Any loss covered by the property policy under Subsection A(1) shall be adjusted with the association, but the insurance proceeds for that loss shall be payable to any insurance trustee designated for that purpose, or otherwise to the association, and not to any mortgagee. The insurance trustee or the association shall hold any insurance proceeds in trust for unit owners and lien holders as their interests may appear. Subject to the provisions of Subsection G, the proceeds shall be disbursed first for the repair or restoration of the damaged common elements and units, and unit owners and lien holders are not entitled to receive payment of any portion of the proceeds unless there is a surplus of proceeds after the common elements and units have been completely repaired or restored, or the condominium is terminated.

E. An insurance policy issued to the association does not prevent a unit owner from obtaining insurance for his own benefit.

F. An insurer that has issued an insurance policy to the association under this Section shall issue certificates or memoranda of insurance, upon request, to any unit owner or mortgagee. The insurance may not be canceled until thirty days after notice of the proposed cancellation has been mailed to the association, each unit owner and each mortgagee to whom certificates of insurance have been issued.

G. Any portion of the condominium damaged or destroyed shall be repaired or replaced promptly by the association unless (1) the condominium is terminated, (2) repair or replacement would be illegal under any state or local health or safety statute or ordinance, or (3) eighty percent, or such other percentage provided in the declaration, of the unit owners vote not to rebuild. The cost of repair or replacement in excess of insurance proceeds and reserves is a common expense. If the entire condominium is not repaired or replaced, (1) the insurance proceeds attributable to the damaged common elements shall be used to restore the damaged area to a condition compatible with the remainder of the condominium, (2) the insurance proceeds attributable to units and limited common elements which are not rebuilt shall be distributed to the owners of those units and the owners of the units to which those limited common elements were assigned, and (3) the remainder of the proceeds shall be distributed to all the unit owners in proportion to their common element interest. If the unit owners vote not to rebuild any unit, that unit's entire common element interest, votes in the association, and common expense liability are automatically reallocated upon the vote as if the unit had been condemned under Section 1121.107, and the association promptly shall prepare, execute, and record an amendment to the declaration reflecting the reallocations. Notwithstanding the provisions of this Subsection, Section 1122.120 governs the distribution of insurance proceeds if the condominium is terminated.

Acts 1979, No. 682, § 1.

§ 1123.113. Fidelity bond or equivalent form of insurance required

A. Any unit owners' association collecting assessments for common expenses shall obtain and maintain a blanket fidelity bond or other equivalent form of insurance covering the officers, directors, and persons employed by the unit owners' association, and any managing agent and employees of the managing agent.

B. The bond or equivalent form of insurance shall provide coverage in an amount equal to the lesser of one million dollars or the amount of reserve balances of the unit owners' association plus one-fourth of the aggregate annual assessment of the unit owners' association. The minimum coverage amount shall be ten thousand dollars.

C. Any unit owners' association whose managing agent maintains its own bond or equivalent form of insurance shall be in compliance with this Section, provided that the managing agent's bond or equivalent form of insurance meets the requirements set forth in this Section, and that the association is named as an additional insured under the managing agent's bond or equivalent form of insurance.

D. (1) The unit owners' association or the managing agent shall maintain proof of the bond or equivalent form of insurance required by this Section on the premises of the condominium at all times.

(2) The unit owners' association or the managing agent shall make the proof available for inspection by a member of the condominium unit owners' association upon request of the member.

(3) The unit owners' association or the managing agent shall also provide every member of the unit owners' association with written or electronic notice of the bond or equivalent form of insurance as well as a statement notifying the member that the member has a right to inspect the proof of the bond or equivalent form of insurance required by this Section.

Added by Acts 2011, No. 84, § 1. Amended by Acts 2012, No. 79, § 1.

Cross References

C.C. arts. 163, 164, 469, 476, 480, 491, 517, 526.

§ 1123.114. [Blank]

§ 1123.115. Privilege on immovables

A. (1) The association shall have a privilege on a condominium parcel for all unpaid or accelerated sums assessed by the association, any fines or late fees in excess of two hundred fifty dollars, and interest thereon at the rate provided in the condominium declaration or, in the absence thereof, at the legal interest rate. This privilege shall also secure reasonable attorney fees incurred by the association incident to the collection of the assessment or enforcement of the privilege. Further, if the unit owner fails to timely pay the assessments for common elements for a period of three months or more during any eight-month period and notice to the delinquent unit owner is provided as set forth in Paragraph (3) of this Subsection, the association may accelerate the assessment on the common elements for a twelve-month period and file a privilege for the accelerated sums. Assessments for common elements are those assessments that are collected on a regular basis by the association for routine expenditures associated with the property.

(2) To be preserved, the privilege shall be evidenced by a claim of privilege, signed and verified by affidavit of an officer or agent of the association, and shall be filed for registry in the mortgage records in the parish in which the condominium is located. The claim of privilege shall include a description of the condominium parcel, the name of its record owner, the amount of delinquent or accelerated assessment, the date on which the assessment became delinquent, and any fines or late fees assessed in excess of two hundred fifty dollars.

(3) The association shall, at least seven days prior to the filing for registry of the privilege, serve upon the delinquent unit owner a sworn detailed statement of its claim for the delinquent or accelerated assessment that includes the date said assessment became delinquent or accelerated, which service shall be effected by personal service, or registered or certified mail.

B. A claim of privilege recorded, as set forth in Subsection A of this Section, shall preserve the privilege against the condominium parcel for a period of one year from the date of recordation. The effect of recordation shall cease and the privilege preserved by this recordation shall perempt unless a notice of filing of suit, giving the name of the court, the title and number of the proceedings and date of filing, a description of the condominium parcel and the name of the unit owner, on said claim is recorded within one year from the date of the recordation of the inscription of the said claim. Such notice of filing suit shall preserve the privilege until the court in which the suit is filed shall order the cancellation of the inscription of the said claim and the notice of filing of suit on said claim or until the claimant authorizes the clerk of court or recorder of mortgages to cancel the said inscriptions.

C. A privilege under this Section is superior to all other liens and encumbrances on a unit except (1) privileges, mortgages, and encumbrances recorded before the recordation of the declaration, (2) privileges, mortgages, and encumbrances on the unit recorded before the recordation of the privilege as provided in Subsection B of this Section, (3) immovable property taxes, and (4) governmental assessments in which the unit is specifically described.

Acts 1979, No. 682, § 1. Amended by Acts 1988, No. 979, § 1; Acts 2006, No. 358, § 1; Acts 2010, No. 245, § 1.

§ 1123.115.1. [Blank]

§ 1123.116. Privilege for utility assessments

A. In addition to the privilege granted to an association on a condominium parcel for unpaid assessments provided in Section 1123.115, the association, provided that the association is in good faith regarding the management of the condominium property, shall have a separate privilege on the condominium parcel for that portion of the unpaid assessment which is assessed for the payment of water, sewerage, electrical, or natural gas utilities on behalf of the condominium parcel. This privilege shall be preserved in the same manner as privileges are preserved under Section 1123.115.

B. Notwithstanding any other provision of law to the contrary, prior to institution of suit by a municipal or parish governing authority or other municipal or parish entity for payment of any tax or fee levied or assessed for providing water, sewerage, electrical, or natural gas services to a condominium property, the authority or entity shall notify the association of its intent to file suit.

C. Upon notification of an intent to file suit for delinquent or past due taxes or fees due, the association shall provide the authority or entity a list of the individual condominium units for which taxes or fees for water, sewerage, electrical, or natural gas services are delinquent or past due. The association shall notify each owner of a condominium unit at the last known address of the owner as reflected in the association records of the fact of institution of suit for payment of past due or delinquent taxes or fees due on the respective unit.

D. If the condominium unit is abandoned property as defined in R.S. 33:4720.12(1), the municipal or parish governing authority may proceed with the sale of the property pursuant to the provisions of Chapter 13–A of Title 33 of the Louisiana Revised Statutes of 1950, relative to the sale of abandoned property.

E. (1) If the condominium unit is determined to be abandoned or blighted housing property as defined in R.S. 33:4720.26(1), the unit may be adjudicated to the municipality or parish for nonpayment of such taxes or assessments.

(2)(a) Abandoned or blighted condominium units which are adjudicated to a municipality or parish may be donated to a nonprofit organization pursuant to R.S. 33:4717.3 or as otherwise provided by law.

(b) In making a donation of abandoned or blighted condominium units the municipality or parish shall offer the association first refusal of the units provided the association forms a nonprofit organization recognized by the Internal Revenue Service as a 501(c)(3) or 501(c)(4) [1] as a nonprofit organization and agrees to renovate and maintain the property until conveyed by the organization.

Added by Acts 2003, No. 770, § 1.

[1] 26 U.S.C.A. §§ 501(c)(3) or 501(c)(4).

§ 1123.117. [Blank]

§ 1124. Repealed by Acts 1979, No. 682, § 3

SUBPART D. PROTECTION OF PURCHASERS

§ 1124.101. Applicability; waiver

A. This Subpart applies to all units subject to this Part, except as provided in Subsection B.

B. A public offering statement need not be prepared or delivered in the case of:

(1) A gratuitous transfer of a unit.

(2) A disposition pursuant to court order.

(3) A disposition by foreclosure or giving in payment, or

(4) A transfer to which Section 1124.107 applies.

Acts 1979, No. 682, § 1.

§ 1124.102. Public offering statement; general provisions

A. Prior to the initial sale or execution of a contract to purchase a condominium unit, the declarant shall provide a purchaser of a unit with a copy of the public offering statement containing or accurately disclosing:

(1) A copy of the condominium declaration.

(2) A copy of articles of incorporation or other documents creating the association.

(3) A copy of the bylaws of the association.

(4) A copy of any predial lease or sublease relating to the condominium property.

(5) A written statement indicating whether the declarant has entered into or intends to enter into a contract for the management of all or a portion of the condominium property. With respect to any such contract, this statement shall specify the services to be rendered, the amount or estimate of the cost to be incurred thereunder and the duration thereof, including any renewal provisions, and any relationship, whether direct or indirect, between the declarant and the person to perform such management services.

(6) A projected operating budget for the association, for the one year period after the date of the first conveyance of a unit to a purchaser and thereafter the current budget of the association, including full details of the estimated monthly charges for maintenance and management of the condominium, including an indication of the amount, or a statement that there is no amount, included in the budget as a reserve for repairs and replacement, monthly charges for the use of any recreational facilities, and of insurance coverage on the condominium, and the estimated premiums therefor.

(7) A brief narrative description of the significant features of the declaration (other than the plats and plans), the articles of incorporation or other documents creating the association, the bylaws, and rules and regulations.

(8) A diagram or other illustration of the floor plan of the unit.

(9) A written statement indicating whether any units remaining unsold subsequent to the filing of the condominium declaration will be exempted from the payment of all or a portion of the common expenses normally accruing to said unsold units and, if so, the period of time of the exemption.

(10) A statement that within fifteen days of receipt of a public offering statement, a purchaser, before conveyance, may cancel any contract to purchase a unit from the declarant.

(11) The terms of any warranties expressly made or limited by the declarant.

(12) A statement of any unsatisfied judgments against the association, the status of any pending suits to which the association is a party, and the status of any pending suits or claims material to the condominium of which the declarant has actual knowledge, and

(13) A description of the insurance coverage provided for the benefit of unit owners.

B. A declarant shall promptly amend the public offering statement to report any material change in the information required by this Section.

C. A cause of action created or recognized under this Section shall in any event prescribe five years after the date of closing of the act transfer.

Acts 1979, No. 682, § 1.

§ 1124.103. [Blank]

§ 1124.104. Public offering statement; conversion condominiums

A. The public offering statement of a condominium containing any building that at any time before recording the declaration was occupied wholly or partially by persons other than purchasers and having greater than ten units, must contain, in addition to the information required by Section 1124.102:

(1) A report prepared by a registered architect or engineer, describing the present condition of all structural components, roof, and mechanical and electrical installations material to the use and enjoyment of the condominium.

(2) A statement by the declarant of the estimated remaining useful life of each item reported on in Paragraph (1) or a statement that no representations are made in that regard, and

(3) A statement by the declarant of any outstanding notices of incurred violations of building codes or other municipal regulations, together with the estimated costs of curing those violations.

B. This Section applies only to units that may be occupied for residential use.

Acts 1979, No. 682, § 1.

§ 1124.105. Public offering statement; condominium securities

If an interest in a condominium is currently registered with the Securities and Exchange Commission of the United States, a declarant satisfies all requirements of this Part relating to the preparation of a public offering statement if he delivers to the purchaser a copy of the public offering statement filed with the Securities and Exchange Commission.

Acts 1979, No. 682, § 1.

§ 1124.106. Purchaser's right to cancel

A. Unless delivery of a public offering statement is not required a declarant shall provide a purchaser of a unit with a copy of the public offering statement before conveyance of that unit, and not later than the date of any contract of sale. Unless a purchaser is given the public offering statement more than fifteen days before execution of a contract for the purchase of a unit, the purchaser, before conveyance, may cancel the contract within fifteen days after first receiving the public offering statement.

B. If a purchaser elects to cancel a contract pursuant to Subsection A, he may do so by hand delivering notice thereof to the declarant or by mailing notice thereof by prepaid United States mail to the declarant, or to his agent for service of process. Cancellation is without penalty, and all payments made by the purchaser before cancellation shall be refunded promptly.

C. Any person who reasonably relies on a materially false, or materially misleading statement in a public offering statement and deposits money or other things of value toward the purchase of a condominium unit shall, in addition to any other rights provided by law, have a cause of action to rescind the contract to purchase or collect damages from the seller prior to the closing of the act of transfer of the unit. After closing of the act to transfer, the purchaser shall have a cause of action against the declarant for damages for one year subsequent to the date upon which the last of the event described in the following paragraph occurs:

(1) The closing of the act of transfer of the unit; or

(2) Sufficient completion by the seller of construction of the building containing the unit sold to allow lawful occupancy of the unit and completion of all common elements and all recreational facilities, whether or not common elements, which the seller is obligated to complete or provide under the contract to purchase the unit or which the seller is represented that he will provide in a sales brochure or similar material.

D. A cause of action created or recognized under this Section shall in any event prescribe five years after the date of closing of the act of transfer.

Acts 1979, No. 682, § 1.

§ 1124.107. Resales of units

A. In the event of a resale of a unit by a unit owner other than a declarant, the unit owner shall furnish to a purchaser before execution of any contract to purchase a unit, or otherwise before conveyance, a copy of the declaration other than plats and plans, the articles of incorporation or documents creating the association, the bylaws, and a certificate containing:

(1) A statement setting forth the amount of any current common expense assessments.

(2) A statement of any capital expenditures approved by the association for the current and two next succeeding fiscal years.

(3) A statement of the amount of any reserves for capital expenditures and of any portions of those reserves designated by the association for any specified projects.

(4) The most recent balance sheet and income and expense statement of the association, if any.

(5) The current operating budget of the association, if any.

(6) A statement of any unsatisfied judgments against the association and the status of any pending suits to which the association is a party.

(7) A statement describing any insurance coverage provided by the association, and

(8) A statement of the remaining term of any ground lease affecting the condominium and provisions governing any extension or renewal thereof.

B. The association, within ten days after a request by a unit owner, shall furnish a certificate containing the information necessary to enable a unit owner to comply with this Section. The unit owner providing a certificate pursuant to Subsection A is not liable to the purchaser for any erroneous information provided by the association and included in the certificate.

C. A unit owner is not liable to a purchaser for the failure or delay of the association to provide the certificate in a timely manner; however, the contract to purchase is voidable by the purchaser until a certificate has been provided and for five days thereafter or until conveyance, whichever first occurs.

Acts 1979, No. 682, § 1.

§ 1124.108. [Blank]

§ 1124.109. Privileges

A. Subsequent to the filing for registry of the condominium declaration, and at all times during which the condominium property remains subject to this Part, no privileges of any nature shall arise or be created against the entire condominium property or the common elements as a whole. During this period a privilege may arise or be created upon or against the individual condominium parcels in the same manner and under the same conditions as a privilege may arise or be created upon or against any other separate parcel of immovable property subject to individual ownership.

B. Labor performed or materials furnished to a unit shall not be the basis for the filing of a claim of privilege pursuant to R.S. 9:4801 through 4820, unless the unit owner expressly requested or consented to the same. Labor performed or materials furnished to the association shall not be the basis for a privilege on the common elements as a whole; however, if the performance of labor or furnishing of materials is expressly authorized by the association, the labor or materials shall be deemed to be performed or furnished with the express consent of each unit owner and shall be the basis for the filing of a claim of privilege against each condominium parcel in the condominium. A single claim of privilege filed against the association shall be deemed to be a separate claim of privilege against each individual unit, but any such claim of privilege against an individual condominium parcel shall be limited in amount to the total charge for the labor performed and materials furnished multiplied by the percentage obligation of the owner of the condominium parcel for common expenses. Each individual owner may thereafter relieve his condominium parcel from any such privilege by payment of the proportionate amount of the claim of privilege attributable to his parcel. Upon such payment, it shall be the duty of the privilege creditor to release the privilege against such condominium parcel.

C. Service or delivery of notices and papers required under R.S. 9:4801 through 4820, on unit owners for or incident to the protection or enforcement of privileges arising from labor performed or materials furnished to the association, may be effected by service on or delivery to an officer of the association.

Acts 1979, No. 682, § 1.

§ 1124.110. [Blank]

§ 1124.111. [Blank]

§ 1124.112. [Blank]

§ 1124.113. [Blank]

§ 1124.114. [Blank]

§ 1124.115. Compliance with condominium declaration, bylaws, and administrative rules and regulations

A. The condominium declaration and bylaws shall have the force of law between the individual unit owners. The remedies for breach of any obligation imposed on unit owners or the declarant shall be damages, injunctions, or other such remedies as provided by law.

For Annotative Materials, see West's Louisiana Statutes Annotated

B. The remedies under Subsection A shall be available by ordinary and summary proceedings.

C. For the purposes of this Section, a unit owner shall be considered an occupant of the condominium property and subject to the provisions of Code of Civil Procedure Articles 4701 through 4735 in an action by the association of unit owners.

Acts 1979, No. 682, § 1. Amended by Acts 1988, No. 979, § 1.

§ 1124.116. [Blank]

§ 1124.117. [Blank]

§§ 1125 to 1131. Repealed by Acts 1979, No. 682, § 3

PART II-A. LOUISIANA TIMESHARING ACT

§ 1131.1. Short title

This Part shall be known as and may be cited as the Louisiana Timesharing Act.

Added by Acts 1983, No. 552, § 1.

§ 1131.2. Definitions

As used in this Part:

(1) "Affiliate" means any person who controls, is controlled by, or is under common control with a developer.

(a) A person "controls" a developer if the person:

(i) is a general partner, officer, director, or employer of the developer;

(ii) directly or indirectly or acting in concert with one or more other persons or through one or more subsidiaries, owns, controls, holds with power to vote, or holds proxies representing more than twenty percent of, the voting interest in the developer or its general partner;

(iii) controls in any manner the selection of a majority of the directors or the general partner of the developer; or

(iv) has contributed more than twenty percent of the capital of the developer.

(b) A person "is controlled by" a developer if the developer:

(i) is a general partner, officer, director, or employer of the person;

(ii) directly or indirectly or acting in concert with one or more other persons or through one or more subsidiaries, owns, controls, holds with power to vote, or holds proxies representing more than twenty percent of, the voting interest in the person;

(iii) controls in any manner the election of a majority of the directors of the person; or

(iv) has contributed more than twenty percent of the capital of the person.

(c) A person is also "controlled by" a developer if such person is a project broker or sales agent for any timeshare property of the developer.

(d) Control does not exist if the powers described in this Paragraph are held solely as security for an obligation and are not exercised.

(2) "Common elements" means all portions of timeshare property other than units.

(3) "Completion of construction" means:

(a)(i) That a certificate of occupancy has been issued for the entire building in which the timeshare interest being sold is located, or for the improvement, or that the equivalent authorization has been issued, by the governmental body having jurisdiction; or

(ii) In a jurisdiction in which no certificate of occupancy or equivalent authorization is issued, that the construction, finishing, and equipping of the building or improvements according to the plans and specifications have been substantially completed; and

(b) That all accommodations of the timeshare unit and facilities of the timeshare plan are available for use in a manner identical in all material respects to the manner portrayed by the promotional material, advertising, and public offering statements filed with the Louisiana Real Estate Commission.

(4) "Conspicuous type" means type in boldfaced capital letters no smaller than the largest type, exclusive of headings, on the page on which it appears and, in all cases, at least 10-point type. Where conspicuous type is required, it must be separated on all sides from other type and print. Conspicuous type may be utilized in purchase contracts or public offering statements only where required by law.

(5) "Contract" includes any agreement conferring the rights and obligations of a timeshare ownership on the purchaser.

(6) "Developer" means the person, or any successor or assignee of such person, who creates the timeshare plan or who is in the business of making sales of timeshare interests which it owns or purports to own.

(7) "Exchange company" means the person operating a program providing any opportunity or procedure for the assignment or exchange of timeshare interests among owners and purchasers in the same or other timeshare plans.

(8) "Lease timeshare interest" means an interest in which a person receives the right to use or occupy, however evidenced or documented, immovable property for a period of time or intervals of time which can be less than a full year during each year, over a period of more than three years.

(9) "Managing entity" means an entity with the duty to manage and operate the timeshare plan and/or the timeshare property.

(10) "Multiple use project" means a project which combines hotel and/or apartment accommodations with timeshare units in which the timeshare interest sold is a lease timeshare interest and the hotel and/or apartment units exceed fifty units in number not subject to a timeshare interest and the timeshare interest units of the development account for less than forty percent of the total square footage of all the units in the project.

(11) "Owner" means any person who owns or is a co-owner of a timeshare interest.

(12) "Ownership timeshare interest" means an interest in which a person receives the right to use or occupy, however evidenced or documented, immovable property for a period of less than a full year during each year, over a period of more than three years, coupled with an ownership interest in immovable property.

(13) "Person" means an individual, partnership, corporation, or other legal entity.

(14) "Project" means immovable property containing more than one unit. "Project" includes but is not limited to condominiums and cooperative housing corporations. A project may include units that are not timeshare units.

(15) "Purchaser" means any person to whom a timeshare interest is offered or who has contracted to purchase a timeshare interest.

(16) "Timeshare association" means a corporation owned by the timeshare interest owners and through which the timeshare interest owners manage and regulate the timeshare property.

(17) "Timeshare declaration" or "declaration" means the instrument by which the timeshare property is made subject to a timeshare plan.

(18) "Timeshare documents" means all of the documents, by whatever names denominated, and any amendments thereto, which establish the timeshare plan, create and govern the rights and relationships of owners, and govern the use and operation of the timeshare property. Such documents include, but are not limited to, the declaration, the articles of incorporation and by-laws of the association, and the rules and regulations for the timeshare plan.

(19) "Timeshare expenses" means any expenditures, fees, charges, or other liabilities for which an owner of a timeshare interest is liable as a result of the ownership of the timeshare interest.

(20) "Timeshare interest" means an ownership "timeshare interest", a lease timeshare interest, a timeshare estate, and a timeshare use unless expressly provided otherwise and includes any of the following:

(a) A "timeshare estate" which is the right to occupy a timeshare property, coupled with present ownership or some right to future ownership in a timeshare property or a specified portion thereof.

(b) A "timeshare use" which is the right to occupy a timeshare property which right is neither coupled with present ownership nor some right to future ownership in a timeshare property or a specified portion thereof.

(c) An "ownership timeshare interest" which is an interest in which a person receives the right to use or occupy immovable property for a period of less than a full year, over a period of more than three years, coupled with an ownership in immovable property.

(d) A "lease timeshare interest" which is an interest in which a person receives the right to use or occupy immovable property for a period of less than a full year, over a period of more than three years.

(21) "Timeshare instrument" means the legal document or documents, by whatever names denominated, that convey a timeshare interest to a purchaser.

(22) "Timeshare plan" means any arrangement, plan, scheme, or similar device, other than an exchange program, whether by membership agreement, sale, lease, license, other act of conveyance, or right-to-use agreement or by any other means, whereby a purchaser, in exchange for consideration, receives ownership rights in or the right to use accommodations for a period of time less than a full year during any given year, but not necessarily for consecutive years. A timeshare plan may be either of the following:

(a) A "single-site timeshare plan" which is the right to use accommodations at a single timeshare property.

(b) A "multisite timeshare plan" which includes either of the following:

(i) A "specific timeshare interest" which is the right to use accommodations at a specific timeshare property together with use rights in accommodations at one or more other component sites created by or acquired through the timeshare plan's reservations system.

(ii) A "nonspecific timeshare interest" which is the right to use accommodations at more than one component site created by or acquired through the timeshare plan's reservation system but including no specific right to use any particular accommodations.

(23) "Timeshare property" means one or more timeshare units subject to the same timeshare plan, together with any common elements or any other immovable property, or rights therein, appurtenant to those units.

(24) "Timeshare unit" means a unit which is the subject of a timeshare plan.

(25) "Unit" means immovable property, or a portion thereof, designated for separate occupancy.

(26) "Use period" means the increments of time into which a timeshare unit or the timeshare property is divided for the purpose of allocating rights of use and occupancy to the owners.

Added by Acts 1983, No. 552, § 1. Amended by Acts 1984, No. 943, § 1, eff. July 20, 1984; Acts 1985, No. 999, § 1; Acts 2003, No. 978, § 1.

Editor's note. Section 4 of Acts 2003, No. 978 provides:

"Section 4. The changes and additions effected by the provisions of this Act shall not apply to any timeshare plan, timeshare project, and/or timeshare developer which or who has filed and been approved to operate a, or as a, timeshare plan and/or project by the Louisiana Real Estate Commission on or before June 1, 1985, and whose developer has not been suspended by the Louisiana Real Estate Commission, and which, if approved prior to July 20, 1984, has been actively and continuously marketed as a timeshare plan and/or timeshare project pursuant to such approval or court decree. Notwithstanding anything to the contrary in this Act, any timeshare developer and timeshare plan and/or timeshare project covered by this Section may elect to be covered by any one or more provision of this Act by giving one hundred eighty days prior written notice of such intention to the Louisiana Real Estate Commission, and any such action shall not be interpreted or construed to constitute a waiver of the rights grants to a timeshare project and/or a timeshare plan and/or a timeshare developer, under this Section. If a developer subject to this Section elects to be subject to any provision under this Act, said developer or successor developer shall thereafter be subject to such provision(s)."

§ 1131.3. Applicability and scope

A. This Part shall apply to the sale, offer to sell, or solicitation of persons for the sale of any timeshare interest in immovable property located in Louisiana, and to the sale, offer to sell, or solicitation of persons in Louisiana for the sale of any timeshare interest in immovable property located in Louisiana and outside Louisiana except as otherwise provided by this Part.

B. The provisions of this Part shall be applicable, from and after the effective date of this Part, to existing timeshare interests created prior to the effective date of this Part; however, the developer of existing timeshare interests or the timeshare association of owners of existing timeshare interests shall have until December 1, 1983 to comply with R.S. 9:1131.4 of this Part. The obligation to provide a public offering statement under this Part or contribution to the fund in R.S. 9:1131.17 shall apply only to sales of timeshare interests after the effective date of this Part. This Part shall not affect or impair any right that is guaranteed or protected by the constitutions of Louisiana or the United States, nor shall this Part be construed to impair or affect any act done or right accruing, accrued, or acquired prior to the effective date of this Part. This Part shall not be construed to impair or cast a cloud upon the titles to units of any timeshare property conveyed prior to the effective date of this Part.

C. The provisions of the Louisiana Condominium Act, R.S. 9:1121.101 et seq., shall be applicable to an ownership timeshare interest created in a condominium to the extent that the provisions do not conflict with the provisions of this Part. However, whenever documents must be filed of record or delivered to purchasers under the Louisiana Condominium Act and this Part, they may be combined to avoid duplication.

D. A developer who sells lease timeshare interests in a multiple use project shall be exempt from the requirements and provisions of Sections 1131.4, 1131.5, 1131.6, 1131.8, 1131.20, 1131.21, 1131.22, and 1131.23 of this Part. The developer shall file an abstract of each lease timeshare interest sold in the conveyance records of the parish in which the timeshare interest is located within thirty days from the date of the sale.

E. The Louisiana Real Estate Commission shall not require a developer of a timeshare plan located outside of this state to make changes in any timeshare instrument to conform to the provisions of this Part regarding the structure of the timeshare regime provided it complies with the law of the state in which the plan is located. The Louisiana Real Estate Commission shall have the power to require disclosure of such provisions as the commission determines is necessary to fairly, meaningfully, and effectively disclose all aspects of the timeshare plan.

F. Each timeshare interest constitutes, for purposes of title, a separate interest in property except for taxes on immovable property in Louisiana.

G. The offer or disposition of a timeshare interest in a timeshare plan which satisfies all the requirements of this Part shall not be deemed to constitute the offer and sale of a security under any other Louisiana law.

H. The commission may grant an exemption from this Part to timeshare plans, whether or not an accommodation is located in Louisiana, under which the prospective purchaser's total contractual financial obligation is less than three thousand dollars during the entire term of the timeshare plan. Added by Acts 1983, No. 552, § 1. Amended by Acts 2003, No. 978, § 1.

Editor's note. For application of Acts 2003, No. 978, see Editor's note following R.S. 9:1131.2.

§ 1131.4. Creation of a timeshare plan

A. (1) No person shall offer for sale, sell, offer to sell, or attempt to solicit any person located in Louisiana to purchase a timeshare interest in a timeshare property unless:

(a) Such timeshare interest offered by such person for sale is pursuant to a timeshare plan registered with and approved by the Louisiana Real Estate Commission, and

(b) Such person has provided the Louisiana Real Estate Commission with proof of its financial ability to complete the timeshare project in accordance with:

(i) The registered timeshare plan.

(ii) The contractual obligations of such person.

(2) No person shall sell, offer to sell, solicit, or attempt to solicit the purchase of a timeshare interest from any location within the state of Louisiana unless such person, or a related entity, has registered with the Louisiana Real Estate Commission a timeshare plan for a timeshare project located in the state of Louisiana consisting of at least forty completed or proposed units, committed to either an ownership timeshare interest or a lease timeshare interest where the initial rights are or were for a period of not less than twenty years provided however, that:

(a) If the person or related entity has not previously registered a timeshare plan in the state of Louisiana consisting of at least forty completed units with the Louisiana Real Estate Commission, as set forth in this Paragraph, but has registered with the Louisiana Real Estate Commission a proposed timeshare plan located in the state of Louisiana, as set forth in this Paragraph, consisting of at least forty units, such person prior to selling, offering to sell, soliciting, or attempting to solicit a person for the purchase of a timeshare interest in a timeshare plan located in the state of Louisiana, shall provide to the Louisiana Real Estate Commission:

(i) A copy of the contract for construction of the initial fifteen units of the timeshare plan,

(ii) A bond for completion of such construction in an amount satisfactory to the Louisiana Real Estate Commission, and

(iii) All applicable permits required by the appropriate local governmental subdivisions, or

(b) In the event such person, or related entity, intends to sell, offer to sell, solicit, or attempt to solicit the purchase of a timeshare interest in a timeshare plan located outside of the state of Louisiana from a location within the state of Louisiana and if the person, or related entity, has not previously registered a timeshare plan located in the state of Louisiana consisting of at least forty completed units with the Louisiana Real Estate Commission, as set forth in this Paragraph, but has registered with the Louisiana Real Estate Commission a proposed timeshare plan located in the state of Louisiana, as set forth in this Paragraph, consisting of at least forty units, such person, prior to selling, offering to sell, soliciting, or attempting to solicit the purchase of a timeshare interest in a timeshare plan located outside the state of Louisiana from a location within the state of Louisiana shall:

(i) Obtain a certificate from the Louisiana Real Estate Commission certifying that a minimum of fifteen units in such hereinabove required timeshare plan are complete for use and occupancy as a timeshare project in accordance with the timeshare plan, and

(ii) Provide the Louisiana Real Estate Commission with a copy of the contract for construction of the remaining units in the timeshare plan, a bond for the completion of such construction, and certified copies of all required permits from the applicable local governmental subdivision.

(3) All timeshare plans approved by the Louisiana Real Estate Commission after August 15, 2003, shall maintain a one-to-one purchaser to accommodation ratio, which means the ratio of the number of purchasers eligible to use the accommodation of a timeshare plan or project on a given day to the number of accommodations available for use within the plan or project on that day, such that the total number of purchasers eligible to use the accommodations of the time-

share plan or project during a given calendar year shall never exceed the total number of accommodations available for use in the timeshare plan or project during that year. For purposes of calculation, each purchaser shall be counted at least once and no individual accommodation may be counted more than three hundred sixty-five times per each calendar year. For purposes of calculating the one-to-one purchaser to accommodation ratio only, a purchaser who is delinquent in the payment of timeshare plan or project assessments shall continue to be considered eligible to use the accommodations of the timeshare plan or timeshare project without regard as to whether such right of use is suspended due to such delinquency.

B. A timeshare plan is created by the execution and recordation of a timeshare declaration and shall be effective upon approval of and shall have legal force and effect in the state of Louisiana as of the date of its approval by the Louisiana Real Estate Commission. The timeshare declaration shall be filed for registry in the conveyance records in the parish or parishes in which the timeshare property is located.

C. A timeshare declaration shall contain the following information:

(1) A legally sufficient description of the timeshare property and the name or other identification of the project, development, or building, if any, within which the timeshare property is located.

(2) A scale drawing showing the boundaries of all timeshare units, all common elements, and a designation by letter, number, name, or combination thereof of all such timeshare units.

(3) A schedule of use periods identifying the use by letter, number, name, or combination thereof for all use periods available in each timeshare unit or, if there are no timeshare units, in the full timeshare property.

(4) A provision for an annual service period for the timeshare property. If the timeshare property is divided into timeshare units, the service period may be different for different timeshare units and need not be for a specifically designated time period or for consecutive days.

(5) A statement that the timeshare property has or has not been made subject to the Louisiana Condominium Act, R.S. 9:1121.101 et seq., and, if the timeshare property is subject to the Louisiana Condominium Act, the date of filing of the condominium declaration required by R.S. 9:1122.101. A timeshare property otherwise subject to the Louisiana Condominium Act will nonetheless be exempt from the provisions of R.S. 9:1122.106(3).

(6) In registering a timeshare plan, the developer shall be responsible for providing information on the following:

(a) The developer's legal name, any assumed names used by the developer, principal office street address, mailing address, primary contact person, and telephone number.

(b) The name of the developer's authorized or registered agent in the state of Louisiana upon whom claims can be served or service of process be had, the agent's street address in Louisiana, and telephone number.

(c) The name, street address, mailing address, primary contact person, and telephone number of any timeshare plan being registered.

(d) The name, street address, mailing address, and telephone number of the managing entity of the timeshare plan.

(e) A public offering statement which complies with the requirements of R.S. 9:1131.9.2, which includes all of the following:

(i) A scale drawing showing the boundaries of all timeshare units, all common elements, and a designation by letter, number, name, or combination thereof of all such timeshare units.

(ii) If it is an ownership timeshare interest, the nature of the timeshare interest and the method for allocating use periods. If it is a lease timeshare interest, the nature of that lease interest and its duration.

(iii) The percentage of timeshare interest expenses and the voting rights assigned to each timeshare interest.

(iv) The method for amendment of the timeshare instrument.

(f) Such other information regarding the developer, timeshare plan, timeshare interest sales persons, acquisition agents, or managing entities as reasonably required by the Louisiana Real Estate Commission.

(7) Repealed by Acts 2003, No. 978, § 3.

(8) Repealed by Acts 2003, No. 978, § 3.

(9) Repealed by Acts 2003, No. 978, § 3.

(10) Repealed by Acts 2003, No. 978, § 3.

(11) Repealed by Acts 2003, No. 978, § 3.

(12) Repealed by Acts 2003, No. 978, § 3.

(13) Repealed by Acts 2003, No. 978, § 3.

D. A timeshare declaration filed after August 30, 1983, shall also include a bond issued by a surety company authorized to do business in this state in the amount of one thousand dollars for each unit week included in the timeshare plan. This bond shall be filed and maintained with the Louisiana Real Estate Commission in favor of the state for the use, benefit, and indemnity of any person who suffers any damage or loss as a result of any unfair or deceptive practice, breach of a contractual duty, or violation of law in connection with the offer or solicitation of a sale or management of a timeshare interest or in connection with the management of a timeshare plan or project by a developer, its agents, employees, sales persons, and others. Said bond shall be maintained until one year following the date of the last timeshare sale made by the filing developer or until January 1, 2008, whichever occurs first. Beginning January 1, 2004, the amount of the bond shall be reduced in an amount by one-quarter in each of the four years following August 15, 2003. On January 1, 2008, this bonding requirement shall be eliminated for all timeshare projects. Thereafter, the developer shall provide to the Louisiana Real Estate Commission proof of its suitability and financial ability to complete its timeshare projects. The commission, by rule and regulation, adopted and promulgated as prescribed by law, shall provide for the kinds of proof that shall be required to be provided.

E. The timeshare declaration must be accompanied by an affidavit or affidavits signed by the chief executive officer or managing partner of the developer and by any natural person having an ownership interest exceeding ten percent in either the developer or entities which control it. The affidavit or affidavits must state under penalty of perjury that the affiant has read the timeshare declaration, and all attached documents and that they are true and complete. Any person who executes an affidavit required under this Section which is not true, or who fails to correct in said affidavit any false statement, false representation of material fact, or omission of material fact made in the timeshare declaration or in documents required to be attached thereto, is guilty of a felony, and shall be imprisoned for not more than five years with or without hard labor or shall be fined not more than five thousand dollars, or both.

F. A person shall not be required to register as a developer under this Part, provided the person performs only the following acts:

(1) The person is an owner of a timeshare interest who has acquired the timeshare interest for his or her own use and occupancy and who later offers it for resale.

(2) A managing entity or an association that is not otherwise a developer of a timeshare plan in its own right, solely while acting as an association or under a contract with an association to offer or sell a timeshare interest transferred to the association through foreclosure, giving in payment, or gratuitous transfer, if such acts are performed in the regular course, or as an incident to, the management of the association for its own account in the timeshare plan.

(3) Offers a timeshare plan in a national publication or by electronic media which is not directed to or targeted to any person located in Louisiana.

(4) A person is conveyed, assigned, or transferred more than seven timeshare interests from a developer in a single voluntary or involuntary transaction and subsequently conveys, assigns, or transfers all of the timeshare interests received from the developer to a single purchaser in a single transaction, which transaction may occur in stages.

Added by Acts 1983, No. 552, § 1. Amended by Acts 1985, No. 999, §§ 1, 3; Acts 2003, No. 978, § 1; Acts 2009, No. 273, § 1.

Editor's note. For application of Acts 2003, No. 978, see Editor's note following R.S. 9:1131.2.

§ 1131.5. Construction and validity of declaration

A. All provisions of the declaration are severable.

B. The effectiveness of the timeshare declaration and merchantability of title to a timeshare interest are not affected by reason of an insubstantial failure of the declaration to comply with this Part.

Added by Acts 1983, No. 552, § 1.

§ 1131.6. Description of timeshare property

A. After the declaration is properly filed for registry, a description of the timeshare property that sets forth the name of the timeshare property, the place of recordation of the declaration, and the parish in which the timeshare property is located is a sufficient legal description of that timeshare property even if the common element interest is not described or referred to therein.

B. The timeshare unit may be legally described by using the identifying designation as set forth in the declaration in conjunction with the legal description of the timeshare property as provided for in this Section.

C. The use period may be legally described by using the identifying designation as set forth in the declaration in conjunction with the legal description of the timeshare property and the timeshare unit as provided in this Section.

Added by Acts 1983, No. 552, § 1.

§ 1131.7. Partition

The timeshare property subject to an ownership timeshare interest shall remain undivided and shall not be subject to partition until the termination of the timeshare plan as provided for in R.S. 9:1131.8(F) or as otherwise provided for in the timeshare documents.

Added by Acts 1983, No. 552, § 1.

§ 1131.8. Termination

A. Except as otherwise provided, a timeshare plan shall terminate at the end of the term of the timeshare plan as set forth in the timeshare declaration, or prior to the end of the term:

(1) As provided in the timeshare documents.

(2) Upon entry of a final judgment by a court of competent jurisdiction brought by an owner or the association declaring that the useful life of the timeshare property has ended.

B. Termination of the timeshare plan shall not terminate the association, which shall continue for so long as is necessary to implement the provisions of the timeshare documents.

C. Unless the timeshare documents expressly provide to the contrary, upon termination of the timeshare plan, the association may sell, convey, transfer, or otherwise dispose of the owners' interests in the timeshare property, upon such terms and conditions as the board of directors, in its sole discretion, shall determine. The timeshare property may be conveyed by deed or other appropriate instrument of conveyance executed and acknowledged by two officers of the association, which instrument recites that it is made pursuant to the authority provided by this Section and, if the timeshare documents provide any procedure therefor, that the procedure set forth in the timeshare documents for the disposition of the timeshare property was followed. After such conveyance, it shall be conclusively presumed that a deed or other instrument of conveyance so executed and acknowledged, and containing such recitals, shall vest good and marketable title in the vendee named therein. No action may be instituted by or on behalf of any owner to set aside or invalidate any conveyance so made.

D. (1) Any proceeds remaining after expenses associated with the termination of a timeshare plan that are received by the association in connection with the sale or other disposition of the owner's interest in the timeshare property shall be distributed to owners in accordance with such owner's percentage ownership in the timeshare property, when a timeshare plan is composed of timeshare estates, and in accordance with the applicable owner's pro rata share of timeshare expenses in the case of a timeshare plan composed of timeshare uses.

(2) If the timeshare plan is a lease timeshare interest plan, such proceeds shall be distributed to owners in the same ratio as they share timeshare expense liability.

E. The association shall notify each owner of the right to receive a pro rata share of the proceeds by certified mail, return receipt requested, sent to the owner's last known address listed in the association records. This notice shall state that the owner shall have one hundred twenty days in which to claim the proceeds, the method for making such claim, and the fact that failure to do so within the allowable time period shall result in the termination of the right to receive the proceeds. Any unclaimed proceeds shall be redistributed to owners who make a claim on a pro rata basis under Subsection D of this Section.

F. If the association fails to act pursuant to Subsection C of this Section within one hundred eighty days from the termination of the timeshare plan, any owner may seek partition of the timeshare property in a court of competent jurisdiction.

Added by Acts 1983, No. 552, § 1. Amended by Acts 2003, No. 978, § 1.

Editor's note. For application of Acts 2003, No. 978, see Editor's note following R.S. 9:1131.2.

§ 1131.9. Tax assessment and payment

A. All kinds of taxes and special assessments authorized by law shall be assessed against the timeshare property as a single entity unless the timeshare property is subject to the Louisiana Condominium Act, R.S. 9:1121.101 et seq., in which case the taxes and special assessments shall be assessed as provided in R.S. 9:1121.105. Each owner shall pay the taxes and assessments in the same ratio as they share the timeshare expenses.

B. The association, through its managing entity, shall collect each owner's share of the taxes or special assessments and shall have responsibility for its payment. For purposes of R.S. 9:1131.22, each owner's share of the taxes or special assessments shall be deemed an assessment for a timeshare interest expense.

C. The assessed value of a timeshare unit shall not exceed the assessed value of a comparable apartment, condominium unit, dwelling, or other accommodation owned by a single owner that is not the subject of a timesharing plan.

Added by Acts 1983, No. 552, § 1. Amended by Acts 2003, No. 978, § 1.

Editor's note. For application of Acts 2003, No. 978, see Editor's note following R.S. 9:1131.2.

§ 1131.9.1. Developer supervisory duties

The developer shall have the duty to supervise, manage, and control all aspects of the offering of the timeshare plan, including but not limited to promotion, advertising, contracting, and closing. The developer shall have responsibility for each timeshare plan approved by the Louisiana Real Estate Commission and for the actions of any timeshare interest sales person utilized by the developer in the offering or selling of any registered timeshare plan. Any violation of this Part which occurs during the offering activities shall be deemed to be a violation by the developer as well as by the timeshare interest salesperson or whoever actually committed such violation.

Added by Acts 2003, No. 978, § 1.

Editor's note. For application of Acts 2003, No. 978, see Editor's note following R.S. 9:1131.2.

§ 1131.9.2. Public offering statement

A. (1) Prior to offering any timeshare interest, the developer shall file a public offering statement with the Louisiana Real Estate Commission for approval. The developer shall fully and accurately disclose those facts concerning the developer and the timeshare plan as hereinafter provided prior to the initial sale of a timeshare interest, and the developer shall furnish each purchaser with a copy of the approved public offering statement. The public offering statement shall be delivered to each prospective purchaser in written format. Written format includes but is not limited to documents delivered on CD–ROM or by other electronic means as approved by the Louisiana Real Estate Commission. The public offering statement shall be dated and shall require the purchaser to certify in writing the receipt thereof. Until the Louisiana Real Estate Commission approves such filing, any contract regarding the sale of the timeshare plan which is subject to the public offering statement is voidable by the purchaser unless otherwise provided by this Section.

(2) The Louisiana Real Estate Commission shall, upon receiving a public offering statement from a developer, mail to the developer an acknowledgment of receipt. The failure of the Louisiana Real Estate Commission to send such acknowledgment will not, however, relieve the developer from the duty of complying with this Section. An applicant for registration under this Act shall submit the necessary information to complete the application, as required by the Louisiana Real Estate Commission, within six months from the date the initial registration application and its supplements were received by the Louisiana Real Estate Commission. If the applicant fails to submit the information necessary to complete the application as required by the Louisiana Real Estate Commission within the six-month period, said application may be voided and a new registration application with applicable fees may be required to be submitted.

(3) All registrations required to be filed with the Louisiana Real Estate Commission under this Act shall be reviewed, and registration shall be effective upon the issuance of a certificate of registration by the Louisiana Real Estate Commission which, in the ordinary course of business, should occur no more than forty-five calendar days after actual receipt by the Louisiana Real Estate Commission of the properly completed application. The Louisiana Real Estate Commission shall provide a list of deficiencies in such application, if any, within thirty calendar days after receipt. If the Louisiana Real Estate Commission fails to either issue a certificate of registration or provide a list of deficiencies within forty-five calendar days after receipt, the registration shall be deemed effective.

(4) Any material change to an approved filing shall be filed with the Louisiana Real Estate Commission for approval as an amendment prior to the changes becoming effective. The Louisiana Real Estate Commission shall have twenty days to approve or cite deficiencies in the proposed amendment. If the Louisiana Real Estate Commission fails to act within twenty days, the amendment will be deemed approved. If the developer fails to file corrections to any deficiency citation within thirty days, the Louisiana Real Estate Commission may reject the amendment.

(5) Upon the filing of a public offering statement, the developer shall pay to the Louisiana Real Estate Commission a filing fee of five hundred dollars or ten dollars for each timeshare unit which is to be part of the proposed timeshare plan, whichever is greater. A developer who files an amendment to a public offering statement already on file with the Louisiana Real Estate Commission shall pay a filing fee of two hundred fifty dollars.

B. Every public offering statement shall contain and accurately disclose the following:

(1) The name of the developer and the principal address of the developer and the name and address of the timeshare plan in which interests are being offered.

(2) A description of the type of timeshare interests being offered.

(3) A general description of the existing and proposed accommodations and amenities of the timeshare plan, including their type and number, personal property furnishing the

accommodations, any use restrictions, and any required fees for use.

(4) A description of any accommodations and amenities that are committed to be built, including without limitation:

(a) The developer's schedule of commencement and completion of all accommodations and amenities.

(b) The estimated number of accommodations per site that may become subject to the timeshare plan.

(5) A brief description of the duration, phases, and operation of the timeshare plan.

(6) The current annual budget, if available, or the projected annual budget for the timeshare plan. The budget shall include without limitation:

(a) A statement of the amount included in the budget as a reserve for repairs and replacement.

(b) The projected common expense liability, if any, by category of expenditures for the timeshare plan.

(c) A statement of any services or expenses not reflected in the budget that the developer provides or pays.

(7) Any initial or special fee due from the purchaser at closing, together with a description of the purpose and method of calculating the fee.

(8) A description of any liens, defects, or encumbrances on or affecting the title to the timeshare interests.

(9) A general description of any purchaser financing offered by or available through the developer.

(10) A statement that within seven calendar days after receipt of the public offering statement or after purchase contract execution, whichever is later, a purchaser may cancel any purchase contract for the purchase of a timeshare interest from a developer, together with a statement providing the name and address to which the purchaser should mail any notice of cancellation. However, if by agreement of the parties by and through the purchase contract the purchase contract allows for cancellation of the purchase contract for a period of time exceeding seven calendar days, then a statement that the cancellation of the purchase contract is allowed for that period of time exceeding seven calendar days.

(11) A statement of any pending suits, adjudications, or disciplinary proceedings material to the timeshare plan of which a developer has knowledge.

(12) Any restrictions on alienation of any number or portion of any timeshare interests.

(13) A statement describing liability and casualty insurance for the timeshare property.

(14) Any current or expected fees or charges to be paid by timeshare purchasers for the use of any amenities related to the timeshare property, including but not limited to all assessments for such use or maintenance.

(15) The extent to which financial arrangements have been provided for completion of all promised improvements.

(16) The developer or managing entity must notify the Louisiana Real Estate Commission of the extent to which an accommodation may become subject to a tax or other lien arising out of claims against other purchasers in the same timeshare plan. The Louisiana Real Estate Commission may require the developer or managing entity to notify a prospective purchaser of any such potential tax or lien which would materially and adversely affect the prospective purchaser.

(17) A statement indicating that the developer and timeshare plan are registered with the Louisiana Real Estate Commission.

(18) Copies of the following documents and plans, to the extent they are applicable, shall be included as exhibits:

(a) A declaration of servitude of properties serving the timeshare accommodations or facilities but not owned by purchasers or leased to them or the association.

(b) A statement of condition of the existing building or buildings, if the offering is of timeshare periods in an existing facility being converted to condominium ownership.

(c) A statement of inspection for termite damage and treatment of the existing improvements, if the timeshare property is a condominium conversion.

(d) The form of agreement for sale of timeshare interests.

(e) The executed agreement for escrow of payments made to the developer prior to closing.

(f) Any documents containing any restrictions on use of the property.

(19) If the timeshare plan provides purchasers with the opportunity to participate in an exchange program, a description of the name and address of the exchange company and the method by which a purchaser accesses the exchange program.

(20) Such other information reasonably required by the Louisiana Real Estate Commission and established by administrative rule necessary for the protection of purchasers of timeshare interests in timeshare plans.

(21) Any other information that the developer, with the approval of the Louisiana Real Estate Commission, desires to include in the public offering statement text.

C. A developer offering a multisite timeshare plan shall also fully and accurately disclose the following information, which information may be disclosed in a written, graphic, or tabular form:

(1) A description of each component site including the name and address of each component site.

(2) The number of accommodations and timeshare periods, expressed in periods of seven-day use availability, committed to the multisite timeshare plan and available for use by purchasers.

(3) Each type of accommodation in terms of the number of bedrooms, bathrooms, sleeping capacity, and whether or not the accommodation contains a full kitchen. For purposes of this description, a full kitchen shall mean a kitchen having a minimum of a dishwasher, range, sink, oven, and refrigerator.

(4) A description of amenities available for use by the purchaser at each component site.

(5) A description of the reservation system, which description shall include the following:

(a) The entity responsible for operating the reservation system.

(b) A summary of the rules and regulations governing access to and use of the reservation system.

(c) The existence of and an explanation regarding any priority reservation features that affect a purchaser's ability to make reservations for the use of a given accommodation.

(6) A description of any right to make any additions, substitutions, or deletions of accommodations or amenities and a description of the basis upon which accommodations

and amenities may be added, substituted, or deleted from the multisite timeshare plan.

(7) A description of the purchaser's liability for any fees associated with the multisite timeshare plan.

(8) The location and the anticipated relative use demand of each component site in a multisite timeshare plan as well as any periodic adjustment or amendment to the reservation system which may be needed in order to respond to actual purchaser use patterns and changes in purchaser use demand for the accommodations existing at that time within the multisite timeshare plan.

(9) Such other information reasonably required by the Louisiana Real Estate Commission and established by administrative rule necessary for the protection of purchasers of timeshare interests in timeshare plans.

(10) Any other information that the developer, with the approval of the Louisiana Real Estate Commission, desires to include in the public offering statement text.

D. If a developer offers a nonspecific timeshare interest in a multisite timeshare plan, the developer shall disclose the information set forth in Subsection B of this Section as to each component site.

E. A developer shall promptly amend the public offering statement to report any material change in the information required by this Section. In the event amendments are made to a public offering statement provided to a purchaser whose transaction has not closed that materially alter or modify the offering in a material and adverse manner to a purchaser, the amendment shall be provided to the purchaser together with a notice containing a statement in conspicuous type in substantially the following form:

"The public offering statement previously delivered to you, together with the enclosed revisions, has been approved by the Louisiana Real Estate Commission. Accordingly, your cancellation right expires seven calendar days after you sign your purchase contract or seven calendar days after you receive these revisions, whichever is later."

F. A purchaser who does not receive a public offering statement prior to or at the time of the act of sale for a timeshare interest may cancel the act of sale for the timeshare interest within one year after the date of the receipt of the public offering statement without penalty or cost of any kind.

Added by Acts 2003, No. 978, § 1.

Editor's note. For application of Acts 2003, No. 978, see Editor's note following R.S. 9:1131.2.

§ 1131.10. Repealed by Acts 2003, No. 978, § 3

Editor's note. For application of Acts 2003, No. 978, see Editor's note following R.S. 9:1131.2.

§ 1131.10.1. Contracts for purchase of timeshare interests

No developer of a timeshare interest shall fail to utilize and furnish each purchaser a fully completed copy of a purchase contract pertaining to the sale, which contract shall include the following information:

(1) The actual date the purchase contract is executed by each party.

(2) The names and addresses of the developer, any owner of the underlying real estate, and the timeshare plan.

(3) The total financial obligation of the purchaser, including the initial purchase price and any additional charges to which the purchaser may be subject, including but not limited to financing, reservation, maintenance, management, and recreation charges.

(4) The estimated date of completion of construction of each accommodation in which the timeshare interest is being purchased that is not completed at the time the purchase contract, unless that information is contained in a public offering statement that incorporates the contract by reference, is executed by the developer and purchaser.

(5) A description of the nature and duration of the timeshare interest being sold, including whether any interest in real property is being conveyed and the specific number of years constituting the term of the timeshare plan.

(6) Immediately prior to the space reserved in the purchase contract for the signature of the purchaser, in conspicuous type, substantially the following statements:

YOU MAY CANCEL THIS PURCHASE CONTRACT WITHOUT ANY PENALTY OR OBLIGATION WITHIN SEVEN DAYS FROM THE DATE YOU SIGN THIS PURCHASE CONTRACT, AND UNTIL SEVEN DAYS AFTER YOU RECEIVE THE PUBLIC OFFERING STATEMENT, WHICHEVER IS LATER. IF YOU DECIDE TO CANCEL THIS PURCHASE CONTRACT, YOU MUST NOTIFY THE DEVELOPER IN WRITING OF YOUR INTENT TO CANCEL. YOUR NOTICE OF CANCELLATION SHALL BE EFFECTIVE UPON THE DATE SENT AND SHALL BE SENT TO...(NAME OF DEVELOPER)...AT...(ADDRESS OF DEVELOPER).... ANY ATTEMPT TO OBTAIN A WAIVER OF YOUR CANCELLATION RIGHT IS UNLAWFUL.

(7) A statement that, in the event the purchaser cancels the purchase contract during a seven-day cancellation period, the developer will refund to the purchaser the total amount of all payments made by the purchaser under the purchase contract, reduced by the proportion of any contract benefits the purchaser has actually received under the purchase contract prior to the effective date of cancellation. The statement shall further provide that the refund will be made within thirty days after receipt of notice of cancellation or within five days after receipt of funds from the purchaser's cleared check, whichever is later.

(8) Unless the developer is, at the time of offering the interest, the owner of the timeshare property free and clear of all liens and encumbrances, a statement that the developer is not the sole owner of the timeshare property and facilities without liens or encumbrances, which statement shall include:

(a) The names and addresses of all persons or entities having an ownership interest or other interest in the timeshare property; and

(b) The actual interest of the developer in the timeshare property.

(9) If the contract is for the sale or transfer of a timeshare interest in which the timeshare property is subject to a lease, the following statement within the text in conspicuous type: THIS TIMESHARE INTEREST IS SUBJECT TO A LEASE (OR SUBLEASE). A copy of the executed lease shall be attached as an exhibit.

Added by Acts 1985, No. 999, § 3. Amended by Acts 2003, No. 978, § 1.

Editor's note. For application of Acts 2003, No. 978, see Editor's note following R.S. 9:1131.2.

§ 1131.11. Public offering statement; when not required

A. The developer shall not be required to prepare and distribute a public offering statement if the developer has registered and there has been issued a public offering statement or similar disclosure document which is provided to purchasers under the Securities and Exchange Act of 1933.

B. A public offering statement need not be prepared or delivered in the case of:

(1) Any transfer of timeshare interest by any timeshare interest owner other than the developer or his or her agent.

(2) Any disposition pursuant to court order.

(3) A disposition by a government or governmental agency.

(4) A disposition by foreclosure or deed in lieu of foreclosure.

(5) A gratuitous transfer of a timeshare interest.

Added by Acts 1983, No. 552, § 1.

§ 1131.12. Regulations of timeshare advertising

A. (1) No person shall intentionally, directly or indirectly, authorize, use, direct, or aid in the dissemination, publication, distribution, or circulation of any statement, advertisement, radio broadcast, or telecast concerning a timeshare property, or promotion thereof, that contains any statement or sketch that is false, misleading, or without substantiation at the time the statement is made.

(2) Nothing in this Section shall be construed to hold the publisher or employee of any newspaper, or any job printer, or any broadcaster or telecaster, or any magazine publisher, or any of the employees thereof, liable for any publication herein referred to unless the publisher, employee, or printer has actual knowledge of the falsity thereof.

B. All advertising materials must be substantially in compliance with this Part and in full compliance with the mandatory provisions of this Part. In the event that any such material is not in compliance, the commission may require any developer to correct the deficiency.

C. The term advertising material includes but is not limited to:

(1) Any promotional brochure, pamphlet, advertisement, or other material to be disseminated to the public in connection with the sale of a timeshare plan.

(2) A transcript of any radio or television advertisement.

(3) Any telephone solicitation.

(4) Any lodging or vacation certificate.

(5) A transcript of any standard oral sales presentation or solicitation, if any.

(6) A picture or proof of any billboard or sign posted on or off the premises.

(7) Any photograph, drawing, or artist's representation of accommodations or facilities of a timeshare plan which exists or which will or may exist.

(8) Any paid publication relating to a timeshare plan which exists or which will or may exist.

(9) Any other promotional device or statement related to a timeshare plan, including any prize and gift promotional offer.

D. The following communications are exempt from the provisions of this Section:

(1) Any stockholder communication such as an annual report, interim financial report, proxy material, registration statement, securities prospectus, registration, property report, or other material required to be delivered to a prospective purchaser by an agency of any other state or the Federal Government.

(2) Any communication addressed to and relating to the account of the person who has previously executed a contract for the sale and purchase of a timeshare period in the timeshare plan to which the communication relates, except when directed to the sale of additional timeshare interests.

(3) Any audio, written, or visual publication or material relating to an exchange company or exchange program.

(4) Any audio, written, or visual publication or material relating to the promotion of the availability of any accommodations for transient rental, provided a mandatory sales presentation is not a term or condition of the availability of such accommodations and provided the failure of any transient renter to take a tour of a timeshare property or attend a sales presentation does not result in any reduction in the level of services which would otherwise be available to such transient renter.

(5) Any oral or written statement disseminated by a developer to broadcast or print media, other than paid advertising or promotional material, regarding plans for the acquisition or development of timeshare property. However, any rebroadcast or any other dissemination of such oral statements to a prospective purchaser by a seller in any manner, or any distribution of copies of newspapers, magazine articles, press releases, or any other dissemination of such written statements to a prospective purchaser by a seller in any manner, shall constitute an advertisement.

(6) Any advertisement or promotion, not clearly directed to Louisiana residents, in any medium to the general public if such advertisement or promotion clearly states that it is not an offer in any jurisdiction in which any applicable registration requirements have not been fully satisfied.

(7) Any communication by a developer to encourage a person who has previously acquired a timeshare interest from the developer to acquire additional use or occupancy rights or benefits, or additional timeshare interests, offered by the same developer or in the same timeshare plan.

E. No advertising or oral statement made by any developer, affiliate, or their agents shall:

(1) Misrepresent a fact or create a false or misleading impression regarding the timeshare plan or property or promotion thereof.

(2) Make a prediction of specific or immediate increases in the price or value of timeshare periods.

(3) Contain a statement concerning future price increases which are non-specific or not bona fide.

(4) Contain any asterisk or other reference symbol as a means of contradicting or substantially changing any previously made statement or as a means of obscuring a material fact.

(5) Describe or portray any improvement to the timeshare plan that is not required to be built or that is uncompleted unless the description or portrayal is conspicuously labeled or identified as "NEED NOT BE BUILT," or "UNDER CONSTRUCTION" with the date of promised completion clearly indicated.

(6) Materially misrepresent the size, nature, extent, qualities, or characteristics of any offered accommodations or facilities or property or the amenities available to the occupant of those facilities or properties.

(7) Misrepresent the amount or period of time during which the accommodations or facilities will be available to any purchaser.

(8) Misrepresent the nature or extent of any facilities or services incident to the timeshare plan.

(9) Make any misleading or deceptive representation with respect to the contents of the timeshare instrument, timeshare documents including the public offering statement and the contract or the rights, privileges, benefits, or obligations of the purchaser under these documents or this Part.

(10) Misrepresent the conditions under which a purchaser may exchange the right to use accommodations or facilities in one location for the right to use accommodations or facilities in another location.

(11) Misrepresent the availability of a resale or rental program offered by or on behalf of the developer.

(12) Contain an offer or inducement to purchase which purports to be limited as to quantity or restricted as to time unless the numerical quantity or time limit applicable to the offer or inducement is clearly stated.

(13) Misrepresent or imply that a facility or service is available for the exclusive use of purchasers if the facility or service may actually be shared by others or by the general public.

(14) Repealed by Acts 2003, No. 978, § 3.

(15) Misrepresent the source of the advertising or statement by leading a prospective purchaser to believe that the advertising material is mailed by a governmental or official agency, credit bureau, bank, or attorney, if that is not the case.

(16) Misrepresent the nature or value of any prize, gift, or other item to be awarded in connection with any prize and gift promotional offer.

(17) Contain any representation as to the availability of a resale program or rental program offered by or on behalf of the developer or its affiliate, unless the resale program and/or rental program has been made a part of the offering, and substantiation is available at the time of the representation to show that a resale market exists.

(18) Repealed by Acts 2003, No. 978, § 3.

(19) Contain any statement that the timeshare interest being offered for sale can be further divided, unless a full disclosure of the legal requirements for further division of the timeshare interest is included.

(20) Misrepresent the conditions under which a purchaser or timeshare interest owner may participate in any exchange program.

(21) Describe any proposed or uncompleted private facilities over which the developer has no control, unless the estimated date of completion is set forth, and completion and operation of the facilities are reasonably assured within the time represented in the advertisement.

F. No written advertising material relating to a timeshare property, including any lodging certificate, gift award, premium, discount, or display booth may be utilized without a disclosure that: "This advertising material is being used for the purpose of soliciting sales of timeshare interests" or a substantially similar disclosure.

G. Prize and gift promotional offers:

(1) As used herein, the term "prize and gift promotional offer" means any advertising material wherein a prospective purchaser may receive goods or services other than the timeshare property itself, either free or at a discount, including, but not limited to, the use of any prize, gift, award, premium, or lodging or vacation certificate.

(2) A developer or other person using a prize and gift promotional offer in connection with the offering of a timeshare interest shall clearly disclose all of the following:

(a) That the purpose of the promotion is to sell timeshare interests, which shall appear in boldface or other conspicuous type.

(b) The name of each developer or other person trying to sell a timeshare interest through the promotion and the name of each person paying for the promotion.

(c) The complete rules of the promotion.

(d) The method of awarding prizes, gifts, vacations, discount vacations, or other benefits under the promotion, a complete and fully detailed description, including approximate retail value of all prizes, gifts, or benefits under the promotion, the quantity of each prize, gift, or benefit to be awarded or conferred, and the date by which each prize, gift, or benefit will be awarded or conferred, and if a game of chance, the odds of winning.

(e) Such other disclosures as provided by rule.

(3) If a person represents that a prize, gift, or benefit will be awarded in connection with a promotion, the prize, gift, or benefit must be awarded or conferred in the manner represented and on or before the date represented.

(4) Repealed by Acts 2003, No. 978, § 3.
(5) Repealed by Acts 2003, No. 978, § 3.
(6) Repealed by Acts 2003, No. 978, § 3.
(7) Repealed by Acts 2003, No. 978, § 3.
(8) Repealed by Acts 2003, No. 978, § 3.

Added by Acts 1983, No. 552, § 1. Amended by Acts 1985, No. 999, § 1; Acts 2003, No. 978, § 1.

Editor's note. For application of Acts 2003, No. 978, see Editor's note following R.S. 9:1131.2.

§ 1131.13. Cancellation

A. Any purchase contract entered into by and between a developer and a purchaser or any purchase contract utilized pursuant to R.S. 9:1131.10.1 and 1131.18 shall be voidable by either party to the purchase contract, without penalty, within seven calendar days after the receipt of the public offering statement from the developer or the execution of the purchase contract, whichever is later. The purchase contract shall provide notice of the seven-day cancellation period together with the name and mailing address to which any notice of cancellation shall be delivered. If either party elects to cancel a purchase contract pursuant to this Section, either party must do so not later than midnight of the seventh calendar day after the receipt of the public offering statement from the developer or the execution of the purchase contract, whichever is later, by hand delivering a written notice of cancellation or by mailing notice of cancellation by certified mail, return receipt requested, to the other party at an address so noted in the purchase contract. Upon such cancellation, the party holding the funds shall refund to the purchaser all payments made by the purchaser less the amount of any benefits actually received pursuant to the purchase agreement. Such refund shall be made within thirty calendar days after receipt of the notice of cancellation, or receipt of funds from the purchaser's cleared check, whichever occurs later.

B. This right of cancellation may not be waived by any purchaser or by any other person on behalf of the purchaser. However, nothing in this Section precludes the execution of documents in advance for delivery after expiration of the cancellation period.

C. Any notice of cancellation shall be considered given on the date postmarked if mailed, or when transmitted from the place or origin if telegraphed. If given by means of writing transmitted other than by mail or telegraph, the notice of cancellation shall be considered given at the time of actual or constructive delivery to the developer.

D. In the event of a timely cancellation, or in the event the plan is a lease timeshare and at any time the accommodations or facilities are no longer available, the developer shall honor the right of any purchaser to cancel the contract which granted the timeshare purchaser rights in and to the plan. Upon such cancellation, the developer shall refund to the purchaser all payments made by the purchaser which exceed the proportionate amount of benefits made available under the plan, using the number of years of the proposed plan as the base.

E. Upon proper cancellation, the developer shall make a full refund to the purchaser of all monies paid and shall return for cancellation all instruments signed by the purchaser. The refund and return of instruments shall be within thirty days after receipt of the notice of cancellation or after receipt by the developer of notice that the purchaser's check has cleared, whichever is later. In no event shall the refund be made later than sixty days after receipt of notice of cancellation from the purchaser. The cancellation provisions of this Section shall not be waivable.

F. Repealed by Acts 2003, No. 978, § 3.

Added by Acts 1983, No. 552, § 1. Amended by Acts 1985, No. 999, § 1; Acts 2003, No. 978, § 1.

Editor's note. For application of Acts 2003, No. 978, see Editor's note following R.S. 9:1131.2.

§ 1131.14. Repealed by Acts 2003, No. 978, § 3

Editor's note. For application of Acts 2003, No. 978, see Editor's note following R.S. 9:1131.2.

§ 1131.15. Repealed by Acts 2003, No. 978, § 3

Editor's note. For application of Acts 2003, No. 978, see Editor's note following R.S. 9:1131.2.

§ 1131.16. Repealed by Acts 2003, No. 978, § 3

Editor's note. For application of Acts 2003, No. 978, see Editor's note following R.S. 9:1131.2.

§ 1131.16.1. Escrow of payments; escrow accounts; nondisturbance agreements; interests, liens, and encumbrances; alternative assurances

A. Prior to the filing of the public offering statement with the Louisiana Real Estate Commission, the developer shall establish an independent escrow account with an escrow agent for the purpose of protecting the payments of purchasers. No developer or seller nor any officer, director, affiliate, subsidiary, or employee thereof may serve the escrow agent in any of the above capacities. An escrow agent shall maintain the accounts prescribed in this Section in such a manner as to be under the direct supervision and control of the escrow agent. A fiduciary relationship shall exist between the escrow agent and the purchaser. The escrow agent shall retain all affidavits received pursuant to this Section for a period of five years. Should the escrow agent receive conflicting demands for the escrowed funds or property, the escrow agent shall immediately, with the consent of all parties, either submit the matter to arbitration or seek an adjudication of the matter from a court of competent jurisdiction.

B. One hundred percent of all funds or other property constituting the purchase payment which is received from or on behalf of purchasers of timeshare interests prior to the occurrence of events required herein shall be deposited pursuant to an escrow agreement approved by the Louisiana Real Estate Commission. The deposit of such funds shall be evidenced by an executed escrow agreement between the escrow agent and the developer, the provisions of which shall include the following:

(1) Funds may be disbursed to the developer by the escrow agent from the escrow account only after expiration of the purchaser's rescission period and in accordance with the purchase contract, subject to Subsection C of this Section.

(2) If a purchaser properly cancels the purchase contract pursuant to its terms, the funds shall be paid to the purchaser or paid to the developer if the purchaser's funds have been previously refunded by the developer.

C. If a developer contracts to sell a timeshare interest and the construction of any property in which the timeshare interest is located has not been completed, the developer, upon expiration of the rescission period, shall continue to maintain in an escrow account all funds received by or on behalf of the developer from the purchaser under a purchase contract. Funds shall be released from escrow as follows:

(1) If a purchaser properly cancels the purchase contract pursuant to its terms, the funds shall be paid to the purchaser or paid to the developer if the purchaser's funds have been previously refunded by the developer.

(2) If a purchaser defaults in the performance of the purchaser's obligations under the purchase contract, the funds shall be paid to the developer.

(3) If the developer defaults in the performance of the developer's obligations under the purchase contract, the funds shall be paid to the purchaser.

(4) If the funds of a purchaser have not been previously disbursed in accordance with the provisions of this Subsection and if no claim of cancellation or default has been received, the funds may be disbursed to the developer by the escrow agent upon the issuance of acceptable evidence of completion of construction as provided herein.

D. In lieu of the provisions of Subsections B and C of this Section, the Louisiana Real Estate Commission may accept from the developer a surety bond, irrevocable letter of credit, or other financial assurance acceptable to the Louisiana Real Estate Commission including, without limitation, any financial assurance posted in another state or jurisdiction, or as provided by rule. Any acceptable financial assurance must be the lesser of an amount equal to or in excess of the funds which would otherwise be placed in escrow, or in an amount equal to the cost to complete the incomplete property in which the timeshare interest is located.

E. The developer shall provide escrow account information to the Louisiana Real Estate Commission and shall execute in writing an authorization consenting to an audit or examination of the account by the Louisiana Real Estate Commission on forms provided by the Louisiana Real Estate Commission. The developer shall make available documents related to the escrow account or escrow obligation to the Louisiana Real Estate Commission upon the Louisiana Real Estate Commission's request. The developer shall maintain any disputed funds in the escrow account until either of the following occurs:

(1) The developer receives written direction agreed to by signature of all parties.

(2) The funds are deposited with a court of competent jurisdiction in which a civil action regarding the funds has been filed.

F. As used in this Section, independent escrow agent means a financial institution whose accounts are insured by a governmental agency or instrumentality, an attorney, or a licensed title insurance company, in which:

(1) The escrow agent is not a relative or an employee of the developer or managing entity or of any officer, director, affiliate, or subsidiary of the developer or managing entity.

(2) There is no financial relationship, other than the payment of fiduciary fees or as otherwise provided in this Section, between the escrow agent and the developer or managing entity or any officer, director, affiliate, or subsidiary of the developer or managing entity.

(3) Compensation paid by the developer to the escrow agent for services rendered is not paid from funds in the escrow account.

G. For purposes of Subsection F of this Section, an independent escrow agent may not be disqualified to serve as escrow agent solely because of any of the following:

(1) The escrow agent provides the developer or managing entity with routine banking services that do not include construction or receivables financing or any other lending activities.

(2) A nonemployee, attorney-client relationship exists between the developer or managing entity and the escrow agent.

(3) The escrow agent performs closings for the developer or issues owner's or lender's title insurance commitments or policies in connection with such closings.

H. If the developer has previously provided a certified copy of any document required by this Section, the developer may, for all subsequent disbursements, substitute a true and correct copy of the certified copy, provided no changes to the document have been made or are required to be made.

I. In lieu of any escrow provisions required by this Section, the director of the Louisiana Real Estate Commission shall have the discretion to permit deposit of funds or other property in an escrow account as required by the jurisdiction in which the sale took place.

J. In lieu of any escrows required by this Section, the director of the Louisiana Real Estate Commission shall have the discretion to accept other assurances, including but not limited to a surety bond issued by a company authorized and licensed to do business in this state as surety or an irrevocable letter of credit in an amount equal to the escrow requirements of this Section.

K. An escrow agent holding funds escrowed pursuant to this Section may invest such escrowed funds in securities of the United States government, or any agency thereof, or in savings or time deposits in institutions insured by an agency of the United States government. Interest generated by any such investments shall be paid to the party to whom the escrowed funds or property are paid unless otherwise specified by contract.

L. Each escrow agent shall maintain separate books and records for each timeshare plan and shall maintain such books and records in accordance with good accounting practices.

M. Developers, sellers, escrow agents, and their employees and agents have a fiduciary duty to purchasers with respect to funds required to be escrowed under this Section. Any developer, seller, escrow agent, or any employee or agent of a developer, seller, or escrow agent who intentionally fails to comply with the requirements of this Section concerning the establishment of an escrow account, deposits of funds, and property into escrow, or withdrawal therefrom, shall be fined not more than three thousand dollars or shall be imprisoned, with or without hard labor, for not more than ten years, or both. The failure to establish an escrow account or to place funds therein as required in this Section is prima facie evidence of an intentional and purposeful violation of this Section.

N. Excluding any encumbrance placed against the purchaser's timeshare interest securing the purchaser's financing for such purchase, the developer shall not be entitled to the release of any funds escrowed under this Section or release of bond or other acceptable financial assurance with respect to each timeshare interest and any other property or rights to property appurtenant to such timeshare interest, including any amenities represented to the purchaser as being part of the timeshare plan until the developer has provided satisfactory evidence to the Louisiana Real Estate Commission of one of the following:

(1) The timeshare interest together with any other property or rights to property appurtenant to such timeshare interest, including any amenities represented to the purchaser as being part of the timeshare plan, are free and clear of any of the claims of the developer, any owner of immovable property, a mortgagee, judgment creditor, other lienholder, or any other person having an interest in or lien or monetary encumbrance against such timeshare interest or appurtenant property or property rights.

(2) The developer, any owner of immovable property, a mortgagee, judgment creditor, other lienholder, or any other person having an interest in or lien or monetary encumbrance against such timeshare interest or appurtenant property or property rights, including any amenities represented to the purchaser as being part of the timeshare plan, has recorded a subordination and notice to creditors document and recorded it among the appropriate public records in the jurisdiction in which the timeshare interest is located. The subordination document shall expressly and effectively provide that the interest holder's right, lien, or encumbrance shall not adversely affect, and shall be subordinate to, the rights of the owners of the timeshare interests in the timeshare plan regardless of the date of purchase, from and after the effective date of such subordination document.

(3) The developer, any owner of immovable property, a mortgagee, judgment creditor, other lienholder, or any other person having an interest in or lien or monetary encum-

brance against such timeshare interest or appurtenant property or property rights, including any amenities represented to the purchaser as being part of the timeshare plan, has transferred the subject accommodations or amenities or all use rights therein to a nonprofit organization or owners' association to be held for the use and benefit of the owners of the timeshare plan. The nonprofit organization or owners' association shall act as a fiduciary to the purchasers, provided that the developer has transferred control of such entity to the owners or does not exercise its voting rights in such entity with respect to the subject accommodations or amenities. Prior to such transfer, any lien or other encumbrance against such accommodation or facility shall be made subject to a subordination and notice to creditors instrument pursuant to Paragraph (2) of this Subsection.

Added by Acts 2003, No. 978, § 1.

Editor's note. For application of Acts 2003, No. 978, see Editor's note following R.S. 9:1131.2.

§ 1131.17. Escrow account; establishment; claims for damages

A. The developer of a lease timeshare interest in a multiple use project in Louisiana and the developer of each timeshare plan that has timeshare property located in Louisiana or who maintains a sales office in Louisiana for the sale of timeshare interests shall deposit in an interest bearing account established in the name of the developer at a financial institution in the parish where the timeshare property or sales office is located, the sum of fifty dollars for each timeshare interest sold. The deposit shall be made within thirty days after each sale of a timeshare interest. The funds in the escrow account shall be available to pay judgments against the developer resulting from a violation of this Part.

B. The fifty dollar deposit shall remain in the escrow account for a period of one year from the date of deposit. At the end of one year from the date of deposit, the developer shall be entitled to withdraw each fifty dollar deposit together with all interest earned on the deposit unless the executive director of the Louisiana Real Estate Commission certifies that the deposit is required to satisfy an existing judgment or that an action has been filed against the developer which may reasonably require the deposit to satisfy a judgment. If the executive director of the Louisiana Real Estate Commission thereafter determines that the deposit, or any portion thereof, is not reasonably required to satisfy a judgment, the deposit or the unused portion together with all interest earned may be withdrawn by the developer.

C. If a purchaser or timeshare interest owner receives a final money judgment against a developer for a violation of this Part, or files suit under this Part, the purchaser or timeshare interest owner shall file a notification with the executive director of the Louisiana Real Estate Commission. This notification shall include appropriate evidence of the judgment or the filing of the cause of action. Upon receipt of such notification, the executive director of the Louisiana Real Estate Commission shall give notice to the financial institution holding the escrow account of the judgment or filing of a cause of action. Upon receipt of the notice by a financial institution, no funds in the escrow account established by the developer under the provisions of this Section shall be disbursed by the financial institution unless approved by the executive director of the Louisiana Real Estate Commission.

D. The Louisiana Real Estate Commission shall have the right to require a developer to give reasonable evidence of the deposits required under the provisions of this Section. The commission shall have the power to seek an injunction to prohibit any further sales by a developer who fails to give the evidence of deposits required herein.

E. The Louisiana Real Estate Commission may adopt reasonable rules and regulations necessary to implement the provisions of this Section.

F. The provisions of this Section shall in no way limit recovery of damages from a developer's assets under any appropriate remedy provided by law.

G. If the Louisiana Real Estate Commission determines that a developer is in compliance with the escrow requirements of R.S. 9:1131.16, it may notify the developer that it will no longer require deposits under this Section, and will return all deposits existing on the date of such notification within one year of such notification, provided no judgment or action exists which the deposits may reasonably be required to satisfy, and provided the developer continues to comply with R.S. 9:1131.16.

Added by Acts 1983, No. 552, § 1. Amended by Acts 1985, No. 999, § 3.

§ 1131.18. Resales of timeshares

A. Except in the case of a sale where delivery of a public offering statement is required or which is subject to the exemptions of R.S. 9:1131.11(A) and (B)(2)–(5), a seller of a timeshare interest in timeshare property in Louisiana shall furnish to the purchaser before execution of any contract for the sale or, if there is no contract for sale, before the transfer of the timeshare interest, a copy of the timeshare documents, including any plats or plans, and a certificate containing:

(1) A statement disclosing the effect on the proposed transfer of any right of first refusal or other restraint on transfer of the timeshare interest or any portion thereof.

(2) A statement setting forth the amount of the periodic timeshare interest expense liability applicable to the timeshare interest to be sold, and any unpaid timeshare expense or special assessment or other sums currently due and payable from the seller as to the timeshare interest to be sold.

(3) A statement of any other fees payable by owners.

(4) A statement of any judgments or other matters that are or may become privileges against the timeshare interest or the timeshare property and the status of any pending suits that may result in those privileges.

B. A managing entity, within ten days after a request by an owner, shall furnish a certificate containing the information necessary to enable the timeshare owner to comply with this Section. An owner providing a certificate pursuant to Subsection A of this Section is not liable to the purchaser for any erroneous information provided by the managing entity and included in the certificate, other than for judgment privileges against the timeshare interest or the timeshare property.

C. A purchaser is not liable for any unpaid timeshare expense liability or fee greater than the amount set forth in a certificate prepared by a managing entity. An owner is not liable to a purchaser for the failure or delay of a managing entity to provide the certificate in a timely manner, but the contract to purchase or the transfer of the timeshare interest is voidable by the purchaser until the certificate has been provided.

Added by Acts 1983, No. 552, § 1. Amended by Acts 1984, No. 943, § 1, eff. July 20, 1984.

§ 1131.19. Privileges

A. In the case of a sale of a timeshare interest in timeshare property in Louisiana when delivery of a public offering statement is required, a developer shall, before transferring a timeshare interest, record, or furnish to the purchaser, releases of all privileges affecting that timeshare interest that the purchaser does not expressly agree to take subject to or assume, or he shall provide a surety bond or substitute collateral.

B. If a privilege other than a mortgage becomes effective against more than one timeshare interest, any owner is entitled to a release of his timeshare interest from the privilege upon payment of his proportionate liability for the privilege in accordance with timeshare expense liability, unless he or his predecessor in interest agreed otherwise with the holder of the privilege. After payment, the managing entity may not assess or have a privilege against that timeshare interest for any portion of the timeshare expenses incurred in connection with that privilege.

C. If a privilege is to be enforced against all timeshare interests in a timeshare property, service of process upon the managing entity, if any, constitutes service thereof upon all the owners for the purposes of foreclosure or enforcement. The managing entity shall forward promptly, by certified or registered mail, a copy thereof to each owner at the last address known to the managing entity. The cost of forwarding must be advanced by the holder of the privilege and may be taxed as a cost of the enforcement proceeding. Such notice does not suffice for the entry of a deficiency or other personal judgment against any owner.

D. A privilege arising from non-payment of taxes may be enforced as provided in Subsection C, despite the fact that it may only attach to a single timeshare interest.

Added by Acts 1983, No. 552, § 1. Amended by Acts 1985, No. 999, § 3.

§ 1131.20. Management and operation of the timeshare plan

A. All timeshare plans having more than twelve timeshare interests shall have an association of owners. If the number of timeshare interests in the timeshare plan is twelve or fewer, the owners may form an association.

B. A required timeshare association shall be organized prior to the first sale of a timeshare interest.

C. The membership of the timeshare association at all times shall include all the timeshare interest owners or, following termination of the timeshare plan, all former timeshare interest owners entitled to distributions of proceeds under R.S. 9:1131.8, or their heirs, successors, or assigns.

D. The timeshare association shall be responsible for and have control over the administration, operation, and maintenance of the timeshare property, except to the extent the timeshare documents vest control of the operation, and maintenance of the common elements in another entity. The timeshare association, through the managing agent, shall assess and collect timeshare expenses and shall establish reserves to provide for maintenance, improvements, replacements, working capital, and other appropriate purposes. The actual management of the timeshare plan and the operation and maintenance of the timeshare property shall be performed by a managing agent or, in the case of a multilocation project, one or more managing agents, selected by the board of directors and engaged by the timeshare association pursuant to a written management agreement. The developer or an affiliate may be a managing agent. Collect and remit all state and local hotel and motel occupancy taxes as those taxes apply to persons renting transient use of accommodations from the association or managing entity. Timeshare owners and persons occupying accommodations through an exchange program are not transient guests and are not subject to occupancy taxes for the use of accommodations, and comply with all applicable state and local health and safety regulations.

E. Repealed by Acts 2003, No. 978, § 3.
F. Repealed by Acts 2003, No. 978, § 3.
G. Repealed by Acts 2003, No. 978, § 3.
H. Repealed by Acts 2003, No. 978, § 3.
I. Repealed by Acts 2003, No. 978, § 3.

J. Managing entities and their agents shall act in the capacity of a fiduciary to the timeshare owners. In this connection they shall:

(1) Provide each year to all owners an itemized annual budget, which shall include all receipts and expenditures.

(2) Maintain all books and records concerning the timeshare plan and make all such books and records reasonably available for inspection by any owner or the authorized agent of such owner.

(3) Arrange for an annual independent audit of all the books and financial records of the timeshare plan by a certified public accountant in accordance with generally accepted auditing standards. A copy of the audit shall be forwarded to the officers of the association; or, if no association exists, the owner of each timeshare interest shall be notified that such audit is available upon request.

(4) Make available for inspection any books and records of the timeshare plan upon request of the Louisiana Real Estate Commission.

(5) Schedule occupancy of the timeshare units, when owners are not entitled to use specific timeshare periods, so that all owners will be provided the use and possession of the accommodations of the timeshare plan which they have purchased.

(6) Perform any other functions and duties which are necessary and proper to maintain the timeshare property as provided in the timeshare documents.

(7) Any person who willfully misappropriates the property or funds of an association shall be guilty of theft.

K. (1) With regard to timeshare plans located within the state of Louisiana, the contract retaining a management company shall be automatically renewable every five years, beginning with the fifth year after the management company is first retained. If the owner's association wishes to terminate the contract, the association must affirmatively vote to discharge the management company. Such a vote shall be conducted by the board of the owners' association, and the management company shall be discharged only if at least sixty-six percent of the purchasers voting, which shall be at least fifty percent of all votes allocated to purchasers, vote to discharge the management company.

(2) In the event the management company is discharged, the board of the owners' association is responsible for obtain-

ing another managing entity. If the board fails to do so, any timeshare owner may apply to the parish district court within the jurisdiction of which the accommodations lie for the appointment of a receiver to manage the affairs of the association. At least thirty days before applying to the said district court, the timeshare owner shall mail to the association and post in a conspicuous place on the timeshare property a notice describing the intended action, giving the association the opportunity to fill any vacancies on the board. If during such time the association fails to fill the vacancies, the timeshare owner may proceed with the petition. If a receiver is appointed, the association is responsible for payment of the salary of the receiver, court costs, and attorney fees. The receiver shall have all powers and duties of a duly constituted board of administration and shall serve until the association fills vacancies on the board sufficient to constitute a quorum.

(3) The management company of a timeshare plan subject to the provisions of any other law may be discharged pursuant to that law.

Added by Acts 1983, No. 552, § 1. Amended by Acts 1984, No. 943, § 1, eff. July 20, 1984; Acts 1985, No. 999, § 3; Acts 2003, No. 978, § 1.

Editor's note. For application of Acts 2003, No. 978, see Editor's note following R.S. 9:1131.2.

§ 1131.21. Assessment for timeshare interest expenses

A. Until timeshare expense assessments are made against the timeshare interests, the developer shall pay all timeshare expenses. After any timeshare expense assessment has been made against the owners, timeshare expense assessments must be made at least annually, based on a budget adopted at least annually by the managing entity.

B. (1) Except for assessments under Subsections C, D, and E of this Section, all timeshare expenses must be assessed against all the timeshare interests in accordance with the allocation set forth in the timeshare documents. The allocation of total common expenses set forth in the timeshare documents may vary on any reasonable basis, including but not limited to timeshare unit size, timeshare unit type, timeshare unit location, specific identification, or a combination of these factors, if the percentage interest in the common elements attributable to each timeshare interest equals the share of the total common expenses allocable to that interest. The share of a timeshare interest in the common expenses allocable to the timeshare interest may vary on any reasonable basis if the timeshare interest's share of its parcel's common expense allocation is equal to that timeshare interest's share of the percentage interest in common elements attributable to such interest.

(2) No owner of a timeshare interest may be excused from the payment of its proportional share of the common expenses, except that the developer may be excused from the payment of such common expenses which would have been assessed against those units during a stated period of time during which the developer has guaranteed in writing to each timeshare interest owner or to the association that the expenses for the common elements would not increase over a stated dollar amount. If such a guarantee is given, the developer is obligated to pay any amount of common expenses incurred during the guarantee period, which was not produced by the assessments at the guarantee level from other timeshare interest owners. Any past due assessment or installment thereof bears interest at the rate established by the managing entity or timeshare documents not to exceed twelve percent per annum.

C. Any timeshare expense benefiting fewer than all of the owners must be assessed exclusively against the owners benefited.

D. Repealed by Acts 2003, No. 978, § 3.

E. If any timeshare interest expense is caused by the misconduct of any owner, the timeshare association may assess that expense exclusively against that owner's timeshare interest.

F. The provisions of this Section shall apply only to timeshare interests in timeshare property located in Louisiana.

G. No owner of a timeshare interest may be excused from the payment of his share of the common expenses unless all owners are likewise excused. Past due assessments may bear interest at the legal rate or some lesser rate established by the managing entity.

Added by Acts 1983, No. 552, § 1. Amended by Acts 1984, No. 943, § 1, eff. July 20, 1984; Acts 1985, No. 999, § 3; Acts 2003, No. 978, § 1.

Editor's note. For application of Acts 2003, No. 978, see Editor's note following R.S. 9:1131.2.

§ 1131.22. Privilege for assessments

A. A person who has a duty to make assessments for timeshare expenses has a privilege on a timeshare interest for any assessment levied against that timeshare interest or fines imposed against its owner from the time the assessment or fine becomes due. The privilege may be foreclosed in like manner as a mortgage on immovable property. Unless the timeshare documents otherwise provide, fees, charges, late charges, fines, and interest charged are enforceable as assessments under this Section. If an assessment is payable in installments, the full amount of the assessment is a privilege from the time the first installment thereof becomes due.

B. A privilege under this Section is superior to all other privileges and encumbrances on a timeshare interest except:

(1) Privileges and encumbrances recorded before the privilege under this Section is perfected;

(2) Mortgages on the timeshare interest securing first mortgage holders and recorded before the due date of the assessment or the due date of the first installment payable on the assessment;

(3) Privileges for property taxes and other governmental assessments or charges against the timeshare interest; and

(4) Privileges securing assessments or charges made by a person managing a project of which the timeshare property is a part.

C. The privilege is perfected upon recordation of a claim of privilege in the parish in which the timeshare unit is situated.

D. A privilege for unpaid assessments is prescribed unless proceedings to enforce the privilege are instituted within three years after the assessments become payable.

E. This Section does not prohibit actions or suits to recover sums for which Subsection A of this Section creates a privilege nor preclude resort to any contractual or other remedy permitted by law.

F. A judgment or decree in any action or suit brought under this Section must include costs and reasonable attorney fees for the prevailing party.

G. A person who has a duty to make assessments for timeshare expenses shall furnish to an owner, upon written request, a recordable statement setting forth the amount of unpaid assessments currently levied against his timeshare interest. The statement must be furnished within ten business days after receipt of the request and is binding in favor of persons reasonably relying thereon.

H. The provisions of this Section shall apply only to timeshare interests in timeshare property located in Louisiana.

Added by Acts 1983, No. 552, § 1.

§ 1131.23. Insurance

A. Commencing not later than the time of the first conveyance of a timeshare interest in timeshare property located in Louisiana to a person other than a developer, the timeshare association shall maintain the following:

(1) Property insurance covering the timeshare property, insuring against all risks of direct physical loss commonly insured against. The total amount of insurance, after application of any deductibles, shall be not less than eighty percent of the actual cash value of the insured property, exclusive of land, excavations, foundations, and other items normally excluded from property insurance policies; and

(2) Comprehensive general liability insurance, including medical payments insurance, in an amount determined by the board of directors of the timeshare association, but not less than any amount specified in the declaration, covering all occurrences commonly insured against for death, bodily injury, and property damage arising out of or in connection with the use, ownership, or maintenance of the timeshare property.

B. (1) If the insurance described in Subsection A is not maintained, the association promptly shall cause notice of that fact to be hand-delivered or sent prepaid by United States mail to all owners.

(2) The declaration may require the timeshare association to carry any other insurance, and the timeshare association in any event may carry any other insurance it deems appropriate, to protect the association or the owners.

C. Insurance policies carried pursuant to Subsection A must provide that:

(1) Each owner is an insured person under the policy with respect to liability arising out of his ownership of a timeshare interest in the timeshare property or his membership in the association.

(2) The insurer waives its right to subrogation under the policy against any owner or members of his household.

(3) No act or omission by any owner, unless acting within the scope of his authority on behalf of the association, will void the policy or be a condition to recovery under the policy.

(4) If, at the time of a loss under the policy, there is other insurance in the name of the owner covering the same property covered by the policy, the policy is primary insurance not contributing with the other insurance.

D. Any loss covered by the property policy under Subsection A(1) of this Section shall be adjusted with the timeshare association, but the insurance proceeds for that loss shall be payable to any insurance trustee designated for that purpose, or otherwise to the timeshare association, and not to any mortgagee. The insurance trustee or the timeshare association shall hold any insurance proceeds in trust for owners and privilege holders as their interest may appear. Subject to the provisions of Subsection G of this Section, the proceeds shall be disbursed first for the repair or restoration of the damaged timeshare property, and owners and privilege holders are not entitled to receive payment of any portion of the proceeds unless there is a surplus of proceeds after the timeshare property has been completely repaired or restored, or the timeshare plan is terminated.

E. An insurance policy issued to the timeshare association does not prevent an owner from obtaining insurance for his own benefit.

F. An insurer that has issued an insurance policy to the timeshare association under this Section shall issue certificates or memoranda of insurance, upon request, to any owner or mortgagee. The insurance may not be cancelled until thirty days after notice of the proposed cancellation has been mailed to the timeshare association, each owner and each mortgagee to whom certificates of insurance have been issued.

G. (1) Any portion of the timeshare property damaged or destroyed shall be repaired or replaced promptly by the timeshare association unless any of the following occur:

(a) The timeshare plan is terminated.

(b) Repair or replacement would be illegal under any state or local health or safety statute or ordinance.

(c) Eighty percent, or such other percentage provided in the declaration, of the owners vote not to rebuild.

(d) The cost of repair or replacement of timeshare property subject to an ownership timeshare interest in excess of insurance proceeds and reserves is a common expense.

(2) In the case of an ownership timeshare interest, if the entire timeshare property is not repaired or replaced:

(a) The insurance proceeds attributable to the damaged timeshare property shall be used to restore the damaged area to a condition compatible with the remainder of the timeshare property.

(b) The insurance proceeds attributable to timeshare property which is not rebuilt shall be distributed to the owners of those timeshare interests and the owners of the timeshare interests to which unrepaired limited common elements were assigned.

(c) The remainder of the insurance proceeds shall be distributed to all the owners in proportion to their interest in the timeshare property.

(3) In the case of a lease timeshare interest, if the entire timeshare property is not repaired or replaced:

(a) The insurance proceeds attributable to the damaged timeshare property shall be used to restore the damaged area to a condition compatible with the remainder of the timeshare property.

(b) The insurance proceeds attributable to the timeshare property which is not rebuilt shall be distributed to the owners of those timeshare interests and the owners of the timeshare interests to which those limited common elements were assigned up to the amount of the owner's purchase price reduced by a sum computed by multiplying the purchase price by a fraction, the numerator of which is the number of years the owner has owned the lease timeshare interest and the denominator of which is the original term of the lease timeshare interests.

(c) The remainder of the proceeds shall be distributed to the developer.

(4) If the owners vote not to rebuild any unit, that unit's entire common element interest, vote in the association, and common expense liability are automatically reallocated upon the vote as if the unit had been condemned. The association promptly shall prepare, execute, and record an amendment to the declaration reflecting the reallocations.

H. The managing entity shall make available for reasonable inspection by purchasers or their authorized agents a copy of each policy of insurance.

Added by Acts 1983, No. 552, § 1. Amended by Acts 1984, No. 943, § 1, eff. July 20, 1984; Acts 1985, No. 999, § 3; Acts 2003, No. 978, § 1.

Editor's note. For application of Acts 2003, No. 978, see Editor's note following R.S. 9:1131.2.

§ 1131.24. Requirements where developer's interest in the timeshare property is a leasehold interest

A. If the interest which the developer holds in the timeshare property is a leasehold interest, the lease, or an amendment or supplement thereto, must contain a purchaser protection clause.

B. The purchaser protection clause shall provide that the lessor cannot terminate the lease by reason of the lessee's default without first giving reasonable notice of the default to the timeshare association and providing the timeshare association with a reasonable opportunity to cure the default.

C. The purchaser protection clause shall also obligate the lessor to enter into a new lease with the association on the same terms and conditions as the old lease so that bankruptcy of the lessee will not disrupt the timeshare interest owner's continued rights of occupancy.

Added by Acts 1983, No. 552, § 1. Amended by Acts 1984, No. 943, § 1, eff. July 20, 1984.

§ 1131.25. Remedies

A. The remedies provided herein shall be in addition to any other remedies provided by law.

B. The timeshare declaration and bylaws shall have the force of law between the individual owners. The remedies for breach of any obligation imposed on owners or the developer shall be damages, injunctions, or any other remedies provided by law.

C. (1) No developer shall have any liability arising out of the use, delivery, or publication by the developer of information provided to it by an exchange company; unless the developer knows the information is false.

(2)(a) Except as provided in this Subsection, no exchange company shall have any liability with respect to:

(i) any representation made by the developer relating to a program for the exchange of timeshare interests or an exchange company; or

(ii) the use, delivery, or publication by the developer of any information relating to a program for the exchange of timeshare interests or an exchange company.

(b) An exchange company shall only be liable for written information provided to the developer by the exchange company.

Added by Acts 1983, No. 552, § 1.

§ 1131.26. Louisiana Real Estate Recovery Fund; exemption

The Louisiana Real Estate Recovery Fund, R.S. 37:1461 et seq., is hereby exempt from and no claim shall be made against the fund for any damages arising from the sale of a timeshare interest to the extent such claim is a claim for which an escrow account is established under R.S. 9:1131.17.

Added by Acts 1983, No. 552, § 1.

§ 1131.27. Repealed by Acts 1984, No. 943, § 5, eff. July 20, 1984

§ 1131.28. Recordation

For timeshare plans located inside and outside the state of Louisiana, the developer shall record the instrument conveying the timeshare interest to the purchaser with the appropriate recording agency within ninety days after the closing of the transaction. Within ninety days after receipt by the developer of the recorded instrument conveying the timeshare interest from the appropriate recording agency, the developer shall mail the recorded instrument bearing its recordation number to the purchaser.

Added by Acts 1984, No. 943, § 3, eff. July 20, 1984. Amended by Acts 1985, No. 999, § 1; Acts 2003, No. 978, § 1.

Editor's note. For application of Acts 2003, No. 978, see Editor's note following R.S. 9:1131.2.

§ 1131.29. Waiver prohibited

The Louisiana Timesharing Act is enacted to protect the public welfare. No person shall solicit any waiver of its provisions which protect the purchaser. Any waiver of its provisions shall be without effect.

Added by Acts 1984, No. 943, § 3, eff. July 20, 1984.

§ 1131.30. Preservation of claims and defenses

A. Any cause of action or defense, for which the remedy of rescission of a sale is provided in the Louisiana Condominium Act,[1] which a purchaser may raise against a timeshare interest seller arising out of a timeshare interest sale is preserved against any assignee or successor to the contract of sale or to any credit contract executed by the purchaser in connection with the timeshare interest sale.

B. Sellers and creditors shall include the following language in promissory notes executed in connection with timeshare interest sales:

NOTICE

ANY HOLDER OF THIS CREDIT CONTRACT IS SUBJECT TO ALL CLAIMS AND DEFENSES FOR WHICH RESCISSION OF THE CONTRACT OF SALE IS PROVIDED IN THE LOUISIANA CONDOMINIUM ACT AND WHICH THE DEBTOR COULD ASSERT AGAINST THE SELLER OF SERVICES OR PROPERTY OBTAINED PURSUANT HERETO OR WITH THE PROCEEDS THEREOF. RECOVERY HEREUNDER BY THE DEBTOR SHALL NOT EXCEED AMOUNTS PAID BY THE DEBTOR HEREUNDER.

Added by Acts 1984, No. 943, § 3, eff. July 20, 1984.

[1] R.S. 9:1121.101 et seq.

§§ 1132 to 1141. Repealed by Acts 1979, No. 682, § 3

PART II–B. LOUISIANA HOMEOWNERS ASSOCIATION ACT

SUBPART A. GENERAL PROVISIONS

§ 1141.1. Short title

This Part shall be known as the "Louisiana Homeowners Association Act".

Added by Acts 1999, No. 309, § 2, eff. June 16, 1999.

§ 1141.2. Definitions

As used in this Part, unless the context clearly indicates otherwise:

(1) "Association property" means all the property either held by the association or commonly held by the members of the association, or both, and lots privately held by members of the association.

(2) "Common area" means property owned or otherwise maintained, repaired, or administered by the association for the benefit, use, and enjoyment of its members.

(3) "Community documents" means the articles of incorporation, bylaws, plat, declarations, covenants, conditions, restrictions, rules and regulations, or other written instruments, including any amendment thereto, by which the association has the authority to exercise any of its powers to manage, maintain, or otherwise affect the association property or which otherwise govern the use of association property.

(4) "Declaration" means any instrument, however denominated, that establishes or regulates, or both, a residential planned community, and any amendment thereto.

(5) "Homeowners association" or "association" means a nonprofit corporation, unincorporated association, or other legal entity, which is created pursuant to a declaration, whose members consist primarily of lot owners, and which is created to manage or regulate, or both, the residential planned community.

(6) "Lot" means any plot or parcel of land designated for separate ownership shown on a recorded subdivision plat for a residential development or the boundaries of which are otherwise described in a recorded instrument, other than common area, within the jurisdiction of the residential community as such area is described in the community documents.

(7) "Residential planned community" or "planned community" means a real estate development, used primarily for residential purposes, in which the owners of separately owned lots are mandatory members of an association by virtue of such ownership.

Added by Acts 1999, No. 309, § 2, eff. June 16, 1999.

§ 1141.3. Applicability

A. The provisions of this Part shall be applicable to existing and future residential planned communities whose declarations have been duly executed and filed for registry. However, this Part shall not be construed to affect the validity or superiority of any provision of a community document. Only to the extent the community documents are silent shall the provisions of this Part apply.

B. (1) This Part shall not apply to condominium property governed by the provisions of Part II of this Chapter.

(2) The provisions of Part II–A of this Chapter shall be applicable to an ownership timeshare interest created in a lot within a planned community to the extent that those provisions do not conflict with the provisions of this Part.

C. This Part shall not impair any right that is guaranteed or protected by the constitution of this state or the United States, nor shall this Part be construed to affect any act done, offense or violation committed, or right accrued.

D. This Part shall not be construed to impair or cast a cloud upon the titles of common areas or lots within a residential planned community.

Added by Acts 1999, No. 309, § 2, eff. June 16, 1999.

SUBPART B. BUILDING RESTRICTIONS

§ 1141.4. Building restrictions; matters of interpretation

The existence, validity, or extent of a building restriction affecting any association property shall be liberally construed to give effect to its purpose and intent.

Added by Acts 1999, No. 309, § 2, eff. June 16, 1999.

§ 1141.5. Building restrictions; generally, affirmative duty, and common areas

A. Building restrictions affecting the building standards, specified uses, or improvements of association property may be established, amended, or terminated in accordance with the provisions of this Part.

B. Such building restrictions may include the imposition of an affirmative duty, including the affirmative duty to pay monthly or periodic dues or fees, or assessments for a particular expense or capital improvement, that are reasonable for the maintenance, improvement, or safety, or any combination thereof, of the planned community.

C. Such building restrictions may also regulate the building standards, specified uses, and improvements of common areas of a homeowners association, including but not limited to the regulation of passage, ingress, and egress upon common areas, streets, and street rights-of-way.

Added by Acts 1999, No. 309, § 2, eff. June 16, 1999.

§ 1141.6. Establishment, amendment, or termination of building restrictions

A. Building restrictions affecting association property, including lots or common areas, or those imposing an affirmative duty may be established, amended, or terminated in accordance with the terms of the applicable community document.

B. In the absence of a provision for the establishment, amendment, or termination of such building restrictions in the community documents:

(1) Building restrictions may be established by agreement of three-fourths of the lot owners.

(2) Existing building restrictions may be made more onerous or increased by agreement of two-thirds of the lot owners.

(3) Existing building restrictions may be made less onerous, reduced, or terminated by agreement of more than one-half of the lot owners.

C. (1) Once established, or amended to be more onerous, building restrictions become a charge on the property and affect all current owners and, once recorded in the public records, affect all subsequent owners. Except for building restrictions relating to assessments or common areas, no new or more onerous building restriction shall impose a duty on the current owner to act affirmatively or remove or renovate any existing structure. All new or replacement structures, however, shall be subject to the new or more onerous building restriction.

(2) Once amended to be less onerous, the building restriction constitutes a reduction of the charge on the property, and once terminated, the property is released of its former charge, affecting all current and subsequent owners.

D. (1) When building restrictions are established under the provisions of Subsection B of this Section, rather than by the community documents, an owner may file with the association and the clerk of court a statement declining to be covered by the building restrictions. Such document must be filed within thirty days of the establishment of such building restrictions.

(2) When building restrictions relative to set-backs or minimum square footage requirements are established or made more onerous under the provisions of Subsection B of this Section, rather than the community documents, the owner of an unimproved lot is exempt from complying with such new or more onerous restrictions.

(3) An "owner" under the provisions of this Subsection means the owner or owners at the time the restriction was established or made more onerous and the waivers of compliance provided in this Subsection are personal to that owner.

Added by Acts 1999, No. 309, § 2, eff. June 16, 1999.

§ 1141.7. Agreement of owners; voting

A. Each lot represents a single vote which can be exercised by the signature or other indication of the registered lot owner or of a single co-owner, the latter of which is presumed to be acting on behalf of the other co-owners. A plot or parcel of unimproved land which is substantially larger than a majority of other lots in the association, however, shall be treated as separate lots, the number of which to be roughly determined by the size of the land in relation to other lots. The ownership interest in common areas, streets, or street rights-of-way does not constitute a voting interest.

B. For purposes of this Subpart, an agreement of lot owners may be obtained by any of the following methods, or a combination thereof:

(1) By a written ballot that states the substance of the issue before the owners and specifies the date by which the return ballot must be received to be counted. The ballot shall be accompanied by the full text of the building restriction being established, amended, or terminated and shall be mailed to the owner by certified mail not less than thirty days prior to the date by which the return ballot must be received.

(2) At a meeting of the owners if written notice of the meeting stating the purpose of the meeting is delivered to each lot owner. The notice shall be accompanied by an agenda of the meeting and the full text of the building restriction being established, amended, or terminated. Such notice shall be mailed to the owner, by certified mail, not less than thirty days prior to the date of the meeting.

Added by Acts 1999, No. 309, § 2, eff. June 16, 1999.

SUBPART C. ENFORCEMENT

§ 1141.8. Community documents; force of law

The community documents of residential planned communities shall have the force of law between the homeowners association and the individual lot owners and as between individual lot owners. The remedies for breach of any obligation imposed on lot owners or the association shall include damages, injunctions, or such other remedies as are provided by law.

Added by Acts 1999, No. 309, § 2, eff. June 16, 1999.

§ 1141.9. Homeowners association privilege

In addition to any other remedies provided by law or by the community documents for nonpayment of assessments, a homeowners association as defined in this Part may utilize the provisions of Part III of this Chapter establishing a privilege on lots of delinquent owners for nonpayment of assessments.

Added by Acts 1999, No. 309, § 2, eff. June 16, 1999.

§ 1142. Repealed by Acts 1979, No. 682, § 3

PART III. PRIVILEGES ON IMMOVABLES FOR CHARGES OR DUES OF ASSOCIATION OF OWNERS

§ 1145. Association of owners; privilege; definition

Upon the filing of a sworn detailed statement in accordance with this Part, an association of owners of lots in a residential or commercial subdivision shall have a privilege upon the lot and improvements thereon of an owner in the subdivision who fails to pay charges, expenses or dues imposed upon such lot and improvements thereon in accordance with recorded restrictions, servitudes, or obligations affecting such subdivision. An association of owners refers to a nonprofit corporation, partnership, association, or other legal entity whose members are owners of lots in the subdivision, and which maintains certain portions of the land or improvements in such subdivision for the use and benefit of the owners of lots in such subdivision. The privilege shall secure unpaid charges, expenses or dues imposed by the association of owners, together with legal interest from the date due and reasonable attorney's fees.

Added by Acts 1979, No. 583, § 1.

§ 1146. Privilege; sworn detailed statement; filing

The sworn detailed statement shall contain the nature and amount of the unpaid charges, expenses, or dues, a description of the lot or lots on which behalf the charges, expenses, or dues have been assessed, shall be signed and verified by an officer or agent of the association, and shall be filed for registry in the mortgage records in the parish in which the residential subdivision is located. The association shall, commensurate with the filing for registry of the privilege, serve upon the delinquent owner a sworn detailed statement of the claim by certified mail, registered mail or personal delivery.

Added by Acts 1979, No. 583, § 1.

§ 1147. Privilege; five year period

A recorded sworn statement shall preserve the privilege against the lot or lots and improvements thereon for a period of five years after the date of recordation. The effect of recordation shall cease and the privilege preserved by this recordation shall perempt unless a suit to enforce the privilege is filed within five years after the date of its recordation and a notice of the filing of such suit is filed in the mortgage records of the parish in which the subdivision is located.

Added by Acts 1979, No. 583, § 1.

§ 1148. Privilege; ranking

The privilege provided in this Part shall be ranked according to its time of recordation.

Added by Acts 1979, No. 583, § 1.

PART IV. MANUFACTURED HOME PROPERTY ACT

§ 1149.1. Short title

This Part shall be known and may be cited as the "Manufactured Home Property Act."

Added by Acts 1982, No. 524, § 1, eff. July 22, 1982.

Cross References

C.C. arts. 463, 464, 467, 468, 472, 490, 491, 493.

§ 1149.2. Definitions

In this Chapter, the following words and phrases shall have the meaning ascribed to them unless the content or subject matter clearly indicates otherwise:

(1) "Person" means any individual, firm, corporation, partnership or association.

(2) "Manufactured home" means a mobile home or residential mobile home.

(3) "Mobile home" means a factory assembled structure or structures transportable in one or more sections, with or without a permanent foundation, and includes the plumbing, heating, air conditioning, and electrical systems contained therein.

(4) "Manufacturer" means any person regularly engaged in the business of assembling manufactured homes, either within or without this state.

(5) "Dealer" means any person engaged in the business of buying, selling, or exchanging manufactured homes which are subject to license under Chapter 4 of the Subtitle II of Title 47 of the Louisiana Revised Statutes of 1950.

(6) "Commissioner" means the director of public safety or his duly assigned assistants, as provided for in R.S. 40:1301, who, in addition to all other powers, shall have all powers granted and perform such duties as are imposed on the commissioner by this Chapter.

(7) "Vehicle" means mobile homes and residential mobile homes.

(8) "Mortgage" shall include any rights under a retail installment contract, a chattel mortgage, a security agreement under Chapter 9 of the Louisiana Commercial Laws (R.S. 10:9–101, et seq.), and mortgages upon immovable property.

(9) "Certificate of title" means a vehicle certificate of title as provided for in R.S. 32:701.

(10) "Residential mobile home" means a manufactured home designed to be used as a dwelling, and may include a mobile home or a residential mobile home that has been declared to be a part of the realty as provided in R.S. 9:1149.4.

(11) "Retail installment contract" means an agreement entered into pursuant to Chapter 10 of Title 6 of the Louisiana Revised Statutes of 1950.

(12) "Manufacturer's certificate of origin" means a certificate on a form to be prescribed by the commissioner, and furnished by the manufacturer, showing the original transfer of a new vehicle from the manufacturer to the original purchaser, and each subsequent transfer between distributor and dealer, dealer and dealer, and dealer to owner, through and including the transfer to the title applicant.

Added by Acts 1982, No. 524, § 1, eff. July 22, 1982. Amended by Acts 1989, No. 137, § 4, eff. Sept. 1, 1989.

Editor's note. Acts 1989, No. 137, § 20 provided:

"It is the intent of the Legislature in enacting this Act to amend the preexisting Louisiana security device laws to accompany and accommodate implementation of Chapter 9 of the Louisiana Commercial Laws (R.S. 10:9–101, et seq.) as previously enacted under Act 528 of 1988. It is further the intent of the legislature that these preexisting Louisiana laws, including without limitation the various statutes and code articles amended and re-enacted under this Act, not be expressly or impliedly repealed by Chapter 9 of the Louisiana Commercial Laws, but that such laws remain in effect and be applied to preexisting secured transactions and, at times when so provided, be applied to secured transactions subject to Chapter 9 of the Louisiana Commercial Laws."

Chapter 9 of the Louisiana Commercial Laws was revised by Acts 2001, No. 128, § 1, effective July 1, 2001, to consist of R.S. 10:9–101 through 10:9–710. This Chapter does not apply to statutory liens and privileges except as expressly provided therein. R.S. 10:9–322(h) provides: "A security interest has priority over a conflicting lien, other than an agricultural lien, in the same collateral except as otherwise provided in this Chapter or except to the extent the lien is created by security interest." The accompanying revision comment states: "For example, see R.S. 9:4501, 9:4502, 9:4521, 9:4758, 9:4870, and 9:4888, each of which provides that certain privileges have priority over certain security interests. See also 9:5001 and 37:218."

Cross References

C.C. arts. 463, 464, 467, 468, 472, 490, 491, 493.

§ 1149.3. Classification

Except as otherwise provided in R.S. 9:1149.4, when any manufactured home shall be moved to and located in or upon any immovable property, or installed therein or thereon in a manner which, under any law, might make the manufactured home an immovable or component part thereof, the manufactured home shall be and will remain a movable subject to the provisions of Chapter 4 of Title 32 of the Louisiana Revised Statutes of 1950 governing its mortgage or sale and subject to the provisions of Chapter 9 of Title 10 of the Louisiana Revised Statutes and Chapter 10 of Title 6 of the Louisiana Revised Statutes of 1950 and Code Book III, Code Title XII, Chapter 2 of Title 9 of the Louisiana Revised Statutes of 1950 governing its financing. Title to the vehicle shall not pass by the sale of the immovable property to which it has been actually or fictitiously attached, whether such sale be conventional or judicial. No sale or mortgage of or lien upon the immovable property shall in any manner affect or impair the rank or privilege of a chattel mortgage or security interest under Chapter 9 of the Louisiana Commercial Laws on such manufactured home, or the remedies of the holder thereof for its enforcement.

Added by Acts 1982, No. 524, § 1, eff. July 22, 1982. Amended by Acts 1989, No. 137, § 4, eff. Sept. 1, 1989.

Editor's note. For § 20 of Acts 1989, No. 137, stating legislative intent, see Editor's note following R.S. 9:1149.2.

Cross References

C.C. arts. 463, 464, 467, 468, 472, 490, 491, 493.

§ 1149.4. Immobilization

A. A manufactured home placed upon a lot or tract of land shall be an immovable when there is recorded in the appropriate conveyance or mortgage records of the parish where the said lot or tract of land is situated an authentic act or a validly executed and acknowledged sale or mortgage or sale with mortgage which contains a description of the manufactured home as described in the certificate of title or manufacturer's certificate of origin and a description of the lot or tract of land upon which the manufactured home is placed, and contains a declaration by the owner of the manufactured home and, when applicable, the holder of a mortgage or security interest under Chapter 9 of the Louisiana Commercial Laws on the manufactured home, that it shall remain permanently attached to the lot or tract of land described in the instrument.

B. Upon recordation of the act described above, the manufactured home shall cease to be subject to the application of Chapter 4 of Title 32 of the Louisiana Revised Statutes of 1950 and the taxes applicable to movables and shall thereafter be subject to all laws concerning immovable property; however, nothing herein shall be construed to affect the rights of the holder of a validly recorded chattel mortgage or previously perfected security interest under Chapter 9 of the Louisiana Commercial Laws duly noted on the certificate of title.

C. (1) Notwithstanding any other law to the contrary, no action to collect a tax applicable to movables which is purported to be due or became due on any purchase made on or after September 1, 2005, through December 31, 2006, of any manufactured home used solely as residential housing in the following parishes which have been severely impacted by Hurricanes Katrina and Rita shall be initiated or continued, if the basis of such action is the date upon which the declaration of immovability provided for in Subsection A of this Section is recorded in the conveyance or mortgage records:

(a) The parishes of St. Helena and Cameron.

(b) The parish of West Feliciana.

(c) The parish of St. James.

(d) The parishes of East Feliciana, Point Coupee, and West Baton Rouge.

(e) The parishes of Allen, Assumption, and Sabine.

(f) The parish of Plaquemines.

(g) The parishes of Beauregard, Evangeline, Iberville, and Jefferson Davis.

(h) The parishes of Acadia, Ascension, Iberia, Lafourche, Livingston, St. Bernard, St. Charles, St. John the Baptist, St. Landry, St. Martin, St. Mary, Vermilion, Vernon, and Washington.

(i) The parishes of Tangipahoa and Terrebonne.

(j) The parishes of Calcasieu, Lafayette, and St. Tammany.

(k) The parishes of East Baton Rouge, Jefferson, and Orleans.

(2) With respect to actions to collect a tax applicable to movables which is purported to be due or became due on those manufactured homes specified in Paragraph (1) of this Subsection, if the basis of such action is the date upon which the declaration of immovability was filed, then the date of immobilization shall relate back to the twentieth day of the month following the month of the delivery of the manufactured home.

(3) The purchaser of a manufactured home who formerly lived at a physical address on or after September 1, 2004 within one of the parishes as provided for in Paragraph 1 of this Subsection, who bought a manufactured home on or after September 1, 2005 through December 31, 2006 for use solely as residential housing, shall also be eligible for the relief provided for in this Subsection if the purchaser submits an Affidavit of Displacement to the Department of Revenue attesting that the purchaser resided in one of the parishes as provided for in Paragraph 1 of this Subsection on or after September 1, 2004.

D. (1) Upon recordation of the act of immobilization provided by this Section, the owner of the manufactured home or his agent shall file with the secretary of the Department of Public Safety and Corrections a certified copy of the act. The secretary of the Department of Public Safety and Corrections shall create an Internet accessible searchable database providing a public record of each such filing, indicating the name of the owner of the manufactured home, the date of recording of the act of immobilization in accordance with Subsection A of this Section, the parish where the act is recorded, the year of manufacture, the name of the manufacturer, the dimensions and the vehicle identification number or numbers of the manufactured home, and the date of the secretary's filing of a copy of the act of immobilization.

(2) The secretary shall return to the owner or his agent an acknowledgment that the act has been received and the public record created. This acknowledgment shall contain information sufficient to allow the location of the public record to be ascertained. For creating this public record, the secretary of the Department of Public Safety and Corrections is authorized to charge and collect the fee provided in R.S. 32:412.1(A)(3)(y). The failure of the owner or his agent to file a certified copy of the immobilization as provided in this Subsection shall not impair the validity or enforceability of the act of immobilization as provided by this Section.

Added by Acts 1982, No. 524, § 1, eff. July 22, 1982. Amended by Acts 1989, No. 137, § 4, eff. Sept. 1, 1989; Acts 2008, No. 463, § 1, eff. July 1, 2008; Acts 2008, No. 924, § 1, eff. Jan. 1, 2009; Acts 2011, 1st Ex.Sess., No. 30, § 1.

Editor's note. Acts 2008, No. 463 enacted subsec. C and Act 924 enacted subsec. D [as redesignated]. Section 2 of Acts 2008, No. 463 declares that the "provisions of this Act shall be retroactive to September 1, 2005." Section 3 of Acts 2008, No. 924 declares that this Act "shall have prospective effect only, and nothing in this Act shall impair any rights existing under law prior to the effective date of this Act by any person claiming an interest in a manufactured home."

Cross References

C.C. arts. 463, 464, 467, 468, 472, 490, 491, 493.

§ 1149.5. Security devices

A. Every retail installment contract, chattel mortgage, or security agreement entered into for the purchase or the refinance of a manufactured home or its contents, or both, shall be effective as against third persons and shall take its rank and priority as provided in Chapter 9 of the Louisiana Commercial Laws, R.S. 10:9–101 et seq. A retail installment contract, chattel mortgage, security agreement or a financing statement in the form approved by the commissioner is filed when received provided the receipt is subsequently validated by the office of the commissioner.

B. Validation of the receipt of the retail installment contract or chattel mortgage, security agreement or financing statement by the commissioner shall affect third persons wherever the manufactured home or the contents thereof are located.

Added by Acts 1982, No. 524, § 1, eff. July 22, 1982. Amended by Acts 1984, No. 574, § 1; Acts 1989, No. 137, § 4, eff. Sept. 1, 1989; Acts 2004, No. 303, § 1.

Editor's note. For § 20 of Acts 1989, No. 137, stating legislative intent, see Editor's note following R.S. 9:1149.2.

Cross References

C.C. arts. 463, 464, 467, 468, 472, 490, 491, 493.

§ 1149.6. Deimmobilization

A. The owner may deimmobilize a manufactured home by detachment or removal. However, to affect third persons, an authentic act or sale or mortgage or sale with mortgage containing a description of the manufactured home as described in the previous certificate of title or manufacturer's certificate of origin, a description of the lot or tract of land upon which the manufactured home has been placed, a statement of intent by the owner that he no longer intends the manufactured home to be an immovable and a description of the document by which the manufactured home was immobilized, including the recording information, must be filed in the appropriate conveyance or mortgage records of the parish where the said lot or tract of land is situated.

B. Thereafter the owner may apply to the commissioner for a certificate of title according to the provisions of Chapter 4 of Title 32 of the Louisiana Revised Statutes of 1950. The commissioner shall issue a certificate of title upon the furnishing of: (a) a certificate of mortgages; (b) a certified copy of the act of deimmobilization as provided in R.S. 9:1149.6(A); and (c) a release of all mortgages previously secured by the manufactured home and/or the immovable property upon which the manufactured home was located.

C. Upon the issuance of a certificate of title by the commissioner, the manufactured home shall be deemed a movable, and shall be subject to all laws concerning movable property.

Added by Acts 1982, No. 524, § 1, eff. July 22, 1982.

Cross References

C.C. arts. 463, 464, 467, 468, 472, 490, 491, 493.

§ 1149.7. Reference to prior law

The provisions of this Part shall replace the provisions of R.S. 32:710(N) and whenever any reference is made in any law to R.S. 32:710(N), said law or laws shall be deemed to refer to the provisions of this Part.

Added by Acts 1982, No. 524, § 1, eff. July 22, 1982.

Cross References

C.C. arts. 463, 464, 467, 468, 472, 490, 491, 493.

CODE TITLE II—OWNERSHIP

CHAPTER 1. ACCESSION

Section
1151. Change in ownership of land or water bottoms as result of action of navigable stream, bay, lake, sea, or arm of the sea; mineral leases.
1152. Grant of mineral servitude on lands acquired by the state from agencies or political subdivisions by subsidence or erosion.

§ 1151. Change in ownership of land or water bottoms as result of action of navigable stream, bay, lake, sea, or arm of the sea; mineral leases

In all cases where a change occurs in the ownership of land or water bottoms as a result of the action of a navigable stream, bay, lake, sea, or arm of the sea, in the change of its course, bed, or bottom, or as a result of accretion, dereliction, erosion, subsidence, or other condition resulting from the action of a navigable stream, bay, lake, sea, or arm of the sea, the new owner of such lands or water bottoms, including the state of Louisiana, shall take the same subject to and encumbered with any oil, gas, or mineral lease covering and affecting such lands or water bottoms, and subject to the mineral and royalty rights of the lessors in such lease, their heirs, successors, and assigns; the right of the lessee or owners of such lease and the right of the mineral and royalty owners thereunder shall be in no manner abrogated or affected by such change in ownership.

Added by Acts 1952, No. 341, § 1. Amended by Acts 2001, No. 963, § 1.

Cross References

C.C. arts. 450, 499, 500, 501, 502, 504, 2728, 3525, 3536.
R.S. 9:1101, 10:9–105.

§ 1152. Grant of mineral servitude on lands acquired by the state from agencies or political subdivisions by subsidence or erosion

A. With regard to lands previously acquired or which may be acquired hereafter by the state of Louisiana from an agency or political subdivision of the state due to subsidence or erosion or other action of a navigable river, stream, bay, or lake or arm of the sea occurring after the effective date of the Louisiana State Constitution of 1921 and which are not subject to a mineral lease granted by the state of Louisiana on the effective date hereof, and which are subject to a mineral lease granted by such agency or political subdivision, or its governmental predecessor, on the effective date hereof, the state of Louisiana hereby grants to the agency or political subdivision, or its governmental successor, from which it acquired or may acquire such lands an imprescriptible and inalienable mineral servitude affecting all minerals underlying the lands so acquired. Any such servitude shall be treated as having been granted on the date of the change in ownership of such lands and the agency or political subdivision holding such servitude is granted the authority to lease or otherwise manage the mineral rights affected thereby in accordance with law.

B. The boundaries of such servitudes shall be fixed as follows:

(1) The state agency or political subdivision having an interest therein may submit to the secretary of the Department of Natural Resources a certified map or plat of survey prepared by a registered land surveyor showing the exact extent of the servitude area, along with such other proof of the boundaries thereof as the secretary may reasonably require. Upon sufficient showing of the boundaries of the servitude area, the secretary shall indicate his assent thereto on said plat and on his certificate evidencing the boundaries of such servitude.

(2) The office of mineral resources of the Department of Natural Resources and the agency or political subdivision holding such servitude may fix the boundaries of such servitudes or otherwise fix their respective interest with respect to such servitude by written agreement.

(3) In the event the boundaries cannot be fixed in either manner provided for above, then the secretary of the Department of Natural Resources, the office of mineral resources of the Department of Natural Resources, or the agency or political subdivision holding such servitude may institute an action in the parish where the property is located to fix the boundaries of such servitude in accordance with applicable law.

(4) A true and certified copy of any certificates, plats, agreements or judgments fixing the boundaries of such servitudes shall be filed with the secretary of the Department of Natural Resources and shall be recorded in the parish where the affected property is located.

C. Nothing contained herein shall have the effect of modifying or repealing R.S. 9:1151.

Added by Acts 1984, No. 839, § 1.

CODE TITLE III—PERSONAL SERVITUDES

CHAPTER 1. FAMILY HOME

Section
1201. Family home.
1202. Form of security for legal usufruct of surviving spouse.

§ 1201. Family home

The rights and obligations of all parties with respect to the family home and contents burdened in whole or in part with a usufruct in favor of the surviving spouse shall be controlled by the provisions of Civil Code Book II, Title III, Personal Servitudes.

Added by Acts 1983, No. 535, § 2.

§ 1202. Form of security for legal usufruct of surviving spouse

If security is owed to the naked owner by the usufructuary who is the surviving spouse, the court may order the execution of notes, mortgages, or other documents as it deems necessary, or may impose a mortgage or lien on either community or separate property, movable or immovable, as security.

Added by Acts 2003, No. 1207, § 1.

Editor's note. Section 3 of Acts 2003, No. 1207 declares that: "The provisions of this Act are interpretative, procedural and remedial." Section 4 of the same Act requests the Louisiana State Law Institute "to write comments to all changes made by this Act."

CODE TITLE IV—PREDIAL SERVITUDES

CHAPTER 1. GENERAL PROVISIONS

Section
1251. Passage to or from waters or recreational sites; servitudes or rights of way or passage not acquired.
1252. Creation of real right for educational, charitable, or historic purposes.
1253. Public transportation servitude.
1254. Enclosed estate; right and servitude of passage on certain waterways.
1255. Solar collectors; right of use.

§ 1251. Passage to or from waters or recreational sites; servitudes or rights of way or passage not acquired

A. Any other provisions of the laws of this state to the contrary notwithstanding, whenever any land owner voluntarily, whether expressly or tacitly, permits passage through or across his land by certain persons or by the public, solely for the purpose of providing a convenience to such persons in the ingress and egress to and from waters for boating, or for the purpose of ingress and egress to and from any recreational site, neither the public nor any person shall thereby acquire a servitude or right of passage, nor shall such passage become a public road or street by reason of upkeep, maintenance, or work performed thereon by any governing authority.

B. The provisions of this section shall not be construed to:

(1) prohibit land owners from entering into enforceable contracts specifically granting servitudes or rights of way or passage;

(2) prohibit land owners from specifically dedicating roads, streets or passages to the public use;

(3) repeal any laws relative to expropriation or appropriation of land or servitudes or laws authorizing the legislature or governing authorities to open, lay out or appoint public roads or streets; nor

(4) repeal any laws creating servitudes along rivers, streams or other waters.

Added by Acts 1958, No. 463, § 1.

Cross References

C.C. arts. 456, 457, 665, 666, 705, 740, 3535, 3536.

§ 1252. Creation of real right for educational, charitable, or historic purposes

A. The owner of immovable property may create a perpetual real right burdening the whole or any part thereof of that immovable property, including, but not limited to, the facade, exterior, roof, or front of any improvements thereon to any corporation, trust, community chest, fund, or foundation, organized and operated exclusively for religious, scientific, literary, charitable, educational, or historical purposes, no part of the net earnings of which inure to the benefit of any private shareholder or individual, or to the United States, the state of Louisiana, or any political subdivision of any of the foregoing. A real right established pursuant hereto may additionally obligate the owner of the immovable property as is necessary to fully execute the rights granted herein.

B. A real right created pursuant to this Section shall be binding on the grantor, his heirs, successors, assigns, and all subsequent owners of the immovable property, regardless of the fact that the grantee does not own or possess any interest in a neighboring estate or the fact that the real right is granted to the grantee and not to the estate of the grantee, the fact that the real right was not created as a part of a common development or building plan, devised by an ancestor in title of the grantor.

C. A real right created under the authority of this Section shall be granted by authentic act and shall be effective against third parties when filed for registry in the conveyance records of the parish in which the immovable property is located. Any right or obligation imposed on the owner of the immovable property by the real right created pursuant hereto, including any affirmative obligation established therein, shall be enforceable by the grantee through judicial proceeding by actions for injunctions or damages brought by the grantee.

D. A real right granted under authority of this Section shall be non-transferable by the grantee except upon dissolution of the grantee in which case the real right shall be transferred to another similar charitable organization or to the state of Louisiana or any political subdivision thereof.

Added by Acts 1977, No. 234, § 1. Amended by Acts 1979, No. 212, § 1.

Cross References

C.C. arts. 639, 646, 775.

§ 1253. Public transportation servitude

Any road or street which becomes a public road or street under R.S. 48:491(B) shall be subject to a servitude of public transportation and utility running in favor of the parish or municipality in which the road or street is located. This servitude shall extend directly above and below the surface of the public road or street and shall grant to the governing authority of the parish or municipality and any public utility authorized by such governing authority the right to construct and maintain all public utilities, including but not limited to, the right to lay water lines, natural gas lines, sewerage lines, and electrical, telecommunications, and cable television lines.

Added by Acts 1986, No. 708, § 1.

Editor's note. Acts 1986, No. 708, § 2, provides that R.S. 9:1253 "shall be retroactive and shall apply to any road or street which became a public road or street under the provisions of R.S. 48:491(B); however, any and all pre-existing public utility servitudes above and below such roads or streets shall be unaffected by this Act."

Cross References

C.C. arts. 639, 641, 645, 646, 659.

§ 1254. Enclosed estate; right and servitude of passage on certain waterways

A. The owner of an enclosed estate who has no access to his estate other than by way of an existing waterway passing through neighboring property shall have a right and servitude of passage on such waterway. The existing waterway passing through the neighboring property shall be directly accessible from a publicly navigable waterway, and shall have been and shall still be capable of use for navigation by the owner of either the dominant or servient estate at the time of acquisition by act of sale, inheritance, or otherwise, by the owner of the dominant estate.

B. If more than one existing waterway is capable of providing access to the enclosed estate pursuant to Subsection A, the passage shall generally be taken along the shortest route of safe passage from the enclosed estate to the nearest publicly navigable waterway at the location least injurious to the intervening lands and waterways. The owner of the dominant estate shall not be required to traverse open waters which may become hazardous for small watercraft during inclement weather.

C. The provisions of this Section shall supersede any other provision of law to the contrary.

D. The provisions of this Section are interpretative and are intended to clarify Civil Code Articles 689, 692, and 705 and any other existing law as to the right and servitude of passage on waterways to enclosed estates which have no means of access other than by way of water due to the lack of sufficient land on which to feasibly construct a road, and shall have retroactive application.

Added by Acts 2004, No. 813, § 1.

§ 1255. Solar collectors; right of use

A. For purposes of this Section, "solar collector" means any device or combination of elements which relies on sunlight as an energy source.

B. No person or entity shall unreasonably restrict the right of a property owner to install or use a solar collector.

C. The provisions of this Section shall not supersede zoning restrictions, servitudes as provided by Civil Code Article 697 et seq., or building restrictions, as provided by Civil Code Article 775 et seq., which require approval prior to the installation or use of solar collectors.

D. The provisions of this Section shall not apply to property or areas which have been identified as historic districts, historical preservations or landmarks by any historic preservation district commission, landmarks commission, or the planning or zoning commission of a governing authority.

Added by Acts 2010, No. 274, § 1.

CHAPTER 2. LOUISIANA CONSERVATION SERVITUDE ACT

Section
1271. Short title.
1272. Definitions.
1273. Creation, conveyance, acceptance and duration.
1274. Judicial actions.
1275. Applicability.
1276. Uniformity of application and construction.

Editor's note. R.S. 9:1271 through 9:1276 were added by Acts 1986, No. 217, § 1. Section 2 declares that the provisions of the Act shall be effective on January 1, 1987.

§ 1271. Short title

This Chapter shall be known as and may be cited as the "Louisiana Conservation Servitude Act".

Added by Acts 1986, No. 217, § 1, eff. Jan. 1, 1987.

Cross References

C.C. arts. 3535, 3536.

§ 1272. Definitions

As used in this Chapter unless the context otherwise requires:

(1) "Conservation servitude" means a nonpossessory interest of a holder in immovable property imposing limitations or affirmative obligations the purposes of which include retaining or protecting natural, scenic, or open-space values of immovable property, assuring its availability for agricultural, forest, recreational, or open-space use, protecting natural resources, maintaining or enhancing air or water quality, or preserving the historical, archaeological, or cultural aspects of unimproved immovable property.

(2) "Holder" means:

(a) A governmental body empowered to hold an interest in immovable property under the laws of this state or the United States; or

(b) A charitable corporation, charitable association, or charitable trust, the purposes or powers of which include retaining or protecting the natural, scenic, or open-space values of immovable property, assuring the availability of immovable property for agricultural, forest, recreational, or open-space use, protecting natural resources, maintaining or enhancing air or water quality, or preserving the historical, archaeological, or cultural aspects of unimproved immovable property.

(3) "Third party right of enforcement" means a right provided in a conservation servitude to enforce any of its terms granted to a governmental body, charitable corporation, charitable association, or charitable trust, which, although eligible to be a holder, is not a holder.

Added by Acts 1986, No. 217, § 1, eff. Jan. 1, 1987.

§ 1273. Creation, conveyance, acceptance and duration

A. Except as otherwise provided in this Chapter, a conservation servitude may be created, conveyed, recorded, assigned, released, modified, terminated, or otherwise altered or affected in the same manner as other servitudes created by contract.

B. No right or duty in favor of or against a holder, and no right in favor of a person having a third party right of enforcement shall arise under a conservation servitude before its acceptance by the holder and a recordation of the acceptance.

C. A conservation servitude is unlimited in duration unless the instrument creating it otherwise provides.

D. Any interest in immovable property in existence at the time a conservation servitude is created is not impaired by the conservation servitude unless the owner of the interest is a party to the conservation servitude or consents to it.

Added by Acts 1986, No. 217, § 1, eff. Jan. 1, 1987.

§ 1274. Judicial actions

Any action affecting a conservation servitude may be brought by any one of the following:

(1) An owner of an interest in the immovable property burdened by the servitude.

(2) A holder of the servitude.

(3) A person having a third party right of enforcement.

(4) A person otherwise authorized by law.

Added by Acts 1986, No. 217, § 1, eff. Jan. 1, 1987.

§ 1275. Applicability

A. This Chapter applies to any interest created after December 31, 1986 which complies with the provisions of this Chapter, whether designated as a conservation servitude or as a covenant, equitable servitude, restriction, or otherwise.

B. This Chapter applies to any interest created before January 1, 1987 if it would have been enforceable had it been created after December 31, 1986 unless retroactive application contravenes the constitution or laws of this state or the United States.

C. This Chapter does not invalidate any interest, whether designated as a conservation or preservation servitude or as a covenant, equitable servitude, restriction, or otherwise, that is enforceable under any other law of this state.

Added by Acts 1986, No. 217, § 1, eff. Jan. 1, 1987.

§ 1276. Uniformity of application and construction

A. This Chapter shall be applied and construed to effectuate its general purpose to make uniform the law with respect to the subject of this Chapter among states enacting similar provisions of law.

B. The provisions of this Chapter shall supercede any conflicting provisions of Civil Code Article 608.

C. This Chapter shall not be applied or construed to allow or permit the holder or owner of such servitude to obstruct or in any way impede the construction, operation, or maintenance of needed public utility facilities as provided by law on the effective date of this Chapter.

Added by Acts 1986, No. 217, § 1, eff. Jan. 1, 1987.

Cross References

C.C. art. 608.

CODE TITLE V—BUILDING RESTRICTIONS [BLANK]
CODE TITLE VI—BOUNDARIES [BLANK]
CODE TITLE VII—OWNERSHIP IN INDIVISION [BLANK]

CODE BOOK III—OF THE DIFFERENT MODES OF ACQUIRING THE OWNERSHIP OF THINGS

CODE TITLE I—OF SUCCESSIONS

CHAPTER 1. SUCCESSIONS

Section
1400. [Blank].

PART I. PROCEDURE

SUBPART A. MISCELLANEOUS PROVISIONS

1421. Repealed.
1422. Certified copies of inventories in Parish of Orleans; admission as proof.
1423. Fees of experts and appraisers.
1424. Affixing of seals on succession property; preservation.
1425. Succession judgments affecting real property in Orleans; attorneys to file with assessor.
1426. Retirement plan; usufruct of surviving spouse.

SUBPART B. SMALL SUCCESSIONS

1431. Repealed.

SUBPART C. PRESUMPTIONS

1441. Presumption of death of military personnel.
1442. Succession of military personnel presumed dead.
1443. Proof of presumption of death of military personnel.

§ 1400. [Blank]

PART I. PROCEDURE

SUBPART A. MISCELLANEOUS PROVISIONS

§ 1421. Repealed by Acts 2001, No. 572, § 2

§ 1422. Certified copies of inventories in Parish of Orleans; admission as proof

Certified copies of original inventories of a succession taken in the parish of Orleans may be returned into the court having jurisdiction and when returned may be admitted as proof in the courts.

Cross References

C.C. arts. 947 to 952.

§ 1423. Fees of experts and appraisers

The fees allowed to experts, notary publics and appraisers appointed to assist in taking inventories of successions, tutorships, interdictions, and other proceedings requiring the taking of inventories, shall be fixed by the court appointing such experts, notary publics and appraisers, and shall be taxed as costs in those proceedings in which the taking of an inventory is required.

Amended by Acts 1970, No. 508, § 1.

§ 1424. Affixing of seals on succession property; preservation

On the application of an interested party, or on its own motion, the court may order the affixing of seals on succession property in the manner and to the extent directed by the court, and may take such other action as the court deems necessary for the preservation of the succession property in the interest of the succession, the heirs, and the creditors.

Added by Acts 1960, No. 31, § 6, eff. Jan. 1, 1961.

Cross References

C.C. arts. 947 to 952, 1100, 3197, 3261, 3263, 3267.

§ 1425. Succession judgments affecting real property in Orleans; attorneys to file with assessor

A. Whenever any real property situated in the parish of Orleans is included in a succession judgment, signed upon the presentation of a petition for simple possession and rendered without opposition, a copy of all such succession judgments shall be filed within fifteen days with the assessor for the parish of Orleans by the attorney at law representing the succession, and it shall be the duty of the attorney representing the successful litigant, if such judgments include any real property situated in the parish of Orleans are signed after opposition and litigation, to so file such judgments with the said assessor within fifteen days from the date the judgments become final.

B. Whoever violates the provisions of this Section shall be fined not more than fifty dollars or imprisoned in the parish jail for not more than sixty days, or both.

Added by Acts 1964, No. 43, §§ 2, 3. Amended by Acts 2006, No. 622, § 1.

§ 1426. Retirement plan; usufruct of surviving spouse

A. (1) If a recurring payment is being made from a public or private pension or retirement plan, an annuity policy or plan, an individual retirement account, a Keogh plan, a simplified employee plan, or any other similar retirement plan, to one partner or to both partners of a marriage, and the payment constitutes community property, and one spouse dies, the surviving spouse shall enjoy a legal usufruct over any portion of the continuing recurring payment which was the deceased spouse's share of their community property, provided the source of the benefit is due to payments made by or on behalf of the survivor.

(2) This usufruct shall exist despite any provision to the contrary contained in a testament of the deceased spouse.

B. The usufruct granted by this Section shall be treated as a legal usufruct and is not an impingement upon the legitime and a naked owner shall not have a right to demand security.

C.C. art. 890.1. Added by Acts 1990, No. 1075, § 1, eff. July 27, 1990. Redesignated as R.S 9:1426 by Acts 1997, No. 1421, § 6, eff. July 1, 1999.

Editor's note. In Boggs v. Boggs, 520 U.S. 833, 117 S.Ct. 1754 (U.S. S.Ct. 1997), the deceased first wife of a pension plan participant bequeathed to the surviving spouse one third of her estate in full ownership and the remaining two thirds to two sons of the marriage subject to a lifetime usufruct in favor of the surviving spouse. That spouse remarried, retired, and when he later died a dispute arose between his sons and the second wife concerning ownership of undistributed benefits in his health plans. It was agreed that, absent preemption, Louisiana law controls and that the first wife could validly dispose by testament of her community property interest in the husband's undistributed pension plan benefits. However, the surviving second wife maintained that the attempted transfer of interests by the testaments of the first wife in the pension plan of her husband was invalid under 29 U.S.C. § 1055 because the Employee Retirement Income Security Act (ERISA) preempts the application of the community property laws of Louisiana.

On certiorari, the United States Supreme Court held that ERISA preempts application of the community property laws of Louisiana in so far as such laws allowed the first wife to make a testamentary transfer of her interest in a survivor's annuity and that ERISA also preempted application of Louisiana's community property laws that would have allowed the first wife to make testamentary transfer to her sons of her interest in participant's retirement benefits consisting of monthly annuity payments made to participant during his retirement, the retirement plan benefits that he had taken as a lump sum and rolled over into his individual retirement account (IRA), and his shares of stock pursuant to employee stock ownership plan (ESOP).

Cross References

C.C. arts. 544, 573, 606, 607, 888 to 890, 894, 2338 et seq.

SUBPART B. SMALL SUCCESSIONS

§ 1431. **Repealed by Acts 1960, No. 31, § 7, eff. Jan. 1, 1961**

SUBPART C. PRESUMPTIONS

§ 1441. **Presumption of death of military personnel**

A person on active duty in one of the armed services of the United States, who has been reported missing under circumstances which have induced the armed service to which he was attached to accept the presumption of his death, shall likewise be presumed dead under the law of this state. Added by Acts 1960, No. 31, § 6, eff. Jan. 1, 1961.

Cross References

C.C. arts. 60, 61, 70, 934.

§ 1442. **Succession of military personnel presumed dead**

A. The succession of a person presumed dead, as provided in R.S. 9:1441, may be opened, administered, and his heirs or legatees sent into absolute possession of his estate, by the district court of the parish where he was domiciled at the time of entering the armed service, and in the same manner as the succession of a deceased person, except as otherwise provided in R.S. 9:1443. His heirs and legatees sent into possession of his property judicially may thereafter deal with such property as the absolute and unconditional owners, and third persons may safely deal with them as such.

B. If it is subsequently discovered that the person presumed dead is alive, and within thirty years of the date of the judgment of possession he demands the return of his property, the persons sent into possession thereof as his heirs or legatees shall return to him all such property which they still own, subject to the mortgages and other encumbrances which they have placed thereon. These persons shall also repay him the value of all property of which they were sent into possession and which they have alienated, and the amount of the mortgages and other encumbrances which they placed on property returned to him. The persons sent into possession as his heirs or legatees shall return to him the annual revenues of his property as follows:

(1) If he reappears within five years, they shall return two-thirds.

(2) If he reappears after five and within seven years, one-half.

(3) But after seven years' absence, the whole of the revenue shall belong to those who shall have been put into possession.

Added by Acts 1960, No. 31, § 6, eff. Jan. 1, 1961. Amended by Acts 1990, No. 989, § 8, eff. Jan. 1, 1991.

Cross References

C.C. arts. 60, 61, 70, 934.

§ 1443. **Proof of presumption of death of military personnel**

In a proceeding to open the succession of a person presumed dead, as provided in R.S. 9:1441, or in any other action or proceeding whatever in which the presumption of his death is an issue, this presumption may be proved by a certified copy of an official certificate of the armed service to which he was attached, or of pertinent excerpts from his service record, indicating that the armed service has accepted the presumption of his death.

Added by Acts 1960, No. 31, § 6, eff. Jan. 1, 1961.

Cross References

C.C. arts. 60, 61, 70, 934.

CHAPTER 2. ADMINISTRATION OF SUCCESSIONS

PART I. IN GENERAL

SUBPART A. PRIVATE SALE; PROCEDURE

Section
1451 to 1454. Repealed.
1454.1. Prescription against informalities of legal procedure.
1455. Repealed.

SUBPART B. DATION EN PAIEMENT; PROCEDURE [REDESIGNATED]

1471 to 1474. [Blank].

Section

SUBPART C. MINERAL LEASES; PROCEDURE [REPEALED]

1491 to 1493. Repealed.

SUBPART D. MISCELLANEOUS PROVISIONS

1511. Option for servitudes or flowage rights; perfecting.
1512. Repealed.
1513. Payment to surviving spouse without court proceedings.
1514. Credit unions; payment to surviving spouse without court proceedings.
1515. Payment to surviving spouse or children of deceased; last wages due by employers.
1516. Transfer or payment of monetary proceeds of minerals or mineral products, rentals, accrued royalties, and other funds related to minerals or mineral contracts belonging or payable to deceased person; authority; discharge of holder.
1517. Certain succession representatives; power of attorney.

SUBPART E. PUBLIC SALE OF SUCCESSION PROPERTY

1521. Public sale of succession property for purposes other than payment of estate debts or legacies.

PART II. BURIAL OF UNCLAIMED BODIES; ADMINISTRATION OF SUCCESSIONS OF $500 OR LESS.

1551. Burial of unclaimed bodies.
1552. Administration of successions of value of five hundred dollars or less.
1553 to 1557. Repealed.

PART III. PUBLIC ADMINISTRATORS

1581. Public administrators; appointment; terms; powers and duties.
1582. Bond.
1583. Administrators of intestate succession; when.
1584. Dative testamentary executors; when.
1585. Repealed.
1586. Curator of vacant succession; disposition of funds.
1587. Repealed.
1588. Power to represent state in court; costs.
1589. Compensation; employees; expense allowance; cost-of-living increases.
1590. Exemptions.

PART IV. STATE SUCCEEDING TO IMMOVABLE PROPERTY

1611. Retention instead of sale; administration.
1612. Compromise of rights and claims.
1613. Disposition of funds; apportionment and allocation.
1614. Special counsel; patents for interests.
1615. Application of sections.

PART I. IN GENERAL

SUBPART A. PRIVATE SALE; PROCEDURE

§§ 1451 to 1454. Repealed by Acts 1960, No. 31, § 7, eff. Jan. 1, 1961

§ 1454.1. Prescription against informalities of legal procedure

Any and all informalities of legal procedure connected with or growing out of any private sale of any succession property by executors or administrators, pursuant to the provisions of R.S. 9:1451 through 9:1454,[1] inclusive, authorized by an order of the courts of this state, to sell at private sale, shall be prescribed against by those claiming under such sale after the lapse of two years from the date of the sale; provided, that where any such informality of legal procedure has existed for a period of two years prior to July 27, 1960, an action to annul because of such informality must be brought within six months from and after July 27, 1960.

Added by Acts 1960, No. 367, § 1.

[1] R.S. 9:1451 to 9:1454 were repealed by Acts 1960, No. 31, § 7 and replaced by corresponding provisions in the Code of Civil Procedure. See C.C.P. Arts. 3261 to 3285. No position is taken regarding the application of the above section to informalities occurring under the new code provisions.

Cross References

C.C. art. 1171.

§ 1455. Repealed by Acts 1960, No. 31, § 7, eff. Jan. 1, 1961

SUBPART B. DATION EN PAIEMENT; PROCEDURE [REDESIGNATED]

§§ 1471 to 1474. [Blank]

SUBPART C. MINERAL LEASES; PROCEDURE [REPEALED]

§§ 1491 to 1493. Repealed by Acts 1974, No. 131, § 3

SUBPART D. MISCELLANEOUS PROVISIONS

§ 1511. Option for servitudes or flowage rights; perfecting

In any case where a person had executed in favor of the United States of America an option for the acquisition of servitudes or flowage rights in any of the spillways in the state and dies prior to the execution of the formal deeds, the administrator, executor, or curator, after having first obtained an order of court authorizing him to sign the deed, may effectuate such option, by deed in the form provided by the United States of America.

§ 1512. Repealed by Acts 1960, No. 31, § 7, eff. Jan. 1, 1961

§ 1513. Payment to surviving spouse without court proceedings

A. Any bank or other depository may pay to the surviving spouse of a depositor a sum not to exceed ten thousand dollars out of the deposits of a decedent or out of deposits of the community between the survivor and the decedent, deposited in the name of decedent or of the survivor or in the name of the decedent jointly with the survivor or otherwise, without any court proceedings, order or judgment authorizing the same or determining whether or not an inheritance tax is due. The surviving spouse shall give to the paying depository an affidavit that the total funds withdrawn do not exceed ten thousand dollars from all depositories.

B. In the event of such payment, the receipt of the surviving spouse to whom it is made is a full release and discharge of the payor bank or other depository for the amount paid and for any inheritance tax determined to be due, and no tax collector, creditor, heir, personal representative, or any other person shall have any right or cause of action against any bank or other depository on account of the payment. R.S. 47:2410 does not apply to such cases.

C. Notwithstanding the provisions of Subsection (A) hereof, in the event a surviving spouse possesses funds which have been deposited in an account listed solely in the name of said surviving spouse, the payor bank or other depository may release such funds in the account of the surviving spouse without liability for any estate, inheritance or succession taxes which may be due the state, provided the payor bank or other depository shall notify the collector of revenue within seven days of the release of any funds in such accounts.

D. Notwithstanding the provisions of this Section or any other provision of law, the provisions of R.S. 6:312 shall establish the exclusive method for payment of funds from an alternative account.

Added by Acts 1952, No. 539, § 1. Amended by Acts 1956, No. 559, § 1; Acts 1958, No. 126, § 1; Acts 1964, No. 194, § 2; Acts 1966, No. 235, § 2; Acts 1974, No. 20, § 1; Acts 1976, No. 316, § 1; Acts 1978, No. 153, § 1; Acts 1984, No. 54, § 1; Acts 1995, No. 1143, § 2.

Cross References

C.C. arts. 889, 890, 891, 935, 957, 1421, 1428, 1598, 2432.

§ 1514. Credit unions; payment to surviving spouse without court proceedings

A. (1) Any credit union in Louisiana may pay to the surviving spouse the value of any shares standing in the name of the decedent in the credit union not in excess of ten thousand dollars without any court proceedings, order or judgment authorizing the same and without determining whether the shares belong to the separate estate of decedent or to the community which existed between the decedent and the surviving spouse. The surviving spouse shall give to the paying depository an affidavit that the total funds withdrawn do not exceed ten thousand dollars from all depositories.

(2) The receipt of the surviving spouse for the payment shall constitute a full release and discharge of the credit union for the amount paid. No person, natural or juridical, shall have any right or cause of action against a credit union because of the payment.

(3) In the event such deceased member of the credit union leaves no surviving spouse, the credit union may pay the balance in the deceased member's share account to the major children of the deceased upon presentment of an affidavit that the total funds withdrawn do not exceed ten thousand dollars from all depositories.

(4) The receipt of a major child of the deceased member for the payment shall constitute a full release and discharge of the credit union for the amount paid. No person, natural or juridical, shall have any right or cause of action against a credit union because of the payment.

B. (1) Any credit union may pay to the surviving spouse of a depositor a sum not to exceed ten thousand dollars out of the deposits of a decedent or out of deposits of the community between the survivor and the decedent, deposited in the name of decedent or of the survivor or in the name of the decedent jointly with the survivor or otherwise, without any court proceedings, order or judgment authorizing the same. The surviving spouse shall give the paying depository an affidavit that the total funds withdrawn do not exceed ten thousand dollars from all depositories.

(2) The receipt of the surviving spouse to whom payment is made is a full release and discharge of the payor credit union for the amount paid, and no tax collector, creditor, heir, personal representative, or any other person shall have any right or cause of action against any credit union on account of the payment.

C. Notwithstanding the provisions of this Section or any other provision of law, the provisions of R.S. 6:664 shall establish the exclusive method for payment of funds from a multiple party account.

Added by Acts 1964, No. 166, § 1. Amended by Acts 1966, No. 235, § 2; Acts 1974, No. 20, § 1; Acts 1978, No. 153, § 1; Acts 1984, No. 54, § 1; Acts 1995, No. 293, § 2; Acts 2010, No. 175, § 2.

Cross References

C.C. arts. 889, 890, 891, 1428, 1598.

§ 1515. Payment to surviving spouse or children of deceased; last wages due by employers

A. Any employer may pay to the surviving spouse of a deceased employee any wages, sick leave, annual leave, or other benefits due to a deceased employee, provided neither spouse has instituted a divorce proceeding. In the event the deceased employee leaves no surviving spouse or if either spouse has instituted a divorce proceeding, the employer may pay the last wages and other benefits to any major child of the deceased employee.

B. Before making such payment to the person requesting same, the employer shall require such person to execute an instrument before two witnesses which shall give the name, address, date and place of death of the deceased employee, the relationship of the person requesting payment to said employee, the name and address of the surviving spouse, or children, if any, of said deceased employee and such other information as the employer may require.

C. The employer may make the payments referred to in this Section, without any court proceedings, order, or judgment authorizing the same and without determining whether or not any inheritance taxes may be due or whether the funds belong to the separate estate of decedent or to the community which existed between the decedent and the surviving spouse, but only if the employer forwards an affidavit stating the name of the deceased, the amount paid, the name of the recipient, and a copy of the release document substantiating the release to the secretary of the Department of Revenue within ten calendar days of the release of the funds.

D. The execution of the instrument referred to in Subsection B and the receipt of such person for such payment shall constitute a full release and discharge of the employer for the amount paid and for all inheritance taxes which may be determined to be due. No person natural or juridical shall have any right or cause of action against such employer because of such payment. R.S. 47:2410 does not apply in such cases.

E. The term "employer" as used in this Section includes the state and any of its political subdivisions which employed such deceased employee and owed him any wages, sick leave, annual leave, or other employment benefits at the time of death.

Added by Acts 1968, No. 253, § 1. Amended by Acts 1974, No. 152, § 1; Acts 1978, No. 96, § 1; Acts 1992, No. 604, § 1; Acts 2005, No. 24, § 1, eff. June 9, 2005.

Cross References

C.C. arts. 889, 890, 891, 1428, 1598, 1857.

§ 1516. Transfer or payment of monetary proceeds of minerals or mineral products, rentals, accrued royalties, and other funds related to minerals or mineral contracts belonging or payable to deceased person; authority; discharge of holder

A. Upon proper authority any holder of monetary proceeds of minerals or mineral products, rentals, accrued royalties or other funds related to minerals or mineral products, belonging or payable to a deceased person, under the terms of a mineral lease or other contract, by operation of law or otherwise, may transfer or pay the same to the decedent's succession representatives, heirs, or the legal representatives of the heirs. The letters of the succession representative or the judgment recognizing and putting the heirs in possession, issued by a Louisiana court of competent jurisdiction, and accompanied by letters of tutorship or curatorship of the heirs who are not sui juris, shall constitute proper authority for making the transfer or payment which when so made shall be full protection to the holder. Conclusive proof to the holder of the letters or judgment and of the jurisdiction of the court rendering them shall result from copies thereof, duly certified.

B. Nothing contained in this section shall be construed as limiting the rights of a holder in making any transfer or payment under the terms and provisions of a mineral lease or other contract, or under existing law.

C. The term "holder" as used in this section means any natural person, corporation, association, partnership, receiver, tutor, curator, executor, administrator, fiduciary, or representative of any kind, in possession of the monetary proceeds of minerals or mineral products, rentals, accrued royalties or other funds related to minerals or mineral contracts, belonging or payable to a deceased person.

D. All laws or parts of laws in conflict herewith are hereby repealed. It is expressly provided however, that R.S. 30:105 through 108 [1] shall not be repealed by the provisions of this section, nor shall this section be construed as altering or affecting the provisions of R.S. 47:2413.

Added by Acts 1970, No. 153, § 1.

[1] R.S. 30:105 to 30:107 were repealed by Acts 1974, No. 50, § 3. See, now, R.S. 31:210, 31:211.

Cross References

C.C. arts. 889, 890, 891.

§ 1517. Certain succession representatives; power of attorney

Any person confirmed as a testamentary executor, or appointed dative testamentary executor, provisional administrator, or administrator of a succession may, by power of attorney, designate a person to manage in his stead. The mandatary may substitute another person to manage in his stead but only if the procuration empowers him to substitute.

Added by Acts 1985, No. 284, § 1.

Editor's note. A prior R.S. 9:1517 was repealed by Acts 1979, No. 709, § 5, eff. January 1, 1980.

SUBPART E. PUBLIC SALE OF SUCCESSION PROPERTY

§ 1521. Public sale of succession property for purposes other than payment of estate debts or legacies

A. The property of a succession, movable, immovable, or both, may be sold at public auction for any purpose. There shall be no priority in the order of sale as between movable and immovable property when succession property is sold for any purpose other than the payment of estate debts or legacies.

B. An administrator or executor desiring to sell succession property at public auction for any purpose other than the payment of estate debts or legacies shall petition the court for authority therefor, describing the property and setting forth the reasons for the sale. When it considers the sale to be in the best interest of the succession, heirs, and succession creditors the court shall render an order authorizing the sale of the property at public auction.

C. Except as otherwise provided in this Section, the property shall be sold in the manner provided for the sale of succession property at public auction to pay estate debts or legacies.

Added by Acts 1956, No. 387, § 1. Amended by Acts 1997, No. 1421, § 4, eff. July 1, 1999.

PART II. BURIAL OF UNCLAIMED BODIES; ADMINISTRATION OF SUCCESSIONS OF $500 OR LESS

§ 1551. Burial of unclaimed bodies

A. (1) Upon oral or written refusal by next of kin, as provided in R.S. 8:655, to bury a decedent, the coroner is authorized to immediately release the remains of the decedent to any interested party who will claim the remains and provide interment for the remains.

(2) The coroner shall have custody of the bodies of all persons who die within the parish and whose bodies are not claimed by friends or relatives. If the decedent had no known property or assets of a sufficient value to defray the expenses of burial, the coroner shall make such disposition of the body of the decedent as is otherwise provided by law for indigents.

B. If a decedent's body is unclaimed by friends or relatives and the decedent had known assets or property of a sufficient value to defray the expenses of burial, the coroner shall cause the body to be interred within thirty days, preferably by a recognized funeral home. The invoices for the expenses of the burial shall be forwarded to the public administrator if there is one in the parish or to the clerk of the district court if there is no public administrator, and the person or official authorized by law to be appointed administrator of the succession of the decedent shall provide for the payment of the burial expenses out of the assets of the decedent in accordance with the existing provisions of law for the administration of successions and in accordance with the provisions of this Part.

Added by Acts 1963, No. 92, § 1. Amended by Acts 2001, No. 326, § 1; Acts 2010, No. 175, § 2.

§ 1552. Administration of successions of value of five hundred dollars or less

A. Upon notification by the coroner of the burial of a person pursuant to the provisions of this Part, the public administrator or the clerk of the district court, as the case may be, shall cause the successions of such persons to be opened judicially in accordance with the existing provisions of law relative to vacant successions if the judicial opening of the succession is required by law and the succession has not been opened judicially by other proceedings within the delays provided by law. If the assets of the succession are of the value of five hundred dollars or less, the person or official who qualifies as administrator of the succession if the succession is opened judicially, or the official authorized by law to be appointed administrator but who does not judicially open the succession when the judicial opening of the succession is not required by law, shall not be entitled to any of the fees or compensation otherwise provided by law for the administration of vacant successions until and unless all expenses of burial have been paid in full and there shall be no costs of court, sheriff's costs, or fees payable out of the assets of the succession other than the costs of advertising when required by law, until and unless all expenses of burial have been paid in full.

B. The administrator of a vacant succession of the value of five hundred dollars or less shall pay the expenses of the burial of the decedent out of the assets of the succession. Any remaining assets of the decedent in such a succession shall be sold in accordance with law and the proceeds delivered by the administrator to the parish coroner to defray the expenses of the office of the coroner in the administration of the provisions of this Part.

C. The officials authorized by law to be appointed administrators of vacant successions shall have authority to administer those successions having assets of a value of five hundred dollars or less, and having no immovable property, in accordance with the procedure in Articles 3431 through 3434 of the Code of Civil Procedure pertaining to small successions. The officials shall execute the affidavits required by Article 3432 of the Code of Civil Procedure for heirs or surviving spouses, setting forth the additional fact that no friends or relatives or heirs of the decedent claimed the body of the decedent and that the decedent's burial was provided by the coroner pursuant to the provisions of this Part. Upon the execution of an affidavit, the official authorized to be appointed administrator of the vacant succession shall have authority to receive all property and funds of the decedent and to execute a receipt and release therefor in accordance with the provisions of Article 3434 of the Code of Civil Procedure applicable to heirs or surviving spouses. No judicial opening of the succession shall be required, and the official authorized hereby to act shall sell any property of the decedent, other than immovables, without inventory, appraisement, advertisement, or judicial authorization at private sale upon the terms and conditions and for a price the official shall determine in his sound discretion. The proceeds of such sales and the funds of the decedent shall be disbursed in accordance with the provisions of this Section.

D. No coroner, public administrator, or clerk of court shall be liable for any good faith acts taken or performed by him or pursuant to his direction in the performance of his duties or in the exercise of his sound discretion pursuant to the provisions of this Part. No bond shall be required of the officials for the faithful performance of the additional duties imposed by this Part.

Added by Acts 1963, No. 92, § 1. Amended by Acts 2010, No. 175, § 2.

Cross References

C.C. art. 1097.

§§ 1553 to 1557. Repealed by Acts 1960, No. 31, § 7, eff. Jan. 1, 1961

PART III. PUBLIC ADMINISTRATORS

§ 1581. Public administrators; appointment; terms; powers and duties

The governor shall appoint public administrators for each parish of the state having a population of fifty thousand or more, according to the last census, whose terms of office shall be concurrent with the term of the governor. Except as is otherwise provided, they shall have the same powers and be subject to the same duties as are provided by law for administrators.

Amended by Acts 1960, No. 497, § 1; Acts 2003, No. 482, § 1.

Cross References

C.C. art. 1097.

§ 1582. Bond

Before entering upon the duties of his office, each public administrator shall file with the governor a bond with security, to be by him approved for the faithful discharge of his duties. Such bond shall be for not less than ten thousand nor more than fifty thousand dollars, at the discretion of the governor, and shall be for the benefit of and may be sued upon by any person interested in any succession administered by the public administrator. The amount of the bond may be increased at any time on the application of any person interested showing an increase to be necessary.

Amended by Acts 1960, No. 497, § 1.

Cross References

C.C. art. 1097.

§ 1583. Administrators of intestate succession; when

They shall be appointed administrators of all intestate succession in their respective parishes when there is no surviving husband or wife or heir present or represented in the state.

The filing of the application of the public administrator for such appointment shall be advertised three times within ten days in a daily newspaper of general circulation in the parish, with notice to any person who may wish to oppose such application to file his opposition thereto within ten days of the date of the first advertisement. If no such opposition is filed timely, or if an opposition thereto is filed but after the trial thereof the court concludes that the opponent has no prior right to the appointment, the court shall appoint the public administrator as administrator of the intestate succession.

Amended by Acts 1960, No. 497, § 1.

Cross References

C.C. art. 1097.

§ 1584. Dative testamentary executors; when

They shall be appointed dative testamentary executors of all testate successions in their respective parishes when, for any cause, the executor cannot discharge the duties of his office and when there is no surviving husband or wife or heir present or represented in the state.

Amended by Acts 1960, No. 497, § 1.

Cross References

C.C. art. 1097.

§ 1585. Repealed by Acts 1972, No. 146, § 2

§ 1586. Curator of vacant succession; disposition of funds

A. They shall administer them until the heirs present themselves and are recognized by the court and placed in possession. If no heir presents himself within one year from the date of the homologation of a final account, the public administrator shall pay the funds realized from the succession into the state treasury.

B. All public administrators shall maintain current records of all transactions involving cash or property. They shall be subject to audit at all times by the legislative auditor and shall furnish the legislative auditor, whenever requested, with statements of all judicial proceedings involving the public administrator and all other information requested by him regarding property received or administered.

Amended by Acts 1960, No. 497, § 1; Acts 2001, No. 1102, § 1.

Cross References

C.C. art. 1097.

§ 1587. Repealed by Acts 1972, No. 146, § 2

§ 1588. Power to represent state in court; costs

Public administrators may appear in court in behalf of the state to assert its claim to any succession in which the state may be interested. They shall not be required to advance or pay any costs of court or sheriff's costs or to give appeal or other bond in any judicial proceeding instituted by or against them in their official capacities.

Amended by Acts 1960, No. 497, § 1.

Cross References

C.C. art. 1097.

§ 1589. Compensation; employees; expense allowance; cost-of-living increases

A. In parishes of less than four hundred twenty-five thousand population public administrators shall receive as a compensation five percent on all funds administered by them, and all necessary expenses incurred in administering and preserving property subject to administration; provided such expenses, other than attorney's fees are authorized by specific court order before they are incurred.

B. In parishes of more than four hundred twenty-five thousand population public administrators shall receive as a compensation ten percent on all funds administered by them, and all necessary expenses incurred in administering and preserving property subject to administration; provided such expenses, other than attorney fees are authorized by specific court order before they are incurred.

Amended by Acts 1950, No. 339, § 2; Acts 1952, No. 200, § 2; Acts 1960, No. 497, § 1; Acts 1966, No. 102, § 1; Acts 1967, No. 76, § 1; Acts 1975, No. 271, § 1; Acts 1979, No. 774, § 1, eff. July 20, 1979; Acts 1985, No. 966, § 1; Acts 1991, No. 111, § 1; Acts 2001, No. 105, § 1.

Cross References

C.C. art. 1097.

§ 1590. Exemptions

R.S. 9:1581 through 9:1586 and R.S. 9:1588 and 9:1589 shall not apply to the parishes of Caddo, Ouachita and Calcasieu.

Added by Acts 1960, No. 497, § 1.

PART IV. STATE SUCCEEDING TO IMMOVABLE PROPERTY

§ 1611. Retention instead of sale; administration

In all cases where the state succeeds to the immovable property of vacant successions, and it shall appear to be advantageous to the state, as determined by the governor, the attorney general, and the executive counsel, or any two of them, for the state to retain the ownership of the property, rather than for the sale thereof to be provoked, these officers, or any two of them, may provide for the administration of the property, upon such terms and conditions as, in their opinion, are in the best interests of the state.

Cross References

C.C. arts. 902, 1095.

§ 1612. Compromise of rights and claims

These officers, or any two of them, may compromise the rights and claims of the state in relation to any immovable property of any vacant succession, upon such terms as they may deem in the best interest of the state.

Cross References

C.C. arts. 902, 1095.

§ 1613. Disposition of funds; apportionment and allocation

Any funds realized from any such administration or compromise shall be paid into the state treasury and credited to the treasurer's special fund for the payment of old age assistance, aid to dependent children, aid to the needy blind, mothers' and child health services, and aid to crippled children, in accordance with law, and may likewise be used in the work of the state hospital board, any such funds to be apportioned and allocated to such purposes by the governor.

Cross References

C.C. arts. 902, 1095.

§ 1614. Special counsel; patents for interests

In any case where the state has, under existing laws, employed special counsel to recover the rights and interest of the state in immovable property of vacant successions belonging to it, and the agreement is that attorneys are to receive a percentage of the property recovered, patents to the attorneys for their interests may be issued in accordance with existing laws, when the rights of the state have been finally determined.

Cross References

C.C. arts. 902, 1095.

§ 1615. Application of sections

R.S. 9:1611 through 9:1614 shall not be deemed to repeal the general provisions of the Civil Code nor the laws relating to the public administrator of the Parish of Orleans [1] and shall be effective only where the claim of the state to property of vacant successions is in dispute.

[1] See R.S. 9:1581 et seq.

Cross References

C.C. arts. 902, 1095.

CHAPTER 3. PARTITIONS

PART I. IN GENERAL

Section
1701. Partition of land in which United States has servitude or real right.
1702. Agreement not to partition by persons holding property in common.

PART I. IN GENERAL

§ 1701. Partition of land in which United States has servitude or real right

Whenever the United States, or any branch or agency thereof, has acquired a servitude, easement, or real right of any kind, nature, or description affecting a piece of land, or a portion thereof, which is owned in indivision, and said servitude, easement, or real right was acquired from less than all the co-owners of said tract of land, or whenever the United States, or any branch or agency thereof, has acquired a servitude, easement, or real right of any kind, nature or description affecting a tract of land, or a portion thereof, which is owned in indivision, and said acquisition having been from a co-owner, or a portion of the co-owners, insofar as his or their undivided interest in the tract of land or portion thereof is concerned, a subsequent suit for a partition thereof among the co-owners shall not affect the rights held by the United States, or any branch or agency thereof, in and to the land sought to be partitioned, nor shall the United States be made a party thereto, but said partition shall be made subject to the rights held by the United States, or any branch or agency thereof.

The provisions of this Section shall be considered remedial, retrospective, and retroactive in operation, as well as prospective in operation.

Cross References

C.C. arts. 646, 797, 807 to 817.

§ 1702. Agreement not to partition by persons holding property in common

Persons holding property in common may agree that there shall not be a partition of the property held in common for a specific period of time, not to exceed fifteen years; however, persons holding in common an electric generating plant or unit, or the site of such plant or unit, located in this state may agree that such plant or unit or site shall not be partitioned for a period of time not to exceed ninety-nine years. Any agreement under the provisions of this Section shall be in writing and shall be valid irrespective of the provisions of Civil Code Article 807.

Added by Acts 1987, No. 477, § 1. Amended by Acts 1989, No. 128, § 1, eff. June 22, 1989; Acts 1991, No. 349, § 2; Acts 2010, No. 221, § 1.

Editor's note. Section 3 of Acts 1991, No. 349 declares that the provisions of this Act "are remedial and shall have both retroactive and prospective effect."

Cross References

C.C. arts. 797, 807 to 817, 3528 to 3534.

CODE TITLE II—OF DONATIONS INTER VIVOS (BETWEEN LIVING PERSONS) AND MORTIS CAUSA (IN PROSPECT OF DEATH)

CHAPTER 1. LOUISIANA TRUST CODE

PART I. PRELIMINARY PROVISIONS

Section
1721. Title.
1722. Express private trusts authorized; application of Code.
1723. Dispositions containing substitutions.
1724. Construction of Code.
1725. Definitions.

Section

PART II. CREATION OF THE TRUST

SUBPART A. GENERAL PROVISIONS
1731. Trust defined.
1732. Inter vivos and testamentary trusts.
1733. Testamentary trust defined.
1734. Inter vivos trust defined.
1735. Gratuitous and onerous trusts.
1736. Conditions.
1737. Dispositions permitted.

SUBPART B. FORM
1751. Form of testamentary trust.

APPENDIX 1—REVISED STATUTES, TITLE 9

Section
- 1752. Form of inter vivos trust.
- 1753. Technical language not required; interpretation of instrument.
- 1754. Incorporation by reference.
- 1755. Acceptance by trustee.

SUBPART C. THE SETTLOR
- 1761. Settlor defined.
- 1762. Number of settlors.
- 1763. Who may be settlor of inter vivos trust.
- 1764. Who may be settlor of testamentary trust.

SUBPART D. THE TRUST PROPERTY
- 1771. General rule.

SUBPART E. THE TRUSTEE
- 1781. Trustee defined.
- 1782. Number of trustees.
- 1783. Who may be trustee.
- 1784. Jurisdiction over the trustee.
- 1785. Manner in which trustee chosen.
- 1786. Provisional trustee.
- 1787. Provisional trustee; security.
- 1788. Resignation of trustee.
- 1789. Removal of trustee.
- 1790. Effect of resignation or removal of trustee.
- 1791. Appeal from judgment appointing or removing trustee.

SUBPART F. THE BENEFICIARY
- 1801. Beneficiary defined.
- 1802. Sufficiency of designation.
- 1803. Requirement that beneficiary be in being and ascertainable.
- 1804. Settlor as beneficiary.
- 1805. One or several beneficiaries; separate beneficiaries.
- 1806. Concurrent beneficiaries.
- 1807. Successive income beneficiaries.
- 1808. Acceptance by beneficiary.
- 1809. Representation upon predecease of named principal beneficiary.

SUBPART G. EFFECTIVE DATE OF CREATION
- 1821. When testamentary trust created.
- 1822. When inter vivos trust created.
- 1823. Retroactive nature of trustee's acceptance.
- 1824. Consequence of trustee's failure to accept.

SUBPART H. TERM OF THE TRUST
- 1831. Limitations upon stipulated term.
- 1832. Effect of stipulation of excessive term.
- 1833. Term in absence of stipulation.
- 1834. Exceptions.
- 1835. Definitions.

SUBPART I. THE LEGITIME IN TRUST
- 1841. General rule.
- 1842. Effect of improper stipulation.
- 1843. Stipulation restraining alienation.
- 1844. Legitime burdened with income interest or usufruct.
- 1845, 1846. Repealed.
- 1847. Invasion of principal; legitime affected.

Section

SUBPART J. MARITAL PORTION IN TRUST
- 1851. General rule.
- 1852. Marital portion in full property.
- 1853. Marital portion in usufruct.
- 1854. Effect of improper stipulation.

SUBPART K. LIFE INSURANCE IN TRUST
- 1881. General rule.

SUBPART L. CLASS TRUSTS

A. GENERAL RULES
- 1891. Creation of class.
- 1892. Class members.
- 1893. Income and principal designations.
- 1894. Representation.
- 1895. Effect of death of class member during the term of the trust.
- 1896. Closing of the class.
- 1897. Term; general rule.
- 1898. Effect of stipulation of excessive term.

B. RULES GOVERNING WHEN MEMBERS OF A CLASS ARE BENEFICIARIES OF INCOME ONLY
- 1899. Distribution of income; forced heirs.
- 1900. Absence of living members before class closes; treatment of income.
- 1901. Closing of class; members living; effect; termination.

C. RULES GOVERNING WHEN MEMBERS OF A CLASS ARE BENEFICIARIES OF PRINCIPAL ONLY
- 1902. Closing of class; continuation of trust.
- 1903. Class not closed; termination of income interests; effect.

D. RULES GOVERNING WHEN MEMBERS OF ONE CLASS ARE BENEFICIARIES OF INCOME AND MEMBERS OF A DIFFERENT CLASS ARE BENEFICIARIES OF PRINCIPAL
- 1904. General rule.

E. RULES GOVERNING WHEN THE MEMBERS OF THE SAME CLASS ARE BENEFICIARIES OF BOTH INCOME AND PRINCIPAL
- 1905. Interests in income.
- 1906. Term.

SUBPART M. TRUSTS FOR EMPLOYEES
- 1921. General rule.
- 1922. Term of trust.

SUBPART N. ADDITIONS TO THE TRUST PROPERTY
- 1931. General rule.
- 1932. Form.
- 1933. Rights of person who adds property.
- 1934. Modification, termination, rescission, or revocation of trust to which property added.
- 1935. When addition by donation inter vivos effected.
- 1936. When addition by donation mortis causa effected.
- 1937. Definition of annual exclusion.

For Annotative Materials, see West's Louisiana Statutes Annotated

APPENDIX 1—REVISED STATUTES, TITLE 9

Section

SUBPART O. TRUSTS FOR MIXED PRIVATE AND CHARITABLE PURPOSES

1951. General rule.
1952. Invasion of principal in mixed trusts.
1953. Assignment of interest in trust and termination of trust for mixed private and charitable purposes.

SUBPART P. COMMUNITY PROPERTY IN TRUST

1955. Power to divide community interests.

PART III. THE INTEREST OF THE BENEFICIARY

SUBPART A. THE INTEREST OF THE INCOME BENEFICIARY

1961. Nature of the interest.
1962. Distribution of income.
1963. Permissible stipulations regulating distribution of income.
1964. Termination of income interest; undistributed income.
1965. Effect of termination of interest.

SUBPART B. THE INTEREST OF THE PRINCIPAL BENEFICIARY

1971. Time of acquisition of interest.
1972. Treatment of interest upon death of principal beneficiary.
1973. Shifting interest in principal.
1974. Substitute beneficiary's interest may be conditional.
1975. Requirement that substitute beneficiary be in being and ascertainable.
1976. Treatment upon death of substitute beneficiary whose interest is not conditioned on survival.
1977. Class as substitute beneficiary.
1978. Shifting interest in principal if beneficiary is descendant of settlor.
1979. Status of potential substitute principal beneficiary.

SUBPART C. REFUSAL

1981. General rule.
1982. Acceptance of interest in inter vivos trust by creditor; effect.
1983. Acceptance of interest in testamentary trust by creditor; effect.
1984. Rights of beneficiary who refuses interest in testamentary trust.
1985. Manner of refusal; effect of conditions.
1986. Retroactive nature of refusal.
1987. Effect of refusal upon trustee.
1988. Partial refusal; refusal in another's favor.
1989. Refusal of addition to trust.
1990. Effect of refusal upon interest refused.

SUBPART D. ALIENATION BY THE BENEFICIARY

2001. General rule.
2002. Restraint upon alienation.
2003. Form.
2004. Seizure by creditor; general rule.
2005. Seizure by creditor; special claims.
2006. Exemption from seizure.
2007. Use of words "spendthrift trust".

Section

SUBPART E. DEFERRED ASCERTAINMENT OF PRINCIPAL BENEFICIARIES OF REVOCABLE TRUSTS

2011. General rule.
2012. Provisional principal beneficiaries.
2013. Settlor as default principal beneficiary.
2014. Number of settlors allowed.

PART IV. MODIFICATION, TERMINATION, REVOCATION, AND RESCISSION OF THE TRUST

SUBPART A. MODIFICATION AND TERMINATION OF THE TRUST

2021. General rule; modification.
2022. Effect of reservation of right to revoke.
2023. Effect of reservation of unrestricted right to modify.
2024. Concurrence of settlors in modification.
2025. Delegation of right to terminate or to modify administrative provisions.
2026. Change of circumstances.
2027. Accomplishment of purposes becoming impossible or illegal.
2028. Concurrence of settlors in termination.
2029. Effect of termination.
2030. Combination and division of trusts.
2031. Delegation of right to amend.

SUBPART B. REVOCATION AND RESCISSION OF THE TRUST

2041. General rule; revocation.
2042. Effect of reservation of right to revoke.
2043. Revocation or rescission under general law.
2044. Concurrence of settlors in revocation; effect.
2045. Delegation of right to revoke.
2046. Effect of revocation or rescission.

SUBPART C. FORMAL REQUIREMENTS

2051. Form.

PART V. DUTIES AND POWERS OF THE TRUSTEE

SUBPART A. GENERAL DISPOSITIONS

2061. General rule.
2062. Limitation of duties by settlor.
2063. Relief from duties by beneficiary.
2064. Judicial permission or direction to deviate from administrative provisions of trust instrument.
2065. Judicial permission to deviate from administrative provisions of this code.
2066. Judicial permission or direction to deviate from investment provisions of trust instrument.
2067. Invasion of principal; action of court.
2068. Invasion of principal; provisions of trust instrument.
2069. Winding-up duty and powers of trustee.

SUBPART B. DUTIES OF THE TRUSTEE

2081. Breach of trust defined.
2082. Administration in interest of beneficiary; duty of impartiality.
2083. Dealing on own account.
2084. Loan by trustee to himself.
2085. Sale by trustee to himself.
2086. Self-dealing by corporate trustee.

For Annotative Materials, see West's Louisiana Statutes Annotated

APPENDIX 1—REVISED STATUTES, TITLE 9

Section
- 2087. Delegating performance.
- 2088. Accounting.
- 2089. Furnishing of information.
- 2090. Prudent administration.
- 2091. Control and preservation of trust property.
- 2092. Recordation of instruments.
- 2093. Defense of actions.
- 2094. Separation of trust property.
- 2095. Bank deposits.
- 2096. Co-trustees.
- 2097. Serving as officer of legal entity in which trust funds invested.

SUBPART C. POWERS OF THE TRUSTEE

- 2111. Extent of powers.
- 2112. Attachment of powers to office.
- 2113. Exercise of powers by two trustees.
- 2114. Three or more trustees; exercise of powers.
- 2115. Control of discretionary powers.
- 2116. Repealed.
- 2117. Expenses that may be incurred.
- 2118. Lease of trust property.
- 2119. Sale of trust property.
- 2120. Mortgage or pledge; borrowing.
- 2121. Compromise, arbitration, and abandonment of claims.
- 2122. Powers with respect to shares of stock.
- 2123. Stock subscription; incorporator; organizer; partnership; joint venture; limited liability company; other legal entities.
- 2124. Holding stock in name of nominee.
- 2124.1. [Blank].
- 2125. Contractual liability of trust.
- 2126. Tort liability of trust.
- 2127. Standard of care in investing and management.
- 2128. Common trust funds.
- 2129. Corporate trustees; deposit of securities in clearing corporation.
- 2130. Transfer of fiduciary accounts.
- 2131. Distributions.

SUBPART D. ALLOCATION TO INCOME AND PRINCIPAL

- 2141. General rule.
- 2142. Allocation to beneficiaries of income and principal.
- 2143. Allocation to beneficiaries of usufruct and naked ownership.
- 2144. Income and principal distinguished.
- 2145. When right to income arises.
- 2146. Apportionment of receipts when right to income arises.
- 2147. Apportionment of receipts when right to income ceases.
- 2148. Succession receipts.
- 2149. Corporate distributions.
- 2150. Bonds.
- 2151. Business operations.
- 2152. Proceeds of mineral interests.
- 2153. Timber.
- 2154. Other property subject to depletion.
- 2155. Underproductive property.
- 2156. Charges.
- 2157. Inventory value defined.

Section

SUBPART E. POWER TO ADJUST

- 2158. Power to adjust.
- 2159. When the power to adjust is denied.
- 2160. Adjustment benefiting trustee.
- 2161. Adjustment beyond percentage limit.
- 2162. General provisions regarding court orders affecting adjustments.
- 2163. Remedies.

SUBPART F. THE TRUSTEE'S BOND

- 2171. Individual and corporate trustees.
- 2172. Security required by court.
- 2173. Increasing, diminishing, or dispensing with trustee's security by court.

PART VI. COMPENSATION AND INDEMNITY OF THE TRUSTEE

SUBPART A. COMPENSATION OF THE TRUSTEE

- 2181. General rule.
- 2182. Effect of breach of trust upon compensation.

SUBPART B. INDEMNITY OF THE TRUSTEE

- 2191. Indemnity for expenses properly incurred.
- 2192. Indemnity for expenses not properly incurred.
- 2193. Liability of beneficiary.
- 2194. Charge on beneficiary's interest.
- 2195. Charge on beneficiary's interest; advance or loan of trust money.
- 2196. Indemnity for tort liability.

PART VII. LIABILITIES OF THE TRUSTEE

- 2201. General rule.
- 2202. Loss not resulting from breach of trust.
- 2203. Balancing losses against gains.
- 2204. Liability of successor trustee.
- 2205. Liability of co-trustee.
- 2206. Relief from liability by trust instrument.
- 2207. Relief from liability by beneficiary.
- 2208. Relief from liability by proper court.

PART VIII. REMEDIES OF THE BENEFICIARY

- 2221. Remedies against trustee.
- 2222. Remedies against third persons.

PART IX. ACTIONS

- 2231. Causes of action; procedure.
- 2232. Injunctive relief.
- 2233. Instructions.
- 2234. Prescription.
- 2235. Proper court.

PART X. DESIGNATION OF ATTORNEY OR REGISTERED AGENT

- 2241. General rule.
- 2242. Registered agent for service of process.

PART XI. VALIDATION

- 2251. Severability of provisions of trust instrument.
- 2252. Saving clause.

For Annotative Materials, see West's Louisiana Statutes Annotated

APPENDIX 1—REVISED STATUTES, TITLE 9

PART I. PRELIMINARY PROVISIONS

§ 1721. Title

This Chapter shall be known and may be cited as the Louisiana Trust Code.

Added by Acts 1964, No. 338, § 2.

Cross References

C.C. arts. 476, 477, 1520, 3528 to 3534.

§ 1722. Express private trusts authorized; application of Code

Express private trusts are hereby authorized subject to the rules prescribed in this Code.

Added by Acts 1964, No. 338, § 2.

Comments—1964

This Code does not treat constructive trusts and does not affect the Louisiana jurisprudence on constructive trusts. See Pascal, Some ABC's About Trusts and Us, 13 La.L.Rev. 555, 558 (1953).

Cross References

C.C. arts. 476, 477, 1520.

§ 1723. Dispositions containing substitutions

A disposition authorized by this Code may be made in trust although it would contain a prohibited substitution if it were made free of trust.

Added by Acts 1964, No. 338, § 2.

Comments—1964

This section makes no change in the law. It, together with Const. [1921], Art. IV, Sec. 16, as amended [see, now, Const. 1974, Art. 12, § 5], removes any doubt engendered by the decisions in Succession of Guillory, 232 La. 213, 94 S.2d 38 (1957), and in Succession of Meadors, 135 S.2d 679 (La.App.1961), concerning the validity of substitutions in trust. Each of these cases may be interpreted as having held a disposition to be invalid because the instrument failed to indicate that the disposition was made in favor of separate beneficiaries of the same trust, but it was feared that the decisions rested upon a broader basis, that all substitutions in trust were prohibited. Art. IV, Sec. 16 of the Constitution states affirmatively that the legislature may authorize substitutions in trust. A disposition in trust which this Code authorizes is valid notwithstanding that it contains a substitution. See Oppenheim, A New Trust Code for Louisiana—Some Steps Toward its Achievement, 37 Tul.L.Rev. 169 (1963).

Cross References

C.C. art. 1520.

§ 1724. Construction of Code

The provisions of this Code shall be accorded a liberal construction in favor of freedom of disposition. Whenever this Code is silent, resort shall be had to the Civil Code or other laws, but neither the Civil Code nor any other law shall be invoked to defeat a disposition sanctioned expressly or impliedly by this Code.

Added by Acts 1964, No. 338, § 2.

Comments—1964

(a) The provisions of this Code should be liberally construed in favor of freedom of disposition so that its purposes may be accomplished.

(b) If no provision is made for a particular situation in the text of this Code, the Civil Code and other laws should be applied. But the rules of the Civil Code and of other laws should be applied only if it is impossible to reach a determination upon the basis of the rules stated in the text of this Code.

(c) A disposition sanctioned by this Code cannot be defeated by a provision of the Civil Code or of other laws of this state. This Code is considered to sanction a disposition in trust if its text expressly or impliedly authorizes the disposition.

Cross References

C.C. arts. 7 to 11, 2045 to 2057.

§ 1725. Definitions

Except when the context clearly indicates otherwise, as used in this Code:

(1) "Affiliate" means a person directly or indirectly controlling or controlled by another person, or a person under direct or indirect common control with another person. It includes a person with whom a trustee has an express or implied agreement regarding the purchase of trust investment by each from the other directly or indirectly, except a broker or stock exchange.

(2) "Income beneficiary" means a beneficiary to whom income is payable, presently, conditionally, or in the future, or for whom it is accumulated, or who is entitled to the beneficial use of principal presently, conditionally, or in the future, for a time before its distribution.

(3) "Person" means an individual, a corporation, a partnership, an association, a joint stock company, a business trust, or two or more persons having a joint or common interest.

(4) "Principal beneficiary" means a beneficiary presently, conditionally, or ultimately entitled to principal.

(5) "Proper court" means the court as determined by the provisions of R.S. 9:2235.

(6) "Relative" means a spouse, ascendant, descendant, brother, or sister.

(7) "Spendthrift trust," when used without other qualifying words, means a trust under which alienation by a beneficiary of an interest in income or principal is restricted to the full extent permitted by this Code.

(8) "Trust instrument" means the written document creating the trust and all amendments and modifications thereof.

Added by Acts 1964, No. 338, § 2. Amended by Acts 1972, No. 656, § 1; Acts 2010, No. 390, § 1.

Comments—1964

(a) Sub-sections (1), (3), (4), (6), and (8) make no change in the law.

(b) The definition of "income beneficiary" that was found in the Trust Estates Law has been changed in this Code to make it clear that there can be successive beneficiaries of income and that a principal beneficiary who is entitled to receive income may be an income beneficiary. *Cf.* R.S. 9:1792(5).

(c) The Trust Estates Law, R.S. 9:1792(11), defined "proper court" as meaning the district court having jurisdiction over the domicile of a resident settlor, if the trust was inter vivos, or the district court having jurisdiction over a resident settlor's succession, if the trust was testamentary. If the trust was established by a non-resident, "proper court" meant a district court that had within its territorial jurisdiction any part of the trust property at the creation of the trust. Arts. 2811, 2812, and 3401, C.C.P., regulate jurisdiction over the opening of a succession.

(d) The Trust Estates Law defined a "spendthrift trust" as one in which the interest of the beneficiary was subject to restraints on alienation. R.S. 9:1923D.

(e) Under this section an adopted child is a relative. Art. 214, R.C.C.

Editor's note. Acts 2010, No. 390, § 2, declares that: "The provisions of this Act shall apply to all trusts, whether created before or after the effective date of this Act [August 15, 2010], but R.S. 9:1895(A)(3) shall apply only to substitutions occurring after the effective date of this Act."

Cross References

C.C. arts. 2045 to 2057.

PART II. CREATION OF THE TRUST

SUBPART A. GENERAL PROVISIONS

§ 1731. **Trust defined**

A trust, as the term is used in this Code, is the relationship resulting from the transfer of title to property to a person to be administered by him as a fiduciary for the benefit of another.

Added by Acts 1964, No. 338, § 2.

Comments—1964

(a) This section makes no change in the law.

(b) The Restatement of Trusts 2d, Sec. 2, defines "a trust," when not qualified by the word "charitable," "resulting," or "constructive," as "a fiduciary relationship with respect to property, subjecting the person by whom the title to the property is held to equitable duties to deal with the property for the benefit of another person, which arises as a result of a manifestation of an intention to create it."

(c) Most of the other provisions of this Code are based upon the principles stated in this section. Because a trust arises out of the transfer of title to property to a trustee, this Code prescribes the manner in which and the circumstances under which such a transfer of title may be effected. Because the trustee holds title for the benefit of another, the office of trustee is surrounded by certain duties that may be prescribed by the terms of the trust instrument or in the text of this Code. Thus, a trustee is under a duty to collect and administer the trust assets, and to exercise that duty he usually may buy, sell, and lease trust property, and enter into contracts, suits, and compromises for its protection. As a fiduciary, he must act solely in the interest of the beneficiary. Sec. 2082; Restatement of Trusts 2d, Secs. 164–196.

Cross References

C.C. arts. 476, 477, 479.

§ 1732. **Inter vivos and testamentary trusts**

A trust is either testamentary or inter vivos.

Added by Acts 1964, No. 338, § 2.

Comments—1964

(a) This section makes no change in the law. All trusts may be classified either as inter vivos trusts or as testamentary trusts.

(b) Donations causa mortis, known in other states, are not permitted under the general law of this state nor under this Code. Succession of Sinnott v. Hibernia National Bank, 105 La. 705, 30 So. 233 (1901). *Cf.* Atkinson on Wills, Sec. 45 (2d ed. 1953).

Cross References

C.C. arts. 586, 587, 1467, 1468, 1469.

§ 1733. **Testamentary trust defined**

A trust is testamentary when it is created by donation mortis causa.

Added by Acts 1964, No. 338, § 2.

Comments—1964

This section makes no change in the law.

Cross References

C.C. arts. 1467, 1469.

§ 1734. **Inter vivos trust defined**

All trusts not testamentary are considered inter vivos, regardless of the time of creation.

Added by Acts 1964, No. 338, § 2.

Comments—1964

The Trust Estates Law provided that an inter vivos trust was created upon its acceptance by the trustee and was intended to take effect during the lifetime of the settlor. R.S. 9:1792(6), 9:1812. Under this Code, all trusts that are not created by donation mortis causa are inter vivos trusts, regardless of the time of creation.

Cross References

C.C. arts. 1467, 1468.

§ 1735. Gratuitous and onerous trusts

A trust may be gratuitous or onerous. It may be gratuitous as to one beneficiary and onerous as to another.

Added by Acts 1964, No. 338, § 2.

Comments—1964

(a) This section makes no change in the law.

(b) *Cf.* Arts. 1523–1526, 1772–1774 [see, now, 1909 and 1910], R.C.C.

Cross References

C.C. arts. 1909, 1910.

§ 1736. Conditions

A trust or a disposition in trust may be made subject to any condition not forbidden in this Code and not against public order or good morals.

Added by Acts 1964, No. 338, § 2.

Comments—1964

(a) The Trust Estates Law did not treat specifically the attaching of conditions to trusts or to dispositions in trust.

(b) This Code, the Civil Code, and the general law apply in determining whether the enforcement of a condition is against public order or good morals. The enforcement of a condition is not contrary to public order or good morals if this Code sanctions the imposition of such a condition.

(c) Except as otherwise provided in this Code, any condition that is not contrary to public order or good morals may be imposed upon an income interest in trust. Sec. 1961.

(d) A condition that may cause an interest in principal to be acquired by the designated beneficiary at a time later than the time prescribed by this Code is invalid, except as permitted by Secs. 1891–1906 (treating class trusts). A condition not forbidden by this Code, the non-fulfillment of which permits the principal beneficiary's acquisition of his interest to be set aside, is valid to the same extent a resolutory condition would be valid out of trust. Sec. 1971.

(e) The provisions of this Code, of the Civil Code, and of the general law apply in determining the effect that the invalidity of a condition imposed upon a trust or upon a disposition in trust has upon the validity of the trust or of the disposition in trust.

(f) The effect of the fulfillment or non-fulfillment of conditions imposed upon a trust or upon a disposition in trust is to be determined through an application of the principles of this Code, of the Civil Code, and of the general law.

Cross References

C.C. arts. 1765 to 1767.

§ 1737. Dispositions permitted

A settlor may dispose of property in trust to the same extent that he may dispose of that property free of trust and to any other extent authorized by this Code. A trust containing a substitution authorized by this Code is valid.

Added by Acts 1964, No. 338, § 2.

Comments—1964

(a) Except as provided in Secs. 1841–1847 treating the legitime in trust, Secs. 1891–1906, treating class trusts, and Secs. 1921, 1922, treating trusts for employees, the rules that treat of collation (Arts. 1227–1288, R.C.C.) and of the legitime (Arts. 1493–1501, R.C.C.) apply to a transfer of an interest made in favor of a particular beneficiary in trust to the same extent that they would apply if a transfer of a comparable interest were made free of trust.

(b) Art. IV, Sec. 16 of the Constitution [of 1921; see, now, Const.1974, Art. 12, § 5] states that the legislature may authorize substitutions in trust. A disposition authorized by this Code is valid although it would contain a prohibited substitution if it were made free of trust. Sec. 1723.

Cross References

C.C. arts. 454, 1520, 1521.

SUBPART B. FORM

§ 1751. Form of testamentary trust

A testamentary trust may be created only in one of the forms prescribed by the laws regulating donations mortis causa.

Added by Acts 1964, No. 338, § 2.

Comments—1964

This section makes no change in the law. A donation mortis causa may be made by the use of one of the testamentary forms authorized in the Civil Code (Arts. 1570–1595, 1597–1604, R.C.C.), by the use of the additional testamentary form given in the Revised Statutes (R.S. 9:2442), or, with respect to testaments executed outside this state, by the use of a testamentary form valid under the law of the place where the will is made or valid under the law of the testator's domicile, if the will is subscribed by the testator and it is in writing (R.S. 9:2401 and Art. 2888, C.C.P.).

Cross References

C.C. arts. 1469, 3528 to 3534.

§ 1752. Form of inter vivos trust

An inter vivos trust may be created only by authentic act or by act under private signature executed in the presence of two witnesses and duly acknowledged by the settlor or by the affidavit of one of the attesting witnesses.

Added by Acts 1964, No. 338, § 2.

Comments—1964

(a) The form for the authentic act is prescribed in Arts. 1536 and 2234 [see, now, 1833], R.C.C. An acknowledgment of an act under private signature may be made by a settlor in the presence of a notary or other authorized officer under the forms prescribed by R.S. 35:511–513, 35:551–555.

(b) Settlors of an inter vivos trust may execute the trust instrument at different times, before different witnesses, and before different notaries, even if the trust property consists partly of immovables.

(c) The Restatement of Trusts 2d recognizes that a writing is not essential to the creation of a trust unless a statute otherwise provides. Most states require that a trust of land either be created by a writing or that its creation be evidenced by a writing. Restatement of Trusts 2d, Secs. 39–50.

Cross References

C.C. arts. 1467, 1468, 1831, 1832, 1837, 1839, 3535, 3536, 3538.

§ 1753. Technical language not required; interpretation of instrument

No particular language is required to create a trust, but it must clearly appear that the creation of a trust is intended.

A trust instrument shall be given an interpretation that will sustain the effectiveness of its provisions if the trust instrument is susceptible of such an interpretation.

Added by Acts 1964, No. 338, § 2.

Comments—1964

(a) This section makes no change in the law.

(b) The purpose of this Code is to authorize express private trusts. The failure of a settlor to use the language of this Code, or other technical language, should not defeat a trust.

Cross References

C.C. arts. 2045 to 2057.

§ 1754. Incorporation by reference

A trust, whether inter vivos or testamentary, may incorporate by reference any or all of the terms of an existing trust. Unless the instrument otherwise provides, all amendments of the existing trust in force on the date of the execution of the instrument creating the new trust shall be deemed incorporated, but neither subsequent modification nor termination of the existing trust shall have any effect on the new trust.

Added by Acts 1964, No. 338, § 2.

Comments—1964

(a) The Trust Estates Law did not contain a similar provision.

(b) The decisions in Succession of Ledet, 170 La. 449, 128 So. 273 (1930), and Hessmer v. Edenborn, 196 La. 575, 199 So. 647 (1940), would render invalid an incorporation by reference in a testamentary disposition. This section creates an exception to the general law in permitting testamentary incorporation by reference. See Note, 26 Tul.L.Rev. 115 (1951).

(c) This section permits a settlor to establish a testamentary trust or an inter vivos trust by incorporating by reference the terms of an existing trust. It is not necessary that the incorporation by reference embrace all of the terms of the existing trust, but the existing trust must be clearly identified. The settlor of the incorporating trust may be someone other than the settlor of the existing trust.

(d) All pertinent amendments of an existing trust in force at the time of the execution of an instrument creating a new trust and purporting to incorporate provisions of the existing trust by reference are considered incorporated. If the existing trust is modified, terminated, revoked, or rescinded after the instrument creating the incorporating trust has been executed, the incorporating trust is not affected.

(e) Testamentary incorporation by reference is permitted in most states. Atkinson on Wills, Sec. 80 (2d ed. 1953).

§ 1755. Acceptance by trustee

The trustee may accept the trust in the trust instrument or in a separate instrument.

Added by Acts 1964, No. 338, § 2.

Comments—1964

(a) A trustee may accept a trust by joining in the signing of the trust instrument or a separate instrument. See Sec. 1824. The Trust Estates Law was not clear in prescribing the form the trustee was to use in accepting the trust.

(b) Unlike this section, the Restatement of Trusts 2d indicates that a trustee's acceptance of a trust may be implied from his words or conduct. Restatement of Trusts 2d, Comment (b) under Sec. 35 and Comments, Sec. 102.

(c) See Secs. 1821–1824 for the trustee's acceptance relative to the creation of the trust.

Cross References

C.C. arts. 1927, 1943.

SUBPART C. THE SETTLOR

§ 1761. Settlor defined

A settlor is a person who creates a trust. A person who subsequently transfers property to the trustee of an existing trust is not a settlor.

Added by Acts 1964, No. 338, § 2.

Comments—1964

Sec. 1931 specifically permits the transfer of property to an existing trust. The Trust Estates Law was uncertain in that respect. This section distinguishes between a settlor and a person who transfers property to an existing trust.

§ 1762. Number of settlors

There may be one or more settlors of an inter vivos trust.

Added by Acts 1964, No. 338, § 2.

Comments—1964

This section makes no change in the law. An inter vivos trust may be created by one settlor or by more than one.

§ 1763. Who may be settlor of inter vivos trust

A person having capacity to contract by onerous title may be a settlor of an onerous inter vivos trust. A person having capacity to contract by gratuitous title may be a settlor of a gratuitous inter vivos trust.

Added by Acts 1964, No. 338, § 2.

Comments—1964

(a) This section makes no change in the law.

(b) Capacity to contract is governed by Arts. 1780–1796 [see, now, 1918 et seq.], R.C.C.

(c) Capacity to make donations inter vivos is governed by Arts. 1470–1492, R.C.C. The incapacity of the settlor may be either relative or absolute. Art. 1471, R.C.C.

(d) A person must have the capacity to make donations inter vivos and the capacity to contract in order to be a settlor of a trust gratuitous as to one beneficiary and onerous as to another.

Cross References

C.C. arts. 1918 to 1926, 3519, 3529, 3535, 3536.

§ 1764. Who may be settlor of testamentary trust

A natural person having capacity to make a donation mortis causa may be the settlor of a testamentary trust.

Added by Acts 1964, No. 338, § 2.

Comments—1964

This section makes no change in the law. A person must possess the capacity to make donations mortis causa to be the settlor of a testamentary trust. Capacity to make donations mortis causa is governed by Arts. 1470–1492, R.C.C. The incapacity of the settlor may be either relative or absolute. Art. 1471, R.C.C.

Cross References

C.C. arts. 1470 et seq., 3519, 3529, 3530.

SUBPART D. THE TRUST PROPERTY

§ 1771. General rule

Property susceptible of private ownership, and any interest in such property may be transferred in trust.

Added by Acts 1964, No. 338, § 2.

Comments—1964

(a) This section makes no change in the law. It follows the rule of the Restatement of Trusts 2d and permits any property that can be voluntarily transferred to be held in trust. Restatement of Trusts 2d, Sec. 78.

(b) Things susceptible of private ownership (Art. 483 [see, now, 453], R.C.C.) and any interest in such things (Art. 487 [see, now, 476], R.C.C.) may be transferred in trust.

(c) A property interest for a definite, indefinite, conditional, or renewable term may be transferred in trust. The types of interests that may be transferred in trust include but are not limited to a lease for a term of years, a lease containing options to renew or extend, a mineral lease for a definite term or for the term of production, a usufruct for a term or for life, a mineral royalty, working interest, production payment, net profits interest, or other similar mineral interest, a patent, license, or other similar right granted by statute for a limited or renewable term, and other terminable interests in property.

(d) A property interest burdened with outstanding rights vested in another for a definite, indefinite, conditional, or renewable term may be an interest transferred in trust, including but not limited to a naked ownership subject to a usufruct for a term or for the usufructuary's life, property burdened with a lease for a term of years, a mineral interest burdened with production payments, net profits, or other similar interests, and other similar burdens terminable at the conclusion of a definite, indefinite, conditional, or renewable term. The termination of the burden affects the title of the trustee with respect to property in trust in the same manner that the termination of the burden would affect the title of a person with respect to property free of trust.

Cross References

C.C. arts. 453, 454.

SUBPART E. THE TRUSTEE

§ 1781. Trustee defined

A trustee is a person to whom title to the trust property is transferred to be administered by him as a fiduciary.

Added by Acts 1964, No. 338, § 2.

Comments—1964

(a) This section makes no change in the law. The title to the trust property is in the trustee. Thus, the trustee has power to sell trust property, and he is under a duty to defend his title unless the trust instrument provides otherwise. Further, a creditor of a beneficiary cannot during the term of the trust seize the trust property itself. As to the seizure of the interest of the beneficiary, see Secs. 2004, 2005.

(b) The Restatement of Trusts 2d defines "trustee" as the person holding property in trust. Restatement of Trusts 2d, Sec. 3(3).

§ 1782. Number of trustees

There may be one or more trustees of a trust.

Added by Acts 1964, No. 338, § 2.

Comments—1964

(a) This section makes no change in the law.

(b) See Comment (c) under Sec. 1783.

§ 1783. Who may be trustee

A. Only the following persons or entities may serve as a trustee of a trust established pursuant to this Code:

(1) A natural person enjoying full capacity to contract who is a citizen or resident alien of the United States, who may be the settlor, the beneficiary, or both.

(2) A federally insured depository institution organized under the laws of Louisiana, another state, or of the United States, or a financial institution or trust company authorized to exercise trust or fiduciary powers under the laws of Louisiana or of the United States.

B. A nonprofit corporation or trust for educational, charitable, or religious purposes that is designated as income or principal beneficiary may serve as trustee of a trust for mixed private or charitable purposes.

Added by Acts 1964, No. 338, § 2. Amended by Acts 1985, No. 534, § 1; Acts 1995, No. 215, § 1; Acts 1997, No. 1400, § 1, eff. July 15, 1997; Acts 2001, No. 684, § 1; Acts 2004, No. 521, § 1.

Comments—1964

(a) This section makes no change in the law.

(b) Capacity to contract is governed by Arts. 1780–1796 [see, now, 1918 to 1926], R.C.C.

(c) A natural person and a bank or trust company meeting the description given in this section may serve as co-trustees.

Cross References

C.C. arts. 29, 1918 to 1926.

§ 1784. Jurisdiction over the trustee

A trustee who accepts a trust established pursuant to this Code submits to the jurisdiction of the courts of this state.

Added by Acts 2001, No. 594, § 2.

Comment—2001

Prior to the enactment of this Section, the Trust Code did not contain any specific provision concerning jurisdiction over the trustee. Instead, the general rules and principles of jurisdiction applied. Under this provision, a trustee who accepts a trust created under Louisiana law consents to the jurisdiction of a Louisiana court. The proper court is determined by R.S. 9:1725. Jurisdiction over the trustee elsewhere, on some other basis, is not precluded.

Editor's note. Acts 2001, No. 594, § 2, enacted R.S. 9:1784, effective August 15, 2001. Section 4 of Acts 2001, No. 594, declares that "The provisions of Section 3 of this Act shall not apply to a transfer in trust made prior to the effective date of this Act."

§ 1785. Manner in which trustee chosen

An original trustee, an alternate trustee, or a successor trustee may be designated in the trust instrument or chosen by the use of a method provided in the trust instrument, but neither failure of the trust instrument to so provide nor disqualification or removal of the trustee for any reason, incompetence or unwillingness to act of the person so designated or chosen shall invalidate the trust. In such a case, the proper court shall appoint one or more trustees.

Added by Acts 1964, No. 338, § 2. Amended by Acts 1978, No. 391, § 1.

Comments—1964

(a) This section makes no change in the law.

(b) The Restatement of Trusts 2d, Sec. 108, permits the proper court or a person designated by the terms of the trust to appoint a trustee if a trustee is not named by the terms of the trust or if a trustee for any reason has ceased to hold his position. Restatement of Trusts 2d.

§ 1786. Provisional trustee

The proper court may appoint a provisional trustee if necessary to preserve, safeguard, and administer the trust property. The appointment may be made summarily upon the application of an interested party or upon the court's own motion.

Added by Acts 1964, No. 338, § 2.

Comments—1964

(a) This section tracks the language of Art. 3111, C.C.P., providing for the appointment of a provisional administrator to the extent that its language is suitable to trusts. It does not contain a phrase similar to the phrase of Art. 3111 that would permit a provisional administrator to be appointed only "... pending the appointment of an administrator or the confirmation of an executor ..." because a phrase of this type would unduly limit the use of a provisional trusteeship.

(b) The appointment of a provisional trustee is temporary and will probably occur: (1) if the trustee has not accepted; (2) if the trustee is temporarily incapacitated or for any reason is unable to serve; or (3) if an action is pending for his removal.

§ 1787. Provisional trustee; security

A provisional trustee shall furnish the security deemed necessary by the proper court.

Added by Acts 1964, No. 338, § 2.

Comments—1964

(a) The Trust Estates Law was silent on this subject.

(b) For provisions relating to the trustee's bond, see Secs. 2171–2173.

§ 1788. Resignation of trustee

A trustee may resign at any time by giving written notice of resignation to each of the beneficiaries or by mailing written notice to each at his last known address. The trust instrument may provide another method of resignation and notice.

Added by Acts 1964, No. 338, § 2.

Comments—1964

(a) This section, unlike the Trust Estates Law, requires a trustee to give written notice of his resignation to each of the beneficiaries or to mail written notice to each of them at his last known address unless the trust instrument provides otherwise.

(b) The Restatement of Trusts 2d, Sec. 106, states that a trustee may resign only with the permission of a proper court and with the consent of all beneficiaries (if all are competent) unless the trust instrument provides otherwise.

§ 1789. Removal of trustee

A. A trustee shall be removed in accordance with the provisions of the trust instrument or by the proper court for sufficient cause.

B. Additionally, a corporate trustee shall be removed upon the petition of a settlor or any current beneficiary, if the court determines that removal is in the best interest of the beneficiaries as a whole, another corporate entity that is qualified to be a trustee has agreed to serve as the trustee, and the trust instrument does not forbid such removal.
Added by Acts 1964, No. 338, § 2. Amended by Acts 2001, No. 594, § 2.

Comments—2001

(a) Subsection B must be coordinated with any provision in the trust instrument designating a successor corporate trustee. See R.S. 9:1785.

(b) Subsection B is designed to allow removal when the beneficiaries have good reason to be dissatisfied with the current corporate trustee but there is not sufficient cause for removal.

Editor's note. Acts 2001, No. 594, § 2, amended R.S. 9:1789, effective August 15, 2001. Section 4 of Acts 2001, No. 594, declares that "The provisions of Section 3 of this Act shall not apply to a transfer in trust made prior to the effective date of this Act."

Cross References

R.S. 9:3801 to 9:3814.

§ 1790. Effect of resignation or removal of trustee

Except as provided in R.S. 9:2069, a trustee who has resigned or who has been removed has no further authority with respect to the trust property. His resignation or removal does not affect his liability for his administration of the trust property.

Added by Acts 1964, No. 338, § 2. Amended by Acts 1995, No. 358, § 1.

Comments—1964

(a) The Trust Estates Law was silent on this subject.

(b) This section is similar to the provisions of Art. 4235, C.C.P., treating the authority and liability of a tutor after resignation or removal.

§ 1791. Appeal from judgment appointing or removing trustee

A judgment or an order of court appointing or removing a trustee shall be executed provisionally. An appeal from an order or judgment appointing or removing a trustee must be taken and the security therefor furnished within thirty days from the date of the order or judgment notwithstanding the filing of an application for a rehearing or a new trial. The appeal shall be docketed and heard by preference.
Added by Acts 1964, No. 338, § 2.

Comments—1964

(a) The Trust Estates Law was silent on this subject. Except for the limited time for taking an appeal provided above, an appeal from an order or judgment appointing or removing a trustee might be taken at any time within ninety days, under Art. 2087, C.C.P. This is much too long a period. *Cf.* Art. 4068, C.C.P.

(b) Under Arts. 2122 and 5251(10), C.C.P., the order or judgment appointing or removing a trustee must be executed provisionally notwithstanding any appeal. Also, *cf.* Arts. 2974, 4068, C.C.P.

(c) This section also applies to the provisional trustee.

SUBPART F. THE BENEFICIARY

§ 1801. Beneficiary defined

A beneficiary is a person for whose benefit the trust is created and may be a natural person, corporation, partnership, or other legal entity having the capacity to receive property. A trustee of a trust, in his capacity of trustee, can be the beneficiary of another trust. Neither the heir, legatee, or assignee of a designated beneficiary, nor a beneficiary by reason of a substitution under Subpart B of Part III of this Chapter, is considered a beneficiary for the purpose of fixing the maximum allowable term of the trust.
Added by Acts 1964, No. 338, § 2. Amended by Acts 1989, No. 110, § 1; Acts 1995, No. 414, § 1.

Comments—1964

(a) The distinction made in this section between a person for whom the trust was created and his heirs, legatees, and assignees is important in fixing the maximum allowable term of a trust. Secs. 1831–1835.

(b) Capacity to receive donations is governed by Arts. 1470–1492, R.C.C. The incapacity of the beneficiary may be either relative or absolute. See Art. 1471, R.C.C. The beneficiary is under a relative incapacity with respect to a settlor if he would be incapable of receiving a donation from the settlor free of the trust of property the equivalent in kind and value of the interest given.

(c) The Restatement of Trusts 2d defines "beneficiary" as "the person for whose benefit property is held in trust." "Person" includes corporations and unincorporated associations. A person incapable of holding title to property is incapable of being a beneficiary. Restatement of Trusts 2d, Sec. 3 and Comments, Secs. 116, 117.

Comments—1989

(a) The new second sentence makes it clear that a trustee of a trust can be a beneficiary of another trust.

(b) The revision of R.S. 9:1973 necessitates revision of the last sentence of this Section, to avoid an indefinite term through successive substitutions of beneficiaries. Without this change, for example, if a grandchild principal beneficiary should die intestate and without descendants and the children of a deceased sibling succeed to part of his interest, their lives would expand the allowed term, and if then one of those nieces or nephews dies intestate and without descendants, and were succeeded by his nieces and nephews or cousins of various generations, the longest lived of them and the previously-designated beneficiaries would govern the term, and so on.

(c) The life of a person who is an original beneficiary of the trust will continue to govern the term of the trust even if he or she also becomes a successor to another beneficiary's interest in the trust.

Cross References

C.C. art. 2801.

§ 1802. Sufficiency of designation

A beneficiary must be designated in the trust instrument, except as otherwise provided in this Code. The designation is sufficient if the identity of the beneficiary is objectively ascertainable solely from standards stated in the trust instrument.

Added by Acts 1964, No. 338, § 2.

Comments—1964

(a) The term "trust instrument" refers to the instrument that establishes the trust, to an instrument that modifies the trust, or to an instrument incorporating by reference provisions of an existing trust.

(b) The trust instrument must designate the beneficiary either by naming him or by stating standards whereby his identity can be objectively ascertained at the proper time. The exceptions referred to in this section are Secs. 1891–1906, 1921–1922, and 1951, treating respectively, class trusts, trusts for employees, and trusts for mixed private and charitable purposes. The Trust Estates Law required that all beneficiaries be ascertainable at the date of the creation of the trust.

(c) If the trust instrument does not designate a beneficiary, the trust fails. If either a beneficiary of income or principal is designated, the trust does not fail.

(d) In other states, a beneficiary may be designated through the exercise of a power of appointment. This section makes it impossible for the settlor to create a trust without a beneficiary or to reserve to himself or confer upon another the power to select a beneficiary subsequently. Restatement of Trusts 2d, Sec. 120 and Comment (c), Sec. 121 and Comment (a).

§ 1803. Requirement that beneficiary be in being and ascertainable

A beneficiary must be in being and ascertainable on the date of the creation of the trust, except as otherwise provided in this Code. An unborn child is deemed a person in being and ascertainable, if he is born alive.

Added by Acts 1964, No. 338, § 2.

Comments—1964

(a) The Trust Estates Law required that all beneficiaries be in being on the date of the creation of the trust except beneficiaries of trusts for the benefit of employees.

(b) The exceptions referred to in this section are Secs. 1891–1906, 1921–1922, and 1951, treating respectively, class trusts, trusts for employees, and trusts for mixed private and charitable purposes.

(c) The Restatement of Trusts 2d states that a beneficiary must be definitely ascertained at the creation of the trust or definitely ascertainable within the period of the Rule Against Perpetuities. The Rule Against Perpetuities is not known to the laws of Louisiana. Restatement of Trusts 2d, Sec. 112.

Cross References

C.C. arts. 26, 939, 940, 1429.

§ 1804. Settlor as beneficiary

A settlor may be the sole beneficiary of income or principal or both, or one of several beneficiaries of income or principal or both.

Added by Acts 1964, No. 338, § 2.

Comments—1964

(a) This section makes no change in the law.

(b) R.S. 9:1901 was identical to the Restatement of Trusts, Sec. 114. This section is similar to Sec. 114 of the Restatement of Trusts 2d.

(c) For example, under this section a settlor could establish a trust, designate himself as income beneficiary, and designate another person as principal beneficiary. Art. 1533, R.C.C., is inapplicable.

§ 1805. One or several beneficiaries; separate beneficiaries

There may be one beneficiary or two or more beneficiaries as to income or principal or both. There may be separate beneficiaries of income and principal, or the same person may be a beneficiary of both income and principal, in whole or in part.

Added by Acts 1964, No. 338, § 2.

Comments—1964

This section makes no change in the law. R.S. 9:1903, the source of this section, was amended by Act 44 of 1962 to remove any doubt engendered by the decision in Succession of Guillory, 232 La. 213, 94 S.2d 38 (1957), concerning the validity of provisions for successive beneficiaries of income or separate beneficiaries of income and principal. Even if some or all of the dispositions in trust authorized by this section contain substitutions, the dispositions are not to be considered invalid. The legislature is given power to authorize substitutions in trust by Const. [1921], Art. IV, Sec. 16 [see, now, Const.1974, Art. 12, § 5].

§ 1806. Concurrent beneficiaries

There may be several concurrent beneficiaries of income or principal or both.

Added by Acts 1964, No. 338, § 2.

Comments—1964

This section makes no change in the law. The principle once stated in R.S. 9:1903 (both before and after its amendment by Act 44 of 1962) and now stated in Sec. 1805 is reaffirmed in this section. Although the decisions in Succession of Guillory, 232 La. 213, 94 S.2d 38 (1957), and in Succession of Meadors, 135 S.2d 679 (La.App.1961), caused doubt to arise concerning the validity of provisions for successive concurrent beneficiaries of income or separate concurrent beneficiaries of income and principal, those decisions did not affect the concurrent enjoyment of interests in trust, as such.

§ 1807. Successive income beneficiaries

Several beneficiaries may be designated to enjoy income successively.

Added by Acts 1964, No. 338, § 2.

Comments—1964

(a) This section removes any doubt engendered by the decisions in Succession of Guillory, 232 La. 213, 94 S.2d 38 (1957), and in Succession of Meadors, 135 S.2d 679 (La.App.1961), and in some degree dispelled by the amending of R.S. 9:1903 in 1962 (see Act 44 of 1962), concerning the validity of provisions for successive beneficiaries of income. Even if some or all of the dispositions in trust authorized by this section contain substitutions, the dispositions are not to be considered invalid. The legislature is given power to authorize substitutions in trust by Const. [1921], Art. IV, Sec. 16 [see, now, Const.1974, Art. 12, § 5].

(b) It is not necessary that later beneficiaries of income succeed earlier beneficiaries of income simultaneously or at regular intervals.

(c) Some beneficiaries may enjoy interests in income successively and other beneficiaries may enjoy interests in income for the duration of the trust.

(d) Income beneficiaries may receive fractional interests in trust income different in size from the interests enjoyed by those who preceded them.

Cross References

C.C. arts. 546, 547.

§ 1808. Acceptance by beneficiary

A beneficiary need not accept the benefit conferred on him; his acceptance is presumed.

Added by Acts 1964, No. 338, § 2.

Comments—1964

(a) This section provides that the beneficiary's acceptance is presumed. The Trust Estates Law contained no rules affecting the matter.

(b) A beneficiary may refuse an interest in trust. Secs. 1981–1990.

(c) The acts of a trustee that occur before a copy of the beneficiary's act of refusal is received by him are valid. Sec. 1987.

(d) The Restatement of Trusts 2d states that acceptance by a beneficiary is not necessary to the creation of a trust, although the beneficiary may "disclaim" if he has not by words or conduct manifested his acceptance. Restatement of Trusts 2d, Sec. 36 and Comments.

Cross References

C.C. arts. 1927, 1942.

§ 1809. Representation upon predecease of named principal beneficiary

When a testamentary trust designates as principal beneficiary a person who is a descendant, a sibling, or a descendant of a sibling of the settlor, and that person does not survive the settlor, the descendants by roots of that person will be principal beneficiaries in his place, unless the trust instrument provides otherwise.

Added by Acts 2003, No. 480, § 1.

Revision Comment—2003

This Section makes the rule for testamentary trusts parallel to the rule for legacies not in trust in certain situations when the principal beneficiary predeceases the settlor. When the principal beneficiary who was a descendant, sibling, or descendant of a sibling of the settlor predeceases the settlor, the disposition of principal to the predeceased beneficiary does not lapse but passes to the descendants of the predeceased principal beneficiary by roots. This is the same result as would obtain under Civil Code Article 1593 if the disposition of principal in trust had been a legacy not in trust. The rules in this Section do not apply when the trust instrument manifests a different intention.

Editor's note. Section 2 of Acts 2003, No. 480 declares that the amendments to "R.S. 9:1809, 1893, 1963, 1965, 1990, and 2068 shall apply only to trusts created after the effective date of this Act. The amendments to R.S. 9:1979, 2051, 2131, 2159(1), and 2241 shall apply to all trusts." Acts 2003, No. 480 became effective on August 15, 2003.

SUBPART G. EFFECTIVE DATE OF CREATION

§ 1821. When testamentary trust created

A testamentary trust is created at the moment of the settlor's death, without awaiting the trustee's acceptance of the trust.

Added by Acts 1964, No. 338, § 2.

Comments—1964

(a) This section makes no change in the law.

(b) The Restatement of Trusts 2d states that a testamentary trust is created at the death of the settlor, and that the trustee's acceptance is not essential. Restatement of Trusts 2d, Secs. 35, 36, and 53, and Comments.

Cross References

C.C. arts. 548, 934, 1429, 1469, 1520.

§ 1822. When inter vivos trust created

An inter vivos trust is created upon execution of the trust instrument, without regard to the trustee's acceptance.

Added by Acts 1964, No. 338, § 2.

Comments—1964

(a) Under the Trust Estates Law, an inter vivos trust was created upon acceptance by the trustee.

(b) The Restatement of Trusts 2d states that an inter vivos trust is created upon a settlor's declaring himself trustee for another or upon his transferring property in trust. The trustee's acceptance is not essential. Restatement of Trusts 2d, Secs. 35, 36, and Comments.

Cross References

C.C. arts. 548, 1468, 1927, 1939, 1942.

§ 1823. Retroactive nature of trustee's acceptance

A trustee's acceptance is retroactive to the date of creation of the trust.

Added by Acts 1964, No. 338, § 2.

Comments—1964

Under the Trust Estates Law, an inter vivos trust was created at the moment of the trustee's acceptance and a testamentary trust at the moment of the testator's death. The Trust Estates Law did not state whether the trustee's acceptance of a testamentary trust was retroactive to the date of its creation.

Cross References

C.C. art. 954.

§ 1824. Consequence of trustee's failure to accept

If the trustee was not a party to the trust instrument, he must accept the trust in writing within a reasonable time after its creation, or the proper court shall appoint a trustee.

Added by Acts 1964, No. 338, § 2.

Comments—1964

(a) The Trust Estates Law provided that if a trust was created and there was no trustee, the trustee could be appointed by the court.

(b) If the person designated or chosen as the original trustee fails to accept the trust within a reasonable time after it is created, the court appoints as alternate trustee the person designated in the trust instrument or chosen by the use of a method provided in the trust instrument. If the trust instrument does not designate a person to serve as alternate trustee or provide a method by which he is to be chosen, or if the person designated or chosen is not competent or willing to act, the court appoints a trustee. Sec. 1785.

(c) The failure of a trustee to accept a trust within a reasonable time after it is created does not cause the trust to fail.

(d) The Restatement of Trusts 2d states that a trustee's acceptance or disclaimer is to be determined on the basis of his words or conduct, but if a trustee to whom property has been transferred fails to accept for a long period of time, he manifests an intention to disclaim. Restatement of Trusts 2d, Sec. 102 and Comment (c).

Cross References

C.C. arts. 979, 988, 1009.

SUBPART H. TERM OF THE TRUST

§ 1831. Limitations upon stipulated term

If the trust instrument stipulates a term and unless an earlier termination is required by the trust instrument, or by the proper court, a trust shall terminate at:

(1) The death of the last surviving income beneficiary or the expiration of twenty years from the death of the settlor last to die, whichever last occurs, if at least one settlor and one income beneficiary are natural persons;

(2) The death of the last surviving income beneficiary or the expiration of twenty years from the creation of the trust, whichever last occurs, if none of the settlors is a natural person but at least one income beneficiary is a natural person;

(3) The expiration of twenty years from the death of the settlor last to die, if at least one settlor is a natural person but none of the income beneficiaries is a natural person;

(4) The expiration of fifty years from the creation of the trust, if none of the settlors and none of the income beneficiaries is a natural person.

Added by Acts 1964, No. 338, § 2. Amended by Acts 1968, No. 132, § 1; Acts 1987, No. 164, § 1, eff. Aug. 1, 1987.

Comments—1964

(a) In other states, the term of the express private trust is usually limited by the Rule Against Perpetuities. As Professor Leach points out in his book upon this subject, "The Rule Against Perpetuities has a reputation for difficulty and abstruseness. It piles its own complexity on top of the feudal terminology and intricate rules of the law of future interests." Since the rule is bound up with common law future interests, it deals with remoteness of vesting and not termination of interests. See Leach and Tudor, The Rule Against Perpetuities (1957).

The Rule Against Perpetuities is foreign to the legal tradition of this state. This Code applies instead the rules of this Sub-part, which are based upon termination of interests. Restatement of Trusts 2d, Sec. 62, Comment (n).

(b) The Trust Estates Law did not make clear which settlor's life was relevant to measuring the term of the trust if a trust was established by more than one natural person.

(c) The Trust Estates Law did not provide a maximum allowable term for a trust of which none of the settlors or income beneficiaries was a natural person.

(d) The Trust Estates Law provided that a ten year term beginning at the settlor's death was the maximum allowable term of a trust if the term was not controlled by the life of a beneficiary.

(e) For the definitions of "beneficiary" and "surviving income beneficiary," see Secs. 1801 and 1835.

(f) For provisions as to the maximum term if the legitime is placed in the trust, see Sec. 1841.

Comments—1968

The purpose of this amendment is to clarify the scope of application of this section and the scope of application of Sec. 1833. The amendment makes it clear that Section 1831 applies only when the trust stipulates a term. A statement in the trust instrument that the term of the trust is the maximum allowable term, is a stipulation of a term. One minor change is made in the section. The fifteen-year period is extended to twenty years in all four subsections. The reason for this change is for tax purposes. Where income is payable to a charity, the Internal Revenue Service in certain situations permits twenty-year arrangements where tax savings are achieved.

Editor's note. Acts 1987, No. 164, § 2 provides that the effective date of the Act is August 1, 1987. Section 3 of the same Act declares: "Section 3. The provisions of this Act shall have both prospective and retroactive effect. The retroactive effect of this Act shall not be effective as to any trust created prior to August 1, 1987, if any settlor, trustee, or beneficiary thereof shall, on or before February 1, 1988, notify in writing all settlors, trustees, and beneficiaries of such trust of its objection to the retroactive application of this Act to such trust. Any such notification shall be filed in each parish in which the trust instrument with respect to such trust was required to be filed pursuant to the provisions of R.S. 9:2092."

Cross References

C.C. art. 1777 et seq.

§ 1832. Effect of stipulation of excessive term

A trust instrument that stipulates a longer term than is permitted shall be enforced as though the maximum allowable term had been stipulated.

Added by Acts 1964, No. 338, § 2.

Comments—1964

This section makes no change in the law.

Cross References

C.C. arts. 7, 1777.

§ 1833. Term in absence of stipulation

If the trust instrument stipulates no term, the trust shall terminate:

(1) Upon the death of the last income beneficiary who is a natural person; or

(2) At the end of the term prescribed by R.S. 9:1831(3) or 9:1831(4), if the income beneficiaries do not include a natural person.

Added by Acts 1964, No. 338, § 2.

Comments—1964

(a) The Trust Estates Law provided that unless an earlier termination was required by the trust instrument or by the proper court, a trust would terminate at the death of the last surviving income beneficiary or at the expiration of ten years from the death of the settlor, whichever was later, if at least one of the income beneficiaries was a natural person.

(b) The Trust Estates Law provided that unless an earlier termination was required by the trust instrument or by the proper court, a trust would terminate at the expiration of ten years from the death of the settlor, if none of the income beneficiaries was a natural person.

(c) The Trust Estates Law did not provide a term for a trust if none of the settlors or income beneficiaries was a natural person.

(d) For the definitions of "beneficiary" and "surviving income beneficiary," see Secs. 1801 and 1835.

Cross References

C.C. arts. 7, 1521.

§ 1834. Exceptions

The provisions of this Sub-part shall not apply to class trusts, to trusts by employers for the benefit of employees, or to charitable dispositions contained in trusts for mixed private and charitable purposes.

Added by Acts 1964, No. 338, § 2.

Comments—1964

(a) The Trust Estates Law did not prescribe a term for a trust established by an employer for the benefit of his employees.

(b) The Trust Estates Law provided that dispositions in favor of non-private beneficiaries were governed by the law regulating trusts for educational, charitable, or religious purposes.

(c) The Trust Estates Law did not permit express private trusts in favor of persons not in being, except trusts established by employers for the benefit of employees.

(d) Trusts established by employers for the benefit of employees and charitable dispositions contained in trusts for mixed private and charitable purposes may be of perpetual duration. Secs. 1921, 1951.

(e) Class trusts are covered in Secs. 1891–1906, trusts by employers for employees in Secs. 1921–1922, and mixed trusts in Sec. 1951.

§ 1835. Definitions

For the purpose of this Sub-part, the term "surviving income beneficiary" means a natural person designated in the trust instrument to enjoy a portion of trust income, whether presently or in the future, or even conditionally; a principal beneficiary who is designated also a beneficiary of income, whether presently or in the future, or even conditionally; and also includes a principal beneficiary who becomes entitled to enjoy income because of the termination of the rights of an income beneficiary. It does not include a beneficiary whose interest in income has terminated.

Added by Acts 1964, No. 338, § 2.

Comments—1964

(a) This section makes clear which lives are to be considered in determining the term of the trust. The Trust Estates Law was not clear as to whether or not the lives of beneficiaries who were to enjoy income in the future or conditionally, or whose interest in income had terminated, were included. This section removes that uncertainty. The lives of beneficiaries who are to enjoy income in the future or conditionally are included.

(b) An illustration of the last sentence of this section follows: "Income to my wife W for the rest of her life, principal to my son A, the trust to continue until my son A attains the age of 21 years." If W dies when A is a minor, the trust does not terminate but continues until A reaches the age of 21.

Cross References

C.C. arts. 550, 551.

SUBPART I. THE LEGITIME IN TRUST

§ 1841. General rule

The legitime or any portion thereof may be placed in trust provided:

(1) The trustee after taking into account all of the other income and support to be received by the forced heir during the year shall distribute to the forced heir, or to the legal guardian of the forced heir, funds from the net income in trust sufficient for the health, maintenance, support, and education of the forced heir.

(2) The forced heir's interest is subject to no charges or conditions except as provided in R.S. 9:1843, 1844, 1891 through 1906 and Subpart B of Part III of this Chapter.

(3) Except as permitted by R.S. 9:1844, the term of the trust, as it affects the legitime, does not exceed the life of the forced heir; and

(4) The principal shall be delivered to the forced heir or his heirs, legatees, or assignees free of trust, upon the termination of the portion of the trust that affects the legitime.

Added by Acts 1964, No. 338, § 2. Amended by Acts 1974, No. 126, § 1; Acts 1979, No. 160, § 1; Acts 1995, No. 414, § 1; Acts 1999, No. 967, § 1.

Comments—1964

(a) This Sub-part sets forth the particular rules that apply if the legitime is placed in trust. The Trust Estates Law in broad language permitted the legitime to be placed in trust. The chief difference between this Sub-part and the comparable provisions of the Trust Estates Law lies in the degree of detail with which problems are treated.

(b) Sub-sections (1) and (4) make no change in the law.

(c) The Trust Estates Law contained no clear provision concerning the matter treated in Subsection (2).

Comment—1974

(d) Sections 1841 and 1844 were amended by Acts 1974, No. 126 to make it clear that, unless otherwise provided in the trust instrument, the term of the trust, as it affects the legitime, is not foreshortened by the death of the forced heir so long as, and to the extent that, the legitime is burdened with a legal usufruct as provided by Article 916 of the Civil Code [see, now, C.C. art. 890] or with an equivalent income interest in favor of the surviving spouse in community. Thus at the death of the forced heir (and assuming that his death would not otherwise terminate the trust) his heirs or legatees would be entitled to a distribution of that portion of the trust property which formerly comprised his legitime unless that trust property is subject either to the legal usufruct provided by Article 916 of the Civil Code or an equivalent income interest. Thereafter when such usufruct or income interest terminates as, for example, by the subsequent death or remarriage of the surviving spouse, the heirs or legatees of the forced heir will be entitled to a distribution of the trust property representing the legitime. Assuming the death or remarriage of the spouse does not terminate the trust, the balance of the trust property will remain in trust.

Subsection 1841(2) was likewise amended to make it clear that the legitime may be placed in a class trust and thereby subjected to any charge arising out of the class trust provisions including the substitution of interest provisions permitted by § 1895.

Comment—1979

(e) Sections 1972 through 1977 were added by Acts 1974, No. 160. Since the conditional substitution is not operative where the original beneficiary is survived by descendants, no charge or condition on descending forced heirship would be created by its use. See, Section 1973. However, the conditional substitution could constitute a charge or condition on the interests of ascending forced heirs of a trust beneficiary. See Comment following Section 1972. The general provisions of Section 1841(4) were not intended to apply where the legitime is placed in a class trust or subject to a conditional substitution. In order to make this clear, Acts 1979 No. 160, Section 1 amended Subsection (2) of Section 1841 by expressly including conditional substitutions as permissible charges or conditions upon the legitime in trust.

At the enactment of the Trust Code in 1964, the question of whether the legitime could be satisfied solely by an interest in usufruct, or solely by naked ownership, was unresolved. Section 1845 was enacted to accommodate the Trust Code to future resolution of this policy question. Subsequently, it was held in Succession of Williams, 184 So.2d 70 (La.App.4th Cir. 1966), writs refused, that the forced portion could not be satisfied solely by a usufruct interest. Accordingly, Section 1845 is now obsolete. In Succession of Hyde, 292 So.2d 693 (La.1974), the Louisiana Supreme Court indicated that the legitime could not be satisfied by naked ownership alone, except as provided by Articles 916 and 916.1, Louisiana Civil Code [see, now, C.C. art. 890]. In light of Section 1844, permitting the legitime in trust to be subjected to an income interest in favor of one who could enjoy the same interest free of trust, Section 1846 appears likewise obsolete. Both sections were repealed by Acts 1979, No. 160, Sections 2 and 3.

Cross References

C.C. arts. 1493, 1499.

§ 1842. Effect of improper stipulation

A provision of a trust instrument that is incompatible with the provisions of this Sub-part shall be reformed to comply herewith.

Added by Acts 1964, No. 338, § 2.

Comments—1964

This section is in accord with the policy of Sec. 1831, which sets forth the general rule regulating the effect of a stipulation of an excessive term for a trust.

Cross References

C.C. art. 7.

§ 1843. Stipulation restraining alienation

A trust instrument may place restraints upon the alienation of the legitime in trust.

Added by Acts 1964, No. 338, § 2.

Comments—1964

(a) The Trust Estates Law contained no clear provision concerning the matter treated in this section.

(b) Alienation may be restrained by spendthrift provisions or by provisions restraining alienation to a lesser extent. Secs. 2001–2007.

Cross References

C.C. arts. 454, 1493, 1495, 1497.

§ 1844. Legitime burdened with income interest or usufruct

The legitime in trust may be burdened with an income interest or with a usufruct in favor of a surviving spouse to the same extent and for the same term that a usufruct of the same property could be stipulated in favor of the same person for a like period.

Added by Acts 1964, No. 338, § 2. Amended by Acts 1974, No. 126, § 1.

Comments—1964

(a) This section makes no change in the general law.

(b) The usufruct provided in favor of the surviving spouse by Art. 916 [see, now, 890], R.C.C., may be confirmed by the other's will, even though the surviving spouse receives also the disposable portion under the will. Succession of Moore, 40 La. Ann. 531, 4 So. 460 (1888); Winsberg v. Winsberg, 233 La. 67, 96 S.2d 44 (1957).

(c) An income interest in a trust is an alternative to a usufruct. While the rights of an income beneficiary may not be precisely the same as the rights of a usufructuary because the nature of the property and consequent rules of administration and apportionment of expenses and income may differ, the vesting of an income interest in a trust as the substantial equivalent of a usufruct complies with the requirements of this section, provided the trust instrument creates no greater rights in the income beneficiary than the rights that would exist under this Code if the trust instrument contained no provisions with respect to administration, contribution of expenses, or apportionment of income.

Comments—1974

See Comment under R.S. 9:1841.

Cross References

C.C. arts. 535, 544, 890, 1428, 1493, 1499, 1514, 1520, 1958.

§§ 1845, 1846. Repealed by Acts 1979, No. 160, §§ 2, 3

§ 1847. Invasion of principal; legitime affected

A trustee may not pay principal to an income beneficiary if the payment would deprive another beneficiary of all or a part of his legitime, notwithstanding any contrary provision of the trust instrument.

Added by Acts 1964, No. 338, § 2.

Comments—1964

Sec. 2068, treating a matter upon which the Trust Estates Law was silent, provides that the trust instrument may direct or permit a trustee to invade principal for the support of an income beneficiary, except as provided in this Sub-part.

Cross References

C.C. arts. 7, 1493, 1520.

SUBPART J. MARITAL PORTION IN TRUST

§ 1851. General rule

The marital portion provided under Article 2432 of the Louisiana Civil Code, whether in full property or usufruct only, or any portion thereof, may be placed in trust, if:

(1) The net income accruing to the surviving spouse therefrom is payable to the surviving spouse not less than once each year;

(2) The surviving spouse's interest is subject to no charges or condition, except that the trust instrument may place restrictions upon the alienation of the marital portion in trust; and

(3) The term of the trust, as it affects the marital portion, does not exceed the life of the surviving spouse.
Added by Acts 1977, No. 67, § 1. Amended by Acts 1979, No. 711, § 2, eff. Jan. 1, 1980.

Cross References

C.C. arts. 890, 2432.

§ 1852. Marital portion in full property

An unconditional principal and income interest in trust, with income payable not less than annually for the life of the beneficiary, satisfies the marital portion to the same extent as would the full ownership not in trust of the same property; however, during the term of the trust, the trustee may pay principal from the trust property for support, maintenance, education, medical expenses, or welfare of the beneficiary and, upon termination of the portion of the trust that affects the marital portion, the principal shall be delivered to the surviving spouse or his heirs, legatees, or assigns free of trust.
Added by Acts 1977, No. 67, § 1.

Cross References

C.C. arts. 477, 2432.

§ 1853. Marital portion in usufruct

A usufruct in trust, or an unconditional income interest in trust, without an interest in principal, payable not less than annually for a term or for the life of the beneficiary satisfies the marital portion to the same extent as would a usufruct not in trust on the same property for the same term.
Added by Acts 1977, No. 67, § 1.

Cross References

C.C. arts. 535, 538, 540, 544, 1520, 2432.

§ 1854. Effect of improper stipulation

A provision of a trust instrument that is incompatible with the provisions of this Subpart shall be reformed to comply herewith.
Added by Acts 1977, No. 67, § 1.

Cross References

C.C. arts. 7, 544.

SUBPART K. LIFE INSURANCE IN TRUST

§ 1881. General rule

A settlor may create an inter vivos or a testamentary trust upon the proceeds of life insurance.

If a policy of life insurance is payable to a named beneficiary of the policy as trustee, the trust is an inter vivos trust and the instrument creating the trust shall be in the form required for an inter vivos trust. The trust is an inter vivos trust although the settlor reserves incidents of ownership with respect to the policy, although the settlor reserves the power to revoke or modify the trust, and although the trustee has no active duties to perform until the death of the settlor.

If the policy of life insurance is payable to the settlor or to his succession or his succession representative, or to a testamentary trustee, the trust is testamentary and the instrument creating the trust shall be in the form required for a testamentary trust.
Added by Acts 1964, No. 338, § 2. Amended by Acts 1972, No. 658, § 1.

Comments—1964

(a) This section makes no substantive change in the law. See Sec. 1752 for the form required for the creation of an inter vivos trust.

(b) See the Restatement of Trusts 2d, Sec. 57, Comment (f), and Scott on Trusts, Sec. 57.3 (2d ed. 1956), where insurance trusts are discussed.

(c) Similarly, in other states an inter vivos insurance trust becomes effective immediately, even though the trustee has no active duties to perform until the death of the settlor. Bogert, Trusts and Trustees, Secs. 235–239 (1953); Scott on Trusts, Sec. 57.3 (2d ed. 1956).

(d) Since under this Code property of any type can be placed in trust, a policy of life insurance can be placed in trust. Sec. 1771.

(e) For provisions as to additions to trusts, see Secs. 1931–1936.

(f) Incidents of ownership would include reserving the power to change the beneficiary of the policy, the power to borrow thereon, and the power to surrender it for its cash value.

(g) In other states, policies may be payable to the settlor's executors, administrators, or assigns or estate or succession. Such designations are sometimes used in Louisiana.

SUBPART L. CLASS TRUSTS

A. General Rules

§ 1891. Creation of class

A. Notwithstanding the provisions of R.S. 9:1803, R.S. 9:1831 through 1835, and R.S. 9:1841 through 1847, but subject to the restrictions stated in this Subpart, a person may create an inter vivos or testamentary trust in favor of a class consisting of some or all of his children grandchildren, great grandchildren, nieces, nephews, grandnieces, grandnephews, and great grandnieces and great grandnephews, or any combination thereof, although some members of the class are not yet in being at the time of the creation of the trust, provided at least one member of the class is then in being. Such a trust is called a class trust. If the trust instrument so provides, the interest of each beneficiary in the class shall be held in a separate trust after the class has closed.

B. If before the application of R.S. 9:1894 the class consists only of members of one generation, the interests of the members of the class shall be equal by roots from their common ancestor, unless the trust instrument provides otherwise. If before the application of R.S. 9:1894 the class consists of persons in more than one generation, their interests shall be equal by heads, unless the trust instrument provides otherwise.

Added by Acts 1964, No. 338, § 2. Amended by Acts 1982, No. 479, § 1; Acts 1989, No. 115, § 1; Acts 1989, No. 339, § 1, eff. June 28, 1989; Acts 1995, No. 274, § 1; Acts 1995, No. 324, § 1; Acts 1995, No. 1038, § 1; Acts 1997, No. 682, § 1; Acts 2001, No. 594, § 3.

Comments—1964

(a) This Sub-part provides for a limited type of donation, i.e., it provides for a donation in trust in favor of a class of descendants. It is important to point out that some members of the class may not be in being at the time of the creation of the trust, provided that one member of the class is then living. While this Sub-part introduces into Louisiana law a limited category of future interests, it takes care of the expressed need for permitting a settlor to make provisions for unborn children or grandchildren.

The Restatement of Property in the Introductory Note to Chapter 22 of Part III of Division III (Future Interests), which is devoted to Class Gifts, states:

"Conveyances frequently describe the intended conveyees thereunder by some group designation such as 'children,' 'grandchildren,' 'brothers,' 'sisters,' 'nephews,' 'nieces,' 'cousins,' 'issue,' 'descendants' of 'family.' The effects of any such conveyance depend upon whether the conveyor is found to have intended his conveyees to be specified persons taking singly or to be the members of a group capable of a future change in number, and taking as a group. If the latter construction is made, the conveyees constitute a 'class' and the conveyance contains a 'class gift.'"

The factor that differentiates a class gift from a gift to individuals singly is the intention of the transferor that there be the possibility of fluctuation in the number of ultimate takers. At common law, the Rule Against Perpetuities plays a role in determining when a class gift vests. Leach and Tudor, The Rule Against Perpetuities, Chapter IV, pp. 82–90 (1957).

(b) Class trusts constitute exceptions to Secs. 1803 (beneficiaries must be in being and definitely ascertainable), 1831–1835 (term of trust), and 1841–1847 (legitime).

(c) Class trusts may be created by either inter vivos or testamentary disposition.

(d) Class trusts may be created only in favor of children or grandchildren. At common law, many other types of class designation are possible. See Restatement of Property, Sec. 279.

(e) In creating a class trust, a settlor may provide for grandchildren coming from different branches. It is also possible to create such trusts if the class consists of children. Thus, a class trust can be created for the children of my marriage to my wife W or for the children of my son A. As long as the group designation constitutes a class of children or grandchildren, it is sufficient under this section. It follows, of course, that a settlor may provide unequal portions for children or for grandchildren coming from different branches.

(f) This section formulates the important limitation not imposed at common law that one member of the class must be living at the time of the creation of the trust. 5 American Law of Property, Secs. 22, 44, n. 377 (1952). In a sense the class must be "open" before it can be provided for under this section. Such a requirement not only simplifies the class trust but also limits the duration of such a trust.

(g) A child conceived but not yet born is in being under the provisions of Sec. 1803. *Cf.* Art. 954, R.C.C.

(h) If a member of a class is a forced heir, the interest given him is subject to the rules of collation and reduction. Arts. 1227–1288, 1502–1518, R.C.C.

Comment—1989

Subsection B of R.S. 9:1891 is new and has the purpose of clarifying the nature of the interests of the members of the two types of class trusts.

Comments—2001

(a) A 1997 amendment to this Section permitted class trusts for unlimited generations. Such a class trust is inconsistent with the vesting requirements of the Trust Code. Under R.S. 9:1972 and 1895, every principal beneficiary, even in a class trust, has a vested and heritable interest. The successors in interest to the designated principal beneficiaries themselves have vested interests in the trust, and their identity has to be tracked as well as the identity of all the later-born or adopted descendants who are members of the class. Yet if the trust never terminates, which could be the case if it never runs out of descendant beneficiaries, those "vested" interests can never be realized.

Furthermore, in the interest of both family harmony and the autonomy of the beneficiary, perpetual class trusts should not be permitted. Beneficiaries who are many generations removed from the settlor are only remotely related to each other. They often have little in common. This can lead to disagreements among the beneficiaries and difficulty in administering the trust to suit all beneficiaries, yet the beneficiaries' interests in the trust are tied together forever. The public policy against perpetual private trusts is similar to the public policy that prohibits substitutions, prohibits co-owned property from being perpetually unpartitionable, and prohibits private donations conditioned on the property's remaining inalienable.

(b) This amendment restores the language that was in effect prior to 1997. It permits the settlor to include three younger generations of beneficiaries within the class but does not require the existence of a member of the youngest permissible generation in order to validate the class as to that generation. The amendment thus permits class trusts that could last longer than 100 years, but not in perpetuity.

(c) As provided in Section 4 of Act 594 of 2001, the amendment to this Section made by that Act does not apply to transfers in trust made prior to the effective date of the amendment. Such a transfer in trust is one that has been effected by a donation inter vivos executed prior to the effective date, or a donation mortis causa occurring upon the death of the transferor prior to the effective date.

Editor's note. Subsection A of R.S. 9:1891 was amended and reenacted by Acts 1989, No. 115, § 1, effective September 3, 1989, and by Acts 1989, No. 339, § 1, effective June 28, 1989. Section 2 of Acts 1989, No. 339 provides that the provisions of this Act are remedial in nature and "shall be applied retroactively to all class trusts created prior to the effective date of this Act."

Subsection B of R.S. 9:1891 was added by Acts 1989, No. 115, § 1, effective September 3, 1989. Section 2 of Acts 1989, No. 115 provides that subsection B of R.S. 9:1891 "shall be effective as to all trusts created on or after the effective date of this Act."

Acts 2001, No. 594, § 3, amended R.S. 9:1891(A), effective August 15, 2001. Section 4 of Acts 2001, No. 594, declares that "The provisions of Section 3 of this Act shall not apply to a transfer in trust made prior to the effective date of this Act."

Cross References

C.C. arts. 1472, 1474, 3530.

R.S. 9:1731 et seq., 9:1801, 9:1803, 9:1831 to 9:1835, 9:1841 to 9:1847, 9:1961.

§ 1892. Class members

A class may include those of the relationship whether by blood or adoption.

Added by Acts 1964, No. 338, § 2. Amended by Acts 1985, No. 582, § 1.

Comments—1964

Adopted children are included in all categories because of amended Art. 214, R.C.C.

Cross References

C.C. art. 3506(8), (12).

§ 1893. Income and principal designations

A class trust may be created with respect to all of or a portion of income or principal, or both, but the members of the class must always be the sole beneficiaries of the portion of the trust of which they are beneficiaries. Subject to R.S. 9:2068, the trustee may invade principal for the benefit of one or more individual income beneficiaries or one or more members of any class of income beneficiaries, even though such income beneficiary may not be a member of the class of principal beneficiaries.

Added by Acts 1964, No. 338, § 2. Amended by Acts 1968, No. 133, § 1; Acts 1974, No. 127, § 1; Acts 2003, No. 480, § 1; Acts 2010, No. 390, § 1.

Comments—1964

(a) No one is permitted to share income or principal with members of a designated class. If a class is beneficiary as to income or principal only, either specified persons or members of a different class will be beneficiaries of the other interest. Thus, it is not possible to leave the income interest to my children and A. The same is true as to any interest in principal.

(b) An undivided interest in property may be transferred in trust under this Sub-part.

Comments—1974

The first sentence of § 1893 was contained in the original Trust Code. It establishes the general rule that members of a class must *always* be the *sole* beneficiaries of their interests. This carries the necessary implication that their interests may not be invaded for the benefit of a nonmember of the class. A second sentence was added by Acts 1968, No. 133 to create an exception to the general rule by permitting invasion of class principal for the benefit of one or more members of a class of income beneficiaries. Some thought that the 1968 amendment authorized the invasion of class principal only where all of the income and principal beneficiaries were members of the identical class, although such limitation was not intended.

There seems to be good reason for permitting the trust instrument to authorize the invasion of class principal for benefit of any income beneficiary, whether or not he is a member of a class of income beneficiaries. For example, if the principal beneficiaries of a trust are the settlor's grandchildren as a class, and the sole income beneficiary is the settlor's wife, there seems to be no valid reason to deny the trustee the power to invade principal for the wife's benefit so long as the trust instrument conforms to the requirements of § 2068 regarding objective standards, etc.

Accordingly, the second sentence was amended by Acts 1974, No. 127 to permit invasion of class principal for the benefit of any income beneficiary whether the income interest accrues to one or more individuals or to a class of individuals, and if it accrues to a class, it is immaterial that the composition of such class may be different from the principal class.

Revision Comment—2003

Since accumulated income is no longer treated as equivalent to principal, there is no longer a need for a special rule about accumulated income in R.S. 9:1893. See, R.S. 9:1963.

Editor's note. Section 2 of Acts 2003, No. 480 declares that the amendments to "R.S. 9:1809, 1893, 1963, 1965, 1990, and 2068 shall apply only to trusts created after the effective date of this Act. The amendments to R.S. 9:1979, 2051, 2131, 2159(1), and 2241 shall apply to all trusts." Acts 2003, No. 480 became effective on August 15, 2003.

Acts 2010, No. 390, § 2, declares that: "The provisions of this Act shall apply to all trusts, whether created before or after the effective date of this Act [August 15, 2010], but R.S. 9:1895(A)(3) shall apply only to substitutions occurring after the effective date of this Act."

§ 1894. Representation

If a person dies before the creation of the trust, who would have been a member of the class if he had not died, his descendants shall be considered members of the class by representation unless the instrument otherwise provides.

Added by Acts 1964, No. 338, § 2. Amended by Acts 1985, No. 582, § 1.

Comments—1964

The operation of the rule of representation in this situation permits the descendants of a predeceased member to share in the class trust. The settlor may change this rule in the trust instrument if he so desires. Under Sec. 296 of the Restatement of Property, a member of the class is excluded if he dies before the effective date of the conveyance. The reason for the rule of this section is that it enables all members of the class to be included within the class trust.

Cross References

C.C. arts. 881, 882.

§ 1895. Effect of death of class member during the term of the trust

A. An interest of a member of the class who dies during the term of the trust vests in his heirs or legatees, unless the trust instrument provides any one of the following:

(1) That the interest of a member of the class who dies intestate and without descendants during the term of the trust vests in the other members of the class .

(2) Except as to the legitime in trust, that the interest of a member of the class who dies without descendants during the term of the trust or at its termination vests in the other members of the class.

(3) Except as to the legitime in trust, that the interest of a member of the class who dies leaving one or more descendants vests in the beneficiary's descendant heirs.

B. For this purpose the term "other members of the class" shall include the successors to the interests of any members of the class who predecease such deceased class member, unless the trust instrument provides otherwise.

Added by Acts 1964, No. 338, § 2. Amended by Acts 1985, No. 582, § 1; Acts 1988, No. 284, § 1; Acts 1997, No. 254, § 1; Acts 2010, No. 390, § 1.

Comments—1964

(a) Under this section, the presumption exists that, upon the creation of the trust, a member of the class in being takes a vested interest and if he dies during the term of the trust, his interest goes to his heirs or legatees. The same rule applies when a class member comes into being after the creation of the trust. This presumption may be changed by the settlor in the trust instrument only if the child or grandchild dies intestate and without descendants. In that case it may be provided that his interest goes to the other members of the class.

(b) This section applies both to interests in income and principal.

(c) For the general rule governing the effect of the termination of an income interest, see Sec. 1965.

(d) This section permits a limited type of substitution of interests. The general rule of this Code is that interests in principal are vested. Sec. 1972. But because of the nature of the class trust, this limited substitution is deemed advisable since other members of the class benefit. This provision does not apply to interests of forced heirs except that in a remote case, the provision can operate as a modification of the forced heir provision in the ascending line. In Succession of Earhart, 220 La. 817, 57 S.2d 695 (1952), the court stated that "forced heirship cannot be done away with wholly, wiped out or destroyed," but that the legislature is not prohibited from regulating or restricting the rights of forced heirs.

(e) In this section the word "interest" includes both principal and undistributed income.

Comments—1988

This provision is intended to make it clear that persons who succeed to a deceased class member's interest in the trust will be included among the successors to the interest of another beneficiary who later dies intestate and without descendants, unless the trust instrument provides otherwise. This is a clarification and is not intended to change the law.

Comments—1997

See comments under Section 9:1978.

Editor's note. Acts 2010, No. 390, § 2, declares that: "The provisions of this Act shall apply to all trusts, whether created before or after the effective date of this Act [August 15, 2010], but R.S. 9:1895(A)(3) shall apply only to substitutions occurring after the effective date of this Act."

Cross References

C.C. arts. 871, 875, 880.

§ 1896. Closing of the class

The trust instrument may state a date or a method for defining a date on which the class shall close. Unless the trust instrument provides otherwise, the class shall close when, because of the definition of the class, members may no longer be added to it.

Added by Acts 1964, No. 338, § 2. Amended by Acts 1978, No. 706, § 1.

Comments—1964

(a) Under this section, the important rule as to when a class closes is formulated. When the members of the class are children, the class closes when the parent or parents, with respect to whom the class is defined, die. When the members of the class are grandchildren, the class closes when the parent or parents and grandparent or grandparents, with respect to whom the class is defined, die. Since adopted children are included, death is the only criterion so far as the closing of the class is concerned.

(b) Under the rule of this section the class closes when the parent or parents, grandparent or grandparents, with respect to whom the class is defined, die. Thus, if a settlor names his children as income beneficiaries and his grandchildren as principal beneficiaries, the class closes as to the income beneficiaries when the settlor dies, while the class closes in regard to the principal beneficiaries, when the children die. A more complicated example is as follows: Suppose a settlor has two children, A and B, and one grandchild, C. With the consent of the children, he sets up a trust in which he names his wife W as income beneficiary and his grandchildren as principal beneficiaries. It should be noted that, in this situation, the measuring lives of the trust are the children of the settlor, not the income beneficiary. If the trust comes into existence, the class, as to grandchildren, does not close until the death of the settlor and his children A and B. Although the effect of this is to prolong the trust for a period of time, it necessarily follows if class trusts of the type envisioned are permitted. At common law, the rule of convenience would close the class at the death of W, but this is not desirable from the point of view of the limited class trust possible under this Sub-part.

(c) A child conceived but not yet born is "in being" under the provisions of Sec. 1803. *Cf.* Art. 954, R.C.C.

Cross References

C.C. art. 454.

§ 1897. Term; general rule

A trust created under the provisions of this Sub-part shall not terminate before the closing of the class. The term of the trust thereafter is determined by the rules prescribed by R.S. 9:1899 through 9:1906.

Added by Acts 1964, No. 338, § 2.

Comments—1964

(a) The general rule for the term of a trust is to be found in sec. 1831.

(b) The rule of this section applies whether the class is sole beneficiary of the trust, or beneficiary as to income or principal only.

Cross References

C.C. art. 1777.

§ 1898. Effect of stipulation of excessive term

The stipulation of an excessive term in a disposition governed by this Sub-part shall not defeat the disposition, but the term shall be reduced to the period allowable under this Sub-part.

Added by Acts 1964, No. 338, § 2.

Comments—1964

This section is in accord with Sec. 1831, the general rule for all trusts wherein an excessive term has been stipulated.

B. Rules Governing When Members of a Class are Beneficiaries of Income Only

§ 1899. Distribution of income; forced heirs

The trust instrument may provide when income shall be distributed, or it may provide that the trustee has discretion to determine the time or frequency of distribution or to accumulate some or all of the income, except as otherwise provided by this Code with respect to the legitime in trust.

Added by Acts 1964, No. 338, § 2.

Comments—1964

The sections that govern the legitime in trust are Secs. 1841–1847. See also Sec. 1963 as to distribution of income.

Cross References

C.C. arts. 454, 1493.

§ 1900. Absence of living members before class closes; treatment of income

If the trust instrument contains a survivorship provision and all members of the class of income beneficiaries die before closing of the class, the income of the trust shall be accumulated until there is a member of the class or the class closes. If the class closes and there is no member of the class, the accumulated income shall be distributed to the beneficiaries of principal in proportion to their interests.

Added by Acts 1964, No. 338, § 2.

Comments—1964

(a) This section applies in the following situation: a trust is created with a class of grandchildren as income beneficiaries. All grandchildren die but a child of the settlor is living. The class has not closed because the living child could adopt or have a child.

(b) If a class member is born, he is entitled to the accumulated income unless the trust instrument provides otherwise. See Sec. 1895. A forced heir is entitled to the income from his forced portion. If the class trust contains no survivorship provision, the heirs and legatees of the deceased succeed to his interest.

Cross References

C.C. arts. 937, 938.

§ 1901. Closing of class; members living; effect; termination

After the class closes, the trust shall continue as to the class until the death of the last surviving member of the class, unless an earlier termination date has been stipulated.

Added by Acts 1964, No. 338, § 2.

Comments—1964

(a) This section is consistent with Sec. 1896 as to the closing of the class.

(b) The trust as to the class cannot be continued after closing of the class for the sole benefit of heirs or legatees of the original beneficiaries.

(c) After the class closes, the settlor may stipulate that the trust will terminate when the members of the class reach a certain age or even upon the happening of a certain condition.

Cross References

C.C. arts. 937, 938.

C. Rules Governing When Members of a Class are Beneficiaries of Principal Only

§ 1902. Closing of class; continuation of trust

When the members of a class are designated beneficiaries of principal only and the beneficiaries of income are not a class as defined in this Sub-part, the trust shall terminate when the class has closed and all interests in income have ceased. The trust instrument may provide that the trust shall continue with respect to the share of a class member for his lifetime.

Added by Acts 1964, No. 338, § 2.

Comments—1964

This section provides for the situation wherein the settlor may have afterborn children or grandchildren. It has been pointed out many times that such afterborns should be permitted to share with other members of their generation.

§ 1903. Class not closed; termination of income interests; effect

If all designated beneficiaries of income have died, or the period of their enjoyment has otherwise lapsed before the class that is beneficiary of the trust principal has closed, the income shall be credited and distributed annually to the beneficiaries of the principal until the trust terminates, in proportion to their interests, unless the trust instrument provides otherwise.

Added by Acts 1964, No. 338, § 2.

Comments—1964

(a) This section is consistent with Sec. 1902 as to termination.

(b) This section is consistent with Sec. 1899 as to distribution of trust income.

(c) If the class trust is in favor of beneficiaries of interests in principal and the income interest is in individuals, all income beneficiaries may die and yet the class of principal beneficiaries may not be closed. Under the theory adopted in this Sub-part there cannot be any distribution until a class closes. Under Sec. 1902 and this section, the trust does not terminate until the class closes, and the income is credited annually to the beneficiaries of the principal in proportion to their interests. If the settlor wants to provide otherwise for an income interest, he may do so.

D. Rules Governing When Members of One Class are Beneficiaries of Income and Members of a Different Class are Beneficiaries of Principal

§ 1904. General rule

If the members of one class of the settlor's children or grandchildren are designated beneficiaries of income and members of a different class of his children or grandchildren are designated as beneficiaries of principal, the class of beneficiaries of income shall be governed by R.S. 9:1899 through 9:1901 and the class of beneficiaries of principal shall be governed by R.S. 9:1902 and 9:1903.

Added by Acts 1964, No. 338, § 2.

Comments—1964

(a) The general rules of Secs. 1891–1898 also apply.

(b) This section applies regardless of which class closes first. Since termination is postponed in all cases at least until the class closes, it is immaterial if the class as to income closes first or the class as to principal closes first.

Cross References

C.C. art. 3506(8), (12).

E. Rules Governing When the Members of the Same Class are Beneficiaries of Both Income and Principal

§ 1905. Interests in income

If members of the same class of the settlor's children or grandchildren are designated beneficiaries of both income and principal, interests in income before the class closes shall be governed by R.S. 9:1899 through 9:1901.

Added by Acts 1964, No. 338, § 2.

Comments—1964

(a) The general rules of Secs. 1891–1898 also apply.

(b) When the class closes all interests will have vested unless the trust contains a survivorship provision as permitted by Sec. 1895.

§ 1906. Term

The trust shall continue with respect to the share of a class member for his lifetime unless the trust instrument stipulates a shorter term, but the trust shall not terminate with respect to any interest until the class is closed.

Added by Acts 1964, No. 338, § 2.

Comments—1964

(a) Regardless of the age of a member of the class, the trust does not terminate as to any interest until the class closes. If all class members have then died, all shares will be immediately distributed since the trust will have terminated.

(b) Should a member of the class die after the class closes even though he not reach an age stated in the trust instrument, the share allocated to him shall be distributed to his heirs or legatees free of the trust unless the trust instrument provides otherwise. Sec. 1895.

Cross References

C.C. art. 1777.

SUBPART M. TRUSTS FOR EMPLOYEES

§ 1921. General rule

An employer may create a trust for the benefit of employees whether or not the beneficiaries are in being and ascertainable at the time of its creation. Several settlors may join in one trust for the benefit of their respective employees.

Added by Acts 1964, No. 338, § 2.

Comments—1964

(a) This section makes no change in the law.

(b) Included within trusts for the benefit of employees are pension trusts, stock-bonus trusts, disability trusts, death-benefit trusts, and profit-sharing trusts.

(c) The Restatement of Trusts 2d notes that many states have eliminated by statute the requirement that a beneficiary of a trust be definitely ascertainable within the period of the Rule Against Perpetuities with respect to beneficiaries of an employee trust. Restatement of Trusts 2d, Sec. 112, and Comment (i).

§ 1922. Term of trust

A trust for employees may be created for any term or for an indefinite term.

Added by Acts 1964, No. 338, § 2.

Comments—1964

(a) This section makes no change in the law.

(b) A trust established by an employer for the benefit of his employees may be established for a definite term of any length or for a term of undefined duration.

Cross References

C.C. art. 1777.

SUBPART N. ADDITIONS TO THE TRUST PROPERTY

§ 1931. General rule

A settlor or any other person may make additions of property to an existing trust by donation inter vivos or mortis causa, with the approval of the trustee. The right to make additions may be restricted or denied by the trust instrument.

Added by Acts 1964, No. 338, § 2.

Comments—1964

(a) This section specifically permits a settlor or another to add property to an existing trust. The Trust Estates Law did not contain specific provisions in that respect. Title to property transferred to an existing trust is held by the trustee of that trust. The trustee, in the exercise of his discretion as a fiduciary, may permit property that is added to the trust to become mingled with the other trust property.

(b) The existing trust to which property is added should be clearly identified.

(c) An incorporation by reference in a new trust of the provisions of an existing trust may be effected in accordance with the provisions of Sec. 1754. The provisions of this sub-part do not apply.

(d) See Sec. 1989.

Cross References

C.C. arts. 454, 1467, 1468, 1469.

§ 1932. Form

An addition of property to an existing trust must be made and accepted in the form required for such a donation free of trust.

Added by Acts 1964, No. 338, § 2. Amended by Acts 2001, No. 594, § 2.

Comments—1964

(a) The Trust Estates Law did not contain specific provisions regulating the addition of property to an existing trust.

(b) Under this section, property may be added to a trust by a manual gift, but the trustee's acceptance must be in writing. *Cf.* Art.1539, R.C.C.

(c) A receipt by the trustee constitutes an acceptance in writing.

Comment—2001

The last sentence requiring the trustee's acceptance of an addition to the property of the trust to be in writing has been deleted. Since it is possible to make a valid donation in some circumstances without any writing (see, e.g., Civil Code Article 1539), the trustee should not always have to accept in writing.

Editor's note. Acts 2001, No. 594, § 2, amended R.S. 9:1932, effective August 15, 2001. Section 4 of Acts 2001, No. 594, declares that "The provisions of Section 3 of this Act shall not apply to a transfer in trust made prior to the effective date of this Act."

Cross References

C.C. arts. 1574 et seq.

§ 1933. Rights of person who adds property

A person who adds property to an existing trust cannot acquire the rights of a settlor by virtue of the transfer, but the addition is subject to the general law of donations.

Added by Acts 1964, No. 338, § 2.

Comments—1964

(a) The Trust Estates Law was silent on this subject.

(b) A settlor who adds property to a trust that he has created cannot, in transferring the property, enlarge his rights as settlor.

(c) A person other than a settlor who adds property to an existing trust cannot, in transferring the property, acquire the rights of a settlor.

(d) For revocation, reduction and collation of donations, see Arts. 1559–1569, 1690–1711, 1502–1518, 1227–1288, R.C.C.

Cross References

C.C. art. 1523.

§ 1934. Modification, termination, rescission, or revocation of trust to which property added

A trust may be modified, terminated, rescinded, or revoked, as provided by law or the trust instrument, without

the consent of a person who has added property to the trust, even though the property that has been added is affected.
Added by Acts 1964, No. 338, § 2.

Comments—1964

(a) The Trust Estates Law was silent on this subject.

(b) For the effect of the revocation or rescission of the trust by a settlor, see Sec. 2046.

(c) For the effect of termination of the trust by a settlor, see Sec. 2029.

§ 1935. When addition by donation inter vivos effected

An addition of property to an existing trust by donation inter vivos is effective upon acceptance by the trustee.
Added by Acts 1964, No. 338, § 2.

Comments—1964

See Comments under Sec. 1931.

Cross References

C.C. arts. 1468, 1927.

§ 1936. When addition by donation mortis causa effected

An addition of property to an existing trust by donation mortis causa is effective at the moment of the donor's death.
Added by Acts 1964, No. 338, § 2.

Comments—1964

(a) See Comments under Sec. 1931.

(b) A trustee may refuse a donation mortis causa. See Sec. 1931.

Cross References

C.C. art. 1969.

§ 1937. Definition of annual exclusion

When a trust anticipates future annual additions and refers to the annual exclusion from federal gift tax without stipulating a dollar limitation, the dollar limitation shall be the amount of the exclusion in effect in the year in which the donation is made to the trust.
Added by Acts 1982, No. 423, § 1.

SUBPART O. TRUSTS FOR MIXED PRIVATE AND CHARITABLE PURPOSES

§ 1951. General rule

A trust may be created for mixed private and charitable purposes. The dispositive provisions of such a trust in favor of private beneficiaries are governed by the provisions of this Code; those in favor of charitable beneficiaries are governed by Parts I through IV of Chapter 2 of Code Title II of Code Book III of this Title. As long as there remains a private beneficiary, the trust shall be administered in accordance with the provisions of this Code.
Added by Acts 1964, No. 338, § 2. Amended by Acts 1972, No. 659, § 1; Acts 2012, No. 742, § 1.

Comments—1964

(a) This section makes no change in the law. R.S. 9:1844 was enacted in 1962 to make clear the validity of trusts for mixed private and educational, charitable, or religious purposes.

(b) The charitable beneficiaries of a mixed trust may receive either income or principal, or private and charitable beneficiaries may concurrently receive income or principal or both.

§ 1952. Invasion of principal in mixed trusts

Invasion of principal in unitrusts and annuity trusts, as defined in the United States Internal Revenue Code, shall be regulated by principles set forth in that Code, unless the trust instrument provides otherwise.
Added by Acts 1972, No. 660, § 1.

§ 1953. Assignment of interest in trust and termination of trust for mixed private and charitable purposes

A. A private beneficiary of a trust for mixed private and charitable purposes, including a spendthrift trust, may at any time gratuitously assign to a charitable principal beneficiary of the trust a fraction or all of his private interest in the trust, unless the trust instrument specifically contains a special needs provision or provides otherwise. An interest that is assignable only to a charitable principal beneficiary of the trust shall not be deemed to be subject to voluntary alienation for purposes of R.S. 9:2004.

B. If the trust instrument provides for the termination of the trust at the end of the specified term of the private interests, the trust may be terminated early as to the portion of the trust that, for any reason, no longer has a private beneficiary.
Added by Acts 2012, No. 742, § 1.

SUBPART P. COMMUNITY PROPERTY IN TRUST

§ 1955. Power to divide community interests

If a married couple transfers property to a trustee of a trust they alone have created, or if the trustee of that trust is designated as the beneficiary of a benefit payable upon a spouse's death under a policy or plan, and the transferred property or the spouses' interest in the policy or plan is wholly or partially their community property, the trust instrument may direct the trustee to divide the trust after the termination of the community into two separate shares or trusts according to the spouses' respective ownership interests in the property, or in the policy or plan. The two separate shares or trusts may be governed by different terms and conditions in the trust instrument, even as to the designation of beneficiaries. A "policy or plan" shall include a life insurance or annuity contract, and an employee benefit plan, individual retirement account, or similar benefit.
Added by Acts 1995, No. 1038, § 2.

Comments—1995

(a) When community property is placed in trust, it is not clear under current law whether the trust document can stipulate that each spouse's share of the community will be governed by different dispositive provisions when the community terminates. An attempt to impose different dispositive provisions would amount to a partition agreed to in advance but not effective until death, and there is no provision of the Civil Code that specifically would authorize such a partition. This amendment makes it clear that such a death-related partition is permitted.

(b) The beneficiaries of each separate share or trust have to be determined as for any other trust, that is, the beneficiaries must be in being and ascertainable as of the date of the creation of the trust except that R.S. 9:2011, *et seq.*, may apply.

Cross References

C.C. art. 2338.

R.S. 9:1731 et seq.

PART III. THE INTEREST OF THE BENEFICIARY

SUBPART A. THE INTEREST OF THE INCOME BENEFICIARY

§ 1961. Nature of the interest

A. An interest in income may be given absolutely or conditionally. It may be given for the life of a beneficiary or for a term, certain or uncertain, not exceeding the life of a beneficiary.

B. A settlor may allocate to a beneficiary of income a portion of income. Any income not allocated to an income beneficiary shall be allocated to principal.

C. Except as otherwise provided with respect to the legitime in trust, a settlor may give a trustee who is not a beneficiary of the trust discretion to allocate income in different amounts among the income beneficiaries or to allocate some or all of the income to principal. The settlor may allow income that is not allocated by the end of the year in which it is received to remain unallocated by the trustee until a future year. Any income unallocated when the trust terminates shall be allocated to principal.

Added by Acts 1964, No. 338, § 2. Amended by Acts 1997, No. 767, § 1; Acts 2001, No. 594, § 2.

Comments—1964

(a) In other states (i.e., in the Anglo-American law) the types of property interests that may be held subject to a trust (in equity) are in general no different from those that may be held free of trust (in law). By the use of various devices, among them shifting interests, interests may be created to be enjoyed successively (either free of trust or subject to a trust). Although this Code permits the approximate equivalent of shifting interests in income, it does not permit shifting interests of the Anglo-American type in principal, except as to class trusts and invasion of principal, Secs. 1891–1906, 2067, 2068. However, a transfer of interests in principal to a principal beneficiary's heirs or legatees may occur. Secs. 1961–1965, 1971, 1972; Restatement of Property, Secs. 153–158.

Although an interest in income terminates upon the death of an income beneficiary, an interest in principal vests in the heirs or legatees of a principal beneficiary under the laws regulating successions and donations. subject to the terms of the trust. The doctrine *le mort saisit le vif* applies in the same manner in which it would apply if there were no trust.

(b) The Trust Estates Law did not specifically treat the attaching of conditions to trusts or to dispositions in trust.

(c) In stating that an interest in income may be given for the life of a beneficiary or for a shorter term, certain or uncertain, this section makes no change in the law.

(d) An interest in trust income may be given absolutely or subject to any condition not forbidden by this Code and not contrary to public order or good morals.

(e) Under this Code interests that are the approximate equivalents of the Anglo-American shifting interest are permitted in income, although they are not permitted in principal, except as to class trusts and invasion of principal. Secs. 1891–1906, 1971, 1972, 2067, 2068; Restatement of Property, Secs. 153–158.

(f) An interest in income may be refused under the provisions of Secs. 1981–2007. Refusal operates retroactively to the date of creation of the trust. Sec. 1986.

Comment—1997

See Comments under Section 9:1964.

Comment—2001

The exercise of discretion given to the trustee pursuant to this Section is subject to review by the court to prevent an abuse of discretion. R.S. 9:2115. With this protection for the beneficiary, it is unnecessary for the discretion to be limited by the standard of the "average reasonable man." The "average reasonable man" standard implies a different standard than that of abuse of discretion. To avoid confusion, the words "average reasonable man" have been removed.

Editor's note. Acts 2001, No. 594, § 2, amended R.S. 9:1961(C), effective August 15, 2001. Section 4 of Acts 2001, No. 594, declares that "The provisions of Section 3 of this Act shall not apply to a transfer in trust made prior to the effective date of this Act."

Cross References

C.C. arts. 1520, 1767, 1768, 1775, 1777, 3530.

§ 1962. Distribution of income

In the absence of a contrary stipulation, income shall be distributed to the designated beneficiary at least every six months.

Added by Acts 1964, No. 338, § 2.

Comments—1964

(a) The Trust Estates Law contained a definite statement on the frequency of payment of income only with respect to the legitime in trust.

(b) In other states the trust instrument cannot provide for accumulation for a period longer than the period of the Rule Against Perpetuities. Restatement of Trusts 2d, Comment (t) under Sec. 62.

§ 1963. Permissible stipulations regulating distribution of income

Except as otherwise provided with respect to class trusts and the legitime in trust, a settlor may stipulate when the income allocated to a beneficiary shall be distributed to him, or may stipulate that the trustee has discretion to determine the time and frequency of distribution. If the trust instrument allows the trust to retain income received in a year of the trust and distribute it in a later year, the income retained at the end of the year is deemed to be accumulated, unless the trust instrument requires the undistributed income to be added to principal. Objective standards are not required for the accumulation of income or for the distribution of accumulated income.

Added by Acts 1964, No. 338, § 2. Amended by Acts 2003, No. 480, § 1.

Comments—1964

(a) The Trust Estates Law was silent on this subject.

(b) Secs. 1841–1847 deal with the legitime in trust, and Secs. 1891–1906 deal with class trusts.

Revision Comments—2003

(a) "Accumulated income" was previously undefined, and had a shadowy status between income and principal. This amendment defines the term in a way that causes its quality as income to be preserved, thereby permitting removal of the requirement of objective standards for its distribution. See also R.S. 9:2068 and 1893. The trust instrument may, however, impose objective standards.

(b) Undistributed income is presumed to be accumulated, but the trust instrument may overcome that presumption and require the undistributed income to be allocated to principal.

Editor's note. Section 2 of Acts 2003, No. 480 declares that the amendments to "R.S. 9:1809, 1893, 1963, 1965, 1990, and 2068 shall apply only to trusts created after the effective date of this Act. The amendments to R.S. 9:1979, 2051, 2131, 2159(1), and 2241 shall apply to all trusts." Acts 2003, No. 480 became effective on August 15, 2003.

Cross References

C.C. arts. 454, 1420, 1493.

§ 1964. Termination of income interest; undistributed income

An interest in income terminates upon the death of the designated beneficiary, or at the expiration of the period of his enjoyment if the interest is for a period less than life. At the termination of an income interest, accumulated or undistributed income that has been or is required to be allocated to the beneficiary shall be paid to the beneficiary or his heirs, legatees, assignees, or legal representatives, except as otherwise provided in this Code.

Added by Acts 1964, No. 338, § 2. Amended by Acts 1997, No. 767, § 1.

Comments—1964

(a) The interest of a designated beneficiary of income does not continue to exist after his death.

(b) The interest of a principal beneficiary is not terminated at his death, but under Sec. 1972 the interest vests in his heirs or legatees. As to class trusts, see Secs. 1891–1906.

Comment—1997

(a) Under the Trust Code as enacted in 1964 an income beneficiary's share of the trust income had to be fixed by the settlor, that is, the share or interest of the income beneficiary had to be determined by an objective standard stated in the trust instrument. The only discretion that the settlor could give to the trustee concerning income was the discretion whether and when to accumulate or distribute the income to the income beneficiary; the settlor could not give the trustee discretion to allocate the income among the various income beneficiaries or discretion to add income to principal. The change to Section 1961 allows the settlor to give the trustee full discretion to allocate income among the income beneficiaries or to add income to principal. It allows a settlor to give the trustee complete flexibility to deal with the changing circumstances of the income beneficiaries. The discretionary provision does not apply to interests in principal.

(b) Since the trustee may already be given the discretion to accumulate income, the addition of discretion to allocate means that the trustee may accumulate income indefinitely without allocating it. Section 1961 provides, however, that any income unallocated when the trust terminates shall be allocated to principal.

(c) The trustee's discretionary power to distribute, apportion, or accumulate income may have tax implications where the trustee is a settlor. See I.R.C. Sections 674, 2036, and 2038.

Cross References

C.C. art. 607.

§ 1965. Effect of termination of interest

Unless the trust instrument provides otherwise:

(1) Termination of the interest of the sole income beneficiary prior to the termination of the trust causes each principal beneficiary to become a beneficiary of income in an amount proportionate to his interest in the principal.

(2)(a) Termination of an interest in income of one of several income beneficiaries causes the other income beneficiaries or their successors to become beneficiaries of that interest in income in proportion to their interests in the balance of trust income.

(b) If, however, termination of the income interest is by death, and if descendants of the deceased income beneficiary are the beneficiaries of an interest in trust principal or succeed to such an interest upon the death of the income beneficiary, such descendants shall become beneficiaries of the deceased beneficiary's interest in trust income in proportion to the descendants' interests in their portion of trust principal.

Added by Acts 1964, No. 338, § 2. Amended by Acts 2003, No. 480, § 1.

Comments—1964

(a) The Trust Estates Law was silent on this subject.

(b) The interest of an income beneficiary terminates upon his death or the expiration of his period of enjoyment. This section is consistent with Sec. 1990 dealing with the effect of refusal.

(c) For the rule governing the vesting of an interest of a deceased class member under a class trust, see Sec. 1895.

Revision Comment—2003

The amendments to R.S. 9:1965 create an exception to the default rule for the destination of the income when the interest of one of several income beneficiaries has terminated. Under the general rule the surviving income beneficiaries are entitled to the income that would have been paid to the beneficiary whose income interest has terminated. By exception, if the income beneficiary's descendants are the beneficiaries of an interest in principal, or succeed to such interest upon the death of the income beneficiary, the descendants, rather than the surviving income beneficiaries, become the successors to his income interest.

Editor's note. Section 2 of Acts 2003, No. 480 declares that the amendments to "R.S. 9:1809, 1893, 1963, 1965, 1990, and 2068 shall apply only to trusts created after the effective date of this Act. The amendments to R.S. 9:1979, 2051, 2131, 2159(1), and 2241 shall apply to all trusts." Acts 2003, No. 480 became effective on August 15, 2003.

Cross References

C.C. arts. 946, 964 to 966.

SUBPART B. THE INTEREST OF THE PRINCIPAL BENEFICIARY

§ 1971. Time of acquisition of interest

The interest of a principal beneficiary is acquired immediately upon the creation of a trust, subject to the exceptions provided in this Code and in Civil Code Article 1521.

Added by Acts 1964, No. 338, § 2. Amended by Acts 1995, No. 413, § 1; Acts 2010, No. 390, § 1.

Comments—1964

(a) See Comment (a) to Sec. 1961.

(b) The Trust Estates Law was silent on this subject.

(c) An interest in principal may be acquired after the trust is created only under the provisions of Secs. 1891–1906 (by the coming into being of a member of a class of descendants that is comprised of principal beneficiaries), or Secs. 2021–2028 (by an effective modification of the trust to create an additional or different interest in principal). Although under this Code interests that are the approximate equivalent of the Anglo-American shifting interest are permitted in income, such interests are not permitted in principal except as to class trusts and invasion of principal. Secs. 1891–1906, 1961–1965, 2067, and 2068; Restatement of Property, Secs. 153–158.

(d) An interest in principal may be refused under the provisions of Secs. 1981–1990. Refusal operates retroactively to the date of the creation of the trust. Sec. 1986.

(e) Secs. 2021, 2026 and 2027 make it possible for an interest in principal to be terminated by an effective modification of the terms of the trust.

(f) Under Secs. 2041 and 2043 an interest in principal ends by an effective revocation or rescission of the trust or of the interest.

(g) See Sec. 1736 and Comment (d) thereto.

Editor's note. Acts 2010, No. 390, § 2, declares that: "The provisions of this Act shall apply to all trusts, whether created before or after the effective date of this Act [August 15, 2010], but R.S. 9:1895(A)(3) shall apply only to substitutions occurring after the effective date of this Act."

Cross References

C.C. arts. 1588, 1590, 1592, 1596, 3530.

§ 1972. Treatment of interest upon death of principal beneficiary

Upon a principal beneficiary's death, his interest vests in his heirs or legatees, subject to the trust; provided, however, that the trust instrument may stipulate otherwise to the extent permitted by the following Sections of this Subpart and R.S. 9:1895.

Added by Acts 1964, No. 338, § 2. Amended by Acts 1974, No. 160, § 1; Acts 1995, No. 414, § 1.

Comments—1964

(a) The interest of a principal beneficiary is not terminated by his death, but vests in his heirs or legatees. The interest of an income beneficiary must terminate at his death although it may terminate at an earlier time. Sec. 1964. For class trusts see Secs. 1891–1906.

(b) The doctrine *le mort saisit le vif* applies upon the death of a principal beneficiary in the same manner in which it would apply if there were no trust.

Comments—1974

Acts 1974 No. 160 amends R.S. 9:1972 and enacts new sections R.S. 9:1973 through R.S. 9:1977 authorizing "conditional substitutions". The Trust Code originally permitted the shifting of principal only where the trust instrument permitted invasion of principal (R.S. 9:2068) and in the class trust where the class beneficiary died both intestate and without descendants (R.S. 9:1895). By utilizing the "conditional substitution trust", the settlor may now provide, under certain circumstances, that the interest of a principal beneficiary who dies *both intestate and without descendants* vests in a named "substitute beneficiary". The substitute beneficiary's interest may be conditioned on his surviving the "original" principal beneficiary. A substitute beneficiary must be *in being and ascertainable* at the creation of the trust (R.S. 9:1803) but may also be a class subject to the provisions on class trusts. Only *one shift* of principal is permitted. Upon the death of a substitute beneficiary his interest, if vested, passes to his heirs or legatees. If the beneficiary is a class, the interest of a deceased member of the class is determined by the rules governing class trusts. (R.S. 9:1891–9:1906) The conditional substitution is predicated in every instance on the requirement that the original principal beneficiary die *both* intestate *and* without descendants. The conditional substitution will have no effect on descending forced heirship, though it may modify forced heirship in the ascending line.

Cross References

C.C. arts. 874, 875.

§ 1973. Shifting interest in principal

A. The trust instrument may provide that the interest of either an original or a substitute principal beneficiary who dies intestate and without descendants during the term of the trust or at its termination vests in some other person or persons, each of whom shall be a substitute beneficiary.

B. Except as to the legitime in trust, the trust instrument may provide that the interest of either an original or a substitute principal beneficiary who dies without descendants during the term of the trust or at its termination vests in some other person or persons, each of whom shall be a substitute beneficiary.

C. The trust instrument may provide that the interest of a designated principal beneficiary of a revocable trust shifts to another person or persons, if the substitution occurs no later than the date when the trust becomes irrevocable.

Added by Acts 1974, No. 160, § 1. Amended by Acts 1989, No. 111, § 1; Acts 1997, No. 254, § 1; Acts 2010, No. 390, § 1.

Comments—1974

See Comment under R.S. 9:1972.

Comments—1989

This change is meant to clarify the Code and overrule the statement in the official comment to Act 160 of 1974 that only one substitution can occur. Allowing successive substitutions makes it possible for all of a beneficiary's interest in trust principal to be treated uniformly. For example, in the case of a trust for several children, if one child dies intestate and without descendants and his interest vests in his siblings, upon the subsequent death intestate and without descendants of one of those siblings the settlor should be able to direct in the trust instrument that the full interest of that second deceased sibling, not just the second sibling's original interest in the trust, vests in the other surviving siblings.

Comments—1997

See comments under Section 1978.

Editor's note. Acts 2010, No. 390, § 2, declares that: "The provisions of this Act shall apply to all trusts, whether created before or after the effective date of this Act [August 15, 2010], but R.S. 9:1895(A)(3) shall apply only to substitutions occurring after the effective date of this Act."

Cross References

C.C. arts. 875, 880, 1588, 1590, 1592.

§ 1974. Substitute beneficiary's interest may be conditional

The interest of a substitute beneficiary may be conditioned upon his surviving the principal beneficiary. The trust instrument may provide for one or more alternative substitute beneficiaries if a substitute beneficiary does not survive the principal beneficiary.

Added by Acts 1974, No. 160, § 1.

Comments—1974

See Comment under R.S. 9:1972.

Cross References

C.C. art. 1520.

§ 1975. Requirement that substitute beneficiary be in being and ascertainable

Except as provided in R.S. 9:1978, a substitute beneficiary must be in being and ascertainable on the date of the creation of the trust; provided, however, that a class may be a substitute beneficiary subject to the requirements of R.S. 9:1891 through R.S. 9:1906.

Added by Acts 1974, No. 160, § 1. Amended by Acts 1982, No. 455, § 1.

Comments—1974

See Comment under R.S. 9:1972.

Cross References

C.C. arts. 548, 939, 1472.

§ 1976. Treatment upon death of substitute beneficiary whose interest is not conditioned on survival

Upon a substitute beneficiary's death, his interest, if not conditioned on survival, vests in his heirs or legatees subject to the trust.

Added by Acts 1974, No. 160, § 1.

Comments—1974

See Comment under R.S. 9:1972.

Cross References

C.C. arts. 937, 938, 1520.

§ 1977. Class as substitute beneficiary

If the substitute beneficiary is a class, the interest of a deceased member of the class is determined by the rules governing class trusts.

Added by Acts 1974, No. 160, § 1.

Comments—1974

See Comment under R.S. 9:1972.

Cross References

C.C. art. 1520.

§ 1978. Shifting interest in principal if beneficiary is descendant of settlor

The trust instrument may provide that the substitute beneficiaries under R.S. 9:1973 are one or more of settlor's descendants who are in being and ascertainable on the date of death of the principal beneficiary.

Added by Acts 1982, No. 455, § 1. Amended by Acts 1997, No. 254, § 1.

Comments—1997

(a) The Trust Code provides that as a general rule the interest of the principal beneficiary must be vested at the creation of the trust and must be heritable. La. R.S. 9:1971, 1972; Martin, Louisiana's Law of Trusts 25 Years After Adoption of the Trust Code, 50 La. L. Rev. 501, 512 (1990). The only exceptions prior to these amendments were the substitutions permitted by R.S. 9:1973, 1978, and 1895, and the survivorship condition permitted by Civil Code Article 1521(A)(2).

The amendments to R.S. 9:1895(A), 1973, and 1978 allow the settlor to name a substitute principal beneficiary in the event the original principal beneficiary has no descendants. Under previous law, the interest of a principal beneficiary with no descendants would go to the legatee under the principal beneficiary's will. Under the Sections as amended, the designation by the settlor of a substitute principal beneficiary will override the original principal beneficiary's will with respect to his interest in the trust if he has no descendants.

(b) The new substitution permitted by R.S. 9:1973(B) and by R.S. 9:1985(A) is inapplicable to the legitime. The substitution permitted by R.S. 9:1973(A) is applicable to the legitime via R.S. 9:1841.

(c) The amendment to R.S. 9:1978 conforms that Section to the change made by R.S. 9:1973(B). It also changes the law in that formerly R.S. 9:1978 was applicable only to trusts where the original principal beneficiary was the settlor's descendant. The amendment to R.S. 9:1978 permits the substitute beneficiary to be one or more of the settlor's descendants who are in being and ascertainable on the date of death of the principal beneficiary whether or not that principal beneficiary was the settlor's descendant.

Cross References

C.C. arts. 875, 880 et seq.

§ 1979. Status of potential substitute principal beneficiary

A person who will be a principal beneficiary of a trust only if a substitution occurs under R.S. 9:1973 is not considered a principal beneficiary until the substitution occurs.

Added by Acts 2003, No. 480, § 1.

Revision Comment—2003

This Section is added to make it clear that a person whose only interest in a trust is as a substitute beneficiary under R.S. 9:1973 has the status of a beneficiary only when the substitution occurs. Until that time such a person has no standing to bring an action on his own behalf with regard to the trust.

Editor's note. Section 2 of Acts 2003, No. 480 declares that the amendments to "R.S. 9:1809, 1893, 1963, 1965, 1990, and 2068 shall apply only to trusts created after the effective date of this Act. The amendments to R.S. 9:1979, 2051, 2131, 2159(1), and 2241 shall apply to all trusts." Acts 2003, No. 480 became effective on August 15, 2003.

SUBPART C. REFUSAL

§ 1981. General rule

A beneficiary, whether of principal or income, may refuse an interest at any time after creation of the trust, provided he does so before accepting any benefit under the trust. A person incapable of contracting cannot refuse an interest in trust, but his representative may refuse for him. The refusal is irrevocable.

Added by Acts 1964, No. 338, § 2.

Comments—1964

(a) The Trust Estates Law was silent on this subject.

(b) The provisions of this Code that concern refusal are in general accord with the Restatement of Trusts 2d, Sec. 31 and Comments (a) and (c) thereunder—which state that, although the beneficiary's acceptance of his interest is presumed, a beneficiary may "disclaim" the interest if he has not accepted any benefit from the trust. See Sec. 1808. Express acceptance by a beneficiary is not necessary to the effectiveness of the trust.

(c) Once a beneficiary has accepted any benefit from a trust he may not refuse an interest in trust. Such acts as the express acceptance of an interest by a declaration in authentic form, acceptance of income from a trust, acceptance of possession of trust principal, the filing of an action as a beneficiary of a trust, or the pledge or assignment of an interest constitute the acceptance of benefit from a trust.

(d) A beneficiary who has not refused an interest is presumed to have accepted it even though he has not accepted any benefit from the trust. Sec. 1808.

(e) Capacity to contract is governed by Arts. 1780–1796, R.C.C. [see, now, generally, C.C. art. 1918 et seq.].

(f) Partial refusal is not permitted. Sec. 1988.

(g) Refusal of an interest in a testamentary trust constitutes a renunciation of a settlor's succession to the extent of that interest. *Cf.* Arts. 1014–1031, R.C.C.

(h) A beneficiary who refuses an interest in a testamentary trust cannot take the interest (or its equivalent) by inheritance free of the trust. Sec. 1984. If a beneficiary were permitted to refuse an interest in a testamentary trust and then to take the property free of the trust the purposes of a testamentary trust could be defeated. Yet his refusal of the interest does not prevent his accepting the rest of the property that he may be entitled to receive in the succession.

(i) For the effect of refusal, see Sec. 1990 and Comments.

Cross References

C.C. arts. 947, 948.

§ 1982. Acceptance of interest in inter vivos trust by creditor; effect

If a beneficiary of a gratuitous inter vivos trust refuses his interest, his creditor cannot accept it in his stead.

Added by Acts 1964, No. 338, § 2.

Comments—1964

(a) The Trust Estates Law was silent on this subject.

(b) It appears that even if a donee refuses or neglects to accept an inter vivos gift in fraud of his creditors, they cannot accept the gift in his stead. *Cf.* Art. 1543, R.C.C. There are no reported cases upon the point. This section applies the principle to the refusal of an interest in an inter vivos trust. It is not necessary to apply the principle to a beneficiary who neglects to accept his interest because his acceptance is presumed. Sec. 1808.

Cross References

C.C. arts. 967, 1418, 1419.

§ 1983. Acceptance of interest in testamentary trust by creditor; effect

If a beneficiary of a testamentary trust refuses his interest to the prejudice of his creditors' rights, the creditors may accept in his stead to the extent that their rights have been prejudiced.

Added by Acts 1964, No. 338, § 2.

Comments—1964

(a) The Trust Estates Law was silent on this subject.

(b) The Civil Code provides that if an heir refuses to accept or renounces an inheritance to the prejudice of his creditors, they can be authorized by the court to accept in the name of the debtor and in his stead according to certain forms. Arts. 1021, 1071–1074, R.C.C. The Civil Code does not contain any specific reference to the acceptance by a legatee's creditors of a legacy that has been refused, nor are there any reported cases on the point. This section applies the provisions of the Civil Code that affect the renunciation of a succession by an heir to the refusal of an interest in a testamentary trust by a beneficiary. A beneficiary's neglect to accept expressly an interest in a testamentary trust does not alter the presumption that he has accepted the interest. Sec. 1808.

(c) The creditors' acceptance of an interest in a testamentary trust is limited to that portion of the interest that he would have been permitted to seize had the beneficiary not refused. See Secs. 2004–2006 on the effect of provisions restricting involuntary alienation.

(d) The creditors' acceptance of an interest in a testamentary trust that has been refused by a beneficiary causes the refusal to be annulled only in favor of the creditors for as much as they are permitted to accept. The refusal remains valid against a beneficiary who has refused. If any balance remains after the payment of the creditors, the rules of Sec. 1990 govern. *Cf.* Art. 1021, R.C.C.

Cross References

C.C. arts. 967, 1418, 1419.

§ 1984. Rights of beneficiary who refuses interest in testamentary trust

A beneficiary who refuses his interest in a testamentary trust cannot take the interest in the property free of the trust.

Added by Acts 1964, No. 338, § 2.

Comments—1964

(a) The Trust Estates Law was silent on this subject.

(b) If a beneficiary were permitted to refuse an interest in a testamentary trust and then to take the property free of the trust, the purposes of the trust would be defeated.

(c) The Civil Code is silent as to whether or not a testator's heir can refuse a legacy and then take as heir the property contained in the legacy.

Cross References

C.C. arts. 947, 962, 964.

§ 1985. Manner of refusal; effect of conditions

The refusal of an interest conferred in an inter vivos trust shall be in authentic form unequivocally disclaiming the interest. The refusal of an interest conferred in a testamentary trust shall be by renunciation of the settlor's succession. Conditions attached to the refusal shall be reputed not written.

Added by Acts 1964, No. 338, § 2.

Comments—1964

(a) The Trust Estates Law was silent on this subject.

(b) See Arts. 1536, 1540, R.C.C.

(c) A renunciation of a succession may be made by authentic act or by judicial declaration. Art. 1017, R.C.C.; Succession of Tertrou, 217 La. 901, 47 So.2d 681 (1950).

Cross References

C.C. arts. 1540, 1542.

§ 1986. Retroactive nature of refusal

A refusal operates retroactively to the date of the creation of the trust, and a beneficiary is considered never to have received an interest.

Added by Acts 1964, No. 338, § 2.

Comments—1964

(a) The Trust Estates Law was silent on this subject.

(b) This section is in accord with Art. 946, R.C.C., which provides that if the heir rejects a succession, he is considered as never having received it. Compare the Restatement of Trusts 2d, Sec. 36, Comment (c), which states that the beneficiary's "disclaimer" has a retroactive effect that frees the beneficiary from any liability as beneficiary. Compare also Arts. 1540, 1541, R.C.C., which concern acceptance of donations inter vivos.

Cross References

C.C. arts. 954, 962, 963.

§ 1987. Effect of refusal upon trustee

A refusal is not effective as to a trustee until a copy of the act of refusal has been received by him. Acts performed by a trustee before a beneficiary's refusal becomes effective as to the trustee are not affected by the refusal.

Added by Acts 1964, No. 338, § 2.

Comments—1964

The Trust Estates Law was silent on this subject.

Cross References

C.C. arts. 1934, 1935.

§ 1988. Partial refusal; refusal in another's favor

A beneficiary may refuse all or any part of an interest in trust. The designation of the person in whose favor the refusal is to operate constitutes acceptance, but such a designation is subject to any restraint placed upon alienation by the trust instrument.

Added by Acts 1964, No. 338, § 2. Amended by Acts 1983, No. 79, § 1.

Comments—1964

(a) The Trust Estates Law was silent on this subject.

(b) The trust instrument may place restraints upon voluntary alienation and, to the extent permitted by Secs. 2001–2007, upon involuntary alienation as well.

Cross References

C.C. arts. 454, 1971, 1978.

§ 1989. Refusal of addition to trust

A beneficiary who has not refused his interest under the trust instrument may refuse an addition of property to the trust.

Added by Acts 1964, No. 338, § 2.

Comments—1964

(a) The Trust Estates Law was silent on this subject.

(b) Property may be added to an existing trust under the provisions of Secs. 1931–1936.

(c) Under Sec. 1988, a beneficiary cannot refuse a part of an interest. By virtue of this section, a refusal of an interest transferred to an existing trust is not a refusal of a part of an interest under Sec. 1988.

§ 1990. Effect of refusal upon interest refused

A settlor may stipulate the effect of refusal. Unless the trust instrument otherwise provides, the following rules govern:

(1) Refusal of the entire interest in trust causes the trust to fail.

(2) Refusal by the sole income beneficiary causes principal beneficiaries, other than the refusing beneficiary, to become income beneficiaries, to the extent of the interest refused, in amounts proportionate to their interests or, in the absence of other principal beneficiaries, such a refusal operates as a substitution of the settlor or his heirs or legatees as beneficiaries of the refused income interest.

(3) Except as provided in Paragraph (4), refusal of an interest by one of several income beneficiaries inures in favor of the other beneficiaries or their successors in proportion to their interests in the balance of the trust income.

(4) If one or more descendants of a refusing income beneficiary are the beneficiaries of an interest in trust principal, either by designation in the instrument or by reason of Paragraph (5), those descendants become the beneficiaries of the refused interest, in proportion to their interests in trust principal.

(5) A principal beneficiary of a testamentary trust who refuses his interest and to whom R.S. 9:1809 would have applied had he predeceased the settlor shall be treated as having predeceased the settlor.

(6) Unless Paragraph (5) applies, refusal by the sole principal beneficiary operates a substitution of the settlor or his heirs or legatees as beneficiary of the principal, to the extent of the interest refused, without affecting the interest of the income beneficiary.

(7) Unless Paragraph (5) applies, refusal of an interest by one of several principal beneficiaries inures in favor of the other beneficiaries or their successors in proportion to their interests in the balance of the trust principal.

Added by Acts 1964, No. 338, § 2. Amended by Acts 1983, No. 79, § 1; Acts 2003, No. 480, § 1.

Comments—1964

(a) The Trust Estates Law was silent on this subject.

(b) Sub-section (1) of this section, which applies to both testamentary and inter vivos trusts, is analogous to Art. 1703, R.C.C., which provides that a testamentary disposition fails if the legatee rejects it.

(c) Sub-section (5) of this section is analogous to the provisions of Arts. 1707–1709, R.C.C., which concern conjoint legacies.

(d) Under the Restatement of Trusts 2d if the settlor transfers property in trust and the beneficiary "disclaims," the trustee holds the property upon a resulting trust in favor of the settlor or his heirs unless there is evidence that the settlor has manifested a contrary intention. Restatement of Trusts 2d, Sec. 36, Comment (d).

Revision Comments—2003

(a) New Paragraph (5) is consistent with R.S. 9:1809, and with Civil Code Articles 965 and 1593, and applies when a principal beneficiary who is a descendant, sibling, or descendant of a sibling of the settlor refuses his interest. Instead of the refused interest passing to the other principal beneficiaries, it passes to the refuser's descendants by roots.

(b) New Paragraph (4) provides for descendants of a refusing income beneficiary to succeed upon a renouncing ancestor's refusal of income, if they have an interest in trust principal. For example, if a trust instrument designates the settlor's children as the income beneficiaries, and the grandchildren, equally by roots as the principal beneficiaries, and if the trust instrument is silent on the effect of a refusal by a settlor's child, the refusal will cause the renouncing child's children to become income beneficiaries in place of their refusing parent. Under prior law, the settlor's other children would have received all the income.

Editor's note. Section 2 of Acts 2003, No. 480 declares that the amendments to "R.S. 9:1809, 1893, 1963, 1965, 1990, and 2068 shall apply only to trusts created after the effective date of this Act. The amendments to R.S. 9:1979, 2051, 2131, 2159(1), and 2241 shall apply to all trusts." Acts 2003, No. 480 became effective on August 15, 2003.

Cross References

C.C. arts. 2045 to 2057.

SUBPART D. ALIENATION BY THE BENEFICIARY

§ 2001. General rule

A beneficiary may transfer or encumber the whole or any part of his interest unless the trust instrument provides to the contrary.

Added by Acts 1964, No. 338, § 2.

Comments—1964

(a) This section states a principle that was implied but not expressly stated in R.S. 9:1923.

(b) A majority of states in some degree restrain alienation of an interest in trust or permit alienation to be restrained by the terms of the trust. Alienation of an interest in trust was once regulated in other states by judicial decision. Most states now have adopted statutes that regulate alienation to some degree. This Code takes the position taken by other states in the absence of statute, that unless the trust instrument contains a stipulation to the contrary, the beneficiary's interest is subject to voluntary and to involuntary alienation. Some state statutes prohibit voluntary and involuntary alienation of interests in income and in principal; some prohibit voluntary and involuntary alienation of an interest in income but permit voluntary and involuntary alienation of an interest in principal; some prohibit voluntary and involuntary alienation of an interest in income and principal in the absence of a stipulation in the trust instrument permitting alienation. Although in England alienation of the beneficiary's interest can be restricted only if the beneficiary is a married woman, in most states that have no statute, and under this Code, the trust instrument can substantially restrict voluntary and involuntary alienation. Secs. 2001, 2002, 2004; Griswold, Spendthrift Trusts, Secs. 53–58 (1957); Scott on Trusts, Secs. 132, 147, 152, 152.1, 153 (2d ed. 1956); Restatement of Trusts 2d, Secs. 132, 147, 152, 153.

Bogert writes that states having authority on the question of whether or not spendthrift trusts are permitted may be divided in four groups; (1) a few that follow the English decisions that provisions restricting alienation are ineffective, (2) some states that sanction the spendthrift trust without limitation as to the size of the income or the needs of the beneficiary, (3) some states that permit spendthrift provisions to the extent necessary to support and educate the beneficiary in the manner of life to which he is accustomed, and (4) some states that limit the spendthrift trust as to the size of corpus or income or the purpose of the trust. Louisiana, under this Code, falls into the fourth group, as it did under the Trust Estates Law. Bogert, Trusts and Trustees, Sec. 222 (1951).

Before statutes concerning alienation of a beneficiary's interest were adopted, a restraint upon the alienation of principal was, in most states, invalid. However, today even the states that have not adopted statutes permit restraint to be placed upon alienation of a right to receive principal in the future. The Restatement of Trusts 2d provides that a restraint upon alienation of an interest in principal is invalid if a principal beneficiary is entitled to have principal conveyed to him immediately or if he is not entitled to have principal conveyed to him during his lifetime. It limits the term "spendthrift trust" to a trust under which the alienation of an interest in income is restrained. This Code makes no distinction between the enforceability of a restraint upon alienation of an interest in income and the enforceability of a restraint upon alienation of an interest in principal. It considers a "spendthrift trust" to be one under which voluntary alienation and involuntary alienation by a beneficiary of an interest in income or principal are restricted to the full extent permitted. The trust instrument may restrict alienation to a lesser extent, but a trust existing under such an instrument is not a "spendthrift trust", as that term is used in this Code. Scott on Trusts, Secs. 152.1, 153 (2d ed. 1956); Restatement of Trusts 2d, Secs. 152, 153.

(c) Capacity to contract is governed by Arts. 1780–1796, R.C.C. [see, now, C.C. arts. 1918 to 1926].

Cross References

C.C. arts. 454, 3530, 3537 to 3541.

§ 2002. Restraint upon alienation

The trust instrument may provide that the interest of a beneficiary shall not be subject to voluntary or involuntary alienation by a beneficiary. A restraint upon voluntary alienation by a beneficiary is valid. But a restraint upon involuntary alienation by a beneficiary is subject to the limitations prescribed by this sub-part.

Added by Acts 1964, No. 338, § 2.

Comments—1964

(a) This section makes only one change in the law. Under the Trust Estates Law a restraint upon voluntary alienation was valid only to the extent that a restraint upon involuntary alienation was valid. This section provides that a restraint upon voluntary alienation is valid.

(b) See Comment (b) under Sec. 2001.

(c) The trust instrument may restrict alienation to a lesser degree than permitted by this Code, but a trust existing under such an instrument is not a "spendthrift trust." For the definition of a spendthrift trust, see Sec. 1725.

Cross References

C.C. arts. 7, 454, 1971.

§ 2003. Form

Except as otherwise provided by Chapter 9 of the Louisiana Commercial Laws, R.S. 10:9–101 et seq., where applicable, a transfer or an encumbrance by a beneficiary of his interest shall be by authentic act or by act under private signature executed in the presence of two witnesses and duly acknowledged by the beneficiary or by the affidavit of one of the attesting witnesses. Except as otherwise provided by Chapter 9 of the Louisiana Commercial Laws, R.S. 10:9–101 et seq., where applicable, the transfer or encumbrance is not effective as to a trustee until a copy of the authentic act or a copy of the acknowledged act is received by him.

Added by Acts 1964, No. 338, § 2. Amended by Acts 1991, No. 665, § 1.

Comments—1964

(a) The Trust Estates Law was silent on this subject.

(b) In other states a writing is not essential to a transfer by a beneficiary of his interest unless a statute provides otherwise. Statutes in most states require the transfer of an interest in a trust of land by a beneficiary to be in writing. Restatement of Trusts 2d, Secs. 39–50, 138, 139.

(c) The form provided by this section is the same as that provided by Sec. 1752 for the creation of an inter vivos trust.

Cross References

C.C. arts. 517, 518, 1833, 1836.

§ 2004. Seizure by creditor; general rule

A creditor may seize only:

(1) An interest in income or principal that is subject to voluntary alienation by a beneficiary.

(2) A beneficiary's interest in income and principal, to the extent that the beneficiary has donated property to the trust, directly or indirectly. A beneficiary will not be deemed to have donated property to a trust merely because he fails to exercise a right of withdrawal from the trust.

Added by Acts 1964, No. 338, § 2. Amended by Acts 1985, No. 581, § 1; Acts 1987, No. 246, § 1, eff. July 3, 1987; Acts 1997, No. 253, § 1; Acts 2010, No. 390, § 1.

Comments—1964

(a) Sub-section (1) makes no change in the law.

(b) Clauses (1) and (4) of R.S. 9:1923A were similar in effect to sub-section (2) of this section. Clause (1) provided that all income due or to accrue in the future in excess of $5,000 per annum was subject to seizure by a creditor of the beneficiary and freely alienable by the beneficiary. Clause (4) provided that the aggregate net income payable to the beneficiary from all spendthrift trusts and insurance policies was considered for the purpose of determining the rights of creditors and assignees. The major changes that this Code effects are to increase to $10,000 the income amount that should be considered in determining the rights of creditors, to remove the limitations that had been placed upon the validity of a restraint of voluntary alienation, and to eliminate income from insurance policies in computing the income amount that should be considered in determining the rights of creditors.

(c) Sub-section (3) of this section makes no change in the law. It follows the laws of other states and the rule of the Restatement in providing that a settlor cannot create a spendthrift trust for his own benefit. Scott on Trusts, Sec. 156 (2d ed. 1956); Restatement of Trusts 2d, Sec. 156.

(d) The trust instrument may restrict alienation to a lesser degree than permitted by this Code, but a trust existing under such an instrument is not a "spendthrift trust," as defined in this Code. For the definition of "spendthrift trust," see Sec. 1725.

Editor's note. Acts 2010, No. 390, § 2, declares that: "The provisions of this Act shall apply to all trusts, whether created before or after the effective date of this Act [August 15, 2010], but R.S. 9:1895(A)(3) shall apply only to substitutions occurring after the effective date of this Act."

Cross References

C.C. arts. 3182, 3183.

§ 2005. Seizure by creditor; special claims

Notwithstanding any stipulation in the trust instrument to the contrary, the proper court, in summary proceedings to which the trustee, the beneficiary, and the beneficiary's creditor shall be parties, may permit seizure of any portion of the beneficiary's interest in trust income and principal in its discretion and as may be just under the circumstances if the claim is based upon a judgment for:

(1) Alimony, or maintenance of a person whom the beneficiary is obligated to support;

(2) Necessary services rendered or necessary supplies furnished to the beneficiary or to a person whom the beneficiary is obligated to support; or

(3) Damages arising from a felony criminal offense committed by the beneficiary which results in a conviction or a plea of guilty.

Added by Acts 1964, No. 338, § 2. Amended by Acts 2010, No. 457, § 1.

Comments—1964

(a) Clause (3) of R.S. 9:1923A provided that the proper court had power to direct the payment of income to a creditor as might be just under the circumstances if the claim was for the support of a husband, wife, or child of the beneficiary, for alimony, for necessary supplies furnished the beneficiary, or for a tort, or if the claim was based upon a judgment for such a claim.

(b) In determining whether or not it is just that a claim for support or for alimony should be satisfied through seizure of a beneficiary's interest, a court should consider the condition of the beneficiary and the claimant.

(c) A person is obligated to support his spouse, his children, and his needy ascendants and descendants. Arts. 119 [see, now, C.C. art. 98], 227, 229, R.C.C.

(d) In other states, even if involuntary alienation is restricted, the interest of the beneficiary can be reached to enforce claims for the support of the wife, children, or other dependents of the beneficiary, claims for necessaries furnished the beneficiary, claims for services that result in increasing or preserving the beneficiary's interest in the trust, claims of the state or federal government, and (so far as there is authority) claims for torts. The Restatement of Trusts 2d is similar to the laws of other states, although it does not list tort claims because, as Scott explains, substantial authority is lacking. Scott on Trusts, Secs. 157–157.5 (2d ed. 1956); Restatement of Trusts 2d, Sec. 157.

Cross References

C.C. arts. 119, 160, 227, 229, 2315.

§ 2006. Exemption from seizure

Exemptions from seizure accorded by law to any kind of property or interest in property are effective with respect to such property in trust to the same extent as if the property were held free of trust.

Added by Acts 1964, No. 338, § 2.

Comments—1964

This section makes no change in the law. It is in general accord with the laws of other states. See Restatement of Trusts 2d, Sec. 149; Scott on Trusts, Sec. 149 (2d ed. 1956).

Cross References

C.C. arts. 3182, 3183.

§ 2007. Use of words "spendthrift trust"

A declaration in a trust instrument that the interest of a beneficiary shall be held subject to a "spendthrift trust" is sufficient to restrain alienation by a beneficiary of the interest to the maximum extent permitted by this Sub-part.

Added by Acts 1964, No. 338, § 2.

Comments—1964

(a) This section makes no change in the law.

(b) Secs. 2004 and 2005 limit the validity of a restraint upon involuntary alienation. A restraint upon voluntary alienation is valid. Sec. 2002. For the definition of "spendthrift trust," see Sec. 1725.

Cross References

C.C. arts. 454, 1971.

SUBPART E. DEFERRED ASCERTAINMENT OF PRINCIPAL BENEFICIARIES OF REVOCABLE TRUSTS

§ 2011. General rule

A revocable trust instrument need not designate the beneficiaries upon the creation of the trust but may instead provide a method whereby they are determined at a later date, but no later than the date when the trust becomes irrevocable. A beneficiary thus determined may be a person who is not in being when the trust is created, as long as he is in being when the beneficiaries are determined. If beneficiaries are thus determined, any provision in this Code that refers to persons in existence at the creation of the trust shall be deemed to refer to persons in existence at the time when the beneficiaries are determined under the trust instrument. The interest of the beneficiary may be conditioned upon the beneficiary surviving the settlor for a period of time permitted by Civil Code Article 1521.

Added by Acts 1988, No. 589, § 1. Amended by Acts 1989, No. 112, § 1; Acts 1995, No. 413, § 1; Acts 2010, No. 390, § 1.

Comments—1988

(a) The provisions of R.S. 9:2011 et seq., allow a settlor to establish and fund a trust during life in a form valid as an inter vivos trust, and to provide in the instrument standards for determining at his death (or at an earlier date when the trust becomes irrevocable) the beneficiaries to succeed him. In this way the inter vivos trust can work like a testament that has vulgar substitutions. Instances of the Civil Code's recognition of the provisional nature of a donation as long as the donor is living can be found in Civil Code Articles 1501–1518, 1534 and 1559–1569.

(b) The provisions of this Section apply only if it is clear that the settlor intends the beneficiaries named in the trust instrument to take only if they are in existence at a later time. For example, a designation of "my children", with nothing more, as the principal beneficiaries has the effect of designating the children of the settlor living at the time the trust is created as the principal beneficiaries, and upon the death of any of them his interest will pass under R.S. 9:1972 et seq. A designation of "my children living at my death" as the principal beneficiaries has the effect of designating as the principal beneficiaries only those children of the settlor living upon the settlor's death. Children born after the creation of the trust and living at the settlor's death will be included; children who die after the creation of the trust and before the settlor's death will not be included, nor do they have a heritable interest at their deaths. This Section allows a trust instrument to designate as the principal beneficiaries some or all of the descendants of the settlor who would be his legal heirs upon his death.

Comment—1989

The "provisions of this Code" referred to in the new sentence include, for example, Sections 1891, 1894, and 1975.

Editor's note. Acts 2010, No. 390, § 2, declares that: "The provisions of this Act shall apply to all trusts, whether created before or after the effective date of this Act [August 15, 2010], but R.S. 9:1895(A)(3) shall apply only to substitutions occurring after the effective date of this Act."

§ 2012. Provisional principal beneficiaries

Until the time when the principal beneficiaries are determined, the persons who would be the principal beneficiaries had that time arrived shall be known as the provisional principal beneficiaries. Provisional principal beneficiaries shall be income beneficiaries in the absence of an effectively designated income beneficiary. A provisional principal beneficiary who is not an income beneficiary is not considered a beneficiary for any purposes under this Code.

Added by Acts 1988, No. 589, § 1.

Comment—1988

For example, if the trust instrument identifies the principal beneficiaries as "settlor's descendant heirs at his death, equally by roots" the persons who would be the settlor's descendant heirs if he were to die at a particular time are the provisional principal beneficiaries at that time.

§ 2013. Settlor as default principal beneficiary

If the trust instrument fails effectively to designate a principal beneficiary at the time when the principal beneficiary is to be determined, the settlor shall be the principal beneficiary, and upon his death his interest shall vest in his heirs or legatees. Likewise, if at any time no provisional principal beneficiary is identifiable under the terms of the trust instrument, the settlor shall be the provisional principal beneficiary.

Added by Acts 1988, No. 589, § 1.

Comment—1988

It can happen that the designation of principal beneficiaries at a later date is ineffectual because of unexpected deaths or otherwise. Any hiatus caused thereby is filled by the settlor. For example, if the trust instrument designates as principal beneficiary "settlor's sister Mary if living at settlor's death otherwise her children living at settlor's death", with no other contingent designation, and Mary dies without issue before the settlor dies, upon Mary's death the settlor becomes the provisional principal beneficiary, and the settlor will ultimately be the principal beneficiary unless the settlor amends the trust to designate someone else as principal beneficiary.

§ 2014. Number of settlors allowed

A. Except as provided in Subsection B, the provisions of this Subpart shall apply only if the trust has but one settlor.

B. If a trust is created by two settlors who are married to each other, and the trust instrument divides community property in the manner described in R.S. 9:1955, and the trust becomes irrevocable as to a spouse's share or trust no later than at the death of that spouse, the beneficiaries of such share or trust may be ascertained under the provisions of this Subpart.

Added by Acts 1988, No. 589, § 1. Amended by Acts 1995, No. 1038, § 3.

Comment—1988

This restriction is necessary to make sure that the delay in ascertaining the principal beneficiaries of the trust does not continue beyond the death of a settlor. A trust having but one settlor cannot be revoked after the death of the settlor and accordingly the interests in the trust become fixed no later than the death of the settlor. If two or more persons could be settlors of a trust under this Subpart, the revocability of the trust could continue after the death of one of them, under R.S. 9:2044, and accordingly the beneficiaries would not be ascertainable at a date no later than that settlor's death.

Comment—1995

The language added by Subsection B is necessary to conform the rules on deferred ascertainment of principal beneficiaries with the new Section 1955 concerning community property in trust. The trust permitted by Section 1955 will have two settlors, the spouses. Prior to this amendment, Section 2014 would not have permitted deferred ascertainment of principal beneficiaries for a trust with more than one settlor. This amendment permits a spouse to defer the ascertainment of the principal beneficiary of his or her respective share or trust; however, the share or trust of a settlor-spouse who wishes to defer the ascertainment of the principal beneficiary must become irrevocable no later than that spouse's death.

Cross References

C.C. art. 2338.

R.S. 9:1731 et seq., 9:1955.

PART IV. MODIFICATION, TERMINATION, REVOCATION, AND RESCISSION OF THE TRUST

SUBPART A. MODIFICATION AND TERMINATION OF THE TRUST

§ 2021. General rule; modification

The settlor may modify the terms of the trust after its creation only to the extent he expressly reserves the right to do so.

Added by Acts 1964, No. 338, § 2.

Comment—1964

This section makes no change in the law. It takes the general position taken by the Restatement of Trusts 2d, Sec. 331, and by other states. Bogert, Trusts and Trustees, Sec. 992 (2d ed. 1962); Scott on Trusts, Secs. 329A, 331 (2d ed. 1956).

Cross References

C.C. arts. 1906, 1983, 1985.

§ 2022. Effect of reservation of right to revoke

Reservation of the right to revoke includes the right to modify the trust.

Added by Acts 1964, No. 338, § 2.

Comments—1964

(a) This section makes no change in the law.

(b) The Restatement of Trusts 2d, Sec. 331, Comment (g), provides that the question of whether or not the reservation of the right to revoke includes the right to modify the trust is a question of interpretation, although ordinarily the reservation of a general right to revoke should be considered to permit modification of the trust. Under this Code, if the settlor has reserved an unrestricted right to revoke the trust, he may modify the trust, unless in the trust instrument the settlor specifically denies himself that right.

§ 2023. Effect of reservation of unrestricted right to modify

If the settlor reserves an unrestricted right to modify the trust, he may change or amend the terms of the trust in any particular, or even revoke or terminate the trust.

Added by Acts 1964, No. 338, § 2.

Comments—1964

(a) This Code draws a distinction between revocation and termination that was not drawn in Trust Estates Law and that is not drawn in the Restatement of Trusts 2d or in Bogert or Scott. Bogert, Trusts and Trustees, Sec. 998 (2d ed. 1962); Scott on Trusts, Sec. 330 (2d ed. 1956); Restatement of Trusts 2d, Secs. 330, 332, 334–345. A termination of a trust causes the dispositive provisions of the trust to accomplish their purpose. A revocation of a trust causes the dispositive provisions of the trust to cease to have effect.

(b) It was not clear under the Trust Estates Law whether or not the reservation of an unqualified right to modify the trust included the right to terminate or to revoke the trust. R.S. 9:2171.

(c) The laws of other states provide that the reservation of an unrestricted right to modify a trust includes the right to revoke the trust. Scott on Trusts, Sec. 331.2 (2d ed. 1956) and the Restatement of Trusts 2d, Sec. 331, Comment (h).

Cross References

C.C. arts. 454, 1971.

§ 2024. Concurrence of settlors in modification

All surviving competent settlors must concur in a modification of the trust.

Added by Acts 1964, No. 338, § 2.

Comments—1964

(a) The Trust Estates Law was silent on this subject.

(b) If there are two or more settlors, the concurrence of only those settlors who are living is required to modify the trust. The concurrence or non-concurrence of the heirs or legatees of the settlors who have died has no legal significance. A surviving competent settlor may modify the trust.

(c) The personal representative of a settlor who has become incompetent cannot exercise the settlor's right of modification. The laws of other states are similar. Bogert, Trusts and Trustees, Sec. 993 (2d ed. 1962).

§ 2025. Delegation of right to terminate or to modify administrative provisions

A settlor may delegate to another person the right to terminate a trust, or to modify the administrative provisions of a trust, but the right to modify other provisions of a trust may not be delegated except as provided in R.S. 9:2031.

Added by Acts 1964, No. 338, § 2. Amended by Acts 2010, No. 390, § 1.

Comments—1964

(a) The Trust Estates Law was silent on this subject.

(b) In other states a settlor can delegate the right to modify a trust to another. Bogert, Trusts and Trustees, Sec. 993 (2d ed. 1962).

(c) Under this Code, the right to revoke a trust can never be delegated. Sec. 2045.

(d) In other states a settlor can reserve the power of revocation or grant the power to terminate to another. This Code draws a distinction between revocation and termination that is not drawn in other states. Bogert, Trusts and Trustees, Secs. 998, 1000 (2d ed. 1962).

Editor's note. Acts 2010, No. 390, § 2, declares that: "The provisions of this Act shall apply to all trusts, whether created before or after the effective date of this Act [August 15, 2010], but R.S. 9:1895(A)(3) shall apply only to substitutions occurring after the effective date of this Act."

Cross References

C.C. art. 1886.

§ 2026. Change of circumstances

The proper court may order the termination or modification of a trust, in whole or in part, if:

(1) The continuance of the trust unchanged would defeat or substantially impair the purposes of the trust.

(2) Except as otherwise provided by the terms of the trust, a trustee has determined that the market value of a trust is less than one hundred thousand dollars and that, in relation to the costs of administration of the trust, the continuance of the trust unchanged would defeat or substan-

tially impair the purposes of the trust. In such a case, the court may provide for the distribution of the trust property, including principal and undistributed income, to the beneficiaries in a manner which conforms as nearly as possible to the intention of the settlor and the court shall make appropriate provisions for the appointment of a tutor in the case of a minor beneficiary. In the event of the termination or modification of a trust under the provisions of this Paragraph, the trustee shall not be subject to liability for such termination or modification.

Added by Acts 1964, No. 338, § 2. Amended by Acts 1991, No. 665, § 1; Acts 1997, No. 252, § 1; Acts 2001, No. 594, § 2.

Comments—1964

(a) This section makes no change in the law, except possibly in one particular. This section provides that the proper court can direct the modification or termination of the trust. On the contrary, former R.S. 9:2175 provided, and the Restatement of Trusts, Sec. 336, and the Restatement of Trusts 2d, Sec. 336, provide, for termination, but not modification.

(b) The Trust Estates Law did not make, and the Restatement of Trusts, Sec. 336 and the Restatement of Trusts 2d, Sec. 336, do not make, the distinction between revocation and termination of a trust. For the distinction between revocation and termination of a trust, see Comment (a) under Sec. 2023.

Comment—1997

As originally written Section 2026(1) allowed termination or modification of a trust only if the court found that the impairment of the trust purpose was due to "circumstances not known to a settlor and not anticipated by him." The settlor's knowledge or anticipation of the change of circumstances is a fact rarely susceptible of objective proof. The requirement invited speculative evidence and unnecessarily restricted the court's power to prevent the trust's purpose from being defeated or impaired. Under the revision a petitioner for modification or termination must still show a change of circumstances.

Editor's note. Acts 2001, No. 594, § 2, amended R.S. 9:2026(2), effective August 15, 2001. Section 4 of Acts 2001, No. 594, declares that "The provisions of Section 3 of this Act shall not apply to a transfer in trust made prior to the effective date of this Act."

Cross References

C.C. arts.1873, 1876.

§ 2027. Accomplishment of purposes becoming impossible or illegal

The proper court may order the termination or modification of the trust if the purpose for which it is created becomes impossible of accomplishment or illegal.

Added by Acts 1964, No. 338, § 2.

Comments—1964

This section makes no change in the law. Its language is taken from R.S. 9:2174, a section of the Trust Estates Law that was identical with Sec. 335 of the Restatement of Trusts. The language of Sec. 335 of the Restatement of Trusts 2d follows that of Sec. 335 of the Restatement of Trusts.

Cross References

C.C. arts. 7, 1769.

§ 2028. Concurrence of settlors in termination

The consent of all settlors, trustees, and beneficiaries shall not be effective to terminate the trust or any disposition in trust, unless the trust instrument provides otherwise.

Added by Acts 1964, No. 338, § 2.

Comments—1964

(a) This section makes no change in the law.

(b) Cf. the Restatement of Trusts 2d, Secs. 337, 338.

(c) See Sec. 2025 on the rights of a settlor to delegate rights to terminate or modify a trust.

§ 2029. Effect of termination

A termination of a trust causes the dispositive provisions of the trust to achieve their ultimate effect. A partial termination of a trust causes some of the dispositive provisions to achieve their ultimate effect. A beneficiary receiving trust property as a result of the whole or partial termination of a trust shall be personally liable for the obligations and liabilities of the trust existing on the date of termination to the extent of the value of the trust property received by such beneficiary unless, in the case of a partial termination, existing trust property is sufficient to satisfy the obligations and liabilities of the trust.

Added by Acts 1964, No. 338, § 2. Amended by Acts 1995, No. 344, § 3.

Comments—1964

(a) The Trust Estates Law was silent on this subject.

(b) For the effect of revocation and rescission, see Sec. 2046.

(c) A termination as to a part of a principal beneficiary's interest will require that the trust principal be considered as having been divided into separate shares, in order to avoid encroachment on the interests of other beneficiaries. Thereafter, that principal beneficiary's interest in income and principal is determined on such separate share basis.

(d) Even if the trust is not revoked, rescinded, or terminated by an outside agency, it must by its own nature terminate, either at the end of the term provided by the trust instrument or at the end of the term provided by this Code. Secs. 1831–1834.

§ 2030. Combination and division of trusts

A trustee may combine two or more trusts into one trust, or divide a trust into two or more trusts, on written notice to all beneficiaries having a current interest in the trust or trusts, if the combination or division does not impair the rights of any beneficiary or adversely affect the accomplishment of the purposes of the trust or trusts. The division of a trust shall be based on the fair market value of the assets of the trust on the effective date of the division and need not result in a uniform interest in each asset. After the division, discretionary distributions need not be made uniformly from each of the separate trusts. A trust instrument may modify these rules, either to expand or to restrict the trustee's authority to combine or divide a trust.

Added by Acts 1995, No. 344, § 2. Amended by Acts 2001, No. 594, § 2.

Comment—2001

The revision extends Section 2030 to permit the combination as well as the division of trusts. Combining trusts may allow for administrative economies. The trusts to be combined and the trusts that result from a division are not required to have identical terms so long as no beneficiary's interest is impaired.

Editor's note. Acts 2001, No. 594, § 2, amended R.S. 9:2030, effective August 15, 2001. Section 4 of Acts 2001, No. 594, declares that "The provisions of Section 3 of this Act shall not apply to a transfer in trust made prior to the effective date of this Act."

§ 2031. Delegation of right to amend

A trust instrument may authorize a person other than the settlor to modify the provisions of the trust instrument in order to add or remove beneficiaries, or modify their rights, if all of the affected beneficiaries are descendants of the person given the power to modify.

Added by Acts 2010, No. 390, § 1.

Comment—2010

A power to amend granted under this Section will not be allowed to the extent that the exercise of the power would impinge on a beneficiary's legitime held in the trust. See R.S. 9:1841.

Editor's note. Acts 2010, No. 390, § 2, declares that: "The provisions of this Act shall apply to all trusts, whether created before or after the effective date of this Act [August 15, 2010], but R.S. 9:1895(A)(3) shall apply only to substitutions occurring after the effective date of this Act."

A prior R.S. 9:2031 was repealed by Acts 1964, No. 338, § 1.

SUBPART B. REVOCATION AND RESCISSION OF THE TRUST

§ 2041. General rule; revocation

Except as otherwise provided in this Code, a settlor may revoke a trust in whole or in part only if he has reserved the right to revoke the trust or an unrestricted right to modify the trust.

Added by Acts 1964, No. 338, § 2.

Comments—1964

(a) This section makes no change in the law. A distinction is drawn in this Code between revocation and termination of a trust, not drawn in the Trust Estates Law and not drawn in Restatement of Trusts 2d or in Bogert or Scott. Bogert, Trusts and Trustees, Sec. 998 (2d ed. 1962); Scott on Trusts, Sec. 330 (2d ed. 1956); Restatement of Trusts 2d, Secs. 330, 332, 334, 345. See Sec. 2029.

(b) This section follows generally the Restatement of Trusts 2d, Sec. 330, and the laws of other states. Bogert, Trusts and Trustees, Secs. 329A, 330 (2d ed. 1962); Scott on Trusts, Sec. 998 (2d ed. 1956). However, in other states a settlor who has not reserved a power of revocation is permitted to revoke a trust if he is the sole beneficiary of the trust. Bogert, Trusts and Trustees, Secs. 992, 1004 (2d ed. 1962). The Restatement of Trusts 2d, Sec. 339, takes a similar position. The position taken by the Restatement of Trusts 2d and by other states is not taken by this Code.

Cross References

C.C. arts. 1606.

§ 2042. Effect of reservation of right to revoke

A reservation by the settlor of the right to revoke includes the right to revoke the interest of any beneficiary, unless otherwise limited by the trust instrument.

Added by Acts 1964, No. 338, § 2.

Comments—1964

This section makes no change in the law. Under the Trust Estates Law, the right to revoke the trust included the right to modify the trust. R.S. 9:2172. By modifying the trust the settlor could revoke the interest of a beneficiary.

Cross References

C.C. arts. 454, 1606, 1983.

§ 2043. Revocation or rescission under general law

An onerous disposition in trust may be rescinded for the causes and under the limitations specified in the general law of contracts. A gratuitous disposition may be revoked for the causes and under the limitations specified in the general law of donations, whether or not the right to revoke has been reserved. For this purpose every disposition in favor of a particular beneficiary shall be treated as a separate donation or contract, as the case may be.

Added by Acts 1964, No. 338, § 2.

Comments—1964

(a) The Trust Estates Law provided that a trust could be "rescinded or revoked" on the same grounds as those upon which a conveyance of immovable property could be "rescinded or revoked," even though the right to revoke was not specifically reserved in the trust instrument. R.S. 9:2173. The language of R.S. 9:2173 was similar to that of Sec. 333 of the Restatement of Trusts and is repeated in the same section of the Restatement of Trusts 2d.

(b) Arts. 1881, 1882, 2221–2231, R.C.C. [see, now, generally, C.C. arts. 1919 to 1924, 2029 to 2033], which treat the rescission of contracts, apply to the rescission of trusts and dispositions in trust.

(c) Arts. 1559–1569, R.C.C., which treat the revocation of donations, apply to the revocation of trusts and dispositions in trust.

(d) If a trust is gratuitous, a revocation of the trust or of a disposition in the trust may be obtained under the proper circumstances. If a trust is onerous, a rescission of the trust may be obtained under the proper circumstances.

Cross References

C.C. arts. 1559, 1606 et seq., 1948, 1959, 1965, 2013, 2029.

§ 2044. Concurrence of settlors in revocation; effect

Revocation of a trust, or of a disposition in trust, pursuant to a reservation of such a right, requires the concurrence of all surviving competent settlors, in the absence of a contrary stipulation.

Added by Acts 1964, No. 338, § 2.

Comments—1964

(a) The Trust Estates Law was silent on this subject.

(b) This section is in accord with Sec. 2024, which requires that all competent settlors who are living concur in a modification of a trust.

§ 2045. Delegation of right to revoke

A settlor who has reserved the right to revoke a trust may delegate the right. The delegation may be accomplished only by an express statement in the trust instrument or in a power of attorney executed by authentic act referring to the trust. The right to amend may not be delegated except as provided in R.S. 9:2025 and 2031.

Added by Acts 1964, No. 338, § 2. Amended by Acts 2001, No. 594, § 2; Acts 2010, No. 390, § 1.

Comments—1964

(a) The Trust Estates Law was silent on this subject.

(b) Although the right to revoke cannot be delegated by the settlor to another person, revocation can sometimes be obtained by someone not a settlor for the causes specified in the general law of donations. *Cf.* Sec. 2043.

(c) This Code provides that the right to terminate or to modify the administrative provisions of a trust may be delegated by the settlor to another person but that the right to modify other provisions may not be delegated. Sec. 2025.

Comment—2001

The revocation of a trust results in the trust property returning to the settlor unless the trust instrument provides otherwise. R.S. 9:2046. A settlor, for example, anticipating his own future incapacity and need for the property, can delegate expressly the power of revoking the trust.

Editor's note. Acts 2001, No. 594, § 2, amended R.S. 9:2045, effective August 15, 2001. Section 4 of Acts 2001, No. 594, declares that "The provisions of Section 3 of this Act shall not apply to a transfer in trust made prior to the effective date of this Act."

Acts 2010, No. 390, § 2, declares that: "The provisions of this Act shall apply to all trusts, whether created before or after the effective date of this Act [August 15, 2010], but R.S. 9:1895(A)(3) shall apply only to substitutions occurring after the effective date of this Act."

Cross References

C.C. arts. 1606.

§ 2046. Effect of revocation or rescission

The settlor may stipulate the effect of revocation or rescission of a disposition. Unless the trust instrument otherwise provides, the following rules shall govern:

(1) Revocation or rescission shall cause the trust to fail and the trust property held by the trustee at the time such revocation or rescission takes effect shall revert to the settlor or his heirs, legatees, or assignees;

(2) Revocation or rescission of a disposition affecting an income beneficiary has the same effect as if the beneficiary had died on the effective date of the revocation or rescission;

(3) Revocation or rescission at any time of a disposition in favor of a principal beneficiary operates a substitution of the settlor, or his heirs, legatees, or assignees as the beneficiary of the interest involved, without affecting the interest of the income beneficiaries; if there are two or more settlors, each disposition affecting principal shall be divided into as many separate dispositions as the number of settlors, and each settlor or his heirs, legatees, or assignees shall receive a share in proportion to the amount of his contribution to the trust principal;

(4) Revocation or rescission affects property added to a trust according to the rules of this section.

(5) Acts of the trustee with regard to the trust property shall not be affected by the subsequent revocation or rescission of a disposition in trust. After a trust has been revoked or rescinded, the trustee shall have only those powers necessary to carry out the effects of the revocation or rescission.

(6) A person receiving trust property as a result of the revocation or rescission of the trust shall be personally liable for the obligations and liabilities of the trust existing on the date of revocation or rescission to the extent of the value of the trust property received by such beneficiary unless existing trust property is sufficient to satisfy the obligations and liabilities of the trust.

Added by Acts 1964, No. 338, § 2. Amended by Acts 1974, No. 128, § 1; Acts 1995, No. 344, § 3.

Comments—1964

(a) The Trust Estates Law was silent on this subject.

(b) In connection with Sub-section (2) of this section, see Secs. 1895, 1965.

(c) In the laws of other states revocation of a trust erases the trust and causes the property to return to the settlor. Bogert, Trusts and Trustees, Sec. 998 (2d ed. 1962); Scott on Trusts, Secs. 329A, 330 (2d ed. 1956).

(d) If the trust is revoked or rescinded, the added property is disposed of in the same manner as the property already in the trust.

Comments—1974

Subsection (1) was amended and subsection (5) was added by Acts 1974, No. 128 to make it clear that the trustee's powers over the trust property are in no way limited by the fact that the trust may be revocable or subject to rescission in the future. So long as the trust has not been revoked or rescinded, third persons may rely upon the actions of the trustee as though the trust were irrevocable and not subject to rescission. Subsequent to revocation or rescission, the trustee may still exercise such powers as may be necessary to carry out its legal consequences. For example, the trustee of a revocable trust may convey good title to trust property until such time as the settlor revokes the trust. The revocation affects only the trust property to which the trustee has title at the time of the revocation.

Comments—1995

(a) R.S. 9:2030 enables the trustee to divide a trust into two or more trusts with identical provisions. The power to divide might be useful when only a fraction of the original trust is subject to a potential transfer tax by operation of Internal Revenue Code Section 2056(b)(7), Section 2632, or some other section.

(b) For the form needed to divide a trust into two or more separate trusts, see R.S. 9:2051.

Cross References

C.C. arts. 454, 966, 1520, 1608, 1609, 1699.

SUBPART C. FORMAL REQUIREMENTS

§ 2051. Form

A. A modification, division, termination, or revocation of a trust shall be by authentic act or by act under private signature executed in the presence of two witnesses and duly acknowledged by the person who makes the modification, division, or termination or by the affidavit of one of the attesting witnesses. The modification, division, termination, or revocation is not effective as to a trustee until a copy of the authentic act or a copy of the acknowledged act is received by him.

B. A modification, division, termination, or revocation of a trust may also be by testament. Such a modification, division, termination, or revocation is not effective as to a trustee until the trustee receives a copy of the testament and of the order probating it or ordering it filed and executed.

Added by Acts 1964, No. 338, § 2. Amended by Acts 1995, No. 344, § 1; Acts 2003, No. 480, § 1.

Comments—1964

(a) The Trust Estates Law was silent on this subject.

(b) The form provided by this section is the same as that provided by Sec. 1752 for the creation of an inter vivos trust and by Sec. 2003 for the alienation or encumbrance of a beneficiary's interest.

Revision Comment—2003

Subsection B allows the settlor of an inter vivos trust, who has reserved the power to modify, divide, terminate, or revoke the trust, to do so by testament. The testament must clearly identify the trust in order to have any effect on it.

Editor's note. Section 2 of Acts 2003, No. 480 declares that the amendments to "R.S. 9:1809, 1893, 1963, 1965, 1990, and 2068 shall apply only to trusts created after the effective date of this Act. The amendments to R.S. 9:1979, 2051, 2131, 2159(1), and 2241 shall apply to all trusts." Acts 2003, No. 480 became effective on August 15, 2003.

Cross References

C.C. arts. 1832, 1833, 1836, 1837.

PART V. DUTIES AND POWERS OF THE TRUSTEE

SUBPART A. GENERAL DISPOSITIONS

§ 2061. General rule

The nature and extent of the duties and powers of a trustee are determined from the provisions of the trust instrument, except as otherwise expressly provided in this Code, and, in the absence of any provisions of the trust instrument, by the provisions of this Part and by law.

Added by Acts 1964, No. 338, § 2.

Comments—1964

(a) This Sub-part contains in modified form the general dispositions made in the Trust Estates Law with respect to the duties and powers of the trustee.

(b) R.S. 9:1941 was based upon the Restatement of Trusts, Sec. 164. This section closely resembles R.S. 9:1941, but it uses the phrase "provisions of the trust instrument" rather than the phrase "terms of the trust" to make it clear that under normal circumstances manifestations of the settlor's intention made outside the trust instrument cannot be considered in determining the powers and duties of the trustee. The Restatement of Trusts 2d, Sec. 4, defines the "terms of the trust" as the "manifestation of intention of the settlor with respect to the trust expressed in a manner which admits of its proof in judicial proceedings."

Cross References

C.C. arts. 1983, 2045 to 2057.

§ 2062. Limitation of duties by settlor

A provision of the trust instrument that purports to limit a trustee's duty of loyalty to the beneficiary is ineffective, except to the extent permitted by this Part.

Added by Acts 1964, No. 338, § 2.

Comments—1964

(a) R.S. 9:2035 contained language that possibly gave the erroneous impression that a settlor who sought to provide a system of powers and duties for a trustee different from that provided by statute was required to define precisely in the trust instrument the nature of his departure from the statutory system.

(b) The Restatement of Trusts 2d states that by the terms of the trust a trustee may be permitted as trustee to sell trust property to himself individually, to buy property from himself individually, to lend to himself money held by him in trust, or otherwise to deal with trust property on his own account, but that the trustee violates his duty of loyalty to the beneficiary if he acts in bad faith regardless of the terms of the trust. Sec. 2062 does not follow the

Restatement rule. Restatement of Trusts 2d, Sec. 170, Comment (t).

Cross References

C.C. art. 7.

§ 2063. Relief from duties by beneficiary

By written instrument delivered to a trustee a competent beneficiary who is acting upon full information may, with respect to himself, and with the trustee's consent, relieve the trustee from duties and restrictions concerning the administration of the trust that are imposed upon the trustee by the trust instrument or by this Code, but no such instrument is effective to the extent that it purports to limit prospectively and in general terms the trustee's duty of loyalty to the beneficiary.

Added by Acts 1964, No. 338, § 2.

Comments—1964

R.S. 9:2036 was based upon the Uniform Trusts Act, Sec. 18.

Cross References

C.C. arts. 7, 454, 1971.

§ 2064. Judicial permission or direction to deviate from administrative provisions of trust instrument

The proper court may direct or permit a trustee to deviate from a provision of the trust instrument concerning the administration of the trust if compliance would defeat or substantially impair the purposes of the trust.

Added by Acts 1964, No. 338, § 2. Amended by Acts 1997, No. 252, § 1.

Comments—1964

(a) This section makes no change in the law.

(b) R.S. 9:1942 was based upon the Restatement of Trusts, Sec. 167. This section is similar to Sec. 167 of the Restatement of Trusts 2d.

Comment—1997

This amendment, which makes a change of circumstances the basis for seeking modification of the administrative provisions of a trust, is consistent with the similar amendment to Section 2026(1) concerning modification or termination of a trust.

§ 2065. Judicial permission to deviate from administrative provisions of this code

The proper court for cause shown may relieve a trustee from duties and restrictions that otherwise would be placed upon him by the administrative provisions of this Code.

Added by Acts 1964, No. 338, § 2.

Comments—1964

(a) This section makes no change in the law.

(b) R.S. 9:2037 was based upon the Uniform Trusts Act, Sec. 19.

§ 2066. Judicial permission or direction to deviate from investment provisions of trust instrument

The proper court, if convinced that adherence to the investments prescribed by the trust instrument would be likely to affect adversely the best interests of a beneficiary to a serious extent, having due regard for the purposes of the trust, may upon application by a trustee or a beneficiary permit or direct the trustee to invest in securities not prescribed by the trust instrument, but a trustee is under no duty to make such an application to the court.

Added by Acts 1964, No. 338, § 2.

Comments—1964

R.S. 9:2062 permitted a trustee to apply for relief. This section makes clear that the court can act not only upon the application of a trustee, but upon the application of a beneficiary.

§ 2067. Invasion of principal; action of court

The proper court may direct or permit a trustee to pay income or principal from the trust property for the necessary support, maintenance, education, medical expenses, or welfare of a beneficiary before the time he is entitled to the enjoyment of that income or principal, if the interest of no other beneficiary of the trust is impaired thereby.

Added by Acts 1964, No. 338, § 2.

Comments—1964

R.S. 9:1943 was based upon the Restatement of Trusts, Sec. 168. This section is similar to Sec. 168 of the Restatement of Trusts 2d.

Cross References

C.C. arts. 98, 160, 227, 229.

§ 2068. Invasion of principal; provisions of trust instrument

A. The trust instrument may direct or permit a trustee to pay principal to an income beneficiary for support, maintenance, education, or medical expenses, or pursuant to an objective standard, for any other purpose. The trust instrument may direct the trustee to pay all or part of the principal to an income beneficiary upon the request of the beneficiary. The trust instrument may direct the trustee to pay a stipulated amount or percentage to an income beneficiary under any trust, including a unitrust or annuity trust as defined in the United States Internal Revenue Code, even if the payments exceed income. The trust instrument may provide the manner in which and the share of the trust to which the payment shall be charged; if it does not, all payments of principal made for the benefit of an income beneficiary shall be charged against such beneficiary's share in the trust as principal beneficiary, or, if there is no such share, proportionately against the shares of all principal beneficiaries. Except as provided in R.S. 9:1841 through 1847, treating the legitime in trust, a payment under this Subsection A may be made even though the payment impairs the interest of another beneficiary.

B. If the same person is beneficiary of both income and principal, the trust instrument may direct or permit the trustee in the trustee's complete discretion to invade principal held for that beneficiary.

Added by Acts 1964, No. 338, § 2. Amended by Acts 1968, No. 133, § 1; Acts 1972, No. 661, § 1; Acts 1974, No. 158, § 1; Acts 1989, No. 113, § 1; Acts 1995, No. 220, § 1; Acts 2003, No. 480, § 1.

Comments—1964

(a) The Trust Estates Law was silent on this subject.

(b) In other states the trust instrument may direct or permit the trustee to invade principal for the benefit of an income beneficiary. Bogert, Trusts and Trustees, Sec. 553 (2d ed. 1960); Scott on Trusts, Sec. 128.7 (2d ed. 1956); Restatement of Trusts 2d, Sec. 128, Comment (i).

Comments—1968

(a) It is important to specify in what manner an invasion of accumulated income or principal shall be charged to the particular beneficiary's share. The settlor may provide otherwise if he so desires.

(b) The foregoing amendment of Subsection B does not change what most trust lawyers believe to be the law, but it removes a possible ambiguity in Sec. 2068 as it formerly read. Sec. 2068 authorized invasion of accumulated income or principal under objective standards set forth in the trust instrument, but the requirement of objective standards was intended to apply only to the situation in which the income and principal beneficiaries are different persons. When there is a sole beneficiary of both principal and income, such as commonly occurs in a trust for a minor or in a marital deduction trust, there is no reason to limit the trustee's discretion to invade, nor to require objective standards, since there is no impairment of the interest of another beneficiary.

Comments—1974

In the amendment of Section 2068 by Acts 1972, No. 661, Section 1, the second sentence of subsection A was inadvertently deleted. That sentence, originally inserted by Acts 1968, No. 133, § 1 was restored by Acts 1974, No. 158.

Comments—1989

(a) Several changes are effected by this revision. First, the wording of Subsection A is modified to make it clear that invasion can be allowed for an income beneficiary for any purpose under objective standards. Support, maintenance, education, and medical expenses are purposes that provide in themselves objective standards. This part is intended as a clarification, not a change in the law.

(b) In many situations a settlor may wish to give an income beneficiary a power to withdraw a portion of corpus. One reason for doing so is to qualify a gift to the trust for the annual exclusion. See *Crummey v. Commissioner*, 398 F.2d 82 (9th Cir. 1968). Subsection A is modified to permit such a withdrawal. A failure to exercise such a withdrawal right may be deemed a taxable gift, under Internal Revenue Code Section 2514(e).

(c) Subsection A is further amended to make it clear that not only annuity trusts and unitrusts but all trusts can be subject to a charge to make annuity payments. This is meant to be a clarification rather than a change in the law. See former R.S. 9:2068(A), last sentence. A charge on a trust to pay an annuity is valid even if the annuitant is not expressly designated as an income beneficiary. See R.S. 9:1736 and 9:1737.

Comments—1995

(a) The language deleted from the first sentence of Subsection A is redundant: It provides the same protection for forced heirs that is provided by the last sentence of the subsection. Furthermore, the redundant language in the first sentence implies that a special rule may have been intended for that sentence and not for the next two sentences, but no such distinction was intended.

(b) By deleting the words "up to a stipulated amount or percentage" the intention is to make it clear that a settlor can allow an income beneficiary to request all of the accumulated income or principal. A settlor can, of course, continue to restrict the withdrawal power of the income beneficiary to a percentage or amount less than 100%.

Revision Comment—2003

Accumulated income is no longer treated as principal for purposes of entitlement to distribution. See, R.S. 9:1963. Although the trust instrument may impose objective standards with regard to the distribution of accumulated income, objective standards are no longer required.

Editor's note. Section 2 of Acts 2003, No. 480 declares that the amendments to "R.S. 9:1809, 1893, 1963, 1965, 1990, and 2068 shall apply only to trusts created after the effective date of this Act. The amendments to R.S. 9:1979, 2051, 2131, 2159(1), and 2241 shall apply to all trusts." Acts 2003, No. 480 became effective on August 15, 2003.

§ 2069. Winding-up duty and powers of trustee

If the trust terminates or is revoked, or if the trustee resigns or is removed, he shall preserve the trust property and deliver it without delay to those persons who are entitled to it. Until he delivers the property, the trustee shall retain the powers that are necessary to preserve and deliver it to those persons who are entitled to it.

Added by Acts 1995, No. 358, § 2.

Comment—1995

This provision states the duty and powers of the trustee when either the trust or the trustee's administration is at an end. The trustee's duty is to preserve and deliver the property to those who are entitled to it without delay. The trustee's powers are limited to the powers that are necessary to carry out the duty.

Cross References

C.C. art. 1493 et seq.

SUBPART B. DUTIES OF THE TRUSTEE

§ 2081. Breach of trust defined

A violation by a trustee of a duty he owes to a beneficiary as trustee is a breach of trust.

Added by Acts 1964, No. 338, § 2.

Comments—1964

(a) This Sub-part is similar to R.S. 9:1961–9:1968 of the Trust Estates Law.

(b) This section makes no change in the law.

(c) R.S. 9:1961 was based upon the Restatement of Trusts, Sec. 201. This section is similar to Sec. 201 of the Restatement of Trusts 2d.

Cross References

C.C. arts. 1983, 1986.

§ 2082. Administration in interest of beneficiary; duty of impartiality

A. A trustee shall administer the trust solely in the interest of the beneficiary.

B. When there is more than one beneficiary, a trustee shall administer the trust impartially, based on what is fair and reasonable to all of the beneficiaries, except to the extent that the trust instrument manifests an intention that the trustee shall or may favor one or more of the beneficiaries.

Added by Acts 1964, No. 338, § 2. Amended by Acts 2001, No. 520, § 1.

Comments—1964

(a) This section makes no change in the law.

(b) R.S. 9:1962(2) was based upon the Restatement of Trusts, Sec. 170. This section is similar to Sec. 170(1) of the Restatement of Trusts 2d.

(c) The fundamental duty that a trustee owes a beneficiary is the duty of loyalty, a duty that all states recognize. Bogert, Trusts and Trustees, Sec. 543 (2d ed. 1960); Scott on Trusts, Sec. 170 (2d ed. 1956).

Comment—2001

Subsection B, derived from Section 103(b) of the Uniform Principal and Income Act (1997), is an express statement of a policy that was previously only implicit in the Trust Code. The duty of impartiality is an important underpinning for the trustee's authority, under R.S. 9:2158, to make adjustments between income and principal.

Editor's note. Acts 2001, No. 520, § 1, amended R.S. 9:2082. Section 7 of Acts 2001, No. 520, declares that "The provisions of Section 1 of this Act shall apply to decisions or actions of the trustee taken on or after the effective date of this Act. The provisions of Sections 2, 3, and 4 of this Act shall apply to all trusts created on or after January 1, 2002. With respect to trusts created before January 1, 2002, the provisions of Sections 2, 3, and 4 of this Act shall apply commencing January 1, 2004. The provisions of Sections 2, 3, and 4 of this Act shall apply to a trust as of an earlier date if that date is either (1) designated in the trust instrument, or (2) designated by all current beneficiaries of the trust in one or more written documents delivered by the trustee."

Cross References

C.C. arts. 1100, 1148, 1171, 1983.

§ 2083. Dealing on own account

A trustee in dealing with a beneficiary on the trustee's own account shall deal fairly with him and communicate to him all material facts in connection with the transaction that the trustee knows or should know.

Added by Acts 1964, No. 338, § 2.

Comments—1964

(a) This section makes no change in the law.

(b) R.S. 9:1962(3) was based upon the Restatement of Trusts, Sec. 170. This section is similar to Sec. 170(2) of the Restatement of Trusts 2d.

(c) Most states distinguish the situation in which a trustee dealing with trust property on his account acts with a beneficiary's consent from the situation in which he acts without a beneficiary's consent. In the latter situation, the transaction is voidable whether or not the trustee acted in good faith and whether or not the transaction is fair and reasonable. In the former situation, the transaction is voidable only if the trustee failed to communicate to the beneficiary all material facts that he knew or should have known, if he used the influence of his position to obtain the beneficiary's consent, or if the transaction was not in all respects fair and reasonable. This section differs from the laws of other states. Scott on Trusts, Sec. 170 (2d ed. 1956).

Cross References

C.C. art. 1759.

§ 2084. Loan by trustee to himself

A corporate trustee shall not lend trust funds to itself or an affiliate, or to a director, an officer or an employee of itself or of an affiliate, unless the trust instrument provides otherwise. An individual trustee shall not lend funds to himself, or to his relative, employer, employee, partner, or other business associate, unless the trust instrument provides otherwise.

Added by Acts 1964, No. 338, § 2.

Comments—1964

(a) R.S. 9:1966 was based upon the Uniform Trusts Act, Sec. 3.

(b) In most states, a trustee cannot lend trust funds to himself, nor can he lend trust funds if he has a substantial personal interest in the loan. Bogert, Trusts and Trustees, Sec. 543(J) (2d ed. 1960); Scott on Trusts, Sec. 170.17 (2d ed. 1956).

Cross References

C.C. arts. 1759, 1983, 2893.

§ 2085. Sale by trustee to himself

A. A corporate trustee shall not directly or indirectly buy or sell property for the trust from or to itself or an affiliate, or from or to a director, officer, or an employee of itself or an affiliate, unless the trust instrument provides otherwise, or unless specifically authorized by a court of competent jurisdiction, after a contradictory hearing. An individual trustee shall not directly or indirectly buy or sell property for the trust from or to himself or his relative, employer, employee, partner, or other business associate, unless the trust instrument provides otherwise, or unless specifically authorized by a court of competent jurisdiction, after a contradictory hearing.

B. No trustee shall, as trustee of one trust, sell property to himself as trustee of another trust, unless the trust instruments concerned expressly provide otherwise, or unless specifically authorized by a court of competent jurisdiction, after a contradictory hearing, except that bonds, notes, bills, and other obligations issued, or fully guaranteed as to both principal and interest by the United States of America, or interests in time deposits or certificates of deposit or other short term investment instruments may be sold from one trust to another only by corporate trustees at the existing current market value.

Added by Acts 1964, No. 338, § 2. Amended by Acts 1978, No. 707, § 1; Acts 1990, No. 359, § 1, eff. July 10, 1990.

Comments—1964

(a) R.S. 9:1967 was based upon the Uniform Trusts Act, Secs. 5, 6.

(b) This section is similar to the laws of most states, Bogert, Trusts and Trustees, Secs. 543(A), 543(C), 543(E) (2d ed. 1960); Scott on Trusts, Secs. 170, 170.10–170.13 (2d ed. 1956).

Cross References

C.C. arts. 1759, 1983, 2439 et seq.

§ 2086. Self-dealing by corporate trustee

A. A corporate trustee shall not purchase for a trust shares of its own stock, or its bonds or other securities, or the stock, bonds, or other securities of an affiliate, unless the trust instrument provides otherwise; but the trustee may retain any such securities, together with any rights pertaining thereto, if acquired other than by purchase by that trustee.

B. A corporate trustee may invest or reinvest in the securities of mutual funds registered under the Investment Company Act of 1940,[1] even if the trustee or an affiliate thereof receives compensation with respect to such mutual fund, provided that the compensation is reasonable and the basis for determining the compensation is disclosed to all beneficiaries affected by the investment.

Added by Acts 1964, No. 338, § 2. Amended by Acts 2001, No. 520, § 1.

[1] Investment Company Act of 1940, see 15 U.S.C.A. § 80a–1 et seq.

Comments—1964

(a) R.S. 9:1968 was based upon the Uniform Trusts Act, Sec. 7.

(b) This section is similar to the laws of most states. In most states a corporate trustee may purchase shares of its own stock, or its bonds or other securities, or the stock, bonds, or other securities of an affiliate if it is granted the power to do so by the trust instrument. Scott on Trusts, Sec. 170.15 (2d ed. 1956).

Comment—2001

This Section is modified by transferring into it the substance of provisions that formerly appeared at R.S. 9:2127(A) and (C)(2).

Editor's note. Acts 2001, No. 520, § 1, amended R.S. 9:2086. Section 7 of Acts 2001, No. 520, declares that "The provisions of Section 1 of this Act shall apply to decisions or actions of the trustee taken on or after the effective date of this Act. The provisions of Sections 2, 3, and 4 of this Act shall apply to all trusts created on or after January 1, 2002. With respect to trusts created before January 1, 2002, the provisions of Sections 2, 3, and 4 of this Act shall apply commencing January 1, 2004. The provisions of Sections 2, 3, and 4 of this Act shall apply to a trust as of an earlier date if that date is either (1) designated in the trust instrument, or (2) designated by all current beneficiaries of the trust in one or more written documents delivered by the trustee."

Cross References

C.C. arts. 1759, 1983, 2439 et seq.

§ 2087. Delegating performance

A. Except as otherwise provided in this Section, a trustee shall not delegate the performance of his duties.

B. A trustee may, by power of attorney, delegate the performance of ministerial duties and acts that he could not reasonably be required to perform personally.

C. A trustee may delegate the selection of specific investments by acquiring mutual funds registered under the Investment Company Act of 1940,[1] or other pooled funds managed by a third party, so long as the portfolio of such a fund consists substantially of investments not prohibited by the trust instrument.

D. (1) A trustee may delegate investment and asset management functions that a prudent trustee of comparable skills could properly delegate under the circumstances. In connection with such delegation, the trustee has the duty to exercise reasonable care, skill, and caution in selecting the agent and establishing the scope and terms of the delegation consistent with the purposes and terms of the trust instrument, to review periodically the actions of the agent, and, in the event of a breach of the agent's duties discovered by the trustee, to take such action to remedy the breach as is reasonable under the circumstances.

(2) In performing a delegated function, an agent owes a duty to the trustee and to the beneficiaries to exercise reasonable care and skill, considering the scope and terms of the delegation. An agreement to relieve the agent from that duty is contrary to public policy and void.

(3) By accepting delegation from a trustee of a trust established pursuant to this Code, an agent submits to the jurisdiction of the courts of this state in all matters relating to the performance of his duties.

Added by Acts 1964, No. 338, § 2. Amended by Acts 2001, No. 520, § 1; Acts 2010, No. 224, § 1.

[1] Investment Company Act of 1940, see 15 U.S.C.A. § 80a–1 et seq.

Comments—1964

(a) This section makes no change in the law.

(b) R.S. 9:1962(4) was based upon the Restatement of Trusts, Sec. 171. This section is similar to Sec. 171 of the Restatement of Trusts 2d, and the laws of most states. Bogert, Trusts and Trustees,

Secs. 555, 556 (2d ed. 1960); Scott on Trusts, Sec. 171 (2d ed. 1956).

(c) Under Sec. 2123 a trustee can act as an incorporator of a corporation or subscribe for the shares of a corporation to be formed. *Cf.* Scott on Trusts, Secs. 171.2, 190.9A (2d ed. 1956).

Comments—2001

(a) The general rule against delegation is retained, but a new exception is set forth at Subsection D. The source of this exception is Section 9 of the Uniform Prudent Investor Act (1994). A trustee who is not an expert investor should have the power to delegate investment responsibilities to someone who is an expert, and indeed may have a duty to do so. Subsection (D)(2) is modeled on the version of Section 9(b) of the Uniform Prudent Investor Act that was adopted in Connecticut.

(b) Subsection C is based on provisions that were formerly found at R.S. 9:2127(B) and (C)(1).

(c) Subsection B reproduces the substance of former R.S. 9:2116, in order to present a coherent set of rules on delegation in this one Section.

Editor's note. Acts 2001, No. 520, § 1, amended R.S. 9:2087. Section 7 of Acts 2001, No. 520, declares that "The provisions of Section 1 of this Act shall apply to decisions or actions of the trustee taken on or after the effective date of this Act. The provisions of Sections 2, 3, and 4 of this Act shall apply to all trusts created on or after January 1, 2002. With respect to trusts created before January 1, 2002, the provisions of Sections 2, 3, and 4 of this Act shall apply commencing January 1, 2004. The provisions of Sections 2, 3, and 4 of this Act shall apply to a trust as of an earlier date if that date is either (1) designated in the trust instrument, or (2) designated by all current beneficiaries of the trust in one or more written documents delivered by the trustee."

Cross References

C.C. arts. 1855, 1886.

§ 2088. Accounting

A. A trustee is under a duty to a beneficiary to keep and render clear and accurate accounts of the administration of the trust. If the trust is revocable, the trustee has a duty to account to the settlor only.

B. A trustee shall render to a beneficiary or his legal representative at least once a year a clear and accurate account covering his administration for the preceding year. His first annual account shall relate to the calendar year during which he became responsible for the trust property, or, at his option, the first accounting period of not more than twelve months and shall be rendered within ninety days after the expiration of that calendar year or accounting period. Each annual account shall show in detail all receipts and disbursements of cash and all receipts and deliveries of other trust property during the year, and shall set forth a list of all items of trust property at the end of the year.

C. A trustee upon the termination, revocation, or rescission of the trust, or upon his resignation or removal, shall render to a beneficiary or his legal representative his final account covering the period elapsed since his most recent annual account (or, should the trust have terminated, or have been revoked or rescinded, during the first year, the period elapsed since he became responsible for the trust property), and setting forth the same information required for annual accounts.

D. A written approval by a beneficiary or his legal representative of an account rendered by a trustee shall be conclusive against the beneficiary with respect to all matters disclosed in the account. If a beneficiary or his legal representative fail or refuse to approve in writing an account rendered by a trustee, a trustee may apply to the proper court for an approval contradictorily with a beneficiary. An approval obtained from the proper court is conclusive against a beneficiary with respect to all matters disclosed in the account so approved.

E. A trustee shall not be under a duty, to file his accounts with the court unless he is expressly required to do so by the trust instrument or by the proper court.

Added by Acts 1964, No. 338, § 2. Amended by Acts 2001, No. 594, § 2.

Comments—1964

(a) Sub-sections A and C of this section make no change in the law. Sub-section A of this section is similar to the introductory clause of the source provision, R.S. 9:1963, and is almost identical with the Restatement of Trusts 2d, Sec. 172. Sub-sections B and C of this section are based upon Sub-sections (1) and (2) of R.S. 9:1963, except that the trustee has been given an optional accounting period.

(b) Sub-section D of this section combines the provisions of R.S. 9:1963(6) and R.S. 9:2193.

(c) R.S. 9:1963, the major source of this section, required all testamentary trustees to file copies of their accounts with the proper court. A trustee is not required by this Code to file a copy of his accounts with the court unless directed to do so by the trust instrument or by the court. In the rendering of accounts, this Code makes no distinction between a trustee of a testamentary trust and a trustee of an inter vivos trust.

(d) Most states require the trustee to render an account to the court. Bogert, Trusts and Trustees, Sec. 963 (2d ed. 1962); Scott on Trusts, Sec. 172 (2d ed. 1956).

Editor's note. Acts 2001, No. 594, § 2, amended R.S. 9:2088(A), effective August 15, 2001. Section 4 of Acts 2001, No. 594, declares that "The provisions of Section 3 of this Act shall not apply to a transfer in trust made prior to the effective date of this Act."

Cross References

C.C. arts. 628, 629, 2369.

§ 2089. Furnishing of information

A trustee shall give to a beneficiary upon his request at reasonable times complete and accurate information as to the nature and amount of the trust property, and permit him, or a person duly authorized by him, to inspect the subject matter of the trust, and the accounts, vouchers, and other documents relating to the trust.

Added by Acts 1964, No. 338, § 2.

Comments—1964

(a) This section makes no change in the law.

(b) R.S. 9:1962(5) was based upon the Restatement of Trusts, Sec. 173. This section is similar to Sec. 173 of the Restatement of Trusts 2d and the laws of most states. Bogert, Trusts and Trustees, Sec. 961 (2d ed. 1962); Scott on Trusts, Sec. 173 (2d ed. 1956).

§ 2090. Prudent administration

A. A trustee shall administer the trust as a prudent person would administer it. In satisfying this standard, the trustee shall exercise reasonable care and skill, considering the purposes, terms, distribution requirements, and other circumstances of the trust.

B. A trustee who has special skills or expertise, or has held himself out as having special skills or expertise, has a duty to use those special skills or expertise.

Added by Acts 1964, No. 338, § 2. Amended by Acts 2001, No. 520, § 1.

Comments—1964

(a) R.S. 9:1962(6) was based upon the Restatement of Trusts, Sec. 174, but differed in policy. It did not require a trustee who had greater skill than a man of ordinary prudence, to exercise such skill as he had. Sec. 174 of the Restatement 2d goes beyond the Restatement in requiring also that a trustee who procures his appointment by representing that he has greater skill than a man of ordinary prudence must exercise such skill as he represents that he has. This section does not follow this additional requirement of the Restatement 2d.

(b) In most states a trustee is under a duty to exercise the skill that an ordinary prudent man would exercise in the management of his own affairs, or, if he has greater skill than a man of ordinary prudence, to exercise the skill he has. Scott suggests that a trustee who procures his appointment by representing that he has greater skill than a man of ordinary prudence should be under a duty to exercise the skill that he represents himself as having, but he admits that there "seem to be" no cases squarely so holding. Bogert, Trusts and Trustees, Sec. 541 (2d ed. 1960); Scott on Trusts, Secs. 174, 174.1 (2d ed. 1956).

(c) See Sec. 2127 with regard to investments.

Editor's note. Acts 2001, No. 520, § 1, amended R.S. 9:2090. Section 7 of Acts 2001, No. 520, declares that "The provisions of Section 1 of this Act shall apply to decisions or actions of the trustee taken on or after the effective date of this Act. The provisions of Sections 2, 3, and 4 of this Act shall apply to all trusts created on or after January 1, 2002. With respect to trusts created before January 1, 2002, the provisions of Sections 2, 3, and 4 of this Act shall apply commencing January 1, 2004. The provisions of Sections 2, 3, and 4 of this Act shall apply to a trust as of an earlier date if that date is either (1) designated in the trust instrument, or (2) designated by all current beneficiaries of the trust in one or more written documents delivered by the trustee."

Cross References

C.C. arts. 539, 576, 2930.

§ 2091. Control and preservation of trust property

A trustee is under a duty to a beneficiary to take reasonable steps to take, keep control of, and preserve the trust property.

Added by Acts 1964, No. 338, § 2.

Comments—1964

(a) This section makes no change in the law.

(b) R.S. 9:1962(7) and R.S. 9:1962(8) were based upon the Restatement of Trusts, Secs. 175 and 176.

(c) This section imposes upon a trustee a duty to take reasonable steps to obtain possession of legacies.

Cross References

C.C. arts. 539, 576.

§ 2092. Recordation of instruments

A. If at any time the trust property of either an inter vivos trust or a testamentary trust includes immovables or other property the title to which must be recorded in order to affect third parties, a trustee shall file the trust instrument, an extract of trust, or a copy of the trust instrument or extract of trust certified by the clerk of court for the parish in which the original trust instrument or extract of trust was filed, for record in each parish in which the property is located.

B. (1) For purposes of recording an extract of a trust instrument, such an extract shall be executed by either the settlor or the trustee and shall include all of the following:

(a) The name of the trust, if any.

(b) A statement as to whether the trust is revocable or irrevocable.

(c) The name of each settlor.

(d) The name of each trustee and name or other description of the beneficiary or beneficiaries.

(e) The date of execution of the trust.

(f) If the trust instrument also contains a transfer of immovable property or other property to the trust, the title to which must be recorded in order to affect third persons, then the extract shall contain a brief legal description of the property.

(2) Unless the trust and abstract of trust recite or otherwise note any modification or restriction of the trustee's power or duties, the trustee shall have all of the powers and duties granted to trustees under the Louisiana Trust Code.

(3) The provisions of this Section authorizing the filing of an extract of the trust instrument or a clerk-certified copy of the trust instrument or extract of trust without a description of the property are remedial and shall be applied retroactively to any trust extract or clerk-certified copy of either the trust instrument or extract of trust theretofore filed for record which is in substantial compliance with the provisions of this Subsection, and such extract or clerk-certified copy shall affect third persons as of the date of recordation. If the extract of an inter vivos trust instrument or clerk-certified copy thereof is recorded, the failure of the trust instrument to be in the form required by R.S. 9:1752 shall not be effective against third parties, who shall be immune

from claims based on the failure of the trust instrument to be in the form required by R.S. 9:1752.

Added by Acts 1964, No. 338, § 2. Amended by Acts 1995, No. 257, § 1; Acts 2003, No. 731, § 1; Acts 2004, No. 491, § 1; Acts 2012, No. 740, § 1.

Comments—1964

(a) This section is broader than R.S. 9:1962(1) since a trustee must record the trust instrument not only if the trust property includes immovables but also if the trust property includes property the title to which must be recorded in order to affect third parties.

(b) The broader rule has been adopted because it is believed that it gives greater protection to beneficiaries as well as to those who deal with a trustee.

Cross References

C.C. arts. 517, 1833, 1837, 1839, 1848.

§ 2093. Defense of actions

A trustee shall defend actions that may result in a loss to the trust estate, unless under all the circumstances it is reasonable not to make a defense.

Added by Acts 1964, No. 338, § 2.

Comments—1964

(a) This section makes no change in the law.

(b) R.S. 9:1962(10) was based upon the Restatement of Trusts, Sec. 178. This section is similar to Sec. 178 of the Restatement of Trusts 2d and the laws of most states. Bogert, Trusts and Trustees, Sec. 594 (2d ed. 1960); Scott on Trusts, Sec. 178 (2d ed. 1956).

Cross References

C.C. arts. 594, 595.

§ 2094. Separation of trust property

A trustee shall keep the trust property separate from his individual property, and, so far as reasonable, keep it separate from other property not subject to the trust, and see that the property is designated as property of the trust, unless the trust instrument provides otherwise.

Added by Acts 1964, No. 338, § 2.

Comments—1964

(a) This section makes no change in the law.

(b) R.S. 9:1962(11) was based upon the Restatement of Trusts, Sec. 179. This section is similar to Sec. 179 of the Restatement of Trusts 2d and the laws of most states. Bogert, Trusts and Trustees, Sec. 596 (2d ed. 1960); Scott on Trusts, Secs. 179–179.3 (2d ed. 1956).

§ 2095. Bank deposits

Although a trustee can properly make a general deposit of trust money in a bank, he shall use reasonable care in selecting the bank and properly earmark the deposit as a deposit of trust funds by him as trustee, unless the trust instrument provides otherwise.

A corporate trustee making a general deposit of trust money with an affiliate or its own banking department has a duty to a beneficiary to obtain as security for the deposit readily marketable bonds or other obligations having and maintaining a market value at least equal to the amount of the deposit, unless dispensed from doing so by specific words in the trust instrument, but such a dispensation shall not be construed as preventing a corporate trustee from putting up security for a deposit of trust money if it desires to do so. No security shall be required for any deposit up to the amount insured by the Federal Deposit Insurance Corporation.

Added by Acts 1964, No. 338, § 2. Amended by Acts 1982, No. 279, § 1.

Comments—1964

(a) The first paragraph of this section follows the Restatement of Trusts 2d, Sec. 180, which does not contain some of the provisions of the corresponding section of the original Restatement followed by R.S. 9:1964. The latter forbade deposits if they were made for an unreasonable time or if restrictions were made on withdrawals. The original provisions had the effect of making all deposits as investments improper. Under this Code a deposit of trust funds in a bank account at interest as an investment is not improper simply because it is a deposit as an investment. However, such an investment must be proper in other respects.

(b) The second paragraph of this section makes no change in the law.

(c) In many states today, a deposit of trust funds in a bank at interest as an investment is not improper, particularly if the deposit is insured by the Federal Deposit Insurance Corporation. Scott on Trusts, Secs. 180–180.4 (2d ed. 1956); cf. Bogert, Trusts and Trustees, Sec. 598 (2d ed. 1960).

§ 2096. Co-trustees

If there are two or more trustees, each shall participate in the administration of the trust and use reasonable care to prevent a co-trustee from committing a breach of trust and shall compel him to redress a breach of trust.

Added by Acts 1964, No. 338, § 2.

Comments—1964

R.S. 9:1962(14) was based upon the Restatement of Trusts, Sec. 184. This section closely resembles Sec. 179 of the Restatement of Trusts 2d and is similar to the laws of most states. Scott on Trusts, Sec. 184 (2d ed. 1956).

§ 2097. Serving as officer of legal entity in which trust funds invested

A. No trustee of any trust created under the laws of this state shall serve as an officer, including without limitation the president, vice president, secretary, treasurer, manager, or managing partner of any legal entity formed after the trust is created, other than a corporate trustee, in which trust funds are invested unless the settlor so authorizes such action in the instrument creating the trust or by a subsequent modification thereof. However, this shall not restrict the investment of trust funds in any bank or savings and loan association with deposits therein insured by the Federal Deposit Insurance Corporation or by any other agency or instrumentality of the federal government.

B. Any trustee who violates the provisions of this section shall be subject to removal for cause by a court of competent jurisdiction. The beneficiary of any such trust may offer proof to the court of competent jurisdiction that a trustee is acting in violation of this section, and upon presentation of such proof, the court shall remove the trustee.

C. All laws or parts of laws in conflict herewith are hereby repealed, but the provisions hereof shall not be construed to repeal R.S. 9:2081 through R.S. 9:2096.

Added by Acts 1968, No. 627, §§ 1 to 3. Amended by Acts 1997, No. 251, § 1.

SUBPART C. POWERS OF THE TRUSTEE

§ 2111. Extent of powers

Except as stated in R.S. 9:2061 through 9:2066, a trustee shall exercise only those powers conferred upon him by the provisions of the trust instrument or necessary or appropriate to carry out the purposes of the trust and are not forbidden by the provisions of the trust instrument.

Added by Acts 1964, No. 338, § 2.

Comments—1964

(a) This Sub-part is similar to R.S. 9:1991–9:2004 in the Trust Estates Law.

(b) R.S. 9:1991 was based upon the Restatement of Trusts, Sec. 186. This section is similar to R.S. 9:1991, but it uses the phrase "provisions of the trust instrument" rather than the phrase "terms of the trust" to make it clear that under normal circumstances manifestations of the settlor's intention made outside the trust instrument cannot be considered in determining the powers of the trustee. The Restatement of Trusts 2d, Sec. 4, defines the "terms of the trust" as the "manifestation of intention of the settlor with respect to the trust expressed in a manner which admits of its proof in judicial proceedings."

Cross References

C.C. arts. 7, 1983.

§ 2112. Attachment of powers to office

All powers of a trustee shall be attached to the office and shall not be personal, unless it is otherwise provided by the trust instrument or by order of the proper court.

Added by Acts 1964, No. 338, § 2.

Comments—1964

(a) This section makes no change in the law.

(b) R.S. 9:1992 was based upon the Uniform Trusts Act, Sec. 10.

Cross References

C.C. art. 1766.

§ 2113. Exercise of powers by two trustees

If there are two trustees, the powers conferred upon them shall be exercised only by both of them, unless it is otherwise provided by the trust instrument or by order of the proper court.

Added by Acts 1964, No. 338, § 2.

Comments—1964

(a) This section makes no change in the law.

(b) This section and its source, R.S. 9:1933, differ from the Restatement of Trusts 1st and 2d, Sec. 194, in not applying to trusts having three or more trustees. Under this Code, as under the Trust Estates Law, if a trust has three or more trustees, the powers of the trustees may be exercised by a majority of the trustees. Sec. 2114; former R.S. 9:1994.

(c) In the absence of a statute, unanimity in the action of trustees of a private trust is universally required. Many states have statutes eliminating the requirement of unanimous action. Bogert, Trusts and Trustees, Sec. 554 (2d ed. 1960); Scott on Trusts, Sec. 194 (2d ed. 1956).

Cross References

C.C. art. 1971.

§ 2114. Three or more trustees; exercise of powers

A power vested in three or more trustees may be exercised by a majority of the trustees, unless the trust instrument provides otherwise. A trustee who has not joined in exercising a power shall not be liable to the beneficiaries or to others for the consequences of that exercise, nor shall a dissenting trustee be liable for the consequences of an act in which he joins at the direction of the majority of trustees, if he expresses his dissent in writing to his co-trustees at or before the time of the joinder. Nothing in this section shall excuse a co-trustee from liability for inactivity in the administration of the trust nor for failure to attempt to prevent a breach of trust.

Added by Acts 1964, No. 338, § 2.

Comments—1964

(a) This section makes no substantial change in the law.

(b) R.S. 9:1994 was based upon the Uniform Trusts Act, Sec. 11.

(c) Unlike this section, the Restatement of Trusts 2d, Sec. 195 states that if a trust has two or more trustees, the powers of trustee shall be exercised by all trustees, unless the terms of the trust provide to the contrary. See Comment (c) under Sec. 2113.

§ 2115. Control of discretionary powers

If discretion is conferred upon a trustee with respect to the exercise of a power, its exercise shall not be subject to control by the court, except to prevent an abuse of discretion by a trustee.

Added by Acts 1964, No. 338, § 2.

Comments—1964

(a) This section makes no change in the law.

(b) R.S. 9:1995 was based upon the Restatement of Trusts, Sec. 187. This section closely resembles Sec. 187 of the Restatement of Trusts 2d.

Cross References

C.C. arts. 1759, 1983.

§ 2116. Repealed by Acts 2001, No. 520, § 5

Editor's note. Acts 2001, No. 520, § 5, repealed R.S. 9:2116, effective August 15, 2001. Section 7 of Acts 2001, No. 520, declares that "The provisions of Section 1 of this Act shall apply to decisions or actions of the trustee taken on or after the effective date of this Act. The provisions of Sections 2, 3, and 4 of this Act shall apply to all trusts created on or after January 1, 2002. With respect to trusts created before January 1, 2002, the provisions of Sections 2, 3, and 4 of this Act shall apply commencing January 1, 2004. The provisions of Sections 2, 3, and 4 of this Act shall apply to a trust as of an earlier date if that date is either (1) designated in the trust instrument, or (2) designated by all current beneficiaries of the trust in one or more written documents delivered by the trustee."

§ 2117. Expenses that may be incurred

A trustee may incur expenses necessary to carry out the purposes of the trust and not forbidden by the provisions of the trust instrument, and other expenses authorized by the provisions of the trust instrument.

Added by Acts 1964, No. 338, § 2.

Comments—1964

(a) This section makes no change in the law.

(b) R.S. 9:1996 was based upon the Restatement of Trusts, Sec. 188. This section is similar to Sec. 188 of the Restatement of Trusts 2d and the laws of most states. Scott on Trusts, Sec. 188 (2d ed. 1956).

Cross References

C.C. arts. 485, 488, 527, 528.

§ 2118. Lease of trust property

Unless the trust instrument provides otherwise, a trustee may enter into leases of trust property, including oil, gas, and mineral leases, either as lessor or lessee, for such periods and with such provisions as are reasonable, whether or not the term of the lease exceeds the term of the trust.

Added by Acts 1964, No. 338, § 2. Amended by Acts 1968, No. 134, § 1.

Comments—1964

(a) The Trust Estates Law required a trustee to obtain judicial approval to lease trust property for a period longer than the period of the trust, unless the terms of the trust provided to the contrary.

(b) The Restatement of Trusts 2d, Sec. 189, permits a trustee to lease property for a reasonable period whether or not that period is longer than the period of the trust.

(c) Scott states that a trustee is ordinarily not justified in making a lease that will extend beyond the period of the trust, if a trust has different persons as beneficiaries of income and principal, even if the lease is in other respects reasonable. This Code does not follow the policy stated in Scott on Trusts, Secs. 189, 189.2 (2d ed. 1956). *Cf.* Bogert, Trusts and Trustees, Secs. 789–792 (2d ed. 1962).

Comment—1968

This section apparently permitted a trustee to enter into a long-term lease for the trust even though the term exceeded the term of the trust, only when the trust was lessor. The added language makes it clear that the trustee may enter into the same arrangement for the trust when the trust is the lessee.

Cross References

C.C. art. 2669 et seq.

§ 2119. Sale of trust property

A trustee may sell trust property unless the sale is forbidden in specific words by the trust instrument or unless it appears from the provisions of the trust instrument that the property is to be retained in kind. A settlor by the provisions of the trust instrument cannot forbid a sale of immovable property for a period beyond fifteen years from his death.

Added by Acts 1964, No. 338, § 2.

Comments—1964

(a) The first sentence of this section differs from Sec. 190 of the Restatement of Trusts 2d. The second sentence finds no counterpart in the Restatement. Under Sec. 190, Restatement of Trusts 2d, the trustee has the power to sell trust property if given the authority in the trust instrument.

(b) The first sentence of this section differs from the laws of most states. Bogert, Trusts and Trustees, Sec. 741 (2d ed. 1960); Scott on Trusts, Secs. 190–190.3 (2d ed. 1956).

Cross References

C.C. arts. 1983, 2439 et seq.

§ 2120. Mortgage or pledge; borrowing

A trustee may mortgage or pledge trust property, or borrow money on the credit of the trust estate and charge the trust estate therefor, unless the trust instrument provides otherwise.

Added by Acts 1964, No. 338, § 2.

Comments—1964

R.S. 9:1999 was based upon the Restatement of Trusts, Sec. 191. This section differs from Sec. 191 of the Restatement of Trusts 2d and from the laws of most states. Bogert, Trusts and Trustees, Sec. 751 (2d ed. 1962); Scott on Trusts, Sec. 191 (2d ed. 1956). Under the Trusts Estates Law, as in most states, the trustee could not mortgage, pledge, or borrow money on the trust property unless authorized to do so by the trust instrument. This section authorizes the trustee to mortgage, pledge, or borrow money on the trust property unless prohibited from doing so by the trust instrument.

Cross References

C.C. arts. 1971, 1983, 2893 et seq., 3133 et seq., 3278 et seq.

§ 2121. Compromise, arbitration, and abandonment of claims

A trustee may compromise, submit to arbitration, or abandon claims affecting the trust property.

Added by Acts 1964, No. 338, § 2.

Comments—1964

(a) This section makes no change in the law.

(b) R.S. 9:2000 was based upon the Restatement of Trusts, Sec. 192. This section resembles Sec. 192 of the Restatement of Trusts 2d.

(c) This section is similar to the laws of most states. Bogert, Trusts and Trustees, Sec. 594 (2d ed. 1960); Scott on Trusts, Sec. 192 (2d ed. 1956).

Cross References

C.C. arts. 3071, 3099, 3101.

§ 2122. Powers with respect to shares of stock

A trustee may exercise all powers of holders of shares of stock or other securities, including the right to vote in person or by proxy.

Added by Acts 1964, No. 338, § 2.

Comments—1964

This section is similar in policy to Restatement of Trusts 2d, Sec. 193, and to the laws of most states. Bogert, Trusts and Trustees, Sec. 556 (2d ed. 1960); Scott on Trusts, Secs. 193–193.3 (2d ed. 1956).

Cross References

C.C. art. 553.

§ 2123. Stock subscription; incorporator; organizer; partnership; joint venture; limited liability company; other legal entities

A trustee may acquire and subscribe for corporate shares, act as an incorporator or organizer, or become a member of a partnership, joint venture, limited liability company, or other legal entity, unless the trust instrument provides otherwise.

Added by Acts 1964, No. 338, § 2. Amended by Acts 1997, No. 251, § 1.

Comments—1964

(a) The Trust Estates Law did not specifically treat the power of the trustee to subscribe for corporate stock or to act as an incorporator.

(b) This section is contrary to the laws of most states. In most states a trustee in not permitted to transfer trust property to a corporation and to receive in exchange shares of the corporation unless authorized by the trust instrument or by the court. Scott on Trusts, Secs. 171.2, 190.9A (2d ed. 1956).

Comment—1997

The phrase "limited liability company" has been added to authorize trustees to utilize this new form of business now recognized in R.S. 12:1301 et seq.

Cross References

C.C. art. 552.

§ 2124. Holding stock in name of nominee

A trustee owning stock may hold it in the name of a nominee, without mention of the trust in the stock certificate or stock registration book, provided that the trust records and all reports or accounts rendered by a trustee clearly show the ownership of the stock and the facts regarding its holding. A trustee shall be personally liable for any loss to the trust resulting from any act of the nominee in connection with stock so held.

Added by Acts 1964, No. 338, § 2.

Comment—1964

R.S. 9:2002 was based upon the Uniform Trusts Act, Sec. 9 [7B Uniform Laws Annotated, Master Edition].

Cross References

C.C. arts. 576, 2315.

§ 2124.1. [Blank]

§ 2125. Contractual liability of trust

A. If a trustee makes a contract that is within his powers as trustee, or if a predecessor trustee has made such a contract, and if a cause of action arises thereon, the party in whose favor the cause of action has accrued may sue the trustee in his representative capacity. A judgment rendered in the action in favor of the plaintiff shall affect or be satisfied out of the trust property.

B. A beneficiary may intervene in such an action for the purpose of contesting the right of the plaintiff to recover.

C. The plaintiff may also hold a trustee who makes a contract personally liable on the contract, if the contract does not exclude personal liability. The addition of the word "trustee" or the words "as trustee" together with language identifying the trust, after the signature of a trustee to a contract, shall be deemed prima facie evidence of an intent to exclude a trustee from personal liability.

Added by Acts 1964, No. 338, § 2.

Comments—1964

(a) This section eliminates the procedural rules that were contained in R.S. 9:2003. Those rules are rendered unnecessary. See Art. 742, C.C.P.

(b) R.S. 9:2003 was based upon the Uniform Trusts Act, Sec. 12 [7B, Uniform Laws Annotated, Master Edition].

Cross References

C.C. arts. 1758, 1765, 1977, 1984, 1994.

§ 2126. Tort liability of trust

A. If a trustee or his predecessor has incurred personal liability for a tort committed in the course of administration, the trustee in his representative capacity may be sued and collection had from the trust property, if the court determines in such an action:

(1) That the tort was a common incident of the kind of business activity in which the trustee or his predecessor was properly engaged for the trust; or

(2) That, although the tort was not a common incident of such an activity, neither a trustee nor his predecessor nor an officer or employee of the trustee or his predecessor was guilty of personal fault in incurring the liability; or

(3) That, although the tort does not fall within paragraphs (1) or (2) above, it increased the value of the trust property.

B. If the tort falls within paragraphs (1) or (2) of Sub-section A above, collection may be had of the full amount of damage proved and, if the tort falls within paragraph (3) of Sub-section A above, collection may be had only to the extent of the increase in the value of the trust property.

C. A beneficiary may intervene in such an action for the purpose of contesting the right of the plaintiff to recover.

D. A trustee may also be held personally liable for any tort committed by him or his agents or employees in the course of their employment, subject to the right of exoneration or reimbursement provided in R.S. 9:2191 through 9:2196.

Added by Acts 1964, No. 338, § 2.

Comment—1964

R.S. 9:2004 was based upon the Uniform Trusts Act, Sec. 14 [7B, Uniform Laws Annotated, Master Edition].

Cross References

C.C. art. 2315.

§ 2127. Standard of care in investing and management

Unless the trust instrument provides otherwise, a trustee shall invest and manage trust property as a prudent investor. In satisfying this standard, the trustee shall consider the purposes, terms, distribution requirements, and other circumstances of the trust. A trustee's investment and management decisions are to be evaluated in the context of the trust property as a whole and as part of an overall investment strategy having risk and return objectives reasonably suited to the trust. In investing within the limitations of the foregoing standard, a trustee is authorized to retain and acquire every kind of property.

Added by Acts 1964, No. 338, § 2. Amended by Acts 1968, No. 135, § 1; Acts 1986, No. 178, § 1; Acts 1991, No. 665, § 2; Acts 2001, No. 520, § 1.

Comments—1964

(a) This section is based upon R.S. 9:2061, as amended by Act 44 of 1962, which abolished the legal list.

(b) This section is similar to the laws of a majority of other states. Bogert, Trusts and Trustees, Secs. 541, 612–614 (2d ed. Scott on Trusts, Secs. 227–227.13, 230, 231 (2d ed. 1956).

Comment—1968

The Trust Estates Law of 1938 gave a trustee the general power to retain assets entrusted to it, but the Trust Code of 1964 deleted the power of retention, making the prudent man rule equally applicable to retention of investments. When there is no specific power of retention in the trust instrument, federal bank examiners have requested banks to divest themselves of their own bank stock. The amendment would eliminate the necessity for a sale in such circumstances. The trustee would still, of course, be subject to the prudent man rule if he decided not to sell.

Comments—2001

(a) The primary source of the new formulation for this Section is Section 2 of the Uniform Prudent Investor Act (1994). It sets forth the "prudent investor rule", which has been widely adopted in the other states in place of the "prudent man rule". The prudent investor rule makes it clear that the trustee's duty is determined by the purposes of the trust and the circumstances of the beneficiaries, not in light of how a prudent man would manage his own property.

(b) The prudent investor rule makes it clear that the prudence of the trustee's actions is determined with respect to the portfolio as a whole: "an investment that might be imprudent standing alone can become prudent if undertaken in sensible relation to other trust assets, or other nontrust assets." (Quote from comment to Uniform Prudent Investor Act (1994) Section 2.)

(c) Diversification usually is necessary to reduce risk. For small trusts this can be accomplished through pooled investments such as mutual funds. See R.S. 9:2087. "Circumstances can, however, overcome the duty to diversify. For example, if a tax-sensitive trust owns an under diversified block of low-basis securities, the tax costs of recognizing the gain may outweigh the advantages of diversifying the holding. The wish to retain a family business is another situation in which the purposes of the trust sometimes override the conventional duty to diversify." (Quote from comment to Uniform Prudent Investor Act (1994) Section 3.)

(d) Rules that had been added in the past to this Section, authorizing investments that might otherwise have been prohibited because of the rules against self-dealing and delegation, have been moved to R.S. 9:2086 and 2087.

Editor's note. R.S. 9:2127 was amended by Acts 2001, No. 520, § 4, effective August 15, 2001. Section 7 of Acts 2001, No. 520, declares that "The provisions of Section 1 of this Act shall apply to decisions or actions of the trustee taken on or after the effective date of this Act. The provisions of Sections 2, 3, and 4 of this Act shall apply to all trusts created on or after January 1, 2002. With respect to trusts created before January 1, 2002, the provisions of Sections 2, 3, and 4 of this Act shall apply commencing January 1, 2004. The provisions of Sections 2, 3, and 4 of this Act shall apply to a trust as of an earlier date if that date is either (1) designated in the trust instrument, or (2) designated by all current beneficiaries of the trust in one or more written documents delivered by the trustee."

Cross References

C.C. arts. 577, 1971, 2930.

§ 2128. Common trust funds

A. A trustee may establish common trust funds for the investment of trust funds of which he is trustee or cotrustee and may invest in such common trust funds, if such investment is not prohibited by the trust instrument, and if the trustee procures the consent of his cotrustees to the investment; provided that:

(1) The records, reports, and accounts of each trust having an interest in the fund clearly show the extent of such interest; and

(2) The trustee himself has no interest in such fund; and

(3) The fractional part of the management fee charged by the trustee proportionate to the interest of each beneficiary shall not, when added to any other compensation charged by a trustee to a beneficiary, exceed the total amount of compensation which would have been charged to the beneficiary if no assets of the beneficiary had been invested in the fund; and

(4) The fund is maintained under a written plan that is on file at the office of the trustee and is available for inspection during business hours by any interested party; and

(5) The trustee has had prepared annually by a certified public accountant and placed on file with the trustee, a statement of the investment changes, income, disbursements, and a list of the current investments with a notation as to defaults, for the period since the last such statement. The trustee shall notify each beneficiary that a copy of the annual statement is available and will be furnished to the beneficiary on request; and

(6) Entrances into, and withdrawals from, such common trust fund are permitted only on those days upon which the assets comprising the fund are valued; and

(7) No funds are admitted to the common trust fund at a time when less than forty per centum of the value of the common trust fund is composed of cash or marketable investments for which quotations are readily available; and

(8) The fund is managed in accordance with any regulations pertaining thereto issued from time to time by the office of financial institutions; and

(9) On the termination of a trust interested in the common trust fund, the trustee shall terminate the interest of that trust and shall pay from cash in the common trust fund to the person or persons then entitled to the trust capital the then market value of the interest of the trust in the common trust fund.

B. If the trustee is restricted to certain investments, then he may invest only in common trust funds limited to such investments.

C. A trustee who has established a common trust fund for the investment of trust funds may also invest therein any other funds that he holds as a fiduciary, provided he procures the consent of his co-fiduciaries.

D. For the purpose of this Section, the term "trustee" shall include two or more trustees who are members of the same "affiliated group" as defined in Section 1504 of the Internal Revenue Code of 1954, as amended, with respect to any fund established pursuant to this Section, of which any of such trustee is trustee or cotrustee.

Added by Acts 1964, No. 338, § 2. Amended by Acts 1968, No. 136, § 1; Acts 1974, No. 159, § 1; Acts 1986, No. 179, § 1.

Comment—1964

This section makes no substantial change in the law.

Comments—1968

(a) Former Sec. 2128(5) and (6) appeared to be in conflict with Sec. 9.18(b) of the Regulations promulgated by the Comptroller of the Currency, which reads (in part):

"Collective investments of funds or other property by national banks under paragraph (a) of this section . . . shall be administered as follows:

. . .

(13) No bank administering a collective investment fund shall issue any certificate of other document evidencing a direct or indirect interest in such fund in any form . . . ."

(b) Since the trustee will also manage the common fund there seems to be little reason to require the trustee to issue a certificate of interest to himself as trustee.

Comments—1974

Subsection (8) formerly permitted entrances into and withdrawals from common trust funds only at quarterly intervals. Regulation 9.8(b)(4), Comptroller of the Currency, requires valuation at least quarterly, but permits entrances or withdrawals on any valuation date. Acts 1974, No. 159 extends the flexibility accorded by the above regulation.

Regulation 9.1(b), Comptroller of the Currency, would accord use of a common trust fund to a bank acting in *any* fiduciary capacity whether as trustee, executor, administrator, tutor, curator of an interdict, managing agent or any other similar capacity. The above amendment permits a bank to utilize its common trust fund in any of such fiduciary capacities.

Subsection C also added by Acts 1974, No. 159 conforms with R.S. 6:322(7) added by Acts 1970, No. 356, Section 1 [see, now, R.S. 6:241 (1984 revision)] which permits a bank to invest the funds of a minor or interdict of which such bank has been appointed tutor or curator in any common trust fund established by such bank under provisions of R.S. 9:2128, such investments to be administered in conformity with such section.

§ 2129. Corporate trustees; deposit of securities in clearing corporation

A. Unless the trust instrument provides otherwise, a corporate trustee may deposit or arrange for deposit in a clearing corporation securities held by it as fiduciary or as agent for a fiduciary or nonfiduciary, provided the records maintained by the corporate trustee with respect to those securities disclose the capacity in which they are held.

B. Securities deposited in a clearing corporation may be registered in the name of either the clearing corporation or its nominee without disclosing the capacity in which they are held.

C. Securities deposited in a clearing corporation may be stored together with other securities of the same class of the same issuer also stored in the clearing corporation, but not the securities of the clearing corporation, and may be combined with such other securities into one or more securities of the same class of the same issuer.

Added by Acts 1983, No. 346, § 1.

Cross References

C.C. art. 2926 et seq.

§ 2130. Transfer of fiduciary accounts

A. Notwithstanding any other provision of this Chapter to the contrary, any two or more banks authorized to exercise fiduciary powers may enter into an agreement under which a bank domiciled in the state of Louisiana is substituted as fiduciary for each existing fiduciary account listed in the agreement. The agreement shall be filed with the commissioner of financial institutions for approval or other disposition within thirty days, and shall be accompanied by a fee to be determined by the commissioner by rule.

B. Following approval by the commissioner and not later than sixty days prior to the effective date of a substitution under this Section, the transferring bank shall send written notice of the substitution of fiduciary to each interested party for each fiduciary account listed in the agreement. For purposes of this Section, an interested party shall include only the following, each as may be appropriate to the respective fiduciary account:

(1) Each adult beneficiary.

(2) Each parent, tutor, or guardian of a minor beneficiary receiving or entitled to receive current distributions of income or principal.

(3) Each co-fiduciary.

(4) Each person who alone or acting in conjunction with others has the power to remove the transferring bank.

(5) Each surviving settlor.

(6) Each issuer of a security for which the transferring bank administers a fiduciary account.

(7) The plan sponsor of each employee benefit plan.

(8) The principal of each agency account.

(9) The curator of the person of each interdict under curatorship.

C. The notice shall be sent by United States mail to the person's current address as shown on the records of the transferring bank. If the transferring bank has no address on its records, the transferring bank shall make a reasonable attempt to ascertain the person's current address. The notice shall disclose the person's rights with respect to objecting to the transfer of the fiduciary account. Intentional failure to send the required notice renders the substitution of fiduciary ineffective, but an unintentional failure to send the required notice shall not impair the validity or effect of the substitution. If a substitution is determined to be ineffective because of a defect in the required notice, the actions taken by the substitute bank before the determination of the invalidity of the substitution shall be valid if the actions would have been valid if performed by the transferring bank.

D. Except as provided by this Subsection, the prospective designation in a will or other instrument of the transferring bank as fiduciary shall be considered designation of the substitute bank. However, the transferring bank and substitute bank may agree in writing to have the designation of the transferring bank as fiduciary of particular fiduciary accounts remain binding, or the creator of the fiduciary account may, by appropriate language in the document creating the fiduciary account, provide that the fiduciary account is not eligible for substitution under this Section.

E. Substitution under this Section shall be effective for all purposes on the effective date stated in the agreement between the two banks unless, not later than fifteen days prior to the effective date:

(1) An interested party entitled to notice under this Section who possesses the lawful authority to designate the trustee or successor trustee sends via certified mail a written objection to the proposed transfer of the particular account. Upon receipt of such objection, the transferring bank shall remove that account from the operation of the agreement. The transferring bank shall, upon the direction of such interested party, transfer the account to a qualified successor.

(2) Any other interested party entitled to notice under this Section files a written petition in a court of competent jurisdiction and venue seeking to have the substitution denied and serves the transferring bank and the substitute bank with a copy of the filed petition. The substitution may be denied if the court, on notice and hearing, determines that the substitution of fiduciary is a material detriment to the account or to the beneficiaries of the account.

F. Subsection E of this Section shall be cumulative to any applicable provisions for removal of a fiduciary or appointment of a successor fiduciary in any other statute or in the instrument creating the fiduciary relationship.

G. On the effective date of the substitution, the substitute bank shall succeed to all rights, title, and interest in all property that the transferring bank holds as fiduciary in the listed accounts, without the necessity of any instrument of transfer or conveyance, and the substitute bank shall, without the necessity of any judicial action or action by the creator of the fiduciary account, become fiduciary and perform all the duties and obligations and exercise all the powers and authority connected with or incidental to the fiduciary capacity in the same manner as if the substitute bank had been originally named or designated fiduciary. However, the transferring bank shall be responsible and liable for all actions taken by it while it acted as fiduciary.

H. A fiduciary account may be removed from the operation of the agreement by an amendment to the agreement filed with the commissioner prior to the effective date stated in the agreement.

Added by Acts 1990, No. 191, § 1. Amended by Acts 1991, No. 665, § 1; Acts 2001, No. 532, § 1, eff. June 21, 2001.

§ 2131. Distributions

A trustee may make a distribution of trust property in full ownership or undivided interests, prorata or non-prorata, after taking into account the values and tax attributes of the trust property.

Added by Acts 2003, No. 480, § 1.

Revision Comment—2003

This Section is adapted from Section 816(22) of the Uniform Trust Code. It allows the trustee flexibility in choosing a method of distributing trust property and lessens the risk that a non-prorata distribution will be treated as a taxable sale. This Section also makes it clear that the trustee who distributes property must take gains and losses for tax purposes into account in valuing the property for distribution. This Section applies to both partial and final distributions, and does not preclude the trustee from selling the property in order to make a distribution.

Editor's note. Section 2 of Acts 2003, No. 480 declares that the amendments to "R.S. 9:1809, 1893, 1963, 1965, 1990, and 2068 shall apply only to trusts created after the effective date of this Act. The amendments to R.S. 9:1979, 2051, 2131, 2159(1), and 2241 shall apply to all trusts." Acts 2003, No. 480 became effective on August 15, 2003.

SUBPART D. ALLOCATION TO INCOME AND PRINCIPAL

§ 2141. General rule

A trust shall be administered with due regard to the respective interests of the beneficiaries in the allocation of receipts and expenditures.

Added by Acts 1964, No. 338, § 2.

Comments—1964

(a) This Sub-part is based upon the Revised Uniform Principal and Income Act [1962 Act]. Departures made from the Revised Uniform Act are noted in the comments.

(b) This section states part of the meaning of R.S. 9:2091 and together with Secs. 2142 and 2143 establishes the principle that allocation to income and principal is a matter that affects the administration of a trust.

(c) This section is similar to the first sentence of Sec. 2(a) of the Revised Uniform Principal and Income Act.

§ 2142. Allocation to beneficiaries of income and principal

A trust receipt shall be credited, or an expenditure charged, to income or principal or partly to each:

(1) In accordance with the terms of the trust instrument, including any provision giving the trustee discretion, notwithstanding contrary provisions of this Subpart; or

(2) In accordance with the provisions of this Subpart, in the absence of contrary provisions of the trust instrument; or

(3) If no rule is provided in the trust instrument or this Subpart, entirely to principal.

Added by Acts 1964, No. 338, § 2. Amended by Acts 1989, No. 114, § 1; Acts 2001, No. 520, § 2.

Comments—1964

(a) This section states part of the meaning of the source provision, R.S. 9:2091. It makes clear that allocation is to be made in accordance with a prudent man rule if neither the provisions of the trust instrument nor those of this Sub-part apply. It helps to establish the principle also advanced in Secs. 2141 and 2143 that allocation is an administrative matter.

(b) This section states substantially the meaning of the Revised Uniform Principal and Income Act, Sec. 2(a). Part of the meaning of Sec. 2(a) of that Act is stated in Sec. 2141 of this Code.

(c) The rules of this Sub-part may be altered or abrogated by the trust instrument. A general statement of abrogation shall be sufficient to render the provisions of this Sub-part inapplicable. The trust instrument may vest the trustee with complete discretion in the allocation of receipts and expenditures.

Comment—1989

This change makes it clear that the trust instrument can vest the trustee with discretion in apportionment of receipts and expenditures, but that such discretion must be exercised equitably. This change is meant to clarify the law, not to change it.

Comments—2001

(a) R.S. 9:2142(3) has provided that allocations between income and principal in the unprovided-for case are to be made according to what is "reasonable and equitable". The new default rule, derived from § 103(a) of the Uniform Principal and Income Act of 1997, is that the receipt is allocated to principal. This is a simple, easy-to-administer rule. Any inequity produced by such an allocation can be cured by the trustee's exercise of his power to adjust under R.S. 9:2158.

(b) The restatement of this Section by Act 520 of the Regular Session of 2001 eliminates the standard under which a trustee's discretion is exercised. The restatement of this Section by Act 520 of the Regular Session of 2001 eliminates the special standard applying to a trustee's exercise of discretion granted in the trust instrument. Therefore, the exercise of that discretion is subject to the standard set forth at R.S. 9:2115.

(c) As provided in Section 7 of Act 520 of the Regular Session of 2001, the modifications of this Section made by that Act shall apply to all trusts created on or after January 1, 2002, and shall apply to trusts created before January 1, 2002, commencing January 1, 2004. However, the modifications made by said Act shall apply to a trust as of any earlier date as of which the provisions of Subpart E of this Part, as included in Act 520 of the Regular Session of 2001, are made effective to the trust.

Editor's note. R.S. 9:2142 was amended by Acts 2001, No. 520, § 2, effective August 15, 2001. Section 7 of Acts 2001, No. 520, declares that "The provisions of Section 1 of this Act shall apply to decisions or actions of the trustee taken on or after the effective date of this Act. The provisions of Sections 2, 3, and 4 of this Act shall apply to all trusts created on or after January 1, 2002. With respect to trusts created before January 1, 2002, the provisions of Sections 2, 3, and 4 of this Act shall apply commencing January 1, 2004. The provisions of Sections 2, 3, and 4 of this Act shall apply to a trust as of an earlier date if that date is either (1) designated in the trust instrument, or (2) designated by all current beneficiaries of the trust in one or more written documents delivered by the trustee."

§ 2143. Allocation to beneficiaries of usufruct and naked ownership

A trust is administered with due regard to the respective interests of beneficiaries of usufruct and naked ownership in the allocation of receipts and expenditures if a receipt is credited or an expenditure is charged to the beneficiary of usufruct or the beneficiary of naked ownership or partly to each:

(1) In accordance with the terms of the trust instrument and the law regulating usufruct, notwithstanding contrary provisions of this Sub-part;

(2) In accordance with the provisions of this Sub-part, in the absence of applicable law regulating usufruct and if the trust instrument contains no provisions to the contrary;

(3) If neither of the preceding rules applies, in accordance with what is reasonable and equitable in view of the interests of those who are beneficiaries of usufruct as well as those who are beneficiaries of naked ownership, and in view of the manner in which men of ordinary prudence, discretion, and intelligence would act in the management of their own affairs.

Added by Acts 1964, No. 338, § 2.

Comments—1964

This section treats allocation under a trust into which a usufruct or naked ownership or both have been placed. It follows the policy of Sec. 2142 of this Code and Sec. 2(a) of the Revised Uniform Principal and Income Act, which provide for allocation under a trust having beneficiaries of income and principal.

Cross References

C.C. art. 535 et seq.

§ 2144. Income and principal distinguished

Receipts paid or delivered in return for the use of money or property forming a part of principal are income, unless this Sub-part expressly provides to the contrary.

Receipts paid or delivered as the consideration for the sale or other transfer of property forming a part of principal or as the replacement of property forming a part of principal are principal unless this Sub-part expressly provides to the contrary.

Added by Acts 1964, No. 338, § 2.

Comments—1964

This section summarizes the meanings of its sources, R.S. 9:2092 and Sec. 3 of the Revised Uniform Principal and Income Act. The listings of types of receipts that are found in Sec. 3 and the specific language that was found in R.S. 9:2092 are unnecessary and inappropriate to the general style of this Code. General principles are stated in this section and specific matters are treated in other sections of this Sub-part. The manner of treatment used in this Code achieves the same effect as that used in the Revised Uniform Principal and Income Act.

Cross References

C.C. arts. 488, 551, 560, 562.

§ 2145. When right to income arises

The right of an income beneficiary to income from property in trust arises at the time prescribed in the trust instrument, or, if no time is prescribed and the person receiving the right to income is the first income beneficiary to receive a right to income from the property, then:

(1) At the time the property becomes subject to the trust, with respect to property transferred by inter vivos disposition;

(2) At the time when, under the laws regulating donations mortis causa, the legatee of the same type of legacy free of trust is entitled to receive income from such a legacy, with respect to property transferred by testamentary disposition.

Added by Acts 1964, No. 338, § 2.

Comments—1964

(a) The Trust Estates Law was silent on this subject.

(b) Although a testamentary trust is created at the death of the settlor, under the laws regulating donations mortis causa the right of the trustee to receive the proceeds or interest from trust property may not arise at the death of the settlor. And although a testamentary addition to an established trust becomes effective at the death of the testator, under the laws regulating donations mortis causa the right of the trustee to receive the proceeds or interest from the property added to the trust may not arise at the death of the testator. In this state the right of an income beneficiary to income from a testamentary trust or from a trust to which property is added by testament cannot always arise at the time provided by the Revised Uniform Principal and Income Act, Sec. 4, i.e., at the time of the testator's death. Rather it must arise at the time a legatee of a similar type of legacy would be entitled to receive income from the property if it were left free of trust. Arts. 1607–1610, 1626–1631, R.C.C.; Secs. 1821, 1936.

(c) Sec. 1962 regulates the distribution of trust income to the income beneficiary.

Cross References

C.C. arts. 934, 954, 1467 to 1469, 1585, 1598.

§ 2146. Apportionment of receipts when right to income arises

A. In the administration of property transferred in trust:

(1) Receipts due but not paid when the right of the first income beneficiary to receive income from the property arises shall be treated as accruing when due;

(2) Receipts in the form of periodic payments, other than corporate distributions to stockholders, not due when the right of the first income beneficiary to receive income from the property arises, shall be treated as accruing from day to day;

(3) Receipts in the form of corporate distributions to stockholders shall be treated as accruing on the date fixed for the determination of stockholders of record entitled to

distribution, or, if no date is fixed, on the date of declaration of the distribution by the corporation;

(4) All other receipts shall be treated as accruing at the time of payment.

B. Receipts treated as accruing after the right of the first income beneficiary to receive income from the property arises, are income if they otherwise are income under the provisions of this Sub-part. Receipts treated as accruing at an earlier time are principal.

Added by Acts 1964, No. 338, § 2.

Comments—1964

(a) R.S. 9:2093 treated the allocation of periodic payments at the time the right of the first income beneficiary arose in the manner in which the allocation of these payments is treated in this section.

(b) R.S. 9:2094E treated the allocation of corporate dividends at the time the right of the first income beneficiary arose in the manner in which the allocation of corporate distributions is treated in this section.

(c) R.S. 9:2093 and the Revised Uniform Principal and Income Act, Sec. 4, treat both allocation at the time the right of the first income beneficiary arises and allocation at the time the right of an income beneficiary ceases. This section treats only allocation at the time the right of the first income beneficiary to receive income arises. Allocation at the time the right of an income beneficiary ceases is treated in Sec. 2147.

(d) The Revised Uniform Principal and Income Act, Sec. 4, provides that receipts from an income-producing asset are income if a trust is inter vivos, whether or not a payment similarly made under a testamentary trust would be income. Under the Revised Uniform Act, initial allocation is to be made between principal and income only if a trust is testamentary. The rules of the Revised Uniform Act governing allocation under a testamentary trust are identical to the rules of this section governing allocation under an inter vivos or a testamentary trust.

Cross References

C.C. arts. 489, 554, 555, 556.

§ 2147. Apportionment of receipts when right to income ceases

Upon the termination of an income interest, the income beneficiary whose interest is terminated (or his heirs, legatees, or assignees) is entitled to:

(1) Income undistributed on the date of termination;

(2) Income due but not paid to the trustee on the date of termination;

(3) Income in the form of periodic payments, other than corporate distributions to stockholders, not due on the date of termination, accrued from day to day;

(4) Corporate distributions to stockholders paid as income after the termination of the interest if the date for determination of stockholders of record entitled to distribution is a date before the termination of the interest, or, in the event no date is fixed, if the date of declaration of the distribution by the corporation is a date before termination of the interest.

Added by Acts 1964, No. 338, § 2.

Comments—1964

(a) R.S. 9:2093 treated the allocation of periodic payments at the time the right of an income beneficiary ceased in the manner provided in this section.

(b) R.S. 9:2094E treated the allocation of corporate dividends at the time the right of an income beneficiary ceased in the same manner in which the allocation of corporate distributions is treated in this section.

(c) R.S. 9:2093 and the Revised Uniform Principal and Income Act, Sec. 4, treat both allocation at the time the right of the first income beneficiary arises and allocation at the time the right of an income beneficiary ceases. This section treats only allocation at the time the right of an income beneficiary ceases. Allocation at the time the right of the first income beneficiary to receive income arises is treated in Sec. 2146.

(d) This section has the same effect as the pertinent provisions of Sec. 4 of the Revised Uniform Principal and Income Act.

Cross References

C.C. arts. 489, 554, 556, 1426.

§ 2148. Succession receipts

Succession receipts shall be credited and succession expenditures shall be charged to a legacy in trust in accordance with the laws regulating donations mortis causa.

Added by Acts 1964, No. 338, § 2.

Comments—1964

(a) The Trust Estates Law was silent on this subject.

(b) The Revised Uniform Principal and Income Act, Sec. 5, contains provisions that allocate succession receipts and expenditures to various legacies in a manner inconsistent with the laws of this state. This section is completely unlike Sec. 5 of the Revised Uniform Act.

Cross References

C.C. art. 1469.

§ 2149. Corporate distributions

A. Corporate distributions of shares of the distributing corporation, including distributions in the form of a stock split or stock dividend, are principal. A right to subscribe to shares or other securities issued by the distributing corporation accruing to stockholders on account of their stock ownership and the proceeds of any sale of the right are principal.

B. Except to the extent that the corporation indicates that some part of a corporate distribution is a settlement of preferred or guaranteed dividends accrued since the trustee became a stockholder or is in lieu of an ordinary cash dividend, a corporate distribution is principal if the distribution is pursuant to:

(1) A call of shares;

(2) A merger, consolidation, reorganization, or other plan by which assets of the corporation are acquired by another corporation; or

(3) A total or partial liquidation of the corporation, including any distribution that the corporation indicates is a distribution in total or partial liquidation, or any distribution of assets, other than cash, pursuant to a court decree or final administrative order by a government agency ordering distribution of the particular assets.

C. Distributions made from ordinary income by a regulated investment company or by a trust qualifying and electing to be taxed under federal law as a real estate investment trust are income. All other distributions made by the company or trust, including distributions from capital gains, depreciation, or depletion, whether in the form of cash or an option to take new stock or cash or an option to purchase additional shares, are principal.

D. All other corporate distributions are income, including cash dividends, distributions of, or rights to subscribe to, shares, securities, or obligations of corporations other than the distributing corporation, and the proceeds of the rights or of the property distributions, except as Sub-sections A, B, or C above provide otherwise.

E. If the distributing corporation gives a stockholder an option to receive a distribution either in cash or in its own shares, the distribution chosen is income, except as provided in Sub-sections B and C of this section.

F. A trustee may rely upon any statement of the distributing corporation as to any fact relevant under any provision of this Sub-part concerning the source or character of dividends or distributions of corporate assets.

Added by Acts 1964, No. 338, § 2.

Comments—1964

(a) Under R.S. 9:2094, corporate distributions made in arrears in settlement of preferred or guaranteed dividends were income, whether or not the trustee was stockholder when the dividends accrued. That provision enabled a trustee who knew that such a distribution would be made to unjustly prefer an income beneficiary by buying stock at an inflated price immediately before the distribution was made. This section protects the principal beneficiary from such conduct.

(b) Under R.S. 9:2094, all distributions that a corporation made in its own shares were principal. Yet a corporation sometimes issues a stock dividend in lieu of a cash dividend. This section provides that a distribution that a corporation makes in its own shares is income if the corporation indicates it is in lieu of an ordinary cash dividend.

(c) This section provides for the allocation of distributions of a regulated investment company. The Trust Estates Law was silent on the subject.

(d) This section provides that a trustee may rely upon a statement of the distributing corporation concerning the nature of distributions. The Trust Estates Law was not clear in that respect.

(e) This section is based upon the Revised Uniform Principal and Income Act, Sec. 6.

Cross References

C.C. art. 552.

§ 2150. Bonds

A. Bonds or other obligations for the payment of money are principal at their inventory value, except as provided in Sub-section B below. No provision shall be made for amortization of bond premiums or for accumulation for discount. The proceeds of sale, redemption, or other disposition of the bonds or obligations are principal.

B. The increment in value of a bond or other obligation for the payment of money payable at a future time in accordance with a fixed schedule of appreciation in excess of the price at which it was issued is income. The increment in value is distributable at the time provided in R.S. 9:1841 through 9:1847, R.S. 9:1891 through 9:1906, and R.S. 9:1961 through 9:1965, from the first principal cash available to the beneficiary who was the income beneficiary at the time of increment. If unrealized increment is distributed as income but out of principal, the principal shall be reimbursed for the increment when realized.

Added by Acts 1964, No. 338, § 2.

Comments—1964

(a) R.S. 9:2095 contained no provision permitting the increment in value of a bond bearing no interest to be considered income.

(b) This section is similar to the Revised Uniform Principal and Income Act, Sec. 7, but, unlike Sec. 7, it makes clear that its provisions do not affect the specific time for distribution of income to an income beneficiary.

§ 2151. Business operations

If a trustee uses any part of the principal in the operation of a business of which, as trustee, he is a proprietor or a partner, the proceeds and losses of the business shall be allocated in accordance with what is reasonable and equitable in view of the interests of those entitled to income as well as of those entitled to principal, and in view of the manner in which men of ordinary prudence, discretion, and intelligence would act in the management of their own affairs.

Added by Acts 1964, No. 338, § 2.

Comments—1964

(a) This section applies in determining income from an agricultural or farming operation, including the raising of animals or the operation of a nursery. Undertakings of those types are businesses within the meaning of this section.

(b) R.S. 9:2096B provided that income from a business consisting of the buying and selling of property should be determined by deducting from the gross returns and inventory value of property at the end of the year the expenses during and inventory value of property at the beginning of the year.

§ 2152. Proceeds of mineral interests

A. If any part of the principal consists of a right to receive royalties or overriding royalties, production from working interests or production payments, proceeds from net profits interests or payments for the right to extract minerals from immovable property, or other interests in oil, gas, and other minerals, the allocation of the proceeds of such interests shall be made as follows:

(1) If received as a delay rental on a lease, extension of payments on a lease, shut-in royalty, or bonus for the execution of a lease, the proceeds shall be allocated to income;

(2) If received from a production payment, then to the extent of any stated factor for interest or its equivalent, the proceeds shall be allocated to income; the balance of such proceeds shall be apportioned between principal and income by allocating to principal the fraction thereof that the unrecovered cost of the production payment bears to the remaining balance due upon the production payment (excluding any factor for interest or its equivalent) and by allocating the remainder of such proceeds to income;

(3) If received from a royalty, overriding royalty, limited royalty, or working interest, net profits interest, or from any other interest in oil, gas, or other minerals, not specifically covered in this section, such proceeds shall be allocated to principal until such time as the cost for such interest (including both tangible and intangible drilling cost) has been fully recovered; thereafter, such proceeds shall be apportioned between principal and income so that twenty-seven and one-half percent of the gross proceeds (but not to exceed fifty percent of the net proceeds remaining after payment of all expenses, direct and indirect, computed without allowances for depletion) shall be allocated to a reserve for depletion to be added to principal and the balance of the gross proceeds, after payment therefrom of all expenses, direct and indirect, shall be allocated to income.

B. This section is not applicable to timber, water, soil, sod, dirt, turf, mosses, shells, gravel, or other natural resources.

Added by Acts 1964, No. 338, § 2.

Comments—1964

(a) This section is based upon Section 9 of the Uniform Revised Principal and Income Act, with modifications. This section eliminates the inconsistencies of the Revised Uniform Principal and Income Act and the Trust Estates Law with respect to bonus payments.

(b) In order to provide consistency, this section treats bonus payments as income in all cases. In Section 9(a)(1) of the Uniform Act, bonus is treated as income, but in Sub-paragraph (3) of the same section, a portion of bonus is allocated to principal. A similar inconsistency existed in the Trust Estates Law. R.S. 9:2098 allocated mineral royalty to principal, whereas R.S. 9:2099 appeared to allocate royalty to income.

(c) In allocating mineral payments between principal and income, it is almost impossible to create homogeneous categories. For example, a bonus is not, strictly speaking, a payment for the permanent severance of minerals from the land. Mineral royalty does constitute such a payment. However, it is possible to negotiate a lease having a large bonus and low royalty thereby making the bonus, for all practical purposes, a payment in part for permanent severance. It would also be possible for a lessor to accept a production payment rather than a royalty and thereby avoid the effects of this section. Despite the possibility of perversion of the intentions of this section, some allocation of mineral payment must be made. Accordingly, this section lumps rentals, extension payments, shut-in royalties, and bonuses together because those payments are more in the nature of income than principal.

(d) Sub-section (2) of this section deals with production payments on the same basis as the Uniform Act.

(e) Sub-section (3) of this section differs from the Uniform Act insofar as working interests are concerned, by permitting recovery of all costs before allocating any proceeds to principal. If that were not done a trustee might be reluctant to invest in working interests because he would be in fact converting principal to income without reimbursement to principal. After the recovery of costs, the section follows the provisions of the Uniform Act by allocating twenty-seven and one-half percent of the gross proceeds to principal.

Cross References

C.C. arts. 488, 551.

§ 2153. Timber

If part of the principal consists of land from which timber may be removed, the receipts from taking the timber from the land shall be allocated in accordance with what is reasonable and equitable in view of the interests of those entitled to income as well as of those entitled to principal, and in view of the manner in which men of ordinary prudence, discretion, and intelligence would act in the management of their own affairs.

Added by Acts 1964, No. 338, § 2.

Comments—1964

(a) R.S. 9:2098 treated timber in the same manner in which minerals were treated, providing that receipts that were the consideration for a lease were income, but that receipts that were the consideration for permanent severance of the timber from the land were principal.

(b) This section is similar to Revised Uniform Principal and Income Act, Sec. 10.

Cross References

C.C. arts. 560, 562.

§ 2154. Other property subject to depletion

Except as provided in R.S. 9:2152 and 9:2153, if the principal consists of property subject to depletion, receipts from the property not in excess of five percent of its inventory value are income, and the balance is principal.

Added by Acts 1964, No. 338, § 2.

Comments—1964

(a) R.S. 9:2099 provided that receipts from property subject to depletion were to be allocated to income if the trustee was not under a duty to change the form of investment, and to be allocated to income to the extent of five percent per annum of its fair inventory value and to principal in the remaining amount, if the trustee was under that duty.

(b) This section is similar to the Revised Uniform Principal and Income Act, Sec. 11.

§ 2155. Underproductive property

A portion of the net proceeds of sale of any part of principal that has not produced an average net income (including the value of any beneficial use of the property by the income beneficiary) of at least one percent per annum of its inventory value for more than a year shall be treated as delayed income to which the income beneficiary is entitled as provided in this section. The net proceeds of sale are the gross proceeds received, including the value of any property received in substitution for the property disposed of, less expenses, including income taxes, incurred in disposition and less carrying charges accrued while the property was underproductive.

The sum allocated as delayed income is the difference between the net proceeds and the amount that, had it been invested at simple interest at four percent per annum while the property was underproductive, would have produced the net proceeds. That sum, plus any carrying charges and expenses previously charged against income while the property was underproductive, less any income received by the income beneficiary from the property and less the value of any beneficial use of the property by the income beneficiary, is income, and the balance is principal.

Property becomes underproductive at the beginning of the year in which it fails to produce an average net income of at least one percent per annum.

If there are successive income beneficiaries, the delayed income shall be divided among them or their heirs, legatees, or assignees according to the length of the period during which each was entitled to income.

If principal subject to this section is disposed of by conversion into property that cannot be apportioned easily, the income beneficiary is entitled to the net income from the substituted property while it is held. If within five years after the conversion the substituted property has not been further converted into easily apportionable property, no allocation as provided in this section shall be made.

This section does not apply to any period during which the trustee is under an express direction not to sell or dispose of the principal or to any period before the income from a legacy begins to accrue to the benefit of the income beneficiary.

Added by Acts 1964, No. 338, § 2.

Comments—1964

(a) The "unproductive property" provision of the Trust Estates Law, R.S. 9:2100, applied only in cases in which the trustee was under a duty to change the form of investment. Delayed income was computed beginning one year from the time the property was received by the trustee, or one year from the time it became unproductive. The rate of interest to be used was five percent per annum.

(b) The underproductive property provision of the Revised Uniform Principal and Income Act, Sec. 12, applies whether or not the trustee was under a duty to change the form of investment. Apparently, delayed income is to be computed from the beginning of the year in which the property became underproductive. The rate of interest to be used is four percent per annum.

(c) This section follows the broad outlines of Sec. 12 of the Revised Uniform Act. This section makes clear that delayed income is to be computed from the beginning of the year in which the property becomes underproductive. This section also makes clear that its provisions do not apply if the trustee is under an express direction to retain the property or if the right of the first income beneficiary to receive income from the property has not yet arisen.

(d) The Revised Uniform Principal and Income Act, Sec. 12, and this section both provide that, if underproductive property is converted into other property that cannot be apportioned easily, no allocation will be made unless the substituted property is converted within five years into property that can be apportioned easily. This provision applies to all types of property, including land and mortgages.

Cross References

C.C. arts. 615, 616.

§ 2156. Charges

A. The following charges shall be made against income:

(1) Ordinary expenses incurred or accrued in connection with the administration, management, or preservation of the trust property;

(2) A reasonable allowance for depreciation on property subject to depreciation under generally accepted accounting principles, but no allowance shall be made for depreciation of that portion of immovable property used by a beneficiary as a residence;

(3) One-half of court costs, attorney's fees, and other fees on periodic accounting, unless the court directs otherwise;

(4) Court costs, attorney's fees, and other fees on other accountings or judicial proceedings if the matter primarily concerns the income interest, unless the court directs otherwise;

(5) One-half of the trustee's regular compensation, whether based on a percentage of principal or income;

(6) Expenses reasonably incurred by the trustee for the management and application of income;

(7) A tax levied upon receipts defined as income under this Sub-part or the trust instrument and payable by the trustee;

(8) Interest accrued on an indebtedness.

B. If charges against income are of unusual amount, the trustee may by means of reserves or other reasonable means charge them over a reasonable period and withhold from distribution sums sufficient to produce substantial regularity in distributions.

C. The following charges shall be made against principal:

(1) Extraordinary expenses incurred or accrued in connection with the administration, management, or preservation of the trust property;

(2) Expenses incurred in making a capital improvement to principal, including special taxes and assessments;

(3) Expenses incurred in investing and reinvesting principal;

(4) One-half of court costs, attorney's fees, and other fees on periodic accounting, unless the court directs otherwise;

(5) Court costs, attorney's fees, and other fees on other accountings or judicial proceedings if the matter primarily concerns the principal interest, unless the court directs otherwise;

(6) Expenses incurred in maintaining or defending an action to construe the trust or to protect the trust or the trust property;

(7) One-half of the trustee's regular compensation, whether based on a percentage of principal or income;

(8) All the trustee's special compensation;

(9) A tax levied upon profit, gain, or other receipts allocated to principal notwithstanding denomination of the tax as an income tax by the taxing authority;

(10) The amount of an estate tax apportioned to the trust, including interest and penalties;

(11) The principal of an indebtedness;

(12) All other expenses not chargeable to income.

D. If the payment of special taxes and assessments produces an addition to the value of the trust property, the trustee shall reserve out of income and add to principal a reasonable allowance for the depreciation of the improvement under generally accepted accounting principles, although the improvement was not made directly to the trust property.

E. Regularly recurring charges shall be apportioned to the same extent and in the same manner that receipts are apportioned under R.S. 9:2145 through 9:2147.

Added by Acts 1964, No. 338, § 2. Amended by Acts 2010, No. 175, § 2.

Comments—1964

(a) R.S. 9:2101 provided that all of the trustee's compensation should be paid out of income except compensation computed on principal. It provided also that all court costs, attorney's fees, and other fees on a regular accounting should be paid out of income.

(b) The Revised Uniform Principal and Income Act, Sec. 13, provides that one-half of the trustee's regular compensation should be charged to income and one-half to principal. Similarly one-half of court costs, attorney's fees, and other fees on a periodic accounting are to be charged to income and one-half to principal. This section follows those provisions.

(c) The Revised Uniform Act also differs from R.S. 9:2101 in providing that a reasonable allowance for depreciation on property subject to depreciation should be charged to principal. This section follows that provision of the Revised Uniform Act.

(d) This section follows R.S. 9:2101 in providing that a reasonable allowance for depreciation of an improvement produced by the payment of special taxes and assessments shall be reserved out of income. The Revised Uniform Act does not contain a similar provision.

Cross References

C.C. arts. 584, 585.

§ 2157. Inventory value defined

The term "inventory value," as used in this Subpart, means the cost of property purchased by the trustee and the market value of other property at the time it became subject to the trust, but in the case of a testamentary trust the trustee may use any value finally determined for the purposes of an estate tax.

Added by Acts 1964, No. 338, § 2. Amended by Acts 2010, No. 175, § 2.

Comments—1964

The Trust Estates Law did not define "inventory value." The definition stated in this section is taken from Sec. 1 of the Revised Uniform Principal and Income Act.

SUBPART E. POWER TO ADJUST

§ 2158. Power to adjust

Subject to the limitations set forth in this Subpart, a trustee may make an adjustment between principal and income when the interest of one or more beneficiaries is defined by reference to the "income" of a trust, and the trustee determines, after taking into account the allocations for the year under Subpart D, that the adjustment is necessary in order for the trustee to satisfy his duty to be fair and reasonable to all the beneficiaries, taking into account the purposes of the trust.

Added by Acts 2001, No. 520, § 4.

Comments—2001

(a) The power to adjust, set forth in this Subpart E, is derived from Section 104 of the Uniform Principal and Income Act (1997). The power to adjust applies to trusts under which the amounts payable to one or more beneficiaries are measured, at least in part, by the "income" of the trust. Income is determined as provided in the preceding Subpart D.

(b) Adjustments are most likely to be appropriate when a trustee invests for total return, including a substantial holding of assets expected to grow but producing little income. While such an investment policy may be best for the trust as a whole, without this Subpart the policy could be unfair to the income beneficiary. The ability to adjust from principal to income helps to enable a trustee to invest as a prudent investor for the good of the trust as a whole while still providing a fair annual benefit for the income beneficiary.

(c) An adjustment from income to principal may be appropriate in some circumstances, for example, when the trustee decides to invest a substantial portion of trust assets in short-term obligations, interest rates are very high, and the failure to allocate some of the interest to principal will cause a reduction of the value of the trust assets when inflation is taken into account.

(d) Including principal in a distribution to the income beneficiary may require selling an asset. The sale may require recognition of a capital gain.

(e) The new rules balance the interests of income and principal beneficiaries who are not the same. The new rules apply equally to trusts for a single beneficiary who is entitled under the trust instrument only to income.

(f) The purposes of the trust may make an adjustment inappropriate. For example, normally it would not be appropriate to adjust from principal to income when the only significant assets of the trust are interests in closely-held businesses or immovables.

(g) As provided in Section 7 of Act 520 of the Regular Session of 2001, this Section and the other Sections of new Subpart E of this Part shall apply to all trusts created on or after January 1, 2002. With respect to trusts created before January 1, 2002, the provisions of this Subpart shall apply commencing January 1, 2004. However, the provisions of this Subpart shall apply to a trust as of an earlier date if that date is either (1) designated in the trust instrument or (2) designated by all current beneficiaries of the trust in one or more written documents delivered to the trustee.

Editor's note. Acts 2001, No. 520, § 4, enacted R.S. 9:2158, effective August 15, 2001. Section 7 of Acts 2001, No. 520, declares that "The provisions of Section 1 of this Act shall apply to decisions or actions of the trustee taken on or after the effective date of this Act. The provisions of Sections 2, 3, and 4 of this Act shall apply to all trusts created on or after January 1, 2002. With respect to trusts created before January 1, 2002, the provisions of Sections 2, 3, and 4 of this Act shall apply commencing January 1, 2004. The provisions of Sections 2, 3, and 4 of this Act shall apply to a trust as of an earlier date if that date is either (1) designated in the trust instrument, or (2) designated by all current beneficiaries of the trust in one or more written documents delivered by the trustee."

§ 2159. When the power to adjust is denied

A trustee shall not make an adjustment under R.S. 9:2158:

(1) If the existence or exercise of the power to adjust would cause ineligibility for the estate-tax or gift-tax marital deduction or charitable deduction.

(2) That diminishes the value for gift-tax purposes of the income interest in a trust to which a person transfers property with intent to qualify for a gift tax exclusion;

(3) If possessing or exercising the power to make an adjustment causes an individual to be treated as the owner of all or part of the trust for income tax purposes, and the individual would not be treated as the owner if the trustee did not possess the power to make an adjustment; or

(4) If the terms of the trust instrument clearly deny the trustee the power to make adjustments.

Added by Acts 2001, No. 520, § 4. Amended by Acts 2003, No. 480, § 1.

Revision Comment—2003

The original wording of Paragraph (1) was too broad, forbidding an adjustment in a trust designed to qualify for the marital deduction under Internal Revenue Code § 2056 even when there would be no adverse tax consequences. It suffices to forbid an adjustment only if the adjustment would prevent qualification for the marital deduction.

Editor's note. Acts 2001, No. 520, § 4, enacted R.S. 9:2159, effective August 15, 2001. Section 7 of Acts 2001, No. 520, declares that "The provisions of Section 1 of this Act shall apply to decisions or actions of the trustee taken on or after the effective date of this Act. The provisions of Sections 2, 3, and 4 of this Act shall apply to all trusts created on or after January 1, 2002. With respect to trusts created before January 1, 2002, the provisions of Sections 2, 3, and 4 of this Act shall apply commencing January 1, 2004. The provisions of Sections 2, 3, and 4 of this Act shall apply to a trust as of an earlier date if that date is either (1) designated in the trust instrument, or (2) designated by all current beneficiaries of the trust in one or more written documents delivered by the trustee."

Section 2 of Acts 2003, No. 480 declares that the amendments to "R.S. 9:1809, 1893, 1963, 1965, 1990, and 2068 shall apply only to trusts created after the effective date of this Act. The amendments to R.S. 9:1979, 2051, 2131, 2159(1), and 2241 shall apply to all trusts." Acts 2003, No. 480 became effective on August 15, 2003.

§ 2160. Adjustment benefiting trustee

A trustee may not make an adjustment under R.S. 9:2158 that benefits himself, directly or indirectly, unless all of the current beneficiaries consent or the proper court authorizes such adjustment after notice to all current beneficiaries.

Added by Acts 2001, No. 520, § 4.

Editor's note. Acts 2001, No. 520, § 4, enacted R.S. 9:2160, effective August 15, 2001. Section 7 of Acts 2001, No. 520, declares that "The provisions of Section 1 of this Act shall apply to decisions or actions of the trustee taken on or after the effective date of this Act. The provisions of Sections 2, 3, and 4 of this Act shall apply to all trusts created on or after January 1, 2002. With respect to trusts created before January 1, 2002, the provisions of Sections 2, 3, and 4 of this Act shall apply commencing January 1, 2004. The provisions of Sections 2, 3, and 4 of this Act shall apply to a trust as of an earlier date if that date is either (1) designated in the trust instrument, or (2) designated by all current beneficiaries of the trust in one or more written documents delivered by the trustee."

§ 2161. Adjustment beyond percentage limit

A. A court order shall be required in order for the trustee to make an adjustment from principal to income under R.S. 9:2158 if the amount of the adjustment from principal, when added to the amount of the net income of the trust for the year, exceeds five percent of the net fair market value of the assets of the trust at the beginning of the year.

B. A court order shall be required in order for the trustee to make an adjustment from income to principal under R.S. 9:2158 if the amount of the adjustment from income reduces the net income for the year below five percent of the net fair market value of the assets of the trust at the beginning of the year.

Added by Acts 2001, No. 520, § 4.

Comment—2001

The limits on adjustments without court supervision are not meant to imply that an adjustment to either limit will always be deemed to be fair and reasonable.

Editor's note. Acts 2001, No. 520, § 4, enacted R.S. 9:2161, effective August 15, 2001. Section 7 of Acts 2001, No. 520, declares that "The provisions of Section 1 of this Act shall apply to decisions or actions of the trustee taken on or after the effective date of this Act. The provisions of Sections 2, 3, and 4 of this Act shall apply to all trusts created on or after January 1, 2002. With respect to trusts created before January 1, 2002, the provisions of Sections 2, 3, and 4 of this Act shall apply commencing January 1, 2004. The provisions of Sections 2, 3, and 4 of this Act shall apply to a trust as of an earlier date if that date is either (1) designated in the trust instrument, or (2) designated by all current beneficiaries of the trust in one or more written documents delivered by the trustee."

§ 2162. General provisions regarding court orders affecting adjustments

A trustee may apply for a court order under R.S. 9:2160 or 2161, or to obtain approval from the court of any other decision to adjust or not to adjust under R.S. 9:2158. The following provisions apply to such an action:

(1) The proceeding shall be governed by R.S. 9:2233(A).

(2) All current beneficiaries of the trust must approve the adjustment or be given the opportunity to oppose it.

(3) A trustee's decision to adjust or not to adjust shall be approved by the court if the trustee's petition sets forth the reasons for the adjustment, or decision not to adjust, the facts upon which the trustee relies, and an explanation of how the income and principal beneficiaries will be affected, unless a beneficiary establishes that the adjustment, or decision not to adjust, would be an abuse of the trustee's discretion.

(4) An order may authorize adjustments, or non-adjustments, for future years as well as the current year, subject to the right of a person in a subsequent year who is at that time a current beneficiary of the trust to apply to the proper court to have the order modified or rescinded.

(5) For purposes of this Subpart, the "current beneficiaries" of a trust as of any date are the persons who are then the principal beneficiaries of the trust and the persons to whom the trustee is then required or permitted to distribute the income of the trust.

Added by Acts 2001, No. 520, § 4.

Comment—2001

Potential beneficiaries who are not current beneficiaries are not required to be parties to any court action under this Subpart. Examples of individuals who are not current beneficiaries are individuals whose only interest is as a potential recipient of income in the future, or as a potential substitute principal beneficiary, or as a potential member of a class of beneficiaries.

Editor's note. Acts 2001, No. 520, § 4, enacted R.S. 9:2162, effective August 15, 2001. Section 7 of Acts 2001, No. 520, declares that "The provisions of Section 1 of this Act shall apply to decisions or actions of the trustee taken on or after the effective date of this Act. The provisions of Sections 2, 3, and 4 of this Act shall apply to all trusts created on or after January 1, 2002. With respect to trusts created before January 1, 2002, the provisions of Sections 2, 3, and 4 of this Act shall apply commencing January 1, 2004. The provisions of Sections 2, 3, and 4 of this Act shall apply to a trust as of an earlier date if that date is either (1) designated in the trust instrument, or (2) designated by all current beneficiaries of the trust in one or more written documents delivered by the trustee."

§ 2163. Remedies

If a court determines that a trustee has abused his discretion in making or failing to make an adjustment under R.S. 9:2158, the court shall restore the beneficiaries to the positions they would have occupied if the trustee had not abused his discretion, according to the following rules:

(1) When the abuse of discretion has resulted in no distribution to a beneficiary or a distribution that is too small, the court shall require the trustee to distribute from the trust to the beneficiary an amount that the court determines will restore the beneficiary to an appropriate economic position.

(2) When the abuse of discretion has resulted in a distribution to a beneficiary that is too large, the court shall require the trustee to withhold an amount from one or more future distributions to the beneficiary or require the beneficiary to return some or all of the distribution to the trust.

(3) When the court is unable, by means of Paragraphs (1) and (2), to restore the beneficiaries, the trust, or both to the positions they would have occupied if the trustee had not abused his discretion, the court may require the trustee to pay an appropriate amount from his own funds to one or more of the beneficiaries or the trust or both.

Added by Acts 2001, No. 520, § 4.

Comments—2001

This Section is based on Section 105 of the Uniform Principal Income Act (2000).

Editor's note. Acts 2001, No. 520, § 4, enacted R.S. 9:2163, effective August 15, 2001. Section 7 of Acts 2001, No. 520, declares that "The provisions of Section 1 of this Act shall apply to decisions or actions of the trustee taken on or after the effective date of this Act. The provisions of Sections 2, 3, and 4 of this Act shall apply to all trusts created on or after January 1, 2002. With respect to trusts created before January 1, 2002, the provisions of Sections 2, 3, and 4 of this Act shall apply commencing January 1, 2004. The provisions of Sections 2, 3, and 4 of this Act shall apply to a trust as of an earlier date if that date is either (1) designated in the trust instrument, or (2) designated by all current beneficiaries of the trust in one or more written documents delivered by the trustee."

SUBPART F. THE TRUSTEE'S BOND

This Subpart, originally designated as Subpart E, was redesignated as Subpart F pursuant to § 3 of Acts 2001, No. 520, and the statutory revision authority of the Louisiana State Law Institute.

§ 2171. Individual and corporate trustees

An individual trustee shall furnish security for the faithful performance of his duties, unless the trust instrument dispenses with security. A corporate trustee need not furnish security unless security is required by the trust instrument.

The amount and type of security shall be approved by the proper court if not provided for in the trust instrument.

Added by Acts 1964, No. 338, § 2.

Comment—1964

This section makes no change in the law.

Cross References

C.C. arts. 571, 573.

§ 2172. Security required by court

On the application of any interested party, the proper court may compel a trustee to furnish security adequate to protect the interests of a beneficiary even if the trustee is not otherwise required to furnish security.

Added by Acts 1964, No. 338, § 2.

Comments—1964

(a) The Trust Estates Law was silent on this subject.

(b) This section is similar to Art. 3154, C.C.P., which provides that forced heirs and the surviving spouse in community of a testator may compel an executor to furnish security.

Cross References

C.C. arts. 571 to 574.

§ 2173. Increasing, diminishing, or dispensing with trustee's security by court

On the application of any interested party, the proper court may increase, diminish, or dispense with the trustee's security.

Added by Acts 1964, No. 338, § 2.

Comments—1964

(a) The Trust Estates Law was silent on this subject.

(b) This section is similar to Art. 4131, C.C.P., which provides that a court may order the security furnished by the tutor to be increased or diminished "at any time as the movable property may increase or diminish in value or for other circumstances which the court may consider proper."

(c) Under the authority of this section and Secs. 1786, 1787, the proper court may appoint a provisional trustee who shall furnish security in an amount adequate to protect the beneficiary. Compare Art. 3152, C.C.P., which provides for the security to be furnished by the provisional administrator.

Cross References

C.C. arts. 571, 572, 573, 890.

PART VI. COMPENSATION AND INDEMNITY OF THE TRUSTEE

SUBPART A. COMPENSATION OF THE TRUSTEE

§ 2181. General rule

A trustee is entitled to reasonable compensation from the trust estate for his services as trustee, unless the trust instrument provides otherwise or unless the trustee waives compensation.

Added by Acts 1964, No. 338, § 2.

Comments—1964

(a) This section makes no change in the law.

(b) A trustee is entitled to receive compensation for his services as a fiduciary unless the trust instrument provides to the contrary. The trust instrument may fix the amount of a trustee's compensation, but if it does not, a trustee may charge a reasonable compensation, subject to review by the proper court. A trustee entitled to receive compensation may waive it. If the amount of compensation fixed by the trust instrument is so inadequate that no duly qualified person can be found who will serve as trustee unless the amount of compensation is increased, the proper court may increase the amount of compensation so that the purposes of the trust will not be defeated or substantially impaired. Even if a trustee receives no compensation, his acceptance of a trust makes him subject to the duties and liabilities of a trustee. Restatement of Trusts 2d, Secs. 169, 242, 243, and Comments.

(c) R.S. 9:2131 was based upon the Restatement of Trusts, Sec. 242. This section is similar to Sec. 242 of the Restatement of Trusts 2d.

(d) In other states a trustee is usually entitled to compensation, either under statute or judicial decision, although the trust instrument does not specifically provide for compensation. In some states, the trustee's compensation is fixed at a percentage of principal or income or both; in others, it is simply a reasonable amount. Bogert, Trusts and Trustees, Sec. 975 (2d ed. 1962); Scott on Trusts, Sec. 242 (2d ed. 1956).

Cross References

C.C. art. 1973.

§ 2182. Effect of breach of trust upon compensation

If a trustee commits a breach of trust, the proper court in its discretion may deny him all compensation, allow him a reduced compensation, or allow him full compensation.

Added by Acts 1964, No. 338, § 2.

Comments—1964

(a) This section makes no change in the law.

(b) R.S. 9:2132 was based upon the Restatement of Trusts, Sec. 243. This section is similar to Sec. 243 of the Restatement of Trusts 2d.

(c) In other states, the effect of breach of trust upon a trustee's compensation is a matter that rests in the discretion of the court. Bogert, Trusts and Trustees, Secs. 861, 980 (2d ed 1962); Scott on Trusts, Sec. 243 (2d ed. 1956).

SUBPART B. INDEMNITY OF THE TRUSTEE

§ 2191. Indemnity for expenses properly incurred

A trustee is entitled to indemnity from the trust estate for expenses properly incurred by him in the administration of the trust, unless the trust instrument provides otherwise.

Added by Acts 1964, No. 338, § 2.

Comments—1964

(a) This section makes no change in the law.

(b) If a trustee properly incurs a liability in the administration of the trust, he is entitled to indemnity. Indemnity takes the form of either exoneration or reimbursement. A trustee is exonerated if trust property is used in discharging a liability. He is reimbursed if he is repaid with trust property after he has discharged a liability with his own property. The trust instrument may provide that only one form of indemnity may be used, but, unless it so provides, either form may be used. Restatement of Trusts 2d, Sec. 244 and Comments.

(c) R.S. 9:2133 was based upon the Restatement of Trusts, Sec. 244. This section is similar to Sec. 244 of the Restatement of Trusts 2d.

(d) In other states a trustee is entitled to indemnity for expenses properly incurred by him in the administration of the trust. Bogert, Trusts and Trustees, Sec. 718 (2d ed. 1960), Sec. 975 (2d ed. 1962); Scott on Trusts, Sec. 244 (2d ed. 1956).

Cross References

C.C. arts. 527, 528, 1973.

§ 2192. Indemnity for expenses not properly incurred

If an expense is not properly incurred in the administration of a trust, a trustee is entitled to indemnity from the trust estate for such an expense to the extent that he has thereby conferred a benefit upon the trust estate, unless the trust instrument provides to the contrary, or unless the circumstances make it inequitable to allow him indemnity.

If an expense is not properly incurred in the administration of a trust, a trustee is entitled to indemnity from the trust estate for the full amount of the expense, if the transaction in which the expense is incurred is of such a character that the beneficiary is in a position either to reject or accept it and he accepts it.

Added by Acts 1964, No. 338, § 2.

Comments—1964

(a) The Trust Estates Law was silent on this subject.

(b) This section follows the language of Restatement of Trusts 2d, Sec. 245, and resembles the laws of most states. Scott on Trusts, Secs. 245–245.2 (ed. 1956).

Cross References

C.C. arts. 527, 528, 1973.

§ 2193. Liability of beneficiary

If the trust estate is not sufficient to indemnify a trustee for expenses properly incurred by him in the administration of a trust, a beneficiary shall be personally liable only if the trustee can show an express or implied contract between that beneficiary and himself that would entitle the trustee to indemnity.

Added by Acts 1964, No. 338, § 2.

Comments—1964

(a) The Trust Estates Law was silent on this subject.

(b) The Restatement of Trusts 2d, Sec. 249(1), does not permit a trustee to obtain indemnity from the beneficiary personally if the trust estate is insufficient to indemnify the trustee unless there is an agreement between the trustee and the beneficiary that the beneficiary is to indemnify the trustee.

(c) The English cases and texts generally agree that a trustee is entitled to obtain indemnity from the beneficiaries personally if the trust estate is insufficient to indemnify him. Generally in the United States, a trustee can obtain indemnity from the beneficiaries only if he can show an express or implied contract between the beneficiaries and himself that would entitle him to indemnity. Bogert, Trusts and Trustees, Sec. 718 (2d ed. 1960); Scott on Trusts, Secs. 249, 249.1 (2d ed. 1956).

Cross References

C.C. arts. 1765, 3182, 3183.

§ 2194. Charge on beneficiary's interest

If a beneficiary is liable to a trustee as such, his interest in the trust estate is subject to a charge for the amount of his liability; but a trustee is not entitled to a charge on a beneficiary's interest in the trust estate to secure a beneficiary's liability not connected with the administration of the trust, unless the beneficiary contracts to give him such a charge.

Added by Acts 1964, No. 338, § 2.

Comments—1964

(a) This section makes no change in the law.

(b) R.S. 9:2134, the source of this section, was based upon the Restatement of Trusts, Secs. 250 and 251. This section is similar to Secs. 250 and 251 of the Restatement of Trusts 2d and the laws of most states. Scott on Trusts, Secs. 250, 251 (2d ed. 1956).

§ 2195. Charge on beneficiary's interest; advance or loan of trust money

If a trustee makes an advance or loan of trust money to a beneficiary, the beneficiary's interest is subject to a charge for the repayment of the amount advanced or lent.

Added by Acts 1964, No. 338, § 2.

Comments—1964

(a) This section makes no change in the law.

(b) R.S. 9:2135 was based upon the Restatement of Trusts, Sec. 255. This section is similar to Sec. 255 of the Restatement of Trusts 2d.

(c) In other states a charge is placed on the beneficiary's interest for the repayment of an amount advanced or lent to the beneficiary by the trustee. Scott on Trusts, Secs. 255, 255.1 (2d ed. 1956).

Cross References

C.C. art. 2893 et seq.

§ 2196. Indemnity for tort liability

A. A trustee who has incurred personal liability for a tort committed in the administration of the trust is entitled to indemnity from the trust estate if:

(1) The tort was a common incident of the kind of business activity in which the trustee was properly engaged for the trust, or,

(2) Although the tort was not a common incident of such activity, if neither the trustee nor an officer or employee of the trustee was guilty of personal fault in incurring the liability.

B. If a trustee has committed a tort that has increased the value of the trust property, he is entitled to indemnity from the trust estate to the extent of the increase in value, even though he would not otherwise be entitled to indemnity.
Added by Acts 1964, No. 338, § 2.

Comments—1964

(a) R.S. 9:2136 was based upon the Uniform Trusts Act, Secs. 13(1) and 13(2).

(b) The Restatement of Trusts 2d, Sec. 247 and Comments, permits a trustee to be indemnified for tort liability if liability was incurred in the proper administration of the trust and the trustee was not personally at fault. It also permits a trustee who committed a tort with the intention of benefiting the trust estate to be indemnified to the extent of the benefit.

(c) This section is similar to the law of most states. Bogert, Trusts and Trustees, Sec. 734 (2d ed. 1960); Scott on Trusts, Sec. 247 (2d ed. 1956).

(d) A trustee is not entitled to receive indemnity from a beneficiary personally for torts for which he becomes liable in the course of administration unless the beneficiary has agreed to indemnify him. *Cf.* Sec. 2193; Bogert, Trusts and Trustees, Sec. 734 (2d ed. 1960).

Cross References

C.C. arts. 1786, 1800, 1804, 2315.

PART VII. LIABILITIES OF THE TRUSTEE

§ 2201. General rule

If a trustee commits a breach of trust he shall be chargeable with:

(1) A loss or depreciation in value of the trust estate resulting from a breach of trust; or

(2) A profit made by him through breach of trust; or

(3) A profit that would have accrued to the trust estate if there had been no breach of trust.

Added by Acts 1964, No. 338, § 2.

Comments—1964

(a) This section makes no change in the law.

(b) R.S. 9:2033 was based upon the Restatement of Trusts, Sec. 205. This section is similar to Sec. 205 of the Restatement of Trusts 2d.

(c) In other states, a trustee is liable for a loss or depreciation in value of the trust estate resulting from a breach of trust, any profit made by him through a breach of trust, and any profit that would have accrued if there had not been a breach of trust. Scott on Trusts, Sec. 205 (2d ed. 1956).

Cross References

C.C. art. 1994 et seq.

§ 2202. Loss not resulting from breach of trust

A trustee is not liable to a beneficiary for a loss or depreciation in value of the trust property, or for a failure to make a profit not resulting from a breach of trust.
Added by Acts 1964, No. 338, § 2.

Comments—1964

(a) This section makes no change in the law.

(b) This section is similar to the laws of most states. Scott on Trusts, Sec. 204 (2d ed. 1956). *Cf.* Bogert, Trusts and Trustees, Sec. 862 (2d ed. 1962).

Cross References

C.C. art. 1996.

§ 2203. Balancing losses against gains

A trustee who is liable for a loss occasioned by one breach of trust cannot reduce the amount of his liability by deducting the amount of a gain that has accrued through another distinct breach of trust; but if the two breaches of trust are not distinct, a trustee is accountable only for the net gain or chargeable only for the net loss resulting therefrom.
Added by Acts 1964, No. 338, § 2.

Comments—1964

(a) The Trust Estates Law was silent on this subject.

(b) This section follows the language of the Restatement of Trusts 2d, Sec. 213.

(c) In other states a trustee is permitted to balance losses from a breach of trust against gains from a breach of trust if the losses and gains result from breaches of trusts that are not separate and distinct. Scott on Trusts, Secs. 213–213.2 (2d ed. 1956).

(d) Comment (e) under Sec. 213 of the Restatement of Trusts 2d gives the following factors in determining whether breaches of trust are distinct:

"In determining whether two breaches of trust are distinct, the following factors may be of importance: (1) whether the breaches of trust relate to the same or to different parts of the trust property; (2) whether the breaches of trust arise out of successive dealings with the same property or its product; (3) the amount of time elapsing between the breaches of trust; (4) whether there has been an accounting between the breaches of trust; (5) how the trustee has dealt with the property or its product between the breaches of trust; (6) whether the trustee intends to misappropriate trust property; or intends to commit a breach of trust, although not intending to misappropriate trust property; or does not intend to commit a breach of trust; (7) whether the breaches of trust are the result of a single policy on the part of the trustee.

"No positive rules can be laid down in respect to the relative weight to be given to these different factors. No one of them is necessarily determinative of the question whether two breaches of trust are distinct or not. Where the breaches of trust relate to different parts of the trust property, they are more likely to be distinct than where they arise out of successive dealings with the same property or its product. The longer the time which elapses between two breaches of trust, the more likely are the breaches to be considered distinct, especially where after committing one breach and before committing the other there has been an accounting by the trustee, or where after he has committed one breach and before he commits another he has turned the property into the trust and dealt with it in accordance with the terms of the trust. Where the trustee engages in successive dealings with the trust property or its product intending to misappropriate it, the successive dealings are more likely to be considered distinct than if he did not intend to misappropriate it."

Cross References

C.C. art. 2002.

§ 2204. Liability of successor trustee

A trustee shall not be liable to a beneficiary for a breach of trust committed by a predecessor trustee, unless he:

(1) Knows or should know of a situation constituting a breach of trust committed by his predecessor and improperly permits it to continue; or

(2) Neglects to take proper steps to compel the predecessor to deliver the trust property to him; or

(3) Neglects to take proper steps to redress a breach of trust committed by the predecessor.

Added by Acts 1964, No. 338, § 2.

Comments—1964

(a) The Trust Estates Law was silent on this subject.

(b) This section is identical in meaning with the Restatement Trusts 2d, Sec. 223.

(c) In most states a trustee is not liable for a breach of trust committed by a predecessor trustee unless he himself is guilty of a breach of trust. That is also the import of this section. Bogert, Trusts and Trustees, Sec. 871 (2d ed. 1962); Scott on Trusts, Secs. 223–223.3 (2d ed. 1956).

Cross References

C.C. arts. 1765, 1824, 2315.

§ 2205. Liability of co-trustee

A trustee shall not be liable to a beneficiary for a breach of trust committed by a co-trustee, unless he:

(1) Participates in a breach of trust committed by his co-trustee;

(2) Delegates improperly the administration of the trust to his co-trustee;

(3) Conceals, approves, or acquiesces in a breach of trust committed by his co-trustee;

(4) Enables his co-trustee to commit a breach of trust by his failure to exercise reasonable care in the administration of the trust; or

(5) Neglects to take proper steps to compel his co-trustee to redress a breach of trust.

Added by Acts 1964, No. 338, § 2.

Comments—1964

(a) Sub-sections (1) through (4) make no change in the law. The Trust Estates Law was silent upon the matter treated in Subsection (5).

(b) This section is identical in meaning with the Restatement of Trusts 2d, Sec. 224.

(c) In other states a trustee is not liable for a breach of trust committed by a co-trustee, unless he himself is guilty of a breach of trust. Bogert, Trusts and Trustees, Secs. 862, 871 (2d ed. 1962); Scott on Trusts, Secs. 224–224.5 (2d ed. 1956).

Cross References

C.C. art. 1786 et seq.

§ 2206. Relief from liability by trust instrument

A. The trust instrument may relieve the trustee from liability, except as provided in Sub-sections B and C of this section.

B. A provision in the trust instrument is not effective to relieve the trustee from liability for breach of the duty of loyalty to a beneficiary or for breach of trust committed in bad faith.

C. A provision in the trust instrument is not effective to relieve the trustee from liability if it is inserted as a result of an abuse by the trustee of a fiduciary or confidential relationship to the settlor.

Added by Acts 1964, No. 338, § 2.

Comments—1964

(a) R.S. 9:2035 was based upon the Uniform Trusts Act, Sec. 17. This section is based upon the Restatement of Trusts 2d, Sec. 222, and renders ineffective a provision of the trust instrument that would relieve the trustee from breach of the duty of loyalty, as well as one that would relieve the trustee from liability for a breach of trust committed in bad faith. The Restatement of Trusts 2d renders ineffective a provision that would relieve the trustee from liability for a breach of trust committed intentionally or with reckless indifference to the interest of a beneficiary or from liability for a profit derived by the trustee from breach of trust. This section uses the term "bad faith" instead of the language of the Restatement because it is more explicit and meaningful.

(b) The trustee's "duty of loyalty to a beneficiary" means the trustee's duty to administer a trust solely in the beneficiary's interest. See Secs. 2082–2086 of this Code; Restatement of Trusts 2d, Sec. 170, Comment (a) under Sec. 206.

Cross References

C.C. arts. 7, 454, 1973.

§ 2207. Relief from liability by beneficiary

A competent beneficiary who is acting with knowledge of the material facts and whose action is not improperly induced by the conduct of a trustee may, by written instrument delivered to a trustee, relieve a trustee from liabilities that otherwise would be imposed upon him. The instrument shall not be effective if it purports to limit a trustee's liability for improperly advancing money or conveying property to a beneficiary of a spendthrift trust or a trust under which a beneficiary's right to alienate is restricted, or if it limits prospectively and in general terms a trustee's liability for breach of the duty of loyalty to a beneficiary, or for breach of trust in bad faith.

Added by Acts 1964, No. 338, § 2.

Comments—1964

(a) R.S. 9:2036 was based upon the Uniform Trusts Act, Sec. 18. This section is based both upon Sec. 18 of the Uniform Trusts Act and upon Secs. 216–218 of the Restatement of Trusts 2d. The Restatement of Trusts 2d, unlike this section, permits a competent beneficiary acting upon full information prospectively to relieve a trustee from liability for dealing with the trust property on his own account, if the transaction was fair and reasonable and if the beneficiary's consent was not improperly induced by the conduct of the trustee.

(b) With respect to a trustee's duty of loyalty to a beneficiary, see Comment (b) under Sec. 2206.

(c) A difference of opinion exists in other states as to whether or not a beneficiary of a spendthrift trust can relieve a trustee from liability for improperly advancing money or conveying property to him. Griswold, Spendthrift Trusts, Secs. 525, 526 (2d ed. 1947); Scott on Trusts, Secs. 216.1, 342.1 (2d ed. 1956).

Cross References

C.C. arts. 7, 454, 1888, 1973.

§ 2208. Relief from liability by proper court

The proper court for cause shown and upon notice to an interested beneficiary may excuse a trustee wholly or partly from liability for a breach of trust if the trustee acted honestly and reasonably.

Added by Acts 1964, No. 338, § 2.

Comments—1964

(a) This section makes no change in the law. R.S. 9:2037 treated duties, restrictions, and liabilities imposed upon a trustee. The scheme of this Code demands that the liabilities of the trustee be treated separately. Sec. 2065 contains the part of R.S. 9:2037 that treated duties and restrictions imposed upon a trustee.

(b) R.S. 9:2037 was based upon the Uniform Trusts Act, Sec. 19.

Cross References

C.C. art. 1759.

PART VIII. REMEDIES OF THE BENEFICIARY

§ 2221. Remedies against trustee

A beneficiary of a trust may institute an action:
(1) To compel a trustee to perform his duties as trustee;
(2) To enjoin a trustee from committing a breach of trust;
(3) To compel a trustee to redress a breach of trust;
(4) To remove a trustee.

Added by Acts 1964, No. 338, § 2.

Comments—1964

(a) This section makes no change in the law.

(b) A trustee may be removed by the proper court for sufficient cause shown. Sec. 1789.

(c) The Restatement of Trusts 1st and 2d differ from this section in permitting a beneficiary to bring an action to appoint a receiver to take possession of the trust property and administer the trust. In other respects, this section follows the Restatement of Trusts 2d, Sec. 199. The Restatement is similar to the laws of most states. Bogert, Trusts and Trustees, Sec. 861 (2d ed. 1962); Scott on Trusts, Secs. 199–199.4 (2d ed. 1956).

(d) A provisional trustee is provided for by Secs. 1786, 1787.

Cross References

C.C. arts. 1758, 1759, 1987, 1994.

§ 2222. Remedies against third persons

A trustee is the proper plaintiff to sue to enforce a right of the trust estate, except that a beneficiary may sue to enforce such a right, in order to protect his own interest, in an action against:

(1) A trustee and an obligor, if the trustee improperly refuses, neglects, or is unable for any reason, to bring an action against the obligor; or

(2) An obligor, if there is no trustee or the trustee cannot be subjected to the jurisdiction of the proper court.

Added by Acts 1964, No. 338, § 2.

Comments—1964

(a) The Trust Estates Law was silent on this subject.

(b) Art. 699, C.C.P., states: "Except as otherwise provided by law, the trustee of an express trust is the proper plaintiff to sue to enforce a right of the trust estate."

Cross References

C.C. arts. 594, 596.

PART IX. ACTIONS

§ 2231. Causes of action; procedure

If a cause or right of action accrues to a beneficiary against a trustee or a settlor or both, to a trustee against a beneficiary or a settlor or both, or to a settlor against a beneficiary or a trustee or both, the action may be by summary proceeding.

Added by Acts 1964, No. 338, § 2.

Comments—1964

(a) This section makes no change in the law.

(b) Summary proceedings brought under this section are governed by Arts. 2591–2596, C.C.P.

§ 2232. Injunctive relief

If irreparable injury, loss, or damage will otherwise result, the injunctive relief authorized by Articles 3601 through 3613 of the Code of Civil Procedure may be granted to a beneficiary as against a trustee or a settlor or both, to a trustee against a beneficiary or a settlor or both, or to a settlor against a beneficiary or a trustee or both.

Added by Acts 1964, No. 338, § 2.

Comments—1964

(a) This section makes no change in the law.

(b) Proceedings brought under this section are governed by Arts. 3601–3613, C.C.P.

Cross References

C.C. art. 1987.

§ 2233. Instructions

A. A trustee, a beneficiary, or a settlor in an ordinary or a summary proceeding may apply to the proper court for instructions concerning the trust instrument, the interpretation of the instrument, or the administration of the trust. An order of a proper court issued pursuant to such an application shall be full authority to act in accordance thereunder, and a trustee shall be fully protected from all claims of any person who has or who may subsequently acquire an interest in the trust property.

B. A trustee may apply for instructions in ex parte proceedings. The order issued therein will protect a third party relying on the order, but will not exonerate a trustee from liability to a settlor or a beneficiary.

Added by Acts 1964, No. 338, § 2.

Comment—1964

In other states a trustee is permitted to apply for instructions and he is protected if he acts in accordance with them. Bogert, Trusts and Trustees, Sec. 559 (2d ed. 1960); Scott on Trusts, Sec. 259 (2d ed. 1956).

§ 2234. Prescription

A. An action for damages by a beneficiary against a trustee for any act, omission, or breach of duty shall be brought within two years of the date that the trustee renders, by actual delivery or mail to the beneficiary, or if the beneficiary lacks legal capacity, the beneficiary's legal representative, to the last known address of the beneficiary and that of the legal representative if any, an accounting for the accounting period in which the alleged act, omission, or breach of duty arising out of the matters disclosed therein occurred. However, such actions shall in all events, even as to actions within two years of disclosure, be filed within three years of the date that the trustee renders an accounting for the accounting period in which the alleged act, omission, or breach of duty occurred. If a beneficiary is a minor when a trustee's accounting for the accounting period in which the alleged act, omission, or breach of duty occurred is rendered, the prescriptive period of two years begins to run from the day he reaches the age of eighteen years.

B. Any action by a beneficiary against a trustee other than those described on Subsection A of this Section is prescribed by two years beginning from the date that the trustee renders his final account to the beneficiary.

C. The provisions of this Section are remedial and apply to all causes of action for damages without regard to the date when the alleged act, omission, or breach of duty occurred. The two-year and three-year periods of limitation provided for in this Section are peremptive periods within the meaning of Civil Code Article 3458, and in accordance with Civil Code Article 3461 may not be renounced, interrupted, or suspended. Notwithstanding the foregoing, a beneficiary shall have one year from July 9, 1999, to bring an action for damages against a trustee arising out of an act, omission, or breach of duty for a transaction disclosed in any prior accounting.

D. Notwithstanding any other provision of law, all actions brought in the state against any trustee, the prescriptive and peremptive period shall be governed exclusively by this Section.

Added by Acts 1964, No. 338, § 2. Amended by Acts 1980, No. 309, § 1; Acts 1999, No. 966, § 1, eff. July 9, 1999.

Comments—1964

(a) This section makes no change in the law.

(b) The Restatement of Trusts 2d, Sec. 219, states that a beneficiary's recovery against a trustee may be barred by laches.

(c) A trustee is under a duty to render an account at least once each year. A written approval by a beneficiary or his legal representative or a judicial approval obtained by the trustee upon failure or refusal of the beneficiary or his legal representative to give written approval is conclusive with respect to all matters disclosed in the account. Sec. 2088.

Cross References

C.C. arts. 3468, 3492, 3499.

§ 2235. Proper court

The proper court for an action under this Chapter shall be determined as follows:

A. (1) In the case of an inter vivos trust, the proper court shall be the district court of any parish that the trust instrument effectively designates as the proper court.

(2) If the trust instrument fails to designate a proper court for an inter vivos trust, any of the following are proper courts:

(a) The district court of the parish in which a settlor was domiciled when the trust was created.

(b) If the trust has a trustee domiciled in Louisiana, the district court of the parish in which a trustee is domiciled.

(c) If the trust has no trustee domiciled in Louisiana, the district court in which the agent for service of process of any nonresident trustee is domiciled.

(3) If the trust instrument fails to designate a proper court for an inter vivos trust, and none of the courts specified in Paragraph (2) of this Subsection are available, the proper court shall be the Nineteenth Judicial District Court.

B. In the case of a testamentary trust, the proper court shall be the district court of the parish having jurisdiction over the settlor's succession, which shall continue as the proper court unless the settlor in the trust instrument has designated a proper court. In that event, the settlor's designation shall be effective after the trustee is put into possession of the entire legacy.

C. The foregoing notwithstanding, in the case of a testamentary trust after the trustee is put into possession of the entire legacy, and in the case of any inter vivos trust, the proper court shall be any court agreed to by all trustees, beneficiaries, and living settlors.

D. Once a matter regarding an inter vivos trust has been litigated in a district court, that court shall continue as the sole proper court absent the agreement described in Subsection C of this Section.

E. Amendments to a trust instrument that attempt to designate a proper court after institution of an action shall have no effect on the selection of the proper court.

Added by Acts 2010, No. 390, § 1.

Editor's note. Acts 2010, No. 390, § 2, declares that: "The provisions of this Act shall apply to all trusts, whether created before or after the effective date of this Act [August 15, 2010], but R.S. 9:1895(A)(3) shall apply only to substitutions occurring after the effective date of this Act."

PART X. DESIGNATION OF ATTORNEY OR REGISTERED AGENT

§ 2241. General rule

The trustee shall select the attorney to handle legal matters relating to the trust. The appointment of an attorney in the trust instrument is not binding on the trustee.

Added by Acts 1964, No. 338, § 2. Amended by Acts 1983, No. 622, § 1; Acts 2003, No. 480, § 1.

Comment—1964

This section makes no change in the law.

Revision Comment—2003

The amendment to this Section conforms the Trust Code to the principle set forth in Succession of Wallace, 574 So. 2d 348 (La. 1991). There the Supreme Court held that an attorney designated in the will as attorney for the estate cannot ethically require the executor to use his services. By the same reasoning a trustee cannot ethically be required to use the services of the attorney designated by the settlor in the trust instrument. The new wording also frees a corporate trustee from being required by the beneficiaries to employ an attorney that the trustee does not want to use, but does not imply that the attorney chosen by the trustee has no duties to the beneficiaries. Since R.S. 9:2241 is an administrative provision, it applies to trusts already in existence. R.S. 9:2252.

Editor's note. Section 2 of Acts 2003, No. 480 declares that the amendments to "R.S. 9:1809, 1893, 1963, 1965, 1990, and 2068 shall apply only to trusts created after the effective date of this Act. The amendments to R.S. 9:1979, 2051, 2131, 2159(1), and 2241 shall apply to all trusts." Acts 2003, No. 480 became effective on August 15, 2003.

Cross References

C.C. art. 1983.

§ 2242. Registered agent for service of process

A. (1) Any trust created to provide for the payment of settlement of claims or judgments as provided in R.S. 22:46(9)(b) or to pool liabilities as provided in R.S. 23:1195 may appoint a registered agent for service of process. The registered agent may be an individual who is a resident of this state or a partnership or professional law corporation which is authorized to practice law in this state. Legal process and other notices or demands may be served on the trust by service upon the registered agent and, if the registered agent is a partnership, upon any partner.

(2) Written notice of the full name and post office address of the registered agent and a notarized affidavit of acknowledgment and acceptance signed by the registered agent shall be delivered by hand or United States mail to the secretary of state. The failure to deliver a notarized affidavit of acknowledgment and acceptance as required by this Subsection shall not be a defense to proper service of process on the trust. The address of the registered agent may be changed by the registered agent or trust filing written notice of the change with the secretary of state. A copy of the change of address shall also be filed with the recorder of mortgages of the parish of the domicile of the trust. Notice of the change of the name of a professional law corporation or partnership as registered agent shall be filed in the same manner within thirty days after the change.

(3) A registered agent may resign and his resignation shall be effective when written notice thereof has been given to the trust, the secretary of state, and the recorder of mortgages of the parish in which the trust is domiciled. When the registered agent resigns, or if the trust ceases to maintain a registered agent, a successor registered agent may be appointed by the trust within thirty days after the resignation or other event which terminated the tenure of the former registered agent. The full name and post office address of the successor registered agent shall be certified in writing, signed in the name of the trust by at least one trustee, and filed with the secretary of state and the appropriate recorder of mortgages. Upon compliance with the provisions of this Section, including the requirement of a notarized affidavit of acceptance, the successor registered agent shall be vested with the powers of the registered agent succeeded.

B. The secretary of state and each recorder of mortgages of the parish where the trust is domiciled shall keep, for public inspection, a permanent record of registered agents, showing all changes and the date thereof.

Added by Acts 2008, No. 325, § 1.

PART XI. VALIDATION

§ 2251. Severability of provisions of trust instrument

If a provision in the trust instrument is invalid for any reason, the intended trust does not fail, unless the invalid provision cannot be separated from the other provisions without defeating the purpose of the trust.

Added by Acts 1964, No. 338, § 2.

Comments—1964

This section provides for severability of trust provisions so that the invalidity of any one provision will not necessarily cause the entire trust to fail.

Cross References

C.C. arts. 1769.

§ 2252. Saving clause

Trusts heretofore created and any provisions or dispositions therein made shall be governed by the laws in effect at the time of their creation. Unless otherwise provided in the trust instrument, trusts created prior to the effective date of this Code shall be governed in all administrative and procedural matters by the provisions of this Code and not by laws in effect at the time of creation of such trusts, and trusts created prior to the adoption of any amendment to this Code shall be governed in administrative and procedural matters by the provisions of the amendment.

Added by Acts 1964, No. 338, § 2. Amended by Acts 1968, No. 137, § 1.

Comment—1964

The purpose of this section is to assure the validity of trusts heretofore created and provisions or dispositions therein authorized by either the Trust Estates Law or this Code.

Comment—1968

As a practical matter, the Trust Code should govern prior trusts in routine administrative matters and court procedures. This should not affect any vested rights and eliminates any question concerning the rule to be applied. In addition, the amendment provides the same rule with regard to future legislation, making it applicable to administrative and procedural matters.

Cross References

C.C. art. 6.

CHAPTER 1–A. UNIFORM CUSTODIAL TRUST ACT

Section
2260.1. Definitions.
2260.2. Custodial trust; general.
2260.3. Custodial trustee for future payment or transfer.
2260.4. Form and effect of receipt and acceptance by custodial trustee; jurisdiction.
2260.5. Transfer to custodial trustee by fiduciary or obligor; facility of payment.
2260.6. Multiple beneficiaries; separate custodial trusts; survivorship.
2260.7. General duties of custodial trustee.
2260.8. General powers of custodial trustee.
2260.9. Use of custodial trust property.
2260.10. Determination of incapacity; effect.
2260.11. Exemption of third person from liability.
2260.12. Liability to third person.
2260.13. Declination, resignation, incapacity, death, or removal of custodial trustee; designation of successor custodial trustee.
2260.14. Expenses, compensation, and bond of custodial trustee.

Section
2260.15. Reporting and accounting by custodial trustee; determination of liability of custodial trustee.
2260.16. Limitations of action against custodial trustee.
2260.17. Distribution on termination.
2260.18. Methods and forms for creating custodial trusts.
2260.19. Applicable law.
2260.20. Uniformity of application and construction.
2260.21. Short title.

§ 2260.1. Definitions

As used in this Chapter:

(1) "Adult" means an individual who has attained the age of eighteen years.

(2) "Beneficiary" means an individual for whom property has been transferred to or held under a declaration of trust by a custodial trustee for the individual's use and benefit under this Chapter.

(3) "Court" means a court of competent jurisdiction.

(4) "Curator" means a person appointed or qualified by a court to manage the estate of an individual or a person legally authorized to perform substantially the same functions.

(5) "Custodial trust property" means an interest in property transferred to or held under a declaration of trust by a custodial trustee under this Chapter and the income from and proceeds of that interest.

(6) "Custodial trustee" means a person designated as trustee of a custodial trust under this Chapter or a substitute or successor to the person designated.

(7) "Incapacitated" means lacking the ability to manage property and business affairs effectively by reason of mental illness, mental deficiency, physical illness or disability, chronic use of drugs, chronic intoxication, confinement, detention by a foreign power, disappearance, minority, or other disabling cause.

(8) "Legal representative" means a personal representative, tutor, or curator.

(9) "Member of the beneficiary's family" means a beneficiary's spouse, descendant, stepchild, parent, stepparent, grandparent, brother, sister, uncle, or aunt, whether of the whole or half blood or by adoption.

(10) "Person" means an individual, corporation, business trust, estate, trust, partnership, joint venture, association, or any other legal or commercial entity.

(11) "Personal representative" means an executor, administrator, or representative of a decedent's estate, a person legally authorized to perform substantially the same functions, or a successor to any of them.

(12) "State" means a state, territory, or possession of the United States, the District of Columbia, or the Commonwealth of Puerto Rico.

(13) "Transferor" means a person who creates a custodial trust by transfer or declaration.

(14) "Trust company" means a financial institution, corporation, or other legal entity, authorized to exercise general trust powers.

(15) "Tutor" means a person appointed or qualified by a court to act as guardian of a minor's property or a person legally authorized to perform substantially the same functions.

Added by Acts 1995, No. 655, § 1, eff. Jan. 1, 1998.

§ 2260.2. Custodial trust; general

A. A person may create a custodial trust of property by a written transfer of the property to another person, evidenced by registration or by other instrument of transfer, executed in any lawful manner naming as beneficiary an individual, who may be the transferor, in which the transferee is designated, in substance, as custodial trustee under the Louisiana Uniform Custodial Trust Act.

B. A person may create a custodial trust of property by a written declaration, evidenced by registration of the property or by other instrument of declaration executed in any lawful manner, describing the property and naming as beneficiary an individual other than the declarant, in which the declarant as titleholder is designated, in substance, as custodial trustee under the Louisiana Uniform Custodial Trust Act. A registration or other declaration of trust for the sole benefit of the declarant is not a custodial trust under this Chapter.

C. Title to custodial trust property is in the custodial trustee and the beneficial interest is in the beneficiary.

D. Except as provided in Subsection E, a transferor may not terminate a custodial trust.

E. The beneficiary, if not incapacitated, or the curator of an incapacitated beneficiary, may terminate a custodial trust by delivering to the custodial trustee a writing signed by the beneficiary or curator declaring the termination. If not previously terminated, the custodial trust terminates on the death of the beneficiary.

F. Any person may augment existing custodial trust property by the addition of other property pursuant to this Chapter.

G. The transferor may designate or authorize the designation of a successor custodial trustee in the trust instrument.

H. This Chapter does not displace or restrict other means of creating trusts. A trust the terms of which do not conform to this Chapter may be enforceable according to its terms under other law.

Added by Acts 1995, No. 655, § 1, eff. Jan. 1, 1998.

§ 2260.3. Custodial trustee for future payment or transfer

A. A person having the right to designate the recipient of property payable or transferable upon a future event may create a custodial trust upon the occurrence of the future event by designating in writing the recipient, followed in substance by: "as custodial trustee for _____ (name of beneficiary) under the Louisiana Uniform Custodial Trust Act".

B. Persons may be designated as substitute or successor custodial trustees to whom the property must be paid or transferred in the order named if the first designated custodial trustee is unable or unwilling to serve.

C. A designation under this Section may be made in a will, a trust, a deed, a multiple-party account, an insurance policy, an instrument exercising a power of appointment, or a writing designating a beneficiary of contractual rights. Otherwise, to be effective, the designation must be registered with or delivered to the fiduciary, payor, issuer, or obligor of the future right.

Added by Acts 1995, No. 655, § 1, eff. Jan. 1, 1998.

§ 2260.4. Form and effect of receipt and acceptance by custodial trustee; jurisdiction

A. Obligations of a custodial trustee, including the obligation to follow directions of the beneficiary, arise under this Chapter upon the custodial trustee's acceptance, express or implied, of the custodial trust property.

B. The custodial trustee's acceptance may be evidenced by a writing stating in substance:

"CUSTODIAL TRUSTEE'S RECEIPT
AND ACCEPTANCE

I, _____ (name of custodial trustee) acknowledge receipt of the custodial trust property described below or in the attached instrument and accept the custodial trust as custodial trustee for _____ (name of beneficiary) under the Louisiana Uniform Custodial Trust Act. I undertake to administer and distribute the custodial trust property pursuant to the Louisiana Uniform Custodial Trust Act. My obligations as custodial trustee are subject to the directions of the beneficiary unless the beneficiary is designated as, is, or becomes incapacitated. The custodial trust property consists of _____.

Dated: _____

_____

(Signature of Custodial Trustee)"

C. Upon accepting custodial trust property, a person designated as custodial trustee under this Chapter is subject to personal jurisdiction of the court with respect to any matter relating to the custodial trust.

Added by Acts 1995, No. 655, § 1, eff. Jan. 1, 1998.

§ 2260.5. Transfer to custodial trustee by fiduciary or obligor; facility of payment

A. Unless otherwise directed by an instrument designating a custodial trustee pursuant to R.S. 9:2260.3, a person, including a fiduciary other than a custodial trustee, who holds property of or owes a debt to an incapacitated individual not having a curator may make a transfer to an adult member of the beneficiary's family or to a trust company as custodial trustee for the use and benefit of the incapacitated individual. If the value of the property or the debt exceeds twenty thousand dollars, the transfer is not effective unless authorized by the court.

B. A written acknowledgment of delivery, signed by a custodial trustee, is a sufficient receipt and discharge for property transferred to the custodial trustee pursuant to this Section.

Added by Acts 1995, No. 655, § 1, eff. Jan. 1, 1998.

§ 2260.6. Multiple beneficiaries; separate custodial trusts; survivorship

A. Beneficial interests in a custodial trust created for multiple beneficiaries are deemed to be separate custodial trusts of equal undivided interests for each beneficiary. Except in a transfer or declaration for the use and benefit of a husband and wife, for whom survivorship is presumed, a right of survivorship does not exist unless the instrument creating the custodial trust specifically provides for survivorship. For purposes of this Section, "survivorship" means right of accretion.

B. Custodial trust property held under this Chapter by the same custodial trustee for the use and benefit of the same beneficiary may be administered as a single custodial trust.

C. A custodial trustee of custodial trust property held for more than one beneficiary shall separately account to each beneficiary pursuant to R.S. 9:2260.7 and 2260.15 for the administration of the custodial trust.

Added by Acts 1995, No. 655, § 1, eff. Jan. 1, 1998.

§ 2260.7. General duties of custodial trustee

A. If appropriate, a custodial trustee shall register or record the instrument vesting title to custodial trust property.

B. If the beneficiary is not incapacitated, a custodial trustee shall follow the directions of the beneficiary in the management, control, investment, or retention of the custodial trust property. In the absence of effective contrary direction by the beneficiary while not incapacitated, the custodial trustee shall observe the standard of care that would be observed by a prudent person dealing with property of another and is not limited by any other law restricting investments by fiduciaries. However, a custodial trustee, in the custodial trustee's discretion, may retain any custodial trust property received from the transferor. If a custodial trustee has a special skill or expertise or is named custodial trustee on the basis of representation of special skill or expertise, the custodial trustee shall use that skill or expertise.

C. Subject to Subsection B, a custodial trustee shall take control of and collect, hold, manage, invest, and reinvest custodial trust property.

D. A custodial trustee at all times shall keep custodial trust property of which the custodial trustee has control, separate from all other property in a manner sufficient to identify it clearly as custodial trust property of the beneficiary. Custodial trust property, the title to which is subject to recordation, is so identified if an appropriate instrument so identifying the property is recorded, and custodial trust property subject to registration is so identified if it is registered, or held in an account in the name of the custodial trustee, designated in substance: "as custodial trustee for _____ (name of beneficiary) under the Louisiana Uniform Custodial Trust Act".

E. A custodial trustee shall keep records of all transactions with respect to custodial trust property, including information necessary for the preparation of tax returns, and shall make the records and information available at reasonable times to the beneficiary or legal representative of the beneficiary.

F. The exercise of a durable power of attorney for an incapacitated beneficiary is not effective to terminate or direct the administration or distribution of a custodial trust.

Added by Acts 1995, No. 655, § 1, eff. Jan. 1, 1998.

§ 2260.8. General powers of custodial trustee

A. A custodial trustee, acting in a fiduciary capacity, has all the rights and powers over custodial trust property which an adult owner has over individually owned property, but a custodial trustee may exercise those rights and powers in a fiduciary capacity only.

B. This Section does not relieve a custodial trustee from liability for a violation of R.S. 9:2260.7.

Added by Acts 1995, No. 655, § 1, eff. Jan. 1, 1998.

§ 2260.9. Use of custodial trust property

A. A custodial trustee shall pay to the beneficiary or expend for the beneficiary's use and benefit so much or all of the custodial trust property as the beneficiary, while not incapacitated, may direct from time to time.

B. If the beneficiary is incapacitated, the custodial trustee shall expend so much or all of the custodial trust property as the custodial trustee considers advisable for the use and benefit of the beneficiary and individuals who were supported by the beneficiary when the beneficiary became incapacitated, or who are legally entitled to support by the beneficiary. Expenditures may be made in the manner, when, and to the extent that the custodial trustee determines suitable and proper, without court order and without regard to other support, income, or property of the beneficiary.

C. A custodial trustee may establish checking, savings, or other similar accounts of reasonable amounts under which either the custodial trustee or the beneficiary may withdraw funds from, or draw checks against, the accounts. Funds withdrawn from, or checks written against, the account by the beneficiary are distributions of custodial trust property by the custodial trustee to the beneficiary.

Added by Acts 1995, No. 655, § 1, eff. Jan. 1, 1998.

§ 2260.10. Determination of incapacity; effect

A. The custodial trustee shall administer the custodial trust as for an incapacitated beneficiary in the event of any of the following:

(1) The custodial trust was created under R.S. 9:2260.5.

(2) The transferor has so directed in the instrument creating the custodial trust.

(3) The custodial trustee has determined that the beneficiary is incapacitated.

B. A custodial trustee may determine that the beneficiary is incapacitated in reliance upon any of the following:

(1) Previous direction or authority given by the beneficiary while not incapacitated, including direction or authority pursuant to a durable power of attorney.

(2) The certificate of the beneficiary's physician.

(3) Other persuasive evidence.

C. If a custodial trustee for an incapacitated beneficiary reasonably concludes that the beneficiary's incapacity has ceased, or that circumstances concerning the beneficiary's ability to manage property and business affairs have changed since the creation of a custodial trust directing administration as for an incapacitated beneficiary, the custodial trustee may administer the trust as for a beneficiary who is not incapacitated.

D. On petition of the beneficiary, the custodial trustee, or other person interested in the custodial trust property or the welfare of the beneficiary, the court shall determine whether the beneficiary is incapacitated.

E. Absent a determination of incapacity of the beneficiary under Subsection B or D, a custodial trustee who has reason to believe that the beneficiary is incapacitated shall administer the custodial trust in accordance with the provisions of this Chapter applicable to an incapacitated beneficiary.

F. Incapacity of a beneficiary does not terminate any of the following:

(1) The custodial trust.

(2) Any designation of a successor custodial trustee.

(3) Rights or powers of the custodial trustee.

(4) Any immunities of third persons acting on instructions of the custodial trustee.

Added by Acts 1995, No. 655, § 1, eff. Jan. 1, 1998.

§ 2260.11. Exemption of third person from liability

A third person in good faith and without a court order may act on instructions of, or otherwise deal with, a person purporting to make a transfer as, or purporting to act in the capacity of, a custodial trustee. In the absence of knowledge to the contrary, the third person is not responsible for determining any of the following:

(1) The validity of the purported custodial trustee's designation.

(2) The propriety of, or the authority under this Chapter for, any action of the purported custodial trustee.

(3) The validity or propriety of an instrument executed or instruction given pursuant to this Chapter either by the person purporting to make a transfer or declaration or by the purported custodial trustee.

(4) The propriety of the application of property vested in the purported custodial trustee.

Added by Acts 1995, No. 655, § 1, eff. Jan. 1, 1998.

§ 2260.12. Liability to third person

A. A claim based on a contract entered into by a custodial trustee acting in a fiduciary capacity, an obligation arising from the ownership or control of custodial trust property, or a tort committed in the course of administering the custodial trust may be asserted by a third person against the custodial trust property by proceeding against the custodial trustee in a fiduciary capacity, whether or not the custodial trustee or the beneficiary is personally liable.

B. A custodial trustee is not personally liable to a third person either:

(1) On a contract properly entered into in a fiduciary capacity unless the custodial trustee fails to reveal that capacity or to identify the custodial trust in the contract.

(2) For an obligation arising from control of custodial trust property or for a tort committed in the course of the administration of the custodial trust unless the custodial trustee is personally at fault.

C. A beneficiary is not personally liable to a third person for an obligation arising from beneficial ownership of custodial trust property or for a tort committed in the course of administration of the custodial trust unless the beneficiary is personally in possession of the custodial trust property giving rise to the liability or is personally at fault.

D. Subsections B and C do not preclude actions or proceedings to establish liability of the custodial trustee or beneficiary to the extent the person sued is protected as the insured by liability insurance.

Added by Acts 1995, No. 655, § 1, eff. Jan. 1, 1998.

§ 2260.13. Declination, resignation, incapacity, death, or removal of custodial trustee; designation of successor custodial trustee

A. Before accepting the custodial trust property, a person designated as custodial trustee may decline to serve by notifying the person who made the designation, the transferor, or the transferor's legal representative. If an event giving rise to a transfer has not occurred, the substitute custodial trustee designated under R.S. 9:2260.3 becomes the custodial trustee, or, if a substitute custodial trustee has not been designated, the person who made the designation may designate a substitute custodial trustee pursuant to R.S. 9:2260.3. In other cases, the transferor or the transferor's legal representative may designate a substitute custodial trustee.

B. A custodial trustee who has accepted the custodial trust property may resign by means of any of the following:

(1) Delivering written notice to a successor custodial trustee, if any, the beneficiary and, if the beneficiary is incapacitated, to the beneficiary's curator, if any.

(2) Transferring, or registering, or recording an appropriate instrument relating to the custodial trust property, in the name of, and delivering the records to, the successor custodial trustee identified under Subsection C.

C. If a custodial trustee or successor custodial trustee is ineligible, resigns, dies, or becomes incapacitated, the successor designated under R.S. 9:2260.2(G) or 2260.3 becomes custodial trustee. If there is no effective provision for a successor, the beneficiary, if not incapacitated, may designate a successor custodial trustee. If the beneficiary is incapacitated, or fails to act within ninety days after the ineligibility, resignation, death, or incapacity of the custodial trustee, the beneficiary's curator becomes successor custodial trustee. If the beneficiary does not have a curator or the curator fails to act, the resigning custodial trustee may designate a successor custodial trustee.

D. If a successor custodial trustee is not designated pursuant to Subsection C, the transferor, the legal representative of the transferor or of the custodial trustee, an adult member of the beneficiary's family, the tutor or curator of the beneficiary, a person interested in the custodial trust property, or a person interested in the welfare of the beneficiary may petition the court to designate a successor custodial trustee.

E. A custodial trustee who declines to serve or resigns, or the legal representative of a deceased or incapacitated custodial trustee, as soon as practicable, shall put the custodial trust property and records in the possession and control of the successor custodial trustee. The successor custodial trustee may enforce the obligation to deliver custodial trust property and records and becomes responsible for each item as received.

F. A beneficiary, the beneficiary's curator, an adult member of the beneficiary's family, a tutor of the person of the beneficiary, a person interested in the custodial trust property, or a person interested in the welfare of the beneficiary may petition the court to remove the custodial trustee for cause and designate a successor custodial trustee, to require the custodial trustee to furnish a bond or other security for the faithful performance of fiduciary duties, or for other appropriate relief.

Added by Acts 1995, No. 655, § 1, eff. Jan. 1, 1998.

§ 2260.14. Expenses, compensation, and bond of custodial trustee

Except as otherwise provided in the instrument creating the custodial trust, in an agreement with the beneficiary, or by court order, a custodial trustee:

(1) Is entitled to reimbursement from custodial trust property for reasonable expenses incurred in the performance of fiduciary services.

(2) Has a noncumulative election, to be made no later than six months after the end of each calendar year, to charge a reasonable compensation for fiduciary services performed during that year.

(3) Need not furnish a bond or other security for the faithful performance of fiduciary duties.

Added by Acts 1995, No. 655, § 1, eff. Jan. 1, 1998.

§ 2260.15. Reporting and accounting by custodial trustee; determination of liability of custodial trustee

A. (1) Upon the acceptance of custodial trust property, the custodial trustee shall provide a written statement describing the custodial trust property and shall thereafter provide a written statement of the administration of the custodial trust property as follows:

(a) Once each year.

(b) Upon request at reasonable times by the beneficiary or the beneficiary's legal representative.

(c) Upon resignation or removal of the custodial trustee.

(d) Upon termination of the custodial trust.

(2) The statements must be provided to the beneficiary or to the beneficiary's legal representative, if any. Upon termination of the beneficiary's interest, the custodial trustee shall furnish a current statement to the person to whom the custodial trust property is to be delivered.

B. A beneficiary, the beneficiary's legal representative, an adult member of the beneficiary's family, a person interested in the custodial trust property, or a person interested in the welfare of the beneficiary may petition the court for an accounting by the custodial trustee or the custodial trustee's legal representative.

C. A successor custodial trustee may petition the court for an accounting by a predecessor custodial trustee.

D. In an action or proceeding under this Chapter or in any other proceeding, the court may require or permit the custodial trustee or the custodial trustee's legal representative to account. The custodial trustee or the custodial trustee's legal representative may petition the court for approval of final accounts.

E. If a custodial trustee is removed, the court shall require an accounting and order delivery of the custodial trust property and records to the successor custodial trustee and the execution of all instruments required for transfer of the custodial trust property.

F. On petition of the custodial trustee or any person who could petition for an accounting, the court, after notice to interested persons, may issue instructions to the custodial trustee or review the propriety of the acts of the custodial trustee or the reasonableness of compensation determined by the custodial trustee for the services of the custodial trustee or others.

Added by Acts 1995, No. 655, § 1, eff. Jan. 1, 1998.

§ 2260.16. Limitations of action against custodial trustee

A. Except as provided in Subsection C, unless previously barred by adjudication, consent, or prescription, a claim for relief against a custodial trustee for accounting or breach of duty is barred as to a beneficiary, a person to whom custodial trust property is to be paid or delivered, or the legal representative of an incapacitated or deceased beneficiary or payee who either:

(1) Has received a final account or statement fully disclosing the matter unless an action or proceeding to assert the claim is commenced within two years after receipt of the final account or statement; or

(2) Has not received a final account or statement fully disclosing the matter unless an action or proceeding to assert the claim is commenced within three years after the termination of the custodial trust.

B. Except as provided in Subsection C, a claim for relief to recover from a custodial trustee for fraud, misrepresentation, or concealment related to the final settlement of the custodial trust or concealment of the existence of the custodial trust is barred unless an action or proceeding to assert the claim is commenced within five years after the termination of the custodial trust.

C. A claim for relief is not barred by this Section if the claimant:

(1) Is a minor, until the earlier of two years after the claimant becomes an adult or dies.

(2) Is an incapacitated adult, until two years after any of the following, whichever occurs first:

(a) The appointment of a curator.

(b) The removal of the incapacity.

(c) The death of the claimant.

(3) Was an adult, now deceased, who was not incapacitated, until two years after the claimant's death if he died less than five years after termination of the custodial trust.

Added by Acts 1995, No. 655, § 1, eff. Jan. 1, 1998.

§ 2260.17. Distribution on termination

A. Upon termination of a custodial trust, the custodial trustee shall transfer the unexpended custodial trust property to one of the following:

(1) To the beneficiary, if not incapacitated or deceased.

(2) To the curator or other recipient designated by the court for an incapacitated beneficiary.

(3) Upon the beneficiary's death, in the following order:

(a) As last directed in a writing signed by the deceased beneficiary while not incapacitated and received by the custodial trustee during the life of the deceased beneficiary.

(b) To the survivor of multiple beneficiaries if survivorship, or right of accretion, is provided for pursuant to R.S. 9:2260.6.

(c) As designated in the instrument creating the custodial trust.

(d) To the estate of the deceased beneficiary.

B. If, when the custodial trust would otherwise terminate, the distributee is incapacitated, the custodial trust continues for the use and benefit of the distributee as beneficiary until the incapacity is removed or the custodial trust is otherwise terminated.

C. Death of a beneficiary does not terminate the power of the custodial trustee to discharge obligations of the custodial trustee or beneficiary incurred before the termination of the custodial trust.

Added by Acts 1995, No. 655, § 1, eff. Jan. 1, 1998.

§ 2260.18. Methods and forms for creating custodial trusts

A. If a transaction, including a declaration with respect to or a transfer of specific property, otherwise satisfies applicable law, the criteria of R.S. 9:2260.2 are satisfied by either of the following:

(1) The execution and either delivery to the custodial trustee or recording of an instrument in substantially the following form:

"TRANSFER UNDER THE LOUISIANA UNIFORM CUSTODIAL TRUST ACT

I, _____ (name of transferor or name and representative capacity if a fiduciary), transfer to _____ (name of trustee other than transferor), as custodial trustee for _____ (name of beneficiary) as beneficiary and _____ as distributee on termination of the trust in absence of direction by the beneficiary under the Louisiana Uniform Custodial Trust Act, the following: (insert a description of the custodial trust property legally sufficient to identify and transfer each item of property).
Dated: _____

_____
(Signature)"

(2) The execution and the recording or giving notice of its execution to the beneficiary of an instrument in substantially the following form:

"DECLARATION OF TRUST UNDER THE LOUISIANA UNIFORM CUSTODIAL TRUST ACT

I, _____ (name of owner of property), declare that henceforth I hold as custodial trustee for _____ (name of beneficiary other than transferor) as beneficiary and _____ as distributee on termination of the trust in absence of direction by the beneficiary under the Louisiana Uniform Custodial Trust Act, the following: (insert a description of the custodial trust property legally sufficient to identify and transfer each item of property).
Dated: _____

_____
(Signature)"

B. Customary methods of transferring or evidencing ownership of property may be used to create a custodial trust, including any of the following:

(1) Registration of a security in the name of a trust company, an adult other than the transferor, or the transferor if the beneficiary is other than the transferor, designated in substance: "as custodial trustee for _____ (name of beneficiary) under the Louisiana Uniform Custodial Trust Act".

(2) Delivery of a certificated security, or a document necessary for the transfer of an uncertificated security, together with any necessary endorsement, to an adult other than the transferor or to a trust company as custodial trustee, accompanied by an instrument in substantially the form prescribed in Paragraph A(1).

(3) Payment of money or transfer of a security held in the name of a broker or a financial institution or its nominee to a broker or financial institution for credit to an account in the name of a trust company, an adult other than the transferor, or the transferor if the beneficiary is other than the transferor, designated in substance: "as custodial trustee for _____ (name of beneficiary) under the Louisiana Uniform Custodial Trust Act".

(4) Registration of ownership of a life or endowment insurance policy or annuity contract with the issuer in the name of a trust company, an adult other than the transferor, or the transferor if the beneficiary is other than the transferor, designated in substance: "as custodial trustee for _____ (name of beneficiary) under the Louisiana Uniform Custodial Trust Act."

(5) Delivery of a written assignment to an adult other than the transferor or to a trust company whose name in the assignment is designated in substance by the words: "as custodial trustee for _____ (name of beneficiary) under the Louisiana Uniform Custodial Trust Act".

(6) Irrevocable exercise of a power of appointment, pursuant to its terms, in favor of a trust company, an adult other than the donee of the power, or the donee who holds the power if the beneficiary is other than the donee, whose name in the appointment is designated in substance: "as custodial trustee for _____ (name of beneficiary) under the Louisiana Uniform Custodial Trust Act".

(7) Delivery of a written notification or assignment of a right to future payment under a contract to an obligor which transfers the right under the contract to a trust company, an adult other than the transferor, or the transferor if the beneficiary is other than the transferor, whose name in the notification or assignment is designated in substance: "as custodial trustee for _____ (name of beneficiary) under the Louisiana Uniform Custodial Trust Act".

(8) Execution, delivery, and recordation of a conveyance of an interest in real property in the name of a trust company, an adult other than the transferor, or the transferor if the beneficiary is other than the transferor, designated in substance: "as custodial trustee for _____ (name of beneficiary) under the Louisiana Uniform Custodial Trust Act".

(9) Issuance of a certificate of title by an agency of a state or of the United States which evidences title to tangible personal property which is either:

(a) Issued in the name of a trust company, an adult other than the transferor, or the transferor if the beneficiary is other than the transferor, designated in substance: "as custodial trustee for _____ (name of beneficiary) under the Louisiana Uniform Custodial Trust Act"; or

(b) Delivered to a trust company or an adult other than the transferor or endorsed by the transferor to that person, designated in substance: "custodial trustee for _____ (name of beneficiary) under the Louisiana Uniform Custodial Trust Act".

(10) Execution and delivery of an instrument of gift to a trust company or an adult other than the transferor, designated in substance: "as custodial trustee for _____ (name of beneficiary) under the Louisiana Uniform Custodial Trust Act".
Added by Acts 1995, No. 655, § 1, eff. Jan. 1, 1998.

§ 2260.19. Applicable law

A. This Chapter applies to a transfer or declaration creating a custodial trust that refers to this Chapter if, at the time of the transfer or declaration, the transferor, beneficiary, or custodial trustee is a resident of or has its principal place of business in this state or custodial trust property is located in this state. The custodial trust remains subject to this Chapter despite a later change in residence or principal place of business of the transferor, beneficiary, or custodial trustee, or removal of the custodial trust property from this state.

B. A transfer made pursuant to an act of another state substantially similar to this Chapter is governed by the law of that state and may be enforced in this state.

Added by Acts 1995, No. 655, § 1, eff. Jan. 1, 1998.

§ 2260.20. Uniformity of application and construction

This Chapter shall be applied and construed to effectuate its general purpose to make uniform the law with respect to the subject of this Chapter among states enacting it.

Added by Acts 1995, No. 655, § 1, eff. Jan. 1, 1998.

§ 2260.21. Short title

This Chapter may be cited as the "Louisiana Uniform Custodial Trust Act".

Added by Acts 1995, No. 655, § 1, eff. Jan. 1, 1998.

CHAPTER 1–B. FOREIGN TRUSTS

Section
2262.1. Definitions.
2262.2. Recordation of instruments.
2262.3. Authority to convey.
2262.4. Form.

§ 2262.1. Definitions

A. As used in this Chapter, "foreign trust" shall mean any of the following:

(1) A trust which by the terms of the trust instrument is governed by the law of a jurisdiction other than Louisiana.

(2) A trust of which the settlor was domiciled in a jurisdiction other than Louisiana at the time the trust was created.

B. As used in this Chapter, "institutional trustee" shall mean an entity entitled to serve as a trustee pursuant to the provisions of R.S. 9:1783(A)(2) and (B).

Added by Acts 2001, No. 890, § 1.

§ 2262.2. Recordation of instruments

A. If at any time the trust property of a foreign trust includes an immovable or other property in Louisiana the title to which must be recorded in order to affect third parties, a trustee shall file the trust instrument, an extract of trust, or a copy of the trust instrument or extract of trust certified by the clerk of court for the parish in which the original trust instrument or extract of trust was filed, for record in each parish in which the property is located.

B. (1) For purposes of recording an extract of a trust instrument, such an extract of a trust instrument either shall be in such form and contain such information as may be lawful under the law of the jurisdiction which the parties have expressly chosen to govern the trust, or shall be executed by either the settlor or the trustee and shall include all of the following:

(a) The name of the trust, if any.

(b) The name of each settlor.

(c) The name of the trustee.

(d) The name or other description of the beneficiary or beneficiaries.

(e) The date of the trust instrument.

(f) A statement whether the trust is revocable or irrevocable.

(g) If the trust instrument also contains a transfer of immovable property or other property to the trust, the title to which must be recorded in order to affect third persons, then the extract shall contain a brief legal description of the property.

(h) Any other provisions of the trust instrument as the party executing the extract deems useful.

(2) Unless the trust and abstract of trust recite or otherwise note any modification or restriction of the trustee's power or duties, the trustee shall have all of the powers and duties granted to trustees under the Louisiana Trust Code.

(3) The provisions of this Section authorizing the filing of an extract of the trust instrument or a clerk-certified copy of the trust instrument or extract of trust without a description of the property are remedial and shall be applied retroactively to any trust extract or clerk-certified copy of either the trust instrument or extract of trust theretofore filed for record which is in substantial compliance with the provisions of this Section, and such extract shall affect third persons as of the date of recordation.

Added by Acts 2001, No. 890, § 1. Amended by Acts 2012, No. 740, § 1.

§ 2262.3. Authority to convey

The authority of a trustee of a foreign trust or his representative to execute and deliver a conveyance of immovable property situated in Louisiana may be evidenced in any manner that is lawful under the law which the parties have expressly chosen to govern the trust.

Added by Acts 2001, No. 890, § 1.

§ 2262.4. Form

A trust instrument executed outside this state in the manner prescribed by, and in conformity with, the law of the place of its execution, or the law of the settlor's domicile, at the time of its execution shall be deemed to be legally executed and shall have the same force and effect in this state as if executed in the manner prescribed by the laws of this state, provided the trust instrument is in writing and subscribed by the settlor.

Added by Acts 2001, No. 890, § 1.

CHAPTER 2. DONATIONS FOR CHARITABLE PURPOSES

PART I. TRUSTS FOR CHARITABLE PURPOSES

Section
2271. Charitable purpose; beneficiary; conditions.
2271.1. Renumbered.
2272. Trustees.
2273. Who may be trustee.
2274. Application of Louisiana Trust Code.
2275. Trust enforcement.
2276 to 2280. Repealed.
2281. Definition of terms used in R.S. 9:2282.
2282. Method of transfer of control of educational, charitable or religious trusts; grounds.
2283. Governing instrument; contents.

PART II. DURATION OF CHARITABLE TRUSTS

2290. Perpetual duration.

Section
2291. Termination of small trust.
2292 to 2295. Repealed.

PART III. DONATIONS TO RELIGIOUS ORGANIZATIONS

2321. Title quieted and perfected by lapse of time.
2322. Rights in property after perfection of title.

PART IV. CY PRES

2331. Circumstances authorizing application of doctrine; jurisdiction; petitioners.
2332. Filing of petition; order; notice; service.
2333. Hearing, evidence.
2334. Judgment.
2335. Immunity of trustee acting pursuant to judgment.
2336. Appeal.
2337. Application of Part.

PART V. UNIFORM PRUDENT MANAGEMENT OF INSTITUTIONAL FUNDS ACT

2337.1. Short title.
2337.2. Definitions.
2337.3. Standard of conduct in managing and investing institutional fund.
2337.4. Appropriation for expenditure or accumulation of endowment fund; rules of construction.
2337.5. Delegation of management and investment functions.
2337.6. Release or modification of restrictions on management, investment, or purpose.
2337.7. Reviewing compliance.
2337.8. Application to existing institutional funds.
2337.9. Relation to Electronic Signatures in Global and National Commerce Act.
2337.10. Uniformity of application and construction.

PART I. TRUSTS FOR CHARITABLE PURPOSES

§ 2271. Charitable purpose; beneficiary; conditions

A charitable trust is created when a person makes a donation inter vivos or mortis causa in trust for the relief of poverty, the advancement of education or religion, the promotion of health, governmental or municipal purposes, or other purposes the achievement of which is beneficial to society. The trust instrument may be specific or general in the statement of its purposes and may include any conditions that are not contrary to law or good morals. The charitable trust may have as its purpose to benefit one or more institutional beneficiaries. An "institutional beneficiary" is a trust, corporation, or other entity that has any of the foregoing purposes and is a current mandatory or discretionary beneficiary. Otherwise, the beneficiaries of the trust shall be selected by the trustee or any other person, pursuant to the terms of the trust instrument.

Acts 2008, No. 637, § 1, eff. Jan. 1, 2009.

Cross References

C.C. arts. 1467, 1468, 1469, 1472, 1520, 3528 to 3534.

§ 2271.1. Renumbered as R.S. 9:2280

§ 2272. Trustees

The trust instrument may designate the trustee or trustees or provide a method for their designation, including provision for the appointment of additional trustees and successor trustees. If the trust has no trustee or fewer trustees than the instrument requires, the vacancy shall be filled in the following order: pursuant to the procedures set forth in the trust instrument; or, if no effective procedure is set forth, by a majority of the remaining trustees; or, if a majority cannot agree or the office of trustee is vacant, by agreement of a majority in interest of the institutional beneficiaries; or, if there are no institutional beneficiaries or they cannot agree, by the proper court upon the application of any person. The trustee appointed by the proper court shall be a person described in R.S. 9:2273(2). Notice and an opportunity to be heard shall be given to the trustees, the institutional beneficiaries, and any person appointed to enforce the trust pursuant to R.S. 9:2275. If there are no trustees, institutional beneficiaries, or persons appointed to enforce the trust, notice shall be given to the attorney general.

Acts 2008, No. 637, § 1, eff. Jan. 1, 2009.

Cross References

C.C. arts. 1467, 1472, 1520, 1971.

§ 2273. Who may be trustee

Only the following persons may serve as a trustee of a trust established by this Part:

(1) A natural person enjoying full capacity to contract who is a citizen or resident alien of the United States.

(2) A federally insured depository institution organized under the laws of Louisiana, another state, or of the United States, or a financial institution or trust company authorized to exercise trust or fiduciary powers under the laws of Louisiana or of the United States.

Acts 2008, No. 637, § 1, eff. Jan. 1, 2009.

Editor's note. Section 2 of Acts 2003, No. 480 [which amended this Section prior to the 2008 revision] declares that the amendments to "R.S. 9:1809, 1893, 1963, 1990, and 2068 shall apply only to trusts created after the effective date of this Act. The amendments to R.S. 9:1979, 2051, 2131, 2159(1), and 2241 shall apply to all trusts." Acts 2003, No. 480 became effective on August 15, 2003.

Cross References

C.C. arts. 1467, 1472, 1520.

§ 2274. Application of Louisiana Trust Code

Whenever the law pertaining to charitable trusts is silent, the Louisiana Trust Code shall apply, but no provision of the Louisiana Trust Code or other law shall be applied to invalidate a trust or any provision thereof permitted by this Part, or to prevent a charitable tax deduction or to affect adversely the trust's tax-exempt charitable status.

Acts 2008, No. 637, § 1, eff. Jan. 1, 2009.

Cross References

C.C. arts. 454, 1467, 1472, 1520, 1973.

§ 2275. Trust enforcement

A. Any of the following persons may petition the court to enforce the trust:

(1) A settlor or a universal successor of a settlor.

(2) A trustee.

(3) An institutional beneficiary.

(4) A person appointed in the trust instrument for this purpose.

(5) The attorney general.

B. Enforcement of the trust includes but is not limited to actions to accomplish any of the following:

(1) Compel a trustee to perform his duties, such as the duty to render an annual account.

(2) Enjoin a trustee from committing a breach of trust.

(3) Compel a trustee to redress a breach of trust.

(4) Remove a trustee.

Acts 2008, No. 637, § 1, eff. Jan. 1, 2009.

Cross References

C.C. arts. 1, 3, 1467, 1472, 1520.

§§ 2276 to 2280. Repealed by Acts 2008, No. 637, § 2, eff. Jan. 1, 2009

Cross References

C.C. arts. 1467, 1472, 1520, 1527, 1549, 1973.

§ 2281. Definition of terms used in R.S. 9:2282

As used in R.S. 9:2282, the following words and phrases shall have the meanings ascribed to them in this Section:

(1) The term "Trust" shall be limited to express or implied trusts created for educational, charitable or religious purposes where all or a substantial part of the corpus thereof shall have been contributed by the local beneficiaries (as hereinafter defined), or by their predecessor beneficiaries; and where said corpus shall consist of real or personal property situated within the state of Louisiana. R.S. 9:2282 shall have no application to private trusts, either express or implied; to trusts administered by any public governmental authority; to Roman Catholic educational, charitable or religious trusts; or to trusts for educational, charitable or religious purposes where all or a substantial portion of the corpus shall not have been contributed by the local beneficiaries thereof, or by their predecessor beneficiaries.

(2) The term "local beneficiaries" shall mean those persons residing within the state of Louisiana who shall have contributed (or whose predecessor beneficiaries shall have contributed) all or a substantial part of the corpus of the trust, as above defined, and who shall locally, immediately, and directly enjoy the benefits of such trust.

(3) The term "majority of beneficiaries" shall be defined as sixty-six and two-thirds per cent of the adult local beneficiaries residing within the state of Louisiana and enjoying locally and immediately and directly the benefits of such trust.

Added by Acts 1960, No. 346, § 1.

Cross References

C.C. art. 1520.

§ 2282. Method of transfer of control of educational, charitable or religious trusts; grounds

When a majority of the local beneficiaries of any educational, charitable or religious Trust (all as defined in R.S. 9:2281) shall determine that there exists a deep-seated and irreconcilable hostility or tension between them and any or all of the trustees or others in authority exercising control over the administration of such Trust; then, and in such event, said majority of the local beneficiaries may file a petition in the District Court of the parish wherein any part of the corpus of said Trust is situated, setting forth the grounds for relief as stated herein and praying for a decree of the court discharging all existing trustees and all others in authority exercising control over the administration of such trust (by whatever name designated) and for the appointment of other trustees who shall, upon their appointment and qualification in conformity with the terms of the decree of the court, thereupon become vested with complete control and authority over the corpus of said Trust. All successor-trustees so appointed and qualified shall be citizens of the state of Louisiana, residing within the jurisdiction of the court appointing them, and who shall be a local beneficiary as defined in R.S. 9:2281(2). However, before entering a decree removing the existing trustees and all others in authority exercising control over the administration of such Trust and appointing successor-trustees, the Court shall first find affirmatively that the conditions set forth in this Section as alleged in the petition actually exist. The acting trustees and all others in authority with respect to said Trust shall be made parties defendant to the petition; shall be summoned in the manner provided by law; and shall be afforded every statutory right to plead, answer or except to the petition filed against them, and to appear and be heard in opposition thereto.

Added by Acts 1960, No. 346, § 2.

§ 2283. Governing instrument; contents

A. Notwithstanding any provision in this Section or in the governing instrument to the contrary (except as provided in Subsection C of this Section), the governing instrument of each trust that is a private foundation described in Section 509 of the Internal Revenue Code (including each nonexempt charitable trust described in Section 4947(a)(1) of the Code that is treated as a private foundation) and the governing instrument of each nonexempt split-interest trust described in Section 4947(a)(2) of the Code (but only to the extent that Section 508(e) of the Code is applicable to such nonexempt split-interest trust under Section 4947(a)(2) of the Code) shall be deemed to contain the following provisions: the trust shall make distributions at such time and in such manner as not to subject the trust to tax under Section 4942 of the Code; the trust shall not engage in any act of self-dealing that would subject it to tax under Section 4941 of the Code; the trust shall not retain any excess business holdings that would subject it to tax under Section 4943 of the Code; the trust shall not make any investments that would subject it to tax under Section 4944 of the Code; and the trust shall not make any taxable expenditures that would subject it to tax under Section 4945 of the Code.

B. The trustee of any trust described in Subsection A of this Section (with the consent of the settlor, if then living and competent to give consent) may, without judicial proceedings, amend the governing instrument to expressly include the provisions required by Section 508(e) of the Code by executing a written amendment to the trust.

C. The trustee of any trust described in Subsection A of this Section (with the consent of the settlor, if then living and competent to give consent) may, without judicial proceedings, amend such trust to expressly exclude the application of Subsection A of this Section by executing a written amendment to the trust instrument.

D. All references in this Section to the "Code" are to the United States Internal Revenue Code of 1986, as amended, and all references in this Section to specific sections of the Code include corresponding provisions of any subsequent federal tax laws.

Acts 2008, No. 637, § 1, eff. Jan. 1, 2009.

PART II. DURATION OF CHARITABLE TRUSTS

§ 2290. Perpetual duration

A charitable trust shall have perpetual duration unless the trust instrument provides otherwise.

Acts 2008, No. 637, § 1, eff. Jan. 1, 2009.

§ 2291. Termination of small trust

If the value of the assets of a charitable trust is less than one hundred thousand dollars, the trustees may terminate the charitable trust. In such a case, the trustees shall distribute the trust property to the institutional beneficiaries or, if there are no institutional beneficiaries, in a manner that conforms as nearly as possible to the purposes of the trust. The trustees shall incur no liability for the termination of the trust in accordance with the provisions of this Section.

Acts 2008, No. 637, § 1, eff. Jan. 1, 2009.

Cross References

C.C. arts. 1520.

§§ 2292 to 2295. Repealed by Acts 2008, No. 637, § 2, eff. Jan. 1, 2009

PART III. DONATIONS TO RELIGIOUS ORGANIZATIONS

§ 2321. Title quieted and perfected by lapse of time

There is hereby quieted and perfected title to real estate donated to church and religious representatives, religious associations or religious corporations, or their successors or religious assigns, where over ten years continuous and uninterrupted possession and use for the purposes intended by the donation have been had and elapsed since the date of the execution of the donation and where the real estate presently is being possessed and used for the purposes intended in the donation and where such donation is of record in the office of the clerk and recorder of the parish in which the donated property is situated.

Added by Acts 1952, No. 462, § 1. Amended by Acts 1960, No. 226, § 1; Acts 1962, No. 439, § 1; Acts 1984, No. 205, § 1.

Cross References

C.C. arts. 3473, 3499.

§ 2322. Rights in property after perfection of title

In all cases the donees or their successors, assigns or representatives may effectively use, mortgage, hypothecate, incumber, alienate and/or dispose of the property donated or any part thereof without regard thereafter to the conditions or changes imposed in the donation, upon declaring the same to have been fully complied with to all intents and purposes by said lapse of time, possession and use in compliance with said conditions or changes, and upon declaring the public policy served thereby to be against restricting property from commerce.

Added by Acts 1952, No. 462, § 2. Amended by Acts 1960, No. 226, § 2; Acts 1962, No. 439, § 1.

Cross References

C.C. arts. 477, 478, 1527, 1550, 1767.

PART IV. CY PRES

§ 2331. Circumstances authorizing application of doctrine; jurisdiction; petitioners

In any case in which circumstances have changed since the execution or probate of a will containing a trust or conditional bequest for charitable, educational or eleemosynary purposes, or since the death of the donor who during his lifetime established a trust or made a conditional donation for any of such purposes, and the change in circumstances is such as to render impractical, impossible or illegal a literal compliance with the terms thereof, the district court having jurisdiction of the succession of the testator or of the domicile of the donee (and in the parish of Orleans, the civil district court) may, upon petition of a trustee, or of the person or corporation having custody or possession of the property subject to said trust, conditional bequest or donation or of any heir, legatee or donee who in the absence or invalidity of such trust, conditional bequest or donation would have been entitled to any part of the property contained therein, in accordance with the procedure hereinafter set forth, enter a judgment directing that such charitable trust, devise or conditional bequest or donation shall be administered or expended in such manner (either generally or specifically defined) as, in the judgment of said court, will most effectively accomplish as nearly as practicable under existing conditions the general purpose of the trust, will or donation, without regard to and free from any specific restriction, limitation or direction contained therein.

Added by Acts 1954, No. 592, § 1. Amended by Acts 1970, No. 43, § 1.

Cross References

C.C. arts. 6, 1769, 1873, 2029, 2034.

§ 2332. Filing of petition; order; notice; service

In the event of the filing of a petition by such trustee or person or corporation having custody or possession of the property, trust or conditional bequest or donation as hereinabove set forth, the court shall thereupon enter an order directing:

(1) That a notice be published stating in general terms the nature of the said trust, devise, conditional bequest or donation and the relief prayed for in said petition, which said notice shall be published in a newspaper of general circula-

tion in the parish once a week for thirty days in the manner provided for judicial advertisements, and

(2) That service of a copy of the petition be made upon any and all persons (including heirs in intestacy of the testator or special or universal legatees or donees) who, in the absence or invalidity of the said trust, devise, conditional bequest or donation would be entitled to the property therein contained; provided, however, that if no heir in intestacy or special or universal legatee or donee is present or can be found within the State of Louisiana, then and in such event such service shall be made upon the attorney general of the State of Louisiana, and in such case proceedings carried on contradictorily with the said attorney general shall, for all purposes, be as fully effective and valid as if the individual heirs in intestacy, legatees or donees had been personally served. In the event such petition has not been brought by the trustee, donee or person or corporation having custody or possession of such property, then service shall also be made upon such trustee, donee or person or corporation having custody or possession of such property. Said order shall further fix a date not less than thirty days subsequent to said order upon which said heir in intestacy, legatee, donee or the attorney general, as the case may be, shall show cause why the prayer in the petition shall not be granted. Service of a certified copy of said petition and order shall be made as aforesaid not later than fifteen days prior to the date set for said hearing.

Added by Acts 1954, No. 592, § 2. Amended by Acts 1970, No. 43, § 1.

§ 2333. Hearing, evidence

Upon the date fixed for the said hearing, or upon any adjournment thereof, the district court shall hear evidence:

(1) As to whether or not there are heirs in intestacy or legatees or donees within the State of Louisiana; provided, however, that the court shall not require more than reasonable efforts to determine the existence and presence of such heirs or legatees or donees.

(2) The terms of the original trust, devise, conditional bequest or donation inter vivos.

(3) The facts and circumstances which, in the opinion of petitioners, render impractical, impossible or illegal the literal compliance with the terms of such trust, devise, conditional bequest or donation inter vivos.

(4) The proposed method or methods of administration or expenditure of the property subject to the trust, devise, conditional bequest or donation in a manner which will most effectively accomplish, as nearly as practical under existing conditions, the general purpose thereof, without regard to and free from any specific restriction, limitation or direction contained therein.

Added by Acts 1954, No. 592, § 3. Amended by Acts 1970, No. 43, § 1.

Cross References

C.C. art. 880 et seq.

§ 2334. Judgment

The said district court shall thereupon enter a judgment in the premises and may direct that such trusts or devises or conditional bequests or donations shall be administered or expended in such a manner or manners as will most effectively accomplish, as nearly as practicable under existing conditions, the general purpose of such trust, devise, conditional bequest or donation, without regard to and free from any specific restriction, limitation or direction contained therein; provided, however, that in the absence of a clearly expressed intention to the contrary no such trust, devise, conditional bequest or donation inter vivos for charitable, educational or eleemosynary purposes shall be invalid because the specific method provided by the testator or donor for the accomplishment of the general purpose indicated by him is or becomes, for any reason, impractical, impossible or unlawful; provided, further, that in the event that the heirs, legatees or donees who in the absence or invalidity of said trust, devise, conditional bequest or donation would be entitled to the property contained therein shall have made recommendations as to the use or expenditure of the property subject to such trust, devise, conditional bequest or donation inter vivos, then and in such event the court, in determining the manner or manners which will most effectively accomplish the general purpose of such trust, devise, conditional bequest or donation inter vivos, shall give preference to the recommendations of such heirs, legatees or donees.

Added by Acts 1954, No. 592, § 4. Amended by Acts 1970, No. 43, § 1.

§ 2335. Immunity of trustee acting pursuant to judgment

In the event that a judgment is entered by the district court directing the administration or expenditure of such trust, conditional bequest or donation inter vivos, in the manner provided hereinabove, and such judgment becomes final without appeal, then no trustee, donee or other person or corporation having custody of the property, subject to such trust, conditional bequest or donation inter vivos, who has administered or expended the said property in accordance with the provisions of said judgment shall ever be liable personally to any person whatsoever for failure to administer said trust, conditional bequest or donation in accordance with the literal terms thereof, and upon a proper showing to said district court that the administration or expenditure thereof in accordance with the terms of said judgment shall have been completed, said trustee, donee or other person or corporation having custody or possession of said property shall be fully and finally discharged from all responsibility in the premises.

Added by Acts 1954, No. 592, § 5. Amended by Acts 1970, No. 43, § 1.

§ 2336. Appeal

No devolutive appeal may be taken from a judgment rendered pursuant to this Part. Any party interested may prosecute a suspensive appeal from such a judgment by filing a petition or motion therefor within thirty days, exclusive of Sundays, from the date of signing of said judgment and posting bond as may be fixed by the court.

Added by Acts 1954, No. 592, § 6. Amended by Acts 1970, No. 43, § 1.

§ 2337. Application of Part

The provisions of this Part shall be applicable to any trust, devise, conditional bequest or donation inter vivos now in being or hereafter created.

Added by Acts 1954, No. 592, § 7. Amended by Acts 1970, No. 43, § 1.

PART V. UNIFORM PRUDENT MANAGEMENT OF INSTITUTIONAL FUNDS ACT

§ 2337.1. Short title

This Part may be cited as the "Uniform Prudent Management of Institutional Funds Act."

Acts 2010, No. 168, § 1, eff. July 1, 2010.

§ 2337.2. Definitions

For the purposes of this Part, the following terms shall have the meanings ascribed to them, unless the context clearly indicates otherwise:

(1) "Charitable purpose" means the relief of poverty, the advancement of education or religion, the promotion of health, the promotion of a governmental purpose, or any other purpose the achievement of which is beneficial to the community.

(2) "Endowment fund" means an institutional fund or part thereof that, under the terms of a gift instrument, is not wholly expendable by the institution on a current basis. The term does not include assets that an institution designates as an endowment fund for its own use.

(3) "Gift instrument" means a record or records, including an institutional solicitation, under which property is granted to, transferred to, or held by an institution as an institutional fund.

(4) "Institution" may mean any of the following:

(a) A person, other than an individual, organized and operated exclusively for charitable purposes.

(b) A government or governmental subdivision, agency, or instrumentality, to the extent that it holds funds exclusively for a charitable purpose.

(c) A trust that had both charitable and noncharitable interests, after all noncharitable interests have terminated.

(5) "Institutional fund" means a fund held by an institution exclusively for charitable purposes. The term does not include any of the following:

(a) Program-related assets.

(b) A fund held for an institution by a trustee that is not an institution.

(c) A fund in which a beneficiary that is not an institution has an interest, other than an interest that could arise upon violation or failure of the purposes of the fund.

(6) "Person" means an individual, any legal or commercial entity, including a corporation, business trust, partnership, limited liability company, association, joint venture, public corporation, government or governmental subdivision, agency, or instrumentality, the trustee of a trust, or the succession representative of a succession.

(7) "Program-related asset" means an asset held by an institution primarily to accomplish a charitable purpose of the institution and not primarily for investment.

(8) "Record" means information that is inscribed on a tangible medium or that is stored in an electronic or other medium and is retrievable in perceivable form.

Acts 2010, No. 168, § 1, eff. July 1, 2010.

§ 2337.3. Standard of conduct in managing and investing institutional fund

A. Subject to the intent of a donor expressed in a gift instrument, an institution, in managing and investing an institutional fund, shall consider the charitable purposes of the institution and the purposes of the institutional fund.

B. In addition to complying with the duty of loyalty imposed by law other than this Part, each person responsible for managing and investing an institutional fund shall manage and invest the fund in good faith and with the care an ordinarily prudent person in a like position would exercise under similar circumstances.

C. In managing and investing an institutional fund, an institution shall be bound by the following obligations:

(1) It may incur only costs that are appropriate and reasonable in relation to the assets, the purposes of the institution, and the skills available to the institution.

(2) It shall make a reasonable effort to verify facts relevant to the management and investment of the fund.

D. An institution may pool two or more institutional funds for purposes of management and investment.

E. Except as otherwise provided by a gift instrument, all of the following rules apply:

(1) In managing and investing an institutional fund, the following factors, if relevant, shall be considered:

(a) General economic conditions.

(b) The possible effect of inflation or deflation.

(c) The expected tax consequences, if any, of investment decisions or strategies.

(d) The role that each investment or course of action plays within the overall investment portfolio of the fund.

(e) The expected total return from income and the appreciation of investments.

(f) Other resources of the institution.

(g) The needs of the institution and the fund to make distributions and to preserve capital.

(h) An asset's special relationship or special value, if any, to the charitable purposes of the institution.

(2) Management and investment decisions about an individual asset must be made not in isolation but rather in the context of the institutional fund's portfolio of investments as a whole and as a part of an overall investment strategy having risk and return objectives reasonably suited to the fund and to the institution.

(3) Except as otherwise provided by law other than this Part, an institution may invest in any kind of property or type of investment consistent with this Section.

(4) An institution shall diversify the investments of an institutional fund unless the institution reasonably determines that, because of special circumstances, the purposes of the fund are better served without diversification.

(5) Within a reasonable time after receiving property, an institution shall make and carry out decisions concerning the retention or disposition of the property or to rebalance a portfolio, in order to bring the institutional fund into compliance with the purposes, terms, and distribution requirements of the institution as necessary to meet other circumstances of the institution and the requirements of this Part.

(6) A person that has special skills or expertise, or is selected in reliance upon the person's representation that the person has special skills or expertise, has a duty to use those

skills or that expertise in managing and investing institutional funds.

Acts 2010, No. 168, § 1, eff. July 1, 2010.

§ 2337.4. Appropriation for expenditure or accumulation of endowment fund; rules of construction

A. Subject to the intent of a donor expressed in the gift instrument, an institution may appropriate for expenditure or accumulate so much of an endowment fund as the institution determines is prudent for the uses, benefits, purposes, and duration for which the endowment fund is established. Unless stated otherwise in the gift instrument, the assets in an endowment fund are donor-restricted assets until appropriated for expenditure by the institution. In making a determination to appropriate or accumulate, the institution shall act in good faith, with the care that an ordinarily prudent person in a like position would exercise under similar circumstances, and shall consider, if relevant, all of the following factors:

(1) The duration and preservation of the endowment fund.

(2) The purposes of the institution and the endowment fund.

(3) General economic conditions.

(4) The possible effect of inflation or deflation.

(5) The expected total return from income and the appreciation of investments.

(6) Other resources of the institution.

(7) The investment policy of the institution.

B. To limit the authority to appropriate for expenditure or accumulate under Subsection A of this Section, a gift instrument must specifically state the limitation.

C. Terms in a gift instrument designating a gift as an endowment, or a direction or authorization in the gift instrument to use only "income", "interest", "dividends", "usufruct", or "rents, issues, or profits", or "to preserve the principal intact", or "to preserve the naked ownership intact", or words of similar import have the following implications:

(1) Create an endowment fund of permanent duration unless other language in the gift instrument limits the duration or purpose of the fund.

(2) Do not otherwise limit the authority to appropriate for expenditure or accumulate under Subsection A of this Section.

Acts 2010, No. 168, § 1, eff. July 1, 2010.

§ 2337.5. Delegation of management and investment functions

A. Subject to any specific limitation set forth in a gift instrument or in law other than this Part, an institution may delegate to an external agent the management and investment of an institutional fund to the extent that an institution could prudently delegate under the circumstances. An institution shall act in good faith, with the care that an ordinarily prudent person in a like position would exercise under similar circumstances, in taking any of the following steps:

(1) Selecting an agent.

(2) Establishing the scope and terms of the delegation, consistent with the purposes of the institution and the institutional fund.

(3) Periodically reviewing the agent's actions in order to monitor the agent's performance and compliance with the scope and terms of the delegation.

B. In performing a delegated function, an agent owes a duty to the institution to exercise reasonable care to comply with the scope and terms of the delegation.

C. An institution that complies with Subsection A of this Section is not liable for the decisions or actions of an agent to which the function was delegated.

D. By accepting delegation of a management or investment function from an institution that is subject to the laws of this state, an agent submits to the jurisdiction of the courts of this state in all proceedings arising from or related to the delegation or the performance of the delegated function.

E. An institution may delegate management and investment functions to its committees, officers, or employees as authorized by law of this state other than this Part.

Acts 2010, No. 168, § 1, eff. July 1, 2010.

§ 2337.6. Release or modification of restrictions on management, investment, or purpose

A. If the donor consents in a record, an institution may release or modify, in whole or in part, a restriction contained in a gift instrument on the management, investment, or purpose of an institutional fund. A release or modification shall not allow a fund to be used for a purpose other than a charitable purpose of the institution.

B. The court, upon application of an institution, may modify a restriction contained in a gift instrument regarding the management or investment of an institutional fund if the restriction has become impracticable or wasteful, if it impairs the management or investment of the fund, or if, because of circumstances not anticipated by the donor, a modification of a restriction will further the purposes of the fund. Notification of interested parties shall be made in accordance with R.S. 9:2332. To the extent practicable, any modification shall be made in accordance with the donor's probable intention.

C. If a particular charitable purpose or a restriction contained in a gift instrument on the use of an institutional fund becomes unlawful, impracticable, impossible to achieve, or wasteful, the court, upon application of an institution, may modify the purpose of the fund or the restriction on the use of the fund in a manner consistent with the charitable purposes expressed in the gift instrument. Notification of interested parties shall be made in accordance with R.S. 9:2332.

D. If all of the following occur, the institution, if there is no written objection within sixty days after giving notice as provided in Subsection E of this Section, may release or modify the restriction, in whole or part:

(1) The institutional fund subject to the restriction has a total value of less than one hundred thousand dollars.

(2) More than twenty years have elapsed since the fund was established.

(3) The institution uses the property in a manner consistent with the charitable purposes expressed in the gift instrument.

(4) The institution determines that a restriction contained in the gift instrument on the management, investment, or purpose of the institutional fund is unlawful, impracticable, impossible to achieve, or wasteful.

E. Notice under Subsection D of this Section shall be made by the institution by certified mail upon all existing donors. If there is no existing donor, notice shall be made upon at least one person who has succeeded to any rights that a donor would have had to the return of the property if the donation had failed or upon a conditional donee who would have had any right to the property if the donation had failed. If, after a reasonable effort, the institution is unable to give notice to any existing donor or successor, or to a conditional donee, then notice by certified mail may be made upon the attorney general.

Acts 2010, No. 168, § 1, eff. July 1, 2010.

§ 2337.7. Reviewing compliance

Compliance with this Part is determined in light of the facts and circumstances existing at the time a decision is made or action is taken, and not by hindsight.

Acts 2010, No. 168, § 1, eff. July 1, 2010.

§ 2337.8. Application to existing institutional funds

This Part applies to institutional funds existing on or established after July 1, 2010. As applied to institutional funds existing on the effective date of this Act, this Part governs only decisions made or actions taken on or after July 1, 2010.

Acts 2010, No. 168, § 1, eff. July 1, 2010.

§ 2337.9. Relation to Electronic Signatures in Global and National Commerce Act

This Part modifies, limits, and supersedes the Electronic Signatures in Global and National Commerce Act, 15 U.S.C. Section 7001 et seq., but does not modify, limit, or supersede Section 101(c) of that Act, 15 U.S.C. Section 7001(c), or authorize electronic delivery of any of the notices described in Section 103(b) of that Act, 15 U.S.C. Section 7003(b).

Acts 2010, No. 168, § 1, eff. July 1, 2010.

§ 2337.10. Uniformity of application and construction

In applying and construing this uniform act, consideration must be given to the need to promote uniformity of the law with respect to its subject matter among states that enact it.

Acts 2010, No. 168, § 1, eff. July 1, 2010.

CHAPTER 2-A. PUBLIC TRUSTS

Section
2341. Public trusts authorized; purposes.
2342. Mode of creation; acceptance of beneficial interest; amendments.
2343. Trustees; appointment; powers; duties; term of office; compliance with Public Bid Law, Public Meetings Law, and Public Records Law; legislative oversight.
2344. Liability of trustees and beneficiary.
2345. Termination of public trusts.
2346. Audits; supervision by legislative auditor; operating budget approval.
2347. Bonds of public trust.

§ 2341. Public trusts authorized; purposes

A. Express trusts may be created or amended to issue obligations and to provide funds for the furtherance and accomplishment of any authorized public function or purpose of the state or of any parish, municipality, political or governmental subdivision or any other governmental unit in the state in real or personal property, or either or both, or in any estate or interest in either or both, with the state, or any such governmental units as the beneficiary thereof by and with the: (1) express approval of the governor and two-thirds of the elected members of each house of the legislature if the state of Louisiana or any state agency is the beneficiary; (2) express approval of a majority of the membership of the governing authority of the beneficiary and the State Bond Commission or its successor if a parish or municipality or a political or governmental subdivision thereof is the beneficiary; and (3) express approval of a majority of the membership of the governing authority of the beneficiary and the State Bond Commission or its successor, in all other cases. The beneficiary of any such trust is authorized to utilize the trust to issue obligations to accomplish any of the foregoing authorized public functions or purposes of the beneficiary. Provided, that no funds of said beneficiary derived from sources other than the trust property, or the operation thereof, shall be charged with or expended for property of or the operation of said trust, except by express action of the legislature or the governing authority of the beneficiary, as the case may be, prior to the charging or expending of the funds. The officers or any other governmental agencies or authorities having the custody, management or control of any property, real or personal or both, of the beneficiary of such trust, or of such a proposed trust, which property shall be used for the execution of the trust purposes, are authorized and empowered to lease such property for said purposes in accordance with law, after the acceptance of the beneficial interest therein by the beneficiary.

B. (1) For purposes of this Chapter, authorized public functions or purposes of the state and of any parish, municipality, political or governmental subdivision or any other governmental unit in this state, except as otherwise and to the contrary provided by the laws of this state, shall mean and include but not be limited to:

(a) Hospital, medical, health, nursery care, nursing care, clinical, ambulance, laboratory, and related services and facilities.

(b) Housing, mortgage finance and related services, activities, facilities, and properties.

(c) Penitentiary, rehabilitation, incarceration, and other correctional services and facilities.

(d) Educational services and facilities and related housing and dormitory services and facilities.

(e) Providing, developing, securing, and improving water storage, treatment, supply, and distribution services and facilities.

(f) Sanitary and storm sewer and other liquid and solid waste collection, disposal, treatment, and drainage services and facilities.

(g) Educational or commercial communication equipment and facilities.

(h) Mass transit, commuting and transportation, and parking services, equipment, and facilities.

(i) Cultural and civic facilities, services and activities.

(j) Community development and redevelopment facilities and activities.

(k) Gas, electric, petroleum, coal and other energy collection, recovery, generation, storage, transportation, and distribution facilities and activities.

(*l*) Industrial, manufacturing, and other economic development facilities and activities.

(m) Antipollution and air, water, ground, and subsurface pollution abatement and control facilities and activities.

(n) Airport and water port and related facilities, services, and activities.

(o) Facilities, property and equipment of any nature for the use or occupancy of the state or the United States, or any agencies or instrumentalities thereof or of any governmental units in the state.

(2) For purposes of this Chapter, authorized public functions or purposes of the state and of any parish, municipality, political or governmental subdivision, or any other governmental unit in this state shall not mean or include casino gaming operations and riverboat gaming operations or any acquisition, construction, demolition, repair, maintenance, or other costs associated directly or indirectly with an official gaming establishment or a riverboat licensed for gaming activities and facilities associated with docking, berthing, or loading and unloading passengers of such riverboats. For purposes of this limitation "casino gaming operations" and "official gaming establishment" shall have the meanings ascribed to them in the Louisiana Economic Development and Gaming Corporation Act, R.S. 27:201 et seq.

C. The trustees of a public trust shall make and adopt bylaws for the due and orderly administration and regulation of the affairs of the public trust. All bylaws of a public trust shall be submitted in writing to the governor of the state of Louisiana, if the state of Louisiana or any state agency is the beneficiary and, in all other cases, the governing authority of the beneficiary. The governor or the governing authority of the beneficiary shall have the power to veto all or part of the proposed bylaws. Failure to approve or veto the proposed bylaws within thirty days shall constitute automatic approval.

D. All public trusts hereafter created or amended under this Chapter shall constitute public corporations of the beneficiary, and as such shall have the powers and duties of such corporations, including the power to incur debt and contract obligations; to sue and be sued; to have a corporate seal; to do and perform all acts in a corporate capacity and in a corporate name. All public trusts created heretofore or hereafter shall be subject to the Public Contracts Law, Public Records Law, Public Meetings Law, Code of Ethics, and the Bond Validation Procedures Law.

E. (1) Upon the application of one or more of the deep-water port commissions or deep-water port, harbor, or terminal districts as defined by Article VI, Section 44 of the Louisiana Constitution of 1974, as authorized by the governing board of such deep-water port commission or deep-water port, harbor, or terminal district, the governor of the state of Louisiana is authorized to create a public trust with the power to issue obligations, to guarantee loans, and to lend money for the purpose of financing and facilitating the import and export of goods, commodities, and services, and the financing of services connected with the import and export of goods, commodities, and services. The beneficiary of such a trust shall be the state of Louisiana. Only one such public trust shall be created in the state by the governor. The trust so created is authorized to issue obligations to accomplish its purposes.

(2)(a) The trust shall have the power and authority to issue and reissue obligations, bonds, notes, or other evidences of indebtedness having a term of fifteen years or less to finance its functions. The functions of the trust shall include but not be limited to: financing and facilitating the import and export of goods, commodities, and services; the financing of services connected with the import and export of goods, commodities, and services; promoting and developing the import and export of goods, commodities, and services; promoting and developing the deep-water ports, harbors, and terminals of the state; guaranteeing loans; and providing funds for the operation, maintenance, and administrative expenses of the trust. All such obligations shall be submitted to and approved by the State Bond Commission prior to the issuance and delivery of such obligations.

(b) All such obligations issued by the trust shall be negotiable instruments, and shall be solely the obligations of the trust and not of the state of Louisiana. The obligations and income thereof shall be exempt from all taxation in the state of Louisiana. The obligations shall be payable out of the income, revenues, and receipts derived or to be derived from the trust properties and facilities maintained and operated by the trust or received by the trust from any other sources whatsoever, including, but not by way of limitation, other monies which, by law or contract, may be made available to the trust. In addition to the pledge of income, revenues, or receipts to secure said obligations, the trust may further secure their payment by any other security authorized in the resolution authorizing the issuance of the obligations. Such obligations shall be authorized and issued by a resolution adopted by a majority vote of the trustees present and voting and shall be of such series, bear such date or dates, mature at such time or times, bear interest at such rate or rates, be in such denominations, be in such form, carry such registration and exchangeability privileges, be payable at such place or places, be subject to such terms of redemption and be entitled to such priorities on the income, revenues, and receipts of the trust and contain such other provisions as such resolution may provide. The obligations shall be executed in the name of the trust in the manner provided in the resolution authorizing the issuance of such obligations. Such obligations may be sold in such manner and from time to time as may be determined by the trust to be most beneficial and the trust may pay all expenses and commissions which it may deem necessary or advantageous in connection with the issuance and sale thereof.

(c) Obligations issued hereunder are hereby declared legal investments and are hereby made securities in which all insurance companies and associations and other persons carrying on an insurance business, trust companies, banks, bankers, banking associations, savings banks, and savings associations, including savings and loan associations, credit unions, building and loan associations, investment companies, executors, administrators, trustees, and other fiduciaries, pension, profit-sharing, retirement funds, and other persons carrying on a banking business, and all other persons who are authorized to invest in revenue bonds may properly and legally invest funds, including capital in their control or belonging to them. Such obligations are hereby made securities which may properly and legally be deposited with and received by any state or municipal or public officer or any agency or political subdivisions of the state for any purpose for which the deposit of revenue bonds is authorized by law.

(d) Any resolution authorizing the issuance of obligations shall be published one time in the official journal of the state of Louisiana; however, it shall not be necessary to publish any exhibits to such resolution if the same are available for public inspection and such fact is stated in the publication. For thirty days after the date of publication, any person in interest may contest the legality of the resolution, any provision of the obligations to be issued pursuant to it, the provisions therein made for the security and payment of the obligations, and the validity of all the provisions and proceedings relating to the authorization and issuance of such obligations. After that time, no person may contest the regularity, formality, legality, or effectiveness of the resolution, any provisions of the obligations to be issued pursuant to it, the provisions for the security and payment of the obligations, and the validity of all other provisions and proceedings relating to their authorization and issuance, for any cause whatever. Thereafter, it shall be conclusively presumed that the obligations are legal and that every legal requirement for the issuance of the obligations has been complied with. The bonds shall not be contestable after the thirty days.

(3) The trust shall have the power to lend money at competitive rates of interest, and to guarantee loans, in order to facilitate the functions of the trust set forth in R.S. 9:2341(E)(2).

(4) The governor shall appoint seven trustees, one from each congressional district in the state and the remaining trustee or trustees from the state at large, and the secretary of the Department of Economic Development shall be a trustee, serving in an ex officio capacity. The appointed trustees shall serve six-year staggered terms; however, of the initial trustees appointed after January 13, 1992, three shall serve terms of two years, three shall serve terms of four years, and two shall serve terms of six years, all as designated by the governor.

(5) The governor shall designate one member of the trust to serve as chairman. The trustees shall elect a vice-chairman and a secretary-treasurer from among the members of the trust.

(6) Except as otherwise provided herein the provisions of this Chapter shall be applicable to the public trust created under this Subsection. The provisions of R.S. 9:2347 shall not be applicable to the public trust created under this Subsection; however, all financial advisors fees and any underwriters discount may be approved in writing by the State Bond Commission and the attorney general's office.

(7) Any attorneys' fees in connection with the issuance of any obligations, notes, or other evidences of indebtedness shall be subject to approval of the attorney general.

(8) All obligations, notes, or other evidences of indebtedness issued by the public trust shall be special obligations of the trust and shall be deemed to have been issued on behalf of the beneficiary of the trust.

(9) In no event shall any obligations, notes, or other evidences of indebtedness of the trust constitute an obligation, either special or general, of the state of Louisiana within the meaning of any constitutional or statutory provision whatsoever, and the obligations shall contain a recital to that effect.

F. Each appointment by the governor shall be submitted to the Senate for confirmation.

Added by Acts 1970, No. 135, § 1. Amended by Acts 1976, No. 699, § 1, eff. Aug. 4, 1976; Acts 1978, No. 778, § 1; Acts 1979, No. 524, § 1, eff. July 17, 1979; Acts 1984, No. 375, § 1, eff. July 6, 1984; Acts 1986, No. 897, § 1; Acts 1986, No. 953, § 1, eff. July 14, 1986; Acts 1986, 1st Ex.Sess., No. 27, § 1, eff. Dec. 24, 1986; Acts 1987, No. 377, § 1, eff. July 7, 1987; Acts 1990, No. 457, § 1; Acts 1991, No. 189, § 1, eff. Jan. 13, 1992; Acts 1993, No. 693, § 1, eff. June 21, 1993; Acts 2012, No. 803, § 2.

Editor's note. Section 4 of Acts 2005, No. 428, provides:

"The Louisiana Imports and Exports Trust Authority created pursuant to R.S. 9:2341 and recognized by House Concurrent Resolution No. 133 of the 1985 Regular Session is hereby abolished."

Section 12 of Act 2012, No. 803 provides:

"Section 12. (A) The provisions of this Act shall not reduce the term of office of any appointee of a board or commission who is lawfully holding such position on or before noon, January 3, 2013, when his position or the overall membership of the board or commission is based upon the number or geographical boundaries of any or all congressional districts.

"(B) Any appointment or reappointment after January 3, 2013, including the naming of a successor to serve an unexpired term, shall be in accordance with the number and new boundaries of congressional districts established pursuant to Act No. 2 of the 2011 First Extraordinary Session of the Legislature. As vacancies occur, the appointing authority shall first make appointments to comply with the congressional district requirements of the membership of the respective board or commission, and, thereafter, the appointing authority may make appointments for membership, if any, from the state at large.

"(C) The action of any board or commission in this state whose membership, in whole or in part, is required by law to be selected from one or more congressional districts shall not be found or held to be unlawful or improper due to the change in the state's congressional district boundaries or number of congressional districts that become effective at noon, January 3, 2013.

"(D) For purposes of this Section, 'board or commission' includes any statutorily created or recognized board, commission, trust, authority, council, committee, or subcommittee."

Cross References

C.C. art. 1520.

§ 2342. Mode of creation; acceptance of beneficial interest; amendments

A. Such trusts shall be created, organized, structured and empowered by written instruments or by will. In the case of written instruments, the same shall be subscribed by the settlor or settlors by authentic act or by act under private signature executed in the presence of two witnesses and duly acknowledged by the settlor or settlors or by the affidavit of one of the attesting witnesses and before the same shall become effective the beneficial interest therein shall be accepted by the governor and two-thirds of the elected members of each house of the legislature if the state of Louisiana or any state agency be the beneficiary, or by the governing body of any other beneficiary named therein, which power and authority of acceptance hereby is conferred upon the governor and the legislature and the governing bodies of the parishes, municipalities and other political and governmental units in the state. Thereupon the said instrument or will, together with the written acceptance of the beneficial interest endorsed thereon, shall be recorded in the official records in the office of the clerk of court of each parish wherein is situated any real estate, or any interest therein, belonging to said trust, as well as the parish wherein is located the trust property or wherein are conducted its principal operations. In the case of any trust of which the state of Louisiana or a state agency thereof shall be the beneficiary, a certified copy of such instrument or will and the instrument of acceptance shall be filed with the secretary of state. Upon the acceptance of the beneficial interest by the beneficiary as hereinabove authorized and provided, the same shall be and constitute a binding contract between the state of Louisiana and the settlor or settlors, or the executor of the estate of the settlor, for the acceptance of the beneficial interest in the trust property by the designated beneficiary and the application of the proceeds of the trust property and its operation for the purposes, and in accordance with the stipulations of the trust instrument or will. Such trusts shall have duration for the term as shall be specified in the instrument or will creating said trust.

B. No public trust in which the state of Louisiana, any state agency, any parish or municipality, or any other political or governmental unit in the state is the beneficiary may be amended without a two-thirds vote of approval of the trustees of such trust. Provided further, that any such amendment shall be subject to approval as provided in Subsection (A) of Section 2341 of this Chapter.

Added by Acts 1970, No. 135, § 2. Amended by Acts 1976, No. 699, § 1, eff. Aug. 4, 1976.

§ 2343. Trustees; appointment; powers; duties; term of office; compliance with Public Bid Law, Public Meetings Law, and Public Records Law; legislative oversight

A. (1) Every person becoming a trustee of a public trust shall be subject to the provisions of R.S. 14:138 and 140 and first shall take the oath of office required of public officials. The oaths of office shall be administered by any person authorized to administer oaths in the state and shall be filed with the secretary of state in the case of trusts wherein the state or a state agency is the beneficiary; in the case of trusts wherein a parish, municipality, political or governmental subdivision, or other governmental units in the state is the beneficiary and in all other cases in the official records in the office of the clerk of court of the parish of the beneficiary's situs.

(2) Every trustee, officer, and employee of a public trust who handles funds of a public trust shall furnish a good and sufficient fidelity bond in an amount and with surety as may be specified and approved by a majority of the trustees, such bond to be in a surety company authorized to transact surety business in the state. The trustees may, at their election, purchase good and sufficient fidelity bonds.

(3) Except as inconsistent with the provisions of this Chapter, trustees shall have those additional duties as are provided by the Louisiana Trust Code [1] for trustees appointed pursuant to such code.

(4) Trustees shall serve without compensation, but may receive per diem not to exceed two hundred dollars and be reimbursed for vouchered expenses incurred in the performance of their duties as trustees at the reimbursement rates applicable to state officers as provided by rules and regulations promulgated by the commissioner of administration.

B. (1) Notwithstanding the terms of any instrument creating a public trust in existence on August 15, 1999, or which creates a public trust after such date, any public trust that names the state of Louisiana or any state agency as a beneficiary shall have seven trustees appointed by the governor of the state of Louisiana, with consent of the Senate.

(2) The initial terms of the trustees shall be as follows: one member shall be appointed for a term of one year; two members shall be appointed for a term of two years; one member shall be appointed for a term of three years; two members shall be appointed for a term of four years; and one member shall be appointed for a term of five years. At the expiration of such initial term of each member and of each succeeding member's term, the governor shall appoint a successor who shall serve for a term of five years.

(3) Whenever a vacancy on such trust shall occur by death, resignation, or otherwise, the governor shall fill the same by appointment, and the appointee shall hold office during the remainder of the unexpired term. Each member shall hold office until his successor shall have been appointed and qualified.

(4) The trustees shall elect a chairman, a vice chairman, and a secretary-treasurer from their own members.

C. Repealed by Acts 1999, No. 1238, § 2.

D. Meetings of the trustees of all public trusts shall be open to the public and the records of all public trusts shall be public records to the same extent as is required by law for the beneficiary.

E. (1) All contracts of a public trust for construction, labor, equipment, material, or repairs shall be awarded to the lowest responsible bidder who has bid according to the contract plans and specifications as advertised, in full accordance with the Public Contract Law, Chapter 10 of Title 38 of the Louisiana Revised Statutes of 1950.

(2) In addition to the requirements provided for in Paragraph (1) of this Subsection, any public trust whose sole beneficiary is a hospital service district is hereby authorized to utilize the sole source purchasing provisions as provided in R.S. 39:1597.

F. (1) Trustees of any public trust hereafter created, not within the scope of R.S. 9:2343(B) shall be the members of the governing authority of the beneficiary or persons appointed by the governing authority of the beneficiary. However, any member of the legislature, all or a portion of whose district lies within the boundaries of the beneficiary of the public trust, shall be an "ex officio" trustee of that public trust if he consents in writing to be a trustee, whether or not that public trust was created prior to January 1, 1985.

(2) Trustees of any public trust hereafter created may be removed from office for cause, including incompetency, neglect of duty, or malfeasance in office, by a district court having jurisdiction.

(3) In the case of persons appointed by the governing authority of the beneficiary or by the governor, as the case may be, such persons shall be appointed for a term not in excess of six years, and shall be subject to removal for cause, as aforesaid, by or at the will of the beneficiary.

(4) In the event of removal of a trustee under this Section, a successor trustee shall be appointed in the same manner as aforesaid except in the case of trusts subject to R.S. 9:2343(B).

(5) However, in the event a trustee is so removed who is also a member of the governing body of a parish or municipal beneficiary, or a legislator who is an ex officio trustee, the successor trustee shall be appointed by the district court wherein the removal occurred. Said successor trustee shall serve only until the removed trustee ceases to serve as a member of the governing body of the parish or municipal beneficiary or as a member of the legislature and his successor on said governing body or in the legislature has qualified.

G. In the proposed adoption, amendment, or repeal of any rule, as defined in R.S. 49:951(6), or the proposed adoption, increasing, or decreasing of any fee, a public trust of which the state is not the beneficiary shall be subject to legislative oversight pursuant to R.S. 49:968. A public trust of which the state is not the beneficiary shall submit the report required by R.S. 40:600.6(D) to the House Committee on Municipal, Parochial, and Cultural Affairs and the Senate Committee on Local and Municipal Affairs.

Added by Acts 1970, No. 135, § 3. Amended by Acts 1976, No. 699, § 1, eff. Aug. 4, 1976; Acts 1978, No. 778, § 1; Acts 1981, No. 239, § 1; Acts 1984, No. 722, § 1, eff. Jan. 1, 1985; Acts 1992, No. 1062, § 1; Acts 1999, No. 1238, § 1; Acts 1999, No. 1323, § 1; Acts 2005, No. 150, § 1.

[1] R.S. 9:1721 et seq.

§ 2344. Liability of trustees and beneficiary

A. No trustee or beneficiary shall be charged personally with any liability whatsoever by reason of any act or omission committed or suffered in the performance of such trust or in the operation of the trust property; but any act, liability for omission or obligation of a trustee or trustees in the execution of such trust, or in the operation of the trust property, shall extend to the whole of the trust estate, or so much thereof as may be necessary to discharge such liability or obligation, and not otherwise.

B. Any obligations issued by a public trust under this Chapter shall not constitute or create any debt or debts, liability or liabilities or a loan of the credit of or a pledge of the faith and credit of the beneficiary of the state or any political or governmental unit thereof but shall be solely the obligation of the public trust.

Added by Acts 1970, No. 135, § 4. Amended by Acts 1976, No. 699, § 1, eff. Aug. 4, 1976.

§ 2345. Termination of public trusts

A. The acceptance of the beneficial interest in any public trust heretofore or hereafter created may be terminated by the beneficiary thereof at any time by the following methods, as applicable. Where the state or any state agency is the beneficiary, the acceptance is terminated by law duly enacted or by Concurrent Resolution of the Senate and House of Representatives. Where another governmental unit be the beneficiary, the acceptance is terminated by duly adopted ordinance or resolution of the governing body of the beneficiary as may be applicable.

B. Notwithstanding the provisions of Subsection A of this Section, the acceptance of the beneficial interest in any public trust heretofore or hereafter created shall not be terminated while there exists outstanding any indebtedness or other contractual obligations chargeable against the trust estate. The termination of the acceptance of the beneficial interest by the beneficiary of a public trust shall not prejudice nor affect any valid indebtedness or obligation of the trust; however, upon termination of the acceptance, the trustee or trustees shall have no powers or authority under the provisions of this Chapter, but shall be governed exclusively by the provisions of the Louisiana Trust Code, exclusive of Chapter 2–A of Title 9 of the Louisiana Revised Statutes, and by the laws of this state pertaining to charitable trusts.

Added by Acts 1970, No. 135, § 5. Amended by Acts 1976, No. 699, § 1, eff. Aug. 4, 1976; Acts 1978, No. 778, § 1.

§ 2346. Audits; supervision by legislative auditor; operating budget approval

A. Any public trust created hereunder shall be subject to the supervision of the legislative auditor of the state of Louisiana, to the same extent as the beneficiary thereof. Should the beneficiary thereof not be subject to the supervision of the legislative auditor, then provision shall be made in the instrument creating the trust for an annual, independent audit of the trust by a certified public accountant. Any such independent audit shall be subject to the authority of the legislative auditor to prescribe and approve the terms and conditions of such audit as set forth in the provisions of R.S. 24:513(A).

B. Any public trust created hereunder in which the state of Louisiana is the beneficiary shall be audited on an annual basis by the legislative auditor as provided in R.S. 24:513 and such public trusts shall annually provide sworn statements of revenues and expenditures in accordance with R.S. 24:514.

C. No later than sixty days before the beginning of its annual operating year, a public trust in which the state of Louisiana is a beneficiary shall submit its proposed annual operating budget to the Joint Legislative Committee on the Budget for its review and approval. The public trust may submit a proposed modification to its approved annual operating budget to the Joint Legislative Committee on the Budget for its review and approval at any time during the course of the annual operating year. At no time shall the public trust incur any expenditures or obligate itself for items which deviate from its approved annual operating budget.

Added by Acts 1970, No. 135, § 6. Amended by Acts 1976, No. 699, § 1, eff. Aug. 4, 1976; Acts 1981, No. 238, § 1; Acts 1999, No. 915, § 1, eff. July 2, 1999.

§ 2347. Bonds of public trust

A. To provide funds for and to fulfill and achieve its authorized public functions or purposes, a public trust may incur debt and issue bonds, notes or other evidences of indebtedness, hereinafter referred to collectively as "bonds" subject to the following:

(1) If the beneficiary of the public trust is a parish, municipality, or a political or governmental subdivision thereof, and such bonds or other debt obligations are issued for the purpose of providing, constructing, expanding, or altering public facilities which are to be operated, maintained, or administered by any such parish, municipality, or political or governmental subdivision thereof, such bonds shall be approved by a vote of a majority of the qualified electors of the beneficiary who vote in a special election held for that purpose in the manner provided by Chapter 6–A of Title 18 (R. S. 18:1281 et seq.) of the Louisiana Revised Statutes of 1950. Furthermore, in all other cases, if the beneficiary of the trust is a parish, municipality, or a political or governmental subdivision thereof, all bonds and other debt obligations shall be issued only after the trust has adopted an appropriate resolution giving notice of its intention to issue such bonds or other debt obligations, which resolution shall include a general description of the bonds or other debt obligations to be issued and the security therefor, and notice of this intention shall be published once a week for four weeks in a newspaper in the locality of the beneficiary or in the parish where it is located, the first publication to appear at least thirty days before the public meeting of the trust at which the trust will meet in open and public session to hear any objections to the proposed issuance of such bonds or other debt obligations. The notice of intent so published shall state the date, time, and place of the public hearing and shall state, and the law is hereby declared to be, that if at such hearing a petition duly signed by electors of the beneficiary in a number not less than five per cent of the electors of the beneficiary voting at the last special or general election object to the issuance of the proposed bonds or other debt obligations, then such bonds or other debt obligations

shall not be issued until approved by a vote of a majority of the qualified electors of the beneficiary who vote in a special election held for the purpose in the manner provided by Chapter 6–A of Title 18 (R.S. 18:1281 et seq.) of the Louisiana Revised Statutes of 1950. Any such petition shall be accompanied by a certificate of the parish registrar of voters certifying that the signers of the petition are qualified electors of the beneficiary and the number of signers amounts to not less than five per cent of the electors in said beneficiary in number, voting at the last special or general election. All bonds and other debt obligations issued hereunder for the purpose of providing, developing, securing and improving the water storage, treatment, supply and distribution services and facilities and sanitary and storm sewer collection, disposal, treatment and drainage services and facilities, shall be issued in accordance with the provisions of Subpart B or C, Part I of Chapter 10, Title 33 of the Louisiana Revised Statutes of 1950 [1], and any and all other laws of the state pertaining to revenue bonds for public utilities.

(2) All such bonds shall be negotiable instruments, and shall be solely the obligations of the trust and not of the state of Louisiana or the beneficiary. The bonds and the income thereof shall be exempt from all taxation in the state of Louisiana. The bonds shall be payable out of the income, revenues and receipts derived or to be derived from the trust properties and facilities maintained and operated by the trust or received by the trust from any other sources whatsoever, including, but not by way of limitation, other monies which, by law or contract, may be made available to the trust. In addition to the pledge of income, revenues or receipts to secure said bonds, the trust may further secure their payment by a conventional mortgage upon any or all of the properties constructed or acquired or to be constructed or acquired by it. Such bonds shall be authorized and issued by resolution adopted by a two-thirds vote of the trustees of the trust and shall be of such series, bear such date or dates, mature at such time or times, bear interest at such rate or rates not exceeding the maximum rate at which revenue bonds of the beneficiary can be issued and sold, be in such denominations, be in such form, either coupon or fully registered without coupons, carry such registration and exchangeability privileges, be payable at such place or places, be subject to such terms of redemption and be entitled to such priorities on the income, revenues and receipts of the trust as such resolution may provide. The bonds shall be signed by such officers as the trust shall determine and one of such signatures may be facsimile. Coupon bonds shall have attached thereto interest coupons bearing the facsimile signatures of such officer or officers as the trust shall designate. Any such bonds may be issued and delivered, notwithstanding that one or more of the officers signing such bonds or the officer or officers whose facsimile signature or signatures may be on the coupons shall have ceased to be such officer or officers at the time such bonds shall actually have been delivered. Such bonds may be sold in such manner and from time to time as may be determined by the trust to be most beneficial and the trust may pay all expenses and commissions which it may deem necessary or advantageous in connection with the issuance and sale thereof subject to the provisions of Subsection (K) of this Section.

(3) Bonds and notes issued hereunder are hereby declared legal investments and are hereby made securities in which all insurance companies and associations and other persons carrying on an insurance business, trust companies, banks, bankers, banking associations, savings banks and savings associations, including savings and loan associations, credit unions, building and loan associations, investment companies, executors, administrators, trustees and other fiduciaries, pension, profit-sharing, retirement funds and other persons carrying on a banking business, and all other persons who are authorized to invest in revenue bonds may properly and legally invest funds, including capital in their control or belonging to them. Such bonds and notes are hereby made securities which may properly and legally be deposited with and received by any state or municipal or public officer or any agency or political subdivisions of the state for any purpose for which the deposit of revenue bonds is authorized by law. Nothing contained herein shall authorize the investment of public pension or retirement funds in public trust bonds or other obligations.

B. The trust may in any resolution authorizing the issuance of such bonds enter into such covenants with the future holder or holders of the bonds as to the management and operation of the trust properties or facilities, the imposition and collection of fees and charges for services and facilities furnished by the trust, the disposition of such fees and revenues, the issuance of future bonds and the creation of future liens and encumbrances against such facilities and the revenues therefrom, the carrying of insurance on the facilities, the keeping of books and records, and other pertinent matters, as may be deemed proper by the trust to assure the marketability of the bonds, provided such covenants are not inconsistent with the provisions of this Chapter. Any holder of the bonds or of any of the coupons thereto attached may by appropriate legal action compel performance of all duties required of the trust and officials by this Chapter or by the resolution authorizing the issuance of bonds if not inconsistent with the provisions of this Chapter. If any bond issued hereunder is permitted to go into default as to principal or interest, any court of competent jurisdiction may pursuant to the application of the holder of the bond, appoint a receiver for the facilities of the trust, which receiver shall be under the duty of operating the facilities and collecting and distributing the revenues thereof pledged to the payment of the bonds, pursuant to the provisions and requirements of this Chapter and the resolution authorizing the bonds. As hereinbefore provided, such bonds may in the discretion of the trust be additionally secured by mortgage on all or any part of the trust properties or facilities acquired, constructed, extended or improved with the proceeds thereof, and the trust shall have full discretion to make such provisions as it may see fit for the making and enforcement of such mortgage and the provisions to be therein contained.

C. If more than one series of bonds is issued hereunder payable from the revenues of any facility, priority of lien on such revenues shall depend on the time of delivery of the bonds, each series enjoying a lien prior and superior to that enjoyed by any series of bonds subsequently delivered, except that where provision is made in the proceedings authorizing any issue or series of bonds for the issuance of additional bonds in the future on a parity therewith pursuant to procedures or restrictions provided in such proceedings, additional bonds may be issued in the future on a parity with such issue or series in the manner so provided in such proceedings.

D. The trust may issue bonds under this Chapter payable from revenues to be derived from two or more facilities owned and operated by the trust (whether or not such facilities are related or used in conjunction) for the purpose of constructing, acquiring, extending or improving any one or more of the facilities, which bonds may be additionally secured by a mortgage upon such facilities; provided, however, in no event shall the bonds constitute a claim against any property or revenue of the trust not specifically pledged or hypothecated for payment of such bonds.

E. Any resolution authorizing the issuance of bonds hereunder shall provide for the creation of a sinking fund into which shall be paid from the revenues of the trust properties and facilities financed by the proceeds of the bonds, subject only to prior payment of the reasonable and necessary expenses of operating and maintaining such properties and facilities, sums fully sufficient to pay the principal and interest of the bonds as the bonds become due and payable, and to create such reserve for contingencies as may be required by the resolution. The monies in the sinking fund shall be applied to the payment of interest on and principal of the bonds or to the purchase of retirement of the bonds prior to maturity in the manner provided in the resolution.

F. The trust may authorize the issuance of refunding bonds of the trust for the purpose of refunding outstanding bonds issued pursuant to this Chapter. Such refunding bonds may either be sold and the proceeds applied to or deposited in escrow for the retirement of the outstanding bonds, or may be delivered in exchange for the outstanding bonds. The refunding bonds shall be authorized in all respects as original bonds are herein required to be authorized, and the authority in authorizing the refunding bonds shall provide for the security of the bonds, the sources from which the bonds are to be paid and for the rights of the holders thereof in all respects as herein provided for other bonds issued under authority of this Chapter. The trust may also provide that the refunding bonds shall have the same priority of lien on the revenues pledged for their payment as was enjoyed by the bonds refunded.

G. It shall be provided in the resolution authorizing any bonds hereunder that such bonds shall recite that they are issued under authority of this Chapter. Such recital shall conclusively import full compliance with all of the provisions of this Chapter and all bonds issued containing such recital shall be incontestable for any cause whatsoever after thirty days from the date of publication of the notice of sale of the bonds as provided for hereinafter.

H. All bond issues of a public trust shall be submitted to and approved by the State Bond Commission prior to the issuance and delivery of said bonds. All bonds of a public trust shall be sold by such public trust except when the state is the beneficiary of the financing. Provided, bonds of a public trust issued in connection with any projects or facilities of the trust for the provisions of industrial, manufacturing, or other economic development facilities and activities shall be sold in accordance with the provisions of R.S. 39:991, et seq., subject to the requirement that a notice of intent to sell such bonds shall be published at least seven days in advance of the sale date. After approval by the State Bond Commission as required herein and at least seven days prior to the sale of such bonds , the public trust shall cause to be published a notice of sale in a newspaper of general circulation in the parish of the beneficiary's situs, or if the state or any state agency be the beneficiary, such publication shall be in the official state journal, and in a financial journal or newspaper containing a section devoted to municipal bond news published in either New Orleans, Louisiana, or New York, New York. This notice of sale shall state if any proposals have been made for the purchase of the bonds and that other proposals will be considered and that the proposal most advantageous to the issuer will be accepted at the time of the sale. After adoption of the resolution or other proceedings authorizing the sale of bonds, the resolution or other proceedings shall be published in a newspaper of general circulation in the parish of the beneficiary's situs, or, if the state or any state agency be the beneficiary, such publication shall be in the official state journal. For a period of thirty days from the date of publication of the notice of sale, any person or persons in interest shall have the right to contest the legality of the notice of sale, resolution or other proceedings authorizing the issuance of the bonds and the legality of the bond issue for any cause, after which time no one shall have any cause or right of action to contest the legality of said resolution or other proceedings or of the bonds authorized thereby for any cause whatsoever. If no suit, action or proceedings are begun contesting the validity of the bonds within the thirty days herein prescribed, the authority to issue the bonds and to provide for the payment thereof, the legality thereof and of all of the provisions of the resolution or other proceedings authorizing the issuance of the bonds shall be conclusively presumed, and no court shall have authority to inquire into such matters. Such bonds shall have all the qualities of negotiable instruments under the law merchant and the commercial laws of the state of Louisiana.

I. All bonds, notes or other evidences of indebtedness issued by a public trust shall be special obligations of the trust and shall be deemed to have been issued on behalf of the beneficiary of the trust. In no event shall any bonds, notes or other evidences of indebtedness of a trust constitute an obligation, either general or special, of the state of Louisiana or the beneficiary of the trust within the meaning of any constitutional or statutory provision whatsoever, and the bonds shall contain a recital to that effect.

J. If the bond issue of the trust requires the expenditure of any state funds in the acquisition of any facilities or properties for use by the trust or if any contractual obligation is to be undertaken or incurred by the state in excess of one year in connection therewith, a two-thirds vote of both the members of the State Bond Commission and the Joint Legislative Committee on the Budget approving such action shall be required as a condition to such action.

K. The trustee or trustees may employ a financial advisor to furnish services in preparing any bond issues for the issuance and may contract for the payment of his services provided however, no continuing fee arrangement with a financial advisor shall exist after the delivery of any bonds and all bond issues upon which the financial advisor provides services shall be sold only at an advertised public sale. All financial advisors fees and any underwriters discount must be approved in writing by the State Bond Commission and the attorney general's office. Any attorneys fees in connection with the financing and the acquisition or construction of the project to be financed shall be subject to approval of the attorney general. Whoever violates this Subsection shall be subject to the imposition of the penalties provided in R.S. 42:264.

L. All bonds heretofore issued under the provisions of Act 135 of the 1970 Regular Session of the Louisiana Legislature are hereby validated, ratified and confirmed and declared to be valid and binding obligations of the public trust in accordance with the terms of their issuance. All proceedings heretofore had in connection with the issuance of such bonds are hereby ratified, validated and confirmed. However, the provisions of this Chapter shall apply to any new or additional bonds issued by any public trusts in existence at the time of the effective date of this Chapter, notwithstanding that said public trusts may have previously issued and have outstanding any bonds and/or notes.

M. The property of any public trust, having as its beneficiary a parish, municipality, or a political or governmental subdivision thereof which is authorized under its trust indenture to engage in or issue bonds to finance projects for substantially all of the public purposes set forth in R.S. 9:2341(B)(1), acquired or held for one or more of said purposes, is hereby declared to be public property used for essential public and governmental purposes. Accordingly, such public trust, and all of its properties at any time owned by it and the income therefrom and all bonds issued by it and the income therefrom, shall be exempt from all taxes of the parish or municipality, the state, or any political subdivision thereof or any other taxing body, provided, however, that such public trust may require the lessee of each of the projects of the public trust to pay annually to parish or municipal taxing authorities or to any other taxing body, through the normal collecting agency, a sum in lieu of ad valorem taxes to compensate such authorities for any services rendered by them to such projects, which sum shall not be in excess of the ad valorem taxes such lessee would have been obligated to pay to such authorities had it been the owner of such project during the period for which such payment is made. Such payments to be made in lieu of taxes together with any fees and charges of such public trust, to the extent in the aggregate they do not exceed the amount of taxes that would be paid if the lessee were the owner, shall constitute statutory impositions within the meaning of R.S. 47:2128. No provision of this Subsection shall become effective until approved by resolution of the parish, municipality, or a political or governmental subdivision thereof which is the beneficiary of such public trust.

Added by Acts 1970, No. 135, § 8. Amended by Acts 1976, No. 699, § 1, eff. Aug. 4, 1976; Acts 1978, No. 778, § 1; Acts 1986, No. 977, § 1, eff. July 14, 1986; Acts 2007, No. 93, § 1, eff. June 22, 2007; Acts 2010, No. 1042, § 1, eff. July 8, 2010; Acts 2011, No. 344, § 1.

1 R.S. 33:4221 et seq. and 33:4251 et seq.

CHAPTER 3. DONATIONS INTER VIVOS

PART I. MARRIED PERSON TO SPOUSE

Section
2351. Donation irrevocable; reservation of right to revoke.
2352. Renouncing right to revoke.
2353. Civil Code Art. 156 unaffected.
2354. [Blank].

PART II. PARENT TO CHILD

2361. Parent's right of usufruct.

PART III. EFFECT ON DONEES AND THIRD PARTIES

2371. Recordation of donations inter vivos; effect.

PART IV. CALCULATION OF MASS, REDUCTION AND COLLATION

2372. Donations inter vivos; exempt from reduction and calculation of succession mass.

Section
2373. Donations inter vivos to spouse of previous marriage; exemption from reduction and calculation of succession mass.

PART I. MARRIED PERSON TO SPOUSE

§ 2351. Donation irrevocable; reservation of right to revoke

Every donation made after twelve o'clock noon, July 29, 1942, by a married person to his or her spouse shall be as irrevocable as if made to a stranger. However, where the donation is made by notarial act the donor may reserve the right of revocation by express stipulation therein. Any right of revocation so reserved unless renounced as provided in R.S. 9:2352, may be exercised at any time during the life of the donor, whether or not the marriage is then in existence, and whether or not the donee is then alive.

Amended by Acts 1950, No. 316, § 1.

Cross References

C.C. arts. 1734, 1736, 1750, 2330, 2343, 2349, 3528.

§ 2352. Renouncing right to revoke

When the donor may revoke a donation previously made to the spouse, either because the donation was made prior to 12 o'clock noon, July 29, 1942, or because the right of revocation was reserved in the act of donation, the donor may renounce this right to revoke, by notarial act, which shall be recorded wherever the act of donation is recorded.

Cross References

C.C. arts. 1736, 1743, 1750, 2330, 2343.

§ 2353. Civil Code Art. 156 unaffected

Nothing contained in R.S. 9:2351 and 9:2352 shall be construed to modify in any way the provisions of Civil Code Article 156.

Editor's note. Article 156 of the Louisiana Civil Code of 1870 has been repealed by Acts 1990, No. 1009, § 9, effective January 1, 1991.

§ 2354. [Blank]

Editor's note. Acts 1995, No. 402, § 1 enacted Part IV, "Calculation of Mass, Reduction and Collation" containing R.S. 9:2372 and 9:2373. The subject matter of this section as added by Acts 1981, No. 881, § 1, "Donations inter vivos to spouse of previous marriage; exemption from reduction and calculation of succession mass" is contained in R.S. 9:2373 as enacted by Act 402. The title of Acts 1995, No. 402 indicated an intent to redesignate R.S. 9:2354 as R.S. 9:2373. Pursuant to the statutory revision authority of the Louisiana State Law Institute, the effect of Acts 1995, No. 402 was to replace the former R.S. 9:2354 with R.S. 9:2373 as enacted by Act 402. See, now, R.S. 9:2373.

PART II. PARENT TO CHILD

§ 2361. Parent's right of usufruct

No parent of a minor child shall have the right of usufruct with respect to any property acquired by such child by donation inter vivos from his or her father or mother, unless such property shall have been donated by written act executed by the father or mother and the right to such usufruct has been reserved therein.

This Section is intended to and does apply to donations inter vivos heretofore made, but any parent who has heretofore made a donation inter vivos to his or her minor child shall have the right, for a period of six months from the effective date hereof, to preserve such right of usufruct with respect to the property so given as such donor had prior to the effective date hereof by executing a notarial act claiming such right and recording the same in the parish of the donor's domicile and wherever the act of donation is recorded.

Added by Acts 1952, No. 266, § 1.

Cross References

C.C. arts. 223, 226, 227, 535, 544.

PART III. EFFECT ON DONEES AND THIRD PARTIES

§ 2371. Recordation of donations inter vivos; effect

Notwithstanding any provision of law to the contrary, a subsequent alienation or encumbrance of an immovable by a donee shall be considered an acceptance in accordance with the provisions of Civil Code Article 1544, and shall be effective against third persons upon recordation of any act or other document which alienates or encumbers the property, regardless of form, filed in the parish in which the immovable is situated.

Added by Acts 1964, No. 122, § 2. Amended by Acts 1995, No. 1031, § 1; Acts 2010, No. 225, § 1.

Editor's note. Subsections A and B of this section were repealed by Acts 2005, No. 169, effective Jan. 1, 2006. That effective date, however, was postponed to July 1, 2006 by emergency legislation, Acts 2005, 1st Ex.Sess., No. 13.

Section 9 of Acts 2005, No. 169 provides:

"Section 9. Nothing in this Act shall be deemed to diminish the effect of, or render ineffective, the recordation of any instrument that was filed, registered, or recorded in the conveyance or mortgage records of any parish before the effective date of this Act. Any instrument that is filed, registered, or recorded before the effective date of this Act, that is not given the effect of recordation by virtue of existing law, shall be given such effect on the effective date of this Act that it would have if it were first filed on that effective date. Any instrument made available for viewing on the Internet by the recorder before the effective date of this Act shall not be subject to the restriction that allows the display of only the last four digits of social security numbers."

Cross References

C.C. arts. 6, 478, 517, 518, 1467, 1468, 1536 et seq., 3473 to 3477.

R.S. 1:2.

Const. 1974, Art. I, § 23.

USCA Const., Art. I, § 10.

PART IV. CALCULATION OF MASS, REDUCTION AND COLLATION

§ 2372. Donations inter vivos; exempt from reduction and calculation of succession mass

No donation inter vivos which is made at least three years prior to the death of the donor shall be subject to reduction under the provisions of Civil Code Articles 1502 through 1518, nor shall the property transferred by such donation be fictitiously added to the aggregate of all property belonging to the donor in calculating the mass of the donor's succession under the provisions of Civil Code Article 1505, nor in calculating the legitime portion under Civil Code Article 1234.

Acts 1995, No. 402, § 1.

Editor's note. Section 2 of Acts 1995, No. 402 provides: "The provisions of this Act shall apply to all donations inter vivos made on or after January 1, 1996."

Cross References

C.C. arts. 870, 871, 1227, 1231, 1234, 1467, 1468, 1503 to 1505, 1513, 1528, 1550, 1726, 1734, 1743 et seq.

§ 2373. Donations inter vivos to spouse of previous marriage; exemption from reduction and calculation of succession mass

No donation inter vivos made by a person to his or her spouse of a previous marriage which was made during the existence of such marriage shall be subject to reduction under the provisions of Civil Code Articles 1502 through 1518, nor shall the property transferred by such donation be fictitiously added to the aggregate of all property belonging to the donor in calculating the mass of the donor's succession under the provisions of Civil Code Article 1505 or in calculating the legitime portion under Civil Code Article 1234.

R.S. 9:2354. Redesignated as R.S. 9:2373 pursuant to Acts 1995, No. 402, § 1.

Editor's note. Acts 1995, No. 402, § 1 enacted Part IV, "Calculation of Mass, Reduction and Collation" containing R.S. 9:2372 and 9:2373. The subject matter of this section as added by Acts 1995, No. 402, § 1, "Donations inter vivos to spouse of previous marriage; exemption from reduction and calculation of succession mass" was formerly contained in R.S. 9:2354 as enacted by Acts 1981, No. 881, § 1. The title of Acts 1995, No. 402 indicated an intent to redesignate R.S. 9:2354 as R.S. 9:2373. Pursuant to the statutory revision authority of the Louisiana State Law Institute, the effect of Acts 1995, No. 402 was to replace the former R.S. 9:2354 with this section (R.S. 9:2373) as enacted by Act 402.

CHAPTER 4. DONATIONS MORTIS CAUSA

PART I. UNIFORM WILLS LAW

Section
2401. Will executed outside state.

PART II. UNIFORM PROBATE LAW

2421. Will probated outside state may be allowed and recorded.
2422. Filing of will and proceedings thereon.
2423. Admission to probate; force and effect.
2424. Probate of will operative under laws of state or country not requiring probate.
2425. Short title; interpretation.

PART II–A. ESTATE TAX APPORTIONMENT LAW

2431. Definitions.
2432. Apportionment of tax liability among persons interested in estate.

APPENDIX 1—REVISED STATUTES, TITLE 9

Section
2433. No apportionment between principal and income beneficiaries of trust and between usufructuaries and naked owners.
2434. Fiduciary's right to withhold or recover proportion of tax attributable to persons interested in estate; security by person interested in estate for payment of tax.
2435. Allowance for exemptions, deductions, and credits.
2436. Action to recover amount of tax or deficiency from person interested in estate; time of filing; liability of fiduciary.
2437. Action by nonresident; reciprocity.
2438. Application of provisions.
2439. Estate tax marital deduction; formula qualifying.

PART III. MISCELLANEOUS PROVISIONS

2440. Continued validity of previously executed testaments.
2441. Duration of usufruct in previously executed testament.
2442 to 2445. Repealed.
2446. Will information registration.
2447. Fees.
2448. Repealed.
2449. Individual retirement accounts; payment of benefits.
2450. Succession representatives; liability for distributions.

PART I. UNIFORM WILLS LAW

§ 2401. Will executed outside state

A will executed outside this state in the manner prescribed by the law of the place of its execution or by the law of the testator's domicile, at the time of its execution shall be deemed to be legally executed and shall have the same force and effect in this state as if executed in the manner prescribed by the laws of this state, provided the will is in writing and subscribed by the testator.

Cross References

C.C. arts. 15, 1573, 3528 to 3534.
R.S. 9:2421 to 9:2425.

PART II. UNIFORM PROBATE LAW

§ 2421. Will probated outside state may be allowed and recorded

A will duly proved, allowed, and admitted to probate outside of this state, may be allowed and recorded in the proper court of any parish in this state, in which the testator shall have left any estate.

Cross References

C.C. arts. 15, 1605, 3528 to 3534.
R.S. 9:2401.

§ 2422. Filing of will and proceedings thereon

When a copy of the will and probate thereof, duly authenticated, shall be presented by the executor or by any other person interested in the will, with a petition for the probate, the same must be filed and proper proceedings had as required by law on a petition for the original probate of a domestic will.

Cross References

C.C. arts. 15, 1605, 3528 to 3534.
R.S. 9:2401.

§ 2423. Admission to probate; force and effect

If upon the hearing, it appears to the satisfaction of the court that the will has been duly proved, allowed, and admitted to probate outside of this state, and that it was executed according to the law of the place in which the same was made, or in which the testator was at the time domiciled, or in conformity with the laws of this state, it must be admitted to probate, which probate shall have the same force and effect as the original probate of a domestic will.

Cross References

C.C. arts. 15, 1605, 1611 et seq., 3528 to 3534.
R.S. 9:2401.

§ 2424. Probate of will operative under laws of state or country not requiring probate

When a duly authenticated copy of a will from any state or country where probate is not required by the laws of such state or country, with a duly authenticated certificate of the legal custodian of such original will that the same is a true copy, and that such will has become operative by the laws of such state or country, and when a copy of a notarial will in possession of a notary in a foreign state or country entitled to the custody thereof (the laws of which state or country require that such will remain in the custody of such notary), duly authenticated by such notary, is presented by the executor or other persons interested to the proper court in this state, such court shall probate the same as in case of an original will presented for probate.

If it appears to the court that the instrument ought to be allowed in this state, as the last will and testament of the deceased the copy shall be filed and recorded, and the will shall have the same effect as if originally proved and allowed in the said court.

Cross References

C.C. arts. 15, 1644, 3528 to 3534.
R.S. 9:2401.

§ 2425. Short title; interpretation

This Part may be cited as the Uniform Probate Law, and shall be so interpreted and construed as to effectuate its general purposes to make uniform the laws of the states which enact it.

Cross References

C.C. arts. 15, 1605, 1611 et seq., 3528 to 3534.
R.S. 9:2401.

PART II–A. ESTATE TAX APPORTIONMENT LAW

§ 2431. Definitions

Unless the context clearly indicates otherwise, the following terms have the meaning ascribed to them in this Section:

(1) "Court" means the court having jurisdiction of the succession of the deceased;

(2) "Estate" means the gross estate of a deceased as determined for the purpose of Federal estate tax;

(3) "Fiduciary" means executor, administrator of any description, and trustee;

(4) "Person" means any individual, partnership, association, joint stock company, corporation, government, political subdivision, governmental agency, or local governmental agency;

(5) "Person interested in the estate" means any person entitled to receive, or who has received, from a deceased person or by reason of his death, any property or interest therein included in the estate of the deceased. It includes a personal representative, tutor, curator, and trustee;

(6) "State" means any state, territory, or possession of the United States, the District of Columbia, and the Commonwealth of Puerto Rico;

(7) "Tax" means the Federal estate tax and the Louisiana estate transfer tax, and includes interest and penalties imposed or accrued thereunder.

Added by Acts 1960, No. 362, § 1. Amended by Acts 2010, No. 175, § 2.

Cross References

C.C. arts. 1421, 1427, 1584 et seq., 1598.

§ 2432. Apportionment of tax liability among persons interested in estate

A. If the deceased has made no provision in his testament for the apportionment of the tax among the persons interested in the estate, the tax shall be apportioned among them by the court in the proportion that the value of the interest of each person interested in the estate bears to the total value of the interests of all persons interested in the estate. The values used in determining the tax shall be used for this purpose.

B. If the deceased has provided in his testament for the apportionment of the tax among all the persons interested in the estate, the court shall apportion the tax as directed by the deceased.

C. If the deceased has provided in his testament for the apportionment of the tax of some, but not of all the persons interested in the estate, the amount of the tax which has not been apportioned shall be apportioned by the court among those as to whom no provision has been made, in the same manner as is provided in Subsection A of this Section.

Added by Acts 2011, No. 346, § 2.

Editor's note. Section 3 of Acts 2011, No. 346, declares that this Act is "remedial, curative, and procedural and therefore it is to be applied retroactively as well as prospectively." The Act is, indeed, "remedial and curative" but it can hardly be considered "procedural." It is substantive legislation that may only be applied retroactively in the absence of constitutional constraints. Under the Louisiana Constitution, retroactive laws that tend to divest vested rights or impair the obligations of contracts violate the Louisiana Constitution. For discussion, see Yiannopoulos, Civil Law System p. 197 (2d ed. 1999); Personal Servitudes, Introduction (5th ed. 2011).

Cross References

C.C. arts. 1427, 1598.

§ 2433. No apportionment between principal and income beneficiaries of trust and between usufructuaries and naked owners

No beneficial interest in income from a trust and no usufruct shall be subject to apportionment as between the principal beneficiary in the case of the trust and the naked owner in the case of the usufruct. The tax on the beneficial interest in income from a trust or the usufruct shall be chargeable against the principal of the trust or the naked ownership of the property in the case of the usufruct. The court shall order that portion of the property subject to the usufruct, or that portion of the trust principal subject to the rights of an income beneficiary, to be sold in whole or in part to pay the tax apportioned in accordance with this Section. Thereafter, only the balance of the property remaining after the sale or the balance of the proceeds of the sale not necessary for the payment of the tax shall be subject to the usufruct or the rights of an income beneficiary of a trust. To avoid the sale or other disposition of property which is subject to a usufruct or an income interest in a trust to satisfy the tax liability, the usufructuary and the naked owner, or the principal beneficiary and the income beneficiary, may agree to the method of and responsibility for payment of the tax.

Added by Acts 2011, No. 346, § 2.

Editor's note. Section 3 of Acts 2011, No. 346, declares that this Act is "remedial, curative, and procedural and therefore it is to be applied retroactively as well as prospectively." The Act is, indeed, "remedial and curative" but it can hardly be considered "procedural." It is substantive legislation that may only be applied retroactively in the absence of constitutional constraints. Under the Louisiana Constitution, retroactive laws that tend to divest vested rights or impair the obligations of contracts violate the Louisiana Constitution. For discussion, see Yiannopoulos, Civil Law System p. 197 (2d ed. 1999); Personal Servitudes, Introduction (5th ed. 2011).

Cross References

C.C. arts. 587, 588, 590, 1427, 1598.

§ 2434. Fiduciary's right to withhold or recover proportion of tax attributable to persons interested in estate; security by person interested in estate for payment of tax

A. The fiduciary or other person in possession of the property of the deceased required to pay the tax may withhold from any property distributable to any person interested in the estate, upon its distribution to him, the amount of tax attributable to his interest. If the property in possession of the fiduciary or other person required to pay the tax and distributable to any person interested in the estate is insufficient to satisfy the proportionate amount of the tax determined to be due from the person, the fiduciary or other person required to pay the tax may recover the deficiency from the person interested in the estate. If the property is not in the possession of the fiduciary or other person required to pay the tax, the fiduciary or other person required to pay the tax may recover from any person interested in the estate, in accordance with R.S. 9:2436, the amount of the tax apportioned to that person as provided in R.S. 9:2432.

B. If property is to be distributed prior to final apportionment of the tax, the court may require, upon application of the fiduciary or other person who may be required to pay the tax, any person who is to share in the distribution of the estate to provide a bond or other security for the apportionment liability in the form and amount prescribed by the court. This application shall be made by contradictory motion or rule to show cause.

Added by Acts 2011, No. 346, § 2.

Editor's note. Section 3 of Acts 2011, No. 346, declares that this Act is "remedial, curative, and procedural and therefore it is to be applied retroactively as well as prospectively." The Act is, indeed, "remedial and curative" but it can hardly be considered "procedural." It is substantive legislation that may only be applied retroactively in the absence of constitutional constraints. Under the Louisiana Constitution, retroactive laws that tend to divest vested rights or impair the obligations of contracts violate the Louisiana Constitution. For discussion, see Yiannopoulos, Civil Law System p. 197 (2d ed. 1999); Personal Servitudes, Introduction (5th ed. 2011).

Cross References

C.C. arts. 1427, 1598.

§ 2435. Allowance for exemptions, deductions, and credits

A. In making an apportionment, allowances shall be made for any exemptions granted, any classification made of persons interested in the estate, and for any deductions and credits allowed by the law imposing the tax.

B. Any exemption or deduction allowed by reason of the relationship of any person to the decedent or by reason of the purposes of the gift shall inure to the benefit of the person bearing such relationship or receiving the gift, except when an interest is subject to a prior present interest which is not allowable as a deduction, the tax apportionable against the present interest shall be paid from principal.

C. Any deduction for property previously taxed and any credit for gift taxes or death taxes of a foreign country paid by the decedent or his estate shall inure to the proportionate benefit of all persons liable to apportionment.

D. Any credit for inheritance, succession or estate taxes, or taxes in the nature thereof in respect to property or interests includable in the estate shall inure to the benefit of the persons or interests chargeable with the payment thereof to the extent that or in proportion as the credit reduces the tax.

E. To the extent that property passing to or in trust for a surviving spouse or any charitable, public, or similar gift or bequest does not constitute an allowable deduction for purposes of the tax solely by reason of an inheritance tax imposed upon and deductible from the property, the property shall not be included in the computation provided for in R.S. 9:2432, and to that extent no apportionment shall be made against the property. This Subsection shall not apply where the result will deprive the estate of a deduction otherwise allowable under Section 2053(d) of the Internal Revenue Code of 1954 of the United States, relating to deduction for state death taxes on transfers for public, charitable, or religious uses.

Added by Acts 2011, No. 346, § 2.

Editor's note. Section 3 of Acts 2011, No. 346, declares that this Act is "remedial, curative, and procedural and therefore it is to be applied retroactively as well as prospectively." The Act is, indeed, "remedial and curative" but it can hardly be considered "procedural." It is substantive legislation that may only be applied retroactively in the absence of constitutional constraints. Under the Louisiana Constitution, retroactive laws that tend to divest vested rights or impair the obligations of contracts violate the Louisiana Constitution. For discussion, see Yiannopoulos, Civil Law System p. 197 (2d ed. 1999); Personal Servitudes, Introduction (5th ed. 2011).

Cross References

C.C. arts. 1427, 1598.

§ 2436. Action to recover amount of tax or deficiency from person interested in estate; time of filing; liability of fiduciary

A. A fiduciary or other person required to pay the tax has a right of action against any person interested in the estate to recover the original amount of the tax apportioned to the person, and any additional amounts based upon the assertion of deficiencies in the amount of the tax, and if the amounts sued for have become uncollectible at the time of the filing of the suit, the tax or the deficiencies shall be equitably apportioned among the other persons interested in the estate and subject to apportionment.

B. This action shall be instituted as an ordinary proceeding. If the action is for the recovery of the original amount of the tax apportioned, it shall be instituted within a reasonable time after the expiration of one year from the date of payment. If the action is for the recovery of a deficiency, it shall be instituted within a reasonable time after the expiration of one year from the date of payment of the deficiency. Unless the action has been timely instituted, the fiduciary or other person required to pay the tax or the deficiency shall not be entitled to reimbursement for any portion of the tax or deficiency which he may have paid or has been required to pay and shall, in addition, be liable to any person interested in the estate for any loss occasioned by the delay.

Added by Acts 2011, No. 346, § 2.

Editor's note. Section 3 of Acts 2011, No. 346, declares that this Act is "remedial, curative, and procedural and therefore it is to be applied retroactively as well as prospectively." The Act is, indeed, "remedial and curative" but it can hardly be considered "procedural." It is substantive legislation that may only be applied retroactively in the absence of constitutional constraints. Under the Louisiana Constitution, retroactive laws that tend to divest vested rights or impair the obligations of contracts violate the Louisiana Constitution. For discussion, see Yiannopoulos, Civil Law System p. 197 (2d ed. 1999); Personal Servitudes, Introduction (5th ed. 2011).

Cross References

C.C. arts. 1427, 1598.

§ 2437. Action by nonresident; reciprocity

A. A fiduciary or any other person required to pay the tax due who is domiciled or residing in a jurisdiction other than Louisiana, has a right of action for the proportionate amount (1) of the federal estate tax, (2) of an estate tax payable to another state, or (3) of a death duty due by the estate of a person deceased to another state, against any person interested in the estate domiciled or residing in Louisiana or who owns property in Louisiana subject to attachment or execution. This action shall be brought as an ordinary proceeding in the domicile of the defendant or, if not domiciled or residing in Louisiana, in the court of the parish where the property of the defendant is situated.

B. For the purposes of this action, the apportionment of the tax liability as determined by the court having jurisdiction of the administration of the estate of the deceased in the other state shall be prima facie correct.

C. With respect to the federal tax, this Section applies only if apportionment of the tax is authorized by congress. In all other respects, this Section applies only if the other state or jurisdiction affords a substantially similar remedy to a Louisiana resident.

Added by Acts 2011, No. 346, § 2.

Editor's note. Section 3 of Acts 2011, No. 346, declares that this Act is "remedial, curative, and procedural and therefore it is to be applied retroactively as well as prospectively." The Act is, indeed, "remedial and curative" but it can hardly be considered "procedural." It is substantive legislation that may only be applied retroactively in the absence of constitutional constraints. Under the Louisiana Constitution, retroactive laws that tend to divest vested rights or impair the obligations of contracts violate the Louisiana Constitution. For discussion, see Yiannopoulos, Civil Law System p. 197 (2d ed. 1999); Personal Servitudes, Introduction (5th ed. 2011).

Cross References

C.C. arts. 1427, 1598.

§ 2438. Application of provisions

R.S. 9:2431 through 2437 shall not apply to taxes due on account of the death of a person dying prior to January 1, 1961.

Added by Acts 2011, No. 346, § 2.

Editor's note. Section 3 of Acts 2011, No. 346, declares that this Act is "remedial, curative, and procedural and therefore it is to be applied retroactively as well as prospectively." The Act is, indeed, "remedial and curative" but it can hardly be considered "procedural." It is substantive legislation that may only be applied retroactively in the absence of constitutional constraints. Under the Louisiana Constitution, retroactive laws that tend to divest vested rights or impair the obligations of contracts violate the Louisiana Constitution. For discussion, see Yiannopoulos, Civil Law System p. 197 (2d ed. 1999); Personal Servitudes, Introduction (5th ed. 2011).

Cross References

C.C. arts. 1427, 1598.

§ 2439. Estate tax marital deduction; formula qualifying

A. In the event of the death of any person after December 31, 1981, if the testament contains a formula expressly providing that the spouse is to receive the maximum amount of property qualifying for the federal estate tax marital deduction allowable by federal law, the formula shall be construed as referring to the federal estate tax marital deduction as allowable by federal law as provided by Section 2056(a) of the Internal Revenue Code as amended by Section 403 of the Economic Recovery Tax Act of 1981.

B. The provisions of this Section shall not apply unless:

(1) The decedent dies after December 31, 1981.

(2) By reason of the death, property is acquired by the decedent's spouse under a formula provided in the testament.

(3) The formula provided in the testament was not amended or otherwise changed as permitted by the laws of this state at any time on or after September 12, 1981, and before the death of the decedent.

C. It is the intention of this Section to allow an increase in the amount of the federal estate tax marital deduction available to certain estates by reason of Section 2056 of the Internal Revenue Code to be conferred upon estates that would have been excluded from the benefits of Section 403 of the Economic Recovery Tax Act of 1981. To the extent necessary, this Section shall be retroactive to January 1, 1982.

D. Nothing contained in the provisions of this Section shall be construed to impinge upon the legitime of a forced heir or to divest the rights of a forced heir to the legitime.

Added by Acts 2011, No. 346, § 2.

Editor's note. Section 3 of Acts 2011, No. 346, declares that this Act is "remedial, curative, and procedural and therefore it is to be applied retroactively as well as prospectively." The Act is, indeed, "remedial and curative" but it can hardly be considered "procedural." It is substantive legislation that may only be applied retroactively in the absence of constitutional constraints. Under the Louisiana Constitution, retroactive laws that tend to divest vested rights or impair the obligations of contracts violate the Louisiana Constitution. For discussion, see Yiannopoulos, Civil Law System p. 197 (2d ed. 1999); Personal Servitudes, Introduction (5th ed. 2011).

Cross References

C.C. arts. 890, 2432.

PART III. MISCELLANEOUS PROVISIONS

§ 2440. Continued validity of previously executed testaments

A testament, testamentary provision, legacy, or other appointment executed prior to January 1, 1998, and valid under the law and jurisprudence prior to that date, when executed, is not invalidated by the passage of Acts 1997, No. 1421.

Added by Acts 1997, No. 1421, § 4, eff. July 1, 1999. Amended by Acts 2003, No. 74, § 1.

Editor's note. Section 2 of Acts 2003, No. 74 declares that: "The provisions of this Act are intended to be remedial and curative."

§ 2441. Duration of usufruct in previously executed testament

When a testament executed prior to June 18, 1996 leaves a usufruct to the surviving spouse without specifying its duration, the law in effect at the time the testament was executed shall govern the duration of the usufruct.

Added by Acts 1996, 1st Ex.Sess., No. 77, § 3.

Cross References

C.C. arts. 573, 890, 1499, 1514.

§§ 2442 to 2445. Repealed by Acts 1997, No. 1421, § 8, eff. July 1, 1999

Editor's note. R.S. 9:2442 through 2445 governed statutory wills. For current texts, see Louisiana Civil Code art. 1756 et seq.

§ 2446. Will information registration

The secretary of state shall establish a registry in which a testator, or his attorney, if authorized by the testator to do so, may register information regarding the execution of the testator's will. Such information shall be kept in strictest confidence until the death of the testator and then it shall be made available to any person who presents a death certificate, or affidavit of death and heirship, or other satisfactory evidence of the death of the testator. Information that may be received, preserved in confidence until death, and reported as indicated is limited to the name, social security or other individual identifying number established by law, address, date, place of birth of the testator, and the intended place of deposit or safekeeping of the instrument pending the death of the testator or the name and address of the attorney or other person having information regarding the place of deposit or safekeeping.

Added by Acts 1981, No. 222, § 1, eff. July 1, 1982.

Cross References

C.C. arts. 952, 1573.

§ 2447. Fees

Fees shall be paid to the secretary of state as provided in R.S. 49:222 for the following:

(1) For registering information regarding a will.

(2) For furnishing information regarding a will.

Added by Acts 1981, No. 222, § 1, eff. July 1, 1982. Amended by Acts 2008, No. 913, § 1.

§ 2448. Repealed by Acts 2012, No. 125, § 1

§ 2449. Individual retirement accounts; payment of benefits

A. Any benefits payable by reason of death from an individual retirement account established in accordance with the provisions of 26 U.S.C. 408, as amended, shall be paid as provided in the individual retirement account agreement to the designated beneficiary of the account. Such payment shall be a valid and sufficient release and discharge of the account holder for the payment or delivery so made and shall relieve the trustee, custodian, insurance company or other account fiduciary from all adverse claims thereto by a person claiming as a surviving or former spouse or a successor to such a spouse.

B. The provisions of this Section shall apply even when the decedent designates a beneficiary by last will and testament.

C. Repealed by Acts 2010, No. 175, § 6.

Added by Acts 1986, No. 600, § 1. Amended by Acts 1987, No. 131, § 1, eff. June 18, 1987; Acts 1988, No. 712, § 1; Acts 2011, No. 346, § 2.

Editor's note. "Of" changed to "or" on authority of the statutory revision authority of the Louisiana State Law Institute; see R.S. 6:766(5)(b), Acts 1986, No. 162, § 1.

Section 3 of Acts 2011, No. 346, declares that this Act is "remedial, curative, and procedural and therefore it is to be applied retroactively as well as prospectively." The Act is, indeed, "remedial and curative" but it can hardly be considered "procedural." It is substantive legislation that may be applied retroactively in the absence of constitutional constraints. Under the Louisiana Constitution, retroactive laws that tend to divest vested rights or impair the obligations of contracts violate the Louisiana Constitution. For discussion, see Yiannopoulos, Civil Law System p. 197 (2d ed. 1999); Personal Servitudes, Introduction (5th ed. 2011).

§ 2450. Succession representatives; liability for distributions

A succession representative shall not be liable to the judgment creditor of a successor for any distributions made to the successor, including a distribution of the proceeds of the sale of immovable property as to which the judgment creditor had a judicial mortgage, unless the judgment creditor seized the interest of the successor in the estate before the representative made the distribution.

Added by Acts 1995, No. 313, § 1.

CHAPTER 5. OF FORCED HEIRS

Section
2501. Repealed.
2502. Disinherison; retroactivity.
2503. Exercise of succession rights; remedial provisions.

§ 2501. Repealed by Acts 2001, No. 560, § 2, eff. June 22, 2001

§ 2502. Disinherison; retroactivity

A. If a person dies after June 22, 2001, leaving an instrument in the form of a testament that was executed prior to June 22, 2001, then a disinherison in that instrument that would be valid under the provisions of Civil Code Articles 1617 through 1626 shall be governed by the provisions of those Articles.

B. If the disinherison would not be valid under the provisions of Civil Code Articles 1617 through 1626, the disinherison shall be governed by the law in effect at the time of the execution of the instrument.

Added by Acts 2001, No. 573, § 2, eff. June 22, 2001.

Comments—2001

(a) This Section is new. It is based in part on the provisions of R.S. 9:2501 for testamentary intent regarding forced heirship.

(b) There are very few instances in which the issue addressed in this Section will be a problem. Disinherisons made in testaments executed prior to July 1, 1999, would have four more grounds for which the testator would have the ability to disinherit a forced heir then those that exist under the 2001 Revision of Civil Code Articles 1617 through 1626. This transitional rule would validate those disinherisons. The likelihood of there being a testament with one of those grounds is extraordinarily slim, since the grounds are very remote and there has never been a reported case for any one of them in nearly 200 years.

(c) The bigger problem, however is what law applies to testaments executed on or after July 1, 1999, and before the effective date of the new Act [Acts 2001, No. 573, eff. June 22, 2001]. There is considerable disagreement over the law in that time period. This transitional rule does not solve the problem, but it provides an opening to the court to conclude that, if the disinherison was valid when executed, it would be valid even though the person dies after the 2001 Revision of Civil Code Articles 1617–1626 is enacted and the new rules may be different. This Section does not propose to impose retroactively any rule that would apply to the interim period between July 1, 1999, and the date that the new law becomes effective to affect testators who die during that period of time.

Editor's note. For temporal conflicts of laws, see Civil Code arts. 870, 1611, as amended by Acts 2001, No. 560, § 1.

§ 2503. Exercise of succession rights; remedial provisions

A. Any alienation, lease, or encumbrance of immovable property made by a successor prior to the date that Civil Code Article 938, as amended and reenacted by Acts 2001, No. 556, becomes effective, that would be valid under the provisions of Civil Code Article 938, is valid.

B. An action to annul an alienation, lease, or encumbrance of immovable property owned by a decedent at his death made by a successor prior to the appointment of a succession representative must be brought within a peremptive period of one year from the effective date of this Section.

Added by Acts 2001, No. 556, § 2, eff. June 22, 2001.

Editor's note. R.S. 9:2503 was enacted by Acts 2001, § 2, as R.S. 9:2502. It has been redesignated as R.S. 9:2503 under the authority of the Louisiana State Law Institute. Acts 2001, No. 556, § 3, declares that "The provisions of this Act are remedial and interpretative and shall be applied retroactively."

CODE TITLE III—OBLIGATIONS IN GENERAL [BLANK]

CHAPTER 1. OF OBLIGATIONS DURING CERTAIN EMERGENCIES AND DISASTERS [BLANK]

Section
2551 to 2553. [Blank].
2554. [Blank].
2555 to 2565. [Blank].

Editor's note. Acts 2005, 1st Ex.Sess., No. 6, enacted Chapter 1, "Of Obligations During Certain Emergencies and Disasters", of Code Title III of Code Book III of Title 9 to be comprised of R.S. 9:2551 to 9:2565. Section 3 of the Act directed the Louisiana State Law Institute to redesignate and renumber the provisions sequentially beginning with R.S. 9:5821 as Part IV, "Suspension of Extension of Prescription, Peremption, and other legal deadlines during Hurricanes Katrina and Rita", of Code Title XXIV of Title 9.

For text of the provisions, see now R.S. 9:5821 et seq.

§§ 2551 to 2553. [Blank]

§ 2554. [Blank]

§§ 2555 to 2565. [Blank]

CODE TITLE IV—CONVENTIONAL OBLIGATIONS OR CONTRACTS

CHAPTER 1. LOUISIANA UNIFORM ELECTRONIC TRANSACTIONS ACT

Section
2601. Short title.
2602. Definitions.
2603. Scope.
2603.1. Electronic applications for all warrants; signatures; electronic judicial records.
2604. Prospective application; exemption from preemption.
2605. Use of electronic records and electronic signatures; variation by agreement.
2606. Construction and application.
2607. Legal recognition of electronic records, electronic signatures, and electronic contracts.
2608. Provision of information in writing; presentation of records.
2609. Attribution and effect of electronic record and electronic signature.
2610. Effect of change or error.
2611. Notarization and acknowledgment.
2612. Retention of electronic records; originals.
2613. Admissibility in evidence.
2614. Automated transaction.
2615. Time and place of sending and receipt.
2616. Transferable records.
2617. Creation and retention of electronic records and conversion of written records by governmental agencies in this state.
2618. Acceptance and distribution of electronic records by governmental agencies in this state.
2619. Interoperability.
2620. Severability clause.

Section
2621. Certification of electronic records.
2622 to 2674. Repealed.

§ 2601. Short title

This Chapter may be cited as the "Louisiana Uniform Electronic Transactions Act".

Added by Acts 2001, No. 244, § 1, eff. July 1, 2001.

§ 2602. Definitions

As used in this Chapter, unless the context otherwise requires:

(1) "Agreement" means the bargain of the parties in fact, as found in their language or inferred from other circumstances and from rules, regulations, and procedures given the effect of agreements under laws otherwise applicable to a particular transaction.

(2) "Automated transaction" means a transaction conducted or performed, in whole or in part, by electronic means or electronic records, in which the acts or records of one or both parties are not reviewed by an individual in the ordinary course of forming a contract, performing under an existing contract, or fulfilling an obligation required by the transaction.

(3) "Computer program" means a set of statements or instructions to be used directly or indirectly in an information processing system in order to bring about a certain result.

(4) "Contract" means the total legal obligation resulting from the agreement of the parties as affected by this Chapter and other applicable law.

(5) "Electronic" means relating to technology having electrical, digital, magnetic, wireless, optical, electromagnetic, or similar capabilities.

(6) "Electronic agent" means a computer program or an electronic or other automated means used independently to initiate an action or respond to electronic records or performances in whole or in part without review or action by an individual.

(7) "Electronic record" means a record created, generated, sent, communicated, received, or stored by electronic means.

(8) "Electronic signature" means an electronic sound, symbol, or process attached to or logically associated with a record and executed or adopted by a person with the intent to sign the record.

(9) "Governmental agency" means an executive, legislative, or judicial agency, department, board, commission, authority, institution, unit, or instrumentality of the federal government or of a state or of a county or parish, municipality, or other political subdivision of a state.

(10) "Information" includes data, text, images, sounds, codes, computer programs, software, and databases, or the like.

(11) "Information processing system" means an electronic system for creating, generating, sending, receiving, storing, displaying, or processing information.

(12) "Person" means an individual, corporation, business trust, estate, trust, partnership, limited liability company, association, joint venture, governmental agency, public corporation, or any other legal or commercial entity.

(13) "Record" means information that is inscribed on a tangible medium or that is stored in an electronic or other medium and is retrievable in perceivable form.

(14) "Security procedure" means a procedure employed for the purpose of verifying that an electronic signature, record, or performance is that of a specific person or for detecting changes or errors in the information in an electronic record. The term includes a procedure that requires the use of algorithms or other codes, identifying words or numbers, encryption, or callback or other acknowledgment procedures.

(15) "State" means this state or another state of the United States, the District of Columbia, Puerto Rico, the United States Virgin Islands, or any territory or insular possession subject to the jurisdiction of the United States. The term includes an Indian tribe or band, or Alaskan native village, which is recognized by federal law or formally acknowledged by a state.

(16) "Transaction" means an action or set of actions occurring between two or more persons relating to the conduct of business, commercial, or governmental affairs.

Added by Acts 2001, No. 244, § 1, eff. July 1, 2001.

Comments—2001

1. "Agreement."

(a) Whether the parties have reached an agreement is determined by their express language and all surrounding circumstances. Although the definition of agreement in this Chapter does not make specific reference to usage of trade and other party conduct, this definition is not intended to affect the construction of the parties' agreement under the substantive law applicable to a particular transaction. Where that law takes account of usage and conduct in informing the terms of the parties' agreement, the usage or conduct would be relevant as "other circumstances" included in the definition under this Chapter.

(b) When the law that is applicable to a given transaction provides that system rules and the like constitute part of the agreement of the parties, these rules will have the same effect in determining the parties agreement under this Chapter. For example, La. R.S. 10:4–103 (2001) provides that Federal Reserve regulations and operating circulars and clearinghouse rules have the effect of agreements. These agreements, by law, properly would be included in the definition of agreement in this Chapter.

(c) The parties' agreement is relevant in determining whether the provisions of this Chapter have been varied by agreement. In addition, the parties' agreement may establish the parameters of the parties' use of electronic records and signatures, security procedures and similar aspects of the transaction. See e.g., Model Trading Partner Agreement, 45 Business Lawyer Supp. Issue (June 1990). *See also* Section 2605B of this Chapter and the comments to that Section.

2. "Automated Transaction."

(a) An automated transaction is a transaction performed or conducted by electronic means in which machines are used without human intervention to form agreements and perform obligations under existing agreements. This broad coverage is necessary because of the diversity of transactions to which this Chapter may apply.

(b) As with electronic agents, this definition addresses the circumstance where electronic records may result in action or performance by a party although no human review of the electronic records is anticipated. Section 2614 of this Chapter provides specific rules to assure that where one or both parties do not review the electronic records, the resulting agreement will still be effective.

(c) The critical element in this definition is the lack of a human actor on one or both sides of a transaction. For example, if a person ordered books from an internet website, the transaction would be an automated transaction because the seller took and confirmed the order by its computers. Similarly, if a manufacturer and a supplier do business through Electronic Data Interchange, the manufacturer's computer, upon receiving information within certain pre-programmed parameters, will send an electronic order to the supplier's computer. If the supplier's computer confirms the order and processes the shipment because the order falls within pre-programmed parameters in the supplier's computer, this would be a fully automated transaction. If, instead, the supplier relies on a human employee to review, accept, and process the manufacturer's order, then only the manufacturer's side of the transaction would be automated. In either case, the entire transaction falls within this definition.

3. "Computer program."

This definition refers to the functional and operating aspects of an electronic, digital system. It relates to operating instructions used in an electronic system such as an electronic agent. (See definition of "Electronic Agent.")

4. "Electronic."

(a) The basic nature of most current technologies and the need for a recognized, single term warrants the use of "electronic" as the defined term. The definition is intended to assure that this Chapter will be applied broadly as new technologies develop. The term must be construed broadly in light of developing technologies in order to fulfill the purpose of this Chapter to validate commercial transactions regardless of the medium used by the parties. Current legal requirements for "writings" can be satisfied by almost any tangible media, whether paper, other fibers, or even stone. The purpose and applicability of this Chapter covers intangible media which are technologically capable of storing, transmitting and reproducing information in human perceivable form, but which lack the tangible aspect of paper.

(b) While not all technologies listed are technically "electronic" in nature, the term "electronic" is the most descriptive term available to describe the majority of current technologies. For example, the development of biological and chemical processes for communication and storage of data, while not specifically mentioned in the definition, are included within the technical definition because these processes operate on electromagnetic impulses. However, whether a particular technology may be characterized as technically "electronic," i.e., operates on electromagnetic impulses, should not be determinative of whether records and signatures created, used and stored by means of a particular technology are covered by this Chapter. This Chapter is intended to apply to all records and signatures created, used and stored by any medium which permits the information to be retrieved in perceivable form.

5. "Electronic agent."

(a) This definition establishes that an electronic agent is a machine. As the term is used in this Chapter, it is limited to the function of a tool. The effect on the party using the agent is addressed in the operative provisions of this Chapter (e.g., Section 2614).

(b) An electronic agent, such as a computer program or other automated means employed by a person, is a tool of that person. As a general rule, the employer of a tool is responsible for the results obtained by the use of that tool since the tool has no independent volition of its own. However, an electronic agent, by definition, is capable within the parameters of its programming, of initiating, responding or interacting with other parties or their electronic agents once it has been activated by a party, without further attention of that party.

(c) While this Chapter presupposes that an electronic agent is capable of performing only within the technical strictures of its preset programming, it is conceivable that in the future, electronic agents may be created with the ability to act autonomously, and not just automatically. That is, through developments in artificial intelligence, a computer may be able to "learn through experience, modify the instructions in their own programs, and even devise new instructions." If these developments occur, the courts may construe the definition of electronic agent accordingly, to recognize such new capabilities.

6. "Electronic record."

(a) An electronic record is a subset of the broader defined term "record." It is any record created, used or stored in a medium other than paper. The defined term is also used in this Chapter as a limiting definition in those provisions in which it is used.

(b) Information processing systems, computer equipment and programs, electronic data interchange, electronic mail, voice mail, facsimile, telex, telecopying, scanning, and similar technologies all qualify as electronic under this Chapter. Accordingly information stored on a computer hard drive or floppy disc, facsimiles, voice mail messages, messages on a telephone answering machine, audio and video tape recordings, among other records, all would be electronic records under this Chapter.

7. "Electronic signature."

(a) The definition requires that the signer execute or adopt the sound, symbol, or process with the intent to sign the record. The act of applying a sound, symbol or process to an electronic record could have differing meanings and effects. The consequence of the act and the effect of the act as a signature are determined under other applicable law. However, the essential attribute of a signature involves applying a sound, symbol or process with an intent to do a legally significant act. It is that intention that is understood in the law as a part of the word "sign", without the need for a definition.

(b) Another important aspect of this definition lies in the necessity that the electronic signature be linked or logically associated with the record. In the paper world, it is assumed that the symbol adopted by a party is attached to or located somewhere in the same paper that is intended to be authenticated, e.g., an allonge firmly attached to a promissory note, or the classic signature at the end of a long contract. These tangible manifestations do not exist in the electronic environment, and accordingly, this definition expressly provides that the symbol must in some way be linked to, or connected with, the electronic record being signed. This linkage is consistent with the regulations promulgated by the Food and Drug Administration. 21 CFR Part 11 (March 20, 1997).

(c) Whether any particular record is "signed" is a question of fact. Proof of that fact must be made under other applicable law. This Chapter simply assures that the signature may be accomplished through electronic means. No specific technology need be used to create a valid signature. One's voice on an answering machine may suffice if the requisite intention is present. Similarly, including one's name as part of an electronic mail communication also may suffice, as may the firm name on a facsimile. A digital signature using public key encryption technology would qualify as an electronic signature, as would the mere inclusion of one's name as a part of an e-mail message—so long as in each case the signer executed or adopted the symbol with the intent to sign. It also may be shown that the requisite intent was not present and accordingly the symbol, sound or process did not amount to a signature. In any case the critical element is the intention to execute or adopt the sound or symbol or process for the purpose of signing the related record.

(d) This definition also includes as an electronic signature the standard webpage click through process if the requisite intent is present. However, the adoption of the process would generally convey the implicit intent to do a legally significant act, the hallmark of a signature.

(e) This Chapter establishes, to the greatest extent possible, the equivalency of electronic signatures and manual signatures. Therefore the term "signature" has been used to connote and convey that equivalency. The purpose is to overcome unwarranted biases against electronic methods of signing and authenticating records. The term "authentication," used in other laws, often has a narrower meaning and purpose than an electronic signature as used in this Chapter. However, an authentication under any of those other laws constitutes an electronic signature under this Chapter.

(f) The precise effect of an electronic signature will be determined based on the surrounding circumstances. See § 2609.

8. "Information processing system."

The term includes computers and other information systems. It is principally used in Section 2615 in connection with the sending and receiving of information, and in that context, the principle aspect of an information processing system is that the information enter a system from which a person can access the information.

9. "Record."

This is a standard definition designed to embrace all means of communicating or storing information except human memory. It includes any method for storing or communicating information, including "writings." A record need not be indestructible or permanent, but the term does not include oral or other communications which are not stored or preserved by some means. Information that has not been retained other than through human memory does not qualify as a record. As in the case of the terms "writing" or "written," the term "record" does not establish the purposes, permitted uses or legal effect which a record may have under any particular provision of substantive law.

10. "Security procedure."

(a) A security procedure may be applied to verify an electronic signature, verify the identity of the sender, or assure the informational integrity of an electronic record. The definition does not identify any particular technology. This permits the use of procedures which the parties select or which are established by law. It permits the greatest flexibility among the parties and allows for future technological development.

(b) The definition in this Chapter is broad and is used to illustrate one way of establishing attribution or content integrity of an electronic record or signature. The use of a security procedure is not accorded operative legal effect, through the use of presumptions or otherwise, by this Chapter. In this Chapter, the use of security procedures is simply one method for proving the source or content of an electronic record or signature.

(c) A security procedure may be technologically very sophisticated. At the other extreme the security procedure may be as simple as a telephone call to confirm the identity of the sender through another channel of communication. It may include the use of a mother's maiden name or a personal identification number. Each of these examples is a method for confirming the identity of a person or accuracy of a message.

11. "Transaction."

The definition has been limited to actions between people taken in the context of business, commercial or governmental activities. The term includes all interactions between people for business, commercial, including specifically consumer, or governmental purposes. However, the term does not include unilateral or non-transactional actions. As such it provides a structural limitation on the scope of the Chapter as stated in the next Section. It is essential that the term "commerce and business" be understood and construed broadly to include commercial and business transactions involving individuals who may qualify as "consumers" under other applicable law.

§ 2603. Scope

A. Except as otherwise provided in Subsection B of this Section, this Chapter applies to electronic records and electronic signatures relating to a transaction.

B. This Chapter shall not apply to:

(1) A transaction to the extent it is governed by a law governing the creation and execution of wills, codicils, or testamentary trusts.

(2) A transaction to the extent it is governed by the provisions of Title 10 of the Louisiana Revised Statutes of 1950, other than R.S. 10:1–107.

(3) (Reserved).

(4)(a) A law governing adoption, divorce, or other matters of family law.

(b) Court orders or notices, or official court documents, including briefs, pleadings, and other writings, required to be executed in connection with court proceedings, except as otherwise provided by law.

(c) Any notice of:

(i) The cancellation or termination of utility services, including water, heat, and power.

(ii) Default, acceleration, repossession, foreclosure, or eviction, or the right to cure, under a credit agreement secured by, or a rental agreement for, a primary residence of an individual.

(iii) The cancellation or termination of health insurance or benefits or life insurance benefits, excluding annuities.

(iv) Recall of a product, or material failure of a product, that risks endangering health or safety.

(d) Any document required to accompany any transportation or handling of hazardous materials, pesticides, or other toxic or dangerous materials.

(e) Publications required by law to be published in the official journals provided for in Chapter 2, 4, or 5 of Title 43 of the Louisiana Revised Statutes of 1950.

C. This Chapter applies to an electronic record or electronic signature otherwise excluded from the application of this Chapter under Subsection B of this Section to the extent it is governed by a law other than those specified by Subsection B of this Section.

D. A transaction subject to this Chapter is also subject to other applicable substantive law.

Added by Acts 2001, No. 244, § 1, eff. July 1, 2001.

Comments—2001

(a) The scope of this Chapter is inherently limited by the fact that it only applies to transactions related to business, commercial, including consumer, and governmental matters. Consequently, transactions with no relation to business, commercial or governmental transactions are not subject to this Chapter. Unilaterally generated electronic records and signatures which are not part of a transaction also are not covered by this Chapter. See § 2602, Comment 11.

(b) This Chapter affects the medium in which information, records and signatures may be presented and retained under current legal requirements. While this Chapter covers all electronic records and signatures which are used in a business, commercial or governmental transaction, the operative provisions of the Chapter relate to requirements for writings and signatures under other laws. Accordingly, the exclusions in Subsection B of this Section focus on those legal rules imposing certain writing and signature requirements which are not affected by this Chapter.

(c) The exclusions listed in Subsection B of this Section provide certainty as to which laws are not affected by this Chapter. This Section provides that transactions subject to specific laws are unaffected by this Chapter and leaves the balance subject to this Chapter.

(d) Paragraph (1) of Subsection B of this Section excludes wills, codicils and testamentary trusts. This exclusion is largely salutary given the unilateral context in which these records are generally created and the unlikely use of these records in a transaction as defined in this Chapter (i.e., actions taken by two or more persons in the context of business, commercial or governmental affairs). Paragraph (2) excludes all of Title 10 of the Louisiana Revised Statutes of 1950, other than R.S. 10:1–107. This Chapter does not apply to these provisions, whether in "current" or "revised" form.

Chapters 3, 4 and 4A of Title 10 of the Louisiana Revised Statutes of 1950 impact payment systems and have specifically been removed from the coverage of this Chapter. The check collection and electronic fund transfer systems governed by Chapters 3, 4 and 4A of Title 10 of the Louisiana Revised Statutes of 1950 involve systems and relationships involving numerous parties beyond the parties to the underlying contract. The impact of validating electronic media in these systems involves considerations beyond the scope of this Chapter. Chapters 5, 8 and 9 of Title 10 of the Louisiana Revised Statutes of 1950 have been excluded from this Chapter because the recent revision of these parts of Title 10 included significant consideration of electronic practices.

(e) The very limited application of this Chapter to Transferable Records in § 2616 does not affect payment systems, and Section 2616 is designed to apply to a transaction only through express agreement of the parties. The exclusion of Chapters 3 and 4 of Title 10 of the Louisiana Revised Statutes of 1950 does not affect this Chapter's coverage of transferable records. Section 2616 of this Chapter is designed to allow for the development of systems which will provide "control" as defined in that Section. This control is necessary as a substitute for the concept of possession which undergirds negotiable instrument law.

The provisions in § 2616 of this Chapter operate as free-standing rules, and those provisions establish the rights of parties using transferable records under this Chapter. The references in § 2616 of this Chapter to La. Rev. Stat. 10:3–302, La. Rev. Stat. 10:7–501, and La. Rev. Stat. 10:9–308 (Revised as La. Rev. Stat. 10:9–330(d)) are designed to incorporate the substance of those provisions into this Chapter for the limited purposes set out in § 2616 of this Chapter. Accordingly, an electronic record which is also a transferable record, would not be used for purposes of a transaction governed by La. Rev. Stat. 10:3–101, et seq., 10:4–101 et seq., and 10:9–101 et seq. but would be an electronic record used for purposes of a transaction governed by § 2616 of this Chapter.

(f) An electronic record or electronic signature may be used for purposes of more than one legal requirement, or may be covered by more than one law. Consequently, it is important to make clear, despite any apparent redundancy, in Subsection C of this Section that an electronic record used for purposes of a law which is not affected by this Chapter under Subsection B of this Section may nonetheless be used and validated for purposes of other laws not excluded by Subsection B. For example, this Chapter does not apply to an electronic record of a check when used for purposes of a transaction governed by La. Rev. Stat. 10:3–101 et seq. Therefore this Chapter does not validate electronic checks. However, for purposes of check retention statutes, the same electronic record of the check is covered by this Chapter, so that the retention of an electronic image or record of a check will satisfy the retention statutes as long as the requirements of § 2612 of this Chapter are fulfilled.

(g) Subsection B(4) of this Section lists the four areas of the law specifically excluded from this Chapter. Subsection B(4)(a) excludes all matters concerning family law matters. Subsection B(4)(b) excludes all court documents and filings from this Chapter, but specifically reserves the possibility that electronic filings and court documents may be provided for in the future by the courts. Subsection B(4)(c) & (d) mirror the consumer protection provisions set forth in the Federal Electronic Signatures in Global and National Commerce Act. The provisions of Subsection B(4)(c) & (d) are applicable under the doctrine of federal preemption, and therefore do not create any new exclusions than already exist. Subsection B(4)(e) of this Section exempts from this Chapter publications required by law to be published in the official journals provided for in Chapter 2, 4, or 5 of Title 43 of the Louisiana Revised Statutes of 1950.

§ 2603.1. Electronic applications for all warrants; signatures; electronic judicial records

A. An application for any warrant or signature utilized by the judicial branch of state government shall not be denied legal effect or enforceability solely because it is in electronic form. Any such application, signature or record in electronic form shall have the full effect of law.

B. If a law requires the application for any warrant to be in writing, an electronic record shall satisfy the law.

C. If a law requires a signature, an electronic signature satisfies the law.

D. Any application used to attach a digital signature to any warrant or affidavit must have security procedures in place that insure the authenticity of the digital signature. The application must also be able to keep an electronic record of the warrant or affidavit, including the time and date of when the signature was attached. The application must also include encryption measures to ensure secure access of the application.

E. Unless otherwise agreed to by a sender of a warrant application and the judiciary, an electronic record is received when:

(1) The record enters an information-processing system that the local court rules have designated and approved for the purpose of receiving electronic applications for warrants and from which the recipient is able to retrieve the electronic record.

(2) It is in a form capable of being processed by the system.

F. In any instance where an affidavit is submitted to a judge or magistrate electronically, the electronic signature of the affiant shall satisfy the constitutional requirement that the testimony of the affiant be made under oath, provided that such signature is made under penalty of perjury and in compliance with Subsection D of this Section. If the requirements of Subsection D of this Section are met, it shall not be necessary for the oath to be made orally for the affidavit to have legal effect.

Added by Acts 2009, No. 401, § 1. Amended by Acts 2010, No. 58, § 1.

Cross References

C.C. art. 1837 et seq.

§ 2604. Prospective application; exemption from preemption

A. This Chapter applies to any electronic record or electronic signature created, generated, sent, communicated, received, or stored on or after July 1, 2001.

B. This Chapter is intended and shall be construed to constitute an enactment or adoption of the Uniform Electronic Transactions Act as approved and recommended for enactment in all states by the National Conference of Commissioners on Uniform State Laws in 1999. If a court of competent jurisdiction finds that any provision of this Chapter is inconsistent with 15 U.S.C. 7002(a)(1) (the Electronic Signatures in Global and National Commerce Act), then any inconsistent provision is intended to comply with 15 U.S.C. 7002(a)(2)(A) and (B).

Added by Acts 2001, No. 244, § 1, eff. July 1, 2001.

Comment—2001

This Section makes clear that the Chapter only applies to validate electronic records and signatures which arise subsequent to the effective date of this Chapter of July 1, 2001. Whether electronic records and electronic signatures arising before the effective date of this Chapter are valid is left to other law.

§ 2605. Use of electronic records and electronic signatures; variation by agreement

A. This Chapter does not require a record or signature to be created, generated, sent, communicated, received, stored, or otherwise processed or used by electronic means or in electronic form.

B. (1) This Chapter applies only to transactions between parties, each of which has agreed to conduct transactions by electronic means.

(2) The context and surrounding circumstances, including the conduct of the parties, shall determine whether the parties have agreed to conduct a transaction by electronic means.

C. (1) A party that agrees to conduct a transaction by electronic means may refuse to conduct other transactions by electronic means.

(2) The right granted by this Subsection may not be waived by agreement.

D. (1) Except as otherwise provided in this Chapter, the effect of any of its provisions may be varied by agreement.

(2) The presence in provisions of this Chapter of the words "unless otherwise agreed", or words of similar import, does not imply that the effect of other provisions may not be varied by agreement.

E. Whether an electronic record or electronic signature has legal consequences is determined by this Chapter and other applicable law.

Added by Acts 2001, No. 244, § 1, eff. July 1, 2001.

Comments—2001

(a) This Section limits the applicability of this Chapter to transactions which parties have agreed to conduct electronically. Broad interpretation of the term agreement is necessary to assure that this Chapter has the widest possible application consistent with its purpose of removing barriers to electronic commerce.

(b) This Section makes clear that this Chapter is intended to facilitate the use of electronic means, but does not require the use of electronic records and signatures. This fundamental principle is set forth in Subsection (A) and elaborated by Subsections (B) and (C), which require an intention to conduct transactions electronically and preserve the right of a party to refuse to use electronics in any subsequent transaction.

(c) The paradigm of this Chapter is two willing parties doing transactions electronically. It is therefore appropriate that the Chapter is voluntary and preserves the greatest possible party autonomy to refuse electronic transactions. The requirement that party agreement be found from all the surrounding circumstances is a limitation on the scope of this Chapter.

(d) If this Chapter is to serve to facilitate electronic transactions, it must be applicable under circumstances not rising to a full fledged contract to use electronics. While absolute certainty can be accomplished by obtaining an explicit contract before relying on electronic transactions, such an explicit contract should not be necessary before one may feel safe in conducting transactions electronically. In fact, such a requirement would itself be an unreasonable barrier to electronic commerce, at odds with the fundamental purpose of this Chapter. Accordingly, the requisite agreement, express or implied, must be determined from all available circumstances and evidence.

(e) Subsection B of this Section provides that the Chapter applies to transactions in which the parties have agreed to conduct the transaction electronically. It is essential that the parties' actions and words be broadly construed to determine whether the requisite agreement exists. Accordingly, the Act expressly provides that the party's agreement is to be found from all circumstances, including the parties' conduct. The critical element is the intent of a party to conduct a transaction electronically. Once that intent is established, this Chapter applies.

Examples of circumstances from which it may be found that parties have reached an agreement to conduct transactions electronically include the following:

A. A manufacturer and a supplier enter into a trading partner agreement setting forth the terms, conditions and methods for the conduct of future business between them that will be conducted electronically.

B. An individual gives out his business card with his business e-mail address during business negotiations. It may be reasonable, under the circumstances, for a recipient of the card to infer that the individual has agreed to communicate electronically for the purposes of the business that was being discussed. However, in the absence of additional facts, it would not necessarily be reasonable to infer an agreement to communicate electronically for purposes outside the scope of the business indicated by use of the business card.

C. If two people are at a meeting and one tells the other to send an e-mail to confirm a transaction—the requisite agreement under Subsection B of this Section would exist.

(f) Just as circumstances may indicate the existence of agreement, express or implied, from the surrounding circumstances, circumstances may also demonstrate the absence of a true agreement. For example:

If a manufacturer were to issue a recall of one of its products by its Internet website, it would not be able to rely on this Chapter to validate that notice in the case of a person who never logged on to the website, or had no ability to do so, notwithstanding a clause in a paper purchase agreement by which the purchaser of the product agreed to receive notices in this manner.

(g) Subsection C of this Section clarifies the ability of a party to refuse to conduct a transaction electronically, even if the person has conducted transactions electronically in the past. The effectiveness of a party's refusal to conduct a transaction electronically will be determined under other applicable law in light of all surrounding circumstances. These circumstances include an assessment of the transaction involved.

A party's right to decline to act electronically under a specific agreement, on the ground that each action under that agreement amounts to a separate "transaction," must be considered in light of the purpose of the agreement and the action to be taken electronically. For example, under an agreement for the purchase of goods, the giving and receipt of notices electronically, as provided in the agreement, should not be viewed as discreet transactions. Allowing one party to require a change of medium in the middle of the transaction evidenced by that agreement is not the purpose of Subsection C of this Section. Subsection C of this Section is intended to preserve the party's right to conduct the next purchase in a non-electronic medium.

(h) Subsection E of this Section is an essential provision in the overall scheme of this Chapter. While this Chapter validates and effectuates electronic records and electronic signatures, the legal effect of these records and signatures is left to existing substantive law outside this Chapter except in very narrow circumstances. See, e.g., § 2616. Even when this Chapter operates to validate records and signatures in an electronic medium, it expressly preserves the substantive rules of other law applicable to the records. See, e.g., § 2611.

For example, beyond validation of records, signatures and contracts based on the medium used, Subsections A and B of this Section should not be interpreted as establishing the legal effectiveness of any given record, signature or contract. Where a rule of law requires that the record contain minimum substantive content, the legal effect of such a record will depend on whether the record meets the substantive requirements of other applicable law.

Section 2608 expressly preserves a number of legal requirements in currently existing law relating to the presentation of information in writing. Although this Chapter now would allow this information to be presented in an electronic record, § 2608 provides that the other substantive requirements of law must be satisfied in the electronic medium as well.

§ 2606. Construction and application

This Chapter shall be construed and applied as follows:

(1) To facilitate electronic transactions consistent with other applicable law.

(2) To be consistent with reasonable practices concerning electronic transactions and with the continued expansion of those practices.

(3) To effectuate its general purpose to make uniform the law with respect to the subject of this Chapter among states enacting it.

Added by Acts 2001, No. 244, § 1, eff. July 1, 2001.

Comments—2001

(a) The purposes and policies of this Chapter are to: facilitate and promote commerce and governmental transactions by validating and authorizing the use of electronic records and electronic signatures; eliminate barriers to electronic commerce and governmental transactions resulting from uncertainties relating to writing and signature requirements; simplify, clarify and modernize the law governing commerce and governmental transactions through the use of electronic means; permit the continued expansion of commercial and governmental electronic practices through custom, usage and agreement of the parties; promote uniformity of the law among the States (and worldwide) relating to the use of electronic and similar technological means of effecting and performing commercial and governmental transactions; promote public confidence in the validity, integrity and reliability of electronic commerce and governmental transactions; and, promote the development of the legal and business infrastructure necessary to implement electronic commerce and governmental transactions.

(b) This Chapter has been drafted to permit flexible application consistent with its purpose to validate electronic transactions. The provisions of this Chapter validating and effectuating the employment of electronic media allow the courts to apply them to new and unforeseen technologies and practices. As time progresses, it is anticipated that what is new and unforeseen today will be commonplace tomorrow. Accordingly, this legislation is intended to set a framework for the validation of media which may be developed in the future and which demonstrate the same qualities as the electronic media contemplated and validated under this Chapter.

§ 2607. Legal recognition of electronic records, electronic signatures, and electronic contracts

A. A record or signature may not be denied legal effect or enforceability solely because it is in electronic form.

B. A contract may not be denied legal effect or enforceability solely because an electronic record was used in its formation.

C. If a law requires a record to be in writing, an electronic record satisfies the law.

D. If a law requires a signature, an electronic signature satisfies the law.

Added by Acts 2001, No. 244, § 1, eff. July 1, 2001.

Comments—2001

(a) This Section sets forth the fundamental premise of this Chapter: namely, that the medium in which a record, signature, or agreement is created, presented or retained does not affect its legal significance. Subsections A and B of this Section are designed to eliminate the single element of medium as a reason to deny effect or enforceability to a record, signature, or agreement. The fact that the information is set forth in an electronic, as opposed to paper, record is irrelevant.

(b) Subsections C and D of this Section provide the positive assertion that electronic records and signatures satisfy legal requirements for writings and signatures. The provisions are limited to the requirements in laws other than found in this Chapter that a record be in writing or be signed. This Section does not address the requirements imposed by the other law in addition to requirements for writings and signatures.

Subsections C and D of this Section are particularized applications of Subsection A of this Section. The purpose of these Subsections is to validate and effectuate electronic records and signatures as the equivalent of writings, subject to all of the rules applicable to the efficacy of a writing, except as such other rules are modified by the more specific provisions of this Chapter.

(c) Section 2608 addresses additional requirements imposed by other law which may affect the legal effect or enforceability of an electronic record in a particular case. For example, in Subsection A of § 2608 the legal requirement addressed is *the provision of information* in writing. The section then sets forth the standards to be applied to determine whether the provision of information by an electronic record is the equivalent of the provision of information in writing. The requirements in § 2608 are in addition to the bare validation that occurs under this section.

(d) Under the substantive law applicable to a particular transaction within this Chapter, the legal effect of an electronic record may be separate from the issue of whether the record contains a signature. For example, where notice must be given as part of a contractual obligation, the effectiveness of the notice will turn on whether the party provided the notice regardless of whether the notice was signed (See § 2615). An electronic record attributed to a party under § 2609 and complying with the requirements of § 2615 would suffice in that case, notwithstanding that it may not contain an electronic signature.

§ 2608. Provision of information in writing; presentation of records

A. (1) If parties have agreed to conduct a transaction by electronic means and a law requires a person to provide, send, or deliver information in writing to another person, the requirement is satisfied if the information is provided, sent, or delivered in an electronic record capable of retention by the recipient at the time of receipt.

(2) An electronic record is not capable of retention by the recipient if the sender or its information processing system

inhibits the ability of the recipient to print or store the electronic record.

B. If a law, other than this Chapter, requires a record to be posted or displayed in a certain manner, to be sent, communicated, or transmitted by a specified method, or to contain information that is formatted in a certain manner, the following rules apply:

(1) The record must be posted or displayed in the manner specified in the other law.

(2) Except as otherwise provided in Paragraph (D)(2) of this Section, the record must be sent, communicated, or transmitted by the method specified in the other law.

(3) The record must contain the information formatted in the manner specified in the other law.

C. If a sender inhibits the ability of a recipient to store or print an electronic record, the electronic record is not enforceable against the recipient.

D. The requirements of this Section may not be varied by agreement, but:

(1) To the extent a law other than this Chapter requires information to be provided, sent, or delivered in writing but permits that requirement to be varied by agreement, the requirement under Subsection A of this Section that the information be in the form of an electronic record capable of retention may also be varied by agreement.

(2) A requirement under a law other than this Chapter to send, communicate, or transmit a record by first class mail, postage prepaid, or by regular United States mail, may be varied by agreement to the extent permitted by the other law.

Added by Acts 2001, No. 244, § 1, eff. July 1, 2001.

Comments—2001

(a) This Section is a savings provision designed to assure, consistent with the fundamental purpose of this Chapter, that otherwise applicable substantive law will not be overridden by this Chapter. The Section makes clear that while the pen and ink provisions of the other law may be satisfied electronically, nothing in this Chapter vitiates the other requirements of such laws. The section addresses a number of issues related to disclosures and notice provisions in other laws.

(b) This Section is independent of the prior section. Section 2607 refers to legal requirements for a writing. This section refers to legal requirements for the provision of information in writing or relating to the method or manner of presentation or delivery of information. This Section addresses more specific legal requirements of other laws, provides standards for satisfying the more particular legal requirements, and defers to other law for satisfaction of requirements under those laws.

(c) Under Subsection A of this Section, to meet a requirement of other law that information be provided in writing, the recipient of an electronic record of the information must be able to get to the electronic record and read it, and must have the ability to get back to the information in some way at a later date. Accordingly, the section requires that the electronic record be capable of retention for later review.

This Section specifically provides that any inhibition on retention imposed by the sender or the sender's system will preclude satisfaction of this section. Use of technological means now existing or later developed which prevents the recipient from retaining a copy the information would result in a determination that the information has not been provided as required under Subsection A of this Section.

The policies underlying laws requiring the provision of information in writing warrant the imposition of an additional burden on the sender to make the information available in a manner which will permit subsequent reference. A difficulty does exist for senders of information because of the disparate systems of their recipients and the capabilities of those systems. However, to satisfy the *legal requirement* of other law to make information available, the sender must assure that the recipient receives and can retain the information. However, it is left for the courts to determine whether the sender has complied with this Subsection if evidence demonstrates that it is something peculiar the recipient's system which precludes subsequent reference to the information.

(d) Subsection B of this Section is a savings provision for laws which provide for the means of delivering or displaying information and which are not affected by the Chapter. For example, if a law requires delivery of notice by first class United States mail, that means of delivery would not be affected by this Chapter. The information to be delivered may be provided in electronic form, but the particular means of delivery must still be by the United States postal service. Display, delivery and formatting requirements will continue to be applicable to electronic records and signatures. If those legal requirements can be satisfied in an electronic medium, this Chapter will validate the use of the medium, leaving to the other applicable law the question of whether the particular electronic record meets the other legal requirements. If a law requires that particular records be delivered together, or attached to other records, this Chapter does not preclude the delivery of the records together in an electronic communication, so long as the records are connected or associated with each other in a way determined to satisfy the other law.

(e) Subsection C of this Section provides incentives for senders of information to use systems which will not inhibit the other party from retaining the information. However, there are circumstances when a party providing certain information may wish to inhibit retention in order to protect intellectual property rights or prevent the other party from retaining confidential information about the sender. In these cases inhibition is understandable, but if the sender wishes to enforce the record in which the information is contained, the sender may not inhibit its retention by the recipient. Unlike Subsection A of this Section, Subsection C of this Section applies in all transactions and simply provides for unenforceability against the recipient. Subsection A of this section applies only where another law imposes the writing requirement, and Subsection A of this

Section imposes a broader responsibility on the sender to assure retention capability by the recipient.

(f) The protective purposes of this section justify the non-waivability provided by Subsection D of this section. However, since the requirements for sending and formatting are imposed by other law, to the extent the other law permits waiver of these protections, there is no justification for imposing a more severe burden in an electronic environment.

§ 2609. Attribution and effect of electronic record and electronic signature

A. (1) An electronic record or electronic signature is attributable to a person if it was the act of the person.

(2) The act of the person may be shown in any manner, including a showing of the efficacy of any security procedure applied to determine the person to which the electronic record or electronic signature was attributable.

B. The effect of an electronic record or electronic signature attributed to a person under Subsection A of this Section is determined from the context and surrounding circumstances at the time of its creation, execution, or adoption, including the agreement of the parties, if any, and otherwise as provided by law.

Added by Acts 2001, No. 244, § 1, eff. July 1, 2001.

Comments—2001

(a) Under Subsection A of this Section, as long as the electronic record or electronic signature resulted from a person's action it will be attributed to that person. The legal effect of the attribution is addressed in Subsection B of this Section. This section does not alter existing rules of law on attribution. This Section assures that these rules will be applied in the electronic environment. A person's actions include actions taken by human agents of the person, as well as actions taken by an electronic agent of the person. Although the rule may appear to state the obvious, it assures that the record or signature is not ascribed to a machine, as opposed to the person operating or programing the machine.

In each of the following cases, both the electronic record and electronic signature would be attributable to a person under Subsection A of this section:

A. The person types his or her name as part of an e-mail purchase order;

B. The person's employee, pursuant to authority, types the person's name as part of an e-mail purchase order;

C. The person's computer, programmed to order goods upon receipt of inventory information within particular parameters, issues a purchase order which includes the person's name, or other identifying information, as part of an e-mail purchase order.

In each of these cases, law other than this Chapter would ascribe both the signature and the action to the person if done in a paper medium. Subsection A of this section expressly provides that the same result will occur when an electronic medium is used.

(b) Nothing in this section affects the use of a signature as a device for attributing a record to a person. In fact, a signature is often the primary method for attributing a record to a person. Once an electronic signature is attributed to the person, the electronic record would also be attributed to the person, unless the person established fraud, forgery, or another invalidating cause. However, a signature is not the only method for attribution.

(c) The use of facsimile transmissions provides a number of examples of attribution using information other than a signature. A facsimile may be attributed to a person because of the information printed across the top of the page that indicates the machine from which it was sent. Similarly, the transmission may contain a letterhead which identifies the sender. Whether the letterhead actually constitutes a signature is determined based on whether it is a symbol adopted by the sender with the intent to authenticate the facsimile. Thus, the signature determination results from the necessary finding of intention.

In the context of attribution of records, normally the content of the record will provide the necessary information for a finding of attribution. It is also possible that an established course of dealing between parties may result in a finding of attribution. Just as with a paper record, evidence of forgery or counterfeiting may be introduced to rebut the evidence of attribution.

(d) Certain information may be present in an electronic environment that does not appear to attribute but which clearly links a person to a particular record. Numerical codes, personal identification numbers, public and private key combinations may serve to establish the party to whom an electronic record should be attributed. Security procedures may be evidence available to establish attribution.

The inclusion of a specific reference to security procedures as a means of proving attribution is salutary because of the unique importance of security procedures in the electronic environment. In certain processes, a technical and technological security procedure may be the best way to show that a particular electronic record or signature was that of a particular person. In certain circumstances, the use of a security procedure to establish that the record and related signature came from the person's business might be necessary to overcome a claim of electronic intervention. The reference to security procedures is not intended to suggest that other forms of proof of attribution should be accorded less persuasive effect. In addition, the particular strength of a given procedure does not affect the procedure's status as a security procedure, but only affects the weight to be accorded the evidence of the security procedure as tending to establish attribution.

(e) This Section applies to determine the effect of a "click-through" transaction. A "click-through" transaction involves a process which, if executed with an intent to "sign," will be an electronic signature as defined in Section 2602(8). In the context of an anonymous "click-through," issues of proof will be paramount.

§ 2610. Effect of change or error

If a change or error in an electronic record occurs in a transmission between parties to a transaction, the following rules apply:

(1) If the parties have agreed to use a security procedure to detect changes or errors and one party has conformed to the procedure but the other party has not, and the nonconforming party would have detected the change or error had that party also conformed, the conforming party may avoid the effect of the changed or erroneous electronic record.

(2) In an automated transaction involving an individual, the individual may avoid the effect of an electronic record that resulted from an error made by the individual in dealing with the electronic agent of another person if the electronic agent did not provide an opportunity for the prevention or correction of the error and, at the time the individual learns of the error, the individual:

(a) Promptly notifies the other person of the error and that the individual did not intend to be bound by the electronic record received by the other person.

(b) Takes reasonable steps, including steps that conform to the reasonable instructions of the other person, to return to the other person or, if instructed by the other person, to destroy the consideration received, if any, as a result of the erroneous electronic record.

(c) Has not used or received any benefit or value from the consideration, if any, received from the other person.

(3) If neither Paragraph (1) nor Paragraph (2) of this Section is applicable, the change or error has the effect provided by other law, including the law of error, and the contract of the parties, if any.

(4) Paragraphs (2) and (3) of this Section may not be varied by agreement.

Added by Acts 2001, No. 244, § 1, eff. July 1, 2001.

Comments—2001

(a) This Section is limited to changes and errors occurring in transmissions between parties B whether person-person (paragraph 1) or in an automated transaction involving an individual and a machine (paragraphs 1 and 2). The Section focuses on the effect of changes and errors occurring when records are exchanged between parties. In cases where changes and errors occur in contexts other than transmission, the law of mistake is expressly made applicable to resolve the conflict.

This Section covers both changes and errors. For example, if a buyer sends a message to a seller ordering 100 items, but the buyer's information processing system changes the order to 1000 items, a "change" has occurred between what the buyer transmitted and what the seller received. However, if the buyer typed in 1000 intending to order only 100, but sent the message before noting the mistake, an error would have occurred which would also be covered by this section.

(b) Paragraph (1) deals with any transmission where the parties have agreed to use a security procedure to detect changes and errors. It operates against the non-conforming party, i.e., the party in the best position to have avoided the change or error, regardless of whether that person is the sender or recipient. The source of the error or change is not indicated in the Section, so both human and machine errors or changes are covered by this Section. For errors or changes that would not be detected by the security procedure even if applied, the parties are left to the general law of mistake to resolve the dispute.

(c) Paragraph (1) applies only in the situation where a security procedure would detect the error or change but one party fails to use the procedure and does not detect the error or change. In this case, consistent with the law of mistake generally, the record is made avoidable at the instance of the party who took all available steps to avoid the mistake.

(d) Paragraph (2), when applicable, allows the mistaken party to avoid the effect of the erroneous electronic record. However, the Subsection is limited to human error on the part of an individual when dealing with the electronic agent of the other party. In a transaction between individuals there is a greater ability to correct the error before parties have acted on it. However, when an individual makes an error while dealing with the electronic agent of the other party, it may not be possible to correct the error before the other party has shipped or taken other action in reliance on the erroneous record.

Because Paragraph (2) applies only to errors made by individuals, if the error results from the electronic agent, it would constitute a system error. In that case, the effect of that error would be resolved under Paragraph (1) if applicable, otherwise under Paragraph (3) and the general law of mistake.

(e) Paragraph (2) also places additional requirements on the mistaken individual before the Paragraph may be invoked to avoid an erroneous electronic record. The individual must take prompt action to advise the other party of the error and the fact that the individual did not intend the electronic record. Whether the action is prompt must be determined from all the circumstances including the individual's ability to contact the other party. The individual should advise the other party both of the error and of the lack of intention to be bound by the electronic record received. Since this provision allows avoidance by the mistaken party, that party should also be required to expressly note that it is seeking to avoid the electronic record i.e., lacked the intention to be bound.

Second, restitution is normally required to undo a mistaken transaction. Accordingly, the individual must also return or destroy any value received, adhering to instructions from the other party in any case. This is to assure that the other party retains control over the consideration sent in error.

Finally, and most important for transactions involving intermediaries which may be harmed because transactions cannot be unwound, the individual cannot have received any benefit from the transaction. This Section prevents a party from unwinding a transaction after the delivery of value which cannot be returned or destroyed. If it is not possible to avoid the benefit conferred, the transaction is not avoidable under this section.

(f) In cases not covered by Paragraphs (1) or (2), where error or change to a record occur, the parties agreement, or other law, specifically including the law of mistake, applies to resolve the dispute. In the event that the parties' agreement and other law would achieve different results, the construction of the parties' contract is left to the other law. If the error occurs in the context of record retention, § 2612 applies and the standard is one of accuracy and retrievability of the information.

(g) Under Paragraph (4), Paragraphs (2) and (3) non-variable. Paragraph (3) is non-variable because this Chapter defers to other substantive law to govern questions of mistake. Paragraph (2) is non-variable because it provides incentives for parties using electronic agents to establish safeguards for individuals dealing with them. It also avoids unjustified windfalls to the individual by erecting stringent requirements before the individual may exercise the right of avoidance under the Paragraph. Therefore, there is no reason to permit parties to avoid the Paragraph by agreement, and instead, parties should satisfy the Paragraph's requirements.

§ 2611. Notarization and acknowledgment

If a law requires a signature or record to be notarized, acknowledged, verified, or made under oath, the requirement is satisfied if the electronic signature of the person authorized to perform those acts, together with all other information required to be included by other applicable law, is attached to or logically associated with the signature or record.

Added by Acts 2001, No. 244, § 1, eff. July 1, 2001.

Comment—2001

This Section permits a notary public and other authorized officers to act electronically. However, the Section does not eliminate any of the other requirements of notarial laws, and consistent with the entire thrust of this Chapter, this Section simply allows the signing and information to be accomplished in an electronic medium. This Section does not provide any guidance for how electronic notarization can be achieved.

§ 2612. Retention of electronic records; originals

A. If a law requires that a record be retained, the requirement is satisfied by retaining an electronic record of the information in the record which:

(1) Accurately reflects the information set forth in the record after it was first generated in its final form as an electronic record or otherwise.

(2) Remains accessible for later reference.

B. A requirement to retain a record in accordance with Subsection A of this Section does not apply to any information the sole purpose of which is to enable the record to be sent, communicated, or received.

C. A person may satisfy Subsection A of this Section by using the services of another person if the requirements of Subsection A of this Section are satisfied.

D. If a law requires a record to be presented or retained in its original form, or provides consequences if the record is not presented or retained in its original form, that law is satisfied by an electronic record retained in accordance with Subsection A of this Section.

E. If a law requires retention of a check, that requirement is satisfied by retention of an electronic record of the information on the front and back of the check in accordance with Subsection A of this Section.

F. A record retained as an electronic record in accordance with Subsection A of this Section satisfies a law requiring a person to retain a record for evidentiary, audit, or like purposes, unless a law enacted after July 1, 2001, specifically prohibits the use of an electronic record for the specified purpose.

G. This Section shall not preclude a governmental agency of this state from specifying additional requirements for the retention of a record subject to the jurisdiction of the agency.

Added by Acts 2001, No. 244, § 1, eff. July 1, 2001.

Comments—2001

(a) This Section deals with the serviceability of electronic records as retained records and originals. As long as there exists reliable assurance that the electronic record accurately reproduces the information, this Section continues the general policy of this Chapter of establishing the functional equivalence of electronic and paper-based records.

(b) Subsection A requires accuracy and the ability to access at a later time. The requirement of continuing accessibility addresses the issue of technology obsolescence and the need to update and migrate information to developing systems. This Section permits parties to convert original written records to electronic records for retention so long as the requirements of Subsection A are satisfied. Accordingly, in the absence of specific requirements to retain written records, written records may be destroyed once saved as electronic records satisfying the requirements of this Section.

Subsection A refers to the information contained in an electronic record, rather than simply relying on the term electronic record, to clarify that the critical aspect in retention is the information itself. What information must be retained is determined by the purpose for which the information is needed.

(c) Subsections B and C simply make clear that certain ancillary information or the use of third parties, does not affect the serviceability of records and information retained electronically.

(d) Subsection D continues the theme of the Chapter as validating electronic records as originals where the law requires retention of an original.

(e) Subsection E addresses check retention requirements in other law. These requirements preclude banks and their customers from realizing the benefits and efficiencies related to truncation processes. The benefits to banks and their customers from electronic check retention are effectuated by this provision.

(f) Subsection F provides relief from existing record retention statutes. As long as the standards in this Section are satisfied, this Section permits all parties to obtain those benefits. The government may require records in any medium, however, Subsection G requires a governmental agency to specifically identify the types of records and requirements that will be imposed.

§ 2613. Admissibility in evidence

In a proceeding, evidence of a record or signature may not be excluded solely because it is in electronic form.

Added by Acts 2001, No. 244, § 1, eff. July 1, 2001.

Comment—2001

This Section prevents the non-recognition of electronic records and signatures solely on the ground of the media in which information is presented. Nothing in this Section relieves a party from establishing the necessary foundation for the admission of an electronic record.

§ 2614. Automated transaction

In an automated transaction, the following rules apply:

(1) A contract may be formed by the interaction of electronic agents of the parties, even if no individual was aware of or reviewed the actions of the electronic agents or the resulting terms and agreements.

(2) A contract may be formed by the interaction of an electronic agent and an individual, acting on the individual's own behalf or for another person, including by an interaction in which the individual performs actions that the individual is free to refuse to perform and which the individual knows or has reason to know will cause the electronic agent to complete the transaction or performance.

(3) The terms of the contract are determined by the substantive law applicable to it.

Added by Acts 2001, No. 244, § 1, eff. July 1, 2001.

Comments—2001

(a) This Section confirms that contracts can be formed by machines functioning as electronic agents for parties to a transaction. This Section negates any claim that lack of human intent, at the time of contract formation, prevents contract formation. When machines are involved, the requisite intention flows from the programming and use of the machine. These provisions are consistent with the fundamental purpose of the Chapter to remove barriers to electronic transactions while leaving the substantive law unaffected to the greatest extent possible.

(b) The process in paragraph (2) validates an anonymous click-through transaction. It is possible that an anonymous click-through process may simply result in no recognizable legal relationship. For example, if a person goes to an Internet website and acquires access without in any way identifying herself, or otherwise indicating agreement or assent to any limitation or obligation, no legal relationship has been created.

On the other hand it may be possible that the person's actions indicate agreement to a particular term. For example, if a person goes to an Internet website and is confronted by an initial screen which advises the person that the information at this site is proprietary, that the person may use the information for her own personal purposes, but that, by clicking below, the person agrees that any other use without the site owner's permission is prohibited. If the person clicks "agree" and downloads the information and then uses the information for other, prohibited purposes, the person is bound by the non-use agreement. If the owner of the website can show that the only way the person could have obtained the information was from the website, and that the process to access the information required that the user must have clicked the "I agree" button after having the ability to see the conditions on use, the user will have assented to the terms of the agreement. The terms of the resulting contract will be determined under general contract principles.

§ 2615. Time and place of sending and receipt

A. Unless otherwise agreed between the sender and the recipient, an electronic record is sent when it:

(1) Is addressed properly or is otherwise directed properly to an information processing system that the recipient has designated or uses for the purpose of receiving electronic records or information of the type sent and from which the recipient is able to retrieve the electronic record.

(2) Is in a form capable of being processed by that system.

(3) Enters an information processing system outside the control of the sender or of a person that sent the electronic record on behalf of the sender or enters a region of the information processing system designated or used by the recipient which is under the control of the recipient.

B. Unless otherwise agreed between the sender and the recipient, an electronic record is received when it:

(1) Enters an information processing system that the recipient has designated or uses for the purpose of receiving electronic records or information of the type sent and from which the recipient is able to retrieve the electronic record.

(2) Is in a form capable of being processed by that system.

C. Subsection B of this Section applies even if the place where the information processing system is located is different from the place where the electronic record is deemed to be received under Subsection D of this Section.

D. Unless otherwise expressly provided in the electronic record or agreed between the sender and the recipient, an electronic record is deemed to be sent from the place of business of the sender and to be received at the place of business of the recipient. For purposes of this Subsection, the following rules apply:

(1) If the sender or recipient has more than one place of business, the place of business of that person is the place having the closest relationship to the underlying transaction.

(2) If the sender or the recipient does not have a place of business, the place of business is the residence of the sender or recipient, as the case may be.

E. An electronic record is received under Subsection B of this Section even if no individual is aware of its receipt.

F. Receipt of an electronic acknowledgment from an information processing system described in Subsection B of this Section establishes that a record was received but, by itself, does not establish that the content sent corresponds to the content received.

G. (1) If a person is aware that an electronic record purportedly sent under Subsection A of this Section, or purportedly received under Subsection B of this Section, was not actually sent or received, the legal effect of the sending or receipt is determined by other applicable law.

(2) Except to the extent allowed by the other law, the requirements of this Subsection may not be varied by agreement.

Added by Acts 2001, No. 244, § 1, eff. July 1, 2001.

Comments—2001

(a) This Section provides default rules regarding when and from where an electronic record is sent and when and where an electronic record is received. It does not address the efficacy of the record that is sent or received. That is, whether a record is unintelligible or unusable by a recipient is a separate issue from whether that record was sent or received. The effectiveness of an illegible record, whether it binds any party, are questions left to other law.

(b) Subsection A furnishes rules for determining when an electronic record is sent. The effect of the sending and its import are determined by other law once it is determined that a sending has occurred.

To have a proper sending, Subsection A requires that information be properly addressed or otherwise directed to the recipient. To send within the meaning of this Section, there must be specific information which will direct the record to the intended recipient.

The record will be considered sent once it leaves the control of the sender, or comes under the control of the recipient. Records sent through e-mail or the Internet will pass through many different server systems. Accordingly, the critical element when more than one system is involved is the loss of control by the sender.

(c) Subsection B provides simply that when a record enters the system which the recipient has designated or uses and to which the recipient has access, in a form capable of being processed by that system, it is received. Tying receipt to a system accessible by the recipient removes the potential for a recipient leaving messages with a server or other service in order to avoid receipt. However, the Section does not resolve the issue of how the sender proves the time of receipt.

To assure that the recipient retains control of the place of receipt, Subsection B requires that the system be specified or used by the recipient, and that the system be used or designated for the type of record being sent. Many people have multiple e-mail addresses for different purposes. Subsection B assures that recipients can designate the e-mail address or system to be used in a particular transaction. For example, the recipient retains the ability to designate a home e-mail for personal matters, work e-mail for official business, or a separate organizational e-mail solely for the business purposes of that organization. If a person sends the recipient a notice at home which relates to business, it may not be deemed received if the recipient designated his business address as the sole address for business purposes. Whether actual knowledge upon seeing it at home would qualify as receipt is determined under the otherwise applicable substantive law.

(d) Subsections C and D provide default rules for determining where a record will be considered to have been sent or received. The focus is on the place of business of the recipient and not the physical location of the information processing system, which may bear absolutely no relation to the transaction between the parties. It is not uncommon for users of electronic commerce to communicate to another without knowing the location of information systems through which communication is operated. In addition, the location of certain communication systems may change without either of the parties being aware of the change. Accordingly, where the place of sending or receipt is an issue under other applicable law such as conflict of laws or tax law, the relevant location should be the location of the sender or recipient and not the location of the information processing system.

Subsection D assures individual flexibility in designating the place from which a record will be considered sent or at which a record will be considered received. Under Subsection D a person may designate the place of sending or receipt unilaterally in an electronic record. This ability, as with the ability to designate by agreement, may be limited by otherwise applicable law to places having a reasonable relationship to the transaction.

(e) Subsection E makes clear that receipt is not dependent on a person having notice that the record is in the person's system. Receipt occurs when the record reaches the designated system whether or not the recipient ever retrieves the record. The paper analog is the recipient who never reads a mail notice.

(f) Subsection F provides legal certainty about the effect of an electronic acknowledgment. It only addresses the fact of receipt, not the quality of the content, nor whether the electronic record was read or "opened."

(g) Subsection G limits the parties' ability to vary the method for sending and receipt provided in Subsections A and B when there is a legal requirement for the sending or receipt. As in other circumstances where legal requirements derive from other substantive law, to the extent that the other law permits variation by agreement, this Chapter does not impose any additional requirements, and provisions of this Chapter may be varied to the extent provided in the other law.

§ 2616. Transferable records

A. In this Section, "transferable record" means an electronic record that:

(1) Would be a note as defined in R.S. 10:3–101 et seq., or a document under R.S. 10:7–101 et seq., if the electronic record were in writing.

(2) The issuer of the electronic record expressly has agreed is a transferable record.

B. A person has control of a transferable record if a system employed for evidencing the transfer of interests in the transferable record reliably establishes that person as the person to which the transferable record was issued or transferred.

C. A system employed for evidencing the transfer of interests in the transferable record satisfies Subsection B of this Section, and a person is deemed to have control of a transferable record, if the transferable record is created, stored, and assigned in such a manner that:

(1) A single authoritative copy of the transferable record exists that is unique, identifiable, and, except as otherwise provided in Paragraphs (4), (5), and (6) of this Subsection, unalterable.

(2) The authoritative copy identifies the person asserting control as:

(a) The person to which the transferable record was issued; or

(b) If the authoritative copy indicates that the transferable record has been transferred, the person to which the transferable record was most recently transferred.

(3) The authoritative copy is communicated to and maintained by the person asserting control or its designated custodian.

(4) Copies or revisions that add or change an identified assignee of the authoritative copy can be made only with the consent of the person asserting control.

(5) Each copy of the authoritative copy and any copy of a copy is readily identifiable as a copy that is not the authoritative copy.

(6) Any revision of the authoritative copy is readily identifiable as authorized or unauthorized.

D. (1) Except as otherwise agreed, a person having control of a transferable record is the holder, as defined in R.S. 10:1-201(20), of the transferable record and has the same rights and defenses as a holder of an equivalent record or writing under Title 10 of the Louisiana Revised Statutes of 1950, including, if the applicable statutory requirements under R.S. 10:3-302(a), 7-501, or 9-308 [1] are satisfied, the rights and defenses of a holder in due course, a holder to which a negotiable document of title has been duly negotiated, or a purchaser, respectively.

(2) Delivery, possession, and endorsement are not required to obtain or exercise any of the rights under this Subsection.

E. Except as otherwise agreed, an obligor under a transferable record has the same rights and defenses as an equivalent obligor under equivalent records or writings under Title 10 of the Louisiana Revised Statutes of 1950.

F. (1) If requested by a person against which enforcement is sought, the person seeking to enforce the transferable record shall provide reasonable proof that the person is in control of the transferable record.

(2) Proof may include access to the authoritative copy of the transferable record and related business records sufficient to review the terms of the transferable record and to establish the identity of the person having control of the transferable record.

Added by Acts 2001, No. 244, § 1, eff. July 1, 2001.

[1] See, now, R.S. 10:9-330, R.S. 10:9-331.

Comments—2001

(a) Paper negotiable instruments and documents are unique in the fact that a tangible piece of paper actually embodies intangible rights and obligations. The difficulty of creating a unique electronic equivalent which embodies the singular attributes of a paper negotiable document or instrument dictates that the rules relating to negotiable documents and instruments not be simply amended to allow the use of an electronic record for the requisite paper writing. However, the desirability of establishing rules by which business parties might be able to acquire some of the benefits of negotiability in an electronic environment is recognized by the inclusion of this Section on transferable records.

This Section provides legal support for the creation, transferability and enforceability of electronic note and document equivalents, as against the issuer or obligor. which may be controlled by the holder, who in turn may obtain the benefits of holder in due course and good faith purchaser status. The certainty created by the Section provides the requisite incentive for industry to develop the systems and processes, which involve significant expenditures of time and resources, to enable the use of electronic documents or instruments.

(b) The definition of transferable record is limited in two significant ways. First, only the equivalent of paper promissory notes and paper documents of title can be created as transferable records. Promissory notes and documents of title do not impact the broad systems that relate to the broader payments mechanisms related, for example, to checks. Impacting the check collection system by allowing for "electronic checks" has ramifications well beyond the ability of this Chapter to address. Accordingly, this Chapter excludes from its scope transactions governed by the law of negotiable instruments as embodied in Chapters 3 and 4 of the Louisiana Commercial Code. The limitation to promissory note equivalents in this Section is quite important in that regard because of the ability to deal with many enforcement issues by contract without affecting such systemic concerns.

Second, not only is this Section limited to electronic records which would qualify as negotiable promissory notes or documents if they were in writing, but the issuer of the electronic record must expressly agree that the electronic record is to be considered a transferable record. The definition of transferable record as "an electronic record that ... the issuer of the electronic record expressly has agreed is a transferable record" indicates that the electronic record itself will likely set forth the issuer's agreement, though it may be argued that a contemporaneous electronic or written record might set forth the issuer's agreement. However, conversion of a paper note would not be possible because the issuer would not be the issuer of an electronic record. The purpose of this restriction is to assure that transferable records can only be created at the time of issuance by the obligor. The possibility that a paper note might be converted to an electronic record and then intentionally destroyed, and the effect of this, was not intended to be covered by this Section.

The requirement that the obligor expressly agree in the electronic record to its treatment as a transferable record does not otherwise affect the characterization of a transferable record because it is a statutory condition. Furthermore, it does not obligate the issuer to undertake to do any other act than the payment of the obligation evidenced by the transferable record. Therefore, it does not make the transferable record "conditional" within the meaning of La. Rev. Stat. 10:3–104(a)(3).

(c) Under this Section, acquisition of "control" over an electronic record serves as a substitute for "possession" for the paper equivalent. "Control" under this Section serves as the substitute for delivery, indorsement and possession of a negotiable promissory note or negotiable document of title. Subsection B allows control to be found so long as "a system employed for evidencing the transfer of interests in the transferable record reliably establishes [the person claiming control] as the person to which the transferable record was issued or transferred." The major point is that a system, whether involving third party registry or technological safeguards, must be shown to reliably establish the identity of *the* person entitled to payment. Subsection C sets forth a safe harbor list of very strict requirements for such a system. The specific provisions listed in Subsection C are derived from La. Rev. Stat.10:9–10:9–105. Generally, the transferable record must be unique, identifiable, and except as specifically permitted, unalterable. That "authoritative copy" must (i) identify the person claiming control as the person to whom the record was issued or most recently transferred, (ii) be maintained by the person claiming control or its designee, and (iii) be unalterable except with the permission of the person claiming control. In addition any copy of the authoritative copy must be readily identifiable as a copy and all revisions must be readily identifiable as authorized or unauthorized.

The control requirements may be satisfied through the use of a trusted third party registry system. These systems are currently in place for the transfer of securities entitlements under Chapter 8 of the Louisiana Commercial Code, La. Rev. Stat. 10:8–101, *et seq.* and in the transfer of cotton warehouse receipts under the program sponsored by the United States Department of Agriculture. This Chapter recognizes the use of these systems as long as the standards of Subsection C are satisfied. In addition, a technological system which meets these exacting standards is also permitted under this Section.

For example, a borrower signs an electronic record which would be a promissory note or document if it were paper. The borrower specifically agrees in the electronic record that it will qualify as a transferable record under this Section. The lender implements a newly developed technological system which dates, encrypts, and stores all the electronic information in the transferable record in a manner which lender can demonstrate reliably establishes lender as the person to which the transferable record was issued. In the alternative, the lender may contract with a third party to act as a registry for all such transferable records, retaining records establishing the party to whom the record was issued and all subsequent transfers of the record. An example of this latter method for assuring control is the system established for the issuance and transfer of electronic cotton warehouse receipts under 7 C.F.R. 735 et seq.

(d) It is important to note what this Section does not provide. Issues related to enforceability against intermediate transferees and transferors (i.e., indorser liability under a paper note), warranty liability that would attach in a paper note, and issues of the effect of taking a transferable record on the underlying obligation, are not addressed by this Section. These matters must be addressed, if at all, by contract between and among the parties in the chain of transmission and transfer of the transferable record. In the event that these matters are not addressed by the contract, the issues would need to be resolved under otherwise applicable law. Other law may include general contract principles of assignment and assumption, or may include rules from Chapter 3 of the Louisiana Commercial Code, La. Rev. Stat. 10:3–101, *et seq.* applied by analogy.

(e) This Section is a stand-alone provision. Although references are made to specific provisions in Chapter 3, Chapter 7, and Chapter 9 of the Louisiana Commercial Code, these provisions are incorporated into this Chapter and made the applicable rules for purposes of this Chapter. The rights of parties to transferable records are established under Subsections D and E. Subsection D provides rules to determine the rights of a party in control of a transferable record. Subsection D makes clear that the rights are determined under this Section, and not under other law, by incorporating the rules on the manner of acquisition into this statute. The last sentence of Subsection D is intended to assure that requirements related to notions of possession, which are inherently inconsistent with the idea of an electronic record, are not incorporated into this statute.

If a person establishes control, Subsection D provides that that person is the "holder" of the transferable record which is equivalent to a holder of an analogous paper negotiable instrument. If the person acquired control in a manner which would make the person a holder in due course of an equivalent paper record, the person acquires the rights of a holder in due course. The person in control would therefore be able to enforce the transferable record against the obligor regardless of intervening claims and defenses. However, by putting these rights into this Section, this Chapter does not validate the wholesale electrification of promissory notes under Chapter 3 of the Louisiana Commercial Code, La. Rev. Stat. 10:3–101, *et seq.*

A transferable record under Section 2616, while having no counterpart under Chapter 3 of the Louisiana Commercial Code, La. Rev. Stat. 10:3–101, *et seq.*, would be an "account," "general intangible," or "payment intangible" under Chapter 9 of the Louisiana Commercial Code, La. Rev. Stat. 10:9–101, *et seq.* Accordingly, two separate bodies of law would apply to that asset of the obligee. A taker of the transferable record under this Section may acquire purchaser rights under Chapter 9 of the Louisiana Commercial Code, La. Rev. Stat. 10:9–101, *et seq.*, however, those rights may be defeated by a trustee in bankruptcy of a prior person in control unless perfection under Chapter 9 of the Louisiana Commercial Code, La. Rev. Stat. 10:9–101, *et seq.*, by filing is achieved. If the person in control also takes control in a manner granting it holder in due course status, of course that person would take free of any claim by a bankruptcy trustee or lien creditor.

(f) Subsection E accords to the obligor of the transferable record rights equal to those of an obligor under an equivalent paper record. Accordingly, unless a waiver of defense clause is obtained in the electronic record, or the transferee obtains holder in due course rights under Subsection D, the obligor has all the rights and defenses available to it under a contract assignment. In addition, the obligor has the right to have the payment noted or otherwise included as part of the electronic record.

(g) Subsection F grants the obligor the right to have the transferable record and other information made available for purposes of assuring the correct person to pay. This will allow the obligor to protect its interest and obtain the defense of discharge by payment or performance. This is particularly important because a person receiving subsequent control under the appropriate circumstances may well qualify as a holder in course who can enforce payment of the transferable record.

(h) This Section actually creates new substantive legal rights and to that extent is an exception to the general purpose of this Chapter which is to simply validate electronic media used in commercial transactions.

§ 2617. Creation and retention of electronic records and conversion of written records by governmental agencies in this state

Each governmental agency of this state shall determine whether, and the extent to which, it will create and retain electronic records and convert written records to electronic records.

Added by Acts 2001, No. 244, § 1, eff. July 1, 2001.

Comment—2001

This Section authorizes state agencies to use electronic records and electronic signatures generally for intra-governmental purposes, and to convert written records and manual signatures to electronic records and electronic signatures. This Section gives the agency the option to use electronic records or convert written records and signatures to electronic records. It also authorizes the destruction of written records after conversion to electronic form.

§ 2618. Acceptance and distribution of electronic records by governmental agencies in this state

A. Except as otherwise provided in R.S. 9:2612(F), each governmental agency of this state shall determine whether, and the extent to which, it will send and accept electronic records and electronic signatures to and from other persons and otherwise create, generate, communicate, store, process, use, and rely upon electronic records and electronic signatures.

B. To the extent a governmental agency uses electronic records and electronic signatures under Subsection A of this Section, the governmental agency, giving due consideration to security, may specify the following:

(1) The manner and format in which the electronic records must be created, generated, sent, communicated, received, and stored and the systems established for those purposes.

(2) The electronic records must be signed by electronic means, the type of electronic signature required, the manner and format in which the electronic signature must be affixed to the electronic record, and the identity of, or criteria that must be met by, any third party used by a person filing a document to facilitate the process.

(3) Control processes and procedures as appropriate to ensure adequate preservation, disposition, integrity, security, confidentiality, and audit ability of electronic records.

(4) Any other required attributes for electronic records which are specified for corresponding nonelectronic records or reasonably necessary under the circumstances.

C. Except as otherwise provided in R.S. 9:2612(F), this Chapter does not require a governmental agency of this state to use or permit the use of electronic records or electronic signatures.

Added by Acts 2001, No. 244, § 1, eff. July 1, 2001.

Comment—2001

This Section broadly authorizes state agencies to send and receive electronic records and signatures in dealing with non-governmental persons. This Section is broad and general to provide the greatest flexibility and adaptation to the specific needs of the State. This Section is permissive and not obligatory (see Subsection C). However, it does provide specifically that for electronic records used for evidentiary purposes, Section 2612 will apply unless a particular agency expressly opts out.

§ 2619. Interoperability

A. The commissioner of administration shall encourage and promote consistency and interoperability with similar requirements adopted by other governmental agencies of this state, other states, the federal government, and nongovernmental persons interacting with governmental agencies of this state.

B. If appropriate, those standards may specify differing levels of standards from which governmental agencies of this state may choose in implementing the most appropriate standard for a particular application.

Added by Acts 2001, No. 244, § 1, eff. July 1, 2001.

Comment—2001

This Section requires governmental agencies or state officers to take account of consistency in applications and interoperability to the extent practicable when promulgating standards. Of paramount importance is the need for the States to assure that whatever systems and rules are adopted, the systems established are compatible with the systems of other governmental agencies and with common systems in the private sector. Without this legislative direction, the myriad systems that could develop independently would be new barriers to electronic commerce, not a removal of barriers. The key to interoperability is flexibility and adaptability. The requirement of a single system may be as big a barrier as the proliferation of many disparate systems.

§ 2620. Severability clause

The provisions of this Chapter are severable as provided in R.S. 24:175.

Added by Acts 2001, No. 244, § 1, eff. July 1, 2001.

Comment—2001

The provisions of this Chapter are severable as provided in R.S. 24:175.

§ 2621. Certification of electronic records

A. Notwithstanding any provision of the law to the contrary, when a governmental agency offers online applications through an Internet interface for any license or permit, and the particular law for such license or permit requires a sworn application for such license or permit, the governmental agency may accept an online certification from the applicant in lieu of the sworn application.

B. (1) The online certification shall require the applicant to certify that all of the information and documentation the applicant submits via the online application through an Internet interface shall be true and correct, and that the applicant has not used a false or fictitious name in such application, and that the applicant has not knowingly made a false statement or has not knowingly concealed any material fact or otherwise committed any fraud in any such application for a license or permit.

(2) Use by a governmental agency of any online certification provisions included in a nationwide online licensing or registration system shall be permissible and deemed in compliance with Paragraph (1) of this Subsection.

C. A governmental agency that elects to accept online applications through an Internet interface, and thus accepting an online certification in lieu of a sworn application, shall promulgate such rules and regulations in accordance with R.S. 9:2619 and the Administrative Procedure Act as are necessary to implement such online certification.

D. The acceptance of an online application with the certification authorized by this Section, in lieu of the sworn application otherwise required by law, shall not result in, or create any liability on the part of the state or the governmental agency.

Added by Acts 2013, No. 176, § 1, eff. June 7, 2013.

§§ 2622 to 2674. Repealed by Acts 1986, No. 471, § 1

CHAPTER 1–A. OF PRESUMPTIONS

Section
2701. Judgment in class action concludes all members of class adequately represented.

§ 2701. Judgment in class action concludes all members of class adequately represented

A definitive judgment on the merits rendered in a class action concludes all members of the class, whether joined in the action or not, if the members joined as parties fairly insured adequate representation of all members of the class.

Added by Acts 1960, No. 31, § 4, eff. Jan. 1, 1961.

CHAPTER 1–B. REQUISITES FOR A VALID AGREEMENT

Section
2711. Definitions; withdrawal of consent to agreement.
2711.1. Consumer's right to cancel noncredit home solicitation sale.
2712. Prohibition; counterletters.
2713. Contract for surrogate motherhood; nullity.
2714. Chiropractors; certain contractual agreements invalid.
2715. Transfer of structured settlement rights.
2716. Contracts with automatic renewal clauses.
2717. Contracts against public policy.

§ 2711. Definitions; withdrawal of consent to agreement

A. For the purposes of this section the following definitions shall apply to the terms used herein:

(1) An "itinerant door-to-door salesman" means as a person who has no fixed place of business and who goes from house to house, or from place to place, selling or offering for sale goods and services.

(2) A "purchase agreement" means a written agreement which obligates a person to accept merchandise or services from another for a stated consideration in excess of one hundred fifty dollars.

B. Any person who signs a purchase agreement with an itinerant door-to-door salesman has a period of three days in which to withdraw his consent to the agreement, the three-day period shall commence on the day following the making of the agreement by the purchaser.

Added by Acts 1970, No. 428, §§ 1, 2.

Cross References

C.C. arts. 1928, 2438, 2441, 2448, 2456, 2474, 2477, 3537 to 3541.

§ 2711.1. Consumer's right to cancel noncredit home solicitation sale

A. For purposes of this Section the following definitions shall apply to the terms used herein:

(1) A "noncredit home solicitation sale" is a consumer sale involving a cash price of twenty-five dollars or more for goods or services or both, in which the seller or a person acting for him engages in a personal solicitation of the sale at any place other than the business establishment of the seller and the purchaser offers to purchase or agrees to the sale at a place other than the business establishment of the seller or his representative. This definition shall also include all telephone solicitations in which the seller has initiated contact regardless of his location, and the consumer's agreement to purchase is made at the consumer's home. It does not

include a consumer credit sale as defined in R.S. 9:3516(11), a sale made pursuant to prior negotiations between the parties at a business establishment at a fixed location where goods or services are offered or exhibited for sale, a catalogue sale, a sale that may have been initiated by the consumer by communication, whether by telephone or in person, with the seller at his business establishment, or policies of insurance.

(2) A "consumer sale" is the sale of a thing or services purchased primarily for personal, family, or household purposes and the purchaser is not an organization; however, a consumer sale shall not include the sale of religious periodicals, books, and other religious materials by a bona fide religious association, a motor vehicle, immovable property, farm equipment, farm services, or any transaction made pursuant to the Motor Vehicle Sales Finance Act, R.S. 6:951 et seq. The parties to a contract may contract with one another that a sale shall be a consumer sale for the purposes of this Section, except those sales subject to the Motor Vehicle Sales Finance Act.

B. Each seller or person acting on behalf of a seller, who makes or attempts to make a noncredit home solicitation sale shall comply with the provisions of R.S. 9:3539 and R.S. 9:3540 and shall provide a written agreement or offer to purchase that complies with the requirements of R.S. 9:3539. Each consumer purchasing or agreeing to purchase as the result of a noncredit home solicitation sale, shall have the right to cancel such sale in accordance with the requirements of R.S. 9:3538 through R.S. 9:3541.

C. It shall be an unfair trade practice for a seller or his representative to fail to comply with the provisions of R.S. 9:3539 and R.S. 9:3540 and the failure to so comply shall subject the seller to the penalties and actions found in the Unfair Trade Practices and Consumer Protection Law, R.S. 51:1401 et seq.

Added by Acts 1982, No. 744, § 1.

§ 2712. Prohibition; counterletters

The use of counterletters that affect the transfer or encumbrance of any public property, the award of any public contract, or the expenditure or receipt of any public funds is prohibited.

Added by Acts 1986, No. 672, § 1.

Cross References

C.C. arts. 1848, 1849, 2025 to 2028, 3538 to 3541.

§ 2713. Contract for surrogate motherhood; nullity

A. A contract for surrogate motherhood as defined herein shall be absolutely null and shall be void and unenforceable as contrary to public policy.

B. "Contract for surrogate motherhood" means any agreement whereby a person not married to the contributor of the sperm agrees for valuable consideration to be inseminated, to carry any resulting fetus to birth, and then to relinquish to the contributor of the sperm the custody and all rights and obligations to the child.

Added by Acts 1987, No. 583, § 1, eff. Sept. 1, 1987.

Cross References

C.C. arts. 3537 to 3541.

§ 2714. Chiropractors; certain contractual agreements invalid

A. The legislature finds that an inequity is foisted on certain chiropractors by the provisions contained in some agreements pertaining to management consultant services to the extent these provisions encourage, promote, facilitate, or require participation in conduct on the part of the chiropractor contrary to the provisions of Chapter 36, Title 37 of the Louisiana Revised Statutes of 1950,[1] governing the licensing and conduct of chiropractors. It is the intent of the legislature by this Section to declare null and void and against public policy of the state of Louisiana any provision in any agreement which encourages, promotes, facilitates, or requires conduct on the part of a chiropractor that is contrary to the provisions of Chapter 36 of Title 37.

B. Any provision contained in, collateral to, or affecting an agreement pertaining to chiropractic management consultant services that encourages, promotes, facilitates, or requires a chiropractor to engage in conduct contrary to the provisions of Chapter 36 of Title 37 of the Louisiana Revised Statutes of 1950 is void and unenforceable to the extent that it encourages, promotes, facilitates, or requires such conduct on the part of a chiropractor.

C. The term "agreement" as it pertains to chiropractic management consultant services, as used in this Section, means any agreement or understanding, written or oral, concerning the provision of chiropractic management consultant services to chiropractors within the state of Louisiana.

D. Any provision in any agreement regarding the provision of chiropractic management consultant services which would frustrate or circumvent the prohibitions of this Section shall be null and void and of no force and effect.

E. Repealed by Acts 1992, No. 473, § 2.

Added by Acts 1991, No. 1047, § 2.

[1] R.S. 37:2801 et seq.

§ 2715. Transfer of structured settlement rights

A. As used in this Section, the following terms shall mean:

(1) "Annuity issuer" means an insurer that has issued an annuity contract to be used to fund periodic payments under a structured settlement.

(2) "Discounted present value" means the fair present value of future payments, as determined by discounting payments to the present using the most recently published applicable federal rate for determining the present value of an annuity, as issued by the United States Internal Revenue Service.

(3) "Independent professional advice" means advice of an attorney, certified public accountant, actuary, or other licensed professional adviser:

(a) Who is engaged by a payee to render advice concerning the legal, tax, and financial implications of a transfer of structured settlement payment rights;

(b) Who is not affiliated with or compensated by the transferee of the transfer; and

(c) Whose compensation is not affected by whether a transfer occurs.

(4) "Interested parties" means the payee, each beneficiary designated under the annuity contract to receive payments following the payee's death, the annuity issuer, the struc-

tured settlement obligor, and any other party that has continuing rights or obligations under a structured settlement.

(5) "Payee" means an individual who receives damage payments that are not subject to income taxation under a structured settlement and proposes to make a transfer of payment rights.

(6) "Structured settlement" means an arrangement for periodic payment of damages for personal injury established by a settlement or judgment in resolution of a tort claim. "Structured settlement" does not include an arrangement for periodic payment of damages for personal injury established by a judgment of confession.

(7) "Structured settlement agreement" means an agreement, judgment, stipulation, or release embodying the terms of a structured settlement.

(8) "Structured settlement obligor" means a party who has the continuing periodic payment obligation to the payee under a structured settlement agreement or a qualified assignment agreement.

(9) "Structured settlement payment rights" means the rights to receive periodic payments, including lump-sum payments under a structured settlement, whether from the settlement obligor or the annuity issuer, if:

(a) The transferee or payee is domiciled in this state;

(b) The structured settlement agreement was approved by a court in this state; or

(c) The settled claim was pending before a court of this state when the parties entered into the structured settlement agreement.

(10) "Terms of the structured settlement" includes the terms of the structured settlement agreement, the annuity contract, a qualified assignment, and an order or approval of a court or responsible administrative authority authorizing or approving a structured settlement.

(11) "Transfer" means a sale, assignment, pledge, hypothecation, or other form of alienation or encumbrance made by a payee for consideration.

(12) "Transfer agreement" means the agreement providing for the transfer of structured settlement payment rights from a payee to a transferee.

(13) "Transferee" means a person who is receiving or will receive structured settlement payment rights from a payee.

B. The direct or indirect transfer of structured settlement payment rights shall not be effective nor shall a structured settlement obligor or annuity issuer be required to make a payment directly or indirectly to a transferee of structured settlement payment rights unless all of the following requirements are met:

(1) The transfer of structured settlement payment rights has been authorized in advance by ex parte order of a court of competent jurisdiction which had jurisdiction over the original tort or workers' compensation claim resolved by the structured settlement or in which the original tort or workers' compensation claim could have been brought, or in the parish where the payee resides at the time of filing the ex parte petition. At least twenty days prior to the issuance of the order, the transferee shall file a petition for transfer with the caption "Ex Parte Petition for Transfer of Structured Settlement Rights by (name of Transferee)."

(2) The transferee shall include with the petition, a copy of the transferee's application, a copy of the transfer agreement, and a disclosure statement to the payee in bold type, no smaller than 14 points, acknowledged by the payee specifying the following:

(a) The amounts and due dates of the structured settlement payments to be transferred.

(b) The aggregate amount of the payments.

(c) The discounted present value of the payments, together with the discount rate used in determining the discounted present value.

(d) The gross amount payable to the payee in exchange for the payments and an itemized listing of all brokers' commissions, service charges, application fees, processing fees, closing costs, filing fees, referral fees, administrative fees, legal fees, notary fees, and other commissions, fees, costs, expenses, and charges payable by the payee or deductible from the gross amount otherwise payable to the payee.

(e) The net amount payable to the payee after deduction of all commissions, fees, costs, expenses, and charges described in Subparagraph (d) of this Paragraph.

(f) The quotient, expressed as a percentage, obtained by dividing the net payment amount by the discounted present value of the payments, which shall be disclosed in the following statement: "The net amount that you will receive from us in exchange for your future structured settlement payments represents ___% of the estimated current value of the payments".

(g) The effective annual interest rate, which rate shall be disclosed in the following statement: "Based on the net amount that you will receive from us and the amounts and timing of the structured settlement payments that you are turning over to us, you will, in effect, be paying interest to us at a rate of ___% per year".

(h) The amount of any penalty and the aggregate amount of any liquidated damages, including penalties, payable by the payee in the event of a breach of the transfer agreement by the payee.

(i) The transferee has given written notice of the transferee's name, address, and taxpayer identification number to the annuity issuer and the structured settlement obligor.

(j) The transfer agreement provides that if the payee is domiciled in this state, any disputes between the parties will be governed, interpreted, construed, and enforced in accordance with the laws of this state and that the domicile state of the payee is the proper place of venue to bring any cause of action arising out of a breach of the agreement.

C. The court shall enter an order approving the transfer based on a finding of all of the following:

(1) That the payee received independent professional advice regarding the legal, tax, and financial implications of the transfer.

(2) That the transferee disclosed to the payee the discounted present value.

D. All costs of court for filing the petition for transfer of structured settlement rights shall be paid by the transferee.

E. If a transfer of structure settlement payment rights has been authorized under this Section, neither the annuity issuer nor the structured settlement obligor shall have any liability to the payee or to any other party for any payment made to the transferee in accordance with the authorization.

F. The provisions of this Section may not be waived.

G. This Section shall not be construed to authorize a transfer of structured settlement payment rights in contravention of applicable law or to give effect to a transfer of structured settlement payment rights that is invalid under applicable law.

H. A provision in a transfer agreement giving a transferee power to confess judgment against a payee is unenforceable to the extent that the amount of the judgment would exceed the amount paid by the transferee to the payee, less any payments received from the structured settlement obligor or the payee.

I. This Section shall not be construed to authorize any transfer of workers' compensation payment rights in contravention of applicable law or to give effect to any transfer of workers' compensation or other payment rights that is invalid under applicable law.

J. Any person who acquires directly or indirectly structured settlement payment rights in a structured settlement factoring transaction in advance of an order required by this Section may be subject to the tax imposed under the Internal Revenue Code, 26 U.S.C. 5891.

Added by Acts 2001, No. 597, § 1. Amended by Acts 2003, No. 569, § 1.

Editor's note. Acts 2001, No. 597, § 2, declares that "The provisions of this Act "shall have prospective application only and shall not apply to transfers occurring before the effective date."

§ 2716. Contracts with automatic renewal clauses

A. Any person, firm, or corporation engaged in commerce that sells, leases, or offers to sell or lease, any products or services to a consumer pursuant to a contract, when the contract automatically renews unless the consumer cancels the contract, shall disclose the automatic renewal clause clearly and conspicuously in the contract or contract offer.

B. Any person, firm, or corporation engaged in commerce that sells, leases, or offers to sell or lease, any products or services to a consumer pursuant to a contract, when the contract automatically renews unless the consumer cancels the contract, shall disclose clearly and conspicuously how to cancel the contract in the initial contract, contract offer, or with delivery of products or services.

C. A person, firm, or corporation that fails to comply with the requirements of this Section is in violation of this Section unless the person, firm, or corporation demonstrates all of the following:

(1) It has established and implemented written procedures to comply with this Section and enforces compliance with the procedures.

(2) Any failure to comply with this Section is the result of error.

(3) When an error has caused the failure to comply with this Section, it, as a matter of routine business practice, provides a full refund or credit for all amounts billed to or paid by the consumer from the date of the renewal until the date of the termination of the contract, or the date of the subsequent notice of renewal, whichever occurs first.

D. The provisions of this Section shall not apply to the following:

(1) The Louisiana Rental–Purchase Agreement Act as provided in R.S. 9:3351 through 3362.

(2) Banks, trust companies, savings and loan associations, savings banks, credit unions, finance or credit companies, industrial loan companies, or any other financial institution licensed or organized under the laws of any state or the United States, or any foreign bank maintaining a branch or agency licensed under the laws of the United States, or any subsidiary or affiliate thereof.

(3) Insurers licensed under Title 22 of the Louisiana Revised Statutes of 1950.

(4) A contract entered into before January 1, 2011.

(5) A contract that allows for cancellation by the consumer by written notice within thirty days or within one month, after the initial period has expired.

E. Any contract automatically renewed in violation of this Section shall revert to a thirty day renewal contract in accordance with the same terms.

Added by Acts 2010, No. 906, § 1.

Cross References

C.C. arts. 2438, 2448, 2474, 2549, 2620, 2623, 2668, 2670, 2678, 2679, 2680, 2720, 2722 , 2724, 2727, 2728.

§ 2717. Contracts against public policy

A. Any contract between a political subdivision and a person or entity entered into as a result of fraud, bribery, corruption, or other criminal acts, for which a final conviction has been obtained, shall be absolutely null and shall be void and unenforceable as contrary to public policy.

B. Any person whose conviction causes the nullity of the contract as provided in Subsection A of this Section shall be responsible for payment of all costs, attorney fees, and damages incurred in the rebidding of the contract.

Added by Acts 2010, No. 970, § 1.

Editor's note. R.S. 9:2717 was enacted by Acts 2010, No. 970, as R.S. 9:2716. It was redesignated by the Louisiana State Law Institute as R.S. 9:2717.

Cross References

C.C. arts. 11, 651, 697, 949, 1968, 2004, 2012, 2035, 2329, 2330, 2679, 2940, 3074, 3082, 3520, 3538, 3540.

CHAPTER 2. REGISTRY OF INSTRUMENTS AFFECTING IMMOVABLES

PART I. GENERAL PROVISIONS

Section
2721. Filing in office of parish recorder.
2721.1, 2722. Repealed.
2723. Operation.
2724. Liens or privileges not dependent upon recordation for existence or priority.
2725. Certificates of redemption under Federal Tax Lien Act; filing and recording.
2726. Attachment and recordation of plats; definitions; penalty.
2727. Attachment and recordation of plats; expropriations.
2728. Repealed.
2729. Presumption of uniform intent and ownership.

PART II. AGREEMENTS FOR EXPLOITATION OF MINERAL INTERESTS [REPEALED]

2731, 2732. [Blank].
2733. Repealed.

PART I. GENERAL PROVISIONS

§ 2721. Filing in office of parish recorder

A. Repealed by Acts 2005, No. 169, § 8, eff. July 1, 2006.

B. An act of sale of immovable property or attachment thereto filed for registry in the office of the parish recorder pursuant to Subsection A of this Section shall designate the name of the person responsible for all property taxes and assessments and include the address where property tax and assessment notices are to be mailed. The person responsible for the taxes and assessments of the immovable being transferred shall provide the above information to the tax assessor for the parish in which the immovable property is located for the purpose of issuing tax and assessment notices.

C. Anyone who acquires immovable property in this state, whether by sale, sheriff's sale, giving in payment, or in any other manner, which property is subject to a recorded lease agreement that is not divested by the acquisition, shall take the property subject to all of the provisions of the lease, including any provision for the payment of a commission to a leasing agent or other third party, provided that the lease was recorded prior to the recordation of the document which establishes the rights of the person who acquires the property. Such document shall include but is not limited to a mortgage, option to purchase, or other writing.

Added by Acts 1950, 2nd Ex.Sess., No. 7, § 1. Amended by Acts 1992, No. 974, § 1; Acts 1999, No. 949, § 1.

Editor's note. Subsection A of this section was repealed by Acts 2005, No. 169, eff. Jan. 1, 2006. That effective date, however, was postponed to July 1, 2006, by emergency legislation, Acts 2005, 1st Ex. Sess., No. 13.

Section 9 of Acts 2005, No. 169 provides:

"Section 9. Nothing in this Act shall be deemed to diminish the effect of, or render ineffective, the recordation of any instrument that was filed, registered, or recorded in the conveyance or mortgage records of any parish before the effective date of this Act. Any instrument that is filed, registered, or recorded before the effective date of this Act, that is not given the effect of recordation by virtue of existing law, shall be given such effect on the effective date of this Act that it would have if it were first filed on that effective date. Any instrument made available for viewing on the Internet by the recorder before the effective date of this Act shall not be subject to the restriction that allows the display of only the last four digits of social security numbers."

Cross References

C.C. arts. 1833, 1839, 1848, 1985, 2035, 2442, 3176, 3320, 3524 to 3527, 3533 to 3535.

§§ 2721.1, 2722. Repealed by Acts 2005, No. 169, § 8, eff. July 1, 2006

§ 2723. Operation

This Chapter is remedial, and is for the benefit of all such third persons or third parties heretofore as well as those hereafter dealing with immovables or real or personal rights therein on the faith of the public records.

Added by Acts 1950, 2nd Ex.Sess., No. 7, § 3.

Cross References

C.C. arts. 6, 1839, 1985, 2442, 3176, 3320.

§ 2724. Liens or privileges not dependent upon recordation for existence or priority

This Chapter shall not derogate from or otherwise affect the existence or priority of any lien or privilege which, under existing law, is not dependent upon recordation for its existence or priority.

Added by Acts 1950, 2nd Ex.Sess., No. 7, § 4.

Cross References

C.C. arts. 1839, 2442, 3176, 3191 et seq., 3216 et seq., 3320.

§ 2725. Certificates of redemption under Federal Tax Lien Act; filing and recording

A. Certificates of redemption under the Federal Tax Lien Act of 1966 (Public Law 89–719 of the United States, Title I, Section 109, Title 26, Section 7425 of the United States Code,[1] as it may from time to time be amended), executed by the secretary of the treasury of the United States or his delegate, certifying the redemption by the United States of real or immovable property on which the United States has or claims a lien for taxes, or a title derived from the enforcement of a lien for taxes, which real or immovable property had been sold pursuant to an instrument creating a lien on such property, pursuant to a confession of judgment on the obligation secured by such an instrument, or pursuant to a nonjudicial sale under a statutory lien on such property, may be filed for record in the office of the register of conveyances of the parish in this state in which such real or immovable property is situated, and, when so filed and recorded, shall have effect as of the time of such filing to the same extent as is given by state law to the filing for record and recording, of acts and deeds conveying real or immovable property in this state.

B. The same fees allowed by law for the recording of acts and deeds conveying real or immovable property in this State shall apply to such certificates of redemption.

C. This section is not intended, and shall not be construed, to create or recognize any right of redemption, the validity and effect of any such right or claimed right of redemption being left to other laws or to the absence of other laws.

Added by Acts 1968, No. 154, §§ 1 to 3.

[1] 26 U.S.C.A. § 7425.

Cross References

C.C. arts. 2567.

§ 2726. Attachment and recordation of plats; definitions; penalty

A. Each person obtaining a servitude or right of way across private property where the servitude or right of way is obtained for the installation of a facility, or facilities, shall attach to the servitude or right of way agreement a plat, sketch or aerial photograph showing the approximate location of the servitude or right of way and the instrument and plat, sketch or aerial photograph shall be recorded in the conveyance records of the parish in which the private property is situated.

B. "Person" as used in this section shall include natural persons, municipalities and parishes and other political subdivisions and agencies and departments thereof, and persons, companies or corporations operating private or public pipelines or private or public utilities.

C. "Facilities" as used in this section include waterways and drainage canals and underground, surface and overhead pipelines, sewerage lines, utility lines and electric power lines.

D. This section shall not apply to any of the following:

(1) public utility servitudes established in a subdivision by the subdivider;

(2) service drop wires.

E. Failure to record the instrument and plat, sketch or aerial photograph herein required shall render the servitude or right of way agreement ineffective except as between grantor and grantee, their heirs, successors and assigns.

F. This section shall apply only to a servitude or right of way obtained after August 1, 1970.

Added by Acts 1970, No. 482, § 1.

Cross References

C.C. arts. 705, 708, 722, 740, 750.

§ 2727. Attachment and recordation of plats; expropriations

A. The state or its political corporations or subdivisions created for the purpose of exercising any state governmental powers, upon obtaining any immovable property, including servitudes or other rights in or to immovable property for the purpose of constructing and maintaining roads or highways class 1 to 3 as defined by the Louisiana Department of Highways Minimum Design Standards for Rural Highways and Roads, shall attach to the instrument evidencing such acquisition a plat of survey showing the location of the acquisition and the instrument and plat of survey shall be recorded in the conveyance records of the parish in which the property is situated. Where there is a plat of record, reference to same shall satisfy the requirements herein.

B. Failure to record the plat of survey herein required shall not render the instrument evidencing such acquisition ineffective.

C. This Section shall apply only to property obtained after September 12, 1975.

Added by Acts 1975, No. 759, § 1.

Cross References

C.C. arts. 450, 455, 457, 646, 659.

§ 2728. Repealed by Acts 2005, No. 169, § 8, eff. July 1, 2006

§ 2729. Presumption of uniform intent and ownership

Co-owners are presumed to acquire in equal portions. For the purposes of this presumption, a husband and wife acquiring together for the community property regime are considered one co-owner.

Added by Acts 2003, No. 722, § 1.

Cross References

C.C. arts. 797 to 818.

PART II. AGREEMENTS FOR EXPLOITATION OF MINERAL INTERESTS [REPEALED]

§§ 2731, 2732. [Blank]

Editor's note. Pursuant to the statutory revision authority of the Louisiana State Law Institute and § 7 of Acts 2005, No. 169, these sections were redesignated as R.S. 31:216 and 31:217, respectively, effective Jan. 1, 2006. That effective date, however, was postponed to July 1, 2006, by emergency legislation, Acts 2005, 1st Ex.Sess., No. 13.

Section 9 of Acts 2005, No. 169 provides:

"Section 9. Nothing in this Act shall be deemed to diminish the effect of, or render ineffective, the recordation of any instrument that was filed, registered, or recorded in the conveyance or mortgage records of any parish before the effective date of this Act. Any instrument that is filed, registered, or recorded before the effective date of this Act, that is not given the effect of recordation by virtue of existing law, shall be given such effect on the effective date of this Act that it would have if it were first filed on that effective date. Any instrument made available for viewing on the Internet by the recorder before the effective date of this Act shall not be subject to the restriction that allows the display of only the last four digits of social security numbers."

§ 2733. Repealed by Acts 2005, No. 169, § 8, eff. July 1, 2006

CHAPTER 2-A. REGISTRY UNDER COMMERCIAL LAWS

Section
2736. Limitation of liability.
2737. Repealed.

§ 2736. Limitation of liability

A person who serves as the secretary of state, a filing officer, or as any of their respective officers, deputies, or employees shall not be individually liable for damages caused by any error, act, or omission in the performance of the duties provided in R.S. 10:9–101, et seq., except for grossly negligent acts or omissions or acts of willful or wanton misconduct.

Added by Acts 1989, No. 137, § 4, eff. Sept. 1, 1989.

Editor's note. Acts 1989, No. 137, § 20 provides:

"Section 20. It is the intent of the Legislature in enacting this Act to amend the preexisting Louisiana security device laws to accompany and accommodate implementation of Chapter 9 of the Louisiana Commercial Laws (R.S. 10:9–101, et seq.) as previously enacted under Act 528 of 1988. It is further the intent of the legislature that these preexisting Louisiana laws, including without limitation the various statutes and code articles amended and reenacted under this Act, not be expressly or impliedly repealed by Chapter 9 of the Louisiana Commercial Laws, but that such laws remain in effect and be applied to preexisting secured transactions and, at times when so provided, be applied to secured transactions subject to Chapter 9 of the Louisiana Commercial Laws."

This section, enacted as R.S. 9:2770.1, was redesignated as R.S. 9:2736 by the Louisiana State Law Institute.

Section 19 of Acts 2001, No. 128, declares that 'it is the intent of the legislature in enacting this Act that R.S. 2736, 4501 and 4502, 4521, 4758, 4770, and 5363.1 not be expressly or impliedly repealed by this Act, but that such laws remain in effect, and, at times when so provided, be applied to secured transactions subject to Chapter 9 of the Louisiana Commercial Law as revised by this Act."

R.S. 9:2736 refers to R.S. 10:9–101 et seq. (Secured Transactions). Chapter 9 of the Louisiana Commercial has been revised by Acts

2001, No. 128, § 1, effective July 1, 2001, to consist of R.S. 10:9–101 through 10:9–710.

§ 2737. Repealed by Acts 2001, No. 128, § 18, eff. July 1, 2001 at 12:01 A.M.

CHAPTER 2–B. REGISTRY

Section
2741. Establishing authenticity.
2742. Notice of lease; requirements and effect.
2743. Certificate of encumbrances; procedure; content; liability.
2744. Repealed.
2745. Repealed.
2746 to 2757. Repealed.
2758. Notarial certified copy of lost original.
2759. Lost original, certified copy from public record.

§ 2741. Establishing authenticity

A. Any interested person may bring an action to:

(1) Establish that a document is an original instrument or that it is a duplicate of an original instrument; or

(2) Obtain the cancellation of a document from the records because it does not bear an original signature and it is not a duplicate of an original instrument.

B. A party who asserts that a recorded document is not an original or a duplicate of an instrument bears the burden of proof.

C. (1) If the court determines that a recorded document is an original instrument or a duplicate of such an instrument, it shall enter a judgment to that effect.

(2) In all other cases, the court shall declare the recordation is without effect and order it cancelled from the records. R.S. 44:113. Added by Acts 2005, No. 169, § 6, eff. July 1, 2006. Redesignated as R.S. 9:2741 pursuant to Acts 2010, No. 284, § 1, eff. Jan. 1, 2011.

Editor's note. Section 1 of Acts 2010, No. 284, directed the Louisiana State Law Institute to redesignate R.S. 44:113 as R.S. R.S. 9:2741.

Section 2 of Acts 2010, No. 284, further directed the Louisiana State Law Institute to make technical changes to any citations and statutory forms, as necessary to reflect the statutory redesignations in Title 9 of the Louisiana Revised Statutes.

Section 3 of Acts 2010, No. 284, declares that: "The redesignation of a statute as provided by this Act shall not invalidate a reference to the former citation of the redesignated statute".

§ 2742. Notice of lease; requirements and effect

A. (1) In lieu of recording a written lease or sublease or any amendment or modification thereof, as provided by Civil Code Article 3338, a party may record a notice of lease or sublease, signed by the lessor and lessee of the lease or sublease.

(2) Recordation of a notice makes the lease or sublease and any subsequent amendment or modification thereof effective as to third persons to the same extent as would recordation of the instrument evidencing it.

(3) The notice of lease must contain the following:

(a) A declaration that the property is leased, and the names and addresses of the lessor and lessee.

(b) A description of the leased property.

(c) The date of the lease, its term, and the provisions of any extensions and renewals of the term provided for in the lease.

(d) A reference to the existence of an option, right of first refusal, or other agreement of the lessor to transfer all or any part of the leased premises.

(e) If of a sublease, the notice shall also contain reference to the recordation information of the primary lease or notice of lease that is subleased; however, the omission of this information does not affect the efficacy of the notice.

B. A notice of lease may also designate a person authorized to certify in writing on behalf of a party the terms of the lease, whether it is in full force and effect, and the extent to which the obligations of the lease have been performed. The certification shall have the same effect that it would have if it were signed by the person on whose behalf it is made.

C. (1) A change in a lease with respect to any matter that is required to be included in a notice of lease is not effective as to a third person unless the parties record a signed amendment to the notice that describes the change.

(2) If the amendment is of a transfer of a party's rights, the notice shall be signed by the transferor and transferee.

(3) If the amendment only designates a different person to certify the matters described in Subsection B of this Section, the amendment need only be signed by the person on behalf of whom the certification is to be made.

D. The effect of recordation of a notice of lease ceases:

(1) Upon recordation of an instrument signed by the parties to the lease or their successors declaring that the lease has terminated; or

(2) On the date that the lease may finally terminate as set forth in the notice of lease.

E. This Section shall apply to mineral leases that are subject to the provisions of the Louisiana Mineral Code. As to mineral leases, in addition to the other requirements provided under this Section, the notice shall include the primary term of the lease, as well as any additional period during which the lease may be maintained by the payment of rentals.

R.S. 44:104. Added by Acts 2005, No. 169, § 6, eff. July 1, 2006. Amended by Acts 2007, No. 8, § 1, eff. June 18, 2007. Redesignated as R.S. 9:2742 pursuant to Acts 2010, No. 284, § 1, eff. Jan. 1, 2011.

Editor's note. Section 1 of Acts 2010, No. 284, directed the Louisiana State Law Institute to redesignate R.S. 44:104 as R.S. R.S. 9:2742.

Section 2 of Acts 2010, No. 284, further directed the Louisiana State Law Institute to make technical changes to any citations and statutory forms, as necessary to reflect the statutory redesignations in Title 9 of the Louisiana Revised Statutes.

Section 3 of Acts 2010, No. 284, declares that: "The redesignation of a statute as provided by this Act shall not invalidate a reference to the former citation of the redesignated statute".

§ 2743. Certificate of encumbrances; procedure; content; liability

A. The recorder shall deliver a certificate of encumbrances to any person who requests it in writing.

B. (1) The certificate shall list all the uncancelled mortgages and instruments evidencing privileges, in the order of their recordation, that appear in the mortgage records and that identify the persons designated in the request as the mortgagor or obligor of the debt secured by the privilege, unless the recorder is supplied with evidence satisfactory to him that such instruments are in fact not those of the person in whose name the certificate is sought.

(2) Satisfactory evidence shall include an affidavit from the Louisiana licensed attorney requesting the certificate, setting forth all of the following information:

(a) A description of the uncancelled mortgages and instruments evidencing privileges.

(b) A statement from the affiant that he or someone under his direction has researched the uncancelled mortgages and instruments evidencing privileges.

(c) A statement that the affiant has determined through due and diligent research that the mortgages and instruments evidencing privileges are not against the person in whose name the certificate is sought.

(d) A statement that the affiant agrees to be personally liable to and indemnify the recorder and any person relying upon the affidavit for any damages they may suffer if the affidavit contains materially false or incorrect statements that cause the recorder to incorrectly list or fail to list instruments in the certificate.

(3) The affidavit provided for in Paragraph (2) of this Subsection shall be recorded in the mortgage records.

C. (1) If no uncancelled mortgage or instrument evidencing a privilege exists, the certificate shall declare that fact.

(2) The certificate shall not list mortgages or privileges arising from the recordation of the ad valorem tax rolls nor shall it list the notices of tax sales filed pursuant to R.S. 47:2180.

D. (1) The recorder is not liable personally or in his official capacity for listing in his certificate an encumbrance in the name of a person who reasonably may be construed to be the person in whose name the certificate is sought.

(2) The recorder is liable in his official capacity for any loss caused by the failure to list a mortgage or privilege in the certificate or by listing a mortgage or privilege that has been cancelled from his records unless the error proceeds from one of the following:

(a) A want of exactness in the description of the property or the name of the mortgagor or obligor of the debt secured by the privilege specifically given to the recorder in the request.

(b) An incorrect statement in an affidavit submitted pursuant to Subsection B of this Section.

R.S. 44:105. Added by Acts 2005, No. 169, § 6, eff. July 1, 2006. Redesignated as R.S. 9:2743 pursuant to Acts 2010, No. 284, § 1, eff. Jan. 1, 2011. Amended by Acts 2012, No. 178, § 1.

Editor's note. Section 1 of Acts 2010, No. 284, directed the Louisiana State Law Institute to redesignate R.S. 44:105 as R.S. R.S. 9:2743.

Section 2 of Acts 2010, No. 284, further directed the Louisiana State Law Institute to make technical changes to any citations and statutory forms, as necessary to reflect the statutory redesignations in Title 9 of the Louisiana Revised Statutes.

Section 3 of Acts 2010, No. 284, declares that: "The redesignation of a statute as provided by this Act shall not invalidate a reference to the former citation of the redesignated statute".

§ 2744. Repealed by Acts 2005, No. 169, § 8, eff. July 1, 2006

§ 2745. Repealed by Acts 2006, No. 621, § 20(B), eff. Jan. 1, 2009; Acts 2006, No. 730, § 2

§§ 2746 to 2757. Repealed by Acts 2005, No. 169, § 8, eff. July 1, 2006

§ 2758. Notarial certified copy of lost original

When the original title or record is no longer in being, a copy is good proof, and supplies the want of the original, when it is certified as being conformable to the record, by the notary who has received it, or by one of his successors, or by any other public officer, with whom the record was deposited and who had authority to give certified copies of it, provided the loss of the original be previously proved.

C.C. art. 2269. Redesignated as R.S. 9:2758 by Acts 1984, No. 331, § 5, eff. Jan. 1, 1985.

Cross References

C.C. arts. 1832, 3320, 3524.

§ 2759. Lost original, certified copy from public record

When an original title, by authentic act, or by private signature duly acknowledged, has been recorded in any public office, by an officer duly authorized, either by the laws of this State, or of the United States, to make such record, the copy of such record, duly authenticated, shall be received in evidence, on proving the loss of the original, or showing circumstances supported by the oath of the party, to render such loss probable.

C.C. art. 2270. Redesignated as R.S. 9:2759 by Acts 1984, No. 331, § 5, eff. Jan. 1, 1985.

Cross References

C.C. arts. 1832, 1840, 3320, 3347, 3392, 3394, 3524.

CHAPTER 3. PERFORMANCE OF OBLIGATIONS

Section
2770, 2770.1. [Blank].
2771. Non-liability of contractor for destruction or deterioration of work.
2772. Peremptive period for actions involving deficiencies in surveying, design, supervision, or construction of immovables or improvements thereon.
2773. Limitations on the responsibility of agents, contractors and representatives.
2774. Guarantees and warranties in construction specifications.
2775. Construction projects; equipment and machinery contracts; certain provisions invalid.
2776. Acceptance of funds to procure legal representation; accounting.
2778. Public contracts; certain provisions invalid.
2779. Construction contracts, subcontracts, and purchase orders; certain provisions invalid.
2780. Certain indemnification agreements invalid.
2780.1. Certain contract provisions invalid; motor carrier transportation contracts; construction contracts.

APPENDIX 1—REVISED STATUTES, TITLE 9

Section
2781. Open accounts; attorney fees; professional fees; open account owed to the state.
2781.1. Real estate broker privilege on commercial real estate; definition; recordation; ranking; collection of open account.
2781.2. Real estate appraiser privilege on commercial real estate; definition; recordation; ranking.
2782. Nonsufficient fund checks; damages, attorney fees.
2782.1. Posting of nonsufficient fund checks.
2782.2. Stop-payment order on checks; damages, attorney fees.
2783. Public parking meters; public and private parking lots and garages.
2784. Late payment by contractors to subcontractors and suppliers; penalties.

§§ 2770, 2770.1. [Blank]

Editor's note. Acts 1989, No. 137, § 4 enacted R.S. 9:2770 and 9:2770.1. Pursuant to the statutory revision authority of the Louisiana State Law Institute, the sections were redesignated as R.S. 9:2737 and 9:2736, respectively, and the redesignated sections were designated as Chapter 2–A of Code Title IV under the heading "Registry Under Commercial Laws".

§ 2771. Non-liability of contractor for destruction or deterioration of work

No contractor, including but not limited to a residential building contractor as defined in R.S. 37:2150.1(9), shall be liable for destruction or deterioration of or defects in any work constructed, or under construction, by him if he constructed, or is constructing, the work according to plans or specifications furnished to him which he did not make or cause to be made and if the destruction, deterioration, or defect was due to any fault or insufficiency of the plans or specifications. This provision shall apply regardless of whether the destruction, deterioration, or defect occurs or becomes evident prior to or after delivery of the work to the owner or prior to or after acceptance of the work by the owner. The provisions of this Section shall not be subject to waiver by the contractor.

Added by Acts 1958, No. 183, § 1. Amended by Acts 1960, No. 84, § 1; Acts 2001, No. 179, § 1.

Cross References

C.C. arts. 2758, 2759, 2760.

§ 2772. Peremptive period for actions involving deficiencies in surveying, design, supervision, or construction of immovables or improvements thereon

A. Except as otherwise provided in this Subsection, no action, whether ex contractu, ex delicto, or otherwise, including but not limited to an action for failure to warn, to recover on a contract, or to recover damages, or otherwise arising out of an engagement of planning, construction, design, or building immovable or movable property which may include, without limitation, consultation, planning, designs, drawings, specification, investigation, evaluation, measuring, or administration related to any building, construction, demolition, or work, shall be brought against any person performing or furnishing land surveying services, as such term is defined in R.S. 37:682, including but not limited to those services preparatory to construction, or against any person performing or furnishing the design, planning, supervision, inspection, or observation of construction or the construction of immovables, or improvement to immovable property, including but not limited to a residential building contractor as defined in R.S. 37:2150.1:

(1)(a) More than five years after the date of registry in the mortgage office of acceptance of the work by owner.

(b) If no such acceptance is recorded within six months from the date the owner has occupied or taken possession of the improvement, in whole or in part, more than five years after the improvement has been thus occupied by the owner.

(c) If, within ninety days of the expiration of the five-year peremptive period described in Subparagraph (a) of this Paragraph, a claim is brought against any person or entity included within the provisions of this Subsection, then such person or entity shall have ninety days from the date of service of the main demand or, in the case of a third-party defendant, within ninety days from service of process of the third party demand, to file a claim for contribution, indemnity or a third-party claim against any other party.

(2) If the person performing or furnishing the land surveying services, as such term is defined in R.S. 37:682, does not render the services preparatory to construction, or if the person furnishing such services or the design and planning preparatory to construction does not perform any inspection of the work, more than five years after he has completed the surveying or the design and planning with regard to actions against that person.

B. (1) The causes which are perempted within the time described above include any action:

(a) For any deficiency in the performing or furnishing of land surveying services, as such term is defined in R.S. 37:682, including but not limited to those preparatory to construction or in the design, planning, inspection, or observation of construction, or in the construction of any improvement to immovable property, including but not limited to any services provided by a residential building contractor as defined in R.S. 37:2150.1(9).

(b) For damage to property, movable or immovable, arising out of any such deficiency.

(c) For injury to the person or for wrongful death arising out of any such deficiency.

(d) Brought against a person for the action or failure to act of his employees.

(2) Deficiency, as used in this Section, includes failure to warn the owner of any dangerous or hazardous condition, regardless of when knowledge of the danger or hazard is obtained or should have been obtained.

(3) Except as otherwise provided in Subsection A of this Section, this peremptive period shall extend to every demand, whether brought by direct action or for contribution or indemnity or by third-party practice, and whether brought by the owner or by any other person.

C. If such an injury to the property or to the person or if such a wrongful death occurs during the fifth year after the date set forth in Subsection A, an action to recover the damages thereby suffered may be brought within one year after the date of the injury, but in no event more than six years after the date set forth in Subsection A, even if the wrongful death results thereafter.

D. Actions for the causes enumerated in Sub-section B of this Section, against the persons enumerated in Sub-section A of this Section, shall prescribe by the applicable prescriptive periods established by law for such actions.

E. The peremptive period provided by this Section shall not be asserted by way of defense by a person in possession or control, as owner, lessor, tenant, or other possessory interest, of such an improvement at the time any deficiency in such an improvement constitutes the proximate cause of the injury, damage, or death sued upon with regard to any cause of action arising out of the alleged delict, quasi delict, or obligation of any such person arising out of his possession or control of the property.

F. Nothing in this Section shall be construed as modifying the liability or responsibility otherwise imposed by law on the owner of an immovable or the possessor, lessor or lessee of an immovable, by reason of the design, planning, supervision, inspection or observation of construction, or construction of improvements to immovable property.

G. Causes of action arising from the performing or furnishing of land surveying services, as such term is defined in R.S. 37:682, if not performed preparatory to construction, which exist prior to September 11, 1981, shall be perempted one year from said date or by the applicable peremptive period established by this Section, whichever is later.

H. (1) The peremptive period provided by this Section shall not apply to an action to recover on a contract or to recover damages against any person enumerated in Subsection A of this Section, whose fraud has caused the breach of contract or damages sued upon. The provisions of this Subsection shall be retroactive.

(2) In any action in which fraud is alleged, that issue shall be decided by trial separate from and prior to the trial of any or all other issues. However, if fraud is alleged in nonresidential contracts in an action commenced after the expiration of the five-year period provided by this Section, and the court determines that the allegation was brought in bad faith and no fraud is found, then the party who made the allegation shall be liable for court costs and attorney fees. If fraud is proven, then the party that has committed the fraud shall be liable for court costs and attorney fees.

(3) Fraud, as used in this Section, shall have the same meaning as provided in Civil Code Article 1953.

I. Nothing in this Section shall be construed as limiting or modifying the non-liability of contractors for destruction or deterioration of, or defects in, any work, as provided in R.S. 9:2771.

Added by Acts 1964, No. 189, § 1. Amended by Acts 1979, No. 329, § 1; Acts 1981, No. 163, § 1; Acts 1985, No. 303, § 1, eff. July 9, 1985; Acts 1990, No. 712, § 1; Acts 1999, No. 1024, § 1; Acts 2001, No. 179, § 1; Acts 2003, No. 279, § 1; Acts 2003, No. 919, § 1; Acts 2010, No. 651, § 1; Acts 2012, No. 762, § 1.

Editor's note. Section 2 of Acts 2003, No. 919 declares that the provisions of this Act "shall become effective only upon the enactment of House Bill 453 of this 2003 Regular Session." That Bill was enacted as Acts 2003, No. 854.

Cross References

C.C. arts. 785, 1953, 3458, 3492, 3493, 3499.

§ 2773. Limitations on the responsibility of agents, contractors and representatives

A. It is the public policy of the state that the responsibility which may be imposed on an agent, contractor, or representative by reason of the responsibility of proprietors under Article 667 of the Louisiana Civil Code shall be limited solely to the obligation of such agent, contractor, or representative to act as the surety of such proprietor in the event the proprietor is held to be responsible to his neighbor for damage caused him and resulting from the work of such agent, contractor, or representative, and only in the event the proprietor is unable to satisfy any claim arising out of such damage. The agent, contractor, or representative who is responsible for damages, as limited by this Section, shall have a right of action against the proprietor for any damages, costs, loss or expense which he may suffer in his capacity as the surety of the proprietor.

B. Nothing in this Section shall be construed to relieve a contractor of any liability which he may incur as a result of his own negligence or the improper performance of the work performed under the construction contract.

C. The provisions of this Section shall apply to all construction agreements entered into after the effective date hereof and may be waived by the contractor.

Added by Acts 1975, No. 602, § 1.

Cross References

C.C. arts. 667, 785, 2315, 2320, 2756 et seq., 3003.

§ 2774. Guarantees and warranties in construction specifications

A. The guarantee and warranty period of all construction contracts shall commence on the date certified by the architect or engineer as the date the prime contract(s) has (have) been substantially completed in accordance with plans and specifications, or beneficially used by the owner, whichever first occurs.

B. The provisions of this Section shall not be subject to waiver by contract.

Added by Acts 1975, No. 675, § 1.

Cross References

C.C. arts. 7, 2756 et seq.

§ 2775. Construction projects; equipment and machinery contracts; certain provisions invalid

A. Any provision in a contract for the sale of equipment or machinery to be incorporated in a construction project, as hereinafter defined, which excludes liability for consequential damages is null and void.

B. (1) For the purposes of this Section the term "construction project" shall mean any residential or commercial project for the improvement, construction, modification, or repair of a fixed land based structure, or commercial project.

(2) The term "construction project" shall not include industrial or agricultural projects including but not limited to:

(a) Shipbuilding.

(b) Energy conversion or generation.

(c) Forestry.

(d) Paper production.

(e) Sugar production.

(f) Chemical or petrochemical production.

(g) Fixed platform fabrication.

(h) Mineral extraction, drilling, production, refining, development, transportation, or fabrication.

(i) Any projects constructed at the sites where such activities are being, or are to be conducted.

(j) Public sewerage, water treatment, or pumping facility.

C. "Consequential damages" are defined as loss of revenue, production, profits, use, rental income, or cost of replacement facilities, equipment and/or product, as may be applicable.

Added by Acts 1983, No. 330, § 1. Amended by Acts 1984, No. 564, § 1; Acts 1988, No. 533, § 1.

Cross References

C.C. arts. 7, 1968, 1971, 2004.

§ 2776. Acceptance of funds to procure legal representation; accounting

Any person who accepts funds to procure representation for another and also owns an interest in the cause of action, upon the written request of any person who advanced funds shall provide that person with a complete accounting in writing within sixty days of receipt of such request.

Added by Acts 1987, No. 565, § 1.

§ 2777. [Blank]

§ 2778. Public contracts; certain provisions invalid

A. The legislature finds that with respect to public contracts involving the state or a political subdivision of the state, provisions in such agreements requiring disputes arising thereunder to be resolved in a forum outside of this state or requiring their interpretation to be governed by the laws of another jurisdiction are inequitable and against the public policy of this state.

B. The legislature hereby declares null, void, unenforceable, and against public policy, any provision in a contract, subcontract, or purchase order, as described in Subsection A, which either:

(1) Requires a suit or arbitration proceeding to be brought in a forum or jurisdiction outside of this state.

(2) Requires interpretation of the agreement according to the laws of another jurisdiction.

C. The provisions of this Section shall apply to public contracts, as described in this Section, entered into on or after June 30, 1992.

Added by Acts 1992, No. 582, § 1, eff. June 30, 1992.

§ 2779. Construction contracts, subcontracts, and purchase orders; certain provisions invalid

A. The legislature finds that, with respect to construction contracts, subcontracts, and purchase orders for public and private works projects, when one of the parties is domiciled in Louisiana, and the work to be done and the equipment and materials to be supplied involve construction projects in this state, provisions in such agreements requiring disputes arising thereunder to be resolved in a forum outside of this state or requiring their interpretation to be governed by the laws of another jurisdiction are inequitable and against the public policy of this state.

B. The legislature hereby declares null and void and unenforceable as against public policy any provision in a contract, subcontract, or purchase order, as described in Subsection A, which either:

(1) Requires a suit or arbitration proceeding to be brought in a forum or jurisdiction outside of this state; rather, such actions or proceedings may be pursued in accordance with the Louisiana Code of Civil Procedure or other laws of this state governing similar actions.

(2) Requires interpretation of the agreement according to the laws of another jurisdiction.

C. The provisions of this Section apply to contracts, subcontracts, and purchase orders, as described in Subsection A, entered into on or after September 6, 1991.

D. Notwithstanding any other provisions of law to the contrary, the provisions of this Section shall not apply to negotiated labor contracts.

Added by Acts 1991, No. 217, § 1.

§ 2780. Certain indemnification agreements invalid

A. The legislature finds that an inequity is foisted on certain contractors and their employees by the defense or indemnity provisions, either or both, contained in some agreements pertaining to wells for oil, gas, or water, or drilling for minerals which occur in a solid, liquid, gaseous, or other state, to the extent those provisions apply to death or bodily injury to persons. It is the intent of the legislature by this Section to declare null and void and against public policy of the state of Louisiana any provision in any agreement which requires defense and/or indemnification, for death or bodily injury to persons, where there is negligence or fault (strict liability) on the part of the indemnitee, or an agent or employee of the indemnitee, or an independent contractor who is directly responsible to the indemnitee.

B. Any provision contained in, collateral to, or affecting an agreement pertaining to a well for oil, gas, or water, or drilling for minerals which occur in a solid, liquid, gaseous, or other state, is void and unenforceable to the extent that it purports to or does provide for defense or indemnity, or either, to the indemnitee against loss or liability for damages arising out of or resulting from death or bodily injury to persons, which is caused by or results from the sole or concurrent negligence or fault (strict liability) of the indemnitee, or an agent, employee, or an independent contractor who is directly responsible to the indemnitee.

C. The term "agreement," as it pertains to a well for oil, gas, or water, or drilling for minerals which occur in a solid, liquid, gaseous, or other state, as used in this Section, means any agreement or understanding, written or oral, concerning any operations related to the exploration, development, production, or transportation of oil, gas, or water, or drilling for minerals which occur in a solid, liquid, gaseous, or other state, including but not limited to drilling, deepening, reworking, repairing, improving, testing, treating, perforating, acidizing, logging, conditioning, altering, plugging, or otherwise rendering services in or in connection with any well drilled for the purpose of producing or excavating, constructing, improving, or otherwise rendering services in connection with any mine shaft, drift, or other structure intended for use in the exploration for or production of any mineral, or an agreement to perform any portion of any such work or services or any act collateral thereto, including the furnishing or rental of equipment, incidental transportation, and other goods and services furnished in connection with any such service or operation.

D. (1) The provisions of this Section do not affect the validity of any insurance contract, except as otherwise provided in this Section, or any benefit conferred by the workers' compensation laws of this state, and do not deprive a full owner or usufructuary of a surface estate of the right to secure an indemnity from any lessee, operator, contractor, or other person conducting operations for the exploration or production of minerals on the owner's land.

(2) Any language in this Section to the contrary notwithstanding, nothing in this Section shall affect the validity of an operating agreement or farmout agreement, as defined herein, to the extent that the operating agreement or farmout agreement purports to provide for defense or indemnity as defined in Subsection B of this Section. This exception shall not extend to any party who physically performs any activities pursuant to any agreement as defined in Subsection C of this Section. For purposes of this Subsection, operating agreement and farmout agreement shall be defined as follows:

(a) "Operating agreement" means any agreement entered into by or among the owners of mineral rights for the joint exploration, development, operation, or production of minerals.

(b) "Farmout agreement" means any agreement in which the holder of the operating rights to explore for and produce minerals, the "assignor", agrees that it will, upon completion of the conditions of the agreement, assign to another, the "assignee", all or a portion of a mineral lease or of the operating rights.

E. This Section shall have no application to public utilities, the forestry industry, or the sulphur industry, so long as the work being performed is not any of the operations, services, or activities listed in Subsection C above, except to the extent those operations, services, or activities are utilized in the sulphur industry.

F. The provisions of this Section do not apply to loss or liability for damages, or any other expenses, arising out of or resulting from:

(1) Bodily injury or death to persons arising out of or resulting from radioactivity; or

(2) Bodily injury or death to persons arising out of or resulting from the retainment of oil spills and clean-up and removal of structural waste subsequent to a wild well, failure of incidental piping or valves and separators between the well head and the pipelines or failure of pipelines, so as to protect the safety of the general public and the environment; or

(3) Bodily injury or death arising out of or resulting from performance of services to control a wild well so as to protect the safety of the general public or to prevent depletion of vital natural resources.

The term "wild well," as used in this Section, means any well from which the escape of salt water, oil, or gas is unintended and cannot be controlled by the equipment used in normal drilling practices.

G. Any provision in any agreement arising out of the operations, services, or activities listed in Subsection C of this Section of the Louisiana Revised Statutes of 1950 which requires waivers of subrogation, additional named insured endorsements, or any other form of insurance protection which would frustrate or circumvent the prohibitions of this Section, shall be null and void and of no force and effect.

H. The provisions of this Act do not deprive a person who has transferred land, with a reservation of mineral rights, of the right to secure an indemnity from any lessee, operator, contractor, or other person conducting operations for the exploration or production of minerals in connection with the reserved mineral rights; provided such person does not retain a working interest or an overriding royalty interest convertible to a working interest in any production obtained through activities described in Subsection C of this Section.

I. This Act shall apply to certain provisions contained in, collateral to or affecting agreements in connection with the activities listed in Subsection C which are designed to provide indemnity to the indemnitee for all work performed between the indemnitor and the indemnitee in the future. This specifically includes what is commonly referred to in the oil industry as master or general service agreements or blanket contracts in whatever form and by whatever name. The provisions of this Act shall not apply to a contract providing indemnity to the indemnitee when such contract was executed before the effective date of this Act and which contract governs a specific terminable performance of a specific job or activity listed in Subsection C.

Added by Acts 1981, No. 427, § 1. Amended by Acts 1981, Ex.Sess., No. 33, § 1; Acts 1982, No. 237, § 1; Acts 1995, No. 240, § 1, eff. June 14, 1995.

Cross References

C.C. arts. 7, 1971, 1983.

§ 2780.1. Certain contract provisions invalid; motor carrier transportation contracts; construction contracts

A. For purposes of this Section, the following terms have the meanings ascribed to them by this Subsection, except where the context clearly indicates otherwise:

(1) "Motor carrier transportation contract" shall mean any contract, agreement, or understanding covering the transportation of property, other than agricultural products as defined in R.S. 9:3306 and timber without limitation, for compensation or hire by a motor carrier, entrance upon property by the motor carrier for the purpose of loading, unloading, or transporting property, other than agricultural products as defined in R.S. 9:3306 and timber without limitation, for compensation or hire, or a service incidental to any such activity, including but not limited to storage of property, other than agricultural products as defined in R.S. 9:3306 and timber without limitation, except the Uniform Intermodal Interchange and Facilities Access Agreement administered by the Intermodal Association of North America or other agreements providing for the interchange, use, or possession of intermodal chassis, containers, or other intermodal equipment.

(2)(a) "Construction contract" shall mean any agreement for the design, construction, alteration, renovation, repair, or maintenance of a building, structure, highway, road, bridge, water line, sewer line, oil line, gas line, appurtenance, or other improvement to real property, or repair or maintenance of a highway, road, or bridge, including any moving, demolition, or excavation, except that no deed, lease, easement, license, or other instrument granting an interest in or the right to possess property will be deemed to be a construction contract even if the instrument includes the right to design, construct, alter, renovate, repair, or maintain improvements on such real property.

(b) "Construction contract" shall not include any design, construction, alteration, renovation, repair, or maintenance of the following:

(i) Any dirt or gravel road used to access oil and gas wells and associated facilities.

(ii) Oil flow lines or gas gathering lines used in association with the transportation of production from oil and gas wells from the point that oil and gas becomes co-mingled for transportation to oil storage facilities or gas transmission lines.

(3) "Indemnitee" means any named party in the contract to whom indemnification is owed pursuant to the terms of the contract.

(4) "Indemnitor" means any party to the contract who obligates himself to provide indemnification pursuant to the terms of the contract.

(5) "Third party" means any party not subject to the contractual obligations between the indemnitee and indemnitor, excluding, however, any party who has otherwise contracted with the indemnitor or is at the indemnitee's facility at the invitation or direction of the indemnitor.

B. Notwithstanding any provision of law to the contrary and except as otherwise provided in this Section, any provision, clause, covenant, or agreement contained in, collateral to, or affecting a motor carrier transportation contract or construction contract which purports to indemnify, defend, or hold harmless, or has the effect of indemnifying, defending, or holding harmless, the indemnitee from or against any liability for loss or damage resulting from the negligence or intentional acts or omissions of the indemnitee, an agent or employee of the indemnitee, or a third party over which the indemnitor has no control is contrary to the public policy of this state and is null, void, and unenforceable.

C. Notwithstanding any provision of law to the contrary and except as otherwise provided in this Section, any provision, clause, covenant, or agreement contained in, collateral to, or affecting a motor carrier transportation contract or construction contract which purports to require an indemnitor to procure liability insurance covering the acts or omissions or both of the indemnitee, its employees or agents, or the acts or omissions of a third party over whom the indemnitor has no control is null, void, and unenforceable. However, nothing in this Section shall be construed to prevent the indemnitee from requiring the indemnitor to provide proof of insurance for obligations covered by the contract.

D. Notwithstanding any contractual provision to the contrary, this Section shall apply to and govern any construction contract to be performed in this state and any motor carrier transportation contract relative to loading or unloading activities, or any services incidental thereto, which occur in this state. Any provision, covenant, or clause in such contracts which conflicts with the provisions of this Section shall be null, void, and unenforceable.

E. The provisions of this Section are not intended to, nor shall they be judicially interpreted, to alter, add to, subtract from, amend, overlap, or affect the provisions of R.S. 9:2780 or R.S. 38:2195.

F. The provisions of this Section shall not apply to prohibited clauses in any motor carrier transportation contract and any construction contract entered into prior to January 1, 2011.

G. Nothing in this Section shall prohibit a motor vehicle operator from securing uninsured motorist coverage.

H. Nothing in this Section shall prohibit any employee from recovering damages, compensation, or benefits under workers' compensation laws or any other claim or cause of action.

I. Nothing in this Section shall invalidate or prohibit the enforcement of the following:

(1) Any clause in a construction contract containing the indemnitor's promise to indemnify, defend, or hold harmless the indemnitee or an agent or employee of the indemnitee if the contract also requires the indemnitor to obtain insurance to insure the obligation to indemnify, defend, or hold harmless and there is evidence that the indemnitor recovered the cost of the required insurance in the contract price. However, the indemnitor's liability under such clause shall be limited to the amount of the proceeds that were payable under the insurance policy or policies that the indemnitor was required to obtain.

(2) Any clause in a construction contract that requires the indemnitor to procure insurance or name the indemnitee as an additional insured on the indemnitor's policy of insurance, but only to the extent that such additional insurance coverage provides coverage for liability due to an obligation to indemnify, defend, or hold harmless authorized pursuant to Paragraph (1) of this Subsection, provided that such insurance coverage is provided only when the indemnitor is at least partially at fault or otherwise liable for damages ex delicto or quasi ex delicto.

Added by Acts 2010, No. 492, § 1. Amended by Acts 2012, No. 684, § 1, eff. June 7, 2012; Acts 2012, No. 780, § 1.

Editor's note. Sections 3 and 4 of Act 780 provide:

"Section 3. The provisions of this Act and the provisions of the Act which originated as Senate Bill No. 693 [Act 684] of the 2012 Regular Session of the Legislature shall have prospective application only.

"Section 4. The provisions of this Act shall supersede and control to the extent of conflict with the provisions of any other Act of the 2012 Regular Session of the Legislature, regardless of the date of enactment."

§ 2781. Open accounts; attorney fees; professional fees; open account owed to the state

A. When any person fails to pay an open account within thirty days after the claimant sends written demand therefor correctly setting forth the amount owed, that person shall be liable to the claimant for reasonable attorney fees for the prosecution and collection of such claim when judgment on the claim is rendered in favor of the claimant. Citation and service of a petition shall be deemed written demand for the purpose of this Section. If the claimant and his attorney have expressly agreed that the debtor shall be liable for the claimant's attorney fees in a fixed or determinable amount, the claimant is entitled to that amount when judgment on the claim is rendered in favor of the claimant. Receipt of written demand by the person is not required.

B. If the demand is forwarded to the person by first class mail to his last known address, a copy of the demand shall be introduced as evidence of written demand on the debtor.

C. If the demand is made by citation and service of a petition, the person shall be entitled to pay the account without attorney fees by delivering payment to the claimant or the claimant's attorney within ten days after service of the petition in city courts and fifteen days after service of the petition in all other courts.

D. For the purposes of this Section and Code of Civil Procedure Articles 1702 and 4916, "open account" includes any account for which a part or all of the balance is past due, whether or not the account reflects one or more transactions and whether or not at the time of contracting the parties expected future transactions. "Open account" shall include debts incurred for professional services, including but not limited to legal and medical services. For the purposes of this Section only, attorney fees shall be paid on open accounts owed to the state.

E. As used in this Section the following terms shall have the following meanings:

(1) "Person" means natural and juridical persons.

(2) "Reasonable attorney fees" means attorney fees incurred before judgment and after judgment if the judgment creditor is required to enforce the judgment through a writ of fieri facias, writ of seizure and sale, judgment debtor examination, garnishment, or other post-judgment judicial process.

F. If the judgment creditor incurs attorney fees after judgment on the principal demand associated with enforcement of the judgment, the judgment creditor may obtain judgment for those attorney fees and additional court costs by filing a rule to show cause along with an affidavit from counsel for the judgment creditor setting forth the attorney fees incurred. If the judgment debtor does not file with the court a memorandum in opposition at least eight days prior to the hearing on the rule, the court may award the attorney fees and court costs as prayed for without the necessity of an appearance in court by counsel for the judgment creditor. The rule to show cause shall include notice to the judgment debtor of the consequences under this Subsection of not timely filing a memorandum in opposition. The amount of any post-judgment award of attorney fees and costs shall be added to the total to be recovered on the principal demand through any existing writ or garnishment proceedings.

Added by Acts 1976, No. 399, § 1. Amended by Acts 1977, No. 647, § 1; Acts 1981, No. 463, § 1; Acts 1983, No. 311, § 1; Acts 1985, No. 701, § 1; Acts 1986, No. 689, § 1; Acts 1987, No. 485, § 1; Acts 2001, No. 1075, § 1; Acts 2010, No. 695, § 1.

Cross References

C.C. arts. 1989, 1994, 2005.

§ 2781.1. Real estate broker privilege on commercial real estate; definition; recordation; ranking; collection of open account

A. A special privilege affecting the interest of the person with whom he has contracted is hereby granted to a licensed real estate broker for the amount of his commission on all commercial real estate for which he negotiates the sale, exchange, purchase, lease, transfer, or other act of conveyance, pursuant to a written agreement between the broker asserting the privilege and a person having legal capacity to transfer or acquire an interest in the real estate.

B. Valid recorded privileges and all mortgages, whether recorded prior or subsequent to, shall have priority over a broker's privilege, including but not limited to:

(1) Valid materialman's or laborer's liens which are recorded subsequent to the broker's privilege but which related back to a date prior to its recordation.

(2) All mortgages, whether to secure revolving credit, future advances, construction loans, including all renewals thereof, even if the renewals are evidenced by an entirely new mortgage and the old mortgage is cancelled.

(3) All vendor's liens.

C. (1) A notice of broker privilege shall be filed at least five days prior to the sale in the parish in which the commercial real estate is located. Such notice shall also be given to the purchaser by certified mail at least five days prior to the sale.

(2) The person claiming a privilege shall commence proceedings by filing a complaint within one year after the filing of the notice. The failure to do so shall extinguish the lien. No subsequent notice shall be given for the same claim, nor shall that claim be asserted in any proceeding under this Section.

(3) A complaint may be withdrawn by the mutual consent of the person claiming the privilege and any other party or parties to the written agreement specified in Subsection A.

(4) The privilege may be released by the posting of a bond or other assets with the court sufficient in value to cover the full value of the claim. This escrowed amount shall be disbursed by the court upon the finality of a judicial decision and in a manner consistent with the decision.

D. The commission owed a real estate broker as provided in Subsection A of this Section is an "open account" for purposes of R.S. 9:2781.

E. As used in this Section, "commercial real estate" means real estate as defined in R.S. 37:1431(6), but does not include single family residential units such as condominiums, townhouses, or houses in a subdivision when sold, leased, transferred, or otherwise conveyed on a unit by unit basis or in units of six or fewer, real estate on which no building or other structure is permanently attached, real estate classified as farmland for assessment purposes, or residential real estate as defined in the federal Real Estate Settlement Procedures Act.

F. If pursuant to this Section a broker acquires rights and receives prepaid commissions and the transaction which gives rise to the right to receive such commissions fails as a result of the fault of the broker, the broker shall return the unearned prepaid commissions.

Added by Acts 1995, No. 770, § 1.

§ 2781.2. Real estate appraiser privilege on commercial real estate; definition; recordation; ranking

A. A special privilege affecting the interest of the person with whom he has contracted is hereby granted to a state-certified real estate appraiser as defined in R.S. 37:3392 for the amount of his fee on all real estate on which he performs an appraisal pursuant to a written agreement between the appraiser asserting the privilege and a person having legal capacity to transfer the real estate or a person having valid title to the real estate as owner.

B. Valid recorded privileges and all mortgages, whether recorded prior or subsequent to, shall have priority over an appraiser's privilege, including but not limited to:

(1) Valid materialman's or laborer's liens which are recorded subsequent to the appraiser's privilege but which relate back to a date prior to its recordation.

(2) All mortgages, whether to secure revolving credit, future advances, construction loans, including all renewals thereof, even if the renewals are evidenced by an entirely new mortgage and the old mortgage is canceled.

(3) All vendor's liens.

C. (1) A notice of appraiser privilege shall be filed at least five days prior to the sale in the parish in which the real estate is located. Such notice shall also be given to the purchaser by certified mail at least five days prior to the sale.

(2) The person claiming a privilege shall commence proceedings by filing a complaint within one year after the filing of the notice. The failure to do so shall extinguish the lien. No subsequent notice shall be given for the same claim, nor shall that claim be asserted in any proceeding under this Section.

(3) A complaint may be withdrawn by the mutual consent of the person claiming the privilege and any other party or parties to the written agreement specified in Subsection A of this Section.

(4) The privilege may be released by the posting of a bond or other assets with the court sufficient in value to cover the full value of the claim. This escrowed amount shall be disbursed by the court upon the finality of a judicial decision and in a manner consistent with the decision.

D. As used in this Section, "real estate" means real estate as defined in R.S. 37:1431(6).

Added by Acts 2003, No. 979, § 1.

§ 2782. Nonsufficient fund checks; damages, attorney fees

A. Whenever any drawer of a check dishonored for nonsufficient funds fails to pay the obligation created by the check within fifteen working days after receipt of written demand for payment thereof delivered by certified or registered mail, the drawer shall be liable to the payee or a person subrogated to the rights of the payee for damages of twice the amount so owing, but in no case less than one hundred dollars plus attorney fees and court costs.

B. The payee, his agent or assignee, or a holder may charge the drawer of the check a service charge not to exceed twenty-five dollars or five percent of the face amount of the check, whichever is greater, when making written demand for payment. The payee shall post a notice indicating the amount to be charged a drawer of a check if the check is returned for nonsufficient funds. Such notice shall be posted on the payee's business premises in a convenient and conspicuous place where persons entering the location will see it.

C. (1) Before any recovery under Subsection A of this Section may be claimed, a written demand in substantially the form which follows shall be sent by certified or registered mail to the drawer of the check at the address shown on the instrument:

"You are hereby notified that a check numbered _____, issued by you on _____ (date), drawn upon_____, (name of bank), and payable to _____, has been dishonored. Pursuant to Louisiana law, you have fifteen working days from receipt of this notice to tender payment in full of the amount of the check plus a service charge of twenty-five dollars or five percent of the face amount of the check, whichever is greater, the total amount due being _____. Unless this amount is paid in full within the fifteen-working-day period, the holder of the check may file a civil action against you for two times the amount of the check or one hundred dollars, whichever is greater, plus any court costs and reasonable attorney fees incurred by the payee in taking the action."

(2) Notice mailed by certified or registered mail evidenced by return receipt to the address printed on the check or given at the time of issuance shall be deemed sufficient and equivalent to notice having been received by the person making the check.

(3) It shall be prima facie evidence that the drawer knew that the instrument would not be honored if notice mailed by certified or registered mail is returned to the sender when such notice is mailed within a reasonable time of dishonor to the address printed on the instrument or given by the drawer at the time of issuance of the check.

Added by Acts 1977, No. 686, § 1. Amended by Acts 1981, No. 464, § 1; Acts 1986, No. 996, § 1; Acts 1995, No. 486, § 1; Acts 1999, No. 690, § 1.

Cross References

C.C. arts. 1958, 1964, 1989, 1994, 2005, 2924, 3498.

§ 2782.1. Posting of nonsufficient fund checks

Whenever a check is dishonored for nonsufficient funds and is returned to anyone who accepted the check from the original maker of the check in exchange for anything of value, the person holding the unpaid check may publicly post the check or a photograph of the maker of the check on the business premises that received the check after six months has elapsed from the date the check was returned dishonored if the check has remained unpaid and the holder of the unpaid check has mailed notice to the maker of the check at the address on the check by registered mail not more than ten days before the elapse of the sixty days that the check remains unpaid and that a copy of the check or a photograph of the maker will be publicly posted on the business premises that received the check.

Added by Acts 1985, No. 577, § 1.

§ 2782.2. Stop-payment order on checks; damages, attorney fees

A. Whenever any drawer of a check stops payment on the check with the intent to defraud or when there is no justifiable dispute as to the amount owed or the existence of the obligation, the drawer shall be liable to a holder in due course as defined in R.S. 10:3–302, or a person subrogated to the rights of such holder, for damages of twice the amount so owing, but in no case less than one hundred dollars, plus attorney fees and court costs, if the drawer fails to pay the obligation created by the check within thirty days after receipt of written demand for payment thereof substantially in the form provided for in Subsection C which notice is delivered by certified or registered mail.

B. The holder in due course may charge the drawer of the check a service charge not to exceed fifteen dollars or five percent of the face amount of the check, whichever is greater, when making written demand for payment.

C. (1) Before any recovery under Subsection A of this Section may be claimed, a written demand in substantially the form which follows shall be sent by certified or registered mail to the drawer of the check at the address shown on the instrument:

"You are hereby notified a stop payment has been ordered by _____ (name of bank) against a check drawn upon such bank, numbered _____ and issued by you on _____ (date), payable to _____, which has been issued and/or negotiated to _____, who is a holder in due course pursuant to R.S. 10:3–302. Pursuant to Louisiana law, you have thirty days from receipt of this notice to tender payment in full of the amount of the check plus a service charge of fifteen dollars or five percent of the face amount of the check, whichever is greater, the total amount due being _____, to such holder in due course. Unless this amount is paid in full within the thirty-day period, the holder in due course of the check may file a civil action against you for two times the amount of the check or one hundred dollars, whichever is greater, plus any court costs and reasonable attorney fees incurred by such holder in taking the action."

(2) Notice mailed by certified or registered mail evidenced by return receipt to the address printed on the check or given at the time of issuance shall be deemed sufficient and equivalent to notice having been received by the drawer of the check.

(3) It shall be prima facie evidence that the drawer has no defenses to the claim of such holder in due course if notice mailed by certified or registered mail is returned to the sender when such notice is mailed within a reasonable time of the stopped payment to the address printed on the instrument or given by the drawer at the time of issuance of the check.

Added by Acts 1997, No. 1198, § 1, eff. July 1, 1997.

Editor's note. Acts 1997, No. 1198, § 2 provides: "This Act shall become effective on July 1, 1997, and shall apply to all checks against which a stop-payment order is issued or dishonored for nonsufficient funds on and after that date."

§ 2783. Public parking meters; public and private parking lots and garages

Notwithstanding any provision of law to the contrary, the leaving or parking of a vehicle by any person at a parking meter operated by any municipality or other political subdivision or at any privately or publicly owned parking lot or garage, when such parking lot or garage has signs prominently displayed informing customers that the lot or garage is unattended, and when the driver retains the keys, shall not give rise to a contract of deposit but only to one of hiring or letting out space, and neither the political subdivision nor the parking lot or garage owner shall thereby incur the obligations or the responsibilities of a depositary for losses as a result of theft, vandalism, or damage to property.

Added by Acts 1983, No. 405, § 1. Amended by Acts 1997, No. 1406, § 1.

Cross References

C.C. arts. 2926, 2927, 2930.

§ 2784. Late payment by contractors to subcontractors and suppliers; penalties

A. When a contractor receives any payment from the owner for improvements to an immovable after the issuance of a certificate of payment by the architect or engineer, or when a contractor receives any payment from the owner for improvements to an immovable when no architect or engineer is on the job, the contractor shall promptly pay such monies received to each subcontractor and supplier in proportion to the percentage of work completed prior to the issuance of the certificate of payment by such subcontractor and supplier, or by the owner if no architect or engineer is on the job. Further, whenever a subcontractor receives payment from the contractor, the subcontractor shall promptly pay such monies received to each sub-subcontractor and supplier in proportion to the work completed.

B. If for any reason the contractor receives less than the full payment from the owner, then the contractor shall be obligated to disperse only the funds received on a prorated basis with the contractor, subcontractors, and suppliers each receiving a prorated portion based on the amount due on the payment.

C. If the contractor or subcontractor without reasonable cause fails to make any payment to his subcontractors and suppliers within fourteen consecutive days of the receipt of payment from the owner for improvements to an immovable, the contractor or subcontractor shall pay to the subcontractors and suppliers, in addition to the payment, a penalty in the amount of one-half of one percent of the amount due, per day, from the expiration of the period allowed herein for payment after the receipt of payment from the owner. The total penalty shall not exceed fifteen percent of the outstanding balance due. In addition, the contractor or subcontractor shall be liable for reasonable attorney fees for the collection of the payments due the subcontractors and suppliers. However, any claim which the court finds to be without merit shall subject the claimant to all reasonable costs and attorney fees for the defense against such claim.

D. The provisions of this Section shall not be applicable to improvements to an immovable that is used for residential purposes.

Added by Acts 1984, No. 720, § 1. Amended by Acts 1986, No. 718, § 1; Acts 1986, No. 750, § 1; Acts 1987, No. 698, § 1.

Cross References

C.C. arts. 493, 496, 498, 2756 et seq.

CHAPTER 4. DEATH OF A PARTY

Section
2785. Death of either party when obligation personal as to both.
2786. Death of legatee before performance of personal obligation imposed on legacy.
2787. Heritable obligations imposed on legacies.

§ 2785. Death of either party when obligation personal as to both

An obligation to pay an annuity to a certain person during the life of the obligor, is personal as to both, and is extinguished by the death of either.

C.C. art. 2004. Redesignated as R.S. 9:2785 by Acts 1984, No. 331, § 4, eff. Jan. 1, 1985.

Editor's note. This section was redesignated as R.S. 9:2785 from former LSA–C.C. art. 2004 by the Louisiana State Law Institute pursuant to Acts 1984, No. 331, § 4, eff. Jan. 1, 1985. Section 4 of Act 331 provided:

"The Louisiana State Law Institute is hereby instructed to transfer and redesignate Civil Code Arts. 2004 through 2006 as R.S. 9:2785 through 2787, as Chapter 4 of Code Title IV of Code Book III, entitled 'Death of a Party'. This redesignation is neither an amendment to nor reenactment of these Articles."

Cross References

C.C. arts. 1764 to 1766, 1986, 2793, 3537 to 3541.

§ 2786. Death of legatee before performance of personal obligation imposed on legacy

A merely personal obligation to do, imposed by testament as the condition on which a legacy is to take effect, is void, if the legatee die before performance, or before he has been put in default; but the legacy will take effect.

C.C. art. 2005. Redesignated as R.S. 9:2786 by Acts 1984, No. 331, § 4, eff. Jan. 1, 1985.

Editor's note. This section was redesignated as R.S. 9:2786 from former LSA–C.C. art. 2005 by the Louisiana State Law Institute pursuant to Acts 1984, No. 331, § 4, eff. Jan. 1, 1985. Section 4 of Act 331 provided:

"The Louisiana State Law Institute is hereby instructed to transfer and redesignate Civil Code Arts. 2004 through 2006 as R.S. 9:2785 through 2787, as Chapter 4 of Code Title IV of Code Book III, entitled 'Death of a Party'. This redesignation is neither an amendment to nor reenactment of these Articles."

Cross References

C.C. arts. 1764 to 1766, 1986.

§ 2787. Heritable obligations imposed on legacies

But if what is to be done, be a thing that can as well be done by the heirs of the legatee as by him, the obligation shall be heritable, and they must perform it before the legacy can take effect. The provisions of this and the preceding article relate only to testamentary dispositions.

C.C. art. 2006. Redesignated as R.S. 9:2787 by Acts 1984, No. 331, § 4, eff. Jan. 1, 1985.

Editor's note. This section was redesignated as R.S. 9:2787 from former LSA–C.C. art. 2006 by the Louisiana State Law Institute pursuant to Acts 1984, No. 331, § 4, eff. Jan. 1, 1985. Section 4 of Act 331 provided:

"The Louisiana State Law Institute is hereby instructed to transfer and redesignate Civil Code Arts. 2004 through 2006 as R.S. 9:2785 through 2787, as Chapter 4 of Code Title IV of Code Book III, entitled 'Death of a Party'. This redesignation is neither an amendment to nor reenactment of these Articles."

Cross References

C.C. arts. 953, 1589, 1764 to 1766.

CHAPTER 5. INTEREST UPON ACCRUED INTEREST; EXCEPTIONS [BLANK]

Section
2788. [Blank].

§ 2788. [Blank]

Editor's note. Added by Acts 1984, No. 331, § 8; Amended by Acts 1986, No. 584, § 3, and redesignated as R.S. 9:3509.2.

CHAPTER 6. INTEREST–BEARING DEPOSIT ACCOUNTS

Section
2789. Interest-bearing deposit accounts.
2789.1 to 2789.10. [Blank].

§ 2789. Interest-bearing deposit accounts

No person other than the owner of the monies deposited in any interest-bearing account funded with deposited monies belonging to third persons as identified in accordance with the provisions of R.S. 6:317 may receive the interest earnings, as provided under Civil Code Art. 510, on those monies.

Added by Acts 1991, No. 546, § 2.

Cross References

C.C. art. 510.

§§ 2789.1 to 2789.10. [Blank]

Editor's note. Acts 1986, No. 676, § 1 enacted R.S. 9:2789.1 to 9:2789.10 to constitute Chapter 6 "New Home Warranty Act" of Title IV of Code Book III. Pursuant to the statutory revision authority of the Louisiana State Law Institute, the sections were redesignated as R.S. 9:3141 to 9:3150 to constitute Chapter 5 of Title VII of Code Book III.

CHAPTER 7. UNIFORM FRAUDULENT TRANSFER ACT [REPEALED]

Section
2790.1 to 2790.4. Repealed.

§§ 2790.1 to 2790.4. Repealed by Acts 2004, No. 447, § 2

Editor's note. R.S. 9:2790.1 to 9:2790.12 were repealed by Acts 2004, No. 447, § 2. However, R.S. 9:2790.5 and R.S. 9:2790.6 have been added as Chapter 1 of Code Title V by Acts 2010, No. 811. R.S. 9:2790.1 to 9:2790.4 and R.S. 9:2790.7 to 9:2790.12 remain repealed.

CODE TITLE V—OF QUASI CONTRACTS, AND OF OFFENSES AND QUASI OFFENSES

CHAPTER 1. DISGORGEMENT

Section
2790.5. Legislative intent.
2790.6. Disgorgement.
2790.7 to 2790.12. Repealed.

§ 2790.5. Legislative intent

The purpose of this Chapter is to provide a civil remedy for the state to recover profits obtained through the commission of certain criminal offenses. Offenses committed against the state cause monetary damage to the state and violate the public trust. To prevent unjust enrichment, the state is hereby authorized to bring an action to recover profits, gains, or other benefits obtained through such criminal activity.

Added by Acts 2010, No. 811, § 2, eff. Aug. 15, 2011.

Editor's note. A prior R.S. 9:2790.5 was repealed by Acts 2004, No. 447, § 2.

§ 2790.6. Disgorgement

A. The state may bring an action for damages against any person who has been convicted of the provisions of R.S.

14:118, 120, 133, 134, 134.3, 138, or 140 to recover the value of any profits, gains, or other benefits obtained through the commission of these crimes. Damages shall include the payment of legal interest at the rate provided in R.S. 13:4202.

B. For purposes of this Section, "state" means the state of Louisiana, or any parish, municipality, district, or other political subdivision thereof, or any agency, board, commission, department, or institution of the state, parish, municipality, district, or other political subdivision.

Added by Acts 2010, No. 811, § 2, eff. Aug. 15, 2011.

Editor's note. A prior R.S. 9:2790.5 was repealed by Acts 2004, No. 447, § 2.

§§ 2790.7 to 2790.12. Repealed by Acts 2004, No. 447, § 2

Editor's note. R.S. 9:2790.1 to R.S. 9:2790.12 were repealed by Acts 2004, No. 447, § 2. However, R.S. 9:2790.5 and R.S. 9:2790.6 have been added as Chapter 1 of Code Title V by Acts 2010, No. 811. R.S. 9:2790.1 to R.S. 9:2790.4 and R.S. 9:2790.7 to R.S. 9:2790.12 remain repealed.

CHAPTER 2. OF OFFENSES AND QUASI OFFENSES

Section	
2791.	Liability of owner or occupant of property not used primarily for commercial recreational purposes.
2792.	Limitation of liability of member, director, trustee or officer of any public, charitable or nonprofit hospital, institution or organization.
2792.1.	Limitation of liability of director, officer, or trustee of nonprofit organization.
2792.1.	Limitation of liability of director, officer, or trustee of nonprofit organization.
2792.2.	Limitation of liability of board member of downtown development district.
2792.3.	Limitation of liability of director, officer, trustee, or volunteer worker for incorporated and unincorporated nonprofit organizations; civic or historical purpose.
2792.4.	Limitation of liability of members of boards, commissions, or authorities of political subdivisions.
2792.5.	Limitation of liability of officer; federal or state credit union.
2792.6.	Limitation of liability of a trustee of a self-insurance trust fund.
2792.7.	Limitation of liability of director, officer, or trustee of certain homeowners associations.
2792.8.	Limitation of liability; employees of certain nonprofit organizations supervising or coordinating community services.
2792.9.	Limitation of liability of volunteers of area agencies on aging and voluntary councils on the aging; definitions; exceptions.
2793.	Gratuitous service at scene of emergency; limitation on liability.
2793.1.	Immunity from liability for public entities; fire department; law enforcement agency; public emergencies; F.B.I. agents.
2793.2.	Gratuitous emergency services rendered by American Red Cross volunteers; limitation of liability.
2793.3.	Gratuitous services rendered by the United Way; limitation of liability.
2793.4.	Gratuitous services rendered by Southern Mutual Help Association; limitation of liability.
2793.5.	Gratuitous services rendered by PRC Compassion, Inc.; limitation of liability.
2793.6.	Gratuitous services rendered by Catholic charities; limitation of liability.
2793.7.	Gratuitous services rendered by the Louisiana Girl Scout Councils; limitation of liability.
2793.8.	Gratuitous services rendered by National Voluntary Organizations Active in Disaster; limitation of liability.
2793.9.	Gratuitous services rendered by religious organizations; limitation of liability.
2794.	Physicians, dentists, optometrists, and chiropractic physicians; malpractice; burden of proof; jury charge; physician witness expert qualification.
2795.	Limitation of liability of landowner of property used for recreational purposes; property owned by the Department of Wildlife and Fisheries; parks owned by public entities.
2795.1.	Limitation of liability of farm animal activity sponsor or professional; exceptions; required warning.
2795.2.	Limitation of liability for the Audubon Commission; the city of New Orleans; other entities operating facilities of the Audubon Commission; exceptions; required warning.
2795.3.	Limitation of liability of equine activity sponsor; exceptions; required warning.
2795.4.	Limitation of liability; motorized off-road vehicle activities; definitions; exceptions; required warning.
2795.5.	Limitation of liability; agritourism activities; definitions; exceptions; required warning.
2796.	Limitation of liability for loss connected with Mardi Gras parades and festivities; fair and festival parades.
2796.1.	Limitation of liability for loss connected with St. Patrick's Day parades or any ethnic parade.
2796.2.	Limitation of liability for loss connected with festivals, programs, or activities sponsored by an animal sanctuary.
2796.3.	Liability for loss related to bonfire presentations on the Mississippi River levee.
2797.	Users of blood or tissue; a medical service.
2797.1.	Certified, nonprofit poison control centers; legislative findings; limitation of liability.
2798.	Limitation of liability of a volunteer athletic coach, manager, team volunteer health care provider, or official; definitions.
2798.1.	Policymaking or discretionary acts or omissions of public entities or their officers or employees.
2798.2.	Limitation of liability for school volunteers.
2798.3.	Limitation of liability for school systems.
2798.4.	Immunity from liability; injuries sustained by persons driving under the influence of alcoholic beverages or drugs.
2798.5.	Limitation of liability; Louisiana Emergency Response Network.
2799.	Limitation of liability for damages from donated food.
2799.1.	Civil liability for theft of goods from merchant.
2799.2.	Institutional vandalism; civil damages.

APPENDIX 1—REVISED STATUTES, TITLE 9

Section	
2799.3.	Limitation of liability of restaurants, schools, churches, civic organizations, and certain food donors for damages from donated food.
2799.4.	Liability for unauthorized release of certain animals, birds, or aquatic species.
2799.5.	Limitation of liability for gratuitous service by a health care provider in a community health care clinic or community pharmacy.
2799.6.	Limitation of liability for damages from long-term consumption of food and nonalcoholic beverages.
2800.	Limitation of liability for public bodies.
2800.1.	Limitation of liability for loss connected with sale, serving, or furnishing of alcoholic beverages.
2800.2.	Psychologist, psychiatrist, marriage and family therapist, licensed professional counselor, and social worker; limitation of liability.
2800.3.	Limitation of liability of persons designing, supervising or performing hazardous waste mitigation, abatement, or cleanup and asbestos removal, abatement, or cleanup services.
2800.4.	Limitation of liability of owner of farm or forest land; owner of oil, gas, or mineral property.
2800.5.	Immunity from liability for owners of block safehouses.
2800.6.	Burden of proof in claims against merchants.
2800.7.	Repealed.
2800.8.	Property adjudicated to local governmental subdivision; liability of owner of record.
2800.9.	Action against a person for abuse of a minor.
2800.10.	Immunity from liability for injuries sustained while committing a felony offense.
2800.11.	Limitation of liability; municipal or parish airport authority; parked aircraft.
2800.12.	Liability for termination of a pregnancy.
2800.13.	Violation of transportation statute or regulation; determination of causation; evidence.
2800.14.	Limitation of liability for damages to oyster leases.
2800.15.	Limitation of liability for commercial and marine contractors, architects, and engineers, and persons licensed by the Louisiana Manufactured Housing Commission; mold and mold damage.
2800.16.	Limitation of liability; Louisiana Public Defender Board members.
2800.17.	Liability for the diminution in the value of a damaged vehicle.
2800.18.	Limitation of liability for volunteer medical transportation pilots.
2800.19.	Limitation of liability for use of force in defense of certain crimes.
2800.20.	Limitation of liability for a nonprofit health care quality improvement corporation; health care providers; health plans; reporting and disclosure of information.
2800.21.	Limitation of liability for curators and undercurators; acts of interdicts.
2800.22.	Limitation of liability for use of school facilities.

§ 2791. Liability of owner or occupant of property not used primarily for commercial recreational purposes

A. An owner, lessee, or occupant of premises owes no duty of care to keep such premises safe for entry or use by others for hunting, fishing, camping, hiking, sightseeing, or boating or to give warning of any hazardous conditions, use of, structure, or activities on such premises to persons entering for such purposes, whether the hazardous condition or instrumentality causing the harm is one normally encountered in the true outdoors or one created by the placement of structures or conduct of commercial activities on the premises. If such an owner, lessee, or occupant gives permission to another to enter the premises for such recreational purposes he does not thereby extend any assurance that the premises are safe for such purposes or constitute the person to whom permission is granted one to whom a duty of care is owed, or assume responsibility for or incur liability for any injury to persons or property caused by any act of person to whom permission is granted.

B. This Section does not exclude any liability which would otherwise exist for deliberate and willful or malicious injury to persons or property, nor does it create any liability where such liability does not now exist. Furthermore the provisions of this Section shall not apply when the premises are used principally for a commercial, recreational enterprise for profit; existing law governing such use is not changed by this Section.

C. The word "premises" as used in this Section includes lands, roads, waters, water courses, private ways and buildings, structures, machinery or equipment thereon.

D. The limitation of liability extended by this Section to the owner, lessee, or occupant of premises shall not be affected by the granting of a lease, right of use, or right of occupancy for any recreational purpose which may limit the use of the premises to persons other than the entire public or by the posting of the premises so as to limit the use of the premises to persons other than the entire public.

Added by Acts 1964, No. 248, §§ 1 to 3. Amended by Acts 1989, No. 534, § 1; Acts 2003, No. 716, § 1.

Cross References
C.C. arts. 660, 2315, 2317, 2322, 2716, 2721.

§ 2792. Limitation of liability of member, director, trustee or officer of any public, charitable or nonprofit hospital, institution or organization

A person serving with or without compensation as a member, director, trustee or officer of any public, charitable or nonprofit hospital, institution or organization shall not be individually liable to any person, firm or entity, public or private, receiving benefits from the hospital, institution or organization for any act or omission to act by any employee or other officer of such public, charitable or nonprofit hospital, institution or organization.

Added by Acts 1972, No. 375, § 1.

Cross References
C.C. arts. 2315 et seq., 3542.

§ 2792.1. Limitation of liability of director, officer, or trustee of nonprofit organization

Text of section as added by Acts 1987, No. 460, § 1

A person who serves as a director, officer, or trustee of a nonprofit organization qualified as a tax-exempt organization under Section 501(c) of the Internal Revenue Code of 1954, as amended,[1] and who is not compensated for such services on a salary basis shall not be individually liable for any act or omission resulting in damage or injury, arising out of the exercise of his judgment in the formation and implementation of policy or arising out of the management of the affairs of the organization while acting as a director, officer, or trustee of that organization, provided he was acting in good faith and within the scope of his official functions and duties, unless such damage or injury was caused by the willful or wanton misconduct of such person.

Added by Acts 1987, No. 460, § 1.

[1] 26 U.S.C.A. § 501(c).

§ 2792.1. Limitation of liability of director, officer, or trustee of nonprofit organization

Text of section as added by Acts 1987, No. 578, § 1, and Acts 1987, No. 859, § 1

A person who serves as a director, officer, or trustee of a nonprofit organization qualified as a tax-exempt organization under Section 501(c) of the Internal Revenue Code of 1954, as amended,[1] and who is not compensated for such services on a salary basis shall not be individually liable for any act or omission resulting in damage or injury, arising out of the exercise of his judgment in the formation and implementation of policy while acting as a director, officer, or trustee of that organization, or arising out of the management of the affairs of that organization, provided he was acting in good faith and within the scope of his official functions and duties, unless such damage or injury was caused by his willful or wanton misconduct.

Added by Acts 1987, No. 578, § 1; Acts 1987, No. 859, § 1.

[1] 26 U.S.C.A. § 501(c).

Editor's note. Acts 1987, No. 568, § 1 added R.S. 9:2792.1 which was redesignated as R.S. 9:2792.3 pursuant to the statutory revision authority of the Louisiana State Law Institute.

§ 2792.2. Limitation of liability of board member of downtown development district

A. A person who serves as a member of the board of commissioners of a downtown development district shall not be individually liable for any act or omission resulting in damage or injury, arising out of the exercise of his judgment in the formation and implementation of policy while acting as a member of the board of commissioners of that downtown development district, provided he was acting in good faith and within the scope of his official functions and duties, unless such damage or injury was caused by his willful or wanton misconduct.

B. "Downtown development district" as used herein means a downtown development district created by law or pursuant to law, and includes the downtown development districts created under the provisions of R.S. 33:2740.3, R.S. 33:2740.8, and R.S. 33:2740.15.

Added by Acts 1987, No. 460, § 1; Acts 1987, No. 859, § 1.

Editor's note. Acts 1987, No. 667, § 1 enacted R.S. 9:2792.2, which was redesignated as R.S. 9:2792.4 pursuant to the statutory revision authority of the Louisiana State Law Institute.

The enactments of this section by Acts 1987, No. 460, § 1 and Acts 1987, No. 859, § 1 were identical, except that, near the end of subsec. A, Act 460 contains "willfull or wanton" [sic] rather than "willful and wanton." The Title of Act 460, however, refers to "willful or wanton." The text of this section as enacted by Acts 1987, No. 859 is printed pursuant to the statutory revision authority of the Louisiana State Law Institute.

§ 2792.3. Limitation of liability of director, officer, trustee, or volunteer worker for incorporated and unincorporated nonprofit organizations; civic or historical purpose

A person who serves as a director, officer, trustee or volunteer worker for any nonprofit organization, whether incorporated or unincorporated, including but not limited to an organization whether incorporated or not, which sponsors a fair or festival, or any nonprofit historical organization, whether incorporated or not, which is organized for civic or historical purposes, whether he serves with or without compensation for such services shall not be individually liable for any act or omission resulting in damage or injury arising out of the exercise of his judgment in the formation and implementation of policy, or arising out of the management of affairs, while acting as a director, officer, trustee or volunteer worker of that organization, provided he was acting in good faith and within the scope of his official functions and duties, unless such damage or injury was caused by his willful or wanton misconduct.

Added by Acts 1987, No. 568, § 1. Amended by Acts 1988, No. 565, § 1.

Editor's note. This section, added as R.S. 9:2792.1 by Acts 1987, No. 568, § 1 was redesignated pursuant to the statutory revision authority of the Louisiana State Law Institute.

Cross References

C.C. art. 2315.

§ 2792.4. Limitation of liability of members of boards, commissions, or authorities of political subdivisions

A. As used in this Section, a "member of a board, commission or authority of a political subdivision" means a person serving as an elected or appointed director, trustee, or member of a board, commission, or authority of a municipality, ward, parish, or special district, board, or commission of the state, including without limitation, a levee district, school board, parish law enforcement district, downtown development district, tourist commission, port commission, publicly owned railroad board or commission, or any other local board, commission, or authority.

B. A person who serves as a member of a board, commission, or authority of a political subdivision as defined in Subsection A, shall not be individually liable for any act or omission resulting in damage or injury, arising out of the exercise of his judgment in the formation and implementation of policy while acting as a member of a board, commission, or authority of that political subdivision, provided he was acting in good faith and within the scope of his official functions and duties, unless the damage or injury was caused by his willful or wanton misconduct.

Added by Acts 1987, No. 667, § 1. Amended by Acts 1988, No. 734, § 1.

Editor's note. This section, added as R.S. 9:2792.2 by Acts 1987, No. 667, § 1 was redesignated pursuant to the statutory revision authority of the Louisiana State Law Institute.

Cross References

C.C. art. 2315.

§ 2792.5. Limitation of liability of officer; federal or state credit union

A person who serves as a director, officer, or committee member of a federally chartered or state chartered credit union, and who is not compensated for such services on a salary basis, shall not be individually liable for any act or omission resulting in damage or injury, arising out of the exercise of his judgment in the formation and implementation of policy while acting as a director, officer, or committee member of that credit union, or arising out of the management of the affairs of that credit union, provided he was acting in good faith and within the scope of his official functions and duties, unless the damage or injury was caused by his willful or wanton misconduct.

Added by Acts 1988, No. 205, § 1.

Cross References

C.C. art. 2315.

§ 2792.6. Limitation of liability of a trustee of a self-insurance trust fund

A person who serves as a trustee of any self-insurance trust fund, whether he serves with or without compensation for such services, shall not be individually liable for any act or omission resulting in damage or injury arising out of the exercise of his judgment in the formation and implementation of policy while acting as a trustee of that organization, or arising out of the management of the affairs of that organization, provided he was acting in good faith and within the scope of his official functions and duties, unless such damage or injury was caused by his willful or wanton misconduct.

Added by Acts 1989, No. 804, § 1.

§ 2792.7. Limitation of liability of director, officer, or trustee of certain homeowners associations

A. A person who serves as a director, officer, or trustee of a homeowners association and who is not compensated for such services on a salary basis shall not be individually liable for any act or omission resulting in damage or injury, arising out of the exercise of his judgment in the formation and implementation of policy while acting as a director, officer, or trustee of that association, or arising out of the management of the affairs of that association, provided he was acting in good faith and within the scope of his official functions and duties, unless such damage or injury was caused by his willful or wanton misconduct.

B. For purposes of this Section, "homeowners association" means any of the following:

(1) A condominium association as defined in the Louisiana Condominium Act, R.S. 9:1121.101 et seq.

(2) A timeshare association as defined in the Louisiana Timesharing Act, R.S. 9:1131.1 et seq.

(3) A homeowners association as defined in the Louisiana Homeowners Association Act, R.S. 9:1141.1 et seq.

(4) An association defined by Section 528(c) of the Internal Revenue Code of 1986, as amended.

Added by Acts 1990, No. 91, § 1. Amended by Acts 1999, No. 88, § 1.

§ 2792.8. Limitation of liability; employees of certain nonprofit organizations supervising or coordinating community services

A. As used in this Section:

(1) "Designated nonprofit organization" means a private, nonprofit, tax-exempt organization under Section 501(c)(3), Internal Revenue Code, pursuant to 26 U.S.C. 501(c)(3), which has been designated by the judges of the judicial district or any city or municipal court within which it is located to coordinate or supervise the utilization of the community service of persons sentenced to perform community service as an alternative to incarceration.

(2) "Employee" means a director, officer, trustee, shareholder, or employee of a designated nonprofit organization, whether or not such person is compensated for his services.

(3) "Community service" means work which has been designated by the sentencing judge to be performed as an alternative to incarceration, and which the sentencing judge deems to be worthwhile to the community as a whole.

(4) "Community service workers" means persons convicted of misdemeanors, or felonies under a state or local ordinance not involving violence, and sentenced to perform community service, or persons who have entered a pretrial diversion agreement with a district attorney's office.

B. The state of Louisiana shall hold harmless and indemnify all designated nonprofit organizations for all acts and omissions of any community service worker which result in damage or injury to the same or any other community service worker and for all acts and omissions of any employee of the nonprofit organization which result in damage or injury to any community service worker, unless such damage or injury was caused by the employee's willful or wanton misconduct.

C. An employee of a designated nonprofit organization shall not be individually liable for any act or omission of his own or of any other employee which results in damage or injury to any community service worker, unless such damage or injury was caused by his willful or wanton misconduct, nor shall such employee be liable for any act or omission of any community service worker which results in damage or injury to any other community service worker or any third person whatsoever, unless such damage or injury was caused by the willful or wanton misconduct of such employee.

D. A community service worker shall have no cause of action for damages, except for the payment of medical expenses, against the entity conducting the program or supervising his participation therein, including a municipality, parish, sheriff, or other entity, nor against any official, employee, or agent of such entity, for any injury or loss suffered by him during or arising out of his participation therein, if such injury or loss is a direct result of the lack of supervision or act or omission of the supervisor, unless the injury or loss was caused by the intentional or grossly negligent act or omission of the entity or its official, employee, or agent.

Added by Acts 1991, No. 682, § 1. Amended by Acts 1996, 1st Ex.Sess., No. 70, § 1, eff. May 10, 1996; Acts 2011, No. 229, § 1.

§ 2792.9. Limitation of liability of volunteers of area agencies on aging and voluntary councils on the aging; definitions; exceptions

A. No volunteer who in good faith and within the scope of his official functions and duties performs services for an area agency on aging or a parish voluntary council on the aging, without compensation, other than reimbursement for actual expenses incurred, shall be liable for any injury, loss, or damage as a result of any act or omission in rendering such service, except when the injury, damage, or loss is caused by the volunteer's willful or wanton misconduct, or the volunteer's gross negligence.

B. Nothing in this Section shall be construed to bar any cause of action against an area agency on aging or a voluntary council on the aging for an act or omission of a volunteer otherwise provided by law.

C. Notwithstanding the provisions of Subsection A of this Section, a person may sue and recover civil damages from a volunteer based upon a negligent act or omission involving the operation of a motor vehicle in performing the volunteer service, except that the amount recovered from the volunteer shall not exceed the limits of applicable insurance coverage maintained by or on behalf of the volunteer with respect to his negligent operation of a motor vehicle. Nothing in this Section shall be construed to limit the right of a person to recover from a policy of uninsured or underinsured motorist coverage available to him as a result of a motor vehicle accident.

D. As used in this Section:

(1) "Area agency on aging" means any area agency on aging designated under the federal Older Americans Act, 42 U.S.C. 3025(a)(2)(A), or a state agency performing the functions of an area agency under the provisions of 42 U.S.C. 3025(b)(5).

(2) "Voluntary council on the aging" means a voluntary council on the aging as designated pursuant to R.S. 46:1601 et seq.

Added by Acts 1995, No. 1288, § 1, eff. June 29, 1995.

§ 2793. Gratuitous service at scene of emergency; limitation on liability

A. No person who in good faith gratuitously renders emergency care, first aid or rescue at the scene of an emergency, or moves a person receiving such care, first aid or rescue to a hospital or other place of medical care shall be liable for any civil damages as a result of any act or omission in rendering the care or services or as a result of any act or failure to act to provide or arrange for further medical treatment or care for the person involved in the said emergency; provided, however, such care or services or transportation shall not be considered gratuitous, and this Section shall not apply when rendered incidental to a business relationship, including but not limited to that of employer-employee, existing between the person rendering such care or service or transportation and the person receiving the same, or when incidental to a business relationship existing between the employer or principal of the person rendering such care, service or transportation and the employer or principal of the person receiving such care, service or transportation. This Section shall not exempt from liability those individuals who intentionally or by grossly negligent acts or omissions cause damages to another individual.

B. The immunity herein granted shall be personal to the individual rendering such care or service or furnishing such transportation and shall not inure to the benefit of any employer or other person legally responsible for the acts or omissions of such individual, nor shall it inure to the benefit of any insurer.

C. For purposes of this Section, rendering emergency care, first aid, or rescue shall include the use of an automated external defibrillator as defined by R.S. 40:1236.12.

Added by Acts 1975, No. 600, § 1. Amended by Acts 2010, No. 459, § 1.

Cross References
C.C. art. 2315.

§ 2793.1. Immunity from liability for public entities; fire department; law enforcement agency; public emergencies; F.B.I. agents

A. No person shall have a cause of action against a public entity or the officers and employees thereof for damage to property at the site of a crime, accident, or fire, including without limitation the destruction or deterioration of property, caused while the officer or employee was acting within the course and scope of his office or employment and while taking reasonable remedial action which is necessary to abate a public emergency, unless such damage was caused by willful or wanton misconduct or gross negligence.

B. (1) As used in this Section, "public entity" means the state, or a political subdivision thereof which maintains a department responsible for fire protection, and its fire department, or a law enforcement agency, office, or department responsible for the prevention and detection of crime and the enforcement of the criminal laws of this state, and its law enforcement agency, office, or department.

(2) For purposes of this Section, the term "public emergency" includes any emergency in which there is a potential threat to life or property requiring immediate or remedial action, in order to insure the safety and health of persons and property, including an emergency created by apparent violation of the criminal laws of this state or an emergency created by fire.

C. Agents of the Federal Bureau of Investigation may raise the defense of qualified immunity if arresting for felonies in progress under the laws of the state of Louisiana or if assisting a peace officer of the state of Louisiana.

Added by Acts 1989, No. 725, § 1. Amended by Acts 1997, No. 126, § 1.

§ 2793.2. Gratuitous emergency services rendered by American Red Cross volunteers; limitation of liability

A. No person who in good faith gratuitously renders any emergency service as a volunteer on behalf of the American Red Cross shall be liable for any civil damages as a result of any act or omission in rendering such care or services or as a result of any act or failure to act or failure to provide or arrange for further services.

B. The limitation of liability provided in Subsection A shall not apply if any of the following exists:

(1) The emergency service provided was inconsistent with or a breach of policies or procedures taught in the current and most advanced national American Red Cross First Aid Training Course or American Red Cross Disaster Nursing Course, or both.

(2) The emergency service provided was not supervised by a duly qualified employee or agent of the American Red Cross, as required by the policy and procedures of the American Red Cross.

(3) The damages were caused by the intentional act or omission or gross negligence or willful or wanton misconduct of the volunteer.

C. As used in this Section:

(1) "Emergency service" means the immediate and temporary care rendered to a victim of injury or sudden illness

consistent with the policies and procedures taught in the current and most advanced American Red Cross First Aid Training Course or the American Red Cross Disaster Nursing Course, or both.

(2) "Volunteer" means a person who has successfully completed first aid training by the American Red Cross or other recognized emergency medical training program and whose certification is current.

Added by Acts 1995, No. 1230, § 1.

§ 2793.3. Gratuitous services rendered by the United Way; limitation of liability

The United Way of America or its licensed member organizations or any officer, employee, or volunteer thereof, who gratuitously renders any evacuation assistance or services of any kind to other persons in advance of a hurricane or tropical storm declared by the United States National Oceanic and Atmospheric Administration's National Weather Service or who gratuitously renders any disaster relief or recovery services following a declared state of emergency, shall not be liable to any person for any injury, death, loss, civil penalty, or damage as a result of any act or omission in rendering assistance, relief, or recovery services or as a result of any act or failure to act or failure to provide or arrange for further services, unless the damage or injury was caused by gross negligence or willful and wanton misconduct.

Added by Acts 2006, No. 836, § 1. Amended by Acts 2007, No. 331, § 1.

§ 2793.4. Gratuitous services rendered by Southern Mutual Help Association; limitation of liability

The Southern Mutual Help Association, Inc., or any officer, employee, or volunteer thereof, who gratuitously renders any evacuation assistance or services of any kind to other persons in advance of a hurricane or tropical storm declared by the United States National Oceanic and Atmospheric Administration's National Weather Service or who gratuitously renders any disaster relief or recovery services following a declared state of emergency, shall not be liable to any person for any injury, death, loss, civil penalty, or damage as a result of any act or omission in rendering assistance, relief, or recovery services or as a result of any act or failure to act or failure to provide or arrange for further services, unless the damage or injury was caused by gross negligence or willful and wanton misconduct.

Added by Acts 2006, No. 836, § 1. Amended by Acts 2007, No. 331, § 1.

§ 2793.5. Gratuitous services rendered by PRC Compassion, Inc.; limitation of liability

PRC Compassion, Inc., or any officer, employee, or volunteer thereof, who gratuitously renders any evacuation assistance or services of any kind to other persons in advance of a hurricane or tropical storm declared by the United States National Oceanic and Atmospheric Administration's National Weather Service or who gratuitously renders any disaster relief or recovery services following a declared state of emergency, shall not be liable to any person for any injury, death, loss, civil penalty, or damage as a result of any act or omission in rendering assistance, relief, or recovery services or as a result of any act or failure to act or failure to provide or arrange for further services, unless the damage or injury was caused by gross negligence or willful and wanton misconduct.

Added by Acts 2006, No. 836, § 1. Amended by Acts 2007, No. 331, § 1.

§ 2793.6. Gratuitous services rendered by Catholic charities; limitation of liability

Any entity or any officer, employee, or volunteer thereof, listed in the Official Catholic Directory published by P.J. Kenedy & Sons who gratuitously renders any evacuation assistance or services of any kind to other persons in advance of a hurricane or tropical storm declared by the United States National Oceanic and Atmospheric Administration's National Weather Service or who gratuitously renders any disaster relief or recovery services following a declared state of emergency, shall not be liable to any person for any injury, death, loss, civil penalty, or damage as a result of any act or omission in rendering assistance, relief, or recovery services or as a result of any act or failure to act or failure to provide or arrange for further services, unless the damage or injury was caused by gross negligence or willful and wanton misconduct.

Added by Acts 2006, No. 836, § 1. Amended by Acts 2007, No. 331, § 1.

§ 2793.7. Gratuitous services rendered by the Louisiana Girl Scout Councils; limitation of liability

The Louisiana Girl Scout Councils or any officer, employee, or volunteer thereof who gratuitously renders any disaster relief or recovery services following a declared state of emergency shall not be liable to any person for any injury, death, loss, civil penalty, or damage as a result of any act or omission in rendering relief or recovery services or as a result of any act or failure to act or failure to provide or arrange for further services, unless the damage or injury was caused by gross negligence or willful and wanton misconduct.

Added by Acts 2006, No. 741, § 1.

§ 2793.8. Gratuitous services rendered by National Voluntary Organizations Active in Disaster; limitation of liability

The National Voluntary Organizations Active in Disaster or its member organizations or any officer, employee, or volunteer thereof, who gratuitously renders any evacuation assistance or services of any kind to other persons in advance of a hurricane or tropical storm declared by the United States National Oceanic and Atmospheric Administration's National Weather Service or who gratuitously renders any disaster relief or recovery services following a declared state of emergency, shall not be liable to any person for any injury, death, loss, civil penalty, or damage as a result of any act or omission in rendering assistance, relief, or recovery services or as a result of any act or failure to act or failure to provide or arrange for further services, unless the damage or injury was caused by gross negligence or willful and wanton misconduct.

Added by Acts 2007, No. 109, § 1, eff. June 22, 2007.

§ 2793.9. Gratuitous services rendered by religious organizations; limitation of liability

Any religious organization qualified as a nonprofit tax-exempt organization under Section 501(c) of the Internal Revenue Code of 1954, as amended, or any officer, employee, or volunteer thereof, who gratuitously renders any evacuation assistance or recovery services of any kind to other persons in advance of a hurricane or tropical storm declared by the United States National Oceanic and Atmospheric Administration's National Weather Service or who gratuitously renders any disaster relief or recovery services during a declared state of emergency, shall not be liable to any person for whom such services are rendered for any injury, death, loss, civil penalty, or damage as a result of any act or omission in rendering assistance, relief, or recovery services or as a result of any act or failure to act or failure to provide or arrange for further services, unless the damage or injury was caused by gross negligence or willful and wanton misconduct.

Added by Acts 2008, No. 318, § 1.

§ 2794. Physicians, dentists, optometrists, and chiropractic physicians; malpractice; burden of proof; jury charge; physician witness expert qualification

A. In a malpractice action based on the negligence of a physician licensed under R.S. 37:1261 et seq., a dentist licensed under R.S. 37:751 et seq., an optometrist licensed under R.S. 37:1041 et seq., or a chiropractic physician licensed under R.S. 37:2801 et seq., the plaintiff shall have the burden of proving:

(1) The degree of knowledge or skill possessed or the degree of care ordinarily exercised by physicians, dentists, optometrists, or chiropractic physicians licensed to practice in the state of Louisiana and actively practicing in a similar community or locale and under similar circumstances; and where the defendant practices in a particular specialty and where the alleged acts of medical negligence raise issues peculiar to the particular medical specialty involved, then the plaintiff has the burden of proving the degree of care ordinarily practiced by physicians, dentists, optometrists, or chiropractic physicians within the involved medical specialty.

(2) That the defendant either lacked this degree of knowledge or skill or failed to use reasonable care and diligence, along with his best judgment in the application of that skill.

(3) That as a proximate result of this lack of knowledge or skill or the failure to exercise this degree of care the plaintiff suffered injuries that would not otherwise have been incurred.

B. Any party to an action shall have the right to subpoena any physician, dentist, optometrist, or chiropractor for a deposition or testimony for trial, or both, to establish the degree of knowledge or skill possessed or degree of care ordinarily exercised as described in Subsection A of this Section without obtaining the consent of the physician, dentist, optometrist, or chiropractor who is going to be subpoenaed only if that physician, dentist, optometrist, or chiropractor has or possesses special knowledge or experience in the specific medical procedure or process that forms the basis of the action. The fee of the physician, dentist, optometrist, or chiropractor called for deposition or testimony, or both, under this Subsection shall be set by the court.

C. In medical malpractice actions the jury shall be instructed that the plaintiff has the burden of proving, by a preponderance of the evidence, the negligence of the physician, dentist, optometrist, or chiropractic physician. The jury shall be further instructed that injury alone does not raise a presumption of the physician's, dentist's, optometrist's, or chiropractic physician's negligence. The provisions of this Section shall not apply to situations where the doctrine of res ipsa loquitur is found by the court to be applicable.

D. (1) In a medical malpractice action against a physician, licensed to practice medicine by the Louisiana State Board of Medical Examiners under R.S. 37:1261 et seq., for injury to or death of a patient, a person may qualify as an expert witness on the issue of whether the physician departed from accepted standards of medical care only if the person is a physician who meets all of the following criteria:

(a) He is practicing medicine at the time such testimony is given or was practicing medicine at the time the claim arose.

(b) He has knowledge of accepted standards of medical care for the diagnosis, care, or treatment of the illness, injury, or condition involved in the claim.

(c) He is qualified on the basis of training or experience to offer an expert opinion regarding those accepted standards of care.

(d) He is licensed to practice medicine by the Louisiana State Board of Medical Examiners under R.S. 37:1261 et seq., is licensed to practice medicine by any other jurisdiction in the United States, or is a graduate of a medical school accredited by the American Medical Association's Liaison Committee on Medical Education or the American Osteopathic Association.

(2) For the purposes of this Subsection, "practicing medicine" or "medical practice" includes but is not limited to training residents or students at an accredited school of medicine or osteopathy or serving as a consulting physician to other physicians who provide direct patient care, upon the request of such other physicians.

(3) In determining whether a witness is qualified on the basis of training or experience, the court shall consider whether, at the time the claim arose or at the time the testimony is given, the witness is board certified or has other substantial training or experience in an area of medical practice relevant to the claim and is actively practicing in that area.

(4) The court shall apply the criteria specified in Paragraphs (1), (2), and (3) of this Subsection in determining whether a person is qualified to offer expert testimony on the issue of whether the physician departed from accepted standards of medical care.

(5) Nothing in this Subsection shall be construed to prohibit a physician from qualifying as an expert solely because he is a defendant in a medical malpractice claim.

Added by Acts 1975, No. 807, § 1. Amended by Acts 1979, No. 545, § 1; Acts 1985, No. 709, § 1; Acts 1995, No. 821, § 1; Acts 1997, No. 623, § 1, eff. July 3, 1997; Acts 2003, No. 581, § 1, eff. June 27, 2003.

Cross References

C.C. art. 2315.

§ 2795. Limitation of liability of landowner of property used for recreational purposes; property owned by the Department of Wildlife and Fisheries; parks owned by public entities

A. As used in this Section:

(1) "Land" means urban or rural land, roads, water, watercourses, private ways or buildings, structures, and machinery or equipment when attached to the realty.

(2) "Owner" means the possessor of a fee interest, a tenant, lessee, occupant or person in control of the premises.

(3) "Recreational purposes" includes but is not limited to any of the following, or any combination thereof: hunting, fishing, trapping, swimming, boating, camping, picnicking, hiking, horseback riding, bicycle riding, motorized, or nonmotorized vehicle operation for recreation purposes, nature study, water skiing, ice skating, roller skating, roller blading, skate boarding, sledding, snowmobiling, snow skiing, summer and winter sports, or viewing or enjoying historical, archaeological, scenic, or scientific sites.

(4) "Charge" means the admission price or fee asked in return for permission to use lands.

(5) "Person" means individuals regardless of age.

B. (1) Except for willful or malicious failure to warn against a dangerous condition, use, structure, or activity, an owner of land, except an owner of commercial recreational developments or facilities, who permits with or without charge any person to use his land for recreational purposes as herein defined does not thereby:

(a) Extend any assurance that the premises are safe for any purposes.

(b) Constitute such person the legal status of an invitee or licensee to whom a duty of care is owed.

(c) Incur liability for any injury to person or property caused by any defect in the land regardless of whether naturally occurring or man-made.

(2) The provisions of this Subsection shall apply to owners of commercial recreational developments or facilities for injury to persons or property arising out of the commercial recreational activity permitted at the recreational development or facility that occurs on land which does not comprise the commercial recreational development or facility and over which the owner has no control when the recreational activity commences, occurs, or terminates on the commercial recreational development or facility.

C. Unless otherwise agreed in writing, the provisions of Subsection B shall be deemed applicable to the duties and liability of an owner of land leased for recreational purposes to the federal government or any state or political subdivision thereof or private persons.

D. Nothing in this Section shall be construed to relieve any person using the land of another for recreational purposes from any obligation which he may have in the absence of this Section to exercise care in his use of such land and in his activities thereon, or from the legal consequences of failure to employ such care.

E. (1) The limitation of liability provided in this Section shall apply to any lands or water bottoms owned, leased, or managed by the Department of Wildlife and Fisheries, regardless of the purposes for which the land or water bottoms are used, and whether they are used for recreational or nonrecreational purposes.

(2)(a) The limitation of liability provided in this Section shall apply to any lands, whether urban or rural, which are owned, leased, or managed as a public park by the state or any of its political subdivisions and which are used for recreational purposes.

(b) The provision of supervision on any land managed as a public park by the state or any of its political subdivisions does not create any greater duty of care which may exist and does not create a duty of care or basis of liability for personal injury or for damage to personal property caused by the act or omission of any person responsible for security or supervision of park activities, except as provided in Subparagraph (E)(2)(d) of this Section.

(c) For purposes of the limitation of liability afforded to parks pursuant to this Section this limitation does not apply to playground equipment or stands which are defective.

(d) The limitation of liability as extended to parks in this Section shall not apply to intentional or grossly negligent acts by an employee of the public entity.

F. The limitation of liability extended by this Section to the owner, lessee, or occupant of premises shall not be affected by the granting of a lease, right of use, or right of occupancy for any recreational purpose which may limit the use of the premises to persons other than the entire public or by the posting of the premises so as to limit the use of the premises to persons other than the entire public.

Added by Acts 1975, No. 615, §§ 2 to 5. Amended by Acts 1986, No. 967, § 1; Acts 1986, No. 976, § 1; Acts 1989, No. 534, § 1; Acts 1995, No. 1092, § 3; Acts 1996, 1st Ex.Sess., No. 75, § 1; Acts 2001, No. 1199, § 1.

Cross References

C.C. arts. 660, 661, 2315, 2322.

§ 2795.1. Limitation of liability of farm animal activity sponsor or professional; exceptions; required warning

A. As used in this Section, the following terms shall have the following meanings, unless the context requires otherwise:

(1) "Engages in a farm animal activity" means riding, training, providing, or assisting in providing medical treatment of, driving, or being a passenger upon a farm animal, whether mounted or unmounted, or any person assisting a participant or show management. The term "engages in a farm animal activity" does not include being a spectator at a farm animal activity, except in cases where the spectator places himself in an unauthorized area and in immediate proximity to the farm animal activity.

(2) "Farm animal" means one or more of the following animals: horse, pony, mule, donkey, hinny, cow, bull, ox or other bovine, sheep, pig, hog, goat, ratite (ostrich, rhea, emu), and chicken or other fowl.

(3) "Farm animal activity" includes any or all of the following:

(a) A farm animal show, fair, competition, performance, or parade that involves any or all farm animals, including but not limited to any dressage, hunter and jumper horse show, grand prix jumping, three-day event, combined training, rodeo, Courir de Mardi Gras, driving, pulling, cutting, polo, steeplechasing, English and western performance riding, endurance trail riding, and western game and hunting.

(b) Training or teaching activities, or both, involving farm animals.

(c) Boarding a farm animal, including daily care.

(d) Riding, inspecting, or evaluating a farm animal belonging to another, whether or not the owner has received some monetary consideration or other thing of value for the use of the farm animal or is permitting a prospective purchaser of the farm animal to ride, inspect, or evaluate the farm animal.

(e) A ride, trip, hunt, or other farm animal activity of any type, however informal or impromptu, that is sponsored by a farm animal activity sponsor.

(f) Placing or replacing horseshoes or trimming the hooves on a farm animal.

(g) Examining or administering medical treatment to a farm animal by a veterinarian.

(4) "Farm animal activity sponsor" means an individual, group, club, partnership, or corporation, whether or not the sponsor is operating for profit or nonprofit, which sponsors, organizes, or provides the facilities for a farm animal activity, including but not limited to: a pony club; 4–H club; Courir de Mardi Gras association; hunt club; riding club; school and college-sponsored class, program, and activity; therapeutic riding program; bull riding activity; and any operator, instructor, and promoter of a farm animal facility.

(5) "Farm animal facility" means any area used for any farm animal activity, including but not limited to a farm, ranch, riding arena, training stable, barn, pasture, riding trail, show ring, polo field, or other area or facility used or provided by a farm animal activity sponsor or where a participant engages in a farm animal activity.

(6) "Farm animal professional" means a person engaged for compensation in any of the following:

(a) Instructing a participant or renting to a participant a farm animal for the purpose of riding, driving, or being a passenger upon the farm animal.

(b) Renting equipment or tack to a participant in a farm animal activity.

(c) Examining or administering medical treatment to a farm animal as a veterinarian.

(d) Veterinarian or farrier services.

(7) "Inherent risks of farm animal activities" means those dangers or conditions which are an integral part of a farm animal activity, including but not limited to:

(a) The propensity of a farm animal to behave in ways that may result in injury, harm, or death to persons on or around them.

(b) The unpredictability of a farm animal's reaction to such things as sounds, sudden movement, and unfamiliar objects, persons, or other animals.

(c) Certain hazards such as surface and subsurface conditions.

(d) Collisions with other farm animals or objects.

(e) The potential of a participant to act in a negligent manner that may contribute to injury to the participant or others, such as failing to maintain control over the farm animal or not acting within his ability.

(8) "Participant" means any person, whether amateur or professional, who engages in a farm animal activity, whether or not a fee is paid to participate in the farm animal activity.

B. Except as provided in Subsection C of this Section, a farm animal activity sponsor, a farm animal professional, or any other person, which shall include a corporation or partnership, shall not be liable for an injury to or the death of a participant resulting from the inherent risks of a farm animal activity and, except as provided in Subsection C of this Section, no participant or participant's representative shall make any claim against, maintain an action against, or recover from a farm animal activity sponsor, a farm animal professional, or any other person for injury, loss, damage, or death of the participant resulting from any of the inherent risks of farm animal activities.

C. Nothing in Subsection B of this Section shall prevent or limit the liability of a farm animal activity sponsor, a farm animal professional, or any other person if the farm animal activity sponsor, farm animal professional, or person either:

(1) Provided the equipment or tack, and knew or should have known that the equipment or tack was faulty, and such equipment or tack was faulty to the extent that it did cause the injury.

(2) Failed to make reasonable and prudent efforts to determine the ability of the participant to engage safely in the farm animal activity and to safely manage the particular farm animal based on the participant's representations of his ability.

(3) Owns, leases, rents, or otherwise is in lawful possession and control of the land or facility upon which the participant sustained injuries because of a dangerous latent condition which was known or should have been known to the farm animal activity sponsor, farm animal professional, or person and for which warning signs have not been conspicuously posted.

(4) Commits an act or omission that constitutes willful or wanton disregard for the safety of the participant, and that act or omission caused the injury.

(5) Intentionally injures the participant.

D. Nothing in Subsection B of this Section shall prevent or limit the liability of a farm animal activity sponsor or a farm animal professional under liability provisions as set forth in the "Louisiana Products Liability Act", R.S. 9:2800.51 through 2800.59.

E. Every farm animal professional and every farm animal activity sponsor shall post and maintain a sign conspicuously located or provide a written warning which contains the warning notice specified in Subsection F of this Section. The sign shall be placed in a clearly visible location on or near any stable, corral, registration area, staging area, or arena where the farm animal professional or the farm animal activity sponsor conducts a farm animal activity or the written warning shall be given to each participant prior to the commencement of the parade or activities. The warning notice specified in Subsection F of this Section shall appear on the sign in black letters, with each letter to be a minimum of one inch in height or shall appear in the written warning in boldfaced capital letters no smaller than 12–point type. Every written contract entered into by a farm animal professional or by a farm animal activity sponsor for the provision of professional services, instruction, or the rental of equipment or tack or a farm animal to a participant, whether or not the contract involves farm animal activities on or off the location or site of the farm animal professional's or the farm animal activity sponsor's business, shall contain in clearly readable print the warning notice specified in Subsection F of this Section.

F. The signs, written warnings, and contracts described in Subsection E of this Section shall contain the following warning notice: "WARNING Under Louisiana law, a farm animal activity sponsor or farm animal professional is not liable for an injury to or the death of a participant in a farm animal activity resulting from the inherent risks of the farm animal activity, pursuant to R.S. 9:2795.1."

G. Failure to comply with the requirements concerning warning notices provided in this Section shall prevent a farm animal activity sponsor or farm animal professional from invoking the privilege of immunity provided by this Section. Added by Acts 1992, No. 351, § 1. Amended by Acts 1999, No. 311, § 1; Acts 2001, No. 504, § 1; Acts 2003, No. 898, § 1.

§ 2795.2. Limitation of liability for the Audubon Commission; the city of New Orleans; other entities operating facilities of the Audubon Commission; exceptions; required warning

A. As used in this Section, the following terms shall have the following meanings, unless the context requires otherwise:

(1) "Audubon Commission" means that public body created by Act 191 of 1914, as amended, and as described in the New Orleans Home Rule Charter Section 5–801 et seq.

(2) "Audubon Golf Course" means the golf course located in Audubon Park.

(3) "Audubon Park" means the public park located in the city of New Orleans operated by the Audubon Commission, including, but not limited to, that property located within the Sixth District of the city of New Orleans, which consists of that property, including the former Foucher Plantation as conveyed by act before M.L. Ainsworth, Notary Public, on August 15, 1871, and registered in the Orleans Parish Conveyance Office in COB 100, folio 187 and 181 on August 16, 1871.

(4) "Hurst Walk" shall mean the walk, walkway, path, or area, which has existed through the Audubon Golf Course between the Western Roadway on the West and the lagoon on the East in Audubon Park.

B. Except as hereinafter provided in this Section, and notwithstanding any other law to the contrary, neither the Audubon Commission, the city of New Orleans, nor any other entity which operates any facilities of the Audubon Commission, including, but not limited to, the Audubon Nature Institute, shall be liable for any loss or damage caused by injury to or the death of any person, resulting from the use of the Hurst Walk area except for intentional or grossly negligent acts by an agent or employee of the Audubon Commission, the city of New Orleans, or any other entity which operates any facilities of the Audubon Commission, including but not limited to the Audubon Nature Institute.

C. (1) Nothing in Subsection B of this Section shall prevent or limit the liability of the Audubon Commission, the city of New Orleans, or any other entity operating any facility of the Audubon Commission, including, but not limited to, the Audubon Nature Institute, unless warning signs are posted as provided in this Subsection. The warning signs provided pursuant to this Subsection shall contain the following warning notice: "You are entering an area which is within the Audubon Golf Course. This area may be dangerous and you risk being struck by golf balls or golf carts. The Audubon Commission, the city of New Orleans, or any other entity which operates any facilities of the Audubon Commission, including but not limited to the Audubon Nature Institute, shall not be liable for your injury or death resulting from your use of this area. Proceed at your own risk." The letters of the sign shall be at least four inches high.

(2) This sign shall be conspicuously located and clearly visible at either end of the Hurst Walk.

D. The limited liability provided under the provisions of this Act shall be applicable to the Audubon Commission and others governed by this legislation, including, but not limited to, all employees and agents of the Audubon Commission, the city of New Orleans, and the Audubon Nature Institute. Added by Acts 2002, 1st Ex.Sess., No. 48, § 1.

§ 2795.3. Limitation of liability of equine activity sponsor; exceptions; required warning

A. As used in this Section, the following terms shall have the following meanings, unless the context requires otherwise:

(1) "Engages in an equine activity" means riding, training, racing, driving, providing farrier services, providing or assisting in providing medical treatment of, or being a passenger upon an equine, whether mounted or unmounted, or any person assisting a participant or show management. The term "engages in an equine activity" does not include being a spectator at an equine activity, except in cases where the spectator places himself in an unauthorized area and in immediate proximity to the equine activity.

(2) "Equine" means a horse, pony, mule, donkey, or hinny.

(3) "Equine activity" includes any or all of the following:

(a) An equine show, auction, fair, race, competition, performance, parade, or carriage ride that involves any or all breeds of equine and any of the equine disciplines, including but not limited to any dressage, hunter and jumper horse show, grand prix jumping, three-day event, combined training, rodeo, driving, pulling, cutting, polo, steeplechasing, English and western performance riding, endurance trail riding and western game, racing, and hunting.

(b) Equine training or teaching activities, or both.

(c) Boarding equine.

(d) Riding, inspecting, or evaluating an equine belonging to another, whether or not the owner has received some monetary consideration or other thing of value for the use of the equine or is permitting a prospective purchaser of the equine to ride, inspect, or evaluate the equine.

(e) A ride, trip, hunt, or other equine activity of any type however informal or impromptu that are sponsored by an equine activity sponsor.

(f) Providing veterinarian or farrier services.

(4) "Equine activity sponsor" means an individual, group, club, partnership, corporation, or other entity, whether or not the sponsor is operating for profit or nonprofit, which sponsors, organizes, or provides the facilities for an equine activity, including but not limited to a pony club; 4–H club; hunt club; riding club; licensed racetrack; licensed training centers; school and college sponsored class, program, and activity; therapeutic riding program; and any operator, instructor, and promoter of an equine facility, including but not limited to a stable, clubhouse, ponyride string, fair, farm, ranch, and arena at which the activity is held.

(5) "Equine professional" means a person engaged for compensation in any of the following:

(a) Instructing a participant or renting to a participant an equine for the purpose of riding, driving, or being a passenger upon the equine.

(b) Renting equipment or tack to a participant.

(c) Providing veterinarian or farrier services.

(6) "Inherent risks of equine activities" means those dangers or conditions which are an integral part of equine activities, including but not limited to:

(a) The propensity of an equine to behave in ways that may result in injury, harm, or death to persons on or around them.

(b) The unpredictability of an equine's reaction to such things as sounds, sudden movement, and unfamiliar objects, persons, or other animals.

(c) Certain hazards such as surface and subsurface conditions.

(d) Collisions with other equine or objects.

(e) The potential of a participant to act in a negligent manner that may contribute to injury to the participant or others, such as failing to maintain control over the animal or not acting within his ability.

(7) "Participant" means any person, whether amateur or professional, who engages in an equine activity, whether or not a fee is paid to participate in the equine activity, and any equine stabled, training, or running on the racetrack or at a licensed training center and any jockey, exercise person, trainer, owner or employee, agent, or independent contractor of each.

B. Except as provided in Subsection C of this Section, an equine activity sponsor, an equine professional, or any other person, which shall include a corporation or partnership, shall not be liable for an injury to or the death of a participant resulting from the inherent risks of equine activities and, except as provided in Subsection C of this Section, no participant or participant's representative shall make any claim against, maintain an action against, or recover from an equine activity sponsor, an equine professional, or any other person for injury, loss, damage, or death of the participant resulting from any of the inherent risks of equine activities.

C. Nothing in Subsection B of this Section shall prevent or limit the liability of an equine activity sponsor, an equine professional, or any other person if the equine activity sponsor, equine professional, or person either:

(1) Provided the equipment or tack, and knew or should have known that the equipment or tack was faulty, and such equipment or tack was faulty to the extent that it did cause the injury.

(2) Failed to make reasonable and prudent efforts to determine the ability of the participant to engage safely in the equine activity and to safely manage the particular equine based on the participant's representations of his ability.

(3) Owned, leased, rented, or otherwise was in lawful possession and control of the land or facility upon which the participant sustained injuries because of a dangerous latent condition which was known or should have been known to the equine activity sponsor, equine professional, or person and for which warning signs have not been conspicuously posted.

(4) Committed an act or omission that constitutes willful or wanton disregard for the safety of the participant, and that act or omission caused the injury.

(5) Intentionally injured the participant.

D. Nothing in Subsection B of this Section shall prevent or limit the liability of an equine activity sponsor or an equine professional under liability provisions as set forth in the Louisiana Products Liability Act, R.S. 9:2800.51 through 2800.59.

E. Every equine professional and every equine activity sponsor shall post and maintain signs which contain the warning notice specified in Subsection F of this Section. Such signs shall be placed in a clearly visible location on or near any stable, corral, or arena where the equine professional or the equine activity sponsor conducts equine activities. The warning notice specified in Subsection F of this Section shall appear on each sign in black letters, with each letter to be a minimum of one inch in height. Every written contract entered into by an equine professional or by an equine activity sponsor for the providing of professional services, instruction, or the rental of equipment or tack or an equine to a participant, whether or not the contract involves equine activities on or off the location or site of the equine professional's or the equine activity sponsor's business, shall contain in clearly readable print the warning notice specified in Subsection F of this Section.

F. The signs and contracts described in Subsection E of this Section shall contain the following warning notice:

WARNING

Under Louisiana law, an equine activity sponsor or equine professional is not liable for an injury to or the death of a participant in equine activities resulting from the inherent risks of equine activities, pursuant to R.S. 9:2795.3.

G. Failure to comply with the requirements concerning warning notices provided in this Section shall prevent an equine activity sponsor or equine professional from invoking the privilege of immunity provided by this Section.

Added by Acts 2003, No. 898, § 1. Amended by Acts 2006, No. 136, § 1.

§ 2795.4. Limitation of liability; motorized off-road vehicle activities; definitions; exceptions; required warning

A. As used in this Section, the following terms shall have the following meanings, unless the context requires otherwise:

(1) "Engages in motorized off-road vehicle activity" means rides or drives, or is a passenger upon a motorized off-road vehicle, or is a person assisting a participant or management. The term "engages in a motorized off-road vehicle activity" does not include being a spectator at a motorized off-road vehicle activity, except in cases where the spectator places himself in an unauthorized area and in immediate proximity to the motorized off-road vehicle activity.

(2) "Inherent risks of motorized off-road vehicle activities" means those dangers or conditions which are an integral part of a motorized off-road vehicle activity, including but not limited to:

(a) The propensity of a motorized off-road vehicle to roll over in ways that may result in injury, harm, or death to persons on or around it.

(b) Certain hazards such as surface and subsurface conditions.

(c) Collisions with other motorized off-road vehicles or objects.

(d) The potential of a participant to act in a negligent manner that may contribute to injury to the participant or others, such as failing to maintain control over the motorized off-road vehicle or not acting within his ability.

(3) "Motorized off-road vehicle" means any two- or four-wheeled vehicle powered by a combustible engine or electric motor and weighing eleven thousand five hundred pounds or less, whether or not such vehicle is required to be registered to operate upon the highways of this state.

(4) "Motorized off-road vehicle activity" includes any or all of the following:

(a) A motorized off-road vehicle show, race, competition, or performance that involves any or all motorized off-road vehicles, including but not limited to any dirt track, paved or unpaved race course, or jump.

(b) Training, teaching, or demonstrating activities involving motorized off-road vehicles.

(c) Driving, inspecting, or evaluating a motorized off-road vehicle belonging to another, whether or not the owner has received some monetary consideration or other thing of value for the use of the motorized off-road vehicle at a motorized off-road vehicle facility.

(d) A ride, trip, hunt, or other motorized off-road vehicle activity of any type, however informal or impromptu, that is sponsored by a motorized off-road vehicle activity sponsor.

(5) "Motorized off-road vehicle activity sponsor" means an individual, group, club, partnership, or corporation, whether or not the sponsor is operating for profit or nonprofit, which sponsors, organizes, or provides the facilities for a motorized off-road vehicle activity, including but not limited to a hunting club; riding club; school or college-sponsored class, program, or activity; therapeutic riding program; or any operator, instructor, or promoter of a motorized off-road vehicle facility.

(6) "Motorized off-road vehicle facility" means any area used for any motorized off-road vehicle activity, including but not limited to a farm, ranch, riding arena, barn, pasture, riding trail, paved or unpaved race course, or other area or facility used or provided by a motorized off-road vehicle activity sponsor or where a participant engages in a motorized off-road vehicle activity.

(7) "Motorized off-road vehicle professional" means a person engaged for compensation in any of the following:

(a) Instructing a participant or renting to a participant a motorized off-road vehicle for the purpose of riding, driving, or being a passenger upon the motorized off-road vehicle.

(b) Renting equipment to a participant in a motorized off-road vehicle activity.

(8) "Participant" means any person, whether amateur or professional, who engages in a motorized off-road vehicle activity, whether or not a fee is paid to participate in the motorized off-road vehicle activity.

B. Except as provided in Subsection C of this Section, a motorized off-road vehicle activity sponsor, a motorized off-road vehicle professional, or any other person, which shall include individuals and all forms of business entities, shall not be liable for an injury to or the death of a participant resulting from the inherent risks of a motorized off-road vehicle activity and, except as provided in Subsection C of this Section, no participant or participant's representative shall make any claim against, maintain an action against, or recover from, a motorized off-road vehicle activity sponsor, a motorized off-road vehicle professional, or any other person for injury, loss, damage, or death of the participant resulting from any of the inherent risks of motorized off-road vehicle activities.

C. Nothing in Subsection B of this Section shall prevent or limit the liability of a motorized off-road vehicle activity sponsor, a motorized off-road vehicle professional, or any other person if the motorized off-road vehicle activity sponsor, motorized off-road vehicle professional, or other person either:

(1) Provided the equipment, and knew or should have known that the equipment was faulty, and such equipment was faulty to the extent that it did cause the injury.

(2) Failed to make reasonable and prudent efforts to determine the ability of the participant to engage safely in the motorized off- road vehicle activity.

(3) Owned, leased, rented, or otherwise was in lawful possession and control of the land or facility upon which the participant sustained injuries because of a dangerous latent condition which was known or should have been known to the motorized off-road vehicle activity sponsor, motorized off-road vehicle professional, or other person and for which warning signs have not been conspicuously posted.

(4) Committed an act or omission that constitutes willful or wanton disregard for the safety of the participant, and that act or omission caused the injury.

(5) Intentionally injured the participant.

D. Nothing in Subsection B of this Section shall prevent or limit the liability of a motorized off-road vehicle activity sponsor or a motorized off-road vehicle professional or other person under liability provisions as set forth in the Louisiana Products Liability Act, R.S. 9:2800.51 through 2800.59.

E. Every motorized off-road vehicle professional and every motorized off-road vehicle activity sponsor shall post and maintain a sign conspicuously located or provide a written warning which contains the warning notice specified in Subsection F of this Section. The sign shall be placed in a clearly visible location on or near any registration area, staging area, or arena where the motorized off-road vehicle professional or the motorized off-road vehicle activity sponsor conducts a motorized off-road vehicle activity, or the written warning shall be given to each participant prior to the commencement of the activities. The warning notice specified in Subsection F of this Section shall appear on the sign in black letters, with each letter to be a minimum of one inch in height or shall appear in the written warning in boldfaced capital letters no smaller than twelve-point type. Every written contract entered into by a motorized off-road vehicle professional or by a motorized off-road vehicle activity sponsor for the provision of professional services, instruction, or the rental of equipment or a motorized off-road vehicle to a participant, whether or not the contract involves motorized off-road vehicle activities on or off the location or site of the motorized off-road vehicle professional's or the motorized off-road vehicle activity sponsor's business, shall contain in clearly readable print the warning notice specified in Subsection F of this Section.

F. The signs, written warnings, and contracts described in Subsection E of this Section shall contain the following warning notice: "WARNING Under Louisiana law, a motorized off-road vehicle activity sponsor or motorized off- road vehicle professional is not liable for an injury to or the death of a participant in a motorized off-road vehicle activity resulting from the inherent risks of the motorized off-road vehicle activity, pursuant to R.S. 9:2795.4."

G. Failure to comply with the requirements concerning warning notices provided in this Section shall prevent a motorized off-road vehicle activity sponsor or motorized off-road vehicle professional from invoking the privilege of immunity provided by this Section.

Added by Acts 2003, No. 1011, § 1. Amended by Acts 2004, No. 912, § 1; Acts 2005, No. 51, § 1.

§ 2795.5. Limitation of liability; agritourism activities; definitions; exceptions; required warning

A. As used in this Section, the following terms shall have the following meanings, unless the context requires otherwise:

(1) "Agritourism" means the travel or visit by the general public to, or the practice of inviting the general public to travel to or visit, a working farm, ranch, or other commercial agricultural, aquacultural, horticultural, or forestry operation for the purpose of enjoyment, education, or participation in the activities of the farm, ranch, or other agricultural, aquacultural, horticultural, or forestry operation.

(2) "Agritourism activities" means those activities related to agritourism as defined in rules and regulations adopted by the commissioner of agriculture and forestry in accordance with the Administrative Procedure Act, and which the conduct of any such activity is set forth in a plan of operation approved by the director of the Louisiana Cooperative Extension Service of the Louisiana State University Agricultural Center or his designee.

(3) "Agritourism professional" means any person and his employees or authorized agents who offers or conducts one or more agritourism activities for agritourism purposes.

(4) "Inherent risks of agritourism activity" means those conditions, dangers, or hazards that are an integral part of an agritourism activity, including surface and subsurface conditions of land and water; natural conditions of vegetation; the behavior of wild or domestic animals; those arising from the form or use of structures or equipment ordinarily used on a working farm, ranch, or other commercial agricultural, aquacultural, horticultural, or forestry operation; and the mistakes or negligent acts of a participant that may contribute to injury to the participant or others, including failing to follow instructions given by the agritourism professional or failing to exercise reasonable caution while engaging in the agritourism activity.

(5) "Participant" means any person, other than an agritourism professional, who engages in an agritourism activity, even if that person did not pay to participate in the agritourism activity.

B. (1) Except as provided in Paragraph (2) of this Subsection, an agritourism professional is not liable for injury to or death of a participant resulting from the inherent risks of agritourism activities, so long as the warning contained in Subsection C of this Section is posted as required and, except as provided in Paragraph (2) of this Subsection, no participant or participant's representative can maintain an action against or recover from an agritourism professional for injury, loss, damage, or death of the participant resulting exclusively from any of the inherent risks of agritourism activities. In any action for damages arising out of an agritourism activity against an agritourism professional, the agritourism professional shall plead the provisions of this Section as an affirmative defense.

(2) Nothing contained in Paragraph (1) of this Subsection prevents or limits the liability of an agritourism professional, if the agritourism professional does any one or more of the following:

(a) Commits an act or omission that constitutes willful or wanton disregard for the safety of the participant and that act or omission caused injury, damage, or death to the participant.

(b) Intentionally injures the participant.

(c) Owns, leases, rents, or otherwise is in lawful possession and control of the land or facility upon which the participant sustained injuries because of a dangerous latent condition, including but not limited to the dangerous propensity of a particular animal used in such activity, which was known or should have been known to the agritourism professional and for which warning signs have not been conspicuously posted.

(d) Any limitation on liability provided in Paragraph (1) of this Subsection to an agritourism professional is in addition to any other limitation of liability otherwise provided by law.

(3) Nothing contained in Paragraph (1) of this Subsection shall prevent or limit the liability of an agritourism professional under liability provisions as set forth in the Louisiana Products Liability Act, R.S. 9:2800.51 through 2800.60.

C. (1) Every agritourism professional shall post and maintain signs that contain the warning notice specified in Paragraph (2) of this Subsection and shall be placed in a clearly visible location at the entrance to the agritourism location and at the site of the agritourism activity. The warning notice shall consist of a sign in black letters, with each letter to be a minimum of one inch in height. Every written contract entered into by an agritourism professional for the providing of professional services, instruction, or the rental of equipment to a participant, whether or not the contract involves agritourism activities on or off the location or at the site of the agritourism activity, shall contain in clearly readable print the warning notice specified in Paragraph (2) of this Subsection.

(2) The signs and contracts described in Paragraph (1) of this Subsection shall contain the following notice of warning:

"WARNING

Under Louisiana law, R.S. 9:2795.5, there is no liability for an injury to or death of a participant in an agritourism activity conducted at this agritourism location if such injury or death results from the inherent risks of the agritourism activity. Inherent risks of agritourism activities include, among others, risks of injury inherent to land, equipment, and animals, as well as the potential for you to act in a negligent manner that may contribute to your injury or death. You are assuming the risk of participating in this agritourism activity."

(3) Failure to comply with the requirements concerning warning signs and notices provided in this Subsection shall prevent an agritourism professional from invoking the limitation of liability provided by this Section.

Added by Acts 2008, No. 591, § 1.

§ 2796. Limitation of liability for loss connected with Mardi Gras parades and festivities; fair and festival parades

A. Notwithstanding any other law to the contrary, no person shall have a cause of action against any krewe or organization, any group traditionally referred to as Courir de Mardi Gras, or any member thereof, which presents Mardi Gras parades, including traditional rural Mardi Gras parades, processions, or runs in which participants ride on horseback, march, walk, or ride on horse-drawn or motordrawn floats, or wheeled beds, or other parades, whether held on a public or private street or waterway, or in a building or other structure, or any combination thereof, connected with pre-Lenten festivities or the Holiday in Dixie Parade, or against any nonprofit organization chartered under the laws of this state, or any member thereof, which sponsors fairs or festivals that present parades or courirs, for any loss or damage caused by any member thereof, during or in conjunction with or related to the parades or courirs presented by such krewe or organization, unless said loss or damage was caused by the deliberate and wanton act or gross negligence of the krewe or organization, or any member thereof as the case may be, or unless said member was operating a motor vehicle within the parade or festival and was a compensated employee of the krewe, organization, or courir. The provisions of this Section shall not be intended to limit the liability of a compensated employee of such krewe or organization for his individual acts of negligence.

B. Any person who is attending or participating in one of the organized parades of floats or persons listed in Subsection A of this Section, when the parade begins and ends between the hours of 6:00 a.m. and 12:00 midnight of the same day, assumes the risk of being struck by any missile whatsoever which has been traditionally thrown, tossed, or hurled by members of the krewe or organization in such parades held prior to the effective date of this Section. The items shall include but are not limited to beads, cups, coconuts, and doubloons unless said loss or damage was caused by the deliberate and wanton act or gross negligence of said krewe or organization.

Added by Acts 1979, No. 361, § 1. Amended by Acts 1987, No. 392, § 1; Acts 1988, No. 877, § 1; Acts 1997, No. 397, § 1, eff. Jan. 1, 1998; Acts 1999, No. 1264, § 1; Acts 2001, No. 504, § 1.

Editor's note. Acts 1997, No. 397, § 2 provides: "The provisions of this Act shall become effective on January 1, 1998, and apply to all causes of action arising on or after that date."

Cross References

C.C. art. 2315.

§ 2796.1. Limitation of liability for loss connected with St. Patrick's Day parades or any ethnic parade

Notwithstanding any other law to the contrary, no person shall have a cause of action against any organization which presents St. Patrick's Day parades or other street parades connected with any ethnic celebration, or against any nonprofit organization chartered under the laws of this state, or any member thereof, which sponsors fairs or festivals that present parades, for any loss or damage caused by any member thereof or related to the parades presented by such organization, unless said loss or damage was caused by the deliberate and wanton act or gross negligence of the organization. The provisions of this Section shall not be intended to limit the liability of a compensated employee of such organization for his individual acts of negligence.

Added by Acts 1991, No. 30, § 1.

Editor's note. Acts 1987, No. 572, § 1 added R.S. 9:2796.1 which was redesignated as R.S. 9:2798 pursuant to the statutory revision authority of the Louisiana State Law Institute.

§ 2796.2. Limitation of liability for loss connected with festivals, programs, or activities sponsored by an animal sanctuary

A. Notwithstanding any other law to the contrary, no person shall have a cause of action against any nonprofit organization which operates or maintains an animal sanctuary, qualified as a tax-exempt organization under Section 501(C) of the Internal Revenue Code of 1954, as amended, or an officer, employee, or volunteer thereof, for any injury, death, loss, or damage in connection with the Chimp Haven Festival, Dixie Chimps art contest, Les Boutiques de Noel, SciPort and Chimp Haven events, Run Wild and Have a Field Day, Eye–20 Art Show Gala, Krewe of Barkus and Meow Paws parade, Krewe of Centaur parade, Krewe of Highland parade, garden tour, ChimpStock, and any other educational and public awareness activities in which the organization sponsors or participates, unless the loss or damage was caused by the deliberate and wanton act or gross negligence of the organization or any officer, employee, or volunteer thereof.

B. As used in this Section, a "nonprofit organization which operates or maintains an animal sanctuary" means an organization authorized to provide a sanctuary system for chimpanzees in accordance with 42 U.S.C. 287a–3a.

C. The provisions of this Section shall not apply to the operation of a vehicle on a public highway by officers, employees, or volunteers of a nonprofit organization which operates or maintains an animal sanctuary.

Added by Acts 2003, No. 691, § 1.

§ 2796.3. Liability for loss related to bonfire presentations on the Mississippi River levee

A. Personal injury, wrongful death, and survivorship actions for damages against a sponsor of a bonfire presentation on the Mississippi River levee in connection with any festival or ethnic or holiday celebration shall be available to the plaintiff if the sponsor of the bonfire failed to obtain and comply with a permit for the bonfire presentation, failed to use only combustible materials approved by the local governing authority, negligently violated an order from the local governing authority, or committed a deliberate and wanton act or gross negligence, and such conduct of the sponsor was the cause in fact of the injury, death, or loss sustained by the plaintiff.

B. Igniting a bonfire by a sponsor prior to receiving specific oral authority from the local governing authority to ignite the bonfire shall constitute the negligent violation of an order of the local governing authority.

C. As used in this Section, the following terms shall have the following meanings, unless the context requires otherwise:

(1) "Bonfire" shall include only those structures which do not exceed a height of twenty feet, a width of twelve feet, and a length of twenty-four feet, and which are roped off by a minimum of twenty- five feet around the entire bonfire structure using nonflammable barricade material.

(2) "Bonfire presentation" means and includes all of the activities of constructing, igniting, and viewing a permitted bonfire on the Mississippi River levee which is being constructed and presented in connection with a festival or ethnic or holiday celebration.

(3) "Sponsor" means any governmental agency, office, or department, or any nonprofit organization, chartered under the laws of this state, or any member thereof, who applies for the bonfire permit or who is specifically listed as a participant on the bonfire permit application.

D. The provisions of this Section provide the exclusive remedies for which a plaintiff may bring a personal injury, wrongful death, or survivorship action against a sponsor of a bonfire presentation.

E. Any action for damages against a sponsor who is covered by the Louisiana Governmental Claims Act shall be subject to the provisions of R.S. 13:5101 et seq. The same limitations on the total amount recoverable provided in R.S. 13:5106(B)(1) and (2) shall be applicable to any action for damages against a nonpublic sponsor.

Added by Acts 2003, No. 1259, § 1.

§ 2797. Users of blood or tissue; a medical service

A. The screening, procurement, processing, distribution, transfusion, or medical use of human blood and blood components of any kind and the transplantation or medical use of any human organ, human tissue, or approved animal tissue by physicians, dentists, hospitals, hospital blood banks, and nonprofit community blood banks is declared to be, for all purposes whatsoever, the rendition of a medical service by each and every physician, dentist, hospital, hospital blood bank, and nonprofit community blood bank participating therein, and shall not be construed to be and is declared not to be a sale. Strict liability and warranties of any kind without negligence shall not be applicable to the aforementioned who provide these medical services.

B. In any action based in whole or in part on the use of blood or tissue by a healthcare provider, to which the provisions of this Section do not apply, the plaintiff shall have the burden of proving all elements of his claim, including defect in the thing sold and causation of his injuries by the defect by a preponderance of the evidence unaided by any presumption.

C. The provisions of Subsections A and B are procedural and apply to all alleged causes of action or other acts, omission, or neglect without regard to the date when the alleged cause of action or other act, omission, or neglect occurred.

D. As used in this Section:

(1) "Healthcare provider" includes all individuals and entities listed in R.S. 9:2797, Civil Code Article 2322.1, R.S. 40:1299.39, and R.S. 40:1299.41, whether or not enrolled with the Patient's Compensation Fund.

(2) "The use of blood or tissue" means the screening, procurement, processing, distribution, transfusion, or any medical use of human blood, blood products, and blood components of any kind and the transplantation or medical use of any human organ, human or approved animal tissue, tissue products, or tissue components by any healthcare provider.

Added by Acts 1981, No. 331, § 1, eff. July 15, 1981. Amended by Acts 1982, No. 204, § 1, eff. July 15, 1982; Acts 1987, No. 567, § 1; Acts 1990, No. 1091, § 2; Acts 1999, No. 539, § 1, eff. June 30, 1999.

Cross References

C.C. art. 2317.

§ 2797.1. Certified, nonprofit poison control centers; legislative findings; limitation of liability

A. The Legislature of Louisiana finds that the lack of a statewide poison control center is a health threat to the citizens of Louisiana. The legislature further finds that the availability of the information provided by such centers could save the lives of many citizens of this state, particularly children. The legislature further finds that liability insurance is unavailable for such centers and that this unavailability of insurance will prevent the provision of this vital service to the citizens of Louisiana.

B. No nonprofit organization established primarily to provide poison information and consultation, collect pertinent data, and deliver professional and public education which is certified as a regional poison center by the American Association of Poison Control Centers or any employee or volunteer of any such center, who in good faith provides information or consultation to any person in need thereof, shall be liable for any civil damages as a result of any act or omission by such person in providing such information or consultation, unless the damages were caused by the gross negligence or willful or wanton misconduct of the organization or employee or volunteer.

Added by Acts 1989, No. 528, § 1, eff. July 5, 1989.

§ 2798. Limitation of liability of a volunteer athletic coach, manager, team volunteer health care provider, or official; definitions

A. Except as provided in Subsection B of this Section, no person shall have a cause of action against any volunteer athletic coach, manager, athletic trainer, team volunteer health care provider, or sports team official for any loss or damage caused by any act or omission to act directly related to his responsibilities as a coach, manager, athletic trainer, team volunteer health care provider, or official, while actively conducting, directing, or participating in the sporting activities or in the practice thereof, unless the loss or damage was caused by the gross negligence of the coach, manager, athletic trainer, team volunteer health care provider, or official.

B. (1) The provisions of this Section shall not be applicable unless the volunteer athletic coach, manager, athletic trainer, team volunteer health care provider, or sports team official has participated in a safety orientation and training program established by the league or team with which he is affiliated. Any safety orientation and training program established in compliance with this Subsection may include, as a condition of satisfactory completion, a course in child cardiopulmonary resuscitation. Participation in a safety orientation and training program by a coach, manager, athletic trainer, team volunteer health care provider, or sports team official may be waived by the league prior to the individual's or person's participation in the sporting activities or in the practice thereof upon submission of appropriate documented evidence as to that individual's or person's proficiency in first aid and safety, which may include a current certification in child cardiopulmonary resuscitation.

(2) Any individual or person who has been tested or trained, and sanctioned or admitted by a recognized league or association shall be deemed to be in compliance with this Subsection. However, compliance with the requirements of this Subsection shall not be construed to create or impose on the volunteer any additional liability or higher standard of care based on participation in safety orientation and training or evidence of proficiency in first aid and safety.

C. The receipt of a small stipend or incidental compensation for volunteer services shall not exclude any individual or person, who is otherwise covered, from the limitation of liability provided in Subsection A of this Section.

D.* For the purposes of this Section, the following phrases shall have the meanings hereafter ascribed to them:

(1) "Actively conducting, directing, or participating in sporting activities or the practice thereof" means the actual preparation, training, and participation in contests or games

of physical skill, including, but not limited to post-practice, post-contest, or post-game treatment and follow-ups at a school facility, pre-season conditioning programs, teaching or other instructional seminars, team meetings, agility drills, and pre-participation fitness evaluations.

(2) "Athletic trainer" means any individual certified pursuant to R.S. 37:3301 et seq.

(3) "Team volunteer health care provider" means any individual or person defined by R.S. 40:1299.41(A) gratuitously providing health care services or treatment to the general membership of a sports team or participants of a sports league or association.

E. Nothing contained in this Section shall extend immunity to any local school system.

Added by Acts 1987, No. 572, § 1. Amended by Acts 1988, No. 420, § 1; Acts 1995, No. 1288, § 1, eff. June 29, 1995; Acts 1999, No. 798, § 1.

Editor's note. This section, enacted as R.S. 9:2796.1 by Acts 1987, No. 572, § 1 was redesignated pursuant to the statutory revision authority of the Louisiana State Law Institute.

Former R.S. 9:2798 was repealed by Acts 1986, No. 669, § 3.

§ 2798.1. Policymaking or discretionary acts or omissions of public entities or their officers or employees

A. As used in this Section, "public entity" means and includes the state and any of its branches, departments, offices, agencies, boards, commissions, instrumentalities, officers, officials, employees, and political subdivisions and the departments, offices, agencies, boards, commissions, instrumentalities, officers, officials, and employees of such political subdivisions.

B. Liability shall not be imposed on public entities or their officers or employees based upon the exercise or performance or the failure to exercise or perform their policymaking or discretionary acts when such acts are within the course and scope of their lawful powers and duties.

C. The provisions of Subsection B of this Section are not applicable:

(1) To acts or omissions which are not reasonably related to the legitimate governmental objective for which the policymaking or discretionary power exists; or

(2) To acts or omissions which constitute criminal, fraudulent, malicious, intentional, willful, outrageous, reckless, or flagrant misconduct.

D. The legislature finds and states that the purpose of this Section is not to reestablish any immunity based on the status of sovereignty but rather to clarify the substantive content and parameters of application of such legislatively created codal articles and laws and also to assist in the implementation of Article II of the Constitution of Louisiana.

Added by Acts 1985, No. 453, § 1. Amended by Acts 1995, No. 828, § 1, eff. Nov. 23, 1995.

Editor's note. Section 5 of Acts 1995, No. 828 provides that this act "shall take effect and become operative if and when the proposed amendment of Article XII, Section 10 of the Constitution of Louisiana, contained in Acts 1995, No. 1328, is adopted at the gubernatorial election to be held in 1995 and becomes effective."

The amendment of Article XII, Section 10 of the Constitution of Louisiana was adopted on October 21, 1995. It became effective on November 23, 1995.

§ 2798.2. Limitation of liability for school volunteers

A. No person working as a school volunteer in any elementary or secondary school, who has been approved for school volunteer work by the principal of the school, shall be personally liable for any loss or damage caused by any act or omission directly related to his responsibilities as a school volunteer, unless the loss or damage was caused by the gross negligence or willful or wanton acts of the school volunteer. The limitation of liability under this Section shall be personal to the school volunteer and shall not extend to any other person or entity who is or may be liable, either vicariously or in contract, for damages caused by the volunteer.

B. The school board or other entity having ownership of or jurisdiction over the elementary or secondary school for which the school volunteer is providing volunteer services shall be liable for any acts or omissions of such volunteer.

Added by Acts 1988, No. 789, § 1. Amended by Acts 1989, No. 288, § 1, eff. June 27, 1989.

Cross References

C.C. art. 2315.

§ 2798.3. Limitation of liability for school systems

No school board or other entity having jurisdiction over a public elementary or secondary school shall be liable for any acts or omissions of any student who has been assigned to perform public work as defined by R.S. 17:416 as a disciplinary measure.

Added by Acts 1994, 3rd Ex.Sess., No. 45, § 1.

§ 2798.4. Immunity from liability; injuries sustained by persons driving under the influence of alcoholic beverages or drugs

A. Neither the state, a state agency, or a political subdivision of the state nor any person shall be liable for damages, including those available under Civil Code Article 2315.1 or 2315.2, for injury, death, or loss of the operator of a motor vehicle, aircraft, watercraft, or vessel who:

(1) Was operating a motor vehicle, aircraft, watercraft, or vessel while his blood alcohol concentration of 0.08 percent or more by weight based on grams of alcohol per one hundred cubic centimeters of blood; or

(2) Was operating a motor vehicle, aircraft, watercraft, or vessel while he was under the influence of any controlled dangerous substance described in R.S. 14:98(A)(1)(c) or R.S. 40:964.

B. The provisions of this Section shall not apply unless:

(1) The operator is found to be in excess of twenty-five percent negligent as a result of a blood alcohol concentration in excess of the limits provided in R.S. 14:98(A)(1)(b), or the operator is found to be in excess of twenty-five percent negligent as a result of being under the influence of a controlled dangerous substance described in R.S. 14:98(A)(1)(c); and

(2) This negligence was a contributing factor causing the damage.

C. For purposes of this Section, "damages" include all general damages, including those otherwise recoverable in a survival or wrongful death action, which may be recoverable for personal injury, death or loss, or damage to property by the operator of a motor vehicle, aircraft, watercraft, or vessel or the category of persons who would have a cause of action for the operator's wrongful death.

D. The provisions of this Section shall not apply if the operator tests positive for any controlled dangerous substance covered by the provisions of R.S. 14:98(A)(1)(c) or R.S. 40:964 and the operator is taking that substance pursuant to a valid prescription for the identified substance or a health care provider verifies that he has prescribed or furnished the operator with that particular substance.

E. Unless the operator's insurance policy provides otherwise, nothing in this Section shall be construed to preclude the operator from making a claim under his or her own policy for first party indemnity coverages.

Added by Acts 1999, No. 1224, § 1, eff. July 9, 1999. Amended by Acts 2004, No. 394, § 1.

§ 2798.5. Limitation of liability; Louisiana Emergency Response Network

A. **Legislative intent.** The provisions of this Section are intended to provide for a limitation of liability for any authorized and duly licensed or certified person or juridical person who specifically acts in accordance with protocols adopted and promulgated by the Louisiana Emergency Response Network Board for the transport of trauma and time-sensitive ill patients. The protocols are developed to facilitate the timely and appropriate delivery of patients to the most appropriate care site for the definitive treatment of injuries.

B. Liability shall not be imposed on any authorized and duly licensed or certified person or juridical person who acts in good faith and within the scope of applicable protocols adopted and promulgated by the Louisiana Emergency Response Network Board (R.S. 40:2842(1)) for the Louisiana Emergency Response Network (R.S. 40:2842(3)), in accordance with the statutory mandates provided in R.S. 40:2842 et seq., for damages from acts or omissions resulting in injury, death, or loss, unless such damage or injury was caused by willful or wanton misconduct or gross negligence.

C. The provisions of this Section shall not supersede the provisions of R.S. 9:2798.1 or apply to claims covered by R.S. 13:5101 et seq., R.S. 40:1299.39 et seq., or R.S. 40:1299.41.

Added by Acts 2007, No. 360, § 1. Amended by Acts 2008, No. 220, § 2, eff. June 14, 2008.

§ 2799. Limitation of liability for damages from donated food

A. (1) No person shall have a cause of action against a food bank and its designated distributor or against any individual, farmer, food service establishment, school, church, civic organization, manufacturer, processor, packer, restaurant, wholesaler, or retailer of food, or vitamins, who donates to food banks perishable, salvageable, or prepared food for gleaning or for free distribution by food banks, for damages caused by the condition of the food or vitamins, unless the damages result from the intentional act or omission or the gross negligence of the food bank, its designated distributor, or donor.

(2) No person shall have a cause of action against a food bank or its designated distributors, or against the donor of wild game, for any damages arising from or caused by the wild game, including the condition of the wild game, which is distributed directly or for redistribution by a food bank or its designated distributors, to the needy, the ill, the handicapped, infants or seniors, or to individuals or families who need emergency food assistance, unless the damages resulted from an intentional act or omission of the food bank, its designated distributor, or donor. For purposes hereof, "wild game" means all game fish, migratory and resident game birds, and game quadrupeds, as defined in R.S. 56:8.

B. For purposes of this Section, words or phrases used in this Section shall have the following meanings:

(1) "Food bank" means a nonprofit entity which operates as a clearinghouse for the purpose of gathering primarily from the food industry those products which, though edible, nutritious, or saleable, are not marketable for various reasons, and distributing those edible products to designated distributors with on-premises feeding programs that serve the needy, the ill, the handicapped, and infants, and to individuals or families who need emergency food assistance rendered in the form of emergency food boxes, provided the entity is inspected and issued permits under the terms of R.S. 40:3 and 5 by the Department of Health and Hospitals.

(2) "Vitamin" means an essential low molecular weight organic compound required in trace amounts for normal growth and metabolic processes which usually serve as components of coenzyme systems. Vitamin shall not include any drug which can be obtained only through a prescription ordered by a medical professional or drug classified as a controlled dangerous substance pursuant to the provisions of R.S. 40:961 et seq.

Added by Acts 1981, No. 705, § 1. Amended by Acts 1988, No. 486, § 1, eff. July 9, 1988; Acts 1989, No. 542, § 1; Acts 1997, No. 375, § 1; Acts 1997, No. 1286, § 1; Acts 2001, No. 494, § 1, eff. June 21, 2001; Acts 2002, 1st Ex.Sess., No. 34, § 1; Acts 2003, No. 475, § 1; Acts 2012, No. 423, § 1.

Cross References

C.C. art. 2315.

§ 2799.1. Civil liability for theft of goods from merchant

A. Any person who unlawfully takes merchandise from a merchant's premises shall be liable to the merchant for the retail value of the merchandise taken, if not recovered in merchantable condition, plus damages of not less than fifty nor more than five hundred dollars.

B. The provisions of this Section shall not be construed to prohibit or limit any other cause of action which a merchant may have against a person who unlawfully takes merchandise from the merchant's premises.

Added by Acts 1985, No. 533, § 1.

§ 2799.2. Institutional vandalism; civil damages

A. The act of institutional vandalism is the engaging in any acts defined in R.S. 14:225.

B. Any person who engages in the act of institutional vandalism shall be liable for general or special compensatory damages, including damages for emotional distress, and costs.

Added by Acts 1986, No. 448, § 1.

Cross References

C.C. art. 2315.

§ 2799.3. Limitation of liability of restaurants, schools, churches, civic organizations, and certain food donors for damages from donated food

No person shall have a cause of action against a restaurant, church, civic organization, or school, or against any individual, farmer, manufacturer, processor, packer, wholesaler, or retailer of food who donates perishable, salvageable food which is prepared and subsequently donated by the restaurant, church, civic organization, or school to a facility which operates an on-premises feeding program for the needy, the ill, the handicapped, infants, or individuals or families in need of assistance for damages caused by the condition of the food, unless the damages result from the intentional act or omission or the negligence of the restaurant or donor.

Added by Acts 1989, No. 698, § 1. Amended by Acts 2012, No. 423, § 1.

§ 2799.4. Liability for unauthorized release of certain animals, birds, or aquatic species

A. Any person who, without permission from the owner or agent in possession, releases or attempts to release an animal, a bird, or an aquatic species which has been lawfully confined for agriculture, science, research, commerce, public propagation, protective custody, or education shall be liable:

(1) To the owner or agent exercising possession of the animal, bird, or aquatic species for damages and replacement costs, including the cost of restoring the animal, bird, or aquatic species to confinement and to its health prior to being released.

(2) For damages to property caused by the release or attempted release of the animal, bird, or aquatic species.

B. If the release or attempted release causes the failure of an experiment, the person causing the release or attempted release shall be liable for all costs of repeating the experiment, including replacement of the animal, bird, or aquatic species.

Added by Acts 1990, No. 205, § 1.

§ 2799.5. Limitation of liability for gratuitous service by a health care provider in a community health care clinic or community pharmacy

A. The Legislature of Louisiana finds that the lack of affordable health care and medication is a health threat to the citizens of Louisiana. The legislature further finds that the rendering of gratuitous services by health care providers in and for community health care clinics and the availability of free medication provide needed medical services and pharmaceuticals which can save the lives of many citizens of this state, particularly children.

B. (1) No health care provider who in good faith gratuitously renders health care services in a community health care clinic or pursuant to an arrangement with a community health care clinic providing that such services will be rendered at the offices of a health care provider shall be liable for any civil damages as a result of any act or omission in rendering such care or services or as a result of any act or failure to act to provide or arrange for further medical treatment or care to any person receiving such services, unless the damages were caused by the gross negligence or willful or wanton misconduct of the health care provider.

(2)(a) The provisions of this Subsection shall be applicable only if the person receiving the health care services receives prior notice from the community health care clinic of the limitation of liability provided for in this Paragraph.

(b) Either at the initial screening of a person or at the time health care services are provided, the community health care clinic or the community health care provider furnishing services shall inform such person of the limitation of liability provided by this Section by: distributing to such person a notice, in a form such person can keep; and have printed and keep posted, at a convenient and conspicuous place where patients entering the clinic will see it, which notice shall read substantially as follows:

"NOTICE - If you are injured here because of things we do or fail to do, you do not have the same legal recourse as you would have against other health care providers."

(c) If the notice is posted, the notice shall be printed in type size sufficient to be easily read by patients upon entering the facility.

(d) Failure to follow notice procedures as provided in this Section negates the limitation of liability provided by this Section.

(3)(a) A community health care clinic or community pharmacy shall conduct a screening to determine whether a prospective patient is enrolled or eligible to be enrolled in a gratuitous medical or dental treatment plan, including enrollment or eligibility to be enrolled for health care benefits in a public entitlement program, including Medicaid, Louisiana Children's Health Insurance Program (LaCHIP), or Medicare.

(b) A community health care clinic or community pharmacy may provide or arrange health care services for a patient who is enrolled or eligible to be enrolled for those services under any gratuitous plan or entitlement program for the immediate or current health condition, illness, injury, or disease and any subsequent medically necessary health care services to diagnose, prevent, treat, cure, or relieve the health condition, illness, injury, or disease. The provision or arrangement for health care services by a community health care clinic or community pharmacy to a patient shall be based on the health care resources of that clinic or pharmacy.

(c) A community health care clinic or community pharmacy shall provide assistance to an eligible patient on enrollment in a gratuitous medical or dental treatment plan or a public entitlement program for which he may qualify within sixty days of screening by the clinic or pharmacy in accordance with Subparagraph (3)(a) of this Subsection.

(d) Nothing in this Section shall be construed to prohibit any individual from receiving health care services provided or arranged by a community health care clinic or community pharmacy.

(4) A community health care clinic that provides or arranges for services at the office of a licensed health care provider after due notice is provided pursuant to Paragraph (2) of this Subsection and appropriate financial screening shall refer a person who is qualified to receive gratuitous health care services to a primary care physician or a general dentist for a medical assessment or examination and treatment, if appropriate, or to determine the necessity to refer such person to a medical or dental specialist for treatment.

C. (1) No pharmacist who gratuitously renders services in a community pharmacy shall be liable for any civil damages as a result of any act or omission in preparing, bottling, or supplying such pharmaceutical products, unless the damages were caused by the gross negligence or willful or wanton misconduct of the pharmacist.

(2) The provisions of this Subsection shall be applicable only if the community pharmacy posts, in a convenient and conspicuous place where persons entering the pharmacy will see it, a notice reading substantially as follows: "NOTICE – If you are harmed by medication which you receive here, you do not have the same legal recourse as you would have against other pharmacies." The notice shall be printed in type size sufficient to be easily read by persons upon entering the facility. Failure to keep such notice posted as provided negates the limitation of liability provided by this Subsection.

D. For purposes of this Section:

(1) "Community health care clinic" means a nonprofit organization qualified or eligible for qualification as a tax-exempt organization under 26 U.S.C. 501, which operates a medical clinic or which provides or arranges for services at the offices of a licensed health care provider solely for educational or charitable purposes, whose principal function is to supply or to make arrangements for the supply of the facilities, volunteer staff, and other support for the rendering of gratuitous medical or dental treatment.

(2) "Community pharmacy" means a nonprofit organization qualified or eligible for qualification as a tax-exempt organization under 26 U.S.C. 501, which operates a pharmacy solely for charitable purposes, whose principal function is to supply gratuitous pharmaceuticals.

(3) "Health care provider" means a clinic, person, corporation, facility, or institution which provides health care or professional services by a physician, clinic, dentist, registered or licensed practical nurse, pharmacist, optometrist, podiatrist, chiropractor, physical therapist, psychologist, or psychiatrist, and any officer, employee, or agent thereof acting in the course and scope of his employment.

(4) "Pharmacist" means a pharmacy, person, corporation, facility, or institution which supplies pharmaceuticals prepared or bottled, or both, by the pharmacists, and otherwise handled by any officer, employee, or agent thereof acting in the course and scope of his service or employment.

E. The provisions of this Section shall not apply to any health care provider rendering services covered by the provisions of R.S. 40:1299.39 et seq.

F. Any health care provider who in good faith gratuitously renders health care services during any evacuation assistance or in advance of a hurricane or tropical storm declared by the United States National Oceanic and Atmospheric Administration's National Weather Service, or who gratuitously renders any health care services, disaster relief or recovery services following a declared state of emergency, in a community health care clinic or community pharmacy, or pursuant to an arrangement with a community health care clinic, shall not be liable for any civil damages as a result of any act or omission in rendering such relief or recovery services or health care services or as a result of any act or failure to act to provide or arrange for further medical treatment, health care services, relief or recovery services to any person receiving such services, unless the damage or injury was caused by the gross negligence or willful or wanton misconduct of the health care provider.

Added by Acts 1995, No. 1230, § 2. Amended by Acts 1997, No. 959, § 1; Acts 1999, No. 1351, § 1; Acts 2001, No. 577, § 1; Acts 2004, No. 405, § 1; Acts 2007, No. 331, § 1.

§ 2799.6. Limitation of liability for damages from long-term consumption of food and nonalcoholic beverages

A. Any manufacturer, distributor, or seller of a food or nonalcoholic beverage intended for human consumption shall not be subject to civil liability for personal injury or wrongful death based on an individual's consumption of food or nonalcoholic beverages in cases where liability is premised upon the individual's weight gain, obesity, or a health condition related to weight gain or obesity and resulting from his long-term consumption of a food or nonalcoholic beverage.

B. For purposes of this Section, the term "long-term consumption" shall mean the cumulative effect of the consumption of food or nonalcoholic beverages, and not the effect of a single instance of consumption.

Added by Acts 2003, No. 158, § 1, eff. June 2, 2003.

Editor's note. Section 2 of Acts 2003, No. 158 declares that the provisions of this Act "shall be applicable to all claims existing or actions pending or filed on or after its effective date, unless a trial or retrial with regard to the civil action has commenced as of the effective date of this Act."

§ 2800. Limitation of liability for public bodies

A. A public entity is responsible under Civil Code Article 2317 for damages caused by the condition of buildings within its care and custody.

B. Where other constructions are placed upon state property by someone other than the state, and the right to keep the improvements on the property has expired, the state shall not be responsible for any damages caused thereby unless the state affirmatively takes control of and utilizes the improvement for the state's benefit and use.

C. Except as provided for in Subsections A and B of this Section, no person shall have a cause of action based solely upon liability imposed under Civil Code Article 2317 against a public entity for damages caused by the condition of things within its care and custody unless the public entity had actual or constructive notice of the particular vice or defect which caused the damage prior to the occurrence, and the public entity has had a reasonable opportunity to remedy the defect and has failed to do so.

D. Constructive notice shall mean the existence of facts which infer actual knowledge.

E. A public entity that responds to or makes an examination or inspection of any public site or area in response to reports or complaints of a defective condition on property of which the entity has no ownership or control and that takes steps to forewarn or alert the public of such defective condition, such as erecting barricades or warning devices in or adjacent to an area, does not thereby gain custody, control, or garde of the area or assume a duty to prevent personal injury, wrongful death, property damage, or other loss as to render the public entity liable unless it is shown that the entity failed to notify the public entity which does have care and custody of the property of the defect within a reasonable length of time.

F. A violation of the rules and regulations promulgated by a public entity is not negligence per se.

G. (1) "Public entity" means and includes the state and any of its branches, departments, offices, agencies, boards, commissions, instrumentalities, officers, officials, employees, and political subdivisions and the departments, offices, agencies, boards, commissions, instrumentalities, officers, officials, and employees of such political subdivisions. Public entity also includes housing authorities, as defined in R.S. 40:384(15), and their commissioners and other officers and employees and sewerage and water boards and their employees, servants, agents, or subcontractors.

(2) "Public site or area" means any publicly owned or common thing, or any privately owned property over which the public's access is not prohibited, limited, or restricted in some manner including those areas of unrestricted access such as streets, sidewalks, parks, or public squares.

H. Terminated by Acts 2006, No. 545, § 1, eff. Aug. 30, 2008.

Added by Acts 1985, No. 454, § 1, eff. July 12, 1985. Amended by Acts 1992, No. 581, § 1; Acts 1995, No. 828, § 1, eff. Nov. 23, 1995; Acts 2003, No. 725, § 1; Acts 2003, No. 1077, § 1, eff. July 2, 2003; Acts 2006, No. 545, § 1.

Editor's note. Section 5 of Acts 1995, No. 828 provides that this act "shall take effect and become operative if and when the proposed amendment of Article XII, Section 10 of the Constitution of Louisiana, contained in Acts 1995, No. 1328, is adopted at the gubernatorial election to be held in 1995 and becomes effective."

The amendment of Article XII Section 10 of the Constitution of Louisiana was adopted on October 21, 1995. It became effective on November 23, 1995.

Section 2 of Acts 2003, No. 725 declares that "the provisions of R.S. 9:2800(B) as enacted by this Act shall be applied prospectively and shall also be applied retroactively to any improvements on state lands or waterbottoms, but shall not apply to any damages that have occurred prior to the effective date of this Act."

Section R.S. 9:2800(H)(4), enacted by Acts 2006, No. 545, declares that "The provisions of this subsection shall be given retroactive application to August 26, 2005." For possible constitutional objections to the retroactive application, see Yiannopoulos, Civil Law System §§ 110–112 (2d ed.1999); *id.*, Civil Law Property § 10 (2001)).

§ 2800.1. Limitation of liability for loss connected with sale, serving, or furnishing of alcoholic beverages

A. The legislature finds and declares that the consumption of intoxicating beverages, rather than the sale or serving or furnishing of such beverages, is the proximate cause of any injury, including death and property damage, inflicted by an intoxicated person upon himself or upon another person.

B. Notwithstanding any other law to the contrary, no person holding a permit under either Chapter 1 or Chapter 2 of Title 26 of the Louisiana Revised Statutes of 1950 [1], nor any agent, servant, or employee of such a person, who sells or serves intoxicating beverages of either high or low alcoholic content to a person over the age for the lawful purchase thereof, shall be liable to such person or to any other person or to the estate, successors, or survivors of either for any injury suffered off the premises, including wrongful death and property damage, because of the intoxication of the person to whom the intoxicating beverages were sold or served.

C. (1) Notwithstanding any other law to the contrary, no social host who serves or furnishes any intoxicating beverage of either high or low alcoholic content to a person over the age for the lawful purchase thereof shall be liable to such person or to any other person or to the estate, successors, or survivors of either for any injury suffered off the premises, including wrongful death and property damage, because of the intoxication of the person to whom the intoxicating beverages were served or furnished.

(2) No social host who owns, leases, or otherwise lawfully occupies premises on which, in his absence and without his consent, intoxicating beverages of either high or low alcoholic content are consumed by a person over the age for the lawful purchase thereof shall be liable to such person or to any other person or to the estate, successors, or survivors of either for any injury suffered off the premises, including wrongful death and property damage, because of the intoxication of the person who consumed the intoxicating beverages.

D. The insurer of the intoxicated person shall be primarily liable with respect to injuries suffered by third persons.

E. The limitation of liability provided by this Section shall not apply to any person who causes or contributes to the consumption of alcoholic beverages by force or by falsely representing that a beverage contains no alcohol.

Added by Acts 1986, No. 18, § 1, eff. June 6, 1986.

[1] R.S. 26:1 et seq. or 26:241 et seq.

Cross References

C.C. arts. 2315, 2315.4, 2315.5.

§ 2800.2. Psychologist, psychiatrist, marriage and family therapist, licensed professional counselor, and social worker; limitation of liability

A. When a patient has communicated a threat of physical violence, which is deemed to be significant in the clinical judgment of the treating psychologist or psychiatrist, or marriage and family therapist, or licensed professional counselor, or social worker, against a clearly identified victim or victims, coupled with the apparent intent and ability to carry out such threat, the psychologist, licensed under R.S. 37:2351 through 2369, the medical psychologist, licensed under R.S. 37:1360.51 through 1360.72, the psychiatrist, licensed under R.S. 37:1261 through 1291, or the social worker, credentialed under R.S. 37:2701 through 2723, treating such patient and exercising reasonable professional judgment, shall not be liable for a breach of confidentiality for warning of such threat or taking precautions to provide protection from the patient's violent behavior.

B. A psychologist's, psychiatrist's, or marriage and family therapist, or licensed professional counselor, or social worker's duty to warn or to take reasonable precautions to provide protection from violent behavior arises only under the circumstance specified in Subsection A of this Section. This duty shall be discharged by the psychologist, psychiatrist, or marriage and family therapist, or licensed professional counselor, or social worker if the treating professional makes a reasonable effort to communicate the threat to the potential victim or victims and to notify law enforcement authorities in the vicinity of the patient's or potential victim's residence.

C. No liability or cause of action shall arise against any psychologist, psychiatrist, or marriage and family therapist, or licensed professional counselor, or social worker based on an invasion of privacy or breach of confidentiality for any confidence disclosed to a third party in an effort to discharge the duty arising under Subsection A of this Section.

Added by Acts 1986, No. 697, § 1, eff. July 8, 1986. Amended by Acts 1987, No. 397, § 1; Acts 1993, No. 764, § 1, eff. June 22, 1993; Acts 2003, No. 870, § 1; Acts 2009, No. 251, § 2, eff. Jan. 1, 2010.

Editor's note. This section became effective on January 1, 2010. See Acts 2009, No. 251, § 14.

Cross References

C.C. art. 2315.

§ 2800.3. Limitation of liability of persons designing, supervising or performing hazardous waste mitigation, abatement, or cleanup and asbestos removal, abatement, or cleanup services

A. There shall be no liability on the part of duly authorized personnel of a state approved educational facility or any duly licensed architect or engineer contracting to design or supervise or any contractor engaged in hazardous waste mitigation, abatement, or cleanup services and asbestos removal, abatement, or cleanup services, for any injury to person or property caused by or related to such services, unless it is shown by a preponderance of the evidence that the design, supervision, or removal was either in violation of procedures established in accordance with applicable state or federal laws relative to such services, and was a proximate cause of the injury, or that the performance of such design, supervision, or removal is found, by a preponderance of evidence, to constitute negligence and was a proximate cause of the injury.

B. The provisions of this Section shall not be construed to alter, amend, or repeal R.S. 30:1148 [1] or R.S. 30:1149.46 [2].

Added by Acts 1986, No. 952, § 1. Amended by Acts 1988, No. 518, § 1, eff. July 8, 1988.

[1] Former R.S. 30:1148 was redesignated as R.S. 30:2204 in 1988.
[2] Former R.S. 30:1149.46 was redesignated as R.S. 30:2276 in 1988.

Cross References

C.C. art. 2315.

§ 2800.4. Limitation of liability of owner of farm or forest land; owner of oil, gas, or mineral property

A. As used in this Section:

(1) "Owner" means the owner and also a tenant, lessee, occupant, or person in control of any farm or forest land or in control of any oil, gas, or mineral property.

(2) "Farm land or forest land" shall mean bona fide agricultural or timberland assessed as such for parish ad valorem taxes.

(3) "Gleaning" means gathering the residue of a crop left in the fields to waste after harvesting is completed.

(4) "Oil, gas, or mineral property" shall mean any land leased for the development and production of oil, gas, or minerals.

B. An owner of farm or forest land shall not be liable to any person, who unlawfully enters upon his farm or forest land, for damages for any injury, death, or loss which occurs while on the farm or forest land of the owner, unless such damage, injury, or death was caused by the intentional act or gross negligence of the owner.

C. An owner of farm or forest land, who allows his land to be used as a landing strip for aerial applications for agricultural purposes, shall not be liable to any person for damages for any injury, death, or loss which occurs during or in connection with such application while on the land of the owner, unless such damage, injury, or death was caused by the intentional act or negligence of the owner.

D. An owner of farm or forest land, who allows his land to be used by a group or individuals for the purpose of gleaning, without compensation to the landowner from the group or individuals, shall not be liable to any person for damages for any injury, death, or loss which occurs during or in connection with such gleaning while on the land of the owner, unless such damage, injury, or death was caused by the intentional act or negligence of the owner.

E. An owner of oil, gas, or mineral property shall not be liable to any person who unlawfully enters upon his oil, gas, or mineral property, for damages for any injury, death, or loss which occurs while on the oil, gas, or mineral property of the owner, unless such damage, injury, or death was caused by the intentional act or gross negligence of the owner.

Added by Acts 1987, No. 580, § 1. Amended by Acts 1989, No. 119, § 1; Acts 1990, No. 828, § 1; Acts 1993, No. 889, § 1.

Editor's note. Acts 1987, No. 605, § 1 enacted R.S. 9:2800.4 which was redesignated as R.S. 9:2800.5 pursuant to the statutory revision of the Louisiana State Law Institute.

§ 2800.5. Immunity from liability for owners of block safe-houses

A. Any owner of a block safe-house shall not be liable for damages for injury, death, or loss to a child using the home under approved guidelines adopted by local authorities as a safe-house or for any act or omission in rendering emergency care, first aid, or rescue, unless such act or omission was intentional or the result of gross negligence.

B. For purposes of this Section, the term "block safe-house" means any residential dwelling which has been designated by the local authorities as a dwelling in which children may seek refuge in time of emergency.

C. For purposes of this Section, the term "owner" includes an owner, tenant, occupant, or person in control of any block safe-house.

Added by Acts 1987, No. 605, § 1.

Editor's note. This section, enacted by Acts 1987, No. 605, § 1 as R.S. 9:2800.4, was redesignated pursuant to the statutory revision authority of the Louisiana State Law Institute.

§ 2800.6. Burden of proof in claims against merchants

A. A merchant owes a duty to persons who use his premises to exercise reasonable care to keep his aisles, passageways, and floors in a reasonably safe condition. This duty includes a reasonable effort to keep the premises free of any hazardous conditions which reasonably might give rise to damage.

B. In a negligence claim brought against a merchant by a person lawfully on the merchant's premises for damages as a result of an injury, death, or loss sustained because of a fall due to a condition existing in or on a merchant's premises, the claimant shall have the burden of proving, in addition to all other elements of his cause of action, all of the following:

(1) The condition presented an unreasonable risk of harm to the claimant and that risk of harm was reasonably foreseeable.

(2) The merchant either created or had actual or constructive notice of the condition which caused the damage, prior to the occurrence.

(3) The merchant failed to exercise reasonable care. In determining reasonable care, the absence of a written or verbal uniform cleanup or safety procedure is insufficient, alone, to prove failure to exercise reasonable care.

C. Definitions:

(1) "Constructive notice" means the claimant has proven that the condition existed for such a period of time that it would have been discovered if the merchant had exercised reasonable care. The presence of an employee of the merchant in the vicinity in which the condition exists does not, alone, constitute constructive notice, unless it is shown that the employee knew, or in the exercise of reasonable care should have known, of the condition.

(2) "Merchant" means one whose business is to sell goods, foods, wares, or merchandise at a fixed place of business. For purposes of this Section, a merchant includes an innkeeper with respect to those areas or aspects of the premises which are similar to those of a merchant, including but not limited to shops, restaurants, and lobby areas of or within the hotel, motel, or inn.

D. Nothing herein shall affect any liability which a merchant may have under Civil Code Arts. 660, 667, 669, 2317, 2322, or 2695.

Added by Acts 1988, No. 714, § 1, eff. July 18, 1988. Amended by Acts 1990, No. 1025, § 1, eff. Sept. 1, 1990; Acts 1996, 1st Ex.Sess., No. 8, § 1, eff. May 1, 1996.

Editor's note. R.S. 9:2800.6 was added by Acts 1988, No. 714, § 1. Section 2 of this act provides that the act "shall become effective upon signature by the governor" and that it "shall apply to all cases tried on or after such date." The act was signed by the governor on July 18, 1988.

Acts 1988, No. 723, § 1 also enacted R.S. 9:2800.6. This statute has been redesignated as R.S. 9:2800.7 pursuant to the statutory revision authority of the Louisiana State Law Institute.

Acts 1990, No. 1025, § 1 amended R.S. 9:2800.6. Section 2 of this act provides that the act "shall become effective September 1, 1990" and that it "shall apply only to causes of action which arise on or after the effective date of this Act."

Section 2 of Act No. 8 of 1996 (1st Extraordinary Session) declares that "the provisions of this Act shall apply only to those causes of action arising on or after the effective date of this Act."

Cross References

C.C. arts. 660, 667, 669, 2315, 2317, 2322, 2695.

§ 2800.7. Repealed by Acts 2010, No. 706, § 2, eff. Jan. 1, 2012

Editor's note. Section 2 of Acts 1988, No. 723 declares that the provisions of this Act "shall become effective on January 1, 1989, except the method of communication established in Subsection A and the provisions of Subsection K which shall become effective on November 1, 1988."

Section 3 declares that the provisions of this Act "shall apply only to actions instituted on or after the effective date of this Act."

This section, enacted by Acts 1988, No. 723, § 1 as R.S. 9:2800.6, was redesignated pursuant to the statutory revision authority of the Louisiana State Law Institute.

Cross References

C.C. art. 2315.

§ 2800.8. Property adjudicated to local governmental subdivision; liability of owner of record

The owner of record of property adjudicated to a local governmental subdivision by means of a tax sale shall be liable for damages occurring on or to the property, or arising from or in connection with the possession or use of the property, until the redemptive and peremptive periods applicable to such property have expired. Nothing herein affects the liability of the local governmental subdivision for its activities in connection with its actual use or possession of the property.

Added by Acts 1989, No. 391, § 1.

§ 2800.9. Action against a person for abuse of a minor

A. An action against a person for sexual abuse of a minor, or for physical abuse of a minor resulting in permanent impairment or permanent physical injury or scarring, is subject to a liberative prescriptive period of ten years. This prescription commences to run from the day the minor attains majority, and this prescription shall be suspended for all purposes until the minor reaches the age of majority. Abuse has the same meaning as provided in Louisiana Children's Code Article 603. This prescriptive period shall be subject to any exception of peremption provided by law.

B. Every plaintiff twenty-one years of age or older at the time the action is filed shall file certificates of merit executed by the attorney for the plaintiff and by a licensed mental health practitioner selected by the plaintiff declaring, respectively, as follows:

(1) That the attorney has reviewed the facts of the case, that the attorney has consulted with at least one licensed mental health practitioner who is licensed to practice and practices in this state and whom the attorney reasonably believes is knowledgeable of the relevant facts and issues involved in the particular action, and that the attorney has concluded on the basis of that review and consultation that there is reasonable and meritorious cause for the filing of the petition. The person consulted may not be a party to the litigation.

(2) That the mental health practitioner consulted is licensed to practice and practices in this state and is not a party to the action, has interviewed the plaintiff and is knowledgeable of the relevant facts and issues involved in the particular action, and has concluded, on the basis of his knowledge of the facts and issues, that in his professional opinion there is a reasonable basis to believe that the plaintiff has been subject to criminal sexual activity or physical abuse during his childhood as defined in this Section.

(3) That the attorney was unable to obtain the consultation required by Paragraph (1) because a statute of limitations would impair the action and that the certificates required by Paragraphs (1) and (2) could not be obtained before the impairment of the action. If a certificate is executed pursuant to this Paragraph, the certificates required by Paragraphs (1) and (2) shall be filed within sixty days after filing the petition.

C. Where certificates are required pursuant to Subsection B of this Section, separate certificates shall be filed for each defendant named in the complaint.

D. A petition filed pursuant to Subsection B of this Section may not name the defendant or defendants until the court has reviewed the certificates of merit filed and has determined, in camera, based solely on those certificates of merit, that there is reasonable and meritorious cause for filing of the action. At that time, the petition may be amended to name the defendant or defendants. The duty to give notice to the defendant or defendants shall not attach until that time.

E. A violation of Subsection B of this Section may constitute unprofessional conduct and may be the grounds for discipline against the attorney.

Added by Acts 1993, No. 694, § 1. Amended by Acts 1995, No. 503, § 1.

Editor's note. Acts 1993, No. 694, § 1, enacted Article 3498.1 of the Louisiana Civil Code. This article has been redesignated as R.S. 9:2800.9 by the Louisiana State Law Institute.

§ 2800.10. Immunity from liability for injuries sustained while committing a felony offense

A. No person shall be liable for damages for injury, death, or loss sustained by a perpetrator of a felony offense during the commission of the offense or while fleeing the scene of the offense.

B. The provisions of this Section shall apply regardless of whether the injury, death, or loss was caused by an intentional or unintentional act or omission or a condition of property or a building. However, the provisions of this Section shall not apply if injury to or death of a perpetrator results from an intentional act involving the use of excessive force.

C. For purposes of this Section "damages" includes all general and special damages which may be recoverable for personal injury, death, or loss of or damage to property, including those otherwise recoverable in a survival or wrongful death action.

Added by Acts 1996, 1st Ex.Sess., No. 46, § 1.

§ 2800.11. Limitation of liability; municipal or parish airport authority; parked aircraft

Notwithstanding any other provision of law to the contrary, except in the parishes of Bossier, Caddo, Jefferson, Orleans, Ouachita, and East Baton Rouge, no municipal or parish airport authority shall be liable for any loss or damage to aircraft parked on an aircraft parking ramp that is operated or maintained by the airport authority, provided that the ramp has signs prominently displayed informing customers or persons using the ramp that the ramp is unattended and that the airport authority is not responsible for losses as a result of theft, vandalism, or damage to property. However, this limitation of liability shall not be applicable if the loss or damage was caused by the gross negligence or willful or wanton misconduct of the airport authority.

Added by Acts 1997, No. 574, § 1.

§ 2800.12. Liability for termination of a pregnancy

A. Any person who performs an abortion is liable to the mother of the unborn child for any damage occasioned or precipitated by the abortion, which action survives for a period of three years from the date of discovery of the damage with a peremptive period of ten years from the date of the abortion.

B. For purposes of this Section:

(1) "Abortion" means the deliberate termination of an intrauterine human pregnancy after fertilization of a female ovum, by any person, including the pregnant woman herself, with an intention other than to produce a live birth or to remove a dead unborn child.

(2) "Damage" includes all special and general damages which are recoverable in an intentional tort, negligence, survival, or wrongful death action for injuries suffered or damages occasioned by the unborn child or mother.

(3) "Unborn child" means the unborn offspring of human beings from the moment of conception through pregnancy and until termination of the pregnancy.

C. (1) The signing of a consent form by the mother prior to the abortion does not negate this cause of action, but rather reduces the recovery of damages to the extent that the content of the consent form informed the mother of the risk of the type of injuries or loss for which she is seeking to recover.

(2) The laws governing medical malpractice or limitations of liability thereof provided in Title 40 of the Louisiana Revised Statutes of 1950 are not applicable to this Section.

Added by Acts 1997, No. 825, § 1.

§ 2800.13. Violation of transportation statute or regulation; determination of causation; evidence

In the trial of any action to recover damages for personal injury, death, or property damages sustained by any party, in which action it is alleged that an owner, agent, shipper, transporter, or carrier of material transported by carrier acted in violation or failed to act in accordance with any provision of any state or federal transportation statute or regulation, such violation or alleged violation of any state or federal transportation statute or regulation shall not be prima facie evidence of negligence or fault. The comparative fault laws of Louisiana shall apply in these cases as in all other cases of negligence.

Added by Acts 2003, No. 1151, § 1, eff. July 2, 2003.

Editor's note. Section 2 of Acts 2003, No. 1151 declares that the provisions of this Act "shall have prospective application only and shall apply only to a cause of action arising on or after its effective date."

§ 2800.14. Limitation of liability for damages to oyster leases

Oil companies, including drilling, exploration, production, pipeline, and marine contractors, and persons performing related services who cause any loss or damage to oyster leases from exploration, excavation, construction, maintenance, remediation, operations, release and response, or events and activities, which include the transportation of materials or equipment to or from existing or proposed drilling sites, well sites, rights of way, or production, storage, and pumping facilities within a designated water route or navigable waters approved by the Department of Natural Resources shall only be liable for the diminution in market value of the oyster leases. Diminution in market value of the oyster leases shall be calculated in accordance with the method used by the Louisiana Oyster Lease Damage Evaluation Board. This Section shall have no effect as to judgments rendered by a court of competent jurisdiction prior to August 15, 2004.

Added by Acts 2004, No. 792, § 1.

§ 2800.15. Limitation of liability for commercial and marine contractors, architects, and engineers, and persons licensed by the Louisiana Manufactured Housing Commission; mold and mold damage

A. Unless the parties otherwise agree in writing, no commercial or marine contractor, architect, or engineer licensed under the laws of this state shall be liable for any personal injuries, property damages or any other damages, losses, or claims whatsoever related to mold or mold damage not caused by defects in workmanship or design.

B. The limitation of liability provided in Subsection A of this Section shall also apply to commercially constructed residential dwellings, also referred to as manufactured homes, and to all persons licensed by the Louisiana Manufactured Housing Commission in accordance with R.S. 51:911.21 et seq. and 912.21 et seq.

C. The limitation of liability provided in Subsection A of this Section shall also apply to real estate licensees representing marine or commercial contractors and who are licensed by the Louisiana Real Estate Commission in accordance with R.S. 37:1437 and 1439.

Added by Acts 2004, No. 844, § 1.

§ 2800.16. Limitation of liability; Louisiana Public Defender Board members

No individual Louisiana Public Defender Board member shall be personally liable for any act or omission resulting in damage, injury, or loss arising out of the exercise of his official functions and duties. However, this limitation of liability shall not be applicable if the damage, injury, or loss was caused by the gross negligence or willful or wanton misconduct of a member.

Added by Acts 2006, No. 326, § 1. Amended by Acts 2007, No. 307, §3, eff. Aug. 15, 2007.

§ 2800.17. Liability for the diminution in the value of a damaged vehicle

Whenever a motor vehicle is damaged through the negligence of a third-party without being destroyed, and if the owner can prove by a preponderance of the evidence that, if the vehicle were repaired to its preloss condition, its fair market value would be less than its value before it was damaged, the owner of the damaged vehicle shall be entitled to recover as additional damages an amount equal to the diminution in the value of the vehicle. Notwithstanding, the total damages recovered by the owner shall not exceed the fair market value of the vehicle prior to when it was damaged, and the amount paid for the diminution of value shall be considered in determining whether a vehicle is a total loss pursuant to R.S. 32:702.

Added by Acts 2010, No. 725, § 1.

Editor's note. R.S. 9:2800.17, was added by Acts 2010, No. 725, effective August 15, 2010. A prior R.S. 9:2800.17 had been enacted by Acts 2006, No. 402, effective August 28, 2008. Its provisions, however, terminated and expired on August 28, 2008. See Acts 2006, No. 402, Section 3.

§ 2800.18. Limitation of liability for volunteer medical transportation pilots

No person acting as a volunteer pilot for Angel Flight or other similar nonprofit organization providing gratuitous transportation for a child or his family to hospital facilities for medical treatment or evaluation shall be personally liable to the child or his family for any loss or damage related to his responsibilities as a pilot, unless the loss or damage was caused by the gross negligence or willful or wanton acts of the pilot.

Added by Acts 2006, No. 495, § 1.

§ 2800.19. Limitation of liability for use of force in defense of certain crimes

A. A person who uses reasonable and apparently necessary or deadly force or violence for the purpose of preventing a forcible offense against the person or his property in accordance with R.S. 14:19 or 20 is immune from civil action for the use of reasonable and apparently necessary or deadly force or violence.

B. The court shall award reasonable attorney fees, court costs, compensation for loss of income, and all expenses to the defendant in any civil action if the court finds that the defendant is immune from suit in accordance with Subsection A of this Section.

Added by Acts 2006, No. 786, § 1.

§ 2800.20. Limitation of liability for a nonprofit health care quality improvement corporation; health care providers; health plans; reporting and disclosure of information

A. A nonprofit health care quality improvement corporation which complies and functions in accordance with R.S. 13:3715.6 and its directors, officers, employees, and agents thereof, acting in good faith, shall not be liable to any person for any injury, damage, or loss as a result of the creation, development, or revision of any quality improvement work product or the disclosure of information, in accordance with R.S. 13:3715.6, unless the injury, damage, or loss was caused by willful or wanton misconduct.

B. Any health care provider or health plan and its directors, officers, employees and agents thereof, acting in good faith, who voluntarily reports or discloses information to a nonprofit health care quality improvement corporation which complies and functions in accordance with R.S. 13:3715.6, shall not be liable to any person for any injury, damage, or loss as a result of reporting or disclosing such information, unless the injury, damage, or loss was caused by willful or wanton misconduct.

Added by Acts 2007, No. 359, § 1.

§ 2800.21. Limitation of liability for curators and undercurators; acts of interdicts

A curator or an undercurator who performs the duties and obligations of his office without compensation shall not be personally liable for any injury, death, damage, civil penalty, or other loss caused by the interdict in his charge unless the injury, death, damage, civil penalty, or other loss was caused by the gross negligence or willful and wanton misconduct of the curator or undercurator in executing the duties and obligations of his office; however, this Section shall not apply if there is applicable insurance to cover such loss, but any recovery shall be limited to the amount of such insurance.

Added by Acts 2010, No. 465, § 1.

§ 2800.22. Limitation of liability for use of school facilities

A. The governing authority of an elementary or secondary school or charter school who enters into a recreational joint-use agreement for use of its facility owes no duty of care to keep such premises safe for entry or use by others, pursuant to a joint-use agreement, outside of regularly scheduled school activities or to give a warning of any hazardous conditions, use of, structure, or activities on the premises. When the governing authority enters into a recreational joint-use agreement, it is not extending any assurance that the premises are safe or a duty of care, or assuming responsibility for or incurring liability for any injury, death, loss, civil penalty, or damages to persons or property caused by any act of a person to whom permission is granted.

B. This Section does not exclude any liability which would otherwise exist for injury or damages caused by gross negligence or willful and wanton misconduct.

C. When entering into a recreational joint-use agreement, the elementary or secondary school or charter school shall require in the agreement that the other entity maintain and provide proof of adequate liability and accident insurance coverage as determined by industry standards.

D. As used in this Section, "recreational joint-use agreement" means a written agreement between the governing authority of an elementary, secondary, or charter school and a public or private entity, authorizing such entity to access the premises of a school under the governing authority's jurisdiction for the purposes of conducting or engaging in recreational activity.

E. The agreement shall set forth the conditions, terms, and requirements under which such authorization and use is granted, including that the entity shall indemnify and hold harmless the governing authority from any liability arising from such use, and that the governing authority may at any time and without cause revoke its authorization to use the premises and terminate the agreement.

Added by Acts 2011, No. 351, § 1, eff. June 29, 2011.

CHAPTER 3. LOUISIANA PRODUCTS LIABILITY ACT

Section
2800.51. Short title.
2800.52. Scope of this Chapter.
2800.53. Definitions.
2800.54. Manufacturer responsibility and burden of proof.
2800.55. Unreasonably dangerous in construction or composition.
2800.56. Unreasonably dangerous in design.
2800.57. Unreasonably dangerous because of inadequate warning.
2800.58. Unreasonably dangerous because of nonconformity to express warranty.
2800.59. Manufacturer knowledge, design feasibility and burden of proof.
2800.60. Liability of manufacturers and sellers of firearms.

§ 2800.51. Short title

This Chapter shall be known and may be cited as the "Louisiana Products Liability Act."

Added by Acts 1988, No. 64, § 1, eff. Sept. 1, 1988.

Cross References

C.C. arts. 2315, 2317.

§ 2800.52. Scope of this Chapter

This Chapter establishes the exclusive theories of liability for manufacturers for damage caused by their products. A claimant may not recover from a manufacturer for damage caused by a product on the basis of any theory of liability that is not set forth in this Chapter. Conduct or circumstances that result in liability under this Chapter are "fault" within the meaning of Civil Code Article 2315. This Chapter does not apply to the rights of an employee or his personal representatives, dependents or relations against a manufacturer who is the employee's employer or against any principal or any officer, director, stockholder, partner or employee of such manufacturer or principal as limited by R.S. 23:1032, or to the rights of a claimant against the following, unless they assume the status of a manufacturer as defined in R.S. 9:2800.53(1):

(1) Providers of professional services, even if the service results in a product.

(2) Providers of nonprofessional services where the essence of the service is the furnishing of judgment or skill, even if the service results in a product.

(3) Producers of natural fruits and other raw products in their natural state that are derived from animals, fowl, aquatic life, or invertebrates, including but not limited to milk, eggs, honey, and wool.

(4) Farmers and other producers of agricultural plants in their natural state.

(5) Ranchers and other producers of animals, fowl, aquatic life, or invertebrates in their natural state.

(6) Harvesters and other producers of fish, crawfish, oysters, crabs, mollusks, or other aquatic animals in their natural state.

Added by Acts 1988, No. 64, § 1, eff. Sept. 1, 1988.

Cross References

C.C. arts. 2315, 2317.

§ 2800.53. Definitions

The following terms have the following meanings for the purpose of this Chapter:

(1) "Manufacturer" means a person or entity who is in the business of manufacturing a product for placement into trade or commerce. "Manufacturing a product" means producing, making, fabricating, constructing, designing, remanufacturing, reconditioning or refurbishing a product. "Manufacturer" also means:

(a) A person or entity who labels a product as his own or who otherwise holds himself out to be the manufacturer of the product.

(b) A seller of a product who exercises control over or influences a characteristic of the design, construction or quality of the product that causes damage.

(c) A manufacturer of a product who incorporates into the product a component or part manufactured by another manufacturer.

(d) A seller of a product of an alien manufacturer if the seller is in the business of importing or distributing the product for resale and the seller is the alter ego of the alien manufacturer. The court shall take into consideration the following in determining whether the seller is the alien manufacturer's alter ego: whether the seller is affiliated with the alien manufacturer by way of common ownership or control; whether the seller assumes or administers product warranty obligations of the alien manufacturer; whether the seller prepares or modifies the product for distribution; or any other relevant evidence. A "product of an alien manufacturer" is a product that is manufactured outside the United States by a manufacturer who is a citizen of another country or who is organized under the laws of another country.

(2) "Seller" means a person or entity who is not a manufacturer and who is in the business of conveying title to or possession of a product to another person or entity in exchange for anything of value.

(3) "Product" means a corporeal movable that is manufactured for placement into trade or commerce, including a product that forms a component part of or that is subsequently incorporated into another product or an immovable. "Product" does not mean human blood, blood components, human organs, human tissue or approved animal tissue to the extent such are governed by R.S. 9:2797.

(4) "Claimant" means a person or entity who asserts a claim under this Chapter against the manufacturer of a product or his insurer for damage caused by the product.

(5) "Damage" means all damage caused by a product, including survival and wrongful death damages, for which Civil Code Articles 2315, 2315.1 and 2315.2 allow recovery. "Damage" includes damage to the product itself and economic loss arising from a deficiency in or loss of use of the product only to the extent that Chapter 9 of Title VII of Book III of the Civil Code, entitled "Redhibition," does not allow recovery for such damage or economic loss. Attorneys' fees are not recoverable under this Chapter.

(6) "Express warranty" means a representation, statement of alleged fact or promise about a product or its nature, material or workmanship that represents, affirms or promises that the product or its nature, material or workmanship possesses specified characteristics or qualities or will meet a specified level of performance. "Express warranty" does not mean a general opinion about or general praise of a product. A sample or model of a product is an express warranty.

(7) "Reasonably anticipated use" means a use or handling of a product that the product's manufacturer should reasonably expect of an ordinary person in the same or similar circumstances.

(8) "Reasonably anticipated alteration or modification" means a change in a product that the product's manufacturer should reasonably expect to be made by an ordinary person in the same or similar circumstances, and also means a change arising from ordinary wear and tear. "Reasonably anticipated alteration or modification" does not mean the following:

(a) Alteration, modification or removal of an otherwise adequate warning provided about a product.

(b) The failure of a person or entity, other than the manufacturer of a product, reasonably to provide to the product user or handler an adequate warning that the manufacturer provided about the product, when the manufacturer has satisfied his obligation to use reasonable care to provide the adequate warning by providing it to such person or entity rather than to the product user or handler.

(c) Changes to or in a product or its operation because the product does not receive reasonable care and maintenance.

(9) "Adequate warning" means a warning or instruction that would lead an ordinary reasonable user or handler of a product to contemplate the danger in using or handling the product and either to decline to use or handle the product or, if possible, to use or handle the product in such a manner as to avoid the damage for which the claim is made.

Added by Acts 1988, No. 64, § 1, eff. Sept. 1, 1988.

Cross References

C.C. arts. 2315, 2315.1, 2315.2, 2317.

§ 2800.54. Manufacturer responsibility and burden of proof

A. The manufacturer of a product shall be liable to a claimant for damage proximately caused by a characteristic of the product that renders the product unreasonably dangerous when such damage arose from a reasonably anticipated use of the product by the claimant or another person or entity.

B. A product is unreasonably dangerous if and only if:

(1) The product is unreasonably dangerous in construction or composition as provided in R.S. 9:2800.55;

(2) The product is unreasonably dangerous in design as provided in R.S. 9:2800.56;

(3) The product is unreasonably dangerous because an adequate warning about the product has not been provided as provided in R.S. 9:2800.57; or

(4) The product is unreasonably dangerous because it does not conform to an express warranty of the manufacturer about the product as provided in R.S. 9:2800.58.

C. The characteristic of the product that renders it unreasonably dangerous under R.S. 9:2800.55 must exist at the time the product left the control of its manufacturer. The characteristic of the product that renders it unreasonably dangerous under R.S. 9:2800.56 or 9:2800.57 must exist at the time the product left the control of its manufacturer or result from a reasonably anticipated alteration or modification of the product.

D. The claimant has the burden of proving the elements of Subsections A, B and C of this Section.

Added by Acts 1988, No. 64, § 1, eff. Sept. 1, 1988.

Cross References

C.C. arts. 2315, 2317.

§ 2800.55. Unreasonably dangerous in construction or composition

A product is unreasonably dangerous in construction or composition if, at the time the product left its manufacturer's control, the product deviated in a material way from the manufacturer's specifications or performance standards for the product or from otherwise identical products manufactured by the same manufacturer.

Added by Acts 1988, No. 64, § 1, eff. Sept. 1, 1988.

Cross References

C.C. arts. 2315, 2317.

§ 2800.56. Unreasonably dangerous in design

A product is unreasonably dangerous in design if, at the time the product left its manufacturer's control:

(1) There existed an alternative design for the product that was capable of preventing the claimant's damage; and

(2) The likelihood that the product's design would cause the claimant's damage and the gravity of that damage outweighed the burden on the manufacturer of adopting such alternative design and the adverse effect, if any, of such alternative design on the utility of the product. An adequate warning about a product shall be considered in evaluating the

likelihood of damage when the manufacturer has used reasonable care to provide the adequate warning to users and handlers of the product.

Added by Acts 1988, No. 64, § 1, eff. Sept. 1, 1988.

Cross References

C.C. arts. 2315, 2317.

§ 2800.57. Unreasonably dangerous because of inadequate warning

A. A product is unreasonably dangerous because an adequate warning about the product has not been provided if, at the time the product left its manufacturer's control, the product possessed a characteristic that may cause damage and the manufacturer failed to use reasonable care to provide an adequate warning of such characteristic and its danger to users and handlers of the product.

B. A manufacturer is not required to provide an adequate warning about his product when:

(1) The product is not dangerous to an extent beyond that which would be contemplated by the ordinary user or handler of the product, with the ordinary knowledge common to the community as to the product's characteristics; or

(2) The user or handler of the product already knows or reasonably should be expected to know of the characteristic of the product that may cause damage and the danger of such characteristic.

C. A manufacturer of a product who, after the product has left his control, acquires knowledge of a characteristic of the product that may cause damage and the danger of such characteristic, or who would have acquired such knowledge had he acted as a reasonably prudent manufacturer, is liable for damage caused by his subsequent failure to use reasonable care to provide an adequate warning of such characteristic and its danger to users and handlers of the product.

Added by Acts 1988, No. 64, § 1, eff. Sept. 1, 1988.

Cross References

C.C. arts. 2315, 2317.

§ 2800.58. Unreasonably dangerous because of nonconformity to express warranty

A product is unreasonably dangerous when it does not conform to an express warranty made at any time by the manufacturer about the product if the express warranty has induced the claimant or another person or entity to use the product and the claimant's damage was proximately caused because the express warranty was untrue.

Added by Acts 1988, No. 64, § 1, eff. Sept. 1, 1988.

Cross References

C.C. arts. 2315, 2317.

§ 2800.59. Manufacturer knowledge, design feasibility and burden of proof

A. Notwithstanding R.S. 9:2800.56, a manufacturer of a product shall not be liable for damage proximately caused by a characteristic of the product's design if the manufacturer proves that, at the time the product left his control:

(1) He did not know and, in light of then-existing reasonably available scientific and technological knowledge, could not have known of the design characteristic that caused the damage or the danger of such characteristic; or

(2) He did not know and, in light of then-existing reasonably available scientific and technological knowledge, could not have known of the alternative design identified by the claimant under R.S. 9:2800.56(1); or

(3) The alternative design identified by the claimant under R.S. 9:2800.56(1) was not feasible, in light of then-existing reasonably available scientific and technological knowledge or then-existing economic practicality.

B. Notwithstanding R.S. 9:2800.57(A) or (B), a manufacturer of a product shall not be liable for damage proximately caused by a characteristic of the product if the manufacturer proves that, at the time the product left his control, he did not know and, in light of then-existing reasonably available scientific and technological knowledge, could not have known of the characteristic that caused the damage or the danger of such characteristic.

Added by Acts 1988, No. 64, § 1, eff. Sept. 1, 1988.

Cross References

C.C. arts. 2315, 2317.

§ 2800.60. Liability of manufacturers and sellers of firearms

A. The legislature finds and declares that the Louisiana Products Liability Act[1] was not designed to impose liability on a manufacturer or seller for the improper use of a properly designed and manufactured product. The legislature further finds and declares that the manufacture and sale of firearms and ammunition by manufacturers and dealers, duly licensed by the appropriate federal and state authorities, is lawful activity and is not unreasonably dangerous.

B. No firearm manufacturer or seller shall be liable for any injury, damage, or death resulting from any shooting injury by any other person unless the claimant proves and shows that such injury, damage, or death was proximately caused by the unreasonably dangerous construction or composition of the product as provided in R.S. 9:2800.55.

C. Notwithstanding any other provision of law to the contrary, no manufacturer or seller of a firearm who has transferred that firearm in compliance with federal and state law shall incur any liability for any action of any person who uses a firearm in a manner which is unlawful, negligent, or otherwise inconsistent with the purposes for which it was intended.

D. The failure of a manufacturer or seller to insure that a firearm has a device which would: make the firearm useable only by the lawful owner or authorized user of the firearm; indicate to users that a cartridge is in the chamber of the firearm; or prevent the firearm from firing if the ammunition magazine is removed, shall not make the firearm unreasonably dangerous, unless such device is required by federal or state statute or regulation.

E. (1) For the purposes of this Chapter, the potential of a firearm to cause serious injury, damage, or death as a result of normal function does not constitute a firearm malfunction due to defect in design or manufacture.

(2) A firearm may not be deemed defective in design or manufacture on the basis of its potential to cause serious bodily injury, property damage, or death when discharged legally or illegally.

F. Notwithstanding any provision of law to the contrary, no manufacturer or seller of a firearm shall incur any liability for failing to warn users of the risk that:

(1) A firearm has the potential to cause serious bodily injury, property damage, or death when discharged legally or illegally.

(2) An unauthorized person could gain access to the firearm.

(3) A cartridge may be in the chamber of the firearm.

(4) The firearm is capable of being fired even with the ammunition magazine removed.

G. The provisions of this Section shall not apply to assault weapons manufactured in violation of 18 U.S.C. § 922(v).[2]

Added by Acts 1999, No. 1299, § 1, eff. July 12, 1999.

[1] R.S. 9:2800.51 et seq.
[2] 18 U.S.C. § 922(v) was repealed in 1994.

CHAPTER 4. LOUISIANA DRUG DEALER LIABILITY ACT

Section
2800.61. Title; legislative intent.
2800.62. Definitions.
2800.63. Action for damages by persons other than the individual user.
2800.64. Action by individual users.
2800.65. Third parties not liable; nonassignment of cause of action.
2800.66. Level of offense; amount of liability.
2800.67. Joinder of actions.
2800.68. Comparative fault.
2800.69. Contribution by tortfeasors.
2800.70. Proof of liability.
2800.71. Defense; exclusion.
2800.72. Writ of attachment.
2800.73. Prescription.
2800.74. Stay of action by governmental entity.
2800.75. Actions between spouses.
2800.76. Exemplary damages.

§ 2800.61. Title; legislative intent

A. This Chapter shall be known and may be cited as the "Louisiana Drug Dealer Liability Act".

B. The purpose of this Chapter is to provide a civil remedy for damages to persons in a community injured by an individual's use of illegal controlled substances. It establishes a cause of action against drug dealers for damages for monetary, noneconomic, and physical losses incurred as a result of an individual's use of an illegal controlled substance. This Chapter will shift the cost of the damage caused by the marketing of illegal drugs to those who illegally profit from that market, as well as deter others from entering the illegal drug market by subjecting them to substantial monetary loss. This Chapter will also provide an incentive for individual users to identify illegal drug marketers and recover from them the costs of their own drug treatment.

Added by Acts 1997, No. 719, § 1.

Editor's note. Acts 1997, No. 719, § 2 provides that "The provisions of this Act shall have prospective application only and shall apply only to a cause of action arising on and after its effective date."

§ 2800.62. Definitions

As used in this Chapter, unless the context requires otherwise:

(1) "Controlled substance" means a controlled dangerous substance as defined and covered by the Uniform Controlled Dangerous Substances Law, R.S. 40:961 et seq.

(2) "Illegal controlled substance" means cocaine, phencyclidine, heroin, or methamphetamine and any other illegal controlled dangerous substance the possession or distribution of which is a violation of the Uniform Controlled Dangerous Substances Law, R.S. 40:961 et seq.

(3) "Individual user" means the individual whose use of an illegal controlled substance, that is not obtained directly from or pursuant to a valid prescription or order of a licensed physician or practitioner, which is the basis of an action brought under this Chapter.

(4) "Level one offense" means the illegal possession with intent to distribute less than four ounces or the illegal distribution of less than one ounce of an illegal controlled substance.

(5) "Level two offense" means the illegal possession with intent to distribute four ounces or more but less than eight ounces, or the illegal distribution of one ounce or more, but less than two ounces, of an illegal controlled substance.

(6) "Level three offense" means the illegal possession with intent to distribute eight ounces or more but less than sixteen ounces, or the illegal distribution of two ounces or more, but less than four ounces, of an illegal controlled substance.

(7) "Level four offense" means the illegal possession with intent to distribute sixteen ounces or more, or the illegal distribution of four ounces or more, of an illegal controlled substance.

(8) "Marketing of an illegal controlled substance" means the possession with intent to distribute or distribution of a specified illegal controlled substance which is a violation of the Uniform Controlled Dangerous Substances Law, R.S. 40:961 et seq.

(9) "Participate in the marketing of an illegal controlled substance" means to transport, import into this state, possess with intent to distribute, distribute an illegal controlled substance or offer to transport, import into this state, possess with the intent to distribute, or distribute an illegal controlled substance. "Participate in the marketing of an illegal controlled substance" does not include the purchase or receipt of an illegal controlled substance for personal use only.

(10) "Period of illegal use" means, in relation to the individual user of an illegal controlled substance, the time from the individual's first illegal use of an illegal controlled substance to the accrual of the cause of action.

(11) "Person" means a natural person, governmental entity, or corporation, partnership, firm, trust, or incorporated or unincorporated association, existing under or authorized by the laws of this state, another state, or a foreign country.

(12) "Place of illegal activity" means, in relation to the individual user of an illegal controlled substance, each parish in which the individual illegally possesses or uses an illegal controlled substance during the period of the individual's use of an illegal controlled substance.

(13) "Place of participation" means, in relation to a defendant in an action brought under this Chapter, each parish in which the person participates in the marketing of illegal

controlled substances during the period of the person's participation in the marketing of illegal controlled substances. Added by Acts 1997, No. 719, § 1.

Editor's note. Acts 1997, No. 719, § 2 provides that "The provisions of this Act shall have prospective application only and shall apply only to a cause of action arising on and after its effective date."

§ 2800.63. Action for damages by persons other than the individual user

A. Any one or more of the following persons may bring an action for damages caused by an individual's use of an illegal controlled substance against those persons enumerated in Subsection B of this Section:

(1) A parent, legal custodian, child, spouse, or sibling of the individual user.

(2) An individual who was exposed to an illegal controlled substance in utero.

(3) An employer of the individual user.

(4) A medical facility, insurer, employer, governmental entity, or other legal entity that funds a drug treatment program or other employee assistance program for or that otherwise expends money on behalf of the individual user.

(5) A person injured as a result of the willful, reckless, or negligent actions of an individual user.

B. A person entitled to bring an action pursuant to Subsection A of this Section may seek damages from one or more of the following:

(1) A person who sold, administered, or furnished an illegal controlled substance to the individual user.

(2) A person who knowingly participated in the marketing of an illegal controlled substance, if all of the following apply:

(a) The place of illegal activity by the individual user is within the municipality, parish, or unincorporated area of the parish in which the defendant's place of participation is situated.

(b) The defendant's participation in the marketing of illegal controlled substances was connected with the same type of illegal controlled substance used by the individual user, and the defendant has been convicted of an offense for that type of specified illegal controlled substance, which he committed in the same parish as the individual user's place of use.

(c) The defendant participated in the marketing of illegal controlled substances at any time during the period in which the individual user used the illegal controlled substance.

C. As used in Paragraph B(2) of this Section, "knowingly participated in the marketing of an illegal controlled substance" means was convicted of possession with the intent to distribute or distribution of an illegal controlled substance in violation of the Uniform Controlled Dangerous Substances Law, R.S. 40:961 et seq.

D. A person entitled to bring an action under this Section may recover all of the following damages:

(1) Economic damages, including but not limited to the cost of treatment and rehabilitation, medical expenses, loss of economic or educational potential, loss of productivity, absenteeism, support expenses, accidents or injury, and any other pecuniary loss proximately caused by the use of an illegal controlled substance.

(2) Noneconomic damages, including but not limited to physical and emotional pain and suffering, physical impairment, emotional distress, mental anguish, disfigurement, loss of enjoyment, loss of companionship, services, and consortium, and other nonpecuniary losses proximately caused by an individual's use of an illegal controlled substance.

(3) Exemplary damages.

(4) Reasonable attorney fees.

(5) Costs of suit, including but not limited to reasonable expenses for expert testimony.

Added by Acts 1997, No. 719, § 1.

Editor's note. Acts 1997, No. 719, § 2 provides that "The provisions of this Act shall have prospective application only and shall apply only to a cause of action arising on and after its effective date."

§ 2800.64. Action by individual users

A. An individual user is entitled to bring an action for damages caused by the use of an illegal controlled substance only if all of the following conditions are met:

(1) Not less than six months before filing the action, the individual personally discloses to narcotics enforcement authorities all of the information known to the individual regarding the individual's sources of illegal controlled substances.

(2) The individual has not used an illegal controlled substance within thirty days before filing the action.

(3) The individual does not use an illegal controlled substance during the pendency of the action.

B. The individual user entitled to bring an action under this Section may recover only the following damages:

(1) Economic damages, including but not limited to the cost of treatment, rehabilitation, and medical expenses, loss of economic or educational potential, loss of productivity, absenteeism, accidents or injury, and any other pecuniary loss proximately caused by the person's use of an illegal controlled substance.

(2) Reasonable attorney fees.

(3) Costs of suit, including but not limited to reasonable expenses for expert testimony.

C. The individual user entitled to bring an action under this Section may seek damages only from a person who distributed or possessed with the intent to distribute the illegal controlled substance actually used by the individual user.

Added by Acts 1997, No. 719, § 1.

Editor's note. Acts 1997, No. 719, § 2 provides that "The provisions of this Act shall have prospective application only and shall apply only to a cause of action arising on and after its effective date."

§ 2800.65. Third parties not liable; nonassignment of cause of action

A. A third party shall not pay damages awarded under this Chapter or provide a defense or the cost of a defense, on behalf of an insured under an obligation of insurance or indemnification.

B. A cause of action authorized by this Chapter shall not be assigned, either expressly, by subrogation, or by any other means, directly or indirectly, to any public or publicly funded agency or institution.

Added by Acts 1997, No. 719, § 1.

Editor's note. Acts 1997, No. 719, § 2 provides that "The provisions of this Act shall have prospective application only and shall apply only to a cause of action arising on and after its effective date."

§ 2800.66. Level of offense; amount of liability

Any person, whose participation in the marketing of illegal controlled substances constitutes the following level of offense, shall be subject to a rebuttable presumption of responsibility in the following amounts:

(1) For a level one offense, twenty-five percent of the damages.

(2) For a level two offense, fifty percent of the damages.

(3) For a level three offense, seventy-five percent of the damages.

(4) For a level four offense, one hundred percent of the damages.

Added by Acts 1997, No. 719, § 1.

Editor's note. Acts 1997, No. 719, § 2 provides that "The provisions of this Act shall have prospective application only and shall apply only to a cause of action arising on and after its effective date."

§ 2800.67. Joinder of actions

A. Two or more persons may join in one action under this Chapter as plaintiffs if their respective actions have at least one market for illegal controlled dangerous substances in common and if any portion of the period of use of an illegal controlled dangerous substance is concurrent with the period of use of an illegal controlled dangerous substance for every other plaintiff.

B. Two or more persons may be joined in one action under this Chapter as defendants, if those persons are liable to at least one plaintiff.

C. A plaintiff need not participate in obtaining and a defendant need not participate in defending against all of the relief demanded. Judgment may be given for one or more plaintiffs according to their respective rights to relief and against one or more defendants according to their respective liabilities.

Added by Acts 1997, No. 719, § 1.

Editor's note. Acts 1997, No. 719, § 2 provides that "The provisions of this Act shall have prospective application only and shall apply only to a cause of action arising on and after its effective date."

§ 2800.68. Comparative fault

A. An action by an individual user pursuant to R.S. 9:2800.64 is governed by the application of comparative fault as provided in Civil Code Article 2323. Comparative fault attributable to the individual user shall not bar recovery but shall reduce the award of compensatory damages proportionally, according to the amount of fault attributable to the individual user.

B. The defendant shall have the burden of proving the comparative fault of the plaintiff, which shall be shown by clear and convincing evidence.

C. Comparative fault shall not be attributable to a plaintiff who is not an individual user, unless that plaintiff intentionally gave the individual user money for the purchase of the illegal controlled substance.

Added by Acts 1997, No. 719, § 1.

Editor's note. Acts 1997, No. 719, § 2 provides that "The provisions of this Act shall have prospective application only and shall apply only to a cause of action arising on and after its effective date."

§ 2800.69. Contribution by tortfeasors

A person subject to liability under this Chapter has a right of action for contribution against another person subject to liability under this Chapter. Contribution may be enforced either in the original action or by a separate action brought for that purpose. A person may seek recovery in accordance with this Chapter and as otherwise provided by law against a person against whom a defendant has asserted a right of contribution.

Added by Acts 1997, No. 719, § 1.

Editor's note. Acts 1997, No. 719, § 2 provides that "The provisions of this Act shall have prospective application only and shall apply only to a cause of action arising on and after its effective date."

§ 2800.70. Proof of liability

A. Proof of liability in an action brought pursuant to this Chapter shall be by clear and convincing evidence. Except as otherwise provided in this Chapter, other elements of the cause of action shall be shown by a preponderance of the evidence.

B. (1) A person against whom recovery is sought who has been convicted of the distribution of an illegal controlled dangerous substance under state law or under the Comprehensive Drug Abuse Prevention and Control Act of 1970, 21 U.S.C. 801 et seq., is precluded from denying participation in the marketing of an illegal controlled dangerous substance. Except as provided in Paragraph (2) of this Subsection, the provisions of this Subsection shall not affect a person's burden of proving the elements required by R.S. 9:2800.63(B)(2)(a) through (c).

(2) A conviction specified in Paragraph (1) of this Subsection shall also be prima facie evidence of the defendant's participation in the marketing of an illegal controlled substance used by the individual user, where the conviction was based upon the person's marketing of that same type of illegal controlled substance.

C. The absence of a criminal conviction of a person pursuant to Paragraph B(1) of this Section against whom recovery is sought does not bar an action against that person in an action pursuant to R.S. 9:2800.63(B)(1) or R.S. 9:2800.64.

Added by Acts 1997, No. 719, § 1.

Editor's note. Acts 1997, No. 719, § 2 provides that "The provisions of this Act shall have prospective application only and shall apply only to a cause of action arising on and after its effective date."

§ 2800.71. Defense; exclusion

A. It is a defense to any action brought pursuant to this Chapter that the person who possessed with the intent to distribute or distributed a controlled substance did so under the authority of law as a licensed physician or practitioner, as an ultimate user of the controlled substance pursuant to a lawful prescription, or as a person otherwise authorized by law.

B. A law enforcement officer or agency, the state, or any person acting at the direction of a law enforcement officer or agency or the state is not liable for participating in the marketing of an illegal controlled substance, if the participation is in furtherance of an official investigation.

Added by Acts 1997, No. 719, § 1.

Editor's note. Acts 1997, No. 719, § 2 provides that "The provisions of this Act shall have prospective application only and shall apply only to a cause of action arising on and after its effective date."

§ 2800.72. Writ of attachment

A person authorized to file an action under this Chapter may seek a writ of attachment pursuant to the provisions of Code of Civil Procedure Articles 3501 et seq. against all assets of a defendant sufficient to satisfy a potential award, except an asset named in or seized pursuant to a forfeiture action by the state or federal agency before a plaintiff commences an action pursuant to this Chapter, unless the asset is released by the agency that seized it.

Added by Acts 1997, No. 719, § 1.

Editor's note. Acts 1997, No. 719, § 2 provides that "The provisions of this Act shall have prospective application only and shall apply only to a cause of action arising on and after its effective date."

§ 2800.73. Prescription

A. Except as otherwise provided in this Subsection, a cause of action prescribes in one year after a defendant furnishes the illegal substance. A cause of action accrues under this Chapter when a person who may recover has reason to know of the harm from the use of an illegal controlled substance that is the basis for the cause of action and has reason to know that the use of an illegal controlled substance is the cause of the harm.

B. Prescription against a defendant is suspended until one year after the individual potential defendant is convicted of a criminal offense involving an illegal controlled dangerous substance or as otherwise provided by law.

Added by Acts 1997, No. 719, § 1.

Editor's note. Acts 1997, No. 719, § 2 provides that "The provisions of this Act shall have prospective application only and shall apply only to a cause of action arising on and after its effective date."

§ 2800.74. Stay of action by governmental entity

A. On motion by a governmental entity involved in an investigation or prosecution involving an illegal controlled dangerous substance, an action brought under this Chapter shall be continued until the completion of the criminal investigation or prosecution that gave rise to the motion for a continuance of the action.

B. Discovery of investigative reports of the state or law enforcement agency shall be available only at the conclusion of the state's prosecution or action against any party in a criminal or civil proceeding, and thereafter only in accordance with R.S. 44:3 et seq.

C. No intelligence file or information regarding illegal drug activity accumulated by a law enforcement agency or the district attorney that does not result in an arrest and bill of information or indictment shall be subject to discovery pursuant to this Chapter.

Added by Acts 1997, No. 719, § 1.

Editor's note. Acts 1997, No. 719, § 2 provides that "The provisions of this Act shall have prospective application only and shall apply only to a cause of action arising on and after its effective date."

§ 2800.75. Actions between spouses

The provisions of this Chapter are not intended to amend, supersede, or repeal the provisions of R.S. 9:291.

Added by Acts 1997, No. 719, § 1.

Editor's note. Acts 1997, No. 719, § 2 provides that "The provisions of this Act shall have prospective application only and shall apply only to a cause of action arising on and after its effective date."

§ 2800.76. Exemplary damages

In addition to general and special damages that may be awarded under this Chapter, exemplary damages may be awarded upon proof that the sale or distribution of an illegal controlled substance or participation in the marketing of an illegal controlled substance was in wanton or reckless disregard for the rights, health, and safety of others.

Added by Acts 1997, No. 719, § 1.

Editor's note. Acts 1997, No. 719, § 2 provides that "The provisions of this Act shall have prospective application only and shall apply only to a cause of action arising on and after its effective date."

CODE TITLE VI—MATRIMONIAL REGIMES

CHAPTER 1. PARTITION OF COMMUNITY PROPERTY

Section
2801. Partition of community property and settlement of claims arising from matrimonial regimes and co-ownership of former community property.
2801.1. Community property; allocation and assignment of ownership.
2801.2. Community property; valuation of goodwill.
2802. Rendition of judgment of partition; prerequisite.
2803, 2804. Repealed.
2805 to 2820. [Blank].
2821, 2822. Repealed.

§ 2801. Partition of community property and settlement of claims arising from matrimonial regimes and co-ownership of former community property

A. When the spouses are unable to agree on a partition of community property or on the settlement of the claims between the spouses arising either from the matrimonial regime, or from the co-ownership of former community property following termination of the matrimonial regime, either spouse, as an incident of the action that would result in a termination of the matrimonial regime or upon termination of the matrimonial regime or thereafter, may institute a proceeding, which shall be conducted in accordance with the following rules:

(1)(a) Within forty-five days of service of a motion by either party, each party shall file a sworn detailed descriptive list of all community property, the fair market value and location of each asset, and all community liabilities. For good cause shown, the court may extend the time period for filing a detailed descriptive list. If a party fails to file a sworn detailed descriptive list timely, the other party may file a rule to show cause why its sworn detailed descriptive list should not be deemed to constitute a judicial determination of the community assets and liabilities. At the hearing of the rule to show cause, the court may either grant the request or, for good cause shown, extend the time period for filing a sworn detailed descriptive list. If the court grants the request, no traversal shall be allowed.

(b) Each party shall affirm under oath that the detailed descriptive list filed by that party contains all of the community assets and liabilities then known to that party. Amendments to the descriptive lists shall be permitted. No inventory shall be required.

(2) Within sixty days of the date of service of the last filed detailed descriptive list, each party shall either traverse or concur in the inclusion or exclusion of each asset and liability and the valuations contained in the detailed descriptive list of the other party. For good cause shown, the court may extend the time period for a party to traverse or concur in the detailed descriptive list of the other party. The trial of the traverses may be by summary procedure. At the trial of the traverses, the court shall determine the community assets and liabilities; the valuation of assets shall be determined at the trial on the merits. The court, in its discretion, may by ordinary procedure try and determine at one hearing all issues, including those raised in the traverses.

(3) The court may appoint such experts pursuant to Articles 192 and 373 of the Louisiana Code of Civil Procedure as it deems proper to assist the court in the settlement of the community and partition of community property, including the classification of assets as community or separate, the appraisal of community assets, the settlement of the claims of the parties, and the allocation of assets and liabilities to the parties.

(4) The court shall then partition the community in accordance with the following rules:

(a) The court shall value the assets as of the time of trial on the merits, determine the liabilities, and adjudicate the claims of the parties.

(b) The court shall divide the community assets and liabilities so that each spouse receives property of an equal net value.

(c) The court shall allocate or assign to the respective spouses all of the community assets and liabilities. In allocating assets and liabilities, the court may divide a particular asset or liability equally or unequally or may allocate it in its entirety to one of the spouses. The court shall consider the nature and source of the asset or liability, the economic condition of each spouse, and any other circumstances that the court deems relevant. As between the spouses, the allocation of a liability to a spouse obligates that spouse to extinguish that liability. The allocation in no way affects the rights of creditors.

(d) In the event that the allocation of assets and liabilities results in an unequal net distribution, the court shall order the payment of an equalizing sum of money, either cash or deferred, secured or unsecured, upon such terms and conditions as the court shall direct. The court may order the execution of notes, mortgages, or other documents as it deems necessary, or may impose a mortgage or lien on either community or separate property, movable or immovable, as security.

(e) In the event that the allocation of an asset, in whole or in part, would be inequitable to a party, the court may order the parties to draw lots for the asset or may order the private sale of the asset on such terms and conditions as the court deems proper, including the minimum price, the terms of sale, the execution of realtor listing agreements, and the period of time during which the asset shall be offered for private sale.

(f) Only in the event that an asset cannot be allocated to a party, assigned by the drawing of lots, or sold at private sale, shall the court order a partition thereof by licitation. The court may fix the minimum bids and other terms and conditions upon which the property is offered at public sale. In the event of a partition by licitation, the court shall expressly state the reasons why the asset cannot be allocated, assigned by the drawing of lots, or sold at private sale.

B. Those provisions of a domestic relations order or other judgment which partitions retirement or other deferred work benefits between former spouses shall be considered interlocutory until the domestic relations order has been granted "qualified" status from the plan administrator and/or until the judgment has been approved by the appropriate federal or state authority as being in compliance with applicable laws. Amendments to this interlocutory judgment to conform to the provisions of the plan shall be made with the consent of the parties or following a contradictory hearing by the court which granted the interlocutory judgment. The court issuing the domestic relations order or judgment shall maintain continuing jurisdiction over the subject matter and the parties until final resolution.

C. In the absence of an agreement between the parties for an extension of time or the granting by the court of an extension for good cause, if a party fails to comply with any time limit provided in this Section, upon motion of the other party or upon its own motion, the court may award reasonable attorney fees and court costs to the other party for the filing of or the response to the motion. If the court rules, pursuant to Subparagraph (A)(1)(a) of this Section, that the other party's sworn detailed descriptive list be deemed to constitute the assets and liabilities of the community, then the court shall not award attorney fees and court costs to the other party.

Added by Acts 1982, No. 439, § 1. Amended by Acts 1986, No. 225, § 1; Acts 1992, No. 825, § 1; Acts 1993, No. 28, § 1; Acts 1995, No. 433, § 2; Acts 1995, No. 1008, § 1; Acts 1997, No. 35, § 2; Acts 2001, No. 493, § 1; Acts 2005, No. 415, § 1.

Editor's note. R.S. 9:2801 was amended by Acts 1986, No. 225, § 1. Section 5 declares that the provisions of the Act "shall not be construed to grant jurisdiction not already granted to any family court, juvenile court, or juvenile division of a district court over proceedings involving partition of community property or over the settlement of claims between spouses arising from a matrimonial regime."

Section 3 of Acts 1995, No. 433 provides:

"This Act applies to former community property that is co-owned by spouses or former spouses on or after January 1, 1996, regardless of when the community regime of the spouses or former spouses terminated. Nothing in this Act shall be construed to change the characterization of assets acquired or fruits and products accrued prior to January 1, 1996, nor to invalidate any act or transaction made prior to January 1, 1996, by a spouse or former spouse according to the law in force at the time of the act or transaction. Nor shall a spouse or former spouse incur an obligation imposed by this Act for any action taken before January 1, 1996, with respect to former community property, unless the spouse or former spouse was obligated according to the law in force at the time the action was taken."

Cross References

C.C. arts. 150, 155, 807 to 817, 2325 et seq., 2336, 2356 et seq., 2375, 3520 to 3527, 3532, 3536.

C.C.P. art. 3942.

§ 2801.1. Community property; allocation and assignment of ownership

When federal law or the provisions of a statutory pension or retirement plan, state or federal, preempt or preclude community classification of property that would have been classified as community property under the principles of the Civil Code, the spouse of the person entitled to such property shall be allocated or assigned the ownership of community property equal in value to such property prior to the division of the rest of the community property. Nevertheless, if such property consists of a spouse's right to receive social security benefits or the benefits themselves, then the court in its discretion may allocate or assign other community property equal in value to the other spouse.

Added by Acts 2001, No. 642, § 1. Amended by Acts 2003, No. 1036, § 1.

§ 2801.2. Community property; valuation of goodwill

In a proceeding to partition the community, the court may include, in the valuation of any community-owned corporate, commercial, or professional business, the goodwill of the business. However, that portion of the goodwill attributable to any personal quality of the spouse awarded the business shall not be included in the valuation of a business.

Added by Acts 2003, No. 837, § 1. Amended by Acts 2004, No. 177, § 1.

§ 2802. Rendition of judgment of partition; prerequisite

An action seeking partition of community property and settlement of claims arising from matrimonial regimes, when asserted as an incident of an action which would result in termination of the matrimonial regime, shall not be deemed premature solely for the reason that the matrimonial regime has not been terminated. No judgment of partition shall be rendered unless rendered in conjunction with, or subsequent to, the judgment which has the effect of terminating the matrimonial regime.

Added by Acts 1986, No. 225, § 3.

Editor's note. R.S. 9:2802 was added by Acts 1986, No. 225, § 3. Section 5 declares that the provisions of the Act "shall not be construed to grant jurisdiction not already granted to any family court, juvenile court, or juvenile division of a district court over proceedings involving partition of community property or over the settlement of claims between spouses arising from a matrimonial regime."

§§ 2803, 2804. Repealed by Acts 1980, No. 237, § 1

§§ 2805 to 2820. [Blank]

§§ 2821, 2822. Repealed by Acts 1978, No. 627, § 8, eff. Jan. 1, 1980; Acts 1979, No. 709, § 3, eff. Jan. 1, 1980

CHAPTER 2. MATRIMONIAL REGIMES [REPEALED]

§§ 2831 to 2856. Repealed by Acts 1979, No. 709, § 5, eff. Jan. 1, 1980

CODE TITLE VII—SALE

CHAPTER 1. SALES IN GENERAL

PART I. RESEARCH CERTIFICATES

SUBPART A. TAX CERTIFICATES; NEW ORLEANS EXCEPTED

Section
2901. Payment of taxes prior to transfer of real property.
2902. Receipt or certificate of collector.
2903. Certificate annexed to act; evidence of payment; officer exonerated for nonpayment.
2904. Repealed.

SUBPART B. TAX, LOCAL IMPROVEMENT ASSESSMENT, AND NONALIENATION CERTIFICATES; NEW ORLEANS

2921. Payment of taxes and past due charges for local improvement assessments prior to transfer of real property.
2922. Receipt or certificate of collector.
2923. Content of certificate.
2924. Certificate annexed to act; evidence of payment; officer exonerated for nonpayment.
2925. Assumption by transferee of taxes for current year.
2926. Assumption by transferee of local improvement assessment charges maturing in future.
2927. Penalty for violation; act prima facie proof.
2928. Nonalienation certificate; penalty for violation.

PART I. RESEARCH CERTIFICATES

SUBPART A. TAX CERTIFICATES; NEW ORLEANS EXCEPTED

§ 2901. Payment of taxes prior to transfer of real property

Any party to an act conveying real property located in this state outside the limits of the city of New Orleans may obtain a certificate showing whether the state, parish, municipal, and levee district taxes due thereon, except those for the year in which the conveyance takes place, have been paid.

Amended by Acts 1978, No. 651, § 1; Acts 2011, 1st Ex. Sess., No. 30, § 1.

§ 2902. Receipt or certificate of collector

Payment shall be shown by the receipt or the certificate of the officer having charge of the collection of the taxes or by the certificate of the state auditor, city controller, or other officer having charge of the accounts.

§ 2903. Certificate annexed to act; evidence of payment; officer exonerated for nonpayment

The certificates so annexed to the act shall be conclusive evidence of the payment of all taxes therein certified to have been paid.

Amended by Acts 1978, No. 651, § 1.

§ 2904. Repealed by Acts 1978, No. 651, § 3

SUBPART B. TAX, LOCAL IMPROVEMENT ASSESSMENT, AND NONALIENATION CERTIFICATES; NEW ORLEANS

§ 2921. Payment of taxes and past due charges for local improvement assessments prior to transfer of real property

No public officer shall execute, pass, or acknowledge any act conveying real property located within the limits of the city of New Orleans unless the state, parish, municipal, and levee district taxes due thereon and the past due charges for local improvement assessments due thereon are paid.

Amended by Acts 2011, 1st Ex.Sess., No. 30, § 1.

§ 2922. Receipt or certificate of collector

Payment shall be shown by the receipt or the certificate of the officer having charge of the collection of the taxes or charges or by the certificate of the state auditor, state tax collector, city controller, or other officer having charge of the accounts.

§ 2923. Content of certificate

When preparing a certificate as provided in R.S. 9:2922, the certifying officer shall examine and report the condition of the tax rolls for thirty years prior to January first of the year in which the certificate is applied for and in the case of local improvement assessments, for ten years prior to January first of the year and for future years during which installments for such charges may become due, reserving to the municipal corporation recourse against its collectors and deputy collectors and their bondsmen for any losses it may sustain by reason of any errors made in the certificate.

The tax certificates shall indicate whether or not the current taxes have been paid, and shall indicate for each separate year the method by which the taxes have been paid or considered paid, whether by the tax debtor, by tax sale, or by any other manner.

The municipal corporation shall fix by ordinance the price to be charged for research certificate.

Amended by Acts 1954, No. 596, § 1.

§ 2924. Certificate annexed to act; evidence of payment; officer exonerated for nonpayment

The certificates shall be annexed to the act, shall be conclusive evidence of the payment of all taxes or past due charges therein certified to have been paid, and shall exonerate the public officer from liability for nonpayment thereof.

§ 2925. Assumption by transferee of taxes for current year

The taxes for the year in which the transfer takes place may be assumed by the transferee if they cannot be paid on the date the act is executed because the collecting officer is not prepared to receive them and to issue an official receipt therefor.

§ 2926. Assumption by transferee of local improvement assessment charges maturing in future

Nothing contained in R.S. 9:2921 pertaining to the local improvement assessments shall prevent the execution, passing, or acknowledgment of any act conveying real property if the act contains a specific assumption of the installment charges which are to mature in the future.

§ 2927. Penalty for violation; act prima facie proof

Any public officer who violates R.S. 9:2921 shall be fined not less than one hundred dollars nor more than two hundred dollars. The act offered in evidence shall be prima facie proof of the violation.

§ 2928. Nonalienation certificate; penalty for violation

No notary or sheriff of the Parish of Orleans shall pass any act conveying real property located in the Parish of Orleans without first obtaining from the register of conveyances a certificate showing that the vendor has not alienated the property. The certificate shall contain a description of the property and shall be annexed to the act.

Any notary or sheriff of the Parish of Orleans who violates this Section shall be fined not less than two hundred and fifty dollars nor more than five hundred dollars.

Cross References

C.C. art. 3393.

CHAPTER 2. CONVENTIONAL SALES

PART I. BOND FOR DEED CONTRACTS

Section
2941. "Bond for deed" defined.
2941.1. Recordation; subsequent filings; interest prohibited; cancellation of mortgage records.
2942. Unlawful to sell encumbered real property by bond for deed without guarantee to release on payment.
2943. Method of payment.
2944. Timely payment of installments precludes foreclosure; change of description upon foreclosure.
2945. Cancellation of bond for deed upon default.
2946. Unlawful to require mortgage notes when property encumbered; act of sale.
2947. Penalty for violations.
2948. Bond for deed buyer deemed owner for purposes of homestead exemption.
2949. [Blank].

PART II. SALES OF MOTOR VEHICLE DEALERSHIPS

2961. Limited availability of revocatory action.
2962 to 2968. Repealed.

PART III. TRANSFER OF LANDS FRONTING WATERWAYS, HIGHWAYS, ETC.

2971. Presumption of grant of all interest; exceptions.
2972. Nature of Part.
2973. Preservation of rights.

PART IV. TRANSFER OF LANDS ABUTTING ABANDONED ROADS, STREETS OR ALLEYS

2981. Presumption of grant of interest in abandoned road.
2982. Part remedial.
2983. Preservation of rights.
2984. Construction.
2985 to 2987. [Blank].

Section
PART V. DUAL OR FRAUDULENT CONTRACTS
2989. Dual contracts; definition; violations; penalties.

PART I. BOND FOR DEED CONTRACTS

§ 2941. "Bond for deed" defined

A bond for deed is a contract to sell real property, in which the purchase price is to be paid by the buyer to the seller in installments and in which the seller after payment of a stipulated sum agrees to deliver title to the buyer.

Cross References

C.C. arts. 3280, 3307.

§ 2941.1. Recordation; subsequent filings; interest prohibited; cancellation of mortgage records

A. Upon the recordation in the mortgage and conveyance records of a bond for deed contract as defined in R.S. 9:2941, any sale, contract, counterletter, lease, or mortgage executed by the bond for deed seller, and any lien, privilege, or judgment relating to or purporting to affect immovable property that has not been filed previously for registry or recorded in the mortgage records shall be subject to the rights created by the bond for deed contract.

B. Following registry of the sale by bond for deed seller to the bond for deed purchaser, his successors or assigns, any such instrument or writing that was filed in the mortgage records after the filing of the bond for deed contract shall be cancelled by the clerk of court or the recorder of mortgages upon request by affidavit of any interested party, but only insofar as it affects the property described in the bond for deed and subsequent sale, after the note holder or lien holder has been given thirty days written notice and fails to execute a release. A copy of the sale by the bond for deed seller to the bond for deed purchaser or his successors or assigns, containing relevant recordation information, shall be attached to the request.

C. The provisions of this Section shall not apply to tax sales or redemptions as provided for by R.S. 47:2171, et seq. Added by Acts 2006, No. 582, § 1. Amended by Acts 2010, No. 386, § 1.

§ 2942. Unlawful to sell encumbered real property by bond for deed without guarantee to release on payment

It shall be unlawful to sell by bond for deed contract, any real property which is encumbered by mortgage or privilege without first obtaining a written guarantee from the mortgage and privilege holders to release the property upon payment by the buyer of a stipulated mortgage release price, with which agreement the secured notes shall be identified. The agreement shall be recorded in the mortgage records of the parish where the property is situated before any part of the property is offered for sale under bond for deed contracts. The provisions of this Part likewise shall apply to any property offered for sale by bond for deed contract which may be subsequently mortgaged or encumbered by a privilege.

Cross References

C.C. arts. 3280, 3307.

§ 2943. Method of payment

All payments by the buyers under bond for deed contracts of property then or thereafter burdened with a mortgage or privilege, shall be made to some bank authorized to do business in this state, which shall have been designated as the escrow agent for all parties interested in the contract. The payments shall be distributed by the escrow agent between the seller and the holder of the mortgage or privilege, in such proportion as the secured obligation shall bear to the purchase price in order to insure the buyer an unencumbered title when all payments have been made as provided in the bond for deed contract.

Cross References

C.C. arts. 3280, 3307.

§ 2944. Timely payment of installments precludes foreclosure; change of description upon foreclosure

The payment as they fall due of all installments by buyers under bond for deed contracts, shall preclude the holder of any secured notes from foreclosure, but the failure of the buyers to make payments as they fall due, shall secure to the holder of the notes the right to foreclose when the notes become due and are unpaid. In the event of a foreclosure under such circumstances, the description as contained in the act of mortgage may be changed so as to leave unaffected those lots or tracts of land on which payments have been kept up and so as to affect and adjudicate under the foreclosure only such lots as may be in default of payments and other lots not sold under bond for deed contracts.

Cross References

C.C. arts. 3280, 3307.

§ 2945. Cancellation of bond for deed upon default

A. If the buyer under a bond for deed contract shall fail to make the payments in accordance with its terms and conditions, the seller, at his option, may have the bond for deed cancelled by proper registry in the conveyance records, provided he has first caused the escrow agent to serve notice upon the buyer, by registered or certified mail, return receipt requested, at his last known address, that unless payment is made as provided in the bond for deed within forty-five days from the mailing date of the notice, the bond for deed shall be cancelled.

B. Where there is no mortgage or privilege existing upon the property, and the buyer shall be in default, the seller shall exercise the right of cancellation in the same manner.

C. The fee of the clerk of court for the registry of the cancellation shall not exceed the legal rate per hundred words fixed for conveyance registries.
Amended by Acts 1999, No. 517, § 1.

Cross References

C.C. arts. 3280, 3307.

§ 2946. Unlawful to require mortgage notes when property encumbered; act of sale

It shall be unlawful for any seller in a bond for deed contract to require promissory notes to represent the purchase price or any portion thereof, if the property should be encumbered with a mortgage or privilege. Upon the payment to the escrow agent of the sum necessary to release the property, the seller shall execute a deed to the buyer and may then exact one or more mortgage notes to represent any portion of the unpaid purchase price. Should the property not be encumbered with a mortgage or privilege, and a note has been executed to represent all or a part of the price under the bond for deed contract, when the buyer shall become entitled to demand a deed, the seller shall execute an authentic sale and the notary passing it shall require the production of the note or notes and shall cancel them at the time of passing the sale.

Cross References

C.C. arts. 3280, 3307.

§ 2947. Penalty for violations

Any person who sells by bond for deed contract any real property encumbered by mortgage or privilege without first obtaining and recording the guarantee required by R.S. 9:2942, shall be fined not more than one thousand dollars, or imprisoned for not more than six months, or both.

Any seller in a bond for deed contract of property encumbered with a mortgage or privilege, who requires promissory notes to represent the purchase price or any portion thereof, shall be fined not more than one thousand dollars, or imprisoned for not more than six months, or both.

Cross References

C.C. arts. 3280, 3307.

§ 2948. Bond for deed buyer deemed owner for purposes of homestead exemption

Notwithstanding any other provisions of law to the contrary, the buyer under a bond for deed contract shall be deemed, for purposes of the homestead exemption only, to own any immovable property he has purchased and is occupying under bond for deed, and may be eligible for the homestead exemption provided in Article VII, Section 20(A) of the Constitution of Louisiana if otherwise qualified. The buyer under a bond for deed contract shall apply for the homestead exemption each year.

Added by Acts 1993, No. 1030, § 1.

§ 2949. [Blank]

PART II. SALES OF MOTOR VEHICLE DEALERSHIPS

Editor's note. R.S. 9:2961 to 9:2968 contained the Bulk Sales Law. These provisions were repealed by Acts 1991, No. 377, § 8, effective January 1, 1992. Section 10 of Acts 1991, No. 377, declares: "The provisions of Section 8 of this Act shall have prospective application only and shall not affect any bulk transfers or sales executed before January 1, 1992, which transfers or sales shall be governed by the law in effect prior to January 1, 1992."

Present R.S. 9:2961 was added by Acts 1992, No. 961, § 1.

§ 2961. Limited availability of revocatory action

A. A revocatory action may not be brought in connection with the sale of a motor vehicle dealership if the requirements of this Part are met.

B. The transferor and the transferee shall, at least ten days before the completion of any such transfer or the payment of any consideration therefor, make a full and detailed inventory showing the quantity and, so far as possible with the exercise of reasonable diligence, the cost price to the transferor of each article to be included in the sale.

C. The transferee shall demand of and receive from the transferor, or if the transferor be a corporation, then from the president, vice president, secretary, or managing agent thereof, a written statement, sworn to substantially as hereinafter provided, of the names and addresses of all of the creditors of the transferor to whom the transferor may be indebted, together with the amount of indebtedness due and owing, and to become due and owing by the transferor to each of the creditors. The transferor shall furnish to the transferee such statement, which shall be verified by an oath to the following effect:

State of Louisiana
Parish of

Before me ___ personally appeared ___ (transferor or agent) who, being by me first duly sworn upon his oath, deposed and said that the foregoing statement contains the names of all the creditors of ___ (name of transferor), together with their addresses, and that the amount set opposite each of their respective names is the amount now due and owing and which shall become due and owing by ___ (transferor) to such creditors, and that there are not creditors holding claims due or which shall become due for or on account of goods, wares, merchandise, or fixtures, or equipment used or to be used in the display, manufacture, care, or delivery of any goods, wares, or merchandise, including movable store and office fixtures, vehicles, or other goods and chattels of the transferor's business purchased upon credit or on account of money borrowed to carry on the business of which the property is a part other than as set forth in said statement, and that the facts set out in this affidavit are within the personal knowledge of the affiant.

———————

Sworn and subscribed to before me this ___ day of ___, 19___.

———————

Title of officer
taking oath

D. The transferee shall, at least ten days before the completion of the transfer or the payment of any consideration therefor, notify personally, by registered mail, or by certified mail, every creditor listed or of whom he has knowledge or can, with reasonable diligence, acquire knowledge, of the time set for the transfer of the property and a copy of the statement of creditors. The transferee shall at least seven days before the completion of the transfer advertise in the official journal of the parish where the motor vehicle dealership is located giving the date, place, and time of the sale. Any creditor whose name has been omitted from the statement may give written notice of his claim to the transferee and shall thereafter be entitled to share equally with the other creditors entitled to the benefits of this Part as to the proceeds of such sale or transfer as are then held by the transferee.

E. No provision of this Part shall be construed as in any way compromising the rights of secured creditors, validly acquired, and their respective rankings as opposed to unsecured creditors, as it relates to their claims against the proceeds of a sale or transfer conducted in conformity with the Part.

F. A buyer of an automobile dealership who complies with the requirements of this Part shall be deemed to have acquired clear title to all of the assets of the acquired dealership, once the proceeds of the sale have been distributed in conformity with the requirements and provisions of this Part.

Added by Acts 1992, No. 961, § 1.

§§ 2962 to 2968. Repealed by Acts 1991, No. 377, § 8, eff. Jan. 1, 1992

PART III. TRANSFER OF LANDS FRONTING WATERWAYS, HIGHWAYS, ETC.

§ 2971. Presumption of grant of all interest; exceptions

It shall be conclusively presumed that any transfer, conveyance, surface lease, mineral lease, mortgage or any other contract, or grant affecting land described as fronting on or bounded by, or as described pursuant to a survey or using a metes and bounds description that shows that it actually fronts on or is bounded by a waterway, canal, highway, road, street, alley, railroad, or other right-of-way, shall be held, deemed and construed to include all of grantor's interest in and under such waterway, canal, highway, road, street, alley, railroad, or other right-of-way, whatever that interest may be, in the absence of any express provision therein particularly excluding the same therefrom; provided, that where the grantor at the time of the transfer or other grant holds as owner the title to the fee of the land situated on both sides thereof and makes a transfer or other grant affecting the land situated on only one side thereof, it shall then be conclusively presumed, in the absence of any express provision therein particularly excluding the same therefrom, that the transfer or other such grant thereof shall include the grantor's interest to the center of such waterway, canal, highway, road, street, alley, railroad, or other right-of-way; provided further, however, that no then existing valid right-of-way upon, across or over said property so transferred or conveyed or so presumed to be conveyed and no warranties with respect thereto shall be in any manner or to any extent impaired, prejudiced, or otherwise affected by any of the terms and provisions of this Part or because of the failure of such grantor or transferor to therein make special reference to such right-of-way or to include or exclude same therefrom.

Added by Acts 1956, No. 555, § 1. Amended by Acts 2003, No. 723, § 1.

Cross References

C.C. arts. 450, 2491, 2495.

§ 2972. Nature of Part

This Part is remedial and is for the benefit of all persons heretofore as well as hereafter acquiring by or under such a transfer or other grant affecting such property, without express exception or reference in the description of such land, rights of way or other property therein set forth.

Added by Acts 1956, No. 555, § 2.

Cross References

C.C. arts. 450, 2491, 2495.

§ 2973. Preservation of rights

Any person who has made a transfer or other grant affecting land so described, their heirs or assigns, whose rights may be affected hereby, shall have a period of one year from August 1, 1956, within which to preserve and protect such rights, by: (a) filing suit in each parish where such land is situated, asserting such rights, or (b) by recording a notarized declaration asserting such rights in the conveyance records of each parish where such land is situated within such one year period; and in case neither said method of preserving such rights is followed within one year from August 1, 1956, said rights shall be forever barred.

Added by Acts 1956, No. 555, § 3.

Cross References

C.C. arts. 450, 2491, 2495.

PART IV. TRANSFER OF LANDS ABUTTING ABANDONED ROADS, STREETS OR ALLEYS

§ 2981. Presumption of grant of interest in abandoned road

It shall be conclusively presumed that any transfer, grant, sale or mortgage of land and property abutting or contiguous to an abandoned road, street or alley, the dedication of which has been revoked, shall be held, deemed and construed to include all of grantor's or mortgagor's interest in and to said abandoned road, street, or alley, in the absence of any express provision therein particularly excluding the abandoned property therefrom; provided further, however, that no then existing valid servitude or rights of third parties in or on the abandoned property shall be in any manner or to any extent impaired, prejudiced, or otherwise affected by any of the terms and provisions of this Part.

Added by Acts 1958, No. 528, § 1.

Cross References

C.C. art. 450.

§ 2982. Part remedial

This Part is remedial and is for the benefit of all persons heretofore as well as hereafter acquiring, or holding mortgages, affecting such property, without express exception or reference to the abandoned road, street, or alley in the description of the property set forth in the instrument of sale, transfer, or mortgage.

Added by Acts 1958, No. 528, § 2.

Cross References

C.C. art. 450.

§ 2983. Preservation of rights

Any person who has made a transfer, grant, sale or mortgage affecting land so described, their heirs or assigns, whose rights may be affected hereby, shall have a period of one year from July 30, 1958 within which to preserve and protect such rights, by (1) filing suit in each parish where such land is situated, asserting such rights, or (2) by recording a notarized declaration asserting such rights in the conveyance records of each parish where such land is situat-

ed within such one year period; and in case neither said method of preserving such rights is followed within one year from July 30, 1958, said rights shall be forever barred.
Added by Acts 1958, No. 528, § 3.

Cross References

C.C. art. 450.

§ 2984. Construction

Nothing in this Part shall be construed to conflict with, affect, or repeal any of the provisions of Act 555 of 1956 and incorporated as R.S. 9:2971, 2972 and 2973.
Added by Acts 1958, No. 528, § 5.

Cross References

C.C. arts. 450, 2495.

§§ 2985 to 2987. [Blank]

PART V. DUAL OR FRAUDULENT CONTRACTS

§ 2989. Dual contracts; definition; violations; penalties

A. As used in this Part the term "dual contracts" means two written contracts entered into between identical contracting parties in identical capacities concerning the same parcel of real property, one of which states the true and actual purchase price and one of which states a purchase price in excess of the true and actual purchase price and is used as an inducement for mortgage investors to make a loan commitment on such real property in reliance upon the stated inflated value.

B. A fraudulent instrument is any paper, document or other form in writing that is intentionally used as a subterfuge or device to induce the making of a loan or the extension of credit as a part of a transaction whereby either the title to real property is transferred or valuable improvements are placed on real property in this state, whether for the benefit of the inducer or another.

C. No person, firm or corporation, or any agent or employee of any such firm or corporation shall, with intent to defraud:

(1) Make or issue a dual contract for the purchase of real property, or

(2) Substitute one instrument in writing for another and by such means cause the making of a loan or the extension of credit, with respect to transactions whereby either the title to real property is transferred or valuable improvements are placed on real property in this state, whether for the benefit of the inducer or another;

(3) Induce by any fraudulent instrument in writing the making of a loan or the extension of credit as a part of a transaction whereby either the title to real property is transferred or valuable improvements are placed on real property in this state, whether for the benefit of the inducer or another.

D. Whoever violates any provision of this Subsection shall be fined not more than one thousand dollars. For the second and all following violations the penalty shall be a fine of not less than one thousand dollars nor more than five thousand dollars.

E. Anything contained herein to the contrary notwithstanding, the provisions of this section shall not apply to loans made by mortgage investors who rely on an independent appraisal of the property in granting such loan.
Added by Acts 1968, No. 415, § 1.

Cross References

C.C. art. 2028.

CHAPTER 3. JUDICIAL SALES

PART I. IN GENERAL

Section
3001. Persons authorized to make judicial sales.
3002. Sales on credit; notes; security.
3003. Notes or bonds to be identified with sales.

PART I. IN GENERAL

§ 3001. Persons authorized to make judicial sales

Judicial sales may be made by the sheriff, by an auctioneer of the parish or city in which the sale is to be made, or by the legal representative of the succession, minor, interdict, or insolvent property owner. In cases where the sale is not to be made by the legal representative, the judge ordering the sale shall direct that it be made by an auctioneer who has been agreed upon by the parties, or if the parties do not agree, by the sheriff or an auctioneer designated by the judge.

Cross References

R.S. 9:3155, 9:3168, 9:3172.

§ 3002. Sales on credit; notes; security

The sheriff, or other person making sales of succession property on credit terms, shall be authorized to receive for the price the notes of the purchasers, and identify them by description in the adjudication. The security on the notes shall in all cases be approved by the vendor or the party representing him.

§ 3003. Notes or bonds to be identified with sales

On the registering of proces verbals of sales in the office of the recorder or register of conveyances of the parish where the property so adjudicated may be situated, the recorder or register shall be authorized to identify with the sales the notes or bonds received, by his paraph, in order that he may cancel the mortgage when they shall have been paid.

CHAPTER 4. ASSIGNMENT OR TRANSFER OF CREDITS OR OTHER INCORPOREAL RIGHTS

PART I. IN GENERAL

Section
3051. Transfer of claims for collection.

PART II. LOUISIANA ASSIGNMENT OF ACCOUNTS RECEIVABLE ACT [REPEALED]

3101 to 3112. Repealed.

Section
PART III. ASSIGNMENT OF PROCEEDS
OF CROP FINANCING
3121. Crop financing; assignment of interest by agricultural producer.

PART IV. LOUISIANA EXCHANGE SALE
OF RECEIVABLES ACT [BLANK]
3131.1 to 3131.9. [Blank].

PART I. IN GENERAL

§ 3051. Transfer of claims for collection

When several parties have claims against the same defendant or defendants, arising out of a common transaction, such as claims of laborers for their wages, they, or any of them, may transfer their claims to any person or persons for collection by suit or otherwise. The transfer need not be supported by a valuable consideration but it shall be sufficient that it be in writing.

PART II. LOUISIANA ASSIGNMENT OF ACCOUNTS RECEIVABLE ACT [REPEALED]

§§ 3101 to 3112. Repealed by Acts 2001, No. 128, § 18, eff. July 1, 2001 at 12:01 A.M.

Editor's note. Acts 2001, No. 128, § 18, effective July 1, 2001, repealed R.S. 9:3101 through 3112. Section 19 of Acts 2001, No. 128, declares that "it is the intent of the legislature in enacting this Act that R.S. 2736, 4501 and 4502, 4521, 4758, 4770, and 5363.1 not be expressly or impliedly repealed by this Act, but that such laws remain in effect, and, at times when so provided, be applied to secured transactions subject to Chapter 9 of the Louisiana Commercial Law as revised by this Act."

PART III. ASSIGNMENT OF PROCEEDS OF CROP FINANCING

§ 3121. Crop financing; assignment of interest by agricultural producer

A. When an agricultural producer, as defined in R.S. 3:3402, obtains financing for the production of a crop, and the total amount of the proceeds of that financing has not been disbursed, the agricultural producer may assign his interest in the undisbursed proceeds of financing for the current crop year to one or more vendors of supplies, materials, or services used in the production or processing of that crop in that crop year. The vendor to whom the assignment is made shall notify the lending institution of the existence of the assignment. The notice shall be transmitted by certified mail, return receipt requested, or by actual delivery receipted for by the lending institution. Upon receipt of the notice, the lending institution shall make any future payments of the undisbursed proceeds jointly, or payable jointly, to the agricultural producer and the vendor until the total amount of the assignment has been paid by such joint payments.

B. The notice of assignment shall contain the following information:

(1) The name and address of the agricultural producer.

(2) The name and address of the lending institution.

(3) The total amount of the proceeds which are assigned.

(4) A description of the crop or crops and the location thereof as furnished to the vendor by the agricultural producer.

(5) The types and amounts of supplies, materials, or services purchased.

(6) The date on which the supplies, materials, or services were purchased.

(7) A copy of the invoice or purchase order for the supplies, materials, or services.

(8) A copy of the contract of assignment.

C. No assignment shall be made for less than one thousand dollars.

D. If the agricultural producer makes multiple assignments, the assignments shall rank in the order they are received by the lending institution.

E. The vendor may terminate an assignment by written instrument transmitted by certified mail, return receipt requested, or by actual delivery receipted for by the lending institution.

F. The assignment shall not abridge or affect any right of offset or compensation which the lending institution may have with respect to any undisbursed proceeds.

G. No lending institution shall incur any liability as a result of compliance with the provisions of this Section. Added by Acts 1986, No. 233, § 1.

Cross References

C.C. arts. 474, 491, 1821, 1984, 2643 et seq., 2705, 3217, 3218.

PART IV. LOUISIANA EXCHANGE SALE OF RECEIVABLES ACT [BLANK]

§§ 3131.1 to 3131.9. [Blank]

CHAPTER 4–A. CORPOREAL IMMOVABLES

Section
3131. Legislative intent.
3132. Definitions.
3133. Private transfer fee; prohibition.
3134. Violations; liability.
3135. Disclosure.
3136. Existing transfer fee obligations; notice requirements.

§ 3131. Legislative intent

The legislature finds and declares that the public policy of this state favors the marketability of immovables and the transferability of interests in immovables free of title defects or unreasonable restraints on alienation. The legislature further finds and declares that private transfer fee obligations violate this public policy by impairing the marketability and transferability of immovables and by constituting an unreasonable restraint on alienation regardless of the duration of the obligation to pay a private transfer fee, the amount of a private transfer fee, or the method by which any private transfer fee is created or imposed. Thus, the legislature finds and declares that a private transfer fee obligation shall not create real rights and shall not be binding on subsequent owners of immovables or other third parties, whether or not evidenced by a recorded instrument.

Added by Acts 2010, No. 938, § 1, eff. July 2, 2010.

Cross References

C.C. arts. 461, 462, 464, 649, 3286, 3291.

§ 3132. Definitions

As used in this Chapter:

(1) "Private transfer fee" means a fee or charge required by a private transfer fee obligation and payable upon the transfer of an interest in an immovable, or payable for the right to make or accept such transfer, regardless of whether the fee or charge is a fixed amount or is determined as a percentage of the value of the immovable, the purchase price, or other consideration given for the transfer. "Private transfer fee" shall not include the following:

(a) Any consideration payable by the buyer to the seller for the interest in the immovable being transferred, including any subsequent additional consideration for the immovable payable by the buyer based upon any subsequent appreciation, development, or sale of the immovable, provided such additional consideration is payable on a one-time basis only and the obligation to make such payment does not bind successors in title to the immovable.

(b) Any commission payable to a licensed real estate broker for the transfer of an immovable pursuant to an agreement between the broker and the seller or the buyer, including any subsequent additional commission for that transfer payable by the seller or the buyer based upon any subsequent appreciation, development, or sale of the immovable.

(c) Any interest, charges, fees, or other amounts payable by a borrower to a lender pursuant to a loan secured by a mortgage against an immovable, including but not limited to any fee payable to the lender for consenting to an assumption of the loan or a transfer of the immovable subject to the mortgage, any fees or charges payable to the lender for estoppel letters or certificates, and any shared appreciation interest or profit participation or other consideration payable to the lender in connection with the loan.

(d) Any rent, reimbursement, charge, fee, or other amount payable by a lessee to a lessor under a lease, including but not limited to any fee payable to the lessor for consenting to an assignment, subletting, encumbrance, or transfer of the lease.

(e) Any consideration payable to the holder of an option to purchase an interest in an immovable or the holder of a right of first refusal or first offer to purchase an interest in an immovable for waiving, releasing, or not exercising the option or right upon the transfer of the immovable to another person.

(f) Any tax, fee, charge, assessment, fine, or other amount payable to or imposed by a governmental authority.

(g) Any fee, charge, assessment, fine, or other amount authorized under Louisiana Condominium Act, R.S. 9:1121.101 et seq.; the Louisiana Timesharing Act, R.S. 9:1131.1 et seq.; or the Louisiana Homeowners Association Act, R.S. 9:1141.1 et seq.

(2) "Private transfer fee obligation" means any obligation arising under any recorded or unrecorded declaration or agreement, whether or not purporting to create a servitude, building restriction or other real right, to pay a private transfer fee to a party to the declaration or agreement, or his successors or assigns, or a third person upon a subsequent transfer of an interest in the immovable.

(3) "Transfer" means the sale, donation, conveyance, assignment, inheritance, or other transfer of an ownership interest in an immovable located in this state.

Added by Acts 2010, No. 938, § 1, eff. July 2, 2010.

Cross References

C.C. arts. 461, 462, 464, 649, 3286, 3291.

§ 3133. Private transfer fee; prohibition

A private transfer fee obligation does not constitute a real right and is not effective or enforceable against third persons, whether or not the declaration or agreement under which it arises is recorded.

Added by Acts 2010, No. 938, § 1, eff. July 2, 2010.

Cross References

C.C. arts. 461, 462, 464, 649, 3286, 3291.

§ 3134. Violations; liability

Any natural or juridical person who records or enters into an agreement imposing a private transfer fee obligation in their favor after July 2, 2010, shall be liable for:

(1) Any and all damages resulting from the imposition of the transfer fee obligation on a transfer of an interest in an immovable, including without limitation the amount of any transfer fee paid by a party to the transfer.

(2) All attorney fees, expenses, and costs incurred by a party to the transfer or mortgagee of the immovable to recover any transfer fee paid or in connection with an action to quiet title or to declare the private transfer fee unenforceable. Where a mandatary acts on behalf of a principal to record or enforce a private transfer fee obligation, both the principal and the mandatary shall be solidarily liable.

Added by Acts 2010, No. 938, § 1, eff. July 2, 2010.

Cross References

C.C. arts. 461, 462, 464, 649, 3286, 3291.

§ 3135. Disclosure

A seller of an immovable shall furnish to any purchaser a written statement disclosing the existence of any private transfer fee obligation. This written statement shall include a description of the private transfer fee obligation and include a statement that private transfer fee obligations are subject to certain prohibitions under this Chapter.

Added by Acts 2010, No. 938, § 1, eff. July 2, 2010.

Cross References

C.C. arts. 461, 462, 464, 649, 3286, 3291.

§ 3136. Existing transfer fee obligations; notice requirements

A. For a private transfer fee obligation imposed prior to July 2, 2010, the person entitled to receive the fee shall record, prior to December 31, 2010, a separate document in the conveyance records of the parish in which the immovable is located that contains all of the following:

(1) A title labeling the document as "Notice of Private Transfer Fee Obligation" in at least fourteen-point boldface type.

(2) The amount, if the fee is a flat amount, or the percentage of the sales price constituting the cost of the transfer fee, or such other basis by which the transfer fee is to be calculated.

(3) If the immovable includes a residential use, actual dollar-cost.

(4) The date or circumstances under which the private transfer fee obligation expires, if any.

(5) The purpose for which the funds from the private transfer fee obligation will be used.

(6) The name of the person or entity to which funds are to be paid and specific contact information regarding where the funds are to be sent.

(7) The acknowledged signature of the person filing the notice.

(8) The legal description of the immovable purportedly burdened by the private transfer fee obligation and the name of the current owner of the immovable.

B. The person or entity to which the transfer fee is to be paid may file an amendment to the notice of transfer fee containing new contact information, but such amendment shall contain the recording information of the notice of transfer fee which it amends and the legal description of the immovable burdened by the private transfer fee obligation.

C. In the absence of timely compliance with Subsection A of this Section, any effect that private transfer fee obligations might otherwise have had against third persons shall cease and shall not be susceptible of revival by a later filing.

D. If the payee fails to provide a written statement of the transfer fee payable within thirty days of the date of a written request for the same sent to the address shown in the notice of transfer fee, then the seller, on recording of the affidavit required under Subsection E of this Section, may convey any interest in the immovable to any buyer without payment of the transfer fee and shall not be subject to any further obligations under the private transfer fee obligation. In such event, the immovable shall be conveyed free and clear of the transfer fee and private transfer fee obligation.

E. An affidavit stating the facts enumerated under Subsection F of this Section shall be recorded in the conveyance records of the parish in which the immovable is located. An affidavit filed under this Subsection shall state that the affiant has actual knowledge of, and is competent to testify to, the facts in the affidavit and shall include the legal description of the immovable burdened by the private transfer fee obligation, the name of the person or entity appearing by the record to be the owner of such corporeal immovable at the time of the signing of such affidavit, and a reference to the instrument of record containing the private transfer fee obligation.

F. When recorded, an affidavit, as described in Subsection E of this Section, shall constitute prima facie evidence that:

(1) A request for the written statement of the transfer fee payable in order to obtain a release of the fee imposed by the private transfer fee obligation was sent to the address shown in the notification.

(2) The person or entity listed on the notice of transfer fee failed to provide the written statement of the transfer fee payable within thirty days of the date of the notice sent to the address shown in the notification.

G. This Section shall apply only to private transfer fee obligations arising under a declaration or agreement entered into prior to July 2, 2010, whether or not recorded; however, neither the provisions of this Section nor compliance by any person with its requirements shall be construed to validate or authorize private transfer fee obligations that were purportedly created prior to July 2, 2010 or to make such private transfer restrictions enforceable against third persons.

Added by Acts 2010, No. 938, § 1, eff. July 2, 2010.

Cross References

C.C. arts. 461, 462, 464, 649, 3286, 3291.

CHAPTER 4–B. LOUISIANA EXCHANGE SALE OF RECEIVABLES ACT

Section
3137.1. Short title.
3137.2. Legislative intent.
3137.3. Definitions.
3137.4. Scope.
3137.5. True sales of receivables; not subject to recharacterization; simulation articles not applicable.
3137.6. Binding effectiveness of Louisiana law.
3137.7. Buyer ownership rights; evidence of ownership.
3137.8. Relationship to the UCC.
3137.9. Prohibition of actions.

§ 3137.1. Short title

This Part shall be known and may be cited as the "Louisiana Exchange Sale of Receivables Act".

Added by Acts 2010, No. 958, § 1, eff. July 6, 2010.

Editor's note. R.S. 9:3137.1 was enacted by Acts 2010, No. 958, as R..S. 9:3131.1. It has been redesignated by the Louisiana State Law Institute as R.S. 9:3137.1.

Cross References

C.C. arts. 2439, 2447, 2450, 2456, 2464, 2467, 2474, 2484, 2485, 2497, 2549, 2601, 2620, 2623, 2642.

§ 3137.2. Legislative intent

A. It is the intent of the legislature to encourage and promote businesses to offer sellers the ability to sell their receivables to qualified buyers over electronic and other types of exchanges located in this state, thereby availing themselves of Louisiana civil law principles not found in common law jurisdictions, and further availing themselves of the true sale provisions of this Part and R.S. 10:9-109(e).

B. The legislature declares the following actions to be the public policy of this state.

(1) All sales of receivables over exchanges located in Louisiana shall be subject to Louisiana law, and specifically subject to this Part and to R.S. 10:9-109(e).

(2) Such sales shall result in true sales for all purposes and not be limited to a bankruptcy context.

(3) Such sales shall not be subject to recharacterization as a simulated sale or as a loan, extension of credit, or other credit accommodation by the buyer to the seller, notwith-

standing that the seller may be obligated to repurchase the receivable, or the buyer may have other recourse against the seller, if the receivable is not timely paid, and further notwithstanding that the seller may be entitled to receive a portion of the collection proceeds.

C. This Part and R.S. 10:9–109(e) specifically reject common law legal theories under which recourse sales of receivables have been recharacterized as loans or credit accommodations, as being contrary to Louisiana civil law principles that apply to sales of receivables over exchanges located in this state.

Added by Acts 2010, No. 958, § 1, eff. July 6, 2010.

Editor's note. R.S. 9:3137.2 was enacted by Acts 2010, No. 958, as R..S. 9:3131.2. It has been redesignated by the Louisiana State Law Institute as R.S. 9:3137.2.

Cross References

C.C. arts. 2439, 2447, 2450, 2456, 2464, 2467, 2474, 2484, 2485, 2497, 2549, 2601, 2620, 2623, 2642.

§ 3137.3. Definitions

A. For the purposes of this Part, the following terms shall have the following meanings unless the context clearly indicates otherwise.

(1) "Buyer" means the person buying a receivable over an exchange located in this state.

(2) "Collection proceeds" means any amounts received or otherwise collected from the person owing the receivable, including the account debtor or a guarantor of the payment obligation.

(3) "Consummate" means to complete all agreements, steps and actions necessary for a sale of receivables to be deemed to be complete under Louisiana law, with ownership of the purchased receivable passing from the seller to the buyer.

(4) "Exchange" means an electronic or other marketplace over which sellers may offer and sell their receivables to qualified buyers.

(5) "Operational employees" means and refers to employees whose work responsibilities are primarily devoted to performing operations-related functions related to the exchange and persons transacting business over the exchange, as compared to employees whose primary work responsibilities are devoted to managerial, marketing, sales, internal accounting and other non-operational functions.

(6) "Receivable" means an account, general intangible, payment intangible, chattel paper or instrument as defined under the UCC. Receivables shall also include third-party payment obligations that are not subject to the UCC. Receivables shall not be limited to United States domestic payment obligations, and shall include receivables owed by non-United States persons and entities as well as receivables originating out of non-United States transactions.

(7) "Seller" means the person offering a receivable for sale over an exchange located in this state.

(8) "True sale" means a consummated sale of all rights, title and interests that the seller may have in a receivable sold over an exchange located in this state, with the buyer acquiring all of the seller's rights and interests, and with the seller not retaining a legal or equitable interest in the receivables sold.

(9) "UCC" means the Uniform Commercial Code of any state and the comparable laws of foreign non-United States jurisdictions. In Louisiana, "UCC" means and refers to Chapter 9 of the Louisiana Uniform Commercial Code, R.S. 10:9–101, et seq.

B. All terms used, but not defined in this Part, shall have the meanings found in the UCC, the Louisiana Revised Statutes of 1950, and the Civil Code.

Added by Acts 2010, No. 958, § 1, eff. July 6, 2010.

Editor's note. R.S. 9:3137.3 was enacted by Acts 2010, No. 958, as R..S. 9:3131.3. It has been redesignated by the Louisiana State Law Institute as R.S. 9:3137.3.

Cross References

C.C. arts. 2439, 2447, 2450, 2456, 2464, 2467, 2474, 2484, 2485, 2497, 2549, 2601, 2620, 2623, 2642.

§ 3137.4. Scope

A. This Part shall apply to all sales of receivables over exchanges located in this state irrespective of whether the buyer or the seller of the receivable is a Louisiana resident, business organization or other entity, provided that the buyer and the seller contractually agree that such sales shall be deemed to be consummated in Louisiana subject to Louisiana law, and contractually agree that the sales of receivables result in true sales for all purposes.

B. An exchange shall be conclusively deemed to be located in this state when the exchange is owned and operated by a Louisiana business organization having fifty percent or more of its operational employees located in this state, and such Louisiana business organization declares in an affidavit filed in the conveyance office of the parish in which the organization has its principal place of business, that the affiant maintains its principal place of business in that parish. An exchange owner or operator located in this state may have additional sales and other offices, as well as managerial, sales, marketing, accounting and other operational and non-operational employees located in other jurisdictions, so long as the company has fifty percent or more of its operational employees in Louisiana. In the case of an electronic exchange conducting exchange business over the Internet or other electronic media, the servers and electronic interchanges of the company need not be physically located in Louisiana.

Added by Acts 2010, No. 958, § 1, eff. July 6, 2010.

Editor's note. R.S. 9:3137.4 was enacted by Acts 2010, No. 958, as R..S. 9:3131.4. It has been redesignated by the Louisiana State Law Institute as R.S. 9:3137.4.

Cross References

C.C. arts. 2439, 2447, 2450, 2456, 2464, 2467, 2474, 2484, 2485, 2497, 2549, 2601, 2620, 2623, 2642.

§ 3137.5. True sales of receivables; not subject to recharacterization; simulation articles not applicable

A. All sales of receivables over exchanges subject to the scope of this Part as provided by R.S. 9:3137.4(A) shall conclusively result in consummated true sales for all purposes, and not be limited to a bankruptcy context, with the buyer acquiring all of the seller's rights, title and interests in and to the traded receivables and the collection proceeds thereof, and with the seller retaining no vestiges of legal or equitable interest in the receivables sold.

B. As true sales, sales of receivables over exchanges located in this state shall not be subject to recharacterization as loans, extensions of credit, or other credit accommodations by the seller to the buyer, notwithstanding that the seller may be obligated to repurchase the receivable, or the buyer may otherwise have recourse against the seller if the receivable is not paid when due, and further notwithstanding that the seller may be entitled to receive a portion of the collection proceeds. Furthermore, sales of receivables over exchanges located in this state shall not be construed, under any circumstance, to be a simulated sale under the simulation articles of the Civil Code.

C. (1) The seller's written agreement in the underlying documents that the seller absolutely, unconditionally, and irrevocably intends that sales of the seller's receivables over an exchange located in this state result in true sales of such receivables for all purposes, shall be definitive and binding on the seller, and may not be subsequently disavowed or refuted by any of the following persons:

(a) The seller.

(b) The seller's successors or assigns, or any person acquiring rights from or through the seller, including the buyer.

(c) Past and future owners, directors, officers, employees, agents, representatives and attorneys of the seller, or of its successors or assigns, or any person acquiring rights from or through the seller.

(d) The account debtor or any other person obligated to pay the receivable.

(e) All other third persons.

(2) Any person, including anyone listed in Paragraph (1) of this Subsection, attempting to recharacterize a sale of a receivable over an exchange located in this state as anything other than a true sale under Louisiana law, shall be personally liable and obligated by operation of law to reimburse the buyer and the buyer's agents for attorney fees, court costs, arbitration costs, expert fees, and out-of-pocket expenses, including but not limited to travel expenses, expended in defense of the status of such sale as a true sale under Louisiana law.

Added by Acts 2010, No. 958, § 1, eff. July 6, 2010.

Editor's note. R.S. 9:3137.5 was enacted by Acts 2010, No. 958, as R..S. 9:3131.5. It has been redesignated by the Louisiana State Law Institute as R.S. 9:3137.5.

Cross References

C.C. arts. 2439, 2447, 2450, 2456, 2464, 2467, 2474, 2484, 2485, 2497, 2549, 2601, 2620, 2623, 2642.

§ 3137.6. Binding effectiveness of Louisiana law

A. Louisiana law, and specifically this Part and R.S. 10:9-109(e), shall apply to all sales of receivables over exchanges located in this state irrespective of the domicile or other location of the buyer or the seller.

B. (1) The seller's written agreement and choice of law covenant in the underlying documents that Louisiana law shall apply to all sales of the seller's receivables over an exchange located in this state, shall be definitive for all purposes, and shall be absolutely, unconditionally and irrevocably binding on the seller, and shall not be subsequently disavowed or refuted by any of the following persons:

(a) The seller.

(b) The seller's successors or assigns, or anyone acquiring rights from or through the seller, including the buyer.

(c) Past and future owners, directors, officers, employees, agents, representatives and attorneys of the seller, or of its successors or assigns, or anyone acquiring rights from or through the seller.

(d) The account debtor or person obligated to pay the receivable.

(e) All other third persons.

(2) Any person, including anyone listed in Paragraph (1) of this Subsection, attempting to contest the applicability of Louisiana law and to apply the laws of another state or jurisdiction to the sale of the seller's receivables over an exchange located in this state, shall be personally liable and obligated by operation of law to reimburse the buyer and the buyer's agents for all attorney fees, court costs, arbitration costs, expert fees, and out-of-pocket expenses, including but not limited to travel expenses expended in defense of the status of such a sale as a true sale under Louisiana law.

C. For the further purpose of applying relevant conflicts of law principles, the legislature declares that Louisiana public policy shall be most seriously impaired to the extent that the laws of another state or jurisdiction might be applied to sales of receivables over exchanges located in Louisiana. As sales of receivables take place in Louisiana over Louisiana-based exchanges, Louisiana shall be deemed to have the most significant contact with the underlying sales transaction.

Added by Acts 2010, No. 958, § 1, eff. July 6, 2010.

Editor's note. R.S. 9:3137.6 was enacted by Acts 2010, No. 958, as R..S. 9:3131.6. It has been redesignated by the Louisiana State Law Institute as R.S. 9:3137.6.

Cross References

C.C. arts. 2439, 2447, 2450, 2456, 2464, 2467, 2474, 2484, 2485, 2497, 2549, 2601, 2620, 2623, 2642.

§ 3137.7. Buyer ownership rights; evidence of ownership

A. The buyer shall be deemed for all purposes, and not be limited to a bankruptcy context, to be the owner of a receivable purchased over an exchange located in this state, with the buyer having the right to all of the following actions:

(1) To collect the receivable from the account debtor or other obligated person.

(2) To resell the receivable to a subsequent buyer.

(3) To pledge or otherwise grant a security interest in the receivable in favor of the buyer's creditor.

(4) To reflect the receivable as an asset on the buyer's books and records.

B. To the extent that the owner or operator of an exchange located in this state maintains records of sales of receivables over the exchange, such records shall serve as the single authoritative record evidencing buyer ownership of traded receivables for all purposes.

Added by Acts 2010, No. 958, § 1, eff. July 6, 2010.

Editor's note. R.S. 9:3137.7 was enacted by Acts 2010, No. 958, as R..S. 9:3131.7. It has been redesignated by the Louisiana State Law Institute as R.S. 9:3137.7.

§ 3137.8. Relationship to the UCC

A. This Part supplements R.S. 10:9–109(e), and shall not be construed to implicitly amend or repeal any provision of the UCC, including but not limited to R.S. 10:1–201(35), 9–102(72)(D), 9–109(e), 9–301, 9–307, 9–310(a), 9–312(a), 9–317 through 9–339, 9–406, 9–501, and 9–607(a)(1).

B. This Part and R.S. 10:9–109(e) provide for and define the true sale status and the state property ownership rights of buyers of receivables purchased over exchanges located in this state, and shall not independently provide for rules governing perfection, the effects of perfection or nonperfection, or the priority rights of buyers of receivables purchased over Louisiana based exchanges within the context of R.S. 10:9–301.

Added by Acts 2010, No. 958, § 1, eff. July 6, 2010.

Editor's note. R.S. 9:3137.8 was enacted by Acts 2010, No. 958, as R..S. 9:3131.8. It has been redesignated by the Louisiana State Law Institute as R.S. 9:3137.8.

Cross References

C.C. arts. 2439, 2447, 2450, 2456, 2464, 2467, 2474, 2484, 2485, 2497, 2549, 2601, 2620, 2623, 2642.

§ 3137.9. Prohibition of actions

A seller shall not maintain an action or have any claim against an owner or operator of an exchange located in this state, or against a buyer of the receivables, unless there is an agreement in writing setting forth the relevant terms and conditions, and the agreement is signed by the seller and the owner or operator on its own behalf and as agent for the buyer.

Added by Acts 2010, No. 958, § 1, eff. July 6, 2010.

Editor's note. R.S. 9:3137.9 was enacted by Acts 2010, No. 958, as R..S. 9:3131.9. It has been redesignated by the Louisiana State Law Institute as R.S. 9:3137.9.

Cross References

C.C. arts. 2439, 2447, 2450, 2456, 2464, 2467, 2474, 2484, 2485, 2497, 2549, 2601, 2620, 2623, 2642.

CHAPTER 5. NEW HOME WARRANTY ACT

Editor's note. This Chapter was enacted as Chapter 6 of Code Title IV of Code Book III, containing R.S. 9:2789.1 to 9:2789.10, and was redesignated pursuant to the statutory revision authority of the Louisiana State Law Institute.

Section
3141. Purpose.
3142. Short title.
3143. Definitions.
3144. Warranties; exclusions.
3145. Required notice.
3146. Peremption.
3147. Insurance.
3148. Transfer of warranty and insurance.

Section
3149. Violations; limitations.
3150. Exclusiveness.

§ 3141. Purpose

The legislature finds a need to promote commerce in Louisiana by providing clear, concise, and mandatory warranties for the purchasers and occupants of new homes in Louisiana and by providing for the use of homeowners' insurance as additional protection for the public against defects in the construction of new homes. This need can be met by providing a warranty for a new home purchaser defining the responsibility of the builder to that purchaser and subsequent purchasers during the warranty periods provided herein. The warranty, which is mandatory in most cases, shall apply whether or not building code regulations are in effect in the location of the structure, thereby promoting uniformity of defined building standards. Additionally, all provisions of this Chapter shall apply to any defect although there is no building standard directly regulating the defective workmanship or materials.

Added by Acts 1986, No. 676, § 1. Amended by Acts 1999, No. 649, § 1.

Cross References

C.C. arts. 2438, 2456, 2475, 2500, 2515, 2520, 2545, 2589, 2756, 2765.

§ 3142. Short title

This Chapter shall be known and may be cited as the "New Home Warranty Act."

Added by Acts 1986, No. 676, § 1.

Cross References

C.C. arts. 2438, 2456, 2475, 2500, 2515, 2520, 2545, 2589, 2756, 2765.

§ 3143. Definitions

For purposes of this Chapter the following words, phrases, and terms shall be defined and construed as follows:

(1) "Builder" means any person, corporation, partnership, limited liability company, joint venture, or other entity which constructs a home, or addition thereto, including a home occupied initially by its builder as his residence. A person, corporation, partnership, limited liability company, joint venture, or other entity which constructs a home, or any addition thereto, is a "builder", whether or not the consumer purchased the underlying real estate with the home.

(2) "Building standards" means the standards contained in the building code, mechanical-plumbing code, and electrical code in effect in the parish, city, or other local political subdivision where a home is to be located, at the time construction of that home is commenced, or, if the parish, city, or other local political subdivision has not adopted such codes, the Standard Building Code, together with any additional performance standards, if any, which the builder may undertake to be in compliance.

(3) "Home" means any new structure designed and used only for residential use, together with all attached and unattached structures, constructed by the builder whether or not the land was purchased from the builder. Such term includes structures containing multiple family dwellings or residences.

(4) "Initial purchaser" means any person for whom a home is built or the first person to whom a home is sold upon completion of construction.

(5) "Major structural defect" means any actual physical damage to the following designated load-bearing portions of a home caused by failure of the load-bearing portions which affects their load-bearing functions to the extent the home becomes unsafe, unsanitary, or is otherwise unlivable:

(a) Foundation systems and footings.

(b) Beams.

(c) Girders.

(d) Lintels.

(e) Columns.

(f) Walls and partitions.

(g) Floor systems.

(h) Roof framing systems.

(6) "Owner" means the initial purchaser of a home and any of his successors in title, heirs, invitees, or assigns to a home during the time the warranties provided under this Chapter are in effect.

(7) "Warranty commencement date" means the date that legal title to a home is conveyed to its initial purchaser or the date the home is first occupied, whichever occurs first. Added by Acts 1986, No. 676, § 1. Amended by Acts 1997, No. 987, § 1; Acts 1999, No. 649, § 1; Acts 2003, No. 333, § 1.

Cross References

C.C. arts. 2438, 2456, 2475, 2500, 2515, 2520, 2545, 2589, 2756, 2765.

§ 3144. Warranties; exclusions

A. Subject to the exclusions provided in Subsection B of this Section, every builder warrants the following to the owner:

(1) One year following the warranty commencement date, the home will be free from any defect due to noncompliance with the building standards or due to other defects in materials or workmanship not regulated by building standards.

(2) Two years following the warranty commencement date, the plumbing, electrical, heating, cooling, and ventilating systems exclusive of any appliance, fixture, and equipment will be free from any defect due to noncompliance with the building standards or due to other defects in materials or workmanship not regulated by building standards.

(3) Five years following the warranty commencement date, the home will be free from major structural defects due to noncompliance with the building standards or due to other defects in materials or workmanship not regulated by building standards.

B. Unless the parties otherwise agree in writing, the builder's warranty shall exclude the following items:

(1) Fences, landscaping, including but not limited to sodding, seeding, shrubs, existing and new trees, and plantings, as well as off-site improvements, all driveways and walkways, or any other improvement not a part of the home itself.

(2) After the first year, the concrete floor of a basement and the concrete floor of an attached or unattached garage that is built separate from a foundation wall or other structural element of the home.

(3) Damage to real property which is not part of the home covered by the warranty and which is not included in the purchase price of the home.

(4) Any damage to the extent it is caused or made worse by any of the following:

(a) Negligence, improper maintenance, neglect or improper operation by anyone other than the builder or any employee, agent, or subcontractor of the builder.

(b) Failure by anyone other than the builder or any employee, agent, or subcontractor of the builder to comply with the warranty requirements of manufacturers of appliances, equipment, or fixtures.

(c) Failure by the owner to give written notice by registered or certified mail to the builder of any defect within the time set forth in R.S. 9:3145. However, the provisions of this Subparagraph shall not be construed to change either the warranty periods enumerated in Subsection A of this Section or the notice requirements provided by R.S. 9:3145.

(d) Any change of the grading of the ground by anyone other than the builder, or any employee, agent, or subcontractor of the builder.

(e) Any change, alteration, or addition made to the home by anyone after the initial occupancy by the owner, except any change, alteration, or addition performed by the builder, or any employee, agent, or subcontractor of the builder.

(f) Dampness, condensation, or other damage due to the failure of the owner to maintain adequate ventilation or drainage.

(5) Any loss or damage which the owner has not taken timely action to minimize.

(6) Any defect in, or any defect caused by, materials or work supplied by anyone other than the builder, or any employee, agent, or subcontractor of the builder.

(7) Normal wear and tear or normal deterioration.

(8) Loss or damage which does not constitute a defect in the construction of the home by the builder, or any employee, agent, or subcontractor of the builder.

(9) Loss or damage resulting from war, accident, riot and civil commotion, water escape, falling objects, aircraft, vehicles, acts of God, lightning, windstorm, hail, flood, mudslide, earthquake, volcanic eruption, wind driven water, and changes in the level of the underground water table which are not reasonably foreseeable.

(10) Any damage caused by soil movement which is covered by other insurance.

(11) Insect damage.

(12) Any loss or damage which arises while the home is being used primarily for a nonresidential purpose.

(13) Any condition which does not result in actual physical damage to the home.

(14) Bodily injury or damage to personal property.

(15) Any cost of shelter, transportation, food, moving, storage, or other incidental expense related to relocation during repair.

(16) Any defect not reported in writing by registered or certified mail to the builder or insurance company, as appropriate, prior to the expiration of the period specified in Subsection A of this Section for such defect plus thirty days.

(17) Consequential damages.

(18) Any loss or damage to a home caused by soil conditions or soil movement if the home is constructed on land

owned by the initial purchaser and the builder obtains a written waiver from the initial purchaser for any loss or damage caused by soil conditions or soil movement.

(19) Mold and mold damage.

C. The provisions of Subsection A of this Section establish minimum required warranties and shall not be waived by the owner or reduced by the builder provided the home is a single or multiple family dwelling to be occupied by an owner as his home.

Added by Acts 1986, No. 676, § 1. Amended by Acts 1997, No. 987, § 1; Acts 1999, No. 649, § 1; Acts 2001, No. 179, § 1; Acts 2003, No. 333, § 1; Acts 2004, No. 45, § 1.

Cross References

C.C. arts. 2438, 2456, 2475, 2500, 2515, 2520, 2545, 2589, 2756, 2765.

§ 3145. Required notice

A. Before undertaking any repair himself or instituting any action for breach of warranty, the owner shall give the builder written notice, by registered or certified mail, within one year after knowledge of the defect, advising him of all defects and giving the builder a reasonable opportunity to comply with the provisions of this Chapter.

B. The builder shall give the owner written notice of the requirements of this Chapter at the time of the closing between the builder and the owner, or if there is no such closing, at the time of the execution of the construction contract between the builder and the owner. The Louisiana State Licensing Board for Contractors shall adopt and promulgate rules and regulations in accordance with the Administrative Procedure Act to implement the provisions of this Subsection.

Added by Acts 1986, No. 676, § 1. Amended by Acts 1997, No. 987, § 1; Acts 2008, No. 387, § 1.

Cross References

C.C. arts. 2438, 2456, 2475, 2500, 2515, 2520, 2545, 2589, 2756, 2765.

§ 3146. Peremption

Any action to enforce any warranty provided in this Chapter shall be subject to a peremptive period of thirty days after the expiration of the appropriate time period provided in R.S. 9:3144.

Added by Acts 1986, No. 676, § 1. Amended by Acts 2001, No. 179, § 1.

Cross References

C.C. arts. 2438, 2456, 2475, 2500, 2515, 2520, 2545, 2589, 2756, 2765.

§ 3147. Insurance

All or part of the builder's obligation under any warranty required in this Chapter may be insured by the builder for the benefit of the purchaser through an insurance company authorized to transact business in this state.

Added by Acts 1986, No. 676, § 1.

Cross References

C.C. arts. 2438, 2456, 2475, 2500, 2515, 2520, 2545, 2589, 2756, 2765.

§ 3148. Transfer of warranty and insurance

Any warranty imposed under the provisions of this Chapter and any insurance benefit shall automatically transfer without charge, to a subsequent owner who acquires title to the home. Any transfer of the home shall not extend the duration of any warranty or insurance coverage.

Added by Acts 1986, No. 676, § 1.

Cross References

C.C. arts. 2438, 2456, 2475, 2500, 2515, 2520, 2545, 2589, 2756, 2765.

§ 3149. Violations; limitations

A. If a builder violates this Chapter by failing to perform as required by the warranties provided in this Chapter, any affected owner shall have a cause of action against the builder for actual damages, including attorney fees and court costs, arising out of the violation. The damages with respect to a single defect shall not exceed the reasonable cost of repair or replacement necessary to cure the defect, and damages with respect to all defects in the home shall not exceed the original purchase price of the home.

B. The parties may provide for the arbitration of any claim in dispute. Any arbitration shall comply with, and may be binding only to the extent provided in R.S. 9:4201 et seq.

Added by Acts 1986, No. 676, § 1.

Cross References

C.C. arts. 2438, 2456, 2475, 2500, 2515, 2520, 2545, 2589, 2756, 2765.

§ 3150. Exclusiveness

This Chapter provides the exclusive remedies, warranties, and peremptive periods as between builder and owner relative to home construction and no other provisions of law relative to warranties and redhibitory vices and defects shall apply. Nothing herein shall be construed as affecting or limiting any warranty of title to land or improvements.

Added by Acts 1986, No. 676, § 1. Amended by Acts 2003, No. 333, § 1.

Cross References

C.C. arts. 2438, 2456, 2475, 2500, 2515, 2520, 2545, 2589, 2756, 2765.

CHAPTER 6. AUCTION SALES, JUDICIAL SALES, AND EXPROPRIATION

PART I. AUCTION SALES

Section	
3151.	Sale by auction, definition.
3152.	Voluntary or forced sale.
3153.	Auction sale by officers of justice.
3154.	General rules governing sales by auction.
3155.	Sale through public officer.

Section
3156. Announcement of conditions of sale and demand for bids.
3157. Adjudication to highest bidder.
3158. Adjudication as completion of sale.
3159. Payment of price before delivery.
3160. Sale of immovable, retention of price until execution of act.
3161. Resale for non-compliance with bid; adjudicatee's liability for deficiency.
3162. Resale, bid by first adjudicatee prohibited.
3163. Rejection of indorser of purchase price notes, effect on adjudication.
3164. Liability of seller refusing to accept solvent indorser.
3165. Liability for unauthorized bidding in name of another.

PART II. JUDICIAL SALES
SUBPART A. IN GENERAL
3166. Kinds of judicial sales.
3167. General rules for judicial sales.

SUBPART B. SEIZURE OR EXECUTION
3168. Execution sale, persons authorized to make.
3169. Rescission for fraud or nullity; redhibition not permitted.
3170. Rights acquired at execution sale.
3171. Rights of buyer in case of eviction.

SUBPART C. SUCCESSION PROPERTY
3172. Authority to order succession sale; persons authorized to sell.
3173. Transfer of title.
3174. Warranties.
3175. Purchase of property by heirs of succession.

PART III. EXPROPRIATION
3176 to 3191. Repealed.
3191.1. Thirty-year prescription; return of expropriated residential property.

PART I. AUCTION SALES

§ 3151. Sale by auction, definition

The sale by auction is that which takes place when the thing is offered publicly to be sold to whoever will give the highest price.

C.C. art. 2601. Redesignated as R.S. 9:3151 pursuant to Acts 1993, No. 841, § 2, eff. Jan. 1, 1995.

Cross References

C.C.P. arts. 3261 to 3264, 3271 to 3273, 3281 to 3284, 4301, 4321, 4322, 4341, 4621 to 4630, 4641.

R.S. 5:1 et seq., 9:603, 9:3152, 9:3167, 9:5622, 37:3105 et seq., 43:202 to 43:203.

§ 3152. Voluntary or forced sale

This sale is either voluntary or forced: voluntary when the owner himself offers his property for sale in this manner; forced, when the law prescribes this mode of sale for certain property, such as that of minors.

C.C. art. 2602. Redesignated as R.S. 9:3152 pursuant to Acts 1993, No. 841, § 2, eff. Jan. 1, 1995.

Cross References

C.C.P. arts. 4271, 4301, 4321, 4322, 4341, 4621 to 4630.

R.S. 9:603, 9:3151.

§ 3153. Auction sale by officers of justice

The sale by auction, as it is made by officers of justice, is treated of separately, under the chapter on *judicial sales*.

C.C. art. 2603. Redesignated as R.S. 9:3153 pursuant to Acts 1993, No. 841, § 2, eff. Jan. 1, 1995.

Cross References

C.C. art. 2589.

C.C.P. arts. 4301, 4321, 4341, 4621 to 4630.

R.S. 9:603, 9:3166 et seq., 9:3172 et seq.

§ 3154. General rules governing sales by auction

The sale by auction, whether made at the will of the seller, or by direction of the law, is subjected to the rules hereafter mentioned.

C.C. art. 2604. Redesignated as R.S. 9:3154 pursuant to Acts 1993, No. 841, § 2, eff. Jan. 1, 1995.

Cross References

R.S. 9:3155 et seq.

§ 3155. Sale through public officer

It can not be made directly by the seller himself, but must be made through the ministry of a public officer, appointed for that purpose.

C.C. art. 2605. Redesignated as R.S. 9:3155 pursuant to Acts 1993, No. 841, § 2, eff. Jan. 1, 1995.

Cross References

C.C.P. arts. 4301, 4321, 4341, 4621 to 4630, 4641.

R.S. 9:603, 9:3001, 9:3154, 9:3156, 9:3168, 9:3172, 13:4350, 13:4406.

§ 3156. Announcement of conditions of sale and demand for bids

This officer, after having received in writing, from the seller, the conditions of the sale, must proclaim them, in a loud and audible voice, and afterwards propose that a bid shall be made for the property thus offered.

C.C. art. 2606. Redesignated as R.S. 9:3156 pursuant to Acts 1993, No. 841, § 2, eff. Jan. 1, 1995.

Editor's note. English translation of French text incomplete; should include "to all the persons present."

Cross References

C.C.P. arts. 2334, 2336.

R.S. 5:3, 9:3155, 9:3157, 13:4344 to 13:4345, 13:4406, 37:3118.

§ 3157. Adjudication to highest bidder

When the highest price offered has been cried long enough to make it probable that no higher will be offered, he who has made the offer is publicly declared to be the purchaser, and the thing sold is adjudicated to him.

C.C. art. 2607. Redesignated as R.S. 9:3157 pursuant to Acts 1993, No. 841, § 2, eff. Jan. 1, 1995.

Cross References

C.C.P. art. 2334.

R.S. 5:3, 5:8, 9:3156, 9:3158, 13:4344 to 13:4345, 13:4406, 37:3118, 37:3125, 37:3128.

§ 3158. Adjudication as completion of sale

This adjudication is the completion of the sale; the purchaser becomes the owner of the article adjudged, and the contract is, from that time, subjected to the same rules which govern the ordinary contract of sale.

C.C. art. 2608. Redesignated as R.S. 9:3158 pursuant to Acts 1993, No. 841, § 2, eff. Jan. 1, 1995.

Cross References

C.C.P. arts. 2342, 2371.

R.S. 5:3, 9:3157, 9:3159 et seq., 9:3165, 9:3170, 9:3173, 13:4354, 37:3118.

§ 3159. Payment of price before delivery

If the adjudication be made on condition that the price shall be paid in cash, the auctioneer may require the price immediately, before delivering possession of the thing sold.

C.C. art. 2609. Redesignated as R.S. 9:3159 pursuant to Acts 1993, No. 841, § 2, eff. Jan. 1, 1995.

Cross References

C.C.P. arts. 2335, 2336.

R.S. 9:3158, 9:3160, 9:3161, 13:4359.

§ 3160. Sale of immovable, retention of price until execution of act

If the object adjudged is an immovable for which the law requires that the act of sale shall be passed in writing, the purchaser may retain the price, and the seller the possession of the thing, until the act be passed.

This act ought to be passed within twenty-four hours after the adjudication, if one of the parties require it; he who occasions a further delay is responsible to the other in damages.

C.C. art. 2610. Redesignated as R.S. 9:3160 pursuant to Acts 1993, No. 841, § 2, eff. Jan. 1, 1995.

Cross References

C.C. arts. 1839, 1994, 2002, 2003.

C.C.P. art. 2342.

R.S. 9:3158, 9:3159, 9:3161, 13:4353.

§ 3161. Resale for non-compliance with bid; adjudicatee's liability for deficiency

In all cases of sale by auction, whether of movables or immovables, if the person to whom adjudication is made, does not pay the price at the time required, agreeably to the two preceding articles, the seller at the end of ten days, and after the customary notices, may again expose to public sale the thing sold, as if the first adjudication had never been made; and if at the second crying, the thing is adjudged for a smaller price than that which had been offered by the person to whom the first adjudication was made, the latter remains a debtor to the vendor, for the deficiency and for all the expenses incurred subsequent to the first sale. But if a higher price is offered for the thing than that for which it was first adjudged, the first purchaser has no claim for the excess.

C.C. art. 2611. Redesignated as R.S. 9:3161 pursuant to Acts 1993, No. 841, § 2, eff. Jan. 1, 1995.

Cross References

C.C.P. arts. 2335, 2336, 2342, 2375.

R.S. 9:3158 et seq., 9:3162, 13:4359.

§ 3162. Resale, bid by first adjudicatee prohibited

At this second crying, the first purchaser can not be allowed to bid, either directly or through the intervention of another person.

C.C. art. 2612. Redesignated as R.S. 9:3162 pursuant to Acts 1993, No. 841, § 2, eff. Jan. 1, 1995.

Cross References

C.C.P. art. 2339.

R.S. 9:3161, 13:4359 to 13:4362.

§ 3163. Rejection of indorser of purchase price notes, effect on adjudication

When a thing is exposed to public sale, with notice that the buyer shall give indorsed notes for the price, he is bound, immediately after the sale, if required, to acquaint the auctioneer or the seller with the name of the person whom he offers for indorser, and if this indorser does not suit the seller, or in his absence the auctioneer, the adjudication is considered as not having been made.

C.C. art. 2613. Redesignated as R.S. 9:3163 pursuant to Acts 1993, No. 841, § 2, eff. Jan. 1, 1995.

Cross References

C.C.P. art. 2336.

R.S. 9:3164.

§ 3164. Liability of seller refusing to accept solvent indorser

The refusal by the seller to receive the indorser whom the purchaser offers, renders him responsible in damages to the latter, if it be proved that the indorser proposed is good and solvent.

C.C. art. 2614. Redesignated as R.S. 9:3164 pursuant to Acts 1993, No. 841, § 2, eff. Jan. 1, 1995.

Cross References

C.C. arts. 1996 to 1998.

R.S. 9:3163.

§ 3165. Liability for unauthorized bidding in name of another

The adjudication can only be made to a bidder present, or properly represented. The person who bids in the name of another, without sufficient authority to bind him, is considered as having bought on his own account, and is answerable for all the consequences of the adjudication.

C.C. art. 2615. Redesignated as R.S. 9:3165 pursuant to Acts 1993, No. 841, § 2, eff. Jan. 1, 1995.

Cross References

C.C. arts. 3008, 3016, 3017, 3019.

R.S. 9:3158.

PART II. JUDICIAL SALES

SUBPART A. IN GENERAL

§ 3166. Kinds of judicial sales

Sales which are made by authority of law are of two kinds:

1. Those which take place when the property of a debtor has been seized by order of a court, to be sold for the purpose of paying the creditor.

2. Those which are ordered in matters of succession or partition.

C.C. art. 2616. Redesignated as R.S. 9:3166 pursuant to Acts 1993, No. 841, § 2, eff. Jan. 1, 1995.

Cross References

C.C.P. arts. 3461, 3501, 4603.

R.S. 5:1 et seq., 5:181 to 5:183, 9:3153, 9:3167 et seq., 9:3172 et seq., 9:5622, 37:3142, 37:3143.

§ 3167. General rules for judicial sales

Judicial sales are subject to the rules laid down above for public sales in general, in all such things as are not contrary to the formalities expressly prescribed for such sales, and with the modifications contained hereafter.

C.C. art. 2617. Redesignated as R.S. 9:3167 pursuant to Acts 1993, No. 841, § 2, eff. Jan. 1, 1995.

Cross References

C.C. arts. 1839, 2447.

C.C.P. arts 2331, 2332, 2340, 2373.

R.S. 9:3151 et seq., 9:3166, 9:3168 et seq., 9:3172, 9:5622, 13:3863, 13:4343 to 13:4346, 13:4406.

SUBPART B. SEIZURE OR EXECUTION

§ 3168. Execution sale, persons authorized to make

The sale on seizure is made at public auction by the sheriff or other officer charged with the execution of the judgment.

C.C. art. 2618. Redesignated as R.S. 9:3168 pursuant to Acts 1993, No. 841, § 2, eff. Jan. 1, 1995.

Cross References

C.C. arts. 2817, 3240.

C.C.P. arts. 2291 to 2299, 2331 to 2348.

R.S. 5:1 et seq., 9:3001, 9:3153, 9:3155, 9:3166, 9:3167, 9:5622, 37:3105 et seq.

§ 3169. Rescission for fraud or nullity; redhibition not permitted

Whatever may be the vices of the thing sold on execution, they do not give rise to the redhibitory action; but the sale may be set aside in the case of fraud, and declared null in cases of nullity.

C.C. art. 2619. Redesignated as R.S. 9:3169 pursuant to Acts 1993, No. 841, § 2, eff. Jan. 1, 1995.

Cross References

C.C. arts. 1918, 1949, 1950, 1953, 1955, 1959, 2029 to 2031, 2033, 2537.

§ 3170. Rights acquired at execution sale

This sale on execution transfers the property of the thing to the purchaser as completely as if the owner had sold it himself; but it transfers only the rights of the debtor such as they are.

C.C. art. 2620. Redesignated as R.S. 9:3170 pursuant to Acts 1993, No. 841, § 2, eff. Jan. 1, 1995.

Cross References

C.C. art. 3477.

C.C.P. art. 2371.

R.S. 9:3158, 9:3166, 9:3173, 13:4353.

§ 3171. Rights of buyer in case of eviction

The purchaser evicted from property purchased under execution shall have his recourse for reimbursement against the debtor and creditor, as provided in Article 2379 of the Code of Civil Procedure.

C.C. art. 2621. Amended by Acts 1960, No. 30, § 1. Redesignated as R.S. 9:3171 pursuant to Acts 1993, No. 841, § 2, eff. Jan. 1, 1995.

Cross References

C.C. arts. 1789, 2500, 2503, 2548.

C.C.P. arts. 2335, 2374, 2379, 2380.

SUBPART C. SUCCESSION PROPERTY

§ 3172. Authority to order succession sale; persons authorized to sell

The judicial sale of succession property is ordered by the judge of the court to which this jurisdiction is specially confided.

Representatives of successions shall have the right to cause sales of the property administered by them to be made either by the sheriff or an auctioneer, or to make it themselves, but in the event of making the sales themselves, they shall receive no commission therefor.

C.C. art. 2622. Redesignated as R.S. 9:3172 pursuant to Acts 1993, No. 841, § 2, eff. Jan. 1, 1995.

Cross References

C.C. arts. 902, 935, 938, 964, 1171, 1421.

C.C.P. arts. 80, 81, 2811, 3261, 3262, 3264, 3285, 3304, 3401, 3461, 4342, 4561, 4565, 4603.

R.S. 9:3001, 9:3153, 9:3155, 9:3166, 9:3167.

§ 3173. Transfer of title

The adjudication made and recorded by the sheriff, auctioneer or representative of the succession, is a complete title to the purchaser, and needs not be followed by an act passed before a notary.

C.C. art. 2623. Redesignated as R.S. 9:3173 pursuant to Acts 1993, No. 841, § 2, eff. Jan. 1, 1995.

Cross References

C.C.P. arts. 2342, 2371.

R.S. 9:3158, 9:3170, 13:4354.

§ 3174. Warranties

All the warranties to which private sales are subject exist against the heir in judicial sales of the property of successions.

C.C. art. 2624. Redesignated as R.S. 9:3174 pursuant to Acts 1993, No. 841, § 2, eff. Jan. 1, 1995.

Cross References

C.C. arts. 2475, 2500, 2503, 2520, 2521, 2537, 2548, 2682.

§ 3175. Purchase of property by heirs of succession

Heirs may purchase the property of the succession to the amount of their proportion, and are not obliged to pay the purchase money, until a liquidation is had, by which it is ascertained what balance there is in their favor or against them.

C.C. art. 2625. Redesignated as R.S. 9:3175 pursuant to Acts 1993, No. 841, § 2, eff. Jan. 1, 1995.

Cross References

C.C. arts. 1343, 1344.

PART III. EXPROPRIATION

§§ 3176 to 3191. Repealed by Acts 2012, No. 702, § 2

§ 3191.1. Thirty-year prescription; return of expropriated residential property

A. If residential property expropriated by the state or a political subdivision of the state remains in the possession of and is maintained by the original owner or his heir for a period of more than thirty years, the expropriated property shall be transferred back to the original owner or his heir upon payment of the fair market value of the property.

B. Upon expiration of the thirty-year period as provided by Subsection A of this Section, the original owner or his heir may tender payment of the fair market value of the property and deliver an act of transfer of ownership to the state or political subdivision of the state that expropriated the residential property. Within thirty days of receipt of the act of transfer of ownership and payment of the fair market value of the property, the state or political subdivision of the state that expropriated the residential property shall execute and return the act of transfer of ownership without additional cost to the original owner or his heir.

C. The state or political subdivision of the state that expropriated the residential property may oppose the act of transfer of ownership by filing an action for injunction within thirty days of receipt of the tendered payment and the act of transfer of ownership in the district court where the property is located.

(1) If the court finds that the original owner or his heir failed to tender fair market value of the property, retain possession of the property, or maintain the property for the requisite thirty-year period, the court shall grant the injunction and the state or political subdivision of the state shall not be required to execute the act of transfer of ownership.

(2) If the court finds that the original owner or his heir tendered the fair market value of the property, retained possession of the property, and maintained the property for the requisite thirty-year period, the court shall order the state or political subdivision of the state to execute the act of transfer of ownership and shall award court costs and attorney fees to the original owner or his heir.

D. (1) The provisions of this Section shall not apply to property expropriated for construction, operation, or maintenance of levees, levee systems, flood control, drainage, hurricane or storm surge protection, or integrated coastal protection.

(2) The provisions of this Section shall not apply to property expropriated by the Department of Transportation and Development.

Added by Acts 2012, No. 445, § 1.

CHAPTER 7. RELATIONSHIP BETWEEN THE CIVIL CODE TITLE ON SALE AND THE COMMERCIAL LAWS

Section
3192. Rule governing conflict between sale and commercial laws.

§ 3192. Rule governing conflict between sale and commercial laws

In case of conflict between the provisions of Title VII of Book III of the Civil Code, governing sales and any provisions of any special legislation, such as those contained in Titles 9 and 10 of the Louisiana Revised Statutes of 1950 and the Louisiana Lease of Movables Act, the latter shall prevail with regard to transactions subject thereto.

Added by Acts 1995, No. 342, § 1; Acts 1995, No. 1201, § 2, eff. June 19, 1995.

Editor's note. Section 3 of Acts 1995, No. 342 declares that "The provision of this Act shall be applied retroactively to January 1, 1995, and shall be applied in conjunction with Acts 1993, No. 841, Section 4."

Cross References

C.C. arts. 8, 13, 2348 et seq.

R.S. 9:2901 et seq., 9:2941 et seq., 9:2961 et seq., 9:2971 et seq., 9:2981 et seq., 9:2989, 9:3301 et seq.

CHAPTER 8. RESIDENTIAL PROPERTY DISCLOSURE

Section
3195. [Blank].
3196. Definitions.
3197. Applicability; exemptions.
3198. Duties of the seller; delivery of property disclosure document; termination of real estate contract; information contained in document and inaccuracies; required disclosure of information relative to homeowners' associations; liability of seller.
3198.1. Duties of governmental entities; contaminated property.
3199. Duty of real estate licensees; liability.
3200. Other statutory disclosure obligations.

§ 3195. [Blank]

§ 3196. Definitions

As used in this Chapter, the following terms shall have the meanings hereinafter ascribed to them:

(1) "Known defect" means a condition found within the property that was actually known by the seller and that results in any of the following:

(a) Has a substantial adverse effect on the value of the property.

(b) Significantly impairs the health or safety of future occupants of the property.

(c) If not repaired, removed, or replaced, significantly shortens the expected normal life of the premises.

(2) "Property disclosure document" means a document in a form prescribed by the Louisiana Real Estate Commission, or a form that contains at least the minimum language prescribed by the commission, which is presented by the seller to the purchaser in the manner set forth in R.S. 9:3198(B) and which discloses, at a minimum, known defects in the residential real property.

(3) "Purchaser" means a transferee or prospective transferee in any of the types of transactions described in R.S. 9:3197(A).

(4) "Real estate contract" means any written agreement, entered into prior to the perfection of the contract of sale or contract to lease or otherwise with an option to purchase, which relates to the sale, offer for sale, purchase, offer to purchase, lease with option to purchase, offer to lease with option to purchase, any other option to purchase, or any other offer which includes an option to purchase any residential real property or improvements thereon.

(5) "Residential real property" means real property consisting of one or not more than four residential dwelling units, which are buildings or structures each of which are occupied or intended for occupancy as single family residences.

(6) "Seller" means an owner of residential real property, whether an individual, partnership, corporation, or trust, who sells or attempts to sell residential real property in a manner described in R.S. 9:3197(A).

Added by Acts 2003, No. 308, § 1, eff. June 13, 2003.

Cross References

C.C. arts. 3458 to 2597, 2620 to 2630.

§ 3197. Applicability; exemptions

A. On and after July 1, 2004, the provisions of this Chapter shall apply to the transfer of any interest in residential real property, whether by sale, exchange, bond for deed, lease with option to purchase, or any other option to purchase, including transactions in which the assistance of a real estate licensee is utilized and those in which such assistance is not utilized.

B. The provisions of this Chapter shall not apply to any of the following:

(1) Transfers ordered by a court, including but not limited to a transfer ordered by a court in the administration of an estate, a transfer pursuant to a writ of execution, a transfer by any foreclosure sale, a transfer by a trustee in bankruptcy, a transfer by eminent domain, and any transfer resulting from a decree of specific performance.

(2) Transfers to a mortgagee by a mortgagor or successor in interest who is in default.

(3) Transfers by a mortgagee who has acquired the residential real property at a sale conducted pursuant to a power of sale under a mortgage or a sale pursuant to decree of foreclosure, or who has acquired the residential property by a deed in lieu of foreclosure.

(4) Transfers by a fiduciary in the course of administration of a decedent's estate, guardianship, conservatorship, or trust.

(5) Transfers of newly constructed residential real property, which has never been occupied.

(6) Transfers from one or more co-owners solely to one or more of the remaining co-owners.

(7) Transfers pursuant to testate or intestate succession.

(8) Transfers of residential real property that will be converted by the purchaser into a use other than residential use.

(9) Transfers of residential real property to a spouse or relative in the line of consanguinity.

(10) Transfers between spouses resulting from a judgment of divorce or a judgment of separate maintenance or from a property settlement agreement incidental to such a judgment.

(11) Transfers or exchanges to or from any governmental entity.

(12) Transfers from an entity that has acquired title or assignment of a real estate contract to a piece of residential real property to assist the prior owner in relocating, as long as the entity makes available to the purchaser a copy of the property disclosure statement, any inspection reports if any furnished to the entity by the prior owner, or both.

(13) Transfers to an inter vivos trust.

(14) Acts that, without additional consideration and without changing ownership or ownership interest, confirm, correct, modify, or supplement a deed or conveyance previously recorded.

Added by Acts 2003, No. 308, § 1, eff. June 13, 2003.

Cross References

C.C. arts. 3458 to 3597, 2620 to 2630.

§ 3198. Duties of the seller; delivery of property disclosure document; termination of real estate contract; information contained in document and inaccuracies; required disclosure of information relative to homeowners' associations; liability of seller

A. (1) The seller of residential real property shall complete a property disclosure document in a form prescribed by the Louisiana Real Estate Commission or a form that contains at least the minimum language prescribed by the commission. The promulgation of this form shall be conducted in accordance with the Administrative Procedure Act no later than April 1, 2004.

(2)(a) Included with the property disclosure documents required by this Section shall be a statement of notification to the purchaser as to whether or not he is obligated to be a member of a homeowners' association as a homeowner in the community in which he is purchasing property.

(b) Included with the property disclosure documents required by this Section shall be a statement of acknowledgment as to whether or not an illegal laboratory for the production or manufacturing of methamphetamine was in operation on the purchasing property.

(c) Included with the property disclosure documents required by this Section shall be a statement of acknowledgment as to whether or not a cavity created within a salt stock by dissolution with water lies underneath the property and whether or not the purchasing property is within two thousand six hundred forty feet of a solution mining injection well.

(3) The statement shall inform the purchaser that the information included in the disclosure statement relative to any homeowners' association is summary in nature and that the covenants and association governing documents are a matter of public record. The statement shall further inform the purchaser how such documents can be obtained.

(4) As used in this Subsection, "homeowners' association" or "association" means a nonprofit corporation, unincorporated association, or other legal entity which is created pursuant to a declaration whose members consist primarily of lot owners, and which is created to manage, maintain, or otherwise affect the association property or which otherwise governs the use of association property.

(5) Forms used for compliance with Paragraph (1) of this Subsection on and after April 1, 2005, shall also include a clause for the seller to indicate whether the property has been zoned commercial or industrial.

B. (1) The seller shall complete the property disclosure document in good faith to the best of the seller's belief and knowledge as of the date the disclosure is completed and signed by the seller. If the seller has no knowledge or information required by the disclosure document, the seller shall so indicate on the disclosure statement and shall be in compliance with this Chapter.

(2) The seller shall deliver or cause to be delivered the completed and signed property disclosure document to the purchaser no later than the time the purchaser makes an offer to purchase, exchange, or option the property or exercises the option to purchase the property pursuant to a lease with an option to purchase.

(3)(a) If the property disclosure document is delivered to the purchaser after the purchaser makes an offer, the purchaser may terminate any resulting real estate contract or withdraw the offer no later than seventy-two hours, excluding federal and state holidays and weekends, after receipt of the property disclosure document. Notwithstanding any other agreement between the purchaser and seller, if the purchaser terminates a real estate contract or withdraws an offer in accordance with this Chapter, the termination or withdrawal of offer is without penalty to the purchaser and any deposit or earnest money shall be promptly returned to the purchaser.

(b) Any rights of the purchaser to terminate the real estate contract provided by this Chapter are waived if not exercised prior to transfer of title or occupancy, whichever is earlier, by the purchaser in the case of a sale or exchange, or prior to the transfer of title in the case of a purchase pursuant to a lease with option to purchase.

(c) A transfer subject to this Chapter is not invalidated solely due to the failure of any person to comply with this Chapter.

(d) The provisions of this Chapter shall not affect any other rights of a purchaser to terminate a real estate contract for reasons other than those set forth in this Chapter.

C. If information disclosed in accordance with this Chapter becomes inaccurate as a result of any action, occurrence, or agreement after delivery of the property disclosure document, the resulting inaccuracy does not constitute a violation of this Chapter.

D. (1) A property disclosure document shall not be considered as a warranty by the seller. The information contained within the property disclosure document is for disclosure purposes only and is not intended to be a part of any contract between the purchaser and seller.

(2) The property disclosure document may not be used as a substitute for any inspections or warranties that the purchaser or seller may obtain. Nothing in this Chapter precludes the rights or duties of a purchaser to inspect the physical condition of the property.

E. A seller shall not be liable for any error, inaccuracy, or omission of any information required to be delivered to the purchaser in a property disclosure document if either of the following conditions exists:

(1) The error, inaccuracy, or omission was not a willful misrepresentation according to the best of the seller's information, knowledge, and belief.

(2) The error, inaccuracy, or omission was based on information provided by a public body or by another person with a professional license or special knowledge who provided a written or oral report or opinion that the seller reasonably believed to be correct and which was transmitted by the seller to the purchaser.

Added by Acts 2003, No. 308, § 1, eff. June 13, 2003. Amended by Acts 2004, No. 452, § 1, eff. July 1, 2005; Acts 2004, No. 546, § 1; Acts 2008, No. 681, § 1; Acts 2013, No. 369, § 1.

§ 3198.1. Duties of governmental entities; contaminated property

A. Whenever a state or local law enforcement agency becomes aware that residential real property has been contaminated by its use as a clandestine methamphetamine drug lab, the agency shall report the contamination to the Department of Environmental Quality, hereinafter referred to as the "department," and to the local sheriff's office.

B. The department shall maintain a listing of residential real property that has been reported as contaminated, and the list shall be made available to the public through a website.

C. If property that is listed as contaminated on the department's website is subsequently seized and sold at a sheriff's sale, the sheriff shall provide notice to all bidders present at the time the sheriff's sale is conducted.

D. The department may promulgate rules and regulations in order to adopt standards for remediating properties contaminated by clandestine methamphetamine drug labs.

E. Upon confirmation by the department that property has been properly remediated to its established standards, the department shall remove the property from the list required in Subsection B of this Section. The department shall provide written notification to the local sheriff and the property owner of record when the documentation shows that the property has been properly remediated.

F. Notwithstanding any other provision of law to the contrary, once the property has been removed from the list required in Subsection B of this Section, the property owner is not required to report or otherwise disclose the past contamination as required in R.S. 9:3198(A)(2)(b).

G. Failure to comply with the provisions of this Section shall not create a cause of action against a governmental entity or the property owner, the owner's agent, the mortgagee, or other person with an interest in the property.

Added by Acts 2008, No. 681, § 1.

§ 3199. Duty of real estate licensees; liability

A. A real estate licensee representing a seller of residential real property shall inform the seller of the duties and rights under this Chapter. A real estate licensee representing a buyer of residential real property shall inform the buyer of the duties and rights under this Chapter.

B. A person representing a seller in the transaction is not liable under this Chapter for any error, inaccuracy, or omission in a property disclosure document, unless the person has actual knowledge of the error, inaccuracy, or omission by the seller.

Added by Acts 2003, No. 308, § 1, eff. June 13, 2003.

§ 3200. Other statutory disclosure obligations

This Chapter shall not limit or modify any obligation between buyers and sellers created by any other statute or that may exist in law.

Added by Acts 2003, No. 308, § 1, eff. June 13, 2003.

CODE TITLE VIII—OF EXCHANGE [BLANK]
CODE TITLE IX—OF LEASE

CHAPTER 1. LEASES

PART I. LIABILITY FOR DAMAGES

Section
3201. Abandonment or failure to cultivate land.
3202. Assisting and enticing lessee to violate lease.
3203. Refusal to permit lessee to occupy or cultivate property.
3204. Lessor's part of crop considered his property; disposition; penalty.

PART II. LIABILITY FOR INJURIES

3221. Assumption of responsibility by lessee; liability of owner.

PART III. LESSOR'S PRIVILEGE

3241. Limitation on lessor's privilege upon failure or death of lessee.

PART IV. LESSEE'S DEPOSIT

3251. Lessee's deposit to secure lease; retention by lessor; conveyance of leased premises; itemized statement by lessor.
3252. Damages; venue.
3253. Costs and attorney's fees.
3254. Waiver of tenant's rights prohibited.

PART V. LESSORS' RIGHTS

3258. Lessor's right to own, control, use, enjoy, protect and dispose of property and things.
3259. Unpaid rent; attorney fees.
3259.1. Unpaid rent; mobile homes or manufactured housing; notification by lessor.
3259.2. Application for or receipt of government funds not a defense to action to evict.

Section

PART VI. OBLIGATIONS AND RIGHTS OF THE LESSEE

3260. Premises rendered uninhabitable; mitigation of damages.
3260.1. Lessee's right to notification of foreclosure action.
3261. Rights of military personnel to terminate lease.

PART I. LIABILITY FOR DAMAGES

§ 3201. Abandonment or failure to cultivate land

Any lessee for cultivation of land, who takes possession of the property leased and fails to cultivate the land or abandons it after the contract has been entered into, is liable to the lessor for damages in an amount equal to the market value of the average crop that could have been grown on the land or on like land located in the immediate vicinity.

Cross References

C.C. art. 2711.

§ 3202. Assisting and enticing lessee to violate lease

Any person who assists and entices a lessee in violating a contract of lease under R.S. 9:3201 and thereby causes damage to the lessor is liable in solido with the lessee to the lessor.

Cross References

C.C. art. 2711.

§ 3203. Refusal to permit lessee to occupy or cultivate property

Any lessor of property to be cultivated who fails to permit the lessee to occupy or cultivate the property leased, is liable to the lessee in an amount equal to the market value of the average crop that could have been grown on the land or on like land located in the immediate vicinity.

Cross References

C.C. art. 2711.

§ 3204. Lessor's part of crop considered his property; disposition; penalty

In a lease of land for part of the crop, that part which the lessor is to receive is considered at all times the property of the lessor.

The lessee or any person acting with his consent who sells or disposes of the part of the crop belonging to the lessor shall be fined not more than one thousand dollars, or imprisoned for not more than one year, or both.

Cross References

C.C. arts. 2671, 2705.

PART II. LIABILITY FOR INJURIES

§ 3221. Assumption of responsibility by lessee; liability of owner

Notwithstanding the provisions of Louisiana Civil Code Article 2699, the owner of premises leased under a contract whereby the lessee assumes responsibility for their condition is not liable for injury caused by any defect therein to the lessee or anyone on the premises who derives his right to be thereon from the lessee, unless the owner knew or should have known of the defect or had received notice thereof and failed to remedy it within a reasonable time.

Amended by Acts 2004, No. 821, § 3, eff. Jan. 1, 2005.

Cross References

C.C. arts. 2004, 2695.

PART III. LESSOR'S PRIVILEGE

§ 3241. Limitation on lessor's privilege upon failure or death of lessee

The lessor's privilege and right of pledge under any lease, on any building used wholly or in part for mercantile purposes, entered into after August 31st, 1926, shall not extend, in the case of the failure or death of the lessee, to secure rent for a term of more than six months after death or failure. Nothing herein shall be construed to deprive the landlord of his privilege upon the effects on the leased premises, belonging to the purchaser of the lease for the unexpired term, at succession, sheriff's, or syndic's sale, except in the case of the insolvency or death of the purchaser. In such case, the provisions of this Section shall apply in full force.

Editor's note. Chapter 9 of the Louisiana Commercial Laws was revised by Acts 2001, No. 128, § 1, effective July 1, 2001, to consist of R.S. 10:9–101 through 10:9–710. This Chapter does not apply to statutory liens and privileges except as expressly provided therein. R.S. 10:9–322(h) provides: "A security interest has priority over a conflicting lien, other than an agricultural lien, in the same collateral except as otherwise provided in this Chapter or except to the extent the lien is created by security interest." The accompanying revision comment states: "For example, see R.S. 9:4501, 9:4502, 9:4521, 9:4758, 9:4870, and 9:4888, each of which provides that certain privileges have priority over certain security interests. See also 9:5001 and 37:218."

Cross References

C.C. arts. 2705, 3218, 3219.

PART IV. LESSEE'S DEPOSIT

§ 3251. Lessee's deposit to secure lease; retention by lessor; conveyance of leased premises; itemized statement by lessor

A. Any advance or deposit of money furnished by a tenant or lessee to a landlord or lessor to secure the performance of any part of a written or oral lease or rental agreement shall be returned to the tenant or lessee of residential or dwelling premises within one month after the lease shall terminate, except that the landlord or lessor may retain all or any portion of the advance or deposit which is reasonably necessary to remedy a default of the tenant or to remedy unreasonable wear to the premises. If any portion of an advance or deposit is retained by a landlord or lessor, he shall forward to the tenant or lessee, within one month after the date the tenancy terminates, an itemized statement accounting for the proceeds which are retained and giving the reasons therefor. The tenant shall furnish the lessor a forwarding address at the termination of the lease, to which such statements may be sent.

B. In the event of a transfer of the lessor's interest in the leased premises during the term of a lease, the transferor shall also transfer to his successor in interest the sum deposited as security for performance of the lease and the transferor shall then be relieved of further liability with respect to the security deposit. The transferee shall be responsible for the return of the lessee's deposit at the termination of the lease, as set forth in Subsection A of this Section.

C. Paragraph A of this Section shall not apply when the tenant abandons the premises, either without giving notice as required by or prior to the termination of the lease.

Added by Acts 1972, No. 696, § 1. Amended by Acts 1974, No. 697, § 1; Acts 1981, No. 499, § 1; Acts 1985, No. 578, § 1.

Cross References

C.C. arts. 567, 2668, 2676, 2692, 2706, 2727.

§ 3252. Damages; venue

A. The willful failure to comply with R.S. 9:3251 shall give the tenant or lessee the right to recover actual damages or two hundred dollars, whichever is greater, from the landlord or lessor, or from the lessor's successor in interest. Failure to remit within thirty days after written demand for a refund shall constitute willful failure.

B. An action for the recovery of such damages may be brought in the parish of the lessor's domicile or in the parish where the property is situated.

Added by Acts 1972, No. 696, § 1. Amended by Acts 1981, No. 499, § 1; Acts 1987, No. 352, § 1.

§ 3253. Costs and attorney's fees

In an action brought under R.S. 9:3252, the court may in its discretion award costs and attorney's fees to the prevailing party.

Added by Acts 1972, No. 696, § 1.

§ 3254. Waiver of tenant's rights prohibited

Any waiver of the right of a tenant under this part shall be null and void.

Added by Acts 1972, No. 696, § 1.

PART V. LESSORS' RIGHTS

§ 3258. Lessor's right to own, control, use, enjoy, protect and dispose of property and things

Every lessor, in accordance with the provisions of Article I, Section 4 of the Louisiana Constitution of 1974, shall have the right to the ownership, control, use, enjoyment, protection and right to dispose of private property including any alienation thereof by lease or otherwise, where a person by law or contract has a legal right to give to another the enjoyment of a thing or property for a valid consideration; which said rights shall include all rights granted to lessors by Title IX of the Louisiana Civil Code [1] dealing with lease, and which said rights shall not be altered, abridged or diminished except by state law, and which said rights are subject to the reasonable exercise of the police power.

Added by Acts 1977, No. 655, § 1, eff. July 20, 1977.

[1] C.C. art. 2668 et seq.

§ 3259. Unpaid rent; attorney fees

A. Whenever any lessee of any apartment building, house, motel, hotel, or other such dwelling fails to pay rent that has become due and delinquent, within twenty days after delivery of written demand therefor made in accordance with the provisions of this Section, correctly setting forth the amount of rent due and owing, the lessee shall be liable for reasonable attorney fees for the prosecution and collection of such claim when judgment on the claim is rendered in favor of the claimant.

B. Delivery of written demand for purposes of this Section may be accomplished by mailing the written demand by certified mail to the last known address of the lessee, by personal delivery to the lessee or by tacking the written demand on the door of the leased premises.

C. The provisions of this Section shall apply to oral leases only.

Added by Acts 1978, No. 478, § 1.

§ 3259.1. Unpaid rent; mobile homes or manufactured housing; notification by lessor

A. As used in this Section the following terms shall have the following meanings:

(1) "Lessor" shall mean the owner of the unsubdivided immovable property on which three or more lots are available for rent for locating a mobile home or manufactured housing.

(2) "Lessee" shall mean the person leasing the immovable property on which a mobile home or manufactured housing is located.

(3) "Mobile home" and "manufactured housing" means a structure, transportable in one or more sections, which, in the traveling mode, is eight body feet or more in width or forty body feet or more in length or, when erected on site, is three hundred twenty or more square feet and which, is built on a permanent chassis and designed to be used as a dwelling with or without a permanent foundation when connected to the required utilities and includes the plumbing, heating, and air conditioning, and electrical systems contained therein; except that such term shall include any structure which meets all the requirements of this Paragraph except the size requirements and with respect to which the manufacturer voluntarily files a certification required by the fire marshal and complies with the standards established by this Part. The terms "mobile home" and "manufactured housing" shall include a manufactured home, a modular home, and a residential mobile home that is no longer declared to be a part of the realty pursuant to R.S. 9:1149.6.

(4) "Mortgagor" shall mean the person executing the security device as the obligor or the transferee if the mobile home or manufactured housing has been transferred and the obligations under the security device assumed by another person with written consent of the holder of the security device.

(5) "Secured party" shall mean the holder of a security interest under Chapter 9 of the Louisiana Commercial Laws (R.S. 10:9–101, et seq.) or a chattel mortgage, the pledgee or assignee of a chattel mortgage or security agreement, or the agent of the holder, assignee, or pledgee of a chattel mortgage or security agreement, or the holder of a promissory note executed for the sale of a mobile home or manufactured housing if that note is sold with recourse against the holder of the note, or the vendor of a retail installment contract as defined in R.S. 6:951 when such retail installment contract is sold with recourse against the vendor.

(6) "Security device" means a security interest under Chapter 9 of the Louisiana Commercial Laws (R.S. 10:9–101, et seq.), a chattel mortgage, or a promissory note executed for the sale of a mobile home or for manufactured housing or a retail installment contract entered into pursuant to Chapter 10 of Title 6 [1] of the Louisiana Revised Statutes of 1950 for the sale of a mobile home or for manufactured housing.

B. When the rental payments for immovable property on which a mobile home or manufactured housing is located are sixty days past the due date for the payment, the lessor shall notify the secured parties and the mortgagor. if the mortgagor is not the lessee or occupant of the mobile home or manufactured housing, in writing by mail that the rental payments are sixty days past the due date. The notice shall include the following information if known or readily available to the lessor or if available from the office of motor vehicles of the Department of Public Safety and Corrections:

(1) The lessor's name.

(2) The lessee's name.

(3) The mortgagor's name.

(4) The location of the mobile home or manufactured housing.

(5) The number of days that the rental payments are overdue, the monthly rental payment, and the total amount past due.

(6) The vehicle identification number of the mobile home or manufactured housing.

(7) A description of the mobile home or manufactured housing including the make, model, year, dimensions, and any identification numbers or marks.

C. Notwithstanding any provision of the law to the contrary, failure of the lessor to provide such notification within thirty days after the rental payments are sixty days past due shall limit the lessor's privilege or right of pledge for rent to the amount of rental payments past due for ninety days.

D. The lessor shall be entitled to collect a fee of twenty-five dollars from the lessee or mortgagor in addition to the rental payments due and any additional fees or charges due the lessor when such notification is made and the lessee or mortgagor subsequently pays the rental payments due.

E. The lessor shall be entitled to collect a fee of twenty-five dollars from the secured parties in addition to all rental or storage payments due at the time the mobile home or manufactured housing is repossessed when such notification is made and the secured party subsequently obtains possession of the mobile home or manufactured housing.

F. The office of motor vehicles in the Department of Public Safety and Corrections shall maintain a record of all mobile homes and manufactured housing for which a vehicle certificate of title has been issued pursuant to Chapter 4 of Title 32 [2] of the Louisiana Revised Statutes of 1950 and which is subject to a security device for a period of ten years or for the period stated for the termination of the security device. The record shall include, if available:

(1) The name and address of the mortgagor or vendee of the mobile home or manufactured housing.

(2) The names and addresses of the primary secured party and any secondary secured party on any security device.

(3) The vehicle identification number of the mobile home or manufactured housing.

(4) A description of the mobile home or manufactured housing including the make, model, year, dimensions, and any identification numbers.

Added by Acts 1985, No. 531, § 1. Amended by Acts 1989, No. 137, § 4, eff. Sept. 1, 1989.

[1] R.S. 6:951 et seq.
[2] R.S. 32:701 et seq.

§ 3259.2. Application for or receipt of government funds not a defense to action to evict

The application for or the receipt of entitlements or funds, under any federal or state rent subsidy program or rent subsidy assistance, shall not be considered payment of rent and shall not be a defense to an action to evict the lessee.

Added by Acts 2004, No. 821, § 3, eff. Jan. 1, 2005.

PART VI. OBLIGATIONS AND RIGHTS OF THE LESSEE

§ 3260. Premises rendered uninhabitable; mitigation of damages

When a lessee or tenant of commercial, residential, or dwelling premises has been constructively evicted from the premises, and when the premises are rendered uninhabitable through no fault of the lessee or tenant, the landlord or lessor shall be required to mitigate his damages.

Added by Acts 1993, No. 906, § 1.

Cross References

C.C. arts. 2710 to 2726.

§ 3260.1. Lessee's right to notification of foreclosure action

A. During, and prior to entering into, a lease agreement for a residential dwelling, the lessor shall disclose in writing to the lessee and any prospective lessee any pending foreclosure action to which the residential dwelling is subject and the right of the lessee to receive a notification of a foreclosure action pursuant to this Section.

B. Within seven calendar days after being served pursuant to Code of Civil Procedure Article 2293 with a notice of seizure in a foreclosure action, a lessor of a residential dwelling subject to a notice of seizure in a foreclosure action shall provide written notice of the seizure to all lessees of the premises.

C. The written disclosure required in Subsection B of this Section shall be signed by the lessor and shall include the name of the district court in which the foreclosure action is pending, the case name and docket number and the following statement: "This is not a notice to vacate the premises. This notice does not mean ownership of the building has changed. All lessees are still responsible for payment of rent and other obligations under the rental agreement. The lessor is still responsible for his obligations under the rental agreement. You will receive additional notice if there is a change in owner."

D. If a lessee in a civil legal proceeding against an owner or lessor establishes that a violation of this Section occurred, the lessee shall be entitled to recover two hundred dollars in damages, in addition to any other damages or remedies and costs to which the lessee may also be entitled.

E. The requirements of this Section shall apply to all lessors in residential leases, including lessors who are leasing residential dwellings subject to a federally-related mortgage loan, as defined in 12 U.S.C. 2602, or who have entered into a housing assistance payments contract with the public housing agency to receive housing subsidies on behalf of a lessee pursuant to Section 8 of the United States Housing Act of 1937, and to all lessees in residential leases, including such lessees receiving vouchers or housing assistance pursuant to Section 8 of the United States Housing Act of 1937.

F. The requirements of this Section shall not apply to a federally insured financial institution that is asserting its rights as an assignee of a lessor whose property is under foreclosure or as a mortgage holder.

Added by Acts 2013, No. 354, § 1.

§ 3261. Rights of military personnel to terminate lease

A. Any active or reserve member of the armed forces of the United States, including the National Guard and the United States Coast Guard, may terminate his residential lease agreement, pursuant to Subsection B of this Section, if any of the following occur:

(1) The member has received initial or permanent change of station orders to depart thirty-five miles or more from the location of the dwelling unit.

(2) The member has received initial or temporary duty orders in excess of three months duration to depart thirty-five miles or more from the location of the dwelling unit.

(3) The member is discharged, released, or retires.

(4) The member is ordered to reside in government-supplied quarters.

(5) The member is notified of the availability of government-supplied quarters which were not available to the mem-

ber at the time the lease was executed, provided that the member notifies the lessor in writing that the member has a pending request or application for government supplied quarters at the time the lease is entered into.

B. Lessees who qualify to terminate a rental agreement pursuant to Subsection A shall do so by serving on the lessor a written notice of termination to be effective on a date stated therein, said date to be not less than thirty days after the date the notice is served on the lessor. The termination shall be no more than sixty days prior to the date of departure necessary to comply with the official orders or any supplemental instructions for interim training or duty prior to the transfer. Prior to the termination date, the lessee shall furnish the lessor with a copy of the official notification of orders, or a signed letter confirming the orders from the lessee's commanding officer, or a statement signed by the housing officer certifying that no government-supplied quarters were available at the time the lease was executed.

C. In consideration of early termination of the lease, the lessee shall not be liable for more than one month's rent if, as of the effective date of the termination, the lessee has completed less than six months of the lease agreement or one-half of the rent for one month if the lessee has completed at least six months of the lease agreement. The lessee shall be entitled to the full return of any security deposit, if such member has otherwise complied with the requirements of the lease.

D. The provisions of this Section may not be waived or modified by the agreement of the parties under any circumstances.

Added by Acts 1999, No. 714, § 1. Amended by Acts 2001, No. 790, § 1.

CHAPTER 2. LEASES OF MOVABLES

Section
3262 to 3272. Repealed.

PART I. IN GENERAL

3301.	Short title.
3302.	Declaration of policy.
3303.	Scope.
3304.	Exclusions.
3305.	Waiver; agreement to forego rights.
3306.	Definitions.
3307.	Terms.
3308.	Construction against implicit repeal.

PART II. CIVIL CODE

3309.	True leases.
3310.	Financed leases.
3310.1.	Constructive delivery and possession in sale/lease-back situations.

PART III. CHARGES

3311.	Interest rate charges; true leases.
3312.	Interest rate charges; financed leases.
3313.	Additional lease related charges.
3314.	Late charges.
3315.	Deferral charges.
3316.	Early termination charges.
3317.	End of lease charges.

Section

PART IV. REMEDIES FOLLOWING LESSEE'S DEFAULT

3318.	Options of lessor following lessee's default.
3319.	Accelerated rental payments.
3320.	Cancellation of lease following lessee's default.
3321.	Surrender of leased property after notice.
3322.	Summary proceeding for surrender of property; rule to show cause; judgment.
3323.	Appeal from judgment on rule.
3324.	Ordinary proceedings in addition to summary proceedings.
3325.	Recovery of liquidated damages.
3326.	Sequestration in ordinary proceedings.
3327.	Release to lessee of sequestered property.
3328.	Release of sequestered property to lessor.
3329.	Prohibition against self-help repossession.
3330.	Lessor's right to protect and preserve leased property.

PART V. INSURANCE

3331.	Requirement of insurance.
3332.	Credit life and credit health and accident insurance.
3333.	Property insurance.
3334.	Choice of insurer.
3335.	Limitations on insurance rates; contract requirements.
3336.	Conditions applying to insurance provided by the lessor.
3337.	Cancellation of insurance; refund or credit upon cancellation.
3338.	Gain from insurance.

PART VI. MISCELLANEOUS

3339.	Referrals.
3340.	Unauthorized collection practices.
3341.	Violations.
3342.	Recordation of leases of movables.

§§ 3262 to 3272. **Repealed by Acts 1985, No. 592, § 6, eff. July 13, 1985**

PART I. IN GENERAL

§ 3301. Short title

This Chapter shall be known and may be cited as the Louisiana Lease of Movables Act.

Acts 1985, No. 592, § 1, eff. July 13, 1985.

Cross References

C.C. arts. 567, 2346, 2371, 2674, 2676, 2678, 2697, 2709, 2710, 2727.

R.S. 10:9–102(b)(6).

§ 3302. Declaration of policy

It is declared to be the policy of this state to encourage and foster the leasing of movable property to individuals and businesses, thus promoting economic growth and development. To this end, financed leases, which have previously been construed as conditional sales transactions, are hereby recognized as valid and enforceable in this state.

Acts 1985, No. 592, § 1, eff. July 13, 1985. Amended by Acts 1986, No. 213, § 1.

Cross References

C.C. arts. 567, 2346, 2371, 2674, 2676, 2678, 2692, 2697, 2709, 2710, 2727.

§ 3303. Scope

A. This Chapter shall apply to all leases of movable property located in this state, whether the property is initially leased in Louisiana or subsequently moved into this state.

B. Subject to the provisions of R.S. 9:3303(D), (E), and (F), a lease agreement affecting movable property located or to be located in Louisiana may provide that the transaction will be governed under the substantive laws of the state in which the lease is entered into or governed under the substantive laws of the state of the lessor's residence, principal office, or incorporation or governed under the substantive laws of any other state having significant contacts with the transaction. As a limited exception to the foregoing, the substantive laws of the chosen forum that would characterize the lease as a type of secured financing transaction under the Uniform Commercial Code shall not apply to a financed lease, provided that the transaction was entered into prior to the time Chapter 9 of the Louisiana Commercial Laws (R.S. 10:9–101, et seq.) became effective. Such a lease shall retain the legal effects of a "financed lease" under this Chapter notwithstanding the fact that the lease may be contractually subject to the substantive laws of another state and may otherwise be classified as a type of secured financing transaction under the Uniform Commercial Code or other laws of the chosen forum. It shall furthermore not be necessary under these limited circumstances for the lessor to perfect any type of security interest on the leased equipment located in Louisiana, again provided that such a financed lease was entered into prior to the time Chapter 9 of the Louisiana Commercial Laws became effective.

C. This Chapter shall not affect the amount of taxes owed to the state of Louisiana, or to any political subdivision, on the purchase, importation, use, storage, lease, or rental of tangible personal property. Tax obligations owed to the state and its political subdivisions shall be levied and collected as provided by law.

D. Whenever a lessor seeks to enforce remedies under any lease of movable property, no matter where consummated, following the lessee's default and the leased property is then located in this state, the lessor shall comply with the remedy provisions under Part IV of this Chapter [1], notwithstanding that the lease agreement may provide that the transaction is to be governed under the laws of another state and further notwithstanding the state of the lessee's residence, domicile, or incorporation.

E. Whenever an action is brought in this state to enforce any rights arising from a lease of movable property located in this state at the time of the lessee's default, the lessor shall, where applicable, reduce the charges sought to be collected from the lessee so that they do not exceed the charges provided in Part III of this Chapter [2].

F. The following agreements by Louisiana lessees are invalid with respect to leases of movable property, or any modifications thereof, to which this Chapter applies:

(1) Agreements in which the lessee consents to the jurisdiction of another state.

(2) Agreements that fix venue.

Acts 1985, No. 592, § 1, eff. July 13, 1985. Amended by Acts 1986, No. 213, § 1; Acts 1989, No. 137, § 4, eff. Sept. 1, 1989; Acts 1990, No. 1079, § 3, eff. Sept. 1, 1990 at 12:01 A.M.

[1] R.S. 9:3318 et seq.
[2] R.S. 9:3311 et seq.

Cross References

C.C. arts. 9 to 13, 2674, 2676, 2678.

§ 3304. Exclusions

A. This Chapter shall not apply to leases of immovable property. This Chapter shall, however, continue to apply to leases of movable property which subsequently becomes a component part of an immovable or which are immobilized by declaration as provided under Articles 466 and 467 of the Louisiana Civil Code, in which case the lessor shall retain all legal rights to and ownership of the leased equipment notwithstanding its immobilization. This Chapter shall also continue to apply to leases of equipment which are subsequently incorporated into other movable property not otherwise subject to the lease, in which case the lessor shall retain all legal rights to and ownership of the leased equipment notwithstanding Article 510 of the Louisiana Civil Code.

B. This Chapter shall not apply to leases of incorporeal movables or licenses of contractual or proprietary rights, such as licenses for the use of computer software, trade names, copyrights, or franchises.

C. R.S. 9:3312, 3331 and 3332 shall not apply to short term leases.

D. R.S. 9:3312 and 3339 through 3341 shall not apply to leases of movable property by or to government or any governmental agency or instrumentality.

E. R.S. 9:3312, 3313, 3314, 3331, 3332, and 3339 through 3341 shall not apply to equipment leases by public utilities, common carriers, or cable television or communication companies if a subdivision or agency of this state or of any municipality or of the United States regulates, approves, or consents to the charges for the services involved.

Acts 1985, No. 592, § 1, eff. July 13, 1985. Amended by Acts 1986, No. 213, § 1.

Cross References

C.C. arts. 466, 467, 510, 2674, 2676, 2678.

R.S. 10:9–102(b)(6).

§ 3305. Waiver; agreement to forego rights

A consumer lessee may not waive or agree to forego any rights or benefits under this Chapter except that a claim, if disputed in good faith, may be settled by compromise or agreement.

Acts 1985, No. 592, § 1, eff. July 13, 1985. Amended by Acts 1986, No. 213, § 1.

Cross References

C.C. arts. 7, 2674, 2676, 2678, 3071 et seq.

§ 3306. Definitions

(1) "Adjusted capitalized cost" means the capitalized cost of the leased equipment less any capitalized cost reduction payments made by the lessee at the inception of the lease.

(2) "Agricultural purpose" means a purpose related to the production, harvest, exhibition, marketing, transportation, processing, or manufacture of agricultural products by a natural person who cultivates, plants, propagates, or nurtures the agricultural products. "Agricultural products" includes products such as horticultural and dairy products, livestock, wildlife, poultry, bees, forest products, fish and

shell fish, and any products thereof, including processed and manufactured products, and any and all products raised or produced on farms and any processed or manufactured products thereof.

(3) "Base term" or "base lease term" of lease means the initial term of the lease as provided under the lease agreement. If a lease is cancelled or terminated for any reason during a renewal period as provided under the lease agreement, "base term" shall mean that renewal period.

(4) "Capitalized cost" means the cost of the leased equipment which is taken into consideration by the lessor in pricing the lease to the lessee.

(5) "Capitalized cost reduction payments" mean any payment or payments made by the lessee at the inception of the lease to reduce the capitalized cost of the leased equipment and therefore to reduce the amount of rental payments which would otherwise be charged under the lease.

(6) "Commercial lease" means a lease to a natural person, corporation, partnership, government, governmental agency or instrumentality, or any other type of entity, primarily for a business, commercial, or agricultural purpose.

(7) "Conditional sale" means a legal arrangement under which a seller sells goods or movable property to a purchaser on a deferred payment or credit basis, with the seller retaining legal title and ownership of the property until such time as the purchase price is paid in full.

(8) "Consumer" means a natural person entering into a lease primarily for a personal, family, or household purpose.

(9) "Consumer lease" means a lease to a consumer as defined in R.S. 9:3306(8), provided that total compensation under the lease over the base lease term does not exceed twenty-five thousand dollars. Where total compensation under the lease exceeds twenty-five thousand dollars, the lease shall be considered a commercial lease for purposes of this Chapter. A lease provided through an employer-sponsored lease program shall not be considered a consumer lease for the purposes of this Chapter.

(10) "Equipment" means movable property.

(11) "Estimated end of term residual value" means the estimated value of the leased property at the end of the base lease term as specified by the lessor at the time the lease is entered into.

(12)(a) "Financed lease" means a lease entered into prior to January 1, 1990 under which:

(i) The lessee is obligated to pay total compensation over the base lease term which is substantially equivalent to or which exceeds the initial value of the leased property; and

(ii) The lessee is obligated to become, or has the option of becoming, the owner of the leased property upon termination of the lease for no additional consideration or for nominal consideration.

(b) After January 1, 1990 a "financed lease" for purposes of this Chapter means a lease entered into on or after that effective date that is classified as a security interest as provided under R.S. 10:1–201(35).

(13) "Initial value" of leased equipment means the price for which the lessee could purchase the leased equipment from the lessor, where appropriate, on an all cash basis in the ordinary course of business. "Initial value" includes the cost of the leased equipment to the lessor plus, where applicable, any increase or markup by the lessor prior to consummation of the lease.

(14) "Interest rate charges" mean interest, time-price differential or time-value of money charges which are capitalized into equipment leases as compensation to the lessor for deferred payment under the lease. Interest rate charges generally represent the difference between (a) total compensation payable to the lessor over the base lease term, less (b) the adjusted capitalized cost of the leased equipment.

(15) "Lease" means a contract or agreement of lease of any movable property, whether for a fixed term or for an indefinite period.

(16) "Lessee" means the lessee under a lease as defined above or his sublessee or assignee.

(17) "Lessor" means the lessor in a lease as defined above, his assignee or designee, or sublessor, assignee, or designee.

(18) "Mandatory purchase price" means the purchase price of the leased equipment which the lessee is obligated to pay at the conclusion of the base lease term, exclusive of official fees and taxes.

(19) "Movable property" or "movables" means corporeal movables, as provided under Civil Code Article 471.

(20) "Nominal consideration" means a sum which is less than twenty-five percent of the fair market value of the leased equipment upon conclusion of the base term of the lease.

(21) "Optional purchase price" of leased equipment means the price for which the lessee has the option to purchase the leased equipment from the lessor at the conclusion of the base term of the lease.

(22) "Property" means any movable subject to a lease.

(23) "Realized value" means:

(a) The price received by the lessor for the leased property at disposition,

(b) The highest offer received for the leased property at disposition, or

(c) The fair market value of the leased property at the conclusion of the lease.

(24) "Short-term lease" means a lease for a term not exceeding four months. Any lease of less than four months containing a provision whereby the term of the lease may be automatically extended or reconducted beyond a period of four months shall not be deemed a short-term lease.

(25) "Total compensation" under the lease means the sum of any capitalized cost reduction payments made at the inception of the lease, plus the total of rental payments payable over the base lease term, exclusive of additional lease related charges, early termination charges, end of lease charges, late charges, deferral charges, and the optional purchase price of the leased equipment as defined herein. Where the lessee is obligated to purchase the leased equipment at the conclusion of the lease term, the mandatory purchase price of the equipment shall be included in the total compensation under the lease.

(26)(a) "True lease" means a lease entered into before January 1, 1990, under which:

(i) The lessee has no obligation to pay total compensation over the base lease term which is substantially equivalent to or in excess of the initial value of the leased property; or

(ii) The lessee does not have the option or obligation to become the owner of the leased property upon termination of the lease for no or nominal consideration.

(b) A true lease also means a lease entered into after January 1, 1990 that is not classified as a security interest as provided under R.S. 10:1–201(35).

(c) Consistent with R.S. 10:9–505, the filing of a financing statement by a lessor under a true lease shall not of itself result in such a lease being classified as a financed lease for purposes of this Chapter or otherwise.

Acts 1985, No. 592, § 1, eff. July 13, 1985. Amended by Acts 1986, No. 213, § 1; Acts 1989, No. 137, § 4, eff. Sept. 1, 1989; Acts 2001, No. 128, § 4, eff. July 1, 2001 at 12:01 A.M.; Acts 2006, No. 533, § 2; Acts 2012, No. 626, § 1, eff. June 7, 2012.

Editor's note. Acts 2001, No. 128, § 4, effective July 1, 2001, amended R.S. 9:3306. Section 19 of Acts 2001, No. 128, declares that "it is the intent of the legislature in enacting this Act that R.S. 2736, 4501 and 4502, 4521, 4758, 4770, and 5363.1 not be expressly or impliedly repealed by this Act, but that such laws remain in effect, and, at times when so provided, be applied to secured transactions subject to Chapter 9 of the Louisiana Commercial Law as revised by this Act."

Cross References

C.C. arts. 471, 567, 2346, 2371, 2674, 2676, 2678, 2692, 2697, 2709, 2710, 2727.

§ 3307. Terms

Whenever applicable in this Chapter, use of the masculine includes the feminine and use of the plural includes the singular and vice versa.

Acts 1985, No. 592, § 1, eff. July 13, 1985.

Cross References

C.C. arts. 567, 2346, 2371, 2674, 2676, 2678, 2692, 2697, 2709, 2710, 2727.

§ 3308. Construction against implicit repeal

This Chapter being a general act is intended as a unified coverage of the subject matter. No part of this Chapter shall be deemed impliedly repealed by subsequent legislation if such construction can be reasonably avoided.

Acts 1985, No. 592, § 1, eff. July 13, 1985.

Cross References

C.C. arts. 567, 2346, 2371, 2674, 2676, 2678, 2692, 2697, 2709, 2710, 2727.

PART II. CIVIL CODE

§ 3309. True leases

Except as specifically provided in this Chapter, true leases are subject to Title IX of Book III of the Civil Code entitled "Of Lease."[1]

Acts 1985, No. 592, § 1, eff. July 13, 1985.

[1] C.C. art. 2668 et seq.

Cross References

C.C. arts. 567, 2346, 2371, 2674, 2676, 2678, 2692, 2697, 2709, 2710, 2727.

§ 3310. Financed leases

A. Except as specifically provided in this Chapter, financed leases are subject to Title IX of Book III of the Civil Code entitled "Lease".[1] Financed leases entered into after Chapter 9 of the Louisiana Commercial Laws[2] becomes effective are a type of secured transaction in favor of the lessor, and thus are additionally subject to R.S. 10:9–101, et seq.

B. Notwithstanding the fact that a financed lease creates a security interest under Chapter 9 of the Louisiana Commercial Laws, the lessor under a properly perfected financed lease shall retain full legal and equitable title and ownership in and to the leased equipment until such time as the lessee exercises his option or complies with his obligation to purchase the leased equipment from the lessor as provided under the lease agreement. The provisions of this Chapter shall further not affect present taxation of financed leases.

Acts 1985, No. 592, § 1, eff. July 13, 1985. Amended by Acts 1989, No. 137, § 4, eff. Sept. 1, 1989.

[1] C.C. art. 2668 et seq.
[2] R.S. 10:9–101 et seq.

Cross References

C.C. arts. 567, 2346, 2371, 2674, 2676, 2678, 2692, 2697, 2709, 2710, 2727.

§ 3310.1. Constructive delivery and possession in sale/lease-back situations

When equipment is sold to, and is contemporaneously leased under a true or financed lease by the vendee/lessor back to the vendor/lessee, the filing of a financing statement as provided in R.S. 9:3342(B) suffices for the transfer of ownership of the equipment as against third persons.

Added by Acts 1989, No. 137, § 4, eff. Sept. 1, 1989.

PART III. CHARGES

§ 3311. Interest rate charges; true leases

Interest rate charges capitalized into both consumer and commercial purpose true leases are unregulated and are not subject to conventional interest rate or usury limitations.

Acts 1985, No. 592, § 1, eff. July 13, 1985.

Cross References

C.C. arts. 567, 2346, 2371, 2674, 2676, 2678, 2692, 2697, 2709, 2710, 2727.

§ 3312. Interest rate charges; financed leases

A. Maximum interest rate charges capitalized into consumer purpose financed leases shall be limited as follows:

(1) The total of:

(a) Twenty-four percent per year on that part of the adjusted capitalized cost under the lease which is not in excess of one thousand seven hundred fifty dollars; and

(b) Eighteen percent per year on that part of the adjusted capitalized cost under the lease which is more than one thousand seven hundred fifty dollars but not in excess of five thousand dollars; and

(c) Twelve percent per year on that part of the adjusted capitalized cost under the lease which is more than five thousand dollars; or

(2) Eighteen percent per year on the adjusted capitalized cost under the lease; or

(3) Any other method of computation which would not yield greater interest rate charges than those computed under Paragraphs (1) or (2) of this Subsection.

B. Interest rate charges capitalized into commercial purpose financed leases are unregulated and are not subject to conventional interest rate or usury limitations.

C. This Section does not limit or restrict the manner of contracting for interest rate charges, whether by way of add-on or otherwise, so long as the rate in connection with consumer purpose financed leases does not exceed that permitted by R.S. 9:3312(A). Interest rates may be calculated on the assumption that all scheduled rental payments will be made when due and the effects of prepayment are governed under the provisions of rebate as provided under R.S. 9:3319(B).

D. For purposes of this Section, the term of a consumer financed lease commences on the date the lease agreement is executed. Differences in lengths of months may be disregarded and a day may be counted as one-thirtieth of a month. Subject to classifications and differentiations, the lessor may reasonably establish a part of a month in excess of fifteen days to be treated as a full month if periods of fifteen days or less are disregarded and if that procedure is not consistently used to obtain a greater yield than would otherwise be permitted under R.S. 9:3312(A).

E. A lessor shall not divide a consumer financed lease into multiple agreements for the purpose of obtaining higher interest rate charges than would otherwise be permitted by R.S. 9:3312(A).

Acts 1985, No. 592, § 1, eff. July 13, 1985. Amended by Acts 1986, No. 213, § 1.

Cross References

C.C. arts. 567, 2346, 2371, 2674, 2676, 2678, 2692, 2697, 2709, 2710, 2727.

§ 3313. Additional lease related charges

A. Both true and financed lease agreements, whether for consumer or commercial purposes, may contractually provide for the assessment, imposition, and collection of the following additional lease related charges:

(1) Taxes, including but not limited to sales, lease, use, excise, and personal property taxes.

(2) Reasonable excess mileage or use charges.

(3) License, title, and registration fees.

(4) Fees for preparation of lease agreements and other documents related to the transaction.

(5) Notarial fees.

(6) Recordation fees.

(7) Repair, maintenance and other fees incident to the use of the leased equipment by the lessee.

(8) Refundable security deposits.

(9) Voluntary credit life and credit accident and disability insurance as provided under R.S. 9:3332.

(10) Property insurance as provided under R.S. 9:3333.

(11) Early termination charges as provided under R.S. 9:3316.

(12) Reasonable excess wear and tear charges.

(13) Reasonable attorney's fees not to exceed twenty-five percent of the total amount payable under the lease.

(14) NSF check charges as provided under R.S. 9:3529.

(15) Late charges as provided under R.S. 9:3314.

(16) Deferral charges as provided under R.S. 9:3315.

(17) Such additional related charges as may be contractually agreed to by the lessee.

B. Such additional lease related charges shall not be considered interest and are exempt from conventional interest rate and usury limitations as well as the limitations of R.S. 9:3312(A).

Acts 1985, No. 592, § 1, eff. July 13, 1985. Amended by Acts 1986, No. 213, § 1.

Cross References

C.C. arts. 567, 2346, 2371, 2674, 2676, 2678, 2692, 2697, 2709, 2710, 2727.

§ 3314. Late charges

A. Lessees under both true and financed consumer lease agreements may contractually agree to pay late charges on any one or more rental payments which are not paid in full within ten days after the scheduled or deferred due dates, in an amount not to exceed five percent of the unpaid amount of such delinquent rental payment, or twenty-five dollars, whichever is greater.

B. Lessees under both true and financed commercial lease agreements may contractually agree to pay late charges in any amount or at any rate on any one or more delinquent rental payments which are not paid in full on the scheduled or deferred due dates.

C. Late charges under R.S. 9:3314(A) may be collected only once on a delinquent rental payment however long it remains in default. No such late charge may be collected on a rental payment that is paid in full within ten days after its scheduled due date for consumer leases, even though an earlier maturing rental payment or a late charge on an earlier rental payment may not have been paid in full. For purposes of this Subsection, payments are deemed to be applied first to current rentals and then to delinquent rentals and then to late charges.

D. No late charge may be collected on a consumer lease payment which has been deferred and a deferral charge has been paid or incurred, provided that the deferred payment is paid within ten days of its deferral date with regard to consumer leases.

E. Late charges may be collected at the time they accrue or at any time thereafter. The lessor is not required to notify the lessee of the assessment of late charges.

F. Late charges may be assessed in addition to interest rate charges as provided under R.S. 9:3311 and 3312.

Acts 1985, No. 592, § 1, eff. July 13, 1985. Amended by Acts 1986, No. 213, § 1.

Cross References

C.C. arts. 567, 2346, 2371, 2674, 2676, 2678, 2692, 2697, 2709, 2710, 2727.

§ 3315. Deferral charges

A. The parties to a true or financed consumer lease may agree, verbally or in writing, before or after default, to a deferral of all or part of one or more unpaid rental payments in consideration for which the lessor may assess, impose, and collect a deferral charge computed by applying a deferral charge rate not to exceed a maximum rate of twenty-five percent per annum, to the amount deferred over the period of deferral, calculated without regard to differences and lengths of months, but proportionately for a part of a month, counting each day as one-thirtieth of a month.

B. The parties to a true or financed commercial lease may agree, verbally or in writing, before or after default, to a deferral of all or part of one or more unpaid rental payments in consideration for which the lessor may assess, impose, and collect a deferral charge computed by applying a deferral charge rate to the amount deferred over the period of deferral, calculated without regard to differences and lengths of months, but proportionately for a part of a month, counting each day as one-thirtieth of a month. For purposes of this Subsection, deferral charges assessed in connection with commercial leases shall be unregulated and exempt from conventional interest rate and usury limitations.

C. A true or financed lease agreement, including in connection with both consumer leases and commercial leases, may provide that if any one or more rental payments are not paid within the time periods specified under the agreement, the lessor may unilaterally grant a deferral of such payments and assess deferral charges as provided in this Section. Deferral charges may not be assessed after the lessor elects to cancel the lease following the lessee's default as provided in R.S. 9:3318(A)(2).

D. A lessor, in addition to deferral charges, may assess appropriate charges for insurance for the extended period. The amount of these additional insurance charges which are not paid in cash may be added to the amount deferred for the purpose of calculating the deferral charge.

E. Deferral charges may be assessed in addition to interest rate charges as provided under R.S. 9:3311 and 3312.

Acts 1985, No. 592, § 1, eff. July 13, 1985. Amended by Acts 1986, No. 213, § 1.

Cross References

C.C. arts. 567, 2346, 2371, 2674, 2676, 2678, 2692, 2697, 2709, 2710, 2727.

§ 3316. Early termination charges

A. Both true and financed lease agreements, whether for consumer or commercial purposes, may contractually provide for the assessment, imposition, and collection of reasonable early termination charges, including but not limited to:

(1) An early termination fee in a fixed amount as contractually agreed to by the lessee.

(2) Excess mileage or use charges as provided under the lease agreement.

(3) Reasonable excess wear and tear charges as provided under the lease agreement.

(4) The difference between (i) the original adjusted capital cost of the leased equipment, less (ii) accumulated depreciation calculated in accordance with the lessor's standard depreciation formula through the date of termination, less (iii) the realized value of the leased equipment following termination of the lease.

(5) Official fees and taxes imposed in connection with termination of the lease.

(6) Current or delinquent rental payments and other charges under the lease which are then due and payable.

(7) Additional reasonable early termination charges which may be contractually provided for under the lease agreement.

B. Early termination charges may be assessed in addition to interest rate charges as provided under R.S. 9:3311 and 3312.

C. Any refundable security deposit held by the lessee may be retained and shall be credited against the lessee's liability for early termination charges.

Acts 1985, No. 592, § 1, eff. July 13, 1985. Amended by Acts 1986, No. 213, § 1.

Cross References

C.C. arts. 567, 2346, 2371, 2674, 2676, 2678, 2692, 2697, 2709, 2710, 2727.

§ 3317. End of lease charges

A. Both true and financed lease agreements, whether in connection with consumer or commercial purpose leases, may contractually provide for the assessment, imposition, and collection of reasonable end of lease charges, including but not limited to:

(1) End of lease fees in a fixed amount as may be agreed to by the lessee.

(2) Excess mileage or use charges as provided under the lease agreement.

(3) Reasonable excess wear and tear charges as provided under the lease agreement.

(4) The difference between (i) the estimated end of term residual value of the leased equipment and (ii) the actual realized value of the leased equipment following termination of the lease.

(5) Official fees and taxes imposed in connection with termination of the lease.

(6) Current or delinquent rental payments and other charges under the lease which are then due and payable.

(7) Any additional reasonable end of lease charges which may be contractually provided for under the lease agreement.

B. End of lease charges may be assessed in addition to interest rate charges as provided under R.S. 9:3311 and 3312.

C. Any refundable security deposit held by the lessor may be retained and shall be credited against the lessee's liability for end of lease charges.

Acts 1985, No. 592, § 1, eff. July 13, 1985. Amended by Acts 1986, No. 213, § 1.

Cross References

C.C. arts. 567, 2346, 2371, 2674, 2676, 2678, 2692, 2697, 2709, 2710, 2727.

PART IV. REMEDIES FOLLOWING LESSEE'S DEFAULT

§ 3318. Options of lessor following lessee's default

A. (1) In the event of default by the lessee under a true lease, or under a financed lease entered into prior to the time Chapter 9 of the Louisiana Commercial Laws [1] becomes effective, the lessor may do any one of the following:

(a) He may file an appropriate collection action against the lessee to recover accelerated rental payments and additional amounts that are then due and outstanding and that will become due in the future over the full base term of the lease, as provided under R.S. 9:3319.

(b) He may cancel the lease, recover possession of the leased property and recover such additional amounts and liquidated damages as may be contractually provided under the lease agreement, as provided under R.S. 9:3320 through 3328.

(2) The above remedies following the lessee's default are not cumulative in nature. The lessor may not seek to collect accelerated rental payments under the lease and also to cancel the lease and recover possession of the leased equipment.

B. In the event of default by the lessee under a financed lease entered into after Chapter 9 of the Louisiana Commercial Laws becomes effective, the lessor may at his option:

(1) Exercise such rights and remedies following default as are provided under this Chapter; or

(2) Exercise such rights and remedies following default as are provided under Chapter 9 of the Louisiana Commercial Laws.

Acts 1985, No. 592, § 1, eff. July 13, 1985. Amended by Acts 1989, No. 137, § 4, eff. Sept. 1, 1989.

1 R.S. 10:9–101 et seq.

Cross References

C.C. arts. 567, 2346, 2371, 2674, 2676, 2678, 2692, 2697, 2709, 2710, 2727.

§ 3319. Accelerated rental payments

A. If the lessor under either a true or financed lease elects to recover accelerated future rental payments and additional amounts that are then due and owing under the lease following the lessee's default, as provided under R.S. 9:3318(A)(1), the lessor shall commence an ordinary collection proceeding against the lessee as provided under the Louisiana Code of Civil Procedure. Any refundable security deposit held by the lessor may be retained and shall be credited against lessee's liability for accelerated rental payments. The lessor under a consumer lease shall not seek to recover full accelerated rental payments from the lessee, but shall grant the lessee an appropriate rebate of unearned interest rate charges capitalized into the lease as required under R.S. 9:3319(B).

B. If the lessor under a consumer lease elects to accelerate future rental payments following the lessee's default, the lessor shall grant the lessee an appropriate rebate of unearned interest rate charges originally capitalized into the lease. This rebate shall represent at least as great a proportion of interest rate charges, after first deducting from those charges a prepayment charge of not more than twenty-five dollars, as the sum of the monthly time balances beginning one month after the month in which payment is accelerated, bears to the sum of all monthly time balances under the schedule of payments under the lease, which method of rebate, upon acceleration, is commonly referred to as the "Rule of 78's" or the "sum of digits" rebate method. If more than one-half of the term of the lease has elapsed, the rebate shall be computed without deducting a prepayment charge. For the purposes of rebate upon acceleration, unearned deferral charges shall be rebated on the same basis as interest rate charges. Following acceleration of rental payments and the filing of suit against the lessee, any unpaid amounts due and owing by the lessee to the lessor shall bear interest at the rate of twenty-five percent per annum until paid in full.

C. If the lessee pays accelerated future rental payments to the lessor, the lessor must permit the lessee to remain in peaceable possession of the leased equipment over the remaining lease term subject to the lessor's rights under R.S. 9:3319(D).

D. If the lessee fails to satisfy a final judgment for accelerated rental payments, the lessor may at any time thereafter judicially seize and sell the lessee's possessory rights to the leased property, as provided under the Louisiana Code of Civil Procedure, in order to satisfy such a final judgment.

E. Prior to obtaining a judgment against the lessee for accelerated future rental payments, the lessor may elect to convert his claim into an action seeking to cancel the lease and to recover possession of the leased property as provided in R.S. 9:3320 through 3324.

Acts 1985, No. 592, § 1, eff. July 13, 1985.

Cross References

C.C. arts. 567, 2346, 2371, 2674, 2676, 2678, 2692, 2697, 2709, 2710, 2727.

§ 3320. Cancellation of lease following lessee's default

A. If the lessor elects to cancel the lease following the lessee's default as provided in R.S. 9:3318(A)(1)(b), the lessor shall forward a written notice to the lessee to that effect, which notice may either be personally delivered to the lessee or mailed to him by registered or certified mail at his address as shown in the lease agreement or at the address mutually agreed upon in writing by the parties, or if there is no such address, then at the lessee's last known address.

B. If the leased property has been subleased or the lease assigned by the lessee and the lessor has been notified in writing of the sublease or assignment, then all notices required under this Section shall also be sent to each known, authorized sublessee or assigned in the same manner as provided for notice to the prime lessee.

Acts 1985, No. 592, § 1, eff. July 13, 1985.

Cross References

C.C. arts. 567, 2346, 2371, 2674, 2676, 2678, 2692, 2697, 2709, 2710, 2727.

§ 3321. Surrender of leased property after notice

Within five days after receipt of the notice of cancellation or within five days after its mailing, whichever is earlier, or if the lease agreement provides for a longer period, then within such longer period, the lessee shall surrender possession of the leased property to the lessor.

Acts 1985, No. 592, § 1, eff. July 13, 1985.

Cross References

C.C. arts. 567, 2346, 2371, 2674, 2676, 2678, 2692, 2697, 2709, 2710, 2727.

§ 3322. Summary proceeding for surrender of property; rule to show cause; judgment

A. If the lessee fails or refuses to surrender the leased property to the lessor within the delays provided in R.S. 9:3321, the lessor may cause the lessee to be cited summarily by a court of competent jurisdiction to show cause why he should not be ordered to surrender possession of the leased property to the lessor, in accordance with the provisions of this Section.

B. (1) The court shall make the rule returnable within five calendar days after the date of the order, at which hearing the court shall try the rule and hear any defense that is made.

(2) When the object of the rule to show cause to surrender possession is to obtain possession of the leased movable from a lessee or sublessee in default of the lease or a third party in possession of the movable, an affidavit by the lessor or his agent shall be prima facie proof of the lessor's entitlement to the relief sought.

(3) The affidavit shall state factual grounds on which the lessee's default is based and shall be accompanied by legible copies of the lease agreement, evidence of ownership of the leased movable, and documents or exhibits which show the mover's right to possession of the leased movable.

(4) The affidavit and exhibits annexed thereto which contain facts to establish a prima facie case shall be admissible and self-authenticating.

(5) The court may, under the circumstances of the case, require additional evidence in the form of oral testimony or documentary evidence before entering judgment on the rule.

C. A hearing in open court shall not be required unless the judge, in his discretion, directs such a hearing to be held. The mover shall submit to the court the proof required by this Section, a certificate indicating the type of service made on the defendant and the date of service, and the original and not less than one copy of the proposed final judgment. The minute clerk shall make an entry showing the dates of receipt of proof, review of the record, and rendition of the judgment. A certified copy of the signed judgment shall be sent to the mover by the clerk of court.

D. If the court finds the lessor entitled to the relief sought, the court shall render immediately a judgment ordering the lessee to surrender possession of the leased property to the lessor.

E. If the lessee does not comply with the judgment within twenty-four hours after its rendition, the clerk of the court that rendered the judgment shall issue, upon written request, a writ of possession directed to and commanding the sheriff, constable, or marshal of any parish where the movable property may be located to seize and deliver possession of the leased property to the lessor.

Acts 1985, No. 592, § 1, eff. July 13, 1985. Amended by Acts 1990, No. 344, § 1.

Cross References

C.C. arts. 567, 2346, 2371, 2674, 2676, 2678, 2692, 2697, 2709, 2710, 2727.

§ 3323. Appeal from judgment on rule

A suspensive appeal shall not be granted unless the lessee has answered the rule under oath, pleading an affirmative defense entitling him to retain possession of the leased movable, and the appeal has been applied for and the appeal bond filed within twenty-four hours after the rendition of the judgment. The amount of the suspensive appeal bond shall be determined by the court in an amount sufficient to protect the appellee against all such damage as he may sustain as a result of the appeal.

Acts 1985, No. 592, § 1, eff. July 13, 1985.

Cross References

C.C. arts. 567, 2346, 2371, 2674, 2676, 2678, 2692, 2697, 2709, 2710, 2727.

§ 3324. Ordinary proceedings in addition to summary proceedings

In addition to the summary proceeding provided above, the lessor may at its option, commence an ordinary proceeding against the lessee to cancel the lease, to recover possession of the leased property or to collect such liquidated damages as may be contractually provided under the lease agreement and as further provided under R.S. 9:3325. The pendency of the summary proceeding permitted above shall not preclude the filing of such ordinary proceeding, nor shall the pendency of an ordinary proceeding preclude the filing of the summary proceeding.

Acts 1985, No. 592, § 1, eff. July 13, 1985.

Cross References

C.C. arts. 567, 2346, 2371, 2674, 2676, 2678, 2692, 2697, 2709, 2710, 2727.

§ 3325. Recovery of liquidated damages

A. The lessor may commence an ordinary proceeding against the lessee, as provided in R.S. 9:3324, to recover amounts then due and owing under the lease as well as such liquidated damages as may be provided under the lease agreement. Any refundable security deposit held by the lessor may be retained and shall be credited against the lessee's liability for liquidated damages and other amounts owed the lessor.

B. The court shall award liquidated damages to the lessor only if it finds the amount thereof to be reasonable. If the court finds the amount of liquidated damages to be unreasonable, or if there is no such stipulation, then the court may, in its discretion, award liquidated damages to the lessor.

Acts 1985, No. 592, § 1, eff. July 13, 1985. Amended by Acts 1986, No. 213, § 1.

Cross References

C.C. arts. 567, 2346, 2371, 2674, 2676, 2678, 2692, 2697, 2709, 2710, 2727.

§ 3326. Sequestration in ordinary proceedings

In an ordinary proceeding, the lessor may also have the leased movable sequestered as provided by the Louisiana Code of Civil Procedure and by furnishing security in an amount determined by the court to be sufficient to protect the lessee against all damage he may sustain.

Acts 1985, No. 592, § 1, eff. July 13, 1985.

Cross References

C.C. arts. 567, 2346, 2371, 2674, 2676, 2678, 2692, 2697, 2709, 2710, 2727.

§ 3327. Release to lessee of sequestered property

The court shall permit the release to the lessee of the sequestered leased property on the lessee's furnishing security in an amount deemed by the court sufficient to protect the rights of the lessor.

Acts 1985, No. 592, § 1, eff. July 13, 1985.

Cross References

C.C. arts. 567, 2346, 2371, 2674, 2676, 2678, 2692, 2697, 2709, 2710, 2727.

§ 3328. Release of sequestered property to lessor

If the lessee does not obtain the release of the sequestered leased property within ten days of its seizure, the court may permit its release to the lessor, without his furnishing additional security unless application for such additional security is made by the lessee and the court finds such additional security to be necessary.

Acts 1985, No. 592, § 1, eff. July 13, 1985.

Cross References

C.C. arts. 567, 2346, 2371, 2674, 2676, 2678, 2692, 2697, 2709, 2710, 2727.

§ 3329. Prohibition against self-help repossession

A. Except as provided in R.S. 9:3330, a lessor is prohibited from attempting to recover possession of the leased property following the lessee's default under any form of self-help repossession.

B. It shall be unlawful for lessors of movable property to enter into, or to cause others to enter into, the premises of any person to whom such property has been leased under the assumption that the lessee has, by agreement, given the right of entry and removal.

C. Any person guilty of entering and removing any property in violation of this Section shall be fined not more than two hundred dollars or imprisoned for not more than three months, or both. Nothing in this Section shall deprive the party injured of his civil action in damages.

D. Nothing in this Section shall be construed to prevent a seizing officer from entering and taking possession of leased property pursuant to proper legal process.

Acts 1985, No. 592, § 1, eff. July 13, 1985.

Cross References

C.C. arts. 567, 2346, 2371, 2674, 2676, 2678, 2692, 2697, 2709, 2710, 2727.

§ 3330. Lessor's right to protect and preserve leased property

A. Notwithstanding the prohibition against self-help repossession in R.S. 9:3329 and under other applicable Louisiana laws, a lessor shall have the right to take possession of leased property wherever it may be found if all of the following conditions are satisfied:

(1) The lessor has knowledge or has the reasonable belief that the lessee has breached his obligations under the lease to maintain insurance on the leased property, or to keep the leased property constantly repaired and in good working order, or to protect and preserve the leased property, or to use the leased property in a proper and lawful manner, and the leased property is then placed in a position of jeopardy of loss, damage, destruction, or seizure.

(2) The lessee is in default under his payment or nonmonetary obligations under the lease.

(3) The lessor has commenced a summary proceeding against the lessee before a court of competent jurisdiction seeking an ex parte order authorizing the lessor to proceed pursuant to this Section. The judge shall sign such an ex parte order only after the lessor has completed all of the following:

(a) Posted a bond.

(b) Executed an affidavit under oath attesting to the facts required under R.S. 9:3330(A)(1) and (A)(2).

(c) Presented to the court all documents necessary to prove that the plaintiff is the lessor and owner of the leased property. Presentation of a certified copy of the lease agreement or an extract of the lease that has been recorded in the manner provided under R.S. 9:3342, shall be sufficient proof for purposes of this Section.

B. If all conditions of R.S. 9:3330(A) are satisfied, the lessor or the lessor's agent or agents may take possession of the leased property, as well as any of the lessee's personal property contained therein or attached thereto, wherever the property may be found, provided the possession is obtained in a peaceable manner without breach of the peace.

C. A lessor who has taken possession of leased property pursuant to R.S. 9:3330(B) shall immediately give notice of the taking to the lessee at such address as specified in the lease or at the lessee's last known address, if different, by registered or certified mail, return receipt requested.

D. Within forty-eight hours after repossession of the leased property, the lessor shall deposit the property into the registry of the court through the sheriff of the parish in which suit is brought.

E. The lessee shall have twenty-one calendar days from the date of the lessor's taking possession of the leased property to reclaim any of the lessee's personal property contained therein or attached thereto.

F. Within seven calendar days following delivery of the leased property to the sheriff, the lessor shall elect between the two remedies provided in R.S. 9:3318(A).

G. If the lessor elects not to cancel the lease and to collect accelerated future rental payments and other charges due and owing under the lease, as provided under R.S. 9:3319, the sheriff shall retain possession of the leased property until such time as:

(1) The lessee satisfies his obligations in full to pay accelerated future rental payments and other amounts due and owing under the lease to the lessor, or

(2) The court shall release the leased property to the lessee on the lessee's furnishing security in an amount deemed by the court sufficient to protect the rights of the lessor.

H. If the lessor elects to cancel the lease as provided under R.S. 9:3320 through 3322, the sheriff shall retain the leased property until such time as the lessor obtains a final judgment against the lessee, as provided under R.S. 9:3322.

I. If the lessor elects to cancel the lease as provided in R.S. 9:3330(H) the lessor shall have an additional right to commence an ordinary proceeding against the lessee to recover liquidated damages and other amounts due and owing under the lease, as provided in R.S. 9:3325.

Acts 1985, No. 592, § 1, eff. July 13, 1985. Amended by Acts 1986, No. 213, § 1.

Cross References

C.C. arts. 567, 2346, 2371, 2674, 2676, 2678, 2692, 2697, 2709, 2710, 2727.

PART V. INSURANCE

§ 3331. Requirement of insurance

A. In any lease transaction made under the authority of this Chapter, including both true leases and financed leases, and whether such leases are entered into for consumer or commercial purposes, the lessor may request or require the lessee to provide credit life insurance and credit health and accident insurance as additional security for such contract or agreement.

B. The cost of such insurance, if required by the lessor in connection with a consumer purpose financed lease, shall be deemed a portion of the interest rate charge imposed under the lease for purpose of computing maximum rates under R.S. 9:3312(A).

C. More than one policy of credit life insurance or policy of health and accident insurance, or both, on any one lessee may be enforced with respect to any one contract or agreement at any time; however, the aggregate coverage of credit life insurance or credit health and accident insurance, or both, on any one lessee with respect to any one contract or agreement cannot exceed the original amount due under such lease.

Acts 1985, No. 592, § 1, eff. July 13, 1985. Amended by Acts 1986, No. 213, § 1.

Cross References

C.C. arts. 567, 2346, 2371, 2674, 2676, 2678, 2692, 2697, 2709, 2710, 2727.

§ 3332. Credit life and credit health and accident insurance

A. On all consumer lease transactions, including both consumer purpose true leases and financed leases, the premium rate for declining balance credit life insurance shall not exceed one dollar per one hundred dollars per annum. The premium rate for joint credit life insurance shall not exceed one dollar and fifty cents per one hundred dollars per annum. The premium rate for level term credit life insurance shall not exceed two dollars per one hundred dollars per annum. The premium rate for joint level term credit life insurance shall not exceed three dollars per one hundred dollars per annum. The amount of credit life insurance issued pursuant to a consumer lease transaction shall not exceed the total sum payable under the lease. Credit life insurance in the amount of the total amount payable not to exceed maximum limits for each individual otherwise provided by law, may be issued on the lives of individuals who are co-obligors with respect to that consumer lease transaction.

B. No policy of health and accident insurance may be issued pursuant to a consumer lease transaction other than seven day, fourteen day, or thirty day retroactive health and accident insurance. The premium rates for retroactive accident and health insurance issued pursuant to a consumer lease transaction shall not exceed the rate set forth in the schedule listed in R.S. 9:3542(C).

Acts 1985, No. 592, § 1, eff. July 13, 1985. Amended by Acts 1986, No. 213, § 1.

Cross References

C.C. arts. 567, 2346, 2371, 2674, 2676, 2678, 2692, 2697, 2709, 2710, 2727.

R.S. 10:9–102(b)(6).

§ 3333. Property insurance

A lessor may request or require a lessee to insure the leased property against loss, damage, destruction, and other contingencies, as well as require the lessee to obtain comprehensive liability insurance with regard to use of the leased property and the lessor's related business activities. The cost of such insurance may also be included at the lessee's option as a separate charge in a lease contract or agreement. Any insurance and the premiums or charges thereon shall bear a reasonable relationship to the amount, term, and condition of the lease contract or agreement, the existing hazards or risks of loss, damage, or destruction, and shall not provide for unusual or exceptional risks or coverages which are not ordinarily included in policies issued to the general public.

Acts 1985, No. 592, § 1, eff. July 13, 1985. Amended by Acts 1986, No. 213, § 1.

Cross References

C.C. arts. 567, 2346, 2371, 2674, 2676, 2678, 2692, 2697, 2709, 2710, 2727.

R.S. 10:9–102(b)(6).

§ 3334. Choice of insurer

A. When insurance is required in connection with a consumer lease made under this Chapter, the lessor shall furnish the lessee with a statement which clearly and conspicuously states that such insurance is required in connection with the lease, and that the lessee has the option of furnishing the required insurance either through existing policies of insurance coverage or through any insurance company authorized to transact business in Louisiana.

B. The lessee shall have the privilege at the time of execution of the lease agreement of purchasing any required insurance from an agent or broker of his own selection and of selecting an insurance company acceptable to the lessor but, in such cases, the inclusion of the insurance premium in the lease contract or agreement shall be at the option of the lessor.

Acts 1985, No. 592, § 1, eff. July 13, 1985. Amended by Acts 1986, No. 213, § 1.

Cross References

C.C. arts. 567, 2346, 2371, 2674, 2676, 2678, 2692, 2697, 2709, 2710, 2727.

R.S. 10:9–102(b)(6).

§ 3335. Limitations on insurance rates; contract requirements

A. Any insurance provided, sold, or obtained through a lessor pursuant to this Chapter shall be written at lawful rates and in accordance with the provisions of the Louisiana Insurance Code by a company authorized to do business in this state but, such insurance may be written in accordance with R.S. 22:432 through 444 if those provisions are applicable.

B. The contract or agreement must briefly indicate the kind, coverage, term, and amount of premium for the insurance.

Acts 1985, No. 592, § 1, eff. July 13, 1985.

Cross References

C.C. arts. 567, 2346, 2371, 2674, 2676, 2678, 2692, 2697, 2709, 2710, 2727.

R.S. 10:9–102(b)(6).

§ 3336. Conditions applying to insurance provided by the lessor

If a lessor under a consumer lease agrees with the lessee to obtain or provide insurance, then such insurance shall be evidenced by an individual policy or certificate of insurance delivered to the lessee, or sent to him at his address as stated by him, within forty-five days after the term of the insurance commences, or the lessor shall promptly notify the lessee of any failure or delay in providing or obtaining the insurance, individual policy, or certificate of insurance.

Acts 1985, No. 592, § 1, eff. July 13, 1985.

Cross References

C.C. arts. 567, 2346, 2371, 2674, 2676, 2678, 2692, 2697, 2709, 2710, 2727.

R.S. 10:9–102(b)(6).

§ 3337. Cancellation of insurance; refund or credit upon cancellation

A. When a consumer lease is cancelled or terminated for any reason, any credit life or credit accident and health insurance paid by the lessee and provided, sold, or obtained through the lessor in connection therewith shall be cancelled. This provision shall not apply where the lessee requests that such insurance remain in force beyond the provision of this Section.

B. When insurance paid by the lessee is cancelled or terminated for any reason, the refund for unearned insurance premiums received by the lessor shall, at the lessor's option, be applied towards payment of the premium for insurance to replace the coverage cancelled, adjusted, or terminated, or towards payment of any unpaid amounts then owing or to be owing in the future under the lease agreement. The order of applying these unearned premiums shall be inverse to the order in which rental payments under the lease agreement are payable according to their terms, beginning with rental payments due on the final due dates and not to the next ensuing rental payment or payments which shall remain payable as originally scheduled. The remaining balance of unearned insurance premiums shall be refunded to the lessee; however, no cash refund shall be required if the amount thereof is less than one dollar.

Acts 1985, No. 592, § 1, eff. July 13, 1985. Amended by Acts 1986, No. 213, § 1.

Cross References

C.C. arts. 567, 2346, 2371, 2674, 2676, 2678, 2692, 2697, 2709, 2710, 2727.

R.S. 10:9–102(b)(6).

§ 3338. Gain from insurance

Any gain, or advantage to the lessor, or any employee, officer, director, agent, general agent, affiliate or associate from such an insurance or its provisions or sale shall not be considered as a further charge nor a further interest rate or markup charge in violation of R.S. 9:3312(A) in connection with any consumer purpose financed lease made under this Chapter.

Acts 1985, No. 592, § 1, eff. July 13, 1985.

Cross References

C.C. arts. 567, 2346, 2371, 2674, 2676, 2678, 2692, 2697, 2709, 2710, 2727.

R.S. 10:9–102(b)(6).

PART VI. MISCELLANEOUS

§ 3339. Referrals

With respect to a consumer lease transaction, the lessor may not give or offer to give a rebate or discount or otherwise pay or offer to pay value to the lessee as an inducement for lease in consideration of his giving to the lessor the names of prospective purchasers or lessees, or otherwise aiding the lessor in making a sale or lease to another person, if the earning of the rebate, discount, or other value is contingent upon the person referred actually purchasing or leasing property from the lessor.

Acts 1985, No. 592, § 1, eff. July 13, 1985. Amended by Acts 1986, No. 213, § 1.

Cross References

C.C. arts. 567, 2346, 2371, 2674, 2676, 2678, 2692, 2697, 2709, 2710, 2727.

R.S. 10:9–102(b)(6).

§ 3340. Unauthorized collection practices

The unauthorized collection practices provisions of R.S. 9:3562 shall apply to consumer lease transactions subject to this Chapter.

Acts 1985, No. 592, § 1, eff. July 13, 1985.

Cross References

C.C. arts. 567, 2346, 2371, 2674, 2676, 2678, 2692, 2697, 2709, 2710, 2727.

R.S. 10:9–102(b)(6).

§ 3341. Violations

A. Unintentional violations of this Chapter by lessors shall be corrected within thirty days following receipt of written notice from the lessee or the attorney general advising of the violation. Each written notice shall specify violations of this Chapter alleged and shall be mailed, certified mail, postage prepaid, to the lessor's designated agent for service of process in this state. Any corrective action by the lessor shall include, but shall not be limited to appropriate revisions to the lease agreement and refunds of any charges in excess of those permitted under this Chapter. For purposes of this Section, unintentional violations shall include good faith errors of fact as well as of law.

B. Intentional violations of this Chapter by lessors shall constitute an unfair or deceptive trade practice subject to R.S. 51:1401 through 1418. Failure to correct an unintentional violation under R.S. 9:3341(A) within thirty days following receipt of the appropriate written notice, shall constitute an intentional violation under this Subsection.

Acts 1985, No. 592, § 1, eff. July 13, 1985.

Cross References

C.C. arts. 567, 2346, 2371, 2674, 2676, 2678, 2692, 2697, 2709, 2710, 2727.

R.S. 10:9-102(b)(6).

§ 3342. Recordation of leases of movables

A. (1) Leases of movables entered into before Chapter 9 of the Louisiana Commercial Laws becomes effective may be recorded in the manner provided under this Subsection. The lease may be recorded by either the lessor or the lessee at their option. There is no requirement that a lease, including a financed lease entered into before the effective date of Chapter 9 of the Louisiana Commercial Laws, be recorded in order to be valid and enforceable as between the lessor and the lessee or with regard to third persons.

(2) A multiple original or photostatic copy of the lease or an extract of the lease may be recorded in the conveyance records of the parish in which the leased property is or will be initially located as well as, where applicable, in the parish in which the lessee is domiciled or maintains its principal or registered office in this state as reflected in the records of the secretary of state at the time the lease is recorded.

(3) For purposes of recording an extract of the lease, such an extract shall include:

(a) The name of the lessor;

(b) The name of the lessee;

(c) The date of the lease;

(d) The base term of the lease;

(e) A brief description of the leased property; and

(f) The location or locations at which the leased property is or will be initially located or kept when not in use elsewhere as provided in the lease.

(4) The extract of the lease shall be executed by a proper officer of the lessor and need not be signed by the lessee or certified before a notary public.

(5) Recorders of conveyances may assess fees for recordation of equipment leases in the same amount as assessed in connection with the recordation of leases of immovable property. Recorders of conveyances are bound to deliver to all persons who may demand it a certificate of recorded leases still in effect which have been filed. If there are none, the certificate shall declare this fact. The cost of the certificate charged by the recorder of conveyances shall be the same as charged for mortgage certificates.

B. Leases of movables entered into after January 1, 1990, may be filed as follows:

(1) Financed leases are subject to the perfection and filing rules as provided in R.S. 10:9-101 et seq.

(2) Other than as provided in R.S. 9:3310.1, there is no requirement that the lessor under a true lease make any type of filing in order for such a true lease to be valid and enforceable as between the lessor and the lessee or with regard to third persons. Notwithstanding this fact, the lessor may at his sole option and discretion choose to file a financing statement with regard to such a true lease in the manner otherwise provided under R.S. 10:9-501 et seq.

(3) Consistent with R.S. 10:9-505, the filing of a financing statement in connection with a true lease not intended for security and not otherwise subject to Chapter 9 of the Louisiana Commercial Laws shall not of itself result in such a lease being classified as a financed lease for purposes of this Chapter or otherwise.

Acts 1985, No. 592, § 1, eff. July 13, 1985. Amended by Acts 1986, No. 213, § 1; Acts 1989, No. 137, § 4, eff. Sept. 1, 1989; Acts 2001, No. 128, § 4, eff. July 1, 2001 at 12:01 A.M.

Editor's note. Acts 2001, No. 128, § 4, effective July 1, 2001, amended R.S. 9:3342. Section 19 of Acts 2001, No. 128, declares that "it is the intent of the legislature in enacting this Act that R.S. 2736, 4501 and 4502, 4521, 4758, 4770, and 5363.1 not be expressly or impliedly repealed by this Act, but that such laws remain in effect, and, at times when so provided, be applied to secured transactions subject to Chapter 9 of the Louisiana Commercial Law as revised by this Act."

Cross References

C.C. arts. 567, 2346, 2371, 2674, 2676, 2678, 2692, 2697, 2709, 2710, 2727.

CHAPTER 3. RENTAL–PURCHASE AGREEMENTS

Section
3351. Short title.
3352. Definitions.
3353. Inapplicability of other laws; exempted transactions.
3354. General requirements of disclosure.
3355. Disclosures.
3356. Prohibited practices.
3357. Reinstatement.
3358. Receipts and accounts.
3359. Renegotiations and extensions.
3360. Advertising.
3361. Enforcement; penalties.
3362. Taxes.

§ 3351. Short title

This Chapter shall be known as and may be cited as the "Louisiana Rental–Purchase Agreement Act".

Added by Acts 1991, No. 204, § 1, eff. Jan. 1, 1992.

§ 3352. Definitions

As used in this Chapter:

(1) "Advertisement" means a commercial message in any medium that aids, promotes, or assists, directly or indirectly, a rental-purchase agreement.

(2) "Cash price" means the price at which the lessor would have sold the property to the consumer for cash on the date of the rental-purchase agreement.

(3) "Consumer" means a natural person who rents personal property under a rental-purchase agreement to be used primarily for personal, family, or household purposes.

(4) "Consummation" means the time when a consumer becomes contractually obligated on a rental-purchase agreement.

(5) "Lessor" means a person who regularly provides the use of property through rental-purchase agreements and to whom rental payments are initially payable on the face of the rental-purchase agreement.

(6) "Rental-purchase agreement" means an agreement for the use of personal property by a natural person primarily for personal, family, or household purposes for an initial period of four months or less, that is automatically renewable with each payment after the initial period, but that does not obligate or require the consumer to continue renting or using the property beyond the initial period, and that permits the consumer to become the owner of the property.

Added by Acts 1991, No. 204, § 1, eff. Jan. 1, 1992.

§ 3353. Inapplicability of other laws; exempted transactions

A. Rental-purchase agreements which comply with this Chapter shall not be governed by the laws relating to the following:

(1) A consumer credit sale as defined in R.S. 9:3516(12) of the Louisiana Consumer Credit Law.

(2) A consumer credit transaction as defined in R.S. 9:3516(13) of the Louisiana Consumer Credit Law.

(3) A consumer loan as defined in R.S. 9:3516(14) of the Louisiana Consumer Credit Law.

(4) A consumer lease as defined in R.S. 9:3306(9) of the Louisiana Lease of Movables Act.

(5) A financed lease as defined in R.S. 9:3306(12) of the Louisiana Lease of Movables Act.

(6) A true lease as defined in R.S. 9:3306(26) of the Louisiana Lease of Movables Act.

(7) A conditional sale as defined in R.S. 9:3306(7) of the Louisiana Lease of Movables Act.

(8) A lease intended for security as defined in R.S. 10:1-201(35) of the Louisiana Commercial Laws.

B. This Chapter shall not apply to the following:

(1) Rental-purchase agreements primarily for business, commercial, or agricultural purposes, or those made with governmental agencies or instrumentalities, or with organizations.

(2) A lease of a safe deposit box.

(3) A lease or bailment of personal property which is incidental to the lease of real property, and which provides that the consumer has no option to purchase the rented property.

(4) A lease of an automobile, van, or truck of less than one ton.

Added by Acts 1991, No. 204, § 1, eff. Jan. 1, 1992. Amended by Acts 2006, No. 533, § 2.

§ 3354. General requirements of disclosure

A. The lessor shall disclose to the consumer the information required by this Chapter. In a transaction involving more than one lessor, only one lessor shall make the disclosures, but all lessors shall be bound by such disclosures.

B. The disclosures shall be made at or before consummation of the rental-purchase agreement.

C. The disclosures shall be made clearly and conspicuously in writing, and a copy of the rental-purchase agreement shall be provided to the consumer. The disclosures required under R.S. 9:3355 shall be made on the face of the contract above the line for the signature of the consumer.

D. If a disclosure becomes inaccurate as the result of any act, occurrence, or agreement by the consumer after delivery of the required disclosures, the resulting inaccuracy shall not be a violation of this Chapter.

Added by Acts 1991, No. 204, § 1, eff. Jan. 1, 1992.

§ 3355. Disclosures

For each rental-purchase agreement, the lessor shall disclose in the agreement the following items, as applicable:

(1) The total number, total amount, and timing of all payments necessary to acquire ownership of the property.

(2) A statement that the consumer will not own the property until the consumer has made the total amount of payments necessary to acquire ownership.

(3) A statement that the consumer is responsible for the fair market value of the property if and as of the time that it is lost, stolen, damaged, or destroyed.

(4) A brief description of the rented property, sufficient to identify the property to the consumer and the lessor, including an identification number, if applicable, and a statement indicating whether the property is new or previously rented. However, a statement that indicates new property is previously rented shall not be a violation of this Chapter.

(5) A statement of the cash price of the property. When the agreement involves two or more items as a set, in one agreement, a statement of the aggregate cash price of all items shall satisfy this requirement.

(6) The total of initial payments paid or required at or before consummation of the agreement or delivery of the property, whichever is later.

(7) A statement that the total of payments does not include other charges, such as late payment, default, pickup, and reinstatement fees, which charges shall be separately disclosed in the contract.

(8) A statement clearly summarizing the terms of the option of the consumer to purchase, including a statement that the consumer has the right to exercise an early purchase option, and the price, formula, or method for determining the price at which the property may be so purchased.

(9) A statement identifying the party responsible for maintaining or servicing the property while it is being rented, together with a description of that responsibility, and a statement that if any part of an express warranty of a manufacturer covers the rented property at the time that the consumer acquires ownership of the property, it shall be transferred to the consumer, if allowed by the terms of the warranty.

(10) The date of the transaction and the identities of the lessor and consumer.

(11) A statement that the consumer may terminate the agreement without penalty by voluntarily surrendering or returning the property in good repair upon expiration of any rental term along with any past due rental payments.

(12) Notice of the right to reinstate an agreement as provided in R.S. 9:3357.

Added by Acts 1991, No. 204, § 1, eff. Jan. 1, 1992.

§ 3356. Prohibited practices

A rental-purchase agreement shall not contain any of the following:

(1) A confession of judgment.

(2) A negotiable instrument.

(3) A security interest or any other claim of a property interest in any goods except those goods delivered by the lessor pursuant to the rental-purchase agreement.

(4) A wage assignment.

(5) A waiver by the consumer of claims or defenses.

(6) A provision authorizing the lessor or a person acting on behalf of the lessor to enter upon the premises of the consumer without contemporaneous permission by the consumer, or to commit any breach of the peace in repossession of goods.

(7) A provision requiring the purchase of insurance or waiver of liability from the lessor for damage to or destruction or loss of the property; however, the lessor may offer to the consumer any such insurance or waiver of liability if it is clearly disclosed to be optional. Nothing in this Chapter shall be construed to prohibit the lessor from requiring the consumer to provide proof of insurance or other similar property protection for the property.

Added by Acts 1991, No. 204, § 1, eff. Jan. 1, 1992.

§ 3357. Reinstatement

A. A consumer who fails to make a timely rental payment may reinstate the agreement, within five days of the renewal date if the consumer pays monthly, or within two days of the renewal date if the consumer pays more frequently than monthly, without losing any rights or options which exist under the agreement, by the payment of all of the following:

(1) All past due rental charges.

(2) If the property has been picked up, the reasonable costs of pickup and redelivery.

(3) Any applicable late fee.

B. In the case of a consumer who has paid less than two-thirds of the total of payments necessary to acquire ownership and when the consumer has returned or voluntarily surrendered the property, other than through judicial process, during the applicable reinstatement period set forth in Subsection A of this Section, the consumer may reinstate the agreement during a period of not less than twenty-one days after the date of the return of the property.

C. In the case of a consumer who has paid two-thirds or more of the total payments necessary to acquire ownership and when the consumer has returned or voluntarily surrendered the property, other than through judicial process, during the applicable reinstatement period set forth in Subsection A of this Section, the consumer may reinstate the agreement during a period of not less than forty-five days after the date of the return of the property.

D. Nothing in this Section shall prevent a lessor from attempting to repossess property during the reinstatement period, but such a repossession shall not affect the right of the consumer to reinstatement. Upon reinstatement, the lessor shall provide the consumer with the same property or substitute property of comparable quality and condition.

Added by Acts 1991, No. 204, § 1, eff. Jan. 1, 1992.

§ 3358. Receipts and accounts

A lessor shall provide the consumer a written receipt for each payment made by cash or money order.

Added by Acts 1991, No. 204, § 1, eff. Jan. 1, 1992.

§ 3359. Renegotiations and extensions

A. A renegotiation shall occur when an existing rental-purchase agreement is satisfied and replaced by a new agreement undertaken by the same lessor and consumer. A renegotiation shall be considered a new agreement requiring new disclosures. However, events such as the following shall not be treated as renegotiations:

(1) The addition or return of property in a multiple-item agreement or the substitution of the rented property, if in either case the average payment allocable to a payment period is not changed by more than twenty-five months.

(2) A deferral or extension of one or more periodic payments, or portions of a periodic payment.

(3) A reduction in charges in the rental-purchase agreement.

(4) A rental-purchase agreement involved in a court proceeding.

B. No disclosures shall be required for any extension of a rental-purchase agreement.

Added by Acts 1991, No. 204, § 1, eff. Jan. 1, 1992.

§ 3360. Advertising

A. If an advertisement for a rental-purchase agreement refers to or states the dollar amount of any payment and the right to acquire ownership for any one specific item, the advertisement shall also clearly and conspicuously state the following items, as applicable:

(1) That the transaction advertised is a rental-purchase agreement.

(2) The total amount of payments necessary to acquire ownership.

(3) That the consumer acquires no ownership rights if the total amount necessary to acquire ownership is not paid.

B. Any owner or personnel of any medium in which an advertisement appears or through which it is disseminated shall not be liable under this Section.

C. The provisions of Subsection A of this Section shall not apply to an advertisement which does not refer to or state the amount of any payment, an advertisement on radio, or an advertisement which is published in the yellow pages of a telephone directory or in any similar directory of business.

Added by Acts 1991, No. 204, § 1, eff. Jan. 1, 1992.

§ 3361. Enforcement; penalties

Any violation of this Chapter shall constitute a prohibited practice under the Unfair Trade Practices and Consumer Protection Act, R.S. 51:1401 et seq., and shall be subject to the enforcement provisions of that Act.

Added by Acts 1991, No. 204, § 1, eff. Jan. 1, 1992.

§ 3362. Taxes

Rental-purchase agreements, as defined by R.S. 9:3352, shall be deemed to be sales for state and local tax purposes only. The tax due on such transactions shall be payable in equal monthly installments over the entire term of the rental-purchase agreement, rather than at the inception of the agreement.

Added by Acts 1991, No. 204, § 1, eff. Jan. 1, 1992.

CHAPTER 4. SALE/LEASE–BACK COMMERCIAL TRANSACTIONS

Section
3370. [Blank].
3371. Validity of sale/lease-back commercial transactions.
3372. Sale/lease-back defined.

§ 3370. [Blank]

§ 3371. Validity of sale/lease-back commercial transactions

Sale/lease-back commercial transactions involving immovable or movable property with a fair market value in excess of twenty-five thousand dollars and located within this state are hereby declared to be valid and enforceable. Such transaction shall produce and result in the legal consequences described in the written sale/lease-back agreement between the parties and shall not be presumed to be a simulation.

Added by Acts 2001, No. 866, § 1.

Editor's note. Acts 2001, No. 866, § 2, declares that "The provisions of this Act shall not invalidate sale/leaseback commercial transactions otherwise permitted by law."

§ 3372. Sale/lease-back defined

As used in this Chapter, a sale/lease-back is a commercial transaction consisting of a contemporaneous sale of property to a person who contemporaneously leases the property back to the vendor, with the original vendor-lessee retaining physical possession of the property at all times pertinent to the transaction.

Added by Acts 2001, No. 866, § 1.

Editor's note. Acts 2001, No. 866, § 2, declares that "The provisions of this Act shall not invalidate sale/leaseback commercial transactions otherwise permitted by law."

CHAPTER 5. REMOVAL AND PRESERVATION OF PROPERTY DURING EMERGENCIES AND DISASTERS [TERMINATED]

Section
3391. Terminated.

§ 3391. Terminated effective June 30, 2006

CODE TITLE X—OF RENTS AND ANNUITIES [BLANK]
CODE TITLE XI—PARTNERSHIP

CHAPTER 1. CENTRAL REGISTRY FOR CONTRACTS OF PARTNERSHIP

Section
3401. Central registry; creation.
3402. Filing.
3403. Contract of partnership; required content.
3404. Contract amendment.
3405. Registration; endorsement; issuance of certificate; effect.
3406. Recorder of mortgages; filings.
3407. Delivery in advance of effective date.
3408. Filing within five days of execution; effect.
3409. Annual report.
3410. Filing and copying fees.

§ 3401. Central registry; creation

A. The secretary of state is hereby directed to create a Central Registry for Contracts of Partnership.

B. For the purposes of Chapters 1 through 4 of this Code Title, any document required to be filed with the secretary of state shall be deemed filed when it is received either physically or electronically in any office designated by the secretary of state for the receipt of such documents.

Added by Acts 1980, No. 151, § 1, eff. Jan. 1, 1981. Amended by Acts 1999, No. 342, § 4.

Cross References

C.C. arts. 2806, 2836.

§ 3402. Filing

A. The contract of partnership or a multiple original thereof, duly executed by the partners, or a certified copy thereof, or statements submitted by foreign partnerships in accordance with R.S. 9:3421 et seq., shall be filed for registry with the secretary of state in accordance with the provisions of this Chapter to affect third persons as provided by Civil Code Articles 2806 and 2841 or when the parties choose to comply with the provisions of this Chapter.

B. (1) The secretary of state may accept any filing authorized by this Title by electronic or facsimile transmission. All electronic filings authorized by this Title shall include an electronic or digital signature.

(2) "Digital signature" means a type of electronic signature that transforms a message using an asymmetric crypt system such that a person having the initial message and the signer's public key can accurately determine:

(a) Whether the transformation was created using the private key that corresponds to the signer's public key.

(b) Whether the initial message has been altered since the transformation was made.

(3) "Electronic signature" means an electronic sound, symbol, or process attached to or logically associated with a record and executed or adopted by a person with the intent to sign the record.

C. A facsimile filing, the process of transmitting printed documents by electronic method to the secretary of state, is deemed to be properly signed when the document received by a facsimile machine in the commercial division, office of the secretary of state, purports to be a copy of the original document, and contains the signatures required by this Section.

Added by Acts 1980, No. 151, § 1, eff. Jan. 1, 1981. Amended by Acts 1999, No. 342, § 4; Acts 2001, No. 1032, § 3.

Editor's note. Acts 2001, No. 1032, § 17, declares that "Nothing contained in this Act shall be construed not prohibit, hinder, affect or alter any records or other information currently available under Title 44 of the Louisiana Revised Statutes of 1950."

Cross References

C.C. arts. 2806, 2836, 2841.

§ 3403. Contract of partnership; required content

A contract of partnership filed for registry with the secretary of state shall contain the name and taxpayer identification number of the partnership, the municipal address of its principal place of business in this state, and the name and the municipal address of each partner, including partners in commendam, if any. The failure to include the taxpayer identification number of the partnership shall not invalidate nor cause the secretary of state to reject the contract.

Added by Acts 1980, No. 151, § 1, eff. Jan. 1, 1981. Amended by Acts 1988, No. 100, § 1; Acts 1990, No. 745, § 1.

Cross References

C.C. art. 2836.

§ 3404. Contract amendment

An amendment to a contract of partnership shall be filed for registry in the same manner as an original contract of partnership. Until filed for registry, such amendment shall not be effective as to third persons. An amendment to a contract of partnership that is not registered with the secretary of state shall be accompanied by an original copy of the contract of partnership, or a certified copy, and all previous amendments.

Added by Acts 1980, No. 151, § 1, eff. Jan. 1, 1981.

Cross References

C.C. art. 2836.

§ 3405. Registration; endorsement; issuance of certificate; effect

When all fees have been paid, the secretary of state shall register the contract of partnership, or a certified copy, or the statement of a foreign partnership, in the Central Registry for Contracts of Partnership created for that purpose, endorse on all documents delivered the month, day, year, and hour of filing, and shall issue a certificate of registry certifying that the contract of partnership or statement of the foreign partnership is filed and registered. The certificate of registry shall be conclusive evidence of due registration. A contract, statement, or amendment that is duly registered is deemed registered as of the time of filing.

Added by Acts 1980, No. 151, § 1, eff. Jan. 1, 1981. Amended by Acts 1999, No. 342, § 4.

Cross References

C.C. arts. 2801 et seq., 2836.

§ 3406. Recorder of mortgages; filings

A multiple original of the contract of partnership, or a copy certified by the secretary of state, and a copy of the certificate of registry, shall be filed for registry with the recorder of mortgages of the parish in which the partnership maintains its principal place of business. Failure to file these documents with the recorder of mortgages as provided by this Section shall not affect the title of immovable property as being in the partnership or the status of a partner in commendam, or a limited partner.

Added by Acts 1980, No. 151, § 1, eff. Jan. 1, 1981.

Cross References

C.C. arts. 2801, 2805, 2836.

§ 3407. Delivery in advance of effective date

Prior to its effective date, a contract of partnership or a statement of a foreign partnership may be delivered to the secretary of state for filing and registration on any specified month, day, year, and hour on or before the thirtieth day after the day of delivery.

Added by Acts 1980, No. 151, § 1, eff. Jan. 1, 1981.

Cross References

C.C. arts. 2801, 2836.

§ 3408. Filing within five days of execution; effect

A contract of partnership or a statement of a foreign partnership filed for registry with the secretary of state within five days of execution, exclusive of legal holidays, is deemed filed for registry on the month, day, year, and hour of execution.

Added by Acts 1980, No. 151, § 1, eff. Jan. 1, 1981.

Cross References

C.C. arts. 2801, 2836.

§ 3409. Annual report

A. Each year on or before the anniversary date of registration with the secretary of state, any partner shall make and sign in the partnership name a report to the secretary of state, stating:

(1) The municipal address, which shall not be a post office box only, of its principal place of business in this state.

(2) The names and municipal addresses, which shall not be post office boxes only, for each partner.

(3) The taxpayer identification number of the partnership. The failure to include the taxpayer identification number of the partnership shall not invalidate nor cause the secretary of state to reject the report.

B. Any partnership registered with the secretary of state prior to August 15, 1997 shall file an annual report on the next anniversary date of registration.

C. The provisions of this Section shall not apply to a partnership which does not have a written agreement.

Added by Acts 1997, No. 989, § 1.

§ 3410. Filing and copying fees

A. The secretary of state shall be paid fees as provided in R.S. 49:222 in advance, for the use and benefit of the state, by every registered partnership:

(1) For filing a contract of partnership.
(2) For certified copies.
(3) For additional certificates.
(4) For filing an annual report.

B. The secretary of state shall be paid fees as provided in R.S. 49:222 in advance, for the use and benefit of the state, by every registered foreign partnership:

(1) For filing partnership registration statements and amended registration statements.
(2) For termination of registration.
(3) For filing an annual report.

Added by Acts 1997, No. 989, § 1. Amended by Acts 2001, No. 1186, § 1; Acts 2008, No. 913, § 1.

CHAPTER 2. QUALIFICATION OF FOREIGN PARTNERSHIPS

Section
3421. Foreign partnership; definition.
3422. Registration.
3423. Ownership of immovable property; limitation of liability.
3424. Service of process.
3425. Effect of registry.
3426. Amendment of statement.
3427. Termination.
3428. Annual report.

§ 3421. Foreign partnership; definition

A foreign partnership is a partnership formed under the laws of any state of the United States, country, territory, possession, province, or commonwealth, other than the state of Louisiana.

Added by Acts 1980, No. 152, § 1, eff. Jan. 1, 1981.

Cross References

C.C. arts. 2801, 2818.

§ 3422. Registration

A. (1) For a foreign partnership to enjoy the rights, privileges and juridical status of a Louisiana partnership, it must file for registry with the secretary of state in the Central Registry for Contracts of Partnership created by R.S. 9:3401 a statement containing the following information:

(a) The name and taxpayer identification number of the partnership;

(b) The jurisdiction of its formation;

(c) The designation of an agent for service of process within this state, including his name and municipal address;

(d) The name and municipal address of at least one of its general partners who gives consent under R.S. 9:3424;

(e) The municipal address of its principal place of business outside of this state;

(f) The municipal address of its principal place of business in this state. If the partnership does not have a principal place of business in this state, then the location at the municipal address of the agent for service of process is deemed to be the partnership's principal place of business in this state;

(g) Whether or not the partnership intends to own immovable property in Louisiana in the partnership name;

(h) If any of the partners are to have limited liability recognized in Louisiana; and

(i) An affidavit executed by a general partner who certifies the correctness of the information and that he has the authority to make the certification.

(2) The articles of partnership shall not be filed with the registration statement; however, by registering the partnership, the partnership agrees to furnish a true copy of its articles of partnership to the secretary of state within thirty days of his written request.

B. If material information contained in the statement was inaccurate when made or if the facts described have changed making the statement inaccurate in any material respect, the foreign partnership shall promptly file with the secretary of state an amended or supplemental statement correcting the inaccurate information.

C. Repealed by Acts 1986, No. 338, § 2.

Added by Acts 1980, No. 152, § 1, eff. Jan. 1, 1981. Amended by Acts 1986, No. 338, § 1; Acts 1990, No. 745, § 1.

Cross References

C.C. arts. 2801, 2818.

§ 3423. Ownership of immovable property; limitation of liability

To own immovable property in this state or to have the limited liability of any partners of a limited partnership recognized, a foreign partnership must be registered in accordance with R.S. 9:3422.

Added by Acts 1980, No. 152, § 1, eff. Jan. 1, 1981. Amended by Acts 1987, No. 479, § 1, eff. July 9, 1987.

Editor's note. R.S. 9:3423 and R.S. 9:3424 were amended and reenacted by Acts 1987, No. 479, § 1. Section 2 of this Act declares that its provisions are "remedial in nature and shall apply retroactively to the registration of any foreign limited partnership prior to the effective date of this Act".

Cross References

C.C. arts. 2801, 2818.

§ 3424. Service of process

A. A foreign partnership registered in accordance with R.S. 9:3422 and the general partner who certified the documents as required by R.S. 9:3422 consent to be served with process in this state through the designated agent for service of process for any purpose permitted by law.

B. Failure to maintain a designated agent for service of process shall constitute appointment of the secretary of state of this state as the designated agent for service of process. Upon receipt of service of process the secretary of state shall ascertain the domiciliary post office address of the foreign partnership, and shall send the original papers served to the foreign partnership by registered or certified mail, or by commercial courier as defined in R.S. 13:3204(D), when the person to be served is located outside of this state. The secretary of state shall retain in his office true copies of these papers, on which he shall note the date, the manner and other particulars of the service, and of the disposition made of the original papers.

Added by Acts 1980, No. 152, § 1, eff. Jan. 1, 1981. Amended by Acts 1987, No. 479, § 1, eff. July 9, 1987; Acts 1999, No. 395, § 1; Acts 2012, No. 544, § 1.

Editor's note. R.S. 9:3423 and R.S. 9:3424 were amended and reenacted by Acts 1987, No. 479, § 1. Section 2 of this Act declares that its provisions are "remedial in nature and shall apply retroactively to the registration of any foreign limited partnership prior to the effective date of this Act".

Cross References

C.C. arts. 2801, 2818.

§ 3425. Effect of registry

The organization, internal affairs, and liability of limited partners of a foreign partnership that is duly registered under this Chapter shall be governed by the laws of the state under which it is organized. A foreign partnership may not be denied registration by reason of any difference between those laws and the laws of this state.

Added by Acts 1980, No. 152, § 1, eff. Jan. 1, 1981. Amended by Acts 1995, No. 847, § 2, eff. June 27, 1995.

Cross References

C.C. arts. 2801 et seq., 2818, 2836 to 2844.

R.S. 9:3422 to 9:3424, 9:3426, 9:3427, 9:3431 et seq.

§ 3426. Amendment of statement

A foreign partnership duly registered under this Chapter shall amend its filings in this state to reflect changes in its certificate of partnership by complying with R.S. 9:3422(A). Until the registration form is filed for registry, such changes or amendments shall not be effective as to third persons.

Added by Acts 1980, No. 152, § 1, eff. Jan. 1, 1981. Amended by Acts 1986, No. 340, § 1.

Cross References

C.C. arts. 2801, 2818.

§ 3427. Termination

A duly registered foreign partnership may terminate its registration by written notification to the secretary of state by a person who certifies that he is a partner of the partnership and has the authority to terminate the registration.

Added by Acts 1980, No. 152, § 1, eff. Jan. 1, 1981.

Cross References

C.C. arts. 2801, 2818.

§ 3428. Annual report

A. Each year on or before the anniversary date of registration with the secretary of state, a partner shall make and sign in the partnership name a report to the secretary of state, stating:

(1) The municipal address of its principal place of business outside of this state.

(2) The name and municipal address, which shall not be a post office box only, of the agent for service of process within this state.

(3) The name and municipal address of the partner who has the authority of the partnership to make this report.

(4) The taxpayer identification number of the partnership.

B. Any foreign partnership registered with the secretary of state prior to August 15, 1997 shall file an annual report on the next anniversary date of registration.

C. The provisions of this Section shall not apply to a partnership which does not have a written agreement.

Added by Acts 1997, No. 989, § 1.

CHAPTER 3. REGISTERED LIMITED LIABILITY PARTNERSHIPS

Section
3431. Nature of partner's liability in ordinary partnership and in registered limited liability partnership.
3432. Registered limited liability partnerships.
3433. Name of registered limited liability partnership.
3434. Restrictions on distributions.
3435. Provisions applicable to registered limited liability partnerships.

§ 3431. Nature of partner's liability in ordinary partnership and in registered limited liability partnership

A. Notwithstanding any other provisions of law to the contrary contained in Civil Code Article 2817, a partner in a registered limited liability partnership shall not be individually liable for the liabilities and obligations of the partnership arising from errors, omissions, negligence, incompetence, malfeasance, or willful or intentional misconduct committed in the course of the partnership business by another partner or a representative of the partnership.

B. Nothing in this Section shall be construed as being in derogation of any rights which any person may have by law against a partner in a registered limited liability partnership because of any fraud practiced upon him, or because of any breach of professional duty or other negligent or wrongful act by such partner, or in derogation of any right which the registered limited liability partnership may have against any such partner because of any fraud practiced upon it by him.

C. Subsection A of this Section shall not affect the liability of a partner for his virile share of liabilities and obligations of the partnership arising from any cause other than those specified in said Subsection A.

D. Subsection A of this Section shall not affect the liability of partnership assets for partnership liabilities and obligations.

E. A partner, which by reason of Subsection A of this Section is not subject to liability, is not a proper party to a proceeding by or against a registered limited liability partnership, the object of which is to enforce the liabilities and obligations described in Subsection A of this Section.

Added by Acts 1992, No. 780, § 1, eff. July 7, 1992. Amended by Acts 1993, No. 475, § 3, eff. June 9, 1993.

§ 3432. Registered limited liability partnerships

A. To become a registered limited liability partnership, a partnership shall file with the secretary of state an application stating the name of the partnership, the address of its principal office, the number of partners, and a brief statement of the business in which the partnership engages.

B. The application shall be executed by a majority in interest of the partners or by one or more partners authorized by a majority in interest of the partners.

C. The application shall be accompanied by a fee as provided in R.S. 49:222 made payable to the secretary of state.

D. The secretary of state shall register or renew any partnership that submits a completed application with the required fee.

E. Registration is effective for one year after the date the registration is filed, unless voluntarily withdrawn by filing with the secretary of state a written withdrawal notice executed by a majority in interest of the partners or by one or more partners authorized by a majority in interest of the partners.

F. The secretary of state may provide forms for application for or renewal of registration.

Added by Acts 1992, No. 780, § 1, eff. July 7, 1992. Amended by Acts 2008, No. 913, § 1.

§ 3433. Name of registered limited liability partnership

A registered limited liability partnership's name shall contain the words "registered limited liability partnership" or the abbreviation "L.L.P." as the last words or letters of its name.

Added by Acts 1992, No. 780, § 1, eff. July 7, 1992.

§ 3434. Restrictions on distributions

A partner that is not liable under R.S. 9:3431(A) shall not be individually liable for the return of a distribution from the partnership to satisfy the liabilities and obligations described in said Subsection A except to the extent that the partner is required to return the distribution in a revocatory action brought in accordance with Chapter 12 of Title IV of Book III of the Civil Code.

Added by Acts 1993, No. 475, § 3, eff. June 9, 1993.

§ 3435. Provisions applicable to registered limited liability partnerships

A registered limited liability partnership is a partnership as defined in Article 2801 of the Civil Code, and the provisions of Title XI of Book III of the Civil Code apply to registered limited liability partnerships to the extent that they are consistent with the provisions of this Chapter. Upon lapse or termination of registration, the affected registered limited liability partnership shall continue as a partnership under Title XI of Book III of the Civil Code, but without application of this Chapter.

Added by Acts 1993, No. 475, § 3, eff. June 9, 1993.

CHAPTER 4. MERGER OR CONSOLIDATION

Section
3441. Terms defined.
3442. Merger or consolidation.
3443. Agreement of merger or consolidation.
3444. Approval of merger or consolidation.
3445. Certificate of merger or consolidation.
3446. Effects of merger or consolidation.
3447. Merger or consolidation with foreign entity.
3448 to 3499. Reserved.

§ 3441. Terms defined

As used in this Chapter, unless the context requires otherwise:

(1) "Constituent entity" means each entity that is a party to a merger or consolidation under this Chapter.

(2) "New entity" means the entity into which constituent entities consolidate, as identified in the agreement or certificate of consolidation provided for in this Chapter.

(3) "Surviving entity" means the constituent entity surviving a merger, as identified in the agreement or certificate of merger provided for in this Chapter.

Added by Acts 1992, No. 780, § 1, eff. July 7, 1992.

§ 3442. Merger or consolidation

Any one or more domestic partnerships or partnerships in commendam may merge or consolidate with or into a domestic business or nonprofit corporation, limited liability company, partnership, or partnership in commendam. Any one or more domestic limited liability companies, or businesses or nonprofit corporations, may merge or consolidate with or into a domestic partnership or partnership in commendam.

Added by Acts 1992, No. 780, § 1, eff. July 7, 1992. Amended by Acts 1995, No. 847, § 2, eff. June 27, 1995.

Cross References

C.C. arts. 2801 et seq., 2836 et seq.

R.S. 9:3441, 3443 to 3447.

§ 3443. Agreement of merger or consolidation

Each constituent entity shall enter into a written agreement of merger or consolidation. The agreement shall state:

(1) The name and state or country of organization of each partnership, partnership in commendam, corporation, or limited liability company which is a constituent entity in the merger or consolidation and the name of the surviving entity into which each other constituent entity proposes to merge or the new entities into which each constituent entity proposes to consolidate.

(2) The terms and conditions of the merger or consolidation.

(3) The manner and basis of converting the interests or shares of stock in each partnership, partnership in commendam, corporation, or limited liability company which is a constituent entity in the merger or consolidation into interests, shares, or other securities or obligations, as the case may be, of the surviving entity or the new entity, or of any other partnership, partnership in commendam, corporation, limited liability company, or other entity, or, in whole or in part, into cash or other property.

(4) In the case of a merger, such amendments to the articles or agreement of partnership or partnership in commendam, articles or certificate of incorporation, or articles of organization, as the case may be, of the surviving entity, as are desired to be effected by the merger, or that no such changes are desired.

(5) In the case of a consolidation, all of the statements required to be set forth in the articles or agreement of partnership or partnership in commendam, articles or certificate of incorporation, or articles of organization, as the case may be, of the new entity.

(6) Such other provisions relating to the proposed merger or consolidation as are deemed necessary or desirable.

Added by Acts 1992, No. 780, § 1, eff. July 7, 1992.

§ 3444. Approval of merger or consolidation

A. The agreement required by R.S. 9:3443 shall be authorized and approved in the manner provided by this Section:

(1) A domestic partnership party to a proposed merger or consolidation shall have the agreement of merger or consolidation authorized and approved by all of the partners, unless otherwise provided in the articles or agreement of partnership.

(2) A domestic partnership in commendam party to a proposed merger or consolidation shall have the agreement of merger or consolidation approved by all general partners and by the limited partners who own more than a majority of the then current percentage or other interest in the profits of the partnership in commendam owned by all of the limited partners, unless otherwise provided in the articles or agreement of limited partnership.

(3) A domestic corporation party to a proposed merger or consolidation shall have the agreement of merger or consolidation approved in the manner provided in Chapter 1 or 2 of Title 12 of the Louisiana Revised Statutes of 1950.[1]

(4) A domestic limited liability company party to a proposed merger or consolidation shall have the agreement of merger or consolidation approved in the manner provided in R.S. 12:1359.

(5) Each constituent entity formed under the laws of a jurisdiction other than this state shall have the proposed agreement of merger or consolidation approved in accordance with the laws of such other jurisdiction.

B. The fact that the agreement has been authorized and approved in accordance with this Section shall be certified on the agreement on behalf of each constituent entity:

(1) In the case of any domestic partnership or partnership in commendam, by any general partner.

(2) In the case of any domestic corporation, in the manner provided in Chapter 1 or 2 of Title 12 of the Louisiana Revised Statutes of 1950.

(3) In the case of any domestic limited liability company, in the manner provided in R.S. 12:1359.

(4) In the case of any constituent entity formed under the laws of any jurisdiction other than this state, in accordance with the laws of such other jurisdiction.

C. After the agreement is authorized and approved, unless the agreement of merger or consolidation provides otherwise, and at any time before the agreement or certificate of merger or consolidation is filed, as provided for in R.S. 9:3445, the agreement of merger or consolidation may be abandoned, subject to any contractual rights, in accordance with the procedure set forth in the agreement of merger or consolidation or, if none is set forth, as follows:

(1) By the partners of each domestic partnership or partnership in commendam that is a constituent entity, in accordance with its articles or agreement of partnership or partnership in commendam, as the case may be.

(2) By each domestic limited liability company that is a constituent entity, in the manner provided in R.S. 12:1359.

(3) By each domestic corporation that is a constituent entity, in the manner provided in Chapter 1 or 2 of Title 12 of the Louisiana Revised Statutes of 1950.

(4) By each constituent entity formed under the laws of any jurisdiction other than this state, in accordance with the laws of such other jurisdiction.

Added by Acts 1992, No. 780, § 1, eff. July 7, 1992.

[1] R.S. 12:1 et seq. or R.S. 12:201 et seq.

§ 3445. Certificate of merger or consolidation

A. After an agreement of merger or consolidation has been authorized, approved, and certified in accordance with R.S. 9:3444, the surviving or new entity shall file the agreement with the secretary of state or, in lieu thereof, the surviving or new entity shall file a certificate of merger or consolidation, duly executed, setting forth:

(1) The name and state or country of organization of each of the constituent entities.

(2) The effective date, and time if desired, of the merger or consolidation if later than the date of filing of the certificate of merger or consolidation.

(3) That an agreement of merger or consolidation has been authorized and approved by each of the constituent entities in accordance with R.S. 9:3444.

(4) The name of the surviving or new entity.

(5) In the case of a merger, such amendments or changes to the certificate, articles or agreement of partnership, partnership in commendam, or limited partnership, articles or certificate of incorporation, or articles of organization, as the case may be, of the surviving entity, as are desired to be effected by the merger, or, if no such amendments or changes are desired, a statement that the certificate, articles or agreement of partnership, partnership in commendam, or limited partnership, articles or certificate of incorporation, or articles of organization, as the case may be, of the surviving entity, shall be its certificate, articles or agreement of partnership, partnership in commendam, or limited partnership, articles or certificate of incorporation, or articles of organization, as the case may be.

(6) In the case of a consolidation, that the certificate, articles or agreement of partnership, partnership in commendam, or limited partnership, articles or certificate of incorporation, or articles of organization, as the case may be, of the new entity shall be as set forth in an attachment to the certificate.

(7) That the executed agreement of merger or consolidation is on file at the principal place of business of the surviving or new entity, stating the address thereof.

(8) That a copy of the agreement of merger or consolidation will be furnished by the surviving or new entity, on request and without cost, to any partner, shareholder, or member of any entity that is a party to the merger or consolidation.

B. (1) The secretary of state, after all taxes, fees, and charges have been paid as required by law, shall record the agreement, or certificate in lieu thereof, in his office, endorse thereon the date and, if requested, the hour of filing thereof with him, and issue a certificate of merger or consolidation, which shall recite the names of all of the merging and consolidating constituent entities, the name of the state or country under the laws of which each was formed, whether a merger or consolidation is involved, the name of the surviving or new entity, the name of the state or country under the laws of which the new entity is formed, the date, and, if endorsed on the agreement or certificate, the hour of filing of the agreement or certificate with him, and the effective date and time of the merger or consolidation, if stated in the agreement or certificate.

(2) The agreement or certificate may be delivered to the secretary of state in advance for filing as of any specified date and, if specified upon such delivery, as of any given time on such date, within thirty days after the date of delivery. A duplicate original of the certificate of merger or consolidation issued by the secretary of state shall, within thirty days after issuance of the certificate, be filed for record in the conveyance records of each parish in this state in which any of the constituent entities has immovable property, title to which will be transferred as a result of the merger or consolidation.

C. A merger or consolidation shall be effective when the agreement or certificate of merger or consolidation has been recorded by the secretary of state and when the requirements for effectiveness of the laws under which any constituent entity was formed have been met, as of the time of filing of the agreement or certificate with the secretary of state. However, if the agreement or certificate was filed within five days, exclusive of legal holidays, after acknowledgment thereof, the merger or consolidation shall be effective as of the time of such acknowledgment, and the merger or consolidation may be made effective as of any later effective date and time if desired, not later than thirty days after the date of such filing, stated in the agreement or certificate of merger or consolidation.

Added by Acts 1992, No. 780, § 1, eff. July 7, 1992. Amended by Acts 1993, No. 475, § 3, eff. June 9, 1993.

§ 3446. Effects of merger or consolidation

A. Consummation of a merger or consolidation has the effects provided in this Section:

(1) The constituent entities party to the agreement of merger or consolidation shall be a single entity which, in the case of a merger, shall be the entity designated in the agreement of merger as the surviving entity and, in the case of a consolidation, shall be the new entity provided for in the agreement of consolidation.

(2) The separate existence of each constituent entity, except the surviving entity or the new entity, shall cease.

(3) The surviving or new entity shall thereupon and thereafter possess all the rights, privileges, immunities, powers, and franchises possessed by each of the constituent entities and shall be subject to all the restrictions, disabilities, and duties of each of such constituent entities to the extent such rights, privileges, immunities, powers, franchises, restrictions, disabilities, and duties are applicable to the form of existence of the surviving entity or the new entity.

(4) All of the property and assets of whatsoever kind or description of each of the constituent entities, and all debts due on whatever account to any of them, including subscriptions for shares, promises to make capital contributions, and all other choses in action, belonging to any of them, shall be taken and be deemed to be transferred to and vested in the surviving or new entity without further act or deed.

(5) The title to all immovables and any interest therein vested in any such constituent entity shall not revert or be in any way impaired by reason of such merger or consolidation.

(6) The surviving or new entity shall thenceforth be responsible and liable for all liabilities and obligations of each of the constituent entities so merged or consolidated. Any claim existing or action or proceeding pending by or against any such constituent entity may be prosecuted as if such merger or consolidation had not taken place, or the surviving or new entity may be substituted in the action.

(7) Neither the rights of creditors nor any liens on the property of any constituent entity shall be impaired by the merger or consolidation.

(8) In the case of a merger, the certificate, articles or agreement of partnership, partnership in commendam, or limited partnership, articles or certificate of incorporation, or articles of organization, as the case may be, of the surviving entity shall be amended to the extent provided in the certificate of merger.

(9) In the case of a consolidation, the statements set forth in the certificate of consolidation and which are required or permitted to be set forth in the certificate, articles or agreement of partnership, partnership in commendam, or limited partnership, articles or certificate of incorporation, or articles of organization, as the case may be, of the new entity shall be deemed to be the original certificate, articles or agreement of partnership, partnership in commendam, or limited partnership, articles or certificate of incorporation, or articles of organization, as the case may be, of the new entity.

(10) The interests in a partnership, partnership in commendam, or limited partnership, shares or other interests in a corporation, or membership interests in a limited liability company that is a constituent entity, as the case may be, that are to be converted or exchanged into interests, shares, or other securities, cash, obligations, or other property under the terms of the agreement of merger or consolidation shall be so converted. The former holders thereof shall be entitled only to the rights provided in the agreement of merger or consolidation or the rights otherwise provided by law.

B. Nothing in this Chapter shall abridge or impair any dissenter's or appraisal rights that may otherwise be available to the members or shareholders or other holders of an interest in any constituent entity.

Added by Acts 1992, No. 780, § 1, eff. July 7, 1992.

§ 3447. Merger or consolidation with foreign entity

A. Any one or more domestic partnerships or partnerships in commendam may merge or consolidate with or into a foreign partnership, limited partnership, limited liability company, or corporation, and any one or more foreign partnerships, limited partnerships, limited liability companies, or corporations may merge or consolidate with or into a domestic partnership or partnership in commendam, if:

(1) The merger or consolidation is permitted by the law of the state or country under whose laws each foreign constituent entity is organized or formed, and each foreign constituent entity complies with that law in effecting the merger or consolidation.

(2) The foreign constituent entity complies with R.S. 9:3445 if it is the surviving entity or the new entity.

(3) Each domestic partnership and partnership in commendam complies with the applicable provisions of R.S. 9:3443 and 3444, and if it is the surviving entity or the new entity complies with R.S. 9:3445.

B. If the surviving entity or new entity is to be governed by the laws of any state other than this state or of a foreign country, then, upon the effectiveness of a merger or consolidation, the surviving entity or new entity shall be subject to service of process in this state in any proceeding for enforcement of any obligation of any constituent entity party to the merger or consolidation that was organized under the laws of this state and for enforcement of any obligation of the surviving entity or new entity arising from the merger or consolidation.

C. The effect of such merger or consolidation shall be as provided in R.S. 9:3446, if the surviving entity or new entity is to be governed by the laws of this state. If the surviving entity or new entity is to be governed by the laws of any jurisdiction other than this state, the effect of such merger or consolidation shall be the same as provided in R.S. 9:3446 except insofar as the laws of such other jurisdiction provide otherwise.

Added by Acts 1992, No. 780, § 1, eff. July 7, 1992. Amended by Acts 1995, No. 847, § 2, eff. June 27, 1995.

Cross References

C.C. arts. 2801 et seq., 2836 et seq.

R.S. 9:3441 to 9:3446.

§§ 3448 to 3499. **Reserved for future legislation**

CODE TITLE XII—OF LOAN

CHAPTER 1. INTEREST

Editor's note. Chapter 9 of the Louisiana Commercial Laws was revised by Acts 2001, No. 128, § 1, effective July 1, 2001, to consist of R.S. 10:9–101 through 10:9–710. This Chapter does not apply to statutory liens and privileges except as expressly provided therein. R.S. 10:9–322(h) provides: "A security interest has priority over a conflicting lien, other than an agricultural lien, in the same collateral except as otherwise provided in this Chapter or except to the extent the lien is created by a statute that expressly provides that the lien has priority over the security interest." The accompanying revision comment states: "For example, see R.S. 9:4501, 9:4502, 9:4521, 9:4758, 9:4870, and 9:48888, each of which provides that certain privileges have priority over certain security interests. See also 9:5001 and 37:218.".

PART I. IN GENERAL

Section
3500. Rates of legal and conventional interest; usury.
3501. Forfeiture of interest.
3502. Statement of policy.
3503. Maximum rate of conventional interest on certain loans.
3504. Certain types of transactions exempt from the application of the laws on usury and interest upon interest; adjustable rate mortgage loan.
3505. Items or charges not considered interest.
3506. Application.
3506.1. Time for accrual of interest; penalties.
3506.2. Repealed.
3507. Maximum interest rate on assessments for public improvements on benefited properties.
3508. Federal Housing Administration insured obligations; interest clause; enforceability.
3509. Rate of interest paid for commercial, business, or agricultural loans; rate upon default.
3509.1. Adjustable rate loans for commercial, business, or agricultural purposes.
3509.2. Interest upon accrued interest; exceptions.
3509.3. Prepayment of loan.
3509.4. Deferment of loan payments during declared disaster.

PART I. IN GENERAL

§ 3500. Rates of legal and conventional interest; usury

A. Interest is either legal or conventional.

B. Legal interest is fixed at the following rates, to wit:

(1) At the rate fixed in R.S. 13:4202 on all sums which are the object of a judicial demand, whence this is called judicial interest; and

(2) On sums discounted at banks at the rate established by their charters.

C. (1) The amount of the conventional interest cannot exceed twelve percent per annum. The same must be fixed in writing; testimonial proof of it is not admitted in any case.

(2) Except in the cases herein provided, if any person shall pay on any contract a higher rate of interest than the above, as discount or otherwise, the same may be sued for and recovered within two years from the time of such payment.

(3)(a) The owner or discounter of any note or bond or other written evidence of debt for the payment of money, payable to order or bearer or by assignment, shall have the right to claim and recover the full amount of such note, bond, or other written evidence of debt and all interest not beyond twelve percent per annum interest that may accrue thereon, notwithstanding that the rate of interest or discount at which the same may be or may have been discounted has been beyond the rate of twelve percent per annum interest or discount.

(b) This provision shall not apply to the banking institutions of this state in operation under existing laws or to a consumer credit transaction as defined by the Louisiana Consumer Credit Law.

(4)(a) The owner of any promissory note, bond, or other written evidence of debt for the payment of money to order or bearer or transferable by assignment shall have the right to collect the whole amount of such promissory note, bond, or other written evidence of debt for the payment of money, notwithstanding such promissory note, bond, or other written evidence of debt for the payment of money may include a greater rate of interest or discount than twelve percent per annum; such obligation shall not bear more than twelve percent per annum after maturity until paid.

(b) This provision shall not apply to a consumer credit transaction as defined by the Louisiana Consumer Credit Law.

(c) Where usury is a defense to a suit on a promissory note or other contract of similar character, it is permissible for the defendant to show the usury whether same was given by way of discount or otherwise, by any competent evidence.

D. The provisions of this Article shall not apply to a loan made for commercial or business purposes or deferring payment of an obligation for commercial or business purposes.

C.C. art. 2924. Amended by Acts 1908, No. 68, § 1; Acts 1970, No. 315, § 1; Acts 1972, No. 454, § 9, eff. Jan. 1, 1973; Acts 1980, No. 402, § 2; Acts 1981, No. 574, § 1; Acts 1981, No. 639, § 1; Acts 1982, No. 142, § 1, eff. July 12, 1982; Acts 1984, No. 458, § 1; Acts 1987, No. 883, § 1; Acts 1989, No. 52, § 1; Acts 1989, No. 774, § 1, eff. July 9, 1989; Acts 1992, No. 1090, § 1, eff. Oct. 1, 1992; Acts 1997, No. 275, § 1, eff. June 17, 1997; Acts 1997, No. 1476, § 2, eff. Sept. 6, 1998. Redesignated from C.C. art. 2924 by Acts 2004, No. 743, § 2, eff. Jan. 1, 2005.

Editor's note. Section 2 of Acts 2004, No. 743, declares that the transfer of Article 2924 of the Louisiana Civil Code to Title 9 of the Revised Statutes and its redesignation as R.S. 9:3500, "is neither an amendment to nor a reenactment of Civil Code Article 2924."

Cross References

C.C. arts. 2000, 2001, 2553, 2922, 2923, 3005, 3014.

C.C.P. art. 1921.

R.S. 3:3414.2, 6:25, 6:242, 6:289, 6:654, 9:170, 9:2782, 9:3501 to 9:3509, 9:3510 to 9:3524, 9:3525 to 9:3536, 9:3538 to 9:3565, 13:4202, 13:5112, 22:936, 23:891, 28:844.1, 30:2025, 33:2718, 33:2740.20, 33:3306, 33:3689.7, 33:3827, 33:3986, 33:4066.11, 33:4160.6, 33:4752, 33:4754, 33:4755.4, 33:4766, 37:780, 39:681, 39:1695, 40:1502.1, 40:1502.3 to 40:1502.9, 46:442, 47:115, 47:120.3, 47:287.657, 47:350, 47:617, 47:1576, 47:1624, 47:2437, 51:1401 to 51:1418.

§ 3501. Forfeiture of interest

Any contract for the payment of interest in excess of that authorized by law shall result in the forfeiture of the entire interest so contracted.

Cross References

C.C. art. 2924.

§ 3502. Statement of policy

It is declared to be the public policy of this state to encourage the free flow of money into Louisiana; to allow this state to compete in the national money market; to promote and stimulate residential construction and to allow those retirement systems who desire it to continue to invest in first mortgage loans.

Added by Acts 1969, No. 28, § 1.

Cross References

C.C. art. 2924.

§ 3503. Maximum rate of conventional interest on certain loans

Unless otherwise provided, the amount of simple conventional interest on obligations bearing interest from date and secured in whole or in part, directly or indirectly, by a mortgage on immovable property, shall not exceed twelve percent per annum. The same must be fixed in writing. Testimonial proof of it is not admitted in any case.

Added by Acts 1969, No. 28, § 2. Amended by Acts 1979, No. 205, § 1, eff. July 6, 1979; Acts 1995, No. 1184, § 2.

Cross References

C.C. art. 2924.

§ 3504. Certain types of transactions exempt from the application of the laws on usury and interest upon interest; adjustable rate mortgage loan

A. Notwithstanding any other law to the contrary, particularly but not exclusively R.S. 9:3500, an obligation secured directly or indirectly, in whole or in part, by a mortgage on immovable property and guaranteed by the Veterans Administration pursuant to the provisions of Public Law 85–857,[1] including any amendments or supplements thereto, or insured by the Federal Housing Administration pursuant to the provisions of Subchapter II of Chapter 13 of Title 12 of the United States Code,[2] including any amendments or supplements thereto, may bear such rate of interest or be discounted at such rate as the parties may agree upon in writing within the maximum limitations permitted under the regulations promulgated from time to time by the Federal Housing Administration or the Veterans Administration. The interest rate may be in excess of the maximum rate of conventional interest authorized by law, and as to any such obligation, the claim or defense of usury, or of the taking of interest in excess of the maximum rate of conventional interest, by the obligor or by any guarantor or endorser of the obligation, is prohibited.

B. Notwithstanding any other law to the contrary, particularly but not exclusively Article 1939[3] of the Louisiana Civil Code and R.S. 9:3500, an obligation secured directly or indirectly, in whole or in part, by a mortgage on immovable property of the form commonly known as a "wrap-around" mortgage shall be exempt from the application of the laws on usury and interest upon interest if the nominal interest of the wrap-around mortgage is not greater than the rate of interest lawfully allowed in a conventional mortgage. For the purposes of this Subsection, the following definitions shall apply:

(1) "Wrap-around mortgage" means any second or lower ranked mortgage that (a) has a face amount that represents not only sums of money advanced by the wrap-around mortgagee but also outstanding balances on mortgages ranked higher than the wrap-around mortgage with respect to the immovable property subject to the wrap-around mortgage, or (b) incorporates provisions for the debt servicing and any other matters relating to the higher ranked mortgages which unpaid balances and charges are represented in the face amount of the wrap-around mortgage.

(2) "Nominal interest" is the interest rate applied to the face amount of the wrap-around mortgage.

C. Notwithstanding any other law to the contrary, particularly but not exclusively Civil Code Art. 1939 and R.S. 9:3500, an obligation secured directly or indirectly, in whole or in part, by a mortgage on immovable property of the form commonly known as "graduated payment" mortgage shall be exempt from the application of the laws on usury and interest upon interest if the nominal interest of the graduated payment mortgage is not greater than the rate of interest lawfully allowed in a conventional mortgage and if the unpaid principal balance does not increase as a result of the addition of deferred interest, exclusive of taxes, insurance, and other nonfinance charges that might be added to the unpaid balance, to an amount greater than one hundred fifty percent of the original face amount of the note and the mortgage. For the purposes of this Subsection, the following definitions shall apply:

(1) "Graduated payment mortgage" means a mortgage which provides for the amortization of the loan by periodic payments which increase one or more times during the term of the mortgage and which provides for the deferring of interest by adding accrued but unpaid interest to the unpaid principal balance.

(2) "Nominal interest" means the interest rate applied to the unpaid principal balance of the graduated payment mortgage.

D. To further promote the objectives of R.S. 9:3502, to encourage the flow of money into Louisiana for homebuilding, home financing, real estate financing, and business development and to assist the citizens of Louisiana in obtaining needed financing at affordable terms and cost, adjustable rate mortgage loans are authorized in accordance with the following terms:

(1) An adjustable rate mortgage loan is any loan of money, credit sale, or extension of credit which provides that the rate of simple interest charged on the unpaid balance may be adjusted from time to time during the term of the loan in accordance with the method of adjustment set forth in the promissory note or other documents evidencing the loan, and which is secured, in whole or in part, directly or indirectly, by a mortgage on leasehold improvements, a mobile home, residential mobile home, or immovable property located in this state.

(2) When the adjustable rate mortgage loan is made for the purpose of financing or refinancing a mobile home, residential mobile home or a one-to-four family dwelling and when applicable to the transaction, either the promissory note or other evidence of the loan shall set forth the following:

(a) The contractual index formula or other basis agreed upon, and any alternate or substitute therefor, upon which changes in the simple interest rate will be based.

(b) The frequency of allowable interest rate adjustments.

(c) Any contractual limitations on interest rate adjustments, such as maximum or minimum interest rates.

(d) The manner and method by which the unpaid balance and, if the loan is to be repaid in installments, the manner and method by which installments will be adjusted periodically to reflect adjustments in the interest rate and the effect, if any, on the number of installments or maturity date of the loan.

(e) The agreement of the parties as to the method by which any changes in the contractual index which are not reflected in a rate adjustment may be carried over to subsequent rate adjustment periods, and be implemented to the extent not offset by opposite movement in the index.

(3) Adjustments in the interest rate shall be based upon changes in the contractual index formula or other basis agreed upon as set forth in either the promissory note or other evidence of the loan. While the parties may agree that the increases in the interest rate caused by increases in the contractual index formula will be made at the option of the lender, notwithstanding any agreement to the contrary, decreases in the interest rate caused by decreases in the contractual index formula shall be implemented at the succeeding adjustment date; provided that no increase or decrease shall be made which would affect any contractual limitations on interest rate adjustments including maximum or minimum interest rates to which the parties have agreed. The parties may agree to use as an index any measurement of interest rates described in either the promissory note or other evidence of the loan, including, but not limited to, the prime or base lending rate of any national or state bank as fixed from time to time by its board of directors or management; the federal reserve discount rate in effect from time to time at any federal reserve bank; the average yield to maturity on United States Treasury obligations of any stipulated terms; or any standard or measurement which may be authorized or permitted in any regulation or statute, or both, for residential mortgage loans by the Federal Home Loan Bank Board or by the Office of the Comptroller of the Currency, Department of the Treasury, or any other federal department, agency, or board.

(4) The provisions of a promissory note evidencing an adjustable rate mortgage loan meeting the requirements of this Subsection shall not impair or destroy the negotiability of the promissory note, nor shall such provisions be deemed potestative conditions.

(5) An adjustable rate mortgage loan shall rank from the date the mortgage is recorded as required by statute, and the priority of the mortgage and all amounts secured thereby shall not be affected by adjustments in the interest rate, or by the effects of such adjustments.

(6) Proof of changes in the interest rate may be made by affidavit of the lender or the holder of the promissory note or other evidence of the loan, or by any officer, partner, or employee of the lender or the holder, if the lender or the holder is not a natural person. Any such affidavit may refer to the contents of an official government publication. In the event of foreclosure by executory process of an adjustable rate mortgage loan, such affidavit shall be authentic evidence of the facts recited therein. Whenever appropriate, proof may also be made by corporate resolution, or by other written instrument. The taking of testimony concerning the content of any affidavit, official government publication, corporate resolution, or other written instrument shall be permitted and shall not be considered a violation of the provisions of R.S. 9:3500 or 9:3503 relative to the taking of testimonial proof of the rate of interest.

(7) The provisions of Louisiana Civil Code Art. 1939 shall not apply to adjustable rate loans.

(8) Except as otherwise provided in either the promissory note or other evidence of the loan, upon the filing of suit for payment of an adjustable rate mortgage loan, the interest rate in effect on the date suit is filed shall be fixed as the interest rate on the loan thereafter and no further adjustment in the rate shall be made; provided that, if the loan is thereafter reinstated, the interest rate may thereafter be adjusted as if no judicial demand had been made.

(9) Nothing herein shall be construed as impairing the validity or enforceability of adjustable rate loans made prior to the effective date hereof. All adjustable rate loans made prior to the effective date of this Act which are not otherwise specifically prohibited by law shall be valid and enforceable.

(10) Except as otherwise provided herein, the provisions of this Subsection shall only be applicable to the types of mortgage loan transactions defined in Paragraph (1) of this Subsection, including, but not limited to, loan transactions made pursuant to the Louisiana Consumer Credit Law R.S. 9:3510, et seq. and the Louisiana Motor Vehicle Sales Finance Act R.S. 6:951, et seq.

E. Notwithstanding any law to the contrary, particularly but not exclusively R.S. 9:3500, an obligation secured by a mortgage on immovable property where the mortgagee is the former owner of said property, may bear such rate of interest or be discounted at such rate as the parties may agree upon in writing within the maximum limitations permitted to be charged by federally insured financial institutions under federal law or regulation. The interest rate may be in excess of the maximum rate of conventional interest authorized by law, and as to any such obligation, the claim or defense of usury, or the taking of interest in excess of the maximum rate of conventional interest, by the obligor or by any guarantor or endorser of the obligation, is prohibited. However, in no instance shall the interest rate exceed seventeen percent.

Added by Acts 1969, No. 28, § 3. Amended by Acts 1978, No. 621, § 1; Acts 1979, No. 764, § 1; Acts 1982, No. 261, § 1; Acts 1982, No. 424, § 1, eff. July 21, 1982; Acts 1982, No. 767, § 1; Acts 1985, No. 984, § 1.

[1] 38 U.S.C.A. § 101 et seq.
[2] 12 U.S.C.A. § 1707 et seq.
[3] For subject matter of former C.C. art. 1939, see, now, C.C. art. 2001.

Cross References

C.C. arts. 1939, 2001, 2924.

§ 3505. Items or charges not considered interest

Notwithstanding any other law to the contrary, particularly but not exclusively R.S. 9:3500, and in addition to those fees, charges, costs and expenses ordinarily not considered interest and not included in the calculation of interest, the following charges, fees, costs and expenses shall not be considered interest on any conventional obligation covered by R.S. 9:3502–9:3506:

(1) Charges for the pre-payment of the loan, or any installment or part thereof, prior to the time fixed for the payment of same;

(2) Charges assessed because of the nonpayment of the loan or any installment or part thereof after said loan or any installment of principal or interest thereof has become delinquent and is not timely paid, including cost of collecting and a reasonable attorney's fee, provided that such charges or the methods of fixing same are provided in writing in either the note or the mortgage securing same;

(3) Brokerage fees, discount fees, service fees, origination fees, commitment fees, warehousing fees, lender's fees, or other similar fees or charges paid by anyone on a loan secured directly or indirectly, in whole or in part, by a mortgage on immovable property;

(4) Fees or charges paid by the borrower to a mortgage broker or agent retained by the borrower to obtain a loan for the borrower from a lender, even though the loan may be closed in the name of such mortgage agent or broker;

(5) Fees, taxes, charges and other expenses incurred in making the loan which are collected from or paid by the borrower or on his behalf, if such fees, taxes, charges and other expenses are actually paid to or are payable to persons other than the lender or the person making the loan or any employee of such lender or person making the loan;

(6) Charges or premiums for credit life insurance actually written on the life of any borrower or endorser;

(7) The listing herein of certain fees and charges shall not be construed as exclusive, but shall be in addition to any fees, charges, costs and expenses not ordinarily considered interest.

Added by Acts 1969, No. 28, § 4.

Cross References

C.C. art. 2924.

§ 3506. Application

The provisions of R.S. 9:3502–9:3506 shall apply only to conventional obligations bearing simple interest from date on the unpaid balance and shall not apply to or affect precomputed interest or discount loans; nor shall it affect the enforceability or collectibility of notes or obligations as provided in R.S. 9:3500. Notwithstanding the twelve percent simple interest rate limitations under R.S. 9:3503, the provisions of R.S. 9:3504 and 3505 shall apply to federally related mortgage loans subject to 12 U.S.C. § 1735f–5 that bear simple interest at rates in excess of twelve percent per annum.

Added by Acts 1969, No. 28, § 5. Amended by Acts 1986, No. 584, § 2, eff. July 2, 1986.

Cross References

C.C. art. 2924.

§ 3506.1. Time for accrual of interest; penalties

A. Notwithstanding the provisions of R.S. 9:3506 or any other law to the contrary, interest on the principal obligation of a promissory note, evidencing a closed-end loan secured by a mortgage on immovable property, including any improvements thereon, shall not commence to accrue prior to the date upon which the loan proceeds have been made available for disbursement. In such case, when funds are to be disbursed to or for the account of a vendor, borrower, or purchaser, the lending institution shall make the loan proceeds available to the notary public or licensed title company for disbursement at the time of execution of the act of sale or act of mortgage.

B. The provisions of Subsection A of this Section shall not apply (a) if the loan proceeds are paid or made available, as the case may be, in cash or by check, cashier's check, share draft, traveler's check, or money order issued by, or drawn on, a financial institution, the accounts of which are insured by an agency or instrumentality of the United States, and which has an office in this state from which payment shall be obtained, or (b) if the notary public or licensed title company fails to comply with the lending institution's written closing instructions. The provisions of Subsection A of this Section also shall not apply to open-end lines of credit, including without limitation, revolving loan accounts, subject to the Louisiana Consumer Credit Law.

C. The provisions of Subsection A of this Section shall not apply to any transaction in which a right of rescission applies pursuant to the provisions of Regulation Z, specifically 12 CFR Section 226.15 and 12 CFR Section 226.23, issued pursuant to the Truth in Lending Act, 15 U.S.C. 1601 et seq.

D. If a lending institution fails to comply with the provisions of Subsection A of this Section, the offending lending institution shall, upon written demand of the borrower, vendor, or purchaser, pay a penalty of one thousand dollars to the borrower, vendor, or purchaser. If a lending institution fails to comply with the provisions of this Subsection within thirty days after receipt of the written demand, the lending institution shall be liable for reasonable attorney fees for the prosecution of the borrower's, vendor's, or purchaser's claim, either amicably or in a judicial proceeding. In the event that a lending institution is liable for the payment of any penalties or attorney fees due to the failure of the notary public or licensed title company to comply with the lending institution's written closing instructions, the notary public or licensed title company shall be liable for any penalties or attorney fees which may be owed to the vendor, borrower, or purchaser.

Added by Acts 1986, No. 972, § 1. Amended by Acts 1987, No. 806, § 1; Acts 1995, No. 674, § 1; Acts 1995, No. 1184, § 2.

Cross References

C.C. arts. 1866, 2000, 2001, 2553, 2923, 2924.

§ 3506.2. Repealed by Acts 1993, No. 458, § 2, eff. July 1, 1993

§ 3507. Maximum interest rate on assessments for public improvements on benefited properties

A. It is the intent and purpose of the legislature in enacting this law to authorize governing bodies of political subdivisions, as herein defined, to provide that local or special assessments for public improvements imposed on benefited properties under laws enacted under authority of Article VI, Section 36 of the Louisiana Constitution of 1974 or prior constitutional provisions, or imposed on benefited properties under the provisions of a home rule charter, may bear such rates of interest as the governing body of such political subdivision may determine, and to provide for the manner and circumstances under which such authority may be exercised.

B. As used in this Section, the words "political subdivision" shall mean parishes, municipalities and other political subdivisions or public corporations, such as, but not limited to sewerage and sub-sewerage districts, waterworks and sub-waterworks districts, and drainage and sub-drainage districts.

C. Any political subdivision authorized to impose local or special assessments on benefited properties under laws enacted under the authority of Article VI, Section 36 of the Constitution of the State of Louisiana of 1974 or prior constitutional provisions, or imposed on benefited properties under the provisions of a home rule charter may, in accordance with the procedure and subject to the limitations provided in the constitution or law or home rule charter authorizing the imposition of such assessments, provide that the maximum interest rate such assessments shall bear shall be the maximum interest rate set forth in the ordinance or instrument levying such assessments or in any ordinance or instrument amendatory thereto, notwithstanding that such law or home rule charter may provide for a lower maximum rate of interest.

D. The right, power and authority conferred herein shall be in addition to any other right, power and authority now conferred upon political subdivisions with reference to the imposition of local or special assessments.

Added by Acts 1970, No. 278, §§ 1 to 4, emerg. eff. July 13, 1970, at 2:36 P.M. Amended by Acts 1976, No. 633, § 1, eff. Aug. 4, 1976; Acts 1980, No. 217, § 1, eff. July 11, 1980.

Cross References

C.C. art. 2924.

§ 3508. Federal Housing Administration insured obligations; interest clause; enforceability

A clause requiring the payment of interest in any obligation secured directly or indirectly, in whole or in part, by a mortgage on immovable property insured by the Federal Housing Administration pursuant to the provisions of Section 245 of the National Housing Act (including any amendments or supplements thereto), or although eligible to be insured by the Federal Housing Administration pursuant to Section 245 of the National Housing Act (including any amendments thereto), but such insurance therefor has been denied by the Federal Housing Administration for reasons other than the rate of interest charged or the manner of collecting such interest, shall be fully enforceable notwithstanding any other law to the contrary.

Added by Acts 1979, No. 582, § 1.

Cross References

C.C. art. 2924. .

§ 3509. Rate of interest paid for commercial, business, or agricultural loans; rate upon default

A. Notwithstanding any other provisions of the law of this state to the contrary, any debtor that is a domestic corporation, a limited liability company formed pursuant to the laws of this or any other state, a foreign corporation, a partnership in commendam formed pursuant to the laws of this state, a registered limited liability partnership formed pursuant to the laws of this or any other state, a foreign limited partnership, or a partnership in which all of the partners are either corporations, limited liability companies formed pursuant to the laws of this or any other state, foreign limited partnerships, partnerships in commendam, or partnerships comprised of corporations, foreign limited partnerships, or partnerships in commendam, or registered limited liability partnerships formed pursuant to the laws of this or any other state, or ordinary partnership or any other person or individual borrowing funds for commercial, business, or agricultural purposes or deferring payment of an obligation for commercial, business, or agricultural purposes, may agree to pay interest in excess of the maximum rate of conventional interest authorized by the laws of this state, whether in connection with unsecured or secured indebtedness and whether the secured indebtedness is secured, in whole or in part, directly or indirectly, by a real estate mortgage or chattel mortgage on property in this state or is otherwise secured, and as to any such agreement such debtor shall be prohibited from asserting a claim or defense of usury or of the taking of interest in excess of the maximum rate of conventional interest, and any person whatsoever signing as co-maker, guarantor, or endorser for such debtor shall also be prohibited from asserting any such claim or defense. The term "foreign limited partnership", as used hereinabove, shall mean any partnership domiciled in any state of the

United States, other than Louisiana or the District of Columbia, which shall have been formed and is existing pursuant to the limited partnership law or Uniform Limited Partnership Law of any such state, and such partnership need not qualify as a partnership in commendam under the laws of this state.

B. (1) Notwithstanding the provisions of Subsection A of this Section, and unless otherwise agreed in writing after the default, a lender may not prospectively increase the simple interest rate under a commercial, business, or agricultural purpose loan following declaration of the obligor's default except as follows:

(a) With respect to obligations having an original principal balance of two hundred fifty thousand dollars or less, the fixed simple interest rate shall not be prospectively increased to a rate greater than eighteen percent per annum or three percentage points over the original, fixed contract rate in effect prior to default, whichever is greater.

(b) With respect to obligations having an original principal balance in excess of two hundred fifty thousand dollars, the fixed simple interest rate shall not be prospectively increased to a rate greater than twenty-one percent per annum or three percentage points over the original, fixed contract rate in effect prior to default, whichever is greater.

(2) This Subsection shall apply only to fixed rate, simple interest commercial, business, and agricultural purpose loans, promissory notes, and other obligations entered into on or after September 7, 1990, which provide for a prospective increase in the interest rate following the obligee's declaration of an obligor's default. This Subsection shall not apply to consumer credit transactions or other consumer obligations, or to loans, notes, or other obligations that do not bear interest at a fixed rate and on a simple interest basis prior to a declaration of default. This Subsection shall also not apply to commercial, business, or agricultural purpose loans, notes, or other obligations which are contractually subject to the laws of another state notwithstanding the fact that the obligor may be located or have facilities in Louisiana or that loan proceeds or a portion thereof may be utilized in Louisiana.

(3) The exclusive remedy that may be asserted against a lender or other obligee for a violation of this Subsection is the return of any excessive post-default interest that may have been assessed and collected. Specifically, the obligor shall have no rights under R.S. 9:3501.

Added by Acts 1981, No. 665, § 1. Amended by Acts 1990, No. 734, § 1; Acts 1990, No. 847, § 1; Acts 1991, No. 697, § 1; Acts 1995, No. 782, § 1; Acts 1997, No. 1295, § 1.

Cross References

C.C. arts. 2924, 2925.

§ 3509.1. Adjustable rate loans for commercial, business, or agricultural purposes

A. Notwithstanding any other provisions of law to the contrary, any person borrowing funds for commercial, business, or agricultural purposes, or deferring payment of an obligation for commercial, business, or agricultural purposes, may agree that the interest rate that is charged on the indebtedness may vary from time to time in accordance with the provisions of either the promissory note or other evidence of the indebtedness. Such conditions in either the promissory note or other evidence of the indebtedness shall not be deemed to rely on the whim of the obligor so as to render them null nor shall such conditions destroy the negotiability of the promissory note or other evidence of the indebtedness.

B. All debts created pursuant to the provisions of this Section shall comply with the provisions of R.S. 9:3504(D)(3) through (7) and (9), and the provisions contained therein shall be applicable to all transactions created pursuant to this Section.

C. All adjustable rate loans made prior to September 3, 1984 shall be valid and enforceable.

Added by Acts 1982, No. 361, § 1, eff. July 21, 1982. Amended by Acts 1984, No. 495, § 1; Acts 1990, No. 847, § 1; Acts 1991, No. 697, § 1.

Cross References

C.C. art. 2924.

§ 3509.2. Interest upon accrued interest; exceptions

The general prohibition against the recovery of interest upon accrued interest, as expressed in Civil Code Article 2001, is subject to the following exceptions:

(1) As provided by the Louisiana Consumer Credit Law,[1] or as specifically provided by law.

(2) In transactions entered into for commercial, business, or agricultural purposes.

(3) In matters preempted by federal law or by rules and regulations of federal agencies, including but not limited to the Federal Home Loan Bank, Comptroller of the Currency, and the Federal Deposit Insurance Corporation.

(4) As provided in rules and regulations promulgated by the commissioner of financial institutions for supervised financial organizations as provided by R.S. 6:242(A)(2).

Added by Acts 1984, No. 331, § 8, eff. Jan. 1, 1985. Amended by Acts 1986, No. 584, § 3, eff. July 2, 1986

[1] R.S. 9:3510 et seq.

Editor's Note. R.S. 9:3509.2 was added by Acts 1986, No. 584, § 3. Previously, the exceptions to the recovery of interest upon accrued interest were found in R.S. 9:2788. Section 3 of Acts 1986, No. 584, amended R.S. 9:2788 and re-enacted it as R.S. 9:3509 2.

Cross References

C.C. art. 2001.

§ 3509.3. Prepayment of loan

In the absence of federal law, rules and regulations of federal agencies, and contractual provisions by the parties to the contrary, including provisions relative to the terms and conditions of prepayment, the debtor in any loan may prepay in full at any time the unpaid balance of all sums due and owing at that point in time. The provisions of this Section shall not be construed to supersede other provisions of law regulating the prepayment of loans.

Added by Acts 1987, No. 670, § 1.

§ 3509.4. Deferment of loan payments during declared disaster

Notwithstanding any other provision of law to the contrary, when the governor declares a state of disaster or emergency pursuant to R.S. 29:721 et seq., and the federal financial regulatory bodies issue guidelines to financial institutions regarding their response thereto, the commissioner of the Office of Financial Institutions is authorized to expend funds in the utilization of all reasonably efficient means of communication to encourage and facilitate communication between Louisiana citizens and their particular financial institution and to inform and educate Louisiana citizens of their potential options under such guidelines. If a lender requires full payment of the deferred principal and interest upon termination of the deferment period, then the lender shall obtain written approval from the borrower prior to the acceptance of the deferment.

Added by Acts 2006, No. 475, § 1, eff. June 22, 2006.

CHAPTER 2. LOUISIANA CONSUMER CREDIT LAW

PART I. GENERAL PROVISIONS AND DEFINITIONS

Section
3510. Short title.
3511. Scope.
3512. Exclusions.
3513. Waiver, agreement to forego rights.
3514. Agreement to contract; disclosures of the contract.
3515. Conduct of certain business other than making consumer loans prohibited.
3516. Definitions.
3517. Terms; construction; additional fees and charges.
3518. Construction against implicit repeal.
3518.1. Records of the Office of Financial Institutions.
3518.2. Credit cards; unsolicited delivery or mailing prohibited; penalty.
3518.3. Credit cards; printing of accounting numbers on sales receipts; liability.

PART II. MAXIMUM CHARGES

3519. Consumer loans.
3520. Consumer credit sale.
3521. Maximum charges after negotiations.
3522. Maximum charges after maturity.
3523. Credit service charge for revolving charge accounts.
3524. Loan finance charge on lender credit card accounts.
3524.1. [Blank].
3524.2. [Blank].
3525. Leap years.
3526. Variable rates.
3526.1. [Blank].
3526.2. [Blank].
3526.3. [Blank].
3527. Maximum delinquency charges; notice of conversion.
3528. Maximum deferral charges.
3529. Installment of consumer credit transaction returned; additional charge to account.
3530. Fees; origination; notary, documentation; over-the-credit-limit fee.
3530.1. [Blank].

PART III. PREPAYMENT OF CONSUMER CREDIT TRANSACTIONS

3531. Right to prepay.

Section
3532. Rebate upon prepayment.
3532.1. Prepayment penalties in connection with simple interest real estate secured loans.
3533. Rebate after acceleration of maturity.

PART IV. LIMITATIONS ON AGREEMENTS AND PRACTICES

3534. Fees; attorney, collection agency.
3534.1. Collection agent; registration; assignment of debt to collector.
3534.5. [Blank].
3535. Use of multiple agreements.
3536. Referral sales.
3537. Repealed.

PART V. HOME SOLICITATION SALES

3538. Consumer's right to cancel.
3538.1. [Blank].
3539. Form of agreement or offer; statement of consumer's right; compliance.
3540. Restoration of down payment; retention of cancellation fee.
3541. Duty of consumer; no compensation for services prior to cancellation.
3541.1. Consumer's right to cancel mail and check solicitation sales.

PART V-A. HOME SOLICITATION OF AGED PERSONS

3541.21. Definitions.
3541.22. Prohibited practices.

PART VI. INSURANCE

3542. Requirement of insurance.
3543. Property insurance.
3544. Existing insurance.
3545. Limitations on insurance rates; contract requirements.
3546. Choice of insurer.
3547. Conditions applying to insurance provided by the extender of credit.
3548. Cancellation of insurance; refund or credit upon cancellation.
3549. Gain from insurance.
3550. Insurance premium finance companies.

PART VII. REMEDIES AND PENALTIES

3551. Unconscionability.
3552. Effect of violations on rights of parties.
3553. Criminal penalties.

PART VIII. ADMINISTRATION

3554. Powers of commissioner.
3554.1. Commissioner's powers; unlicensed persons.
3554.2. Reapplication after revocation of a license.
3554.3. Cost of appeal; effect of final decision.
3555. Injunctions; investigations; enforcement actions; civil penalties; costs.
3556. Method of procedure.
3556.1. Records; rules.
3556.2. Guidance by commissioner; advisory opinions.
3556.3. Violations; penalties.

PART IX. LICENSING PROVISIONS

Section	
3557.	Authority to make consumer loans.
3558.	License to make consumer loans.
3559.	Continuation of licensing.
3559.1.	Regulation of former licensees.
3560.	Licenses not required.
3561.	Single place of business; additional licenses.
3561.1.	License; examination; renewal fees; records.

PART X. COLLECTION PRACTICES

3562.	Unauthorized collection practices.

PART XI. NOTIFICATION AND FEES

3563.	Applicability.
3563.1.	Financial institutions exempt.
3564.	Notification.
3565.	Notification fee.
3566.	Repealed.
3567.	Repealed.

PART XII. IDENTITY THEFT

3568.	Identity theft.

PART XIII. DISCLOSURE OF PERSONAL CREDIT INFORMATION

3571.	Dissemination of specific credit information; subpoena of records; requirements; penalties.
3571.1.	Credit reporting agency information and reports; consumer access to files; right of correction; dissemination or maintenance of untrue or misleading credit information by credit reporting agency; investigation; right to recovery.
3571.2.	Limitations on use of consumer's credit report.

PART XIV. LOAN BROKERS

3572.1.	Loan broker defined.
3572.2.	Exemptions; licensing and bonding; loan broker.
3572.3.	Licensure required.
3572.4.	Corporation.
3572.5.	Application form.
3572.6.	Restrictions; records.
3572.7.	Examination; rules.
3572.8.	Bond or trust account required.
3572.9.	Rebate upon prepayment.
3572.10.	Right of cancellation.
3572.11.	Loan brokerage statement; disclosure statement required.
3572.12.	Violations; penalties.

PART XV. CREDIT REPAIR SERVICES ORGANIZATIONS ACT

3573.1.	Short title; purpose.
3573.2.	Definitions; exemptions.
3573.2–A.	[Blank].
3573.3.	Prohibited conduct.
3573.4.	Bond; trust account.
3573.5.	Repealed.
3573.6.	Disclosure statement.
3573.7.	Form and terms of contract.
3573.8.	Waiver.
3573.9.	Repealed.
3573.10.	Action for damages.
3573.11.	Orders, injunctions, and publication.
3573.12.	Statute of limitations.
3573.13.	Criminal penalty.
3573.14.	Burden of proving exemption.
3573.15.	Remedies cumulative.
3573.16.	Civil money penalties.
3573.17.	Repealed.

PART XVI. ADVANCE FEE LOANS

3574.1.	Short title.
3574.2.	Definitions.
3574.3.	Advance fees; prohibited acts.
3574.4.	Responsibility of principals.
3574.5.	Investigations; cease and desist orders; administrative fines.
3574.6.	Investigations; examinations; subpoenas; hearings; witnesses.
3574.7.	Injunction to restrain violations.
3574.8.	Criminal penalties.
3574.9.	Actions for damages.
3574.10.	Duties and powers of the office.
3575.	[Blank].

PART XVII. REFUND ANTICIPATION LOANS [REPEALED]

3575.1 to 3575.4.	Repealed.
3575.5.	Repealed.
3575.6 to 3575.10.	Repealed.

PART XVIII. COLLECTION AGENCY REGULATION ACT [REPEALED]

3576.1 to 3576.24.	Repealed.

PART XIX. COLLEGE CAMPUS CREDIT CARD SOLICITATION LAW

3577.1.	Short title.
3577.2.	Definitions.
3577.3.	Registration prior to solicitation; inducements prohibited.
3577.4.	Debt collection against parent or guardian prohibited.
3577.5.	Violations; penalties.
3577.6 to 3577.8.	[Blank].

Editor's note. Chapter 9 of the Louisiana Commercial Laws was revised by Acts 2001, No. 128, § 1, effective July 1, 2001, to consist of R.S. 10:9-101 through 10:9-710. This Chapter does not apply to statutory liens and privileges except as expressly provided therein. R.S. 10:9-322(h) provides: "A security interest has priority over a conflicting lien, other than an agricultural lien, in the same collateral except as otherwise provided in this Chapter or except to the extent the lien is created by a statute that expressly provides that the lien has priority over the security interest." The accompanying revision comment states: "For example, see R.S. 9:4501, 9:4502, 9:4521, 9:4758, 9:4870, and 9:48888, each of which provides that certain privileges have priority over certain security interests. See also 9:5001 and 37:218.".

PART I. GENERAL PROVISIONS AND DEFINITIONS

§ 3510. Short title

This chapter shall be known and may be cited as the Louisiana Consumer Credit Law.

Added by Acts 1972, No. 454, § 1, eff. Jan. 1, 1973.

Cross References

C.C. arts. 2923, 2924.

§ 3511. Scope

A. Subject to the provisions of R.S. 9:3511(B), the parties to a consumer credit transaction may agree that the law of the place wherein the consumer credit transaction was entered into or the law of the residence of the buyer or debtor shall apply. For the purposes of this Chapter the residence of a buyer or debtor is the address given by him as his residence in any writing signed by him in connection with a consumer credit transaction. Until he notifies the creditor of a new or different address, the given address is presumed to be unchanged.

B. Whenever an action is brought in this state to enforce rights arising from consumer credit transactions wherever made the creditor shall, where applicable, reduce the charges so that they do not exceed those provided in Part II and/or III of this chapter.

C. Except as otherwise provided herein, the following agreements by a consumer are invalid with respect to consumer credit transactions, or modifications thereof, to which this chapter applies:

(1) by which the consumer consents to the jurisdiction of another state; and

(2) that fix venue.

D. All fees and charges authorized under this Chapter, whether or not such fees and charges constitute or are considered to be loan finance charges, shall be deemed to be "material to the determination of the interest rate" for purposes of exportation to borrowers residing in other states under the most favored lender doctrine of federal law.

E. All consumer credit transactions shall comply with federal Regulation Z of the Board of Governors of the Federal Reserve System. Failure to comply with Regulation Z is a violation of this Chapter.

F. The Louisiana S.A.F.E. Residential Mortgage Lending Act, R.S. 6:1081, et seq., is the primary law governing residential mortgage loans as defined in the Louisiana S.A.F.E. Residential Mortgage Lending Act. A residential mortgage lender, broker, and a natural person who is a residential mortgage loan originator shall comply with the licensing provisions of the Louisiana S.A.F.E. Residential Mortgage Lending Act, R.S. 6:1081, et seq., unless otherwise exempt by the Act. Notwithstanding any other law to the contrary, parties to a consumer loan, as defined in this Part, which is secured by a mortgage, deed of trust, or other equivalent consensual security interest on a dwelling as defined in 15 U.S.C. 1602(v), or on residential immovable property upon which is constructed or intended to be constructed a dwelling, whether or not such a loan includes any additional security interest in movable property, may agree by contract that such a loan shall be governed by the Louisiana Consumer Credit Law, provided the lenders, brokers, and originators are properly licensed under this Part and the Louisiana S.A.F.E. Residential Mortgage Lending Act or otherwise exempt under R.S. 6:1081 et seq.

Added by Acts 1972, No. 454, § 1, eff. Jan. 1, 1973. Amended by Acts 1985, No. 592, § 2, eff. July 13, 1985; Acts 1988, No. 629, § 1; Acts 1999, No. 1315, § 1, eff. Jan. 1, 2000; Acts 2007, No. 13, § 1, eff. June 18, 2007; Acts 2009, No. 522, § 2, eff. July 31, 2009.

Cross References

C.C. arts. 2923, 2924.

§ 3512. Exclusions

This law does not apply to:

(1) Extensions of credit to organizations, including government or governmental agencies or instrumentalities.

(2) The sale of insurance by an insurer, except as otherwise provided in the part on insurance; however, this law shall apply to the sale of insurance by an insurance agent in which such agent charges a credit service charge and the insured is permitted to defer all or part of the amount due such agent in two or more installments excluding the down payment, and which otherwise constitutes a "consumer credit sale".

(3) Transactions under public utility or common carrier tariffs if a subdivision or agency of this state or of the United States regulates, approves, or consents to the charges for the services involved, the charges for delayed payment, and any discount allowed for early payment.

(4) Motor vehicle credit transactions, including refinancings, subject to the Motor Vehicle Sales Finance Act, R.S. 6:969.1 et seq.

(5) Federally chartered and state chartered credit unions and transactions between credit unions and the members thereof.

(6) Pawn brokerage services.

(7) Credit transactions involving extensions of credit for business, commercial, or agricultural purposes.

(8) Federally related mortgage loans. This exclusion does not apply to loans secured by residential property made specifically subject to the Louisiana Consumer Credit Law by contract.

Added by Acts 1972, No. 454, § 1, eff. Jan. 1, 1973. Amended by Acts 1974, No. 144, § 1; Acts 1974, No. 466, § 2; Acts 1980, No. 694, § 1; Acts 1983, No. 365, § 1; Acts 1986, No. 584, § 1, eff. July 2, 1986; Acts 1990, No. 847, § 1; Acts 2001, No. 877, § 2; Acts 2003, No. 340, § 2; Acts 2006, No. 213, § 1.

§ 3513. Waiver, agreement to forego rights

A consumer may not waive or agree to forego rights or benefits under this chapter except that a claim, if disputed in good faith, may be settled by compromise or agreement.

Added by Acts 1972, No. 454, § 1, eff. Jan. 1, 1973.

§ 3514. Agreement to contract; disclosures of the contract

A. The parties to a transaction other than a consumer credit transaction may contract with one another that such transaction shall be subject to the provisions of this Chapter, in which event the transaction shall be a consumer credit transaction within the provisions of this Chapter. Notwithstanding the foregoing, the parties to a consumer credit transaction otherwise subject to the Motor Vehicle Sales Finance Act, R.S. 6:969.1 et seq. may not contract to become subject to the provisions of this Chapter. Unless a creditor is exempt from the licensing requirements of this Chapter under R.S. 9:3560, a creditor may not contract more than four transactions under the provisions of this Chapter over any calendar year without first complying with the licensing requirements under Part IX of this Chapter.

B. Written credit contracts and agreements shall accurately reflect the actual terms, conditions, applicable amount of fees, and repayment schedule agreed to by the parties. If a loan is to be repaid on demand, in a lump sum, or at undefined intervals of time, interest on the loan shall be computed by the actuarial or simple interest method when allocating payments made on the loan.

Added by Acts 1972, No. 454, § 1, eff. Jan. 1, 1973. Amended by Acts 1980, No. 694, § 1; Acts 1980, 2nd Ex.Sess., No. 16, § 1, eff. Sept. 16, 1980; Acts 1986, No. 584, § 1, eff. July 2, 1986; Acts 1988, No. 244, § 2; Acts 1995, No. 1184, § 2; Acts 1999, No. 1315, § 1, eff. Jan. 1, 2000; Acts 2001, No. 877, § 2; Acts 2003, No. 340, § 2; Acts 2010, No. 668, § 1.

§ 3515. Conduct of certain business other than making consumer loans prohibited

A. (1)(a) A licensed lender shall not engage in the business of making sales of goods at any location where consumer loans are made. The sale and financing of a home protection plan, thrift and buying club memberships, auto club memberships, insurance authorized by the Louisiana Insurance Code, similar consumer benefit club memberships, or financial and tax services, including the use of stored value cards or electronic cash for loan disbursement, shall not be deemed a violation of this Chapter. The word "location" as used in this Section means the entire space in which consumer loans are made, and said location must be separated from any location in which merchandise is sold or displayed by walls that may be broken only by a passageway to which the public is not admitted.

(b) In addition, the cost of any home protection plan, club membership, insurance, or service offered pursuant to this Section may, at the option of the consumer, be payable from the proceeds of consumer loans and included on the amount financed, provided that:

(i) The sale of a home protection plan, club membership, or service is not a factor in the approval and this fact is clearly disclosed in writing to the consumer.

(ii) In order to obtain a home protection plan, club membership, insurance, or service, the consumer gives a specific affirmative written indication of his desire to purchase it after receiving written disclosure of the cost.

(2) Nothing contained herein shall be construed to prohibit a licensed lender from conducting the business of making consumer loans under this Chapter on the same premises where a person, not an affiliate of said licensed lender, is engaged in the business of making sales of goods, provided that such licensed lender is not an affiliate.

B. A sale of goods or services made with the use of a seller credit card or lender credit card or other credit arrangement at a location other than that of the licensee does not violate this section. Formal application for a loan must be made at the location of the licensed lender; however, when a loan application is taken by persons not employed by the licensed lender, such application shall not be deemed a violation of this section.

C. An occasional sale of property used in the ordinary course of the business of the licensee does not violate this section.

D. A sale of property seized or legally recovered by the licensed lender does not violate this Section.

E. No licensed lender shall conduct the business of making consumer loans under this Chapter under any name and from or at any place of business within this state, other than that stated in the license. The closing of a consumer loan on immovable property in the office of a notary public shall not violate this Section. Loans made by mail where credit approval is given at the location of the lender and loans made with the use of a lender credit card shall not violate this Section. Loans governed by R.S. 9:3550 that are closed at an insurance agent/broker's location shall not violate this Section provided the loan shall be accepted by a licensed lender.

F. The commissioner may issue a permit to persons licensed and regulated by the Office of Financial Institutions under the provisions of R.S. 37:1781 through 1808 to conduct the sale of goods and services at a location where consumer loans are made pursuant to the provisions of this Chapter. The commissioner shall have the authority to deny the permit or suspend or terminate the permit for violations of this Chapter. The commissioner may adopt rules to implement the provisions of this Subsection. Such rules shall require the commissioner to grant or deny the permit within thirty days from the date the application for a permit is filed with the Office of Financial Institutions.

Added by Acts 1972, No. 454, § 1, eff. Jan. 1, 1973. Amended by Acts 1974, No. 466, § 1; Acts 1980, No. 694, § 1; Acts 1986, No. 584, § 1, eff. July 2, 1986; Acts 1991, No. 693, § 1; Acts 1992, No. 218, § 1; Acts 1995, No. 1184, § 2; Acts 2003, No. 578, § 1; Acts 2004, No. 346, § 1; Acts 2004, No. 347, § 1; Acts 2005, No. 101, § 1; Acts 2006, No. 213, § 1.

§ 3516. Definitions

(1) "Affiliate", as used in this Chapter, means a specific person who is directly or indirectly, through one or more intermediaries, controlled by, or controls, or is under common control with the person specified.

(2) "Agricultural purpose" means a purpose related to the production, harvest, exhibition, marketing, transportation, processing, or manufacture of agricultural products by a natural person who cultivates, plants, propagates or nurtures the agricultural products. "Agricultural products" includes products such as horticultural, and dairy products, livestock, wildlife, poultry, bees, forest products, fish and shell fish, and any products thereof, including processed and manufactured products, and any and all products raised or produced on farms and any processed or manufactured products thereof.

(3) "Amount deferred" means the cash price, subtracting any down payment, under a consumer credit sale, revolving charge or seller credit card account, plus any other charges, fees and closing costs authorized by law, that are financed by the creditor under the transaction or included in or added to the balance of the consumer's indebtedness subject to credit service charges.

(4) "Amount financed" means the amount borrowed under a consumer loan, revolving loan or lender credit card account, plus any other charges, fees, and closing costs authorized by law, that are financed by the creditor under the transaction, or included in or added to the balance of the consumer's indebtedness subject to loan finance charges. Amount financed also includes premiums payable for insurance procured in lieu of perfecting a security interest otherwise required by the creditor in connection with the sale, lease, or loan if the premiums do not exceed the fees and charges which would otherwise be payable, and premiums payable for any insurance authorized by the Louisiana Insurance Code purchased by the consumer, at rates set forth

herein or, when no rate is specified herein, at lawful rates in accordance with the provisions of the Louisiana Insurance Code.

(5) "Billing period" or "billing cycle" means the time interval between regular periodic billing statement dates. Such intervals may be considered equal intervals of time unless a billing date varies more than four days from the regular date.

(5.1) "Cash advance" means an advance of cash or a cash equivalent under a lender credit card account including but not limited to the purchase of a money order, wire transfer services, or the use of a convenience check to purchase goods or services.

(6) "Cash price" of goods and services means the price for which the seller would have sold to the consumer and the consumer would have bought from the seller, the thing that is the subject matter of the consumer credit transaction, if such sale had been a sale for cash instead of a consumer credit transaction. The cash price may include any taxes and charges for delivery, installation, servicing, processing, repairs, alterations or improvements.

(7) "Check" means any check, draft, item, orders or requests for payment of money, negotiable orders, withdrawal or any other instrument used to pay a debt or transfer money from one to another.

(8) "Closing costs" with respect to a debt secured by a mortgage, lien, or privilege on immovable property includes:

(a) fees or premiums for title examination, title curative expenses, title insurance, or similar purposes including surveys, and essential public certificates,

(b) fees for preparation of an act, settlement statement, or other documents,

(c) escrows for future payments of taxes and insurance,

(d) notarial fees,

(e) recording fees,

(f) appraisal fees, and

(g) credit reports.

(9) "Commissioner" means the commissioner of financial institutions.

(10) "Consumer" means a natural person who purchases goods, services, or movable or immovable property or rights therein, for a personal, family, or household purpose and includes a purchaser or buyer in a consumer credit sale or transaction made with the use of a seller credit card or otherwise, or a borrower or debtor in a consumer loan, revolving loan account, or a lender credit card.

(11) "Consumer credit insurance" means insurance, other than insurance on property, by which the satisfaction of debt in whole or in part is a benefit provided, but does not include

(a) insurance issued as an isolated transaction on the part of the insurer not related to an agreement or plan for insuring debtors of the creditor; or

(b) insurance indemnifying the creditor against loss due to the debtor's default.

(12) A "consumer credit sale" is the sale of a thing, other than the sale of religious periodicals, books, and other religious materials by bona fide religious associations, or immovable property, in which a credit service charge is charged and the purchaser is permitted to defer all or part of the purchase price or other consideration in two or more installments excluding the down payment when the thing is purchased primarily for personal, family, or household purposes, and the purchaser is a person other than an organization. "Consumer credit sale" shall not include a lease of movable property under which the lessee agrees to pay as compensation for use a sum substantially equivalent to, or in excess of, the initial value of the leased property and under which the lessee will become, or has the option to become, for no additional consideration or for nominal consideration, the owner of the leased property upon compliance with the agreement.

(13) "Consumer credit transaction" means a consumer loan or a consumer credit sale but does not include a motor vehicle credit transaction made pursuant to R.S. 6:969.1 et seq.

(14) "Consumer loan" means a loan of money or its equivalent made by a supervised financial organization, a licensed lender, or lender in which the debtor is a consumer, and the loan is entered into primarily for personal, family, or household purposes and includes debts created by the use of a lender credit card, revolving loan account, or similar arrangement, as well as insurance premium financing.

(15) "Credit card" means any card, plate, coupon book, or other single credit device that may be used from time to time to obtain credit.

(16)(a) "Credit service charge" means the sum of the following:

(i) All charges payable directly or indirectly by the consumer and imposed directly or indirectly by the seller as an incident to the extension of credit, including any of the following types of charges that are applicable: time price differential; service; carrying or other charge, however denominated; premium or other charge for any guarantee or insurance protecting the seller against the consumer's default or other credit loss; and

(ii) Charges paid by the consumer for investigating the collateral or credit worthiness of the consumer or for commissions or brokerage for obtaining the credit, irrespective of the person to whom the charges are paid or payable, unless the seller had no notice of the charges when the credit was granted.

(b) The term does not include default charges, delinquency charges, deferral charges, N.S.F. check charges as set forth in R.S. 9:3529, origination fees as set forth in R.S. 9:3530, or any of the items enumerated in R.S. 9:3516(3).

(17) "Down payment" means an amount, including the value of any property used as a trade-in, paid to a seller to reduce the cash price of goods or services purchased under a consumer credit sale.

(18) The term "extender of credit" or "creditor" as used in this Chapter includes a seller in a consumer credit sale, revolving charge account, or transaction made with the use of a seller credit card or otherwise, or a lender in a consumer loan, a revolving loan account, or a lender credit card transaction. "Creditor" also includes a subsequent assignee or transferee of the consumer's obligation, but does not include a bona fide pledgee.

(19) "Federally related mortgage loan" as used in this Chapter shall have the same meaning as defined in the Residential Mortgage Lending Act, specifically R.S. 6:1083(3.1).

(19.1) "Home protection plan" means a contract between the homeowner and a warranty or service company wherein the company is obligated to pay or reimburse the cost to repair or replace the covered built-in appliances or major mechanical systems of the consumer's home in the event of a breakdown.

(20) A "home solicitation sale" is a consumer credit sale of goods or services or both, other than motor vehicles, farm equipment, or services, in which the seller or a person acting for him engages in a personal solicitation of the sale at any place other than the business establishment of the seller and consumer's agreement or offer to purchase is there given to the seller or a person acting for him. This definition shall also include all telephone sales in which the seller has initiated contact regardless of his location, and the consumer's agreement to purchase is made at the consumer's home. It does not include a sale made pursuant to a preexisting revolving charge account, a catalogue credit sale, a preexisting consumer credit sale agreement providing for a series of sales, or a sale made pursuant to prior negotiations between the parties at a business establishment at a fixed location where goods or services are offered or exhibited for sale, or a sale that may have been initiated by the consumer by communication with the seller at his business establishment.

(21) "Lender credit card" means a revolving loan account that may be accessed by use of a credit card. For limited purposes of R.S. 9:3516(23)(b), 3517(B), 3524(D), 3527, 3529, and 3530, a "lender credit card" includes a travel and entertainment credit card account that is not subject to loan finance charges or credit service charges.

(22) "Licensed lender" means a person licensed by the commissioner to make consumer loans pursuant to this Chapter.

(23)(a) "Loan finance charge" means the sum of the following:

(i) All charges payable directly or indirectly by the consumer and imposed directly or indirectly by the lender as a requirement of the extension of credit, including any of the following types of charges that are applicable: interest or any amount payable under a point, discount, or other system of charges, however denominated; and

(ii) Charges paid by the consumer for investigating the collateral or credit worthiness of the consumer.

(b) The term does not include default charges, deferral charges, delinquency charges, N.S.F. check charges as set forth in R.S. 9:3529, reasonable membership charges in connection with an open-end credit plan, origination and other fees as set forth in R.S. 9:3530, any of the items enumerated in Subparagraph (8)(b) of this Section, or other fees and charges that are not considered to be a finance charge under the Federal Truth in Lending Act and Regulation Z of the Board of Governors of the Federal Reserve System.

(24) "Organization" means corporation, government or governmental subdivision or agency, trust, estate, partnership, cooperative, or association.

(24.1) "Person" as used in this Chapter means an individual or corporation, partnership, trust, association, joint venture pool, syndicate, sole proprietorship, unincorporated organization, or any other form of entity not specifically listed herein.

(25) "Precomputed consumer credit transaction" means a consumer credit transaction under which loan finance charges or credit service charges are computed in advance over the entire scheduled term of the transaction and capitalized into the face amount of the debtor's promissory note or other evidence of indebtedness.

(26) "Prepaid finance charge" in connection with a simple interest transaction means any loan finance charge or credit service charge paid separately in cash or by check before or at consummation of the transaction, or withheld from the proceeds of the transaction at any time. Prepaid finance charges may be funded under the loan at the borrower's request by increasing the original amount financed or amount deferred under the borrower's note, with such increased amount, including prepaid finance charges, being subject to simple interest over the loan term.

(27) "Principal" means the amount financed or amount deferred under a consumer credit transaction.

(28) "Pro rata" as used in this chapter refers to a method of computing deferral charges by dividing the precomputed loan finance charge or precomputed credit service charge by the total number of days in the contract and multiplying the sum by the number of days that are deferred.

(29) "Revolving charge account" means an arrangement between a seller or issuer of a seller credit card honored by the seller and a consumer pursuant to which:

(a) The creditor permits the consumer to purchase goods or services on a preauthorized basis;

(b) The creditor reasonably contemplates repeated transactions;

(c) The creditor may impose a credit service charge from time to time on the outstanding unpaid balance of the consumer's account;

(d) The amount of credit that may be extended to the consumer, up to any limit set by the creditor, is generally made available to the extent that any outstanding balance is repaid; and

(e) No credit service charges may be imposed upon the consumer for a billing period if the account is paid in full within a period of twenty-five days from the billing date.

(30)(a) "Revolving loan account" means an arrangement between a lender and a consumer pursuant to which:

(i) The creditor may permit the consumer to obtain consumer loan advances on a preauthorized basis;

(ii) The creditor reasonably contemplates repeated transactions;

(iii) The creditor may impose a loan finance charge from time to time on the outstanding unpaid balance of the consumer's account; and

(iv) The amount of credit that may be extended to the consumer under the account, up to any limit set by the creditor, is generally made available to the extent that any unpaid balance is repaid.

(b) The amount borrowed under a revolving loan account may include, if required by the creditor, an amount not greater than ninety-nine dollars and ninety-nine cents exceeding the draft or similar order if said amount is immediately credited to the consumer's deposit account with the creditor or with the creditor's agent.

(31) "Seller credit card" means a revolving charge account that may be accessed by use of a credit card.

(32) "Simple interest transaction" means a consumer credit transaction under which loan finance charges or credit service charges are assessed by application of a contractual simple interest rate or rates to the unpaid balance of the

debtor's promissory note, account or other evidence of indebtedness.

(33) "Supervised financial organization" means either of the following:

(a) A banking or similar organization organized, certified, and supervised by an agency of either the United States of America or the state of Louisiana or any other state pursuant to the banking, currency, and related laws of the United States of America or of the state of Louisiana or any other state.

(b) An organization which is an approved lender under the rules and regulations of the Federal Housing Administration, the Veterans Administration, or the Federal Home Loan Mortgage Corporation.

(34) Repealed by Acts 1995, No. 1184, § 4.

(35) "Thing" as used in the chapter is as defined by law and includes movable and immovable property and rights therein, goods, or services.

(36) "Unconscionable". A contract or clause is unconscionable when at the time the contract is entered into it is so onerous, oppressive or one-sided that a reasonable man would not have freely given his consent to the contract or clause thereof in question; provided, however, for the purposes of this chapter, an agreement, clause, charge or practice expressly permitted by this chapter or any other law or regulation of this state or of the United States or subdivision of either, or an arrangement, clause, charge or practice necessarily implied as being permitted by this chapter or any other law or regulation of this state or the United States or any subdivision of either is not unconscionable.

(37) "Unpaid debt" as used in this Chapter means the total of the amount financed, loan finance charges, default charges, and delinquency charges including the amount due at the time of default plus all interest which may accrue from the time of default until the entire balance is paid.

Added by Acts 1972, No. 454, § 1, eff. Jan. 1, 1973. Amended by Acts 1974, No. 466, § 1; Acts 1978, No. 636, § 1; Acts 1978, No. 761, § 1; Acts 1980, No. 502, § 1, eff. July 22, 1980; Acts 1980, No. 694, § 1; Acts 1980, 2nd Ex.Sess., No. 16, § 1, eff. Sept. 16, 1980; Acts 1981, No. 473, § 1; Acts 1982, No. 258, § 1; Acts 1982, No. 434, § 1; Acts 1983, No. 365, § 1; Acts 1984, No. 384, § 1; Acts 1985, No. 592, § 2, eff. July 13, 1985; Acts 1985, No. 808, § 1, eff. July 22, 1985; Acts 1986, No. 584, § 1, eff. July 2, 1986; Acts 1987, No. 870, § 1; Acts 1988, No. 629, § 1; Acts 1990, No. 709, § 2, eff. July 20, 1990; Acts 1991, No. 480, § 1; Acts 1991, No. 697, § 1; Acts 1992, No. 100, § 1; Acts 1995, No. 1184, § 2; Acts 1997, No. 1033, § 1; Acts 2000, 1st Ex.Sess., No. 34, § 2, eff. April 14, 2000; Acts 2001, No. 877, § 2; Acts 2005, No. 101, § 1; Acts 2007, No. 13, § 1, eff. June 18, 2007; Acts 2008, No. 50, § 1, eff. Jan. 1, 2009.

Editor's note. Section 2 of Acts 2008, No. 50 declares that "This Act shall apply prospectively only, and shall not affect any loans originated prior to the effective date of this Act."

§ 3517. Terms; construction; additional fees and charges

A. upload Wherever applicable in this Chapter, use of the masculine includes the feminine and use of the plural includes the singular and vice versa.

B. As a general rule of construction, persons may look to comparable rules, definitions, and principles under the Federal Real Estate Settlement Procedures Act [1] and Regulation X of the Office of the Secretary of the Department of Housing and Urban Development, the Federal Truth in Lending Act,[2] and Regulation Z of the Board of Governors of the Federal Reserve System for guidance in further defining and interpreting terms and concepts that are not otherwise defined or specified under the provisions of this Chapter. For example, those fees and charges that are not classified as or considered to be finance charges for Federal Truth in Lending purposes are not considered to be loan finance charges for purposes of this Chapter. In addition, nothing contained in the provisions of this Chapter shall be construed to prohibit the imposition of fees and charges which are otherwise permissible under R.S. 6:548.

C. The commissioner shall prescribe, by rule not inconsistent with the provisions of this Chapter, additional fees and charges which may be imposed and collected by an extender of credit if such fees and charges have been contractually provided for in the consumer's promissory note, or credit contract or agreement.

Added by Acts 1972, No. 454, § 1, eff. Jan. 1, 1973. Amended by Acts 1988, No. 629, § 1; Acts 1995, No. 1184, § 2; Acts 1999, No. 1315, § 1, eff. Jan. 1, 2000.

[1] 12 U.S.C.A. § 2601 et seq.
[2] 15 U.S.C.A. § 1601 et seq.

§ 3518. Construction against implicit repeal

This chapter being a general act intended as a unified coverage of its subject matter, no part of it shall be deemed impliedly repealed by subsequent legislation if such construction can reasonably be avoided.

Added by Acts 1972, No. 454, § 1, eff. Jan. 1, 1973.

§ 3518.1. Records of the Office of Financial Institutions

A. Except as otherwise provided, all records of the office of financial institutions shall be kept strictly confidential within the office, and such records and reports shall not be subject to subpoena or other legal process.

B. The commissioner, in his sole discretion, when requested in writing, may disclose or cause the employees of the office of financial institutions to disclose records of the office of financial institutions concerning any person governed by this Chapter when such records are requested by another state or federal agency having authority to investigate or license such person governed by this Chapter, or are requested by a bankruptcy trustee or any law enforcement agency in connection with an investigation to recover assets of a current or former licensee.

C. Confidential records of either the office of financial institutions or of one of its supervised entities licensed under this Chapter, produced by discovery or introduced into evidence as part of a public hearing conducted under the Louisiana Administrative Procedure Act shall remain confidential and not be deemed public.

D. Notwithstanding any provision of law to the contrary, except for documents or information of other federal or state regulatory or law enforcement agencies in the possession of the office of financial institutions, any federal or state district court within Louisiana may order the office of financial institutions to disclose information and produce documents belonging to the office of financial institutions which are relevant to claims or issues at dispute in a lawsuit subject to the following conditions:

(1) The requesting party shall file the appropriate motion in the proper federal or state court setting forth the docu-

ments or information requested with sufficient specificity and the basis for such request.

(2) The requesting party shall provide the office of financial institutions with a copy of any such filing prior to any scheduled proceeding designed to resolve the motion to allow the office a reasonable period of time within which to respond to such filing in an adequate manner, but in no event fewer than ten days prior to such scheduled hearing date.

(3) When no other source for such information requested is available, and upon a showing by the requesting party of good cause and substantial need, the court may require the disclosure of all or a part of the information requested subject to a protective order. The contents and terms of such protective order shall be determined solely by the office of financial institutions with the approval of the court.

E. Notwithstanding any other provision of law to the contrary, including but not limited to R.S. 49:956(8)(c), there shall be no liability on the part of, and no cause of action shall rise against, the Office of Financial Institutions or its agents or employees for any good faith release or disclosure of information or for statements made in good faith in any administrative hearings or in any reports or communications concerning regulatory issues and the supervision and regulation of all entities under the jurisdiction of the Office of Financial Institutions.

Added by Acts 1997, No. 366, § 2. Amended by Acts 2004, No. 587, § 2, eff. June 29, 2004.

§ 3518.2. Credit cards; unsolicited delivery or mailing prohibited; penalty

A. As used in this Section, "credit card" means any credit card as defined in R.S. 9:3516(15) and any other document or device intended or adopted for the purpose of establishing the identity and credit of any person in connection with the purpose of renting on credit goods or services, or obtaining loans.

B. (1) Except as provided in Subsection C of this Section, it shall be unlawful for any financial institution, retail merchant, or other person to mail or otherwise deliver any credit card in this state.

(2) Whoever violates this Subsection may, upon conviction, be sentenced to pay a fine of not more than one thousand dollars per occurrence.

C. This Section shall not apply to any credit card when mailed or otherwise delivered either:

(1) In response to a request or application for a credit card.

(2) As a replacement for a credit card previously issued to the person to whom the credit card is shipped or mailed.

D. If any credit card is issued to a person who has not requested or accepted by use the issuance of such credit card, the issuer shall be liable to the person whose name appears on the credit card for any damages and expenses or either, including attorney fees, which the person incurs due to the use of such credit card without permission of the person to whom it is issued.

Added by Acts 1999, No. 664, § 1.

§ 3518.3. Credit cards; printing of accounting numbers on sales receipts; liability

A. As used in this Section, the following terms shall have the following meanings:

(1) "Cardholder" means the person named on the face of a credit card to whom or for whose benefit the credit card is issued by an issuer and shall include any employee or other agent or authorized user of the card.

(2) "Credit card" means any instrument or device, whether known as a credit card, credit plate, bank service card, bank card, check guarantee card, debit card, or by any other name, including an account number, issued with or without fee by an issuer for the use of a cardholder in obtaining money, goods, services, or anything else of value or for use in an automated banking device to obtain any of the services offered through the device.

(3) "Issuer" means the financial institution or other business organization which issues a credit card or its duly authorized agent.

(4) "Person" means an individual or corporation, partnership, trust association, joint venture pool, syndicate, sole proprietorship, unincorporated organization, or any other legal entity.

(5) "Provider" means a person who furnishes money, goods, services, or anything else of value upon presentation, whether physically, in writing, verbally, electronically, or otherwise of a credit card by the cardholder, or any agent or employee of such person.

B. Except as otherwise provided in this Section, no provider shall print or otherwise produce or reproduce, or permit the printing or other production or reproduction of either of the following:

(1) Any part of the credit card account number, other than the last five digits or other characters on any receipt provided or made available to the cardholder.

(2) The credit card expiration date on any receipt provided or made available to the cardholder.

C. (1) This Section shall not apply to a credit card transaction in which the sole means available to the provider of recording the credit card account number is by handwriting or by imprint of the card.

(2) This Section shall not apply to receipts issued for transactions on the electronic benefits transfer card system in accordance with 7CFR 274.12(g)(3).

D. Any provider who violates the provisions of this Section shall be liable to the cardholder and the issuer for any damages or expenses, or both, including attorney fees, which the cardholder or issuer incurs due to the use of the cardholder's credit card without the permission of the cardholder.

E. (1) The provisions of this Section shall become operative on January 1, 2004, with respect to any cash register or other machine or device that electronically prints receipts for credit card transactions that is in use prior to January 1, 2002.

(2) The provisions of this Section shall become operative on January 1, 2002, with respect to any cash register or other machine or device that electronically prints receipts for credit card transactions that is first put into use on or after January 1, 2002.

Added by Acts 2001, No. 584, § 1.

PART II. MAXIMUM CHARGES

§ 3519. Consumer loans

A. The maximum loan finance charge for any consumer loan other than one made with a lender credit card that may be charged, contracted for or received by a licensed lender or supervised financial organization may equal but not exceed:

(a) Thirty-six percent per year for that portion of the unpaid principal amount of the loan not exceeding one thousand four hundred dollars;

(b) Twenty-seven percent per year for that portion of the unpaid principal amount of the loan exceeding one thousand four hundred dollars and not exceeding four thousand dollars;

(c) Twenty-four percent per year for that portion of the unpaid principal amount on the loan exceeding four thousand dollars and not exceeding seven thousand dollars; and

(d) Twenty-one percent per year for that portion of the unpaid principal amount of the loan exceeding seven thousand dollars.

B. This Section does not limit or restrict the manner of contracting for loan finance charges under a consumer loan, whether by way of precomputed interest, simple interest, or otherwise, so long as the annualized loan finance charge rate computed on an actuarial or U.S. Rule basis over the entire scheduled term of the transaction, assuming that all payments will be made when due and disregarding the possible effects of early prepayment or acceleration of maturity, does not exceed the maximum rates permitted in this Chapter. Demand loans shall have presumed term of five years.

C. For the purposes of this section, the term of a loan commences with the date the loan is made. Differences in the lengths of months are disregarded and a day may be counted as one-thirtieth of a month. Subject to classifications and differentiations the lender may reasonably establish, a part of a month in excess of fifteen days may be treated as a full month if periods of fifteen days or less are disregarded and if that procedure is not consistently used to obtain a greater yield than would otherwise be permitted.

D. With respect to a consumer loan made pursuant to a revolving loan account

(1) the loan finance charge shall be deemed not to exceed the maximum annual rates if the loan finance charge contracted for and received does not exceed a charge in each monthly billing cycle which is one-twelfth of the maximum annual rates computed on an amount no greater than

(a) the average daily balance of the debt;

(b) the unpaid balance of the debt on the 1st day of the billing cycle, or,

(c) the median amount within a specified range within which the average daily balance or the unpaid balance of the debt, on the first day of the billing cycle, is included; for the purposes of this subparagraph and subparagraph (b), a variation of not more than four days from month to month is "the first day of the billing cycle";

(2) if the billing cycle is not monthly, the loan finance charge shall be deemed not to exceed the maximum annual rates if the loan finance charge contracted for and received does not exceed a percentage which bears the same relation to the maximum annual rates as the number of days in the billing cycle bears to 360.

E. Notwithstanding any provision of Subsection A the extender of credit may contract for and receive a minimum loan finance charge of not more than fifteen dollars when the amount advanced does not exceed two hundred dollars or twenty-five dollars when the amount advanced exceeds two hundred dollars; such charge shall be in lieu of all other finance charges.

Added by Acts 1972, No. 454, § 1, eff. Jan. 1, 1973. Amended by Acts 1974, No. 466, § 2; Acts 1980, No. 501, § 1, eff. July 22, 1980; Acts 1980, No. 694, § 1; Acts 1986, No. 584, § 1, eff. July 2, 1986.

§ 3520. Consumer credit sale

A. Except as otherwise provided by R.S. 9:3521, the maximum credit service charge for any consumer credit sale other than one made pursuant to a revolving charge account, may not exceed the equivalent of the greater of any of the following:

(1) the total of

(a) twenty-four percent per year on that part of the unpaid balances of the amount deferred which is not in excess of $1,750.00; and

(b) eighteen percent per year on that part of the unpaid balances of the amount deferred which is more than $1,750.00 and not exceeding $5,000.00;

(c) twelve percent per year on that part of the unpaid balance of the amount deferred which is more than $5,000.00; or

(2) eighteen percent per year on the unpaid balances of the amount deferred; or

(3) any other method of computation which would not yield a greater credit service charge than (1) or (2) of this section.

B. Notwithstanding Subsection A, the seller may contract for and receive a minimum credit service charge of not more than five dollars when the amount deferred does not exceed seventy-five dollars, or seven dollars and fifty cents when the amount deferred exceeds seventy-five dollars.

C. This Section does not limit or restrict the manner of contracting for credit service charges under a consumer credit sale, whether by way of precomputed interest, simple interest, or otherwise, so long as the annualized credit service charge rate computed on an actuarial or U.S. Rule basis over the entire scheduled term of the transaction, assuming that all payments will be made when due and disregarding the possible effects of early prepayment or acceleration of maturity, does not exceed the maximum rates permitted in this Chapter.

D. It shall be unlawful for a seller to charge a consumer a fee for sending an initial billing statement; however, the seller may charge a fee for any additional billing statement sent at the request of the consumer.

Added by Acts 1972, No. 454, § 1, eff. Jan. 1, 1973. Amended by Acts 1986, No. 584, § 1, eff. July 2, 1986; Acts 1997, No. 327, § 1.

§ 3521. Maximum charges after negotiations

A. The obligation arising out of any consumer credit sale, including a revolving charge account, may be evidenced by a written agreement which may provide for a credit service charge not in excess of the maximum loan finance charge which could be charged, contracted for, or received by a supervised financial organization, lender who files notification pursuant to R.S. 9:3564, or licensed lender in a consumer loan transaction where the principal is the same as the amount financed and the term is a corresponding term.

B. Such written agreement must be transferred or assigned to a supervised financial organization, lender who files notification pursuant to R.S. 9:3564, or a licensed lender within thirty-five days from the date of making. If such written agreement is not so transferred or assigned within the said time limit, the seller or holder shall:

(1) Notify the maker that the written agreement was not transferred or assigned.

(2) Credit the obligation with any amounts contracted for in excess of the credit service charge authorized by R.S. 9:3520 and 9:3521. Such computation shall be made as of the date of making and the debtor shall be notified of such credit.

(3) Provide the debtor, prior to the first installment due date, with a new payment schedule reflecting the change in terms.

(4) Notify the debtor of the address where payments are to be made if such address is different from the address previously given to the debtor.

Added by Acts 1972, No. 454, § 1, eff. Jan. 1, 1973. Amended by Acts 1980, No. 694, § 1; Acts 1990, No. 685, § 1; Acts 1999, No. 1315, § 1, eff. Jan. 1, 2000.

§ 3522. Maximum charges after maturity

In the case of a precomputed consumer credit transaction which is unpaid at contractual maturity, the rate of the loan finance charge or the credit service charge for the period beginning as of contractual maturity until payment in full may not exceed the rate of the loan finance charge or the credit service charge previously agreed to by the extender of credit and the debtor at the time the consumer credit transaction was entered into. Provided however, beginning one year after contractual maturity, the rate shall not exceed 18% per annum.

Added by Acts 1972, No. 454, § 1, eff. Jan. 1, 1973. Amended by Acts 1980, No. 694, § 1.

§ 3523. Credit service charge for revolving charge accounts

On a revolving charge account, the extender of credit, issuer of a seller credit card honored by the extender of credit, or their assignee, may charge and collect a credit service charge in each billing period at a rate

(1) not in excess of one and one-half percent per month computed on (a) the average daily balance of the account or (b) the balance of the account on the first day of each billing period without regard to transactions affecting the account during the billing period; provided, however, that a minimum credit service charge not in excess of fifty cents per month may be charged and collected; and provided further that no credit service charge shall be charged unless the bill is mailed no later than ten days (Saturdays, Sundays and legal holidays excluded) after the billing date stated on the bill; or

(2) any other method of computation which would not yield a greater credit service charge than subsection (1) of this section.

Added by Acts 1972, No. 454, § 1, eff. Jan. 1, 1973.

§ 3524. Loan finance charge on lender credit card accounts

A. (1) On a revolving loan account made with a lender credit card, an extender of credit or an assignee or a transferee thereof may receive or contract to receive and collect a loan finance charge in an amount not in excess of one and one-half percent per month computed in accordance with the following:

(a) For the period ending December 31, 1974, on either:

(i) The average daily unpaid balance of the principal of the debt during the billing period; or

(ii) The balance of the account on the first day of each billing period without regard to transactions affecting the account during the billing period.

(b) Commencing January 1, 1975 and thereafter:

(i) On the average daily unpaid balance of the principal of the debt during the billing period; or

(ii) Any method of loan finance charge computation which may produce yield not in excess of the average daily balance method of loan finance charge calculation as provided for in (1)(b)(i) above.

(2) For purposes of the foregoing computation, a month shall be deemed as any time of thirty consecutive days, or alternatively, any calendar month.

(3) An extender of credit may impose such a loan finance charge from the date that goods, property, or services are purchased or cash advances are obtained under a lender credit card plan; however, an extender of credit may not impose or collect a loan finance charge on goods, property, or services purchased under a lender credit card plan for the first twenty-five days of any billing cycle when the borrowing consumer pays the entire billed balance of his account within said initial twenty-five day period.

B. Repealed by Acts 1988, No. 629, § 2.

C. If the billing period is more frequent than monthly, the maximum loan finance charge for such billing period shall be the percentage which bears the same relation to the monthly percentage provided for in Subsection A of this section as the number of days in the billing period bears to thirty.

D. In addition to the loan finance charge provided for in Subsection A of this section, extenders of credit under a lender credit card plan may lawfully receive, contract for and collect a fee for the privilege of receiving cash advances under such a lender credit card plan. The fee shall not exceed four percent of the amount of the cash advance.

E. Where an account has the attributes of both a revolving loan account and a lender credit card account, the creditor may elect to treat such an account as either a revolving loan account subject to R.S. 9:3519(D), or as a lender credit card account subject to this Section. Examples of such accounts include, without limitation:

(1) Overdraft lines of credit that may be accessed by use of an automated teller machine.

(2) An independent line of credit issued by a supervised financial organization in conjunction with a travel and entertainment credit card account offered by a third party creditor.

Added by Acts 1972, No. 454, § 1, eff. Jan. 1, 1973. Amended by Acts 1974, No. 466, § 1; Acts 1986, No. 584, § 1, eff. July 2, 1986; Acts 1990, No. 709, § 2, eff. July 20, 1990.

§ 3524.1. [Blank]

§ 3524.2. [Blank]

§ 3525. Leap years

The effects of a leap year may be disregarded for purposes of determining whether the annualized loan finance charge rate or credit service rate under a consumer credit transaction exceeds the maximum rate limitations provided in this Part.

Added by Acts 1986, No. 584, § 1, eff. July 2, 1986.

§ 3526. Variable rates

A. Licensed lenders and supervised financial organizations may enter into variable rate consumer credit transactions under this Chapter in the manner provided under R.S. 6:242(A)(2) and regulations issued by the commissioner.

B. Licensed lenders and supervised financial organizations may also enter into graduated payment mortgage loans and adjustable rate mortgage loans under this Chapter in the manner provided under R.S. 9:3504(C) and 3504(D), respectively.

Added by Acts 1986, No. 584, § 1, eff. July 2, 1986.

§ 3526.1. [Blank]

§ 3526.2. [Blank]

§ 3526.3. [Blank]

§ 3527. Maximum delinquency charges; notice of conversion

A. The parties to a consumer credit transaction may contract for the payment of a delinquency charge on any installment or other regular payment not paid in full within ten days after its scheduled or deferred due date in either one of the following amounts:

(1) Five percent of the unpaid amount of the delinquent installment, or ten dollars, whichever is greater.

(2) The deferral charge that would be permitted to defer the unpaid amount of the installment or other regular payment for the period that it is delinquent.

B. The parties to a revolving loan account or lender credit card account may contract for the payment of a delinquency charge not to exceed fifteen dollars on any regularly scheduled payment not paid in full within ten days of the payment due date.

C. (1) A delinquency charge may be collected only once on an installment or other payment however long it remains delinquent. No such delinquency charge may be collected if the installment or other payment has been deferred and a deferral charge has been paid or incurred, provided that the deferred payment is paid within ten days of its deferred date. Such a delinquency charge may be collected at the time it accrues or at any time thereafter.

(2) No such delinquency charge may be collected on an installment or other regular payment that is paid in full within ten days after its scheduled due date even though an earlier maturing installment, other payment, or delinquency charge on an earlier installment or other payment may not have been paid in full. For purposes of determining delinquency, payments are deemed to be applied first to current installments or other payments due and then to delinquent installments or other payments and then to delinquent and other charges.

(3) An extender of credit is prohibited from levying or collecting any delinquency charge on a payment when the only delinquency is attributable to late fees or delinquency charges assessed on earlier installments, and the payment is otherwise a full payment for the applicable period and is paid on its due date or within an applicable grace period.

(4) Nothing in this Subsection shall be construed to prohibit the extender of credit from assessing and collecting a finance charge on any delinquency or deferral charges not paid when due. Such finance charges shall not exceed the contract rate charged on the consumer transaction.

D. If two installments or other regular payments or parts thereof of a precomputed consumer credit transaction are in default for ten days or more, the extender of credit may, upon first giving the consumer written notice, elect to convert the precomputed consumer credit transaction into a simple interest transaction. The notice must state the exact date on which the conversion will occur, the interest rate to be charged under the simple interest transaction, the balance due on the loan at the time of the conversion, and whether or not there will be a balloon payment. In this event he shall make a rebate pursuant to the provisions on rebate upon prepayment as of the maturity date of a delinquent installment or other regular payment, and thereafter may make a loan finance charge or credit service charge as authorized by this Part. The amount of the rebate shall not be reduced by the amount of any minimum loan finance charge or minimum credit service charge as provided in R.S. 9:3519(E) and 3520(B); however, the extender of credit may deduct a prepayment charge as provided in R.S. 9:3532.

E. A creditor may contractually reserve the right to prospectively increase the simple interest rate under a consumer loan transaction upon or at any time following the borrower's default. However, such a default interest rate shall not exceed the loan finance charge rate or rates authorized under R.S. 9:3519(A).

Added by Acts 1972, No. 454, § 1, eff. Jan. 1, 1973. Amended by Acts 1980, No. 694, § 1; Acts 1982, No. 370, § 1; Acts 1986, No. 584, § 1, eff. July 2, 1986; Acts 1988, No. 629, § 1; Acts 1993, No. 726, § 1; Acts 1995, No. 1184, § 2; Acts 1997, No. 227, § 1; Acts 1997, No. 1033, § 1; Acts 2003, No. 337, § 2; Acts 2004, No. 763, § 1, eff. July 6, 2004.

§ 3528. Maximum deferral charges

A. (1) With respect to a precomputed consumer credit transaction payable in more than one installment, the parties before or after default may agree in writing to a deferral of all or part of one or more unpaid installments, and the extender of credit may make and collect a charge not exceeding the rate previously stated to the consumer calculated without regard to differences in the lengths of months, but proportionately for a part of a month, counting each day as one-thirtieth of a month. A deferral charge may be collected at the time it is assessed or at any time thereafter. Deferral charges on a precomputed consumer credit transaction may be computed on a pro rata basis or any other method of calculation that does not yield a greater sum than the maximum rates permitted in this Chapter.

(2) In lieu of a deferral charge, the entire unpaid balance of the transaction may be deferred by charging an amount equal to the rate previously stated to the consumer times the balance at the time of deferral for the period of deferral. In such a case, the transaction maturity date will be extended by the number of months that the balance is deferred.

B. The parties may agree in writing at the time of a precomputed consumer credit transaction that if an installment is not paid within ten days after its due date, the extender of credit may unilaterally grant a deferral and make charges as provided in this Section, provided the transaction consists of more than one installment. No deferral charge may be made for a period after the date that the extender of credit elects to accelerate the maturity of the agreement. A delinquency charge made by the extender of credit on an installment may not be retained if a deferral charge is made pursuant to this Section with respect to the period of delinquency.

C. In addition to the lawful rate of loan finance charges that may be assessed on the outstanding balance of a simple interest consumer credit transaction, the parties may before or after default agree in writing to a deferral of all or part of one or more unpaid installments, and the extender of credit may make and collect an additional deferral charge in an amount not to exceed twenty-five dollars. This deferral charge may be collected at the time it is assessed or at any time thereafter. Whether accrued interest is designated as "loan finance charges" or "interest to date", payment of interest shall not constitute payment of a deferral charge.

D. The extender of credit, in addition to the deferral charge, may make appropriate charges for insurance for the extended period and the amount of these charges which is not paid in cash may be added to the amount for the purpose of calculating the deferral charge.

Added by Acts 1972, No. 454, § 1, eff. Jan. 1, 1973. Amended by Acts 1974, No. 466, § 1. Redesignated from R.S. 9:3526 to R.S. 9:3528 on authority of Acts 1986, No. 584, § 5, eff. July 2, 1986. Amended by Acts 1991, No. 697, § 1; Acts 1995, No. 1184, § 2; Acts 1997, No. 67, § 1; Acts 1997, No. 1033, § 1; Acts 1999, No. 1315, § 1, eff. Jan. 1, 2000.

§ 3529. Installment of consumer credit transaction returned; additional charge to account

The parties in a consumer credit transaction may contract for an additional charge to be assessed against the consumer's account if the consumer tenders a check or makes an electronic debit in payment on such account and such check or electronic debit is returned from any bank, savings and loan association, thrift institution, or credit union or any other organization or institution authorized by the state of Louisiana or the United States to issue checks, drafts, or similar negotiable instruments or payments by electronic means, due to insufficient credit or funds in the account for payment of such check or electronic payment in full upon its presentation, or due to account closure, stop payment, drawn on uncollected funds, or any other reason for which the instrument or electronic payment is not paid. The additional charge shall not exceed twenty-five dollars or five percent of the amount of the check or electronic payment, whichever is greater. The charge shall be in addition to any delinquency charge assessed under the provisions of R.S. 9:3527. For the purposes of this Section, the phrase "due to insufficient credit or funds" means a check or electronic payment returned unpaid for any reason.

Added by Acts 1981, No. 473, § 1. Redesignated from R.S. 9:3526.1 to R.S. 9:3529 in 1986 on authority of Acts 1986, No. 584, § 5, eff. July 2, 1986. Amended by Acts 1999, No. 690, § 1; Acts 2004, No. 65, § 2; Acts 2005, No. 132, § 1; Acts 2008, No. 476, § 2.

§ 3530. Fees; origination; notary, documentation; over-the-credit-limit fee

A. (1) A lender may charge an origination fee that does not exceed fifty dollars on a consumer loan or revolving loan account.

(2) The origination fee may be charged only once in connection with a single loan to one borrower over any consecutive thirty-day period, regardless of the number of renewals or refinances during the same thirty-day period. An origination fee may be charged on any new loan made during a prior loan's consecutive thirty-day period provided the new loan is not a renewal, refinance, or rollover of the prior loan. When a loan is paid in full, an origination fee may be charged on any subsequent new loan without regard to the prior loan's consecutive thirty-day period.

(3) Notwithstanding any other law to the contrary, an origination fee shall not be considered a loan finance charge and shall not be subject to refund upon prepayment or acceleration of maturity.

(4) Repealed by Acts 2003, No. 633, § 2.

B. Non-real estate related notary fees assessed in connection with consumer credit transactions subject to this Chapter are limited to a maximum of fifteen dollars.

C. (1) A lender may charge a documentation fee in an amount not to exceed one-half of the amount authorized in Paragraph (4) of this Subsection, in connection with a non-real estate consumer loan transaction.

(2) Notwithstanding any other law to the contrary, a documentation fee shall not be considered as interest nor shall it be included in the calculation of interest.

(3) An insurance premium finance company may not charge a documentation fee under this Subsection.

(4) In lieu of the documentation fee provided in Paragraph (1) of this Subsection, a lender may charge a documentation fee, not to exceed twenty dollars, in connection with any non-real estate consumer loan not subject to R.S. 9:3578.1 through 3578.8.

D. A lender upon entering into a revolving loan or lender credit card account that is secured by a collateral mortgage or equivalent security interest on immovable (real) property, may assess an origination fee in an amount not to exceed two percent of the consumer's established credit limit. Such origination fees may be assessed in addition to permissible loan finance charges and are not subject to rebate upon cancellation or termination of the consumer's account.

E. (1) A lender may contract for and receive reasonable over-the-credit-limit fees in connection with revolving loan, lender credit card, revolving charge and seller credit card accounts that are payable whenever the consumer exceeds the credit limit established for the account.

(2) A lender shall cease the assessment of over-the-credit-limit fees in connection with lender credit card and seller credit card accounts upon termination of the contract.

F. (1) A lender may charge the consumer the convenience fee authorized by R.S. 47:532.1(C) for services performed by a public license tag agent as well as any E.L.T. fees pursuant to R.S. 32:707.2. Such fees shall not be charged to the consumer more than once.

(2) Notwithstanding any other law to the contrary, the convenience fee authorized by R.S. 47:532.1(C) as well as any E.L.T. fees shall not be considered as interest nor shall they be included in the calculation of interest.

G. Notwithstanding the limitations set in this Section or any other law to the contrary, a federally insured depository institution entering into a consumer credit transaction as defined in R.S. 9:3516(13) may contract for and receive the types of fees provided for in Subsections A, C, and D of this Section in any amount agreed to in a written agreement signed by the consumer. Fees charged under this Subsection by a federally insured depository institution shall not be considered loan finance charges or credit service charges under this Chapter.

Added by Acts 1982, No. 434, § 1. Amended by Acts 1986, No. 584, § 1, eff. July 2, 1986. R.S. 9:3526.2 redesignated as subsec. A on authority of Acts 1986, No. 584, § 5, eff. July 2, 1986. Amended by Acts 1987, No. 498, § 1; Acts 1988, No. 629, § 1; Acts 1995, No. 153, § 1; Acts 1995, No. 1184, § 2; Acts 1999, No. 514, § 1; Acts 1999, No. 1315, § 1, eff. Jan. 1, 2000; Acts 2004, No. 89, § 1; Acts 2005, No. 123, § 1, eff. June 22, 2005; Acts 2007, No. 31, § 1; Acts 2010, No. 96, § 1; Acts 2010, No. 668, § 1; Acts 2011, No. 115, § 1.

§ 3530.1. [Blank]

PART III. PREPAYMENT OF CONSUMER CREDIT TRANSACTIONS

§ 3531. Right to prepay

A. Notwithstanding any contrary provision of a consumer credit transaction, the consumer may prepay in full the unpaid balance at any time. An extender of credit may within its discretion accept the amount tendered by the consumer to be a prepayment in full of a simple interest loan if the amount tendered is within one dollar, or to the extent provided by federal law, more or less, of the amount actually owed. Under such circumstances, the extender of credit may retain any excess amount tendered by the consumer provided that the amount tendered does not exceed the amount actually owed by more than one dollar, or to the extent provided by federal law.

B. (1) The extender of credit shall provide the consumer, within five days of the date a written request is received from the consumer, with the amount necessary to prepay the account in full; and if the amount disclosed includes an amount which is required to be refunded under this Section with respect to such prepayment, the amount of such refund.

(2) A consumer shall be entitled to receive one such disclosure of information statement each year without charge. Thereafter, the extender of credit may impose a reasonable fee to cover the cost of providing an additional disclosure statement; however, the charge imposed must be disclosed to the consumer before furnishing such disclosure statement.

Added by Acts 1972, No. 454, § 1, eff. Jan. 1, 1973. Redesignated from R.S. 9:3527 to 9:3531 on authority of Acts 1986, No. 584, § 5, eff. July 2, 1986. Amended by Acts 1991, No. 697, § 1; Acts 1997, No. 237, § 1; Acts 1999, No. 1315, § 1, eff. Jan. 1, 2000.

§ 3532. Rebate upon prepayment

A. Upon prepayment in full of a precomputed consumer credit transaction, the extender of credit shall refund unearned loan finance charges or credit service charges and such refund shall represent at least as great a proportion of the loan finance charge or credit service charge after first deducting from such charge a prepayment charge of not more than twenty-five dollars as the sum of the monthly time balances beginning one month after the month in which prepayment is made, bears to the sum of all the monthly time balances under the schedule of payments in the contract; this method of rebate upon prepayment is commonly referred to as the "Rule of 78's" or the "Sum of Digits" rebate method. If more than one-half of the term of the installment contract has elapsed, the rebate shall be computed without deducting a prepayment charge. For the purposes of rebate upon prepayment, deferral charges are not required to be rebated. No rebate less than one dollar, or to the extent provided for by federal law is required.

B. (1) There is no requirement that prepaid finance charges be rebated upon prepayment in full of a simple interest transaction prior to maturity, provided that all of the following conditions are satisfied:

(a) The original amount financed under the transaction was ten thousand dollars or more.

(b) The original scheduled term of the transaction was thirty-six months or longer.

(c) Prepaid finance charges assessed under the transaction did not exceed five percent of the original amount financed or amount deferred.

(2) Where any one or more of the foregoing conditions are not satisfied, prepaid finance charges shall be subject to rebate upon prepayment in full of a simple interest transaction under the same method in Subsection A of this Section.

C. Compliance with the provisions of this Section shall constitute compliance with the provisions of R.S. 9:3519.

Added by Acts 1972, No. 454, § 1, eff. Jan. 1, 1973. Amended by Acts 1978, No. 761, § 1; Acts 1986, No. 584, § 1, eff. July 2, 1986. Redesignated from R.S. 9:3528 to 9:3532 on authority of Acts 1986, No. 584, § 5, eff. July 2, 1986. Amended by Acts 1990, No. 685, § 1; Acts 1990, No. 796, § 1; Acts 1995, No. 1184, § 2; Acts 1997, No. 237, § 1.

§ 3532.1. Prepayment penalties in connection with simple interest real estate secured loans

A. As a condition of the consumer's being permitted to prepay a consumer loan secured by a mortgage on immovable property in full prior to the loan's maturity, an extender of credit may contract for and receive a prepayment penalty in an amount not to exceed:

(1) Five percent of the unpaid principal balance if the loan is prepaid in full during the first year of its term.

(2) Four percent of the unpaid principal balance if the loan is prepaid in full during the second year of its term.

(3) Three percent of the unpaid principal balance if the loan is prepaid in full during the third year of its term.

(4) Two percent of the unpaid principal balance if the loan is prepaid in full during the fourth year of its term.

(5) One percent of the unpaid principal balance if the loan is prepaid in full during the fifth year of its term.

B. No prepayment penalties shall be assessed if the loan is prepaid in full after the fifth year of its term. Prepayment penalties may be assessed under this Section only with respect to consumer real estate secured loans that bear simple interest, and that have an original principal balance of twenty-five thousand dollars or more, and that are payable over a term of seven years or longer.

C. Notwithstanding any other provision of law to the contrary, no prepayment penalty or similar fee or charge shall be due, assessed, charged, collected, paid, held in escrow, or contracted to be paid if all or part of a prepayment of all or part of an outstanding loan balance is made from proceeds paid in full or partial satisfaction of a claim or claims made under a policy or policies of insurance insuring against casualty, flood, or other loss or damage to property securing the loan being prepaid in connection with a gubernatorially declared disaster.

Added by Acts 1995, No. 1184, § 2. Amended by Acts 2006, No. 188, § 2.

§ 3533. Rebate after acceleration of maturity

Except as provided in R.S. 9:3527, if the maturity of a consumer credit transaction is accelerated for any reason and suit is filed, the obligation shall be credited with the same rebate required under R.S. 9:3532(A) or (B), as applicable, as if prepayment in full had been made as of the date the maturity of the obligation is accelerated at the creditor's election, except that any credit life insurance and health and accident insurance in force at such time shall not be rebated until payment is made in full; thereafter the obligation sued upon shall be deemed to bear a loan finance charge or credit service charge on the amount due at the annualized rate previously agreed to by the consumer until the transaction is paid in full.

Added by Acts 1972, No. 454, § 1, eff. Jan. 1, 1973. Amended by Acts 1983, No. 365, § 1; Acts 1986, No. 584, § 1, eff. July 2, 1986. Redesignated from R.S. 9:3529 to R.S. 9:3533 on authority of Acts 1986, No. 584, § 5, eff. July 2, 1986.

PART IV. LIMITATIONS ON AGREEMENTS AND PRACTICES

§ 3534. Fees; attorney, collection agency

A. Any consumer credit transaction agreement may provide for the payment by the consumer of attorney's fees not in excess of twenty-five per cent of the unpaid debt after default and referral to an attorney for collection.

B. An extender of credit may not contract with a consumer for the reimbursement of fees paid to a collection agency employed to collect the consumer's indebtedness.

Added by Acts 1972, No. 454, § 1, eff. Jan. 1, 1973. Amended by Acts 1974, No. 466, § 1; Acts 1986, No. 584, § 1, eff. July 2, 1986. R.S. 9:3530 redesignated as subsec. A on authority of Acts 1986, No. 584, § 5, eff. July 2, 1986.

§ 3534.1. Collection agent; registration; assignment of debt to collector

A. For purposes of this Section, "collection agency" and "debt collector" are synonymous and interchangeable terms and mean any person, other than a licensed Louisiana attorney, who uses any instrumentality of intrastate or interstate commerce or the mails in any business the principal purpose of which is the collection of any debts, or who regularly collects or attempts to collect, directly or indirectly, debts owed or due or asserted to be owed or due another, and relative to Louisiana clients, notwithstanding the fact that such person has no employees, offices, equipment, or other physical facilities in this state, or any person who regularly attempts to collect, directly or indirectly, debts owed or due, or asserted to be owed or due another, and who is located in the state regardless of whether the person has Louisiana clients.

B. Any collection agency or debt collector doing business in this state shall register with the secretary of state. The secretary of state shall promulgate rules and regulations necessary to provide for the registration required by this Section.

C. In any suit brought by a collection agency or debt collector to collect a debt acquired from a client or customer via assignment, an agreement in writing by the such collector to expend time, effort, money, or other resources in pursuit of such debt, and to pay the credit grantor a net percentage of the amount collected on the debt shall be deemed a valid and enforceable assignment pursuant to this Section, and all other applicable laws of Louisiana.

D. When such collector attempts the collection of a debt owed a credit grantor, the representation of the credit grantor by such collector shall in all instances be deemed as an assignment and authorization for the purpose of allowing such collector to bring legal action to collect the debt. When such legal action is brought through an attorney licensed to practice law by the Supreme Court of Louisiana it shall not be a violation of any state law, rule, or regulation including but not limited to R.S. 37:212.

E. In any suit brought by a collection agency or debt collection to collect the debt of a client or customer, the formal assignment of the debt to such collector shall be presumed valid if a copy of the assignment is filed in court with the petition. If the defendant fails to object to the validity of the assignment prior to the filing of an answer, then the assignment shall be conclusively presumed valid.

F. Subsections C and D of this Section shall apply in all instances whether or not the debt is assigned for valuable consideration; whether or not the services performed by the attorney were for the collector alone; whether or not the collector hired the attorney; and whether or not the collector's fees are contingent upon the amount collected by the attorney.

Added by Acts 2006, No. 534, § 1, eff. June 22, 2006.

Editor's note. Section 2 of Acts 2006, No. 534 declares: "The provisions of this Section are remedial in nature and shall be applied retroactively in application. For possible constitutional objections to the retroactive application, see Yiannopoulos, Civil Law System §§ 110–112 (2d ed. 1999; id., Civil Law property § 10 (2001)).

§ 3534.5. [Blank]

§ 3535. Use of multiple agreements

An extender of credit shall not divide a consumer credit transaction into multiple agreements for the purpose of obtaining a higher credit service charge, loan finance charge, or any other additional fee or charge permitted by this Chapter.

Added by Acts 1972, No. 454, § 1, eff. Jan. 1, 1973. Redesignated from R.S. 9:3531 to R.S. 9:3535 on authority of Acts 1986, No. 584, § 5, eff. July 2, 1986. Amended by Acts 1997, No. 50, § 1.

§ 3536. Referral sales

With respect to a consumer credit transaction, the extender of credit may not give or offer to give a rebate or discount or otherwise pay or offer to pay value to the consumer as an inducement for a sale in consideration of his giving to the extender of credit the names of prospective purchasers or otherwise aiding the extender of credit in making a sale to another person, if the earning of the rebate, discount or other value is contingent upon the occurrence of an event subsequent to the time the consumer agrees to buy. If a consumer is induced by a violation of this Section to enter into a consumer credit transaction, the agreement is unenforceable by the extender of credit and the consumer, at his option, may rescind the agreement or retain the goods delivered and the benefit of any services performed, without any obligation to pay for them.

Added by Acts 1972, No. 454, § 1, eff. Jan. 1, 1973. Amended by Acts 1985, No. 592, § 2, eff. July 13, 1985.

§ 3537. Repealed by Acts 1980, No. 694, § 2

PART V. HOME SOLICITATION SALES

§ 3538. Consumer's right to cancel

A. Except as provided in subsection (E) of this section, in addition to any right otherwise to revoke an offer, the consumer has the right to cancel a home solicitation sale until midnight of the third business day after the day on which the consumer signs an agreement or offer to purchase.

B. Cancellation occurs when the consumer gives written notice of cancellation to the seller at the address stated in the agreement or offer to purchase.

C. Notice of cancellation, if given by mail, is given when it is deposited in a mailbox properly addressed and postage prepaid.

D. Notice of cancellation given by the consumer need not take a particular form and is sufficient if it indicates by any form of written expression the intention of the consumer not to be bound by the home solicitation sale.

E. The consumer may not cancel a home solicitation sale if the consumer requests the seller to provide goods or services without delay because of an emergency, and

(1) the seller in good faith makes a substantial beginning of performance of the contract before the consumer gives notice of cancellation, and

(2) in the case of goods, the goods cannot be returned to the seller in substantially as good condition as when received by the consumer.

F. The term "home solicitation sale" as used in this Part, shall be defined as provided in R.S. 9:2711.1 and R.S. 9:3516(20).

Added by Acts 1972, No. 454, § 1, eff. Jan. 1, 1973. Amended by Acts 1982, No. 744, § 1.

§ 3538.1. [Blank]

§ 3539. Form of agreement or offer; statement of consumer's right; compliance

A. In a home solicitation sale, unless the consumer requests the seller to provide goods or services without delay in an emergency, the seller must present to the consumer and obtain his signature to a written agreement or offer to purchase that designates as the date of the transaction the date on which the consumer actually signs and contains a statement of the consumer's rights that complies with subsection B of this section.

B. The statement must

(1) appear under the conspicuous caption: "CONSUMER'S RIGHT TO CANCEL", and

(2) read as follows: "If this agreement was solicited at your residence and you do not want the goods or services, you may cancel this agreement by mailing a notice to the seller. The notice must say that you do not want the goods or services and must be mailed before midnight of the third business day after you sign this agreement. The notice must be mailed to: (Insert name and mailing address of seller). If you cancel, the seller must return all of your cash down payment."

C. Until the seller has complied with this section the consumer may cancel the home solicitation sale by notifying the seller in any manner and by any means of his intention to cancel.

D. Compliance with the notice requirements of the consumer's right to cancel a home solicitation sale of the Code of Federal Regulations Title 12, Part 226, commonly known as Regulation Z of the Consumer Credit Protection Act, 15 United States Code, Sections 1601 through 1681 or the Federal Trade Commission trade regulation providing for a cooling-off period for door-to-door sales of the Code of Federal Regulations, Title 16, Part 429 shall constitute compliance with this Section.

Added by Acts 1972, No. 454, § 1, eff. Jan. 1, 1973. Amended by Acts 1974, No. 466, § 1; Acts 1978, No. 373, § 1.

§ 3540. Restoration of down payment; retention of cancellation fee

A. Except as provided in this section, within ten days after a home solicitation sale has been cancelled or an offer to purchase revoked the seller must tender to the consumer any payments made by the consumer and any note or other evidence of indebtedness.

B. If the down payment includes goods traded in, the goods must be tendered in substantially as good condition as when received by the seller. If the seller fails to tender the goods as provided by this section, the consumer may elect to recover an amount equal to the trade-in allowance stated in the agreement.

C. The seller may retain as a cancellation fee five percent of the cash price but not exceeding the amount of the cash down payment. If the seller fails to comply with an obligation imposed by this section, or if the consumer avoids the sale on any ground independent of his right to cancel provided by the provisions on the consumer's right to cancel (R.S. 9:3538) or revokes his offer to purchase, the seller is not entitled to retain a cancellation fee.

D. Until the seller has complied with the obligations imposed by this section the consumer may retain possession of goods delivered to him by the seller and has a privilege on the goods in his possession or control for any recovery to which he is entitled.

Added by Acts 1972, No. 454, § 1, eff. Jan. 1, 1973.

§ 3541. Duty of consumer; no compensation for services prior to cancellation

A. Except as provided by the provisions on retention of goods by the consumer (R.S. 9:3540(D)), within a reasonable time after a home solicitation sale has been cancelled or an offer to purchase revoked, the consumer upon demand must tender to the seller any goods delivered by the seller pursuant to the sale but he is not obligated to tender at any place other than his residence. If the seller fails to demand possession of goods within a reasonable time after cancellation or revocation, the goods become the property of the consumer without obligation to pay for them. For the purpose of this section, forty days is presumed to be a reasonable time.

B. The consumer has a duty to take reasonable care of the goods in his possession before cancellation or revocation and for a reasonable time thereafter, during which time the goods are otherwise at the seller's risk.

C. If the seller has performed any services pursuant to a home solicitation sale prior to its cancellation, the seller is entitled to no compensation except the cancellation fee provided in this part.

Added by Acts 1972, No. 454, § 1, eff. Jan. 1, 1973.

§ 3541.1. Consumer's right to cancel mail and check solicitation sales

A. (1) In addition to any right otherwise to revoke an offer, a consumer shall have the right to cancel a mail and check solicitation sale, except when the sale is made to and accepted by a customer who has an existing loan, revolving account, or other line of credit with the party making the mail and check solicitation sale.

(2) For purposes of this Section, a "mail and check solicitation sale" means a consumer credit sale of a thing or service, a consumer credit transaction, a revolving loan account, or a credit card, if such sale, transaction, loan, or the use of such credit card is contracted:

(a) Pursuant to a solicitation received by the consumer through the mail.

(b) Through the cashing of a check by the consumer that was sent to him with the solicitation.

B. The consumer has the right to cancel such mail and check solicitation sale for at least sixty days and receive a refund for the return of unused and undamaged goods or cancellations of unused services.

C. (1) Cancellation occurs when the consumer gives notice of cancellation to the person making such solicitation.

(2)(a) Notice of cancellation given by the consumer need not take a particular form and is sufficient if it indicates by any form of expression the intention of the consumer not to be bound by the check and mail solicitation sale.

(b) Notice of cancellation, if given by mail, is given when it is deposited in a mailbox properly addressed and postage prepaid.

D. The cancellation of the mail and check solicitation sale shall occur even if the consumer has cashed the check or utilized the credit, loan account, or credit card.

E. In addition, such a check shall contain the following language as a conspicuous caption: "WARNING: THE CASHING OF THIS CHECK WILL ENROLL YOU IN A PROGRAM OR A LOAN, OR WILL CAUSE YOU TO BE BOUND TO REPAY THE LOAN OR PURCHASE GOODS OR SERVICES WHICH MAY COST YOU ADDITIONAL MONEY."

Added by Acts 1999, No. 67, § 1. Amended by Acts 2001, No. 1038, § 1.

PART V–A. HOME SOLICITATION OF AGED PERSONS

§ 3541.21. Definitions

In this Part, the following words and terms have these meanings:

(1) "Aged person" means a natural person who is sixty-five years of age or older.

(2) "Consumer" means a natural person who purchases goods, services, or movable or immovable property or rights therein, for a personal, family, household, or agricultural purpose and includes a purchaser or buyer in a consumer credit sale or transaction made with the use of a seller credit card or otherwise, or a borrower or debtor in a consumer loan, revolving loan account, or a lender credit card.

(3) "Disabled person" means a natural person who has a physical or mental impairment which substantially limits one or more major life activities.

(4) "Goods" means tangible objects bought or leased for use primarily for a personal, family, or household purpose, including certificates or coupons exchangeable for these goods which, at the time of the sale or subsequently, are to be so affixed to immovable property as to become a part of the immovable property whether or not severable therefrom.

(5) A "home solicitation sale" is a consumer credit sale of goods or services or both, other than motor vehicles, farm equipment, or services, in which the seller or a person acting for him engages in a personal solicitation of the sale at any place other than the business establishment of the seller and a consumer's agreement or offer to purchase is given to the seller or a person acting for him. This definition shall include all telephone sales in which the seller has initiated contact regardless of his location, and the consumer's agreement to purchase is made at the consumer's home. It does not include a sale made pursuant to a preexisting revolving charge account, a catalogue credit sale, a preexisting consumer credit sale agreement providing for a series of sales, or a sale made pursuant to prior negotiations between the parties at a business establishment at a fixed location where goods or services are offered or exhibited for sale, or a sale that may have been initiated by the consumer by communication with the seller at his business establishment.

(6) "Person" means an individual, partnership, corporation, limited liability company, association, or other group, however organized.

(7) "Services" means work, labor, and services for other than a commercial or business and including services furnished in connection with the sale or repair of goods.

(8) "Transaction" means an agreement between a consumer and any other person, whether or not the agreement is a contract enforceable by action, and includes the making of, and the performance pursuant to, that agreement.

Added by Acts 1997, No. 194, § 1.

§ 3541.22. Prohibited practices

A. The home solicitation of any consumer where a loan is made encumbering the primary residence of that consumer for the purposes of paying for home improvements and where the transaction is part of a pattern or practice in violation of either Subsection (h) or (i) of Section 1639 of Title 15 of the United States Code or Subsection (e) of Section 226.32 of Title 12 of the Code of Federal Regulations is prohibited.

B. A third party holder in due course of a loan made in violation of Subsection A of this Section shall not be in violation of the prohibitions in this Section unless there was an agency relationship between the person who engaged in home solicitation and the third party holder, or the third party holder had actual knowledge of or participated in the transaction.

Added by Acts 1997, No. 194, § 1. Amended by Acts 2003, No. 514, § 1.

PART VI. INSURANCE

§ 3542. Requirement of insurance

A. In any consumer credit transaction made under the authority of this Chapter, other than insurance premium financing, an extender of credit may request or require a consumer to provide credit life insurance, credit dismemberment insurance, and credit health and accident insurance as additional security for such contract or agreement. If the extender of credit provides credit life insurance, credit dismemberment insurance, or credit health and accident insurance to a consumer, he shall disclose to the consumer at the time of contracting his option to purchase such insurance coverage or shall make such disclosures as are required by Regulation Z of the Board of Governors of the Federal Reserve System, 12 C.F.R. 226.1 et seq. The cost of such insurance, if required by the extender of credit, is deemed to be a portion of the credit service charge or loan finance charge for the purpose of computing maximum rates. More than one policy of credit life insurance, policy of credit dismemberment insurance, or policy of credit health and accident insurance, or any combination thereof, on any one consumer may be in force with respect to any one contract or agreement at any one time; however, the coverage of credit life insurance, credit dismemberment insurance, or credit health and accident insurance on any one consumer with respect to any one contract or agreement may not exceed the total sum payable under such contract including all loan finance charges and credit service charges.

B. (1) On all consumer credit transactions, entered into on or after January 1, 1998, the premium rates shall be as follows:

(a) The premium rate for declining balance credit life insurance shall not exceed ninety cents per one hundred dollars per annum.

(b) The premium rate for joint credit life insurance coverage shall not exceed one dollar and thirty-five cents per one hundred dollars per annum.

(c) The premium rate for level term credit life insurance shall not exceed one dollar and eighty cents per one hundred dollars per annum.

(d) The premium rate for joint level term credit life insurance shall not exceed two dollars and seventy cents per one hundred dollars per annum.

(2) Beginning on or after January 1, 1999, on all consumer credit transactions entered into, the premium rates shall be as follows:

(a) The premium rate for declining balance credit life insurance shall not exceed eighty cents per one hundred dollars per annum.

(b) The premium rate for level term credit life insurance shall not exceed one dollar and sixty cents per one hundred dollars per annum.

(c) The premium rate for joint credit life insurance shall not exceed one dollar and twenty cents per one hundred dollars per annum.

(d) The premium rate for joint level term credit life insurance shall not exceed two dollars and forty cents per one hundred dollars per annum.

(3) The amount of credit life insurance issued pursuant to a consumer credit transaction shall not exceed the total sum payable under such contract including all loan finance and credit service charges. However, credit life insurance in the amount of the total amount payable not to exceed the maximum limits for each individual otherwise provided by law, may be issued on each of the lives of individuals who are co-obligors with respect to that consumer credit transaction.

(4) The premium rate for credit dismemberment insurance shall not exceed twenty-five cents per one hundred dollars per annum.

C. No policy of health and accident insurance may be issued pursuant to a consumer credit transaction other than seven day, fourteen day or thirty day retroactive health and accident insurance. The premium rates for retroactive accident and health insurance issued pursuant to a consumer credit transaction shall not exceed the rates set forth in the following schedule:

Months	Amount per $100.00		
	7-Day Retro	14-Day Retro	30-Day Retro
0–6	$ 1.75	$1.10	$ .85
more than 6 through 12	3.50	2.20	1.70
more than 12 through 24	4.30	3.00	2.50
more than 24 through 36	5.10	3.80	3.30
more than 36 through 48	5.60	4.60	4.10
more than 48 through 60	6.00	5.40	4.90
more than 60 through 72	6.80	6.20	5.70
more than 72 through 84	7.60	7.00	6.50
more than 84 through 96	8.40	7.80	7.30
more than 96 through 108	9.20	8.60	8.10
more than 108 through 120	10.00	9.40	8.90

D. An extender of credit may offer credit life insurance in connection with a revolving loan account, lender credit card account, revolving charge account, or seller credit card account. The premium rate for individual credit life insurance offered in connection with such accounts shall not exceed .154 dollars per one hundred dollars, or portion thereof, per thirty day billing period that coverage is afforded. The premium rate for joint credit life insurance offered in connection with such accounts shall not exceed .231 dollars per one hundred dollars, or portion thereof, per thirty day billing period that the coverage is afforded. The charge for the revolving credit life insurance premium for each billing period shall not be due and payable until the end of the billing period that it insures.

E. An extender of credit may offer any credit insurance authorized by the Louisiana Insurance Code in connection with a revolving loan account, lender credit card account, revolving charge account, or seller credit card account. The premium rate for these insurances shall not exceed the actuarial equivalent of the maximum rates allowed by law. Such rates shall have prior approval by the appropriate state agency. The charge for the revolving credit insurance premium for each billing period shall not be due and payable until the end of the billing period that it insures.

F. In connection with a single consumer credit transaction, an extender of credit may not request or require a consumer to provide any credit insurance that provides duplicate or substantially the same protection against a single peril or loss as that furnished by any other credit insurance provided in connection with the same consumer credit transaction.

G. Notwithstanding any other provision of law to the contrary, an extender of credit may offer any credit insurance authorized by the Louisiana Insurance Code in connection with any extension of credit authorized by this Chapter.

Added by Acts 1972, No. 454, § 1, eff. Jan. 1, 1973. Amended by Acts 1974, No. 466, § 2; Acts 1980, No. 694, § 1; Acts 1982, No. 630, § 1; Acts 1986, No. 584, § 1, eff. July 2, 1986; Acts 1987, No. 288, § 1; Acts 1987, No. 908, § 2; Acts 1988, No. 629, § 1; Acts 1991, No. 480, § 1; Acts 1991, No. 697, § 1; Acts 1992, No. 1013, § 1, eff. July 13, 1992; Acts 1992, No. 1087, § 1, eff. July 14, 1992; Acts 1993, No. 726, § 2; Acts 1995, No. 1184, § 2; Acts 1997, No. 143, § 1, eff. Jan. 1, 1998.

§ 3543. Property insurance

A. An extender of credit may, in addition, request or require a consumer to insure property, all or part of which is involved in a contract or agreement, made under the authority of this Chapter, and include the cost of the insurance as a separate charge in the contract or agreement. The property shall be described so as to readily identify it and such description shall be included as part of the contract or agreement. This insurance and the premiums or charges thereon shall bear a reasonable relationship to the amount, term, and conditions of the contract or agreement, and to the existing hazards or risk of loss, damage, or destruction. This insurance and the premiums or charges thereon shall also bear a reasonable relationship to the character and value of the property insured or to be insured, when, in the event of loss, such insurance policy does not pay off the entire balance of the loan. Such insurance shall not provide for unusual or exceptional risks or coverages which are not ordinarily included in policies issued to the general public.

B. Where a consumer fails to maintain required property insurance or fails to provide the creditor with timely notice of the purchase or renewal of such insurance coverage, the creditor may, after notice to the consumer and expiration of a fifteen day curative period from the mailing of said notice, purchase insurance on the customer's property, including insurance protecting only the creditor's interest in such property. Such insurance premiums may be added to the outstanding balance of the customer's indebtedness and made subject to additional loan finance charges or credit service charges at the rate previously agreed to by the consumer.

Added by Acts 1972, No. 454, § 1, eff. Jan. 1, 1973. Amended by Acts 1985, No. 554, § 1; Acts 1986, No. 584, § 1, eff. July 2, 1986; Acts 1992, No. 146, § 1; Acts 1999, No. 1315, § 1, eff. Jan. 1, 2000.

§ 3544. Existing insurance

When consumer credit insurance is required in connection with such a contract or agreement made under this chapter, the extender of credit shall furnish the consumer a statement which shall clearly and conspicuously state that consumer credit insurance is required in connection with the contract, and that the consumer shall have the option of furnishing the required insurance either through existing policies of insurance coverages through any insurance company authorized to transact business in Louisiana.

Added by Acts 1972, No. 454, § 1, eff. Jan. 1, 1973.

§ 3545. Limitations on insurance rates; contract requirements

Any insurance provided, sold, or obtained through an extender of credit shall be written at lawful rates and in accordance with the provisions of the Louisiana Insurance Code by a company authorized to do business in this state which is not under a court-ordered rehabilitation, conservation, liquidation, or dissolution; provided, however, that such insurance may be written in accordance with R.S. 22:432 through 444 if the provisions thereof are applicable. Any extender of credit which writes insurance in compliance with the preceding requirements shall not be liable to any insured as a result of the insurer's inability to pay any claim to an insured due to insolvency, or pursuant to any court-ordered rehabilitation, conservation, liquidation, or dissolution. The contract or agreement must briefly indicate the kind, coverage, term, and amount of premium of such insurance.

Added by Acts 1972, No. 454, § 1, eff. Jan. 1, 1973. Amended by Acts 1991, No. 697, § 1.

§ 3546. Choice of insurer

The consumer shall have the privilege at the time of execution of the contract or agreement of purchasing any required or requested insurance from an agent or broker of his own selection and of selecting an insurance company acceptable to the extender of credit but, in such cases, the inclusion of the insurance premium in the contract or agreement shall be optional with the extender of credit. However, any licensed admitted property and casualty insurer possessing a valid certificate of authority to transact property and liability insurance coverage in the state of Louisiana shall be deemed to be an acceptable insurer for the provisions of this Chapter. The extender of credit may refuse any otherwise acceptable insurer which is under court-ordered rehabilitation, conservation, liquidation, or dissolution.

Added by Acts 1972, No. 454, § 1, eff. Jan. 1, 1973. Amended by Acts 1988, No. 166, § 2, eff. June 29, 1988; Acts 1990, No. 692, § 2, eff. July 20, 1990.

§ 3547. Conditions applying to insurance provided by the extender of credit

If a creditor agrees with a debtor to obtain or provide insurance

(1) the insurance shall be evidenced by an individual policy or certificate of insurance delivered to the debtor, or sent to him at his address as stated by him, within forty-five days after the term of the insurance commences; or

(2) the creditor shall promptly notify the debtor of any failure or delay in providing or obtaining the insurance, individual policy or certificate of insurance.

Added by Acts 1972, No. 454, § 1, eff. Jan. 1, 1973.

§ 3548. Cancellation of insurance; refund or credit upon cancellation

A. When a consumer credit transaction is paid in full for any reason, the insurance paid by the debtor and provided, sold, or obtained through the extender of credit in connection therewith shall be cancelled; however, this provision shall not apply to credit life insurance and property insurance other than contents insurance which is the subject of a specific written request by the consumer requesting that such insurance remain in force beyond the provision of this Section.

B. When insurance paid by the debtor is canceled, or terminated for any reason, the refund for unearned insurance premiums received by the extender of credit shall, at the extender's option, be applied toward payment of the premium for insurance to replace the coverage canceled, adjusted, or terminated, or toward payment of the unpaid balance of the consumer credit transaction. The order of applying said unearned premium shall be inverse to the order in which the installments of the consumer credit transaction are payable according to its terms, beginning with the installment due on the final due dates and not to the next ensuing installment which shall remain payable as originally scheduled. The remaining balance of unearned insurance premiums, if any, shall be refunded to the consumer; however, no cash refund shall be required if the amount thereof is less than one dollar, or to the extent provided for by federal law.

Added by Acts 1972, No. 454, § 1, eff. Jan. 1, 1973. Amended by Acts 1980, No. 694, § 1; Acts 1995, No. 1184, § 2; Acts 1997, No. 237, § 1.

§ 3549. Gain from insurance

Any gain, or advantage to the extender of credit, or any employee, officer, director, agent, general agent, affiliate or associate from such insurance or its provisions or sale shall not be considered as a further charge nor a further credit service charge or loan finance charge in violation of this chapter in connection with any contract or agreement made under this part.

Added by Acts 1972, No. 454, § 1, eff. Jan. 1, 1973.

§ 3550. Insurance premium finance companies

A. This Section shall apply to any person engaged in the business of financing insurance premiums for consumers entering into premium finance agreements or otherwise acquiring premium finance agreements.

B. For purposes of this Section:

(1) "Insurance premium finance company" means a person engaged in the business of entering into premium finance agreements.

(2) "License" means an insurance premium finance company holding a license issued under this Section.

(3) "Person" includes an individual, limited liability company, partnership, association, business corporation, nonprofit corporation, common law trust, joint-stock company, or any other group of individuals however organized.

(4) "Premium finance agreement" means an agreement by which an insured or prospective insured promises to pay to an insurance premium finance company the amount advanced or to be advanced under the agreement to an insurer or to an insurance agent or broker in payment of premiums on an insurance contract together with a service charge as authorized and limited by this Section. A premium finance agreement shall not include an agreement on the part of an extender of credit to finance credit life, credit disability, and credit property insurance coverage as an incident to a consumer credit transaction subject to this Chapter or subject to any other applicable provision of Louisiana or federal law.

C. (1) No person, unless otherwise exempt from the licensing requirement of this Chapter, shall engage in the business of financing insurance premiums in this state or out of this state with Louisiana consumers, entering into premium finance agreements, or otherwise acquiring premium finance agreements subject to the Louisiana Consumer Credit Law, without first having obtained a license as an insurance premium finance company from the commissioner as provided in Subsection A of this Section.

(2) The commissioner may in his discretion give prior written approval for an unlicensed person to acquire insurance premium finance agreements in connection with securitized financing arrangements.

(3) The commissioner may issue insurance premium finance licenses for a temporary period, or subject to any restrictions or conditions he deems necessary. The application, license, examination, survey, renewal, and change of name or location fees shall be the same as those for a licensed lender as provided in R.S. 9:3561.1.

D. (1) Premium finance agreements shall:

(a) Be dated and signed by the insured or by its agent under a validly executed power of attorney.

(b) Contain the name and place of business of the insurance agent who negotiated the related insurance contract, and a brief description of the insurance contract involved.

(c) Include, either as part of the insurance premium finance agreement or refer to a separate document which shall be made a part of the insurance premium finance agreement by reference, an itemized listing of the premium cost, and each charge, fee, or other amount that is part of the total cost of obtaining the insurance coverage sought by the insured.

(d) Contain the address of the insured and other persons who are entitled to receive all notices required under this Chapter. The address may be in the form of an electronic address or a physical address.

(2) Upon accepting, funding, or declining a premium finance agreement of a related insurance contract primarily for personal, family, or household use, when the premiums were paid or were to be paid to the providing insurance agent, the premium finance company shall deliver or mail accountable written or electronic notification within five business days advising the insurer, managing general agent, or general agent of its action to accept, fund, or decline the premium finance agreement. The notification shall state the insured's full name and address, the producing insurance agent's full name and address, the total policy cost, and the premiums that were paid to the producing insurance agent, or that the payment of premium was declined. With respect to commercial policies, the insurer, managing general agent, or general agent receiving notification shall deliver or mail accountable written or electronic notification within ten business days advising the premium finance company that an insurance contract or contracts or endorsements listed in and related to the premium finance agreement was not issued.

E. An insurance premium finance company shall not charge, contract for, receive, or collect a loan finance charge or credit service charge, or any other fee or charge other than as provided in this Subsection or in Subsection F:

(1) The loan finance charge or credit service charge shall be computed on the balance of the premium due, less the down payment made by the insured in accordance with the premium finance agreement. Loan finance charges or credit service charges accrue from the effective date of the insurance coverage for which the premiums are being advanced to and including the date when the final installment of the premium finance agreement is paid.

(2) The loan finance charge or credit service charge shall not exceed the charges permitted under this law. The loan

finance charge or credit service charge permitted by this Subsection anticipates repayment in consecutive monthly installments equal in amount for a period of one year. For repayment in greater or lesser periods or in unequal, irregular, or other than monthly installments, the credit service charge may be computed at an equivalent effective rate having due regard for the installments as scheduled.

(3) Notwithstanding the provisions of any premium finance agreement, any insured may prepay the obligation in full at any time. In such an event he shall receive a refund credit consisting of precomputed finance charges or credit service charges that shall represent at least as great a proportion of the loan finance charge or credit service charge as the sum of the periodic balances after the month in which prepayment is made bears to the sum of all periodic balances under the schedule of installments in the agreement. Where the amount of the refund credit is less than one dollar, or to the extent provided for by federal law, no refund need be made.

F. A premium finance agreement may provide for the payment by the insured of the delinquency charge in accordance with R.S. 9:3527, the N.S.F. check charge in accordance with R.S. 9:3529, an origination fee in accordance with R.S. 9:3530(A), attorney collection fees in accordance with R.S. 9:3534, and any charges as provided in this Subsection and in Subsection E. If the nonpayment by the consumer results in default and subsequently, results in cancellation of any insurance contract listed in the agreement, the agreement may provide for the payment by the insured of a cancellation charge not to exceed twenty-five dollars, which need not be rebated or credited to the consumer in the event that the premium finance agreement is subsequently reinstated.

G. Insurance contracts may be canceled upon default as follows:

(1) When a premium finance agreement contains a power of attorney enabling the insurance premium finance company to cancel any insurance contract, or contracts, or endorsements listed in the agreement, the insurance contract, or contracts, or endorsements shall not be canceled by the insurance premium finance company unless such cancellation is effectuated in accordance with this Subsection.

(2) Upon default of the insurance premium finance agreement by the debtor, the premium finance company shall mail or send an electronic notice of cancellation to the insured, at his last known mailing or electronic address as shown on the records of the insurance premium finance company. In the event the default is timely cured, the premium finance company shall, within three business days from the time the default was cured, mail or send electronic notice of rescission of the cancellation notice to the insured, at his last known mailing or electronic address as shown on the records of the premium finance company and to all other parties who had previously been sent notice of cancellation. In the event the default is not timely cured as provided herein and the insurance policy is canceled pursuant to the terms of the insurance premium finance agreement, a copy of the notice of cancellation of the insurance contract shall also be sent to the insurance agent negotiating the related insurance contract whose name and place of business appears on the insurance premium finance agreement. Such notice of cancellation shall also state the name of any governmental agency, holder of a security interest in the insured property, or third party also requiring notice of cancellation as shown on the insurance premium finance agreement.

(3)(a) Ten days after notice of cancellation has been mailed to the insured, or fourteen days when notice is sent from outside of this state, if the default has not been cured, the insurance premium finance company may thereafter effect cancellation of such insurance contract, or contracts, or endorsements by sending to the insurer, by depositing in the mail or with a private carrier, or via electronic mail, within five business days after the date of cancellation, except when the payment has been returned uncollected, a copy of the notice of cancellation together with a statement certifying that:

(i) The premium finance agreement contains a valid power of attorney as provided in Paragraph (1) of this Subsection.

(ii) The premium finance agreement is in default and the default has not been timely cured.

(iii) Upon default, a notice of cancellation was sent to the insured as provided in Paragraph (2) of this Subsection, specifying the date of sending by the premium finance company to the insured.

(iv) Copies of the notice of cancellation were sent to all persons shown by the premium finance agreement to have an interest in any loss which may occur thereunder, specifying the names and addresses of any governmental agencies, holders of a security interest in the insured property, or third parties to whom the insurance premium finance company has sent notice of cancellation.

(b)(i) Upon receipt of such notice of cancellation and statement from the premium finance company, the insurer shall consider that cancellation of the insurance contract or contracts has been requested by the insured but without requiring the return of the insurance contract or contracts and the insurer may proceed to cancel such contract or contracts as provided in R.S. 22:885. The effective date of cancellation shall be as of 12:01 a.m. on the tenth day after the date of sending of the notice of cancellation as shown in said statement furnished to the insurer by the premium finance company.

(ii) The time period between the date of the late notice and notice of cancellation was sent shall commence upon the date the late notice is sent.

(iii) Payment of an insurance premium installment by the insured, or on behalf of the insured, with a check or other instrument, which is returned to the premium finance company by the financial institution or other entity upon which it is drawn for insufficient funds available in the account, lack of credit, closed account, stopped payment, or for any other reason, shall be deemed grounds for the premium finance company to cancel the insurance policy pursuant to the terms of the power of attorney from the date the insurance policy could have been canceled upon default for nonpayment.

(c) The receipt of such notice of cancellation and statement by the insurer shall create a conclusive presumption that the facts stated in said notice and statement are correct, that the insurer is entitled to rely on such facts and that the cancellation of the insurance contract or contracts is concurred in and authorized by the insured. No liability of any nature whatsoever either in favor of the insured, any governmental agency, holder of a security interest in the insured property, or third party shall be imposed upon the insurer as a result of any misstatement of fact contained in said notice of cancellation or statement furnished by the insurance premium finance company to the insurer, or as a result of failure by the insured, any governmental agency, holder of a security interest in the insured property, or third party to receive the notice of cancellation required by Paragraph (2) of this Subsection, or as a result of failure of the insurance premium finance company to comply with any of the requirements of this Subsection. Upon mailing of any unearned premium and unearned commission to the insurance premium finance company as soon as practicable following such cancellation, the insurer shall be fully discharged from all liability under the insurance contract or contracts for any loss occurring subsequent to the effective date of cancellation.

(4) Upon receipt of the notice of cancellation, the insurer shall give notice to any governmental agency, holder of a security interest in the insured property, or other third party as shown in the records of the insurer requiring statutory, regulation, or contractual notice and which were not given by the premium finance company as provided in Paragraph (3) of this Subsection. The insurer shall give the prescribed notice on behalf of itself or the insured to any governmental agency, holder of a security interest in the insured property, or third party on or before the fifth business day after the day it receives a copy of the notice of cancellation from the insurance premium finance company and shall determine the effective date of cancellation taking into consideration the number of days notice required to complete the cancellation if such notice is given by the insurer, otherwise the effective date of cancellation shall be calculated from the date the premium finance company sent the notice to such governmental agency, holder of a security interest in the insured property, or other third party taking into consideration the number of days notice required to complete the cancellation.

H. Whenever the financed insurance contract, or contracts, or endorsements are canceled, the insurer shall return whatever unearned premiums and unearned commissions that are due under the insurance contract to the insurance premium finance company for the account of the insured or insureds as soon as reasonably possible but in no event shall the period for payment exceed sixty days after the effective date of cancellation. In the event that the crediting of return premiums and commissions to the account of the insured results in a surplus over the amount due from the insured, the insurance premium finance company shall refund such excess to the insured within sixty days of receipt of the proceeds from the insurer unless the commissioner grants, upon a showing of good cause, an extension pursuant to a request for additional time, provided that no such refund shall be required if it amounts to less than one dollar, or to the extent provided by federal law. The parties to an insurance premium finance agreement may agree that the unearned premiums and unearned commissions may be retained by or paid to the insurance company in order to purchase continued coverage under the insurance contract. In such event, the insurance premium finance company shall only retain the funds necessary to pay the amount required to pay the insurance premium finance agreement in full and shall transfer such excess funds to the insurance company in a timely manner to assure that the insurance coverage is not terminated. When the insurance agent provides proof that any check, money order, bank draft, or other means of payment used to pay the down payment was returned by the financial institution for whatever reason, the refund of surplus funds shall be made from the lender to the agent. The refund shall be made payable to both the agent and the insured.

I. No filing of the premium finance agreement shall be necessary to perfect the validity of such agreement as a secured transaction as against creditors, subsequent purchasers, pledges, encumbrances, successors, or assigns.

J. No insurer or its agent may refuse to issue a policy of insurance solely because the premiums therefor have been advanced by a premium finance company licensed in Louisiana. Nor shall any insurer or its agent discriminate, intimidate, or retaliate against a producing agent/broker who uses premium financing by denying him the same rights accorded agents/brokers whose insureds pay their policies in a different manner.

Added by Acts 1980, No. 694, § 1. Amended by Acts 1985, No. 333, § 1, eff. July 9, 1985; Acts 1985, No. 808, § 1, eff. July 22, 1985; Acts 1988, No. 629, § 1; Acts 1991, No. 697, § 1; Acts 1992, No. 354, § 1; Acts 1992, No. 355, § 1; Acts 1995, No. 1184, § 2; Acts 1997, No. 237, § 1; Acts 1999, No. 941, § 1; Acts 2003, No. 633, § 1; Acts 2003, No. 645, § 1; Acts 2010, No. 1016, § 1.

PART VII. REMEDIES AND PENALTIES

§ 3551. Unconscionability

With respect to a consumer credit transaction, if the court as a matter of law finds the agreement or any clause of the agreement to have been unconscionable at any time it was made the court may refuse to enforce the agreement, or it may enforce the remainder of the agreement without the unconscionable clause, or it may so limit the application of any unconscionable clause as to avoid any unconscionable result; provided, however, for the purposes of this chapter, an agreement, clause, charge or practice expressly permitted by this chapter or any other law or regulation of this state or of the United States or subdivision of either, or an agreement, clause, charge or practice necessarily implied as being permitted by this chapter or any other law or regulation of this state or the United States or any subdivision of either is not unconscionable.

Added by Acts 1972, No. 454, § 1, eff. Jan. 1, 1973.

§ 3552. Effect of violations on rights of parties

A. Violations discovered as a result of written consumer complaint

(1) Intentional violations or violations not caused by good faith errors.

(a) If the court finds that the extender of credit has intentionally or as a result of error not in good faith violated the provisions of this chapter, the consumer is entitled to a refund of all loan finance charges or credit service charges and has the right to recover three times the amount of such loan finance charge or credit service charge together with reasonable attorney's fees. The right to recover the civil penalty under this subsection accrues only after

(i) written notice is given to the extender of credit by certified mail addressed to the extender of credit's place of business in which the consumer credit transaction arose;

(ii) a copy of such notice is mailed to the extender of credit's agent for service of process; and

(iii) thirty days have elapsed since receipt of such notice by the extender of credit, and the violation has not been corrected.

(b) Except as otherwise provided herein, if the notices provided for in Subsection A(1)(a) of this section have been given by the consumer, the following acts by the extender of credit shall be presumed to be an intentional violation or a violation not resulting from good faith error:

(i) Failure to return or give credit for an overcharge in the loan finance charge or credit service charge or, failure to return a deficiency in the rebate within the time period set forth in Subsection A(1)(a)(iii) of this section when such overcharge or deficiency exceeds the greater of (1) ten percent of such loan finance charge, credit service charge or rebate; or (2) fifteen dollars.

(c) If the extender of credit fails to return or give credit for an overcharge or deficiency as provided in Subsection A(1)(b) of this section, in addition to the penalties in Subsection A(1)(a) of this section, the consumer executing the consumer credit transaction and giving the required notices shall be entitled to collect from the extender of credit up to one hundred dollars of his actual documented out-of-pocket expenses incurred as a direct result of such failure to act.

(d) In the case of multiple violations involving an overcharge in the loan finance charge, credit service charge or rebate of the size described in Subsection A(1)(b)(i) of this section, the extender of credit must notify the commissioner of the existence of such multiple violation and must give the commissioner a reasonable description of such multiple violation within thirty days after the receipt of the written notice from the complaining consumer, and the extender of credit must correct such multiple violation as to each consumer affected thereby within thirty days of the receipt of the written notice from the complaining consumer. Upon good cause shown, the commissioner may grant up to two thirty day extensions within which the extender of credit must correct the violation. If the extender of credit fails to give the commissioner the required notice or fails to correct such multiple violation as required herein, then from such failure it shall be presumed that such multiple violation was intentional or not in good faith.

(2) Unintentional violations or violations caused by good faith errors.

(a) If a violation of this chapter is not intentional or is made in good faith on the part of the extender of credit the court may require the extender of credit to correct the violation, but the consumer is not entitled to the civil remedies granted by this section; provided however the provisions hereof shall not protect the extender of credit if the provisions of Subsections A(1)(b) and A(1)(d) of this section are applicable.

(b) If the complaining consumer gives the extender of credit written notice as provided in Subsections A(1)(a)(i) and A(1)(a)(ii) of this section of an alleged violation of the provisions of this chapter, although such violation was unintentional or resulted from good faith error or did not in fact exist, the extender of credit must give the complaining consumer a reasonable response to the complaint in writing within thirty days of the receipt of written notice from the complaining consumer. If the extender of credit fails to give such response timely, the complaining consumer shall be entitled to collect from the extender of credit up to one hundred dollars of his actual documented out-of-pocket expenses incurred as a direct result of the failure of the extender of credit to comply with the provisions hereof.

B. Self-discovered violations

(1) An extender of credit has no liability for the civil remedies granted by this section in all instances other than multiple violations and whether intentional or resulting from good faith error or not, if: (a) within fifteen days after discovering a violation and prior to receipt of written notice of such violation from a consumer, or (b) within fifteen days after the occurrence of such violation, regardless of receipt of such notice from a consumer, the extender of credit gives written notice to the consumer or his designated agent of the violation and corrects the violation. If the violation consists of a prohibited agreement, giving the consumer a corrected copy of the writing containing the violation is sufficient notification and correction. If the violation consists of an excess charge, correction shall be made by an adjustment or refund.

(2) In the case of all self discovered multiple violations whether intentional or resulting from good faith error or not, the extender of credit shall have no liability for the civil remedies granted by this section if: (a) within fifteen days after discovering such violations the commissioner is notified of the existence of such multiple violation and given a reasonable description thereof, and (b) such violations are corrected as to each consumer affected thereby within thirty days after discovering such violations. Upon good cause shown the commissioner may grant up to two thirty day extensions within which the extender of credit may correct the violation. If a consumer delivers written notice of such violation at any time after the commissioner is notified by the extender of credit, it shall not affect the rights of the extender of credit to be relieved of liability as provided herein.

C. No act done or omitted in conformity with any advisory opinion or interpretation issued by the office of financial institutions at the time of the act or omission or subsequent to the act or omission shall constitute a violation of this Chapter, notwithstanding that after such act or omission has occurred, such advisory opinion or interpretation is amended, rescinded, or determined by judicial or other authority to be invalid for any reason. Advisory opinions and interpretations of the office of financial institutions shall not be considered rules requiring compliance with the rulemaking process of the Louisiana Administrative Procedure Act. The commissioner and the employees of the office of financial institutions shall have no liability to any person with respect to an advisory opinion or interpretation issued in connection with this Chapter.

D. Except as otherwise provided herein, any written notice required in this section may be mailed by registered, certified, first class, or air mail at the sender's option. Proof of receipt by the extender of credit may consist of a return receipt executed by an employee of the extender of credit. Proof of receipt by the consumer may be a return receipt executed by the consumer. Proof of mailing any written notice may be a postmarked registered mail receipt, a postmarked certified mail receipt, or a post office certificate of mailing.

The written notice shall identify the contract, state the names of the extender of credit and the consumer, and shall include the date and a reasonable description of the violation.

In any case where the extender of credit must respond in writing to a complaining consumer, the written notice or other required written response shall be mailed to the last address contained in the extender of credit's file on that consumer, unless the consumer specifies a different address in his written notice sent to the extender of credit.

E. Any civil action under this section must be brought within sixty days of final payment of the consumer credit contract, or in the case of a revolving loan or revolving charge account, within one year of the date of the violation.

F. Definitions of terms used in this section:

(1) The term "civil remedies" as used herein shall include civil penalties, attorney's fees and out-of-pocket expenses.

(2) The term "good faith error" as used herein shall include errors of law as well as errors of fact.

(3) The term "multiple violation" as used herein means a violation which has recurred more than one hundred times as a result of a common error.

G. Attorney fees shall be measured by the time reasonably expended by the consumer's attorney and not by the amount of recovery.

Added by Acts 1972, No. 454, § 1, eff. Jan. 1, 1973. Amended by Acts 1995, No. 1184, § 2; Acts 2000, 1st Ex.Sess., No. 34, § 2, eff. April 14, 2000.

§ 3553. Criminal penalties

A. (1) An extender of credit and any individual directly involved in the extension of credit who willfully makes charges in excess of those permitted by the provisions of this chapter is guilty of a misdemeanor and upon conviction may be sentenced to pay a fine not less than two hundred fifty dollars or more than five thousand dollars, or to imprisonment not exceeding one year, or both.

(2) A person, other than a supervised financial organization, who willfully engages in the business of making or taking assignments of consumer loans without a license in violation of the provisions of this Chapter applying to authority to make consumer loans is guilty of a misdemeanor and upon conviction may be sentenced to pay a fine not less than two hundred fifty dollars nor more than five thousand dollars, or to imprisonment not exceeding one year, or both.

(3) A person who willfully engages in the business of making consumer credit transactions, or of taking assignments of rights against consumers arising therefrom and undertakes direct collection of payments or enforcement of these rights, without complying with the provisions of this Chapter concerning notification (R.S. 9:3563–3565), is guilty of a misdemeanor and upon conviction may be sentenced to pay a fine not exceeding one thousand dollars, or to imprisonment not exceeding four months, or both.

(4) A person who willfully engages in the business of consumer loan brokering without complying with the provisions of this Chapter concerning registration (R.S. 9:3572.1 et seq.) is guilty of a misdemeanor, and upon conviction may be sentenced to pay a fine not exceeding five thousand dollars, or to imprisonment not exceeding one year, or both.

B. When the extender of credit is a corporation, its officers, directors or stockholders who are not personally involved in violations of this Chapter, shall not be subject to the criminal penalties of this Section.

Added by Acts 1972, No. 454, § 1, eff. Jan. 1, 1973. Amended by Acts 1992, No. 147, § 1; Acts 1995, No. 1184, § 2.

PART VIII. ADMINISTRATION

§ 3554. Powers of commissioner

A. In addition to other powers granted by this Chapter, the commissioner within the limitations provided by law may:

(1) Receive and act on complaints, take action designed to obtain voluntary compliance with this Chapter, including entering into voluntary consent or compliance agreements with persons conducting activities regulated by this Chapter without the necessity of a hearing or order, or commence proceedings on his own initiative;

(2) counsel persons and groups on their rights and duties under this chapter;

(3) establish programs for the education of consumers with respect to credit practices and problems;

(4) make studies appropriate to effectuate the purposes and policies of the chapter and make the results available to the public; and

(5) adopt, amend, and repeal substantive rules when specifically authorized by this chapter, and adopt, amend, and repeal procedural rules to carry out the provisions of this chapter.

B. The commissioner shall have the power to promulgate rules and regulations necessary for the enforcement of but not inconsistent with this chapter. Such rules and regulations shall be referenced to the sections or subsections which they interpret or apply. Copies of rules and regulations shall be sent to all persons who have filed notification with the commissioner at least thirty days prior to the effective date of the rule or regulation.

C. (1) The commissioner is hereby authorized to request and obtain from any other department or agency of the state and such are hereby authorized to furnish to the commissioner any records or information relevant to any consumer complaint or consumer credit transaction investigation or hearing by the commissioner, but excluding records or information otherwise provided by law to be privileged. The commissioner, in his sole discretion, when requested in writing, may disclose or cause the employees of the office of financial institutions to disclose records of the office of financial institutions concerning any person governed by Title 9, when such records are requested by another state or federal agency having authority to investigate or license such person governed by Title 9, or are requested by a bankruptcy trustee or any law enforcement agency in connection with an investigation to recover assets of a current or former licensee.

(2) If the lender's records are located outside the state, the lender, at the commissioner's option, shall make those records available to the commissioner at a location within the state convenient to the commissioner, or pay the reasonable and necessary expenses for the commissioner or his representatives to examine them at the place where they are maintained. The commissioner may designate representatives, including comparable officials of the state in which the records are located, to inspect them on his behalf.

D. The commissioner shall have the power to subpoena any person for the purpose of discovering violations of this chapter.

E. The commissioner may, upon notice to a person regulated by this Chapter and reasonable opportunity to be heard at an administrative hearing, revoke or suspend the license, notification, or registration if:

(1) The person has violated any provisions of this Chapter or any rule or order lawfully made by the commissioner under this Chapter.

(2) The person has violated any provisions of a voluntary consent or compliance agreement which has been entered into with the commissioner.

(3)(a) The person has intentionally or knowingly provided or caused to be made any false or fraudulent information or financial statements to the commissioner.

(b) The person has intentionally or knowingly failed to state in any application for a license, registration, or notification any material fact which is required to be stated therein.

(c) The commissioner finds any fact or condition exists which, if it had existed at the time of the original application for licensure, notification, or registration, would have warranted the refusal of its issuance.

(4) The person fails to maintain records as required by the commissioner by rule, after being given written notice and thirty days within which to correct the failure to maintain such records. Upon good cause shown, the commissioner may grant up to two thirty-day extensions within which the recordkeeping violations may be corrected.

(5) The person violates any provision of a regulatory or prohibitory statute, and has been found to have violated such statute by the governmental agency responsible for determining such violations.

(6) The person engages in fraudulent conduct, including a finding of civil fraud.

(7) The person has been permanently or temporarily enjoined by any court of competent jurisdiction from engaging in or continuing any conduct or practice involving any aspect of the business of making loans.

(8) A license, notification, or registration the person holds in any other state to engage in the business of making consumer loans or consumer credit sales is revoked or suspended for acts or practices which also violate the provisions of this Chapter.

(9) The person violates the written restrictions or conditions under which his license, registration, or notification was issued.

(10) The person transfers consumer loans to an unlicensed or non-exempt person, without the prior written approval of the commissioner, except in accordance with the provisions of this Chapter or any rule pursuant thereto.

(11) The person has abandoned the physical location for which the license, registration, or notification was issued, has not applied for a change of location, and fails to respond within thirty days to a certified mail notice sent to his registered agent for service of process and to his mailing address.

(12) A person which is a business entity is used as a means of furthering a criminal act or a civil fraud.

(13) Another consumer loan license held by the same person or his parent company is revoked for serious and repeated violations of the Louisiana Consumer Credit Law.

(14) A person fails, after notice and without lawful excuse, to obey an order or subpoena issued by the commissioner.

F. The commissioner may, if he finds that the public safety or welfare requires emergency action, order an immediate suspension of a license, registration, or notification under this Chapter, or order a person to immediately cease and desist from an act or practice regulated by this Chapter and to take affirmative action to prevent the continuance of such act or practice pending a hearing, whenever it appears that any person has engaged in or is engaging in any act or practice which is prohibited by this Chapter, or by any rule, regulation, or order promulgated or issued thereunder, or any person has failed to act under any affirmative duty imposed by this Chapter, or rule or regulations promulgated or issued thereunder, subject to the right of such person to a hearing as provided in the Administrative Procedure Act. Such order shall become effective upon service upon such person and shall provide for a hearing and opportunity to be heard within ten days of the order, unless extended by mutual consent of the parties. An order of immediate suspension shall be temporary and shall expire automatically if the commissioner fails to afford notice and an opportunity for hearing pursuant to the Administrative Procedure Act. Such temporary order shall remain effective and enforceable pending the completion of such administrative proceedings or until such time as the commissioner shall dismiss the charges specified in such notice.

G. The commissioner shall conduct a hearing for the purpose of revoking or suspending the license of a licensed lender when three aggrieved parties not related by marriage to each other have filed affidavits stating facts reasonably showing that the licensed lender has engaged in fraudulent conduct.

H. The commissioner may, upon notice to a person engaging in activities regulated under this Chapter and a reasonable opportunity to be heard at an administrative hearing, do one or more of the following:

(1) Place permanent or temporary restrictions upon a person's exercise of any of the privileges granted by this Chapter, if the person is found to have violated any of the provisions of this Chapter or of any rule promulgated by the commissioner.

(2) Issue and serve upon a person an order requiring such person to cease and desist and take corrective action whenever the commissioner finds that such person is violating or has violated any provisions of this Chapter, any rule or order adopted under this Chapter, or any written agreement entered into with the office of financial institutions.

(3) Issue a public reprimand.

I. (1) The commissioner may remove from office any individual with power to direct the management or policies of a person regulated by this Chapter, including but not limited to any officer, director, or manager, if any such individual is convicted of, pleads guilty to, or is found guilty after a plea of nolo contendere, of any felony under any state or federal law, or of a misdemeanor of which fraud is an essential element or which involves any aspect of the business of making loans. Prior to such removal, the commissioner shall serve written notice upon such individual and upon the person regulated by this Chapter, of his intent to remove such individual from office. If such individual remains in office thirty days after such written notice, the commissioner may revoke the license or other privileges granted by this Chapter without any further notification or a hearing.

(2) The commissioner may, upon notice to an individual with the power to direct the management or policies of a person regulated by this Chapter, including but not limited to any officer, director, or manager, and after reasonable opportunity to be heard at an administrative hearing, remove the individual from participating in the affairs of a licensee if that individual has been prohibited, temporarily or permanently, by any other state or federal regulator from participating in activities for which he is licensed under this Chapter.

J. If it is found, after an administrative hearing, that consumers who have done business with the extender of credit have been aggrieved by an improper loan finance charge, credit service charge, deferral charge, delinquency charge, or improper rebate, or the inclusion of an improper item in the amount financed, the commissioner may institute a civil action on behalf of such consumers in any form which he deems appropriate to effectuate the provisions of this Subsection, in order to recover any such money improperly exacted from the consumer by the extender of credit, provided that sixty days have passed after giving notice by certified mail of his intentions. All monies recovered shall be returned to the aggrieved consumer in a manner deemed to be reasonable and which shall assure prompt and expeditious payment to the consumer, in whole or in part, and is calculated to minimize the expenses associated with the distribution of such monies.

K. Whenever an alleged violation has occurred under this Section which necessitates action on the part of the commissioner, and the person has arbitrarily refused to cooperate with the commissioner after due notice, the commissioner may send an investigator to investigate the alleged violation.

(1) The commissioner, after investigation of a complaint and after a proper opportunity for hearing and after finding that a provision of this Chapter has been violated, may issue an order to cease and desist from further violations of a like nature; or

(2) The commissioner, upon notice to the extender of credit and after reasonable opportunity to be heard, provided that he finds that the extender has willfully failed to comply with the provisions of this Chapter to an extent to warrant belief that the business will not be operated honestly and fairly within the purposes of this Chapter, may revoke the privileges granted under this Chapter.

L. The commissioner shall have authority to examine the books, records, and accounts of all persons regulated under or making loans subject to the Louisiana Consumer Credit Law. Such examination shall not occur more frequently than once a year unless there arises the necessity for an additional examination based on a probable cause.

M. If any part of the regulations promulgated is declared invalid, all parts that are severable from the invalid parts shall remain in effect.

Added by Acts 1972, No. 454, § 1, eff. Jan. 1, 1973. Amended by Acts 1974, No. 466, § 2; Acts 1991, No. 700, § 1, eff. July 18, 1991; Acts 1992, No. 139, § 1; Acts 1992, No. 149, § 1; Acts 1992, No. 150, § 1, eff. June 5, 1992; Acts 1999, No. 261, § 2; Acts 1999, No. 1315, § 1, eff. Jan. 1, 2000.

§ 3554.1. Commissioner's powers; unlicensed persons

A. For the purpose of discovering violations of this Chapter or securing information lawfully required by it hereunder, the commissioner may at any time investigate the loans and business and examine the books, accounts, records, and files used therein of every person engaged in or believed to be engaged in any business regulated by this Chapter, whether such person shall act or claim to act as principal or agent or within or without the authority of this Chapter. For such purpose the commissioner shall have free access to the offices and places of business, books, accounts, papers, records, files, safes, and vaults of such persons. The commissioner may require the attendance of and examine under oath all persons, may administer oaths or affirmations, and, upon his own motion or upon request of any party, may subpoena witnesses, compel their attendance, adduce evidence, and require the production of any matter which is relevant to the investigation, including the existence, description, nature, custody, condition, and location of any books, documents, or other tangible things and the identity and location of persons having knowledge of relevant facts, or any other matter reasonably calculated to lead to the discovery of admissible evidence.

B. No person, except as authorized by the provisions of this Chapter, shall, directly or indirectly, charge, contract for or receive any interest, charge, or consideration upon the loan, use, or forbearance of money or credit for a consumer purpose.

C. If any individual without lawful excuse fails to obey a subpoena or to give testimony when directed to do so by the commissioner or obstructs the proceedings by any means, whether or not in the presence of the commissioner that individual is guilty of contempt. The commissioner may file a complaint in a district court setting forth the facts constituting the contempt and requesting an order returnable in not less than two days or more than five days, directing the alleged offender to show cause before the court why he should not be punished for contempt. If the court determines that the respondent has committed any alleged contempt, the court shall punish the offender for contempt.

D. If an investigation or examination by the commissioner shall disclose that any person has violated the provisions of this Chapter relative to licensing requirements other than as a result of a bona fide error, the costs of such investigation or examination shall be borne by the person investigated or examined and the commissioner may maintain an action in any court to recover such costs.

E. Whenever the commissioner has reasonable cause to believe that any person is violating, is threatening to violate, or is about to violate any provision of this Chapter relative to licensing, notification, or registration requirements, he may in addition to all actions provided for in this Chapter, and without prejudice thereto, order such person to cease and desist from such violation, and/or may order such person to cease collecting or enforcing such consumer loans subject to the Louisiana Consumer Credit Law, unless and until such person is licensed to make consumer loans pursuant to this Chapter. An action may be brought by the commissioner or by the attorney general of Louisiana to enjoin such person from engaging in or continuing such violation or from doing any act or acts in furtherance thereof. In any such action an order or judgment may be entered awarding such preliminary or final injunction as may be deemed proper. In addition to all other means provided by law for the enforcement of a restraining order or injunction, the court in which such action is brought shall have power and jurisdiction to impound, and to appoint a receiver for the property and business of the defendant, including books, papers, documents, and records pertaining thereto or so much thereto as the court may deem reasonably necessary to prevent violations of the licensing, notification, or registration provisions of this Chapter through or by means of the use of said property and business. Such receiver, when appointed and qualified, shall have such powers and duties as to custody, collection, administration, winding up, and liquidation of such property and business as shall from time to time be conferred upon him by the court.

F. In addition to any other authority conferred, the commissioner may impose a fine or penalty not exceeding one thousand dollars upon any person required to be licensed under this Chapter who, at an administrative proceeding is determined to have violated the licensing provisions of this Chapter. Such fines may be imposed by a court in which the commissioner has brought an action authorized by this Section. For the purposes of this Section, each day that an unlicensed person engages in the activities regulated by this Chapter shall constitute a separate violation.

Added by Acts 1992, No. 1013, § 1, eff. July 13, 1992; Acts 1992, No. 1112, § 1, eff. July 14, 1992.

§ 3554.2. Reapplication after revocation of a license

A. Any person whose licensure under this Chapter has been revoked for any reason may not reapply for a license under this Chapter until after at least five years from the date of the order of suspension or revocation unless the commissioner, in his sole discretion, prescribes an earlier or later date.

B. For purposes of this Section:

(1) The term "order" shall mean the commissioner's notification of revocation of the person's license.

(2) The term "person" shall include the applicant, its owners, and its members if the applicant is a limited liability company, its partners if the applicant is a partnership, its officers and directors if the applicant is a corporation, and any other person determined by the commissioner, in his sole discretion, to be closely related to the person.

Added by Acts 2006, No. 213, § 1.

§ 3554.3. Cost of appeal; effect of final decision

A. Subject to the provisions of R.S. 13:4521 and 4581, all estimated costs of appeal, including those involved in preparation of the administrative record for appeal, taken by a person in connection with an adverse ruling of an administrative law judge in connection with a hearing held pursuant to this Chapter and the Administrative Procedure Act,[1] shall be paid by that person within sixty days of the filing of the petition for appeal in the district court. Failure to pay such estimated costs within the time specified herein shall result in said appeal being dismissed with prejudice and without the necessity of any further action being taken by any party.

B. Any final and definitive decision of an administrative law judge, or in the case such decision is appealed, a final and definitive judgment of an appellate court, issued in connection with any hearing held pursuant to this Chapter and the Administrative Procedure Act[1] shall be considered a valid and final judgment that may be made executory by the commissioner in accordance with the Code of Civil Procedure.

Added by Acts 2006, No. 213, § 1.

[1] R.S. 49:950 et seq.

§ 3555. Injunctions; investigations; enforcement actions; civil penalties; costs

A. The commissioner may bring a suit in a court of competent jurisdiction and venue to restrain and enjoin an extender of credit or a person acting on his behalf or both from engaging in future violations of this Chapter or from engaging in a course of fraudulent conduct in inducing consumers to enter into fraudulent consumer credit transactions or in the collection of debts in violation of law.

B. If the court finds that there is reasonable cause to believe that the respondent is engaging in or is likely to engage in fraudulent conduct or in conduct that violates this Chapter, it may grant injunctive relief as otherwise provided by law but without the furnishing of a bond by the commissioner.

C. If an investigation or examination conducted by the commissioner discloses that any person has violated an order of the commissioner under the provisions of this Chapter, or has violated a consent agreement entered into with the commissioner, other than as a result of a bona fide error, the cost of such investigation or examination shall be borne by the person investigated or examined. If the commissioner is granted an injunction pursuant to this Section, or is granted a court order enforcing an order of the commissioner or enforcing any provision of a consent agreement, the commissioner may recover from the defendant or defendants costs and reasonable attorney fees incurred in bringing such action.

D. Civil penalties paid to the commissioner, and overcharge violations of five dollars or less per consumer ordered by the commissioner to be refunded, and paid to the commissioner, shall be deposited in the state treasury and, after compliance with the requirements of Article VII, Section 9(B) of the Constitution of Louisiana relative to the Bond Security and Redemption Fund shall be designated as self-generated revenues of the agency.

Added by Acts 1972, No. 454, § 1, eff. Jan. 1, 1973. Amended by Acts 1992, No. 138, § 1, eff. June 5, 1992; Acts 1995, No. 1184, § 2; Acts 1999, No. 1315, § 1, eff. Jan. 1, 2000; Acts 2001, No. 1182, § 1, eff. July 1, 2001.

§ 3556. Method of procedure

A. The commissioner may, in his discretion, conduct such investigations and hearings as he deems necessary to ascertain possible violations of this Chapter or any rule or order promulgated or issued hereunder. Such hearings may be private, if the commissioner, in his sole discretion, so determines after considering the interests of the person afforded the hearing and the need to protect the public interest. If a public hearing is held and any confidential records of the office of financial institutions are produced by discovery or introduced into evidence at the hearing, such records shall not become public but shall be sealed.

B. The Louisiana Administrative Procedure Act shall supplement this Chapter for the purpose of administrative hearings.

Added by Acts 1972, No. 454, § 1 eff. Jan. 1, 1973. Amended by Acts 1991, No. 700, § 1, eff. July 18, 1991.

§ 3556.1. Records; rules

A. Each person regulated by this Part shall maintain records of its consumer credit sales or loans as required by the commissioner or by rule. Persons who make consumer credit sales and do not transfer or assign their agreements to a supervised financial organization, a lender who files notification pursuant to R.S. 9:3564, or a licensed lender within thirty-five days, as provided by R.S. 9:3521, shall comply with the Records Retention Rule for licensed lenders, and shall promptly notify the commissioner that such person is collecting or otherwise enforcing consumer sales agreements or consumer loans and shall further retain copies of all such documents and contracts on file for examination by the commissioner.

B. Any records to be retained pursuant to this Section or regulations promulgated hereunder may be reproduced by any photographic, photostatic, microfilm, microcard, or miniature or microphotographic process, or by any mechanical or electronic recording or re-recording electronic or optical imaging, chemical process, or other process or technique which accurately reproduces the original or forms or creates a durable medium for accurately reproducing the original record.

C. Each reproduction shall be treated for all purposes as if it were the original record, item, or instrument.

D. The commissioner may promulgate such rules and regulations in accordance with the Administrative Procedure Act as he deems necessary to effect the purposes of this Part.

Added by Acts 1995, No. 1184, § 2. Amended by Acts 1997, No. 63, § 1; Acts 1999, No. 1315, § 1, eff. Jan. 1, 2000.

§ 3556.2. Guidance by commissioner; advisory opinions

A. Advisory opinions and interpretations of the office shall not be considered rules requiring compliance with the rulemaking process under the Louisiana Administrative Procedure Act.

B. This Section shall only have prospective application.

Added by Acts 1997, No. 58, § 2.

§ 3556.3. Violations; penalties

A person subject to this Part who violates a provision of this Chapter may be fined up to one thousand dollars for each violation. The commissioner may maintain a civil action in a court of competent jurisdiction to recover such fines, together with his costs and attorney fees incident to such action.

Added by Acts 1997, No. 63, § 1.

PART IX. LICENSING PROVISIONS

§ 3557. Authority to make consumer loans

A. Unless a person has first obtained a license from the commissioner as provided under this Part, he shall not engage in the business of:

(1) Making consumer loans; or

(2) Making loans with the use of a lender credit card or similar arrangement.

B. Provided that the creditor has one or more offices in this state, a creditor may not take assignments of and undertake direct collection of payments from or enforce rights against consumers arising from consumer loans, without first having obtained a license from the commissioner as provided under this Part. A creditor may, however, collect and enforce consumer loan obligations of which he has taken assignment for three months without a license if he notifies the commissioner in writing of his intention to take assignments of consumer loans, including the name and address of the proposed assignee and assignor, the number of loans assigned, the dollar amount of the assignment, and other information the commissioner requires at least ten days prior to the time the assignment is made, and the commissioner has not objected, and such creditor promptly applies for a license and his application has not been denied.

C. Any person licensed under this Part shall not engage in the business of originating, lending, or brokering any loan primarily for personal, family, or household use that is secured by a mortgage, deed of trust, or other equivalent consensual security interest on a dwelling as defined in 15 U.S.C. 1602(v) or on residential immovable property upon which is constructed or intended to be constructed a dwelling, unless such person has also obtained a license pursuant to the Louisiana S.A.F.E. Residential Mortgage Lending Act, R.S. 6:1081 et seq.

Added by Acts 1972, No. 454, § 1, eff. Jan. 1, 1973. Amended by Acts 1986, No. 584, § 1, eff. July 2, 1986; Acts 1992, No. 370, § 1; Acts 1995, No. 1184, § 2; Acts 2009, No. 522, § 2, eff. July 31, 2009.

§ 3558. License to make consumer loans

A. The commissioner shall receive and act on all applications for licenses to make consumer loans under this Chapter. Applications shall be filed in the manner prescribed by the commissioner and shall contain the information the commissioner requires to make an evaluation of the financial responsibility, character, and fitness of the applicant.

B. No license shall be issued unless the commissioner, upon investigation, finds that the financial responsibility, character and fitness of the applicant, and of the members thereof (if the applicant is a partnership or association) and of the officers and directors thereof (if the applicant is a corporation), are such as to warrant belief that the business will be operated honestly and fairly within the purposes of this chapter.

C. Upon written request, the applicant is entitled to a hearing on the question of his qualifications for a license if (1) the commissioner has notified the applicant in writing that his application has been denied, or (2) the commissioner has not issued a license within sixty days after the application for the license was filed. A request for a hearing may not be made more than fifteen days after the commissioner has mailed a written notice to the applicant notifying him that the application has been denied and stating in substance the commissioner's findings supporting denial of the application.

D. The commissioner may grant restricted or conditional licenses. Violation of such restrictions or conditions by the licensee may constitute grounds for suspension or revocation of such license.

E. (1) Any person whose application or renewal application for licensure under this Chapter has been denied for any reason may not reapply for a license under this Chapter until after at least three years from the date of the order of denial, unless the commissioner, in his sole discretion, prescribes an earlier or later date.

(2) For purposes of this Subsection:

(a) The term "order" shall mean the date of the commissioner's notification of denial of the person's application.

(b) The term "person" shall include the applicant, its owners, and its members if the applicant is a limited liability company, its partners if the applicant is a partnership, its officers and directors if the applicant is a corporation, and any other person determined by the commissioner, in his sole discretion, to be closely related to the person.

Added by Acts 1972, No. 454, § 1, eff. Jan. 1, 1973. Amended by Acts 1992, No. 370, § 2; Acts 1995, No. 1184, § 2; Acts 2006, No. 213, § 1.

§ 3559. Continuation of licensing

A. All persons licensed or otherwise authorized under the provisions of the Louisiana Small Loan Act (R.S. 6:571–593) [1], the Motor Vehicle Sales Finance Act or Direct Vehicle Loan Companies Act (R.S. 6:951–964; R.S. 6:970–976) [2] and who have an occupational license to make loans not regulated by the above acts on January 1, 1973, are licensed to make consumer loans, and the commissioner shall, upon request, within forty-five days, deliver evidence of licenses to the person so previously licensed or authorized.

B. All persons previously licensed as set forth in Subsection A of this section desiring to become licensed lenders pursuant to this provision shall file notice of such intent with the commissioner within thirty days after the effective date of this chapter and shall be deemed a licensed lender within the meaning of this chapter from January 1, 1973, provided that notice is timely filed. Failure to file notice within the allotted time shall constitute a waiver of the rights granted under this section.

Added by Acts 1972, No. 454, § 1, eff. Jan. 1, 1973. Amended by Acts 1997, No. 38, § 1.

[1] R.S. 6:571 to 6:593 was repealed by Acts 1972, No. 454, § 2. For "Louisiana Small Loan Act", see now, R.S. 9:3577.1 et seq. as added by Acts 1997, No. 41.

[2] R.S. 6:970 to 6:976 was repealed by Acts 1972, No. 454, § 3.

§ 3559.1. Regulation of former licensees

A. A licensed lender whose license has been revoked, suspended, or canceled may, with the prior written consent of the commissioner, continue to collect payments on or enforce such loans without a license so long as it complies with each of the following:

(1) The record keeping requirements for licensed lenders.

(2) All other provisions of this Chapter.

(3) Pays the commissioner's costs for conducting compliance examinations or investigations of its records.

(4) The terms of any valid order of the commissioner or of a court relative to provisions of this Chapter.

(5) All consent agreements entered into with the commissioner.

B. The commissioner may require such unlicensed persons to enter into a consent agreement containing the provisions of this Section and may require additional restrictions and conditions therein, as determined by the commissioner, as a condition to the former licensee's continued collection or enforcement of consumer loans.

C. The commissioner may assess civil money penalties of up to one thousand dollars per violation for violations of this Section. Such penalties may be recovered by the commissioner in a civil action brought in a court of competent jurisdiction, together with reasonable attorney fees and costs incurred in bringing such action.

Added by Acts 1992, No. 148, § 1, eff. June 5, 1992.

§ 3560. Licenses not required

A. Notwithstanding R.S. 9:3557, the following persons shall be exempt from the consumer loan licensing requirements under this Part:

(1)(a) A bank, savings and loan association, or similar financial institution organized, certified, and supervised by an agency of either the United States of America or the state of Louisiana pursuant to the banking, currency and related laws of the United States of America or the state of Louisiana.

(b) A subsidiary of any state-chartered entity described in Subparagraph (a) of this Paragraph in which eighty percent or more of the ownership rests with such parent entity.

(2) A trust administered by a bank or a bank trust department.

(3) A governmental agency, instrumentality, or public entity organized by act of congress or the Legislature of Louisiana.

(4) An insurance company when entering into a life insurance loan to a policyholder.

(5) A qualified pension plan when entering into an extension of credit to a plan participant.

(6) A bona fide pledgee of a consumer credit transaction to secure a bona fide loan thereon.

(7) A seller or other creditor refinancing a retail installment transaction subject to the Motor Vehicle Sales Finance Act.

(8) A creditor having no office within this state offering credit to Louisiana consumers through the mails and other means of interstate commerce.

(9) Unless otherwise provided by rule or regulation of the commissioner, persons whose lending activities pertain to federally related mortgage loans, and who are subject to licensing, supervision or auditing by the Federal National Mortgage Association, the Federal Home Loan Mortgage Corporation, the Governmental National Mortgage Association, the Veterans Administration, or the United States Department of Housing and Urban Development. Such lenders may also make loans secured by a second or junior lien or mortgage on owner-occupied one-to-four family residential immovable property made contemporaneously with federally related mortgage loans or as part of a mortgage revenue bond loan program, or sold on the secondary market to the Federal National Mortgage Association, the Federal Home Loan Mortgage Corporation, or the Governmental National Mortgage Association, and the entity sells ten or fewer of such loans over any calendar year.

(10) Repealed by Acts 2009, No. 522, § 3, eff. July 31, 2009.

B. The commissioner is authorized to waive the consumer loan licensing and examination requirements for a subsidiary of an entity as described in Subparagraph (A)(1)(a) of this Section where the holding company thereof has one or more state-chartered subsidiaries. In lieu of such licensure and examination, the commissioner may review relevant reports or portions thereof prepared by any subsidiary agency described in Subparagraph (A)(1)(a) of this Section.

C. The commissioner may enter into a supervisory agreement with any supervisory agency described in Subparagraph (A)(1)(a) of this Section where such supervisory agency agrees to periodically examine the entity which is subject to its jurisdiction for compliance with this Chapter. Where such an agreement has been entered into, the commissioner may accept relevant reports or portions thereof prepared by such supervisory agency in lieu of the licensing and examination requirements of this Chapter.

Added by Acts 1972, No. 454, § 1, eff. Jan. 1, 1973. Amended by Acts 1986, No. 584, § 1, eff. July 2, 1986; Acts 1988, No. 629, § 1; Acts 1995, No. 1184, § 2; Acts 1997, No. 1432, § 1; Acts 2000, 1st Ex.Sess., No. 34, § 2, eff. April 14, 2000; Acts 2001, No. 617, § 2, eff. June 22, 2001.

§ 3561. Single place of business; additional licenses

A. Each licensee shall maintain a place of business in the state and, unless otherwise provided by rule, shall maintain records of its consumer loans at that location. Not more than one place of business shall be maintained under the same license, but the commissioner shall issue additional licenses to the same licensed lender upon his compliance with all the provisions of this Part governing issuance of a license.

B. A licensed lender may change the location of the business only after written approval of the commissioner. The application to change the location shall be filed at least thirty days prior to the proposed relocation date. Upon receipt of the application, the commissioner may cause a survey to be made to determine if the proposed location meets the requirements imposed for a new licensed location. If the requirements are met, the application shall be approved.

C. A license to make consumer loans may not be sold or otherwise transferred. However, all accounts and other assets may be sold or transferred to another licensed lender, upon prior written approval of the commissioner. After the sale or transfer of all accounts, the license of the selling or transferring licensee shall be surrendered to the commissioner as cancelled.

D. (1) No person shall acquire or control a consumer loan license through the acquisition or control of more than fifty percent of the ownership interest in a licensee without first having obtained written approval from the commissioner, pursuant to an application for a change of control in ownership of the licensee filed in the manner and on a form prescribed by the commissioner and accompanied by a fee of three hundred dollars. Any person who acquires controlling interest in a licensee without first having filed an application for change of control with the commissioner shall be deemed to be operating without proper authority under this Chapter and is subject to the penalties of R.S. 9:3554.1.

(2) For the purposes of this Section, a person acquires or controls the licensee when the person directly or acting through one or more other persons owns a majority interest in the licensee, or exercises a controlling influence over the management or the policies of the licensee as determined by the commissioner after notice and an opportunity for an informal meeting, not subject to the Administrative Procedure Act, regardless of whether the acquisition or control occurs incrementally over a period of time or as one transaction.

(3) Any person who acquires or anticipates acquiring a seventy-five percent interest in a licensee shall file for a new license prior to acquiring ownership of said interest either incrementally over a period of time or as one transaction.

E. A licensed lender may change its name only after written application to and approval by the commissioner.

F. (1) Unless prior written approval is obtained from the commissioner, a licensed lender may not assign or otherwise transfer ownership of consumer loans, including insurance premium financing agreements, to a person who is not a licensed lender, or who has not complied with R.S. 9:3557(B), or who is not exempt from the licensing requirements as provided in R.S. 9:3560.

(2) A licensee shall keep a record or list of all consumer loans which it has purchased, sold, assigned, or otherwise transferred or acquired. The records shall include the name and address of the persons from which the loans were acquired or to whom the notes were transferred, indicate any affiliation between the seller and buyer, the date and dollar amount of each such transaction, and account names and numbers.

Added by Acts 1972, No. 454, § 1, eff. Jan. 1, 1973. Amended by Acts 1974, No. 466, § 1; Acts 1985, No. 808, § 1, eff. July 22, 1985; Acts 1991, No. 215, § 1, eff. July 2, 1991; Acts 1991, No. 697, § 1; Acts 1992, No. 370, § 3; Acts 1993, No. 458, § 1, eff. July 1, 1993; Acts 1995, No. 1184, § 2; Acts 2003, No. 1233, § 1; Acts 2006, No. 213, § 1.

§ 3561.1. License; examination; renewal fees; records

A. The initial application, survey, and license fee for a license to make consumer loans shall be five hundred fifty dollars payable in a form acceptable to the commissioner when the application is filed. Such application, survey, and license fee shall be nonrefundable. If the license is not issued for any reason, upon written request of the applicant, the fee shall be applied to the submission of a new application.

B. The annual renewal fee, including examination, shall be four hundred fifty dollars, payable on or before December thirty-first of each year.

C. (1) The survey fee for an application to change the location of a licensed lender shall be one hundred dollars. If the change in location is approved by the commissioner of financial institutions, no additional fee shall be required for the transfer of the existing license to the new location.

(2) The fee to change the name or the mailing address of a licensed lender that does not involve the relocation of the lender shall be fifty dollars.

(3) However, a fee of fifty dollars shall be assessed if a licensed lender changes locations without complying with the provisions of R.S. 9:3561(B) or changes its name without complying with the provisions of R.S. 9:3561(E). Whenever the commissioner learns that a licensed lender has changed locations or name without complying with the provisions of R.S. 9:3561(B) or (E), he shall notify the licensed lender by certified mail, return receipt requested, that the fee has been assessed.

D. If the commissioner has not received the assessed fee within thirty days after the date the licensed lender received his notification of assessment, he shall revoke the licensed lender's license without hearing or further notification. The license shall not be reinstated. However, the former licensee may apply for a new license.

E. No fee shall be prorated.

F. (1) If the commissioner has not received the annual renewal fee from a licensed lender on or before December thirty-first, he shall notify the licensed lender and assess a late fee of one hundred dollars.

(2) If the commissioner has not received the annual renewal fee and late fee before March first of the following year, the license to make consumer loans and insurance premium finance loans shall lapse without a hearing or notification, and the license shall not be reinstated; however, the person whose license has lapsed may apply for a new license.

G. (1) If the lender's records are located outside this state, the lender, at the commissioner's option, shall make them available to the commissioner at a location within this state convenient to the commissioner, or pay the reasonable and necessary expenses for the commissioner or his representatives to examine them at the place where they are maintained. The commissioner may designate representatives, including comparable officials of the state in which the records are located, to inspect them on his behalf.

(2) The commissioner shall have the authority to examine the books, records, and accounts of any former licensed lender or other permit holder which is being liquidated or is engaging in the collection or enforcement of consumer loans.

(3) Persons regulated by this Chapter, including persons engaged in the collection or enforcement of consumer loans who have not paid an examination fee for any reason, including revocation, suspension, cancellation, relinquishment, or

non-renewal of permit, shall, upon examination, pay an examination fee to the commissioner of fifty dollars per hour per examiner. If the examination fee is not paid within thirty days after its assessment, the person examined is subject to an administrative penalty of not more than one hundred dollars each day that it is late. The penalty, together with the amount due, may be recovered by the commissioner in a civil action brought in any court of competent jurisdiction.

H. The commissioner may promulgate rules or regulations to reduce the fees described in Subsections A and B of this Section with respect to their application to automated loan machines.

I. Any person required to be licensed by this Chapter shall pay all applicable fees to utilize any electronic database licensing system as described in R.S. 6:121.8.

Added by Acts 1985, No. 808, § 1, eff. July 22, 1985. Amended by Acts 1988, No. 936, § 1; Acts 1990, No. 227, § 1, eff. July 3, 1990; Acts 1992, No. 114, § 1, eff. June 5, 1992; Acts 1992, No. 145, § 1; Acts 1995, No. 1184, § 2; Acts 1997, No. 284, § 1; Acts 1997, No. 1432, § 1; Acts 1999, No. 1315, § 1, eff. Jan. 1, 2000; Acts 2003, No. 1233, § 1; Acts 2010, No. 33, § 1, eff. May 26, 2010; Acts 2012, No. 220, § 2, eff. May 22, 2012.

PART X. COLLECTION PRACTICES

§ 3562. Unauthorized collection practices

Except as otherwise provided by law or this section, the creditor, including, but not limited to the creditor in a consumer credit transaction, shall not contact any person other than an extender of credit or credit reporting agency who is not living, residing, or present in the household of the debtor regarding the debtor's obligation to pay a debt.

(1) Notwithstanding R.S. 9:3513 the debtor may waive the benefits of this section at any time by giving consent, provided such consent is given at a time subsequent to the date the debt arises.

(2) The creditor may contact any person without the debtor's consent:

(a) To ascertain information bearing on a debtor's credit worthiness, credit standing, credit capacity, character, general reputation, personal characteristics or mode of living which is used or expected to be used or collected in whole or in part for the purpose of serving as a factor in establishing the debtor's eligibility for credit or insurance provided such contacts are not designed to collect a delinquent debt, or

(b) To ascertain the whereabouts of the debtor when the creditor has reason to believe the debtor has changed his employment or has moved from his last known address.

(3) If the debtor has defaulted on his promise to pay, and if he has given specific notice in writing by registered or certified mail, instructing the creditor to cease further contacts with the debtor in regard to the indebtedness, the creditor shall thereafter limit mail contacts to one notice per month so long as the notice is not designed to threaten action not otherwise permitted by law. If the debtor has instructed the creditor to cease further contact, as heretofore provided, the creditor may make a maximum of four personal contacts with the debtor for the purpose of settling the obligation provided such contacts are not designed to threaten action not otherwise permitted by law.

(4) This section shall not prohibit the extender of credit from

(a) contacting any person in order to discover property belonging to the debtor that may be seized to satisfy a debt that has been reduced to judgment;

(b) making amicable demand and filing suit on the debt; or

(c) contacting persons related to the debtor if permission is specifically given in writing at the time the debt arises or at any time thereafter, provided that such contacts are reasonable.

(5) This section shall not limit a debtor's right to bring an action for damages provided by Article 2315 of the Louisiana Civil Code.

(6) Notwithstanding the provisions of Paragraph (3), when the extender of credit has filed suit and obtained judgment he shall be permitted to resume contacts with the consumer against whom judgment has been obtained.

Added by Acts 1972, No. 454, § 1, eff. Jan. 1, 1973. Amended by Acts 1974, No. 466, § 2.

Cross References

C.C. art. 2315.

PART XI. NOTIFICATION AND FEES

§ 3563. Applicability

This Part applies to a person engaged in this state in making consumer credit sales or consumer loans and to a person who takes assignments of and undertakes direct collection of payments from or enforcement of rights against debtors arising from these sales or loans. This Part shall not apply to a licensed lender or to any person whose only act of extending credit is the making of a sale to a consumer by honoring a credit card issued by a supervised financial organization subject to regulation, supervision, or auditing by any state or federal agency, and where such seller receives payment for the sale from the credit card issuer and retains neither an interest in the extension of the credit nor a right of recourse against the buyer in the event of nonpayment of the account.

Acts 1985, No. 808, § 2, eff. July 22, 1985. Amended by Acts 1986, No. 584, § 1, eff. July 2, 1986; Acts 1992, No. 366, § 1.

§ 3563.1. Financial institutions exempt

Notwithstanding the provisions of R.S. 9:3563, banks, savings and loan associations, savings banks, credit unions, and any nonpublic elementary and secondary schools that finance their tuition, shall be exempt from the notification filing requirements under this Part. Such institutions, except as provided in R.S. 9:3512, shall be subject to the provisions of this Chapter on all consumer credit transactions made by the institution. "Consumer credit transactions" is as defined in R.S. 9:3516(13).

Added by Acts 1993, No. 932, § 2, eff. Sept. 1, 1993. Amended by Acts 1995, No. 255, § 1; Acts 1995, No. 292, § 1; Acts 2003, No. 372, § 1.

§ 3564. Notification

A. Persons subject to this Part shall file notification with the commissioner within thirty days after commencing business in this state, and thereafter, on or before April first of each year. The notification shall state:

(1) The name of the person.

(2) The name in which business is transacted if different from (1).

(3) The address of the principal office, which may be located outside this state.

(4) The address of each office or retail store in this state, if any, at which consumer credit sales or consumer loans are made. If a person takes assignments of obligations, the notification shall state the offices or places of business within this state at which business is transacted.

(5) If consumer credit sales or consumer loans are made otherwise than at an office or retail store in this state, a brief description of the manner in which they are made.

(6) The address of the designated agent upon whom service of process may be made in this state.

(7) Whether or not consumer loans are made.

(8) Any other information that may be required by the commissioner.

B. If information in a notification becomes inaccurate after filing, the filer shall correct the inaccurate information within sixty days by written notice to the commissioner.

C. Each branch or location of a business shall be considered as a separate entity, notification shall be filed for each entity.

Acts 1985, No. 808, § 2, eff. July 22, 1985. Amended by Acts 1986, No. 584, § 1, eff. July 2, 1986; Acts 1992, No. 366, §§ 1, 2; Acts 1997, No. 38, § 1.

§ 3565. Notification fee

A. Each entity required to file notification with the commissioner shall remit with that notification a fee as set forth in Subsection B of this Section.

B. (1) The notification fee for each entity engaged in making consumer credit sales shall be as follows:

(a) An entity with a preceding calendar year consumer credit sales total of not more than five hundred thousand dollars shall pay seventy-five dollars.

(b) An entity with a preceding calendar year consumer credit sales total of more than five hundred thousand but less than one million dollars shall pay one hundred fifty dollars.

(c) An entity with a preceding calendar year consumer credit sales total of more than one million but less than two million dollars shall pay three hundred seventy-five dollars.

(d) An entity with a preceding calendar year consumer credit sales total of more than two million dollars shall pay seven hundred fifty dollars.

(2) Repealed by Acts 1992, No. 282, § 1.

(3) Repealed by Acts 1986, No. 584, § 4, eff. July 2, 1986.

(4) Each entity that takes assignments and undertakes direct collection of payments from or enforcement of rights against debtors arising from consumer credit sales or loans shall pay seventy-five dollars.

C. If the required notification and notification fee are not received by the commissioner, postmarked by April sixteenth of each year, a late fee of fifty dollars shall be assessed. If the required notification, notification fee, and late fee are not received by the commissioner, postmarked by May thirtieth of that year, the commissioner shall notify the person that if the notification and fees are not received by the commissioner, postmarked by June sixteenth of that year, the person shall forfeit his right to engage in the privileges provided for in this Part.

D. A person shall not be authorized to engage in the activities regulated by this Part unless such person has complied with the notification provisions of this Part and the notification filing has not been suspended or revoked by the commissioner as provided for in this Chapter.

E. No new license shall be issued upon the filing of a new application by any person against whom any penalty or fee has been imposed unless and until such penalty or fee previously accrued under this Section has been paid.

Acts 1985, No. 808, § 2, eff. July 22, 1985. Amended by Acts 1992, No. 366, §§ 1, 2; Acts 1997, No. 284, § 1; Acts 2001, No. 620, § 1, eff. June 22, 2001.

§ 3566. Repealed by Acts 1997, No. 48, § 1

§ 3567. Repealed by Acts 1997, No. 63, § 3

PART XII. IDENTITY THEFT

§ 3568. Identity theft

A. **Police reports.** Notwithstanding the fact that jurisdiction may lie elsewhere for investigation and prosecution of a crime of identity theft, victims of identity theft may file police reports about the identity theft with the Louisiana Department of Justice, office of the attorney general, or in the municipality or parish in which the victim is domiciled, or both. The Louisiana Department of Justice, office of the attorney general, or the municipal police department or sheriff's office shall receive and file any report of identity theft filed by victims as authorized under this Subsection. For the purposes of this Subsection, "police report" means a loss or other similar report filed with the Louisiana Department of Justice, office of the attorney general, or the municipal police department, or with a sheriff's department, or with a similar law enforcement agency.

B. **Creditors to make information available.** (1) Each creditor who grants credit as a result of information which was obtained through an identity theft shall make available to the victim of the identity theft application information and transactional information, such as a copy of one or more complete monthly billing statements prepared in the regular course of business by a financial institution, in the possession of the creditor which the victim needs to undo the effects of the identity theft. Prior to providing information to the victim, the creditor or its representative may require the victim to submit a written statement, dated and signed by the victim of identity theft, which (a) provides information sufficient to verify the identity of the victim and the existence of an identity crime, including a copy of the police report and a copy of the victim's state-issued identification card, and (b) states that the consumer authorizes disclosure of the information, and (c) identifies the information the victim requests to be disclosed.

(2) No creditor may be held liable for an action taken in good faith to provide information regarding potential or actual violations of this Part to other financial information repositories, financial service providers, merchants, law enforcement authorities, victims, or any person alleging to be a victim who complies with Paragraph (1) of this Subsection, or to assist a victim in recovery of fines, restitution, and rehabilitation of the victim's credit, or such other relief as may be appropriate.

C. **Security alerts.** (1) A person who receives notification of a security alert under R.S. 9:3571.1 in connection with a request for a consumer report for the approval of a credit-based application, including an application for a new extension of credit, a purchase, lease, or rental agreement for goods, or for an application for a noncredit-related service, shall not lend money, extend credit, or authorize an application without taking reasonable steps to verify the consumer's identity. For the purposes of this Section, "extension of credit" does not include an increase in an existing open-end credit plan, as defined in Regulation Z of the Federal Reserve System (12 C.F.R. 226.2), or any change to or review of an existing credit account.

(2) If a consumer has included with a security alert a specified telephone number to be used for identity verification purposes, a person who receives that number with a security alert shall contact the consumer using that number or take reasonable steps to verify the consumer's identity and confirm that the application for an extension of credit is not the result of financial theft before lending money, extending credit, or completing any purchase, lease, or rental of goods, or approving any noncredit-related services.

(3) If a person uses a consumer report to facilitate the extension of credit or for any other transaction on behalf of a subsidiary, affiliate, agent, assignee, or prospective assignee, that person, rather than the subsidiary, affiliate, agent, assignee, or prospective assignee, may verify the consumer's identity.

D. Damages. Effective January 1, 2004, each creditor, potential creditor, credit reporting agency, or other entity which violates the provisions of this Part shall be liable to the victim of an identity theft for all of the documented out-of-pocket expenses caused by such creditor, potential creditor, credit reporting agency, or other entity and suffered by the victim as a result of the identity theft, plus reasonable attorney fees.

Added by Acts 2003, No. 934, § 1.

PART XIII. DISCLOSURE OF PERSONAL CREDIT INFORMATION

§ 3571. Dissemination of specific credit information; subpoena of records; requirements; penalties

A savings bank, a savings and loan association, a company issuing credit cards, or a business offering credit shall disclose financial records of its customers only pursuant to R.S. 6:333.

Added by Acts 1976, No. 252, § 1. Amended by Acts 1980, No. 806, § 1; Acts 1989, No. 157, § 1; Acts 1989, No. 779, § 2, eff. July 9, 1989; Acts 1990, No. 694, § 1, eff. July 20, 1990; Acts 1993, No. 1018, § 1; Acts 1997, No. 44, § 2.

Editor's note. Section 4 of Acts 1989, No. 779 provides that the provisions of Section 2 of the same Act amending R.S. 9:3571, subsection A, shall supersede and take precedence over the provisions of R.S. 9:3571, as amended by Acts 1989, No. 157 of the 1989 Regular Session of the Legislature. Accordingly, subsection A of R.S. 9:3571 is printed as amended by Acts 1989, No. 779, § 2.

§ 3571.1. Credit reporting agency information and reports; consumer access to files; right of correction; dissemination or maintenance of untrue or misleading credit information by credit reporting agency; investigation; right to recovery

A. (1) Each credit reporting agency shall, within five business days of receipt of a written request from a consumer, mail, first class, to that consumer a copy of his credit report, including the nature and substance of any information being provided to credit reporting agency customers of the agency.

(2) Any consumer appearing in person during normal business hours at the office of a full service credit reporting agency location which offers customer service shall, upon presentation of clear and proper identification, be immediately given a copy of his report unless the agency has reason to believe the requestor is an impostor.

(3) The credit reporting agency may charge the consumer a fee not to exceed eight dollars for each requested copy of his credit report, whether the request is made in person or in writing. The eight dollar fee maximum may be increased each year on August twenty-first by an amount not to exceed the annual percentage increase in the retail Consumer Price Index in the preceding year. Such annual adjustment shall be rounded to the nearest half-dollar.

B. Any credit reporting agency doing business in this state shall maintain reasonable procedures to comply with the federal Fair Credit Reporting Act, the Consumer Credit Protection Act, and all provisions of this Section. Each credit reporting agency shall use reasonable care to insure the maximum possible accuracy of the credit reports it disseminates.

C. Upon written notification by the affected consumer disputing the completeness or accuracy of any item so maintained or disseminated, a credit reporting agency shall initiate an investigation of the disputed item. Within forty-five calendar days of receipt of such written notification, the credit reporting agency shall either promptly correct the disputed item or shall provide a written update of the current status of the disputed file items after investigation of said items. When the consumer provides evidence substantiating his claim, the credit reporting agency shall consider such information. If the investigation does not resolve the dispute, the consumer may file a brief statement setting forth the nature of the dispute. The credit reporting agency may limit such statements to not more than one hundred words if it provides the consumer with assistance in writing a clear summary of the dispute. Whenever a dispute statement is filed, unless there are compelling grounds to believe such dispute is frivolous or irrelevant, the credit reporting agency shall in any subsequent report containing the information in question clearly note that it is disputed and provide either the consumer's statement or a clear and accurate summary thereof.

D. Any consumer who is denied credit, insurance, or employment on the whole or partial basis of information provided by a credit reporting agency shall be entitled to a copy of his credit report without charge, provided that he requests such report in writing from the agency within sixty days of being denied credit by a third party. The third party shall upon request by the consumer provide the name of the credit reporting agency which provided information used in the credit denial decision.

E. Each credit reporting agency shall maintain a record of the recipients of any credit report which was furnished for employment consideration purposes in the two years preceding the request, and such agency shall also maintain a record of the recipients of a report requested for any other purpose during the six-month period preceding the request.

F. Any person damaged by an intentional or negligent violation of Subsections A through E may bring an action for and shall be entitled to recovery of actual damages, plus reasonable attorney fees, court costs, and other reasonable costs of prosecution of the suit.

G. (1) Any person who is denied credit, insurance, or employment on the basis of erroneous or inaccurate information furnished by a credit reporting agency is entitled to the recovery from such agency of his actual damages, plus reasonable attorney fees and court costs, if both of the following exist:

(a) The erroneous or inaccurate information was a significant material cause of the denial of credit, insurance, or employment.

(b) The credit reporting agency failed to use ordinary care in obtaining or amassing the information or failed to exercise due diligence in discovering such error.

(2) Any person who is required to have erroneous or inaccurate information removed from his credit report as a condition to having his credit, insurance, or employment application approved is entitled to the recovery of his actual damages, plus reasonable attorney fees and court costs, if both of the following exist:

(a) The erroneous or inaccurate information was a significant material cause of the request for the removal of such information.

(b) The credit reporting agency failed to use ordinary care in obtaining or amassing the information or failed to exercise due diligence in discovering such error.

(3) For purposes of this Subsection, the failure to use ordinary care or exercise due diligence shall mean the failure to comply with the federal Fair Credit Reporting Act, the Consumer Credit Protection Act, or any provision of this Section. Such failure to comply shall be presumptive evidence that the credit reporting agency failed to use ordinary care or exercise due diligence.

H. For the purposes of this Section:

(1) "Clear and proper identification" means information generally deemed sufficient to identify a person.

(2) "Credit report" means any written, oral, or other communication of any credit information by a credit reporting agency, as defined in the federal Fair Credit Reporting Act, which operates or maintains a database of consumer credit information bearing on a consumer's credit worthiness, credit standing, or credit capacity.

(3) "Credit reporting agency" means any person who, for monetary fees, dues, or on a cooperative nonprofit basis, regularly engages in whole or in part in the practice of assembling or evaluating consumer credit information or other information on consumers for the purpose of furnishing consumer reports to third parties, and who uses any means or facility of interstate commerce for the purpose of preparing or furnishing consumer reports. For the purposes of this Section, "Credit Reporting Agency" shall not mean a check acceptance service which provides check approval and guarantees services to merchants.

(4) "Security alert" means a notice placed on a consumer file, at the request of the consumer, that is sent to a recipient of a consumer report involving that consumer file, signifying the fact that the consumer's identity may have been used without the consumer's consent to fraudulently obtain goods or services in the consumer's name.

(5) "Security freeze" means a notice placed on a consumer file, at the request of the consumer and subject to certain exceptions, that prohibits a credit reporting agency from releasing the consumer's credit report or credit score without the express authorization of the consumer.

I. Upon a request by a consumer in writing or by telephone, with proper identification provided by the consumer, a consumer reporting agency shall place a security alert on the consumer's file not later than five business days after the date the agency receives the request. The security alert must remain in effect for not less than ninety days after the date the agency places the security alert on file. There is no limit on the number of security alerts a consumer may request. At the termination of the security alert, upon written request or telephone authorization by the consumer, and with proper identification provided by the consumer, the agency shall provide the consumer with a copy of the consumer's file.

J. A consumer reporting agency shall send an alert to each person who requests a consumer report if a security alert is in effect for the consumer file involved regardless of whether a full credit report, or summary report is requested.

K. A consumer reporting agency that compiles and maintains files on a nationwide basis, as defined by 15 U.S.C. § 1681a(p) shall maintain a toll-free telephone number that will accept security alert requests from consumers twenty-four hours a day, seven days a week, subject to reasonable maintenance, or service outages beyond the control of the consumer reporting agency.

L. The following persons are not required to place a security alert or a security freeze on a credit report in accordance with this Part:

(1) A check services or fraud prevention services company, which issues reports on incidents of fraud or authorizations for the purpose of approving or processing negotiable instruments, electronic funds transfers, or similar methods of payments.

(2) A deposit account information service company, which issues reports regarding account closures due to fraud, substantial overdrafts, ATM abuse, or similar negative information regarding a consumer, to inquiring banks or other financial institutions for use only in reviewing a consumer request for a deposit account at the inquiring bank or financial institution.

(3) A reseller of credit information that assembles or merges information contained in the database of another consumer reporting agency or multiple consumer reporting agencies, and does not maintain a permanent database of credit information from which new consumer reports are produced.

(4) Any database or file which consists solely of any information adverse to the interests of the consumer, including but not limited to criminal record information, which is used for fraud prevention or detection, tenant screening, employment screening, or any purpose permitted by the federal Fair Credit Reporting Act, 15 U.S.C. § 1681b.

(5) A person to the extent such person offers fraud prevention services that issues reports on incidents of fraud or reports used primarily in the detection or prevention of fraud.

(6) A bank, as defined in 12 U.S.C. 1813(a) and Title 6 of the Louisiana Revised Statutes of 1950.

M. (1) A consumer may elect to place a security freeze on his credit report by any of the following methods:

(a) By written request, sent by standard or certified mail, that includes clear and proper identification, to a credit reporting agency.

(b) Telephone call.

(c) Electronically by secure website.

(2) A credit reporting agency shall place a security freeze on a consumer's credit report no later than five business days after receiving a written request for the security freeze from the consumer by mail. A credit reporting agency that receives such a request electronically by secure website or by telephone shall comply with the request within twenty-four hours of receiving the request.

(3) When a security freeze is in place, information from a consumer's credit report shall not be released to a third party without prior express authorization from the consumer. This Subsection does not prevent a credit reporting agency from advising a third party that a security freeze is in effect with respect to the consumer's credit report.

N. The credit reporting agency shall, no later than five business days after the date the agency receives the request for a security freeze, provide the consumer with a unique personal identification number or password to be used by the consumer when providing authorization for the access to his credit file for a specific period of time. In addition, the credit reporting agency shall simultaneously provide to the consumer in writing the process of placing, removing, and temporarily lifting a security freeze and the process for allowing access to information from the consumer's credit file for a specific period while the security freeze is in effect.

O. A consumer may request a replacement personal identification number or password. The request shall comply with the requirements for requesting a security freeze under Subsection M of this Section. The credit reporting agency shall, not later than the fifth business day after the date the agency receives the request for a replacement personal identification number or password, provide the consumer with a new, unique personal identification number or password to be used by the consumer instead of the number or password that was provided under Subsection N of this Section.

P. A credit reporting agency shall notify a person who requests a consumer report or score if a security freeze is in effect for the consumer file involved in that report or score.

Q. If a third party requests access to a consumer credit report on which a security freeze is in effect, and this request is in connection with an application for credit or any other use, and the consumer does not allow his credit report to be accessed for that specific period of time, the third party must treat the application as incomplete.

R. If the consumer wishes to allow his credit report or score to be accessed for a specific period of time while a freeze is in place, he shall contact the credit reporting agency by a method provided for in Subsection M of this Section and request that the freeze be temporarily lifted, and provide the following:

(1) Clear and proper identification.

(2) The unique personal identification number or password provided by the credit reporting agency pursuant to Subsection N or O.

(3) The proper information regarding the time period for which the report shall be available to users of the credit report.

S. A credit reporting agency that receives a request by mail from a consumer to temporarily lift a freeze on a credit report pursuant to Subsection R of this Section shall comply with the request no later than three business days after receiving the request. A credit reporting agency that receives such a request electronically by secure website or by telephone shall comply with the request within twenty-four hours of receiving the request.

T. A credit reporting agency shall remove or temporarily lift a freeze placed on a consumer's credit report only in the following cases:

(1) Upon consumer request as provided in this Section.

(2) If the consumer's credit report was frozen due to a material misrepresentation of fact by the consumer. If a credit reporting agency intends to remove a freeze upon a consumer's credit report pursuant to this Paragraph, the credit reporting agency shall notify the consumer in writing prior to removing the freeze on the consumer's credit report.

U. A security freeze shall remain in place until the consumer requests that the security freeze be temporarily lifted for a specific period of time or removed. A credit reporting agency shall remove a security freeze within three business days of receiving a written request for removal from the consumer or within twenty-four hours of receiving an electronic request by secure website or telephonic request for removal from the consumer, who provides both of the following:

(1) Clear and proper identification.

(2) The unique personal identification number or password provided by the credit reporting agency.

V. A security freeze does not apply to a consumer report provided to:

(1) A federal, state, or local governmental entity, including a law enforcement agency, or court, or their agents or assigns.

(2) A private collection agency for the sole purpose of assisting in the collection of an existing debt of the consumer who is the subject of the credit report requested.

(3) A person or entity, or a subsidiary, affiliate, or agent of that person or entity, or an assignee of a financial obligation owing by the consumer to that person or entity, or a prospective assignee of a financial obligation owing by the consumer to that person or entity in conjunction with the proposed purchase of the financial obligation, with which the consumer has or had prior to assignment an account or contract, including a demand deposit account, or to whom the consumer issued a negotiable instrument, for the purposes of reviewing the account or collecting the financial obligation owing for the account, contract, or negotiable instrument. For purposes of this Paragraph, "reviewing the account" includes activities related to account maintenance, monitoring, credit line increases, and account upgrades and enhancements.

(4) A subsidiary, affiliate, agent, assignee, or prospective assignee of a person to whom access has been granted under Subsection R for the purposes of facilitating the extension of credit.

(5) A person, for the purposes of prescreening as provided by the federal Fair Credit Reporting Act.

(6) A credit reporting agency for the purposes of providing a consumer with a copy of his own report on his request.

(7) A child support enforcement agency.

(8) A credit reporting agency that acts only as a reseller of credit information by assembling and merging information contained in the database of another credit reporting agency or multiple credit reporting agencies and does not maintain a permanent database of credit information from which new credit reports are produced. However, a credit reporting agency acting as a reseller shall honor any security freeze placed on a credit report by another credit reporting agency.

(9) A check services or fraud prevention services company, which issues reports on incidents of fraud or authorizations for the purpose of approving or processing negotiable instruments, electronic funds transfers, or similar methods of payments.

(10) A deposit account information service company, which issues reports regarding account closures due to fraud, substantial overdrafts, ATM abuse, or similar negative information regarding a consumer, to inquiring banks or other financial institutions for use only in reviewing a consumer request for a deposit account at the inquiring bank or financial institution.

W. A credit reporting agency may impose a reasonable charge on a consumer for initially placing a security freeze on a consumer file. The amount of the charge may not exceed ten dollars. The charge to temporarily lift the security freeze may not exceed eight dollars per request. At no time shall the consumer be charged for revoking the freeze. On January first of each year, a credit reporting agency may increase the charge for placing a security alert based proportionally on changes to the Consumer Price Index of All Urban Consumers as determined by the United States Department of Labor with fractional changes rounded to the nearest twenty-five cents. An exception shall be allowed whereby the consumer will be charged zero dollars by the consumer reporting agency placing the security freeze if any of the following applies:

(1) If the consumer is a victim of identity theft and, upon the request of the consumer reporting agency, provides the credit reporting agency with a police report described in R.S. 9:3568.

(2) If the consumer is sixty-two years of age or older.

X. If a security freeze is in place, a credit reporting agency shall not change any of the following official information in a consumer credit report without sending a written confirmation of the change to the consumer within thirty days of the change being posted to the consumer's file: name, date of birth, social security number, and address. Written confirmation is not required for technical modifications of a consumer's official information, including name and street abbreviations, complete spellings, or transposition of numbers or letters. In the case of an address change, the written confirmation shall be sent to both the new address and to the former address.

Y. Any consumer damaged by an intentional or negligent violation of Subsections M through U may bring an action for and shall be entitled to recovery of actual damages, plus reasonable attorney fees, court costs, and other reasonable costs of prosecution of the suit.

Z. A credit reporting agency is not required to place, remove, or temporarily lift a security freeze within the time periods provided in this Section, only for such time as the occurrences prevent compliance, if any of the following occurrences apply:

(1) The consumer fails to provide information required by this Section or commits or attempts to commit a fraud or misrepresentation.

(2) The credit reporting agency's ability to place, remove, or temporarily lift the security freeze is prevented by any of the following circumstances:

(a) An act of God, including fire, earthquakes, hurricanes, storms, or similar natural disaster or phenomena.

(b) Unauthorized or illegal acts by a third party, including terrorism, sabotage, riot, vandalism, labor strikes or disputes disrupting operations, or similar occurrence.

(c) Operational interruption, including electrical failure, unanticipated delay in equipment or replacement part delivery, computer hardware or software failures inhibiting response time, or similar disruption.

(d) Governmental action, including emergency orders or regulations, judicial or law enforcement action, or similar directives.

(e) Regularly scheduled maintenance, during other than normal business hours, of, or updates to, the credit reporting agency's systems.

(f) Commercially reasonable maintenance of, or repair to, the credit reporting agency's systems that is unexpected or unscheduled.

Added by Acts 1990, No. 671, § 1. Amended by Acts 1992, No. 592, § 1; Acts 1993, No. 243, § 1; Acts 2003, No. 934, § 1; Acts 2004, No. 766, § 1, eff. July 1, 2005; Acts 2010, No. 998, § 1.

§ 3571.2. Limitations on use of consumer's credit report

A. No motor vehicle dealer shall request, obtain, or review a consumer's credit report in connection with the following activities unless, prior to the activity, the dealer has received an application from the consumer to lease or finance a motor vehicle or a written authorization from the consumer for such request or review:

(1) A request to test drive or the test driving of a motor vehicle.

(2) A request for information concerning pricing or financing.

(3) Negotiating with a consumer.

B. Whoever violates the provisions of this Section shall be subject to civil penalties not to exceed two thousand five hundred dollars per violation.

Added by Acts 1999, No. 1239, § 1.

PART XIV. LOAN BROKERS

§ 3572.1. Loan broker defined

A "loan broker" is defined as any person who, for compensation or the expectation of compensation, obtains or offers to obtain a consumer loan from a third party either for another person domiciled in Louisiana, or for another person wherever domiciled, if the broker is operating in Louisiana.

Added by Acts 1986, No. 729, § 1. Amended by Acts 1992, No. 353, § 1, eff. June 17, 1992; Acts 1997, No. 1419, § 1; Acts 2006, No. 213, § 1.

Cross References

C.C. arts. 2913, 3494.

§ 3572.2. Exemptions; licensing and bonding; loan broker

A. The following shall be excepted from the licensing and bonding provisions of this Part:

(1) A supervised financial organization that is exempt from the requirement of licensure as a licensed lender.

(2) A lender licensed by the commissioner of financial institutions to make consumer loans pursuant to the Louisiana Consumer Credit Law.

(3) An officer, director, or employee of the entities listed in Paragraph (1) or (2) of this Subsection when such person is acting within the scope of his duties to that supervised financial organization or licensed lender.

(4) Persons subject to licensing, supervision, or auditing by the Federal National Mortgage Association, the Federal Home Loan Mortgage Corporation, the Government National Mortgage Association, the Veterans Administration, or the United States Department of Housing and Urban Development as an approved seller, servicer, or issuer, provided that all brokered loans comply with a program administered by a federal agency in which the broker is approved, licensed, supervised, or audited and provided further that all broker's loans are subject to oversight by the approving federal agency.

B. The following shall be excepted from the definition of a loan broker:

(1) An attorney licensed to practice law in the state of Louisiana when such attorney is not actively engaged in the business of brokering consumer loans or federally related mortgage loans and when the brokering is incidental to the provision of other legal services.

(2) A person licensed by the Louisiana Real Estate Commission who arranges financing in the normal course of representation of a client for the purchase, sale, lease, or rental of real estate.

(3) A person licensed as an insurance agent or broker by the Louisiana Department of Insurance who arranges for the financing of insurance premiums with a financial institution or licensed insurance premium finance company, when the compensation received or expected to be received is paid only by the financial institution or insurance premium finance company.

(4) Any real estate broker or a real estate salesman who is not actively and principally engaged in negotiating, placing, or finding mortgage loans when rendering professional services.

(5) Any real estate investment trust.

(6) Any securities broker-dealer registered with the federal Securities and Exchange Commission and the securities law division of the office of financial institutions, and the registered agents of the broker-dealer, when such persons are not principally engaged in negotiating, placing, or finding mortgage loans when rendering professional services.

(7) Any manufactured home dealer licensed pursuant to the provisions of R.S. 51:911.24 who arranges or assists in arranging for a customer a direct or indirect consumer of federally related mortgage loan secured in whole or in part by a manufactured home, when such dealer's business is not primarily that of a consumer loan broker.

(8) Any person who is licensed pursuant to the Residential Mortgage Lending Act and whose primary business is that of a mortgage broker, mortgage lender, or both.

(9) An income tax preparer who is an authorized Internal Revenue Service e-file provider and whose only brokering activity is facilitating refund anticipation loans. For purposes of this Paragraph, "refund anticipation loan" means a loan whereby the creditor arranges to be repaid directly by the Internal Revenue Service from the anticipated proceeds of the debtor's income tax refund.

Added by Acts 1986, No. 729, § 1. Amended by Acts 1992, No. 353, § 1, eff. June 17, 1992; Acts 1997, No. 1419, § 1; Acts 1999, No. 704, § 1; Acts 1999, No. 1160, § 1; Acts 2000, 1st Ex.Sess., No. 34, § 2, eff. April 14, 2000; Acts 2003, No. 665, § 2, eff. June 27, 2003.

Cross References

C.C. arts. 2913, 3494.

§ 3572.3. Licensure required

A. (1) Unless a person has first been licensed by the commissioner as provided in this Part, he shall not engage in the business of loan brokering, and shall not advertise or solicit, whether in print, by letter, in person, or otherwise in Louisiana, that he will find lenders for consumer loans or federally related mortgage loans. The initial license and annual renewal fee shall be five hundred dollars. However, a natural person through whom a corporation brokers loans pursuant to R.S. 9:3572.4 shall pay an initial license and annual renewal fee of one hundred dollars. No portion of the fee shall be refunded if the application is denied.

(2) The annual renewal application and fee are due on or before January first of each year. The form and content of renewal applications shall be determined by the commissioner of financial institutions, and a renewal application may be denied upon the same grounds as would justify denial of an initial application, or may be denied if administrative proceedings to suspend or revoke the license have begun. If the commissioner has not received the annual renewal application and fee postmarked on or before January sixteenth, he shall notify the loan broker by United States mail and assess a late fee of one hundred dollars.

(3) If the commissioner has not received the annual renewal application, renewal fee and late fee postmarked on or before March thirty-first, the license shall automatically lapse without a hearing or notification, and any consumer loan or federally related mortgage loan brokered after that date shall be a violation and punishable pursuant to R.S. 9:3572.12(B).

B. (1) In the event that a broker wishes to change its name, location, or mailing address, it shall notify the commissioner by written notice within thirty days prior to such change and submit a fee of fifty dollars. If the broker fails to notify the commissioner or remit the required fee within the required thirty days, the commissioner may assess the licensee one hundred dollars as a penalty.

(2) If any information furnished by the broker becomes inaccurate after its filing, the broker shall correct the inaccuracy by written notice to the commissioner within thirty days after the information becomes inaccurate. No additional fee shall be required.

Added by Acts 1986, No. 729, § 1. Amended by Acts 1992, No. 353, § 1, eff. June 17, 1992; Acts 1997, No. 1419, § 1; Acts 1999, No. 1124, § 2.

Cross References

C.C. arts. 2913, 3494.

§ 3572.4. Corporation

A corporation that is a loan broker shall be licensed and shall act as a loan broker only through natural persons who are licensed loan brokers.

Added by Acts 1986, No. 729, § 1. Amended by Acts 1997, No. 1419, § 1.

Cross References

C.C. arts. 2913, 3494.

§ 3572.5. Application form

A. The commissioner of financial institutions shall provide an application form that requires at least the following information which shall be given by the applicant:

(1) For a natural person:

(a) Full name.

(b) Date of birth.

(c) Place of birth.

(d) Business address.

(e) Home address.

(f) Name and address of employer.

(g) Names and addresses of the lenders through which the principal amount of the consumer loans or federally related mortgage loans are brokered.

(h) Number of consumer loans or federally related mortgage loans brokered in the past one-year period.

(i) A certified copy of the bond or of the formal notification by the depository of the establishment of the trust account required by R.S. 9:3572.8.

(2) For a corporation:

(a) Name.

(b) Copy of the certificate of incorporation if a Louisiana corporation.

(c) Copy of certificate authorizing the corporation to do business in Louisiana, if a foreign corporation.

(d) Address of the corporation in Louisiana.

(e) Address of the main corporate office, if outside of Louisiana.

(f) Name and address of president, secretary, and treasurer of the corporation.

(g) Name of each licensed loan broker through which it will conduct business.

(h) Names and addresses of the lenders through which the principal amount of consumer loans or federally related mortgage loans are brokered.

(i) Number of consumer loans or federally related mortgage loans brokered in the past one-year period.

(j) A certified copy of the bond or of the formal notification by the depository of the establishment of the trust account required by R.S. 9:3572.8.

B. (1) The commissioner may deny an application if he finds that the financial responsibility, character, and fitness of the applicant and its principals, owners, officers, directors, partners, and members, and the character and fitness of its managers are such as to warrant a belief that the business will not be operated honestly and fairly within the purposes of this Part.

(2) Upon written request, the applicant is entitled to a hearing on the question of his qualifications for a loan broker license if either of the following occurs:

(a) The commissioner has notified the applicant in writing that his application has been denied.

(b) The commissioner has not issued a permit within sixty days after the application therefor was filed.

(3) A request for a hearing may not be made more than fifteen days after the commissioner has mailed a written notice to the applicant notifying him that the application has been denied and stating in substance the commissioner's findings supporting denial of the application.

Added by Acts 1986, No. 729, § 1. Amended by Acts 1992, No. 353, § 1, eff. June 17, 1992; Acts 1997, No. 1419, § 1.

Cross References

C.C. arts. 2913, 3494.

§ 3572.6. Restrictions; records

A. A loan broker shall broker a consumer loan or federally related mortgage loan only to a lender licensed by the office of financial institutions, or to a supervised financial organization or a lender that is exempt from licensure.

B. (1) Each loan broker shall maintain a copy of all Federal Disclosure Statements from each loan that he brokers and a copy of the signed "Loan Brokerage Agreement and Disclosure Statement" given to each person pursuant to R.S. 9:3572.11, which shall be available for inspection.

(2) If the records of the loan broker are located outside this state, the broker shall, at the option of the commissioner, make such records available to the commissioner at a specified location within this state convenient to the commissioner, or the broker shall pay the reasonable and necessary expenses for the commissioner to examine the records at the location specified in the records of the office. The commissioner may designate representatives from his office or, if available and more practical, officials serving in similar capacity in the state in which the records are located to inspect them on his behalf.

C. Except as specified by this Part, no loan broker may assess, contract for, or receive any type of fee, interest, or other charge in advance, except for expense deposits under conditions specified in this Subsection, from a potential borrower for the procurement of a loan. A loan broker may accept an advance expense deposit, but such deposit shall not exceed the good faith estimate of the actual cost of any appraisal, title search, credit reports performed by an independent person and required by the originating lender for the evaluation of the potential borrower's loan application, or the actual cost of any charge of no more than twenty-five dollars assessed to a loan broker by Fannie Mae for "Desktop Underwriter" or Freddie Mac for "Loan Prospector". Any expense deposit that exceeds the actual cost of any appraisal, title search, credit reports, or charge assessed to a loan broker by Fannie Mae for "Desktop Underwriter" or Freddie Mac for "Loan Prospector" must be promptly refunded to the borrower or credited to the borrower's account at the time of the loan closing.

Added by Acts 1986, No. 729, § 1. Amended by Acts 1992, No. 353, § 1, eff. June 17, 1992; Acts 1997, No. 1419, § 1; Acts 1999, No. 1160, § 1; Acts 2003, No. 924, § 2.

Cross References

C.C. arts. 2913, 3494.

§ 3572.7. Examination; rules

A. The commissioner of financial institutions, through his employees, may examine the records of a loan broker at any time during normal business hours without prior notice.

B. The commissioner may issue rules and regulations to implement this Part and may require that additional information be disclosed in the licensure form.

Added by Acts 1986, No. 729, § 1. Amended by Acts 1997, No. 1419, § 1.

Cross References

C.C. arts. 2913, 3020, 3494.

§ 3572.8. Bond or trust account required

A. Every loan broker, except those loan brokers employed by a corporation with a valid loan broker's license, must obtain a surety bond issued by a surety company authorized to do business in Louisiana, or establish a trust account with a federally insured bank or savings institution located in Louisiana. The amount of the bond or trust account shall be twenty-five thousand dollars. The bond or trust account shall be in favor of the state of Louisiana. Any person damaged by the loan broker's breach of contract or of any obligation arising therefrom, or by any violation of law, or the attorney general seeking additional relief from R.S. 51:1408, may bring an action against the bond or trust account to recover monies therefrom. The aggregate liability of the surety or trustee shall be only for actual damages or additional relief under R.S. 51:1408 and in no event shall exceed the amount of the bond or trust account.

B. The term of the bond shall be continuous, but it shall be subject to termination by the surety upon giving sixty days written notice to the principal and to the commissioner. The bond shall continue in effect during the sixty-day period.

C. A copy of said bond shall be conspicuously posted at any business location of the broker near the location where payments are received.

D. It shall be unlawful for any loan broker or its agent or employee to post an expired bond or a bond which does not meet the requirements of this Section.

Added by Acts 1986, No. 729, § 1. Amended by Acts 1997, No. 1419, § 1.

Cross References

C.C. arts. 2913, 3494.

§ 3572.9. Rebate upon prepayment

Whenever a lender that funded a brokered consumer loan or federally related mortgage loan is required to rebate unearned loan finance charges or credit service charges to the consumer due to prepayment or the acceleration of maturity, the loan broker shall refund to the lender the proportion of the broker's fee that must be rebated by the lender. This refund shall be made within seven days of the lender's furnishing proof to the broker of the required rebate.

Added by Acts 1986, No. 729, § 1. Amended by Acts 1997, No. 1419, § 1.

Cross References

C.C. arts. 2913, 3494.

§ 3572.10. Right of cancellation

An applicant for a consumer or federally related mortgage loan shall have the right to cancel a "Loan Brokerage Agreement and Disclosure Statement" required by R.S. 9:3572.11 within five business days of signing such agreement. The applicant may exercise the right to cancel until midnight of the fifth business day following his signing of such statement. The applicant borrower shall have been considered to have exercised his right of cancellation when written notification has been postmarked or otherwise delivered to the loan broker's designated place of business within the prescribed time.

Added by Acts 1986, No. 729, § 1. Amended by Acts 1997, No. 1419, § 1; Acts 1999, No. 1160, § 1.

Cross References

C.C. arts. 2913, 3494.

§ 3572.11. Loan brokerage statement; disclosure statement required

A. (1) Each application for a consumer or federally related mortgage loan in which a loan broker is involved shall be accompanied by a written "Loan Brokerage Agreement and Disclosure Statement" which shall be signed by all contracting parties. A copy of the signed agreement shall be presented to the applicant at the time of signing.

(2) The initial paragraph of the "Loan Brokerage Agreement and Disclosure Statement" shall be entitled in at least ten point bold-face capital letters "DISCLOSURE REQUIRED BY LOUISIANA LAW". Under this title shall appear the statement in at least ten point type that "The state of Louisiana does not approve or disapprove any loan brokerage contract. The information contained in this disclosure has not been verified by the state. If you have any questions see an attorney before you sign a contract agreement."

B. The "Loan Brokerage Agreement and Disclosure Statement" shall contain the following information:

(1) The name of the loan broker; whether the loan broker is doing business as an individual, partnership, limited liability company, or corporation; the names under which the loan broker has done, is doing, or intends to do business; and the name of any parent or affiliated companies providing a settlement service.

(2) Repealed by Acts 1999, No. 1160, § 2.

(3) The length of time the loan broker has conducted business as a loan broker.

(4) A full and detailed description of the actual services that the loan broker undertakes to perform for the prospective borrower.

(5) One of the following statements, whichever is appropriate:

(a) "As required by Louisiana law, this loan broker has secured a bond by ––––––, a surety authorized to do business in this state. A certified copy of this bond is filed with the commissioner of financial institutions. Before signing a contract with this loan broker, you should check with the surety company to determine the bond's current status.", or

(b) "As required by Louisiana law, this loan broker has established a trust account (number of account) with (name/address of bank or savings institution). Before signing a contract with this loan broker you should check with the bank or savings institution to determine the current status of the trust account."

Added by Acts 1986, No. 729, § 1. Amended by Acts 1997, No. 1419, § 1; Acts 1999, No. 1160, § 1.

Cross References

C.C. arts. 2913, 3494.

§ 3572.12. Violations; penalties

A. A loan made in violation of this Part shall not be invalid solely for that reason.

B. A person who violates a provision of this Part may be assessed a civil penalty of not more than one thousand dollars for each violation. The commissioner may maintain a civil action in a court of competent jurisdiction to recover such a civil penalty, together with his costs and attorney fees incident to such action.

C. (1) The commissioner may, after a hearing pursuant to the Administrative Procedure Act,[1] suspend or revoke the license of a loan broker, upon a finding that any fact or condition exists which, if it had existed at the time of the original application for licensure, would have warranted the denying of its issuance.

(2) The commissioner may, after a hearing pursuant to the Administrative Procedure Act, suspend or revoke the license of a loan broker, upon a finding that the loan broker violated a provision of this Part or a rule or regulation of the commissioner issued pursuant thereto, or that the loan broker willfully, either orally or in writing, misrepresented the terms, benefits, privileges, or provisions of any service contract issued or to be issued by the loan broker or by any lender.

D. The contracting to receive any fee, interest, or other charge in violation of this Chapter shall result in forfeiture by the loan broker to the benefit of the aggrieved person of the entire fee, plus damages in the amount of twice the fee. In case the fee has been paid, the person by whom it has been paid may recover from the loan broker the amount of the fee thus paid, plus damages in the amount of twice the fee.

E. Whenever it shall appear to the commissioner, either upon complaint or otherwise, that any person has engaged in, is engaging in, or is about to engage in any act, practice, or transaction which is prohibited by this Part or by any order of the commissioner issued pursuant to any Section of this Part, or which is declared to be illegal in this Part, the commissioner may, in his discretion:

(1) Issue any order, including but not limited to cease and desist orders, which he deems necessary or appropriate in the public interest or for the protection of the public. Any person aggrieved by an order issued pursuant to this Subsection may request a hearing before the commissioner if such request is made within ten days after receipt of the order. Any such hearing or appeal therefrom shall be held in accordance with the Administrative Procedure Act.

(2) Apply to the district court of any parish in this state for an injunction restraining such person and the agents, employees, partners, officers, and directors of such person from continuing such act, practice, or transaction or engaging therein or doing any acts in furtherance thereof, and for such other and further relief as he deems necessary.

Added by Acts 1986, No. 729, § 1. Amended by Acts 1992, No. 353, § 1, eff. June 17, 1992; Acts 1997, No. 1419, § 1; Acts 1999, No. 1160, § 1.

[1] R.S. 49:950 et seq.

Cross References

C.C. arts. 2913, 3494.

PART XV. CREDIT REPAIR SERVICES ORGANIZATIONS ACT

Editor's note. Acts 1987, No. 838, § 1 enacted a Part XV containing R.S. 9:3575.1 to 9:3575.8. Pursuant to the statutory revision authority of the Louisiana State Law Institute, the sections of Part XV were redesignated as R.S. 9:3573.1 to 9:3573.8.

§ 3573.1. Short title; purpose

A. This Part shall be known and may be cited as the "Credit Repair Services Organizations Act."

B. The Legislature of Louisiana recognizes the right of the citizens of the state to utilize the services of qualified credit repair organizations for advice and assistance in improving their credit matters. The Legislature of Louisiana does hereby declare that it is in the best interest of the citizens of the state to protect consumers in their efforts to improve their credit record, history, and rating. The purpose of this Part is to promote the safety and welfare of the people of this state by providing a statutory structure in an area in which unqualified or unscrupulous individuals may injure or mislead the public.

Added by Acts 1992, No. 345, § 1. Amended by Acts 2003, No. 1027, § 1, eff. Dec. 31, 2003; Acts 2006, No. 190, § 1; Acts 2008, No. 858, § 1, eff. July 9, 2008.

Editor's note. A prior R.S. 9:3573.1 was repealed by Acts 1992, No. 345, § 2.

§ 3573.2. Definitions; exemptions

A. As used in this Part, the following terms shall have the following meanings:

(1) "Buyer" means an individual who is solicited to purchase or who purchases the services of a credit repair services organization.

(2) "Consumer reporting agency" shall have the meaning assigned by Section 603(f), Fair Credit Reporting Act (15 U.S.C. Section 1681 et seq.).

(3) "Credit repair services organization" means a person who, with respect to a buyer, in return for the payment of money or other valuable consideration, directly or indirectly, provides or represents that he can or will, directly or indirectly, provide any of the following services:

(a) Improving a buyer's credit record, history, or rating.

(b) Advice or assistance to a buyer with regard to improving a buyer's credit record, history, or rating, including the sale of a self-help instructional guide.

(4) "Person" means an individual, corporation, partnership, trust, association, joint venture pool, syndicate, sole proprietorship, unincorporated organization, or any other form of entity not specifically listed herein.

B. The following are exempt from this Part:

(1) Repealed by Acts 2004, No. 79, § 2, eff. May 28, 2004.

(2) A licensed lender or other person authorized to make or broker loans or extensions of credit under the laws of this state or the United States who is subject to regulation and supervision by this state or the United States, or a lender approved by the United States Secretary of Housing and Urban Development for participation in a mortgage insurance program under the National Housing Act (12 U.S.C. Section 1701 et seq.), provided the credit repair service is in connection with a loan and no additional fee is charged.

(3) A bank or savings association whose deposits or accounts are federally insured or a wholly-owned subsidiary of such a bank or savings association.

(4) A credit union doing business in this state.

(5) A person licensed to practice law in this state while acting within the course and scope of the person's practice as an attorney, and when such attorney is not actively and principally engaged as a credit repair services organization and such attorney's credit repair services are ancillary to the providing of other legal services. The exemption provided for in this Paragraph does not apply when an attorney is paid a fee by a client solely for the purposes of providing services, directly or indirectly, as a credit repair services organization as defined in Paragraph (A)(4) of this Section.

(6) A consumer reporting agency.

(7) Certified public accountants licensed to practice their profession in the state of Louisiana, while acting within the course and scope of their practice as a certified public accountant, and when such certified public accountant is not actively and principally engaged as a credit repair services organization and such certified public accountant's credit repair services are ancillary to the providing of other accounting services. The exemption provided for in this Paragraph does not apply when a certified public accountant is paid a fee by a client solely for the purposes of providing services, directly or indirectly, as a credit repair services organization defined in Paragraph (A)(4) of this Section.
Added by Acts 1992, No. 345, § 1. Amended by Acts 1995, No. 332, § 1; Acts 2003, No. 1027, § 1, eff. Dec. 31, 2003; Acts 2006, No. 190, § 1; Acts 2008, No. 858, § 1, eff. July 9, 2008.

Editor's note. A prior R.S. 9:3573.2 was repealed by Acts 1992, No. 345, § 2.

§ 3573.2–A. [Blank]

§ 3573.3. Prohibited conduct

A credit repair services organization or a salesperson, agent, or representative of a credit repair services organization, who sells or attempts to sell the services of a credit repair services organization shall not:

(1) Charge a buyer or receive from a buyer money or other valuable consideration unless the credit repair services organization has obtained, in accordance with R.S. 9:3573.4, a surety bond issued by a surety company authorized to do business in this state.

(2) Make or use a false or misleading representation in the offer or sale of the services of a credit repair services organization, including guaranteeing to "erase bad credit" or words to that effect unless the representation clearly discloses that this can be done only if the credit history is inaccurate or obsolete.

(3) Engage, directly or indirectly, in a fraudulent or deceptive act, practice, or course of dealing in connection with the offer or sale of the services of a credit repair services organization.

(4) Make or advise a buyer to make a statement with respect to a buyer's credit worthiness, credit standing, or credit capacity that is false or misleading or that should be known by the exercise of reasonable care to be false or misleading to a consumer reporting agency or to a person who has extended credit to a buyer.

(5) Advertise or cause to be advertised, in any manner whatsoever, the services of a credit repair services organization without filing a registration statement with the attorney general, unless otherwise provided by this Part.

(6) Make nonessential requests for credit information relating to a buyer from any source providing such information for no cost.

(7) Repealed by Acts 2008, No. 858, § 2, eff. July 9, 2008.

(8) Structure a transaction with a buyer in such a manner as to attempt to circumvent the provisions of this Part.

(9) Divide a transaction into multiple transactions, such as by attempting to sell or selling any publication, including but not limited to any book, pamphlet, or electronic or computer guide, related in any way to improving a buyer's credit record, history, or rating, to a buyer and, directly or indirectly, through any affiliate, subsidiary, related person, or otherwise, providing services to the buyer to assist him in utilizing or implementing the information or directions contained therein, unless all charges and fees related to such sale and service combined do not exceed the bona fide costs for publishing the copy of such publication.

(10) Violate any provision of the federal Credit Repair Organizations Act, 15 U.S.C. 1679 et seq., as amended. Any violation of such Act shall constitute a violation of state law.
Added by Acts 1992, No. 345, § 1. Amended by Acts 1995, No. 332, § 1; Acts 2003, No. 1027, § 1, eff. Dec. 31, 2003; Acts 2008, No. 858, § 1, eff. July 9, 2008; Acts 2009, No. 76, § 1.

Editor's note. A prior R.S. 9:3573.3 was repealed by Acts 1992, No. 345, § 2.

§ 3573.4. Bond; trust account

A. All credit repair services organizations shall obtain a surety bond issued by a company licensed to do business in Louisiana.

B. The bond shall be filed with the attorney general of Louisiana.

C. The bond must be in favor of the state of Louisiana for the benefit of any person who is damaged by any violation of this Part.

D. Any persons claiming against the bond for a violation of this Part may maintain an action at law against the credit repair services organization and against the surety or trustee. The surety or trustee shall be liable only for damages awarded under R.S. 9:3573.10 and not the punitive damages permitted under that Section. The aggregate liability of the surety or trustee to all persons damaged by a credit repair services organization's violation of this Part shall not exceed the amount of the bond or trust account.

E. The bond shall be in the amount of one hundred thousand dollars.

F. The credit repair services organization shall notify the attorney general in writing within thirty days after it has ceased to do business in this state.

G. The failure to obtain or file the bond as required by this Section shall constitute a violation of this Part for purposes of civil or criminal remedies or penalties.

Added by Acts 1992, No. 345, § 1. Amended by Acts 2003, No. 1027, § 1, eff. Dec. 31, 2003; Acts 2004, No. 79, § 1, eff. May 28, 2004; Acts 2006, No. 190, § 1; Acts 2008, No. 858, § 1, eff. July 9, 2008; Acts 2009, No. 76, § 1.

Editor's note. A prior R.S. 9:3573.4 was repealed by Acts 1992, No. 345, § 2.

§ 3573.5. Repealed by Acts 2006, No. 190, § 2

§ 3573.6. Disclosure statement

A. Before executing a contract or agreement with a buyer or receiving money or other valuable consideration, a credit repair services organization shall provide the buyer with a statement in writing, containing:

(1) A complete and detailed description of the services to be performed by the credit repair services organization for the buyer and the total cost of the services.

(2) A statement explaining the buyer's right to proceed against the bond required by R.S. 9:3573.4.

(3) The name and address of the surety company that issued the bond or the name and address of the depository and the trustee and the account number of the trust account.

(4) A complete and accurate statement of the buyer's right to review any file on the buyer maintained by a consumer reporting agency, as provided by the Fair Credit Reporting Act (15 U.S.C. Sec. 1681 et seq.).

(5) A statement that the buyer's file is available for review from the consumer reporting agency at no charge, under certain circumstances, if requested by the consumer within thirty days of receiving notice of a denial of credit and as provided in the federal Fair Credit Reporting Act.

(6) A complete and accurate statement of the buyer's right to dispute directly with the consumer reporting agency the completeness or accuracy of an item contained in a file on the buyer maintained by that consumer reporting agency.

(7) A statement that accurate information cannot be permanently removed from the files of a consumer reporting agency.

(8) A complete and accurate statement of when consumer information becomes obsolete and of when consumer reporting agencies are prevented from issuing reports containing obsolete information.

(9) A complete and accurate statement of the availability of nonprofit credit counseling services.

B. The credit repair services organization shall maintain on file, for a period of four years after the date the statement is provided, an exact copy of the statement, signed by the buyer, acknowledging receipt of the statement.

Added by Acts 1992, No. 345, § 1. Amended by Acts 2008, No. 858, § 1, eff. July 9, 2008; Acts 2009, No. 76, § 1.

Editor's note. A prior R.S. 9:3573.6 was repealed by Acts 1992, No. 345, § 2.

§ 3573.7. Form and terms of contract

A. Each contract between the buyer and a credit repair services organization for the purchase of the services of the credit repair services organization must be in writing, dated, signed by the buyer, and must include:

(1) A statement in type that is boldfaced, capitalized, underlined, or otherwise set out from surrounding written materials so as to be conspicuous, in immediate proximity to the space reserved for the signature of the buyer, as follows: "You, the buyer, may cancel this contract at any time before midnight of the fifth day after the date of the transaction. See the attached notice of cancellation form for an explanation of this right."

(2) The terms and conditions of payment, including the total of all payments to be made by the buyer, whether to the credit repair services organization or to another person.

(3) A full and detailed description of the services to be performed by the credit repair services organization for the buyer, including all guarantees and all promises of full or partial refunds, and the estimated length of time, not to exceed one-hundred eighty days, for performing the services.

(4) The address of the credit repair services organization's principal place of business and the name and address of its agent in the state authorized to receive service of process.

B. The contract must have attached two easily detachable copies of a notice of cancellation. The notice must be in boldfaced type and in the following form:

"Notice of Cancellation

You may cancel this contract, without any penalty or obligation, within five days after the date the contract is signed.

If you cancel, any payment made by you under this contract will be returned within ten days after the date of receipt by the seller of your cancellation notice.

To cancel this contract, send by registered or certified mail, return receipt requested, or deliver in person, a signed dated copy of this cancellation notice, or other written notice to:

(Name of seller) at (address of seller) (place of business) not later than midnight (date).

I hereby cancel this transaction.

(date)

(purchaser's signature)"

C. The credit repair services organization shall give to the buyer a copy of the completed contract and all other documents the credit repair services organization requires the buyer to sign at the time they are signed.

D. The breach by a credit repair services organization of a contract under this Part, or of any obligation arising from a contract under this Part, is a violation of this Part.

Added by Acts 1992, No. 345, § 1.

Editor's note. A prior R.S. 9:3573.7 was repealed by Acts 1992, No. 345, § 2.

§ 3573.8. Waiver

A. A credit repair services organization shall not attempt to cause a buyer to waive a right under this Part.

B. A waiver by a buyer of any part of this Part is void.

Added by Acts 1992, No. 345, § 1.

Editor's note. A prior R.S. 9:3573.8 was repealed by Acts 1992, No. 345, § 2.

§ 3573.9. Repealed by Acts 2008, No. 858, § 2, eff. July 9, 2008

§ 3573.10. Action for damages

A. A buyer injured by a violation of this Part or by a credit repair services organization's breach of contract subject to this Part may maintain an action in a court of competent jurisdiction for recovery of actual damages plus costs of suit and reasonable attorney fees, which shall be measured by the time reasonably expended by the consumer's attorney and not by the amount of recovery. In case of an action brought by a buyer, actual damages shall not be less than the amount paid by the buyer to the credit repair services organization.

B. In the event of a willful violation by a credit repair services organization of this Part or of a contract subject to this Part, a person who is injured thereby shall be awarded, in addition to the damages allowable under Subsection A of this Section, an additional amount equal to twice the actual damages awarded under Subsection A of this Section.

C. A person who is entitled to recover damages, costs, or attorney fees from a credit repair services organization may petition the attorney general of Louisiana for relief under any surety bond established pursuant to R.S. 9:3573.4.

Added by Acts 1992, No. 345, § 1. Amended by Acts 2003, No. 1027, § 1, eff. Dec. 31, 2003; Acts 2008, No. 858, § 1, eff. July 9, 2008.

§ 3573.11. Orders, injunctions, and publication

A. A buyer may bring an action in a court to enjoin a violation of this Part.

B. The attorney general may, in his discretion, conduct such investigations as he deems necessary to ascertain possible violations of this Part. Any person who is engaged in or is engaging in or is about to engage in any act or practice which is prohibited by this Part or any rule, regulation, or order promulgated or issued pursuant to this Chapter, or any person who has failed to act or is failing to act or is about to fail to act under any affirmative duty imposed by this Part, shall be subject to appropriate action by the attorney general. Such action shall include but shall not be limited to the issuance of orders to cease and desist, entering into compliance agreements, seeking injunctive relief from a court of competent jurisdiction, or any combination thereof.

C. Repealed by Acts 2009, No. 76, § 2.

Added by Acts 1992, No. 345, § 1. Amended by Acts 2003, No. 1027, § 1, eff. Dec. 31, 2003; Acts 2006, No. 190, § 1; Acts 2008, No. 858, § 1, eff. July 9, 2008; Acts 2009, No. 76, § 1.

§ 3573.12. Statute of limitations

An action shall not be brought under R.S. 9:3573.10 or 3573.11 after four years after the date of the execution of the contract for services to which the action relates.

Added by Acts 1992, No. 345, § 1.

§ 3573.13. Criminal penalty

A. A person who willfully violates any provision of this Part is guilty of a misdemeanor and upon conviction may be sentenced to pay a fine of not less than two hundred fifty dollars nor more than five thousand dollars, or to imprisonment not exceeding one year, or both.

B. The attorney general through an administrative action, or the district attorney of any judicial district may maintain an action to enjoin violations of this Part.

C. Costs and reasonable attorney fees shall be awarded to the attorney general or a district attorney in all injunctive actions where the attorney general or district attorney successfully enforces this Part.

Added by Acts 1992, No. 345, § 1. Amended by Acts 2008, No. 858, § 1, eff. July 9, 2008.

§ 3573.14. Burden of proving exemption

A. In an action under this Part, the burden of proving an exemption under R.S. 9:3573.2(B) shall be on the person claiming the exemption.

B. Repealed by Acts 2004, No. 79, § 2, eff. May 28, 2004.

Added by Acts 1992, No. 345, § 1. Amended by Acts 2003, No. 1027, § 1, eff. Dec. 31, 2003.

§ 3573.15. Remedies cumulative

The remedies provided by this Part are in addition to any other remedies provided by law.

Added by Acts 1992, No. 345, § 1.

§ 3573.16. Civil money penalties

A person who violates a provision of this Part may be fined up to one thousand dollars for each violation. The attorney general may maintain a civil action in a court of competent jurisdiction to recover such fines, together with his costs and attorney fees incident to such action.

Added by Acts 1992, No. 345, § 1. Amended by Acts 2008, No. 858, § 1, eff. July 9, 2008.

§ 3573.17. Repealed by Acts 2008, No. 858, § 2, eff. July 9, 2008

PART XVI. ADVANCE FEE LOANS

§ 3574.1. Short title

This Part shall be known and may be cited as the "Louisiana Advance Fee Loan Law".

Added by Acts 1992, No. 346, § 1, eff. June 17, 1992.

§ 3574.2. Definitions

As used in this Part, unless the context otherwise requires:

(1) "Advance fee" means any consideration which is assessed or collected prior to the issuance of a written commitment to make a loan that is binding on the lender, provided that certain conditions precedent are satisfied.

(2) "Borrower" means a person obtaining or desiring to obtain a loan of money, a credit card, or a line of credit.

(3) "Loan originator or broker" means any person, except any regulated or supervised financial organization, credit union, licensed commercial or consumer lender, insurance company, consumer loan broker, or mortgage broker or lender, provided that the person excepted is licensed or registered with and subject to regulation or supervision by an agency of the United States or any state and is acting within the scope of the license, charter, or other permit, who:

(a) For, or in expectation of, consideration paid by the borrower, directly or indirectly arranges or attempts to arrange, or offers to fund or make a loan of money, a credit card, or a line of credit.

(b) For, or in expectation of, consideration paid by the borrower, assists or advises a borrower, wherever located, in obtaining or attempting to obtain a loan of money, a credit card, a line of credit, or a related guarantee, enhancement, or collateral of any kind or nature.

(c) Acts for, or on behalf of, a loan broker for the purpose of soliciting borrowers.

(d) Holds himself out as a loan broker.

(4) "Office" means the Office of Financial Institutions in the office of the governor.

(5) "Person" means an individual or corporation, partnership, trust, association, joint venture pool, syndicate, sole proprietorship, unincorporated organization, or any other form of entity not specifically listed herein. A "person" shall not include an agency or instrumentality established or chartered under the laws of the United States.

(6) "Principal" means any officer, director, owner, sole proprietor, partner, member, joint venturer, manager, or other person with similar managerial or supervisory responsibilities for a person who makes or offers to make or broker loans, whatever his job title.

Added by Acts 1992, No. 346, § 1, eff. June 17, 1992. Amended by Acts 1993, No. 283, § 1, eff. July, 1, 1993; Acts 2001, No. 8, § 4, eff. July 1, 2001; Acts 2001, No. 9, § 2, eff. July 1, 2001.

Editor's note. Acts 2001, No. 9, § 13, declares that "All assets, liabilities, and fund balances of the Small Business Surety Bonding Fund created pursuant to R.S. 51:1766 shall be transferred to the Small Business Bonding Fund created pursuant to R.S. 51:942(1) upon the effective date of this Act."

§ 3574.3. Advance fees; prohibited acts

No loan originator or broker shall:

(1) Assess or collect an advance fee from a borrower to provide services as a loan originator or broker. Notwithstanding the foregoing, a person who originates or brokers commercial loans may accept from a potential borrower an advance expense deposit for commercial loans, but such deposit shall not exceed the good faith estimate of the actual cost of any appraisal, title search, or credit reports performed by a person independent of the loan originator or broker, and required by the originating lender for the evaluation of the potential borrower's commercial loan application. Any expense deposit which exceeds the actual cost of any appraisal, title search, or credit reports shall be promptly refunded to the borrower or credited to the borrower's account at the time of the commercial loan closing. For purposes of this Part, a "commercial loan" means any loan the purpose of which is not for personal, family, or household use.

(2) Make or use any false or misleading representations or omit any material fact in the offer or sale of his services, or engage, directly or indirectly, in any act that operates or would operate as fraud or deception upon any person in connection with the offer or sale of the services of a loan originator or broker, notwithstanding the absence of reliance by the buyer.

(3) Make or use any false or deceptive representation in its business dealings.

(4) Make or use any false or deceptive representation to the office or conceal a material fact from the office.

Added by Acts 1992, No. 346, § 1, eff. June 17, 1992.

§ 3574.4. Responsibility of principals

Each principal of a loan originator or broker may be sanctioned for actions by the loan originator or broker, including its agents or employees, engaged in during the course of business of the loan originator or broker.

Added by Acts 1992, No. 346, § 1, eff. June 17, 1992.

§ 3574.5. Investigations; cease and desist orders; administrative fines

A. The office may investigate the actions of any person for compliance with this Part.

B. The office may order a person to cease and desist whenever the office determines that the person has violated, is violating, or will violate any provision of this Part, any rule or order promulgated by the office, or any written agreement entered into with the office.

C. The office may impose and collect an administrative fine against any person found to have violated any provision of this Part, any rule or order promulgated by the office, or any written agreement entered into with the office in an amount not to exceed five thousand dollars for each such violation. Each loan originated or brokered may be considered a separate violation. All fines collected hereunder shall be deposited in the Louisiana Consumer Credit Education Fund, provided such fund is in existence at the time of payment of the fine.

Added by Acts 1992, No. 346, § 1, eff. June 17, 1992.

§ 3574.6. Investigations; examinations; subpoenas; hearings; witnesses

A. The office may make investigations and examinations upon reasonable suspicion, within or outside of this state as it deems necessary, to determine whether a person has violated or is about to violate any provision of this Part, or any rule or order promulgated thereunder.

B. The office may gather evidence in the matter in any legally appropriate manner. The office may administer oaths, examine witnesses, and issue subpoenas.

C. Subpoenas for witnesses whose evidence is deemed material to any investigation or examination may be issued by the office under the seal of the office commanding such witnesses to appear before the office at a time and place to be therein named, and to bring such books, records, and documents as may be specified, or to submit such books, records, and documents to inspection. Such subpoenas may be served by an authorized representative of the office.

D. (1) In the event of substantial noncompliance with a subpoena or subpoena duces tecum issued by the office, the office may petition the district court of the parish in which the person subpoenaed resides or has its principal place of business for an order requiring the person to appear and fully comply with the subpoena. The court may grant injunctive relief restraining the violation of this Part and may grant such other relief including, but not limited to, the restraint, by injunction or appointment of a receiver, of any transfer, pledge, assignment, or other disposition of such person's assets or any concealment, alteration, destruction, or other disposition of subpoenaed books, records, or documents, as the court deems appropriate, until such person has fully complied with such subpoena or subpoena duces tecum and the office has completed its investigation or examination. The office is entitled to use summary proceedings as provided in the Louisiana Code of Civil Procedure, and the court shall advance the cause on its calendar. Costs incurred by the office to obtain an order granting, in whole or in part, such petition for enforcement of a subpoena or subpoena duces tecum shall be taxed against the subpoenaed person, and failure to comply with such order shall be a contempt of court.

(2) When it shall appear to the office that the compliance with a subpoena or subpoena duces tecum issued by the office is essential to an investigation or examination, the office, in addition to the other remedies provided for in this Part, may, by verified petition setting forth the facts, apply

to the district court of the parish in which the subpoenaed person resides or has its principal place of business for any and all appropriate writs. The court may thereupon direct the issuance of the appropriate writ against the subpoenaed person requiring sufficient bond conditioned on compliance with the subpoena or subpoena duces tecum. The court shall cause to be endorsed on the writ a suitable amount of bond on payment of which the person named in the writ shall be freed, having a due regard to the nature of the case.

E. Witnesses shall be entitled to the same fees and mileage as they may be entitled to by law for attending as witnesses in the district court, except where such examination or investigation is held at the place of business or residence of the witness.

F. The material compiled by the office in an investigation or examination under this Part is confidential and not subject to the Public Records Act until the investigation or examination is complete. The investigation or examination is not deemed complete if the office has submitted the material or any part of it to any law enforcement agency or other regulatory agency for further investigation, or for the filing of criminal or civil prosecution, and such investigation and prosecution have not been completed or become inactive.

Added by Acts 1992, No. 346, § 1, eff. June 17, 1992.

§ 3574.7. Injunction to restrain violations

A. Whenever the office determines, from evidence satisfactory to it, that any person has engaged, is engaged, or is about to engage in an act or practice constituting a violation of this Part, or a rule or order promulgated thereunder, the office may bring action in the name and on behalf of the state against such person and any other person concerned in or in any way participating in or about to participate in such practice, or engaging therein, or doing any act or acts in furtherance thereof or in violation of this Part to enjoin the person or persons from continuing the violation or acts in furtherance thereof. In such court proceedings, the office may apply for, and on due showing be entitled to have issued, the court's subpoena requiring the appearance of any defendant and his employees or agents, and the production of documents, books, and records that may appear necessary for the hearing of such petition, to testify or give evidence concerning the acts or conduct or things complained of in such application for injunction.

B. In addition to all other means provided by law for the enforcement of any temporary restraining order, temporary injunction, or permanent injunction issued in such court proceedings, the court shall have the power and jurisdiction, upon application of the office, to impound and to appoint a receiver or administrator for the property, assets, and business of the loan originator or broker, including but not limited to the books, records, documents, and papers appertaining thereto. Such receiver or administrator, when appointed and qualified, shall have all powers and duties as to custody, collection, administration, winding up, and liquidation of said property and business as shall from time to time be conferred upon him by the court. In such action, the court may issue orders and decrees staying all pending suits and enjoining any further suits affecting the receiver's or administrator's custody or possession of the said property, assets, and business or, in its discretion, may, with the consent of the presiding judge of the district, require that all such suits be assigned to the district court judge appointing the said receiver or administrator.

C. In addition to any other remedies provided by this Part, the office may apply to the court hearing this matter for an order of restitution whereby the defendants in such action shall be ordered to make restitution of those sums shown by the office to have been obtained by them in violation of any of the provisions of this Part. Such restitution shall, at the option of the court, be payable to the administrator or receiver appointed pursuant to this Section or directly to the persons whose assets were obtained in violation of this Part.

Added by Acts 1992, No. 346, § 1, eff. June 17, 1992.

§ 3574.8. Criminal penalties

Whoever violates any provision of this Part commits a felony and shall be fined not more than fifty thousand dollars, or imprisoned with or without hard labor for not more than ten years, or both.

Added by Acts 1992, No. 346, § 1, eff. June 17, 1992.

§ 3574.9. Actions for damages

A. Any borrower injured by a violation of this Part may bring an action for recovery of damages. Judgment shall be entered for actual damages, but in no case less than the amount paid by the borrower to the loan originator or broker, plus reasonable attorney fees and costs. A penalty not to exceed three times the amount of actual damages may also be assessed the loan originator or broker and be awarded to the borrower.

B. Any borrower injured by a violation of this Part may bring an action against the surety bond or trust account, if any, of the loan originator or broker.

C. The remedies provided under this Part are in addition to any other procedures or remedies for any violation or conduct provided for in any other law.

Added by Acts 1992, No. 346, § 1, eff. June 17, 1992.

§ 3574.10. Duties and powers of the office

A. The office shall be responsible for the administration and enforcement of this Part. The attorney general for the state of Louisiana may assist and cooperate in and have coordinate investigation and enforcement powers in actions seeking to remedy violations of this Part.

B. The office may adopt such rules as it may deem necessary in the administration of this Part and not inconsistent therewith.

Added by Acts 1992, No. 346, § 1, eff. June 17, 1992.

§ 3575. [Blank]

PART XVII. REFUND ANTICIPATION LOANS [REPEALED]

§§ 3575.1 to 3575.4. Repealed by Acts 1997, No. 798, § 1

§ 3575.5. Repealed by Acts 1993, No. 506, § 2; Acts 1993, No. 856, § 2

§§ 3575.6 to 3575.10. Repealed by Acts 1997, No. 798, § 1

PART XVIII. COLLECTION AGENCY REGULATION ACT [REPEALED]

§§ 3576.1 to 3576.24. Repealed by Acts 2003, No. 638, § 1

PART XIX. COLLEGE CAMPUS CREDIT CARD SOLICITATION LAW

§ 3577.1. Short title

This Part may be cited as the "College Campus Credit Card Solicitation Act".

Added by Acts 1999, No. 1110, § 1.

§ 3577.2. Definitions

The following words and phrases when used in this Part shall have the meanings ascribed to them below:

(1) "College campus" means the premises and grounds of an institution of postsecondary education.

(2) "Commissioner" means the commissioner of financial institutions.

(3) "Credit card" means a writing, number, or other evidence of an undertaking to pay for property or services delivered or rendered to or upon the order of a designated person or bearer.

(4) "Institution of postsecondary education" means any institution under the management of the Board of Supervisors for the University of Louisiana System, the Board of Supervisors of Louisiana State University and Agricultural and Mechanical College, the Board of Supervisors of Southern University and Agricultural and Mechanical College, and the Board of Supervisors of Community and Technical Colleges or any private or accredited college in the state.

(5) "Solicitation" means an act of asking, enticing, or requesting a student to read, review, or consider materials relating to an application for a credit card or to complete an application for a credit card.

(6) "Student" means a person who is under twenty-one years of age and who attends an institution of postsecondary education, whether enrolled on a full-time or part-time basis.

Added by Acts 1999, No. 1110, § 1.

§ 3577.3. Registration prior to solicitation; inducements prohibited

A. Prior to engaging in the solicitation of a student on a college campus, a credit card issuer shall register its intent to solicit the student for that purpose with an appropriate official of the institution of postsecondary education.

B. The registration shall include the principal place of business of the credit card issuer and shall be in such form as required by regulation of the commissioner.

C. It shall be unlawful for any credit card issuer to give or offer to give, directly or indirectly, orally or in writing, any gratuity or other thing of value, or advertise the offering of such as an inducement for a student to read, review, or consider materials relating to an application for a credit card or to complete an application for a credit card, unless the student has been provided a credit card debt education brochure.

Added by Acts 1999, No. 1110, § 1. Amended by Acts 2003, No. 1010, § 1.

§ 3577.4. Debt collection against parent or guardian prohibited

It shall be unlawful for a credit card issuer to take any debt collection action, including but not limited to telephone calls or demand letters against the parent or legal guardian of a student for whom a credit card has been issued, unless the parent or legal guardian has agreed in writing to be liable for the debts of the student under the credit card agreement.

Added by Acts 1999, No. 1110, § 1.

§ 3577.5. Violations; penalties

A person who violates any provision of this Part may be fined up to one thousand dollars for each violation. The commissioner may maintain a civil action in a court of competent jurisdiction to recover such fines, together with his costs and attorney fees incident to such action.

Added by Acts 1999, No. 1110, § 1.

§§ 3577.6 to 3577.8. [Blank]

PART XX. [BLANK]

CHAPTER 2–A. LOUISIANA DEFERRED PRESENTMENT AND SMALL LOAN ACT

Section
3578.1. Short title.
3578.2. Legislative intent.
3578.3. Definitions.
3578.4. Finance charge and fees.
3578.5. Rebate upon prepayment.
3578.6. Prohibited acts.
3578.7. Posting of notice; toll-free number.
3578.8. Powers of the commissioner; adoption of rules and regulations.

§ 3578.1. Short title

This Chapter shall be known and may be cited as the "Louisiana Deferred Presentment and Small Loan Act".

Added by Acts 1999, No. 1315, § 1, eff. Jan. 1, 2000.

§ 3578.2. Legislative intent

It is the intent of the legislature to regulate deferred presentment transactions and small loans. These loans meet a legitimate credit need for many consumers; however, in order to protect consumers from excessive charges, it is the intent of the legislature to put certain restrictions on lenders who make these loans.

Added by Acts 1999, No. 1315, § 1, eff. Jan. 1, 2000.

§ 3578.3. Definitions

As used in this Chapter, the following terms have the following meanings ascribed to them:

(1) "Commissioner" means the commissioner of the office of financial institutions.

(2) "Deferred presentment transaction" means a transaction made pursuant to a written agreement whereby a licensee:

(a) Accepts a check from the issuer dated as of the date it was written;

(b) Agrees to hold the check for a period of time not to exceed thirty days prior to negotiation or presentment; and

(c) Pays to the issuer of the check the amount of the check less the fee permitted in R.S. 9:3578.4(A). The amount paid to the issuer of the check may not exceed three hundred fifty dollars.

(3) "Licensee" means a person licensed pursuant to this Chapter that offers deferred presentment transactions or small loans, or both.

(4) "Partial payment" means a payment of fifty dollars or more on a deferred presentment transaction or small loan.

(5) "Prepayment" means payment in full of the deferred presentment transaction or small loan amount prior to the end of the term of that transaction or loan.

(6) "Small loan" means a consumer loan, as defined in R.S. 9:3516(14), of three hundred fifty dollars or less, made for a term of sixty days or less.

Added by Acts 1999, No. 1315, § 1, eff. Jan. 1, 2000.

§ 3578.4. Finance charge and fees

A. (1) In conjunction with a deferred presentment transaction or small loan, a licensee may charge a fee not to exceed sixteen and seventy-five one hundredths percent of the face amount of the check issued or in the case of a small loan, the equivalent rate of interest, provided however that such fee or interest does not exceed forty-five dollars, regardless of the name or type of charge.

(2) However, if the loan remains unpaid at contractual maturity, the licensee may charge one of the following:

(a) An amount equal to the rate of thirty-six percent per annum for a period not to exceed one year and beginning one year after contractual maturity, the rate shall not exceed eighteen percent per annum.

(b) A one-time delinquency charge as authorized in R.S. 9:3527(A)(1).

B. A licensee may contract with the borrower for reimbursement of the actual fee assessed to the licensee by the licensee's depository institution as a result of a borrower's check being returned for any reason. The fee shall be reimbursed to the licensee only once per check, regardless of the number of times the check was returned by the depository institution.

C. Except for reasonable attorney fees and costs awarded by a court, and fees allowed under R.S. 9:3529 and 3530(C), no other fees or charges may be assessed or collected on a deferred presentment transaction or small loan, including any other fees as may be provided for under Chapter 2 of this Code Title or any other law.

Added by Acts 1999, No. 1315, § 1, eff. Jan. 1, 2000. Amended by Acts 2003, No. 1283, § 1; Acts 2010, No. 668, § 1.

§ 3578.5. Rebate upon prepayment

Upon the prepayment in full of a deferred presentment transaction or small loan, during the first five days of the term of such transaction or loan only, the licensee shall refund any and all unearned charges by a method no less favorable to the consumer than the actuarial method, less twenty dollars of the original fee, which shall be considered earned and shall not be subject to refund. Should the consumer make prepayment after the first five days of the term of the transaction or loan, the licensee shall not be required to make any refund.

Added by Acts 1999, No. 1315, § 1, eff. Jan. 1, 2000.

§ 3578.6. Prohibited acts

A. A licensee shall not:

(1) Except for reasonable attorney fees and costs awarded by a court, charge, contract for, receive, or collect a loan finance charge or credit service charge, or any other fee or charge other than as provided in R.S. 9:3578.4.

(2) Sell any goods when those goods are financed with the proceeds of the loan or sell insurance in connection with a deferred presentment transaction or small loan. The sale and financing of services, including but not limited to utility payment services, financial or tax services, or the sale of prepaid telephone services and telephone-related products which are not financed with the proceeds of the loan, shall not be deemed a violation of this Chapter.

(3) Refuse a partial loan payment of fifty dollars or greater.

(4) Divide a deferred presentment transaction or small loan into multiple agreements for the purpose of obtaining a higher fee or charge.

(5) Threaten any customer with prosecution or refer for prosecution any check accepted as payment of a deferred presentment transaction and returned by the lender's depository institution for reason of insufficient funds.

(6) Structure the repayment of a loan in such a manner as to attempt to circumvent the provisions of this Chapter.

(7) Renew or roll over a deferred presentment transaction or small loan. However, a licensee may accept a partial payment of twenty-five percent of the amount advanced plus fees charged and enter into a new deferred presentment transaction or renew the small loan for the remaining balance owed. Once a deferred presentment transaction or small loan has been completed, a consumer may enter into a new transaction or loan with the licensee. A deferred presentment transaction or small loan shall be considered completed when the amount advanced has been paid in full by the consumer.

(8) Take any direct or indirect interest, possessory or otherwise, whether perfected or unperfected, in any property in connection with a small loan, or a deferred presentment transaction.

B. It shall be unlawful for any small loan lender, for any reason and by any means, including but not limited to direct deposit and personal tender, to accept as payment, offer to accept as payment, or require for use as security any check issued pursuant to the federal Social Security Act. In addition, it shall be unlawful for any lender making small loans to act as a depository institution for the acceptance of any check issued pursuant to the federal Social Security Act, unless such lender is a federally insured financial institution.

Added by Acts 1999, No. 542, § 1; Acts 1999, No. 1315, § 1, eff. Jan. 1, 2000. Amended by Acts 2003, No. 1272, § 1; Acts 2003, No. 1283, § 1; Acts 2005, No. 99, § 1.

§ 3578.7. Posting of notice; toll-free number

The commissioner may provide a notice, which includes a toll-free number to the commissioner's office, which shall be posted, along with the fees as allowed under this Chapter, in a conspicuous manner by the licensee at the lending location.

Added by Acts 1999, No. 1315, § 1, eff. Jan. 1, 2000.

§ 3578.8. Powers of the commissioner; adoption of rules and regulations

A. The commissioner may apply the provisions of Parts I, VII, VIII, IX, and X of Chapter 2 of this Code Title, the Louisiana Consumer Credit Law, for purposes of administering and regulating the activities of licensees and the provisions of this Chapter.

B. The commissioner may adopt rules and regulations as he deems necessary to implement the purposes and provisions of this Chapter.

C. (1) Beginning January 1, 2013, for a period of one year, the commissioner shall collect and compile information and data from licensees concerning the operation, function, and customers of deferred presentment transactions and small loan businesses.

(2) The information and data collected by the commissioner from a licensee shall include but not be limited to the following:

(a) The number of deferred presentment transactions and small loans issued quarterly.

(b) The fees collected quarterly on deferred presentment transactions and small loans.

(c) The location of the licensee's business.

(d) The number of checks returned unpaid for any reason and the amount of the fee charged by the licensee for such checks.

D. The commissioner shall compile and submit to the legislature, in an aggregate format, the information and data collected by April 1, 2014.

Added by Acts 1999, No. 1315, § 1, eff. Jan. 1, 2000. Amended by Acts 2012, No. 234, § 1.

CHAPTER 2–B. LOUISIANA TAX REFUND ANTICIPATION LOAN ACT

Section
3579.1. Short title.
3579.2. Definitions.
3579.3. Restriction on acting as facilitator.
3579.4. Disclosure requirements.

§ 3579.1. Short title

This Chapter shall be known and may be cited as the "Louisiana Tax Refund Anticipation Loan Act".

Added by Acts 2010, No. 975, § 1, eff. Jan. 1, 2011.

§ 3579.2. Definitions

(1) "Borrower" means an individual who receives the proceeds of a refund anticipation loan.

(2) "Facilitator" means a person who, for compensation from a borrower or any other person, assists the borrower in applying for or obtaining a refund anticipation loan. "Facilitator" does not include a lender that makes a refund anticipation loan, an affiliate that is a servicer for such a lender, or any person who does not have direct contact with a borrower in connection with applying for or obtaining a refund anticipation loan. For the purposes of this Chapter, a "facilitator" shall also mean the individual or entity that signs the tax return on which the refund anticipation loan is based.

(3) "Lender" means a person who extends credit to a borrower in the form of a refund anticipation loan.

(4) "Refund anticipation loan" means a loan obtained by a taxpayer based on the taxpayer's anticipated federal income tax refund.

(5) "Refund anticipation loan fee" means a fee imposed or other consideration required by the facilitator or the lender for a refund anticipation loan. The term does not include a fee usually imposed or other consideration usually required by the facilitator in the ordinary course of business for services not related to the making of loans, including a fee imposed for tax return preparation or for the electronic filing of a tax return.

Added by Acts 2010, No. 975, § 1, eff. Jan. 1, 2011.

§ 3579.3. Restriction on acting as facilitator

A. A person may not, individually or in conjunction or cooperation with another person, act as a facilitator unless he complies with all of the following requirements:

(1) Is engaged in the business of preparing tax returns, or employed by a person engaged in the business of preparing tax returns.

(2) Is primarily involved in financial services or tax preparations.

(3) Is authorized by the Internal Revenue Service as an e-file provider.

B. This Chapter shall not apply to any of the following entities:

(1) Federally insured financial institution.

(2) An affiliate that is a servicer of an entity described in Paragraph (1) of this Subsection, operating under the name of that entity.

(3) Any person or entity that acts solely as an intermediary and does not interact directly with a taxpayer in the making of the refund anticipation loan.

Added by Acts 2010, No. 975, § 1, eff. Jan. 1, 2011.

§ 3579.4. Disclosure requirements

A. A facilitator shall discuss with and clearly disclose to a borrower, after the borrower's tax return has been prepared and before the loan is closed, all of the following items:

(1) The refund anticipation loan fee schedule.

(2) A written statement disclosing all of the following items:

(a) That a refund anticipation loan is a loan and is not the borrower's actual income tax refund.

(b) That the taxpayer may file an income tax return electronically without applying for a refund anticipation loan.

(c) That the borrower is responsible for repayment of the loan and related fees if the tax refund is not paid or is insufficient to repay the loan.

(d) Any fee that will be charged if the loan is not approved.

(e) The average time, as published by the Internal Revenue Service, within which a taxpayer can expect to receive a refund for an income tax return filed by either of the following methods:

(i) Electronically, and the refund is delivered by either of the following methods:

(aa) Deposited directly into the taxpayer's bank account.

(bb) Mailed to the taxpayer.

(ii) By mail, and the refund is delivered by either of the following methods:

(aa) Deposited directly into the taxpayer's financial institution account.

(bb) Mailed to the taxpayer.

(f) That the Internal Revenue Service does not make either of the following guarantees:

(i) Payment of the full amount of the anticipated refund.

(ii) A specific date on which it will mail a refund or deposit the refund into a taxpayer's financial institution account.

(g) The estimated time within which the proceeds of the refund anticipation loan will be paid to the borrower if the loan is approved.

(3) All of the following information, specific to the borrower:

(a) The estimated total fees for the loan.

(b) The estimated annual percentage rate for the loan, calculated using the guidelines established under the Truth in Lending Act, 15 U.S.C. 1601 et seq.

B. A refund anticipation loan fee schedule required by Paragraph (A)(1) of this Section, shall be a listing or table of refund anticipation loan fees charged by the lender for refund anticipation loan amounts. The schedule shall include all of the following:

(1) Each fee imposed related to the making of a refund anticipation loan listed separately.

(2) The total amount of fees imposed related to the making of a refund anticipation loan.

(3) For each stated loan amount, the estimated annual percentage rate for the loan, calculated using the guidelines established under the Truth in Lending Act, 15 U.S.C. 1601 et seq.

C. Tax preparers who facilitate refund anticipation loans shall post the schedule of fees imposed by the facilitator for making refund anticipation loans in a conspicuous manner at the tax preparer's location.

Added by Acts 2010, No. 975, § 1, eff. Jan. 1, 2011.

CHAPTER 3. LOUISIANA EQUAL CREDIT OPPORTUNITY LAW

Section
3581. Short title.
3582. Scope.
3583. Discrimination prohibited.
3584, 3585. Repealed.

§ 3581. Short title

This Act shall be known and may be cited as the Louisiana Equal Credit Opportunity Law.

Added by Acts 1975, No. 705, § 1.

§ 3582. Scope

The provisions of this Chapter shall apply to all loans or extensions of credit made or executed in the state of Louisiana between any natural person and any extender of credit.

Added by Acts 1975, No. 705, § 1.

§ 3583. Discrimination prohibited

It shall be unlawful for any extender of credit to refuse to extend credit to any major or emancipated minor solely because of that person's race, color, religion, national origin, sex, or marital status.

It shall also be unlawful for any extender of credit to require any major or emancipated minor to meet credit qualification standards not required of other persons similarly situated.

Added by Acts 1975, No. 705, § 1. Amended by Acts 1978, No. 161, § 1.

§§ 3584, 3585. Repealed by Acts 1979, No. 709, § 3, eff. Jan. 1, 1980

CHAPTER 4. CONFESSION OF JUDGMENT

PART I. IN GENERAL

Section
3590. Limitations on confession of judgment.

PART I. IN GENERAL

§ 3590. Limitations on confession of judgment

Except for the purposes of executory process, confessions of judgment, prior to the maturity of the obligation sued on, are hereby prohibited.

Added by Acts 1978, No. 518, § 1.

CODE TITLE XIII—OF DEPOSIT AND SEQUESTRATION

CHAPTER 1. DEPOSIT IN GENERAL

Section
3601. Payment of interest by newspapers on deposits required of their distributors or dealers.

§ 3601. Payment of interest by newspapers on deposits required of their distributors or dealers

Whenever any person or corporation engaged in the newspaper business shall demand of its distributors or dealers a cash security to protect the furnisher of the newspapers from loss by reason of extending to such dealers or distributors credit on papers advanced for sale, the furnisher shall pay to that distributor or dealer, interest at the rate of four per cent per annum upon the amount of the deposit so long as it continues to hold or exact the deposit. The balance of the deposit together with earned interest shall be returned to the depositor, within ninety days after termination of the dealership or distributorship whenever the dealership or distributorship is discontinued, and any refusal or neglect to return the balance shall subject the furnisher of said newspapers to the penalty of paying the dealer or distributor 20 per cent per annum interest upon the deposit not returned to the depositor within said ninety days.

Added by Acts 1960, No. 490, § 1.

APPENDIX 1—REVISED STATUTES, TITLE 9

CODE TITLE XIV—OF ALEATORY CONTRACTS [BLANK]
CODE TITLE XV—OF MANDATE

CHAPTER 1. UNIFORM FIDUCIARIES LAW

Section
3801. Definitions.
3802. Payment or transfer to fiduciary; responsibility for proper application.
3803. Repealed.
3804. Endorsement of negotiable instrument; duty and liability of endorsee.
3805. Payee of check or bill of exchange; duties and liability.
3806. Check or bill of exchange payable to, or transferred to, fiduciary; duties and liability of transferee.
3807. Bank paying check; liability of.
3808. Check upon principal's account; liability of bank paying.
3809. Deposit by fiduciary to his personal credit; duties and liabilities of bank.
3810. Check upon deposit in name of two or more trustees; duties of bank and holder.
3811. Transactions prior to January 1, 1925.
3812. Cases not provided for; rules applicable.
3813. Uniform construction.
3814. Short title.

§ 3801. Definitions

For the purposes of this Chapter, unless the context or subject matter otherwise requires:

(1) "Bank" includes any person or association of persons, whether incorporated or not, carrying on the business of banking.

(2) "Fiduciary" includes a trustee under any trust, expressed, implied, resulting or constructive, executor, administrator, guardian, conservator, curator, receiver, trustee in bankruptcy, assignee for the benefit of creditors, partner, agent, officer of a corporation, public or private, public officer, or any other persons acting in a fiduciary capacity for any person, trust or estate.

(3) "Person" includes a corporation, partnership, or other association, or two or more persons having a joint or common interest.

(4) "Principal" includes any person to whom a fiduciary as such owes an obligation.

(5) A thing is done "in good faith" within the meaning of this Chapter when it is in fact done honestly, whether it be done negligently or not.

Cross References

R.S. 9:1789.

§ 3802. Payment or transfer to fiduciary; responsibility for proper application

A person who in good faith pays or transfers to a fiduciary any money or other property which the fiduciary as such is authorized to receive, is not responsible for the proper application thereof by the fiduciary; and any right or title acquired from the fiduciary in consideration of such payment or transfer is not invalid in consequence of a misapplication by the fiduciary.

Cross References

R.S. 9:1789.

§ 3803. Repealed by Acts 1960, No. 444, § 2

§ 3804. Endorsement of negotiable instrument; duty and liability of endorsee

If any negotiable instrument payable or endorsed to a fiduciary as such is endorsed by the fiduciary, or if any negotiable instrument payable or endorsed to his principal is endorsed by a fiduciary empowered to endorse such instrument, on behalf of his principal, the endorsee is not bound to inquire whether the fiduciary is committing a breach of his obligation as fiduciary in endorsing or delivering the instrument and is not chargeable with notice that the fiduciary is committing a breach of his obligation as fiduciary unless he takes the instrument with actual knowledge of such breach or with knowledge of such facts that his action in taking the instrument amounts to bad faith. If, however, such instrument is transferred by the fiduciary in payment of or as security for a personal debt of the fiduciary to the actual knowledge of the creditor, or is transferred in any transaction known by the transferee to be for the personal benefit of the fiduciary, the creditor or other transferee is liable to the principal if the fiduciary in fact commits a breach of his obligation as fiduciary in transferring the instrument.

Cross References

R.S. 9:1789.

§ 3805. Payee of check or bill of exchange; duties and liability

If a check or other bill of exchange is drawn by a fiduciary as such or in the name of his principal by a fiduciary empowered to draw such instrument in the name of his principal, the payee is not bound to inquire whether the fiduciary is committing a breach of his obligation as fiduciary in drawing or delivering the instrument and is not chargeable with notice that the fiduciary is committing a breach of his obligation as fiduciary unless he takes the instrument with actual knowledge of such breach or with knowledge of such facts that his action in taking the instrument amounts to bad faith. If, however, such instrument is payable to a personal creditor of the fiduciary and delivered to the creditor in payment of, or as security for, a personal debt of the fiduciary, to the actual knowledge of the creditor, or is drawn and delivered in any transaction known by the payee to be for the personal benefit of the fiduciary, the creditor or other payee is liable to the principal if the fiduciary in fact commits a breach of his obligation as fiduciary in drawing or delivering the instrument.

Cross References

R.S. 9:1789.

§ 3806. Check or bill of exchange payable to, or transferred to, fiduciary; duties and liability of transferee

If a check or other bill of exchange is drawn by a fiduciary as such, or in the name of his principal by a fiduciary empowered to draw such instrument in the name of his principal, payable to the fiduciary personally, or payable to a third person and by him transferred to the fiduciary, and is thereafter transferred by the fiduciary, whether in payment of a personal debt of the fiduciary or otherwise, the transferee is not bound to inquire whether the fiduciary is committing a breach of his obligation as fiduciary in transferring the instrument and is not chargeable with notice that the fiduciary is committing a breach of his obligation as fiduciary, unless he takes the instrument with actual knowledge of such breach, or with the knowledge of such facts that his action in taking the instrument amounts to bad faith.

Cross References
R.S. 9:1789.

§ 3807. Bank paying check; liability of

If a deposit is made in a bank to the credit of the fiduciary as such, the bank is authorized to pay the amount of the deposit or any part thereof, upon the check of the fiduciary, signed with the name in which such deposit is entered, without being liable to the principal, unless the bank pays the check with actual knowledge that the fiduciary is committing a breach of his obligation as fiduciary in drawing the check, or with the knowledge of such facts that its action in paying the check amounts to bad faith. If, however, such check is payable to the drawee bank and is delivered to it in payment of, or as, security for a personal debt of the fiduciary to it, the bank is liable to the principal if the fiduciary in fact commits a breach of his obligation as fiduciary in drawing or delivering the check.

Cross References
R.S. 9:1789.

§ 3808. Check upon principal's account; liability of bank paying

If a check is drawn upon the account of his principal in a bank by a fiduciary who is empowered to draw checks upon his principal's account the bank is authorized to pay any such check without being liable to the principal, unless the bank pays the check with actual knowledge that the fiduciary is committing a breach of his obligation as fiduciary in drawing such check, or with the knowledge of such facts that its action in paying the check amounts to bad faith. If, however, such a check is payable to the drawee bank and is delivered to it in payment of, or as security for, a personal debt of the fiduciary to it, the bank is liable to the principal, if the fiduciary in fact commits a breach of his obligation as fiduciary in drawing or delivering the check.

Cross References
R.S. 9:1789.

§ 3809. Deposit by fiduciary to his personal credit; duties and liabilities of bank

If a fiduciary makes a deposit in a bank to his personal credit of checks drawn by him upon an account in his own name as fiduciary or of checks payable to him as fiduciary, or of checks drawn by him upon an account in the name of his principal if he is empowered to draw checks thereon, or of checks payable to his principal and endorsed by him, if he is empowered to endorse such checks, or if he otherwise makes a deposit of funds held by him as fiduciary, the bank receiving such deposit is not bound to inquire whether the fiduciary is committing thereby a breach of his obligation as fiduciary; and the bank is authorized to pay the amount of the deposit or any part thereof upon the personal check of the fiduciary without being liable to the principal, unless, the bank receives the deposit or pays the check with actual knowledge that the fiduciary is committing a breach of his obligation as fiduciary in making such deposit or in drawing such check, or with knowledge of such facts that its action in receiving the deposit or paying the checks amounts to bad faith.

Cross References
R.S. 9:1789.

§ 3810. Check upon deposit in name of two or more trustees; duties of bank and holder

When a deposit is made in a bank in the name of two or more persons as trustees and a check is drawn upon the trust account, by any trustee or trustees, authorized by the other trustee or trustees to draw checks upon the trust account, neither the payee nor other holder, nor the bank, is bound to inquire whether it is a breach of trust to authorize such trustee or trustees to draw checks upon the trust account, and is not liable unless the circumstances be such that the action of the payee or other holder or the bank amounts to bad faith.

Cross References
R.S. 9:1789.

§ 3811. Transactions prior to January 1, 1925

The provisions of this Chapter shall not apply to transactions taking place prior to January 1, 1925.

§ 3812. Cases not provided for; rules applicable

In any case not provided for in this Chapter the rules of law and equity, including the law merchant and those rules of law and equity relating to trusts, agency, negotiable instruments and banking, shall continue to apply.

§ 3813. Uniform construction

This Chapter shall be so interpreted and construed as to effectuate its general purpose to make uniform the law of those states which enact it.

§ 3814. Short title

This Chapter may be cited as the Uniform Fiduciaries Law.

CHAPTER 2. UNIFORM LAW FOR SIMPLIFICATION OF FIDUCIARY SECURITY TRANSFERS

Section
3831. Definitions.
3832. Registration in the name of a fiduciary.
3833. Assignment by a fiduciary.

APPENDIX 1—REVISED STATUTES, TITLE 9

Section
3834. Evidence of appointment or incumbency.
3835. Adverse claims.
3836. Non-liability of corporation and transfer agent.
3837. Non-liability of third persons.
3838. Territorial application.
3839. Tax obligations.
3840. Uniformity of interpretation; short title.
3841 to 3849. [Blank].
3850. Express mandate between spouses; revocation.

§ 3831. Definitions

In this Chapter, unless the context otherwise requires:

(1) "Assignment" includes any written stock power, bond power, bill of sale, deed, declaration of trust or other instrument of transfer;

(2) "Claim of beneficial interest" includes a claim of any interest by a decedent's legatee, distributee, heir or creditor, a beneficiary under a trust, a ward, a beneficial owner of a security registered in the name of a nominee, or a minor owner of a security registered in the name of a custodian, or a claim of any similar interest, whether the claim is asserted by the claimant or by a fiduciary or by any other authorized person on his behalf, and includes a claim that the transfer would be in breach of fiduciary duties;

(3) "Corporation" means a private or public corporation, association or trust issuing a security;

(4) "Fiduciary" means an executor, administrator, trustee, guardian, committee, conservator, curator, tutor, custodian or nominee;

(5) "Person" includes an individual, a corporation, government or governmental subdivision or agency, business trust, estate, trust, partnership or association, two or more persons having a joint or common interest, or any other legal or commercial entity;

(6) "Security" includes any share of stock, bond, debenture, note or other security issued by a corporation which is registered as to ownership on the books of the corporation;

(7) "Transfer" means a change on the books of a corporation in the registered ownership of a security;

(8) "Transfer agent" means a person employed or authorized by a corporation to transfer securities issued by the corporation.

Added by Acts 1960, No. 444, § 1.

Cross References

C.C. art. 3008.

§ 3832. Registration in the name of a fiduciary

A corporation or transfer agent registering a security in the name of a person who is a fiduciary or who is described as a fiduciary is not bound to inquire into the existence, extent, or correct description of the fiduciary relationship, and thereafter the corporation and its transfer agent may assume without inquiry that the newly registered owner continues to be the fiduciary until the corporation or transfer agent receives written notice that the fiduciary is no longer acting as such with respect to the particular security.

Added by Acts 1960, No. 444, § 1.

§ 3833. Assignment by a fiduciary

Except as otherwise provided in this Chapter, a corporation or transfer agent making a transfer of a security pursuant to an assignment by a fiduciary

(1) may assume without inquiry that the assignment, even though to the fiduciary himself or to his nominee, is within his authority and capacity and is not in breach of his fiduciary duties;

(2) may assume without inquiry that the fiduciary has complied with any controlling instrument and with the law of the jurisdiction governing the fiduciary relationship, including any law requiring the fiduciary to obtain court approval of the transfer; and

(3) is not charged with notice of and is not bound to obtain or examine any court record or any recorded or unrecorded document relating to the fiduciary relationship or the assignment, even though the record or document is in its possession.

Added by Acts 1960, No. 444, § 1.

§ 3834. Evidence of appointment or incumbency

A corporation or transfer agent making a transfer pursuant to an assignment by a fiduciary who is not the registered owner shall obtain the following evidence of appointment or incumbency:

(1) In the case of a fiduciary appointed or qualified by a court, a certificate issued by or under the direction or supervision of that court or an officer thereof and dated within sixty days before the transfer; or

(2) In any other case, a copy of a document showing the appointment or a certificate issued by or on behalf of a person reasonably believed by the corporation or transfer agent to be responsible or, in the absence of such a document or certificate, other evidence reasonably deemed by the corporation or transfer agent to be appropriate. Corporations and transfer agents may adopt standards with respect to evidence of appointment or incumbency under this paragraph (2) provided such standards are not manifestly unreasonable. Neither the corporation nor transfer agent is charged with notice of the contents of any document obtained pursuant to this paragraph (2) except to the extent that the contents relate directly to the appointment or incumbency.

Added by Acts 1960, No. 444, § 1.

§ 3835. Adverse claims

A. A person asserting a claim of beneficial interest adverse to the transfer of a security pursuant to an assignment by a fiduciary may give the corporation or transfer agent written notice of the claim. The corporation or transfer agent is not put on notice unless the written notice identifies the claimant, the registered owner and the issue of which the security is a part, provides an address for communications directed to the claimant and is received before the transfer. Nothing in this Chapter relieves the corporation or transfer agent of any liability for making or refusing to make the transfer after it is so put on notice, unless it proceeds in the manner authorized in Subsection B of this Section.

B. As soon as practicable after the presentation of a security for transfer pursuant to an assignment by a fiduciary, a corporation or transfer agent which has received notice of a claim of beneficial interest adverse to the transfer may send notice of the presentation by registered or certified mail to the claimant at the address given by him. If the corporation or transfer agent so mails such a notice it shall withhold the transfer for thirty days after the mailing and shall then make the transfer unless restrained by a court order.

Added by Acts 1960, No. 444, § 1.

§ 3836. Non-liability of corporation and transfer agent

A corporation or transfer agent incurs no liability to any person by making a transfer or otherwise acting in a manner authorized by this Chapter.

Added by Acts 1960, No. 444, § 1.

§ 3837. Non-liability of third persons

A. No person who participates in the acquisition, disposition, assignment or transfer of a security by or to a fiduciary including a person who guarantees the signature of the fiduciary is liable for participation in any breach of fiduciary duty by reason of failure to inquire whether the transaction involves such a breach unless it is shown that he acted with actual knowledge that the proceeds of the transaction were being or were to be used wrongfully for the individual benefit of the fiduciary or that the transaction was otherwise in breach of duty.

B. If a corporation or transfer agent makes a transfer pursuant to an assignment by a fiduciary, a person who guaranteed the signature of the fiduciary is not liable on the guarantee to any person to whom the corporation or transfer agent incurs no liability by reason of this Chapter.

C. This Section does not impose any liability upon the corporation or its transfer agent.

Added by Acts 1960, No. 444, § 1.

§ 3838. Territorial application

A. The rights and duties of a corporation and its transfer agents in registering a security in the name of a fiduciary or in making a transfer of a security pursuant to an assignment by a fiduciary are governed by the law of the jurisdiction under whose laws the corporation is organized.

B. This Chapter applies to the rights and duties of a person other than the corporation and its transfer agents with regard to acts and omissions in Louisiana in connection with the acquisition, disposition, assignment or transfer of a security by or to a fiduciary and of a person who guarantees in Louisiana the signature of a fiduciary in connection with such a transaction.

Added by Acts 1960, No. 444, § 1.

§ 3839. Tax obligations

This Chapter does not affect any obligation of a corporation or transfer agent with respect to taxes imposed by the laws of Louisiana.

Added by Acts 1960, No. 444, § 1. Amended by Acts 2010, No. 175, § 2.

§ 3840. Uniformity of interpretation; short title

This Chapter shall be so construed as to effectuate its general purpose to make uniform the law of those states which enact it, and it may be cited as the Uniform Law for Simplification of Fiduciary Security Transfers.

Added by Acts 1960, No. 444, § 1.

§§ 3841 to 3849. [Blank]

§ 3850. Express mandate between spouses; revocation

An express mandate from one spouse to another authorizing transactions with a specified creditor may be revoked only by delivery of written revocation to the creditor.

Added by Acts 1978, No. 511, § 1.

CHAPTER 3. LOUISIANA MILITARY POWERS OF ATTORNEY

Section
3861. Application; military personnel.
3862. Illustrative form; military power of attorney.
3863. Requirements for legally sufficient power of attorney; federal preemption.
3864. Initialed lines on form or designation as general or special; no limitation of powers.
3865. Repealed.
3867. Additional form of power of attorney; application of this Chapter.
3868. Short title.
3869. Application and construction of Chapter.
3870. Powers granted.
3871. Tangible personal property transactions; powers granted.
3872. Stock and bond transactions; powers granted.
3873. Commodity and option transactions; powers granted.
3874. Banking and other financial institution transactions; powers granted.
3875. Business operating transactions; powers granted.
3876. Insurance and annuity transactions; powers granted.
3877. Estate, trust, and other beneficiary transactions; powers granted.
3878. Claims and litigations; powers granted.
3879. Personal and family maintenance; powers granted.
3879.1. Care, custody, and control of minor child.
3880. Social security; civil or military benefits; powers granted.
3881. Retirement plan transactions; powers granted.
3882. Tax matters; powers granted.
3882.1. Real or immovable property transactions; powers granted.
3883. After-acquired property; state where property is located or where power is executed.
3884. Trust instruments; power to modify or revoke.
3885. Liability of person acting in good faith reliance upon power of attorney.
3886. Application of power of attorney to all or portion of property of principal; description of items or parcels.
3887. Acceptance of military power of attorney.

§ 3861. Application; military personnel

A. The military power of attorney provided in this Chapter may be executed by:

(1) Military personnel.

(2) Other persons eligible for legal assistance under the provisions of 10 U.S.C. 1044 or regulations of the Department of Defense.

B. "Military personnel" shall apply to members of any of the branches of the armed forces of the United States as defined by 10 U.S.C. 101(a)(4), the reserve components of the armed forces of the United States as defined by 10 U.S.C. 10101, or the Louisiana National Guard.

Added by Acts 1991, 1st Ex.Sess., No. 5, § 1, eff. April 17, 1991. Amended by Acts 1995, No. 1131, § 1; Acts 1997, No. 849, § 1; Acts 1999, No. 227, § 1.

Cross References

C.C. arts. 27, 1918, 2985 et seq., 2989, 3001, 3030.

R.S. 9:3862 to 9:3864, 9:3867 to 9:3887.

10 U.S.C.A. § 1044.

§ 3862. Illustrative form; military power of attorney

The following is an illustrative form of a military power of attorney suggested for use by military personnel or other eligible persons who reside or own immovable property in the state of Louisiana:

LOUISIANA'S MILITARY

POWER OF ATTORNEY

STATE OF LOUISIANA

PARISH OF _____

This is a MILITARY POWER OF ATTORNEY prepared pursuant to Title 10, United States Code, Section 1044b and executed by a person authorized to receive legal assistance from the military services. Federal law exempts this power of attorney from any requirement of form, substance, formality, or recording that is prescribed for powers of attorney under the laws of a state, the District of Columbia, or a territory, commonwealth, or possession of the United States. Federal law specifies that this power of attorney shall be given the same legal effect as a power of attorney prepared and executed in accordance with the laws of the jurisdiction where it is presented.

Additionally, this form is specifically designed for use under Louisiana law, including transactions involving immovable property. It is suggested for use by any person authorized to receive legal assistance from the military service in accordance with federal or state law, who by these presents represents and warrants that he is so eligible. Any person to whom this form is presented may conclusively rely on the authority purportedly granted hereunder.

BE IT KNOWN THAT on this ___ day of _____ in the year of our Lord nineteen hundred and _____, before me, Notary Public in and for said parish and state, duly commissioned and qualified as such, personally came and appeared _____, who declared that he is a member of the _____, a branch of the military designated in R.S. 9:3861, or is otherwise included thereunder, and did execute and sign the following Military Power of Attorney.

NOTICE: THE POWERS GRANTED BY THIS DOCUMENT ARE BROAD AND SWEEPING. THEY ARE EXPLAINED IN THE LOUISIANA MILITARY POWERS OF ATTORNEY ACT, R.S. 9:3861 ET SEQ. IF YOU HAVE ANY QUESTIONS ABOUT THESE POWERS, OBTAIN COMPETENT LEGAL ADVICE. THIS DOCUMENT DOES NOT AUTHORIZE ANYONE TO MAKE MEDICAL AND OTHER HEALTH-CARE DECISIONS FOR YOU, BUT IT MAY AUTHORIZE YOUR AGENT TO MAKE MEDICAL DECISIONS ON BEHALF OF YOUR MINOR CHILD. YOU MAY REVOKE THIS POWER OF ATTORNEY IF YOU LATER WISH TO DO SO.

I, _____

(YOUR NAME AND ADDRESS)

appoint _____

(NAME AND ADDRESS OF THE PERSON APPOINTED, OR OF EACH PERSON APPOINTED IF YOU WANT TO DESIGNATE MORE THAN ONE) as my agent (attorney-in-fact) to act for me in any lawful way with respect to the following initialed subjects:

I. GENERAL POWERS

TO GRANT OR WITHHOLD ANY OF THE FOLLOWING POWERS, INITIAL THE LINE IN FRONT OF IT IN THE APPROPRIATE COLUMN ("YES" OR "NO"). (THE GRANTING OF POWERS AFFECTING IMMOVABLE PROPERTY IS PROVIDED IN A SEPARATE SECTION.)

YES	NO		
___	___	(A)	Tangible personal property transactions.
___	___	(B)	Stock and bond transactions.
___	___	(C)	Commodity and option transactions.
___	___	(D)	Banking and other financial institution transactions.
___	___	(E)	Business operating transactions.
___	___	(F)	Insurance and annuity transactions.
___	___	(G)	Estate, trust, and other beneficiary transactions.
___	___	(H)	Claims and litigation.
___	___	(I)	Personal and family maintenance.
___	___	(J)	Care, custody, and control of a minor child.
___	___	(K)	Benefits from social security, Medicare, Medicaid, or other governmental programs, or civil or military service.
___	___	(L)	Retirement plan transactions.
___	___	(M)	Tax matters.
___	___	(N)	ALL OF THE POWERS LISTED ABOVE.

YOU NEED NOT INITIAL ANY OTHER LINES IF YOU INITIAL IN THE APPROPRIATE COLUMN ("YES" OR "NO") OF LINE (N).

II. POWERS AFFECTING IMMOVABLE PROPERTY

TO GRANT THE POWER TO AFFECT IMMOVABLE OR REAL PROPERTY WHICH YOU OWN, SUCH AS SELL, LEASE, OR MORTGAGE REAL ESTATE, INITIAL IN THE APPROPRIATE COLUMN ("YES" OR "NO") OF LINE (P) AND PROVIDE LOCATION OF PROPERTY.

YES NO
___ ___ (P) Real property transactions affecting the following property: _____

III. SPECIAL INSTRUCTIONS

ON THE FOLLOWING LINES YOU MAY GIVE SPECIAL INSTRUCTIONS LIMITING OR EXTENDING THE POWERS GRANTED TO YOUR AGENT.

_____

UNLESS YOU DIRECT OTHERWISE ABOVE, THIS POWER OF ATTORNEY IS EFFECTIVE IMMEDIATELY AND WILL CONTINUE UNTIL IT IS REVOKED.

This power of attorney will:

____ Continue to be effective even though I become incapacitated.
____ Terminate when I become incapacitated.

EXERCISE OF POWER OF ATTORNEY WHERE MORE THAN ONE AGENT DESIGNATED

If I have designated more than one agent, the agents are to act:
____ separately or ____ jointly.

I agree that any third party who receives a copy of this document may act under it. I agree that any transaction entered into by any third party in reliance on this document shall be binding upon me and I hereby waive all rights I may have to challenge the authority of the named agent, except to recover against him. Revocation of the power of attorney is not effective as to a third party until the third party has actual knowledge of the revocation.

_____
(Signature)   (SSN—optional)

Done and passed at the Parish of _____, Louisiana, on the day and date first above written, in the presence of _____ and _____, competent witnesses, (two witnesses preferred, but only required if line (P) is initialed) who sign with appearer and me, officer, after due reading of the whole.

WITNESSES:

_____

_____
                  (address)

_____
                  (address)

NOTARY SEAL _____
         (SIGNATURE OF NOTARY PUBLIC)

Added by Acts 1991, 1st Ex.Sess., No. 5, § 1, eff. April 17, 1991. Amended by Acts 1993, No. 24, § 1, eff. May 18, 1993; Acts 1995, No. 1131, § 1.

Cross References

C.C. arts. 1833 to 1835, 2985 et seq., 2989, 3001, 3030.
R.S. 9:3861, 9:3863, 9:3864, 9:3867 to 9:3887.

§ 3863. Requirements for legally sufficient power of attorney; federal preemption

A. In accordance with 10 U.S.C. 1044b, a military power of attorney is exempt from any requirement of form, substance, formality, or recording that is provided for powers of attorney under the laws of Louisiana or any other state. Any such military power of attorney shall be given the same legal effect as a power of attorney prepared and executed in accordance with the laws of the state of Louisiana.

B. For purposes of this Chapter, a military power of attorney is any general or special power of attorney that:

(1) Contains a statement that sets forth the provisions of Subsection A.

(2) Is notarized in accordance with 10 U.S.C. 1044a or other applicable state or federal law.

Added by Acts 1991, 1st Ex.Sess., No. 5, § 1, eff. April 17, 1991. Amended by Acts 1995, No. 1131, § 1.

Cross References

C.C. arts. 1832 to 1834, 2985 et seq., 2989, 3003, 3030.
R.S. 9:3861, 9:3862, 9:3864, 9:3867 to 9:3887.
10 U.S.C.A. §§ 1044a, 1044b.

§ 3864. Initialed lines on form or designation as general or special; no limitation of powers

A. If the line in front of (N) of the statutory form under R.S. 9:3862 is initialed, an initial on the line in front of any other power does not limit the powers granted by line (N).

B. The designation of any section or powers as "general" or "special" are not used to correspond to any provision of the Louisiana Civil Code, Code of Civil Procedure, or the Louisiana Revised Statutes of 1950, nor does it limit or expand the powers listed thereunder or the technical requirements thereof.

Added by Acts 1991, 1st Ex.Sess., No. 5, § 1, eff. April 17, 1991. Amended by Acts 1993, No. 24, § 1, eff. May 18, 1993; Acts 1995, No. 1131, § 1.

Cross References

C.C. art. 2994.
R.S. 9:3861 to 9:3863, 9:3867 to 9:3887.

§ 3865. Repealed by Acts 1995, No. 1131, § 2

§ 3866. Reserved

§ 3867. Additional form of power of attorney; application of this Chapter

A. Nothing in this Chapter affects or limits the use of:

(1) Any other military power of attorney prepared and executed in accordance with the provisions of 10 U.S.C. 1044b, regardless of form, substance, formality, or recording.

(2) Any other form for a power of attorney authorized by Civil Code Articles 2985 through 3034.

B. Any form that complies with the requirements of any law other than the provisions of this Chapter may be used in lieu of the form set forth in R.S. 9:3862, except that none of the provisions of this Chapter apply if such other form is used. This Chapter provides an additional form for granting a power of attorney and is governed by the provisions contained herein and does not affect, limit, or invalidate any other form or requirements for a power of attorney provided in Civil Code Articles 2985 through 3034 or any other provision of law.

Added by Acts 1991, 1st Ex.Sess., No. 5, § 1, eff. April 17, 1991. Amended by Acts 1995, No. 1131, § 1.

Cross References

C.C. arts. 2985 to 3032.

R.S. 9:3861 to 9:3864, 9:3868 to 9:3887.

10 U.S.C.A. § 1044b.

§ 3868. Short title

This Chapter may be cited as the "Louisiana Military Power of Attorney Act".

Added by Acts 1991, 1st Ex.Sess., No. 5, § 1, eff. April 17, 1991. Amended by Acts 1995, No. 1131, § 1.

Cross References

R.S. 9:3861 to 9:3864, 9:3867, 9:3869 to 9:3887.

§ 3869. Application and construction of Chapter

This Chapter shall be applied and construed to effectuate its general purpose to make uniform the law with respect to the subject of this Chapter among states enacting it.

Added by Acts 1991, 1st Ex.Sess., No. 5, § 1, eff. April 17, 1991.

§ 3870. Powers granted

By executing a military power of attorney with respect to a subject listed in R.S. 9:3862, the principal, except as limited or extended by the principal in the power of attorney, empowers the agent, for that subject, to do all of the following:

(1) Demand, receive, and obtain by litigation or otherwise, money or other thing of value to which the principal is, may become, or claims to be entitled, and conserve, invest, disburse, or use anything so received for the purposes intended.

(2) Contract in any manner with any person, on terms agreeable to the agent, to accomplish a purpose of a transaction, and perform, rescind, reform, release, or modify the contract or another contract made by or on behalf of the principal.

(3) Execute, acknowledge, seal, and deliver a sale, transfer, assignment, revocation, mortgage, lease, notice, check, release, security agreement, or other instrument the agent considers desirable to accomplish a purpose of a transaction.

(4) Prosecute, defend, submit to arbitration, settle, and propose or accept a compromise with respect to, a claim existing in favor of or against the principal or intervene in litigation relating to the claim.

(5) Seek on the principal's behalf the assistance of a court to carry out an act authorized by the power of attorney.

(6) Engage, compensate, and discharge an attorney, accountant, expert witness, or other assistant.

(7) Keep appropriate records of each transaction, including an accounting of receipts and disbursements.

(8) Prepare, execute, and file a record, report, or other document the agent considers desirable to safeguard or promote the principal's interest under a statute or governmental regulation.

(9) Reimburse the agent for expenditures properly made by the agent in exercising the powers granted by the power of attorney.

(10) In general, do any other lawful act with respect to the subject.

Added by Acts 1991, 1st Ex.Sess., No. 5, § 1, eff. April 17, 1991. Amended by Acts 1995, No. 1131, § 1.

Cross References

C.C. arts. 476, 1756 et seq., 2985 et seq., 2989, 3001, 3030, 3287 et seq.

R.S. 9:3861 to 9:3864, 9:3867 to 9:3869, 9:3871 to 9:3887.

§ 3871. Tangible personal property transactions; powers granted

In a military power of attorney, the language granting power with respect to tangible personal property transactions empowers the agent to do all of the following:

(1) Accept as a gift or as security for a loan, reject, demand, buy, receive, or otherwise acquire ownership or possession of tangible personal property or an interest in tangible personal property.

(2) Sell, exchange, convey with or without covenants, release, surrender, mortgage, encumber, pledge, hypothecate, create a security interest in, pawn, grant options concerning, lease, sublease to others, or otherwise dispose of tangible personal property or an interest in tangible personal property.

(3) Release, assign, satisfy, or enforce by litigation or otherwise, a mortgage, security interest, encumbrance, lien, or other claim on behalf of the principal, with respect to tangible personal property or an interest in tangible personal property.

(4) Do an act of management or conservation with respect to tangible personal property or an interest in tangible personal property on behalf of the principal, including all of the following:

(a) Insuring against casualty, liability, or loss.

(b) Obtaining or regaining possession, or protecting the property or interest, by litigation or otherwise.

(c) Paying, compromising, or contesting taxes or assessments or applying for and receiving refunds in connection with taxes or assessments.

(d) Moving from place to place.

(e) Storing for hire or on a gratuitous bailment.

(f) Using, altering, and making repairs or alterations.

Added by Acts 1991, 1st Ex.Sess., No. 5, § 1, eff. April 17, 1991. Amended by Acts 1995, No. 1131, § 1.

Cross References

C.C. arts. 476, 1756 et seq., 2985 et seq., 2909, 3001, 3030, 3186 et seq., 3287 et seq.

R.S. 9:3861 to 9:3864, 9:3867 to 9:3870, 9:3872 to 9:3887.

§ 3872. Stock and bond transactions; powers granted

In a military power of attorney, the language granting power with respect to stock and bond transactions empowers the agent to do all of the following:

(1) Buy, sell, and exchange stocks, bonds, mutual funds, and all other types of securities and financial instruments

except commodity futures contracts and call and put options on stocks and stock indexes.

(2) Receive certificates and other evidence of ownership with respect to securities.

(3) Exercise voting rights with respect to securities in person or by proxy, enter into voting trusts, and consent to limitations on the right to vote.

Added by Acts 1991, 1st Ex.Sess., No. 5, § 1, eff. April 17, 1991. Amended by Acts 1995, No. 1131, § 1.

Cross References

C.C. arts. 476, 2985 et seq., 2989, 3001, 3030.

R.S. 9:3861 to 9:3864, 9:3867 to 9:3871, 9:3873 to 9:3887, 12:31, 12:121, 12:135, 12:140.11.

§ 3873. Commodity and option transactions; powers granted

In a military power of attorney, the language granting power with respect to commodity and option transactions empowers the agent to do all of the following:

(1) Buy, sell, exchange, assign, settle, and exercise commodity futures contracts and call and put options on stocks and stock indexes traded on a regulated option exchange.

(2) Establish, continue, modify, and terminate option accounts with a broker.

Added by Acts 1991, 1st Ex.Sess., No. 5, § 1, eff. April 17, 1991. Amended by Acts 1995, No. 1131, § 1.

Cross References

C.C. arts. 2438 et seq., 2985 et seq., 2989.

R.S. 9:3861 to 9:3864, 9:3867 to 9:3871, 9:3874 to 9:3886.

§ 3874. Banking and other financial institution transactions; powers granted

In a military power of attorney, the language granting power with respect to banking and other financial institution transactions empowers the agent to do all of the following:

(1) Continue, modify, and terminate an account or other banking arrangement made by or on behalf of the principal.

(2) Establish, modify, and terminate an account or other banking arrangement, including any investment, annuity, or other financial product or service, with or through a bank, trust company, savings and loan association, credit union, thrift company, industrial loan company, brokerage firm, or other financial institution selected by the agent.

(3) Hire or close a safe deposit box or space in a vault.

(4) Contract to procure other services available from a financial institution as the agent considers desirable.

(5) Withdraw by check, order, or otherwise money or property of the principal deposited with or left in the custody of a financial institution.

(6) Receive bank statements, vouchers, notices, and similar documents from a financial institution and act with respect to them.

(7) Enter a safe deposit box or vault and withdraw or add to the contents.

(8) Borrow money at an interest rate and on such terms and conditions as may be agreeable to the agent in his or her sole discretion, and may grant a security interest in or mortgage or other security device upon any property of the principal necessary in order to borrow, pay, renew, or extend the time of payment of a debt of the principal, provided the principal has initialed line (P) of the power of attorney authorizing the agent to so act and the power of attorney includes a reasonable description of the affected property.

(9) Make, assign, draw, endorse, discount guarantee, and negotiate promissory notes, checks, drafts, and other nonnegotiable paper of the principal, or payable to the principal or the principal's order, receive the cash or other proceeds of those transactions, and accept a draft drawn by a person upon the principal and pay it when due.

(10) Receive for the principal and act upon a sight draft, warehouse receipt, or other negotiable or nonnegotiable instrument.

(11) Apply for and receive letters of credit, credit cards, and traveler's checks from a financial institution, and give an indemnity or other agreement in connection with letters of credit.

(12) Consent to an extension of the time of payment with respect to commercial paper or a financial transaction with a financial institution.

Added by Acts 1991, 1st Ex.Sess., No. 5, § 1, eff. April 17, 1991. Amended by Acts 1995, No. 1131, § 1.

Cross References

C.C. arts. 2985 et seq., 2989.

R.S. 9:3861 to 9:3864, 9:3867 to 9:3873, 9:3875 to 9:3887.

§ 3875. Business operating transactions; powers granted

In a military power of attorney, the language granting power with respect to business operating transactions empowers the agent to do all of the following:

(1) Operate, buy, sell, enlarge, reduce, and terminate a business interest.

(2) To the extent that an agent is permitted by law to act for a principal and subject to the terms of the partnership agreement:

(a) Perform a duty or discharge a liability and exercise a right, power, privilege, or option that the principal has, may have, or claims to have, under a partnership agreement, whether or not the principal is a partner.

(b) Enforce the terms of a partnership agreement by litigation or otherwise.

(c) Defend, submit to arbitration, settle, or compromise litigation to which the principal is a party because of membership in the partnership.

(3) Exercise in person or by proxy, or enforce by litigation or otherwise, a right, power, privilege, or option the principal has or claims to have as the holder of a bond, share, or other instrument of similar character, and defend, submit to arbitration, settle, or compromise litigation to which the principal is a party because of a bond, share, or similar instrument.

(4) With respect to a business owned solely by the principal:

(a) Continue, modify, renegotiate, extend, and terminate a contract made with an individual or a legal entity, firm, association, or corporation by or on behalf of the principal with respect to the business before execution of the power of attorney.

(b) Determine the policy of the business as to:

(i) The location of its operation.

(ii) The nature and extent of its business.

(iii) The methods of manufacturing, selling, merchandising, financing, accounting, and advertising employed in its operation.

(iv) The amount and types of insurance carried.

(v) The mode of engaging, compensating, and dealing with its accountants, attorneys, and other agents and employees.

(c) Change the name or form of organization under which the business is operated and enter into a partnership agreement with other persons or organize a corporation to take over all or part of the operation of the business.

(d) Demand and receive money due or claimed by the principal or on the principal's behalf in the operation of the business, and control and disburse the money in the operation of the business.

(5) Put additional capital into a business in which the principal has an interest.

(6) Join in a plan or reorganization, consolidation, or merger of the business.

(7) Sell or liquidate a business or part of it at the time and upon the terms the agent considers desirable.

(8) Represent the principal in establishing the value of a business under a buy-out agreement to which the principal is a party.

(9) Prepare, sign, file, and deliver reports, compilations of information, returns, or other papers with respect to a business which are required by a governmental agency or instrumentality or which the agent considers desirable, and make related payments.

(10) Pay, compromise, or contest taxes or assessments and do any other act which the agent considers desirable to protect the principal from illegal or unnecessary taxation, fines, penalties, or assessments with respect to a business, including attempts to recover in any manner permitted by law, money paid before or after the execution of the power of attorney.

Added by Acts 1991, 1st Ex.Sess., No. 5, § 1, eff. April 17, 1991. Amended by Acts 1995, No. 1131, § 1.

Cross References

C.C. arts. 1757 et seq., 2801 et seq., 2808 et seq., 2814 et seq., 2818 et seq., 2985 et seq., 2989.

R.S. 9:3861 to 9:3864, 9:3867 to 9:3874, 9:3867 to 9:3887.

§ 3876. Insurance and annuity transactions; powers granted

In a military power of attorney, the language granting power with respect to insurance and annuity transactions empowers the agent to do all of the following:

(1) Continue, pay the premium or assessment on, modify, rescind, release, or terminate, a contract procured by or on behalf of the principal which insures or provides an annuity to either the principal or another person, whether or not the principal is a beneficiary under the contract.

(2) Procure new, different, and additional contracts of insurance and annuities for the principal and the principal's spouse, children, and other dependents, and select the amount, type of insurance of annuity, and mode of payment.

(3) Pay the premium or assessment on, modify, rescind, release, or terminate a contract of insurance or annuity procured by the agent.

(4) Designate the beneficiary of the contract, but the agent may be named a beneficiary of the contract, or an extension, renewal, or substitute for it, only to the extent the agent was named as a beneficiary under a contract procured by the principal before executing the power of attorney.

(5) Apply for and receive a loan on the security of the contract of insurance or annuity.

(6) Surrender and receive the cash surrender value.

(7) Exercise an election.

(8) Change the manner of paying premiums.

(9) Change or convert the type of insurance contract or annuity as to any insurance contract or annuity with respect to which the principal has or claims to have a power described in this Section.

(10) Change the beneficiary of a contract of insurance of annuity, but the agent may not be designated a beneficiary except to the extent permitted by Paragraph (4).

(11) Apply for and procure government aid to guarantee or pay premiums of a contract of insurance on the life of the principal.

(12) Collect, sell, assign, hypothecate, borrow upon, or pledge the interest of the principal in a contract of insurance or annuity.

(13) Pay from proceeds or otherwise, compromise or contest, and apply for refunds in connection with, a tax or assessment levied by a taxing authority with respect to a contract of insurance or annuity or its proceeds or liability accruing by reason of the tax or assessment.

Added by Acts 1991, 1st Ex.Sess., No. 5, § 1, eff. April 17, 1991. Amended by Acts 1995, No. 1131, § 1.

Cross References

C.C. arts. 2985 et seq., 2989.

R.S. 9:3861 to 9:3864, 9:3867 to 9:3875, 9:3877 to 9:3887, 22:1791 to 22:1802, 22:200 to 22:202, 22:1015, 22:1097.

§ 3877. Estate, trust, and other beneficiary transactions; powers granted

In a military power of attorney, the language granting power with respect to estate, trust, and other beneficiary transactions, empowers the agent to act for the principal in all matters that affect a trust, probate estate, guardianship, conservatorship, escrow, custodianship, or other fund from which the principal is, may become, or claims to be entitled, as a beneficiary, to a share of payment, including the power to do all of the following:

(1) Accept, reject, disclaim, receive, receipt for, sell, assign, release, pledge, exchange, or consent to a reduction in or modification of a share in or payment from the fund.

(2) Demand or obtain by litigation or otherwise money or other thing of value to which the principal is, may become, or claims to be entitled by reason of the fund.

(3) Initiate, participate in, and oppose litigation to ascertain the meaning, validity, or effect of a deed, will, declaration of trust, or other instrument or transaction affecting the interest of the principal.

(4) Initiate, participate in, and oppose litigation to remove, substitute, or surcharge a fiduciary.

(5) Conserve, invest, disburse, and use anything received for an authorized purpose.

(6) Transfer an interest of the principal in real or immovable property, stocks, bonds, accounts with financial institutions, insurance, and other property, to the trustee of a revocable trust created by the principal as settlor.

Added by Acts 1991, 1st Ex.Sess., No. 5, § 1, eff. April 17, 1991. Amended by Acts 1995, No. 1131, § 1.

Cross References

C.C. arts. 2895 et seq., 2989.

R.S. 9:1731 et seq., 9:3861 to 9:3864, 9:3867 to 9:3876, 9:3878 to 9:3880.

§ 3878. Claims and litigations; powers granted

In a military power of attorney, the language with respect to claims and litigation empowers the agent to do all of the following:

(1) Assert and prosecute before a court or administrative agency a claim, claim for relief, cause of action, counterclaim, cross-complaint, or offset, and defend against an individual, a legal entity, or government, including suits to recover property or other thing of value, to recover damages sustained by the principal, to eliminate or modify tax liability, or to seek an injunction, specific performance, or other relief.

(2) Bring an action to determine adverse claims, intervene in litigation, and act as amicus curiae.

(3) In connection with litigation:

(a) Procure an attachment, garnishment, libel, order of arrest, or other preliminary, provisional, or intermediate relief and use any available procedure to effect, enforce, or satisfy a judgment, order, or decree.

(b) Perform any lawful act, including acceptance of tender, offer of judgment, admission of facts, submission of a controversy on an agreed statement of facts, consent to examination before trial, and binding the principal in litigation.

(4) Submit to arbitration, settle, and propose or accept a compromise with respect to a claim of litigation.

(5) Waive the issuance and service of process upon the principal, accept service of process, appear for the principal, designate persons upon whom process directed to the principal may be served, execute and file or deliver stipulations on the principal's behalf, verify pleadings, seek appellate review, procure and give surety and indemnity bonds, contract and pay for the preparation and printing of records and briefs, receive and execute and file or deliver a consent, waiver, release, confession of judgment, satisfaction of judgment, notice, agreement, or other instrument in connection with the prosecution, settlement, or defense of a claim of litigation.

(6) Act for the principal with respect to bankruptcy or insolvency proceedings, whether voluntary or involuntary, concerning the principal or some other persons, or with respect to reorganization proceedings, or with respect to an assignment for the benefit of creditors, receivership, or application for the appointment of a receiver or trustee which affects an interest of the principal in property or other thing of value.

(7) Pay a judgment against the principal or a settlement made in connection with litigation and receive and conserve money or other thing of value paid in settlement of or as proceeds of a claim or litigation.

Added by Acts 1991, 1st Ex.Sess., No. 5, § 1, eff. April 17, 1991. Amended by Acts 1995, No. 1131, § 1.

Cross References

C.C. arts. 1756, 3071 et seq., 3099 et seq.

R.S. 9:3861 to 9:3864, 9:3867 to 9:3877, 9:3879 to 9:3887.

§ 3879. Personal and family maintenance; powers granted

In a military power of attorney, the language granting power with respect to personal and family maintenance empowers the agent to do all of the following:

(1) Do the acts necessary to maintain the customary standard of living of the principal, the principal's spouse, children, and other individuals customarily or legally entitled to be supported by the principal, including providing living quarters by purchase, lease, or other contract, or paying the operating costs, including interest, amortization payments, repairs, and taxes on premises owned by the principal and occupied by those individuals.

(2) Provide for the individuals described in Paragraph (1) all of the following:

(a) Normal domestic help.

(b) Usual vacations and travel expenses.

(c) Funds for shelter, clothing, food, appropriate education, and other current living costs.

(3) Pay for the individuals described in Paragraph (1) necessary medical, dental, and surgical care, hospitalization, and custodial care.

(4) Continue any provision made by the principal, for the individuals described in Paragraph (1), for automobiles or other means of transportation, including registering, licensing, insuring, and replacing them.

(5) Maintain or open charge accounts for the convenience of the individuals described in Paragraph (1) and open new accounts the agent considers desirable to accomplish a lawful purpose.

(6) Continue payments incidental to the membership or affiliation of the principal in a church, club, society, order, or other organization and continue contributions to those organizations.

Added by Acts 1991, 1st Ex.Sess., No. 5, § 1, eff. April 17, 1991. Amended by Acts 1995, No. 1131, § 1.

Cross References

C.C. arts. 2895 et seq., 2989.

R.S. 9:3861 to 9:3864, 9:3867 to 9:3878, 9:3880 to 9:3887.

§ 3879.1. Care, custody, and control of minor child

In a military power of attorney, the language granting power with respect to the care, custody, and control of a minor child empowers the agent to do all of the following:

(1) The general functions, powers, and duties accorded to tutors pursuant to Chapter 8 of Title VI of Book VII of the Code of Civil Procedure, except those that require court approval.

(2) Consenting to and authorizing such medical care, treatment, or surgery as may be deemed necessary for the health, safety, and welfare of the child or children.

(3) Enrolling the child or children in such schools or educational institutions as may be deemed necessary for his due and proper education.

(4) Disciplining the child in such reasonable manner as may be necessary for his proper rearing, supervision, and training.

Added by Acts 1993, No. 24, § 1, eff. May 18, 1993. Amended by Acts 1995, No. 1131, § 1.

Cross References

C.C. arts. 2318, 2320, 2985 et seq., 2989.

C.C.P. arts. 4261 to 4275.

R.S. 9:3861 to 9:3864, 9:3867 to 9:3879, 9:3880 to 9:3887.

§ 3880. Social security; civil or military benefits; powers granted

In a military power of attorney, the language granting power with respect to benefits from social security, Medicare, Medicaid or other governmental programs, or civil or military service, empowers the agent to do all of the following:

(1) Execute vouchers in the name of the principal for allowances and reimbursements payment by the United States or a foreign government or by a state or subdivision of a state to the principal, including allowances and reimbursements for transportation of the individuals described in R.S. 9:3879(1), and for shipment of their household effects.

(2) Take possession and order the removal and shipment of property of the principal from a post, warehouse, depot, dock, or other place of storage or safekeeping, either governmental or private, and execute and deliver a release, voucher, receipt, bill of lading, shipping ticket, certificate, or other instrument for that purpose.

(3) Prepare, file, and prosecute a claim of the principal to a benefit or assistance, financial or otherwise, to which the principal claims to be entitled, under a statute or governmental regulation.

(4) Prosecute, defend, submit to arbitration, settle, and propose or accept a compromise with respect to any benefits the principal may be entitled to receive.

(5) Receive the financial proceeds of a claim of the type described in this Section, conserve, invest, disburse, or use anything received for a lawful purpose.

Added by Acts 1991, 1st Ex.Sess., No. 5, § 1, eff. April 17, 1991. Amended by Acts 1995, No. 1131, § 1.

Cross References

C.C. arts. 2985 et seq., 2989, 3071 et seq., 3099 et seq.

R.S. 9:2861 to 9:2864, 9:2867 to 9:3879.1, 9:3881 to 9:3887.

§ 3881. Retirement plan transactions; powers granted

In a military power of attorney, the language granting power with respect to retirement plan transactions empowers the agent to do all of the following:

(1) Select payment options under any retirement plan in which the principal participates, including plans for self-employed individuals.

(2) Designate beneficiaries under those plans and change existing designations.

(3) Make voluntary contributions to those plans.

(4) Exercise the investment powers available under any self-directed retirement plan.

(5) Make rollovers of plan benefits into other retirement plans.

(6) If authorized by the plan, borrow from, sell assets to, and purchase assets from the plan.

(7) Waive the right of the principal to be a beneficiary of a joint or survivor annuity if the principal is a spouse who is not employed.

Added by Acts 1991, 1st Ex.Sess., No. 5, § 1, eff. April 17, 1991. Amended by Acts 1995, No. 1131, § 1.

Cross References

C.C. art. 2985, 2989.

R.S. 9:3861 to 9:3864, 9:3867 to 9:3880, 9:3882 to 9:3887.

§ 3882. Tax matters; powers granted

In a military power of attorney, the language granting power with respect to tax matters empowers the agent to do all of the following:

(1) Prepare, sign, and file federal, state, local, and foreign income, gift, payroll, Federal Insurance Contributions Act returns, and other tax returns, claims for refunds, requests for extension of time, petitions regarding tax matters, and any other tax-related documents, including receipts, offers, waivers, consents (including consents and agreements under Internal Revenue Code Section 2032A or any successor section), closing agreements, and any power of attorney required by the Internal Revenue Service or other taxing authority with respect to a tax year upon which the statute of limitations has not run and to the tax year in which the power of attorney was executed and any subsequent tax year.

(2) Pay taxes due, collect refunds, post bonds, receive confidential information, and contest deficiencies determined by the Internal Revenue Service or other taxing authority.

(3) Exercise any election available to the principal under federal, state, local, or foreign tax law.

(4) Act for the principal in all tax matters for all periods before the Internal Revenue Service and any other taxing authority.

Added by Acts 1991, 1st Ex.Sess., No. 5, § 1, eff. April 17, 1991. Amended by Acts 1995, No. 1131, § 1.

Cross References

C.C. arts. 2985 et seq., 2989.

R.S. 9:3861 to 9:3864, 9:3867 to 9:3881, 9:3882.1 to 9:3887.

I.R.C. (Internal Revenue Code) § 2032A.

§ 3882.1. Real or immovable property transactions; powers granted

In a military power of attorney, the language granting power with respect to real or immovable property transactions empowers the agent to do all of the following:

(1) Accept as a gift or as security for a loan, reject, demand, buy, lease, receive, or otherwise acquire an interest

in real property or a right incidental to real or immovable property.

(2) Sell, exchange, convey with or without covenants, quitclaim, release, surrender, mortgage, encumber, partition, consent to partitioning, subdivide, apply for zoning, rezoning, or other governmental permits, plat or consent to platting, develop, grant options concerning, lease, sublease, give in payment, or otherwise dispose of an interest in real or immovable property or a right incidental to real or immovable property.

(3) Release, assign, satisfy, and enforce by litigation or otherwise a mortgage, deed of trust, encumbrance, lien, or other claim to real or immovable property which exists or is asserted.

(4) Do any act of management or of conservation with respect to an interest in real or immovable property, or a right incidental to real or immovable property, owned or claimed to be owned, by the principal, including all of the following:

(a) Insuring against a casualty, liability, or loss.

(b) Obtaining or regaining possession, or protecting the interest or right, by litigation or otherwise.

(c) Paying, compromising, or contesting taxes or assessments, or applying for and receiving refunds in connection with them.

(d) Purchasing supplies, hiring assistance or labor, and making repairs or alterations in the real or immovable property.

(5) Use, develop, alter, replace, remove, erect, or install structures or other improvements upon real or immovable property in or incidental to which the principal has, or claims to have, an interest or right.

(6) Participate in a reorganization with respect to real or immovable property or a legal entity that owns an interest in or right incidental to real or immovable property and receive and hold shares of stock or obligations received in a plan of reorganization, and act with respect to them, including all of the following:

(a) Selling or otherwise disposing of them.

(b) Exercising or selling an option, conversion, or similar right with respect to them.

(c) Voting them in person or by proxy.

(7) Change the form of title of an interest in or right incidental to real or immovable property.

(8) Dedicate to public use, with or without consideration, servitudes, easements, or other rights or interests in and to real or immovable property in which the principal has, or claims to have, an interest or right.

Added by Acts 1995, No. 1131, § 1.

Cross References

C.C. arts. 462 et seq., 476, 2439, 2491, 2492, 2494, 2495, 2589 et seq., 2655, 2989, 2994.

C.C.P. arts. 422, 3651 et seq., 3655 et seq., 3691 et seq.

R.S. 9:3861 to 9:3864, 9:3867 to 9:3881, 9:3883 to 9:3887.

§ 3883. After-acquired property; state where property is located or where power is executed

The powers described in this Chapter are exercisable equally with respect to an interest the principal has when the military power of attorney is executed or acquires later, whether or not the property is located in this state, and whether or not the powers are exercised or the power of attorney is executed in this state.

Added by Acts 1991, 1st Ex.Sess., No. 5, § 1, eff. April 17, 1991. Amended by Acts 1995, No. 1131, § 1.

Cross References

C.C. arts. 2985 et seq., 2989, 3535, 3536.

R.S. 9:3861 to 9:3864, 9:3867 to 9:3882.1, 9:3884 to 9:3887.

§ 3884. Trust instruments; power to modify or revoke

A military power of attorney under this Chapter does not empower the agent to modify or revoke a trust created by the principal unless that power is expressly granted by the power of attorney. If a military power of attorney under this Chapter empowers the agent to modify or revoke a trust created by the principal, the trust may be modified or revoked by the agent only as provided in the trust instrument.

Added by Acts 1991, 1st Ex.Sess., No. 5, § 1, eff. April 17, 1991. Amended by Acts 1995, No. 1131, § 1.

Cross References

C.C. arts. 2895 et seq., 2989.

R.S. 9:1731 et seq., 9:3861 to 9:3864, 9:3867 to 9:3883, 9:3885 to 9:3887.

§ 3885. Liability of person acting in good faith reliance upon power of attorney

A. Any person, firm, corporation, financial institution, or other entity who acts in good faith reliance upon a military power of attorney is not liable to the principal or to any other person for so acting if all of the following requirements are satisfied:

(1) The power of attorney is presented to the person by the attorney in fact named in the power of attorney.

(2) The power of attorney appears on its face to be valid.

(3) The power of attorney includes either:

(a) A notary public's certificate of acknowledgment.

(b) The signature of any person acting as notary, together with the title of that person's office, provided he is authorized to perform a notarial act pursuant to 10 U.S.C. 1044a.

B. Nothing in this Section is intended to create an implication that a person is liable for acting in reliance upon a power of attorney under circumstances where the requirements of Subsection A are not satisfied. Nothing in this Section affects any immunity that may otherwise exist apart from this Section.

C. A military power of attorney appears on its face to be valid if it contains the language provided by R.S. 9:3862, and all signature spaces thereon including those for the principal, notary public, and witnesses, where applicable, have been completed.

D. Any banking institution or other third person acting in good faith may conclusively rely on the power apparently conferred under a military power of attorney executed in accordance with the provisions of this Chapter or military power of attorney as defined in 10 U.S.C. 1044b and all acts or transactions by any banking institution or other third person in reliance on such military power of attorney shall be valid, binding, and of full force and effect as entered into for any and all purposes. No cause of action shall lie against any banking institution or third person which relies in good faith on such military power of attorney, nor shall any transaction entered into by any person in reliance on a military power of attorney be subject to attack for any reason as a result of the reliance placed upon such military power of attorney, and the sole recourse by the principal shall be a claim for damages against the agent.

Added by Acts 1991, 1st Ex.Sess., No. 5, § 1, eff. April 17, 1991. Amended by Acts 1995, No. 1131, § 1.

Cross References

C.C. arts. 2895 et seq., 2989.

R.S. 9:3861 to 9:3864, 9:3867 to 9:3884, 9:3886 to 9:3887.

§ 3886. Application of power of attorney to all or portion of property of principal; description of items or parcels

A. A military power of attorney may by its terms apply to all or a portion of the personal or movable property of the principal, whether owned by the principal at the time of the giving of the power of attorney or thereafter acquired, whether located in this state or elsewhere, without the need for a description of each item of property.

B. A military power of attorney conferring power to act with respect to immovable (real) property of the principal located in Louisiana must contain a reasonable description of the property with respect to which the agent is authorized to act, but need not be accompanied by a detailed legal description of such property.

Added by Acts 1991, 1st Ex.Sess., No. 5, § 1, eff. April 17, 1991. Amended by Acts 1995, No. 1131, § 1.

Cross References

C.C. arts. 2985 et seq.

R.S. 9:3861 to 9:3864, 9:3867 to 9:3885, 9:3887.

§ 3887. Acceptance of military power of attorney

A. No state bank, trust company, national bank, savings bank, federal mutual savings bank, savings and loan association, federal savings and loan association, federal mutual savings and loan association, credit union or federal credit union or branch of a foreign banking corporation, or any other supervised financial organization or licensed lender as provided in R.S. 9:3516, each of the foregoing referred to in this Section as "banking institution", located in this state shall refuse to honor a military power of attorney properly executed in accordance with R.S. 9:3862 or a military power of attorney as defined in 10 U.S.C. 1044b.

B. The failure of a banking institution to honor a properly executed military power of attorney executed in accordance with R.S. 9:3862 or a military power of attorney as defined in 10 U.S.C. 1044b, shall be deemed unlawful.

C. No banking institution receiving and retaining a military power of attorney presented to it as provided in Subsection A of this Section nor any officer, agent, or employee of such institution shall incur any liability by reason of acting upon the authority thereof unless the institution shall have actually received, at the office where the account is located, written notice of the revocation or termination of such power of attorney.

Added by Acts 1991, 1st Ex.Sess., No. 5, § 1, eff. April 17, 1991. Amended by Acts 1995, No. 1131, § 1.

Cross References

C.C. art. 2985, 2989.

R.S. 9:3516, 9:3861 to 9:3864, 9:3867 to 9:3886.

10 U.S.C.A. § 1044b.

CHAPTER 3–A. CONDITIONAL PROCURATION

Section
3890. Conditional procuration.

§ 3890. Conditional procuration

A. The term "conditional procuration" means a written document stating that the procuration becomes effective upon the disability of the principal.

B. In a conditional procuration, the disability of a principal shall be established by an authentic act as described in Subsection C, stating that due to any infirmity, the principal is unable consistently to make or to communicate reasoned decisions regarding the care of the principal's person or property.

C. The authentic act shall be signed by two physicians licensed to practice medicine by the Louisiana Sate Board of Medical Examiners who have personally examined the principal. However, if the executed conditional procuration so provides, the authentic act may be signed by the attending physician who is licensed to practice medicine by the Louisiana State Board of Medical Examiners and the agent appointed in the conditional procuration.

D. A conditional procuration which has been entered into under the provisions of this Section and which has become effective as provided in this Section, shall have the same effectiveness as any other procuration.

E. Except as otherwise specifically provided in this Chapter, a conditional procuration which becomes effective upon a determination of disability shall be subject to all of the provisions of the Louisiana Civil Code and all other provisions of law which govern procuration.

Added by Acts 1999, No. 1083, § 1.

CHAPTER 4. AGENCY RELATIONS IN REAL ESTATE TRANSACTIONS

Section
3891. Definitions.
3892. Relationships between licensees and persons.
3893. Duties of licensees representing clients.
3894. Licensee's relationship with customers.
3895. Termination of agency relationship.
3896. Compensation; agency relationship.
3897. Dual agency.
3898. Subagency.
3899. Vicarious liability.

§ 3891. Definitions

(1) "Agency" means a relationship in which a real estate broker or licensee represents a client by the client's consent, whether express or implied, in an immovable property transaction.

(2) "Broker" means any person licensed by the Louisiana Real Estate Commission as a real estate broker.

(3) "Brokerage agreement" means an agreement for brokerage services to be provided to a person in return for compensation or the right to receive compensation from another.

(4) "Client" means one who engages the professional advice and services of a licensee as his agent.

(5) "Commission" means the Louisiana Real Estate Commission.

(6)(a) "Confidential information" means information obtained by a licensee from a client during the term of a brokerage agreement that was made confidential by the written request or written instruction of the client or is information the disclosure of which could materially harm the position of the client, unless at any time any of the following occurs:

(i) The client permits the disclosure by word or conduct.

(ii) The disclosure is required by law or would reveal serious defect.

(iii) The information becomes public from a source other than the licensee.

(b) Confidential information shall not be considered to include material information about the physical condition of the property.

(c) Confidential information can be disclosed by a designated agent to his broker for the purpose of seeking advice or assistance for the benefit of the client.

(7) "Customer" means a person who is not being represented by a licensee but for whom the licensee is performing ministerial acts.

(8) "Designated agency" means the agency relationship that shall be presumed to exist when a licensee engaged in any real estate transaction, except as otherwise provided in this Chapter, is working with a client, unless there is a written agreement providing for a different relationship.

(9) "Designated agent" means a licensee who is the agent of a client.

(10) "Dual agency" means an agency relationship in which a licensee is working with both buyer and seller or both landlord and tenant in the same transaction. However, such a relationship shall not constitute dual agency if the licensee is the seller of property that he owns or if the property is owned by a real estate business of which the licensee is the sole proprietor and agent. A dual agency relationship shall not be construed to exist in a circumstance in which the licensee is working with both landlord and tenant as to a lease which does not exceed a term of three years and the licensee is the landlord.

(11) "Licensee" means any person who has been issued a license by the commission as a real estate salesperson or a real estate broker.

(12) "Ministerial acts" means those acts that a licensee may perform for a person that are informative in nature. Examples of these acts include but are not limited to:

(a) Responding to phone inquiries by persons as to the availability and pricing of brokerage services

(b) Responding to phone inquiries from a person concerning the price or location of property.

(c) Conducting an open house and responding to questions about the property from a person.

(d) Setting an appointment to view property.

(e) Responding to questions from persons walking into a licensee's office concerning brokerage services offered or particular properties.

(f) Accompanying an appraiser, inspector, contractor, or similar third party on a visit to a property.

(g) Describing a property or the property's condition in response to a person's inquiry.

(h) Completing business or factual information for a person represented by another licensee on an offer or contract to purchase.

(i) Showing a person through a property being sold by an owner on his or her own behalf.

(j) Referral to another broker or service provider.

(13) "Person" means and includes individuals and any and all business entities, including but not limited to corporations, partnerships, trusts and limited liability companies, foreign or domestic.

(14) "Substantive contact" means that point in any conversation where confidential information is solicited or received. This includes any specific financial qualifications of the consumer or the motives or objectives in which the consumer may divulge any confidential, personal, or financial information, which, if disclosed to the other party to the transaction, could harm the party's bargaining position. This includes any electronic contact, electronic mail, or any other form of electronic transmission.

Added by Acts 1997, No. 31, § 1, eff. March 1, 1998. Amended by Acts 1999, No. 452, § 1; Acts 2010, No. 247, § 1.

§ 3892. Relationships between licensees and persons

Notwithstanding the provisions of Civil Code Articles 2985 through 3032 or any other provisions of law, a licensee engaged in any real estate transaction shall be considered to be representing the person with whom he is working as a designated agent unless there is a written agreement between the broker and the person providing that there is a different relationship or the licensee is performing only ministerial acts on behalf of the person.

Added by Acts 1997, No. 31, § 1, eff. March 1, 1998.

§ 3893. Duties of licensees representing clients

A. A licensee representing a client shall:

(1) Perform the terms of the brokerage agreement between a broker and the client.

(2) Promote the best interests of the client by:

(a) Seeking a transaction at the price and terms stated in the brokerage agreement or at a price and upon terms otherwise acceptable to the client.

(b) Timely presenting all offers to and from the client, unless the client has waived this duty.

(c) Timely accounting for all money and property received in which the client has, may have, or should have had an interest.

For Annotative Materials, see West's Louisiana Statutes Annotated

(3) Exercise reasonable skill and care in the performance of brokerage services.

B. A licensee representing a client does not breach a duty or obligation to the client by showing alternative properties to prospective buyers or tenants or by showing properties in which the client is interested to other prospective buyers or tenants.

C. A licensee representing a buyer or tenant client does not breach a duty or obligation to that client by working on the basis that the licensee shall receive a higher fee or compensation based on a higher selling price.

D. A licensee shall not be liable to a client for providing false information to the client if the false information was provided to the licensee by a customer unless the licensee knew or should have known the information was false.

E. Nothing in this Section shall be construed as changing a licensee's legal duty as to negligent or fraudulent misrepresentation of material information.

F. Nothing in this Chapter or in Chapter 17 of Title 37 of the Louisiana Revised Statutes of 1950 shall be construed as to require agency disclosure with regard to a lease that does not exceed a term of three years and under which no sale of the subject property to the lessee is contemplated.

Added by Acts 1997, No. 31, § 1, eff. March 1, 1998. Amended by Acts 1999, No. 452, § 1.

§ 3894. Licensee's relationship with customers

A. Licensees shall treat all customers honestly and fairly and when representing a client in a real estate transaction may provide assistance to a customer by performing ministerial acts. Performing those ministerial acts shall not be construed in a manner that would violate the brokerage agreement with the client, and performing those ministerial acts for the customer shall not be construed in a manner as to form a brokerage agreement with the customer.

B. A licensee shall not be liable to a customer for providing false information to the customer if the false information was provided to the licensee by the licensee's client or client's agent and the licensee did not have actual knowledge that the information was false.

Added by Acts 1997, No. 31, § 1, eff. March 1, 1998.

§ 3895. Termination of agency relationship

Except as may be provided in a written agreement between the broker and the client, neither a broker nor any licensee affiliated with the broker owes any further duties to the client after termination, expiration, or completion of performance of the brokerage agreement, except to account for all monies and property relating to the transaction and to keep confidential all confidential information received during the course of the brokerage agreement.

Added by Acts 1997, No. 31, § 1, eff. March 1, 1998.

§ 3896. Compensation; agency relationship

The payment or promise of payment of compensation to a broker is not determinative of whether an agency relationship has been created.

Added by Acts 1997, No. 31, § 1, eff. March 1, 1998.

§ 3897. Dual agency

A. A licensee may act as a dual agent only with the informed written consent of all clients. Informed consent shall be presumed to have been given by any client who signs a dual agency disclosure form prepared by the commission pursuant to its rules and regulations. The form prepared by the commission shall include the following language:

"What a licensee shall do for clients when acting as a dual agent:

(1) Treat all clients honestly.

(2) Provide information about the property to the buyer or tenant.

(3) Disclose all latent material defects in the property that are known to the licensee.

(4) Disclose financial qualification of the buyer or tenant to the seller or landlord.

(5) Explain real estate terms.

(6) Help the buyer or tenant to arrange for property inspections.

(7) Explain closing costs and procedures.

(8) Help the buyer compare financing alternatives.

(9) Provide information about comparable properties that have sold so both clients may make educated decisions on what price to accept or offer."

B. A licensee shall not disclose to clients when acting as a dual agent:

(1) Confidential information that the licensee may know about either of the clients, without that client's permission.

(2) The price the seller or landlord will take other than the listing price without the permission of the seller or landlord.

(3) The price the buyer or tenant is willing to pay without the permission of the buyer or tenant.

C. The written consent required in Subsection A of this Section shall be obtained by a licensee from the client at the time the brokerage agreement is entered into or at any time before the licensee acts as a dual agent.

D. No cause of action shall arise on behalf of any person against a dual agent for making disclosures allowed or required by this Section, and the dual agent does not terminate any agency relationship by making the allowed or required disclosures.

E. In the case of dual agency, each client and licensee possess only actual knowledge and information. There shall be no imputation of knowledge or information among or between the clients, brokers, or their affiliated licensees.

F. In any transaction, a licensee may without liability withdraw from representing a client who has not consented to a disclosed dual agency. The withdrawal shall not prejudice the ability of the licensee to continue to represent the other client in the transaction or limit the licensee from representing the client in other transactions. When a withdrawal occurs, the licensee shall not receive a referral fee for referring a client to another licensee unless written disclosure is made to both the withdrawing client and the client that continues to be represented by the licensee.

G. A licensee shall not be considered as acting as a dual agent if the licensee is working with both buyer and seller, if the licensee is the seller of property he owns, or if the property is owned by a real estate business of which the licensee is the sole proprietor and agent. A dual agency shall not be construed to exist in a circumstance in which the licensee is working with both landlord and tenant as to a lease which does not exceed a term of three years and the licensee is the landlord.

Added by Acts 1997, No. 31, § 1, eff. March 1, 1998. Amended by Acts 1999, No. 452, § 1.

§ 3898. Subagency

Subagency can only be created by a written agreement. A licensee is not considered to be a subagent of a client or another broker solely by reason of membership or other affiliation by the broker in a multiple listing service or other similar information source.

Added by Acts 1997, No. 31, § 1, eff. March 1, 1998.

§ 3899. Vicarious liability

A client shall not be liable for the acts or omissions of a licensee in providing brokerage services for or on behalf of the client.

Added by Acts 1997, No. 31, § 1, eff. March 1, 1998.

CODE TITLE XVI—SURETYSHIP

CHAPTER 1. SURETYSHIP

PART I. IN GENERAL

Section
3901. Premium on bond, expense of administration.
3902. Failure of surety to pay; recovery of attorney's fees.
3903. Subrogation in favor of surety on twelve months' bond.
3904. Agreement with surety as to deposit of moneys.

PART II. SURETY FOR LEGAL REPRESENTATIVE

3911. Withdrawal of surety from bond of administrator, executor, curator or tutor.
3912. Procedure for release of judicial surety.

PART I. IN GENERAL

§ 3901. Premium on bond, expense of administration

Any executor, administrator, curator, tutor, liquidator, receiver, syndic, or other similar officer appointed or confirmed by any court of the state who is required to give bond, may charge among the expenses of his administration the premium paid therefor to any surety company authorized to do business in this state, provided that the amount of the premium does not exceed one-half of one per centum upon the amount of the bond.

Cross References

C.C. art. 3035 et seq.

§ 3902. Failure of surety to pay; recovery of attorney's fees

If the surety on a bond fails to pay his obligation and it becomes necessary for the creditor to sue thereon, the latter shall be entitled to ten per cent attorney's fees on the amount recovered, provided he has employed an attorney for the purpose, has made written amicable demand on the principal and surety and thirty days have elapsed from their receipt thereof without payment being made, and the full amount claimed in the demand is recovered.

This Section shall not affect the right to recover interest and costs as otherwise provided by law.

Cross References

C.C. arts. 3035, 3045, 3065.

§ 3903. Subrogation in favor of surety on twelve months' bond

Whenever a person bound as surety upon a twelve months' bond has paid the same, he shall be subrogated to all the rights which the original creditor had at the time such bond was given, or at the time the bond is paid by such surety. This section shall only apply where the property has been adjudicated to the defendant in the judgment, and he is the principal upon such twelve months' bond.

Cross References

C.C. arts. 3048, 3049.

§ 3904. Agreement with surety as to deposit of moneys

It shall be lawful for any party of whom a bond, undertaking or other obligation is required, to agree with his surety or sureties for the deposit of any or all moneys and assets for which he and his surety or sureties are or may be held responsible, with a bank, savings bank, safe-deposit or trust company, authorized by law to do business as such, or with other depository approved by the court or a judge thereof, if such deposit is otherwise proper, for the safekeeping thereof, and in such manner as to prevent the withdrawal of such money or assets or any part thereof, without the written consent of such surety or sureties, or an order of court, or a judge thereof, made on such notice to such surety or sureties as such court or judge may direct; provided, however, that such agreement shall not in any manner release from or change the liability of the principal or sureties as established by the terms of the said bond.

Added by Acts 1958, No. 356, § 1.

Cross References

C.C. arts. 3035, 3040.

PART II. SURETY FOR LEGAL REPRESENTATIVE

§ 3911. Withdrawal of surety from bond of administrator, executor, curator or tutor

Sureties on the bond of any administrator, executor, curator or tutor, shall have the right to be released from any further liability on such bond, by causing their principal to be cited into the court having jurisdiction over the appointment of such administrator, curator, executor or tutor, by petition, setting forth their fears that such administrator, curator, executor or tutor is mismanaging the property under his charge, and that they are in danger of being injured seriously by his conduct, and praying that he shall be required to give new security.

C.C. art. 3069. Redesignated as R.S. 9:3911 by Acts 1987, No. 409, § 3, eff. Jan. 1, 1988.

Cross References

C.C. arts. 3035 et seq., 3055 to 3062.

R.S. 42:190 to 42:192.

§ 3912. Procedure for release of judicial surety

On due proof being made of maladministration by any curator, administrator, executor or tutor cited, the court shall require him to give a new bond, with other sufficient security, for the faithful administration of the property; and upon failure to do so within three days after such order, he shall be forthwith removed from the administration thereof, and the judge shall proceed at once to the appointment of another curator, administrator, executor or tutor, who shall be required to give security in manner and form as now required by law; and this being done, the former sureties on the bond shall be released from all liability for any maladministration of such administrator, curator, executor or tutor, from and after execution of the new bond with security as aforesaid.

C.C. art. 3070. Redesignated as R.S. 9:3912 by Acts 1987, No. 409, § 3, eff. Jan. 1, 1988.

Cross References

C.C. arts. 3055 to 3062.

C.C.P. arts. 75, 4254, 4265.

R.S. 42:190 to 42:192.

CODE TITLE XVII—OF TRANSACTION OR COMPROMISE

CHAPTER 1. TRANSACTION OR COMPROMISE

Section
3921. Remission, transaction, compromise, or other conventional discharge of obligations.

§ 3921. Remission, transaction, compromise, or other conventional discharge of obligations

A. Notwithstanding any provision in Title III of Code Book III of Title 9 of the Louisiana Revised Statutes of 1950 to the contrary, every master or employer is answerable for the damage occasioned by his servant or employee in the exercise of the functions in which they are employed. Any remission, transaction, compromise, or other conventional discharge in favor of the employee, or any judgment rendered against him for such damage shall be valid as between the damaged creditor and the employee, and the employer shall have no right of contribution, division, or indemnification from the employee nor shall the employer be allowed to bring any incidental action under the provisions of Chapter 6 of Title I of Book II of the Louisiana Code of Civil Procedure [1] against such employee.

B. The provisions of this Section are remedial and shall be applied retrospectively and prospectively to any cause of action for damages arising prior to, on, or after the effective date of this Section.

Added by Acts 1982, No. 803, § 1. Amended by Acts 1984, No. 331, § 10, eff. July 2, 1984; Acts 1988, No. 401, § 1.

[1] C.C.P. art. 1031 et seq.

Cross References

C.C. arts. 2316, 3071.

CODE TITLE XVIII—OF RESPITE [BLANK]
CODE TITLE XIX—OF ALTERNATIVE DISPUTE RESOLUTION

CHAPTER 1. LOUISIANA MEDIATION ACT

Section
4101. Short title; purpose; definitions.
4102. Discussion of mediation with clients.
4103. Referral of a case for mediation; exceptions.
4104. Selection of mediator.
4105. Approved register of mediators.
4106. Qualifications of mediators.
4107. Standard of conduct; disclosure.
4108. Required attendance and participation in mediation.
4109. Cost of mediation.
4110. Nonbinding effect.
4111. Written settlement agreements.
4112. Confidentiality.

§ 4101. Short title; purpose; definitions

A. This Chapter shall be known and may be referred to as the "Louisiana Mediation Act".

B. The purpose of this Chapter is to provide encouragement and support for the use of mediation to promote settlement of legal disputes.

C. For purposes of this Chapter:

(1) "ADR Section" means the Louisiana State Bar Association, Alternative Dispute Resolution Section.

(2) "Approved register" means the register of qualified mediators prepared and maintained by the ADR Section.

(3) "Cost of mediation" includes the mediator's fee, administrative fees, and expenses.

(4) "Mediation" is a procedure in which a mediator facilitates communication between the parties concerning the matters in dispute and explores possible solutions to promote reconciliation, understanding, and settlement.

(5) "MCLE Committee" means the Louisiana State Bar Association, Mandatory Continuing Legal Education Committee.

Added by Acts 1997, No. 1451, § 1.

Editor's note. Acts 1997, No. 1451, § 5 declares: "The provisions of this Act shall apply to all civil cases pending on, and all civil cases filed on or after, January 1, 1998. However, the Pilot Mediation Program in Orleans, originally created in accordance with House Concurrent Resolution No. 76 of 1992 and a resolution of the Louisiana Supreme Court dated September 3, 1992, shall continue uninterrupted in the Civil District Court for the Parish of Orleans and in the First City Court of the City of New Orleans until August 31, 1999 and all provisions of this Act which are inconsistent with the Resolution of the Louisiana Supreme Court, Rule 18 of the Civil District Court for the Parish of Orleans, or the rules of the First City Court of the City of New Orleans, as may be amended, are not applicable to such Pilot Mediation Program. The Louisiana State Bar Association, Alternative Dispute Resolution Section shall study the Pilot Mediation Program and issue its report to the Louisiana Legislature before the commencement of the 1999 Regular Legislative Session."

§ 4102. Discussion of mediation with clients

Counsel are encouraged to discuss with their clients the appropriateness of using mediation in any civil case pending in the courts.

Added by Acts 1997, No. 1451, § 1.

Editor's note. Acts 1997, No. 1451, § 5 declares: "The provisions of this Act shall apply to all civil cases pending on, and all civil cases filed on or after, January 1, 1998. However, the Pilot Mediation Program in Orleans, originally created in accordance with House Concurrent Resolution No. 76 of 1992 and a resolution of the Louisiana Supreme Court dated September 3, 1992, shall continue uninterrupted in the Civil District Court for the Parish of Orleans and in the First City Court of the City of New Orleans until August 31, 1999 and all provisions of this Act which are inconsistent with the Resolution of the Louisiana Supreme Court, Rule 18 of the Civil District Court for the Parish of Orleans, or the rules of the First City Court of the City of New Orleans, as may be amended, are not applicable to such Pilot Mediation Program. The Louisiana State Bar Association, Alternative Dispute Resolution Section shall study the Pilot Mediation Program and issue its report to the Louisiana Legislature before the commencement of the 1999 Regular Legislative Session."

§ 4103. Referral of a case for mediation; exceptions

A. On motion of any party, a court may order the referral of a civil case for mediation. Upon filing of an objection to mediation by any party within fifteen days after receiving notice of the order, the mediation order shall be rescinded.

B. The following types of proceedings shall not be referred to mediation pursuant to this Chapter:

(1) Actions brought pursuant to the Post Separation Family Violence Relief Act, R.S. 9:361 et seq., or the Domestic Abuse Assistance Act, R.S. 46:2131 et seq.

(2) Actions for child custody or visitation, which are subject to mediation pursuant to the provisions of R.S. 9:332 et seq.

(3) Actions governed by the Code of Criminal Procedure or the Children's Code.

Added by Acts 1997, No. 1451, § 1. Amended by Acts 1999, No. 952, § 1.

Editor's note. Acts 1997, No. 1451, § 5 declares: "The provisions of this Act shall apply to all civil cases pending on, and all civil cases filed on or after, January 1, 1998. However, the Pilot Mediation Program in Orleans, originally created in accordance with House Concurrent Resolution No. 76 of 1992 and a resolution of the Louisiana Supreme Court dated September 3, 1992, shall continue uninterrupted in the Civil District Court for the Parish of Orleans and in the First City Court of the City of New Orleans until August 31, 1999 and all provisions of this Act which are inconsistent with the Resolution of the Louisiana Supreme Court, Rule 18 of the Civil District Court for the Parish of Orleans, or the rules of the First City Court of the City of New Orleans, as may be amended, are not applicable to such Pilot Mediation Program. The Louisiana State Bar Association, Alternative Dispute Resolution Section shall study the Pilot Mediation Program and issue its report to the Louisiana Legislature before the commencement of the 1999 Regular Legislative Session."

§ 4104. Selection of mediator

A. Once an order referring a case for mediation has been signed, the parties are encouraged to mutually agree upon a person to be appointed as the mediator. Upon submission of the chosen person's name to the court, the court shall issue an order making such appointment.

B. If the parties do not agree on a mediator within fifteen days after the signing of the referral order, each party shall submit to the opposing party or parties a list of four names of mediators from the approved register, and each party may strike any names on this list. The parties shall then submit the lists to the court. If any names remain after the parties have exercised their strikes, the court shall appoint a mediator from the names not struck. If all names are stricken, the court shall appoint a mediator from the approved register, excluding any person whose name was previously stricken by any party.

C. After an order referring a case for mediation has been signed in a complicated or complex case, a court may appoint as mediator a person who has professional training or experience in the subject matter of the dispute and in dispute resolution procedures.

D. A person appointed pursuant to Subsection A or C hereof need not be listed on the approved register of mediators nor possess the qualifications of a mediator, as required pursuant to R.S. 9:4105 and 4106, respectively, and for purposes of this Chapter, is considered a "mediator" during the tenure of his appointment.

Added by Acts 1997, No. 1451, § 1.

Editor's note. Acts 1997, No. 1451, § 5 declares: "The provisions of this Act shall apply to all civil cases pending on, and all civil cases filed on or after, January 1, 1998. However, the Pilot Mediation Program in Orleans, originally created in accordance with House Concurrent Resolution No. 76 of 1992 and a resolution of the Louisiana Supreme Court dated September 3, 1992, shall continue uninterrupted in the Civil District Court for the Parish of Orleans and in the First City Court of the City of New Orleans until August 31, 1999 and all provisions of this Act which are inconsistent with the Resolution of the Louisiana Supreme Court, Rule 18 of the Civil District Court for the Parish of Orleans, or the rules of the First City Court of the City of New Orleans, as may be amended, are not applicable to such Pilot Mediation Program. The Louisiana State Bar Association, Alternative Dispute Resolution Section shall study the Pilot Mediation Program and issue its report to the Louisiana Legislature before the commencement of the 1999 Regular Legislative Session."

§ 4105. Approved register of mediators

A. The ADR Section shall prepare and maintain a register of those persons qualified under criteria established pursuant to R.S. 9:4106. A mediator denied listing in the approved register may request a review of that decision by a panel of three members of the ADR Section.

B. The ADR Section shall make available to participating courts and parties the approved register of mediators and a summary of their professional qualifications.

C. The ADR Section may assess such reasonable fees as are necessary to perform the functions associated with administering the provisions of this Chapter and creating and maintaining the approved register of qualified mediators.

Added by Acts 1997, No. 1451, § 1.

Editor's note. Acts 1997, No. 1451, § 5 declares: "The provisions of this Act shall apply to all civil cases pending on, and all civil cases filed on or after, January 1, 1998. However, the Pilot Mediation Program in Orleans, originally created in accordance with House Concurrent Resolution No. 76 of 1992 and a resolution of the Louisiana Supreme Court dated September 3, 1992, shall continue uninterrupted in the Civil District Court for the Parish of Orleans and in the First City Court of the City of New Orleans until August 31, 1999 and all provisions of this Act which are inconsistent with the Resolution of the Louisiana Supreme Court, Rule 18 of the Civil District Court for the Parish of Orleans, or the rules of the First City Court of the City of New Orleans, as may be amended, are not applicable to such Pilot Mediation Program. The Louisiana State Bar Association, Alternative Dispute Resolution Section shall study the Pilot Mediation Program and issue its report to the Louisiana Legislature before the commencement of the 1999 Regular Legislative Session."

§ 4106. Qualifications of mediators

A. To qualify for appointment as a mediator under this Chapter:

(1)(a) A person must have completed a minimum of forty classroom hours of training in mediation in a course conducted by an individual or organization approved by the MCLE Committee or the ADR Section and must be licensed to practice law in any state for not less than five years. Any previous mediation training approved by the MCLE Committee can be used to satisfy the requirements of this Section; or

(b) A person, whether or not licensed to practice law, must have completed a minimum of forty classroom hours of training in mediation in a course conducted by an organization or individual approved by the MCLE Committee or the ADR Section, and must have mediated more than twenty-five disputes or must have engaged in more than five hundred hours of dispute resolutions. The ADR Section shall determine the proper method by which to certify the requirements hereof.

(2) A person must have served as a Louisiana district, appellate, or supreme court judge for at least ten years and no longer be serving as a judge.

B. In order to maintain a listing in the approved register of qualified mediators, a mediator must be willing to accept two annual pro bono appointments and participate in ten hours of training in alternative dispute resolutions in a continuing education course approved by the MCLE Committee or the ADR Section every two years.

Added by Acts 1997, No. 1451, § 1. Amended by Acts 1999, No. 713, § 1, eff. July 1, 1999; Acts 1999, No. 997, § 1.

Editor's note. Acts 1997, No. 1451, § 5 declares: "The provisions of this Act shall apply to all civil cases pending on, and all civil cases filed on or after, January 1, 1998. However, the Pilot Mediation Program in Orleans, originally created in accordance with House Concurrent Resolution No. 76 of 1992 and a resolution of the Louisiana Supreme Court dated September 3, 1992, shall continue uninterrupted in the Civil District Court for the Parish of Orleans and in the First City Court of the City of New Orleans until August 31, 1999 and all provisions of this Act which are inconsistent with the Resolution of the Louisiana Supreme Court, Rule 18 of the Civil District Court for the Parish of Orleans, or the rules of the First City Court of the City of New Orleans, as may be amended, are not applicable to such Pilot Mediation Program. The Louisiana State Bar Association, Alternative Dispute Resolution Section shall study the Pilot Mediation Program and issue its report to the Louisiana Legislature before the commencement of the 1999 Regular Legislative Session."

§ 4107. Standard of conduct; disclosure

A. The Standards of Conduct for Mediators adopted by the American Arbitration Association, the American Bar Association, and the Society of Professionals in Dispute Resolution shall apply to the professional conduct of mediators appointed under this Chapter unless the ADR Section adopts an alternative code of conduct.

B. Upon receiving notice of appointment as a mediator in a particular proceeding, the mediator shall make available to all parties a list of his professional qualifications, curriculum vitae, and fee schedule and disclose to the parties all past or present conflicts or relationships with the parties or their counsel.

Added by Acts 1997, No. 1451, § 1.

Editor's note. Acts 1997, No. 1451, § 5 declares: "The provisions of this Act shall apply to all civil cases pending on, and all civil cases filed on or after, January 1, 1998. However, the Pilot Mediation Program in Orleans, originally created in accordance with House Concurrent Resolution No. 76 of 1992 and a resolution of the Louisiana Supreme Court dated September 3, 1992, shall continue uninterrupted in the Civil District Court for the Parish of Orleans and in the First City Court of the City of New Orleans until August 31, 1999 and all provisions of this Act which are inconsistent with the Resolution of the Louisiana Supreme Court, Rule 18 of the Civil District Court for the Parish of Orleans, or the rules of the First City Court of the City of New Orleans, as may be amended, are not applicable to such Pilot Mediation Program. The Louisiana State Bar Association, Alternative Dispute Resolution Section shall study the Pilot Mediation Program and issue its report to the Louisiana Legislature before the commencement of the 1999 Regular Legislative Session."

§ 4108. Required attendance and participation in mediation

A. A court order referring a case to mediation may require any or all of the following:

(1) Attendance of parties, including those persons with authority to negotiate and enter into binding settlement agreements.

(2) Advance submission to other parties and the mediator of a position paper and relevant documents or information.

(3) Minimal meaningful participation by parties and their counsel during the procedure.

B. Mediation shall be completed within ninety days of notice of appointment of the mediator, unless extended by agreement of all parties.

Added by Acts 1997, No. 1451, § 1.

Editor's note. Acts 1997, No. 1451, § 5 declares: "The provisions of this Act shall apply to all civil cases pending on, and all civil cases filed on or after, January 1, 1998. However, the Pilot Mediation Program in Orleans, originally created in accordance with House Concurrent Resolution No. 76 of 1992 and a resolution of the Louisiana Supreme Court dated September 3, 1992, shall continue uninterrupted in the Civil District Court for the Parish of Orleans and in the First City Court of the City of New Orleans until August 31, 1999 and all provisions of this Act which are inconsistent with the Resolution of the Louisiana Supreme Court, Rule 18 of the Civil District Court for the Parish of Orleans, or the rules of the First City Court of the City of New Orleans, as may be amended, are not applicable to such Pilot Mediation Program. The Louisiana State Bar Association, Alternative Dispute Resolution Section shall study the Pilot Mediation Program and issue its report to the Louisiana Legislature before the commencement of the 1999 Regular Legislative Session."

§ 4109. Cost of mediation

A. The cost of mediation shall be agreed in writing by the parties and the mediator prior to commencement of mediation. If there is no agreement on such cost, the court shall rescind the appointment and the selection of a mediator shall commence anew.

B. (1) Unless otherwise ordered by the court in its referral order or unless the parties agree to some other allocation of cost:

(a) The cost of mediation shall be taxed as costs of court, to be shared equally by the parties.

(b) If the case is not settled by mediation, the costs of mediation shall be taxed as costs of court upon rendition of a final judgment.

(2) No later than the conclusion of the mediation, whether or not successful, the parties shall pay the cost of mediation, unless the parties and the mediator have agreed otherwise. The mediator may intervene in any pending civil case between the parties to the mediation to enforce payment of the cost of the mediation. An intervention to enforce payment of the cost of the mediation shall be disposed of as a summary proceeding.

C. Any court filings by the mediator appointed under this Chapter shall be accepted by the clerk of court without a filing fee.

Added by Acts 1997, No. 1451, § 1.

Editor's note. Acts 1997, No. 1451, § 5 declares: "The provisions of this Act shall apply to all civil cases pending on, and all civil cases filed on or after, January 1, 1998. However, the Pilot Mediation Program in Orleans, originally created in accordance with House Concurrent Resolution No. 76 of 1992 and a resolution of the Louisiana Supreme Court dated September 3, 1992, shall continue uninterrupted in the Civil District Court for the Parish of Orleans and in the First City Court of the City of New Orleans until August 31, 1999 and all provisions of this Act which are inconsistent with the Resolution of the Louisiana Supreme Court, Rule 18 of the Civil District Court for the Parish of Orleans, or the rules of the First City Court of the City of New Orleans, as may be amended, are not applicable to such Pilot Mediation Program. The Louisiana State Bar Association, Alternative Dispute Resolution Section shall study the Pilot Mediation Program and issue its report to the Louisiana Legislature before the commencement of the 1999 Regular Legislative Session."

§ 4110. Nonbinding effect

Mediation procedures are nonbinding unless all the parties specifically agree otherwise in writing.

Added by Acts 1997, No. 1451, § 1.

Editor's note. Acts 1997, No. 1451, § 5 declares: "The provisions of this Act shall apply to all civil cases pending on, and all civil cases filed on or after, January 1, 1998. However, the Pilot Mediation Program in Orleans, originally created in accordance with House Concurrent Resolution No. 76 of 1992 and a resolution of the Louisiana Supreme Court dated September 3, 1992, shall continue uninterrupted in the Civil District Court for the Parish of Orleans and in the First City Court of the City of New Orleans until August 31, 1999 and all provisions of this Act which are inconsistent with the Resolution of the Louisiana Supreme Court, Rule 18 of the Civil District Court for the Parish of Orleans, or the rules of the First City Court of the City of New Orleans, as may be amended, are not applicable to such Pilot Mediation Program. The Louisiana State Bar Association, Alternative Dispute Resolution Section shall study the Pilot Mediation Program and issue its report to the Louisiana Legislature before the commencement of the 1999 Regular Legislative Session."

§ 4111. Written settlement agreements

A. If, as a result of a mediation, the parties agree to settle and execute a written agreement disposing of the dispute, the agreement is enforceable as any other transaction or compromise and is governed by the provisions of Title XVII of Book III of the Civil Code, to the extent not in conflict with the provisions of this Chapter.

B. The court in its discretion may incorporate the terms of the agreement in the court's final decree disposing of the case.

Added by Acts 1997, No. 1451, § 1.

Editor's note. Acts 1997, No. 1451, § 5 declares: "The provisions of this Act shall apply to all civil cases pending on, and all civil cases filed on or after, January 1, 1998. However, the Pilot Mediation Program in Orleans, originally created in accordance with House Concurrent Resolution No. 76 of 1992 and a resolution of the Louisiana Supreme Court dated September 3, 1992, shall continue uninterrupted in the Civil District Court for the Parish of Orleans and in the First City Court of the City of New Orleans until August 31, 1999 and all provisions of this Act which are inconsistent with the Resolution of the Louisiana Supreme Court, Rule 18 of the Civil District Court for the Parish of Orleans, or the rules of the First City Court of the City of New Orleans, as may be amended, are not applicable to such Pilot Mediation Program. The Louisiana State Bar Association, Alternative Dispute Resolution Section shall study the Pilot Mediation Program and issue its report to the Louisiana Legislature before the commencement of the 1999 Regular Legislative Session."

§ 4112. Confidentiality

A. Except as provided in this Section, all oral and written communications and records made during mediation, whether or not conducted under this Chapter and whether before or after the institution of formal judicial proceedings, are not subject to disclosure, and may not be used as evidence in any judicial or administrative proceeding.

B. (1) The parties, counsel, and other participants therein shall not be required to testify concerning the mediation proceedings and are not subject to process or subpoena, issued in any judicial or administrative procedure, which requires the disclosure of any communications or records of the mediation, except with respect to the following:

(a) Reports made by the mediator to a court, pursuant to that court's order, only as to whether the parties appeared as ordered, whether the mediation took place, and whether a settlement resulted therein.

(b) In connection with a motion for sanctions made by a party to the mediation based on a claim of a party's noncompliance with the court's order to participate in the mediation proceedings; however, the disclosure of any communications and records made during the course of the mediation shall be strictly limited to the issue of noncompliance with the court's order.

(c) A judicial determination of the meaning or enforceability of an agreement resulting from a mediation procedure if the court determines that testimony concerning what occurred in the mediation proceeding is necessary to prevent fraud or manifest injustice.

(2) The mediator is not subject to subpoena and cannot be required to make disclosure through discovery or testimony at trial except in a judicial or administrative procedure with respect to Subparagraph B(1)(a) of this Section.

C. The confidentiality provisions of this Section do not extend to statements, materials and other tangible evidence, or communications that are otherwise subject to discovery or are otherwise admissible, merely because they were presented in the course of mediation, if they are based on proof independent of any communication or record made in mediation.

D. If this Section conflicts with other legal requirements for disclosure of communications or materials, the issue of confidentiality may be presented to the court having jurisdiction of the proceedings to determine, in camera, whether the facts, circumstances, and context of the communications or materials sought to be disclosed warrant a protective order or whether the communications or materials are subject to disclosure.

E. Confidentiality, in whole or in part, may be waived when all parties and the mediator specifically agree in writing.

Added by Acts 1997, No. 1451, § 1.

Editor's note. Acts 1997, No. 1451, § 5 declares: "The provisions of this Act shall apply to all civil cases pending on, and all civil cases filed on or after, January 1, 1998. However, the Pilot Mediation Program in Orleans, originally created in accordance with House Concurrent Resolution No. 76 of 1992 and a resolution of the Louisiana Supreme Court dated September 3, 1992, shall continue uninterrupted in the Civil District Court for the Parish of Orleans and in the First City Court of the City of New Orleans until August 31, 1999 and all provisions of this Act which are inconsistent with the Resolution of the Louisiana Supreme Court, Rule 18 of the Civil District Court for the Parish of Orleans, or the rules of the First City Court of the City of New Orleans, as may be amended, are not applicable to such Pilot Mediation Program. The Louisiana State Bar Association, Alternative Dispute Resolution Section shall study the Pilot Mediation Program and issue its report to the Louisiana Legislature before the commencement of the 1999 Regular Legislative Session."

CHAPTER 2. LOUISIANA BINDING ARBITRATION LAW

Section
4201. Validity of arbitration agreements.
4202. Stay of proceedings brought in violation of arbitration agreement.
4203. Remedy in case of default; petition and notice; hearing and proceedings.
4204. Appointment of arbitrators.
4205. Application heard as motion.
4206. Witnesses; summoning; compelling attendance; evidence.
4207. Depositions.
4208. Award.
4209. Motion to confirm award; jurisdiction; notice.
4210. Motion to vacate award; grounds; rehearing.
4211. Motion to modify or correct award; grounds.
4212. Judgment upon award.
4213. Notice of motions; when made; service; stay of proceedings.
4214. Record; filing; judgment; effect and enforcement.
4215. Appeals.
4216. Limitation of application of Chapter.
4217. Short title.

§ 4201. Validity of arbitration agreements

A provision in any written contract to settle by arbitration a controversy thereafter arising out of the contract, or out of the refusal to perform the whole or any part thereof, or an agreement in writing between two or more persons to submit to arbitration any controversy existing between them at the time of the agreement to submit, shall be valid, irrevocable, and enforceable, save upon such grounds as exist at law or in equity for the revocation of any contract.

Cross References

C.C. arts. 3099, 3100, 3102, 3104.

§ 4202. Stay of proceedings brought in violation of arbitration agreement

If any suit or proceedings be brought upon any issue referable to arbitration under an agreement in writing for arbitration, the court in which suit is pending, upon being satisfied that the issue involved in the suit or proceedings is referable to arbitration under such an agreement, shall on application of one of the parties stay the trial of the action until an arbitration has been had in accordance with the terms of the agreement, providing the applicant for the stay is not in default in proceeding with the arbitration.

Cross References

C.C. arts. 3099, 3102.

§ 4203. Remedy in case of default; petition and notice; hearing and proceedings

A. The party aggrieved by the alleged failure or refusal of another to perform under a written agreement for arbitration, may petition any court of record having jurisdiction of the parties, or of the property, for an order directing that the arbitration proceed in the manner provided for in the agreement. Five days' written notice of the application shall be served upon the party in default. Service shall be made in the manner provided by law for the service of a summons.

B. The court shall hear the parties, and upon being satisfied that the making of the agreement for arbitration or the failure to comply therewith is not an issue, the court shall issue an order directing the parties to proceed to arbitration in accordance with the terms of the agreement. If the making of the arbitration agreement or the failure or refusal to perform is an issue, the court shall proceed summarily to the trial thereof.

C. If no jury trial is demanded, the court shall hear and determine the issue. Where such an issue is raised, either party may, on or before the return day of the notice of application, demand a jury trial of the issue, and upon such demand the court shall issue an order referring the issue or issues to a jury called and empanelled in the manner provided by law.

D. If the jury finds that no agreement in writing for arbitration was made or that there is no default in proceeding thereunder, the proceeding shall be dismissed. If the jury finds that an agreement for arbitration was made in writing and that there is a default in proceeding thereunder, the court shall issue an order summarily directing the parties to proceed with the arbitration in accordance with the terms thereof.

E. Failure to pay within ten business days any deposit, fee, or expense required under the arbitration process shall constitute default in the arbitration proceeding. A party aggrieved by the default shall be entitled to remove the matter under arbitration in its entirety to a court of competent jurisdiction and shall be entitled to attorney fees and costs in addition to other remedies as provided in this Section.

Amended by Acts 2010, No. 545, § 1.

Cross References

C.C. arts. 3099, 3102.

§ 4204. Appointment of arbitrators

If, in the agreement, provision is made for a method of naming or appointing an arbitrator or arbitrators or an umpire, this method shall be followed. If no method is provided or if a method is provided and a party thereto fails to avail himself of the method or if for any other reason there shall be a lapse in the naming of an arbitrator or arbitrators or an umpire, or in filling a vacancy, then, upon the application of either party to the controversy, the court aforesaid or the court in and for the parish in which the arbitration is to be held shall designate and appoint an arbitrator or arbitrators or umpire, as the case may require, who shall act under the agreement with the same force and effect as if he or they had been specifically named therein. Unless otherwise provided in the agreement, the arbitration shall be by a single arbitrator.

Cross References

C.C. arts. 3099, 3118.

§ 4205. Application heard as motion

Any application to the court under this Chapter shall be made and heard in the manner provided by law for the making and hearing of motions, except as otherwise herein expressly provided.

Cross References

C.C. art. 3099.

§ 4206. Witnesses; summoning; compelling attendance; evidence

A. When more than one arbitrator is agreed to, all the arbitrators shall sit at the hearing of the case unless, by consent in writing, all parties agree to proceed with the hearing with a less number. The arbitrators, selected either as prescribed in this Chapter or otherwise, or a majority of them, may, at the request of a party or independently, summon in writing any person to attend before them or any of them as a witness and in a proper case to bring with him or them any book, record, document, or paper which may be deemed material as evidence in the case. The fees for attendance shall be the same as the fees of witnesses in courts of general jurisdiction.

B. The summons shall issue in the name of the arbitrator or arbitrators, or a majority of them, and shall be signed by the arbitrator, arbitrators, or a majority of them, and shall be directed to the person and shall be served in the same manner as subpoenas to appear and testify before the court. If any person or persons summoned to testify refuses or neglects to obey the summons, upon petition, the court in and for the parish in which the arbitrators are sitting may compel the attendance or punish the person or persons for contempt in the same manner provided by law for securing the attendance of witnesses or their punishment for neglect or refusal to attend in the courts of this state.

C. (1) The parties to the arbitration may offer evidence as is relevant and material to the dispute and shall produce evidence as the arbitrator may deem necessary to an understanding and determination of the dispute. Strict conformity to the Code of Evidence shall not be required, except for laws pertaining to testimonial privileges.

(2) The arbitrator shall determine the admissibility, relevance, and materiality of the evidence offered, including the admissibility of expert evidence, and may exclude evidence deemed by the arbitrator to be cumulative or irrelevant.

Amended by Acts 2010, No. 545, § 1.

Editor's note. Section 2 of Acts 2010, No. 545, declares that: "The provisions of this Act shall not apply to any cause of action or claim in existence on or prior to the effective date of this Act."

Cross References

C.C. arts. 3099, 3115, 3126, 3172.

§ 4207. Depositions

Upon petition, approved by the arbitrators or by a majority of them, any court of record in and for the parish in which the arbitrators are sitting may direct the taking of depositions to be used as evidence before the arbitrators, in the same manner and for the same reasons provided by law for the taking of depositions in suits or proceedings pending in the courts of record in this state.

Cross References

C.C. arts. 3099, 3115.

§ 4208. Award

The award shall be in writing and shall be signed by the arbitrators or by a majority of them.

Cross References

C.C. arts. 3099, 3123, 3126.

§ 4209. Motion to confirm award; jurisdiction; notice

At any time within one year after the award is made any party to the arbitration may apply to the court in and for the parish within which the award was made for an order confirming the award and thereupon the court shall grant such an order unless the award is vacated, modified, or corrected as prescribed in R.S. 9:4210 and 9:4211. Notice in writing of the application shall be served upon the adverse party or his attorney five days before the hearing thereof.

C.C. arts. 3099, 3129.

§ 4210. Motion to vacate award; grounds; rehearing

In any of the following cases the court in and for the parish wherein the award was made shall issue an order vacating the award upon the application of any party to the arbitration.

A. Where the award was procured by corruption, fraud, or undue means.

B. Where there was evident partiality or corruption on the part of the arbitrators or any of them.

C. Where the arbitrators were guilty of misconduct in refusing to postpone the hearing, upon sufficient cause shown, or in refusing to hear evidence pertinent and material to the controversy, or of any other misbehavior by which the rights of any party have been prejudiced.

D. Where the arbitrators exceeded their powers or so imperfectly executed them that a mutual, final, and definite award upon the subject matter submitted was not made.

Where an award is vacated and the time within which the agreement required the award to be made has not expired, the court may, in its discretion, direct a rehearing by the arbitrators.

Cross References

C.C. arts. 3099, 3129, 3130.

§ 4211. Motion to modify or correct award; grounds

In any of the following cases the court in and for the parish wherein the award was made shall issue an order modifying or correcting the award upon the application of any party to the arbitration.

A. Where there was an evident material miscalculation of figures or an evident material mistake in the description of any person, thing, or property referred to in the award.

B. Where the arbitrators have awarded upon a matter not submitted to them unless it is a matter not affecting the merits of the decision upon the matters submitted.

C. Where the award is imperfect in matter of form not affecting the merits of the controversy.

The order shall modify and correct the award so as to effect the intent thereof and promote justice between the parties.

Cross References

C.C. arts. 3099, 3129, 3130.

§ 4212. Judgment upon award

Upon the granting of an order confirming, modifying, or correcting an award, judgment may be entered in conformity therewith in the court wherein the order was granted.

Cross References

C.C. arts. 3099, 3129, 3130.

§ 4213. Notice of motions; when made; service; stay of proceedings

Notice of a motion to vacate, modify, or correct an award shall be served upon the adverse party or his attorney within three months after the award is filed or delivered, as prescribed by law for service of a motion in an action. For the purposes of the motion any judge, who might issue an order to stay the proceedings in an action brought in the same court may issue an order, to be served with the notice of motion, staying the proceedings of the adverse party to enforce the award.

Cross References

C.C. arts. 3099, 3129.

§ 4214. Record; filing; judgment; effect and enforcement

Any party to a proceeding for an order confirming, modifying, or correcting an award shall, at the time the order is filed with the clerk for the entry of judgment thereon, also file the following papers with the clerk:

(1) The agreement, the selection or appointment, if any, of an additional arbitrator or umpire, and each written extension of the time, if any, within which to make the award.

(2) The award.

(3) Each notice, affidavit, or other paper used upon an application to confirm, modify, or correct the award, and a copy of each order of the court upon such an application.

The judgment shall be docketed as if it were rendered in an action.

The judgment so entered shall have the same force and effect, in all respects, as, and be subject to all the provisions of law relating to, a judgment in an action, and it may be enforced as if it had been rendered in an action in the court in which it is entered.

Cross References

C.C. arts. 3099, 3129.

§ 4215. Appeals

An appeal may be taken from an order confirming, modifying, correcting, or vacating an award, or from a judgment entered upon an award, as from an order or judgment in an action.

Cross References

C.C. arts. 3099, 3129, 3130.

§ 4216. Limitation of application of Chapter

Nothing contained in this Chapter shall apply to contracts of employment of labor or to contracts for arbitration which are controlled by valid legislation of the United States or to contracts made prior to July 28, 1948.

Cross References

C.C. art. 3099.

§ 4217. Short title

This Chapter may be referred to as the "Louisiana Arbitration Law."

CHAPTER 3. ARBITRATION OF MEDICAL AND DENTAL SERVICES OR SUPPLIES CONTRACTS

Section
4230. Definitions.
4231. Voluntary arbitration; medical or dental practitioner and patient.
4232. Voluntary arbitration; patient and medical institution.
4233. Selection of arbitrators; qualifications; restrictions.
4234. Arbitration procedure; controversies involving medical contracts and dental contracts.
4235. Notification to patient.
4236. Expiration of contract.

§ 4230. Definitions

As used in this Chapter, the terms listed below shall mean the following:

(1) "Medical practitioner" means anyone issued a permit or licensed to practice under the provisions of Chapters 11, 13, or 15 of Title 37,[1] when engaged in such practice, and shall include professional medical corporations and partnerships, pharmacists, optometrists, podiatrists, chiropractors, physical therapists, and psychologists.

(2) "Dental practitioner" means anyone issued a permit or licensed to practice under the provisions of Chapter 9 of Title 37,[2] when engaged in such practice, and shall include professional dental corporations and partnerships.

(3) "Medical institution" means any hospital as defined in R.S. 40:2102; any nursing home or home as defined in R.S. 40:2009.2; or any physician's or dentist's offices or clinics containing facilities for the examination, diagnosis, treatment, or care of human illnesses.

(4) "Medical contract" means a) with respect to employment for services entered into by a patient and a medical practitioner, any written agreement, a sample of which is provided in R.S. 9:4231 below b) with respect to agreement between a medical institution and a patient, any contract of employment for services (including all equipment, supplies or personnel employed in connection therewith) described or regulated by Chapters 11, 13, and 15 of Title 37 [1] or Chapter 11 of Title 40,[3] whether entered into directly or indirectly by the patient, on the one hand, and the medical institution, on the other hand.

(5) "Dental contract" means any employment for services including all equipment, supplies or personnel employed in connection therewith described or regulated by Chapter 9 of Title 37,[2] whether entered into directly or indirectly by the patient, on the one hand, and the dental practitioner or medical institution, on the other hand.

(6) "Professional corporation" means any professional medical corporation created under the provisions of R.S. 12:901, any professional dental corporation created under the provisions of R.S. 12:981.

Added by Acts 1975, No. 371, § 1.

[1] R.S. 37:911 et seq., 37:1101 et seq., and 13:1261 et seq.
[2] R.S. 37:751 et seq.
[3] R.S. 40:2001 et seq.

Cross References

C.C. arts. 3099, 3104, 3107, 3118, 3129.

§ 4231. Voluntary arbitration; medical or dental practitioner and patient

The decisions to enter into a medical or dental contract shall be voluntary on the part of the patient, and on the part of the medical or dental practitioner. If both parties voluntarily agree to enter such a contract, the following but not necessary or exclusive provisions of such contract shall be valid, irrevocable, and enforceable, save upon such grounds as exist at law or in equity for the revocation of any contract. The following contract is merely a sample and the provisions therein are not required as a matter of law to be included in arbitration agreements under this Chapter.

ARBITRATION AGREEMENT

_____, hereinafter called "Patient", engages _____, hereinafter called "Medical or Dental Practitioner", to render medical care and service. For and in partial consideration of the rendition of any and all present and future medical care and service, the patient agrees that in the event of any controversy arising out of claims based on negligence or medical malpractice, between patient, whether a minor or an adult, or the heirs at law or personal representatives of a patient, as the case may be, and medical or dental practitioner, including his agents or employees, the same shall be submitted to arbitration. Within fifteen days after any of the above named parties shall give notice to the other of demand for arbitration of said controversy, the parties to the controversy shall each appoint an arbitrator and give notice of such appointment to the other. Within fifteen days after such notices have been given, the two arbitrators so selected shall select a neutral arbitrator who is an attorney, licensed to practice in the state of Louisiana, and give notice of the selection thereof to the parties. The arbitrators shall hold a hearing within ninety days of the date of notice of selection of the neutral arbitrator. All notices or other papers required to be served shall be served by certified United States mail. Except as herein provided, the arbitration shall be conducted and governed by the provisions of the Louisiana Arbitration Law, R.S. 9:4201 et seq. The taking of testimony and presentation of evidence at the arbitration hearing shall be governed by the general rules of evidence applied in the courts of Louisiana.

This agreement shall become effective on the _____ day of _____ 19___, and expire five years thereafter. Nevertheless, any dispute arising from an act or omission occurring during the term of this contract shall be resolved in accordance with this contract regardless of when the dispute arises. This agreement applies to the rendition of all present and future medical or dental care and service by medical or dental practitioner within the term of this contract.

___, 19___ By_____
                Medical or Dental Practitioner
___, 19___ By_____
                Patient
         By_____
         Parent or Guardian if patient is a Minor

Added by Acts 1975, No. 371, § 1.

Cross References

C.C. arts. 3099, 3104, 3107, 3118, 3129.

§ 4232. Voluntary arbitration; patient and medical institution

A provision in any medical contract between a patient and medical institution, under which the parties agree to settle by arbitration a controversy thereafter arising out of the contract, or out of the refusal to perform the whole or any part thereof, or a provision to submit to arbitration any controversy existing between them at the time of the agreement to submit, shall be valid, irrevocable, and enforceable, save upon such grounds as exist at law or in equity for the revocation of any contract, and except as herein provided.

Added by Acts 1975, No. 371, § 1.

Cross References

C.C. arts. 3099, 3104, 3107, 3118, 3129.

§ 4233. Selection of arbitrators; qualifications; restrictions

If an arbitration contract contains a provision which permits a physician, dentist, or medical institution to appoint one or more arbitrators, then the contract shall also provide that the patient shall have the right to appoint an equal number of arbitrators. There shall be no restriction in the arbitration agreement as to whom the patient can appoint as an arbitrator and specifically the arbitration agreement shall not require the patient to appoint a physician or dentist as members of the arbitration panel. If the agreement provided for the appointment of one or more neutral arbitrators by arbitrators chosen by the parties and said arbitrators cannot agree on the neutral arbitrators, then the neutral arbitrators shall be appointed by the court in accordance with the provisions of R.S. 9:4204.

Any agreement under this Chapter is voidable by either party or parties within thirty days from the date of execution of said contract, provided, however, that if an act or acts of negligence and/or medical malpractice is committed by the medical or dental practitioner or medical institution prior to the revocation date, the contract shall be binding as to that act.

Added by Acts 1975, No. 371, § 1.

Cross References

C.C. arts. 3099, 3104, 3107, 3118, 3129.

§ 4234. Arbitration procedure; controversies involving medical contracts and dental contracts

Proceedings in arbitration of controversies involving medical contracts and dental contracts shall be governed by the provisions of the Louisiana Arbitration Law, R.S. 9:4201 et seq.

Added by Acts 1975, No. 371, § 1.

Cross References

C.C. arts. 3099, 3104, 3107, 3118, 3129.

§ 4235. Notification to patient

Prior to obtaining a patient's signature on an arbitration agreement, the medical or dental practitioner or medical institution shall inform the patient in writing that:

(1) the patient has the right to void the agreement within thirty days of execution thereof, and that

(2) if an act or acts of negligence and/or medical malpractice is committed prior to the revocation date the arbitration agreement shall be binding with respect to said act or acts, and that

(3) notification of revocation of the said arbitration agreement must be in writing and mailed by certified mail, return receipt requested.

Added by Acts 1975, No. 371, § 1.

Cross References

C.C. arts. 3099, 3104, 3107, 3118, 3129.

§ 4236. Expiration of contract

A medical or dental contract provided in this Chapter shall expire no later than five years from the date of inception. Nevertheless any dispute arising from an act or omission occurring during the term of this contract shall be resolved in accordance with the contract regardless of when the dispute arises. This contract shall neither extend or reduce the prescriptive period provided by law.

Added by Acts 1975, No. 371, § 1.

Cross References

C.C. arts. 3099, 3104, 3107, 3118, 3129.

CHAPTER 4. INTERNATIONAL COMMERCIAL ARBITRATION ACT

Section
4241. Scope of application.
4242. Definitions and rules of interpretation.
4243. Receipt of written communications.
4244. Waiver of right to object.
4245. Extent of court intervention.
4246. Court; functions of arbitration assistance and supervision.
4247. Definition and form of arbitration agreement.
4248. Arbitration agreement and substantive claim before court.
4249. Arbitration agreement and interim measures by court.
4250. Number of arbitrators.
4251. Appointment of arbitrators.
4252. Grounds for challenge.
4253. Challenge procedure.
4254. Failure or impossibility to act.
4255. Appointment of substitute arbitrator.
4256. Competence of arbitral tribunal to rule on its jurisdiction.
4257. Power of arbitral tribunal to order interim measures.
4258. Equal treatment of parties.
4259. Determination of rules of procedure.
4260. Place of arbitration.
4261. Commencement of arbitral proceedings.
4262. Language.
4263. Statements of claim and defense.
4264. Hearings and written proceedings.
4265. Default of a party.
4266. Expert appointed by arbitral tribunal.
4267. Court assistance in taking evidence.
4268. Rules applicable to substance of dispute.
4269. Decisionmaking by panel of arbitrators.
4270. Settlement.
4271. Form and contents of award.
4272. Termination of proceedings.
4273. Correction and interpretation of award; additional award.
4274. Application for setting aside as exclusive recourse against arbitral award.
4275. Recognition and enforcement.
4276. Grounds for refusing recognition or enforcement.

§ 4241. Scope of application

A. This Chapter applies to international commercial arbitration, subject to any agreement in force between the United States and any other country or countries.

B. The provisions of this Chapter, except R.S. 9:4248, 4249, 4275, and 4276, apply only if the place of arbitration is in the territory of this state.

C. An arbitration is international if:

(1) The parties to an arbitration agreement have, at the time of the conclusion of that agreement, their places of business in different countries; or

(2) One of the following places is situated outside the country in which the parties have their places of business:

(a) The place of arbitration if determined in, or pursuant to, the arbitration agreement;

(b) Any place where a substantial part of the obligations of the commercial relationship is to be performed or the place with which the subject matter of the dispute is most closely connected; or

(3) The parties have expressly agreed that the subject matter of the arbitration agreement relates to more than one country.

D. For the purposes of Subsection C of this Section:

(1) If a party has more than one place of business, the place of business is that which has the closest relationship to the arbitration agreement.

(2) If a party does not have a place of business, reference is to be made to his habitual residence.

E. This Chapter shall not affect any other law of this state by virtue of which certain disputes may not be submitted to arbitration or may be submitted to arbitration only according to provisions other than those of this Chapter.

Added by Acts 2006, No. 795, § 1.

§ 4242. Definitions and rules of interpretation

A. For the purposes of this Chapter:

(1) "Arbitration" means any arbitration whether or not administered by a permanent arbitral institution.

(2) "Arbitral tribunal" means a sole arbitrator or a panel of arbitrators.

(3) "Court" means a body or organ of the judicial system of a country.

B. When a provision of this Chapter, except R.S. 9:4268, leaves the parties free to determine a certain issue, that freedom includes the right of the parties to authorize a third party, including an institution, to make that determination.

C. When a provision of this Chapter refers to the fact that the parties have agreed or that they may agree or in any other way refers to an agreement of the parties, the agreement includes any arbitration rules referenced in that agreement.

D. When a provision of this Chapter, other than R.S. 9:4265(A) and 4272(B)(1), refers to a claim, it also applies to a counterclaim, and when it refers to a defense, it also applies to a defense to a counterclaim.

Added by Acts 2006, No. 795, § 1.

§ 4243. Receipt of written communications

A. Unless otherwise agreed by the parties:

(1) Any written communication is deemed to have been received if it is delivered to the addressee personally or if it is delivered at his place of business, habitual residence, or mailing address. If none of these locations can be found after making a reasonable inquiry, a written communication is deemed to have been received if it is sent to the addressee's last known place of business, habitual residence, or mailing address by registered letter or any other means which provides a record of the attempt to deliver it.

(2) Any written communication is deemed to have been received on the day it is delivered.

B. The provisions of this Section do not apply to communications in court proceedings.

Added by Acts 2006, No. 795, § 1.

§ 4244. Waiver of right to object

A party who knows that any provision of this Chapter from which the parties may derogate or any requirement under the arbitration agreement has not been complied with and yet proceeds with the arbitration without stating his objection to the noncompliance without undue delay or, if a time limit is provided therefor, within the period of time, shall be deemed to have waived his right to object.

Added by Acts 2006, No. 795, § 1.

§ 4245. Extent of court intervention

In matters governed by this Chapter, no court shall intervene except when provided for in this Chapter.

Added by Acts 2006, No. 795, § 1.

§ 4246. Court; functions of arbitration assistance and supervision

The procedures provided in R.S. 9:4251(C) and (D), 4253(C), 4254, 4256(C), and 4274(B) shall be performed by a state or federal district court in this state with jurisdiction over civil actions in which the arbitral tribunal sits.

Added by Acts 2006, No. 795, § 1.

§ 4247. Definition and form of arbitration agreement

A. An arbitration agreement is an agreement by the parties to submit to arbitration all or certain disputes which have arisen or which may arise between them in respect of a defined legal relationship, whether contractual or not. An arbitration agreement may be in the form of an arbitration clause in a contract or in the form of a separate agreement.

B. The arbitration agreement shall be in writing. An agreement is in writing if it is contained in a document signed by the parties or in an exchange of letters, telex, telegrams, or other means of telecommunication which provide a record of the agreement, or in an exchange of statements of claim and defense in which the existence of an agreement is alleged by one party and not denied by another. The reference in a contract to a document containing an arbitration clause constitutes an arbitration agreement provided that the contract is in writing and the reference makes that clause part of the contract.

Added by Acts 2006, No. 795, § 1.

§ 4248. Arbitration agreement and substantive claim before court

A. A court before which an action is brought in a matter which is the subject of an arbitration agreement shall, if a party so requests not later than when submitting his first statement on the substance of the dispute, refer the parties to arbitration unless it finds that the agreement is null and void, inoperative, or incapable of being performed.

B. When an action referred to in Subsection A of this Section has been brought, arbitral proceedings may nevertheless be commenced or continued, and an award may be made while the issue is pending before the court.

Added by Acts 2006, No. 795, § 1.

§ 4249. Arbitration agreement and interim measures by court

It is not incompatible with an arbitration agreement for a party to request, before or during arbitral proceedings, from a court an interim measure of protection and for a court to grant the measure.

Added by Acts 2006, No. 795, § 1.

§ 4250. Number of arbitrators

The parties are free to determine the number of arbitrators. However, if they do not make a determination, the number of arbitrators shall be three.

Added by Acts 2006, No. 795, § 1.

§ 4251. Appointment of arbitrators

A. No person shall be precluded by reason of his nationality from acting as an arbitrator, unless otherwise agreed by the parties.

B. The parties are free to agree on a procedure of appointing the arbitrator or arbitrators, subject to the provisions of Subsections D and E of this Section.

C. Failing an agreement:

(1) In an arbitration with three arbitrators, each party shall appoint one arbitrator, and the two arbitrators thus appointed shall appoint the third arbitrator; if a party fails to appoint the arbitrator within thirty days of receipt of a request to do so from the other party, or if the two arbitrators fail to agree on the third arbitrator within thirty days of their appointment, the appointment shall be made, upon request of a party, by the court.

(2) In an arbitration with a sole arbitrator, if the parties are unable to agree on the arbitrator, he shall be appointed, upon request of a party, by the court.

D. When, under an appointment procedure agreed upon by the parties:

(1) A party fails to act as required; or

(2) The parties, or two arbitrators, are unable to reach an agreement expected of them; or

(3) A third party, including an institution, fails to perform any function entrusted to it, any party may request the court to take the necessary measure, unless the agreement on the appointment procedure provides other means for securing the appointment.

E. A decision on a matter entrusted to the court by Subsections C and D of this Section shall be subject to no appeal. The court, in appointing an arbitrator, shall have due regard to any qualifications required of the arbitrator by the agreement of the parties and to the considerations as are likely to secure the appointment of an independent and impartial arbitrator and, in the case of a sole or third arbitrator, shall take into account as well the advisability of appointing an arbitrator of a nationality other than those of the parties.

Added by Acts 2006, No. 795, § 1.

§ 4252. Grounds for challenge

A. When a person is approached in connection with his possible appointment as an arbitrator, he shall disclose any circumstances likely to give rise to justifiable doubts as to his impartiality or independence. An arbitrator, from the time of his appointment and throughout the arbitral proceedings, shall without delay disclose any circumstances to the parties unless they have already been informed of them by him.

B. An arbitrator may be challenged only if circumstances exist that give rise to justifiable doubts as to his impartiality or independence or if he does not possess qualifications agreed to by the parties. A party may challenge an arbitrator appointed by him, or in whose appointment he has participated, only for reasons of which he becomes aware after the appointment has been made.

Added by Acts 2006, No. 795, § 1.

§ 4253. Challenge procedure

A. The parties are free to agree on a procedure for challenging an arbitrator, subject to the provisions of Subsection C of this Section.

B. Failing an agreement, a party who intends to challenge an arbitrator shall, within fifteen days after becoming aware of the constitution of the arbitral tribunal or after becoming aware of any circumstance provided in R.S. 9:4252(B), send a written statement of the reasons for the challenge to the arbitral tribunal. Unless the challenged arbitrator withdraws from his office or the other party agrees to the challenge, the arbitral tribunal shall decide on the challenge.

C. If a challenge under any procedure agreed upon by the parties or the procedure of Subsection B of this Section is not successful, the challenging party may request, within thirty days after having received notice of the decision rejecting the challenge, the court to decide on the challenge, which decision shall be subject to no appeal. While a request is pending, the arbitral tribunal, including the challenged arbitrator, may continue the arbitral proceedings and make an award.

Added by Acts 2006, No. 795, § 1.

§ 4254. Failure or impossibility to act

A. If an arbitrator becomes de jure or de facto unable to perform his functions or for other reasons fails to act without undue delay, his mandate terminates if he withdraws from his office or if the parties agree on the termination. Otherwise, if a controversy remains concerning any of these grounds, any party may request the court to decide on the termination of the mandate, which decision shall be subject to no appeal.

B. If, in accordance with this Section or R.S. 9:4253(B), an arbitrator withdraws from his office or a party agrees to the termination of the mandate of an arbitrator, this does not imply acceptance of the validity of any ground referred to in accordance with this Section or R.S. 9:4252(B).

Added by Acts 2006, No. 795, § 1.

§ 4255. Appointment of substitute arbitrator

When the mandate of an arbitrator terminates in accordance with R.S. 9:4253 or 4254 or because of his withdrawal from office for any other reason or because of the revocation of his mandate by agreement of the parties or in any other case of termination of his mandate, a substitute arbitrator shall be appointed according to the rules that were applicable to the appointment of the arbitrator being replaced.

Added by Acts 2006, No. 795, § 1.

§ 4256. Competence of arbitral tribunal to rule on its jurisdiction

A. The arbitral tribunal may rule on its own jurisdiction, including any objections with respect to the existence or validity of the arbitration agreement. For that purpose, an arbitration clause which forms part of a contract shall be treated as an agreement independent of the other terms of the contract. A decision by the arbitral tribunal that the contract is null and void shall not entail ipso jure the invalidity of the arbitration clause.

B. A plea that the arbitral tribunal does not have jurisdiction shall be raised not later than the submission of the statement of defense. A party is not precluded from raising a plea by the fact that he has appointed, or participated in the appointment of, an arbitrator. A plea that the arbitral tribunal is exceeding the scope of its authority shall be raised as soon as the matter alleged to be beyond the scope of its authority is raised during the arbitral proceedings. The arbitral tribunal may, in either case, admit a later plea if it considers the delay justified.

C. The arbitral tribunal may rule on a plea in Subsection B of this Section either as a preliminary question or in an award on the merits. If the arbitral tribunal rules as a preliminary question that it has jurisdiction, any party may request, within thirty days after having received notice of that ruling, the court in accordance with R.S. 9:4246, to decide the matter and that decision shall be subject to no appeal; while a request is pending, the arbitral tribunal may continue the arbitral proceedings and make an award.

Added by Acts 2006, No. 795, § 1.

§ 4257. Power of arbitral tribunal to order interim measures

Unless otherwise agreed by the parties, the arbitral tribunal may, at the request of a party, order any party to take interim measures of protection as the arbitral tribunal may consider necessary in respect of the subject matter of the dispute. The arbitral tribunal may require any party to provide appropriate security in connection with the measure.

Added by Acts 2006, No. 795, § 1.

§ 4258. Equal treatment of parties

The parties shall be treated with equality and each party shall be given a full opportunity of presenting his case.

Added by Acts 2006, No. 795, § 1.

§ 4259. Determination of rules of procedure

A. Subject to the provisions of this Chapter, the parties are free to agree on the procedure to be followed by the arbitral tribunal in conducting the proceedings.

B. Failing an agreement, the arbitral tribunal may, subject to the provisions of this Chapter, conduct the arbitration in a manner it considers appropriate. The power conferred upon the arbitral tribunal includes the power to determine the admissibility, relevance, materiality, and weight of any evidence.

Added by Acts 2006, No. 795, § 1.

§ 4260. Place of arbitration

A. The parties are free to agree on the place of arbitration. Failing an agreement, the place of arbitration shall be determined by the arbitral tribunal having regard to the circumstances of the case, including the convenience of the parties.

B. Notwithstanding the provisions of Subsection A of this Section, the arbitral tribunal may, unless otherwise agreed by the parties, meet at any place it considers appropriate for consultation among its members, for hearing witnesses, experts, or the parties, or for inspection of goods, other property, or documents.

Added by Acts 2006, No. 795, § 1.

§ 4261. Commencement of arbitral proceedings

Unless otherwise agreed by the parties, the arbitral proceedings in respect of a particular dispute commence on the date on which a request for that dispute to be referred to arbitration is received by the respondent.

Added by Acts 2006, No. 795, § 1.

§ 4262. Language

A. The parties are free to agree on the language or languages to be used in the arbitral proceedings. Failing an agreement, the arbitral tribunal shall determine the language or languages to be used in the proceedings. This agreement or determination, unless otherwise specified therein, shall apply to any written statement by a party, any hearing and any award, decision, or other communication by the arbitral tribunal.

B. The arbitral tribunal may order that any documentary evidence shall be accompanied by a translation into the language or languages agreed upon by the parties or determined by the arbitral tribunal.

Added by Acts 2006, No. 795, § 1.

§ 4263. Statements of claim and defense

A. Within the period of time agreed by the parties or determined by the arbitral tribunal, the claimant shall state the facts supporting his claim, the points at issue and the relief or remedy sought, and the respondent shall state his defense in respect of these particulars, unless the parties have otherwise agreed as to the required elements of the statements. The parties may submit with their statements all documents they consider to be relevant or may add a reference to the documents or other evidence they will submit.

B. Unless otherwise agreed by the parties, either party may amend or supplement his claim or defense during the course of the arbitral proceedings, unless the arbitral tribunal considers it inappropriate to allow an amendment having regard to the delay in making it.

Added by Acts 2006, No. 795, § 1.

§ 4264. Hearings and written proceedings

A. Subject to any contrary agreement by the parties, the arbitral tribunal shall decide whether to hold oral hearings for the presentation of evidence or for oral argument or whether the proceedings shall be conducted on the basis of documents and other materials. However, unless the parties have agreed that no hearings shall be held, the arbitral tribunal shall hold hearings at an appropriate stage of the proceedings, if so requested by a party.

B. The parties shall be given sufficient advance notice of any hearing and of any meeting of the arbitral tribunal for the purposes of inspection of goods, other property, or documents.

C. All statements, documents, or other information supplied to the arbitral tribunal by one party shall be communicated to the other party. Also any expert report or evidentiary document on which the arbitral tribunal may rely in making its decision shall be communicated to the parties.

Added by Acts 2006, No. 795, § 1.

§ 4265. Default of a party

Unless otherwise agreed by the parties, if, without showing sufficient cause:

(1) The claimant fails to communicate his statement of claim in accordance with R.S. 9:4263(A), the arbitral tribunal shall terminate the proceedings.

(2) The respondent fails to communicate his statement of defense in accordance with R.S. 9:4263(A), the arbitral tribunal shall continue the proceedings without treating the failure in itself as an admission of the claimant's allegations.

(3) Any party fails to appear at a hearing or to produce documentary evidence, the arbitral tribunal may continue the proceedings and make the award on the evidence before it.

Added by Acts 2006, No. 795, § 1.

§ 4266. Expert appointed by arbitral tribunal

A. Unless otherwise agreed by the parties, the arbitral tribunal:

(1) May appoint one or more experts to report to it on specific issues to be determined by the arbitral tribunal.

(2) May require a party to give the expert any relevant information or to produce, or to provide access to, any relevant documents, goods, or other property for his inspection.

B. Unless otherwise agreed by the parties, if a party so requests or if the arbitral tribunal considers it necessary, the expert shall, after delivery of his written or oral report, participate in a hearing where the parties have the opportunity to put questions to him and to present expert witnesses in order to testify on the points at issue.

Added by Acts 2006, No. 795, § 1.

§ 4267. Court assistance in taking evidence

The arbitral tribunal or a party with the approval of the arbitral tribunal may request from a competent court of this state assistance in taking evidence. The court may execute the request within its competence and according to its rules on taking evidence.

Added by Acts 2006, No. 795, § 1.

§ 4268. Rules applicable to substance of dispute

A. The arbitral tribunal shall decide the dispute in accordance with the rules of law as chosen by the parties as applicable to the substance of the dispute. Any designation of the law or legal system of a given country shall be construed, unless otherwise expressed, as directly referring to the substantive law of that country and not to its conflict of law rules.

B. Failing any designation by the parties, the arbitral tribunal shall apply the law determined by the conflict of law rules which it considers applicable.

C. The arbitral tribunal shall decide *ex aequo et bono* or as amiable compositeur only if the parties have expressly authorized it to do so.

D. In all cases, the arbitral tribunal shall decide in accordance with the terms of the contract and shall take into account the usages of the trade applicable to the transaction.

Added by Acts 2006, No. 795, § 1.

§ 4269. Decisionmaking by panel of arbitrators

In arbitral proceedings with more than one arbitrator, any decision of the arbitral tribunal shall be made, unless otherwise agreed by the parties, by a majority of all its members. However, questions of procedure may be decided by a presiding arbitrator, if so authorized by the parties or all members of the arbitral tribunal.

Added by Acts 2006, No. 795, § 1.

§ 4270. Settlement

A. If, during arbitral proceedings, the parties settle the dispute, the arbitral tribunal shall terminate the proceedings and, if requested by the parties and not objected to by the arbitral tribunal, record the settlement in the form of an arbitral award on agreed terms.

B. An award on agreed terms shall be made in accordance with R.S. 9:4271 and shall state that it is an award. An award has the same status and effect as any other award on the merits of the case.

Added by Acts 2006, No. 795, § 1.

§ 4271. Form and contents of award

A. The award shall be made in writing and shall be signed by the arbitrators. In arbitral proceedings with more than one arbitrator, the signatures of the majority of all members of the arbitral tribunal shall suffice, provided that the reason for any omitted signature is stated.

B. The award shall state the reasons upon which it is based, unless the parties have agreed that no reasons are to be given or the award is an award on agreed terms in accordance with R.S. 9:4270.

C. The award shall state its date and the place of arbitration as determined in accordance with R.S. 9:4260(A). The award shall be deemed to have been made at that place.

D. After the award is made, a copy signed by the arbitrators in accordance with Subsection A of this Section shall be delivered to each party.

Added by Acts 2006, No. 795, § 1.

§ 4272. Termination of proceedings

A. The arbitral proceedings are terminated by the final award or by an order of the arbitral tribunal in accordance with Subsection B of this Section.

B. The arbitral tribunal shall issue an order for the termination of the arbitral proceedings when:

(1) The claimant withdraws his claim, unless the respondent objects thereto and the arbitral tribunal recognizes a legitimate interest on his part in obtaining a final settlement of the dispute.

(2) The parties agree on the termination of the proceedings.

(3) The arbitral tribunal finds that the continuation of the proceedings has for any other reason become unnecessary or impossible.

C. The mandate of the arbitral tribunal terminates with the termination of the arbitral proceedings, subject to the provisions of R.S. 9:4273 and 4274(D).

Added by Acts 2006, No. 795, § 1.

§ 4273. Correction and interpretation of award; additional award

A. Within thirty days of receipt of the award, unless another period of time has been agreed upon by the parties:

(1) A party, with notice to the other party, may request the arbitral tribunal to correct in the award any errors in computation, any clerical or typographical errors, or any errors of similar nature.

(2)(a) A party, with notice to the other party, may request the arbitral tribunal to give an interpretation of a specific point or part of the award.

(b) If the arbitral tribunal considers the request to be justified, it shall make the correction or give the interpretation within thirty days of receipt of the request. The interpretation shall form part of the award.

B. The arbitral tribunal may correct any error of the type referred to in Paragraph (A)(1) of this Section on its own initiative within thirty days of the date of the award.

C. Unless otherwise agreed by the parties, a party, with notice to the other party, may request, within thirty days of receipt of the award, the arbitral tribunal to make an additional award as to claims presented in the arbitral proceedings but omitted from the award. If the arbitral tribunal considers the request to be justified, it shall make the additional award within sixty days.

D. The arbitral tribunal may extend, if necessary, the period of time within which it shall make a correction, interpretation, or an additional award in accordance with Subsections A and C of this Section.

E. The provisions of R.S. 9:4271 shall apply to a correction or interpretation of the award or to an additional award.

Added by Acts 2006, No. 795, § 1.

§ 4274. Application for setting aside as exclusive recourse against arbitral award

A. Recourse to a court against an arbitral award may be made only by an application for setting aside in accordance with Subsections B and C of this Section.

B. An arbitral award may be set aside by the court specified in R.S. 9:4246 only if:

(1) The party making the application furnishes proof that:

(a) A party to the arbitration agreement in accordance with R.S. 9:4247 was under some incapacity; or the agreement is not valid under the law to which the parties have subjected it or, failing any indication thereon, under the law of this state; or

(b) The party making the application was not given proper notice of the appointment of an arbitrator or of the arbitral proceedings or was otherwise unable to present his case; or

(c) The award deals with a dispute not contemplated by or not falling within the terms of the submission to arbitration, or contains decisions on matters beyond the scope of the submission to arbitration, provided that, if the decisions on matters submitted to arbitration can be separated from those not so submitted, only that part of the award which contains decisions on matters not submitted to arbitration may be set aside; or

(d) The composition of the arbitral tribunal or the arbitral procedure was not in accordance with the agreement of the parties, unless the agreement was in conflict with a provision of this Chapter from which the parties cannot derogate, or, failing an agreement, was not in accordance with this Chapter; or

(2) The court finds that:

(a) The subject matter of the dispute is not capable of settlement by arbitration under the law of this state or of the United States of America; or

(b) The award is in conflict with the public policy of this state.

C. An application for setting aside may not be made after three months have elapsed from the date on which the party making that application had received the award or, if a request had been made in accordance with R.S. 9:4273, from the date on which that request had been disposed of by the arbitral tribunal.

D. The court, when asked to set aside an award, may, where appropriate and so requested by a party, suspend the setting aside proceedings for a period of time determined by it in order to give the arbitral tribunal an opportunity to resume the arbitral proceedings or to take other action as in the arbitral tribunal's opinion will eliminate the grounds for setting aside.

Added by Acts 2006, No. 795, § 1.

§ 4275. Recognition and enforcement

A. An arbitral award, irrespective of the country in which it was made, shall be recognized as binding and, upon application in writing to the competent court, shall be enforced in accordance with this Section and R.S. 9:4276.

B. The party relying on an award or applying for its enforcement shall supply the duly authenticated original award or a duly certified copy thereof, and the original arbitration agreement provided for in R.S. 9:4247 or a duly certified copy thereof. If the award or agreement is not made in the English language, the party shall supply a duly certified translation thereof into that language.

Added by Acts 2006, No. 795, § 1.

§ 4276. Grounds for refusing recognition or enforcement

A. Recognition or enforcement of an arbitral award, irrespective of the country in which it was made, may be refused only:

(1) At the request of the party against whom it is invoked, if that party furnishes to the competent court where recognition or enforcement is sought proof that:

(a) A party to the arbitration agreement provided in R.S. 9:4247 was under some incapacity; or the agreement is not valid under the law to which the parties have subjected it or, failing any indication thereon, under the law of the country where the award was made; or

(b) The party against whom the award is invoked was not given proper notice of the appointment of an arbitrator or of the arbitral proceedings or was otherwise unable to present his case; or

(c) The award deals with a dispute not contemplated by or not falling within the terms of the submission to arbitration, or it contains decisions on matters beyond the scope of the submission to arbitration, provided that, if the decisions on matters submitted to arbitration can be separated from those not so submitted, that part of the award which contains decisions on matters submitted to arbitration may be recognized and enforced; or

(d) The composition of the arbitral tribunal or the arbitral procedure was not in accordance with the agreement of the parties or, failing an agreement, was not in accordance with the law of the country where the arbitration took place; or

(e) The award has not yet become binding on the parties or has been set aside or suspended by a court of the country in which, or under the law of which, that award was made; or

(2) If the court finds that:

(a) The subject matter of the dispute is not capable of settlement by arbitration under the law of this state; or

(b) The recognition or enforcement of the award would be contrary to the public policy of this state.

B. If an application for setting aside or suspension of an award has been made to a court provided in Subparagraph (A)(1)(e) of this Section, the court where recognition or enforcement is sought may, if it considers it proper, adjourn its decision and may also, on the application of the party claiming recognition or enforcement of the award, order the other party to provide appropriate security.

Added by Acts 2006, No. 795, § 1.

CODE TITLE XX—OF PLEDGE

CHAPTER 1. PLEDGES

PART I. RIGHTS UNDER MINERAL LEASES AND CONTRACTS [REPEALED]

Section
4301 to 4304. Repealed.
4305. [Blank].

PART II. INCORPOREAL RIGHTS NOT EVIDENCED IN WRITING [REPEALED]

4321 to 4323.1. Repealed.

PART II–A. DISPOSITION OF PLEDGED INCORPOREAL BY PLEDGOR [REPEALED]

4324. Repealed.

PART II–B. SECURITIZED FINANCINGS [REPEALED]

4330 to 4334. Repealed.

PART III. CROP PLEDGES [REPEALED]

SUBPART A. IN GENERAL [REPEALED]

4341 to 4343. Repealed.

SUBPART B. RECORDATION [REPEALED]

4361. Repealed.
4362. Repealed.
4363. Repealed.

SUBPART C. LIABILITY FOR VIOLATIONS [REPEALED]

4381, 4382. Repealed.

SUBPART D. RELATION TO CHAPTER 9 OF THE LOUISIANA COMMERCIAL LAWS [REPEALED]

4391. Repealed.

PART IV. PLEDGE OR ASSIGNMENT OF LEASES AND RENTS

4401. Conditional or collateral assignment of leases or rents.

PART V. PLEDGE OR ASSIGNMENT OF SECURED INSTRUMENTS

4421. Repealed.
4422. Obligations secured by mortgages or privileges; signatures and writings deemed authentic for purposes of foreclosure.
4423 to 4450. [Blank].
4451. [Blank].

PART I. RIGHTS UNDER MINERAL LEASES AND CONTRACTS [REPEALED]

§§ 4301 to 4304. Repealed by Acts 1989, No. 137, § 19, eff. Sept. 1, 1989

§ 4305. [Blank]

PART II. INCORPOREAL RIGHTS NOT EVIDENCED IN WRITING [REPEALED]

§§ 4321 to 4323.1. Repealed by Acts 2001, No. 128, § 18, eff. July 1, 2001 at 12:01 A.M.

Editor's note. Acts 2001, No. 128, § 18, effective July 1, 2001, repealed R.S. 9:4321 through 9:4391. Section 19 of Acts 2001, No. 128, declares that "it is the intent of the legislature in enacting this Act that R.S. 2736, 4501 and 4502, 4521, 4758, 4770, and 5363.1 not be expressly or impliedly repealed by this Act, but that such laws remain in effect, and, at times when so provided, be applied to secured transactions subject to Chapter 9 of the Louisiana Commercial Law as revised by this Act."

PART II–A. DISPOSITION OF PLEDGED INCORPOREAL BY PLEDGOR [REPEALED]

§ 4324. Repealed by Acts 2001, No. 128, § 18, eff. July 1, 2001 at 12:01 A.M.

Editor's note. Acts 2001, No. 128, § 18, effective July 1, 2001, repealed R.S. 9:4321 through 9:4391. Section 19 of Acts 2001, No. 128, declares that "it is the intent of the legislature in enacting this Act that R.S. 2736, 4501 and 4502, 4521, 4758, 4770, and 5363.1 not be expressly or impliedly repealed by this Act, but that such laws remain in effect, and, at times when so provided, be applied to secured transactions subject to Chapter 9 of the Louisiana Commercial Law as revised by this Act."

PART II–B. SECURITIZED FINANCINGS [REPEALED]

§§ 4330 to 4334. Repealed by Acts 2001, No. 128, § 18, eff. July 1, 2001 at 12:01 A.M.

Editor's note. Acts 2001, No. 128, § 18, effective July 1, 2001, repealed R.S. 9:4321 through 9:4391. Section 19 of Acts 2001, No. 128, declares that "it is the intent of the legislature in enacting this Act that R.S. 2736, 4501 and 4502, 4521, 4758, 4770, and 5363.1 not be expressly or impliedly repealed by this Act, but that such laws remain in effect, and, at times when so provided, be applied to secured transactions subject to Chapter 9 of the Louisiana Commercial Law as revised by this Act."

PART III. CROP PLEDGES [REPEALED]

SUBPART A. IN GENERAL [REPEALED]

§§ 4341 to 4343. Repealed by Acts 2001, No. 128, § 18, eff. July 1, 2001 at 12:01 A.M.

Editor's note. Acts 2001, No. 128, § 18, effective July 1, 2001, repealed R.S. 9:4321 through 9:4391. Section 19 of Acts 2001, No. 128, declares that "it is the intent of the legislature in enacting this Act that R.S. 2736, 4501 and 4502, 4521, 4758, 4770, and 5363.1 not be expressly or impliedly repealed by this Act, but that such laws remain in effect, and, at times when so provided, be applied to secured transactions subject to Chapter 9 of the Louisiana Commercial Law as revised by this Act."

SUBPART B. RECORDATION [REPEALED]

§ 4361. Repealed by Acts 2001, No. 128, § 18, eff. July 1, 2001 at 12:01 A.M.

Editor's note. Acts 2001, No. 128, § 18, effective July 1, 2001, repealed R.S. 9:4321 through 9:4391. Section 19 of Acts 2001, No. 128, declares that "it is the intent of the legislature in enacting this Act that R.S. 2736, 4501 and 4502, 4521, 4758, 4770, and 5363.1 not be expressly or impliedly repealed by this Act, but that such laws remain in effect, and, at times when so provided, be applied to secured transactions subject to Chapter 9 of the Louisiana Commercial Law as revised by this Act."

§ 4362. Repealed by Acts 1988, No. 370, § 2

Editor's note. Acts 2001, No. 128, § 19, effective July 1, 2001, repealed R.S. 9:4321 through 9:4391. Section 19 of Acts 2001, No. 128, declares that "it is the intent of the legislature in enacting this Act that R.S. 2736, 4501 and 4502, 4521, 4758, 4770, and 5363.1 not be expressly or impliedly repealed by this Act, but that such laws remain in effect, and, at times when so provided, be applied to secured transactions subject to Chapter 9 of the Louisiana Commercial Law as revised by this Act."

§ 4363. Repealed by Acts 2001, No. 128, § 18, eff. July 1, 2001 at 12:01 A.M.

Editor's note. Acts 2001, No. 128, § 18, effective July 1, 2001, repealed R.S. 9:4321 through 9:4391. Section 19 of Acts 2001, No. 128, declares that "it is the intent of the legislature in enacting this Act that R.S. 2736, 4501 and 4502, 4521, 4758, 4770, and 5363.1 not be expressly or impliedly repealed by this Act, but that such laws remain in effect, and, at times when so provided, be applied to secured transactions subject to Chapter 9 of the Louisiana Commercial Law as revised by this Act."

SUBPART C. LIABILITY FOR VIOLATIONS [REPEALED]

§§ 4381, 4382. Repealed by Acts 2001, No. 128, § 18, eff. July 1, 2001 at 12:01 A.M.

Editor's note. Acts 2001, No. 128, § 18, effective July 1, 2001, repealed R.S. 9:4321 through 9:4391. Section 19 of Acts 2001, No. 128, declares that "it is the intent of the legislature in enacting this Act that R.S. 2736, 4501 and 4502, 4521, 4758, 4770, and 5363.1 not be expressly or impliedly repealed by this Act, but that such laws remain in effect, and, at times when so provided, be applied to secured transactions subject to Chapter 9 of the Louisiana Commercial Law as revised by this Act."

SUBPART D. RELATION TO CHAPTER 9 OF THE LOUISIANA COMMERCIAL LAWS [REPEALED]

§ 4391. Repealed by Acts 2001, No. 128, § 18, eff. July 1, 2001 at 12:01 A.M.

Editor's note. Acts 2001, No. 128, § 18, effective July 1, 2001, repealed R.S. 9:4321 through 9:4391. Section 19 of Acts 2001, No. 128, declares that "it is the intent of the legislature in enacting this Act that R.S. 2736, 4501 and 4502, 4521, 4758, 4770, and 5363.1 not be expressly or impliedly repealed by this Act, but that such laws remain in effect, and, at times when so provided, be applied to secured transactions subject to Chapter 9 of the Louisiana Commercial Law as revised by this Act."

PART IV. PLEDGE OR ASSIGNMENT OF LEASES AND RENTS

§ 4401. Conditional or collateral assignment of leases or rents

A. Any obligation may be secured by an assignment by a lessor or sublessor of leases or rents, or both leases and rents, pertaining to immovable property. Such assignment may be expressed as a conditional or collateral assignment, and may be effected in an act of mortgage, by a separate written instrument of assignment, or by a separate written instrument of pledge, and may be referred to, denominated, or described as a pledge or an assignment, or both. The instrument shall state the amount of the obligation secured thereby or the maximum amount of the obligation that may be outstanding at any time from time to time that such assignment secures. If such conditional or collateral assignment is made, it shall become absolute upon the assignor's default in respect to the obligation thereby secured or in accordance with the terms of the instrument creating such assignment, and shall become operative as to the debtor upon written notice to the debtor from or on behalf of the assignee or the assignor that such assignment has so become absolute.

(1) An assignment relating to a lease or rent of an immovable is given the effect of recordation when an original or a certified copy of the instrument creating the assignment is filed in the conveyance records of the parish in which the immovable is situated; however, an assignment contained in an act of mortgage filed in the mortgage records of such parish on or after September 1, 1995, shall be given the effect of recordation when, to the extent, and for so long as the act of mortgage is given such effect, without the need for separate recordation in the conveyance records. An assignment given the effect of recordation has such effect with regard to all obligations, present and future, secured thereby notwithstanding the date of the incurrence of such obligations or the nature of such obligations.

(2) Such assignment may include all or any portion of the assignor's presently existing and anticipated future leases and rents pertaining to the described immovable property. As future leases or rents of an immovable come into existence the assignee's rights as to such leases and rents shall have effect as to third persons from the date of the filing of the instrument. It shall not be necessary to specifically describe the presently existing or future arising leases or rents; to affect the assignor, the assignee, the debtor, or other third parties the instrument shall suffice if it contains a general description of the leases and rents together with a description of the immovable affected by the lease. The immovable property description shall be the kind of description which, if contained in a mortgage of the immovable, would cause such mortgage to be effective as to third persons if the mortgage were properly filed for record under the laws of this state.

(3) Once an assignment relating to leases or rents of an immovable is so filed, the assignee shall have a superior claim to the leases and rents assigned and their proceeds as

against all other creditors whose claims or security interests arise or are perfected after the filing of the assignment, notwithstanding the fact that the debtor is not notified of or does not consent to the assignment or that the assignee is not in possession of the immovable property.

(4) Except for purposes of Subsection G, the term "lease" as used in this Section includes a sublease.

B. This Section is intended to recognize one method of securing obligations, and shall not have the effect of repealing any other provision of law in respect to pledge, pawn, and assignment of incorporeal rights.

C. This Section is remedial and shall be retroactive. All assignments of leases or rents heretofore made in compliance with the provisions of this Section are hereby validated.

D. A landowner or mineral servitude owner may make a conditional or collateral assignment pursuant to this Section of rents, royalties, delay rentals, shut-in payments, and other payments which are rent or rentals under Title 31 of the Louisiana Revised Statutes attributable to the landowner's sale, lease, or other disposition of his right to explore and develop his land for production of minerals or to the mineral servitude owner's sale, lease, or other disposition of his mineral right. This Section shall not otherwise apply to rents, royalties, overriding royalties, bonuses, and other payments and other rights under mineral leases and other contracts relating to minerals.

E. This Section shall apply to assignments of leases of movable property subject to the Louisiana Lease of Movables Act entered into prior to the time Chapter 9 of the Louisiana Commercial Laws (R.S. 10:9–101, et seq.) becomes effective, including without limitation those assignments of leases that affect rights arising after the effective date of Chapter 9 and those continuing assignments that may secure future obligations, lines of credit, and other ongoing credit facilities. This Section shall further apply to assignments of leases of immovable property located in this state without regard to the time Chapter 9 becomes effective.

F. (1) Except as otherwise agreed to by the parties, the assignee's interest in the leases or rents assigned continues in any identifiable proceeds including collections received by the assignor.

(2) In the event of insolvency proceedings instituted by or against an assignor, the assignee has a perfected security interest in proceeds of the leases or rents or both leases and rents assigned, as follows:

(a) In identifiable noncash proceeds and in separate deposit accounts containing only proceeds.

(b) In identifiable cash proceeds in the form of money which is neither commingled with other money nor deposited in a deposit account prior to the insolvency proceedings.

(c) In identifiable cash proceeds in the form of checks and the like which are not deposited in a deposit account prior to the insolvency proceedings.

(d) In all cash and deposit accounts of the assignor in which proceeds have been commingled with other funds, but the perfected security interest under this Section is subject to any right of set-off. It is further limited to an amount not greater than the amount of any cash proceeds received by the assignor within ten days before the institution of the insolvency proceedings, less the sum of:

(i) the payments to the assignee on account of cash proceeds received by the assignor during such period; and

(ii) the cash proceeds received by the assignor during such period to which the assignee is entitled under Paragraphs (a) through (c) of Subsection F(2).

G. (1) The rights of an assignee against the debtor shall be subject to any dealing by the debtor with the assignor, any other assignee, or other successor in interest of the assignor until the debtor receives written notice from or on behalf of the assignee or the assignor that the assignment of the particular lease or rent of which he is debtor has become absolute. A notification which does not reasonably identify the rights assigned is ineffective. If requested by the debtor, the assignee must seasonably furnish reasonable proof that the assignment has been made and unless he does so the debtor may pay the assignor.

(2) Except as provided in this Subsection (G), a debtor who has received written notice that the assignment has become absolute will not be discharged from his debt if he pays anyone other than the assignee. In any case in which a debtor is not notified of the assignment made in compliance with the provisions of this Section and, in good faith, makes payment of rent in whole or in part to the assignor or the assignor's successor, or to a subsequent assignee of the rent who shall have notified the debtor of that assignment, then to the extent of payment, the debtor shall be exonerated of liability to make payment to the first assignee; however, the person to whom payment was made shall be accountable and liable to the assignee for the sums received. The debtor may, at its option, commence concursus proceedings instead of making payment to the assignor or the assignee.

(3) Notwithstanding the debtor's receipt of written notice of the assignment, a modification of or substitution for the lease made in good faith and in accordance with reasonable commercial standards is effective against an assignee, unless the debtor has otherwise agreed with the assignee. In either event the assignee acquires rights under the modified or substituted lease corresponding to the assignee's rights under the original lease. No termination or modification of or substitution for a lease shall be effective against an assignee as to the right to the payment of rent or a part thereof under an assigned lease which has been fully earned by performance. The assignment may provide that modification of or substitution for the lease is a default by the assignor.

(4) A term in any lease between a debtor and an assignor is ineffective if it prohibits assignment of rent or prohibits creation of a security right in rent due or to become due or requires the debtor's consent to such assignment of rent or security interest in rent.

(5) The mere existence of a conditional or collateral assignment does not impose contract or tort liability upon the assignee for the assignor's acts or omissions relating to such leases.

H. (1) The effect of recordation of all assignments recorded on or after September 1, 1990, ceases ten years after the date of the instrument creating the assignment, except, that if an instrument creating an assignment describes the maturity of an obligation secured thereby and if any part of the described obligation matures nine years or more after the date of the instrument, the effect of recordation ceases six years after the described maturity date. A recorded instrument creating an assignment may be reinscribed by filing a signed, written notice of reinscription. The notice shall state the name of the assignor as it appears in the recorded instrument and recordation number or other appropriate recordation information of the instrument or of a prior notice of reinscription and shall declare that the instrument is reinscribed. A notice of reinscription that is filed before the effect of recordation ceases continues that effect for ten years from the date the notice is filed. A notice of reinscription that is filed after the effect of recordation ceases produces the effects of recordation, but only from the date the notice is filed. The method of reinscription provided in this Section is exclusive, and neither an amendment of an instrument creating an assignment nor an acknowledgment of the existence of an assignment by the assignor constitutes a reinscription of the instrument. Notwithstanding the foregoing, the effect of recordation of an assignment contained in an act of mortgage filed on or after September 1, 1995, continues for so long as the act of mortgage is given the effect of recordation. In such cases, reinscription of the act of mortgage constitutes reinscription of the assignment contained therein.

(2) Notwithstanding the foregoing provisions, the effect of registry of all assignments recorded on or before August 31, 1990, shall be determined by the other laws of registry applicable thereto.

(3) The recordation of an assignment may be cancelled by the consent of the assignee evidenced by any written release, under private signature or otherwise. Cancellation or erasure of an act of mortgage containing an assignment constitutes cancellation of the assignment contained therein, whether the act of mortgage was recorded in the mortgage records or conveyance records, or both.

I. The provisions of R.S. 9:4401(A), as amended and reenacted, and the provisions of R.S. 9:4401(G) and (H) as enacted by Acts of the 1990 Regular Session are remedial and shall, wherever possible, be given retroactive effect. All assignments of present and future leases or rents heretofore made in compliance herewith are hereby validated.

Added by Acts 1980, No. 321, § 1. Amended by Acts 1985, No. 592, § 5, eff. July 13, 1985; Acts 1987, No. 130, § 1, eff. June 18, 1987; Acts 1989, No. 137, § 4, eff. Sept. 1, 1989; Acts 1990, No. 1079, § 3, eff. Sept. 1, 1990 at 12:01 A.M; Acts 1995, No. 1087, § 3.

Editor's note. Section 7 of Acts 1985, No. 592 provided:

"R.S. 9:3303(A) through (D), 3305, 3309 through 3311, 3313 through 3319, 3325, 3329, 3330 and 3342 are hereby declared to be remedial in nature and shall apply to leases of movables in existence as of the effective date of this Act. Sections 2 through 6 of this Act are also declared to be remedial in nature and shall apply to leases of movables in existence as of the effective date of this Act."

For § 20 of Acts 1989, No. 137, stating legislative intent, see note preceding R.S. 9:4301.

Cross References

C.C. arts. 1984, 2643, 2645, 2646, 2648, 2669, 2670, 2673, 2674, 2676, 2744, 2779, 2780, 2782 to 2784, 2787.

PART V. PLEDGE OR ASSIGNMENT OF SECURED INSTRUMENTS

§ 4421. Repealed by Acts 2001, No. 128, § 18, eff. July 1, 2001 at 12:01 A.M.

Editor's note. Acts 2001, No. 128, § 18, effective July 1, 2001, repealed R.S. 9:4421. Section 19 of Acts 2001, No. 128, declares that "it is the intent of the legislature in enacting this Act that R.S. 2736, 4501 and 4502, 4521, 4758, 4770, and 5363.1 not be expressly or impliedly repealed by this Act, but that such laws remain in effect, and, at times when so provided, be applied to secured transactions subject to Chapter 9 of the Louisiana Commercial Law as revised by this Act."

§ 4422. Obligations secured by mortgages or privileges; signatures and writings deemed authentic for purposes of foreclosure

The following shall apply when foreclosure by executory process is instituted by the transferee, assignee, or pledgee of any promissory note, whether negotiable or not, and any negotiable instrument:

(1) All signatures of the following persons or entities are presumed to be genuine and no further evidence is required of those signatures for the purposes of executory process: endorsers, guarantors, and other persons whose signatures appear on or are affixed to such instrument secured by the mortgage or privilege.

(2) The assignment, pledge, negotiation, or other transfer of any obligation secured by a mortgage or privilege may be proven by any form of private writing, and such writing shall be deemed authentic for the purposes of executory process.

(3) The holder of any promissory note, whether negotiable or not, and any negotiable instrument under this Section may enforce the mortgage or privilege securing such instrument without authentic evidence of the signatures, assignment, pledge, negotiation, or transfer thereof.

Added by Acts 1989, No. 292, § 1. Amended by Acts 2012, No. 400, § 1.

§§ 4423 to 4450. [Blank]

§ 4451. [Blank]

Editor's note. Acts 1987, No. 129, § 1 enacted Part V, containing R.S. 9:4451, which section was redesignated, pursuant to the statutory revision authority of the Louisiana State Law Institute, as R.S. 9:4421.

CODE TITLE XXI—OF PRIVILEGES

CHAPTER 1. PRIVILEGES ON MOVABLES

PART I. MAKING AND REPAIRING MOVABLES

Section
4501. Repairman's privilege on automobiles and other machinery.
4502. Privilege for making or repairing movable goods, commodities, equipment, merchandise, machinery, and other movable objects.

Section

PART I–A. AIRCRAFT

4511. Privilege; aircraft.
4512. Notice of privilege.
4513. Privilege; storage of aircraft.

PART II. CROPS

4521. Repealed.
4522. Water furnished to grow crops.
4522.1. Water furnished under crop share agreement; exempt.

APPENDIX 1—REVISED STATUTES, TITLE 9

Section
- 4523. Threshermen's, combinemen's, and grain drier's privilege.
- 4524. Repealed.

PART III. VENDOR'S PRIVILEGE
SUBPART A. IN GENERAL
- 4541. Seller of agricultural products in chartered cities and towns.
- 4542. Seller of cotton seed on manufactured products.
- 4543. Seller of sugar cane on manufactured products.
- 4544. Vegetables, seafood, and other perishable items.

SUBPART B. SEWING MACHINES AND PIANOS
- 4561. Sewing machines and pianos subject to seizure.
- 4562. Repealed.
- 4563. Entry and removal of property.
- 4564. Penalty for violation.

SUBPART C. PAYMENTS UNDER POLICIES OF INSURANCE
- 4581. Holder of vendor's privilege on property destroyed by fire, privilege on insurance.
- 4582. Notice to insurer and to assured; deposit in court.

PART IV. CARRIER'S CHARGES
- 4601. Hauling or trucking.

PART V. LOGS AND LUMBER
- 4621. Logs and products manufactured therefrom.
- 4622. Effective period; rank; sequestration.

PART VI. MOSS
- 4641. Laborers and furnishers of supplies.

PART VII. HORSES
- 4661. Feed, medicine, and veterinary services for horses.

PART VIII. RUGS, CARPETS, CLOTHING, AND HOUSEHOLD GOODS
- 4681. Carpets and rugs, cleaning and storage.
- 4682. Loss of privilege.
- 4683. Other remedies.
- 4684. Satisfaction of privilege; procedure; sale.
- 4685. Proceeds, disposition of.
- 4686. Claimant may pay charges and acquire possession.
- 4687. Clothing or household goods; procedures for sale.
- 4688. Proceeds, disposition of.
- 4689. Clothing or household goods; disposition of other than by sale.

PART IX. JEWELRY, GEMS, AND WATCHES
- 4701. Private sale of unclaimed goods of less than $10.
- 4702. Notice to owner.
- 4703. Proceeds, disposition of.

PART X. SUGAR, SYRUP, AND MOLASSES
- 4721. Sugar refinery and mill employees.

PART XI. SHIPS AND OTHER VESSELS
- 4741. Canal toll fees.

PART XII. PROCEEDS RECOVERED BY INJURED PERSON
- 4751. Definitions.

Section
- 4752. Privilege on net proceeds collected from third party in favor of medical providers for services and supplies furnished injured persons.
- 4753. Written notice.
- 4754. Failure to pay over monies after notice.
- 4755. Itemized statements.

PART XIII. SELF–SERVICE STORAGE FACILITIES
- 4756. Short title.
- 4757. Definitions.
- 4758. Privilege.
- 4759. Options of owner upon lessee's default.
- 4760. Supplemental nature of act.

PART XIV. RELATION TO UNIFORM COMMERCIAL CODE
- 4770. Conflicts with Chapter 9 of the Uniform Commercial Code.

PART XV. MARINA AND BOATYARD STORAGE FACILITIES
- 4780. Short title.
- 4781. Definitions.
- 4782. Privilege.
- 4783. Notice of privilege.
- 4784. Enforcement of privilege.
- 4785. Cessation of enforcement actions.

PART XVI. OTHER PRIVILEGES ON MOVABLES
- 4790. Child support arrearages; privilege on motor vehicles.

PART XVII. TOWED AND STORED VESSEL ACT
- 4791. Short title.
- 4792. Definitions.
- 4793. Privilege.
- 4794. Vessel owner information.
- 4795. Notice of privilege and default.
- 4796. Advertisement: enforcement of privilege.
- 4797. Sale and purchasers.
- 4798. Regulations.

PART I. MAKING AND REPAIRING MOVABLES

§ 4501. Repairman's privilege on automobiles and other machinery

A. Any person operating a garage or other place where automobiles or other machinery are repaired, or parts therefor are made or furnished, has a privilege upon the automobile or other machinery for the amount of the cost of repairs made, parts made or furnished, and labor performed. If an estimate was given by the repairman for the repairs, then in order for the amount of the privilege to exceed the amount of the estimate, the repairman must secure authorization to exceed the amount of the estimate. This privilege is effective for a period of one hundred twenty days from the last day on which materials were furnished or labor was performed if the thing affected by such privilege is removed from the place of business where such labor was performed or materials were furnished; provided that if the thing affected by such privilege remains in the place of business of the person who furnished such materials or performed such

For Annotative Materials, see West's Louisiana Statutes Annotated

labor, such privilege continues as long as such thing remains in such place of business. For the purposes of this Section, it is immaterial where the automobile or other machinery may have been located at the time or by whom the parts may have been attached.

B. This privilege may be enforced by the writ of sequestration, without the repairman having to furnish security therefor; and the exemptions from seizure granted by R.S. 13:3881 shall not be applicable to objects or property subject to this privilege for purposes of enforcing the privilege. This privilege is superior to all other privileges except for a vendor's privilege, a chattel mortgage previously recorded, a previously perfected security interest under Chapter 9 of Louisiana Commercial Laws,[1] or against a bona fide purchaser to whom possession has been delivered and who has paid the purchase price without previous notice of the existence of the privilege.

C. If the automobile or other machinery is seized and sold by the holder of a vendor's privilege or previously recorded chattel mortgage, then any proceeds over and above the balance due on the vendor's privilege and previously recorded chattel mortgage, plus costs of court including costs of the sheriff, constable, or marshal, shall be paid to the garage or repairman, not to exceed the amount of the repairman's privilege.

Amended by Acts 1960, No. 31, § 1, eff. Jan. 1, 1961; Acts 1976, No. 102, § 1; Acts 1977, No. 369, § 1; Acts 1979, No. 93, § 1; Acts 1983, No. 359, § 1; Acts 1988, No. 949, § 1; Acts 1989, No. 137, § 4, eff. Sept. 1, 1989.

[1] R.S. 10:9–101 et seq.

Cross References

C.C. arts. 3186, 3216, 3217, 3224.

§ 4502. Privilege for making or repairing movable goods, commodities, equipment, merchandise, machinery, and other movable objects

A. (1) Any person engaged in the making or repairing of movable goods, furniture, upholstery, commodities, equipment, merchandise, machinery, marine vessels, trailers used in transporting marine vessels, equipment or motors used on marine vessels, or movable objects or movable property of any type or description, has a privilege on the thing for the debt due him for materials furnished or labor performed. This privilege is effective for a period of one hundred twenty days from the last day on which materials were furnished or labor was performed, if the thing affected by such privilege is removed from the place of business where such labor was performed or materials furnished; provided that if the thing affected by such privilege remains in the place of business of the person who furnished such materials or performed such labor, such privilege continues as long as such thing remains in such place of business.

(2) This privilege is effective for a period of twelve months from the last day on which materials were furnished or labor was performed on any farm equipment or machinery, if said thing affected by such privilege is removed from the place of business where such labor was performed or materials furnished; provided, further, that this special farm privilege shall not be effective for more than one hundred twenty days as against third parties who purchase the equipment or machinery, or who lend money secured by the equipment or machinery, in good faith without knowledge of the existence of any privilege.

B. This privilege may be enforced by the writ of sequestration, without the necessity of the creditor furnishing security therefor, if the debtor is first given ten days' written notice by registered mail, and the exemptions from seizure granted by R.S. 13:3881 shall not be applicable to objects or property subject to this privilege for purposes of enforcing this privilege. This privilege is inferior to a vendor's privilege, a chattel mortgage previously recorded, a previously perfected security interest under Chapter 9 of the Louisiana Commercial Laws,[1] or against a bona fide purchaser to whom possession has been delivered and who has paid the purchase price without previous notice of the existence of the privilege.

C. In addition to the remedy above granted, when the thing affected by the privilege remains in the place of business of the person having such privilege and the debt due thereon remains unpaid for more than ninety days from the date on which the last labor was performed or last material was furnished, the holder of such privilege may sell such property at private sale and without appraisement, after advertising such property for ten days as provided by law in case of judicial sales of movables. If the thing affected by such privilege and subject to such sale is of a value of ten dollars or less, to be shown by written estimate made and signed by two disinterested appraisers, then it shall not be necessary to advertise such property for sale, but in lieu thereof the privilege holder shall, at least ten days prior to such sale, mail by registered mail to the owner or apparent owner at his last known address a notice stating the intention to sell such property and giving the date, time and place of the sale. From the proceeds of any such sale, the amount of the debt secured by such privilege shall be satisfied, including all reasonable charges for registered notices, advertisement or charges for appraisers and costs of the sale; and the balance, if any, shall be held for the benefit of the owner for a period of six months, after which time, if it remains unclaimed, it shall be paid to the state treasury.

D. This Section shall not be construed as repealing any of the provisions of R.S. 9:4501 or of any other law which grants a privilege, or grants another remedy for the enforcement thereof. However, the remedy granted by Subsection C of this Section is not available to any person who is granted a remedy for the enforcement of his privilege under any other Section of this Title. When property to which the privilege granted by R.S. 9:4501 does not apply, but for which a certificate of title from the office of motor vehicles of the Department of Public Safety is required, is sold at private sale pursuant to Subsection C, the office of motor vehicles shall issue a new certificate of title to the purchaser, if the application therefor is accompanied by an authentic act of sale and proof of compliance with the advertisement or notice requirement, as the case may be.

Amended by Acts 1952, No. 427, §§ 1, 2; Acts 1960, No. 31, § 1, eff. Jan. 1, 1961; Acts 1972, No. 518, § 1; Acts 1979, No. 94, § 1; Acts 1981, No. 252, § 1; Acts 1983, No. 359, § 1; Acts 1989, No. 137, § 4, eff. Sept. 1, 1989; Acts 2004, No. 179, § 1.

[1] R.S. 10:9–101 et seq.

Editor's note. "Lien and privilege" was changed to "privilege" throughout the section. Section 2 of Act No. 341 of 1946 was deleted. This Section provided that "This Act shall not be construed to conflict with any of the provisions of Act No. 209 of 1926 (R.S. 9:4501)." The deletion of this section is not intended to be construed as changing the original legislative intent.

Cross References

C.C. arts. 3186, 3216, 3217.

PART I-A. AIRCRAFT

§ 4511. Privilege; aircraft

Any person who repairs, restores, performs maintenance work or other services to or on an aircraft, or provides fuel or materials in connection therewith has the privilege on the aircraft for either of the following:

(1) The amount due under the contract for the repairs or maintenance performed and the fuel or materials in connection therewith.

(2) If no amount is specified by contract, an amount that is reasonable under the circumstances.

Added by Acts 2001, No. 899, § 1.

§ 4512. Notice of privilege

A. (1) Any person claiming a privilege on an aircraft under R.S. 9:4511 may record the privilege on the aircraft by filing a notice or a claim with the Federal Aviation Administration - Aircraft Registry not later than the ninetieth day after the labor, services, fuel, and materials were furnished.

(2) Any privilege claimed on an aircraft under R.S. 9:4511 is enforceable when a verified notice of privilege has been recorded with the recorder of mortgages for the parish where the aircraft was located at the time of labor, services, fuel, or materials were last furnished.

(3) The notice shall state the names of the person asserting the privilege, the name of the owner of the aircraft, a description of the aircraft upon which the person is asserting the privilege, the amount expended for labor, services, fuel, or material for which the privilege is being claimed, and the date the repairs or changes were furnished.

(4) The privilege may be enforced by writ of sequestration, without the necessity of the creditor furnishing security therefor, if the debtor is first given fifteen days written notice by registered mail. This privilege is inferior to a vendor's privilege, a chattel mortgage, or security interest recorded prior to the commencement of work or services on the aircraft or the provision of fuel and materials in connection therewith, or against the bona fide purchaser to whom possession has been delivered and who has paid the purchase price without previous notice of the existence of the privilege. Recordation of the notice of privilege in any manner provided for in this Section shall constitute the requisite notice to prospective purchasers of the aircraft.

B. In addition to the remedy provided in this Section, when the aircraft remains in the possession of the privilege holder, and the debt due thereon remains unpaid for more than ninety days from the date on which the last labor was performed or last fuel or material was furnished, the holder of such privilege may sell such property at private sale and without appraisement, after advertising such property for ten days as provided by law in case of judicial sale of movables. From the proceeds of any such sale, the amount of the debts secured by such privilege shall be satisfied, including all reasonable charges for registered notices, advertisement or charges for appraisers and cost of the sale, including reasonable attorney fees incurred by the privilege holder in connection therewith; and the balance, if any, shall be held for the benefit of the owner for a period of six months, after which time, if it remains unclaimed, it shall be paid to the clerk of court for the parish in which the sale took place.

C. The privilege holder may retain possession of the aircraft subject to the privilege until the amount due is paid in full.

D. Upon payment of the debt owed to the privilege holder by or on behalf of the registered owner of the aircraft or other property subject to the privilege, or by the customer, the privilege holder shall cause to be filed with the Federal Aviation Administration-Aircraft Registry a notice of cancellation of the privilege. The filing of this notice of cancellation shall terminate all interest of the privilege holder. The privilege holder shall not be foreclosed from asserting an additional privilege against the aircraft for the payment of amounts owed for work or services performed, or fuel materials furnished to the aircraft after the cancellation.

Added by Acts 2001, No. 899, § 1.

§ 4513. Privilege; storage of aircraft

A. Any person who stores an aircraft, whether or not in connection with the performance of repairs, restoration, or maintenance work on said aircraft, has a privilege on the aircraft for either of the following:

(1) The amount due under the contract for storage.

(2) If no amount was specified by contract, the reasonable and usual compensation for the storage.

B. The rights and remedies provided to the privilege holder under this provision shall be identical to those provided in R.S. 9:4511 and R.S. 9:4512 with the exception that the amount due to the privilege holder under this provision shall include storage costs or fees up to the day judgment is obtained, the aircraft is sold, or the possession of the aircraft is relinquished, whichever first occurs. However, in the event the aircraft remains in the possession of the privilege holder, the privilege holder shall not be precluded from asserting the same privilege for any subsequent storage fees or costs incurred.

Added by Acts 2001, No. 899, § 1.

PART II. CROPS

§ 4521. Repealed by Acts 2010, No. 378, § 4

§ 4522. Water furnished to grow crops

Any person who furnishes water to another for the purpose of assisting him in growing or maturing a crop has a privilege coequal with the privilege for supplies upon the crop to secure the payment of the agreed compensation therefor.

Cross References

C.C. arts. 3186, 3216, 3217.

§ 4522.1. Water furnished under crop share agreement; exempt

In all cases where an agreement exists for the supplying of irrigation water to any farmer in consideration for a share of the crop, the portion of the crop which the water supplier is to receive under the terms of such agreement shall be considered at all times the property of the water supplier and

no privilege for any debt of the farmer shall affect the agreed share of the water supplier.
Added by Acts 1972, No. 202, § 1.

Cross References

C.C. arts. 3186, 3216, 3217, 3259.

§ 4523. Threshermen's, combinemen's, and grain drier's privilege

Threshermen, combinemen and grain driers have a privilege for services rendered on the crop which they have threshed, combined or dried.
Amended by Acts 1950, No. 170, § 1.

Cross References

C.C. arts. 474, 3186, 3216, 3217.

§ 4524. Repealed by Acts 2010, No. 378, § 4

PART III. VENDOR'S PRIVILEGE

SUBPART A. IN GENERAL

§ 4541. Seller of agricultural products in chartered cities and towns

Any person who sells agricultural products of the United States in any chartered city or town of this state has a privilege thereon to secure the payment of the purchase money for five days after the day of delivery, within which time the vendor may seize the same in whatever hands or place it may be found, and his claim for the purchase money has preference over any warehouse privilege or claim for warehouse charges, or any privilege or claim by the holder of any warehouse receipt. If the vendor gives a written order for the delivery of any such produce and says therein that it is to be delivered without vendor's privilege, then no privilege attaches thereto.
Amended by Acts 1991, No. 539, § 2, eff. Jan. 1, 1992 at 12:01 A.M.

Cross References

C.C. arts. 3186, 3216, 3227.

§ 4542. Seller of cotton seed on manufactured products

In addition to the other privileges accorded by law, the seller of cotton seed to any manufacturer has a privilege for the amount of the unpaid purchase price of the cotton seed on all the cotton seed products manufactured by the purchaser during the season to the amount of the value of the cotton seed sold. This privilege bears upon the products as long as they remain upon the premises where manufactured.

This privilege is concurrent in favor of all unpaid vendors of cotton seed and is next in rank to the laborer's privilege.

Cross References

C.C. arts. 3186, 3216, 3227.

§ 4543. Seller of sugar cane on manufactured products

In addition to the other privileges accorded by law, the seller of sugar cane to any manufacturer of sugar has a privilege for the amount of the unpaid purchase price on the syrup, sugar, and molasses manufactured during the season by the purchaser to the amount of the product of the cane sold, which quantity is fixed as that portion of the products of the season which bears the same proportion to the entire product of the season as the cane sold and unpaid for bears to the entire quantity of cane manufactured during the season. This privilege exists as long as the said syrup, sugar, and molasses remain in the possession and custody of the manufacturer.

This privilege is concurrent in favor of all unpaid sellers of sugar cane during the season and is next in rank to the laborer's privilege given by R.S. 9:4721.

Cross References

C.C. arts. 3186, 3216, 3227.

§ 4544. Vegetables, seafood, and other perishable items

No vendor's privilege or lien shall be applicable to any fresh or frozen vegetables, seafood, or other perishable food products.
Added by Acts 1978, No. 609, § 1.

Cross References

C.C. arts. 3186, 3216.

SUBPART B. SEWING MACHINES AND PIANOS

§ 4561. Sewing machines and pianos subject to seizure

Sewing machines and pianos may be seized to enforce the vendor's privilege thereon.

Cross References

C.C. arts. 3186, 3216, 3227.

§ 4562. Repealed by Acts 1985, No. 592, § 5, eff. July 13, 1985

§ 4563. Entry and removal of property

It is unlawful for the vendors or transferors of any movable property exempt from general seizure to enter the premises of any person to whom such property has been sold or transferred with the object of removing the property under the assumption that the buyer or transferee has by agreement given the right of entry or removal.

Cross References

C.C. arts. 3186, 3216.

§ 4564. Penalty for violation

Any person guilty of entering and removing any property in violation of R.S. 9:4563 shall be fined not more than two hundred dollars or imprisoned for not more than three months or both. Nothing in this Section shall deprive the party injured of his civil action in damages. Nothing in R.S. 9:4561 through 9:4563 shall be construed to prevent the seizing officer from entering and taking under proper legal process, property not exempt from seizure, and which, although exempt from general seizure, is liable to be levied on for the enforcement of the vendor's privilege when existing.

Cross References

C.C. arts. 3186, 3216, 3227.

SUBPART C. PAYMENTS UNDER POLICIES OF INSURANCE

§ 4581. Holder of vendor's privilege on property destroyed by fire, privilege on insurance

The holder of a vendor's privilege on movable property which is destroyed by fire has a privilege to the amount of the unpaid portion of the purchase price on the claim or money due the owner or vendee under policies of insurance covering that property. This privilege has the rank of a vendor's privilege on the thing sold and is superior in rank to any privilege growing out of the attachment, garnishment, or seizure of the claim or money.

Cross References

C.C. arts. 3186, 3216, 3227, 3277.

§ 4582. Notice to insurer and to assured; deposit in court

In order to protect the privilege provided in R.S. 9:4581, the vendor, his heirs, or assigns shall give, at any time prior to the payment of the amount due under the policies, written notice to the insurer of the existence of the claim and state under oath the amount thereof. On the receipt of this notice the insurer shall give written notice to the assured of the filing of the vendor's claim, and in the event of a dispute between the vendor and his vendee, or of any one claiming adverse interest under oath, the insurer shall deposit, subject to the right of all parties in interest, the amount due under the policies in the registry of the court having jurisdiction in any suit that may be brought on the policies to recover the amount due thereunder. Having made the deposit, the insurer shall be relieved of further responsibility.

Cross References

C.C. arts. 3186, 3216, 3277.

PART IV. CARRIER'S CHARGES

§ 4601. Hauling or trucking

A. Any person engaged in the business of hauling has a privilege on the property hauled for the charges or labor performed in connection therewith for a period of one hundred eighty days from the last day of hauling or performing such labor.

B. This privilege may be enforced by the writ of sequestration, without the necessity of furnishing security therefor. This privilege is inferior to a vendor's privilege, a chattel mortgage previously recorded, a previously perfected security interest under Chapter 9 of the Louisiana Commercial Laws,[1] or against a bona fide purchaser to whom possession has been delivered and who has paid the purchase price without previous notice of the existence of the privilege. Amended by Acts 1960, No. 31, § 1, eff. Jan. 1, 1961; Acts 1985, No. 296, § 1; Acts 1989, No. 137, § 4, eff. Sept. 1, 1989.

[1] R.S. 10:9–101 et seq.

Cross References

C.C. arts. 3186, 3216, 3217, 3265.

PART V. LOGS AND LUMBER

§ 4621. Logs and products manufactured therefrom

The debts which are privileged on logs and on products manufactured therefrom, are the following:

(1) The debt due any land owner or stumpage owner for the price, on the logs sold and on the poles and cross ties manufactured therefrom.

(2) The debt due any person for money advanced or supplies furnished to enable another to deaden, cut, load, or transport any logs or to manufacture poles or cross ties, on the logs and on the poles and cross ties manufactured therefrom.

(3) The debt due any person for the price of his labor or services in deadening, cutting, loading, or transporting any logs, staves, poles, or cross ties, or in manufacturing poles, cross ties, lumber, staves, hoops, boxes, shingles, doors, blinds, or window sashes, as well as the debt due any person cooking for persons so engaged, on the logs and on the poles, ties, lumber, and other manufactured products.

Cross References

C.C. arts. 3186, 3205, 3208, 3216, 3217.

§ 4622. Effective period; rank; sequestration

The privileges conferred by R.S. 9:4621 are effective for a period of ninety days from the maturity of the debt, are concurrent, and may be enforced by the writ of sequestration, without the necessity of furnishing security therefor. These privileges have no effect against a bona fide purchaser to whom possession has been delivered and who has paid the purchase price without previous notice of the existence of the privilege. In no event shall the seizing officer seize more than is sufficient to satisfy the claim and all probable costs. Amended by Acts 1960, No. 31, § 1, eff. Jan. 1, 1961.

Cross References

C.C. arts. 3186, 3205, 3208, 3216, 3217.

PART VI. MOSS

§ 4641. Laborers and furnishers of supplies

Laborers engaged in gathering, saving, and preparing moss for market, have a privilege on the moss for their wages. Persons advancing money or furnishing supplies to enable another to gather, save, and prepare moss for market, have a privilege on the moss for the advances and supplies.

The laborer's privilege ranks first and that of the furnisher of supplies second.

Cross References

C.C. arts. 3186, 3216, 3217.

PART VII. HORSES

§ 4661. Feed, medicine, and veterinary services for horses

Any person who furnishes feed or medicines for a horse or horses, or any licensed veterinarian who furnishes medical services for a horse or horses, to or upon the order of the owner, has a privilege for the unpaid portion of the price thereof upon the horse or horses of the owner, which received the feed, medicine, or medical services. This privilege is effective for a period of six months from the dates of the respective deliveries and may be enforced by the writ of sequestration. This privilege is superior to all claims, privileges, and mortgages, whether recorded or unrecorded, which theretofore may have been or thereafter may be created against such horse or horses, and to the claims of any and all purchasers thereof.

Amended by Acts 1985, No. 843, § 1; Acts 1987, No. 829, § 1; Acts 1988, No. 838, § 1.

Cross References

C.C. arts. 3186, 3208, 3216, 3217.

PART VIII. RUGS, CARPETS, CLOTHING, AND HOUSEHOLD GOODS

§ 4681. Carpets and rugs, cleaning and storage

Any person conducting the business of cleaning carpets and rugs and storing them at his place of business after cleaning until delivery to the owner, has a privilege upon the carpets and rugs for all lawful charges for services rendered in the cleaning, storage, and preservation of the goods, as well as for all lawful claims for money advanced, interest, insurance, transportation, labor, and other charges and expenses in relation to the goods, and also for all reasonable charges and expenses in advertisements of sale and for the sale of the goods where default has been made in satisfying the privilege.

Cross References

C.C. arts. 3186, 3216, 3217.

§ 4682. Loss of privilege

The privilege holder loses the privilege by surrendering possession of the goods, or by refusing to deliver them when demand is made with which he is bound to comply under the provisions of R.S. 9:4686. However, he may refuse to deliver the goods until the privilege is satisfied.

Cross References

C.C. arts. 3186, 3216, 3217.

§ 4683. Other remedies

Whether or not the person has a privilege upon the goods, he is entitled to all remedies allowed by law for the collection from the depositor of all charges and advances which the depositor has expressly or impliedly contracted with him to pay.

Cross References

C.C. arts. 3186, 3216, 3217.

§ 4684. Satisfaction of privilege; procedure; sale

Whenever any carpets or rugs are left for cleaning and storage until delivery, with any person engaged in the business of cleaning carpets and rugs, and the charges which have accrued thereon are due and unpaid for a period of six months, the person in whose custody the rugs or carpets are deposited for cleaning and storage, may satisfy the privilege as follows: By giving written notice to the person on whose account the goods are held, either by delivery in person or by registered letter addressed to his last known place of business or residence. This notice shall contain:

(1) An itemized statement of the claim, showing the sum due at the time of the notice and the date or dates when it became due.

(2) A demand, that the amount of the claim as stated in the notice, and of such further claim as shall accrue shall be paid on or before a day mentioned, not less than ten days from the delivery of the notice if it is personally delivered, or from the time when the notice should reach its destination according to the due course of the mails, if the notice is sent by mail.

(3) A statement that unless the claim is paid within the time specified, the goods will be sold.

In accordance with the terms of the notice, the goods may then be sold to satisfy any valid claim for which there may be a privilege, either at private sale or public auction, at the option of the privilege holder, without appraisement, and without limit or reserve.

If the sale should be at public auction, it may be cried by the privilege holder.

Cross References

C.C. arts. 3186, 3216, 3217.

§ 4685. Proceeds, disposition of

From the proceeds of the sale, the amount of the privilege shall be satisfied, including all reasonable charges of notice, advertisement, and sale. The balance if any, shall be credited on the books of the seller to the person who deposited the goods for storing and cleaning.

Cross References

C.C. arts. 3186, 3216, 3217.

§ 4686. Claimant may pay charges and acquire possession

Any time before the goods are sold, any person claiming the right of property or possession therein may pay the amount necessary to satisfy the privilege, including reasonable expenses incurred in serving notice, advertising, and preparing for the sale up to the time of payment. Upon tender of this amount, the goods shall be delivered to the person making the demand, if he should be entitled to the possession, upon payment of the charges. Otherwise, the goods shall be retained according to the terms of the original contract, and shall be sold as specified.

Cross References

C.C. arts. 3186, 3216, 3217.

§ 4687. Clothing or household goods; procedures for sale

A. As used in this Section, the term "person" means a natural person, partnership, corporation or other legal entity.

B. Any garment, clothing, wearing apparel or household goods which have been repaired, altered, dyed, cleaned, pressed, glazed or laundered, which remain in the possession of a person for a period of ninety days or more, may be sold to pay reasonable or agreed charges, together with any costs or expenses provided for in this Section; provided, however, that the person to whom such charges are due and payable shall first notify the owner or owners of the proposed sale of the articles belonging to them and the amount of the charges due thereon, and provided, further, that no property that is to be placed in storage after any of the services or labors mentioned herein have been performed shall be subject to sale under the provisions of this Subsection.

C. All garments, clothing, wearing apparel or household goods placed in storage or on which any of the services or labors mentioned in Subsection B of this Section have been performed and which then are placed in storage by agreement which remain in the possession of a person without the reasonable or agreed charges having been paid for a period of twelve months, may be sold to pay said charges, provided, however, that the person with whom any of these is stored first shall notify the owner or owners thereof of the time and place of such sale, and provided, further, that the provisions of this Subsection shall not apply to any person operating as a warehouse or warehouseman.

D. Where any of the articles listed in the Subsection B of this Section are in possession of any person on July 27, 1966, for the purpose of being repaired, altered, dyed, cleaned, pressed, glazed or laundered, and such services have been performed and the charges therefor have become due and are unpaid and the possession thereof for that purpose has continued or shall continue for ninety days or more, and where, on July 27, 1966, such articles are in the possession of any person for the purposes stated in Subsection C, and such services have been performed and the charges therefor have become due and are unpaid, and such possession has continued or shall continue for a period of twelve months or more, then the person so holding such articles may, after ninety days from July 27, 1966 in the case of those articles already held for the periods above prescribed, and after ninety days from the time such periods shall expire in each case as above prescribed, proceed to give the notices and to sell such articles for the purposes and pursuant to the terms and provisions of this Section, and dispose of the proceeds of such sales as provided in R.S. 9:4688.

E. The mailing by United States mail of a letter, with a return address marked thereon, addressed to the owner or owners at their address given at the time of delivery of such articles to the person shall constitute notice under the provisions of this Section. Said notice shall be mailed at least ten days before the articles belonging to the owner or owners may be sold for charges due thereon. The cost of mailing said letter shall be added to the charges.

If the chattel or chattels are not redeemed prior to the date set for the sale, the person may sell such articles on the day and at the time and place specified in such letter. Such sales may be made either at public auction or by private sale.

F. All persons taking advantage of the provisions of this Section must keep posted at all times, in a prominent place in their receiving office or offices, two notices which shall read as follows: "All articles cleaned, pressed, glazed, laundered, washed, altered, dyed or repaired, and not called for in ninety days, will be sold to pay charges," and "All articles which are stored by agreement and upon which the charges are not paid for twelve months, will be sold to pay charges."

G. The purpose and intent of this Section is to provide an inexpensive means of enforcing liens for small amounts, and to that end the provisions of this Section shall be deemed to create a lien in addition to, but shall not exclude, any liens which may exist by virtue of any other statute of the State of Louisiana.

Amended by Acts 1966, No. 43, § 1.

Cross References

C.C. arts. 3186, 3216.

§ 4688. Proceeds, disposition of

The proceeds of the sale in excess of the charges and necessary expenses of the procedure required by this Section, shall be held by the person for a period of six months, and if not reclaimed by the owner thereof within that time shall escheat to the parish and shall be paid over to the parish treasurer and shall be placed by him in the general fund of the parish in which the sale was held.

Amended by Acts 1966, No. 43, § 1.

Cross References

C.C. arts. 3186, 3216.

§ 4689. Clothing or household goods; disposition of other than by sale

Any unclaimed garments, clothing, wearing apparel or household goods which the person holding them feels could not be sold for an amount sufficient to pay the charges and expenses involved in the procedure for sale provided for in R.S. 9:4687 and 9:4688 of this Part plus the amount owed to the cleaning or laundry establishment may be given by the person holding them to any charitable organization willing to accept them.

Added by Acts 1966, No. 43, § 1.

Cross References

C.C. arts. 3186, 3216.

PART IX. JEWELRY, GEMS, AND WATCHES

§ 4701. Private sale of unclaimed goods of less than $10

Whenever any goods, jewelry, gems, precious stones, watches, or any other article or articles usually handled, sold, or made by jewelers, jewelry manufacturers, watchmakers, and dealers are deposited with any person so engaged for repairing, cleaning, inspection, or appraisement, and are repaired, cleaned, inspected, or appraised and are not claimed by their owners within six months from the date of deposit, the person with whom they are deposited may offer by private sale any or all of the unclaimed goods for a price of not less than the amount due for the services, provided the goods are appraised at less than ten dollars by two sworn disinterested appraisers.

Cross References

C.C. arts. 3186, 3216.

§ 4702. Notice to owner

The person with whom the goods are deposited shall first notify the apparent owner by registered mail at his last known address that the unclaimed goods are to be placed on sale. The notice shall be given at least thirty days prior to the sale and shall set forth the date, time, and place of the sale.

Cross References

C.C. arts. 3186, 3216.

§ 4703. Proceeds, disposition of

All money derived from such sales shall be placed in separate accounts and the seller shall only deduct the amount due him for his services, labor, and materials used in repairing, cleaning, inspecting, and appraising the particular article or goods sold. Any balance shall be credited on the books of the seller to the former owner. If unclaimed after the expiration of one year, from the date of sale the amount shall be paid into the state treasury.

Cross References

C.C. arts. 3186, 3216.

PART X. SUGAR, SYRUP, AND MOLASSES

§ 4721. Sugar refinery and mill employees

All managers, mechanics, or laborers employed in sugar refineries, sugar mills, or syrup mills have a privilege on all sugar, syrup, or molasses manufactured during the season by the refineries or mills where they are employed for the payment of their salaries or wages for a period of thirty days from the maturity of the debt.

This privilege may be enforced by the writ of sequestration, without the necessity of furnishing security therefor. This privilege has no effect against bona fide purchasers, but it is superior to the privilege granted by R.S. 9:4543 to unpaid vendors of sugar cane during the season.

Amended by Acts 1960, No. 31, § 1, eff. Jan. 1, 1961.

Cross References

C.C. arts. 3186, 3216, 3217.

PART XI. SHIPS AND OTHER VESSELS

§ 4741. Canal toll fees

The owners of private canals within the state have a privilege on all vessels for the payment of the toll or canal fees. This privilege is of equal rank with those granted by Civil Code Article 3237.

This privilege exists for six months from the date the toll becomes due.

Cross References

C.C. arts. 3186, 3216.

PART XII. PROCEEDS RECOVERED BY INJURED PERSON

§ 4751. Definitions

As used in this Part:

(1) "Ambulance service" means any person who through the use of one or more ambulances and certified emergency medical technicians as defined in R.S. 40:1231, provides transportation of sick or injured persons as a part of a regular course of conduct or business.

(2) "Health care provider" means a person, partnership, corporation, facility, or institution licensed by this state to provide health care or professional services as a physician, dentist, chiropractor, podiatrist, optometrist, pharmacist, dietician, physical therapist, occupational therapist, or psychologist.

(3) "Hospital" means an institution licensed as such by the state of Louisiana.

(4) "Person" means any individual, partnership, association, corporation, government, political subdivision, or governmental agency.

Added by Acts 1970, No. 409, § 1. Amended by Acts 1989, No. 328, § 1, eff. June 27, 1989; Acts 1990, No. 792, § 1; Acts 1995, No. 886, § 1; Acts 2001, No. 288, § 1; Acts 2003, No. 444, § 1.

Cross References

C.C. arts. 3186, 3217.

§ 4752. Privilege on net proceeds collected from third party in favor of medical providers for services and supplies furnished injured persons

A health care provider, hospital, or ambulance service that furnishes services or supplies to any injured person shall have a privilege for the reasonable charges or fees of such health care provider, hospital, or ambulance service on the net amount payable to the injured person, his heirs, or legal representatives, out of the total amount of any recovery or sum had, collected, or to be collected, whether by judgment or by settlement or compromise, from another person on account of such injuries, and on the net amount payable by any insurance company under any contract providing for indemnity or compensation to the injured person. The privilege of an attorney shall have precedence over the privilege created under this Section.

Added by Acts 1970, No. 409, § 2. Amended by Acts 1989, No. 328, § 1, eff. June 27, 1989; Acts 1990, No. 792, § 1.

Cross References

C.C. arts. 3186, 3217.

§ 4753. Written notice

A. The privilege created by R.S. 9:4752 shall become effective if, prior to the payment of insurance proceeds, or to the payment of any judgment, settlement, or compromise on account of injuries, a written notice containing the name and address of the injured person and the name and location of the interested health care provider, hospital, or ambulance service is delivered by certified mail, return receipt requested, or by facsimile transmission with proof of receipt of transmission by the interested health care provider, hospital, or ambulance services, or the attorney or agent for the interested health care provider, hospital, or ambulance service, to the injured person, to his attorney, to the person alleged to be liable to the injured person on account of the injuries sustained, to any insurance carrier which has insured such person against liability, and to any insurance company obligated by contract to pay indemnity or compensation to the injured person. This privilege shall be effective against all persons given notice according to the provisions of this Section and shall not be defeated nor rendered ineffective as against any person that has been given the required notice because of failure to give the notice to all those persons named in this Subsection.

B. If delivery of the notice required by this Section is made by facsimile transmission, and the sender fails to obtain a signed proof or receipt within seven days, then delivery shall be made by certified mail, return receipt requested, and costs of mailing shall be taxed as court costs. Added by Acts 1970, No. 409, § 3. Amended by Acts 1989, No. 328, § 1, eff. June 27, 1989; Acts 1990, No. 792, § 1; Acts 1995, No. 886, § 1; Acts 2003, No. 873, § 1; Acts 2003, No. 979, § 2; Acts 2008, No. 611, § 1.

Cross References
C.C. arts. 3186, 3217.

§ 4754. Failure to pay over monies after notice

Any person who, having received notice in accordance with the provisions hereof, pays over any monies subject to the privilege created herein, to any injured person, or to the attorney, heirs, or legal representatives of any injured person, shall be liable to the licensed health care provider, hospital, or ambulance service having such privilege for the amount thereof, not to exceed the net amount paid.
Added by Acts 1970, No. 409, § 4. Amended by Acts 1989, No. 328, § 1, eff. June 27, 1989; Acts 1990, No. 792, § 1.

Cross References
C.C. arts. 3186, 3217.

§ 4755. Itemized statements

A. Upon receipt of a written request, mailed by certified mail, return receipt requested, from any person who has been given notice, the licensed health care provider, hospital, or ambulance service having the privilege shall, within thirty days after receipt of such request, furnish an itemized statement of all charges having reference to the injured person.

B. If such licensed health care provider, hospital, or ambulance service fails to comply with the provisions of this Section, the privilege created shall be dissolved and ineffective.
Added by Acts 1970, No. 409, § 5. Amended by Acts 1989, No. 328, § 1, eff. June 27, 1989; Acts 1990, No. 792, § 1.

Cross References
C.C. arts. 3186, 3217.

PART XIII. SELF-SERVICE STORAGE FACILITIES

§ 4756. Short title

This Act shall be known as the "Self-Service Storage Facility Act."
Added by Acts 1981, No. 506, § 1.

Cross References
C.C. art. 3186.

§ 4757. Definitions

As used in this Part, unless the context clearly requires otherwise:

(1) "Self-service storage facility" means any real property designed and used for the purpose of renting or leasing individual storage space to lessees who are to have access to such for the purpose of storing and removing movable property. No lessee shall use a self-service storage facility for residential purposes. A self-service storage facility shall not be considered as a warehouse subject to the provisions of Title 10 of the Louisiana Revised Statutes; however, if an owner issues any warehouse receipt, bill of lading, or other document of title for the movable property stored, the owner and the lessees shall be subject to the provisions of Title 10 of the Louisiana Revised Statutes and the provisions of this Part shall not apply.

(2) "Owner" means the owner, operator, lessor, or sublessor of a self-service storage facility, his agent, or any other person authorized by him to manage the facility or to receive rent from a lessee under a rental agreement.

(3) "Lessee" means a person, his sublessee, successor, or assign, entitled to the use of storage space at a self-service storage facility under a rental agreement, to the exclusion of others.

(4) "Rental agreement" means any agreement or lease, written or oral, entered into between the owner and a lessee, that establishes or modifies the terms, conditions, rules, or any other provisions concerning the use of self-service storage facility.

(5) "Last known address" means that address provided by the lessee in the most recent rental agreement or the address provided by the lessee in a subsequent written notice of a change of address.
Added by Acts 1981, No. 506, § 1.

Cross References
C.C. art. 3186.

§ 4758. Privilege

The owner of a self-service storage facility, his heirs, executors, administrators, successors, and assigns has a privilege upon all movable property stored at a self-service storage facility for the debt due him for rent, and for all reasonable charges and expenses necessary for the preservation of movable property stored at a self-service storage facility, and for expenses reasonably incurred in the enforcement of this privilege, including, but not limited to, the cost of removing and replacing any locks, preparing a brief and general description of the movable property upon which the privilege is claimed, sending notices, and advertising, by sale of movable property or other disposition pursuant to this Part. The privilege granted herein attaches as of the date the movable property is brought to the self-service storage facility. This privilege is superior to and shall take priority over any other privileges or security interests, except the privilege shall be inferior to a vendor's privilege, or a chattel mortgage previously issued and recorded in the manner provided by law, or a previously perfected security interest under Chapter 9 of the Louisiana Commercial Laws (R.S.

10:9–101, et seq.). The exemption from seizure granted by R.S. 13:3881 shall not be applicable to property subject to this privilege.

Added by Acts 1981, No. 506, § 1. Amended by Acts 1989, No. 137, § 4, eff. Sept. 1, 1989.

Editor's note. For priority of a possessory lien, see Acts 2001, No. 128, § 1, effective July 1, 2001, now, R.S. 10:9–333: "A possessory lien on goods has priority over a security interest in the goods unless the lien is created by statute that expressly provides otherwise."

Cross References

C.C. art. 3186.

§ 4759. Options of owner upon lessee's default

In the event of default by the lessee, the owner of a self-service storage facility has the option to enforce judicially all of his rights under the rental agreement, including, if the agreement so provides, his right to accelerate all rentals that will become due in the future for the full term of the lease or to cancel the lease and enforce his privilege for the debt due him, as follows:

(1) Upon default by the lessee, the owner shall be authorized to remove any lock on the rented self-service storage space in order to compile a brief and general description of the movable property upon which a privilege is claimed and shall be entitled to place his own lock upon such space until his privilege is satisfied.

(2) The lessee shall be notified of the owner's intention to enforce his privilege.

(3) The notice shall be delivered in person to the lessee or sent by certified mail to the last known address of the lessee.

(4) The notice shall include:

(a) A copy of any written rental agreement between the owner and defaulting lessee, or, if the rental agreement is verbal, a summary of its terms and conditions.

(b) An itemized statement of the owner's claim, showing the sum due at the time of the notice and the date when the sum became due.

(c) A brief and general description of the movable property upon which a privilege is claimed. The description shall be reasonably adequate to permit the person notified to identify it, except that any container, including, but not limited to, a trunk, valise, or box that is locked, fastened, sealed, or tied in a manner which deters immediate access to its contents may be described as such without describing its contents.

(d) Notification that the lessee has been or shall be denied access to the movable property, if such denial is permitted under the terms of the rental agreement, with the name, street address, and telephone number of the owner or his designated agent whom the lessee may contact to respond to the notice.

(e) A demand for payment within a specified time not less than ten days after the date of mailing or delivery of the notice.

(f) A statement that the contents of the lessee's rented space are subject to the owner's privilege and that, unless the claim is paid within the time stated in the notice, the movable property is to be advertised for sale or other disposition and to be sold or otherwise disposed of to satisfy the owner's privilege for rent due and other charges at a specified time and place.

(5) Actual receipt of the notice made pursuant to this Section shall not be required. Within ten days after receipt of the notice, or within ten days after its mailing, whichever is earlier, an advertisement of the sale or other disposition of movable property subject to the privilege shall be published on at least one occasion in a newspaper of general circulation where the self-service storage facility is located. The advertisement shall include:

(a) A brief and general description of the movable property reasonably adequate to permit its identification as provided for in Paragraph (4)(c) of this Section.

(b) The address of the self-service storage facility and the number, if any, of the space where the movable property is located and the name of the lessee.

(c) The time, place, and manner of the sale or other disposition.

(6) The sale or other disposition of movable property shall take place not sooner than ten days following publication as required herein.

(7) Any sale or other disposition of the movable property shall conform to the terms of the notification as provided for in this Section.

(8) Any sale or other disposition of the movable property shall be held at the self-service storage facility, or at the nearest suitable place to where the movable property is held or stored, as indicated in the notice required herein. The owner shall sell the movable property to the highest bidder, if any. If there are no bidders, the owner may purchase the movable property for a price at least sufficient to satisfy his claim for rent due and all other charges, or he may donate the movable property to charity.

(9) Prior to any sale or other disposition of movable property to enforce the privilege granted by this Section, the lessee may pay the amount necessary to satisfy the privilege, including all reasonable expenses incurred under this Section, and thereby redeem the movable property. Upon receipt of such payment, the owner shall have no liability to any person with respect to such movable property.

(10) A purchaser in good faith of movable property sold by an owner to enforce the privilege granted herein takes the property free of any claims or rights of persons against whom the privilege was valid, despite noncompliance by the owner with the requirements of this Section.

(11) In the event of a sale held pursuant to this Section, the owner may satisfy his privilege from the proceeds of the sale, but shall hold the balance, if any, as a credit in the name of the lessee whose property was sold. The lessee may claim the balance of the proceeds within two years of the date of sale, without any interest thereon, and if unclaimed within the two year period, the credit shall become the property of the owner, without further recourse by the lessee. If the sale or other disposition of movable property made pursuant to this Part does not satisfy the owner's claim for rent due and other charges, the owner may proceed by ordinary proceedings to collect the balance owed.

Added by Acts 1981, No. 506, § 1.

Cross References

C.C. art. 3186.

§ 4760. Supplemental nature of act

Nothing in this Part shall be construed as in any manner impairing or affecting the right of parties to create additional privileges by special contract or agreement, nor shall it in any manner affect or impair other privileges created by any other law of this state.

Added by Acts 1981, No. 506, § 1.

Cross References

C.C. art. 3186.

PART XIV. RELATION TO UNIFORM COMMERCIAL CODE

§ 4770. Conflicts with Chapter 9 of the Uniform Commercial Code

A. This Code Title (Code Title XXI of Code Book III, R.S. 9:4501 et seq.), Part 8 of Chapter 7 of the Louisiana Mineral Code (R.S. 31:146 through 148), and Title XXI of Book III of the Louisiana Civil Code (Arts. 3182 through 3277) shall be interpreted and applied in a manner consistent with Chapter 9 of the Uniform Commercial Code. Any conflict between the priority ranking of privileges under this Title, Part 8 of Chapter 7 of the Louisiana Mineral Code, or Title XXI of Book III of the Louisiana Civil Code with the priority rules of Chapter 9 of the Uniform Commercial Code shall be resolved by application of the priority rules of Chapter 9 of the Uniform Commercial Code.

B. The rights of a vendor under Civil Code Articles 2561, 3217(7), and 3227 or of a lessor under Civil Code Article 2707 or Mineral Code Article 146 are subordinate to the rights of a secured party with a security interest under Chapter 9 of the Uniform Commercial Code except as otherwise provided by R.S. 10:9–322(g).

Added by Acts 1989, No. 137, § 5, eff. Sept. 1, 1989. Amended by Acts 1990, No. 1079, § 3, eff. Sept. 1, 1990 at 12:01 A.M; Acts 1991, No. 539, § 2, eff. Jan. 1, 1992 at 12:01 A.M; Acts 1993, No. 948, § 2, eff. Jan. 1, 1994; Acts 1997, No. 1295, § 1; Acts 2006, No. 533, § 2; Acts 2010, No. 378, § 2.

Cross References

C.C. arts. 2561, 2705, 3187, 3188, 3191, 3214, 3217, 3237, 3238, 3247, 3254, 3270, 3276.

PART XV. MARINA AND BOATYARD STORAGE FACILITIES

§ 4780. Short title

This Act shall be known as the "Marina and Boatyard Storage Act".

Added by Acts 2003, No. 840, § 1, eff. July 1, 2003.

§ 4781. Definitions

For the purposes of this Part, the following terms shall have the following meanings unless the context clearly requires otherwise:

(1) "Default" means the failure to pay obligations incurred by the storage of a boat, boat motor, boat trailer, or any other accessories thereto.

(2) "Last known address" means that address provided by the lessee in the most recent rental agreement or the address provided by the lessee in a subsequent written notice of a change of address.

(3) "Lessee" means a person, his sub-lessee, successor, or assign, entitled to the use of a space in a marina under a rental agreement, to the exclusion of others.

(4) "Lienholder" means a person who claims an interest in or privilege on the property pursuant to a mortgage properly recorded in the parish wherein the marina is located.

(5) "Marina" means a marina, boatyard, or marine repair yard that provides, as part of its commercial operation, the storage of boats, boat motors, or boat trailers.

(6) "Owner" means the owner, operator lessor, or sub-lessor of a marina, his agent, or any other person authorized by him to manage the facility or to receive rent from a lessee under a rental agreement.

(7) "Property" means a boat, boat motor, boat trailer, or any other boat accessories in storage at a marina.

(8) "Rental agreement" means any written agreement or lease, entered into between the marina owner and a lessee that establishes or modifies the terms, conditions, rules, or any other provisions concerning use of the marina.

Added by Acts 2003, No. 840, § 1, eff. July 1, 2003. Amended by Acts 2012, No. 752, § 1.

§ 4782. Privilege

A. Privilege created. A marina owner has a privilege on property stored at that marina for rent, labor, or other charges and for expenses reasonably incurred in the sale of that property under the provisions of this Part.

B. Exclusion. This Part does not create a privilege on a documented vessel subject to a preferred ship mortgage or other preferred maritime privilege pursuant to 46 U.S.C. Chapter 131.

Added by Acts 2003, No. 840, § 1, eff. July 1, 2003.

§ 4783. Notice of privilege

A. A property owner must be notified of the privilege created by this Part before enforcement of the privilege by a marina owner. Notification of the privilege created by this Part is satisfied by:

(1) **Written storage agreement.** A written rental agreement signed by the property owner that includes a notice of the privilege created by this Part; or

(2) **Written notice of privilege.** Written notification of the privilege sent by the marina owner to the property owner.

B. A marina owner who does not have a written rental agreement that includes a notice of the privilege created by this Part may not initiate an enforcement action under R.S. 9:4784 until thirty days after the written notice of a privilege required by Paragraph (A)(2) of this Section is delivered to the property owner.

Added by Acts 2003, No. 840, § 1, eff. July 1, 2003. Amended by Acts 2012, No. 752, § 1.

§ 4784. Enforcement of privilege

A. A marina owner may enforce a privilege created by this Part only if the property owner has been notified of the privilege as required by R.S. 9:4783.

(1) **Sale; use of proceeds.** If a property owner is in default for a period of more than one hundred eighty days, a marina owner may enforce a privilege by selling the stored

property at a commercially reasonable public sale for cash. As used in this Section, "commercially reasonable" has the same meaning as in the Commercial Laws, R.S. 10:1–101 through 9–710. The proceeds of the sale must be applied in the following order:

(a) To the reasonable expenses of the sale incurred by the marina owner including, to the extent not prohibited by law, reasonable attorney's fees and legal expenses.

(b) To the satisfaction of all superior mortgages on the property held by mortgage holders of record to be paid in the order of priority.

(c) To the satisfaction of the privilege created by this Part.

(d) To the satisfaction of all other mortgages and privileges on the property held by all lienholders of record to be paid in the order of priority.

(e) To the extent that the proceeds of sale exceed the sum of the foregoing, the surplus must be paid by the marina owner to the property owner.

(2) If proceeds of the sale are not sufficient to satisfy the property owner's outstanding obligations to the marina owner or any lienholder of record, the property owner remains liable to the marina owner or lienholder for the deficiency.

B. Advertisement; notice of default. Before conducting a sale under this Section, the marina owner shall:

(1) Send a notice of default to the property owner. The marina owner shall provide a copy of the notice to each lienholder of record. The notice must include:

(a) A statement that the property is subject to a privilege held by the marina owner.

(b) A statement of the marina owner's claim indicating the charges due on the date of the notice, the amount of any additional charges that will become due before the date of sale, and the date those additional charges will become due.

(c) A demand for payment of the charges due within a specified time not less than thirty days after the date the notice is delivered to the property owner.

(d) A statement that unless the claim is paid within the time stated, the property will be sold, specifying the time and place of the sale.

(e) The name, street address, and telephone number of the marina owner, or the marina owner's designated agent, whom the property owner may contact to respond to the notice.

(2) After the expiration of the thirty day period set forth in Subparagraph (1)(c) of this Subsection, publish an advertisement of the sale once a week for two consecutive weeks in a newspaper of general circulation in the area where the sale is to be held. The advertisement must include a general description of the property, the name of the property owner, and the time and place of the sale. The date of the sale must be more than fifteen days after the date the first advertisement of the sale is published.

C. Location of sale. A sale under this Part must be held at the marina or at the nearest suitable location.

D. Purchasers. A purchaser of property sold at a commercially reasonable sale pursuant to this Part takes the property free and clear of any rights of persons against whom the privilege was valid and all other lienholders of record. The purchase of a boat sold pursuant to this Part shall require a notarized bill of sale signed by the buyer and a representative of the marina, clearly identifying the marina as the seller, and shall state that the boat was sold pursuant to the Marina and Boatyard Storage Act. The marina shall attach to the bill of sale the proof of notice and sale requirements, including proof of all publications.

E. Marina owner liability. If the marina owner complies with the provisions of this Part, the marina owner's liability is as follows:

(1) To a lienholder of record, the marina owner's liability is limited to payment from the net proceeds received from the sale of the property.

(2) To the property owner, the marina owner's liability is limited to the net proceeds received from the sale of the property after payment in full of all lienholders of record.

F. Denying access to marina. A marina owner may deny a property owner who has been notified under Subsection B of this Section access to the marina, except that the property owner is entitled to access to the marina during normal business hours for the purpose of satisfying the privilege or viewing and verifying the condition of the property.

G. Notices. Except as otherwise provided, all notices required by this Part must be sent by registered or certified mail, return receipt requested, or by commercial courier as defined by R.S. 13:3204(D). Notices sent to a marina owner must be sent to the owner's business address or to the address of the owner's designated representative. Notices to a property owner must be sent to the property owner at the property owner's last known address. Notices to a lienholder of record must be sent to the address of the lienholder as provided in the public record that serves to perfect the lienholder's interest in the property. Notices are considered delivered on either of the following dates:

(1) The date the recipient of the notice signs the return receipt or, if the notice is undeliverable, the date the post office last attempts to deliver the notice.

(2) The date of delivery as indicated on the signed receipt of delivery obtained by the commercial courier.

Added by Acts 2003, No. 840, § 1, eff. July 1, 2003. Amended by Acts 2012, No. 752, § 1.

§ 4785. Cessation of enforcement actions

A marina owner shall cease enforcement actions immediately if:

(1) Payment by owner. The property owner pays the marina owner the full amount necessary to satisfy the privilege. At any time before the conclusion of a sale conducted under this Part, the property owner may redeem the property by paying the full amount necessary to satisfy the privilege; or

(2) Payment by other lienholders. A person other than the marina owner who has a lien on the property pays the marina owner the full amount necessary to satisfy the privilege held by the marina owner. Upon payment by a lienholder of record, the marina owner shall hold the property for the benefit of and at the direction of that lienholder and may not deliver possession of the property to the property owner. Unless the marina owner and the lienholder enter into a new rental agreement, the lienholder shall arrange removal of the property from the marina.

Added by Acts 2003, No. 840, § 1, eff. July 1, 2003.

PART XVI. OTHER PRIVILEGES ON MOVABLES

§ 4790. Child support arrearages; privilege on motor vehicles

An obligee who has a judgment ordering the payment of past due child support may file the judgment with the office of motor vehicles in accordance with R.S. 32:708.1 and subject to the provisions of R.S. 13:3881. The judgment, when filed, shall operate as privilege on any titled motor vehicle, as defined in R.S. 10:9–102(d)(19), owned by the support obligor at the time deficient child support judgment is filed with the office of motor vehicles, and shall not affect liens, privileges, chattel mortgages, or security interests as provided in R.S. 10:9–101 et seq. or mortgages already affecting or encumbering the motor vehicle at the date of the filing. The motor vehicle shall be subject to seizure and sale for the payment of the judgment according to the preference and rank of the privilege securing its payment. The privilege for child support shall be legally subordinate to motor vehicle purchase money security interests.

Added by Acts 2006, No. 772, § 1.

PART XVII. TOWED AND STORED VESSEL ACT

§ 4791. Short title

This Part shall be known as the "Towed and Stored Vessel Act".

Added by Acts 2012, No. 752, § 1.

§ 4792. Definitions

For the purposes of this Part, the following terms shall have the following meanings:

(1) "Department" means the Department of Wildlife and Fisheries.

(2) "Licensed storage facility" means a lot, yard, or other storage, parking, or repair facility licensed by the Department of Public Safety and Corrections, office of state police, to store towed vehicles as provided by R.S. 32:1714.

(3) "Tow truck" means any motor vehicle equipped with a boom or booms, winches, slings, tilt beds, or similar equipment designed for the towing or recovery of vehicles and other objects which cannot operate under their own power or for other reason is required to be transported by means of towing and licensed by the Department of Public Safety and Corrections pursuant to R.S. 32:1711 et seq.

(4) "Towed vessel" means any vessel titled under the Vessel and Motor Titling Act, R.S. 34:852.1 et seq., or required to be registered pursuant to R.S. 34:851.1 et seq., towed by a tow truck and being held at a licensed storage facility. "Towed vessel" does not include any vessel with a valid or expired registration number awarded pursuant to federal law or a federally approved numbering system of another state, unless subsequently registered in Louisiana.

Added by Acts 2012, No. 752, § 1.

§ 4793. Privilege

A licensed storage facility has a privilege on a vessel, including any inboard or outboard motor attached to the vessel, towed and stored at that facility for the towing charges and storage fees. However, this Part shall not create a privilege on a documented vessel subject to a preferred ship mortgage or other preferred maritime privilege pursuant to 46 U.S.C. Chapter 313.

Added by Acts 2012, No. 752, § 1.

§ 4794. Vessel owner information

The licensed storage facility shall provide the department or its authorized agent, within three business days of the vessel being towed and stored, the vessel's registration numbers, hull identification number (HIN), motor serial number, and any other identifying factors requested by the department. The department or its authorized agent shall provide to a licensed storage facility holding a towed vessel the name and address of the last registered owner of the vessel and lienholders as listed in the official records of the agency.

Added by Acts 2012, No. 752, § 1.

§ 4795. Notice of privilege and default

A. The towed vessel owner and any lienholders shall be notified of the privilege created by this Part before enforcement of the privilege by the licensed storage facility. Notification of the privilege created by this Part shall be satisfied by the following:

(1) For owners and lienholders identified by the department pursuant to R.S. 9:4794, written notification of the privilege sent by the licensed storage facility, using a certificate of mailing within ten business days from the date the department or its authorized agent sends the owner and lienholder information of the stored vessel to the licensed storage facility. If the department or its authorized agent sends the information electronically, the licensed storage facility shall send notice within five business days.

(2) After compliance with R.S. 9:4794, for those vessels for which no records exist in the official records of the department, publishing notification of the privilege in the official newspaper of the parish in which the towed vessel was towed on two separate occasions.

B. Notification shall include the following:

(1) As applicable, registration numbers, a general description of the towed vessel, including the make, length, type of vessel, whether inboard or outboard motors, and make and horsepower, registration numbers, motor serial number, and hull identification number (HIN).

(2) The date and location where the vessel was found, the present location, charges due on the date of the notice, and name, street address, and telephone number of the licensed storage facility, which the owner may contact to respond to the notice.

(3) A statement that the vessel is subject to the privilege held by the licensed storage facility and that the vessel owner is in default.

(4) A statement that unless the claim is paid within the time stated the property will be sold at a commercially reasonably public sale, and the location and date of the sale, which shall not be earlier than thirty days after the date notice is mailed to the owner or thirty days after the last date of notification as provided in this Section. As used in this Part, "commercially reasonably" has the same meaning as in the Commercial Laws, R.S. 10:1–101 through 9–710.

Added by Acts 2012, No. 752, § 1.

§ 4796. Advertisement: enforcement of privilege

After the expiration of the thirty-day period set forth in R.S. 9:4795(B)(4), the licensed storage facility shall publish an advertisement of the sale once a week for two consecutive weeks in the official newspaper of the parish where the sale is to be held. The date of the sale shall be more than fifteen days after the date of the first advertisement of the sale is published. The advertisement shall include the following:

(1) The name of the last registered owner of the vessel, if known.

(2) The date and location where the vessel was found.

(3) As applicable, the registration numbers, a general description of the towed vessel, including the make, length, type of vessel, whether inboard or outboard motors, and make and horsepower, outboard motor serial number, and hull identification number (HIN).

Added by Acts 2012, No. 752, § 1.

§ 4797. Sale and purchasers

A. A sale under this Part shall be held at the location of the licensed storage facility or at the nearest suitable location.

B. The vessel shall be sold to the highest bidder and shall require a notarized bill of sale signed by the buyer and a representative of the licensed storage facility, clearly identifying the licensed storage facility as the seller, and shall state the boat was sold pursuant to this Part. The licensed storage facility shall attach to the bill of sale the proof of notice and sale requirements, including proof of all publications, without which the bill of sale shall be null and void.

C. The proceeds of the sale shall be applied in the following order:

(1) To the reasonable expenses of the sale including, to the extent not prohibited by law, reasonable attorney fees and legal expenses.

(2) To the satisfaction of all superior mortgages on the vessel held by holders of record to be paid in order of priority.

(3) To the satisfaction of the privilege created by this Part.

(4) To the satisfaction of all other mortgages and privileges on the vessel held by all lienholders of record to be paid in the order of priority.

(5) To the extent the proceeds of the sale exceed the sum of the foregoing, the surplus shall be paid to the owner of the vessel. However, if the funds so credited are not claimed by the owner within six months from the date of the sale, the funds shall be transferred to the administrator of the Uniform Unclaimed Property Act of 1997 as unclaimed property.

(6) If proceeds of the sale are not sufficient to satisfy the vessel owner's outstanding obligations to the licensed storage facility or any lienholder of record, the vessel owner remains liable to the licensed storage facility for the deficiency.

D. A purchaser of the vessel sold at a commercially reasonable sale pursuant to this Part takes the vessel free and clear of any rights of persons against whom the privilege was valid and all other lienholders of record.

E. The vessel owner shall be entitled access to the licensed storage facility during normal business hours for the purpose of satisfying the privilege or viewing and verifying the condition of the vessel.

F. Except as otherwise provided, all notices required by this Part shall be sent by certificate of mailing. Notices sent to the licensed storage facility shall be sent to the business address or to the address of the designated representative. Notices to the vessel owner shall be sent to the vessel owner's address as identified in the official records of the department. Notices to a lienholder of record shall be sent to the address of the lienholder as provided in the public record that serves to perfect the lienholder's interest in the vessel.

Added by Acts 2012, No. 752, § 1.

§ 4798. Regulations

The department may promulgate rules and regulations to implement the provisions of this Part.

Added by Acts 2012, No. 752, § 1.

CHAPTER 2. PRIVILEGES ON IMMOVABLES

PART I. PRIVATE WORKS ACT

SUBPART A. LIABILITY OF OWNERS AND CONTRACTORS FOR THE IMPROVEMENT OF AN IMMOVABLE

Section
4801. Improvement of immovable by owner; privileges securing the improvement.
4802. Improvement of immovable by contractor; claims against the owner and contractor; privileges securing the improvement.
4803. Amounts secured by claims and privileges.

SUBPART B. DEFINITIONS

4806. Owner defined; interest affected.
4807. Contractor, general contractor, subcontractor defined.
4808. Work defined.

SUBPART C. WORK PERFORMED BY GENERAL CONTRACTORS

4811. Notice of a contract with a general contractor to be filed.
4812. Bond required; terms and conditions.
4813. Liability of the surety.
4814. Contractors; misapplication of payments prohibited; civil penalties; payment of claims, attorney fees and costs.
4815. Escrow of funds due under contract; procedures.

SUBPART D. CLAIMS AND PRIVILEGES; EFFECTIVENESS; PRESERVATION; RANKING; EXTINGUISHMENT

4820. Privileges; effective date.
4821. Ranking of privileges.
4822. Preservation of claims and privileges.
4823. Extinguishment of claims and privileges.

SUBPART E. FILING; CANCELLATION; PEREMPTION

4831. Filing; place of filing; contents.
4832. Cancellation of notice of contract.
4833. Request to cancel the inscription of claims and privileges; cancellation; notice of pendency of action.
4834. Notice of contract; cessation of effect, reinscription.

APPENDIX 1—REVISED STATUTES, TITLE 9

Section
4835. Filing of bond or other security; cancellation of statement of claim or privilege or notice of pendency of action.

SUBPART F. PROCEDURE FOR ENFORCEMENT; BURDEN OF PROOF

4841. Enforcement of claims and privileges; concursus.
4842. Delivery of notice or other documents and materials; burden of proof.

SUBPART G. RESIDENTIAL TRUTH IN CONSTRUCTION ACT

4851. Scope; definition.
4852. Notice.
4853. Copies of notice.
4854. Lien rights unaffected.
4855. Penalty for violation.

PART II. OIL, GAS, AND WATER WELLS

SUBPART A. IN GENERAL

4861. Definitions.
4862. Privilege for labor, services, or supplies.
4863. Property subject to the privilege.
4864. When the privilege is established and when it is extinguished.
4865. Cessation of effect as to certain third persons.
4866. Extinction as to movable property.
4867. Notice to operator.
4868. Statement of privilege; form and content.
4869. Purchaser of hydrocarbons; effect of privilege and notices required.
4870. Ranking of privileges.
4871. Enforcement of claims and privileges.
4872. Filing of bond or other security; cancellation of statement of privilege or notice of pendency of action.
4873. Delivery of movables to well site; burden of proof.
4874 to 4880. [Blank].

SUBPART B. PRIVILEGES AND OTHER RIGHTS OF OPERATORS AND NON–OPERATORS

4881. Definitions.
4882. Privilege of the operator and non-operator.
4883. Property subject to the privilege.
4884. When the privilege is established and when it is extinguished.
4885. Cessation of effect as to certain third persons.
4886. Extinction as to movable property.
4887. Statement of privilege; form and content.
4888. Ranking of privileges.
4889. Enforcement of privileges.

PART III. RAILROADS

SUBPART A. IN GENERAL

4901. Railroad tracks, road-beds, etc., privilege for material or labor.
4902. Recordation unnecessary; effective period.
4903. Rank.

PART IV. PUBLIC WORKS

SUBPART A. IN GENERAL

4921. Feed for livestock used on public works; filing claims for.
4922. Statement of amount due.

Section
4923. Feed claims have same rights as those for labor or materials.

SUBPART B. BONDING CLAIMS

4941. Contractor may bond claims.

PART V. MISCELLANEOUS

4961. Attorney's fees, limitation for recordation of lien.
4962 to 4965. Repealed.

PART I. PRIVATE WORKS ACT

SUBPART A. LIABILITY OF OWNERS AND CONTRACTORS FOR THE IMPROVEMENT OF AN IMMOVABLE

§ 4801. Improvement of immovable by owner; privileges securing the improvement

The following persons have a privilege on an immovable to secure the following obligations of the owner arising out of a work on the immovable:

(1) Contractors, for the price of their work.

(2) Laborers or employees of the owner, for the price of work performed at the site of the immovable.

(3) Sellers, for the price of movables sold to the owner that become component parts of the immovable, or are consumed at the site of the immovable, or are consumed in machinery or equipment used at the site of the immovable.

(4) Lessors, for the rent of movables used at the site of the immovable and leased to the owner by written contract.

(5) Registered or certified surveyors or engineers, or licensed architects, or their professional subconsultants, employed by the owner, for the price of professional services rendered in connection with a work that is undertaken by the owner. A "professional subconsultant" means a registered or certified surveyor or engineer or licensed architect employed by the prime professional, as described in this Paragraph. In order for the privilege of the professional subconsultant to arise, the subconsultant must give notice to the owner within thirty days after the date that the subconsultant enters into a written contract of employment. The notice shall include the name and address of the subconsultant, the name and address of his employer, and the general nature of the work to be performed by the subconsultant.
Acts 1981, No. 724, § 1, eff. Jan. 1, 1982. Amended by Acts 1987, No. 685, § 1; Acts 1988, No. 713, § 1.

Comments—1981

(a) This section incorporates the privileges found in the former R.S. 9:4801 securing the direct obligations of the owner to the persons named for amounts arising out of work done for the owner. It presupposes a direct contractual relationship between the privilege holder and the owner. The privilege is thus accessory to the conventional obligation of the owner. Although the description of the persons given a privilege has been simplified, no substantive changes to the prior law are intended. The obligations secured must arise out of a work (see Section 4808, *infra*) and must be of the nature described with respect to each claimant.

For Annotative Materials, see West's Louisiana Statutes Annotated

(b) Subsection (1) must be read in conjunction with Section 4811D, *infra*, which in certain cases denies the privilege to a general contractor who does not properly and timely file notice of his contract. This is consistent with the existing law. See Officer v. Combre, 194 So. 441 (La.App.1st Cir. 1940); Glassell, Taylor & Robinson v. John Harris, 26 So.2d 1 (La.1946); Gauguin Inc. v. Addison, 288 So.2d 893 (La.App.1st Cir. 1973); and Dickson v. Moran, 344 So.2d 102 (La.App.2d Cir. 1977).

(c) Subsection (2) contemplates that the obligations secured must be for the price of labor or services of an employee. A contractor who renders personal services in the course of performing his contract is not included in this category. The owner is not liable to him for such services but only for the price of the contract. This distinction is significant, primarily because of the priority given to the privileges of employees by Section 4821, *infra*.

(d) Subsection (3) recognizes the distinction articulated in Heard v. Southwest Steel Products, 124 So.2d 211 (La.App.2d Cir. 1960), between a contract of sale and a contract for the performance of work. See also Leonard B. Hebert, Jr. & Co. v. Kinler, 336 So.2d 922 (La.App.4th Cir. 1976). It is largely irrelevant to the person dealing with the owner. If he is a contractor he has a privilege under Subsection (1); if he is a seller he has a privilege under Subsection (3). The distinction becomes important in that a seller to a contractor is given rights under the act by Section 4802 but a seller to a seller is not. Subsection (3) also incorporates the interpretation given the former act that the things sold must be physically incorporated into the immovable or consumed in the work. See Hortman-Salmen Co., Inc. v. White, 123 So. 711 (La.1929); Trouard v. Calcasieu Building Materials, 62 So.2d 81 (La.1952); Century National Bank v. Parent, 341 So.2d 1371 (La. App.4th Cir. 1977). See also Section 4842B, *infra*. Electricity is a movable for the purposes of this Part.

(e) Subsection (4) incorporates part of the former R.S. 9:4801.1. The additional requirements of R.S. 9:4801.1 are found in Sections 4802G and 4803B, *infra*.

(f) Subsection (5) restates part of the former R.S. 9:4813. It recognizes the privilege only exists if the work done by surveyor or engineer relates to a work on the property. See Construction Eng. Co. of La. v. Village Shop Ctr., 168 So.2d 826 (La. App.2d Cir. 1964). Other provisions of the former R.S. 9:4813 regulating this privilege are found in Section 4822D, *infra*. This act requires the surveyor or engineer to be either certified or registered under the provisions of R.S. 37:681 et seq.

Cross References
C.C. arts. 3186, 3230, 3231, 3249, 3250, 3251, 3267, 3268, 3272.

§ 4802. Improvement of immovable by contractor; claims against the owner and contractor; privileges securing the improvement

A. The following persons have a claim against the owner and a claim against the contractor to secure payment of the following obligations arising out of the performance of work under the contract:

(1) Subcontractors, for the price of their work.

(2) Laborers or employees of the contractor or a subcontractor, for the price of work performed at the site of the immovable.

(3) Sellers, for the price of movables sold to the contractor or a subcontractor that become component parts of the immovable, or are consumed at the site of the immovable, or are consumed in machinery or equipment used at the site of the immovable.

(4) Lessors, for the rent of movables used at the site of the immovable and leased to the contractor or a subcontractor by written contract.

(5) Prime consultant registered or certified surveyors or engineers, or licensed architects, or their professional subconsultants, employed by the contractor or a subcontractor, for the price of professional services rendered in connection with a work that is undertaken by the contractor or subcontractor.

(a) A "professional subconsultant" means a registered or certified surveyor or engineer, or licensed architect employed by the prime consultant.

(b) For the privilege under this Subsection to arise, a prime consultant or professional subconsultant shall give written notice to the owner within thirty working days after the date that the prime consultant or professional subconsultant is employed. The notice shall include the name and address of the prime consultant or professional subconsultant, the name and address of his employer, and the general nature of the work to be performed by the prime consultant or professional subconsultant.

B. The claims against the owner shall be secured by a privilege on the immovable on which the work is performed.

C. The owner is relieved of the claims against him and the privileges securing them when the claims arise from the performance of a contract by a general contractor for whom a bond is given and maintained as required by R.S. 9:4812 and when notice of the contract with the bond attached is properly and timely filed as required by R.S. 9:4811.

D. Claims against the owner and the contractor granted by this Part are in addition to other contractual or legal rights the claimants may have for the payment of amounts owed them.

E. A claimant may assert his claim against either the contractor, his surety, or the owner without the joinder of the others. The claim shall not be subject to a plea of discussion or division.

F. A contractor shall indemnify the owner for claims against the owner arising from the work to be performed under the contract. A subcontractor shall indemnify the owner, the contractor, and any subcontractor from or through whom his rights are derived, for amounts paid by them for claims under this part arising from work performed by the subcontractor.

G. (1) For the privilege under this Section or R.S. 9:4801(4) to arise, the lessor of the movables shall deliver notice to the owner and to the contractor not more than ten days after the movables are first placed at the site of the immovable for use in a work. The notice shall contain the name and mailing address of the lessor and lessee and a description sufficient to identify the movable property placed at the site of the immovable for use in a work. The notice shall state the term of rental and terms of payment and shall be signed by the lessor and lessee.

(2) For the privilege under this Section or R.S. 9:4801(3) to arise, the seller of movables shall deliver a notice of nonpayment to the owner at least ten days before filing a statement of his claim and privilege. The notice shall be served by registered or certified mail, return receipt requested, and shall contain the name and address of the seller of movables, a general description of the materials provided, a description sufficient to identify the immovable property against which a lien may be claimed, and a written statement of the seller's lien rights for the total amount owed, plus interest and recordation fees. The requirements of this Paragraph (G)(2) shall apply to a seller of movables sold for use or consumption in work on an immovable for residential purposes.

(3) In addition to the other provisions of this Section, if the seller of movables has not been paid by the subcontractor and has not sent notice of nonpayment to the general contractor and the owner, then the seller shall lose his right to file a privilege or lien on the immovable property. The return receipt indicating that certified mail was properly addressed to the last known address of the general contractor and the owner and deposited in the U.S. mail on or before seventy-five days from the last day of the month in which the material was delivered, regardless of whether the certified mail was actually delivered, refused, or unclaimed satisfies the notice provision hereof or no later than the statutory lien period, whichever comes first. The provisions of this Paragraph shall apply only to disputes arising out of recorded contracts.

Acts 1981, No. 724, § 1, eff. Jan. 1, 1982. Amended by Acts 1989, No. 41, § 1, eff. June 15, 1989; Acts 1991, No. 1024, § 1, eff. Jan. 1, 1992; Acts 1999, No. 1134, § 1; Acts 2013, No. 357, § 1.

Comments—1981

(a) This Section consolidates the provisions of the former law regulating the rights of persons who supply services or materials to a contractor or subcontractor of an owner and who thus have no direct contractual relationship with the owner or, in the case of the suppliers to subcontractors, with the contractor, under various provisions of former Sections 9:4801, 4802, 4806 and 4812. Personal liability to these persons was imposed upon the owner and a privilege was imposed upon the immovable for the amounts owed the claimants. The owner was relieved of liability and could obtain cancellation of the privilege if the work was performed by a general contractor under a written and properly recorded contract to which was attached a proper bond. (See former R.S. 9:4812 and 4806.) Former Section 9:4803 was interpreted as imposing a statutory liability upon the contractor to persons dealing with his subcontractor, if they either filed their claims timely or gave notice to the contractor. (See former R.S. 4814C.) The position of the contractor to such persons where no contract was filed or bond provided was not expressly provided for under the former law. Subsection A continues the basic pattern of the former law but modifies and clarifies the relationship of the statutory liability and privilege it creates to the contractual obligation of the contractor or subcontractor giving rise to the claim. Thus, the personal liability imposed upon the owner and that imposed upon the contractor are distinct and may be separately extinguished. (See R.S. 9:4823, *infra.*) The statutory liability imposed upon the contractor includes not only claims arising from work done for subcontractors but for those arising out of work done directly for the contractor. While the extinguishment of the statutory liability of the contractor in the latter case will not relieve him, or his surety, of their contractual liabilities, it may affect the priority of the claim vis a vis those claimants who preserve such statutory liability as against the surety. (See R.S. 9:4813, *infra.*)

(b) Although the personal liability imposed upon the owner and the personal liability imposed upon the contractor are not those of sureties the claims are clearly obligations of security and are accessory to the primary contractual obligations of the claimants. Thus, extinguishment of the primary contractual obligation extinguishes the statutory liability. (See Section 4823A(3), *infra.*) It is intended that the owner or contractor who is required to pay a claimant will be legally subrogated to the claimant's contractual rights. See Civil Code Article 2161(3) [see, now, C.C. arts. 1804, 1829].

(c) Subsection B gives a privilege on the immovable to those persons to whom the owner is made liable by Subsection A. Although, under the former law the personal liability of the owner for the obligations of his contractors or their subcontractors to persons supplying services or materials to the immovable and the privilege on the immovable were separately provided for, it was not possible for one to exist without the other, except perhaps in the case where the claimant filed notice of his claim but did not serve notice of it upon the owner. The present section makes it clear that the privilege given under this section is accessory to and only secures the personal liability of the owner imposed by Subsection A. Thus, under both this section and Section 4801 the privilege upon the owner's property secures the liability of the owner.

(d) Subsection C continues the rule implicit in the former law that the statutory liability of the owner and the privilege securing it is extinguished if the work is performed by a general contractor who timely and properly files the bond and notice of contract. The contractor, in such a case, enjoys a privilege under Section 4801, *supra*, for the price of the contract.

(e) Subsections D and E make it clear that the liability of the owner, contractor, and surety are distinct from and supplemental to any contractual obligations that may exist. Although each may be liable to the claimant who takes steps to perfect his rights, such liabilities are not expressed as being solidary, and are in fact solidary only in the imperfect sense. It is not intended that the technical rules regulating the obligations of principals bound in solido prescribed by Civil Code Articles 2091 et seq. [see, now, generally, C.C. art. 1794 et seq.] apply to such relationships.

(f) Subsection F insures that responsibility for the obligations giving rise to the claims and privileges regulated by the act is ultimately imposed upon the person who is in the first instance contractually bound for it. If there is a surety bond, Section 4812C(1), *infra*, also makes the surety liable to the owner who is required to pay a claim under this section. The surety who so pays will, under the general rules of suretyship, be subrogated to the owner's rights of indemnity. (See Civil Code Article 3053 [see, now, C.C. art. 3048].)

(g) Subsection G incorporates and modifies slightly the requirements of former R.S. 9:4801.1. The purpose of the provision is to give notice to the owner and contractor (in case of a lease to a subcontractor) that equipment being used upon the premises by a contractor or subcontractor is leased and thus potentially creating liability under the act, and to disclose the nature and extent of such potential liability. This subsection should not be construed to require that a copy of the lease will have to be separately delivered to the contractor or owner who is for some reason already a party to it. Nor is such delivery required for a lease made directly to the owner and giving rise to a privilege under Section 4801, *supra*.

Cross References

C.C. arts. 3186, 3219, 3230, 3231, 3249, 3250, 3251, 3267, 3268, 3272.

§ 4803. Amounts secured by claims and privileges

A. The privileges granted by R.S. 9:4801 and the claims granted by R.S. 9:4802 secure payment of:

(1) The principal amounts of the obligations described in R.S. 9:4801 and R.S. 9:4802(A), interest due thereon, and fees paid for filing the statement required by R.S. 9:4822.

(2) Expenses incurred by the claimant or other person having a privilege, for the cost of delivering movables that become component parts of the immovable, or are consumed at the site of the immovable, or are consumed in machinery or equipment used at the site of the immovable, if the amounts are owed by the owner, contractor, or subcontractor to the claimant or person having the privilege.

(3) Amounts owed under collective bargaining agreements with respect to a laborer's or employee's wages or other compensation for which a claim or privilege is granted and which are payable to other persons for vacation, health and welfare, pension, apprenticeship and training, supplemental unemployment benefits, and other fringe benefits considered as wages by the secretary of labor of the United States in determining prevailing wage rates, unless the immovable upon which the work is performed is designed or intended to be occupied primarily as a residence by four families or less. Trustees, trust funds, or other persons to whom the employer is to make such payments may assert and enforce claims for the amounts in the same manner and subject to the same procedures provided for other amounts due laborers or employees granted a claim or privilege under this Part.

B. The claim or privilege granted the lessor of a movable by R.S. 9:4801(4) or R.S. 9:4802(A)(4) is limited to and secures only that part of the rentals accruing during the time the movable is located at the site of the immovable for use in a work. A movable shall be deemed not located at the site of the immovable for use in a work after:

(1) The work is substantially completed or abandoned; or

(2) A notice of termination of the work is filed; or

(3) The lessee has abandoned the movable, or use of the movable in a work is completed or no longer necessary, and the owner or contractor gives written notice to the lessor of abandonment or completion of use.

Acts 1981, No. 724, § 1, eff. Jan. 1, 1982.

Comments—1981

(a) Subsection A incorporates the substance of the former law and makes no major change in it.

(b) Subsection B incorporates the substance of former Section 4801.1. It limits the amount of the rent incurred under the lease that the act protects.

Cross References

C.C. arts. 3186, 3230, 3231, 3249, 3250, 3251, 3267, 3268.

SUBPART B. DEFINITIONS

§ 4806. Owner defined; interest affected

A. An owner, co-owner, naked owner, owner of a predial or personal servitude, possessor, lessee, or other person owning or having the right to the use or enjoyment of an immovable or having an interest therein shall be deemed to be an owner.

B. The claims against an owner granted by R.S. 9:4802 are limited to the owner or owners who have contracted with the contractor or to the owner or owners who have agreed in writing to the price and work of the contract of a lessee, wherein such owner or owners have specifically agreed to be liable for any claims granted by the provisions of R.S. 9:4802. If more than one owner has contracted each shall be solidarily liable for the claims.

C. The privilege granted by R.S. 9:4801 and 4802 affects only the interest in or on the immovable enjoyed by the owner whose obligation is secured by the privilege.

D. The privilege granted by this Part upon a lessee's rights in the lease or buildings and structures shall be inferior and subject to all of the rights of, or obligations owed to, the lessor, including the right to resolve the lease for nonperformance of its obligations, to execute upon the lessee's rights and to sell them in satisfaction of the obligations free of the privilege. If a sale of the lease is made in execution of the claims of the lessor, the privilege attaches to that portion of the sale proceeds remaining after satisfaction of the claims of the lessor.

Acts 1981, No. 724, § 1, eff. Jan. 1, 1982. Amended by Acts 1985, No. 903, § 1.

Comments—1981

(a) This section substantially follows the jurisprudence interpreting the former R.S. 9:4811. See Fruge v. Muffoletto, 137 So.2d 336 (La.1962); Abbeville Lumber Co. v. Richard, 350 So.2d 1292 (La. App. 3rd Cir. 1977); and McCulley v. Dublin Construction Co., 234 So.2d 257 (La.App. 4th Cir. 1970). The reference to mineral leases formerly found in R.S. 9:4811 has been suppressed since the privileges given for such work are now regulated by R.S. 9:4861.

(b) Subsection D restates the principle of the former R.S. 9:4811 relative to the rights of lessors whose lessees improve the leased property. It does not change the law.

Cross References

C.C. arts. 3186, 3230, 3231, 3249, 3250, 3251, 3267, 3268.

§ 4807. Contractor, general contractor, subcontractor defined

A. A contractor is one who contracts with an owner to perform all or a part of a work.

B. A general contractor is a contractor:

(1) Who contracts to perform all or substantially all of a work; or

(2) Who is deemed to be a general contractor by R.S. 9:4808(B).

C. A subcontractor is one who, by contract made directly with a contractor, or by a contract that is one of a series of contracts emanating from a contractor, is bound to perform all or a part of a work contracted for by the contractor. Acts 1981, No. 724, § 1, eff. Jan. 1, 1982.

Comments—1981

(a) The provisions of Section 4807 are new but articulate rules implicit in the former law. The former R.S. 9:4802 required the filing of every contract (and bond) entered into for "the repair ... or, improvement of any work on immovable property by any undertaker, general contractor, master mechanic, or engineer or other person undertaking *such general contract* with the owner". (emphasis added) The courts construed this to mean that only a contract with a "general" contractor could be filed in compliance with the act. Executive House Building v. Demarest, 248 So.2d 405 (La.App. 4th Cir. 1971); Gifford Hill & Co. v. Harper, 262 So.2d 843 (La.App. 2d Cir. 1972); and Wilson v. Centennial Homes, Inc., 329 So.2d 893 (La.App. 2d Cir. 1976). The jurisprudence left open, however, the question of precisely who a "general contractor" was. (See also the Comment to Section 4808A, *infra.*) If a general contractor does not file his contract in a proper and timely manner he loses his privilege. (See Section 4811D, *infra.*)

(b) Subsection B resolves a problem that existed under the former law. When read in light of Section 4808, *infra*, defining a work it has the following effect. If a contract is entered into by an owner for work on an immovable, and the notice of contract is filed for record with a bond in proper amount attached to it, the work to be performed under the contract is conclusively deemed to be a separate work even though it may be part of a larger project being carried out by the owner. Accordingly, with respect to such work the time for filing claims, the liability of the surety, and all other aspects of the act, will be determined independently even though in the absence of such filing the work might be considered part of a larger and single work. It thus gives assurance to the owner, contractor, surety, and third persons that work undertaken by a contractor under a single contract can be considered and dealt with without regard to its relationship to other work being carried on by the owner. If a notice of contract and bond are not filed, then the question of whether work done by several contractors or partly by the owner and partly by contractors is so substantially interrelated as to be one work will be left to the determination of the courts in light of Section 4808A, *infra*.

(c) Subsection C adopts the present rule that the term "subcontractor" includes a contractor of a subcontractor so that laborers and suppliers of material to a sub-subcontractor are protected by the act. (See Comment. (d) to Section 4801(3), *supra.*)

Cross References

C.C. arts. 3186, 3230, 3231, 3249, 3250, 3251, 3267, 3268.

§ 4808. Work defined

A. A work is a single continuous project for the improvement, construction, erection, reconstruction, modification, repair, demolition, or other physical change of an immovable or its component parts.

B. If written notice of a contract with a proper bond attached is properly filed within the time required by R.S. 9:4811, the work to be performed under the contract shall be deemed to be a work separate and distinct from other portions of the project undertaken by the owner. The contractor, whose notice of contract is so filed, shall be deemed a general contractor.

C. The clearing, leveling, grading, test piling, cutting or removal of trees and debris, placing of fill dirt, leveling of the land surface, demolition of existing structures, or performance of other work on land for or by an owner or the owner's contractor, in preparation for the construction or erection of a building or other construction thereon to be substantially or entirely built or erected by a contractor, shall be deemed a separate work to the extent the preparatory work is not a part of the contractor's work for the erection of the building or other construction. The privileges granted by this Part for the work described in this Subsection shall have no effect as to third persons acquiring rights in, to, or on the immovable before the statement of claim or privilege is filed.

D. This Part does not apply to:

(1) The drilling of any well or wells in search of oil, gas, or water, or other activities in connection with such a well or wells for which a privilege is granted by R.S. 9:4861.

(2) The construction or other work on the permanent bed and structures of a railroad for which a privilege is granted by R.S. 9:4901.

(3) Public works performed by the state or any state board or agency or political subdivision of the state.

Acts 1981, No. 724, § 1, eff. Jan. 1, 1982. Amended by Acts 2003, No. 729, § 1.

Comment—1981

(a) Subsection A expressly defines what the former law largely left to implication. The definition of a "work" is essentially that established by the jurisprudence. See W. C. Gaston v. H. R. Stover, 126 So.2d 360 (La.App. 2d Cir. 1960); Bernard

Lumber Co. v. John F. Cerise Co., 148 So.2d 819 (La.App. 4th Cir. 1963); McGill Corporation v. Dolese Concrete Co., 201 So.2d 125 (La.App. 1st Cir. 1967); Anderson Dunham, Inc. v. John P. Cryer Construction Co., 349 So.2d 1304 (La.App. 1st Cir. 1977); and Daigrepont v. Welch, 358 So.2d 1302 (La.App. 3d Cir. 1978). The concept of a "work" is critical to the administration of the act. Its relevancy is found in the following. The contract of a "general contractor" must be recorded to protect the owner from personal liability and to preserve a privilege for the price of work. (See Section 4802C, *supra* and 4811, *infra*.) A contract with an owner who is constructing a work "acting as his own general contractor" or that is otherwise not a "general" one is not required to be filed and the bond, if any, given is not covered by the act. (See Section 4801, *supra*.) To determine whether a contractor is a "general" one requires a determination of what "the work" is. (See Section 4807A, *supra*.) The beginning of "the work" may determine the priority between persons having claims under the act and mortgagees or others obtaining rights in the immovable, (see Section 4820, *infra*) and will determine when a contract is "timely filed" which then fixed whether the owner is personally liable for claims under the act. (See Sections 4811A, *infra* and 4802C, *supra*.) The completion of the "work" determines when a notice of termination may be filed (see Section 4822, *infra*) and when the period for filing claims begins if no contract is filed.

(b) Subsection B is new. Its effect is discussed in the comments to Section 4807, *supra*.

(c) Subsection C incorporates the substance of prior R.S. 9:4819 added by Acts 1979, No. 163. It changes the effect of the provision to some extent. Under the former law the provision apparently regulated only the effect of such preliminary site work upon the priority of other privileges or mortgages. It thus created the possibility that for other purposes (such as determining whether the contract of the owner with a contractor was timely filed) work "had begun". The present act considers such site work to be in substance a separate work, unless it is performed by a contractor who is to construct a building or other improvement following the site work. The last sentence of Subsection C is an exception to Section 4820A which provides that the filing of a notice of contract, or the commencement of work fixes the time when the privileges given by the act become effective as to third persons. Although the privileges for preliminary site work are effective under Subsection C, above, only when a statement of claim or privilege is filed (see Section 4822), the rank of the privilege remains unchanged. (See Section 4821.) Thus, when the privilege becomes effective, it ranks equally with others of the same nature. The proviso does have relevance to the ranking of nonlabor privileges with mortgages and vendor's privileges. Under Section 4821 the ranking in such cases is dependent upon the relative order in which such privileges become effective as to third persons. See Comment (b) to Section 4821.

Cross References

C.C. arts. 3186, 3230, 3231, 3249, 3250, 3251, 3267, 3268.

SUBPART C. WORK PERFORMED BY GENERAL CONTRACTORS

§ 4811. Notice of a contract with a general contractor to be filed

A. Written notice of a contract between a general contractor and an owner shall be filed as provided in R.S. 9:4831 before the contractor begins work, as defined by R.S. 9:4820, on the immovable. The notice:

(1) Shall be signed by the owner and contractor.

(2) Shall contain the legal property description of the immovable upon which the work is to be performed and the name of the project.

(3) Shall identify the parties and give their mailing addresses.

(4) Shall state the price of the work or, if no price is fixed, describe the method by which the price is to be calculated and give an estimate of it.

(5) Shall state when payment of the price is to be made.

(6) Shall describe in general terms the work to be done.

B. A notice of contract is not improperly filed because of an error in or omission from the notice in the absence of a showing of actual prejudice by a claimant or other person acquiring rights in the immovable. An error or omission of the identity of the parties or their mailing addresses or the improper identification of the immovable shall be prima facie proof of actual prejudice.

C. A notice of contract is not improperly filed because a proper bond is not attached.

D. A general contractor shall not enjoy the privilege granted by R.S. 9:4801 if the price of the work stipulated or reasonably estimated in his contract exceeds twenty-five thousand dollars unless notice of the contract is timely filed.

E. If a notice of contract is mutually released by the owner and contractor, then the contract will have no effect, provided no work has begun on the land or materials placed on the site. The recorder of mortgages shall immediately cancel the contract upon the filing of the mutual release and an affidavit made by a registered or certified engineer or surveyor, licensed architect, or building inspector employed by the city or parish or by a lending institution chartered under federal or state law, that states he inspected the immovable at a specified time subsequent to the filing of the contract and work had not been commenced and no materials placed at the site. If the contract, or a certified copy, is then refiled, the refiling date shall become the effective date for privilege for work done pursuant to the contract in accordance with R.S. 9:4820(A)(1).

Acts 1981, No. 724, § 1, eff. Jan. 1, 1982. Amended by Acts 1988, No. 685, § 1, eff. Jan. 1, 1989; Acts 2003, No. 729, § 1.

Comments—1981

(a) This Section incorporates the substance of the former law. (See R.S. 9:4802.) In lieu of requiring the contract itself to be filed, it permits the filing of a notice disclosing those terms of the contract necessary for the functioning of the act. The notice is not required to be authenticated. Current practice is to execute an abbreviated form of the contract containing the essential elements described for the notice and adopting by reference general plans, terms, and conditions, for the work that are contained in separate documents. The filing of such a contract will comply with the act if it contains the required information. The former law (R.S. 9:4802) required the filing of the contract before work was commenced *and* within thirty days after its execution. The thirty day limitation has been suppressed as being of no value. The place of filing all documents under the act is regulated by R.S. 9:4831, *infra*.

(b) Subsection A(4) clarifies the former law. It was not clear that cost-plus or other contracts containing flexible pricing arrangements could be utilized under the former law since the amount of the contract was required to be stated and the amount of the bond fixed with reference to that price.

(c) Subsection B is new. The owner is made personally liable, and the contractor may lose his privilege if the notice is not properly filed. A form of notice that substantially complies with the act will avoid imposition of these penalties unless actual prejudice to a claimant can be demonstrated.

(d) Subsection C recognizes that the filing of the notice of contract serves as notice of the potential existence of the privileges and fixes their priorities over subsequent mortgages. The absence of a bond does not affect this. The failure to attach a bond will give rise to the claim against the owner and make the privileges securing those claims valid (Section 4802C, *supra*).

(e) Subsection D changes the law in one respect. Formerly a "general" contractor lost his privilege if he did not file his contract. (See the Comments to Section 4808, *supra*.) The jurisprudence was not entirely clear as to the distinction between a "general contractor" for a work and one who might be a "contractor", but not a general one. Section 4807, *supra*, now provides the distinction. It means however that if the "work" is a relatively minor one, as where a plumber is called to repair a sink or a contractor is retained to make repairs to a window or door, that the privilege for the price of the work, given by R.S. 9:4801(1) would not exist in the absence of the filing of a written contract. Subsection D avoids this result by excluding contracts of relatively minor amounts from the filing requirements. However, the failure to file such a contract will still impose personal liability on the owner under Section 4802, *supra*, to persons dealing with the contractor.

Cross References

C.C. arts. 3186, 3230, 3231, 3249, 3250, 3251, 3267, 3272.

§ 4812. Bond required; terms and conditions

A. To be entitled to the benefits of the provisions of R.S. 9:4802(C), every owner shall require a general contractor to furnish and maintain a bond of a solvent, legal surety for the work to be performed under the contract. The bond shall be attached to the notice of the contract when it is filed.

B. The amount of the bond shall not be less than the following amounts or percentages of the price of the work stipulated or estimated in the contract:

(1) If the price is not more than ten thousand dollars the amount of the bond shall be one hundred percent of the price.

(2) If the price is more than ten thousand dollars but not more than one hundred thousand dollars the amount of the bond shall be fifty percent of the price, but not less than ten thousand dollars.

(3) If the price is more than one hundred thousand dollars but not more than one million dollars the amount of the bond shall be thirty-three and one-third percent of the price, but not less than fifty thousand dollars.

(4) If the price is more than one million dollars the amount of the bond shall be twenty-five percent of the price, but not less than three hundred thirty-three thousand three hundred thirty-three dollars.

C. The condition of the bond shall be that the surety guarantees:

(1) To the owner and to all persons having a claim against the contractor, or to whom the contractor is conventionally liable for work done under the contract, the payment of their claims or of all amounts owed them arising out of the work performed under the contract to which it is attached or for which it is given.

(2) To the owner, the complete and timely performance of the contract unless such guarantee is expressly excluded by the terms of the bond.

D. The bond of a legal surety attached to and filed with the notice of contract of a general contractor shall be deemed to conform to the requirements of this part notwithstanding any provision of the bond to the contrary, but the surety shall not be bound for a sum in excess of the total amount expressed in the bond.

E. The bond given in compliance with this Part shall be deemed to include the following conditions:

(1) Extensions of time for the performance of the work shall not extinguish the obligation of the surety but the surety who has not consented to the extensions has the right of indemnification under the original terms of the contract as provided by Article 3057 of the Civil Code.[1]

(2) No other amendment to the contract, or change or modification to the work, or impairment of the surety's rights of subrogation made without the surety's consent shall extinguish the obligations of the surety, but if the change or action is materially prejudicial to the surety, the surety shall be relieved of liability to the owner, and shall be indemnified by the owner, for any loss or damage suffered by the surety.

(3) A payment by the owner to the contractor before the time required by the contract shall not extinguish the obligation of the surety, but the surety shall be relieved of liability to the owner, and shall be indemnified by the owner for any loss or damage suffered by the surety.

Acts 1981, No. 724, § 1, eff. Jan. 1, 1982.

[1] See, now, C.C. art. 3053.

Comments—1981

(a) This Section consolidates in one place a number of provisions found throughout the former act and incorporates a number of rules established by the jurisprudence. It does not change their substance.

(b) Subsection A reproduces the provisions of the former R.S. 9:4802.

(c) Subsection B slightly modifies the amounts of the bond required so that increasing the price of the contract will in no case decrease the amount of the bond as was formerly the case with R.S. 9:4802.

(d) Subsection C recognizes the difference between a "performance and payment" bond and a "payment" bond. The courts have recognized that only the latter is required to comply with the act. It establishes a presumption that a bond given to a contractor comprehends both by requiring the express exclusion of the performance conditions.

(e) Subsection D is new. It resolves the continuing controversy as to whether a bond is a "legal" one or not. See Bowles and Edens Co. v. H & H Sewer Systems, Inc., 324 So.2d 528 (La.App. 1st Cir. 1975); and Jimco, Inc. v. Gentilly Terrace Apts., 230 So.2d 281 (La.App. 4th Cir. 1970). It adopts the policy that the bond given to comply with the act is in effect a legal suretyship. It also creates a presumption that a bond for a contractor is intended to comply with the act if it is filed with the notice of contract. It is implicit that such filing would have to be made with the knowledge or consent of the surety. This subsection is not intended to change the law of the cases of Avant v. Submersible Rig Peter Duncan, 447 F.2d 478 (1971), and McCall v. United Bonding Ins. Co., 197 So.2d 400 (La.App. 4th Cir. 1967).

(f) Subsection E incorporates rules that have been jurisprudentially developed or are presently provided for by the act. It is not intended to change the law. As to (1), See Electrical Supply Co. v. Eugene Freeman, Inc., 152 So. 510 (La.1933); and the former R.S. 9:4806. As to (2), See Central Louisiana Electric Company v. Giant Enterprises, Inc., 371 So.2d 641 (La.App. 3rd Cir. 1979); E. Rabalais & Son, Inc. v. United Bonding Ins. Co., 226 So.2d 528 (La.App. 3rd Cir. 1969); and the former R.S. 9:4806. Subsection E(3) reproduces the substance of the former R.S. 9:4806.

Cross References

C.C. arts. 3186, 3230, 3231, 3249, 3250, 3251, 3267, 3268, 3272, 3274.

§ 4813. Liability of the surety

A. The surety is liable without benefit of discussion or division.

B. If the total amount owed to persons to whom the surety is liable exceeds the total amount of the bond, the surety's liability shall be discharged in the following order:

(1) First, and pro rata, to persons who preserve their claims in the manner required by R.S. 9:4822.

(2) Second, and in the order in which they present their obligations to the surety, to persons who do not preserve their claims as required by R.S. 9:4822 but to whom the contractor is otherwise liable.

(3) Third, to the owner.

C. The liability of the surety is not extinguished by a deficiency in the amount of the bond, the failure to attach the bond to the notice of contract, or the failure to file the notice as required by R.S. 9:4811.

D. An action shall not be brought against a surety, other than by the owner, before the expiration of the time specified by R.S. 9:4822 for claimants to file statements of their claims, unless a statement of the claim in the form required by R.S. 9:4822(G) is delivered to the surety at least thirty days prior to the institution of the action.

E. The surety's liability, except as to the owner, is extinguished as to all persons who fail to institute an action asserting their claims or rights against the owner, the contractor, or the surety within one year after the expiration of the time specified in R.S. 9:4822 for claimants to file their statement of claim or privilege.

Acts 1981, No. 724, § 1, eff. Jan. 1, 1982.

Comments—1981

(a) The liability of the surety is made unconditional through the eliminations of the pleas of division and discussion. (See also Section 4802E, supra.) However, the liability remains that of a surety and is regulated by the rules of the suretyship (as modified by this act) not those of principal solidary obligors. See Wisconsin Capital Corp. & Trans. World Land Title Corp., 378 So.2d 495 (La. App. 4th Cir. 1979); Louisiana Bank & Trust Co. v. Boutte, 309 So.2d 274 (La.1975); and Aiavolasiti v. Versailles Gardens Land Dev. Co., 371 So.2d 755 (La.1979).

(b) Subsection B incorporates the present order of priority of payment by the surety established by the act. (See the former R.S. 9:4809.) One minor change has been effected in Subsection B(2). The former act made the surety liable to persons who had not filed a claim, in the order in which they filed suit. (R.S. 9:4814B). This has been changed to make the priority dependent upon when the claims are presented to the surety. If a valid, undisputed claim is presented the surety, a suit should not be required to permit him to safely pay it.

(c) Subsection C incorporates the provisions of the former R.S. 9:4807. It does not change the law.

(d) Subsection D incorporates the provisions of the former R.S. 9:4814. It does not change the law.

(e) Subsection E incorporates the substance of the former R.S. 9:4814B but makes one alteration. The time for filing suit on a claim is made one year from the expiration from the time for filing claims rather than from the filing of the claim as was formerly the case. Since a concursus may be instituted by any person before such claims expire, one period of time is provided in which to file a suit on a claim, rather than having the period expire at different times for different claims. The filing of a concursus joining a claimant and an owner or contractor is deemed to be the institution of such an action. (See Section 4841, *infra*.)

Cross References

C.C. arts. 3045, 3186, 3230, 3231, 3249, 3250, 3267, 3268, 3272.

§ 4814. Contractors; misapplication of payments prohibited; civil penalties; payment of claims, attorney fees and costs

A. No contractor, subcontractor, or agent of a contractor or subcontractor, who has received money on account of a contract for the construction, erection, or repair of a building, structure, or other improvement, including contracts and mortgages for interim financing, shall knowingly fail to apply the money received as necessary to settle claims to sellers of movables or laborers due for the construction or under the contract. Any seller of movables or laborer whose claims have not been settled may file an action for the amount due, including reasonable attorney fees and court costs, and for civil penalties as provided in this Section.

B. When the amount misapplied is one thousand dollars or less, the civil penalties shall be not less than two hundred fifty dollars nor more than seven hundred fifty dollars.

C. When the amount misapplied is greater than one thousand dollars, the civil penalties shall be not less than five hundred dollars nor more than one thousand dollars, for each one thousand dollars in misapplied funds.

D. A contractor, subcontractor, or agent of a contractor or subcontractor who is found by the court to have knowingly failed to apply construction contract payments as required in Subsection A shall be ordered by the court to pay to plaintiff the penalties provided in Subsection B or C, as may be applicable, and the amount due to settle the claim, including reasonable attorney fees and court costs.

Added by Acts 1997, No. 861, § 1.

§ 4815. Escrow of funds due under contract; procedures

A. When, under the provisions of this Part, a contract in the amount of fifty thousand dollars or more is entered into between an owner and a contractor and if in accordance with the terms of such contract funds earned by the contractor are withheld as retainage by the owner from periodic payments due to the contractor then such funds shall be deposited by the owner into an interest bearing escrow account. The provisions of this Section shall not apply to a contract for a single family residence or double family residence. The provisions of this Section also shall not apply to a contract for the construction or improvement of the following types of industrial facilities that are, or will be, engaged in activities defined or classified under one or more of the following subsectors, industry groups, or industries of the 1997 North American Industry Classifications System (NAICS):

(1) 22111 electric power generation.
(2) 321 wood products manufacturing.
(3) 322 paper manufacturing.
(4) 324 petroleum and coal products manufacturing.
(5) 325 chemical manufacturing.
(6) 326 plastics and rubber products manufacturing.
(7) 331 primary metals manufacturing.
(8) 562211/562212 hazardous and solid waste landfills.
(9) 422710 bulk stations and materials.
(10) 486110 crude oil pipelines.
(11) 486910 refined petroleum products pipelines.
(12) 486210 natural gas pipelines.
(13) 486990 other pipelines.
(14) 211112 natural gas processing plants.

B. An escrow account under the provisions of this Section shall be located at a qualified financial institution and shall be under the control of an escrow agent. The escrow account and escrow agent shall be selected by mutual agreement between the owner and the contractor.

C. Upon completion of the work that is the subject of the contract, the funds, including any interest located in the escrow account shall be released from escrow under the following conditions:

(1) If there are no existing claims by the owner, the whole amount shall be paid to the contractor within three business days upon receipt by the escrow agent of a written release signed by the contractor and the owner.

(2) If there is a dispute between the owner and contractor and the contract does not provide for binding arbitration of such dispute:

(a) Undisputed amounts shall be released by the escrow agent within three business days of receipt of a notarized request of the contractor.

(b) Disputed amounts that are the subject of a judicial proceeding shall be released by the escrow agent within three business days of the receipt of a final order by the court. Upon receipt of the order of the court, the escrow agent shall pay the contractor or owner such amounts as are determined by the court.

(3) If there is a dispute between the owner and contractor and the contract provides for binding arbitration of such dispute, the following shall occur:

(a) Undisputed amounts shall be released by the escrow agent within three business days of receipt of a notarized request of the contractor.

(b) Disputed amounts that are the subject of binding arbitration under the contract shall be released by the escrow agent within three business days of the receipt of a final order by the arbitrator who has been selected by mutual agreement between the owner and the contractor. Upon receipt of the order of the arbitrator, the escrow agent shall pay the contractor or owner such amounts as are determined by the arbitrator under the rules as defined in the contract between the owner and the contractor.

D. Receipt by the escrow agent or the qualified financial institution in which the escrow account is maintained of what purports to be a written release signed by the contractor and owner, or an order by a court or arbitrator, shall be a full release and discharge of the escrow agent for transfer of funds to the contractor. Neither the escrow agent nor the qualified financial institution in which the escrow account is maintained shall be held liable to any party based on any claim that the written release is unauthorized, forged, or otherwise fraudulent.

E. Neither the escrow agent nor the qualified financial institution in which the escrow account is maintained pursuant to the provisions of this Section shall have any liability to the owner, contractor, or any other person when complying with the provisions of this Section.

Added by Acts 2010, No. 638, § 1.

SUBPART D. CLAIMS AND PRIVILEGES; EFFECTIVENESS; PRESERVATION; RANKING; EXTINGUISHMENT

§ 4820. Privileges; effective date

A. The privileges granted by this Part arise and are effective as to third persons when:

(1) Notice of the contract is filed as required by R.S. 9:4811; or

(2) The work is begun by placing materials at the site of the immovable to be used in the work or conducting other work at the site of the immovable the effect of which is visible from a simple inspection and reasonably indicates that the work has begun. For these purposes, services rendered by a surveyor, architect, or engineer, or the driving of test piling, cutting or removal of trees and debris, placing of fill dirt, demolition of existing structures, or leveling of the land surface shall not be considered, nor shall the placing of materials having an aggregate price of less than one hundred dollars on the immovable be considered. For these purposes, the site of the immovable is defined as the area within the boundaries of the property.

B. If the work is for the addition, modification, or repair of an existing building or other construction, that part of the work performed before a third person's rights become effective shall, for the purposes of R.S. 9:4821, be considered a distinct work from the work performed after such rights become effective if the cost of the work done, in labor and materials, is less than one hundred dollars during the thirty-day period immediately preceding the time such third person's rights become effective as to third persons.

C. A person acquiring or intending to acquire a mortgage, privilege, or other right, in or on an immovable may conclusively rely upon an affidavit made by a registered or certified engineer or surveyor, licensed architect, or building inspector employed by the city or parish or by a lending institution chartered under federal or state law, that states he inspected the immovable at a specified time and work had not then been commenced nor materials placed at its site, provided the affidavit is filed within four business days after the execution of the affidavit, and the mortgage, privilege, or other document creating the right is filed before or within four business days of the filing of the affidavit. The correctness of the facts recited in the affidavit may not be controverted to affect the priority of the rights of the person to whom or for whom it is given, unless actual fraud by such person is proven. A person who gives a false or fraudulent affidavit shall be responsible for any loss or damage suffered by any person whose rights are adversely affected.

D. A person acquiring or intending to acquire a mortgage, privilege, or other right under Subsection C of this Section shall have priority in accordance with R.S. 9:4821, regardless of whether work has begun or materials were delivered to the job site after the effective date and time of the affidavit, but prior to the recordation of the mortgage, privilege, or other right, provided that the document creating the right was filed before or within four business days of the filing of the affidavit.

Acts 1981, No. 724, § 1, eff. Jan. 1, 1982. Amended by Acts 1986, No. 424, § 1; Acts 1988, No. 904, § 1; Acts 1988, No. 999, § 1; Acts 1991, No. 370, § 1; Acts 1995, No. 666, § 1; Acts 2003, No. 729, § 1; Acts 2012, No. 425, § 1.

Comments—1981

(a) This section establishes when the privileges given under the act became effective as to third persons who deal with an immovable. It does not regulate the priority of such privileges although it serves as a foundation for determining the question which is regulated by Section 4821. Subsection A(2) incorporates the substance of former R.S. 9:4819A(1).

(b) Subsection B incorporates the substance of former R.S. 9:4819A(2). It clarifies certain aspects of the former provision. This section is irrelevant if a notice of contract for a work has been previously filed since under Subsection A(1) such filing fixes the effectiveness of the privileges as to all work done under its terms. In the absence of a filed contract, if a work of repair or renovation is suspended for more than thirty days, then as to third persons acquiring rights in or over the immovable (including mortgages) that part of the work done prior to the thirty day period will be considered a separate work from that conducted thereafter. The former law was unclear as to the effect of the previous work. If persons performing such work file their claims within sixty days of the date the prior activities cease they will enjoy priority over subsequent mortgages in the same manner as if the work had been completed. The provisions do not prevent them from awaiting final completion of the work to file their claims, but they may lose priority over intervening rights acquired during the time the work is temporarily suspended. Furthermore, the existence of such prior activity and the filing of claims for it will not give retroactive effect to work performed after the suspension ends insofar as the rights of third persons may have intervened.

(c) Subsection C incorporates the substance of former R.S. 47:4819A(3). It makes it clear that the filing of the affidavit does not of itself give the mortgage or other right priority over a privilege. It only provides that the facts recited in the affidavit as to the nonperformance of work at the time of the inspection are conclusive and may not be controverted. The effect of such facts will be determined under the other provisions of the act.

Cross References

C.C. arts. 3186, 3230, 3231, 3249, 3250, 3251, 3267, 3268.

§ 4821. Ranking of privileges

A. The privileges granted by R.S. 9:4801 and 4802 rank among themselves and as to other mortgages and privileges in the following order of priority:

(1) Privileges for ad valorem taxes or local assessments for public improvements against the property, liens, and privileges granted in favor of parishes for reasonable charges imposed on the property under R.S. 33:1236, liens and privileges granted in favor of municipalities for reasonable charges imposed on property under R.S. 33:4752, 4753, 4754, 4766, 5062, and 5062.1, and liens and privileges granted in favor of a parish or municipality for reasonable charges imposed on the property under R.S. 13:2575 are first in rank and concurrent regardless of the dates of recordation or notation of such liens and privileges in any public record, public office, or public document.

(2) Privileges granted by R.S. 9:4801(2) and 4802(A)(2) rank next and equally with each other.

(3) Bona fide mortgages or vendor's privileges that are effective as to third persons before the privileges granted by this Part are effective rank next and in accordance with their respective rank as to each other.

(4) Privileges granted by R.S. 9:4801(3) and (4) and 4802(A)(1), (3), and (4) rank next and equally with each other.

(5) Privileges granted by R.S. 9:4801(1) and (5) rank next and equally with each other.

(6) Other mortgages or privileges rank next and in accordance with their respective rank as to each other.

B. A person acquiring or intending to acquire a mortgage, privilege, or other right under R.S. 9:4820(D) shall have priority in accordance with the provisions of this Section, regardless of whether work has begun or materials were delivered to the jobsite after the effective date and time of the affidavit, but prior to the recordation of the mortgage, privilege, or other right, provided that the document creating the right was filed before or within four business days of the filing of the affidavit.

Acts 1981, No. 724, § 1, eff. Jan. 1, 1982. Amended by Acts 1990, No. 952, § 1; Acts 1991, No. 353, § 1; Acts 1995, No. 31, § 2; Acts 1995, No. 1155, § 1, eff. June 29, 1995; Acts 2004, No. 209, § 1, eff. June 14, 2004; Acts 2012, No. 425, § 1.

Comments—1981

(a) This section regulates the priority of the privileges. It expresses the existing order and does not change the law.

(b) The preceding Section 4820 establishes when the privileges become effective as to third persons. (See the Comments to Section 4820, *supra*. Note also the exception contained in the last sentence to Section 4808(c), *supra*.) Whether a privilege is effective and in what order it may rank as to other privileges or mortgages are different questions. The first is relevant to the rights of nonsecurity holders. Only an owner may impose a privilege upon property. Consequently the sale or other alienation of an immovable will render a previously created privilege of no consequence if it is not effective as to third persons when the alienation occurs. The term "privilege" ordinarily refers to a hypothecation which enjoys some preference or priority over ordinary hypothecations that take their rank by the order in which they are created. Consequently, once a privilege is validly imposed upon property, its rank may be superior to existing privileges or hypothecations. The privileges given by this act have a mixed character. The laborer's privilege is given priority over all other hypothecations except those securing payment of ad valorem taxes or assessments. The other privileges rank, with respect to mortgages or the vendor's privilege, in the order in which they become effective. They are thus treated as ordinary mortgages in this respect. Among themselves they rank by nature. Thus, all claims of materialmen, subcontractors and lessors of movables rank equally (whether or not they arise out of the same work) and ahead of the privilege of the contractor and surveyors, architects, and engineers which also rank equally.

(c) Any system that permits creation of a variety of hypothecations that rank by different criteria implicitly permits the possibility of circular priorities (i.e. the so-called "vicious circle"). This is possible under the present system. It is likely to arise only rarely. If no claimant conclusively establishes a prior claim to a fund superior to other claimants it is assumed Civil Code Article 3183 would require a pro rata distribution.

(d) Subsection 3 is not intended to change the law, although it does not adopt the detailed language of the former law regulating when a mortgage or vendor's privilege had priority over nonlabor privileges. It leaves to the general law the matter of determining when a mortgage or vendor's privilege is effective and thus has priority over the nonlabor privileges given by the act. In essence, if such a mortgage or privilege is effective as against a subsequent mortgage or purchaser of the property when the nonlabor privileges are effective (i.e. when the contract is recorded or work begins) then it will have priority over them. Otherwise, it will be inferior to such privileges. This appears to be the interpretation given the former law and no change is intended. See American Bank & Trust Co. v. F & W Const., 357 So.2d 1226 (La.App.2nd Cir. 1978).

Cross References

C.C. arts. 3186, 3230, 3231, 3249, 3250, 3251, 3267, 3268.

§ 4822. Preservation of claims and privileges

A. If a notice of contract is properly and timely filed in the manner provided by R.S. 9:4811, the persons to whom a claim or privilege is granted by R.S. 9:4802 shall within thirty days after the filing of a notice of termination of the work:

(1) File a statement of their claims or privilege.

(2) Deliver to the owner a copy of the statement of claim or privilege. If the address of the owner is not given in the notice of contract, the claimant is not required to deliver a copy of his statement to the owner.

B. A general contractor to whom a privilege is granted by R.S. 9:4801 of this Part, and whose privilege has been preserved in the manner provided by R.S. 9:4811, shall file a statement of his privilege within sixty days after the filing of the notice of termination or substantial completion of the work.

C. Those persons granted a claim and privilege by R.S. 9:4802 for work arising out of a general contract, notice of which is not filed, and other persons granted a privilege under R.S. 9:4801 or a claim and privilege under R.S. 9:4802 shall file a statement of their respective claims and privileges within sixty days after:

(1) The filing of a notice of termination of the work; or

(2) The substantial completion or abandonment of the work, if a notice of termination is not filed.

D. (1) Notwithstanding the other provisions of this Part, the time for filing a statement of claim or privilege to preserve the privilege granted by R.S. 9:4801(5) expires sixty days after the latter of:

(a) The filing of a notice for termination of the work that the services giving rise to the privilege were rendered; or,

(b) The substantial completion or abandonment of the work if a notice of termination is not filed. This privilege shall have no effect as to third persons acquiring rights in, to, or on the immovable before the statement of claim or privilege is filed.

(2) Notwithstanding the provisions of this Part, the seller of movables sold for use or consumption in work on an immovable for residential purposes, if a notice of contract is not filed, shall file a statement of claim or privilege within seventy days after:

(a) The filing of a notice of termination of the work; or

(b) The substantial completion or abandonment of the work, if a notice of termination is not filed.

E. A notice of termination of the work:

(1) Shall reasonably identify the immovable upon which the work was performed and the work to which it relates. If the work is evidenced by notice of a contract, reference to the notice of contract as filed or recorded, together with the names of the parties to the contract, shall be deemed adequate identification of the immovable and work.

(2) Shall be signed by the owner or his representative, who contracted with the contractor, or, if the owner has conveyed the immovable, then it may also be signed by the new owner, or his representative.

(3) Shall certify that:

(a) The work has been substantially completed; or

(b) The work has been abandoned by the owner; or

(c) A contractor is in default under the terms of the contract.

(4) Shall be conclusive of the matters certified if it is made in good faith by the owner, his representative, or his successor.

F. A notice of termination or substantial completion may be filed from time to time with respect to a specified portion or area of work. In that case, the time for preserving privileges or claims as specified in Subsection A or C of this Section shall commence with the filing of the notice of termination or substantial completion as to amounts owed and arising from the work done on that portion or area of the work described in the notice of termination. This notice shall identify the portion or area of the land and certify that the work performed on that portion of the land is substantially completed or has been abandoned. Once the period for preserving claims and privileges has expired and no liens have been timely filed, the portion or area of work described in the notice of termination shall be free of the claims and privileges of those doing work on the area described in the notice of termination, as well as those doing work elsewhere on the immovable being improved.

G. A statement of a claim or privilege:

(1) Shall be in writing.

(2) Shall be signed by the person asserting the same or his representative.

(3) Shall reasonably identify the immovable with respect to which the work was performed or movables or services were supplied or rendered and the owner thereof.

(4) Shall set forth the amount and nature of the obligation giving rise to the claim or privilege and reasonably itemize the elements comprising it including the person for whom or to whom the contract was performed, material supplied, or services rendered. The provisions of this Paragraph shall not require a claimant to attach copies of unpaid invoices unless the statement of claim or privilege specifically states that the invoices are attached.

H. A work is substantially completed when:

(1) The last work is performed on, or materials are delivered to the site of the immovable or to that portion or area with respect to which a notice of partial termination is filed; or

(2) The owner accepts the improvement, possesses or occupies the immovable, or that portion or area of the immovable with respect to which a notice of partial termination is filed, although minor or inconsequential matters remain to be finished or minor defects or errors in the work are to be remedied.

I. A work is abandoned by the owner if he terminates the work and notifies persons engaged in its performance that he no longer desires to continue it or he otherwise objectively and in good faith manifests the abandonment or discontinuance of the project.

J. Before any person having a direct contractual relationship with a subcontractor, but no contractual relationship with the contractor, shall have a right of action against the contractor or surety on the bond furnished by the contractor, he must record his claim as provided in this Section and give written notice to the contractor within thirty days from the recordation of notice of termination of the work, stating with substantial accuracy the amount claimed and the name of the party to whom the material was furnished or supplied or for whom the labor or service was done or performed. Such notice shall be served by mailing the same by registered or certified mail, postage prepaid, in an envelope addressed to the contractor at any place he maintains an office in the state of Louisiana.

K. (1) Any person to whom a privilege is granted by R.S. 9:4802 may give notice to the owner of an obligation to that person arising out of the performance of work under the contract. The notice shall be given prior to:

(a) The filing of a notice of termination of the work; or

(b) The substantial completion or abandonment of the work, if a notice of termination is not filed.

(2) The method of notice shall be under R.S. 9:4842(A). The notice shall set forth the nature of the work or services performed by the person to whom the obligation is owed and shall include his mailing address.

L. (1) When notice under Subsection K has been given by a person to the owner, the owner shall notify that person as required by R.S. 9:4842(A) within three days of:

(a) Filing a notice of termination of the work; or

(b) The substantial completion or abandonment of the work, if a notice of termination is not filed.

(2) The owner who fails to give notice to the person under the provisions of this Subsection within ten days of commencement of the period for preservation of claims and privileges shall be liable for all costs and attorney's fees for the establishment and enforcement of the claim or privilege.

M. (1) The contractor may elect to furnish at the contractor's cost and without off-set of the cost against the retainage amount a retainage bond equal to and in lieu of the amount of the retainage required by the contract whenever a contract between an owner and a contractor for the construction, alteration, or repair of any work requires the withholding of sums for retainage until after the recordation of formal acceptance of such work, or notice of default by the contractor or subcontractor, or substantial completion or final payment exclusive of nonconforming work.

(2) If the contractor elects to furnish a retainage bond, it shall be in a form designated by the contracting agency from

a surety, within their underwriting limits, with at least an A-rating in the latest printing of the A.M. Best's Key Rating Guide.

Acts 1981, No. 724, § 1, eff. Jan. 1, 1982. Amended by Acts 1987, No. 897, § 1; Acts 1988, No. 685, § 1, eff. Jan. 1, 1989; Acts 1991, No. 1024, § 1, eff. Jan. 1, 1992; Acts 2001, No. 1105, § 1, eff. June 28, 2001; Acts 2003, No. 729, § 1; Acts 2010, No. 601, § 1; Acts 2013, No. 277, § 1.

Comments—1981

(a) This Section establishes the procedure which persons having claims or privileges under the act must follow if they wish to preserve those claims and privileges. It continues, in principle, the dual time period for filing provided by the prior law but makes a number of changes in it. Section 4802 of the prior law provided that claimants (other than the general contractor) had to file an affidavit of their claim within 30 days after a notice of acceptance of the job was filed. Section 4812 provided that if no written contract existed or if it was not filed when and as required the claimants could file their claims within 60 days after the furnishing of the last materials or performance of the last work on the job. Later the act was amended (Acts 1964, No. 317) to provide that where a contract was not filed, a notice of completion could be filed by an owner upon "substantial completion" of the work, thus starting the 60 day limit upon filing. "Substantial completion" was defined by R.S. 9:4802.1. The jurisprudence also developed the rule that abandonment of the work would start the 60 day filing period. The necessity for reconciling these rules gave rise to considerable litigation.

The present Section, while maintaining the basic 30–60 day pattern for filing, adopts the following structure: The contract no longer has to be "timely filed" (i.e. filed before beginning of work) to bring into play the basic 30 day filing period. If a notice of contract is filed, a notice of termination is always required to commence the 30 day time for filing. Where no notice of contract is filed the owner may still file a notice of termination. If he does so, the period for filing a statement of claim or privilege expires 60 days thereafter. If a notice of termination is not filed, the filing period expires 60 days after the work is substantially completed or abandoned. In as much as the filing of the notice of contract no longer has to be made before work beings there appears to be nothing in the act that would preclude the simultaneous filing of the contract and a notice of completion to start the running of the 30 day period for filing rather than the 60 day one. A general contractor is in all cases given 60 days to file a statement of privilege. See, however, Section 4811(D), denying the contractor a privilege if the amount of the contract exceeds $25,000 and notice of the contract is not timely filed.

(b) Subsection A(2) requires as a prerequisite to the preservation of a privilege delivery to the owner of a copy of the statement of claim or privilege, whenever a notice of contract is filed, whether timely or not. The former law required such delivery only when the contract was timely recorded,

Derbes v. Marshall, 183 So. 74 (La.App. 2d Cir. 1938); Lawrence v. Wright, 124 So. 697 (Orl.App.1929); and Madison Lumber Co. v. Wright, 137 So. 221 (Orl.App.1931); or if there was a defect in the bond, La. Glass and Mirror Works v. Irwin, 52 So. 765 (1910); and Casey v. Allain, 120 So. 420 (Orl.App.1929).

(c) Paragraph D reproduces the substance of the former R.S. 9:4813. It is not intended to change the law. See Capital Bank & Trust Co. v. Broussard Paint & Wallpaper Co., 198 So.2d 204 (La.App. 1st Cir. 1967); and National Bank of Com. v. Southern Land Title Corp., 244 So.2d 685 (La.App. 4th Cir. 1971).

(d) This Section adopts the term "notice of termination" for the notice to be filed rather than notice of acceptance or notice of completion as being more nearly descriptive of its function.

(e) The last sentence in Subsection E partially resolves the problem occasionally encountered when the owner prematurely files a notice of termination. This was especially critical under the former act in the case of works for which no contract was filed. R.S. 9:4812 originally provided that the period for filing expired sixty days after completion of the work. Because of the extensive and continuing litigation, the act was amended to define when the work was completed (R.S. 9:4802.1). Later the act was amended to permit the owner to file an affidavit of completion (R.S. 9:4812). The obvious purpose of the latter amendment was to give some certainty to the time for the filing of claims. However, the act left open the question of what would happen if the work was not in fact completed when the notice is filed. The current rule seems to be that if it is prematurely filed it becomes effective when the work is completed. See Keller Bldg. Products of Baton Rouge v. Siegen Dev., Inc., 312 So.2d 182 (La.App. 1st Cir. 1975). This is also equivalent to declaring the premature filing totally ineffective since, in the absence of such a filing the time for filing claims would begin upon completion of the work. Subsection E(4) makes the test of a notice's validity the good faith of the owner. It does not attempt to specifically regulate the question of what happens if the notice is filed in bad faith. Since the filing period of Subsections A and B do not expressly depend upon whether the notice is filed in good or bad faith, it is assumed they will have effect if third persons rights are involved (such as one who takes a mortgage after the apparent time for filing has expired). At the same time since one ordinarily cannot assert his own misconduct as a defense, the early filing should be ineffective as to the owner himself.

(f) Subsection F expands the provisions of former R.S. 9:4802.1 somewhat. It permits the filing of a notice of termination if work over a specific geographic area is completed and the parties, as to that work, wish to be certain the contractor has paid his laborers, suppliers and others. This will facilitate the contracting for major work in phases without requiring separate contracts to be entered into (which could be accomplished under Section 4808B). It should be noticed that although privileges arising out of the work must be filed within the time given it does not free the immovable (including the part completed) from the privilege of those who are doing work elsewhere. The privilege in all cases affects all of the immovable being improved.

(g) Subsection G is new but does not change the law. It incorporates the rules developed by the courts concerning the content of the statement of claim. See Hughes v. Will, 35 So.2d 241 (Orl.App.1948); and Paul E. Riviere v. Universal Excavator, Inc., 358 So.2d 670 (La.App. 1st Cir. 1978). The requirement that the statement be sworn to has been abrogated. The purpose of a statement of claim or privilege is to give notice to the owner (and contractor) of the existence of the claim and to give notice to persons who may deal with the owner that a privilege is claimed on the property. See Mercantile Nat. Bank of Dallas v. J. Thos. Driscoll, Inc., 195 So. 497 (La.1940). Technical defects in the notice should not defeat the claim as long as the notice is adequate to serve the purposes intended.

(h) Subsection H incorporates the substance of the rules interpreting the term "substantial completion". The test formerly found in Section 4812 for the beginning of the filing period upon the last delivery of material or the last furnishing of services or performance of labor has been suppressed. The interpretation given that Section by the courts was in fact practically the same as substantial completion. No substantial change in the law is intended.

(i) Subsection I is new. It recognizes and adopts the interpretation given the former act that abandonment of the work is equivalent to completion and starts the time for filing of claims as to works for which no contract is filed. See Jonesboro State Bank v. Tucker, 381 So.2d 578 (La.App. 2nd Cir. 1980).

Editor's note. Acts 2001, No. 1105, § 2, effective June 28, 2002, declares that this Act "shall apply prospectively only to contracts entered into after the effective date of this Act and shall not apply to any contract existing on the effective date of this Act."

Cross References

C.C. arts. 3186, 3230, 3231, 3249, 3250, 3251, 3267, 3268.

§ 4823. Extinguishment of claims and privileges

A. A privilege provided by R.S. 9:4801, a claim against the owner and the privilege securing it provided by R.S. 9:4802, or a claim against the contractor provided by R.S. 9:4802 is extinguished if:

(1) The claimant or holder of the privilege does not preserve it as required by R.S. 9:4822; or

(2) The claimant or holder of the privilege does not institute an action against the owner for the enforcement of the claim or privilege within one year after filing the statement of claim or privilege to preserve it; or

(3) The obligation which it secures is extinguished.

B. A claim against a contractor granted by R.S. 9:4802 is not extinguished by the failure to file a statement of claim or privilege as required by R.S. 9:4822 if a statement of the claim or privilege is delivered to the contractor within the period allowed for its filing by R.S. 9:4822. The failure to file an action against the owner as required by R.S. 9:4823(A)(2) shall not extinguish a claim against a contractor if an action for the enforcement of the claim is instituted against the contractor or his surety within one year after the expiration of the time given by R.S. 9:4822 for filing the statement of claim or privilege to preserve it.

C. The extinguishment of a claim or privilege shall not affect other rights the claimant or privilege holder may have against the owner, the contractor, or the surety.

D. A privilege granted by this Part is extinguished if a bond is filed by the owner as provided by R.S. 9:4835.

E. A claim against the owner and the privilege securing it granted by this Part are extinguished if a bond is filed by the contractor as provided by R.S. 9:4835.

F. In a concursus proceeding brought under R.S. 9:4841, the joinder of the owner and a person who has a privilege or a claim against the owner, or the joinder of the contractor or surety and a person who has a claim against the contractor constitutes the institution of an action for the enforcement of the claim or privilege against the owner, contractor, or surety as the case may be.

Acts 1981, No. 724, § 1, eff. Jan. 1, 1982. Amended by Acts 2012, No. 394, § 1, eff. Aug. 1, 2013.

Comments—1981

(a) This section incorporates the substance of the prior law requiring the timely filing of notices of claims and the institution of suits for their enforcement. The effect of failing to take such action results in the extinguishment of the claims or privileges given under the act. Under Subsection A preserving the claim against the owner also prevents its extinguishment against the contractor or surety. Such extinguishment would be irrelevant in light of the owner's rights of indemnity. (See R.S. 9:4802F, *Supra*.)

(b) Subsection B provides that the extinction of the claim against the owner will not necessarily extinguish the statutory claims against the contractor. It thus serves the same function as former Section R.S. 9:4814C.

(c) Although Subsections D and E only refer to the filing of a surety bond, Section 4835, *supra*, permits the filing of a bond or the pledging of certain other funds to guarantee payment of the claims. In light of the provisions of 4835, authorizing the clerk to cancel the privileges upon giving of such security, the term "bond" in this Section should be deemed to include not only a "surety bond" but the other forms of security in lieu of such a bond permitted to be given by Section 4835.

Editor's note. Acts 2012, No. 394, Section 1, has amended R.S. 9: 4823 and Section 2 of the same Act has amended R.S. 9: 4831, 4833, 4835, 4862, 4865, 4872, and 4885. Section 3 of Acts 2012, No. 394, declares that the provisions of Section 1 of this Act shall become effective on August 1, 2013, and the provisions of Section 2 of this Act shall become effective on August 1, 2012.

Cross References

C.C. arts. 3186, 3230, 3231, 3249, 3250, 3251, 3267, 3268.

APPENDIX 1—REVISED STATUTES, TITLE 9

SUBPART E. FILING; CANCELLATION; PEREMPTION

§ 4831. Filing; place of filing; contents

A. The filing of a notice of contract, notice of termination, statement of a claim or privilege, or notice of pendency of action required or permitted to be filed under the provisions of this Part is accomplished when it is filed for registry with the recorder of mortgages of the parish in which the work is to be performed. The recorder of mortgages shall inscribe all such acts in the mortgage records.

B. For purposes of this Part, the recorder of mortgages includes the office of the clerk of court and ex officio recorder of mortgages.

C. Each filing made with the recorder of mortgages pursuant to this Part which contains a reference to immovable property shall contain a description of the property sufficient to clearly and permanently identify the property. A description which includes the lot and/or square and/or subdivision or township and range shall meet the requirement of this Subsection. Naming the street or mailing address without more shall not be sufficient to meet the requirements of this Subsection.

Acts 1981, No. 724, § 1, eff. Jan. 1, 1982. Amended by Acts 1983, No. 589, § 1; Acts 2012, No. 394, § 2, eff. Aug. 1, 2012.

Comment—1981

This does not change the law. It consolidates in one section the various provisions of the former act relative to filing in the public records. It makes the filing of the documents the significant time, rather than recordation. This is consistent with the law generally prevailing for the public records. See Civil Code Article 3358.

Editor's note. The effective date of Section 2 of Acts 2012, No.394 that has amended R.S. 9:4831, 4833, 4835, 4862, 4865, 4872, and 4885 is August 1, 2013. Section 3 of Acts 2012, No. 394, declares that the provisions of Section 1 of this Act "shall become effective on August 1, 2013, and the provisions of Section 2 of this Act shall become effective on August 1, 2012."

Cross References

C.C. arts. 3186, 3230, 3231, 3249, 3250, 3251, 3267.

§ 4832. Cancellation of notice of contract

A. The recorder of mortgages shall cancel from his records a notice of contract upon written request of any person made more than thirty days after the filing of a notice of termination of work performed under the contract if:

(1) A statement of claim or privilege with respect to the work was not filed within the thirty day period; and

(2) The request contains or has attached to it the written concurrence of the contractor or a written receipt from the contractor acknowledging payment in full of all amounts due under the contract.

B. If the request for cancellation of a notice of contract does not contain or is not accompanied by the written concurrence or receipt of the contractor, but a statement of claim or privilege was not filed within the thirty day period, the recorder of mortgages shall cancel the notice of contract as to all claims and privileges except that of the contractor. The recorder of mortgages shall completely cancel the notice of contract from his records upon written request of any person if:

(1) The request is made more than sixty days after the filing of the notice of termination and the contractor did not file a statement of his claim or privilege within that time; or

(2) The request contains or is accompanied by the written concurrence of or a written receipt from the contractor acknowledging payment in full of all amounts due under the contract.

Acts 1981, No. 724, § 1, eff. Jan. 1, 1982.

Comment—1981

This section does not change the law. It provides for cancellation of the notice of contract. Erasure of a claim or privilege is regulated by Section 4833. It is implicit that if a statement of claim or privilege is timely filed but later erased the notice of contract could also be cancelled because the records would then not disclose any statement filed within the period required. The erasure or cancellation of a claim or privilege eliminates them from the records and they should then be considered as having never been filed for purposes of cancellation of the notice of contract.

Cross References

C.C. arts. 3186, 3230, 3231, 3249, 3250, 3251, 3267, 3268.

§ 4833. Request to cancel the inscription of claims and privileges; cancellation; notice of pendency of action

A. If a statement of claim or privilege is improperly filed or if the claim or privilege preserved by the filing of a statement of claim or privilege is extinguished, an owner or other interested person may require the person who has filed a statement of the claim or privilege to give a written request for cancellation in the manner provided by law directing the recorder of mortgages to cancel the statement of claim or privilege from his records. The request shall be delivered within ten days after a written request for it is received by the person filing the statement of claim or privilege.

B. One who, without reasonable cause, fails to deliver a written request for cancellation in proper form to cancel the claim or privilege as required by Subsection A of this Section shall be liable for damages suffered by the owner or person requesting the authorization as a consequence of the failure and for reasonable attorney fees incurred in causing the statement to be cancelled.

C. A person who has properly requested a written request for cancellation shall have an action pursuant to R.S. 44:114 against the person required to deliver the written request to obtain a judgment declaring the claim or the privilege extinguished and directing the recorder of mortgages to cancel the statement of claim or privilege if the person required to give the written request fails or refuses to do so within the time required by Subsection A of this Section. The plaintiff may also seek recovery of the damages and attorney fees to which he may be entitled under this Section.

D. The recorder of mortgages shall cancel a statement of a claim or privilege from his records upon the filing with him by any person of a written request for cancellation in proper form or when he is ordered to do so by judgment of the court.

E. The effect of filing for recordation of a statement of claim or privilege and the privilege preserved by it shall cease as to third persons unless a notice of pendency of action in accordance with Article 3752 of the Code of Civil Procedure, identifying the suit required to be filed by R.S. 9:4823 is filed within one year after the date of filing the statement of claim or privilege. In addition to the requirements of Article 3752 of the Code of Civil Procedure, the notice of pendency of action shall contain a reference to the notice of contract, if one is filed, or a reference to the recorded statement of claim or privilege if a notice of contract is not filed.

Acts 1981, No. 724, § 1, eff. Jan. 1, 1982. Amended by Acts 1985, No. 711, § 1; Acts 2005, No. 169, § 4, eff. July 1, 2006; Acts 2012, No. 394, § 2, eff. Aug. 1, 2012.

Comments—1981

(a) This section is new but does not change the law. It adopts the substance of the former R.S. 9:4821 but expands its provisions. Many construction projects contemplate or are dependent upon financing arrangements, leases, or conveyances that are to be consummated shortly after completion of the work. This section is designed to discourage the filing of a claim that is clearly unjustified, late, or otherwise made without reasonable cause for believing it is valid in the hope that economic pressure may be placed upon the owner or contractor to extract a settlement or other payment as the price of a release. Thus, the delay for delivering authorization to cancel the lien after request has been reduced from thirty days to ten days.

(b) The evidentiary provisions in the former Section 4821 are now included in R.S. 9:4842, *infra*, which regulates delivery of notices and other documents.

(c) Subsection F reproduces the requirements for the contents of a notice of lis pendens that were scattered throughout the former act. (See former R.S. 9:4802, 4806 and 4812). However, it does make one important change. Since the purpose of lis pendens is to protect third persons who may be dealing with the property, the failure to file notice of lis pendens does not extinguish the privilege as against the owner but makes the privilege ineffective as to third persons. This is analogous to an unrecorded mortgage that is good between the parties but not good against third persons. Thus, the decisions in Robins v. Pavone, 224 So.2d 541 (La. App. 4th Cir. 1969), and Lafayette Woodworks v. Boudreaux, 255 So.2d 176 (La.App. 1st Cir. 1971) would be different if decided under this revision.

Editor's note. This section has been amended by Acts 2005, No. 169, § 8, effective Jan. 1, 2006. That effective date, however, was postponed to July 1, 2006, by emergency legislation, Acts 2005, 1st Ex.Sess., No. 13.

Section 9 of Acts 2005, No. 169 provides:

"Section 9. Nothing in this Act shall be deemed to diminish the effect of, or render ineffective, the recordation of any instrument that was filed, registered, or recorded in the conveyance or mortgage records of any parish before the effective date of this Act. Any instrument that is filed, registered, or recorded before the effective date of this Act, that is not given the effect of recordation by virtue of existing law, shall be given such effect on the effective date of this Act that it would have if it were first filed on that effective date. Any instrument made available for viewing on the Internet by the recorder before the effective date of this Act shall not be subject to the restriction that allows the display of only the last four digits of social security numbers."

The effective date of Section 2 of Acts 2012, No. 394 that has amended R.S. 9:4831, 4833, 4835, 4862, 4865, 4872, and 4885 is August 1, 2013. Section 3 of Acts 2012, No. 394, declares that the provisions of Section 1 of this Act "shall become effective on August 1, 2013, and the provisions of Section 2 of this Act shall become effective on August 1, 2012."

Cross References

C.C. arts. 3186, 3230, 3231, 3249, 3250, 3251, 3267, 3268.

§ 4834. Notice of contract; cessation of effect, reinscription

The effect of filing a notice of contract ceases five years after it is filed, unless a written request for its reinscription, in the manner provided for the reinscription of mortgages, is properly and timely made by an interested person to the recorder of mortgages in whose office the notice of contract is filed. A request for reinscription may not be made after the effect of the filing of the notice of the contract has ceased. The effect of reinscription shall cease five years after the request for reinscription is filed.

Acts 1981, No. 724, § 1, eff. Jan. 1, 1982. Amended by Acts 2005, No. 169, § 4, eff. July 1, 2006.

Comment—1981

This section reproduces the substance of the former Section 4818. It is not intended to change the law.

Editor's note. This section has been amended by Acts 2005, No. 169, § 8, effective Jan. 1, 2006. That effective date, however, was postponed to July 1, 2006, by emergency legislation, Acts 2005, 1st Ex.Sess., No. 13.

Section 9 of Acts 2005, No. 169 provides:

"Section 9. Nothing in this Act shall be deemed to diminish the effect of, or render ineffective, the recordation of any instrument that was filed, registered, or recorded in the conveyance or mortgage records of any parish before the effective date of this Act. Any instrument that is filed, registered, or recorded before the effective date of this Act, that is not given the effect of recordation by virtue of existing law, shall be given such effect on the effective date of this Act that it would have if it were first filed on that effective date. Any instrument made available for viewing on the Internet by the recorder before the effective date of this Act shall not be subject to the restriction that allows the display of only the last four digits of social security numbers."

Cross References

C.C. arts. 3186, 3230, 3231, 3249, 3250, 3251, 3267, 3268.

§ 4835. Filing of bond or other security; cancellation of statement of claim or privilege or notice of pendency of action

A. If a statement of claim or privilege or a notice of pendency of action is filed, any interested party may deposit with the recorder of mortgages either a bond of a lawful surety company authorized to do business in the state or cash, certified funds, or a federally insured certificate of deposit to guarantee payment of the obligation secured by the privilege or that portion as may be lawfully due together with interest, costs, and attorney fees to which the claimant may be entitled up to a total amount of one hundred twenty-five percent of the principal amount of the claim as asserted in the statement of claim or privilege or such a suit. A surety shall not have the benefit of division or discussion.

B. If the recorder of mortgages finds the amount of the cash, certified funds, or certificate of deposit or the terms and amount of a bond deposited with him to be in conformity with this Section, he shall note his approval on the bond and make note of either the bond or of the cash, certified funds, or certificate of deposit in the margin of the statement of claim or privilege or notice of pendency of action as it is recorded in the mortgage records and cancel the statement of claim or privilege or the notice of pendency of action from his records by making an appropriate notation in the margin of the recorded statement or notice. The bond shall not be recorded but shall be retained by the recorder of mortgages as a part of his records.

C. Any party who files a bond or other security to guarantee payment of an obligation secured by a privilege in accordance with the provisions of R.S. 9:4835(A) shall give notice to the owner of the immovable, the holder of the lien, and the contractor of the improvements to the immovable by certified mail to the address of the immovable or to the lienholder's address in the case of notice to the lienholder.

Acts 1981, No. 724, § 1, eff. Jan. 1, 1982. Amended by Acts 1984, No. 388, § 1; Acts 1985, No. 556, § 1; Acts 2012, No. 394, § 2, eff. Aug. 1, 2012.

Comment—1981

This Section clarifies and consolidates into one Section the provisions of former Sections 9:4841 and 4842 permitting the filing of security as a substitute for the privilege given to a particular claimant. The Section permits any "interested person" to either give a surety bond or to "deposit" (i.e. pledge) cash or bank funds for the same purpose. Sections 4823 D and E draw a distinction between the effect of such security given to secure an owner's obligation which only extinguishes the privilege against the property and a contractor's obligation, in which case the privilege on the property and the statutory liability imposed on the owner by Section 4802 are both extinguished. The section also clarifies the responsibility of the recorder and requires notation of his approval of the formal requisites of the bond before it will have the effect provided by R.S. 9:4823D and E, *infra*.

Editor's note. The effective date of Section 2 of Acts 2012, No. 394 that has amended R.S. 9:4831, 4833, 4835, 4862, 4865, 4872, and 4885 is August 1, 2013. Section 3 of Acts 2012, No. 394, declares that the provisions of Section 1 of this Act "shall become effective on August 1, 2013, and the provisions of Section 2 of this Act shall become effective on August 1, 2012."

Cross References

C.C. arts. 3186, 3230, 3231, 3249, 3250, 3251, 3267, 3268.

SUBPART F. PROCEDURE FOR ENFORCEMENT; BURDEN OF PROOF

§ 4841. Enforcement of claims and privileges; concursus

A. After the period provided by R.S. 9:4822 for the filing of statements of claims or privileges has expired, the owner or any other interested party may convoke a concursus and shall cite all persons who have preserved their claims against the owner or their privileges on the immovable, and shall cite the owner, the contractor and the surety if they are not otherwise parties to establish the validity and rank of their claims and privileges.

B. The owner who convokes or is made a party to the concursus may deposit into the registry of the court the amounts owed by him to the contractor.

C. The owner may by rule order the other parties to the action to show cause why a judgment should not be entered discharging and cancelling their claims and privileges or discharging the owner from further responsibility to them. The rule shall be tried and appealed separately from the main cause of action and shall be limited to a consideration of the following matters:

(1) Whether the proper amounts have been deposited by the owner into the registry of the court.

(2) Whether the asserted claims or privileges have been properly preserved.

(3) Whether a notice of the contract and a bond for the work were properly and timely filed as required by R.S. 9:4811 and R.S. 9:4812.

(4) Whether the bond complies with the requirements of this Part.

D. If the court determines that the owner has properly deposited all sums owed by him to the contractor; that the owner has complied with this Part by properly and timely filing notice of a contract and bond as required by R.S. 9:4811 and R.S. 9:4812; that the bond complies with the requirements of this Part, or if it finds that any of the claims or privileges have not been preserved, it shall render a judgment on the rule directing the claims or privileges to be cancelled by the recorder and declaring the owner discharged from further liability for such claims or limiting the claims and privileges to the amounts as may be owed by the owner or otherwise granting such relief to the owner as may be proper.

E. The surety who convokes a concursus proceeding shall deposit into the registry of the court an amount equal to the lesser of:

(1) The full amount of the bond; or

(2) One hundred and twenty-five percent of the total amount claimed by persons who have filed a timely statement of claim or privilege for work arising out of the contract for which the bond is given.

After answer by or judgment of default against all claimants, the surety, upon motion and order may withdraw from the registry of the court any sums so deposited to the extent they exceed one hundred twenty-five percent of the aggregate amount of the claims then asserted against the contractor and surety by such claimants.

F. The attorney for the owner, who convokes a concursus under this Section, or the attorney for a claimant or privilege holder who convokes the concursus where more than ninety days have elapsed from the expiration of the time given by R.S. 9:4822 for claimants or privilege holders to file statements of their claim and such a concursus has not been convoked, shall be entitled to recover from the contractor and his surety a reasonable fee for his services in convoking the concursus. The fees awarded may be paid out of the funds deposited into the registry of the court but only after satisfaction of all valid claims and privileges.

G. The costs of the concursus taxable to the person who convokes it shall be paid in preference to other claims asserted.

Acts 1981, No. 724, § 1, eff. Jan. 1, 1982.

Comments—1981

(a) This Section restates and clarifies the concursus proceeding contemplated by the former R.S. 9:4804, 4805 and 4810. It does not make any substantial change in the law but does clarify and expand the procedures available. The Code of Civil Procedure supplements this Section. Federal Nat. Bank & Trust Co. v. Calsim, Inc., 340 So.2d 611 (La.App. 4th Cir. 1977).

(b) The phrase "after answer by or judgment of default against" in Subsection E is used in place of "after the case is at issue" to make the concept consistent with the Code of Civil Procedure. See Comment (a) to Article 928 of the Code of Civil Procedure.

(c) The provisions of former R.S. 9:4805 have been suppressed. The owner can no longer escape personal liability or have the privileges on his property cancelled if the claimants do not object to the sufficiency of the surety within ten days after the concursus is filed. This rule created an inequitable situation if the surety appeared solvent when the concursus was filed but later became insolvent. See Magnon Electric, Inc. v. J. P. Van Way Eng. Contr., Inc., 256 So.2d 851 (La.App. 3rd Cir. 1971). Under Subsections C and D the owner remains personally liable until he proves the bond is sufficient. He bears the risk of the insolvency of the surety until the rule is decided.

Cross References

C.C. arts. 3186, 3230, 3231, 3249, 3250, 3251, 3267, 3268.

§ 4842. Delivery of notice or other documents and materials; burden of proof

A. A notice required or permitted to be given by this Part or any document required or permitted to be delivered by this Part shall be deemed to have been given or delivered when it is delivered to the person entitled to receive it, or when the notice or document is properly deposited in the United States mail for delivery by certified or registered mail to that person. The mailing may be addressed to an owner, contractor, or surety at the address given in a notice of contract or attached bond filed in accordance with this Part, or to a claimant at the address given in the statement of claim or privilege filed by the claimant or a notice given by the claimant under the provisions of R.S. 9:4822.

B. Proof of delivery at the site of the immovable by a claimant asserting a claim or privilege under the provisions of R.S. 9:4801(3) or R.S. 9:4802(3) is prima facie evidence that the movables became component parts of the immovable, or were used on the immovable, or in machinery or equipment used at the site of the immovable in performing the work.

Acts 1981, No. 724, § 1, eff. Jan. 1, 1982. Amended by Acts 1988, No. 685, § 1, eff. Jan. 1, 1989.

Comments—1981

(a) Subsection A consolidates into one Section the provisions specifying how delivery of documents are to be made and when such delivery has been accomplished.

(b) Subsection B is new but does not change the law. It reproduces the jurisprudential rule developed in Derbes v. Marshall, 183 So. 74 (La.App. 2nd Cir. 1938); Romero & Sons Lumber Co. v. Babineaux, 151 So.2d 714 (La.App. 3rd 1963) and Century National Bank v. Parent, 341 So.2d 1371 (La. App. 4th Cir. 1977).

Cross References

C.C. arts. 3186, 3230, 3231, 3249, 3250, 3251, 3267, 3268.

SUBPART G. RESIDENTIAL TRUTH IN CONSTRUCTION ACT

§ 4851. Scope; definition

A. The provisions of this Subpart and the notice required to be given herein shall be nonwaivable and shall be applicable to all residential home improvements and shall be read and construed in pari materia with the other provisions of this Part.

B. For the purposes of this Subpart, residential home improvements shall include all improvements or construction which enhance the value or enjoyment of any real property occupied by the owner thereof principally as a single-family dwelling or residence if such works would entitle any person to lien rights against the property under the provisions of R.S. 9:4801 through 9:4842.

Added by Acts 1976, No. 237, § 1.

Cross References

C.C. arts. 3186, 3230, 3231, 3249, 3250, 3251, 3267, 3268.

§ 4852. Notice

A. Prior to or at the time of entering into a contract for residential home improvements under the provision of this Subpart, the contractor shall deliver to the owner or his authorized agent, for such owner's or agent's signature, written notice in substantially the following form:

NOTICE OF LIEN RIGHTS

Delivered this _____ day of _____, 19___, by _____, Contractor.

I, the undersigned owner of residential property located at

_____(street address)_____ in the city of _____, parish of _____, Louisiana, acknowledge that the abovenamed contractor has delivered this notice to me, the receipt of which is accepted, signifying my understanding that said contractor is about to begin improving my residential property according to the terms and conditions of a contract, and that in accordance with the provisions of law in Part I of Chapter 2 of Code Title XXI of Title 9 of the Louisiana Revised Statutes of 1950, R.S. 9:4801, et seq.:

(1) A right to file a lien against my property and improvements is granted to every contractor, subcontractor, architect, engineer, surveyor, mechanic, cartman, truckman, work-

man, laborer, or furnisher of material, machinery or fixtures, who performs work or furnishes material for the improvement or repair of my property, for the payment in principal and interest of such work or labor performed, or the materials, machinery or fixtures furnished, and for the cost of recording such privilege.

(2) That when a contract is unwritten and/or unrecorded, or a bond is not required or is insufficient or unrecorded, or the surety therefor is not proper or solvent, I, as owner, shall be liable to such subcontractors, materialmen, suppliers or laborers for any unpaid amounts due them pursuant to their timely filed claims to the same extent as is the hereinabove designated contractor.

(3) That the lien rights granted herein can be enforced against my property even though the contractor has been paid in full if said contractor has not paid the persons who furnished the labor or materials for the improvement.

(4) That I may require a written contract, to be recorded, and a bond with sufficient surety to be furnished and recorded by the contractor in an amount sufficient to cover the cost of such improvements, thereby relieving me, as owner, and my property, of liability for any unpaid sums remaining due and owing after completion to subcontractors, journeymen, cartmen, workmen, laborers, mechanics, furnishers of material or any other persons furnishing labor, skill, or material on the said work who record and serve their claims in accordance with the requirements of law.

I have read the above statement and fully understand its contents.

_____
Owner or Agent

_____
Date

B. The notice herein required shall not be considered a condition of the construction contract.

Added by Acts 1976, No. 237, § 1.

Cross References

C.C. arts. 3186, 3230, 3231, 3249, 3250, 3251, 3267, 3268.

§ 4853. Copies of notice

A. A copy of the signed notice shall be given to the owner or agent who has affixed his signature thereto.

B. Every person who may be entitled to lien rights against the residential property for work to be done or material to be furnished pursuant to this Subpart shall be furnished a copy of the signed notice by the contractor upon request.

Added by Acts 1976, No. 237, § 1.

Cross References

C.C. arts. 3168, 3230, 3231, 3249, 3250, 3251, 3267, 3268.

§ 4854. Lien rights unaffected

Nothing contained in this Subpart shall abrogate or interfere with the lien rights of any person otherwise entitled thereto pursuant to the provisions of this Part.

Added by Acts 1976, No. 237, § 1.

Cross References

C.C. arts. 3186, 3230, 3231, 3249, 3250, 3251, 3267, 3268.

§ 4855. Penalty for violation

In the event any liens are perfected under the provisions of this Part against any immovable property for work or improvements covered under the provisions of this Subpart and the contractor has failed to comply with the provisions of this Subpart, or, if having technically complied with this Subpart, has willfully, knowingly, and unlawfully falsified any statements or fraudulently obtained the signature of the owner or his agent, such owner shall have a civil cause of action therefor, and shall be entitled to reasonable damages and attorney fees. The penalty provided for herein shall not apply if the contractor or subcontractor obtains a bond from a good and solvent surety in favor of the owner of the property on which the lien is placed pursuant to R.S. 9:4841, or reimburses the property owner in an amount sufficient to satisfy the lien, either in the form of a deduction from the original contract price or other refund and the owner so acknowledges receipt in writing.

Added by Acts 1976, No. 237, § 1.

Cross References

C.C. arts. 3186, 3230, 3231, 3249, 3250, 3251, 3267, 3268.

PART II. OIL, GAS, AND WATER WELLS

SUBPART A. IN GENERAL

§ 4861. Definitions

For purposes of this Part:

(1) A "claimant" is a person who is owed an obligation secured by the privilege established by R.S. 9:4862.

(2) "Hydrocarbons" are oil and gas occurring naturally in the earth and any other valuable liquid or gaseous substance found and produced in association with them.

(3) A "well" is one that is intended to:

(a) Explore for or produce hydrocarbons.

(b) Inject or dispose of substances, whether useful or not, produced from a well that is intended to explore for or produce hydrocarbons.

(c) Inject hydrocarbons or other substances into the earth to enhance or facilitate the production of hydrocarbons.

(d) Produce water for use in the operations of a well that is intended to explore for or produce hydrocarbons.

(4)(a) "Operations" are every activity conducted by or for a lessee on a well site for the purpose of:

(i) Drilling, completing, testing, producing, reworking, or abandoning a well.

(ii) Saving, treating, or disposing of hydrocarbons or other substances produced from a well.

(iii) Injecting substances into the earth to produce or enhance the production of hydrocarbons.

(b) "Operations" do not include an activity conducted for the purpose of transporting, handling, processing, treating, or otherwise dealing with:

(i) Liquid hydrocarbons produced or separated at the well site after being removed from a leasehold tank and delivered into a truck, barge, pipeline, or other facility for transportation away from the well site.

(ii) Hydrocarbons produced in gaseous form, or produced in association with those produced in gaseous form and not separated at the well site, after being delivered into a pipeline for transportation away from the well site or delivered to a plant at the well site for processing or manufacturing.

(iii) Salt water or another waste substance produced in association with hydrocarbons, after it is placed in a truck, rail-car, pipeline, or other means of transportation for disposal away from the well site.

(5)(a) An "operating interest" is a mineral lease or sublease of a mineral lease, or an interest in a lease or sublease that gives the lessee, either singly or in association with others, the right to conduct the operations giving rise to the claimant's privilege.

(b) A mineral lease or sublease or an interest in the lease or sublease, is not an operating interest if an owner has divested himself of the right to conduct the operations giving rise to the claimant's privilege by assignment, sublease, or another form of mineral right before the claimant's privilege is established.

(c) A contract, such as one which commonly is referred to in the industry as a "farm-out" or "farm-in", by which a lessee agrees to sublease or transfer all or part of his rights in a lease to another person, commonly referred to as a "farmee", upon the drilling of a well or completion of some other operations, but which does not then vest such interest in the farmee, is not an operating interest until the sublease or transfer is made, and until then the farmee is a contractor of the lessee for the purposes of this Part.

(6) A "lessee" is a person who owns an operating interest.

(7) An "operator" is a lessee who is personally bound by contract to the claimant or to a contractor from whom the claimant's activities giving rise to the privilege emanate.

(8) A "participating lessee" is a lessee who is not the operator, but who is personally bound by contract to the operator to pay or reimburse the operator for any part of the obligation secured by the privilege or for any part of the price of the contract of the contractor from whom the operations giving rise to the claimant's privilege emanate.

(9) A "non-participating lessee" is a lessee who is neither an operator nor a participating lessee. A non-participating lessee does not become a participating lessee because an operator, contractor, or the claimant has the right to recover all or part of the obligation secured by the privilege out of hydrocarbons attributable to the interest of the lessee in the operating interest or from the lessee's share of the proceeds derived from such hydrocarbons, or out of other property of the lessee.

(10) A "contractor" is a person, other than a lessee, who contracts with an operator to perform the operations giving rise to the claimant's privilege or who, by subcontract with a contractor of the operator or through a series of subcontracts emanating from such a contractor, contracts to perform all or part of the operations contracted for by the operator.

(11) A "third person" is a person, including a lessee or operator, who is not contractually bound to the claimant for the obligation secured by a privilege or who has not expressly assumed the obligation.

(12) A "well site" is the area covered by:

(a) The operating interest.

(b) A unit in which the operating interest participates.

(c) A tract of land or the area covered by a servitude or predial lease of the lessee on which is located a well drilled to, producing from, or injecting substances into the area covered by the operating interest.

Acts 1995, No. 962, § 1.

§ 4862. Privilege for labor, services, or supplies

A. The following persons have a privilege over the property described in R.S. 9:4863 to secure the following obligations incurred in operations:

(1) A contractor for the price of his contract for operations.

(2) A contractor for the price of his contract for providing services or facilities to persons performing labor or services on a well site located in the waters of the state.

(3) A laborer or employee of an operator or contractor, for the price of his labor performed at the well site.

(4) A person who performs trucking, towing, barging, or other transportation services for an operator or contractor, for the price of transporting movables to the well site.

(5) A person who transports, to or from a well site located in the waters of the state, persons who are employed in rendering labor or services on the well site, for the price of transporting those persons.

(6) A seller for the price of a movable sold to an operator or contractor that is:

(a) Incorporated in a well or in a facility located on the well site.

(b) Consumed in operations.

(c) Consumed at the well site by a person performing labor or services on a well site located in the waters of the state.

(7) A lessor for the rent of a movable leased to an operator or contractor used in operations and that accrues while the movable is located on the well site.

B. The privilege created by this Part is accessory to and secures only the following:

(1) The amount of the obligation described in Subsection A of this Section.

(2) Interest due on the amount of the obligation.

(3) The cost of preparing and filing the statement of privilege and notice of pendency of action authorized by this Part.

(4) The amount of reasonable attorney fees not to exceed ten percent if an attorney is employed to enforce obligations.

Acts 1995, No. 962, § 1. Amended by Acts 2012, No. 394, § 2, eff. Aug. 1, 2012.

Editor's note. The effective date of Section 2 of Acts 2012, No. 394 that has amended R.S. 9:4831, 4833, 4835, 4862, 4865, 4872, and 4885 is August 1, 2013. Section 3 of Acts 2012, No. 394, declares that the provisions of Section 1 of this Act "shall become effective on August 1, 2013, and the provisions of Section 2 of this Act shall become effective on August 1, 2012."

§ 4863. Property subject to the privilege

A. Except as limited by Subsections B, C, and D of this Section, the privilege given by R.S. 9:4862 is established over:

(1) The operating interest under which the operations giving rise to the claimant's privilege are conducted together with the interest of the lessee of such interest in a:

(a) Well, building, tank, leasehold pipeline, and other construction or facility on the well site.

(b) Movable on a well site that is used in operations, other than a movable that is only transiently on the well site for repair, testing, or other temporary use.

(c) Tract of land, servitude, and lease described in R.S. 9:4861(12)(c) covering the well site of the operating interest.

(2) Drilling or other rig located at the well site of the operating interest if the rig is owned by the operator or by a contractor from whom the activities giving rise to the privilege emanate.

(3) The interest of the operator and participating lessee in hydrocarbons produced from the operating interest and the interest of a non- participating lessee in hydrocarbons produced from that part of his operating interest subject to the privilege.

(4) The proceeds received by, and the obligations owed to, a lessee from the disposition of hydrocarbons subject to the privilege.

B. The privilege that results from operations on a voluntary or compulsory unit affects only that part of a non-participating lessee's interest in the operating interest located within the boundaries of the unit and only insofar as the unit covers and affects the unitized zone or formation. The privilege affects only the interest of the non-participating lessee in the other property described in Subsection (A)(1) and (2) of this Section that is used in the operations of the unit well.

C. The privilege does not affect:

(1) That part of hydrocarbons produced from an operating interest that is owned by a lessor, sublessor, overriding royalty owner, or other person who is not a lessee of the operating interest.

(2) The obligations or proceeds arising from the disposition of such hydrocarbons that are owned by or payable to such persons.

D. The lien and privilege provided for in this Subpart shall not attach or apply to any rigs, machinery, appurtenances, appliances, equipment, or other related equipment moved onto the lease for the purpose of plugging and abandoning the well or wells and closing associated pits thereon in compliance with an order issued by the commissioner of conservation after public hearing in accordance with the provisions of R.S. 30:1 et seq. Additionally, the lien and privilege provided for in this Subpart shall not attach or apply to any casing, tubing, pipe, and other tubular goods recovered from the drill hole as a result of such plugging and abandoning operations.

Acts 1995, No. 962, § 1. Amended by Acts 1997, No. 533, § 1.

§ 4864. When the privilege is established and when it is extinguished

A. The privilege in favor of a claimant is established and is effective as to a third person when:

(1) The claimant, who is a contractor, laborer, or employee begins rendering services at the well site.

(2) Movables sold by the claimant to an operator or contractor are delivered to the well site.

(3) The claimant begins transporting movables to, or persons to or from, the well site.

(4) Property leased by the claimant to an operator or contractor is placed on the well site for use in operations.

B. The privilege is extinguished:

(1) Upon extinction of the obligation it secures.

(2) By written consent of the claimant.

(3) As otherwise provided in this Part.

C. All obligations owed to a claimant arising from operations on the same operating interest, without a lapse of more than ninety consecutive days between an activity or event that establishes the privilege as described in Subsection A of this Section, are secured by a single privilege whether or not such activities are performed or events occur at different times and under several contracts with different operators or contractors. If more than ninety consecutive days elapse between such activities or events, the privileges established before and those established after such time are separate.

Acts 1995, No. 962, § 1.

§ 4865. Cessation of effect as to certain third persons

A. A privilege ceases to have effect against a third person one hundred- eighty days after the last activity or event which gives rise to the privilege unless:

(1) The property subject to the privilege is not a drilling or other rig and the claimant files a statement of privilege in the mortgage records of the parish where the operating interest subject to the privilege is located; or

(2) The property subject to the privilege is a drilling or other rig and the claimant files, in the place specified in R.S. 10:9–501, a financing statement conforming to the requirements of R.S. 10:9–502. Notwithstanding R.S. 10:9–509(a), the claimant may file such a financing statement without the debtor's authorization so long as the claimant holds the privilege at the time of filing and the financing statement covers only a rig covered by the claimant's privilege.

B. A privilege shall also cease to have effect against a third person unless the claimant institutes an action for the enforcement of the privilege within one year after the date of the filing of the statement of privilege or financing statement.

C. The privilege shall also cease to have effect against third persons who are not parties to the action instituted pursuant to the provisions of Subsection B of this Section unless the claimant files a notice of pendency of action in the mortgage records of the parish where the property is located or lawfully seizes the property subject to the privilege within thirty days after institution of the action unless the property subject to the privilege is a drilling or other rig.

Acts 1995, No. 962, § 1. Amended by Acts 2001, No. 128, § 4, eff. July 1, 2001 at 12:01 A.M; Acts 2012, No. 394, § 2, eff. Aug. 1, 2012.

Editor's note. Acts 2001, No. 128, § 4, effective July 1, 2001, amended R.S. 9:3342. Section 19 of Acts 2001, No. 128, declares that "it is the intent of the legislature in enacting this Act that R.S. 2736, 4501 and 4502, 4521, 4758, 4770, and 5363.1 not be expressly or impliedly repealed by this Act, but that such laws remain in effect, and, at times when so provided, be applied to secured transactions subject to Chapter 9 of the Louisiana Commercial Law as revised by this Act."

The effective date of Section 2 of Acts 2012, No. 394 that has amended R.S. 9:4831, 4833, 4835, 4862, 4865, 4872, and 4885 is August 1, 2013. Section 3 of Acts 2012, No. 394, declares that the provisions of Section 1 of this Act "shall become effective on August 1, 2013, and the provisions of Section 2 of this Act shall become effective on August 1, 2012."

§ 4866. Extinction as to movable property

A privilege, if not otherwise extinguished, is extinguished as to movable property other than hydrocarbons, the obligations and proceeds derived from the disposition of hydrocarbons, and drilling or other rigs, when the property is transferred by an onerous transaction to a third person who is in good faith and it is removed from the well site.

Acts 1995, No. 962, § 1.

§ 4867. Notice to operator

A. A privilege is extinguished over the property upon which it is established, other than a drilling or other rig not owned by the operator, unless a statement of the claimant's privilege is delivered to the operator within the time specified in R.S. 9:4865(A) for the filing of a statement of privilege or unless the operator is contractually bound to the claimant for the obligation secured by the privilege.

B. A privilege established over a drilling or other rig, not owned by the operator, is extinguished at the time specified in R.S. 9:4865(A) for the filing of a statement of privilege unless a statement of the claimant's privilege is delivered to the owner of the rig within that time or unless the owner of the rig is contractually bound to the claimant for the obligation secured by the privilege.

Acts 1995, No. 962, § 1.

§ 4868. Statement of privilege; form and content

A. A statement of privilege must be in writing, signed by or on behalf of the claimant, and contain all of the following information:

(1) The name and address of the claimant.

(2) The amount and nature of the obligation for which the privilege is claimed.

(3) The name and address of the person owing such amount.

(4) The name of the operator of the well as shown by the records of the commissioner of conservation.

(5) A description of the operating interest upon which the privilege is claimed, or of the well with respect to which the operations giving rise to the claimant's privilege were performed.

B. (1) A well is adequately identified if the statement of privilege gives the name and serial or other identification number of the well and the name of the field where it is located as these are designated by the records of the commissioner of conservation.

(2) A notice is properly delivered to the operator if it is delivered to the operator who is properly identified in the statement of privilege.

C. A notice is delivered when:

(1) It is mailed by certified or registered mail properly addressed with sufficient postage affixed.

(2) If not mailed by certified or registered mail when either:

(a) It is received by the person to whom it is sent.

(b) It is received at the office of the person to whom it is addressed.

D. A return receipt, indicating delivery to a person or to his place of business, of a U.S. Postal Service registered or certified letter transmitting a notice, is prima facie proof of its mailing. A proof of mailing issued by the U.S. Postal Service is prima facie proof of mailing of the document to which it relates. The burden of proving that the notice was not received by the person or at the time and place indicated by the return receipt is upon the person denying it.

E. A statement of privilege is not invalid if it fails to contain all of the information required by Subsection A of this Section, but fairly apprises the recipient or person against whom the privilege is asserted of the privilege claimed and of the operating interest, hydrocarbons, or other property upon which the privilege is claimed.

Acts 1995, No. 962, § 1.

§ 4869. Purchaser of hydrocarbons; effect of privilege and notices required

A. The privilege established by R.S. 9:4863(A)(3) and (4) over hydrocarbons, the amount due for their price, and their proceeds is extinguished or becomes ineffective as to a third person in the manner provided in R.S. 9:4864, 4865, and 4867, and also in the following ways:

(1)(a) The privilege is extinguished as to hydrocarbons that are sold or otherwise transferred in a bona fide onerous transaction by the lessee or other person who severed or owned them at severance if the transferee pays for them before he is notified of the privilege by the claimant.

(b) After the transferee is notified of the privilege, the claimant may either enforce his privilege against hydrocarbons in the hands of the transferee or against the amount owed for their price, as he so elects.

(2) The privilege over hydrocarbons is extinguished when the hydrocarbons have become so commingled with, processed with, or transformed into other hydrocarbons or substances not subject to the privilege as to no longer be reasonably identifiable.

(3) The privilege over the proceeds from the disposition of hydrocarbons attributable to an interest of the lessee is extinguished when the proceeds have become so commingled with other funds not subject to the privilege as to no longer be reasonably identifiable.

B. A purchaser of hydrocarbons who is notified of the claim to a privilege over them may retain the amounts owed for them without liability to the claimant or the transferor from whom he received them until he is:

(1) Directed in writing by the claimant to release them or is advised by the claimant that the claimant no longer asserts a privilege over them.

(2) Directed in writing to deliver them to the claimant by the person to whom the purchaser owes the obligation.

(3) Directed in writing by the claimant and the person to whom the purchaser owes the obligation to deliver them to a third person or otherwise to dispose of them.

(4) Ordered to make some disposition of them by the judgment of a court in an action in which the claimant and the person to whom the purchaser owes the obligation are parties.

Acts 1995, No. 962, § 1.

§ 4870. Ranking of privileges

A. The privileges given by this Part are of equal rank and priority, except that the privilege of a contractor is inferior to that of a person to whom the contractor is contractually bound or to whom a contractor or subcontractor of such a contractor is bound.

B. The privileges granted by this Part are superior in rank and priority to all other privileges, security interests, or mortgages against the property they encumber except the following which are of superior rank and priority:

(1) Privileges for ad valorem taxes against the property subject to the privilege.

(2) Mortgages and vendor's privileges on the operating interest and other property affected by such mortgages or privileges that are effective as to a third person before the privilege is established.

(3) Security interests in collateral subject to the privilege that are perfected before the privilege is established or that are perfected by a financing statement covering the collateral filed before the privilege is established if there is no period thereafter when there is neither filing nor perfection.

(4) The lien and privilege of the commissioner of conservation as provided in R.S. 30:32, 74(A)(3), and 91(B)(2).

Acts 1995, No. 962, § 1. Amended by Acts 1997, No. 532, § 1; Acts 2001, No. 128, § 4, eff. July 1, 2001 at 12:01 A.M; Acts 2004, No. 303, § 1.

Editor's note. Acts 2001, No. 128, § 4, effective July 1, 2001, amended R.S. 9:4870. Section 19 of Acts 2001, No. 128, declares that "it is the intent of the legislature in enacting this Act that R.S. 2736, 4501 and 4502, 4521, 4758, 4770, and 5363.1 not be expressly or impliedly repealed by this Act, but that such laws remain in effect, and, at times when so provided, be applied to secured transactions subject to Chapter 9 of the Louisiana Commercial Law as revised by this Act."

§ 4871. Enforcement of claims and privileges

A claimant may enforce his privilege by a writ of sequestration, without the necessity of furnishing security.

Acts 1995, No. 962, § 1.

§ 4872. Filing of bond or other security; cancellation of statement of privilege or notice of pendency of action

A. If a statement of privilege or a notice of pendency of action is filed, any interested person may deposit with the recorder of mortgages of the parish where the operating interest is located a bond of a lawful surety company authorized to do business in the state or cash, certified funds, or a federally insured certificate of deposit. The bond or deposit shall be not less than one hundred twenty-five percent of the principal amount of the obligation claimed in the notice and shall guarantee payment up to such amount of the claimant's obligations secured by the privilege or such portion thereof as is lawfully due.

B. If the recorder of mortgages finds that the terms and amount of the bond or deposit is in conformity with this Section, he shall note his approval of the bond or of the deposit, in the margin of the claimant's statement of privilege and in the margin of the notice of pendency of action where they are recorded and shall then cancel them from his records by making an appropriate notation in the margins of their recordation. A bond deposited with the recorder shall not be recorded but shall be retained by the recorder of mortgages as a part of his records.

C. A claimant's privilege is extinguished upon acceptance and approval by the recorder of the bond or deposit given for it.

Acts 1995, No. 962, § 1. Amended by Acts 2012, No. 394, § 2, eff. Aug. 1, 2012.

Editor's note. The effective date of Section 2 of Acts 2012, No. 394 that has amended R.S. 9:4831, 4833, 4835, 4862, 4865, 4872, and 4885 is August 1, 2013. Section 3 of Acts 2012, No. 394, declares that the provisions of Section 1 of this Act "shall become effective on August 1, 2013, and the provisions of Section 2 of this Act shall become effective on August 1, 2012."

§ 4873. Delivery of movables to well site; burden of proof

Proof of delivery of movables to a well site by a claimant asserting a privilege under the provisions of R.S. 9:4862(A)(5) is prima facie evidence that the movables were incorporated in a well or in a facility located on the well site, or were consumed on the well site.

Acts 1995, No. 962, § 1.

§§ 4874 to 4880. [Blank]

SUBPART B. PRIVILEGES AND OTHER RIGHTS OF OPERATORS AND NON-OPERATORS

§ 4881. Definitions

For purposes of this Subpart:

(1) The terms defined in R.S. 9:4861 have the same meaning in this Subpart, unless they are differently defined in this Section.

(2) A "non-operator" is a lessee other than the operator.

(3) An "operator" is a lessee who is conducting operations with respect to a well.

Added by Acts 1997, No. 1040, § 1.

Editor's note. A prior Subpart B, "Miscellaneous provisions" consisting of R.S. 9:4881 to 9:4887 was repealed by Acts 1950, No. 200, § 1.

§ 4882. Privilege of the operator and non-operator

A. The operator has a privilege over the property described in R.S. 9:4883 to secure payment of all obligations incurred in the conduct of operations which the non-operator is personally bound to pay or reimburse.

B. A non-operator has a privilege over the property described in R.S. 9:4883 to secure payment of all obligations owed to him by the operator from the sale or other disposition of hydrocarbons of the non-operator produced from the well.

Added by Acts 1997, No. 1040, § 1.

§ 4883. Property subject to the privilege

A. A privilege given by this Subpart is established over the interest of the operator or non-operator in the following property:

(1) The operating interests under which the operations are conducted.

(2) A well, building, tank, leasehold pipeline, and other construction or facility on the well site.

(3) A movable on a well site that is used in the operations, other than a movable that is only transiently on the well site for repair, testing, or other temporary use.

(4) A tract of land, servitude, and lease described in R.S. 9:4861(12)(c) covering the well site of the operating interest.

(5) The hydrocarbons produced from the well site.

(6) The proceeds received by, and the obligations owed to, the operator or non-operator from the disposition of hydrocarbons subject to the privilege.

B. The privilege given by this Subpart does not affect:

(1) The hydrocarbons produced from the well site that are owned by the lessor, sublessor or overriding royalty owner.

(2) The obligations or proceeds arising from the disposition of such hydrocarbons that are owned by or payable to such persons.

Added by Acts 1997, No. 1040, § 1.

§ 4884. When the privilege is established and when it is extinguished

A. A privilege given by this Subpart is established and is effective as to a third person when the obligation it secures is incurred.

B. The privilege is extinguished:

(1) Upon extinction of the obligation it secures.

(2) By written consent of the person in whose favor the privilege exists.

(3) As otherwise provided in this Subpart.

Added by Acts 1997, No. 1040, § 1.

§ 4885. Cessation of effect as to certain third persons

A. A privilege given by this Subpart ceases to have effect against a third person to the extent it secures an obligation due more than one hundred eighty days or incurred more than one year before a statement of privilege is filed in the mortgage records of the parish where the operating interest subject to the privilege is located. The filing of the statement of privilege preserves the effect as to a third person for all obligations incurred thereafter.

B. The privilege ceases to have effect against a third person unless the creditor institutes an action for the enforcement of the privilege within one year after the date of the filing of the statement of privilege.

C. The privilege ceases to have effect against a third person who is not a party to the action instituted pursuant to the provisions of Subsection B of this Section unless the creditor files a notice of pendency of action in the mortgage records of the parish where the property is located or lawfully seizes the property subject to the privilege within thirty days after institution of the action.

D. The provisions of R.S. 9:4869 apply to the privileges given by this Subpart.

Added by Acts 1997, No. 1040, § 1. Amended by Acts 2012, No. 394, § 2, eff. Aug. 1, 2012.

Editor's note. The effective date of Section 2 of Acts 2012, No. 394 that has amended R.S. 9:4831, 4833, 4835, 4862, 4865, 4872, and 4885 is August 1, 2013. Section 3 of Acts 2012, No. 394, declares that the provisions of Section 1 of this Act "shall become effective on August 1, 2013, and the provisions of Section 2 of this Act shall become effective on August 1, 2012."

§ 4886. Extinction as to movable property

A privilege given by this Subpart is extinguished as to movable property other than hydrocarbons and the obligations and proceeds derived from the disposition of hydrocarbons when the property is transferred by an onerous transaction to a third person who is in good faith and it is removed from the well site.

Added by Acts 1997, No. 1040, § 1.

§ 4887. Statement of privilege; form and content

A. A statement of privilege given by this Subpart must be in writing, signed by or on behalf of the creditor, and contain all of the following information:

(1) The name and address of the creditor and whether he is filing as an operator or non-operator.

(2) The amount of the obligation due as of the date of the statement.

(3) The name and address of the person owing such amount.

(4) The name of the operator of the well as shown by the records of the commissioner of conservation.

(5) A description of the operating interest over which the privilege is claimed.

B. The statement of privilege is not invalid if it fails to contain all of the information required by Subsection A of this Section, but fairly apprises the person against whom the privilege is asserted of the privilege claimed and of the operating interest, hydrocarbons, or other property upon which the privilege is claimed.

Added by Acts 1997, No. 1040, § 1.

§ 4888. Ranking of privileges

A. The privileges given by this Subpart are of equal rank.

B. The privileges given by this Subpart are superior in rank to all other privileges, security interests, or mortgages against the property they encumber except the following which are of superior rank:

(1) Privileges for ad valorem taxes against the property subject to the privilege and the privileges provided in R.S. 30:32, 74(A)(3), and 91(B)(2).

(2) Privileges given by Subpart A of this Part.

(3) Mortgages and vendor's privileges on the operating interest and other property affected by such mortgages or privileges that are effective as to a third person before the privilege is established.

(4) Security interests in collateral subject to the privilege that are perfected before the privilege is established or that are perfected by a financing statement covering the collateral filed before the privilege is established if there is no period thereafter when there is neither filing nor perfection.

Added by Acts 1997, No. 1040, § 1. Amended by Acts 2001, No. 128, § 4, eff. July 1, 2001 at 12:01 A.M; Acts 2004, No. 303, § 1.

Editor's note. Acts 2001, No. 128, § 4, effective July 1, 2001, amended R.S. 9:4888. Section 19 of Acts 2001, No. 128, declares that "it is the intent of the legislature in enacting this Act that R.S. 2736, 4501 and 4502, 4521, 4758, 4770, and 5363.1 not be expressly or impliedly repealed by this Act, but that such laws remain in effect, and, at times when so provided, be applied to secured transactions subject to Chapter 9 of the Louisiana Commercial Law as revised by this Act."

§ 4889. Enforcement of privileges

The provisions of R.S. 9:4871 and 4872 apply, for purposes of enforcement, to the privileges given by this Subpart. Added by Acts 1997, No. 1040, § 1.

PART III. RAILROADS

SUBPART A. IN GENERAL

§ 4901. Railroad tracks, road-beds, etc., privilege for material or labor

Any person who furnishes supplies, materials, or labor which enters into the construction, maintenance, or repair of the permanent road bed and structures of a railroad, has a privilege upon the road beds, tracks, rights of way, and franchises of the railroad for the amount due for the supplies, materials, or labor.

Cross References

C.C. arts. 3186, 3230, 3231, 3249, 3250, 3251, 3267, 3268.

§ 4902. Recordation unnecessary; effective period

This privilege exists without the necessity of recordation, and is effective for a period of twelve months from the date upon which the materials or supplies are delivered or the labor is performed. In case of a running account of twelve months, the period is calculated from the date of the delivery or performance of the last item upon the account.

Cross References

C.C. arts. 3186, 3230, 3231, 3249, 3250, 3251, 3267, 3268.

§ 4903. Rank

The privilege is a first privilege upon the road-beds, tracks, rights of way, and franchises of the railroad, and has priority over all other mortgages or encumbrances and shall be paid by preference out of the proceeds of the sale of the road-beds, tracks, rights of way, and franchises of the railroad, under foreclosure or otherwise.

Cross References

C.C. arts. 3186, 3230, 3231, 3249, 3250, 3251, 3267, 3268.

PART IV. PUBLIC WORKS

SUBPART A. IN GENERAL

§ 4921. Feed for livestock used on public works; filing claims for

Any person, to whom any money is due on account of having furnished feed for mules or other livestock used by any contractor or subcontractor in the construction, erection, alteration, or repair of any public roads or other public works, under a contract in excess of five hundred dollars at the expense of the state or any parish, city, town, village, public board or body, may file with the authority having the work done and record in the office of the recorder of mortgages of the parish in which the work is being done any time after the maturity of his claim, a sworn statement of the amount due him. Any payments made thereafter by the authority without deducting the amount of the claim so served on it shall be at its own risk.

Cross References

C.C. arts. 3186, 3230, 3231, 3249, 3250, 3251, 3267, 3268.

§ 4922. Statement of amount due

Any person, to whom any money is due on account of having supplied and furnished feed for mules or other livestock used by any contractor or subcontractor in the construction, erection, alteration, or repair of such roads or public works shall, within forty five days after the acceptance of the work by the state, parish, city, town, village, public board or body, or within forty five days after the default of the contractor or subcontractor, file with the authority a sworn statement of the amount due and record a sworn statement thereof with the recorder of mortgages of the parish in which the work is done or being done. The forty five days does not begin to run until the authorities record in the mortgage office an acceptance of the work or notice of the default of the contractor.

Cross References

C.C. arts. 3186, 3230, 3231, 3249, 3250, 3251, 3267, 3268.

§ 4923. Feed claims have same rights as those for labor or materials

Any person, who furnishes feed to mules or other livestock under the provisions of this Sub-part has the same rights and privileges as those accorded by law to any laborer or furnisher of material in the construction, erection, alteration, or repair of any public building, public road, public work or public improvement.

Cross References

C.C. arts. 3186, 3230, 3231, 3249, 3250, 3251, 3267, 3268.

SUBPART B. BONDING CLAIMS

§ 4941. Contractor may bond claims

When any contractor shall have entered into a contract to perform public works under the laws of this state governing the letting and awarding of such contracts and in conformity with the requirements thereof, the contractor shall have the right to bond any claim or claims which may be filed or recorded against said work by depositing with the clerk of court of the parish in which such claims are filed or recorded a bond with surety signed by any surety company authorized to do business in the state for an amount equal to the claim plus one-fourth. The bond shall be approved by the clerk of court conditioned that in the event the legality of such claim or claims is established by suit or otherwise, the bond shall remain in full force and effect to protect the interest of the claimant in the premises.

Cross References

C.C. arts. 3168, 3230, 3231, 3249, 3250, 3251, 3267, 3268.

PART V. MISCELLANEOUS

§ 4961. Attorney's fees, limitation for recordation of lien

When, under any provision of this chapter there is authority for ten percent attorney's fees in the event it becomes necessary to employ an attorney to enforce collection, the fee shall be limited to five hundred dollars when the services of the attorney are limited to recording the lien.

This section shall not apply when it is necessary to institute judicial action to enforce the lien.

Added by Acts 1960, No. 217, § 1.

Cross References

C.C. arts. 3186, 3230, 3231, 3249, 3250, 3251, 3267, 3268, 3274.

§§ 4962 to 4965. Repealed by Acts 1950, No. 200, § 2

CHAPTER 3. PRIVILEGES ON MOVABLES AND IMMOVABLES

PART I. PRIVILEGE FOR ATTORNEY FEES

Section
5001. Privilege for fees.

PART II. PRIVILEGES TO EFFECT SEPARATION OF PATRIMONY

5011. Privilege of succession creditor and particular legatee.
5012. Privilege of creditor of heir or legatee.
5013. Effect of privileges.
5014. Enforcement of privilege on immovables alienated by heirs or legatees.
5015. Peremption of inscription of privilege of succession creditor or particular legatee.
5016. Peremption of inscription of privilege of creditor of heir or legatee.

PART III. PRIVILEGE FOR PRODUCERS OF AGRICULTURAL AND DAIRY PRODUCTS

5021. Privilege on assets of purchaser when purchaser becomes insolvent or bankrupt.

PART IV. RIGHTS OF LIEN OR PRIVILEGE HOLDER

5031. Preservation of rights of lien or privilege holder in sales held in certain proceedings.

PART I. PRIVILEGE FOR ATTORNEY FEES

§ 5001. Privilege for fees

A. A special privilege is hereby granted to attorneys at law for the amount of their professional fees on all judgments obtained by them, and on the property recovered thereby, either as plaintiff or defendant, to take rank as a first privilege thereon superior to all other privileges and security interests under Chapter 9 of the Louisiana Commercial Laws.

B. The term "professional fees", as used in this Section, means the agreed upon fee, whether fixed or contingent, and any and all other amounts advanced by the attorney to or on behalf of the client, as permitted by the Rules of Professional Conduct of the Louisiana State Bar Association.

Amended by Acts 1989, No. 78, § 1, eff. June 16, 1989; Acts 2001, No. 128, § 4, eff. July 1, 2001 at 12:01 A.M.

Editor's note. Acts 2001, No. 128, § 4, effective July 1, 2001, amended R.S. 9:5001. Section 19 of Acts 2001, No. 128, declares that "it is the intent of the legislature in enacting this Act that R.S. 2736, 4501 and 4502, 4521, 4758, 4770, and 5363.1 not be expressly or impliedly repealed by this Act, but that such laws remain in effect, and, at times when so provided, be applied to secured transactions subject to Chapter 9 of the Louisiana Commercial Law as revised by this Act."

Cross References

C.C. arts. 3186, 3197, 3230, 3231, 3250, 3251, 3252, 3267, 3268.

PART II. PRIVILEGES TO EFFECT SEPARATION OF PATRIMONY

§ 5011. Privilege of succession creditor and particular legatee

A creditor of the succession of a deceased person has a privilege on all of the property left by the deceased, if the heirs or legatees have accepted the succession without an administration thereof. The creditor enjoys this privilege whether his claim is demandable or not, and whether it is liquidated or not.

A particular legatee who has not received the delivery of his legacy has a privilege on all of the property left by the deceased, if the residuary heirs or legatees have accepted the succession without an administration thereof.

The privileges provided by this section entitle the succession creditor to be paid out of the proceeds of the judicial sale of the property left by the deceased, and the particular legatee to compel the delivery of his legacy, with preference over the creditors of the heirs or legatees.

Added by Acts 1960, No. 31, § 5, eff. Jan. 1, 1961.

Cross References

C.C. arts. 3186, 3230, 3231, 3250, 3251, 3252, 3267, 3268, 3276, 3306.

§ 5012. Privilege of creditor of heir or legatee

A creditor of an heir or residuary legatee who has accepted the succession of a deceased person without an administration thereof has a privilege on all of the property owned by the heir or legatee which was not acquired through the succession. The creditor enjoys this privilege whether his claim is demandable or not, and whether it is liquidated or not.

The privilege provided by this section entitles the creditor of the heir or residuary legatee to be paid out of the proceeds of the judicial sale of the property affected thereby, with preference over the succession creditors.

Added by Acts 1960, No. 31, § 5, eff. Jan. 1, 1961.

Cross References

C.C. arts. 3186, 3230, 3231, 3250, 3251, 3252, 3267, 3268, 3276, 3306.

§ 5013. Effect of privileges

A. The privilege provided by R.S. 9:5011 or R.S. 9:5012, for a period of three months after the death of the deceased and whether recorded or not, shall affect the movables owned by the heirs or legatees at, but shall be subordinate to any mortgage granted or other privilege existing thereon prior to, the time the privilege to effect a separation of patrimony is sought to be enforced.

B. If the succession creditor, particular legatee, or creditor of the heir or legatee, as the case may be, files an affidavit of his claim for recordation in the mortgage office of the parish where the immovable property is situated within three months of the death of the deceased:

(1) The privileges provided by R.S. 9:5011 shall affect all immovables left by the deceased, including those alienated by the heirs or legatees, as provided by R.S. 9:5014; and

(2) The privilege provided by R.S. 9:5012 shall affect immovables not acquired through the succession and owned by the heir or legatee at, but shall be subordinate to any mortgage granted or other privilege existing thereon prior to, the time the privilege to effect a separation of patrimony is sought to be enforced.

Added by Acts 1960, No. 31, § 5, eff. Jan. 1, 1961.

Cross References

C.C. arts. 3186, 3230, 3231, 3250, 3251, 3252, 3267, 3268, 3276, 3306.

§ 5014. Enforcement of privilege on immovables alienated by heirs or legatees

If an affidavit of his claim of privilege under R.S. 9:5011 has been filed for recordation as provided by R.S. 9:5013, a succession creditor or a particular legatee may enforce the privilege claimed against the immovable left by the deceased and alienated within three months of the death of the deceased, by a suit filed prior to the peremption of the inscription of his privilege against the then owner of the immovable and the heirs or legatees who have accepted the succession of the deceased.

Added by Acts 1960, No. 31, § 5, eff. Jan. 1, 1961.

Cross References

C.C. arts. 3186, 3230, 3231, 3250, 3251, 3252, 3267, 3268, 3276, 3306.

§ 5015. Peremption of inscription of privilege of succession creditor or particular legatee

If no suit has been filed to enforce the privilege before, the inscription of either of the privileges provided by R.S. 9:5011 perempts three months from the date of any judgment of possession rendered without an administration of the succession of the deceased, or three months after the recordation of the privilege if the succession has not been opened judicially.

Added by Acts 1960, No. 31, § 5, eff. Jan. 1, 1961.

Cross References

C.C. arts. 3186, 3230, 3231, 3250, 3251, 3252, 3267, 3268, 3276, 3306.

§ 5016. Peremption of inscription of privilege of creditor of heir or legatee

Unless the creditor institutes a suit to enforce his claim before, the inscription of the privilege provided by R.S. 9:5012 perempts three months after the date of any judgment of possession rendered without an administration of the succession of the deceased, or three months after the recordation of the privilege if the succession has not been opened judicially.

Added by Acts 1960, No. 31, § 5, eff. Jan. 1, 1961.

Cross References

C.C. arts. 3186, 3230, 3231, 3250, 3251, 3252, 3267, 3268, 3276, 3306.

PART III. PRIVILEGE FOR PRODUCERS OF AGRICULTURAL AND DAIRY PRODUCTS

§ 5021. Privilege on assets of purchaser when purchaser becomes insolvent or bankrupt

When any corporation formed under the provisions of the laws of the State of Louisiana, or any corporation doing business in this state, or any partnership, firm or individual doing business in this state, becomes insolvent or bankrupt, the producers of agricultural and dairy products, including cooperative marketing associations of such producers, shall have a special privilege upon the assets, whether immovable, movable, or mixed, of such corporation, partnership, firm or individual for the amount of payments for agricultural and dairy products due them, not exceeding six months payments for such products which shall have accrued prior to the adjudication of the insolvency or bankruptcy of such corporation, partnership, firm or individual, which privilege shall rank ahead of all other privileges, debts, charges, or claims against said corporation, partnership, firm or individual, except: (1) those arising out of taxes due the United States government or the State of Louisiana, and (2) bona fide vendor's privileges or mortgages if the vendor's privileges or mortgages exist and have been recorded before the purchase of the agricultural and dairy products for which payment is due, and, (3) laborer's privileges, and (4) lessor's privileges; provided, however, that the privilege of producers of agricultural and dairy products shall take effect and its rank or order of priority established only from the date and time that an affidavit asserting such indebtedness and privilege is recorded in the mortgage records of the parish in which the bankrupt or insolvent debtor is domiciled, if domiciled in the State of Louisiana, or in the parish where the bankrupt or insolvent debtor has its principal place of business in Louisiana, if its domicile is out of the State of Louisiana.

Added by Acts 1968, No. 461, § 1.

Cross References

C.C. arts. 3186, 3230, 3231, 3250, 3251, 3252, 3267, 3268.

PART IV. RIGHTS OF LIEN OR PRIVILEGE HOLDER

§ 5031. Preservation of rights of lien or privilege holder in sales held in certain proceedings

No lien or privilege shall be cancelled, removed from the public records, or in any manner affected by any public or private sale of property subject thereto in any succession, liquidation, insolvency, receivership, bankruptcy, or partition proceeding. However, the provisions of this Section shall not apply to the execution of judgments governed by Book IV of the Louisiana Code of Civil Procedure, Article 2251 et seq., or to judicial sales in executory proceedings under the Louisiana Code of Civil Procedure, Articles 2631 et seq.

Added by Acts 1980, No. 356, § 1. Amended by Acts 1981, No. 894, § 1.

Cross References

C.C. arts. 813, 815, 3186, 3230, 3231, 3250, 3251, 3267, 3268.

CODE TITLE XXII—MORTGAGES

CHAPTER 1. MORTGAGES IN GENERAL

PART I. PROPERTY SUBJECT TO MORTGAGE

SUBPART A. IN GENERAL

Section
5101. Repealed.
5102. Repealed.
5103. Newspaper plant, equipment, name, and good will.
5104. Repealed.
5105. Repealed.
5106 to 5110. [Blank].

SUBPART B. HOME APPLIANCES AND EQUIPMENT [REPEALED]

5121 to 5126. Repealed.

SUBPART C. MINERAL MORTGAGES—APPOINTMENT OF KEEPER

5131. Appointment by court.
5132. Designation in mortgage.
5133. Powers, duties and compensation.
5134. Security.
5135. Requests to court for instructions.

SUBPART D. CONVENTIONAL MORTGAGES, APPOINTMENT OF RECEIVER OR KEEPER

5136. Designation in mortgage or other instrument of keeper of property.
5137. Appointment of person designated by parties.
5138. Powers, duties, and compensation.
5139. Security.
5140. Requests to court for instructions.
5140.1. Effect of Subpart on other provisions of law.
5140.2. Security interests under Chapter 9 of Louisiana Commercial Laws.

PART II. DUTIES OF RECORDERS

SUBPART A. INSCRIPTION

5141. Repealed.
5142. Parish wherein state capitol is located, special mortgages.
5143. Parish wherein state capitol is located, vendor's mortgages or sales with mortgage.

SUBPART B. ERASURE OR CANCELLATION

5161, 5162. Repealed.

Section
5163. United States agencies mortgagees of record; no cancellation or subordination without notice.
5164. Service of notice.
5165. Issuance of release of mortgage by current mortgagee.
5166. Cancellation of mortgage and vendor's lien inscriptions; uniform cancellation affidavit; requirements and effects.
5167. Cancellation of mortgage or vendor's privilege by affidavit of notary or title insurer where paraphed note or other evidence is lost or destroyed.
5167.1. Cancellation of mortgage inscription by affidavit; penalties.
5167.2. Cancellation of mortgage inscription.
5168. Promissory notes; loss or destruction; proof by affidavit.
5169. Cancellation of mortgages and privileges not securing paraphed obligations.
5169.1. Repealed.
5170. Cancellation of mortgages and privileges securing paraphed obligations.
5171. Cancellation; certified copy of order, decree or other instrument.
5172. Cancellation; licensed financial institution.
5173. Mortgage or privilege cancellation by financial institution-standard form.
5174. Liability for incorrect or false request for cancellation.
5175. Order of discharge in bankruptcy; effect.
5176. Extinction of certain rights; acknowledgment by owner or holder.
5177 to 5180.1. Repealed.
5180.2. Repealed.
5180.3, 5180.4. Repealed.

SUBPART C. CERTIFICATES [REPEALED]

5181. Repealed.
5182. Repealed.
5183. Repealed.

SUBPART D. NOTICE OF TAX SALES [REPEALED]

5201 to 5203. Repealed.

SUBPART E. THE OFFICE OF MORTGAGES

5206, 5207. Repealed.
5208. Registers kept by recorder of mortgages in Orleans parish.
5209. Authentication of registers in Orleans parish.
5210. Registers and authentication outside Orleans parish.
5211. Register with title of acts and time of filing.

For Annotative Materials, see West's Louisiana Statutes Annotated

APPENDIX 1—REVISED STATUTES, TITLE 9

Section
5212. Prompt recordation and certificate of encumbrances.
5213. Method of recordation; certificate of encumbrances.
5214 to 5216. Repealed.
5217. Recorder's fees for multiple indebtedness mortgages; form.

PART III. RIGHTS OF MORTGAGE HOLDER
5251. Preservation of rights of mortgage holder in sales held in certain proceedings.

PART I. PROPERTY SUBJECT TO MORTGAGE

SUBPART A. IN GENERAL

Editor's note. Acts 1989, No. 137, which amends or enacts numerous sections within this Code Title, provided in § 20:

"It is the intent of the Legislature in enacting this Act to amend the preexisting Louisiana security device laws to accompany and accommodate implementation of Chapter 9 of the Louisiana Commercial Laws (R.S. 10:9–101, et seq.) as previously enacted under Act 528 of 1988. It is further the intent of the legislature that these preexisting Louisiana laws, including without limitation the various statutes and code articles amended and reenacted under this Act, not be expressly or impliedly repealed by Chapter 9 of the Louisiana Commercial Laws, but that such laws remain in effect and be applied to preexisting secured transactions and, at times when so provided, be applied to secured transactions subject to Chapter 9 of the Louisiana Commercial Laws."

Chapter 9 of the Louisiana Commercial Laws was revised by Acts 2001, No. 128, § 1, effective July 1, 2001, to consist of R.S. 10:9–101 through 10:9–710. This Chapter does not apply to statutory liens and privileges except as expressly provided therein. R.S. 10:9–322(h) provides: "A security interest has priority over a conflicting lien, other than an agricultural lien, in the same collateral except as otherwise provided in this Chapter or except to the extent the lien is created by a statute that expressly provides that the lien has priority over the security interest." The accompanying revision comment states: "For example, see R.S. 9:4501, 9:4502, 9:4521, 9:4758, 9:4870, and 9:4888, each of which provides that certain privileges have priority over certain security interests. See also 9:5001 and 37:218.".

§ 5101. Repealed by Acts 1974, No. 50, § 3, eff. Jan. 1, 1975; Acts 1974, No. 546, § 2, eff. Jan. 1, 1975

§ 5102. Repealed by Acts 1991, No. 652, § 4, eff. Jan. 1, 1992

§ 5103. Newspaper plant, equipment, name, and good will

Any person engaged in the publication and circulation of a newspaper may issue bonds, notes, or other evidences of debt and secure them by the hypothecation of the plant and equipment of the newspaper and the name and good will of its business.

The act of mortgage shall be made in the form provided by law for other acts of mortgage, shall have the same legal effects, and shall be recorded in the mortgage records of the parish in which the newspaper is published. The foreclosure and sale of the property shall be made as is provided by law for the foreclosure and sale of mortgaged immovables.

Cross References
C.C. arts. 3281, 3287, 3320.

§ 5104. Repealed by Acts 1978, No. 728, § 3, eff. Jan. 1, 1979

§ 5105. Repealed by Acts 1978, No. 728, § 3, eff. Jan. 1, 1979

§§ 5106 to 5110. [Blank]

SUBPART B. HOME APPLIANCES AND EQUIPMENT [REPEALED]

§§ 5121 to 5126. Repealed by Acts 1978, No. 728, § 3, eff. Jan. 1, 1979

SUBPART C. MINERAL MORTGAGES— APPOINTMENT OF KEEPER

§ 5131. Appointment by court

If a mineral right affected by a mortgage executed under the provisions of R.S. 31:203 is seized as an incident to an action for the enforcement of such mortgage, the court issuing the order under which the seizure is to be effected shall direct the sheriff or other officer making the seizure to appoint as keeper of the mineral right such person as the parties may have designated as herein provided.

Added by Acts 1974, No. 546, § 1, eff. Jan. 1, 1975.

§ 5132. Designation in mortgage

The parties to a mortgage of a mineral right may designate the keeper of property to be appointed as provided by R.S. 9:5131 by expressly naming or identifying the person who is to serve as keeper or by describing the method by which he is to be selected. The parties may designate the mortgagee or his agent as the keeper or permit the mortgagee to name the keeper at the time the seizure is effected.

Added by Acts 1974, No. 546, § 1, eff. Jan. 1, 1975.

§ 5133. Powers, duties and compensation

A keeper appointed under the provisions of R.S. 9:5131 through 9:5135 shall have full powers of administration and may operate the mineral right and all wells or facilities located thereon covered by the mortgage in the ordinary course of business and produce and dispose of minerals accruing to such interest without further or express authority. All revenues or other amounts received by the keeper during the course of his administration shall be first applied to the costs and expenses incurred by him in the administration or preservation of the property and the balance, if any, shall be applied to the debt secured by the mortgage. The keeper shall render an accounting of his administration at such time or times as the court before whom the proceedings are pending may direct and all costs and expenses necessarily incurred by him in the course of his administration shall be taxed as a part of the costs of the proceedings to the extent they have not been satisfied out of revenues previously received by the keeper. Costs and expenses of administration shall not include any compensation to a keeper appointed under the provisions of R.S. 9:5131 through 9:5135 for his services unless he was particularly identified by the parties in the act of mortgage and the manner of determining such compensation is therein agreed to. The mortgagee or any employee of the mortgagee shall not be entitled to compensation as keeper, even if he is expressly designated in the mortgage to act as keeper. The court may reduce the amount of compensation of the keeper as fixed by the terms of the mortgage if the court determines the amount to be unreasonable in light of the services actually rendered by him.

Added by Acts 1974, No. 546, § 1, eff. Jan. 1, 1975.

§ 5134. Security

No bond shall be required of the keeper of the person provoking the seizure beyond that which may otherwise be required by law in such proceedings. The sheriff or other officer seizing the property shall have no responsibility for the property seized or the actions of the keeper after custody of the property has been delivered to the keeper.

Added by Acts 1974, No. 546, § 1, eff. Jan. 1, 1975.

§ 5135. Requests to court for instructions

If the keeper or the mortgagor or the mortgagee is of the opinion that some action, beyond the ordinary course of administration of the property, is required to preserve or protect the property or if in the event the mortgagor or mortgagee believes the keeper is acting beyond his authority or is failing to act in accordance with his authority, such party may apply to the court before whom the proceedings are pending in a summary proceeding with notice to the mortgagor and mortgagee if they are not a party to such application, for instructions as to the proper course that should be taken by the keeper and the court may issue orders or instructions deemed necessary or appropriate for the protection of the property and the interests of the parties therein. An order of the proper court issued pursuant to such an application shall be full authority for the keeper to act in accordance therewith and he shall be fully protected from all claims of any person as a result thereof.

Added by Acts 1974, No. 546, § 1, eff. Jan. 1, 1975.

SUBPART D. CONVENTIONAL MORTGAGES, APPOINTMENT OF RECEIVER OR KEEPER

§ 5136. Designation in mortgage or other instrument of keeper of property

The parties to a mortgage of either immovable property or movable property, or both, or the parties to a security agreement under Chapter 9 of the Louisiana Commercial Laws (R.S. 10:9–101, et seq.), may designate a keeper of the property to be appointed pursuant to R.S. 9:5137 by expressly naming or identifying in the mortgage or security agreement the person who is to serve as keeper or by describing the method by which he is to be selected. The parties may designate the mortgagee, or secured party, or his agent as the keeper or may permit the mortgagee or secured party to name the keeper at the time the seizure is effected. If the designation of the keeper by the parties to the mortgage or security agreement is not made in the original instrument, it may be made by any other instrument executed by them, either concurrently with or subsequent to the act of mortgage or security agreement, which in the case of a mortgage on immovable property shall be by an instrument duly acknowledged by the parties in the presence of a notary public and two witnesses.

Added by Acts 1976, No. 315, § 1. Amended by Acts 1977, No. 226, § 1; Acts 1986, No. 974, § 1; Acts 1989, No. 137, § 5, eff. Sept. 1, 1989.

Editor's note. For § 20 of Acts 1989, No. 137, stating legislative intent, see note preceding R.S. 9:5101.

§ 5137. Appointment of person designated by parties

A. If any immovable or any movable property, or both immovable and movable property, affected by a mortgage is seized as an incident to an action for the recognition or the enforcement of the mortgage, whether by executory process, writ of fieri facias, sequestration, or otherwise, the court issuing the order under which the seizure is to be effected shall, if such order is petitioned for by the seizing creditor, direct the sheriff or other officer making the seizure to appoint as keeper of the seized property such person as the parties may have designated as herein provided. The designation of a keeper of the property in accordance with the provisions of R.S. 9:5136 is for the benefit of the seizing creditor, but such designation shall not be deemed to require the seizing creditor to provoke the appointment of any such keeper.

B. If the parties have not designated a keeper of the property in accordance with the provisions of R.S. 9:5136, and if the sheriff or other officer making the seizure fails, refuses, or declines to operate or administer the seized property or for any reason wishes to have the court appoint a keeper, then upon application of either the seizing creditor, the mortgagor, or the sheriff and in a summary proceeding, with notice to the mortgagor, the mortgagee, and the sheriff or other officer making the seizure if they are not party to such application, the court before whom the proceedings are pending shall direct the sheriff or other officer making the seizure to appoint as keeper of the property a person whom the court designates.

Added by Acts 1976, No. 315, § 1.

§ 5138. Powers, duties, and compensation

A. The keeper or receiver shall perform his duties as a prudent administrator, and neither the keeper nor the seizing creditor shall be liable to the mortgagor or the owner of the seized property or any other person for any financial or pecuniary loss or damage claimed to have been suffered by the mortgagor or owner of the seized property or any other person by reason of the administration or management of the property by the keeper or receiver acting as a prudent administrator. A keeper appointed under the provisions of R.S. 9:5136 through 5140.2 shall have full powers of management and administration of the property and may operate the property seized, whether immovable, movable, or both, in the ordinary course of business.

B. All revenues or other amounts received by the keeper during his administration first shall be applied to the costs and expenses incurred by him in the administration or preservation of the property, including meeting any obligations the owner might have to provide services, amenities, or other obligations as provided in the prior recorded existing leases of the tenants or lessees of the property, and any balance shall be applied to the debt secured by the mortgage.

C. The keeper shall render an accounting of his administration at such time or times as the court before whom the proceedings are pending may direct, and all costs and expenses necessarily incurred by him in the course of his administration shall be taxed as a part of the costs of the proceedings to the extent they have not been satisfied out of revenues previously received by the keeper. Costs and expenses of administration shall not include any compensation to a keeper appointed under R.S. 9:5136 through 5140.2

for his services, unless he was particularly identified by the parties in the act of mortgage and the manner of determining such compensation is therein agreed to, or unless the keeper was appointed by the court pursuant to the provisions of R.S. 9:5137(B).

Added by Acts 1976, No. 315, § 1. Amended by Acts 1992, No. 972, § 1.

§ 5139. Security

A. No bond shall be required of the keeper appointed pursuant to R.S. 9:5137(A) by the person provoking the seizure other than any bond otherwise required by law in such proceedings.

B. The keeper appointed pursuant to R.S. 9:5137(B) shall give such bond for the faithful performance of his duties as the court may fix, which shall be at such reasonable sum as the nature of the case justifies.

C. The sheriff or other officer seizing property shall have no responsibility for the property seized or the actions of the keeper after custody of the property has been delivered to the keeper, and shall not be entitled to receive any commission on the rents, revenues, or other fruits of the property delivered to the keeper.

Added by Acts 1976, No. 315, § 1.

§ 5140. Requests to court for instructions

If the keeper or the mortgagor or the mortgagee is of the opinion that some action beyond the ordinary course of administration or management of the property is required to preserve or protect the property, or if, in the event the mortgagor or mortgagee believes the keeper is acting beyond his authority or is failing to act in accordance with his authority, such party may apply to the court before whom the proceedings are pending, in a summary proceeding with notice to the mortgagor and mortgagee if they are not a party to such application, for instructions as to the proper course that should be taken by the keeper. The court may issue orders or instructions deemed necessary or appropriate for the protection of the property and the interests of the parties therein. An order of the proper court issued pursuant to such an application shall be full authority for the keeper to act in accordance therewith, and he shall be fully protected from all claims of any person as a result thereof.

Added by Acts 1976, No. 315, § 1.

§ 5140.1. Effect of Subpart on other provisions of law

Nothing in this Subpart shall affect or be construed to affect any rights conferred by R.S. 9:5131 through R.S. 9:5135 and R.S. 6:826(D).

Added by Acts 1976, No. 315, § 1.

§ 5140.2. Security interests under Chapter 9 of Louisiana Commercial Laws

The provisions of this Subpart shall apply to security interests subject to Chapter 9 of the Louisiana Commercial Laws (R.S. 10:9–101, et seq.).

Added by Acts 1989, No. 137, § 5, eff. Sept. 1, 1989.

Editor's note. For § 20 of Acts 1989, No. 137, stating legislative intent, see note preceding R.S. 9:5101.

PART II. DUTIES OF RECORDERS

SUBPART A. INSCRIPTION

§ 5141. Repealed by Acts 2005, No. 169, § 8, eff. July 1, 2006

§ 5142. Parish wherein state capitol is located, special mortgages

In the parish wherein the state capitol is located in the inscription of special mortgages on real estate, including building and loan and homestead association mortgages and federal savings and loan association mortgages, but excluding railroad mortgages, it shall be sufficient to inscribe the following:

(1) The date of execution;

(2) The name and domicile of the notary, if an authentic act;

(3) The full appearance of the mortgagor, giving his name, marital status and residence;

(4) The name of the mortgagee;

(5) The amount of the mortgage and a concise statement of the payments;

(6) Complete description of the mortgaged property with its acquisition by the mortgagor, if stated in the act;

(7) The following clause shall be inserted in the inscription of the act by the recorder, "For the balance of this act see the original (recorded as Original _____ Bundle _____)."

(8) The closing paragraph of the mortgage;

(9) Copy of the signatures of the parties as signed to the act, including the names of the witnesses and the name of the notary as written in the act.

Added by Acts 1950, No. 279, § 1.

Cross References

C.C. art. 3320.

§ 5143. Parish wherein state capitol is located, vendor's mortgages or sales with mortgage

In the parish wherein the state capitol is located in the inscription both in the conveyance and in the mortgage records of vendor's mortgages or sales with mortgage, including building and loan and homestead association mortgages and federal savings and loan association mortgages, it shall be sufficient to inscribe the following portions thereof only, to-wit:

(1) The date of execution;

(2) The name and domicile of the notary, if an authentic act;

(3) The full appearance of the vendor and of the purchaser with their full names, marital status and residence;

(4) The clause containing warranty, substitution and subrogation as written in the act;

(5) Complete description of the property conveyed with acquisition, as stated in the act;

(6) The purchase price with a concise statement of the payments;

(7) The following clause shall be inserted in the inscription of the act by the recorder, "For the balance of this act see

the original; recorded as Original _____ Bundle _____;"

(8) The closing paragraph of the sale;

(9) Copy of the signatures of the parties as signed to the act; including the names of the witnesses and the name of the notary, as written in the act.

Added by Acts 1950, No. 279, § 2.

Cross References

C.C. art. 3320.

SUBPART B. ERASURE OR CANCELLATION

§§ 5161, 5162. Repealed by Acts 2005, No. 169, § 8, eff. July 1, 2006

§ 5163. United States agencies mortgagees of record; no cancellation or subordination without notice

Mortgages and the recordation in which any agency or instrumentality of the United States, lending on mortgages secured by real estate is the mortgagee of record, cannot be cancelled, removed from the public records, or in any manner affected, by any sale in any succession, liquidation, insolvency, receivership, or partition proceeding, in any court, unless previous to the application or petition for sale, written notice thereof is given to the agency or instrumentality of the United States, the mortgagee of record. The notice unless waived in writing by the agency or instrumentality of the United States, the mortgagee of record, before or after the sale, must be filed in the proceeding, and a certified copy thereof served on the agency or instrumentality, the mortgagee of record, not less than ten days previous to the filing of the petition or application for the sale. In no event shall the mortgage held by the agency or instrumentality be made secondary to, or ranked or primed by any costs or fees in the proceedings, with the exception of the costs immediately and directly incident to the advertising and selling of the property.

§ 5164. Service of notice

The notice to be given to the agency or instrumentality of the United States shall be served by the sheriff, or other appropriate officer, on an agent resident in the state, designated for the service of notice by the agency or instrumentality, and the agency or instrumentality shall record in the mortgage records of each parish wherein mortgages are recorded in which it is the mortgagee of record, the name and address in the state of the agent designated by the agency or instrumentality for service of the notice, and upon failure of the agency or instrumentality to record the name and address of the agent, service of the notice shall be made upon the agency or instrumentality by serving same on the Secretary of State or someone in his office during his absence he may designate.

Amended by Acts 1954, No. 141, § 1.

§ 5165. Issuance of release of mortgage by current mortgagee

A. The provisions of this Section shall apply only to residential mortgages, where a mortgage has been granted by a consumer on a one-to-four family residential immovable property, including a mortgage to finance the initial construction of the one-to-four family residential immovable property. The provisions of this Section shall apply only to mortgages recorded on and after January 1, 2012.

B. (1) Upon extinction of the mortgage in accordance with Civil Code Article 3319, the mortgagor, his successor in ownership or settlement agent may submit a written request, signed by the mortgagor to the mortgagee, to issue a written act of release directing the appropriate recorder of mortgages to cancel the inscription of the mortgage from the mortgage records. The written request that the mortgage be cancelled shall extinguish any obligation on the part of the mortgagee and all additional lenders, on whose behalf the mortgagee may be representing or acting for the benefit of, to make any further loan or advance that would be secured by the mortgage.

(2) If the mortgagee has assigned, transferred, or delegated the servicing rights to a third party, then the duties and liabilities of the mortgagee pursuant to this Section shall apply solely to the third party.

(3) The written request shall be delivered to the mortgagee at the address designated by the mortgagee to be used for such written requests. If the request is accompanied by a payoff check from a settlement agent, the written request shall be delivered to the same address where the payoff check is delivered.

(4) The mortgagee shall issue within forty-five days after receipt from the mortgagor or settlement agent of a written request for cancellation of the mortgage accompanied by the fees required by Paragraph (5) of this Subsection, the act of release along with a request for cancellation that complies with Civil Code Article 3366.

(5) The mortgagee shall submit the act of release of the mortgage directly to the settlement agent if a written request was received by the mortgagee from a settlement agent. The written request to issue an act of release of the mortgage shall be accompanied by sufficient payment to the mortgagee to pay the mortgagee a fee for this service. The mortgagee may charge a fee to the mortgagor or his agent for all services and costs to prepare and execute the act of release and request for cancellation that complies with Civil Code Article 3366, in an amount not to exceed forty dollars, plus postage. Any fees charged by the mortgagee pursuant to this Subsection shall be clearly itemized to the requesting mortgagor or settlement agent in the payoff letter or statement or other communication.

(6) If the mortgagee receives a signed written request, in accordance with Paragraph (1) of this Subsection, directly from the mortgagor or the successor in ownership, and there is no settlement agent involved in forwarding the request, and the required fees in an amount not to exceed one hundred dollars are received by the mortgagee for all services and costs to prepare, execute, and deliver the act of release and request for cancellation that complies with Civil Code Article 3366, along with the appropriate cancellation fees for the recorder of mortgages, then the mortgagee shall, within forty-five days of receiving such request and fees, prepare and submit to the appropriate recorder of mortgages an act of release along with the request for cancellation that complies with Civil Code Article 3366.

(7) A mortgagor may obtain a complimentary copy of the act of release from the mortgagee when there is no settlement agent involved.

C. Upon receipt of the act of release and request for cancellation, the settlement agent shall file them with the appropriate recorder of mortgages within forty-five days.

(1) The mortgagee shall not be liable for damages, fees, or costs caused by the failure of the settlement agent to timely file the act of release and request for cancellation, if the act of release and request for cancellation are in compliance with the law and sufficient to cancel the inscription of the mortgage from the mortgage records.

(2) If the settlement agent fails to timely file the release, he shall be liable for the statutory and actual damages, costs, and fees provided for in Subsection E of this Section.

D. In the event either the mortgagee or settlement agent has failed to comply with the requirements of this Section, the mortgagee and settlement agent shall be provided with written notice of noncompliance identifying the mortgage at issue and the explanation of how they failed to comply with the requirements of this Section, and then the mortgagee and settlement agent shall be given an opportunity to prepare and submit an act of release of mortgage and request for cancellation to the appropriate recorder of mortgages within fifteen days of receiving the notice before any rights accrue pursuant to Subsection E of this Section.

E. If the mortgagee fails to perform the duty required by this Section, the mortgagor or his successor in ownership may, by summary proceedings instituted against the mortgagee, in the parish where the mortgaged property is located, obtain a judgment ordering the mortgage inscription to be cancelled from the records and for the costs, reasonable attorney fees, statutory damages in the amount of five hundred dollars, and actual damages he has suffered from the failure to comply with this Section. Any judgment for damages may be awarded individually, but not in a representative capacity. The rights to recover damages provided by this Section are personal to the mortgagor or his successor in ownership of the property and may not be assigned.

F. A mortgagee complying with the provisions of this Section shall not be subject to the requirements of R.S. 9:5167.2.

Added by Acts 2011, No. 342, § 1, eff. Jan. 1, 2012.

§ 5166. Cancellation of mortgage and vendor's lien inscriptions; uniform cancellation affidavit; requirements and effects

A. A uniform cancellation affidavit as provided in this Section may be used to cancel a mortgage or vendor's lien inscription, except for judgments or legal mortgages. The uniform cancellation affidavit may be in lieu of any other affidavit otherwise required by law, and no additional affidavit shall be necessary for cancellation.

B. The uniform cancellation affidavit shall:

(1) Contain the information required by this Section.

(2) Recite the statutory authorization for the cancellation, any other recitations as may be required by law for cancellation, and a declaration that the affiant has complied with all requirements of law for the cancellation.

(3) Be sworn to and subscribed in the presence of a notary public or other properly authorized official, but shall not be required to be an authentic or witnessed act.

C. The filing with the clerk of court and ex officio recorder of mortgages of a uniform cancellation affidavit containing a request to cancel, together with any additional documents as may otherwise be required by law, shall operate as a release and authorization to the clerk of court and ex officio recorder of mortgages to cancel and erase from the mortgage records any mortgage or vendor's lien inscription described in the uniform cancellation affidavit.

D. Liability

(1) The clerk of court as ex officio recorder of mortgages shall not be liable for any damages resulting to any person or entity as a consequence of canceling a mortgage in reliance upon a uniform cancellation affidavit complying with this Section.

(2) The affiant shall be liable to and indemnify the clerk of court as ex officio recorder of mortgages and any person relying upon the cancellation for any claims or damages suffered if the uniform cancellation affidavit contains materially false or incorrect statements.

(3) The preparing, signing, or filing of a uniform cancellation affidavit with the knowledge that it contains materially false or incorrect statements shall subject the offender to civil and criminal liability under Louisiana law, including R.S. 9:5174, R.S. 14:125, and R.S. 14:133.

E. The provisions of this Section shall not be construed to invalidate, prohibit, restrict or limit the use of any other method or form otherwise authorized by law for the cancellation of a mortgage or vendor's lien inscription.

F. A uniform cancellation affidavit shall satisfy the requirements of this Section if it provides all the information set forth in the following form:

UNIFORM CANCELLATION AFFIDAVIT
(FOR MORTGAGES AND VENDOR'S LIENS)
STATE OF _____
PARISH OF _____

BE IT KNOWN THAT before me, the undersigned Notary Public, appeared:

(Name)_____(Corporate Title and Name of Entity if Applicable)_____, its duly authorized agent hereinafter referred to as affiant, who after first being sworn declares that affiant is:

CHECK ONE BOX ONLY:

[ ] *A notary public requesting cancellation under R.S. 9:5167(A)(1)*, herein declaring that affiant or someone under his direction did satisfy the promissory note, and that the affiant or someone under his direction (1) received the note marked "Paid in Full" from the last holder of the note, and that the note was lost or destroyed while in the affiant's custody; or (2) has confirmed that the last holder of the paraphed note received payment in full and sent the note but the note was never received, and that the affiant has made a due and diligent search for the note, the note cannot be located, and sixty days have elapsed since payment or satisfaction of the note.

[ ] *A duly authorized officer of a Louisiana licensed title insurer as defined in R.S. 22:46 of the Louisiana Insurance Code, requesting cancellation under R.S. 9:5167(B)(1)*, herein declaring that all obligations secured by the mortgage or vendor's privilege have been satisfied, and that affiant has made a due and diligent search for the lost or destroyed instrument which was sufficient to cause a cancellation of the mortgage or vendor's privilege, that the lost or destroyed instrument cannot be located, and that sixty days have elapsed since payment or satisfaction of the secured obligation.

[ ] *An authorized officer of a title insurance business, the closing notary public, or the attorney for the person or entity*

APPENDIX 1—REVISED STATUTES, TITLE 9

R.S. 9:5166

which made the payment requesting cancellation under R.S. 9:5167.1, herein declaring on behalf of the mortgagor or an owner of the property encumbered by the mortgage that the mortgagee provided a payoff statement with respect to the loan secured by the mortgage and that the mortgagee has received payment of the loan secured by the mortgage in accordance with the payoff statement, as evidenced by (1) a bank check, certified check, or escrow account check which has been negotiated by or on behalf of the mortgagee, or (2) other documentary evidence of the receipt of payment by the mortgagee, including but not limited to verification that the funds were wired to the mortgagee, that more than sixty days have elapsed since the date payment was received by the mortgagee and that the mortgagee has not returned documentary authorization for cancellation of the mortgage; and that the mortgagee has been given at least fifteen days notice in writing of the intention to execute and record an affidavit in accordance with R.S. 9:5167.1, with a copy of the proposed affidavit attached to the written notice. *Affiant declares that he has attached all evidence required by law.*

[ ] *An obligee of record requesting cancellation under R.S. 9:5168*, herein declaring that affiant is the obligee of record of the mortgage or vendor's privilege securing a paraphed promissory note and that the note has been lost or destroyed and cannot be presented; that the note is paid, forgiven, or otherwise satisfied; and that affiant has not sold, transferred, or assigned the note to any other person or entity. *If affiant is not the Original Obligee of Record, but an Obligee of Record by recorded Assignment of the inscription to be cancelled, a list of recorded assignments is attached.*

[ ] *An obligee of record requesting release under R.S. 9:5169*, declaring that affiant is herein acknowledging the satisfaction, releasing or acknowledging the extinction of the mortgage or privilege. If affiant is not the Original Obligee of Record, but an Obligee of Record by recorded Assignment of the inscription to be cancelled, affiant has attached a list of recorded assignments. JUDGMENTS OR LEGAL MORTGAGES MAY NOT BE CANCELLED USING THIS FORM.

[ ] *An affiant requesting cancellation under R.S. 9:5170*, herein declaring that he is attaching herewith

_____ The paraphed obligation marked "PAID" or "CANCELLED"; or

_____ An authentic act of release conforming to the requirements of R.S. 9:5170(A)(2).

[ ] *A duly authorized officer of a Licensed Financial Institution under R.S. 9:5172*, herein declaring that the institution was the obligee or the authorized agent of the obligee of the obligation secured by the mortgage or privilege when the obligation was extinguished and that the secured obligation has been paid or otherwise satisfied or extinguished; or that the institution is the obligee or authorized agent of the obligee of the secured obligation and that it releases the mortgage or privilege and directs the recorder to cancel its recordation.

AFFIANT HEREBY EXPRESSLY REQUESTS, AUTHORIZES, AND DIRECTS, in accordance with the provisions of the applicable statute indicated by the checked box above and in accordance with the provisions of Civil Code Article 3366, that the Clerk of Court and ex officio Recorder of Mortgages for the Parish of _____ to [ ] FULLY CANCEL, or [ ] PARTIALLY CANCEL the following:

A mortgage or Vendor's privilege:
Granted/Made by: _____
In favor of: _____
Instrument dated _____ Recorded in Parish;
Recorded in FOLIO _____ INSTRUMENT MOB _____ _____, NO. _____;

[LEGAL DESCRIPTION OF PROPERTY: SEE ATTACHMENT HERETO MADE A PART HEREOF.]

AFFIANT DECLARES that he has attached property descriptions as required by law, and that he is aware that if no property description is attached, this Affidavit will be rejected.

AFFIANT FURTHER DECLARES that if this Affidavit is intended to cancel related inscriptions, such as assignments or subordinations, in a parish where the clerk allows such cancellations, he has attached a separate list of related inscriptions.

AFFIANT WARRANTS that affiant has complied with all requirements of applicable law, including full or partial discharge of the obligation where the law requires.

AFFIANT AGREES to be liable to and to indemnify the Clerk of Court as ex officio recorder of mortgages and any person relying upon the cancellation by this affidavit for any claims or damages suffered as a consequence of such reliance if this affidavit contains materially false or incorrect statements.

AFFIANT ACKNOWLEDGES BY HIS SIGNATURE BELOW that the contents of this affidavit are true and correct to the best of his knowledge, information, and belief, and further that he is aware that knowingly preparing, signing, or filing a uniform cancellation affidavit containing materially false or incorrect statements shall subject the affiant to civil and criminal liability under Louisiana law, including the provisions of R.S. 9:5174, R.S. 14:125, and R.S. 14:133.

Affiant's Signature: _____ Printed Name: _____
Company Name: _____ Title: _____
(Its duly authorized agent)
Mailing Address: _____
City: _____ State: _____ ZIP: _____
Telephone #: _____
Email: _____

SWORN TO AND SUBSCRIBED before me this _____ day of _____, 20___.
Notary Signature and Seal:
Printed Name of Notary: _____
State of Appointment: _____
Notary or Bar No.: _____
Commission expires: _____

FILER: Fill out below if filer is NOT the affiant:
REQUEST TO CANCEL

In accordance with the provisions of Civil Code Article 3366, the undersigned filer requests the Clerk of Court and ex officio Recorder of Mortgages to file this Uniform Cancellation Affidavit and hereby requests the cancellation referenced therein.

Signature: _____
Printed Name: _____
Company: _____
Title: _____ (Its duly authorized agent)
Mailing Address: _____
City: _____ State: ____ ZIP: ____
Telephone #: _____ Email: ____
Added by Acts 2011, No. 124, § 1.

Cross References

C.C. arts. 3278 to 3313, 3315 to 3337, 3338 to 3368.

§ 5167. **Cancellation of mortgage or vendor's privilege by affidavit of notary or title insurer where paraphed note or other evidence is lost or destroyed**

A. (1) When a promissory note paraphed for identification with a mortgage or act creating a vendor's privilege on immovable property has been lost or destroyed after receipt by the notary public who satisfied the promissory note out of the proceeds of an act of sale or mortgage executed before him, or with funds given to him for that purpose, the clerk of court or recorder of mortgages may cancel the mortgage or vendor's privilege upon receipt of an affidavit from the notary public. The affidavit shall set forth all of the following:

(a) The name of the mortgagor or obligor of the privilege as it appears in the recorded mortgage or vendor's privilege and recordation information.

(b) A description of the paraphed promissory note and the property.

(c) A statement that the affiant or someone under his direction did satisfy the promissory note.

(d) That the affiant or someone under his direction:

(i) Received the note marked "Paid in Full" from the last holder of the note, and that the note was lost or destroyed while in the affiant's custody; or

(ii) Has confirmed that the last holder of the paraphed note received payment in full and sent the note and the note was never received.

(e) That the affiant agrees to be personally liable to and indemnify the recorder of mortgages and any person relying upon the cancellation by affidavit for any damages that they may suffer as a consequence of such reliance if the recorded affidavit contains materially false or incorrect statements that cause the recorder to incorrectly cancel the recordation of a mortgage or privilege.

(f) A statement that the affiant has made a due and diligent search for the note, the note cannot be located, and sixty days have elapsed since payment or satisfaction of the note.

(2) No mandamus proceeding is required to use the provisions of this Subsection.

(3) A person who signed an affidavit that is provided to the recorder of mortgages pursuant to this Subsection and that contains materially false or incorrect statements causing the recorder to incorrectly cancel the recordation of a mortgage or privilege is liable to and shall indemnify the recorder and any person relying upon the cancellation for any damages that they may suffer as a consequence of such reliance.

(4) The recorder of mortgages shall not be liable for any damages resulting to any person or entity as a consequence of canceling a mortgage or vendor's privilege pursuant to an affidavit which complies with this Subsection.

B. (1) When a paraphed promissory note or other evidence sufficient to cause a cancellation of a mortgage or vendor's privilege is lost or destroyed, and all obligations secured by the mortgage or vendor's privilege have been satisfied, the recorder of mortgages shall cancel the mortgage or vendor's privilege upon receipt of an affidavit from an officer of a licensed title insurer that has issued or issues a title insurance policy covering the immovable property encumbered by the mortgage or vendor's privilege. The affidavit shall set forth all of the following:

(a) A description of the instrument that was lost or destroyed and an affirmative statement that the instrument has been lost or destroyed.

(b) The name of the mortgagor or obligor of the privilege as it appears in the recorded mortgage or vendor's privilege, and recordation number or other appropriate recordation information.

(c) A statement that all obligations secured by the mortgage or vendor's privilege have been satisfied.

(d) A declaration that the title insurer agrees to be liable to and indemnify the recorder of mortgages and any person relying upon the cancellation by affidavit for any damages that they may suffer as a consequence of such reliance if the recorded affidavit contains materially false or incorrect statements that cause the recorder to incorrectly cancel the recordation of a mortgage or privilege.

(e) A statement that the affiant has made a due and diligent search for the lost or destroyed instrument, the lost or destroyed instrument cannot be located, and sixty days have elapsed since payment or satisfaction of the secured obligation.

(2) No mandamus proceeding is required to use the provisions of this Subsection.

(3) A title insurer whose officer has signed an affidavit that is provided to the recorder of mortgages pursuant to this Subsection and that contains materially false or incorrect statements causing the recorder to incorrectly cancel the recordation of a mortgage or privilege is liable to and shall indemnify the recorder and any person relying upon the cancellation for any damages that they may suffer as a consequence of such reliance.

(4) The recorder of mortgages shall not be liable for any damages resulting to any person or entity as a consequence of canceling a mortgage or vendor's privilege pursuant to an affidavit which complies with this Subsection.

Added by Acts 1974, No. 579, § 1. Amended by Acts 1987, No. 684, § 1; Acts 1988, No. 986, § 1; Acts 2007, No. 337, § 1.

§ 5167.1. **Cancellation of mortgage inscription by affidavit; penalties**

A. A mortgagee shall execute and deliver sufficient acceptable documentation, as required by the clerk of court and ex officio recorder of mortgages for the cancellation of a mortgage, to the mortgagor or the mortgagor's designated agent within sixty days after the date of receipt of full payment of the balance owed on the debt secured by the mortgage in accordance with a payoff statement. The payoff statement shall be furnished by the mortgagee or its mortgage servicer. If the mortgagee fails to execute and deliver acceptable documentation, an authorized officer of a title insurance business, the closing notary public, or the notary public for the person or entity which made the payment may, on behalf of the mortgagor or an owner of the property encumbered by the mortgage, execute an affidavit that complies with the requirements of this Section and record the affidavit in the mortgage records of each parish in which the mortgage was recorded.

B. An affidavit executed under this Section shall state that:

(1) The affiant is an authorized officer of a title insurance business, the closing notary public, or the attorney for the person or entity which made the payment.

(2) The affidavit is made on behalf of the mortgagor or an owner of the property encumbered by the mortgage.

(3) The mortgagee provided a payoff statement with respect to the loan secured by the mortgage.

(4) The affiant has ascertained that the mortgagee has received payment of the loan secured by the mortgage in accordance with the payoff statement, as evidenced by:

(a) A bank check, certified check, or escrow account check which has been negotiated by or on behalf of the mortgagee; or

(b) Other documentary evidence of the receipt of payment by the mortgagee including but not limited to verification that the funds were wired to the mortgagee.

(5) More than sixty days have elapsed since the date payment was received by the mortgagee and the mortgagee has not returned documentary authorization for cancellation of the mortgage.

(6) The mortgagee has been given at least fifteen days notice in writing of the intention to execute and record an affidavit in accordance with this Section, with a copy of the proposed affidavit attached to the written notice.

C. The affidavit shall include the names of the mortgagor and the mortgagee, the date of the mortgage, and the book and page, or folio, or clerk's file number of the immovable property records where the mortgage is recorded, together with similar information for a recorded assignment of the mortgage.

D. The affiant shall attach to the affidavit the documentary evidence that payment has been received by the mortgagee including a copy of the payoff statement. Evidence of payment may include a copy of the canceled check indicating endorsement by the mortgagee or other documentary evidence described in Subsection B.

E. An affidavit executed and recorded as provided by this Section shall constitute a release of and an authority to cancel the mortgage described in the affidavit. The clerk of court and ex officio recorder of mortgages may rely on the sworn statements contained within the affidavit and has no duty to traverse the contents thereof.

F. The clerk of court and ex officio recorder of mortgages shall index the affidavit in the names of the original mortgagee and the last assignee of the mortgage appearing of record as the grantors and in the name of the mortgagor as grantee, and shall cancel the inscription of the mortgage and assignments from the mortgage records.

G. The intentional falsification of information by the affiant in an affidavit filed in the office of the recorder of mortgages is subject to the provisions of R.S. 14:132, governing the crime of injuring public records. The affiant shall also be liable for any damages, attorney fees, and expenses occasioned by a fraudulently executed affidavit.

H. As used in this Section:

(1) "Attorney for the person or entity making payment" is an attorney licensed to practice law in this state who certifies in the affidavit that he is authorized to make the affidavit on behalf of the person or entity making payment.

(2) "Closing" shall have the same meaning as provided in R.S. 22:512(2) and (15).

(3) "Closing notary public" is the duly commissioned notary public who executes the required documents or performs notarial functions at the closing.

(4) "Payoff statement" is the statement of the following:

(a) The unpaid balance of a loan secured by a mortgage, including principal, interest, and other charges properly assessed under the loan documentation of the mortgage.

(b) The interest on a per diem basis for the unpaid balance.

(5) "Title insurance business" shall have the same meaning as provided in R.S. 22:512(17).

Added by Acts 1999, No. 869, § 1.

§ 5167.2. Cancellation of mortgage inscription

A. A mortgagee servicing agent or any holder of the note shall execute and deliver sufficient acceptable documentation, including the original note or notes, and instructions regarding the cancellation of mortgage inscriptions to the mortgagor or the mortgagor's designated agent within sixty days after the date of receipt of full payment of the balance owed on the debt secured by the mortgage in accordance with a payoff statement. The payoff statement shall be furnished by the mortgagee or its mortgage servicer.

B. The provisions of this Section shall apply only to residential mortgages, where a mortgage has been granted by a consumer on one-to-four family residential immovable property, including a mortgage to finance the initial construction of the one-to-four family residential immovable property.

C. This Section shall not apply to collateral mortgages as defined in R.S. 9:5550 nor to mortgages to secure future advances as defined in Civil Code Article 3298.

Added by Acts 2003, No. 494, § 1. Amended by Acts 2004, No. 294, § 1.

§ 5168. Promissory notes; loss or destruction; proof by affidavit

A. When a promissory note paraphed for identification with a mortgage or act creating a vendor's privilege on immovable property has been lost or destroyed, the maker of such note or any other interested party may prove its payment by presentation of the sworn affidavit of the obligee of record of the mortgage or vendor's privilege specifically attesting to and testifying as to the truth of all of the allegations required by this Section.

B. The affidavit shall set forth all of the following:

(1) The name of the mortgagor or obligor of the privilege as it appears in the recorded mortgage or vendor's privilege and the recordation information.

(2) A description of the paraphed promissory note and the encumbered immovable property.

(3) The affiant is the obligee of record of the paraphed promissory note.

For Annotative Materials, see West's Louisiana Statutes Annotated

(4) The note has been lost or destroyed and cannot be presented.

(5) The note is paid, forgiven, or otherwise satisfied.

(6) The affiant authorizes the clerk of court and ex officio recorder of mortgages to cancel the inscription of the mortgage or vendor's privilege.

(7) The affiant has not sold, transferred, or assigned the note to any other person or entity.

(8) The affiant agrees to be personally liable to and indemnify the clerk of court and ex officio recorder of mortgages and any person relying upon the cancellation by affidavit for any damages that they may suffer as a consequence of such reliance if the recorded affidavit contains incorrect statements that cause the recorder to incorrectly cancel the recordation of a mortgage or privilege.

C. An affidavit executed according to the provisions of this Section may be substituted for the original paraphed note as is otherwise required in R.S. 9:5170. No mandamus proceeding is required to use the provisions of this Section. Neither the clerk of court and ex officio recorder of mortgages nor his surety on his official bond shall have any liability for any damages resulting to any person or entity as a consequence of canceling the inscription of a mortgage or vendor's privilege pursuant to an affidavit which complies with this Section.

D. The clerk of court and ex officio recorder of mortgages shall not refuse to accept an affidavit which complies with this Section and shall not require the filing of a mandamus proceeding as a condition of canceling the inscription of a mortgage or vendor's privilege.

E. Any person in whose favor a cancelled inscription was recorded shall have a cause of action against the affiant in the event the note was not paid, forgiven, or otherwise satisfied and the mortgage or vendor's privilege cancelled from the mortgage records was legally enforceable. The cause of action created by this Subsection shall prescribe on the same date that the cause of action to enforce the underlying mortgage or vendor's privilege prescribes.

F. An affiant who has signed an affidavit that is provided to the clerk of court or the recorder of mortgages pursuant to this Section and that contains incorrect statements causing the recorder to incorrectly cancel the inscription of a mortgage or privilege from his certificate is liable to and shall indemnify the clerk of court or the recorder of mortgages, the sheriff, and any person relying upon the cancellation for any damages that they may suffer as a consequence of such reliance.

Added by Acts 2008, No. 651, § 1.

Editor's note. Section 2 of Acts 2008, No. 651 declares: "The provisions of this Act are declared to be curative and remedial and therefore shall be applied retroactively as well as prospectively."

§ 5169. Cancellation of mortgages and privileges not securing paraphed obligations

A. If a mortgage or privilege does not secure a note or other written obligation that is paraphed for identification with it, the request for cancellation shall have attached to it an act executed before a notary public or duly acknowledged before a notary public with or without witnesses or any act that is otherwise self-proving under the provisions of Code of Evidence Article 902(1), (2), (3), or (8), signed by the obligee of record of the mortgage or privilege that acknowledges the satisfaction or extinction of the secured obligation, releases or acknowledges the extinction of the mortgage or privilege, or directs the recorder to cancel its recordation.

B. A request for cancellation by an assignee must also provide the name of the mortgagor or obligor of the privilege as it appears in the recorded instrument and registry number or other appropriate recordation information of the instrument.

R.S. 44:106. Added by Acts 2005, No. 169, § 6, eff. July 1, 2006. Amended by Acts 2007, No. 337, § 2. Redesignated as R.S. 9:5169 pursuant to Acts 2010, No. 284, § 1, eff. Jan. 1, 2011.

Editor's note. Section 1 of Acts 2010, No. 284, directed the Louisiana State Law Institute to redesignate R.S. 44:106 as R.S. 9:5169.

Section 2 of Acts 2010, No. 284, further directed the Louisiana State Law Institute to make technical changes to any citations and statutory forms, as necessary to reflect the statutory redesignations in Title 9 of the Louisiana Revised Statutes of 1950.

Section 3 of Acts 2010, No. 284, provides that the redesignation of a statute as provided by that Act shall not invalidate a reference to the former citation of the redesignated statute.

Cross References

C.C. art. 3337.

§ 5169.1. Repealed by Acts 2005, No. 169, § 8, eff. July 1, 2006

§ 5170. Cancellation of mortgages and privileges securing paraphed obligations

A. If a mortgage or privilege secures a note or other written obligation paraphed for identification with it, there shall be attached to the request for cancellation:

(1) The paraphed obligation duly marked "paid" or "cancelled"; or

(2) An authentic act describing the paraphed obligation with sufficient particularity to reasonably identify it as the one paraphed for identification with the act of mortgage or privilege and containing:

(a) The appearer's declaration that he is the holder and owner of the paraphed obligation and that he releases or acknowledges extinction of the mortgage or privilege or directs the recorder to cancel its recordation; and

(b) A declaration by the notary that the appearer presented him with the paraphed obligation and that he paraphed it for identification with his act.

B. When a person requests cancellation and the original paraphed obligation is attached to the request or is presented to the recorder with it, the recorder shall, upon that person's request, make a duplicate of the original paraphed obligation, attach it to the request for cancellation, and note upon it that it is a duplicate of the paraphed obligation that was presented. The recorder shall then paraph the original obligation for identification with the request for cancellation and return it to the person presenting the request.

R.S. 44:107. Added by Acts 2005, No. 169, § 6, eff. July 1, 2006. Redesignated as R.S. 9:5170 pursuant to Acts 2010, No. 284, § 1, eff. Jan. 1, 2011.

Editor's note. Section 1 of Acts 2010, No. 284, directed the Louisiana State Law Institute to redesignate R.S. 44:107 as R.S. 9:5170.

Section 2 of Acts 2010, No. 284, further directed the Louisiana State Law Institute to make technical changes to any citations and statutory forms, as necessary to reflect the statutory redesignations in Title 9 of the Louisiana Revised Statutes of 1950.

Section 3 of Acts 2010, No. 284, provides that the redesignation of a statute as provided by that Act shall not invalidate a reference to the former citation of the redesignated statute.

Cross References

C.C. art. 3337.

§ 5171. Cancellation; certified copy of order, decree or other instrument

If a cancellation is to be effected pursuant to a certificate by a sheriff, marshal, or other officer as a consequence of a judicial sale, or other decree or action, the request for cancellation shall have attached to it a certified copy of the order, decree, or other instrument evidencing the extinction or directing the cancellation.

R.S. 44:108. Added by Acts 2005, No. 169, § 6, eff. July 1, 2006. Redesignated as R.S. 9:5171 pursuant to Acts 2010, No. 284, § 1, eff. Jan. 1, 2011.

Editor's note. Section 1 of Acts 2010, No. 284, directed the Louisiana State Law Institute to redesignate R.S. 44:108 as R.S. 9:5171.

Section 2 of Acts 2010, No. 284, further directed the Louisiana State Law Institute to make technical changes to any citations and statutory forms, as necessary to reflect the statutory redesignations in Title 9 of the Louisiana Revised Statutes of 1950.

Section 3 of Acts 2010, No. 284, provides that the redesignation of a statute as provided by that Act shall not invalidate a reference to the former citation of the redesignated statute.

Cross References

C.C. art. 3337.

§ 5172. Cancellation; licensed financial institution

A. In lieu of complying with the provisions of R.S. 9:5169, 5170, and 5171, a request for cancellation may have attached to it the signed, written act of a licensed financial institution executed before a notary public or duly acknowledged before a notary public with or without witnesses or any act that is otherwise self-proving under the provisions of Code of Evidence Article 902(1), (2), (3), or (8), declaring that the obligee is a licensed financial institution as defined in Subsection C of this Section and that the institution:

(1) Was the obligee or the authorized agent of the obligee of the obligation secured by the mortgage or privilege when the obligation was extinguished and that the secured obligation has been paid or otherwise satisfied or extinguished; or

(2) Is the obligee or authorized agent of the obligee of the secured obligation and that it releases the mortgage or privilege and directs the recorder to cancel its recordation.

B. When a request for cancellation is made by the licensed financial institution, in lieu of attaching a separate act of release, the financial institution may include the information required by R.S. 9:5169, 5170, and 5171 if the request is in authentic or authenticated form.

C. For purposes of this Section, a "licensed financial institution" is any person licensed or regulated by the Louisiana Office of Financial Institutions, or any bank, credit union, lending agency, or other person conducting such a business that is licensed or regulated by another state or the United States.

R.S. 44:109. Added by Acts 2005, No. 169, § 6, eff. July 1, 2006. Amended by Acts 2007, No. 337, § 2. Redesignated as R.S. 9:5172 pursuant to Acts 2010, No. 284, § 1, eff. Jan. 1, 2011.

Editor's note. Section 1 of Acts 2010, No. 284, directed the Louisiana State Law Institute to redesignate R.S. 44:109 as R.S. 9:5172.

Section 2 of Acts 2010, No. 284, further directed the Louisiana State Law Institute to make technical changes to any citations and statutory forms, as necessary to reflect the statutory redesignations in Title 9 of the Louisiana Revised Statutes of 1950.

Section 3 of Acts 2010, No. 284, provides that the redesignation of a statute as provided by that Act shall not invalidate a reference to the former citation of the redesignated statute.

Cross References

C.C. art. 3337.

§ 5173. Mortgage or privilege cancellation by financial institution-standard form

A financial institution seeking to cancel a mortgage or privilege inscription pursuant to R.S. 9:5172 may use, and the recorder of mortgages for each and every parish in the state of Louisiana shall accept, the following form as fully compliant as a request for cancellation and act of release. The form contained in this Section is not the exclusive form to be accepted for filing, and any other form meeting the requirements of R.S. 9:5172 may be used and filed for canceling the recordation of a mortgage or privilege:

R.S. 9:5172 FORM:

REQUEST FOR CANCELLATION OF MORTGAGE OR PRIVILEGE AND RELEASE BY LICENSED FINANCIAL INSTITUTION PURSUANT TO R.S. 9:5172

State of _____

Parish or County of _____

BE IT KNOWN THAT on this ___ day of _____, 20___, before me, the undersigned Notary Public, appeared _____ (name of financial institution) herein represented by its undersigned duly authorized representative, which declared that it is a licensed financial institution as defined in R.S. 9:5172 et seq. and that one of the following statements is true and correct:

(1) The institution was the obligee or the authorized agent of the obligee of the obligation secured by the mortgage or privilege described below when the obligation was extinguished, and the secured obligation has been paid or otherwise satisfied or extinguished; or

(2) The institution is the obligee or authorized agent of the obligee of the secured obligation, and it releases the mortgage or privilege described below.

The Clerk of Court and Ex-Officio Recorder of Mortgages for the Parish identified below is hereby expressly requested, authorized, and directed to cancel the recordation of the mortgage or privilege described as follows:

A mortgage or privilege granted by:

In favor of: _____

Date of Instrument: _____

Parish of Recordation: _____

Recording Data: _____

Legal description is as follows or is hereby attached as Exhibit "A": ___

_____
_____
_____

(3) The recorder of mortgages shall not be liable for any damages resulting to any person or entity as a consequence of canceling a mortgage or vendor's privilege pursuant to this form.

THUS DONE AND PASSED before me, Notary Public, on the date set forth above.

_____

Name of officer and title
Name of financial institution
Requested mailing address
City, state, and zip code

_____

Notary Public
(Printed name of notary and bar roll or notary number)

R.S. 44:109.1. Added by Acts 2007, No. 337, § 2. Redesignated as R.S. 9:5173 pursuant to Acts 2010, No. 284, § 1, eff. Jan. 1, 2011.

Editor's note. Section 1 of Acts 2010, No. 284, directed the Louisiana State Law Institute to redesignate R.S. 44:109.1 as R.S. 9:5173.

Section 2 of Acts 2010, No. 284, further directed the Louisiana State Law Institute to make technical changes to any citations and statutory forms, as necessary to reflect the statutory redesignations in Title 9 of the Louisiana Revised Statutes of 1950.

Section 3 of Acts 2010, No. 284, provides that the redesignation of a statute as provided by that Act shall not invalidate a reference to the former citation of the redesignated statute.

Cross References

C.C. art. 3337.

§ 5174. Liability for incorrect or false request for cancellation

A. Any person who requests the recorder to cancel recordation of a mortgage or privilege and who knows or should have known that an act or declaration that he provided to the recorder pursuant to this Title contains materially false or incorrect statements that cause the recorder to incorrectly cancel the recordation of a mortgage or privilege is personally liable to and shall indemnify the recorder and any person relying upon the cancellation for any damages suffered as a consequence of such reliance.

B. Any person signing any act or declaration that is presented to the recorder pursuant to this Title containing materially false or incorrect statements causing the recorder to incorrectly cancel the recordation of a mortgage or privilege is personally liable to and shall indemnify the recorder and any person relying upon the cancellation for any damages suffered as a consequence of such reliance.

C. Any person who knowingly provides or executes the materially false or incorrect statement is also guilty of false swearing under the provisions of R.S. 14:125.

R.S. 44:110. Added by Acts 2005, No. 169, § 6, eff. July 1, 2006. Amended by Acts 2007, No. 337, § 2. Redesignated as R.S. 9:5174 pursuant to Acts 2010, No. 284, § 1, eff. Jan. 1, 2011.

Editor's note. Section 1 of Acts 2010, No. 284, directed the Louisiana State Law Institute to redesignate R.S. 44:110 as R.S. 9:5174.

Section 2 of Acts 2010, No. 284, further directed the Louisiana State Law Institute to make technical changes to any citations and statutory forms, as necessary to reflect the statutory redesignations in Title 9 of the Louisiana Revised Statutes of 1950.

Section 3 of Acts 2010, No. 284, provides that the redesignation of a statute as provided by that Act shall not invalidate a reference to the former citation of the redesignated statute.

Cross References

C.C. art. 3337.

§ 5175. Order of discharge in bankruptcy; effect

A. A judgment debtor in whose favor a United States Bankruptcy Court has entered an order of discharge, or any person whose rights are or may be affected by the order, may bring an action in accordance with the provisions of R.S. 44:114, against the recorder of mortgages of a parish in which the judgment is recorded to declare the judicial mortgage created by its recordation extinguished and order the recordation of the judgment cancelled from the records of the parish and any other parish in which the judgment is recorded.

B. (1) Upon proof of the order of discharge, and that the judgment is for a claim that has been discharged, the court shall declare extinguished the judicial mortgage evidenced by the recordation of the judgment and order the recordation of the judgment cancelled unless the judgment creditor, or any other party to the action whose rights are or may be adversely affected by the cancellation, proves that the judgment creditor or such other person possesses equity in property as a result of the judicial mortgage over and above superior liens, in which case the order of cancellation shall expressly exclude its effect as to that property.

(2) If a bankruptcy court order authorizing the sale of property free and clear of all judgments, mortgages, and privileges does not specify the discharged judgments, mortgages, or privileges to be cancelled, the trustee or former trustee in the proceedings, or his attorney of record, may specify by affidavit which discharged judgments, mortgages, or privileges are to be partially cancelled as to the particular property subject to the order. The affidavit and a Request to Cancel shall be filed with the bankruptcy court order. The affidavit shall contain all of the following information:

(a) A statement that the debtor filed a petition under the United States Bankruptcy Code.

(b) The name of the court where the bankruptcy proceeding was filed.

(c) The date on which the petition was filed.

(d) A statement that the debt or debts upon which the judgment, mortgage, or privilege is based were listed in the bankruptcy proceeding.

(e) A description of the particular property to be released and a statement that the property is free and clear of all judgments, mortgages, or privileges.

(f) A listing of the judgments, mortgages, or privileges, including the clerk's office identification by instrument number, book, or folio.

(g) A certified copy of the bankruptcy court order.

C. (1) A judgment debtor may obtain a partial cancellation of the inscription of a judgment as it affects property not owned by the judgment debtor on the date of his filing a petition under Chapter 7 of the United States Bankruptcy

Code upon the filing of an affidavit in accordance with this Subsection.

(2) The affidavit shall contain all of the following:

(a) A statement that the judgment debtor filed a petition under Chapter 7 of the United States Bankruptcy Code.

(b) The name of the court where the bankruptcy proceeding was filed.

(c) The date on which the petition was filed.

(d) A statement that the debt or debts upon which the judgment is based were listed in the bankruptcy proceeding and that the debtor was subsequently released from personal liability on the debt or debts by virtue of a discharge in bankruptcy.

(e) A description of any particular property to be partially released and a statement that the property was not owned by the debtor at the time of filing the bankruptcy proceeding.

(f) A copy of the schedule or schedules listing the debt.

(g) A copy of the discharge order.

(3) Upon the filing of an affidavit in compliance with this Subsection, the recorder shall partially cancel the judgment insofar as it affects the property described in the affidavit and any property that may have been acquired after the date stated in Subparagraph (2)(c) of this Subsection that the debtor filed his petition for bankruptcy.

(4) For purposes of this Subsection, a debtor is deemed to own inherited property as of the date of death of the decedent from whom he inherited the property.

R.S. 44:111. Added by Acts 2005, No. 169, § 6, eff. July 1, 2006. Redesignated as R.S. 9:5175 pursuant to Acts 2010, No. 284, § 1, eff. Jan. 1, 2011. Amended by Acts 2012, No. 179, § 1.

Editor's note. Section 1 of Acts 2010, No. 284, directed the Louisiana State Law Institute to redesignate R.S. 44:111 as R.S. 9:5175.

Section 2 of Acts 2010, No. 284, further directed the Louisiana State Law Institute to make technical changes to any citations and statutory forms, as necessary to reflect the statutory redesignations in Title 9 of the Louisiana Revised Statutes of 1950.

Section 3 of Acts 2010, No. 284, provides that the redesignation of a statute as provided by that Act shall not invalidate a reference to the former citation of the redesignated statute.

Cross References

C.C. art. 3337.

§ 5176. Extinction of certain rights; acknowledgment by owner or holder

A. Within thirty days after receipt of a written request from the owner of an immovable to do so, the following persons shall deliver to the owner a written instrument, in proper form, acknowledging that the rights of that person are extinguished:

(1) The lessee of an immovable or the owner of a predial or personal servitude, servitude of right-of-use, or usufruct of an immovable whose rights have become extinguished by the expiration of their term, from the happening of a resolutory or other condition, or from the failure to timely renew, extend, or otherwise modify them according to their terms.

(2) A person who had an option, right of first refusal, or other contractual or legal right to acquire an immovable, a right in or over it, or the lease of an immovable and whose rights have become extinguished by virtue of the expiration of their term, the failure to exercise them timely, or the happening of a condition or other occurrence.

B. If the person required to deliver an acknowledgment fails or refuses to do so, or if he cannot be located after diligent effort, the owner of the immovable may bring an action to declare that the rights are extinguished or ineffective and to direct the recorder to record in his records the judgment so rendered.

C. A return receipt showing delivery by registered or certified mail of a letter addressed to the person required to give the acknowledgment shall be presumptive evidence of receipt of the notice. Proof that the person to whom the notice is to be given could not be located after a diligent search shall suffice in lieu of the giving of the notice and an attorney shall be appointed to represent the absent defendant.

D. The prevailing party in an action pursuant to this Section may be awarded reasonable attorney fees in addition to the costs of the action from the person who demanded or refused delivery of the written acknowledgment.

E. This Section shall not apply to mineral rights or to a petitory or possessory action.

R.S. 44:112. Added by Acts 2005, No. 169, § 6, eff. July 1, 2006. Redesignated as R.S. 9:5176 pursuant to Acts 2010, No. 284, § 1, eff. Jan. 1, 2011.

Editor's note. Section 1 of Acts 2010, No. 284, directed the Louisiana State Law Institute to redesignate R.S. 44:112 as R.S. 9:5176.

Section 2 of Acts 2010, No. 284, further directed the Louisiana State Law Institute to make technical changes to any citations and statutory forms, as necessary to reflect the statutory redesignations in Title 9 of the Louisiana Revised Statutes of 1950.

Section 3 of Acts 2010, No. 284, provides that the redesignation of a statute as provided by that Act shall not invalidate a reference to the former citation of the redesignated statute.

Cross References

C.C. art. 3337.

§§ 5177 to 5180.1. Repealed by Acts 2005, No. 169, § 8, eff. July 1, 2006

§ 5180.2. Repealed by Acts 1995, No. 1087, § 5

§§ 5180.3, 5180.4. Repealed by Acts 2005, No. 169, § 8, eff. July 1, 2006

SUBPART C. CERTIFICATES [REPEALED]

§ 5181. Repealed by Acts 2005, No. 169, § 8, eff. July 1, 2006

§ 5182. Repealed by Acts 1992, No. 1132, § 3, eff. Jan. 1, 1993

§ 5183. Repealed by Acts 1978, No. 651, § 3

SUBPART D. NOTICE OF TAX SALES [REPEALED]

§§ 5201 to 5203. Repealed by Acts 1997, No. 584, § 1

SUBPART E. THE OFFICE OF MORTGAGES

R.S. 9:5208 to 9:5213 are redesignated provisions of the Louisiana Civil Code of 1870, Book II, Title XXII of the Louisiana Civil Code of 1870 (Of Mortgages) was revised by Acts 1991, No. 632, § 1 and by Acts 1992, No. 1132, § 2. Acts 1992, No. 1132, § 4, effective January 1, 1993, instructed the Louisiana State Law Institute to redesignate Articles 3371 through 3385.1 of the Louisiana Civil Code of 1870 as R.S. 9:5169 through 9:5180.4. Section 4 of Acts 1992, No. 1132 provides that "the resignation is neither a repeal nor a reenactment of the redesignated provisions." Section 7 of Acts 1992, No. 1132 declares that "the provisions of this Act relative to the time for reinscription of mortgages are applicable only to those mortgages created on or after January 1, 1993. Mortgages and privileges created before January 1, 1993 shall continue to be regulated by the laws in existence before January 1, 1993. The procedure for reinscription of mortgages and privileges as set forth in Civil Code Articles 3328 through 3331 shall be effective as to all requests for reinscription filed on or after the effective date of this Act." Articles 3328 through 3331 of the Louisiana Civil Code have been repealed by Acts 2005, No. 169, effective January 1, 2006 [postponed to July 1, 2006, by Acts 2005, 1st Ex.Sess., No. 13]. The procedures for reinscription are now governed by Articles 3362 through 3365, as revised by Acts 2005, No. 169, effective January 1, 2006 [postponed to July 1, 2006, by Acts 2005, 1st Ex.Sess., No.13].

§§ 5206, 5207. Repealed by Acts 2005, No. 169, § 8, eff. July 1, 2006

§ 5208. Registers kept by recorder of mortgages in Orleans parish

The recorder of mortgages for the parish of Orleans has his office in the city of New Orleans, and must keep two registers:

(1) The first, to record all acts from which there results a conventional, judicial or legal mortgage, or privilege.

(2) The second, to record all donations which have to undergo that formality.

C.C. art. 3388. Redesignated as R.S. 9:5208 pursuant to Acts 1992, No. 1132, § 4, eff. Jan. 1, 1993.

Cross References

C.C. arts. 3299, 3303, 3320, 3325.

§ 5209. Authentication of registers in Orleans parish

These registers shall be numbered at each page and signed *ne varietur* on the first and last page, by one of the judges or a justice of the peace for the parish of Orleans.

C.C. art. 3389. Redesignated as R.S. 9:5209 pursuant to Acts 1992, No. 1132, § 4, eff. Jan. 1, 1993.

Cross References

C.C. art. 3325.

R.S. 9:5208, 9:5210, 44:261 to 44:262, 44:321, 44:361.

§ 5210. Registers and authentication outside Orleans parish

The parish recorders must keep the same number of registers as the recorder of mortgages for the parish of Orleans, and shall number their pages, and have them signed *ne varietur* on the first and last page by the parish judge of their parish or two justices of the peace for their parish.

C.C. art. 3390. Redesignated as R.S. 9:5210 pursuant to Acts 1992, No. 1132, § 4, eff. Jan. 1, 1993.

Cross References

R.S. 9:5211, 44:131, 44:133, 44:161 to 44:162, 44:261 to 44:262, 44:321, 44:361.

§ 5211. Register with title of acts and time of filing

A. Besides the registers above mentioned, the recorder of mortgages, and the parish recorders performing the same duties in the different parishes, shall keep a separate register, in which they shall set down from day to day, and according to their date, the title of the different acts transmitted to them to be recorded, for the purpose of establishing with exactness the time of such transmission.

B. This register shall be open to the inspection of all persons who may wish to examine it, during the hours at which the office is kept open, but it can not be removed.

C.C. art. 3391. Redesignated as R.S. 9:5211 pursuant to Acts 1992, No. 1132, § 4, eff. Jan. 1, 1993.

Cross References

C.C. arts. 1839, 2021, 2035, 3273.

R.S. 9:5208, 9:5210, 9:5212, 9:5391, 44:32, 44:102, 44:131, 44:136, 44:161 to 44:162, 44:261 to 44:262.

§ 5212. Prompt recordation and certificate of encumbrances

Except as provided in R.S. 35:12(D), in no case can the recorder of mortgages and the parish recorders fulfilling the same duties refuse or delay the recording of the acts which are presented to them for that purpose, or the delivery of the certificates which are required of them, as hereafter stated.

C.C. art. 3392. Redesignated as R.S. 9:5212 pursuant to Acts 1992, No. 1132, § 4, eff. Jan. 1, 1993. Amended by Acts 2004, No. 62, § 1.

Cross References

C.C. art. 3273.

R.S. 9:5211, 9:5213, 44:102, 44:131, 44:135 to 44:136, 44:161 to 44:162.

§ 5213. Method of recordation; certificate of encumbrances

These officers shall record on their register the acts which are presented to them, in the order of their date, and without leaving any intervals or blank space between them; and they are bound also to deliver to all persons who may demand them, a certificate of the mortgages, privileges or donations, which they may have thus recorded; if there be none, their certificate shall declare that fact.

C.C. art. 3393. Redesignated as R.S. 9:5213 pursuant to Acts 1992, No. 1132, § 4, eff. Jan. 1, 1993.

Cross References

C.C. arts. 3273.

C.C.P. art. 2234.

R.S. 5:3 to 5:4, 9:2928, 9:5208, 9:5212, 13:4406, 13:4344 to 13:4345, 37:3118, 38:1504, 44:32, 44:102, 44:136, 44:263.

§§ 5214 to 5216. Repealed by Acts 2005, No. 169, § 8, eff. July 1, 2006

§ 5217. Recorder's fees for multiple indebtedness mortgages; form

A. The uniform filing fee that a recorder in any parish of this state is authorized to charge for the filing and recordation of a multiple indebtedness mortgage executed in accordance with Civil Code Article 3298 is twenty-five dollars, plus ten dollars for each subsequent page, and five dollars for each name after the first name that is required to be indexed. Notwithstanding the provisions of R.S. 13:844, R.S. 44:234, or any similar provision or any other law to the contrary, the provisions of this Section establish the sole and exclusive method of determining the filing and recordation fee for a multiple indebtedness mortgage executed in accordance with Civil Code Article 3298, regardless of the length of such mortgage.

B. For purposes of establishing the recordation fee, every multiple indebtedness mortgage filed for recordation shall be captioned as a "multiple indebtedness mortgage" or "multiple obligations mortgage" on the first page, and shall have on the first page a margin of two inches at the top and one inch at the bottom and on each side, and all subsequent pages shall have a margin requirement of one inch on all sides. In addition, the type size shall be not less than eight point.

C. For any document not in compliance with the requirements of Subsection B there shall be an additional noncompliance fee of ten dollars per document.

Added by Acts 1997, No. 1474, § 1. Amended by Acts 2001, No. 770, § 1.

PART III. RIGHTS OF MORTGAGE HOLDER

§ 5251. Preservation of rights of mortgage holder in sales held in certain proceedings

Except as otherwise provided in Civil Code Articles 813 and 815, no conventional or judicial mortgage, or chattel mortgage, or security interest under Chapter 9 of the Louisiana Commercial Laws (R.S. 10:9–101 et seq.), shall be cancelled, removed from the public records, or in any manner affected by any public or private sale of property subject thereto in any succession, liquidation, insolvency, receivership, bankruptcy, or partition proceeding. The provisions of this Section shall not apply to the execution of judgments governed by Book IV of the Louisiana Code of Civil Procedure, Article 2251 et seq., or to judicial sales in executory proceedings under the Louisiana Code of Civil Procedure, Article 2631 et seq.

Added by Acts 1980, No. 356, § 1. Amended by Acts 1981, No. 894, § 1; Acts 1989, No. 137, § 5, eff. Sept. 1, 1989; Acts 1995, No. 768, § 1.

Editor's note. For § 20 of Acts 1989, No. 137, stating legislative intent, see note preceding R.S. 9:5101.

Cross References

C.C. arts. 813, 815, 3307.

CHAPTER 2. CONVENTIONAL MORTGAGES

PART I. MORTGAGES SECURING SEVERAL OBLIGATIONS

Section
5301. Conventional mortgage to secure several obligations.

Section
5302. Fiduciary as mortgagee in trust for creditors.
5303. Creditors' interests under mortgage.
5304. Enforcement of mortgage; limitations.
5305. Paraph unnecessary; proviso.
5306. Act of mortgage may include pledge.
5307. Substitutions, fidei commissa, or trust dispositions; laws not applicable.

PART II. MORTGAGES ON RURAL PROPERTY

5321. Definitions.
5322. Repealed.
5323. Repealed.
5324. Schedule of penalties.
5325. Exclusions.
5326. Repealed.

PART III. CHATTEL MORTGAGES

5351 to 5352. Repealed.
5352.1. Repealed.
5353 to 5363. Repealed.
5363.1. Abandoned mobile homes; secured parties.
5364 to 5366.2. Repealed.

PART IV. MORTGAGE OF MOVABLES USED IN COMMERCIAL OR INDUSTRIAL ACTIVITY [REPEALED]

5367 to 5373. Repealed.

PART V. MISCELLANEOUS PROVISIONS

5381. Ships and other vessels, hypothecation and conveyance; record; effect.
5382. Right of mortgage holder to recover for disposal or conversion of property.
5383. Transfers of more than one parcel of immovable property.
5384. Assumption of a mortgage on immovable property by a third person.
5385. Satisfaction of mortgage; production of promissory note or release for cancellation; liability.
5386. Mortgage including collateral assignment and pledge of certain incorporeal rights.
5387. Repealed.
5388. Authority to carry out and enforce rights.
5389. Additional funds advanced under mortgage or security agreement.
5390. Amendment, renewal, or refinancing of mortgage and mortgage note.
5391. Additions, accessions, and natural increases subject to mortgage.
5392. Continuation of mortgage after judgment.
5393. Combination forms.
5394. Applicability.
5395. Protection of mortgage lenders and fiduciaries from state environmental liability; parity with federal law.
5396. Maintenance of abandoned mortgaged property.

PART I. MORTGAGES SECURING SEVERAL OBLIGATIONS

§ 5301. Conventional mortgage to secure several obligations

A conventional mortgage may be given to secure the payment of the principal and interest of two or more notes, bonds, or other obligations of the mortgagor or of any third person.

Cross References

C.C. arts. 3280, 3287, 3290, 3298, 3307.

§ 5302. Fiduciary as mortgagee in trust for creditors

A fiduciary for the holders of the obligations secured by the mortgage may be named in the act as mortgagee in trust for the benefit of the creditors. He shall be irrevocably appointed special attorney-in-fact for the holders of the obligations and vested with full power in their behalf to effect and enforce the mortgage for their benefit.

Cross References

C.C. arts. 3280, 3287, 3290, 3298, 3307.

§ 5303. Creditors' interests under mortgage

The interest of the holders of the obligations shall be in common and indivisible, and in case of the enforcement of the mortgage, the holders shall be entitled to participate pro rata in the proceeds of the mortgaged property.

Cross References

C.C. arts. 3280, 3287, 3290, 3298, 3307.

§ 5304. Enforcement of mortgage; limitations

In case of default, the mortgage may be enforced by seizure and sale or otherwise, as the fiduciary shall deem expedient for the protection of the debt. However, the act of mortgage may provide that in the event of default, the fiduciary shall not be obliged to proceed to sell the property unless the holders of a designated portion of the obligations secured shall request the fiduciary to enforce the mortgage and agree to indemnify him against all costs and expenses incurred. The mortgagor may restrict the right of the fiduciary to foreclose or sell in the event of default.

Cross References

C.C. arts. 3280, 3287, 3290, 3298, 3300, 3307.

§ 5305. Paraph unnecessary; proviso

The notes, bonds, or other obligations secured by the mortgage need not be paraphed if the act of mortgage identifies them by date, number, amount, and date when payable.

Cross References

C.C. arts. 3280, 3287, 3290, 3298, 3307.

§ 5306. Act of mortgage may include pledge

The act of mortgage may include a pledge of incorporeal movables and may provide for the deposit thereof with the fiduciary.

Cross References

C.C. arts. 3280, 3287, 3290, 3298, 3307.

§ 5307. Substitutions, fidei commissa, or trust dispositions; laws not applicable

The laws relative to substitutions, fidei commissa, or trust dispositions shall not apply to or in any manner affect conventional mortgages executed in conformity with the provisions of this Part, and all laws or parts of laws conflicting with the provisions of this Part are repealed insofar as regards the purposes of this Part, but not otherwise.

Cross References

C.C. arts. 3280, 3287, 3290, 3298, 3307.

PART II. MORTGAGES ON RURAL PROPERTY

§ 5321. Definitions

As used in this Part:

(1) "Instrument" means any instrument, whether or not negotiable, which evidences the indebtedness of one or more persons.

(2) "Rural Property" means a tract of land which is at least forty acres in area and from which at least seventy-five percent of the income derived is from agricultural or livestock purposes or mineral income and which is not located within the territorial limits of any incorporated municipality.

Added by Acts 1977, No. 251, § 1.

§ 5322. Repealed by Acts 1995, No. 1201, § 6, eff. June 19, 1995

§ 5323. Repealed by Acts 1995, No. 1201, § 6, eff. June 19, 1995

§ 5324. Schedule of penalties

No penalty for the prepayment of any indebtedness evidenced by an instrument which is secured by a mortgage on rural property may exceed:

(1) Five percent of the unpaid principal balance if prepaid during the first year from the date of the instrument;

(2) Four percent of the unpaid principal balance if prepaid during the second year from the date of the instrument;

(3) Three percent of the unpaid principal balance if prepaid during the third year from the date of the instrument;

(4) Two percent of the unpaid principal balance if prepaid during the fourth year from the date of the instrument;

(5) One percent of the unpaid principal balance if prepaid during the fifth year from the date of the instrument;

(6) No prepayment penalty shall be assessed if prepaid more than five years from the date of the instrument.

Added by Acts 1977, No. 251, § 1.

§ 5325. Exclusions

The provisions of this Part shall not apply to any instrument which is secured by a conventional mortgage on rural property if that instrument provides that it is a consumer credit transaction within the provisions of the Louisiana Consumer Credit Law, R.S. 9:3510 through R.S. 9:3568.

Added by Acts 1977, No. 251, § 1.

§ 5326. Repealed by Acts 1995, No. 1184, § 4; Acts 1995, No. 1201, § 6, eff. June 19, 1995

PART III. CHATTEL MORTGAGES

§§ 5351 to 5352. Repealed by Acts 2001, No. 128, § 18, eff. July 1, 2001 at 12:01 A.M.

Editor's note. Acts 2001, No. 128, § 18, effective July 1, 2001, repealed R.S. 9:5351 to 9:5373. Section 19 of Acts 2001, No. 128, declares that "it is the intent of the legislature in enacting this Act that R.S. 2736, 4501 and 4502, 4521, 4758, 4770, and 5363.1 not be expressly or impliedly repealed by this Act, but that such laws remain in effect, and, at times when so provided, be applied to secured transactions subject to Chapter 9 of the Louisiana Commercial Law as revised by this Act."

§ 5352.1. Repealed by Acts 1988, No. 528, § 2, eff. July 1, 1989; Acts 1988, No. 920, § 2, eff. July 26, 1988

Editor's note. Acts 2001, No. 128, § 4, effective July 1, 2001, repealed R.S. 9:5351 to 9:5373. Section 19 of Acts 2001, No. 128, declares that "it is the intent of the legislature in enacting this Act that R.S. 2736, 4501 and 4502, 4521, 4758, 4770, and 5363.1 not be expressly or impliedly repealed by this Act, but that such laws remain in effect, and, at times when so provided, be applied to secured transactions subject to Chapter 9 of the Louisiana Commercial Law as revised by this Act."

§§ 5353 to 5363. Repealed by Acts 2001, No. 128, § 18, eff. July 1, 2001 at 12:01 A.M.

Editor's note. Acts 2001, No. 128, § 4, effective July 1, 2001, repealed R.S. 9:5351 to 9:5373. Section 19 of Acts 2001, No. 128, declares that "it is the intent of the legislature in enacting this Act that R.S. 2736, 4501 and 4502, 4521, 4758, 4770, and 5363.1 not be expressly or impliedly repealed by this Act, but that such laws remain in effect, and, at times when so provided, be applied to secured transactions subject to Chapter 9 of the Louisiana Commercial Law as revised by this Act."

§ 5363.1. Abandoned mobile homes; secured parties

A. Definitions

(1) "Mobile home" means a structure, transportable in one or more sections, which is eight body feet or more in width and is thirty-two body feet or more in length, designed to be used as a dwelling with or without a permanent foundation when connected to the required utilities, and includes the plumbing, heating, air conditioning, and electrical systems contained therein. The term "mobile home" shall include a modular home, a mobile home, and a residential mobile home that is no longer declared to be part of the realty pursuant to R.S. 9:1149.6.

(2) "Abandoned" or "abandonment" shall mean that the secured party has been notified by the mortgagor or by the owner of the immovable property on which the mobile home is located that the mortgagor no longer intends to remain in the mobile home, or when a reasonable person would conclude that the mobile home is no longer being occupied and from all appearances substantially all of the mortgagor's personal belongings have been removed from the mobile home.

(3) "Mortgagor" shall mean the person executing the chattel mortgage or security agreement under Chapter 9 of the Louisiana Commercial Laws (R.S. 10:9–101, et seq.) or, if the mobile home has been transferred and the chattel mortgage or security interest under Chapter 9 of the Louisiana Commercial Laws assumed by a new purchaser with written consent of the holder of the chattel mortgage or security agreement, the transferee.

(4) "Secured party" shall mean the holder of the chattel mortgage or security interest under Chapter 9 of Louisiana Commercial Laws, the pledgee or assignee of the chattel mortgage or security interest, or the agent of the holder, assignee, or pledgee of the chattel mortgage or security interest.

B. (1) In addition to those remedies provided in R.S. 9:5363, the holder of a chattel mortgage enforceable against third parties pursuant to Chapter 4 of Title 32 of the Louisiana Revised Statutes of 1950[1] or pursuant to this Part or the secured party under a perfected security interest subject to Chapter 9 of Louisiana Commercial Laws, shall have the right to take possession of the mobile home on default if all of the following criteria are met:

(a) The mobile home has been abandoned.

(b) The mortgagor has not paid a minimum of two consecutive monthly payments on the date due pursuant to the terms of the chattel mortgage or security agreement.

(c) A petition has been filed in a court of competent jurisdiction seeking an ex parte order authorizing the secured party to proceed pursuant to this Section. The judge shall sign the order only after the secured party has completed the following:

(i) Posted a bond in an amount fixed by the judge, which shall be the amount stated in the suit;

(ii) Executed an affidavit stating that the mobile home has been abandoned;

(iii) Presented to the court all documents necessary to prove that the secured party is the holder of the first mortgage on the mobile home.

(2) If the above criteria are satisfied the holder or holder's agent may take possession of the mobile home only after a ten day period following the placing of written notice on the front door of the mobile home by the sheriff, or his designee. The written notice shall contain the name of the debtor, the fact that the secured party shall take possession of the mobile home in accordance with the provisions of R.S. 9:5363.1, the citation and docket number of the case wherein a court authorized the secured party to proceed in accordance with this Section, and the name and telephone number of the secured party or his agent. In addition, the secured party shall also advertise once in the official publication or newspaper in the parish in which the mobile home is located at the time that the secured party takes possession. The advertisement only need state the names of the debtors, the fact that the secured party shall take possession of the mobile home, and the name and telephone number of the individual to contact for further information. The sheriff shall be paid a fee of twenty-five dollars for the placing of the written notice as provided by this Paragraph.

(3) When the mortgagor has notified the secured party in writing that he no longer intends to occupy the mobile home and has requested that the secured party retake possession thereof, the judge may issue an order waiving the provisions of this Section and may issue an order directing the Department of Public Safety to issue a new certificate of title to the secured party or any other person that purchases the abandoned mobile home at a private sale. When such an order is granted by the judge, the entire indebtedness shall be cancelled.

C. A secured party who has taken possession of a mobile home pursuant to Subsection B of this Section shall immediately give notice to the debtor at such address as specified in the chattel mortgage and at the debtor's last known address, if different, by registered or certified mail, return receipt requested.

D. The debtor shall have twenty-one calendar days from the date of the secured party's taking possession to reclaim any personal property contained in the mobile home or to redeem the mobile home by the paying to the secured party in cash the entire amount of delinquent payments, all interest and late charges due pursuant to the chattel mortgage, all costs of transporting and housing the mobile home, and all advertisement costs. Nothing herein shall prevent the secured party from reinstating the promissory note and chattel mortgage or security agreement for a lesser amount at the sole option of the secured party.

E. After the expiration of the twenty-one calendar days from the date of taking possession provided for in Subsection D of this Section:

(1) The secured party may sell the mobile home at public or private sale and apply the proceeds to the indebtedness. If there are mortgages or other security interests superior to that held by the secured party, the proceeds of the sale shall be paid first to those superior security interests; then the remaining balance, if any, shall be applied to the secured creditor's debt. Any funds received which are in excess of the indebtedness and superior security interests, including principal, interest, costs of repossession, and costs of sale, as each is provided for in the chattel mortgage or note, shall be delivered to the debtor, or if he cannot be found, shall be deposited with the clerk of court of the parish in which the mobile home was located prior to the secured party obtaining possession of the mobile home.

(2) The secured party shall obtain two appraisals of the mobile home from two qualified appraisers, and the average of both appraisals shall be the established value of the mobile home.

(3) If the amount of the entire indebtedness due pursuant to the chattel mortgage or security agreement which shall be deemed accelerated at the time of the sale plus the costs of transporting and storing the mobile home and advertisement costs exceeds the established value of the mobile home, the secured party shall have the right to bid at any public sale, without paying cash, up to the amount of the total indebtedness including the costs of transporting and storing the mobile home and advertisement costs or sell the mobile home to itself for the amount of said indebtedness.

(4) A secured party that sells the mobile home subject to a chattel mortgage entered into prior to the time Chapter 9 of the Louisiana Commercial Laws becomes effective at either public or private sale shall not have the right to seek a deficiency judgment from any debtor or other person, including any guarantor, liable on the promissory note or chattel mortgage. Provided, that nothing herein shall be construed to affect any agreement between the mortgagee and the selling dealer.

F. A debtor or a third party seeking to recover for damages occasioned by a reclaiming of a mobile home in violation of this Section shall be entitled to recover from the seizing secured party all costs and expenses incurred in the prosecution of such action, including reasonable attorney's fees as determined by the court. If such an action for damages is dismissed by the court, the court may grant reasonable attorney's fees to the creditor.

G. After the secured party has fulfilled the requirements of this Section and has taken possession of the mobile home, the court that issued the ex parte order provided for in Subparagraph (c) of Paragraph B(1) of this Section shall order the Department of Public Safety to issue a new certificate of title to the party that purchases the abandoned mobile home at the sale provided for by this Section.

Added by Acts 1983, No. 367, § 1. Amended by Acts 1985, No. 715, § 1; Acts 1989, No. 137, § 5, eff. Sept. 1, 1989.

[1] R.S. 32:701 et seq.

Editor's note. Acts 2001, No. 128, § 1 revised, in Title 10, Chapter 9, "Secured Transactions" containing R.S. 10:9–101 to 10:9–710. Sections 2 through 17 of Acts 2001, No. 128 made conforming amendments and enactments in Titles 3, 6, 9, 10, 12, 23, 32, 37, 39, 40, 46 of the Louisiana Revised Statutes of 1950 and in the Code of Civil Procedure. Section 21 of Act 128 provided for an effective date of 12:01 A.M. on July 1, 2001.

This section was included within a range (R.S. 9:5351 through 9:5373) of sections repealed pursuant to § 18 of Acts 2001, No. 128. However, § 19 of Acts 2001, No. 128 provides:

"Section 19. It is the intent of the legislature in enacting this Act that R.S. 9:2736, 4501 and 4502, 4521, 4758, 4770, and 5363.1 not be expressly or impliedly repealed by this Act, but that such laws remain in effect, and, at times when so provided, be applied to secured transactions subject to Chapter 9 of the Louisiana Commercial Law as revised by this Act."

Pursuant to § 19 of Acts 2001, No. 128 and the statutory revision authority of the Louisiana State Law Institute, this section remains live text.

Cross References

C.C. arts. 3216, 3278, 3286, 3287, 3320.

§§ 5364 to 5366.2. Repealed by Acts 2001, No. 128, § 18, eff. July 1, 2001 at 12:01 A.M.

Editor's note. Acts 2001, No. 128, § 18, effective July 1, 2001, repealed R.S. 9:5351 to 9:5373. Section 19 of Acts 2001, No. 128, declares that "it is the intent of the legislature in enacting this Act that R.S. 2736, 4501 and 4502, 4521, 4758, 4770, and 5363.1 not be expressly or impliedly repealed by this Act, but that such laws remain in effect, and, at times when so provided, be applied to secured transactions subject to Chapter 9 of the Louisiana Commercial Law as revised by this Act."

PART IV. MORTGAGE OF MOVABLES USED IN COMMERCIAL OR INDUSTRIAL ACTIVITY [REPEALED]

§§ 5367 to 5373. Repealed by Acts 2001, No. 128, § 18, eff. July 1, 2001 at 12:01 A.M.

Editor's note. Acts 2001, No. 128, § 18, effective July 1, 2001, repealed R.S. 9:5351 to 9:5373. Section 19 of Acts 2001, No. 128, declares that "it is the intent of the legislature in enacting this Act that R.S. 2736, 4501 and 4502, 4521, 4758, 4770, and 5363.1 not be expressly or impliedly repealed by this Act, but that such laws remain in effect, and, at times when so provided, be applied to secured transactions subject to Chapter 9 of the Louisiana Commercial Law as revised by this Act."

PART V. MISCELLANEOUS PROVISIONS

§ 5381. Ships and other vessels, hypothecation and conveyance; record; effect

In addition to the conveyances and securities otherwise allowed by law, all hypothecations and conveyances of ships, steamboats, and other vessels, or parts thereof, made in good faith and for a valuable consideration, shall be valid, and the record thereof, if of vessels of the United States, according to the laws of the United States, or if of a foreign state, according to the laws of such state, shall be notice to all persons.

Cross References

C.C. arts. 3286, 3287, 3292.

§ 5382. Right of mortgage holder to recover for disposal or conversion of property

The holder of a conventional mortgage shall have the same rights, privileges, and actions as the mortgagor land owner to recover against any person who, without the written consent of the mortgagee, buys, sells, cuts, removes, holds, disposes of, changes the form of, or otherwise converts to the use of himself or another, any trees, buildings, or other immovables covered by the mortgage.

Recovery by the mortgagee may not be for more than the unpaid portion of the secured indebtedness, plus interest, advances, court costs, and attorney's fees, provided such recovery may be had severally or jointly with the mortgagor land owner.

Amended by Acts 1980, No. 107, § 1.

Cross References

C.C. arts. 3286, 3307.

§ 5383. Transfers of more than one parcel of immovable property

In a transfer of more than one parcel of immovable property, no assumption in globo is created by the assumption by a purchaser of more than one vendor's privilege and/or mortgage, unless the contrary is expressed in said transfer. In such cases, whenever separate parcels of immovable property are transferred to a purchaser who expressly assumes the payment of the vendors' privileges and/or mortgages bearing against the immovable property purchased, each vendor's privilege and/or mortgage shall be deemed to have each been assumed separately and distinctly as if only one parcel of immovable property had been transferred, and each such vendor's privilege and/or mortgage shall continue to affect and bear against only the specific immovable property described in the instrument by which the vendor's privilege and/or mortgage was originally created. Likewise, unless the contrary is expressed in said transfer, any resolutory condition or right to rescind arising in favor of the vendor as a result of the failure to pay any of the vendors' privileges and/or mortgages shall be deemed to apply only to the immovable property affected by its respective vendor's privilege and/or mortgage.

Added by Acts 1976, No. 338, § 1. Amended by Acts 1999, No. 875, § 1.

§ 5384. Assumption of a mortgage on immovable property by a third person

An original vendor's privilege or first mortgage, or both, is not extinguished nor is its ranking subordinated to any other mortgage, lien, privilege, or encumbrance when the obligation it secures is assumed by a new obligor, notwithstanding the release of the original obligor.

Added by Acts 1980, No. 585, § 1.

§ 5385. Satisfaction of mortgage; production of promissory note or release for cancellation; liability

A. When the obligation secured by a mortgage has been fully satisfied, the mortgagee, the servicing agent, or any holder of the note shall, within thirty days of receipt of written demand by the person providing full satisfaction, produce the satisfied promissory note or an instrument of release in a form sufficient to bring about the cancellation of the inscription of the recorded mortgage to the person providing full satisfaction. However, if the note is held by a federal agency or instrumentality, or a federally sponsored or supported lender, or any nonoriginating secondary mortgage market lender domiciled outside the state of Louisiana, the holder of the note shall, within sixty days after receipt of notice of the satisfaction from the servicing agent, produce the satisfied promissory note or an instrument of release to the servicing agent.

B. If the mortgagee, the servicing agent, or any holder of the note fails to produce the satisfied promissory note or an instrument of release in a form sufficient to bring about cancellation of the mortgage within thirty days after receipt of written demand by the person providing full payment of the balance of the note, the mortgagee and the servicing agent or the mortgagee and any holder of the note shall be liable in solido to the person providing full satisfaction for all damages and costs resulting therefrom, including reasonable attorney fees. However, if the note is held by a federal agency or instrumentality, or a federally sponsored or supported lender, or any nonoriginating secondary mortgage market lender domiciled outside the state of Louisiana, the servicing agency shall, within thirty days of receipt of the satisfied promissory note or an instrument of release from the holder of the note, produce the note or instrument to the person providing full satisfaction.

C. For purposes of this Section, "person" shall include the mortgagor acting in his own behalf, or a notary public or any person, firm, or corporation acting in place of or on behalf of the mortgagor.

Added by Acts 1986, No. 974, § 1. Amended by Acts 1987, No. 705, § 1; Acts 1992, No. 647, § 1; Acts 1995, No. 1087, § 3.

§ 5386. Mortgage including collateral assignment and pledge of certain incorporeal rights

A. A mortgage of immovable property may provide for the collateral assignment or pledge of the right to receive proceeds attributable to the insurance loss of the mortgaged property. Such collateral assignment or pledge shall have effect, other than between the immediate parties, or those on whose behalf or for whose benefit they act, and shall be deemed perfected by the proper recordation of the mortgage in the mortgage records of the parish in which the immovable is situated.

B. The rights of the mortgagee against the insurer shall be subject to any dealing by the insurer with the mortgagor, any other assignee or pledgee, or other successor in interest of the mortgagor until the insurer receives written notice from or on behalf of the mortgagee or the mortgagor of the collateral assignment or pledge of the right to receive the insurance proceeds. In any case in which an insurer is not notified in writing of the assignment or pledge of the right to receive insurance proceeds made in compliance with the provisions of this Section and, in good faith, makes payment of the insurance proceeds attributable to the loss of the mortgaged property in whole or in part to the mortgagor, any other assignee or pledgee, or other successor in interest of the mortgagor, then, to the extent of payment, the insurer shall be exonerated of liability to make payment to the mortgagee; however, the person to whom payment was made shall be accountable and liable to the mortgagee for the sums received. Nothing contained in this Section shall be construed to modify the obligations of any insurer under any simple or standard or other loss payee clause of its insurance policy or endorsement.

C. A mortgage shall not be deemed to be invalid, ineffective or fraudulent against other creditors by reason of the mortgagor's freedom to use, commingle or dispose of proceeds from the insurance loss of the mortgaged property, or by reason of the mortgagee's failure to require the mortgagor to account therefor.

Added by Acts 1988, No. 985, § 1. Amended by Acts 1989, No. 137, § 5, eff. Sept. 1, 1989; Acts 1990, No. 1079, § 3, eff. Sept. 1, 1990 at 12:01 A.M.

Editor's note. Section 2 of Acts 1988, No. 985 provides: "The provisions of this Act are hereby declared to be remedial and shall, wherever possible, be given retroactive effect. Nothing under this Act shall be construed to affect the effectiveness, validity, and enforceability of existing mortgages and chattel mortgages or to call existing mortgage practices into question or to affect the effectiveness or recording of mortgages, whether on movable or immovable property, or pledges or other forms of security under R.S. 12:701 and 702. With the exception of R.S. 9:5387(B) and 5390(C), the provisions of this Act merely confirm and codify established customs and practices and therefore shall apply to existing mortgages and chattel mortgages."

For § 20 of Acts 1989, No. 137, stating legislative intent, see note preceding R.S. 9:5101.

Acts 1990, No. 1079, § 10, declares that the provisions of Section 3 of this act, which amend R.S. 9:5386, "shall not impair or invalidate any collateral assignment or pledge of incorporeal rights provided in mortgage agreements entered into prior to the effective date of this Act."

Cross References

C.C. arts. 463, 466 to 475, 483 to 489, 490 to 497, 504, 508, 517 to 519, 526, 550, 559, 563, 743, 1913, 2367.2, 2461, 2645, 3133, 3154, 3280, 3287, 3292, 3298, 3307, 3319.

§ 5387. Repealed by Acts 1990, No. 1079, § 8, eff. Sept. 1, 1990 at 12:01 a.m.

§ 5388. Authority to carry out and enforce rights

A mortgage or security agreement may contain provisions granting the mortgagee or secured party and its agents the power to carry out and enforce all or any specified portion of the incorporeal rights collaterally assigned or pledged by the mortgagor or on which the mortgagor/debtor has granted a security interest under Chapter 9 of the Louisiana Commercial Laws (R.S. 10:9–101, et seq.). The grant of authority may be phrased in the form of a mandate or power of attorney, coupled with an interest or otherwise. The grant of authority may not be revoked by the mortgagor or debtor so long as the mortgage or security interest remains in effect.

Added by Acts 1988, No. 985, § 1. Amended by Acts 1989, No. 137, § 5, eff. Sept. 1, 1989.

Editor's note. For the remedial and retroactive effect of Acts 1988, No. 985: See Editor's note under R.S. 9:5386.

For § 20 of Acts 1989, No. 137, stating legislative intent, see note preceding R.S. 9:5101.

Cross References

C.C. arts. 463, 466 to 475, 483 to 489, 490 to 497, 504, 508, 517 to 519, 526, 550, 559, 563, 743, 1913, 2367.2, 2461, 2645, 3133, 3154, 3280, 3287, 3292, 3298, 3307, 3319.

§ 5389. Additional funds advanced under mortgage or security agreement

A. A mortgage or security interest shall secure additional funds that may be advanced by the mortgagee or secured party for the protection, preservation, repair, or recovery of the mortgaged or encumbered property, or the protection and preservation of the mortgagee's mortgage or secured party's security interest thereunder. A mortgage or security agreement may provide that the mortgagee or secured party may, at its sole election, purchase insurance or pay taxes on the mortgaged or encumbered property should the mortgagor or debtor fail to comply with its contractual obligations to do so.

B. Unless the mortgage or security agreement provides otherwise, all additional sums advanced by the mortgagee or secured party under the provisions of Subsection A are deemed to bear interest at the rate provided under the mortgage note or other secured indebtedness from the date of each such advance until repaid in full by the mortgagor or debtor.

C. Unless the mortgage or security agreement provides otherwise, the mortgage or security interest is deemed without further action to secure additional funds advanced by the mortgagee or secured party under the provisions of Subsection A, together with interest thereon.

Added by Acts 1988, No. 985, § 1. Amended by Acts 1989, No. 137, § 5, eff. Sept. 1, 1989; Acts 1991, No. 377, § 3, eff. Jan. 1, 1992.

Editor's note. For the remedial and retroactive effect of Acts 1988, No. 985: See Editor's note under R.S. 9:5386.

For § 20 of Acts 1989, No. 137, stating legislative intent, see note preceding R.S. 9:5101.

Cross References

C.C. arts. 463, 466 to 475, 483 to 489, 490 to 497, 504, 508, 517 to 519, 526, 550, 559, 563, 743, 1913, 2367.2, 2461, 2645, 3133, 3154, 3280, 3286, 3287, 3292, 3298, 3307, 3319.

§ 5390. Amendment, renewal, or refinancing of mortgage and mortgage note

A. The effectiveness, validity, enforceability, and priority of a conventional mortgage, conventional chattel mortgage, or security agreement are not adversely affected by a change in the terms of the note or notes secured thereby, including but not limited to such changes as an extension of the maturity of the note or notes, an increase or decrease of the interest rate stipulated in the note or notes, or the agreement that the unpaid accrued interest of the note or notes would be converted to principal and thereafter bear interest. It shall not be necessary to amend the mortgage or security agreement to reflect such changes in the terms of the note or notes secured thereby in order to foreclose thereunder through executory process or otherwise. However, if the mortgage or security agreement is amended to reflect such changes, the effectiveness, validity, enforceability, and priority thereof shall not be adversely affected.

B. When the mortgage so provides, a conventional mortgage or conventional chattel mortgage automatically secures payment of a renewal or refinancing note or notes delivered in substitution for the note or notes then secured by the mortgage even though the renewal or refinancing note or notes reflect a change in the terms of such note or notes, including but not limited to such changes as an extension of the maturity of the note or notes, an increase or decrease of the interest rate stipulated in such note or notes, or the fact that the unpaid accrued interest under the note or notes has been converted to principal and will thereafter bear interest, and the effectiveness, validity, enforceability, and priority of the mortgage shall not be affected by the delivery of such renewal or refinancing note or notes. To the extent that the renewal or refinancing note or notes evidence an increase in the secured principal indebtedness (other than the increase that results from the conversion of unpaid accrued interest to principal), the mortgage with respect to the increase in the secured principal indebtedness shall rank from the date of the filing of an amendment to the mortgage reflecting the execution and delivery of such renewal or refinancing note or notes.

Added by Acts 1988, No. 985, § 1. Amended by Acts 1989, No. 137, § 6, eff. June 22, 1989; Acts 2001, No. 541, § 1.

Editor's Note. For the remedial and retroactive effect of Acts 1988, No. 985: See Editor's note under R.S. 9:5386.

For § 20 of Acts 1989, No. 137, stating legislative intent, see note preceding R.S. 9:5101.

Cross References

C.C. arts. 463, 466 to 475, 483 to 489, 490 to 497, 504, 508, 517 to 519, 526, 550, 559, 563, 743, 1913, 2367.2, 2461, 2645, 3133, 3154, 3280, 3287, 3292, 3298, 3307, 3319.

§ 5391. Additions, accessions, and natural increases subject to mortgage

A mortgage of immovable property without further action attaches to present and future component parts thereof and accessions thereto, without further description and without the necessity of subsequently amending the mortgage agreement.

Added by Acts 1988, No. 985, § 1. Amended by Acts 1989, No. 137, § 7, eff. Sept. 1, 1989; Acts 1990, No. 1079, § 3, eff. Sept. 1, 1990 at 12:01 A.M.

Editor's note. For the remedial and retroactive effect of Acts 1988, No. 985: See Editor's note under R.S. 9:5386.

For § 20 of Acts 1989, No. 137, stating legislative intent, see note preceding R.S. 9:5101.

Cross References

C.C. arts. 463, 466 to 475, 483 to 489, 490 to 497, 504, 508, 517 to 519, 526, 550, 559, 563, 743, 1913, 2367.2, 2461, 2645, 3133, 3154, 3280, 3287, 3292, 3298, 3307, 3319.

§ 5392. Continuation of mortgage after judgment

A mortgage shall continue when the mortgagee has reduced to judgment any obligation thereby secured, and shall secure such judgment without interruption, whether it expressly recognizes the mortgage, except to the extent that the judgment expressly provides to the contrary.

Added by Acts 1988, No. 985, § 1. Amended by Acts 1991, No. 377, § 3, eff. Jan. 1, 1992.

Editor's note. Remedial and retroactive effect of Acts 1988, No. 985: See Editor's note under R.S. 9:5386.

Cross References

C.C. arts. 463, 466 to 475, 483 to 489, 490 to 497, 504, 508, 517 to 519, 526, 550, 559, 563, 743, 1913, 2367.2, 2461, 2645, 3133, 3154, 3280, 3287, 3292, 3298, 3307, 3319.

§ 5393. Combination forms

A. A mortgage note and mortgage or a promissory note and security agreement under Chapter 9 of the Louisiana Commercial Laws (R.S. 10:9–101, et seq.) may be combined under a single form, with the maker/mortgagor or debtor signing in one location on the face of the form, agreeing to the note and mortgage or security agreement covenants on the face and reverse sides thereof.

B. When one form combines the mortgage and mortgage note under the provisions of Subsection A, it is not necessary to paraph the mortgage note "Ne Varietur" for identification with the mortgage.

C. The combining of the mortgage note and mortgage or the note and security agreement under one form, with only one combined signature by the maker/mortgagor/debtor, has no effect on the validity or enforceability of the note or the mortgage or security agreement, or on the mortgagee's or secured party's rights to foreclose under the mortgage or security agreement by means of executory process.

Added by Acts 1988, No. 985, § 1. Amended by Acts 1989, No. 137, § 7, eff. Sept. 1, 1989.

Editor's note. For the remedial and retroactive effect of Acts 1988, No. 985: See Editor's note under R.S. 9:5386.

For § 20 of Acts 1989, No. 137, stating legislative intent, see note preceding R.S. 9:5101.

Cross References

C.C. arts. 463, 466 to 475, 483 to 489, 490 to 497, 504, 508, 517 to 519, 526, 550, 559, 563, 743, 1913, 2367.2, 2461, 2645, 3133, 3154, 3280, 3287, 3292, 3298, 3307, 3319.

§ 5394. Applicability

To the extent not otherwise governed under Chapter 9 of the Louisiana Commercial Laws (R.S. 10:9–101, et seq.), R.S. 9:5386 through R.S. 9:5393 shall apply to all mortgages and security interests, including collateral mortgages, chattel mortgages, and collateral chattel mortgages, and further including without limitation, blanket equipment collateral chattel mortgages previously subject to R.S. 9:5367, et seq., Louisiana ship mortgages subject to R.S. 9:5521, et seq., and motor vehicle chattel mortgages and floor plan collateral chattel mortgages subject to R.S. 32:710. The provisions of R.S. 9:5388 also apply to other types of security agreements, including pledge agreements and collateral assignments.

Added by Acts 1988, No. 985, § 1. Amended by Acts 1989, No. 137, § 7, eff. Sept. 1, 1989.

Editor's note. For the remedial and retroactive effect of Acts 1988, No. 985: See Editor's note under R.S. 9:5386.

For § 20 of Acts 1989, No. 137, stating legislative intent, see note preceding R.S. 9:5101.

Cross References

C.C. arts. 463, 466 to 475, 483 to 489, 490 to 497, 504, 508, 517 to 519, 526, 550, 559, 563, 743, 1913, 2367.2, 2461, 2645, 3133, 3154, 3280, 3287, 3292, 3298, 3307, 3319.

§ 5395. Protection of mortgage lenders and fiduciaries from state environmental liability; parity with federal law

It is the intent of the legislature that financial institutions, fiduciaries, and other secured lenders shall have no greater exposure to environmental liability and financial responsibility under state law than they would under federal law, in any way arising from or associated with property on which they hold any mortgage, lien, or privilege, or in which they may have any security interest, or which they hold or administer in a fiduciary capacity. Therefore, notwithstanding any other law to the contrary, to the extent that financial institutions and other secured lenders may be exempt, excluded, made immune, or otherwise protected from liability or financial responsibility under federal law or regulation for environmental conditions or events with respect to property on or in which they may have any mortgage, lien, privilege, or security interest, or other similar interest, or which they hold or administer in a fiduciary capacity, or with respect to borrowers to whom they may extend credit or who may be otherwise indebted or obligated to them, financial institutions and other secured lenders shall be entitled to the same exemptions, exclusions, immunities, and protections from environmentally related liability and financial responsibility under the laws of this state.

Added by Acts 1995, No. 1087, § 3. Amended by Acts 1997, No. 1295, § 1.

§ 5396. Maintenance of abandoned mortgaged property

A. If a mortgagee or loan servicer receives a notice from a governing authority in accordance with R.S. 33:5062 or R.S. 33:5065 et seq., identifying certain maintenance required on the mortgaged property, the mortgagee and loan servicer shall have the right to directly or through third parties enter onto the property to perform maintenance.

B. If any abandoned residential property, as defined by R.S. 33:5066, affected by a mortgage is unoccupied or abandoned, the mortgagee and loan servicer shall each have the legal right, directly or through third parties, to enter onto the property and to perform maintenance to protect and preserve the property until it can be sold at private sale or sheriff's sale.

C. The mortgagee, loan servicer, and any third parties hired by them to perform maintenance on the property, as defined by R.S. 33:5066, shall not be liable to the mortgagor or the owner of the seized property or any other person for any financial or pecuniary loss or damage claimed to have been suffered by the mortgagor or owner of the property or any other person by reason of the maintenance of the property.

D. Any costs and expenses incurred by the mortgagee or loan servicer for maintaining the property may be added to any loan balance secured by the mortgage and recoverable from proceeds received from a sale of the property.

Added by Acts 2012, No. 692, § 1, eff. Oct. 1, 2012.

CHAPTER 3. LEGAL MORTGAGES

PART I. IN GENERAL

Section
5501. Affidavit of distinction; acknowledgment; contents; damages.
5501.1. Sworn affidavit; form.
5502. Repealed.
5503. Affidavit of identity; content; effect; penalty for falsifying.
5504. Privileges and liens in favor of state, parish, or municipal bodies.

PART I. IN GENERAL

§ 5501. Affidavit of distinction; acknowledgment; contents; damages

A. (1) An owner of immovable property with a name similar to that of a debtor against whom a judgment has been obtained and recorded may execute an affidavit of distinction before a notary public or before any authorized employee of the clerk of court's office on a form provided by the clerk of court to clarify that he is not the same person as named in the judgment. The affidavit shall be duly recorded and thereafter the judgment shall not affect title to any property the person may own or acquire.

(2) The notary public or clerk of court or any employee of the clerk shall be immune from civil or criminal liability as a result of providing the affidavit, assisting in the completion of the affidavit, or recording of the affidavit form as prescribed in R.S. 9:5501.1.

B. The judgment creditor shall sign the acknowledgment in the affidavit of distinction as provided in R.S. 9:5501.1 within ten days after the date of receipt of the affidavit, after ascertaining that the affiant is not the debtor named in the judgment. The judgment creditor shall be liable for any damages, attorney fees, and expenses arising out of his failure to sign the acknowledgment without good cause. The affiant shall be liable for any damages, attorney fees, and expenses occasioned by a fraudulently executed affidavit of distinction.

C. The procedure established in this Section for executing an affidavit of distinction shall not be the exclusive means of clarifying that an owner of immovable property with a name similar to that of a judgment debtor is not the same person as such judgment debtor.

Added by Acts 1985, No. 839, § 1. Amended by Acts 1997, No. 1200, § 1.

Editor's note. A prior R.S. 9:5501 was repealed by Acts 1960, No. 31, § 7, effective January 1, 1961.

§ 5501.1. Sworn affidavit; form

A. Notwithstanding the provisions of R.S. 13:841 et seq. the clerks of the several district courts shall provide to any person who makes a request the following affidavit and acknowledgment form and shall notarize and record the affidavit subject to a fee to be established by the clerk or the recorder of mortgages.

B. The affidavit and the acknowledgment concerning the distinction or identity of a person shall comply with the requirements of R.S. 9:5501 and 5503 if it provides all the information required or set forth in the following form:

STATE OF LOUISIANA PARISH OF _____

AFFIDAVIT

Before me, the undersigned authority _____, personally came and appeared:

_____(Affiant)_____, (marital status and mailing address), who after being duly sworn, deposed as follows:

I, _____(Affiant)_____, being of sound mind acknowledge and understand that any intentional falsification of information I am about to provide shall subject me to penalties for the crime of injuring public records and false swearing.

My full name is _____. I am ____ years old and I was born on _____(Month) (Day) (Year)_____ at _(City, Parish/County and State of Birth)_. My social security number is _____. I presently reside at _____ and my previous addresses for the preceding 10 years were _____, _____. Name and address of my employer _____; Name and address of location of employment _____; Occupation _____; Marital status _____, If married full name of spouse _(Maiden name if applicable)_; spouse's social security number _____.

I HEREBY AFFIRM AND ATTEST, under penalty of law, that I am not the same person as the debtor or debtors named in the following described recorded judgments, liens, privileges, or mortgages:

(1) (Identification of recorded judgments, liens, privileges, or mortgages.)

I HEREBY FURTHER AFFIRM AND ATTEST, that on the ____ day of _____, _____, I mailed a copy of the affidavit to each judgment creditor listed in the affidavit at his last known address by registered mail and hereby submit proof of said certified mailing.

I HEREBY FURTHER AFFIRM AND ATTEST, that the Judgment Creditor has failed to comply with R.S. 9:5501 and I hereby execute this affidavit of identity to establish that I am not the same person identified as the debtor in the said recorded judgments, liens, privileges, mortgages or other such documents itemized above.

Thus done, read and signed at _____, State of Louisiana, this ____ day of _____.

WITNESSES:
_____
_____ Affiant

_____
Notary Public
Acknowledgment

I,(we), _____(Name of Judgment Creditor)_____ hereby acknowledge that the above named affiant is not the same person identified or named in the above identified or described (judgment, lien, privilege, or mortgage) and that the property of the affiant is not subject to the judicial mortgage resulting from the judgment.

Thus done, read and signed at _____, State of Louisiana, this day of the month of____, ____.

Judgment Creditor

_____
Notary Public

Added by Acts 1997, No. 1200, § 1.

§ 5502. Repealed by Acts 2005, No. 169, § 8, eff. July 1, 2006

§ 5503. Affidavit of identity; content; effect; penalty for falsifying

A. If the judgment creditor cannot be located or does not comply with R.S. 9:5501, any person may execute before a notary public or any authorized employee of the clerk's office on a form provided by the clerk of court and file for record in the office of clerk of court or the office of the recorder of mortgages an affidavit of identity as set forth in R.S. 9:5501.1 to establish that he is not the same person identified as the debtor in one or more recorded judgments, liens, privileges, mortgages, or other such documents.

B. The affiant shall mail a copy of the affidavit to each judgment creditor listed in the affidavit at his last known address by registered mail. The clerk of court or recorder of mortgages shall not record the affidavit unless the affiant can show proof of mailing.

C. The intentional falsification of information by the affiant in an affidavit of identity filed in the office of a recorder of mortgages constitutes the crime of injuring public records. The affiant shall also be liable for any damages, attorney fees, and expenses occasioned by a fraudulently executed affidavit of identity.

D. The procedure established in this Section for executing the affidavit of identity shall not be the exclusive means of clarifying that an individual with a name similar to that of a judgment debtor is not the same person as such judgment debtor.

E. The clerk of court or recorder of mortgages may not charge more than eighteen dollars to prepare and record the first page of the affidavit filed by a single affiant including the acknowledgment returned by those judgment creditors designated by the affiant, executed pursuant to R.S. 9:5501 or this Section, plus six dollars for each subsequent page, and three dollars for each name after the first name that is required to be indexed.

Added by Acts 1991, No. 559, § 1. Amended by Acts 1997, No. 1200, § 1.

§ 5504. Privileges and liens in favor of state, parish, or municipal bodies

Liens and privileges against property granted in favor of parishes or municipalities for assessments for public improvements or for reasonable charges imposed on property pursuant to the provisions of R.S. 33:1236, 4752, 4753, 4754, 4766, 5062, or 5062.1, or R.S. 13:2575 are not effective against third parties until filed in the mortgage records. If the liens or privileges are placed on the ad valorem property tax bill, the sheriff shall remove them upon request of an interested party whose interest in the property was acquired prior to the recording of the lien in the mortgage records.

Added by Acts 2010, No. 279, § 1.

APPENDIX 1—REVISED STATUTES, TITLE 9

CHAPTER 4. SHIP MORTGAGE LAW

Section
5521. Short title.
5522. Definitions.
5523. Identifying numbers.
5524. Title to work; materials and components.
5525. Mortgage of ships; materials and components.
5526. Mortgage to be in writing; description and content.
5527. Authentication; filing; fee.
5528. Effect of filing; rights and privileges retained.
5529. Ship mortgage book; form.
5530. Cancellation; reinscription; fee.
5531. Failure to affix hull number; removal of hull number; penalty.
5532. Mortgaging with fraudulent intent; penalty.
5533. Disposal of mortgaged ship with fraudulent intent; penalty.
5534. Acceleration of maturity date, grounds for.
5535. Fraudulent release of mortgage; penalty.
5536. Remedies of creditors.
5537. Ship mortgage certificates; fee.
5538. Relation to Chapter 9 of the Louisiana Commercial Laws.

§ 5521. Short title

This Chapter shall be known and may be cited as the Ship Mortgage Law.

Added by Acts 1975, No. 368, § 1.

Cross References

C.C. arts. 3133, 3134, 3158, 3286, 3287.
R.S. 9:5386 to 9:5394.

§ 5522. Definitions

In this Chapter unless the context otherwise requires:

(a) "Contract" means a written agreement for the construction of a ship.

(b) "Ship" means a tug, pushboat, pullboat, barge, dredge, or other vessel or watercraft of more than fifty tons gross weight to be constructed within the state of Louisiana.

(c) "Work" means in the case of a ship having a keel, the keel, and in the case of a ship not having a keel, the bottom plates, and all materials, machinery, equipment, components, and fabrications forming a part of the ship when permanently installed in place.

(d) "Builder" means the person undertaking or contracting to build a ship pursuant to a contract or otherwise.

(e) "Purchaser" means the person for whom a ship is to be constructed pursuant to a contract.

(f) "Person" includes an individual, corporation, trust, partnership, joint venture, or other organization.

(g) "Materials" means all materials (other than piping, cables, fittings, and other materials taken out of builder's stock), all items of machinery, and all items of equipment (other than equipment taken out of builder's stock) which are purchased or acquired for use in the construction of the ship, which will, when so used, form a part of the ship and which have been delivered to the shipyard.

(h) "Components" means all parts and components of a ship which are fabricated by the builder for use in the construction of the ship, which will, when so used, form a part of the ship and the fabrication of which is commenced at the shipyard.

(i) "Hull Number" means the number assigned to a ship by the builder.

(j) "Shipyard" means the shipyard or place of business where a ship is to be constructed.

Added by Acts 1975, No. 368, § 1. Amended by Acts 1976, No. 374, § 1.

Cross References

C.C. arts. 3133, 3134, 3158, 3286, 3287.

§ 5523. Identifying numbers

A. Every builder shall assign a hull number to each ship to be constructed by such builder.

B. The builder shall affix a plaque showing the name of the builder, the hull number, and the parish in which the ship is to be constructed, to the keel of the ship, if the ship has a keel, or to the bottom plates, if the ship does not have a keel, when laid, so as to be clearly visible at all times during the performance of the work and until the decking is laid. At such time as the decking is laid, the aforementioned plaque shall be removed and permanently affixed to the weather deck so as to be clearly visible at all times during continuance of the work and after completion.

C. The builder shall mark or stamp on all materials, title to which is in the purchaser, and all materials, title to which is in the builder and on which the builder has granted a mortgage pursuant to this Chapter, the hull number of the ship of which such materials will form a part, upon the delivery of such materials to the shipyard, or alternatively, maintain records which will identify with certainty all such materials with the hull number of the ship under construction.

D. The builder shall mark or stamp on all components, title to which is in the purchaser, and all components, title to which is in the builder and on which the builder has granted a mortgage pursuant to this Chapter, the hull number of the ship of which such components will form a part, upon commencement of the fabrication thereof, or alternatively, maintain records which will identify with certainty all such components with the hull number of the ship under construction.

E. Each contract shall state the hull number of the ship to be constructed pursuant to the contract.

Added by Acts 1975, No. 368, § 1. Amended by Acts 1976, No. 374, § 2.

Cross References

C.C. arts. 3133, 3134, 3158, 3286, 3287.

§ 5524. Title to work; materials and components

A. Whenever a contract provides that the purchaser shall be the owner of the ship to be constructed pursuant to the contract and title to the work shall vest in the purchaser as and when performed, the work shall be deemed to have been delivered to, and title to the work shall be vested in, the purchaser as and when performed, and title to the ship shall be vested in the purchaser upon completion thereof.

B. If the contract provides that the purchaser shall be the owner of the ship to be constructed pursuant to the contract and title to the work shall vest in the purchaser as and when performed, and provides that title to the materials shall vest in the purchaser as and when delivered to the shipyard, the materials shall be deemed to have been delivered to the purchaser and title thereto shall vest in the purchaser as and when delivered to the shipyard.

C. If the contract provides that the purchaser shall be the owner of the ship to be constructed pursuant to the contract and title to the work shall vest in the purchaser as and when performed, and provides that title to the components shall vest in the purchaser as and when fabricated, the components shall be deemed to have been delivered to the purchaser and title thereto shall vest in the purchaser as and when fabricated.

D. No other person shall acquire any rights in the work, materials, components, or completed ship, title to which is vested in the purchaser, by purchase from the builder and no such work, materials, components, or ship shall be liable to seizure and attachment in behalf of the creditors of the builder, but nothing contained in this Chapter shall affect any rights or privileges granted by law to sellers, laborers, and suppliers of materials in the construction of the ship or to the builder.

E. If a contract does not provide that the purchaser shall be the owner of the ship to be constructed pursuant to the contract or if there is no contract for the construction of the ship, the purchaser shall not acquire any title to the work or any materials or components or the completed ship prior to the completion of the ship and the delivery thereof to the purchaser, notwithstanding any agreement or arrangement to the contrary.

Added by Acts 1975, No. 368, § 1.

Cross References

C.C. arts. 3133, 3134, 3158, 3286, 3287.

§ 5525. Mortgage of ships; materials and components

A. Whenever a contract provides that the purchaser shall be the owner of the ship to be constructed pursuant to the contract and title to the work shall vest in the purchaser as and when performed, it shall be lawful for the purchaser, by complying with the provisions of this Chapter, to mortgage, and after Chapter 9 of the Louisiana Commercial Laws (R.S. 10:9-101, et seq.) becomes effective, to grant a security interest on the ship, either before construction thereof has commenced or during the construction thereof, to secure the performance of any obligation, including future advances, and such mortgage or security interest under Chapter 9 of the Louisiana Commercial Laws shall attach to the work, and to any and all materials and components title to which is vested in the purchaser, as and when the title thereto vests in the purchaser, and to the ship upon completion.

B. If a contract does not provide that the purchaser shall be the owner of the ship to be constructed pursuant to the contract and title to the work shall vest in the purchaser as and when performed, or if there is no contract for the construction of the ship, it shall be lawful for the builder, by complying with the provisions of this Chapter, to mortgage, and after the time Chapter 9 of the Louisiana Commercial Laws becomes effective, to grant a security interest on the ship, either before the construction thereof has commenced or during the construction thereof, to secure the performance of any obligation, including future advances, and such mortgage or security interest under Chapter 9 of the Louisiana Commercial Laws shall attach to the work as and when performed, the materials as and when delivered to the shipyard and the components as and when fabricated, and to the ship upon completion. However, the mortgage or security interest shall not attach to any materials or components expressly excluded from the mortgage or security agreement.

Added by Acts 1975, No. 368, § 1. Amended by Acts 1989, No. 137, § 7, eff. Sept. 1, 1989.

Editor's note. For § 20 of Acts 1989, No. 137, stating legislative intent, see note preceding R.S. 9:5101.

Cross References

C.C. arts. 3133, 3134, 3158, 3286, 3287.

§ 5526. Mortgage to be in writing; description and content

Every mortgage of a ship subject to this Chapter entered into prior to the time Chapter 9 of the Louisiana Commercial Laws becomes effective shall be in writing and shall state the hull number of the mortgaged ship, and the location of the shipyard at which the mortgaged ship will be or is being constructed. The obligation secured by the mortgage shall be described, the exact sum secured thereby shall be stated or, if the same is to secure future advances, then the maximum amount thereof shall be stated, and there shall also be stated whether the sum is payable on demand or at which fixed or determinable future time. Every security agreement affecting a ship subject to this Chapter entered into after Chapter 9 of the Louisiana Commercial Laws becomes effective shall comply with the requirements otherwise applicable under Chapter 9.

Added by Acts 1975, No. 368, § 1. Amended by Acts 1989, No. 137, § 7, eff. Sept. 1, 1989.

Editor's note. For § 20 of Acts 1989, No. 137, stating legislative intent, see note preceding R.S. 9:5101.

Cross References

C.C. arts. 3133, 3134, 3158, 3286, 3287.

§ 5527. Authentication; filing; fee

In order to affect third persons, every mortgage of a ship subject to this Chapter entered into prior to the time Chapter 9 of the Louisiana Commercial Laws becomes effective shall be by authentic act, or by private act, duly authenticated in any manner provided by law. A multiple original of every such act of mortgage shall be filed in the office of the recorder of mortgages of the parish where the mortgaged ship is to be constructed according to the terms of the mortgage instrument and also in the office of the recorder of mortgages for the parish of the mortgagor's domicile, if the mortgagor is domiciled in the state. If the mortgagor is not domiciled in the state, filing in the office of the recorder of mortgages of the parish where the ship is to be constructed according to the terms of the mortgage instrument will be sufficient. Upon receipt of the instrument the recorders of mortgages shall note thereon the date, hour, and minute of receiving it and shall record it in their respective offices. The recorder of mortgages immediately shall cause to be endorsed on the instrument his certificate of recordation. For these services each recorder of mortgages shall receive two dollars. Every security interest affecting a ship subject to this Chapter entered into after Chapter 9 of the Louisiana Commercial Laws (R.S. 10:9-101, et seq.) becomes effective shall be created and perfected in the manner provided under Chapter 9.

Added by Acts 1975, No. 368, § 1. Amended by Acts 1989, No. 137, § 7, eff. Sept. 1, 1989.

Editor's note. For § 20 of Acts 1989, No. 137, stating legislative intent, see note preceding R.S. 9:5101.

Cross References

C.C. arts. 3133, 3134, 3158, 3286, 3287.

§ 5528. Effect of filing; rights and privileges retained

Every mortgage of a ship shall be effective as against third persons from the time of filing in the proper offices, and the filing shall be notice to all parties of the existence of the mortgage, which shall be superior in rank to any privilege or preference arising subsequent thereto, but nothing contained in this Chapter shall affect any rights or privileges granted by law to sellers, laborers, and suppliers of materials in the construction of the ship or to the builder.

Added by Acts 1975, No. 368, § 1.

Cross References

C.C. arts. 3133, 3134, 3158, 3286, 3287.

§ 5529. Ship mortgage book; form

For the purposes of this Chapter, it shall be sufficient for the recorders of mortgages each to keep a book to be known as the ship mortgage book, which shall be ruled off into columns, with the headings as follows:

Time of filing for Recordation; Name of Mortgagor; Name of Mortgagee; Date of Instrument; Amount secured; When Due; Hull number of Ship mortgaged; Builder; Remarks.

Added by Acts 1975, No. 368, § 1.

Cross References

C.C. arts. 3133, 3134, 3158, 3286, 3287.

§ 5530. Cancellation; reinscription; fee

A. When any mortgage of a ship under this Chapter shall have been fully paid or satisfied the mortgage may be cancelled in any manner provided by law for the cancellation of mortgages on immovable property. The effect of a mortgage of a ship shall cease if the inscription thereof has not been renewed in the same manner in which it was first made by the recorder of mortgages within one year after the date of the last installment provided for in such mortgage or within five years after the date of execution of the act of mortgage, whichever is later. Reinscription shall renew the effect of the mortgage for the amount unpaid for a period of two years from the date of the reinscription and further renewals may be made thereafter from time to time, the effect of each new reinscription being for two years from its date. The recorder of mortgages shall each receive one dollar for each cancellation and two dollars for each reinscription of a mortgage under this Chapter.

B. Recorders of mortgages may destroy the records of mortgages of ships in their respective offices two years after the date of the last installment provided for in such mortgage or six years after the date of execution of the act of mortgage, whichever is later, unless they have been reinscribed in the form and manner herein provided.

Added by Acts 1975, No. 368, § 1.

Cross References

C.C. arts. 3133, 3134, 3158, 3286, 3287.

§ 5531. Failure to affix hull number; removal of hull number; penalty

If the builder shall fail to affix a plaque or to mark or stamp any materials or components, or fail to maintain records as an alternative to marking or stamping any materials or components, as provided in R.S. 9:5523, or if any person removes, other than for the purpose of repair of the ship, obliterates or defaces, or having removed for the purpose of repair of the ship fails to promptly replace a plaque affixed as provided in R.S. 9:5523, or if any person removes, obliterates or defaces the hull number marked or stamped on any materials or components as provided in R.S. 9:5523, prior to the time such materials are incorporated into the work or the components or the components are incorporated into the work, as the case may be, he shall be fined not more than five hundred dollars, or imprisoned for not more than six months, or both.

Added by Acts 1975, No. 368, § 1. Amended by Acts 1976, No. 374, § 3.

Cross References

C.C. arts. 3133, 3134, 3158, 3286, 3287.

§ 5532. Mortgaging with fraudulent intent; penalty

If any person shall fraudulently give or attempt to give a mortgage or a security interest under Chapter 9 of the Louisiana Commercial Laws on a ship subject to this Chapter without being the owner thereof or without having the proper authority to represent the owner thereof or if any person shall fraudulently give a mortgage or security interest on a ship subject to this Chapter without fully disclosing in writing or causing to be written into the act of mortgage the description and the amount, if known, of any existing liens, privileges, or encumbrances on the ship mortgaged, he shall be fined not more than five hundred dollars, or imprisoned for not more than six months, or both.

Added by Acts 1975, No. 368, § 1. Amended by Acts 1989, No. 137, § 7, eff. Sept. 1, 1989.

Editor's note. For § 20 of Acts 1989, No. 137, stating legislative intent, see note preceding R.S. 9:5101.

Cross References

C.C. arts. 3133, 3134, 3158, 3286, 3287.

§ 5533. Disposal of mortgaged ship with fraudulent intent; penalty

Any person who, having executed a mortgage or security agreement under Chapter 9 of the Louisiana Commercial Laws on a ship subject to this Chapter, sells, assigns, exchanges, injures, destroys, conceals, or otherwise disposes of the work or the completed ship with fraudulent intent to defeat the mortgage or security interest, or removes the work or the completed ship from the location designated in the act of mortgage or security agreement at which the ship is to be constructed without the written consent of the mortgagee or secured party and with fraudulent intent to defeat the mortgage or security interest, shall be fined not more than five hundred dollars, or imprisoned for not more than six months, or both.

Added by Acts 1975, No. 368, § 1. Amended by Acts 1989, No. 137, § 7, eff. Sept. 1, 1989.

Editor's note. For § 20 of Acts 1989, No. 137, stating legislative intent, see note preceding R.S. 9:5101.

Cross References
C.C. arts. 3133, 3134, 3158, 3286, 3287.

§ 5534. Acceleration of maturity date, grounds for

The obligation secured by the act of mortgage shall, at the option of the creditor or holder of the mortgage note, forthwith mature and become due and payable and the mortgagee shall be entitled to enforce the collection of the obligation secured by the mortgage immediately and in the manner provided, in any case where the mortgagor shall have committed any of the practices denounced by R.S. 9:5531, R.S. 9:5532, and R.S. 9:5533. These provisions for acceleration of the mortgage debt shall not be construed as excluding the operation of any other statutory provision, or any lawful stipulation between the parties, accelerating the maturity of the obligation secured by the mortgage.

Added by Acts 1975, No. 368, § 1.

Cross References
C.C. arts. 3133, 3134, 3158, 3286, 3287.

§ 5535. Fraudulent release of mortgage; penalty

If any mortgagee named in a mortgage of a ship, and not being at the time the owner and holder of the debt secured, shall fraudulently execute a release or satisfaction of said mortgage, he shall be fined not more than five hundred dollars, or imprisoned for not more than six months, or both.

Added by Acts 1975, No. 368, § 1.

Cross References
C.C. arts. 3133, 3134, 3158, 3286, 3287.

§ 5536. Remedies of creditors

All laws and rules and all remedies and processes now or hereafter made available to creditors for the protection or enforcement of their rights under mortgages affecting immovables shall be available to creditors of obligations secured by mortgages affecting ships; the right of executory process is hereby specifically granted to all creditors on work, materials, and components and completed ships as hereinabove set forth whether their rights shall arise under the terms of authentic act or acts under private signature duly acknowledged.

Added by Acts 1975, No. 368, § 1.

Cross References
C.C. arts. 3133, 3134, 3158, 3286, 3287.

§ 5537. Ship mortgage certificates; fee

When so requested recorders of mortgages shall furnish a certificate in the name or names requested showing all uncancelled mortgages on a ship which operate upon the ship described in the request, and shall receive as a fee therefor the sum of three dollars for the first name and the sum of one dollar for each additional name. Whenever said certificate contains more than one hundred fifty words, he shall charge thirty-five cents for each additional one hundred words or fraction thereof.

Added by Acts 1975, No. 368, § 1.

Cross References
C.C. arts. 3133, 3134, 3158, 3286, 3287.

§ 5538. Relation to Chapter 9 of the Louisiana Commercial Laws

A. This Chapter shall apply to Louisiana ship mortgages that were entered into prior to the time Chapter 9 of the Louisiana Commercial Laws (R.S. 10:9–101, et seq.) became effective, including without limitation those continuing mortgages that affect a property acquired after the effective date and those mortgages that may secure future obligations, lines of credit and other ongoing credit facilities.

B. The provisions of R.S. 9:5522, 5523, 5524, 5525, 5531, 5532, 5533, and 5534 shall continue to apply to the security interests and agreements concerning ships under construction that are entered into under Chapter 9 of the Louisiana Commercial Laws.

Added by Acts 1989, No. 137, § 7, eff. Sept. 1, 1989.

Editor's note. For § 20 of Acts 1989, No. 137, stating legislative intent, see note preceding R.S. 9:5101.

Cross References
C.C. arts. 3133, 3134, 3158, 3286, 3287.

CHAPTER 5. COLLATERAL MORTGAGES AND VENDOR'S PRIVILEGES: EFFECTIVE DATE OF COLLATERAL MORTGAGES, RELATIONSHIP OF COLLATERAL MORTGAGES TO CHAPTER 9 OF THE LOUISIANA COMMERCIAL LAWS AND DEFENSES TO ENFORCEMENT

Section
5550. Definitions.
5551. Effective date of a collateral mortgage.
5552. Defenses to enforcement of a collateral mortgage.
5553. Defenses to enforcement of a vendor's privilege.
5554. No requirement of registry of transfer, assignment, pledge, or security interest in or of the written obligation, collateral mortgage, or vendor's privilege.
5555. Executory process in the case of notes or other obligations not paraphed for identification with the mortgage.
5556. Repealed.
5557. Obligation to grant release of mortgage.
5558 to 5600. Reserved.

§ 5550. Definitions

The following words, phrases, and terms as used in this Part shall be defined and construed as follows:

(1) "Collateral mortgage" shall mean a mortgage that is given to secure a written obligation, such as a collateral mortgage note, negotiable or nonnegotiable instrument, or other written evidence of debt, that is issued, pledged, or otherwise used as security for another obligation. A collateral mortgage or collateral chattel mortgage may provide on its face that the mortgage is granted in favor of a designated mortgagee and any future holder or holders of the collateral mortgage note.

(2) "Vendor's privilege" shall mean a vendor's lien or vendor's privilege on immovable property that secures a written obligation, such as a collateral mortgage note, negotiable or nonnegotiable instrument, or other written evidence of debt.

Added by Acts 1989, No. 137, § 7, eff. Sept. 1, 1989. Amended by Acts 1991, No. 377, § 3, eff. Jan. 1, 1992.

Editor's note. For § 20 of Acts 1989, No. 137, stating legislative intent, see note preceding R.S. 9:5101.

Cross References

C.C. arts. 2792, 3251, 3268, 3269, 3278, 3280, 3282, 3283, 3307.

§ 5551. Effective date of a collateral mortgage

A. A collateral mortgage becomes effective as to third parties, subject to the requirements of registry of the collateral mortgage, when a security interest is perfected in the obligation secured by the collateral mortgage in accordance with the provisions of Chapter 9 of the Louisiana Commercial Laws, R.S. 10:9–101 et seq.

B. A collateral mortgage takes its rank and priority from the time it becomes effective as to third parties. Once it becomes effective, as long as the effects of recordation continues in accordance with Articles 3328 through 3334 of the Civil Code, a collateral mortgage remains effective as to third parties (notwithstanding any intermediate period when the security interest in the secured obligation becomes unperfected) as long as the secured party or his agent or his successor retains possession of the collateral mortgage note or other written obligation, or the obligation secured by the mortgage otherwise remains enforceable according to its terms, by the secured party or his successor.

C. As long as the effects of registry of the collateral mortgage continue, in accordance with Articles 3328 through 3334 of the Civil Code, if there is a termination, remission, or release of possession of the written obligation, a collateral mortgage takes its rank and priority from the time a new security interest is perfected in the written obligation, regardless of whether the secured party is the original secured party, his successor, or a new or different secured party.

D. The provisions of this Section shall become effective on January 1, 1990.

Added by Acts 1989, No. 137, § 7, eff. Sept. 1, 1989; Acts 1989, No. 598, § 1, eff. Sept. 1, 1989. Amended by Acts 1990, No. 1079, § 3, eff. Sept. 1, 1990, at 12:01 A.M.; Acts 1991, No. 377, § 3, eff. Jan. 1, 1992; Acts 1995, No. 1087, § 3; Acts 2001, No. 128, § 4, eff. July 1, 2001 at 12:01 A.M.

Editor's note. Article 3369 of the Louisiana Civil Code of 1870 to which R.S. 9:5551 refers has been repealed by Acts 1992, No. 1132, § 1. For corresponding provision of the 1992 revision, see Civil Code art. 3328, as revised by Acts 1992, No. 1132, § 2.

Acts 2001, No. 128, § 19, effective July 1, 2001, amended R.S. 9:5551. Section 4 of Acts 2001, No. 128, declares that "it is the intent of the legislature in enacting this Act that R.S. 2736, 4501 and 4502, 4521, 4758, 4770, and 5363.1 not be expressly or impliedly repealed by this Act, but that such laws remain in effect, and, at times when so provided, be applied to secured transactions subject to Chapter 9 of the Louisiana Commercial Law as revised by this Act."

Cross References

C.C. arts. 2792, 3251, 3268, 3269, 3278, 3280, 3282, 3283, 3307.

§ 5552. Defenses to enforcement of a collateral mortgage

A. If the obligor of the written obligation that the collateral mortgage secures does not raise the following defenses or claim the extinction of the collateral mortgage, then the mortgagor may not raise as a defense to the enforcement or claim the extinction of the collateral mortgage for any cause, other than forged signatures, based on the invalidity or unenforceability of the written obligation, or the extinction of the written obligation.

B. If neither the obligor of the written obligation that the collateral mortgage secures nor the mortgagor raises the following defenses or claims the extinction of the collateral mortgage, then, as long as the effects of registry continue in accordance with Article 3369 of the Civil Code, third persons may not raise as a defense to the enforcement or claim the extinction of the collateral mortgage for any cause, other than forged signatures, based on the invalidity or unenforceability of the written obligation, or the extinction of the written obligation.

Added by Acts 1989, No. 137, § 7, eff. Sept. 1, 1989.

Editor's note. For § 20 of Acts 1989, No. 137, stating legislative intent, see note preceding R.S. 9:5101.

Article 3369 of the Louisiana Civil Code of 1870 to which R.S. 9:5552 refers has been repealed by Acts 1992, No. 1132, § 1. For corresponding provision of the 1992 revision, see Civil Code art. 3328, as revised by Acts 1992, No. 1132, § 2.

Cross References

C.C. arts. 2792, 3251, 3268, 3269, 3278, 3280, 3282, 3283, 3307.

§ 5553. Defenses to enforcement of a vendor's privilege

If the obligor of the written obligation that the vendor's privilege secures does not raise the following defenses or claim the extinction of the vendor's privilege, then, as long as the effects of recordation continue in accordance with Articles 3328 through 3334 of the Civil Code, third persons may not raise as a defense to the enforcement or claim the extinction of the vendor's privilege for any cause, other than forged signatures, based on: the invalidity of the written obligation; the extinction of the written obligation; or the lack of registry or any deficiency in registry of any transfer, assignment, or pledge of the written obligation from the original vendee.

Added by Acts 1989, No. 137, § 7, eff. Sept. 1, 1989; Acts 1989, No. 598, § 1, eff. Sept. 1, 1989. Amended by Acts 1995, No. 1087, § 3.

Editor's note. Article 3369 of the Louisiana Civil Code of 1870 to which R.S. 9:5553 refers has been repealed by Acts 1992, No. 1132, § 1. For corresponding provision of the 1992 revision, see Civil Code art. 3328, as revised by Acts 1992, No. 1132, § 2.

Cross References

C.C. arts. 2792, 3251, 3268, 3269, 3278, 3280, 3282, 3283, 3307.

§ 5554. No requirement of registry of transfer, assignment, pledge, or security interest in or of the written obligation, collateral mortgage, or vendor's privilege

There is no requirement that there be registry of:

(1) Any evidence of pledge of the written obligation secured by a collateral mortgage or a vendor's privilege.

(2) Any transfer or assignment of the written obligation secured by a collateral mortgage or a vendor's privilege, or of the collateral mortgage or vendor's privilege.

(3) Any security interest in a collateral mortgage or vendor's privilege or written obligation secured by either.

Added by Acts 1989, No. 137, § 7, eff. Sept. 1, 1989. Amended by Acts 1990, No. 1079, § 3, eff. Sept. 1, 1990 at 12:01 A.M.

Editor's note. For § 20 of Acts 1989, No. 137, stating legislative intent, see note preceding R.S. 9:5101.

Cross References

C.C. arts. 2792, 3251, 3268, 3269, 3278, 3280, 3282, 3283, 3307.

§ 5555. Executory process in the case of notes or other obligations not paraphed for identification with the mortgage

A. In accordance with Code of Civil Procedure Article 2636(8), there is no requirement that a note or other written obligation secured by a mortgage be paraphed for identification with the mortgage in order for the mortgagee to have the right to foreclose under the mortgage utilizing Louisiana executory process procedures. For purposes of executory process, the existence, amount, terms, and maturity of the note or other written obligation not evidenced by an instrument paraphed for identification with the act of mortgage or privilege may be proved by affidavit or verified petition.

B. The affidavit or verified petition may be based upon personal knowledge or upon information and belief derived from the records kept in the ordinary course of business of the mortgagee, the creditor whose claim is secured by the privilege, or any other person. The affidavit or verified petition need not particularize or specifically identify the records or date upon which such knowledge, information or belief is based.

C. The affidavit shall be deemed to provide authentic evidence of the existence, amount, terms, and maturity of the obligation for executory process purposes.

Added by Acts 1991, No. 652, § 2, eff. Jan. 1, 1992. Amended by Acts 1993, No. 948, § 2, eff. Jan. 1, 1994; Acts 1995, No. 1087, § 3.

§ 5556. Repealed by Acts 2005, No. 169, § 8, eff. July 1, 2006

§ 5557. Obligation to grant release of mortgage

A. The provisions of this Section shall apply only to mortgages recorded prior to January 1, 2012.

B. Upon extinction of the mortgage, the mortgagor or his successor may request the mortgagee to provide a written act of release directing the recorder to erase the mortgage from his records. The mortgagee shall deliver the act of release to the mortgagor within sixty days of receiving the request. If the mortgagee fails to deliver the act timely and in a form susceptible of recordation, the mortgagor may, by summary proceedings instituted against the mortgagee in the parish where the mortgaged property is located, obtain a judgment ordering the mortgage to be erased from the records and for the costs, reasonable attorneys fees, and any damages he has suffered from the mortgagee's default.

C. This Section does not apply to a mortgage insofar as it secures payment of a note or other instrument paraphed for identification with the act of mortgage by the notary before whom it is executed.

Added by Acts 1991, No. 652, § 2, eff. Jan. 1, 1992. Amended by Acts 2011, No. 342, § 1, eff. Jan. 1, 2012.

§§ 5558 to 5600. Reserved for future legislation

CODE TITLE XXIII—OCCUPANCY AND POSSESSION [BLANK]
CODE TITLE XXIV—PRESCRIPTION

CHAPTER 1. PRESCRIPTION

PART I. PERIODS OF PRESCRIPTION

SUBPART A. ONE YEAR

Section	
5601.	Crops; injury, destruction, or loss of profits; non-delivery or non-acceptance.
5602.	Contracts for work and labor; New Orleans.
5603.	Public ways; damages due to grading.
5604.	Actions for professional accounting liability.
5605.	Actions for legal malpractice.
5605.1.	Theft of client funds; prescription.
5606.	Actions for professional insurance agent liability.
5607.	Actions against a professional engineer, surveyor, professional interior designer, architect, real estate developer; peremptive periods.
5608.	Actions against home inspectors.
5609.	Contracts to buy or sell; peremption of the effect of recordation; prescription for actions.

SUBPART B. TWO YEARS

Section	
5621.	Acts of succession representative.
5622.	Informalities in auction sales, two and five year prescription.
5623.	Acts of sheriff; overpayments.
5624.	Actions for damages to property damaged for public purposes.

APPENDIX 1—REVISED STATUTES, TITLE 9

Section
5625. Violation of zoning restriction, building restriction, or subdivision regulation.
5626. Actions and claims for lands and improvements used or destroyed for levees or levee drainage purposes.
5627. Building encroaching on public way.
5628. Actions for medical malpractice.
5628.1. Actions for liability from the use of blood or tissue.
5629. Uninsured motorist insurance claims.
5630. Actions by unrecognized successor against third persons.
5631. Minors, interdicts, and posthumous children.
5632. Actions against succession representatives, tutors, and curators; defect in private sales or mortgages.

SUBPART B–1. THREE YEARS

5633. Blighted property; acquisitive prescription.

SUBPART C. FIVE YEARS

5641. Sale under attachment against foreign corporation.
5642. Sheriffs' deeds.
5643. Right to probate testament.
5644. Prescription of actions involving asbestos abatement.
5645. Prescription of actions involving contract to sell or transfer immovable property.
5646. Sale of immovable property by domestic or foreign corporation or unincorporated association.
5647. Power of attorney; action to set aside under certain conditions.

SUBPART D. SIX YEARS

5661. Land patents.

SUBPART E. TEN YEARS

5681. Redesignated.
5682. Redesignated.
5683, 5684. Repealed.
5685. Prescription against the state.

SUBPART F. THIRTY YEARS

5701. Debts due charitable or educational institution or fund.

PART II. INTERRUPTION AND SUSPENSION

5801. Involuntary dismissal; failure to timely request service of citation.
5802. Fugitive from justice.
5803. Property adjudicated to state for non-payment of taxes.
5804. Immovable property of municipal corporation.
5805. Minerals, mineral or royalty rights; liberative prescription not suspended by minority or other disability.
5806. Repealed.
5807. Interruption of prescription on pledged obligations by payment on obligation secured by pledge.

PART III. ALTERATION OF PRESCRIPTIVE PERIODS

5811. Prescription of action of revendication.

Section
PART IV. SUSPENSION OR EXTENSION OF PRESCRIPTION, PEREMPTION, AND OTHER LEGAL DEADLINES DURING HURRICANES KATRINA AND RITA

5821. Purpose; ratification.
5822. Suspension and extension of prescription and peremption; exceptions.
5823. Suspension of legal deadlines; extension of legal deadlines; contradictory hearing.
5824. Purpose; certain courts; suspension and extension of prescription and peremption and other legal deadlines.
5825. Applicability.
5826 to 5835. [Reserved].

PART I. PERIODS OF PRESCRIPTION

SUBPART A. ONE YEAR

§ 5601. Crops; injury, destruction, or loss of profits; non-delivery or non-acceptance

The following actions are prescribed by one year:

(1) That for damages for the injury to or destruction of or the profits lost on a crop, in whole or in part, reckoning from the day the act occurred, or from the day the cause ceased if the cause was a continuing one.

(2) That for damages for the value of the whole or a portion of a crop contracted to be sold, resulting from the non-delivery or non-acceptance of the crops, reckoning from the day by which the crops were to have been delivered or accepted, or from the last day of the period, if the crops were to have been delivered or accepted over a period.

Cross References

C.C. arts. 463, 474, 483 et seq., 3492, 3493, 3549.

§ 5602. Contracts for work and labor; New Orleans

The following actions are prescribed by one year:

(1) Those for the enforcement of any contract entered into with the municipal corporation of New Orleans for work and labor to be performed, reckoning from the expiration of the time within which the contract was required to be performed.

(2) Those for the recovery of damages in favor of the contractors for breach of any such contract on the part of such municipal corporation, reckoning from the day the damages are alleged to have arisen.

Cross References

C.C. arts. 2762, 3493, 3494.

§ 5603. Public ways; damages due to grading

Actions for the recovery of damages to person or property by reason of the grading of any public way by any municipality are prescribed by one year, reckoning from the time the damage was sustained.

Cross References

C.C. arts. 450, 457, 3493.

§ 5604. Actions for professional accounting liability

A. No action for damages against any accountant duly licensed under the laws of this state, or any firm as defined in R.S. 37:71, whether based upon tort, or breach of contract, or otherwise, arising out of an engagement to provide professional accounting service shall be brought unless filed in a court of competent jurisdiction and proper venue within one year from the date of the alleged act, omission, or neglect, or within one year from the date that the alleged act, omission, or neglect is discovered or should have been discovered; however, even as to actions filed within one year from the date of such discovery, in all events such actions shall be filed at the latest within three years from the date of the alleged act, omission, or neglect.

B. The provisions of this Section are remedial and apply to all causes of action without regard to the date when the alleged act, omission, or neglect occurred. However, with respect to any alleged act, omission, or neglect occurring prior to September 7, 1990, actions must, in all events, be filed in a court of competent jurisdiction and proper venue on or before September 7, 1993, without regard to the date of discovery of the alleged act, omission, or neglect. The one-year and three-year periods of limitation provided in Subsection A of this Section are peremptive periods within the meaning of Civil Code Article 3458 and, in accordance with Civil Code Article 3461, may not be renounced, interrupted, or suspended.

C. Notwithstanding any other law to the contrary, in all actions brought in this state against any accountant duly licensed under the laws of this state, or any firm as defined in R.S. 37:71, whether based on tort or breach of contract or otherwise arising out of an engagement to provide professional accounting service, the prescriptive and peremptive period shall be governed exclusively by this Section and the scope of the accountant's duty to clients and nonclients shall be determined exclusively by applicable Louisiana rules of law, regardless of the domicile of the parties involved.

D. The provisions of this Section shall apply to all persons whether or not infirm or under disability of any kind and including minors and interdicts.

E. The peremptive period provided in Subsection A of this Section shall not apply in cases of fraud, as defined in Civil Code Article 1953.

F. The peremptive periods provided in Subsections A and B of this Section shall not apply to any proceedings initiated by the State Board of Certified Public Accountants of Louisiana.

Added by Acts 1990, No. 683, § 1. Amended by Acts 1992, No. 611, § 1; Acts 1995, No. 190, § 1.

Cross References

C.C. art. 1953.

§ 5605. Actions for legal malpractice

A. No action for damages against any attorney at law duly admitted to practice in this state, any partnership of such attorneys at law, or any professional corporation, company, organization, association, enterprise, or other commercial business or professional combination authorized by the laws of this state to engage in the practice of law, whether based upon tort, or breach of contract, or otherwise, arising out of an engagement to provide legal services shall be brought unless filed in a court of competent jurisdiction and proper venue within one year from the date of the alleged act, omission, or neglect, or within one year from the date that the alleged act, omission, or neglect is discovered or should have been discovered; however, even as to actions filed within one year from the date of such discovery, in all events such actions shall be filed at the latest within three years from the date of the alleged act, omission, or neglect.

B. The provisions of this Section are remedial and apply to all causes of action without regard to the date when the alleged act, omission, or neglect occurred. However, with respect to any alleged act, omission, or neglect occurring prior to September 7, 1990, actions must, in all events, be filed in a court of competent jurisdiction and proper venue on or before September 7, 1993, without regard to the date of discovery of the alleged act, omission, or neglect. The one-year and three-year periods of limitation provided in Subsection A of this Section are peremptive periods within the meaning of Civil Code Article 3458 and, in accordance with Civil Code Article 3461, may not be renounced, interrupted, or suspended.

C. Notwithstanding any other law to the contrary, in all actions brought in this state against any attorney at law duly admitted to practice in this state, any partnership of such attorneys at law, or any professional law corporation, company, organization, association, enterprise, or other commercial business or professional combination authorized by the laws of this state to engage in the practice of law, the prescriptive and peremptive period shall be governed exclusively by this Section.

D. The provisions of this Section shall apply to all persons whether or not infirm or under disability of any kind and including minors and interdicts.

E. The peremptive period provided in Subsection A of this Section shall not apply in cases of fraud, as defined in Civil Code Article 1953.

Added by Acts 1990, No. 683, § 1. Amended by Acts 1992, No. 611, § 1.

Cross References

C.C. art. 1953.

§ 5605.1. Theft of client funds; prescription

A. Notwithstanding the provisions of R.S. 9:5605, prescription of a claim of theft or misappropriation of funds of a client by the client's attorney shall be interrupted by the filing of a complaint with the Office of Disciplinary Counsel, Louisiana Attorney Disciplinary Board, by the client alleging the theft or misappropriation of the funds of the client.

B. The record of the hearing of the Office of Disciplinary Counsel, Louisiana Attorney Disciplinary Board, held to review the claim of theft or misappropriation of the funds of the client may be admissible as evidence in the civil action brought to recover the stolen or misappropriated funds, and in such action, the court may award reasonable attorney fees to the client.

Added by Acts 2003, No. 1154, § 1.

§ 5606. Actions for professional insurance agent liability

A. No action for damages against any insurance agent, broker, solicitor, or other similar licensee under this state, whether based upon tort, or breach of contract, or otherwise, arising out of an engagement to provide insurance services shall be brought unless filed in a court of competent jurisdiction and proper venue within one year from the date of the alleged act, omission, or neglect, or within one year from the date that the alleged act, omission, or neglect is discovered or should have been discovered. However, even as to actions filed within one year from the date of such discovery, in all events such actions shall be filed at the latest within three years from the date of the alleged act, omission, or neglect.

B. The provisions of this Section shall apply to all persons whether or not infirm or under disability of any kind and including minors and interdicts.

C. The peremptive period provided in Subsection A of this Section shall not apply in cases of fraud, as defined in Civil Code Article 1953.

D. The one-year and three-year periods of limitation provided in Subsection A of this Section are peremptive periods within the meaning of Civil Code Article 3458 and, in accordance with Civil Code Article 3461, may not be renounced, interrupted, or suspended.

Added by Acts 1991, No. 764, § 1. Amended by Acts 1999, No. 905, § 1.

Cross References

C.C. art. 1953.

§ 5607. Actions against a professional engineer, surveyor, professional interior designer, architect, real estate developer; peremptive periods

A. No action for damages against any professional engineer, surveyor, engineer intern, surveyor intern, or licensee as defined in R.S. 37:682, or any professional architect, landscape architect, architect intern, or agent as defined in R.S. 37:141, or professional interior designer, or licensee as defined in R.S. 37:3171, or other similar licensee licensed under the laws of this state, or real estate developer relative to development plans which have been certified by a professional engineer or professional architect, whether based upon tort, or breach of contract, or otherwise arising out of an engagement to provide any manner of movable or immovable planning, construction, design, or building, which may include but is not limited to consultation, planning, designs, drawings, specifications, investigation, evaluation, measuring, or administration related to any building, construction, demolition, or work, shall be brought unless filed in a court of competent jurisdiction and proper venue at the latest within five years from:

(1) The date of registry in the mortgage office of acceptance of the work by owner; or

(2) The date the owner has occupied or taken possession of the improvement, in whole or in part, if no such acceptance is recorded; or

(3) The date the person furnishing such services has completed the services with regard to actions against that person, if the person performing or furnishing the services, as described herein, does not render the services preparatory to construction, or if the person furnishes such services preparatory to construction but the person furnishing such services does not perform any inspection of the work.

B. The provisions of this Section shall apply to all persons whether or not infirm or under disability of any kind and including minors and interdicts.

C. The five-year period of limitation provided for in Subsection A of this Section is a peremptive period within the meaning of Civil Code Article 3458 and in accordance with Civil Code Article 3461, may not be renounced, interrupted, or suspended.

D. The provisions of this Section shall take precedence over and supersede the provisions of R.S. 9:2772 and Civil Code Articles 2762 and 3545.

E. The peremptive period provided in Subsection A of this Section shall not apply in cases of fraud, as defined in Civil Code Article 1953.

F. The peremptive periods provided in Subsections A and B of this Section shall not apply to any proceedings initiated by the Louisiana Professional Engineering and Land Surveying Board or the State Board of Architectural Examiners.

Added by Acts 2003, No. 854, § 1. Amended by Acts 2006, No. 732, § 1.

Cross References

C.C. arts. 1953, 2762, 3458 to 3461, 3545.

§ 5608. Actions against home inspectors

A. No action for damages against any home inspector duly licensed under the laws of this state or against any home inspection company, whether based in tort, breach of contract, or otherwise, arising out of a home inspection or report performed or prepared by the home inspector shall be brought unless filed in a court of competent jurisdiction and proper venue within one year from the date the act, omission, or neglect is alleged to have occurred.

B. The prescriptive period provided in Subsection A of this Section shall not apply in cases of fraud, as defined in Civil Code Article 1953.

C. The prescriptive period provided in Subsection A of this Section shall not apply to any proceedings initiated by the Louisiana State Board of Home Inspectors.

D. The provisions of this Section shall not apply to the inspection of new homes which are subject to the provisions of R.S. 9:3141 et seq.

Added by Acts 2004, No. 437, § 1.

§ 5609. Contracts to buy or sell; peremption of the effect of recordation; prescription for actions

A. The effect of recording in the conveyance records of a contract to buy or sell an immovable shall cease one year from the date of its recordation, unless prior thereto one of the parties to the contract causes it to be reinscribed in the same manner as the reinscription of a mortgage as provided by Article 3362 of the Civil Code. Such a reinscription shall continue the effect of recordation for one year and its effect may be renewed from time to time thereafter in the same manner. Except as provided in Paragraph B, the effect of recordation shall thereafter cease upon the lapse of any continuous twelve-month period during which the contract is not reinscribed.

B. The filing of a notice of lis pendens of a suit to enforce a recorded contract to buy or sell the immovable that is then effective as provided in Paragraph A shall continue the effect of recordation in the manner and to the extent prescribed by Articles 3751 through 3753 of the Code of Civil Procedure, and reinscription of the contract shall thereafter not be required or have effect.

C. A contract recorded pursuant to Paragraph A shall be canceled from the records by the recorder upon the written request of any person after the effect of its inscription has ceased as herein provided or as provided by Article 3753 of the Code of Civil Procedure.

Added by Acts 2006, No. 701, § 1, eff. Aug. 15, 2007.

SUBPART B. TWO YEARS

§ 5621. Acts of succession representative

Actions against any person who has served as curator of a vacant succession or as administrator, testamentary executor, or dative testamentary executor of a succession in this state, or against the surety on his bond, arising out of any act the succession representative, as such, may have done or failed to do, are prescribed by two years, reckoning from the day of the judgment homologating the final account.

This prescription shall not be suspended or interrupted because of the incapacity of the person who might bring the action, reserving to him his recourse against his tutor or curator.

This prescription does not apply to actions for the recovery of any funds or other property misappropriated by the succession representative nor to actions for any amount not paid in accordance with the proposed payments shown on the final account.

Cross References

C.C. arts. 47, 389, 390, 392, 394, 395, 3042, 3060.

§ 5622. Informalities in auction sales, two and five year prescription

All informalities of legal procedure connected with or growing out of any sale at public auction or at private sale of real or personal property made by any sheriff of the Parishes of this State, licensed auctioneer, or other persons authorized by an order of the courts of this State, to sell at public auction or at private sale, shall be prescribed against by those claiming under such sale after the lapse of two years from the time of making said sale, except where minors or interdicted persons were owners or part owners at the time of making it, and in the event of such ownership or part ownership by said minors or interdicted persons, the prescription thereon shall accrue after five years from the date of public adjudication or private sale thereof.

C.C. art. 3543. Amended by Acts 1932, No. 231; Acts 1960, No. 407, § 1. Redesignated as R.S. 9:5622 by Acts 1983, No. 173, § 2, eff. Jan. 1, 1984.

Editor's note. Article 3543 of the Louisiana Civil Code of 1870, as amended by Acts 1932, No. 231 and Acts 1960, No. 407, § 1, was redesignated as R.S. 9:5622 by Acts 1983, No. 173, § 2, eff. Jan. 1, 1984.

Cross References

R.S. 9:3152 et seq.

§ 5623. Acts of sheriff; overpayments

The following actions against sheriffs and their sureties are prescribed by two years, reckoning from the day of the act of omission or commission:

(1) Those for the recovery of damages arising out of any act of misfeasance or nonfeasance by the sheriff.

(2) Repealed by Acts 1978, No. 710, § 1.

(3) Those for the recovery of costs overpaid to the sheriff.

Cross References

C.C. arts. 3492, 3494.

§ 5624. Actions for damages to property damaged for public purposes

When private property is damaged for public purposes any and all actions for such damages are prescribed by the prescription of two years, which shall begin to run after the completion and acceptance of the public works.

Added by Acts 1950, No. 421, § 1. Amended by Acts 1987, No. 339, § 1.

Cross References

R.S. 9:3176 et seq.

§ 5625. Violation of zoning restriction, building restriction, or subdivision regulation

A. (1) All actions civil or criminal, created by statute, ordinance, or otherwise, except those actions created for the purpose of amortization of nonconforming signs and billboards enacted in conformity with the provisions of R.S. 33:4722, which may be brought by parishes, municipalities, or their instrumentalities or by any person, firm or corporation to require enforcement of and compliance with any zoning restriction, building restriction, or subdivision regulation, imposed by any parish, municipality, or an instrumentality thereof, and based upon the violation by any person, firm, or corporation of such restriction or regulation, must be brought within five years from the first act constituting the commission of the violation.

(2) Where a violation has existed for a period of two years prior to August 1, 1956, except those actions created for the purpose of amortization of nonconforming signs and billboards enacted in conformity with the provisions of R.S. 33:4722, the action must be brought within one year from and after August 1, 1956.

(3) With reference to violations of use regulations all such actions, civil or criminal, except those actions created for the purpose of amortization of nonconforming signs and billboards in conformity with the provisions of R.S. 33:4722, must be brought within five years from the date the parish, municipality, and the properly authorized instrumentality or agency thereof if such agency has been designated, first had been actually notified in writing of such violation.

(4) Except as relates to nonconforming signs and billboards, any prescription heretofore accrued by the passage of two years shall not be interrupted, disturbed, or lost by operation of the provisions of this Section.

B. In all cases where the prescription provided for herein has accrued, the particular property involved in the violation of the zoning restriction, building restriction or subdivision regulation shall enjoy the same legal status as land uses, construction features of buildings or subdivisions made nonconforming by the adoption of any zoning restriction, building restriction or subdivision regulation. However, the governing authority may provide for the removal of nonconforming signs and billboards in accord with the provisions of R.S. 33:4722.

C. Notwithstanding the provisions of Subsection A of this Section, the following provisions shall be applicable only to the parishes of East Baton Rouge and Jefferson or their instrumentalities. All actions, civil or criminal, created by statute, ordinance, or otherwise, except those actions created for the purpose of amortization of nonconforming signs and billboards enacted in conformity with the provisions of R.S. 33:4722, which may be brought by such parishes or their instrumentalities or by any person, firm, or corporation to require enforcement of and compliance with any zoning restriction, building restriction, or subdivision regulation, imposed by any such parish or their instrumentalities, and based upon the violation by any person, firm, or corporation of such restriction or regulation, must be brought within three years from the date such parish or its properly authorized instrumentality or agency, if such agency has been designated, received actual notice in writing of such violation, and except for violations of use regulations, all such actions, civil or criminal, must be brought within five years from the date of the first act constituting the commission of the violation. However, in the parish of East Baton Rouge, and municipalities included within such parish, all actions, civil or criminal, for violations of use regulations must be brought within five years from the date of the first act constituting the commission of the violation.

D. In the parishes of East Baton Rouge and Jefferson, in cases where the parish or its instrumentality, after receiving notification of violation, institutes an investigation or other administrative or judicial proceeding in order to seek a cessation of the violation and during the course of such investigation or proceeding makes the determination that the violation has in fact ceased, prescription shall be interrupted and if any recurrence or new violation commences thereafter, prescription will begin to accrue anew upon the date the parish or its properly authorized instrumentality or agency, if such agency has been designated, receives actual notice in writing of such recurrence or new violation. Except for violations of use regulations, all such actions, civil or criminal, must be brought within five years from the date of the recurrence or new act constituting the commission of the violation. However, in the parish of East Baton Rouge, and municipalities included within such parish, all actions, civil or criminal, for violations of use regulations must be brought within five years from the date of the first act constituting the commission of the violation.

E. The provisions of this Section shall supersede any other provisions of law inconsistent herewith.

F. The provisions of Subsections C and D of this Section shall not apply in the parish of Orleans or the city of New Orleans.

G. (1) The provisions of this Section shall not apply to property or areas which have been identified as historic districts, historical preservations or landmarks by any historic preservation district commission, landmarks commission, or the planning or zoning commission of a governing authority; however, the prescriptive period within which to bring an action to enforce a zoning restriction or regulation or a violation thereof shall be ten years from the first act constituting the commission of the violation.

(2) The provisions of this Subsection shall apply only to zoning or planning restrictions made by a municipality or parish, or other municipal or parish entity responsible for zoning, planning, or building restrictions.

(3)(a) Notwithstanding the provisions of Paragraph (1) of this Subsection, the prescriptive period set forth therein regarding any action to enforce a zoning restriction or regulation or a violation thereof in the Vieux Carre section of the city of New Orleans shall begin to run on the date the properly authorized agency of the city actually receives written notice of the violation.

(b) The provisions of Subparagraph (a) of this Paragraph shall not divest a person of any right obtained as a result of prescription that accrued prior to August 15, 2007.

Added by Acts 1956, No. 455, §§ 1, 2. Amended by Acts 1962, No. 415, §1; Acts 1972, No. 54, § 1; Acts 1993, No. 1025, § 1, eff. June 27, 1993; Acts 1997, No. 491, § 1, eff. July 3, 1997; Acts 1997, No. 1146, § 1; Acts 2001, No. 871, § 1; Acts 2007, No. 263, § 1; Acts 2011, 1st Ex.Sess., No. 30, § 1.

Cross References

C.C. art. 775 et seq.

§ 5626. Actions and claims for lands and improvements used or destroyed for levees or levee drainage purposes

Notwithstanding any other law to the contrary, when lands are appropriated for levees or levee drainage purposes all claims and actions for payment for lands and improvements thereon actually used or destroyed for levees or levee drainage purposes shall prescribe within two years from the date on which the property was actually occupied and used or destroyed for construction of levees or levee drainage works. This prescription shall run against all those persons otherwise excepted by law.

Added by Acts 1958, Ex.Sess., No. 11, § 1. Amended by Acts 1999, No. 739, § 1, eff. July 2, 1999.

Editor's note. In Wynat Development Company v. Board of Levee Commissioners for the Parish of Orleans, 719 So. 2d 783 (La. 1998), the court held that the two year prescription under R.S. 9:5626 has been impliedly repealed by R.S. 13:5111. Accordingly, the applicable prescription is that for taking under R.S. 13:5111 (three years).

Cross References

C.C. arts. 450, 455, 456, 665.

§ 5627. Building encroaching on public way

A. A building that merely encroaches on a public way without preventing its use and which cannot be removed without causing substantial damage to its owner shall be permitted to remain. If it is demolished from any cause the owner shall be bound to restore to the public the part of the way upon which the building stood.

All actions to remove such a building shall be barred by prescription two years from the date of the commencement of said building or six months from the effective date of this Section, whichever occurs later; provided that all actions to remove such a building which became barred by prescription under Act No. 684 of 1970 [1] shall remain barred.

B. This Section shall not apply where the encroachment is on public servitudes of drainage, levees, waterways, or on rights-of-way for public highways.

Added by Acts 1979, No. 350, § 1, eff. July 10, 1979.

[1] Former R.S. 9:5627.

Cross References

C.C. art. 459.

§ 5628. Actions for medical malpractice

A. No action for damages for injury or death against any physician, chiropractor, nurse, licensed midwife practitioner, dentist, psychologist, optometrist, hospital or nursing home duly licensed under the laws of this state, or community blood center or tissue bank as defined in R.S. 40:1299.41(A), whether based upon tort, or breach of contract, or otherwise, arising out of patient care shall be brought unless filed within one year from the date of the alleged act, omission, or neglect, or within one year from the date of discovery of the alleged act, omission, or neglect; however, even as to claims filed within one year from the date of such discovery, in all events such claims shall be filed at the latest within a period of three years from the date of the alleged act, omission, or neglect.

B. The provisions of this Section shall apply to all persons whether or not infirm or under disability of any kind and including minors and interdicts.

C. The provisions of this Section shall apply to all healthcare providers listed herein or defined in R.S. 40:1299.41 regardless of whether the healthcare provider avails itself of the protections and provisions of R.S. 40:1299.41 et seq., by fulfilling the requirements necessary to qualify as listed in R.S. 40:1299.42 and 1299.44.

Added by Acts 1975, No. 808, § 1. Amended by Acts 1976, No. 214, § 1; Acts 1987, No. 915, § 1, eff. Sept. 1, 1987; Acts 1990, No. 501, § 1; Acts 1995, No. 818, § 1; Acts 1995, No. 983, § 1, eff. June 29, 1995; Acts 2001, No. 95, § 1.

Editor's note. R.S. 9:5628 was amended and reenacted by Acts 1987, No. 915, § 1. Section 3 of this Act declares that "Nothing in this Act shall be construed to supersede the provisions of R.S. 17:7.1(D)," and Section 4 of the same Act provides that the Act shall become effective on September 1, 1987.

Cross References

C.C. arts. 2315, 3492, 3549.

§ 5628.1. Actions for liability from the use of blood or tissue

A. No action for damages against any healthcare provider as defined in this Section, whether based upon negligence, products liability, strict liability, tort, breach of contract, or otherwise, arising out of the use of blood or tissue as defined in this Section shall be brought unless filed in a court of competent jurisdiction within one year from the date of the alleged cause of action or other act, omission, or neglect, or within one year from the date that the alleged cause of action or other act, omission, or neglect is discovered or should have been discovered; however, except as provided in Subsection B, even as to actions filed within one year from the date of such discovery, in all events such actions shall be filed at the latest within three years from the date of the act, omission, or neglect.

B. The provisions of this Section are remedial and apply to all causes of action without regard to the date when the alleged cause of action or other act, omission, or neglect occurred. However, with respect to any cause of action or other act, omission, or neglect occurring prior to July 1, 1997, actions against any healthcare provider as defined in this Section, must, in all events, be filed in a forum of competent jurisdiction on or before July 1, 2000. The three-year period of limitation provided in Subsection A of this Section is a peremptive period within the meaning of Civil Code Article 3458 and, in accordance with Civil Code Article 3461, shall not be renounced, interrupted, or suspended.

C. Notwithstanding any other law to the contrary, in all actions brought in this state against any healthcare provider as defined in this Section, whether based on strict liability, products liability, tort, breach of contract or otherwise arising out of the use of blood or tissue as defined in this Section, the prescriptive and peremptive periods shall be governed exclusively by this Section.

D. The provisions of this Section shall apply to all persons whether or not infirm or under disability of any kind and including minors and interdicts.

E. The peremptive period provided in Subsection A of this Section shall not apply in cases of intentional fraud or willful concealment.

F. As used in this Section:

(1) "Healthcare provider" includes those individuals and entities provided for in R.S. 9:2797, Civil Code Article 2322.1, R.S. 40:1299.39, and R.S. 40:1299.41 whether or not enrolled with the Patient's Compensation Fund.

(2) "The use of blood or tissue" means the screening, procurement, processing, distribution, transfusion, or any medical use of human blood, blood product and blood components of any kind and the transplantation or medical use of any human organ, human or approved animal tissue, tissue products or tissue components by any healthcare provider.

Added by Acts 1999, No. 539, § 3, eff. June 30, 1999.

§ 5629. Uninsured motorist insurance claims

Actions for the recovery of damages sustained in motor vehicle accidents brought pursuant to uninsured motorist provisions in motor vehicle insurance policies are prescribed by two years reckoning from the date of the accident in which the damage was sustained.

Added by Acts 1977, No. 444, § 1, eff. July 1, 1978.

Cross References

C.C. arts. 2315, 3492.

§ 5630. Actions by unrecognized successor against third persons

A. An action by a person who is a successor of a deceased person, and who has not been recognized as such in the judgment of possession rendered by a court of competent jurisdiction, to assert an interest in an immovable formerly owned by the deceased, against a third person who has acquired an interest in the immovable by onerous title from a person recognized as an heir or legatee of the deceased in the judgment of possession, or his successors, is prescribed in two years from the date of the finality of the judgment of possession.

B. This Section establishes a liberative prescription, and shall be applied both retrospectively and prospectively; however, any person whose rights would be adversely affected by this Section, shall have one year from the effective date of this Section within which to assert the action described in Subsection A of this Section and if no such action is instituted within that time, such claim shall be forever barred.

C. "Third person" means a person other than one recognized as an heir or legatee of the deceased in the judgment of possession.

D. For the purposes of this Section, after thirty years from the date of recordation of a judgment of possession there shall be a conclusive presumption that the judgment was rendered by a court of competent jurisdiction.

Added by Acts 1981, No. 721, § 1. Amended by Acts 1982, No. 37, § 1; Acts 1984, No. 394, § 1, eff. July 6, 1984; Acts 1988, No. 312, § 1.

Revision Comment—1982

The amendment to R.S. 9:5630(B) conforms with the policy objectives adopted by the legislature in 1981. The purpose of the amendment is to correct an anomaly and to extend the rights of persons who have acquired property in conformity with the statute. In Louisiana, property rights are acquired by acquisitive prescription rather than liberative prescription. The amendment strengthens the position of acquirers of property as it affords protection to them not only against suits of omitted heirs but also against suits by third persons.

Cross References

C.C. arts. 876, 1832, 2480, 3423, 3447, 3473.

§ 5631. Minors, interdicts, and posthumous children

The prescription herein provided shall accrue against all persons including minors, interdicts, and posthumous children.

Added by Acts 1981, No. 721, § 1.

Cross References

C.C. art. 3468.

§ 5632. Actions against succession representatives, tutors, and curators; defect in private sales or mortgages

A. When the legal procedure is defective or does not comply with the requisites of law in the alienation, encumbrance, or lease of movable or immovable property made by a legal representative of a succession, minor, or interdict, provided an order of court has been entered authorizing such alienation, encumbrance, or lease, any action shall be prescribed against by those claiming such defect or lack of compliance after the lapse of two years from the time of making such alienation, encumbrance, or lease.

B. This Section shall be applied both retrospectively and prospectively, however, any person whose rights would be adversely affected by this Section, shall have six months from July 10, 1990 within which to assert the action described in Subsection A of this Section and if no such action is instituted within that time, such claim shall be forever barred.

Added by Acts 1990, No. 374, § 1, eff. July 10, 1990.

§ 5632.1. [Blank]

SUBPART B–1. THREE YEARS

§ 5633. Blighted property; acquisitive prescription

A. Ownership of an immovable may be acquired by the prescription of three years without the need of just title or possession in good faith. The requirements for the acquisitive prescription of three years are as follows:

(1) The land and all improvements thereon shall be located in a municipality having a population of three hundred thousand or more, according to the latest federal decennial census, and shall have been declared or certified blighted after an administrative hearing, pursuant to R.S. 13:2575 or 2576.

(2) The following shall be filed in the conveyance records for the parish where the immovable property is situated:

(a) An affidavit by the possessor stating the name and address of the possessor, stating the intention of the possessor to take corporeal possession of the immovable property for the possessor's own account in accordance with this Section, stating that such corporeal possession shall commence no sooner than sixty calendar days from the date of filing of the affidavit and giving a short legal description of the immovable property intended to be possessed; and

(b) There shall be annexed to and filed with the affidavit described in Subparagraph (A)(2)(a) of this Section a certified copy of the judgment declaring or certifying the property as blighted and the following certificate or proof:

(i) In the event an appeal has not been timely filed in the district court appealing the judgment or declaration of blight, a certificate of the clerk of court of the district court showing that thirty days have elapsed since the date of the judgment or declaration of blight and certifying that an appeal has not been filed in the district court appealing the judgment or declaration of blight; or

(ii) In the event an appeal has been timely filed in the district court appealing the judgment or declaration of blight, a certificate of the clerk of court certifying that the district court has affirmed the judgment declaring or certifying the property as blighted or the case has been abandoned and showing that more than sixty days have elapsed from either:

(aa) The expiration of the delay for applying for a new trial or judgment notwithstanding the verdict, as provided by Code of Civil Procedure Articles 1974 and 1811, and certifying that such application was not filed within such delays as allowed by law, or

(bb) The date of the mailing of notice of the refusal of the district court to grant a timely application for a new trial or judgment notwithstanding the verdict as provided by Code of Civil Procedure Article 1914, in the event an application for a new trial or judgment notwithstanding the verdict was timely filed as provided by Code of Civil Procedure Articles 1974 and 1811; and further certifying that no order has been rendered or signed by such district court allowing an appeal from such judgment of the district court to the respective appellate court of this state.

(iii) If, within the time allowed by Code of Civil Procedure Article 2087 or 2123, an order is rendered or signed by such district court allowing an appeal from the judgment of the district court to the respective appellate court of this state, a certificate of the clerk of the court of appeal certifying either that the appeal has been abandoned, or that the judgment of the court of appeal affirming the district court has become final and definitive in accordance with Code of Civil Procedure Article 2166 may be filed in lieu of the certificate required by Item (A)(2)(b)(i) or (ii) of this Section.

(iv) In the event the Supreme Court of Louisiana grants an application for certiorari to review such judgment of the court of appeal, written proof that the Supreme Court of

Louisiana has affirmed such judgment of the court of appeal and that a writ of certiorari to the United States Supreme Court has not been made within the time allowed for such application may be filed in lieu of the certificates required by Item (A)(2)(b)(i) or (ii) of this Section.

(v) In the event an application for certiorari to review such judgment of the Supreme Court of Louisiana is timely filed, proof that such application was denied may be filed in lieu of the certificates required by Item (A)(2)(b)(i) or (ii) of this Section.

(vi) In the event the United States Supreme Court grants an application for certiorari to review such judgment of the Supreme Court of Louisiana, written proof that the United States Supreme Court has affirmed such judgment of the Supreme Court of Louisiana may be filed in lieu of the certificates required by Item (A)(2)(b)(i) or (ii) of this Section.

(vii) In the event the clerk of the district court fails or refuses to issue any certificates required by this Section within ten days following a written request for same, the requesting party may cause the clerk of court to be cited summarily by a court of competent jurisdiction to show good cause why the certificate has not been issued. If the court shall deem that good cause has not been shown, the clerk of court shall pay all reasonable attorney fees and costs incurred by the party bringing such rule.

(c) An affidavit by the New Orleans Redevelopment Authority stating that all appeals and appeal delays have run, and that the judgment declaring or certifying the property as blighted is final, filed together with a copy of the judgment declaring or certifying the property as blighted prior to August 29, 2005, shall satisfy the requirements of Subparagraph (A)(2)(b) and Paragraph (A)(11) of this Section. However, any property acquired pursuant to this Subparagraph by the New Orleans Redevelopment Authority and which is still in its possession on or after January 1, 2010, shall again become subject to the provisions of Paragraph (A)(11) of this Section.

(3) Within one week after the judgment, certificate or proof and affidavit are filed as described in Paragraph (A)(2) of this Section, said judgment, certificate or proof and affidavit shall be sent certified mail, return receipt requested, to the address of the owner shown on the tax rolls of the assessor, to the addresses of owners of immovable property having common boundaries with the immovable shown on the tax rolls of the assessor and to all parties having an interest in the immovable, as shown by the mortgage and conveyance records, at the address of each party as may be reasonably ascertained.

(4) Within one week after the judgment, certificate or proof and affidavit are filed as described in Paragraph (A)(2) of this Section, a notice shall be affixed in a prominent location on the immovable, stating the name and address of the possessor, stating that the possessor intends to take corporeal possession of the immovable for the possessor's own account and stating the date that the notice is so affixed.

(5) An owner of immovable property having common boundaries with the immovable shall have a first right of possession to such immovable. In the event more than one owner of immovable property having common boundaries with the immovable files the judgment, certificate or proof and affidavit as described in Paragraph (A)(2) of this Section, the owner of property having common boundaries who first files the judgment, certificate or proof, and affidavit as described in Paragraph (A)(2) of this Section shall secure the first right to assert possession of the immovable. An owner of immovable property having common boundaries with the immovable may, within the earlier of thirty days of receipt or forty-five days of mailing of the notice required by Paragraph (A)(3) of this Section, file the judgment, certificate or proof and affidavit as described in Paragraph (A)(2) of this Section, fulfill all requirements of Paragraphs (A)(3) and (4) and notify the intended possessor of his own intent to possess the immovable in writing by certified mail, return receipt requested. The owner of immovable property having common boundaries with the immovable shall adhere to the time restraints of the provisions of this Section, and the original intended possessor's time limits shall be suspended during the time the owner of immovable property having common boundaries with the immovable is attempting to assert possession. If the owner of immovable property having common boundaries with the immovable does not comply with the provisions of this Section, then the original party who filed the judgment, certificate or proof and affidavit as described in Paragraph (A)(2) of this Section shall exclusively have thirty days from the failure of the owner of immovable property having common boundaries with the immovable to comply to reassert his intention to possess the immovable by complying with all provisions of this Section, except that notice to the owners of property having common boundaries with the immovable property shall not be again required. After this exclusive thirty-day period has elapsed, any interested party may avail themselves of the provisions of this Section.

(6) Within ninety calendar days after the date on which the affidavit described in Subparagraph (A)(2)(a) of this Section is filed in the conveyance records as required by Paragraph (A)(2) of this Section, the possessor shall request from the recorder of mortgages a mortgage certificate, setting forth the full legal description of the immovable property, to be run in the name of the owner of the immovable property for a period of time commencing with the date of the acquisition of the immovable property by the said owner and ending sixty days following the date of the filing of the affidavit described in Subparagraph (A)(2)(a) of this Section.

(7) The possessor shall take corporeal possession peaceably and no sooner than the date the mortgage certificate described in Paragraph (A)(6) of this Section is generated by the recorder of mortgages and no later than sixty calendar days following the date of such generation.

(8) The following shall be filed in the conveyance records for the parish where the immovable property is situated within ten days after the possessor has taken corporeal possession of the immovable property:

(a) An affidavit by the possessor stating the name and address of the possessor, stating that the possessor has taken corporeal possession of the immovable for the possessor's own account, stating the date that the possessor took corporeal possession, stating the acts taken by the possessor to effect corporeal possession, and giving a short legal description of the immovable; and

(b) There shall be annexed to and filed with the affidavit described in Subparagraph (A)(8)(a) of this Section the mortgage certificate of the recorder of mortgages described in Paragraph (A)(6) of this Section, showing that sixty days have elapsed from the date of the filing of the affidavit described in Subparagraph (A)(2)(a) of this Section and showing that no notice of lis pendens has been filed against the immovable property and that the immovable property has not been seized under a writ of fieri facias or seizure and sale.

(9) Within one week after the affidavit and certificate are filed as described in Paragraph (A)(8) of this Section, said affidavit and certificate shall be sent certified mail, return receipt requested, to the address of the owner shown on the tax rolls of the assessor and to all parties having an interest in the immovable, as shown by the mortgage and conveyance records, at the address of each party as may be reasonably ascertained.

(10) Within one week after the affidavit and certificate are filed as described in Paragraph (A)(8) of this Section, a notice shall be affixed in a prominent location on the immovable, stating the name and address of the possessor, stating that the possessor has taken corporeal possession of the immovable for the possessor's own account, and stating the date that the possessor took corporeal possession.

(11) All ad valorem taxes, interest, and penalties due and payable shall be paid in full.

(12) If there are any improvements on the immovable, they shall be demolished or certificates of use and occupancy shall be obtained within two hundred seventy calendar days after the date that corporeal possession was taken.

B. In the event a judgment is rendered finding that a violation of any public health, housing, fire code, environmental or historic district ordinance of the municipality where the property is situated has occurred with respect to the immovable after the date that the possessor took corporeal possession, or should any possessor seeking to acquire hereunder fail to satisfy any of the requisites for acquisitive prescription listed in Subsection A of this Section, then possession and the running of prescription and the effect of the affidavits hereunder shall cease, and all rights which may have accrued thereunder shall be null and void ab initio. The fact that there has been no judgment rendered finding that any such violation has occurred on the immovable after the date that the possessor took corporeal possession may be established by an affidavit of a hearing officer appointed pursuant to R.S. 13:2575 or 2576.

C. The possessor may not demolish any structure on the immovable unless the hearing officer appointed pursuant to R.S. 13:2575 or 2576 finds the structure to be a public nuisance and unless the possessor obtains all permits required by law. Any garage, shed, barn, house, building, or structure shall be deemed to be a public nuisance if:

(1) By reason of being dilapidated, decayed, unsafe or unsanitary, it is detrimental to health, morals, safety, public welfare, and the well-being of the community, endangers life or property or is conducive to ill health, delinquency, and crime.

(2) It is a fire hazard.

(3) By reason of the conditions which require its continued vacancy, it and its surrounding grounds are not reasonably or adequately maintained, thereby causing deterioration and creating a blighting influence or condition on nearby properties and thereby depreciating the value, use, and enjoyment to such an extent that is harmful to the public health, welfare, morals, safety, and the economic stability of the area, community, or neighborhood in which such a public nuisance is located.

D. If the possessor has met the requisites listed in Subsection A of this Section, the possessor shall not be liable to the owner of the immovable for any tortious act related to the possession of the possessor which may have occurred on or after the date that corporeal possession was taken, including but not limited to trespass and demolition of the improvements, and such possessor shall not be subject to criminal prosecution for trespass upon the immovable or for demolition of the improvements. However, nothing provided in this Subsection shall prevent the owner from instituting and prosecuting a real action against the possessor pursuant to Code of Civil Procedure Article 3651 et seq.

E. (1) In the event that the owner is successful in bringing a real action against the possessor pursuant to Code of Civil Procedure Article 3651 et seq., the owner shall reimburse the possessor for all monies advanced by the possessor for attorney fees and costs, tax statements or researches, mortgage or conveyance certificates, title abstracts, filing fees, postage, copies, printing, the payment or satisfaction of mortgages, judgments, liens, and other encumbrances, plus costs and expenses for cancellation thereof, and for all ad valorem taxes, interest, and penalties paid by the possessor on the immovable, the value of the improvements made or done on the immovable by the possessor after the date that corporeal possession was taken, and the cost or value of any repairs, rehabilitation, maintenance, removal, or demolition to the extent not otherwise included in the value of the improvements and for any other reasonable costs incurred or work done by the possessor in connection with the acquisitive prescription provided for in this Section.

(2) In addition to the foregoing reimbursements, all monies advanced by the possessor shall earn, and the possessor shall be entitled to receive, conventional interest at the highest rate allowed pursuant to Civil Code Article 2924(C).

(3) To prove the cost or value of repairs, rehabilitation, maintenance, removal, or demolition made or done on the immovable, the possessor shall provide written receipts for the payments of said costs from the persons who performed the work or from whom the materials were purchased or affidavits establishing the hourly rate generally charged for such work in the parish in which the immovable subject to possession pursuant to this Section is located and the number of hours spent on such work.

(4) In the event that the owner contests the validity of such documentation, appraisers shall be appointed and shall proceed in the manner set forth in R.S. 47:2223 to determine the cost or value of said repairs, rehabilitation, maintenance, removal, or demolition.

F. If the possessor has met the requirements set forth in Subsection A of this Section, all expenses and monies itemized in Subsection E of this Section advanced by the possessor, plus all accrued interest as provided by Subsection E of this Section, shall be secured by a first lien and privilege on the immovable property described in the affidavit filed under Subparagraph (A)(2)(a) of this Section, which lien shall be superior in rank to all prior and subsequent recorded mortgages, judgments, liens, privileges and security interests. Such lien shall be in favor of the possessor and, as such, it may be pledged or assigned to secure any loan or loans made to the possessor for the purpose of financing the acquisition of the immovable property by the acquisitive prescription provided for in this Section or for the rehabilitation, demolition or for the construction of improvements on or to the immovable property, or both.

G. (1) If the possessor or possessors of any immovable property possessed pursuant to this Section have met the requirements of Paragraphs (A)(1) through (A)(10) of this Section, the holder or holders of any mortgage, lien, privilege, judgment, or security interest encumbering the immovable property described in the affidavit provided for in Subparagraph (A)(2)(a) of this Section, may not enforce such mortgage, lien, privilege, judgment, or security interest by seizure and sale or other in rem action against such immovable property, and such mortgage, lien, privilege, judgment, or other security interest shall have no effect whatsoever against such immovable property, the possessor thereof under this Section, or any other third party while the possessor or possessors are in corporeal or civil possession of the immovable, and the effect of recordation of the document creating the security interest shall cease as to the immovable upon the possessor acquiring the property by the acquisitive prescription described in this Section. Notwithstanding the foregoing, if the possessor does not comply with the requisites of Paragraphs (A)(11) and (12) of this Section or if a judgment described in Subsection B of this Section is rendered, the enforcement of a security interest shall no longer be prohibited.

(2) Paragraph (G)(1) of this Section shall not apply to liens imposed by or in favor of the municipality or parish in which the immovable property is located.

(3) Upon presentation of evidence to the clerk of court or the recorder of mortgages attached to or made part of an affidavit of any interested party that a possessor under this Section has met all the requirements of this Section and has acquired immovable property pursuant to this Section, the clerk of court or the recorder of mortgages shall cancel and erase all mortgages, judgments, liens, privileges, and security interests, from the records of his office, except liens imposed by or in favor of the municipality or parish in which the immovable property is located.

H. The provisions governing acquisitive prescription of ten years and of thirty years apply to the prescription of three years to the extent that their application is consistent with the prescription of three years.

I. Notwithstanding the provisions of Subsection A of this Section, in the event that the possessor rehabilitates or constructs a residential or commercial structure in accordance with Paragraph (A)(12) of this Section, ownership of the immovable may be acquired by prescription without the need of just title or possession in good faith on the date that a certificate of use and occupancy shall be obtained by the possessor. For the purposes of this Subsection, "residential or commercial structure" shall not include garages, sheds, barns, or other outbuildings.

J. In the event that the possessor does not comply with the provisions of Subsection A of this Section or if a judgment described in Subsection B of this Section is rendered, any interested party may execute and file in the conveyance records an affidavit describing the instance or instances of the possessor's failure to comply with the provisions of Subsection A of this Section or may file in the mortgage records a certified copy of the notice of the judgment described in Subsection B of this Section. Said filed affidavit or filed certified notice of judgment shall be conclusive evidence of the failure of the possessor to comply with the requirements necessary to acquire the immovable by the prescription provided for in this Section and shall act to nullify the filed affidavit of intent to possess described in Paragraph (A)(2) of this Section and the filed affidavit of possession described in Paragraph (A)(8) of this Section as if the said affidavits were never filed, without any need to have said affidavits canceled or released of record.

K. The filing or depositing in the conveyance or mortgage records of any forged affidavit, notice of judgment, certificate or proof, or mortgage certificate described herein, wrongfully altered affidavit, notice of judgment, certificate or proof, or mortgage certificate described herein, or any affidavit, notice of judgment, certificate or proof, or mortgage certificate described herein containing a false statement or false representation of a material fact, shall be a felony pursuant to R.S. 14:133 and shall be actionable under Civil Code Article 2315. Notwithstanding the foregoing, a possessor may not file an action against a third person who has acquired an interest in an immovable by onerous title from a person who has acquired the immovable by the acquisitive prescription provided by this Section based upon an executed or filed false affidavit, notice of judgment, certificate or proof, or mortgage certificate described herein.

Added by Acts 2001, No. 1226, § 1. Amended by Acts 2003, No. 1188, § 1, eff. July 3, 2003; Acts 2006, 1st Ex.Sess., No. 30, § 1; Acts 2011, 1st Ex.Sess., No. 30, § 1.

SUBPART C. FIVE YEARS

§ 5641. Sale under attachment against foreign corporation

Any action to set aside a public sale of land made under attachment proceedings against a foreign corporation as record title holder, instituted in the court of the parish where the land is situated and maintained by judgment of that court, is prescribed by five years, reckoning from the day the act of sale was recorded in the conveyance records.

Cross References

C.C. art. 3497.

§ 5642. Sheriffs' deeds

Actions to set aside sheriffs' deeds are prescribed by five years, reckoning from their date. This prescription applies only where the owner knew that the sheriff was proceeding to sell his property and where the purchaser or those claiming under him went into possession under the deed and remained in actual, open, and peaceable possession as owner for five years, and where the purchaser paid consideration for the property which was then paid over by the sheriff to the creditors of the real owner of the property.

This prescription does not apply to any attempted sale of property, not belonging to the defendant in execution, nor does it apply to minors and interdicts.

Cross References

C.C. art. 3497.

§ 5643. Right to probate testament

The right to probate a purported testament in a succession proceeding shall prescribe five years after the date of the judicial opening of the succession of the deceased.

Added by Acts 1960, No. 31, § 6, eff. Jan. 1, 1961. Amended by Acts 1981, No. 316, § 2, eff. Sept. 1, 1983; Acts 1986, No. 247, § 2.

Cross References

C.C. arts. 934, 944, 1605, 3497, 3499.

§ 5644. Prescription of actions involving asbestos abatement

A. Asbestos abatement shall include any of the following:

(1) The removal of asbestos or materials containing asbestos from any building.

(2) Any other measures taken to detect, correct, or ameliorate any problem related to asbestos in a building.

(3) Reimbursement for the removal, correction, or amelioration of asbestos or materials containing asbestos.

B. Notwithstanding any other provision of law to the contrary, any time limitation or prescriptive period which may be applicable to any action to recover for asbestos abatement work shall not apply or expire until five years after the date on which the party seeking to recover has completed the abatement work or discovered the identity of the manufacturer of the materials which require abatement, whichever is later.

C. Any person who has an action to recover for asbestos abatement work under the provisions of this Section but whose action is barred by the prescriptive period provided in R.S. 9:5644 shall have one year from the effective date of this Act within which to bring an action or be forever barred.

D. Nothing in this Section is intended to nor shall it have the effect of changing in any respect the applicable prescription periods fixed by law for benefits under the worker's compensation law for claims for damages due to asbestos related injury or disease.

Added by Acts 1985, No. 728, § 1.

§ 5645. Prescription of actions involving contract to sell or transfer immovable property

An action for the breach or other failure to perform a contract for the sale, exchange, or other transfer of an immovable is prescribed in five years.

Added by Acts 2006, No. 701, § 1, eff. Aug. 15, 2007.

§ 5646. Sale of immovable property by domestic or foreign corporation or unincorporated association

A. (1) Any action to set aside a sale, transfer, lease, mortgage, encumbrance, or any other document by any legal entity or unincorporated association affecting any immovable property located in this state on the ground that the officer, agent, or other representative of the legal entity or unincorporated association signing the document was without authority to do so is prescribed by five years, reckoning from the day the document was recorded in the mortgage or conveyance records, or both, as applicable, of the parish in which the immovable property is located. Nothing contained in this Section shall be construed to limit or to establish a prescriptive period as to any proceeding which may arise between the legal entity or unincorporated association and the person acting in a representative position.

(2) Any action to set aside a sale, transfer, or other conveyance to or from any legal entity or unincorporated association affecting any immovable property located in this state on the ground that the documents establishing or evidencing the legal entity or unincorporated association have not been filed for registry as otherwise required by law is prescribed in five years, reckoning from the day the document was recorded in the conveyance or mortgage records, or both, as applicable, of the parish in which the immovable property is located. Nothing contained in this Section shall be construed to limit or to establish a prescriptive period as to any proceeding which may arise between the legal entity or unincorporated association and any person acting in a representative capacity of the legal entity or unincorporated association.

B. As used herein, "legal entity" means and includes any corporation, partnership, limited liability company, trust, or any other legal entity, whether public or private, whether business or nonprofit, and whether domestic or foreign.

C. The prescriptive period established by this Section shall run whether or not any resolution or other evidence of authority to act in a representative capacity is attached to the document or is otherwise previously or subsequently filed of record, and whether or not, even if such authorization is attached or filed of record, that authorization is invalid or is defective.

D. The prescriptive periods established in Subsection A of this Section shall be retroactive and shall apply to all such documents whether recorded prior to or after August 15, 2008; however, as to any documents as to which prescription has not already run and become final, this prescriptive period shall not become final and complete until ten years from the date the document was recorded or August 15, 2013, whichever occurs first.

E. Upon the expiration of the prescriptive period established by Paragraph A(2) of this Section and the filing of an affidavit by the then current owner of the property or as of the date of the affidavit, it shall be conclusively presumed that any sale, transfer, or other conveyance to or from the legal entity or unincorporated association shall have vested title in and to or from the legal entity or unincorporated association as of the date of recordation of the sale, transfer, or other conveyance in the office of the clerk and recorder for the parish in which the immovable property is located. Redesignated from R.S. 9:5681. Amended by Acts 1979, No. 595, § 1; Acts 1995, No. 1087, § 3; Acts 1999, No. 1133, § 1; Acts 2008, No. 367, § 1.

Editor's note. R.S. 9:5681 has been redesignated by the Louisiana State Law Institute as R.S. 9:5646.

Cross References

C.C. arts. 3499, 3549.

§ 5647. Power of attorney; action to set aside under certain conditions

A. Any action to set aside a document or instrument on the ground that the party executing the document or instrument under authority of a power of attorney was without authority to do so, or that the power of attorney was not valid, is prescribed by five years, beginning from the date on which the document or instrument is recorded in the conveyance records, or the mortgage records if appropriate. Nothing contained in this Section shall be construed to limit or prescribe any action or proceeding which may arise between a principal and the person acting under authority of a power of attorney.

B. The prescriptive period established by Subsection A of this Section shall be retroactive and shall apply to all such documents whether recorded prior to or after August 15, 2008; however, as to any documents recorded prior to August 15, 2008, as to which prescription has not already run and become final, the prescriptive period established by Subsection A of this Section shall become final and complete ten years from the date the document was recorded or August 15, 2013, whichever occurs first.

Redesignated from R.S. 9:5682. Added by Acts 1982, No. 481, § 1. Amended by Acts 2008, No. 371, § 1; Acts 2010, No. 196, § 1.

Editor's note. R.S. 9:5632.1 has been redesignated by the Louisiana State Law INstitute as R.S. 9:5647.

Section 2 of Acts 2010, No. 196, declares that this Act is remedial, curative, and procedural and that, therefore, is to be applied prospectively and retroactively to August 15, 2010.

Cross References

C.C. arts. 2985, 2989, 2996, 3024, 3025, 3026, 3027.

SUBPART D. SIX YEARS

§ 5661. Land patents

Actions, including those by the State of Louisiana, to annul any patent issued by the state, duly signed by the governor and the register of the state land office, and of record in the state land office, are prescribed by six years, reckoning from the day of the issuance of the patent.

Cross References

C.C. arts. 450, 453, 477, 481.

SUBPART E. TEN YEARS

§ 5681. Redesignated as R.S. 9:5646 by Acts 2008, No. 367, § 2

§ 5682. Redesignated as R.S. 9:5647 by Acts 2008, No. 371, § 2

Editor's note. R.S. 9:5682 enacted by Acts 2008, No. 371 has been redesignated under the authority of the Louisiana State Law Institute as R.S. 9:5647.

§§ 5683, 5684. Repealed by Acts 1981, No. 721, § 2

§ 5685. Prescription against the state

A. All judgments in favor of the state against all persons and the effect of recordation thereof shall be prescribed by the lapse of ten years from the date of the signing of the judgment if rendered by a trial court or from its rendition if rendered by an appellate court. Nevertheless, only a political subdivision or municipality, as defined in Louisiana Constitution Article VI, Section 44, may reinscribe the judgment as provided by law.

B. All liens and privileges in favor of the state securing a claim and the effect of recordation thereof shall be prescribed by the lapse of ten years from the date of recordation of such privilege or lien or by the lapse of a shorter prescriptive period applicable to the claim secured by the lien or privilege. Nevertheless, the liens and privileges may be reinscribed only by a political subdivision or municipality, as defined in Louisiana Constitution Article VI, Section 44, in the same manner as an instrument creating a mortgage in accordance with Civil Code Article 3362.

C. As used in Subsections A and B of this Section, "state" shall include departments, agencies, and political subdivisions of the state. "Political subdivision" shall have the same meaning as provided in Louisiana Constitution Article VI, Section 44(2), and "municipality" as used in that definition shall have the same meaning as provided in Louisiana Constitution Article VI, Section 44(3).

Added by Acts 1974, No. 386, § 1. Amended by Acts 1977, No. 311, § 1; Acts 1984, No. 407, § 1; Acts 2008, No. 848, § 1.

Cross References

C.C. art. 3499.

SUBPART F. THIRTY YEARS

§ 5701. Debts due charitable or educational institution or fund

A. Except as provided in Subsection B of this Section, actions for debts including student loans, stipends, or benefits due to any charitable or educational institution in the state or to any fund bequeathed for charitable or educational purposes, or educational obligations owed to the state or its agencies, other than obligations created under the Federal Family Education Loan Program, are prescribed by thirty years, provided the debt is evidenced in writing.

B. Actions for debts, due to public institutions of higher education in this state, other than student loans, stipends, or benefits are prescribed by ten years, provided the debt is evidenced in writing.

Amended by Acts 1999, No. 1011, § 1; Acts 2003, No. 184, § 1, eff. June 5, 2003.

Cross References

C.C. art. 3502.

PART II. INTERRUPTION AND SUSPENSION

§ 5801. Involuntary dismissal; failure to timely request service of citation

Notwithstanding the provisions of Civil Code Article 2324(C), interruption is considered never to have occurred as to a person named as a defendant who is dismissed from a suit because service of citation was not timely requested and the court finds that the failure to timely request service of citation was due to bad faith. Nonetheless, as to any other defendants or obligors, an interruption of prescription, as provided in Civil Code Article 3463, shall continue.

Added by Acts 1997, No. 518, § 3, eff. Jan. 1, 1998.

Editor's note. Acts 1997, No. 518, § 5 declares: "The provisions of this Act shall be applicable only to suits filed on and after its effective date."

§ 5802. Fugitive from justice

Prescription does not run against the action of a citizen of this state against a former citizen or resident of this state who is a fugitive from justice and is without a representative in this state upon whom judicial process may be served.

Prescription begins to run from the day the fugitive returns to the state or from the day his power of attorney appointing a representative upon whom judicial process may be served is filed in the office of the clerk of court of the parish of his former residence.

Cross References

C.C. art. 3467 et seq.

§ 5803. Property adjudicated to state for non-payment of taxes

In all cases where immovable property has been, or may be, adjudicated or forfeited to the state for non-payment of taxes and has been or is subsequently redeemed by a purchaser in good faith and by just title, or by the heirs or assigns of such purchaser, prescription shall not be interrupted or suspended during the period that title is vested in the state. This Section shall not apply to or affect the three-year prescription provided by law for tax privileges, and in all cases where immovable property has been adjudicated to the state for non-payment of taxes, such property shall only be redeemed upon paying the amounts provided by law.

Cross References

C.C. arts. 3467 et seq., 3473 et seq.

§ 5804. Immovable property of municipal corporation

Any municipal corporation owning alienable immovable property may prevent the running of prescription acquirendi causa against it in favor of any third possessor, by recording a notice with the clerk of court of the parish where the property is situated, or with the register of conveyances in the Parish of Orleans insofar as property in that parish is concerned. This notice shall contain a description of the property and a declaration that it is public property belonging to the municipality and the recording shall suspend the running of prescription during the time the ownership of the property shall remain vested in the name of the municipality.

The recordation of the written act by which a municipal corporation shall acquire alienable immovable property likewise shall be deemed sufficient notice in order to suspend the term of prescription.

Cross References

C.C. arts. 453, 3467 et seq.

§ 5805. Minerals, mineral or royalty rights; liberative prescription not suspended by minority or other disability

The accrual of the liberative prescription against the ownership, use, or development of minerals, or mineral or royalty rights shall not be suspended or interrupted because of the minority or other legal disability of any owner.

This Section is intended to and does affect presently existing mineral or royalty rights; however, any minor or other person under legal disability, whose rights are affected hereby, shall have a period of one year from the effective date hereof within which to exercise such rights.

Amended by Acts 1950, No. 510, § 1.

Cross References

C.C. art. 3468.

§ 5806. Repealed by Acts 1974, No. 50, § 3, eff. Jan. 1, 1975

§ 5807. Interruption of prescription on pledged obligations by payment on obligation secured by pledge

A payment by a debtor of interest or principal of an obligation shall constitute an acknowledgement of all other obligations including promissory notes of such debtor or his codebtors in solido pledged by the debtor or his codebtors in solido to secure the obligation as to which payment is made. In all cases the party claiming an interruption of prescription of such pledged obligation including a promissory note as a result of such acknowledgement shall have the burden of proving all of the elements necessary to establish the same. For purposes of this Section, a "pledged obligation" shall include any obligation, including a promissory note, in which a security interest has been granted under Chapter 9 of the Louisiana Commercial Laws or the corresponding provisions of the Uniform Commercial Code as adopted in any other state, to the extent applicable.

Added by Acts 1970, No. 354, § 1. Amended by Acts 1975, No. 119, § 1, eff. July 7, 1975; Acts 1990, No. 1079, § 3, eff. Sept. 1, 1990 at 12:01 A.M.; Acts 1991, No. 377, § 3, eff. Jan. 1, 1992.

PART III. ALTERATION OF PRESCRIPTIVE PERIODS

§ 5811. Prescription of action of revendication

A. The changes in the action of revendication of an immovable arising out of the obligation of collation provided in Civil Code Articles 1264, 1270, 1281, 1516, 1517, and 1518, as amended by Act No. 739 of the 1981 Regular Session of the Legislature of Louisiana are hereby made retroactive in application from the effective date of that Act No. 739.

B. A person who has a right to exercise an action of revendication which is not prescribed or otherwise extinguished or barred on September 10, 1982 and who is adversely affected by the provisions of this Section shall have one year from September 10, 1982 to initiate proceedings on the action or otherwise be forever barred from exercising such right or cause of action.

Added by Acts 1982, No. 535, § 1.

Cross References

C.C. arts. 1264, 1270, 1281, 1513.

PART IV. SUSPENSION OR EXTENSION OF PRESCRIPTION, PEREMPTION, AND OTHER LEGAL DEADLINES DURING HURRICANES KATRINA AND RITA

Editor's note. Acts 2005, 1st Ex.Sess., No. 6, § 1 enacted Chapter 1, "Of Obligations During Certain Emergencies and Disasters", of Code Title III of Code Book III of Title 9 to be comprised of R.S. 9:2551 to 9:2565.

Section 3 of Act 6 directed the Louisiana State Law Institute to redesignate and renumber the provisions sequentially beginning with

APPENDIX 1—REVISED STATUTES, TITLE 9

R.S. 9:5821 as Part IV, "Suspension or Extension of Prescription, Peremption, and Other Legal Deadlines during Hurricanes Katrina and Rita", of Code Title XXIV of Code Book III of Title 9. These sections have been reproduced here in accordance with the redesignation pursuant to § 3.

Sections 2 and 4 of Acts 2005, 1st Ex.Sess., No. 6 provide:

"Section 2. (A) The provisions of this Act shall preempt and supersede but not repeal any conflicting provision of the Civil Code or any other provision of law to the extent that such provision conflicts with the provisions of this Act.

"(B) However, notwithstanding the provisions of Paragraph A of this Section, nothing contained in this Act shall be construed as to invalidate, supersede, or modify the provisions of House Bill No. 92 of this 2005 First Extraordinary Session if it is subsequently enacted into law."

"Section 4. This Act is declared to be interpretative, curative, and procedural and therefore is to be applied retroactively as well as prospectively.

Executive Orders KBB 2005–32, 48, and 67 provide, respectively:

EXECUTIVE ORDER NO. KBB 2005–32
EMERGENCY SUSPENSION OF PRESCRIPTION, PEREMPTION AND OTHER LEGAL DEADLINES

"**WHEREAS,** the Louisiana Homeland Security and Emergency Assistance and Disaster Act, R.S. 29:721, *et seq.*, confers upon the governor of the state of Louisiana emergency powers to deal with emergencies and disasters, including those caused by fire, flood, earthquake or other nature or man-made causes;

"**WHEREAS,** Hurricane Katrina struck the state of Louisiana causing severe flooding and damage to the southeastern part of the state, which has threatened the safety and security of the citizens in the affected areas, along with private property and public facilities;

"**WHEREAS,** pursuant to Proclamation No. 48 KBB 2005, a state of emergency was declared for the entire state and is currently in effect;

"**WHEREAS,** as a direct consequence of the disaster and evacuation, attorneys throughout the state have clients whom they cannot contact due to client's evacuation outside of their home parishes and in many cases, outside the state of Louisiana;

"**WHEREAS,** similarly, there are client's who can not contact their counsel due to counsel's evacuation as well as the extreme challenges to communication networks resulting from the hurricane and subsequent flooding;

"**WHEREAS,** in addition, attorneys from areas affected by Hurricane Katrina have clients and cases in parishes not directly affected by this extreme disaster, but because the attorney's office is either destroyed or not accessible, the attorney is not reasonably able to timely file claims or responses on behalf of their clients;

"**WHEREAS,** La. Constitution Art. I, Section 22 provides that all courts shall be open, and every person shall have an adequate remedy by due process of law and justice, administered without denial, partiality, or unreasonable delay, for injury to him in his person, property, reputation, or other rights;

"**WHEREAS,** Hurricane Katrina has also rendered several of the court houses temporarily inoperable and/or not fit for occupancy;

"**WHEREAS,** the destruction and disruption of services and infrastructure to our system of justice caused by Hurricane Katrina will have a profound impact on the basic rights to an untold number of persons unless action is taken to suspend the effects of the tolling of legal delays during the period of this emergency; and

"**WHEREAS,** the Louisiana State Bar Association, the Louisiana Trial Lawyers Association, and the Louisiana Association of Defense Counsel jointly requested the governor to suspend all deadlines applicable to legal proceedings, including prescription and peremption, in all Louisiana state courts, administrative agencies and boards;

"**NOW THEREFORE I, KATHLEEN BABINEAUX BLANCO,** Governor of the state of Louisiana, by virtue of the authority vested by the Constitution and laws of the state of Louisiana, do hereby order and direct as follows:

"**SECTION 1:** All deadlines in legal proceedings, including liberative prescriptive and peremptive periods in all courts, administrative agencies, and boards are hereby suspended until at least September 25, 2005, including, but not limited to, any such deadlines set for in the following:

"A. Louisiana Civil Code;

"B. Louisiana Code of Civil Procedure;

"C. La. R.S. Title 9, Civil Code Ancillaries;

"D. La. R.S. Title 13, Courts and Judicial Procedure;

"E. La. R.S. Title 23, Chapter 10, Worker's Compensation;

"F. La. R.S. Title 40, Chapter 5 Part XXI–A, Malpractice Liability for State Services; and

"G. La. R.S. Title 40, Chapter 5, Part XXIII, Medical Malpractice.

"**SECTION 2:** This Order is effective upon signature and shall apply retroactively from Monday, August 29, 2005, through Sunday, September 25, 2005, unless amended, modified, terminated, or rescinded by the governor, or terminated by operation of law prior to such time.

"**IN WITNESS WHEREOF,** I have set my hand officially and caused to be affixed the Great Seal of Louisiana, at the Capitol, in the city of Baton Rouge, on the 6th day of September, 2005.

"/S/Kathleen Babineaux Blanco

"**GOVERNOR OF LOUISIANA**"

"EXECUTIVE ORDER NO. KBB 2005–48
"EXTENSION OF EXECUTIVE ORDER NO. KBB 2005–32 EMERGENCY SUSPENSION OF PRESCRIPTION, PEREMPTION AND OTHER LEGAL DEADLINES

"**WHEREAS,** Executive Order No. KBB 2005–32, issued on September 6, 2005, suspended all deadlines applicable to legal proceedings, including prescription and peremption, in all Louisiana state courts, administrative agencies and boards;

"**WHEREAS,** Executive Order No. KBB 2005–32 is in effect until September 25, 2005; and

"**WHEREAS,** the Louisiana State Bar Association, the Louisiana Trial Lawyers Association, and the Louisiana Association of Defense Counsel jointly requested that Executive Order No. 2005–32 be extended for an additional thirty (30) days;

"**NOW THEREFORE I, KATHLEEN BABINEAUX BLANCO,** Governor of the state of Louisiana, by virtue of the authority vested by the Constitution and laws of the state of Louisiana, do hereby order and direct as follows:

"**SECTION 1:** Section 1 of Executive Order No. KBB 2005–32, issued on September 6, 2005, is amended as follows:

"A. All deadlines in legal proceedings, including liberative prescriptive and peremptive periods in all courts, administrative agencies, and boards are hereby suspended until at least October 25, 2005, including, but not limited to, non-constitutionally mandated deadlines in criminal proceedings and any such deadlines set for in the following:

"1. Louisiana Civil Code;

"2. Louisiana Code of Civil Procedure;

"3. R.S. Title 9, Civil Code Ancillaries;

"4. La. R.S. Title 13, Courts and Judicial Procedure;

"5. La. R.S. Title 23, Chapter 10, Workers Compensation;

"6. La. R.S. Title 40, Chapter 5 Part XXI–A, Malpractice Liability for State Services; and

"7. La. R.S. Title 40, Chapter 5, Part XXIII, Medical Malpractice.

"B. The suspension of laws as provided in Subsection 1(A) of this Executive Order shall apply statewide and in all matters, except to the extent that the suspension of deadlines in legal proceedings may hereafter be shortened or lifted, in whole or in part, by an order issued by the Louisiana Supreme Court acting in accordance with the power vested pursuant to Article V of the Constitution.

"**SECTION 2:** This Order is effective upon signature and shall remain in effect until Tuesday, October 25, 2005, unless amended, modified, terminated, or rescinded by the governor, or terminated by operation of law prior to such time.

APPENDIX 1—REVISED STATUTES, TITLE 9

"IN WITNESS WHEREOF, I have set my hand officially and caused to be affixed the Great Seal of Louisiana, at the Capitol, in the city of Baton Rouge, on this 23rd day of September, 2005.

"/S/Kathleen Babineaux Blanco
"GOVERNOR OF LOUISIANA"

"EXECUTIVE ORDER NO. KBB 2005–67
"EMERGENCY SUSPENSION OF PRESCRIPTION, PEREMPTION AND OTHER LEGAL DEADLINES

"**WHEREAS**, the Louisiana Homeland Security and Emergency Assistance and Disaster Act, R.S. 29:721, *et seq.*, confers upon the governor of the state of Louisiana emergency powers to deal with emergencies and disasters, including those caused by fire, flood, earthquake or other nature or man-made causes;

"**WHEREAS**, Hurricane Katrina and its aftermath, and Hurricane Rita struck the state of Louisiana causing severe damage and flooding to the southern part of the state, which has threatened the safety, health, and security of the citizens of the state of Louisiana, along with private property and public facilities;

"**WHEREAS**, pursuant to the Louisiana Homeland Security and Emergency Assistance and Disaster Act, R.S. 29:721, *et seq.*, a state of emergency/disaster was declared through Proclamation No. 48 KBB 2005, as amended by Proclamation No. 54 KBB 2005, and Proclamation No. 53 KBB 2005, as amended by Proclamation No. 60 KBB 2005;

"**WHEREAS**, as a direct consequence of these disasters and evacuations, attorneys throughout the state had clients whom they could not contact due to the client's evacuation and similarly, there were clients who could not contact their counsel due to counsel's evacuation;

"**WHEREAS**, in addition to challenges resulting from displacement and access to office and personal files and records, the storms and their aftermaths resulted in extreme challenges to communication networks and disruption of mail service;

"**WHEREAS**, Hurricanes Katrina and Rita also rendered several court houses temporarily inoperable and/or not fit for occupancy;

"**WHEREAS**, La. Constitution Art. I, Section 22 provides that all courts shall be open, and every person shall have an adequate remedy by due process of law and justice, administered without denial, partiality, or unreasonable delay, for injury to him in his person, property, reputation, or other rights;

"**WHEREAS**, the destruction and disruption of services and infrastructure to our system of justice caused by Hurricanes Katrina and Rita would have had a profound impact on the basic rights to an untold number of persons unless action was taken to suspend the effects of the tolling of legal delays during the period of these emergencies;

"**WHEREAS**, based on the above, on September 6, 2005, Executive Order No. KBB 2005–32, suspending deadlines in legal proceedings, was issued at the request of the Louisiana State Bar Association, the Louisiana Trial Lawyers Association, and the Louisiana Association of Defense Counsel, and in the interest of fairness and justice for all parties;

"**WHEREAS**, on September 23, 2005, Executive Order No. KBB 2005–32, was amended to extend the suspension for an additional thirty days and to recognize the Louisiana Supreme Court's authority to lift the suspension, in whole or in part, by Order;

"**WHEREAS**, on October 3, 2005, the Louisiana Supreme Court issued a Resolution and Temporary Rule that provided a procedure to have a judge consider allowing legal proceedings to proceed where justice and equity mandate the shortening or lifting of the suspension;

"**WHEREAS**, it has been announced that the Louisiana Legislature will be called into a special session from November 6, 2005, to November 18, 2005, which will be the first opportunity for legislative action on these issues;

"**WHEREAS**, as the immediacy of the emergency passes and as the state begins to move toward a recovery and rebuilding phase, it is necessary to provide notice and begin the process of returning legal affairs to their normal processes as soon as practical in an effort to restore commerce; and

"**WHEREAS**, the attorney general will issue, to judges and Justice of the Peace Courts in the affected areas, recommended eviction guidelines according to current law but taking into consideration the emergency circumstances that occurred over the last several weeks, so that as these proceedings begin in the parishes affected by Hurricane Katrina, the authorities have legal guidance as to the rights and privileges of both the lessees and lessors;

"**NOW THEREFORE I, KATHLEEN BABINEAUX BLANCO**, Governor of the state of Louisiana, by virtue of the authority vested by the Constitution and laws of the state of Louisiana, do hereby order and direct as follows:

"**SECTION 1:** Section 1 of Executive Order No. KBB 2005–32, issued on September 6, 2005 as amended by Executive Order No. KBB 2005–48, issued on September 23, 2005, is hereby amended as follows:

"A. Liberative prescriptive and peremptive periods are hereby suspended statewide until at least Friday, November 25, 2005.

"B. Except as provided in Subsection A of this Section, the suspension of deadlines in legal proceedings, as provided in Executive Order No. KBB 2005–32, as amended by Executive Order No. KBB 2005–48, in all courts, administrative agencies, and boards unaffected by Hurricane Rita, as defined as those parishes not identified in Subsection C of Section 1 of this Order, shall end as of Tuesday, October 25, 2005.

"C. Deadlines in legal proceedings in courts, administrative agencies, and boards affected by Hurricane Rita, defined as the parishes of Calcasieu, Cameron, Jefferson Davis, and Vermilion are hereby suspended until at least Friday, November 25, 2005, including but not limited to, non-constitutionally mandated deadlines in criminal proceeding and any such deadlines as follows:

"1. Louisiana Civil Code;
"2. Louisiana Code of Civil Procedure;
"3. La. R.S. Title 9, Civil Code Ancillaries;
"4. La. R.S. Title 13, Courts and Judicial Procedure;
"5. La. R.S. Title 23, Chapter 10, Workers' Compensation;
"6. La. R.S. Title 40, Chapter 5 Part XXI–A, Malpractice Liability for State Services; and
"7. La. R.S. Title 40, Chapter 5, Part XXIII, Medical Malpractice.

"D. Paragraph C of this Section shall not be interpreted so as to prohibit the parties from proceeding in accordance with the Louisiana Supreme Court's Resolution and Temporary Rules issued on October 3, 2005, as amended, including but not limited to, landlord-tenant disputes, evictions proceedings, and lease disputes regarding immovable property, provided such proceedings are carried out in the manner provided for by the Louisiana Supreme Court Resolution and Temporary Rule, as amended.

"E. Nothing in Subsection C of this Section shall prohibit an owner of immovable property from reclaiming leased property if abandoned as provided for by law, or entering leased property to make necessary repairs as provided for by law.

"**SECTION 2:** This Order is effective upon signature and shall remain in effect until Friday, November 25, 2005, unless amended, modified, terminated, or rescinded by the governor, or terminated by operation of law prior to such time.

"IN WITNESS WHEREOF, I have set my hand officially and caused to be affixed the Great Seal of Louisiana, at the Capitol, in the city of Baton Rouge, on this 19th day of October, 2005.

"/S/Kathleen Babineaux Blanco
"GOVERNOR OF LOUISIANA"

§ 5821. Purpose; ratification

A. The legislature finds that Hurricanes Katrina and Rita created a statewide emergency disrupting and forcing the closure of certain courts and public offices and further resulting in the displacement of courts, offices, clients, and counsel. This Chapter is enacted for the benefit and protection of the state as a whole and its citizens, and to prevent injustice, inequity, and undue hardship to persons who were prevented by these hurricanes from timely access to courts and offices in the exercise of their legal rights, including the filing of documents and pleadings as authorized or required by law. Therefore, this Chapter shall be liberally construed to effect its purposes.

B. The action of the governor of this state in issuing Executive Orders KBB 2005–32, 48, and 67 is hereby approved, ratified, and confirmed subject to the provisions of R.S. 9:5822 through 5825.

Added by Acts 2005, 1st Ex.Sess., No. 6, § 1, eff. Nov. 23, 2005.

Editor's note. For text of Executive Orders KBB 2005–32, 48 and 67, see Editor's note preceding R.S. 9:5821.

§ 5822. Suspension and extension of prescription and peremption; exceptions

A. All prescriptions, including liberative, acquisitive, and the prescription of nonuse, and all peremptive periods shall be subject to a limited suspension and/or extension during the time period of August 26, 2005, through January 3, 2006; however, the suspension and/or extension of these periods shall be limited and shall apply only if these periods would have otherwise lapsed during the time period of August 26, 2005, through January 3, 2006. This limited suspension and/or extension shall terminate on January 3, 2006, and any right, claim, or action which would have expired during the time period of August 26, 2005, through January 3, 2006, shall lapse on January 4, 2006.

B. The provisions of Subsection A shall not apply to any matter concerning the prescription of nonuse applicable to mineral servitudes, mineral royalty interests, and executive rights and shall be governed by the Louisiana Mineral Code and are not subject to the suspension provisions in this Section.

Added by Acts 2005, 1st Ex.Sess., No. 6, § 1, eff. Nov. 23, 2005.

Editor's note. For text of Executive Orders KBB 2005–32, 48 and 67, see Editor's note preceding R.S. 9:5821.

§ 5823. Suspension of legal deadlines; extension of legal deadlines; contradictory hearing

A. All deadlines in legal proceedings, which were suspended by Executive Orders KBB 2005–32, 48, and 67, shall be subject to a limited suspension and/or extension during the time period of November 25, 2005, through January 3, 2006; however, the suspension and/or extension of these deadlines shall be limited and shall apply only if these deadlines would have otherwise lapsed during the time period of November 25, 2005, through January 3, 2006. This limited suspension and/or extension shall terminate on January 3, 2006, and any deadline in legal proceedings which would have expired during the time period of November 25, 2005, through January 3, 2006, shall lapse on January 4, 2006.

B. Notwithstanding the provisions of Subsection A and to the extent that deadlines in legal proceedings were not suspended by Executive Orders KBB 2005–48 and 67, if a deadline in a legal proceeding lapsed during the time period of October 25, 2005, through November 25, 2005, a party shall have the right to seek an extension or suspension of that deadline by contradictory motion or declaratory judgment. The party seeking the extension shall bear the burden of proving that either the party or his attorney was adversely affected by Hurricane Katrina or Rita and but for the catastrophic effects of Hurricane Katrina or Rita, the legal deadline would have been timely met. For good cause shown, the court shall extend the deadline in the legal proceeding, but in no instance shall the extension be later than January 3, 2006.

Added by Acts 2005, 1st Ex.Sess., No. 6, § 1, eff. Nov. 23, 2005.

Editor's note. For text of Executive Orders KBB 2005–32, 48 and 67, see Editor's note preceding R.S. 9:5821.

§ 5824. Purpose; certain courts; suspension and extension of prescription and peremption and other legal deadlines

A. The legislature finds that Hurricanes Katrina and Rita created a statewide emergency which affected the entire judicial system in this state and all legal communities, and prohibited the court system from functioning as required by law. The legislature acknowledges that the proper functioning of this state's judicial system is essential to the administration of justice for all citizens. The legislature also recognizes that the courts in Cameron, Orleans, Plaquemines, St. Bernard, Jefferson, and Vermilion, the legal communities, and the citizens were so severely devastated and although the courts may be open on a limited basis, the massive destruction of these areas continues to endanger and infringe upon the normal functioning of the judicial system, the ability of persons to avail themselves of the judicial system and the ability of litigants or others to have access to the courts or to meet schedules or time deadlines imposed by court order or rule or statute. The majority of residents and attorneys domiciled in these areas have been displaced and numerous client files, witnesses, evidence, records and documents have been lost, damaged, or destroyed. The legislature hereby declares that there is a compelling governmental interest in protecting the rights, claims, or actions of parties and the attorneys who represent them by granting additional time and access to these courts provided in this Section.

B. (1) Notwithstanding the provisions of R.S. 9:5822 or 5823, a party who is domiciled within the parishes of Cameron, Orleans, Plaquemines, St. Bernard, Jefferson, or Vermilion, or whose cause of action arose within such parishes or whose attorney is domiciled within or has a law office within such parishes, may seek in any court of competent jurisdiction in this state a limited suspension and/or extension of prescription or peremption periods or other legal deadlines, beyond the termination dates provided in R.S. 9:5822 and 5823, by contradictory motion or declaratory judgment. The party seeking an additional suspension and/or extension, in accordance with the provisions of this Section, shall bear the burden of proving by a preponderance of the evidence that the motion was filed at the earliest time practicable and but for the catastrophic effects of Hurricane Katrina or Rita, the legal deadline would have been timely met. If the court grants the motion, the prescription or peremptive period or other legal deadline shall be suspended or extended for a period not to exceed thirty days from the date of the granting of the motion. This limited suspension or extension shall terminate on June 1, 2006, and any right, claim, or action which would have expired during the time period of January 4, 2006, through May 31, 2006, shall lapse on June 1, 2006.

(2) The failure to file the motion authorized in Paragraph (1) of this Subsection shall not preclude a party from using

the basis of the motion as a defense to an exception of prescription.

Added by Acts 2005, 1st Ex.Sess., No. 6, § 1, eff. Nov. 23, 2005.

Editor's note. For text of Executive Orders KBB 2005–32, 48 and 67, see Editor's note preceding R.S. 9:5821.

§ 5825. Applicability

Notwithstanding any other provision of law, R.S. 9:5822 through 5824 shall not apply to landlord-tenant disputes, evictions proceedings, and lease disputes regarding immovable property, provided the proceedings are carried out in accordance with Executive Order KBB 2005–67.

Added by Acts 2005, 1st Ex.Sess., No. 6, § 1, eff. Nov. 23, 2005.

Editor's note. For text of Executive Orders KBB 2005–32, 48 and 67, see Editor's note preceding R.S. 9:5821.

§§ 5826 to 5835. [Reserved]

CODE TITLE XXV—OF THE SIGNIFICATION OF SUNDRY TERMS OF LAW EMPLOYED IN THIS CODE [BLANK]

CODE BOOK IV—CONFLICT OF LAWS

CODE TITLE I—OF FOREIGN LAW

CHAPTER 1. APPLICATION OF FOREIGN LAW

Section
6000. [Blank].
6001. Application of foreign law.

§ 6000. [Blank]

§ 6001. Application of foreign law

A. "Foreign law" means any law, rule, or legal code or system established and used or applied in a jurisdiction outside of the states or territories of the United States.

B. The legislature finds that it shall be the public policy of this state to protect its citizens from the application of foreign laws when the application of a foreign law will result in the violation of a right guaranteed by the constitution of this state or of the United States, including but not limited to due process, freedom of religion, speech, or press, and any right of privacy or marriage as specifically defined by the constitution of this state.

C. A court, arbitrator, administrative agency, or other adjudicative, mediation, or enforcement authority shall not enforce a foreign law if doing so would violate a right guaranteed by the constitution of this state or of the United States.

D. If any contractual provision or agreement provides for the choice of a foreign law to govern its interpretation or the resolution of any dispute between the parties, and if the enforcement or interpretation of the contractual provision or agreement would result in a violation of a right guaranteed by the constitution of this state or of the United States, the agreement or contractual provision shall be modified or amended to the extent necessary to preserve the constitutional rights of the parties.

E. If any contractual provision or agreement provides for the choice of venue or forum outside of the states or territories of the United States, and if the enforcement or interpretation of the contract or agreement applying that choice of venue or forum provision would result in a violation of any right guaranteed by the constitution of this state or of the United States, that contractual provision or agreement shall be interpreted or construed to preserve the constitutional rights of the person against whom enforcement is sought. Similarly, if a natural person subject to personal jurisdiction in this state seeks to maintain litigation, arbitration, agency, or similarly binding proceedings in this state, and if a court of this state finds that granting a claim of forum non conveniens or a related claim violates or would likely lead to the violation of the constitutional rights of the nonclaimant in the foreign forum with respect to the matter in dispute, the claim shall be denied.

F. Any contractual provision or agreement incapable of being modified or amended in order to preserve the constitutional rights of the parties pursuant to the provisions of this Section shall be null and void.

G. Without prejudice to any other legal right, the provisions of this Section shall not apply when a juridical person as defined by Civil Code Article 24 is a party to the contract or agreement.

H. The public policies expressed in the provisions of this Section shall apply only to actual or foreseeable violations of the constitutional rights of a person caused by the application of the foreign law.

Added by Acts 2010, No. 714, § 1.

Editor's note. Acts 2010, No. 714 and Acts 2010, No. 886 enacted Chapter 1 of Code Book IV of Title 9 of the Louisiana Revised Statutes of 1950 to be comprised of R.S. 9:6000. The Louisiana State Law Institute noted the conflict between the two Acts. Pursuant to 24:252(B), the Legislature certified Act 714 as last enacted. Then, the Louisiana State Law Institute redesignated R.S. 9:6000 as R.S. 9:6001 and instructed the West Publishing Company to print in the 2011 Louisiana Statutes Annotated only Acts 2010, No. 714.

There are legal questions concerning the effect of Acts 2010, No. 886. According to the Louisiana Constitution, Acts 2010, No. 886, became law as soon as it was enacted in accord with constitutional provisions and procedures. See La.Const. Article 3, § 18 (1974): "[a] bill, except a joint resolution, *shall become law* if the Governor signs it or if he fails to sign or veto it within ten days after delivery to him if the legislature is in session, or within twenty days if the legislature is adjourned" [emphasis added]. Accordingly Acts 2010, No. 886 became law on August 15, 2010. On the same date, Acts 2010, No. 714 also became law and was certified by the Legislature as last enacted. Acts 2010, No. 886 has been noted in the 2011 Louisiana Statutes Annotated but has not been printed.

According to the civilian tradition, a law becomes obligatory and binding on citizens after it is promulgated, that is, made public. See Yiannopoulos, Civil Law System 193-195 (2d ed. 1999). In accord, Article 3, § 19 of the Louisiana Constitution of 1974 declares: "All laws shall take effect on the sixtieth day after final adjournment of the session in which they were enacted, *and shall be published* [emphasis added] prior thereto in the official journal of the state as provided by law."

In light of the above, the question of the effect of Acts 2010, No. 886, is a question of implied repeal of the statute by a subsequently enacted statute on the same subject matter. Questions of implied repeal are matters of statutory interpretation. See Yiannopoulos, Civil Law System 236-238 (2d ed. 1999). According to Article 8 of the Louisiana Civil Code, repeal is implied "when the new law contains provisions contrary to, or irreconcilable with those of the former law." The solution to the questions of conflict and implied repeal, or no conflict and repeal, depends on an objective judicial search for the intent of the legislature and on the determination of whether the new law contains provisions contrary to, or irreconcilable with, those of the former law. To the extent that a new law contains such provisions, the intent of the legislature to repeal the previous law should be regarded as established. As a general rule, "[r]epeals by implication, according to our jurisprudence, are not favored." Wenck v. Anisman, 211 La. 41, 651, 30 So.2d 567, 571 (1947). The Louisiana Supreme Court stated emphatically in Chappuis v. Reggie 222 La. 35, 43-44, 62 So.2d 92, 95 (1952): "The uniform jurisprudence is to the effect that all statutory provisions are to be given effect whenever possible. . . . If acts can be reconciled by a fair and reasonable interpretation, it must be done, since the repeal of a statute by implication is not favored and will not be indulged in if there is any other reasonable construction. . . ."

As enacted by Act 886, R.S. 9:6000 reads:

"§ 6000. Application of foreign law

"A. "Foreign law" means any law, rule, or legal code or system established and used or applied in a jurisdiction outside of the states or territories of the United States.

"B. The legislature finds that it shall be the public policy of this state to protect its citizens from the application of foreign laws when the application of a foreign law will result in the violation of a right guaranteed by the constitution of this state or of the United States, including but not limited to due process, freedom of religion, speech, or press, and any right of privacy or marriage as specifically defined by the constitution of this state.

"C. A court, arbitrator, administrative agency, or other adjudicative body, mediator, or enforcement authority shall not enforce a foreign law if doing so would violate a right guaranteed by the constitution of this state or of the United States.

"D. If any contractual provision or agreement provides for the choice of a foreign law to govern its interpretation or the resolution of any claim or dispute between the parties, and if the enforcement or interpretation of the contractual provision or agreement would result in a violation of a right guaranteed by the constitution of this state or of the United States, the contractual provision or agreement shall be interpreted, modified, amended, or construed to the extent necessary to preserve the constitutional rights of the person against whom enforcement is sought.

"E. If any contractual provision or agreement provides for the choice of venue or forum outside of the states or territories of the United States, and if the enforcement or interpretation of the contract or agreement applying that choice of venue or forum provision would result in a violation of any right guaranteed by the constitution of this state or of the United States, the contractual provision or agreement shall be interpreted, modified, amended, or construed to preserve the constitutional rights of a person against whom enforcement is sought. Similarly, if a natural person subject to personal jurisdiction in this state seeks to maintain litigation, arbitration, agency, or similarly binding proceedings in this state, and if a court of this state finds that granting a claim of forum non conveniens or a related claim violates or would likely lead to the violation of the constitutional rights of the nonclaimant in the foreign forum with respect to the matter in dispute, such claim shall be denied.

"F. Any contractual provision or agreement incapable of being interpreted, modified, amended, or construed in order to preserve the constitutional rights of the parties pursuant to the provisions of this Section shall be null and void.

"G. Without prejudice to any other legal right, the provisions of this Section shall not apply when a juridical person as defined by Civil Code Article 24 is a party to the contract or agreement.

"H. The public policies expressed in the provisions of this Section shall apply only to actual or foreseeable violations of the constitutional rights of a person caused by the application of the foreign law."

Cross References

C.C. arts. 24, 3515 to 3549.

APPENDIX 2
REPEALED AND REDESIGNATED PROVISIONS

Since 1976 and through 2013, many parts of the Louisiana Civil Code have been revised and the 1870 texts have been repealed on the recommendation of the Louisiana State Law Institute. Generally, the revised texts have been intended to apply both prospectively and retroactively, unless constitutional provisions protecting vested rights and the obligations of contracts exclude retroactive application. Repealed texts may thus still continue to apply in certain cases. The repealed texts of the Louisiana Civil Code of 1870 are found in Volumes 16, 17 and 17A of LSA–Civil Code (Compiled Edition) and in earlier editions of this pamphlet.

This Appendix lists the Titles of the Civil Code that have been revised.

1. Louisiana Civil Code, Preliminary Title (1870)

The Preliminary Title of the Louisiana Civil Code of 1870 "Of the General Definitions of Law and the Promulgation of the Laws", consisting of Articles 1 through 23, was revised by Acts 1987, No. 124, § 1, effective January 1, 1988, to consist of Article 1 through 15. Articles 14 and 15 of the new Preliminary Title were formerly Articles 9 and 10 of the Louisiana Civil Code of 1870 that have been redesignated as Articles 14 and 15 under the authority of the Louisiana State Law Institute.

Acts 1991, No. 923, § 1, effective January 1, 1992, revised Chapter 3 of the Preliminary Title of the Civil Code, comprising redesignated Articles 14 and 15, to consist of Articles 14 through 49. Articles 15 through 49 of the 1991 legislation have been redesignated under the authority of the Louisiana State Law Institute as Articles 3515 through 3549 to form Book IV—Conflict of Laws. For the texts of Articles 14 and 15 as they existed at the time of the 1991 revision, see Volume 16 of LSA–Civil Code (Compiled Edition).

2. Louisiana Civil Code, Book I, Title I (1870)

Book I, Title I "Of the Distinction of Persons" of the Louisiana Civil Code of 1870, consisting of Articles 24 through 37, was revised by Acts 1987, No. 125, § 1, effective January 1, 1988, to consist of Articles 24 through 29. For prior texts of the articles, see Volume 16 of LSA–Civil Code (Compiled Edition).

3. Louisiana Civil Code, Book I, Title II (1870)

Book I, Title II, of the Louisiana Civil Code of 1870, "Of Domicile and the Manner of Changing the Same", consisting of Articles 38 through 46, has been revised, amended, and re-enacted by Acts 2008, No. 801, § 1, effective January 1, 2009, under the heading "Domicile" to consist of Articles 38 through 46. For prior texts of the articles, see Volume 16 of LSA Civil Code (Compiled Edition).

4. Louisiana Civil Code, Book I, Title III (1870)

Book I, Title III "Of Absentees" of the Louisiana Civil Code of 1870, consisting of Articles 47 through 85, was revised by Acts 1990, No. 989, § 1, effective January 1, 1991, to consist of Articles 17 through 59. Article 84 of the Louisiana Civil Code of 1870 was redesignated by Acts 1990, No. 989, § 6 as R.S. 9:195. For prior texts of the articles and of the redesignated provision, see Volume 16 of LSA–Civil Code (Compiled Edition).

5. Louisiana Civil Code, Book I, Title IV (1870)

Book I, Title IV "Of Husband and Wife" of the Louisiana Civil Code of 1870, consisting of Articles 86 through 137, was revised by Acts 1987, No. 886, § 1, effective January 1, 1988, to consist of Articles 86 through 101. For prior texts of the articles, see Volume 16 of LSA–Civil Code (Compiled Edition).

6. Louisiana Civil Code, Book I, Title V (1870)

Title V of Book I of the Louisiana Civil Code of 1870, "Of the Causes of Separation from Bed and Board and of Divorce" is now styled "Title V—Divorce". This title was revised, amended, and re-enacted by a series of acts. See Acts 1990, No. 1088, § 2, effective January 1, 1991; Acts 1990, No. 1009, § 2, effective January 1, 1991; Acts 1993, No. 108, § 1, effective January 1, 1994; Acts 1993, No. 261, § 1, effective January 1, 1994.

Chapter 1 of Book I, Title V, of the Louisiana Civil Code of 1870 was revised, amended, and re-enacted by Acts 1990, No. 1009, § 2, as "Chapter 1.—The Divorce Action", consisting of Articles 102 to 105, effective January 1, 1991.

APPENDIX 2—REPEALED AND REDESIGNATED PROVISIONS

Chapter 2 of Book I, Title V, of the Louisiana Civil Code of 1870 was revised, amended, and re-enacted by a series of Acts. Section 1 "Spousal Support" of this Chapter has been revised, amended, and re-enacted by Acts 1997, No. 1078, § 1 to consist of Articles 111 to 117, effective January 1, 1998, Section 2 "Claim for Contributions to Education and Training" has been enacted by Acts 1990, No. 1008, § 2, to consist of Articles 117 to 120, effective January 1, 1991. These articles have been redesignated as Articles 121 to 124 by the Louisiana State Law Institute. Section 3 "Child Custody", has been revised, amended, and re-enacted by Acts 1993, No. 261, § 1, to consist of Articles 131 to 136, effective January 1, 1994. Section 4 "Child Support" has been enacted by Acts 1993, No. 261, § 6, to consist of Articles 141 and 142, effective January 1, 1994. Section 5 "Provisional and Incidental Proceedings in Actions of Nullity" has been enacted by Acts 1993, No. 108, § 1, to consist of Articles 151 and 152, effective January 1, 1994.

Chapters 3, 4, and 5 of Book I, Title V, of the Louisiana Civil Code of 1870 were restructured under the authority of the Louisiana State Law Institute to consist of Chapter 2 "Provisional and Incidental Proceedings" and Chapter 3 "Effects of Divorce", containing Article 159.

For prior texts of the articles, see Volume 16 of LSA–Civil Code (Compiled Edition).

7. Louisiana Civil Code, Book I, Title VII (1870)

Chapters 1, 2, and 3 of Book I, Title VII of the Louisiana Civil Code of 1870, consisting of Articles 178 to 211, were revised, amended, and reenacted by Acts 2005, No. 192, effective June 29, 2005, to consist of Articles 184 to 198. For prior texts of the articles, see Volume 16 of LSA–Civil Code (Compiled Edition).

Chapter 4 of Book I, TItle VII, of the Louisiana Civil Code of 1870, "Of Adoption", consisting of Article 214, has been revised, amended, and re-enacted by Acts 2008, No. 351, § 1, effective January 1, 2009, under the heading "Adult Adoption" to consist of Articles 212 through 214.

Chapters 1, 2, 3, and 4 of Book I, Title VII of the Louisiana Civil Code of 1870, consisting of Articles 178 to 214, were revised, amended, and reenacted by Acts 2009, No. 3, effective June 9, 2009, to consist of Articles 178 to 214. Acts 2009, No. 3 also renamed and redesignated the Chapter, Section, and Subsection headings. For prior text of Chapters 1 to 4, see Volume 16 of LSA–Civil Code (Compiled Edition).

8. Louisiana Civil Code, Book I, Title VIII (1870)

Chapter 2 of Book I, Title VIII, of the Louisiana Civil Code of 1870, "Of Emancipation", consisting of Articles 365 through 385, has been revised, amended, and re-enacted by Acts 2008, No. 351, § 1, effective January 1, 2009, under the heading "Emancipation" to consist of Articles 365 through 371. For prior texts of the articles, see Volume 16 of LSA–Civil Code (Compiled Edition).

9. Louisiana Civil Code, Book I, Title IX (1870)

Title IX of Book I of the Louisiana Civil Code of 1870 "Of Persons Incapable of Administering Their Estates, Whether on Account of Insanity or Some Other Infirmity, and of Their Interdiction and Curatorship", consisting of Articles 389 to 426, was revised, amended, and reenacted by Acts 2000, 1st Ex.Sess., No. 25, § 1, effective July 1, 2001, to consist of Articles 389 to 399. For prior texts of the articles, see Volume 16 of LSA–Civil Code (Compiled Edition).

10. Louisiana Civil Code, Book II, Titles I–VI (1870)

The entire Book II of the Louisiana Civil Code of 1870, "Of Things, and of the Different Modifications of Ownership", consisting of Titles I through VI (Articles 448 through 869) was revised by a series of acts in 1976, 1977, 1978, and 1979. See

Title I—Of Things, revised by Acts 1978, No. 728, effective January 1, 1979.

Title II—Of Ownership, revised by Acts 1979, No. 180, effective January 1, 1980.

Title III—Of Usufruct, Use and Habitation, revised by Acts 1976, No. 103, effective January 1, 1977.

Many of the provisions of Book II, Title III, Chapter 2, of the Louisiana Civil Code have been amended and reenacted by Acts 2010, No. 881, effective July 2, 2010. For prior texts of the articles, see Volume 16 of LSA–Civil Code (Compiled Edition).

Title IV—Of Predial Servitudes or Servitudes on Land, revised by Acts 1977, No. 514, effective January 1, 1978.

Title V—Of Fixing the Limits, and Of Surveying of Lands, repealed by Acts 1977, No. 170, effective January 1, 1978.

Title VI—Of New Works, the Erection of Which Can Be Stopped or Prevented, repealed by Acts 1977, No. 169, effective January 1, 1978.

APPENDIX 2—REPEALED AND REDESIGNATED PROVISIONS

Title VII—Ownership in Indivision, was added by Acts 1990, No. 890, effective January 1, 1991.

For prior texts of the articles, see Volume 16 of LSA–Civil Code (Compiled Edition).

11. Louisiana Civil Code, Book III, Preliminary Title

Book III, Preliminary Title "General Dispositions" of the Louisiana Civil Code of 1870, consisting of Article 870, was revised by Acts 1981, No. 919, effective January 1, 1982, to consist of new Article 870. For prior texts of the article, see Volume 16 of LSA–Civil Code (Compiled Edition).

12. Louisiana Civil Code, Book III, Title I

Book III, Title I "Of Successions", Chapters 1, 2, and 3, of the Louisiana Civil Code of 1870, consisting of Articles 871 through 933, were revised by Acts 1981, No. 919, effective January 1, 1982, to consist of Articles 871 through 902. For prior texts of the articles, see Volume 16 of LSA–Civil Code (Compiled Edition).

Book III, Title I "Of Successions" of the Louisiana Civil Code of 1870, Chapters 4, 5, 6, and 13, consisting of Articles 934 through 1074 and 1415 through 1466 were revised by Acts 1997, No. 1421, § 1, eff. July 1, 1999, to consist of Articles 934 to 968 and 1415 to 1429. For prior texts of the articles, see Volume 16 of LSA–Civil Code (Compiled Edition).

13. Louisiana Civil Code, Book III, Title II

Book III, Title II, "Of Donation Inter Vivos (Between Living Persons) and Mortis Causa (in Prospect of Death)" of the Louisiana Civil Code of 1870, Chapter 1, "General Dispositions", consisting of Articles 1467 through 1469, has been revised, amended, and reenacted by Acts 2008, No. 204, § 1, effective January 1, 2009, under the heading "General Dispositions" to consist of Articles 1467 through 1469. For prior text of articles, see Volume 17 of LSA–Civil Code (Compiled Edition).

Book III, Title II "Of Donation Inter Vivos (Between Living Persons) and Mortis Causa (in Prospect of Death)" of the Louisiana Civil Code of 1870, Chapter 2 "Of the Capacity Necessary for Disposing of and Receiving by Donation Inter Vivos or Mortis Causa", consisting of Articles 1470 through 1492, was revised by Acts 1991, No. 363, § 1, effective September 6, 1991, to consist of Articles 1479 through 1483. For prior texts of the articles, see Volume 17 of LSA–Civil Code (Compiled Edition).

Book III, Title II "Of Donations Inter Vivos (Between Living Persons) and Mortis Causa (in Prospect of Death)" of the Louisiana Civil Code of 1870, Chapter 3 "Of the Disposable Portion, and of its Reduction in Case of Excess", consisting of Articles 1493 through 1518, was revised by Acts 1996, No. 77, § 1 (1st Extraordinary Session 1996), effective June 18, 1996, to consist of Articles 1493 through 1514. For prior texts of the articles, see Volume 17 of LSA–Civil Code (Compiled Edition).

Book III, Title II, "Donations" of the Louisiana Civil Code of 1870, Chapter 5, "Of Donations Inter Vivos (Between Living Persons)", consisting of Articles 1523 through 1568.1, has been revised, amended, and re-enacted by Acts 2008, No. 204, § 1, effective January 1, 2009, under the heading "Donations Inter Vivos" to consist of Articles 1523 through 1469.1. These texts have been redesignated under the authority of the Louisiana State Law Institute as Articles 1526 through 1569. For prior text of articles, see Volume 17 of LSA–Civil Code (Compiled Edition).

Book III, Title II "Of Donations Inter Vivos (Between Living Persons) and Mortis Causa (in Prospect of Death" of the Louisiana Civil Code of 1870, Chapter 6 "Of Dispositions Mortis Causa (in Prospect of Death)", consisting of Articles 1570 through 1723 was revised by Acts 1997, No. 1421, § 1, effective July 1, 1999, to consist of Articles 1570 through 1616. For prior texts of the articles, see Volume 17 of LSA–Civil Code (Compiled Edition).

Book III, Title II "Donations" of the Louisiana Civil Code of 1870, Chapter 8 "Of Donations made by Marriage Contract to the Husband or Wife, and to the Children to Be Born of the Marriage," and Chapter 9 "Of Donations Between Married Persons, Either by Marriage Contract or During the Marriage," consisting of Articles 1734 to 1755 were revised by Acts 2004, No. 619, § 1, effective September 1, 2005, to consist of Articles 1734 to 1751. For prior texts of the articles, see Volume 17 of LSA—Civil Code (Compiled Edition).

14. Louisiana Civil Code, Book III, Titles III and IV (1870)

Book III, Title III "Of Obligations" and Title IV "Of Conventional Obligations" of the Louisiana Civil Code of 1870, Articles 1756 through 2291, were revised by Acts 1984, No. 331, effective January 1, 1985, to consist of Articles 1756 through 2057.

Articles 2004 through 2006 of the Louisiana Civil Code of 1870 have been redesignated as R.S. 9:2785 through 2787; Articles 2251 through 2267, 2269 and 2270 have been redesignated as R.S. 9:2741 through

APPENDIX 2—REPEALED AND REDESIGNATED PROVISIONS

2759; and Article 2286 has been redesignated as R.S. 13:4231. For prior texts of the articles, see Volume 17 of LSA–Civil Code (Compiled Edition).

15. Louisiana Civil Code, Book III, Title V (1870)

Book III, Title V "Of Quasi Contracts, and Of Offenses and Quasi Offenses", of the Louisiana Civil Code of 1870 has been renamed "Obligations Arising Without Agreement". See Acts 1995, No. 1041, § 3, effective January 1, 1996.

Book III, Title V of the Louisiana Civil Code of 1870, Article 2292 and Chapter 1, consisting of Articles 2293 through 2313, were revised by Acts 1995, No. 1041, § 1, effective January 1, 1996, to consist of Chapter 1—"Management of Affairs (Negotiorum Gestio)", Articles 2292 through 2297, and Chapter 2—"Enrichment Without Cause", Articles 2298 through 2305. The Louisiana State Law Institute was instructed to redesignate Chapter 2 of Title V of Book II of the Louisiana Civil Code of 1870 as Chapter 3 "Of Offenses and Quasi–Offenses". See Acts 1995, No. 1041, § 2, effective January 1, 1996. For prior texts of the articles, see Volume 17 of LSA–Civil Code (Compiled Edition).

16. Louisiana Civil Code, Book III, Title VI (1870)

Book III, Title VI "Of the Marriage Contract, and of the Respective Rights of the Parties in Relation to Their Property" of the Louisiana Civil Code of 1870, consisting of Articles 2325 through 2437, was repealed by Acts 1979, No. 709, effective January 1, 1980. Acts 1979, No. 709, § 1, effective January 1, 1980, enacted the first three chapters of the new Title VI, "Matrimonial Regimes", consisting of Articles 2325 to 2376. Acts 1979, No. 710, § 1, effective January 1, 1980, added Chapter 4, "Marital Portion", consisting of Articles 2432 to 2437. For prior texts of the articles, see Volume 17 of LSA–Civil Code (Compiled Edition).

17. Louisiana Civil Code, Book III, Title VII (1870)

Book III, Title VII "Of Sale" of the Louisiana Civil Code of 1870, consisting of articles 2438 through 2659, was revised by Acts 1993, No. 841, effective January 1, 1995, to consist of new Articles 2438 through 2659. Articles 2601 through 2641 of the 1870 Code have been redesignated by Acts 1993, No. 841, as R.S. 9:3151 through 3191. For prior texts of the articles, see Volume 17 of LSA–Civil Code (Compiled Edition).

18. Louisiana Civil Code, Book III, Title VIII (1870)

Book III, Title VIII, of the Louisiana Civil Code of 1870, "Of Exchange", consisting of Articles 2660 through 2667, has been revised, amended, and reenacted by Acts 2010, No. 186, effective August 15, 2010, to consist of Articles 2660 through 2667 under the heading "Exchange". For the prior texts of the articles, see Volume 17 of LSA- Civil Code (Compiled Edition).

19. Louisiana Civil Code, Book III, Title IX (1870)

Book III, Title IX "Of Lease," of the Louisiana Civil Code of 1870, Chapters 1 and 2, consisting of Articles 2668 to 2744 were revised by Acts 2004, No. 821, § 1, effective January 1, 2005, to consist of Articles 2668 to 2729. For prior texts of the articles, see Volume 17 of LSA–Civil Code (Compiled Edition).

20. Louisiana Civil Code, Book III, Title X

Book III, Title X of the Louisiana Civil Code of 1870, "Of Rents and Annuities", consisting of Articles 2778 through 2800 was revised by Acts 2012, No. 258, effective January 1, 2013, to consist of Articles 2778 through 2791. The prior texts of Articles 2778 through 2800, effective until December 31, 2012, are reproduced here.

Art. 2778. Rent of land and rent of money

There are two species of rent; that of land which is properly called rent, and that of money.

Art. 2779. Rent of lands, definition

The contract of *rent of lands* is a contract by which one of the parties conveys and cedes to the other a track [tract] of land, or any other immovable property, and stipulates that the latter shall hold it as owner, but reserving to the former an annual rent of a certain sum of money, or of a certain quantity of fruits, which the other party binds himself to pay him.

Art. 2780. Perpetual duration essential; lease distinguished

It is of the essence of this conveyance that it be made in perpetuity. If it be made for a limited time, it is a lease.

Art. 2781. Sale and rent distinguished

A contract of sale, in which it is stipulated that the price shall be paid at a future time, but that it bears interest from the day of sale, is not a contract of rent.

On the contrary, a contract made bearing the name of a sale in which the seller does not stipulate the payment of the price, but at a capital bearing interest forever, is a contract of rent.

APPENDIX 2—REPEALED AND REDESIGNATED PROVISIONS

Art. 2782. Elements of sale and lease in rent contract

The contract of rent partakes of the nature of sale and of lease.

Of sale, inasmuch as it transfers the ownership of the thing, and subjects the party to the same warranty which is imposed on the vendor.

And of lease, inasmuch as it subjects the rentee to the payment of rent.

Art. 2783. Applicability of rules of sale

The contract of rent is subjected to the same rules as the contract of sale, except in the cases hereafter specified.

Art. 2784. Preservation of property by purchaser under reservation of rent

The thing sold with reservation of rent, becomes the property of the person receiving it, in the same manner as a thing sold becomes the property of the purchaser; but whereas the purchaser may make what use he pleases of the thing bought and may even destroy it, when he has paid the price, the purchaser under reservation of rent is bound to preserve the thing in good condition that it may continue capable of producing wherewith to pay the rent.

Art. 2785. Total or partial destruction of property, rights and obligations of parties

When a thing sold is destroyed from unforeseen accident, the loss falls entirely on the purchaser; in case of a sale reserving rent, the loss is sustained by both parties; for on one side the lessee loses the enjoyment of the thing, and on the other the lessor loses the right to demand the rent which is extinguished.

But in order that the rent be extinguished, the thing must have perished entirely; if it be lost only in part, the rent is only reducible in proportion to the loss.

Art. 2786. Perpetual nature of rent charge

A thing sold and paid for may be alienated absolutely and unconditionally; but if it be sold with a rent reserved, it remains perpetually subject to the rent, into whatsoever hands it may pass.

Art. 2787. Rent as charge on the property

The price of a thing sold is a debt personal to the purchaser. But where there has been rent reserved, it is a charge imposed on the property, and the person alienating it is only answerable for the arrears which become due while he was in the possession.

Art. 2788. Redeemable nature of contract

The rent charge, although stipulated to be perpetual, is essentially redeemable. But the seller may determine the terms of the redemption and stipulate that it shall not take place until after a certain time, which can never exceed thirty years.

Art. 2789. Price of redemption when valued in contract

If the value of the property has been determined by the contract, the possessor who wishes to redeem can not be made to pay anything beyond that value.

Art. 2790. Determination of price in absence of valuation

If there has been no valuation, the rent is considered as fixed at the rate of six per cent. on the value and the lessee may pay the capital at that valuation.

Art. 2791. Mortgage on property for payment of rent

The rentor has for the payment of this rent a right of mortgage on the property, commencing from the date of the contract. But he can not have it seized and sold, unless there be at least one entire year's rent due.

Art. 2792. Mortgageability of rent charge

The rent, charged, [rent charge] being inherent to the property burdened with it, is itself susceptible of being mortgaged, except when it has been gratuitously established, for the benefit of a third person, on condition that it should not be liable to seizure.

Acts 1871, No. 87.

Art. 2793. Annuity, definition

The contract of *annuity* is that by which one party delivers to another a sum of money, and agrees not to reclaim it so long as the receiver pays the rent agreed upon.

Art. 2794. Perpetual or life annuities

This annuity may be either perpetual or for life.

Art. 2795. Limitation on rate of interest

The amount of annuity for life can in no case exceed the double of the conventional interest.

The amount of perpetual annuity can not exceed the conventional interest.

Art. 2796. Redeemable nature of contract

Constituted annuity is essentially redeemable.

The parties may only agree that the same shall not be redeemed prior to a time which can not exceed ten years, or without having warned the creditor a time before, which they shall limit.

Art. 2797. Compulsory redemption against debtor

The debtor of a constituted annuity may be compelled to redeem the same:

1. If he ceases fulfilling his obligations during three years.

2. If he does not give to the lender the securities promised by the contract.

Art. 2798. Insolvency of debtor, effect

If the debtor should fail, or be in a state of insolvency, the capital of the constituted annuity becomes exigible; but only up to the amount at which it is rated, according to the order of contribution amongst the creditors.

Art. 2799. Right of debtor's surety to compel redemption

The debtor may be compelled by his security to redeem the annuity within the time which has been fixed in the contract, if any time has been fixed, or after ten years, if no mention be made of the time in the act.

APPENDIX 2—REPEALED AND REDESIGNATED PROVISIONS

Art. 2800. Interest on sums lent and on arrears of annuity

The interest of the sums lent and the arrears of constituted and life annuity can not bear interest but from the day a judicial demand of the same has been made by the creditor and when interest is due for at least one whole year.

21. Louisiana Civil Code, Book III, Title XI (1870)

Book III, Title XI "Of Partnership" of the Louisiana Civil Code of 1870, consisting of Articles 2801 through 2890, was revised by Acts 1980, No. 150, effective January 1, 1981, to consist of Articles 2801 through 2848. For prior texts of the articles, see Volume 17A of LSA–Civil Code (Compiled Edition).

22. Louisiana Civil Code, Book III, Title XII (1870)

Book III, Title XII "Of Loan," of the Louisiana Civil Code of 1870, consisting of Articles 2891 through 2925 was revised by Acts 2004, No. 743, § 1, effective January 1, 2005, to consist of Articles 2891 through 2913. For prior texts of the articles, see Volume 17A of LSA–Civil Code (Compiled Edition).

23. Louisiana Civil Code, Book III, Title XIII (1870)

Book III, Title XIII "Of Deposit and Sequestration" of the Louisiana Civil Code of 1870, consisting of Articles 2926 through 2981, was revised by Acts 2003, No. 491, § 1, effective January 1, 2004, to consist of Articles 2926 through 2951. For prior texts of the articles, see Volume 17A of LSA–Civil Code (Compiled Edition).

24. Louisiana Civil Code, Book III, Title XV (1870)

Book III, Title XV "Of Mandate" of the Louisiana Civil Code of 1870, consisting of Articles 2985 to 3034, was revised by Acts 1997, No. 261, § 1, effective January 1, 1998, to consist of Articles 2985 to 3032. For prior texts of the articles, see Volume 17A of LSA–Civil Code (Compiled Edition).

25. Louisiana Civil Code, Book III, Title XVI (1870)

Book III, Title XVI "Of Suretyship" of the Louisiana Civil Code of 1870, consisting of Articles 3035 through 3070, was revised by Acts 1987, No. 409, § 1, effective January 1, 1988, to consist of new Articles 3035 through 3070. Articles 3069 and 3070 of the 1870 Code have been redesignated as R.S. 9:391 and R.S. 9:3912. For prior texts of the articles, see Volume 17A of LSA–Civil Code (Compiled Edition).

26. Louisiana Civil Code, Book III, Title XVII (1870)

Book III, Title XVII of the Louisiana Civil Code of 1870, "Of Transaction or Compromise," consisting of Articles 3071 through 3083, was revised, amended and reenacted by Acts 2007, No. 138, effective August 15, 2007, to consist of Articles 3071 through 3083. For prior texts of the articles, see Volume 17A of LSA–Civil Code (Compiled Edition).

27. Louisiana Civil Code, Book III, Title XXII (1870)

Book III, Title XXII, of the Louisiana Civil Code of 1870 "Of Mortgages" was revised by Acts 1991, No. 652, § 1 and Acts 1992, No. 1132, § 2.

Articles 3278 through 3298 were revised, amended and re-enacted by Acts 1991, No. 652, § 1, effective January 1, 1992. Acts 1991, No. 652, § 4, effective January 1, 1992, repealed Articles 3299 through 3310 of the Louisiana Civil Code of 1870.

Articles 3311 through 3337 were revised, amended, and re-enacted by Acts 1992, No. 1132, § 2, and effective January 1, 1993. Acts 1992, No. 1132, § 4, effective January 1, 1993, instructed the Louisiana State Law Institute to redesignate Articles 3371 through 3385.1 of the Louisiana Civil Code of 1870 as R.S. 9:5169 through R.S. 9:5180.4 and Articles 3386 through 3396 of the Louisiana Civil Code of 1870 as R.S. 9:5206 through R.S. 9:5216. Acts 1992, No. 1132, § 1, effective January 1, 1993, repealed Articles 3311 through 3370 of the Louisiana Civil Code of 1870 and Articles 3397 through 3411 of the same Code.

Articles 3308 to 3310, 3314, 3321 to 3324, and 3327 to 3336 were repealed by Acts. 2005, No. 169, effective January 1, 2006. The effective date of Act 169 was postponed to July 1, 2006, pursuant to emergency legislation, Acts 2005, 1st Ex.Sess., No. 13.

For prior texts of the articles, see Volume 17A of LSA–Civil Code (Compiled Edition).

28. Louisiana Civil Code, Book III, Title XXII–A

Articles 3338 to 3668 were enacted by Acts 2005, No. 169, effective January 1, 2006, under the heading of Title XXII–A—"Of Registry". The effective date of Act 169 was postponed to July 1, 2006, pursuant to emergency legislation, Acts 2005, 1st Ex.Sess., No. 13.

APPENDIX 2—REPEALED AND REDESIGNATED PROVISIONS

29. Louisiana Civil Code, Book III, Title XXIII (1870)

Book III, Title XXIII "Of Occupancy, Possession and Prescription" of the Louisiana Civil Code of 1870 was revised in part by Acts 1982, No. 187, and in part by Acts 1983, No. 173. Title XXIII, Chapters 1 and 2, and Chapter 3, Sections 1 and 2 (Articles 3412 through 3527), were revised by Acts 1982, No. 187. Title XXIII, Chapter 3, Section 3 (Articles 3528 through 3531, 3533 through 3542, and 3544 through 3554) was revised by Acts 1983, No. 173. By the same act, Article 3532 was redesignated as an unnumbered paragraph of Article 10 (which article was subsequently redesignated as Article 15 pursuant to Acts 1987, No. 124, § 2) and Article 3543 was redesignated as R.S. 9:5622. For prior texts of the articles, see Volume 17A of LSA–Civil Code (Compiled Edition).

30. Louisiana Civil Code, Book IV

The Preliminary Title of the Louisiana Civil Code of 1870 "Of the General Definitions of Law and the Promulgation of the Laws", consisting of Articles 1 through 23, was revised by Acts 1987, No. 124, § 1, effective January 1, 1988. Articles 9 and 10 of the Louisiana Civil Code of 1870 were redesignated as Articles 14 and 15 of new Chapter 3—"Conflict of Laws" under the authority of the Louisiana State Law Institute.

Acts 1991, No. 923, § 1, effective January 1, 1992, revised Chapter 3 of the Preliminary Title of the Civil Code, comprising redesignated Articles 14 and 15, to consist of Articles 14 through 49. Further, Articles 15 through 49 of the 1991 legislation were redesignated under the authority of the Louisiana State Law Institute as Articles 3515 through 3549 to form a new Book IV—"Conflict of Laws". For the texts of Articles 14 and 15 as they existed at the time of the 1991 revision, see Volume 16 of LSA–Civil Code (Compiled Edition).

*

APPENDIX 3

CIVIL LAW TERMS AND DEFINITIONS FOUND IN TEXTS OF THE LOUISIANA CIVIL CODE AND IN REVISION COMMENTS*

* This Appendix contains terms and definitions found in provisions of the Louisiana Civil Code and in Revision Comments in typical 'definition form' as well as in descriptions of a word's meaning established by example or particular usage. These terms and definitions, however, do not necessarily provide all inclusive meanings of words and sentences. The Appendix is merely a reference guide to the particular, and sometimes peculiar, usage of words and sentences found in the pamphlet edition of the Louisiana Civil Code.

Abandoned thing, CC 3418
Absent person, CC 47
    Spouse, CC 2355, Comment 1990
Absolute nullity, CC 2030
    Simulation, CC 2026
Absolutely null marriage, CC 94
Acceptance of a succession, formal or informal, CC 957
Accession, CC 482, Comment (b); *cf.*, CC. 482, 483
    Above and below the surface of land, CC 490
Accessory, Contract, CC 1913; CC 3035, Comment (b)
    Real rights, CC 3536, Comment (a)
    Rights (servitudes), *see*, CC 743
    Thing, CC 508; *cf.*, CC 559, Comment (b)
Accident (destruction of property subject to usufruct), CC 613, Comment (e)
Accretion,
    On the bank of a river or stream, CC 499
    Testamentary, CC 1590–1593, 1595, 1956
    Upon renunciation of succession, CC 964, 965, 966
Acknowledgment, CC 3464; *id.*, Comment (b); 3449, Comment (c)
Acquets, CC 2327, Comment (b)
Acquisitive prescription, CC 3446, 3473–3491
Act, Contracts, CC 2036, Comment (d)
    Authentic, CC 1833
    Conservatory, CC 1771, 1783
    Last will, CC 1570, Comment (c); *cf.*, 1573
    Negotiorum gestio, CC 2292, Comment (b)
    Testament, CC 1570
    Translative of ownership, CC 3483, Comment (b); *see also*, CC 487, Comment (b); CC 517, Comment (c)
Active mass (successions), CC 1356
Administration expenses, probate, CC 1415
Administrators of vacant successions, CC 1097
Affirmative servitude, CC 706
Aleatory contract, CC 1912; *see also*, CC 2982
Alienation, see, CC 2305
Alimony, CC 230(a) and (b)
Alluvion, CC 499, 500
Alternative obligation, CC 1808
Amicable compounders, CC 3110

APPENDIX 3—CIVIL LAW TERMS

Animals, CC 551, Comment (f)
    Domestic, CC 3417, Comment (d)
    Wild ("wildlife"), CC 3412, Comment (e); *see also*, CC 3413; CC 3417, Comment (d)
Annual charges, CC 584, Comments (b) and (c)
Annuity, CC 2778
Antichresis, CC 3135; CC 3176
Apparent servitude, CC 707
Approval (sales); right of view and trial, CC 2460, Comment (c); *cf.* CC 2605; *id.*, Comment (c)
Arbitrators, CC 3110
Assignment of rights without warranty, CC 2502, Comment (c)
Assigns, CC 3506(5)
Authentic act, CC 1833
Author (in title), CC 3483, Comment (f)
Bad faith (contracts), CC 1997, Comment (c)
Banks, navigable river or stream, CC 456; *see also*, Comments (b) and (f)
Beneficiary successors, CC 879
Bilateral (or synallagmatic) contract, CC 1908; *cf.* CC 1993, Comment (b)
Bilateral error, CC 1949, Comment (d)
Bon père de famille, CC 576, Comment (b)
Bornage, CC 784, Comment (b)
Boundary, CC 784
Boundary marker, CC 784
Breach of contract, CC 1994, Comment (b)
Building materials (movable or immovable), CC 472
Building restrictions, CC 775
Caretaker, CC 3469
Cas fortuit, CC 1873, Comment (c)
Cause, CC 1967; *cf.*, CC 1950
    Unlawful, CC 1968
Certain term, CC 1778
Children, CC 3506(8)
Chronic sickness, CC 3200
Civil,
    Fruits, CC 551
    Possession, CC 3431
Clandestine possession, CC 3436; *cf.*, CC 3476, Comment (g)
Clause pénale, CC 2005, Comment (c)
Clear and convincing evidence, CC 1482, Comment (c)
Collateral line, CC 901
Collation, CC 1227
    By taking less, CC 1253
    In kind, CC 1252
Commencement de preuve par écrit, CC 1837, Comment (b)
Commendam, partnership in, CC 2837
Commercial suretyship, CC 3042
Commercial symbols, *see, e.g.*, CC 2616, Comment (b)
Commodatum, CC. 2891, 2893
Common things, CC 449
Common wall servitude, CC 673
Communauté d'acquets ou de gains, CC 2327, Comment (b)
Community,
    Enterprise, CC 2369.3
    Obligation, CC 2360
    Of acquets and gains, *see*, CC 2327; CC 2336, Comments (c) and (d)
    Property, CC 2338

APPENDIX 3—CIVIL LAW TERMS

Commutative contract, CC 1911
Compensatory damages (contracts), *see*, CC 1989, Comment (b)
Component part, *see*, CC 463, 465, 466
Compromise, CC 3071
Conditio legis, *see*, CC 1767, Comment (f)
Condition, *see*, CC 1767, Comment (f)
    Obligation, CC 1767; *see also, id.*, Comment (e)
    Resolutory, CC 1767
    Suspensive, CC 1767
Confidential relationship, CC 1483, Comment (c)
Confirmation, CC 1842; *cf.*, CC 1883, Comment (d)
Confusion, *see*, CC 1903; *see, e.g.*, CC 622 and 765
Conjunctive obligation, CC 1807; *cf.*, CC 2019
Consent, Contracts, *see*, CC 1927
Conservatory acts, CC 1771, 1783
Consignation, CC 1869, Comment (f)
Constructions, CC 463, Comment (c)
Constructions, transfer or encumbrance, CC 469, Comment (d)
Constructive possession, CC 3426
Consumable things, CC 536
Contract, CC 1906
    Aleatory, CC 1912
    Bilateral or synallagmatic, CC 1908
    Commutative, CC 1911
    Gratuitous, CC 1910
    Nominate and innominate, CC 1914
    Null, CC 2029
    Onerous, CC 1909
    Option, CC 1933
    Principal and accessory, CC 1913
    To build by a plot, CC 2756
    To sell, CC 2623
    To work by the job, CC 2756
    Unilateral, CC 1907
Contrats spéciaux, CC 1914, Comment (b)
Contributory negligence, CC 2323
Conventional,
    Interest, CC 2924
    Mortgage, CC 3284
    Servitude, CC 654
    Usufruct, CC 544; *cf., id.*, Comment (b)
Co-ownership, CC 480
Corporeal,
    Movable, CC 471
    Possession, CC 3425
    Thing, CC 461
Co-sureties, CC 3055
Counteroffer, CC 1943
Custom, CC 3
Damages,
    Contracts, CC 1995
    Tort, CC 2315

APPENDIX 3—CIVIL LAW TERMS

Dans la mesure, CC 1857, Comment (b)
Debts of the estate, CC 1415
Deduction (successions), CC 1358
Definitive partition, CC 1295 and 1296
Degree (propinquity of consanguinity), CC 900
Deimmobilization, *see*, CC 468
Delictual liability, CC 3492, Comment (b)
Deposit, CC 2926
    Contract to sell, CC 2624
    Conventional, CC 2926
    Judicial, CC 2949
Depositary, *see, e.g.,* CC 2617, Comment (d)
Dereliction, CC 499
Destination of the owner, CC 741
Détenteur, CC 3437, Comment (b)
Detention, CC 3437; *id.*, Comment (b); *cf.*, CC 3477, Comments (b) and (c)
Dies interpellat pro homine, CC 1990, Comment (a)
Diligent effort (lost things), CC 3419, Comment (d)
Direct line, CC 901
Discontinuous possession, CC 3436
Dissolution, *see*, CC 2536, Comment (d)
Divisible obligation, CC 1815
Dol, CC 1953, Comment (c); *see also*, CC 1958, Comment (b); CC 1997, Comment (c); CC 2004, Comment (a)
Domestic animals, CC 3417, Comment (d)
Domestics, CC 3205
Domicile, CC 38
    Of a juridical person, *see*, CC 3518
Dominant estate CC 646, Comment (d)
Dommage moral, CC 1998, Comment (b)
Donation,
    Onerous, CC 1523; *see also*, CC 1524
    Inter vivos, CC 1468
    Mortis causa, CC 1469
    Of entire patrimony, ("of all good things" or "*omnium bonorum*"), CC 1497(a)
    Purely gratuitous, CC 1523
    Remunerative, CC 1523; *see also*, CC 1525
Duress, CC 1959; *id.*, Comment (b)
Earnest money, CC 2624
Earth, CC 551, Comment (f)
Emancipation, kinds of, CC 365
Enclosed estate, CC 689
Enrichment (without cause), CC 2298, Comment (b)
Equivocal possession, CC 3436
Error,
    Contracts, CC 1949
    Bilateral, CC 1949, Comment (d)
    Unilateral, CC 1949, Comment (d)
Estate,
    Dominant, CC 646, Comment (b); CC 698, Comment (b)
    Of a deceased, CC 872
    Servient, CC 646
Estate debts, CC 1415
Étendue, CC 1912, Comment (f)

APPENDIX 3—CIVIL LAW TERMS

Eviction, CC 2500 (sales warranty); *cf.*, CC 3433, Comment (d) (loss of possession)
Ex tunc, CC 2019, Comment (c)
Exceptio non adimpleti contractus, CC 2022 and Comment (b); *see also*, CC 1911, Comment (c)
Exchange, CC 2660; *see, e.g.*, CC 1382; *cf.*, CC 1909, Comment (c)
Expenses
    Necessary, CC 527, Comment (b); CC 1259; *cf.* CC 2577, Comment (b)
    For mere pleasure, CC 1259; *cf.* CC 2577, Comment (b)
    Useful, CC 528, Comment (b); CC 1259; *cf.* CC 2577, Comment (b)
Exploitation of the things, CC 581, Comment (b)
Express acceptance,
    Successions, CC 957
    Consent, Sales, CC 2457, Comment (b)
Extraordinary,
    Charges, CC 585, Comment (b), CC 585, Comment (b)
    Repairs, CC 578
Facultative compensation, CC 1901, Comment (a)
Failure to perform, CC 1994
Family, CC 3506(12)
Favor matrimonii, CC 3520, Comment (b)
Favor testamenti, see, CC 3528, Comments (b) and (c)
Fidelity in marriage, CC 98, Comment (b)
Filiation, CC 178
First refusal, right of, CC 2625
Fixing of the boundary, CC 785, 789
Force majeure, CC 1873, Comment (c)
Forced heirs, CC 1493(a)
Foreseeable, CC 1996, Comment (b)
Former community (enterprise), CC 2369.3, Comment (b)
Fortuitous event, CC 1875
Fraud, CC 1953
Fraude, CC 1958, Comment (b)
Fruits, CC 551
Funeral charges, CC 3192
Future thing, sale of, CC 2450
Gain, CC 2327, Comment (b)
General legacy, CC 1586
General mortgage, CC 3285
Giving in payment ("*dation*"), CC 2655
Good faith,
    Acquisitive prescription, CC 3480
    Accession, CC 487, Comments (b) and (c)
    Acquisition of corporeal movable, CC 523
    Marriage, CC 96, Comment (d)
Gratuitous,
    Donation, CC 1523
    Contract, CC 1910; *cf.*, CC 1967, Comment (c)
Habitation, CC 630; *see also*, Comment (b)
Heir, CC 876
    Ab intestato, CC 1096, *cf.*, CC 876
    Incapacity, CC 950
Heritable obligation, CC 1765; *see, e.g.*, CC 2315.1(c); CC 2315.2(c); CC 2364, Comment (b); CC 2369, Comment (b); CC 2600; *see also*, CC 1765, Comment (9b); CC 1933, Comment (c); CC 1984
Héritage, CC 646, Comment (b); CC 698, Comment (b)

APPENDIX 3—CIVIL LAW TERMS

Hire, CC 2669
Homo diligens et studiosus paterfamilas, CC 576, Comment (b)
Hope, sale of, CC 2451
Hors du commerce, CC 2448, Comment (b)
Immovables, *see*, CC 462
    By declaration, CC 467
    By destination (obsolete), CC 466, Comment (b)
    By nature (obsolete), CC 466, Comment (d)
    Incorporeal, CC 470
Imperfect obligation, (obsolete), CC 1760, Comment (d)
Imperfect usufruct (obsolete), CC 535, Comment (c)
Implied consent (sales), CC 2457, Comment (b)
Impossibility of performance (obligations), CC 1873, Comment (d)
Improvements,
    Inseparable, CC 497, Comment (c)
    Separable, CC 497, Comment (c)
Imputation of payments, *see*, CC 1864
In pari causa turpitudinem potior est conditio possidentis, CC 2033, Comment (c)
In rem mortgage, *see*, CC 3297
In solido (obligations in general), CC 1790, 1794
    Torts, CC 2324
Incapacity of heirs, CC 941, Comment (c)
Incorporeal,
    Immovables, CC 470; *cf., id.*, Comment (b)
    Movables, CC 473
    Things, CC 461
Indivisibility (mortgage), CC 3280, Comment (a)
Indivisible obligation, CC 1815
Indivision, ownership in, CC 797
Ingratitude (revocation of donations), *see*, CC 1560
Innkeepers, CC 3232
Innominate contract, CC 1914
Insolvency, CC 2037
Inspection (sales), *see*, CC 2604, 2605; *id.*, Comment (c); CC 2460, Comment (c)
Intended use (sales), CC 2475, Comment (b)
Inter vivos, CC 1468
Interest (loan), CC 2923, 2924
Interpretation (contracts), CC 2045
Interrupted possession, *see, e.g.*, CC 3434; *cf.*, CC 3465
Interruption of prescription, *see*, CC 3462, 3463, and 3466; *see, e.g.*, CC 2534 (redhibition)
Intestate,
    Succession, CC 875; CC 1096
    Successor, CC 876; *see also*, CC 1096
Irresistible force, CC 1873, Comment (d)
Irrevocable offer, *see*, CC 1928
Items of performance, *see*, CC 1808, Comment (b)
Joint,
    Obligations, CC 1788
    Joint legacy, CC 1588
Judicial,
    Deposit, CC 2979
    Mortgage, CC 3284; CC 3299
    Partition, CC 1296

APPENDIX 3—CIVIL LAW TERMS

Juridical,
    Act, CC 492, Comment (b); CC 3471, Comment (c)
    Person, CC 24; CC 479, Comment (c)
Just title, CC 3483; *id.*, Comment (b)
Last sickness, CC 3199
Law,
    Sources of, CC 1
    Charges, CC 3195
Lease, CC 2669
    Of labor or industry, CC 2675
    Of things, CC 2674
Legal,
    Bad faith (obsolete), *see*, CC 3481, Comment (c)
    Interest, CC 2924
    Mortgage, CC 3284; CC 3299
    Servitude, CC 654; *see also*, CC 659
    Suretyship, CC 3043
    Usufruct, CC 544
Legatee, CC 876
    Under particular title, CC 1587
    Under universal title, CC 1586, Comment (a)
    Universal, CC 1595
Leges causae, see, CC 3549, Comment (k)
Legislation, CC 2
Legitime, CC 1494
Lesion,
    Among co-owners, CC 814; *cf.*, CC 1406
    Beyond moiety, CC 2589; *cf.*, CC 2665
Lessee, CC 2677
Lessor, CC 2677
Lessor's privilege, CC 2705; CC 3218
Lex causae, CC 3549, Comment (b); *see also*, CC 3538, Comment (d)
Lex fori, CC 3549, Comment (b)
Liberative prescription, CC 3447
Licitation, partition by, CC 811, Comment (b)
Limited personal servitude, CC 639, Comment (c)
Line, Successions, CC 901
    Collateral, CC 901
    Direct, CC 901
Litigious right, CC 2652
Loan,
    For consumption, CC 2891, 2910
    For use, CC 2891, 2893
Lost thing, *see*, CC 3419 and comments thereto
Management of affairs, CC 2292
Mandate, CC 2989
Mandatory law, CC 2802, Comment (b)
Manual gift, CC 1539
Marital portion, *see*, CC 2432 and 2433
Marriage, CC 86
    Absolutely null, CC 94
    Contract (1870) CC 2328, Comment (c); CC 2328, Comment (c)

APPENDIX 3—CIVIL LAW TERMS

    Putative, CC 96
    Relatively null, CC 95
Masters of boarding homes, CC 3211
Material alteration (offer and acceptance), CC 2601, Comment (g), *cf.* CC 1943
Matrimonial,
    Agreement, CC 2328
    Regime, CC 2325
Mentally infirm, CC 1482, Comment (b)
Merchant (offer and acceptance), CC 2601, Comment (g)
Mode of use, *cf.*, CC 803 and 2369.3; *id.*, Comment (d)
Moratory damages, CC 1989, Comments (a) and (b)
More probable than not, CC 1482, Comment (c)
Mortgage, CC 3278
    Conventional, CC 3284
    General, CC 3285
    Judicial, CC 3284; CC 3299
    Legal, CC 3284; CC 3299
    Special, CC 3285
Mortgagee, CC 3279, Comment (a)
Mortis causa, CC 1469
Multilateral contract, *see*, CC 2020, Comment (b)
Mutuum, CC. 2891, 2910
Naked ownership, CC 478
Natural,
    Fruits, CC 551
    Obligation CC 1760; *see also*, CC 3447, Comment (b); CC 3448, Comment (c)
    Deposit, CC 2964
    Expenses CC 527, Comment (b); CC 1259; *cf.* CC 2577, Comment (b)
    Person, CC 24
    Servitude, CC 654
Negative servitude, CC 706
Negotiorum gestio, CC 2292, Comment (a); see also, CC 2608, Comment (b)
Neminem res sua servit, CC 622, Comment (b), CC 646, Comment (f)
Nemo est heres viventis, CC 876, Comment (b)
Nemo propriam terpitudinem, allegare potest, CC 1762, Comment (d); CC 2033, Comment (c)
Nominate contract, CC 1914
Nonapparent servitude, CC 707
Nonconsumable things, CC 537
Nonpecuniary loss, CC 1998, Comment (b)
Nonuse, prescription of, CC 3448
Novation, CC 1879; *cf.*, CC 1826, Comment (b)
    Subjective, *see*, CC 1882
Null contract, CC 2029
Nullity,
    Absolute, CC 2030
    Relative, CC 2031
Obligation, CC 1756
    Alternative, CC 1808
    Civil (obsolete) CC 1756, Comment (b); CC 1760, Comment (b)
    Community, CC 2360
    Conditional, CC 1767
    Conjunctive, CC 1807

APPENDIX 3—CIVIL LAW TERMS

    Divisible, CC 1815

    Heritable CC 1765; *see, e.g.*, CC 2315.1(c); CC 2315.2(c); CC 2364, Comment (b); CC 2369, Comment (b); CC 2600; *see also*, CC 1765, Comment (b); CC 1933, Comment (c); CC 1984

    Imperfect, (obsolete), CC 1760, Comment (d)

    Indivisible, CC 1815

    In general, (obsolete phraseology), CC 1756, Comment (b) Natural CC 1760; *see also*, CC 3447, Comment (b); CC 3448, Comment (c)

    Real, CC 1763

    Separate, CC 2363

    Strictly personal, CC 1766

Obligee, CC 1756, Comment (c)

Obligor, CC 1756, Comment (c)

Occupancy, CC 3412

Offers, revocable and irrevocable, *see*, CC 1928, 1930

Offres réelles, CC 1869, Comment (g)

Olographic testament, CC 1575

Onerous,

    Contract, CC 1909

    Donation, CC 1523; *see also*, CC 1524

Open mine doctrine, CC 561, Comments (b), (c)

Option contract, CC 1933

    To buy or sell, CC 2620

Ordinary,

    Partnership (obsolete), CC 2814, Comment (a); *cf.* CC 2817, Comment (c)

    Repairs, CC 578; *cf.* CC 577, Comment (c)

    Suretyship, CC 3044

Out of commerce, CC 2448, Comment (b)

Owed not, CC 2300; CC 2301

Owners in common, CC 480, Comment (b)

Ownership, CC 477; *cf., id.*, Comments (b), (c); *see also*, CC 481, 490,

    In indivision, CC 797

Particular,

    Revocation, CC 1691

    Successor, CC 3506(28)

    Usufruct under, CC 587

    Particular title, legacy, CC 1625

Partition, *see*, CC 1382

    By licitation, CC 811, Comment (b)

    Definitive, CC 1295 and 1296

    Of a succession, CC 1293

    Provisional, CC 1295 and 1296

Partnership, CC 2801; *cf.*, 2815, Comment

    In commendam, CC 2837

Patrimony, *see, e.g.*, CC 2358.1, Comment (a)

Paulian action, CC 2036, Comment (c)

Pawn, CC 3135; CC 3154 and 3157

Payment (imputation), CC 1864, Comment (b)

Pedis possessio, CC 3426, Comment (d)

Penal clause, CC 1808, Comment (d)

Peremption, CC 3458

Perfect usufruct (obsolete), CC 535, Comment (c)

APPENDIX 3—CIVIL LAW TERMS

Performance, *see*, CC 1756; CC 1854; *id.*, Comment (b)
    Items of, *see*, CC 1808, Comment (b)
Personal,
    Injury (separate property), CC 2344, Comment (a)
    Rights, CC 476, Comment (b)
    Servitude, CC 534
Persons,
    Juridical, CC 24
    Kinds of, CC 24
    Natural, CC 24
Pledge, CC 3133
Porte-fort, *see*, CC 1977, Comments (b), (c)
Possesseur précaire, CC 3437, Comment (b)
Possession, CC 3421; *cf.*, CC 3437, Comment (b); CC 3412, Comments (b) and (c); CC 481 (distinguished from ownership); CC 531, Comment (a) (immovable property)
    Civil, CC 3431
    Clandestine, CC 3436
    Constructive, CC 3426
    Corporeal, CC 3425
    Discontinuous, CC 3436
    Equivocal, CC 3436
    Precarious, CC 3437
    Vices of, CC 3435
    Violent, CC 3436
Possessor in good faith (accession), CC 487; *cf.*, *id.*, Comments (b), (c)
Potestative condition, *see*, CC 1770, Comment (c); *cf.*, CC 1529
Praediis inhaerent, CC 650, Comment (b)
Precarious possessor CC 3429, Comment (b); *cf.*, CC 3437, Comment (b); CC 3477, Comments (b) and (c)
Predial servitude, CC 646; *see also*, *id.*, Comment (b)
Preference, lawful causes of, CC 3184
Preparatory acts, Successions, CC 959
Prescription,
    Acquisitive, CC 3446
    Interruption of, *see*, CC. 3462, 3463, and 3466; *see, e.g.*, CC 2534 (redhibition)
    Liberative, CC 3447
    Nonuse, CC 3448
    Of nonuse, CC 3448
    Renunciation of, CC 3449, Comment (c)
    Suspension of, *see*, CC 3472; *cf.*, CC 3463, Comment (b)
Presumption, rebuttable and conclusive, CC 1851
Price, CC 2464
Principal, Contract, CC 1913
    Real rights, CC 3536, Comment (a)
    Thing (accession), CC 509; *cf.*, CC 508
Prior tempore, potior jure, CC 620, Comment (b)
Private roads, CC 457
Private things, CC 453
Privilege, CC 3186
Prize, see, CC 3412, Comment (f)
Procuration, CC 2987
    Marriage by, CC 92, Comment (b)
Product (conflict of laws), CC 3545, Comment (a)
Products, CC 488; see also, CC 551, Comment (c); CC 2339, Comment (c)

APPENDIX 3—CIVIL LAW TERMS

Prohibited substitution, CC 1520
Promesse de porte-fort, CC 1976, Comment (b)
Promise of sale, CC 2623
Property, CC 2325, Comment (b)
Proprietor, undivided, CC 1292
Propter rem, Obligation, CC 746, Comment (b)
Provisional partition, CC 1295 and 1296
Prudent administrator, CC 576, Comment (b)
Prudent owner, CC 576, Comment (b)
Public property, CC 450, Comment (b)
Public roads, CC 457
Public things, CC 450
Putative,
    Marriage, CC 96
    Title, CC 3483, Comment (e)
Quasi-possession, CC 3421
Quitclaim deed, CC 2502; Comments (b), (c) and (d)
Ratification, CC 1834; *cf.*, CC 1883, Comment (d)
Real,
    Deposit, CC 2963
    Accessory, CC 3536, Comment (a)
    Obligation, CC 1763
    Principal, CC 3536, Comment (a)
    Rights, CC 476, Comment (b); CC 535, Comment (b); CC 812, Comment (d)
    Subrogation, CC 2341, Comment (c)
    Tender (obligations), CC 1869, Comment (g)
Reasonable efforts (mitigation), CC 2002, Comment (c)
Reciprocal, CC 1993, Comment (b)
Reconduction, CC 2688, 2689
Redemption (sales), CC 2567, Comment (c)
Redhibitory defect, CC 2520
Rejection of goods (sales), CC 2605; *id.*, Comment (c)
Relative nullity, CC 2031
    Simulation, CC 2027
Relatively null marriage, CC 95
Relativity of contracts, CC 1985, Comment (a)
Remunerative donation, CC 1523; *see also*, CC 1525
Rendition of medical services, *see, e.g.*, CC 2322.1
Renunciation of prescription, CC 3449, Comment (c)
Renunciation of successions, CC 947, 960, 964–966
Renunciation, tacit or express, (prescription), CC 3450
Renvoi, *see*, CC 3517; *id.*, Comment (a)
Repairs,
    Extraordinary, CC 577, 578
    Ordinary, CC 577, 578
Representation, CC 881, 2985
Res nullius, CC 3412, Comment (d); *cf.*, CC 3413, Comment (b)
Resiliation, CC 2019, Comment (c)
Resolutory,
    Condition, CC 1767
    Term CC 1777, Comment (d); *cf.*, CC 1778, Comment (c) ("term of duration" or "extinctive term")
Respite, CC 3084

APPENDIX 3—CIVIL LAW TERMS

Revocation of testament, CC 1607, 1608
    Forced or voluntary, CC 3085
Retail dealers, CC 3208
Revendication, CC 526, Comment (b)
Revocable offer, *see*, CC 1930
Revocation, Testaments, CC 1607, 1608
Revocatory action, CC 2036
Rich (marital portion), CC 2342, Comment (c)
Right, CC 2625
    Of first refusal, CC 2625
    Of use, CC 639
    To possess, CC 3422
Roads, CC 457
Rule of validation (conflict of laws) *see*, CC 3528, Comment (c); CC 3538, Comment (b)
Sale, CC 2439
    Future things, CC 2450
    Of a hope, CC 2451
    On approval, (right of view and trial), CC 2460, Comment (c)
Seashore, CC 451
Security (subrogation), CC 1826, Comment (d)
Seizin, see, CC. 935
Separate,
    Immovables, *see*, CC 464
    Legacy, CC 1588
    Obligation, CC 2363
    Property, CC 2341
Separation of property regime, CC 2370
Sequestration, CC 2946, 2949
    Conventional, CC 2946
    Judicial, CC 2949
Servants, CC 3205
Servient estate, CC 646, Comment (d)
Servitude,
    Affirmative and negative, CC 706
    Apparent and nonapparent, CC 707
    By destination of the owner, CC 741
    Limited personal, CC 639, Comment (c)
    Of light, CC 703
    Of passage, CC 705
    Of prohibition of light, CC 704
    Of prohibition of view, CC 702
    Of support, CC 700
    Of view, CC 701
    Personal, CC 534
    Predial, CC 646
Servitudes, kinds of, CC 533
Servitus utilis esse debet, CC 647, Comment (b)
Several obligations, CC 1787
Simulation, CC 2025; *see also*, CC 2569
    Absolute, CC 2026
    Relative, CC 2027
Situs rule (conflict of laws),*see*, CC 3535; *id.*, Comment (d)
Solidary obligations,

APPENDIX 3—CIVIL LAW TERMS

  In general, CC 1790, 1794
  Torts, CC 2324
Sources of law, CC 1
Special mortgage, CC 3285
Spondet peritiam artis, CC 2545, Comment (b)
Spouse (marital regimes), CC 2369.1, Comment (d)
State (conflict of laws), CC 3516
Status, CC 3519, Comment (a)
Stipulated damages, CC 2005 and comments thereto
Stipulation pour autrui, CC 1978; *cf.*, CC 1882, Comment (c); CC 1977, Comment (c)
Stolen thing, CC 521
Strictly personal obligation, CC 1766
Subjective novation, *see*, CC 1882
Subjects of the obligations, CC 1882, Comment (b)
Submission (to arbitrate), CC 3099
Subrogation, CC 1825; *cf.*, CC 1826, Comment (b); CC 2341, Comment (c)
Subrogatum capit naturam subrogati, CC 2341, Comment (c)
Substitute goods (sales), CC 2609, Comment (b)
Substitution (obligations), CC 1881, Comment (c)
Successeur, CC 875, Comment (b)
Succession, CC 871
  Intestate, CC 875
  Partition, CC 1293
  Testate, CC 874
  Vacant, CC 1095
Successor CC 3506(28); *see also*, 875, Comment (b); CC 3298, Comment (e)
  Partnerships, CC 2823, Comment (b)
  Intestate, CC arts. 876; *see also*, 1096
  Particular, CC 3506(28)
  Testate, CC 876
  Universal, CC 3506(28)
Suppletive law, CC 2802, Comment (b)
Suretyship, CC 3035
  Commercial, CC 3042
  Legal, CC 3043
  Ordinary, CC 3044
Suspension of prescription, *see*, CC 3463, Comment (b)
Suspensive,
  Condition, CC 1767
  Term, CC 1777, Comment (d)
Synallagmatic (or bilateral), contract, CC 1908; *cf.* CC 1993, Comment (b)
Tacit,
  Acceptance (successions), CC 957
  Renunciation (prescription), CC 3450
  Revocation, CC 1691
Tenant, CC 2677
Tender (obligations), CC 1869; *cf., id.*, Comment (g)
Term, CC 1777, Comment (b)
  Certain or uncertain, CC 1778
  For deliberating, CC 2033
  Resolutory CC 1777, Comment (d); *cf.*, CC 1778, Comment (c) ("term of duration" or "extinctive term")
  Suspensive, CC 1777, Comment (d)

APPENDIX 3—CIVIL LAW TERMS

Termination, *see*, CC 2536, Comment (d)
Testament, CC 1570, 1571
    Olographic, CC 1575
Testamentary accretion, CC 1590
Testate, Succession, CC 874
Testate, Successor, CC 876
Theft, in continental systems, CC 521, Comment (b)
Things,
    Abandoned, CC 3418
    Consumable (usufruct), CC 536
    Division of, CC 448
    In commerce, CC 2448, Comment (b)
    Lost, *see*, CC 3419 and comments thereto
    Nonconsumable, CC 537
    Not owed, CC 2300; CC 2301
    Obligations; technical usage, *see*, CC 1808, Comment (b)
    Principal and accessory, CC 508, 509; *cf.*, CC 559, Comment (b)
    Private, CC 453
    Public, CC 450
    Stolen, CC 521
Third,
    Person, CC 3506(32)
    Possessor, CC 3315
Title
    Acts translative of ownership, CC 532; *cf., id.*, Comment (c); CC 740, Comment (b); CC 3426, Comment (b)
    Description, CC 793; *cf., id.*, Comment (c)
    Ownership, CC 531, Comment (b)
Transferable right (assignment) CC 1765, Comment (b); see also, "heritable obligation," this Appendix
Travelers, CC 3235
Treasure, CC 3420; *id.*, Comment (c)
Umpire, CC 3116
Uncertain term, CC 1778
Unconditional successors, CC 878
Undertakers (contractors), CC 2771
Undivided proprietor, CC 1292
Undue influence, *see*, CC 1479; *cf.*, Comments (b) and (c)
Unilateral, Contract, CC 1907
    Error, CC 1949, Comment (d)
Universal,
    Legacy, CC 1595
    Successor, CC 3506(28)
    Title, legacy under, CC 1586
    Usufruct, CC 587
Unlawful cause, CC 1968
Unworthiness, CC 941
Use,
    Right of, CC 639
    Of property, CC 581, Comment (b)
Useful expenses CC 528, Comment (b); CC 1259; *cf.* CC 2577, Comment (b),
Usufruct, CC 535, 540
    Conventional, CC 544; *cf., id.*, Comment (b)
    Imperfect (obsolete), CC 535, Comment (c)

APPENDIX 3—CIVIL LAW TERMS

    In divided portions, CC 541, Comment (b)
    In undivided portions CC 541, Comment (b); *see also*, CC 547 and Comments (b) and (c) thereto
    Legal, CC 544
    Perfect (obsolete), CC 535, Comment (c)
    Under particular title, CC 587
    Under universal title, CC 587
Utility, CC 696.1
Vacant succession, CC 1095
Vendor's privilege, CC 3227; CC 3249 and 3250
Vices,
    Of consent, *see, e.g.*, CC 1948
    Of possession, CC 3435
View and trial (sales), CC 2460, Comment (c); *cf.*, CC 2605; *id.*, Comment (c)
Vinculum juris, see, CC 1763, Comment (b)
Violent possession, CC 3436
Virile portion, CC 1804
Voluntary,
    Respite, CC 3085
Voyage, CC 3245
Wall, CC 673, Comment (e)
Warranty of portions, CC 1384
Wildlife, CC 3412, Comment (e); *see also*, CC 3413; CC 3417, Comment (d)
Without cause (enrichment), CC 2298
Writing, CC 3038, Comment (b)

*

TABLES

TABLE 1—DISPOSITION

This table shows the continuing revision of the Louisiana Civil Code of 1870 and the *disposition* of the articles of that Code, that is, where the subject-matter of prior articles may be found after revision.

1. Former Articles 1 to 23, and Revision of the Preliminary Title, Articles 1 to 15:

Prior Art. No.	1987 Revision Art. No. (Act No. 124)	Prior Art. No.	1987 Revision Art. No. (Act No. 124)	Prior Art. No.	1987 Revision Art. No. (Act No. 124)
1	2	7	5	13	9
2	—	8	6	14	11
3	1, 3	9	14*	15	11
4	—	10	15*	16	12
5	—	11	7	17	13
6	—	12	7	18	10
				19	—
				20	—
				21	4
				22	8
				23	8

* For the disposition of Articles 14 and 15 in the 1991 Conflict of Laws Revision, see editor's notes preceding Articles 14 and 3515.

2. Former Articles 24 to 37, and Revision of Book I, Title I, Articles 24 to 31:

Prior Art. No.	1987 Revision Art. No. (Act No. 125)	Prior Art. No.	1987 Revision Art. No. (Act No. 125)	Prior Art. No.	1987 Revision Art. No. (Act No. 125)
24	—	27	—	30	—
25	—	28	26	31	—
26	—	29	26	32	—
				33	—
				34	—
				35	—
				36	—
				37	29

3. Former Articles 38 to 46, and Revision of Book I, Title II, Articles 38 to 46:

Prior Art. No.	2008 Revision Art. No. (Act No. 801)	Prior Art. No.	2008 Revision Art. No. (Act No. 801)	Prior Art. No.	2008 Revision Art. No. (Act No. 801)
38	cf. 38	40	—	41	cf. 39
39	cf. 41, 42, 43	40.1	CCP 11	42	cf. 45
				43	cf. 45
				44	cf. 46
				45	cf. 46
				46	cf. 46

TABLE 1—DISPOSITION

4. Former Articles 47 to 85, and Revision of Book I, Title III, Articles 47 to 59:

Prior Art. No.	1990 Revision Art. No. (Act No. 989)	Prior Art. No.	1990 Revision Art. No. (Act No. 989)	Prior Art. No.	1990 Revision Art. No. (Act No. 989)
47	—	58	—	72	—
48	—	59	—	73	—
49	—	60	—	74	—
50	—	61	—	75	—
51	—	62	—	76	—
52	—	63	—	77	—
53	—	64	—	78	—
54	—	65	—	79	—
55	—	66	—		
		67	—	81	—
		68	—	82	—
		69	—	83	—
		70	—	84	[R.S. 9:195]
57	—	71	—	85	—

5. Former Articles 86 to 119, and Revision of Book I, Title IV, Chapters 1 to 5, Articles 86 to 101:

Prior Art. No.	1987 Revision Art. No. (Act No. 886)	Prior Art. No.	1987 Revision Art. No. (Act No. 886)	Prior Art. No.	1987 Revision Art. No. (Act No. 886)
86	86	96	—	106	—
87	86	97	—	107	—
88	86, 91	98	—	108	—
89	86	99	91	109	—
90	87	100	—	110	95
91	93	101	—	111	95
92	87	102	—	112	—
93	88	103	—	113	—
94	90	104	—	114	94
95	90	105	—	115	—
				116	94
				117	96, 97
				118	96, 97
				119	98

6. Former Articles 111 to 120, and Revision of Book I, Title V, Chapter 2, Section 1, Articles 111 to 117:

Prior Art. No.	1997 Revision Art. No.	Prior Art. No.	1997 Revision Art. No.
111	111	112	111, 112, 231

7. Former Articles 131 to 135, 138 to 145, and Revision of Book I, Title V, Chapters 1 and 2:

Prior Art. No.	1993 Revision Art. No. (Act No. 261)	Prior Art. No.	1993 Revision Art. No. (Act No. 261)	Prior Art. No.	1990 Revision Art. No. (Act No. 1009)
131	131 to 135	135	—	139	103
132	136		1990 Revision Art. No. (Act No. 1009)	140	—
133	—	Prior Art. No.		141	—
134	—	138	—	142	—
				143	—
				144	—
				145	—

TABLE 1—DISPOSITION

8. Former Article 178 to 211 and Revision of Book I, Title VII, Chapters 1 and 2

Prior Art. No.	2005 Revision Art. No.	Prior Art. No.	2005 Revision Art. No.	Prior Art. No.	2005 Revision Art. No.
178	—	188	188	200	—
179	—	189	189	201	—
180	—	190	190	202	—
181	—	191	—	203	—
182	—	192	—	204	—
183	—	193	—	205	—
184	185	194	—	206	—
185	186	195	—	207	—
186	—	196	—	208	—
187	187	197	—	209	—
		198	—	210	—
		199	—	211	—

9. Former Article 214 and Revision of Book I, Title VII, Chapter 4, Articles 212 to 214

Prior Art. No.	2008 Revision Art. No. (Act No. 351)
214	—

10. Former Articles 365 to 385 and Revision of Book I, Title VIII, Chapter 2, Articles 365 to 371

Prior Art. No.	2008 Revision Art. No. (Act No. 786)	Prior Art. No.	2008 Revision Art. No. (Act No. 786)	Prior Art. No.	2008 Revision Art. No. (Act No. 786)
365	cf. 365	372	—	379	cf. 367
366	cf. 368	373	—	380	—
367	—	374	—	381	—
368	—	375	—	382	cf. 367
369	—	376	—	383	—
370	—	377	—	384	—
371	—	378	—	385	—

11. Former Articles 389 to 426, and Revision of Book I, Title IX, Articles 389 to 399:

Prior Art. No.	2000 Revision Art. No. (Act No. 25, 1st Ex. Sess.)	Prior Art. No.	2000 Revision Art. No. (Act No. 25, 1st Ex. Sess.)	Prior Art. No.	2000 Revision Art. No. (Act No. 25, 1st Ex. Sess.)
389	389	401	394, 396	414	—
389.1	390, 392, 395	402	394	415	—
390	—	403	cf. 394, 396	416	—
391	—	404	cf. 392	417	—
392	—	405	cf. 392	418	—
393	—	406	cf. 393	419	399
394	391	407	cf. 393	420	397, 398
395	—	408	cf. 393	421	cf. 397
396	—	409	cf. 393	422	389
397	—	410	cf. 393	423	—
398	—	411	cf. 393	424	—
399	—	412	—	425	—
400	396	413	—	426	cf. 389

TABLE 1—DISPOSITION

12. Former Articles 448 to 855, and Revision of Book II, Articles 448 to 796:

Prior Art. No.	1978 Revision Art. No.
448	—
449	448, 453
450	449
451	451
452	452
453	450, 452
454	450
455	456
456	—
457	456
458 (par. 1)	—
458 (par. 2)	450(3)
458 (par. 3)	453
459	453
460 (par. 1)	448
460 (par. 2)	461
460 (par. 3)	461
461	448
462	—
463	—
464	462
465	463
466	—
467	466
468 (par. 1)	467
468 (par. 2)	466
469	466
470	470
471	470
472	—
473	471
474	473
475	471, 473, 475
476	472
477	—
478	—
479	—
480	—
481	449, 450, 453
482 (par. 1)	449
482 (par. 2)	450, 455
483	453
484	454
485	—
486	—
487	476

Prior Art. No.	1979 Revision Art. No.
488	477
489	—
490(2), (3)	478
491(1)	477
491(2)	10
492	—
493	479
494	480
495	—
496	481
497	—
498	482
499	483
500	484
501	485
502	486
503	487
504	—
505	490
506	491
507	494
508	491–498
509	499
510(1)	499
510(2)	500
511	502
512	505
513	506
514	506
515	506
516	501
517	503
518	504
519	—
520	507
521	510
522	508
523	510
524	509
525	511
526	511
527	513
528	514
529	514
530	—
531	515
532	516

Prior Art. No.	1976 Revision Art. No.
533	539
534	535
534 (par. 1)	537
534 (par. 2)	536
535	539, 628
536	538
537	540
538	541
539	541
540	544
541	544
542	545
543	549
544	550
545	551
546 (par. 1)	554
546 (par. 2)	555
547	556
548	559
549	538, 629
550	569
551 (par. 2)	560
552	561
553 (sent. 1)	563
553 (par. 2)	564
554	565
555	567
556	566
557 (sent. 1)	557
557	570
558	571
559 (par. 1)	572
559 (par. 2)	573
560	573
561	567
562	572
563	575
564	575
565	—
566	554, 574
567 (par. 1)	539
567 (par. 2)	567, 628
568	558
569	558
569 (par. 3)	545
569 (par. 3)	601
570	581
571	577
572	578
573	579
574	580
575	582
576	579
577	583
578	584
579	585
580	593
581	586, 587, 588
582	586
583	587, 589
584	587, 590
585	587, 591, 592
586	587, 591
587	587
587 (par. 1)	591
587 (par. 2)	592
588	594
588 (par. 2)	596
589	595
590	597
591	598
592	600
593	599, 600
594	601
595	602
596	—
597	—
598	—
599	557
600	605
601	606
601 (par. 2)	605
602	604
603	605
604	—
605	603
606	607

TABLE 1—DISPOSITION

Prior Art. No.	1976 Revision Art. No.
607	609
608	610
609	546, 611
610	612
611	—
612	608
613	613, 614
614	614
615	614, 615
616	619
617	620
618	621
619	622
620	622
621 (par. 1)	623
621 (par. 2)	624
622	624
623	625
624	626
625	627
625 (par. 1)	628
626	—
627	630
628	631
629	—
630	—
631 (par. 1)	632
632	632
633	—
634	—
635	—
636	—
637	—
638	637
639	638
640	633
641	634
642	3556(12)
643	637
644	635
645	636

Prior Art. No.	1977 Revision Art. No.
646	646
647	646
648	646
649	646, 741
650	647
651	648
652	649
653	650
654	650
655	651
656	652
657	653
658	—
659	654
660 (par. 1)	655
660 (pars. 2, 3)	656
661 (par. 1)	657
661 (par. 2)	658
662	684
663	—

Prior Art. No.	1977 Revision Art. No.
664	659
665	665
666	659
667	667
668	668
669	669
670	660
671	661
672	671
673	—
674	672
675	673
676	674
677	675
678	678
679	679
680	680
681	682
682	682
683	683
684	676
685	680
686	685
687	685
688	685
689	686
690	686
691	688
692	662
693	662
694	662
695	662
696	681
697	663
698	664
699	689, 691
700	692
701	694
702	690
703	695
704	—
705	—
706	—
707	666
708	696
709	697
710	698
711	699
712 (pars. 1, 2)	700
713 (par. 1)	664
714	—
715	—
716	701, 702
717	703, 704
718	—
719	705
720	—
721	699
722	705
723	—
724	—
725	—
726	—

Prior Art. No.	1977 Revision Art. No.
727	—
728	707
729	708
730	710
731 (par. 1)	708
732	—
733	709
734	—
735	713
736 (sent. 1)	712
737	711
738	714
739	715
740	716
740	717
741 (1870)	718
742	719
743	722
744	723
745	724
746 (par. 1)	725
747	726
748	727
749	720
750	721
751	728
752	729
753	730
754	731
755	732
756	733
757 (pars. 1, 3)	734
758	—
759	735, 736
760	735
760	738
761	737
762	735
763 (par. 1)	735
763 (par. 2)	737, 738
764	735
765	740, 742
766	739
767	741
768	741
769	741
770	—
771 (par. 1)	743
772	744
773	744
774	745
775	746
776	747
777	748
778	—
779	750
780	749
781	—
782	—
783(1)	751
783(2)	753
783(3)	765
783(4)	770

TABLE 1—DISPOSITION

Prior Art. No.	1977 Revision Art. No.	Prior Art. No.	1977 Revision Art. No.	Prior Art. No.	1977 Revision Art. No.
783(5)	771	806	766	830	786
783(6)	773	807	—	831	787
783(7)	774	808	—	832	789
784	751	809	—	833	789
785	752	810	767	834	—
786	752	811	768	835	—
787	756	812	769	836	—
788	756	813	770	837	—
789	753	814	746, 770	838	—
790	754 (par. 1)	815	770	839	—
791	754 (par. 2)	816	771	840	—
792	755	817	771	841	—
793	757	818	772	842	—
794	757	819	—	843	—
795	758	820	—	844	—
796	—	821	773	845	792
797	760	822	774	846	793
798	759	823	785	847	793
799	761	823	786	848	—
800	—	824	788	849	—
801	762	825	788	850	—
802	763	826	784	851	—
803	762	827	785	852	794, 796
804	764	828	—	853	—
805	765	829	786	854	—
				855	791

13. Former Articles 870 to 933, and Revision of Book III, Preliminary Title and Title I, Chapters 1 through 3, Articles 870 to 902:

Prior Art. No.	1981 Revision Art. No.	Prior Art. No.	1981 Revision Art. No.	Prior Art. No.	1981 Revision Art. No.
870	870	892	901	914	896
871	871	893	—	915	889
872	872	894	881	916	890
873	872	895	882	916.1	890
874	871	896	883	917	—
875	873	897	884	918	—
876	874	898	885	919	—
877	875	899	886	920	—
878	875	900	887	921	—
879	876	901	—	922	—
880	—	902	888	923	—
881	877	903	891	924	894
882	878	904	891	925	—
883	879	905	895	926	—
884	—	906	895	927	—
885	—	907	895	928	—
886	880	908	897	929	902
887	880	910	898	930	—
888	899	911	—	931	—
889	900	912	892	932	—
890	901	913	893	933	—
891	901				

TABLE 1—DISPOSITION

14. Former Articles 934 to 1074, and Revision of Book III, Title I, Chapters 4, 5, and 6, Articles 934 to 968. Articles repealed prior to the 1997 Revision are identified by an asterisk:

Prior Art. No.	1997 Revision Art. No.	Prior Art. No.	1997 Revision Art. No.	Prior Art. No.	1997 Revision Art. No.
934	934	980	950	1027	—
935	*	981	952	1028	—
936	—	982	952	1029	—
937	—	983	950	1030	—
938	—	984	951	1031	—
938	*	985	But see 953	1032	—
940	935	986	947	1033	—
941	935	987	954	1034	—
942	936	988	957	1035	—
943	935, 936	989	957	1036	—
944	937	990	957	1037	—
945	935	991	958	1038	—
946	954	992	958	1039	—
947	954	993	—	1040	—
948	954	994	959	1041	*
949	—	995	—	1042	*
950	—	996	959	1043	*
951	—	997	959	1044	*
952	—	998	—	1045	*
953	939	999	959	1046	*
954	940	1000	959	1047	*
955	940	1001	959	1048	*
956	940	1002	959	1049	*
957	—	1003	960	1050	—
958	—	1004	*	1051	*
959	—	1005	*	1052	—
960	—	1006	*	1053	*
961	—	1007	—	1054	—
962	—	1008	—	1055	—
963	—	1009	—	1056	—
964	941	1010	—	1057	—
965	941	1011	*	1058	—
966	941	1012	*	1059	—
967	914, 942	1013	961	1060	—
968	—	1014	962	1061	—
969	945	1015	963	1062	—
970	945	1016	—	1063	*
971	945	1017	963	1064	*
972	—	1018	948	1065	*
973	cf. 946	1019	—	1066	*
974	—	1020	—	1067	—
975	943	1021	967	1068	—
976	—	1022	964	1069	*
977	947, 948	1023	—	1070	*
978	949	1024	—	1071	967
979	949	1025	—	1072	967
		1026	—	1073	967
				1074	967

15. Former Articles 1415 to 1466, and Revision of Book III, Title I, Chapter 13, Articles 1415 to 1429. Articles repealed prior to the 1997 Revision are identified by an asterisk:

Prior Art. No.	1997 Revision Art. No.	Prior Art. No.	1997 Revision Art. No.	Prior Art. No.	1997 Revision Art. No.
1415	1420	1422		1429	
1416	1420	1423		1430	
1417		1424		1431	
1418		1425	1416	1432	
1419		1426	1416	1433	
1420		1427	1416	1434	
1421		1428		1435	

TABLE 1—DISPOSITION

Prior Art. No.	1997 Revision Art. No.	Prior Art. No.	1997 Revision Art. No.	Prior Art. No.	1997 Revision Art. No.
1436		1445	*	1454	*
1437		1446	*	1455	*
1438		1447	*	1456	*
1439		1448	*	1457	*
1440		1449	*	1458	*
1441		1450	*	1459	*
1442		1451	*	1460	*
1443		1452	*	1461	*
1444	*	1453	*	1462	*
				1463	*
				1464	*
				1465	
				1466	

16. Former Articles 1467 to 1469, and Revision of Book III, Title II, Chapter 1, Articles 1467 to 1469:

Prior Art. No.	2008 Revision Art. No. (Act No. 204)	Prior Art. No.	2008 Revision Art. No. (Act No. 204)	Prior Art. No.	2008 Revision Art. No. (Act No. 204)
1467	1467	1468	1468	1469	1469

17. Former Articles 1470 to 1492, and Revision of Book III, Title II, Chapter 2, Articles 1470 to 1483; Former Articles 1493 to 1518, and Revision of Book III, Title II, Chapter 3, Articles 1493 to 1514:

Prior Art. No.	1991 Revision Art. No.	Prior Art. No.	1991 Revision Art. No.	Prior Art. No.	1996 Revision Art. No. (Act No. 77, 1st Extraordinary Session)
1470	1470	1488	—	1502	1503
1471	—	1489	—	1503	
1472	1471	1490	—	1504	1504
1473	1472	1491	1475	1505	1505
1474	1473	1492	—	1506	—
1475	1477		**1996 Revision Art. No. (Act No. 77, 1st Extraordinary Session)**	1507	1507, 1508
1476	1476			1508	1509
1477	1476			1509	—
1478	—	1493	1493	1510	—
1479	—	1494	1494	1511	1507, 1508
1480	—	1495	1495	1512	—
1481	—	1496	1497	1513	1510
1482	1474	1497	1498	1514	1511
1483	—	1498	—	1515	1512
1484	—	1499	—	1516	1513
1485	—	1500	—	1517	1513
1486	—	1501	—	1518	1513
1487	—				

18. Former Articles 1523 to 1569, and Revision of Book III, Title II, Chapter 5, Articles 1526 to 1567:

Prior Art. No.	2008 Revision Art. No. (Act No. 204)	Prior Art. No.	2008 Revision Art. No. (Act No. 204)	Prior Art. No.	2008 Revision Art. No. (Act No. 204)
1523	—	1528	1529	1533	—
1524	1526	1529	1530	1534	1532
1525	cf. 1527	1530	1531	1535	1533
1526	1527	1531	—	1536	1541; cf. 1550
1527	1528	1532	—	1537	—

TABLE 1—DISPOSITION

Prior Art. No.	2008 Revision Art. No. (Act No. 204)	Prior Art. No.	2008 Revision Art. No. (Act No. 204)	Prior Art. No.	2008 Revision Art. No. (Act No. 204)
1538	1541	1549	—	1560	1557
1539	1543	1550	1551	1561	1558
1540	1544	1551	1549	1562	1559
1541	1544	1552	—	1563	1560
1542	1545	1553	—	1564	—
1543	1544, 1547	1554	—	1565	1562
1544	1546	1556	—	1566	1563
1546	1548	1557	—	1567	1564
1547	—	1558	—	1568	cf. 1565
1548	—	1559	1556	1569	1566

19. Former Articles 1570 to 1723, and Revision of Book III, Title II, Chapter 6, Articles 1570 to 1616. Articles repealed prior to the 1997 Revision are identified by an asterisk:

Prior Art. No.	1997 Revision Art. No.	Prior Art. No.	1997 Revision Art. No.	Prior Art. No.	1997 Revision Art. No.
1570	1573	1614	But see 1598	1659	*
1571		1615		1660	*
1572	1571	1616		1661	
1573	1571, 1572	1617		1662	
1574		1618		1663	
1575		1619		1664	*
1576		1620		1665	
1577		1621		1666	*
1578		1622		1667	*
1579		1623	*	1668	*
1580		1624		1669	*
1581		1625	1587	1670	*
1582		1626	1598	1671	*
1583		1627	1598	1672	
1584		1628	1598	1673	*
1585		1629	1598	1674	*
1586		1630	1598	1675	*
1587		1631	1598	1676	*
1588	1575	1632	1598	1678	*
1589	1575	1633	1602	1679	*
1590	1570	1634	1600	1680	
1591	1581	1635	1601	1681	*
1592	1582	1636		1682	*
1593		1637		1683	*
1594		1638		1684	*
1595	1573	1639		1685	*
1596	*	1640		1686	*
1597		1641	1616	1687	*
1598		1642		1688	*
1599		1643	1597	1689	*
1600		1644	1605	1690	1606
1601		1645	1605	1691	1607, 1608
1602		1646	1605	1692	1607
1603		1647	1605	1693	1608
1604		1648	*	1694	1607, 1608
1605		1649	*	1695	1608
1606	1585	1650	*	1696	1608
1607		1651	*	1697	1589
1608	1598	1652	*	1698	1589
1609		1653	*	1699	1589
1610		1654	*	1700	
1611		1655	*	1701	
1612	1586	1656	*	1702	
1613		1657	*	1703	1589
		1658		1704	1591

TABLE 1—DISPOSITION

Prior Art. No.	1997 Revision Art. No.	Prior Art. No.	1997 Revision Art. No.	Prior Art. No.	1997 Revision Art. No.
1705		1711		1717	1613
1706	1590	1712	1611	1718	
1707	1588, 1590, 1592	1713	1612	1719	1615
1708	1598, 1590	1714		1720	1614
1709	1596	1715	1611	1722	1614
1710		1716	1613	1723	1615

20. Former Articles 1734 to 1755 and Revision of Book III, Title II, Chapters 8 and 9, Articles 1734 to 1751. Articles repealed prior to the 2004 Revision are identified by an asterisk:

Prior Art. No.	2004 Revision Art. No.	Prior Art. No.	2004 Revision Art. No.	Prior Art. No.	2004 Revision Art. No.
1734	—	1740	—	1746	—
1735	—	1741	—	1747	—
1736	—	1742	—	1748	—
1737	—	1743	—	1749	*
1738	—	1744	—	1750	—
1739	—	1745	—	1751	*
				1752	*
				1753	*
				1754	—
				1755	—

21. Former Articles 1756 to 2291, and Revision of Book III, Titles III and IV, Articles 1756 to 2057:

Prior Art. No.	1984 Revision Art. No.	Prior Art. No.	1984 Revision Art. No.	Prior Art. No.	1984 Revision Art. No.
1756	1756	1787	—	1817	1927, 1942
1757	1760	1788	1918, 1919, 1925, 1926	1818	—
1758	1762	1789	1925	1819	1934, 1948
1759	1761	1790	—	1820	—
1760	1757	1791	2031, 2033	1821	—
1761	1906	1792	1921, 1924, 2033	1822	—
1762	—	1793	1921, 1924, 2033	1823	1949, 2034
1763	1984, 1985	1794	1920	1824	—
1764	—	1795	2031, 2035	1825	1949
1765	1907, 1908	1796	—	1826	1949
1766	—	1797	1927	1827	—
1767	—	1798	1927	1828	—
1768	1911	1799	—	1829	—
1769	—	1800	—	1830	—
1770	—	1801	1929, 1931	1831	—
1771	1913	1802	1928, 1929, 1931	1832	—
1772	—	1803	—	1833	—
1773	1910	1804	—	1834	—
1774	1909	1805	1943	1835	—
1775	—	1806	1943	1836	—
1776	1912	1807	—	1837	—
1777	1915	1808	1943	1838	—
1778	1916	1809	1928, 1934	1839	—
1779	—	1810	1932	1840	—
1780	—	1811	—	1841	—
1781	—	1812	1927	1842	—
1782	1918	1813	—	1843	—
1783	—	1814	—	1844	—
1784	1919	1815	—	1845	—
1785	1922, 1923	1816	1927	1846	—
1786	—			1847	1953, 1955, 1956

TABLE 1—DISPOSITION

Prior Art. No.	1984 Revision Art. No.	Prior Art. No.	1984 Revision Art. No.	Prior Art. No.	1984 Revision Art. No.
1848	1957	1911	1991	1973	2042
1849	—	1912	—	1974	—
1850	1959	1913	—	1975	—
1851	1959	1914	—	1976	—
1852	1961	1915	—	1977	2043
1853	1960	1916	—	1978	—
1854	—	1917	—	1979	2038
1855	—	1918	—	1980	2038
1856	1962	1919	—	1981	2038
1857	1962	1920	—	1982	2038
1858	1963	1921	—	1983	—
1859	—	1922	—	1984	—
1860	1965	1923	—	1985	2037
1861	1965	1924	—	1986	2040
1862	—	1925	—	1987	—
1863	1965	1926	1986	1988	2043
1864	—	1927	1986	1989	—
1865	—	1928	1987	1990	—
1866	1923	1929	1987	1991	—
1867	—	1930	1994	1992	—
1868	—	1931	1994	1993	—
1869	—	1932	—	1994	2041
1870	—	1933	1874, 1989	1995	—
1871	—	1934	1995, 1996, 1997, 1999, 2003	1996	—
1872	—			1997	1765, 1766
1873	—	1935	2000	1998	—
1874	—	1936	—	1999	1765
1875	—	1937	—	2000	1766
1876	—	1938	—	2001	1766
1877	—	1939	2001	2002	—
1878	—	1940	2000	2003	—
1879	—	1941	—	2004	R.S. 9:2785
1880	—	1942	—	2005	R.S. 9:2786
1881	—	1943	—	2006	R.S. 9:2787
1882	—	1944	—	2007	—
1883	—	1945	—	2008	—
1884	1971	1946	2047	2009	1765
1885	1971	1947	2047	2010	1763
1886	1971, 1973	1948	—	2011	—
1887	1976	1949	2045	2012	—
1888	1976	1950	2045	2013	—
1889	1977	1951	2049	2014	—
1890	1978	1952	2048	2015	—
1891	1971, 1972	1953	2053	2016	—
1892	2030	1954	—	2017	—
1893	1966	1955	2050	2018	—
1894	1969	1956	—	2019	—
1895	1968	1957	2057	2020	1767
1896	—	1958	2057	2021	1767
1897	—	1959	2051	2022	—
1898	—	1960	—	2023	—
1899	—	1961	—	2024	1770
1900	1970	1962	2052	2025	—
1901	1983	1963	—	2026	1768
1902	1978, 1985	1964	2055	2027	—
1903	—	1965	2055	2028	—
1904	—	1966	2055	2029	—
1905	—	1967	—	2030	—
1906	—	1968	—	2031	1769
1907	—	1969	—	2032	1769
1908	—	1970	2036	2033	1769
1909	1986	1971	2037	2034	1770
1910	1992	1972	—	2035	1770

TABLE 1—DISPOSITION

Prior Art. No.	1984 Revision Art. No.	Prior Art. No.	1984 Revision Art. No.	Prior Art. No.	1984 Revision Art. No.
2036	—	2099	—	2162	—
2037	—	2100	—	2163	1864
2038	1773	2101	—	2164	1866
2039	1774	2102	—	2165	1867
2040	1772	2103	1804, 1805	2166	1868
2041	1775	2104	1804, 1806	2167	1869
2042	1771	2105	1806	2168	1869
2043	1767	2106	1804	2169	—
2044	—	2107	1796	2170	—
2045	1767	2108	1815	2171	—
2046	2013	2109	1815	2172	—
2047	2013	2110	1820	2173	—
2048	1777	2111	1816, 1817	2174	—
2049	1777	2112	1819	2175	—
2050	1777, 1778	2113	1789, 1818, 1819	2176	—
2051	—	2114	1819	2177	—
2052	1781	2115	1819	2178	—
2053	1779	2116	1819	2179	—
2054	1782	2117	2005	2180	—
2055	1783	2118	—	2181	—
2056	—	2119	—	2182	—
2057	1784	2120	2008	2183	—
2058	1784	2121	—	2184	—
2059	—	2122	—	2185	1879
2060	—	2123	2006	2186	1883
2061	—	2124	2007	2187	1881
2062	1807	2125	2007	2188	1883
2063	1807	2126	2010	2189	1881, 1882
2064	—	2127	2011	2190	1880
2065	1807	2128	—	2191	1882
2066	1808	2129	—	2192	1886
2067	—	2130	1854	2193	—
2068	1809	2131	1854	2194	—
2069	1811	2132	1756	2195	1884
2070	—	2133	—	2196	1884
2071	1812, 1814	2134	1855	2197	—
2072	1812	2135	—	2198	—
2073	1813	2136	1855	2199	1888, 1889
2074	1808	2137	1855	2200	—
2075	—	2138	—	2201	1890
2076	—	2139	—	2202	—
2077	1786	2140	1857	2203	—
2078	1787	2141	1857	2204	1891
2079	1787	2142	1857	2205	1892
2080	1788	2143	1857	2206	1892
2081	1788	2144	1857	2207	1893
2082	—	2145	—	2208	1893
2083	—	2146	1857	2209	1893
2084	1787	2147	1858	2210	1894
2085	1789	2148	—	2211	1897, 1898
2086	1789	2149	1859	2212	1900
2087	1789	2150	—	2213	1895
2088	1790	2151	—	2214	1896
2089	1791, 1792	2152	—	2215	1899
2090	1793	2153	1861	2216	1899
2091	1794	2154	—	2217	1903
2092	1798	2155	—	2218	1904, 1905
2093	1796	2156	1860	2219	1813, 1876
2094	1795	2157	1862	2220	—
2095	1795	2158	1863	2221	2032
2096	—	2159	—	2222	—
2097	1799	2160	1828	2223	—
2098	1801	2161	1829	2224	1924

TABLE 1—DISPOSITION

Prior Art. No.	1984 Revision Art. No.	Prior Art. No.	1984 Revision Art. No.	Prior Art. No.	1984 Revision Art. No.
2225	—	2248	—	2270	1841, R.S. 9:2759
2226	—	2249	—	2271	—
2227	—	2250	—	2272	1842, 1843
2228	—	2251	R.S. 9:2741	2273	1845, 2030
2229	—	2252	R.S. 9:2742	2274	—
2230	—	2253	1841, R.S. 9:2743	2275	1832, 1839
2231	—	2254	R.S. 9:2744	2276	1848
2232	1831	2255	R.S. 9:2745	2277	1846
2233	—	2256	R.S. 9:2746	2278	1832, 1847
2234	1833	2257	1841, R.S. 9:2747	2279	1832
2235	1834	2258	R.S. 9:2748	2280	1832
2236	1835	2259	R.S. 9:2749	2281	—
2237	—	2260	R.S. 9:2750	2282	—
2238	—	2261	R.S. 9:2751	2283	—
2239	2021, 2028, 2035	2262	R.S. 9:2752	2284	1849
2240	1836	2263	R.S. 9:2753	2285	—
2241	1837	2264	1839, R.S. 9:2754	2286	R.S. 13:4231
2242	1836	2265	1839, R.S. 9:2755	2287	1850, 1851, 1857
2243	—	2266	1839, 2021, 2035, R.S. 9:2756	2288	1852
2244	1838	2267	1841, R.S. 9:2757	2289	—
2245	1838	2268	1840	2290	—
2246	—	2269	R.S. 9:2758	2291	1853
2247	—				

22. **Former Articles 2292 to 2313, and Revision of Book III, Title V, Articles 2292 to 2305:**

Prior Art. No.	1995 Revision Art. No. (Act No. 1041)	Prior Art. No.	1995 Revision Art. No. (Act No. 1041)	Prior Art. No.	1995 Revision Art. No. (Act No. 1041)
2292	—	2298	2295	2304	2300
2293	—	2299	2297	2305	2300
2294	—	2300	2296	2306	—
2295	2292, 2293	2301	2299	2307	—
2296	—	2302	—	2308	2301
2297	—	2303	—	2309	—
				2310	2302
				2311	2303
				2312	2304
				2313	2305

23. **Former Articles 2325 to 2437, and Revision of Book III, Title VI, Articles 2325 to 2437:**

Prior Art. No.	1979 Revision Art. No.	Prior Art. No.	1979 Revision Art. No.	Prior Art. No.	1979 Revision Art. No.
2325	2327, 2328	2337	—	2352	—
2326	2329, 2330	2338	—	2353	—
2327	2329, 2330	2339	—	2354	—
2328	2331	2340	—	2355	—
2329	2331, 2332	2341	—	2356	—
2330	2333	2342	—	2357	—
2331	—	2343	—	2358	—
2332	2327, 2328, 2329, 2330	2344	—	2359	—
2333	—	2345	—	2360	—
2334	2335, 2336, 2338, 2339, 2341, 2342, 2344	2346	—	2361	—
		2347	—	2362	—
		2348	—	2363	—
		2349	—	2364	—
2335	2335	2350	—	2365	—
2336	—	2351	—	2366	—

TABLE 1—DISPOSITION

Prior Art. No.	1979 Revision Art. No.
2367	—
2368	—
2369	—
2370	—
2371	—
2372	—
2373	—
2374	—
2375	—
2376	—
2377	—
2378	—
2379	—
2380	—
2381	—
2382	2432, 2434, 2435, 2437
2383	—
2384	—
2385	—
2386	2336, 2338, 2339
2387	—
2388	—
2389	—
2390	—

Prior Art. No.	1979 Revision Art. No.
2391	—
2392	2339, 2370
2393	2371
2394	2371
2395	2373
2396	—
2397	—
2398	2336, 2346
2399	2327, 2328
2400	10
2401	2329, 2334
2402	2338, 2339
2403	2345, 2357
2404	2346, 2347, 2348
2405	2340
2406	—
2407	—
2408	2364, 2365, 2367, 2368
2409	2357, 2361
2410	—
2411	—
2412	—
2413	—
2414	—

Prior Art. No.	1979 Revision Art. No.
2415	—
2416	—
2417	—
2418	—
2419	—
2420	—
2421	—
2422	—
2423	—
2424	2327, 2328, 2329, 2330
2425	2356, 2374
2426	—
2427	2331, 2332, 2370
2428	—
2429	—
2430	—
2431	—
2432	2375
2433	—
2434	2376
2435	2373
2436	2371
2437	—

24. **Former Articles 2438 to 2659, and Revision of Book III, Title VII, Articles 2438 to 2659:**

Prior Art. No.	1993 Revision Art. No. (Act No. 841)
2438	2438
2439	2439
2440	2440
2441	—
2442	2442
2443	2443
2444	2444
2445	—
2446	—
2447	2447
2448	2448
2449	2448
2450	2450
2451	2451
2452	2452
2453	2453
2454	—
2455	—
2456	2456
2457	—
2458	2457, 2458
2459	2458
2460	2460
2461	2461
2462	2620, 2623
2463	2624
2464	2464
2465	2465

Prior Art. No.	1993 Revision Art. No. (Act No. 841)
2466	2463
2467	2467
2468	—
2469	—
2470	—
2471	—
2472	—
2473	—
2474	2474
2475	2475
2476	2475
2477	2477
2478	2477
2479	2477
2480	2480
2481	2481
2482	2482
2483	2483
2484	2484
2485	2485
2486	2485
2487	2487
2488	2487
2489	2489
2490	—
2491	2491
2492	2492
2493	2492
2494	2494, 2495

Prior Art. No.	1993 Revision Art. No. (Act No. 841)
2495	2495
2496	2494
2497	2497
2498	2498
2499	—
2500	2500
2501	2500
2502	2500
2503	2503, 2548
2504	2503
2505	2503
2506	2506
2507	2507
2508	2507
2509	2509
2510	2509
2511	2511
2512	2512
2513	2513
2514	2511
2515	—
2516	—
2517	2517
2518	2517
2519	2517
2520	2520
2521	2521
2522	2521
2523 to 2529	—

TABLE 1—DISPOSITION

Prior Art. No.	1993 Revision Art. No. (Act No. 841)	Prior Art. No.	1993 Revision Art. No. (Act No. 841)	Prior Art. No.	1993 Revision Art. No. (Act No. 841)
2530	2530	2574	2574	2616	R.S. 9:3166
2531	2531	2575	2575	2617	R.S. 9:3167
2532	2532	2576	2577	2618	R.S. 9:3168
2533	2532	2577	2577	2619	R.S. 9:3169
2534	2534	2578	2578	2620	R.S. 9:3170
2535	—	2579	—	2621	R.S. 9:3171
2536	2532	2580	2584, 2600	2622	R.S. 9:3172
2537	2537			2623	R.S. 9:3173
2538	2538	2581	2584, 2600	2624	R.S. 9:3174
2539	2538			2625	R.S. 9:3175
2540	2540	2582 to 2586	—	2626	R.S. 9:3176
2541	2541	2587	2587	2627	R.S. 9:3177
2542	—	2588	2588	2628	R.S. 9:3178
2543	2541	2589	2589	2629	R.S. 9:3179
2544	—	2590	2590	2630	R.S. 9:3180
2545	2545	2591	2591	2631	R.S. 9:3181
2546	2534	2592	2592	2632	R.S. 9:3182
2547	—	2593	2589	2633	R.S. 9:3183
2548	2548	2594	2589	2634	R.S. 9:3184
2549	2549	2595	—	2635	R.S. 9:3185
2550	2550	2596	—	2636	R.S. 9:3186
2551	—	2597	2597	2637	R.S. 9:3187
2552	—	2598	2597	2638	R.S. 9:3188
2553	2553	2599	2599	2639	R.S. 9:3189
2554	2553	2600	2584, 2600	2640	R.S. 9:3190
2555	2555			2641	R.S. 9:3191
2556	2612	2601 to 2641	Redesignated as R.S. 9:3151 to 9:3191	2642	—
2557	2557			2643	2643
2558	2557			2644	2644
2559	2557	2601	R.S. 9:3151	2645	2645
2560	2560	2602	R.S. 9:3152	2646	2646
2561	2561	2603	R.S. 9:3153	2647	2646
2562	2562	2604	R.S. 9:3154	2648	2648
2563	2563	2605	R.S. 9:3155	2649	2649
2564	2564	2606	R.S. 9:3156	2650	2650
2565	—	2607	R.S. 9:3157	2651	—
2566	—	2608	R.S. 9:3158	2652	2652
2567	2567	2609	R.S. 9:3159	2653	2652
2568	2568	2610	R.S. 9:3160	2654	2652
2569	2571	2611	R.S. 9:3161	2655	2655
2570	2570	2612	R.S. 9:3162	2656	2656
2571	2571	2613	R.S. 9:3163	2657	—
2572	2572	2614	R.S. 9:3164	2658	—
2573	—	2615	R.S. 9:3165	2659	2659

25. Former Articles 2660 to 2667 and Revision of Book III, Title VIII, Articles 2660 to 2667:

Prior Art. No.	2010 Revision Art. No.	Prior Art. No.	2010 Revision Art. No.	Prior Art. No.	2010 Revision Art. No.
2660	2660	2662	2662, 2663	2664	2663
2661	2660	2663	2662, 2663	2665	—
				2666	2663
				2667	2661

TABLE 1—DISPOSITION

26. Former Articles 2668 to 2744 and Revision of Book III, Title IX, Chapters 1 and 2, Articles 2668 to 2729:

Prior Art. No.	2004 Revision Art. No.	Prior Art. No.	2004 Revision Art. No.	Prior Art. No.	2004 Revision Art. No.
2668	2669	2692	2682	2718	—
2669	2668	2693	2684, 2691	2719	—
2670	2668	2694	2694	2720	—
2671	2675, 2676	2695	2692, 2697	2721	2687
2672	2676	2696	2700, 2701	2722	2687
2673	—	2697	2714, 2715	2723	2687
2674	2668, 2678	2698	2690	2724	cf. 2688
2675	—	2699	2715	2725	2713
2676	—	2700	2693	2726	2695
2677	2668	2701	2685	2727	2720
2678	2673	2702	2689	2728	2714
2679	2673	2703	2702	2729	2719
2680	650	2704	2700, 2701	2730	2716
2681	2674	2705	2707	2731	2717
2682	2682, 2700	2706	2708	2732	2718
2683	2681	2707	2709	2733	2711
2683.1	—	2708	2709	2734	—
2684	2678	2709	2710	2735	2712, 2718
2685	2680	2710	2683	2736	—
2686	2727; cf. 2728	2711	2686	2737	—
2687	2678, 2680	2712	2704	2738	—
2688	2721, 2722	2713	—	2739	—
2689	2721, 2723	2714	—	2740	—
2690	cf. 2724	2715	2692	2741	—
2691	2721	2716	2692	2742	—
		2717	2691, 2692	2743	2705
				2744	2705

27. Former Articles 2778 to 2800 and Revision of Book III, Title X, Articles 2779 to 2791:

Prior Art. No.	2012 Revision Art. No.	Prior Art. No.	2012 Revision Art. No.	Prior Art. No.	2012 Revision Art. No.
2778	—	2785	—	2792	—
2779	—	2786	—	2793	—
2780	—	2787	—	2794	—
2781	—	2788	—	2795	—
2782	—	2789	—	2796	—
2783	—	2790	—	2797	—
2784	—	2791	—	2798	—
				2799	—
				2800	—

28. Former Articles 2801 to 2890, and Revision of Book III, Title XI, Articles 2801 to 2848:

Prior Art. No.	1980 Revision Art. No.	Prior Art. No.	1980 Revision Art. No.	Prior Art. No.	1980 Revision Art. No.
2801	2801	2814	2815	2827	—
2802	2801	2815	—	2828	2837
2803	2802	2816	—	2829	—
2804	—	2817	—	2830	—
2805	2801	2818	—	2831	—
2806	—	2819	—	2832	—
2807	—	2820	—	2833	—
2808	—	2821	—	2834	—
2809	2801	2822	—	2835	—
2810	—	2823	2832	2836	2806
2811	2803, 2804	2824	—	2837	2805
2812	—	2825	—	2838	2805
2813	2803, 2804	2826	—	2839	2837, 2840

TABLE 1—DISPOSITION

Prior Art. No.	1980 Revision Art. No.	Prior Art. No.	1980 Revision Art. No.	Prior Art. No.	1980 Revision Art. No.
2840	2837	2857	—	2874	2816
2841	2840	2858	—	2875	2807, 2814
2842	2840	2859	—	2876	2826
2843	2842	2860	—	2877	2826
2844	2843	2861	—	2878	2827
2845	2841	2862	2809	2879	—
2846	2840	2863	—	2880	—
2847	—	2864	2811	2881	—
2848	—	2865	2803, 2804	2882	—
2849	2838, 2839, 2844	2866	—	2883	2826
2850	2839	2867	2807, 2814	2884	2822
2851	2842	2868	2807, 2814	2885	2822
2852	—	2869	2807	2886	—
2853	—	2870	2807, 2814	2887	2821
2854	—	2871	2812	2888	—
2855	—	2872	—, 2817	2889	—
2856	2808	2873	2817	2890	2834

29. Former Articles 2891 to 2925 and Revision of Book III, Title XII, Articles 2891 to 2913:

Prior Art. No.	2004 Revision Art. No.	Prior Art. No.	2004 Revision Art. No.	Prior Art. No.	2004 Revision Art. No.
2891	—	2902	2895	2913	2907
2892	—	2903	—	2914	2907
2893	cf. 2891	2904	2899	2915	2907
2894	cf. 2891	2905	2900	2916	2908
2895	cf. 2891	2906	2901	2917	cf. 2909
2896	2893	2907	2901	2918	cf. 2909
2897	—	2908	2899	2919	—
2898	2894	2909	2902	2920	2910
2899	2896	2910	2904	2921	2911
2900	2897	2911	2905	2922	2912
2901	2898	2912	—	2923	—
				2924	R.S. 9:3500
				2925	2913

30. Former Articles 2926 to 2981 and Revision of Book III, Title XIII, Articles 2926 to 2951:

Prior Art. No.	2003 Revision Art. No.	Prior Art. No.	2003 Revision Art. No.	Prior Art. No.	2003 Revision Art. No.
2926	2926	2944	2933	2962	—
2927	2926, 2946	2945	2934	2963	—
2928	2926	2946	2934	2964	—
2929	cf. 2928, 2942, 2951	2947	—	2965	2941
2930	2929	2948	2935	2966	2930, 2942, 2944
2931	2926, 2941	2949	2926	2967	2942, 2944
2932	2927	2950	2936	2968	cf. 2943
2933	2927	2951	—	2969	2943
2934	2927	2952	—	2970	—
2935	2927	2953	2937	2971	2945
2936	2927	2954	2937	2972	2946, 2949
2937	2930	2955	2938	2973	2946
2938	2930	2956	2939	2974	2928, 2947
2939	2930	2957	—	2975	2928, 2947
2940	2931	2958	—	2976	2946
2941	2932	2959	—	2977	2946
2942	—	2960	2940	2978	2948
2943	—	2961	—	2979	2949

TABLE 1—DISPOSITION

Prior Art. No.	2003 Revision Art. No.
2980	—
2981	2951

31. Former Articles 2985 to 3034, and Revision of Book III, Title XV, Articles 2985 to 3032:

Prior Art. No.	1997 Revision Art. No.	Prior Art. No.	1997 Revision Art. No.	Prior Art. No.	1997 Revision Art. No.
2885	2989	3002	3001, 3030	3018	—
2986	2991	3003(1)	3001	3019	—
2987	—	3003(2)	3002	3020	—
2988	—	3004	3032	3021	3010
2989	—	3005	3004	3022	3012
2990	—	3006	—	3023	3004
2991	2992	3007	3007	3024	3013
2992	2993	3008	3007	3025	3014
2993	—	3009	3007	3026	3015
2994	2994	3010	3008	3027(A)	3024
2995	2994, 2995	3011	3011	3027(B)	3026, 3027
2996	2996	3012	cf. 3016, 3017	3028	3025
2997	2996, 2997	3013	cf. 3016, 3017, 3019	3029	3028
2998	2997	3014	3009	3030	—
2999	2997	3015	3005	3031	3029
3000	2995	3016	3000	3032	3031
3001	2999	3017	—	3033	3031
				3034	—

32. Former Articles 3035 to 3070, and Revision of Book III, Title XVI, Articles 3035 to 3070:

Prior Art. No.	1987 Revision Art. No. (Act No. 409)	Prior Art. No.	1987 Revision Art. No. (Act No. 409)	Prior Art. No.	1987 Revision Art. No. (Act No. 409)
3035	3035	3046	—	3057	3053
3036	3036	3047	—	3058	3055, 3056
3037	—	3048	—	3059	3058, 3059
3038	—	3049	—	3060	3046
3039	3038, cf. 3044	3050	—	3061	cf. 3062
3040	—	3051	—	3062	—
3041	—	3052(1)	3049(1)	3063	—
3042(1)	3065	3053	3048	3064	3065
3043	3070	3054	3049(2)	3065	3068
3044	—	3055	3051	3066(1)	3045, 3069
3045	cf. 3045	3056	cf. 3049, 3050	3067	—
				3068	3064
				3069	R.S. 9:3911
				3070	R.S. 9:3912

33. Former Articles 3071 to 3083, and Revision of Book III, Title XVII:

Prior Art. No.		Prior Art. No.		Prior Art. No.	
3071	3071, 3072	3076	—	3081	—
3072	cf. 3073	3077	cf. 3075	3082	—
3073	3076; cf. 3072	3078	3080	3083	—
3074	3078	3079	3082		
3075	—	3080	cf. 3082		

TABLE 1—DISPOSITION

34. Former Articles 3278 to 3411, and Revision of Book III, Title XXII, Chapter 1, Articles 3278 to 3337: (1991 Revision)

Prior Art. No.	1991 Revision Art. No.
3278	3278, 3279
3279	—
3280	—
3281	—
3282	3280
3283	3281
3284	3278, 3282
3285	3282, 3298
3286	3283
3287	3284
3288	3283, 3285
3289	3286, 3291
3290	3287
3291	3293, 3297
3292	3293, 3298
3293	3298
3294	—
3295	3295
3296	3295
3297	3295
3298	—
3299	3282, 3295
3300	3290
3301	—
3302	—
3303	—
3304	3292
3305	3287
3306	3288
3307	3288
3308	3292
3309	3288
3310	3280
3311	3301
3312	3301
3313	3302, 3303
3314	—
3315	—
3316	—
3317	—
3318	—
3319	—
3320	3302, 3303
3321	3299
3322	3300, 3308
3323	3304
3324	3304
3325	—
3326	3305
3327	3306
3328	3302, 3303
3329	3308
3330	—
3331	—
3332	—
3333	—
3334	—
3335	—
3336	—
3337	—
3338	—
3339	—
3340	—
3341	—
3342	3308
3343	3309, 3315
3344	3309, 3310
3345	3308
3346	3308, 3320
3347	3308, 3320
3348	3320, 3321
3349	—
3350	—
3351	—
3352	—
3353	—
3354	—
3355	—
3356	—
3357	3320
3358	3308
3359	—
3360	—
3361	—
3362	—
3363	3326
3364	—
3365	—
3366	3321
3367	3321
3368	3321
3369	3328, 3329, 3330, 3331, 3332, 3333, 3334, 3335, 3336
3370	—
3371	Redesignated as R.S. 9:5169
3372	Redesignated as R.S. 9:5170
3373	Redesignated as R.S. 9:5171
3374	Redesignated as R.S. 9:5172
3375	Redesignated as R.S. 9:5173
3376	Redesignated as R.S. 9:5174
3377	Redesignated as R.S. 9:5175
3378	Redesignated as R.S. 9:5176
3379	Redesignated as R.S. 9:5177
3380	Redesignated as R.S. 9:5178
3381	Redesignated as R.S. 9:5179
3382	Redesignated as R.S. 9:5180
3383	Redesignated as R.S. 9:5180.1
3384	Redesignated as R.S. 9:5180.2
3385	Redesignated as R.S. 9:5180.3
3385.1	Redesignated as R.S. 9:5180.4
3386	Redesignated as R.S. 9:5206
3387	Redesignated as R.S. 9:5207
3388	Redesignated as R.S. 9:5208
3389	Redesignated as R.S. 9:5209
3390	Redesignated as R.S. 9:5210
3391	Redesignated as R.S. 9:5211
3392	Redesignated as R.S. 9:5212
3393	Redesignated as R.S. 9:5213
3394	Redesignated as R.S. 9:5214
3395	Redesignated as R.S. 9:5215
3396	Redesignated as R.S. 9:5216
3397	3307
3398	—
3399	—
3400	—
3401	—
3402	—
3403	—
3404	—
3405	—
3406	—
3407	3316, 3318
3408	—
3409	—
3410	—
3411	3319

TABLE 1—DISPOSITION

35. Former Articles 3308 to 3310, 3314, 3321 to 3324, 3327 to 3336 of Title XXII (2005 Revision):

3308	3340, cf. 3338, 3343, 3356	3323	3355	3330	3359
3309	3343	3324	R.S. 44:111, R.S. 44:113	3331	3360
3310	3343	3327	R.S. 44:111, R.S. 44:113	3332	3361
3314	3356			3333	3362
3321	cf. 3340, 3346	3328	3357	3334	3364
3322	3355	3329	3358	3335	3365
				3336	3363

36. Former Articles 3412 to 3554, and Revision of Book III, Titles XXIII and XXIV, Articles 3412 to 3504:

Prior Art. No.	1982 Revision Art. No.	Prior Art. No.	1982 Revision Art. No.	Prior Art. No.	1982 Revision Art. No.
3412	3412	3459	3447	3508	—
3413	3412	3460	3449	3509	3491
3414	3412	3461	3450	3510	3477
3415	3413	3462	3451	3511	3477
3416	3414	3463	3452	3512	3478
3417	3416	3464	—	3513	3479
3418	3417	3465	—	3514	3477
3419	3417	3466	3453	3515	3478
3420	3412	3467	3467	3515(3)	3478
3421	3418	3468	3455	3516	—
3422	3419	3469	3456	3517	3434, 3465
3423	3420	3470	3457	3518	3462
3424	—	3471	—	3519	3463
3425	—	3472	—	3520	3464
3426	3421, 3437	3473	—	3521	3467
3427	—	3474	3473	3522	3468
3428	3425	3475	3486	3523	3469
3429	3431	3476	3489	3524	—
3430	3421	3477	—	3525	—
3431	—	3478	3473, 3474	3526	3470
3432	3421	3479	3475	3527	3470
3433	3429, 3437	3480	3481	3528	3447
3434	—	3481	3481	3529	3448
3434(2)	3422	3482	3482	3530	3447
3435	—	3483	3483	3531	—
3436	3421, 3424	3484	3483	3532	10
3437	3426	3485	3483	3533	—
3438	3428	3486	3483	3534	3494
3439	—	3487	3435, 3436, 3476	3535	3495
3440	3430	3488	3427	3536(1)	3492
3441	—	3489	3438	3536(2)	C.C.P. 3658
3442	3431	3490	3477	3536(3), (4)	3492
3443	3432	3491	3435, 3436, 3477	3537(1), (2)	3492
3444	—	3492	3443	3537(3)	3493
3445	3428	3493	3441	3538	3494
3446	3438	3494	3442	3539	3496
3447	3433	3494(2)	3441	3540	3498
3448	3433	3495	3442	3541	3468
3449	3433	3496	3441	3542	3497
3449(2)	3434	3497	3485	3543	R.S. 9:5622
3450	—	3498	3426	3544	3499
3451	3480	3499	3486	3545	3500
3452	3481	3500	3435, 3436, 3486	3546	3448
3453	—	3501	3431, 3432	3547	3501
3454	—	3502	3431, 3432	3548	3502
3454(1)	3423	3503	3487	3549	—
3455	—	3504	—	3550	—
3456	—	3505	3488, 3489	3551	3462–3466
3457	3445, 3447	3506	3490	3552	3503
3458	3446	3507	—	3553	3504

TABLE 1—DISPOSITION

Prior Art. No.	1982 Revision Art. No.
3554	3469
3555	—
3556	3506

TABLE 2—DERIVATION

This table shows the continuing revision of the Louisiana Civil Code of 1870 and the *derivation* of the revised articles, that is, where the subject-matter of the revised articles may be found in corresponding provisions of the Louisiana Civil Code of 1870.

1. **Revision of the Preliminary Title, Articles 1 through 15, and Former Articles 1 to 23:**

New (1987) Art. No. (Act No. 124)	Corresponding Provisions: Prior Art. No.	New (1987) Art. No. (Act No. 124)	Corresponding Provisions: Prior Art. No.	New (1987) Art. No. (Act No. 124)	Corresponding Provisions: Prior Art. No.
1	1, 3	6	8	11	14, 15
2	1	7	11, 12	12	16
3	3	8	22, 23	13	17
4	21	9	13	14	9*
5	7	10	18	15	10*

* Article 14 of the 1987 Revision was again "revised" in the 1991 Conflict of Laws Revision, although the substance of Article 14 was not reproduced within the revision. Article 15 of the 1987 Revision was vacated by the 1991 Conflict of Laws Revision. For the derivation of the present Article 14, see editor's note preceding that article.

2. **Revision of Book I, Title I, Articles 24 to 31, and Former Articles 24 to 37:**

New (1987) Art. No. (Act No. 125)	Corresponding Provisions: Prior Art. No.	New (1987) Art. No. (Act No. 125)	Corresponding Provisions: Prior Art. No.	New (1987) Art. No. (Act No. 125)	Corresponding Provisions: Prior Art. No.
24	—cf. 479, 2801	26	28, 29 cf. 252, 955, 956, 1482	27	—
25	—cf. 955, 956, 965			28	—cf. 1782, 1918, 1926
				29	37
				30	—
				31	76

3. **Revision of Book I, Title II, Articles 38 to 46, and Former Articles 38 to 46:**

New (2008) Art. No. (Act No. 801)	Corresponding Provisions: Prior Art. No.	New (2008) Art. No. (Act No. 801)	Corresponding Provisions: Prior Art. No.	New (2008) Art. No. (Act No. 801)	Corresponding Provisions: Prior Art. No.
38	new; cf. 38	40	new	42	new; cf. 39
39	new; cf. 38 (2)	41	new; cf. 39	43	new; cf. 38
				44	new; cf. 41
				45	new; cf. 38, 42, 43
				46	new; cf. 44, 45, 46

4. **Revision of Book I, Title III, Articles 47 to 59, and Former Articles 47 to 85:**

New (1990) Art. No. (Act No. 989)	Corresponding Provisions: Prior Art. No.	New (1990) Art. No. (Act No. 989)	Corresponding Provisions: Prior Art. No.	New (1990) Art. No. (Act No. 989)	Corresponding Provisions: Prior Art. No.
47	—	51	—	55	—
48	—	52	—	56	—
49	—	53	—	57	—
50	—	54	—	58	—

TABLE 2—DERIVATION

New (1990) Art. No. (Act No. 989)	Corresponding Provisions: Prior Art. No.
59	—

5. Revision of Book I, Title IV, Chapters 1 through 5, Articles 86 to 100 and Former Articles 86 to 119:

New (1987) Art. No. (Act No. 886)	Corresponding Provisions: Prior Art. No.	New (1987) Art. No. (Act No. 886)	Corresponding Provisions: Prior Art. No.	New (1987) Art. No. (Act No. 886)	Corresponding Provisions: Prior Art. No.
86	86, 87, 88, 89	90	94, 95, 96, but cf. 214	93	90, 91
87	90	91	99, 100, 102 to 105	94	113, 114, 116
88	93	92	109	95	110, 111
89	88			96	117, 118
				97	—
				98	119
				99	—
				100	—

6. Revision of Book I, Title V, Chapter 2, Section 1, Articles 111 to 117, and Former Articles 111 to 120:

New (1997) Art. No. (Act No. 1078)	Corresponding Provisions Prior Art. No.	New (1997) Art. No. (Act No. 1078)	Corresponding Provisions Prior Art. No.	New (1997) Art. No. (Act No. 1078)	Corresponding Provisions Prior Art. No.
111	111, 112, 231	112	112	113	111
				114	112
				115	112
				116	New
				117	New

7. Revision of Book I, Title V, Chapters 1 and 2, Articles 102 to 105, 131 to 136, 141, 142, 151, 152, and Former Articles 131 to 158:

New (1990) Art. No. (Act No. 1009)	Corresponding Provisions: Prior Art. No.	New (1993) Art. No. (Act No. 261)	Corresponding Provisions: Prior Art. No.	New (1993) Art. No. (Act No. 261)	Corresponding Provisions: Prior Art. No.
102	—	131	131	135	131(G)
103	139	132	131(A)	136	132
104	152, 154	133	131(A) & (B)	141	—
105	—	134	131(C)(2)	142	—
				151	—
				152	—

8. Revision of Book I, Title VII, Articles 184 to 198 and Former Articles 178 to 211

New Art. No.	Prior Art. No.	New Art. No.	Prior Art. No.	New Art. No.	Prior Art. No.
184	193, 196, 197	189	189	194	New
185	184	190	190	195	New; cf. 190, 198
186	185	191	New	196	New
187	187	192	New	197	New; cf. 209
188	188	193	New	198	190

TABLE 2—DERIVATION

9. Revision of Book I, Title VII, Chapter 4, Articles 212 to 214, and Former Article 214:

New (2008) Art. No. (Act No. 351)	Corresponding Provisions: Prior Art. No.
212	new
213	new
214	new

10. Revision of Book I, Title VIII, Chapter 2, Articles 365 to 371, and Former Articles 365 to 385:

New (2008) Art. No. (Act No. 786)	Corresponding Provisions: Prior Art. No.
365	new; cf. 365
366	new; cf. 366
367	new; cf. 379
368	new; cf. 371, 373
369	new; cf. 366
370	new
371	new

11. Revision of Book I, Title IX, Articles 389 to 399, and Former Articles 389 to 426:

New (2000) Art. No. (Act No. 25)	Corresponding Provisions: Prior Art. No.
389	cf. 389, 422
390	cf. 389.1
391	cf. 394
392	cf. 389.1, 404, 405, 2985
393	cf. 406, 407, 409, 410
394	cf. 402, 403
395	cf. 28, 389.1, 1918, 2031
396	400
397	cf. 420, 421
398	420
399	419

12. Revision of Book II, Articles 448 to 818, and Former Articles 448 to 855:

New (1978) Art. No. (Act No. 728)	Corresponding Provisions: Prior Art. No.
448	449, 460 (par. 1), 461
449	450, 481, 482 (par. 1)
450	453, 454, 458 (par. 2), 481, 482 (par. 2)
451	451
452	452, 453
453	449, 458 (par. 3), 459, 481, 483
454	484
455	482 (par. 2), 658, 664
456	455, 457
457	704, 705, 706, 658(2)
458	861
459	862
460	863
461	460
462	464
463	464, 465
464	—
465	464, 465, 467, 468 (par. 2), 469
466	467, 468 (par. 2), 469
467	468 (par. 1)
468	—
469	—
470	470, 471
471	473, 475
472	476
473	474, 475
474	—
475	475
476	487

New (1979) Art. No. (Act No. 180)	Corresponding Provisions: Prior Art. No.
477	488, 491(1)
478	490(2), (3)
479	493
480	494
481	496
482	498
483	499
484	500
485	501
486	502, 3453(1)
487	503
488	—
489	—
490	505
491	506
492	—
493	—
494	507
495	—
496	508(4)
497	508(1)–(3)
498	—
499	509, 510(1)
500	510(2)
501	516
502	511
503	517
504	518
505	512
506	513–515
507	520
508	522
509	524
510	521, 523
511	525, 526
512	—

TABLE 2—DERIVATION

New (1979) Art. No. (Act No. 180)	Corresponding Provisions: Prior Art. No.
513	527
514	528, 529
515	531
516	532
517	—
518	—
519	—
520	—
521	—
522	—
523	—
524	3507, 3508
525	—
526	3453(1), (2)
527	2314
528	2314
529	3453(2)
530	—
531	—
532	—

New (1976) Art. No. (Act No. 103)	Corresponding Provisions: Prior Art. No.
533	646 (par. 1)
534	646 (par. 2)
535	490 (par. 2), 534
536	534 (par. 2)
537	534 (par. 1)
538	536, 549
539	533, 535, 567 (par. 1)
540	537
541	538, 539
542	—
543	—
544	540, 541
545	542, 569 (par. 3)
546	609
547	—
548	—
549	543
550	544
551	545
552	—
553	—
554	566, 546 (par. 1)
555	546 (par. 2)
556	547
557	557 (sent. 1), 599
558	568, 569
559	548
560	551 (par. 2)
561	552 (as reinstated 1975)
562	—
563	553 (sent. 1)
564	553 (par. 2)
565	554
566	556
567	555, 561
568	—
569	550

New (1976) Art. No. (Act No. 103)	Corresponding Provisions: Prior Art. No.
570	557
571	558
572	559 (par. 1), 562
573	559 (par. 2), 560
574	566
575	563, 564
576	567 (par. 2)
577	571
578	572
579	573, 576
580	574
581	570
582	575
583	577
584	578
585	579
586	582, 581
587	581, 583–587
588	581
589	583
590	584
591	585, 586, 587 (par. 1)
592	585, 587 (par. 2)
593	580
594	588
595	589
596	588 (par. 2)
597	590
598	591
599	593
600	592, 593
601	569 (par. 3), 594
602	595
603	605
604	602
605	599, 600, 601 (par. 2), 603
606	601
607	606
608	612
609	607
610	608
611	609
612	610
613	613
614	613–615
615	615
616	—
617	—
618	—
619	616
620	617
621	618
622	619, 620
623	621 (par. 1)
624	621 (par. 2), 622
625	623
626	624
627	625
628	535, 567 (par. 2), 625 (par. 1)

New (1976) Art. No. (Act No. 103)	Corresponding Provisions: Prior Art. No.
629	549
630	627
631	628
632	631 (par. 1), 632
633	640
634	641
635	644
636	645
637	638, 643
638	639
639	—
640	—
641	—
642	—
643	—
644	—
645	—

New (1977) Art. No. (Act No. 514)	Corresponding Provisions: Prior Art. No.
646	646, 647, 648, 649
647	650
648	651
649	652
650	653, 654
651	655
652	656
653	657
654	659
655	660 (par. 1)
656	660 (pars. 2, 3)
657	661 (par. 1)
658	661 (par. 2)
659	664, 666
660	670
661	671
662	692 to 695
663	697
664	698, 713 (par. 1)
665	665
666	707
667	667
668	668
669	669
670	—
671	672
672	674
673	675
674	676
675	677
676	684
677	—
678	678
679	679
680	680, 685
681	696
682	681, 682
683	683
684	662
685	686, 687, 688
686	689, 690
687	—
688	691

TABLE 2—DERIVATION

New (1977) Art. No. (Act No. 514)	Corresponding Provisions: Prior Art. No.
689	699
690	702
691	699
692	700
693	—
694	701
695	703
696	708
697	709
698	710
699	711, 721
700	712 (pars. 1, 2)
701	716
702	716
703	717
704	717
705	719, 722
706	—
707	728
708	729, 731 (par. 1)
709	733
710	730
711	737
712	736 (sent. 1)
713	735
714	738
715	739
716	740
717	740
718	741 (1870)
719	742
720	749
721	750
722	743, 2481
723	744
724	745
725	746 (par. 1)
726	747
727	748
728	751
729	752
730	753
731	754
732	755
733	756

New (1977) Art. No. (Act No. 514)	Corresponding Provisions: Prior Art. No.
734	757 (pars. 1, 3)
735	759, 760, 762, 763 (par. 1), 764
736	759
737	761, 763 (par. 2)
738	760, 763 (par. 2)
739	766
740	765
741	649, 767, 768, 769
742	765 (sent. 1), 3504
743	771 (par. 1)
744	772, 773
745	774
746	775, 814
747	776
748	777
749	780
750	779
751	783(1), 784
752	785, 786
753	783(2), 789
754	790, 791
755	792
756	787, 788
757	793, 794
758	795
759	798
760	797
761	799
762	801, 803
763	—
764	804
765	783(3), 805
766	806
767	810
768	811
769	812
770	783(4), 813, 814, 815
771	783(5), 816, 817
772	818
773	783(6), 821
774	783(7), 822

New (1977) Art. No. (Act No. 170)	Corresponding Provisions: Prior Art. No.
775–783	—

New (1977) Art. No. (Act No. 169)	Corresponding Provisions: Prior Art. No.
784	826
785	823, 827
786	823, 829, 830
787	831
788	824, 825
789	832, 833
790	663
791	855
792	845
793	846, 847
794	852
795	—
796	852

New (1990) Art. No. (Act No. 990)	Corresponding Provisions: Prior Art. No.
797	—
798	—
799	—
800	—
801	—
802	—
803	—
804	—
805	—
806	—
807	1289, 1297–1301, 1303
808	1303
809	1294, 1322, 1323
810	1339, 1340
811	C.C.P. 4614
812	1338, 1383
813	1338, 1383
814	1398
815	1338
816	1384, 1385, 2501
817	1304
818	—

13. **Revision of Book III, Preliminary Title and Title I, Chapters 1 through 3, Articles 870 to 902 and Former Articles 870 to 933:**

New (1981) Art. No. (Act No. 919)	Corresponding Provisions: Prior Art. No.
870	870
871	871, 874
872	872, 873
873	875
874	876
875	877, 878
876	879
877	881
878	882
879	883

New (1981) Art. No. (Act No. 919)	Corresponding Provisions: Prior Art. No.
880	886, 887
881	894
882	895
883	896
884	897
885	898
886	899
887	900
888	902

New (1981) Art. No. (Act No. 919)	Corresponding Provisions: Prior Art. No.
889	915
890	916, 916.1
891	903, 904
892	912
893	913
894	924
895	905, 906, 907
896	914
897	908

TABLE 2—DERIVATION

New (1981) Art. No. (Act No. 919)	Corresponding Provisions: Prior Art. No.	New (1981) Art. No. (Act No. 919)	Corresponding Provisions: Prior Art. No.	New (1981) Art. No. (Act No. 919)	Corresponding Provisions: Prior Art. No.
898	910	899	888	900	889
				901	890, 891, 892
				902	929

14. Revision of Book III, Title I, Articles 934 to 968, and former Articles 934 to 1074:

New (1997) Art. No. (Act No. 1421)	Corresponding Provisions: Prior Art. No.	New (1997) Art. No. (Act No. 1421)	Corresponding Provisions: Prior Art. No.	New (1997) Art. No. (Act No. 1421)	Corresponding Provisions: Prior Art. No.
934	934	945	969, 970, 971	956	cf. 1059
935	940, 941	946	see 973	957	cf. 988, 989, 999
936	942, 943	947	977(1), 986	958	991
937	944	948	977(2), 1018	959	994, 996, 997; cf. 990, 1000, 1001, 1002
938	—	949	978, 979		
939	953	950	980, 983	960	1003
940	954, cf. 955, 956	951	984	961	1013
941	cf. 964–967	952	981, 982	962	—
942	cf. 967–974	953	But see 985	963	cf. 1017
943	975	954	987; cf. 946–948	964	1028; cf. 1022, 1027
944	—	955	—	965	cf. 1704, 1709
				966	1024
				967	cf. 1021, 1071
				968	—

15. Revision of Book III, Title I, Articles 1415 to 1429, and Former Articles 1415 to 1466:

New (1997) Art. No. (Act No. 1421)	Corresponding Provisions: Prior Art. No.	New (1997) Art. No. (Act No. 1421)	Corresponding Provisions: Prior Art. No.	New (1997) Art. No. (Act No. 1421)	Corresponding Provisions: Prior Art. No.
1415	—	1420	1415, 1416	1425	—
1416	1425, 1426, 1427	1421	—	1426	—
1417	—	1422	—	1427	—
1418	—	1423	—	1428	—
1419	—	1424	—	1429	—

16. Revision of Book III, Title II, Chapter 1, Articles 1467 to 1469, and Former Articles 1467 to 1469:

New (2008) Art. No. (Act No. 204)	Corresponding Provisions: Prior Art. No.	New (2008) Art. No. (Act No. 204)	Corresponding Provisions: Prior Art. No.	New (2008) Art. No. (Act No. 204)	Corresponding Provisions: Prior Art. No.
1467	1467	1468	1468	1469	1469

17. Revision of Book III, Title II, Chapter 2, Articles 1470 to 1483 and Former Articles 1470 to 1492; Chapter 3, Articles 1493 to 1514 and Former Articles 1493 to 1518:

New (1991) Art. No. (Act No. 363)	Corresponding Provisions: Prior Art. No.	New (1991) Art. No. (Act No. 363)	Corresponding Provisions: Prior Art. No.	New (1991) Art. No. (Act No. 363)	Corresponding Provisions: Prior Art. No.
1470	1470	1474	1482	1478	—
1471	1472	1475	1491	1479	—
1472	1473	1476	1476, 1477	1480	—
1473	1474	1477	1475	1481	—

TABLE 2—DERIVATION

New (1991) Art. No. (Act No. 363)	Corresponding Provisions: Prior Art. No.
1482	—
1483	—

New (1996) Art. No. (Act No. 77, 1st Extraordinary Session)	Corresponding Provisions: Prior Art. No.
1493	1493
1494	1494
1495	1495
1496	1710

New (1996) Art. No. (Act No. 77, 1st Extraordinary Session)	Corresponding Provisions: Prior Art. No.
1497	1496
1498	1497
1500	—
1501	—
1502	—
1503	1502
1504	1504
1505	1505
1506	—

New (1996) Art. No. (Act No. 77, 1st Extraordinary Session)	Corresponding Provisions: Prior Art. No.
1507	1507; cf. 1511, 1634, 1635
1508	1507; cf. 1511, 1634
1509	1508
1510	1513
1511	1514
1512	1515
1513	1516, 1517, 1518
1514	890

18. Revision of Book III, Title II, Chapter 5, Articles 1526 to 1567, and Former Articles 1523 to 11569:

New (2008) Art. No. (Act No. 204)	Corresponding Provisions: Prior Art. No.
1526	new; cf. 1524
1527	new; cf. 1525, 1526
1528	1527
1529	151528
1530	1529
1531	1530
1532	1534
1533	1535
1541	1536

New (2008) Art. No. (Act No. 204)	Corresponding Provisions: Prior Art. No.
1542	new
1543	1539
1544	new; cf. 1540
1545	1542
1546	1543, 1544
1547	new; cf. 1543
1548	1546
1549	1551
1550	new; cf. 1536

New (2008) Art. No. (Act No. 204)	Corresponding Provisions: Prior Art. No.
1551	1550
1556	1559
1557	11560
1558	1561
1559	1562
1560	new; cf. 1563, 1568
1561	new; cf. 1565, 1566
1562	new; cf. 1565
1563	1566
1564	new; cf. 1567
1565	new
1566	1569
1567	new

19. Revision of Book III, Title II, Articles 1570 to 1616, and Former Articles 1570 to 1723:

New (1997) Art. No. (Act No. 1421)	Corresponding Provisions: Prior Art. No.
1570	1570, 1590
1571	1572, 1573
1572	1573
1573	1570, 1595
1574	—
1575	1588, 1589
1576	—
1577	—
1578	—
1579	—
1580	—
1581	1591
1583	—
1584	cf. 1605
1585	—

New (1997) Art. No. (Act No. 1421)	Corresponding Provisions: Prior Art. No.
1586	1612
1587	cf. 1625
1588	1707, 1708
1589	1691 to 1694, 1703
1590	1706 to 1708
1591	1704
1592	1707
1593	—
1594	—
1595	1606
1596	1709
1597	1643
1598	cf. 1608, 1614, 1626, 1628 to 1632
1599	—

New (1997) Art. No. (Act No. 1421)	Corresponding Provisions: Prior Art. No.
1600	1634
1601	1635
1602	1633
1603	—
1604	—
1605	1644 to 1647
1606	1690
1607	1691, 1692, 1694
1608	1691, 1693 to 1696
1609	—
1610	—
1611	1712, 1715
1612	1713
1613	1716, 1717
1614	1720 to 1722
1615	1719, 1723
1616	1641

TABLE 2—DERIVATION

20. Revision of Book III, Title II, Chapters 8 and 9, Articles 1734 to 1751 and Former Articles 1734 to 1755:

New Art. No.	Corresponding Provisions Prior Art. No.
1734	—
1735	—
1736	—
1737	—
1738	—
1739	—
1740	—
1741	—
1742	—
1743	—
1744	—
1745	—
1746	—
1747	—
1748	—
1749	—
1750	—
1751	—

21. Revision of Book III, Titles III and IV, Articles 1756 to 2057 and Former Articles 1756 to 2291:

New (1984) Art. No. (Act No. 331)	Corresponding Provisions: Prior Art. No.
1756	1756, 1761, 2132
1757	1760
1758	—
1759	—
1760	1757
1761	1759
1762	1758
1763	2010
1764	—
1765	1997, 1999, 2009
1766	1997, 2000, 2001
1767	2020, 2021, 2043, 2045
1768	2026
1769	2031, 2032, 2033
1770	2024, 2034, 2035
1771	2042
1772	2040
1773	2038
1774	2039
1775	2041
1776	—
1777	2048, 2049, 2050
1778	2050
1779	2053
1780	—
1781	2052
1782	2054
1783	2055
1784	2057, 2058
1785	—
1786	2077
1787	2078, 2079, 2084
1788	2080, 2081
1789	2085, 2086, 2087, 2113
1790	2088
1791	2089(1)
1792	2089(2)
1793	2090
1794	2091
1795	2094, 2095
1796	2093, 2107
1797	—
1798	2092
1799	2097
1800	—
1801	2098
1802	—
1803	—
1804	2103, 2104, 2106
1805	2103(2)
1806	2104, 2105
1807	2062, 2063, 2065
1808	2066, 2074
1809	2068
1810	—
1811	2069
1812	2071, 2072
1813	2073, 2219
1814	2071
1815	2108, 2109
1816	2111(1)
1817	2111(2)
1818	2113
1819	2112–2116
1820	2110
1821	—
1822	—
1823	—
1824	—
1825	—
1826	—
1827	—
1828	2160(2)
1829	2161
1830	—
1831	2232
1832	2275, 2278(4), 2279, 2280
1833	2234
1834	2235
1835	2236
1836	2240, 2242
1837	2241
1838	2244, 2245
1839	2264, 2265, 2266, 2275
1840	2268
1841	—
1842	2272
1843	2272
1844	—
1845	2273
1846	2277
1847	2278
1848	2276
1849	2284
1850	2287(1)
1851	2287(2)
1852	2288
1853	2291
1854	2130, 2131
1855	2134, 2136, 2137
1856	—
1857	2140, 2141, 2142, 2143, 2144, 2146
1858	2147
1859	2149
1860	2156
1861	2153
1862	2157
1863	2158
1864	2163
1865	—
1866	2164
1867	2165
1868	2166
1869	2167, 2168
1870	—
1871	—
1872	—
1873	—
1874	1933(4)
1875	—
1876	2219
1877	—
1878	—
1879	2185
1880	2190
1881	2189(1), 2187
1882	2189(2), 2191
1883	2186, 2188
1884	2195, 2196
1885	—
1886	2192
1887	—
1888	2199
1889	2199
1890	2201
1891	2204
1892	2205, 2206
1893	2207, 2208, 2209
1894	2210

TABLE 2—DERIVATION

New (1984) Art. No. (Act No. 331)	Corresponding Provisions: Prior Art. No.
1895	2213
1896	2214
1897	2211
1898	2211
1899	2215, 2216
1900	2212
1901	—
1902	—
1903	2217
1904	2218
1905	2218
1906	1761
1907	1765
1908	1765
1909	1774
1910	1773
1911	1768
1912	1776
1913	1771
1914	—
1915	1777
1916	1778
1917	—
1918	1782, 1788
1919	1784, 1788, 1791
1920	1794
1921	1792
1922	1785
1923	1785, 1866
1924	2224
1925	1789
1926	1788(5)–(11)
1927	1797, 1798, 1812, 1816, 1817
1928	1802, 1809
1929	1801, 1802
1930	—
1931	1801, 1802
1932	1810
1933	—
1934	1809, 1819
1935	—
1936	—
1937	—
1938	—
1939	—
1940	—
1941	—
1942	1817
1943	1805, 1806, 1808
1944	—
1945	—
1946	—
1947	—
1948	1819
1949	1823, 1825, 1826
1950	—
1951	—
1952	—
1953	1847(6)
1954	—
1955	1847
1956	1847(9)
1957	1848
1958	—
1959	1850, 1851
1960	1853
1961	1852
1962	1856, 1857
1963	1858
1964	—
1965	1860, 1861, 1863
1966	1893
1967	—
1968	1895
1969	1894
1970	1900
1971	1884, 1885, 1886, 1891
1972	1891
1973	1886
1974	—
1975	—
1976	1887, 1888
1977	1889
1978	1890, 1902
1979	—
1980	—
1981	—
1982	—
1983	1901
1984	1763
1985	1763, 1902
1986	1909, 1926, 1927
1987	1928, 1929
1988	—
1989	1933(1)
1990	—
1991	1911
1992	1910
1993	—
1994	1930, 1931
1995	1934(1)
1996	1934(1)
1997	1934(1)
1998	—
1999	1934(3)
2000	1935, 1940
2001	1939
2002	—
2003	1934(4)
2004	—
2005	2117
2006	2123
2007	2124, 2125
2008	2120
2009	—
2010	2126
2011	2127
2012	—
2013	2046, 2047
2014	—
2015	—
2016	—
2017	—
2018	—
2019	—
2020	—
2021	—
2022	—
2023	—
2024	—
2025	—
2026	—
2027	—
2028	2239
2029	—
2030	1892
2031	1791, 1795
2032	2221
2033	1791, 1792, 1793
2034	1823
2035	1795
2036	1970
2037	1971, 1985
2038	1979, 1980, 1981, 1982
2039	—
2040	1986
2041	1994
2042	1973
2043	1977, 1988
2044	—
2045	1949, 1950
2046	—
2047	1946, 1947
2048	1952
2049	1951
2050	1955
2051	1959
2052	1962
2053	1953
2054	—
2055	1964, 1965, 1966
2056	—
2057	1957, 1958

TABLE 2—DERIVATION

22. Revision of Book III, Title V, Articles 2292 to 2305, and Former Articles 2291 to 2313:

New (1995) Art. No. (Act No. 1041)	Corresponding Provisions: Prior Art. No.
2292	2295(1)
2293	2295(2)
2294	—
2295	2298
2296	2300
2297	2299
2298	—
2299	2301
2300	2304, 2305
2301	2308, 2309
2302	2310
2303	2311
2304	2312
2305	2313

23. Revision of Book III, Title VI, Articles 2325 to 2437, and Former Articles 2325 to 2437:

New (1979) Art. No. (Act No. 709)	Corresponding Provisions: Prior Art. No.
2325	—
2326	—
2327	2325, 2332, 2399, 2424
2328	2325, 2332, 2424
2329	2326, 2327, 2332, 2392, 2424
2330	2326, 2327, 2332, 2392, 2424
2331	2328, 2329, 2427
2332	2328, 2329, 2427
2333	2330
2334	2399, 2400, 2401
2335	2334
2336	2334, 2386, 2398, 2402
2337	—
2338	2334, 2386, 2398, 2402
2339	488, 2334, 2386, 2398, 2402
2340	2405
2341	488, 2334, 2386
2342	2334, 2386
2343	—
2344	2334
2345	—
2346	2387, 2393, 2394, 2404
2347	2404
2348	—
2349	2404
2350	—
2351	—
2352	—
2353	—
2354	2404
2355	—
2355.1	—
2356	136, 155, 2425
2357(1)	2409
2357(2)	2409
2358	—
2358.1	—
2359	—
2360	—
2361	—
2362	—
2362.1	—
2363	—
2364	—
2365	—
2366	—
2367	—
2368	2408
2369	—
2369.1	—
2370	2392, 2427
2371	2393, 2394, 2436
2372	—
2373	2395, 2435
2374	2425
2375	2432
2376	2433, 2434
2432	2382
2433	—
2434	2382
2435	2382
2436	—
2437	2382

24. Revision of Book III, Title VII, Articles 2438 to 2659, and Former Articles 2438 to 2659:

New (1993) Art. No. (Act No. 841)	Corresponding Provisions: Prior Art. No.
2438	2438
2439	2439
2440	2440, 2462; cf. 1839 (Rev.1984)
2441	(Reserved)
2442	2442
2443	2443
2444	2444
2445	(Reserved)
2446	(Reserved)
2447	2447
2448	2448, 2449
2449	(Reserved)
2450	2450
2451	2451
2452	2452
2453	2453
2454	(Reserved)
2455	(Reserved)
2456	2456; 517, 518 (Rev.1979)
2457	1909, 1915, 2458
2458	2458, 2459
2459	(Reserved)
2460	2460
2461	2461, 2490
2462	(Reserved)
2463	2466
2464	2464
2465	2465; 1974 (Rev. 1984)
2466	1816; 1927 (Rev. 1984)
2467	2467, 2552
2468 to 2473	(Reserved)
2474	2474; cf. 1759, 1983

TABLE 2—DERIVATION

New (1993) Art. No. (Act No. 841)	Corresponding Provisions: Prior Art. No.
2475	2475, 2476
2476	(Reserved)
2477	2477 to 2479; cf. 2642
2478	(Reserved)
2479	(Reserved)
2480	2480
2481	2481, 2642; 473 (Rev.1978)
2482	2482, 2483
2483	2483
2484	2484
2485	2485, 2486; cf. 1986, 2013 to 2023 (Rev.1984)
2486	(Reserved)
2487	2487, 2488; cf. 2022, 2023 (Rev. 1984)
2488	(Reserved)
2489	2489; 1860 (Rev. 1984); cf. 1907, 1908
2490	(Reserved)
2491	2491
2492	2492, 2493
2493	(Reserved)
2494	2494, 2496
2495	2494, 2495
2496	(Reserved)
2497	2497
2498	2498
2499	(Reserved)
2500	2500 to 2502, 2515
2501	(Reserved)
2502	——; cf. 2451, 2500 to 2505, 2593, 2642; 487 (Rev.1979); 3480, 3481, 3483 (Rev.1982)
2503	2503 to 2505; 1759, 1983 (Rev.1984)
2504	(Reserved)
2505	(Reserved)
2506	2506
2507	2507, 2508
2508	(Reserved)
2509	1259, 2509, 2510; 496, 497 (Rev.1979)
2510	(Reserved)
2511	2511, 2514; 1966 (Rev.1984)
2512	2512; cf. 551 (Rev. 1976)
2513	2513
2514 to 2516	(Reserved)
2517	2517 to 2519
2518	(Reserved)
2519	(Reserved)
2520	2520; cf. 65 (Digest of 1808); 2496 (C.C.1825)
2521	2521, 2522
2522	——; cf. 2521, 2522
2523	(Reserved)
2524	——
2525 to 2528	(Reserved)
2529	——
2530	2530
2531	2531
2532	2532, 2533, 2536; 1992, 1993, 2018, 2033 (Rev.1984)
2533	(Reserved)
2534	2534, 2546
2535	(Reserved)
2536	(Reserved)
2537	2537, 2616, 2624
2538	2538, 2539; 1815 to 1820 (Rev.1984)
2539	(Reserved)
2540	2540
2541	2541, 2543
2542 to 2544	(Reserved)
2545	2545
2546	(Reserved)
2547	(Reserved)
2548	2548, 2503; 2004 (Rev.1984)
2549	2549
2550	2550; 1777, 1778 (Rev.1984)
2551	(Reserved)
2552	(Reserved)
2553	2553, 2554
2554	(Reserved)
2555	2555; 1989 to 1993 (Rev.1984)
2556	(Reserved)
2557	2557 to 2559; 1869 to 1872 (Rev.1984)
2558	(Reserved)
2559	(Reserved)
2560	2560
2561	2561; 2013 to 2024 (Rev.1984)
2562	2562
2563	2563; 1990, 1991, 2017 (Rev.1984)
2564	2564; cf. 2013 to 2024 (Rev.1984)
2565	(Reserved)
2566	(Reserved)
2567	2567
2568	2568
2569	——; cf. 2480
2570	2570
2571	——; cf. 2568, 2570, 2571; 3458 (Rev.1982)
2572	2572; 522 (Rev. 1979)
2573	(Reserved)
2574	2574; cf. 2042, 2044 (Rev.1984)
2575	2575; cf. 551 (Rev. 1976); 488 (Rev. 1979)
2576	(Reserved)
2577	2576, 2577; cf. 483 to 516 (Rev.1979)
2578	2468, 2578
2579 to 2583	(Reserved)
2584	2600
2585	(Reserved)
2586	(Reserved)
2587	2587
2588	2588
2589	2589, 2593, 2594; cf. 1860, 1869, 1871
2590	2590
2591	2591
2592	2592
2593	(Reserved)
2594	
2595	——; cf. 2595
2596	
2597	2531, 2597, 2598
2598	(Reserved)
2599	2599
2600	2580 to 2582; 1788, 1789 (Rev.1984)
2601	——
2602	——
2603	——; cf. 2053, 2054 (Rev.1984)
2604	——
2605	——
2606	——
2607	——; cf. 2018 (Rev. 1984)
2608	——; cf. 2298, 2468
2609	——
2610	——
2611	——; cf. 2555, 2565; 2002 (Rev. 1984)
2612	2556; cf. 1869 to 1872 (Rev.1984)
2613	——
2614	——; cf. 2488
2615	2564
2616	——

TABLE 2—DERIVATION

New (1993) Art. No. (Act No. 841)	Corresponding Provisions: Prior Art. No.	New (1993) Art. No. (Act No. 841)	Corresponding Provisions: Prior Art. No.	New (1993) Art. No. (Act No. 841)	Corresponding Provisions: Prior Art. No.
2617	——	2628	——; cf. 1839 (Rev. 1984)	2648	2648
2618	(Reserved)			2649	2649; 1759 (Rev. 1984); cf. 2545, 2547, 2548
2619	(Reserved)	2629	——; cf. 1815 to 1820 (Rev.1984)		
2620	——; cf. 2440, 2456, 2462; 1839, 1933 (Rev.1984)	2630	——	2650	2650
		2631 to 2641	(Reserved)	2651	(Reserved)
2621	——; cf. 1934 (Rev. 1984)	2642	——; cf. 1766, 1825 to 1830 (Rev.1984)	2652	2652 to 2654, 3556(18)
2622	——; cf. 2646, 2647			2653	——
2623	——2462	2643	2643	2654	——
2624	——; cf. 2463	2644	2644	2655	2655
2625	——	2645	2645	2656	2656
2626	——	2646	2646, 2647	2657	——
2627	——; cf. 2019 (Rev. 1984)	2647	(Reserved)	2658	(Reserved)
				2659	2659

25. Revision of Book III, Title VIII, Articles 2660 to 2667, and Former Articles 2660 to 2667:

New (2010) Art. No. (Act No. 186)	Corresponding Provisions: Prior Art. No.	New (2010) Art. No. (Act No. 186)	Corresponding Provisions: Prior Art. No.	New (2010) Art. No. (Act No. 186)	Corresponding Provisions: Prior Art. No.
2660	2660	2661	2660, 2667	2662	2662 to 2664, 2667
				2663	2662, 2663
				2664	2667
				2665	(Reserved)
				2666	(Reserved)
				2667	(Reserved)

26. Revision of Book III, Title IX, Articles 2668 to 2729 and Former Articles 2668 to 2744:

New Art. No.	Corresponding Provisions Prior Art. No.	New Art. No.	Corresponding Provisions Prior Art. No.	New Art. No.	Corresponding Provisions Prior Art. No.
2668	2669, 2670, 2674, 2677	2686	2711	2708	2706
2669	2668	2687	2721, 2722, 2723	2709	2707, 2708
2670	New; cf. 1971, 1976	2688	New; cf. 2724	2710	2709
2671	New	2689	2702	2711	2733; cf. 2682
2672	New	2690	2698	2712	New; cf. 2735
2673	2678, 2679	2691	2693, 2717, 2718	2713	2725
2674	2681, 2682	2692	2715, 2716, 2717	2714	2697, 2728
2675	2671	2693	2700	2715	2697, 2699
2676	2671, 2672	2694	2694	2716 (par. 1)	567, 2730
2677	R.S. 9:3204	2695	2726	2716 (par. 2)	2730
2678 (sent. 1)	2674	2696	2692, 2695	2717	2731
2678 (sent. 2)	2685, 2687	2697	2695	2718	2732, 2735
2679	New	2698	New	2719	2729
2680 (subpar. 1)	2687	2699	New	2720	2686, 2727
2680 (subpar. 2)	2685	2700	2682, 2692, 2696, 2704	2721	2688, 2689, 2691
2680 (subpar. 3)	New	2701	2692, 2696, 2704	2722	2688
2681 (sent. 1)	2683	2702	2703	2723	2689
2681 (sent. 2)	1839	2703	New	2724	New
2682	2692	2704	2712	2725	New
2683	2710; cf. 2719, 2720	2705	2743, 2744	2726	New
2684	2693	2706	R.S. 9:3204	2727	2024, 2686
2685	2701	2707	2705	2728	New; cf. 2024, 2686
				2729	New; cf. 2686

TABLE 2—DERIVATION

27. Revision of Book III, Title X, Articles 2778 to 2791, and Former Articles 2778 to 2800:

New (2012) Art. No. (Act No. 258)	Corresponding Provisions: Prior Art. No.	New (2012) Art. No. (Act No. 258)	Corresponding Provisions: Prior Art. No.	New (2012) Art. No. (Act No. 258)	Corresponding Provisions: Prior Art. No.
2778	New	2781	New	2784	New
2779	New	2782	New	2785	New
2780	New	2783	New	2786	New
				2787	New
				2788	New
				2789	New
				2790	New
				2791	New

28. Revision of Book III, Title XI, Articles 2801 to 2848, and Former Articles 2801 to 2890:

New (1980) Art. No. (Act No. 150)	Corresponding Provisions: Prior Art. No.	New (1980) Art. No. (Act No. 150)	Corresponding Provisions: Prior Art. No.	New (1980) Art. No. (Act No. 150)	Corresponding Provisions: Prior Art. No.
2801	2801, 2805, 2809	2816	2874	2832	2823
2802	2803	2817	2872, 2873, 2975	2833	—
2803	2811, 2813, 2865	2818	—	2834	2890
2804	2865	2819	—	2835	—
2805	2837, 2838	2820	—	2836	—
2806	2836	2821	—	2837	2828, 2839, 2840
2807	2867, 2868, 2869, 2870	2822	—	2838	2849
2808	2856(1)	2823	—	2839	2849, 2850
2809	2862	2824	—	2840	2839, 2842
2810	—	2825	—	2841	2845
2811	2864	2826	2876, 2877	2842	2843, 2851
2812	2871	2827	2878	2843	2844
2813	—	2828	—	2844	2849(2)
2814	2870	2829	—	2845	—
2815	2814	2830	—	2846	—
		2831	—	2847	—
				2848	—

29. Revision of Book III, Title XII, Articles 2891 to 2913 and Former Articles 2891 to 2925:

New Art. No.	Corresponding Provisions Prior Art. No.	New Art. No.	Corresponding Provisions Prior Art. No.	New Art. No.	Corresponding Provisions Prior Art. No.
2891	New; cf. 2893, 2894, 2895	2898	2901	2906	New; cf. 1828
2892	New; cf. 2438, 2990	2899	2904, 2908	2907	2913, 2914, 2915
2893	2896; cf. 2448	2900	2905	2908	2916
2894	2898	2901	2906, 2907	2909	New; cf. 1777, 2917, 2918
2895	2902	2902	2909	2910	2920
2896	New; 1874, cf. 2899	2903	New	2911	2921
2897	2900	2904	2910	2912	2922
		2905	2911	2913	2925

TABLE 2—DERIVATION

30. Revision of Book III, Title XIII, Articles 2926 to 2951, and Former Articles 2926 to 2981:

New (2003) Art. No. (Act No. 491)	Corresponding Provisions: Prior Art. No.	New Art. No.	Corresponding Provisions: Prior Art. No.	New Art. No.	Corresponding Provisions: Prior Art. No.
2926	2926	2933	2944	2942	—
2927	—	2934	2945, 2946	2943	2969
2928	cf. 2929	2935	2948	2944	cf. 2966, 2967
2929	2930	2936	2950	2945	2971
2930	2937 to 2939	2937	2953, 2954	2946	2973 to 2977
2931	2940	2938	2955	2947	—
2932	2941	2939	2956	2948	2978
		2940	2960	2949	2979
		2941	2965, 2968	2950	—
				2951	2981

31. Revision of Book III, Title XV, Articles 2985 to 3032, and Former Articles 2985 to 3034:

New (1997) Art. No. (Act No. 261)	Corresponding Provisions: Prior Art. No.	New (1997) Art. No. (Act No. 261)	Corresponding Provisions: Prior Art. No.	New (1997) Art. No. (Act No. 261)	Corresponding Provisions: Prior Art. No.
2985	New	3001	3002(1)	3016	New; cf.i 3012, 3013
2986	New	3002	3003	3017	New; cf. 3012, 3013
2987	New	3003	New	3018	New
2988	New	3004	3005, 3023	3019	New; cf. 3013
2989	New	3005	3015	3020	3021
2990	New	3006	New	3021	New
2991	2986	3007	New, in part 3007, 3008, 3009	3022	New
2992	2991			3023	New
2993	2992	3008	3010	3024	3027(A)
2994	2994, 2995	3009	3014	3025	New; cf. 3028
2995	3000	3010	New; ¤.3021	3026	3027(B)
2996	2996, 2997	3011	3011	3027	3027(B)
2997	2997	3012	3022	3028	3029
2998	New	3013	3024	3029	3031
2999	3001	3014	3025	3030	3002
3000	New; cf. 3016	3015	3026	3031	3032, 3033
				3032	3004

32. Revision of Book III, Title XVI, Articles 3035 to 3070, and Former Articles 3035 to 3070:

New (1987) Art. No. (Act No. 409)	Corresponding Provisions: Prior Art. No.	New (1987) Art. No. (Act No. 409)	Corresponding Provisions: Prior Art. No.	New (1987) Art. No. (Act No. 409)	Corresponding Provisions: Prior Art. No.
3035	3035	3046	3060	3057	—
3036	3036	3047	—	3058	3059
3037	—	3048	3053	3059	—
3038	3039	3049	3052, 3054	3060	—
3039	—	3050	cf. 3056	3061	—
3040	—	3051	3055	3062	3061
3041	—	3052	—	3063	—
3042	—	3053	3057	3064	3060(3), 3068
3043	—	3054	—	3065	3042, 3064
3044	cf. 3039	3055	3058	3066	—
3045	cf. 3045	3056	3058	3067	—
				3068	3065
				3069	3066
				3070	3043

TABLE 2—DERIVATION

33. Revision of Book I, Title XVII, Articles 3071 to 3083, and Former Articles 3071 to 3083:

New Art. No.	Prior Art. No.	New Art. No.	Prior Art. No.	New Art. No.	Prior Art. No.
3071	3071(1)	3076	3073	3080	3078
3072	3071(2)	3077	(Reserved)	3081	New
3073	New; cf. 3072	3078	3074	3082	3979, 3080
3074	New	3079	New	3083	New
3075	3077				

34. Revision of Book III, Title XXII, Articles 3278 to 3337 and Former Articles 3278 to 3411:*(1991 Revision)

New (1991) Art. No. (Act No. 652)	Corresponding Provisions: Prior Art. No.	New (1991) Art. No. (Act No. 652)	Corresponding Provisions: Prior Art. No.	New (1991) Art. No. (Act No. 652)	Corresponding Provisions: Prior Art. No.
3278	3278, 3284	3292	3304, 3307, 3308	3306	3327
3279	3278	3293	3291, 3292	3307	3397
3280	3282, 3310	3294	—	3311	—
3281	3283	3295	3295, 3296, 3297, 3299	3312	cf. 2645
3282	3284, 3285, 3299	3296	—	3313	—
3283	3286, 3288	3297	3291	3315	3343
3284	3287	3298	3292, 3293	3316	3407
3285	3288	3299	3321	3317	—
3286	3289	3300	3322	3318	3407
3287	3290, 3305	3301	3311	3319	3411
3288	3306, 3309	3302	3313, 3320, 3328	3320	3346, 3347, 3348, 3357
3289	—	3303	3313, 3320, 3328	3325	3384 [Redesignated as R.S. 9:5180.2]
3290	3300, 3301	3304	3323, 3324		
3291	3289	3305	3326	3326	3363

* See Table 33 for new articles of the 2005 revision.

35. Revision of Book III, Title XXII, Articles 3338 to 3368 and Former Articles 3308 to 3310, 3314, 3321 to 3324, 3327 to 3337 (2005 Revision):

New Art. No.	Prior Art. No.	New Art. No.	Prior Art. No.	New Art. No.	Prior Art. No.
3338	3308	3349	New	3359	3330
3339	New	3350	New	3360	3331
3340	3338	3351	New	3361	3332
3341	New	3352	New	3362	3333
3342	3309, 3310	3353	New	3363	New
3344	New	3354	New	3364	3334
3345	New	3355	3322, 3323	3365	3335
3346	New	3356	3314	3366	New
3347	New	3357	New	3367	3337
3348	New	3358	3329	3368	New

36. Revision of Book III, Title XXIII and Title XXIV, Articles 3412 to 3504, and Former Articles 3412 to 3554:

New (1982) Art. No. (Act No. 187)	Corresponding Provisions: Prior Art. No.	New (1982) Art. No. (Act No. 187)	Corresponding Provisions: Prior Art. No.	New (1982) Art. No. (Act No. 187)	Corresponding Provisions: Prior Art. No.
3412	3412, 3413, 3414	3422	3434(2)	3433	3447, 3448, 3449
3413	3415	3423	3454(1)	3434	3449(2), 3517
3414	3416	3424	3436	3435	3487, 3491, 3500
3415(1)	—	3425	3428	3436	3487, 3491, 3500
3415(2)	519	3426	3437	3437	3426, 3433
3416	3417	3427	3488	3438	3446, 3489
3417	3419	3428	3438, 3445	3439	—
3418	3421	3429	3433	3440	—
3419	3422	3430	3440	3441	3493, 3494(2), 3496
3420	3423	3431	3429, 3442, 3501, 3502	3442	3493, 3494, 3495
3421	3426, 3430, 3433, 3436	3432	3443, 3501, 3502	3443	3492
				3444	3458(2), 3455, 3456

TABLE 2—DERIVATION

New (1982) Art. No. (Act No. 187)	Corresponding Provisions: Prior Art. No.	New (1982) Art. No. (Act No. 187)	Corresponding Provisions: Prior Art. No.	New (1983) Art. No. (Act No. 173)	Corresponding Provisions: Prior Art. No.
3445	3457, 3546	3469	3523	3492	3536(1), 3537(2)
3446	3458	3470	3526, 3527	3493	3537(3)
3447	3457, 3459	3471	—	3494	3534, 3538
3448	—	3472	—	3495	3535
3449	3460	3473	3474, 3478 (sent. 1)	3496	3539
3450	3461	3474	3478 (sent. 2)	3497	3542
3451	3462	3475	3479	3498	3540
3452	3463	3476	3487	3499	3544
3453	3466	3477	3510, 3511	3500	3545
3454	3467	3478	3512, 3515(3)	3501	3547
3455	3468	3479	3513	3502	3548
3456	3469	3480	3451	3503	2097, 3552
3457	3470	3481	3452, 3480, 3481	3504	3553
3458	—	3482	3482		
3459	—	3483	3483, 3484, 3485, 3486	**New (2013) Art. No. (Act No. 88)**	
3460	—	3484	—		
3461	—	3485	3497	3505	—
3462	3518	3486	3499	3505.1	—
3463	3519	3487	3503	3505.2	—
3464	3520	3488	3505	3505.3	—
3465	3517	3489	3476, 3505, 3509	3505.4	—
3466	—	3490	3506		
3467	3521	3491	3509		
3468	3522				

37. Book IV, Titles I-VIII, Articles 3515 to 3549:

New (1991) Art. No. (Act No. 923)	Corresponding Provisions: Prior Art. No.
3515-3549	—

TABLE 3—REVISION

This table shows the 1976–2013 Revision of the Louisiana Civil Code of 1870 and changes after revision. For changes in the law effected by the revision, see Tables 1 and 2.

Preliminary Title:
Articles
1 to 13	1987, No. 124	Revised
14	1987, No. 124	Revised
	1991, No. 923	Revised
15	1987, No. 124	Revised
	1991, No. 923	Vacated

Book I, Title I:
24 to 29	1987, No. 125	Revised
30, 31	1990, No. 989	Added

Book I, Title II:
38	2008, No. 801	Revised
	2012, No. 713	Amended
39 to 46	2008, No. 801	Revised

Book I, Title III:
47 to 53	1990, No. 989	Revised
54	1990, No. 989	Revised
	2006, No. 258	Amended
55 to 59	1990, No. 989	Revised
212 to 214	2008, No. 351	Revised
365 to 371	2008, No. 786	Revised

Book I, Title IV:
86 to 88	1987, No. 886	Revised
89	1987, No. 886	Revised
	1999, No. 890	Amended
90 to 100	1999, No. 886	Revised
	2004, No. 26	Amended
101	1987, No. 886	Renumbered from Article 136
	1987, No. 886	Amended
	1990, No. 1009	Amended

Book I, Title V:
Articles
102	1990, No. 1009	Revised
	1991, No. 367	Amended
	1993, No. 107	Amended
	1995, No. 386	Amended
	2006, No. 743	Amended
103	1990, No. 1009	Revised
	1991, No. 918	Amended
	2006, No. 743	Amended
103.1	2006, No. 743	Added
	2010, No. 604	Amended
104, 105	1990, No. 1009	Revised
111	1997, No. 1078	Revised
	2006, No. 749	Amended
112	1997, No. 1078	Revised
	2006, No. 749	Amended
113	1997, No. 1078	Revised

Book I, Title V:
Articles
	2001, No. 738	Amended
	2003, No. 1092	Amended
114	1997, No. 1078	Revised
	2001, No. 1049	Amended
115 to 117	1997, No. 1078	Revised
121	1990, No. 1008	Added
	1991, No. 367	Amended
122 to 124	1990, No. 1008	Added
131	1990, Nos. 1008, 1009	Renumbered from Article 146
	1993, No. 261	Revised
132	1990, Nos. 1008, 1009	Renumbered from Article 146.1
	1992, No. 782	Amended
	1993, No. 261	Revised
133	1990, Nos. 1008, 1009	Renumbered from Article 147
	1993, No. 261	Revised
134	1990, Nos. 1008, 1009	Renumbered from Article 157
	1993, No. 261	Revised
	2012, No. 627	Comment added
135	1990, Nos. 1008, 1009	Renumbered from Article 158
	1993, No. 261	Revised
136	1993, No. 261	Revised
	2009, No. 379	Amended
	2012, No. 763	Amended
137	1970, No. 108	Repealed
	2001, No. 499	Added
	2010, No. 873	Amended
	2012, No. 763	Amended
141, 142	1993, No. 261	Revised
151, 152	1993, No. 108	Revised

Book I, Title VII, Chapters 1, 2, 3, and 4:
178	2009, No. 3	Revised
179	2009, No. 3	Revised
184 to 186	1976, No. 430	Revised
	2005, No. 192	Revised
187	1976, No. 430	Revised
	1989, No. 790	Amended
	2005, No. 192	Revised
188	1976, No. 430	Revised
	1989, No. 790	Amended
	2005, No. 192	Revised
189	1976, No. 430	Revised
	1999, No. 790	Amended

TABLE 3—REVISION

Book I, Title VII, Chapters 1, 2, 3, and 4:
     2005, No. 192 .... Revised
190 .... 1976, No. 430 .... Revised
     1999, No. 790 .... Amended
     2005, No. 192 .... Revised
191 .... 2004, No. 530 .... Enacted
     2005, No. 192 .... Revised
192 to 195 .... 2005, No. 192 .... Revised
196 .... 2005, No. 192 .... Revised
     2006, No. 344 .... Amended
197 to 198 .... 2005, No. 192 .... Revised
199 .... 2009, No. 3 .... Revised
200 .... 2009, No. 3 .... Revised

Book I, Title IX:
389 to 394 .... 2000, No. 25 (1st
     Ex.Sess.) .... Revised
395 .... 2000, No. 25 (1st
     Ex.Sess.) .... Revised
     2001, No. 509 .... Amended
     2003, No. 1008 .... Amended
396 to 426 .... 2000, No. 25 (1st
     Ex.Sess.) .... Revised

Book II:
448 to 465 .... 1978, No. 728 .... Revised
466 .... 1978, No. 728 .... Revised
     2005, No. 301 .... Amended
     2006, No. 765 .... Amended
467 to 476 .... 1978, No. 728 .... Revised
477 .... 1979, No. 180 .... Revised
     1995, No. 640 .... Amended
478 to 516 .... 1979, No. 180 .... Revised
517 .... 1979, No. 180 .... Revised
     2005, No. 169 .... Amended
518 .... 1979, No. 180 .... Revised
     1984, No. 331 .... Amended
519 to 532 .... 1979, No. 180 .... Revised
533 to 537 .... 1976, No. 103 .... Revised
538 .... 1976, No. 103 .... Revised
     2010, No. 881 .... Amended
539 to 542 .... 1976, No. 103 .... Revised
543 .... 1976, No. 103 .... Revised
     1983, No. 535 .... Amended
544 to 548 .... 1976, No. 103 .... Revised
549 .... 1976, No. 103 .... Revised
     2010, No. 881 .... Amended
550 to 552 .... 1976, No. 103 .... Revised
553 .... 1976, No. 103 .... Revised
     2010, No. 881 .... Amended
554 to 557 .... 1976, No. 103 .... Revised
558 .... 1976, No. 103 .... Revised
     2010, No. 881 .... Amended
559 to 566 .... 1976, No. 103 .... Revised
567 .... 1976, No. 103 .... Revised
     2010, No. 881 .... Amended
568 .... 1976, No. 103 .... Revised
     1986, No. 203 .... Amended
     2010, No. 881 .... Amended
568.1 .... 2010, No. 881 .... Added
568.2 .... 2010, No. 881 .... Added
568.3 .... 2010, No. 881 .... Added
569 .... 1976, No. 103 .... Revised
     2010, No. 881 .... Amended
570 .... 1976, No. 103 .... Revised
571 .... 1976, No. 103 .... Revised

Book II:
     2004, No. 158 .... Amended
572 .... 1976, No. 103 .... Revised
573 .... 1976, No. 103 .... Revised
     2004, No. 158 .... Amended
     2010, No. 881 .... Amended
574 .... 1976, No. 103 .... Revised
     2010, No. 881 .... Amended
575 .... 1976, No. 103 .... Revised
     2010, No. 881 .... Amended
576 .... 1976, No. 103 .... Revised
577 .... 1976, No. 103 .... Revised
     1979, No. 157 .... Amended
     2010, No. 881 .... Amended
578 .... 1976, No. 103 .... Revised
579 .... 1976, No. 103 .... Revised
580 .... 1976, No. 103 .... Revised
     2010, No. 881 .... Amended
581 .... 1976, No. 103 .... Revised
     2010, No. 881 .... Amended
582 .... 1976, No. 103 .... Revised
583 .... 1976, No. 103 .... Revised
     2010, No. 881 .... Amended
584 .... 1976, No. 103 .... Revised
     2010, No. 881 .... Amended
585 .... 1976, No. 103 .... Revised
586 .... 1976, No. 103 .... Revised
     2010, No. 881 .... Amended
587 .... 1976, No. 103 .... Revised
     2010, No. 881 .... Amended
588 .... 1976, No. 103 .... Revised
     2010, No. 881 .... Amended
589 .... 1976, No. 103 .... Revised
     2010, No. 881 .... Amended
590 .... 1976, No. 103 .... Revised
     2010, No. 881 .... Amended
591 .... 1976, No. 103 .... Revised
     2010, No. 881 .... Amended
592 .... 1976, No. 103 .... Revised
     2010, No. 881 .... Amended
593 .... 1976, No. 103 .... Revised
     1990, No. 706 .... Amended
     2010, No. 881 .... Amended
594 .... 1976, No. 103 .... Revised
     2010, No. 881 .... Amended
595 to 600 .... 1976, No. 103 .... Revised
601 .... 1976, No. 103 .... Revised
     2010, No. 881 .... Amended
602 .... 1976, No. 103 .... Revised
603 .... 1976, No. 103 .... Revised
     1990, No. 706 .... Amended
     2010, No. 881 .... Amended
604 .... 1976, No. 103 .... Revised
     2010, No. 881 .... Amended
605 to 607 .... 1976, No. 103 .... Revised
608 .... 1976, No. 103 .... Revised
     2010, No. 881 .... Amended
609 to 612 .... 1976, No. 103 .... Revised
613 .... 1976, No. 103 .... Revised
     2010, No. 881 .... Amended
614 .... 1976, No. 103 .... Revised
615 .... 1976, No. 103 .... Revised
     2010, No. 881 .... Amended
616 .... 1976, No. 103 .... Revised
     1983, No. 535 .... Amended

TABLE 3—REVISION

Book II:

	2010, No. 881	Amended
617	1976, No. 103	Revised
618	1976, No. 103	Revised
	2010, No. 881	Amended
619	1976, No. 103	Revised
	2010, No. 881	Amended
620	1976, No. 103	Revised
	2010, No. 881	Amended
621 to 622	1976, No. 103	Revised
623	1976, No. 103	Revised
	2010, No. 881	Amended
624	1976, No. 103	Revised
	2010, No. 881	Amended
625	1976, No. 103	Revised
	2010, No. 881	Amended
646 to 649	1977, No. 514	Revised
650	1977, No. 514	Revised
	2004, No. 821	Amended
651	1977, No. 514	Revised
	2010, No. 938	Amended
652 to 659	1977, No. 514	Revised
660	1996, No. 77 (1st Ex.Sess.)	Amended
660 to 664	1996, No. 77 (1st Ex.Sess.)	Revised
665	2006, No. 776	Amended
666	1977, No. 514	Renumbered from 707
667 to 669	Unaffected by Revision	
670 to 688	1977, No. 514	Revised
689	2012, No. 739	Amended
690	1977, No. 514	Revised
	2012, No. 739	Amended
691	1977, No. 514	Revised
	2012, No. 739	Amended
692	1977, No. 514	Revised
	2012, No. 739	Amended
693	1977, No. 514	Revised
694	1977, No. 514	Revised
	2012, No. 739	Amended
695 to 696	1977, No. 514	Revised
696.1	2012, No. 739	Added
697 to 704	1977, No. 514	Revised
705	1977, No. 514	Revised
	2012, No. 739	Amended
706 to 738	1977, No. 514	Revised
739	1977, No. 514	Revised
	1978, No. 479	Amended
740	1977, No. 514	Revised
741	1977, No. 514	Revised
	1978, No. 479	Amended
742 to 766	1977, No. 514	Revised
767	1977, No. 514	Revised
	2001, No. 572	Amended
768 to 774	1977, No. 514	Revised
775	1977, No. 170	Revised
776	1977, No. 170	Revised
	1999, No. 309	Amended
777	1977, No. 170	Revised
778	1977, No. 170	Revised
	2010, No. 938	Amended
779	1977, No. 170	Revised
780	1977, No. 170	Revised
	1980, No. 310	Amended

Book II:

	1983, No. 129	Amended
	1999, No. 309	Amended
781, 782	1977, No. 170	Revised
783	1977, No. 170	Revised
	1999, No. 309	Amended
784 to 796	1977, No. 169	Revised
797 to 806	1990, No. 990	Added
807	1990, No. 990	Added
	1991, No. 349	Amended

Book III, Preliminary Title:

870	1981, No. 919	Revised

Book III, Title I, Chapters 1 through 6 and Chapter 13:

871, 876	1981, No. 919	Revised
877 to 879	1981, No. 919	Revised
	2001, No. 572	Repealed
880, 881	1981, No. 919	Revised
882	1981, No. 919	Revised
	1990, No. 147	Amended
883 to 889	1981, No. 919	Revised
890	1981, No. 919	Revised
	1996 (1st Ex.Sess.)	Amended
891	1981, No. 919	Revised
	2004, No. 26	Amended
892 to 902	1981, No. 919	Revised
934 to 937	1997, No. 1421	Revised
938	1997, No. 1421	Revised
	2001, No. 556	Amended
939 to 941	1997, No. 1421	Revised
942	1997, No. 1421	Revised
	2001, No. 824	Amended
943 to 945	1997, No. 1421	Revised
946	1997, No. 1421	Revised
	2001, No. 824	Amended
947 to 951	1997, No. 1421	Revised
952	1997, No. 1421	Revised
	2001, No. 824	Amended
953 to 964	1997, No. 1421	Revised
965	1997, No. 1421	Revised
	2001, No. 824	Amended
966, 967	1997, No. 1421	Revised
1415	1997, No. 1421	Revised
1416	1997, No. 1421	Revised
	2001, No. 824	Amended
1417 to 1466	1997, No. 1421	Revised

Book III, Title II, Chapter 1:

1467 to 1469	2008, No. 204	Revised

Book III, Title II, Chapters 2 and 3:

1470 to 1481	1991, No. 363	Revised
1482	1991, No. 363	Revised
	2001, No. 509	
	2003, No. 1008	Amended
1483	1991, No. 363	Revised
1484	2001, No. 560	Enacted
1493	1996, No. 77 (1st Ex.Sess.)	Revised
1493(E)	2003, No. 1297	Added
1494 to 1498	1996, No. 77 (1st Ex.Sess.)	Revised
1499	1996, No. 77 (1st Ex.Sess.)	Revised
	2003, No. 548	Amended

TABLE 3—REVISION

Book III, Title II, Chapters 2 and 3:
1500	1996, No. 77 (1st Ex.Sess.)	Revised
1501	1996, No. 77 (1st Ex.Sess.)	Revised
	1997, No. 706	Repealed
1502 to 1513	1996, No. 77 (1st Ex.Sess.)	Revised
1514	1996, No. 77 (1st Ex.Sess.)	Revised
	2003, No. 1207	Amended

Book III, Title II, Chapter 5:
1526 to 1567	2008, No. 204	Revised

Book III, Title II, Chapter 6:
1570 to 1574	1996, No. 77 (1st Ex.Sess.)	Revised
1575	1996, No. 77 (1st Ex.Sess.)	Revised
	2001, No. 824	Amended
1576	1996, No. 77 (1st Ex.Sess.)	Revised
	1999, No. 745	Amended
1577 to 1582	1997, No. 1421	Revised
1582.1	2003, No. 707	Added
	2004, No. 231	Amended
1583 to 1592	1997, No. 1421	Revised
1593	1997, No. 1421	Revised
	2001, No. 824	Amended
1594 to 1596	1997, No. 1421	Revised
1597	1997, No. 1421	Revised
	2001, No. 824	Amended
1598 to 1610	1997, No. 1421	Revised
1610.1	2001, No. 824	Added
1611	1997, No. 1421	Revised
	2001, No. 560	Amended
1617 to 1626	2001, No. 573	Added

Book III, Title II, Chapters 8 and 9:
1734 to 1751	2004, No. 619	Revised

Book III, Title III:
1756 to 1825	1984, No. 331	Revised
1826	1984, No. 331	Revised
	2001, No. 305	Amended
1827 to 1828	1984, No. 331	Revised
1829	1984, No. 331	Revised
	1989, No. 137	Amended
	2001, No. 572	Amended
1830 to 1832	1984, No. 331	Revised
1833	1984, No. 331	Revised
	2003, No. 965	Amended
1834 to 1847	1984, No. 331	Revised
1848	1984, No. 331	Revised
	2012, No. 277	Amended
1849	1984, No. 331	Revised
	1997, No. 577	Repealed
	2012, No. 277	Added
1850 to 1852	1984, No. 331	Revised
	1997, No. 577	Repealed
1853 to 1905	1984, No. 331	Revised

Book III, Title IV:
1906 to 1912	1984, No. 331	Revised
1913	1984, No. 331	Revised
	1989, No. 137	Amended
1914 to 1999	1984, No. 331	Revised
2000	1984, No. 331	Revised

Book III, Title IV:
	1985, No. 137	Amended
	1987, No. 883	Amended
2001 to 2020	1984, No. 331	Revised
2021	1984, No. 331	Revised
	2005, No. 169	Amended
2022 to 2027	1984, No. 331	Revised
2028	1984, No. 331	Revised
	2012, No. 277	Amended
2029 to 2034	1984, No. 331	Revised
2035	1984, No. 331	Revised
	2005, No. 169	Amended
2036	1984, No. 331	Revised
	2003, No. 552	Amended
	2004, No. 447	Amended
2037	1984, No. 331	Revised
	2003, No. 552	Amended
	2004, No. 447	Amended
2038 to 2040	1984, No. 331	Revised
2041	1984, No. 331	Revised
	2013, No. 88	Amended
2042 to 2057	1984, No. 331	Revised

Book III, Title V:
2292 to 2305	1995, No. 1041	Revised
2315.3	2009, No. 382	Added
2319	2000, No. 25 (1st Ex.Sess.)	Amended

Book III, Title VI:
2325 to 2328	1979, No. 709	Revised
2329	1979, No. 709	Revised
	1980, No. 565	Amended
2330 to 2334	1979, No. 709	Revised
2335	1979, No. 709	Revised
	1991, No. 329	Amended
2336	1979, No. 709	Revised
	1981, No. 921	Amended
	1982, No. 282	Amended
2337 to 2338	1979, No. 709	Revised
2339	1979, No. 709	Revised
	1980, No. 565	Amended
2340	1979, No. 709	Revised
2341	1979, No. 709	Revised
	1981, No. 921	Amended
2341.1	1991, No. 329	Added
2342	1979, No. 709	Revised
	1980, No. 565	Amended
	1982, No. 453	Amended
2343	1979, No. 709	Revised
	1981, No. 921	Amended
2343.1	1981, No. 921	Added
2344 to 2346	1979, No. 709	Revised
2347	1979, No. 709	Revised
	2001, No. 558	Amended
2348	1979, No. 709	Revised
	1981, No. 132	Amended
	1984, Nos. 554, 622	Amended
2349 to 2354	1979, No. 709	Revised
2355	1979, No. 709	Revised
	1990, No. 989	Amended
2355.1	1990, No. 989	Added
2356	1979, No. 709	Revised
	1990, No. 989	Amended
2357	1979, No. 709	Revised

TABLE 3—REVISION

Book III, Title VI:

	1990, No. 989	Amended
2358	1979, No. 709	Revised
	1990, No. 989	Amended
	2009, No. 204	Amended
2358.1	1990, No. 991	Added
2359 to 2362	1979, No. 709	Revised
2362.1	1990, No. 1009	Added
	1990, No. 1009	Amended
	2009, No. 204	Amended
2363	1979, No. 709	Revised
	2009, No. 204	Amended
2364	1979, No. 709	Revised
	2009, No. 204	Amended
2364.1	1997, No. 499	Added
	2009, No. 204	Repealed
2365	1979, No. 709	Revised
	1990, No. 991	Amended
	2009, No. 204	Amended
2366	1979, No. 709	Revised
	1984, No. 933	Amended
	2009, No. 204	Amended
2367	1979, No. 709	Revised
	1984, No. 933	Amended
	1990, No. 991	Amended
	2009, No. 204	Amended
2367.1	1984, No. 933	Added
	1990, No. 991	Amended
	2009, No. 204,	Amended
2367.2	1984, No. 933	Added
	2009, No. 204,	Amended
2367.3	2009, No. 204,	Added
2368, 2369	1979, No. 709	Revised
2369.1	1981, No. 751	Added
	1982, No. 439	Repealed
	1990, No. 991	Added
	1995, No. 433	Amended
2369.2 to 2369.8	1995, No. 433	Added
2370 to 2373	1979, No. 709	Revised
2374	1979, No. 709	Revised
	1990, No. 989	Amended
	1992, No. 295	Amended
	1993, No. 25	Amended
	1993, No. 627	Amended
	2010, No. 603	Amended
2375	1979, No. 709	Revised
	1990, No. 989	Amended
	1992, No. 295	Amended
	1993, No. 25	Amended
	1993, No. 627	Amended
	2010, No. 603	Amended
2376	1979, No. 709	Revised
2432 to 2433	1979, No. 710	Revised
2434	1979, No. 710	Revised
	1987, No. 289	Amended
2435 to 2437	1979, No. 710	Revised

Book III, Title VII:

2438 to 2441	1993, No. 841	Revised
2442	1993, No. 841	Revised
	2005, No. 169	Amended
2443	1993, No. 841	Revised
2444	1993, No. 841	Revised
	2012, No. 277	Repealed
2445 to 2553	1993, No. 841	Revised

Book III, Title VII:

2534	1993, No. 841	Revised
	1995, No. 172	Amended
	1997, No. 266	Amended
2535 to 2627	1993, No. 841	Revised
2628	1993, No. 841	Revised
	2003, No. 1005	Amended
2629 to 2659	1993, No. 841	Revised

Book III, Title VIII:

2660 to 2667	2010, No. 186	Revised

Book III, Title IX:

2668 to 2744	2004, No. 821	Revised

Book III, Title X:

2778 to 2791	2012, No. 258	Revised

Book III, Title XI:

2801 to 2813	1980, No. 150	Revised
2814	1980, No. 150	Revised
	1981, No. 888	Amended
	1989, No. 137	Amended
2815 to 2817	1980, No. 150	Revised
2818	1980, No. 150	Revised
	2004, No. 827	Amended
2819 to 2825	1980, No. 150	Revised
2826	1980, No. 150	Revised
	1981, No. 797	Amended
	1982, No. 273	Amended
2827 to 2838	1980, No. 150	Revised
2839	1980, No. 150	Revised
	1984, No. 429	Amended
2840 to 2843	1980, No. 150	Revised
2844	1980, No. 150	Revised
	1995, No. 847	Amended
2845	1980, No. 150	Revised
	1995, No. 847	Repealed
2846	1980, No. 150	Revised
	1984, No. 429	Amended
	1995, No. 847	Repealed
2847, 2848	1980, No. 150	Revised
	1995, No. 847	Repealed

Book III, Title XII:

2891 to 2913	2004, No. 743	Revised

Book III, Title XIII:

2926 to 2981	2003, No. 491	Revised

Book III, Title XV:

2985 to 2996	1997, No. 261	Revised
2997	1997, No. 261	Revised
	2001, No. 594	Amended
2998 to 3032	1997, No. 261	Revised

Book III, Title XVI:

3035 to 3070	1987, No. 409	Revised

Book III, Title XXII:

3278 to 3297	1991, No. 652	Revised
3298	1991, No. 652	Revised
	1995, No. 1087	Amended
	2010, No. 385	Amended
3299 to 3307	1992, No. 1132	Revised

TABLE 3—REVISION

Book III, Title XXII:
3308 to 3310	1992, No. 1132	Revised
	2005, No. 169	Repealed
3311 to 3313	1992, No. 1132	Revised
3314	1992, No. 1132	Revised
	2005, No. 169	Repealed
3315 to 3318	1992, No. 1132	Revised
3319	1992, No. 1132	Revised
	1995, No. 1087	Amended
3320	1992, No. 1132	Revised
	2005, No. 169	Amended
3321 to 3324	1992, No. 1132	Revised
	2005, No. 169	Repealed
3325	1992, No. 1132	Revised
	1995, No. 1087	Amended
3326 to 3336	1992, No. 1132	Revised
	2005, No. 169	Repealed
3337	1992, No. 1132	Revised
	2005, No. 169	Amended
3338 to 3368	2005, No. 169	Added

Book III, Title XXIII:
3412 to 3462	1982, No. 187	Revised

Book III, Title XXIV:
3463	1982, No. 187	Revised
	1999, No. 1263	Amended
3464 to 3467	1982, No. 187	Revised
3468	1982, No. 187	Revised

Book III, Title XXIV:
	1983, No. 173	Amended
	1991, No. 107	Amended
3469	1982, No. 187	Revised
	1988, No. 676	Amended
3470 to 3473	1982, No. 187	Revised
3474	1982, No. 187	Revised
	1991, No. 107	Amended
3475 to 3491	1982, No. 187	Revised
3492 to 3493	1983, No. 173	Revised
3493.1	1999, No. 832	Added
3494	1983, No. 173	Revised
	1984, No. 147	Amended
	1986, No. 1031	Amended
3495 to 3496	1983, No. 173	Revised
3496.1	1988, No. 676	Added
3497	1983, No. 173	Revised
	2009, No. 107	Amended
3497.1	1984, No. 147	Added
	1990, No. 1008	Amended
3498 to 3504	1983, No. 173	Revised
3505 to 3505.4	2013, No. 88	Added

Book IV:
3515 to 3519	1991, No. 923	Revised
3520	1991, No. 923	Revised
	1999, No. 890	Amended
3521 to 3548	1991, No. 923	Revised
3549	1991, No. 923	Revised
	2005, No. 213	Amended

TABLE 4— CHANGE—CIVIL CODE OF 1870

This table shows changes in the provisions of the Louisiana Civil Code of 1870 until their repeal, revision, or redesignation. "Redesignated" or "renumbered" are used to indicate the transfer of a Civil Code provision to the Revised Statutes or the change of the number of a Civil Code article. "Added" is used to indicate enactment of new articles, usually to fill vacant numbers of long-repealed articles of the 1870 Civil Code.

For the work of Revision, see Tables 1—Disposition and 2—Derivation. For changes after Revision, see Table 3.

Preliminary Title arts. 1–23 (1870):
The Preliminary Title of the Louisiana Civil Code of 1870, containing Articles 1 to 23, has been revised. This Table traces the provisions of the 1870 Code until their repeal. For the work of revision, see Tables 1 and 2.

Art.	Act	Action
1 to 8	1987, No. 124	Repealed
9	1987, No. 124	Renumbered as Article 14
	1991, No. 923	Repealed
10	1979, No. 711	Amended
	1987, No. 124	Renumbered as Article 15
	1991, No. 923	Repealed
11 to 23	1987, No. 126	Repealed

Book I, arts. 24–447 (1870):

Art.	Act	Action
24	1921, Ex.Sess., No. 44	Amended
	1987, No. 125	Repealed
25	1921, Ex.Sess., No. 33	Amended
	1987, No. 125	Repealed
26 to 35	1987, No. 125	Repealed
36	1974, No. 134	Repealed
37	1972, No. 98	Amended
	1974, No. 91	Amended
	1987, No. 125	Repealed
38	2008, No. 801	Repealed
39	1985, No. 272	Amended
	2008, No. 801	Repealed
40	2008, No. 801	Repealed
40.1	1984, No. 494	Added
	2008, No. 801	Repealed
42 to 46	2008, No. 801	Repealed
47	1990, No. 989	Repealed
48	1979, No. 711	Amended
	1990, No. 989	Repealed
49 to 63	1979, No. 989	Repealed
64	1979, No. 711	Amended
	1990, No. 989	Repealed
65 to 67	1990, No. 989	Repealed
68	1978, No. 457	Amended
	1986, No. 270	Amended
	1990, No. 989	Repealed
69	1990, No. 989	Repealed
70	1946, No. 377	Amended
	1948, No. 343	Amended
	1978, No. 457	Amended
	1986, No. 270	Amended
	1990, No. 989	Repealed

Book I, arts. 24–447 (1870):

Art.	Act	Action
71 to 77	1990, No. 989	Repealed
78	1956, No. 533	Amended
	1990, No. 989	Repealed
79	1956, No. 532	Amended
	1990, No. 989	Repealed
80	1916, No. 211	Amended
	1938, No. 357	Repealed
81 to 83	1990, No. 989	Repealed
84	1990, No. 989	Redesignated
85	1990, No. 989	Repealed
86 to 87	1987, No. 886	Repealed
88	1975, No. 361	Amended
	1987, No. 886	Repealed
89 to 91	1987, No. 886	Repealed
92	1934, No. 140	Amended
	1954, No. 398	Amended
	1956, No. 289	Amended
	1987, No. 886	Repealed
93	1987, No. 886	Repealed
94	1972, No. 256	Amended
	1984, No. 54	Amended
	1987, No. 886	Repealed
95	1902, No. 9	Amended
	1972, No. 230	Amended
	1974, No. 533	Amended
	1977, No. 365	Amended
	1981, No. 647	Amended
	1987, No. 886	Repealed
96 to 98	1987, No. 886	Repealed
99	1882, No. 25	Amended
	1948, No. 312	Amended
	1987, No. 886	Repealed
100	1987, No. 886	Repealed
101	1944, No. 23	Amended
	1987, No. 886	Repealed
	1990, No. 1009	Amended
102	1952, No. 229	Amended
	1958, No. 331	Amended
	1987, No. 886	Repealed
103	1987, No. 886	Repealed
103.1	1990, No. 1009	Added
	2010, No. 604	Amended
104	1979, No. 677	Amended
	1980, No. 351	Amended
	1987, No. 886	Repealed
105	1984, No. 61	Amended
	1987, No. 886	Repealed
106 to 112	1987, No. 886	Repealed
113	1904, No. 129	Amended

TABLE 4—CHANGE—CIVIL CODE OF 1870

Book I, arts. 24–447 (1870):

	1912, No. 54	Amended
	1938, No. 426	Amended
	1950, No. 242	Amended
	1987, No. 886	Repealed
114 to 115	1987, No. 886	Repealed
116	1906, No. 150	Amended
	1987, No. 886	Repealed
117 to 119	1987, No. 886	Repealed
120	1985, No. 271	Repealed
121 to 130	1974, No. 89	Repealed
131	1979, No. 709	Repealed
132 to 135	1974, No. 89	Repealed
136	1987, No. 886	Renumbered as Article 101
136	1993, No. 261	Added
	1995, No. 57	Amended
	2009, No. 379	Amended
137	1970, No. 108	Repealed
	2001, No. 499	Added
	2010, No. 873	Amended
138	1954, No. 617	Amended
	1956, No. 303	Amended
	1977, No. 735	Amended
	1986, No. 210	Amended
	1990, No. 1009	Repealed
139	1877, Ex.Sess., No. 122	Amended
	1954, No. 618	Amended
	1990, No. 1009	Repealed
140	1990, No. 1009	Repealed
141	1960, No. 30	Repealed
	1976, No. 495	Added
	1990, No. 99	Amended
	1990, No. 1009	Repealed
142	1920, No. 113	Amended
	1934, No. 1	Amended
	1946, No. 347	Amended
	1960, No. 30	Amended
	1974, No. 164	Amended
	1990, No. 1009	Repealed
143	1958, No. 154	Amended
	1990, No. 1009	Repealed
144	1990, No. 1009	Repealed
145	1928, No. 271	Amended
	1932, No. 73	Amended
	1958, No. 82	Amended
	1990, No. 1009	Repealed
146	Renumbered as 131	
	1888, No. 124	Amended
	1979, No. 718	Amended
	1981, No. 283	Amended
	1982, No. 307	Amended
	1983, No. 695	Amended
	1984, Nos. 133, 786	Amended
	1986, No. 950	Amended
	1989, No. 188	Amended
	1993, No. 261	Repealed
146.1	Renumbered as 132	
	1988, No. 817	Added
	1992, No. 782	Amended
	1993, No. 261	Repealed
147	Renumbered as 133	
	1928, No. 65	Repealed
	1986, No. 966	Added

Book I, arts. 24–447 (1870):

	1989, No. 546	Amended
	1993, No. 261	Repealed
148	Renumbered as 111	
	1928, No. 130	Amended
	1979, No. 72	Amended
	1990, No. 361	Amended
149	1979, No. 711	Amended
	1990, No. 1009	Repealed
150	1979, No. 709	Repealed
	1986, No. 225	Added
	1990, No. 1009	Repealed
151 to 154	1990, No. 1009	Repealed
155	1944, No. 200	Amended
	1950, No. 304	Amended
	1962, No. 178	Amended
	1977, No. 483	Amended
	1979, No. 711	Amended
	1985, No. 525	Amended
	1990, No. 1009	Repealed
156	1990, No. 1009	Repealed
157	Renumbered as 134	
	1921, No. 38	Amended
	1924, No. 74	Amended
	1970, No. 436	Amended
	1977, No. 448	Amended
	1979, No. 718	Amended
	1981, No. 283	Amended
	1982, No. 307	Amended
	1988, No. 817	Amended
	1990, No. 361	Amended
	1993, No. 261	Repealed
158	Renumbered as 135	
	1990, No. 361	Amended
	1993, No. 261	Repealed
159	1977, No. 483	Amended
	1979, No. 711	Amended
	1990, No. 361	Amended
160	Renumbered as 112	
	1916, No. 247	Amended
	1928, No. 21	Amended
	1934, 2nd Ex.Sess., No. 27	Amended
	1964, No. 48	Amended
	1979, No. 72	Amended
	1982, Nos. 293, 580	Amended
	1986, No. 229	Amended
	1993, No. 261	Repealed
161	1958, No. 340	Amended
	1962, No. 271	Amended
	1966, No. 182	Amended
	1968, No. 591	Amended
	1970, No. 739	Amended
	1972, No. 625	Repealed
	1986, No. 780	Added
	1990, No. 1008	Repealed
162 to 165	1990, No. 705	Repealed
166	1974, No. 89	Repealed
167	1964, No. 355	Amended
	1990, No. 705	Repealed
168	1964, No. 383	Amended
	1990, No. 705	Repealed
169 to 175	1990, No. 705	Repealed
176	1990,	Redesignated as Art. 2320(A)

TABLE 4—CHANGE—CIVIL CODE OF 1870

Book I, arts. 24–447 (1870):
177	1990, No. 705	Repealed
178	1979, No. 607	Amended
	2009, No. 3	Revised
179	1979, No. 607	Amended
	2009, No. 3	Revised
180	1979, No. 607	Amended
181	1979, No. 607	Amended
182	1979, No. 607	Repealed
183	1979, No. 607	Repealed
184 to 190	1976, No. 430	Repealed
191	1968, No. 158	Amended
	1976, No. 430	Repealed
192	1968, No. 159	Amended
	1976, No. 430	Repealed
198	1944, No. 50	Amended
	1948, No. 482	Amended
	1979, No. 607	Amended
199	1979, No. 607	Amended
	2009, No. 3	Revised
200	1972, No. 391	Amended
	1979, No. 607	Amended
	2009, No. 3	Revised
	1983, No. 480	Amended
202	1979, No. 607	Repealed
203	1979, No. 607	Amended
204	1948, No. 483	Amended
	1979, No. 607	Repealed
206	1979, No. 607	Amended
	1983, No. 480	Repealed
207	1979, No. 607	Amended
208	1979, No. 607	Amended
	1980, No. 549	Amended
	1981, No. 720	Amended
209	1980, No. 549	Amended
	1981, No. 720	Amended
	1982, No. 527	Amended
	1984, No. 810	Amended
210	1980, No. 549	Repealed
212	1980, No. 549	Repealed
	2008, No. 351	Added
213	1948, No. 227	Repealed
	2008, No. 351	Added
214	1948, No. 454	Amended
	1958, No. 514	Amended
	1978, No. 458	Amended
	1990, No. 147	Amended
	2008, No. 351	Amended
214.1 to 214.8	1948, No. 454	Added
	1958, No. 514	Repealed
218	1974, No. 134	Amended
221	1916, No. 41	Amended
	1920, No. 252	Amended
	1924, No. 197	Amended
222	1960, No. 30	Repealed
223	1986, No. 303	Amended
225	1990, No. 361	Repealed
226	1952, No. 265	Amended
	1985, No. 714	Amended
229	1970, No. 436	Amended
	1972, No. 668	Amended
	1979, No. 249	Amended
230	1985, No. 173	Amended
245	1979, No. 607	Repealed
	1983, No. 215	Added

Book I, arts. 24–447 (1870):
246	1924, No. 72	Amended
248	1960, No. 30	Amended
250	1924, No. 196	Amended
	1981, No. 283	Amended
	1982, No. 307	Amended
	1983, No. 695	Amended
251	1960, No. 30	Repealed
253	1974, No. 163	Repealed
254	1960, No. 30	Repealed
255	1882, No. 18	Amended
	1960, No. 30	Repealed
256	1964, No. 90	Amended
	1979, No. 536	Amended
	1983, No. 215	Amended
257	1974, No. 142	Amended
258	1960, No. 30	Amended
	1983, No. 695	Amended
260	1960, No. 30	Repealed
261	1979, No. 607	Amended
263	1976, No. 429	Amended
264	1976, No. 429	Repealed
265	1960, No. 30	Amended
	1976, No. 429	Repealed
266	1976, No. 429	Repealed
267	1960, No. 30	Amended
	1976, No. 429	Repealed
268, 269	1976, No. 429	Repealed
270	1960, No. 30	Amended
271	1952, No. 141	Amended
	1960, No. 30	Repealed
272	1952, No. 141	Repealed
273	1960, No. 30	Amended
274 to 277	1960, No. 30	Repealed
279	1960, No. 30	Repealed
281 to 291	1960, No. 30	Repealed
298	1974, No. 163	Amended
301	1974, No. 163	Amended
302 to 304	1960, No. 30	Repealed
305	1880, No. 82	Amended
	1960, No. 30	Repealed
306 to 307	1960, No. 30	Repealed
309	1974, No. 163	Amended
312 to 321	1960, No. 30	Repealed
322	1960, No. 30	Amended
323 to 332	1960, No. 30	Repealed
333	1960, No. 30	Amended
334, 335	1960, No. 30	Repealed
336	1960, No. 30	Repealed
	1966, No. 496	Renumbered from Art. 345
337	1960, No. 30	Repealed
	1966, No. 496	Renumbered from Art. 352
	2001, No. 572	Repealed
338	1960, No. 30	Repealed
	1966, No. 496	Renumbered from Art. 360
339	1960, No. 30	Repealed
	1966, No. 496	Renumbered from Art. 361
340	1960, No. 30	Repealed
	1966, No. 496	Renumbered from Art. 362
341, 342	1960, No. 30	Repealed

TABLE 4—CHANGE—CIVIL CODE OF 1870

Book I, arts. 24–447 (1870):

Art.	Act	Change
343	1914, No. 78	Amended
	1960, No. 30	Repealed
344	1960, No. 30	Repealed
345	1966, No. 496	Renumbered as Art. 336
346	1876, No. 65	Amended
	1960, No. 30	Repealed
347	1960, No. 30	Repealed
348	1940, No. 370	Amended
	1952, No. 508	Amended
	1958, No. 75	Amended
	1960, No. 30	Repealed
349 to 351	1960, No. 30	Repealed
352	1966, No. 496	Renumbered as Art. 337
353	1960, No. 30	Repealed
354	1960, No. 30	Repealed
	1966, No. 496	Added
355	1928, No. 170	Amended
	1960, No. 30	Repealed
	1966, No. 496	Added
	1974, No. 714	Amended
	1991, No. 107	Amended
356	1960, No. 30	Repealed
	1966, No. 496	Added
	1974, No. 714	Amended
357	1960, No. 30	Repealed
	1966, No. 496	Added
358	1960, No. 30	Repealed
	1966, No. 496	Added
	1979, No. 216	Amended
359	1960, No. 30	Repealed
	1966, No. 496	Added
	1974, No. 714	Amended
360	1966, No. 496	Renumbered as Art. 338
	1966, No. 496	Added
361	1966, No. 496	Renumbered as Art. 339
	1966, No. 496	Added
362	1966, No. 496	Renumbered as Art. 340
	1966, No. 496	Added
363	1920, No. 251	Amended
	1960, No. 30	Repealed
364	1960, No. 30	Repealed
365 to 366	2008, No. 786	Revised
367	1972, No. 346	Repealed
	2008, No. 786	Revised
368	2008, No. 786	Revised
369	1960, No. 30	Repealed
	2008, No. 786	Revised
370 to 372	2008, No. 786	Revised
373	1966, No. 17	Amended
	1972, No. 346	Amended
	2008, No. 786	Repealed
374	2008, No. 786	Repealed
375	1960, No. 30	Repealed
376 to 379	2008, No. 786	Repealed
380	1979, No. 711	Amended
	2008, No. 786	Repealed
381	2008, No. 786	Repealed
382	1908, No. 224	Amended
	1966, No. 17	Amended

Book I, arts. 24–447 (1870):

Art.	Act	Change
	1972, No. 346	Amended
	1978, No. 73	Amended
	2008, No. 786	Repealed
383, 384	2008, No. 786	Repealed
385	1950, No. 418	Amended
	1960, No. 30	Amended
	1972, No. 346	Repealed
	1976, No. 155	Added
	2008, No. 786	Repealed
386	1940, No. 308	Amended
	1960, No. 30	Repealed
387 to 388	1960, No. 30	Repealed
389	2000, No. 25 (1st Ex.Sess.)	Repealed
389.1	1981, No. 167	Added
	2000, No. 25 (1st Ex.Sess.)	Repealed
390	2000, No. 25 (1st Ex.Sess.)	Repealed
391	948, No. 321	Amended
	2000, No. 25 (1st Ex.Sess.)	Repealed
392, 393	2000, No. 25 (1st Ex.Sess.)	Repealed
394	1997, No. 1117	Amended
	2000, No. 25 (1st Ex.Sess.)	Repealed
395	1961, No. 23	Repealed
396, 397	2000, No. 25 (1st Ex.Sess.)	Repealed
398	962, No. 70	Repealed
399	2000, No. 25 (1st Ex.Sess.)	Repealed
400	1997, No. 1117	Amended
	2000, No. 25 (1st Ex.Sess.)	Repealed
401 to 404	2000, No. 25 (1st Ex.Sess.)	Repealed
405	1997, No. 1117	Amended
	2000, No. 25 (1st Ex.Sess.)	Repealed
406, 407	2000, No. 25 (1st Ex.Sess.)	Repealed
408	1960, No. 30	Repealed
409 to 411	2000, No. 25 (1st Ex.Sess.)	Repealed
412, 413	1964, No. 48	Repealed
414	2000, No. 25 (1st Ex.Sess.)	Repealed
415	1960, No. 30	Repealed
416	1979, No. 709	Repealed
417 to 426	2000, No. 25 (1st Ex.Sess.)	Repealed
427 to 442	1987, No. 126	Repealed
443	1942, No. 43	Repealed
444 to 445	1987, No. 126	Repealed
446	1987, No. 126	Redesignated
	1977, No. 489	Amended
	1978, No. 388	Amended
	1978, No. 459	Amended
	1979, No. 356	Amended
	1980, No. 352	Amended
	1987, No. 126	Redesignated as R.S. 9:1051

TABLE 4—CHANGE—CIVIL CODE OF 1870

Book II, arts. 448–869 (1870):

Article	Act	Change
448 to 451	1978, No. 728	Repealed
452	1914, No. 173	Amended
	1978, No. 728	Repealed
453 to 466	1978, No. 728	Repealed
467	1912, No. 51	Amended
	1978, No. 728	Repealed
466 to 487	1978, No. 728	Repealed
488 to 494	1979, No. 180	Repealed
495	1871, No. 87	Amended
	1979, No. 180	Repealed
496 to 532	1979, No. 180	Repealed
533 to 551	1976, No. 103	Repealed
552	1974, No. 50	Repealed
	1975, No. 588	Added
	1976, No. 103	Repealed
553 to 559	1976, No. 103	Repealed
560	1871, No. 87	Amended
	1976, No. 103	Repealed
561 to 579	1976, No. 103	Repealed
580	1871, No. 87	Amended
	1976, No. 103	Repealed
581 to 645	1976, No. 103	Repealed
646	1976, No. 431	Amended
	1977, No. 514	Repealed
647 to 664	1977, No. 514	Repealed
666	1977, No. 514	Repealed
667	1996, No. 77 (1st Ex.Sess.)	Amended
670 to 698	1977, No. 514	Repealed
699	1916, No. 197	Amended
	1970, No. 672	Amended
	1977, No. 514	Repealed
700 to 706	1977, No. 514	Repealed
707	1977, No. 514	Renumbered as 666
708 to 730	1977, No. 514	Repealed
731	1974, No. 89	Amended
	1977, No. 514	Repealed
732 to 740	1977, No. 514	Repealed
741	1940, No. 336	Amended
	1950, No. 521	Amended
	1974, No. 50	Repealed
	1975, No. 588	Added
	1977, No. 514	Repealed
742 to 764	1977, No. 514	Repealed
765	1904, No. 25	Amended
	1977, No. 514	Repealed
766 to 822	1977, No. 514	Repealed
823 to 832	1977, No. 170	Repealed
833	1968, No. 156	Amended
	1977, No. 170	Repealed
834 to 855	1977, No. 170	Repealed
856 to 862	1977, No. 169	Repealed
863	1932, No. 129	Amended
	1977, No. 169	Repealed
864 to 869	1977, No. 169	Repealed

Book III, arts. 870–3556 (1870):

Article	Act	Change
870 to 908	1981, No. 919	Repealed
909	1979, No. 709	Repealed
910 to 914	1981, No. 919	Repealed
915	1910, No. 57	Amended
	1916, No. 80	Amended
	1920, No. 160	Amended
	1938, No. 408	Amended
	1942, No. 82	Amended
	1979, No. 607	Amended
	1981, No. 919	Repealed
916	1975, No. 680	Amended
	1979, No. 678	Amended
	1981, No. 911	Amended
	1981, No. 919	Repealed
916.1	1976, No. 227	Added
	1981, No. 919	Repealed
917	1979, No. 607	Amended
	1981, No. 919	Repealed
918	1979, No. 607	Amended
	1981, No. 919	Repealed
919	1979, No. 607	Amended
	1981, No. 919	Repealed
920	1979, No. 607	Repealed
921	1979, No. 607	Amended
	1981, No. 919	Repealed
922	1979, No. 607	Amended
	1981, No. 919	Repealed
923	1979, No. 607	Amended
	1981, No. 919	Repealed
924	1979, No. 607	Amended
	1981, No. 919	Repealed
925	1979, No. 607	Amended
	1981, No. 919	Repealed
926	1979, No. 607	Amended
	1981, No. 919	Repealed
927	1979, No. 607	Amended
	1981, No. 919	Repealed
928	1979, No. 607	Amended
	1981, No. 919	Repealed
929	1979, No. 607	Amended
	1981, No. 919	Repealed
930 to 933	1981, No. 919	Repealed
935	1960, No. 30	Repealed
937	1985, No. 526	Amended
938	1938, No. 418	Amended
	1985, No. 526	Amended
939	1938, No. 418	Amended
	1985, No. 526	Repealed
966(1)	1987, No. 354	Amended
974	1991, No. 678	Amended
986	1981, No. 249	Amended
1005	1974, No. 89	Repealed
1006	1979, No. 709	Repealed
1011, 1012	1960, No. 30	Repealed
1019	1960, No. 30	Repealed
1024	1986, No. 239	Amended
1041 to 1046	1960, No. 30	Repealed
1048	1924, No. 117	Amended
	1960, No. 30	Repealed
1049	1960, No. 30	Repealed
1051	1960, No. 30	Repealed
1053	1960, No. 30	Repealed
1063, 1064	1960, No. 30	Repealed
1065	1898, No. 193	Amended
	1960, No. 30	Repealed
1066	1960, No. 30	Repealed
1069, 1070	1960, No. 30	Repealed
1075 to 1094	1960, No. 30	Repealed
1097	1960, No. 30	Amended
1098, 1099	1960, No. 30	Repealed

TABLE 4—CHANGE—CIVIL CODE OF 1870

Book III, arts. 870–3556 (1870):

Article	Act	Change
1101, 1102	1960, No. 30	Repealed
1103	1980, No. 150	Repealed
1104 to 1109	1960, No. 30	Repealed
1110	1921, Ex.Sess., No. 43	Amended
	1960, No. 30	Repealed
1111 to 1126	1960, No. 30	Repealed
1127	1922, No. 86	Amended
	1960, No. 30	Repealed
1128 to 1137	1960, No. 30	Repealed
1138 to 1145	1980, No. 150	Repealed
1146	1912, No. 197	Amended
	1950, No. 431	Amended
	1960, No. 30	Repealed
1147	1960, No. 30	Repealed
1149 to 1170	1960, No. 30	Repealed
1172 to 1183	1960, No. 30	Repealed
1184	1896, No. 51	Amended
	1960, No. 30	Repealed
1185 to 1187	1960, No. 30	Repealed
1189	1960, No. 30	Repealed
1190	1900, No. 53	Amended
	1960, No. 30	Repealed
1191	1960, No. 30	Repealed
1192	1981, No. 254	Amended
1193 to 1210	1960, No. 30	Repealed
1211	1871, No. 87	Amended
	1960, No. 30	Repealed
1212 to 1220	1960, No. 30	Repealed
1221 to 1223	1877, No. 86	Repealed
	1894, No. 130	Added
	1960, No. 30	Repealed
1224 to 1226	1960, No. 30	Repealed
1232	1986, No. 246	Amended
1235	1996, No. 77 (1st Ex.Sess.)	Amended
1236	1990, No. 147	Repealed
	1995, No. 1180	Repealed
1238	1990, No. 147	Amended
1239	1990, No. 147	Amended
1242	1980, No. 565	Amended
1243	1979, No. 711	Amended
1264	1981, No. 739	Amended
1270	1981, No. 739	Amended
1281	1981, No. 739	Amended
1289	1991, No. 689	Repealed
1294	1991, No. 689	Repealed
1298	1991, No. 689	Repealed
1302	1982, No. 448	Amended
1303	1991, No. 689	Repealed
1304	1991, No. 689	Repealed
1308	1871, No. 87	Amended
1316, 1317	1960, No. 30	Repealed
1322	1991, No. 689	Repealed
1323	1991, No. 689	Repealed
1324	1960, No. 30	Repealed
1327	1960, No. 30	Repealed
1338	1896, No. 86	Amended
	1991, No. 689	Repealed
1339	1991, No. 689	Repealed
1340	1991, No. 689	Repealed
1340	1991, No. 689	Repealed
1348	1960, No. 30	Amended
1364	1938, No. 407	Amended
1368	1960, No. 30	Repealed
1369	1962, No. 70	Repealed
1373	1979, No. 711	Amended
	1991, No. 107	Amended
1374 to 1377	1960, No. 30	Repealed
1381	1990, No. 989	Repealed
1383	1991, No. 689	Repealed
1397	1991, No. 689	Repealed
1398	1991, No. 689	Repealed
1399	1991, No. 107	Amended
1400	1991, No. 107	Amended
1434	1896, No. 72	Amended
1444 to 1464	1960, No. 30	Repealed
1467	2008, No. 204	Amended
1468	1871, No. 87	Amended
	2008, No. 204	Amended
1469	2008, No. 204	Amended
1470 to 1479	1991, No. 363	Repealed
1480	1974, No. 89	Repealed
1481	1987, No. 468	Repealed
1482	1991, No. 363	Repealed
	2000, No. 25 (1st Ex.Sess.)	Amended
1483	1979, No. 607	Repealed
1484	1979, No. 607	Amended
	1990, No. 147	Repealed
	1995, No. 1180	Repealed
1485	1979, No. 607	Amended
	1990, No. 147	Repealed
	1995, No. 1180	Repealed
1486	1979, No. 607	Repealed
1487	1979, No. 607	Repealed
1488	1978, No. 362	Repealed
1489 to 1491	1991, No. 363	Repealed
1492	1990, No. 147	Repealed
	1995, No. 1180	Repealed
1493	1981, No. 884	Amended
	1990, No. 147	Amended
	1996, No. 77 (1st Ex.Sess.)	Repealed
1494	1956, No. 313	Amended
	1979, No. 778	Amended
	1981, No. 442	Repealed
	1990, No. 147	Added
	1995, No. 1180	Amended
	1996, No. 77 (1st Ex.Sess.)	Repealed
1495	1981, No. 442	Amended
	1990, No. 147	Amended
	1996, No. 77 (1st Ex.Sess.)	Repealed
1496	1981, No. 442	Amended
	1990, No. 147	Amended
	1996, No. 77 (1st Ex.Sess.)	Repealed
1497	1982, No. 641	Amended
	1985, No. 522	Amended
	1996, No. 77 (1st Ex.Sess.)	Repealed
1498	1981, No. 645	Amended
	1990 No. 147	Amended
	1996, No. 77 (1st Ex.Sess.)	Repealed
1501	1986, No. 246	Amended

TABLE 4—CHANGE—CIVIL CODE OF 1870

Book III, arts. 870–3556 (1870):

Article	Source	Action
	1996, No. 77 (1st Ex.Sess.)	Repealed
1502	1981, No. 765	Amended
	1996, No. 77 (1st Ex.Sess.)	Repealed
1505	1981, Nos. 646, 909	Amended
	1982, No. 356	Amended
	1983, No. 656	Amended
	1990, No. 147	Amended
	1996, No. 77 (1st Ex.Sess.)	Repealed
1516	1981, No. 739	Amended
	1996, No. 77 (1st Ex.Sess.)	Repealed
1517	1981, No. 739	Amended
	1996, No. 77 (1st Ex.Sess.)	Repealed
1518	1981, No. 739	Amended
	1996, No. 77 (1st Ex.Sess.)	Repealed
1520	1962, No. 45	Amended
1521	1972, No. 628	Amended
	1984, No. 957	Amended
	1985, No. 583	Amended
1521(A)(2)	1987, No. 680	Amended
1523 to 1525	2008, No. 204	Repealed
1526 to 1532	2008, No. 204	Revised
1533	1974, No. 210	Amended
	2008, No. 204	Revised
1534	2008, No. 204	Repealed
1535	1979, No. 711	Amended
	2008, No. 204	Repealed
1536 to 1540	2008, No. 204	Repealed
1541 to 1544	2008, No. 204	Revised
1545	1974, No. 89	Repealed
	2008, No. 204	Revised
1546	1966, No. 44	Amended
	2008, No. 204	Repealed
1547	2008, No. 204	Repealed
1548	1988, No. 546	Amended
	2008, No. 204	Repealed
1549 to 1553	2008, No. 204	Repealed
1554	1981, No. 798	Amended
	2008, No. 204	Repealed
1555	1974, No. 89	Repealed
1556, 1557	2008, No. 204	Repealed
1558	1979, No. 711	Amended
	2008, No. 204	Repealed
1568	1871, No. 87	Amended
	1985, No. 527	Amended
1573	1982, No. 448	Amended
1581	1871, No. 87	Amended
1584	1898, No. 88	Amended
1589	1871, No. 87	Amended
1591	1908, No. 30	Amended
	1979, No. 711	Amended
	1983, No. 198	Amended
1592	1986, No. 709	Amended
	1989, No. 6	Amended
1596	1960, No. 30	Repealed
1621	1983, No. 566	Amended
	1985, No. 456	Amended
1622	1983, No. 566	Amended
	1984, No. 445	Amended

Book III, arts. 870–3556 (1870):

Article	Source	Action
	1985, No. 456	Amended
	1987, No. 334	Amended
1623	1990, No. 147	Repealed
	1995, No. 1180	Repealed
1624	1985, No. 456	Amended
	1989, No. 82	Amended
	1989, No. 307	Amended
1644	1979, No. 709	Repealed
1648, 1649	1960, No. 30	Repealed
1650	1936, No. 317	Amended
	1960, No. 30	Repealed
1651 to 1654	1960, No. 30	Repealed
1655	1896, No. 119	Amended
	1960, No. 30	Repealed
1656, 1657	1960, No. 30	Repealed
1659, 1660	1960, No. 30	Repealed
1664	1980, No. 565	Repealed
1666 to 1671	1960, No. 30	Repealed
1672	1960, No. 30	Amended
1673 to 1679	1960, No. 30	Repealed
1681 to 1689	1960, No. 30	Repealed
1691	1928, No. 114	Amended
	1987, No. 354	Amended
1705	1948, No. 334	Amended
	1966, No. 471	Amended
1705	1974, No. 209	Amended
1725	1982, No. 448	Amended
1729	1871, No. 87	Amended
1734 to 1740	2004, No. 619	Repealed
1741	1871, No. 87	Amended
	2004, No. 619	Repealed
1742 to 1748	2004, No. 619	Repealed
1749	1942, No. 187	Repealed
1750	1990, No. 147	Amended
	1995, No. 1180	Amended
	2004, No. 619	Repealed
1751	1979, No. 709	Repealed
1752	1882, No. 13	Amended
	1916, No. 116	Amended
	1990, No. 147	Repealed
	1995, No. 1180	Repealed
1753	1918, No. 238	Repealed
1754	2004, No. 619	Repealed
1755	2004, No. 619	Repealed
1764	1968, No. 301	Amended
1764(B)	1977, No. 723	Amended
1782	1924, No. 45	Amended
1786	1979, No. 709	Repealed
1787	1944, No. 49	Amended
	1979, No. 709	Repealed
1790	1978, No. 627	Amended
	1979, No. 711	Amended
1791	1978, No. 627	Amended
	1979, No. 711	Amended
1794	1871, No. 87	Amended
1844	1871, No. 87	Amended
1846(3)	1982, No. 187	Repealed
1862	1978, No. 728	Amended
1863	1940, No. 280	Amended
1888	1979, No. 711	Amended
1935	1983, No. 483	Amended
1936	1972, No. 454	Amended
1938	1970, No. 315	Amended
	1980, No. 402	Amended

TABLE 4—CHANGE—CIVIL CODE OF 1870

Book III, arts. 870–3556 (1870):

	1981, Nos. 574, 639	Amended
	1982, No. 142	Amended
1939	1924, No. 161	Amended
	1972, No. 454	Amended
	1981, No. 822	Amended
	1982, No. 673	Amended
1945	1871, No. 87	Amended
1957	1871, No. 87	Amended
1992	1979, No. 711	Amended
2004 to 2006	1984, No. 331	Redesignated as R.S. 9:2785 to 9:2787
2061	1871, No. 87	Amended
2103	1960, No. 30	Amended
	1979, No. 431	Amended
2142	1979, No. 711	Amended
2218	1871, No. 87	Amended
2221	1979, No. 711	Amended
	1980, No. 308	Amended
2226	1979, No. 711	Amended
2229	1979, No. 711	Amended
2234	1920, No. 171	Amended
2239	1884, No. 5	Amended
2251	1890, No. 48	Amended
2251 to 2267, 2269 to 2270	1984, No. 331	Redesignated as R.S. 9:2741 to 9:2759
2265	1979, No. 711	Amended
2278	1886, No. 121	Amended
2280	1970, No. 382	Amended
	1979, No. 365	Amended
2281	1888, No. 59	Amended
	1898, No. 190	Amended
	1916, No. 157	Repealed
2286	1984, No. 331	Redesignated as R.S. 13:4231
2292 to 2313	1995, No. 1041	Repealed
2314	1979, No. 180	Repealed
2315	1884, No. 71	Amended
	1908, No. 120	Amended
	1918, No. 159	Amended
	1932, No. 159	Amended
	1948, No. 333	Amended
	1960, No. 30	Amended
	1982, No. 202	Amended
	1984, No. 397	Amended
	1986, No. 211	Amended
2315.1	1976, No. 217	Added
	1980, No. 324	Repealed
	1986, No. 211	Added
	1987, No. 675	Amended
2315.2	1986, No. 211	Added
2315.3	1984, No. 335	Added
	1990, No. 302	Amended
	1996, No. 77 (1st Ex.Sess.)	Repealed
	2009, No. 382	Added
2315.4	1984, No. 511	Added
2315.5	1987, No. 690	Added
	1991, No. 180	Amended
2315.6	1991, No. 782	Added
2317.1	1996, No. 77 (1st Ex.Sess.)	Added

Book III, arts. 870–3556 (1870):

2318	1984, No. 578	Amended
2319	2000, No. 25 (1st Ex.Sess.)	Amended
2322	1996, No. 77 (1st Ex.Sess.)	Amended
2322.1	1981, No. 611	Added
	1990, No. 1091	Amended
2323	1979, No. 431	Amended
	1996, No. 77 (1st Ex.Sess.)	Amended
2324	1979, No. 431	Amended
	1987, No. 373	Amended
	1988, No. 430	Amended
	1996, No. 77 (1st Ex.Sess.)	Amended
2324.1	1984, No. 331	Added
2324.2	1989, No. 771	Added
2325 to 2328	1979, No. 709	Repealed
2329	1910, No. 236	Amended
	1979, No. 709	Repealed
2330 to 2333	1979, No. 709	Repealed
2334	1920, No. 186	Amended
	1962, No. 353	Amended
	1976, No. 679	Amended
	1979, No. 709	Repealed
2335 to 2357	1979, No. 709	Repealed
2358	1979, No. 709	Revised
	2009, No. 204	Amended
2359 to 2362	1979, No. 709	Revised
2362.1	1990, No. 1009	Added
	2009, No. 204	Amended
2363	1979, No. 709	Revised
	2009, No. 204	Amended
2364	1979, No. 709	Revised
	2009, No. 204	Amended
2364.1	1997, No. 499	Added
	2009, No. 204	Repealed
2365	1979, No. 709	Revised
	2009, No. 204	Amended
2366	1979, No. 709	Revised
	2009, No. 204	Amended
2367	1979, No. 709	Revised
	2009, No. 204	Amended
2367.1	1984, No. 933	Added
	2009, No. 204	Amended
2367.2	1984, No. 933	Added
	2009, No. 204	Amended
2367.3	2009, No. 204	Added
2368 to 2381	1979, No. 709	Repealed
2382	1926, No. 113	Amended
	1974, No. 115	Amended
2383 to 2385	1979, No. 709	Repealed
2386	1944, No. 286	Amended
	1979, No. 709	Repealed
2387 to 2397	1979, No. 709	Repealed
2397	1974, No. 89	Repealed
	1979, No. 709	Repealed
2398	1974, No. 89	Repealed
	1976, No. 444	Added
	1979, No. 709	Repealed
2399 to 2401	1979, No. 709	Repealed
2402	1902, No. 68	Amended
	1979, No. 709	Repealed
2403	1979, No. 709	Repealed

TABLE 4—CHANGE—CIVIL CODE OF 1870

Book III, arts. 870–3556 (1870):

Article	Act	Change
2404	1926, No. 96	Amended
	1979, No. 709	Repealed
2405 to 2419	1979, No. 709	Repealed
2420	1926, No. 49	Repealed
	1979, No. 709	Repealed
2436	1974, No. 89	Repealed
2437	1979, No. 709	Repealed
2438 to 2659	1993, No. 841	Repealed
2446	1979, No. 709	Repealed
2447 to 2448	1993, No. 841	Repealed
2449	1888, No. 126	Amended
	1993, No. 841	Repealed
2450 to 2452	1993, No. 841	Repealed
2453	1878, No. 3	Amended
	1993, No. 841	Repealed
2454 to 2461	1993, No. 841	Repealed
2462	1910, No. 249	Amended
	1910, 2d Ex.Sess. No. 3	Amended
	1920, No. 27	Amended
	1993, No. 841	Repealed
2463 to 2494	1993, No. 841	Repealed
2495	1871, No. 87	Amended
	1993, No. 841	Repealed
2496 to 2502	1993, No. 841	Repealed
2503	1924, No. 116	Amended
	1993, No. 841	Repealed
2594 to 2530	1993, No. 841	Repealed
2531	1974, No. 673	Amended
	1993, No. 841	Repealed
2532 to 2544	1993, No. 841	Repealed
2545	1968, No. 84	Amended
	1993, No. 841	Repealed
2546	1993, No. 841	Repealed
2547	1968, No. 84	Amended
	1993, No. 841	Repealed
2548 to 2553	1993, No. 841	Repealed
2554	1972, No. 454	Amended
	1993, No. 841	Repealed
2555 to 2560	1993, No. 841	Repealed
2561	1924, No. 108	Amended
	1993, No. 841	Repealed
2562 to 2565	1993, No. 841	Repealed
2566	1871, No. 87	Amended
	1993, No. 841	Repealed
2567 to 2589	1993, No. 841	Repealed
2590	1950, No. 154	Amended
	1993, No. 841	Repealed
2591	1871, No. 87	Amended
	1993, No. 841	Repealed
2592	1993, No. 841	Repealed
2593	1985, No. 222	Amended
	1993, No. 841	Repealed
2594 to 2600	1993, No. 841	Repealed
2601 to 2620	1993, No. 841	Redesignated as R.S. 9:3151 to 9:3170
2621	1960, No. 30	Amended
	1993, No. 841	Redesignated as R.S. 9:3171
2622 to 2631	1993, No. 841	Redesignated as R.S. 9:3172 to 9:3181
2632	1936, No. 276	Amended

Book III, arts. 870–3556 (1870):

Article	Act	Change
	1940, No. 187	Amended
	1993, No. 841	Redesignated as R.S. 9:3182
2633	1993, No. 841	Redesignated as R.S. 9:3183
2634	1954, No. 705	Amended
	1960, No. 92	Amended
	1993, No. 841	Redesignated as R.S. 9:3184
2635	1954, No. 47	Amended
	1993, No. 841	Redesignated as R.S. 9:3185
2636	1960, No. 93	Amended
	1993, No. 841	Redesignated as R.S. 9:3186
2637 to 2638	1993, No. 841	Redesignated as R.S. 9:3187 to 9:3188
2639	1979, No. 711	Amended
	1993, No. 841	Redesignated as R.S. 9:3189
2640 to 2641	1993, No. 841	Redesignated as R.S. 9:3190 to 9:3191
2642	1993, No. 841	Repealed
2643	1984, No. 921	Amended
	1985, No. 97	Amended
	1993, No. 841	Repealed
2644 to 2659	1993, No. 841	Repealed
2660 to 2664	2010, No. 186	Repealed
2665	1871, No. 87	Amended
	2010, No. 186	Repealed
2666 to 2667	2010, No. 186	Repealed
2668 to 2683	2004, No. 821	Repealed
2683.1	1992, No. 973	Added
	2004, No. 821	Repealed
2684	2004, No. 821	Repealed
2685	2004, No. 821	Repealed
2686	1924, No. 9	Amended
	2004, No. 821	Repealed
2687 to 2704	2004, No. 821	Repealed
2705	1934, No. 197	Amended
	1979, No. 711	Amended
	2004, No. 821	Repealed
2706	2004, No. 821	Repealed
2707	1984, No. 66	Amended
	2004, No. 821	Repealed
2708	2004, No. 821	Repealed
2709	1960, No. 30	Amended
	1990, No. 942	Amended
	2004, No. 821	Repealed
2710	2004, No. 821	Repealed
2711	2004, No. 821	Repealed
2712	1992, No. 1108	Amended
	2004, No. 821	Repealed
2713	1981, No. 713	Amended
	2001, No. 289	Amended
	2004, No. 821	Repealed
2714 to 2725	2004, No. 821	Repealed
2726	1984, No. 933	Amended
	2004, No. 821	Repealed
2727 to 2739	2004, No. 821	Repealed
2740	1871, No. 87	Amended
	2004, No. 821	Repealed

TABLE 4—CHANGE—CIVIL CODE OF 1870

Book III, arts. 870–3556 (1870):

2741 to 2774	2004, No. 821	Repealed
2778 to 2800	2012, No. 258	Repealed
2792	1871, No. 87	Amended
2801 to 2824	1980, No. 150	Repealed
2825	1932, No. 150	Amended
	1980, No. 150	Repealed
2826 to 2838	1980, No. 150	Repealed
2839	1968, No. 304	Amended
	1980, No. 150	Repealed
2840 to 2890	1980, No. 150	Repealed
2891 to 2923	2004, No. 743	Repealed
2924	1908, No. 68	Amended
	1970, No. 315	Amended
	1972, No. 454	Amended
	1980, No. 402	Amended
	1981, Nos. 574, 639	Amended
	1982, No. 142	Amended
	1984, No. 458	Amended
	1987, No. 883	Amended
	1989, No. 52	Amended
	1989, No. 774	Amended
	1992, No. 1090	Amended
	1997, No. 275	Amended
	1997, No. 1476	Amended
	2004, No. 743	Redesignated as R.S. 9:3500
2925	2004, No. 743	Repealed
2926 to 2950	2003, No. 491	Repealed
2951	1979, No. 711	Amended
	2003, No. 491	Repealed
2952	1979, No. 711	Amended
	2003, No. 491	Repealed
2953 to 2970	2003, No. 491	Repealed
2971	1912, No. 231	Amended
	1982, No. 382	Amended
	2003, No. 491	Repealed
2972 to 2976	2003, No. 491	Repealed
2977	1871, No. 87	Amended
	2003, No. 491	Repealed
2978 to 2979	2003, No. 491	Repealed
2980	1979, No. 711	Amended
	2003, No. 491	Repealed
2981	2003, No. 491	Repealed
2985	1997, No. 261	Repealed
2986	1871, No. 87	Amended
	1997, No. 261	Repealed
2987 to 2996	1997, No. 261	Repealed
2997	1981, No. 572	Amended
	1990, No. 184	Amended
	1997, No. 261	Repealed
2998 to 3000	1997, No. 261	Repealed
3001	1979, No. 711	Amended
	1997, No. 261	Repealed
3002 to 3026	1997, No. 261	Repealed
3027	1882, No. 19	Amended
	1981, No. 303	Amended
	1997, No. 261	Repealed
3028	1882, No. 19	Amended
	1997, No. 261	Repealed
3029 to 3034	1997, No. 261	Repealed
3035	1987, No. 409	Repealed
3036	1979, No. 711	Amended
	1987, No. 409	Repealed
3037 to 3041	1987, No. 409	Repealed

Book III, arts. 870–3556 (1870):

3042	1876, No. 67	Amended
	1908, No. 235	Amended
	1987, No. 409	Repealed
3043 to 3068	1987, No. 409	Repealed
3069 to 3070	1987, No. 409	Redesignated as R.S. 9:3911, 9:3912
3071	1981, No. 782	Amended
	2007, No. 138	Revised
3072 to 3083	2007, No. 138	Revised
3093	1888, No. 134	Amended
3095	1979, No. 711	Amended
3101	1979, No. 711	Amended
3105	1984, No. 782	Amended
3108	1979, No. 709	Repealed
3125	1871, No. 87	Amended
3128	1985, No. 571	Amended
3133.1	1989, No. 137	Added
	1990, No. 1079	Amended
3151	1980, No. 150	Repealed
3156	1981, No. 315	Amended
3158	1900, No. 157	Amended
	1952, No. 290	Amended
	1989, No. 137	Amended
3159	1900, No. 157	Amended
3160	1900, No. 157	Amended
	1988, No. 243	Repealed
3161	1900, No. 157	Repealed
3165	1872, No. 9	Amended
3191	1979, No. 711	Amended
3194	1954, No. 114	Amended
3215	1979, No. 709	Repealed
3218	2004, No. 821	Repealed
3233	1896, No. 29	Amended
	1898, No. 110	Amended
3234	1896, No. 35	Amended
3236	1896, No. 28	Amended
	1974, No. 713	Amended
3251	1989, No. 538	Amended
3252	1917, Ex.Sess., No. 17	Amended
	1918, No. 242	Amended
	1979, No. 711	Amended
3254	1979, No. 711	Amended
3260	1871, No. 87	Amended
3274	1877, No. 45	Amended
3275	1960, No. 30	Repealed
	1995, No. 1295	Added
3276	1979, No. 711	Amended
3278 to 3288	1991, No. 652	Repealed
3289	1979, No. 180	Amended
	1991, No. 652	Repealed
3290	1991, No. 652	Repealed
3291	1980, No. 238	Amended
	1991, No. 652	Repealed
3292 to 3298	1991, No. 652	Repealed
3299	1979, No. 711	Amended
	1991, No. 652	Repealed
3300, 3301	1991, No. 652	Repealed
3302	1991, No. 107	Amended
	1991, No. 652	Repealed
3303, 3304	1991, No. 652	Repealed
3305	1916, No. 105	Amended
	1991, No. 652	Repealed
3306, 3307	1991, No. 652	Repealed

TABLE 4—CHANGE—CIVIL CODE OF 1870

Book III, arts. 870–3556 (1870):

Article	Act	Change
3308 to 3310	2005, No. 169	Repealed
	1992, No. 1132	Revised
3314	2005, No. 169	Repealed
	1992, No. 1132	Revised
3321 to 3324	2005, No. 169	Repealed
	1992, No. 1132	Revised
3327 to 3336	2005, No. 169	Repealed
	1992, No. 1132	Revised
3338 to 3368	2005, No. 169	Added
3369	1918, No. 227	Amended
	1924, No. 50	Amended
	1938, No. 322	Amended
	1940, No. 247	Amended
	1942, No. 213	Amended
	1948, No. 453	Amended
	1988, No. 986	Amended
	1989, No. 598	Amended
	1992, No. 1132	Repealed
3369(6)	1979, No. 709	Repealed
3370	1987, No. 666	Amended
	1992, No. 1132	Repealed
3371 to 3385	1992, No. 1132	Redesignated as R.S. 9:5169 to R.S. 9:5180.3
3385.1	1980, No. 569	Added
	1992, No. 1132	Redesignated as R.S. 9:5180.4
3386	1985, No. 457	Amended
	1992, No. 1132	Redesignated as R.S. 9:5206
3387 to 3393	1992, No. 1132	Redesignated as R.S. 9:5207 to R.S. 9:5213
3394	1970, No. 609	Amended
	1992, No. 1132	Redesignated as R.S. 9:5214
3395, 3396	1992, No. 1132	Redesignated as R.S. 9:5215, R.S. 9:5216
3397, 3398	1992, No. 1132	Repealed
3399	1960, No. 30	Amended
	1992, No. 1132	Repealed
3400 to 3404	1960, No. 30	Repealed
3405 to 3410	1992, No. 1132	Repealed
3411	1991, No. 652	Amended
	1992, No. 1132	Repealed
3412 to 3441	1982, No. 187	Repealed
3442	1871, No. 87	Amended
	1982, No. 187	Repealed
3443 to 3452	1982, No. 187	Repealed
3453	1979, No. 180	Repealed
3454	1979, No. 180	Amended
	1982, No. 187	Repealed
3455 to 3477	1982, No. 187	Repealed
3478	1920, No. 161	Amended
	1924, No. 64	Amended
	1972, No. 346	Amended
	1979, No. 711	Amended
	1982, No. 187	Repealed
3479 to 3496	1982, No. 187	Repealed
3497	1983, No. 173	Revised
	2009, No. 107	Amended
3498 to 3503	1982, No. 187	Repealed
3504	1979, No. 158	Repealed

Book III, arts. 870–3556 (1870):

Article	Act	Change
3505	1982, No. 187	Repealed
	2013, No. 88	Added
3505.1	2013, No. 88	Added
3505.2	2013, No. 88	Added
3505.3	2013, No. 88	Added
3505.4	2013, No. 88	Added
3506	1982, No. 187	Redesignated
3506(4)	1999, No. 503	Repealed
3506(6)	1999, No. 503	Repealed
3506(7)	1999, No. 503	Repealed
3506(9)	1999, No. 503	Repealed
3506(10)	1999, No. 503	Repealed
3506(11)	1999, No. 503	Repealed
3506(13)	1999, No. 503	Repealed
3506(14)	1999, No. 503	Repealed
3506(15)	1999, No. 503	Repealed
3506(16)	1999, No. 503	Repealed
3506(17)	1999, No. 503	Repealed
3506(18)	1999, No. 503	Repealed
3506(19)	1999, No. 503	Repealed
3506(20)	1999, No. 503	Repealed
3506(21)	1999, No. 503	Repealed
3506(22)	1999, No. 503	Repealed
3506(24)	1999, No. 503	Repealed
3506(25)	1999, No. 503	Repealed
3506(26)	1999, No. 503	Repealed
3506(27)	1999, No. 503	Repealed
3506(29)	1999, No. 503	Repealed
3506(30)	1999, No. 503	Repealed
3506(31)	1999, No. 503	Repealed
3507, 3508	1979, No. 180	Repealed
	1982, No. 187	Repealed
3509 to 3517	1982, No. 187	Repealed
3518	1954, No. 532	Amended
	1982, No. 187	Repealed
3519	1898, No. 107	Amended
	1954, No. 615	Amended
	1960, No. 30	Amended
	1982, No. 187	Repealed
3520 to 3523	1982, No. 187	Repealed
3524, 3525	1979, No. 709	Amended
	1982, No. 187	Repealed
3526, 3527	1982, No. 187	Repealed
3528 to 3531	1983, No. 173	Repealed
3532	1960, No. 30	Amended
	1983, No. 173	Redesignated as a paragraph of Article 10
3533 to 3536	1983, No. 173	Repealed
3537	1902, No. 33	Amended
	1983, No. 173	Repealed
3538	1888, No. 78	Amended
	1983, No. 173	Repealed
3539 to 3540	1983, No. 173	Repealed
3541	1920, No. 146	Amended
	1922, No. 17	Amended
	1954, No. 736	Amended
	1958, No. 341	Amended
	1979, No. 711	Amended
	1983, No. 173	Repealed
3542	1980, No. 308	Amended
	1983, No. 173	Repealed
3543	1932, No. 231	Amended
	1960, No. 407	Amended
	1983, No. 173	Redesignated as R.S. 9:5622

TABLE 4—CHANGE—CIVIL CODE OF 1870

Book III, arts. 870–3556 (1870):

3544 to 3546	1983, No. 173	Repealed
3547	1936, No. 278	Amended
	1942, No. 73	Amended
	1960, No. 30	Amended
	1983, No. 173	Repealed
3548 to 3554	1983, No. 173	Repealed
3555	1979, No. 709	Repealed
3556	1991, No. 923	Redesignated as Article 3506
3556(3)	1990, No. 988	Repealed
3556(8)	1979, No. 607	Amended
	1981, No. 919	Amended
	1991	Redesignated as Article 3506(8)
3556(12)	1979, No. 711	Amended
3556(23)	1987, No. 125	Repealed

Book IV, arts. 3515–3556:

Articles 3515 to 3549 are redesignated provisions of the Preliminary Title, Chapter 3, of the Civil Code. That Title was revised, amended, and re-enacted by Acts 1991, No. 923, § 1. The substantive Conflict of Laws provisions of that Act were redesignated by the Louisiana State Law Institute as new Book IV of the Civil Code, consisting of Articles 3515 to 3549.

3515 to 3549	1991, No. 923	Added
3550 to 3554	1983, No. 173	Repealed
3555	1979, No. 709	Repealed
3556	1991, No. 923	Redesignated

TABLE 5—CONCORDANCE FOR THE 1976–2013 REVISION, THE CIVIL CODE OF 1870, CIVIL CODE OF 1825, PROJET, CIVIL CODE OF 1808, AND CODE NAPOLÉON

This Concordance shows where the subject matter of *present* articles of the Louisiana Civil Code is found in the Civil Code of 1825, the 1825 Projet, the Civil Code of 1808, and the Code Napoléon (the French Civil Code of 1804). In areas in which the Louisiana Civil Code has been revised, reference is also made to the corresponding provisions of the 1870 Code. There is no concordance for provisions of the Louisiana Civil Code that are no longer in force. One interested in historical research should consult the Concordance Table in the Compiled Edition of the Louisiana Civil Codes (Volumes 16, 17, and 17A, West's Louisiana Statutes Annotated, Civil Code) which provides a concordance for all articles of the Louisiana Civil Code of 1870.

1976–2013 Revision of the Civil Code Art.	Civil Code 1870 Art.	Civil Code 1825 Art.	Projet Civil Code 1825 Page	Civil Code 1808 Page	Civil Code 1808 Art.	Code Napoléon 1804 Art.
			Preliminary Title			
1	1	1	1	2	1	
	3	3	1	2	3	
2	1	1	1	2	1	
3	3	3	1	2	3	
4	21	21		6	21	
			2	6	22	
5	7	7	1			
6	8	8		4	7	2
			2	4	8	
7	11	11	2	4	11	6
	12	12		4	12	
8	22	22		6	23	
	23	23		6	24	
9	13	13		4	13	
10	18	18		4	18	
11	14, 15	14		4	14	
		15		4	15	
12	16	16		4	16	
13	17	17		4	17	
			Book I—Of Persons			
24						
25						
26	28, 29	28		8	5	
			3	8	6	
		29	3	8	7	
27						
28						
29	37	41		10	19	388
30						
31						
38						
39						
40						
41						
42						
43						
44						
45						
46						
	47					

TABLE 5—CIVIL CODE OF 1870 TO CODE NAPOLÉON

1976–2013 Revision of the Civil Code Art.	Civil Code 1870 Art.	Civil Code 1825 Art.	Projet Civil Code 1825 Page	Civil Code 1808 Page	Civil Code 1808 Art.	Code Napoléon 1804 Art.
		Book I—Of Persons				
		48				
		49				
		50				
		51				
		52				
		53				
		54				
		55				
		56				
		57				
		58				
		59				
86	86	87		24	1	
	87	88	8			
	88	89		24	2	
	89	90		24	3	
87	90	91		24	4	
88	93	94		24	7	147
89	88	89		24	2	
90	94	95, 96		24	8, 9	161
	95	97		26	10	162, 163
	96	98	8			
91	99					
	100	106	9			
	102	101	8			
	103	102	9			
	104	103	9			
	105	107	9			75
92	109	111	9			
93	90	91		24	4	
	91	92		24	5	146
94	113	115		26	16	184
	114	117		26	17	187
	116	118		26	18	188
95	110	112		26	13	180
	111	113		26	14	181
96	117	119	10			201
	118	120	10			202
97						
98	119	121		26	19	212
99						
100						
101	136	133		10	30	227
102						
103						
104						
105						
111	148	146		32	12	268, 269
112	160					301
113	148	146		32	12	268
114	160					301
115	160					
116						
117						
121						
122						
123						
124						
131						

TABLE 5—CIVIL CODE OF 1870 TO CODE NAPOLÉON

1976–2013 Revision of the Civil Code Art.	Civil Code 1870 Art.	Civil Code 1825 Art.	Projet Civil Code 1825 Page	Civil Code 1808 Page	Civil Code 1808 Art.	Code Napoléon 1804 Art.
Book I—Of Persons							
132						
133						
134						
135						
136						
141						
142						
151						
152						
159						301
	178	197		44	1	
184						
185						
186						
187						
188						
189						
190						
191						
192						
193						
194						
195						
196						
197						
198						
212						
213						
214						
	215	233		52	36	371
	216	234	18	52	37	372, 373
	217	235	18	52	38	
	218	236		52	39	374, 375
	219	237	19	52	40	
	220	238	19	52	41	
	221	267		58	5	389
	223	239		52	42	384
	224	240		52	43	385
	226	242		52	45	387
	227	243		52	46	203
	228	244		52	47	204
				52	48	
	229	245	19			205, 207
				54	58(3)	
	230	246	19	54	49	
	231	247		54	50	208
	232	248		54	51	209
	233	249	19	54	52	210
	234	250		54	53	211
			19	54	54	
	235	251		54	55	
	236	252		54	56	
	237	253		54	57	
			19	54	58(1, 2, 4, 5)	
	238	254		56	59	
	239	255		56	60	

TABLE 5—CIVIL CODE OF 1870 TO CODE NAPOLÉON

1976–2013 Revision of the Civil Code Art.	Civil Code 1870 Art.	Civil Code 1825 Art.	Projet Civil Code 1825 Page	Civil Code 1808 Page	Civil Code 1808 Art.	Code Napoléon 1804 Art.
		Book I—Of Persons				
	240	256		56	61	
	241	257		56	62	
	242	258		56	63	
		259	20	56	64	
	243	260		56	65	764
	244	261		56	66	
	246	263		58	1	
	247	264		58	2	
	248	265		58	3	
	249	266		58	4	
	250	268		58	6	302, 390
				82	32	
	252	415, 270				393
				58	8	
	256	274	21			
	257	275		60	11	397, 398
	258	276		60	12	399
	259	277		60	13	401
	261	279	21			
	262	280	21			
	263	281		60	15	402
	270	288		62	20	405
	273	300	22	64	32	420(1), 421(1), 422
	278					
	280	304		64	35	425
	292	312	23	64	36	427, 428
	293	313	23	64	37	430
	294	314	23	64	38	431(1)
	295	315	23	66	39	432
	296	316	24	66	40	433
	297	317		66	41	434
	298	318		66	42	435
			24	66	43	436
			24	66	44	437
	299	319		66	45	438, 439
	300	320		66	46	440
	301	321	24			
	308	290	21	62	23	406
	309	291	21	62	24	
	310	292	21	62	25	
	311	293	21	62	26	
	322					
	333					
	336—formerly 345	339	27			460(1)
	338—formerly 360	353		72	74	474
	339—formerly 361	355		72	76	472
	340—formerly 362	356		72	77	475
	354					
	355					
	356					
	357					
	358					
	359					
	360					

TABLE 5—CIVIL CODE OF 1870 TO CODE NAPOLÉON

1976–2013 Revision of the Civil Code Art.	Civil Code 1870 Art.	Civil Code 1825 Art.	Projet Civil Code 1825 Page	Civil Code 1808 Page	Civil Code 1808 Art.	Code Napoléon 1804 Art.
	361					
	362					
365						
366						
367						
368						
369						
370						
371						
	372	375		76	93	484(2)
	373	376		76	94	484(1)
	374	377		76	95	
	376	379		76	97	487
	377	380	30			485
	378	381	30			486
	379	367		74	87	476
	380	368	29			482
	381					
	382					
	383					485
	384					
	385					
389						
390						
391						
392						
393						
394						
395						
396						
397						
398						
399						

Book II—Things And Different Modifications Of Ownership

1976–2013 Revision of the Civil Code Art.	Civil Code 1870 Art.	Civil Code 1825 Art.	Projet Civil Code 1825 Page	Civil Code 1808 Page	Civil Code 1808 Art.	Code Napoléon 1804 Art.
448	449	440		94	2	
448	460	451		96	11	
448	461	452		96	12	516
449	450	441	35	94	3	538
449	481	473	41			
449	482	474	41			
450	453	444		94	6	538
450	454	445	35	94	7	542
450	458	449	37	96	9	542
450	481	473	41			
450	482	474	41			
451	451	442		94	4	
452	452	443		94	5	
452	453	444		94	6	538
453	449	440		94	2	
453	458	449	37	96	9	542
453	459	450		96	10	
453	481	473	41			
453	483	475	41			
454	484	476	41	100	32	537
455	482	474	41			
455	658	654	70			
455	664	660		128	12	649
456	455	446	35	96	8	

TABLE 5—CIVIL CODE OF 1870 TO CODE NAPOLÉON

1976–2013 Revision of the Civil Code Art.	Civil Code 1870 Art.	Civil Code 1825 Art.	Projet Civil Code 1825 Page	Civil Code 1808 Page	Civil Code 1808 Art.	Code Napoléon 1804 Art.
\multicolumn{7}{c}{**Book II—Things And Different Modifications Of Ownership**}
456	457	448	36			
457	658	654	70			
457	704	700	74			
457	705	701	74			
457	706	702	74			
457	708	704		136	48	685
458	861	857	103			
459	862	858	103			
460	863	859	103			
461	460	451		96	11	
462	464	455	37	96	15, 16	518, 519
463	464	455	37	96	15, 16	518, 519
463	465	456	37	96	17	520
464						
465	464	455	37	96	15, 16	518, 519
465	465	456	37	96	17	520
465	467	458		98	18	523
465	468	459		98	20	524
465	469	460	38	98	21	525
466	467	458		98	18	523
466	468	459		98	20	524
466	469	460	38	98	21	525
467	468	459		98	20	524
468						
469						
470	470	462	38			
470	471	463	38	98	22	526
471	473	465		98	24	528
471	475	467	40	100	27	531
472	476	468	40	100	28	532
473	474	466	39	98	25	529
			39	100	26	530
473	475	467	40	100	27	531
474						
475	475	467	40	100	27	531
476	487	479		100	34	543
477	488	480	42			
477	491	483	43	102	1	544
478	490	482	42			
479	493	485	43			
480	494	486	43			
481	496	488	44			
	3435	3398	400	478	20	
482	498	490	45	102	3	546
483	499	491	45	102	4	547
484	500	492	45			
485	501	493		102	5	548
486	502	494		102	6	549
486	3453	3416	402	480	30	
487	503	495	45	102	7	550
488						
489						
490	505	497	46	104	9	552
491	506	498	46	104	10	553
492						
493						
493.1						

TABLE 5—CIVIL CODE OF 1870 TO CODE NAPOLÉON

1976–2013 Revision of the Civil Code Art.	Civil Code 1870 Art.	Civil Code 1825 Art.	Projet Civil Code 1825 Page	Civil Code 1808 Page	Civil Code 1808 Art.	Code Napoléon 1804 Art.
\multicolumn{7}{c}{Book II—Things And Different Modifications Of Ownership}
493.2						
494	507	499	47	104	11	554
495						
496	508	500		104	12	555
497	508	500		104	12	555
498						
499	509	501	47	106	13	556
499	510	502		106	14	557
500	510	502		106	14	557
501	516	508	48			
502	511	503		106	15	559
503	517	509		106	16	562
504	518	510		106	17	563
505	512	504	47			560
506	513	505	47			561
506	514	506	47			561
506	515	507	48			561
507	520	512		106	19	565
508	522	514		106	21	567
509	524	516		108	23	569
510	521	513		106	20	566
510	523	515		108	22	568
511	525	517		108	24	570
511	526	518		108	25	571
512						
513	527	519		108	26	572
514	528	520		108	27	573
514	529	521		108	28	574
515	531	523		108	30	576
516						
517						
518						
519						
521						
522						
523						
524	3507	3473	409	488	76	2280
524	3508	3474	409			
525						
526	3453	3416	402	480	30	
527	2314	2292	320	320	15	1381
528	2314	2292	320	320	15	1381
529	3453	3416	402	480	30	
530						
531						
532						
533	646	642	68			
534	646	642	68			
535	490	482	42			
536	534	526	48	110	2, 3	
537	534	526	48	110	2, 3	
538	536	528	49	110		
538	549	542	51	112	15	587
539	533	525	48	110	1	578
539	535	527	49	110	2	
539	567	560		116	27	
540	537	529	49			
541	538	530	50			
541	539	531	50			
542						

TABLE 5—CIVIL CODE OF 1870 TO CODE NAPOLÉON

1976–2013 Revision of the Civil Code Art.	Civil Code 1870 Art.	Civil Code 1825 Art.	Projet Civil Code 1825 Page	Civil Code 1808 Page	Civil Code 1808 Art.	Code Napoléon 1804 Art.
Book II—Things And Different Modifications Of Ownership						
543						
544	540	532		110	4	579
544	541	533		110	5	581
545	542	534		112	6	580
545	569	563	55			
546	609	604		120	53	
547						
548						
549	543	535		112	7	
550	544	536	50	112	8	582
551	545	537	50	112	9, 10	583, 584
552						
553						
554	566	559		116	26	604
554	546	538		112	11	585
555	546	538		112	11	585
				112	13	586
556	547	540	51	114	17	588
557	557	550	53	114	22	600
557	599	594		120	44	
558	568	561	54	116	28	
558	569	563	55			
559	548	541		112	14	
560	551	544	51	114	18	592–594
561	552	545	52			598
562						
563	553	546	52	114	19	596, 598(2)
564	553	546	52	114	19	596, 598(2)
564	554	547		114	20	597
565	554	547		114	20	597
566	556	549	52			
567	555	548	52	114	21	595
567	561	554	54			
568						
569	550	543		112	16	589
570	557	550	53	114	22	600
571	558	551	53	114	23(1)	601
572	559	552	53	114	23(1, 2)	601
572	562	555	54			
573	559	552	53	114	23(1, 2)	601
573	560	553		114	23(3)	601
574	566	559		116	26	604
575	563	556	54	114	24	602
575	564	557		116	25	603
576	567	560		116	27	
577	571	565		116	30	605
578	572	566	55	116	31	606
579	573	567	55			
579	576	570	56			
580	574	568	56			
581	570	564	55	116	29	
582	575	569	56			
583	577	571	56	116	32	607
584	578	572	57	116	33	608
585	579	573	57	116	34	609
586	582	576	58	118	37(1)	612(1)

TABLE 5—CIVIL CODE OF 1870 TO CODE NAPOLÉON

1976–2013 Revision of the Civil Code Art.	Civil Code 1870 Art.	Civil Code 1825 Art.	Projet Civil Code 1825 Page	Civil Code 1808 Page	Civil Code 1808 Art.	Code Napoléon 1804 Art.
\multicolumn{7}{c}{Book II—Things And Different Modifications Of Ownership}
586	581	575		118	36	611
587	581	575		118	36	611
587	583	577	58			
587	584	578	58			
587	585	579	58			
587	586	580	58			
587	587	581	58	118	37(2, 3)	612(2–4)
588	581	575		118	36	611
589	583	577	58			
590	584	578	58			
591	585	579	58			
591	586	580	58			
591	587	581	58	118	37(2, 3)	612(2–4)
592	585	579	58			
592	587	581	58	118	37(2, 3)	612(2–4)
593	580	574		118	35	610
594	588	582	59	118	38	613
595	589	583	60			
596	588	582	59	118	38	613
597	590	584	60			
598	591	585		118	39	614
599	593	587		118	41	616
600	592	586		118	40	615
600	593	587		118	41	616
601	569	563	55			
601	594	589	60	118	43	599(2, 3)
602	595	590	60			
603	605	600	61	120	50	
604	602	597		120	47	
605	599	594		120	44	
605	600	595		120	45	599(1)
605	601	596		120	46	
605	603	598		120	48	
606	601	596		120	46	
607	606	601		120	51	617(1, 2)
608	612	607	62	122	55	619
609	607	602	61			
610	608	603		120	52	617(1, 3)
611	609	604		120	53	
612	610	605		120	54	620
613	613	608	62	122	56	617(1, 6), 624
614	613	608	62	122	56	617(1, 6), 624
614	614	609		122	57	623
614	615	610	62			
615	615	610	62			
616						
617						
618						
619	616	611	62			
620	617	612		122	58	621

TABLE 5—CIVIL CODE OF 1870 TO CODE NAPOLÉON

1976–2013 Revision of the Civil Code Art.	Civil Code 1870 Art.	Civil Code 1825 Art.	Projet Civil Code 1825 Page	Civil Code 1808 Page	Civil Code 1808 Art.	Code Napoléon 1804 Art.
\multicolumn{7}{c}{**Book II—Things And Different Modifications Of Ownership**}
621	618	613	62	122	59	617(1, 5)
622	619	614	63	122	60	617(1, 4)
622	620	615	63			
623	621	616	63	122	61	618(1, 3)
624	621	616	63	122	61	618(1, 3)
624	622	617	64			
625	623	618	64			618(2)
626	624	619	64			622
627	625	620	64	122	62	
628	535	527	49	110	2	
628	567	560		116	27	
628	625	620	64	122	62	
629	549	542	51	112	15	587
630	627	622		124	64	
631	628	623		124	65	625
632	631	626	65	124	67	628
632	632	627	66	124	68	629
633	640	636	67			632
634	641	637	67	126	77	633
635	644	640	67			627
636	645	641		126	80	635
637	638	634		126	75	631
637	643	639	67	126	79	634
638	639	635		126	76	
639						
640						
641						
642						
643						
644						
645						
646	646	642	68			
646	647	643	68	126	1	637
646	648	644	68			
646	649	645	69			
647	650	646	69			
648	651	647	69			
649	652	648	69			
650	653	649	69			
650	654	650	69			
651	655	651	70			
652	656	652	70			
653	657	653	70			
654	659	655		126	3	639
655	660	656		128	4	640
656	660	656		128	4	640
657	661	657	71	128	8	644
658	661	657	71	128	8	644
659	664	660		128	12	649
659	666	662		130	14	651
660	670	666		130	18	
661	671	667		130	19	
662	692	688		134	38	674
662	693	689		134	39	
662	694	690		134	40	
662	695	691		136	41	

TABLE 5—CIVIL CODE OF 1870 TO CODE NAPOLÉON

1976–2013 Revision of the Civil Code Art.	Civil Code 1870 Art.	Civil Code 1825 Art.	Projet Civil Code 1825 Page	Civil Code 1808 Page	Civil Code 1808 Art.	Code Napoléon 1804 Art.
Book II—Things And Different Modifications Of Ownership							
663	697	693	73			678
664	698	694		136	45	681
664	713	709	75			
665	665	661		128	13	650
666	707	703	74			
667	667	663		130	15	
668	668	664		130	16	
669	669	665		130	17	
670						
671	672	668	71	130	20	
672	674	670		132	22	652(2)
673	675	671		132	23	
674	676	672		132	24	
675	677	673		132	25	653
676	684	680		134	32	661
677						
678	678	674		132	26	655
679	679	675		132	27	656
680	680	676		132	28	657
680	685	681		134	33	662
681	696	692		136	42	675
682	681	677		132	29	658
682	682	678		132	30	659
683	683	679		134	31	660
684	662	658		128	10	647
685	686	682	72	134	34	663
685	687	683	72	134	35	
685	688	684	73			670
686	689	685		134	36	666
686	690	686		134	37	669
687						
688	691	687	73			671, 672
689	699	695		136	46	682
690	702	698	74			
691	699	695		136	46	682
692	700	696	73	136	47	683, 684
693						
694	701	697	74			
695	703	699	74			
696	708	704		136	48	685
697	709	705		138	49	686
698	710	706		138	50	687
699	711	707	75			
699	721	717	77			
700	712	708	75			
701	716	712	76			
702	716	712	76			
703	717	713	76			
704	717	713	76			
705	719	715	77			
705	722	718	77			
706						
707	728	724		138	52	689
708	729	725	78			
708	731	727	78			
709	733	729	79			
710	730	726	78			
711	737	733	79			

TABLE 5—CIVIL CODE OF 1870 TO CODE NAPOLÉON

1976–2013 Revision of the Civil Code Art.	Civil Code 1870 Art.	Civil Code 1825 Art.	Projet Civil Code 1825 Page	Civil Code 1808 Page	Art.	Code Napoléon 1804 Art.
Book II—Things And Different Modifications Of Ownership							
712	736	732	79			
713	735	731	79			
714	738	734	80			
715	739	735	80			
716	740	736	80			
717	740	736	80			
718	741	737	80			
719	742	738	81			
720	749	745	82			
721	750	746	82			
722	743	739	81			
722	2481	2457	306	350	31	1607
723	744	740	81			
724	745	741	81			
725	746	742	81			
726	747	743	81			
727	748	744	81			
728	751	747	82			
729	752	748	82			
730	753	749	82			
731	754	750	82			
732	755	751	82			
733	756	752	83			
734	757	753	83			
735	759	755	83			
735	760	756	84			
735	762	758	84			
735	763	759	84			
735	764	760	85			
736	759	755	83			
737	761	757	84			
737	763	759	84			
738	760	756	84			
738	763	759	84			
739	766	762	85	138	54	691(1)
740	765	761	85	138	53	690
741	649	645	69			
741	767	763	85	138	55	692
741	768	764		138	56	693
741	769	765		140	57	694
742	765	761	85	138	53	690
742	3504	3470	409			
743	771	767	86	140	59	696
744	772	768		140	60	697
744	773	769		140	61	698
745	774	770	86			
746	775	771		140	62	699
746	814	810	94			
747	776	772		140	63	700
748	777	773		140	64	701
749	780	776	87			
750	779	775	86			
751	783	779	88			
751	784	780	88	142	66	703
752	785	781	88	142	67	704
752	786	782	89			665
753	783	779	88			
753	789	785	89	142	68	706
754	790	786	89	142	69	707
754	791	787	90			

635

TABLE 5—CIVIL CODE OF 1870 TO CODE NAPOLÉON

1976–2013 Revision of the Civil Code Art.	Civil Code 1870 Art.	Civil Code 1825 Art.	Projet Civil Code 1825 Page	Civil Code 1808 Page	Civil Code 1808 Art.	Code Napoléon 1804 Art.
\multicolumn{7}{c}{Book II—Things And Different Modifications Of Ownership}					
755	792	788	90			
756	787	783	89			
756	788	784	89			
757	793	789	90			
757	794	790	90			
758	795	791	91			
759	798	794	91			
760	797	793	91			
761	799	795	91			
762	801	797		142	71	709
762	803	799	92			
763						
764	804	800	92			
765	783	779	88			
765	805	801	92			705
766	806	802	92			
767	810	806	93			
768	811	807	93			
769	812	808	94			
770	783	779	88			
770	813	809	94			
770	814	810	94			
770	815	811	94			
771	783	779	88			
771	816	812	94			
771	817	813	94			
772	818	814	94			
773	783	779	88			
773	821	817	95			
774	783	779	88			
774	822	818	95			
775						
776						
777						
778						
779						
780						
781						
782						
783						
784	826	822	96			
785	823	819	96			
785	827	823	96			
786	823	819	96			
786	829	825	97			
786	830	826	97			
787	831	827	97			
788	824	820	96			
788	825	821	96			
789	832	828	97			
789	833	829	97			
790	663	659		128	11	646
791	855	851	101			
792	845	841	99			
793	846	842	100			
	847	843	100			
794	852	848	101			
795						
796	852	848	101			
797						

TABLE 5—CIVIL CODE OF 1870 TO CODE NAPOLÉON

1976–2013 Revision of the Civil Code Art.	Civil Code 1870 Art.	Civil Code 1825 Art.	Projet Civil Code 1825 Page	Civil Code 1808 Page	Art.	Code Napoléon 1804 Art.
Book II—Things And Different Modifications Of Ownership						
798	....	....	....	....	....	....
799	....	....	....	....	....	....
800	....	....	....	....	....	....
801	....	....	....	....	....	....
802	....	....	....	....	....	....
803	....	....	....	....	....	....
804	....	....	....	....	....	....
805	....	....	....	....	....	....
806	....	....	....	....	....	....
807	1289	1215	165	184	156	815(1)
	1298	1221	167	....	....	815(2)
808	1303	1226	167	....	....	....
809	1294	1217	166	....	....	....
	1322	1245	171	186	166(1)	819(1)
	1323	1246	171	186	166(2)	823, 838
810	1339	1261	173	188	171	827
			174	188	172	....
	1340	1262	174	188	173	....
			174	188	174	....
811	....	....	....	....	....	....
812	1338	....	....	....	....	....
813	1338	....	....	....	....	....
	1383	1434	202	206	249	883
814	1398	1436	....	206	250(3)	887(2)
815	1338	....	....	....	....	....
816	1384	1421	200	202	238	....
				204	239(1)	884(1)
	1385	1422	201	204	239(2)	884(2)
817	1304	1227	167	....	....	....
818	....	....	....	....	....	....
Book III—Of The Different Modes Of Acquiring The Ownership Of Things						
870	870	866	106	144	1	711, 712
871	871	867	106	144	1	....
	874	870	....	144	3	....
872	872	868	106	144	2	....
	873	869	107	....	....	....
873	875	871	....	144	4	....
874	876	872	....	146	5	....
875	877	873	....	146	6	....
	878	874	....	146	7	....
876	879	875	107	....	....	....
880	886	882	....	146	10	....
	887	883	....	146	11	....
881	894	890	....	148	18	739
882	895	891	....	148	19	740
883	896	892	....	148	20	741
884	897	893	108	148	21	742
885	898	894	109	148	23	743
886	899	895	....	148	24	744(1)
887	900	896	....	148	25	744(2)
888	902	898	109	150	27–29	745
889	915	....	....	....	....	....
890	916	....	....	....	....	....
	916.1	....	....	....	....	....
891	903	899	110	....	....	748

TABLE 5—CIVIL CODE OF 1870 TO CODE NAPOLÉON

1976–2013 Revision of the Civil Code Art.	Civil Code 1870 Art.	Civil Code 1825 Art.	Projet Civil Code 1825 Page	Civil Code 1825 Page	Civil Code 1808 Art.	Code Napoléon 1804 Art.
Book III—Of The Different Modes Of Acquiring The Ownership Of Things							
	904	900	110			749
892	912	908	111	152	35–37	750
893	913	909	112	152	34, 38	
				154	40	
894	924	918		156	50	767
895	905	901	110			
	906	902	110	150	30(1)	746(1.3)
	907	903	110	150	30(2–5)	746(2)
896	914	910	112	154	39, 41, 42	753
897	908	904	110			747
898	910	906	111			
899	888	884		146	12	
900	889	885		146	13	735
901	890	886		146	14	736
	891	887		146	15	737
	892	888		148	16	738
902	929	923		156	51	767, 768
934	934	928		158	58	718
	987	981	123	160	72	777
			123	162	73	
			123	162	74	
			123	162	75	774
935	940	934	115			724, 1004, 1006, 1011, 1014(2)
	941	935	115			
	943	937	115			
936	942	936	115			
	943	937	115			
937	944	938	116			
938						
939	953	947	117	158	65	725
940	954	948	117			
	955	949	118			
	956	950	118			
941	964	958	119			
	965	959	119			
	966	960	119	160	66	727
	967	961	119			
942	967	961	119			
943	975	969	121			
944						
945	969	963	120	160	68	729
	970	964	120			
	971	965	120			
946						
947	977	970		160	71	775
	986	980	123			
948	977	970		160	71	775
	1018	1011		164	90	
949	978	972	121			
	979	973	122			
950	980	974	122			
	983	977	122			
951	984	978	123			
952	981	975	122			
	982	976	122			
953						

TABLE 5—CIVIL CODE OF 1870 TO CODE NAPOLÉON

1976–2013 Revision of the Civil Code Art.	Civil Code 1870 Art.	Civil Code 1825 Art.	Projet Civil Code 1825 Page	Civil Code 1808 Page	Civil Code 1808 Art.	Code Napoléon 1804 Art.
		Book III—Of The Different Modes Of Acquiring The Ownership Of Things				
954	946	940	116			785
	947	941	116	160	72	
	948	942	116			
955						
956						
957	988	982	123			
				162	77	778
	989	983	124			
	990	984	124			
958	992	986	124			
959	996	990	125			
	997	991		162	78	779
	999	993	125			
	1000	994				
	1001	995	125			
	1002	996		162	79(1)	780(1)
960	1003	997		162	79(2)	780(2), (3)
961	1013	1006	127			
				164	86	
962						
963	1015	1008	127			
	1017	1010	128	164	88, 89	784
964	1022	1015	128			786
965						
966						
967	1021	1014	128	162	83	788
	1071	1064	135			
	1072	1065	136			
	1073	1066	136			
	1074	1067	136			
968						
	1095	1088	139	172	118(1)	811
	1096	1089	139	172	119	
	1097	1090	140	172	118(2), 121(1)	812
	1100					
	1148	1141	149	176	135(1)	
	1171					
	1188	1176	156	178	139(1)	
	1192	1180	158	180	142	
	1227	1305		192	192	
	1228	1306	181	192	193(1, 2)	843
	1229	1307		192	194	
	1230	1308		192	195	
	1231	1309	181	192	196(1)	844
	1232	1310	181	192	196(2)	919(2)
	1233	1311	182		197	
	1234	1312		192		
	1235	1313	182	192	198	857
	1237	1315		194	200	845
	1238	1316		194	201	846
	1239	1317		194	202	847
	1240	1318		194	203	848
	1241	1319		194	204	
	1242	1320	182			850
	1243	1321	182	196	208(1)	851
			182	196	208(2)	
	1244	1322	183	196	207(1–3)	852
	1245	1323	183	196	107(4)	852
	1246	1324	183	196	206(2)	853

TABLE 5—CIVIL CODE OF 1870 TO CODE NAPOLÉON

1976–2013 Revision of the Civil Code Art.	Civil Code 1870 Art.	Civil Code 1825 Art.	Projet Civil Code 1825 Page	Civil Code 1808 Page	Civil Code 1808 Art.	Code Napoléon 1804 Art.
	\multicolumn{6}{l}{Book III—Of The Different Modes Of Acquiring The Ownership Of Things}					
	1247	1325	183	196	206(1)	854
	1248	1326	183	194	205(1, 2)	
			182	194	205(3)	
	1249	1327	183			
	1250	1328	183	196	212	855
	1251	1329	184			858
	1252	1330	184			
	1253	1331	184			
	1254	1332	184	196	209	
	1255	1333	184	196	210	859, 860
	1256	1334	185	196	211, 213	861
	1257	1335	185			862
	1258	1336	185			
	1259	1337	185			
	1260	1338	185	198	214	863
	1261	1339	186	196	212	855
	1262	1340	186			
	1263	1341	186			
	1264	1342		198	217	865
	1265	1343	186			
	1266	1344	186	198	218(1)	866(1)
	1267	1345	187	198	218(2)	866(2)
	1268	1346	187	198	219	867
	1269	1347	187			
	1270	1348	187	198	215(1, 3)	
	1271	1349	186	198	215(2)	
	1272	1350	188	198	216	864
	1273	1351	188			
	1274	1352	188			
	1275	1353	188			
	1276	1354	188			
	1277	1355	189			
	1278	1356	189			
	1279	1357	189			
	1280	1358	189			
	1281	1359	189			
	1282	1360	190			
	1283	1361, 1363	190, 191	200	220	868
	1284	1362	190			
	1285	1364	191	200	221	869
			190	200	222	856
	1286	1365	191			
	1287	1366	191			
	1288	1367	191			
	1290	1304	180			
	1291					
	1292	1214	165	184	155	
	1293	1216	166	184	157	
	1295	1218		184	158	
	1296	1219	166			
	1297	1220	166	186	159	815(1)
	1299	1222	167			
	1300	1223	167			815(2)
	1301	1224	167			
	1302	1225		186	161	
	1305	1228	168			
	1306	1229	168			
	1307	1230	168			
	1308	1231	168			

TABLE 5—CIVIL CODE OF 1870 TO CODE NAPOLÉON

1976–2013 Revision of the Civil Code Art.	Civil Code 1870 Art.	Civil Code 1825 Art.	Projet Civil Code 1825 Page	Civil Code 1808 Page	Civil Code 1808 Art.	Code Napoléon 1804 Art.
	\multicolumn{6}{l}{Book III—Of The Different Modes Of Acquiring The Ownership Of Things}					
	1309	1232	168			
	1310	1233	169			
	1311	1234	169			
	1312	1235	169	186	162	817(1), 465
	1313	1236	169			
	1314	1237	169			465
	1315	1238	169			817(2)
	1318	1241		186	164	
	1319	1242	170			
	1320	1243	171			
			171	186	165	
	1321	1244	171	186	160	816
	1325	1248	171			
	1326	1249	172			
	1328	1251	172			
	1329	1252	172			
	1330	1253	172			
	1331	1254	172			
	1332	1255	172			
	1333	1256	172			
	1334	1257	173			
	1335	1258	173			
	1336	1259	173			
			173	186	168	824(2)
			173	188	169	
	1337	1260		188	170	826
	1341	1263	174			
	1342	1264	174			
	1343	1265	174			
	1344	1266	174			
	1345	1267	175	188	176	828(1)
	1346	1268	175	188	175	
	1347	1269	175			
	1348	1270	175			
	1349	1271	175			
	1350	1272	175			
	1351	1273	176			
	1352	1274	176			
	1353	1275	176			
	1354	1276	176	188	179(1)	830(1)
	1355	1277	176	188	177	828(2)
	1356	1278	176	188	178	829
	1357	1279	177			
	1358	1280	177			
	1359	1281	177			
	1360	1282	177			
	1361	1283	177			
	1362	1284	177	188	179(2)	830(2)
	1363	1285	178			
	1364	1286	178	190	180, 181	831
	1365	1287		190	182	832
	1366	1288		190	183	833
	1367	1289	178	190	184	834
	1370	1292		190	187	836
	1371	1293	179			
	1372	1294		190	188	840
	1373	1295	179			
	1378	1300	180			
	1379	1301		190	189	842

TABLE 5—CIVIL CODE OF 1870 TO CODE NAPOLÉON

1976–2013 Revision of the Civil Code Art.	Civil Code 1870 Art.	Civil Code 1825 Art.	Projet Civil Code 1825 Page	Civil Code 1808 Page	Civil Code 1808 Art.	Code Napoléon 1804 Art.
	Book III—Of The Different Modes Of Acquiring The Ownership Of Things					
	1380	1302		190	190	
	1382	1420		202	237	
	1384	1421	200	202	238	
				204	239(1)	884(1)
	1385	1422	201	204	239(2)	884(2)
	1386	1423	201	204	239(2)	884(2)
	1387	1424	201	204	240	885(1)
	1388	1425	201			
	1389	1426		204	241	885(2)
	1390	1427		204	242	886
	1391	1428	201	204	243	
	1392	1429	201			886
	1393	1430		204	244	
	1394	1431		204	245	
	1395	1432	201	204	246	
			202	204	247	
	1396	1433	202	206	248	
	1399	1437	203	206	251(1)	
	1400	1438	203	206	251(2)	
	1401	1439		206	252	887(2)
	1402	1440		206	253(1)	888(1)
	1403	1441		206	253(2)	888(2)
	1404	1442		206	254	889
	1405	1443	203			
	1406	1444	203			
	1407	1445	203			
	1408	1446	203	206	255	891
	1409	1447	204			
	1410	1448		206	256	892
	1411	1449		206	257	
	1412	1450		206	258	
	1413	1451	204	206	259	
	1414	1452	204	206	259	
1415						
1416	1425	1374	192			
	1426	1374	192			
	1427	1376	192			
1417						
1418						
1419						
1420	1415	1393	196			
	1416	1393	196			
1421						
1422						
1423						
1424						
1425						
1426						
1427						
1428						
1429						
1467	1467	1453		208	1	893
1468	1468	1454		208	2	894
1469	1469	1455		208	3	895
1470	1470	1456		208	4	902
1471	1472	1458	204			
1472	1473	1459	205			
1473	1474	1460	205			
1474	1482	1469	205	210	11	906
1475	1491	1478		212	17	911

TABLE 5—CIVIL CODE OF 1870 TO CODE NAPOLÉON

1976–2013 Revision of the Civil Code Art.	Civil Code 1870 Art.	Civil Code 1825 Art.	Projet Civil Code 1825 Page	Civil Code 1808 Page	Art.	Code Napoléon 1804 Art.
		Book III—Of The Different Modes Of Acquiring The Ownership Of Things				
1476	1476	1463		208	6	903
	1477	1464		208	7	904
1477	1475	1461	205	208	5(1)	901
		1462	205	208	5(2)	
1478						
1479						
1480						
1481						
1482						
1483						
	1493	1480	206	212	19	913, 914
1493	1493	1480	206	212	19	913, 914
1494						
1495	1495	1482		212	22	
1496	1710	1703		259	198	1046
1497	1496	1483	207	212	21	916
1498	1497	1484	207			
1499	890	916				
1500						
1502						
1503	1502	1489		214	26	920
1504	1504	1491		214	28	921
1505	1505	1492		214	29	922
1507	1507	1494		216	30	923
	1511	1498		216	33	926
1508	1507	1494		216	30	923
	1511	1498		216	33	926
1509	1508	1495	208			
1510	1513	1500	208			
1511	1514	1501	208			
1512	1515	1502		216	35	928
1513	1516	1503		216	36	929
	1517	1504		216	37	930
	1518	1505		216	38	930
1514	890	916				
	1519	1506		216	39	900
	1520	1507		216	40	896
	1521	1508		218	41	898
	1522	1509		218	42	899
1526	1524	1511	209			
1527	1526	1513	209			
1528	1527	1515	209			
1529	1528	1514		218	43	943
1530	1529	1516		218	44	944
1531	1530	1517		218	45	945
1532	1534	1521		220	51	951
1533	1535	1522		220	52	952
1541	1536	1523	209	220	53	931
	1538	1525	210	218	48	948
1542						
1543	1539	1526	210			
1544	1540	1527		220	54	932
1545	1542	1529		220	55	933
1546	1543	1530	210			
	1544	1531	210			
1547	1543	1530	210			
1548	1546	1533		220	57	935
1549	1551	1538	210			

TABLE 5—CIVIL CODE OF 1870 TO CODE NAPOLÉON

1976–2013 Revision of the Civil Code Art.	Civil Code 1870 Art.	Civil Code 1825 Art.	Projet Civil Code 1825 Page	Civil Code 1808 Page	Civil Code 1808 Art.	Code Napoléon 1804 Art.
\multicolumn{7}{c}{Book III—Of The Different Modes Of Acquiring The Ownership Of Things}
1550						
1551	1550	1537		222	61	938
1556	1559	1546	211	222	66	953
1557	1560	1547		222	67	955
1558	1561	1548		222	68	957
1559	1562	1549		222	69	958(1)
1560	1563	1550		224	70	958(2)
1561						
1562						
1563	1569	1562	211			
1564						
1565						
1566						
1567						
1570	1590	1583	214	230	104	
1571	1572	1565	211	226	87	968
	1573	1566	211	226	88	
1572	1573	1566	211	226	88	
1573	1570	1563	211	226	81	967
	1595	1588	211	232	108	1001
1574						
1575	1588	1581	213	230	103	970
	1589	1582	214			
1576						
1577						
1578						
1579						
1580						
1581	1591	1584	215	230	105	980
1582	1592	1585	215	232	106	975
1583						
1584						
1585						
1586	1612	1604	217	232	115	1010(1)
1587	1625	1618	218	232	116	1010(2)
			218	238	139	
1588	1707	1700		250	195	1044
1589	1697	1690		250	188	1039
	1698	1691		250	189	1040
	1699	1692		250	190	1041
	1703	1696		250	193	1043
1590	1706	1699		250	194	
	1707	1700		250	195	1044
	1708	1701		250	196	1045
1591	1704	1697		233		
1592	1707	1700		250	195	1044
1593						
1594						
1595	1606	1599	216	232	114	1003
			211	232	117	
			216	234	118	
			216	234	119	
			216	234	120	
			216		121	
1596	1709	1702		250	197	
1597	1643	1636	219			
1598	1608	1601	217	234	123	1005
	1626	1619	218	238	140	1014
	1627	1620	218			
	1628	1621	218			

TABLE 5—CIVIL CODE OF 1870 TO CODE NAPOLÉON

1976–2013 Revision of the Civil Code Art.	Civil Code 1870 Art.	Civil Code 1825 Art.	Projet Civil Code 1825 Page	Civil Code 1808 Page	Civil Code 1808 Art.	Code Napoléon 1804 Art.
	\multicolumn{6}{l}{Book III—Of The Different Modes Of Acquiring The Ownership Of Things}					
	1629	1622	218			
	1630	1623	219			
	1631	1624		238	141	1015
	1632	1625		240	142	1016(1)
	1708	1701		250	196	1045
1599						
1600	1634	1627	219			
1601	1635	1628	219			
1602	1633	1626		240	143	1017
1603						
1604						
1605	1644	1637	211	242	153	1007(1)
	1645	1638	211	242	154	
	1646	1639	211	242	155	
	1647	1640	211	242	156	
			220	244	164	
1606	1690	1683	211	248	182	
1607	1691	1684	222			
	1692	1685	222	250	184	1035
	1694	1687	211	250	186	1037
1608	1691	1684	222			
	1693	1686	211	250	185	1036
	1694	1687	211	250	186	1037
			222	248	183	
	1695	1688		250	187	1038
1609						
1610						
1611	1712	1705	223	252	200	
	1715	1708	224			
1612	1713	1706	223	252	201	
1613	1716	1709	224			
	1717	1710	224			
1614	1720	1713	224			
	1721	1714	224			
	1722	1715	224			
1615	1719	1712	224			
	1723	1716	224			
1616	1641	1634		240	149	1023
	1724	1717		252	202	1075
	1725	1718		252	203	1076(1)
	1726	1719		252	204	1076(1)
	1727	1720		254	205(1)	1076(1)
			211	254	205(2)	
	1728	1721		254	206	1077
	1729	1722		254	207	1078
	1730	1723	224	254	208	1079
	1731	1724	225	254	209	1080
	1732	1725	225			
	1733	1726	225			
1734						
1735						
1736						
1737						
1738						
1739						
1740						
1741						
1742						
1743						
1744						

TABLE 5—CIVIL CODE OF 1870 TO CODE NAPOLÉON

1976–2013 Revision of the Civil Code Art.	Civil Code 1870 Art.	Civil Code 1825 Art.	Projet Civil Code 1825 Page	Civil Code 1808 Page	Art.	Code Napoléon 1804 Art.
Book III—Of The Different Modes Of Acquiring The Ownership Of Things						
1745						
1746						
1747						
1748						
1749						
1750						
1751						
1756	1756	1749	226			
	2132	2128	281			
1757	1760	1753	227			
1758						
1759						
1760	1757	1750	226			
1761	1759	1752	226			
1762	1758	1751	226			
1763	2010	2005	271			
1764						
1765	1997	1992	269			
	1999	1994	269			
	2009	2004	270			
1766	1997	1992	269			
	2000	1995	269			
	2001	1996	270			
1767	2020	2015	273			
	2021	2016	273	272	68	1168
	2043	2038	274	274	81	1181
	2045	2040	274	274	83	1183
1768	2026	2021	273			
1769	2031	2026		272	72	1172
	2032	2027		272	73	1173
	2033	2028	274			
1770	2024	2019		272	70	1170
	2034	2029		272	74	1175
	2035	2030	274			
1771	2042	2037		274	80	1180
1772	2040	2035		274	78	1178
1773	2038	2033		272	76	1176
1774	2039	2034		272	77	1177
1775	2041	2036		274	79	1179
1776						
1777	2048	2043	275			
	2049	2044	275			
	2050	2045	275			
1778	2050	2045	275			
1779	2053	2048		276	87	1187
1780						
1781	2052	2047		276	86	1186
1782	2054	2049	276	276	88	1188
1783	2055	2050	276			
1784	2057	2052	276			
	2058	2053	276			
1785						
1786	2077	2072	278			
1787	2078	2073	278			
	2079	2074	278			
	2084	2079	278			
1788	2080	2075	278			
	2081	2076	278			
1789	2085	2080	279			
	2086	2081	279			

TABLE 5—CIVIL CODE OF 1870 TO CODE NAPOLÉON

1976–2013 Revision of the Civil Code Art.	Civil Code 1870 Art.	Civil Code 1825 Art.	Projet Civil Code 1825 Page	Civil Code 1808 Page	Civil Code 1808 Art.	Code Napoléon 1804 Art.
		2087	2082	279		
		2113	2109		284	122	1222
1790	2088	2083		278	97	1197
1791	2089	2084		278	98	1198
1792	2089	2084		278	98	1198
1793	2090	2085		278	99	1199
1794	2091	2086		278	100	1200
1795	2094	2089		278	103	1203
	2095	2090		280	104	1204
1796	2093	2088		278	102	1202
	2107	2103	279			
1797						
1798	2092	2087		278	101	1201
1799	2097	2092		280	106	1206
		2093		280	107	1207
1800						
1801	2098	2094		280	108	1208
1802						
1803						
1804	2103	2099		280	113	1213
	2104	2100		280	114	1214
	2106	2102		282	116	1216
1805	2103	2099		280	113	1213
1806	2104	2100		280	114	1214
	2105	2101		280	115	1215
1807	2062	2057	277			
	2063	2058	277			
	2065	2060	277			
1808	2066	2061	277			
	2074	2069		278	96	1196
1809	2068	2063		276	90	1190
1810						
1811	2069	2064		276	91	1191
1812	2071	2066		276	93	1193
	2072	2067		276	94	1194
1813	2073	2068	277	278	95	1195
	2219	2216		300	202	1302
1814	2071	2066		276	93	1193
1815	2108	2104		282	117	1217
	2109	2105		282	118	1218
1816	2111	2107		282	120	1220
1817	2111	2107		282	120	1220
1818	2113	2109		284	122	1222
1819	2112	2108		282	121	1221
	2113	2109		284	122	1222
	2114	2110		284	123	1223
	2115	2111		284	124	1224
	2116	2112		284	125	1225
1820	2110	2106		282	119	1219
1821						
1822						
1823						
1824						
1825						
1826						
1827						
1828	2160	2156		288	150	1250
1829	2161	2157		290	151	1251
1830						
1831	2232	2229		304	215	1315

Book III—Of The Different Modes Of Acquiring The Ownership Of Things

TABLE 5—CIVIL CODE OF 1870 TO CODE NAPOLÉON

1976–2013 Revision of the Civil Code Art.	Civil Code 1870 Art.	Civil Code 1825 Art.	Projet Civil Code 1825 Page	Civil Code 1808 Page	Civil Code 1808 Art.	Code Napoléon 1804 Art.
	**Book III—Of The Different Modes Of Acquiring The Ownership Of Things**					
1832	2275	2255	288	310	241	
	2278					
	2279	2258	289	312	247	1348(2)
	2280	2259	289			
1833	2234	2231		304	217	1317
1834	2235	2232		304	218	1318
1835	2236	2233		304	219	1319
1836	2240	2237		306	222	
	2242	2239		306	224	1322
1837	2241	2238		306	223	1326
1838	2244	2240		306	225	1323
	2245	2241	287	306	226	1324
			287	306	227	1325
1839	2264					
	2265					
	2266					
	2275	2255	288	310	241	
1840	2268	2247		308	234	1334
1841	2253	2250	288			
	2257					
	2267					
	2270	2249	288	308	236	1336
1842	2272	2252		310	238	1338
1843	2272	2252		310	238	1338
1844						
1845	2273	2253		310	239	1339
1846	2277	2257	289	310	243, 244	1341, 1347
				310	244(2)	1347
			289	310	245	
			289	312	246	1348(1), 1348(2)
1847	2278					
1848	2276	2256	289	310	242	
1853	2291	2270		314	257	1356
			290	316	258	
			290	316	259	
			290	316	260	
			290	316	261	
			290	316	262	
			290	316	263	
			290	316	264	
1854	2130	2126		286	134	1234
	2131	2127	281			
1855	2134	2130		286	136	1236
	2136	2132		286	137	1237
	2137	2133	281			
1856						
1857	2140	2136		288	139	1239
	2141	2137	283			
	2142	2138	283			
	2143	2139	283			
	2144	2140	283			
	2146	2142	283			
	2287	2266		314	253	1352
1858	2147	2143	282	288	141	1241
1859	2149	2145	283	288	142	1242
1860	2156	2152		288	146	1246
1861	2153	2149		288	144	1244(1)
1862	2157	2153		288	147	1247

TABLE 5—CIVIL CODE OF 1870 TO CODE NAPOLÉON

1976–2013 Revision of the Civil Code Art.	Civil Code 1870 Art.	Civil Code 1825 Art.	Projet Civil Code 1825 Page	Civil Code 1808 Page	Civil Code 1808 Art.	Code Napoléon 1804 Art.
Book III—Of The Different Modes Of Acquiring The Ownership Of Things							
1863	2158	2154		288	148	1248
1864	2163	2159		290	153	1253
1865						
1866	2164	2160	284	290	154	1254
1867	2165	2161		290	155	1255
1868	2166	2162		290	156	1256
1869	2167	2163		292	157	1257
	2168	2164		292	158	1258
			284	292	159	1259
			284	292	160	1259
			284	292	161	1260
			284	292	162	1261
			284	292	163	1262
			284	294	164	1263
			284	294	165	1264
1870						
1871						
1872						
1873						
1874	1933	1927	257	268	46–48	1146–1148
1875						
1876	2219	2216		300	202	1302
1877						
1878						
1879	2185	2181	286			
1880	2190	2186	286	296	174	1272, 1273
1881	2187	2183	286			
	2189	2185		296	173	1271
1882	2189	2185		296	173	1271
	2191	2187		296	175	1274
1883	2186	2182	286			
	2188	2184	286			
1884	2195	2191		296	179	1278
	2196	2192		296	180	1279
1885						
1886	2192	2188		296	176	1275
1887						
1888	2199	2195		296	183	1282
1889	2199	2195		296	183	1282
1890	2201	2197	286			
1891	2204	2200		298	186	1286
1892	2205	2201		298	187	1287
	2206	2202		298	188	1288
1893	2207	2203		298	189	1289
	2208	2204		298	190	1290
	2209	2205, 2206		298	191, 192	1291(1), 1292
1894	2210	2207		298	193	1293
1895	2213	2210		300	196	1296
1896	2214	2211		300	197	1297
1897	2211	2208		298	194	1294
1898	2211	2208		298	194	1294
1899	2215	2212		300	198	1298
	2216	2213		300	199	1299
1900	2212	2209		298	195	1295
1901						
1902						
1903	2217	2214		300	200	1300

TABLE 5—CIVIL CODE OF 1870 TO CODE NAPOLÉON

1976–2013 Revision of the Civil Code Art.	Civil Code 1870 Art.	Civil Code 1825 Art.	Projet Civil Code 1825 Page	Civil Code 1808 Page	Civil Code 1808 Art.	Code Napoléon 1804 Art.
\multicolumn{7}{c}{Book III—Of The Different Modes Of Acquiring The Ownership Of Things}
1904	2218	2215		300	201	1301
1905	2218	2215		300	201	1301
1906	1761	1754	227	260	1	1101
1907	1765	1758	228	260	2, 3	1102, 1103
1908	1765	1758	228	260	2, 3	1102, 1103
1909	1774	1767	229	260	6	1106
1910	1773	1766	229	260	5	1105
1911	1768	1761	228	260	4(1)	1104(1)
1912	1776	1769	229	260	4(2)	1104(2)
1913	1771	1764	229			
1914						
1915	1777	1770	229	260	7(1)	1107(1)
1916	1778	1771	229	260	7(2)	1107(2)
1917						
1918	1782	1775	230	264	23, 24	1123, 1124
	1783	1781	231			
1919	1783	1781	231			
	1784	1777	230			
1920	1794	1788	233			
1921	1792	1786	233			
	1793	1787	233			
1922	1785	1778	230	264	25(1)	1125(1)
1923	1785	1778	230	264	25(1)	1125(1)
	1866	1860	246			
1924	1792	1786	233			
	1793	1787	233			
	2224	2221		302	207	1307
1925	1783	1781	231			
	1789	1782	232			
		1783	232			
1926	1783	1781	231			
1927	1797	1791	234			
	1798	1792	234			
	1812	1806	236			
	1816	1810	236			
	1817	1811	237			
1928	1802	1796	234			
	1809	1803	235			
1929	1801	1795	234			
	1802	1796	234			
1930						
1931	1801	1795	234			
	1802	1796	234			
1932	1810	1804	236			
1933						
1934	1809	1803	235			
	1819	1813	237	262	9	1109
1935						
1936						
1937						
1938						
1939						
1940						
1941						
1942	1817	1811	237		9	1109
1943	1805	1799	235			
	1808	1802	235			

TABLE 5—CIVIL CODE OF 1870 TO CODE NAPOLÉON

1976–2013 Revision of the Civil Code Art.	Civil Code 1870 Art.	Civil Code 1825 Art.	Projet Civil Code 1825 Page	Civil Code 1808 Page	Civil Code 1808 Art.	Code Napoléon 1804 Art.
Book III—Of The Different Modes Of Acquiring The Ownership Of Things							
1944						
1945						
1946						
1947						
1948	1819	1813	237	262	9	1109
1949	1823	1817	238	262	10(1)	1110(1)
	1825	1819	238			
	1826	1820	238			
1950						
1951						
1952						
1953	1847	1841	242	262	16(1)	1116(1)
1954						
1955	1847	1841	242	262	16(1)	1116(1)
1956	1847	1841	242	262	16(1)	1116(1)
1957	1848	1842	244	262	16(2)	1116(2)
1958						
1959	1850	1844	244			
	1851	1845	244	262	12	1112
1960	1853	1847	244	262	13	1113
1961	1852	1846	244	262	11	1111
1962	1856	1850	245			
	1857	1851	245			
1963	1858	1852	245			
1964						
1965	1860	1854	246			
	1861	1855	246			
	1863	1857	246			
1966	1893	1887		264	31	1131
1967						
1968	1895	1889		264	33	1133
1969	1894	1888		264	32	1132
1970	1900	1894	251			
1971	1884	1878		264	27	1127
	1885	1879	249	264	28	1128
	1886	1880		264	29	1129
	1891	1885	250			
1972	1891	1885	250			
1973	1886	1880		264	29	1129
1974						
1975						
1976	1887	1881		264	30	1130
	1888	1882	250			
1977	1889	1883	250	262	19, 20	1119, 1120
1978	1890	1884	250	262	21	1121
				264	22	1122
	1902	1896	251			
1979						
1980						
1981						
1982						
1983	1901	1895		266	34	1134
1984	1763	1756	227			
1985	1763	1756	227			
	1902	1896	251			
1986	1909	1903	252	266	38	1138
	1926	1920	256	268	42	1142
	1927	1921	256			
1987	1928	1922	256	268	43	1143

TABLE 5—CIVIL CODE OF 1870 TO CODE NAPOLÉON

1976–2013 Revision of the Civil Code Art.	Civil Code 1870 Art.	Civil Code 1825 Art.	Projet Civil Code 1825 Page	Civil Code 1808 Page	Art.	Code Napoléon 1804 Art.
	Book III—Of The Different Modes Of Acquiring The Ownership Of Things					
	1929	1923	257	268	45	1145
1988						
1989	1933	1927	257	268	46–48	1146–1148
1990						
1991	1911	1905	253	266	39	1139
1992	1910	1904	252	266	38(2)	1138(2)
1993						
1994	1930	1924	257			
	1931	1925	257			
1995	1934	1928	258	268	49, 51, 52	1149, 1151, 1152
1996	1934	1928	258	268	49, 51, 52	1149, 1151, 1152
1997	1934	1928	258	268	49, 51, 52	1149, 1151, 1152
1998						
1999	1934	1928	258	268	49, 51, 52	1149, 1151, 1152
2000	1935	1929	259	270	53	1153
	1940	1935	260			
2001	1939	1934	260	270	54	1154
2002						
2003	1934	1928	258	268	49, 51, 52	1149, 1151, 1152
2004						
2005	2117	2113	280	284	126	1226
2006	2123	2119		284	127	1227
2007	2124	2120		284	128	1228
	2125	2121		284	129	1229
2008	2120	2116	280			
2009						
2010	2126	2122		284	130	1230
2011	2127	2123		284	131	1231
2012						
2013	2046	2041	275	274	84	1184
	2047	2042	275	275	84	1184
2014						
2015						
2016						
2017						
2018						
2019						
2020						
2021	2239	2236	287	304	221	1321
2022						
2023						
2024						
2025						
2026						
2027						
2028	2239	2236	287	304	221	1321
2029						
2030	1892	1886	250			
	2273	2253		310	239	1339

TABLE 5—CIVIL CODE OF 1870 TO CODE NAPOLÉON

1976–2013 Revision of the Civil Code Art.	Civil Code 1870 Art.	Civil Code 1825 Art.	Projet Civil Code 1825 Page	Civil Code 1808 Page	Art.	Code Napoléon 1804 Art.
	**Book III—Of The Different Modes Of Acquiring The Ownership Of Things**
2031	1791	1785	233	264	25(2)	1125(2)
	1795	1789	233			
2032	2221	2218		302	204	1304
2033	1791	1785	233	264	25(2)	1125(2)
	1792	1786	233			
	1793	1787	233			
2034	1823	1817	238	262	10(1)	1110(1)
2035	1795	1789	233			
	2239	2236	287	304	221	1321
2036	1970	1965	264			
2037	1971	1966	265			
	1985	1980	267			
2038	1979	1974	266			
	1980	1975	266			
	1981	1976	266			
	1982	1977	266			
2039						
2040	1986	1981	267			
2041	1994	1989	268			
2042	1973	1968	265			
2043	1977	1972	265			
	1988	1983	267			
2044						
2045	1949	1944	261			
	1950	1945	261	270	56	1156
2046						
2047	1946	1941	261			
	1947	1942	261			
2048	1952	1947		270	58	1158
2049	1951	1946		270	57	1157
2050	1955	1950		270	61	1161
2051	1959	1954		270	63	1163
2052	1962	1957	262	270	64	1164
			263	270	65	1165
2053	1953	1948		270	59	1159
2054						
2055	1964	1959	263			
	1965	1960	263			
	1966	1961	263			
2056						
2057	1957	1952		270	62	1162
2057	1958	1953	262			
2292	2295(1)	2274	291	318	5	1372
2293	2295(2)	2276	291	318	5	1372
2294						
2295	2298	2277		318	8	1374
2296	2300	2298	292			
2297	2299	2278		320	9	1375
2298						
2299	2301	2279		320	10	1376
2300	2304	2282	291			
	2305	2283	292			
2301	2308	2286	292			
	2309	2287	292			
2302	2310	2288	292	320	11	1377
2303	2311	2289	292	320	12	1378
2304	2312	2290	292	320	13	1379
2305	2313	2291	292	320	14	1380
			290	318	4	

TABLE 5—CIVIL CODE OF 1870 TO CODE NAPOLÉON

1976–2013 Revision of the Civil Code Art.	Civil Code 1870 Art.	Civil Code 1825 Art.	Projet Civil Code 1825 Page	Civil Code 1808 Page	Civil Code 1808 Art.	Code Napoléon 1804 Art.
	Book III—Of The Different Modes Of Acquiring The Ownership Of Things					
	2315	2294	293	320	16	1382
			293	320	17	
			293	320	18	
	2316	2295	293	320	19	1383
	2317	2296	293	320	20(1)	1384(1)
	2318	2297	293	320	20(2)	1384(2)
	2319	2298	293			
	2320	2299	293	320	20(3–6)	1384(3–5)
		2300	293	322	21	
	2321	2301	293	320	20(7)	1385
	2322	2302	294	322	22	1386
	2323	2303	294			
	2324	2304	294			
2325						
2326						
				322	1	1387
2327	2325	2305	294			
				324	8	
2327	2332	2312	295	324	10	
2327	2399	2369	299	336	63	
2327	2424	2393	300			
				322	1	1387
2328	2325	2305	294			
				324	8	
2328	2332	2312	295	324	10	
2328	2424	2393	300			
2329	2326	2306	294	324	3	1389
2329	2327	2307	294	324	4	1388
2329	2332	2312	295	324	10	
2329	2392	2394	301			
2329	2424	2393	300			
2330	2326	2306	294	324	3	1389
2330	2327	2307	294	324	4	1388
2330	2332	2312	295	324	10	
2330	2392	2394	301			
2330	2424	2393	300			
2331	2328	2308		324	5	1394
2331	2329	2309		324	5	1394
2331	2427	2401		342	87	1443(2)
2332	2328	2308		324	5	1394
2332	2329	2309		324	6	1395
2332	2427	2401		342	87	1443(2)
2333	2330	2310	294	324	7	1398
2334	2399	2369	299	336	63	
2334	2400					
2334	2401	2370	299			
2335	2334	2314	295	324	13, 14	
2336	2334	2314	295	324	13, 14	
2336	2386	2363	298	334	60	1578
2336	2398	2412	302			
2336	2402	2371	299	336	64	1401
2337						
2338	2334	2314	295	324	13, 14	
2338	2386	2363	298	334	60	1578
2338	2398	2412	302			
2338	2402	2371	299	336	64	1401
2339	488	480	42			
2339	2334	2314	295	324	13, 14	
2339	2386	2363	298	334	60	1578
2339	2398	2412	302			

TABLE 5—CIVIL CODE OF 1870 TO CODE NAPOLÉON

1976–2013 Revision of the Civil Code Art.	Civil Code 1870 Art.	Civil Code 1825 Art.	Projet Civil Code 1825 Page	Civil Code 1808 Page	Art.	Code Napoléon 1804 Art.
Book III—Of The Different Modes Of Acquiring The Ownership Of Things						
2339	2402	2371	299	336	64	1401
2340	2405	2374		336	67	1402
2341	488	480	42			
2341	2334	2314	295	324	13, 14	
2341	2386	2363	298	334	60	1578
2342	2334	2314	295	324	13, 14	
2342	2386	2363	298	334	60	1578
2343						
2343.1						
2344	2334	2314	295	324	13, 14	
2345						
2346	2387	2364	299			
2346	2393	2395	301			1536
2346	2394	2396	301			1538
2346	2404	2373	299	336	66	1421, 1422
2347	2404	2373	299	336	66	1421, 1422
2348						
2349	2404	2373	299	336	66	1421, 1422
2350						
2351						
2352						
2353						
2354	2404	2373	299	336	66	1421, 1422
2355						
2355.1						
2356	136	133	10	28	30	227
2356	155	151		34	17	311
2356	2425	2399		340	86	1443(1)
2357(1)	2409	2378		338	71	1482
2357(2)	2409	2378		338	71	1482
2358						
2358.1						
2359						
2360						
2361						
2362						
2362.1						
2363						
2364						
2365						
2366						
2367						
2367.1						
2367.2						
2367.3						
2368	2408	2377		338	70	1437
2369						
2369.1						
2369.2 to 2369.8						
2370	2392	2394	301			
2370	2427	2401		342	87	1443(2)
2371	2393	2395	301			1536
2371	2394	2396	301			1538
2371	2436	2410		342	97	1449
2372						
2373	2395	2397	301			1537

TABLE 5—CIVIL CODE OF 1870 TO CODE NAPOLÉON

1976–2013 Revision of the Civil Code Art.	Civil Code 1870 Art.	Civil Code 1825 Art.	Projet Civil Code 1825 Page	Civil Code 1808 Page	Civil Code 1808 Art.	Code Napoléon 1804 Art.
	Book III—Of The Different Modes Of Acquiring The Ownership Of Things						
2373	2435	2409		342	96	1448
2374	2425	2399		340	86	1443(1)
2375	2432	2406		342	93	1445(2)
2376	2433	2407		342	94	1446
2376	2434	2408		342	95	1447
2432	2382	2359		334	55	
2433						
2434	2382	2359		334		
2435	2382	2359		334	55	
2436						
2437	2382	2359		334	55	
2438	2438	2413	302			
2439	2439	2414		344	1	1582(1)
2440	2440	2415		344	2(1,2)	1582(2)
	2462	2437		346	9	1589
2442	2442	2417	302	344	3	
2443	2443	2418	303			
2444	2444	2419	303			
2447	2447	2422	303			1597
2448	2448	2423		348	16	1598
	2449	2424		348	17	
2450	2450	2425		348	18	
2451	2451	2426		348	19	
2452	2452	2427		348	20	1599
2453	2453	2428	303			
2456	2456	2431		346	4	1583
2457						
2458	2458	2433		346	6	1585
	2459	2434		346	7	1586
2460	2460	2435		346	8	1587
2461	2461	2436		304		1588
	2490	2466		352	39	1615
2463	2466	2441		346	13	1593
2464	2464	2439	304	346	11	1591
2465	2465	2440		346	12	1592
2466						
2467	2467	2442	304	352	48	1624
	2552	2530	312			
2474	2474	2449		348	23	1602
2475	2475	2450		348	24	1603
	2476	2451		348	25	1625
2477	2477	2452		350	26	2604
	2478	2453		350	27	1606
		2454		350	28	
	2479	2455	305	350	29	1605
			306	350	30	
2480	2480	2456	306			
2481	2481	2457	306	350	31	1607
	2642	2612		368	121	1689
2482	2482	2458	306			
2483	2483	2459		350	32	1608
2484	2484	2460		350	33	1609
2485	2485	2461		350	34	1610
	2486	2462		350	35	1611
2487	2487	2463		350	36	1612
	2488	2464		352	37	1613
2489	2489	2465	306	352	38	1614
2491	2491	2467		352	40	1616
2492	2492	2468		352	41	1617
	2493	2469		352	42	1618

TABLE 5—CIVIL CODE OF 1870 TO CODE NAPOLÉON

1976–2013 Revision of the Civil Code Art.	Civil Code 1870 Art.	Civil Code 1825 Art.	Projet Civil Code 1825 Page	Civil Code 1808 Page	Civil Code 1808 Art.	Code Napoléon 1804 Art.
Book III—Of The Different Modes Of Acquiring The Ownership Of Things						
2494	2494	2470	306	352	43	1619
	2496	2472		352	44	1620
2495	2494	2470	306	352	43	1619
	2495	2471	307			
	2496	2472		352	44	1620
2497	2497	2473		352	45	1621
2498	2498	2474		352	46	1622
2500	2500	2476		354	50	
	2501	2477		354	49	1626
	2502	2478	307			
	2515	2491		356	62	1638
2502						
2503	2503	2479		354	51	1627
	2504	2480		354	52	1628
	2505	2481		354	53	1629
2506	2506	2482		354	54	1630
2507	2507	2483		354	55	1631
	2508	2484		354	56	1632
			307	354	57	1633
2509	2509	2485		354	58	1634
	2510	2486		354	59	1635
2511	2511	2487		354	60	1636
	2514	2490	307	356	61	1637
2512	2512	2488	307			
2513	2513	2489	307			
				356	61	1637
2517	2517	2493	308			
	2518	2494	308	356	64	1640
	2519	2495	308			
2520	2520	2496	308	356	65, 67	1641
				356	68	1643
2521	2521	2497	308	356	69	1642
	2522	2498	309	356	69	
2522						
	2524	2500	309	358	78	
2524						
2529						
2530	2530	2508	310	358	76	
2531	2531	2509	310	358	72	1646
2532	2532	2510	310	358	73(1)	1647(1)
	2533	2511	310	358	73(2)	1647(2)
	2536	2514	310			
2534	2534	2512	310	358	75	1648
	2546	2524	311			
2537	2537	2515	310	358	74	1649
	2616	2594	316			
	2624	2602	317			
2538	2538	2516	310			
	2539	2517	310			
2540	2540	2518	310			
2541	2541	2519	311	356	70	1644
	2543	2521	311			
2545	2545	2523	311	356	66	1645
2548	2548	2526	311			
	2503	2479	354		51	1627
2549	2549	2527	312	360	82	1650
2550	2550	2528	312	360	82, 83	1650, 1651
2553	2553	2531		360	84	1652
	2554	2532	312			

TABLE 5—CIVIL CODE OF 1870 TO CODE NAPOLÉON

1976–2013 Revision of the Civil Code Art.	Civil Code 1870 Art.	Civil Code 1825 Art.	Projet Civil Code 1825 Page	Civil Code 1808 Page	Civil Code 1808 Art.	Code Napoléon 1804 Art.
Book III—Of The Different Modes Of Acquiring The Ownership Of Things							
2555	2555	2533	312			
	2556	2534	312			
2557	2557	2535	313	360	85	1653
	2558	2536	313			
	2559	2537	313			
2560	2560	2538	313			
2561	2561	2539		360	86	1654
2562	2562	2540		360	87	1655
2563	2563	2541		362	88	1656
2564	2564	2542		362	89	1657
2567	2567	2545		362	91	1659
2568	2568	2546		362	92	1660
2569						
2570	2570	2548		362	94	1662
2571	2569	2547		362	93	1661
	2571	2549		362	95	1663
2572	2572	2550		362	96	1664
2574	2574	2552		362	98	1666
2575	2575	2553	313			
2577	2576	2554	313			
	2577	2555	314			
2578	2468	2443	304			
	2478	2556	314			
2584	2600	2578		366	117	1685
			316	366	118	1686
			316	366	119	1687
			316	366	120	1688
2587	2587	2565		364	107	1673(1)
2588	2588	2566		364	108	1673(2)
2589	2589	2567		364	109	1674
	2593	2571		366	113	1683
	2594	2572		366	114	1684
2590	2590	2568		366	110	1675
2591	2591	2569		366	111	1681
2592	2592	2570		366	112	1682
2594						
2595						
2596						
2597	2531	2509	310	358	72	1646
	2597	2575	314			
	2598	2576	314			
2599	2599	2577	314			
2600						
	2580	2558		364	100	1668
	2581	2559		364	101	1669
	2582	2560		364	102	1670
2601						
2602						
2603						
2604						
2605						
2606						
2607						
2608						
2609						
2610						
2611						
2612	2556	2534	312			
2613						
2614						

TABLE 5—CIVIL CODE OF 1870 TO CODE NAPOLÉON

1976–2013 Revision of the Civil Code Art.	Civil Code 1870 Art.	Civil Code 1825 Art.	Projet Civil Code 1825 Page	Civil Code 1808 Page	Art.	Code Napoléon 1804 Art.
	**Book III—Of The Different Modes Of Acquiring The Ownership Of Things**
2615	2564	2624		368	132	1701
2616						
2617						
2618						
2619						
2620						
2621						
2622						
2623	2462	2437		346	9	1589
2624						
2625						
2626						
2627						
2628						
2629						
2630						
2642						
2643	2643	2613		368	122	1690
2644	2644	2614		368	123	1691
2645	2645	2615		368	124	1692
2646	2646	2616		368	125	1693
	2647	2617		368	126	1694
2648	2648	2618		368	127	1695
2649	2649	2619	318			
2650	2650	2620		368	128	1696
2652	2652	2622		368	130	1699
	2653	2623		368	131	1700
	2654	2624		368	132	1701
2653						
2654						
2655	2655	2625	318			
2656	2656	2626	318			
2657						
2659	2659	2629	319			
2660						
2661						
2662						
2663						
2664						
2665						
2666						
2667						
2668	2669	2639	319			
	2670	2640	319			
	2677	2647	320	372	6	
2669	2668	2638	319	372	8	
2673	2678	2648	320	372	7	1713
	2679	2649	320			
2674	2681	2651	320			
2675	2671	2641	319			
2676	2671	2641	319			
	2672	2642	320			
2678	2674	2644		372	2	1709
	2684	2654		374	10	
	2685	2655	321	374	11(1)	1736
	2687	2657		374	12	1774(1)
2680	2685	2655	321	374	11(1)	1736
	2687	2657		374	12	1774(1)
2682	2682	2652	321			
	2692	2662		374	17	1719

TABLE 5—CIVIL CODE OF 1870 TO CODE NAPOLÉON

1976–2013 Revision of the Civil Code Art.	Civil Code 1870 Art.	Civil Code 1825 Art.	Projet Civil Code 1825 Page	Civil Code 1808 Page	Art.	Code Napoléon 1804 Art.
\multicolumn{7}{l}{Book III—Of The Different Modes Of Acquiring The Ownership Of Things}
2683	2683	2653		372	8	1714
	2710	2680		376	26	1728
	2721	2691		378	35	1732
2684	2693	2663		374	18	1720
2685	2701	2671		376	23	1765
2686	2711	2681		376	27	1729, 1760
2687	2722	2692		378	36	1735
	2723	2693		378	37	1733
2688	2724	2694		378	38	1768(1)
		2695		378	39	
2689	2702	2672	322			
2690	2698	2668		376	21	1723
2691	2693	2663		374	18	1720
	2717	2687		378	31	1755
2692	2695	2665	322	374	19	1721
	2715	2685		378	29	
	2716	2686		378	30	1754
	2717	2687		378	31	1755
2693	2700	2670		376	22	1724
2694	2694	2664	321			
2695	2726	2697	324			
2696	2692	2662		374	17	1719
2697	2695	2665	322	374	19	1721
2700	2682	2652	321			
	2692	2662		374	17	1719
	2696	2666	322			
	2704	2674		376	25	1727
2701	2692	2662		374	17	1719
	2696	2666	322			
	2704	2674		376	25	1727
2702	2703	2673		376	24	1725
2704	2712	2682		378	28	
2705	2743	2714		380	54	1769, 1770, 1772, 1773
						1771(1)
	2744	2715	324			
2707	2705	2715	322	468	74	2102
2708	2706	2676	323			1753
2709	2707	2677	323			
	2708	2678	323			
2710	2709	2679	322	468	74	2102
2711	2733	2704		380	44	1743
2712	2735	2706		380	46	1744
2713	2725	2696	324	374	9	1717
2714	2697	2667	322	376	20	1722
	2728	2699	324	378	40	1741
2715	2697	2667	322	376	20	1722
	2699	2669	322			
2716	2730	2701		380	41	
2717	2731	2702		380	42	1742
2718	2732	2703		380	43	1761
	2735	2706		380	46	1744
2719	2729	2700	324	378	40	1741
2720	2686	2656	321	374	11(2)	1736
2721	2688	2658	321	374	14	1776
	2689	2659	321	374	15	1738, 1759
	2691	2661	321			1739

TABLE 5—CIVIL CODE OF 1870 TO CODE NAPOLÉON

1976–2013 Revision of the Civil Code Art.	Civil Code 1870 Art.	Civil Code 1825 Art.	Projet Civil Code 1825 Page	Civil Code 1808 Page	Art.	Code Napoléon 1804 Art.
	**Book III—Of The Different Modes Of Acquiring The Ownership Of Things**						
2722	2688	2658	321	374	14	1776
2723	2689	2659	321	374	15	1738, 1759
2727	2686	2656	321	374	11(2)	1736
2728	2727	2698	324	374	13	1737
	2745	2716		382	55	1779
	2746	2717		382	56	1780
	2747	2718		382	57	
	2748	2719		382	58	
	2749	2720		382	59	
	2750	2721		382	60	
	2751	2722		384	61	1782
	2752	2723	325			1783
	2753	2724		384	62	
	2754	2725		384	63	1784
	2755	2726	325			
			325	384	64	1786
	2756	2727		384	65	1711(6)
	2757	2728		384	66	1787
	2758	2729		384	67	1788
	2759	2730		384	68	1789
	2760	2731		384	69	1790
	2761	2732		384	70	1791
	2762	2733		384	71	1792
	2763	2734		386	72	1793
	2764	2735	325			
	2765	2736	325	386	73	1794
	2766	2737		386	74	1795
	2767	2738		386	75	1796
	2768	2739		386	76	1797
	2769	2740		386	77	
	2770	2741		386	78	1798
	2771	2742		386	79	1799
	2772	2743	325			
	2773	2744	326			
	2774	2745	326			
	2775	2746	326			
	2776	2747	326			
	2777	2748	326			
2778						
2779						
2780						
2781						
2782						
2783						
2784						
2785						
2786						
2787						
2788						
2789						
2790						
2791						
	2792					
	2793					
	2794					
	2795					
	2796					
	2797					
	2798					

TABLE 5—CIVIL CODE OF 1870 TO CODE NAPOLÉON

1976–2013 Revision of the Civil Code Art.	Civil Code 1870 Art.	Civil Code 1825 Art.	Projet Civil Code 1825 Page	Civil Code 1808 Page	Civil Code 1808 Art.	Code Napoléon 1804 Art.
		Book III—Of The Different Modes Of Acquiring The Ownership Of Things				
	2799					
	2800					
2801	2801	2772	329	388	1, 2(3)	1832
2801	2805	2776	329	388	2(2)	
2801	2809	2780	330	388	3	1833(2)
2802	2803	2774	329	388	5	1834
2803	2811	2782	330	388	3	
2803	2813	2784	330			
2803	2865	2836	338	394	31	1853(1)
2804	2865	2836	338	394	31	1853(1)
2805	2837	2808	333			
2805	2838	2809	334			
2806	2836	2807	333			
2807	2867	2838	338	394	34	1856
2807	2868	2839		394	35	1857
2807	2869	2840		394	36	1858
2807	2870	2841	339	394	37	1859, 1860
2808	2856	2827	337	392	22	1845
2809	2862	2833	337	394	28	1850
2810						
2811	2864	2835	338	394	30	1852
2812	2871	2842		396	38	1861
2813						
2814	2870	2841	339	394	37	1859, 1860
2815	2814	2785	330	394	33	1855
2816	2874	2845	340	398	45	1864
2817	2872	2843	340	398	43	1862
2817	2873	2844	340	398	44	1863
2817	2875	2846	340			
2818						
2819						
2820						
2821						
2822						
2823						
2824						
2825						
2826	2876	2847	340	398	46	1865
2826	2877	2848		398	47	
2827	2878	2849		398	48	1866
2828						
2829						
2830						
2831						
2832	2823	2794	331			
2833						
2834	2890	2861		400	60	1872
2835						
2836						
2837	2828	2799	332			
2837	2840	2811	334			
2837	2839	2810	334	390	17	
2838	2849	2830	335			
2839	2849	2830	335			
2839	2850	2821	336			
2840	2839	2810	334	390	17	
2840	2842	2813	334			
2841	2845	2816	335			

TABLE 5—CIVIL CODE OF 1870 TO CODE NAPOLÉON

1976–2013 Revision of the Civil Code Art.	Civil Code 1870 Art.	Civil Code 1825 Art.	Projet Civil Code 1825 Page	Civil Code 1808 Page	Art.	Code Napoléon 1804 Art.
\multicolumn{7}{c}{**Book III—Of The Different Modes Of Acquiring The Ownership Of Things**}
2842	2843	2814	334			
2842	2851	2822	336			
2843	2844	2815	335			
2844	2849	2830	335			
2891	2893	2864	342	402	3	1875
	2894	2865		402	4	1876
	2895	2866		402	5	1877
2893	2896	2867		402	6	1878
2894	2898	2869	342	402	8	1880
2895	2902	2873		404	12	1884
2896	2899	2870		402	9	1881
2897	2900	2871		402	10	1882
2898	2901	2872		404	11	1883
2899	2904	2875		404	14	1886
	2908	2879		404	17	1890
2900	2905	2876	342			1887
2901	2906	2877		404	15	1888
	2907	2878		404	16	1889
2902	2909	2880	343			1891
2904	2910	2881		402	18	1892
2905	2911	2882		404	19	1893
2907	2913	2884		406	21	1895
	2914	2885		406	22	1896
	2915	2886		406	23	1897
2908	2916	2887	343	406	24	1898
2909	2917	2888		406	25	1899, 1900
	2918	2889		406	26	
2910	2920	2891	343	406	28	1902
2911	2921	2892		406	29	1903
2912	2922	2893		406	30	1904
2913	2925	2896	344			1908
2926	2926	2897	344	410	1(1)	1915
2927						
2928	2929	2900		410	4	1917
2929	2930	2901	344			1919
			344	410	2(1)	
2930	2937	2908	345	412	11(1)	1927
2931	2940	2911	346	412	12	1930
2932	2941	2912	346			
2933	2944	2915	346	412	14	1932
2934	2945	2916	346	412	15	1933
2935	2948	2919		414	18	1936
2936	2950	2921		414	20	1938
2937	2953	2924		414	23	1942
	2954	2925		414	24	1943
2938	2955	2926		414	25	1944
2939	2956	2927	346	414	28(3)	1948
2940	2960	2931		414	28(1, 2)	1947
2941	2965	2936		416	30	1952
2942						
2943	2969					
2944	2967	2938		416	32	1953
2945	2971	2940		416	34	
2946	2973	2942		416	36	1956
2947						
2948	2978	2947		418	41	1960
2949	2979	2948	347	418	42	1961
2950						
2951	2981	2950	348	418	44	1963

TABLE 5—CIVIL CODE OF 1870 TO CODE NAPOLÉON

1976–2013 Revision of the Civil Code Art.	Civil Code 1870 Art.	Civil Code 1825 Art.	Projet Civil Code 1825 Page	Civil Code 1808 Page	Civil Code 1808 Art.	Code Napoléon 1804 Art.
		Book III—Of The Different Modes Of Acquiring The Ownership Of Things				
	2982	2951	348	420	1	1964
	2983	2952		420	2	1965, 1966
	2984	2953		420	3	1967
2986						
2989	2985	2954		420	1	1984(1)
2986						
2987						
2988						
2990						
2991	2986	2955	348			
2992	2991	2960		422	5	1986
2993	2992	2961		422	6	1985(1)
2994	2994	2963		422	8	1987
	2995	2964		422	9	
2995	3000	2969	349	422	13	
2996	2996	2965	349			1988
	2997	2966	349	422	10	
2997	2997	2966	329	422	10	
2998						
2999	3001	2970	349	422	14, 15	1990
3000	cf. 3016	2985	350			
3001	3002	2971	350	422	16	1991
3002	3003	2972	350	424	17	1992
3003						
3004	3005	2974		424	19	1993
	3023	2992		351		
3005	3015	2984		424	26	1996
3006						
3007	cf. 3007	2976		424	21	1994(1)
3008	2977			424	22	1994(1)
3009	2978			424	23	1994(2)
3008	3010	2979		424	24	
3009	3014	2983		424	25	1995
3010	cf. 3021	2990	351	424	27	1998
3011	3011	2980	350			
3012	3022	2991	351	424	29	1999
3013	3024	2993		426	30	2000
3014	3025	2994		426	31	2001
3015	3026	2995		426	32	2002
3016	cf. 3012	2981	350	424	28	1997
3013	2982		350			
3012	2981		350	424	23	1997
3017	3013	2982	350			
3018						
3019	cf. 3013					
3020	3021					
3021						
3022						
3023						
3024	3027	2996	352	426	33	2003
3025	cf. 3028	2997	352	426	34	2004
3026	3027	2976		424	21	1994(1)
3027	3027					
3028	3029	2998		426	35	2005
3029	3031	3000	352	426	37, 38	2007
			352	426	39	
3030	3002	2971	350	422	16	1991
3031	3032	3001	353	426	40	2008
	3033	3002	353			2009

TABLE 5—CIVIL CODE OF 1870 TO CODE NAPOLÉON

1976–2013 Revision of the Civil Code Art.	Civil Code 1870 Art.	Civil Code 1825 Art.	Projet Civil Code 1825 Page	Civil Code 1808 Page	Art.	Code Napoléon 1804 Art.
	Book III—Of The Different Modes Of Acquiring The Ownership Of Things						

1976–2013 Revision of the Civil Code Art.	Civil Code 1870 Art.	Civil Code 1825 Art.	Projet Civil Code 1825 Page	Civil Code 1808 Page	Art.	Code Napoléon 1804 Art.
3032	3004	2973		424	18	1993
3035	3035	3004	353	428	1	2011
3036	3036	3005		428	2	2012
3037						
3038	3039	3008		428	5	2015
3039						
3040						
3041						
3042						
3043						
3044						
3045	3045	3014		428	7	2021
	3066	3035		434	29	2042
3046	3060	3029		432	21	2036
3047						
3048	3053	3022		430	15	2029
3049(1)	3052(1)	3021		430	14	2028
3049(2)	3054	3023		430	16	2030
3050	3056	3025	355			2031(2)
3051	3055	3024		430	17	2031(1)
3052						
3053	3057	3026		430	18	2032
3054						
3055	3058	3027		432	19	2033
3056	3058	3027		432	19	2033
3057						
3058	3059	3028		432	20	2034, 2035
3059	3059	3028		432	20	2034, 2035
3060						
3061						
3062	3061	3030		432	22	2037
3063						
3064	3068	3037	356			
3065	3042(1)	3011	353	432	25	2018
	3064	3033	355	432	25	2040(1)
3066						
3067						
3068	3065	3034	356	434	28	2041
3069	3066	3035		434	29	2042
3070	3043	3012	353	434	27	2020
3071	3071	3038		434	1	2044
3072	3071	3038		434	1	2044
3073	3072	3039		434	2	2045(1, 2)
3074						
3075	3077	3044		436	9	2051
3076	3073	3040		434	3	2048, 2049
			356	434	4	
			356	436	5	
3077						
3078	3074	3041		436	6	2050
3079						
3080	3078	3045		436	10	2052, 2058
3081						
3082	3079	3049	566	436	14	2056
	3080	3047		436	12	2054

TABLE 5—CIVIL CODE OF 1870 TO CODE NAPOLÉON

1976–2013 Revision of the Civil Code Art.	Civil Code 1870 Art.	Civil Code 1825 Art.	Projet Civil Code 1825 Page	Civil Code 1808 Page	Civil Code 1808 Art.	Code Napoléon 1804 Art.
		Book III—Of The Different Modes Of Acquiring The Ownership Of Things				
3083						
	3084	3051	356	438	1	
	3085	3052		438	2	
	3086	3053	357	438	3	
	3087	3054	357	438	4	
	3088	3055	358			
	3089	3056	358			
	3090	3057	358			
	3091	3058		438	5	
	3092	3059	358			
	3093	3060	358			
	3094	3061	358			
	3095	3062	358	440	6	
	3096	3063		440	7	
	3097	3064		440	8	
	3098	3065	359			
	3099	3066		440	1	
	3100	3067		440	2	
	3101	3068		440	3	
	3102	3069		440	4	
	3103	3070		440	5	
	3104	3071		440	6	
	3105	3072		442	7	
	3106	3073		442	8	
	3107	3074		442	9	
	3108	3075		442	10	
	3109	3076		442	11	
	3110	3077		442	12	
	3111	3078		442	13	
	3112	3079		442	14	
	3113	3080		442	15	
	3114	3081	359	442	16, 18	
	3115	3082	359	442	17	
	3116	3083		442	19	
	3117	3084		442	20	
	3118	3085		444	21	
	3119	3086		444	22	
	3120	3087		444	23	
	3121	3088	360	444	24	
	3122	3089	360	444	25	
	3123	3090		444	26	
	3124	3091		444	27	
	3125	3092		444	28	
	3126	3093		444	29	
	3127	3094		444	30	
	3128	3095		444	31	
	3129	3096		444	32	
	3130	3097		444	33	
	3131	3098		446	34	
	3132	3099		446	35	
	3133	3100		446	1	2071
	3134	3101		446	2	2072
	3135	3102		446	3	2072
	3136	3103	360			
	3137	3104	360			
	3138	3105	360			
	3139	3106	360			
	3140	3107	360			
	3141	3108	360	446	9	
	3142	3109	360			

TABLE 5—CIVIL CODE OF 1870 TO CODE NAPOLÉON

1976–2013 Revision of the Civil Code Art.	Civil Code 1870 Art.	Civil Code 1825 Art.	Projet Civil Code 1825 Page	Civil Code 1808 Page	Civil Code 1808 Art.	Code Napoléon 1804 Art.
	Book III—Of The Different Modes Of Acquiring The Ownership Of Things					
	3143	3110	361			
	3144	3111	361			
	3145	3112	361			
	3146	3113	361			
	3147	3114	361			
	3148	3115	361			
	3149	3116	361			
	3150	3117	361			
	3152	3119	362			
	3153	3120	362			
	3154	3121	362	446	4	
	3155	3122	362			
	3156	3123	362			
	3157	3124	362	446	5	2073
	3158	3125	362	446	6	2074(1)
	3159	3126	362			
	3162	3129	363	446	8	2076
	3163	3130		448	10	
	3164	3131		448	11	2082(1)
	3165	3132	363	448	12	2078
	3166	3133		448	13	2079
	3167	3134		448	14	2080
	3168	3135		448	15	
	3169	3136		448	16	2081
	3170	3137	364			
	3171	3138		448	17	2083
	3172	3139		448	18	
	3173	3140		448	19	
	3174	3141		448	20	
	3175	3142		448	21	
	3176	3143		448	22	2085
	3177	3144		450	23	2086
	3178	3145		450	24	2087
	3179	3146		450	25	2088
	3180	3147		450	26	2089
	3181	3148		450	27	2091
	3182	3149	364			2092
	3183	3150	364	468	67(1)	2093
	3184	3151	365	468	67(2)	2094
	3185	3152	365			
	3186	3153	365	468	68	2095
	3187	3154		468	69	2096
	3188	3155		468	70	2097
	3189	3156	365	468	71	2099
	3190	3157		468	72	2100
	3191	3158	365	468	73	2101
	3192	3159	366			
	3193	3160	366			
	3194	3161	366			
	3195	3162	366			
	3196	3163	366			
	3197	3164	366			
	3198	3165	367			
	3199	3166	367			
	3200	3167	367			
	3201	3168	367			
	3202	3169	367			
	3203	3170	367			
	3204	3171	367			
	3205	3172	368			

TABLE 5—CIVIL CODE OF 1870 TO CODE NAPOLÉON

1976–2013 Revision of the Civil Code Art.	Civil Code 1870 Art.	Civil Code 1825 Art.	Projet Civil Code 1825 Page	Civil Code 1808 Page	Art.	Code Napoléon 1804 Art.
	Book III—Of The Different Modes Of Acquiring The Ownership Of Things					
	3206	3173	368			
	3207	3174	368			
	3208	3175	368			
	3209	3176	368			
	3210	3177	368			
	3211	3178	368			
	3212	3179	368			
	3213	3180	369			
	3214	3181	369			
	3215	3182	369			
	3216	3183	369			
	3217	3184	369	468	74	2102
			370	468	74	2102
	3218	3185	370			
	3219	3186	370			
	3220	3187	370			
	3221	3188	370			
	3222	3189	370			
	3323	3190	371			
	3224	3191	371			
	3225	3192	371			
	3226	3193	371			
	3227	3194	371			
	3228	3195	371			
	3229	3196	372	468	74	2102
	3230	3197	372			
	3231	3198	372			
	3232	3199	372			
	3233	3200	372			
	3234	3201	372			
	3235	3202	372			
	3236	3203	372			
	3237	3204	373			
	3238	3205	373			
	3239	3206	374			
	3240	3207	374			
	3241	3208	374			
	3242	3209	374			
	3243	3210	374			
	3244	3211	374			
	3245	3212	374			
	3246	3213	374			
	3247	3214	374			
	3248	3215	375			
	3249	3216	375	470	75	2103
	3250	3217	376	470	75	
	3251	3218	376	470	75	2103
	3252	3219	376	470	76	2104
	3253	3220	376	470	77	2105
	3254	3221	377			
	3255	3222	377			
	3256	3223	377			
	3257	3224	377			
	3258	3225	377			
	3259	3226	377			
	3260	3227	377			
	3261	3228	378			
	3262	3229	378			
	3263	3230	378	468	74	2102
	3264	3231	378			

TABLE 5—CIVIL CODE OF 1870 TO CODE NAPOLÉON

1976–2013 Revision of the Civil Code Art.	Civil Code 1870 Art.	Civil Code 1825 Art.	Projet Civil Code 1825 Page	Civil Code 1808 Page	Art.	Code Napoléon 1804 Art.
		Book III—Of The Different Modes Of Acquiring The Ownership Of Things				
	3265	3232	378			
	3266	3233	378			
	3267	3234	378			
	3268	3235	378			
	3269	3236	379			
	3270	3237	379			
	3271	3238	379			2108
	3272	3239	379			2110
	3273	3240	380			
	3274	3241	380			2113
	3276	3243	380			2107
	3277	3244	380	472	81	2180(1, 2, 3)
3278	3278	3245	381			
	3284	3251	382			
3279	3278	3245	381			
3280	3282	3249	381	452	3	2114
	3310	3278	385			2133
3281	3283	3250	382			2115
3282	3284	3251	382			
	3285	3252	382			
	3299	3266	383			
3283	3286	3253	382	452	4	2116
	3288	3255	382	456	30	
3284	3287	3254	382	452	4	2117
3285	3288	3255	382	456	30	
3286	3289	3256	382	458	36, 38	2118, 2120
3287	3290	3257	382	452	1	
	3305	3272	384	452	5	2127
				458	38	2120
			381	452	6	
3288	3306	3273	384			2129(1)
		3274	384			
	3309	3277	385			2132
3289						
3290	3300	3267	384	458	32	2124
	3301	3268	384	452	7	2125
3291						
3292	3304	3271	384			
	3307	3275	384			
	3308	3276	384			2129(2)
3293	3291	3258	383			
	3292	3259	383			
3294						
3295	3295	3262	383			
	3296	3263	383			
	3297	3264	383			
	3299	3266	383			
3296						
3297	3291	3258	383			
3298	3292	3259	383			
	3293	3260	383			
3299	3321	3289	386	452	8	2123(1)
3300	3322	3290	386	454	9	
3301	3311	3279	385	454	15(1)	
	3312	3280	385	454	16	
3302	3313	3281	385	454	15(2)	2121
			381	454	18	
	3320	3288	386			2122

669

TABLE 5—CIVIL CODE OF 1870 TO CODE NAPOLÉON

1976–2013 Revision of the Civil Code Art.	Civil Code 1870 Art.	Civil Code 1825 Art.	Projet Civil Code 1825 Page	Civil Code 1808 Page	Art.	Code Napoléon 1804 Art.
		Book III—Of The Different Modes Of Acquiring The Ownership Of Things				
	3328	3296	387			2123(2)
3303	3313	3281	385	454	15(2)	2121
	3320	3288	386			2122
	3328	3296	387			2123(2)
3304	3323	3291	386	454	9	
	3324	3292	386	454	10	
3305	3326	3294	386	454	12	2123(4)
3306	3327	3295	387	454	13	
3307	3397	3360		460	39	
3311						
3312						
3313						
3315	3343	3315	389			
	3344	3316	390			
3316	3407	3370		462	48	2175
3317						
3318	3407	3370		462	48	2175
3319	3411	3374	398	472	81	2180
	3320	3346	3318	390		2146(1)
	3347					
	3348					
	3357					
		3319	390	464	53(1, 2)	
		3320	390	464	53(3)	
3321	3348					
	3366	3330	392	466	63	2148(1)
	3367	3331	392			
	3368	3332	392	464	54	
3337						
3338						
3339						
3340						
3341						
3342						
3343						
3344						
3345						
3346						
3347						
3348						
3349						
3350						
3351						
3352						
3353						
3354						
3355						
3356						
3357						
3358						
3359						
3360						
3361						
3362						
3363						
3364						
3365						
3366						
3367						
3368						

TABLE 5—CIVIL CODE OF 1870 TO CODE NAPOLÉON

1976–2013 Revision of the Civil Code Art.	Civil Code 1870 Art.	Civil Code 1825 Art.	Projet Civil Code 1825 Page	Civil Code 1808 Page	Civil Code 1808 Art.	Code Napoléon 1804 Art.
	**Book III—Of The Different Modes Of Acquiring The Ownership Of Things**						
3412	3412	3375		472	1	
	3413	3376		472	2	
	3414	3377		474	3	
	3420	3383		474	9	
3413	3415	3378		474	4	
3414	3416	3379		474	5	
3415(1)						
3415(2)	519	511		106	18	564
3416	3417	3380		474	6	
3417	3418	3381		474	7	
	3419	3382		474	8	
3418	3421	3384		474	10	
3419	3422	3385(1)	398	476	11	
		3385(2)	398			
3420	3423	3386		476	12	716
3421	3426	3389	399	476	16	2228
	3430	3393	399			
	3432	3395	399	476	17	
	3436	3399	400			
3422	3434	3397	400	476	19	
3423	3450	3413	402			
	3454	3417	402	478	23	
				480	29, 31	
3424	3436	3399	400			
3425	3428	3391	399			
3426	3437	3400	400			
	3498	3464	408			
3427	3488	3454	407	482	39	2230
3428	3438	3401	400			
	3445	3408	401			
3429	3433	3396	399	476	18	
3430	3440	3403	400			
3431	3427	3390	399			
	3429	3392	399			
	3442	3405	401			
	3444	3407	401			
3432	3443	3406	401			
3433	3447	3410	401			
	3448	3411	401			
	3449	3412	402			
3434	3449(2)	3412	402			
	3456	3419	403	480	27	
				480	28	
	3517	3483		484	51	2243
3435	3487	3453	407	482	38	2229
	3491	3457	407	482	41	2233
	3500	3466	408			
3436	3487	3453	407	482	38	2229
	3491	3457	407	482	41	2233
	3500	3466	408			
3437	3426	3389	399	476	16	2228
	3433	3396	399	476	18	
3438	3446	3409	401			
	3489	3455	407	482	39	2231
3439	3441	3404	400			
	3440					
3441	3493	3459	408	484	43	2235
	3496	3462	408			
3442	3493	3459	408	484	43	2235
	3494	3460	408			

TABLE 5—CIVIL CODE OF 1870 TO CODE NAPOLÉON

1976–2013 Revision of the Civil Code Art.	Civil Code 1870 Art.	Civil Code 1825 Art.	Projet Civil Code 1825 Page	Civil Code 1808 Page	Civil Code 1808 Art.	Code Napoléon 1804 Art.
\multicolumn{7}{c}{Book III—Of The Different Modes Of Acquiring The Ownership Of Things}					
	3495	3461	408	484	44	
3443	3492	3458	407	484	42	2234
3444	3455	3418	403	478	26	
3445	3457	3420	403	482	32	2219
3446	3458	3421	403			
3447	3457	3420	403	482	32	2219
	3459	3422	404			
	3528	3494	412			
	3530	3496	412			
3448	3546	3511	414			
	3529	3495	412			
3449	3460	3423		482	33	2220
3450	3461	3424		482	34	2221
3451	3462	3425		482	35	2222
3452	3463	3426	404			2223
	3464	3427	404	482	36	2224
3453	3466	3429		482	37	2225
3454	3467	3430	404	486	64	2260
3455	3468	3431	404			
3456	3469	3432	404			
3457	3470	3433	404			
3458						
3459						
3460						
3461						
3462	3518	3484		484	52	2244, 2246
3463	3519	3485	411			2247
3464	3520	3486		484	53	2248
3465	3517	3483		484	51	2243
3466						
3467	3521	3487	411			2251
3468	3522	3488		486	56	2252
3469	3523	3489		486	57	2253
			411	486	61	2257
3470	3526	3492		486	62	2258
	3527	3493		486	63	2259
3471						
3472						
3473	3474	3437	405			
3474	3478	3442	405	486	67	2265
		3443	405	488	69	2266
		3444	406			
3475	3479	3445	406			
3476	3487	3453	407	482	38	2229
3477	3490	3456	407	482	40	2232
	3491	3457	407	482	41	2233
	3510	3476		484	45	2236
	3511	3477		484	46	2237
	3514	3480	410	484	48	2240
3478	3512	3478	410			2238
	3515	3481	410			
3479	3513	3479		484	47	2239
3480	3451	3414	402	478	21(1, 2)	
3481	3452	3415	402	478	21(3)	
				478	22	
				478	24	
				478	25	
	3480	3446	406			
	3481	3447	406	488	71	2268

TABLE 5—CIVIL CODE OF 1870 TO CODE NAPOLÉON

1976–2013 Revision of the Civil Code Art.	Civil Code 1870 Art.	Civil Code 1825 Art.	Projet Civil Code 1825 Page	Civil Code 1808 Page	Art.	Code Napoléon 1804 Art.
	Book III—Of The Different Modes Of Acquiring The Ownership Of Things						
3482	3482	3448	406	488	72	2269
3483	3483	3449	406			
	3484	3450	406			
	3485	3451	406	488	68	
	3486	3452	406	488	70	2267
3484						
3485	3497	3463	408			
3486	3475	3438	405			
		3439	405	488	74	
	3499	3465	408	486	66	
	3500	3466	408			
	3501	3467	409			
	3502	3468	409			
3487	3503	3469	409			
3488	3505	3471	409			
3489	3476	3440	405			
	3505	3471	409			
3490	3506	3472	409	488	75	2279
3491	3509	3475	410			
3492	3536(1)	3501(1)	413			
	3537(2)	3502(2)	413			
3493	3537(3)	3502(3)	413			
3494	3534	3499	412		77	2271
	3538	3503	413		78	2272, 2273, 2277
3495	3535	3500	412	488	77	2274
3496	3539	3504	413			2276(1)
	3556	3522	416			
				490	1	
				490	2	
				490	3	
				490	4	
				490	5	
				490	6	2205
				490	7	
3497	3542	3507	414			
3498	3540	3505	413			
3499	3544	3508	414			
3500	3545	3509		488	73	2270
		3510	414			
3501	3547					
3502	3548	3512	414	486	65	2262
		3513	414			
3503	3552	3517	415	484	54	2249
3504	3553	3518	415	486	55	2250
3505						
3505.1						
3505.2						
3505.3						
3505.4						
3506	3556	3522	416			
				490	1	
				490	2	
				490	3	
				490	4	
				490	5	
				490	6	2205
				490	7	

TABLE 5—CIVIL CODE OF 1870 TO CODE NAPOLÉON

1976–2013 Revision of the Civil Code Art.	Civil Code 1870 Art.	Civil Code 1825 Art.	Projet Civil Code 1825 Page	Civil Code 1808 Page Art.	Code Napoléon 1804 Art.
\multicolumn{6}{c}{Book IV—Conflict of Laws}
3515					
3516					
3517					
3518					
3519					
3520					
3521					
3522					
3523					
3524					
3525					
3526					
3527					
3528					
3529					
3530					
3531					
3532					
3533					
3534					
3535					
3536					
3537					
3538					
3539					
3540					
3541					
3542					
3543					
3544					
3545					
3546					
3547					
3548					
3549					

INDEX TO TITLE 9

ABANDONED OR UNCLAIMED PROPERTY
    Generally, **9:151 et seq.**
Administrator, **9:167**
Agents, property held by, **9:163**
Application of law, foreign transactions, **9:178**
Auction, public sale, **9:164**
Bank deposits, **9:154, 9:155**
Blighted property, acquisitive prescription, **9:5633**
Certificates of ownership, relieving holder of liability, **9:162**
Certified checks, presumptions, **9:154**
Claims, **9:166 et seq.**
Clocks, **9:4701 et seq.**
Compensation and salaries, **9:166**
Costs, examination of records, **9:172**
Courts holding property, **9:154**
Credit unions, deposits, **9:154**
Custody of state, **9:162, 9:166**
Defenses, good faith payment or delivery by holder, **9:162**
Delivery of property, **9:160**
Deposits, **9:155, 9:165**
    Banks, **9:155**
    Courts, **9:164**
    State treasury, **9:165**
    Utilities, **9:154**
Destruction or disposition, property having insubstantial commercial value, **9:170**
Dissolution of business associations, **9:164**
Dividends,
    Bank deposits, **9:154, 9:163**
    Business associations, **9:163, 9:173**
    Crediting, **9:163**
    Owner entitlement, **9:163**
Dry cleaners, **9:4687 et seq.**
Endowment insurance policies, **9:158**
Escrows and escrow accounts, **9:165**
Examination, records, **9:172**
Federal courts holding property, **9:164**
Fiduciaries, property held by, **9:163**
Filing of claims, **9:167**
Fines and penalties, **9:176**
Foreign countries, application of law, **9:178**
Gift certificates, **9:154**
Gold, **9:4701 et seq.**
Governmental custody, prescription, **9:171**
Income, **9:154**
Increments, owner entitlement, **9:163**
Intangible interests, business associations, **9:154**
Intangible personal property, taking custody, **9:156**
Interest,
    Bank deposits, **9:154**
    Business associations, **9:173**
    Claims, **9:167**
    Failure to pay or deliver property, **9:176**
    Owner entitlement, **9:163**
    Remittance under protest, action to recover, **9:168**
    Utility deposits, **9:154**
Investment companies, **9:153, 9:154**
Joint stock associations, **9:153, 9:154**

ABANDONED OR UNCLAIMED PROPERTY—Cont'd
Jurisdiction, actions to recover, protest, **9:170**
Laundries, sale, **9:4687 et seq.**
Liability of holder, relief, **9:160**
Life insurance policies, **9:154**
Lists, notice and publication, **9:161, 9:164**
Mechanic's privileges and liens, **9:4803**
    Work, **9:4822**
Money orders, **9:154**
    Report of abandoned property, **9:159**
    Retention of records, **9:182**
Municipally owned utilities, deposits of consumers, **9:154**
Payment of property, **9:160**
Payroll checks, **9:154**
Political subdivisions holding property, **9:154**
Prescription, **9:171**
Presumptions, **9:154 et seq.**
Proceeds from public sale, deposit of funds, **9:165**
Protest, remittance under protest, actions to recover, **9:168**
Public authorities or public corporations holding property, **9:154**
Public sale, **9:164 et seq.**
Publication,
    Lists of abandoned property, **9:161, 9:169**
    Notice of public sale, **9:164**
Refusal of administrator to receive property, **9:167 et seq.**
Reimbursement, holder paying claims, **9:162**
Rents, **9:154**
Reports, **9:172**
    Failure to render, fines and penalties, **9:172**
    Requests, **9:172**
Repositories for safe keeping, contents, **9:155**
Royalties, **9:154**
Rules and regulations, **9:156, 9:180**
Safe deposit boxes, **9:155**
State agencies holding property, **9:156, 9:165**
State, custody of, **9:156**
Tailor shops, **9:4687 et seq.**
Taxidermists, disposition, **9:191, 9:192**
Time deposits, **9:154**
Travelers checks, **9:154**
    Report of abandoned property, **9:159**
    Retention of records, **9:173**
United States agencies and institutions holding property, **9:154**
Utility deposits, **9:154**
Wages, **9:154**

ABANDONMENT
Consumer credit, licensee's physical location, **9:3554**
Covenant marriage, divorce, **9:307**
Trust property claim, trustee's authority, **9:2121**

ABORTION
Damages, **9:2800.12**

ABUSE
Animals, this index
Domestic Abuse, generally, this index

INDEX TO TITLE 9

ACCESSION, ACCRETION AND AVULSION
Generally, 9:1101
Acquisition of property by alluvion not affected in certain cases, 9:1102
Change in ownership of land or water bottoms, minerals, oil and gas, leases, 9:1151

ACCOUNTANTS
Certified public accountants, boards and commissions, proceedings, prescription, 9:5604

ACCOUNTS AND ACCOUNTING
Abandoned or unclaimed property, escrow account, 9:165
Condominiums, 9:1123.116
Consumer credit,
    Examination of persons regulated, 9:3554, 9:3554.1, 9:3561.1
    Sales and transfers, licensees, 9:3561
Mortgages, keeper of property in foreclosure proceedings, 9:5138
Open accounts, collection, 9:2781.1

ACKNOWLEDGMENT
See, also, Authentic Acts, generally, this index
Electronic transactions, 9:2611
Illegitimate Children, this index
Negotiable instruments, interruption of prescription, 9:5807

ACQUISITIVE PRESCRIPTION
Blighted property, 9:5633

ACTION EN DESAVEU
Paternity, blood or tissue test, 9:396 et seq.

ACTS OF SALE AND CONVEYANCES
Bond for deed, generally, 9:2421 et seq.
    Cancellation,
        Default, 9:2945
            Foreclosure, holders of secured notes, 9:2944
            Notes for purchase price, 9:2946
        Encumbered property, 9:2942
            Escrow agent, payments to, 9:2943
            Mortgage notes, requiring from purchaser, 9:2946
            Release of encumbrance, 9:2946
        Escrow agent,
            Notice of default, service, 9:2945
            Payments to on encumbered property, 9:2943
        Foreclosure, 9:2944
        Guarantee, payment of mortgage or privilege, 9:2942
        Homestead exemption, 9:2948
        Offenses, encumbered real property, sales, 9:2942
        Payment, 9:2943 et seq.
            Authentic sale, 9:2946
            Encumbrance, balance to release, 9:2946
        Penalties, 9:2947
        Release, encumbrances, 9:2942, 9:2946
Curators, perfecting servitudes or flowage rights, 9:1511
Custodial trusts, designations, 9:2260.3
Dual contracts, 9:2989
Foreign trusts, records and recordation, 9:2262.2
Fraudulent contracts, 9:2989
Land fronting on or bounded by waterway, canal, etc., 9:2971 et seq.
Leases, security deposits, transfers, 9:3251
Legitime in trust, trust instrument restraining, 9:1843
Manufactured homes, recordation, immobilization, 9:1149.4
Navigable waters and beds by state to levee district, rescission and cancellation, 9:1101

ACTS OF SALE AND CONVEYANCES—Cont'd
New home warranties, transfer, 9:3148
Offenses, Orleans Parish, nonalienation certificate, notary or sheriff passing, 9:2928
Payment of taxes prior to transfer, 9:2901 et seq.
Power of attorney, military forces, 9:3871, 9:3882.1
Records and recordation,
    Foreign trusts, 9:2262.2
    Third parties protected, 9:2721
Taxation, payment, necessity, 9:2901 et seq.
Trusts and trustees, foreign trusts, records and recordation, 9:2262.3

ADJOINING LANDOWNERS
Agents causing damages, remedies, 9:2773
Contractors causing damages, remedies, 9:2773
Damages, construction work, public policy, 9:2773

ADOPTION
Generally, 9:461 et seq.
Age of person adopted or adopting, 9:461
Birth certificate, 9:464
Change of names. Names, post
Class trusts, members, 9:1892
Confidential or privileged information, 9:461
Electronic transactions, exemptions, 9:2603
In vitro human ova, adoptive implantation, 9:130
Names, change of name, 9:462
Notarial acts, 9:461
Persons over seventeen, 9:461
Persons who may adopt, 9:461
Recordation of adoption, 9:463
Records and recordation,
    Inspection, 9:461
    Notarial Act, adoption of person over seventeen, 9:461
Signature, notarial act of adoption, person over seventeen, 9:461

ADULT ADOPTION
Generally, 9:461 to 9:464
Birth certificate, 9:464
Recordation of adoption, 9:463

ADULTS
Adoption, 9:461, 9:462
Definitions,
    Custodial trusts, 9:2260.1
    Uniform Transfers to Minors Act, 9:751

ADVANCE FEE LOAN LAW
Generally, 9:3574.1 et seq.

ADVERTISEMENTS
Carpets and rugs, sale to satisfy privilege, 9:4681, 9:4685
Credit repair services organizations, 9:3573.3
Definitions, rental purchase agreements, 9:3352
Public administrator, appointment, 9:1583
Real estate timesharing, regulation, 9:1131.12
Rental purchase agreements, 9:3360
Self-service storage facilities, sales, privileges and liens, satisfaction, 9:4759

AERIAL PHOTOGRAPHS OR MOSAICS
Servitudes, attaching and recording, 9:2726

AFFIDAVITS
Arbitration, filing, 9:4214
Blood tests, paternity, 9:397.3

AFFIDAVITS—Cont'd
Child custody or visitation orders, violation, return of child, **9:343**
Compensation and salaries, deceased employees, surviving spouse and children, **9:1515**
Executory process, mortgages, obligations not paraphed for identification, **9:5555**
Inter vivos trust creation, attesting witnesses, **9:1752**
Mechanic's privileges and liens, inspections, **9:4820**
Mobile homes, remedies of mortgagees, **9:5363.1**
Name similarity, judgment mortgages, affidavits of distinction, **9:5501**
    Form, **9:5501.1**
Partition, community property, **9:2801**
Partnerships, foreign partnerships, registration statement, accompanying affidavit, **9:3422**
Real estate timesharing, declarations, **9:1131.4**
Surviving spouse, bank or credit union deposit payments, **9:1513**, **9:1514**
Trust interests, transfer or encumbrance of interest by beneficiary, **9:2003**

AFTERBORN CHILDREN
Persons in being and ascertainable, beneficiary status, **9:1803**

AGE
Adoption, person adopted or adopting, **9:461**
Definitions, home solicitation, **9:3541.21**
Volunteers, privileges and immunities, area agencies and councils, **9:2792.9**

AGENTS
Abandoned or unclaimed property, property held by agents, **9:163**
Definitions, real estate brokers and salespersons, **9:3891**
Power of attorney, military personnel, **9:3861 et seq.**

AGRICULTURAL LABOR AND EMPLOYMENT
Privileges, **9:5021**
    Thresherman's privilege on crops,
        Right of privilege, **9:4523**

AGRICULTURAL PRODUCTS
Assignment, proceeds of crop financing, **9:3121**
Cotton, generally, this index
Damages, breach of lease, **9:3201**, **9:3203**
Donated food, limitation of liability, **9:2799.3**, **9:2799.6**
Financing proceeds, assignment, **9:3121**
Fines and penalties,
    Disposal or sale by lessee of lessor's share, **9:3204**
Injury, destruction or loss of profits, prescription, **9:5601**
Ownership, lessor and lessee, **9:3204**
Privileges,
    Chartered cities and towns, **9:4541**
    Threshermen, combinemen, etc., **9:4523**
    Vendor, **9:4541 et seq.**
    Water furnisher, **9:4522**
        Crop share agreement, **9:4522.1**
Producers, privilege on assets of insolvent or bankrupt purchasers, **9:5021**
Sales of movables, lessor's share, **9:3204**
Sugar Cane, generally, this index
Warehouses and Warehousemen, generally, this index
Water supplier, crop share agreement, **9:4522.1**

AGRICULTURE
Assignment, crop financing proceeds, **9:3121**
Consumer credit, exemptions, **9:3512**

AGRICULTURE—Cont'd
Donated food, limitation of liability, **9:2799.3**, **9:2799.6**
Gleaning, privileges and immunities, **9:2800.4**
Leases,
    Abandonment, lease for cultivation of land, lessee's liability, **9:3201**
    Breach, **9:3201 et seq.**
    Crop, ownership, **9:3204**
    Cultivation of land, lessee's failure, liability, **9:3201**, **9:3203**
    Damages, **9:3202**
    Refusal to permit cultivation, damages, **9:3203**
Loans,
    Accrued interest, recovery of interest upon, **9:3509.2**
    Adjustable interest rate loans, **9:3509.1**
Privileges and immunities, landowners, **9:2800.4**
Trespass, liability of owner, injury, death or loss from unauthorized entry, **9:2800.4**

AIR CONDITIONING
New home warranties, **9:3141 et seq.**

AIR POLLUTION
Public trust, purposes, **9:2341 et seq.**

AIRCRAFT
Operating under influence of alcohol or drugs,
    Injury or death of operator, privileges and immunities, **9:2798.4**
    Privileges and immunities, injury or death of operator, **9:2798.4**
Photographs, servitudes, attaching and recording, **9:2726**
Priorities and preferences, privileges, **9:4512**
Privileges,
    Maintenance and repairs, **9:4511**, **9:4512**
    Records and recordation, privileges, **9:4512**
    Sales, privileges, **9:4512**
    Storage, **9:4513**

AIRPORTS
Public trust, purposes, **9:2341 et seq.**

ALCOHOLIC BEVERAGES
Damages, limitation of liability, injuries or losses connected with sale, **9:2800.1**
Dram Shop Act, limitation of liability, **9:2800.1**

ALIENS
Trustees, resident aliens, qualifications, **9:1783**

ALIMONY
See, also, Support, generally, this index
Actions between spouses, **9:291**
Arrearages, actions for, attorney fees and costs, **9:375**
Orders, retroactive effect, **9:310**
Spousal support. Support, this index
Trust property, seizure of beneficiary's interest, **9:2005**

ALTERNATIVE DISPUTE RESOLUTION
Children and minors, custody, parenting coordinators, **9:358.1 et seq.**

AMBULANCES
Definitions, privileges, services and supplies, **9:4751**
Privileges, proceeds from insurance for third party, **9:4751 et seq.**
Public trust, purposes, **9:2341 et seq.**

INDEX TO TITLE 9

AMUSEMENTS AND SPORTS
Medical care and treatment, volunteers, liability, **9:2798**

ANHYDROUS AMMONIA
Tanks, placing on land for storage, movable property, **9:1106**

ANIMALS
Consumer credit, **9:3510 et seq.**
Cruelty, scientific research, unauthorized release, **9:2799.4**
Exhibitions, privileges and immunities, **9:2795.1**
Fish and Game, generally, this index
Laboratories, unauthorized release, **9:2799.4**
Privileges,
    Feed for livestock used on public works, **9:4921 et seq.**
    Horses, feed and medicine, **9:4661**
Sanctuaries, limitation of liability, **9:2796.3**

APARTMENTS
Construction projects, machinery and equipment, limiting liability, **9:2775**
Residential Truth in Construction Act, **9:4851 et seq.**

APPORTIONMENT OF TAXES
Estate Tax Apportionment Law, **9:2431 through 2439**
    Action by nonresident, reciprocity, **9:2437**
    Action to recover amount of tax or deficiency from person interested in estate, **9:2436**
        Time of filing, liability of fiduciary, **9:2436**
    Allowance for exemptions, deductions and credits, **9:2435**
    Application of provisions, **9:2438**
    Apportionment of tax liability among persons interested in estate, **9:2432**
    Fiduciary right to withhold or recover proportion of tax attributable to person interested in estate, **9:2434**
    Security by person interested in estate for payment of tax, **9:2434**

APPRAISERS
Community property, partition, **9:2801**
    Valuation of goodwill, **9:2801.2**
Interdiction proceedings, inventories, fees, **9:1423**
Jewelry, gems and watches, unclaimed, private sale for charges, **9:4701**

ARBITRATION
    See, also, Mediation, generally, this index
    Generally, **9:4201 et seq.**
Affidavits, filing, **9:4214**
Agreements, **9:4201**
    Enforcement, **9:4201, 9:4203**
    Federal legislation, exemption from state act, **9:4216**
    Filing, **9:4214**
    Irrevocability, **9:4201**
    Stay of proceedings brought in violation of, **9:4202**
    Trial of issue, **9:4203**
Appeals, **9:4215**
Application heard as motion, **9:4205**
Application of act, restriction, **9:4216**
Arbitrators,
    Appointment, **9:4204, 9:4214**
    Award upon matter not submitted, correction, **9:4211**
    Consent to proceeding with less than all arbitrators, **9:4206**
    Misconduct, vacation of award, **9:4210**
    Partiality or corruption, vacation of award, **9:4210**
    Selection of appointment of additional arbitrator or umpire, filing record, **9:4214**
Books, papers, memoranda, etc., use as evidence, **9:4206**

ARBITRATION—Cont'd
Citation, **9:4217**
Confirmation of award, **9:4209**
Corruption, award procured by, vacation, **9:4210**
Custody of children, **9:331 et seq.**
Default,
    Application for stay of trial, **9:4202**
    Remedy, **9:4203**
Dental services or supplies contracts, **9:4230 et seq.**
Depositions, **9:4207**
Divorce, postseparation family violence relief, **9:363**
Evidence,
    Books, etc., **9:4206**
    Refusal of arbitrators to hear, vacation of award, **9:4210**
Filing award or orders, **9:4214**
Form of award imperfect, modification, **9:4211**
Formalities of award, **9:4208**
Fraud, vacation of award, **9:4210**
Hearing,
    Application for order directing arbitration, **9:4203**
    Less than full number of arbitrators, **9:4206**
    Refusal to postpone, vacating award, **9:4210**
Judgments and decrees, **9:4212**
    Appeal, **9:4215**
    Docketing, **9:4214**
    Enforcement, **9:4214**
Jury trial, right to arbitration, **9:4203**
Medical services or supplies contracts, **9:4230 et seq.**
Miscalculation of figures, correction of award, **9:4211**
Misconduct, vacation of award, **9:4210**
Modifying or correcting award, **9:4211**
Motions,
    Application heard as, **9:4205**
    Confirm award, jurisdiction, notice, **9:4209**
    Modify or correct award, **9:4211**
    Service of notice of motion, **9:4209, 9:4213**
    Stay of proceedings, **9:4213**
    Vacate award, **9:4210**
New home warranties, **9:3149**
Orders,
    Appeal, **9:4215**
    Confirming award, **9:4209**
    Directing, **9:4203**
    Filing, **9:4214**
    Modifying or correcting award, **9:4211**
    Vacation of award, **9:4210**
Partiality, vacating award, **9:4210**
Petition for, **9:4203**
Power of attorney, military personnel, powers granted, **9:3870**
Record of proceedings, filing, **9:4214**
Rehearing, direction for, **9:4210**
Signatures,
    Award, **9:4208**
    Summons to witness, **9:4206**
Stay of proceedings, **9:4213**
Undue means, award procured by, vacation, **9:4210**
Vacation of award, **9:4210**
Visitation, children, **9:331 et seq.**
Witnesses,
    Contempt, **9:4206**
    Fees, **9:4206**
    Summoning, **9:4206**
Writing,
    Agreement, **9:4201 et seq.**
    Award, **9:4208**

ARBITRATION—Cont'd
Writing—Cont'd
　Consent to proceeding with less than all arbitrators, **9:4206**
　Extension of time, filing, **9:4214**
　Notice of application to confirm award, **9:4209**
　Summoning witnesses, **9:4206**

ARCHITECTS
Fraud, affidavits of inspection, mechanic's privileges and liens, **9:4820**
Hazardous waste, limitation of liability, **9:2800.3**
Mechanic's privileges and liens, **9:4801 et seq.**
Privileges,
　Immovables, **9:4801 et seq.**
　Private works, **9:4801 et seq.**

ASBESTOS
Abatement, prescription, actions and proceedings, **9:5644**
Limitation of liability, removal, abatement, or clean-up services, **9:2800.3**

ASSIGNMENTS
Application of law, secured transactions, **9:4401**
Chattel mortgages, incorporeal rights, **9:5386 et seq.**
Claims for collection, **9:3051**
Collateral assignments, leases or rents, **9:4401**
Conditional assignments, leases or rents, **9:4401**
Controlled dangerous substances, dealer liability, **9:2800.65**
Creditors. Insolvency, generally, this index
Credits, collection, **9:3051**
Crop financing proceeds, **9:3121**
Definitions, Uniform Law for Simplification of Fiduciary Security Transfers, **9:3831**
Evidence, fiduciary's authority to make, **9:3834**
Foreclosure, signatures on obligations presumed authentic, **9:4422**
Gas and oil. Minerals, Oil and Gas, this index
Insolvency of assignor, perfected security interests, **9:4401**
Military forces, power of attorney, **9:3870**
　Immovables, **9:3882.1**
Notice, proceeds of crop financing, **9:3121**
Rents, **9:4401**

ASSIGNMENTS FOR BENEFIT OF CREDITORS
Stock registered in name of assignee of fiduciary, **9:3832**

ASSOCIATIONS AND SOCIETIES
Appearance in court, **9:1051**
Consumer credit, exclusions, **9:3512**
Directors, tort liability, **9:2792**
Donations, immovable property, **9:1051**
Estates, power to acquire and possess, **9:1051**
Holiday in Dixie parades, limitation of liability, **9:2796**
Homeowners Association Act, **9:1141.1 et seq.**
Homeowners associations, privileges and immunities, **9:2792.7**
Immovables, transfer of title, **9:1051**
Incorporation, transfer of title, notice, exemption, **9:1051**
Investment of funds, **9:2337.1 et seq.**
Liabilities, **9:1051**
Mardi Gras parades, limitation of liability, **9:2796**
Mineral rights, transfer of title, **9:1051**
Mortgages, immovable property, **9:1051**
Parades, ethnic parades, limitation of liability, **9:2796.1**
Powers and liabilities, **9:1051**
Predial leases, transfer of title, **9:1051**
Predial servitudes, transfer of title, **9:1051**
Quasi offenses, liability of officers or directors, **9:2792**

ASSOCIATIONS AND SOCIETIES—Cont'd
Saint Patrick's Day parade, damages, limitation of liability, **9:2796.1**
Sales, immovables, prescription, **9:5681**
Tort liability, officers or directors, **9:2792**

ASSUMED OR FICTITIOUS NAMES
Consumer credit, **9:3515**

ATHLETICS
Medical care and treatment, volunteers, liability, **9:2798**

ATTACHMENT
　See, also, Seizures, generally, this index
Controlled dangerous substances, dealer liability, **9:2800.72**
Foreign corporation, sale, prescription, **9:5641**
Warehouse Receipts, generally, this index

ATTORNEY FEES
Abandoned or unclaimed property, agreements to locate reported property, **9:177**
Accounts and accounting, acceptance of funds to procure legal representation, **9:2776**
Aircraft, privileges, sales of movables, **9:4512**
Checks,
　Nonsufficient funds, collection, **9:2782**
　Stop payment, **9:2782.2**
Condominiums, **9:1121.104**
Consumer loan brokers, fine recoveries, **9:3572.12**
Covenant marriage, separation from bed and board, **9:309**
Credit cards,
　Liabilities, receipts, **9:3518.3**
　Unsolicited cards, mail and mailing, damages, **9:3518.2**
Credit repair services organization, **9:3573.10**
　District attorneys, criminal proceedings, **9:3573.13**
Credit reporting agencies, **9:3571.1**
Debtors and creditors, open accounts, collection, **9:2781**
Insurance, consumer credit, **9:3555**
Leases, action for deposit, **9:3253**
Mechanic's privileges and liens, **9:4833**
Mobile homes and manufactured housing, repossession, **9:5363.1**
Negotiable Instruments, this index
New home warranties, violations, **9:3149**
Open accounts, collection, **9:2781**
Paternity actions, **9:398.1**
Public administrators, **9:1589**
Separation from bed and board, covenant marriage, **9:309**
Stop payment, checks, **9:2782.2**
Successions and succession proceedings, designation of attorney by testator, **9:2448**
Sureties, failure to pay obligations, bonds, **9:3902**
Trusts and trustees, charges against income, **9:2156**
Wells, privileges, **9:4862**

ATTORNEY GENERAL
State succeeding to immovable property,
　Compromise of rights and claims, **9:1612**
　Disposition of funds, **9:1613**
　Retention instead of sale, **9:1611**

ATTORNEYS
Accounts and accounting, acceptance of funds to procure legal representation, **9:2776**
Central registry, will information, **9:2446**
Checks, nonsufficient funds, collection, fees, **9:2782**
Debtors and creditors, open accounts, collection, fees, **9:2781**

INDEX TO TITLE 9

ATTORNEYS—Cont'd
Disbarment, discipline or suspension, abuse of children, certificate of merit, 9:2800.9
Mechanic's privileges and liens, fees, 9:4833
Mediation, 9:4101 et seq.
Military forces, power of attorney, powers granted, 9:3870
Mortgages, affidavits, cancellation, 9:5167.1
Prescription, malpractice actions, 9:5605
Theft of client funds, 9:5605.1
Trusts and trustees, 9:2241
Visitation, protective and remedial measures, 9:345

AUCTIONS AND AUCTIONEERS
Abandoned or unclaimed property, public sale, 9:173
Act of sale of immovable executed within 24 hours, 9:3160
Adjudication to bidder, 9:3157 et seq.
    Auction sales not under order of court, 9:3157 et seq., 9:3163, 9:3165
    Authority of persons bidding in name of another, liability for consequences, 9:3165
    Completion of sale by adjudication, 9:3158
    Indorsement, validity of adjudication when seller does not accept indorser, 9:3163
    Presence or representation of bidder to whom adjudication made, 9:3165
    Price before delivery, payment in cash, 9:3159
    Retention of price and possession until act of sale passes, 9:3160
    Second sale, bidder's failure to pay, 9:3161, 9:3162
    Time act of sale passes, 9:3160
    Title to purchaser, completion on recording adjudication, 9:3173
Delivery, payment of price as condition, 9:3159
Forced sale defined, auction, 9:3152
General rules governing, 9:3154
Indorsement of notes,
    Purchaser required to give name of indorser, 9:3163
    Vendor refusing to accept solvent indorser, liability of, 9:3164
Laundries, unclaimed property, 9:4687
Manner of conducting sale, 9:3156, 9:3157
Prescription, judicial sales, 9:5622
Presence of person at sale, 9:3165
Resale, 9:3161, 9:3162
Voluntary sale, definitions, 9:3152, 9:3154

AUDITS AND AUDITORS
Electronic transactions, 9:2612
Public administrator's records, 9:1586
Public trusts, 9:2346

AUTHENTIC ACTS
Bond for deed, satisfaction of requirements, 9:2946
Copies, foreign judgment or decree of emancipation, 9:901
Family home, designation, 9:2801
Foreign testament, 9:2424
Judicial sale, succession property, act passed before notary not required, 9:3173

BAIL
Abandoned or unclaimed property, presumptions, cash bill bonds, 9:154

BANK DEPOSITS AND COLLECTIONS
Generally, 9:2095
Clearing houses, food banks, donations, limitation of liability, 9:2799.3

BANK DEPOSITS AND COLLECTIONS—Cont'd
Fiduciaries,
    Authority of tutor or curator, 9:734
    Deposit to personal credit, duties and liabilities of bank, 9:3809
    Liability of bank for checks drawn on account, 9:3807
    Trustees, check in name of two or more, duties of bank and holder, 9:3810
Interest-bearing accounts, payments to other than owner, 9:2789
Joint deposits, payment to surviving spouse without court proceedings, 9:1513

BANKRUPTCY
Fiduciary, trustee as, 9:3801
Mortgages, sales of property, 9:5251
Privileges,
    Assets of purchaser, producers of agricultural and dairy products, 9:5021
    Sales of property, 9:5031

BANKS AND BANKING
Adverse claims, stock transfer by bank as fiduciary, 9:3835
Assignment of stock held as fiduciary, 9:3833
Confidential or privileged information, personal credit information, 9:3571
Credit information, confidentiality, 9:3571
Crop financing proceeds, assignment, 9:3121
Exemptions, notification filing requirements, 9:3563.1
Fiduciaries,
    Bank as, 9:3801 et seq.
    Checks upon principal's account, 9:3808
    Deposit of funds to personal credit, duties and liabilities of bank, 9:3809
    Discharging personal obligation of fiduciary, use of fiduciary funds, 9:3807
Instruments issued or certified by bank, abandoned or unclaimed property, 9:154
Interest-bearing accounts, payments to other than owner, 9:2789
Investments, trust funds, 9:2097
Personal credit information, confidentiality, 9:3571
Records and recordation, customers, financial records, disclosure, 9:3571
Securities, registration in name of as fiduciary, 9:3832
Subpoenas, dissemination of credit information, 9:3571
Successions and succession proceedings, surviving spouse, account, release, 9:1513
Sureties, deposits, joint control, 9:3904
Transfer of fiduciary accounts, 9:2130

BATTURE
See, also, Accession, Accretion and Avulsion, generally, this index
Cities and towns, 9:1102
Riparian owner's action for batture not necessary for public use, 9:1102

BAYOUS
Beds and waters, state ownership, 9:1101

BAYS
Change in ownership of land or water bottoms, minerals, oil and gas, leases, 9:1151
State ownership, 9:1101

BEDDING AND UPHOLSTERED FURNITURE
Privilege, making or repairs, 9:4502

I–6

INDEX TO TITLE 9

BEES
Consumer credit, 9:3510 et seq.

BENEFICIARIES
Generally, 9:1801 et seq.
Charge on interest, indemnification of trustee, 9:2194
Class trusts, 9:1893
Conditions, interest of beneficiary, 9:1961
Definitions, custodial trusts, 9:2260.1
Income beneficiary, 9:1961 et seq.
    Definitions, 9:1725
Military forces, power of attorney, 9:3861 et seq.
Principal beneficiaries, definitions, 9:1725

BICYCLES
Private property, personal injuries, limiting liability, 9:2795

BIDS AND BIDDING
Deep water port commission, lease or sublease of commission property, 9:1102.2
Judicial Sales, this index
Public sales, demand for bids, 9:3156
Unclaimed property, public sale, 9:164

BILLS OF LADING
Self-service storage facilities, exemption, 9:4757

BIOTECHNOLOGY
Human embryos, in vitro fertilized human ovum, 9:121 et seq.

BLOCK SAFE-HOUSES
Damages, liability, 9:2800.5

BLOOD
Community blood centers, malpractice, prescription, 9:5628
Liability, users of blood, organs or tissue, 9:2797
Nonprofit community blood banks, limitation of liability, 9:2797

BLOOD BANKS
Limitation of liability, 9:2797
Malpractice, prescription, 9:5628

BLOOD TESTS
Illegitimate Children, this index
Paternity, 9:396 et seq.
    Affidavits, 9:397.3
    Chain of custody, 9:397.2
    Disavowal, 9:398.2
    Reports, 9:397.3

BOARDS AND COMMISSIONS
Actions and proceedings, limitation of liability, 9:2800
Definitions,
    Manufactured homes, 9:1149.2
    Real estate brokers and salespersons, 9:3891
    Support of persons, 9:315.31
Limitation of liability, board or commission of political subdivision, 9:2792.4
Notice, condition of things within care and custody, limitation of liability, 9:2800

BOND FOR DEED CONTRACTS
Generally, 9:2941 et seq.

BONDS
Institutional funds, investments, 9:2337.1 et seq.
Military forces, power of attorney, powers granted, 9:3872

BONDS—Cont'd
Public trust,
    Issuance, 9:2347
    Purposes, 9:2341
Uniform Law for Simplification of Fiduciary Security Transfers, 9:3831 et seq.

BONDS (OFFICERS AND FIDUCIARIES)
Actions and proceedings, public administrator, Orleans Parish, 9:1588
Child visitation orders, compliance, 9:342
Consumer loan brokers, 9:3572.8
Credit repair services organizations, 9:3573.4
Custodial trusts, 9:2260.13, 9:2260.14
Lis pendens, cancellation upon furnishing of security, 9:4835
Mobile homes, remedies of mortgagees, 9:5363.1
Newspapers,
    Distributors and dealers, interest on security bond, 9:3601
    Security by mortgage on plant equipment, name and good will, authority, 9:5103
Private works, bonding claims against, 9:4841
Public administrators, 9:1582, 9:1588
Real estate timesharing, 9:1131.4
    Escrow, 9:1131.16
Uniform Transfers to Minors Act, custodians, 9:765
Visitation orders, compliance, 9:342

BONFIRES
Limitation of liability, 9:2996.3

BOUNDARIES
Condominiums, relocation, 9:1122.114
False River, title of property, 9:1110
Servitudes, land acquired by state due to erosion or subsidence, mineral servitude, 9:1152

BRANDS, MARKS AND LABELS
Products liability, manufacturers, 9:2800.5

BROKERS
Consumer loan brokers, 9:3572.1 et seq.
Definitions,
    Real estate brokers and salespersons, 9:3891
    Uniform Transfers to Minors Act, 9:751
Military forces, power of attorney, powers granted, 9:3873

BUILDER'S LIEN ACT
Generally, 9:4801 et seq.

BUILDING CONTRACTS
Privileges and liens, 9:4801 et seq.
    Enforcement of privilege, procedure, 9:4802
Real estate appraiser privilege, 9:2781.2

BUILDING RESTRICTIONS
Homeowners association, 9:1141.4 et seq.

BUILDING STANDARDS
Definitions, new home warranties, 9:3143

BUILDINGS
Asbestos abatement, prescription, 9:5644
Blighted property, acquisitive prescription, 9:5633
Demolition, blighted property, 9:5633
Disposal or conversion, mortgagee's right of action, limitation of recovery, 9:5382
Encroachment on public places, 9:5627

INDEX TO TITLE 9

BUILDINGS—Cont'd
Inspection and inspectors, cities over 15,000, fraud, mechanic's privileges and liens, **9:4820**
Oil and gas wells, connected with, privilege, labor, services or supplies, **9:4861 et seq.**
Prescription,
    Action to remove encroachment on public places, **9:5627**
    Asbestos abatement, **9:5644**
    Encroachment on public way, **9:5627**
Real estate appraiser privilege, **9:2781.2**
Recreation, owner's duty of care, **9:2791**
Repairs, landlord's liability for injuries, failure to repair, **9:3221**
Riparian owners, construction and use, **9:1102.2**
Roads and highways, encroachment, removal, **9:5627**
Water wells, connected with, privilege for labor, services or supplies, **9:4861 et seq.**
Work, mechanic's privileges and liens, **9:4808**

BUSINESS AND COMMERCE
Consumer credit, exemptions, **9:3512**
Licenses and permits, support of persons, suspension, **9:315.30 et seq.**
Loans, adjustable interest rate loans, **9:3509.1**
Military forces, power of attorney, powers granted, **9:3875**
Personal injuries, liability, merchant, persons on premises, **9:2800.6**
Trustees, **9:2151**

BUTANE GAS
Tanks placed on land for storage as movable property, **9:1106**

CAMPS AND CAMPING
Private property, personal injuries, limiting liability, **9:2795**
Recreation, landowner, duty of care, **9:2791**

CANALS
Curators, sale or lease of right of way over and of ward, **9:731**
Servitudes, recording, **9:2726**
Toll canals, privilege on ships and vessels, **9:4741**
Transfer, land fronting or bounded by, effect, **9:2971 et seq.**
Tutors, sale or lease of right of way over land of ward, **9:731**

CARPETS AND RUGS
Cleaning and storage,
    Delivery on payment of charges, **9:4686**
    Remedies for unpaid charges, **9:4683**
Privilege, on, **9:4681 et seq.**
Unclaimed carpets or rugs, **9:4685**
    Payment to state, **9:4688**
    Recovery by owner, **9:4686**
Sale to satisfy privilege for cleaning or storage, **9:4684**

CARRIERS
See, also, Motor Carriers, generally, this index
Privileges, **9:4601**
    Water wells, trucking, towing or barging, **9:4861 et seq.**

CEMETERIES AND DEAD BODIES
Unclaimed bodies, burial, **9:1551, 9:1552**
Vandalism, institutional vandalism, damages, **9:2799.2**

CENTRAL REGISTRY FOR CONTRACTS OF PARTNERSHIP
Generally, **9:3401 et seq.**

CERTIFICATES AND CERTIFICATION
See, also, specific index headings

CERTIFICATES AND CERTIFICATION—Cont'd
Abuse of children, certificate of merit, **9:2800.9**
Birth certificates. Vital Statistics, this index
Common trust funds, **9:2128**
Fiduciary, appointment or authority, **9:3834**
Redemption, Federal Tax Lien Act, recordation and filing, **9:2725**

CERTIFICATES OF INDEBTEDNESS
Adjustable rate certificates, business, commerce, agriculture, **9:3509.1**

CERTIFICATES OF TITLE
Definitions, manufactured homes, **9:1149.2**

CERTIFIED COPIES
Authentic acts, certified copies as evidence, **9:2759**
Birth certificates, short form certification cards, **9:226**
Interdiction of veterans, medical examination records, **9:1021**
Inventories, succession, Orleans Parish, **9:1422**
Notice, cancellation or subordination of federal mortgage, service, **9:5163, 9:5164**
Partnership certificates,
    Fee, **9:3404**
    Use as proof, **9:3403**

CHARITIES
Curators, donations, **9:1023**
Cy pres doctrine, **9:2331 et seq.**
Debts due, prescription, **9:5701**
Directors, tort liability, **9:2792**
Donations,
    Inter vivos, exemptions, reduction and calculation of succession mass, **9:2372**
    Trusts and trustees, **9:2271**
Investments, **9:2337.1 et seq.**
Officers and employees, tort liability, **9:2792**
Servitudes, granting, **9:1252**

CHILDREN AND MINORS
    Generally, **9:391 et seq.**
Abuse of children,
    Actions and proceedings, **9:2800.9**
Accounts and accounting, Uniform Transfers to Minors Act, custodians, **9:769**
Actions and proceedings,
    Controlled dangerous substances, dealer liability, **9:2800.63**
    Restrictions on actions against parents, **9:571**
Adult children or grandchildren, abuse of parents or grandparents, protection, **9:575**
Alternative dispute resolution, custody, parenting coordinators, **9:358.1 et seq.**
Appointments, custody, parenting coordinators, **9:358.1**
    Domestic abuse, exemptions, **9:358.2**
    Termination, **9:358.8**
Attorney fees,
    Custody or visitation proceedings, **9:345**
    Visitation rights, enforcement, **9:375**
Best interests of child, joint custody, **9:335**
Block safe-houses, damages, liability, **9:2800.5**
Certificates and certification, abuse of children, certificate of merit, **9:2800.9**
Contracts,
    Surrogate motherhood contracts, **9:2713**
Controlled dangerous substances, dealer liability, **9:2800.63**
Costs,
    Custody, parenting coordinators, **9:358.1**

INDEX TO TITLE 9

CHILDREN AND MINORS—Cont'd
Costs—Cont'd
    Visitation, enforcement, **9:375**
Credit, discrimination, **9:3583**
Custody, **9:758 et seq.**
    Actions between spouses, authority, **9:291**
    Attorneys, appointment, protective and remedial measures, **9:345**
    Burdens, family violence perpetrators, **9:364**
    Continuing jurisdiction, relocation, **9:355.17**
    Death of mother, **9:195**
    Drug tests, **9:331.1**
    Duration, provisional custody by mandate, **9:952**
    Evaluation and mediation, **9:331 et seq.**
    Evidence, relocation hearing, burden of proof, **9:355.13**
    Factors determining best interest of child, relocation hearing, **9:355.12**
    Family violence perpetrators, **9:364**
    Foreign states, relocation, **9:355.1 et seq.**
    Forms, provisional custody by mandate, **9:954**
    Frivolous or unwarranted relocation request, **9:355.16**
    Joint custody, **9:335 et seq.**
    Jurisdiction, relocation, continuing jurisdiction, **9:355.17**
    Mediation, **9:351 et seq.**
    Moving, **9:355.1 et seq.**
    Notice, relocation, **9:355.1 et seq.**
    Orders,
        Drug tests, **9:331.1**
        Family violence, injunctions, **9:366**
    Parenting coordinators, **9:358.1 et seq.**
    Preference of child, relocation hearing, **9:355.12**
    Presumptions, family violence perpetrators, **9:364**
    Provisional custody, mandate, **9:951 et seq.**
    Relocation, **9:355.1 et seq.**
    Sanctions, frivolous or unwarranted relocation request, **9:355.16**
    Support of persons, raising issues, **9:315.25, 9:356**
    Temporary orders, relocation, **9:355.10**
Death of parent, credit unions, payment without court proceedings, **9:1514**
Dentists, records, access, parents, **9:351**
Discipline,
    Power of attorney, military personnel, **9:3879.1**
    Provisional custody by mandate, powers and duties of agent, **9:953**
Disclosure, parenting coordinators, custody, **9:358.7**
Discrimination, credit, **9:3583**
Domestic abuse, custody, parenting coordinators, appointments, exemptions, **9:358.2**
Donations,
    Inter vivos, exemptions, reduction and calculation of succession mass, **9:2372**
Education,
    Power of attorney, military personnel, **9:3879.1**
    Provisional custody by mandate, powers and duties of agent, **9:953**
Emancipation,
    Foreign judgments and decrees, full faith and credit, **9:901**
Ex parte proceedings, parenting coordinators, custody, **9:358.6**
Exemptions, custody, parenting coordinators, appointments, domestic abuse, **9:358.2**
Expropriation judgments, binding effect, **9:3189**
Forms,
    Power of attorney, military personnel, **9:3862 et seq.**
    Provisional custody by mandate, **9:954**

CHILDREN AND MINORS—Cont'd
Frivolous or unwarranted relocation request, custody of children, **9:355.16**
Hearings,
    Immovables, Uniform Transfers to Minors Act, creating custodial property, **9:759**
    Relocation hearing, custody of children, **9:355.9 et seq.**
    Temporary custody of children, orders, relocation hearing, **9:355.9 et seq.**
Injunctions, family violence, **9:366**
Joint custody, **9:335 et seq.**
Judicial sales, person authorized to make, **9:3001**
Mandate, provisional custody, **9:951 et seq.**
Mediation, custody, parenting coordinators, **9:358.1 et seq.**
Medical care and treatment,
    Power of attorney, military personnel, **9:3879.1**
    Privileges and immunities, health care providers, gratuitous services, **9:2799.5**
    Provisional custody by mandate, powers and duties of agent, **9:953**
Medical records, access, parents, **9:351**
Mental health practitioners, certificate of merit, abuse of children, **9:2800.9**
Military Parent Child Custody Protection Act, **9:359 to 9:359.13**
Moving, custody of children, **9:355.1 et seq.**
Orders, custody,
    Family violence, injunctions, **9:366**
    Relocation, **9:355.10**
Parenting coordinators, custody, **9:358.1 et seq.**
Prescription,
    Abuse of children, **9:2800.9**
Presumptions, paternity, blood test to determine paternity, **9:397.3**
Private sale of immovable property, concurrence of under tutor, validation, **9:675**
Privileges and immunities, parenting coordinators, custody, **9:358.9**
Records and recordation,
    Parents, access, **9:351**
Relocation, custody of children, **9:355.1 et seq.**
Reports, custody, parenting coordinators, **9:358.5**
School records, access, parents, **9:351**
Sexual abuse, custody or visitation,
    Attorney, appointment, **9:345**
    Restrictions, **9:341**
Surrogate motherhood contracts, **9:2713**
Temporary custody of children, orders, relocation, **9:355.10**
Test tube babies, **9:121 et seq.**
Training programs, custody dispute mediators, qualifications, **9:334**
Uniform Transfers to Minors Act, **9:751 et seq.**
Witnesses, custody, parenting coordinators, **9:358.5**

CHIROPRACTORS
Arbitration and award, services or supplies contracts, **9:4230 et seq.**
Contracts,
    Breach of contract, prescription, **9:5628**
    Management consultants, **9:2714**
    Services, arbitration and award, **9:4230 et seq.**
Damages, medical care and treatment, gratuitous services, **9:2799.5**
Depositions, malpractice, **9:2794**
Negligence, burden of proof, **9:2794**
    Medical care and treatment, gratuitous services, **9:2799.5**

INDEX TO TITLE 9

CIVIC ORGANIZATIONS
Limitation of liability, director, officer or trustee, nonprofit organizations, **9:2792.3**

CLASS ACTIONS
Consumer credit, **9:3554**
Judgments and decrees, conclusiveness, **9:2701**

CLEANING AND DYEING ESTABLISHMENTS
Privilege, **9:4687, 9:4688**
Unclaimed property, disposition, **9:4687 et seq.**

CLERKS OF COURTS
Arbitration proceedings, filing record, **9:4214**
Fees and charges,
    Partnership certificates, filing and indexing, **9:3410**
    Registry, cancellation of bond for deed, **9:2945**
Mortgages, cancellation, **9:5167**
Vendor's privilege, cancellation, **9:5167**

CLINICS
Contracts for services, arbitration and award, **9:4230 et seq.**
Damages, medical care and treatment, gratuitous services, **9:2799.5**
Public trust, purposes, **9:2341 et seq.**
Supplies contracts, arbitration and award, **9:4230 et seq.**

CLOCKS
Unclaimed clocks,
    Notice to owner of sale, **9:4702**
    Private sale for repairing, cleaning, inspection or appraisal charges, **9:4701**
    Proceeds of sale, disposition, **9:4703**

COACHES
Liability, volunteer athletic coaches, **9:2798**

COLLATERAL ASSIGNMENTS
Application of law, secured transactions, **9:4401**
Leases or rents, **9:4401**

COLLATERAL MORTGAGES
    Generally, **9:5550 et seq.**
Definitions, mortgages, **9:5550**
Mortgages, this index

COLLATION
Immovables, prescription, revendication, **9:5811**

COLLEGES AND UNIVERSITIES
Immovables, real rights created for benefit of organization, **9:1252**
Investments, **9:2337.1 et seq.**
Student loans, prescription, **9:5701**

COMBINEMEN
Privilege for services rendered on crop, **9:4523**

COMMERCIAL LAW
Law merchant, fiduciaries, laws governing, **9:3812**

COMMERCIAL PROJECTS
Construction projects, machinery and equipment, limiting liability, **9:2775**

COMMERCIAL REAL ESTATE
Definitions, privileges, real estate brokers, unpaid commissions, **9:2781.1**
Real estate appraiser privilege, **9:2781.2**

COMMISSIONER
Definitions,
    Credit repair services organizations, **9:3573.2**
    Manufactured homes, **9:1149.2**
    Small loans, **9:3578.3**

COMMODITIES
Privilege for making or repairing, creation, duration enforcement, **9:4502**

COMMUNITY CENTERS
Institutional vandalism, damages, **9:2799.2**

COMMUNITY OF ACQUETS AND GAINS
    Generally, **9:2801 et seq.**
Alienation, injunctions, divorce proceedings, **9:371**
Application of law, married women, **9:105**
Deposits in banks, etc., payment to surviving spouse, **9:1513, 9:1514**
Divorce,
    Injunctions, **9:371**
    Possession and use, **9:374**
Emancipation and powers of married women, **9:101 et seq.**
Goodwill, evaluation, **9:2801.2**
Injunctions, **9:371**
Law governing not affected by law on powers of married women, **9:105**
Married women, power to dispose of property for benefit of community, **9:103**
Partition, **9:2801**
    Judgments and decrees, **9:2802**
    Retirement and pensions, **9:2801.1**
        Evaluation of goodwill, **9:2801.2**
Privileges, injunctions, divorce, **9:371**
Spousal property division, trusts and trustees, **9:1955**
    Principal beneficiary, deferred ascertainment, **9:2014**

COMMUNITY PROPERTY
See Community of Acquets and Gains, this index

COMMUNITY SERVICES
Definitions, nonprofit organizations, limitation of liability, **9:2792.8**

COMPENSATION AND SALARIES
Abandoned or unclaimed property, **9:166**
Assignment of wages,
    Claims for collection of wages, **9:3051**
    Rental purchase agreements, prohibited provisions, **9:3356**
Custodial trusts, **9:2260.14**
Custodians, Uniform Transfers to Minors Act, **9:765**
Laborers or suppliers, contractors, misapplication of payments, **9:4814**
Liens. Privileges on wages, generally, post
Mechanic's privileges and liens, **9:4803**
Minerals, oil and gas, keeper, enforcement of mortgage on mineral rights, **9:5133**
Payment,
    Misapplication, laborers or suppliers, contractors, **9:4814**
    Penalty for violations, laborers or suppliers, contractors, **9:4814**
    Surviving spouse and children of deceased employee, **9:1515**
Privileges on wages,
    Logs and lumber, working with, **9:4621**
    Moss, **9:4641**
    Private works, **9:4803**

INDEX TO TITLE 9

COMPENSATION AND SALARIES—Cont'd
Privileges on wages—Cont'd
    Sequestration, enforcement by, **9:4721**
Public administrators, **9:1589**
    Clerks, **9:1589**
Sugar refinery and mill employees, privilege on product, **9:4721**

COMPROMISE AND SETTLEMENT
Consumer credit, **9:3513**
Hospital privilege for charges, personal injury settlement, **9:4751 et seq.**
Labor and employment, employers right to contribution or indemnification, **9:3921**
Leases, movables, **9:3305**
Military forces, power of attorney, powers granted, **9:3870**
Structured settlements, transfer, **9:2715**
Trust property claims, **9:2121**
Wrongful death, compromises prior to death, **9:3921**

COMPTROLLER OF THE CURRENCY
Accrued interest, recovery of interest upon, **9:3509.2**

CONCURSUS PROCEEDINGS
Mechanic's privileges and liens, **9:4841**
    Extinguished, **9:4823**

CONDITIONAL SALES
Definitions, leases, movable property, **9:3306**
Financed leases, **9:3301 et seq.**
Repossession, exempt property, restrictions, penalties, **9:4563**, **9:4564**

CONDOMINIUMS
    Generally, **9:1121.101 et seq.**
  Acts of sale and conveyances,
    Cancellation, **9:1124.106**
    Management association, **9:1123.102**
    Protection of purchasers, **9:1124.101 et seq.**
    Resale of units, **9:1124.107**
    Rescission of purchase contract, **9:1124.106**
    Rules and regulations, **9:1122.105**
  Alteration of units, **9:1122.113**
  Application of law, **9:1121.102**
    Ordinances, zoning and building restrictions, **9:1121.106**
  Assessments, **9:1121.105**
    Common area expenses, **9:1123.102**
    Imposition, **9:1123.102**
    Insurance, **9:1123.112**
  Association,
    Management association, **9:1123.101 et seq.**
    Unit owners, charges or dues, privileges, **9:1145 et seq.**
  Attorney fees, **9:1121.104**
  Boundaries, relocation, **9:1122.114**
  Building Code, application of law, **9:1121.106**
  Bylaws, **9:1122.103**
    Amendment, **9:1122.119**
    Compliance, **9:1124.115**
    Governing authority, **9:1123.106**
    Resale of units, **9:1124.107**
  Charges or dues, privileges, **9:1145 et seq.**
  Common areas,
    Alteration of units, **9:1122.113**
    Designation, **9:1122.105**
    Expropriation, allocation, **9:1121.107**
    Insurance, **9:1123.112**
    Percentage interest, allocation, **9:1122.106**
    Reapportionment, **9:1122.106**

CONDOMINIUMS—Cont'd
Common areas—Cont'd
    Subdivision or conversion of units, **9:1122.115**
    Taxation, **9:1121.105**
    Voting rights, **9:1122.108**
Common elements, **9:1121.105 et seq.**
Contracts,
    Purchaser,
        Cancellation, **9:1124.106**
        Disclosure, **9:1124.102**
    Purchases, **9:1124.102**
    Resale of units, **9:1124.107**
    Termination, **9:1123.105**
Conversion, **9:1122.115**
    Advertisements, **9:1124.104**
Damages, breach of contract, **9:1124.115**
Declaration of creation, **9:1122.101 et seq.**
    Amendment, **9:1122.119**
        Additional immovable property, **9:1122.105**
    Construction, **9:1122.103**
    Contents, **9:1122.105**
    Validity, **9:1122.103**
Definitions, **9:1121.103**
Description of units, **9:1122.104**
Disclosure, public offering statement, **9:1124.101 et seq.**
Dues or charges, privileges and liens, **9:1145 et seq.**
Expropriation, **9:1121.107**
    Common areas, reallocation, **9:1122.108**
    Zoning and planning, **9:1121.106**
Fines and penalties, delinquent assessments, **9:1123.102**
Fraud, cancellation of deed by purchaser, **9:1124.106**
Improvements,
    Alteration of units, **9:1122.113**
    Privileges against unit owners, **9:1145 et seq.**
    Rules and regulations, **9:1123.102**
Indemnity and indemnification, management association, **9:1123.102**
Injunction, rules and regulations, **9:1124.115**
Insurance, **9:1123.112**
    Purchasers, disclosure, **9:1124.102**
    Resale of units, **9:1124.107**
Leases,
    Application of law, **9:1122.101 et seq.**
    Establishment on leased land, **9:1122.107**
    Limitations, **9:1122.105**
    Resale of units, **9:1124.107**
    Termination, **9:1123.105**
Management association, **9:1123.101 et seq.**
Maps and plats,
    Amendment of declaration, **9:1122.119**
    Contents, **9:1122.110**
    Contents of declaration, **9:1122.105**
    Purchasers, **9:1124.102**
    Relocation of boundaries, **9:1122.114**
    Resale, **9:1124.107**
Mortgages, withdrawal, **9:1122.112**
Name, **9:1122.105**
Ordinances, **9:1121.106**
Partition,
    Alteration of units, **9:1122.113**
    Common areas, **9:1122.108**
    Withdrawal, **9:1122.112**
Plats. Maps and plats, generally, ante
Powers and duties, management association, **9:1123.102**
Privileges, **9:1124.109**, **9:1124.115**, **9:1124.116**
    Associations of owners, charges or dues, **9:1145 et seq.**
    Authorization, **9:1123.116**

CONDOMINIUMS—Cont'd
Privileges—Cont'd
    Materialmen's lien, 9:1124.109
    Mechanic's liens, 9:1124.109
    Purchasers, disclosure, 9:1124.102
    Utility assessments, 9:1122.116
    Withdrawal, 9:1122.112
Public offering statement, 9:1124.101 et seq.
Records and recordation, 9:1122.101 et seq.
    Assessments, 9:1123.102
    Financial records, 9:1123.108
    Privileges and liens, 9:1123.115, 9:1124.109
        Association charges or dues, 9:1145 et seq.
    Subdivision or conversion of units, 9:1122.115
Repairs and maintenance, 9:1123.107
Rescission of purchase contract, 9:1124.106
Residential Truth in Construction Act, 9:4851 et seq.
Rules and regulations, 9:1123.102
    Enforcement, 9:1124.115
Sale of units, escrow accounts, 9:1121.108
Securities, purchaser, disclosure, 9:1124.105
Subdividing units, 9:1122.115
Subdivision regulations, application of law, 9:1121.106
Summary proceedings, 9:1124.115
Tax liens, 9:1121.105
Taxation, 9:1121.105
    Privileges and liens, priorities, 9:1123.115
    Resale of units, disclosure, 9:1124.107
Termination, 9:1122.101 et seq.
Title of act, 9:1121.101
Voting rights, 9:1122.108
    Amendment of declaration, 9:1122.119
Withdrawal, 9:1122.112
Zoning and planning, application of law, 9:1121.106

CONFESSION OF JUDGMENT
Limitations, 9:3590
Rental purchase agreements, prohibited provisions, 9:3356

CONFLICT OF LAWS
Application of foreign law, 9:6001
Compromise and settlement, structured settlements, transfer, 9:2715
Construction contracts, invalid provisions, 9:2779
Consumer credit, 9:3511
Controlled dangerous substances, dealer liability, 9:2800.75
Electronic transactions, 9:2604
Emergency response network, privileges and immunities, 9:2798.5
Fiduciary's transfer of stock, 9:3838
Leases, 9:3303
    Civil Code, 9:3192
Sales of movables, Civil Code and revised statute provisions, application of law, 9:3192
Vessels, hypothecation and conveyance, 9:5381

CONSERVATION SERVITUDE
Definitions, 9:1272

CONSTRUCTION CONTRACT ACT (PRIVILEGES)
Generally, 9:4801 et seq.

CONSTRUCTION PROJECTS
Machinery and equipment, limiting liability for consequential damages, 9:2775

CONSTRUCTIVE NOTICE
Definitions, merchant liability, 9:2800.6

CONSUMER CREDIT
    Generally, 9:3510 et seq.
Acceleration, rebate, 9:3533
Accounts and accounting, 9:3554, 9:3554.1, 9:3561.1
Accrued interest, recovery of interest upon, 9:3509.2
Administrative law and procedure, 9:3556
Agreement, transaction be subject to provisions, 9:3514
Application of law, 9:3511, 9:3563
Assets, sales or transfers, licensees, 9:3561
Assignments,
    Fines and penalties, 9:3553
    Licenses and permits, 9:3557
    Records and recordation, 9:3556.1
Attorney fees, 9:3530, 9:3556.3, 9:3567
    Credit reporting agencies, 9:3571.1
    Injunctions, 9:3555
    Insurance, 9:3550
    Unlicensed lenders, payment collection and loan enforcement, 9:3559.1
Branch offices, 9:3561, 9:3564
Brokers, consumer loans, 9:3572.1 et seq.
Business purposes, exemptions, 9:3512
Casualty insurance, 9:3543
Catalogue credit sale, home solicitation sale, 9:3516
Cease and desist orders, 9:3554, 9:3554.1
Change of name or location by licensee, notice, 9:3561
Checks,
    Definitions, 9:3516
    Mail and check solicitation sale, 9:3541.1
    Nonsufficient fund checks, fees and charges, 9:3529
Citation of act, 9:3510
Class action, 9:3554
Closing of loan on immovable property, using office of notary public, 9:3515
Club memberships, payment, 9:3515
    Collection practices, 9:3562 et seq.
    Unauthorized practices, leases, 9:3340
    Unlicensed lenders, 9:3559.1
Commercial purposes, exemptions, 9:3512
Compromise and settlement, 9:3513
Conditional licenses, 9:3558
Confidential or privileged information, personal credit information, 9:3571
Conflict of laws, 9:3511
Consent agreements, violations, attorney fees, 9:3555
Construction of act, 9:3517, 9:3518
Consumer, definitions, 9:3516
Contempt orders, 9:3554.1
Contracts,
    Subjecting transaction to law, 9:3514
Corporations, fines and penalties, 9:3553
Costs,
    Civil actions, 9:3556.3
    Credit reporting agencies, 9:3571.1
    Investigations or injunctions, 9:3555
    Unlicensed lenders, payment collection and loan enforcement, 9:3559.1
Credit reporting agencies, 9:3571.1
Creditor, definitions, 9:3516
Damages,
    Credit reporting agencies, 9:3571.1
    Treble damages, 9:3552
Default,
    Collection practices, 9:3562
    Interest rate, 9:3524
    Notice, conversion to simple interest transaction, 9:3527

INDEX TO TITLE 9

CONSUMER CREDIT—Cont'd
Deferral charges, 9:3528
    Prepayment, 9:3532
Delinquency charges, 9:3527
    Insurance premium finance companies, 9:3550
Disclosure,
    Credit life and health insurance, optional nature, 9:3542
    Personal information, 9:3571
    Terms and conditions, 9:3514
Discounts, referral sales, 9:3536
    Leases, movable property, 9:3339
Dismemberment insurance, 9:3542
Documentation fee, 9:3530
Domicile and residence, 9:3511
Duplicative insurance, 9:3542
Education, 9:3554
Emergencies, home solicitation sales, cancellation, 9:3538
Enforcement, 9:3554
    Unconscionable agreement, 9:3551
Enforcing loans, unlicensed lenders, 9:3559.1
Exclusions from law, 9:3512
Exemptions, licenses, 9:3560
Extender of credit,
    Definitions, 9:3516
    Insurance, 9:3542
Fees and charges, 9:3517, 9:3521
    Accrued interest, recovery of interest upon, 9:3509.2
    Attorneys fees, 9:3530
    Casualty insurance, 9:3543
    Computation, credit cards, 9:3524
    Credit cards, 9:3524
    Credit insurance, 9:3542
    Credit sale, 9:3520
    Default interest rate, 9:3524
    Deferral charges, 9:3528
        Prepayment, 9:3532
    Delinquency charges, 9:3527
    Dismemberment insurance, 9:3542
    Documentation fee, 9:3530
    Examinations, records, 9:3561.1
    Home solicitation sale, cancellation, 9:3540
    Insurance, 9:3542, 9:3545
    Insurance premium finance companies, 9:3550
    Interest, credit life, health and accident insurance premiums, 9:3331
    Leap year, 9:3525
    Licensed lenders, name changes, 9:3561.1
    Loan, 9:3519
    Maximum, 9:3519 et seq.
    Nonsufficient fund checks, 9:3529
    Notaries public, 9:3530
    Notification, 9:3565
    Origination fees, 9:3530
    Over-the-credit-limit fees, 9:3530
    Overcharges, intentional violations, 9:3552
    Prepayment charges, 9:3532.1
    Public license tag agents, convenience fees, 9:3530
    Rate after maturity, 9:3522
    Renewal, origination fees, 9:3530
    Service charge, 9:3521
    Variable rate, 9:3526
    Written agreements, 9:3521
Fines and penalties, 9:3553, 9:3554.1, 9:3556.3
    Licenses and permits, 9:3565
    Overcharges, 9:3552
    Unlicensed persons, 9:3554.1
        Payment collection and loan enforcement, 9:3559.1

CONSUMER CREDIT—Cont'd
Foreign lenders, examination of records, 9:3561.1
Form of agreement or offer, 9:3539
Formal applications, loans, location, 9:3515
Former licensed lenders, examination of records, 9:3561.1
Fraud,
    License suspension or revocation, 9:3554
Hearings, 9:3554, 9:3556
Home solicitation sales,
    Aged persons, 9:3541.21, 9:3541.22
    Cancellation, 9:2711.1, 9:3538
        Mail and check solicitation sale, 9:3541.1
        Restoration of down payment, 9:3540
        Tender of goods, 9:3541
    Contents of agreement, 9:3539
    Definitions, 9:3516
    Down payment, restoration, 9:3540
    Mail and check solicitation sale, 9:3541.1
    Noncredit home solicitation sales, cancellation, 9:2711.1
Immovable property, closing of loan on, using office of notary public, 9:3515
Information, credit reporting agencies, 9:3571.1
Injunctions, 9:3555
    Attorney fees, 9:3555
    Unlicensed persons, 9:3554.1
Insurance, 9:3542
    Cancellation, 9:3548
    Casualty insurance, 9:3543
    Choice of insurer, 9:3334, 9:3546
    Dismemberment insurance, 9:3542
    Duplicative coverage, 9:3542
    Exemptions, 9:3512
        Life insurance loans, 9:3560
    Existing insurance, 9:3544
    Extender of credit, 9:3542
    Gain from insurance, application of law, 9:3549
    Leases, movable property, 9:3331 et seq.
    Payment, 9:3515
    Policy conditions, 9:3547
    Premiums, rates, 9:3542
    Rates and charges, 9:3545
Insurance agents, brokers and salespersons, closing of loans, 9:3515
Insurance premium finance companies, 9:3550
Investigations and investigators,
    Alleged violations, 9:3554, 9:3554.1
    Unlicensed persons, 9:3554.1
Jurisdiction, 9:3511
Leap years, finance charge rates, 9:3525
Lender credit cards, finance charges, 9:3524
Licenses and permits, 9:3557
    Application, 9:3558
    Branch offices, 9:3561
    Collection agencies, ante
    Continuation of licensing, 9:3559
    Contracts, subjecting transaction to law, licensing requirement, 9:3514
    Exemptions, 9:3560
    Fees or charges, 9:3561.1, 9:3565
    Grandfather clause, 9:3559
    Insurance premium finance companies, 9:3550
        Lapse, 9:3561.1
    Restricted or conditional licenses, 9:3558
    Revocation, 9:3554
    Suspension or revocation, 9:3554, 9:3554.1
        Fees, failure to pay, 9:3561.1
        Unlicensed loan collection and enforcement, 9:3559.1

INDEX TO TITLE 9

CONSUMER CREDIT—Cont'd
Licenses and permits—Cont'd
    Unlicensed persons, investigations, **9:3554.1**
Life insurance, **9:3542**
Limitation of actions, **9:3552**
Mail and check solicitation sale, **9:3541.1**
Mail and mailing,
    Licenses and permits, **9:3560**
    Notices, **9:3552**
Maximum deferral charges, **9:3528**
Mortgages, this index
Motor carriers, exemptions, **9:3512**
Motor Vehicles, this index
Movable property, **9:3301 et seq.**
Multiple agreements, movable property, interest, **9:3312**
Multiple violations, **9:3552**
N.S.F. checks, fees and charges, **9:3529**
Names, changes,
    Licensed lenders, fees, **9:3561.1**
Negotiable instruments, **9:3516, 9:3521**
    Assignments, crimes and offenses, **9:3553**
Organizations and societies, exemptions, **9:3512**
Origination fees, **9:3530**
Overdraft credit lines, **9:3524**
Pawnbrokers, exclusion from law, **9:3512**
Pension plans, exemptions, **9:3560**
Personal information,
    Confidential, disclosure, **9:3571**
    Credit reporting agencies, **9:3571.1**
    Untrue or misleading information, maintenance or dissemination, **9:3571.1**
Place of business, **9:3515**
    Licensees, **9:3561**
Pledges, exemptions, licenses, **9:3560**
Political subdivisions, exemptions, **9:3560**
Powers and duties, **9:3554, 9:3554.2**
Premium finance agreements, insurance premium finance companies, **9:3550**
    Licenses and permits, lapse, **9:3561.1**
Premiums,
    Insurance, cancellation, refund, **9:3548**
    Property insurance, **9:3543**
Prepayment, **9:3527 et seq., 9:3531**
    Rebates, **9:3532**
Prescription, **9:3552**
    Home solicitation sales, **9:3540**
    Restrictions, **9:3554**
Production of books and papers,
    Unlicensed persons, investigations, **9:3554.1**
Public reprimands, **9:3554**
Public utilities, exemptions, **9:3512**
Rates and charges. Fees and charges, generally, ante
Rebates,
    Acceleration, **9:3533**
    Delinquent installments, conversion of transaction into simple interest, **9:3527**
    Prepayment, **9:3532**
    Referral sales, **9:3536**
        Leases, movable property, **9:3339**
Referral sales, **9:3536**
    Leases, movable property, **9:3339**
Refinancing,
    New sale or loan, fees, **9:3565**
    Origination fees, **9:3530**
Refunds, cancellation of insurance, **9:3548**
Registration, brokers, crimes and offenses, **9:3553**
Renewal, origination fees, **9:3530**

CONSUMER CREDIT—Cont'd
Reproduction of records, **9:3556.1**
Rescission, referral sales, **9:3536**
Restricted licenses, **9:3558**
Revolving charge accounts,
    Fees and charges, **9:3523**
    Over-the-credit-limit charges, **9:3530**
    Prescription, **9:3552**
    Service charges, **9:3523**
Revolving loan accounts,
    Accounts with credit card and revolving loan attributes, **9:3524**
    Delinquency charges, **9:3527**
Rural property, mortgages, exclusions, **9:5325**
Sales,
    Definitions, **9:3516**
    Exemption, transactions pursuant to Motor Vehicle Sales Finance Act, **9:3516**
Sales of movables, assets, accounts and shares, licensees, **9:3561**
Savings and loan associations, exemptions, licenses, **9:3560**
Self discovered violations, **9:3552**
Services, payment, **9:3515**
Shares and shareholders, sales and transfers, licensees, **9:3561**
Subpoenas, **9:3554, 9:3554.1**
    Unlicensed persons, **9:3554.1**
Surveys and surveyors, change of location, licensees, **9:3561, 9:3561.1**
Suspension or revocation, unlicensed loan collection and enforcement, **9:3559.1**
Thrift and buying club memberships, **9:3515**
Trade-in allowances, home solicitation sale, cancellation, **9:3540**
Transfers,
    Licensees, **9:3561**
    Records and recordation, **9:3556.1**
Unauthorized collection practices, **9:3562**
    Leases, **9:3340**
Unintentional violations, **9:3552**
United States agencies, exemptions, **9:3560**
Unlicensed lenders, **9:3559.1**
Unlicensed persons, investigations, **9:3554.1**
Variable rate transactions, **9:3526**
Venue, **9:3511**
Waiver of rights, **9:3513**
    Collection practices, **9:3562**
Withdrawals, **9:3516**
Written agreements, **9:3521**

CONSUMER CREDIT REPORTS
Fines and penalties, motor vehicle dealers, **9:3571.2**

CONSUMER LOAN BROKERS
Generally, **9:3572.1 et seq.**

CONSUMER PROTECTION
    See, also, Monopolies and Unfair Trade, generally, this index
Cancellation, consumer loan brokers, contracts, **9:3572.10**
Contracts, noncredit home solicitation sales, cancellation, **9:2711.1**
Deferred Presentment and Small Loan Act, **9:3578.1 et seq.**
Fines and penalties, home solicitation sales, unfair trade practices, **9:2711.1**
Home solicitation sales, **9:2711.1**
Loans, small loans, **9:3578.1 et seq.**
Noncredit home solicitation sales, **9:2711.1**

INDEX TO TITLE 9

CONSUMER PROTECTION—Cont'd
Payday loans, **9:3578.1 et seq.**
Rental purchase agreements, **9:3351 et seq.**
Small loans, **9:3578.1 et seq.**
Telephone solicitations, noncredit home solicitation sales, cancellation, **9:2711.1**
Unfair trade practices, noncredit home solicitation sales, **9:2711.1**

CONSUMERS
Definitions,
  Consumer transactions, **9:3516**

CONTAINERS
Privileges on movables, boxes, **9:4621, 9:4622**

CONTEMPT
Arbitration proceedings, **9:4206**
Consumer credit, unlicensed persons, **9:3554.1**

CONTINUING EDUCATION
Parenting coordinators, child custody, **9:358.3**

CONTRACT FOR SURROGATE MOTHERHOOD
Definitions, **9:2713**

CONTRACTORS
Attorney fees, late payment of subcontractors and suppliers, **9:2784**
Bonding claims, **9:4841**
  Public works, **9:4941**
Bonds (officers and fiduciaries),
  Approval, **9:4941**
  Claims against public works, **9:4941**
  Mechanic's privileges and liens, **9:4812**
  Privilege on immovables, recording, **9:4802**
  Retainage bonds, **9:4822**
Claims against public works contractors, livestock feed, **9:4921 et seq.**
Defects in work, immunity from liability, **9:2771**
Destruction of work, immunity from liability, **9:2771**
Electronic transactions, retention, **9:2612**
Fines and penalties,
  Late payment of subcontractors and suppliers, **9:2784**
  Misapplication of payments, **9:4814**
Guaranty, beginning of period, **9:2774**
Immovables, improvements, mechanic's privileges and liens, **9:4802**
Immunity from liability, **9:2771**
Indemnity,
  Mechanic's privileges and liens, **9:4802**
  Minerals, oil, gas or water, development, exploration and exploitation, **9:2780**
Insurance, new home warranties, **9:3147**
  Subsequent owners, transfer of warranty and insurance, **9:3148**
Notice, nonpayment, delivery before filing claim, **9:4802**
Prime consultants, privileges on immovables, recording, **9:4802**
Private works, **9:4801 et seq.**
Professional subconsultants, privileges on immovables, recording, **9:4802**
Residential Truth in Construction Act, **9:4851 et seq.**
Retainage bonds, **9:4822**
Subcontractors,
  Definitions, mechanic's privileges and liens, **9:4807**
  Misapplication of payments, **9:4814**
  Payment by contractors, **9:2784**

CONTRACTORS—Cont'd
Subcontractors—Cont'd
  Professional subconsultants, mechanic's privileges, **9:4801 et seq.**
Suppliers, payment, **9:2784**
Waiver, destruction or deterioration of work, provisions relating to, **9:2771**
Warranties,
  Beginning of period, **9:2774**
  New home warranties, **9:3141 et seq.**
Water supply, development, exploration and exploitation, indemnity, invalidity, **9:2780**

CONTRACTS
Application of law, credit, **9:3514**
Central registry for contracts of partnership, **9:3401 et seq.**
Consumer loan brokers, **9:3572.1 et seq.**
Consumer protection, home solicitation sales, cancellation, **9:2711.1**
Contracts against public policy, **9:2717**
Damages, construction machinery and equipment, **9:2775**
Object of contracts, recording, **9:2721**
Records and recordation, **9:2721**
  Improvements on immovables, **9:4802**
Rental purchase agreements, **9:3351 et seq.**
Self-service storage facilities, **9:4756 et seq.**
Sureties, deposits, joint control, **9:3904**
Surrogate motherhood contracts, **9:2713**
Women, **9:101**

CONTROLLED DANGEROUS SUBSTANCES
Dealer liability, **9:2800.61 et seq.**
  Assignments, **9:2800.65**
  Attachment, **9:2800.72**
  Comparative fault, **9:2800.68**
  Confidential or privileged information, **9:2800.74**
  Conflict of laws, **9:2800.75**
  Cumulation of actions, **9:2800.67**
  Damages, **9:2800.61 et seq.**
  Defenses, **9:2800.71**
  Discovery, **9:2800.74**
  Evidence,
    Burden of proof, comparative fault, **9:2800.68**
    Dealer liability, **9:2800.70**
  Indemnity, **9:2800.65**
  Insurance, **9:2800.65**
    Health and accident insurance, **9:2800.63**
  Joinder of actions, **9:2800.67**
  Labor and employment, **9:2800.63**
  Negligence, **9:2800.63**
  Prescription, **9:2800.73**
  Privileges and immunities, **9:2800.71**
  Public policy, **9:2800.61**
  Quasi offenses, **9:2800.63**
    Contribution, **9:2800.69**
  Relatives, **9:2800.63**
  Stay of proceedings, **9:2800.74**
  Subrogation, **9:2800.65**
  Third parties, **9:2800.65**

CONVENTIONAL SALES
Generally, **9:2941 et seq.**

CONVERSION
Mortgaged property, mortgagee's right of action, limitation on recovery, **9:5382**

INDEX TO TITLE 9

COOPERATIVE APARTMENTS
Residential Truth in Construction Act, **9:4851 et seq.**

CORONERS
Death, reports, **9:111**
Judicial Sales, generally, this index

CORPORATIONS
Acts of sale and conveyances, prescription, **9:5681**
Assets, quieting title, land title based on private sale of minor's property, **9:675**
Bankruptcy, privilege on assets, producers of agriculture and dairy products, **9:5021**
De facto corporation, **9:1051**
Dividends,
    Corporate distributions, trust, allocation to income and principal, **9:2149**
    Trust income, corporate distributions, **9:2149**
Insolvency, privilege on assets, producers of agriculture and dairy products, **9:5021**
Institutional funds, investments, **9:2337.1 et seq.**
Interest, exceeding maximum conventional rate, **9:3509**
Literary, trust, incorporation of, **9:2275**
Officers and employees, fiduciary relation, **9:3801**
Prescription, acts of sale or conveyances, **9:5681**
Presumptions, abandoned or unclaimed property, **9:153**
Registration, consumer loan brokers, **9:3572.4**
Religious trust, incorporation, **9:2275**
Scientific, trust, incorporation, **9:2275**
Shares and shareholders,
    Adverse claims to transfer by fiduciary, **9:3835**
    Evidence, fiduciary's authority to make assignment, **9:3834**
    Fiduciaries,
        Adverse claim to transfer by, **9:3835**
        Stock registered in name of, **9:3832**
        Transfer agents, liability for transfer of stock held by fiduciaries, **9:3836**
    Investments, institutional funds, **9:2337.1 et seq.**
    Transfer agent, stock registered in name of fiduciary, **9:3831**
    Transfers, adverse claims to transfer by fiduciary, **9:3835**
    Tutors and tutorship, stock registered in name of fiduciary, **9:3832**
    Uniform Law for Simplification of Fiduciary Security Transfers, **9:3831 et seq.**
Transfer agents,
    Assignment by fiduciaries, **9:3833**
    Liability for transfer of stock held by fiduciaries, **9:3836**
    Stock registered in name of fiduciary, duties, **9:3832**
Unauthorized corporations, rights and powers, **9:1051**
Unfair trade. Monopolies and Unfair Trade, generally, this index
Zoning, prescription of actions, **9:5625**

CORPOREAL IMMOVABLES
Private transfer fee obligations,
    Definitions, **9:3132**
    Marketability, **9:3131**
    Prohibition of private transfer fee obligations, **9:3133**

COSTS
Children and minors, custody, parenting coordinators, **9:358.1**
Compromise and settlement, structured settlements, petitions, transfer, **9:2715**
Consumer loan brokers, fine recoveries, **9:3572.12**
Covenant marriage, separation from bed and board, **9:309**

COSTS—Cont'd
Credit repair services organizations,
    Action for damages, **9:3573.10**
    Criminal proceedings, **9:3573.13**
Credit reporting agencies, **9:3571.1**
Custody, mediation, **9:332**
Leases, action for deposit, **9:3253**
Mediation, **9:4101, 9:4109**
New home warranties, actions for violations, **9:3149**
Paternity, blood or tissue test to determine, **9:397.1**
Public administrators, payment, **9:1588**
Stop payment, checks, **9:2782.2**
Structured settlements, petitions, transfer, **9:2715**

COTTON
Privileges, vendor, cotton seed, privilege on manufactured products, **9:4542**
Sales of movables, privilege of seller on manufactured product, **9:4542**
Seeds, seller's privilege on manufactured products, **9:4542**

COUNTERLETTERS
Recording, **9:2721**
Use, affecting transfer or encumbrance of public property, award of public contracts or expenditure or receipt of public funds, **9:2712**

COVENANT MARRIAGE
Generally, **9:272 et seq.**

CREDIT
Advance fee loans, **9:3574.1 et seq.**
Confidential or privileged information, disclosure, **9:3571**
Disclosure of personal credit information, banks, businesses, etc., **9:3571**
Discrimination, **9:3583**
Equal Credit Opportunity Law, **9:3581 et seq.**
Personal information, confidential, **9:3571**

CREDIT CARDS
Accounts with revolving loan and credit card attributes, **9:3524**
Advance fee loans, **9:3574.1 et seq.**
Advance fees, **9:3574.1 et seq.**
Attorney fees,
    Liabilities, receipts, **9:3518.3**
    Unsolicited cards, mail and mailing, damages, **9:3518.2**
Colleges and universities,
    Issuers, **9:3577.1 et seq.**
        Fines and penalties, **9:3577.5**
        Registration, **9:3577.4**
    Solicitation, **9:3577.1 et seq.**
Confidential information, **9:3571**
Conforming to Consumer Credit Law, **9:3515**
Damages, unsolicited cards, mail and mailing, **9:3518.2**
Definitions, **9:3516**
Delinquency charges, **9:3527**
Disclosure, issuing companies, customer financial records, **9:3571**
Fees and charges, **9:3524**
Licenses and permits, **9:3557**
Mail and check solicitation sale, **9:3541.1**
Mail and mailing, unsolicited cards, damages, **9:3518.2**
Power of attorney, military personnel, powers granted, **9:3874**
Receipts, liabilities, **9:3518.3**
Revolving charge accounts, generally. Consumer Credit, this index

INDEX TO TITLE 9

CREDIT CARDS—Cont'd
Service charges, 9:3524
Travel and entertainment credit cards, 9:3524

CREDIT REPAIR SERVICES ORGANIZATIONS
    Generally, 9:3573.1 et seq.
Actions and proceedings, 9:3573.10
Advertisements, 9:3573.3
Attorney fees, 9:3573.10
    District attorneys, criminal proceedings, 9:3573.13
Bonds (officers and fiduciaries), 9:3573.4
    Commissioner, definitions, 9:3573.2
Conduct, prohibitions, 9:3573.3
Costs, criminal proceedings, 9:3573.13
Cumulative remedies, 9:3573.15
Damages, 9:3573.10
Definitions,
    Buyer, 9:3573.2
    Consumer reporting agency, 9:3573.2
Disclosure statements, 9:3573.6
District attorneys, criminal proceedings, 9:3573.13
Evidence, exemption, 9:3573.14
Exemptions, 9:3573.2
    Burden of proof, 9:3573.14
Fines and penalties, 9:3573.16
Form, contracts, 9:3573.7
Fraud, 9:3573.3
Information, nonessential requests, no cost sources, prohibition, 9:3573.3
Injunctions, 9:3573.11
Limitation of actions, 9:3572.12
Notice,
    Cancellation, contracts, 9:3573.7
    Trust accounts, establishment, 9:3573.4
Prohibited conduct, 9:3573.3
Punitive damages, 9:3573.10
Signatures, contracts, 9:3573.7
Terms, contracts, 9:3573.7
Trust accounts, 9:3573.4
Waiver, buyers rights, 9:3573.8
Written contracts, 9:3573.7

CREDIT REPAIR SERVICES ORGANIZATIONS ACT
Generally, 9:3573.1 et seq.

CREDIT REPORTING AGENCIES
Generally, 9:3571.1

CREDIT SERVICES ORGANIZATIONS
Costs, action for damages, 9:3573.10
Exemplary damages, 9:3573.10

CREDIT UNIONS
Consumer credit, application of law, 9:3514
    Transactions, 9:3563.1
Deposits,
    Abandoned or unclaimed property, 9:155, 9:165
    Surviving spouse, payments without court proceedings, 9:1514
Directors, liability, federal or state unions, 9:2792.5
Exemptions, notification filing requirements, 9:3563.1
Liabilities, directors and officers, federal or state unions, 9:2792.5
Military forces, power of attorney, powers granted, 9:3874
Officers and employees, liability, federal or state unions, 9:2792.5
Surviving spouse, payments without court proceedings, 9:1514

CREDITORS
Definitions, consumer credit transactions, 9:3516

CRIMES AND OFFENSES
Consumer credit, 9:3553
Curators, removal from office, 9:1025
Dual contracts, sale of realty, 9:2989
Injuring public records, false affidavit of identity, 9:5503
Marriage, false entries, licenses or certificates, 9:256
Negligence, privileges and immunities, injuries sustained during felonies, 9:2800.10
Personal injuries, privileges and immunities, injuries sustained during felonies, 9:2800.10
Prescription of prosecutions, zoning restrictions, etc., 9:5625
Privileges and immunities, felonies, injuries sustained during commission, 9:2800.10
Separation from bed and board, covenant marriage, 9:307
Shoplifting, 9:2799.1
Trust property, seizure of beneficiary's interest, 9:2005
Unfair trade. Monopolies and Unfair Trade, generally, this index

CURATORS
Adverse claim to transfer of stock by, 9:3835
Appointment,
    Undercurators, 9:602
    Without convocation of family meeting, 9:602
Assignment of stock held as fiduciary, 9:3833
Authority to receive mineral proceeds, 9:1516
Bonds (officers and fiduciaries),
    Dispensing with, sale of property, absent interdict owning undivided interest, 9:603
    Premium as expense, 9:3901
Confirmation, without convocation of family meeting, 9:602
Curators and undercurators, liability for acts of interdicts, 9:2800.21
Definitions, custodial trusts, 9:2260.1
Donation inter vivos, 9:1022
Donations,
    Charitable or nonprofit corporations, 9:1023
    Interdiction, 9:1022 et seq.
Embezzlement, removal, 9:1025
Embryos, in vitro fertilized human ovum, 9:126
Estate Tax Apportionment Law, 9:2431 et seq.
Fiduciary, 9:3801
Foreign curators, sale of property, minor or interdict holding undivided interest, 9:603
Gross negligence, removal, 9:1025
Hospital charges of decedent, privilege of hospital, 9:4751 et seq.
Investments,
    Deposit of money in bank, 9:734
    Federal obligations, 9:733
Judicial sales, authority to make, 9:3001
Mineral proceeds, authority to withdraw, 9:1516
Misconduct, 9:1025, 9:3911, 9:3912
Oaths and affirmations, absent minor or interdict, special representation, 9:603
Prescription, defective sale or mortgage or property, 9:5632
Privilege, hospital charges against decedent, 9:4751 et seq.
Ratification of minor interdict's sale, 9:732
Recognition without convocation of family meeting, 9:602
Removal from office, 9:1025
    Abuse of interdict, 9:1025
    Accounts and accounting, failure to render accounts, 9:1025
    Incarceration, 9:1025
    Incompetence, 9:1025

INDEX TO TITLE 9

CURATORS—Cont'd
Removal from office—Cont'd
    Misconduct, **9:1025**
    Mismanagement, **9:1025**
Sales of movables,
    Ratification, **9:732**
    Right of way, **9:731**
Security, release of surety on request, **9:3911, 9:3912**
Servitudes or flowage, rights, option to United States, perfecting, **9:1511**
Stock registered in name of as fiduciary, **9:3832**
Undercurators,
    Appointment, recognition or confirmation, **9:602**

CY PRES ACT
    Generally, **9:2331 et seq.**
Institutional funds, investments, application of law, **9:2337.7**

DAIRIES AND DAIRY PRODUCTS
Consumer credit, **9:3510 et seq.**
Privilege, assets of bankrupt purchasers, **9:5021**

DAMAGE
Diminution of value, damaged vehicle, **9:2800.17**
Dwellings, neighbors, public policy, **9:2773**
Emergency medical services, privileges and immunities, volunteers, **9:2793.2**
Emotional distress, institutional vandalism, **9:2799.2**
First aid, emergency care, **9:2793**
Food banks, donations, limitation of liability, **9:2799, 9:2799.6**
Health care providers, privileges and immunities, gratuitous services, **9:2799.5**
Holiday in Dixie parades, limitation of liability, **9:2796**
Hospitals, privilege for charges, **9:4751 et seq.**
Housing authorities, limitation of liability, **9:2800**
Institutional vandalism, **9:2799.2**
Insurance commissioner, notice, submission of information, mobile homes, repossession, **9:5363.1**
Mortgages, affidavits, cancellation, **9:5167.1**
New home warranties, **9:3149**
Parades,
    Ethnic parades, limitation of liability, sponsors, **9:2796.1**
    Mardi Gras parades, limitation of liability, **9:2796**
    Saint Patrick's Day parade, sponsors, limitation of liability, **9:2796.1**
Poison control centers, immunity, quasi offenses, **9:2797.1**
Punitive damages,
    Consumer loan brokers, **9:3572.12**
    Controlled dangerous substances, dealer liability, **9:2800.63, 9:2800.76**
    Credit repair services organizations, **9:3573.10**
    Loan brokers and others, advance fees, **9:3574.9**
Real estate timesharing,
    Actions, fraud in public offering statement, **9:1131.13**
    Escrow accounts, **9:1131.17**
Real rights, charitable purposes, enforcement, **9:1252**
Research, release of animal subjects, **9:2799.4**
Shoplifting, **9:2799.1**
Social hosts, serving alcoholic beverages, limitation of liability, **9:2800.1**
Special damages, institutional vandalism, **9:2799.2**
Stop payment, checks, **9:2782.2**
Surveys and surveyors, preemptive periods, **9:2772**
Treble damages, consumer credit, **9:3552**

DEATH
Definitions, **9:111**
Divorce, presumption of death, authority to remarry, **9:301**

DEATH—Cont'd
Merchants, liability, **9:2800.6**
Mother, provisional tutorship of children, **9:195**
Oil, gas, or mineral property, landowner's liability, **9:2800.4**
Trespass, liability of owner, farm or forestland, **9:2800.4**
Uniform Transfers to Minors Act, custodian, successor, **9:768**

DEATH TAX APPORTIONMENT STATUTE
Generally, **9:2431 et seq.**

DEBTORS AND CREDITORS
Affidavit of identity, filing, **9:5503**
Assignments, claims for collection, **9:3051**
Attorney fees, open accounts, collection, **9:2781**
Collection, unauthorized practices, **9:3562**
Credit reporting agencies, **9:3571.1**
Demand for payment, open accounts, **9:2781**
Fiduciary as mortgagee in trust for creditors, **9:5302**
Information, credit reporting agencies, **9:3571.1**
Judgment creditors, affidavits of distinction, mortgages, similar names, **9:5501, 9:5501.1**
Judgment debtors, affidavits of distinction, mortgages, similar names, **9:5501, 9:5501.1**
Leases, movable property, **9:3318 et seq.**
Obligations secured by mortgage, fiduciary as mortgagee in trust, **9:5302**
Open accounts, demand for payment, **9:2781**
Physician's fees, open accounts, collection, **9:2781**
Prepayment of loans, **9:3509.3**
Records and recordation,
    Affidavit of identity, filing, **9:5503**
Reports, credit reporting agencies, **9:3571.1**
Transfer of claims for collection, **9:3051**
Unauthorized collection practices, **9:3562**

DECEDENT'S ESTATES
Successions and Succession Proceedings, generally, this index

DECLARATIONS
Definitions, Homeowners Association Act, **9:1141.2**
Illegitimate children, declaration of acknowledgment, **9:392**
Minerals, oil and gas, filing in lieu of agreement for joint exploration, **9:2732**

DEEP WATER PORT COMMISSION
Bids and bidding, lease or sublease of commission property, **9:1102.2**
Expropriations, wharves, buildings or improvements, **9:1102.1**
Leases, riparian lands, **9:1102.2**
Riparian owners, use of commission lands, **9:1102.2**
Wharves, buildings or improvements, expropriations, **9:1102.1**

DEFERRED PRESENTMENT AND SMALL LOAN ACT
Generally, **9:3578.1 et seq.**

DENTISTS
Arbitration and award, services or supplies contracts, **9:4230 et seq.**
Contracts,
    Arbitration and award, **9:4230 et seq.**
    Breach of contract, prescription, **9:5628**
    Services, arbitration and award, **9:4230 et seq.**
Depositions, malpractice, **9:2794**
Fees and charges, depositions in malpractice actions, **9:2794**
Limitation of liability, use of blood, organs or tissues, **9:2797**
Negligence,
    Burden of proof, **9:2794**
    Medical care and treatment, gratuitous services, **9:2799.5**

I–18

INDEX TO TITLE 9

DENTISTS—Cont'd
Privileges and immunities, medical care and treatment, gratuitous services, **9:2799.5**
Professional Dental Corporations, generally, this index

DEPOSITIONS
Arbitration proceedings, **9:4207**
Evidence, use as, arbitration proceedings, **9:4207**

DEPOSITS
Consumer loan brokers, advance expenses, **9:3572.6**
Lessees, **9:3251 et seq.**
Mechanic's privileges and liens, concursus proceedings, **9:4841**
Newspaper dealers and distributors, interest rate on cash bond or security, **9:3601**
Savings and Loan Associations, this index
Sureties, joint control, **9:3904**
Tenants, **9:3251 et seq.**
Trust companies. Bank Deposits and Collections, generally, this index

DEPOSITS IN COURTS
Abandoned property, **9:164**
Bonding claims of contractor,
　Private works, **9:4841**
　Public works, **9:4941**
Fire insurance proceeds, claim of seller's privilege on property destroyed by fire, **9:4582**
Unclaimed property, **9:164**

DEVELOPER
Definitions, real estate timesharing, **9:1131.2**

DIRECTORS
Associations and societies, tort liability, **9:2792**
Downtown development districts, limitation of liability, **9:2792.2**
Quasi offenses, liability, **9:2792**
　Nonprofit corporations, **9:2792.1**
Tort liability, **9:2792**

DISASTERS
Privileges and immunities,
　Health care providers, gratuitous services, **9:2799.5**
　National Voluntary Organizations Active in Disaster, **9:2793.8**

DISCLOSURE
Children and minors, parenting coordinators, custody, **9:358.7**

DISTRICT COURTS
Chambers, emancipation, recognition of foreign judgment or decree, **9:901**

DIVORCE
Affidavits, return of child kept in violation of custody or visitation order, **9:343**
Attorney fees, **9:345**
　Family violence cases, **9:367**
　Support or contributions arrearages, **9:375**
　Visitation, **9:375**
Attorneys, appointment, child custody or visitation proceedings, **9:345**
Compromise and settlement, mediation, custody or visitation actions, **9:331 et seq.**
Conflict of laws, Revision Act, pending actions, **9:381**
Coparenting seminars, **9:306**
Covenant marriage, **9:272 et seq., 9:307 et seq.**

DIVORCE—Cont'd
Custody of children,
　Actions between spouses, **9:291**
　Affidavit, return of child kept in violation of order, **9:343**
　Appointment of attorney, **9:345**
　Attorneys, appointment, protective and remedial measures, **9:345**
　Best interest of child,
　　Joint custody, **9:335**
　　Relocation hearing, **9:355.12**
　Coparenting seminars, **9:306**
　Evaluation and mediation, **9:331 et seq.**
　Evidence, relocation hearing, burden of proof, **9:355.13**
　Fines and penalties, frivolous or unwarranted relocation request, **9:355.16**
　Foreign states, relocation, **9:355.1 et seq.**
　Frivolous or unwarranted relocation request, **9:355.16**
　Joint custody, **9:335 et seq.**
　Jurisdiction, relocation, **9:355.17**
　Mandate, provisional custody, **9:951 et seq.**
　Mediation, **9:331 et seq.**
　Mediators, qualifications, **9:334**
　Moving, **9:355.1 et seq.**
　Notice, relocation, **9:355.1 et seq.**
　Postseparation family violence relief, **9:361 et seq.**
　Presumption, family violence perpetrators, **9:364**
　Priority, relocation, hearing, **9:355.9**
　Protective and remedial measures, **9:343, 9:345**
　Provisional custody, mandate, **9:951 et seq.**
　Records, access, **9:351**
　Relocation, **9:355.1 et seq.**
　Return of child kept in violation of order, **9:343**
　Sanctions, frivolous or unwarranted relocation request, **9:355.16**
　Sexual abuse, appointment of attorney, **9:345**
　Temporary orders, relocation, **9:355.10**
　Training, mediators, **9:334**
　Violence, postseparation family violence relief, **9:361 et seq.**
Death, presumption of, authority to remarry, **9:301**
Domestic violence, covenant marriage, **9:307**
Electronic transactions, exemptions, **9:2603**
Evidence,
　Custody of children, relocation hearing, burden of proof, **9:355.13**
　Mediation, custody or visitation proceedings, **9:332**
　Sexual abuse, child custody or visitation, **9:364**
Frivolous or unwarranted relocation request, custody of children, **9:355.16**
Hearings,
　In chambers, **9:302**
　Relocation hearing, custody of children, **9:355.9 et seq.**
　Temporary custody of children, orders, relocation hearing, **9:355.9 et seq.**
High test marriage, **9:272 et seq.**
Injunctions, **9:371 et seq.**
　Domestic abuse, injunctions, **9:372**
　Family violence, relief, **9:361 et seq.**
Joint custody of children, **9:335 et seq.**
Mediation,
　Custody of children, **9:331 et seq., 9:351 et seq.**
　Postseparation family violence relief, **9:363**
　Qualifications, mediators, custody and visitation, **9:334**
　Visitation, **9:351 et seq.**
Medical care and treatment, family violence victims, costs, **9:367**

I–19

DIVORCE—Cont'd
Military forces, presumption of death, authority to remarry, **9:301**
Movable property, removal, **9:373**
Moving, custody of children, **9:355.1 et seq.**
Notice, relocation, custody of children, **9:355.3 et seq.**
Orders,
    Child custody or visitation,
        Bond (officers and fiduciaries), compliance, **9:342**
        Family violence, injunctions, **9:366**
        Return of child kept in violation of order, **9:343**
            Mediation, **9:332**
    Family violence, injunctions, **9:366**
    Joint custody, children, **9:335 et seq.**
    Temporary custody of children, relocation, **9:355.10**
Pending actions, conflict of laws, Revision Act, **9:381**
Records and recordation, children, access, **9:351**
Relocation, custody of children, **9:355.1 et seq.**
Reports,
    Custody or visitation proceedings, mental health professionals, **9:331**
    Mediation, custody of children, fees, **9:351**
Temporary custody of children, orders, relocation, **9:355.10**
Violence, postseparation family violence relief, **9:361 et seq.**
Visitation,
    Affidavit, return of child kept in violation of order, **9:343**
    Coparenting seminars, **9:306**
    Evaluation and mediation, **9:331 et seq.**
        Qualifications, mediators, **9:334**
    Grandparents, rights, **9:344**
    Protective and remedial measures, **9:341 et seq.**
    Siblings, rights, **9:344**
    Violence, postseparation family violence relief, **9:361 et seq.**
Witnesses,
    Custody or visitation proceedings, evaluations, mental health professionals, **9:331**
    Family violence, **9:364, 9:365**
        Fees, **9:367**

DOMESTIC ABUSE
Covenant marriage, divorce, **9:307**
Grandparents and grandchildren, protection, **9:575**
Parenting coordinators, child custody, appointments, exemptions, **9:358.2**
Postseparation family violence relief, **9:361 et seq.**
Separation from bed and board, covenant marriage, **9:307**

DOMICILE AND RESIDENCE
Consumer credit, **9:3511**
Definitions, uniform disposition of unclaimed property, **9:153**
Electronic transactions, exemptions, **9:2603**
Trustee, qualification to act as, **9:1783**

DONATIONS
    See, also, Testaments, generally, this index
Associations and societies, immovable property, **9:1051**
Conditional donations, cy pres doctrine, **9:2331 et seq.**
Cy pres doctrine, **9:2331 et seq.**
    Educational purposes, **9:2331 et seq.**
    Eleemosynary donations, **9:2331 et seq.**
Educational institutions, **9:2271**
Literary institutions, **9:2271**
Notarial acts, married person to spouse, reservation of right to revoke, **9:2351**
Power of attorney, military forces, immovables, **9:3882.1**
Real estate timesharing, prize and gift promotional offers, **9:1131.12**

DONATIONS—Cont'd
Records and recordation, **9:2371**
    Religious organizations, quieting title by lapse of time, **9:2321**
Reduction and calculation of succession mass,
    Exemptions, educational charitable or religious organizations, **9:2372**
    Inter vivos donations, made to spouse of previous marriage, **9:2354, 9:2373**
Registration, inter vivos donations of mortgageable property, effect, **9:2371**
Religious organizations and societies, successors, **9:2321, 9:2322**

DONATIONS FOR CHARITABLE PURPOSES
Generally, **9:2290, 9:2321** See **9:2771 et seq.**

DONKEYS
Sponsors, equine activities, immunities, **9:2795.1**

DOOR-TO-DOOR SALESMEN
Purchase agreement, withdrawal of consent, **9:2711**

DOORS
Privilege, **9:4621, 9:4622**

DOWNTOWN DEVELOPMENT DISTRICTS
Board members, liability, quasi offenses, **9:2792.2**
Definitions, liability, board members, **9:2792.2**
Directors, limitation of liability, **9:2792.2**

DOWNTOWN DISTRICTS
Limitation of liability, directors or trustees, **9:2792.4**

DRAINAGE DISTRICTS
Interest, assessments for improvements, **9:3507**
Subdrainage districts,
    Assessments, interest, **9:3507**
    Interest, assessments for improvements, **9:3507**

DRAINS AND DRAINAGE
Building encroachments, prescription, **9:5627**
Public trust, purposes, **9:2341 et seq.**
Servitudes, recording, **9:2726**

DRUG DEALER LIABILITY ACT
Generally, **9:2800.61 et seq.**

DRUGS AND MEDICINE
Dealers, liability, **9:2800.61 et seq.**
Tests,
    Custody, **9:331.1**
    Visitation, **9:331.1**
Treatment, substance abuse, dealer liability, **9:2800.63**

DUAL AGENCY
Definitions, real estate brokers and salespersons, **9:3891**

DWELLINGS
Aged persons, home solicitation sales, **9:3541.21, 9:3541.22**
Attorney fees, collection of rent, **9:3259**
Blighted property, prescription, **9:5633**
Construction or repair,
    Encroachment on public places, **9:5627**
    Machinery and equipment, consequential damages, limiting liability, **9:2775**
    New home warranties, **9:3141 et seq.**
Expropriation, exemptions, **9:3187**
Homeowners Association Act, **9:1141.1 et seq.**

INDEX TO TITLE 9

DWELLINGS—Cont'd
New home warranties, **9:3141 et seq.**
    Defects, **9:3141 et seq.**
    Insurance, **9:3147**
        Transfer of warranty and insurance, subsequent owners, **9:3148**
    Major structural defects, **9:3141 et seq.**
    Peremption, enforcement, **9:3146**
    Waiver, **9:3144**
Prescription,
    Blighted property, **9:5633**
    New home warranties, enforcement, **9:3146**
Rent, collection, attorneys fees, **9:3259**
Residential Truth in Construction Act, **9:4851 et seq.**

EDUCATION
Donations,
    Cy pres doctrine, **9:2331 et seq.**
    Exemptions, reduction and calculation of succession mass, **9:2372**
    Inter vivos donations, exemptions, reduction and calculation of succession mass, **9:2372**
Mediators, child custody disputes, qualifications, **9:334**
Parenting coordinators, child custody, **9:358.3**
Public trust, purposes, **9:2341 et seq.**
Schools and School Districts, generally, this index
Trusts and trustees,
    Mixed trusts, educational trust acting as trustee, **9:1783**

EDUCATIONAL CORPORATIONS
Nonprofit corporations, servitudes, granting, **9:1252**

EDUCATIONAL TELEVISION AND RADIO
Public trust, purposes, **9:2341 et seq.**

ELECTRICITY
    See, also, Public Utilities, generally, this index
New home warranties, **9:3141 et seq.**
Nuclear electric generating plants, partition, agreements against, duration, **9:1702**
Poles and wires, servitudes, recording, **9:2726**
Public trust, purposes, **9:2341 et seq.**
Servitudes,
    Public roads or streets, **9:1253**
    Recording, **9:2726**
Warranties, new home warranties, **9:3141 et seq.**

ELECTRONIC TRANSACTIONS
    Generally, **9:2601 et seq.**
Acknowledgments, **9:2611**
Agents and agencies. Electronic agents, post
Application of law, **9:2604, 9:2605**
Applications, **9:2603.1**
Attributions, **9:2609**
Audits and auditors, **9:2612**
Automated transactions,
    Electronic agents, **9:2614**
    Errors, **9:2610**
Checks, retention, **9:2612**
Conflict of laws, **9:2604**
Consideration, transmissions, errors, return, **9:2610**
Construction of law, **9:2605, 9:2606**
Contractors, retention, **9:2612**
Contracts,
    Automated transactions, electronic agents, **9:2614**
    Enforcement, **9:2607, 9:2608**
    Mistakes, transmissions, **9:2610**
    Notaries public, **9:2611**

ELECTRONIC TRANSACTIONS—Cont'd
Contracts—Cont'd
    Variation, **9:2605**
Control processes, state agencies, **9:2618**
Definitions, **9:2602**
Digital signatures. Signatures, generally, post
Electronic agents,
    Automated transactions, **9:2614**
    Errors, **9:2610**
Electronic signatures. Signatures, generally, post
Enforcement, **9:2607, 9:2608**
    Transferable records, **9:2616**
Evidence, **9:2613**
    Retention, **9:2612**
    State agencies, **9:2617**
Exemptions, **9:2603, 9:2612**
    Adoption, **9:2603**
    Commercial Code, **9:2603**
    Divorce, **9:2603**
    Domicile and residence, **9:2603**
    Eviction, **9:2603**
    Foreclosure, **9:2603**
    Hazardous substances and waste, transportation, **9:2603**
    Health and accident insurance, cancellation, **9:2603**
    Life insurance, cancellation, **9:2603**
    Orders, **9:2603**
    Public utilities, **9:2603**
    Trusts and trustees, **9:2603**
    Water supply, **9:2603**
    Wills, **9:2603**
Forms, **9:2612**
Holder, transferable records, **9:2616**
Identity and identification,
    Security, **9:2609**
    Transferable records, **9:2616**
Judicial records, **9:2603.1**
Lost or destroyed property, **9:2610**
Mail and mailing, **9:2608**
Negotiable Instruments, this index
Notaries public, **9:2611**
Notice,
    Courts, exemptions, **9:2603**
    Transmissions, errors, **9:2610**
Oaths and affirmations, **9:2611**
Originals, retention, **9:2612**
Posting, **9:2608**
Purported transmissions, legal effect, **9:2615**
Receipt, **9:2615**
Reciprocity, state agencies, **9:2619**
Scope, **9:2603**
Security,
    Identity and identification, **9:2609**
    Transmissions, **9:2618**
        Errors, **9:2610**
Sending, **9:2615**
Signatures, **9:2603.1**
    Enforcement, **9:2607**
    Identity and identification, **9:2609**
    Oaths and affirmations, **9:2611**
    State agencies, **9:2618**
State agencies, **9:2617**
    Reciprocity, **9:2619**
    Signatures, **9:2618**
Storage, **9:2617**
Transactions, automated, electronic agents, **9:2614**
Transferable records, **9:2616**
    Authoritative copies, **9:2616**

ELECTRONIC TRANSACTIONS—Cont'd
Transferable records—Cont'd
    Control, **9:2616**
    Copies, **9:2616**
    Defenses, **9:2616**
    Enforcement, **9:2616**
    Holder, **9:2616**
    Identity and identification, **9:2616**
    Obligor, **9:2616**
    Rights, **9:2616**
Transmissions,
    Business office, **9:2615**
    Changes, **9:2610**
    Errors, **9:2610**
    Methods, variation by agreement, **9:2608**
    Mistakes, **9:2610**
    Purported, legal effect, **9:2615**
    Security, **9:2618**
Variation by agreement, **9:2605**
    Transmissions, methods, **9:2608**
Verification, **9:2611**
Warrants, **9:2603.1**
Writing, enforcement, **9:2607**, **9:2608**

EMBRYOS
Human embryos, in vitro fertilized human ovum, **9:121 et seq.**

EMERGENCIES
First aid, tort liability, **9:2793**
Food assistance, liability, **9:2799**

EMERGENCY MEDICAL SERVICES
Privileges and immunities,
    Response network, **9:2798.5**
    Volunteers, **9:2793.2**

EMERGENCY RESPONSE NETWORK
Privileges and immunities, **9:2798.5**

EMPLOYEES
Definitions, nonprofit organizations, limitation of liability, **9:2792.8**
Labor and Employment, generally, this index

ENCROACHMENT
Public places, buildings encroaching upon, **9:5627**

ENERGY
Public trust, purposes, **9:2341 et seq.**
Solar collectors, right of use, **9:1255**

ENGINEERS AND ENGINEERING
    See, also, Surveys and Surveyors, generally, this index
Asbestos, limitation of liability, **9:2800.3**
Fraud, affidavits of inspection, mechanic's privileges and liens, **9:4820**
Hazardous substances and waste, limitation of liability, **9:2800.3**
Mechanic's privileges and liens, **9:4801 et seq.**
Privileges,
    Immovables, **9:4801 et seq.**
    Private works, **9:4801 et seq.**

ENVIRONMENTAL PROTECTION
Servitudes, conservation, **9:1271 et seq.**

EQUAL CREDIT OPPORTUNITY LAW
Generally, **9:3581 et seq.**

ESCHEAT
Carpets, proceeds from sale, **9:4688**
Clothing left for washing, cleaning or repair, proceeds of sale, **9:4688**
Gold, unclaimed, proceeds of sale, **9:4703**
Immovable property, vacant successions, **9:1611 et seq.**
Jewelry, unclaimed, proceeds of sale, **9:4703**
Silver and silverware, unclaimed, proceeds of sale, **9:4703**
Tailors, unclaimed property, proceeds of sale, **9:4688**
Watches, unclaimed, proceeds of sale, **9:4703**

ESCROWS AND ESCROW AGENTS
    See, also, Sequestration, generally, this index
Abandoned or unclaimed property,
    Administrator's escrow account, **9:165**
    Remittance under protest, action to recover, **9:168**
Bond for deed contract, **9:2941 et seq.**
Military forces, power of attorney, powers granted, **9:3877**
Real estate timesharing,
    Accounts, claims for damages, **9:1131.17**
    Deposits, **9:1131.16**

ESTATE TAX
Estate Tax Apportionment Law, **9:2431 through 2439**
    Action by nonresident, reciprocity, **9:2437**
    Action to recover amount of tax or deficiency from person interested in estate, **9:2436**
        Time of filing, liability of fiduciary, **9:2436**
    Allowance for exemptions, deductions and credits, **9:2435**
    Application of provisions, **9:2438**
    Apportionment of tax liability among persons interested in estate, **9:2432**
    Fiduciary right to withhold or recover proportion of tax attributable to person interested in estate, **9:2434**
    Security by person interested in estate for payment of tax, **9:2434**

ESTATE TAX APPORTIONMENT LAW
    Generally, **9:2431 et seq.**
Action by nonresident, reciprocity, **9:2437**
Action to recover amount of tax or deficiency from person interested in estate, **9:2436**
    Time of filing, liability of fiduciary, **9:2436**
Allowance for exemptions, deductions and credits, **9:2435**
Application of provisions, **9:2438**
Fiduciary right to withhold or recover proportion of tax attributable to person interested in estate, **9:2434**
Security by person interested in estate for payment of tax, **9:2434**

EVICTION
Constructive eviction, uninhabitable premises, mitigation of damages, **9:3260**
Electronic transactions, exemptions, **9:2603**
Mitigation of damages, uninhabitable premises, **9:3260**
Warranties, title against eviction, succession sale, **9:3174**

EVIDENCE
Burden of proof,
    Credit repair services organizations, exemption, **9:3573.14**
    Malpractice, **9:2794**
    Mechanic's privileges and liens, **9:4841**
    Merchants, liability, **9:2800.6**
Chain of custody, blood or tissue samples, determining paternity, **9:397.2**
Checks, stop payment, **9:2782.2**

INDEX TO TITLE 9

EVIDENCE—Cont'd
Copies and duplicates,
    Authenticated copies as evidence, **9:2759**
Credit repair services organizations, exemption, **9:3573.14**
Debtors and creditors, open accounts, demand for payment, receipt, **9:2781**
Documents, mechanic's privileges and liens, **9:4842**
Electronic transactions, **9:2613**
Fiduciary, appointment or incumbency, **9:3834**
Interest, maximum rate, conventional interest, **9:3503**
Partnership, registry certificate, conclusive evidence of registration, **9:3405**
Partnership certificate, certified copy, **9:3403**
Paternity,
    Blood tests, **9:396 et seq.**
    Tissue test, **9:396 et seq.**
Payment, taxes, **9:2902, 9:2903, 9:2922, 9:2924**
Premium finance companies, consumer credit, insurance, **9:3550**
Presumptions,
    Conclusive presumptions, bounded by waterway, highway, etc., **9:2971 et seq.**
    Premium finance companies, consumer credit, insurance, **9:3550**
    Roads, abandonment, **9:2981 et seq.**
    Successions and Succession Proceedings, this index
    Trust, acceptance by beneficiary, **9:1808**
Privileges and liens, private works, burden of proof, **9:4841**
Successions and Succession Proceedings, this index

EX PARTE PROCEEDINGS
Children and minors, parenting coordinators, custody, **9:358.6**

EXCHANGE OF PROPERTY
Military forces, power of attorney, powers granted, **9:3871**

EXECUTORY PROCESS
Affidavits, mortgages, obligations not paraphed for identification, **9:5555**
Confession of judgment, **9:3590**
Mortgages,
    Foreclosure, keeper of property, designation, **9:5136 et seq.**
    Obligations not paraphed for identification, **9:5555**
Verified petition, mortgages, obligations not paraphed for identification, **9:5555**

EXEMPTIONS
Consumer credit, **9:3512**
    Licenses, **9:3560**
Consumer loan brokers, **9:3572.2**
Credit repair services organizations, **9:3573.2**
    Burden of proof, **9:3573.14**
Expropriation, **9:3187**
Parenting coordinators, child custody, appointments, domestic abuse, **9:358.2**
Trusts, seizure, **9:2006**

EXPERTS
Fees and charges,
    Interdiction proceedings, inventories, **9:1423**
    Successions, Orleans Parish, preparation of inventory, **9:1423**
    Tutorships, inventories, **9:1423**

EXPORTS AND IMPORTS
Harbors and ports, public trusts, creation to improve facilities, **9:2341**

EXPORTS AND IMPORTS—Cont'd
Public trusts, purposes, **9:2341**

EXPROPRIATION
Damages,
    Municipalities over 5,000, wharves, buildings or improvements, **9:1102.1**
    Port of New Orleans, wharves, buildings and improvements, **9:1102.1**
Deep water port commission, wharves, buildings or improvements, **9:1102.1**
Port of New Orleans, **9:1102.1**
Prescription, private property damaged for public purposes, **9:5624**
Riparian lands, buildings or improvements, **9:1102.2**
Servitudes, highways and roads, recording plats, **9:2727**
Surveys, plats, recording, **9:2727**
Wharves, buildings or improvements, deep water port commission, **9:1102.1**

FAIRS AND EXPOSITIONS
Animal sanctuary, limitation of liability, **9:2796.2**
Farm animal activities, privileges and immunities, **9:2795.1**

FALSE RIVER
    See, also, Rivers and Streams, generally, this index
Boundaries, title of property, **9:1110**

FAMILY HOME
    Generally, **9:2801 et seq.**
Community property, **9:2801 et seq.**
Consent to sale or mortgage, **9:2801**
Declaration, **9:2801**
Description, **9:2801**
Homesteads, generally, this index
Mortgage, consent of wife, **9:2801**
Records, description and declaration, **9:2801**
Sale, consent of wife, **9:2801**
Usufruct, surviving spouse, **9:1201**

FAMILY MEETINGS
Recognition of confirmation of tutors or curators without meeting, **9:602**

FARM ANIMAL ACTIVITIES
Definitions, privileges and immunities, **9:2795.1**

FARMLAND
Definitions, liability of owner, unauthorized entry, **9:2800.4**

FARMOUT AGREEMENT
Definitions, mineral rights, **9:2780**

FAULT
Presumption, violation of transportation, statute, **9:2800.13**

FEDERAL BUREAU OF INVESTIGATION
Privileges and immunities, agents, **9:2793.1**

FEDERAL CREDIT UNIONS
Liability, directors and others, **9:2792.5**

FEDERAL DEPOSIT INSURANCE CORPORATION
Interest, accrued interest, **9:3509.2**

FEDERAL ESTATE TAX
Apportionment, Estate Tax Apportionment Law, **9:2431 et seq.**
Inheritance Tax, this index

INDEX TO TITLE 9

FEDERAL GIFT TAX
Annual exclusion, trusts and trustees, 9:1937

FEDERAL HOME LOAN BANKS
Accrued interest, recovery of interest upon, 9:3509.2

FEDERAL HOUSING ADMINISTRATION
Mortgages, interest, 9:3504
Obligations insured by, interest rate, 9:3504

FEDERAL SAVINGS AND LOAN ASSOCIATIONS
Mortgages, inscription in parish wherein state capitol is located, 9:5142, 9:5143

FEDERAL SAVINGS AND LOAN INSURANCE CORPORATION
Accrued interest, recovery of interest upon, 9:3509.2
Interest, accrued interest, recovery of interest upon, 9:3509.2

FEDERAL TAX LIEN ACT
Certificates of redemption, filing and recording, 9:2725

FERTILIZERS
Liquid fertilizers, storage tank, movable property, 9:1106

FIDEI COMMISSA
Mortgages securing several obligations not governed by, 9:5307

FIDUCIARIES
Generally, 9:3801 et seq.
Abandoned property, 9:163
Assignee for benefit of creditors, 9:3801
Assignments, securities, stock, etc., 9:3833
Breach of duty, knowledge or bad faith of persons dealing with fiduciaries, 9:3805, 9:3808
Citation of act, 9:3814
Definitions, 9:3801
    Estate tax apportionment, 9:2431
    Uniform Law for Simplification of Fiduciary Security Transfers, 9:3831
Estate Tax Apportionment Law, 9:2431 through 2439
    Action by nonresident, reciprocity, 9:2437
    Action to recover amount of tax or deficiency from person interested in estate, 9:2436
        Time of filing, liability of fiduciary, 9:2436
    Allowance for exemptions, deductions and credits, 9:2435
    Fiduciary right to withhold or recover proportion of tax attributable to person interested in estate, 9:2434
    Security by person interested in estate for payment of tax, 9:2434
Evidence, appointment or incumbency, 9:3834
Investigations, duty of persons dealing with, 9:3809
Mandatary, 9:3801
Military forces, power of attorney, 9:3861 et seq.
Money, payment to, responsibility for proper application, 9:3802
Obligations, breach of, duties and liabilities of bank, 9:3809
Officers, 9:3801
Partners, 9:3801
Property transferred to, responsibility for proper application, 9:3802
Rules applicable, cases not provided for, 9:3812
Securities, transfer, Uniform Law, 9:3831 et seq.
Third persons, nonliability for participation in fiduciary's breach of duty, 9:3837
Unclaimed property, 9:163
Uniform construction, 9:3813

FIDUCIARIES—Cont'd
Uniform Law for Simplification of Fiduciary Security Transfers, 9:3831 et seq.

FIDUCIARY SECURITY TRANSFERS ACT
Generally, 9:3831 et seq.

FINANCED LEASES
    Generally, 9:3310
Definitions, leases, movable property, 9:3306
Sale/lease-back, secured transactions, application of law, 9:3310.1
Secured transactions, application of law, 9:3310

FINANCIAL INSTITUTIONS
Confidential or privileged information, personal credit information, 9:3571
Consumer credit transactions, application of law, 9:3563.1
Exemptions, notification filing requirements, 9:3563.1
Military forces, power of attorney, powers granted, 9:3874

FINANCIAL INSTITUTIONS COMMISSIONER
Advisory opinions, 9:3556.2
Interpretations of office, 9:3556.2

FINANCIAL INSTITUTIONS OFFICE
Confidential or privileged information, 9:3518.1
Copies, records and reports, confidentiality, 9:3518.1
Disclosure, records or reports, 9:3518.1
Examinations of institutions, records, disclosure, 9:3518.1
Motions, disclosure, 9:3518.1
Orders, disclosure, production, 9:3518.1
Records and recordation, 9:3518.1
Subpoenas, records and reports, 9:3518.1

FIREFIGHTERS AND FIRE DEPARTMENTS
Privileges and immunities, damages to property resulting from actions taken in course and scope of employment, 9:2793.1

FIRST AID
Emergency treatment,
    Privileges and immunities, volunteers, 9:2793.2
    Tort liability, 9:2793
Privileges and immunities, volunteers, 9:2793.2

FISH AND GAME
Consumer credit, 9:3510 et seq.
Injunctions, laboratories, unauthorized release, 9:2799.4
Landowners, duty of care, 9:2791
Licenses and permits,
    Support of persons, suspension or revocation, 9:315.30 et seq.
Private property, use for recreational area, limiting liability for personal injuries, 9:2795
Recreation area, owner, duty of care, 9:2791
Taxidermists, abandoned or unclaimed specimens, disposition, 9:191, 9:192

FOOD
Donations, food banks, limitation of liability, 9:2799
Limitation of liability, donated food, 9:2799.3, 9:2799.6
Vendor's privilege, exemption, perishable food products, 9:4544

FORCED HEIRS
Successions and Succession Proceedings, this index

FORCED PUBLIC SALE
Definitions, auctions, 9:3152

INDEX TO TITLE 9

FORECLOSURE
Bond for deed contract, **9:2944**
Electronic transactions, exemptions, **9:2603**
Mortgages, this index

FOREIGN CORPORATIONS
Attachment, sale under attachment against, prescription, **9:5641**
Immovable property, sale, action to set aside, prescription, **9:5681**
Receivers and Receivership, generally, this index

FOREIGN LIMITED PARTNERSHIP
Definitions, commercial loans, interest, agreements exceeding maximum conventional rate, **9:3509**
Interest, exceeding maximum conventional rate, **9:3509**

FOREIGN STATES
Abandoned or unclaimed property,
  Claim of foreign state, **9:166, 9:175**
  Claim to recover, **9:166**
  Reciprocal agreements and cooperation, **9:175**
Custodial trusts, **9:2260.19**
Estate Tax Apportionment Law, **9:2431 et seq.**
Money orders, unclaimed property, claim of foreign state, **9:176**
Public contracts, interpretation and dispute resolution, **9:2778**
Reciprocal agreements, abandoned and unclaimed property, **9:175**
Traveler's checks, abandoned or unclaimed property, claim of foreign state, **9:154, 9:166**
Trusts and trustees, **9:2262.1 et seq.**

FORESTLAND
Definitions, liability of owner, unauthorized entry, **9:2800.4**

FORESTS AND FORESTRY
Airports and landing fields, immunity from liability for death or injury, **9:2800.11**
Gleaning, privileges and immunities, **9:2800.4**
Indemnity, oil, minerals and gas, drilling and wells, **9:2780**
Minerals, oil and gas, indemnity agreements, drilling and wells, **9:2780**
Privileges and immunities, landowners, **9:2800.4**
Trespass, liability of owner, injury, death, or loss from unauthorized entry, **9:2800.4**

FORFEITURES
Interest, **9:3501**

FOUNDATIONS
Immovables, real rights created for benefit of organization, **9:1252**
Religious Organizations and Societies, generally, this index

FRAUD
Arbitration award, vacating for, **9:4210**
Condominiums, purchaser, cancellation of contract, **9:1124.106**
Credit repair services organizations, **9:3573.3**
Fines and penalties, contracts, sales of realty, **9:2989**
Limited liability partnerships, **9:3431**
Loan brokers, advance fees, **9:3574.3**
Mechanic's privileges and liens, affidavits, inspections, **9:4820**
Privileges and liens, private works, affidavits, inspections, **9:4820**
Real estate timesharing, advertisements, **9:1131.12**
Residential Truth in Construction Act, **9:4851 et seq.**
Stop payment, checks, **9:2782.2**

FRAUD—Cont'd
Uniform Fraudulent Transfer Act, **9:2790.1 et seq.**

FUNERAL DIRECTORS AND EMBALMERS
Unclaimed bodies, burial, **9:1551, 9:1552**

FURNITURE
Privileges, making or repairs, **9:4502**

GARAGEMAN'S PRIVILEGE ACT
  Generally, **9:4501**
Privileges, repairmen, automobiles and machinery, **9:4501**

GEMS
Unclaimed, **9:4701**
  Proceeds of sale, disposition, **9:4703**

GIFT CERTIFICATES
Abandoned or unclaimed property, **9:165**

GIFT TAX
Trusts and trustees, annual exclusion, federal gift tax, **9:1937**

GOING OUT OF BUSINESS SALES
Proceeds, application, responsibility, **9:3802**

GOOD FAITH
Definitions, abandoned or unclaimed property, defense and indemnification of holder, **9:162**
Fiduciary, **9:3801**

GOOD SAMARITAN LAW
Privileges and immunities, **9:2793**

GOODWILL
Community property, valuation, **9:2801.2**

GOVERNOR
Appointments,
  Public administrators, **9:1581**
Bonds (officers and fiduciaries), public administrators, **9:1582**
Discretion, public administrators bond, **9:1582**
Executive counsel, compromise and settlement, state succeeding to immovable property, rights and claims, **9:1612**
Public administrators, bonds, **9:1582**

GRADUATED PAYMENT MORTGAGES
Interest, **9:3504**

GRANDPARENTS AND GRANDCHILDREN
Class trusts, **9:1891 et seq.**
Domestic abuse, protection, **9:575**
Great grandparents and great grandchildren, class trusts, **9:1891 et seq.**
Visitation rights, **9:344**

GRATUITOUS TRUSTS
Classification as, **9:1735**

HABITATION
Attorney fees, collection of rent, **9:3259**

HANDICAPPED PERSONS
Child support, guidelines, deviations, **9:315.1**
Food banks, donations, limitation of liability, **9:2799, 9:2799.6**
Support of persons, guidelines, deviations, **9:315.1**

HARBORS AND PORTS
Bonds, public trusts improvement of import and export facilities, **9:2341**
Exports and imports, improvements, public trusts, **9:2341**

INDEX TO TITLE 9

HARBORS AND PORTS—Cont'd
Improvements, export and import facilities, public trusts, 9:2341
Municipalities over 5,000, wharves, buildings or improvements, 9:1102.1
Port, harbor and terminal districts, public trust for handling imports and exports, 9:2341
Port commissions, limitation of liability, 9:2792.4
Port of New Orleans,
    Compensation, expropriation, 9:1102.1
    Consent, wharves, buildings or improvements, riparian owners, 9:1102.1
    Constitutional provisions continued in force, building or improvements, 9:1102.1
    Expropriation, 9:1102.1
Public trusts,
    Improvement of import and export facilities, 9:2341
    Purposes, 9:2341 et seq.
Public use, riparian owners, improvements of property on navigable waters, 9:1102.1
Riparian owners, use of land, 9:1102.2

HAWKERS AND PEDDLERS
Drugs and medicine, withdrawal of consent to agreement, 9:2711
Purchase agreement, withdrawal of consent, 9:2711

HAZARDOUS SUBSTANCES AND WASTE
Abatement, limitation of liability, persons designing, supervising or performing, 9:2800.3
Cleanup, limitation of liability, persons designing, supervising or performing, 9:2800.3
Electronic transactions, exemptions, transportation, 9:2603
Liability, limitation of liability, mitigation, abatement or clean-up services, 9:2800.3
Mortgages, liability of lenders, 9:5395
Negligence, liability, mitigation, abatement or clean-up services, 9:2800.3
Remedial actions, recreational areas, private owners, limitation of liability, 9:2795
School asbestos abatement, limitation of liability, 9:2800.3
Transportation, electronic transactions, exemptions, 9:2603

HEALTH CARE FACILITIES
    See, also, Hospitals, generally, this index
Damages, privileges and immunities, gratuitous services, 9:2799.5
Negligence, gratuitous services, 9:2799.5
Notice, gratuitous services, limitation of liability, 9:2799.5
Privileges and immunities, gratuitous services, 9:2799.5

HEALTH CARE PROVIDERS
Damages, medical care and treatment, gratuitous services, 9:2799.5
Negligence, medical care and treatment, gratuitous services, 9:2799.5
Privileges and immunities,
    Medical care and treatment, gratuitous services, 9:2799.5
    Nonprofit health care quality improvement corporations, reports, 9:2800.20
    services, 9:4751 et seq.

HEAT AND HEATING COMPANIES
New home warranties, 9:3141 et seq.
Warranties, new home warranties, 9:3141 et seq.

HIGHWAYS AND ROADS
    See, also, Streets and Alleys, generally, this index

HIGHWAYS AND ROADS—Cont'd
Abandonment,
    Abutting property, sale or transfer, 9:2981 et seq.
    Actions, 9:2983
    Mortgages, remedial provisions of act, 9:2982
    Prescription, right, title and interest in abandoned roads, 9:2983
    Presumptions, 9:2981 et seq.
    Sales, remedial provisions of act, 9:2982
    Third parties, 9:2981
    Transfer of lands fronting highways, 9:2984
Actions and proceedings, removal of encroachments, 9:5627
Boating or recreational sites, 9:1251
Buildings, encroachment, 9:5627
    Prescription, 9:5627
Cable television, servitudes, 9:1253
Curators, sale or lease of right of way over land of ward, 9:731
Damages, grading, prescription, 9:5603
Electric transmission lines, construction, servitudes, 9:1253
Encroachments, 9:5627
Plank roads, expropriation, petition, 9:3180
Prescription,
    Abandonment, ante
    Damages due to grading, 9:5603
    Removal of encroachments, 9:5627
Privileges, feed for livestock used in construction, alteration or repair, 9:4921 et seq.
Public transportation servitudes, 9:1253
Public utilities and facilities, servitudes, 9:1253
Purchases and sales, abandoned highways and roads, abutting property, 9:2981 et seq.
Records and recordation, abandonment, notarized declarations, 9:2983
Recreation and recreational facilities, owner duty of care, 9:2791
Tramroads, right of way, tutors or curators selling or leasing over land of ward, 9:731
Transfer of land fronting or bounding by,
    Abandonment of roads, 9:2984
    Effect, 9:2971 et seq.
Tutors, sale or lease of right of way over land of ward, 9:731

HIKING
Landowner, duty of care, 9:2791

HINNY
Sponsors, equine activities, immunities, 9:2795.1

HISTORICAL ASSOCIATION
Limitation of liability, directors, officers or trustees, nonprofit organizations, 9:2792.3

HISTORICAL SITES
Outdoor advertising, amortization, nonconforming billboards, 9:5625
Prescription, amortization, nonconforming billboards, 9:5625
Private property, personal injuries, limiting liability, 9:2795

HOLIDAY IN DIXIE PARADES
Associations and societies, damages, limitation of liability, 9:2796

HOME APPLIANCES AND EQUIPMENT
Unclaimed goods, disposition, 9:4687 et seq.

HOMEOWNERS ASSOCIATION ACT
    Generally, 9:1141.1 et seq.

HOMEOWNERS ASSOCIATION ACT—Cont'd
Privileges and immunities, directors and officers and trustees, 9:2792.7

HOMESTEADS
Bond for deed contracts, 9:2948, 9:2949
Declaration and description, 9:2801
Exemptions, bond for deed contracts, 9:2948
Matrimonial regimes, divorce, possession and use of family residence, 9:374
Mortgage,
    Consent of wife, 9:2801
    Foreclosure proceedings, keeper of property, appointment, 9:5136 et seq.
Sale, consent of wife, 9:2801
Taxation, exemptions, bond for deed contract holders, 9:2948

HORSE RACING
Privileges and immunities, feed and medicine, 9:4661
    Limitation of liability, 9:2795.3

HORSEBACK RIDING
Private property, personal injuries, limiting liability, 9:2795

HORSES
Farm animal activities, privileges and immunities, 9:2795.1
Privileges, feed and medical services, 9:4661
Shows, farm animal activities, privileges and immunities, 9:2795.1
Sponsors, equine activities, immunities, 9:2795.1
    Limitation of liability, 9:2795.3

HORTICULTURE
Consumer credit, 9:3510 et seq.

HOSPITALS
    See, also, Health Care Facilities, generally, this index
Accident insurance proceeds, privilege for charges and supplies, 9:4751 et seq.
Charges, privilege, 9:4751 et seq.
Clinics, generally, this index
Contracts,
    Arbitration and award, 9:4230 et seq.
    Breach of contract, prescription, 9:5628
Definitions, privilege for services and supplies furnished patient, 9:4751
Directors, tort liability, 9:2792
Emergency response network, privileges and immunities, 9:2798.5
Fees, privilege, 9:4751 et seq.
First aid, emergencies, tort liability, 9:2793
Judgment proceeds, patient receiving, privilege for charges and supplies, 9:4751 et seq.
Lien for charges and supplies, 9:4751 et seq.
Limitation of liability, users of blood, organs or tissue, 9:2797
Negligence, blood, organs or tissue, limitation of liability, 9:2797
Officers and employees, tort liability, 9:2792
Organ transplants, limitation of liability, 9:2797
Priority, privilege for charges and supplies, 9:4752
Privilege for charges and supplies, 9:4751 et seq.
Privileges and immunities, emergency response network, 9:2798.5
Public trust, purposes, 9:2341 et seq.
Quasi offenses, liability of officers or directors, 9:2792
Rates and charges, privilege, 9:4751 et seq.
Services contracts, arbitration and award, 9:4230 et seq.

HOSPITALS—Cont'd
State hospitals, New Orleans charity hospital, generally.
    Charity Hospitals, this index
Supplies,
    Contracts, arbitration and award, 9:4230 et seq.
    Privilege for supplies furnished patients, 9:4751 et seq.
Tissue transplants, limitation of liability, 9:2797
Tort liability,
    Officers or directors, 9:2792
    Trustees, 9:2792

HOTCHPOT
Immovables, revendication, alteration of prescriptive period, 9:5811

HOTELS AND MOTELS
Rent, collection, attorney fees, 9:3259

HOUSING
Aged persons, home solicitation sales, 9:3541.21, 9:3541.22
Attorney fees, rent, 9:3259
Blighted property, prescription, 9:5633
Construction projects, limiting liability, 9:2775
New Home Warranty Act, 9:3141 et seq.
Public trust, purposes, 9:2341 et seq.
Residential Property Disclosure Act, 9:3196 et seq.
Residential Truth in Construction Act, 9:4851 et seq.

HOUSING AUTHORITIES
Damages, limitation of liability, 9:2800
Limitation of liability, 9:2800

HUMAN EMBRYOS
Definitions, in vitro fertilized human ovum, 9:121

HUMAN TISSUE OR ORGANS
Malpractice, 9:5628
    Paternity tests, 9:396 et seq.

HURRICANES
Health care providers, privileges and immunities, medical care and treatment, gratuitous services, 9:2799.5

HUSBAND AND WIFE
    Generally, 9:101 et seq.
Actions and proceedings, 9:102
    Between husband and wife, 9:291
    By and against wife, husband's authority unnecessary, 9:102
Attorney in fact, sale or mortgage of family home, consent, 9:2801
Civil rights and duties, 9:51
Community of Acquets and Gains, this index
Consumer credit, insurance, 9:3542
Contracts, actions between husband and wife, 9:291
Credit discrimination, 9:3583
Deposits in bank, payments to survivor without court proceeding, 9:1513
Disabilities and incapacities, emancipation from 9:101
Donations, 9:2351 et seq.
    Inter vivos,
        Exemptions, reduction and calculation of succession mass, 9:2372
        Made to spouse of previous marriage, reduction, 9:2373
    Irrevocable, 9:2351
    Renouncing right to revoke, 9:2352
    Revocability, reservation of right, 9:2351
Emancipation, 9:101

HUSBAND AND WIFE—Cont'd
Legitimation of children, **9:391**
Matrimonial Regimes, generally, this index
Nonsupport. Support, generally, this index
Obligations, validity, authority of husband or judge not required, **9:101**
Personal obligation for benefit of husband or community, **9:103**
Property of married persons, power to dispose for benefit of husband or community, **9:103**
Surname of married person, **9:0292**
Trusts and trustees, spousal property division, **9:1955**
  Principal beneficiary, deferred ascertainment, **9:2014**
Widows and widowers. Surviving Spouses, generally, this index

HYDROCARBONS
Definitions, privileges, wells, **9:4861**

ICE SKATING
Private property, personal injuries, limiting liability, **9:2795**

IDENTIFICATION
Electronic transactions,
  Security, **9:2609**
  Transferable records, **9:2616**
Marriage, license applications, social security numbers, **9:224**

IDENTITY THEFT
Credit reporting agency information and reports, **9:3571.1**
Police report, **9:3568 et seq.**

ILLEGAL CONTROLLED SUBSTANCE
Definitions, dealer liability, **9:2800.62**

ILLEGITIMATE CHILDREN
See, also, Legitimate Filiation, generally, this index
Acknowledgments,
  Declaration of acknowledgment, **9:392**
  Full faith and credit, **9:393**
Adjudication, paternity, putative father registry, **9:400**
Affidavits, uncontested paternity proceedings, proof by affidavit, **9:572**
Attorney fees, paternity actions, **9:398.1**
Blood tests,
  Determining paternity, **9:396 et seq.**
  Disavowal of paternity, **9:398.2**
Child support following judgment of paternity, **9:399**
Costs, blood or tissue test to determine paternity, **9:397.1**
Death of husband, artificial insemination, **9:391.1**
Disavowal of paternity, generally Legitimate Filiation, this index
Disclosure, putative father registry, agencies and courts, **9:400**
Evidence,
  Blood test to determine paternity, **9:396 et seq.**
  Putative father registry, **9:400**
  Tissue test to determine paternity, **9:396 et seq.**
Expert witnesses, blood or tissue test, determining paternity, **9:396 et seq.**
Filing, putative father registry, **9:400**
Genetic tests, rights of parties, **9:392**
Hearings, rescinding acknowledgment of paternity, **9:392**
Inheritance rights, acknowledgment of paternity, **9:392**
Injunctions, **9:396**
Legitimation, **9:391**
Mandate, provisional custody, **9:951 et seq.**

ILLEGITIMATE CHILDREN—Cont'd
Military Parent Child Custody Protection Act, **9:359 to 9:359.13**
Notarial acts, acknowledgments, paternity, **9:392**
Paternity proceeding,
  Address, **9:395**
  Drivers license numbers, **9:395**
  Information, state case registry, **9:395**
  Telephone numbers, **9:395**
Presumptions,
  Legitimacy of child, blood test to determine paternity, **9:397.3**
Putative father registry, **9:400**
Reports, blood test to determine paternity, **9:397.3**
Rights of children, acknowledgment of paternity, **9:392**
Rights of parties, declaration of acknowledgment, paternity, **9:392**
Support, acknowledgments, obligations, **9:392**
Tests,
  Disavowal of paternity, **9:398.2**
  Genetic tests, rights of parties, **9:392**
Tissue test, determining paternity, **9:396 et seq.**
Tutors and tutorship, provisional custody by mandate, **9:951 et seq.**
Uncontested paternity proceedings, proof by affidavit, **9:572**
Visitation, acknowledgment of paternity, **9:392**
Voiding acknowledgment of paternity, **9:392**
Witnesses, experts, blood or tissue test to determine paternity, **9:396 et seq.**

IMMOVABLES
Generally, **9:1101 et seq.**
Abandoned or Unclaimed Property, generally, this index
Associations and societies, transfer of title, **9:1051**
Auctions, sale for purposes other than payment of debts or legacies, **9:1521**
Bankruptcy, privilege of buyers from producers of agricultural and dairy products, **9:5021**
Beneficial interests in trust, owners, classification, **9:1111**
Blighted property, prescription, **9:5633**
Carbon sequestration on surface or water bottoms, **9:1103**
Classification, manufactured homes, **9:1149.3**
Consumer credit, closing of loan on using office of notary public, **9:3515**
Contracts, recording, third parties protected, **9:2721**
Dual contracts for sales, **9:2989**
Fraudulent contracts for sales, **9:2989**
Homeowners Association Act, **9:1141.1 et seq.**
Improvements by third persons,
  Actions involving deficiencies in design, prescription, **9:2772**
  Contractor payments to subcontractors and suppliers, **9:2784**
Improvements, private works, privileges, **9:4801 et seq.**
Institutional funds, investments, **9:2337.1 et seq.**
Instruments affecting, recording, **9:2721**
Interest in trust, classification, **9:1111**
Judgments and decrees,
  Recording, third parties protected, **9:2721**
Manufactured Home Property Act, **9:1149.1 et seq.**
Orleans Parish, succession judgment, recording, **9:1425**
Partition of joint ownership, agreements against, duration, **9:1702**
Personal injuries, prescription, **9:2772**
Planned community, Homeowners Association Act, **9:1141.1 et seq.**
Real rights, creation, **9:1252**

IMMOVABLES—Cont'd
Recreation, owner, duty of care, **9:2791**
Rent, assignment, **9:4401**
Residential planned community, Homeowners Association Act, **9:1141.1 et seq.**
Revendication, collation, **9:5811**
Riparian owners, use of surface water, fees prohibited, legislative finding, **9:1104**
Special privilege, assets of bankrupt purchaser, **9:5021**
Succession judgment, recording, **9:1425**
Surface leases, recording, third parties protected, **9:2721**
Surveys, deficiency, preemptive periods, **9:2772**
Tanks placed upon for storage of gases, movables, declared to be, **9:1106**
Third parties,
    Recording law, **9:2721**
Wrongful death, prescription, actions for deficiencies and design, **9:2772**

IMPROVEMENTS
Construction projects, machinery and equipment, limiting liability, **9:2775**
Military forces, power of attorney, immovables, **9:3882.1**
Nonprofit health care quality improvement corporations, privileges and immunities, **9:2800.20**
Residential Truth in Construction Act, **9:4851 et seq.**
Riparian owners, construction and use, **9:1102.2**

IN FORMA PAUPERIS
Support of persons, collection, **9:304.1**

IN VITRO FERTILIZED HUMAN OVUM
Generally, **9:121 et seq.**

INCOME TAX--FEDERAL
Deductions, support of persons, entitlement, **9:315.18**

INCOME TAX--STATE
Deductions from gross income, support of persons, entitlement, **9:315.18**
Federal taxes, charitable, benevolent, or eleemosynary trusts, **9:2283**

INCOMPETENCY
Curators, removal from office, **9:1025**
Interdiction, generally, this index
Trustee, effect, **9:1785**

INCORPOREALS
Conventional mortgage to secure several obligations, authorization, **9:5306**

INDEBTEDNESS
Advance fee loans, **9:3574.1 et seq.**
Common defendant, assignment of claims for collection, **9:3051**
Surety, failure to pay, award of attorneys fees, **9:3902**
Trustees, breach, checks on trust funds, **9:3810**
Women, **9:103**

INDEMNITY
Abandoned or unclaimed property, holder, indemnification by administrator, **9:162**
Controlled dangerous substances, dealer liability, **9:2800.65**
Fiduciary, costs and expenses, foreclosing mortgage securing several obligations, **9:5304**
Forests and forestry, minerals, oil and gas, drilling and wells, **9:2780**

INDEMNITY—Cont'd
Good faith, definitions, defense and indemnification of holder, **9:162**
Labor and employment, remitted, compromised or discharged employee liability, **9:3921**
Minerals, oil and gas, development, exploration and exploitation, agreements, **9:2780**
Oilfield Indemnity Act, **9:2780**
Public utilities, minerals, oil and gas, drilling and wells, **9:2780**
Sulphur, drilling and wells, **9:2780**
Trustees, **9:2191 et seq.**

INDIGENT PERSONS
Interdiction, curators and tutors, nonprofit corporations, **9:1031 et seq.**

INDIVIDUAL RETIREMENT ACCOUNTS
Benefits payable by reason of death, payment to beneficiary of account, **9:2449**
Liability of account holder, payments to beneficiaries, **9:2449**
Taxes, liability of account holder, payments to beneficiaries, **9:2449**

INHERITANCE TAX
Bank deposits and collections, payments to surviving spouse, **9:1513**, **9:1514**
Credit unions, payments to surviving spouse, **9:1514**
Estate transfer tax,
    Apportionment, **9:2431 et seq.**
    Fiduciary security transfers, **9:3839**
Federal estate tax,
    Apportionment, **9:2431 et seq.**
    Fiduciary security transfers, **9:3839**
Joint deposits, payment to surviving spouse without court proceeding, **9:1513**
    Credit unions, **9:1514**

INJUNCTIONS
Attorney fees, consumer credit, **9:3555**
Condominiums, rules and regulations, **9:1124.115**
Consumer credit, **9:3555**
    Unlicensed persons, **9:3554.1**
Covenant marriage, separation from bed and board, **9:308**
Credit repair services organizations, **9:3573.11**
Definitions, postseparation family violence relief, **9:362**
Family violence, **9:366**
Loans, advance fees, **9:3574.6**, **9:3574.7**
Paternity, **9:396**
Real rights, charitable purposes, enforcement, **9:1252**

INNOCENT PURCHASERS
Movable goods, etc., priority over repairmen's or manufacturer's privilege, **9:4502**

INSOLVENCY
Federal mortgage, **9:5163**
Judicial sales, persons authorized to make, **9:3001**
Lessee, limitation on lessor's privilege, **9:3241**
Privilege on assets, purchasers from producers of agriculture and dairy products, **9:5021**
Privileges, sale of property, **9:5031**

INSTITUTIONAL VANDALISM
Damages, **9:2799.2**

INSURANCE
Alcoholics and intoxicated persons, liability, injury of third persons, **9:2800.1**

INDEX TO TITLE 9

INSURANCE—Cont'd
Annuities,
    Death, extinguishment of obligation, **9:2785**
    Military forces, power of attorney, powers granted, **9:3876**
    Uniform Transfers to Minors Act, creating custodial property, **9:759**
Attorney fees, consumer credit, **9:3555**
Cancellation, Premium finance companies, consumer credit, **9:3550**
Contractors, new home warranties, **9:3147**
Controlled dangerous substances, dealer liability, **9:2800.65**
    Health and accident insurance, **9:2800.63**
Credit property insurance, **9:3543**
Custodial trusts, designations, **9:2260.3**
Discrimination, premium finance companies, **9:3550**
Dismemberment insurance, consumer credit, **9:3542**
Emergency medical treatment, privileges and immunities, application of law, **9:2793**
Fidelity and surety insurance, lis pendens, cancellation upon furnishing security, **9:4835**
Fire insurance, proceeds, privilege of seller of property destroyed by fire, **9:4581**
Food banks, donations, limitation of liability, **9:2799**, **9:2799.6**
Health and accident insurance,
    Cancellation, electronic transactions, exemptions, **9:2603**
    Children and minors, support obligations, **9:315.4**
    Controlled dangerous substances, dealer liability, **9:2800.63**
    Hospitals, privilege for proceeds received by patients, **9:4751 et seq.**
    Premiums, child support obligations, **9:315.4**
    Privileges, hospital charges, insurance proceeds received by patients, **9:4751 et seq.**
    Proceeds, patient receiving, privilege for charges and supplies, **9:4751 et seq.**
    Support, this index
Homeowners insurance, new home warranties, **9:3147**
Liability insurance,
    Military forces, power of attorney, immovables, **9:3882.1**
Licenses and permits, premium finance companies, consumer credit, **9:3550**
    Lapse, **9:3561.1**
Life insurance,
    Cancellation, electronic transactions, exemptions, **9:2603**
    Cash value, abandoned or unclaimed property, **9:154**
    Consumer credit, **9:3542**
    Credit life, health and accident insurance, **9:3542**
    Custodial property, creating, Uniform Transfers to Minors Act, **9:759**
    Trust created upon proceeds, **9:1881**
Military forces, power of attorney,
    Immovables, **9:3882.1**
    Powers granted, **9:3871**
New home warranties, **9:3147**
Premium finance companies, consumer credit, **9:3550**
    Licenses and permits, lapse, **9:3561.1**
Premiums,
    Credit property insurance, **9:3543**
    Health and accident insurance, ante
Prescription, uninsured motorist claims, **9:5629**
Property damage insurance, rental purchase agreements, prohibited provisions, **9:3356**
Real estate timesharing, **9:1131.23**
Rental purchase agreements, liability insurance, prohibited provisions, **9:3356**

INSURANCE—Cont'd
Self insurance,
    Trust funds, trustee, limitation of liability, **9:2792.6**
Support of persons, health and accident insurance, child support obligations, **9:315.4**
Water supply, development and exploration, indemnity agreements, **9:2780**

INSURANCE AGENTS, BROKERS AND SALESPERSONS
Prescription, **9:5606**

INTERDICTION
Absentees, curator and undercurator, appointment in proceedings to sell property, **9:603**
Confidential or privileged information, indigent adults, fines and penalties, **9:1033**
Corporations, nonprofit, curators and tutors, indigent adults, **9:1031 et seq.**
Costs,
    Exemption, indigent adults, **9:1034**
    Fees for inventories, **9:1423**
Curators,
    Absentees, appointment, **9:603**
    Appointments,
        Nonprofit corporations, indigent adults, **9:1031 et seq.**
        Proceedings to sell property, **9:603**
        Recognition or confirmation without convocation of family meeting, **9:602**
    Charitable contributions, **9:1023**
    Donations, **9:1022 et seq.**
    Indigent adults, nonprofit corporations, **9:1031 et seq.**
    Sale or lease of right of way over land of ward, **9:731**
Donations, siblings and sibling descendants, **9:1024**
Experts, inventories, fees, **9:1423**
Fees,
    Exemption, indigent adults, **9:1034**
    Inventories by experts, appraisers and notaries public, **9:1423**
Indigent adults, curators and tutors, nonprofit corporations, **9:1031 et seq.**
Inventories, fees of experts, appraisers and notaries public, **9:1423**
Judicial sales, persons authorized to make, **9:3001**
Leases, right of way, **9:731**
Nurses, **9:1021**
Sale of property,
    Absentee interdict, special representation, **9:603**
    Ratification, **9:732**
    Right of way, **9:731**
Taxation of costs, fees for inventories, **9:1423**
Testaments, donations, **9:1022**
Tutors,
    Appointments, will of spouse of interdict as tutor of child, **9:601**
    Indigent adults, nonprofit corporations, **9:1031 et seq.**
    Nonprofit corporations, indigent adults, **9:1031 et seq.**
Undercurators, donations inter vivos, **9:1022**
Venue, undivided interest, proceedings for sale of property, **9:603**
Veterans in government institutions, **9:1021**

INTEREST
Acceleration, corporations and partnerships, **9:3509**
Accrued interest, recovery of interest upon, **9:3509.2**
Assessments for improvements, **9:3507**
Collection charges, **9:3505**

INDEX TO TITLE 9

INTEREST—Cont'd
Conventional interest,
    Maximum rate, **9:3503 et seq.**
    Rate, **9:3503 et seq.**
Corporations, exceeding maximum conventional rate, **9:3509**
Costs and expenses not considered interest, **9:3505**
Definitions, leases, movable property, **9:3306**
Delinquency, collection charges, **9:3505**
Evidence, maximum rate, **9:3503**
Federal housing administration insured loans, enforcement, **9:3508**
Federal housing administration, obligations guaranteed by, **9:3504**
Fees, etc., not considered interest, **9:3505**
Forfeiture for usury, **9:3501**
Graduated payment mortgages, application of law, **9:3504**
Items not considered interest, **9:3505**
Maximum conventional rate, corporations and partnerships, interest in excess of, **9:3509**
Maximum rate, conventional interest, **9:3503 et seq.**
Mechanic's privileges and liens, **9:4803**
Newspaper dealers and distributors, cash bond or security deposited, **9:3601**
Payment, prepayment charges not considered interest, **9:3505**
Privileges and liens, private works, **9:4803**
Tax assessments, **9:3507**
Trusts, charge against income, **9:2156**
Variable rates,
    Agriculture loans, **9:3509.1**
    Business loans, **9:3509.1**
    Commercial loans, **9:3509.1**
Veteran's administration, obligation guaranteed by, **9:3504**
Wrap-around mortgages, application of law, **9:3504**

INVENTORIES
Admission as proof, Orleans Parish, **9:1422**
Orleans Parish, successions, **9:1422, 9:1423**

INVESTMENTS
Federal farm loan bonds, tutors and curators, **9:733**
Institutional funds, **9:2337.1 et seq.**
Interdicts, **9:733**
Military forces, power of attorney, powers granted, **9:3870**
Public trust obligations, **9:2341**

IRRIGATION
Children and minor's property, sale or lease of right of way, **9:731**
Crop share agreement, **9:4522.1**
Privilege on crops, **9:4522**

JEWELERS
Privilege, **9:4701 et seq.**
Unclaimed jewelry, **9:4702**

JOINT ACCOUNTS
Credit unions, payments to surviving spouse without court action, **9:1514**

JOINT CUSTODY OF CHILDREN
Generally, **9:335 et seq.**

JOINT TENANCY
Agreements against partition of property, duration, **9:1702**
Agreements not to alienate, encumber or lease, duration, **9:1112**

JOINT VENTURES
Trustees, powers, **9:2123**

JUDGES
Jurisdiction, marriage, authority to perform, **9:203**

JUDGMENTS AND DECREES
Affidavits, identity, filing, **9:5503**
Class actions, conclusiveness, **9:2701**
Mobile homes, repossession, **9:5363.1**
Paternity, child support following judgment, **9:399**
Records and recordation, **9:2721**
    Third parties protected, **9:2721**
Third parties protected, recording law, **9:2721**
Trustees contract, action on, **9:2125**

JUDICIAL RECORDS
Electronic applications, **9:2603.1**

JUDICIAL SALES
    See, also, Execution, generally, this index
    Generally, **9:3001 et seq.**
Act of sale, time allowed for making, **9:3160**
Adjudicatee's liability for deficiency on resale, **9:3161**
Adjudication, completion of sale, **9:3158**
Announcement of conditions of sale and demand for bids, **9:3156**
Authority to make, **9:3001**
Bids and bidding,
    Adjudication to highest bidder, **9:3157**
    Announcement of conditions of sale and demand for bids, **9:3156**
    First adjudicatee prohibited from bidding at resale, **9:3162**
    Resale for noncompliance with bid, **9:3161, 9:3162**
    Unauthorized bidding for another, **9:3165**
Buyer's right in case of eviction, **9:3171**
Completion, adjudication as completion, **9:3158**
Conditions of sale, announcement, **9:3156**
Credit sales, notes, security, **9:3002**
Debtor's property, seized by order of court, to be sold for purpose of paying creditor, **9:3166**
Definitions, sales by auction, public sales, **9:3151, 9:3152**
Delivery,
    Payment of price as condition, **9:3159**
    Time for making, **9:3160**
Failure to comply with bid, resale, **9:3161, 9:3162**
First adjudicatee prohibited from bidding at resale, **9:3162**
Forced sale, definition, auction, **9:3152**
General rules governing, **9:3154**
Highest bidder, adjudication to, **9:3157**
Informalities, prescription, **9:5622**
Judge, designating person to make, **9:3001**
Kinds, **9:3166**
Lessor's privilege, **9:3241**
Liability of seller refusing to accept solvent indorser, **9:3164**
Method of making, **9:3155 et seq.**
Mortgages, cancellation, **9:3003**
Noncompliance with bid. Resale, post
Notes, identification, **9:3002, 9:3003**
Offer for sale, method of making, **9:3156**
Officers of justice, **9:3153**
Partition sale, procedure, **9:3166, 9:3172 et seq.**
Payment,
    Cash sales, **9:3159**
    Indorsed notes, **9:3163, 9:3164**
        Indorsers not suitable to seller or auctioneer, effect, **9:3163**

I–31

INDEX TO TITLE 9

JUDICIAL SALES—Cont'd
Payment—Cont'd
  Indorsed notes—Cont'd
    Purchaser's duty to supply indorsers, **9:3163**
    Seller's refusal to accept indorsers, liability for damages, **9:3164**
  Retention by auctioneer until payment of price, **9:3159**
  Time for making, **9:3160**
Persons authorized to make, **9:3001**
Prescription, informalities, **9:5622**
Prices,
  Retention by auctioneer until payment of price, **9:3159**
  Retention of price until execution of act on sale of immovable, **9:3160**
Public auction, sale at, **9:3168**
Public officer, sale through, **9:3155**
Records and recordation,
  Credit sales, identification of notes or bonds, **9:3003**
  Mortgage cancellation, **9:3003**
Redhibition, **9:3169**
Reimbursement, procedure, **9:3171**
Rejection of indorser of purchase price notes, effect on adjudication, **9:3163**
Resale, noncompliance with bid, **9:3161, 9:3162**
  Bid by first adjudicatee, **9:3162**
  First purchaser's liability for deficiency, **9:3161**
  First purchaser's right to,
    Bid, **9:3162**
    Excess, **9:3161**
  Procedure, **9:3161**
Rescission,
  Fraud, **9:3169**
  Nullity, **9:3169**
Retention,
  By auctioneer until payment of price, **9:3159**
  Price until execution of act on sale of immovable, **9:3160**
Rights acquired, **9:3170**
Rules applicable, **9:3167**
Security, approval by vendor, **9:3002**
Seller prohibited from making, **9:3155**
Transfer,
  Ownership, **9:3158**
  Title, **9:3173**
Unauthorized bidding for another, **9:3165**
Voluntary sale, definition, auction, **9:3152**
Warranties attaching, **9:3174**

JURY
Arbitration, proceedings to compel, **9:4203**
Instructions to jury, malpractice, burden of proof, **9:2794**

JUSTICES OF THE PEACE
Jurisdiction, marriage, authority to perform, **9:203**

LABOR AND EMPLOYMENT
Actions and proceedings, master's right of action for injury by servant, **9:3921**
Automobiles, repairmen's privilege, **9:4501**
Compromise of damages, employee liability, employer's right of contribution, **9:3921**
Contracts, exclusion from arbitration, **9:4216**
Contribution, employee liability for damages, employer's right of contribution, **9:3921**
Damages, employer action against employee, **9:3921**
Definitions, payment of wages of deceased employees to surviving spouse, **9:1515**
Exclusion of employment contract from Arbitration Law, **9:4216**

LABOR AND EMPLOYMENT—Cont'd
Fiduciary, **9:3801**
Indemnity and indemnification, compromised or discharged employee liability, **9:3921**
Payment, wages due payable to surviving spouse or others, **9:1515**
Power of attorney, military forces, immovables, **9:3882.1**
Prescription, action for wages, New Orleans, **9:5602**
Remission of damages, employee liability, employer right of contribution, **9:3921**
Respondeat superior, employer's right of contribution, **9:3921**
Sick leave, payment to surviving spouse without judgment of court, **9:1515**
Trusts and trustees, employees, **9:1921**
  Term of trust, **9:1834, 9:1922**

LABOR DISPUTES
Collective bargaining, mechanic's privileges and liens, amounts owed, **9:4803**
Mediation and arbitration, exemption from arbitration law, **9:4216**

LABORATORIES
Animals, research, unauthorized release, **9:2799.4**
Birds, research, unauthorized release, **9:2799.4**
Public trust, purposes, **9:2341 et seq.**

LAFAYETTE PARISH
Health care providers, privileges and immunities, gratuitous services, **9:2799.5**
Medical care and treatment, privileges and immunities, gratuitous services, **9:2799.5**

LAGOONS
Beds and waters, state ownership, **9:1101**

LAKES
Riparian owners, use of land, **9:1102.2**

LAW MERCHANT
Fiduciaries, rules governing, **9:3812**

LEASES
Generally, **9:3201 et seq., 9:3301 et seq.**
Accelerated rental payments,
  Lessor's right to protect and preserve leased property, **9:3330**
  Remedies upon lessee's default, movable property, **9:3319**
Acts of sale, security deposits, transfers, **9:3251**
Advance of money by tenant, **9:3251 et seq.**
Alienation of property, rights of lessor, **9:3258**
Appeal and review, judgment on rule to show cause to surrender possession, **9:3323**
Application of law, **9:3303**
Assignments, **9:4401**
  Notice, cancellation following lessee's default, **9:3320**
Associations and societies, predial leases, **9:1051**
Attorney fees,
  Action for deposit, **9:3253**
  Collection of rent, **9:3259**
Cancellation,
  Insurance, refund or credit, **9:3337**
  Lessee's default, **9:3320 et seq.**
  Lessor's right to protect and preserve leased property, movable property, **9:3330**
Collection,
  Late charges, movable property, **9:3314**
  Liquidated damages, **9:3324**

INDEX TO TITLE 9

LEASES—Cont'd
Collection—Cont'd
    Practices, consumer leases, **9:3340**
Compromise and settlement, movables, **9:3305**
Conflict of laws, **9:3303**
    Civil Code, **9:3192**
Construction of law, **9:3307, 9:3308**
Control of property, rights of lessor, **9:3258**
Costs, actions and proceedings, action for deposit, **9:3253**
Credit life, health and accident insurance,
    Cancellation, refund or credit, **9:3337**
    Gain from insurance, **9:3338**
    Retroactivity, **9:3332**
Crimes and offenses, self-help repossession, **9:3329**
Curators, right of way, **9:731**
Damages, **9:3221**
    Deposit not returned, **9:3252**
    Enticing lessee to violate lease, **9:3202**
    Liability for, **9:3201 et seq.**
    Liquidated damages, recovery, **9:3325**
    Mitigation, constructive eviction, uninhabitable premises, **9:3260**
    Occupancy or cultivation, lessor's refusal to permit, liability, **9:3203**
    Solidary liability, lessee and person enticing breach of lease, **9:3202**
Debtors and creditors, movable property, **9:3318 et seq.**
Deep water port commission, riparian land, **9:1102.2**
Default, movable property, **9:3318 et seq.**
Defects, knowledge of lessor, **9:3221**
Definitions, movable property, **9:3306**
Deposit, tenants, **9:3251 et seq.**
Deprivation of property, lessor's possession for protection of property, **9:3330**
Disposal of property, rights of lessor, **9:3258**
Enjoyment of property, rights of lessor, **9:3258**
Enticement of breach, solidary liability, **9:3202**
Equipment, application of law, **9:3304**
Exclusions, **9:3304**
Fees and charges,
    Additional lease-related charges, movable property, **9:3313 et seq.**
    Deferral charges, movable property, **9:3315**
        Rebates, accelerated rental payment remedy, movable property, **9:3319**
    Early termination charges, movable property, **9:3316**
    End-of-lease charges, movable property, **9:3317**
    Late charges, movable property, **9:3314**
    Movable property, **9:3311 et seq.**
    Property insurance, movable property, **9:3333**
    Records and recordation, **9:3342**
Financed leases, **9:3310**
    Interest, **9:3312**
    Validity and enforcement, **9:3302**
Fines and penalties, self help repossession, movable property, **9:3329**
Immovables, application of law, **9:3304**
Insolvency, proceedings against assignor, security interests of assignee, **9:4401**
Insurance, **9:3331 et seq.**
    Choice of insurer, **9:3334**
    Movable property, **9:3331 et seq.**
Intentional violations, movable property, **9:3341**
Interdict's property, right of way, **9:731**
Interest,
    Consumer-financed lease, **9:3312**
    Movable property, **9:3311 et seq.**

LEASES—Cont'd
Interest—Cont'd
    Rebates, accelerated rental payment remedy, movable property, **9:3319**
Invalid agreements, jurisdiction and venue, **9:3303**
Irrigation canal, etc., right of way, minor's property, **9:731**
Jurisdiction, invalid agreements, **9:3303**
Liquidated damages, actions and proceedings, **9:3324, 9:3325**
Mechanics, privileges, **9:4801 et seq.**
Mitigation of damages, uninhabitable premises, **9:3260**
Monopolies and unfair trade, intentional violations, **9:3341**
Ownership of property, rights of lessor, **9:3258**
Pledges, **9:4401**
    Right of pledge of lessor, unpaid rent, **9:3259.1**
Possession,
    Accelerated rental payment remedy, **9:3319**
    Lessor's right to protect and preserve leased property, **9:3330**
    Recovery, movable property, **9:3324**
    Self-help repossession, **9:3329**
Power of attorney, military forces, immovables **9:3882.1**
Predial leases, associations and societies, **9:1051**
Premiums, insurance, limitations, movable property, **9:3335**
Prescription, setting aside leases of immovables, legal entities, lack of authority, **9:5681**
Presumption, lands bounded by waterways, highways, etc., **9:2971 et seq.**
Privileges of, **9:4811**
    Business property, **9:3241**
    Prescription, death or insolvency of lessee, **9:3241**
    Private works, **9:4801 et seq.**
    Unpaid rent, **9:3259.1**
Property insurance, movable property, **9:3333**
Protection of property, rights of lessor, **9:3258**
Rebates, accelerated rental payment remedy, movable property, **9:3319**
Records and recordation,
    Movable property, **9:3342**
Recreation, duty of care, **9:2791**
Release, sequestration of property to lessee, security, **9:3327, 9:3328**
Remedies, lessee's default, movable property, **9:3318 et seq.**
Rental purchase agreements, **9:3351 et seq.**
Repairs, failure to make, liability for injuries, **9:3221**
Repossession, **9:3329**
Retaining deposit by landlord, **9:3251**
Rights of lessor, **9:3258**
Riparian lands, deep water port commissions or municipalities over 5,000, **9:1102.2**
Sale and lease-back, commercial transactions, **9:3370**
Sales or transfers of leases,
    Security deposits, **9:3251**
    Unexpired term, lessor's privilege, **9:3241**
Security, sequestration, movable property, **9:3326, 9:3327**
Seized property,
    Accelerated rental payment remedy, lessee's failure to satisfy final judgment, **9:3319**
    Rule to show cause to surrender possession, cancellation following default, **9:3322**
Self help, repossession, **9:3329**
Self-service storage facility, **9:4756 et seq.**
Sequestration, movable property, **9:3326 et seq.**
Storage facilities, self-service storage facilities, **9:4756 et seq.**
Subleases, notice, cancellation following lessee's default, **9:3320**
Summary proceedings, cancellation of lease, lessee's default, **9:3320 et seq.**

INDEX TO TITLE 9

LEASES—Cont'd
Surface leases, recording, third parties protected, **9:2721**
Surrender, cancellation following lessee's default, **9:3321**
    Rule to show cause, **9:3322**
Taxation, application of law, **9:3303**
Tenancy in common, agreements against leases, duration, **9:1112**
Third parties,
    Right upon acquisition of immovable property, **9:2721**
Timesharing, **9:1131.1 et seq.**
True leases, **9:3309**
    Interest, **9:3311**
Unauthorized collection practices, consumer leases, **9:3340**
Unintentional violations, movable property, **9:3341**
Use of property, rights of lessor, **9:3258**
Venue, **9:3252**
    Invalid agreements, **9:3303**
Waivers,
    Lessee's rights, movables, **9:3305**
    Right of tenant to deposit, **9:3254**

LEGAL REPRESENTATIVES
Definitions,
    Custodial trusts, **9:2260.1**

LEGAL USUFRUCT
Surviving spouse, security, form, **9:1202**

LEGITIMATE FILIATION
Acknowledgment,
    Paternity, **9:392**
    Putative father registry, **9:400**
Affidavits, uncontested paternity proceedings, proof by affidavit, **9:572**
Artificial insemination, death of husband, **9:391.1**
Attorney fees, **9:398.1**
Blood tests, **9:396 et seq.**
    Chain of custody, **9:397.2**
    Disavowal of paternity, **9:398.2**
    Reports, **9:397.3**
Contempt of court, licenses and permits, suspension or revocation, **9:315.30, 9:315.33**
Death of husband, artificial insemination, **9:391.1**
Disavowal of paternity,
    Blood tests, **9:398.2**
    Husband, death, artificial insemination, **9:391.1**
    Testing, **9:398.2**
    Time limit, suspension, support proceedings, **9:402**
Evidence, hospital bills, **9:394**
Evidence test to determine paternity, **9:396 et seq.**
Injunctions, **9:396**
Military Parent Child Custody Protection Act, **9:359 to 9:359.13**
Presumptions, legitimacy of child, blood test to determine paternity, **9:397.3**
Putative father registry, **9:400, 9:400.1**
Registry, putative father registry, **9:400, 9:400.1**
Tests,
    Disavowal of paternity, **9:398.2**
    Genetic tests, bills, evidence, **9:394**
Uncontested paternity proceedings, proof by affidavit, **9:572**
Witness fees, **9:397.1**

LENDER CREDIT CARD
Definitions, consumer credit, **9:3516**

LERN
Emergency response network, privileges and immunities, **9:2798.5**

LESSEE
Definitions,
    Leases, movable property, **9:3306**
    Privileges, wells, **9:4861**
    Self-service storage facilities, **9:4757**

LESSORS
Definitions,
    Leases, movable property, **9:3306**
    Rental purchase agreements, **9:3352**

LETTERS OF CREDIT
Military forces, power of attorney, powers granted, **9:3874**

LEVEE AND DRAINAGE DISTRICTS
Boards and commissions,
    Authority not diminished, **9:1102.1**
    Limitation of liability, **9:2792.4**
Expropriation, wharves, buildings or improvements, **9:1102.1**
Limitation of liability, directors, trustees or members, **9:2792.4**

LEVEES AND FLOOD CONTROL
Building encroachments, prescription, **9:5627**
Drainage, actions and claims for lands and improvements used or destroyed for, **9:5626**
Flowage rights, option to United States, by executor, administrator or curator, **9:1511**
Prescription, actions and claims for lands and improvements used or destroyed for, **9:5626**

LICENSES AND PERMITS
Definitions, insurance premium finance companies, **9:3550**
Food banks, donations, limitation of liability, **9:2799, 9:2799.6**
Revocation and suspension,
    Consumer loan brokers, **9:3572.12**
    Support of persons, **9:315.30 et seq.**
Support of persons, suspension, **9:315.30 et seq.**

LIENS AND PRIVILEGES
Privileges and liens in favor of the state, **9:5504**

LIMITATION OF LIABILITY
Abatement, persons designing, supervising or performing, **9:2800.3**
Actions and proceedings, **9:2800**
Alcoholic beverages, damages or losses connected sale, serving or furnishing, **9:2800.1**
Animal sanctuary, **9:2796.2**
Associations and societies, damages, **9:2796**
Blood banks, **9:2797**
Boards and commissions, **9:2792.4**
City boards, **9:2792.4**
Civic or historic purposes, **9:2792.3**
Cleanup, persons designing, supervising or performing, **9:2800.3**
Commission plan, **9:2792.4**
Community service organizations, **9:2792.8**
Community services, nonprofit organizations, **9:2792.8**
Construction projects, machinery and equipment, contracts or terms of sale, **9:2775**
Damages,
    Community service organizations, **9:2792.8**
    Condition of things within care and custody, **9:2800**
    Injuries or losses connected with sale, **9:2800.1**

INDEX TO TITLE 9

LIMITATION OF LIABILITY—Cont'd
Definitions, **9:2792.8**
    Nonprofit corporations, **9:2792.8**
Directors, **9:2792.1**
    Officers or trustees, nonprofit organizations, **9:2792.3**
    Trustees, etc., **9:2792.4**
Donated food, **9:2799.3, 9:2799.6**
Downtown development districts, **9:2792.2**
Dram Shop Act, **9:2800.1**
Ethnic parades, sponsors, **9:2796.1**
Food banks, donations, **9:2799.6**
Hazardous waste, **9:2800.3**
Holiday in Dixie parades, damages, **9:2796**
Housing authorities, **9:2800**
Human tissue transplant, **9:2797**
Injuries, community service organizations, **9:2792.8**
Law enforcement districts, **9:2792.4**
Liability, mitigation, abatement or clean-up services, **9:2800.3**
Limited liability partnerships, **9:3431**
Machinery and equipment, consequential damages, **9:2775**
Mardi Gras parades, damages, **9:2796**
Medical care and treatment, **9:2797**
Members of boards, commissions or authorities, **9:2792.4**
Negligence, gratuitous services, **9:4861 et seq.**
Nonprofit community blood banks, viral diseases, **9:2797**
Nonprofit organizations, **9:2792.1**
Notice,
    Condition of things within care and custody, **9:2800**
    Gratuitous services, **9:2799.5**
Officers and agents, **9:2792.1**
Officers and employees, community service organizations, **9:2792.8**
On premises feeding program, food banks, donations, **9:2799**
Organ transplants, **9:2797**
Parish school boards, **9:2792.4**
Parks, personal injuries, **9:2795**
Political subdivision, **9:2792.4**
    Quasi offenses, **9:2795**
Port commissions, **9:2792.4**
Private property, personal injuries, **9:2795**
Public bodies, **9:2800**
Quasi offenses, **9:2795**
    Users of blood, organs or tissue, **9:2797**
Recreation areas, private owners, **9:2795**
Registration statement, **9:3422**
Remedial actions, recreational areas, private owners, **9:2795**
Saint Patrick's. Day parade, damages, **9:2796.1**
Sanctuaries, **9:2796.3**
School asbestos abatement, **9:2800.3**
Self insurance, trust funds, **9:2792.6**
Shares and shareholders, community service organizations, **9:2792.8**
Social hosts, serving alcoholic beverages, **9:2800.1**
Trust funds, trustees, **9:2792.6**
Users of blood, organs or tissue, **9:2797**
Vitamin, food banks, donations, **9:2799**
Wild game, food banks, donations, **9:2799, 9:2799.6**

LIMITED LIABILITY COMPANIES
Interest, commercial loans, agreements exceeding maximum conventional rate, **9:3509**
Loans, interest, agreements exceeding maximum conventional rate, **9:3509**
Trustees, powers, **9:2123**
Usury, agreements exceeding maximum conventional interest rate, **9:3509**

LIMITED LIABILITY PARTNERSHIPS
Generally, **9:3431 et seq.**

LIQUIDATION AND LIQUIDATORS
Federal mortgage, effect upon, **9:5163**
Mortgages, sale of property, **9:5251**
Privileges and liens, sale of property, **9:5031**
Surety bond, premium as expense, **9:3901**

LIQUIFIED PETROLEUM GASES
Tanks placed on land for storage as movable property, **9:1106**

LIS PENDENS
Cancellation upon furnishing bond, **9:4835**
Mechanic's privileges and liens, **9:4831**
Third parties, **9:4833**

LITERARY ORGANIZATIONS
Immovables, real rights created for benefit of organization, **9:1252**
Trusts to promote, **9:2271**

LOAN BROKERS
Advance fees, **9:3574.1 et seq.**
    Actions and proceedings, **9:3574.9**
    Cease-and-desist orders, **9:3574.5**
        Crimes and offenses, **9:3574.8**
        Damages, **9:3574.9**
        Examinations and examiners, **9:3574.6**
        Fees, **9:3574.1 et seq.**
        Fines and penalties, **9:3574.5**
        Fraud, **9:3574.3**
        Hearings, **9:3574.6**
        Injunctions, **9:3574.6, 9:3574.7**
        Investigations and investigators, **9:3574.5, 9:3574.6**
        Punitive damages, **9:3574.9**
        Restitution, **9:3574.7**
        Subpoenas, **9:3574.6**
        Supersedeas or stay, **9:3574.7**
        Witnesses, **9:3574.6**
Confidential or privileged information, investigations or examinations, **9:3574.6**
Consumer loan brokers, **9:3572.1 et seq.**

LOANS
Advance fee loans, **9:3574.1 et seq.**
    Cease-and-desist orders, **9:3574.5**
    Consumption, restitution by borrower, **9:3574.7**
    Crimes and offenses, **9:3574.8**
    Damages, **9:3574.9**
    Examinations and examiners, **9:3574.6**
    Fees, **9:3474.1**
    Fines and penalties, **9:3574.5**
    Hearings, **9:3574.6**
    Injunctions, **9:3574.6, 9:3574.7**
    Investigations and investigators, **9:3574.5, 9:3574.6**
    Originator, **9:3574.1 et seq.**
    Punitive damages, **9:3574.9**
    Subpoenas, **9:3574.6**
    Supersedeas or stay, **9:3574.7**
    Witnesses, **9:3574.6**
Aged persons, home solicitation sales, **9:3541.21, 9:3541.22**
Business loans, adjustable rate loans, **9:3509.1**
Commercial loans, adjustable rate loans, **9:3509.1**
Confidential or privileged information, investigations or examinations, **9:3574.6**
Consumer loan brokers, **9:3572.1 et seq.**
Deferred Presentment and Small Loan Act, **9:3578.1 et seq.**

INDEX TO TITLE 9

LOANS—Cont'd
Discrimination, extension of credit, **9:3583**
Equal Credit Opportunity Law, **9:3581 et seq.**
Examinations and examiners, advance fees, **9:3574.6**
Fees,
    Advance fees, **9:3574.1 et seq.**
    Deferred presentment and small loans, **9:3578.4**
Guaranty, public trusts, purposes, **9:2341**
Injunctions, advance fees, **9:3574.6, 9:3574.7**
Louisiana Tax Refund Anticipation Loan Act, **9:3579.1 to 9:3579.4**
Notice, deferred presentment and small loans, toll free telephone number, **9:3577.7**
Prepayment, **9:3509.3**
    Brokers, unearned loan finance charges or credit service charges, **9:3572.9**
    Deferred presentment and small loans, **9:3578.5**
Prohibited practices, deferred presentment and small loans, **9:3578.6**
Public trusts, port commissions, improvement of export and import facilities, **9:2341**
Rebates, loan finance charges or credit service charges, **9:3572.9**
    Prepayment, deferred presentment and small loans, **9:3578.5**
Social security, lenders, checks received as payment, **9:3578.7**
Unearned loan finance charges or credit service charges, rebate upon prepayment, **9:3572.9**
Variable rates,
    Agriculture loans, **9:3509.1**
    Business loans, **9:3509.1**
    Commercial loans, **9:3509.1**
    Mortgages, **9:3504**

LOCKS
Self-service storage facilities, removing or replacing, **9:4759**

LOST OR DESTROYED INSTRUMENTS
Certified copies, evidence, **9:2758**
Mortgages, promissory notes,
    Affidavits, cancellation, **9:5167**
Negotiable Instruments, this index
Vendor's privilege, promissory notes, affidavits, cancellation, **9:5167**

LOTS
Definitions, Homeowners Association Act, **9:1141.2**

LOUISIANA EMERGENCY RESPONSE NETWORK
Privileges and immunities, **9:2798.5**

LOUISIANA EXCHANGE SALE OF RECEIVABLES ACT
Generally, **9:3137.1 to 9:3137.9**

MACHINERY AND EQUIPMENT
Construction projects, contracts or terms of sale, limiting liability, **9:2775**
Definitions, leases, movable property, **9:3306**
Oil, gas and water wells, privilege for labor, services or supplies, **9:4861 et seq.**
Privileges,
    Immovables, **9:4801 et seq.**
    Making or repairing, **9:4501, 9:4502**
Recreation areas, owner's duty of care, **9:2791**
Recreation, owner's duty of care, **9:2791**
Repairman's privilege, seizures, exemptions, **9:4502**

MAIL
Bonds, deed, cancellation upon default, notice, **9:2945**

MAIL—Cont'd
Certified or registered mail,
    Adverse claim to transfer brought by fiduciary, notice of, **9:3835**
    Bond for deed, cancellation notice, **9:2945**
    Mechanic's privileges and liens, notice or other documents and materials, **9:4842**
    Privileges, movables, **9:4502**
    Stop payment, checks, **9:2782.2**
    Unclaimed property, notice, **9:4702**
Credit cards, unsolicited cards, damages, **9:3518.2**

MALPRACTICE
Accountants, **9:5604**
Prescription, attorneys, **9:5605**
Theft of client funds, **9:5605.1**

MANAGED CARE PLAN
Health and accident insurance, generally. Insurance, this index

MANAGERS
Athletic managers, volunteers, liability, **9:2798**
Chiropractors, consultants, contracts, **9:2714**
Military forces, power of attorney, immovables, **9:3882.1**
Real estate timesharing, **9:1131.20**

MANDATE
Commercial paper. Negotiable Instruments, generally, this index
Conditional procuration, **9:3890**
Custodial trusts, **9:2260.7**
Custody of children, provisional custody, **9:951 et seq.**
Divorce, provisional custody of children, **9:951 et seq.**
Durable power of attorney, custodial trusts, **9:2260.7**
Express mandate, husband and wife, revocation, **9:3850**
Fiduciary, **9:3801**
Married women,
    Revocation, express mandate, **9:3850**
    Sale or mortgage of family home, consent, **9:2801**
Powers of attorney,
    Action to set aside document, **9:5647**
    Prescription periods, **9:5647**
Provisional custody of children, **9:951 et seq.**
Separation from bed and board, provisional custody of children, **9:951 et seq.**
Special attorney in fact, fiduciary for holders of obligations secured by mortgage, **9:5302**
Trusts and trustees, revocation, **9:2088**

MANUFACTURED HOME PROPERTY ACT
Generally, **9:1149.1 et seq.**

MANUFACTURERS
Construction equipment, contracts, limiting liability, **9:2775**
Definitions,
    Manufactured homes, **9:1149.2**
    Products liability, **9:2800.53**
Manufactured Home Property Act, **9:1149.1 et seq.**

MAPS AND PLATS
Expropriation, highway property, recording, **9:2727**
Military forces, power of attorney, immovables, **9:3882.1**
Servitudes,
    Attaching and recording, **9:2726**
    Land acquired by state from political subdivision due to erosion or subsidence, mineral servitude of subdivision, **9:1152**
Surveys and Surveyors, this index

INDEX TO TITLE 9

MARDI GRAS
Associations and societies, damages, limitation of liability, 9:2796
Assumption of risk, 9:2796
Limitation of liability, damages, 9:2796

MARINA AND BOATYARD STORAGE ACT
Generally, 9:4780 et seq.

MARITAL PORTION
Trust as satisfying, 9:1851 et seq.

MARRIAGE
Affidavits,
    Covenant marriage, 9:273
    Verification, license application, 9:224
Annulment, actions between spouses, authority, 9:291
Application of law, covenant marriage, 9:274
Ceremony,
    Authority to perform, 9:202, 9:203
    Delay after license issuance, 9:241 et seq.
    Officiants, 9:201 et seq.
    Witnesses, 9:244
Certificates and certification, 9:245
    Consolidated form, 9:251
    Covenant marriage, 9:245
    Disposition, 9:253, 9:254
    Fines and penalties, false entries, 9:256
Clergy,
    Authority to perform, 9:202
    License to celebrate marriage, 9:205
Collateral relations, 9:211
Consent, covenant marriage, 9:273
Costs, opposition to marriage, overruling, 9:263
Counseling, covenant marriage, 9:272
Covenant marriage, 9:272 et seq.
    Attestation, 9:273.1
    Certificates and certification, 9:245
    Couples already married, 9:275
        Declaration of intent, 9:275.1
    Licenses and permits, 9:224, 9:225
    Summary, matrimonial regimes, 9:237
Credit, discrimination, 9:3583
Crimes and offenses, false entries, licenses or certificates, 9:256
Declaration of intent, covenant marriage, 9:224, 9:225, 9:272 et seq., 9:273.1, 9:275.1
Declarations. Declaration of intent, generally, ante
Dissolution, restriction on suit by child against parent entitled to custody and control, 9:571
Emancipation, 9:101 et seq.
Fines and penalties,
    False entries, licenses or certificates, 9:256
    License duplicates, filing, 9:252
    Premature ceremony, 9:243
    Recordkeeping violations, 9:254
Form,
    Consolidated form, license, authorization and marriage certificate, 9:251
    Licenses, 9:223 et seq.
Hearing, opposition to marriage, 9:262
High test marriage, 9:272 et seq.
Judges,
    Authority to perform, 9:202, 9:203
    Children and minors, authorization to marry, license application, 9:225
    License to perform, 9:205

MARRIAGE—Cont'd
Jurisdiction, judges and justices of the peace, authority to perform, 9:203
Justices of the peace,
    Authority to perform, 9:202, 9:203
    License to perform, 9:205
Licenses and permits, 9:221 et seq.
    Affidavit of verification, 9:224
    AIDS testing, application, summary of matrimonial regimes, 9:237
    Applications, information, 9:224
    Authority to issue, 9:221
    Birth certificate, 9:225 et seq.
    Children and minors, consent or authorization, accompanying application, 9:225
    Clergymen, license to celebrate, 9:205
    Consolidated form, 9:251
    Covenant marriage, 9:224, 9:225, 9:272 et seq.
    Delay before ceremony, 9:241 et seq.
    Domicile or residence, license issuance, 9:222
    Duplicate records, 9:252
    Fines and penalties, false entries, 9:256
    Form, 9:223 et seq.
    Identification, social security numbers, 9:224
    Issuance, 9:221
    Officiants, 9:205
    Place of issuance, 9:222
    Records and recordation, 9:252
        Birth certificates, retention by recorder, 9:226
    Reissuance, 9:236
    Time,
        Issuance and celebration of marriage, 9:234
        Validity, 9:235
    Unavailable birth certificate, alternate proof, 9:227
    Waiver, birth certificate, 9:228
Notice, opposition to marriage, 9:261
Officiants, 9:201 et seq.
    Certificate, signature, 9:245
    Fines and penalties, recordkeeping violations, 9:254
    License, 9:205
Opposition to, 9:261 et seq.
Premature ceremonies, 9:241
Records and recordation, 9:251 et seq.
Regimes of matrimony, summary, license application, 9:237
Registration, officiant other than judge, 9:204
Reissuance, expired license, 9:236
Relations of the fourth degree, 9:211
Separation of property, interspousal immunity, 9:291
Summary, matrimonial regimes, 9:237
Surname of married person, 9:0292
Time,
    Delay between license and ceremony, 9:241 et seq.
    Issuance of license, 9:234
    Licenses and permits, ante
    Validity of license, 9:235
Waiver, premature ceremony prohibition, 9:242
Witnesses, ceremony, 9:244

MARRIAGE CONTRACTS
Surname of married person, 9:0292

MASS TRANSPORTATION
Public trust, purposes, 9:2341 et seq.

MATERIAL CHANGE IN CIRCUMSTANCES
Definitions, support of persons, 9:311

I-37

MATRIMONIAL REGIMES
See, also, Community of Acquets and Gains, this index
Actions and proceedings, **9:291**
Affidavits, partition, community property, **9:2801**
Alienation. Community of Acquets and Gains, this index
Appraisal and appraisers, partition, community property, **9:2801**
Community of Acquets and Gains, generally, this index
Divorce,
    Injunctions, alienation or encumbrance, community property, **9:371**
    Partition, community property, **9:2801**
    Possession and use, community property, **9:374**
Fraud, actions between spouses, **9:291**
Good faith, actions between spouses, administering community property, **9:291**
Homesteads, divorce, possession and use, **9:374**
Injunctions, divorce proceedings, alienation or encumbrance, **9:371**
Judicial authorization, acting without consent of spouse, **9:291**
Leases, actions between spouses, **9:291**
Movable property, removal, divorce proceedings, **9:373**
Partition,
    Community property, **9:2801**
    Retirement and pensions, community property, **9:2801.1**
Privileges,
    Actions between spouses, **9:291**
    Injunctions, divorce proceedings, community property, **9:371**
Restitution, separate property, actions between spouses, **9:291**
Retirement and pensions, partition, community property, **9:2801, 9:2801.1**
Separate property, restitution, actions between spouses, **9:291**
Solicitation, partition, community property, **9:2801**
Suits between spouses, **9:291**
Unauthorized alienation, actions between spouses, **9:291**

MECHANIC'S PRIVILEGES
Generally, **9:4801**
Abandoned or unclaimed property, **9:4803**
Actions and proceedings, **9:4823**
Affidavits, inspections, **9:4820**
Aged persons, improvements, home solicitation sales, **9:3541.21, 9:3541.22**
Agricultural machinery and equipment, **9:4502**
Architects, **9:4801 et seq.**
Assessments, taxation, ranking, **9:4821**
Attorney fees, **9:4833**
Automobiles, **9:4501**
Bonds (officers and fiduciaries),
    Contractors, **9:4812**
    Extinguishment of claim or privilege, **9:4823**
    Filing, in lieu of privilege, **9:4835**
Claims,
    Copies and duplicates, **9:4802**
    Extinguishment, **9:4823**
    Preservation, **9:4822**
Clothing, etc., cleaning and pressing, **9:4687, 9:4688**
Collective bargaining agreements, amounts owed, **9:4803**
Compensation and salaries, **9:4803**
Concursus proceedings, **9:4841**
    Deposits, **9:4841**
    Extinguishment of liens, **9:4823**
Contracts,
    General contractors, notice, **9:4811**

MECHANIC'S PRIVILEGES—Cont'd
Contracts—Cont'd
    Notice,
        Cancellation, **9:4832**
        Filing, **9:4831**
        General contractors, **9:4811**
        Prescription, **9:4834**
Cook, privilege on logs and lumber, **9:4621**
Damages, failure to cancel, **9:4833**
Definitions, **9:4806 et seq.**
Delivery, movables, **9:4803**
Demolition, work, **9:4808**
Description, references to immovables, records and recordations, **9:4831**
Documentary evidence, **9:4842**
Engineers and engineering, **9:4801 et seq.**
Evidence,
    Burden of proof, **9:4841**
    Documentary evidence, **9:4842**
    Prima facie evidence, **9:4842**
Expenses, **9:4803**
Extinguishment of claims, **9:4823**
Filing, **9:4831**
    Bonds, in lieu of privilege, **9:4835**
    General contractors, contracts, notice, **9:4811**
Fraud, affidavits, inspections, **9:4820**
Furniture, making or repairing, **9:4502**
Garageman, **9:4501**
General contractor,
    Definitions, **9:4807**
    Notice of contract, filing, **9:4811**
Guaranty, condition of bond, **9:4812**
Hauling or trucking, **9:4601**
Home solicitation sales, aged persons, improvements, **9:3541.21, 9:3541.22**
Immovables, **9:4801 et seq.**
Indemnity, contractors, **9:4802**
Interest, **9:4803**
Interests affected, **9:4806**
Jewelry, gems and watches, **9:4701 et seq.**
Leases, **9:4801 et seq.**
Liability of surety, **9:4813**
Lis pendens, **9:4831**
Logs and lumber, **9:4621, 9:4622**
Machinery, **9:4501, 9:4502**
Mail and mailing, notice or documents, **9:4842**
Making movable goods, **9:4502**
Merchandise, making or repairing, **9:4502**
Molasses, refinery and mill employees, **9:4721**
Mortgages, ranking, **9:4821**
Moss, **9:4641**
Oil, gas and water wells, **9:4861 et seq.**
Ownership, definitions, **9:4806**
Prescription, **9:4823**
    Notice of contract, **9:4834**
    Sureties, liability, **9:4813**
Preservation of claims, **9:4822**
Prima facie evidence, **9:4842**
Prime consultants, contractors, **9:4802**
Private works, **9:4801 et seq.**
Professional subconsultants, **9:4801 et seq.**
Rank, **9:4821**
    Immovables, **9:4801**
    Moss, **9:4641**
    Movable goods, manufacturer, repair, etc., **9:4502**
    Repairmen, **9:4501, 9:4502**
    Sugar, refinery and mill employees, **9:4721**

INDEX TO TITLE 9

MECHANIC'S PRIVILEGES—Cont'd
Records and recordation, **9:4801**, **9:4812**
Refinery and mill employees, sugar, syrup, and molasses, **9:4721**
Repairing movables, **9:4501**, **9:4502**
Sales of immovables, **9:4801 et seq.**
Sequestration,
    Automobiles and machinery, **9:4501**
    Movable goods, commodities, etc., repairs, **9:4502**
Site of immovable, definitions, **9:4820**
Statements,
    Claim or privilege, residential housing work, **9:4822**
    Filing, claims or privileges, **9:4831**
    Preservation of claims, **9:4822**
Subconsultants, professional subconsultants, **9:4801 et seq.**
Subcontractors,
    Claims against contractor, preservation, **9:4822**
    Definitions, **9:4807**
    Privileges and liens, **9:4807**
Sugar refinery and mill employees, **9:4721**
Summary proceedings, failure to cancel, **9:4833**
Suppliers, claims against contractor, preservation, **9:4822**
Suretyship and guaranty, **9:4812**
    Actions and proceedings, **9:4813**
    Claims against owners, **9:4802**
    Condition of bond, **9:4812**
    Liability of surety, **9:4813**
Surveys and surveyors, **9:4801 et seq.**
Syrup, refinery and mill employees, **9:4721**
Tax assessments, ranking, **9:4821**
Tax assessments--special, ranking, **9:4821**
Third parties, **9:4820 et seq.**
    Lis pendens, **9:4833**
Wells, **9:4861 et seq.**
    Exception, **9:4808**
    Privilege on immovables, **9:4861 et seq.**
Work, definitions, **9:4808**

MEDIATION
    See, also, Arbitration and Award, generally, this index
    Generally, **9:4101 et seq.**
Attorneys, discussion with clients, **9:4102**
Confidential or privileged information, **9:4112**
Costs, **9:4109**
Discussion with clients, attorneys, **9:4102**
Labor Disputes, this index
Mediator,
    Approved register, **9:4105**
    Qualifications, **9:4106**
    Selection, **9:4104**
    Standard of conduct, **9:4107**
Nonbinding effect, **9:4110**
Objections, **9:4103**
Parenting coordinators, child custody, **9:358.1 et seq.**
Referral of case for, **9:4103**
Settlement agreements, **9:4111**
Waiver, confidential or privileged information, **9:4112**

MEDICAL CARE AND TREATMENT
Arbitration and award, contracts for services and supplies, **9:4230 et seq.**
Contracts, arbitration and award, **9:4230 et seq.**
Damages, privileges and immunities,
    Gratuitous services, **9:2799.5**
    Volunteers, emergency medical services, **9:2793.2**
Divorce, family violence victims, costs, **9:367**
Fees, open accounts, demand for payment, **9:2781**

MEDICAL CARE AND TREATMENT—Cont'd
Limitation of liability, users of blood, organs or tissue, **9:2797**
Medical Malpractice, generally, this index
Negligence, gratuitous services, limitation of liability, **9:4861 et seq.**
Notice, gratuitous services, limitation of liability, **9:2799.5**
Privileges and immunities,
    Emergency response network, **9:2798.5**
    Gratuitous services, **9:2799.5**
    Hospital services and supplies furnished, **9:4751 et seq.**
    Nonprofit health care quality improvement corporations, **9:2800.20**
    Volunteers, emergency medical services, **9:2793.2**
Public trust, purposes, **9:2341 et seq.**

MEDICAL MALPRACTICE
Blood or tissue banks, prescription, **9:5628**
Burden of proof, **9:2794**
Contracts, services or supplies, arbitration and award, **9:4230 et seq.**
Damages,
    Gratuitous services, **9:2799.5**
    Physicians and surgeons, prescription, **9:5628**
Prescription, **9:5628**
Privileges and immunities, gratuitous services, **9:2799.5**
Subpoenas, **9:2794**
Users of blood, organs, or tissue, limitation of liability, **9:2797**

MERCANTILE LAW
Law merchant, fiduciaries, laws governing, **9:3812**

MICROFILM
Mortgages, cancellation, erasure or partial release, alternative methods, **9:5810.4**
Privileges and liens, cancellation, erasure or partial release, alternative methods, **9:5810.4**

MILITARY FORCES
Acts of sale and conveyances,
    Adjutant general, powers and duties, **9:3871**
    Power of attorney,
        Immovables, **9:3882.1**
        Powers and duties, **9:3871**
Death, member, presumptions, **9:1441**
    Divorce, authority to remarry, **9:301**
    Proof, **9:1443**
    Successions, **9:1442**
Military Parent Child Custody Protection Act, **9:359 to 9:359.13**
National guard,
    Leases, termination of lease, **9:3261**
Power of attorney,
    Acceptance, **9:3887**
    Accountant, employment, **9:3870**
    Actions and proceedings,
        Immovables, **9:3882.1**
        Powers granted, **9:3870**, **9:3878**
    Acts of sale and conveyances, immovables, **9:3882.1**
    Additional form, **9:3867**
    After-acquired property, **9:3883**
    Annuity transactions, powers granted, **9:3876**
    Application, **9:3861**
        Personal property, **9:3886**
    Application of chapter, **9:3869**
        Additional form, **9:3867**
    Arbitration, powers granted, **9:3870**
    Assignments, **9:3870**
        Immovables, **9:3882.1**

INDEX TO TITLE 9

MILITARY FORCES—Cont'd
Power of attorney—Cont'd
    Assistants, powers granted, **9:3870**
    Attorney, employment, **9:3870**
    Banking transactions, powers granted, **9:3874**
        Privileges and immunities, **9:3885**
    Beneficiary transactions, powers granted, **9:3877**
    Benefits, **9:3880**
    Bond transactions, **9:3872**
    Business operating transactions, **9:3875**
    Casualty insurance, immovables, **9:3882.1**
    Checks, powers granted, **9:3870**
    Children and minors, **9:3862**
    Civil benefits, **9:3880**
    Claims, **9:3878**
    Commodity transactions, **9:3873**
    Compromise, **9:3870**
    Conservation, immovables, **9:3882.1**
    Construction of chapter, **9:3869**
    Contracts, **9:3861**
    Damages, reliance, **9:3885**
    Description, immovables, **9:3886**
    Donations, immovables, **9:3882.1**
    Enforcement, powers granted, **9:3870**
    Estate transactions, **9:3887**
    Exchanges, immovables, **9:3882.1**
    Execution, **9:3861**
    Exemptions, forms, **9:3863**
    Expenses, **9:3870**
    Family maintenance, **9:3879**
    Financial institution transactions, **9:3874**
    Forms, **9:3862**
        Initialed lines, **9:3864**
    Good faith reliance on power, liability, **9:3885**
    Immovables, **9:3882.1 et seq.**
    Improvements, immovables, **9:3882.1**
    Insurance, **9:3876**
        Immovables, **9:3882.1**
    Labor and employment, immovables, **9:3882.1 et seq.**
    Leases, immovables, **9:3882.1**
        Powers granted, **9:3870**
    Legal sufficiency, requirements, **9:3863**
    Liabilities, **9:3885**
    Liability insurance, immovables, **9:3882.1**
    Licenses and permits, immovables, **9:3882.1**
    Limitation of powers, **9:3864**
    Litigation, powers, **9:3878**
    Loans, immovables, **9:3882.1**
    Location of property, scope of power, **9:3883**
    Management, immovables, **9:3882.1**
    Maps and plats, immovables, **9:3882.1**
    Military benefits, powers, **9:3880**
    Modification of trust, **9:3884**
    Mortgages,
        Immovables, **9:3882.1**
        Powers granted, **9:3870**
    Movables, **9:3871**
    Notice, powers granted, **9:3870**
    Option transactions, **9:3873**
    Personal maintenance, **9:3879**
    Personal property, **9:3871**
        Application of power, **9:3886**
        Powers granted, **9:3871**
    Powers, **9:3870**
    Privileges, immovables, **9:3882.1**
    Records and recordation, powers granted, **9:3870**
    Release, powers granted, **9:3870**

MILITARY FORCES—Cont'd
Power of attorney—Cont'd
    Reports, powers granted, **9:3870**
    Retirement plan transactions, **9:3881**
    Revocation,
        Powers granted, **9:3870**
        Trust, **9:3884**
    Sales, **9:3870**
    Scope of power, after-acquired property, location of property, **9:3883**
    Secured transactions, **9:3870**
        Immovables, **9:3882.1**
    Security interest, **9:3874**
    Servitudes, immovables, **9:3882.1**
    Settlement and compromise, powers granted, **9:3870**
    Shares and shareholders, immovables, **9:3882.1**
    Social security, **9:3880**
    Stock transactions, **9:3872**
    Subdivisions, **9:3882.1**
    Tangible personal property transactions, **9:3871**
    Tax assessments, immovables, **9:3882.1**
    Tax matters, powers granted, **9:3882**
    Transfers, **9:3870**
    Trust transactions, powers granted, **9:3877**
    Trusts and trustees, modification or revocation, **9:3884**
    Validity, **9:3885**
    Witnesses, employment, **9:3870**
    Zoning and planning, immovables, **9:3882.1**

MILITARY POWER OF ATTORNEY ACT
Generally, **9:3861 et seq.**

MINERALS, OIL, AND GAS
Accounts and accounting, keeper, enforcement of mortgage of mineral rights, **9:5133**
Actions and proceedings,
    Indemnity agreements, **9:2780**
    Mortgage of mineral rights, enforcement, **9:5131 et seq.**
Assignments, rents, **9:4401 et seq.**
Associations and societies, transfer of title, **9:1051**
Bonds, keeper, enforcement of mortgage on mineral rights, **9:5134**
Certificates and certification, declarations filed in lieu of agreement for joint exploration, development, etc., **9:2732**
Children and minors, mineral or royalty rights, liberative prescription, **9:5805**
Compensation and salaries, keeper enforcement of mortgage of mineral rights, **9:5133**
Contractors, indemnity, invalidity, **9:2780**
Contracts,
    Declaration in lieu of agreement for joint exploration, filing, **9:2732**
    Indemnity agreements, **9:2780**
    Joint exploration, development, etc., **9:2731 et seq.**
    Third persons, binding effect, joint exploration, **9:2731**
Coproprietors, prescription, suspension as to one, **9:5805**
Curators, authority to receive mineral proceeds, **9:1516**
Damages, indemnity agreements, exploration and development, **9:2780**
Deceased persons, payments to representatives, **9:1516**
Designation, keeper of property, enforcement of mortgage, **9:5132**
Development and operation, exploration and exploitation, indemnity agreements, **9:2780**
Easements, Servitudes, generally, post
Expenses, administration or preservation of property, **9:5133**

MINERALS, OIL, AND GAS—Cont'd
Exploration and prospecting,
    Contracts, joint exploration, **9:2731 et seq.**
    Indemnity agreements, **9:2780**
    Insurance, indemnity agreements, **9:2780**
    Joint exploration of minerals, agreements, **9:2731 et seq.**
    Liens for, **9:4861 et seq.**
    Privilege, **9:4861 et seq.**
    Rigs, machinery, privilege for labor, services or supplies, **9:4861 et seq.**
Farm-out agreements, mineral rights, **9:2780**
Fees and charges,
    Declarations filed in lieu of agreement for joint exploration, **9:2732**
Filing,
    Agreements for joint exploration, development, etc., **9:2731**
    Declaration in lieu of agreement for joint exploration, development, etc., **9:2732**
Forests and forestry, indemnity agreements, drilling and wells, **9:2780**
Holder, definitions, payments for deceased persons, **9:1516**
Indemnity agreements, development, exploration, and exploitation, **9:2780**
Insurance, indemnity agreements, development, and exploration, **9:2780**
Joint operating contracts or agreements, exploitation of mineral interest, **9:2731 et seq.**
Keeper, mortgage of mineral rights, enforcement of mortgage, **9:5131 et seq.**
Landowner's liability, **9:2800.4**
Leases,
    Deceased persons, payments to representatives, **9:1516**
    Interest conveyed, presumption, **9:2971 et seq.**
    Navigable stream, bay, or lake, change in ownership of water bottoms, **9:1151**
    Political subdivisions, land acquired by state from subdivision, **9:1152**
    Privileges and liens, labor, services, or supplies, **9:4861 et seq.**
    Recording, **9:2721**
    State agencies, land acquired by state from agency, **9:1152**
    Successions and succession proceedings, payment to representatives, **9:1516**
    Surface leases, recording, third parties protected, **9:2721**
    Third parties protected, recording law, **9:2721**
    Trust property, **9:2118**
Machinery and equipment, privilege on oil or gas produced, **9:4861 et seq.**
Mechanic's liens, drilling wells, exception, **9:4808**
Mortgages, mineral rights, **9:5131 et seq.**
    Enforcement of mortgage, **9:5131 et seq.**
Negligence, indemnity agreements, **9:2780**
Oil Field Indemnity Act, **9:2780**
Operating agreements, validity, mineral rights, **9:2780**
Prescription, mineral or royalty rights, liberative prescription, **9:5805**
Privileges, **9:4861 et seq.**
    Leases, ante
    Pipelines, **9:4861**
    Wells, **9:4861 et seq., 9:4881 et seq.**
Provisional seizure, enforcement of lien of privilege in connection with drilling, **9:4861**
Public trust, purposes, **9:2341 et seq.**
Registration, agreements for joint exploration, development, etc., **9:2731**

MINERALS, OIL, AND GAS—Cont'd
Rent, deceased persons, payments to representatives, **9:1516**
Repairs, privilege on oil or gas produced from well, **9:4861 et seq.**
Revenues, mortgaged mineral rights, enforcement of mortgage, disposition, **9:5133**
Royalties,
    Change of ownership of land or water bottoms, **9:1151**
    Deceased persons, payments to representatives, **9:1516**
    Liberative prescription, minority as affecting, **9:5805**
    Rights, prescription, co-proprietors, **9:5805**
Searches and seizures, mineral rights, enforcement of mortgage, **9:5131**
Servitudes,
    Expropriation, plats, recording, **9:2727**
    Highways and roads, **9:1253**
    State agencies, land acquired, mineral servitude of agency, **9:1152**
    Streets and alleys, **9:1253**
Signatures, declaration filed in lieu of agreement for joint exploration, **9:2732**
Successions and succession proceedings,
    Payments to representatives, **9:1516**
Sulphur, indemnity agreements, wells or drilling, **9:2780**
Third persons, binding agreements, joint exploration of minerals, **9:2731**
Trusts and trustees, allocation of proceeds to income or principal, **9:2152**
Wells,
    Buildings, appurtenant to wells, privilege, **9:4861 et seq.**
    Indemnity agreements, bodily injury or death, **9:2780**
    Mechanic's privileges and liens, exception, **9:4808**
    Pipes and pipelines, privileges and liens, **9:4861 et seq.**
    Privileges, **9:4861 et seq., 9:4881 et seq.**
    Tanks, appurtenant to wells, privilege for labor, services or supplies, **9:4861 et seq.**
Workers' compensation, indemnity agreements, contractors, **9:2780**

MIXED PRIVATE AND CHARITABLE TRUSTS
General rule, **9:1951**

MOBILE HOMES AND MANUFACTURED HOUSING
Acts of sale and conveyance, recordation, immobilization, **9:1149.4**
Bonds (officers and fiduciaries), remedies of mortgagees, **9:5363.1**
Certificates of title,
    Abandoned mobile homes, **9:5363.1**
Deimmobilization, **9:1149.6**
Immobilization, **9:1149.4**
Immovables, classification, **9:1149.3**
Leases, unpaid rent, mortgagor, notice, **9:3259.1**
Manufactured Home Property Act, **9:1149.1 et seq.**
Mortgages,
    Delinquent rent, notice, **9:3259.1**
    Recordation, immobilization, **9:1149.4**
Movable property, classification, **9:1149.3**
Notice, repossession, mortgagees, **9:5363.1**
Privileges and liens, **9:1149.3**
Rent, delinquent rent, privileges and liens, **9:3259.1**
Repossession by secured parties, **9:5363.1**
Retail installment contracts, **9:1149.5**
Secured parties, repossession, **9:5363.1**
Secured transactions, **9:1149.3 et seq.**
Security, retail installment contracts or chattel mortgages, **9:1149.5**
Title to property, **9:1149.3**

INDEX TO TITLE 9

MOLASSES
Privilege,
  Refinery and mill employees, **9:4721**
  Seller of sugar cane, **9:4543**

MONEY
Custodial property, creating, Uniform Transfers to Minors Act, **9:759**
Minors, custodial property, creating, Uniform Transfers to Minors Act, **9:759**
Privileges,
  Advances for,
    Gathering moss, **9:4641**
    Logs and lumber, **9:4621**
  Purchase money,
    Agricultural products in chartered cities and towns, **9:4541**
    Cotton seed, **9:4542**
    Sugar cane, **9:4543**
Sureties, joint control of deposits, **9:3904**
Uniform Transfers to Minors Act, creating custodial property, **9:759**

MORTGAGES
Accessions, attachment, **9:5391**
Accrual of interest, time, **9:3506.1**
Actions and proceedings, failure to release upon satisfaction, **9:5385**
Additions, attachment, **9:5391**
Adjustable rates, **9:3504**, **9:3526**
Affidavits,
  Cancellation, **9:5167.1**
  Identity, filing, **9:5503**
  Names, similar names, affidavits of distinction, **9:5501**
    Form, **9:5501.1**
Application of law, **9:5140.2**
  Collateral assignment and incorporeal rights, **9:5386**
  Consumer credit, **9:3511**
  Secured transactions, **9:4401**
Assignments,
  Collateral mortgages, registry, no requirement, **9:5554**
  Foreclosure, signatures, presumed authenticity, **9:4422**
  Incorporeal rights, **9:5386 et seq.**
  Leases or rents, **9:4401**
Associations and societies, immovable property, **9:1051**
Assumption in globo, transfer of more than one parcel of property, **9:5383**
Assumption, rank of subordination, **9:5384**
Attachment, additions and accessions, **9:5391**
Attorney fees,
  Affidavits, cancellation, **9:5167.1**
  Failure to release upon satisfaction, **9:5385**
  Recovery, actions for disposal or conversion of mortgaged property, **9:5382**
Attorney in fact, fiduciary for obligation holders, irrevocable appointment, **9:5302**
Attorneys, affidavits, cancellation, **9:5167.1**
Bankruptcy,
  Sale of property, effect on mortgage, **9:5251**
Bonds,
  Keeper of property in foreclosure proceedings, **9:5139**
  Payment of release price, method, **9:2943**
  Release price, stipulation for, recording, **9:2942**
  Securing several bonds, **9:5301**
Cancellation, **9:5167**, **9:5385**
  By financial institution, standard form, **9:573**
  Certified copy of order, decree or other instrument, **9:5171**

MORTGAGES—Cont'd
Cancellation—Cont'd
  Federal agencies as mortgagees, **9:5163**, **9:5164**
  Judicial sale, **9:3003**
  Licensed financial institution, **9:5172**
  Lost or destroyed notes, affidavits, **9:5167**
  Mortgages and privileges,
    Not securing paraphed obligations, **9:5169**
    Securing paraphed obligations, **9:5170**
  Notice, service of agency or instrumentality of United States, **9:5164**
  Records and recordation,
    Description, **9:5167**
    Federal agencies as mortgagees,
      Notice, **9:5163**
      Service of notice, **9:5164**
  Sales of property, effect on mortgages, **9:5251**
Collateral assignment, incorporeal rights, **9:5386 et seq.**
Collateral mortgages, **9:5550 et seq.**
  Defenses, **9:5552**
  Effective date, **9:5551**
  Registry, transfer, assignment, pledge of security interest, no requirement of, **9:5554**
  Vendor's privilege, **9:5550**
    Defenses, **9:5553**
Common interest of obligation holders, **9:5303**
Confidential nature of personnel records, **9:5175**
Consumer credit, application of law, **9:3511**
Conversion of property, **9:5382**
Costs,
  Failure to release upon satisfaction, **9:5385**
  Foreclosure,
    Keeper of property, **9:5138**
Damages, affidavits, cancellation, **9:5167.1**
Defenses, collateral mortgages, enforcement, **9:5552**
Donations, mortgageable property, registration, effect on donees and third parties, **9:2371**
Dual contracts for sale of real property, **9:2989**
Environmental liability, lenders, immunities, **9:5395**
Execution, keeper of property, appointment, **9:5136 et seq.**
Exemptions, usury and interest, **9:3504**
Extinction of rights, acknowledgement by owner or holder, **9:5176**
Family home, consent of wife, **9:2801**
Federal housing administration insured loans, interest, enforcement, **9:3508**
Federally related mortgaged loans,
  Consumer credit, exemptions, **9:3512**, **9:3516**
  Usury, application of law, **9:3506**
Fees and charges,
  Designation as interest, **9:3505**
  Multiple indebtedness mortgages, **9:5217**
Fidei commissa, law relating to, **9:5307**
Fiduciaries,
  Mortgagee in trust for creditors, **9:5302**
  Mortgages securing several obligations,
    Enforcement, limitations on power, **9:5304**
    Pledge, inclusion under mortgage and deposit with fiduciary, **9:5306**
Fines and penalties,
  Accrual of interest, noncompliance, **9:3506.1**
  Affidavits, cancellation, **9:5167.1**
  Prepayment, **9:3532.1**
  Rural property, **9:5324**
Floating rates, **9:3504**

MORTGAGES—Cont'd
Foreclosure,
    Expenses, mortgages, indemnity of fiduciary by obligation holders, 9:5304
    Newspaper, 9:5103
    Prorating proceeds, mortgages securing several obligations, 9:5303
    Signatures, obligations, presumed authenticity, 9:4422
Fraud, contracts for sale of realty, 9:2989
Future obligations, executory process, 9:5555
Graduated payment mortgages, 9:3526
    Definitions, 9:3504
    Interest, 9:3504
Hazardous substances and waste, liability of lenders, 9:5395
Homestead, foreclosure, keeper of property, designation, 9:5136 et seq.
Husband and wife, 9:103
    Family home, consent of wife, 9:2801
Incorporeal rights, assignment, 9:5386 et seq.
Insolvency, sale of property, effect on mortgage, 9:5251
Institutional funds, investments, 9:2337.1 et seq.
Interest, 9:3502 et seq., 9:3504
    Adjustable rates, 9:3504, 9:3526
    Federally related mortgage loans, usury, application of law, 9:3506
    Graduated payment mortgages, 9:3504, 9:3526
    Mortgagee, action for disposal or conversion of mortgaged property, 9:3582
    Property insured by federal housing administration, enforcement, 9:3508
    Rural property, prepayment, 9:5324
    Secured by mortgage, 9:5301
    Time for accrual of interest, 9:3506.1
    Usury,
        Application of law, 9:3506
        Exemptions, graduated payment mortgages, 9:3504
Judicial mortgages,
    Affidavit of distinction, name similarity, 9:5501
    Names, similarity, affidavit of distinction, 9:5501
        Form, 9:5501.1
    Sales of property, effect on mortgage, 9:5251
Judicial sales, effect on mortgages, 9:5251
Keeper of property,
    Accounting, 9:5138
    Application of law, 9:5140.1
    Appointment, 9:5137
    Bonds, 9:5139
    Designation, 9:5136 et seq.
    Mineral rights, enforcement of mortgage, 9:5131 et seq.
    Powers and duties, 9:5138
    Request for instructions, 9:5140
Legal mortgages, affidavits of distinction, judgment debtor, similar names, 9:5501, 9:5501.1
Liability for incorrect or false request for cancellation, 9:5174
Liquidation, sale of property, effect on mortgage, 9:5251
Loan proceeds, availability, time for accrual of interest, 9:3506.1
    Affidavits, cancellation, 9:5167
Manufactured housing, delinquent rent, notice, 9:3259.1
Mechanic's privileges and liens, ranking, 9:4821
Military forces, power of attorney,
    Immovables, 9:3882.1
    Powers granted, 9:3870
Multiple indebtedness mortgages, fees and charges, 9:5217
Multiple pieces of property, assumption in globo, 9:5383
Names,
    Newspapers, mortgages, 9:5103

MORTGAGES—Cont'd
National Housing Act, insured loans, interest, enforcement, 9:3508
Newspaper plant, equipment, name and good will, 9:5103
Notaries public, affidavits, cancellation, 9:5167.1
Obligations not paraphed for identification,
    Executory process, 9:5555
Obligations, release, 9:5557
Oil and gas. Minerals, Oil and Gas, this index
Open-end loans, interest, 9:3506.1
Orleans Parish, this index
Owners of property, affidavits, cancellation, 9:5167.1
Paraph unnecessary if obligation identified in mortgage, 9:5305
Partition, sale of property, effect on mortgages, 9:5251
Penalties. Fines and penalties, generally, ante
Pledges,
    Collateral mortgages, registry, no requirement, 9:5554
    Incorporeal rights, 9:5386 et seq.
    Property pledged to fiduciary under mortgage securing several obligations, 9:5306
    Securing several obligations, inclusion of pledge within, 9:5306
Power of attorney, military forces,
    Immovables, 9:3882.1
    Powers granted, 9:3870
Prepayment, 9:3509.3
    Fines and penalties, 9:3532.1
Prescription, setting aside, legal entities, lack of authority, 9:5681
Presumptions, interest conveyed in lands bounded by waterways, highways, 9:2971 et seq.
Priorities and preferences,
    Assumption of first mortgage by third person, 9:5384
    Collateral mortgages, 9:5551
    Federal agency as mortgagee, 9:5163
    Labor and materials, 9:4801
    Tax assessments--special, 9:4821
Private works, ranking, 9:4821
Privileges and immunities, environmental liability, lenders, 9:5395
Proceeds available for disbursement, time for accrual of interest, 9:3506.1
Prorating proceeds, enforcement of mortgage, 9:5303
Public trust, purposes, 9:2341 et seq.
Purchase money mortgages,
    Interest, 9:3504
    Release of prior encumbrances under bond for deed, 9:2946
Real estate timesharing, 9:1131.28
Records and recordation, 9:2721
    Affidavit of identity, 9:5503
    Cancellation, ante
    Manufactured homes, immobilization, 9:1149.4
    Multiple indebtedness mortgages, 9:5217
    Newspaper plant equipment, name and good will, 9:5103
    Partnership contracts, filing at principal place of business, 9:3406
    Release price, 9:2942
    Removal,
        Mortgages held by federal agencies, notice, waiver, service, 9:5163, 9:5164
        Sale of property, 9:5251
    Title of acts and time of filing, 9:5211
    Wells, privileges, notice, 9:4865, 9:4885
Registry, collateral mortgages, transfers, no requirement, 9:5554

INDEX TO TITLE 9

MORTGAGES—Cont'd
Release,
    Instruments, 9:5385
    Obligations, 9:5557
Revolving loan accounts, interest, 9:3506.1
Roads, abandonment, 9:2981 et seq.
    Remedial provisions of act, 9:2982
Rural property, 9:5321 et seq.
Sales, continuation of mortgage, 9:5251
Satisfaction, 9:5385
Seizure of collateral,
    Keeper of property, designation, 9:5136 et seq.
    Mineral rights, enforcement of mortgage, 9:5131
Several notes, 9:5301
Several obligations, securing, 9:5301 et seq.
Ships and watercraft, this index
Substitutions, law relating to, 9:5307
Successions and Succession Proceedings, this index
Summary proceedings, keeper of property, appointment in foreclosure proceedings, 9:5137
Third parties,
    Recording law, protection, 9:2721
Time, accrual of interest, 9:3506.1
Title insurance officers, affidavits, cancellation, 9:5167.1
Transfers, collateral mortgages, registry, no requirement, 9:5554
Trusts and Trustees, this index
United States agencies, cancellation,
    Notice, 9:5163
    Service of notice, 9:5164
Usury, 9:3502 et seq.
    Exemptions, graduated payment mortgages, 9:3504
    Variable rates, 9:3504
Vendor's privilege, 9:5550 et seq.
    Defenses, enforcement, 9:5553
Wells, privileges, notice, 9:4865, 9:4885
Wrap-around mortgages,
    Definitions, 9:3504
    Interest, 9:3504

MOSS
Privilege, laborers and furnishers of supplies, 9:4641

MOTOR CARRIERS
Consumer credit, exemptions, 9:3512
Drivers licenses, generally. Motor Vehicles, this index
Licenses and permits, drivers licenses, generally. Motor Vehicles, this index
Privileges, 9:4601

MOTOR VEHICLE INSURANCE
Limitation of actions, uninsured motorist claims, 9:5629
Prescription, uninsured motorist claims, 9:5629

MOTOR VEHICLES
Certificates of title, repairman's privilege, 9:4502
Chattel mortgages, priority, repairman's privilege, 9:4501
Consumer credit, exemptions, 9:3512, 9:3516
    Licenses, 9:3560
Contracts, consumer credit sales, exemptions, 9:3516
Dealers and distributors,
    Consumer credit, reports, 9:3571.2
    Notice, sale of dealerships, 9:2961
    Reports, consumer credit, 9:3571.2
    Sale of dealerships, 9:2961
Drivers licenses, support of persons, number, providing, 9:313

MOTOR VEHICLES—Cont'd
Driving under influence of alcohol or drugs. Traffic Rules and Regulations, this index
Leases, records and recordation, 9:3342
Licenses and permits,
    Revocation or suspension, support of persons, 9:315.30 et seq.
    Temporary license, support of persons, compliance, 9:315.33, 9:315.34
Mobile Homes and Manufactured Housing, generally, this index
Notice, sale of dealerships, 9:2961
Oaths and affirmations, dealerships, sale, 9:2961
Prescription, accidents, uninsured motorists, 9:5629
Privileges, rank of vendor's privilege, 9:4501
Records and recordation, leases, 9:3342
Repairs, privilege, 9:4501
Sale and distribution,
    Bona fide buyer, priority over repairmen's privilege, 9:4501
    Dealers and distributors, generally, ante
    Distributors. Dealers and distributors, generally, ante
Searches and seizures, repairman's privilege, exemptions, application of law, 9:4501
Support of persons, licenses and permits, revocation or suspension, 9:315.30 et seq.

MOVABLE PROPERTY
Certificates of title, repairman's privileges, 9:4502
Chattel Mortgages, generally, this index
Classification, manufactured homes, 9:1149.3
Covenant marriage, separation from bed and board, 9:308
Damages, property adjudicated to political subdivision, liability of owner, 9:2800.8
Definitions, leases, 9:3306
Delivery, mechanic's privileges and liens, 9:4803
Insolvency, privilege of purchaser from producers of agricultural and dairy products, 9:5021
Institutional funds, investments, 9:2337.1 et seq.
Intangibles, abandoned or unclaimed property, taking custody, 9:154
Manufactured Home Property Act, 9:1149.1 et seq.
Military forces, power of attorney, powers granted, 9:3871
Owner's liability, damages, property adjudicated to political subdivision, 9:2800.8
Records and recordation, leases, 9:3342
Repairman's privilege, seizures, exemptions, 9:4502
Self-Service Storage Facilities Act, 9:4756 et seq.
Tanks placed on land for storage of liquified gases, 9:1106

MUNICIPAL BUILDINGS AND GROUNDS
Liability for damages, 9:2800

MUNICIPAL OFFICERS AND EMPLOYEES
Limitation of liability, members of boards, commissions or authorities, 9:2792.4

MUNICIPALITIES
Beneficiaries to trust, 9:2341 et seq.
Blighted property, prescription, 9:5633
Boards and commissions, limitation of liability, 9:2792.4
Building restriction or subdivision regulation, limitation of action, 9:5625
Claims against,
    Buildings, liability, 9:2800
    Policymaking or discretionary acts, 9:2798.1
Crimes and offenses, policy making or discretionary acts, liability, 9:2798.1

I–44

MUNICIPALITIES—Cont'd
Expropriation, municipalities over 5,000, wharves, buildings or improvements, **9:1102.1**
Home rule charters,
    Assessments, interest, **9:3507**
    Interest, assessments for improvements, **9:3507**
Interest, assessments for improvements, **9:3507**
Leases, riparian lands, municipalities over 5,000, **9:1102.2**
Limitations of liability, members of board, commission or authority, **9:2792.4**
Prescription,
    Blighted property, **9:5633**
    Prevention of running, recording notice, **9:5804**
Quasi offenses,
    Buildings, liability, **9:2800**
    Policymaking or discretionary acts, liability, **9:2798.1**
Records and recordation, claim to public property, effect upon prescription, **9:5804**
Riparian owners, wharves, buildings or improvements, cities over 5,000, **9:1102.1**
Wards, limitation of liability, boards, commissions or authorities, **9:2792.4**

MUNICIPALITIES OF 325,000 OR MORE
Building restriction or subdivision regulation, limitation of action, **9:5625**

MUNICIPALITIES OF 500,000 OR MORE
Riparian owners, use of municipal land, **9:1102.2**

MUNICIPALLY OWNED UTILITIES
Abandoned deposits, **9:154**
Deposits by consumers, abandonment, **9:154**
Sewers and Sewer Systems, generally, this index
Water Supply, generally, this index

MUTUAL FUNDS
Institutional funds, investments, **9:2337.1 et seq.**

NAMES
Change of name, consumer credit licensee, notice, **9:3561**
Consumer credit lenders, changes, fees, **9:3561.1**
Judicial mortgages, similar names, affidavits of distinction, **9:5501**
    Form, **9:5501.1**
Limited liability partnerships, **9:3433**
Newspaper, mortgage on, **9:5103**

NATIONAL SERVICE LIFE INSURANCE
Beneficiary, interdiction, **9:1021**

NATIONAL VOLUNTARY ORGANIZATIONS ACTIVE IN DISASTER
Privileges and immunities, **9:2793.8**

NATIONALITY
Credit, discrimination, **9:3583**

NATURAL RESOURCES
Conservation servitudes, **9:1271 et seq.**
Forests and Forestry, generally, this index
Minerals, Oil and Gas, generally, this index
Servitudes, conservation, **9:1271 et seq.**

NEGLIGENCE
Architects, hazardous waste, abatement or clean up services, liability, **9:2800.3**
Children and minors, actions against parents, **9:571**
Chiropractors, burden of proof, **9:2794**

NEGLIGENCE—Cont'd
Controlled dangerous substances, dealer liability, **9:2800.63**
Crimes and offenses, injuries sustained during felonies, **9:2800.10**
Curators, gross negligence, removal from office, **9:1025**
Dentists and dentistry, burden of proof, **9:2794**
Emergency medical services, volunteers, privileges and immunities, **9:2793.2**
Engineers, hazardous waste, abatement, clean up or removal services, liability, **9:2800.3**
First aid, medical treatment, damages, **9:2793**
Health care providers, medical care and treatment, gratuitous services, **9:2799.5**
Holiday in Dixie parades, damages, limitation of liability, **9:2796**
Insurance agents, brokers and salespersons, prescription, **9:5606**
Limited liability partnerships, **9:3431**
Mardi Gras parades, damages, limitation of liability, **9:2796**
Minors, actions against parents, **9:571**
Nonprofit community blood banks, viral diseases, limitation of liability, **9:2797**
Optometrists, burden of proof, **9:2794**
Political subdivision boards, commissions or authorities, limitation of liability, **9:2792.4**
Recreation areas, private owners, limiting liability, **9:2795**
Recreation, landowner, **9:2791**

NEGOTIABLE INSTRUMENTS
Abandoned or unclaimed property, **9:151 et seq.**
Acknowledgments, actions to enforce, interruption of prescription, **9:5807**
Actions and proceedings, prescription, pledge notes, interruption of prescription, **9:5807**
Adjustable rate instruments,
    Agriculture, **9:3509.1**
    Business, **9:3509.1**
    Commerce, **9:3509.1**
    Mortgage notes, **9:3504**
Attorney fees, checks, stop payment, **9:2782.2**
Bad checks. Nonsufficient funds checks, generally, post
Bad faith, indorsement by fiduciary, **9:3804**
Certified checks, abandoned property, **9:151 et seq.**
Checks,
    Attorney fees,
        Nonsufficient funds, collections, **9:2782**
        Stop payment, **9:2782.2**
    Certified or registered mail, stop payment, **9:2782.2**
    Consumer credit transactions, nonsufficient fund checks, fees and charges, **9:3529**
    Costs, stop payment, **9:2782.2**
    Damages,
        Nonsufficient funds, collection, **9:2782**
        Stop payment, **9:2782.2**
    Evidence, stop payment, **9:2782.2**
    Fees and charges, nonsufficient funds checks, consumer credit transactions, **9:3529**
    Fiduciaries,
        Breach of obligations, **9:3805, 9:3806**
        Deposit to personal credit of checks drawn on fiduciary funds, **9:3809**
        Liability of bank, **9:3807, 9:3808**
        Payee's duties and liability, **9:3805**
        Personal benefit, **9:3807**
        Transferee's duties and liability, **9:3806**
    Holder, check on trust funds, duty, **9:3810**

NEGOTIABLE INSTRUMENTS—Cont'd
Checks—Cont'd
  Military forces, power of attorney, powers granted, **9:3870**
  Posting, nonsufficient funds, **9:2782.1**
  Service charges, stop payment, **9:2782.2**
  Stop payment, **9:2782.2**
Credit memos, abandoned or unclaimed property, **9:153**
Electronic transactions, retention, **9:2612**
Evidence,
  Burden of proof, interruption of prescription on pledged notes, **9:5807**
  Checks, stop payment, **9:2782.2**
Fiduciaries,
  Bills of exchange drawn by and payable to,
    Payee's duties and liabilities, **9:3805**
    Transferee's duties and liabilities, **9:3806**
  Breach of fiduciary obligations, **9:3805, 9:3806**
    Indorsements, **9:3804**
    Personal benefit, **9:3807**
    Principal's account, liability of bank paying, **9:3808**
  Duties and liabilities,
    Indorsee, **9:3804**
    Transferee, **9:3806**
  Indorsements, **9:3804**
  Notices,
    Breach of obligation, **9:3806**
    Payee of check or bill of exchange, **9:3805**
  Payee's duties and liabilities, **9:3805**
Fraud, stop payment, **9:2782.2**
Gift certificates, abandoned or unclaimed property, **9:154**
Indorsements, fiduciary, duty and liability of indorsee, **9:3804**
Military forces, power of attorney, powers granted, **9:3874**
Mortgages, generally, this index
Newspaper, security by mortgage on plant equipment, name and good will, **9:5103**
Nonsufficient funds checks,
  Attorney fees, collections, **9:2782**
  Consumer credit transactions, fees and charges, **9:3529**
  Fees and charges, consumer credit transactions, **9:3529**
  Notice, fees and charges, **9:2782**
  Posting, **9:2782.1**
Posting, nonsufficient fund checks, **9:2782.1**
Prescription, actions to enforce, interruption, prescription on pledged notes, **9:5807**
Real estate timesharing, form of promissory notes, **9:1131.30**
Records and recordation, electronic transactions, retention, **9:2612**
Rental purchase agreements, negotiable instruments, prohibited provisions, **9:3356**
Stop payment, checks, **9:2782.2**
Subrogation, checks, stop payment, **9:2782.2**
Trust Companies, generally, this index
Trusts and trustees, sales, **9:2085**
Unclaimed property, **9:151 et seq.**
Variable rate loans,
  Agriculture, **9:3509.1**
  Business, **9:3509.1**
Warehouse Receipts, generally, this index
Worthless checks. Nonsufficient funds checks, generally, ante

NETWORKS
Emergency response network, privileges and immunities, **9:2798.5**

NEW HOME WARRANTY ACT
Generally, **9:3141 et seq.**

NEW ORLEANS
Contracts, work and labor, prescription, **9:5602**
Improvement assessments Tax assessments, generally, post
Local improvement assessments, payment prior to conveyance, **9:2921**
Officers and employees, conveyances, delinquent taxes or assessments, **9:2921, 9:2927**
Payment, local improvement assessments, etc., on transfer of immovables, **9:2921 et seq.**
Prescription, zoning and planning, **9:5625**
Recorder of mortgages for Parish of Orleans, office, **9:5208**
Sales of immovables, tax assessments, payment prior to conveyance, **9:2921**
Tax assessments,
  Future maturity, assumption by transferee of property, **9:2926**
  Officers,
    Execution or passing act of conveyance without payment, **9:2921**
    Liability for nonpayment, exoneration, **9:2924**
  Payment before transfer of immovable property, **9:2921 et seq.**
  Receipt, payment showing by, **9:2922**
  Research certificates, **9:2921 et seq.**
Tax sales,
  Current taxes, assumption by transferee, **9:2925**
  Officers,
    Execution or passing act of conveyance without payment, **9:2921**
    Liability for nonpayment, exoneration, **9:2924**
  Payment before transfer of immovable property, **9:2921 et seq.**
  Receipt, payment showing by, **9:2922**
  Research certificates, **9:2921 et seq.**
  Transferee, assumption of current taxes, **9:2925**
Zoning and planning, prescription, **9:5625**

NEWSPAPERS
Dealers and distributors, cash bond or security, interest on deposit, **9:3601**
Mortgage, plant equipment, name and good will, **9:5103**
Publication of notices, etc. Publication, generally, this index

NONPROFIT CORPORATIONS
Actions and proceedings, community service workers, limitation of liability, **9:2792.8**
Charities, generally, this index
Community service organizations, limitation of liability, **9:2792.8**
Curators,
  Donations, **9:1023**
  Interdiction, indigent adults, **9:1031 et seq.**
Damages, community service organizations, limitation of liability, **9:2792.8**
Definitions, limitation of liability, **9:2792.8**
Directors,
  Limitation of liability, **9:2792.1**
    Community service organizations, **9:2792.8**
  Tort liability, **9:2792**
Donations,
  Exemptions, reduction and calculation of succession mass, **9:2372**
  Food banks, limitation of liability, **9:2799, 9:2799.6**
Educational corporations, servitudes, granting, **9:1252**
Food banks, donations, limitation of liability, **9:2799, 9:2799.6**
Historical corporations, servitudes, granting, **9:1252**
Hospitals, generally, this index
Indemnity, community service organizations, **9:2792.8**

INDEX TO TITLE 9

NONPROFIT CORPORATIONS—Cont'd
Indigent adults, curators and tutors, interdiction, **9:1031 et seq.**
Injuries, limitation of liability, community service organizations, **9:2792.8**
Institutional funds, investments, **9:2337.1 et seq.**
Inter vivos donations, exemptions, reduction and calculation of succession mass, **9:2372**
Interdiction, curators and tutors, indigent adults, **9:1031 et seq.**
Liabilities. Limitations of liability, generally, post
Limitations of liability,
    Civic or historic purposes, **9:2792.3**
    Directors, officers or trustees, **9:2792.1, 9:2792.8**
    Fair and festival parades, **9:2796**
    Food banks, donations, **9:2799**
    Trusts and trustees, post
Medical care and treatment, nonprofit health care quality improvement corporations, privileges and immunities, **9:2800.20**
Officers and agents,
    Limitation of liability, **9:2792.1**
    Tort liability, **9:2792**
Officers and employees, limitation of liability, community service organizations, **9:2792.8**
On-premises feeding programs, food banks, donations, limitation of liability, **9:2799**
Poison control centers, immunity from liability, **9:2797.1**
Privileges and immunities, nonprofit health care quality improvement corporations, **9:2800.20**
Quasi offenses, liability of officers or directors, **9:2792**
Servitudes, granting, educational, charitable or historical purposes, **9:1252**
Shares and shareholders, limitation of liability, community service organizations, **9:2792.8**
Tort liability, officers or directors, **9:2792**
Trusts and trustees, **9:1783**
    Limitations of liability, **9:2792.1**
        Community service organizations, **9:2792.8**
    Mixed trusts, qualification to act as trustee, **9:1783**
    Tort liability, **9:2792**
Tutors, interdiction, indigent adults, **9:1031 et seq.**
Water supply corporations, abandoned deposits, **9:154**

NONPROFIT ORGANIZATIONS
Community blood banks, limitation of liability, **9:2797**

NOTARIAL ACTS
Adoption, persons over seventeen, **9:461**
Copies, certification, **9:2758**
Donations, married person to spouse, reservation of right to revoke, **9:2351**
Parent's usufruct in estate donated to child, preservation by executing, **9:2361**

NOTARIES PUBLIC
Donations,
    Married person to spouse, reservation of right to revoke, **9:2351**
Electronic transactions, **9:2611**
Fees and charges,
    Interdictions, inventories, **9:1423**
    Successions, inventories, **9:1423**
    Tutorships, inventories, **9:1423**
Fines and penalties,
    Closing instructions, noncompliance, **9:3506.1**
Interdiction proceedings, inventories, fees, **9:1423**
Legitimation acts, natural children, **9:391**

NOTARIES PUBLIC—Cont'd
Orleans Parish,
    Nonalienation certificate, necessity to pass act of conveyance, **9:2928**
Tutorships, inventories, fees, **9:1423**
Women, **9:51**

NOTICE
Adverse claim, stock transferred by fiduciary **9:3835**
Cancellation,
    Bond for deed, **9:2945**
    Federal mortgage, proceedings, **9:5164**
Carpet and rug cleaner, sale to satisfy privilege, **9:4684**
Constructive notice, definitions, public entities, condition of things within care and custody, liability, **9:2800**
Consumer loan brokers, registration, **9:3572.3**
    Denials, **9:3572.5**
Contractors, this index
Custodial trusts, trustee resignation, **9:2260.13**
Designation as public property, effect upon prescription, **9:5804**
Farm animal activities, privileges and immunities, **9:2795.1**
Fiduciaries, deposit of fiduciary funds to personal credit, **9:3809**
Fire insurance, claim of seller's privilege against proceeds, **9:4582**
Interest, abandoned or unclaimed property, claims allowed, **9:167**
Military forces, powers of attorney, powers granted, **9:3870**
Mobile Homes and Manufactured Housing, this index
New home warranties, advising builder of defects, **9:3145**
Paternity, reports, blood test to determine paternity, **9:397.3**
Power of attorney, military personnel, powers granted, **9:3870**
Premium finance companies, consumer credit, insurance, **9:3550**
Products liability, unreasonably dangerous, inadequate warning, **9:2800.57**
Public administrators, appointment, **9:1583**
Public sale, abandoned or unclaimed property, **9:164**
Repossession, mobile homes and manufactured housing, mortgagees, **9:5363.1**
Residential Truth in Construction Act, **9:4851 et seq.**
Self-service storage facilities, privileges and liens, **9:4758, 9:4759**
Service,
    Agency or instrumentality of United States, **9:5164**
    Federal mortgage, notice of cancellation or subordination, **9:5163, 9:5164**
United States, cancellation or subordination of mortgage held by agency, **9:5163**

NUCLEAR ELECTRIC GENERATING PLANTS
Partition, agreements against, duration, **9:1702**

NUISANCES
Blighted property, acquisitive prescription, **9:5633**

NURSES
Damages, privileges and immunities, gratuitous services, **9:2799.5**
Negligence, medical care and treatment, gratuitous services, **9:2799.5**
Privileges and immunities, gratuitous services, **9:2799.5**
Veterans, interdiction, **9:1021**

NURSING HOMES
Contracts for services, arbitration and award, **9:4230 et seq.**

NURSING HOMES—Cont'd
Public trust, purposes, **9:2341 et seq.**
Services contracts, arbitration and award, **9:4230 et seq.**
Supplies contracts, arbitration and award, **9:4230 et seq.**

OATHS AND AFFIRMATIONS
Electronic transactions, **9:2611**
Feed for livestock used on public works, statement of amount due, **9:4922**

OBLIGATIONS
    See, also, Contracts, generally, this index
Annuities, extinguishment, death of party, **9:2785**
Class actions, conclusiveness of judgments, **9:2701**
Contractors, nonliability of contractor, destruction of deterioration of work, **9:2771**
Custodial trusts, transfers to trustees, **9:2260.5**
Death,
    Extinguishment, payment of annuity, **9:2785**
    Personal obligation imposed by testament, before performance of obligation, **9:2786**
Extinguishment, annuities, death of party, **9:2785**
Heritable obligations, legacies, **9:2787**
Judgments and decrees, class actions, conclusiveness, **9:2701**
Married women, **9:103**
Performance, **9:2771 et seq.**
Personal obligations,
    Annuities, extinguishment by death, **9:2785**
    Imposed by testament, death of legatee before performance, **9:2786**
Prohibition of private transfer fee obligations, **9:3133**
    Liability for violations, **9:3134**
Transfers, custodial trusts, transfers to trustees, **9:2260.5**
Women, **9:101**, **9:103**

OBLIQUE ACTIONS
Child support enforcement, **9:315.24**

OILFIELD INDEMNITY ACT
Generally, **9:2780**

OPPOSITION
Marriage, **9:261 et seq.**

OPTOMETRISTS
Contracts for services, arbitration and award, **9:4230 et seq.**
Contracts, breach, prescription, **9:5628**
Damages, medical care and treatment, gratuitous services, **9:2799.5**
Depositions, malpractice, **9:2794**
Medical Malpractice, generally, this index
Negligence,
    Burden of proof, **9:2794**
    Medical care and treatment, gratuitous services, **9:2799.5**
Privileges and immunities, medical care and treatment, gratuitous services, **9:2799.5**
Quasi offenses, prescription, **9:5628**
Services contracts, arbitration and award, **9:4230 et seq.**
Supplies contracts, arbitration and award, **9:4230 et seq.**

ORDINANCES
    See, also, specific index headings
Condominiums, **9:1121.106**

ORGANS
Limitation of liability, medical care and treatment, **9:2797**

ORLEANS PARISH
Acts of sale and conveyances,
    Nonalienation certificate, **9:2928**
    Register of conveyances, generally, post
Bonds (officers and fiduciaries). Recorder of mortgages, post
Cancellation of instruments. Recorder of mortgages, post
Fines and penalties, succession judgments, recording, **9:1425**
Immovables, succession judgment, recording, **9:1425**
Mortgages,
    Cancellation of mortgage, **9:5167**
    Recorder of mortgages, generally, post
Officers and employees,
    Recorder of mortgages, generally, post
    Register of conveyances, generally, post
Recorder of mortgages,
    Authentication, **9:5210**
    Registers, **9:5209**
    Cancellation of mortgage, **9:5167**
    Registers to be kept by, kinds, **9:5208 et seq.**
Records and recordation,
    Immovables, succession judgments, **9:1425**
Register of conveyances,
    Nonalienation certificate, **9:2928**
    Partnership certificate,
        Certified copy as evidence, **9:3403**
        Fee for filing and indexing, **9:3404**
        Filing and indexing, **9:3401**, **9:3404**
Successions and Succession Proceedings, this index
Tax assessors, succession judgments, filing, **9:1425**
Vendor's privilege, cancellation, **9:5167**

OUTDOOR ADVERTISING
Actions, amortization of nonconforming billboards, **9:5625**
Historical sites, amortization, nonconforming billboards, **9:5625**
Nonconforming billboards, actions for amortization, **9:5625**
Removal, nonconforming billboards, **9:5625**

OWNERSHIP
Carbon sequestration on surface or water bottoms, **9:1103**
Children and minors, private sale of property without issuance of rule nisi, **9:675**
Crops, lessor's share, **9:3204**
Custodial trusts, trust property, **9:2260.2**
Expropriation, generally, this index
False river boundaries, **9:1110**
Fiduciaries, misapplication of proceeds, effect upon title, **9:3802**
Financed leases, **9:3310**
Manufactured homes, **9:1149.3**
Married women, **9:103**
Military forces, presumed dead, **9:1442**
Private sale of minor's property without issuance of rule nisi, quieting title, **9:675**
Rental purchase agreements, reinstatement, **9:3357**
Women, **9:103**

OWNERSHIP TIMESHARE INTERESTS
Definitions, real estate timesharing, **9:1131.2**

PACKERS
Food banks, donations, limitation of liability, **9:2799**, **9:2799.6**

PARADES
Associations and societies, damages, limitation of liability, **9:2796**
Equine activity sponsors, immunities, **9:2795.1**

PARADES—Cont'd
Ethnic parades, sponsors, limitation of liability, **9:2796.1**
Farm animal activities, privileges and immunities, **9:2795.1**
Saint Patrick's Day parade, damages, limitation of liability, **9:2796.1**

PARAPH
See, also, Signatures, generally, this index
Notes, etc.,
    Identified with judicial sales for cancellation of mortgage, **9:3003**
    Secured by mortgage, unnecessary if identified by mortgage, **9:5305**

PARENTING COORDINATORS
Child custody, **9:358.1 et seq.**

PARISH OFFICERS AND EMPLOYEES
Boards and commissions, limitation of liability, **9:2792.4**
Commission plan, limitation of liability, **9:2792.4**
Limitation of liability, members of boards, commissions or authorities, **9:2792.4**

PARISH RECORDERS AND REGISTERS
Cancellation of mortgage, **9:5167**
Certificates,
    Inscription, duty to supply, **9:5213**
    Prompt delivery, **9:5212**
Delays in registering acts, **9:5212**
Inspection, records kept by, **9:5211**
Method of recording acts, **9:5213**
Mortgages, cancellation, **9:5167**
Order of recordation, **9:5213**
Paraph, identification of notes or bonds with judicial sales, **9:3003**
Prompt recordation and issuance of certificates, **9:5212**
Registers to be kept by recorders, kinds, **9:5208 et seq.**

PARISHES
Beneficiaries to trust, **9:2341 et seq.**
Boards and commissions, limitation of liability, members, **9:2792.4**
Building restriction or subdivision regulation, limitation of action, **9:5625**
Buildings, liability for damages, **9:2800**
Canals, generally, this index
Claims against political subdivisions,
    Buildings, liability, **9:2800**
    Policy making or discretionary acts, **9:2798.1**
Commission plan,
    Board of commissioners. Parish Officers and Employees, this index
    Parish Officers and Employees, this index
Contracts,
    See, also, Public Contracts, generally, this index
Crimes and offenses,
    Buildings, liability, **9:2800**
    Policy making or discretionary acts, liability, **9:2798.1**
Interest, assessments for improvements, **9:3507**
Limitation of liability, members of boards, commissions, or authority, **9:2792.4**
Officers and employees. Parish Officers and Employees, generally, this index
Quasi offenses, policy making or discretionary acts, liability, **9:2798.1**
Trust instruments, recording, **9:2092**
Trusts and trustees,
    Beneficiaries, **9:2341 et seq.**

PARISHES—Cont'd
Trusts and trustees—Cont'd
    Public trusts, generally. Trusts and Trustees, this index

PARISHES OVER 325,000
Building restriction or subdivision regulation, limitation of action, **9:5625**

PARKING LOTS AND FACILITIES
Contracts of deposit, liability, **9:2783**
Liability, contracts of deposit, **9:2783**

PARKING METERS
Contracts of deposit, liability, **9:2783**

PARKS
Limitation of liability, personal injuries, **9:2795**
Political subdivisions, quasi offenses, limitation of liability, **9:2795**
Quasi offenses, limitation of liability, **9:2795**

PARTIES
Claims against, defendant, assignment, **9:3051**
Limited liability partnerships, actions to enforce debts and obligations, **9:3431**

PARTITION
Agreements against, duration, **9:1702**
Federal mortgage, **9:5163**
Joint ownership, arguments against, duration, **9:1702**
Judicial sale to effect, **9:3166, 9:3172 et seq.**
Mortgages, sale of property, **9:5251**
Nuclear electric generating plants or units, agreements against, duration, **9:1702**
Privileges and liens, sale of property, **9:5031**
Real estate timesharing, **9:1131.7**
Retirement and pensions, matrimonial regimes, community property, **9:2801**
Retrospective operation, United States having servitude or real right, **9:1701**
Solicitation, community property, **9:2801**
Time, agreements against partition, duration, **9:1702**
United States, servitude, easement or real right, **9:1701**

PARTNERSHIP
Generally, **9:3401 et seq.**
Addresses, contracts filed for registry, **9:3403**
Affidavit, general partner, accompanying registration statement, **9:3422**
Amendments,
    Partnership contract, central registry for contracts of partnership, **9:3404**
    Registration statement, foreign partnerships, **9:3426**
Application of law, limited liability partnerships, **9:3435**
Applications, limited liability partnerships, **9:3432**
Assignment of stock held by partner as fiduciary, **9:3833**
Bankruptcy, purchaser from producers of agriculture and dairy products, **9:5021**
Central registry for contracts of partnership, **9:3401 et seq.**
Certificates and certification, **9:3401 et seq.**
    Certified copy,
        Evidence, **9:3403**
        Filing fees, **9:3404**
        Proof, **9:3403**
Fee, filing and indexing, **9:3404**
Index, **9:3404**
Merger or consolidation, **9:3445**
Proof, certified copy as, **9:3403**

INDEX TO TITLE 9

PARTNERSHIP—Cont'd
Certificates and certification—Cont'd
    Registry,
        Central registry for contracts of partnership, **9:3405**
        Statement, certificate accompanying, **9:3422**
Conflict of laws, foreign partnerships, registration, **9:3425**
Consent, foreign partnerships, general partner, service of process, **9:3424**
Contracts,
    Central registry for contracts of partnership, **9:3401 et seq.**
    Contents, **9:3403**
Copying, fees, state, **9:3410**
Delivery, partnership contracts or foreign partnership statements, filing, **9:3407**
Distributions, restrictions, limited liability partnerships, **9:3434**
Evidence, certificate of registry, conclusive evidence of registration, **9:3405**
Fees,
    Certificate, certified copy, filing and indexing, **9:3404**
    Filing and copying, state, **9:3410**
    Limited liability partnerships, applications, **9:3432**
Fiduciary, partner, **9:3801**
Filing,
    Contracts of partnership, **9:3402**
    Fees, state, **9:3410**
Fines and penalties, name, improper use, **9:3406**
Foreign partnerships, **9:3421 et seq.**
    Limited, registration, **9:3423**
    Merger or consolidation, **9:3447**
    Registration, **9:3425**
    Reports, annual informational reports, **9:3428**
    Service of process, consent and agent, **9:3424**
Fraud, limited liability partnerships, **9:3431**
Indebtedness,
    Limited liability partnerships, **9:3431**
    Merger or consolidation, effects, **9:3446**
Informational annual reports, **9:3409**
Institutional funds, investments, **9:2337.1 et seq.**
Interest, exceeding maximum conventional rate, **9:3509**
Liability,
    Distributions, limited liability partnership, **9:3434**
    Limited liability partnerships, **9:3431 et seq.**
Limitation of liability, registration statement, **9:3422**
Merger and consolidation, **9:3441 et seq.**
    Agreement, **9:3443**
    Approval, **9:3444**
    Certificate, **9:3445**
    Effects, **9:3446**
    Foreign entities, **9:3447**
    Indebtedness, effects, **9:3446**
Military forces, power of attorney, powers granted, **9:3875**
Names,
    Designation of and Company or & Co., restriction on use, **9:3406**
    Limited liability partnerships, **9:3433**
    Partner not interested in firm, **9:3406**
Negligence, limited liability partnerships, **9:3431**
Parties, limited liability partnerships, actions to enforce debts and obligations, **9:3431**
Partnership stock, registered in name of partner as fiduciary, **9:3832**
Personal liability, distributions, limited liability partnerships, **9:3434**
Process, foreign partnerships, consent and appointment of agent, **9:3424**

PARTNERSHIP—Cont'd
Property, foreign partnerships, ownership, **9:3423**
Recorder of mortgages partnership contracts and registry certificates, filing, **9:3406**
Registered limited liability partnerships, **9:3431 et seq.**
Registration,
    Conflict of laws, foreign partnerships, **9:3425**
    Foreign partnerships, **9:3425**
    Lapse or termination, limited liability partnerships, **9:3435**
    Limited foreign partnerships, **9:3423**
    Limited liability partnerships, **9:3431 et seq.**
    Partnership contracts, central registry for contracts of partnership, **9:3405**
Reports,
    Annual informational reports, **9:3409**
    Foreign partnerships, annual informational reports, **9:3428**
    Informational annual reports, **9:3409**
Restrictions, distributions, limited liability partnerships, **9:3434**
State, fees, filing and copying, **9:3410**
Termination, foreign partnerships, registration, **9:3427**
Trustees, powers, **9:2123**
Unclaimed property. Abandoned or Unclaimed Property, generally, this index

PATENTS
Navigable waters and beds, void, **9:1108**
Special counsel for state, interest in vacant successions, **9:1614**

PAWNBROKERS
Consumer credit, exclusion from law, **9:3512**

PAYDAY LOANS
Generally, **9:3577.1 et seq.**

PAYMENT
Bond for deed contracts. Acts of Sale and Conveyances, this index
Custodial trusts, transfers to trustees, **9:2260.5**
Demand, surety on bond, prerequisite to award of attorney fees, **9:3902**
Real estate timesharing, tax assessments, **9:1131.9**
Rental purchase agreements, reinstatement, **9:3357**
Surety's obligation, failure to pay, award of attorney fees, **9:3902**

PEREMPTION
New home warranties, enforcement, **9:3146**
Warranties, new home warranties, enforcement, **9:3146**

PEREMPTIVE PERIODS
Surveys, damages, **9:2772**

PERISHABLES
Food products, vendor's privilege, exemption, **9:4544**

PERSONAL INJURIES
Actions and proceedings, deficiencies in design, supervision or construction of improvements, prescription, **9:2772**
Alcoholic beverages, limitation of liability, serving or furnishing, **9:2800.1**
Block safe-houses, liability, **9:2800.5**
Crimes and offenses, privileges and immunities, sustained during commission, **9:2800.10**
Deficiencies in design, supervision or construction of improvements, prescription, **9:2772**

PERSONAL INJURIES—Cont'd
Farmland, liability of owner, unauthorized entry, **9:2800.4**
Forestland, unauthorized entry, liability of owner, **9:2800.4**
Immovables, actions involving deficiencies in design or construction, prescription, **9:2772**
Lessee, assumption of liability by, **9:3221**
Merchants, liability, persons on premises, **9:2800.6**
Oil, gas, or mineral property, landowner's liability, **9:2800.4**
Prescription, deficiencies in design, supervision or construction of improvements, **9:2772**
Privileges and immunities, felonies, sustained during commission, **9:2800.10**
Recreational areas, private owners, limiting liability, **9:2795**
Trespass, liability of owner, farm or forestland, **9:2800.4**
Unauthorized entry, liability of owner, farm or forestland, **9:2800.4**

PERSONAL REPRESENTATIVE
Definitions,
    Custodial trusts, **9:2260.1**
    Uniform Transfers to Minors Act, **9:751**

PHARMACISTS
Arbitration and award, services or supplies contracts, **9:4230 et seq.**
Contracts for services, arbitration and award, **9:4230 et seq.**
Definitions, gratuitous medical services, **9:2799.5**
Negligence, medical care and treatment, gratuitous services, **9:2799.5**
Privileges and immunities, medical care and treatment, gratuitous services, **9:2799.5**
Services contracts, arbitration and award, **9:4230 et seq.**

PHOTOGRAPHS AND PICTURES
Aerial photographs, servitudes, attaching and recording, **9:2726**
Servitudes, attaching and recording, **9:2726**

PHYSICAL THERAPISTS
Arbitration and award, services or supplies contracts, **9:4230 et seq.**
Contracts for services, arbitration and award, **9:4230 et seq.**
Damages, medical care and treatment, gratuitous services, **9:2799.5**
Negligence, medical care and treatment, gratuitous services, **9:2799.5**
Privileges and immunities, medical care and treatment, gratuitous services, **9:2799.5**
Services contracts, arbitration and award, **9:4230 et seq.**
Supplies contracts, arbitration and award, **9:4230 et seq.**

PHYSICIANS AND SURGEONS
Athletic team physicians, volunteers, liability, **9:2798**
Blood banks, limitation of liability, **9:2797**
Contracts for services, arbitration and award, **9:4230 et seq.**
Damages, privileges and immunities, gratuitous services, **9:2799.5**
Death, definitions, **9:111**
Defenses, controlled dangerous substances, dealer liability, **9:2800.71**
Fees and charges,
    Depositions, malpractice actions, **9:2794**
    Open accounts, collection, **9:2781**
Human tissue transplant, limitation of liability, **9:2797**
Immunities. Privileges and immunities, generally, post
In vitro fertilization, **9:121 et seq.**
Liability,
    Embryos, in vitro fertilized human ovum, **9:132**

PHYSICIANS AND SURGEONS—Cont'd
Liability—Cont'd
    Volunteer athletic team physicians, **9:2798**
Limitation of liability,
    Blood, organs or tissue, **9:2797**
    Users of blood, organs or tissues, **9:2797**
Malpractice. Medical Malpractice, generally, this index
Medical Malpractice, generally, this index
Narcotics. Controlled Dangerous Substances, generally, this index
Negligence,
    Burden of proof, **9:2794**
    Gratuitous services, **9:2799.5**
Organ transplants, limitation of liability, **9:2797**
Privileges and immunities,
    Athletics, volunteer team physicians, **9:2798**
    Gratuitous services, **9:2799.5**
    In vitro fertilized human ovum, **9:132**
Professional Medical Corporations, generally, this index
Psychiatrists and Psychiatry, generally, this index
Quasi offenses, users of blood, organs or tissue, limitation of liability, **9:2797**
Service contracts, arbitration and award, **9:4230 et seq.**
Strict liability, blood, organs or tissue, **9:2797**
Supplies contracts, arbitration and award, **9:4230 et seq.**
Team physicians, volunteers, liability, **9:2798**
Tissue transplant, limitation of liability, **9:2797**
Volunteer athletic team physicians, liability, **9:2798**

PIANOS
Seller's privilege, **9:4561 et seq.**

PICNICS
Private property, personal injuries, limiting liability, **9:2795**

PIPES AND PIPELINES
Curators, sale or lease of right of way over land of ward, **9:731**
Natural gas, servitudes, roads or streets, **9:1253**
Privileges and liens, gas, oil and water wells, **9:4861 et seq.**
Secured Transactions, this index
Servitudes, roads or streets, **9:1253**
Tutors or curators, sale or lease of right of way over land of ward, **9:731**

PLAQUEMINE
Grass, cutting or removal, property owner's liability, privileges, rank, **9:4821**
Noxious weeds, cutting or removal, property owner's liability, privileges, rank, **9:4821**
Privileges, grass and noxious weeds, property owner's liability, rank, **9:4821**
Weeds, cutting or removal, property owner's liability, privileges, rank, **9:4821**

PLEDGES
Application of law, secured transactions, **9:4401**
Associations and societies, immovable property, **9:1051**
Chattel mortgages, incorporeal rights, **9:5386 et seq.**
Consumer credit, exemptions, licenses, **9:3560**
Fiduciaries, deposit of pledged property under mortgage securing obligations, **9:5306**
Foreclosure, signatures on obligations, presumed authenticity, **9:4422**
Leases, **9:4401**
    Unpaid rent, lessor's right of pledge, **9:3259.1**
Married women, **9:103**
Military forces, power of attorney, powers granted, **9:3871**

INDEX TO TITLE 9

PLEDGES—Cont'd
Rents, **9:4401**
Signatures, foreclosure, presumed authenticity on obligations, **9:4422**
Trust property, **9:2120**

PLUMBERS AND PLUMBING
Warranties, new home warranties, **9:3141 et seq.**

PODIATRISTS
Arbitration and award, services or supplies contracts, **9:4230 et seq.**
Contracts for services, arbitration and award, **9:4230 et seq.**
Damages, medical care and treatment, gratuitous services, **9:2799.5**
Privileges and immunities, medical care and treatment, gratuitous services, **9:2799.5**
Services contracts, arbitration and award, **9:4230 et seq.**

POLICE
Controlled dangerous substances, dealer liability, privileges and immunities, **9:2800.71**
Damages to property caused during course and scope of employment, **9:2793.1**

POLITICAL SUBDIVISIONS
Abandoned or unclaimed property, **9:164**
Beneficiaries to trusts, **9:2341 et seq.**
Buildings, liability for damages, **9:2800**
Claims against,
  Buildings, liability, **9:2800**
  Policy making or discretionary acts, **9:2798.1**
Consumer credit, exemptions, **9:3560**
Crimes and offenses, policymaking or discretionary acts, liability, **9:2798.1**
Damages, condition of things within care and custody, limitation of liability, **9:2800**
Discretionary acts, liability, **9:2798.1**
Interest, assessments for improvement, **9:3507**
Investments, **9:2337.1 et seq.**
Limitation of liability, members of boards, commissions or authorities, **9:2792.4**
Minerals, oil and gas, grant of mineral servitude to subdivisions, **9:1152**
Notice, condition of things within care and custody, limitation of liability, **9:2800**
Officers. Public Officers and Employees, generally, this index
Policymaking acts, liability, **9:2798.1**
Privileges and immunities,
  Damages to property caused by employees, **9:2793.1**
  Driving under influence of alcohol or drugs, injury or death of operator, **9:2798.4**
  Policy making or discretionary acts, **9:2798.1**
Servitudes, land acquired from subdivision due to subsidence or erosion, **9:1152**
Unclaimed property, **9:164**

POLO
Sponsors, equine activities, immunities, **9:2795.1**

PONY CLUBS
Farm animal activities, privileges and immunities, **9:2795.1**

POSTSEPARATION FAMILY VIOLENCE RELIEF ACT
Generally, **9:361 et seq.**

POWERS OF ATTORNEY
Action to set aside document, **9:5647**
  Prescription periods, **9:5647**

PREDIAL SERVITUDES
Associations and societies, transfer of title, **9:1051**

PREMIUM FINANCE COMPANIES
Consumer credit, insurance, **9:3550**

PRESCRIPTION
  Generally, **9:5601 et seq.**
Abandoned or unclaimed property, **9:171**
Abatement, asbestos, actions and proceedings, **9:5644**
Abuse of children, **9:2800.9**
Acquisitive prescription,
  Blighted property, **9:5633**
  Foreign corporation, immovables sold by, **9:5681**
  Land patents, **9:5661**
  Restriction, title to land, **9:5622**
  Sale under attachment against foreign corporation, **9:5641**
Asbestos abatement, actions, **9:5644**
Associations and societies, sales of immovables, **9:5681**
Attachment, sale, foreign corporation, **9:5641**
Attorneys, malpractice actions, **9:5605**
Auctions and auctioneers, judicial sales, **9:5622**
Billboards, amortization of nonconforming billboards, **9:5625**
Blighted property, **9:5633**
  Acquisitive prescription, **9:5633**
Building restriction or subdivision regulation, **9:5625**
Collation, revendication, **9:5811**
Construction of improvements, deficiencies, **9:2772**
Consumer credit, **9:3552**
Credit repair services organizations, **9:3573.12**
Crops, injury, destruction or loss of profits, nondelivery or nonacceptance, **9:5601**
Curators,
  Defective private sales or mortgages, **9:5632**
  Vacant succession, **9:5621**
Debts due charitable or educational institutions or funds, **9:5701**
Design, improvements, deficiencies, **9:2772**
Encroachments, public places, removal action, **9:5627**
Failure to warn, surveys, **9:2772**
Foreign corporations, sales by, setting aside, **9:5681**
Heirs or legatees, action for title to property, **9:5682 et seq.**
Historical sites, amortization, nonconforming billboards, **9:5625**
Hotchpot, revendication, **9:5811**
Insurance agents, brokers and salespersons, **9:5606**
Interruption and suspension,
  Dismissal and nonsuit, involuntary, citation, service, **9:5801**
  Fugitive from justice, **9:5802**
  Immovable property of municipality, **9:5804**
  Mineral or royalty right, suspension as to one coproprietor, **9:5805**
  Pledged notes, **9:5807**
  Property adjudicated to state for nonpayment of taxes, **9:5803**
Judicial sales, informalities, **9:5622**
Land patents, **9:5661**
Leases, setting aside leases of immovables, legal entities, lack of authority, **9:5681**
Legal malpractice, **9:5605**
Levees or levee drainage, actions and claims for lands used or destroyed for, **9:5626**

INDEX TO TITLE 9

PRESCRIPTION—Cont'd
Liberative prescription,
    Covenants running with land, termination, 9:5622
    Mineral or royalty rights, minority as suspending, 9:5805
    Recovery in expropriation suits, 9:3180
    Restrictive covenants, termination, 9:5622
New Orleans, zoning and planning, 9:5625
Outdoor advertising, amortization of nonconforming signs, 9:5625
Periods of, 9:5601 et seq.
Personal injuries, actions for deficiencies in design, supervision or construction, 9:2772
Pledged promissory notes, interruption, 9:5807
Powers of attorney,
    Action to set aside document, 9:5647, 9:5682
    Prescription periods, 9:5647
Private property damaged for public purposes, 9:5624
Probate of testament, proceeding, 9:5643
Prosecutions, zoning restrictions, etc., 9:5625
Public places, encroachments, removal action, 9:5627
Quieting title, donations of real estate to religious organizations, 9:2321
Restrictions in title to land, 9:5622
Revendication, collation, 9:5811
Right to probate testaments, 9:5643
Sales, judicial sales, 9:5622
Signs, amortization of nonconforming signs, 9:5625
Student loans, 9:5701
Supervision of improvements, deficiencies, 9:2772
Surveys and surveyors, 9:2772
Suspension. Interruption and suspension, generally, ante
Testaments,
    Proceeding to probate, 9:5643
    Right to probate, 9:5643
Tutors and tutorship, defective sale or mortgage of property, 9:5632
Uninsured motorist, motor vehicles, accidents, 9:5629
Wells, privileges, effect on third persons, 9:4865, 9:4885
Work and labor, New Orleans, city of, 9:5602
Zoning actions, civil or criminal, 9:5625

PRIORITIES AND PREFERENCES
Aircraft, privileges, 9:4512
Assets of purchaser from producers of agricultural and dairy products, 9:5021
Attorney fees, medical services privileges, 9:4752
Hospitals, privilege for services and supplies furnished, 9:4752
Manufactured homes, mortgages, certificate of title, 9:1149.5
Self-service storage facilities, vendor's liens, 9:4758

PRIVACY
Psychologists, patient threats against victims, duty to warn, 9:2800.2

PRIVATE WORKS ACT
    Generally, 9:4801 et seq.
Escrow of funds due under contract procedure, 9:4815

PRIVILEGES
    Generally, 9:4501 et seq., 9:4801 et seq.
Affidavits,
    Identity, filing, 9:5503
    Judicial mortgages, name similarity, affidavit of distinction, 9:5501
        Form, 9:5501.1
    Private works, inspections, 9:4820

PRIVILEGES—Cont'd
Aged persons, improvements, home solicitation sales, 9:3541.21, 9:3541.22
Ambulances, services and supplies, 9:4751 et seq.
Application of law, secured transactions, 9:4401
Assessments of taxes. Tax Privilege or Lien, generally, this index
Assumption, rank of subordination, first mortgage, 9:5384
Bankruptcy,
    Privilege on assets of purchaser from producers of agricultural products, 9:5021
    Sale of property, effect on privilege or lien, 9:5031
Bond for deed contracts,
    Payment of release price, method, 9:2943
    Release price, agreement, recording, 9:2942
Bonds (officers and fiduciaries),
    Claims by contractor, immovables, 9:4841, 9:4941
    Wells, 9:4872
Canal toll fees, 9:4741
Cancellation,
    Sale of property, 9:5031
Certificates and certification,
    Duty of recorder of mortgages to furnish, 9:5213
    Prompt delivery, 9:5212
Clothing, 9:4681 et seq.
Commercial real estate, real estate brokers, unpaid commissions, 9:2781.1
Commodities, making or repairing, 9:4502
Conflict of laws, secured transactions, 9:4770
Consumer credit, home solicitation sales, 9:3540
Counterletters, public property, 9:2712
Drilling rigs,
    Property subject to well privileges, 9:4863
    Well privileges, effect on third persons, 9:4865
Enforcement, 9:4502
    Hauling or trucking privilege, 9:4601
Environmental liability, lenders, immunities, 9:5395
Equipment suppliers. Mechanic's privileges, generally, this index
Estimates, repairs exceeding, automobiles and other machinery, 9:4501
Federal Tax Lien Act, recording and filing, 9:2725
Fees and charges,
    Hospital charges, 9:4751 et seq.
    Privilege for law charges, generally. Costs, this index
Franchises, railroads, 9:4901
Gems, 9:4701 et seq.
Grass, cutting, city of Plaquemine, property owners liability, rank, 9:4821
Hauling, charges or labor performed, 9:4601
Home solicitation sales, aged persons, improvements, 9:3541.21, 9:3541.22
Horses, feed and medical services, 9:4661
Hospitals, services and supplies, 9:4751 et seq.
Improvements, aged persons, home solicitation sales, 9:3541.21, 9:3541.22
Injunctions, divorce proceedings, 9:371
Insolvency, sale of property, effect on privilege or lien, 9:5031
Irrigation, privilege on crops, water supplier, 9:4522.1
Judicial sale subject to lien, effect on privileges or liens, 9:5031
Liquidation, sale of property, effect on privilege or lien, 9:5031
Logs and lumber, 9:4621, 9:4622
Maintenance and repairs, aircraft, 9:4511, 9:4512
Manufactured homes, 9:1149.3

I–53

INDEX TO TITLE 9

PRIVILEGES—Cont'd
Materialman's privilege. Mechanic's privileges, generally, this index
Military forces, power of attorney,
    Immovables, **9:3882.1**
    Powers granted, **9:3871**
Mills, **9:4721**
Minerals, Oil and Gas, this index
Motor carriers, wells, **9:4862**
Movable property, wells, sales or leases, right to privilege, **9:4862**
Noxious weeds, city of Plaquemine, property owner's liability, rank, **9:4821**
Partition, sale of property, effect on privilege or lien, **9:5031**
Payment, bond for deed contract, **9:2943**
Perishable food products, exemption, vendor's privilege, **9:4544**
Pianos, **9:4561 et seq.**
Power of attorney, military forces,
    Immovables, **9:3882.1**
    Powers granted, **9:3871**
Prescription, **9:4802**
    Private works, **9:4823**
        Surety, liability, **9:4813**
    Real estate brokers, commercial real estate, unpaid commissions, **9:2781.1**
    Setting aside, legal entities, lack of authority, **9:5681**
    State, **9:5685**
    Wells, effect on third persons, **9:4865**, **9:4885**
Priorities and preferences,
    Aircraft, **9:4512**
    Rank, generally, post
    Real estate brokers, commercial real estate, unpaid commissions, **9:2781.1**
    Wells, **9:4870**, **9:4888**
Private sale, **9:4502**
Private works, immovables, **9:4801 et seq.**
Privileges and immunities, environmental liability, lenders, **9:5395**
Public works, feed for livestock used on public works, immovables, **9:4921 et seq.**
Rank,
    Canal toll fees, **9:4741**
    Conflicting privileges, **9:4502**
    Fire insurance proceeds, sellers, **9:4581**
    Immovables, **9:4812**, **9:4813**
        Railroad tracks, road beds, etc., privilege for material or labor, **9:4903**
    Logs and lumber, **9:4622**
    Machinery, conflicting privileges upon, **9:4501**
    Moss, **9:4641**
    Motor vehicles, conflicting privileges upon, **9:4501**
    Recording statute, effect upon liens not dependent upon recording, **9:2724**
    Tax assessments--special, **9:4821**
    Vendor's privilege, generally, this index
    Wood products, **9:4622**
Real estate brokers and salespersons, commercial real estate, unpaid commissions, **9:2781.1**
Real estate timesharing, **9:1131.19**
Receiverships, sale of property, effect on privilege or lien, **9:5031**
Refineries, **9:4721**
Release,
    Real estate brokers, commercial real estate, unpaid commissions, **9:2781.1**
Residential Truth in Construction Act, **9:4851 et seq.**

PRIVILEGES—Cont'd
Roads, feed of livestock used, **9:4921 et seq.**
Self-service storage facilities, **9:4758 et seq.**
Separation of patrimony, **9:5011 et seq.**
Sequestration, security, necessity, **9:4622**, **9:4866**
Sewing machines, vendor's privilege, **9:4561 et seq.**
Storage, aircraft, **9:4513**
Subcontractor's privilege on immovables, **9:4801**
Tax assessments, wells, priority, **9:4870**, **9:4888**
Tenancy in common, agreement not to encumber, duration, **9:1112**
Transportation services, wells, **9:4862**
Trucking, charges or labor performed, **9:4601**
Upholstery, making or repairing, **9:4502**
Waiver, seller's privilege, **9:4541**
Watches, **9:4701 et seq.**
Wells, **9:4861 et seq.**, **9:4881 et seq.**
    Attorney fees, **9:4862**
    Bonds (officers and fiduciaries), **9:4872**
    Claims of privilege, notice, **9:4867**, **9:4887**
    Definitions, **9:4861**
    Delivery, evidence, **9:4873**
    Drilling rigs,
        Effect on third persons, **9:4865**
        Property subject to privilege, **9:4863**
    Drilling supplies and equipment, filing privilege, **9:4863**, **9:4864**
    Effective period, **9:4864**
    Enforcement, **9:4871**, **9:4888**
    Extinguishment, **9:4864**, **9:4883**, **9:4884**
        Transfers, **9:4866**, **9:4886**
    Hydrocarbons,
        Effect of privilege, **9:4869**
        Property subject to privilege, **9:4863**
    Leases, right to privilege, **9:4862**
    Mortgages, priority, **9:4870**, **9:4888**
    Notice, **9:4868**
        Claims of privilege, **9:4867**, **9:4887**
    Prescription, effect on third persons, **9:4865**, **9:4885**
    Priorities and preferences, **9:4870**, **9:4888**
    Property subject to privilege, **9:4863**, **9:4882**
    Records and recordation, mortgages, notice, **9:4865**, **9:4885**
    Right to privilege, **9:4862**, **9:4882**
    Secured transactions, priority, **9:4870**, **9:4888**
    Services, supplies and equipment, **9:4862**
    Statements of privilege, **9:4868**, **9:4887**
    Tax assessments, priority, **9:4870**, **9:4888**
    Third persons, effect on, **9:4865**, **9:4885**
    Transportation services, **9:4862**
    Vendor's privileges, priority, **9:4870**, **9:4888**
    Venue, **9:4867**
Wood products,
    Effective period, rank, enforcement, **9:4622**
    Right of privilege, **9:4621**

PRIVILEGES AND IMMUNITIES
Aged persons, volunteers, area agencies and councils, **9:2792.9**
Athletics, volunteers, **9:2798**
Banks and Banking, this index
Cancellation,
    Sale of property, **9:5031**
Children and minors, parenting coordinators, custody, **9:358.9**
Compromise and settlement, structured settlements, transfer, **9:2715**
Consumer credit information, dissemination, **9:3571**

INDEX TO TITLE 9

PRIVILEGES AND IMMUNITIES—Cont'd
Contractors, defective work, **9:2771**
Controlled dangerous substances, dealer liability, **9:2800.71**
Crimes and offenses, injuries sustained during felonies, **9:2800.10**
Emergency response network, **9:2798.5**
Fairs and festivals, parades, **9:2796**
Farm animal activities, **9:2795.1**
Firefighters and fire departments, damages to property, **9:2793.1**
First aid, emergency care, **9:2793**
Food banks, donations, limitation of liability, **9:2799, 9:2799.6**
Gleaning, landowner liability, **9:2800.4**
Holiday in Dixie parades and festivities, **9:2796**
Homeowners associations, directors and officers and trustees, **9:2792.7**
Mardi Gras parades and festivities, **9:2796**
Medical Care and Treatment, this index
Mortgages, environmental liability and financial responsibility, lenders, **9:5395**
National Voluntary Organizations Active in Disaster, **9:2793.8**
Nonprofit corporations, fair and festival parades, **9:2796**
Nonprofit health care quality improvement corporations, **9:2800.20**
Oil, gas, or mineral property, landowners liability, **9:2800.4**
Parades, fairs and festivals, **9:2796**
Personal injuries, felonies, sustained during commission, **9:2800.10**
Poison control centers, nonprofit organizations, liability for damages, **9:2797.1**
Polling places, liability, owner of property, **9:2800**
Privilege for utility assessment, **9:1123.16**
Public officers and employees, policy making or discretionary acts, **9:2798.1**
Quasi offenses, felonies, injuries sustained during commission, **9:2800.10**
Real estate appraiser privilege, **9:2781.2**
Real estate timesharing, assessments, **9:1131.22**
Secured transactions, collection of fees, filing officers and secretary of state, **9:2736**
Security interest, environmental liability and financial responsibility, lenders, **9:5395**
Structured settlements, transfer, **9:2715**
Volunteers,
    Emergency medical services, **9:2793.2**
    Schools and school districts, **9:2798.2**
Women, **9:51**

PROCESS
Agents for service, fugitive from justice, **9:5802**
Arbitration proceedings, **9:4206**
Citations,
    Dismissal and nonsuit, involuntary, service, prescription, interruption, **9:5801**
    Service of process,
        Dismissal and nonsuit, involuntary, prescription, interruption, **9:5801**
        Interdiction, veterans in government institutions, **9:1021**
        Veterans in government institutions, interdiction, **9:1021**
Form, arbitration proceedings, **9:4206**
Secretary of state,
    Federal agency, **9:5164**
    United States agency, **9:5164**
Seller's privilege, enforcement, **9:4564**
Service of process,
    Citations, ante

PROCESS—Cont'd
Service of process—Cont'd
    Credit repair services organizations, **9:3573.9**
    Demand for payment, open accounts, **9:2781**
Signatures, arbitrator, **9:4206**
Veteran in government institution, interdiction, service, **9:1021**

PROCURATION
Conditional procuration, disability, **9:3890**

PRODUCTS LIABILITY
Generally, **9:2800.51 et seq.**
Definitions, **9:2800.53**
Firearms, **9:2800.60**
Medical care and treatment, users of blood, organs or tissue, **9:2797**
Notice, unreasonably dangerous, inadequate warning, **9:2800.57**
Unreasonably dangerous, **9:2800.54 et seq.**

PROFESSIONAL DENTAL CORPORATIONS
Contracts for services, arbitration and award, **9:4230 et seq.**

PROFESSIONAL MEDICAL CORPORATIONS
Contracts for services, arbitration and award, **9:4230 et seq.**

PSYCHIATRISTS AND PSYCHIATRY
Damages, medical care and treatment, gratuitous services, **9:2799.5**
Disclosure, threats of violence against clearly identified victims, duty to warn, **9:2800.2**
Negligence, medical care and treatment, gratuitous services, **9:2799.5**
Privileges and immunities, medical care and treatment, gratuitous services, **9:2799.5**

PSYCHOLOGISTS
Contracts for services and supplies, arbitration and award, **9:4230 et seq.**
Damages, gratuitous services, **9:2799.5**
Duty to warn, patients' threats against clearly identified victims, **9:2800.2**
Malpractice, prescription, **9:5628**
Negligence, medical care and treatment, gratuitous services, **9:2799.5**
Privacy, threats by patients against clearly identified victims, warning, **9:2800.2**
Privileges and immunities, medical care and treatment, gratuitous services, **9:2799.5**

PUBLIC CONTRACTS
Arbitration and award, foreign forum, **9:2778**
Counterletters, affecting award, **9:2712**
Foreign jurisdiction, interpretation and dispute resolution, **9:2778**
Interpretation, foreign jurisdictions, **9:2778**

PUBLIC DEFENDER BOARD
Limitation of liability, **9:2800.16**

PUBLIC LANDS
Actions and proceedings,
    Patents, setting aside, prescription, **9:5661**
    Removal of encroachments, **9:5627**
Acts of sale and conveyances, counterletters, **9:2712**
Batture in cities and towns, **9:1102**
Encroachment, **9:5627**
Erosion, grant of mineral servitude to subdivision, **9:1152**

INDEX TO TITLE 9

PUBLIC LANDS—Cont'd
Leases, riparian lands, **9:1102.2**
Patents, actions to set aside, prescription, **9:5661**
Prescription,
    Patents, setting aside, **9:5661**
    Removal of encroachments, **9:5627**
Real rights created for benefit of organization, **9:1252**
Riparian land, use, **9:1102.2**
Subsidence, grant of mineral servitude to subdivision, **9:1152**
Succeeding to, **9:1611 et seq.**

PUBLIC OFFICERS AND EMPLOYEES
Discretionary acts, liability, **9:2798.1**
Fiduciary, **9:3801**
    Stock registered in name of, **9:3832**
Policy making acts, liability, **9:2798.1**

PUBLIC POLICY
Contracts against public policy, **9:271**

PUBLIC REGISTRY ACT
Generally, **9:2721**

PUBLIC UTILITIES
Consumer credit, exemptions, **9:3512**
Deposits, abandoned or unclaimed property, **9:154**
Electronic transactions, exemptions, **9:2603**
Expropriation, **9:3180 et seq.**
Municipally Owned Utilities, this index
Prescription,
    Attachment sale, **9:5641**
    Set aside sale of immovable property, **9:5681**
Indemnity,
    Agreements, drilling and wells, **9:2780**
    Minerals, oil and gas, drilling and wells, **9:2780**
Minerals, oil and gas, indemnification agreements, drilling and wells, **9:2780**
Public trust, purposes, **9:2341 et seq.**
Servitudes,
    Public roads or streets, **9:1253**
    Recording, **9:2726**
Streets and alleys, servitudes, **9:1253**

PUBLIC WORKS AND IMPROVEMENTS
Actions involving deficiencies in design, supervision or construction, prescription, **9:2772**
Bonding claims, **9:4941**
Interest on assessments, **9:3507**
Limitation of actions, deficiency in design, supervision or construction, **9:2772**
Livestock used on, privilege for feed, **9:4921 et seq.**
Prescription, actions involving deficiencies in design, supervision or construction, **9:2772**
Privileges and liens, **9:4801 et seq., 9:4921 et seq.**
Time of actions, deficiencies in design, supervision or construction, **9:2772**
Wrongful death, prescription, deficiencies in design, supervision or construction, **9:2772**

PUTATIVE FATHER REGISTRY
Illegitimate children, **9:400**

QUASI OFFENSES
Accountants, liability, prescription, **9:5604**
Alcoholic beverages, limitation of liability, injuries or losses connected with sale, **9:2800.1**
Associations, officers or directors, **9:2792**
Block safe-houses, liability, **9:2800.5**
Blood banks, limitation of liability, **9:2797**

QUASI OFFENSES—Cont'd
Blood users, limitation of liability, **9:2797**
Chiropractors, prescription, **9:5628**
Controlled dangerous substances, dealer liability, **9:2800.63**
    Contribution, **9:2800.69**
Crimes and offenses, injuries sustained during commission, **9:2800.10**
Curators and undercurators liability for acts of interdicts, **9:2800.21**
Custodial trusts, trustee liability, **9:2260.12**
Dentists, prescription, **9:5628**
Diminution of value of damaged vehicle, **9:2800.17**
Directors,
    Associations and societies, **9:2792**
    Nonprofit organizations, limitation of liability, **9:2792.1**
Discretionary acts or omissions, public officers and employees, **9:2798.1**
Downtown development districts, board members, **9:2792.2**
First aid, emergency situations, **9:2793**
Hospital directors or officers, **9:2792**
Hospitals,
    Prescription, **9:5628**
    Users of blood, organs or tissue, limitation of liability, **9:2797**
Liability,
    Downtown development districts, board members, **9:2792.2**
    Nonprofit organizations, directors, officers or trustees, **9:2792.1**
Mardi Gras parades, limitation of liability, **9:2796**
Nonprofit corporations, officers, **9:2792**
Officers and employees,
    Associations and societies, **9:2792**
    Nonprofit organizations, **9:2792.1**
Optometrists, prescription, **9:5628**
Organ transplants, limitation of liability, **9:2797**
Parks, personal injuries, limited liability, **9:2795**
Poison control centers, immunity from liability, **9:2797.1**
Policymaking acts or omissions, public officers and employees, **9:2798.1**
Privileges and immunities, injuries sustained during felonies, **9:2800.10**
Psychologists, prescription, **9:5628**
Public bodies, limitation of liability, **9:2800**
Public entities or officers and employees, discretionary acts or omissions, **9:2798.1**
Public officers and employees, policy making or discretionary acts or omissions, **9:2798.1**
Public trustees, application of law, **9:2344**
Recreation and recreational facilities,
    Personal injuries, limitation of liability, **9:2795**
    Premises used for, **9:2791**
Recreation areas, private owners, limiting liability, **9:2795**
Remedy for the state to recover profits,
    Obtained through commission of criminal offenses, **9:2790.5**
    To prevent unjust enrichment, **9:2790.5**
Self-insurance trust funds, trustees, limitation of liability, **9:2792.6**
Tissue transplants, limitation of liability, **9:2797**

QUIETING TITLE
Minors' property, private sale, **9:675**
Religious organizations, lapse of time, **9:2321**

RAILROADS
Curators, selling or leasing right of way over land of ward, **9:731**

INDEX TO TITLE 9

RAILROADS—Cont'd
Expropriation,
    Prescription of claims for damages, **9:3180**
    Property exempt from, **9:3187**
Franchises, privilege against for materials, labor or supplies, **9:4901 et seq.**
Labor and employment. Privileges, generally, post
Liens. Privileges, generally, post
Mechanic's privileges. Privileges, generally, post
Privileges, **9:4901 et seq.**
    Effective period, **9:4902**
    Exception, **9:4808**
    Rank, **9:4903**
    Recordation of claim, **9:4902**
    Tracks and roadbeds, **9:4901 et seq.**
Records and recordation, privilege for material or labor, **9:4902**
Repairs, tracks, road beds, structures, etc., privilege, **9:4901 et seq.**
Right of way,
    Privilege against for materials in construction and maintenance, **9:4901 et seq.**
    Tutors or curators selling or leasing over land of ward, **9:731**
Ties, privilege, **9:4621, 9:4622**
Transfer, etc., of land fronting or bounded by, effect, **9:2971 et seq.**
Tutors, selling or leasing right of way over land of ward, **9:731**

REAL ESTATE BROKERS AND SALESPERSONS
Agency relationship with clients, **9:3891 et seq.**
Clients, relationship, **9:3891 et seq.**
Commercial real estate, liens, unpaid commissions, **9:2781.1**
Commission, privileges, commercial real estate, unpaid commissions, **9:2781.1**
Consent, dual agency, **9:3897**
Disclosure, dual agency, **9:3897**
Dual agency, **9:3897**
Duties to clients, **9:3893**
Forms, dual agency, **9:3897**
Open accounts, unpaid commissions, commercial real estate liens, **9:2781.1**
Privileges, commercial real estate, unpaid commissions, **9:2781.1**
Relationship with clients, **9:3891 et seq.**
Subagency, **9:3898**
Termination, agency relationship, **9:3895**
Vicarious liability, clients, **9:3899**
Withdrawal, dual agency, **9:3897**

REAL ESTATE INVESTMENT TRUSTS
Corporate distributions, income, **9:2149**
Institutional funds, investments, **9:2337.1 et seq.**

REAL ESTATE TIMESHARING
Generally, **9:1131.1 et seq.**
Accounts and accounting, escrow accounts, **9:1131.17**
Actions and proceedings,
    Preservation of claims and defenses, **9:1131.30**
    Public offering statements that do not comply with regulations, damages, **9:1131.13**
Acts of sale or conveyances, public offering statements, **9:1131.9.2**
Advertisements, regulation, **9:1131.12**
Affidavits, declarations, **9:1131.4**
Application of law, **9:1131.3**
Assessment of the interest expenses, **9:1131.21**

REAL ESTATE TIMESHARING—Cont'd
Assessments,
    Interest, expenses, **9:1131.21**
    Privileges, **9:1131.22**
    Tax assessments, **9:1131.9**
Bonds (officers and fiduciaries), **9:1131.4**
    Escrow, **9:1131.16**
Cancellation,
    Conveyance within certain time period, **9:1131.13**
    Preservation of claims and defenses, **9:1131.30**
Claims,
    Damages, escrow account, **9:1131.17**
    Preservation, **9:1131.30**
Collection, owner share of tax assessments, **9:1131.9**
Construction, declarations, **9:1131.5**
Contract for purchase of timeshare interests, **9:1131.10.1**
Creation of timesharing plan, **9:1131.4**
Damages,
    Escrow accounts, **9:1131.17**
    Misleading or false public offering statements, actions, **9:1131.13**
Declarations,
    Construction and validity, **9:1131.5**
    Filing, **9:1131.4**
Deeds and conveyances, owners interest, **9:1131.8**
Defenses, preservation, **9:1131.30**
Definitions, **9:1131.2**
Deposits, escrow, **9:1131.16**
Description of property, **9:1131.6**
Developer supervisory duties, **9:1131.9.1**
Developer's interest, leasehold interest, requirements, **9:1131.24**
Donations, prize and gift promotional officers, **9:1131.12**
Escrow,
    Accounts, **9:1131.17**
    Deposits, **9:1131.16**
Escrow of payments, **9:1131.16.1**
Exemption, real estate recovery fund, **9:1131.26**
Expenses and expenditures, assessments for timeshare interest expenses, **9:1131.21**
Fraud, advertisements, **9:1131.12**
Funds, real estate recovery fund, **9:1131.26**
Injunctions, sales by developers, state, failure to give evidence of deposits, **9:1131.17**
Inspections and inspectors, records, **9:1131.20**
Insurance, **9:1131.23**
Interest expenses, assessments, **9:1131.21**
Leases, **9:1131.10.1 et seq.**
    Developers, requirements, **9:1131.24**
    Plans, disposition of proceeds upon sale, **9:1131.8**
Liability insurance, **9:1131.23**
Management and operation of timeshare plans, **9:1131.20**
Misrepresentation, advertisements, **9:1131.12**
Mortgages, **9:1131.28**
Notice,
    Cancellation, **9:1131.13**
    Owner's right, share of proceeds from sales, **9:1131.8**
    Public offering statements, **9:1131.9.2**
Owners associations, management, **9:1131.20**
Partition, **9:1131.7**
Payment, tax assessments, **9:1131.9**
Plans and planning, **9:1131.4**
Preservation of claims and defenses, **9:1131.30**
Privileges and liens, **9:1131.19**
    Assessments, **9:1131.22**
Prize and gift promotional offers, **9:1131.12**
Proceeds, sales, disposition, **9:1131.8**

INDEX TO TITLE 9

REAL ESTATE TIMESHARING—Cont'd
Promissory notes, form, **9:1131.30**
Property insurance, **9:1131.23**
    Actions and proceedings, misleading or fraudulent statements, **9:1131.12**
    Exemptions, **9:1131.11**
Real estate recovery fund, exemption, **9:1131.26**
Records and recordation, **9:1131.4**, **9:1131.28**
    Advertisements, **9:1131.12**
    Declarations, **9:1131.4**
    Description of timeshare property, **9:1131.6**
    Inspections, **9:1131.20**
Refunds, cancellation, **9:1131.13**
Regulation of timesharing advertising, **9:1131.12**
Remedies, **9:1131.25**
    Preservation of claims and defenses, **9:1131.30**
Resale, timeshares, **9:1131.18**
Rescission, preservation of claims and defenses, **9:1131.30**
Right of cancellation, timeshare purchase, **9:1131.13**
Rules and regulations, advertisements, **9:1131.12**
Sales,
    Disposal of owner's interest, **9:1131.8**
    Resales, **9:1131.18**
Special assessments, **9:1131.9**
Statement. Public offering statement, generally, ante
Tax assessment of payment, **9:1131.9**
Tax assessments, **9:1131.9**
Termination of plan, **9:1131.8**
Validity, declarations, **9:1131.5**
Waiver, **9:1131.29**
Warranties, **9:1131.14**
    Implied warranties, **9:1131.15**

REAL RIGHTS
Creation in immovables for charitable purposes, **9:1252**

RECEIVERS AND RECEIVERSHIP
Assignment, stock held as fiduciary, **9:3833**
Bonds (officers and fiduciaries), premium, expense, **9:3901**
Federal mortgage, **9:5163**
Fiduciary, **9:3801**
Mortgages, sale of property, **9:5251**
Privileges, sale of property, **9:5031**
Shares and shareholders, registered in name of as fiduciary, **9:3832**

RECIPROCITY
Electronic transactions, state agencies, **9:2619**
Estate Tax Apportionment Law, **9:2431 through 2439**
    Action by nonresident, reciprocity, **9:2437**
    Action to recover amount of tax or deficiency from person interested in estate, **9:2436**
        Time of filing, liability of fiduciary, **9:2436**
    Allowance for exemptions, deductions and credits, **9:2435**
    Application of provisions, **9:2438**

RECORDS AND RECORDATION
Abandoned or unclaimed property, examination of records, **9:172**
Aerial photographs, servitudes, **9:2726**
Affidavit of identity, filing, **9:5503**
Agents, service of notice, federal agency, **9:5164**
Alimony judgment or order, **9:324 et seq.**
Arbitration, papers to be filed, **9:4214**
Consumer Credit, this index
Consumer loan brokers, **9:3572.6**
    Examination, **9:3572.7**
Contracts, improvements on immovables, **9:4808**

RECORDS AND RECORDATION—Cont'd
Delays in registry, **9:5212**
Duties of recorders,
    Loss or destruction of promissory notes,
        Proof by affidavit, **9:5168**
Electronic judicial records, **9:2603.1**
Evidence, electronic transactions, **9:2613**
Expropriation, property acquired for highways, plats, **9:2727**
Federal Tax Lien Act, **9:2725**
Fees and charges, leases, **9:3342**
Injuring public records, crimes and offenses, false affidavit of identity, **9:5503**
Instruments affecting immovable property, place, **9:2721**
Judgments and Decrees, this index
Leases,
    Movable property, **9:3342**
Liens. Privileges, this index
Lis pendens, cancellation, furnishing of bond or other security, **9:4835**
Manufactured homes. Mobile Homes and Manufactured Housing, this index
Medical examination, veteran in government institution, interdiction proceeding, **9:1021**
Paraphing of registers, **9:5209 et seq.**
Plats, servitudes, **9:2726**
Public administrators, parishes over 100,000, **9:1586**
Real rights and immovables for charitable purposes, **9:1252**
Servitudes,
    Nonprofit corporations, granted to, **9:1252**
    Plats, sketches or aerial photographs, **9:2726**
Sketches, servitudes, **9:2726**
Successions and Succession Proceedings, this index
Surveys and Surveyors, this index
Testament probated out of state, **9:2421**
Third parties protected, **9:2723**
Unclaimed property, examination of records, **9:172**
Vessels, hypothecation and conveyance, **9:5381**

RECREATION AND RECREATIONAL FACILITIES
Limitation of liability, **9:2795**
Private property, personal injuries, limiting liability, **9:2795**
Property owner, duty of care, **9:2791**
Sites, passageway, servitudes, **9:1251**

REDHIBITION
Judicial sale, **9:3169**

REFINERIES
Privilege on sugar, syrup or molasses, **9:4721**

REGISTERED LIMITED LIABILITY PARTNERSHIPS
Generally, **9:3431 et seq.**

REGISTRATION
Adoption of adults, **9:461**
Consumer loan brokers, **9:3572.3 et seq.**
    Crimes and offenses, **9:3553**
Corporations, this index
Donations, inter vivos donations of mortgageable property, effect, **9:2371**
Gas, oil and minerals, agreements for joint exploration, development, etc., **9:2731**

REGULATED INVESTMENT COMPANIES
Institutional funds, investments, **9:2337.1 et seq.**

RELATIVES
Controlled dangerous substances, dealer liability, **9:2800.63**
Definitions, Trust Code, **9:1725**

INDEX TO TITLE 9

RELATIVES—Cont'd
Grandparents and Grandchildren, generally, this index
Visitation rights, **9:344**

RELIGION
Credit, discrimination, **9:3583**

RELIGIOUS ORGANIZATIONS AND SOCIETIES
Consumer credit, exemptions, **9:3516**
Directors, tort liability, **9:2792**
Donations,
    Disposal of property, **9:2322**
    Exemptions, reduction and calculation of succession mass, **9:2372**
    Title to donated real estate quieted and perfected, **9:2321**
Immovables, real rights created for benefit of organization, **9:1252**
Institutional vandalism, damages, **9:2799.2**
Inter vivos donations, exemptions, reduction and calculation of succession mass, **9:2372**
Investment of funds, **9:2337.1 et seq.**
Officers and employees, tort liability, **9:2792**
Quasi offenses, liability of officers or directors, **9:2792**
Quieting title, lapse of time, **9:2321**
Tort liability, officers or directors, **9:2792**
Trusts and trustees,
    Incorporation, **9:2275**
    Mixed trusts, religious trust acting as trustee, **9:1783**
    Tort liability, **9:2792**

RENT
Abandoned or unclaimed property, **9:154**
Assignment, **9:4401**
Attorney fees, collection of rent, **9:3259**
Crop, ownership, **9:3204**
Pledges, **9:4401**
Self-Service Storage Facilities Act, **9:4756 et seq.**

REPORTS
Health care providers, nonprofit health care quality improvement corporations, privileges and immunities, **9:2800.20**
Parenting coordinators, child custody, **9:358.5**

REPRESENTATION
Class trust, descendant of child or grandchild, **9:1894**
Representation upon predecease of principal beneficiary, **9:1202**

RES IPSA LOQUITUR
Malpractice, burden of proof, application of law, **9:2794**

RESCUE
Emergencies, tort liability, **9:2793**

RESIDENTIAL MOBILE HOME
Definitions, manufactured homes, **9:1149.2**

RESIDENTIAL PLANNED COMMUNITY
Definitions, Homeowners Association Act, **9:1141.2**
Homeowners Association Act, **9:1141.1 et seq.**

RESIDENTIAL TRUTH IN CONSTRUCTION ACT
Generally, **9:4851 et seq.**

RESPONDEAT SUPERIOR
Emergency first aid treatment, privileges and immunities, application of law, **9:2793**
Remission, compromise or discharge of obligations, employers rights, **9:3921**

RESTAURANTS
Donated food, limitation of liability, **9:2799.3, 9:2799.6**

RETAIL INSTALLMENT CONTRACT
Definitions, manufactured homes, **9:1149.2**

RETIREMENT AND PENSIONS
Community of acquets and gains, partition, **9:2801.1**
Consumer credit, exemptions, qualified pension plans, **9:3560**
Matrimonial regimes, partition, community property, **9:2801, 9:2801.1**
Partition,
    Community of acquets and gains, **9:2801.1**
    Matrimonial regimes, community property, **9:2801**
Power of attorney, military personnel, powers granted, **9:3881**

REVENDICATION
Collation, alteration of prescriptive period, **9:5811**

REVOCATORY ACTION
Child support enforcement, **9:315.24**

REVOLVING CHARGE ACCOUNTS
Definitions, **9:3516**

REVOLVING LOAN ACCOUNTS
Definitions, consumer credit, **9:3516**

RIDING CLUBS
Horses, farm animal activities, privileges and immunities, **9:2795.1**

RIGHT OF WAY
Boating or recreational sites, **9:1251**
Building encroachments, prescription, **9:5627**
Railroads, this index
Transfer, etc., of land fronting or bounded by, effect, **9:2971 et seq.**
Tutors or curators, sale or lease of right of way over land of ward, **9:731**

RIPARIAN OWNERS
Actions, batture not necessary for public use, **9:1102**
Beds of nonnavigable waters, **9:1115.1 et seq.**
Buildings, construction and use, **9:1102.2**
Deep water port commission, construction of wharves, buildings or improvements, **9:1102.1**
Expropriation, buildings or improvements, **9:1102.2**
Fees and charges, buildings or improvements used for public purposes, **9:1102.2**
Improvements,
    Construction and maintenance, **9:1102.1**
    Construction and use, **9:1102.2**
Joint use, land on public waterways, **9:1102.2**
Leases, riparian lands on public waters, **9:1102.2**
Non-navigable waters, beds, ownership, **9:1115.1 et seq.**
Public lands, use, **9:1102.2**

RIVERS AND STREAMS
Change in ownership of land or water bottoms, minerals, oil and gas, leases, **9:1151**
Ownership, **9:1101**
Riparian owners,
    Use of land, **9:1102.2**
    Use of surface water, fees prohibited, legislative finding, **9:1104**

RODEOS
Sponsors, equine activities, immunities, **9:2795.1**

INDEX TO TITLE 9

ROYALTIES
Abandoned or unclaimed property, 9:154
Minerals, Oil and Gas, this index
Trust, allocation to income or principal, 9:2152

SAFE DEPOSIT BOXES AND COMPANIES
Military forces, power of attorney, powers granted, 9:3874
Sureties, deposits, joint control, 9:3904
Trustee, authority to act as, 9:2273
Unclaimed property, Abandoned or Unclaimed Property, generally, this index

SAFE HOUSES
Damages, liability, 9:2800.5

SAINT PATRICK'S DAY PARADE
Sponsors, limitation of liability, 9:2796.1

SALES AND USE TAX
Rental purchase agreements, 9:3362

SALES OF IMMOVABLES
Associations and societies, prescription, 9:5681
Bond for deed contracts, generally. Acts of Sale and Conveyances, this index
Children and minors, private sales, validation, 9:675
Conventional sales, 9:2941 et seq.
Corporations, prescription, 9:5681
Escrow to insure unencumbered title, 9:2943
Family home, consent of wife required, 9:2801
Federal mortgage, property subject to, petition, 9:5163
Foreign trusts, records and recordation, 9:2262.3
Fraud, 9:2989
Joint tenants, agreements against, duration, 9:1112
Local improvement assessments, payment, 9:2921 et seq.
Mechanic's privileges and liens, 9:4801 et seq.
Military forces, power of attorney, 9:3870, 9:3882.1
Noncredit home solicitation sales, cancellation, 9:2711.1
Payment of past-due charges, tax assessments prior to conveyance, New Orleans, 9:2921
Privileges, water wells, 9:4861 et seq.
Records and recordation,
  Foreign trusts, 9:2262.3
  Third parties protected, 9:2721
Sale and lease-back, commercial transactions, 9:3371
Tenancy in common, agreements against, duration, 9:1112
Third parties, protected, recording, 9:2721
Timesharing, resales, 9:1131.18
Trusts and trustees, foreign trusts, records and recordation, 9:2262.3
Tutors and Tutorship, this index

SALES OF MOVABLES
  Generally, 9:2901 et seq., 9:3137.1 to 9:3137.9
Application of law, Civil Code and revised statutes conflicts, 9:3192
Carpets, cleaning and storage charges, 9:4684
Carriers, privilege, priority over buyer, 9:4601
Civil Code, conflict of laws, revised statutes, 9:3192
Claims for collection, transfer, 9:3051
Cleaning and pressing establishments, unclaimed property, 9:4687
Contractors,
  Fines and penalties, misapplication of payments, 9:4814
  Misapplication of payments, fines and penalties, 9:4814
Conventional sales, 9:2941 et seq.
Fire insurance, privilege of vendor, 9:4581

SALES OF MOVABLES—Cont'd
Itinerant vendors, withdrawal of consent to agreement, 9:2711
Louisiana Exchange Sale of Receivables Act, 9:3137.1 to 9:3137.9
Nonalienation certificates, 9:2928
Noncredit home solicitation sales, cancellation, 9:2711.1
Notice, unclaimed property, 9:4702
Power of attorney, military forces, 9:3870, 9:3871
Prescription, attachment against foreign corporation, 9:5641
Purchase agreement, withdrawal of consent, 9:2711
Rental purchase agreements, 9:3351 et seq.
Residential Property Disclosure Act, 9:3196 et seq.
Sale and lease-back, commercial transactions, 9:3371
Taxidermists, abandoned or unclaimed specimens, 9:191, 9:192
Withdrawal of consent to purchase agreement, 9:2711

SAVINGS AND LOAN ASSOCIATIONS
Agricultural products, proceeds of financing, assignment, 9:3121
Assignments, crop financing proceeds, 9:3121
Confidential or privileged information, personal credit information, 9:3571
Consumer credit,
  Exemptions, licenses, 9:3560
  Transactions, application of law, 9:3563.1
Crop financing proceeds, assignment, 9:3121
Deposits, abandoned or unclaimed property, 9:155
Exemptions, notification filing requirements, 9:3563.1
Financial Institutions Office, generally, this index
Military forces, power of attorney, powers granted, 9:3874
Personal credit information, confidentiality, 9:3571
Powers of attorney, military personnel, powers granted, 9:3874
Privileges and immunities, disclosure of personal credit information, liability, 9:3571
Records and recordation, customer financial records, disclosure, 9:3571
Subpoenas, dissemination of credit information, 9:3571

SAVINGS BANKS
Confidential or privileged information, personal credit information, 9:3571
Consumer credit,
  Application of law, 9:3514
  Transactions, application of law, 9:3563.1
Exemptions, notification, filing requirements, 9:3563.1
Personal credit information, confidentiality, 9:3571
Privileges and immunities, disclosure of personal credit information, civil or criminal liability, 9:3571
Records and recordation, customer financial records, disclosure, 9:3571
Subpoenas, dissemination of credit information, 9:3571
Sureties, deposits, joint control, 9:3904
Trusts and trustees, authority to act as, 9:2273

SCENIC AREAS
Private property, personal injuries, limiting liability, 9:2795

SCHOOL BUILDINGS AND GROUNDS
Damages, liability, 9:2800
Liability, damages caused by, 9:2800

SCHOOLS AND SCHOOL DISTRICTS
Asbestos, limitation of liability, removal, abatement or clean up services, 9:2800.3
Boards and commissions, limitation of liability, 9:2792.4

INDEX TO TITLE 9

SCHOOLS AND SCHOOL DISTRICTS—Cont'd
City boards, limitation of liability, **9:2792.4**
Claims against,
    Buildings and grounds, liability, **9:2800**
    Policy making or discretionary acts, **9:2798.1**
Conditional bequests, cy pres doctrine, **9:2331 et seq.**
Crimes and offenses,
    Buildings and grounds, liability, **9:2800**
    Policy making or discretionary acts, liability, **9:2798.1**
Discipline, liability of school systems, work performed as disciplinary measure, **9:2798.3**
Immovables, servitudes nonprofit corporations, **9:1252**
Indebtedness, due, prescription, **9:5701**
Institutional vandalism, damages, **9:2799.2**
Investment of funds, **9:2337.1 et seq.**
Nonprofit corporations, servitudes, granting, **9:1252**
Parish school boards, limitation of liability, **9:2792.4**
Privileges and immunities, claims against, volunteers, **9:2798.2**
Quasi offenses,
    Buildings and grounds, liability, **9:2800**
    Policy making or discretionary acts, liability, **9:2798.1**
Records and recordation, parents, access, **9:351**
Servitudes, granting to nonprofit corporations, **9:1252**
Trusts and trustees, **9:2271**
    Cy pres doctrine, **9:2331 et seq.**
    Invasion of principal for education of beneficiary, **9:2067, 9:2068**
    Mixed private and educational trust, **9:1951**
Vandalism, institutional vandalism, damages, **9:2799.2**
Volunteers, privileges and immunities, **9:2798.2**

SCIENTIFIC ORGANIZATIONS
Immovables, real rights created for benefit of organization, **9:1252**

SCIENTIFIC RESEARCH
Animals, cruelty, unauthorized release, penalties, **9:2799.4**

SECURED TRANSACTIONS
Application of law,
    Assignments, pledges and privileges, **9:4401**
    Mechanic's privileges, **9:4502**
    Mortgages, **9:5140.2**
    Privileges, conflict of laws, **9:4770**
Assignments, master assignments, **9:4401**
Conflict of laws,
    Leases, **9:3303**
    Privileges, **9:4770**
Finance leases, **9:3310**
Leases,
    Assignments, application of law, **9:4401**
    Conflict of laws, **9:3303**
Manufactured homes, **9:1149.3**
Military forces, power of attorney, **9:3870**
    Immovables, **9:3882.1**
Mobile homes and manufactured housing, **9:1149.3 et seq.**
    Remedies of mortgagees, **9:5363.1**
Mortgages, application of law, **9:5140.2**
Power of attorney, military forces, **9:3870**
    Immovables, **9:3882.1**
Sale/lease-back, finance leases, application of law, **9:3310.1**
Seizure of collateral, keeper of property, designation, **9:5136 et seq.**
Ships and watercraft, **9:5525 et seq.**
Wells, priority, **9:4870, 9:4888**
Writ, carrier's privilege, hauling or trucking, **9:4601**

SECURITIES
Children and minors, custodial property, creating, Uniform Transfers to Minors Act, **9:759**
Condominiums, purchaser, disclosure, **9:1124.105**
Dealers, brokers or salespersons, exemptions, consumer loan brokers, **9:3572.2**
Definitions, Uniform Law for Simplification of Fiduciary Security Transfers, **9:3831**
Institutional funds, investments, **9:2337.1 et seq.**
Manufactured homes, retail installment contracts or chattel mortgages, **9:1149.5**
Military forces, power of attorney, powers granted, **9:3872**
Uniform Law for Simplification of Fiduciary Security Transfers, **9:3831 et seq.**
Uniform Transfers to Minors Act, creating custodial property, **9:759**

SECURITY
Assignment, leases or rents, **9:4401**
Electronic transactions,
    Identity and identification, **9:2609**
    Transmissions, errors, **9:2610**
Leases, assignments or pledges, **9:4401**
Military forces, power of attorney, powers granted, **9:3871**
Newspaper dealers and distributors, interest on security deposit, **9:3601**
Pledges, leases or rents, **9:4401**
Transmissions, electronic transactions, errors, **9:2610**

SECURITY INTEREST
Environmental liability, lenders, immunities, **9:5395**
Military forces, power of attorney, **9:3871, 9:3874**
Rental purchase agreements, prohibited provisions, **9:3356**

SEIZURES
Exemptions,
    Motor vehicle repairman's privilege, application of law, **9:4501**
    Repairman's privilege, application of law, **9:4502**
Interest of beneficiary, **9:2004 et seq.**
Judicial Sales, generally, this index
Mortgage foreclosure, keeper of property, designation, **9:5136 et seq.**
Repairman's privilege, exemptions, application of law, **9:4502**
Trust interests of beneficiaries, **9:2004 et seq.**

SELF-SERVICE STORAGE FACILITIES
Generally, **9:4756 et seq.**

SEPARATION FROM BED AND BOARD
Adultery, covenant marriage, **9:307**
Alimony, retroactive effect, **9:310**
Costs, covenant marriage, **9:309**
Covenant marriage, **9:307 et seq.**
Custody of children,
    Covenant marriage, **9:308**
    Mandate, provisional custody, **9:951 et seq.**
Injunctions, covenant marriage, **9:308**
Judgments and decrees, effect, **9:382**
Postseparation family violence relief, **9:361 et seq.**
Reconciliation, community property, effect, **9:384**
Venue, covenant marriage, **9:308**
Violence, postseparation family violence relief, **9:361 et seq.**
Visitation, covenant marriage, **9:308**

SEQUESTRATION
Carbon sequestration on surface or water bottoms, **9:1103**

SEQUESTRATION—Cont'd
Carrier's charges for hauling or trucking, enforcement of, **9:4601**
Logs and lumber, enforcement of privilege on, **9:4622**
Molasses, enforcement of refinery and mill employees' privilege, **9:4721**
Mortgage foreclosure, keeper of property, designation, **9:5136 et seq.**
Sugar, enforcement of refinery and mill employees' privilege, **9:4721**
Syrup, enforcement of refinery and mill employees' privilege, **9:4721**

SERVITUDES
Aerial photograph, attaching to servitude, **9:2726**
Associations and societies, predial servitudes, transfer of title, **9:1051**
Boundaries, land acquired by state due to erosion, mineral servitude of subdivision, **9:1152**
Building encroachments, prescription, **9:5627**
Canals, recording, **9:2726**
Charitable nonprofit corporations, **9:1252**
Conservation, **9:1271 et seq.**
Duration, conservation servitudes, **9:1273**
Educational nonprofit corporations, **9:1252**
Electric power lines, recording, **9:2726**
Facilities, definitions, plats, **9:2726**
Highways and Roads, this index
Historical nonprofit corporations, granting to, **9:1252**
Military forces, power of attorney, immovables, **9:3882.1**
Nonprofit corporations, educational, charitable or historical purposes, **9:1252**
Overhead lines, recording, **9:2726**
Photographs, attaching to servitude, **9:2726**
Pipes and pipelines,
　Public roads or streets, **9:1253**
　Recording, **9:2726**
Plats, attaching to servitude, **9:2726**
Poles and wires, public roads or streets, **9:1253**
Public lands, grant of mineral servitudes to political subdivisions, **9:1152**
Recording, plat, sketch or aerial photograph, **9:2726**
Sewerage lines, recording, **9:2726**
Sketch, attaching to servitude, **9:2726**
Surface lines, recording, **9:2726**
Underground lines, recording, **9:2726**
Utility lines, recording, **9:2726**
Water supply, public roads or streets, **9:1253**

SEWERS AND SEWER SYSTEMS
Construction projects, machinery and equipment, limiting liability, **9:2775**
Interest, assessments for improvements, **9:3507**
Public trust, purposes, **9:2341 et seq.**
Servitudes,
　Public roads or streets, **9:1253**
　　Recording, **9:2726**
　　　Interest, **9:3507**

SEWING MACHINES
Seller's privilege, **9:4561 et seq.**

SEXUAL ABUSE
Child custody or visitation proceedings, appointment of attorney, **9:345**
Definitions, postseparation family violence relief, **9:362**
Visitation, restrictions, **9:341**

SHERIFFS
Acts of and overpayments to, prescription, **9:5623**
Costs, public administrators, payment, **9:1588**
Fees, mobile homes, placing notice of repossession, **9:5363.1**
Law enforcement districts, limitation of liability, **9:2792.4**
Payment, overpayment of costs, prescription, **9:5623**
Prescription,
　Acts of sheriff, **9:5623**
　Judicial sales, informalities, **9:5622**
　Overpayments, **9:5623**

SHINGLES
Privilege, **9:4621, 9:4622**

SHIP MORTGAGE LAW
Generally, **9:5521 et seq.**

SHIPS AND WATERCRAFT
Driving under influence of alcohol or drugs,
　Injury or death of operator, privileges and immunities, **9:2798.4**
　Privileges and immunities, injury or death of operator, **9:2798.4**
Hulls, number, construction of ships, **9:5523**
Hypothecation, validity, record as notice, **9:5381**
Identifying numbers, construction of ships, **9:5523**
Landowner, duty of care, **9:2791**
Materials and supplies, construction of ship, title, **9:5523**
Mortgages, **9:5381, 9:5521 et seq.**
　Acceleration, **9:5534**
　Authentication, **9:5527**
　Cancellation, **9:5530**
　Certificates of recorders, **9:5537**
　Citation of act, **9:5521**
　Contents, **9:5526**
　Definitions, **9:5522**
　Description, **9:5526**
　Disposal of mortgaged ship with fraudulent intent, **9:5533**
　Executory process, **9:5536**
　Failure to affix hull number, **9:5531**
　Fees, recording certificates, **9:5537**
　Filing, rights and privileges, **9:5528**
　Filing fees, **9:5527**
　Fines and penalties,
　　Disposal of mortgaged ship with fraudulent intent, **9:5533**
　　Fraudulent release, **9:5535**
　Forms, **9:5529**
　Fraud, **9:5532**
　　Acceleration, **9:5534**
　　Release of mortgage, **9:5535**
　Identifying numbers, **9:5523**
　Materials and components, **9:5525**
　Recorders, certificates, **9:5537**
　Release, fraudulent release, **9:5535**
　Remedies of creditors, **9:5536**
　Title to property, **9:5524**
Private property, personal injuries, limiting liability, **9:2795**
Privileges, **9:4741**
　Canal toll fees, **9:4741**
Records, identifying numbers, materials and supplies, construction of ship, **9:5523**
Sales of movables, validity, record as notice, **9:5381**
Secured transactions, **9:5525 et seq.**
Title to property, construction of ships, **9:5523 et seq.**

INDEX TO TITLE 9

SHOPLIFTERS
Damages, 9:2799.1

SHOPPING CENTERS
Construction projects, machinery and equipment, limiting liability, 9:2775

SHORT FORM BIRTH CERTIFICATE CARDS
Certified copies, 9:226

SHORT TERM LEASES
Definitions, leases, movable property, 9:3306

SICK LEAVE
Deceased employee, payment of benefits due to survivors, 9:1515

SIDEWALKS
Actions, removal of encroachments, 9:5627
Buildings, encroachment by, 9:5627
Encroachment upon public places, 9:5627
Houses, encroachment by, 9:5627
Prescription, removal of encroachments, 9:5627

SIGHTSEEING
Landowner, duty of care, 9:2791

SIGNATURES
Credit repair services organizations, contracts, 9:3573.7
Electronic signatures. Electronic Transactions, this index
Married women, consent to sale or mortgage of family home, 9:2801
Minerals, oil and gas, declaration in lieu of agreement for joint exploration, 9:2732
Register of conveyances, identification of notes or bonds with judicial sales, 9:3003

SIMPLIFICATION OF FIDUCIARY SECURITY TRANSFERS ACT
Generally, 9:3831 et seq.

SKIING
Private property, personal injuries, limiting liability, 9:2795

SLEDS
Private property, personal injuries, limiting liability, 9:2795

SMALL LOAN ACT
Generally, 9:3577.1 et seq.

SMALL LOANS
Generally, 9:3577.1 et seq.
Deferred Presentment and Small Loan Act, 9:3577.1 et seq.
Social security, lenders, checks received as payment, 9:3577.7

SNOWMOBILES
Private property, personal injuries, limiting liability, 9:2795

SOCIAL SECURITY
Military forces, power of attorney, powers granted, 9:3880
Small loans, lenders, checks received as payment, 9:3578.7

SOCIAL SECURITY NUMBERS
Divorce, attachment to proceedings, 9:313
Marriage, license applications, 9:224
Support of persons, providing, 9:313

SOCIAL SERVICES
Allocation of funds, state succeeding to immovable property of vacant successions, 9:1613

SOCIAL SERVICES—Cont'd
Apportionment of funds, state succeeding to immovable property, 9:1613
Food banks, donations, limitation of liability, 9:2799, 9:2799.6
Medical assistance,
    Military forces, power of attorney, powers granted, 9:3880
    Power of attorney, military personnel, powers granted, 9:3880
State succeeding to immovable property of vacant successions, 9:161

SOLAR COLLECTORS
Right of use, 9:1255

SPECIAL DISTRICTS
Limitation of liability, directors, trustees, etc., 9:2792.4

SPENDTHRIFT TRUSTS
Definitions, 9:1725
Trusts and Trustees, this index

SPILLWAYS
Servitudes or flowage rights, conveyance to United States, 9:1511

STATE
Actions and proceedings,
    Claims against state, generally, post
    Limitation of liability, condition of things within care and custody, 9:2800
Beneficiary to trust, 9:2341 et seq.
Claims against state,
    Buildings, liability, 9:2800
    Condition of things within care and custody, limitation of liability, 9:2800
    Immovable property of vacant successions, compromise, 9:1612
    Policy making or discretionary acts, 9:2798.1
Compromise, immovable property of vacant succession, rights of state, 9:1612
Crimes and offenses, policy making or discretionary acts, liability, 9:2798.1
Damages, condition of things within care and custody, limitation of liability, 9:2800
Discretionary acts, claims against state, liability, 9:2798.1
Judgments and decrees, prescription, 9:5685
Land patents, actions by state to annul, prescription, 9:5661
Liens, prescription, 9:5685
Notice, condition of things within care and custody, limitation of liability, 9:2800
Policy making, claims against state, liability, 9:2798.1
Prescription,
    Judgments and decrees, 9:5685
    Liens and privileges, 9:5685
Privileges and immunities,
    Driving under influence of alcohol or drugs, injury or death of operator, 9:2798.4
    Policy making or discretionary acts, 9:2798.1
Privileges and liens, prescription, 9:5685
Quasi offenses,
    Buildings, liability, 9:2800
    Policy making or discretionary acts, liability, 9:2798.1

STATE AGENCIES
Abandoned or unclaimed property, 9:164

STATE AGENCIES—Cont'd
Claims against political subdivisions, constructive notice, things within care and custody, limitation of liability, **9:2800**
Condition of things within care and custody, limitation of liability, **9:2800**
  Limitations and recovery, condition of things within care and custody, **9:2800**
Constructive notice, things within care and custody, limitation of liability, **9:2800**
Damages, condition of things within care and custody, limitation of liability, **9:2800**
Leases, mineral rights, land acquired by state due to erosion or subsidence, **9:1152**
Notice, condition of things within care and custody, limitation of liability, **9:2800**
Privileges and immunities, injury or death of operator, **9:2798.4**
Servitudes, lands acquired from agency due to subsidence or erosion, **9:1152**
Unclaimed property, **9:164**

STATE BUILDINGS
Damages, liability, **9:2800**
Institutional vandalism, damages, **9:2799.2**

STATE CONTRACTS
Awards, counter letters affecting, **9:2712**
Counter letters affecting award, **9:2712**

STATE OFFICERS AND EMPLOYEES
Governor, generally, this index
Policymaking acts, liability, **9:2798.1**
Privileges and immunities, policy making or discretionary acts, **9:2798.1**
Quasi offenses, policymaking or discretionary acts or omissions, **9:2798.1**

STATE TREASURER
Abandoned property, money or property, public administrators, payment into, **9:1586**
Crippled children aid fund, disposition, **9:1613**
Dependent child aid fund, immovable property to which state succeeds, **9:1613**
Mother and child health services fund, disposition, **9:1613**
Needy blind aid fund, disposition, **9:1613**
Old age assistance fund, disposition, **9:1613**
State hospital board, disposition of funds, **9:1613**
Vacant successions, funds payable to, **9:1586**

STATUTES
Construction,
  Custodial trusts, **9:2260.19**
  Military forces, power of attorney, **9:3869**

STAVES
Privilege for labor, supplies or transportation, **9:4621**

STAY OF PROCEEDINGS
Arbitration,
  Enforcement of award, **9:4213**
  Pendency of, **9:4202**
Controlled dangerous substances, dealer liability, **9:2800.74**
Loans, advance fees suits, **9:3574.7**

STEEPLECHASING
Sponsors, equine activities, immunities, **9:2795.1**

STREETS AND ALLEYS
Actions and proceedings, removal of encroachments, **9:5627**
Boating or recreational sites, servitudes, **9:1251**
Buildings, encroaching upon, **9:5627**
Cable television lines, servitudes, **9:1253**
Damages, grades and grading, prescription, **9:5603**
Electrical lines, servitudes, **9:1253**
Encroachments upon, **9:5627**
Housing, encroaching upon, **9:5627**
Improvements, privileges, feed for livestock used in construction or repair, **9:4921 et seq.**
Livestock used in street work, privilege for feed, **9:4921 et seq.**
Natural gas lines, servitudes, **9:1253**
Pipes and pipelines, public utilities servitudes, **9:1253**
Poles and wires, servitudes, **9:1253**
Prescription, removal of encroachments, **9:5627**
Privileges. Improvements, ante
Public transportation servitudes, **9:1253**
Public utilities, servitudes, **9:1253**
Servitudes, public transportation and utility servitudes, **9:1253**
Sewerage lines, servitudes, **9:1253**
Telecommunications lines, servitudes, **9:1253**
Transfer of lands fronting or bounded by, **9:2971 et seq.**
Water lines, servitudes, **9:1253**

SUBMERGED AND OVERFLOWED LANDS
Nonnavigable waters, ownership of beds, **9:1115.1 et seq.**
Ownership, **9:1101**
  Nonnavigable waters, beds, **9:1115.1 et seq.**
  Public policy of state, navigable waters, **9:1107**
  Transfer of title, navigable waters, **9:1108**
State ownership, **9:1101**

SUBPOENAS
Banks and banking, dissemination of credit information, **9:3571**
Consumer Credit, this index
Financial institutions, dissemination of credit information, **9:3571**
Loan brokers, advance fees, **9:3574.6**
Savings and loan associations, dissemination of credit information, **9:3571**
Savings banks, dissemination of credit information, **9:3571**

SUBROGATION
Generally, **9:3903**
Checks, stop payment, **9:2782.2**
Controlled dangerous substances, dealer liability, **9:2800.65**

SUCCESSIONS AND SUCCESSION PROCEEDINGS
Generally, **9:1422 et seq.**
Acts of sale and conveyances, servitudes or flowage, conveying to United States, **9:1511**
Apportionment, Estate Tax Apportionment Law, **9:2431 et seq.**
Appraisal and appraisers, fees, inventories, **9:1423**
Assignments, shares of stock, held as fiduciary, **9:3833**
Auctions and auctioneers, purposes other than payment of debts or legacies, **9:1521**
Authentic acts, judicial sale, act passed before notary not required, **9:3173**
Banks and banking, surviving spouse, account, release, **9:1513**
Calculation, donations inter vivos made to spouse of previous marriage, **9:2373**

INDEX TO TITLE 9

SUCCESSIONS AND SUCCESSION PROCEEDINGS
—Cont'd
Claims, hospital charges against decedent, privilege, **9:4751 et seq.**
Class trust member dying intestate without descendants, **9:1895**
Compensation and salaries, deceased employee, payment to survivors, **9:1515**
Costs, inventory fees, taxation as costs, **9:1423**
Credit union deposits, etc., payment to surviving spouse, **9:1514**
Creditors, succession representatives, liability for distributions, **9:2450**
Dative testamentary executor. Executors and administrators, post
Deposits, bank, etc., payments to surviving spouse without court proceeding, **9:1513**
Distribution, representatives, liability to judgment creditor, **9:2450**
Donations, inter vivos made to spouse of previous marriage, reduction, **9:2373**
Embryos, in vitro fertilized human ovum, inheritance rights, **9:133**
Estate Tax Apportionment Law, **9:2431 through 2439**
    Action by nonresident, reciprocity, **9:2437**
    Action to recover amount of tax or deficiency from person interested in estate, **9:2436**
        Time of filing, liability of fiduciary, **9:2436**
    Allowance for exemptions, deductions and credits, **9:2435**
    Application of provisions, **9:2438**
    Apportionment of tax liability among persons interested in estate, **9:2432**
    Fiduciary right to withhold or recover proportion of tax attributable to person interested in estate, **9:2434**
    Security by person interested in estate for payment of tax, **9:2434**
Executors and administrators,
    Attorney, designation by testator, **9:2448**
    Authority, mineral proceeds, receiving, **9:1516**
    Bonds (officers and fiduciaries),
        Premium as expense, **9:3901**
        Public administrators, **9:1582**
        Sureties, **9:3911, 9:3912**
    Dative testamentary executor,
        Mandatary, designation, **9:1517**
        Public administrator, appointment as, **9:1584**
    Definitions, **9:3801**
    Distributions, judgment creditors, liability to, **9:2450**
    Hospital charges of decedent, privilege of hospital, **9:4751 et seq.**
    Judgment creditors, distributions, liability for, **9:2450**
    Mandataries, **9:1517**
    Mineral proceeds, authority to receive, **9:1516**
    Misconduct, surety's right to release, **9:3911, 9:3912**
    Power of attorney, mandatary, **9:1517**
    Prescription, **9:5621**
        Proceeding to probate testament, **9:5643**
        Sales, **9:1454.1**
    Privilege, hospital charges against decedent, **9:4751 et seq.**
    Provisional administrators, mandatary, designation, **9:1517**
    Public administrators, **9:1581 et seq.**
        Absence, surviving spouse or heirs, administrator appointment, **9:1583**
        Appointment, **9:1581**
        Bonds (officers and fiduciaries), **9:1582**

SUCCESSIONS AND SUCCESSION PROCEEDINGS
—Cont'd
Executors and administrators—Cont'd
    Public administrators—Cont'd
        Bonds (officers and fiduciaries)—Cont'd
            Appeal, **9:1582**
        Clerks, employment of, **9:1589**
        Compensation, **9:1589**
        Costs, not required to advance, **9:1588**
        Dative testamentary executor, when, **9:1584**
        Expenses, **9:1589**
        Notice, appointment, **9:1583**
        Parishes exempted from act, **9:1590**
        Parishes over 100,000, **9:1581 et seq.**
        Powers and duties, **9:1581**
        Sheriff's costs, not required to pay, **9:1588**
        State, power to represent succession in which state is interested, **9:1588**
        State treasury, payment of proceeds of vacant successions into, **9:1586**
        Term, **9:1581**
        Unclaimed bodies, burial, **9:1551, 9:1552**
        Vacant successions, **9:1552, 9:1586**
    Representation, designation of attorney by testator, upon predecease of principal beneficiary, **9:1202**
    Security, release, **9:3911, 9:3912**
    Self-service storage facilities, privileges and liens, **9:4758**
Exemptions, inter vivos donations, **9:2372**
Exercise of rights, **9:2503**
Experts, inventories, fees, **9:1423**
Federal mortgage, effect upon, **9:5163**
Fees, inventories, taxation as costs, **9:1423**
Flowage rights, spillways, **9:1511**
Forced heirs, legitime in trust, **9:1841**
Foreign probate, allowance and recording, **9:2421**
Heritable obligations, legacies, **9:2787**
Hospital charges against decedent, privilege of hospital, **9:4751 et seq.**
Human embryos, in vitro fertilized human ovum, inheritance rights, **9:133**
Illegitimate children, acknowledgment of paternity, **9:392**
In vitro fertilized human ovum, inheritance rights, **9:133**
Individual retirement accounts, payment of benefits to beneficiary of account, **9:2449**
Instrument from state or country where probate not required, **9:2424**
Inter vivos donations, exemptions, calculation of succession mass, **9:2372**
Intestate succession, trusts, death of beneficiary during term of trust, **9:1973, 9:1978**
Inventories,
    Fees for, taxation as costs, **9:1423**
    Orleans Parish, fees of experts and appraisers, **9:1423**
Judicial sales, **9:3172 et seq.**
    Heir's right to purchase, **9:3175**
    Method of making, **9:3172**
    Payment, heirs buying, **9:3175**
    Persons authorized to make, **9:3001**
    Recording, **9:1425**
        Persons charged with making, **9:3173**
    Representative's right to require, **9:3172**
    Transfer of title, **9:3173**
    Warranties attaching, **9:3174**
Legitime, calculation, donations inter vivos to spouse of previous marriage, **9:2373**
Lessor's privilege, **9:3241**
Marital portion, trusts, **9:1851 et seq.**

INDEX TO TITLE 9

SUCCESSIONS AND SUCCESSION PROCEEDINGS
—Cont'd
Mass, calculation, donations inter vivos to spouse of previous marriage, 9:2373
Military forces,
    Power of attorney, powers granted, 9:3877
    Presumed dead, 9:1442
        Proof, 9:1443
Notaries public, inventories, fees, 9:1423
Obligations,
    Death of legatee before performance of personal obligation on legacy, 9:2786
    Heritable obligations, legacies, 9:2787
Options, servitudes or flowage rights, perfecting, 9:1511
Orders, servitudes or flowage rights to United States, authorizing, 9:1511
Payment,
    Public sale of property for purposes other than, 9:1521
    Vacant successions and absent heirs, post
Petitions,
    Charitable trust or bequest, effectuation of purpose, 9:2331
    Foreign testament, 9:2422
    Testament previously probated out of state, 9:2422
Prescription, 9:5621
    Defective sale or mortgage of property, 9:5632
    Executors and administrators, ante
    Exercise of rights, 9:2503
    Liberative prescription, unrecognized, actions against third persons, 9:5630
    Private sales, 9:1454.1
    Proceeding to probate testament, 9:5643
    Right to probate testament, 9:5643
    Unrecognized successors, actions against third persons, 9:5630, 9:5631
Presumption of death, military forces, 9:1442
Presumptions, judgment of possession, court of competent jurisdiction, 9:5630
Private sales, prescription, 9:1454.1
Public administrators, 9:1581 et seq.
Public sales, purposes other than payment of debts or legacies, 9:1521
Purchase of property of succession, 9:3175
Receipts, mortis causa laws regulating donations, 9:2148
Reduction, donations made to spouse of previous marriage, 9:2373
Sales,
    Prescription, 9:1454.1
    Without priority for purposes other than payment of debt or legacies, 9:1521
Sealing succession effects, affixing seals on property, 9:1424
Seizin of heirs and legatees, exercise of rights, 9:2503
Self-service storage facilities, privileges, 9:4758
Separation of patrimony, privileges to effect separation of patrimony, 9:5011 et seq.
Servitudes,
    Option to United States, perfecting, 9:1511
    Spillways, 9:1511
Shares of stock, registered in name of fiduciary, 9:3831, 9:3832
Sick leave of deceased employee, payment to survivors, 9:1515
Small successions,
    Administrator, vacant successions, 9:1552
    Vacant successions, 9:1551, 9:1552
Special counsel for state, patents for interests, 9:1614

SUCCESSIONS AND SUCCESSION PROCEEDINGS
—Cont'd
State succeeding to immovable property,
    Administration, 9:1611
    Application of statute, 9:1615
    Compromise of rights and claims, 9:1612
    Disposition of funds, 9:1613
    Retention instead of sale, 9:1611
    Special counsel, patents for interests, 9:1614
Taxation,
    Costs, fees for inventories, 9:1423
    Estate Tax Apportionment Law, 9:2431 et seq.
    Inheritance Tax, generally, this index
Third persons,
    Actions by unrecognized successors, 9:5630
    Liberative prescriptions, actions by unrecognized successors, 9:5630
Title to property, actions, prescriptions, 9:5682 et seq.
Trusts and trustees,
    Beneficiary death, intestacy, 9:1973, 9:1978
    Marital portion,
        Satisfaction, 9:1851 et seq.
        Trust as satisfying, 9:1851 et seq.
Uniform Law, 9:2421 et seq.
Usufruct, marital portion, satisfaction, 9:1853
Vacant successions and absent heirs, 9:1586
    Claims to immovable property, compromise, 9:1612
    Funds, disposition, 9:1613
    Immovables, state succession, 9:1611
    Patents for interests, 9:1614
    Public administrators, appointment as curator, 9:1586
    Rights to immovable property, compromise, 9:1612
    Small successions, 9:1551, 9:1552
    Special counsel, 9:1614
    Succeeding to immovable property, state, 9:1611 et seq.
    Succession to immovable property, 9:1611
    Trusts, death of beneficiary intestate, 9:1978
Vacation pay due deceased, payment to survivors, 9:1515

SUGAR
Privilege,
    Refinery and mill employees, 9:4721
    Seller of sugar cane, 9:4543

SUGAR CANE
Manufacturers and manufacturing, seller's privilege on manufactured products, 9:4543

SUMMARY PROCEEDINGS
Arbitration, making of agreement or failure to perform in issue, 9:4203
Condominiums, 9:1124.115
Leases, cancellation, default by lessee, 9:3320 et seq.
Mechanic's privileges and liens, failure to cancel, 9:4833
Privileges and liens, private works, failure to cancel, 9:4833

SUPPORT
Generally, 9:315 et seq., 9:315.30 et seq.
Absent parties, notice, subsequent proceedings, 9:313
Accounts and accounting, 9:312
Actions and proceedings,
    Between spouses, 9:291
    Guidelines for determination, 9:315 et seq.
Addresses, providing, 9:313
Age of majority, termination, 9:315.22
Alimony, generally, this index
Appeal and review,
    Guidelines, deviations, standard of review, 9:315.17

SUPPORT—Cont'd
Appeal and review—Cont'd
    Periodic review, **9:311**
Arrearages, attorney fees and costs, **9:375**
Assignments, earnings, **9:303**
Attorney fees,
    Accounts and accounting, **9:312**
    Arrearages, **9:375**
    Material change in circumstances, **9:311**
Attorneys, fees. Attorney fees, generally, ante
Business and commerce, licenses and permits, suspension or revocation, **9:315.30 et seq.**
Calculation,
    Basic obligations, guidelines, **9:315.2**
    Shared custody, **9:315.9**
    Split custody, **9:315.10**
    Total child support obligation worksheet, **9:315.8, 9:315.20**
Changes,
    Material change in circumstances, reduction or increase in support, **9:311**
    Medical support, **9:311**
Child care, net cost, addition to basic guideline obligation, **9:315.3**
Contempt, licenses and permits, suspension or revocation, **9:315.30, 9:315.33**
Costs,
    Accounts and accounting, **9:312**
    Arrearages, **9:375**
    In forma pauperis, collection, **9:304.1**
Covenant marriage, **9:308**
Credits,
    Child support following judgment of paternity, **9:399**
    Joint custody, **9:315.8**
Custody, children and minors, raising issues, **9:315.25, 9:356**
Deductions, **9:315.7**
Definitions,
    Guidelines, **9:315**
    Income assignments, **9:303**
Determination, guidelines for determination, **9:315 et seq.**
Developmentally disabled persons, **9:315.22**
Disabled obligors, guidelines, deviations, **9:315.1**
Disavowal of paternity, time limit, suspension, **9:402**
Disclosure, licenses and permits, suspension, **9:315.32**
Drivers license numbers, providing, **9:313**
Emancipation of child, termination, **9:315.22**
Expenses and expenditures,
    Accounts and accounting, **9:312**
    Basic obligations, guidelines, **9:315.2**
    Extraordinary expenses, **9:315.6**
Extraordinary medical expenses,
    Addition to basic obligation, **9:315.5**
    Modification of support guidelines, **9:315.1**
Fish and game, licenses and permits, suspension or revocation, **9:315.30 et seq.**
Forms, guideline worksheet for calculation, **9:315.20**
Frivolous actions,
    Accounts and accounting, **9:312**
    Attorney fees, **9:311**
Guidelines, **9:315.21 et seq.**
    Determination, **9:315 et seq.**
    Increased payments, **9:315.19**
Handicapped obligors, guidelines, deviations, **9:315.1**
Health and accident insurance, child support obligations, **9:315.4**
Hearings, accounts and accounting, **9:312**
Illegitimate Children, this index

SUPPORT—Cont'd
In forma pauperis, collection, **9:304.1**
Income schedule, guidelines, **9:315.19**
Income tax--federal, deductions, entitlement, **9:315.18**
Income tax--state, deductions, entitlement, **9:315.18**
Increase or decrease, change in circumstances, **9:311**
Interim child support, **9:399**
Joint custody, adjustments for time with nondomiciliary parties, **9:315.8**
Judgments and decrees,
    Past due support, change in circumstances, **9:311**
    Paternity, child support following judgment of paternity, **9:399**
    Retroactivity, child support judgments, **9:315.21**
Licenses and permits, suspension or revocation, **9:315.30 et seq.**
Mandatory minimums, **9:315.14**
Medical support orders, change in circumstances, **9:311**
Mentally retarded and developmentally disabled persons, **9:315.22**
Motor vehicles, licenses and permits, revocation or suspension, **9:315.30 et seq.**
Multiple families, **9:315.1**
Notice,
    Licenses and permits, suspension, **9:315.33**
    Subsequent proceedings, absent party, **9:313**
Orders of court,
    Accounts and accounting, **9:312**
    Assignments, earnings, **9:303**
    Income tax, deductions, entitlement, **9:315.18**
    Licenses and permits, suspension, **9:315.32**
    Retroactive effect, **9:310**
Other dependents, adjustments to guidelines schedule, **9:315.1**
Overtime, subsequent families, **9:315.12**
Paternity,
    Child support following judgment of paternity, **9:399**
    Disavowal, time limit, suspension, **9:305**
    Interim child support, **9:399**
Payment, income assignment orders, **9:402**
Presumptions, guidelines, rebuttable presumptions, **9:315.1**
Professions and occupations, licenses and permits, suspension, **9:315.30 et seq.**
Reduction in support, change in circumstances, **9:311**
Retroactive effect, orders of court, **9:310**
Retroactivity,
    Child support judgments, **9:315.21**
    Judgments, **9:315.21**
Schedules, basic child support schedule, **9:315.19**
Schools and school districts, expenses and expenditures, **9:315.6**
Second jobs, subsequent families, **9:315.12**
Secreting of child, suspension or modification of support obligation, **9:315.23**
Shared custody, **9:315.9**
Social security numbers, providing, **9:313**
Split custody, **9:315.10**
Spousal support, **9:321 et seq.**
    Application of law, **9:386**
    Cancellation of record, judgments or orders, payments, **9:324**
    Grace period, **9:387**
    Recording judgment or order, **9:322, 9:323**
    Retroactivity of judgment, **9:321**
    Separation from bed and board, effect of present judgment, **9:382**
Standard of review, guidelines, deviations, **9:315.17**

SUPPORT—Cont'd
Stipulations, between parties, effect on guidelines, **9:315.1**
Subsequent families, **9:315.12**
Suspension,
> Definitions, **9:315.30, 9:315.31**
> Secreting of child, **9:315.23**

Table, child support schedule, **9:315.19**
Tax deductions, entitlement, **9:315.18**
Telephone numbers, providing, **9:313**
Termination, **9:315.22**
> Child support, **9:315.22**
> Majority or emancipation, **9:315.22**

Transportation, expenses and expenditures, **9:315.6**
Trust property, seizure of beneficiary's interest, **9:2005**
Unemployment, voluntary, **9:315.11**
Visitation, children and minors, raising issues, **9:315.25, 9:356**
Worksheet, calculating guideline obligations, **9:315.20**

SURETYSHIP AND GUARANTY
> Generally, **9:3901 et seq.**

Attorney's fee, liability of surety, **9:3902**
Contractors, beginning of period, **9:2774**
Demand on principal and surety for payment, **9:3902**
Deposits, joint control, **9:3904**
Fiduciaries, guarantor of signature, nonliability, **9:3837**
Judicial proceedings, petition for release of judicial surety, **9:3911, 9:3912**
Legal suretyship, release, grounds and procedure, **9:3911, 9:3912**
Married women, **9:103**
Mortgage release, bond for deed contract, **9:2942**
Prescription, mechanic's privileges and liens, **9:4813**
Privileges, private works, **9:4812**
Release, deposits, joint control, **9:3904**
Women, **9:103**

SURROGATE PARENTS
Contracts, enforceability, **9:2713**

SURVEYS AND SURVEYORS
Actions and proceedings, damages, prescription, **9:2772**
Consumer credit, change of location, licensees, **9:3561, 9:3561.1**
Damages, preemptive period, **9:2772**
Expropriation of land for highways, plats, recording, **9:2727**
Fraud, affidavits of inspection, mechanic's privileges and liens, **9:4820**
Maps and plats, expropriation of land for highways, recording, **9:2727**
Mechanic's privileges and liens, **9:4801 et seq.**
Prescription, **9:2772**
Privileges and immunities, private works, **9:4801 et seq.**
Records and recordation, expropriated property for highways, **9:2727**

SURVIVING SPOUSES
Bank accounts, release of funds, **9:1513**
Compensation due payment, **9:1515**
Credit unions, payment to survivor, **9:1514**
Deposits in bank or depository, payment to widow, **9:1513**
Employees wages payable to surviving spouse without judgment of court, **9:1515**
Estate tax marital deduction, formula qualifying, **9:2439**
> Action by nonresident, reciprocity, **9:2437**
> Action to recover amount of tax or deficiency from person interested in estate, **9:2436**
> > Time of filing, liability of fiduciary, **9:2436**
>
> Allowance for exemptions, deductions and credits, **9:2435**

SURVIVING SPOUSES—Cont'd
Estate tax marital deduction, formula qualifying—Cont'd
> Application of provisions, **9:2438**
> > Apportionment of tax liability among persons interested in estate, **9:2432**
> > Security by person interested in estate for payment of tax, **9:2434**

Family home, usufruct, **9:1201**
Legitime in trust, interest or usufruct, **9:1844**
Marital portion of surviving spouse, trust as satisfying, **9:1851 et seq.**
Sick benefits due, payment, **9:1515**
Usufruct,
> Family home, **9:1201**
> Previously executed testaments, application of law, **9:2441**
> Security, **9:1202**

Vacation pay due, payment, **9:1515**

SURVIVORSHIP
Custodial trusts, **9:2260.6**
Definitions, custodial trusts, **9:2260.1**

SWIMMING
Private property, personal injuries, limiting liability, **9:2795**

SYNDICS
Adverse claim to transfer of stock held by, **9:3835**
Assignment, stock held as fiduciary, **9:3833**
Bonds (officers and fiduciaries), premium as expense, **9:3901**
Fiduciaries, **9:3801**
Judicial sales, authority to make, **9:3001**
Sales, lessor's privilege, **9:3241**
Stock registered in name of as fiduciary, **9:3832**

SYRUPS
Privilege,
> Refinery and mill employees, **9:4721**
> Seller of sugar cane, **9:4543**

TAILORS
Privilege, **9:4687, 9:4688**
Unclaimed property, sale, **9:4687, 9:4688**

TANKS
Liquid fertilizer, storage, movable property, **9:1106**
Water wells, appurtenant to, privilege for labor, services or supplies, **9:4861 et seq.**

TAX ASSESSMENTS
Benefited property, interest, **9:3507**
Drainage districts, interest, benefited property, **9:3507**
Home rule cities, interest, **9:3507**
Interest, **9:3507**
Mechanic's privileges and liens, ranking, **9:4821**
Military forces, power of attorney, immovables, **9:3882.1**
New Orleans, this index
Payment, conveyance of free property, **9:2921 et seq.**
Power of attorney, military forces, immovables, **9:3882.1**
Privileges and liens, private works, ranking, **9:4821**
Real estate timesharing, **9:1131.9**
Sales of immovables, past due charges, payment prior to conveyance, New Orleans, **9:2921**
Waterworks districts, interest, benefited property, **9:3507**

TAX CERTIFICATES
Generally, **9:2922 et seq.**

INDEX TO TITLE 9

TAX REDEMPTION
After adjudication to state for nonpayment, effect upon prescription, 9:5803
Certificates of redemption, federal tax liens, 9:2725

TAX SALES
Certificate, payment of taxes, 9:2901 et seq.
Owner's liability, damages, property adjudicated to political subdivision, 9:2800.8
Research certificate, 9:2901 et seq.

TAXATION
Certificate of payment, 9:2902, 9:2922
Estate Tax Apportionment Law, 9:2431 through 2439
    Action by nonresident, reciprocity, 9:2437
    Action to recover amount of tax or deficiency from person interested in estate, 9:2436
        Time of filing, liability of fiduciary, 9:2436
    Allowance for exemptions, deductions and credits, 9:2435
    Application of provisions, 9:2438
    Apportionment of tax liability among persons interested in estate, 9:2432
    Fiduciary right to withhold or recover proportion of tax attributable to person interested in estate, 9:2434
    Security by person interested in estate for payment of tax, 9:2434
Evidence, certificates, 9:2903
Fiduciaries, transfer of securities, 9:3839
Fines and penalties, payment of taxes before transfer of immovable property, 9:2927
Louisiana Tax Refund Anticipation Loan Act, 9:3579.1 to 9:3579.4
Mechanic's privileges and liens, ranking, 9:4821
Payment, before transfer of immovable property, 9:2901
    Act of conveyance, officers not to execute or pass until payment, 9:2901
    New Orleans, 9:2921
    Officer,
        Liability for nonpayment, exoneration, 9:2903, 9:2924
        Not to execute or pass without payment, 9:2901, 9:2921
    Penalty for violation, 9:2927
    Receipt, 9:2902, 9:2922
    Research certificate, 9:2902, 9:2903, 9:2924
Power of attorney, military personnel, powers granted, 9:3871
Research certificates, 9:2901 et seq.
Sales of immovables, past due charges, payment prior to conveyance, New Orleans, 9:2921
Uniform Law for Simplification of Fiduciary Security Transfers, 9:3839

TAXIDERMISTS
Abandoned and unclaimed property, disposition, 9:191, 9:192

TELECOMMUNICATIONS
Expropriation,
    Petition, 9:3180
    Prescription, claims for damages, 9:3180
Highways and roads, lines, servitudes, 9:1253
Home solicitation sales, telephone solicitations, cancellation, 9:2711.1
Internet. Electronic Transactions, generally, this index
Numbers, support, 9:313
Rights of way, tutors or curators selling or leasing over land of ward, 9:731
Servitudes, public roads or streets, 9:1253

TELEVISION AND RADIO
Cable television, servitudes, public roads or streets, 9:1253

TENANCY IN COMMON
Alienation of property, agreement against, 9:1112
Leases, agreements against, 9:1112
Liens and encumbrances, agreements against, 9:1112
Mortgages securing several obligations, interest of obligation holders, 9:5303

TEST TUBE BABIES
Generally, 9:121 et seq.

TESTAMENTS
Application of law, disinherison, forced heirs, 9:2502
Attorneys, central registry system, 9:2446
Authenticated copy, foreign testament, filing, 9:2422
Central registry, 9:2446
    Fees and charges, 9:2447
    Information, 9:2446
Charitable, educational or eleemosynary purposes, cy pres doctrine, 9:2331 et seq.
Children and minors, testamentary transfers, Uniform Act, 9:755
Conditional legacies, charitable, education or eleemosynary purposes, 9:2331 et seq.
Confidential or privileged information, central registry, 9:2446
Continued validity, 9:2440
Custodial trusts, designations, 9:2260.3
Cy pres doctrine, 9:2331 et seq.
Disinherison, forced heirs, application of law, 9:2502
Educational purposes, cy pres doctrine, 9:2331 et seq.
Electronic transactions, exemptions, 9:2603
Eleemosynary purposes, cy pres doctrine, 9:2331 et seq.
Execution of testament,
    Foreign testament, law governing, 9:2423
    Prior to 1998, continued validity, 9:2440
Exemptions, inter vivos donations, reduction and calculation of succession mass, 9:2372
Fees and charges, central registry, 9:2447
Foreign testament,
    Admission to probate, force and effect, 9:2423
    Allowance and recording, 9:2421
    Authenticated copy, filing, proceedings, 9:2422
    Effect, 9:2401
    Execution, law governing, 9:2423
    Petition, filing authenticated copy of testament and foreign probate, 9:2422
    Probated out of state, allowance and recording, 9:2421
    Recording, foreign testament, 9:2421
    State or country not requiring probate, authentication, 9:2424
    Venue, 9:2421
Individual retirement accounts, payment of benefits to beneficiary of account, 9:2449
Interdiction, donations, 9:1022
Notaries public,
    Foreign, authentication, 9:2424
Prescription,
    Proceeding to probate testament, 9:5643
    Right to probate, 9:5643
Reduction of donations,
    Inter vivos donations,
        Exemptions, calculation of succession mass, 9:2372
        Spouse of previous marriage, 9:2373
Registry, will information, fees and charges, 9:2447
Search for testament. Notaries public, ante

TESTAMENTS—Cont'd
Surviving spouses, usufruct, previously executed testament, application of law, **9:2441**
Transfers to minors, Uniform Act, **9:755**
Uniform Probate Law, **9:2421 et seq.**
Uniform Transfers to Minors Act, transfers by testaments, **9:755**
Uniform Wills Law, **9:2401**
Usufruct, surviving spouses, previously executed testaments, application of law, **9:2441**
    Security, form, **9:1202**
Validity, continued, **9:2440**

THEFT
Identity theft, **9:3568**
Storekeepers, damages, **9:2799.1**

THIRD PARTIES
Controlled dangerous substances, dealer liability, **9:2800.65**
Custodial trusts, exemption from liability, **9:2260.11**
Definitions,
    Privileges, wells, **9:4861**
    Succession and succession proceedings, **9:5630**
Donations, inter vivos donations, immovables, recordation, **9:2371**
Manufactured homes,
    Deimmobilization, **9:1149.6**
    Security devices, **9:1149.5**
Mechanic's privileges and liens, **9:4820 et seq.**
Mortgages, this index
Recording law, protection, **9:2721**
Registry laws, protection under, **9:2723**
Roads, etc., abandonment, easements, **9:2981**
Trusts and trustees,
    Custodial trusts, exemption from liability, **9:2260.11**
    Remedies against, **9:2222**

TIMBER AND LUMBER
Consumer credit, **9:3510 et seq.**
Privilege, **9:4621, 9:4622**
Trust, allocation of proceeds to income or principal, **9:2153**

TOURISTS AND TOURISM
Commissions, **9:2792.4**

TRAFFIC RULES AND REGULATIONS
Driving under influence of alcohol or drugs,
    Injury or death of operator, privileges and immunities, **9:2798.4**

TRAINING PROGRAMS
Parenting coordinators, child custody, **9:358.3**

TRANSFEROR
Definitions,
    Custodial trusts, **9:2260.1**
    Uniform Transfers to Minors Act, **9:751**

TRANSFERS
Definitions,
    Uniform Law for Simplification of Fiduciary Security Transfers, **9:3831**
    Uniform Transfers to Minors Act, **9:751**
Fiduciaries, claims adverse to transfer of stock by, **9:3835**
Land, fronting or bounding on waterway, etc., **9:2971 et seq.**
Navigable waters and beds by state to levee district, rescission and cancellation, **9:1101**
Private transfer fee obligations,
    Existing transfer fee, notice requirement, **9:3136**

TRANSFERS—Cont'd
Private transfer fee obligations—Cont'd
    Liability for violations, **9:3134**
    Prohibition of private transfer fee obligations, **9:3133**
Uniform Fraudulent Transfer Act, **9:2790.1 et seq.**
Uniform Law for Simplification of Fiduciary Security Transfers, **9:3831 et seq.**

TRANSIENT MERCHANTS
Door-to-door salesman, withdrawal of consent to agreement, **9:2711**
Purchase agreement, withdrawal of consent, **9:2711**

TRANSPORTATION STATUTE
Violation, presumption of fault, **9:2800.13**

TREES
Disposal or conversion, mortgagee's right of action, limitation of recovery, **9:5382**

TRUST ACCOUNTS
Consumer loan brokers, **9:3572.8**
Credit repair services organizations, **9:3573.4**

TRUST COMPANIES
Assignment of stock held as fiduciary, **9:3832**
Charitable, benevolent and eleemosynary trusts,
    Authority to act as trustee, **9:2273**
Definitions,
    Custodial trusts, **9:2260.1**
    Uniform Transfers to Minors Act, **9:751**
Deposits. Bank Deposits and Collections, generally, this index
Military forces, power of attorney, powers granted, **9:3874**
Shares and shareholders, registered in name of fiduciary, **9:3832**
Sureties, deposit, joint control, **9:3904**
Sworn financial statements, public trusts, **9:2346**
Trustee, authority to act as, **9:1783, 9:2273**

TRUSTS AND TRUSTEES
    Generally, **9:1721 et seq.**
Abandonment of claim, trustees, **9:2121**
Abuse of discretion, trustees, **9:2115**
Acceptance, **9:1755, 9:1808, 9:1824**
    Addition to trust property, **9:1932, 9:1935**
    Creditors of beneficiaries, powers of acceptance, **9:1982, 9:1983**
    Custodial trusts, **9:2260.4**
    Designation of person in whose favor refusal operates, **9:1988**
    Retroactive to date of creation, **9:1823**
Accounts and accounting, **9:2088**
    Charges against income or principal, **9:2156**
    Common trust fund, **9:2128**
    Custodial trusts, post
    Dealing on own account, trustees, **9:2083**
    Inspection, **9:2089**
    Ownership of stock held in name of nominee, **9:2124**
Accumulated income,
    Payment to beneficiary, **9:1964**
    Standards for payment, **9:2068**
Acknowledgment, modification, termination or revocation, **9:2051**
Actions and proceedings, **9:2191 et seq., 9:2231 et seq.**
    Beneficiaries, **9:2191 et seq., 9:2221**
    Construe or protect, expenses charged against principal, **9:2156**

INDEX TO TITLE 9

TRUSTS AND TRUSTEES—Cont'd
Actions and proceedings—Cont'd
    Contracts, **9:2125**
    Custodial trusts, trustee liability, **9:2260.12**
    Defense by trustee, **9:2093**
    Enforcing right of trust estate, **9:2222**
    Torts, **9:2126**
Acts of trustees performed before beneficiary's refusal of interest, **9:1987**
Additional property, **9:1931 et seq.**
    Approval, trustees, **9:1931**
    Effective date,
        Donation inter vivos, **9:1935**
        Donation mortis causa, **9:1936**
    Form, **9:1932**
    Modification, termination, rescission or revocation of trust, **9:1934**
    Refusal by beneficiary, **9:1989**
    Revocation or rescission, **9:2046**
    Rights of person adding property, **9:1933**
Administration in interest of beneficiary, **9:2082**
Administrative matters, saving clause, **9:2252**
Advance of trust money, charge on beneficiary's interest, **9:2195**
Adverse claim to transfer of stock by trustee, **9:3835**
Affidavits, attesting witnesses, **9:1752**
Affiliate, definitions, **9:1725**
Alienation by beneficiary, **9:2001 et seq.**
Alienation of legitime in trust, restraints, **9:1843**
Aliens, resident aliens, qualifications, **9:1783**
Alimony judgments, seizure of beneficiary's interest, **9:2005**
Allocations to income and principal, **9:2141 et seq., 9:2142**
    Apportionment of receipts, right to income ceasing, **9:2147**
    Business operations of trustee, **9:2151**
    Corporate distributions, **9:2149**
    Depletion, property subject to, **9:2154**
    Distinction between income and principal, **9:2144**
    Inventory value, definitions, **9:2157**
    Naked ownership, beneficiary, **9:2143**
    Prudent man rule, usufruct and naked ownership of beneficiaries, **9:2143**
    Right to income,
        Apportionment of receipts, **9:2146**
        Time arising, **9:2145**
    Succession receipts, **9:2148**
    Timber, **9:2153**
    Underproductive property, **9:2155**
    Use of beneficiaries, **9:2143**
Amendment, incorporation in trust instrument, **9:1754**
Amortization of bond premium, allocation to income or principal, **9:2150**
Annual accounting, **9:2088**
Annual exclusion, federal gift tax, **9:1937**
Annuity trusts,
    Accumulated income or principal, payment, **9:2068**
    Invasion of principal, **9:1952**
    Mixed trust, **9:1951**
Appeals, appointment or removal, **9:1791**
Appointment of trustee, **9:1785, 9:1786**
    Appeal, **9:1791**
    Failure of trustee to accept, **9:1785, 9:1824**
    Provisional trustee, **9:1786**
Apportionment of receipts, right to income ceasing, **9:2147**
Approval of trustee's account, **9:2088**
Arbitration, claims affecting trust property, **9:2121**

TRUSTS AND TRUSTEES—Cont'd
Ascertainment of beneficiaries, deferred ascertainment, **9:2011 et seq.**
Associations and societies, tort liability, **9:2792**
Attachment of powers to office of trustee, **9:2112**
Attorneys, **9:2241**
Audits and auditing, public trusts, **9:2346**
Balancing losses against gains, **9:2203**
Bank deposits and collections, **9:2095**
    Federal Deposit Insurance Corporation, security requirements, **9:2095**
Banks and banking,
    Charitable trustee, authority to act, **9:2273**
    Qualification to act as trustee, **9:1783**
    Transfers, fiduciary accounts, **9:2130**
Beneficiaries,
    Absolute interest in income, **9:1961**
    Acceptance of benefit, **9:1808**
    Accumulated income, **9:1964**
    Actions by or against, **9:2191 et seq.**
        Remedy against trustee, **9:2221**
    Addition of property, refusal, **9:1989**
    Administration in interest of, **9:2082**
    Alienation, **9:2001 et seq.**
    Allocation of receipts and expenditures, **9:2141 et seq.**
    Annual accounting by trustee, **9:2088**
    Approval of trustee's account, **9:2088**
    Attorney, selection, **9:2241**
    Causes of action, **9:2231**
    Charge on interest, advance of loan of trust money, **9:2195**
    Class trusts, generally, post
    Concurrent beneficiaries, **9:1806**
    Conditional interest,
        Beneficiaries rights conditioned on surviving settlor, **9:2011**
        Income, **9:1961**
    Conditions attached to refusal of interest, **9:1985**
    Consent to termination, **9:2028**
    Death, **9:1831, 9:1833, 9:1964**
        Intestacy, shifting interest, **9:1973, 9:1978**
        Principal beneficiary, **9:1972**
        Status of potential substitute principal beneficiary, **9:1979**
    Debtors and creditors,
        Accepting refused interest, **9:1982**
        Testamentary trust, **9:1983**
        Seizure of interest, **9:2004 et seq.**
    Definitions, **9:1801**
    Designation,
        Person in whose favor refusal operates, **9:1988**
        Sufficiency, **9:1802**
    Disclaiming interest, **9:1985**
    Distribution of income, **9:1962**
    Effect of refusal of interest, trustees, **9:1990**
    Encumbrance of interest, **9:2001**
    Enforcing right of trust estate, **9:2222**
    Estate tax apportionment, **9:2431 et seq.**
    Exemption from seizure, **9:2006**
    Form, transfer or encumbrance of interest, **9:2003**
    Governmental subdivisions, **9:2341 et seq.**
    Income beneficiaries, **9:1961 et seq.**
        Definitions, **9:1725**
        Several beneficiaries, **9:1805**
        Successive beneficiaries, **9:1807**
    Indemnity of trustee, **9:2193**
    Information, request to trustee, **9:2089**

INDEX TO TITLE 9

TRUSTS AND TRUSTEES—Cont'd
Beneficiaries—Cont'd
    Injunctions against trustee or settlor, 9:2232
    Instructions, application to court, 9:2233
    Interdicts, investments, 9:2066
    Interest of beneficiary, 9:1961 et seq.
        Beneficiaries interest conditioned on surviving settlor, 9:2011
        Custodial trusts, 9:2260.6
        Principal beneficiary, 9:1971, 9:1972
    Intervention,
        Action on to trustee's contract, 9:2125
        Tort actions, 9:2126
    Invasion of principal to benefit, 9:2067, 9:2068
    Life policy, beneficiary as trustee, 9:1881
    Manner of refusing interest, 9:1985
    Municipalities, 9:2341 et seq.
    Obligations, partial termination, liability, 9:2029
    Parishes, 9:2341 et seq.
    Partial refusal of interest, 9:1988
    Partial termination, liability for obligations, 9:2029
    Person in being and ascertainable, 9:1803
    Political subdivisions, 9:2341 et seq.
    Prescription, action against trustee, 9:2234
    Presumption of acceptance, 9:1808
    Principal beneficiary, 9:1971, 9:1972
        Death, intestate, substitute beneficiary, 9:1973, 9:1978
        Deferred ascertainment, 9:2011 et seq.
        Definitions, 9:1725
        Several beneficiaries, 9:1805
        Status of potential substitute principal beneficiary, 9:1979
        Termination of income beneficiary interest, 9:1965
    Public trusts, 9:2341 et seq.
    Refusal of interest, 9:1981 et seq.
    Relief of trustees, 9:2063
        Liability, 9:2207
    Remedies against trustee, 9:2221
    Renunciation of settlor's succession, 9:1985
    Representative, beneficiary incapable of contracting, refusal of interest, 9:1981
    Reservation of right to revoke interest, 9:2042
    Resignation of trustee, notice, 9:1788
    Restraint upon alienation, 9:2002
    Retroactive refusal of interest, 9:1986
    Revocation or rescission of trusts, obligations, personal liability, 9:2046
    Right to income, time arising, 9:2145
    Separate beneficiaries, 9:1805
    Settlor as beneficiary, 9:1804
    Several beneficiaries, 9:1805
    Sole income beneficiary,
        Refusal of trust, 9:1990
        Termination of interest, 9:1965
    Spendthrift trust, effect of use of words, 9:2007
    State, 9:2341 et seq.
    Substitute beneficiaries, intestate death of principal beneficiary, 9:1973, 9:1978
        Status of potential substitute principal beneficiary, 9:1979
    Substitution of settlor or heirs as beneficiary of principal, 9:1990
    Successive income beneficiaries, 9:1807
    Sufficiency of designation, 9:1802
    Summary proceedings against trustee or settlor, 9:2231
    Surviving income beneficiary, definitions, 9:1835

TRUSTS AND TRUSTEES—Cont'd
Beneficiaries—Cont'd
    Termination, interest of income beneficiary, 9:1965
    Testamentary trusts, post
    Transfer of interest, 9:2001
Bonds,
    Allocation to income or principal, 9:2150
    Issuance, 9:2347
    Official, trustees, 9:2171 et seq.
    Sales, 9:2085
    Trustee purchasing bonds from self, 9:2086
Bonds (officers and fiduciaries), custodial trusts, 9:2260.13, 9:2260.14
Borrowing, credit of trust estate, 9:2120
Breach of trust, 9:2081, 9:2201
    Balancing losses against gains, 9:2203
    Compensation of trustee, 9:2182
    Cotrustees, 9:2096, 9:2205
        Excuse for failure to prevent, 9:2114
    Definitions, 9:2081
    Enjoining trustee, 9:2221
    Excuse for failure to prevent, 9:2114
    Extent to which trustee liable, 9:2201
    Relief of trustee from liability, 9:2208
    Successor trustee, liability, 9:2204
Business operation, trustees, 9:2151
Certificates of deposit, sales, 9:2085
Charge on beneficiary's interest,
    Advance or loan of trust money, 9:2195
    Indemnification of trustee, 9:2194
Charging income and principal payments against beneficiary's share, 9:2068
Charitable, benevolent or eleemosynary trusts, 9:2271 et seq.
    Board of trustees,
        Corporate body, succession, duration, powers, 9:2275
    Conditions, 9:2271
    Corporate trustee, 9:2273
    Cy pres doctrine, 9:2331 et seq.
    Definitions, 9:2281
    Donations, 9:2271
        Administration and objects, prescribing, 9:2274
    Donor prescribing manner of administering, 9:2274
    Duration, 9:2291 et seq.
    Federal taxation, amendment of governing instrument to avoid, 9:2283
    Incorporation, 9:2275
    Intent, perpetual duration, 9:2295
    Jurisdiction to effect purpose of trust or will, 9:2331
    Local beneficiary, definitions, 9:2281
    Majority of beneficiaries, definitions, 9:2281
    Mixed private and charitable trust, 9:1951
        Charitable trust acting as trustee, 9:1783
    Objects, donor to prescribe, 9:2274
    Perpetual duration, 9:2291 et seq.
    Procedure to effectuate purpose of trust or will, 9:2331 et seq.
    Property, requirement of alienability, 9:2274
    Purposes, 9:2271
    Regulations governing trustees, authority to prescribe, 9:2272
    Removal of trustees, 9:2282
    Sale of property, donor to prescribe manner, 9:2274
    Substitutions, law relating to inapplicable, 9:2279
    Term, exception, 9:1834
    Tort liability, 9:2792
    Trust, definitions, 9:2281

INDEX TO TITLE 9

TRUSTS AND TRUSTEES—Cont'd
Charitable, benevolent or eleemosynary trusts—Cont'd
    Trust dispositions, law relating to inapplicable, 9:2279
Check upon deposit in name of two or more trustees, duties of bank and holder, 9:3810
Choice of law, custodial trusts, 9:2260.19
Citizenship of trustee, 9:1783
Class trusts, 9:1891 et seq.
    Adoption, members, 9:1892
    Closing of class, 9:1896
        Continuance of trust, 9:1901
        Death, before, 9:1900, 9:1903
        Termination of trust, 9:1902
    Continuation of trust, 9:1902
    Creation of class, 9:1891
    Death, 9:1900 et seq.
        Before creation of trust, representation by descendants, 9:1894
            Representation upon predecease of principal beneficiary, 9:1202
        Intestate succession, 9:1895
        Last surviving member of class, 9:1901
        Member of class during term of trust, 9:1895
        Principal beneficiary, class as substitute beneficiary, 9:1977
        Status of potential substitute principal beneficiary, 9:1979
    Descendant of child or grandchild, representation, 9:1202, 9:1894
    Distribution of income, 9:1899
        Class closing without members, 9:1900
        Stipulations by settlor, 9:1963
    Effect on legitime, 9:1841
    Income and principal beneficiaries, 9:1904, 9:1905
    Income designation, 9:1893
    Interest in income beneficiaries of both income and principal, 9:1905
    Intestate member of class without descendants, 9:1895
    Invasion, principal and income, 9:1893
    Lapse of period of enjoyment before closing of class, 9:1903
    Members,
        Blood or adoption, 9:1892
        Different classes, 9:1904 et seq.
    Possibility of admitting other members of class, 9:1896
    Principal beneficiary's death, 9:1972
        Status of potential substitute principal beneficiary, 9:1979
    Principal, designation, 9:1893
    Representation, descendant of child or grandchild, 9:1894
        Upon predecease of principal beneficiary, 9:1202
    Term of trust, 9:1897, 9:1898, 9:1906
        Exception, 9:1834
        Stipulation of excessive term, 9:1898
    Termination of trust, 9:1902
Classification of trust, 9:1732, 9:1735
    Exclusion from classification as immovable property, 9:1111
Clearing corporations, corporate trustee, deposits, securities, 9:2129
Closing of class. Class trusts, ante
Co-trustees, 9:2096
    Breach of trust, 9:2114, 9:2205
    Excuse for inactivity in administering trust, 9:2114
    Exercise of power, 9:2113
Combination, 9:2030

TRUSTS AND TRUSTEES—Cont'd
Commercial paper. Negotiable Instruments, this index
Common trust fund, investments, 9:2128
Community of acquets and gains, division of spousal property, 9:1955
    Principal beneficiary, deferred ascertainment, 9:2014
Compensation and salaries, 9:2181, 9:2182
    Charges against income and principal, 9:2156
    Custodial trusts, 9:2260.14
Compromise of claims, 9:2121
Concurrence of settlors, revocation, 9:2044
Concurrent beneficiaries, 9:1806
Conditional interest in income, beneficiary, 9:1961
Conditions, 9:1736
    Custodial trusts, 9:2260.3
    Interest of beneficiary, 9:1961
        Beneficiaries rights conditioned on surviving settlor, 9:2011
    Refusal of interest by beneficiary, 9:1985
Consent to termination, 9:2028
Construction of code, 9:1724
Construction of trust instrument, 9:1753
    Custodial trusts, 9:2260.2
Contracts,
    Actions by trustee, 9:2125
    Custodial trusts,
        Designations, 9:2260.3
        Trustee liability, 9:2260.12
Control of trust property, 9:2091
Corporate distributions,
    Allocation to income and principal, 9:2149
    Apportionment of receipts, 9:2146, 9:2147
Corporate trustees,
    Charitable, etc., trust, 9:2273
    Deposits in own banking department, 9:2095
    Loans, purchases or sales to self, 9:2084 et seq.
    Mutual funds, investments, 9:2086
    Securities, deposits, clearing corporation, 9:2129
    Security, 9:2171
    Self-dealing, 9:2086
Corporations,
    Charitable trusts. Charitable, benevolent or eleemosynary trusts, ante
    Dividends, corporate distribution, 9:2149
    Incorporation, 9:2275
    Removal, 9:1789
    Sale to self, 9:2085
    Trustee as officer in corporation in which funds are invested, 9:2097
    Trustees, acting as incorporator, 9:2123
Creation, 9:1731 et seq., 9:1822
    Class trust, 9:1891
    Custodial trusts, 9:2260.2, 9:2260.18
    Testamentary trust, 9:1821
Crimes and offenses, seizure of beneficiary's interest, 9:2005
Custodial trusts, 9:2260.1 et seq.
    Acceptance, 9:2260.4
    Accounts and accounting,
        Multiple beneficiaries, 9:2260.6
        Multiple party accounts, designations, 9:2260.3
        Trustees, 9:2260.15
    Actions and proceedings, trustee liability, 9:2260.12
    Application of law, 9:2260.19
    Augmentation, 9:2260.2
    Bonds (officers and fiduciaries), 9:2260.13, 9:2260.14
    Choice of law, 9:2260.19
    Compensation and salaries, 9:2260.14

INDEX TO TITLE 9

TRUSTS AND TRUSTEES—Cont'd
Custodial trusts—Cont'd
    Conditions, **9:2260.3**
    Construction of trust instrument, **9:2260.2**
    Contracts,
        Designations, **9:2260.3**
        Trustee liability, **9:2260.12**
    Creation, **9:2260.2**
    Deeds, designations, **9:2260.3**
    Designation, recipient and transfer, **9:2260.3**
    Distribution of property, **9:2260.9**
    Durable powers of attorney, **9:2260.7**
    Duties of trustee, **9:2260.7**
    Expenses and expenditures, trustee, **9:2260.14**
    Forms,
        Acceptance, **9:2260.4**
        Creation, **9:2260.18**
        Execution, **9:2260.18**
    Incapacity, **9:2260.10**
    Interruption and suspension, **9:2260.16**
    Jurisdiction of trustee, **9:2260.4**
    Mandates, **9:2260.7**
    Multiple beneficiaries, **9:2260.6**
    Multiple party accounts, designations, **9:2260.3**
    Notice, trustee resignation, **9:2260.13**
    Obligors, transfers to trustee, **9:2260.5**
    Payments, transfers to trustee, **9:2260.5**
    Power of appointment, **9:2260.3**
    Powers of trustee, **9:2260.8**
    Prescription, **9:2260.16**
    Quasi offenses, trustee liability, **9:2260.12**
    Receipt and acceptance, **9:2260.4**
    Records and recordation, trust property, **9:2260.7**
    Removal of trustee, **9:2260.13**
    Reports, **9:2260.15**
        Custodial trusts, **9:2260.15**
    Resignation of trustee, **9:2260.13**
    Right of survivorship, **9:2260.6**
    Standard of care, trustee, **9:2260.7**
    Substitute trustees, **9:2260.3, 9:2260.13**
    Successor trustee, **9:2260.2, 9:2260.3, 9:2260.13**
    Termination, **9:2260.2, 9:2260.17**
        Distribution, **9:2260.17**
    Third persons, exemption from liability, **9:2260.11**
    Title to property, **9:2260.2**
    Transfers to trustee, **9:2260.5**
    Trustee liability, **9:2260.12**
    Use of property, **9:2260.9**
    Wills, designations, **9:2260.3**
Cy pres doctrine, **9:2331 et seq.**
Dealings on own account, trustees, **9:2083**
Death,
    Addition to trust property, effective date, **9:1936**
    Beneficiary, **9:1831, 9:1833, 9:1964**
    Last income beneficiary, termination of trust, **9:1833**
    Principal beneficiary, vesting of interest in substitute beneficiary, **9:1972 et seq.**
        Status of potential substitute principal beneficiary, **9:1979**
Decrease of trustee's security, **9:2173**
Deeds, custodial trusts, designations, **9:2260.3**
Defense of actions by trustee, **9:2093**
Deferred ascertainment of principal beneficiaries, **9:2011 et seq.**
Definitions, **9:1731**
    Annual exclusion, federal gift tax, **9:1937**
    Custodial trusts, **9:2260.1**

TRUSTS AND TRUSTEES—Cont'd
Definitions—Cont'd
    Inter vivos trusts, **9:1734**
    Trustee, **9:1781**
Delegation of authority, **9:975**
    Right to revoke, **9:2045**
    Termination or modification, **9:2025**
Deposits in banks, **9:2095**
Designation,
    Attorney, **9:2241**
    Beneficiary, **9:1802**
    Person in whose favor refusal of interest operates, **9:1988**
    Property of trust, **9:2094**
    Trustee, **9:1785**
Deviations by trustee,
    Code, **9:2065**
    Trust provisions, **9:2064, 9:2066**
Diminution, trustees bond, **9:2173**
Disclaiming of interest, beneficiaries, manner, **9:1985**
Discretion of trustee, **9:1961**
    Control, **9:2115**
    Distribution of income, **9:1963**
    Invading principal and income, **9:2068**
Disposition containing substitution, authorization, **9:1723**
Dispositions permitted, **9:1737**
Dissenting trustee, liability, **9:2114**
Distribution of income, **9:1962, 9:1963**
    Class trusts, ante
    Direction to trustee, **9:1961**
    Discretion of trustee, **9:1963**
    Stipulation by settlor, **9:1963**
Distribution of property, custodial trusts, **9:2260.9**
Distributions, power to adjust, **9:2158 et seq.**
Division of trusts, trustee powers, **9:2030**
Domicile or residence of trustee, **9:1783**
Donations for charitable purposes, **9:2271 et seq., 9:2290**
    Application of Louisiana Trust Code, **9:274**
    Governing instrument,
        Contents, **9:2283**
    Perpetual duration, **9:2290**
    Termination of small trusts, **9:2271**
    Trust enforcement, **9:2275**
    Trustees, **9:2272**
    Who may be trustee, **9:2273**
Donations mortis causa,
    Additions to trust property, **9:1733, 9:1931, 9:1936**
    Capacity to make, settlor of testamentary trust, **9:1764**
    Form of testamentary trust, **9:1751**
Donations. Charitable, benevolent or eleemosynary trusts, ante
Durable powers of attorney, custodial trusts, **9:2260.7**
Duration, **9:2291 et seq.**
Duties and powers, **9:2061 et seq.**
Duties of trustee, custodial trusts, **9:2260.7**
Effective date,
    Creation, **9:1821 et seq.**
    Donation inter vivos, **9:1935**
    Donation mortis causa, **9:1936**
    Modification, termination or revocation, **9:2051**
    Principal beneficiary's interest, acquisition, **9:1971**
Electronic transactions, exemptions, **9:2603**
Eleemosynary trusts. Charitable, benevolent or eleemosynary trusts, generally, ante
Employees,
    Trust for, **9:1921, 9:1922**

INDEX TO TITLE 9

TRUSTS AND TRUSTEES—Cont'd
Employees—Cont'd
    Trustee as officer of legal entity in which funds invested, **9:2097**
Estate Tax Apportionment Law, **9:2431 through 2439**
    Action by nonresident, reciprocity, **9:2437**
    Action to recover amount of tax or deficiency from person interested in estate, **9:2436**
        Time of filing, liability of fiduciary, **9:2436**
    Allowance for exemptions, deductions and credits, **9:2435**
    Application of provisions, **9:2438**
    Apportionment of tax liability among persons interested in estate, **9:2432**
    Fiduciary right to withhold or recover proportion of tax attributable to person interested in estate, **9:2434**
    Security by person interested in estate for payment of tax, **9:2434**
Estate Tax Apportionment Law, **9:2431 et seq.**
Ex parte proceedings, trustees, court instructions, **9:2233**
Exceptions, term of trust, **9:1834**
Execution, custodial trusts, **9:2260.18**
Exemptions,
    Electronic transactions, **9:2603**
    Public trusts, gaming operations, **9:2341**
Exoneration,
    Court instructions issued in ex parte proceedings, **9:2233**
    Trustee liable for torts, **9:2126**
Expenses and expenditures, **9:2117, 9:2191**
    Allocation, **9:2117, 9:2141**
    Beneficiaries, invasion of principal, **9:2067**
    Charges against income or principal, **9:2156**
    Custodial trusts, **9:2260.14**
    Indemnity, **9:2191, 9:2192**
    Not properly incurred, indemnity, **9:2192**
Express disposition, application of law, **9:1724**
Express private trust, authorization, **9:1722**
Extent of powers, **9:2111**
Extracts, trust instruments, recording, immovables, **9:2092**
Failure of trust,
    Refusal of entire interest in trust, **9:1990**
    Revocation or rescission, **9:2046**
Federal Deposit Insurance Corporation, bank deposits, security requirements, **9:2095**
Federal gift tax, annual exclusion, **9:1937**
Fees and charges,
    Charges against income, **9:2156**
    Indemnification of trustee, **9:2194**
Filing,
    Foreign trusts, **9:2262.1**
    Trustee's accounts with court, **9:2088**
Final accounts of trustee, **9:2088**
Financial institutions, **9:1783**
Financial statements, public trusts, **9:2346**
Foreign states, custodial trusts, **9:2260.19**
Foreign trusts, **9:2262.1 et seq.**
Forms,
    Addition of property, **9:1932**
    Custodial trusts, ante
    Inter vivos trust, **9:1752**
Gains, balancing losses against, **9:2203**
Gift tax, federal gift tax, annual exclusion, **9:1937**
Good morals, trusts or dispositions against, **9:1736**
Governmental subdivisions, beneficiaries, **9:2341 et seq.**
Gratuitous disposition, revocation, **9:2043**
Gratuitous trust, **9:1735, 9:1763**
Illegality of accomplishment, termination or modification, **9:2027**

TRUSTS AND TRUSTEES—Cont'd
Immovables,
    Classification of interest in trust, **9:1111**
    Forbidding sale, **9:2119**
    Foreign trusts, filing, **9:2262.2**
    Public trusts, **9:2341 et seq.**
    Real rights created for benefit of organization, **9:1252**
    Recordation of instruments, **9:2092**
Implied disposition, **9:1724**
Incapacitated beneficiaries, custodial trusts, **9:2260.10**
Incidents of ownership, reservation by settlor, life insurance policy, **9:1881**
Income,
    Accumulated income,
        Payment, income interest in termination, **9:1964**
        Standards for payment, **9:2068**
    Adjustments, **9:2158 et seq.**
    Allocations, **9:2142**
    Allocations to, **9:1961, 9:2141 et seq.**
    Charges against, **9:2156**
    Class trust, **9:1893, 9:1899, 9:1900**
    Distinguished from principal, **9:2144**
    Legitime in trust, **9:1844**
    Principal beneficiary, **9:1971, 9:1972**
    Time right to arises, **9:2145**
Incompetence of trustee, **9:1785**
Incorporation, **9:2275**
Incorporation by reference, **9:1754**
Incorporator acting as trustee, **9:2123**
Increase, trustee's security, **9:2173**
Increment in value of bond or other obligation, income, **9:2150**
Indefinite term, employees benefit trust, **9:1922**
Indemnity, trustees, **9:2191 et seq.**
Information to beneficiary, **9:2089**
Injunctions, **9:2232**
    Breach of trust, **9:2221**
Institutional funds, investments, **9:2337.1 et seq.**
Instructions by court, trustees, **9:2233**
Insurance, this index
Interest in property, beneficiary, **9:1961 et seq.**
Interpretation, **9:1753**
    Instructions from court, **9:2233**
Interruption and suspension, custodial trusts, **9:2260.16**
Invalidity of provisions, **9:2251**
Invasion, class trusts, income and principal, **9:1893**
Invasion of principal,
    Accumulated income, beneficiary, **9:2068**
    Court action, **9:2067**
    Legitime in trust, **9:1847**
    Mixed trust, **9:1952**
    Trust provisions, **9:2068**
Investments,
    Banks or savings and loan association, **9:2097**
    Charges against principal, **9:2156**
    Common trust funds, **9:2128**
    Delegation of authority, **9:975**
    Deviation, **9:2066**
    Other fiduciary funds in common trust, **9:2128**
    Power to adjust, **9:2158 et seq.**
    Prudent persons, **9:2127**
    Standard of care, **9:2127**
    Trust provisions, **9:2066**
    Trustee as officer of corporation in which funds invested, **9:2097**
Involuntary alienation by beneficiary, restraint subject to limitations, **9:2002**

INDEX TO TITLE 9

TRUSTS AND TRUSTEES—Cont'd
Joinder of settlors, trust for employees, **9:1921**
Joint venture, trustees, **9:2123**
Judgments,
    Action on contracts, **9:2125**
    Appointing or removing trustee, **9:1791**
Judicial permission, trustee, deviations, **9:2064, 9:2065**
    Investment provisions of trust, **9:2066**
Jurisdiction, **9:1784**
    Custodial trusts, **9:2260.4**
Labor and Employment, this index
Language used, **9:1753**
Law governing, class trust,
    Beneficiaries of both income and principal, **9:1905**
    Beneficiaries of income and beneficiaries of principal, **9:1904**
Leases, **9:2118**
    Allocation of proceeds to income or principal, **9:2152**
Legal term, trusts stipulating longer than legal term, enforcement, **9:1832**
Legitime in trust, **9:1841**
    Burdened with income interest or usufruct, **9:1844**
    Distribution of income, stipulations by settlor, **9:1963**
    Effect of class trust, **9:1841**
    Forced heirs, **9:1841**
    Incompatible trust provisions, reformation to comply, **9:1842**
    Invasion of principal, **9:1847**
        Exception, **9:2068**
    Payment to beneficiary depriving another beneficiary, **9:1847**
    Restraints upon alienation, **9:1843**
    Surviving spouse, interest or usufruct, **9:1844**
        Security, form, **9:1202**
Liability of trustees, **9:2201 et seq.**
    Contracts, **9:2125**
    Custodial trusts, **9:2260.12**
    Nonjoining trustee in exercising power, **9:2114**
    Stock held in name of nominee, lost trust, **9:2124**
Liberal construction, code, **9:1724**
Life insurance beneficiary, trustees, **9:1881**
Life interest, income beneficiary, **9:1961**
Limitation, trust term, **9:1831**
Limitation of trustee duties by settlor, **9:2062**
Limited liability companies, powers, **9:2123**
Loans,
    Charge on beneficiary's interest, **9:2195**
    Trustee to self, **9:2084**
Losses,
    Balancing against gains, **9:2203**
    Business operations by trustees, **9:2151**
    Not resulting from breach of trust, liability of trustee, **9:2202**
Maintenance judgments, seizure of beneficiary's interest, **9:2005**
Maintenance of beneficiary, invasion of principal, **9:2067, 9:2068**
Majority of trustees, exercise of powers, **9:2114**
Management,
    Fees, common trust funds, **9:2128**
    Standard of care, **9:2127**
Mandates,
    Custodial trusts, **9:2260.7**
    Revocation, **9:2088**
Marital portion, succession and succession proceeding, trust as satisfying, **9:1851 et seq.**
Medical expenses, invasion of principal, **9:2067, 9:2068**

TRUSTS AND TRUSTEES—Cont'd
Mixed trust,
    Invasion of principal, **9:1952**
    Trustees, nonprofit corporations or trusts for educational, charitable or religious purposes acting as, **9:1783**
Modification, **9:2021 et seq.**
    Adding property, **9:1934**
    Change of circumstances, **9:2026**
    Concurrence of settlors, **9:2024**
    Copy of act, **9:2051**
    Delegation of rights, **9:2025**
    Express reservation of right, **9:2021**
    Form, **9:2051**
    Illegality or impossibility of accomplishment, **9:2027**
    New trust, **9:1754**
    Power of attorney, military personnel, **9:3884**
    Reservation,
        Life insurance policy, **9:1881**
        Right to revoke, **9:2022**
        Unrestricted right to modify, **9:2023, 9:2041**
Monopolies and Unfair Trade, generally, this index
Mortgages, **9:2120**
    Fiduciary as mortgagee in trust for creditors, **9:5302**
    Securing obligations, not governed by law relating to trust dispositions, **9:5307**
Multiple beneficiaries, custodial trusts, **9:2260.6**
Multiple party accounts, custodial trusts, designations, **9:2260.3**
Municipalities, beneficiaries, **9:2341 et seq.**
Necessaries, creditor's seizure of beneficiary's interest, **9:2005**
Obligations,
    Beneficiaries personal liability, partial termination, **9:2029**
    Revocation or rescission of trusts, personal liability, beneficiary, **9:2046**
Obligors, custodial trusts, transfers to trustee, **9:2260.5**
Officers and employees,
    Trust for, **9:1921, 9:1922**
    Trustee as officer of legal entity in which funds invested, **9:2097**
Onerous disposition, revocation, **9:2043**
Onerous trust, **9:1735**
Order, appointing or removing trustee, appeal, **9:1791**
Partial refusal of interest by beneficiary, **9:1988**
Partial revocation, **9:2041**
Partial termination, **9:2029**
Partnership member, trustee, **9:2123**
Payments, custodial trusts, transfers to trustee, **9:2260.5**
Person,
    Definitions, **9:1725**
    In being and ascertainable, beneficiary, **9:1803**
Personal liability of trustee, **9:2193**
    Tort liability, **9:2196**
Pledge of trust property, **9:2120**
Political subdivisions, beneficiaries, **9:2341 et seq.**
Power of appointment, custodial trusts, **9:2260.3**
Powers of trustees, **9:2111 et seq.**
    Adjustments, **9:2158 et seq.**
    Custodial trusts, **9:2260.8**
    Revocation or rescission, **9:2046**
    Winding up, trust property, **9:2069**
Predecessor trustee, breach of trust committed by, **9:2204**
Prescription,
    Action by beneficiary, **9:2234**
    Custodial trusts, **9:2260.16**
    Interruption and suspension, custodial trusts, **9:2260.16**

INDEX TO TITLE 9

TRUSTS AND TRUSTEES—Cont'd
Preservation of trust property, **9:2091**
Presumptions, benefit acceptance by beneficiary, **9:1808**
Principal,
    Accumulated principal, standards for payment, **9:2068**
    Adjustments, **9:2158 et seq.**
    Allocations to, **9:1961, 9:2141 et seq.**
    Charges against, **9:2156**
    Class trusts, **9:1893**
    Designation, **9:1893**
    Distinguished from income, **9:2144**
Prior laws, saving clause, **9:2252**
Private trust, express private trust, authorization, **9:1722**
Proper court, **9:2235**
    Definitions, **9:1725**
Provisional principal beneficiaries, revocable trusts, **9:2012**
Provisional trustee, **9:1786, 9:1787**
Provisions incompatible with legitime in trust, reformation, **9:1842**
Proxy vote, trusts, **9:2122**
Prudent administration, **9:2090**
    Allocation to beneficiaries of usufruct and naked ownership, **9:2143**
    Business operations by trustees, **9:2151**
    Investment and management, **9:2127**
    Timber, allocations to income or principal, **9:2153**
Public order, trust or disposition against, **9:1736**
Public trusts, **9:2341 et seq.**
    Amendment of trust, **9:2342**
    Annual operating budget, **9:2346**
    Auditing, **9:2346**
    Beneficiaries, **9:2341 et seq.**
    Bonds (officers and fiduciaries), **9:2343**
    Creation, **9:2341**
    Financial statements, **9:2346**
    Investments, obligations of trusts, **9:2341**
    Method of creation, **9:2342**
    Number of trustees, **9:2343**
    Oath of office, **9:2343**
    Obligations, issuance, **9:2341**
    Per diem, **9:2343**
    Powers and duties, **9:2341, 9:2343**
    Sworn financial statements, **9:2346**
    Termination, **9:2345**
    Tort liability, **9:2344**
Purchase by trustee from self, **9:2086**
Purpose for which created, **9:2271 et seq.**
Qualifications, trustees, **9:1783**
Quasi offenses, **9:2126, 9:2792**
    Custodial trusts, trustee liability, **9:2260.12**
    Indemnity of trustees, **9:2196**
    Liability, **9:2792**
        Nonprofit organizations, directors, officers or trustees, **9:2792.1**
    Seizure of beneficiary's interest, **9:2005**
Receipt and acceptance, custodial trusts, form, **9:2260.4**
Records and recordation,
    Common trust funds, **9:2128**
    Custodial trusts, ante
    Ownership of stock held in name of nominee, **9:2124**
    Trust instruments, **9:2092**
Reduced compensation, trustees, breach of trust, **9:2182**
Reformation,
    Provisions incompatible with legitime in trust, **9:1842**
    Provisions incompatible with marital portion, **9:1854**
Refusal of interest by beneficiary, **9:1981 et seq.**
Reimbursement, trustee liable for tort, **9:2126**

TRUSTS AND TRUSTEES—Cont'd
Relative, definitions, **9:1725**
Relief of trustee,
    Duties, **9:2063**
    Liability, beneficiary relieving, **9:2207**
Religious Organizations and Societies, this index
Removal of trustee, **9:1789, 9:1790**
    Accounting, **9:2088**
    Appeal, **9:1791**
    Beneficiary's remedy, **9:2221**
    Custodial trusts, **9:2260.13**
    Invalidation of trust, **9:1785**
    Officer of corporation in which trust funds invested, **9:2097**
    Winding up, powers and duties, **9:2069**
Renunciation, settlor's succession, testamentary trust, **9:1985**
Reports of trustee, ownership of stock held in name of nominee, **9:2124**
Rescission, **9:2043**
    Accounting by trustee, **9:2088**
    Addition of property, **9:1934**
    Obligations, liability, beneficiary, **9:2046**
    Onerous disposition, **9:2043**
    Stipulating effect, **9:2046**
Reservation,
    Life insurance policy, **9:1881**
    Modify trust, **9:2021, 9:2023**
    Revocation of trust, **9:2022, 9:2041, 9:2042**
        Concurrence of settlors, **9:2044**
Resident aliens, qualifications, **9:1783**
Resignation of trustee, **9:1788, 9:1790**
    Accounting, **9:2088**
    Custodial trusts, **9:2260.13**
    Winding up, powers and duties, **9:2069**
Restraint on alienation,
    Beneficiary, **9:2002**
    Designation of person in whose favor refusal operates, **9:1988**
    Legitime in trust, **9:1843**
Restrictions, right to make additions, **9:1931**
Retroactive acceptance by trustee, **9:1823**
Retroactive refusal of interest by beneficiary, **9:1986**
Reversion, settlor or heirs, effect of revocation or rescission, **9:2046**
Revocation, **9:2041 et seq.**
    Accounting by trustee, **9:2088**
    Addition of property, **9:1934**
    Beneficiaries, obligations, personal liability, **9:2046**
    Concurrence of settlors, **9:2044**
    Copy of act, **9:2051**
    Deferred ascertainment of principal beneficiaries, **9:2011 et seq.**
    Delegation of right, **9:2045**
    Effect on trustee's powers, **9:2046**
    Form, **9:2051**
    Gratuitous disposition, **9:2043**
    Obligations, beneficiaries, personal liability, **9:2046**
    Power of attorney, military personnel, **9:3884**
    Reservation,
        Power by settlor, life insurance policy, **9:1881**
        Right to revoke, **9:2022, 9:2041, 9:2042**
        Unrestricted right to modify, **9:2023**
    Stipulating effect, **9:2046**
    Trustee,
        Notice, **9:2051**
        Winding up, powers and duties, **9:2069**
Winding up, trustees, powers and duties, **9:2069**

INDEX TO TITLE 9

TRUSTS AND TRUSTEES—Cont'd
Right of representation, class trusts, **9:1891**
Right of survivorship, custodial trusts, **9:2260.6**
Sale of trust property, **9:2119**
    Trustees, sale to self, **9:2085**
    Underproductive property, allocation to income or principal, **9:2155**
Savings clause, prior law, **9:2252**
Securities, **9:2122**
    Corporate trustees, deposits in clearing corporation, **9:2129**
    Trustees, purchase from self, **9:2086**
Security, **9:2171 et seq.**
    Appeal from judgment appointing or removing, **9:1791**
    Corporate trustee depositing in own bank, **9:2095**
    Interested party, application of, **9:2172**
    Provisional trustee, **9:1787**
    Requirement by court, **9:2172**
Seizures, trust interests of beneficiaries, creditors, **9:2004**
Self insurance, trust funds, limitation of liability, **9:2792.6**
Separate trusts, division of trust into, trustee powers, **9:2030**
Separation of trust property, **9:2094**
Settlors,
    Beneficiary, settlors as, **9:1804**
    Causes of action, **9:2231**
    Concurrence,
        Modification, **9:2024**
        Revocation, **9:2044**
    Consent to termination, **9:2028**
    Definitions, **9:1761**
    Employees benefit, joinder of several settlors, **9:1921**
    Gratuitous inter vivos trusts, **9:1763**
    Injunction against beneficiary or trustee, **9:2232**
    Instructions, application to court, **9:2233**
    Inter vivos trust, **9:1762, 9:1763**
    Modification, **9:2021 et seq.**
    Number, **9:1762**
    Onerous inter vivos trust, **9:1763**
    Refusal, stipulating effect, **9:1990**
    Revocable trusts, **9:2014**
    Stipulations,
        Distribution of income, **9:1963**
        Effect of revocation or rescission, **9:2046**
        Excessive term, class trust, **9:1898**
    Summary proceeding against beneficiary or trustee, **9:2231**
    Testamentary trust, **9:1764**
Shares and shareholders,
    Allocation of stock to income and principal, **9:2149**
    Holding in name of nominee, **9:2124**
    Income and principal payments, **9:2068**
    Powers, **9:2122, 9:2123**
    Purchasing stock from self, trustees, **9:2086**
    Registered in name of trustee as fiduciary, **9:3832**
    Subscription, **9:2123**
    Trustee, purchases from self, **9:2086**
Sole income beneficiary, termination of interest, **9:1965**
Solicitation of business for attorney, **9:2241**
Spendthrift trusts,
    Definitions, **9:1725**
    Restraint of alienation by fiduciary, **9:2007**
Spousal property division, **9:1955**
    Principal beneficiary, deferred ascertainment, **9:2014**
Standard of care,
    Custodial trusts, **9:2260.7**
    Investment and management, **9:2127**
State, beneficiary, **9:2341 et seq.**

TRUSTS AND TRUSTEES—Cont'd
Statement, investment changes, **9:2128**
Stipulated amounts, income and principal payments, **9:2068**
Stipulating effect of revocation or rescission, **9:2046**
Stipulations,
    Class trust continuance after closing of class, **9:1901**
    Excessive term, class trust, **9:1898**
    Settlors, ante
    Term, **9:1831 et seq.**
Subsequent laws, saving clause, **9:2252**
Substitute beneficiaries, death of principal beneficiary, **9:1972 et seq.**
    Status of potential substitute principal beneficiary, **9:1979**
Substitute trustees, custodial trusts, **9:2260.3, 9:2260.13**
Substitutions, **9:1737**
    Disposition containing, authorization, **9:1723**
    Settlor or heirs as beneficiary of principal, **9:1990**
Successions and Succession Proceedings, this index
Successive income beneficiaries, **9:1807**
    Division of delayed income from underproductive property, **9:2155**
Successor trustees,
    Custodial trusts, **9:2260.2, 9:2260.3, 9:2260.13**
    Liability, **9:2204**
    Manner chosen, **9:1785**
Summary proceedings,
    Against beneficiary or settlor, **9:2231**
    Provisional trustee, appointment, **9:1786**
    Seizure of beneficiary's interest, **9:2005**
Support and maintenance of judgment, seizure of beneficiary's interest, **9:2005**
Support of beneficiary, invasion of principal, **9:2067, 9:2068**
Surviving income beneficiary, definitions, **9:1835**
Taxation, charges against income or principal, **9:2156**
Term of trust,
    Absence of stipulation, **9:1833**
    Class trusts, ante
    Employees benefit trust, **9:1922**
    Exceptions, **9:1834**
    Limitations on stipulated term, **9:1831**
    Stipulating longer than legal term, **9:1832**
Termination of trust, **9:1754, 9:1831 et seq., 9:2029**
    Accounting by trustee, **9:2088**
    Addition of property, **9:1934**
    Change of circumstances, **9:2026**
    Class trust, **9:1897**
        Closing of class, **9:1902**
    Common trust funds, **9:2128**
    Consent of settlor, trustees and beneficiaries, **9:2028**
    Copy of act, **9:2051**
    Custodial trusts, **9:2260.2, 9:2260.17**
    Delegation of right, **9:2025**
    Dispositive provisions of trust achieving ultimate effect, **9:2029**
    Form, **9:2051**
    Illegality or impossibility of accomplishment, **9:2027**
    Income interest, **9:1964**
    Interest of income beneficiary, **9:1965**
    Notice, trustees, **9:2051**
    Partial termination, **9:2029**
    Reservation of unrestricted right to modify, effect, **9:2023**
    Trustee, winding up, powers and duties, **9:2069**
Testamentary trusts, **9:1732**
    Beneficiaries,
        Acceptance of interest by creditors, **9:1983**

INDEX TO TITLE 9

TRUSTS AND TRUSTEES—Cont'd
Testamentary trusts—Cont'd
    Beneficiaries—Cont'd
        Refusal of interest, 9:1983, 9:1984
        Renunciation of settlor's succession, 9:1985
    Class trusts, 9:1891 et seq.
    Classification, 9:1732
    Creation, 9:1821
    Definition, 9:1733
    Donation mortis causa, 9:1733
    Form, 9:1751
    Life insurance proceeds, 9:1881
    Settlor, 9:1764
    Time of creation, 9:1821
Third parties,
    Court instructions, 9:2233
    Custodial trusts, exemption from liability, 9:2260.11
Three or more trustees, exercise of powers, 9:2114
Time deposits, sales, 9:2085
Time, trustee acceptance of trust, 9:1824
Title to property, custodial trusts, 9:2260.2
Transfers, 9:1771
    Banks, 9:2130
    Custodial trusts, 9:2260.5
    Interest by beneficiary, 9:2001
        Form, 9:2003
    Property susceptible of private ownership, 9:1771
Trust instrument, definitions, 9:1725
Two trustees, exercise of powers, 9:2113
Unborn child, person in being and ascertainable, beneficiary status, 9:1803
Underproductive property, allocation to income or principal, 9:2155
United States obligations, issued or guaranteed by, sales, 9:2085
Unitrusts,
    Accumulated income or principal, payment, 9:2068
    Invasion of principal, 9:1952
    Mixed trust, 9:1951
Unrealized increment distributed as income out of principal, 9:2150
Unwillingness to act, trustees, 9:1785
Use of property, custodial trusts, 9:2260.9
Usufruct,
    Beneficiaries, allocation of receipts and expenditures, 9:2143
    Burdening legitime in trust with, 9:1844
    Surviving spouse, security, 9:1202
Vacancies in office of trustee, charitable trusts, 9:2275
Waiver of compensation trustees, 9:2181
Welfare of beneficiary, invasion of principal, 9:2068
Wills, custodial trusts, designations, 9:2260.3
Winding up, trustees, powers and duties, 9:2069
Withdrawals, common trust fund, 9:2128
Witnesses,
    Inter vivos trust, 9:1752
    Modification, termination or revocation, 9:2051
    Transfer or encumbrance of interest by beneficiary, 9:2003

TRUSTS FOR CHARITABLE PURPOSES
    Generally, 9:2290, 9:2321 See 9:2271 et seq.
Application of Louisiana Trust Code, 9:274
Governing instrument,
    Contents, 9:2283
Perpetual duration, 9:2290
Termination of small trust, 9:2291

TRUSTS FOR CHARITABLE PURPOSES—Cont'd
Trust enforcement, 9:2275
Trustees, 9:2272
Who may be trustee, 9:2273

TUTORS AND TUTORSHIP
    Generally, 9:601 et seq.
Absence and absentees, appointment in proceedings to sell property, 9:603
    Validation, 9:675
Adoption, signing notarial act of adoption by tutor, 9:461
Adverse claim to transfer of stock by, tutor, 9:3835
Appointment or confirmation,
    Parent's right to appoint, spouse insane, 9:601
    Without convocation of family meeting, 9:602
Assignment, stock held as fiduciary, 9:3833
Banks for cooperative, bonds, investment, 9:733
Bonds (officers and fiduciaries),
    Premium as expense, 9:3901
    Sale of property, absent minor holding undivided interest, 9:603
Costs, fees for inventory and appraisement, taxation as costs, 9:1423
Custody, provisional custody by mandate, 9:951 et seq.
Definitions,
    Custodial trusts, 9:2260.1
    Uniform Transfers to Minors Act, 9:751
Divorce, provisional custody by mandate, 9:951 et seq.
Embryos, in vitro fertilized human ovum, 9:126
Estate tax apportionment, 9:2431 et seq.
Experts, inventories, fees, 9:1423
Federal farm loan bonds, investment, 9:733
Fees, inventories, taxation as costs, 9:1423
Fiduciary capacity, 9:3801
Foreign tutorship, sale of property, minor or interdict owning undivided interest, 9:603
    Validation, 9:675
Forms, provisional custody by mandate, 9:954
Hospital charges of decedent, privilege of hospital, 9:4751 et seq.
Human embryos, in vitro fertilized human ovum, 9:126
Illegitimate children, provisional custody by mandate, 9:951 et seq.
Insanity of spouse, other parent's right to appoint, 9:601
Interdiction, this index
Interstate Compact on Juveniles, fees for, taxation as costs, 9:1423
Investments,
    Deposit of money in bank, 9:734
    Federal obligations, 9:733
Judicial sales, authority to make, 9:3001
Leases, right of way over land of ward, 9:731
Limited tutorship by nature, 9:196
Mandate,
    Military personnel, powers granted, 9:3877
    Provisional custody of children, 9:951 et seq.
Military forces, power of attorney, powers granted, 9:3877
Misconduct of tutor, surety's right to release, 9:3911, 9:3912
Natural tutors, limited tutorship by nature, 9:196
Notaries public, inventories, fees, 9:1423
Oaths and affirmations, absent minor or interdict, special representation, 9:603
Petition. Bonds (officers and fiduciaries), ante
Prescription, this index
Privileges, hospital charges against decedent, 9:4751 et seq.
Quieting title, private sale of property, 9:675
Ratification, minor interdict's sale, 9:732

I–79

TUTORS AND TUTORSHIP—Cont'd
Recognition without convocation of family meeting, **9:602**
Right of way over lands of ward, **9:731**
Sales,
    Absent minor or interdict, special representation, **9:603**
        Validation, **9:675**
    Quieting title, private sale of property, **9:675**
    Ratification by curator after interdiction of minor, **9:732**
    Right of way over land of ward, **9:731**
Securities, registration in tutor's name, **9:3832**
Separation of parents, tutorship of children, provisional custody by mandate, **9:951 et seq.**
Shares and shareholders. Corporations, this index
Signature of tutor, notarial act of adoption, child over seventeen, **9:461**
Statutory form power of attorney, military personnel, **9:3879.1**
Taxation of costs, fees for inventories, **9:1423**
Testamentary tutors,
    Spouse interdict or insane, **9:601**
    Vacating tutorship, restoration to reason of interdicted or insane parent, **9:601**
Undertutors, appointment without convocation of family meeting, **9:602**
Vacating of tutorship, appointment by other parent, restoration to sanity, **9:601**

UNBORN CHILDREN
Human embryos, in vitro fertilized human ovum, **9:121 et seq.**
Trusts, person in being and ascertainable, **9:1803**

UNCLAIMED BODIES
Burial, **9:1551, 9:1552**

UNCLAIMED PROPERTY
Uniform Unclaimed Property Act, **9:151 to 9:181**

UNIFORM FRAUDULENT TRANSFER ACT
Generally, **9:2790.1 et seq.**

UNIFORM LAWS
Custodial Trust Act, **9:2260.1 et seq.**
Fiduciaries, **9:3801 et seq.**
Fiduciary security transfers, simplification, **9:3831 et seq.**
Louisiana Military Power of Attorney Act, **9:3861 et seq.**
Management of institutional funds, **9:2337.1 et seq.**
Probate Law, **9:2421 et seq.**
Simplification of fiduciary security transfers, **9:3831 et seq.**
Transfers to minors, **9:751 et seq.**
Unclaimed Property Act, **9:151 et seq.**
Uniform Electronic Transactions Act, **9:2601 et seq.**
Uniform Fraudulent Transfer Act, **9:2790.1 et seq.**
Wills, **9:2401**

UNIFORM TRANSFERS TO MINORS ACT
    Generally, **9:751 et seq.**
Accounts and accounting, **9:769**
Annuity contracts, creating custodial property, **9:759**
Bonds (officers and fiduciaries), custodians, **9:765**
Compensation and salaries, custodians, **9:765**
Contractual rights,
    Annuities, creating custodial property, **9:759**
    Corporeal movable property, creating custodial property, **9:759**
    Immovable property, creating custodial property, **9:759**
    Movable property, creating custodial property, **9:759**

UNIFORM TRANSFERS TO MINORS ACT—Cont'd
Contractual rights—Cont'd
    Present right to future payment, creating custodial property, **9:759**
Custodial property, **9:758 et seq.**
Custodians, **9:759 et seq.**
    Jurisdiction, **9:752**
    Nomination, **9:753**
Death of custodian, successor, **9:768**
Definitions, **9:751**
Endowment contracts, creating custodial property, **9:759**
Expenses and expenditures, custodians, **9:765**
Fiduciaries, transfers by, **9:756**
Forms, **9:759**
Future rights, creating custodial property, **9:759**
Gifts, transfers by, **9:754**
Insurance, creating custodial property, **9:759**
Jurisdiction, custodianship, **9:752**
Liability,
    Custodians, **9:767, 9:769**
    Third persons, **9:766**
Life insurance, creating custodial property, **9:759**
Money, creating custodial property, **9:759**
Obligor, transfers by, **9:757**
Property, custodial property, **9:758 et seq.**
Receipt, custodial property, **9:758**
Removal of custodian, successor, **9:768**
Renunciation of custodianship, successor, **9:768**
Resignation of custodian, successor, **9:768**
Securities, creating custodial property, **9:759**
Successor custodians, **9:768**
Termination of custodianship, **9:770**
Testaments, transfers by, **9:755**

UNIFORM UNCLAIMED PROPERTY ACT
Generally, **9:151 et seq.**

UNITED STATES
Arbitration, contracts controlled by federal law, exclusion from state act, **9:4216**
Bonds and obligations, investments, tutors and curators, purchases, **9:733**
Immovables, real rights created for benefit of organization, **9:1252**
Institutional vandalism, damages, **9:2799.2**
Mortgage erasure or cancellation, service of notice, **9:5164**
Navigation, supremacy acknowledged, **9:1101**
Real rights, partition not to affect, **9:1701**
Servitudes,
    Flowage and spillway, perfecting option to United States, **9:1511**
    Partition not to affect, **9:1701**
    Spillway, perfecting option to United States, **9:1511**
Social Security, generally, this index
Waters and Watercourses, this index

UNITED STATES AGENCIES AND INSTITUTIONS
Abandoned or unclaimed property, **9:154**
Consumer credit, exemptions, **9:3560**
Mortgagees of record, cancellation or subordination of mortgage, notice, **9:5163, 9:5164**
Service of notice, recording name and address, **9:5164**

UNJUST ENRICHMENT
Remedy for the state to recover profits,
    Disclosure of fees, **9:3135**
    Legislative purpose, **9:2790.5**
    Liability for violations, **9:3134**

INDEX TO TITLE 9

UNJUST ENRICHMENT—Cont'd
Remedy for the state to recover profits—Cont'd
    Prevention of unjust enrichment, **9:2790.6**
    Profits obtained through commission of criminal offenses, **9:2790.5**

URBAN RENEWAL
Prescription, **9:5633**

USUFRUCT
Estate Tax Apportionment Law, **9:2431 through 2439**
    Action to recover amount of tax or deficiency from person interested in estate, **9:2436**
        Time of filing, liability of fiduciary, **9:2436**
    Allowance for exemptions, deductions and credits, **9:2435**
    Application of provisions, **9:2438**
    Apportionment of tax liability among persons interested in estate, **9:2432**
    No apportionment between usufructuaries and naked owners, **9:2433**
Family home, surviving spouse, **9:1201**
Maintenance, marital portion, usufruct in trust as satisfying, **9:1853**
Successions and Succession Proceedings, this index
Surviving spouse security, form, **9:1202**

USURY
Conventional interest, **9:3503 et seq.**
Exemptions, **9:3504**
Forfeiture of interest, **9:3501**
Graduated payment mortgages, application of law, **9:3504**
Loans exceeding maximum conventional rates, **9:3509**
Mortgages, this index
Purchase money mortgages, application of law, **9:3504**

VANDALISM
Institutional vandalism, damages, **9:2799.2**

VEGETABLES
Vendors, lien, exemption, **9:4544**

VENDOR'S PRIVILEGE
Assignments, registry, **9:5554**
Cancellation, **9:5167**
Definitions, collateral mortgages, **9:5550**
Priorities and preferences, wells, privileges, **9:4870, 9:4888**
Tax assessments--special, ranking, **9:4821**

VENUE
Consumer credit, **9:3511**
Covenant marriage, separation from bed and board, **9:308**
Probate, testament probated out of state, **9:2421**
Separation from bed and board, covenant marriage, **9:308**

VETERANS
Interdiction, **9:1021**
Mortgages, guaranteed by veterans administration, interest, **9:3504**
Obligations guaranteed, interest rate, **9:3504**

VETERINARIANS
Privileges, horses, medical services, **9:4661**

VISITATION
Attorney fees, **9:375**
Attorneys, appointment, protective and remedial measures, **9:345**
Bonds (officers and fiduciaries), orders, compliance, **9:342**
Costs, protective and remedial measures, **9:341**

VISITATION—Cont'd
Evaluation and mediation, **9:331 et seq.**
    Mediators, qualifications, **9:334**
Grandparents, rights, **9:344**
Illegitimate children, acknowledgment of paternity, **9:392**
Mediation, **9:331 et seq.**
Orders, drug tests, **9:331.1**
Postseparation family violence relief, **9:361 et seq.**
Protective and remedial measures, **9:341 et seq.**
Relatives, rights, **9:344**
Sexual abuse or exploitation,
    Appointment of attorney, **9:345**
    Restrictions on visitation, **9:341**
Siblings, rights, **9:344**
Support of persons, children and minors, raising issues, **9:315.25, 9:356**

VITAL STATISTICS
Birth certificates,
    Certified copies, short form certification cards, **9:226**
    Forms, short form certification cards, **9:226**
    Marriage licenses,
        Application, **9:225 et seq.**
        Retention of birth certificates by recorder, **9:226**
    Short form certification cards, **9:226**
Certified copies, birth certificates, short form certification cards, **9:226**
Marriage certificates, **9:245**
    Duplication and recordation, **9:253, 9:254**
Marriage records, **9:255**
Short form birth certificate cards, **9:226**

VOCATIONAL REHABILITATION
Public trust, purposes, **9:2341 et seq.**

VOLUNTEERS
Athletics, privileges and immunities, **9:2798**
Definitions, emergency medical services, privileges and immunities, **9:2793.2**
Privileges and immunities,
    Emergency medical services, **9:2793.2**
    Health care providers, gratuitous services, **9:2799.5**

WAREHOUSE RECEIPTS
Privileges and liens,
    Sale to enforce, self-service storage facilities, **9:4759**
    Self-service storage facilities, **9:4759**

WAREHOUSES AND WAREHOUSEMEN
Abandoned or unclaimed property, disposition, **9:4687 et seq.**
Default, self-service storage facilities, **9:4759**
Movable property, self-service storage facilities, **9:4756 et seq.**
Options, default by lessee, self-service storage facilities, **9:4759**
Privileges,
    Notice, self-service storage facilities, **9:4759**
    Sales to enforce, self-service storage facilities, **9:4759**
    Self-service storage facilities, **9:4758, 9:4759**
    Subordination to seller's privilege, agricultural products, **9:4541**
Self-Service Storage Facilities Act, **9:4756 et seq.**
Storage and handling charges, self-service storage facilities, **9:4758**
    Default, **9:4759**

WARRANTIES
Contractors, beginning of period, **9:2774**

WARRANTIES—Cont'd
Eviction, this index
Express warranties, **9:1131.14**
    Definitions, products liability, **9:2800.53**
    Products liabilities, unreasonably dangerous, **9:2800.58**
Implied warranties, real estate timesharing, **9:1131.15**
New Home Warranty Act, **9:3141 et seq.**
Peremption, new home warranties, enforcement, **9:3146**
Prescription, new home warranties, enforcement, **9:3146**
Real estate timesharing, **9:1131.14, 9:1131.15**
Waiver, new home warranties, **9:3144**

WARRANTS
Electronic applications, **9:2603.1**

WATCHES AND WATCHMAKERS
Abandoned or unclaimed property,
    Notice to owner of sale, **9:4702**
    Private sale, **9:4701 et seq.**
    Proceeds of sale, disposition, **9:4703**
Privilege, **9:4701 et seq.**

WATER POLLUTION
Public trust, purposes, **9:2341 et seq.**

WATER SUPPLY
Construction projects, machinery and equipment, limiting liability, **9:2775**
Electronic transactions, exemptions, **9:2603**
Exploration and development, indemnity agreements, bodily injury or death, **9:2780**
Indemnity, contractors, minerals, oil, gas or water, development exploration and exploitation, invalidity, **9:2780**
Privileges, crops, **9:4522**
Public trust, purposes, **9:2341 et seq.**
Rates and charges, use for municipal, agricultural or domestic purposes, **9:1101**
Riparian owners, use of surface water, fees prohibited, legislative finding, **9:1104**
Servitudes, public roads or streets, **9:1253**
Unclaimed property. Abandoned or Unclaimed Property, generally, this index

WATER WELLS
Indemnity agreements, contractors, **9:2780**
Negligence, indemnity agreements, contractors, **9:2780**

WATERS AND WATERCOURSES
Boating areas, servitudes, **9:1251**
Building encroachments, prescription, **9:5627**
Change in ownership of land or water bottoms, minerals, oil and gas, leases, **9:1151**
Nonnavigable waters, ownership of beds, **9:1115.1 et seq.**
Ports. Harbors and Ports, generally, this index
Privilege on crops, right to privilege, **9:4522**
Public policy, ownership, **9:1107**
Recreation, owner's duty of care, **9:2791**
Riparian owners,
    Use of land, **9:1102.2**
    Use of surface water, fees prohibited, legislative finding, **9:1104**
Servitudes, facilities, recording, **9:2726**
Submerged and Overflowed Lands, generally, this index
Title, **9:1101**
    Beds, non-navigable waters, **9:1115.1 et seq.**
Transfer of title, **9:1108**
United States,
    Control, acknowledgment of, **9:1101**

WATERS AND WATERCOURSES—Cont'd
United States—Cont'd
    Flowage rights and spillways perfecting option, **9:1511**
Waterbottoms. Submerged and Overflowed Lands, generally, this index

WATERSKIING
Private property, personal injuries, limiting liability, **9:2795**

WATERWAYS
Transfer, etc., of land fronting or bounded by, effect, **9:2971 et seq.**

WEAPONS
Dealers and distributors, firearms, products liability, **9:2800.60**
Manufacturers and manufacturing, firearms, products liability, **9:2800.60**
Products liability, **9:2800.60**
    Firearms, **9:2800.60**

WEARING APPAREL
Privileges, **9:4681 et seq.**
Unclaimed property, disposition, **9:4687 et seq.**

WELLS
Definitions, privileges, **9:4861**

WHARVES, DOCKS AND PIERS
Public trust, purposes, **9:2341 et seq.**
Riparian owners, right to construct and maintain, **9:1102.1**

WHOLESALERS
Donations, food banks, limitation of liability, **9:2799, 9:2799.6**
Food banks, donations, limitation of liability, **9:2799, 9:2799.6**
Limitation of liability, food banks, donations, **9:2799, 9:2799.6**

WITNESSES
Confidential or Privileged Information, generally, this index
Divorce, family violence, **9:364, 9:365**
Fees, **9:367**
Fees and charges,
    Opinion and expert testimony, post
    Paternity, **9:397.1**
    Physicians and surgeons, malpractice, **9:2794**
Immunities. Privileges and Immunities, generally, this index
Legitimation of natural children, **9:391**
Loans, advance fees, **9:3574.6**
Marriage, ceremony, **9:244**
Military forces, power of attorney, powers granted, **9:3870**
Opinion and expert testimony,
    Blood test to determine paternity, **9:396 et seq.**
    Fees and charges, paternity proceedings, blood or tissue test, **9:397.1**
    Tissue test to determine paternity, **9:396 et seq.**
Parenting coordinators, child custody, **9:358.5**
Privileged information. Confidential or Privileged Information, generally, this index
Privileges and Immunities, generally, this index
Testimonial privileges. Confidential or Privileged Information, generally, this index

WOMEN
    Generally, **9:51 et seq.**
Actions and proceedings, **9:102**
Civil rights and duties, **9:51**
Contracts, **9:101**
Credit, discrimination, **9:3583**
Emancipation and powers, **9:101 et seq.**

INDEX TO TITLE 9

WOMEN—Cont'd
Husband and Wife, generally, this index
Hypothecating property for benefit of husband or community, **9:103**
Obligations, **9:101**, **9:103**

WORDS AND PHRASES
Abandoned, mobile homes, **9:5363.1**
Abused parent, postseparation family violence relief, **9:362**
Actively participating in sporting activities, privileges and immunities, volunteers, **9:2798**
Administrator,
    Abandoned or unclaimed property, **9:167**
    Child support, licenses and permits, suspension or revocation, **9:315.40**
ADR Section, mediation, **9:4101**
Advance fee, loans, **9:3574.2**
Advertisements, rental purchase agreements, **9:3352**
Advertising material, real estate time sharing, **9:1131.12**
Aged persons, home solicitation, **9:3541.21**
Agency, real estate brokers and salespersons, **9:3891**
Agricultural products, leases, movable property, **9:3306**
Agricultural purpose, leases, movable property, **9:3306**
Ambulance service, privilege for services and supplies furnished patient, **9:4751**
Apparent owner,
    Abandoned or unclaimed property, **9:153**
    Uniform disposition of unclaimed property, **9:152**
Assignment, Uniform Law for Simplification of Fiduciary Security Transfers, **9:3831**
Association, Homeowners Association Act, **9:1141.2**
Athletic trainer, privileges and immunities, volunteers, **9:2798**
Attorney for the person or entity making payment, mortgages, cancellation, **9:5167.1**
Auction, sale, **9:3151**
Automated transactions, electronic transactions, **9:2602**
Bank, **9:3801**
Base term, leases, movable property, **9:3306**
Beneficiary,
    Custodial trusts, **9:2260.1**
    Trusts, **9:1801**
Billing period, consumer credit, **9:3516**
Block safe-houses, liability, **9:2800.5**
Bond for deed, **9:2941**
Borrower, advance fee loans, **9:3574.2**
Breach of trust, Trust Code, **9:2081**
Broker,
    Real estate brokers and salespersons, **9:3891**
    Uniform Transfers to Minors Act, **9:751**
Builder,
    New home warranties, **9:3143**
    Ship mortgages, **9:5522**
Building standards, new home warranties, **9:3143**
Capitalized cost, leases, movable property, **9:3306**
Cardholder, credit cards, receipts, liabilities, **9:3518.3**
Cash advance, consumer credit, **9:3516**
Cash price, rental purchase agreements, **9:3352**
Certificate of title, manufactured homes, **9:1149.2**
Checks, consumer credit transactions, **9:3516**
Claimant,
    Privileges, wells, **9:4861**
    Products liability, **9:2800.53**
Class trust, **9:1891**
Closing notary public, mortgages, cancellation, **9:5167.1**
Collateral mortgages, **9:5550**
College campus, credit cards, **9:3577.2**
Commercial lease, movable property, **9:3306**

WORDS AND PHRASES—Cont'd
Commercial loan, advance fees, **9:3574.3**
Commercial real estate, brokers, unpaid commissions, **9:2781.1**
Commission, real estate brokers and salespersons, **9:3891**
Commissioner,
    Credit cards, **9:3578.2**
    Credit repair services organizations, **9:3573.2**
    Small loans, **9:3578.3**
Common area, Homeowners Association Act, **9:1141.2**
Common elements, real estate timesharing, **9:1131.2**
Community health care clinics, gratuitous health care services, **9:2799.5**
Community pharmacies, gratuitous medical services, **9:2799.5**
Community services, nonprofit organizations, limitation of liability, **9:2792.8**
Compliance with an order of support, suspension or revocation, **9:315.40**
Computer program, electronic transactions, **9:2602**
Conditional sales, leases, movable property, **9:3306**
Condominiums, **9:1121.103**
Conservation servitude, **9:1272**
Constituent entity, merger or consolidation, partnerships, **9:3441**
Constructive notice,
    Limitation of liability for public entities, **9:2800**
    Merchant's liability, **9:2800.6**
Consumer,
    Consumer credit, **9:3516**
    Home solicitation, aged persons, **9:3541.21**
    Leases, movable property, **9:3306**
    Rental purchase agreements, **9:3352**
Consumer credit,
    Remedies, **9:3552**
    Sale, **9:3516**
Consumer credit transaction, **9:3516**
Consumer lease, movable property, **9:3306**
Consumer loan, **9:3516**
Consumer loan brokers, **9:3572.1**
Consumer reporting agency, credit repair services organizations, **9:3573.2**
Consummation, rental purchase agreements, **9:3352**
Contempt of court, support of persons, **9:315.31**
Contract for surrogate motherhood, **9:2713**
Contractor,
    Mechanic's privileges and liens, **9:4807**
    Privileges, wells, **9:4861**
Controlled substance, dealer liability, **9:2800.62**
Corporation, Uniform Law for Simplification of Fiduciary Security Transfers, **9:3831**
Court,
    Custodial trusts, **9:2260.1**
    Estate tax apportionment, **9:2431**
    Postseparation family violence relief, **9:362**
    Support of persons, **9:315.31**
    Uniform Transfers to Minors Act, **9:751**
Credit cards, **9:3516**
    College Campus Credit Card Solicitation Act, **9:3577.2**
    Receipts, liabilities, **9:3518.3**
    Unsolicited cards, mail and mailing, **9:3518.2**
Credit repair services organization, **9:3573.2**
Credit report, **9:3571.1**
Credit reporting agency, **9:3571.1**
Credit service charge, consumer credit transactions, **9:3516**
Curator, custodial trusts, **9:2260.1**
Custodial property, Uniform Transfers to Minors Act, **9:751**
Custodial trust property, **9:2260.1**

INDEX TO TITLE 9

WORDS AND PHRASES—Cont'd
Custodian, Uniform Transfers to Minors Act, **9:751**
Customer,
    Real estate brokers and salespersons, **9:3891**
Damages,
    Abortion, **9:2800.12**
    Privileges and immunities, felonies, injuries during commission, **9:2800.10**
    Products liability, **9:2800.53**
Dealer, manufactured homes, **9:1149.2**
Death, **9:111**
Declaration,
    Homeowners Association Act, **9:1141.2**
    Real estate timesharing, **9:1131.2**
Deferred presentment transactions, small loans, **9:3577.3**
Designated nonprofit organization, limitation of liability, **9:2792.8**
Developer, real estate timesharing, **9:1131.2**
Disabled person, home solicitation, aged persons, **9:3541.21**
Domicile,
    Abandoned or unclaimed property, **9:153**
    Uniform disposition of unclaimed property, **9:152**
Down payment, consumer credit, **9:3516**
Dual agency, real estate brokers and salespersons, **9:3891**
Electronic record, electronic transactions, **9:2602**
Electronic signature, electronic transactions, **9:2602**
Emergency services, volunteers, privileges and immunities, **9:2793.2**
Equipment, leases, **9:3306**
Estate, tax apportionment, **9:2431**
Exchange company, real estate timesharing, **9:1131.2**
Express warranty, products liability, **9:2800.53**
Facilities, servitudes, recording, **9:2726**
Family violence, postseparation family violence relief, **9:362**
Farm animal activity, privileges and immunities, **9:2795.1**
Farm land or forest land, unauthorized entry, liability of owner, **9:2800.4**
Fiduciaries, **9:3801**
    Estate tax apportionment, **9:2431**
    Uniform Law for Simplification of Fiduciary Security Transfers, **9:3831**
Financial institutions, Uniform Transfers to Minors Act, **9:751**
Food bank, donations, limitation of liability, **9:2799, 9:2799.6**
Foreign limited partnership, commercial loans, interest, maximum conventional rate, **9:3509**
Foreign partnerships, **9:3421**
Foreign trust, **9:2262.1**
General contractor, mechanic's privileges and liens, **9:4807**
Gleaning, privileges and immunities, **9:2800.4**
Governmental agency, electronic transactions, **9:2602**
Health care provider,
    Gratuitous health care services, **9:2799.5**
    Privileges, **9:4751**
    Users of blood, organs or tissue, **9:2797**
Holder,
    Abandoned or unclaimed property, **9:153**
    Conservation servitude, **9:1272**
    Mineral proceeds, payments for deceased persons, **9:1516**
Home solicitation sale, **9:3516**
    Aged persons, **9:3541.21**
Homeowners association, **9:1141.2, 9:2792.7**
Hospitals, privilege for services and supplies furnished patient, **9:4751**
Illegal controlled substance, dealer liability, **9:2800.62**
Incapacitated, custodial trusts, **9:2260.1**

WORDS AND PHRASES—Cont'd
Income beneficiary, trusts, **9:1725**
Independent professional advice, compromise, structured settlements, transfer, **9:2715**
Information processing system, electronic transactions, **9:2602**
Initial purchaser, new home warranties, **9:3143**
Injunction, post-separation, family violence relief, **9:362**
Institutional trustee, foreign trusts, **9:2262.1**
Insurance company,
    Abandoned or unclaimed property, **9:153**
    Uniform disposition of unclaimed property, **9:152**
Insurance premium finance company, **9:3550**
Intangible personal property, uniform disposition of unclaimed property, **9:153**
Inter vivos trust, **9:1734**
Issuer, credit card, receipts, liabilities, **9:3518.3**
Itinerant door-to-door salesman, **9:2711**
Joint custody, support, **9:315.8**
Last known address,
    Self-service storage facilities, **9:4757**
    Uniform disposition of unclaimed property, **9:152**
Lease timeshare interest, real estate timesharing, **9:1131.2**
Leases, movable property, **9:3306**
Legal entity, sales of immovables, lack of authority, **9:5681**
Legal representative,
    Custodial trusts, **9:2260.1**
    Uniform Transfers to Minors Act, **9:751**
Lender credit card, **9:3516**
Lessee,
    Movable property, **9:3306**
    Privileges, wells, **9:4861**
    Self-service storage facilities, **9:4757**
Lessor,
    Movable property, **9:3306**
    Rental purchase agreements, **9:3352**
Level one offense, controlled dangerous substances, dealer liability, **9:2800.62**
License,
    Child support, licenses and permits, suspension or revocation, **9:315.40**
    Insurance premium finance companies, **9:3550**
Licensee,
    Child support, licenses and permits, suspension or revocation, **9:315.40**
    Real estate brokers and salespersons, **9:3891**
    Small loans, **9:3578.3**
Licensing authority, child support, licenses and permits, suspension or revocation, **9:315.40**
Loan finance charge, consumer credit, **9:3516**
Loan originator or broker, advance fee loans, **9:3574.2**
Mail and check solicitation sale, consumer credit, **9:3541.1**
Major structural defect, new home warranties, **9:3143**
Manufacturer,
    Manufactured homes, **9:1149.2**
    Products liability, **9:2800.53**
Manufacturer's certificate of origin, manufactured homes, **9:1149.2**
Material change in circumstances, support of persons, **9:311**
Material, ship mortgages, **9:5522**
MCLE committee, mediation, **9:4101**
Mediator, mediation, **9:4104**
Military personnel, power of attorney, **9:3861**
Military power of attorney, **9:3863**
Mineral proceeds, abandoned or unclaimed property, **9:153**
Ministerial acts, real estate brokers and salespersons, **9:3891**

INDEX TO TITLE 9

WORDS AND PHRASES—Cont'd
Mobile homes,
    Abandoned mobile homes, **9:5363.1**
    Manufactured Home Property Act, **9:1149.2**
Mortgage, manufactured homes, **9:1149.2**
Mortgagor, abandoned mobile homes, **9:5363.1**
Movables, leases, **9:3306**
Nominal consideration, leases, movable property, **9:3306**
Noncredit home solicitation sale, consumer's right to cancel, **9:2711.1**
Nonoperator, privileges, wells, **9:4881**
Nonparticipating lessee, privileges, wells, **9:4861**
Officiant, marriage, **9:201**
Oil, gas or mineral property, landowner's liability, **9:2800.4**
Open account,
    Professional services, **9:2781**
    Real estate brokers, unpaid commissions, commercial real estate liens, **9:2781.1**
Operating agreement, mineral rights, **9:2780**
Operating interest, oil, gas or water wells, privileges, **9:4861**
Operations, privileges, wells, **9:4861**
Operator, privileges, wells, **9:4861, 9:4881**
Owners,
    Abandoned or unclaimed property, **9:153**
    Block safe houses, liability, **9:2800.5**
    Mechanic's privileges and liens, **9:4806**
    New home warranties, **9:3143**
    Real estate timesharing, **9:1131.2**
    Recreational areas, private owners, limitation of liability, **9:2795**
    Self-service storage facilities, **9:4757**
    Unauthorized entry, farm or forestland, liability of owner, **9:2800.4**
Ownership timeshare interests, real estate timesharing, **9:1131.2**
Payoff statement, mortgages, cancellation, **9:5167.1**
Person,
    Consumer credit, **9:3516**
    Credit card, receipts, liabilities, **9:3518.3**
    Credit repair services organization, **9:3573.2**
    Custodial trusts, **9:2260.1**
    Electronic transactions, **9:2602**
    Estate tax apportionment, **9:2431**
    Fiduciaries Law, **9:3801**
    Hospital's privilege for services and supplies furnished patient, **9:4751**
    Insurance premium finance companies, **9:3550**
    Open accounts, **9:2781**
    Real estate timeshare, **9:1131.2**
    Recreational areas, private owners, limiting liability, **9:2795**
    Servitudes, recording, **9:2726**
    Trust Code, **9:1725**
    Unclaimed clothing and household goods, **9:4687**
Personal representative,
    Custodial trusts, **9:2260.1**
    Uniform Transfers to Minors Act, **9:751**
Pharmacists, gratuitous medical services, **9:2799.5**
Pledged obligation, prescription, interruption, **9:5807**
Precomputed consumer credit transaction, **9:3516**
Premises, recreation, owner's duty of care, **9:2791**
Prepaid finance charge, consumer credit, **9:3516**
Prepayment, small loans, **9:3577.3**
Principal, **9:3801**
    Advance fee loans, **9:3574.2**
    Consumer credit, **9:3516**

WORDS AND PHRASES—Cont'd
Principal beneficiary, Trust Code, **9:1725**
    Status of potential substitute principal beneficiary, **9:1979**
Pro rata, consumer credit, **9:3516**
Products, products liability, **9:2800.53**
Professional fees, attorney fees, **9:5001**
Professional subconsultant, mechanic's privileges, **9:4801, 9:4802**
Provider, credit card, receipts, liabilities, **9:3518.3**
Public emergency, police and firefighter immunity from liability, **9:2793.1**
Public entities,
    Claims against, policy making or discretionary acts, **9:2798.1**
    Immunity from liability, **9:2793.1**
    Limitation of liability, conditions of things within care and custody, **9:2800**
    Political subdivision buildings, liability, **9:2800**
    Quasi offenses, liability for discretionary acts or omissions, **9:2798.1**
Purchase agreement, itinerant door-to-door salesman, **9:2711**
Purchaser,
    Real estate timeshare, **9:1131.2**
    Ship mortgages, **9:5522**
Reasonably anticipated use, products liability, **9:2800**
Recreational purposes, private owners of recreational areas, limiting liability, **9:2795**
Rental agreement, self-service storage facilities, **9:4757**
Residential mobile home, manufactured homes, **9:1149.2**
Residential planned community, Homeowners Association Act, **9:1141.2**
Retail installment contract, manufactured homes, **9:1149.2**
Revolving charge account, **9:3516**
Revolving loan account, consumer credit, **9:3516**
Sale/lease-back, **9:3516**
Secured party, mobile homes, **9:5363.1**
Security, Uniform Law for Simplification of Fiduciary Security Transfers, **9:3831**
Security procedure, electronic transactions, **9:2602**
Self-service storage facility, **9:4757**
Seller, products liability, **9:2800.53**
Seller credit card, consumer credit, **9:3516**
Settlor, Trust Code, **9:1761**
Shared custody, support, **9:315.9**
Ship, mortgages, **9:5522**
Short term lease, movable property, **9:3306**
Simple interest transaction, consumer credit, **9:3516**
Site of the immovable, mechanic's privileges and liens, **9:4820**
Spendthrift trust, **9:1725**
State,
    Abandoned or unclaimed property, **9:153**
    Custodial trusts, **9:2260.1**
    Electronic transactions, **9:2602**
    Estate tax apportionment, **9:2431**
    Uniform disposition of unclaimed property, **9:153**
    Uniform Transfers to Minors Act, **9:751**
Structured settlement, compromise and settlement, **9:2715**
Student, College Campus Credit Card Solicitation Act, **9:3577.2**
Subcontractor, mechanic's privileges and liens, **9:4807**
Surviving income beneficiary, trusts, **9:1835**
Survivorship, custodial trusts, **9:2260.6**
Tax, estate tax apportionment, **9:2431**
Taxidermists, disposition of abandoned property, **9:191**
Team volunteer health care provider, privileges and immunities, **9:2798**

WORDS AND PHRASES—Cont'd
Terms of the structured settlement, compromise and settlement, transfer, **9:2715**
Testamentary trust, **9:1733**
Third party right of enforcement, conservation servitudes, **9:1272**
Third person,
    Privileges, wells, **9:4861**
    Successions and succession proceedings, **9:5630**
Timeshare association, real estate timeshare, **9:1131.2**
Title insurance business, mortgages, cancellation, **9:5167.1**
Transaction,
    Electronic transactions, **9:2602**
    Home solicitation, aged persons, **9:3541.21**
Transfer,
    Compromise and settlement, structured settlements, **9:2715**
    Uniform Law for Simplification of Fiduciary Security Transfers, **9:3831**
    Uniform Transfers to Minors Act, **9:751**
Transfer agent, Uniform Law for Simplification of Fiduciary Security Transfers, **9:3831**
Transferable record, electronic transactions, **9:2616**
Transferees, compromise and settlement, structured settlements, **9:2715**
Transferor,
    Custodial trusts, **9:2260.1**
    Uniform Transfers to Minor Act, **9:751**
Trust company,
    Custodial trusts, **9:2260.1**
    Uniform Transfers to Minors Act, **9:751**
Trust instrument, **9:1725**
Trustee, **9:1781**
Trusts, **9:1731**
    Charitable trusts, **9:2281**
Tutor,
    Custodial trusts, **9:2260.1**
    Uniform Transfers to Minor Act, **9:751**
Unborn child, abortion, **9:2800.12**
Unconscionable, consumer credit, **9:3516**
Unit, real estate time sharing, **9:1131.2**
Unpaid debt, consumer credit, **9:3516**
Unreasonably dangerous, products liability, **9:2800.54**

WORDS AND PHRASES—Cont'd
Use of blood or tissue, medical care and treatment, **9:2797**
Utility, abandoned or unclaimed property, **9:153**
Vehicle, manufactured homes, **9:1149.2**
Vendor's privilege, collateral mortgage, **9:5550**
Vitamin, food banks, donations, limitation of liability, **9:2799**
Voluntary council on the aging, privileges and immunities, **9:2792.9**
Voluntary sale, auction, **9:3152**
Volunteer, emergency medical services, privileges and immunities, **9:2793.2**
Warranty commencement date, new home warranties, **9:3143**
Well, privileges, **9:4862**
Wild game, food banks, donations, limitation of liability, **9:2799**, **9:2799.6**
Wild well, indemnity, mineral, oil and gas development and exploration, **9:2780**
Work,
    Mechanic's privileges and liens, **9:4808**
    Ship mortgages, **9:5522**
Written agreement, support, income assignments, **9:303**

WORKERS COMPENSATION
Structured settlements, transfer, **9:2715**
Voluntary settlement of claims, structured settlements, transfer, **9:2715**

WRONGFUL DEATH
Alcoholic beverages, limitation of liability, damages or losses connected with sale, serving or furnishing, **9:2800.1**
Compromises prior to death, **9:3921**
Deficiencies in design, supervision or construction of improvements, prescription, **9:2772**
Immovables, actions involving deficiencies in design or construction, prescription, **9:2772**
Physicians and surgeons, malpractice, prescription, **9:5628**
Prescription, deficiencies in design, supervision or construction of improvements, **9:2772**

ZONING AND PLANNING
Condominiums, application of law, **9:1121.106**
Limitation of action, **9:5625**
New Orleans, prescription, **9:5625**